BEARDMORE

CARLETON LIBRARY SERIES

The Carleton Library Series publishes books about Canadian economics, geography, history, politics, public policy, society and culture, and related topics, in the form of leading new scholarship and reprints of classics in these fields. The series is funded by Carleton University, published by McGill-Queen's University Press, and is under the guidance of the Carleton Library Series Editorial Board, which consists of faculty members of Carleton University. Suggestions and proposals for manuscripts and new editions of classic works are welcome and may be directed to the Carleton Library Series Editorial Board c/o the Library, Carleton University, Ottawa K1S 5B6, at cls@carleton.ca, or on the web at www.carleton.ca/cls.

For Crawford

Contents

Acknowledgments

This book had its genesis in the research for my doctoral dissertation, "Stone of Power" (York University, 2015). As I gathered evidence for the misappropriation of Indigenous cultural materials in support of spurious ideas of early European voyages to the Americas, I amassed several files on dubious claims of Viking voyages. In 2013, I had my first, intrigued look at materials on the Beardmore hoax in the archives of the Royal Ontario Museum and Trent University. As the hoax did not fit my thesis, I set the case aside, knowing I would return to it if I ever had the chance. After completing my PhD, I began chipping away at the small mountain of Beardmore evidence in what turned out to be several collections in several archives. Hard as it might be to believe, noodling around in the Beardmore mystery became my way of relaxing during my postdoctorate at the University of Waterloo, when I was also preparing my dissertation for publication (as *The Place of Stone*, with University of North Carolina Press, in October 2017). When my postdoctorate ended in the spring of 2017, I began focussing almost exclusively on completing the manuscript for *Beardmore*. I owe thanks to innumerable people in my doctoral and postdoctoral years who listened to my tangential musings about this scandal. Their feedback helped me to appreciate how the story mattered to archaeologists, historians, and museologists. As well, without the support of the Social Sciences and Humanities Research Council during my doctoral and postdoctoral years, and the government of Canada when I held a Vanier Canada graduate scholarship, I never would have been able to devote the initial time I did to probing the Beardmore case.

This book exists because of the enthusiasm and support of editor Jonathan Crago and the staff and editorial board at McGill-Queen's University Press, who green-lit the project on the basis of an outline and a sample chapter. The anonymous referees who read and commented on the first draft (which was more of a work in progress) provided invaluable guidance for refining my effort to tell as well as contextualize a vexatiously complex story. K. Joanne Richardson was the able copyeditor who gave my words a final polish.

While I visited in person the archives of the Royal Ontario Museum, Trent University, the Fisher Collection at the University of Toronto, and the United Church of Canada, the aid of archivists at other collections saved me from making prohibitively expensive trips in hope of finding one letter that could shed more light on the hoax. A former York classmate and tireless task-tackler, Keri-Lyn Durant, ran down newspaper articles and pages in city directories for me in Thunder Bay.

The unfailing assistance of Charlotte Chaffey and the rest of the archives staff of the Royal Ontario Museum spread to other parts of the museum. Craig Cipolla, newly arrived as associate curator, North American archaeology, reached out to me when he heard what I was up to. Through him I was able to inspect the Beardmore "bits" not on display – and most importantly, examine documents beyond the archives, in the accession file – with the assistance of Jennifer Kinnaird, a technician in the museum's European section. Craig also put me in touch with the museum's senior metals conservator, Susan Stock, whose curiosity about the relics was boundless. Susan shared with me photographs and X-rays of the sword as she prepared it for inclusion in the touring "Vikings" exhibition that opened at the museum in November 2017. With the museum's blessing, I shared these images with experts in Europe in an effort to settle questions about the sword's provenance – including whether it was even authentic. David Edge, head of conservation, and metallurgist Alan Williams of the Wallace Collection at London's Hatfield House, and Vegard A. Vike, archaeological conservator at Oslo's Museum of Cultural History, responded promptly and authoritatively to those questions. Archaeologist Birgitta Wallace, renowned for her work at L'Anse aux Meadows, in addition to sharing with me her letter from Edmund Carpenter in September 1965, was generous in our email exchanges about all things Viking and archaeological.

I must thank two members of Beardmore "families" for their cooperation. Susan MacLatchie provided reminiscences about her father, O.C. "Teddy" Elliott. John Garner recalled for me his grandfather, James Hansen, and combed through his grandfather's business records to cull for me important facts about his life and enterprises.

Finally, I am indebted to my wife, Debbie, whose support and patience had already seen me through three decades of research and writing when this project began to dominate my waking hours.

List of Recurring Characters

Barbeau, Marius: ethnologist with Dominion Geological Survey of Canada and National Museum.

Beamish, Royd E.: reporter for Port Arthur *Daily News-Chronicle*, Toronto *Globe and Mail*.

Beeman, Harry H.: lawyer in Fort William, Ontario.

Bell, Robert: travelling salesman, Port Arthur, Ontario; husband of Teddy Elliott's sister-in-law, Pearl.

Bjorke, C.J.: Norwegian vice-consul in Vancouver.

Black, Mary: librarian in Fort William, Ontario.

Bloch, Andreas: Norwegian artist and collector; father of John (Jens).

Bloch (Block), John (Jens): Norwegian immigrant to Port Arthur, Ontario; tenant of James Hansen; presumed source of the Beardmore relics.

Bohan, Patrick J.: CNR foreman, friend of Eddy Dodd.

Bolduc, Joseph: engineer in provincial mining record office in Port Arthur, Ontario; brother of Leo.

Bolduc, Leo (Leonidas): partner in Port Arthur, Ontario, real estate business with Walter S. Ruttan; brother of Joseph.

Bovey, Wilfrid: director of extra-mural relations and extensions, McGill University; author of Royal Society of Canada paper on Vinland voyages.

Brett, Gerard: C.T. Currelly's successor as director of archaeology division of Royal Ontario Museum

Brøgger, Anton Wilhelm (A.W.): archaeologist; University of Oslo professor; director of Museum of Cultural History.

Brøndsted, Johannes: archaeology professor, University of Copenhagen; curator at, later director of, National Museum of Denmark.

Brooks, Carey M.: mining professional and leading citizen of Beardmore, Ontario.

Brown, George: History professor, University of Toronto; editor of the *Canadian Historical Review*.

Brownell, George McLeod: professor of geology and mineralogy, University of Manitoba.

Burpee, Lawrence J.: Canadian civil servant; historian; president of Royal Society of Canada (1936–37).

Burwash, Nathanael: chancellor of Victoria College, University of Toronto; father of Ned and Lachlan Taylor.

Burwash, "Professor" Ned (Edward Moore Jackson): Ontario government geologist; childhood friend of C.T. Currelly.

Cameron, Duncan: director of publicity, Royal Ontario Museum; later a museologist, director of Brooklyn Museum and Glenbow Museum.

Carpenter, Edmund: archaeologist; anthropologist; University of Toronto professor; later anthropology professor, San Fernando Valley State.

Creighton, Donald G.: history professor, University of Toronto; associate editor, the *Canadian Historical Review.*

Cross, Julian: Port Arthur, Ontario, mining engineer; brother of William.

Cross, William: Port Arthur, Ontario, machinist; brother of Julian.

Curran, James Watson (Jim): owner and publisher/editor of *Sault Daily Star*; author of *Here Was Vinland.*

Currelly, Charles Trick: director of Royal Ontario Museum of Archaeology; professor of archaeology, University of Toronto.

Dear, Colonel L.S.: militia commander; naturalist; brewery manager in Port Arthur, Ontario.

Delbridge, Tom: log scaler with Ontario Department of Lands and Forests, Port Arthur, Ontario.

Dodd, Eddy (James Edward): CNR employee; itinerant prospector; perpetrator of Beardmore hoax.

Dodd, Ellen: spouse of Eddy Dodd.

Dodd, Walter: adopted son of Eddy and Ellen Dodd.

Eakins, Dr George Edwin: Port Arthur, Ontario, physician; historical enthusiast.

Einarsson, Stefán: specialist in Icelandic literature, Johns Hopkins University.

Elliott, Kate (née Jarvis): spouse of Teddy Elliott.

Elliott, Teddy (Otho Christopher): schoolteacher and investigator of Beardmore hoax.

Emerson, J. Norman: archaeologist; University of Toronto professor.

Feltham, William: erstwhile commercial fisherman; associate of Eddy Dodd.

Fleming, James Henry (J.H.): honorary curator of ornithology, zoology division of Royal Ontario Museum.

Fraser, A.D.: professor in archaeology division of University of Virginia's school of ancient languages.

Gathorne-Hardy, Geoffrey Malcolm (G.M.): librarian of House of Lords, London; proponent of Kensington stone.

Gill, Fletcher: CNR employee; prospecting partner of Eddy Dodd.

Godfrey Jr, William S.: graduate student at Peabody Museum; archaeology professor at Balliol College.

Godsell, Philip H.: former Hudson's Bay Company factor; popular historian.

Gould, Chester N.: University of Chicago linguist and Scandinavianist.

Gowe, Robert L.: *Globe and Mail* reporter.

Greenaway, Ethlyn: assistant to C.T. Currelly.

Grieg, Sigurd: Norwegian archaeologist, colleague of A.W. Brøgger at University of Oslo and Museum of Cultural History.

Hansen, James (Jens): Norwegian immigrant; contractor and property owner, Port Arthur, Ontario.

Hartvik, Os: civil engineer, Port Arthur, Ontario.

Hastings, Shana Block: widow of John Bloch; former Shana Lyons; former Christina/Kristana Grimson.

Hermannsson, Halldór: curator of Fiske Icelandic Collection, Cornell University.

Holand, Hjalmar R.: Wisconsin fruit farmer; avocational historian; chief proponent of Kensington stone.

Hynes (Hines), George: log scaler with Ontario Department of Lands and Forests, Port Arthur.

Innis, Harold: professor of political economy, University of Toronto.

Jacob, John Drew: homesteader; naturalist; game warden (1930–34) in Ontario's District 6.

Jenness, Diamond: chief anthropologist, Dominion Geological Survey of Canada and National Museum.

Kenney, James: Director of Historical Research and Publicity, Public Archives of Canada.

Kidd, Kenneth E.: curator of ethnology, Royal Ontario Museum.

Lechler, George: archaeologist and anthropologist; art and archeology instructor, Detroit Institute of Arts.

Lindqvist, Sune: archaeologist, Uppsala University.

Lougheed, Aaron: retired land surveyor, Port Arthur, Ontario.

MacKay, E. Ross: associate editor of *Sault Daily Star.*

McArthur, Duncan: former Queen's University historian; Ontario's deputy minister of education; minister of education in wartime cabinet.

McComber, Judge Alexander J.: lawyer; avocational historian; senior justice in Thunder Bay District.

McGugan, John: mining engineer, Port Arthur, Ontario.

McIlwraith, Thomas F.: professor of anthropology, University of Toronto; curator of ethnology, Royal Ontario Museum; later assistant director of archaeology division.

Mann, James Gow (J.G.): director of Wallace Collection at Hertford House, London.

Means, Philip Ainsworth: American archaeologist and historian specializing in Spanish Americas.

Nash, Philleo: archaeologist, lecturer in anthropology department, University of Toronto.

Ohlgren, Roy: Fort William, Ontario, clerk.

Ohman, Olof: "discoverer" of Kensington stone.

Olson, Robert: Canadian journalist; *Maclean's* writer.

Petersen, Jan: creator of Norse weapons typology, in *De Norske Vikingesverd* (1919).

Petrie, Flinders: British archaeologist of ancient Egypt and Palestine.

Pierce, Lorne: editor, Ryerson Press.

Prowse, George Robert Farrar (G.R.F.): retired Winnipeg school principal; cartologist.

Rafn, Carl Christian: secretary of Royal Society of Northern Antiquaries in Copenhagen; editor of *Antiquitates Americanae* (1837).

Ragotte, Eli: CNR employee in Winnipeg, Manitoba, and Port Arthur, Ontario.

Robins, John D.: professor of English, Victoria College, University of Toronto.

Robinson, Percy J.: private school instructor, historian of Ontario during the French regime.

Ross, James F.W.: law partner of Harry Beeman in Beeman and Ross, Fort William, Ontario.

Ruttan, Colonel Henry A.: partner in Ruttan family real estate business in Port Arthur, Ontario.

Ruttan, Walter S.: partner in in Port Arthur, Ontario, real estate business with Leo Bolduc.

Samuel, Sigmund: Toronto industrialist and philanthropist; source of funds for acquisitions by the Royal Ontario Museum.

Scheel, Knut (Knud): Winnipeg associate of G.R.F. Prowse

Scott, Harry: retired railway baggageman, Port Arthur, Ontario.

Simonsen, G.A.: Port Arthur, Ontario, grocer.

Snyder, Leslie (L.L.): technologist, later curator of ornithology, zoology division of Royal Ontario Museum.

Sorensen, Carl: Norwegian vice-consul, Fort William, Ontario.

Stefansson, Vilhjalmur: Arctic explorer and anthropologist.

Strandwold, Olof: school superintendent in Prosser, Washington; avocational proponent of North American runestones.

Tanton, T.L. (Thomas Leslie): geologist with Dominion Geological Survey of Canada.

Thórdarson, Matthias: curator of National Museum of Iceland.

Todd, William: preparator, later chief conservator, Royal Ontario Museum.

Trotter, Reginald G.: Douglas professor of Canadian and colonial history, Queen's University.

Tushingham, A.D.: Gerard Brett's successor as director of archaeology division of Royal Ontario Museum.

Wade, Gerald: manager of Western Municipal News, Winnipeg; friend of J.H. Fleming.

Walker, Sir Byron Edmund: Canadian banker; founder of numerous cultural institutions; lead proponent of Royal Ontario Museum.

Wallace, Birgitta: archaeologist; curator at Carnegie Museum of Natural History; later chief Parks Canada archaeologist at L'Anse aux Meadows.

Wallace, W.S. (Stewart): history professor, chief librarian, University of Toronto; managing editor, *Canadian Historical Review*; honorary editor, Royal Society of Canada.

Wintemberg, William: archaeologist with Dominion Geological Survey of Canada and National Museum.

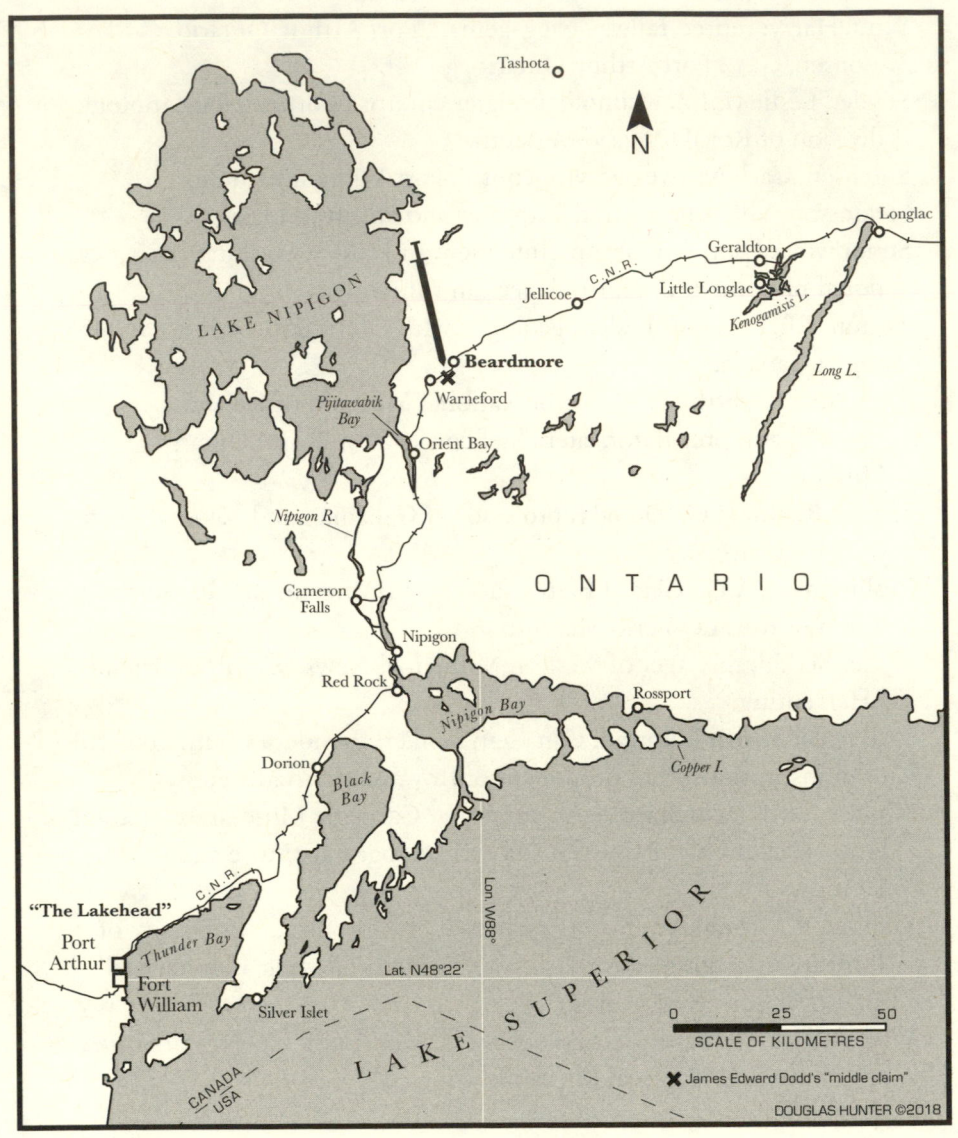

Tashota

N

Longlac

Geraldton

LAKE NIPIGON

C.N.R.

Jellicoe

Little Longlac

Kenogamisis L.

Long L.

Beardmore

Pijitawabik Bay

Warneford

Orient Bay

Nipigon R.

O N T A R I O

Cameron Falls

Nipigon

Red Rock

Rossport

Nipigon Bay

Dorion

Black Bay

Copper I.

"The Lakehead"

C.N.R.

Port Arthur

Thunder Bay

Lon. W88°

Lat. N48°22'

Fort William

Silver Islet

L A K E   S U P E R I O R

CANADA
USA

0   25   50
SCALE OF KILOMETRES

✖ James Edward Dodd's "middle claim"

DOUGLAS HUNTER ©2018

Fletcher Gill (*left*) and Eddy Dodd at the Beardmore middle-claim cabin, date unknown (ROM 12.9.2.5; ROM2018_16184_1)

Fletcher Gill (*right*) and Eddy Dodd in the middle-claim trench, photographer unknown, taken 14 November 1938 (ROM 12.9.2.5; ROM2018_16184_2)

Teddy Elliott prospecting at Little Longlac in the 1930s (Courtesy Susan MacLatchie)

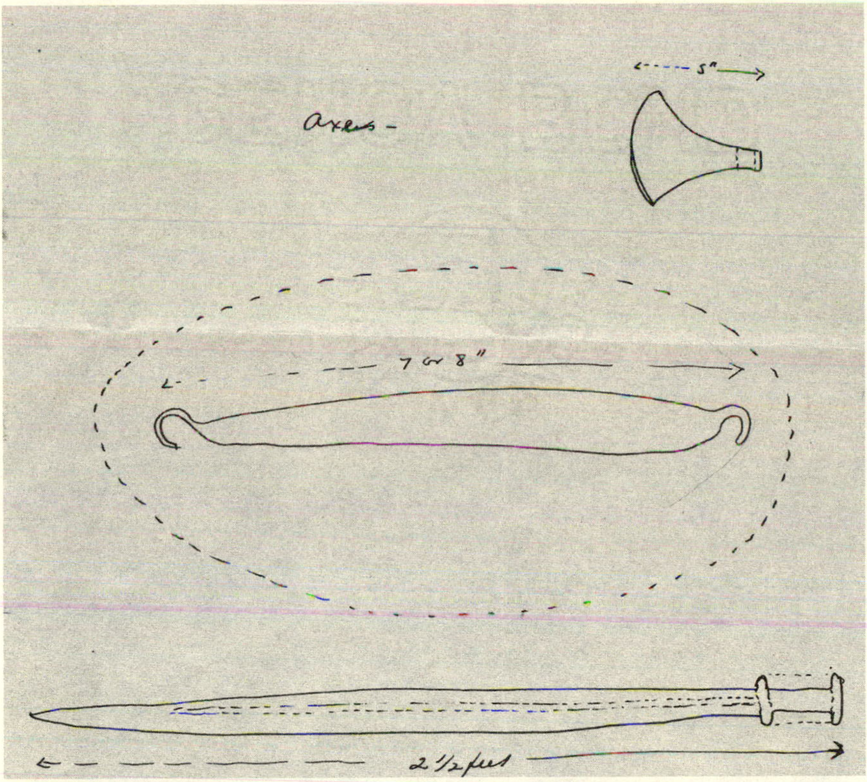

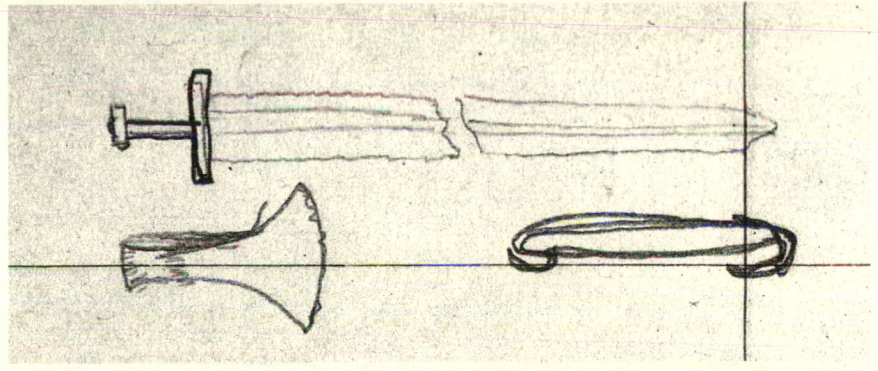

E.M. "Ned" Burwash's sketch of the Beardmore relics on the second page of his letter to C.T. Currelly, 14 February 1934 (ROM RG12.9.1.6; ROM2018_16184_10)

Teddy Elliott's small sketch of the Beardmore relics on the first page of his stenographer's notebook, August 1936 (ROM SC9, Box 2; ROM2018_16184_8)

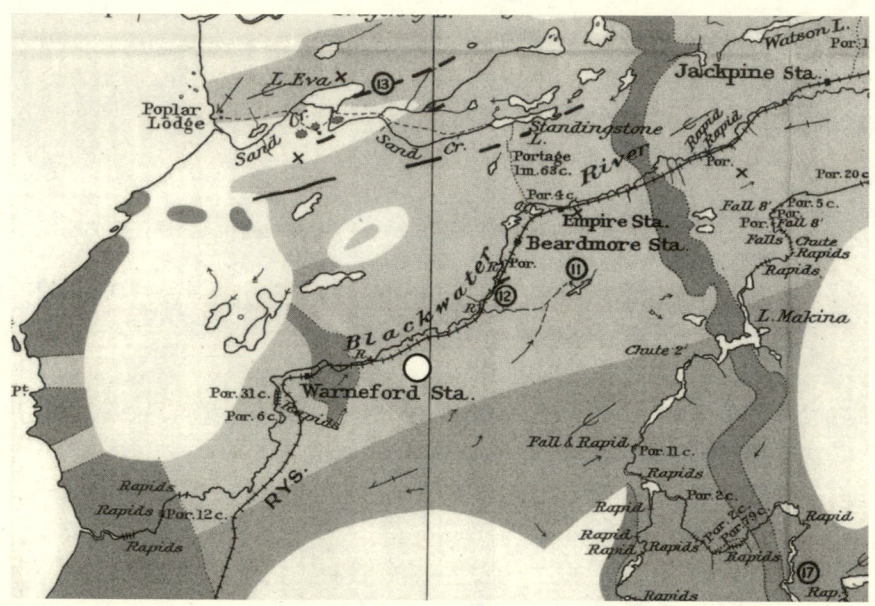

Detail of Dominion Geological Survey Map 312A, with circle indicating the location of Eddy Dodd's discovery, according to coordinates provided by Dodd to Teddy Elliott in August 1936.

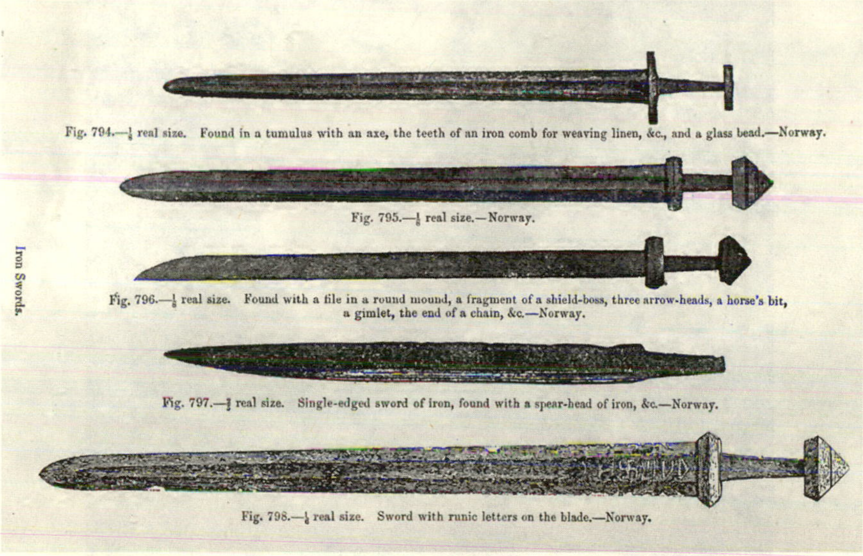
Fig. 794.—1/8 real size. Found in a tumulus with an axe, the teeth of an iron comb for weaving linen, &c., and a glass bead.—Norway.
Fig. 795.—1/8 real size.—Norway.
Iron Swords.
Fig. 796.—1/8 real size. Found with a file in a round mound, a fragment of a shield-boss, three arrow-heads, a horse's bit, a gimlet, the end of a chain, &c.—Norway.
Fig. 797.—2/9 real size. Single-edged sword of iron, found with a spear-head of iron, &c.—Norway.
Fig. 798.—1/8 real size. Sword with runic letters on the blade.—Norway.

Page 70 in volume 2 of Paul Bellini Du Chaillu's *The Viking Age*. Teddy Elliott was struck by the similarity of Eddy Dodd's broken sword to the Norse sword depicted at the top (fig. 794).

Charles Trick Currelly, by Ashley and Crippen photographers, 1930s (ROM2008_9806_1)

Southwest mural of the ROM Armour Court (now Currelly Hall), depicting a 1475 jousting tournament, with museum staff as spectators. C.T. Currelly is the presiding noble, second from the right. Thomas F. McIlwraith is seated on his right. (ROM2004_1306_6)

Thomas F. McIlwraith (*right*) and Kenneth E. Kidd confer at the ROM excavation of Fort Ste Marie, 1941 (ROM RG140-09-0-2; ROM2018_16184_12)

Thomas F. McIlwraith photo of the middle-claim discovery trench, September 1937. The piece of paper fastened to the stick marks the height of the original overburden (ROM RG12.9.2.4; ROM2018_16184_3)

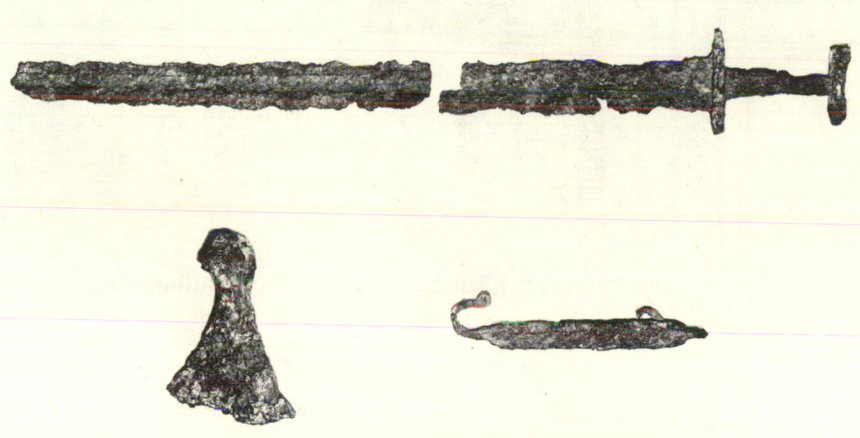

Official ROM photo of Beardmore sword, axe, and "shield handle," 1937 (black and white negative ROMA 1989; ROM2018_16184_4)

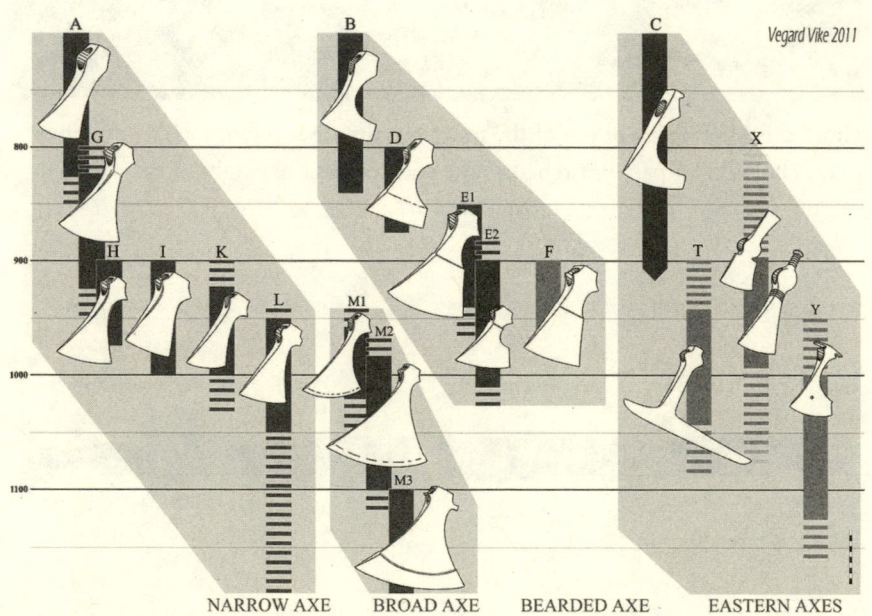

Viking axe types, according to the Petersen typology. The Beardmore axe conforms to the M1 type. (Courtesy Vegard A. Vike)

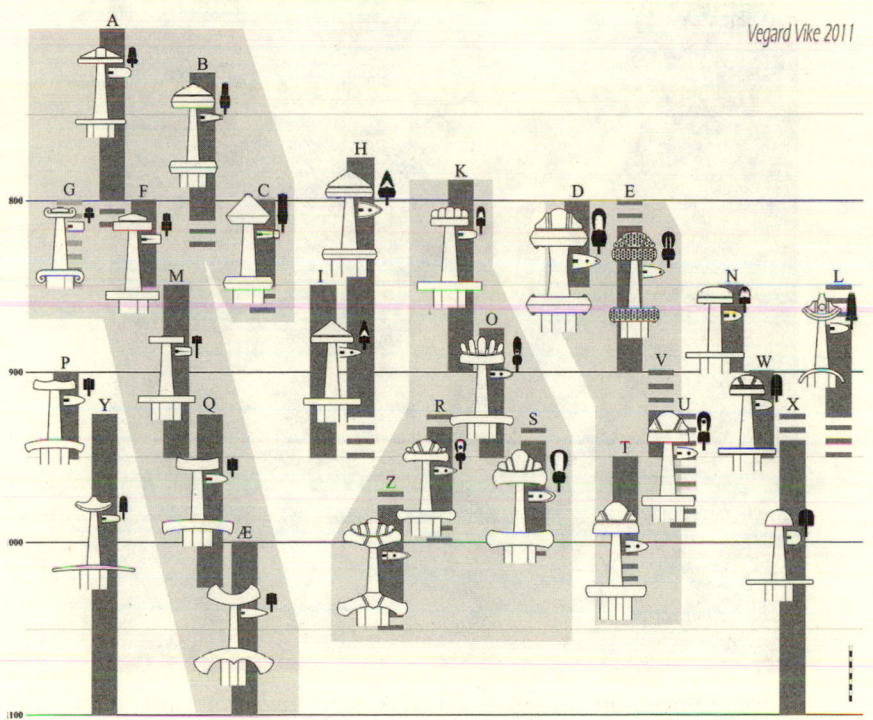

Viking sword types, according to the Petersen typology. The Beardmore sword conforms to the M type. (Courtesy Vegard A. Vike)

Anton Wilhelm Brøgger, 1935 (copyright 2017 Kulturhistorisk museum, UiO)

James W. "Jim" Curran (Trent University, James W. Curran fonds, Accession 74-0006, Box 1, Folder 57)

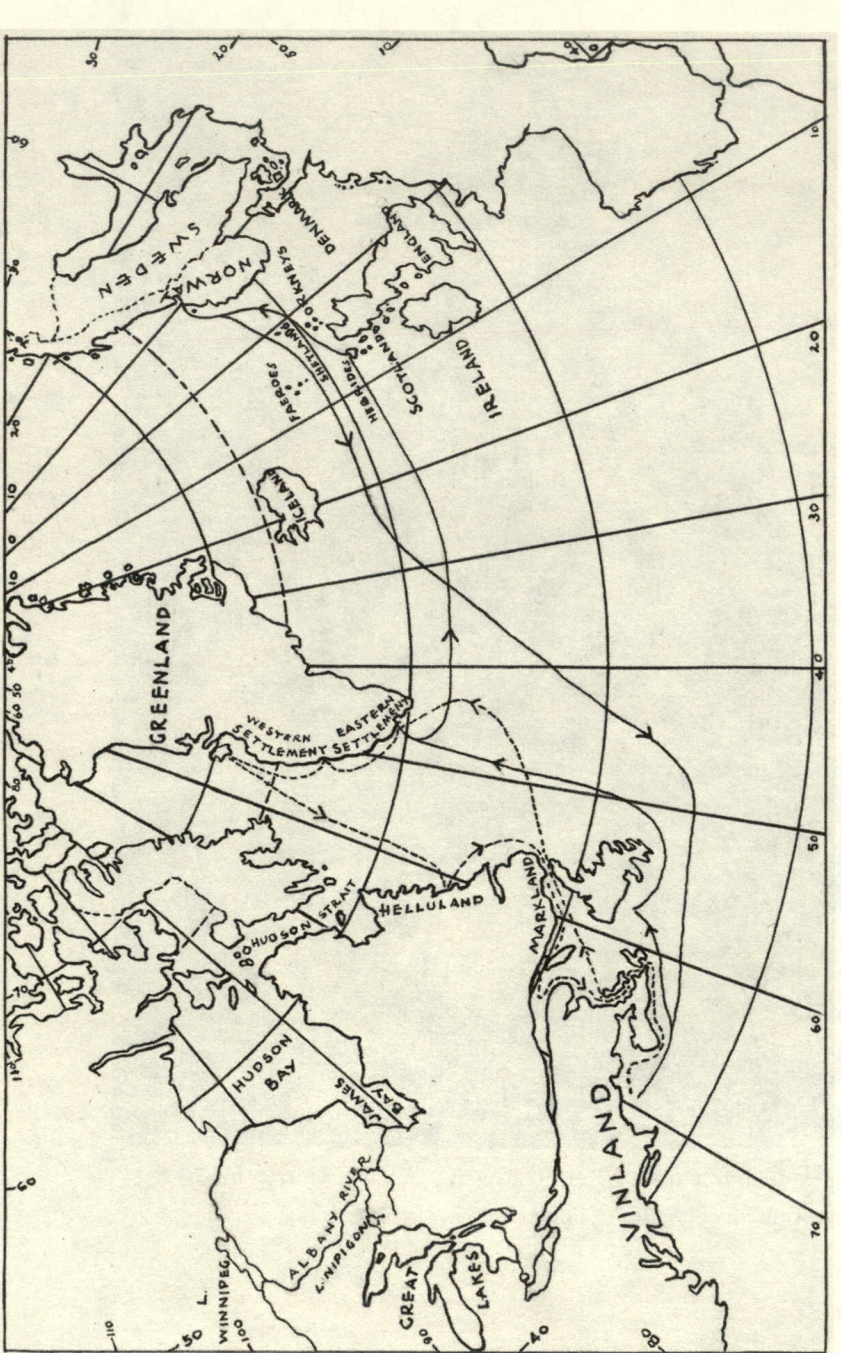

Ink drawing of a lantern slide used by C.T. Currelly in a lecture to teachers on 6 October 1938, "The Norse Sea Rovers." In addition to showing likely Viking exploration routes of the Atlantic seaboard, the map allowed Currelly to trace the presumed route of the Beardmore-relic Vikings across Hudson Strait, down Hudson Bay to James Bay, up the Albany River, and through portages to Lake Nipigon and the Beardmore River. (ROM RG12.9.2.4; ROM2018_16184_5)

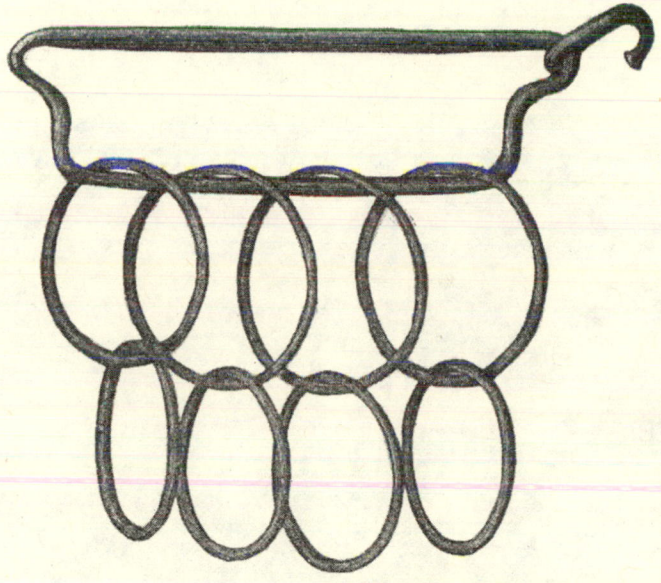

Ranglene (pagan sleigh rattle) illustration (fig. 50) in Petersen's *De Norske Vikingesverd*, which conforms to the Beardmore "shield handle."

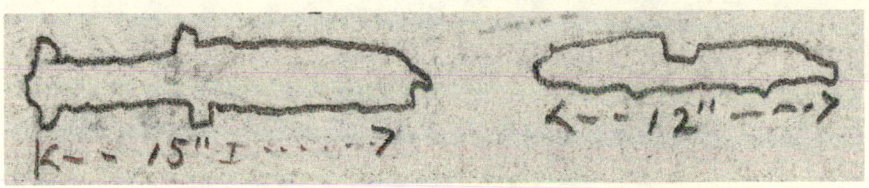

Sketch of the broken sword, in copy of a letter from Aaron Lougheed to T.L. Tanton, 22 April 1940, re: Dods Sword (ROM SC9, Box 1; ROM2018_16208_1)

T.L. Tanton (*left*) and James Hansen, Fort William, Ontario, 18 June 1940
(Courtesy family of James Hansen)

BEARDMORE

Introduction

Arms and armour no longer dominate the visitor experience at the Royal Ontario Museum (ROM) in Toronto. After the original 1914 building was greatly expanded from 1931 to 1933, visitors entering the museum through the new main entrance on Avenue Road passed through a stone rotunda, its barrel-vaulted ceiling decorated with Venetian glass and faux gilt paint. Stretching before them, beyond the stairwells housing two enormous totem poles, was the two-story spectacle of the Armour Court. Full suits of European armour stood as silent sentries amid displays of fierce weapons. Along with early gunpowder arms were swords, pikes, and halberds whose gleaming polish defied the brutal violence of battlefields. On the upper level of the far wall was a mural, created in the early 1940s by staff artist Sylvia Hahn, of a 1475 jousting tournament. Its two dozen faces depicted staff members, and none of them was more important than the presiding noble, Charles Trick Currelly, director of what was then known as the Royal Ontario Museum of Archaeology, the largest of the museum's five founding divisions.[1] Currelly was the institution's preeminent personality, from his hiring in 1906 (to accumulate artefacts for the envisioned public museum) until his retirement in 1946. Because of Currelly, and the generosity of Toronto industrialist Sigmund Samuel, a display dedicated to ancient implements of war dominated the visitors' experience on their arrival. "The arts of man through all the ages," as an inscription at the new museum entrance promised, on first glance seemed very bloody indeed.

All that changed in 1982, when the ROM completed its next significant expansion. The Armour Court still existed in physical fact, but the jousting mural was boarded over and not restored to view until 1997. The court was repurposed as a "theme" gallery called Mankind Discovering, designed to introduce visitors to the many interconnected riches of the museum. Some armour remained on display, but otherwise the terrible metal was packed off to more distant, less high-priority display spaces. Today, what was once the Armour Court and then the Mankind Discovering Gallery is a special-events space that, on Friday nights, features DJs, live music, drinks, and dancing. The European armour and weapons have been compressed into a surprisingly efficient space full of display cabinets on the third floor, as part of the Samuel (for Sigmund Samuel) European Galleries.

The tour of European weapons begins with a display case labelled "Europe in Conflict, 400–1100," which features four swords from the Norse Viking period.[2] At the bottom of the case, laid out horizontally on a shelf beneath a scene from the Bayeaux Tapestry depicting the Norman invasion of England in 1066, is a small and badly corroded example, broken in two, about thirty inches long. The sword is labelled "Steel blade," and "Distinctive Norwegian-type hilt," and is assigned the date range of 775 to 900. Above it is another badly corroded survival, a "Viking Battle Axe," with the label "Iron, of East Norwegian type, 900–1025." The axe head is paired with a sword that is heftier and in much better condition than the small, broken one – an intact steel blade with copper inlay on the hilt and dated, like the axe, to 900–1025 AD.

Museums are still fundamentally object-oriented. They gather, preserve, and display physical items according to what Steven Conn calls an "object-based" epistemology, a means of organizing and describing the world.[3] Presentation styles and technologies may have changed, but museums are still a place where, generally, physical objects are relics displayed in glass cabinets, visible but untouchable. A museum's interface between curatorial knowledge and public consumption takes the form of labels and other explanatory text, augmented perhaps by maps and other graphics and contextual imagery, video displays, and audio guides, but the interface can also include how objects are arranged and associated with one another. Basic display information conveys what are considered an object's necessary details: precisely what it is, its cultural affinity, its material(s), when it was made, and how it was used. (At least to a degree: nothing in this display case of Viking relics tells you what body parts were aimed at with these weapons, or what sort of fearful and messy damage they could do by cutting, thrusting, or whacking.)

History multiplies before your eyes as you examine the Viking weapons in the third-floor display case. When we consider the history of objects displayed in museums according to their history *as objects in museums*, we want to understand what a public interface consisting largely of text labels, crafted by curators, does not or cannot convey. I have already introduced elements of a history that is invisible to the casual visitor but that has a bearing on objects displayed: the history of the museum itself. Within that institutional history are multiple histories: of an institution's founding, expansion, funding, personnel, and its rationale as a place of research and education. Curators within this history make acquisition and display choices based on relative desirability or priority, the interests of private benefactors, and the sheer good luck of chance opportunities. And, over time, those priorities can change. Within institutions, the value and educative utility of certain objects rise and fall for myriad reasons. In the case of the Viking weapons, they have migrated from what was once a place of priority, the Armour Court, to a third-floor gallery. In the process, as this book explores, the broken sword and axe shed virtually all the history (at the level of public interface) that makes them extraordinary in the museum world. For decades, they were not on display at all. Objects that were once among the most notorious artefacts in any leading museum subsided into a kind of curatorial anonymity. Visitors literally have no idea what they are looking at. These objects have a history more recent, and even more compelling, than the unknowable history attached to their original use. It is a history that the museum display does not appear to tell, but there are hints within the labels.

In 1971, the provocative and sometimes controversial museum professional Duncan F. Cameron – who got his start in the museum field in 1956 as the ROM's publicity director and would have his own role in the story of the broken sword and the axe head above it – delivered an influential address in which he conceived of the public museum as a "temple" of truth. If an object was on display in a museum, the public accepted that "it was not only real but represented a standard of excellence. If the museum said that this and that was so, then that was a statement of truth."[4] The bedrock of truth for any museum object is an individual history called a provenance – a chain of possession as best as can be reconstructed. If that chain of possession is not unbroken from the date of an object's creation, then we at least trust that the institution knows when and how the object was acquired. If it was not unearthed before a staff archaeologist's eyes, then we hope a plausible history can account for its existence before the institution acquired it. The provenance can be its own window into a fascinating timeline of owners, fortunes, and misfortunes. Above all, provenance helps insulate an institution, scholars, and a trusting public against fakes.

Fakes, of necessity, involve fakery: an act of deception in creation or interpretation (or both). Malicious intention is what separates fakery from errors in scholarship, which can misidentify authentic objects, assigning them an incorrect purpose, culture, typology, or origin. When we think of fakes, we usually think of forgeries, but there are other, perhaps more insidious and dangerous, fakes: objects that are authentic as artefacts but inauthentic in how and where they were purportedly found. Authentic ancient Roman coins allegedly excavated on the bank of the Ohio River would have massive implications for the history of North America (not to mention of ancient Rome) if accepted as a genuine discovery. Similarly, if authentic Viking relics were said to have been unearthed in a grave in the wilds of northern Ontario, the history of North America and Norse voyaging would require a serious overhaul. Rewriting history at such a fundamental level would be a scholarly catastrophe if it proved to be based on a hoax that professionals had failed to detect – even worse, if they had defended the find against compelling contrary evidence and even aided and abetted the fraud. It would betray what Duncan Cameron argued was a public museum's responsibility "to admit to the things that are not known, are not understood, as well as to argue with confidence for those things that are held to be true and for those things that are the considered judgments of time."[5]

The typical curatorial information that is packaged for public consumption is not intended to convey the multilayered metahistories of historical objects as objects in museums. We cannot know the history of the object's display – of how its presentation has changed, in location and information. We may not be informed about how an object was acquired, and when, and why. Where was it excavated? Was it purchased from a dealer or a private collector? Who was involved in that acquisition? (These are questions for which the museum may not have answers.) Who decided over the years how it should be displayed and interpreted? Who wrote the current display label? In short, how has this object come to be in this place of display with this interpretation? And, over the years, how (if at all) has the interpretation influenced our understandings of history at various scholarly levels, from microhistories of individual lives to the longue durée of cultures and empires?

Beyond their presence in the same display case of Viking relics, there is nothing obvious to connect a small broken sword, dated 775–900, to an axe head above it, which is paired with another sword and dated 900–1025. But, by more closely examining the display case, we can start to suspect unelaborated histories. The labels do tell us that *something* must link these objects, beyond a general Viking provenance: the axe has accession number 936.55.2 and the broken sword has number 936.55.1 (the sword pieces are 936.55.1a and 936.55.1b), whereas the sword with which the axe is paired is 925.49.32.[6] The first three numbers refer to the accession year.[7] The accession number for the intact sword paired with the axe begins with 925 and so, according to the ROM system, was taken into inventory in 1925. The broken sword and axe were acquired eleven years later, in 1936. The broken sword and axe also share the same second set of numbers, 55, which means that they were part of a single acquisition, the fifty-fifth recorded by the ROM for that year. The final digits indicate that the sword was item one and that the axe was item two in that acquisition. We might rightly suspect that they were indexed in their order of perceived value, with the sword having been the more prized of the two objects. What we cannot know is that there was a third object acquired in that acquisition, 936.55.3, which was taken to be a shield handle but is nowhere on display. We do not know why this phantom third object was removed from display, let alone that it was once grouped with the broken sword and axe head in a place in the Armour Court so prominent that it inspired a Viking-themed wall mural in the space where children enrolled in the museum's Saturday-morning club gathered. Nor do we know that in storage with the once-celebrated shield handle are three small fragments of metal, labelled 936.55.1c-d-e, that came to the museum in 1937 and 1938, two of which were once on display and were thought to represent pieces of the shield handle and a shield boss.

Oddly, the labels for the broken sword and the axe give no indication of how they were discovered. In contrast, the label for an 800–900 sword in the display says: "Reportedly found in the River Seine, France," while the 900–1025 sword paired with the axe says: "Found in London, England." For some reason, there is an omitted provenance with two objects in this case that also happen to be linked by their accession codes. We don't know where they came from. We don't know how they got here.

I was intrigued by the provenance of the broken Viking sword and axe head long before I was aware they were even on display on the third floor of the ROM. I knew they had been removed from display in late 1956 (along with the other pieces mentioned), after almost twenty controversial years of public exhibition. I did not know they had gone back on display, probably in the late 1970s, denatured of their controversial provenance. While researching their acquisition in the museum's archives, I asked an employee where these objects could now be found. He told me he wasn't sure. I assumed they were somewhere deep in storage, and I didn't bother to check the current displays. The museum had recently found

an entire barosaurus skeleton in its architectural bowels, and I wondered
how much effort would be required to track down a few scraps of ancient
metal. In September 2015, I arrived early for a public lecture I was to give
at the museum on Samuel de Champlain, and I decided to tour the upper
galleries. There, in the cabinet of Viking relics on the third floor, I recognized immediately the broken sword and the axe head. They were hiding
in plain view before a public oblivious to their infamy.

These two survivals of Norse life, more than one thousand years old, in a
poor if presumably stable state of preservation, would not give a visitor to a
major Viking museum collection much pause. Even in the ROM, the small
broken sword hardly inspires the visceral shudders encouraged by the larger, later, bone-smashing broadswords nearby. But as a historian whose specialty is not Viking history but, rather, the history of history, or of ideas in
history, I was looking at two of the most significant objects in the annals of
museology, public history, and the conceptualization of the European "discovery" and colonization of the Americas. These were the Beardmore relics.
By then, I had learned enough from research in various archives and other
documentary sources to begin to untangle the complex provenance of the
broken sword and axe head, and to realize why they are so important to our
understanding of how history is shaped and presented, of how public history – the space occupied by popular writers, the general media, and museums devoted to public education – formulates and propagates ideas.

The story accepted as true by the Royal Ontario Museum when it acquired
the relics was that an itinerant prospector named James Edward ("Eddy")
Dodd found them after blasting a birch stump out of a trench on a mining claim near Beardmore, Ontario, on the east side of Lake Nipigon, north
of Lake Superior. Exactly when he found them – 1930? 1931? 1933? – would
be a fundamental issue in the authenticity case. In December 1936, Dodd
and his relics travelled eight hundred miles south to the ROM, home to one
of the world's leading archaeological collections. Dodd sold them for five
hundred dollars to Charles Trick Currelly, the renowned founding director
of the museum's dominant archaeology division and excavator of relics of
Egypt and Crete. From there, the Beardmore relics entered a wider world
of historical notoriety, school textbooks, and, ultimately, infamy.

Housed in a respected museum, the relics became Viking grave goods.
They satisfied a scholarly yearning, by then at least a century old, to

produce hard evidence that voyages described in the Vinland sagas and later records were more than legends and entertainments – that Vinland existed as surely as did Troy in the poems of Homer, that hardy Norse adventurers had set foot in the New World centuries before the arrival of early modern Europeans like Columbus, Cabot, and Verrazano. What is more, the Norse had not merely grazed Newfoundland or New England and made temporary settlements there on the voyages of Leif Eiriksson and Thorfinn Karlsefni, as most Vinland theorists argued, but had ventured deep into the heart of the continent. The relics immediately brought to mind a controversial discovery in Minnesota in 1898, the Kensington rune stone, which recounted a violent clash between a party of Christian Norsemen and Indigenous Americans in the fourteenth century. Together, the Beardmore relics and the Kensington stone became compelling proof that, for centuries, the Norse had been visiting the western Great Lakes region by sailing from Iceland or Greenland across Davis Strait, westward along Hudson Strait, then southward into Hudson Bay and James Bay. Using the rivers and lakes of the Laurentian Shield, Norsemen had made epic journeys inland. Some of them had carved the runic record in Minnesota. At least one of them, from a circa 1000 venture, had left behind his weapons, and presumably his body (dragged away by animals), in a grave on the east side of Lake Nipigon.

C.T. Currelly thought, with good reason, that the Beardmore relics were the greatest historical discovery in North America. They certainly were one of the greatest archaeological mysteries of the twentieth century. They engaged the curiosity and criticism of leading scholars in Canada, the United States, and Europe. They also brought a schoolteacher named O.C. (Teddy) Elliott a notoriety far beyond what he could ever have imagined, embroiling him in a controversy in which his adversaries were far above his professional station. Elliott had heard the prospector Eddy Dodd's discovery story in July 1934 and inspected the relics in Dodd's Port Arthur home in August 1936. In November 1936, Elliott alerted Currelly, who then eagerly bought them for the ROM. But after Currelly put the relics on display, Elliott's support of their authenticity turned dramatically and aggressively negative. For Elliott, in partnership with Thomas Leslie Tanton, a respected scientist with the Dominion Geological Survey of Canada, proving the Beardmore relics were fakes – or, more correctly, were authentic Norse relics that had been used to perpetrate a hoax – became a remarkable crusade involving amateur scholarship and detective work. Opposing them was Currelly, the hoax's outward victim, and his scholarly allies. Elliott and Tanton did what they could, but it would take a final push from Edmund Carpenter, a star anthropologist at the University of Toronto and the ROM, fifteen years after Elliott and Tanton retired from their investigation, to bring about the collapse of the Beardmore hoax.

In a hoax of this complexity, exercises of power make it difficult to distinguish the perpetrators from the victims. Foucauldian and Gramscian interpretations of how museums exercise coercive powers of the state, and organize public consent to these powers, have been explored by authors like Tony Bennett in *The Birth of the Museum* and Susan M. Pearce in *On Collecting* – and rejected by Steven Conn in *Museums and American Intellectual Life, 1876–1926*. One can argue that the ROM was flexing such powers in its collecting priorities and founding objectives (see chapter 4). But I am most interested in how the Beardmore story illustrates other exercises of power. The case for (and against) the authenticity of the Beardmore relics was not decided solely on objective facts. The dispute shows how institutional and professional power can function in ways that are unpleasantly counter to determining historical truths.

The Beardmore case involved issues of social class and professional status, both of which figure in the dynamics of power. C.T. Currelly had a complex personal relationship with class, and he framed the authenticity dispute along class lines. In his mind, it was a contest between, on the one hand, the discreditable testimonies of a drunk railway brakeman and a mentally unstable tradesman and, on the other hand, the unimpeachable evidence of his star witness to Eddy Dodd's find, John Jacob, a "government man" from a "good family" – despite abundant problems relating to Jacob's character and motivations. Edmund Carpenter became intrigued by the Beardmore case because of his interest in the 1953 collapse of British paleontology's "Piltdown Man" hoax, whose endurance for more than forty years he attributed in part to the class system. Duncan Cameron had scarcely begun his museum career as the ROM's publicity director when, in 1956, Carpenter revived the Beardmore scandal. The scandal is an unacknowledged personal trauma in Cameron's seminal 1971 address on public museums as "temples" of truth. Public museums, Cameron argued, were shrines of authenticity overseen by a new class of elites – curators – who took over from wealthy private collectors as society's arbiters of what is real and what is true. Currelly was the foremost member of that elite class in Canada and was backed by the wealth of private donors in acquiring what he desired and declared to be real and true. For the elites who defended the relics, the lower-class status of Dodd – a desperately poor railway man with an unrecognized reputation for low-grade cons and thievery – became an argument for their authenticity: he was too simple and uncultured a man to have pulled off a hoax that could fool the likes of Currelly, who never failed to remind people how trained he was in spotting fakes.

Where professional status is concerned, there were complex tensions (and alliances) between scholarly "insiders" and avocational "outsiders" as well as within the scholarly world. A centre of academic authority like the conjoined institutions of the University of Toronto (especially Victoria College) and the ROM enjoyed considerable control of historical discourse in Canada, far beyond anything possible today. That control was exercised through internal hierarchies of authority; the gatekeeping of a scholarly journal like the *Canadian Historical Review* (CHR), published by University of Toronto Press; and the innumerable levers that could be pulled through constricted professional networks, including positions of power and influence within the Royal Society of Canada (RSC). The general media were complicit in enabling this power by deferring to institutional and individual authority, refusing to run articles or letters to the editor that questioned the museum's purchase (routinely, it seems, by seeking and heeding Currelly's advice). Such was the scope of Currelly's influence that the artefacts remained on prominent display in the museum for ten years after his retirement in 1946, altering the historical relationship between Europe and North America all the while. Exercises of power to defend a scholarly position (and reputation) ultimately became mechanisms to maintain that power.

The power exercised in defence of the Beardmore acquisition went largely unchallenged within a scholarly world that was, at best, collegially deferential. At worst, for a myriad of personal, professional, and institutional reasons, that world was loath to give offence. Despite misgivings, no professional historian or archaeologist in Canada was willing to publicly question the ROM's claim of having found a Viking grave in northern Ontario, leaving the debunking of the hoax to a vocational high school teacher and a government geologist.

Elliott and Tanton's struggle to expose the hoax was all uphill. Scholarly opinions were so conflated with reputation that, where the Beardmore relics were concerned, open exchanges of opinion in the pursuit of historical truth were impossible. The University of Toronto's chief librarian, Stewart Wallace, a Currelly ally, perfectly expressed this dysfunctional state in Canadian letters by conveying Currelly's objections to the paper that Elliott was about to present at the RSC's annual meeting in May 1940. As Wallace explained to the secretary of the RSC's Section 2, Currelly "naturally regards the paper as an attack on the Royal Ontario Museum and its management, since the Museum has bought the relics and vouches for their authenticity."[8] Wallace's actions in the Beardmore case demonstrate how scholarly authority can metastasize into abuse of authority when the power afforded to professional hierarchies and networks goes unchallenged.

Only in the mid-1950s would a scholar who was willing to publicly challenge the Beardmore find finally emerge. Ironically, anthropologist Edmund Carpenter was from within the University of Toronto and the ROM, but because he was an American who was not a product of either of those institutions, he was also an outlier. Even after the hoax had collapsed completely (at least to any impartial observer) in 1956–57, the museum continued, for at least a decade, to cling to the possibility of the find's authenticity. In 1961, after returning to the United States, Carpenter lambasted former colleagues at the university and the ROM for committing a multitude of alleged archaeological frauds, the Beardmore find foremost among them, and accused them of succumbing to the corruption of "identification with institutional power." He charged that museum staff privately admitted to him that the discovery was a fraud but were compelled to defend it publicly out of loyalty to the museum and its leading figures.

While various writers and scholars have remarked upon the Beardmore controversy, the full scope of the documentary record has never been explored. Most accounts rely on O.C. Elliott's article in the *CHR* of September 1941 (with its rebuttal by C.T. Currelly) and Robert Olson's article in *Maclean's* magazine of 13 April 1957. Neither writer had access to all the documents available today, which extend beyond the considerable trove of materials available in the ROM archives (which include Elliott's papers, donated in 1972) and in files elsewhere in the museum. Missing from standard accounts altogether, for example, is the critical personal relationship between Eddy Dodd and J.W. (Jim) Curran, a Sault Ste Marie newspaper publisher whose papers, housed in the Trent University Archives, document how Curran's investigations upheld the authenticity of Dodd's find and show how he propagandized the idea of a Norse presence in the Great Lakes, to the gratitude of Currelly. Other archival sources, including the papers of the indefatigable advocate for the Kensington stone, Hjalmar Holand, and of the arctic explorer, author, and anthropologist Vilhjalmur Stefansson, fill in key behind-the-scenes roles of an array of well-known and lesser-known figures and scholars. The cast of characters from both sides of the Atlantic that emerge in the documentary record include the American Peruvianist Philip Ainsworth Means; Langdon Warner of Harvard's Fogg Museum; an array of eminent Scandinavian archaeologists, including Norwegian colleagues A.W. Brøgger and Sigurd Grieg; the editors of *Antiquity* and the *Geographical Journal*; and a *Who's Who* of scholars of Scandinavian studies. On the Canadian front, an impressive roll-call of scholars and academics is drawn into the controversy: Lawrence J. Burpee, Harold Innis, Donald Creighton, Stewart Wallace, James Kenney, William Kaye Lamb, Reginald Trotter, Thomas McIlwraith, William Wintemberg, Diamond Jenness, and George Brown, editor of the CHR, to name a few. The Beardmore story tells us much (not all of it pretty) about how, particularly during the late 1930s and early 1940s, scholarship and academia functioned through personal relationships and professional organizations like the Canadian Historical Association and the Royal Society of Canada. The story also makes us ask if such a hoax could happen today.

The Beardmore story is complex, and not because the hoax was a sophisticated crime – it was not. Teddy Elliott, in his final analysis, suspected Eddy Dodd never set out to perpetrate a hoax on the museum – or on any other potential purchaser of the relics – and there may be much value in this conclusion. In striving to disentangle the case, I have benefited from almost an embarrassment of primary materials, including literally thousands of pages of vital correspondence, which renders the scandal both unusually well documented and difficult to condense. The story as I tell it involves an ever-growing cast of characters. The hoax is elusive, if undeniable, but there is no definitive explanation of how it transpired. There may have been more than one set of relics, or at least more than one broken sword. Most of the evidence is circumstantial, relying on personal recollections. It is a story of stories, and those stories kept changing. Witnesses were unreliable, their motivations sometimes inscrutable, and, not infrequently, they were lying. The case against the authenticity of Dodd's find depended on testimony that was as fallible, sometimes as incoherent, and sometimes as deceitful, as that of Dodd and his supporters. Few people in the Beardmore case *ever* told the truth consistently. Even when people were *trying* to be truthful, their memories failed them. The relics also factored in the mysterious disappearance of one key figure in the controversy, another committed suicide, and I believe the scandal's dramatic unravelling brought on the death of Currelly, who was as cursed by the Beardmore find as was anyone who had disturbed Tut's tomb.

It is impossible to summarize the Beardmore case as a set of facts for and facts against; this is because the facts kept changing and, in many instances, never crystallized into an indisputable form. A fact as elemental as *when* Eddy Dodd came upon the relics is open to debate. The only way to understand and learn from the Beardmore case is to approach it as narrative, as a detective story – to watch it unfold and to appreciate how the discovery story was shaped and reshaped, how individuals on both sides of the authenticity argument responded to evidence and to each other.

This process of understanding is the most informative aspect of delving into the Beardmore case. In a way, the Beardmore story is not about Viking relics nearly as much as it is about the evolution of scholarship on Vinland and Norse voyages, including scholarly responses to the Kensington stone and the Newport Tower. The sword, the centrepiece of the Beardmore relics, is what Alfred Hitchcock calls the "maguffin," the plot device that sets the story rolling. It is the Maltese Falcon of a museum scandal that exposed the behaviours of an array of characters in the scholarly world, in popular media, and in the ranks of ordinary people struggling to survive during the crushing 1930s Depression.

Some people may have believed the Beardmore story well past the point of reasonable doubt: in 1957, Carpenter argued that accepting Dodd's find after 1938 required "a naiveté beyond the capacity of ordinary minds."[9] While much of the case against Dodd's find had difficulty holding water, there was also much about Currelly's response to the relics that, from the day of their acquisition, indicates a determination to believe in them and to eschew normal avenues of inquiry and verification. Worse, Currelly began manipulating the provenance evidence within weeks of the purchase and otherwise withheld key components from the public.

The Beardmore scandal had something of the quality of a runaway train, answerable only to its own irresistible momentum, impossible to stop once it had gathered a sufficient head of steam. But the fact was that people who could have stopped it had no interest in doing so, or at least believed that it could not be stopped unless they threw themselves under its wheels. Charles Trick Currelly not only did not attempt to stop it, he actively stoked its engine from the moment he heard its siren-like whistle emanating from Ontario's northern wilds. He rode it, with haughty, defiant bravado, right into the final, fatal curve. It's best that we now board it, when it was still on the tracks and two of its key figures were first brought together.

PART ONE

1

The Middle Claim

On the hot summer night of 16 July 1934, a Canadian National Railways (CNR) train clattering through the boreal gloom of northern Ontario was brought to a sharp halt about four miles southwest of the whistle stop of Beardmore Station, on the east side of Lake Nipigon. There was a fire on the track. Someone had lit a pile of newspaper to interrupt the train's run to Port Arthur, the CNR grain port at the head of the Great Lakes, at Thunder Bay on Lake Superior, some 120 miles down the track to the southwest. The engineer understood this makeshift signal and stopped the steam locomotive long enough to allow a man labouring under an enormous packsack to clamber aboard one of the day coaches.

The new passenger was stocky, about five and a half feet tall, forty-nine years old, and prematurely silver-haired. "Mind if I slip in here, buddy?" he asked a balding, thirty-five-year-old schoolteacher of about the same height. "Make yourself at home," replied the teacher, who was travelling alone. He helped the newcomer store the packsack on the luggage rack.[1]

The teacher's full name was Otho Christopher Elliott, but everyone called him Teddy and he was otherwise formally known by his initials, O.C. His new travel companion was James Edward – usually Eddy, sometimes Jimmy – Dodd. Eddy Dodd worked for the CNR when the jobs were there, which was not always the case during the hard times of the Depression. Dodd was fond of telling stories, and he told them to all sorts of people in all sorts of places, the beverage room of the Mariaggi Hotel in downtown Port Arthur being a favourite spot. As the train resumed its spine-jarring run through a night-shrouded forest, the two men relieved the fidgeting discomfort of the bench seats with a wide-ranging conversation. They were two very different people, but they could find common ground in at least two subjects: their experiences in the Canadian army during the First World War and their interests in prospecting for mineral wealth.

James Edward Dodd was baptized in 1885 at Portage du Fort, Quebec, on the upper Ottawa River, the fifth of eight children in a family of Irish Catholic heritage. Like two of his brothers, Eddy found work in the railways. In January 1916, when Dodd was a month shy of his thirty-first birthday and employed at Rainy River as a CNR brakeman, he enlisted in the 94th Overseas Battalion, formed the previous October to receive volunteers from northwestern Ontario. On arrival in England the 94th was broken up. Dodd was sent to France in late August, and after a few days with the 2nd Entrenching Battalion he was taken on strength by the 28th (Northwest) Battalion, which included other men from Port Arthur. Whatever tales Dodd might have told of his war experience were never written down, but he probably served as a labourer as he also spent some time assigned to the Royal Engineers in November 1917. Other than a good conduct badge received on 1 January 1918 (and two instances of having his pay docked before he got overseas), Dodd's record would reveal nothing about his experiences of the front, but he was on hand for some of the war's most brutal episodes. For about twenty months, Private Dodd was with the 28th as it saw action in a string of major engagements, from the Somme to Vimy Ridge to Passchendaele.[2]

In late April 1918, as the 28th was preparing to relieve the 26th in the front lines south of Arras, Dodd was evacuated by field ambulance to the No. 5 general hospital in Rouen, where he was diagnosed with PUO – pyrexia (fever) of an unknown origin – and general myalgia, or muscle pain. It was the end of Dodd's frontline service. He moved through an assortment of hospitals before at last being assigned to Camp Bramshott in Hampshire. His diagnosis expanded to include DAH (disordered action of the heart) and wheezing in the chest. A medical officer's assessment in Camp Bramshott on 22 October 1918 portrayed an all but broken man. "Patient states he was healthy prior to enlistment … states breath has been short and he has had a smothering sensation when lying down for last 6 months." Dodd was only thirty-three, but the officer noted he "looks much over forty years of age – hair quite grey, and face drawn, as if he had endured considerable hardship." Dodd would always look much older than his years. "No visible swelling of joints or muscles, but the long bones are very sensitive to the least pressure. There is a decided grating sensation in knee joints on manipulation. Knee jerk accentuated. All movts normal but very laboured." His resting pulse was an elevated 128, and the medical officer judged his arterial walls thickened. He was not fit for duty in the field but could serve on base in training.

The war by then was all but over. On 1 November, Dodd was granted permission to marry, and a week after the 11 November armistice he travelled some 150 miles north to Birmingham to take as his bride Ellen (Helena) Palmer, from North Budley, Wales, who was about twenty-four; they had probably met while he was hospitalized in Birmingham in May 1918. Ellen Palmer had agreed to marry a man with serious, chronic health problems whose ability to support a family must have been in doubt. She would prove to be fiercely loyal.

Dodd and his bride sailed for Canada in January 1919; their first daughter, Margaret, was baptized in November 1919, in Bristol, a village near Portage du Fort in the Pontiac region of Quebec, where Dodd had grown up. Eddy and Ellen soon relocated to Port Arthur, where a second daughter, Helena (Leona), was baptized in January 1921. Soon after, a son, Walter, who was born about 1917, was adopted by the Dodds around the age of five.[3] Eddy managed to resume his railway work as well as part-time prospecting, which had first engaged him before the war, but it is probable that he never fully recovered the health he had once enjoyed. He was old before his time, with physical labour that pained him being his only option for keeping his family afloat during the Depression. The heavy packsack he had slung aboard the day coach, a physical manifestation of his last opportunity to find some comfort in life, was a burden a younger man would have had difficulty bearing.

Teddy Elliott had a much different résumé and war experience. Born in 1898, he was the son of a prominent Baptist preacher (also named O.C. Elliott) who had moved his family around southern Ontario, from Teddy's birthplace of Peterborough to Belleville to St Thomas and finally to Toronto. Elliott had enlisted in the Canadian Overseas Expeditionary Force in St Thomas in May 1918 after finishing his first year of theology studies at his father's alma mater, the Baptist university, McMaster, which was then affiliated with the University of Toronto and located on the west side of the new Royal Ontario Museum. Elliott had military roots: his father was born in 1867 in the barracks at Kingston, Ontario, where his own parents lived as part of the British garrison following the Crimean War.[4] On enlistment, Teddy Elliott asserted he had tried to join the Royal Air Force – the No. 4 School of Military Aeronautics had begun cadet training at the University of Toronto in 1917 – but had been turned down because of his eyesight. The British Empire insinuated itself into the Russian Revolution, and, as a private with the 11th Stationary Hospital, Elliott served with the Canadian Siberian Expeditionary Force (CSEF) in Vladivostok. The CSEF saw little action, and Elliott returned to Canada in May 1919 to complete his studies at McMaster, serve as the athletics editor of the university's monthly student publication, and sit on the executive of the intercollegiate debating union. Elliott then trained at the Ontario College of Education and landed his first teaching job in Fort William, the Canadian Pacific port and rail terminus in Thunder Bay on the west side of Port Arthur. He also had enjoyed a spell as a cub reporter at the *Globe and Mail*, where an uncle was an editor, and, for a few years in the early 1930s, he kept a hand in journalism by writing a short weekly advice column for parents ("Chats with a Teacher") in that newspaper.[5]

Teddy Elliott oversaw the commercial department at Fort William's high school. He met Lillian Catherine (Kate) Jarvis, the daughter of a local railway switchman, who had graduated from nursing school in 1927. Teddy and Kate married in 1928, in a ceremony in Teddy's parents' living room in the Toronto suburb of Etobicoke, presided over by Teddy's father. The couple then moved to Hamilton, where Teddy taught at Westdale Secondary School, two blocks from their house in the new Hamilton suburb of Westdale, which had taken root around McMaster when the university relocated there in 1930. The couple returned to the Thunder Bay area every summer to visit with Kate's extended family.[6]

Teddy Elliott and Eddy Dodd might have had much to share about medical care in the military, but they otherwise talked about the world of railways, and about prospecting, as these were subjects on which Dodd could hold forth without end. When Dodd wasn't employed by the CNR he prospected for gold, as so many men in northwestern Ontario had taken to doing. Since 1925, Dodd had been working several claims off and on near Beardmore. Setting some newspaper alight had secured him a ride home to Port Arthur from his latest visit to the claims. Elliott never mentioned in any recollections of his dealings with Eddy Dodd that he, too, had been bitten by the gold bug. He was prospecting (and otherwise enjoying the outdoors) in the area of the 1917 strike at Little Longlac (Kenogamisis Lake), in a partnership that included the local CNR telegraph agent Jack Gervais. He was on his way back from Little Longlac, about sixty-five miles east of where Dodd had boarded the train, to rejoin his wife at the Lakehead. In 1933, a company had finally been organized to exploit the 1917 Little Longlac find, and a shaft was dug to two levels in 1934, but Elliott never enjoyed prospecting success. By 1939, his Little Longlac claims would be owned by a company called Jowato Gold.[7]

According to Elliott, for no other reason than to keep the conversation flowing, he asked Dodd: "Did you ever find anything strange in your claims?" The button that was waiting to be pushed had been engaged. As Elliott would recall, Dodd's blue eyes looked straight into his own. "Strange that you should ask me that, young fellow."

In February 1934, five months before Teddy Elliott met Eddy Dodd on the train, Dodd happened upon Edward Moore Jackson Burwash on the streets of Port Arthur. For someone like Dodd, "Ned" Burwash was a leading authority on wealth buried in the ground. Burwash was sixty-one years old, four years from retirement as a geologist with Ontario's Department of Mines. He specialized in the rocks of the Laurentian Shield, which were yielding vast profits in gold, silver, platinum, cobalt, nickel, copper, and other metallic and non-metallic minerals, and were attracting investment capital from around the world. Burwash had long been a prospecting celebrity. In 1896, freshly equipped with a master's degree from the University of Toronto (he would also earn a doctorate from the University of Chicago in 1915), Burwash was hired by Ontario's Bureau of Mines. Scouring the land in Shaw Township in the Porcupine District, about 140 miles north of Sudbury, Burwash found traces of gold in quartz veins. For a time, after a gold rush swept the area in 1909, the Porcupine District was the largest gold producer in the world.[8]

From 1905 to 1915, Ned Burwash was a professor of natural science at Columbian Methodist College in New Westminster, British Columbia, which was affiliated with the University of Toronto's Victoria College and was a forerunner of the University of British Columbia (UBC). After serving as a Canadian army chaplain in the First World War, he taught at UBC and the University of Manitoba in the 1920s. He was thereafter known as Professor Burwash and, in 1927, began running the prospecting schools of Ontario's Department of Mines.[9] Burwash roamed the province between November and April, visiting as many as sixteen communities, equipped with 250 mineral specimens and an array of lantern slides for his eight-day course. Port Arthur was home to Thunder Bay District's mining registry office and hosted one of Burwash's best-attended schools. In 1934, between 14 January and 1 February, Burwash held two sessions of classes, in Port Arthur and Fort William, before heading west to Kenora for a session. He was back in Port Arthur on 13 February and was about to depart by train to his next session, in the mining centre of Haileybury, when he ran into Dodd.

Dodd had staked three adjoining Beardmore claims in 1925, two years before Burwell took charge of the prospecting course.[10] Dodd may have continued to attend classes into the 1930s, and he was otherwise a fixture of the local prospecting community as, by now, he had worked two of the claims a few miles down the track from Beardmore Station for almost nine years. Unfortunately, Dodd's energies had yielded nothing of mineral promise. His desire to strike pay dirt was now being driven by a combination of the hard times of the Depression and a gold price that had leapt overnight, two weeks before Dodd and Burwash met on the street. American monetary policy had caused the unprecedented spike in the value of gold. Burwash was wrapping up his prospector's classes in Fort William on 30 January 1934, when the United States reinstated the gold standard it had suspended in April 1933. The Gold Reserve Act raised the official gold price overnight by almost 70 percent, from \$20.67 to \$35.00.[11]

Thunder Bay District was already one of mining's investment hotspots. A 1921 geological map for the lands explored along the CNR route from the Sturgeon River westward to Lake Nipigon, when updated in 1934, featured Xs across the Beardmore area. Every X, like a mark on a treasure map, denoted a gold discovery. One such X being aggressively exploited was just east of Beardmore Station. In 1933, the Northern Empire mines operation sank a shaft an additional 350 feet and made numerous improvements. Already, an average of fifty-six men had jobs there, twenty-two of them underground.[12] This period also saw the Little Longlac discovery of 1917 at last enter production, which gave rise to the boom town of Geraldton, incorporated in 1937.[13] These mines were either mocking Dodd's long-standing efforts to cash in on this mineral bonanza or were extending the tantalizing hope of his finding an X of his own to place on the geology map. Mining, especially gold mining, was one of the few bright spots in a bleak Depression economy. Canada's gross national product had fallen by more than half between 1929 and 1933. The official unemployment rate was almost 20 percent in 1933, but actual joblessness was more like 32 percent. The economic crisis was exacerbated by drought on the southern Prairies, which created a net outmigration of a quarter-million people between 1931 and 1941. The collapse in grain production had a knock-on effect on the railways and Great Lakes shipping, the industries essential to the prosperity of Fort William and Port Arthur.[14]

Men like Eddy Dodd were struggling to find or hold steady employment and avoid the quasi-voluntary last resort of reporting to the relief camps that had sprung up in the bush across northern Ontario, where they could build aerodromes for twenty cents a day. But hard times for railway men had set in long before the Depression. When the federal government merged the assets of the Grand Trunk Railway and the Canadian Northern Railway to create the Canadian National Railways in 1923, most of the Canadian Northern facilities in Port Arthur were closed. Two years later, Dodd had begun his prospecting while securing whatever railway work he could. Holding on to a claim meant, every six months, filing a report that met ministry milestones totalling two hundred eight-hour days of labour over a five-year period. Keeping a claim active required time, personnel, and money.

Dodd was carrying a custom-made wood case when Burwash met him on the street in mid-February 1934. The provincial geologist might have expected to see quartzite chunks flecked with promises of gold. But Dodd was hauling around a different sort of buried treasure: three badly corroded pieces of metal. Dodd agreed to bring the items to Burwash's room at the CNR's Prince Arthur Hotel. What Burwash saw and heard compelled him to contact Charles Trick Currelly, director of the Royal Ontario Museum of Archaeology.

The social strata of Canada were so shallow and broad as to make it improbably easy for an itinerant prospector like Eddy Dodd in Port Arthur to be linked to an internationally renowned museum director like Charles Trick Currelly, some eight hundred miles away in Toronto. Ned Burwash provided that connection.

Where some men monitored the province's hinterlands as part-time scouts for professional hockey teams, Ned Burwash practised a more specialized bird-dogging. While executing his geologist's duties, he kept an eye peeled for items that might belong in the ROM, including whatever might intrigue C.T. Currelly, the first and only director of its largest division, archaeology. The two men had been close friends since meeting in high school at Toronto's Harbord Collegiate. Together they had attended Victoria College, the Wesleyan Methodist institution at the University of Toronto overseen by Burwash's father, Nathanael. Ned Burwash proved to be a doppelganger of his celebrated father, sporting the same style of beard and pursuing the same dual career in theology and natural sciences. (At Columbian Methodist College, Ned had investigated Pleistocene volcanism while also delivering sermons and publishing *The New Theology* in 1910.) Chancellor Nathanael Burwash, Victoria College, and Methodism figured significantly in Currelly's early career and his rise to the museum directorship (see chapter 4). At this point, it is important to appreciate how closely knit the Burwash and Currelly worlds were. Beyond their personal connections, Burwash worked for a provincial ministry, and Ontario's legislature and bureaucracy were centred in Queen's Park in the heart of Toronto. At the northwest edge of Queen's Park was the ROM, which, as a division of the University of Toronto, answered to the Ministry of Education, and that made Currelly a civil servant of sorts. Created by an act of the legislature in 1912 as five museums under one roof, dedicated to archaeology, paleontology, mineralogy, zoology, and geology, each division had its own director, and they were all University of Toronto professors. Cross-postings at the university and the museum were routine for professors and curators until the two institutions were formally separated in 1955 (indeed, the practice continues today). Government, museum, and university thus were firmly interconnected and within short walking distance of each other.

The Royal Ontario Museum(s) had just completed a major two-year expansion, reopening in October 1933 after closing entirely in March 1932. After meeting with Eddy Dodd at the Prince Arthur Hotel on 13 February 1934, Burwash thought Dodd might have something to enliven the display cases in the museum's new Armour Court, which connected the new east wing to the original west wing in the renovation's H-shaped plan. Burwash telephoned Currelly after the meeting, before departing on the train for Haileybury. The following day, 14 February, Burwash committed what he had seen and learned from Dodd to four pages of hotel letterhead he had taken with him from Port Arthur.[15]

As Burwash explained, Dodd had found the items in his case about three years earlier on a mining claim, 48TB4895, that he had staked about five miles east of Lake Nipigon. Burwash did not elaborate, but this was Dodd's "middle claim" as it lay between two other claims he had first staked in 1925. Having dynamited clear an old birch stump about fifteen inches in diameter, Dodd had begun excavating an underlying gravel bed that may have been deposited in some distant age when the course of a nearby stream ran there. Three feet down, Dodd discovered the three objects, arranged as Burwash drew them.

At the top was an axe head that Burwash indicated was five inches long, its blade facing left. In the middle was an odd length of metal, seven or eight inches long, with hooks on both ends, that was the handle of a shield. Burwash's drawing placed this piece of metal in the middle of a dashed ellipse, which represented what Dodd said was a small shield about one foot in diameter. The shield fell to pieces as Dodd attempted to remove it, as it was nothing more than a layer of rust; Burwash would later recall Dodd's telling him that he was left with only the handle in his hand as he pulled.[16] Dodd ventured to Burwash that the dynamite blast must have shaken it up. At the bottom of the page was a simple sword, two and a half feet long. The sword Burwash inspected was in two pieces, but he drew it with an intact blade.

Burwash thought Dodd would agree to send the items to the museum for inspection. He reported that Dodd had already been offered fifty dollars by an unnamed engineer. Burwash assured Currelly that Dodd didn't know the price of such things. "From researches made by himself & a friend in the public library here," Burwash advised, "he believes the material to be norse."

Exactly when and how Eddy Dodd became aware his relics might be Norse lies in a tangle of observations and recollections that involved two men in the Thunder Bay area: Aaron Lougheed and John Drew Jacob.

Aaron Lougheed was an enigmatic, elusive character. Born in 1863 in Heathcote, a small community on Ontario's Bruce Peninsula, Lougheed worked with construction engineers on the Canadian Pacific Railway (CPR) line north of Lake Superior in 1883. He was certified as an Ontario land surveyor in 1888 and opened a practice in Port Arthur in 1890. The expansion of Port Arthur kept him busy with subdivision surveys, and, on the side, he pursued gold prospecting, which, in 1902, seems to have taken him all the way to British Columbia and California. In 1913, he sold his surveying practice. Never marrying, he began a quasi-retirement of almost forty years.[17]

Lougheed was associated with two prominent Port Arthur families, Ruttan and Bolduc, that would figure in the Beardmore relics story. The Ruttan family originated in Cobourg, Ontario, and two brothers, Robert A. (a former secretary to the premier of Manitoba) and Walter S. (who had started out as an engineer) became involved in real estate in Port Arthur at the turn of the twentieth century. In 1909, the Ruttans built the two-story Ruttan Building, also known as the Ruttan Block, which anchored Port Arthur's civic affairs and repeatedly surfaced as a locale in the Beardmore case.[18] Lougheed formed a long-standing relationship with Walter S. Ruttan and Leonidas (Leo) Bolduc, who were partners in real estate as well as in a mortgage and insurance brokerage business. One of the properties Ruttan Estates managed was a home on 296 Wilson that was occupied by Eddy Dodd at a crucial moment in the Beardmore story. Over the years, Lougheed, Ruttan, and Bolduc either shared an office in the Ruttan

Building or occupied spaces next door to each other.[19] Leo Bolduc's younger brother, Joseph, would figure in the Beardmore story as an engineer overseeing prospecting claims in the local mining record office. Their brother Adolphe, a railway conductor who died in 1915, would also figure tangentially in the story.[20]

After selling his surveying business, Lougheed busied himself with two incongruous passions: prospecting and socialism. Lougheed surveyed claims for prospectors, and he could have marked out Dodd's Beardmore claims in July 1925. He developed a reputation for radical politics that extended well beyond the Thunder Bay District. Hewlett Johnson, the dean of Canterbury who was known as the "red bishop" for his Marxist views, purportedly made a point of travelling to Port Arthur to meet Lougheed during one of his visits to Canada, even though Lougheed had no known affiliation with the Anglican Church – he gave his religion as "agnostic" in the 1921 census.[21] Lougheed's politics must have been a source of controversy within the Ruttan ranks. Colonel Henry A. Ruttan, who joined his uncles Robert and Walter in business in Port Arthur, was a First World War veteran who, in 1930, resuscitated the local militia unit, the Lake Superior Regiment, amid rising fears of Communism.[22]

John Drew Jacob – known to his friends as Jack – may have shared Aaron Lougheed's philosophical enthusiasms. In July 1940, Harry Beeman, a prominent Fort William lawyer who said he knew Jacob well, would advise C.T. Currelly that the museum's key witness in the Dodd find "was a sort of dreamer [who] had most unusual views on many subjects, including politics and religion." Born in 1881, John Drew Jacob was the son of a barrister in the agricultural mill town of Elora in southwestern Ontario. His middle name came from prominent relations, the Drews. His uncle, Judge George Alexander Drew, was the grandfather of a namesake lawyer who was made master of the Ontario Supreme Court in 1929, chair of the Ontario Securities Commission in 1931, and leader of the Conservative Party of Ontario in 1938; George A. Drew would serve as both premier and as minister of education from 1943 to 1948.[23]

John Drew Jacob did not follow in the legal footsteps of his father, John Charles Jacob, and so many Drew relatives. He arrived in Thunder Bay District no later than 1904, apparently after teaching school in northern Minnesota. In 1907, in Port Arthur, he married Edith Chambers, whom he had known from childhood and whose father, a cooper, had decided to leave Elora to try homesteading in O'Connor Township, on the west side of Thunder Bay District, at some point after 1901. John and Edith were burned out of their first homestead farm, and the 1921 census found them on their second farm in the township, raising four children, ages three to eleven; two more children would follow.[24]

Jacob's reputation in the eyes of the ROM was burnished by his close association with a prominent birder and leading Port Arthur citizen, Lionel Sextus Dear. An accountant by training, L.S. Dear managed the local brewery, the Port Arthur Beverage Company. Born in England in 1883, Dear had arrived in the Lakehead area in 1905.[25] He was not a large man, standing five feet, six inches, but he spent most of his adult life as a military leader, after being certified in October 1905 as a sergeant with the local militia unit, the 96th Lake Superior Regiment (LSR).[26] Dear was a captain with the LSR when he enlisted in the Canadian Overseas Expeditionary Force in January 1915. He was sickened by gas at Ypres in April 1915 and, a month later, was knocked out of front-line service when the horse he was riding collided with a truck. Back home, Dear resumed his militia activities with the LSR and rose to lieutenant-colonel when he succeeded Henry A. Ruttan as the regiment's commander in 1933, the same year that he helped to found the Thunder Bay Field Naturalists Club.[27] Thereafter, he was invariably known as Colonel Dear. In July 1940, Port Arthur's city council appointed Dear the commander of the Volunteer Civic Guard, whose ranks were filled by fellow veterans.

During Dear's wanderings as he hunted, fished, and studied birds, he came upon John Drew Jacob at his second O'Connor Township homestead. Jacob was "extremely interested in birds and bird life and was very well versed. He made an extensive collection of eggs which he gave to me."[28] According to Dear, Jacob was not cut out for farming, any more it seems than he was for teaching in Minnesota; after trying his hand at a few jobs he moved to Toronto to work for a time in his brother Henry's engineering office and, later, for a mining company.[29] Around February 1930, Jacob was hired as a game warden on a monthly basis by the District 6 office of the provincial Department of Game and Fisheries in Fort William. He was taken on full time, at twelve hundred dollars a year, in 1930–31. His busiest year was 1931–32, when, in addition to his salary, he received almost $840 in travel expenses. He was gone by the autumn of 1934 as drastic cutbacks began and salaried employees were replaced with temporary or seasonal hires.[30] Events would prove that Jacob managed to have more irons in the fire, including prospecting. He lived part of the year with his wife at a home on Eglinton Avenue in Toronto. Anyone who wanted to know Jacob's whereabouts or how to reach him consulted Dear.

In 1959, Dear would recount that John Drew Jacob's great-grandfather was the younger son of a titled Scottish family and had fought in the Napoleonic Wars. Presumably denied a handsome inheritance by primo-geniture, the great-grandfather, after the Battle of Waterloo, was granted a tract of land along the St Lawrence River. This story was pure fancy. Jacob's grandfather was a Newfoundland merchant, John Jacob, who was born in Hampshire, England, around 1799; his grandmother, Hannah Garland, was born in Newfoundland.[31] John Drew Jacob's younger brother, Fred (who died of a heart attack at forty-six in 1928), was a sports reporter with the Toronto *Mail and Empire*. Fred Drew was also a poet and novelist who scandalized his hometown of Elora with the thinly dis-guised characters of *Day Before Yesterday*.[32] A gift for storytelling appar-ently ran in the family. Unfortunately, so did a possible streak of mental instability. John Drew Jacob's father died at sixty-eight of "senile decay" (possibly early onset Alzheimer's) in a York County insane asylum.[33] Thunder Bay lawyer Harry Beeman would advise C.T. Currelly that John Drew Jacob "was generally regarded locally as a man who did not have a well-balanced mind."[34]

Jacob was regularly in touch with the Royal Ontario Museum of Zool-ogy. In February 1938, J.H. Fleming, honorary curator of ornithology, would recount for a friend the zoology division's use of amateur infor-mants like Jacob. "The Royal Ontario Museum of Zoology ... believes in making friends, and in the various collecting expeditions made for zoo-logical research in northern Ontario a connection has been set up in the north country that has proved very valuable. Surveyors[,] miners[,] engi-neers[,] prospectors, any man who is intelligent and becomes interested in the museum's work in the field becomes a source of information[. I]f a strange owl hoots in the north country the museum hears of it. If any of these men come to Toronto they receive a genuine welcome at the muse-um [–] at least in zoology."[35]

John Jacob gave his Beardmore relics story in a series of statements to the ROM.[36] The elaborations, as we will see, were problematic, but, in sum, Jacob recalled Eddy Dodd's showing the retired surveyor Aaron Lougheed the freshly discovered sword in Port Arthur, in May or June 1930, right after find-ing it. (The year of the find would be fundamental in the authenticity dis-pute.) Lougheed told Jacob about the find a few days later. Jacob and Lougheed then went over to Dodd's house and examined the sword and other items. According to Jacob, Lougheed suspected the items were French.

Jacob and Lougheed next visited a local library to research Dodd's objects. It was probably Port Arthur's library, which was in the Ruttan Building, where Lougheed lived. "Mr. Lougheed and I interested ourselves in discoveries of this nature," Jacob would state, "and immediately looked up reference books [and] from the data we came to the conclusion the relics were probably Norse." Whether Dodd participated in the library research, and whatever Lougheed's actual involvement, it is reasonable to conclude that the friend Burwash heard about from Dodd who had identified the relics as Norse was Jacob.

"At that time I was Game and fisheries overseer in that district," Jacob would assert in June 1937, and "only a matter of days after the discovery had been made" he was en route to Jellicoe, about twenty miles east of Beardmore on the CNR line, and made a stop to inspect the discovery trench with Dodd. He saw a clear, rusted impression left by the sword in the underlying rock as well as a clump of birch roots that had covered the find, which testified to its antiquity. On his return from viewing the discovery site, Jacob wrote to the ROM. Jacob did not recall whether he addressed someone in zoology or archaeology, but he never received a reply, and no such letter survives.[37] Jacob would recall that, on a visit to the ROM in 1934, he mentioned Dodd's find to "Prof. Snyder," an erroneous reference to Leslie Snyder, a technologist and bird expert with the museum's zoology division who would be named the curator of ornithology in 1935.[38] Jacob was one of Snyder's sources for bird specimens, and Snyder purportedly introduced him to another museum staffer – Jacob believed it was the curator of ethnology, Thomas F. McIlwraith, who was also a capable amateur naturalist. (Oddly, neither the museum nor anyone else ever secured a statement from Snyder on the matter.) Jacob said he shared with McIlwraith the news of the Beardmore find and assured him that Dodd's sword was the "exact counterpart" of a Viking sword already in the ROM's collection. In 1925, the ROM had acquired a Viking sword that had been the private property of Sir Guy Francis Laking, first keeper of the London Museum. It was larger and in far better condition than Dodd's sword; C.T. Currelly would rhapsodize about its exquisite quality, including inlay "incredible in its fineness."[39] Still, Dodd's find did resemble its general shape. Jacob also recalled trying to persuade Dodd to send the items to the ROM. Dodd told Jacob he wanted fifty dollars for them, or perhaps just for the sword. But Jacob's efforts went nowhere. "When no one at the museum seemed interested," Jacob recalled, "I let the matter rest." According to C.T. Currelly in 1939, Jacob's attempt to alert him to Dodd's find was carried out by word of mouth and the message never reached him.[40]

Jacob probably did try to alert the museum to Dodd's relics, if not by letter as he claimed, then in person, either before or after Burwash saw them. Dodd certainly had already benefited from homework on medieval weapons when he met with Burwash, and Jacob, as noted, was likely the friend who searched the library stacks. Dodd's description to Burwash of the shield, with a diameter of only about twelve inches and a rusty residue, suggests he was describing a buckler, squashed perhaps into an ovoid shape. A medieval buckler was about the size of a dinner plate, was made of metal, and had a dome or boss to protect the hand on the front and a metal grip or handle on the back. The ROM coincidentally was about to acquire a later example of a buckler, from the time of Henry VIII, in its June 1934/June 1935 operations year.

Dodd had enough sense of the relics' value to house them in a custom wooden case when he showed them to Burwash, which makes it difficult to understand why he was ever willing to part with one of the world's great archaeological finds, one that any leading museum in Europe or North America would be eager to own, for just fifty dollars (or even less, by one account), regardless of their sorry condition. To a man like Dodd, struggling to find steady work and oblivious to the true market value of such items, a windfall of seven hundred dollars in today's money may have been a handsome payday.[41] But there was no overt indication in Burwash's letter to Currelly that Dodd was actively trying to sell them, only that he had almost sold them. Eddy liked to show off and talk about his relics, which also meant talking about his mining claim. An important, unanswerable question is whether Dodd was aware of Burwash's informal bird-dogging for Currelly when he waylaid the government geologist in February 1934. Certainly, by 1936, in recounting to Teddy Elliott how he had shown the relics to Burwash, Dodd understood that the latter was associated with the ROM. Still, showing the relics to Burwash could have been a gambit to talk up the potential of his prospecting efforts in the hope that Burwash could connect him to investors right after the value of gold soared. The day Dodd sold the relics, to a museum or a private collector, was the day he no longer had a conversation-starter that would allow him to bend a stranger's ear about the mineral promise of the middle claim.

Alerted by Ned Burwash to Eddy Dodd's extraordinary weapons cache, C.T. Currelly wrote Dodd on 16 February 1934.[42] Currelly would recall that he did not receive a reply, which may not have been the case. He was labouring under the burden of his director's duties in a greatly expanded museum facility that had only reopened a few months earlier. He simply may have lost track of Dodd's response. Currelly's letter does not survive, but he seems to have asked Dodd to ship the artefacts to Toronto for inspection, which Dodd would not do. Dodd promised to bring them to Toronto on a "business trip," but he failed to do so.[43] Dodd was thought to be afraid of losing control of the relics if he did not bring them in person, but he was also probably reluctant to part with them. Currelly did comment: "the whole thing seemed so utterly impossible that I did not go to Port Arthur to follow it up."[44] On a radio program in December 1938, Currelly would mention he had been ill at the time and unable to travel. He was in a constant struggle with his mental health, taking periodic rest leaves for episodes of what Lovat Dickson described as "nervous prostration" that could leave him bedridden for more than a month.[45]

Then, on a hot July night in 1934, Dodd halted the CNR train with burning newspaper and drew Teddy Elliott into the saga of the Beardmore relics. Dodd told Elliott on the train much the same discovery story that he had told Burwash in February, with one exception. Dodd made no mention of Vikings, instead proposing: "I think they're French armour or Indian relics. If you get a chance, come on up to the house and I'll show them to you."[46] Elliott took down Dodd's address: 74 South Algoma Street in Port Arthur, about two blocks from the station and the nearby hotel watering holes. Elliott watched Dodd disappear into the crowd as the day coach of prospectors, each one clinging to a dream of buried riches amid a brutal Depression, emptied onto the Port Arthur platform. Because Dodd had been drinking, Elliott wasn't sure how much to believe him. Elliott passed on paying Dodd a visit, and the relics entered another lull of notoriety.

The following winter, Ned Burwash was back in Thunder Bay delivering his prospecting lessons. Burwash had just dined with Norman Paterson, a

Fort William grain-shipping magnate, when he wrote Currelly on 25 January 1935.[47] After noting Paterson had four Chinese paintings on rice paper that he was interested in selling or donating to the museum, Burwash added: "I met the man who had the battle axe, sword and shield handle in Port Arthur a few days ago. He sold them to a coin collector from the States who comes here trout fishing. He got $50. This was before he heard from the museum I believe he said." Burwash would recall in 1940 that the buyer was from St Paul, Minnesota.[48] But the sale did not go through. A Toronto physician, Matthew John Haffey, would recall that, in the autumn of 1935, Dodd's older brother, Joseph, who lived in the city and was a railway baggageman when he married in 1907, "came to me as a patient and told me that his brother had found in his mining claim at Beardmore a sword & axe and that they thought they were French. He said his brother had arranged to sell them to an American for $25 but the American had not paid, so he had them still. I suggested that he get in touch with the Royal Ontario Museum."[49] Dodd's brother did not take the doctor's advice. For someone purportedly angling to cash in on a major archaeological find, Eddy Dodd wasn't trying very hard.

It is unclear when Eddy Dodd thought – or began telling people – the relics were French and perhaps had been possessed by Indians, and even that they had been in an Indian grave on the middle claim. According to John Jacob, the French provenance originated with Aaron Lougheed, soon after the relics were found. But, contrary to Jacob's story, Lougheed encountered the relics much later, recalling in April 1940 that he first saw them about five years earlier.[50] Lougheed probably entered the picture soon after Burwash did, around the spring or summer of 1934, suggesting the French-and-Indian provenance *after* Dodd, with Jacob's help, had arrived at a Norse one. Lougheed probably proposed a French manufacture for no other reason than that he doubted any metal object could have survived in Dodd's soggy mining claim for almost one thousand years. Then, in July 1934, Dodd told Teddy Elliott that the objects were either French or had been possessed by Indians, and Dodd's brother told the same story to Dr Haffey in Toronto in October 1935. But, by 1936, Dodd would be back to favouring the Norse provenance, without entirely abandoning the French/Indian option. The idea of an Indian grave at least held open the possibility that Indians had gained the objects from the Norse.

In suggesting the relics were French or Indian and omitting mention of Vikings, Dodd may have been affecting an unsophisticated air that encouraged people to investigate, with his being confident that research would lead them to the more spectacular Norse provenance. It would have been a good con to allow others to make an emotional investment in the discovery by "solving" the provenance. If that were the case, the approach worked time and again as people who considered themselves more sophisticated than Dodd – who thought him too simple, too unschooled, too working class to have engineered a hoax that could fool the likes of C.T. Currelly – busied themselves constructing a plausible historical scenario.

In January 1938, Dodd would volunteer that people had accused him of perpetrating a hoax "several years ago."[51] He may have put the relics away for good after Dr. Haffey failed to bite, the discovery story having been told with too many variations and been met with too much derision among people who knew him all too well. The Beardmore relics story could well have ended there, had not Teddy Elliott indulged his lingering curiosity during another visit to Thunder Bay in August 1936.

Elliott was about to begin a new job as director of the commercial department of Kingston Collegiate and Vocational Institute in Kingston, Ontario. He was probably also keen to begin writing again. His weekly *Globe and Mail* column "Chats with a Teacher," which he had begun in October 1932, had ended in December 1933. Elliott had dispensed gentle, progressivist advice through novelistic scenarios involving vexed children and parents. His final column of 16 December 1933 had begun in typical style: "The December breeze whirled the snow from the top of the drifts into dancing wraiths which sparkled in the afternoon sunlight. Dick idly watched them as he moped by the window."[52] As Elliott looked up Dodd on 12 August 1936 at the address he had been given on the train in 1934, he was about to confront an entirely different interleaving of fiction and truth – one that would preoccupy him for more than five years.

The Viking Age

"Not a little self-consciously," Teddy Elliott would recall of his initial visit to Eddy Dodd's home on 12 August 1936, "I knocked on the Dodds' door and Mrs. Dodd, a bright little woman, answered my query. 'No, he's out on his run.'"[1] Elliott explained that Eddy had invited him to inspect the relics two years earlier. Ellen had become accustomed to Eddy's arriving home with strangers to whom he wished to show them off. She directed Elliott into the parlour and went to fetch them.

One of Elliott's teenage daughters, fifteen-year-old Helena or sixteen-year-old Margaret, brought him the relics.[2] Wrapped in a towel were a heavily corroded sword in two pieces, which, he judged, reassembled to be about thirty-four inches long – four inches longer than what Burwash had accurately estimated in 1934. The history of contradictory first impressions of the Beardmore sword had begun.[3] In addition to the axe head, there was the strange iron object, which "was like nothing I had ever seen. It was flat, about six inches long by three-quarters of an inch wide," with hooks on either end. As Ellen Dodd would not let Elliott photograph the items, he made a rough sketch. A notebook he had purchased for his investigation of Dodd's relics preserves a truly thumbnail-sized ink sketch of the items at the top of the first page, with the broken sword idealized, as if new (see illustrations).

Elliott returned on 15 August, hoping to see Dodd and photograph the relics. Finding the house empty, he tried again the next day. Dodd, who was alone, welcomed Elliott, but, after a "desultory" search for the relics came up empty-handed, he said he couldn't find where his wife had left them.[4] A newspaper article in October 1938 would contend the relics migrated all over the house as Ellen tried to keep them out of her way.[5]

Eddy Dodd otherwise wasn't shy about revisiting his story. He produced map 312A, Sturgeon River Area, issued in 1934 by the Geological Survey of Canada. It depicted the basic features of a landscape he and Elliott had individually prospected. The map mainly described the abstruse world of geology and mineralogy, a realm overburdened with terminology and features alien to all but the initiated who could see past the muskeg, boreal forest, rapids-riven rivers, and outcroppings of Precambrian rock. There were scattered indications of iron formations, glacial striae (direction of glacial flow), and vertical schistosity (a type of cleavage in metamorphic rocks that is a clue to finding gold veins). Splashes of colour marked different geological zones. A swath of willow green traversed the middle of the map, called the Pre-Windigokan zone, which the legend defined as *Volcanic rocks in large part altered to hornblende, chlorite, and sericite schists; tuff; small amounts of iron formation and sediment.* The Blackwater River flowed eccentrically through this green dominion – first eastward, into the south end of Blackwater Lake, and then out of the north end of the lake, back westward, parallel to the course of its own upper reaches before making a final meandering passage confounded by rapids into Lake Nipigon on the map's left margin. The map showed the CNR line following closely the river's westward run from Blackwater Lake towards Lake Nipigon, through Beardmore and Warneford Stations. Dodd indicated for Elliott the precise location of the find, and Elliott measured its coordinates with a ruler to the thirty-second of an inch (see illustrations). The simplest way to reach Dodd's middle claim was to get off the train at the sign marking one mile to Warneford Station for Port Arthur-bound trains. The spot was about four miles southwest of Beardmore Station, near the banks of the westward-flowing leg of the Blackwater River. From there, Dodd only had to walk about a quarter-mile eastward into the wilds to reach his prospecting cabin. Dodd would have lit his newspaper on the tracks at the sign where, on that hot summer night, he came aboard the day coach and drew Elliott into his discovery story.

Dodd was as talkative as Elliott had found him on the train in 1934. Unfortunately, Elliott did not write any of it down; instead, he reconstructed Dodd's soliloquy from memory. In quoting from his notebook in the *Canadian Historical Review* in 1941, Elliott would assert he had secured Dodd's "statements ... on which he made notes immediately after the interview."[6] Elliott's questions and Dodd's replies do not begin in his stenographer's notebook until the twenty-fourth page, after notes he had made researching exploration history and weapons at two Thunder Bay libraries and back home in Kingston at the Queen's University library. Thus, unless Elliott was working from a set of notes now lost, Dodd's words were composed many days after Elliott heard them. Also, they were not "statements" in the sense of an affidavit that Dodd reviewed and signed, which was what became the basis for amassing the mounting and conflicting eyewitness testimony in the Beardmore case. While the fact that Elliott was composing entire paragraphs of dialogue from memory after several days brings their verbatim reliability into question, the information he recorded was largely substantiated by other people's encounters with Dodd.

Elliott described Dodd in the notebook as "a man of medium build, with the blue eyes of a visionary with an expressive face that is always ready to light up with an appreciative smile of one who is in touch with the fun and realities of life." Dodd reminisced about his prospecting. He had staked at Little Longlac with several other men in 1912. When he returned from overseas military service, he heard about Tony Okland and Tom Johnson's big gold find in 1917. "I went to Mileage 180 on the Long Lac branch, got a canoe and went in to where I had staked in 1912.[7] I found the posts, but Johnson and Okland's stakings surrounded me. That's the way it goes." Elliott let this sensational claim about having lost the Little Longlac strike to Okland and Johnson go unchallenged. Dodd said he next tried his luck in the Tashota District, on the northeast side of Nipigon, before trying again a little south, at Beardmore. "Mr. Dodds [sic] and two other partners have 16 gold claims in the Beardmore gold area," Elliott recorded. "He claims to have uncovered 117 different veins on his property and many of them show traces of gold up to assays of startling value." Dodd now had "a nice showing in the midst of a rapidly growing area. It's only a matter of time before things come my way." Mining office records at least would show that Dodd secured a mining licence required for prospecting in Ontario (which expired annually on 31 March) on 15 July 1925, and that he had promptly staked the three Beardmore claims (the maximum permitted a provincial licence holder in one territory) on 25 July, registering them in the mining recorder's office in Port Arthur on 27 July as 48TB-4894-95-96. As for his two partners, Dodd would attest in 1939 to having started his prospecting in 1925 with a building contractor named Tom Halls and a CNR engineer named Fletcher Gill.[8] Gill was assigned a half-interest in the three Beardmore claims on 26 February 1926 and was still associated with Dodd as his prospecting partner.

On the matter of the relics' discovery, Elliott had Dodd testifying:

It was the 24th of May 1933 that I found the sword and other things. I was doing my assessment work on my claims and was blasting out a trench across the side of a low hill. After the blast I saw the sword sticking out of the schist. In trying to get the rest of it out where it was embedded in the rock I broke the sword in two. Thinking maybe that it was some Indian sword I threw it up on top of the dump of rubble and it lay there for almost two months before I brought it home. The axe was found right close to the sword, also embedded in the schist formation. Where the axe came from was a depression as clean cut as if you had made a mold for it. The handle of the shield was lying right across the middle of an oval shaped brownish depression about 10 ins long and 5 ins wide.

They certainly must have been lying there some time because there was a big birch stump over the spot that was well-rotted and about 14 inches in diameter directly above the spot.

Elliot asked him what he thought the objects were. Dodd replied: "Well I don't know but archaeologists from the Royal Ontario Museum in Toronto who have seen them think they belonged to the Norsemen, but whether they were buried there with some Norsemen, or belonged to some Indians who received them in trade is hard to say. Certainly the Indians themselves didn't make weapons like that." The idea the relics might be French in origin had been dispensed with. The Norse relics were back, with Dodd's crediting professionals from the ROM. C.T. Currelly may well have told Dodd the relics appeared to be from the Viking age in the now-lost 1934 letter he wrote Dodd after being alerted to the relics by Ned Burwash. Dodd otherwise was clever, but he was not sophisticated, and, to him, Burwash was probably as much an archaeologist as a geologist, an educated expert who dug things out of the ground and was associated in some way with the museum. Dodd's assertion was also true to his wont to shift responsibility for the determination of Norse provenance as far from himself as possible. He was maintaining a role as a simple man who knew nothing of such things. From this point forward in Dodd's retellings, experts from the museum came up with the Norse attribution, even though Burwash had already told Currelly in February 1934 that Dodd was sure he had Norse relics.

Elliott would report that autumn that Dodd told him a man connected with the ROM who was lecturing at the Prospectors' Classes in Port Arthur the previous winter saw the relics and told him they might be of Norse origin. Dodd thought it was either Burwash or a man named Coleman.[9] He made no mention to Elliott of Aaron Lougheed or John Jacob.

Ned Burwash had seen the relics around the time of the annual prospecting classes in February 1934, not in February 1935. Was it possible Arthur P. Coleman, a retired geology professor at the University of Toronto and past director of the geology division of the ROM, had also suggested the Norse provenance? Coleman had worked as a geologist for the provincial government from 1931 to 1934.[10] Although nothing in Coleman's papers relates to work in the Lakehead area, Eddy Dodd certainly knew who Coleman was, and so, at some point, Coleman could have delivered a guest lecture at one of the prospecting classes conducted by his former student, Ned Burwash, and have been shown the relics by Dodd.

The date of discovery recorded by Elliott – 24 May 1933 – would become a factor in Elliott's eventual crusade to expose a hoax. He would insist that Dodd gave him this date in August 1936, along with saying that there was a two-month period during which the relics were lying in the rubbish after blasting. In future statements, Dodd would retain a discovery date of 24 May (or thereabouts), regardless of the exact year. A further dating complication is that at the top of his notebook's first page, under the small drawing of the relics, Elliott wrote: "Found on Jas Dodds claims in 1934 April while blasting out the rock for assessment purposes." Where did that date come from? Was it given to Elliott by Ellen Dodd, or one of the daughters, on that first viewing?

Teddy Elliott sketched an outline for an article, and for the two days that followed his meeting with Eddy Dodd, Monday 17 August and Tuesday 18 August, he holed up in local libraries, beginning with the Port Arthur library in the Ruttan Building. He assuredly did not know he was retracing the steps of John Jacob in seeking proof of the relics' Norse provenance, nor did he know that Aaron Lougheed, who lived in the building, purportedly had suggested to Dodd the relics might be French. In a crash course in early exploration history, Elliott filled his notebook with voyage details, beginning with John Cabot in 1497. He jotted down a mass of information about fur trading history into the eighteenth century. He still hadn't reached the Norse.

Elliott's breakthrough came after passing through the oversized limestone pillars marking the entrance to the public library in neighbouring Fort William. If the idea that Dodd possessed Norse relics had been around the Thunder Bay area since at least early 1934, it wasn't well known until Elliott became involved. It was news at least to Fort William's librarian, Mary Joanna Louise Black. Fifty-seven years old, Black was one of the more prominent public librarians in North America and was active in the Thunder Bay Historical Society, serving as president from 1928 to 1932. Elliott already would have known her from his teaching days in Fort William.[11]

From the library's stacks, Black provided Elliott with a list of books on weapons. One source was *The Viking Age* by a French-American explorer named Paul Belloni Du Chaillu.[12] On page 70 of volume 2, Elliott found an illustration of five iron swords. One of them looked strikingly like the one Dodd had found, particularly in the grip and the guard (see illustrations).

Through Black, word of a Norse weapons discovery leaked immediately. The local tourism bureau was holding campfire meetings at Chippewa Park on Fort William's waterfront, and it was Black's turn to give a chat on behalf of the local historical society on the evening of 18 August.[13] Black's talk, delivered mere hours after Elliott identified what appeared to be Dodd's sword in Du Chaillu's book, received front-page coverage in the Fort William *Daily Times-Journal* on 19 August.[14]

It's impossible to be certain of who was responsible for which facts and misstatements in the confused article. "Early Viking Armor Found in Beardmore" reads like a nameless newspaper reporter's half-understood version of Black's address, which was a half-understood version of what she had gathered from Elliott. Eddy Dodd was erroneously identified as a nameless "mining company employee" who had unearthed the relics that summer while working at Beardmore, thus creating the impression that not only had the items just been discovered but also that they were associated with the Empire mine. The only identified figure, other than Black, was Elliott, a former staff member of Fort William Collegiate Institute who had seen the relics while at Beardmore – another error. The relics themselves were misidentified: "Three pieces of armor were discovered, including a long sword and a steel chest protector. These have the same markings on them, and are of the same type, as those worn by Vikings six or seven hundreds [sic] years ago and on display in museums." Elliott may have been on hand for the talk, as the newspaper paraphrased his stating that the relics "are identical in appearance to those worn by Vikings in the twelfth and thirteenth centuries." Whatever role Black might have played in crafting the provenance story would never be known. Struck by illness in 1937, she resigned her library position and moved to Vancouver to live with her brother Norman, a physician. She died of a stroke under his care in January 1939.[15]

"Previous discoveries have proven that the Vikings had wandered into Minnesota and parts of Manitoba, but this is the first conclusive proof that the hardy Norsemen had ventured into the hinterlands of Thunder Bay district," the *Daily-Times Journal* reported. "The theory is held at present that the men wearing the pieces of armor discovered this summer at

Beardmore may have been cut off from the main party that entered west of the lakehead, and have become lost in what is now the Beardmore district and died there."[16] The Beardmore relics had staked their initial public claim to a place of prominence in the evolving saga of Norsemen in the New World. They had also been linked to one of the most contentious items of evidence: the Kensington stone.

Until the discovery of a small settlement at L'Anse aux Meadows in northern Newfoundland in 1960, there was no widely accepted archaeological evidence for the Norse presence in North America that the Vinland sagas promised. The two main family narratives, the Greenlander's Saga and Eirik the Red's Saga, recounted the bold and sometimes bloody adventures of the Norse in finding and attempting to colonize lands to the west of Greenland around AD 1000. The nineteenth century witnessed a fluorescing of purported physical evidence for the settlement attempts of two key saga figures, Leif Eiriksson and Thorfinn Karlsefni. None of it could withstand scrutiny.

In 1837, the Royal Society of Northern Antiquaries in Copenhagen published *Antiquitates Americanae*, one of the century's most influential works of history. In addition to providing transcriptions (in old Norse, modern Danish, and Latin) of the relevant sagas, the editor, society secretary Carl Christian Rafn, and his associate, the Icelandic scholar Finn Magnussén, argued for Vinland's location in southern New England. They offered a borderline fraudulent interpretation of an Indigenous petroglyph, Dighton Rock in southeastern Massachusetts, as an inscription by Karlsefni. Aided by a credulous American antiquarian, Thomas Webb, Rafn used the society's journal, *Mémoires*, to propagate the idea the Norse had remained in the area for centuries. Rafn turned the stone shell of a seventeenth-century windmill in Newport, Rhode Island, into the ruins of a Norse church, and a typical seventeenth-century Indigenous burial at Fall River, Massachusetts, into a Bronze Age European grave, which Henry Wadsworth Longfellow recast as the last resting place of a Viking adventurer with his poem "The Skeleton in Armor."[17] In the 1890s, Eben Norbert Horsford (a former Rumford Professor of Chemistry at Harvard who secured independent wealth through the Rumford Chemical Works) claimed to have found the remains of Leif Eriksson's settlement, Leifsbooths, on the shore of Boston's Charles

River.[18] Then, in 1898, evidence for Norsemen in North America came from an entirely novel direction.

A Swedish immigrant, Olof Ohman, claimed he was pulling a stump on his farm in Kensington county, about 130 miles north-northwest of Minneapolis, when his ten-year-old son, Edward, noticed a curious stone covered in runes on one side and along one edge.[19] The Kensington stone would become the most significant artefact in the debate over proof of a Norse presence in North America. Inevitably, Hjalmar Rued Holand, the Kensington stone's greatest advocate, would be drawn into the Beardmore case, along with his scholarly supporters and critics.

The Kensington stone got off to an inauspicious start as an archaeological wonder. Olaus Breda, who taught Scandinavian languages at the University of Minnesota, concluded it was probably a hoax. In February 1899, the stone was shipped to George Oliver Curme, a philologist at Northwestern University in Illinois. Professor Curme specialized in German and English, and he assessed it with the help of scholars in Scandinavia who were sent photos. Curme proposed that some numerals Breda could not read included a date, AD 1362. And so with Curme the essential translation of the inscription was set:

Eight Goths and twenty-two Norwegians upon a journey of discovery from Vinland westward. We had a camp by two skerries one day's journey north from this stone. We were out fishing one day. When we returned home, we found ten men red with blood and dead. A.V.M., save us from evil.
Have ten men by the sea to look after our vessels fourteen days' journey from this island. Year 1362.[20]

Curme, however, noted that some runes featured umlauts, which did not come into use until the seventeenth century. Like Breda, Curme considered the stone a fake. Not even Rasmus Anderson, one of the most polemical advocates of a Norse America, who taught for a time at the University of Wisconsin, believed it was real.

Probably nothing more would have been heard of the stone were it not for Hjalmar Holand, a Scandinavian-American fruit farmer in Wisconsin.[21] Born in Norway in 1872, Holand earned a bachelor's degree from the University of Wisconsin, where he studied under Anderson. In 1902, he began serving as the archivist of the Norwegian Society, a literary club in Minneapolis concerned with preserving the state's Norwegian roots.

While travelling rural Minnesota in 1907 to gather materials for the society (materials that, in 1908, became his first book, *De Norske Settlementers Historie*, a history of Scandinavian settlement in the region), Holand either chanced upon Olof Ohman's stone or deliberately sought it out. Ohman allowed Holand to have the stone on the condition that he deposit it, on Ohman's behalf, with the Minnesota Historical Society. Instead, Holand kept the stone and tried to sell it to the society for five thousand dollars. Holand wrote articles for *Harper's Weekly* and the *Journal of American History* asserting the stone's authenticity. He also co-authored a preliminary report on the stone by the historical society's museum committee, which was published in December 1910.

A runic message with the date 1362 could have nothing to do with the Vinland sagas. Holand found a reference in Gustav Storm's *Studier over Vinlandsreiserne* (1887) to an expedition by Paul Knutson from Bergen, Norway, in 1355. In 1354, Magnus Smek, the king of Norway and Sweden, had purportedly commanded Knutson to make a voyage to the Greenland settlements to "not allow it to perish in our days." The original command was destroyed in a fire in 1728 and existed only in what Kirsten Seaver calls "a dubious sixteenth-century copy."[22] It said nothing explicit about defending Christians (presumably from the Inuit) or about sailing beyond Greenland, as Holand and the many investigators he inspired would contend. But Holand leaned on the slender reed of Knutson evidence to construct an epic voyage scenario. He argued that the Knutson party had travelled beyond Greenland, westward along Hudson Strait in the Canadian subarctic, to penetrate deep into Hudson Bay. The Nelson River led them inland, to Lake Winnipeg, and from there they pressed southwards along the Red River, until misadventure with Native Americans claimed ten men at Kensington, seven years after the expedition began.

Gustav Storm, who inspired Holand with the Knutson evidence, declared the Kensington stone a "crude fraud" in 1899 and, for good measure, a "clumsy fraud" in 1911, as Holand tried to revive its credibility.[23] Response to Holand's efforts to rally scholarly support for the stone can best be summarized by the title of an article by philologist George T. Flom of the University of Illinois, published in June 1910 by the Illinois Historical Society: "The Kensington Rune Stone, a Modern Inscription from Douglas County, Minnesota." Holand took the stone to Scandinavia in 1911, where its authenticity was rejected by expert runologists.

Holand was not done. He sold the stone for four thousand dollars to the chamber of commerce of Alexandria, Minnesota, where it remains housed in its own museum. The success of *De Norske Settlementers Historie* and sub-sequent works of local history brought Holand scholarly credibility. A position on the board of curators of the State Historical Society of Wisconsin added some scholarly gravitas to his persistent support for the stone. In a privately published pamphlet in 1919, Holand criticized the earlier dismissals of the relic and insisted on the stone's authenticity.[24] Holand had created a new pre-Columbian Norse presence deep in North America, where Scandinavian immigrants had flocked in the nineteenth century.

In 1932, Holand expanded his 1919 pamphlet into a self-published book, *The Kensington Stone*.[25] It received an impressive degree of careful consideration and outright support in academic circles, although Scandinavianists with expertise in runes and early texts tended to dismiss it. Laurence M. Larson, chair of the history department at the University of Illinois at Urbana-Champaign, set the tone for *Minnesota History*'s consistent scepticism with a politely dubious review in June 1932. Larson recommended the inscription be submitted to a committee of competent Scandinavian philologists in hope of ending the controversy over it, "which otherwise is likely to continue its irritating course."[26] But enough academics were sufficiently dazzled by Holand's professed knowledge of historical sources, scholarly literature, runes, and languages to keep it on course. They either accepted his evidence for a fourteenth-century Norse visit to Minnesota or concluded that he had at least revived the possibility the stone was genuine. "No impartial person will deny, at least, that this book reopens to debate a question which had been generally regarded as a *res judicata*," Frank Stanton Cawley, a professor of Scandinavian languages and literature at Harvard, concluded an otherwise critical review in the *New England Quarterly* (NEQ).[27] Reviewers like Mary Wilhelmine Williams in the *Mississippi Valley Historical Review* accepted that Holand was an expert in early Scandinavian languages and allowed him to overturn some linguistic evidence for fakery made by the stone's initial critics.[28] The Canadian-born arctic explorer, anthropologist, and author Vilhjalmur Stefansson was a prominent champion, as was Richard Hennig, a professor of geography at the technical university of Dusseldorf.[29] No one did more to advance Holand's ideas than Geoffrey Malcolm Gathorne-Hardy, librarian of the House of Lords in London. Gathorne-Hardy had been in Norway when it gained independence from the Danish Crown in 1905 and had learned Norwegian as well as some Icelandic. He travelled in Labrador and put his language skills and experiences to use in writing *The Norse Discoverers of America: The Wineland Sagas* (1921).[30] Gathorne-

Hardy championed Holand's findings in the *Geographical Journal*, *Antiquity*, the *English Historical Review*, and the *Scandinavian Review*. Gathorne-Hardy would also provide Holand a letter endorsing the stone's authenticity for his forthcoming *Westward from Vinland* (1940). His endorsement ventured: "If your case is not conclusive many men must be hanged annually on insufficient evidence."[31] Like Holand, Gathorne-Hardy believed that Indigenous peoples of alleged mixed ancestry were proof of a Norse presence in North America.[32] Gathorne-Hardy and Hennig would make appearances in the Beardmore story, as, in more prominent roles, would Holand and Stefansson.

After the initial wave of at least polite reviews of *The Kensington Stone*, Holand began to experience critical pushback. Finding Cawley's earlier scepticism in NEQ too respectful, Michigan historian Milo M. Quaife denounced Holand's work in NEQ in December 1934.[33] His thirty-three-page dismantling of every aspect of Holand's scholarship (and other Norse American delusions besides) employed such terms as "preposterous" and "balderdash" in asserting that the stone was a hoax and that Holand's translation and his case for the Knutson expedition was shoddy. Holand was allowed to reply in the March 1935 issue, as well as to publish an article in *Minnesota History* in June 1936 that fired back at both Quaife's NEQ review and the earlier "attack" by Larson.[34] But as support appeared to flag for Holand's besieged Kensington ideas, Eddy Dodd's relics surfaced with fortuitous timing.

In support of the rune stone, Holand presented as evidence five purported finds: a fire-steel, a spear point, and three battle axes (he would add two more axes in *Westward from Vinland*). When, in 1936, the Fort William *Daily Times-Journal* reported a single set of weapons, discovered independently of Holand, east of Lake Nipigon, surely this additional physical evidence was proof positive of a historic Norse presence in the upper Great Lakes and the American Midwest. The Kensington stone and the Beardmore relics became more plausible as they created a larger, collective body of evidence. Scholars who were inclined to believe in the authenticity of the Kensington stone were quick to embrace the Beardmore find, regardless of its own evidentiary problems. Among the scholars who accepted Hjalmar Holand's contentious findings was Vilhjalmur Stefansson's friend, Charles Trick Currelly, director of the Royal Ontario Museum of Archaeology.

3

"Everything Is Conjecture"

On Friday, 21 August 1936, three days after librarian Mary Black revealed Eddy Dodd's discovery during her evening lecture at Chippewa Park, Teddy Elliott wrote (care of the ROM) either Arthur P. Coleman or Ned Burwash, the two people whom Dodd said had suggested to him that the items were Norse. Elliott may have written both, such was the confusion in his recollections.[1] "At that time I humbly expressed the opinion that, incredible as it seemed, the articles appeared to be of Norse origin," Elliott recalled around 1957.[2] He included a "crude sketch" of the items. There was no reply – not surprising, as Coleman had retired and Burwash had no position at the museum.

Elliott left the Lakehead in late August for Kingston, Ontario, where he was about to start his first teaching year as head of the commercial department at Kingston Collegiate and Vocational Institute. He worked up a set of ink drawings of the relics and, after further research in the Queen's University library, produced a draft of an article, "Were Vikings in Northern Ontario?" A story drawn from the Fort William *Daily Times-Journal* article went out on the Canadian Press (CP) wire on 7 September (and was "scalped" by AP the same day); on 8 or 9 September, a CP reporter contacted Elliott at home, wanting to know more about the Viking relics. A *Toronto Star* writer also contacted him. Elliot declined to comment to either reporter. He would recall he was waiting to hear back from the ROM and wanted to be confident of what Dodd had found before making any statement of his own, but he certainly also wanted to preserve his scoop, under his own byline.[3]

On 10 September, Thomas Wheeler, an editor at the *Toronto Star*, wrote Elliott, asking to see a thirty-five-hundred-word article he understood the schoolteacher had written on the Beardmore find.[4] Elliott submitted the draft immediately.[5] Wheeler passed the article on to Main Johnson, editor of the newspaper's weekend magazine, the *Star Weekly*. The rejection was swift. As Johnson explained: "In the first place there seems to be quite a bit of uncertainty as to just what James Dodds [sic] found in Beardmore, it not appearing certain by any means that the material was Norse. In the second place, for the particular needs of the *Star Weekly* there is too much history in your article. We are not criticizing you nor your article for this but we are merely saying that it doesn't fit in with *Star Weekly* policy to have so much historical material."[6]

The rejection was a revealing beginning to Elliott's efforts to tell the Beardmore relics story – which, by mid-1939, would become an effort to tell the story of what he was convinced was a hoax. Johnson's "too much history" comment appeared to encapsulate the popular media's general aversion to scholarship and nuance. News outlets wanted a sensational, unequivocal story, but Elliott was wrestling with uncertainties in the Dodd story and the many possible historical explanations. He was also showing himself to be a determined researcher, albeit one without any experience publishing in the historical field. Unfortunately, he began pursuing the Beardmore case without fully documenting his activities. He had no carbon of the 21 August letter to the ROM, and he contradicted himself about to whom he wrote it. Most of the initial drawings he produced disappeared. He would learn to gather, preserve, sift, and evaluate evidence with precision. Teddy Elliott would become as much a detective as a historian, as concerned with human motivations as he was with documentary evidence.

Teddy Elliott's notoriety spread rapidly. Word of the Beardmore find worked like chum ladled into the ocean, attracting the bigger fish in the world of Scandinavian Americans who took ethnic pride in the Norse as North America's original European discoverers. Hjalmar Holand's championing of the Kensington stone did not happen in a cultural vacuum. The propagandizing of a Norse past in North America by Scandinavian Americans is one of the "home-making myths" for ethnic groups of European origins described by immigration historian Orm Øverland. Through these myths, immigrants could claim the United States was a place they rightfully belonged.[7] These myths fall into three main Øverland categories.[8] First, the "foundation myth" made Scandinavians the original colonizers, as Leif Eiriksson settled the New World five hundred years before Columbus. For Chicago's 1893 Columbian Exposition, which was supposed to mark (had it opened on time in 1892) the four hundredth anniversary of the first Columbus voyage, Norwegian citizens launched a daring counter-programming strike through public subscription: a seventy-six-foot replica Norse longship, the *Gaia*, crossed the Atlantic to be on hand in Chicago.[9] Second, the "blood sacrifice myth," embodied by the Norse losses at the hands of the *skraelings* (the Indigenous people encountered in North America and

Greenland) in the Vinland sagas and in the record of the Kensington stone, was repeated by nineteenth-century Scandinavian homesteaders killed in skirmishes with Indigenous peoples. And third, "myths of ideological gifts or an ideological relationship" were found in the republican tradition of the Althing, the assembly that had governed Iceland as a commonwealth from about AD 930 to 1262 and was restored in 1843.[10]

These Scandinavian-American homemaking myths were writ large on the Norse American Immigration Centennial Celebration of 1925 at Minnesota's state fairgrounds, which marked the centenary of the arrival of the first ship of Norwegian immigrants. President Calvin Coolidge spoke to a crowd estimated at more than eighty thousand (more than 160,000 tickets were sold to attendees from Canada and the United States).[11] Norse mania carried its momentum into 1926, through another longship voyage. A Norwegian merchant seaman, Gerhard Folgero, fashioned a half-scale (forty-six-foot) longship out of a ship's lifeboat, christened it the *Leif Erikson*, and sailed from Bergen to North America. The *Leif Erikson* wended its way to Chicago for the dedication of Leif Erikson Drive and finally took up residence in a special park in Duluth, Minnesota, in 1927. Folgero went home to build a bigger replica ship, the sixty-two-foot *Roald Amundsen*, and repeated the proselytizing trip in 1930 on the nine-hundredth anniversary of the founding of Iceland's Althing (a major celebration in Iceland attended by international dignitaries), with the ship hauled by flatbed truck to Minneapolis-St Paul for the last leg of the tour.[12]

Thunder Bay had its own Scandinavian community, whose members would take pride in the Beardmore find as proof their ancestors were the first Europeans to have set foot in their newly adopted land. The community's rise began with a Port Arthur Board of Trade appeal in 1901 to the minister of the interior for more immigrants experienced in "wood cutting and timber floating," which meant Finns and Scandinavians; most recruits arrived after the First World War.[13] Some community members arrived initially in Minnesota or Wisconsin, which was charged with homemaking myths, before trying their luck in Canada. In the 1931 census, 3.5 percent of Thunder Bay (1,631 of 46,095) was of Scandinavian heritage (Danish, Swedish, Norwegian, Icelandic), with most of them (1,009) living in Port Arthur.[14] There were enough Scandinavians to warrant a Norwegian vice-consul, and the community contributed to the celebrations (and assertions) of a heroic Norse past in North America. One month after Folgero's *Leif Erikson* was installed in a Duluth park, Thunder Bay's Norwegian community entered a Leif Eiriksson longboat float in the local Do-

minion Day parade, marking the diamond jubilee of Canada's Confeder-
ation in 1927. The float's designer was a Norwegian immigrant, John
(Jens) Bloch. Two months after Teddy Elliott interviewed Eddy Dodd at
his Port Arthur home, Bloch died in Vancouver. John Bloch would haunt
Eddy Dodd's discovery to the end of his days.

In October 1936, the most important figure in Elliott's quest to understand Dodd's discovery entered the Beardmore narrative. If Thomas Leslie
Tanton was not the most gifted geologist Canada ever produced, he was
one of the most productive. Born in London, Ontario, in 1890, T.L. Tanton was the son of a Baptist pattern maker who had emigrated from England in 1871.[15] He was such an exceptional undergraduate student in geology and mineralogy at the University of Toronto that he won the Sir
Edward Blake scholarship in physical sciences three years running. After
earning his master's degree in 1912, he studied in Vienna for a year before
moving on to the University of Wisconsin, where he taught physiography
and secured a doctorate in economic geology in 1915 under C.K. Leith.
Like Ned Burwash, whom he knew well, Tanton specialized in the Precambrian geology of Canada, and he was hired by the Dominion Geological Survey's (DGS's) Bureau of Economic Geology. A tireless field geologist who used the new rail lines to explore and map the mineral resources
of the shield country, Tanton produced or contributed to forty-six DGS reports and maps issued between 1915 and 1944.[16] Most of that work covered northwestern Ontario and, especially, the Thunder Bay District. He
was elected an honoured fellow of the Geological Society of America in
1927, and his activities in the Royal Society of Canada – which would have
a direct bearing on the Beardmore case – would lead to his presidency of
Section 4 (geological sciences) in 1949–50.

Gordon A. Gross would remember Tanton as "an energetic and enthusiastic field man devoted to his scientific work and interested in the problems faced by the pioneer residents" as well as "a popular public servant
who gave expert advice freely to the host of prospectors, developers, and
others who consulted him and sought his counsel."[17] Married with two
daughters, Tanton lived in Ottawa when he wasn't prowling Precambrian
geology. For itinerant prospectors like Eddy Dodd and Teddy Elliott, Tanton (who had lived in Beardmore and Fort William) was *the* authority on
mineral wealth in their claim stakes. Among Tanton's first DGS reports

was a 1917 survey of the resources along the Canadian Northern line between Nipigon and Longlac. The legend of Map 312A, on which Dodd had pinpointed the discovery location for Elliott, noted that it depicted geological features determined in part by Tanton's fieldwork in 1917. Elliott would have possessed his own copy of this essential prospecting tool as well as 313A for Little Longlac, both of which had been updated by Tanton in 1934. Tanton needed no introduction when he wrote Elliott, and they probably already knew each other.

Tanton was an active community member in Ottawa, with eclectic interests; he would serve as president of the Ottawa Centre of the Royal Astronomical Society in 1943–44. Closer to the spadework of his profession was his curiosity about archaeology. His interest was plain in his most ambitious work, *Memoir 167*, a 222-page DGS report on the geology of the Fort William–Port Arthur and Thunder Cape areas published in 1931, which included a short section on "Relics of Prehistoric Man." Tanton had access to the best archaeological minds and resources the country could offer, right within the DGS.

From its beginning in 1842, the DGS had been concerned not only with geology but also with flora, fauna, and fossils.[18] With the opening of the Victoria Memorial Museum in 1912, the DGS became both a federal research operation and a public museum. In 1910, it hired its first chief anthropologist, an American protégé of Franz Boas, Edward Sapir, who quickly built an impressive team. Sapir hired the American archaeologist Harlan I. Smith, the New Zealand anthropologist Diamond Jenness (about whom we will hear more), and the Quebec ethnologist-folklorist-ethnomusicologist Marius Barbeau. Another critical early hiring, who would become involved alongside Jenness in the Beardmore controversy and the overarching question of Vikings in the Great Lakes, was William Wintemberg, who specialized in sites yielding the cultural materials of Canada's Indigenous peoples.[19]

From his office in room 304 in the Victoria Memorial Museum building, Tanton could consult the small but gifted DGS team of archaeologists and anthropologists. In 1927, the building had also become home to the National Museum, which was affiliated with the DGS. Tanton was a collegial and influential educator and colleague whose contacts ranged across the sciences and humanities, well beyond the Ottawa museum's walls. When he read press reports of Dodd's find, he got in touch with Mary Black, who steered him towards Elliott. Tanton jotted a quick letter on 13 October 1936, asking for details about the discovery.[20]

Elliott promptly provided a detailed briefing on his dealings with Dodd and his activities to date.[21] He expressed his embarrassment that Mary Black leaked the news of the discovery before there was definite proof of the relics' origins. The Norse provenance, Elliott assured Tanton, "is still a matter of conjecture." He dated his initial encounter with Dodd on the train to 25 July 1933, which, in 1938, he would revise to 16 July 1934. It was an early warning of the difficulties people caught up in the Beardmore case would have in recalling the precise timing of events. Elliott shared what he understood from Dodd of the ROM's efforts to get him to bring the relics to Toronto, and he gave Tanton the ruler measurements to locate the find on map 312A. He enclosed a copy of his draft article, which mentioned the discovery date of 24 May 1933, which Dodd had given him, and an image of the Thames River sword featured in the 1929 issue of the ROM *Bulletin* (the only Viking sword ever to appear in the publication), which he advised bore some resemblance to Dodd's find.

"Some one who is really competent to judge should have a look at Dodds' [sic] collection for the sake of determining their true origin," Elliott advised. He admitted it was possible that Dodd's claim "may prove to be just another farce. In any event an investigation is warranted. If you can assist in any way it would be of great benefit. You know the district much better than I and will probably be at the head of the lakes before me."

After reading Elliott's letter and article, which he found "very entertaining," Tanton suspected fraud. "Your suggestion that the reported find by Mr. Dodds at Beardmore may prove to be a hoax seems to be clearly indicated from the circumstances of the discovery as described," he replied.[22] Tanton did not share his specific misgivings, but he had found absurd Dodd's assertion to Elliott that the sword had been fused with the underlying schist and that the axe head had been set in a space in the rock moulded to its shape. There was no conceivable way a metal implement perhaps one thousand years old could become intermingled with hard Precambrian schist more than 600 million years old.

Tanton suggested that if Elliott thought the relics were of great antiquity, regardless of how Dodd had acquired them, the director of the Royal Ontario Museum of Archaeology might want to hear from him. It seems odd that Tanton did not think the National Museum would be interested in Dodd's find as, conceivably, the relics could have been part of an Indigenous site, acquired through long-distance trade or some conflict. An Indian grave, after all, was a scenario Dodd had put to Elliott and Elliott had communicated to Tanton. It is not known whether Tanton consulted any of his colleagues in anthropology and archaeology at the DGS and the museum at this point. Perhaps he did, and was met with eye rolls; perhaps Jenness and Wintemberg thought Norse relics were things best left to the ROM. The anthropology division in any case was very much the poor cousin of geology within the DGS, chronically underfunded and overextended;[23] Tanton's research in support of mining, in contrast, was considered an engine of national prosperity. But the anthropology division would not be able to avoid (or resist) being drawn into the Beardmore controversy.

Tanton composed his reply to Elliott on 19 October but held off sending it (as he explained in a handwritten postscript) because he had written Dodd the same day seeking "some plausible explanation." When Dodd did not reply, Tanton finally mailed the letter to Elliott on 27 October. For now, Tanton was done with the puzzle of Dodd's relics. He would not reappear in the Beardmore debate for another two years.

As news of the Beardmore discovery spread, Teddy Elliott's mailbox began to fill with enquiries from the Scandinavian-American community. Anna Fuhr of the Fuhr Printing and Publishing Co. in Duluth, Minnesota, was one correspondent. The company operated one of the largest newspaper printing plants in North America, and its stable of Scandinavian-language weeklies included *Dominion Skandinav* and *Dansk-Skandinav* in Winnipeg.[24] Leif Erikson Day in Minnesota, 9 October, was approaching, and the Norwegian ambassador was to speak at the celebrations in Duluth. As Fuhr noted, in 1935, President Roosevelt had encouraged all states in the United States to declare the holiday. She had gathered from Mary Black that the find was authentic, and she asked Elliott to contribute an article to a special "Leif Erikson issue" of the company's newspapers, which would be distributed freely at all gatherings that day. Elliott was cautious about the provenance, but he was willing to provide a three-thousand-word story, based on the incomplete evidence. Fuhr did not reply.[25]

Just as T.L. Tanton mailed his letter to Elliott, the leading figure in Scandinavian-American enthusiasm for Norse America contacted the Kingston teacher. Hjalmar Holand wrote on 29 October, introducing himself as the author of a book on the Kensington stone and assuring him: "For years I have been specializing in pre-Columbian American history."[26] Holand was hoping to secure photographs of the Beardmore relics, and his initial enquiry bespoke caution as he wanted to know if a seventeenth-century French attribution could be excluded.

Soon after, another Scandinavian American with an interest in purported evidence for Norse visits surfaced. In September, the *Washington Post* had published an article on claims to the Norse discovery of North America that discussed "Prof. Olof Strandwold" and Nova Scotia's Yarmouth rune stone, a dubious relic that had been debated since the 1880s.[27] Strandwold, in truth, was a school superintendent in Prosser, Washington, with an exaggerated sense of his own expertise in Old Norse and runic writing. He never came closer to the Yarmouth stone than a photograph, but he declared it to be an inscription by Leif Eiriksson.[28] Strandwold informed Elliott that he was writing a book on the Yarmouth Stone and other New England runic inscriptions, and that he wanted to secure images of the Beardmore relics.[29]

Elliott set aside Strandwold's letter and replied on 5 November to Holand, whom he held in great respect.[30] Elliott even sent Holand his research notes, which he had not yet copied, along with some sketches, asking only that Holand return them at his convenience. In a long and frank letter, Elliott reviewed his encounter with Dodd that summer. He suspected Dodd deliberately avoided showing him the relics when he called on him: "He is not a very learned man and is very jealous lest the government confiscate them." He shared what he understood from Dodd of the ROM's past effort to get Dodd to send or bring the relics to the ROM, and he mentioned an otherwise unknown detail from Dodd – a purported enquiry from an official of the Canadian government that Dodd left unanswered.

As for the Norse provenance, Elliott directed Holand to page 70 in Du Chaillu's *The Viking Age* for a sword that was "practically identical" to Dodd's and to T.R. Kendrick's *A History of the Vikings* (1930) for an "identical" axe. Elliott nevertheless advised Holand: "Everything is conjecture. They may be French, English or Norse. They may even be merely trade weapons given to Indians by a trading company. Your guess is as good, maybe better than mine." They only had Dodd's word on where the relics had been found, and under what circumstances. "Certainly, though, [the relics] bear a strong resemblance to early Norse weapons of Norse manufacture about the year 1000 A.D. Should this fact be proved, then how did they get up in that part of the country? and be buried in the rock. Certainly a long time must have elapsed if they were buried in the schist as Dodds [sic] claims. Should all this be finally proven to be correct, then it lends a tremendously favorable light to your own contentions that a

Norse expedition traversed the north country." He told Holand he had written the ROM but had not yet heard back.

Holand appreciated Elliott's assistance. "It is too early to draw any conclusion as to the home and date of the articles found," he replied, returning Elliott's notes.[31] "If I could see a photograph of the axe or the sword handle I could tell you at once their home and date as I have specialized in this field for years." He asked if Elliott could secure photographs from Dodd and to be kept informed of any developments. Elliott had been enlisted in the ranks of Holand's contacts in the speculative world of Norse visits to North America.

On 5 November, the same day he replied to Hjalmar Holand, Teddy Elliott took up T.L Tanton's suggestion and tried again with the ROM, this time writing the director of the archaeology division, not knowing Currelly's name.[32] Elliott essentially repeated what he had written to Tanton and Holand, enclosing pencil sketches of Dodd's rusty objects, a photostat of the material on Norse weapons from *The Viking Age*, and a copy of his unpublished draft article. An Elliott drawing of a fourth object Dodd claimed to have found also reached Currelly.[33] During their conversation on 16 August, Elliott had asked Dodd if he had made other, similar findings. As Elliott quoted him: "Well, not right there, although the boys in the camp always joked about finding the owner's shoes and coat. As a matter of fact I did find a half-moon shaped tool like a prospector's pick that had a hole in the centre for a handle." He had found it about five hundred yards west of the other relics. Dodd said he fitted a handle into it and used it for a prospector's pick for weeks. "It was as hard as any pick you ever saw. No amount of banging and chopping on the rocks would dull or break it." But he had lost it when it fell out of his packsack as he walked through the bush.[34] Elliott's drawing was based on Dodd's description.

Elliott repeated the observation he had made to Tanton. "Someone who is really competent to judge should have a look at the Dodd collection. Either it is just another hoax or, if the Norse manufacture be correct, then the whole case of their origin, and location[,] is of tremendous historical interest." He concluded by remarking: "The clearing up of this case would be an interesting project." He could not know how long it would take for that to happen, how indispensable an ally T.L. Tanton would be to his cause, and how deeply opposed to one another he and Charles Trick Currelly (and Hjalmar Holand) would become.

4

Carlo

It would be wrong to say that no public museum devoted to teaching, research, and public enlightenment would exist in Toronto today were it not for Charles Trick Currelly, as that would ignore the superior organizing role of Sir Byron Edmund Walker. But it is also true that no museum quite like the Royal Ontario Museum, dominated by its superb archaeology division, would have existed without Currelly. It is hard to imagine a director of Currelly's flair and overseas experience emerging in his absence to collect for and shape the archaeology division, as he did from 1906, as a salaried antiquities buyer for the University of Toronto eight years before its opening, until his retirement as director of the archaeology division in 1946. It is also hard to imagine a scandal like the Beardmore purchase shaking the ROM without Currelly. Frauds and fakes are standard risks in museum acquisitions. What matters is how they are handled. Anyone could have bought Dodd's relics, but not anyone could have brought the resultant scandal upon the institution (and himself) in quite the way Currelly did.

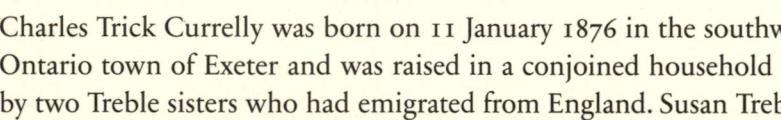

Charles Trick Currelly was born on 11 January 1876 in the southwestern Ontario town of Exeter and was raised in a conjoined household bound by two Treble sisters who had emigrated from England. Susan Treble had married John Trick, a native of Cornwall; in January 1872, Mary Ann Treble married in Exeter a miller, John Currelly, from Port Hope in Northumberland County. Their husbands likely were in business together. Charles was the only child born to either Treble sister, and he seems to have enjoyed a collective parental hope for his success.[1]

The source of Charles Currelly's lifelong curiosity in trade and craft is suggested in his memoir: "I spent much of my free time watching men at work, until I knew a good deal about the different trades that were practiced in the village: blacksmithing, woodworking, stone cutting and stone polishing."[2] A local minister was hired to tutor him in Latin, and in 1885 his parents – perhaps both couples – moved to Toronto to give Charles the opportunity for a better education. The relocation was short-lived: Currelly would recall that Toronto was not to his family's liking. In 1892, when Charles was sixteen, his parents tried again. The Currellys moved into a house on the south side of Bloor Street West, at the intersection of St Thomas Street.[3] That same year, Victoria University, a Wesleyan Methodist institution in Cobourg, Ontario, relocated to Toronto and became a college federated with the University of Toronto, the province's public seat of higher learning. The new, red sandstone Victoria College was but a short walk south of the Currelly home. John and Mary Ann Currelly had their sights on Charles's attending the new college. Charles's grandfather, Thomas, had attended Victoria University and sent his sons there; its chancellor, Nathanael Burwash, was a family friend.[4] Chancellor Burwash succeeded Egerton Ryerson as the leading figure in the Methodist Church in Ontario in the late nineteenth century, and he shared Ryerson's devotion to public education.[5] He typified the Canadian intellectual elite's late nineteenth-century struggle with a global evolution in science that left no place for supernatural design or influence as he taught geology and biology alongside theology.[6] Victoria College remained a Methodist institution under Chancellor Burwash, who continued to teach while also serving on the university's senate in the new century.

Before enrolling at Victoria College in 1894, Currelly attended Harbord Collegiate.[7] In addition to making probably his closest, lengthiest friendship there, with Nathanael Burwash's son Ned, Currelly also became close to a younger student, Edmund Murton Walker, son of Sir Byron Edmund Walker, the banker, civic dynamo, and philanthropist from Hamilton.[8] Currelly would join Edmund for sketching trips with the artist Lucius Richard O'Brien, and he took his own lessons from other artists, including Farquhar McGillvray-Knowles.[9] Currelly shared the Walker and Burwash interest in natural sciences and would collect butterflies and learn to stuff bird specimens under the tutelage of Dr William Brodie at Victoria College.[10] Sir Byron Edmund Walker also knew James Mavor, a professor of political economy at the University of Toronto, through the "Round Table Club" Mavor helped found in 1896, at which twelve men dined and discussed issues of the day.[11] Mavor would become a major influence in Currelly's university education.

Another prominent family, the Masseys, completed the circle of influence that advanced Currelly's fortunes. Currelly attended Bible studies conducted by Walter Edward Hart Massey at Central Methodist Church. W.E.H. Massey was a son of Hart Massey, the wealthy farm-machinery manufacturer and patron of various Methodist charitable endeavours. The classes, which included lantern slides and relics that Massey brought back from his travels to Palestine, fired Currelly's enthusiasm for the Bible as literature and for archaeology – especially the archaeology of the biblical lands. Massey's classes showed how artefacts could anchor history and validate narrative tradition. The same use of artefacts to bring biblical narrative to life was on display at Victoria College when Currelly attended.

Around 1896, Susan and John Trick moved to Toronto, into a large detached home on Avenue Road at the intersection of Yorkville Avenue, two blocks north of Bloor Street and the future site of the ROM. Charles appeared with them in the city directory that year as a student, and his parents joined the household in 1898. John Trick seems to have been independently wealthy, while John Currelly sold goods acquired from bankruptcies.[12] In 1897, Currelly's family forged a significant connection to the Masseys through the marriage of Lillian Massey to a cousin of the Treble sisters, a Toronto men's wear dealer, John Treble.[13] The couple settled in Euclid Hall, the mansion Lillian's late father, Hart, had purchased on Jarvis Street. Lillian and her brothers had been left the family fortune and the responsibility for dispensing more than $1 million in funds earmarked for philanthropy.

In 1902, Lillian Massey Treble persuaded Nathanael Burwash to convince the University of Toronto to create a degree-granting school of industrial arts for women. In 1907, the university established the Faculty of Household Science, and in 1913 an impressive three-story building, the Lillian Massey Department of Household Science (now home to the university's classics department and centre for medieval studies) opened just south of the Currelly-Treble home, through a $500,000 donation from Lillian Massey Treble. (That same year, Burwash Hall, named in honour of Nathanael Burwash, opened as a residence for Victoria College.) Its main entrance faced west, across Avenue Road, towards the new Royal Ontario Museum, which would open in another year with C.T. Currelly as the director of its archaeology division. Currelly secured a requisite university professorship in the history of industrial art, and it was attached to the facility across the road, which was brought to life by Lillian Massey Treble.

The course of C.T. Currelly's life, which was carefully plotted by his conjoined family, was not supposed to lead to a museum of archaeology. In 1898, Currelly completed a bachelor's degree at Victoria College and was all but commanded by Chancellor Burwash to serve the Methodist Church by heading to Manitoba, as his own son Ned was doing, to train as a minister with a remote territory of 750 square miles. After a year of privation and frustrations with church hierarchy that saw him temporarily barred, Currelly abandoned his ministerial training and returned to Victoria College, where he completed a master's degree and prepared to tackle a doctorate under James Mavor, who had taught him wood-carving and had inspired a youthful embrace of socialism. For his doctoral dissertation, Currelly planned to work as an ornamental wood carver for two years in Europe to research socialism and religion among the working class; after that he would begin theology studies that would lead to his ordination in the Methodist Church. In 1902, Mavor supplied him with a letter of introduction to the Russian anarchist Peter Kropotkin, who was living in London.[14]

An elaborate chain of happenstance sent Currelly's life on a wildly improbable trajectory. Visiting an antiquities dealer near the British Museum to look at coins, Currelly bought an ushabti, a small Egyptian funerary figurine, as it reminded him of one that Lillian Massey Treble had brought back from Egypt. He rolled it in a handkerchief. When he pulled out the handkerchief the next day while in the coin room at the British Museum, the ushabti tumbled out.[15]

"Hello, are you interested in Egypt?" asked Herbert Grueber, assistant keeper of coins and medals, who had recommended the dealer to Currelly. This casual enquiry was the definitive moment in setting the course of the twenty-six-year-old Currelly's life as a museum director and antiquities buyer. "Enormously," Currelly replied. Ancient Egypt had figured in his master's thesis. Grueber was the honorary treasurer of the Egypt Exploration Fund (EEF), and he suggested that Currelly meet Flinders Petrie, the forty-nine-year-old professor of Egyptology at University College London and an archaeologist with the fund. Petrie happened to be back in London.

Currelly raced to University College and found Petrie. After a brief interview, which satisfied the archaeologist that Currelly could produce drawings and surveys, Petrie invited him to spend a few weeks with the EEF as it prepared for another sailing to Egypt. Currelly so impressed Petrie that he became a house guest and was taken on staff as an assistant for a one-year term. It was an extraordinary break: Petrie's assistants typically had two years of university education in Egyptology under him at University College. Currelly had no sooner stepped off a cattle boat from Canada (the working transatlantic passage choice of students) than he had dazzled or charmed his way into the close company and employment of a leading Egyptologist and renowned field archaeologist. One of Petrie's past assistants, Howard Carter, would go on to discover Tut's tomb, and Petrie trained many other leading members of the field.

Currelly was bright, and credited with impressive powers of memory, and Petrie was not the only leading figure in England who was taken with him. Currelly became close to the artist William Holman Hunt, a co-founder of the Pre-Raphaelite movement and a popular painter of lush religious scenes steeped in an Orientalism that was informed by four trips to Palestine and Egypt.[16] Hunt was in his eighties, his eyesight failing, when Currelly became a regular house guest. "I shall have a week to ten days' holiday again on the river with the Holman Hunts," Currelly wrote Ned Burwash from London in the summer of 1906. "We are going to take a week's canoe trip."[17] When Hunt died in 1910 and his sons, being abroad, were unavailable, Hunt's widow turned to Currelly to carry her husband's ashes before a crowd of thousands into St Paul's Cathedral, where Hunt's friends had lobbied for them to be interred in the crypt next to J.M.W. Turner.

Currelly strove to learn from everyone he encountered, whether the skill was making moccasins and mitts and working with moose hide, which he gleaned from a family of "Scotch half-breeds" (Home Guard Cree) in Manitoba, or the art of spying fakes, which he absorbed from leading archaeologists on the Egyptian scene, Petrie above all.[18] Currelly also had a gift for ingratiating himself with people in positions of influence, both at home and abroad. Some of the most important figures in his life were older men like Petrie, Hunt, and Sir Byron Edmund Walker, who had had humble beginnings and had bootstrapped themselves into their successes. Currelly's advantages of class, of privilege, would be a source of omission and contradiction in his memoir. There was something about his own social status that he found wanting, as he conjured a heritage more romantic than the prosaic reality of a grandfather who had emigrated from England to farm in southern Ontario's Northumberland County. The Currelly family, he asserted in his memoir, was descended from "the ancient *gens Corelea* of Rome."[19] He went so far as to record his ethnicity as "Italian" in the 1911 Canadian census (a fiction he abandoned in the 1921 census) and was known to friends as "Carlo." He affected a theatrical appearance, wearing a cape and a broad-brimmed hat throughout his ROM years. His tolerance of privation during his Manitoba sojourn and in the field with Petrie did not prevent him, in late 1910, from bringing home to Toronto (along with his English wife, Ada Mary Newton, their newborn daughter, and his sister-in-law) an Egyptian youth as an "attendant," whose salary he expected the university's museum, not yet built, to pay. (This youth appears to have been Aûd, the son of an important chieftain in the Sinai, and he had served as a messenger and emissary for Currelly.[20]) Currelly also glossed over the depth of his connections to the Masseys, which served to further his career; he instead cultivated a narrative of personal fortitude blessed by chance encounters and opportunities so providential that he entertained the idea of actual divine intervention. Holman Hunt wrote in the autobiography he was composing when the young Currelly met him: "It is remarkable that when circumstances outwardly seemed most unpromising, a special fate always kept open my artistic prospects."[21] It was as if the formative examples of Hunt, Petrie, and Walker compelled Currelly to mould his own story to the spirit of theirs.

In Currelly's mind, the origin of the Royal Ontario Museum of Archaeology lay in his surprise encounter with Nathanael Burwash, shortly after he was taken on by Flinders Petrie in 1902.[22] Ned Burwash was also in England, and his father, at home in Canada, heard a rumour that his son was deathly ill. Chancellor Burwash dropped everything and hurried across the Atlantic to find Ned in perfect health and Charles Currelly in the short-term employ of Petrie. Chancellor Burwash thought the EEF represented a wonderful opportunity and that Currelly should make more than a one-year commitment. He envisioned Currelly's developing expertise as an archaeologist of the biblical lands and then completing his training as a minister. After ordination, he could teach biblical archaeology at Victoria College, thus fusing scholarly studies of artefacts and sites with furthering the Lord's work, in much the way that Chancellor Burwash and his son Ned were combining theology and geology.

Chancellor Burwash also thought Currelly's role in the EEF could help revive the dormant antiquities collection at Victoria College and establish a far more ambitious institution.[23] The EEF operated on a subscription basis: participating institutions received artefacts in proportion to the funds they provided for excavations. Burwash felt the University of Toronto, more specifically Victoria College, could join the fund, and it did. "It seems to me that this is our chance to start a museum in the university," the chancellor told Currelly.[24]

Currelly duly informed Petrie that he wanted to make a permanent switch to archaeology in his studies. Petrie agreed. Neither the doctoral dissertation Currelly planned with Mavor nor the minister's training Burwash envisioned came to pass. Instead, a career in antiquities was born.

Currelly came to Flinders Petrie's attention at an opportune time as the archaeologist needed a replacement for Arthur Weigell, who was moving to a new position with the German Egyptologist Friedrich Wilhelm von Bissing.[25] However much Currelly owed his opportunities to class, privilege, and pure chance, he delivered impressive results. In his first season, he found the tomb of an eighteenth-century dynasty ruler; Ahmes I. Petrie would recall how, in December 1903, Currelly (who was only beginning his second season) arrived at his camp "with twenty-seven men from Koptos, having marched them more than eighty miles to the Red Sea, got a mining company's steamer to carry them over, and then marched up to Wady Maghara."[26] Currelly was twenty-seven years old. He seemed unstoppable.

Before the second season was under way, Currelly was determined to build a museum collection for the university. "I now have hundreds of Greek and Roman coins ready to go over and hope by next year I have thousands as I have been admitted into the Datari coin ring," Currelly revealed to Ned Burwash from Crete on 21 May 1903, an observation that makes one wonder how much of Currelly's early collecting was for his own profit. "So I am deadly earnest about the collections. This year I have spent every cent I had and have stuff of enormous value … There are few people in the world [who] have the chances for picking up stuff that I have, as I know most of the centers and am up and down through the countries twice a year … [T]he number of people who wish me to buy for them is getting rather large." He had already sent Victoria College twelve cases of material, with more to come, and he relied on Ned Burwash to sort the material as it arrived.[27]

Petrie's 1903–04 digs were frustratingly unproductive, but Currelly made his first contributions to scholarship in heady company. In the EEF report on the 1903–04 season at Ehnasya, Currelly wrote a chapter and co-authored another with Petrie, while also contributing unspecified plates of photographs and illustrations to the volume.[28] In a supplemental volume on the EEF's Abydos digs published that year, Currelly contributed four of eight chapters, relating his exploits in his first season.[29] His gift as a raconteur, which would make him popular in Toronto society and among the staff at the ROM and faculty at the University of Toronto, was already on display. Currelly recounted how local Egyptians feared his work party would dig under the tomb of a sheikh, or even pull it down. "Just as we had exhausted the cemetery, a select deputation of the biggest men in the district, armed with clubs, came up to ask us not to go any nearer. The request was granted at once."[30]

Petrie was a font of knowledge, and Currelly's enviable hands-on education was augmented by the contacts Petrie made possible with many leading British scholars. Currelly knew Sir William Ridgeway at Cambridge and, in 1903, he roomed in Crete with Sir Arthur Evans, keeper of the Ashmolean Museum, who was making ground-breaking digs at Knossos. He shared their fervour in acquiring everything possible while artefacts were in abundance and prices were cheap.[31] His formal education was over, but Currelly would be awarded an honorary doctorate by Queen's University, which was the basis of his status as "Dr Currelly." Along with fellowships in the Royal Canadian Academy and the Royal Geographical Society, Currelly could unspool a formidable title: Dr C.T. Currelly, BA, MA, LLD, RCA, FRGS.

The ROM was the culmination of six decades of fits-and-starts initiatives to create a public museum in the provincial capital that would serve (as Harold J. Needham described) the three main functions that had inspired their creation in the Western world since the seventeenth century: "preservation (collecting knowledge), education (collating and transmitting 'old' knowledge) and research (developing 'new' knowledge)."[32] Education Minister Egerton Ryerson's Normal School Museum, also known as the Museum of Natural History and Fine Arts, began in 1853 in a second-floor display room for teaching supplies. It was dismantled in 1881 and its collection dispersed. In 1897, the Normal School became home to another museum initiative, which arose from the enthusiasms of David Boyle, a blacksmith turned school principal in Elora, Ontario, who became a respected international figure in archaeology and ethnology. The self-taught Boyle's interests extended to geology and natural history, but he was mainly concerned with the Indigenous cultures of the province, past and present. In 1897, his private collection was given a home on a newly built third floor of the Normal School; in 1902, the floor was grandly named the Ontario Provincial Museum.[33] But the cramped museum did not satisfy the ambitions of leading citizens and collectors like Sir Byron Edmund Walker, or of C.T. Currelly, and the germ of an idea of an archaeology museum devoted foremost to Old World artefacts, already planted by Chancellor Burwash in 1902, began to grow in 1905.

In the 1904–05 EEF season, Currelly provided "valuable help" to the major excavation of the XI Dynasty temple complex at Deir el Bahari, and he was entrusted with producing the plan.[34] Flinders Petrie broke with the EEF in August 1905, feeling deeply betrayed by the executive's management decisions. Rather than stay with Petrie, who established the British School of Archaeology in Egypt in 1906, Currelly chose to remain with the EEF while also freelancing as a collector for various museums. He developed a reputation for being a little fast and loose, and answerable only to himself. In April 1906, the secretary of the Royal Scottish Museum (RSM) wrote the EEF to complain about a terse note from Currelly in Cairo "in which he tells me that he has bought for us a number of things in Egypt & asking me to have a considerable sum paid, at once, into the Canadian Bank of Commerce." The RSM felt "quite in the dark" about Currelly's activities on its behalf. "Mr. Currelly gives absolutely no details as to the sort of things he has got & without even the name of the objects for which the money is wanted the department could not be asked to provide it."[35]

On a return visit to Toronto in the autumn of 1905, Currelly pitched Walker on a university-based public museum devoted to archaeology. Currelly was already making antiquities purchases for Walker's private collection, and his enticing stories of treasures to be had by opportunistic buyers persuaded Walker to arrange his salaried appointment as an official collector for the University of Toronto in January 1906. Walker was one of seven members of a Royal Commission struck in 1904 to assess the state of the University of Toronto, and its 1906 report advised: "One of the necessary features of a great modern University is a properly equipped Museum."[36]

Sir Byron Edmund Walker was determined to raise the cultural quality of life not only of Toronto but also of the nation as a whole through public institutions like the ROM and the University of Toronto, with which he had been associated since 1890; Walker served as the university's chairman of the board from 1910 to 1923, when he was made chancellor, a year before his death.[37] Walker was also instrumental in founding or guiding the Champlain Society, the National Gallery, the Art Gallery of Toronto (which became the Art Gallery of Ontario in 1966), and the Guild of Civic Art in Toronto. He was never singularly focused on archaeology as the basis of the new, university-affiliated museum. He would donate a large paleontology collection of specimens and books to the ROM; his son Edmund, Currelly's childhood friend, was a leading entomologist who became head of zoolo-

gy at the University of Toronto in 1934 and was largely responsible for the
ROM's invertebrate collection. Edmund served as assistant director of the
invertebrate collection from 1918 to 1931 and as honorary director thereafter until his death in 1969.[38] But from the beginning of the planning for
the ROM, Currelly's collecting, backed by private donors, was considered a
key element of the public museum that Walker envisioned.

Walker successfully lobbied Ontario's Conservative premier, James
Whitney, to create the museum as an adjunct of the university. A dazzling
exhibit of antiquities mounted by Currelly at the University of Toronto in
1909 promised the museum's potential in archaeology. In April 1912, a
provincial act creating the ROM received royal assent; the building was already under construction in 1911. The second bylaw passed by the board
of trustees, under the chair of Walker, in November 1912 created the first
of the museum's five divisions – archaeology – with C.T. Currelly named
its director.[39] The new museum opened in March 1914.

Walker deserved enormous credit for bringing the museum plan to
fruition as well as for soothing the bruised egos of the university professors appointed directors of the museum's other divisions. When he married in London in August 1909, Currelly described himself on the licence
as "Director of Museum at Toronto" three years before there was a museum with a board.[40] Currelly wrote in the March 1911 issue of the *University of Toronto Monthly* about the coming museum, giving the impression
that the ROM would be his museum. The other division directors "were
understandably upset by the assumption in the article that the sole attraction of the 'New Museum' would be Currelly's collections."[41] When
tensions became unbearable, in the spring of 1913 Walker dispatched Currelly on a speaking tour of the American southwest.[42] As Lovat Dickson
has noted, "Tact was not one of Currelly's finer points."[43]

The ROM could draw on an array of models in Europe and the United
States for inspiration, but it most closely resembled British examples. Currelly's archaeology division embraced the general spirit of the Victoria and
Albert Museum (which arose from the Great Exhibition of 1851 and was
initially known as the South Kensington Museum). Currelly already had
this museum model in mind when he wrote Ned Burwash from Crete in
1903: "I do *so* want the arrangement to be on a uniform plan and on a
plan that is the outcome mostly of the South Kensington Directors experience."[44] However much Currelly was even aware of (or sympathetic to)
larger purposes of exercising state power, of crafting new relations of
power and knowledge, the envisaged museum fulfilled what Tony Ben-

nett calls the Gramscian "ethical and educative function of the modern state."[45] A nineteenth-century museum was one of a set of cultural technologies that included art galleries and exhibitions that, in Foucauldian terms, were intended to organize a self-improving, self-regulating citizenry.[46] The museum space was meant to be "a place in which the working classes would acquire more civilized habits by imitating their betters" – that is, the middle class with whom they would mingle.[47] According to Barbara Ruth Marshall, Walker believed that museums like the ROM "would function as 'shopwindows' in which Canadians and foreigners could comprehend, at a single glance, the vast resource potential of the nation. Displays in museums of manufactured articles of a high level of workmanship would increase, he thought, demands for fine things, thereby, raising the level of craftsmanship in Canada."[48] Currelly's fascination with craftsmanship and materials, and his initial university appointment as a professor of industrial art, reflected this institutional objective. Currelly also saw Canada, as did Walker, within a British Imperial system. Britain to Currelly was home for Canadians, even if, like him, you were not born there. In fact, Canadians were legally considered British subjects until 1947.[49] The Scottish travel writer John Foster Fraser, visiting Toronto in 1904, found it "the most ultra British city on earth ... Its patriotism is ever on the bubble ... Englishmen suffering from laxity in loyalty should hasten to Toronto, where they can be so impregnated with patriotism that they will want to wear shirt fronts made of the Union Jack."[50] The museum of archaeology strove to reinforce Canada's Imperial association and instill it in the school children who were such an important audience. In the 1930s, the British Imperial sentiment of the museum remained strong because Currelly believed in its importance, as did much of the city and the province. After the First World War, Britain remained "the ultimate arbiter of Canadian tastes" in high culture, according to John Herd Thompson.[51] Percy J. Robinson wrote in *Toronto during the French Regime* (1933) that "British traditions [were] immovably established" in Ontario and that Toronto was "the citadel of British sentiment in America, and Ontario, the most British of all the Provinces."[52]

Currelly showed some interest in North American ethnology, but he was mainly concerned with depicting the rise of Western civilization and, above all, British civilization. As he wrote in 1913, history as it pertained to that rise "does not come from within our sphere. For example, Montcalm's flag is interesting to us as a piece of weaving, but is of no interest from the sentimental side, i.e., as a historical object."[53] His general focus was on the Old World of Europe, ancient Egypt, Greece, Rome, Crete, and the biblical lands, which provided a progressivist narrative of Western civilization leading to the British Empire. China was included in Currelly's collecting in part because Sir Byron Edmund Walker saw Canada's economic future tied to east Asia.

By the time the Beardmore relics surfaced, Charles Trick Currelly had built the ROM's archaeology division into a marvel of breadth and depth. Its east Asian holdings were considered to rival if not better those of the British Museum. Currelly would be justly saluted by the *Report on Survey of Royal Ontario Museum 1953–1954*, by Clarkson, Gordon and Co. (a.k.a. the Glassco Report). The ROM had "reaped the fruits of an astute and energetic collector armed with much more money than most museum directors and operating in the period when large quantities of valuable objects became available."[54]

Currelly bridged two worlds in his collecting – that of private clients and that of public museums – and fused them by having private benefactors underwrite acquisitions for the ROM. At the same time, as large public museums superseded private collections as centres of acquisition, they created new elites – the curators and directors – who passed judgment on significance, value, and meaning. Some, like Currelly, were crossposted to a university. In 1971, the museum professional Duncan Cameron (who got his start in museums at the ROM in 1956, just as the Beardmore provenance finally collapsed in scandal) called public museums "an exclusive, private club of curators" who selected and presented materials according to "the value systems of the middle class if not an upper-middle-class elite."[55] These curators and directors indeed wielded considerable cultural power in determining what was (and was not) displayed and how it was interpreted. At the ROM, Currelly was the embodiment of that cultural power. The authority of the museum's archaeology division was *his* authority. No one in the country, let alone in the conjoined institutions of museum and university, could compete with his reputation or openly question his judgment.

C.T. Currelly was a font of stories about his collecting experiences, which were an essential part of his charm, charisma, and authority. The museum's private benefactors (some of whom had spent time with him in the field on their own trips to Egypt) and colleagues around the museum and the

University of Toronto were regaled by tales of his adventures in exotic locales, especially of brushes with death and unsavory characters. Of a desert crossing on which hostile tribesmen were feared, Currelly would write: "As we got quite close to the pass I rode back along the line telling the men to keep two abreast and that if any were shot they must be left, as it would be impossible to stop."[56] The fact that no shootout occurred hardly mattered to the thrill of the tale. "Am rather tired as this last expedition has been the hardest and most dangerous I have ever had," Currelly wrote Ned Burwash from Cairo in June 1905, "but thanks to a kind Providence I did not lose a man though I nearly lost eleven, the closest-shave thing [I] will ever have."[57] In the same letter, Currelly said he had just heard at government house that he was being considered by the Khedivate (as the de jure Ottoman province of Egypt was known) for a knighthood, the Turkish Order of the Medjedie. "Say not a word of this as it may not happen," Currelly instructed, while allowing it was fine for Ned to tell his parents. The knighthood never materialized, but the mere thought of it would have astounded Chancellor and Mrs Burwash.

"Everyone was dazzled by Currelly," Lovat Dickson notes of staid and provincial Toronto's response to its man in Egypt.[58] Other Currelly tales upheld his ability to spot fakes that fooled other museum types and academics, and delivered the backstories of objects he had managed to secure through shrewd negotiation. All of it was interlaced with effortless historical asides. Margaret Tushingham, who began working for the museum as a secretary around 1939 (and married A.D. Tushingham, a successor of Currelly as museum director, who would figure in the Beardmore story), would recall Currelly's treating staff to a new story at every rigorously observed 3:30 p.m. tea break.[59] The editor of his memoirs, the literary scholar Northrop Frye, recalled first hearing many of Currelly's stories with colleagues as they regularly took lunch with him in the Senior Common Room of Victoria College. Frye called Currelly's life story "one of the most amazing to come out of Ontario."[60]

With Currelly, stories of how an object came into the hands of a dealer (and of how Currelly himself recognized its authenticity and bargained his way to ownership) became part of an object's provenance. Sometimes it was about all the provenance an object possessed. Currelly told good stories, and a story well told, much like one from the Bible, had an authenticity no scientific process could measure – or challenge. When Eddy Dodd walked into the rotunda of the ROM in December 1936, he was bearing not only an assemblage of intriguing metal objects but also a story of discovery that Currelly could not resist.

"The Biggest Historical Find ... in America"

On 7 September 1936, a small Canadian Press story that related the news out of Fort William of Viking relics caught the eye of an unknown Henry Morgan executive in Montreal. He glued the clipping "Historic Armor Stirs Interest" to a sheet of letterhead, jotted beside it "Can these things be?" and mailed it to C.T. Currelly.[1] The director of the Royal Ontario Museum of Archaeology responded on 9 September. Although no reply is preserved, the clipping indicates that Teddy Elliott's subsequent letter of 5 November 1936, revealing Dodd's weapons cache, could not have come as a complete surprise.

The contents of Elliott's letter electrified Currelly. The enclosed drawings of Dodd's relics, he would recall, "sent me right up into the air."[2] They suggested to Currelly that Dodd possessed "one of the early types of the Norse sword, 10th to 11th century. The axe could very well also be Norse, and the pick-like piece might be a good many things."[3] Currelly wondered if Elliott would write Dodd "to beg him to send the things down here," if only for the sake of preservation. But instead of mailing the letter, Currelly, like T.L. Tanton before him, decided to set aside his reply to the schoolteacher and to write Eddy Dodd directly on 12 November.[4]

From the beginning of his collecting activities, Currelly had struggled with two opposing tensions. One was the fear of missing out on opportunities by not acting quickly and decisively, which caused much personal and financial anxiety in his early acquisition years. Currelly routinely encountered what he considered once-in-a-lifetime chances in a market dominated by major institutions and private collectors with far larger budgets than what was available to him. The other tension was the fear of being duped by fakes.

Throughout his career, Currelly had to make snap decisions on acquisition opportunities. There was no time for prolonged investigations of provenance, and all museum directors of his generation had to contend with the ephemeral if not nonexistent archaeological documentation for many of the objects they collected. Currelly had been fortunate to work under Flinders Petrie, a pioneering figure in scientific archaeology in Egypt and Palestine.[5] But most of Currelly's collecting from the beginning of his career involved dealers as well as ordinary people who appeared at excavations with purportedly ancient items to sell. His archaeology experience ended in 1907; thereafter, he was exclusively a buyer, not an excavator, of relics. Currelly could not know for certain the origins of items, and his memories of collecting in Egypt and the Mediterranean were animated by an ever-present and understandable concern that he would be duped. The rise of public museums along with private collectors in the late nineteenth century created a ravenous market for relics, which could only encourage fakes. As Currelly advised Sir Byron Edmund Walker at the start of his 1903–04 season with Petrie, forgeries outnumbered authentic items on the market by a margin of ten to one.[6] Currelly considered Petrie to be one of the best at spotting fakes, and he learned everything he could from him. After Currelly's first season in Egypt, he passed a key test with Sir William Ridgeway, Disney Professor of Archaeology at Cambridge, by correctly identifying some Egyptians scarabs as exquisite fakes because he saw that they were made from labradorite.[7] The Ridgeway test was one of Currelly's stories, and the wealthy philanthropists who funded Currelly's museum acquisitions must have been comforted by the idea that his exceptional eye spared them from underwriting worthless acquisitions. However, there was a difference between items that were forgeries and items that were authentic but had been planted in a sensational location to increase their significance and value. New World archaeology had a long history of both authentic and fraudulent items that people claimed to have dug up and that proved the presence of ancient Romans, Phoenicians, and other Old World peoples. Discoveries of authentic ancient coins were easy to fake, their being readily available from numismatists. Other items, like the weapons Hjalmar Holand presented as evidence of Norsemen, could be brought to North America by immigrants as heirlooms and then proclaimed as remarkable discoveries.[8]

Currelly explained to Dodd that Elliott had sent "some quite good drawings of a sword, an axe, and a couple of other things that he saw in your house. They are intensely interesting, because if his drawings are right, they may very well be Norse." He asked Dodd to send the items to the museum at the ROM's expense so that, at the very least, they could be preserved. "If you can give or obtain proof that these were not planted there by some Norwegian or Swede in recent years, we will be willing to give you a very good price for them." Despite his caution about the possibility of fraud, Currelly volunteered circumstantial evidence to support Dodd's find, including the Kensington stone. "It is known that the

Norsemen came down into Minnesota and left an inscription, and of course Indians may have brought the pieces long ago down into the Long Lac, or Norsemen themselves may have come down there. The last is rather unlikely, I think, though Mr. Stefansson [Currelly's friend, Vilhjalmur Stefansson] told me that he had every reason to feel sure the Norsemen had landed in the Hudson Bay and had not come up from the east coast of America." Initially, then, Currelly doubted Norsemen had been anywhere near Beardmore; rather, he suspected the relics had some relation to the Kensington stone.

Currelly's remarks call to mind an exchange of letters the previous year with Knute Haddeland of the League of Norsemen in Canada. Haddeland had sent Currelly a clipping of an article he had published in the *Winnipeg Tribune Magazine* on 16 November 1935, "Viking Colonies Predated Columbus," which endorsed Holand's Kensington stone theorizing and included a map showing the route the Knutson party took deep into the continent via Hudson Bay – a route that in Haddeland's interpretation employed the Albany River, which empties into James Bay in northern Ontario. "The explorations of the intrepid early Norsemen were primarily within the border of what is now Canada and, therefore, should be of particular interest to Canadians," Haddeland had lectured Currelly. In reply, Currelly noted: "My friend Stefansson has been very much interested in the matter of the Norsemen in America, and has talked a good deal about the Minnesota inscribed stone, which he found most interesting."[9] Currelly informed Haddeland that the museum had just acquired another Viking sword. It was from a private collection in Paris and was said to have been found in the Seine. Currelly presumed that it had been lost in the great Viking siege of the city in the late tenth century.[10] A year after buying the Paris sword, Currelly had the opportunity to acquire relics that would endorse the view of Norse explorations that Stefansson propounded and that was otherwise contentiously supported by the Kensington stone.

Currelly's interest in the Beardmore weapons tapped several undercurrents of historical interest, museum policy, and cultural framing. The archaeology division placed a strong emphasis on European history, which Currelly believed could be taught through its wars. In an object-based educational setting there was no better way to teach wars than with weapons. Currelly knew that a key audience for his museum's collection was schoolboys – perhaps more than schoolgirls – and that weaponry sparked imaginations with a glorious if violent past across the Atlantic. Norse weapons carried deep ethnohistorical connotations. The letter from

Knute Haddeland of the League of Norsemen in Canada was a reminder of the continued strength of the home-making myth in Scandinavian communities, which the museum's sword purchases fed, even if they were not North American relics. But Currelly was more interested in what Norse artefacts said to most museum goers, who had a British heritage. Since the nineteenth century, Norse fascinations in North America, especially among Anglo-Americans in New England, had been buoyed by a view of race, culture, and history that scholars call Gothicism. Gothicism embodies a mélange of paganism, a hardy warrior ethos, freedom-loving republicanism, chivalry, Protestant morality, and white racial superiority. It constantly shifts shape to suit the needs of its advocates, but in its essential form it contends that white people from northern Europe are the finest human race, descended from Japheth, a son of Noah favoured by God. These northern European whites hailed from the wellspring of modern civilization and overthrew the southern tyrannies of the imperial Romans and Roman Catholicism. Gothicism encoded and legitimized powerful notions of race-based entitlement and privilege where colonization in the Americas was concerned.[11]

Carl Christian Rafn had appealed to the American subscribers upon whom he relied to produce *Antiquitates Americanae* in 1837 with allusions to a Gothicist sensibility of a racial/cultural heritage shared by Angles, Saxons, Jutes, Scandinavians, and Scottish Highlanders.[12] The relationship was propagandized by Rasmus Anderson in his efforts to build a bridge between Scandinavian-American home-making myths and Anglo-American white heritage. As Anderson enthused in *America Not Discovered by Columbus* (1874): "Yes, the Norsemen were truly a great people! Their spirit found its way into the Magna Charta of England and into the Declaration of Independence in America. The spirit of the Vikings still survives in the bosoms of Englishmen, Americans and Norsemen, extending their commerce, taking bold positions against tyranny, and producing wonderful internal improvements in these countries."[13] April Schultz calls the First World War "a moment of profound crisis in the Norwegian-American community," with the Norse American centennial of 1925 in Minnesota aimed at countering nativist sentiments that Norwegian immigrants were hyphenated Americans who had opposed American participation in the First World War.[14] The celebration was an exercise in Gothicist revisionism as the hated German enemies of the war were excluded from the ideal white northern European population. According to Schultz, the Norwegian-American historian O.M. Norlie asserted in the centennial's souvenir program that "the Anglo-Saxon ancestors of Americans of the dominant culture were closely related to Norwegians. In fact, he argued, the English, Irish, and French counties that supplied the most immigrants to America were once ruled by Norwegians – 'the Pilgrim Fathers themselves were mainly of Norwegian descent.'"[15] In an America increasingly obsessed with eugenicist racial fitness, the ancestors of Scandinavian immigrants were positioned as the biological wellspring of white America, the inspiration for its republican values, and the immigrants themselves as the most racially desirable source of new Americans.[16]

The Gothicist appeal of Norsemen to New Englanders remained so powerful that Oscar J. Falnes was compelled to devote an essay to its historic roots in the *New England Quarterly* in 1937.[17] In Canada, Gothicism fused the lore of Vikings with the British heritage and allegiance of the country's dominant class. The Gothicist sentiment within the ROM in the 1930s was such that Viking relics were more important than anything that survived from the ancien régime of French Canada, and Indigenous materials were a low acquisition and display priority. The distinction between the British as a biological race and as a culture and nation was as ephemeral as were the distinctions applied to other peoples in the Western worldview, and racial fitness was a bedrock notion of immigration policies in Canada and the United States.

"White racism ... was a universal feature of Britannic nationalism in the settlement colonies," John Herd Thompson writes of Canada in the first decades of the twentieth century.[18] C.T. Currelly, to his credit, never stooped to the Aryanist racism of Hjalmar Holand in extolling the superior nature of Norse adventurers (especially where Indigenous peoples were concerned). Currelly's claims of ancient Italian roots defied the blatant racism that infected the most virulent strain of Gothicism and its intertwined sentiments of British Imperialism, and his respect for craftsmanship inoculated him against a blindered devotion to Britishness at the expense of other cultures. Still, Currelly's public discussions of the Beardmore relics would have an undeniable if lightly wielded Gothicist edge. Norse weapons of any origin were freighted with connotations of a deep cultural heritage claimed by the British and their Imperial descendants in Canada through the Norman invasion of England. In January 1938, Currelly would state that the Vikings "to a certain degree are our own ancestors (because we must all have a bit of Norse blood in us if we are British)."[19] The Beardmore relics were an unparalleled opportunity to bridge the Old and New Worlds through weaponry, one of Currelly's favourite instructive tools, within a complex ethnic and imperialist context. The relics placed the Vikings in the landscape with a sword, which was always treated with the greatest priority by anyone discussing Eddy Dodd's find. A sword conveyed power, authority, and daring. It conjured the sweep of a Norseman's arm in claiming a new land for the Gothicist descendants who ultimately would settle it.

C.T. Currelly concluded his 12 November letter to Eddy Dodd: "As these are Ontario finds, we are naturally very eager to keep them in the province, so we shall be very glad if you will set a price on them … I should be very glad indeed to hear from you all the details you know of the finding of them. If you are quite unwilling to sell them, we will of course return them to you as soon as we can properly treat them for you, and at no expense to you."[20]

Dodd replied on 19 November.[21] He was "doubtful" of shipping the relics to Toronto "as I am afraid they may be broken up," and he suggested he bring them in person "and I could give you Better details and [a] Blue Print of my workings on claims." Dodd also warned: "I have been offered good substancel sum's from some american mining Engers and also one fellow from the newyork arts of archaeology what do you think you could give me for them, kindly let me know by Return of mail, and I would be able to judge if it was worth my while to Bring them down."

What Currelly made of Dodd's semiliterate bluff about eager American collectors is unknown. When he received Dodd's letter, he headed to Queen's Park to secure permission to pay for Dodd to bring the relics to the museum.[22] Currelly probably sought permission directly from the deputy minister, Duncan McArthur. That Currelly had to make such a request indicates how thin a shoestring the museum was operating on in the Depression years. Currelly informed Dodd by telegram on 23 November that he had secured the approval to pay his expenses. They could discuss a "possible purchase" when he arrived.[23] Dodd cabled the following day that he would leave at the "earliest convenience."[24] Currelly replied: "I sincerely hope that you will not ask more for the objects than we can pay. If they are all right, we are naturally willing to pay all we can, as we are very anxious to keep all Ontario finds in the province, and at the same time we do not wish to make anyone suffer for helping in such a matter."[25]

On Tuesday, 1 December, Dodd cabled Currelly: WILL BE IN TORONTO THURSDAY MORNING. Currelly alerted the deputy minister that Dodd was on his way.[26] On 3 December 1936, Eddy Dodd mounted the steps of the Avenue Road entrance of the ROM, bearing his rusty metal objects. The octagonal rotunda provided a dramatic view towards the Armour Court, where, if all went well, Dodd's relics were destined.

Currelly was joined by Thomas F. McIlwraith, curator of ethnology, in examining Dodd's relics.[27] Currelly prided himself on his knowledge of materials and methods, and he already had some experience in acquiring Viking swords, but they had come to him through conventional acquisition channels, the milieu of European dealers and private collectors, with little potential controversy in their provenance. The story of the museum's Viking sword from the Laking collection having been fished out of the Thames by a dredger working on the Vauxhall Bridge was a lovely story, but no one was much concerned with the name of the workman who supposedly sold it for a shilling or exactly what day he found it. Dodd's relics, in comparison, had an extraordinary story that was fundamental to their value. Their poor condition was to their credit as authentic survivals that appeared to be about one thousand years old. But were they unearthed as Dodd claimed?

Currelly would recall asking Dodd about the "handle bar," or shield handle. If there was a shield, Currelly suspected that an iron "boss," or dome, at the centre of a Viking shield would have survived. The museum already owned a circa AD 500 Anglo-Saxon shield boss, acquired in 1927. Dodd readily agreed that there had been just such a thing in the blasted trench, in the form of a dome of rust. This detail impressed Currelly. "That proved it for me!" he would tell the *Toronto Star* in 1938. "Because every shield of this kind would have a 'boss,' or protector, over the hand-grip. And a freight conductor wouldn't know anything about such things as that!"[28]

Currelly questioned Dodd on the details of the discovery; McIlwraith was probably the one who jotted down his replies in pencil on a personalized notepad. This small sheaf of paper, written on both sides, was the verbatim basis of a statement that was typed up and signed by Dodd.

3 ½ ft. down
¼ m. south of Blackwater

3 ½ m. from mth of Blackwater
Under big birch stub [sic]*, 2 ½ ft diameter*
Would be on line to headwaters of Jackpine R., on route to Superior
Map 312A of Bureau of Economic Geol. on second r of Warneford Sta.
gravel & muck on top.
Blackwater may have shifted course, so that this may have been on bank.
Dome of rust, slightly flat, about size of goose-egg, over "handle bar"
Dug out after loosening with dynamite.
Lying on vein of quartz.
No bones noticed, i.e. not obvious.

The note continued on the opposite side:

Rough country, unlikely that L. Nipigon spread in there.
Thrown out & left on surface of ground till 1933.

The heading of the typed statement, signed by Dodd, asserted he discovered the sword, axe, and shield handle on 24 May 1931.[29]

According to an affidavit sworn out by Dodd in February 1939, Currelly did not question him on the details of the discovery, particularly the shield boss, until after agreeing to make the purchase.[30] The mere sight of the relics seemed to convince Currelly he simply had to own them. He surely had already secured the promise of purchase funds from philanthropist Sigmund Samuel. Between 1921 and 1948, the province provided the museum with a total of $993,333 for acquisitions, but annual amounts steadily declined over that period, and private donors like Samuel were vital. Before the museum existed in physical fact, and long afterwards, Currelly depended on philanthropists on both sides of the Atlantic: private donors provided $558,411 for acquisitions between 1921 and 1948.[31] By the 1930s, Sigmund Samuel was one of the most important financial friends the museum had. According to Lovat Dickson, Sigmund Samuel, Sarah T. (Mrs H.D.) Warren, and Sir Robert Mond "formed a protective ring around Currelly, often saving him at the last moment from the consequence of some expensive purchase he had not been authorized to make." In Currelly's early years of collecting for the museum, Sarah Warren provided a cheque to cover a purchase he had insisted on making on personal credit after he asked her: "Do you want me to go to jail?"[32]

Sigmund Samuel was sole proprietor of a metals company, Samuel, Son & Co. (as it was incorporated in 1931). His prominence in a major philanthropic cause like the ROM was exceptional in a city that still permitted real estate covenants barring Jews. Sigmund's father, Lewis, was an orthodox Jew from a family that had lived in England since the time of Cromwell. He immigrated to the United States in 1844 and endured as a tailor's assistant in New York City, then as an itinerant peddler, and finally as the proprietor of a dry goods store in Syracuse. Lewis Samuel arrived in Toronto in 1856, establishing with his brother Mark a wholesale hardware business. The family enterprise diversified, mainly in metals, and prospered as Canada industrialized in the late nineteenth century. Like Sir Byron Edmund Walker, who recruited him as a museum patron, Sigmund Samuel was never able to secure a university education. Born in 1867, he had gone to work for his father as a child and took over the enterprise when his father died in 1887. Determined to build a life as an English gentleman, he divided his time between Toronto and London, and twice ran unsuccessfully for the British Parliament.[33]

Samuel funded ROM acquisitions across the collecting spectrum. He made his ROM debut in spectacular fashion in 1920, pledging three thousand pounds for the purchase of the Sturge Collection, which included more than four hundred Greek vases. He would pay for more than one thousand Japanese prints as well as silk brocades and numerous acquisitions for the Armour Court. With Sir Robert Mond, he reimbursed the nine thousand dollars that Bishop William Charles White, keeper of the museum's east Asiatic collection, paid for the H.H. Mu Library, which comprised more than forty thousand Chinese volumes; Samuel also funded paleontology acquisitions.[34] The University of Toronto granted Samuel an honorary doctorate in 1933 (Mond received one as well), and he took the award seriously enough that he insisted his grandchildren address him as "Dr Samuel."[35] His growing interest in Canadiana (he published a collection of documents and images from the Seven Years' War in Canada in 1934[36]) helped to turn the archaeology division away from a predominantly Old World focus, although, like Currelly, he was a Britophile. As Samuel had funded the ROM's previous purchases of Viking swords in 1925 and 1935, Currelly naturally turned to him when Eddy Dodd's find at last arrested his attention in late 1936.

According to a newspaper account in October 1938, when Currelly asked Dodd what he wanted for the relics, Dodd proposed he suggest a price. When Currelly replied that a museum could not do that, Dodd requested four hundred dollars. Currelly responded by saying the museum was prepared to give him five hundred dollars, which was ten times what

Dodd allegedly had tried to get for at least the sword from a Minnesota tourist.[37] It is not known how much Samuel might have authorized, but Currelly's offer was a fraction of what the relics would likely fetch if their provenance was indisputable.

Dodd was fine with that price. His collection of Norse relics that day became the property of the Royal Ontario Museum of Archaeology.[38]

With the Beardmore relics now in hand, C.T. Currelly at last responded to Teddy Elliott's correspondence on 10 December, enclosing the earlier response he had been holding since 11 November.[39] "I am glad to say that we just bought the sword, axe and shield handle," Currelly reported. "We owe you a very deep debt of gratitude. I don't quite know how we are going to be able to show it. One thing is, of course, that a full statement of how we got the things will go to the Minister of Education and to the Kingston papers, but it will have to wait until we can get certain details ready." Currelly made it clear that he did not want Elliott to write anything about the discovery. "This is the biggest historical find, I believe, that has ever been made in America, and it will be to our advantage as a Province to have it come out in as thoroughly scientific a form as possible."

The author of Currelly's envisioned report would be Duncan McArthur, the deputy minister of education. McArthur had held the Douglas Chair in Canadian and Colonial History at Queen's University and rose to head of the history department before being named deputy minister in July 1934 in the new Liberal government of Mitchell Hepburn.[40] But McArthur was not known for his scholarly output. Before accepting the posting in the Hepburn government, McArthur had made one contribution to the *Canadian Historical Review*, "Some Problems of Canadian Historical Scholarship," in 1927, a brief article that, in part, revisits his early work at the Dominion Archives in Ottawa under his mentor, social scientist Adam Shortt, and is otherwise concerned with the state of scholarship.[41] That same year he published the first edition of his only book, *History of Canada for High Schools*.

There is no evidence of what McArthur thought of Currelly's publication plan or, indeed, if he was even aware of it at this stage.[42] Currelly's choice of author to produce the "scientific publication" on the Beardmore relics appears to have been political. If the relics indeed represented the biggest historical find ever made in America, writing the definitive report would be a professional plum for McArthur, who was Currelly's ultimate boss. The report apparently was to be issued by the Ministry of Education, but this probably meant a new issue of the ROM's *Bulletin*. The annual publication's moribund state was another indicator of the museum's desperate finances. It was suspended after the 1929 issue, which featured the Viking sword from London. Only one issue, in 1932, had been produced since then.

To preserve the scholarly scoop for the deputy minister, Currelly needed to dissuade Elliott from pursuing his own article. "I strongly advise your not publishing anything just now, or, in fact, till after the Deputy Minister has brought out the full scientific publication," Currelly wrote, promising that McArthur's report would give him full credit for bringing the Beardmore items to the museum's attention and that the Kingston *Whig-Standard* would also be notified. To further dissuade him, Currelly criticized Elliott's scholarship. He advised Elliott on 10 December that his drawings were "so much idealized that they are useless as illustrations of the objects." He further warned: "Your drawings are made so much from memory and from looking at a book, that they would tend to bring discredit on you when the photographs of the objects are published." Whether Elliott's drawings were as bad as Currelly claimed is unknowable. But Currelly had also informed Dodd that Elliott's drawings were "quite good," certainly good enough for him to realize that the sword was probably tenth-century Norse.[43] Currelly also observed: "There are also certain inaccuracies in your information. Dr. Burwash has at no time had any connection with the Royal Ontario Museum." That was an overly literal reading of Elliott's understanding from Dodd that Burwash was associated with the ROM. Currelly also noted that some details of Elliott version of Dodd's discovery differed from Dodd's signed statement. The date of discovery would have been foremost as Elliott had understood from Dodd the find was in 1933, not 1931, but the size of the birch stump was another problem. Elliott had been told it was fourteen inches in diameter; Burwash, in 1934, had reported it as fifteen inches. Dodd's statement made it an outlandish two and a half feet. Discrepancies that could have been an early warning about Dodd's truthfulness instead moved Currelly, in an attempt to dissuade Elliott from publishing, to assert that he had a poor grasp of facts.

"This may seem as if I am trying to deprive you of a chance of a certain amount of kudos from the publication," Currelly continued. "You will notice I am not attempting to gain any myself. I am particularly anxious to have no attacks made that may queer the thing rather badly. When anything of this kind is found, a great many people immediately try to see if they cannot display great superiority by disproving it; and it would be a great pity, I think, for any preliminary paper to appear without all the information possible, photographs and everything else of this kind." Currelly closed on a warm and generous note. "I want to express the deep debt of gratitude we owe to you, in fact, I think I may say, that the Province owes to you, for having been such an important link in this chain of events."

Elliott replied immediately, on 13 December.[44] He said nothing about the supposed flaws in his drawings, and he was not willing to concede carelessness or error with respect to Dodd's discovery story: "Discrepancies were bound to occur between my version of Dodd's story and his own. With me he was chatting informally while with you he was probably much more careful in his statements." Elliott otherwise was charmed and deferential. He agreed not to publish, assuring Currelly: "I will do nothing to embarass [sic] the project." It was kind of Currelly to suggest that, in due time, both the Kingston *Whig-Standard* and the deputy minister would be notified of his contribution. "I am not seeking publicity, but I shall look forward with pleasure to the publication of Dr. McArthur's report." He allowed himself a sense of collegiality in the effort to prove a Norse presence deep in North America: "I thank you for your generous expressions of gratitude. If scientific investigation vindicates our suspicion of Norse origin (with all the historical significance that implies) then I shall be amply repaid for any small part I have been permitted to play."

Elliott also wrote T.L. Tanton, Hjalmar Holand, and (finally) Olof Strandwold that day. He shared with Tanton the news of the museum's purchase and the plan for McArthur to produce a report.[45] He quoted Currelly's statement about the relics promising to be the biggest historical find ever made in America and stressed the secret nature of the purchase. "I need hardly add that I am passing the information on to you in confidence because of your kindly interest in the matter." To Holand he was less revealing but similarly informed him that the museum had bought Dodd's relics "and [was] making a thorough investigation of the whole matter." Photographs would not be available until after the government report was published, and he promised to be sure Holand received a copy. "Till the report appears I am not in a position to add anything more to what I have already told you," but he allowed: "I have reason to believe that report will be very interesting from your standpoint."[46]

Elliott was less collegial with Strandwold, not even mentioning that the museum had purchased the relics. "I have handed the whole matter off to the Director of the Royal Ontario Museum who is making a thorough investigation of the whole matter."[47] In his letter to Strandwold especially, El-liott wrote in a slightly officious, proprietary tone. He took a not unjustified pride in having brought the relics to Currelly's attention and, despite his earlier hesitancy about the provenance, was becoming excited by the possi-bility, even the likelihood, they represented a new chapter in exploration history that aligned with Holand's theorizing. Elliott presumed for himself a continuing, central role. He expected to be recognized for his contribu-tions and to be kept informed by the museum. For that, he was prepared to be the good foot soldier of scholarship and maintain his public silence.

On 29 December, Teddy Elliott took advantage of the holiday school break to visit C.T. Currelly at the museum. Currelly shared that, since mak-ing the purchase, he had discussed the relics with Ned Burwash and John Jacob. Elliott would recall how Currelly "maintained that Dr. Burwash had never mentioned the matter to him at all and that his first intimation was when I wrote. Further, he said that he checked with Dr. Burwash as to why he had not mentioned the fact to him long before, and that Dr. Bur-wash had stated that he did not think the matter of sufficient importance to warrant mention. The Doctor then continued to mention another sim-ilar instance of the same type."[48] This was a strange assertion for Currelly to make as Burwash had addressed the relics in two letters and a telephone call. Otherwise there was never any doubt in the minds of Burwash and Currelly that the former had alerted the latter to the find.

If Currelly was being misleading about Burwash's role within a few weeks of the purchase, then he was already engineering their authenticity. While Currelly would come to credit Burwash with having alerted him to the find, he would never reveal the contents of Burwash's letters, especially the one of February 1934 in which Burwash sketched the items and related Dodd's impression of them. Dodd's supposed naiveté about the presence of a shield boss when Currelly questioned him would be fundamental to the latter's assertions of his belief in Dodd's discovery story. But if Dodd knew in February 1934, from a research trip to the library, that the find included a Norse shield, as Burwash had reported to Currelly, then Dodd certainly knew that a Norse shield had a metal boss more than two years before he brought the relics to the ROM and was questioned by Currelly.

John Jacob's appearance at the ROM on 9 December 1936 was another peculiar episode in the young history of the museum's acquisition. Elliott would recall Currelly's telling him in his meeting with the museum director later that month that Jacob had come by the museum and mentioned to him some Viking relics he ought to consider acquiring, and being surprised to learn that Currelly had just purchased the very same.[49] Jacob had made a suspiciously chance visit to the museum, only six days after the sale, to offer corroborating evidence for the discovery that Dodd knew the museum would seek. It is probable that Jacob, who lived for part of the year in Toronto, had met with Dodd in the city in that first week of December and learned of the sale (if he did not already know Dodd was taking the relics to the museum). Had Dodd then sent Jacob to Currelly? Or had Jacob taken the initiative?

Jacob provided a short statement to Currelly on 9 December: "When the find of the Viking sword, axe and shield handle was made, I, John Drew Jacob, game warden, visited the place where they were found, within a very short time, and saw the impression of the iron rust on the rock. A big group of birch trees covered the immediate area and no digging could have been done without showing."[50] In saying there was a "big group" of birch trees, Jacob probably meant that the tree Dodd removed was a clump of dwarf birch, as he would later attest. It might explain why Dodd had stated to Currelly that the tree was two and a half feet in diameter, not the fourteen- or fifteen-inch stump to which he had previously attested. This detail suggests that Dodd and Jacob had discussed the discovery story before Dodd met Currelly. But, as we will see, Jacob does not appear to have been an ongoing accomplice of Dodd. Jacob valued his connections in the museum's zoology division, and he was probably determined to forge one with the archaeology division by making himself useful to Currelly. While Jacob seemed to have been involved in researching the Norse origins of the relics with or for Dodd, he now appeared to be freelancing his corroboration. By April 1938 it would become clear that Jacob was operating independently of Dodd, to his own ends, even while working to Dodd's advantage. The idea that there was an "impression" of rust in the schist sounded like the "dome of rust" Dodd had described for Currelly, which was taken to be the crumbled boss, but Jacob was attesting to the condition of the discovery site *after* the relics had been removed. The assertion of the existence of a rust impression would belong to Jacob alone, and this impression would become an outline of the sword, with nothing to do with the shield or its boss. In his brief statement, Jacob did not provide a date for his visit to the site, gave no details about the nature of the rust mark, and said nothing about his role in identifying the relics as Norse.

In asserting that he had visited the site "within a very short time" of the find, Jacob was creating complications for Dodd's discovery story. If that were the case, how could the relics have remained tossed aside at the mining claim for two years, ignored by Dodd, as Dodd's statement six days earlier to Currelly indicated? Why would Jacob have travelled to the site and made a prompt inspection of the hole in which the relics had just been found, if Dodd wasn't paying any attention to them?

John Jacob's statement, which was offered the day before the museum director wrote Elliott to report the purchase, assured Currelly of the find's authenticity – or, rather, assured him that he could defend its authenticity. If Jacob had come forward not to assist Dodd but to ingratiate himself with Currelly, he succeeded splendidly. Currelly needed more than Dodd's word to justify his tremendous acquisition, and Jacob's eyewitness corroboration proved hugely important. As significant problems with the provenance case emerged, Currelly turned to Jacob to provide an additional, lengthy statement (which was further amended) that buttressed Dodd's discovery story and eliminated timing problems. The fact that Jacob was no longer a game warden when he appeared at the museum to endorse Dodd's find tended to be glossed over. Jacob became Currelly's unimpeachable witness, a "government man" from a "good family" as Currelly made class and character a central issue in the reliability of conflicting testimonies. Currelly would also turn to Jacob as an investigator as the hoax counternarrative emerged. In the final, astounding chapter of Jacob's involvement in the Beardmore affair, Jacob would vanish into thin air, if not actually into dark waters.

Eddy Dodd's signed statement for C.T. Currelly had its own complication, independent of John Jacob's version of events. The original notes said: *Thrown out & left on surface of ground till 1933.* Nothing indicated how long the relics lay there, which indicates that Dodd did not volunteer a discovery date at the time of sale. Currelly may have added the typed headline with the date of 24 May 1931 to Dodd's signed statement much later, to tidy up the provenance, after Dodd volunteered the discovery date to the press in January 1938 (see chapter 9), when he also said the relics had been left at the claim for two years.

Otherwise, the first time a 1931 discovery year (but not the full date) was stated in a museum document is found in Thomas McIlwraith's report on his visit to the middle claim with Eddy Dodd in September 1937 (see chapter 6). Ned Burwash's February 1934 letter, which reported that Dodd found the relics "some three years ago," did support a 1931 discovery, but for some reason Dodd, in 1936, was limiting his recollection of discovery events to 1933. Teddy Elliott had understood back in August that Dodd discovered the relics in May 1933 and left them at the camp for almost two months before bringing them home. Currelly knew this because Elliott had sent him a draft of his article, but nothing in the museum's notes of the meeting with Dodd indicate that Currelly interrogated Dodd on the timing details. An enquiring mind might have wondered what had occurred between 1931 and 1933 that Dodd, in his constantly shifting story, was trying to avoid.

6

The Norse Grave

At the turn of the twentieth century, preservation and restoration of rusted iron antiquities invited an assortment of strategies, some of them alarming. One prescribed heating an artefact in a furnace and then plunging it in water or a weak sulphuric acid bath to violently remove the rust. Krefting's Method, first published in 1892 by the Norwegian archaeologist Otto Krefting, took a less pyrotechnic approach. An artefact was wrapped in zinc strips and immersed in an electrolytic solution of caustic soda. A voltaic cell was thus created, with the iron object the negative pole and the zinc strips the positive pole. As an electrical current naturally flowed between the poles through galvanic action, oxygen was freed from the iron oxide rust and combined with the zinc to form zinc oxide, which then dissolved in the electrolytic solution. The electrochemical process of rust removal usually took twenty-four hours but could last several weeks, depending on the artefact.[1]

Krefting's Method was not without risks or harm. Harder, underlying rust (*edelrost*) that was not eliminated by the process was removed with a chisel, and the galvanic process could cause great and irreversible damage. As Krefting warned, Iron Age weapons removed from the earth with a distinctive form could "be unrecognizable when removed from the electrolytic bath."[2] Krefting's process was not recommended for rust incrustations of greater than one-eighth of an inch (three millimetres) or with objects with precious metal inlays.

C.T. Currelly had seen Krefting's Method employed in Munich, and the ROM adopted what Currelly called the Munich Method for preserving iron acquisitions. This method gave Currelly the confidence to acquire and treat heavily rusted antiquities that other museum directors shied away from. However, he defied Krefting's warning not to use the method on items with more than one-eighth of an inch of rust. "In one case," Currelly recalled, "a big ball of rusted iron yielded us a beautifully made axe, in which a Roman had cut his initials."[3] The treatment of the Beardmore relics was overseen by the museum's preparator, William Todd, who had no formal training: he had joined the staff in 1927, when he was seventeen, and may have started out as a carpenter. Todd would become chief conservator and, according to S. James Gooding, for many years was "the only conservator working in the Canadian historical museum field."[4] The young preparator subjected the Beardmore relics to this electrochemical treatment over an unknown period, leaving the museum with three heavily pitted and eroded relics that were then sealed in paraffin.

How much damage might have been inflicted on the relics is one of the great unknowns of the Beardmore saga. When ROM conservator Sarah Stock cleaned and prepared the sword for exhibition in 2017, she found that glue had been applied at an unknown time to strengthen a grip that was so weakened the metal sagged.[5] The lack of a documented treatment process complicates the issue of contradictory recollections of the sword's size and condition before the ROM acquired it. The relics were probably already in precarious condition when they were subjected to what seems to have been an aggressive treatment. X-rays in 2017 revealed the treated sword had a pattern of round pitting that was produced by corrosion having pushed off surface flakes of iron. The pattern was typical of other Norse finds that had been removed from the ground and had not been treated to remove salts from the metal, and the process could have been exacerbated by humid conditions after unearthing.[6]

The electrochemical treatment of the Beardmore relics might have lasted a few weeks, but Currelly was in no hurry to announce the find or put the items on display. As Currelly had advised Teddy Elliott, he expected any announcement of Norse weapons blasted out of a prospector's trench east of Lake Nipigon to be a target for criticism. "From the first I have warned archaeology this thing will rip the museum up the back," J.H. Fleming over in the zoology division would advise a friend in February 1938.[7] Currelly and Elliott both knew before the ROM acquired the relics that they could be a hoax – authentic in being Norse weapons but fake in not having been found in the manner and location Dodd claimed. Currelly would assert that, after the purchase, he remained concerned about unpleasant surprises. "When I bought the weapons, I kept quiet about them for a while to see if anything could be found out as to any possibility of their having been brought from the old world," he explained to the editor of *Antiquity* in January 1940.[8]

In the 1930s, there was no broadly accepted evidence for a Norse presence anywhere in North America. Dubious rune stones proliferated and were dismissed as fakes. Only Hjalmar Holand's indefatigable advocacy was keeping the Kensington stone alive as an historical find that was accepted by professionals like Currelly. In her talk at Chippewa Park, Mary

Black had placed the Beardmore relics in the twelfth or thirteenth century, between the circa 1000 Vinland sagas and the 1362 Kensington stone.
Currelly thought they might be associated with the Kensington expedition, but, on first glance, the weapons looked tenth century. It was hard to
imagine how such weapons, if they were indeed circa 900 to 1000, would
have been carried by someone associated with the Knutson expedition
some four hundred years later. Instead, they could be from an expedition
described in the Vinland sagas, but Vinland was supposed to be on the Atlantic coast. Otherwise they must have been part of an expedition made
around the same time as those in the Vinland sagas. Not every family saga,
which were oral traditions, had survived in written form, and it was possible that there were contemporary voyages that had been lost to recorded memory. Some scholars, Vilhjalmur Stefansson especially, were open to
the idea that Greenland Norse would have probed Hudson Strait had they
become aware of it in crossing Davis Strait. Conceivably, these adventurers could have followed Hudson Strait all the way to Hudson Bay and
James Bay, although plunging from there into the heart of North America in an overland/riverine expedition, as in the case of Holand's Kensington stone expedition, was another matter. Currelly himself had doubted
to Dodd that the Beardmore relics got to his middle claim in the hands of
Norsemen. Whatever scenario Currelly chose to advance, he could not expect leading scholars to accept Eddy Dodd's relics without a strong provenance. But if Currelly could present one – or assure scholars there *was* one
– history would have to be rewritten to accommodate them.

On 20 January 1937, word leaked to the press of the Beardmore discovery through Currelly's friend, Ned Burwash, during his final tour as a
prospecting instructor. While Burwash was delivering classes in Sault Ste
Marie from 14 to 22 January,[9] he revealed to E. Ross MacKay, associate editor of the *Sault Daily Star*, that, "about two years ago," Dodd had found in
a gravel bed near Warneford "an iron sword, an iron axe and part of a
shield, which investigation had shown to be definitely of Norse workmanship of the Viking period."[10] Burwash's dating of the find to 1934–35 was
surprising, but MacKay may have confused the time Burwash recalled seeing the relics with when Dodd found them, given that other article details
were not perfect: for example, they included Dodd's showing the articles
to Burwash on a visit to Toronto and a sword length of a mere fifteen inches, which would have been accurate for a broken portion. MacKay further
stated that, on Burwash's suggestion, the relics were sent to Currelly, whose
investigations had established that they were Norse. The story, while

inaccurate, defied Currelly's telling Elliott less than a month earlier that Burwash had failed to do anything about Dodd's find. And while the article did not say that the museum had purchased the relics, it was the first word in print of a connection between Dodd's sensational find and the ROM. But, unlike the news of Mary Black's talk the previous August, the *Daily Star* article never gained traction through the wire services.

Currelly shared news of the relics with colleagues, perhaps to informally seek their opinion on their authenticity or to pick their brains on how they might have reached Dodd's middle claim. One of these colleagues was Wilfrid Bovey, director of extra-mural relations and extensions at McGill, who had delivered a paper on the Vinland sagas before the Royal Society of Canada in 1936 proposing that Thorfinn Karlsefni's settlement, Høp, was in Chaleur Bay in the Gulf of St Lawrence.[11] The Beardmore find, Bovey wrote Currelly on 4 January 1937, "fits in entirely with that of the rune stone at Kensington to which I referred in my paper. I have always believed that the Hudson Bay route as well as the Gulf of St. Lawrence was part of northern sailor lore and this seems to put a most important piece of evidence into the case ... The Kensington stone has been described by its finder [sic] in a book and I have seen some interesting letters by European experts agreeing to its authenticity." [12]

Currelly also shared the news with John D. Robins, a professor of English at Victoria College, who, in turn, informed Chester N. Gould, a prominent linguist and Scandinavianist at the University of Chicago and a past president (1929–31) of the Society for Advancement of Scandinavian Study. Gould had been a harsh critic of Hjalmar Holand's Kensington ideas since 1910. Robins, in his letter to Gould, must have drawn a parallel between the Kensington stone and the Beardmore acquisition. In reply, Gould launched into several pages of cheerful condemnation of the scholarship of Holand, the stone's "apostle in chief." Gould, in part, advised: "His book sounds good if you do not look between the lines, then it shows up as worthless. To the non-specialist, it reads better than a detective novel, and more convincing, but it is tricky at every step. He appeals to manuscript passages which he can not read correctly. He could not pass my first quarter examination in Old Icelandic, so far as his grammatical forms go ... yet he assumes to speak with authority on matters of manuscript readings and linguistic history. He reproduces bits of medieval latin manuscripts as a basis for some of his argumentation. Show them to a man who is accustomed to reading medieval latin manuscripts and watch him smile at the argumentation."[13]

While the Kensington stone was "an amusing fake," Gould counselled that "the possibility of a fairly extensive Scandinavian commerce via Hudson Bay or the Atlantic Coast is a very reasonable thing to discuss" and should be considered "quite apart from the question of the [Kensington] inscription." Robins forwarded the letter to Currelly as it found its way into the museum's Beardmore files. Gould's opinion may not have moderated Currelly's enthusiasm for the Kensington stone, but it would have assured him that a leading Scandinavianist (and withering Holand critic) thought the Beardmore find could stand on its own merits as evidence for a Norse presence deep in the continent.

Having been informed of the museum acquisition by Teddy Elliott, Hjalmar Holand wrote Currelly on 16 December 1936 to introduce himself and to request photographs of the relics.[14] As much as Currelly was enchanted by the Kensington stone, he ignored Holand's letter. There was a limit to how voluble he was willing to be about the acquisition, especially with strangers. Holand did not give up. His circle of supporters included Graham Carey, the architect, artist, and liturgical art critic associated with Harvard's Fogg Art Museum. Carey was charged with the idea of pre-Columbian visitors to North America, and, on 24 February, he informed Holand that Langdon Warner, an archaeologist and the curator of Oriental art at the Fogg, was writing Currelly "to see if he can get us some advance info on the Nipigon finds."[15] The ROM and the Fogg had magnificent examples of Chinese wall paintings, and, through Warner, Currelly had recently secured the help of the Fogg's conservator, George Leslie Stout, to prepare for exhibition the ROM's thirteenth-century Buddhist fresco from the Hsing-Hua monastery in Shansi Province, which had been carted off in eighty pieces.

Warner wrote Currelly on 23 February 1937, on behalf of his friend Carey, who "has become convinced that the whole subject of the Norsemen in America has fallen into undeserved disrepute. He has spent the last year or so collecting the available evidence in an attempt to satisfy his own mind. He tells me that you and your friends have dug up a sword, a shield and an axe near Lake Nipigon." Carey wanted photographs of the items for "study and comparison," and Warner said he would "cheerfully assume responsibility that Carey will not rush into print on the subject or permit anyone else to do so." Carey otherwise wanted to know when publication on the find was planned.[16]

"I am really sorry that I cannot fall in with your request," Currelly replied.[17] Currelly feared published leaks, and as Carey was corresponding with Holand, who was writing a follow-up book to *The Kensington Stone*, the fear was justified. Currelly explained the Beardmore relics case had been turned over to Duncan McArthur, "who is also my ultimate chief. He will publish them when he can get all the information he wants, and a preliminary publication of any kind would be very unwise. The demand for photographs has been very great, as we have quietly talked about the find to a great many people."

Warner was disappointed, and cautioning. "I quite understand that this Viking material must be jealously guarded from unauthorized publications – or any publication at all if you hope for more definite proofs," he replied. "However, I'm sorry in this case because Carey has no ambition to print and it is always well to have several minds mulling over the available material."[18] However, from the beginning Currelly was determined to limit the number of people, expert and otherwise, whom the museum consulted before revealing the find. Even with those in whom he chose to confide, he provided minimal information.

Word otherwise continued to spread through academic circles, and Currelly's assistant, Ethlyn Greenaway, would find herself handling a mass of correspondence on the Beardmore acquisition over the next few years. Born in 1894 in Toronto, Greenaway was the daughter of a foundry core-maker.[19] Her brother Roy was a crime reporter for the *Toronto Star*. She graduated from Victoria College in arts in 1916 and spent a year in museum work in England after the war before being hired by Currelly around 1921. Never marrying, Greenaway was a tireless assistant who conducted her own correspondence with museum contacts. In February 1937, she was called upon to soothe the bruised feelings of A.D. Fraser, a professor in the archaeology division of the University of Virginia's school of ancient languages. Fraser had favourably reviewed the ROM's two-volume work on its Greek vases in 1932,[20] but he was now operating well outside his expertise in Greek and Roman art in preparing an article for the *Dalhousie Review* on evidence for Norse voyages to North America, one hundred years after the publication of *Antiquitates Americanae*.

Fraser had written Currelly to learn more about the Beardmore find; evidently, Currelly's response was brusque and unforthcoming. Greenaway crossed paths with Norman W. De Witt, a former dean of the Faculty of Arts at Victoria College, and learned from him of Fraser's treatment. As Greenaway related to Fraser, the reply "had made you wonder if we had discovered they are not genuine. No, there can be no possible doubt about the weapons themselves, and we have been able to check the story of their discovery and we believe the find to have been absolutely genuine as described to us." Because of the find's historical importance, an official publication would be made by the minister of education, "probably late this spring or in early autumn."[21]

Greenaway was overly optimistic as no publication appeared, if for no other reason than that there was nothing scientific to report. Currelly had brief, signed statements from Eddy Dodd and John Jacob on the discovery and nothing else with which McArthur could work. Fraser meanwhile proceeded to publish "The Norsemen in Canada" in the July 1937 issue of the *Dalhousie Review*. He cast aside the various purported rune stones that had emerged in New England and Nova Scotia, as well as one more recently announced near Winnipeg, observing: "The runic inscription has long served as a pitfall for the ignorant and the learned alike."[22] Fraser then advised: "a mass of rubbish has now been cleared away, and we are beginning to lay our hands on a few things that are of certain origin."[23] He was among the academics who accepted the Kensington stone as the one genuine gem among the inscribed dross, thanks to Hjalmar Holand's work, and also accepted as authentic the assortment of purported Norse iron relics that Holand had rounded up. Those finds failed to impress Chester Gould. "Most of these are such things as our great-grandfathers would have taken along on a lengthy canoe voyage in the wilds, even the spear from Wisconsin does not impress me," Gould had written Robins. "Most of the things are so unspecialized that they could be found anywhere." Holand's Norse fire-steel, he continued, "is the duplicate as to size, form … of one I saw used by an Irish farm-hand in Minnesota in my youth."[24]

Having been assured by Greenaway of the museum's absolute confidence, Fraser presented the Beardmore relics as an authentic Norse find. "A discovery of the highest importance has been announced only a few months ago in Ontario," Fraser reported, although the ROM had made no formal announcement. A "Viking grave" had been blasted by a prospector out of a mineral deposit, its contents consisting of "a sword, a battle-axe and a shield" in "a remarkably good state of preservation." The material had "escaped the clutches of private collectors" by being purchased by the Royal Ontario Museum of Archaeology, and Fraser incorrectly reported that the relics were already on display. "The importance of the Nipigon discovery would be difficult to exaggerate," Fraser declared, "arising as it does from the consideration that we have here the first undoubted example of undisturbed Norse remains ever found in North America."[25] Fraser was getting ahead of himself: no one had said anything about human remains, especially "undisturbed" ones, but his assertion indicated that the discovery was already being whispered about within the ROM as a gravesite, which was a great leap forward from Currelly's initial doubt that Norsemen had even transported the relics to the middle claim. To Fraser, the Beardmore find suggested an "entirely obvious" exploration route for the Norse, through Hudson Strait to Hudson Bay, James Bay, and then into the continent via the Albany River and an unnamed tributary of Lake Nipigon.[26]

Fraser's article was a significant scholarly endorsement of the ROM's acquisition, although Currelly would be exercised by the leak (and the inaccuracies). Yet the mainstream press missed the revelation that these astounding artefacts were in the museum's possession, if not actually in a display case. For the second time in seven months, a premature announcement of the acquisition had failed to find traction in the wider media.

The key point in Greenaway's letter to Fraser, and in Fraser's article, was that, before performing any corroborative research, the museum – or, rather, Currelly – had become convinced of the relics' authenticity and that they might even represent Norse grave goods in northern Ontario. The museum still needed to examine the discovery site and determine the weapons typology – their place in the standard classification system found in Jan Petersen's *De Norske Vikingesverd* (1919), which catalogued the Norse weapons in Scandinavian museum collections and identified sword, axe, and spear types by letter codes. The Beardmore weapons could be modern fakes. They could be authentic, but individually from significantly different eras or geographic origins, as some weapons types were known mostly or exclusively in particular regions of the Norse world and had been assigned specific date ranges. Incongruities would make their alleged discovery as a single deposit of artefacts more than a little suspect. The discovery story would collapse, regardless of what any site investigation suggested.

For some reason, Currelly did not initiate any serious research into the weapons typology. The University of Toronto or the ROM held a copy of Sir Guy Francis Laking's multi-volume *A Record of European Armour and Arms through Seven Centuries*, and Currelly consulted it.[27] But libraries at the ROM and the University of Toronto were so thin on reference books that they did not hold Du Chaillu's *The Viking Age*, which Elliott had found in the stacks of the Fort William Public Library. And despite Currelly's having now acquired three Viking swords, neither the museum nor the university owned a copy of Petersen's *Der Norske Vikingesverd*. Indeed, there was not a single copy of Petersen anywhere in Canada.

Currelly needed to complete the preservation treatment and photograph the weapons before seeking informed opinions. He also may have left aside the weapons typology so as not to expose the claim to outside experts whom he did not know personally before he was confident about the discovery site. That aspect of the research he could manage internally. He asked John Jacob to provide a more detailed statement on his examination of the site. Availing himself of a typewriter and some letterhead at his brother's engineering firm in Toronto, Jacob hammered out a one-page statement. Although he did not date it, the one assigned by the museum, of June 1937, is likely correct.[28]

For the first time, Jacob told of encountering the relics through Aaron Lougheed and of the two of them researching their Norse character in the library. He then wrote of visiting Dodd's middle claim "only a matter of days after the discovery was made," but he still did not provide a year. As he explained:

Dodd had made the discovery in the process of stripping a mineral vein[.] I saw that there had been about four feet of earth over the rock at this point. The imprint of the sword was very distinct on the rockso [sic] clear was it that you [would] almost think the sword had been imbedded in the rock. I am not certain that [the] imprint of the ax was not there to [sic] but I was so taken up with the sword impression that I would not say for certain that it was not visable [sic] however this would not be surprising as the ax was probably laid in the buckler and dirt would in this way have gotten under it and prevented it from resting on the rock[.] No trace of buckles or c [sic] clothing remains were found but that was not surprising either as they may have needed his clothes and removed them or what is much more likely wild animals dug him up as the grave would be very shalow [sic]. There was not much overburden in this neighborhood and any way it is hard to say what the conditions were surrounding the burial as burial it undoubtedly was.

Jacob concluded by recounting his efforts to alert the museum and to persuade Dodd to send the relics to the ROM for examination.

Jacob seemed to be playing up to Currelly in rationalizing the site as a Norse grave, justifying how the relics could be there without the body. For the first time, the sword was said to have left a vivid rust impression on the underlying rock. Jacob's reference to a "buckler" recalled the small-diameter shield Ned Burwash had drawn in his February 1934 letter to Currelly. Dodd may have gathered an impression of a buckler style of shield and handle from research Jacob had conducted in the local library prior to February 1934. In avowing that the sword almost seemed to be "imbedded" in the rock, Jacob in June 1937 was echoing the story Teddy Elliott had heard from Dodd in August 1936. Otherwise, Jacob blazed an independent factual trail. He asserted that the axe did not leave a rust mark on the rock because it would have been contained inside the buckler, whereas Dodd had told Elliott that the underlying rock appeared to be moulded to the outline of the axe. As well, Dodd would never mention Lougheed (or, for that matter, Jacob) in his various accounts of the discovery, or any sort of rust mark in the schist.

As outwardly valuable as Jacob's latest statement was in authenticating the Beardmore find, Currelly remained determined to keep the purchase under wraps. He left the find unmentioned in his summary of acquisitions by the museum's archaeology division for the 1937 President's Report of the University of Toronto (which addressed the fiscal year ending in June 1937). He instead made plans to examine the discovery site. In June 1937, he began arranging for Thomas F. McIlwraith, the museum's curator of ethnology and chair of the University of Toronto's anthropology department, to head north by train to inspect the middle claim with Eddy Dodd.

"I Think He Is Honest"

Thomas Forsyth McIlwraith V, the man chosen by C.T. Currelly to investigate the discovery site at Eddy Dodd's middle claim, was literally the museum director's right-hand man; Sylvia Hahn would place him at Currelly's side in the jousting mural in the Armour Court, where Dodd's relics came to be displayed. He was raised in the Victorian milieu of amateur natural science in Hamilton, Ontario, which also produced Sir Byron Edmund Walker. Thomas III, his grandfather, owned a commercial wharf and was an ardent birdwatcher. Grandfather Thomas's treatise, *The Birds of Ontario*, was "a landmark in the maturing of avian biology as a discipline," and he was well known among North American naturalists. He taught Ernest Thomson Seton taxidermy (some of Thomas III's stuffed birds became part of the display collection of the ROM), and he was one of the founders of the American Ornithologists Union.[1] Thomas V, born the youngest of three children in Hamilton in 1899, received a private school education and tracked towards academia and museum work. He was a capable field naturalist,[2] and by training and profession an expert on human culture, but it was his skill in judging human nature that would be tested by Eddy Dodd.

McIlwraith was four months younger than Teddy Elliott. Like Elliott, he was a late entry in the fighting ranks of the Great War. At eighteen, having already completed a year of studies in the arts at McGill, he entered officer's training with the Canadian Overseas Expeditionary Force in June 1917. He was a small man, five feet, four-and-a-half inches tall, with a thirty-three-inch chest and a "sallow" complexion on enlistment, but keen to serve, having already been rejected as too young at sixteen. To his disappointment, he never saw action, only arriving in France as a lieutenant with the King's Own Scottish Borderers (an infantry regiment in the British Army) in October 1918, shortly before the armistice.[3]

After the war, McIlwraith was an outstanding anthropology student at Cambridge University, winning scholarships and completing his studies with first class standing. He was preparing for field studies in New Guinea when his promise brought him to the attention of Edward Sapir at the Dominion Geological Survey, who was looking for additional hires.

McIlwraith wrote Sapir, expressing his desire "to do field work among the dying races."[4]

Sapir could not offer McIlwraith a permanent position, but he steered him away from New Guinea, where Diamond Jenness had done his field-work at Oxford. McIlwraith accepted from Sapir a contract of a few months' duration for fieldwork among the Bella Coola (Nuxalk) of British Columbia. Before heading west, McIlwraith met with C.T. Currel-ly and museum trustee Julian Falconer about possible positions at the ROM and the University of Toronto. He conducted his fieldwork over the course of eleven months, from 1922 to 1924. The result was "one of the finest ethnographies ever written about a Northwest Coast people ... a splendidly comprehensive and thematically coherent study," according to the editors of his field letters.[5]

McIlwraith completed a draft of his massive dissertation, married Beu-lah Gillet Knox of Ohio, and started a family of three children. In 1925, he accepted a cross-posting as the keeper of ethnology at the ROM under Cur-relly and a lecturer in anthropology at the University of Toronto. "It was for many years a demanding and lonely post," the editors of his field let-ters have observed.[6] Until a second hiring was made – the ethnologist Charles "Steve" W.M. Hart in 1932 – McIlwraith *was* the anthropology program at the University of Toronto, and he had the additional duties of overseeing the ethnology collection of the museum. He was also bedev-iled by his dissertation, which he had been striving to publish with the DGS and the National Museum since turning in a draft in March 1925. Di-amond Jenness, promoted to head of anthropology at the DGS and the Na-tional Museum with Sapir's retirement in 1925, assumed the Sisyphean task of bringing the dissertation to a publishable form. In addition to its length (more than two thousand manuscript pages), its publication was complicated by the specialized typography required for the Nuxalk lan-guage and the sexually explicit nature of Nuxalk traditions, which scan-dalized DGS geologists on the editorial board. Jenness and McIlwraith were forced to cut the most explicit passages and convert other passages into Latin. Although a first volume was finally prepared and approved for publication, it died at press in 1930, a victim of Depression cutbacks. It would not be published until 1948, by the University of Toronto Press, as the two-volume *The Bella Coola Indians*, with all excised passages restored and Latin obfuscation eliminated. [7] Although John Barker argues that it "must be regarded as one of the most authoritative ethnographies we have on a traditional Northwest-Coast society," he also notes that, by the time it was published, McIlwraith's dissertation was "curiously out-of-date, an example of 'salvage anthropology.'"[8]

A delay of more than twenty years in bringing his dissertation to press did not help McIlwraith's standing as an anthropologist, nor did the lack of funds for anthropology at the university (a problem also faced by the DGS and the National Museum in the 1920s and 1930s). "One can only imagine what might have happened had McIlwraith become established early in his career as a leading ethnographer," Barker wonders. "As it was, he turned his energies towards administration, an area in which his talents proved less impressive."[9] In 1936, the University of Toronto created one of the first anthropology departments at any Canadian university, with McIlwraith promoted to professor and placed in charge while continuing as the museum's curator of ethnology. "McIlwraith was consistently cautious, conservative, and somewhat secretive – and not always effective," as well as "somewhat myopic and stubborn on fundamentals," Barker writes of McIlwraith as an administrator.[10] Soon after his promotion, McIlwraith was embroiled in the Beardmore case.

There is an important difference between archaeology conducted in the lab – the careful cleaning, preserving, identifying, sorting, and describing of artefacts – and field, or "dirt," archaeology, which involves conducting excavations and includes not only recovering artefacts but also recording stratigraphy, identifying remnants of physical structures and other signs of occupation, and describing it all in accurate field surveys. Expertise in field archaeology in Canada was restricted to the National Museum, but it was in short supply, and, while experienced, it was also aging. The DGS's original hiring, Harlan I. Smith, retired in 1937, and while William Wintemberg was promoted to associate archaeologist that year, his chronic poor health limited his fieldwork.[11]

The University of Toronto and the ROM were bereft of expertise in field archaeology. Nominally, C.T. Currelly was the department's professor of archaeology, a title switch from his original university affiliation as a professor of the history of industrial arts. But Currelly was in no way, shape, or form an active field archaeologist. He had performed no work of the kind since 1907 in Egypt, where his assignments had mainly involved overseeing large labour parties moving sand and rubble in cemeteries, tombs, and temple complexes. As for McIlwraith, he had conducted no serious fieldwork in ethnology since his time among the Nuxalk (whom he never again visited), and, in 1937, he had no experience in field archaeology.[12]

McIlwraith addressed the university anthropology department's deficit in field archaeology in 1937, soon after Currelly purchased the Beardmore relics, by hiring an American lecturer. Philleo Nash had received his doctorate in anthropology from the University of Chicago for a dissertation on Native American religious revivalism, but he also had archaeology experience.[13] He had published a report on an excavation of the Ross Mound group in his native Wisconsin in 1933, and he launched both the University of Toronto and the ROM into a fresh engagement with the archaeology of Ontario's Indigenous peoples. He was, in fact, the first person hired by any Canadian university to conduct and teach field archaeology.[14] In 1938 and 1939, Nash oversaw a dig at the Pound site, near Aylmer, Ontario, an Ontario Iroquoian village that would help to define the "Middleport" Late Woodland period of pottery and pipe typologies.[15]

McIlwraith, as head of the university's anthropology department and as assistant director of the ROM's archaeology division after Currelly's retirement in 1946, would oversee the expansion of their intertwined archaeology programs and would himself participate, to some degree, in the field. (Archaeologist Kenneth C.A. Dawson would remember McIlwraith from his time investigating stone pit formations near Marathon, Ontario, on northern Lake Superior in the 1950s as "small of stature, assertive and rather fussy but pleasant."[16]) However, even in these later years, before his death in 1964, McIlwraith was more an administrative supervisor than an archaeologist.

Another year might have made all the difference in the Beardmore saga, had Nash become sufficiently established to be entrusted with investigating the Beardmore relics' discovery site. Currelly began pressing Eddy Dodd to cooperate with an examination of the site in June 1937, several months before Nash started his job. Ethlyn Greenaway wrote Dodd on 8 June, hoping to arrange a visit by McIlwraith on 19 June. Dodd replied on 14 June, saying it wasn't possible for him to do so until late August, and besides, he wrote, "the flies are terrible this month and July." Currelly assured him the timing "suits us very well" as McIlwraith would be available between 25 August and 20 September, before the start of classes. On 26 August, Dodd wrote with instructions for a visit on 30 August but promptly cancelled the plan by telegram: "UNAVOIDABLY DETAINED UNTIL AROUND THE FIFTEENTH OF SEPTEMBER." Currelly pressed him again by telegram on Monday, 13 September, to confirm a date. They were almost out of time. Dodd replied immediately by telegram: he would meet "your man" on Sunday.[17] The rendezvous was moved up, and at 7:15 in the morning on Friday, 17 September, Thomas McIlwraith left Beardmore with Eddy Dodd to inspect the trench in which Dodd said the relics had come to light. McIlwraith was carrying a camera and a trowel, and a much heavier burden of expectation that the discovery had been made as described by Dodd and as endorsed by John Jacob, and that his museum superior, C.T. Currelly, had not squandered the five hundred dollars provided by Sigmund Samuel.

On Monday, 20 September 1937, three days after inspecting the discovery site with Eddy Dodd, Thomas McIlwraith was aboard a train, hurrying back to Toronto for the start of the new school year and composing his findings on the way. His typed report barely reached five double-spaced pages. While McIlwraith had taken some photographs and gathered a soil sample at the middle claim, no survey or drawing was attempted, place names in the report were left incomplete, and his few site measurements sounded like educated guesses. Much of the report featured McIlwraith's trying to understand – and ultimately trying to rationalize – how Viking weapons ended up being dynamited out of the earth in such a confounding place. According to John Jacob's June 1937 statement, Dodd had found a Norse grave.

About four miles westbound along the track from Beardmore, around mile 24 on the Dorion subdivision, and within a few yards of the sign announcing the approach to Warneford Station, McIlwraith and Dodd had ventured into the rising terrain east of the track.[18] McIlwraith's skill as a field naturalist was on display as he recounted his visit to the discovery site. They pressed through "moderately dense second-growth of spruce and brich [sic], with occasional badly rotted stumps, reputedly pine, and alder and tamarack in the hollows. The country has undoubtedly been burnt over, but is said not to have been lumbered."[19]

They came to a ridge or knoll a little more than a quarter mile from the CNR line, running northeast-southwest and marked by outcroppings of schist and quartz veins. On the north side, a steep wall of about seven feet at its greatest height displayed the vertical schistocity that prospectors hoped could point to gold seams. Through the use of dynamite, the base of the wall had been exposed for about twenty yards. "The artefacts were found when clearing away the debris from the explosion. They must have been lying close to the rock, about 2 ½ feet underground." Another trench had been gouged from the rock opposite the find, to a depth of about three feet, and still another trench had been cleared by Dodd purportedly within the last year, two or three feet down along the face of the schist wall, about thirty feet west of the find. McIlwraith took a photograph with a branch planted in the trench, a poor substitute for a graduated surveying rod. Two pieces of paper were attached: the lower one indicating where the relics were found, the upper one indicating the ground level before blasting. Nothing in the photograph indicates scale (see illustrations).

McIlwraith spent several hours scraping the schist wall east of the find with a trowel, cutting a vertical section of an unknown dimension. "Though I examined the earth very carefully, I found nothing to indicate intrusion either ancient or recent. I brought back samples of discoloured earth for analysis of the stain, but I doubt it is other than natural." He could see no evidence of a human settlement and thought the chance of finding more objects "limited" and "negligible." Yet Dodd managed to find something new: a small fragment of iron "in the mud and leaves of a small depression on top of the rock where, he said, he had thrown the finds at the time of their discovery." This thin, somewhat rectangular bit of metal, about an inch long, located half a dozen years after the initial claimed discovery, was brought back to the museum by McIlwraith.

The site perplexed McIlwraith. It was clear how its vertical wall would attract a gold prospector. It was far less clear how it would have attracted a party of armed Norsemen. McIlwraith may not have been an archaeologist, but he read the landscape capably. The location made no sense as a permanent camp or settlement. Apart from the fact that no supportive artefacts for an occupation had come to light (and McIlwraith doubted they ever would), the middle claim's schist wall was too far from the Blackwater River, where building sites were available on sloping ground, near its bank. Dodd, in his December 1936 statement, had asserted that the site lay near an ancient water course, but an older channel marked by sand and gravel was almost a quarter mile away. "I feel sure that this could not have had any appreciable amount of water within geologically recent times. North of the knoll is another small valley with a tiny stream, ultimately reaching the Blackwater; I doubt if this could have been significant."

If a settlement or camp near the old course of the Blackwater River was unlikely, what else could explain how the relics got into Eddy's Dodd's prospecting trench? "A purely accidental loss cannot be ruled out, although the finding of *three* articles makes this unlikely. The relatively steep edge of the knoll would give protection, admittedly from the south, making this a desirable camping place. It is not unreasonable to think of a wayfarer abandoning his equipment in such a place or, perhaps more probably, being buried with it." As an archaeological site, the middle claim had been seriously disturbed by prospecting. Dynamite and trenching "has destroyed any possibility of recognizing disturbance of the soil above the find, nor can I judge whether an accumulation of approximately 2 ½ feet is likely to have occurred in 900 years ... It is impossible to judge whether the articles were laid on the surface, or buried; perhaps a shallow hole which later became covered more deeply is the best hypothesis."

McIlwraith now blazed a speculative trail as to "*why* a camp should have been pitched at this point." And he did so without making any investigation of the landscape:

A logical route from Lake Nipigon to Lake Superior would be up the Blackwater River to Lake N[blank], on the height of land; from this lake the M[blank] River flows south about 27 miles to Lake Superior. The Blackwater winds so much that an overland portage of about 7 miles near the find would cut off about 70 miles of river. Map No. [blank] of the Geological Survey of Canada does not show the shortest portage as passing close to the find, but Mr. Dodds [sic] tells me that a lake about 3 miles long has been found since this map was made, and that is shown (as Dodds Lake) on the forestry air survey maps (q.v.). By traversing this lake, the portage distance would be shortened; the shortest route from the Blackwater to Dodds Lake would pass the location of the find. Furthermore, as far as I could judge – and this was substantiated by Mr. Dodds – there is wet ground both to the east and west, while in the small valley north of the knoll, as well as to the immediate east of it, there is (to-day) growth of birch and spruce. Under existing conditions, anyone leaving the Blackwater in this vicinity and travelling in a south-easterly direction would find the easiest course around the eastern edge of the knoll. The protected slope under the edge of the knoll would provide a good and obvious camping place, and it was here that the find was made. I do not know the possibilities of this route further from the river. On the basis of birch and spruce instead of alder and tamerack [sic], I think this route would be suitable in winter, if the river valleys were being followed.

McIlwraith had produced a tour de force of conjecture that turned the discovery site into a "good and obvious" place for Norsemen to have camped en route from Lake Nipigon (presumably as they worked their way south from some landing point in Hudson Bay or James Bay) to Lake Superior. He made no attempt to justify why a detour upstream into the small, rapids-riven Blackwater River on the east side of Lake Nipigon would have suggested itself to Norsemen in the first place. He had no time to trace the Blackwater River for a few miles downstream through its rapids and twists to the shore of Lake Nipigon. Instead, McIlwraith, with no small amount of advice from Dodd, had constructed a scenario of convoluted bush-whacking through the difficult terrain east of Lake Nipigon, for some reason partly in winter. The journey the Norsemen anticipated involved a large unmapped lake Dodd had named for himself and helpfully inserted into the blank space of DGS map 312A.[20] The route lay on a seven-mile portage that Norsemen (who had never been here before) somehow knew would save them seventy miles of river travel in an unknown type of vessel, with a camp at the middle claim along the way, and a destination – Lake Superior – they somehow knew existed and wished to reach. If the explanation was that they had Indigenous guides, then surely those guides would never have led them into the confounding terrain around the Blackwater River when they could have continued down Lake Nipigon to the deep southerly indentation of Pijitawabik Bay or the Nipigon River to its west and followed either one to Lake Superior.

As McIlwraith left the names of several water bodies incomplete in this, the only version of the report he ever produced, it is difficult to reconstruct exactly what route he had in mind for the Norsemen. Nothing on 312A or a modern topographic map suggests a passage on the Blackwater River through a lake starting with "N," followed by a twenty-seven-mile run to Lake Superior on a river starting with "M." The "N" may have been a mistaken reference to Lake Makina, from which the Blackwater River flowed and is just east of the middle claim. The "M" was probably a keystroke error as McIlwraith missed the letter "J" above it as Dodd had avowed in his statement for Currelly that the Jackpine River provided a course to the lake. But the Jackpine is a small tributary that feeds Nipigon Bay on the north shore of the lake and hardly provided a course from the middle claim area, far to the north. The country south of the Blackwater River was a confusion of lakes, small rivers, streams, and uncooperative terrain, with no easy or obvious route – if you even knew enough to seek one – to Lake Superior.

In 1981, L.M. "Buzz" Lein, who was instrumental in founding the Nipigon Historical Museum and had no doubt Dodd's discovery was a hoax, recounted his personal experience of the Beardmore site. "In the 1950s we were logging and road building in that area around Warneford. I spent some time looking around to see if I could spot the discovery site but there was no way anyone could find anything in that fly infested jungle of young growth. All my looking around did was to convince me that no one in his right mind would be wandering around in that area – let alone a seafaring Viking. The Blackwater River leads to nowhere and unless you know where you are going, you could wander around for a long time."[21]

"It is extremely unfortunate that no trace of the find could be located *in situ*," McIlwraith concluded. "Everything rests on the veracity of Mr. Dodds [sic], substantiated to a limited extent, by Mr. Jacobs [sic]. The fragment found in my presence proves nothing; if the objects had been 'planted,' this could likewise have been 'planted.'" The site's authenticity came down to whether you found Eddy Dodd credible. And Thomas McIlwraith did. "I talked at great length with Mr. Dodds and am convinced that the articles were found at this place in 1931. He is vague as to the exact depth below the surface, but I believe the facts to be substantially as reported by him. In brief, I think he is honest."

McIlwraith's mention of a 1931 discovery would have been the first time the year appeared in museum documents since the acquisition, if we consider it likely that the heading of Dodd's signed statement of 6 December 1936, asserting a discovery date of 24 May 1931, was only added after Dodd announced that date to the press in January 1938. McIlwraith further noted: "Mr Dodds is anxious (for sufficient reasons which he confided to me) to have his name kept out of any type of publication." McIlwraith declined to share what those reasons might have been.

Absent from McIlwraith's analysis is any consideration of *how* the Norse travelled. They were seafaring people, employing large, shallow-draught wooden vessels equipped with sails and oars. As traders, raiders, and farmers with grazing animals seeking new homestead sites, they would negotiate navigable rivers and fjords. While the Norse owned smaller vessels that could be portaged, their ocean-going vessels were incapable of such travel, and they were otherwise neither inclined nor equipped to make epic inland journeys that employed small lakes, rivers, streams, and portages in difficult boreal terrain. The route McIlwraith conjured made no sense, unless the Norse had helped themselves to Indigenous canoes (and Indigenous guides). Even at that, the journey was daunting, and McIlwraith's willingness to entertain it, absent any personal experience of the route, was typical of armchair speculation in which maps reduced hundreds of miles of forbidding landscape to a few tame inches of ink on paper. Critics of Hjalmar Holand's Kensington stone scenario stressed the horrendous challenges anyone faced in attempting to make an ascent of the rapids-riven Nelson River on a twenty-two hundred-mile foray into the continent's interior.[22] The museum would conclude that the Beardmore Norsemen had journeyed from the mouth of the Albany River on James Bay to the discovery site, via Lake Nipigon, covering three hundred-odd crow-flight miles. That was a less daunting proposition than Holand's Kensington route, but it still entailed a trail-blazing, mostly upstream journey through the taiga of the Hudson Bay lowlands and the difficult boreal forest to the south, and encounters with Indigenous people whose lands they were transgressing. McIlwraith, however, may have entertained the notion of a friendly encounter as he would alert W.S. (Stewart) Wallace to Christoph Girtanner's idea (published in 1796) that there were Native Americans of mixed Norse descent.[23]

McIlwraith also gave no consideration to *why* Vikings would have been making such a journey. What possessed them to abandon all known patterns of travel, trade, timber harvesting, raiding, and coastal home-steading? No purpose would ever suggest itself, whereas Holand's scenario for the Kensington stone was a sort of ethno-religious quest by Knutson to locate the so-called lost Christian Greenland colonists. It may have been significant that McIlwraith was confronting the Beardmore riddle a few years after Ned Burwash's brother, Lachlan Taylor, made some of the most productive investigations into traces of the Franklin expedition. He had gathered an array of evidence for the doomed men who had abandoned their ships for an overland quest to reach salvation to the south.[24] Perhaps all one needed to accept the logic of the Beardmore relics was a conviction that hardy northern Europeans were capable of epic, heroic journeys into the unknown.

The ROM's curator of ethnology and head of the University of Toronto's Department of Anthropology had concluded that Eddy Dodd was credible and that the discovery site was plausible, even logical, as a Viking encampment en route to Lake Superior. There, the weapons were either accidentally left behind or buried in a shallow grave with their owner. McIlwraith did not address the issue of what happened to the body, but John Jacob had proposed it had been scavenged by animals that somehow removed a Norseman from his final resting place while leaving the neat assemblage of weapons that would have lain across his body. When McIlwraith disembarked from the train at Toronto's Union Station and delivered his sparse and confidential report to C.T. Currelly, the museum's interpretation of the relics as an authentic Viking grave was so firmly set as to be incapable of derailment.

8

Troublesome Typology

About one month after Thomas McIlwraith returned to the Royal Ontario Museum with his report, C.T. Currelly's plan to publicly announce the museum's purchase of relics of a Viking grave in northern Ontario encountered a considerable roadblock. The chairman of the museum's board of trustees, James B. O'Brien (who was also chair of the university's board of governors) had spoken recently with Duncan McArthur, the deputy minister of education. As the secretary of the museum board informed Currelly, McArthur had not yet received McIlwraith's report. "Dr. McArthur also stated that it would be impossible for him to write the contemplated article on [the relics] and that he was strongly of the opinion that Professor McIlwraith should write it."[1] T.L. Tanton would note in December 1939 that "some time ago" McArthur had discussed the relics with Currelly as well as with Lawrence J. Burpee, president of the Royal Society of Canada in 1936–37. Tanton gathered from Burpee that McArthur "was not convinced that the find was genuine."[2]

Whether by McIlwraith's choice or Currelly's decision, McArthur's suggestion that McIlwraith should write the article was not going to happen. Certainly, McIlwraith's site report was unpublishable: it was inadequate as an archaeological investigation and overly speculative. It would never be published or otherwise be made available. Although Currelly would rely on McIlwraith's (unattributed) analysis, the museum director must have understood that he would have to establish the Beardmore provenance and publish the evidence himself.

Meanwhile, someone who was interested in publishing – eventually – on the Beardmore find had re-emerged. Hjalmar Holand had decided to give the museum another try after his initial letter of 13 December 1936 was ignored by Currelly. He wrote a fresh letter of inquiry on 20 August 1937, now asking to view the relics rather than simply to receive a photograph. "As I have been making a special study of late medieval weapons and armor, and have visited every museum in western Europe north of the Alps, this is a field in which I am quite at home ... I have, of course, no desire to make any public report or comment on the find until your report is ready."[3]

Holand's Kensington scholarship had been under duress as of late. In the March 1937 issue of *Minnesota History*, Milo M. Quaife (who had already excoriated Holand's work in the *New England Quarterly* in 1934) argued that his fire-steel relic found near Climax, Minnesota, was modern, not Norse, as Chester Gould had also recently assured John Robins. *Minnesota History* granted Holand a rebuttal in the June 1937 issue. However, in that same issue, John M. Armstrong argued that whoever carved the numerals in the Kensington stone was following a modern numbering system and didn't understand how runic numbers functioned.[4] If the mounting scholarly pushback on Holand's ideas registered with Currelly, it did not deter him from welcoming Holand into an inner sanctum of associates allowed to view relics still hidden from public view and knowledge. While the relics would not be exhibited until after the planned publication, Currelly replied on 24 August, "we shall be glad to let you examine them at any time that you come to Toronto."[5] For some reason this open invitation did not reach Holand until late October. Holand held off on a planned trip to the western United States to make a dedicated visit in the first week of November.

Another interested party was Philip Ainsworth Means, a leading scholar in Peruvian archaeology who had served as national director of the National Museum of Archaeology in Lima and then as an associate in anthropology at Harvard's Peabody Museum from 1921 to 1927.[6] His *Ancient Civilization of the Andes* (1931) "became the standard textbook on Inca society and for the first time made him as famous in the United States as abroad."[7] After producing several more important works on the Inca and the Spanish Empire, Means's interest shifted to early European voyages to North America, and, in 1937, he made research visits to Denmark, Norway, Iceland, and Germany. As he explained to Currelly on 28 October 1937: "For two years now I have all but abandoned my normal field of research (Spanish American archaeology and history) in order to devote myself to a book which I hope to finish (Deo Volente) by 1940. Its subject (not its title) is: Voyages from Europe and Africa towards, to, and into the Western Hemisphere before 1494."[8] As Means told Currelly, he had initially assumed the Kensington stone was a fake but, two years earlier, had begun to study the case more closely. "The arguments put forth by the sustainers of the KS's falsity struck me as unconvincing. Moreover, some of the writers on that side seemed to be seething with unholy venom against a gentleman named Holand." He read Holand's book and struck up a correspondence. "I have the very highest admiration for his diligence, his intelligence, and his invariable good manners and good sportsmanship under often most unmannerly attack. He is, in short, both a gentleman and a scholar." Means would make his own stab at relic revivalism with a study of the Newport Tower, which, in 1839, Carl Christian Rafn, aided by the American antiquarian Thomas H. Webb, had interpreted as the ruins of a Norse church. Its far more plausible origin as a mid-seventeenth-century colonial windmill had quickly been asserted in 1851.[9] In 1942, Means would publish a defence of the tower as a medieval Norse church in a book with an introduction by Currelly's friend, Vilhjalmur Stefansson.[10] Before 1937 was out, Stefansson, too, was drawn into the Beardmore controversy. Eddy Dodd's relics were turning the ROM into a point of convergence for a network of theorists interested in Viking explorations and colonization in North America. Stefansson would be a moderator, investigator, sceptic, and enabler.

Vilhjalmur Stefansson's parents emigrated from Iceland in 1876, helping to found the Icelandic community of Arnes, on the west side of Lake Winnipeg, where Stefansson was born in 1879.[11] He was christened with the anglicized name William Stephenson but, when he was twenty, asserted the Icelandic Vilhjalmur Stefansson. When he was two the family moved to another Icelandic community, this one in the Dakota territory. His childhood was marked by hardship (his father died in 1892) and outdoor vigour that prepared him for Arctic travel. He earned a scholarship to Harvard, where he was to train as a Unitarian minister, but he stayed with divinity studies for only a year before switching to anthropology and becoming a graduate student at the Peabody Museum. After two years in Iceland conducting studies of dentition (which led to a lifelong fascination with diet), he joined the Anglo-American Polar Expedition as an anthropologist in 1906. The expedition failed to rendezvous with him, and he spent two years living with the Inuit in the western Arctic. In 1908, with a classmate from the University of Iowa, zoologist Rudolph Anderson, Stefansson secured the sponsorship of the American Museum of Natural History for a four-year expedition in the western Arctic, which he recounted in *My Life with the Eskimo* (1913). During the expedition, he fathered a child with an Inuk, Fannie Pannigabuk. He never publicly acknowledged their son, Alex, but did provide for him financially.[12]

Stefansson and Anderson next commanded the Canadian Arctic Expedition of 1913-18, a major enterprise whose misfortunes and controversies almost ended Stefansson's career. Stefansson had chartered an old whaler, the *Karluk*, as the main expedition vessel, which (after he disembarked) drifted helplessly westward in the ice of the Beaufort Sea, ultimately claiming eleven lives. Stefansson's performance was harshly criticized at the end of the expedition, and among his detractors was his erstwhile partner, Anderson, the leader of the expedition's Southern Party, who had clashed with Stefansson over the deployment of personnel and resources after the *Karluk*'s loss. Although Stefansson's reputation in Canada suffered, he escaped professional ruination in part through the support of Canada's prime minister, Robert Borden. Although he never returned to the Arctic, he became one of its great living experts, maintaining his reputation in part through an instinct for self-promotion from his base in New York City.

Stefansson also positioned himself as an expert in human error. *The Standardization of Error* (1927), a slim volume in W.W. Norton's New Science Series, was republished as the first two chapters in *Adventures in Error* (1936), which otherwise mostly addressed misconceptions about the Arctic and its people. *The Standardization of Error* (and much of *Adventures in Error*) was less a work of scholarship than an exercise in dry wit worthy of Stephen Leacock.[13] Stefansson, in *The Standardization of Error*, nevertheless foreshadowed fundamental issues in the Beardmore controversy. He compared the ostrich of fact, the bird species known to scientists, to the ostrich of literature, or of "definition." The latter was famous for burying its head in the sand, a behaviour never observed in the wild. Yet despite the ostrich-by-definition having no basis in the ostrich-of-fact, the former was inestimably valuable. "Can you imagine any real attribute more instructive than the head burying of the ostrich-by-definition? As a text for moralists, as an epithet that politicians use for opponents, as a figure of speech generally, what could serve as well?"[14] Stefansson would have ample opportunities to consider whether advocates of Eddy Dodd's find were more enamoured with the Beardmore-by-definition, of fearless Vikings slogging through Ontario's northern forests, than with the Beardmore-of-fact, and whether these advocates were behaving as ostriches-by-definition, in burying their heads in the sand and refusing to recognize the truth about the relics' origins. Stefansson would struggle with which Beardmore ostrich he preferred.

Philip Ainsworth Means had been visiting Montreal in October 1937 when he learned from an acquaintance (possibly Wilfrid Bovey) about the Beardmore find in the ROM's possession. "All this is simply splendid!"

Means gushed to Currelly.[15] He had also learned that Hjalmar Holand was about to visit the ROM and examine the relics. Means was desperate to see them and to at last meet Holand. Currelly hosted both Means and Holand on 3 and 4 November, and they were joined by Thomas McIlwraith, fresh from his examination of Dodd's trench, as well as the newly hired archaeologist, Philleo Nash, and Currelly's assistant, Ethlyn Greenaway.

It was a meeting of great consequence for the relics and the museum. Means had never visited the ROM, and he proclaimed it "one of the very greatest Museums in the world – and, in Chinese art, *the* greatest."[16] Currelly and his staff had given Means "one of the greatest experiences of [his] life." As for Holand, "to meet him under such pleasant auspices was for me an event of the first importance. He is obviously a careful, devoted, and very intelligent scholar whom we must all respect greatly." Currelly offered to treat for preservation the relics Holand had collected, the supposedly Norse iron tools and weapons as well as the Kensington stone (which wasn't in Holand's possession as he had long ago sold it to the chamber of commerce of Alexandria, Minnesota). As Means wrote Currelly: "The last certainly should be cast, as you suggested." With this meeting in early November 1937, Currelly's attitude towards the Beardmore relics as well as the Kensington stone was firmly cast, with no small credit to Means, a respected authority in New World archaeology who was also trying to engineer a relationship between the ROM and the National Museum of Archaeology in Lima. Currelly had begun imagining a museum exhibit that featured the Beardmore grave goods alongside castings of the Kensington stone and other purported relics – a cabinet of curiosities of Viking meanderings in the Great Lakes region.

Holand received a collegial and generous welcome from Currelly – Holand would write the following March how "I enjoyed that day with you very much."[17] Holand could be charming and personable, especially if you agreed with his Kensington theory. ("I know Holand rather well," Chester Gould had informed John Robins the previous January. "He used to come to see me until he found he could not impress me. I like him personally."[18]) Holand knew the names and works of the leading figures in Norse-Icelandic scholarship, even if some of them had no enthusiasm for his Kensington ideas. For Currelly, Holand must have been a welcome guest, a walking encyclopaedia of Scandinavian sources and Nordic lore. Holand would claim in 1938: "I was the first to tell Dr. Currelly that [the relics] were of the eleventh century. I have seen scores of them in European museums."[19] Holand would later assert that Currelly had thought the weapons were from the Knutson expedition.[20] Currelly, however, knew enough about Norse armour to recognize that the sword was probably tenth century or earlier, which was much older than the Kensington stone. By the time Holand visited the museum, Currelly had Jacob's more elaborate second statement and McIlwraith's report, which together suggested a Norse grave and an expedition from the north, employing the Albany River and Lake Nipigon. But Currelly still needed to establish the weapons typology, and Holand would write that "these weapons represented a field of research with which Dr. Currelly's staff had very little contact, and considerable correspondence and study were a preliminary necessity."[21] Holand set Currelly on the proper course for determining the weapons typology by providing a list of leading scholars to contact.[22]

On 24 November 1937, another figure involved in north Atlantic voyage history entered the Beardmore discussion, and he remained part of a private debate and enquiry that carried on for several years. Born in St John's, Newfoundland, in 1860, George Robert Farrar (G.R.F.) Prowse was a retired Winnipeg school principal who, since 1892, had been delving into cartology (the history of cartography), studying maps in collections in the Boston Public Library, the British Museum, and Paris. He produced several monographs on John Cabot as well as a work on early explorations of the Gulf of St Lawrence.[23] As he explained to Stefansson in March 1939, "The Norsemen have always been present in my mind for half a century."[24]

Prowse's knowledge of sources recommended him to Stefansson, who maintained a private library dedicated to Arctic matters so massive he had to rent a second apartment in New York to house it and employ assistants to catalogue and run it. Stefansson gathered people like Prowse assiduously and benefited from their ability to keep him grounded in his scholarly impulses, however much he embraced Holand's Kensington theorizing. The fact Prowse lived in Winnipeg would prove critical to his role in the private discussions and investigations of the Beardmore relics.

Stefansson and Prowse began corresponding no later than 1935.[25] Stefansson was embarking on a writing tear, Arctic-wise. He was about to publish the two-volume *The Three Voyages of Martin Frobisher* (1938). He would soon publish *Iceland: The First American Republic* (1939) and *Unsolved Mysteries of the Arctic* (1939), with *Ultima Thule* (1940) and *Greenland* (1942) on the near horizon. Stefansson was serving a term as president of the Explorer's Club of New York when he visited Prowse in Winnipeg in March 1937, gathering from him copies of documents that could aid him with his forthcoming Frobisher book's introduction, in which he weighed evidence for early transat-

lantic voyages. Stefansson wrote Prowse on 5 November 1937, with his belated thanks; a few weeks later, on 24 November, Prowse was writing Currelly, whom he had come to know, wondering if he had yet published on the
Beardmore relics, as Fraser's *Dalhousie Review* article in July had promised.[26]

Having heard back from Currelly, Prowse informed Stefansson on 4 December that the museum planned to publish on the Beardmore relics in
"the late winter or early spring."[27] The earliest publishing date seemed
wildly optimistic. Although a museum photo of the relics, taken after the
rust removal process was completed, existed by 1 December (as Currelly
reported to Means that day[28]), Currelly had yet to secure any outside expertise on the weapons typology.

Currelly had taken a tentative step in that direction on 30 November
with a letter to "My dear Mann" – James Gow Mann, director of the Wallace Collection of arms and armour at Hertford House in London.[29] Without giving any particulars as to his curiosity, Currelly directed Mann to
figure 23 in the first volume of Sir Guy Francis Laking's *A Record of European Armour and Arms through Seven Centuries*.[30] The small photograph
showed the grip and guard of a Viking sword tentatively dated to the
ninth or even eighth century. "Is there any more known about this type,"
Currelly asked. "Our poverty has prevented our having anything like a decent library, and regarding Norse things we are completely hopeless." Currelly admitted the museum did not even own a copy of Mann's "very in-
tensive history of the sword," by which he probably meant the arms and
armour catalogue of the Wallace Collection, originally written by Laking
in 1901 and updated by Mann. "If you can give me any information about
this type of sword, I shall be extremely grateful."

Ten days after Currelly wrote Mann, the *Toronto Star* published an article
on Norse voyaging that revealed the presence of the Beardmore relics at the
ROM.[31] The newspaper was responding to a London report that the Icelandic poet and novelist Guðmundur Kamban had found in the library of
the University of Copenhagen a mention of the Icelandic discovery of Vinland in 1017.[32] For comment the *Star* had turned to William Stewart (W.S.)
Wallace, chief librarian since 1922 at the University of Toronto, as well as
C.T. Currelly. Born in Georgetown, Ontario, in 1884, Stewart Wallace (as he
was known to colleagues) was one of Canada's leading figures in historical
publishing. He was not a formally trained historian, holding a master's degree in library sciences, but nevertheless was a professor of history at the
University of Toronto at a time when the emerging discipline welcomed
the contributions of academics in an array of fields in the humanities and

social sciences. In the 1920s, Wallace had decried the course that the historical profession was charting, with its rising emphasis on doctorates and what he regarded as overly narrow theses that made no real contribution to knowledge and failed to achieve the standard of literature.[33] As managing editor, he launched the *Canadian Historical Review* as a quarterly journal in 1920, and under his guidance it "functioned as the chief vehicle for the historical profession in English Canada."[34] He was also general editor of the Champlain Society from 1923 to 1943. When the Beardmore relics emerged, he had just completed the six-volume *Encyclopedia of Canada*, for which he was general editor while writing most of the entries.

Wallace's prolific output encompassed two dominant if potentially antagonistic approaches to history. He considered himself a practitioner of dispassionate, methodological history, and he was inspired by an American movement in the 1920s to debunk legends and purge them from textbooks.[35] In *The Story of Laura Secord* (1932) he concluded that Canada's War of 1812 heroine was a self-serving mythologizer.[36] At the same time, he sympathized with a conviction in Canadian academia that the country's history should be accessible and engaging to the general reader, which carried the risk of writing material that was stirring rather than strictly factual and that was driven by heroic personality – precisely the sort of thing demythologizers like himself wanted to eradicate. His papers contain a mass of letters documenting his dealings with trade publishers, including impressive royalty statements, and pitches for books and magazine articles. Among his works for general readers was *By Star and Compass: Tales of the Explorers of Canada* (1922) and *Murders and Mysteries* (1931). Wallace would serve as president of Section 2 (English literature, history, and archaeology, among other disciplines) of the Royal Society of Canada in 1938–39. He would also be a staunch ally of Currelly in defending the Beardmore relics.

As the *Star* reported, Wallace "stated that at the Royal Ontario Museum there was on exhibit a Norseman's sword which had been found in a northern Ontario mining property, and this was probably something in the belief that the Norsemen had come to America by way of Hudson Bay." Wallace only seemed to know what was in A.D. Fraser's recent *Dalhousie Review* article as Fraser, too, had mistakenly reported the relics were on display. It is remarkable that Wallace, whose library was a brief stroll from the museum's Armour Court, would make such an error. Currelly said nothing to the *Star* about the Beardmore relics but, like Wallace, commented favourably on the Kensington stone. "I have an open mind about the matter," Currelly said, before holding forth approvingly on the "facts."

Clearly, Currelly (a month after Hjalmar Holand's visit) accepted the rune stone as authentic.[37] The article's passing mention of the Beardmore find allegedly on display at the ROM failed to generate further media curiosity. For Currelly, who was still trying to keep a public lid on the acquisition, the *Star* article was a very near-run thing.

The 10 December *Toronto Star* article likely spurred Currelly to get on with the long-delayed typology research by casting a much wider net of professional opinion than J.G. Mann, from whom he had not yet received a reply. On 14 December, Currelly composed a standard request for assistance.[38] The mailing list of ten experts was probably based on names Hjalmar Holand and Philip Ainsworth Means would recall providing. Most were Scandinavian scholars, and two of the Anglo-American ones had penned favourable reviews of *The Kensington Stone*. All but two would respond. Every expert received a copy of the closely guarded museum photograph of the sword, axe head, and shield handle.

Of the letters sent out on 14 December, only J.G. Mann received a personalized one, acknowledging the earlier missive from Currelly. Otherwise, they contained the same wording: "We have recently received the contents of a Norse grave, of which I am sending you a photograph, showing the sword, axe, and the grip of the shield. We have only a fragment of the boss as it was destroyed completely getting it out. I shall be most grateful if you can give me as accurately as possible the date, as our library is very weak in Norse archaeology."

The letter was silent on who had excavated the grave, and when, and above all *where* it was. Otherwise, it showed how Currelly's interpretation of Eddy Dodd's find had crystallized. The possibility of Dodd's trench having contained a grave was now a certainty. The chunk of metal recovered by Dodd and McIlwraith in September 1937 (which was not included in the photograph) was initially interpreted as the point of a knife or sword, as we will see. But in Currelly's letter, it became a fragment of the shield boss. Currelly had acquired for the ROM such a metal boss from a circa AD 500 Anglo-Saxon shield in 1927. The mysterious third bit of metal was absolutely the handle or grip of the shield that Dodd said had crumbled. Currelly's casual phrasing made it sound like the shield boss had been destroyed in the course of a museum excavation and that the presence of a shield was unquestionable.

The day Currelly dispatched the letters, his friend Stefansson composed one to him from New York. Stefansson had recently visited the ROM and viewed the relics, and the day before writing Currelly, he had written A.D. Fraser to secure a copy of his *Dalhousie Review* article. (Fraser, in reply, allowed: "My own field being Greek Archaeology, I really have no business transgressing in this Scandinavian-American preserve."[39]) Stefansson now provided Currelly with "some notes that could possibly prove useful in connection with the fascinating mystery of which you gave me some glimpse at the Museum."[40] With Stefansson's entrance, a private circle of debate around the Beardmore relics was completed. Its informal membership included Holand, Means, and Prowse, with Fraser on the periphery, and all were in touch with Currelly.

Like Holand, Stefansson pressed Currelly to consult leading Scandinavian experts before publishing anything, unaware that Currelly had sent out his letters that day. Foremost, Stefansson had in mind Matthias Thórdarson, curator of the National Museum housed in the National Library in Reykjavik, Iceland. Stefansson understood that Iceland had more examples of Norse weapons after 870 than any other country, and Thórdarson "has long been a specialist in the study of Norse armour from the ninth to thirteenth centuries." Further, around the National Library "is grouped a small body of experts in these studies who are among the very best authorities in Europe – in some respects the best. No doubt Mr. Thórdarson will consult some of these before replying." As a matter of tact, he recommended that Currelly refer to Thórdarson's *The Vinland Voyages*, for which Stefansson had written the foreword in the 1930 English translation. Stefansson told Currelly he could locate a copy in the University of Toronto's library. The book contained photos of an axe head and two swords in the National Museum of Iceland. The axe head was superficially like the Beardmore find, and one sword (intact and in much better condition) bore a reasonable similarity to Dodd's. The weapons were presented without any typology beyond a general date of "the year 1000."[41]

Stefansson also advised Currelly to consult Halldór Hermannsson, curator of the Fiske Icelandic Collection in the Cornell University Library and editor of its annual journal, *Icelandica*. Thórdarson had cited Hermannsson repeatedly in *The Vinland Voyages*. Stefansson assured Currelly that Hermannsson was "much the best scholar in these matters resident in America" and that he "undoubtedly ranks with the foremost half dozen in the world when Viking studies generally are considered, though he is not exactly a specialist in armour." But Stefansson warned Currelly that, if he wrote Hermannsson, he should make no reference to Holand, "for Hermannsson took from the start an attitude of violent antipathy [towards the Kensington stone]. He is a keen and precise scholar but emotional."[42] Finally, Stefansson pointed out: "One of the best men of Sweden happens to be in this country now," Dag Strömbäck, a folklorist in the Department of Germanic Languages and Literature at the University of Chicago. "Wouldn't it be grand to get Hermannsson and Strömbäck, either or both, to run up to Toronto and have a look at your finds?"

As it happened, Hermannsson was among the ten experts to whom Currelly wrote on the day Stefansson composed his letter. If Holand had recommended Hermannsson, he gracefully overlooked his "violent antipathy." It is a mystery as to why Thórdarson was not already among the letter recipients. Currelly, having sent his ten letters, did not act on Stefansson's recommendations, save for writing Thórdarson an odd courtesy letter about a year later to notify the expert of his imminent plan to publish on the Beardmore find, without inviting Thórdarson's opinion of the relics.[43] Hermannsson, while already among the letter recipients, was not, as Stefansson had suggested, invited by Currelly to view the relics in person. Strömbäck was ignored, perhaps because he was a folklorist, although other scholars contacted also had no weapons expertise. Stefansson had warned Currelly that Thórdarson could be slow to respond to letters and suggested "impressing him with the fact that you must soon go to press and that you can use only opinions which you receive immediately." The museum director was in a rush to publish in the ROM's *Bulletin,* as Prowse had learned, which meant that he was unwilling to canvas experts as thoroughly as Stefansson advised. Currelly had no patience for anything other than a firm and prompt reply to his batch of letters. After a year of inaction on typing the weapons, Currelly was hurrying what he regarded as the biggest historical find in America through its scholarly assessment.

Replies to C.T. Currelly's 14 December 1937 letter began arriving on the museum director's desk over the Christmas holidays.[44] One by one, they produced a gathering consensus on a tenth-century antiquity for the weapons. But they also raised concerns.

J.G. Mann (replying to Currelly's initial letter of 30 November) advised that the sword was illustrated in Laking's first volume of *European Armour and Arms.* Figure 23 showed a simple sword, dated to the eighth century, which would have been extremely early for a voyage to North America as Iceland was only settled by the Norse beginning around 870. The ROM sword "is not an uncommon type," Mann wrote, "but its appearance is altered by the fact that the rounded top to the pommel is missing." Mann enclosed a sketch of how this semicircular cap would have fit atop the short bar, or pommel, at the top of the grip. Mann was the only expert to suggest a missing cap to the pommel, and he must have done so because he assumed the sword was a later example of the one illustrated. Otherwise Mann advised the sword type could be found in the standard reference work by Jan Petersen. "I think he dates it a little later than Laking, and puts it between the IXth and Xth centuries," Mann advised. As the ROM library did not contain Petersen's essential volume, Currelly could not follow up.

Stefán (Steve) Einarsson of Johns Hopkins University in Baltimore was the first expert to respond to the 14 December letter. Einarsson was an Icelander, a specialist in Old Norse who had been a member of the Johns Hopkins faculty since 1927 and would be made a professor of Scandinavian philology in 1945.[45] He had authored a polite review of Holand's *The Kensington Stone*, which was nevertheless devastating in its critique of Holand's knowledge (and, by implication, that of the inscription's forger) of Old Norse.[46] Not being a weapons expert, Einarsson had gone straight to Petersen's book and concluded that the sword was an M type, which Einarsson explained was "the second most common type of the Viking age swords, it is also the simplest of the types." It was most common, he explained, in eastern Norway, although one was known from Iceland and a few from other locales, and belonged to the second half of the ninth century, surviving a little into the tenth century, when it was superseded by the Q type. As for the axe, Petersen's guide indicated it was an M type from the mid-tenth into the eleventh century (see illustrations).

Although Einarsson showed no curiosity about where the relics had been discovered, he was puzzled that the sword and axe were found together in one grave. As Einarsson noted, M-type axes had been found with well-developed examples of the more recent Q-type sword, but not with the older M-type swords. Even if the axe were interpreted as an L type, it would still be from about the same, more recent, era as the M-type axe. An older type of axe, K, was sometimes found with the M-type sword, but Einarsson didn't think it was much like Currelly's axe. As for the shield grip or handle, "I have found no references – not being an archaeologist, I am not so well versed in the literature." What Einarsson did not say was that there were *no* shield handles in Petersen's authoritative study, for the simple reason that no examples existed in any museum collection. In closing, Einarsson advised that the grave belonged to the tenth century, perhaps about 950.

Halldór Hermannsson at Cornell replied on 21 December. He wondered if the grave was in Ontario, then refused to say anything about the weapons. "In the first place, I am not an archaeologist, and secondly, I believe, it would be extremely difficult, if not impossible, to determine the age and origin of such articles from a photograph. The material of which they are made and all the circumstances connected with the finding of them would be essential for that purpose." Hermannsson suggested Currelly send photographs showing the items from different angles to Poul Nørlund, an archaeologist with the National Museum in Copenhagen, and include "a minute description of the finding place of them." It was an inspired suggestion. In 1921, Nørlund had made a sensational discovery: at Herjolfsnes in Greenland's Eastern Settlement he found a number of bodies dressed in fifteenth-century clothing, which proved that the Greenland Norse had not, as commonly believed, vanished in the fourteenth century – a revelation problematic to Holand's idea that, in 1362, Knutson had wound up in Minnesota in his search for "lost" colonists. Holand ignored Nørlund's major discovery. Currelly never contacted Nørland.

The next expert heard from was Geoffrey Malcolm Gathorne-Hardy, librarian of the House of Lords in London and one of the most prolific scholars in support of Holand's Kensington theories. Chester Gould, in his 1937 letter to John Robins, had derided Gathorne-Hardy as "that very dumb person." Gathorne-Hardy confessed to Currelly in his 30 December reply: "I can lay no claim to sufficient archaeological knowledge to be able to answer your question. I should guess early Viking period – early tenth century." He was incurious about the grave's location and forwarded Currelly's query to Haskon Shetelig of Norway's Bergens Museum, "who ought to be able to settle the matter authoritatively. I do not think there is anyone in the world who knows more about these things than he does."

Shetelig was already one of the ten experts to whom Currelly had written on 14 December, and he replied on 3 January 1938: "The sword is of a type which covers a rather long period comprising the late 9th. century and a greater part of the 10th. cent. The axe is more distinct and certainly belongs to the later 10th. century. The grave consequently must be dated by the later object." Shetelig did not give any letter types but directed Currelly to Petersen's volume to look up the relevant information himself, which of course Currelly could not do. In closing, Shetelig wrote: "You will greatly oblige me by some information about the locality of the grave where the antiquities were found." Currelly did not reply.

Four days later, Anton Wilhelm Brøgger posted his reply. Brøgger was an archaeologist and professor at Royal Frederick University (as the University of Oslo was known until 1938) and the director of Universitetets Old-saksamling, the university's celebrated Museum of Cultural History, which held the world's largest collection of Viking artefacts and operated the Viking Ship Museum. Brøgger enjoyed the highest possible standing in his profession. He was a member of the Royal Norwegian Society of Sciences and Letters, the chair of the Norwegian Museums Federation from 1918 to 1934, and a co-founder in 1936 of the Norwegian Archaeological Society, for which he served as secretary-general until his death in 1951.[47]

Brøgger was not going to flip through the pages of Petersen for Currelly. Instead, he wrote: "I should be very obliged if you will let me know where from you have got these objects, which I suppose have come from one of the Northern countries. Have you bought them from anyone here and have you got sure informations about *where they have been found* – in Norway or Sweden? For any information about this matter I shall thank you very much and after getting it I shall have the pleasure to give you all the dates I can afford." Brøgger most certainly was concerned that the relics had left Norway after its independence in 1905, when, without an export permit, such removals of cultural materials became illegal.

At the beginning of his collecting efforts, at least, Currelly viewed export restrictions as things to be evaded. "Most of the stuff I bought in Palestine is in England," Currelly informed Ned Burwash from Crete in November 1904, "and I sent it to different people for fear of suspicion as it was known in Jerusalem that I was a Canadian and they do not allow anything to leave the country."[48] Margaret Tushingham would recall Currelly confiding that he "bootlegged" some Minoan figurines out of Crete. "Fearing they might be confiscated or stolen, he put them in the bottom of his riding boots when he packed," Tushingham explained.[49] There was a hue and cry from Chinese authorities after the ROM secured the forty thousand volumes that formed the H.H. Mu Library in 1933. Several volumes from the private collection were donated back to Chinese institutions, and the Chinese government thereafter imposed strict controls on the export of books (including a ban on any published before 1851).[50]

Currelly cut off any further discussion of the Beardmore relics with Brøgger on 22 January. "I do not think there will be time to receive another answer from you. The answers I have already received from similar enquiries have so definitely agreed on the date of our Viking weapons that I am hoping we may be able to publish the matter shortly." The reply verged on an affront to curatorial courtesy. After asking someone of Brøgger's stature for his assistance, Currelly would not assure him the items had not been removed illegally from Norway – perhaps because he still feared that they might have been brought to Canada and used to perpetrate a hoax.

Despite Currelly's assurance to Brøgger that he had secured a definitive answer on the weapons from other experts, he had received no such thing. Without a copy of Petersen, he was unable to confirm for himself the guidance his experts provided. Einarsson (who was a philologist, not a weapons expert) provided the most detailed synopsis of what the standard reference work suggested, and his conclusion that the grave contained an M-type sword and an M-type axe has stood up well. But Einarsson's assessment should have flagged the basic problem of the so-called Beardmore grave. Petersen had worked out chronologies for weapons typologies by noting how examples were (and were not) found in association, as Viking weapons overwhelmingly were known from grave goods. Dodd's sword did not occur in association with his axe in any known burial. As Einarsson accepted in good faith that the grave was a genuine archaeological discovery, he had resolved the incongruity of an M-type sword's turning up with an M-type axe from a more recent period by choosing a date of 950 for the grave.[51] But he could not find an example of a shield handle or grip, and no other expert so far heard from had mentioned it. No informed archaeologist had pronounced on the weapons to a degree they would have considered satisfactory. A.W. Brøgger, one of the greatest experts in Viking materials, had refused to cooperate unless he was told where the grave was located. And Currelly had refused to tell him.

Two more replies were on the way when Currelly dismissed Brøgger with his assurance that he already had the definitive answer on the date and type of weapons. He had written Frank Stanton Cawley, the Harvard professor of Scandinavian languages and literature who had sceptically if politely reviewed Holand's *The Kensington Stone*. Rather than reply, Cawley took Currelly's query to Hugh O'Neill Hencken, curator of European archaeology at Harvard's Peabody Museum, whose fieldwork, involving Vikings, was mainly in Ireland. Hencken's brief note to Currelly on 22 January added little: "as far as I know, these objects belong to the Late Viking Age, 11th century. A.D." He gave no explanation of how he had arrived at this late date. Before the final reply from Currelly's list of experts could arrive, the Beardmore discovery erupted in public controversy.

"One of the Greatest Hoaxes of All Times"

Teddy Elliott strove to be the good soldier of scholarship for C.T. Currelly, maintaining his publishing silence, but if the Kingston schoolteacher thought he was part of a team of discovery, he had been left out of the loop since meeting Currelly at the Royal Ontario Museum on 29 December 1936. Elliott knew nothing about Thomas McIlwraith's investigation in September 1937. He continued to assume well into 1938 that Duncan McArthur was working on a government report. After a year of waiting for the museum's acquisition to be announced, Elliott could no longer contain his silence about the relics. On 13 December 1937 – the day before Currelly sent his letters to the ten chosen experts – Elliott wrote a letter that triggered the public scandal that broke just as Currelly was concluding, however preemptively, his fact-finding on the weapons typology.

Elliott had written to Philip Henry Godsell. Born in England, Godsell had arrived at Manitoba's York Factory at sixteen as an apprentice clerk in the Hudson's Bay Company. He worked for the HBC until 1929, and his various assignments took him to the Lake Superior region, where he was the factor at the HBC post at Longlac.[1] Whether or not Elliott ever crossed paths with Godsell around Longlac, they knew many of the same people in the area. From 1929 to 1936, Godsell served as an HBC auditor in Winnipeg, and he was made a fellow of the Royal Geographical Society in 1933. He then turned full time to writing, with his tremendous output drawing on his experiences as a fur trader and HBC inspector. In addition to books, lectures, and radio material, he cranked out true-crime stories for the detective pulp trade. As Carolyn Strange and Tina Merrill Loo describe, Godsell "never met an adjective he didn't like. His stories were full of 'mahogany-face' savages and 'steely-eyed' Mounties matching wits with each other in the 'empurpled dusk of the prairie skies' or in the 'shade of the saw-toothed mountains' of British Columbia. As an auditor by trade, he preferred to be known as 'Philip H. Godsell, FRGS, Arctic Traveller, Author, and Explorer.'"[2] He posed for promotional photos in Inuit clothing and Plains regalia complete with an elaborate war bonnet.

Elliott's letter of 13 December 1937 is no longer extant, but, as Godsell's reply of 14 January 1938 described, it was "interesting and very newsy," full of details about characters they had both known at Longlac.[3] "I have given up trying to dig up history," Godsell professed. "You can dig up all the history you like but magazines and newspapers have an utter horror of anything approaching 'history,' as they call it." Godsell recounted having a story about the first masquerade dance at Fort Smith in the Northwest Territories returned by an unnamed publication "with the comments that it was very interesting but 'too historical'!!!" Elliott, having had his original Beardmore story rejected by the *Toronto Star* for having "too much history," would have silently commiserated.

One particular bit of Elliott gossip caught Godsell's eye: "I read with the most intense interest the story of the discovery of a Norse axe, sword and shield handle uncovered as a result of assessment work near Beardmore." Elliott had revealed that Eddy Dodd was the discoverer and that C.T. Currelly was planning an official publication by Duncan McArthur: "The historical association of this find is unquestionably of tremendous importance, and I shall be most interested to hear what Dr. Currelly has to say about it."

Godsell did not wait to hear what Dr Currelly had to say. On 24 January 1938, Godsell announced Dodd's discovery in an address to the Canadian Club in Winnipeg. It was the fourth time that word of the find had leaked to the world. The Godsell address was the most consequential. He had already provided a *Winnipeg Free Press* reporter with a statement, on 22 January.[4] The revelation went out on the Canadian Press wire before the *Free Press* could even run a story. The news appeared on the front page of the *Globe and Mail* and in a slew of other Canadian newspapers on Tuesday, 25 January, and in the *Free Press* the following day.[5]

Elliott was sure he had asked Godsell to keep the information confidential. Godsell credited an anonymous informant, and he appears to have had no other source than Elliott's letter, augmented by his own imagination.[6] "This find definitely links the hardy Vikings with the forests of Northern Ontario," Godsell announced, "and proves that the followers of Eric the Red and his successors penetrated into the heart of the North American continent." As the *Free Press* reported, the relics had been found on "James Dodds [sic] gold claim, north [sic] of Beardmore." The newspaper further alleged: "The relics, through the efforts of the department of education of Ontario, were removed to the Royal Ontario Museum in Toronto, and according to Mr. Godsell, have been pronounced by competent authorities as genuine Norse weapons of the eleventh century. Prof. D. McArthur, deputy minister of education, is at present preparing a government report on the find. Mr. Godsell's informant did not state who the competent authorities were." A callout box within the Winnipeg story reported from Toronto that "[the relics] have been in the Royal Ontario Museum for two years, officials stated Tuesday, but they declined to make any comment about them."

Godsell proposed that Vikings had travelled up Hudson Strait into Hudson Bay and landed near the mouth of the Albany River. Knowing Norse vessels were totally unsuitable to the inland journey before them, Godsell proposed that they secured canoes from the Cree to venture up either the Albany River or the Pagwachewan River. In the longer CP article of 25 January, based on a Godsell handout, Godsell held forth in his best pulp fiction style: "I can picture the Norsemen holding councils with the red men, accompanying them on deer and moose hunts in the forests of Northern Ontario and reverting to the barbaric life of earlier ancestors through force of circumstances." Alternately, the Beardmore relics originated with a group of Norsemen who had penetrated further westward and left a rune stone found in 1933 at Sandy Hook, a Lake Winnipeg beach resort area just south of the Icelandic community of Gimli – a discovery no historian or archaeologist took seriously. In still another scenario, Godsell proposed that Beardmore "may have been the scene of some Woodland fight between these hardy warriors and Redmen who for the first time gazed upon the palefaces who were eventually to bring about their downfall. The Indians may have looked upon them as Weetigoes, cannibal spirits or visitors from another world." However, Godsell also cautioned that, as a former factor of the HBC post at Longlac who had travelled extensively through the province's north, he knew of no Indian tradition of Norse visitors.[7]

Godsell's address had notable omissions. Beyond ignoring Hjalmar Holand's overlapping Kensington stone theory for a Norse arrival via Hudson Bay, Godsell had not said the items were from a grave. But his mention of the "James Dodds" gold claims was enough for Royd E. Beamish, a reporter for Port Arthur's *Daily News-Chronicle*, to surprise Dodd with Godsell's revelation. Beamish had just turned twenty-seven. Born in Port Arthur, he had broken into the newspaper business with the *Daily News-Chronicle* at nineteen. By January 1938, Beamish was a well-rounded reporter who knew how to investigate a story.[8] In addition to his reports in the *Daily News-Chronicle*, he filed "specials" on the Beardmore find with the *Globe and Mail* and performed so well that he quickly landed a job with the Toronto newspaper.

"There's really nothing to say," Dodd told Beamish when informed of Godsell's address.[9] "We found a few things while doing assessment work on mining claims some years ago. We found more last summer and we think we may make further discoveries next summer, too." When pressed by Beamish on what sort of discoveries, Dodd replied: "Well, the archaeology fellow tells me they're weapons used by the Vikings some time in the tenth or eleventh century. We found a piece of a sword, part of a shield and a battle axe among other things." But they were in poor shape. "Just a few odds and ends of rusty metal, you might say." It was odd that Dodd claimed they had only found a "piece" of a sword rather than a sword in two pieces. Perhaps Beamish had misunderstood him or there was an editing error.

Dodd professed he was otherwise sworn to secrecy: "I promised the archaeologist fellow who was up here last year I wouldn't say anything about it until we had further proof, and he promised me the same thing. I don't know how the newspapers got hold of it at all." C.T. Currelly was no less mystified. "How Godsell in Winnipeg got his information I don't know," he confessed to Hjalmar Holand in March, "although Dodd is a great talker."[10] Currelly had no idea Elliott had leaked the find to Godsell, and Elliott was not about to confess to having done so.

Despite his avowed reluctance to address the find, Dodd naturally warmed to his subject: "We were cross-trenching on our claims about six years ago when we turned up the first piece. I forget what it was at the moment, but I mentioned it to Professor Burwash one time and he became interested. Then some experts found that they compared identically with weapons used by the Norsemen." Beamish reported Dodd's asserting "other articles were found in subsequent years, and last year the sword and part of a shield were uncovered." The shield part could have been the piece recovered for McIlwraith that Currelly had decided was part of the boss, but the idea that the sword was found within the past year made no sense. Dodd suggested there were more discoveries to come: "There's a heavy overburden on the property, and almost anything might be buried under it. We made our early finds when we weren't expecting them, but now we intend to really get over the ground and see if anything else is there."

The interest arising from Godsell's speech was "a lot of fuss about nothing," Dodd declared: "We were going to keep the whole thing quiet until we had gone over the property to see what else could be found. The big question seems to be whether the Vikings reached this part of Canada from the east or from the west, and we hoped that other discoveries might prove it one way or another."

Dodd would not reveal the exact location of the claim. He said his biggest worry was that news of the find would bring out the treasure hunters: "if everyone else gets in there, they won't leave much for me" – a complaint that reinforced the likelihood Dodd intended to bring further relics to light. Nor would he describe the articles found in detail. "That's up to the archaeology people," he said. "They know what those things are and I don't. All I know is that they look pretty old and rusty and they may be of some historical value." He had nothing further to say: "You'll have to get in touch with the Ontario Museum or Professor McIlwraith. I didn't want to have anything in the papers at all." He did assert that a party from Toronto planned to visit the site in the summer and search for more articles.

Beamish's initial interview with Dodd was crucial for establishing how the latter chose to describe and date his discovery (or, rather, discoveries) for the media, for the first time. The find had been made "about six years ago," which could have meant the spring or summer of 1931 or 1932. Instead of a single discovery, Dodd stated that there had been a series, and he could not even remember what the first item was, which was at odds with his standard story of having found the three items sold to the museum in one fortuitous blast of dynamite.

Before Beamish's article could go to type, a telegram arrived from the *Winnipeg Free Press* on the morning of 26 January, alerting the *Daily News-Chronicle* to a fresh development. Among the readers of the article on Godsell's address that the *Winnipeg Free Press* had just published was Eli Ragotte. Dodd's discovery was "one of the greatest hoaxes of all times," he told the newspaper. Ragotte "declared that the rusty sword and shield now resting in the Royal Ontario Museum were hauled not from a mining property but from a pile of ashes in the basement of Dodds' home. 'And I ought to know', Mr. Ragotte, rocking with laughter, declared, 'for I was the man who actually discovered the rusty sword and dragged it from its resting place in a pile of clinkers" – the slag-like residue in coal furnaces. As early as 1928, Ragotte claimed, he had produced the sword as well as a shield from the furnace ashes in the basement of Eddy Dodd's Port Arthur home on Wilson Street.[11]

The coming clash over the Beardmore provenance, being so reliant on anecdote or personal testimony rather than on hard physical evidence, would hinge on the credibility of individuals. As in any courtroom drama, credibility relied on perceptions of character, and those perceptions were at times driven by class. To the end of his life C.T. Currelly would cast Eli

Ragotte as human trash, the "drunk brakes-man" whose evidence was worthless, in contrast to the bird-spotter John Jacob, the "government man" from a "good family" who offered unimpeachable testimony. It was natural for Currelly to privilege the testimony of a man with a fine British-Canadian pedigree and a government job over men like Ragotte and (as we will see) James Hansen – labourers or tradesmen with ethnic names and rumoured problems with the bottle or mental health.

Currelly, to be sure, cast Ragotte as a discreditable low-life, but no one who took an interest in the Beardmore relics, not even Currelly, ever appreciated how complex and messy the private life of Eli Ragotte actually was. As the person who ignited the crisis in the Beardmore provenance that roiled for almost two decades, and whose assertions changed with exasperating and baffling regularity, Ragotte's personal story must be understood. It also must be remembered that John Jacob, who was granted immediate high standing and credibility, did not have his privileged voice questioned or the more problematic aspects of his life probed.

Since the mid-nineteenth century, the Ragotte family's story was defined by hardship and mobility. Eli Ragotte's grandparents, Pierre Rajotte ("Peeter Rashot" in the 1861 census) and Basilice Cournoyer, had been forced off their farm on Isle de Grace in Lac St-Pierre, in the township of Sorel, Quebec, by flooding and had moved on to homestead in Ontario's Hastings County. Pierre and Basilice already had eight children when Eli's father Charles, the ninth and final offspring, was born in 1859.[12] Charles was nineteen and his bride, Harriet Hott, was seventeen when they married in 1877, and they and Charles's brother Joseph moved to Michigan. Charles landed work in a sawmill in Pine River in Bay County, Michigan, where mills and shipbuilding abounded. Harriet would bear ten children in eighteen years, most of whom survived to adulthood. Eli, their sixth child, was born in Bay City in the summer of 1888.[13]

In 1890, the family moved to Wisconsin's Green Bay area, probably chasing the lumber boom. Life for the family of Eli Ragotte (as Charles's branch of the family spelled the surname) was a persistent struggle. In the 1900 US census of Marinette County, Wisconsin, Charles had no occupation and the household included nine children. In March 1903, the Ragottes started over as homesteaders east of Dauphin, Manitoba, near the francophone community of Ste-Rose-du-Lac.[14] It was the same remote area to which the Methodist minister-in-training, C.T. Currelly, had been assigned five years earlier. One wonders if, on the one occasion they met, Eli Ragotte and Currelly were aware of this coincidence.

Soon after arriving, the Ragotte family began to disintegrate. A family genealogy records Harriet's dying in Ste-Rose-du-Lac in June 1903.[15] Her husband Charles made three dollars in improvements to his grant, but the following October he secured an eighty-acre homestead back in Marinette County, and he remained in the United States.[16] Charles and his oldest son, Albert, eventually settled in Idaho, where Charles died in November 1936.[17] Eli Ragotte was seventeen when he secured a Ste-Rose-du-Lac homestead in February 1906, but he never patented the grant.[18] While Eli's brothers Mitchell and Edward became local farmers, Eli and his brother George found work with the Canadian Northern Railway.[19]

Four of the Ragotte brothers served in the Canadian army in the First World War. Eli was a Canadian Northern engineer, living in Port Arthur, when he joined the Independent Forestry Company in April 1917.[20] Eli was a compact, powerful man, standing five feet, seven inches with a forty-inch chest on enlistment. He had married Olive Hallet, who went by the name Violet, in January 1912, and they had a daughter, Violet Harriet May, in November 1913.[21] But when Eli Ragotte enlisted, he noted he was sep-arated and gave his daughter as his next of kin. He arranged for his pay to go to May (Mary) Bolduc in Port Arthur, whom he listed as Violet's guardian.[22] That small detail created an interesting complication in the Beardmore story. Mary Bolduc's husband, Adolphe, was a railway conduc-tor who died in 1915, and Ragotte presumably knew him.[23] Adolphe's brother was Leo, who, as we saw in chapter 1, was a business partner of Walter S. Ruttan. One of the properties Bolduc and Ruttan managed was 296 Wilson, where Eddy Dodd lived until June 1931. Bolduc and Ruttan were also closely associated with Aaron Lougheed when Eli Ragotte came forward with his claim of having found the relics in the basement of 296 Wilson. The many Bolduc connections to key figures in the Beardmore controversy remain unknowable factors in the hoax.

All four Ragotte brothers survived the war, although Eli's experience wasn't much different from that of Eddy Dodd. After transferring to the Canadian Railway Troops, from June 1918 onwards he was in and out of military hospitals, with pleurisy and chronic bronchitis, before being dis-charged from service after leaving hospital for the last time in May 1919. Eli and his brother George took advantage of land grants for veterans to register neighbouring homesteads in Saskatchewan, but neither man seems to have done much (if any) farming, and they resumed their railway work out of Winnipeg.[24] In Henderson city directories for Winnipeg, Eli was always some kind of Canadian Northern (and, after the railway merger of 1923, Canadian National) employee, usually a brakeman, but also a fireman or engineer.

In 1921 Eli married for the second time, to Violet Muriel Clements.[25] The relationship seems to have been short-lived, possibly because the second Violet discovered Eli was still married to the first Violet. In September 1924, the first Violet pre-cleared immigration to the United States, giving Eli (at a separate address in Winnipeg) as her next of kin. Violet was planning to take their not quite eleven-year-old daughter to Los Angeles, but the daughter does not seem to have accompanied her. Violet knew no one in Los Angeles and had no occupation. Had she imagined film stardom for herself? Eli (who retained American citizenship) showed up at immigration in Blaine, Washington, in January 1925 with $150 (about $1,650 today) and a stated plan to visit his wife in LA's beachside community of Santa Monica for three months.[26]

If this trip was Eli's attempt at a reconciliation, it didn't stick. He returned to Canada that July, and his daughter Violet became the concern of other Ragotte family members and friends. In 1935, his daughter, now twenty-two, was living in Winnipeg with Eli's sister Margaret and her husband Edwin Ferguson.[27] When Eli ignited the controversy surrounding the true origins of Eddy Dodd's relics in January 1938, he was approaching fifty, was working as a CNR brakeman (but had applied for a US social security registration the previous October), and was living in one of a series of apartments he occupied after leaving the Brandon Avenue home he had shared with the second Violet in the 1920s.[28] He gives the impression of having been a hard-living, alienating man – a description to which Eddy Dodd's wife Ellen was only too happy to attest. How much Eli Ragotte ever truly knew about Dodd's relics became an enduring mystery, to himself as much as to others.

At noon on January 26, Royd Beamish shared Eli Ragotte's published claims with Eddy Dodd, who called them "false and malicious." He continued: "That fellow's word isn't good anywhere. I see he claims I found the relics in the basement of a house on Wilson Street. Well, I didn't live on Wilson Street until 1934 and I made my first discovery on May 24, 1931. He never saw the relics until three years later, so what does he know about it?"[29] Later in the story, Beamish quoted Dodd as saying: "When I first ran across the stuff after we had blasted on a cross-trench,

I thought so little of it I threw it up on the bank and left it there for two years."

Dodd was free to argue that Ragotte did not see the relics until 1934, three years after he discovered them, but not when he was living on Wilson Street: Dodd had lived at 296 Wilson for many years *before* his claimed discovery date, and so was living there, as Ragotte stated, in 1928. Royd Beamish may have been confused by the mélange of dates.[30] Otherwise, Dodd had fixed in the public record a timeline of discovery that the provenance case now had to accommodate: he found the relics on 24 May 1931 and had left them ignored at the middle claim until 1933. That meant that no one could have seen them in Port Arthur before 1933, and, as Dodd insisted, that Ragotte did not see them until 1934. As we have seen, in 1936 Teddy Elliott had understood Dodd to say he discovered them (and left them on the claim for up to two months) on 24 May 1933, but Elliott had also made a note that the find was in April 1934. Currelly's notes at the time of purchase similarly said that the relics were left at the claim until 1933, but not for how long. As mentioned, it is possible Currelly added the heading with the discovery date of 24 May 1931 to Dodd's 3 December 1936 statement after Dodd made this published assertion to Royd Beamish. John Jacob had provided two affidavits to the museum (which had not been made public) that said he inspected the discovery trench right after the relics were found, which was impossible to square with Dodd's assertion to Beamish that the relics had been ignored at the claim for two years. The discovery date of 24 May 1931 that Dodd now asserted to Beamish was at least supported by Ned Burwash's report to Currelly in February 1934 that Dodd had found the relics three years earlier. As well, Thomas McIlwraith had recorded in the suppressed report of his visit to the middle claim in September 1937 that Dodd had found the relics in 1931.

This wasn't the first time that Dodd had been accused of engineering a hoax with the relics. "They started a story like that several years ago," Dodd told Beamish, "but I have my son and another man to prove that I found them while cross-trenching on my property. Not only that, but a university professor himself dug up part of a Viking sword in the same area last year." That was not quite true: Dodd had found the additional piece of metal, not McIlwraith. There is evidence that this item was initially thought to be a knife or sword point; Dodd didn't know that Currelly was interpreting it as a fragment of the shield boss. Dodd's mention of part of a sword being recovered in 1937 may have been the source of confusion in Beamish's reportage that Dodd had only ever found a partial sword.

The Beardmore story was moving so quickly that Royd Beamish could scarcely keep pace. Eli Ragotte must have shared an important additional detail that the *Winnipeg Free Press* had given to the *Daily News-Chronicle* to chase down: the house Dodd occupied, where Ragotte found the relics, was owned by a man named James Hansen. The *Daily News-Chronicle* had all but gone to press on 26 January, having combined Beamish's Dodd interviews into one story, when the typesetters had to insert fresh copy at the top of the story. James Hansen had emerged that afternoon with his own claim to Dodd's relics.

James M. Hansen had a far less peripatetic backstory than Ragotte. He was born Jens Martin Blix Hansen in 1882 on Vestvågøya in the Lufoten Islands, a stark Norwegian fishing archipelago located above the Arctic Circle. (In 1983, archaeologists on Vestvågøya would find the largest Viking chieftain's longhouse yet discovered.) In 1901, Hansen emigrated from Norway to Minnesota and began working as a carpenter and plasterer; in 1903, he moved on to Port Arthur to pursue the same trades. There, in October 1907, he married Lise (Laese) Irene Gunhelde, who arrived from Vestvågøya on her wedding day. They bought a house at 159 Secord Street and, in 1911, were living there with two young children and nine boarders who had emigrated from Norway and Sweden in the past two years and paid four to five dollars a month for their rooms. In 1913, Hansen purchased and moved into a home at 33 Machar Avenue. Except for a brief period around the end of the First World War, when the family lived on a farm Hansen had purchased in McIntyre Township, the Hansens resided uninterrupted at 33 Machar until 1931. The property would prove central to the Beardmore case. Hansen was a building contractor, and he "owned, bought/sold/traded and rented out numerous residential and commercial properties, and land parcels, across the region from rural Fort William/Port Arthur to Lake Helen on the Nipigon River," his grandson John Garner recalls.[31] A surviving business ledger indicates that Hansen was active in communities along the north shore of Lake Superior, in particular Red Rock, after the Lake Sulphite Pulp Company purchased property for a mill that included a townsite in 1936.[32] Hansen otherwise was a busy purchaser, renovator, and landlord of Port Arthur properties in the 1920s and 1930s, and in addition to several other town residential properties he came to own three neighbouring houses on Machar, at 33, 37 (on the south side of 33, purchased in 1921), and 39 (purchased in 1924).[33] He mortgaged and remortgaged properties as he improved them, making him no stranger to bankers and lawyers in the community, and he took in boarders at 33 Machar into the early 1930s.

Rushed into the top of the *Daily News-Chronicle*'s 26 January story was an allegation by Hansen that "he had accepted a collection of old relics from a Norwegian named Black, in settlement of an account. A native of Norway himself, Mr. Hanson [sic] said he recognized the articles as of historical importance, and that he valued them at $150." He had left them in the basement of a house he owned, where two years ago Dodd had been his tenant.[34]

The "grizzled little prospector" Eddy Dodd was not happy either to have had his role as the discoverer of the relics revealed or to be confronting mounting allegations of fraud. "I don't like seeing my name in black lines all over the front pages of the newspapers," Dodd told Beamish, after the 26 January article unfurled a front-page banner headline "DENIES VIKING RELICS 'PLANTED' AT BEARDMORE," with the subhead "James E. Dodd Says He Has Good Proof Discovery Genuine." Dodd refused to provide Beamish with an affidavit swearing to his story details, and he announced that he was heading to Beardmore. "I won't give any statements or any photos or any affidavits to any newspapers. I'm lying low from now on, and if anybody libels me they're going to pay for it. You can ask Professor McIlwraith all about it and he will vouch for me. This fellow Ragotte is just sore at me and is trying to make trouble. But he's all wrong about finding any relics in the basement of Hanson's house in 1928. In the first place I didn't live in Hanson's house until 1931 and in the second place I didn't even know Ragotte in 1928."[35]

Dodd was correct to say he had not become a tenant of Hansen until 1931, and the newspaper was wrong to report he had still been a tenant in 1936. Whether Dodd knew Ragotte in 1928 was not yet established (and never would be), but the hoax case was emerging in a haphazard and easily discredited way. Dodd found an apparently unimpeachable supporter in Carl Sorensen, an insurance adjustor in Fort William who served as the Norwegian vice-consul at the Lakehead. Sorensen had emigrated from Norway to the United States and secured citizenship, in Minnesota, in 1898. He then moved to Canada, arriving in Port Arthur in December 1912 and setting up business in Fort William.[36] About to turn seventy, Sorensen was understood to be a widower and was a leading member of the local Scandinavian community. He also knew Vilhjalmur Stefansson from the explorer's youth, when both had lived in the Dakota territory.

The man from whom Hansen had supposedly received the relics, initially reported as "Black," Sorensen informed Beamish, was "Lieut. John Bloch, a retired officer of the Norwegian reserve army." Bloch had anglicized his surname to Block, and, while Sorensen did not explain, his original given name was Jens. "I saw as much of him as anyone else while he was here, and he did not at any time mention having any Norse relics in his possession. I'm sure he would have told me if he had." Sorensen explained that Bloch's father was a well-known artist in Norway who was "keenly interested in the historical lore of his country, particularly in the Viking period." Bloch had shown Sorensen several of his father's paintings of Norsemen (which were probably reproductions in a book), "but I never saw a single weapon or piece of armor that might have belonged to that period or any other ancient period in his possession. I do not recall him ever mentioning that his father had a collection of such weapons, and if he had any himself he certainly did not mention it to me."[37]

Beamish sought additional witnesses. One person who might have been able to speak volumes was Eddy Dodd's younger brother, Stephen, a railway conductor who lived in Fort William, but no one pursuing the truth about the Beardmore relics ever seemed to be aware of him.[38] Beamish did come up with Dodd's prospecting partner, Fletcher Gill, who said he was as surprised as anyone when he read about the discovery of Norse relics on the claim.

"I certainly wasn't with Mr. Dodd when he found the relics, and in fact I did not know he had made the discovery until it appeared in the newspapers," Gill confessed. "I do recall an incident some time ago when Mr. Dodd and I were talking to some other men and he said to me: 'Remember that stuff I found on the property, Fletcher.' I didn't pay much attention to it, thinking he had found an old jack-knife or a saw, or something like that." Fletcher did his best to explain how he could have been so in the dark about a discovery on a claim he had been working with Dodd for the last twelve years. It wasn't always possible for of them to be at their claims at the same time, he offered. "He might easily have found the stuff when he was there without me. That would account for my not having heard of it. Mr. Dodd was never inclined to talk a great deal about things like that anyway."[39]

C.T. Currelly could only have watched the erupting controversy at a distance with helpless dread and fascination. There was nothing he could do about Dodd's extemporizing, and the characters in the controversy were multiplying with every passing day. When the *Globe and Mail* ran a "special" from Beamish on 27 January, it included a vague statement about the status of the relics. "Archaeologists in Toronto who have been informed of the find more than a year ago, refrained from comment beyond stating that the relics in question were now in the Royal Ontario Museum and that they had been identified with the Viking period of the eleventh century."[40] It wasn't clear from the report that the museum owned the items.

On 27 January, Currelly received a lengthy telegram from the *Winnipeg Free Press*, outlining the allegations made by Ragotte and other "associates" of Dodd.[41] The Dodd provenance was clearly in trouble, and the published statements of Ragotte, Hansen, Dodd, and Sorensen, while contradictory and confusing, raised issues of the ROM's competence – his own competence – in acquiring the relics. On 28 January, Currelly issued a formal statement for the Toronto press to protect the ROM (and himself) from any fallout arising from Hansen's or Ragotte's allegations being proven correct:

About a year ago, Mr. Dodd of Port Arthur brought to the Museum the Norse articles under discussion. I saw at once that they were a set much as one man would have. In my thirty years of hunting, this was the first set that I had ever seen offered for sale. We paid Mr. Dodd a price that I would have been willing to pay had he bought the things on King Street, in London, or in Norway. Every museum man knows one thing, that the story costs nothing; but the chance of getting a Viking set had never come before, and anything connected with these people who took charge of Russia, Northern France, Southern Italy and Sicily, and to a certain degree are our own ancestors (because we must all have a bit of Norse blood in us if we are British), has a tremendous teaching value.

Now, the question of their finding was also very important, and that is why the Museum for a year has said nothing and for a year has been doing its level best to find out about it. Photographs were sent to certain Norse scholars in northern Europe and their agreement was complete that the articles are all of the same period. The attack on Mr. Dodd's honesty by Mr. Ragotte is, after all the word of one man against another, but it is not safe to take one man's word against another's in a scientific question. We have been doing our best to find out all we can, and we hope before long to make a statement to the press of all that we know.

During my whole period of hunting, nothing has been more constantly on my mind than to show our students and adults from the day they first read any English history, the extraordinarily efficient equipment of these marvellous Norsemen, who seemingly introduced the mailed shirt into Russia, England, France, etc., and were looked upon as absolutely irresistible. Either they were amazing mechanics themselves or got their material at that very early time by way of the Russian rivers from Constantinople. During this whole time, three swords, as far as I can remember, have been offered for sale in England and New York, till these things appeared. I never saw any other part of the equipment for sale, and I am very, very glad to say that thanks largely to the generosity of Mr. Sigmund Samuel, every one of the swords I have seen for sale are in the Museum;[42] I have managed not to let one piece slip. So that this set, no matter where they came from, is a matter of vital importance to the Museum.

It would seem as if Mr. Dodd and the man on the next mining claim to him, are not on the best of terms.[43]

Currelly did not reveal what the museum had paid, but he asserted that Dodd's story was immaterial to the relics' value. Currelly made no mention of McIlwraith's September 1937 investigation (and McIlwraith's endorsement of Dodd's honesty); nor did he confirm or deny plans for further fieldwork. Although he had advised that it was "not safe to take one man's word against another's in a scientific question," he had decided that the provenance question in fact was going to hinge on statements by individuals whose characters could be disparaged or uplifted. His own concluding statement was a careless shot at Ragotte and Hansen as neither man was a prospecting neighbour of Dodd. Currelly was pulling aspersions out of thin air to discredit the men who were accusing Dodd of engineering a hoax, even as he left Dodd dangling as a possible hoaxer.

Currelly was wrong to state that the ROM was "doing the best to find out all we can" about the weapons typology. Days before the controversy broke, Currelly had informed A.W. Brøgger at Oslo's Museum of Cultural History that the ROM had gathered everything it needed to know and required no further input from him. Currelly had not acted on any recommendations to pursue further opinions from authorities in Viking arms and armour. He had not bothered to contact Matthias Thórdarson, despite Stefansson's urging. He still had not heard back from three of the experts he had written when he issued his statement. While two would never respond, one remaining reply was posted the day Currelly issued his statement. It was among the most authoritative, and it ought to have been deeply concerning.

Otto von Friesen was a linguist and runologist who had been a professor at the University of Uppsala in Sweden until 1935. The professor emeritus submitted Currelly's photograph to an Uppsala colleague, the prominent archaeologist Sune Lindqvist, who consulted Petersen's guide and provided Currelly with a review of its evidence, much as Stefán Einarsson had. Lundqvist agreed with Einarsson's assessment that the sword was a type M and that the axe, too, was a type M. The sword type mainly belonged to the 850 to 900 period, he explained, but some examples from the early tenth century were known, when the Q type otherwise became prevalent. The axe belonged to the most recent Viking period, 950 to the beginning of the eleventh century. The presence of the older style sword with the newer style axe troubled Lundqvist. Unlike Einarsson (who was not an archaeologist), Lundqvist was not willing to imagine a very late example of the sword type having been used by a warrior at the same time as a very early example of the axe type. However, in a postscript Friesen explained: "By word of mouth professor Lundqvist has said [to] me, that it is possible that the grave belongs to the time about 1000 A.D. One has observed that often very aged objects have been given with the dead in the grave."[44] The sword thus would have been an heirloom when it went into the ground with an axe contemporary with the burial. It would be harder to explain why a Norseman in the North American hinterland would have been relying on a "very aged" weapon like the sword along with a new axe. As for the burial, Friesen could not help but ask: "Has the grave from which the weapons come been found in Canada? And if so, where? Has the discovery been made under scientifically safe circumstances? Indeed a norse [sic] find from the Viking age in Canada should be of the greatest historical interest." These were pointed questions that Currelly would not answer.

There was one more item of interest in Lundqvist's assessment. "The third object is scarcely any handle of a shield. The photo gives me no guidance to say to what it served. The end next to the sword-hilt is secondarily deformed, perhaps also the other." With the Friesen-Lundqvist assessment, Currelly had received the daunting opinion of experts in Scandinavian archaeology that not only did the sword and axe belong to two different eras (as other experts had also surmised from Petersen) but also that Dodd's shield handle was no such thing. John Jacob had proposed the shield was a small metal "buckler," but the wooden shields used by Vikings did not have metal handles. If the object wasn't a handle, then Dodd's story of finding a shield, essential to Currelly's conviction of the find's authenticity, ought to have crumbled like the shield itself. Incredibly, the answer for the true nature of the "shield handle" was right in Petersen, and none of the experts had spotted it. More than twelve years would pass before the item was properly identified.

Currelly ignored Lundqvist's learned opinion where the handle was concerned. And as far as the public knew, based on Currelly's 28 January statement, the Norse experts of northern Europe were in complete agreement that the relics were all from the same period. One of those experts, however, was not letting the matter of the relic's discovery location rest. Currelly had ended discussions with A.W. Brøgger on 22 January, but it must have been inconceivable to this prominent Norwegian museum director that a literally *provincial* museum in Canada would treat him so discourteously. Many of the weapons that were the basis of Petersen's standard typology were housed in his Oslo museum. He wrote Currelly again on 8 February.[45] "It interests me very much to learn that you are going to publish Your Viking weapons, but besides this I should be very interested into [sic] the special question to which I did get no answer: where have they come from, and do [you] know more specially *the locality in Scandinavia* where they have been found? As a director of the largest collection in Scandinavia of Viking weapons this special question would be of great interest to me, and I should be very grateful for getting any information you could afford."

It was unlikely that Brøgger had caught wind of the controversy in the Canadian press in late January. He assumed the relics must have come from Scandinavia, and he continued to seek assurance that they hadn't been illegally removed from Norway. The possibility that this was precisely how they had arrived in Canada – not at some time in the early tenth century but, rather, in the early twentieth century – was much greater than when Brøgger last wrote, now that Ragotte and Hansen had made their admittedly uneven allegations. Currelly again ignored Brøgger. It was a fateful error.

10

Ripped Right Up the Back

Royd Beamish could see that the statements made for and against Eddy Dodd's Beardmore discovery were a mass of contradictions. To clarify the record, the Port Arthur newspaper reporter asked the main figures in the dispute to swear out affidavits. Eli Ragotte, James Hansen, and Carl Sorensen did so in late January; Dodd refused and so, apparently, did Fletcher Gill. With the collecting of affidavits, the Beardmore story began to mirror that of the Kensington stone, which relied on affidavits of purported eyewitnesses to its unearthing in 1898. The Beardmore find's authenticity, too, would come to rely on an increasing mass of such statements bearing witness to Dodd's discovery or his display of the relics at a critical date.

Ragotte's 28 January affidavit stated that, in 1929 or 1930, he had lived in a Port Arthur house on Wilson Street (he could not recall the number) owned by James Hansen.[1] Hansen was renting it to Eddy Dodd, who in turn was Ragotte's landlord at the house. Hansen told Ragotte he had left "various articles in and on the said premises." At some time between 1928 and 1930, while helping Dodd clean up the Wilson Street property, Ragotte found "an old rusty sword in the basement." About six weeks later, Dodd told him he had blasted it out of the middle claim, along with a shield and an axe. Ragotte never saw the axe but was shown "a rusted piece of steel which Mr. Dodds told me was a shield." Whether this piece of metal was the shield handle or was supposed to be the shield (perhaps the boss) Ragotte did not clarify, but this was a different story than the one the *Winnipeg Free Press* had reported, of Ragotte dragging a sword and shield from furnace ashes. Ragotte said that Dodd had also shown the sword to a prospector named Dolbridge (sic; Tom Delbridge), a prospector and blacksmith named Smith, and a railway engineer named Fletcher Gill, all of Port Arthur, and had told them he had found it on his claim. The sword was "twenty-six to thirty inches long, the blade being well rusted." It had a handle, "but I do not recollect what the handle was like." The sword he saw in the Wilson Street basement, Ragotte said in closing, was the same one Dodd had been showing around Port Arthur and saying he had found at the middle claim.

Ragotte's assertion that Dodd had shown the relics to Fletcher Gill, Dodd's prospecting partner, contradicted Gill's statement to Royd Beamish that the recent press revelations were the first he had heard of the relics. Ragotte's statement otherwise posed a fundamental problem for Dodd's story. If Ragotte was correct in saying he said he had seen the sword in the basement on Wilson Street no later than 1930, Dodd could not have found the relics in the Beardmore claim on 24 May 1931, as he had now stated. Ragotte also would have seen them long before 1933, which is when Dodd had separately told Beamish and C.T. Currelly he had brought them home from the claim – which was also long before the date Dodd had given Teddy Elliott for the discovery (May 1933). But as Currelly was not making public the statement Dodd made at the time of the museum's purchase, the seriousness of the discrepancy was not readily apparent. One person who did take notice of conflicting statements was T.L. Tanton, the geologist at the DGS who had suspected a hoax from the moment Elliott had shared what Dodd had told him. Tanton knew that Dodd had told Elliott he found the relics in May 1933, and he began assembling a clipping file.

James Hansen's affidavit told a different story than did Eli Ragotte's.[2] Hansen said he came to know John Bloch shortly after Bloch's arrival in Port Arthur at an unstated date and that he had employed him for a short time. Through "numerous conversations" with Bloch, Hansen learned "he had in his possession certain relics identified with the Viking period of the 11th century." Bloch owed Hansen twenty-five dollars, and to settle the account "he offered me some of the said relics which I accepted." Hansen stored the relics in the basement of a house he owned at 33 Machar in Port Arthur. Later, Eddy Dodd became Hansen's tenant there. While Dodd was living there, Hansen discovered that the Viking relics he had received from Bloch were missing. Hansen believed then and now that the relics were genuine and "although I had no knowledge of what value authorities would place them at, I personally valued them at One Hundred and Fifty Dollars ($150.00)." The relics that went missing from the Machar Avenue house "answer in general to the description of the relics which were reported to have been found on Dodd's mining claim near Beardmore."

Hansen and Ragotte were telling two contradictory yet intertwined stories. There was a house owned by Hansen that was rented by Dodd, and a basement in which the sword, at least, had been stored. But whereas Ragotte said the house was on Wilson Street, Hansen said it was on Machar Avenue, and Hansen never owned a Wilson Street property. The Henderson's city directory of Winnipeg would have shown Ragotte at addresses there from 1922 to 1931, which would rule out his having lived regularly with Dodd at any home in Port Arthur between 1928 and 1930. Dodd insisted that he did not know Ragotte at the time Ragotte claimed to have found the relics in the basement and that Ragotte did not see them until 1934. Hansen offered no dates for the events.

More problematic perhaps was the fact that neither Ragotte nor Hansen noted that the sword was in two pieces – a striking omission. Had they done so, their personal knowledge of the relics would have been more persuasive as no photograph had circulated in the press and the media reports had not revealed this essential condition. Dodd had been careful not to describe the relics in any detail, although Beamish's reportage had left the impression that only a partial sword was found. Ragotte's affidavit had the overall length of the broken sword generally correct, but one would expect that if he had found a broken sword, he would have remembered that the handle was a separate piece and not simply have said that he could not recall what it looked like. On the other hand, Ragotte may have been fudging the truth: he had only seen part of the sword and had contrived a story about finding an entire sword – not knowing the actual sword was in two pieces.[3]

To square their stories, Hansen wrote Ragotte on 31 January, thanking him "for advising the Manitoba Free Press re my relic there was at 33 Machar Ave."[4] If Ragotte had lived in a Port Arthur house Dodd was renting from Hansen, then Hansen implied it must have been 33 Machar, not 296 Wilson. Hansen attempted to craft a version of events that he and Ragotte could agree on for 33 Machar:

As you were speaking that the relics were among the clinkers, I kinda remember that I was down at 33 Machar looking for my fishing tackle that I lost and Dodds went down the basement to look for them and I went down and you came also then *I asked for my norse relics* you remember the bench they were standing left along the east wall in the basement and Dodds said he saw some old iron and junk that he threw amongst the clinkers that were left in the basement at the time and *you went over and rooted amongst the ashes* and found some of them and you remember also that I told Dodds to get them up and

put oil on them as I had did which he promised. As I [had] several
calls to make that night and you both promised me to get them out
for me. I do suppose that you remember the ackation [occasion] the
same as I do? According to what I found out last night the relics was
sold to the Royal Museum by Dodds? Of course the fishing tackle and
rod that he claims you have I suppose are lost. You don't remember
what became of the grine [sic] stone that was standing in the back.
The frame was left but the stone end [and?] handle were gone this I almost forgot perhaps you remember?

Hansen also reported to have recently called on Fletcher Gill, who lived
around the corner from Dodd. Unbeknownst to anyone trying to make
sense of the Beardmore discovery story, the now-infamous middle claim at
this point belonged to Gill. Mining office records indicated that Dodd
had not filed an account of any work at the middle claim, 48TB4895, and
the adjoining 4894 since November 1932, although he apparently continued to visit the site, to which his encounter on the train with Teddy Elliott
in July 1934 attests. The leases for both claims were not renewed; instead,
Gill re-staked the pair of claims on 4 December 1937 and secured fresh
registrations in his name, as TB25788 and TB25787, on 6 December. Any
further plans to probe claim 25788 for relics would have required Gill's
knowledge and permission. The overhanging question is how Dodd had
managed to sell the relics to the ROM not only without telling Gill but
also without sharing the proceeds of a find on their claim.

Fletcher Gill was born in Cornwall, England, in 1889; his father was a
foreman and engine driver on the Great Western Railway (GWR). Gill
began working for the GWR when he was sixteen and rose to the position
of fireman. He married Beatrice Mitchell in 1910, and in 1912, the couple
came to Canada with an infant son, Alfred. A daughter born in Toronto
in 1913 did not survive infancy, and they relocated that year to Port
Arthur. In January 1922, double tragedy struck. Beatrice died in childbirth
and so did the infant.[5] Now a single father, Gill continued to work as a locomotive engineer for the CNR and, by 1926, was prospecting on the side
as Dodd's partner.

Dodd and Gill were an odd couple. Dodd was the gregarious hustler, and
he wrote in a semi-literate scrawl. Gill was a devoted freemason, belonging
to chapters in Port Arthur and Winnipeg as well as to the Shriners, and his
elegant, almost archaic penmanship might have reflected a role as a lodge
scribe. Gill's handwriting and diction suggested far more education than

his partner had managed, although he was not a particularly sophisticated man. His knowledge of the truth about Dodd's find was inscrutable. Deferential in his correspondence, Fletcher Gill projected a guilelessness concerning the relics, and he was probably yet another mark in Eddy's life of hustling. As a partner, he presented a more polished front in seeking funds for prospecting – that is, when Gill himself was not a source.

By the time Hansen wrote Ragotte in an attempt to square their stories, the credibility of Hansen's claim that he had acquired relics from Bloch had been seriously challenged by a third affidavit, gathered by Beamish on 29 January from the Norwegian vice-consul Carl Sorensen.[6] Sorensen attested that he had met Bloch in Winnipeg around 1922, and he believed that Bloch had moved to Port Arthur around 1922 or 1923, where Sorensen met him again in 1926. Bloch had indeed been employed by the builder and contractor Hansen, Sorensen said, and had excavated a basement for him in a house on Machar Avenue. Sorensen also agreed that Dodd was later a tenant of that house. But Sorensen gave no credence to Hansen's assertion that Bloch had Norse relics, let alone that he used them to settle a debt with Hansen.

Sorensen and Bloch "spent many evenings together," during which Bloch said he was a reserve lieutenant in the Norwegian army, and he showed Sorensen some of his military equipment ("belts, caps, insignia, and other such things") that he had brought from Norway. Bloch told him that his father "was a noted painter in Norway, and had been commissioned by the Norwegian Government on various occasions to reproduce on canvas the costumes, wearing apparel, and fighting equipment that the Vikings used during their time. He also told me that his father was quite an authority on Viking lore and studied it a great deal, and that he also had quite a private collection of Viking relics." Bloch showed Sorensen some reproductions of his father's paintings, and they "had many discussions of Viking lore." But "never at any time during my numerous discussions with Lieutenant Bloch, did he ever mention having brought with him any relics." Bloch "gave no impression of being a man of any wealth, and had he disposed of any Viking relics which he may have brought with him, he would, without a doubt, have mentioned that fact to me." Bloch "was a well educated man and from life associations with his father, would have been able to recognize any authentic Viking relics, and would have known the value of same." In closing, Sorensen noted that Bloch had then moved to Winnipeg and later to Vancouver, where he had died in 1931 or 1932. In fact, Bloch did not die in Vancouver until October 1936, two months before Dodd sold the relics to the ROM.

Sorensen may have been convinced that John Bloch never owned Viking relics, but where Beamish had quoted Sorensen saying that Bloch's father never owned Norse artefacts, Sorensen, in his affidavit one day later, said that the elder Bloch had "quite a private collection of Viking relics." And despite his effort to discredit Hansen, Sorensen affirmed that Dodd had been a tenant of Hansen's in a house on Machar Avenue where Bloch had done work. Dodd himself, in his interview with the *Daily News-Chronicle*, had said he had lived at 33 Machar in 1931 – the same year that he said he found the relics in the middle claim.

As the initial flurry of activity surrounding the hoax allegations ended, C.T. Currelly appeared to be open to the possibility of fraud. E. Ross MacKay, the associate editor of the *Sault Daily Star*, who had interviewed Ned Burwash and published the article about the find on 20 January 1937, contacted Currelly to gather his perspective. Currelly did not want to make a public statement but advised MacKay: "When the Norse weapons, which are undoubtedly Norse and all of the same date, were brought to me, I hoped that we might be able to find out for sure what their more recent history has been; and I hope that through a rather strange accident [i.e., the public controversy], we are still going to be able to know definitely. At the present time, there is nothing to be said. Mr. Dodd makes a certain statement, another man calls him a cheat and a liar; and it's the word there of two men who evidently were closely connected and now have quarrelled. There is of course a question of probability which cannot be allowed to enter as historical fact, but I hope we will have the matter pretty clear before long, and that it will be at once given out to the press."[7]

The hoax case hinged on several questions. Did John Bloch bring to Canada Norse artefacts that had once belonged to his father? Could anyone or anything prove those relics ended up in James Hansen's hands and were left in 33 Machar before Eddy Dodd moved in? And could Dodd in his own defence prove he had found the relics at Beardmore before he moved into 33 Machar? In the coming months, Currelly would strive to secure the answers.

When the Beardmore scandal erupted in the press in late January 1938, an important perspective from within the ROM was committed to paper. James Henry (he always signed himself J.H.) Fleming was one of the world's leading bird experts. The son of James Fleming, a pioneering seed merchant and amateur scientist in Toronto, J.H. Fleming appears never to have held a paying job, instead devoting his life to ornithology.[8] He was the first Canadian to serve as president of the American Ornithological Union (1933–35), and he kept the organization afloat during the Depression with his own money. He turned part of his home on Toronto's Rusholme Road into one of the world's great private collections of mounted birds, skins, and eggs. In 1920 he donated the collection, along with its superb reference library and his personal journals, to the ROM's zoology division. More than thirty-two thousand specimens and the library made the ROM's Fleming Collection one of the finest in the world. In 1927, the museum made him its honorary curator of ornithology, which came with an office to oversee the collection.

Fleming enjoyed an unusual, multidimensional perspective on the Beardmore controversy, as distant as ornithology might have seemed from Norse weapons and archaeology. He had a curator's view of the museum's activities and politics as well as the perspective of a major donor. As an ornithologist whose studies relied on specimens sent to him from around the world, he appreciated the importance of provenance. He had to be confident that a skin or egg truly was sourced in a specific location.

When the Beardmore scandal broke, Fleming rose to the defence of the museum, convinced the find was genuine. On 27 January, he wrote his friend Gerald Wade, manager of Western Municipal News in Winnipeg.[9] "Today the relics were brought out of a Port Arthur cellar in an ash can," Fleming noted sarcastically after the claims of Ragotte and Hansen surfaced, "but don't you believe it[,] the relics are absolutely authentic and as Godsell states. The controversy will rip the whole story of the discovery of North America up the back. The Royal Ontario Museum has been keeping the announcement back till such time as further investigation on the site can be made. Prof. McIlwraith got a knife point there this past summer." Thomas McIlwraith's report had only indicated that he and Dodd had come up with a piece of iron, which Currelly decided was a piece of the shield boss. Fleming's letter indicates that, within the museum, there was a different initial interpretation of the find, which was reinforced by Dodd's recent assertion in the press that McIlwraith had found part of a sword.

Fleming was close to McIlwraith, having been a co-founder with McIlwraith's grandfather of the American Ornithological Union. As a skilled taxidermist, the elder McIlwraith had mounted birds in the ROM's collection. Because Thomas McIwraith became a keen field naturalist in his youth, he may have known Fleming since childhood. The ornithologist in zoology empathized with the ethnologist over in archaeology and explained to Wade, "I have just written him a letter of sympathy for he will be attacked on all sides for believing such a fable."

Fleming felt McIlwraith's predicament keenly as he was enduring a similar ordeal. In 1935, the ROM had published an occasional paper by Fleming on a new genus and species of flightless teal, *Xenonetta nesiotis* (which Fleming further declared to be extinct), based on a specimen a sailor had bludgeoned with an oar at New Zealand's subantarctic Campbell Island in 1886.[10] A notice of Fleming's paper appeared in the international ornithology journal *Ibis* in October 1935, with the comment: "The discovery of a flightless duck in 1935 is certainly an unexpected event."[11] Fleming's coup was met by accusations from New Zealand that the specimen and Fleming's analysis were bogus. "They have dug up an engineer who was on the boat and even sheep farmers," Fleming complained to Wade, "and this was in 1884 [sic; 1886] anyway I and the duck are being ripped right up the back it is not a good genus or species and did not come from Campbell Island, me not knowing anything about ducks."[12]

In a second letter to Wade on 19 February, Fleming reviewed what he understood of how Dodd's relics were brought to the museum's attention, which more or less agreed with John Jacob's account. Most informative was what he had heard from within the ROM about the actual discovery: "Two men were working a claim[,] one a railroad man who supplied the money and worked in his off time, the other doing most of the work, both names are in print." This was an informed assessment of the partnership between Gill (who mainly provided the money) and Dodd (who mainly did the work). "These men were trenching alongside or around a low knoll[. O]ne night there was a storm, one of the men returning to the claim next morning found the clump of dwarf birches that covered the knoll had been blown over carrying all the roots and soil with it and exposing the decomposed gneiss of the knoll. It was on this knoll the prospector found the relics. I do not know in what order they were, but the museum informant hearing of the find visited the claim and he saw he could distinguish the impressions of the weapons in the soft gneiss."

"Last summer some effort was made to go over the site of the find," Fleming continued, referring to McIlwraith's September 1937 investigations. "I rather think some corroborative evidence was found but I do not care to get mixed up in the controversy so have not enquired. Archaeology is in a difficult position[. B]oth of the prospectors [Dodd and Gill] are unreliable and they are out of touch with the one reliable man [Jacob] who informed Zoology." Clearly, after the scandal broke, Dodd especially was written off by the museum as an untrustworthy source on his own find. John Jacob was now the lone, dependable eyewitness. His name had not yet appeared in the press and Fleming was not willing to share it with his friend Wade, who was in the news business.

The discovery story Fleming reported is certainly the one the museum's zoology division initially heard from Jacob, as Jacob would repeat the detail of the exposed roots of a windblown clump of birch later that year. Fleming's account suggests that John Jacob helped Dodd craft a discovery story, with a clump of birch blown over by the wind and an impression left by the weapons in crumbled gneiss. Dodd then complicated the story by adding a tree stump more than a foot in diameter and garbling the crumbled gneiss into Precambrian rock moulded to the shape of the relics. Jacob alternately could have heard Dodd's improbable detail of moulded rock and given it a more credible spin in his own telling. Why Jacob then would have changed or elaborated his story to stress the presence of a sword-shaped rust stain on the underlying rock (which Dodd never mentioned and Fleming did not hear) is unknowable. Jacob simply may have been trying to improve his own version of the story with every telling.

"I am satisfied of the genuineness of the find," Fleming continued, "it consists of the nearly full equipment of one man, the weapons are 10th Century as I saw at once, though the museum till recently attributed them to the 11th Century. I am familiar with Norse relics in Copenhagen and Oslow [sic]. From the first I have warned archaeology this thing will rip the museum up the back, it is curious how any statement of fact if in archaeology or zoology is promptly contradicted as I told you in my last letter of the reception of the new duck in New Zealand."

Fleming again wrote Wade, on 27 February. Currelly, he vowed, "is an astute person, and realises he must keep clear of any controversy for the present at least, he has the armament of one Norseman, sword, axe, and handle of the shield, as yet he lacks the knife." The idea persisted that the so-called grave should yield a knife, and Fleming's letter suggests the museum indeed hoped to return to the middle claim that summer to find what was presumed to be the final item in a dead Norseman's burial armory.

Most illuminating was Fleming's observation that the ROM "has to depend on private donors for its material added to the museum and donors are easily scared by publicity of an unfavourable character such as arose over some of the Greek vases some are claimed they were forged [i.e., forgeries]." Ancient Greek ceramics were one of the most hazardous collecting

areas as the market had been flooded with fakes in response to high demand. Currelly had been dazzled by a private collection in England,
owned by Dr William Allen Sturge, a Bristol physician and archaeologist,
that included "about four hundred Greek vases." When the collection became available to Currelly during the First World War for "about a third
of what such things had fetched when the war broke out," he was frantic
to make the deal.[13] Sigmund Samuel pledged three thousand pounds in
1920 for the Sturge Collection, which provided most of the museum's
holding of Greek vases. Whispering after a two-volume work dedicated to
the museum's Greek vases appeared in 1930 may have suggested that the
collection contained forgeries.[14] Currelly could have just tapped Samuel
for a second purchase of questionable relics.[15]

On 24 February, Harold Innis, professor of political economy at the University of Toronto, wrote Currelly in his capacity as chair of Section 2 of
the Royal Society of Canada, inviting him to give a paper on the Beardmore find at the society's next meeting, in Ottawa, in late May. Wilfrid
Bovey's paper on the Vinland voyages had been a highlight of the 1936
meeting. "It was the unanimous opinion of the Executive that this paper
might provide the most interesting contribution for the session."[16] Currelly left the letter unanswered. He could say nothing further publicly
until he had unequivocal answers to the hoax allegations. For the sake of
his own credibility, especially with Sigmund Samuel, Currelly was not
prepared to back down on the Beardmore purchase if there was any
chance the hoax accusations could be challenged, as Fleming was determined to do with regard to the accusations of his flightless duck critics.

For Eddy Dodd, the burst of publicity about the Beardmore relics bore a
silver lining: it attracted interest in his prospecting efforts. In February, the
Norse-Beardmore Syndicate was incorporated in Toronto under president
Percy Herron, with $35,000 in capital and an option on a Dodd mining
claim. If the syndicate involved the middle claim, Fletcher Gill would have
been involved as the claim was staked in his name. Diamond drilling was
announced in the *Globe and Mail* on 14 February, with a further announcement on 15 March that Howey Gold Mines, which had producing
mines around Kenora and Red Lake, had taken an option on the property, subject to drilling results. At last, Dodd appeared to be poised to capitalize on the real wealth he had been digging for near Beardmore.[17]

John Drew Jacob Investigates

Philip Godsell continued to milk the scoop of the Beardmore discovery he had filched from Teddy Elliott. He made an address on the Winnipeg radio station CKY, and Gerald Wade passed along to the station his 27 January 1938 letter from J.H. Fleming to encourage Godsell. Darby Coats, the station's publicity manager, replied to Wade: "I believe he is going to get somewhere with this thing, though, of course, I have no scientific knowledge of the subject."[1]

Godsell was indeed determined to get somewhere with this thing. On 12 February 1938, the *Winnipeg Free Press* published a Godsell letter criticizing a 27 January editorial, "Improbable Immigrant Imprints," that had dismissed the relics based on Ragotte's revelation. Godsell disparaged Ragotte (unnamed) as an "irresponsible rail roader" and advised: "While discoveries of this nature, having such important historical significance, have naturally to be received with great caution and all aspects subjected to close investigation as to their authenticity I point out that the information was received by me from unquestionably reliable sources, with the added assertion that the articles in question had been submitted to competent authorities who had pronounced them genuine Norse weapons of the 11th century." Leaving aside the matter of Currelly's incomplete typology queries, Godsell's only apparent source was his chatty letter from Teddy Elliott.

On 5 March, Godsell published a Saturday-edition feature article, "Viking Footprints," in the *Winnipeg Tribune*, stirring in his own hypothesizing and facts (reliable and otherwise) gleaned from recent press coverage. The article opened with a dramatic account, borne of his detective-fiction imagination, of the Beardmore discovery – or, rather, discoveries – as Godsell had accepted the scenario Eddy Dodd had offered to Royd Beamish in his first interview of a series of finds, beginning with a "rusty piece of metal" that had been revealed by his gold pick and that he had ignored for two years. "Probably it would have lain there till the corroded metal fell apart but for the visit of Professor Burwash. Led to the spot by a chance word of the miner, his astonished eyes rested upon this piece of rusty armour worn by some Viking warrior long before the days of

Christopher Columbus." Godsell then had Burwash, "fearful that this information might get into irresponsible hands before its period and authenticity could be determined," swear Dodd to secrecy. Next came the discoveries of the rest of the relics "at different times and by four different people, including Prof. McIlwraith of Toronto."

Fictionalizing aside, Godsell performed a valuable service to the ROM by endorsing the find's authenticity. He reiterated C.T. Currelly's confident assurance that a thorough investigation had produced a unanimous endorsement from experts. Godsell's account had Currelly anxiously awaiting the responses of "leading Norse scholars throughout Europe" to the relics photograph he sent them before he made the purchase. "All agreed – they were genuine Viking weapons of one period, dating from 950 A.D. to 1000 A.D." Godsell briefly addressed the hoax claim made by "a former Port Arthur man" (the again unnamed Ragotte) but gave Dodd the final word, having him note he had not lived at the house on Wilson Street in which Ragotte said he saw the relics until three years after he had unearthed them in the presence of two witnesses – a timing error of residence that Godsell perpetuated by cribbing from Beamish's articles. Accepting Dodd's declaration that the relics' discovery had been independently witnessed (even though no witnesses had gone on record), Godsell ventured, "since the burying of these valuable articles in an Ontario claim would not have added a dollar to their value, but would only lead to the place being overrun by irresponsible people bent on digging up further specimens, it is difficult to see what advantage could have accrued to anyone attempting to perpetrate such a hoax." Godsell was incapable of understanding that a hoax founded on a discovery while prospecting was incomplete without a discovery while prospecting.

Not everyone was content with the dismissal of Ragotte's (and Hansen's) allegations, or with Dodd's reliability. Vilhjalmur Stefansson still believed in the likelihood of a Norse penetration of the continent via Hudson Strait, but he had turned cautious about his friend Currelly's relics purchase. On 3 February, G.R.F. Prowse in Winnipeg had alerted Stefansson to the public controversy: "Some news lately in the Free Press rather blows upon the Nipigon find of Norse remains."[2] Stefansson wrote Currelly on 7 March to learn more. "You are quoted by the Free Press of January 28th to the effect that you are sure the articles are genuine Norse but that you are not sure as to the other point of the controversy – whether a hoax has been perpetrated by the deliberate planting of the said relics. If you are in a position to tell anybody, please tell me."[3]

Currelly's equivocation on the authenticity of Dodd's story in his January statement to the Toronto press had since hardened to certainty. Currelly had managed to acquire the original affidavits that Ragotte, Hansen, and Sorensen provided to Royd Beamish, and he could see the contradictions and inconsistencies in the statements of the "two worthies," Ragotte and Hansen, which he reviewed for Stefansson.[4] "Two workmen quarreled [sic] and one has tried to damn the other," he explained, referring to Ragotte and Dodd. He did not find credible Hansen's claim that he had left valuable relics in the basement of a rental house: "it is not customary in Canada for poor men to leave $150's worth of property lying in a house into which a tenant is moving." Sorensen was "quite positive" that Bloch never owned Norse relics, and Currelly doubted if Hansen would ever have come forward with his story if he had not known that Bloch was dead. "Altogether, I do not think there is a shadow of doubt about the things having been found as Dodd told us, but we will have to run the matter down a little more thoroughly before we can give anything out to the public."

Currelly found a silver lining in the dispute. "I am extremely glad that this controversy came out before we had published the Viking things. Up to the present I think of it only as nastiness, particularly as a man of some importance" – John Jacob – "heard about the things immediately after they were found and went and examined the site. He saw the imprint on the rock of the iron rust from the sword." For Currelly, the authenticity case was overwhelmingly dependent on the word of Jacob. Yet he was determined to protect Jacob as his corroborating witness to Dodd's discovery: Currelly would not even tell Stefansson Jacob's name. It was enough that Stefansson understood that "a man of some importance" could refute the dubious claims of "two worthies" and two quarrelling workmen.

Eli Ragotte was not backing down, whatever the contradictions in his and Hansen's stories. On 17 March, he wrote to the editor of the *Winnipeg Free Press* to protest Godsell's categorization of him as an "irresponsible rail roader."[5] Ragotte responded with eloquence and dignity. "As I cannot write F.R.G.S. after my name I will not attempt to match Mr. Godsell's remarks. I would like to remind this learned gentleman that the person who descends to abuse has no case. I am a rail-roader. I have no wish and will not enter into a controversy with him. I made a statement of fact. These facts I can corroborate." He quoted in part from Hansen's recent letter to him and enclosed the entire letter for the editor's perusal. In closing, Ragotte advised: "Only a very simple person would be taken in by such a stupid hoax. The average Canadian is not simple."

At some point in March – probably after Ragotte's letter was published on 23 March – Prowse met with Ragotte in Winnipeg. "He gave me the impression of being an honest fellow," Prowse would recount for Currelly the following January. Ragotte provided Prowse with a copy of his letter from Hansen. "I gathered Ragotte regarded Dodd as a crook."[6] Stefansson, evidently not content with Currelly's assurances, wrote Ragotte around this time; Prowse likely provided an address. The Stefansson correspondence with Ragotte does not survive, but clearly he was making his own investigations.

Stefansson was not the only scholar who doubted that the hoax allegations were much ado about nothing. A.D. Fraser of the University of Virginia had endorsed the authenticity of the Beardmore find in his July 1937 article in the *Dalhousie Review*. Hell assuredly hath no fury like an academic exposed to ridicule through his own credulousness, not to mention his trust in the ROM's thoroughness. After Prowse shared with Fraser a copy of Hansen's letter to Ragotte, Fraser wrote Ragotte on 30 March, hoping to learn more. Ragotte in turn wrote Hansen on 4 April, quoting in part from Fraser's letter. Fraser had wanted to know if Ragotte or Hansen had seen the relics now in the museum and if they could positively identify them as the ones they saw in the basement of the house Hansen owned. Fraser had written to Ragotte: "If either you or Hansen are sure that they are the arms in question from having examined them closely, that would settle the matter as far as I am concerned. And Hansen ought certainly to take legal action for the recovery of what apparently is his. But of course the real question is; were these weapons found underground, near Beardmore, or not? And if you should be mistaken about the identity of them, this would not prove they were found where Dodd declares they were."[7] Ragotte also revealed he had received "another letter from Vilhjalmur Stefansson, the great explorer, and gave him your address so you most likely have heard from him." (Unfortunately, no copies of letters between Stefansson and Hansen survive in Stefansson's papers either.)

"If I were you," Ragotte continued to Hansen, "I would take up Mr. Fraser's advice in regard to the weapons & take legal action and concentrate on the weapons alone and dismiss the fishing pole episode." Ragotte was not angling for compensation, and at any rate he had no way to claim any interest in the relics. Some desire for vengeance on Dodd for past wrongs seems to have been Ragotte's motivation for advising and assisting Hansen. Ragotte had decided Eddy Dodd needed to be cut down to size; whether he had genuine evidence was another matter.

Ragotte wrote his own reply to Fraser on 4 April.[8] He had concluded he had been living with Dodd at 33 Machar Avenue, not on Wilson Street as he had previously stated, when the relics were found in 1929–30. The house belonged, then and now, to Hansen, he told Fraser. "The sword was found amongst the clinkers in the basement," he reiterated, and he said he could positively identify it, "along with the shield and axe." He was willing to go to the ROM and identify the relics as the ones found in the basement, "but due to financial difficulties, [I] could not afford the trip at present."

Ragotte went far beyond his circumspect affidavit, returning to his forthright assertions of a hoax. "Mr. Dodds has also picked up picks, etc., that I had personally brought to Port Arthur and was always under the impression he had found something valuable which upon very little investigation proved absolutely worthless." As well, Hansen had left other items, such as fishing poles, axes, picks, and grindstones, in the basement at 33 Machar. They turned up on the mining claim where Dodd and three others, including Ragotte, worked, "and knowing the property very well, [I] am quite sure the disputed relics were never found upon it." Ragotte's mention of "picks" was significant. He could not have known that Dodd had told Teddy Elliott in August 1936 about finding an iron object on his claim that he had used as a pick but then lost.

However, whereas Hansen had claimed he had received the relics from Bloch as settlement for a debt, Ragotte now informed Fraser that Hansen had once told him he had personally brought them from Norway, which made Bloch irrelevant and gave Hansen undisputed ownership. As suspicious as Eddy Dodd's inconsistent story was about finding the relics on his mining claim, the stories of Ragotte and Hansen were fraught with incongruities. Fraser gave up on anything credible ever coming from Hansen.

Ragotte's 4 April letter to Fraser was shared by the latter with Hjalmar Holand, who in turn provided a copy to Currelly. Currelly can be forgiven for suspecting that Ragotte and Hansen were scheming to con the museum out of the relics or, at least, to seize from Dodd the money he had been paid. But the irregularities of the Hansen-Ragotte stories in no way forgave Currelly's poor effort in researching the provenance of the relics. Even before the scandal broke, he was determined to prematurely conclude the weapons typology research, with minimal input from experts. None of the experts was told the "grave" was in northern Ontario, or even in North

America. Hermannsson had advised that "all the circumstances connected
with the finding of them would be essential" to establishing the weapons
types, and Otto von Friesen had more pointedly asked whether the relics
had been found "under scientifically safe circumstances." Such requests for
more details had been met with silence and probably not a little professional anxiety. Initially, in his statement to the Toronto press when the hoax
case had erupted, Currelly suggested the relics were valuable to the people
of Ontario, regardless of the story of where they came from, and he had not
defended the Dodd discovery claim in writing E. Ross MacKay on 3 February. Had he maintained this course, Currelly could have agreed that
Dodd's find was questionable and still defended the purchase while pursuing further investigations of Dodd's story as well as the weapons typology. But, enamoured with the idea of their historical significance and assured by the affidavits secured by Royd Beamish of the unreliability of
Hansen and Ragotte, Currelly resolved to stand by Dodd's discovery – and
rewrite continental history in the process.

The ROM's case for the authenticity of the Beardmore find received its first
scholarly boost through a report in the April 1938 issue of the Royal Geographical Society's *Geographical Journal*, filed by society fellow Philip Godsell. The item was reprinted with permission in *Antiquity* that June, further
bolstering the find's authenticity.[9] Godsell drew on his Canadian Club address, which relied on unacknowledged and garbled information from
Teddy Elliott, and he leavened it with details (reliable and otherwise) that
emerged during the late January news frenzy. The museum's photographs
of the relics had been "submitted to authorities on Norse archaeology in
Europe. According to Dr. Currelly, the Director, there is complete agreement that they are of one period, and are to be dated between A.D. 950 and
1000. Professor D. McArthur, Deputy Minister of Education, is preparing a
report for submission to the Legislature." Godsell, however, had never been
in touch with Currelly. And he said nothing about the hoax allegations.

James Hansen, whom Currelly believed was perpetrating a hoax of his
own in alleging a Dodd hoax, would not withdraw from the field. On 8
April, Hansen wrote "The Royal Museum, Toronto, Ontario."[10] The letter
found its way to Currelly's desk. Hansen identified himself as the owner
of relics that had been left in a house he had rented to Eddy Dodd, and he
said that they sounded like the relics that newspapers had reported Dodd

to have found on his Beardmore mining claim. "Would it be possible to give me a photograph or drawing of the relics in your possession received from Mr. Dodds. Did he receive any money for these relics as I have been told he received a payment from the Royal Museum for them. I presume you are anxious to have this situation cleared up. We know by history that the Norsemen were in Canada before Columbus discovered America and that the two ships which went northward from Vinland penetrated into the Hudson Bay. Of course, I hope that these relics are not my lost relics but as it is, I believe you would do the same if you were in my position, as my relics cost me over Thirty Dollars as a loan."

Currelly added Hansen's letter to his growing collection of unanswered correspondence on the Beardmore relics. Hansen was unhappy at being ignored. He wrote the museum again, on 11 May. "My letter to you on April 8th. I have not had a reply; what can be the delay? I stated plainly enough to you in my letter, and I have been looking forward to a letter from you long ago. Are Mr. Dodd's Norse relics in your possession yet? Kindly let me hear from you regarding same."[11]

Currelly continued to leave Hansen's letters unanswered. Hansen wanted a photograph or drawing, and Currelly suspected that he was on a fishing expedition. No images of the relics had been published, nor had they been described in detail in the press. If Hansen had never seen the relics, he needed museum images on which to base any further claims that they were his stolen property. By 11 May, Currelly was becoming confident to the point of certainty that Hansen had concocted the story about relics in the basement of 33 Machar. For the past two weeks, John Jacob had been making enquiries in Port Arthur on Currelly's behalf and securing testimonials to the authenticity of Dodd's discovery and the unreliability of Hansen.

On Sunday, 24 April 1938, John Jacob arrived in Port Arthur and began working with impressive zeal on the Beardmore file for Currelly. The first man he looked up was Wilmington (William) Cross, a machinist who worked on mining equipment. William Cross had been born in 1871 at Silver Islet, where his father James, a millwright, was the manager of the local mine; a younger brother, Julian (Jules), was a mining engineer who would come to figure in the Beardmore story.[12] According to Jacob (writing Currelly on 28 April) William Cross doubted Hansen's story and "[said] Hansen is as big a liar as Dodds."[13] Still, Cross found Eddy Dodd credible where the find was concerned. He had visited Dodd's claim three or four months after the discovery. "Dodds took him over and showed him where he found the sword axe etc he did not look at all closely at the striping [i.e., rust marks] but is positive that Dodds found the relics there. Cross says that he thinks that Dodds brought them to him first when he brought them up from Beardmore immediately after finding them and the relics were dirty and rusty." Cross "was not sure (offhand) whether it was in 30 or 31 he visited Dodds claims but may be able to set the date." Cross appeared willing to attest to having seen the rust stains that, so far, only Jacob had mentioned, and Jacob hoped he would write a statement.

John Jacob's account of William Cross's recollection was the first inkling that Dodd's discovery date might be moved back, from 1931 to 1930. A discovery in the spring of 1930, if endorsed by persuasive witnesses, would crush James Hansen's claims as Dodd would have had the relics more than a year before he moved into 33 Machar. Whether backdating the discovery was the objective of Jacob's investigations or whether it emerged by chance because of Cross (or what Jacob claimed to have learned from Cross), is unknowable. Whatever the case, the idea of changing the discovery from May 1931 to May 1930 did not originate with Dodd.

Jacob dropped in on William Nuttall, a fifty-nine-year-old Port Arthur tug captain so consumed by mining that, in the 1935 voter's list, he gave his profession as "prospector."[14] According to Jacob, "His opinion re the sword is Hansen is a liar Dodds is a nut and the sword find is probably genuine." Jacob also met with Dr George Edwin Eakins, who was trying to get to the bottom of the Beardmore story himself. Fifty years old, Dr Eakins was one of the Lakehead's leading citizens. A past president of the Ontario College of Physicians and Surgeons, he sat on Port Arthur's municipal council from 1921 to 1923 as well as on the Board of Education, the Parks Board, and the Board of Health. He was a leading member of the Thunder Bay Historical Society, serving as president from 1933 to 1934. Dr Eakins was also the Dodd family's physician, and it seems remarkable that he was not aware of Dodd's relics prior to 1938, considering his known association with the historical society and the fact that Dodd's brother had shared the news of the relics with his own physician in Toronto in 1935. According to Jacob, Dr Eakins thought little of Dodd but even less of Hansen. William Cross and Dr Eakins "say Dodds is to [sic] dumb to frame anything but Hansen is fairly clever."

Dr Eakins, Jacob explained, "is trying to get Mr. Dodds story[.] I haven't seen Dodds yet either." The most persuasive evidence for the fact that

Jacob was not actively collaborating with Dodd in perpetrating a hoax (beyond his volunteering credible opinions that Dodd was a liar and a nut) is that he didn't know where Dodd lived and couldn't locate him. As Jacob reported to Currelly on 28 April, "Dodds has moved twice lately is somewhere on Bay st now haven't found him yet Hansen I can find when I want him." As it happened, Jacob never did speak with Hansen.

Jacob understood correctly that Dodd was living on Wilson Street in 1930 and moved to Machar Avenue later; he was going to check the dates with property managers. Meanwhile, Jacob assured Currelly on 28 April: "The opinion among those I've spoken to who really know is that Hansen's story is spite work and laugh at the idea that he got relics as valuable as that from a Norwegian who would know their value for $25 or that Block would be toting such relics all over Canada and that Hanson would buy relics from anyone for any reason and after doing so leave them 'in the cellar' to rot."

Jacob was off to meet with the Norwegian vice-consul, Carl Sorensen, later that day. Sorensen agreed to provide Jacob with a written statement on what he knew about Bloch.[15] He reviewed what was already in his affidavit of 29 January but added he heard that Hansen was telling people Bloch had found the relics while digging out a basement in a house that Hansen owned on Machar; Hansen had then purchased the relics from Bloch and left them in the basement when he moved out. In other words, the relics still proved Vikings had visited the area, but they had visited the future site of Hansen's house at 33 Machar, not of Eddy Dodd's middle claim. This was the third version of the story allegedly heard from Hansen regarding how the relics ended up at 33 Machar.

"I have the following reasons for not believing this story," Sorensen wrote of the most recent version. "In the first place Mr. Hansen would never had paid Block any money, in the second place Block never found such articles, in the third place I do not believe that any such articles had ever been buried in that particular place by any Vikings or Indians, as this was old ground, where the timber was heavy up to 50 years ago." "Finally," Sorensen stated, crushing Hansen's credibility, "I would not believe James Hansen's statement given under oath, and he should be made to retract this pipe dream."

Jacob met another member of the Norwegian community, the Port Arthur grocer G.A. Simonsen, who provided a statement on 30 April.[16] Simonsen reiterated that he and Sorensen, as well as a Fort William man named "Ohlgreen" (a clerk, Roy Ohlgren) knew Bloch very well and that "he never at any time mentioned that he had ever had or ever seen any Norwegian relics in this country. I am convinced that had Mr. Block had or known of any such relics here he certainly would have mentioned them." Bloch was "an educated man of good character[,] reliable and well regarded by people here and [I] feel sure had he had any relics of this description he would have known how to dispose of them to the best advantage." Simonsen also mentioned a photo in Sorensen's possession of the Leif Eiriksson longboat float constructed for the 1927 Dominion Day parade. Simonsen confirmed that Bloch, who appeared in the photo, had designed and partly built the float. "If he had possessed any Norse relics or known of any being here he would have had them on hand at this time."

As for Hansen, Simonsen knew him "very well and [I have] no hesitation in stating that I do not regard him as being very reliable. He never at any time mentioned having or seeing any Norse relics here and his statement to the press I do not regard as serious. In my conversation with Hansen since regarding his action in this connection I told him plainly that I and other Norwegians here were convinced that his action was altogether foolish and ill considered and should be retracted. He stated that it had gotten him some publicity. I do not think by his admissions to me that he had any idea of the seriousness of his action in this affair."

Jacob's Norwegian sources painted Hansen as a certifiable lunatic. As Jacob reported to Currelly: "Sorensen says that he and other Norse citizens here for some time tried to give Hansen all the assistance they could by giving him jobs at his trade and small contracts but that he constantly fell down on his assignments and they were in a state of constant annoyance at him until they gave him up but now they thing [sic] it is past a trifle and that he ought to be 'put away' or be compelled to make a public retraction of his statments [sic] and even then he has cast a shadow on what is to them an exceedingly important find." The categorization of Hansen as a troubled man dependent on the kindness of the Norwegian community for small jobs is defied by the sheer number of commercial, residential, agricultural, and vacation properties he was purchasing, renovating, and renting out.[17] Jacob otherwise had made a crucial observation, even if he did not appreciate it. The local Norwegian community was proud of Dodd's discovery and was unhappy with Hansen for trying to debunk a thrilling home-making myth: the Norse had been in the neighbourhood about one thousand years before Scandinavian immigrants began arriving over the last few decades, and centuries before the British or French. On 1 May, Jacob reported to

Currelly that Sorensen thought the community "may get Hansen to retract[,] that he is just a 'big child.'"

The following Thursday evening, 5 May, Jacob met with Os Hartvik, a
Norwegian civil engineer who immigrated to Port Arthur in 1924, at age
twenty-four, and knew both Hansen and Bloch.[18] In a written statement,
Hartvik recalled boarding with Hansen in a Port Arthur house between
1924 and about 1928, which was when Hansen was living at 33 Machar.[19]
Hansen "showed me his stamps and coins and other trinkets on which he
apparently set value," but he had nothing resembling a sword or any other
Norse relics, and Hartvik could not recall his mentioning where such
items might be in Port Arthur. "I feel sure he would have mentioned
knowing if he had." Granted, none of this mattered if Hansen had acquired Bloch's relics after Hartvik was boarding with him. Hartvik admitted to not being well informed on the business connections between
Hansen and Bloch, "but from what little I do know I think Mr. Hansen
might find himself at [a] loss to explain how Mr. Block came to owe him
money." Hartvik said he knew Bloch very well "and conversed with him on
subjects of interest pertaining to Norway[,] Norwegian relics being one of
the subjects of special interest. He never mentioned possessing or having
ever possessed any Norse relics nor did [he] mention having seen any here
or knowing where there was any here and Im [sic] certain had he done so
he would have mentioned it." Bloch did show him a Norwegian book that
contained illustrations by his father. "I know very well that Mr Block was
well aware of the value of Norse relics, and if he had ever possessed any he
knew very well where to dispose of them to advantage."

On Friday, 6 May Jacob came upon information "which when followed
up will put Hansen on the spot," he promised Currelly. Jacob had run into
William Feltham, whom he had known very well for some time and who
had held for years the commercial fishing licence on Whitefish Lake, which
was west of Thunder Bay, near Jacob's homestead farm. Feltham "was at
Dodds mining claims at his camp in the spring of 1930 immediately after
Dodds found the sword. I talked to Feltham for a few minutes on the street
he is a man whose word is good to all who know him and is accepted without reserve here." Jacob paraphrased Feltham's recollections, which Feltham
would commit to paper on 9 May.[20] Feltham asserted he was "at Thos.
Dodds [sic] camp on his claims near Beardmore in the late spring of 1930
and saw some relics which he had recently dug up laying on the banking
that was around his camp. These relics were all metal there was a sword or
part of a sword an ax and a couple of other scraps[.] I had no idea what ori-

gin they were and we did not place any particular value on them but thought them rather unusual to be found out there but did not doubt that Dodd had dug them up while working on his claim and feel certain he had no idea of what they were these claims are about one hundred miles from Port Arthur I thought some of the iron was part of a shield."[21]

On Saturday, 7 May, Jacob at last caught up with Dodd. Jacob had been focused on finding eyewitnesses who could move the discovery date back to 1930 as Cross's and Feltham's recollections had already suggested. Dodd, naturally, was the crucial one, and he did not disappoint: "His boy [Walter] says the relics were found the spring of 1930 fastens the date by a sickness he had Dodds admits he is probably correct," Jacob reported. It is not clear if Jacob heard this from Walter Dodd or from Eddy Dodd. Jacob himself was now testifying to the 1930 date for Currelly: "I saw those relics at Dodds place on Wilson St 1930 I knew I could recognize the house Hansen never owned this house."

Jacob also began to form a clearer picture of Dodd's address changes. He understood that Dodd had lived at 296 Wilson Street for sixteen years prior to moving to Machar Avenue. This was not exactly the case, but Dodd had been there for some time, and not *after* the relics were discovered, as Beamish had erroneously reported and as Godsell had repeated. It also turned out that Dodd had lived in two neighbouring houses on Machar Avenue in 1931, both owned by Hansen. Dodd told Jacob he had moved initially to 37 Machar in June or July of 1931, then next door to 33 Machar, where Bloch had lived, that October or November. Dodd said he did not know Hansen until midsummer 1931 and that he left 33 Machar after a dispute with Hansen over rent for outbuildings. Furthermore, Ragotte's "spite" was due to the fact Dodd had thrown him out of his mining camp.

Dodd gave Jacob the names of at least two more people who could verify 1930 as the discovery year. Tom Delbridge, a log scaler with the local forestry branch of the provincial Department of Lands and Forests, apparently had seen the relics that spring, although Jacob cautioned Currelly that Delbridge was "not very reliable I know him well." (This was the "Dolbridge" mentioned by Ragotte in his affidavit for Beamish.) A more critical witness was Patrick J. ("Pat" or "Paddy") Bohan of Dorion, whom Dodd said was the section manager (foreman) for the CNR at Beardmore Station in 1930–31. Dodd claimed to have shown Bohan the relics in the spring of 1930. Bohan, like Dodd, was of Irish Catholic heritage; Bohan was born around 1900 in Quyon, Quebec, and the two men had grown up in the same area of the Ottawa River.[22] Although they did not know each other until they moved to Port Arthur, they became friends in the early 1920s and were closer than anyone who was sorting through the Beardmore evidence would ever realize. In June 1936, Bohan's son, John Patrick, was baptized at Orient Bay, with Eddy and Ellen Dodd as his godparents.[23]

Jacob advised Currelly that he had "several other rumors I can follow up later if you wish," but he was going to be away for seven or eight months. While he didn't secure statements from Cross, Bohan, or Delbridge, in exchange for his basic expenses Jacob had performed an invaluable service to Currelly.

During Jacob's sleuthing, Colonel L.S. Dear visited the ROM, having left Port Arthur on 1 May for a meeting with the museum's ornithologist, L.L. Snyder. Jacob advised Currelly: "if you ask Dr. [sic] Snyder to have [Dear] see you I am sure you will find him a very fine type of man and very willing to assist you in any way he could up here." Currelly was able to meet Dear, and whatever endorsement Dear gave for Jacob would have carried enormous weight. Currelly would have been impressed by any burnishing by Dear of Jacob's membership in a venerable family. The connection to George Drew would have been pointed out (if not already known), and Dear, as noted, had garnered from Jacob a romantic lineage, complete with a hero of the Napoleonic Wars descended from a titled Scottish family. Jacob's fanciful pedigree would have appealed to a museum director so fretful about his own class status that he conjured a descent from the *gens Corelea* of ancient Rome. When combined with his status as a government employee (at least at the time he purportedly visited the middle claim and saw the rust mark), Jacob was, in Currelly's estimation, unimpeachable as a witness compared to the feuding "worthies" and quarrelling labourers that included Dodd himself. If the ROM remained confident of Jacob, the museum could also remain confident that, one way or another, Eddy Dodd had found the Norse relics east of Lake Nipigon.

Unfortunately, Eddy still had not found gold. On 14 May, Howey Gold Mines announced it had dropped the option on Dodd's Norse-Beardmore Syndicate claim and was focusing instead on the Yellowknife area. The drilling results obviously had not met expectations.[24] It was the end of the Norse-Beardmore venture. Dodd would have to find some other way to get wealth out of the ground.

12

James Watson Curran to the Rescue

In late April 1938, a fresh attack on the Beardmore discovery came to C.T. Currelly's attention as Philip Ainsworth Means alerted him to an article published in an Oslo newspaper, *Tidens Tegn,* on 9 April.[1] Means couldn't quite make out what the article was about, and he sent it to Hjalmar Holand for translation. Means passed on the result to Currelly on 21 May, "in order that you may be informed as to the sort of irresponsible chatter that seems to be going on in Oslo with respect to your Viking finds. As you will readily understand, I do this simply out of friendship for you and for the Museum, as well as out of faith in the objects themselves."[2]

The unnamed writer of "Fraudulent American Viking Finds Smuggled in from Norway" had come upon A.D. Fraser's 1937 *Dalhousie Review* article, which upheld the authenticity of the Kensington stone and the Beardmore relics. "This is the old story once more – the American desire to provide itself with history, ancient history," the writer complained. Again and again, so-called "finds" surfaced to show that Norsemen settled in America. The Kensington stone was a fraud whose perpetrator was known to be its discover, Olof Ohman. For the Beardmore find, the writer sought out A.W. Brøgger for comment. Brøgger revealed he had received a request not long ago from the director of the ROM to identify the relics based on a photograph. Brøgger said the sword was from the eleventh century, "but it was not found in America. In some way or other it must have been smuggled in from Norway. The University Museum has informed the Ontario museum to this effect, but quite characteristically we have received no reply. [These] kind of 'finds' are deplorable – they continually compromise the real facts concerning the Vinland journeys, and it is a sin that such legends are continually fabricated concerning a real historical event."

Ethlyn Greenaway replied to Means on behalf of Currelly, who was about to depart to Philadelphia for the annual meeting of the American Museums Association, with a stop planned in New York before attending the annual meeting of the Royal Society of Canada in Ottawa. She advised Means that Brøgger's remarks "as quoted give a somewhat inaccurate impression of our correspondence with him; he refused any opinion as to date unless Dr. Currelly would first tell him where the weapons had been found." Greenaway continued: "We have been having a merry time over the weapons recently, thanks to some more unofficial and premature publicity such as Professor Fraser gave us last summer in his article in the DAL-HOUSIE REVIEW, which has been a great source of annoyance to Dr. Currelly ever since it appeared."[3] Greenaway offered to send Means a copy. She was silent on the Ragotte-Hanson allegations that had so animated the daily press in late January.

Means confirmed that he had never heard of the *Dalhousie Review* article and asked to borrow a copy. "Probably I am extremely ignorant," he confessed, having no idea of just how ignorant he remained of the active Beardmore controversy. "I suspect that this Fraser must be the chappie with whom Dr. Currelly was distinctly nettled last Autumn on account of his having spilled the beans before they were cooked, so to speak. Personally I think that Dr. Brøgger's attitude is fundamentally wrong: As do many otherwise sapient Scandinavian scientists, he persists in assuming that there *can* be no authentic traces of the early Northmen in this continent."[4]

For all Means's cheerleading, Currelly was still not ready to make any further official comment on Dodd's relics, especially now that the director of the museum with the largest collection of Viking relics in the world was condemning the find and the ROM. Currelly had ignored at his own peril Brøgger's repeated requests for further information about the Beardmore discovery. But Brøgger's condemnation would prove to be contained: his allegations did not find their way into the English-language press.

As Currelly prepared to leave on his trip on 21 May, he realized he had forgotten to respond to Harold Innis's invitation to address the Royal Society of Canada on the Beardmore find. A paper presented at the RSC meeting was automatically considered for inclusion in the society's annual *Transactions*. Currelly had Greenaway deliver his regrets. It was doubtful he would be able to attend the RSC meeting as he had planned, and, in any case, "there remain a few details to settle before any official publication of the Viking weapons would be advisable."[5] Currelly also had Greenaway send an identical letter to all the scholars (including Brøgger) who had responded to his December 1937 request to identify the weapons. The 23 May letter thanked them for their assistance and noted that, for reasons unexplained, the anticipated publication on the relics had been delayed.[6]

Back from his trip, Currelly finally replied on 30 May to James Hansen's letters.[7] He did not air his conviction that Hansen had no credible claim to the relics and had probably never seen them. There had been a "tremendous demand" for photographs of the Norse relics, Currelly wrote curtly, "but till the matter is published, no photographs will be sent out." Not publishing anything on the discovery for the time being would have the bonus of keeping photographs out of circulation and away from Hansen's eyes.

Currelly also wrote Teddy Elliott on 30 May. Elliott had made his return to the Beardmore story on 24 May, after being stung by Philip Godsell's indiscreet use of his Beardmore revelations. Thinking Duncan McArthur was still producing an official publication, Elliott wrote the deputy minister of education that day with additional information on Dodd's discoveries.[8] Elliott observed that, in one of the *Globe and Mail* stories in January, Dodd had claimed that other unnamed relics had been found on the site. Elliott typed out the part of the conversation he had composed in his notes after meeting Dodd on 16 August 1936 that addressed the "half moon shaped tool like a prospector's pick." He enclosed a drawing he had made of the item. Elliott planned to be in the Lakehead and Longlac areas again that summer, following up leads suggested by media coverage. "Any service I can render would be a pleasure," he informed the deputy minister. Rather than respond, McArthur passed along the letter and drawing to Currelly, who then replied to Elliott.

"The rather stupid row between Dodd and other men has made it very necessary for me to keep very quiet till the row should clear itself," Currelly explained, without revealing that McArthur was no longer writing the planned article.[9] "I think things are rapidly taking shape now. I'd be most grateful, of course, for any information you could get. The man who really, I think, started the trouble [Ragotte], when put on oath simply backed down." This was not true: Ragotte was still agitating. "There is a man called Hansen, however, who has tried to claim that the weapons were his and therefore that they could not have come from Beardmore. Any hurried action on our part I think would have been extremely unwise, as we are not anxious to prove anything but simply to find out what are the real facts." Currelly wrote in closing: "I have not forgotten that when the matter comes to publication, full credit is to be given you as the first person who brought the weapons to our attention." Elliott would continue to be the good soldier of scholarship, not publishing anything until he had Currelly's blessing.

As the summer of 1938 approached, Currelly could not make a compelling argument for the authenticity of the discovery, regardless of the discredited state of Ragotte's and Hansen's stories. The archaeological evidence was essentially non-existent and irrecoverable. If ever there was a plan to make another investigation of the site, it failed to materialize. One of the foremost authorities on Viking weapons in Norway was calling the find a hoax, although the English-language press had not noticed. Eddy Dodd's discovery story was a shape-shifting shambles. The only bright spot was John Jacob's eyewitness testimony and his sleuthing in Port Arthur. Through witnesses, including Dodd, Jacob had laid the groundwork for asserting the discovery had occurred in May 1930. It wouldn't matter if Bloch had relics and pawned them to Hansen. A credible 1930 discovery date would make it impossible for Dodd to have found *his* relics in a house he began renting from Hansen in 1931. Still, Currelly appeared unsure of how to proceed, beyond postponing any article and hoping the Ragotte-Hansen controversy subsided. Then a crusading newspaperman unexpectedly rode to Currelly's and Dodd's rescue.

James Watson (J.W.) "Jim" Curran, editor and publisher of the *Sault Daily Star*, arrived in Port Arthur on 12 September 1938 – on vacation, he would state, with "no faith at all in the Dodd story on the account of the scornful stories in the newspapers but unable to keep from doing a little digging to put in the time on the off chance that the Dodd yarn was really true."[10] But this visit was no vacation. By the time Curran plunged into the Beardmore controversy, he was already committed to a series of twenty-six articles, beginning 13 August, that would lay out his case that the Vinland described in the sagas began on the shore of James Bay and extended into the Great Lakes, with Lake Nipigon at its heart. It was true that Curran had at least expressed caution about the Beardmore find in the first article in his series: "There has been some dispute as to whether [the relics] were actually found in the spot claimed and that point has not yet been entirely cleared up. As to the Norse origin of the relics, however, there does not appear to be any doubt."[11] Beardmore would come to provide the central evidence for his Vinland theory, and Curran, in turn, became central to the effort to discredit the hoax charges against Dodd.

Where C.T. Currelly was able to discourage Teddy Elliott from writing about the relics until an official publication was made, there was no stopping a force like Jim Curran. Currelly quickly realized that Curran was an indispensable ally. He had the time, energy, and resources – and publicity savvy – that Currelly and the ROM lacked to mount the counterattack on Dodd's critics and to clear the way for the relics to go on display as a genuine discovery. Currelly could then proceed with publishing on the find.

Seventy-three years old when he took on the Beardmore story, Jim Curran was raised in the newspaper trade. Born in Ireland in 1865, he had immigrated to Ontario with his family at age eight; his father bought the *Essex Chronicle* and then, in 1884, the *Orillia News-Letter*. The family settled in Orillia, and Jim became the family newspaper's news editor. The hands-on training launched a journalism career that took him to Toronto in 1890, as a reporter and then as city editor for the *Toronto Empire*, and then to Montreal in 1895, as the city editor for the *Montreal Herald*. A visit to Sault Ste Marie in 1901 convinced Curran of the future of Ontario's north – and of his own future in it. He bought the weekly newspaper, the *Star*, and by 1912 he had transformed it into the *Daily Star*.[12] Curran was an able storyteller with an interest in history as well as a determined promoter of northern Ontario. Those qualities found a perfect point of convergence in the Beardmore story.

As we have seen, E. Ross MacKay, Curran's associate editor, had published the first word of the ROM's Beardmore acquisition, as related by Ned Burwash, on 20 January 1937. Currelly had declined to say anything on the record when MacKay wrote him on 31 January 1938, as the Ragotte-Hanson allegations lit up the media. MacKay did not pursue the story, but some seven months later his boss Jim Curran assumed the leading role in asserting the authenticity of the Beardmore find. Curran built relationships with almost everyone determined to defend Eddy Dodd's find, including Dodd himself and his prospecting partner Fletcher Gill.

Curran was well connected with captains of industry in the province's north, and one of them, John McPhail, president of Great Lakes Power Co. in Sault Ste Marie, provided him with an introduction to Alexander J. McComber, a prominent lawyer who had just been appointed senior justice for Thunder Bay District. Judge McComber was an authority on local history stretching back through the fur trade to the earliest explorers; his essay "Some Early History of Thunder Bay and District" was cited by Harold Innis in his seminal "staple thesis" for the economic and territorial evolution of Canada.[13] Judge McComber, in turn, introduced Curran to a friend and fellow member of the Thunder Bay Historical Society, Dr George Eakins, who, as we have seen, was already probing the Beardmore case when John Jacob made enquiries for Currelly in the spring of 1938. As Curran would relate, "The first thing the three of us knew we were up to our necks in 'Dodd vs. The Public.'"[14] Together, Curran, Dr Eakins, and Judge McComber formed a Thunder Bay investigative committee, with Judge McComber at its head. Curran was the crusader for Dodd; the other two, while supportive, were more concerned with gathering evidence. Judge McComber became the most important figure at the Lakehead in the effort to determine the truth about the Beardmore relics.

Judge Alexander J. McComber's father worked in various mines (and inspired the name for McComber Township), while his mother at times ran a boarding house. Alexander worked in local silver mines while continuing his education. He was only sixteen when he began articling in 1887 and was called to the bar a year later. In 1895, he married Georgina Guerard of Port Arthur, whose family was from Quebec; they would have seven children. In the 1920s, operating the law firm McComber and Mc-Comber with his son Jarvis, Alexander J. McComber was active in various ventures, including mining and a short-lived film production company. McComber twice ran unsuccessfully for public office, losing a close three-way federal race in 1921 as a Liberal and in 1926 on the Liberal-Labour ticket. McComber otherwise was busy in local affairs, serving as secretary and chair of the Port Arthur Separate School Board in addition to his historical society duties.[15]

The sixty-seven-year-old judge's local renown, broad and deep connections, prominence in the local historical society, experience with mining and prospecting, and legal gravitas proved indispensable to the cause of authenticating the Dodd discovery. No less indispensable was the degree to which Jim Curran charmed Judge McComber and his wife Georgina. "Mrs. McComber and I certainly enjoyed your visit very much," Mc-Comber would write Curran on 22 December 1938, "and we trust that you will be able to come again soon, so that we can again have the pleasure of your company. Mrs. McComber often speaks of you, and she thought you were one of the most delightful men she had ever met. Of course, I told her it was the way you had blarneyed her, but she won't believe this."[16] In time, Judge McComber's professional dedication to dispassionately weighing evidence would overcome Curran's charm.

When Jim Curran arrived in Thunder Bay to launch his Beardmore investigations, the third article in his Norsemen series was about to be published. The first, published on 13 August 1938, "Who Were the Wooden Boat Men?," had argued that the word *wemistikose* for "white man" originated with the Moose River Cree of James Bay through their contact with the Norse. It was abbreviated to *mistikose*, and was one and the same word as *mistigoche*, which

Champlain and other French on the St Lawrence in the early seventeenth century heard Algonquian-speaking people use to describe Europeans. The French understood it to mean someone who travels in a wooden canoe or vessel.[17] Even though Europeans in wooden ships had been a fact of Indigenous life on the eastern seaboard since Cabot's visit in 1497, Curran was insistent that the word made its way into their vocabulary from the James Bay Cree. Curran had not consulted the James Bay Cree himself and, instead, relied on testimony from members of the Ojibwa community at Garden River near Sault Ste Marie, who also provided evidence for his second article, "'White' Indians of James Bay" (6 September 1938), which contended that a mixed-heritage people in James Bay must have been the result of interbreeding with the Norse. Curran as well as Hjalmar Holand were perpetuating old and at times frankly racist notions that proof of early European visitors to the New World could be found in so-called "White Indians," whom the superior newcomers had improved through interbreeding and who had left additional clues to their presence in Indigenous languages and technologies. Carl Christian Rafn had relied considerably on such evidence in making the case for an extended Norse presence in New England.[18] Holand and Curran had their own White Indians, the Mandans on the Missouri, the supposed product of beneficial interbreeding with the Norse.

Curran was following the basic blueprint of Holand's Kensington stone scenario, in which the fourteenth-century Knutson expedition, searching for the lost Greenland colony's members, left their ships behind on Hudson Bay and reached the site of the Kensington stone via rivers and portages. When Curran began to weigh the evidence for the Beardmore relics, a new Norse narrative leapt to mind, set centuries earlier than Holand's scenario, in the time of the Vinland sagas. His third article, "The Tragic Story of the Castaways" (13 September 1938), drew largely on Poul Nørland's *Viking Settlers in Greenland* (1935) to suggest that the so-called lost colony, long before it was ever lost, might have provided Norsemen that reached Hudson Bay. The Beardmore relics would provide the proof that they got there. Curran's results were so authoritative, and so supportive of the Dodd provenance, that Curran gained instant respectability in the mainstream press as an expert on Vikings in the New World.

Jim Curran possessed relentless curiosity and a journalist's tradecraft, along with his own printing press and an attentive audience in other newsrooms. With the aid of Dr Eakins and Judge McComber, he performed basic sleuthing on Eddy Dodd's story. On his visit to Port Arthur, Curran headed to Dodd's house with Dr Eakins, who, according to Curran, had been the Dodd family's physician for twenty-eight years. On their first visit, they found only Ellen, who was voluble on the matter of the relics. "Her indignation at the doubts cast on 'Eddie' punctuated the interview," Curran told his readers on 4 October.[19] "She answered without hesitation every question. As the conversation progressed I found myself thinking that if she were making up the story she must have an extraordinary mind. Her directness and simple truthfulness (as it appeared to me) did not belong to an imaginative or a brilliant intellect. I left her with a great respect for her story, her devotion to her husband and her implicit faith in him. Outside I said to the doctor: 'That woman is telling the truth as she knows it. She couldn't make up a long yarn like that.' I felt then that the whole Dodd story was true."[20]

On 16 September, Curran, Dr Eakins, Dodd, and Gill visited the middle claim, where Eddy revealed that, around June, he had found another piece of metal that was like the one he had found when McIlwraith had visited the previous September. Dodd told Curran he had left it where he had found it, explaining, "There has been so much criticism and fault finding, and so much doubt expressed by people, I just thought I would leave it for somebody else to pick up."[21] The fragment was still in the trench. "He had apparently forgotten the exact spot as he found it 6 or 8 inches from where he first began to disturb the earth."[22] The piece of metal was less than an inch wide and about two and a half inches long and was taken to be a remnant of the crumbled shield boss. It did not occur to Curran that Dodd may have arranged for his guests the privilege of witnessing the only discovery of a Norse relic *in* the trench (and not tossed in the rubbish heap, as was the case with the McIlwraith find). On Dr Eakins's recommendation Curran took the fragment to the ROM, where he handed it over to Currelly and secured a receipt for it as Dodd's property. There is no record of Dodd's ever being paid for this find, or for the one brought back by McIlwraith.[23]

Curran was persuaded that all the finds made at the middle claim were authentic, but he knew that the allegations of James Hansen and Eli Ragotte still had to be addressed. Curran travelled to Winnipeg and spoke with Ragotte on 20 September. According to the account Curran published on 6 October 1938, when he asked Ragotte about the initial story in the *Winnipeg Free Press*,

"I only said it as a joke," he said.

"Then you looked on the report in the newspaper as a joke?"

"Yes, of course. As a matter of fact I had seen what looked like a sword or just an old piece of rusted iron in his cellar, – I wouldn't be sure which it was – and am sorry I got into the yarn. I never saw the shield or axe. Of course it was my own fault. I didn't know it might hurt Eddie, and I have no desire to hurt him or anybody else. He has a heart as big as a house."[24]

Ragotte's capitulation and effusive goodwill towards Dodd was a strange reversal, and it would not be his last one. Curran moved decisively to eliminate the obstacle Ragotte posed to Dodd's discovery story. He had Ragotte swear an affidavit to what he had told him, and he called in a favour from the president of the Canadian Pacific Railway, Sir Edward Wentworth Beatty, who covered the return trip of a CNR brakeman to Toronto. Currelly agreed to show Ragotte the relics in the company of Curran so that he could say positively whether or not he had seen them in Hansen's house.

On 28 September 1938, Judge McComber cabled Curran at Toronto's Royal York Hotel: IN HIS WINNIPEG AFFIDAVIT RAGOTTE SAYS SAW ARTICLES BEFORE 1930 IF HE DID THEY CANNOT BE SAME AS OTHERS FOUND FOLLOWING YEAR [1931] AND HE SHOULD SAY DEFINITELY THEY ARE NOT SAME.[25] Events would prove that the initiative to backdate Dodd's discovery to 1930 was unknown to Curran's investigative trio. Judge McComber's telegram does suggest that the investigators were open to the possibility that there were two sets of relics: Bloch had brought one set from Norway, and Dodd had unearthed a second set at Beardmore.

The events at the ROM on 30 September would become another source of controversy. Currelly would recall laying out the relics on a table for Ragotte to examine; Ragotte would recall that they were behind glass in a display case. Ragotte nevertheless agreed to sign two statements for the museum and for Curran.[26] One addressed Hansen's claim:

Mr. J. M. Hansen told me he had brought certain Viking objects from Norway, though he now says he obtained them from Lieutenant Bloch. As far as I know, Mr. Hansen made no claim to the Viking objects owned by Mr. J. E. Dodds until January 25, 1938, after he had learned that Mr. Dodds had sold his pieces to the Royal Ontario Museum of Archaeology.

The other statement addressed his own claim to have found the sword that Dodd then sold to the ROM:

When cleaning out Mr. J. E. Dodds' cellar at 33 Machar Avenue, Port Arthur, I saw a piece of iron much like a rusty butcher knife. Later Mr. Dodds showed me a rusted hand-axe and a piece of metal like the handle of a curling stone.

I have now seen the Viking objects that the Royal Ontario Museum of Archaeology bought from Mr. Dodds. I have never seen any of them before, and I am sure that they are not the pieces that I saw in Mr. Dodds' house.

Since John Jacob had filed his reports from the Lakehead the previous spring, the museum director had been confident that Hansen's and Ragotte's stories had no credibility. Now Ragotte, who had started the entire controversy with his claims in the *Winnipeg Free Press*, had fully recanted. Whatever he had seen in the basement of 33 Machar was not in the possession of the ROM.

Jim Curran was a skilled publicist, issuing statements of what he planned to publish as well as "specials" that covered his *Sault Daily News* stories in other newspapers. On 4 October 1938, back home in Sault Ste Marie, Curran announced (as the *Globe and Mail* reported the following day) that his next story would show that Dodd's find was "a preposterous, unbelievable story that turns out to be true."[27] As Curran wrote in his first article to address the Beardmore find: "I have no more doubt that James Edward Dodd … found Norse relics in 1931 at the spot near Beardmore where he says he found them than that Hudson Bay exists where people tell me it is located. I have the profoundest conviction that James Edward Dodd and a number of men and women who testify to the details of his story are right and honest." Curran claimed to have "talked to and cross-examined everybody who I considered might be able to throw some light on Dodd's claim. There are no flaws in their testimony." He stressed: "I accept Mr. Dodd as a truthful man, and so accept his story as true and exact. There is no question in my mind but that he found the Norse relics where he said he did."[28]

"In the minds of many of his fellow citizens," Curran continued, "James Edward Dodd is probably looked on as a liar and a cheat. But the fact is he is an honest man who when the jeers broke, didn't know what to do about it. And like so many of us who find a situation beyond us he just relapsed into a silent indignation. It looked to him as if everybody had conspired to defame him – the newspapers with their 'big heads' as he called them, and 'silly items,' the people he met daily who smiled knowingly at him."

In Curran's skilled editorial hands, in his second Beardmore story (6 October), Eddy and Ellen Dodd became empathetic characters, each exasperated in his or her own way by the burdens of the discovery. Ellen was the besieged spouse who had to put up with the visitors Eddy would bring home to show off the relics and who endured the clutter and inconvenience of the chunks of metal that migrated around the house. She alternated between tossing them outside and suggesting that Eddy have them gilded and hung on the wall. "You don't know how old things like that clutter up a place and make work," Curran quoted Ellen. "Of course," Curran commented, "men don't know how trying a few old iron relics can be to a housewife."[29]

As for Eddy's persistent efforts to show off the relics at home and in the Mariaggi Hotel, "his friends seem in fact to have grown a little weary of him talking about them." His "pals" on the CNR, who were also part-time prospectors, didn't want to hurt his feelings, and so would agree to come home with him and inspect the relics. His friend Patrick Bohan supposedly said to him: "What squaw gave them to you?" when he first saw them at the claim. "They joked about James Edward and his find and at last as one put it 'thought he was bugs.' No wonder James E. retired within himself."[30] Friends turned from indulgence to diffidence, and Dodd began to hear taunts.

In the same article, Curran reported Ragotte's complete capitulation at the museum, and also noted that he, Judge McComber, and Dr Eakins had met with James Hansen on 22 September 1938. Hansen, Curran asserted, told them he "had never seen" Dodd's relics, which was true in the sense that he had never seen the artefacts in the possession of the ROM. Curran further reported that Hansen had written Currelly, asking for photographs of the purchased relics, which we know to be true. However, it was not true that "Dr. Currelly wrote back that as long as the ownership of the Dodd relics were in dispute he would not furnish photos of them," although that was a fair assessment of why Currelly refused to hand any over to Hansen.

The trio of investigators also visited with Carl Sorensen, who acted as a spokesperson for members of the Norwegian community scoffing at the idea Bloch ever owned such relics. The vice-consul repeated the essential

assertions of his 29 January 1938 affidavit and covered the same arguments he had made for John Jacob.[31] Sorensen conceded that Bloch, in
need of money, may have helped Hansen excavate a cellar for a home on
Machar. But Sorensen could "hardly believe" Bloch would have brought
Norse relics to Canada or that he would not have mentioned it to him if
he had. "No I don't believe any of the stories now told about that. Some
of Lieut. Bloch's other friends and myself have discussed these reports and
we all think them utterly without foundation … Lieut. Bloch certainly
had nothing of value in his possession. He had been compelled to sell
some little personal possessions to live. No relics at all. All he possessed
was a college cap and a belt outside of his few necessities … Neither myself nor any other of Bloch's friends ever heard of him having Norse relics
till after his death." Sorensen said Bloch was well known in the community, and among his friends was Colonel L.S. Dear, who, as we have seen,
was close to John Jacob. It was another strange, seeming coincidence, on
par with Eli Ragotte's having named Mary Bolduc the guardian of his
daughter, that had linked Ragotte to Aaron Lougheed's circle. Jacob, as it
happened, was the only significant figure in the Dodd discovery story
other than Lougheed whom Curran, in his ongoing investigations, was
never able to reach.

On 6 October, Dr Eakins publicly professed his inclination to believe
Dodd's story.[32] "I am strongly of the opinion that the story is correct." The
story "seemed a little incredible at first," but Eakins had investigated the allegations against the find and concluded: "I probably believe Dodd's story
is right. After checking up, I can't see how a fellow like Dodd could make
up a story of this kind unless it were true. He is a smart fellow and would
know that such a thing would be subject to verification. The contradictory story that a man named Bloch brought the relics from Norway is, to my
mind, a myth. Bloch was a highly educated and cultured fellow. He would
have had a keen appreciation of the value of such articles and would not
have permitted them to be cast as rubbish in somebody's basement."

Jim Curran and his investigative committee had cleared all seeming
obstacles to a broad acceptance that Eddy Dodd had found the relics in
the middle claim. On 6 October, the contents of a Viking grave in northern Ontario were, for the first time, wheeled onto display at the Royal
Ontario Museum.

PART TWO

13

"The Whole Story Is Perfectly Clear Now"

Jim Curran's 6 October 1938 declaration of the Beardmore find's authenticity and the ROM's public revealing of the relics were closely coordinated. A custom-built case was wheeled onto display that day, containing five items: the sword (mounted as a unified weapon), the axe head, the shield handle, and the two metal fragments recovered during the site visits by Thomas McIlwraith in September 1937 and by Curran and Dr Eakins only a few weeks earlier. McIlwraith's item, once interpreted as the tip of a knife or sword, was now interpreted as a remnant of the shield boss. Curran's and Dr Eakins's find, initially thought to be another piece of the boss, was now part of the shield handle. The label identified:

A VIKING SWORD, AXE, AND WHAT PROBABLY IS
A SHIELD HANDLE AND A PIECE OF THE SHIELD BOSS
ABOUT 1000 A.D.
FOUND NEAR BEARDMORE CLOSE TO LAKE NIPIGON, ONTARIO
THE BURIAL WAS ON A PORTAGE ON THE ROUTE FROM HUDSON BAY
DOWN TO LAKE SUPERIOR.[1]

"The sparkling showcase looked like a million dollars. The corroded scraps of iron inside looked like nothing at all," quipped the *Toronto Star*. "But, nearby stood the white-haired gentleman who paid $500 for them, and who knows they are likely worth many times more."[2] C.T. Currelly was delivering a lecture, "The Norse Sea Rovers," to a group of schoolteachers. Included in his talk was a lantern slide showing a map of the northern hemisphere. The presumed routes of voyages in the Vinland sagas to Atlantic Canada were shown, and details delineating Hudson Bay and James Bay, the Albany River, Lake Nipigon, and the lower reaches of the Blackwater River allowed Currelly to trace the route of the Beardmore Norsemen (see illustrations).

"These are the Beardmore relics – genuine Viking armour found in Ontario," Currelly announced to his audience of educators. "And when a reporter for The Star first came and told me about this find, several years ago, I said, 'It can't be!'" Currelly had made a strange revision to the discovery story that completely eliminated Teddy Elliott and Ned Burwash. "This is the first time we have put them on display because before we were not sure of their origin," he continued. "But because Mr. Jim Curran of Sault Ste. Marie is an intelligent and restless man, we now have proof." Currelly was "very grateful to Mr. Curran and his friends, Judge Alexander McComber and Dr. George E. Eakins, for making this investigation. The inquiry has cost a great deal of money and the museum never could have afforded such an undertaking."[3]

"I am perfectly satisfied that the relics are authentic," Curran further told the *Toronto Star*. "Our mass of evidence gathered from a wide area under legal direction is unassailable."[4] Currelly, referring to Ragotte, declared: "The man who threw the monkey wrench into the works has now admitted he was joking. The whole story is perfectly clear now. As soon as the evidence has all been presented the story told by James Dodd of his finding the relics will be justified."[5]

Currelly was deeply indebted to the Thunder Bay investigative committee, but he had suffered public opprobrium at the hands of Curran in his *Sault Daily Star* article the same day. Curran felt that the museum director had taken advantage of Dodd. He told Dodd's story of having asked for four hundred dollars and his being offered five hundred by Currelly. Curran asserted the money was quickly eaten up by medical bills. "Dodd probably could today get enough for his relics to keep himself and family in comfort for the rest of their lives. That is if he hadn't sold them to Dr. Currelly, after having them lie around the house for years." Curran also criticized Currelly for not unequivocally standing behind Dodd and his story when the controversy erupted in January 1938.[6]

Curran assured his readers that Dodd had forgiven Currelly. In truth, the idea that he had sold the relics for far too little would gnaw at Dodd in the coming months, especially as railway work was elusive. "There is a lot of people very jealous now up here afraid that I am going to make two mutch money if I do make half a million I aint half paid for any Discovery," Dodd wrote Curran on 2 November.[7] Dodd's resentment was a bit rich, given how the Beardmore case would ultimately play out. Also, Curran had not heard that Dodd purportedly had almost sold the sword, the showpiece of his relics, for as little as twenty-five dollars. To be fair to Currelly, the museum director had gambled on the authenticity, paying what an art gallery might for a painting attributable to the studio of Rembrandt and hoping that further research would prove it to be by Rembrandt himself and thus far more valuable. Dodd's wife Ellen would sound a more conciliatory note in a letter written to Currelly on Eddy's behalf on 16 November, asking if the museum director could protect any rights Dodd might have to his story, as told in books or elsewhere. "I am only a working man and only am working about three months of the year, and anything I could make on this find would indeed be grateful."[8]

Currelly was in no position to complain about Curran's barbs. Beyond having made such a persuasive public case for authenticity, which allowed the relics to at last go on display, Curran had written a misinformed but beneficial account of how Currelly had come to acquire the relics. Following Philip Godsell's example, he had Currelly first sending photographs of the relics to experts in Norway to verify their authenticity, only then buying them from Dodd.[9] This version of Currelly's actions was repeated a few weeks later in *Time* magazine. While some would suspect Currelly wrote the item, the content indicates that Curran was the likely source.[10]

In a Curran "special" carried by the *Globe and Mail* on 7 October 1938, more details were revealed about the timing of Dodd's discovery, and these seemed to erase any doubts about the truth of his claims.[11] Dodd had told Curran he moved to 37 Machar on 29 June 1931 and that the relics were discovered before that, in "early June," which was a slight change from his previous statements pinning the find to 24 May 1931. Curran did not yet fully grasp Dodd's series of movements in 1931 as Judge McComber was still investigating Dodd's moves, and the details of James Hansen's properties were not yet understood. As noted, Hansen owned three neighbouring homes, at 33, 37, and 39 Machar, at the time Dodd said he found the relics at Beardmore. Rental records at Ruttan Estates, which managed the 296 Wilson property, were incomplete, but they would confirm that Dodd was living there in 1930. Hansen would confirm that Dodd signed a lease on 23 June 1931 for 37 Machar, and utility records showed that Dodd had his telephone service moved there from Wilson Street on 29 June. Curran thought that Hansen had alleged that the Bloch relics were at 37 Machar. Hansen, however, had said that they were next door in 33 Machar, where he had lived, moving out as Dodd moved in; Dodd's telephone service was moved from 37 to 33 Machar on 18 September. Dodd remained at 33 Machar until March 1933; his telephone service was moved to 74 South Algoma on 9 March.

If Dodd found the relics on the middle claim on 24 May 1931 (as he had stated to Royd Beamish in January 1938) or in early June 1931 (as Curran had reported in the 7 October *Globe and Mail* "special"), then Dodd was living at 296 Wilson at the time, just as he claimed. That was about a month before he moved to 37 Machar and almost four months before he shifted next door to 33 Machar, where Bloch's relics according to Hansen were supposedly awaiting his actual discovery.

The provenance case would have seemed closed but for doubts raised by Royd Beamish, now with the *Globe and Mail*. In running the Curran "special" on 7 October, the *Globe and Mail* included a bylined critique by Beamish.[12] Beamish greatly admired Curran, whom he would call "one of the few men on small city newspapers who nevertheless were not only abreast of their metropolitan contemporaries but carried within them the spark of life and understanding that makes an editor great."[13] Beamish's 7 October commentary was respectful, even salutary. "If ever an investigator had to track his quarry over a more complicated trail, or through a greater mass of contradicting facts than J.W. Curran, editor of the *Sault Daily Star*, has done in his investigation of the famous Norse Relics, I'd like to meet him." Beamish had "sought out the same elusive truth" the previous January. "I wound through the same maze of facts and fallacy, distorted by passing years, and I encountered the same inconsistencies of speech and record which he has so patiently winnowed through to isolate the facts he now presents as 'unassailable evidence' of the discovery."

Salutes to Curran dispensed with, Beamish pointed out unresolved problems. Curran had asserted that records supported Dodd's claim that he had discovered the relics a month before he moved to Machar Avenue, but Beamish noted that when he interviewed Dodd the previous January, Dodd said he found the relics in 1931 and left them at the claim for two years before telling anyone about them. If the relics had been left ignored on the middle claim's trash heap until 1933, how, then, could there be records of anyone's having seen the relics at 296 Wilson in 1931? Beamish did not know that, at the time of sale, Dodd had also signed a statement for the ROM saying the relics had been left at the site until 1933 and that Dodd also had told Elliott in August 1936 that he had not discovered the relics until 1933 and had brought them to Port Arthur after about two months. Dodd had made three statements that made it impossible for anyone to have seen the relics at 296 Wilson. These statements also meant that no one could have seen the relics until Dodd was about to move out of Hansen's house at 33 Machar in March 1933 or, more likely had already done so.

Dodd had also stated to Beamish in January 1938 that his son and "another man" saw him dig up the relics. Walter Dodd had never been heard from, and while Dodd did not name the other man, Beamish had assumed that he must have been Dodd's partner, Fletcher Gill – who then told Beamish he knew nothing of the relics until the news had broken a few days earlier. Apart from the fact that this left the second eyewitness unaccounted for, Beamish found it hard to believe that Dodd would never have told Gill. As for Curran's assertion that Dodd had "hawked them here and there and had people coming to his house to see what at first were supposed to be Indian relics," Dodd had told Beamish that he had not spoken to anyone about the find "because they would have wanted to share in anything I made from their sale," by which Dodd as much as admitted that he had cut his prospecting partner Gill out of the windfall. And where Dodd had refused in January to provide Beamish with an affidavit, Hansen had done so willingly. Beamish assured readers that he did not intend to discredit Dodd or Curran, that he only wanted to point out "the maze of conflicting facts which must still be sifted through before any one can say with assurance just what were the facts behind the discovery of those taunting, puzzling, bewildering Viking relics."

Remarkably, C.T. Currelly cleared up the identity of the mysterious second eyewitness to Dodd's discovery in an article that ran in the *Toronto Star* on the same day that Beamish shared his misgivings in the *Globe and Mail*. Currelly stated that he had heard about the man from Dodd himself. "Likely riding a freight car or living in a hobo jungle somewhere between Halifax and Vancouver is the one man who is said to have seen James Edward Dodd unearth the Norse relics," the *Star* reported. "Even his name is unknown. He dropped off a freight train at Beardmore, east of Port Arthur, and came upon Dodd digging in his mining claim." Currelly explained: "Dodd offered him a day's work helping him and he accepted. Dodd says the man was there when the sword, axe and shield handle were uncovered. But he went on his way and Dodd has had no word of him since."[14]

Jim Curran elaborated on the second discovery witness the next day, 8 October, in his own newspaper; a matched story (assuredly provided by Curran) ran that day in the *Toronto Star*. The two people present with Dodd were his son, Walter, who was now twenty-two, and a nameless Ukrainian youth, "who had come along the C.N.R. track close by and asked for food. He spent two days with Dodd and was given 50 cents and his meals for the little work he did."[15]

The sudden appearance of the nameless Ukrainian youth/hobo/man eyewitness in the *Toronto Star*, just as Beamish was wondering in the *Globe and Mail* about the second person present at the discovery, cannot have been a coincidence. Curran and Currelly must have been made aware of

Beamish's scepticism before the *Globe and Mail* went to press on 7 October, and they produced an eyewitness for the rival *Toronto Star* (where the brother of Currelly's assistant, Ethlyn Greenaway, was a reporter). No one questioned why a Ukrainian hobo would have struck out from CNR tracks in the middle of nowhere to wander the bush until he stumbled on Dodd's mining camp.

On 11 October, C.T. Currelly issued a press statement defending the Beardmore find. Any suggestion that Dodd had buried the relics on his claim "is ridiculous," he declared. As the *Globe and Mail* further reported on 12 October, "[Currelly] is satisfied the weapons were buried along with the owner when he died while making a portage from James Bay to Lake Superior." The discovery of additional relics in 1937 and 1938 "definitely settled any doubt as to the authenticity of the story."[16]

On the day Currelly issued his statement, the *Toronto Star* carried a "special" from Curran in which he presented his theory that James Bay was Vinland and that the Norse had reached the site of the Beardmore grave and Lake Superior via the Moose or Albany Rivers.[17] The article included the museum's photo of the weapons; the *Globe and Mail* also ran the photo the following day.[18] Finally, an image of the relics, which revealed that the sword was in two pieces, had appeared in the press.

After Jim Curran sent Eddy Dodd the issue of his newspaper that contained the article declaring Dodd an honest man, Dodd wrote him on 6 October: "glad I have one friend in the world that knows that I was telling the truth."[19] As a friend, Dodd now had a favour to ask. Curran evidently had promised he would help financially with work on the middle claim. "Well I hear there is some one going to watch if we do the work on those claims we got two [sic] the 15 day of Nov 1938 two [sic] record work," Dodd shared.

This deadline was not correct. The two claims staked the previous December by Fletcher Gill, TB25787 and TB25788 (the middle claim), had faced imminent cancellation in the summer of 1938 due to the lack of work (which suggests that they had nothing to do with the Norse-Beardmore syndicate initiative that had fizzled in May). On 16 July, Dodd restaked the claims, and the middle claim became TB26737. He did not record them at the mining office in Port Arthur until 4 August, the day Gill's claims were cancelled, which bought him some time in performing required work.

Under the 1937 Mining Act, Dodd had to report at least thirty days of work (in minimum eight-hour days) within three months of recording a claim or face cancellation. Dodd thus only had until 4 November (not 15 November) to do so. That was less than a month away. Dodd told Curran he already had William Feltham at the mining camp, and so some work may already have been performed, but it is suspicious that Dodd overstated the number of days left. Dodd explained that his son, Walter, wasn't working and was available. "Do you sujest we have [Walter] down on the claim two [sic] get in the number of days work I ain't any millionaire and it costs money and I *will not* lose these claims. But as you said if I needed any assistance you would glaldly [sic] help me, all we want is a little money for groceries and a little heater for camp."

Curran opened an account, furnished with an unknown sum, at the Royal Bank in Port Arthur on which Dodd and Fletcher Gill could draw. Within a few weeks, Curran received disturbing news from Gill. On 30 October, Gill reported that he had told Eddy they didn't need Curran's money and that Eddy had promised him he wouldn't touch the account.[20] Gill had also reminded Eddy that Curran "had done a lot for us." Gill revealed that, for site work, the partners had already received one hundred dollars a few weeks earlier from Thomas Falls, a sixty-three-year-old timber merchant and prominent Port Arthur citizen who served as a municipal councillor and a schoolboard trustee, and as public utilities commissioner. On the day Gill wrote Curran, Dodd admitted to his partner that he had taken money out of the Curran account, but only nine dollars. Gill went to the bank and learned Dodd had in fact withdrawn sixty-three dollars.

"I was certainly surprised," Gill confessed to Curran. "So when I see him I am afraid we are going to have a good scrap because I am certainly going to ball him out." Falls, according to Gill, also objected to Dodd's having drawn on the Curran account, given that Falls had already sunk ample funds into the operation. Gill, for his part, had just paid for a new stove that he had shipped to the site as well as a grub stake, an outlay of twenty-one dollars. Gill did not know it, but he had paid for everything that, on 6 October, Dodd had told Curran they needed money for.

Three days later, Gill was writing Curran again.[21] "I guess I was rather too hasty in writing you" about the money, Gill advised: "[Dodd] explained everything to me well I am satisfied it's OK. I did not know his financial position and am pleased to think you were kind enough to help us out." Dodd had told Gill that three men were working on the property and, as Gill faithfully reported, "hard working young men eat quite a bit and it does cost money. The money that Eddy had from Mr. Falls was used for wages, railway fare etc. and Mr. Dodd has bought them a good supply of food. So it will last them quite a while yet. Mr. Dodd was up today and recorded the work on the claims. So they are in good standing."

That same day, 2 November, Dodd, too, wrote the newspaper editor: "I have been pretty busy on the Road and did not have mutch time to write."[22] Dodd said nothing about prospecting work, but, on that day, he did file a report with the mining office in Port Arthur, asserting he had performed exactly thirty days of work on the middle claim, the minimum required to hold onto it. Jim Curran had just been initiated into the slippery world of Eddy Dodd and his credulous partner, Fletcher Gill. If Curran suspected Dodd had scammed him, no record remains.

14

From Thirty-One to Thirty

C.T. Currelly may have been satisfied to have Eddy Dodd's relics in a museum display case, but Jim Curran saw Dodd's middle claim, the site of a Viking grave, as a historic artefact worthy of preservation. Curran persuaded the CNR that something should be done to preserve and protect the site (under what authority it is not clear). A 5 October 1938 editorial in the *Kingston Whig-Standard* asserted that CNR vice-president W.A. Kingsland "ha[d] given instructions for the location and protection" of Dodd's discovery site.[1] On 16 November, Ellen Dodd, writing on behalf of Eddy, would report to Curran that "the Canadian Nat. Engineers were down last week to run lines out from the trench where relics were found ... running a line straight north to the railway track, they are making blue print of same no doubt you will get a copy."[2]

Curran also lobbied for the site to be protected by the federal government. On 6 October, Professor Fred Landon of the University of Western Ontario wrote C.T. Currelly in his capacity as a member of the Historical Sites and Monuments Board of Canada.[3] "Editor Curran's interest seems to be in the protection of the place where the relics are alleged to have been found until such time as the site can be scientifically examined," Landon noted, and he asked Currelly for any information on the site that he could pass on to Ottawa.

Currelly immediately replied, aggressively discouraging any thought of further investigation. "I cannot possibly see that when a man is buried on a portage, there is any likelihood of anything being found in the neighbourhood. I may be hopelessly wrong, but my opinion is that the site might be marked, but that any excavations would be a waste of money."[4] Currelly was echoing Thomas McIlwraith's opinion in his site report that there was little chance of anything else turning up at the claim, but it seemed as though Currelly *feared* having professional archaeologists take a more careful look. A few days later, Currelly followed up with a rehash of the discovery controversy, even though Landon had expressed no qualms. "As far as my judgment goes," he concluded, "there is no possible doubt about the question [of authenticity], and I have been as skeptical as I could possibly be, and have tried to follow down every possible scrap of evidence."[5]

C.T. Currelly knew that the Beardmore find had loose ends and that they were largely related to timing. Eddy Dodd's publicly stated discovery date of 24 May 1931 was uncomfortably close to Dodd's move from 296 Wilson to a home owned by James Hansen on Machar Avenue one month later. John Jacob had already begun to line up people willing to attest to a 1930 date, including Dodd himself, which would steer the find well clear of Hansen and Bloch. Dodd's recollections of the relics remaining on a rubbish heap at the middle claim until 1933 could be written off as an imperfect memory or a harmless penchant for gilding his story.

Jacob was willing to personally attest to the 1930 discovery date, and he made a handwritten amendment to his typed statement of June 1937 to that effect.[6] As Jacob had informed Currelly from Port Arthur in May 1938 that he would be going away for seven or eight months, the earliest Jacob could have provided this critical amendment to the museum's document was in the autumn of 1938. Although Jacob's amendment was undated, Currelly had it in hand no later than 13 October, when he told the Toronto *Telegram* that Jacob had visited the middle claim between 17 and 21 June, as the amendment contended. The *Telegram* story, however, still stated that the discovery was in 1931, which could have been a reporter's or editor's adherence to the standard timing repeatedly stated and lately reinforced by Curran.

While Jacob provided a few more details about the rust stain, the most important aspect of his amendment was dating the find, which he did for the first time, on his third try:

> In consulting my memorandum notes I find that on my visit to Port Arthur at the end of May or early June 1930 I called on Aaron Lougheed who told me that a few days before Dodds had brought him a sword which he said he had just recently taken out of his mining claim. I went right down to Dodds house and saw it and the other things also he told me the impression of the sword was stained in the rock on which it had been lying. Within a few days (between the 17th and 21st of June) I went to the locality and saw the impression of the staining on the rock.
>
> The stain of the complete shape of the sword as it had lain was very plainly marked on the rock and this stain could not have been made unless the metal had lain on the rock for a long period of time.

The trees (a large clump of Bushes) had such a wide root system that they would have prevented the planting of these relics there within a generation and I can safely say that they (the trees) had not been uprooted for more than two months or since the frost had come out.

As a prospector I have had years of experience in examining rock stains and would unquestionably state that this sword had lain on the rock for many years in order to cause a stain such as I saw where it had been laying.

If Jacob was a game warden, as he asserted when he saw the rust stain, the province's public accounts placed a firm limit on how far back Dodd's discovery could be dated: Jacob had worked his first nine months for the enforcement office of District 6 in Fort William in the year ending 31 October 1930, which meant that he was hired in February 1930. He had barely started his Department of Games and Fisheries job when he now alleged to have visited the middle claim. And while Jacob's recollections reinforced the certitude of the new, earlier discovery date, they continued to complicate the essential story. He reiterated Aaron Lougheed's crucial role in the discovery narrative, but Lougheed (and Jacob, for that matter) still had not appeared anywhere in the narrative offered by Curran and Dodd. And nowhere in Curran's and Dodd's accounts was there a rust stain of the sword on the underlying rock, even though Jacob said that Dodd had told him there was a stain before he visited the middle claim.

There was also the matter of the shape-shifting tree. Jacob's birch was a clump of bushes with a wide root system. Dodd's statement to the ROM at the time of purchase mentioned a stump with a diameter of two and a half feet. That was improbable for a single tree but consistent with a clump of dwarf birch. But Dodd was also continuing to describe a single, thick stump. Ned Burwash, in February 1934, said the stump was fifteen inches in diameter; Teddy Elliott had been told in August 1936 that it was fourteen inches. Curran, in his *Toronto Star* "special" of 8 October 1938, described a rotted birch stump twelve to eighteen inches in diameter. As for how the relics were exposed, Jacob said that the birch clump had been uprooted that spring, but he did not say how. His account echoed the story related by J.H. Fleming the previous February, in which the exposed roots of a clump of dwarf birches had been blown over in a storm, a version that most certainly originated with Jacob. Jacob made no mention of dynamite's being the cause of the tree's removal, which was Dodd's explanation. Dodd and Jacob were telling stories of two different kinds of birch trees, with two different causes for their uprooting.

The contentious issue of the tree stump recalled a key element of the Kensington stone story that no one engaged with the Beardmore case noticed. Olof Ohman and his eyewitnesses had asserted that the stone had been unearthed from beneath a poplar stump; the age of the tree, estimated at seventy years, was considered proof that the stone must have been there at least since the 1820s, before any mischievous Scandinavian settler could have arrived. The discovery of relics beneath (or entangled in) tree roots was an established trope in Ohman's time. In 1894, a sword, said to belong to Samuel de Champlain, was reportedly found entangled in tree roots on the shore of Ontario's Balsam Lake.[7] It should have struck sceptics as highly coincidental that Dodd claimed to have found his Norse relics beneath the roots of a birch tree, whatever the species or dimension.

The ROM would have had Jacob's amendment in hand when Eddy Dodd and Fletcher Gill visited the museum on 17 October. Thomas McIlwraith may have refreshed Dodd's memory with Jacob's May report, in which he had noted that Dodd was willing to shift the discovery to 1930, based on his son's illness. Dodd seemed agreeable to the date change. McIlwraith jotted in pencil on a slip of paper, with the general date of October 1938: "Date was probably May 1930, based on memory of his son, then 13 years old."[8]

Dodd came to the museum bearing a surprise: another metal fragment, slightly larger but similar to the small, thin, rectangular bits retrieved during McIlwraith's visit to the site in September 1937 and Curran's in 1938. Nothing was ever said publicly about this latest find, nor are there any documents indicating how or when Dodd recovered it. Dodd's penchant for coming up with more items, more than half a dozen years after the alleged initial find, may have been worrying. The fact that Dodd continued to find things also defied Currelly's insistence that any archaeological investigation of the site would be pointless. The latest discovery was inventoried as: "Fragment of iron from trench at base of the rock a few inches west of the spot where the other remains were found." If Eddy Dodd was bitter about the price he had received for the relics, he made no apparent effort to lever more money out the museum with this find. The museum's trustees issued Eddy and Ellen Dodd a certificate on 10 November acknowledging their donation.[9] The museum now had three additional fragments of metal from Dodd's middle claim. Despite the museum's efforts to interpret the McIlwraith and Curran finds variously as pieces of the shield boss, shield handle, or tip of a knife, metallurgical testing would eventually suggest that they were all fragments from the break area of the sword.[10]

On 6 October 1938, Jim Curran had allowed to the *Toronto Star* that his research would soon be complete. "I need only one more affidavit."[11] He did not say from whom, but it was probably from Eddy Dodd. On 20 October – three days after Dodd met with McIlwraith at the ROM and seemed agreeable to changing the discovery year to 1930 – Judge McComber reported to Curran that Dodd had called on him that morning and had provided him with a statement. McComber sent Curran a copy. Dodd's October statement would never enter the printed record. Its contents are unknown, but, as he had not given McIlwraith a signed statement attesting to a 1930 discovery, he probably stayed with the 1931 date for McComber and Curran. Eddy was having trouble managing the different versions of the story and was not prepared to complicate it further with competing versions under his own signature.

On 21 October, Judge McComber took a statement from Fletcher Gill. The original would not surface, but based on a later description by the judge, it was no different than an affidavit Gill would sign the following February.[12] Gill backtracked from his admission to reporter Royd Beamish in January 1938 that he knew nothing of the relics until the story had made the papers in recent days. Gill now recalled working at Hornepayne (about ninety miles east-southeast of Longlac) as a CNR engineer when he received a letter from Dodd, "the exact wording of which I do not remember, but which in a general way informed me of the work he had been doing on the said claim, and after mentioning the work the letter went on to say that whilst trenching on the dyke on the claim he had found an old Indian cemetery but that he had not yet come across any tombstones. I did not attach any importance to this at the time, and I destroyed the letter." Gill received the letter "some time during the summer of 1931." As Gill had just been at the ROM with Dodd in October 1938, when Dodd allowed that the discovery may have been in May 1930, it is difficult to imagine Gill's offering 1931 for the letter timing if he knew Dodd was going to tell McComber the discovery year was now 1930. But it is also possible that Gill never grasped the importance of a discovery in 1930 versus a discovery in 1931.

Judge McComber also sent Curran a statement by Dodd's close friend, Patrick Bohan. John Jacob had informed Currelly in May 1938 that Dodd claimed he had shown Bohan the relics in the spring of 1930, but Jacob never spoke with Bohan. Curran had reported in his 6 October article that Bohan saw the relics at Dodd's cabin "right after" they were discovered in 1931, but he had not spoken with Bohan either. Bohan's statement for McComber in October 1938 does not survive, but it appears to have been the same as an affidavit he signed the following February.[13] Bohan strove to nail down the date he (or anyone else) allegedly saw the sword at Dodd's camp: "In 1931 I was foreman at Warnford [sic], one mile from Dodd's camp and I used to visit Dodd at his camp. On one of those visits – between the 15th of May and the 1st of July, 1931 – (I take these dates from my staff records, which show that I was stationed at Warnford between these dates) – I saw the handle part of the sword pictured in the Globe newspaper [on 12 October 1938], lying on the ground outside on the left hand side (south side) of Dodd's camp."[14]

As well, Tom Delbridge had shown Judge McComber a letter from a man named Smith, who was probably the prospector and blacksmith mentioned by Eli Ragotte in his January 1938 affidavit. The judge quoted in part from Smith: "I don't remember the year, but we went to a house on Machar Avenue. I am sure of it. It is quite a while ago now."[15] This was not the sort of corroboration Curran was looking for, and Smith's letter never entered the printed record.

The statements by Gill and Bohan, who were close to Dodd, endorsed Dodd's repeated assertion, amplified in the press by Curran, that he had found the relics in the spring of 1931. Dodd had probably attested to the same for Judge McComber. But they all did so at the very time the ROM was determined to change the discovery date to the spring of 1930, thinking it had Dodd's blessing. Curran and McComber were clearly unaware of the museum initiative. Currelly continued to withhold his Jacob evidence (including Jacob's statements, the keystone of his faith in Dodd's discovery) from Curran and his investigative committee, a strategy so counter-productive that Currelly must have wanted to shield Jacob himself. Consequently, in the *Time* article of 24 October, which likely originated with Curran, the year of discovery was reiterated as 1931. The provenance case was careening into chaos.

In handing over the latest affidavits to Jim Curran, Judge McComber shared what he had learned about John Bloch.[16] Bloch had rented Room 9 in the Ruttan Building no later than 18 March 1927 and had left on 22 November 1927, owing rent. Bloch thus had a history of money troubles that would at least make it possible that he would borrow money from James Hansen. Still, Judge McComber confessed to Curran that he was "very forcibly" struck by one element of Hansen's story. "If Bloch took the trouble to bring these articles out from Norway, he must have known their value." Yet Hansen said Bloch handed them over to satisfy a mere twenty-five-dollar debt. The judge thought it was more likely Bloch had provided the relics as security for a loan, and ought to have tried to retrieve them, especially as he had enough money later to get married in Winnipeg and move to Vancouver. "But Hansen said nothing about Bloch ever trying to get them back." The judge had not been able to question Hansen about this, and Hansen otherwise had become frosty. Dr Eakins had reported to the judge that Hansen had called him up, "and said he would hold the Doctor responsible for some of the articles in the paper." Hansen was furious with Dr Eakins's public assertion that the story that the relics originated with Bloch was a "myth."

"Mr. Curran has pretty thoroughly stolen Dr. Currelly's thunder as far as publicity is concerned," Ethlyn Greenaway informed Philip Ainsworth Means on 14 October.[17] "On the other hand, the Museum has been saved the expense of an investigation that we could ill have afforded." Greenaway did not mention the considerable investigative work done in Port Arthur on Currelly's behalf by John Jacob the previous spring. She advised Means that Currelly planned to submit an article of his own to the *New York Times* the following week. *Time* magazine instead ran its story on 24 October, which, as noted, probably originated with Curran, and no item ever appeared in the *New York Times*.

Currelly did not endorse all of Curran's published ideas. He rejected Curran's assertion that the Norse had interbred with Indigenous people and left behind "White Indians" in the James Bay region. As the *Globe and Mail* reported on 7 October: "There is no trace of Norse blood among the people of America, claimed Dr. Currelly. Any story of Norse blood discovered in Indian, Eskimo or any other American people is without a scrap of foundation, he said."[18] Currelly was reiterating his friend Vilhjalmur Stefansson's effort to distance himself from his sensational claims, made in 1912, of having discovered "blond Eskimos" in Coronation Gulf. Stefansson insisted that his comments to a New York journalist about blond hair and blue eyes among a few Inuit had been wildly inflated and sensationalized. On 24 October, Stefansson sent Curran a copy of his book *My Life with the Eskimos* to familiarize him with his revised opinion.[19]

Even while Currelly withheld his Jacob materials and rejected Curran's White Indians notions, the relationship between Currelly and Curran was friendly and cooperative. Curran had become the unofficial publicity arm of the museum's acquisition, and his independent investigative committee's findings (as Greenaway explained to Means) "convince them beyond doubt that the story of the man from whom we bought the weapons is true, and that they were found as he told us."[20] Curran's investigations had also brought him into the corresponding circle of Holand and Stefansson, and he was beginning to send to Currelly old weapons (akin to those of Holand) from around the Great Lakes for identification, preservation, and casting.

By early November 1938, the ROM, Curran, and Dodd were singing from the same song sheet on the discovery timing. A letter from Currelly to Curran on 31 October is no longer extant, but Currelly had likely squared Curran on the ticklish point of the discovery year. In reply, on 3 November, Curran informed Currelly that William Feltham had provided a statement endorsing the 1930 discovery date and that there may be another "one or two."[21] Feltham had already provided such a letter to Jacob in May. Without realizing it, Curran and his committee were ploughing the same ground of evidence already covered by Jacob for the museum.

On 8 November, Currelly delivered a talk at the ROM entitled "The Coming of the Norsemen." Seated in a Roman chair, he shared his thoughts in advance with Thelma Craig of the *Globe and Mail*:

> It is true that the Viking visit to our northland led to nothing; the Norsemen never followed it up. Their visit did not add an ounce of ore or a bushel of grain. But it is as a great poem. Everyone is bucked up by the thought of a 16-man boat pushing its way from Norseland to Iceland, on to Greenland, down through the icy waters of Hudson Bay and into James Bay and on into the Long Lac country. Theirs was the spirit of skilled adventure, not of foolhardiness. In the minds of every one there is the love of romance and big achievement. Materially it does not matter whether the Vikings came here or not, but from the viewpoint of inspirational value this saga of the Norseman contributes a great deal.[22]

Currelly did not explain why he thought the Beardmore voyagers had travelled all the way from "Norseland," when the known circa 1000 Vinland voyages, which were coincident with the age of the Beardmore weapons, involved Norse from Iceland and Greenland. He had otherwise implicitly divided the Beardmore story into Stefansson's knowledge categories of scientific fact and literature, having come close to saying that whether there really was a Viking grave near Beardmore was irrelevant. In the same interview, Currelly regretted that children were not raised on Bible stories as he was. For Currelly, his earliest exposure to archaeology, relics of the Middle East, provided him with a tactile connection to stories of the divine. Beardmore provided the physical evidence that made for an inspiring story. Two large paintings on Viking subjects were soon being executed by Sylvia Hahn for the museum's Children's Room. They became the conclusion of a tour Hahn would deliver, with historical commentary to students, along a "Norse trail" leading from the Armour Court.[23] The paintings "have already proved their value as teaching material," Currelly remarked in his contribution to the 1939 report by the president of the University of Toronto. "'The Vikings' is a subject frequently requested by school classes, and the galleries provide no illustrations other than weapons."[24] (Currelly again managed not to mention the actual Beardmore acquisition: he never recognized it in his contributions to the president's report.) Currelly imagined the museum's Viking relics would allow boys to appreciate their British heritage, even if, like him, they had not been born there. As he had told the press the previous January, "we must all have a bit of Norse blood in us if we are British." For Currelly, the story that could be attached to the Viking grave by definition, according to Stefansson's knowledge scheme, was more important than whatever science could say about the Viking grave in fact. The evidence only mattered insofar as it could support the story, and Currelly had all the evidence he desired.

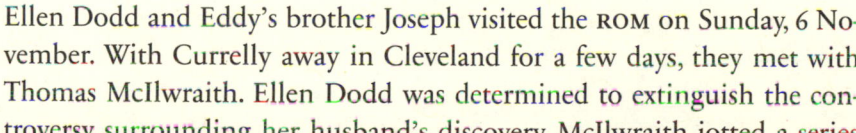

Ellen Dodd and Eddy's brother Joseph visited the ROM on Sunday, 6 November. With Currelly away in Cleveland for a few days, they met with Thomas McIlwraith. Ellen Dodd was determined to extinguish the controversy surrounding her husband's discovery. McIlwraith jotted a series of pencil notes:

Dodd had specimens & showed them to friends when living on Wilson St before going to Machar Ave.

Hanson [sic] owned house on Machar Ave & had rented it to another man before renting to Dodd. I.e., relics (if left by Hanson) were left when house occupied by more than one family.

Much bad blood between Hanson, who is grasping, & Dodd re rent.

Bad blood between Dodd (& wife) and Rigotte [sic] who roomed with Dodd about women & drink

---

About 3 weeks ago Hanson met Dodd on street & admitted before a retired railwayman named Scott that the Beardmore relics were not the ones he (Hanson) had owned.

Mrs. Dodd was warned by Father McLennan, a parish priest, that Rigotte was crooked, harsh to his sister & morally bad.[25]

Largely through Jim Curran's publicity efforts, news of the Beardmore find was spreading, free of Ragotte's and Hansen's claims and A.W. Brøgger's condemnation. Articles that appeared in the Danish press on 30 October and 13 November were clipped by Hjalmar Holand and forwarded to Curran.[26] Curran continued to steal C.T. Currelly's thunder as he addressed the Empire Club in Toronto on 10 November.

Curran was in fine form in delivering "A Norseman Died in Ontario 900 Years Ago." He began: "I once read that a gentleman was a person who, knowing all about a subject, listened with great courtesy to another who didn't know anything about it. I am sure I can depend on your indulgence this afternoon."[27] All introductory self-effacement aside, Curran congratulated himself for turning the liar Dodd into an honest man in the court of public opinion. "When I arrived in Port Arthur, I hadn't found anyone who believed that they were genuine Norse relics. By the time I got through everyone accepted. So I think we can take Mr. James Edward Dodd, as an honest man, telling the exact truth when he says he found the sword, the handgrip of a shield and a battle axe exactly where he says he did."[28]

Curran sarcastically suggested that Norse relics in the Great Lakes region were the work of an energetic joker. After he planted the Kensington stone, "he came over to Ontario, and you know what he did here. I think the joker must have been Dodd's Norseman. You see what this fellow did. He dug a hole, put an axe and a sword and a shield in it and then he crawled in himself."[29] The line would have generated laughter, but Curran declined to note that this Viking grave had not yielded the dead Viking that had crawled into it.

The most important statement Curran made before that audience was a basic assertion of fact. "James Edward Dodd found the armour of a Norseman seven miles from Lake Nipigon in 1930."[30] He had made the first public pronouncement of the new discovery year: and he did so without acknowledging that, up until the preceding month, the discovery year had repeatedly been asserted, by himself as much as by Dodd, as 1931.

Thomas Leslie Tanton Takes on the Case

"Have you had any more snarls and yappings, beyond those of Dr. Brøgger as to which I wrote you months ago, from abroad or from this country?" Philip Ainsworth Means asked C.T. Currelly's assistant, Ethlyn Greenaway, in October 1938. "Have you even received favorable comments, besides those of Mr. Curran?"[1]

Stewart Wallace, chief librarian of the University of Toronto, as noted, would prove to be a Currelly stalwart on the Beardmore find. George Lechler, who taught ancient art and archaeology at the Detroit Institute of Arts and had an interest in pre-Columbian voyages to the Americas, wrote Currelly on 28 August, plainly accepting the authenticity of the find.[2] Frank Johnson, curator of American archaeology at the Phillips Academy in Andover, Massachusetts, wrote Currelly after reading the 24 October *Time* article. "Your report is particularly interesting in view of the Kensington stone in Minnesota and also it seems to me because it is the most definite proof of the presence of the Norse of which I know."[3] On 4 November, Sir Charles Marston, an amateur archaeologist and British businessman who bankrolled digs in Palestine, viewed the ROM display and publicly pronounced the Beardmore relics genuine.[4]

The considerable surviving Beardmore correspondence in the ROM archives is otherwise bereft of supportive messages from leading scholars – especially Scandinavian scholars with Norse expertise – in the months after the relics were put on display. Currelly did have an awkward letter exchange with Halfdan Hebo, a Danish engineer based in New York who was a member of Denmark's Royal Society of Northern Antiquaries. Hebo proposed to subject the bones of the Beardmore grave to spectrophotometry, as the presence of rare metals in bone structures could reveal where the person had lived. "I have access to the most powerful spectrographs in existence," Hebo assured Currelly somewhat ominously, "and I am at present building one of still greater dispersion." Currelly was forced to reply that his celebrated Viking grave did not actually contain a Viking.[5]

In 1937, Chester Gould, the Chicago Scandinavianist, had advised John Robins that the possibility of a Norse voyage into Hudson Bay and the authenticity of the Kensington stone needed to be maintained as distinct issues. The Beardmore relics now fell into a similar position, with not even Hjalmar Holand completely at ease with their authenticity in the wake of the Ragotte and Hansen allegations. Holand exhibited a combination of impossibly romantic notions of Viking incursions into North America for the Kensington stone and salutary caution with evidence for theories advanced by anyone else. He was beginning to pursue evidence of "mooring holes" in northern Minnesota, absurdly convinced that the Knutson expedition drilled holes in rocks to set pins for securing the "light war vessels" that Holand conjured for its inland exploration.[6] Apparently, the vessels were light enough to be portaged but not light enough to simply be beached or tied to a tree overnight.

More concerned with the laborious measures the Knutson party used to prevent its vessels from floating away than with how it overcame forty-seven rapids on the tortuous journey up the Nelson River, Holand would eventually find fourteen mooring stones, one for each day of the journey inland enumerated on the Kensington stone.[7] Yet towards the Beardmore find he remained rigorously sceptical, if hopeful. "I am extremely anxious that the Beardmore find be proven genuine," Holand confessed to Jim Curran on 17 October, "and I think you are doing a most excellent job in the matter. But one thing has not yet been cleared up."[8] Holand was bothered by the fact that, in initial reportage, Eddy Dodd said he did not take the relics home from his Beardmore claim until 1933, which meant that they would have first been seen at the house he rented from James Hansen (actually, most likely after he moved out of it that March). "This matter should be thoroughly elucidated. I would also like to hear what this Mr. Hansen has to say. So far he has not appeared on the witness stand." Holand cautioned in closing: "You are doing fine and I hope you will succeed. But don't let any evidence be overlooked as it will later come out like a boomerang."

It was not exactly true that Hansen had been silent, but he had not been extended the same courtesy as had Eli Ragotte, who had been brought to the ROM to inspect the relics. Holand decided to write Hansen himself. Hansen replied on 1 November, in Norwegian. According to a translation Holand provided C.T. Currelly in 1941, Hansen said that Dodd is "a big B.S. and known as such by all here."[9] But Hansen could not say if Dodd found the relics at Beardmore or if the ones at the ROM were the ones John Bloch brought from Norway without seeing the ROM's artefacts for himself. Hansen continued: "The other side of the matter is that you are Norwegian and you know our history from the old days and you are convinced that [the Norsemen] were here. If I should see [the relics] there in the Museum, I would say that they were not the same as those that I had even if they were." Holand would inform Currelly in 1941 that Hansen "is unscrupulous and unreliable because he frankly states that he will give false evidence because he thinks this might please me."[10] Holand also had the 4 April 1938 letter from Eli Ragotte to A.D. Fraser, in which Ragotte said that Hansen had once told him he had brought the relics personally from Norway. "In my opinion, Hansen's story of Bloch's ancient weapons is an invention by him made with the hope of being reimbursed for the money loaned to Bloch."[11]

It seemed that Hansen was so distressed by his alienation from Thunder Bay's Scandinavian community that he was willing to abandon his claim to the relics and say whatever would ingratiate him with community members as well as with Holand, whose writing was so revered by them – Hansen included. At the same time, personal pride would not allow Hansen to tolerate being called a liar.[12] Claiming that he did receive relics from Bloch, but that they weren't the ones the ROM had on display, would make for a face-saving exit. As it happened, Dodd informed Curran on 2 November: "I met this man hanson on the street and he wanted two [sic] shake hands with me and said the Pieces of his sword was not as long as the ones he seen in the Papers, so I don't think they would grow."[13] Heartened by Dodd, Curran immediately informed Currelly that Hansen might be prepared to back down.[14] As we have seen, Ellen Dodd and her brother-in-law Joseph then told Thomas McIlwraith on 6 November of this meeting between Hansen and Eddy Dodd, with Hansen's volunteering that the sword in the museum photograph was not the one he had obtained from John Bloch.

Despite his misgivings about the evidence for Eddy Dodd's find, Hjalmar Holand provisionally accommodated the Beardmore relics within his own scenario of epic and repeated Norse efforts to explore (or, rather, to circumnavigate) the lands to the west of Greenland, but he balked at Jim Curran's scenario of Lake Nipigon's being the heart of Vinland. The Kensington stone inscription maintained that Knutson's party ventured westward *from* Vinland. "I think you are completely in error in locating Vinland on the shore of Hudson Bay or anywhere inland from it," Holand wrote Curran on 17 October 1938, the first of several such blunt declarations.[15] He added: "I feel confident that no student of the Vinland voyages will support you in your contention that Vinland was in the vicinity of Lake Nipigon."

"Why bother with Vinland at all?" Holand posed to Curran. "To me the Beardmore find, if genuine, is more remarkable without your Vinland theory. It shows that the early Norse voyages to America were far more extensive than anyone has thought. It shows that among these explorers there were men who conceived the bold but very natural idea of circumnavigating this new land." Beardmore was "the grave of one of the probably many men who lost their lives on this great journey. The dead man was no doubt buried by his companions for if he had been alone or with Indians he would not have been buried in this way."

An indefatigable networker, Vilhjalmur Stefansson positioned himself astride the debate surrounding Norse voyages that Curran was animating, and he strove to shape its outcome. In effusive letters, Stefansson encouraged Curran in the autumn of 1938 and suggested that he publish his ongoing series of newspaper articles in book form rather than simply selling reprints. Stefansson offered to introduce Curran to his own publisher, Macmillan; Curran, however, would decide to self-publish.[16] But Curran's ideas about Vinland were a non-starter with Stefansson as well. As Stefansson advised C.T. Currelly in November 1938: "Curran is taking upon himself unnecessary trouble. It takes a whole lot less evidence to prove that Norsemen were in the region between James Bay and Lake Superior than to prove that that region is Vinland." Stefansson believed (as he advised Curran) that Norse voyages to James Bay, if they occurred, were probably in the twelfth, thirteenth, and fourteenth centuries.[17] But Curran was unshakeable. The Beardmore relics were proof positive that the Vinland of Leif Eiriksson was in his beloved northern Ontario.

With the Beardmore relics on display, C.T. Currelly began formalizing plans to tell the museum's story and not to leave the discovery exclusively to Curran, Godsell, Fraser, and whoever else came along. Foremost, Currelly planned to employ the ROM *Bulletin*. As he informed a staff member of *Time* on 11 November 1938: "We hope to issue a Museum BULLETIN shortly, with as full a statement as possible regarding these Viking weapons."[18] On 15 November, Currelly also proposed an article to the *Canadian Historical Review*, which was published by University of Toronto Press.[19] Editor George Brown welcomed it; he already appears to have been preparing an article by Stewart Wallace, his predecessor as CHR's editor, on the Vinland sagas, and he wanted the two items to appear in the same issue.

On 18 November, Currelly wrote Matthias Thórdarson, some eleven months after Stefansson had advised him to seek the Icelandic expert's opinion on the weapons typology.[20] "I have sent a photograph to several Norse archaeologists," Currelly wrote. "My friend Stefansson has told me of the fine collection of 9th to 13th century weapons in your Museum, and of your own highly specialized knowledge of this period. I was therefore delighted to find my dating of our sword and axe confirmed by an illustration in your very interesting book, THE VINLAND VOYAGES, in which you show a sword and axe of the same type as ours, and date them 1000. I hope to publish full details of these weapons in a Museum BULLETIN to appear next month, a copy of which we shall be very pleased to send you." It was an odd letter. Even though Currelly sent Thórdarson a photo of the relics under separate cover, he had as much as served notice that Thórdarson had already typed the weapons for him through *The Vinland Voyages* and that he had no interest in securing his professional opinion.

On 26 November, Currelly shared with Teddy Elliott his two-step publishing plan.[21] The Beardmore account would appear in the *Bulletin* before the end of the year, with CHR "probably" being given an article after the latter had appeared. As he prepared to publish, Currelly could be confident that Hjalmar Holand was now safely onside. Ethlyn Greenaway had sent Holand the photograph of the relics he had long desired, and, in reply, Holand reported he had been in touch with James Hansen. "I have found he is *more than careless with the truth*."[22]

"The amusing thing about Mr. Hansen's claim that he left the Viking things in a house that Dodd rented," Currelly replied to Holand on 30 November, "is that several people were shown the things – including a govt servant – whose notes we had – dated eighteen months before Dodd moved into the house where Hansen claimed he had left them."[23] Currelly was overreaching in his defence of the acquisition. There is no indication Currelly ever saw the "notes" that John Jacob purportedly possessed. He further assured Holand: "Northern Ontario fits your stone completely and also is going to bring a quantity of 'finds' of all sorts of things. I want a cast of the Kensington stone and of your axes very badly." All sorts of things indeed were beginning to percolate out of various corners of the Great Lakes. Jim Curran was gathering and sending them to the ROM for identification, preservation, and casting. Holand, in reply, informed Currelly that Hansen, in his recent letter, "proved himself a liar twice – all about the Beardmore find. It proves the old saying that a man must be very clever to lie consistently."[24]

Currelly jotted another note to Holand on 7 December, unsure if he had covered all his main points.[25] "I hope I mentioned that the Viking things were seen by scores 18 months before Dodd moved into Hansen's house." Again, Currelly was exaggerating. In no way did such witnesses number in the "scores," although he may have been aware of two more statements somewhat in support of the new discovery timing that were gathered by Judge McComber in mid-November. John McGugan, who was probably a mining engineer of that name in Port Arthur, asserted he had known Dodd since moving to Port Arthur in 1921.[26] He recalled sitting in the Mariaggi Hotel when Dodd came in "about seven years ago," showed him two pieces of iron, and asked: "What do you think of these?" Dodd spoke of them as Indian relics and said he had found them on his claim near Beardmore. McGugan recognized them as the pieces of the sword that had appeared in the *Globe and Mail* of 12 October 1938. Soon after, he dined at Dodd's home at 296 Wilson Street and saw the sword pieces again.[27] George Hynes (or Hines), a log scaler with the Port Arthur branch of the province's Department of Lands and Forests, attested to the same experience of visiting Dodd at his home on 296 Wilson "about seven years ago" and seeing the sword pieces that appeared in the *Globe and Mail*.[28] Both affidavits were firm in stating that Dodd possessed the broken sword before he moved to Machar Avenue. But they were also so similar in content that they seemed coordinated, perhaps even based on a template someone had provided.

Currelly continued to Holand: "The Norwegians of Port Arthur under the influence of the Norse Consul [Sorensen] has [sic] gone into the matter and are sure no things were ever brought from the home land of Norway-Sweden. The pictures [rust stains] seen by John Jacob a govt inspector is a final confirmation for me. Many thanks for your letters. I shall be glad of casts of your axes at any time and for a cast of the Kensington stone also."

Not everyone in Currelly's circle was satisfied that the Beardmore provenance was settled in Dodd's favour. Vilhjalmur Stefansson remained infuriatingly sceptical with Currelly. In a letter on 29 November, Stefansson allowed that one could imagine a series of voyages by Greenland Norse through Hudson Strait and southward into James Bay between 1030 and 1347, provided "the Beardmore relics were not planted but are a genuine find."[29] Currelly drafted a long tirade defending the Beardmore provenance, then decided not to mail it.[30]

The promised *Bulletin* featuring the Beardmore acquisition failed to materialize in December. In a belated reply on 15 December to repeated requests from archaeologist George Lechler for a photograph of the relics for an article he was preparing for the *Art Quarterly*, Currelly said that the issue of the *Bulletin* had been held up; however, he assured him: "We have been steadily getting more information on the find, so that it is as well attested as any archaeological find that I know of."[31] Currelly had made an extraordinarily exaggerated statement to an archaeologist who was preparing to publish on the find. Far from pursuing a rigorous site investigation, Currelly had actively dissuaded any closer consideration of Dodd's mining claim.

G.R.F. Prowse was another member of Currelly's inner circle who balked at Curran's theorizing and was not convinced that the Beardmore provenance was settled. In early January 1939 Prowse complained to Currelly that Curran's determination to place Vinland in the Nipigon region was "bunk." Prowse also shared the fact that, in March 1938, he had interviewed Eli Ragotte in Winnipeg, made a copy of the initial letter he had received from Hansen, gathered that Ragotte thought Dodd was a crook, and personally thought Ragotte to be honest.[32]

Currelly assured Prowse that there was nothing to the claims against the Dodd find. "I am sorry that Ragotte vented his spleen, because of course now everybody *knows* the things are not right, and no amount of proof to the contrary will have any effect on a large number of people. However, that will eventually die out." As for Hansen's claims, the ROM had no worries there, either, "because twenty or thirty people had seen the Beardmore weapons about a year and a half before Mr. Dodd lived in a house belonging to Hansen. So we can dismiss both Ragotte and Hansen from the matter altogether. Of the verification of the finding of the weapons there is no question whatever, as we now have the evidence of three different men."[33]

Despite Currelly's confidence, *CHR*'s 15 January 1939 deadline for confirming a Beardmore article for the March issue passed without a word from the museum, and still no *Bulletin* had appeared.[34] Currelly seemed to be suffering another lapse in the confidence to move ahead with formal publication, regardless of his statements in the daily press, a radio address on Vikings and the relics on CBC on 23 December 1938, and his bravura assertions in letters. A scholarly audience was different than a public one, and he must have understood that the evidence for the Dodd discovery was barely enough to support even a short article. Certainly, with Thomas McIlwraith's site report effectively suppressed, there was scarcely anything scientific to share. Currelly did discuss possible metallurgy tests on the sword after a chance meeting with Henry Craig Richardson of Republic Steel at the Cleveland Museum of Art in early November 1938, but he would inform Richardson in February 1939 that the amount of material required from the sword was "pretty appalling," and the tests never proceeded.[35]

Currelly also may have hoped to bring to bear in print some of the archaeological relics Curran was gathering from sources around the Great Lakes and sending to the museum for inspection and preservation, but they were a dubious, even embarrassing assortment of so-called finds. Curran, in his Empire Club address, conceded that Currelly had just rejected as Norse a spear point that two boys had supposedly discovered under a rock along the shore of Lake Superior. And in addition to being pestered by Stefansson's and Prowse's nagging doubts, Currelly may have gathered that the case against the Beardmore find was gaining quiet but determined support within the Dominion Geological Survey and the National Museum in Ottawa.

On 28 November, Vilhjalmur Stefansson wrote Diamond Jenness, Canada's chief anthropologist at the DGS and National Museum, for advice on what he should be reading "to get the lowdown" on Curran's ideas about the Norse having reached James Bay.[36] Stefansson and Jenness were friends who corresponded regularly, despite a precarious start to their relationship. As a young, Oxford-trained anthropologist from New Zealand, Jenness had accepted a position in 1912 with the Canadian government's Canadian Arctic Expedition, which Stefansson co-commanded. Serendipity saw Stefansson remove Jenness from the doomed *Karluk*. Jenness ended up with the expedition's Southern Party, under Rudolph Anderson. Jenness feared the ship would be destroyed by ice, and he lost a close colleague, the French anthropologist Henri Beuchat, when the *Karluk* was crushed.[37]

Jenness was drawn into the fray over Stefansson's performance as co-commander of the expedition. When Stefansson published a popular account of the expedition, *The Friendly Arctic* (1921), with a one-sided rendering of its controversies, Jenness wrote a critical review for the journal *Science*.[38] He also objected to Stefansson's 1912 claims of having met "blond Eskimos" in Coronation Gulf. Jenness had lived with these very people during his time with the Southern Party, and, in 1921, he published in *American Anthropologist* a firm rebuttal of the idea that European (perhaps Norse) genes had resulted in a people of mixed ethnicity.[39]

Stefansson and Jenness managed to repair and maintain a long friendship. During the early years of the Beardmore controversy, Stefansson was writing Jenness regularly for his advice on matters of Arctic anthropology. When Stefansson asked for resources on Curran's ideas about the Norse reaching James Bay, Jenness went straight to the heart of the matter – which, to his mind, was the Beardmore find. Jenness notified Stefansson on 29 November that he had passed his inquiry along to the DGS geologist, T.L. Tanton, "[who] has kept a complete file of the published statements concerning the Norse find, and knows personally one or two of the principals. It may be several days before he is able to write you, but I think you will find his letter interesting. Apart from these finds on Lake Superior I know of no evidence that the Norsemen ever reached James Bay other than what one can conclude from a critical examination of the old sagas."[40]

Jenness's reply indicated that Tanton was the point man in critically examining the Beardmore find inside the DGS and the National Museum. Jenness would not shy away from engaging directly with key figures in the controversy, but it was to his institutional and professional advantage that a department geologist had taken such an ardent interest. By deferring to Tanton (and providing whatever support he required), Jenness avoided a direct confrontation between the anthropology division of the DGS and the National Museum, on the one side, and the archaeology division of the ROM and the anthropology department of the University of Toronto, on the other – and between himself and Currelly and McIlwraith. The National Museum and the ROM collaborated in exchanges of collection items, and Jenness had enjoyed a close relationship with McIlwraith as the editor of the stillborn published version of his dissertation. (Whether Jenness and McIlwraith ever discussed the Beardmore relics is unknown.)

Tanton's six-page letter to Stefansson of 6 December does not survive, but Stefansson found it "long and informative."[41] The government geologist would have touched on the same points he would make in a letter to James Hansen in early 1939 and in a memo he wrote for Julian Cross on 7 February, after Hansen recommended Tanton speak with the Port Arthur mining engineer.[42] Tanton remained struck by what he had learned from Teddy Elliott in the autumn of 1936: Dodd had told Elliott he found the sword firmly embedded in the schist of the Keewatin zone

– a ridiculous scenario. Tanton recognized that Dodd had since changed his story to indicate that the relics had been uncovered by blasting in gravel. Tanton also recognized that the discovery timing was key to any investigation. He was aware that, in August 1936, Dodd had told Elliott he discovered the relics on 24 May 1933, and he thought the recent public statements that the discovery was in May 1931 were meant to predate the find to Dodd's occupancy of Hansen's home at 33 Machar. (Tanton did not yet know of the efforts to further backdate the discovery to 1930.) Tanton suspected that Dodd had always known the relics were Norse, regardless of what he had said about French and Indians, and that he had directed everyone towards recognizing this.

Tanton possessed a peerless sense of the landscape, having mapped the country that included Dodd's middle claim. As he would note for Julian Cross, Norsemen approaching from the north would have first encountered the large Sturgeon River system, which flowed almost parallel to the Blackwater River and was a much better canoe route. Tanton thought it "highly improbable" that any European travellers from Hudson Bay would end up in the vicinity of Beardmore.[43]

Tanton considered it significant that Bloch's father was a Norwegian painter of scenes showing Vikings in armour, and he found Hansen's version of events plausible. The geologist's emergence as a critical investigator of Dodd's story reinvigorated Hansen's insistence that Dodd had stolen the relics he received from Bloch, just as Hansen was trying to find a face-saving exit from the controversy. Hansen made a wandering reply on 26 December to a Tanton enquiry of 5 December, saying he had possessed five relics from Bloch but only saw four (counting both pieces of the sword) in the photograph that appeared in newspapers in October. They all seemed to be the same as those he had possessed, except for one.[44] Hansen did not say which one that was, but it was probably the so-called shield handle. Hansen asked Tanton how the relics could have been in the ground since 1000 and be in such good condition – which they were not, but it is possible that they were in much better condition before the museum subjected them to aggressive galvanic action. The unlikelihood of their survival in the wet ground of the Beardmore discovery site was an argument Tanton would make. Hansen thought that the ROM should send the relics to him so that he could inspect them, "as I am the only one and the wife that could say if they were the ones I had." An inveterate collector, Hansen also said he had "some relics from the stone age which I think are very important to see." Jenness then wrote Hansen himself, to follow up on the "stone age" relics.[45]

If Dodd found Bloch's relics in Hansen's house, Tanton reasoned, then Dodd would have known that their value lay in their antiquity, which he could best prove by satisfying the common knowledge that items of antiquity tended to be dug out of the ground. That January Tanton proposed to Julian Cross the following: "Where could Dodd report a discovery during excavation better than on his Beardmore claim? There was opportunity for him to visit the claims, to plant the relics and later uncover them."[46]

Tanton's determination to expose the hoax was complicated by the fact that the victim, the ROM, was buttressing Dodd's innocence. Others may have been questioning the Beardmore provenance, but Tanton was becoming as central to the cause of revealing a hoax as were Jim Curran, C.T. Currelly, and T.F. McIlwraith to defending Dodd's discovery.

As well as writing Diamond Jenness to ask his opinion of Jim Curran's ideas, Vilhjalmur Stefansson, on 6 December, sent a batch of Curran's articles to A.W. Brøgger, inviting the Oslo museum director's opinion.[47] Stefansson told Curran that Brøgger was "one of the most active and imaginative students of the Viking period."[48] It would have been more accurate to call Brøgger, who had pronounced the Kensington stone and Beardmore relics hoaxes in the Norwegian press, one of the most vehement critics of claims for Norse relics in North America. Stefansson was cultivating and milking contacts on all sides of the debate. It would have been difficult for anyone corresponding with him to be certain exactly who or what he was supporting.

On 8 December, Stefansson informed Brøgger he had received the letter from Tanton, "one of the most thorough students of the Beardmore situation."[49] Stefansson briefly reviewed the evidence that the relics originated with John Bloch via a loan by James Hansen, and he acknowledged Carl Sorensen's scepticism. He thought Brøgger might be able to help by tracing members of Bloch's family, possibly in Norway, to find out if the relics were known to them. Stefansson sent Sorensen a carbon copy of his letter to Brøgger, hoping the vice-consul would assist, whatever he thought of Hansen's story.

As Stefansson waited for replies from Brøgger and Sorensen, Jenness received a request from Jim Curran to render an opinion on the Beardmore find. As Canada's chief anthropologist, Jenness's job included fielding every sort of inquiry from the public on Indigenous cultures and the prehistory of the nation. It was only a matter of time before Curran turned to him for help with his pursuit of Norse relics in the Great Lakes.[50]

"I am really not qualified to express an opinion on your Beardmore discovery," Jenness began his 21 December reply, which was typical: he was wont to downplay his expertise in archaeology, despite having performed some first-class work in the western Arctic.[51]

It has two sides: first, the authenticity of the find; and, second, its interpretation in relation to Norse voyages. My sympathies lie with you and with the Royal Ontario Museum; I should be delighted to see all your claims in the matter confirmed. Theoretically, however, it seems to me very improbable that Norse sailors should have directed their course to the bottom of James Bay, then abandoned their boats, which were impracticable for rivers, and travelled overland to Beardmore, which does not lie on any canoe route; and I should like stronger evidence than is yet forthcoming. But I am not an authority on the Norsemen and their voyages, and sometimes it is the seemingly impossible that proves to be true.

Jenness was being politely dissuasive, but he did not suggest that Curran touch base with Tanton.

On 3 January 1939, A.W. Brøgger replied to Stefansson, assuring him he already knew a "great deal" about the Beardmore find.[52] C.T. Currelly may not have been interested in hearing what Brøgger thought of Eddy Dodd's relics, but Vilhjalmur Stefansson was determined to bring the expert on Viking weapons and culture into a debate he regarded as unresolved.

16

"He Is a Damned Liar"

Through late 1938 and early 1939, Jim Curran and the Thunder Bay investigation committee continued to assemble evidence for Eddy Dodd's discovery. Curran also published the remainder of his series of twenty-six newspaper articles about his vision of Vinland, which concluded in late February. Along the way, Curran continued to hear from Dodd and his partner, Fletcher Gill.

Dodd and Gill hoped they could sell the rights to their mining claim, to capitalize on its historic nature. They thought the Canadian or Norwegian governments should purchase it as a historic site and otherwise pressed Curran on the idea of a Hollywood film. Dodd strove to exercise some control over his story, without quite understanding how to monetize it. He first broached the idea of a feature film in an undated letter Curran received on 2 November 1938, and he returned to the theme on 24 November: "Don't you think you should get Hollywood interested in the Place two take the movies and Talkies of the Place and you could be in on it your self and for a Picture of a place like that would be well worth seeing what do you think, and we could obtain so mutch Royalty on the same, and if any books be written on the same so don't lett any one steal our Rights."[1]

With little railway work available out of Port Arthur, Dodd let Curran know on 3 December 1938 that he was going to try his luck with the CNR terminal in Melville, Saskatchewan. Curran could notify his wife Ellen if "the Government or the Historical socity [sic]" had any interest in the Beardmore claim.[2] Dodd's Melville sojourn landed him only a week of work. "I think I will have to go and dig up some more Relics," he informed Curran in mid-December. "But I will make shure they will not get them for nothing. I think I can get more [money] from the United states if I get any more ... I think I will get down two [sic] the Property and take a case of dynamite and loosening up the soil around the spot I may get quiet [sic] a few more it might start some thing so as two [sic] get some one Interested in it we might be able too [sic] sell a few claims."[3] To anyone concerned that Dodd had been capable of salting the middle claim with his earlier finds, this would have been an alarming letter.

There is no indication that Dodd ever headed to the middle claim in the dead of winter with a case of dynamite to shake out a few more Norse relics, but his letter raised the question of where he would have found the items necessary for the salting. While metallurgy tests would conclude the three additional pieces found in September 1937 and September 1938 and turned in by Dodd in October 1938 were likely fragments of the sword, Dodd could have had additional items that belonged to John Bloch, given that James Hansen was insisting to T.L. Tanton there had been five objects, not four.

Without any railway work available, Eddy Dodd, with Fletcher Gill's help, was focused on finding Curran more relics.[4] In early January, Gill was making a wooden model of the pick-like object that Dodd claimed to have found and then lost on the property to send to Curran.[5] (Evidently this was nothing more than a pick that Dodd had liberated from Hansen or Eli Ragotte.) Dodd was tracking down Joseph G. Molinski, who operated a sawmill in Rossport on the north shore of Lake Superior. When the Beardmore controversy erupted in the local press the previous winter, Molinski wrote a letter to the *Daily News-Chronicle*, reporting he had found a sword while skidding logs on Copper Island a few years earlier.[6] Molinski wrote Dodd on 16 January to confirm he still had the sword, which had a blade three feet long but no handle, only a tapered tang.[7] Dodd forwarded the letter to Curran, imagining the ROM would want the sword, and he told Curran he was writing Molinksi to "put him wise so as they will not fool him the way they fooled me on the Price of the same." Dodd also noted he was sending this letter by registered mail "as I don't seem to get any word from you to any of my letters."[8] Curran was spurred to respond in a series of letters between 19 and 22 January. While none of these survive, Curran informed Dodd he had been told the Norse did not use copper for their spears. On 24 January Dodd replied: "What would you do if you Ran out of iron and found native copper would you make any spear heads out of them, according to history the Norse built boats out of oak. But if there [sic] boats got Broke up and were out do you think they might use cedar, spruce, Pine, ash, Elm, tamarack or many other wood that we have in this continent." Dodd closed by noting that he had been out of work since 8 December 1938.[9] In his 30 January 1939 article, "Mystery of the Copper Tools," Curran made precisely Dodd's argument (without giving him any credit) that the Norse would have substituted copper for iron when they lost their weapons in the new lands. Curran thus turned ancient Copper Culture items into Norse relics.

As for the Rossport sword, Curran got in touch with Molinski, who reported that several people had expressed interest in buying it, including someone in Port Arthur, which may have been an overstatement of Dodd's interest.[10] The prospective purchasers all thought it was Norse, but for Molinski's part: "personally I don't think it is." Molinski had found a series of letters on the blade and a number, 1701, that was possibly a date. He agreed to ship the sword to Curran so that the latter could send it to the ROM for preservation. Curran thought it was a French rapier, but he forwarded it to C.T. Currelly anyway.[11] The museum shipped it back to Molinski, untreated. Currelly explained that it was a late seventeenth-century rapier, probably French but possibly English. "We regret being unable to clean the blade for you, but our offer to clean iron finds by the electric method applies only to Norse material. The cost of cleaning is much too high to permit its use with objects of very small value."[12]

Currelly's letter captured perfectly his narrow view of the material culture of Canada's colonial period. A sword of this date could have been associated with Pierre-Esprit Radisson and Médard Chouart, Sieur des Groseilliers, or the French trading efforts of the Sieur de Cadillac, yet to Currelly it was a near-valueless object, not worth cleaning, let alone acquiring. To Currelly, Canadian history was still British history, and English Canadian historians as a whole were slow to come to grips with the French fact of the nation's history.[13] "Only the most stubborn and insular patriotism would reject the rich legacy of romance bequeathed by the pioneers of New France," Percy J. Robinson had groused in his history of the French regime in the province in 1933.[14] Six years later, Currelly had no interest in preserving that rich legacy in the province's museum. Before the Conquest of Quebec, only the Norse in Canada mattered because it was they who captured the Gothicist spirit of adventure that the Normans had brought to Britain with the 1066 conquest.

On 5 January 1939, the Norwegian vice-consul Carl Sorensen took Vilhjalmur Stefansson's advice and wrote A.W. Brøgger in Oslo on what he knew about John Bloch.[15] He revisited what he had already stated in affidavits and in the press, with one correction. "John Bloch was not a lieutenant, he told me he was a cadet for one year; he never seemed to get started in something worth while." Writing to a fellow Norwegian, Sorensen thus was less effusive about "Lieutenant" Bloch's upstanding nature. Sorensen said he agreed with

Jim Curran that the Vikings could have reached Lake Superior from Hudson Bay, and he enclosed a map of the Beardmore area, probably the Geological Survey's 312A based on T.L. Tanton's fieldwork. In closing he noted: "Dr. Tanton has I believe covered that part of the country thoroughly as Government Minerologist [sic], and is a man of considerable standing in Canada."

Brøgger let Stefansson know on 23 January that he had heard from Sorensen.[16] The vice-consul's report did not seem "particularly important and anyhow it is difficult to judge the case until I know more of the entire discovery history." Brøgger asked Stefansson to send him a copy of the letter from Tanton that he had mentioned, along with anything the ROM had published. Brøgger confessed that he was "extremely skeptical," but he assured Stefansson that this should not prevent him from treating the Beardmore case without prejudice, if all the evidence could be obtained.

Brøgger's attitude was a seeming retreat from his public declaration that the find was a hoax. On 3 February Stefansson was pleased to hear that "in spite of the circumstances which reasonably promote skepticism you [Brøgger] are nevertheless wanting to study thoroughly and with an open mind the Beardmore problem."[17] He sent Brøgger the requested copy of Tanton's 6 December letter. "This is about as strong a case as I have seen of those presented against the good faith of the central figures in the Beardmore situation," Stefansson advised. "It seems conclusive, so far as it goes." But he warned Brøgger that there was much support for the find among leading figures. At the recent annual meeting of the American Anthropological Association in New York, 27 to 30 December, Stefansson had spoken with several Canadian and American anthropologists

who have made a specialty of the region between Hudson Bay and Lake Superior and most of them are inclined to believe in the good faith of the chief Beardmore figures, considering that there is a strong probability that the finds were made approximately as stated by Dodd. Nearly quite all these students, however, consider weak [he crossed out "between weak and ridiculous"] those arguments of Mr. Curran which are based on Cree linguistics and other linguistic sources; and they are of the opinion, too, that his knowledge of the Old Norse sources is amateurish. But most of them close by saying that we must not be distracted by the enthusiasm of poor linguistic scholarship of Curran from the main problem of whether the relics were actually found substantially as stated by Mr. Dodd. For this part most of the anthropologists felt Curran had made out a good case.

Stefansson also wanted Brøgger to be aware that most supporters of the Beardmore find were

> partly swayed by their growing confidence in the authenticity of the Kensington stone. As a simple matter of counting noses, you will find that among anthropologists (including archaeologists), geologists, and historians, the Kensington Stone is steadily winning converts. There has even been some weakening among the linguists, nearly all of whom at first agreed with the contemptuous views expressed by Professor Flom[18] ... All the more because of the swing towards favoring the Kensington authenticity it becomes desperately important to investigate thoroughly, and while most of the protagonists are still living, every angle of the Beardmore problem.

Given the postwar enthusiasm some leading archaeologists would show for the Kensington stone, Stefansson's anecdotal report may have been an accurate reflection of opinions, although it would be unwise to attribute any such shift to Stefansson's friend, Diamond Jenness, who was elected president of the American Anthropological Association at the New York meeting. But it may be more accurate to consider Stefansson's letter to Brøgger a reflection of what Stefansson thought. Stefansson considered it likely that the Norse ventured into Hudson Bay and he wanted to take the Kensington stone seriously, and, despite his misgivings, he had not given up on the Beardmore find as authentic. His letter to Brøgger may have been an attempt to manufacture scholarly consent. Stefansson promised to keep Brøgger informed of "any progress in these studies which comes to my attention," but his 3 February letter is the last surviving item of correspondence between them. The Oslo expert's opinions of the Kensington stone and the Beardmore relics were not about to bend, much less break.

In early 1939, Judge Alexander McComber made a final push to secure all the affidavits in support of Eddy Dodd's find that Jim Curran desired. Harry Scott, a retired railway baggage handler in Port Arthur, provided one on 24 January. He was most certainly the man named "Scott" about whom Ellen and Joseph Dodd had told Thomas McIlwraith the previous October; they had said Scott was present when James Hansen met Eddy Dodd on the street and told him his own relics weren't the Beardmore ones. Vague in his recollections, Scott said nothing about this meeting. He instead recalled examining three rusty metal objects at Dodd's house at 296 Wilson, but he couldn't remember what they looked like or whether Dodd had told him where he had found them.[19]

On 3 February, Eddy Dodd, his son Walter, and William Feltham all met at Fletcher Gill's house and walked with Gill to the Whalen Building in Port Arthur, where they read their prepared affidavits in the presence of lawyer R. Lloyd Seaman and signed them accordingly.[20] An affidavit was also prepared for Patrick Bohan in Dorion, and Gill mailed it to him for his signature.

William Feltham had already written a letter for the ROM in May 1938 at John Jacob's request. Feltham now told a similar story. He had stayed at Dodd's mining camp overnight as he considered staking a neighbouring claim and, while there, saw on the banked earth around the camp "an old sword in two pieces and what looked like the handle of a shield with three prongs, and an axe head of some sort about 9 or 10 inches long. It was rough made. The sword was a rusted skeleton of what it had been. I thought the objects very old. The sword had some kind of guard as I remember it. It was about 3 feet long. I am positive it was in May or June, 1930. I fish in the spring but not before the end of May, but couldn't get a permit that year."[21]

Curran had requested a fresh affidavit from Eddy Dodd in December. Dodd had balked: "I don't understand you about avidaits as I gave McComber my story long ago and also ontario museum so I don't quite understand what else you want."[22] But Curran was insistent. He wanted an affidavit that incorporated all the key elements of Dodd's discovery story as Curran had related them in his newspaper articles the previous autumn, along with a firm statement about the 1930 discovery. Dodd's earlier statement to Judge McComber (no longer extant) in October 1938 was likely unsatisfactory because he probably stuck to the standard discovery date of 24 May 1931. Judge McComber agreed to secure a new, consolidated Dodd affidavit for Curran, and Gill took care of organizing it.[23] Because of its importance to the authenticity case, most of the affidavit is worth quoting.[24]

About the end of May, 1930, I sank a trench on the claim contiguous to a quartz vein in a 12-foot dike of rock to see if the vein continued out from the dike. My son Walter, then 14 years of age, was with me at the time. I first dug about 2 ½ feet of overburden close to the dike and as I then saw the vein continued out from the dike I blasted the rock for two or three feet down. Standing in the hole thus made I loosened the overburden out from the trench with a stick and further loosened it with some dynamite. While shovelling out this loosened earth to lengthen the trench, my shovel struck some pieces of old iron, which were thrown out on top of the dump. I paid no attention to these scraps at the time, merely wondering if they were Indian relics.

A Ukrainian youth unknown to me, who had come along the C.N.R. track looking for work, asked me for food. I gave him 50c and his meals for a day's work. He was at the trench when I dug out the relics. He never told me his name. The lad was hungry and that was the reason I gave him a little work.

The relics lay on the dump for a day or two and were carried to the cabin on the claim where they lay on the banking of the cabin till I left for Port Arthur in a few days. I showed these to many people but nobody could tell me what they were. Finally in 1936 I think it was, Dr. C. T. Currelly of the Royal Ontario Museum said they were the armor of a Norseman of the 11th century. The pieces were a sword, which broke in two as I was taking it out of the ground, a Norse axe, and the handle of a shield. I had seen in the trench what looked like a shallow bowl but this shattered when my spade touched it. Dr. Currelly told me when I remembered about this bowl during questioning after the sale that it was "the boss of a shield." Dr. MacIlwraith [sic] of the Ontario Museum found a small piece of the supposed "boss" when he visited the trench in the fall of 1937. I sold the relics to Dr. Currelly for $500 and they are now at the Royal Ontario Museum. In September, 1938, J. W. Curran of the Soo and Dr. C. E. Eakins of Port Arthur, were at the trench with me when another piece of the "boss" was found. This was taken to Dr. Currelly by J. W. Curran.

While the relics were at my cabin, P. J. Bohan, C.N.R. section man at Dorion[25] saw them, also Wm. Feltham.

I took the relics to my home at 296 Wilson Street, Port Arthur, in May or June 1930, and they were never out of my possession till I sold them to Dr. Currelly.

Dodd's admission that he showed the relics to "many people" at least left room for Jacob and Lougheed in the discovery narrative, although Dodd insisted no one could tell him what the relics were. Crediting Currelly with identifying them as Norse relics was contradicted by Ned Burwash's February 1934 letter, which made it clear that Dodd then knew the relics were Norse. But no one interested in the Beardmore provenance (other than Currelly) knew about Burwash's letter.

For the first time, Eddy's son Walter was also heard from on the discovery. His affidavit was brief:[26]

> I was with my father, James Edward Dodd, about May 24, 1930, when he found some old iron pieces in a trench he was digging on the claim 48TB4895, which has since been restaked as TB26737. I saw the pieces thrown out on the dump. I have read my father's affidavit and can testify to its correctness. The old iron pieces looked like a broken sword, an axe and another piece of iron. They were taken to our cabin on the claim, and afterwards taken to our home at 296 Wilson Street, Port Arthur. They were always in my father's possession and when he moved he took them with him. He sold them to Dr. Currelly.

Fletcher Gill's affidavit was as brief as Walter Dodd's.[27] It was assuredly the same statement he had given to McComber the previous autumn, now typed up and ready for signature. Gill recalled receiving the letter from Dodd mentioning some sort of Indian graveyard "some time during the summer of 1931."

Considering that Gill, Eddy Dodd, Walter Dodd, and William Feltham – all involved in the middle claim the previous autumn – swore their affidavits in a single visit to a lawyer's office organized by Gill, it is amazing that Gill failed to corroborate his partner Dodd's account on its most essential element: that the discovery was made in the spring of 1930. But the problem was only compounded by the affidavit Gill mailed on 4 February to Bohan for signing, which Bohan obligingly did before a justice of the peace in Dorion on 7 February. Bohan, too, appears to have signed essentially the same statement he had given to McComber on 20 October, in which he claimed to have checked his CNR employment records and determined that he had seen the sword (but no other relics) on a visit to Dodd's camp "between the 15th of May and the 1st of July, 1931" when he was stationed at Warneford.[28]

Bohan's affidavit (backed by Gill) threw the entire effort to backdate Dodd's discovery to 1930 into disarray. One can only conclude that Dodd, who was tired (and wary) of making signed statements, had not impressed upon his good friend Bohan the importance of *not* documenting his own presence at Warneford in the spring of 1931. Judge McComber probably had no idea of any backdating scheme (and would never have tolerated one) and had drawn up for Bohan's signature an affidavit based on his statement the previous October. Gill seemed as oblivious as ever. It was as if, on 3 February, two different affidavit plans were being carried out among the members of the same small group on their visit to the Whalen Building. Only a few months later would Gill realize the trouble his own affidavit caused and try to craft a new narrative for himself and the discovery.

On 6 February, James Hansen paid Judge McComber a visit. He respected the judge. As he would shortly explain to T.L. Tanton: "I have known him and done business with him for many years and is a man I would trust among a hundred."[29] Hansen had promised Jim Curran's investigative committee the previous autumn that if he could find the promissory notes for the John Bloch loan, he would show them. He had at last found the notes – or had decided to find them, after Tanton contacted him in December and treated his widely discredited story as believable.

In a letter of 10 January, Hansen had already reviewed for Tanton the story of his dealings with Bloch and his loss of the relics.[30] In addition to the promissory notes, Hansen now showed Judge McComber Tanton's letter in reply, which made clear the geologist's belief that a hoax had been perpetrated. Judge McComber, in turn, allowed Hansen to examine affidavits he had gathered in support of Dodd's story. Hansen agreed to go over his own story, and, as he took down Hansen's words, Judge McComber considered them a formal statement. Hansen's letter to Tanton and his statement to Judge McComber can be treated as a single recounting of his story.[31] His claim emerged in a more coherent, consistent narrative.

For reasons unknown (and unstated by Hansen), Bloch had needed money. Hansen told Tanton that Bloch wanted to sell him the relics for twenty-five dollars, but they settled on a loan of thirty dollars, with the relics pledged as security, just as Judge McComber had suspected. Now that Hansen had found the promissory notes, the details were slightly adjusted. To begin, the loan was from the Imperial Bank of Canada in Port Arthur to Bloch, with Hansen's serving as Bloch's guarantor. In this way, Hansen did not have to advance Bloch any of his own money but would be out of pocket if the latter failed to retire the debt. Thus, Hansen had taken the relics as personal collateral. Bloch's promissory note for the bank loan made no mention of collateral, but that was not surprising as Hansen wasn't the one lending the money. The note did prove that

Hansen as guarantor had been involved in a Bloch debt, contrary to assertions from members of the Norwegian community that no debt agreement could have existed between them.

On 16 April 1928, Bloch borrowed forty-five dollars and agreed to pay the bank back within eighteen days. Seventeen days later, on 3 May, Bloch paid back ten dollars and promised to retire the remaining thirty-five dollars by 15 May. Bloch failed to settle the outstanding balance, which the bank charged to Hansen's account.

Judge McComber did not have all the evidentiary pieces – no one did. For example, Judge McComber knew that John Bloch had skipped on his Ruttan Building rent on 22 November 1927. But the judge did not know that Os Hartvik had told John Jacob he had boarded with James Hansen. Hartvik had married Agnes Louise Carlson on 4 September 1927.[32] The newlywed Hartvik thus probably moved out of Hansen's home at 33 Machar, allowing Bloch to move in, doing jobs for Hansen that included excavating the cellar. The judge now had proof that Bloch had left Hansen on the hook for an unpaid bank debt in May 1928. Regardless of how insistent members of the Norwegian community were about Bloch's fine character, he had left a trail of money woes in Port Arthur over a short period before leaving town for Winnipeg.

Hansen also shared with Tanton critical details about Bloch's explanation of where he got the relics. At first, Bloch "said he had found [the relics] in Canada and I told him if he had he had made his fortune. But as far as I can remember that was only a joke on me as he brought them from Norway and also said it was unlegal to take such things out of the country." Hansen's recollection explained why no one else in the Norwegian community had ever heard of the relics: Bloch knew when he immigrated to Canada that, since Norway gained its independence in 1905, it had been illegal to remove cultural materials without an export permit. He would have been loath to talk about them, above all to the vice-consul, Carl Sorensen, and Sorensen's circle of friends. Hansen recalled Bloch's saying that his father was an artist. "I do think it was either his father or some other relations that had found them. He was always saying to me that he was [a] spoiled boy of a wealthy family with two sisters."[33]

As for how the relics found their way into Dodd's hands, Hansen explained to Tanton and Judge McComber that he had owned neighbouring properties on Machar Avenue. Dodd had signed a lease for 37 Machar Avenue on 23 June 1931. Hansen was living next door, at 33 Machar, and after a few months decided to move into an upstairs apartment in a home he had remodelled about one mile away, at 240 St. James, where he would live for the remainder of his life. Hansen did not go into the details, but he had bought the St James property in 1928 and had spent considerably on renovations, which included adding three garages and converting the single-family home into upper and lower units.[34] As the apartment lacked space, Hansen left some of his belongings behind at the vacated 33 Machar; the relics were on a shelf in the basement.[35] In September 1931, Dodd moved into 33 Machar, and Hansen allowed him to continue as a tenant under the terms for 37 Machar without issuing a new lease. "Not knowing Dodds personally and not believing what other people told me I soon found out I had made a mistake," he told Tanton.

On a return visit to 33 Machar, Hansen found Dodd's children, who ranged from about eleven to thirteen, playing with his walking stick. He had stored it on the back porch, which was padlocked, with the only key in his possession. Disturbed, Hansen started removing his belongings from the property, visiting repeatedly after the working day. He could not recall precisely when this was. It might have been the same autumn in which Dodd moved in or the following spring. In the basement, he could not find his fishing tackle or a grindstone – or Bloch's relics.

On a subsequent visit, Hansen found Dodd with Eli Ragotte, who was boarding with him. "I told them I had missed the relics. I also had a box in the basement in which I used to throw pieces of old iron for future use. Dodd said he had thrown all these things in the ashes, as he thought they were all the same thing, that is, that the relics were part of the iron scraps. I didn't examine the ashes, but I told him he had better find these relics, and that I would hold him responsible, as they were valuable." Hansen recalled Ragotte "kicking amongst the ashes, and I think one piece was found. I don't know what piece it was. I left it there, and I told them he had better find the rest. He said he would look for the other pieces. I never got the piece that was kicked up by Ragotte out of the ashes."

Hansen said Dodd moved out of 33 Machar to a home on South Algoma before the terms of the original 37 Machar lease had expired – probably three months early – leaving him with a loss. "I billed Dodd several times for this, and I am going to sue him." As for his fishing tackle, Hansen asked about it several times, and Dodd said Ragotte must have it. Hansen then met Ragotte at the Prince Arthur Hotel, after Dodd had moved out of 33 Machar. "Dodd claims you stole my fishing tackle," Hansen said. Ragotte replied, "He is a damned liar," and added, "Dodd has your relics." Ragotte promised Hansen he would make an affidavit to that effect. "Ragotte and

Dodd had locked horns about something," Hansen said. "Ragotte claimed that Dodd owed him some money and that Dodd had kept his trunk."

Hansen's story, while more coherent than what had been reported to date, left Judge McComber perplexed. He still could not understand why, if Hansen already knew the relics were valuable, he would have left them behind when he moved out of 33 Machar. And why did Hansen not take with him the one piece Ragotte kicked out of the ashes? Regardless, McComber thought Hansen's story important enough to share in detail with Curran in a letter the following day.[36] He further reported that Hansen refused to provide the affidavit Curran desired, which would say the relics he received from Bloch were not the ones that belonged to Dodd. Hansen first needed to examine the ones in the ROM, as he had repeatedly insisted. Hansen suggested that either he should be paid his expenses (as Ragotte had been) to travel to Toronto or the museum should send the relics to Port Arthur (as Hansen had also proposed to Tanton). Curran would report none of this in his forthcoming book.

There was a surprise for Judge McComber when Hansen showed him the letter he had received from Tanton. Julian Cross's brother, the machinist William (as McComber related to Curran), "visited the dump on Dodd's claim and found what he supposed to be part of a relic, and he is inclined to accept Dodd's story." McComber confessed to Curran: "This is the first I have heard of [William] Cross visiting the property and making any discovery. Have you heard anything of this?" Curran wrote in the margin "no." Whatever the truth to William Cross's recollection, Judge McComber now understood an enterprising, respected, and disbelieving DGS geologist was excavating evidence right in his judicial backyard.

Judge McComber met with Eddy Dodd soon after Hansen's visit and showed him Hansen's statement. Dodd "says they are all lies," the judge reported to Curran.[37] Judge McComber had also seen an item in the latest *Toronto Star* announcing that Curran would soon publish a book version of his researches, tentatively titled *The Tragic Story of Vinland*. "I will want a copy of this, so please put me down for a subscription." His relationship with Curran remained warm and supportive, but McComber's confidence that the Beardmore provenance was a closed case was beginning to waver, if it had ever solidified. Curran himself was aware that significant loose ends remained, writing in the margin of McComber's letter that no replies had been received from letters to John Jacob and Eli Ragotte. But C.T. Currelly had no such qualms. He was about to pronounce the provenance of the relics settled in the pages of the *Canadian Historical Review*.

Doctor Currelly Publishes

On 27 January 1939, twelve days after editor George Brown's stated deadline for materials for the March issue of the *Canadian Historical Review*, Ethlyn Greenaway informed Brown that an article on the Beardmore find was on the way from C.T. Currelly, who, she explained, had been down with the flu. Currelly expected Brown to publish it in the coming issue.[1] That Currelly got his way spoke volumes about his authority.

Currelly was still planning something larger in the museum's *Bulletin*. In early February, he jotted a note to Hjalmar Holand: "In a couple of weeks I hope we shall have a bulletin out and give all the information we have. Find 24 May '30 Inspector of Fisheries & Game saw print on rock in July of same year."[2] On 22 February, Currelly informed Frank Johnson, the Phillips Academy's curator of American archaeology, that the *Bulletin* "was unfortunately delayed, but it will be out in a few weeks" and promised to send him a copy. "We have made the most careful investigations regarding the find," he assured Johnson, "and I have not the slightest doubt the weapons mark the burial of a Viking in northern Ontario about the year 1000."[3] No *Bulletin* appeared. Currelly was increasingly gambling his reputation, and that of the Royal Ontario Museum of Archaeology, on unequivocal assurances.

Currelly was pursuing his publishing plans despite persistent doubts about Dodd's find among his correspondents. G.R.F. Prowse was not letting up. He informed Currelly on 23 January that a Danish friend in Winnipeg, Knut (or Knud) Scheel, had just told him that John Bloch "knew Dodd."[4] Further, Bloch "was a very crooked gambler, came on here when it was too hot for him in Port Arthur and had to skip from here to Vancouver where he died." Also, Scheel did not believe the relics could have survived all those years in a burial at Beardmore, unlike relics buried in proper graves in Norway: "he suggests Bloch brought them over."

"I think we have run down every line of approach," Currelly advised Prowse on 13 February.[5] There was "no question" the relics had been found by Dodd at his mining claim. "By extraordinary good fortune, a man of extremely good repute happened along and saw them lying on the edge of where Mr. Dodd was digging." This outstanding citizen was presumably William Feltham, whose character Jacob had praised. In addition to having provided a letter to the ROM in support of a 1930 discovery, Feltham had just sworn out a similar affidavit for Curran. But, as Feltham had been employed by Dodd at the mining claim the previous autumn (which Currelly probably did not know), he was hardly a disinterested witness.

Currelly continued: "More important still, a government servant [Jacob], who is a very accurate observer of birds, saw the rust stain on the rock where the sword had been lying." But Dodd had just signed an affidavit for Curran in which he had again failed to make any mention of a rust stain, or of Jacob. For that matter, Dodd had failed to make any mention of the birch tree that supposedly had to be dynamited clear, thus exposing the relics. In the oddly secretive state of relations between the museum and Curran, Currelly doubtless knew nothing about what Dodd had attested to the newspaper publisher. Currelly assured Prowse the museum had "no hesitation" about the truth to claims that Bloch was the source of the relics. Scheel's perspective on Bloch's character "does not quite agree with the opinion of the Port Arthur Norwegians who knew him, but the point is that his great friend [Sorensen], to whom he showed all his treasures, is positive that he at no time owned any Viking ones." Currelly reiterated that Dodd did not move into 33 Machar until eighteen months after he had been showing the weapons "to many people."

Prowse's doubts and criticisms persisted. "I do not think he is wise to write in such a flamboyant style," Prowse wrote to Currelly on 21 February about Curran's newspaper series.[6] "Mr. Curran is a great missionary for the north country," Currelly replied, "and everything he does must be looked on in the light of an evangelist who is trying to boom the north country. He has been a most useful man, and the future is going to owe him a great deal. He has got the north country talked about more than any other five men in existence."[7]

Prowse was not finished. The random weapons that were the supposed proof of an extended Norse presence around the Great Lakes were the sort of things that collectors treasured and that immigrants brought with them as heirlooms or mementos of the old country, and they could easily be planted. Prowse quite reasonably wanted to see a more prosaic type of evidence for a prolonged period of settlement: trash, in the form of kitchen middens.[8] At this time, coincidentally, Hjalmar Holand shared with Jim Curran his puzzlement that no archaeological fieldwork was planned at the Beardmore site. Dodd after all had told the press in January 1938 that the site could be rich in material – "almost anything might be buried under it," Dodd had assured Beamish – and that further investigations were planned.⁹ Holand asked Curran on 13 February: "Has any thorough search been made up at Dodd's diggings for bone remains, shield parts and other things? A competent archaeologist should undertake that work. Photographs of the rust spots (from the sword and axe) should be taken."¹⁰ More pointedly, Holand asked Curran on 21 February: "Why doesn't Mr. Currelly take charge of the investigation? It should be done by a competent archaeologist. The museum, according to its official name, is the archaeological body of the Province."¹¹ But, as Currelly's 7 October 1938 letter to Frank Landon of the monuments board had made clear, Currelly insisted that any further investigation of the site would be a waste of time. No one outside the museum knew that, ten days later, Dodd had brought yet another purported artefact from the claim to the museum – something that should have mandated a proper archaeological investigation. But by avoiding any further site studies, Currelly could ensure that Dodd had no opportunities to clumsily salt the site with more "discoveries" that could discredit the initial find. So far, whenever anyone went near the site with Dodd, he managed to come up with another relic for them.

Another doubting voice reached Currelly in late February. Geologist Jack Satterly signed a note for the museum in which he contended "that a prospector, who wished to keep his name out of the case, told him that Dodds [sic] was a liar and a kleptomaniac. A brakeman informed him that Dodds had found the objects in the cellar of a house rented by Dodds, that Dodds took them and salted them in his claim, later finding them in the presence of two men. J.S. believes his informant is truthful, but of course the story reached him, the prospector, through an unknown (to us) brakeman." It sounded like Satterly's informant had been speaking with Ragotte. Currelly paid the note no mind.¹²

Currelly's exasperation with the persistent claims for the credibility of Hansen and Ragotte may be understandable, given Hansen's apparently erratic stance in the past and what had appeared to be Ragotte's complete capitulation at the museum in September 1938. But Prowse had brought forward another view of Bloch that demanded more careful consideration than Currelly was willing to give. Scheel had provided a possible explanation for Bloch's money woes: gambling debts. Scheel's further observation that Bloch knew Dodd was of potentially huge significance. According to Carl Sorensen, Bloch worked for a time at the Mariaggi Hotel, where Dodd was known to drink. Scheel had drawn a direct line between Dodd and Bloch that had nothing to do with Hansen's properties on Machar Avenue. Dodd could have acquired the relics (or *some* relics) from Bloch while living at 296 Wilson. The entire debate around when and where Dodd lived and Bloch's debt to Hansen could be a red herring. But Currelly wasn't interested. Proving Dodd got the relics directly from Bloch instead of stealing them from Hansen would not advance the museum's authenticity case.

On 28 February, Currelly wrote Curran with disquieting news.[13] A young woman had veritably stormed his office to demand a photograph of the relics for Hansen. She was Evelyn Tanton, the geologist's nineteen-year-old daughter, who was studying home economics at the University of Toronto. Not only did she demand a photograph (which Currelly apparently did not surrender) but she also announced that the proof that Hansen had loaned Bloch money had surfaced. Hansen evidently had informed her father that he had found the promissory-note documents. Currelly thought Curran should know. He was unaware that Curran had just been informed of the evidence by Judge McComber, who had been shown the notes by Hansen.

Above and beyond the news of proof for a loan involving Bloch and Hansen, Currelly now understood that the Dodd provenance case had a fresh and formidable critic in the form of an esteemed geologist. Tanton's aggressive interest, personified by his daughter's brazen demand, might have suggested the possibility of a more widespread infestation of hostility within the DGS and the National Museum. The news about the loan also came at an inconvenient time for Currelly. The March issue of CHR, which contained his Beardmore article, was going to press; editor George Brown sent him the article's final page proofs on 6 March.[14] There was fresh fuel for a fire Currelly thought he was about to extinguish.

The March 1939 issue of CHR offered readers two articles addressing the Beardmore relics. The lead article was C.T. Currelly's long-awaited statement on the Beardmore discovery. The one following it, by Stewart Wallace, was a review of scholarly efforts to determine the location of places explored and settled in the Vinland sagas.

Wallace's article was the longer one (nine pages), and it credited the Beardmore find with helping to revive interest in Viking voyages to North America. Wallace also gave due consideration to Hjalmar Holand's *The Kensington Stone*, which he found "difficult to characterize. While using the language of impartial history, he is in reality a special pleader: he reminds one of the lawyer who seeks to squeeze out of the evidence every ounce of weight he can in favour of his client. His conjectures, and even his assertions, often go far beyond established facts."[15] Wallace was "profoundly skeptical" of some of Holand's evidence for a Norse presence in North America.[16] "But it must be confessed that he builds up an impressive argument in favour of the authenticity of the Kensington rune-stone itself."[17] The Beardmore find had attracted similar doubt and suspicion, and Jim Curran "has done a valuable service in clearing up the circumstances under which they were found and their history prior to their acquisition in 1936 by the Royal Ontario Museum."[18] Wallace vowed not to engage the Beardmore authenticity question in the article. "But I venture to ask the question: Is there any valid à priori reason why the Beardmore weapons should not be genuine?"[19] He found plausible the scenario of Vikings reaching the heart of the continent via Hudson Strait. "If the Kensington rune-stone and the Beardmore sword and axe are genuine, they may have gone into Hudson bay. Then it is possible that they, or others, may have penetrated from the shores of Hudson bay to northern Ontario and to Minnesota, perhaps by way of Lake Nipigon."[20]

Currelly's article was full of gaping holes and the rounding of factual corners. Totalling fewer than fifteen hundred words and illustrated by the museum's photo of the sword, axe head, and "shield handle" as well as a map of the discovery area, the article sprinted through the details of Dodd's discovery and the museum's acquisition. Currelly began with the words "On May 24, 1930," thus unequivocally establishing the museum's new position on the discovery date.[21] The article otherwise was largely bereft of dates – in a provenance case that was inordinately reliant upon them.

Currelly depended particularly on the statements of John Jacob, who made his debut in the public record. A subtextual struggle was apparent in Currelly's description of Dodd's discovery as Currelly attempted to reconcile Dodd's account with Jacob's. As we have seen, Dodd had described dynamiting clear a large birch stump, where Jacob had described a clump of dwarf birch blown over by the wind. Currelly struck a happy compromise (without citing either source) by creating "a rotted stump surrounded by a group of young trees sprung from the roots. Birch is a very hard wood, and to cut through such a mass of tangled roots promised to be a serious undertaking. Consequently Mr. Dodd put in a considerable charge of dynamite and blew over the whole tangled clump. The big mass went over all together, and the rock which lay about three and a half feet below the surface was exposed. Lying on the rock were some pieces of iron. Mr.

Dodd threw these out and went on with his work."[22] Currelly had created a new, hybrid species of birch tree and an explosion that knocked over the clump like a blast of wind. He did not know that Dodd had just signed a new affidavit for Jim Curran that said nothing about a tree of any kind being in the way of his trenching efforts.

Currelly next had William Feltham ("a well-known man of the district") appear at the camp "a few days later" and discuss what the objects might be as well as the "great mass of trees over them."[23] But there was nothing in Feltham's written statement, provided to Jacob for the museum, about the trees, and, in any case, Currelly did not quote from it. "A little later," Dodd took the relics to Port Arthur and showed them to Aaron Lougheed, who then involved Jacob in the library research that determined they were Norse.[24] These new details in the printed record came from Jacob's chain of statements. Currelly burnished Jacob's status as an employee of "the game and fisheries service of the province of Ontario, and a brother of the late Fred Jacob who was well known in Canadian journalism."[25] Jacob, however, had not been employed by the department since 1934. Dragooning Fred Jacob into the Beardmore case, as if his repute somehow endorsed his brother's reliability, was symptomatic of Currelly's desperate effort to make John Jacob an eyewitness of the highest calibre – a man from a good family with a government job who also had a naturalist's eye for detail. "Mr. Jacob has been for a number of years in touch with the Royal Ontario Museum of Zoology," Currelly explained, "and is an extremely accurate observer of birds."[26]

Currelly continued his review of how Dodd's objects came to the museum: of how Jacob tried to send word but the message never reached him; of how "some time later" Dodd showed the relics to Burwash, who did alert him; of how Currelly wrote Dodd but never heard back and then did not follow up because "the whole thing seemed so utterly impossible"; and of how "later" O.C. Elliott saw them and sent him drawings that caused him to write Dodd and at last bring the relics into the museum's collection.

"It was obvious to me that the weapons were a set, that is, to be about 1000 A.D.," Currelly recounted of seeing them for the first time.[27] He had queried Dodd about whether there was anything lying over the "metal bar," and Dodd had replied that there was "something like a bowl that was rusted into little fragments. He had just shovelled them out. This bit of evidence was as it should have been, and since no one unacquainted with Viking things would have known of this iron boss that covered the hand on the Viking shield, I felt, therefore, that there was no question that these things had been found as was described."[28] Currelly did not report that no one *acquainted* with Viking things had ever seen a metal shield handle and that the experts he had consulted had alerted him to this incongruity. Nor did he mention that Ned Burwash had already informed him in February 1934 that Dodd was sure he had found, among other things, a Norse shield. Currelly had contradicted his own description of Dodd's discovery as he had established (relying on John Jacob) that Dodd had already performed library research that told him the relics were Norse. While Dodd's statement for the museum when he sold the relics supported the scenario of a crumbled boss positioned atop the handle, Currelly had told the *Toronto Star* in October 1938 that, in questioning Dodd when he brought the relics to the museum, Dodd had told him "there was a small metal bowl, across which lay the handle."[29] The shield, in other words, was upside down in that version of the story, with the handle exposed, which was a version that Ned Burwash would also recall hearing from Dodd.[30]

Currelly testified to his own professional caution. "As suspicion of nearly everything has to go with all archaeological work, I had been suspicious as to whether the weapons had been brought from Norway or Denmark and the Beardmore locality given to them in recent times; but the story as I have just told it dispelled this suspicion."[31] But as Dodd had just attested to Curran (which no one yet knew), Currelly had only questioned him about the shield *after* agreeing to buy the relics.

Currelly then explained how Jacob had called on him "shortly afterwards" and "gave me a written statement as to his and Mr. Lougheed's part in the matter."[32] Currelly was greatly telescoping what transpired with Jacob. Jacob's initial statement of 9 December 1936 said nothing about Aaron Lougheed, and the full statement consisted of additional typed and handwritten statements in June 1937 and the autumn of 1938. Reading between the lines, one could surmise that Currelly had neither sought nor received the corroboration of Aaron Lougheed. But the key part of Currelly's summary of Jacob's contribution was Jacob's inspection of the discovery trench: "he saw that the clump of trees had been recently turned over, and that on the rock there was a picture of the sword in iron rust, just as it had been laying."[33] Currelly then mentioned Thomas McIlwraith's visit to the site at an unstated date, when another scrap of metal was found that "could very well be a part of the boss of the shield." Later, another piece was found (Currelly did not say when or by whom), "which could also be from the thicker edge of the boss."[34] Neither item was photographed for the article, although they were included in the museum display. He said nothing about the third additional piece donated to the museum by Dodd in October 1938.

Currelly moved on to the preservation of the relics and the typology research. "Photographs of them were sent to a number of well-known Norse archaeologists, who agreed that the sword and axe could well be of the same period, and that from 900 to 1000 would be a general statement of date."[35]. He did not identify any of these experts or quote their specific assessments, including their concerns, nor did he address the fact that he had not told them that the relics had supposedly been unearthed in North America. He only mentioned that there was a similar sword and axe dated to 1000 illustrated in Thórdarson's *The Vinland Voyages*, without noting that Thórdarson (the sole expert identified) was not among the well-known Norse archaeologists he said he had consulted.

As for the controversy raised by Ragotte and Hansen, Currelly flew through the details in a paragraph without naming either man. Dodd had not moved into the house where the relics supposedly were stored until eighteen months after he discovered them, and the man who started the controversy with a story to a reporter "said he had meant it only as a joke, and signed a statement that he had never seen the things."[36]

Currelly concluded: "Now we are met with the seemingly incredible fact that a Viking was buried near Lake Nipigon."[37] This was the first time in the story Currelly referred to the find as a grave, and he made no mention of the presence or absence of an actual body. He raised the possibility the relics were acquired from the James Bay or Labrador shores by Indigenous people, but he considered it "inconceivable" that the items would have remained together if traded by them inland, much as McIlwraith had concluded.[38] Currelly noted that scholarship on the Vinland sagas had always presumed that the Vikings landed at some place on the Atlantic coast. He ignored Jim Curran's Vinland theory in observing: "It does not seem to have occurred to anyone that the Vikings might have come into Hudson bay and down to James bay, and from there southward and westward to Lake Superior, as this find suggests." As for how the Vikings might have gotten there, Currelly advised that there was "a well-known Indian trade route from James Bay to Lake Nipigon." He conceded that the most obvious route from there to Lake Superior was down the Nipigon River, but there was an "alternate way" up the Blackwater River. Relying on McIlwraith's uncited field report, Currelly asserted the relics were found close to a "short cut" that avoided an eastward loop of the Blackwater River of some seventy miles of river and rapids by using a "small, unnamed lake" – the lake that Eddy Dodd told McIlwraith was called Dodd's Lake – to reach Lake Nakina, "from which a portage leads to the headwaters of a stream flowing southward to Lake Superior."[39] The article's map of the discovery area did not show how the alleged portage connected the discovery site to Lake Superior, which lurked somewhere well south of its lower border.

The article's breezy self-confidence was vintage Currelly. Published almost two and a half years after he purchased Dodd's relics, it was remarkable for how much it did not say. The discovery cried out for a more detailed assessment, which the ROM *Bulletin* presumably would deliver. But the short, casual narrative of the CHR story would have to stand as Currelly's (and the museum's) only statement. Ethlyn Greenaway would blame the repeated failure to publish the planned edition of the *Bulletin* on a lack of funds in the fiscal year ending in June 1939, which delayed the anticipated issue until the autumn of 1939, at which time the issue was killed altogether by wartime austerity measures.[40] It was true that no *Bulletin* appeared until issue 13, in December 1945. But it was also true that, once the ROM returned to publishing after the war, no issue addressed the Beardmore relics. Currelly's unfulfilled promises of a *Bulletin*, along with his beyond-deadline confirmation of an article for the March 1939 CHR, suggest larger issues than dollars and cents.

On 1 March 1939, Jim Curran replied to C.T. Currelly's 28 February letter in which he had shared news that proof of a loan by James Hansen to John Bloch had surfaced.[41] "I don't think you have anything to worry about," Curran assured the anxious museum director. "I have a bunch of affidavits covering everything and a couple of stories regarding Hansen's manouevres which couldn't be used unless in court." Curran proposed to deliberately risk libelling Hansen in his newspaper to provoke him to file suit. The discovery process of a libel case would carry far more risk for Hansen and his statements than any signed affidavit, and it could compel him to tell the truth. "I hate to go to the expense and trouble of publishing that Hansen's claims are unjustified, but that would be the way to have a court pass on them."

Curran saw no merit in Hansen's story. "The man is, I think, irresponsible, poor fellow. Judge McComber has had long talks (fresh) with Hansen & then with Dodd. The latter says Dodd [sic; Hansen's] statements to the judge are 'all lies' … I have always felt that Bloch got some loan from Hansen, but the man has been so confused and evasive with me that I think he unproves the 'incident.' I have a hunch that I can get him to see the light first time I get up to Port Arthur." Curran also promised in a margin note that he would give Currelly "all the affidavits." If he hoped this would encourage Currelly to reciprocate with his own materials, it didn't work. Currelly had not quoted from Jacob's statements in his CHR article, and they remained sealed within the public museum. Despite his best efforts, Curran was never able to contact Jacob. The most important witness to Dodd's discovery remained a phantom even to those who believed Dodd. And perhaps the second most important witness, Aaron Lougheed – who could vouch for Jacob – had never been interviewed by anyone.

C.T. Currelly's CHR article appeared as Jim Curran was preparing the book version of his series of newspaper articles. Curran moved to tidy up the hoax controversy by securing a final affidavit from Eli Ragotte that combined in a single document what he had previously stated to Curran in Winnipeg and at the museum on September 1938.[42] In the affidavit sworn out in Winnipeg on 6 March, Ragotte asserted that, while rooming with Dodd at his house in Port Arthur prior to 1930, the two were cleaning the cellar "and I saw what looked like a rusty piece of iron on a pile of cinders, the same probably having fallen from a cellar rafter. The object looked something like a sword but it may have been something else." As for the news item in the *Winnipeg Free Press* in January 1938 in which he said that he, not Dodd, had found the relics: "I only said this to the reporter as a joke and looked on the paper report as a joke. I know nothing about the axe and shield." And as for the relics he viewed at the ROM at Curran's request: "I never saw any of them before and I am sure the sword is not the piece of iron I saw in Dodd's cellar. I signed a statement to that effect for the museum." Hansen may have come up with a more coherent story for T.L. Tanton and Judge McComber, but there was no support for it now from Ragotte, who was central to Hansen's recollection of Dodd's taking the relics from 33 Machar.

The ROM's authenticity case received a boost from George Lechler of the Detroit Institute of Arts with his article in the Spring 1939 edition of the *Art*

Quarterly. Lechler (who was also inclined to believe the Kensington stone was authentic) accepted the Beardmore find unconditionally, quoting Currelly's overreaching assurance to him regarding the archaeological integrity of the discovery site. Lechler confessed that the discovery "appeared in a region where we would have least expected it," but he nevertheless declared "the weapons now represent the oldest European documents on the American continent, and as such they deserve a place in history beside the voyages of Columbus and the Pilgrim fathers."[43] Consulting Petersen's guide, Lechler concluded the sword was early eleventh century.

C.T. Currelly's unwavering confidence in the Beardmore discovery was winning over G.R.F. Prowse, who moved on to helping figure out how the relics got there. As Prowse wrote Vilhjalmur Stefansson on 8 March, he had advised Currelly to keep the relics issue and the location of Vinland separate, and he intended to advise Jim Curran to do the same. Prowse saw no reason to move Vinland to northern Ontario. He doubted the Vikings ever reached Hudson Bay, and he opposed a suggestion from Stefansson that they might have wandered the Gulf of St Lawrence and farther south; instead, Prowse believed the Beardmore party went up the Hamilton River on the Labrador coast "and then down into James Bay and so on to Nipigon and Minnesota." This was an epic journey of almost insane determination and fortitude.[44] In reply, Stefansson noted that he, too, had told Curran to keep the issue of the Beardmore relics separate from the location of Vinland. Prowse forwarded a copy of Stefansson's letter to Currelly and annotated Stefansson's comment: "But [Curran] has paid no attention."[45]

While support for the Beardmore find was consolidating among scholars, T.L. Tanton was forging ahead in his solitary effort to expose a hoax. He was continuing to correspond with James Hansen, who wrote him twice on 10 March. Hansen promised to get him copies of the bank notes for the Bloch loan and was trying to track down Bloch's widow.[46] Hansen had comments on the shield handle; his persistent perplexity regarding its present condition was a strong indication that he had once possessed the relics. But he refused to say whether any of the museum relics were his unless he could inspect them first-hand.

Tanton decided it was time he returned to his own beginnings in the Beardmore controversy. On 21 March, he wrote Teddy Elliott to ask the schoolteacher if he had read Currelly's *CHR* article and what he thought of it.[47]

PART THREE

Doctor Tanton and Mr Elliott Investigate

For Teddy Elliott, the Beardmore discovery had become an interminable frustration. Elliott wanted to be written about *and* to write about the Beardmore find. He wanted his own role publicly recognized and to tell the story of his dealings with Eddy Dodd and share his ideas about how Vikings reached the Nipigon region. He had maintained his public silence in accordance with C.T. Currelly's wishes, only to see Philip Godsell betray his confidence and reveal the find and then have his key role in the museum's acquisition glossed over when Jim Curran proclaimed the find's authenticity. Curran acknowledged him once in his articles, as a nameless schoolteacher. Worse, when Currelly did announce the find on 6 October, he made no mention of Elliott and credited the *Toronto Star* with having first alerted him to the relics.

In late October 1938, Elliott delivered an essay on Queen's University radio describing his role in bringing the Beardmore discovery to light and endorsed its authenticity.[1] Elliott rejected a panoply of purported archaeological evidence for Norse voyagers and colonists. Only the Beardmore relics offered compelling proof, although he wavered on the Kensington stone. Elliott assured listeners that two men he declined to name (Eli Ragotte and James Hansen) who challenged Dodd's story had no credibility. "If time sustains the truth of Dodd's story (and we have no reason to believe it will not) some authorities say that this is the first, authentic evidence, of Norsemen being in America." He also placed an article in the *Kingston Whig-Standard*, advancing the idea (endorsed by Fridtjof Nansen) that the Indigenous game of lacrosse originated in the ancient Icelandic game of *knattleikr*.[2]

The autumn otherwise brought dispiriting rejections. Jim Curran cheerfully rebuffed Elliott's efforts to share his research and probably did not appreciate Elliott's unsolicited criticisms of points in his articles.[3] The *Toronto Star* rejected a Beardmore article with a form letter.[4] On 21 November 1938, he sent to Macmillan in Toronto a book proposal endorsing the Beardmore find. The rejection came so swiftly, via a standard printed card, on 24 November that an editor must not have even read his proposal.[5] Elliott's frustrations were evident when, in an almost lawyerly manner, he reminded C.T. Currelly on 24 November of the promises the museum director had made to him: "It has been difficult to maintain silence in the face of all the recent publicity re Dodd's find," he stated, not admitting to his overtures to publishers or his radio address. "I am anticipating the redemption of your promises made by letter and conversation: (1) To send a copy of the Government's report; (2) To give me a copy of a picture of the relics; and (3) To send a statement to the Kingston Whig-Standard."[6]

Currelly responded collegially, enclosing a photo of the relics.[7] "There is no need for you to maintain silence regarding your part in our acquiring them, though I should like the photograph withheld from publication for a little while." This was a strange request as the photo had already appeared in the Toronto daily press in October. Currelly advised Elliott that the official account would appear in the museum's *Bulletin*, hopefully before year-end, and confided that CHR was "very anxious to have an article." The *Bulletin* of course did not appear, and Elliott was left waiting for the public acknowledgment of his role that he kept expecting Currelly to deliver.

He decided to try again with a book proposal, submitting to Ryerson Press in February an outline for a broader work on the Norse in North America. Editor Lorne Pierce turned it down but thought Elliott might have a "small and interesting book" if he focused on Beardmore.[8] Elliott at once took up the suggestion, drafting a manuscript of about twenty-five thousand words that could be published as a pamphlet. He was nearing completion when T.L. Tanton's letter of 21 March arrived, asking him what he thought of Currelly's CHR article. It was the first Elliott knew the article existed.[9]

Elliott replied to Tanton on 1 April with his comments on Currelly's article.[10] "I do not maintain that [Currelly] is wrong in any particular instance, since he, no doubt, has had access to records that are not available to me. I do believe, however, that my comments show that he is leaving himself open to attack." Elliott was foremost perturbed by the date of discovery in the article's opening sentence: 24 May 1930. He did not know that this new date had made its debut in Curran's 10 November 1938 Empire Club address. He reiterated that, in August 1936, Dodd had told him the date was 24 May 1933. "In view of the many dates [Dodd] has committed himself to, I doubt if this particular one has any more weight in truth than the others."

"I cannot prove that the story as given me is false," Elliott continued. "Currelly, Curran, Judge McComber and Eakins are too shrewd to be taken in easily. But I think that if some one were to attempt to offer a different explanation there are enough facts to build up such a plausible story. I may try it myself just to show that it could be done." Elliott's willingness to change from a supporter to a sceptic with regard to the Beardmore find seemed remarkably mercurial, but, in his Queen's radio address the previous October, he had otherwise rejected, with sound reasoning, other purported Norse evidence in North America. At this point, the provenance problem appealed to him as an intellectual exercise. As a university debater he had learned to hone lawyerly skills by defending both the pro and the con of any position assigned to him on any subject, and Tanton's suspicions of the Beardmore relics reignited his penchant for this sort of competitive challenge.

In reply, Tanton stressed the valuable contribution Elliott had made to his understanding of the provenance case, reiterating how he had been struck by Dodd's claim to Elliott that he had broken the sword trying to extract it from the schist in which it was embedded.[11] "To any student of geology it is obviously impossible that Precambrian rocks could contain human relics." Tanton reminded Elliott that he had been sure Dodd's find was a hoax from the moment the schoolteacher had provided the details to him in 1936. Tanton wanted a full explanation for the change in the reported date of discovery as well as its circumstances. He had hoped that Curran's newspaper articles might produce convincing evidence for the find's authenticity, but "the statements, and the glaring omissions," especially with respect to Hansen's claims, "serve to confirm my tentatively formed opinion of 1936." As it happened, one of the criticisms of the authenticity case that Elliott had made to Curran the previous autumn was the fact that Hansen had not been given the same opportunity as had Ragotte to examine the relics in Toronto.

By the time Tanton replied to Elliott, the geologist had probably received two letters Hansen wrote him on 2 April.[12] Hansen decided that he could rely on the published photograph of the ROM's relics to say that they were very similar to the ones he had received from Bloch, and he affirmed that the sword was in two pieces when he received it. An additional relic, which he did not see in the ROM photograph, had been used to hang a pot, and he drew for Tanton a squashed, C-shaped curve. Hansen had decided that this was a different object than the so-called shield handle. Hansen also allowed he had not responded the previous autumn to Jim Curran's assertions that his story was not believable because he had been unable to find the notes proving the Bloch loan. Now that the evidence was in hand, "I must answer it as it is more [or] less a personal challenge to me." Hansen at last provided Tanton with a statement from the Imperial Bank of Canada in Port Arthur for the Bloch loan.[13]

Teddy Elliott finished typing his manuscript, "The Viking Relics of Beardmore," on the night of 5 April.[14] The next day, he decided to set aside the third and final part to mail to T.L. Tanton for comment, and he was preparing to send the rest of it to Ryerson Press when a note from Tanton arrived, sharing news of the loan evidence and the contents of Hansen's recent letters.[15] Tanton outlined for Elliott a hoax scenario consistent with Hansen's claims. "If you had not brought the subject to light while the people competent to supply the essential facts are still living," Tanton assured Elliott, "it would have been a very difficult matter to clear up. Your contribution was very good. The manner in which the case has been investigated and officially reported leaves much to be desired."

Elliott replied to Tanton immediately. He had planned to acknowledge but minimize the problem Hansen's allegations posed in his manuscript, but: "when I read your information to-day it was as if a promising showing had petered out – as if all the work of the past was nullified. In the interests of truth I feel that something should be done about the matter."[16] He asked Tanton for his permission to use his materials to write a final chapter "which would tell a story nearer to the truth." He was willing to travel to Ottawa to make notes from the documents Tanton had gathered.

While waiting to hear from Tanton, Elliott went back to the typewriter and composed an addition to his Ryerson manuscript, a novelistic imagining of how Eddy Dodd would have committed a hoax – not that he was saying he did. He accounted for all the known discovery details while also maintaining the existing manuscript's rejection of James Hansen's and Eli Ragotte's claims. In 1929, John Bloch, down on his luck and drowning his sorrows in the Mariaggi Hotel, encounters Dodd and agrees to sell the beloved relics of his late father. Dodd then visits the middle claim and buries them. Returning the next spring with his son, Dodd hurries to execute his plan before Fletcher Gill arrives and learns what he is up to. The Ukrainian youth turns up, and Dodd agrees to feed him and pay him for a day's work. Dodd then sets off the dynamite charge in the trench that blows over the birch stump and reveals the relics to his son and the youth. Later that year, John Jacob drops by and sees the rust marks.

It was an eccentric narrative turn and an unpublishable libel, no matter how much Elliott insisted it was fiction. He mailed off the entire fifty-six pages to Ryerson Press on 8 April. "Just as the typing was completed information was received of decidedly damaging nature to the present accepted story," he explained to Pierce.[17] Elliott also wrote Hjalmar Holand to secure a photograph of the Kensington stone for the anticipated publication, but mainly to secure his opinion on Currelly's CHR article.[18] Elliott and Holand had resumed a collegial correspondence after the relics were made public in October 1938. In Holand, Elliott seemed to have found a kindred spirit who believed in the authenticity of the Beardmore relics but still questioned the way the ROM and Curran were establishing the provenance. "I trust the museum report will be better supported by affidavits and other corroborative evidence than Mr. Curran's reports has [sic] been," were Holand's comments to Elliott in a letter of 10 December.[19]

Elliott detailed his concerns for Holand in a dense, multi-page letter. It was a far better effort at analysis than what he had sent Ryerson Press, and it revealed how much disquiet had been stewing inside the schoolteacher as he strove to believe in the Beardmore find's authenticity. Virtually every questionable aspect of the Dodd provenance was laid out. On the discovery date alone, going through his records, Elliott had found thirty-five mentions, ranging from 24 May 1930 to April 1934. He had determined that the 24 May 1931 date had been offered as late as 22 October 1938 by Curran and Currelly, and that the new date of 24 May 1930 was first used by Curran in his Empire Club address on 10 November 1938 and had now been used by Currelly in CHR. Currelly had "glossed over" the basic question of whether the relics had been left at the claim for two months or two years.

Tanton meanwhile was encouraging Elliott to join him in probing the Beardmore case. The geologist saw Elliott's potential as a collaborator, as someone who was willing to make the hoax crusade a public one. He had paid Elliott compliments that assured him he was capable of dismantling the ROM's ramshackle provenance case. Elliott took advantage of Easter break to meet with Tanton on 14 April in his office at the National Museum.[20] It was the beginning of their effort to coordinate research and to build individual databases of evidence. From this point forward, they made copies of each other's correspondence and the responses received from witnesses and experts.

Lorne Pierce rejected Elliott's submission to Ryerson Press. "The more I think of it, the more certain I feel that we would have no luck with a

book on this subject," Pierce informed him on 24 April.[21] "The whole
episode is fantastic." The speculative ending was "a grotesque anticlimax.
It is difficult to make a theft romantic, and the letdown from a Viking trek
through the Hudson Bay country to what actually happened scarcely warrants book publication. It is in the 'news' class." He suggested Elliott instead write a feature article for *Maclean's*, or the *Star Weekly*, which could
syndicate the story in some newspapers and "pay you rather well for it."

By the time Elliott had heard from Pierce, the rejection seemed not to
matter. Although he was not yet persuaded beyond a reasonable doubt
that Dodd had committed fraud, he was energized by the suspicion that
he had become ensnarled in a hoax and had aided the hoaxer by connecting him with Currelly and the ROM. Elliott was now working with
Tanton to compile the evidence that Eddy Dodd had duped C.T. Currelly
and Thomas McIlwraith (and Jim Curran and his investigative committee), and that the ROM, through its lack of due diligence, was abetting the
fraud – and, in the process, falsely rewriting history.

Teddy Elliott was transformed by his new association with T.L. Tanton. He
lost the desire for public recognition that had moved him the previous autumn to write a lawyerly reminder to C.T. Currelly of the promises the
museum director had made to publicize his role in the ROM's acquisition.
Unfortunately, Elliott had experienced this profound change just as Currelly made good on those promises.

Elliott reaped, with embarrassment and regret, the praise that Currelly
showered on him in the spring of 1939. Currelly mailed him a copy of the
CHR article, which recounted: "Mr. O.C. Elliott of the Collegiate Institute
in Kingston, Ontario, saw the things and made an extremely good drawing. This he sent to me, together with an excellent description of the objects. I saw at once that they were without doubt Viking."[22] On 15 April,
Elliott's role in the museum's acquisition was saluted in an editorial in the
Kingston Whig-Standard; Currelly had been true to his word and notified
Elliott's local newspaper of his role. Elliott was "probably the most important link between the finding of the articles by Dodd and the changes
that will have to be made in the history books. Kingston and the
[Kingston Collegiate and Vocational Institute] can be extremely proud of
the credit that has been assigned to him by Canada's greatest archaeologist."[23] Having craved this recognition for almost two and a half years, El-

liott was mortified to be celebrated as a hero of the find just as he was overcome by doubt.

"Frankly, I am in a very embarrassing position," Elliott informed Currelly on 15 April.[24] He now had "grave misgivings regarding the truth of Dodd's story. Upon close examination many points give rise to reasonable doubts." Elliott did not offer the broad and detailed critique he had submitted to Holand. He only addressed one issue, and weakly at that: the discovery date Currelly gave of 24 May 1930. If, as Currelly stated, Dodd found the relics eighteen months prior to moving into Hansen's home, presumably 33 Machar, then the discovery was on 24 March 1930, not 24 May 1930. And if the house in question was 37 Machar, then Dodd would have found the relics on 24 December 1929. He did not ask Currelly why the discovery date had been moved back a year, and he made no mention of Dodd's having told him the discovery was made on 24 May 1933. "There is no doubt as to the authenticity of the weapons," Elliott granted, "but the many inconsistencies in the accepted Dodd story make it apparent that something is definitely awry, or that all the facts have not been made public." While Elliott thanked Currelly "for so ably fulfilling your promises to me," he confessed: "I am still in a quandary."

Elliott was more than in a quandary: he was actively investigating the evidence for Dodd's find. He wrote John Jacob on 15 April, Patrick Bohan and Judge McComber on 16 April, and Fletcher Gill and Eli Ragotte on 22 April. As well, on 18 April, Elliott wrote W.R. Davies, editor of the *Kingston Whig-Standard*, expressing in confidence his conviction "the Beardmore incident is by no means closed. I believed that eventually Dr. Currelly's statement [in CHR] will prove to be inaccurate in details and fundamentals."[25] He offered to chat if Davies was interested, but there is no evidence the editor accepted the invitation. On 18 April, Elliott also took the bold step of writing George Brown, asking the CHR's editor the latest date he would accept an article critiquing Currelly's contribution, as he was keen to make the next issue.[26] Brown replied that the next issue (June) was dedicated to the centennial of Lord Durham's report and would have no room for another article but that he would be "pleased … to have further information as to what you have in mind."[27] Elliott replied that he planned something "rather lengthy" and that, as the June issue was full, he would delay submission.[28]

Elliott would have been naive to think he could criticize Currelly's scholarship to individuals like W.R. Davies and George Brown and not have word get back to the renowned museum director. Currelly enjoyed a panoramic deference to his authority, as Elliott would discover. On 10 April, for example, the *Star Weekly* sent Currelly proofs of an article it was about to run by Frederick Griffin on Currelly's CHR article.[29] The general and scholarly press was not in the habit of publishing about Currelly without consulting Currelly himself.

Currelly replied to Elliott with palpable exasperation that someone who had been so determined to receive public credit for the museum's acquisition appeared to be turning against it. "I think you misread what I have written," he began stonily.[30] He wasn't about to tangle over a rough statement of eighteen months if sixteen months would have been more precise. Suspecting Elliott had more on his mind than that, he quickly reviewed the Hansen evidence and shared that Dodd had discovered he had made a mistake of a year in the discovery date and had notified the museum. "Hansen's claim is simply silly, because we have traced the dates down for the occupation of his houses, and if Dodd was showing the things around even a month before he moved into Hansen's house, it disposes of Hansen's claim completely." Currelly closed with a whiff of disdain for the schoolteacher's ingratitude: "I was anxious to give you the credit for bringing the things to my attention: that is all."

Elliott was not the only correspondent plaguing Currelly. Finding the CHR article wanting, Vilhjalmur Stefansson had corresponded with Hansen and appeared to consider him more credible than did Currelly. "This question of Mr. Hansen seems most peculiar," Currelly began in reply to a now-lost letter from Stefansson.[31] He ran through the Hansen evidence, with John Jacob's investigations his trump card. "Owing to the need of government men putting in reports, John Jacob had his notebook of a visit to Port Arthur when he saw the things. So that seems to me to dispose of Mr. Hanson [sic] completely." Currelly, however, was asserting the existence of a government report he had never seen. As for Hansen's having produced proof of the Bloch loan, Currelly baldly suggested fraud: "The finding of a note in his box at the bank is very easy to do. A prominent doctor stated that Mr. Hanson is definitely a mental case, and in his writing to me I would have felt the same, as his letters do not agree." Currelly, however, had no letters from Hansen that were in contradiction – Hjalmar Holand said he had received such. Currelly insisted: "I do not think that there is one question that has not been covered, and if my judgment is worth anything, there is no doubt that those things were dug up near Beardmore. Naturally all kinds of people have come to the office with all kinds of ideas, and every possible clue I think has been followed,

and I can find no question. We were able to eliminate Hansen early because of the dates, and because of certain letters coming to say not to
worry about him as he was a mental case. He was frantically eager to get
hold of a photograph of the objects, as he was quite unable to give any description of them, and wanted to see a photograph of them so that he
could describe them from the photograph." Stefansson nevertheless persisted with questions in a follow-up letter. Currelly did not reply.[32]

In May 1939, the letter-writing efforts of Teddy Elliott and T.L. Tanton
began to yield results. Elliott had a prompt reply from Fletcher Gill to his
letter of 22 April. Dodd's prospecting partner was voluble and apparently
unguarded. Which is not to say he was necessarily being truthful.

Gill realized that he had messed up in his duties to produce the affidavits by himself and Patrick Bohan. There was nothing he could do now
about Bohan's memory, but in writing Elliott on 30 April, Gill offered a
fresh narrative that not only endorsed the 1930 discovery but also gave
himself a more prominent role.[33] Gill related essentially the same story to
Jim Curran in an undated letter that included a few more details about
the prospecting operation and that was tinged with resentment. "Ever
since the Norse relics were discovered my partner Mr. Dodds gets all the
credit for it. I really don't think it's fair. So I am going to tell you how the
relics were found."[34]

Gill explained that he had been Dodd's prospecting partner since 1925
and that they had worked the middle claim together every chance they
had. They had dug away the base of the wall of schist, which they called
the dyke, to trace a promising vein. Realizing it went still deeper, they
blasted. The dyke base filled with water as fast as they could bail it with a
pail. Gill told Dodd that, to drain it, they needed to make a cross trench.
At that point, prospecting work paused, as did paying work with the CNR
out of Port Arthur. To find work, Gill told Elliott that he went to Hornepayne "after the snow was gone in the spring of 1930."[35] Dodd had no
work at all, and he offered to resume activities at the middle claim with
his son Walter if Gill would pay for the grub stake. Gill agreed. While Gill
was away, Eddy and Walter cut the trench that Gill had recommended and
found the relics. "So you see I paid for the discovery of the Norse relics and
get no credit for it," Gill complained to Curran, adding: "Everything
should be Dodds [sic] and Gill."

Gill told Elliott that he was at Hornepayne when Dodd wrote him about the find. "I did not pay much attention to it as I though[t] it was some old stuff belong[ing] to some Indian years ago, and Mr. Dodd though[t] the same." They otherwise saw each other infrequently, and "there was not anything said much about the find all this time he had it laying about the house." Gill believed he returned to Port Arthur for a short period in 1932 but otherwise remained in Hornepayne until 1934. At that point, "I had forgotten all about the find as I heard no more about it."

Gill tried to explain to Elliott how he had told reporter Royd Beamish in January 1938 that he had known nothing about the discovery until he read about it in the newspaper. "You see Sir I did not want to get mixed up in anything and did not want to say anything that Mr. Beamish might print. So when I told Mr. Beamish I knew nothing about it, I meant Mr. Ragotte['s] Statement and Mr. Hansen['s] Statement. I did not mean anything about the relics. The first time I seen the relics was in October 1938, when we went to Toronto." But in Beamish's reportage, Gill was specific about not knowing anything about the discovery. As for the pick-like object, Gill recounted: "I brought it to Port Arthur, had it sharpened and a handle put in it, as it was very rusty. Later we lost this pick on the property." Gill informed Elliott they had sent Curran a wooden model of the pick "but haven't heard about it." Eli Ragotte had claimed picks belonging to him and Hansen turned up at Dodd's camp.

Elliott sent Tanton a copy of the Gill correspondence and asked that Diamond Jenness receive a copy as well.[36] Thus, from an early stage in his investigative relationship with Tanton, Elliott understood that Canada's chief anthropologist was in the background, lending support; in fact, Elliott already may have met Jenness on his visit to Tanton in mid-April.

Elliott then received a long and considerate reply from Judge Alexander McComber, who shared details of Dodd's address changes around the purported discovery period and provided summaries of affidavits gathered from Harry Scott, Fletcher Gill, John McGugan, George Hynes, and Patrick Bohan.[37] McComber did not have access to the affidavits by Eddy and Walter Dodd, which Gill had arranged, but he summarized the affidavits of Gill and Bohan from the statements they had provided him the previous October. Elliott could now see how Gill was changing and elaborating his story about the discovery year while, at the same time, Bohan's recollection of having been stationed at Warneford in 1931, purportedly backed by employment records, made a 1930 discovery impossible.

Judge McComber recounted how James Hansen told him he intended to sue Dodd for back rent and that Dodd denied owing Hansen money: "Evidently they are not friendly to each other." Hansen's story otherwise abounded in incongruities that suggested to the judge that Hansen, if he indeed ever possessed the relics, only thought they had significant value after the news broke of the museum's acquisition. Furthermore, "Hansen is very undecided as to whether he got these articles before or after he made a loan, or rather a note of $45 – for Bloch." The judge reiterated the Norwegian vice-consul Carl Sorensen's repeated insistence that his friend Bloch never mentioned having such relics. Finally, there was the confusion over the precise identity of the four items on display at the museum and the five Hansen said he had possessed. Hansen "also said that he had never actually claimed that the Dodd relics were his, but that they looked like his." Judge McComber closed with: "I will be glad to hear from you after you have considered the above." The judge at least had signalled his willingness to hear counter-arguments.

On 9 May, Eli Ragotte replied to a letter from Tanton.[38] The railway brakeman did not so much change his story as refine it. Sometime after he moved in with Dodd at 33 Machar, which Hansen had vacated, he and Dodd were in the basement when Ragotte found what looked like a rusty knife, about fourteen inches long. That was all he found, he stressed: he did not find the axe or shield, and he had no idea where Dodd got them. About a month after Ragotte found the knife, Dodd showed him the same knife as well as the axe and a piece of metal he called the shield, and he told Ragotte he had found them on his claims at Beardmore. Ragotte knew Dodd was lying because Dodd had not been to his claims, and it was the same knife Ragotte had found in the basement. "This story is nothing new for Mr. Dodd for every time you meet Mr. Dodds [sic] he has bin [sic] finding something. And everybody that knew Mr. Dodd in Port Arthur took it as a joke."

Hansen's missing fishing gear was "another one of Mr. Dodd['s] stunts." Ragotte found the gear in the basement of 33 Machar. He put it aside "and a few days later we were down to Beardmore when Mr. Dodd produced the fishing rods: telling me that he had bought them, which I knew was not the truth … Mr. Tanton I could tell you stories all day about stunts Mr. Dodd pulled off, and I do not believe that Mr. Dodd ever found any relics or any thing else on his claims at Beardmore."

For all that, Ragotte advised: "The Norse relics now in the museum in Tronto [sic] is not the rusted knife and axe and the piece Mr. Dodd called a shield that Mr. Dodd showed me at 33 Machar Ave. and just where Mr. Dodd did get the relics that he sold to the Museum in Tronto I could not say." But Ragotte wondered aloud if the rusted knife he found was, indeed, part of the sword: "I might of seen the Piece with the handle on." When he saw the sword at the museum he could not tell if it was in two pieces because it was mounted in a rack in a glass case. Thus, Ragotte did not realize the museum's sword was in two pieces until *after* he viewed it on 30 September and signed his statements.

Ragotte had little good to say to Tanton about Hansen. Hansen was not, as he had claimed, in the basement when Ragotte found the knife or the fishing gear, "and I didn't find the knife and rods at the same time for when I found the fishing rods I was by my self and when I found the rusted knife Mr. Dodd was with me." Later, after Hansen and Dodd had some dispute, Hansen asked Ragotte to give him a written statement that Dodd had taken his fishing gear to the Beardmore claims along with some other items Hansen said were his. Ragotte could not have disagreed, but he had declined the request. "Mr. Hansen and Mr. Dodd are both about the same (they would sell their soul or anything else for a fue [sic] dollars.) So I kept out of trouble and away from both of them and let them fight it out their selves." When he mentioned to Hansen the old knife he had found in the basement, "he just laughed, and said they were some old relics he had brought from the old countary [sic]." After Ragotte set off the public controversy and Hansen learned Dodd had gotten money for the relics, "he wanted me to say that he was in the basement when I found the knife, which he was not" – a reference to Hansen's letter to Ragotte of 31 January 1938.

Ragotte's rounding on Hansen was a dramatic change from his earlier positions. When he wrote the *Winnipeg Free Press* to complain about Philip Godsell's comments in 1938, Ragotte assured its editor he could prove his claims, and he submitted (and quoted from) Hansen's letter to him. Now, Hansen's letter was proof that Dodd's old landlord had tried to talk him into making a false statement. By the time Ragotte had concluded his letter to Tanton, the provenance of the relics was an impossible mess. On the one hand, Dodd appeared to be a thief and had likely helped himself to some of Hansen's belongings at 33 Machar, as both Hansen and Ragotte alleged. On the other hand, Ragotte strongly suggested Hansen was contriving a claim to the museum's purchase. And while Ragotte was no longer telling his original story about finding a sword twenty-seven to thirty inches long as well as a shield, which he had disowned as a "joke," he now wavered between saying that nothing he saw at 33 Machar was in the ROM display case and entertaining the idea that maybe he saw part of the sword. It did not help (unbeknownst to Tanton) that, on 6 March, in a fresh affidavit for Jim Curran, Ragotte had sworn that he was sure that the sword he saw at the ROM was not the piece of iron that he saw in the basement of 33 Machar.

Elliott thought that Hansen might have told Ragotte that the knife was among some relics he had brought from the old country to protect Bloch from the consequences of having taken them out of Norway illegally; otherwise, Hansen's explanation had just been "an easy avoidance of the truth."[39] Elliott conceded it was possible there was "no connection whatever between the 'knife' Ragotte found and what he saw." Then again, he wondered if Dodd had concealed the relics in the furnace ashes from Hansen until he could decide how to dispose of them, which was how Ragotte stumbled on a piece of the sword.

Tanton was prepared to believe Hansen. His version of events was "clear and consistent. It provides a more reasonable explanation for the existence of Viking relics in Canada at this date than does any one of the versions of the Dodd story I have heard as yet."[40] Given that Dodd was the comparative standard, this was faint praise, but Tanton was now sure of the general narrative of the hoax. John Bloch had emigrated from Norway with relics that had belonged to his late father. He knew it was illegal to do so, which was why he never told his friend, the vice-consul Sorensen, and other members of the Norwegian community that he had them. (Tanton accepted that the relics were genuine Viking weapons and presumed that Currelly had performed due diligence on the typology with leading experts.) Bloch fell on hard times and used them as collateral for a bank loan backed by his landlord, Hansen. Hansen was a collector who knew, as did Bloch, that taking the relics out of Norway was illegal. That greatly discounted their market value as they could never be sold publicly, but they were valuable enough to Hansen as mementos of the old country for him to accept them as collateral in guaranteeing a small bank loan for Bloch. Hansen kept the relics when Bloch left him obligated for the bank debt, but, like Bloch, he told no one in the Norwegian community about them, Sorensen above all. Bloch moved away and died. Hansen stored the relics in the basement of 33 Machar and moved out. (No one, Tanton included, considered that Hansen left the relics there so that he could not be directly associated with property that had been illegally removed from Norway. If the relics were ever found at 33 Machar, he could just say they must have belonged to Bloch.) Dodd moved in and started making off with possessions that Hansen had been forced to leave behind when he moved to an apartment. Ragotte may have embellished his story of finding the sword and shield in Hansen's basement in the initial telling, but Tanton felt that there was an essential truth to his account. Ragotte found *something* in the basement – a rusty old knife that sounded like part of the sword. Why Ragotte would ever have said to Jim Curran that he never meant Dodd any harm, when there was such obvious bad blood between them, was still difficult to understand.

Tanton was sure Dodd had taken Hansen's relics to the Beardmore claim and planted them so he could claim he had dug them up. The extra bits of iron found by McIlwraith in 1937 and Curran's party in 1938 were later planted to sway key opinions in favour of the authenticity of the original find. Dodd's discovery had been backdated from 1931 to 1930 to avoid the problem of his move to Hansen's Machar properties, but Patrick Bohan's statement seemed unequivocal in dating the planting of the relics at the claim to 1931. And if what Dodd had said to reporter Royd Beamish was taken to be true – that he had left the relics ignored at his prospecting camp for two years after finding them in May 1931 – then Elliott was correct in recognizing that "all affidavits are out."[41]

Patrick Bohan's statement was problematic for Elliott's and Tanton's investigation. Rather than treating Dodd's August 1936 statement to Elliott that he had found the relics in May 1933 as the version of the discovery story nearest the truth, the pair regarded it as just another careless variation. They provisionally accepted that Bohan must have seen the relics at the middle claim between 15 May and 1 July 1931, presuming that Bohan's employment records would back him up. But if the relics were indeed seen in the spring of 1931, how did Dodd get them from Hansen if he didn't move into 33 Machar until September 1931? No one on either side of the provenance debate had a bird's-eye view of all the evidence; everyone was drawing conclusions in a fog of ignorance. No one outside the museum, for example, knew that Dodd had signed a statement for Currelly at the time of purchase saying he had left the relics at the claim until 1933, which was equally disqualifying of Curran's batch of affidavits.

Regardless of the 1931 timing problems, by early May 1939, a government geologist and a schoolteacher had crafted the basic hoax hypothesis that guided the coming years of efforts to expose a fraud that was perpetrated upon – and perpetuated by – a leading public museum.

19

"The More Confused I Get"

On 8 May 1939, Hjalmar Holand replied to Teddy Elliott's long list of concerns with Currelly's CHR article.[1] "I agree with you that it is decidedly superficial. Some of the things that you emphasize are, however, of minor importance." These "minor" issues included the disputed discovery date. "Most men find it practically impossible to recall the date or the year when certain events took place." He was unconcerned about the preservation of buried metals and John Jacob's singular observation of the rust stain. Elliott's questioning of why the supposed dead Norseman's companions did not take his weapons with them rather than bury them launched Holand into imaginative throes. They "probably had their own weapons to carry. They would not therefore burden themselves with unnecessary weapons. The Indians, if hostile, would prefer their own weapons with which they were familiar rather than use new weapons even if they found them, which would not be likely."

Holand then raised a major issue: "The mutilation of weapons was a pagan custom." Elliott already knew that Vikings were buried with broken weapons, and even expected the Beardmore grave would contain an authentic broken sword, not one broken by Dodd. But Holand made an important point: "These men were presumably Christian and had given up this custom." The known circa 1000 Vinland voyages were mounted by Christian Norse from Greenland and Iceland. If the sword was already broken when Dodd found it – and Tanton thought Dodd's story of breaking it while trying to extract it from schist was nonsense – how did a pagan Norseman come to be buried (without a surviving body) near Lake Nipigon? Holand made no effort to rationalize this striking incongruity. Perhaps he concluded there was a pagan among the travel party. After all, Christianity was new among these people, and Thorfinn Karlsefni's voyage included a known pagan, Thorhall the Hunter. Holand did grant that Elliott's points about Currelly's lack of reference to statements by Fletcher Gill, James Hansen, and others were well made. Beyond Currelly's article, Elliott had also expressed his doubt that the pick-like object supposedly found on the middle claim could be one thousand years old and in such fine condition that Dodd could have used it.

Holand agreed that the "pick (if it is a pick) can not have anything to do with the Viking grave."

Elliott felt that Holand's earlier scepticism about the Beardmore find was abating in the aftermath of Currelly's article. He did not know that Holand had pronounced Hansen a liar to Currelly some six months earlier. There had been a limit to how collegial Holand was willing to be with Elliott in sharing information. The ranks of active doubters were narrowing.

However, a breakthrough came quickly, from A.W. Brøgger, whom Tanton had written, updating him on his investigation and wondering if Brøgger could enlighten him on John Bloch's father and on the nature of the weapons. When Tanton shared Brøgger's reply with Elliott on 18 May, the schoolteacher became as certain as the geologist that Dodd's discovery could only have been a hoax.[2]

Brøgger reported that Bloch's father was Andreas Schelven Schroeter Bloch (1860–1917). He was "a very able designer and painter, whose works covered a large field. His special interests were heraldry and war-history, he had a profound knowledge of ancient weapons and costumes and have performed [sic] a lot of designs of equipment of every kind from the Viking age to modern times." As for the weapons typology, Brøgger had shared the photo C.T. Currelly had sent him in December 1937 with a museum colleague, the prominent archaeologist Sigurd Grieg. Brøgger only passed along information from Grieg about the sword, but it was enough to confirm for Brøgger his initial suspicions about Dodd's find.

According to Grieg, the relics "belong to a rather typical Viking-milieu from the eastern-most part of Norway," the Ostfold region around Oslo, and dated to the mid-tenth century. Grieg recommended examining figure 111 in Petersen's *De Norske Vikingesverd*, which Tanton could not do. It was a Q type sword in Petersen's scheme, a development of the M type that had been chosen by scholars whom Currelly had consulted. There were 122 known examples in museum collections. It was a curious conclusion, as the Q type had a distinctive downward curve or droop to the guard, which is absent from the ROM's sword. By opting for a later sword type that would agree with the younger axe's period, Grieg (and Brøgger) may have been trying to rationalize how the sword and axe could appear together in the same Norwegian grave.[3] Perhaps they thought the guard of the badly corroded weapon had been straightened. But advancing the Q type allowed Brøgger to assert that the Beardmore relics could not possibly be associated with the Vinland voyages. If so, the Oslo scholars were overreaching in an effort to condemn the Beardmore find.

The sword, Brøgger explained, "is a typical Norwegian form and has never been found in Iceland nor in Sweden-Denmark," which could not be said of an M type. Brøgger made a more crucial point: "You will never find, neither on Iceland nor in Greenland, heathen burials from the 11th century like the Beardmore relics. They correspond in [sic] the contrary extremely well with the common custom of Ostfold in the 10th century." Brøgger did not provide details, but Elliott knew the pagan custom of breaking the sword and that the Vinland voyages from Iceland and Greenland were mounted by Christian Norse. "I have personally no doubt that the Beardmore relics belong to some collection of the Bloch senior," Brøgger advised.

The typology assessment by Brøgger and Grieg was flawed, but the Norwegian archaeologists had established that the broken sword was typical of a pagan burial in Ostfold, regardless of whether it was an M or a Q type. Overall, Brøgger had increased the likelihood that Andreas Bloch had been the source of the weapons. Now the challenges before Tanton and Elliott were (1) persuading others that Dodd's relics originated with Jens Bloch's father and (2) building a strong case for how a hoax would have been perpetrated.

T.L. Tanton and Teddy Elliott knew from C.T. Currelly's CHR article that John Jacob was key to the authenticity case, but neither man had any success in contacting him. Tanton had better luck flushing out Aaron Lougheed, after mining engineer Julian Cross provided him with an address.[4] The seventy-six-year-old retired surveyor wrote Tanton a teasing note on 20 May 1939 that admitted nothing about his role but that strongly suggested he did not believe Dodd: "I saw this sword & heard his statement reguarding [sic] the finding thereof & etc. How much of a sword would you expect to find after laying on or in porous ground for 900 years. Call when you come this way."[5] But Tanton was not able to visit with him as he headed to northern Manitoba for his summer of fieldwork, and Lougheed was set aside as an enticing, unexploited lead.

Julian Cross also put Tanton in touch with his brother, William. As we have seen, in the spring of 1938 John Jacob had thought the Port Arthur machinist would state he had seen the relics in Dodd's possession in 1930. But, in a letter to Tanton, William Cross offered a different account than the one Jacob had related to Currelly.[6] He had first visited the middle claim in 1926, on behalf of a prominent local businessman, James Whalen (of Port Arthur's Whalen Building fame), presumably to assess its investment potential. The trench where the relics were found had not yet been dug. He did not see the sword (or, implicitly, any other relics) until 1931. "At that time Dodds [sic] was moving from Algoma St. to Machen [sic] Avenue and came to the shop to borrow pipe wrenches to change the hot water pipes on his sto[v]e. Dobbs [sic] had mentioned several times about finding this sword and as he was moving close to the shop I asked him to bring it down. He went home and brought the sword wrapped up in an old news paper. We had it in the shop for about two hours when he returned the wrenches and took the sword away." Cross said "several persons [saw] the relic at that time."

Reading between the lines, William Cross had asked for the sword as security for the loan of pipe wrenches. Cross may not have trusted Dodd with his tools, but he believed that Dodd had found the relics as claimed. Cross recalled visiting the middle claim with Dodd on 20 May 1933, which was the Saturday of the Victoria Day long weekend. Cross inspected a trench about four feet deep, partly filled with leaves and muck. Some blasting had been performed and stumps of about sixteen inches had been removed. Dodd pointed out where the sword was found.

William Cross sounded honest, but his account did not provide proof for a 1930 discovery. If anything, it pointed to 1933 as the year Dodd began claiming he had found the relics. Cross was wrong to say that Dodd had been moving from South Algoma to Machar, but he did move from Machar to South Algoma in March 1933. William Cross's recollections were part of an evidence pattern that suggests Dodd did not start showing the relics to people until he moved out of 33 Machar, in March 1933, which reinforced the likelihood he stole them from Hansen. But because no one had access to all the statements, including different statements made by a single person, it was impossible to see this evidence trend. Tanton did not know that William Cross had told John Jacob in April 1938 that Dodd had shown him the relics immediately after the find and that he had visited the middle claim three or four months later. That roughly agreed with a scenario of Dodd's claiming in March 1933 that he had just found the relics and showing Cross the sword, Cross's lending Dodd pipe wrenches as he moved out of 33 Machar and into 74 South Algoma, and then Cross's visiting the middle claim to inspect the discovery trench on 20 May 1933. When Dodd told Elliott in 1936 that he had found the relics on 24 May 1933, he may have been recalling the Victoria Day long weekend on which he showed William Cross the discovery trench. This timing scenario would also explain why Dodd only showed the relics to Ned Burwash in February 1934. Burwash had been running the local prospecting classes every winter for seven years by then. Why did it take so long for Dodd to get around to waylaying Burwash with the relics on the street, if he had found them in 1930 or even 1931? Furthermore, a May 1933 "discovery" would explain why Dodd never shared the proceeds (or the news) of the find with Fletcher Gill. The middle claim was effectively dead, as they had filed no further work reports after 1932, and it would not be restaked (by Gill) until December 1937.

Elliott and Tanton, however, would continue to presume that, as per Patrick Bohan's statement, which supposedly was backed by employment records, Dodd had the relics in the spring of 1931. Elliott devoted considerable mental energy to conjuring scenarios for how anyone could have seen the relics at 296 Wilson, before Dodd moved to Machar Avenue, if Dodd had stolen them from Hansen as he believed. Elliott also suspected that Jacob really did see a rust mark from the sword. "I think [Dodd] laid the sword on the rock and watered it to give the distinct impression that Jacob saw."[7] Otherwise Elliott wondered if John Bloch had two sets of relics. Perhaps Bloch sold one set to Dodd while he was a clerk at the Mariaggi Hotel and Dodd was a customer of its beverage room, as he had speculated in his Ryerson Press manuscript, which would explain how people would have seen the relics at 296 Wilson in 1930. There was another set, which Hansen had acquired from Bloch. "Dodd, finding Hansen's relics at #33, which he had previously heard about from Bloch, shoveled them into the furnace, and threw them out with the ashes to remove a competing set," he proposed to Tanton. Elliott did not return to this somewhat desperate scenario. But Dodd's having acquired the relics (or *some* relics) directly from Bloch around 1928 was not an unreasonable proposition. Elliott had brushed up against the possibility that Bloch had, at the least, owned two broken swords and that Dodd came to possess both.

Elliott made a second round of enquiry with Judge McComber and Fletcher Gill in late May. He provided the judge with five single-spaced typed pages of cogent analysis of statements, events, and timing problems.[8] He proposed that C.D. Howe, the federal member of Parliament for Port Arthur and minister of transport, be approached to pay for Hansen's visit to Toronto to confront the museum's relics. Elliott had also heard that Judge T.E. Godson of the Mining Court of Ontario had forbidden Dodd's claims to be sold or transferred without written consent from his court. "Surely the Province of Ontario is not going to permit this incident to be exploited without an adequate investigation into the validity of Dodd's story!"[9]

Elliott deftly cultivated Gill as a credulous source of potentially self-incriminating evidence, praising Gill for his cooperation. Could Gill provide any evidence for his employment at Hornepayne in 1930? Could he suggest anyone who saw the relics at 296 Wilson? And why did he not want to "get mixed up in anything"? Had Gill wanted to keep his name out of the press, "or was there really some more to the story that you did not wish to be quoted as the one who mentioned it?"[10]

Gill was not about to confess to complicity in a hoax, but on 30 May he wrote how pleased he was to hear again from Elliott: "and as I told you in my first letter any other information you would want, I would be only too glad to help you."[11] To vouch for his time at Hornepayne, Gill recalled further purported details of his employment movements, which indicated that Dodd wrote him there in late May 1930 to tell him of the find. Gill, however, offered no documentary support. Gill said that he could name up to nine men who had seen the relics at the middle claim before Dodd brought them home and that "about a dozen affidavits" had been made out to support the discovery. But they had all been sent to Jim Curran, who "is going to print them later. Mr. Curran don't want for us to give anyone else any affidavits." Gill also confessed that Dodd would not allow him to give Elliott the names of anyone who saw the relics at 296 Wilson. "Myself of course I would tell you." Gill suggested that Elliott write Dodd at his most recent address, 334 Bay Street, or contact Curran.

Gill wondered why the American, Canadian, and Norwegian governments hadn't come together to "pay us a nice sum" for the middle claim "and put up a monument there with a fence around it to protect it. Anything you can do in this line we would appreciate it." Gill had been pressing the idea of a multinational government purchase for commemorative purposes since late March, when he sought Curran's advice on what to do about the middle claim.[12] Eddy Dodd had written a similar letter to Curran at the end of April. By then, Dodd was out of work and had no telephone service.[13]

Gill "does not seem too happy in his partnership," Elliott ventured to Tanton on 3 June, "and apparently would like to talk if it could be done without straining relations with Dodd whose refusal to co-operate is true to form." Elliott thought the hoax had been perpetrated not to sell relics to a museum but, rather, "to attract attention and money to the claims."[14] Elliott began to hear rumours that the new Trans-Canada Highway, which ran close to the CNR line, was going to have its route diverted so that it would pass by the middle claim, which would be made a National Historic Site; he also heard that archaeologists from American universities would be digging at the claim.[15] When Gill asked Elliott for help in having the middle claim purchased as a historic site, Elliott was happy to set the trap that could expose the hoax.

Elliott provided Gill with three people in Canada, the United States, and Norway, respectively, to whom he could write to make the case for government-funded preservation. The Canadian was Diamond Jenness. The Norwegian was Sigurd Grieg, the colleague of A.W. Brøgger, who had identified the relics as a typical pagan burial from Ostfold. The American was Clark Wissler of the American Museum of Natural History, an anthropologist specializing in Plains tribes. Wissler assuredly was suggested by Jenness, who knew him well.[16] All three scholars must have been enlisted in a plan to draw out Dodd and Gill on the discovery, to secure details that would undermine the archaeological case for the relics. When Gill wrote Jenness on 7 July, asking for his assistance, Jenness replied: "The Canadian government is hardly likely to consider the purchase of your Beardmore claim without a full statement from Mr. Dodds [sic] himself."[17] Jenness laid out a list of details he trusted Dodd would provide.

Dodd, in reply, unfortunately said little if anything that could be used against him.[18] The position in which the relics were found, he advised Jenness, "is Quite difficult to explain." He told a short version of the discovery story and asserted the date was the "24 day of May 24th 1930." The rest of the letter was a rant on the failure of the federal government to acquire the site. "I can not understand why the government of Canada do not take any interest in it as it Proceeds [sic] Christer Colums 500 years, as I have had quiet [sic] a lot of correspondence from USA. and nothing from Canada," which got the relics "cheap from us." If the government wanted to place a monument on the site "for turist [sic] extraction me and my Partner we will sell the surface Rights to them." Dodd thought the Norwegian government would be interested "as we have had some correspondence to this effect." Gill and Dodd thus may have heard from Grieg. Whether the partners wrote to or heard from Wissler is unknown.

In the meantime, Teddy Elliott had written his wife Kate's cousin, Mona Oliver, who worked for the forestry branch of the provincial Department of Lands and Forests in Port Arthur, hoping she could help track down John Jacob and others. A department deputy at Beardmore, Oscar Gulin, made enquiries about Dodd's relics at her request.[19] Gulin did not have much luck, but according to him Beardmore residents thought the discovery had been made four years before the news broke in January 1938, which meant about 1934. It was another clue (overlooked) that Dodd did not start making his relics claims until after he moved out of 33 Machar. "Most people doubt that Dodds did find them there," Gulin wrote, "and I am one of them."

"It might be a good idea for you to come up and visit the scene of action for yourself," Oliver advised Elliott. "Everyone around this neck of the woods seems to think that Mr. Dodds [sic] put something over but no one has any proof." Elliott, unfortunately, was not visiting the Lakehead as planned with Kate that summer. Oliver informed Elliott that George Hynes, one of the affidavit writers who supported the 1930 discovery, "doesn't work here any more but if you can ever catch him sober he might know something. However, I think this very unlikely. He just got into a row with someone when in his cups and has a broken collar bone and jaw. The other guy has 6 months in Stoney Mountain." Elliott would never hear from Hynes.

Oliver somehow secured a museum photograph of the relics. Word spread that she had the photo, "and pretty soon in comes Mr. Dodds [sic] and Fletcher Gill," she reported to Elliott. "You know all the railroad men ride Mr. Dodds all the time and he's as cranky as a bear. I thought he was going to have me pinched. He thought I had a picture of the property and evidently no one is allowed to go in on it. He said there were signs all over."[20]

Gill and Dodd were in a public state of apoplexy about unauthorized visitors to the middle claim. While they were likely creating an air of alarm about treasure seekers invading the claim so as to promote the idea that some government authority ought to buy their mining rights and protect it as a historic site, actual would-be treasure hunters did indeed appear to be afoot there. Gill had informed Jim Curran that he did not want a woman who wished to take photographs to know the location of the claim site "because all Beardmore will be there digging and the place will be all dug up and spoiled and then if they find any more relics they are looking to take them away and who knows they might say they found them in their garden at Beardmore."[21] Gill seemed to believe Dodd's discovery story as much as did Curran.

On 23 June, Thomas McIlwraith addressed the annual meeting of the Ontario Historical Society on the Beardmore find. He assured his audience that the relics had been authenticated by experts and that, while there had

been an effort to show that the relics had been planted, he was satisfied with Dodd's story.[22]

On 29 June, Elliott submitted his Currelly rejoinder to George Brown at CHR. "You are hesitant, no doubt, in giving space to one who has no standing as an historian. Inspection of the documents used in this article is invited. My only desire is to arrive at the truth."[23] By the time Elliott had finished reviewing the accumulating mass of contrary evidence, the manuscript reached twenty-seven pages, which was at least three times as long as the original Currelly article. Elliott received a printed card acknowledging receipt on 4 July and, in reply, submitted some minor corrections.[24] He heard nothing back, but he waited hopefully for his comments to appear in the next issue, in September.

Elliott was otherwise trying to get his criticism of the museum's authenticity case into the mainstream press before Jim Curran's book came out in support of Dodd's claims. He had submitted an article to *Time* on 27 May but never received a reply.[25] *Maclean's* then rejected his "rather libellous" submission.[26] He next tried the *Globe and Mail*, volunteering that his article as written might be libellous, and suggesting that the package be given to reporter Royd Beamish to use for a story of his own. The managing editor declined the offer due to "space limitations."[27] Elliott immediately wrote a letter to the *Toronto Star* for its "Voice of the People" section.[28] It never ran; Elliott would hear indirectly that the *Star* had shared it with Currelly, who pronounced it "rot."[29]

At least there was encouraging news from T.L. Tanton, who wrote Elliott on 27 July from a camp on Athapaskan Lake in northern Manitoba.[30] He had met Eli Ragotte in Winnipeg en route to his fieldwork. Ragotte stood by what he had stated in his letter to Tanton and was warming to the resemblance between the sword on display at the ROM and the piece of iron he saw in the basement at 33 Machar. "He made it clear that he did not know that the sword in the museum case was in 2 pieces & hence did not identify the haft ½ as the same as the long knife. He now recalls the resemblance." Ragotte insisted he had told Curran and others that he did not believe Dodd's story, "and seemed surprised his connection with the affair could be used to bolster the case for the Beardmore Viking."

Tanton had also received a promotional card for Curran's forthcoming book, which was to be called *Here Was Vinland*. "Poor chap his efforts were worthy of a better cause," he commented to Elliott. "No doubt he has done a deal of valuable research." Tanton had also heard from Vilhjalmur Stefansson, who had written C.T. Currelly a letter "that had indicated the outstanding questions regarding the accuracy of the 'official' statement." Stefansson had no reply. Stefansson and Currelly were now estranged on the Beardmore question.

Diamond Jenness, too, had received the book promotion, and he mailed it to Stefansson. "Newspaper editors may walk boldly where scholars fear to tread," Jenness quipped.[31] Stefansson was concerned that Curran had overreached in his enthusiasm for Vinland in northern Ontario, with Beardmore at its heart, despite his own efforts to steer the newspaperman in a less flamboyant interpretive direction. Based on what he had read in Curran's articles, he told Jenness, "it seems to me he is riding for more than one fall."[32]

Thwarted in his efforts to publish, Teddy Elliott's one outstanding success came with Carl Sorensen. The vice-consul had earlier agreed to find him a photo of the 1927 Viking ship parade float, which could show that a Viking shield would not have been unknown to Dodd or his possible accomplices. Sorensen had taken the opportunity to disparage Hansen's credibility, adding: "I do not know Dodd, but I believe that Mr. James Curran is on the right track."[33] Elliott decided to have another try with Sorensen.[34] He dismantled the case for Dodd and the case against Hansen, and strove to get inside the mind of Bloch on terms Sorensen could appreciate. Even though Sorensen and Bloch were friendly, would Bloch have admitted to a Norwegian vice-consul he had Viking relics from his father that he had brought here illegally? The relics were probably a sentimental reminder of his father and his home country. He probably hoped to return to Norway someday, which would mean asking Sorensen to arrange a passport or visa. Could Sorensen do so if he knew Bloch had broken Norwegian law by bringing the relics to Canada? Elliott suggested the relics were a "nest egg" Bloch could dispose of in some way if he was ever so hard up, but he could never sell them to the logical market – a government museum outside Norway – because they had been exported illegally. Consequently, Bloch could never get a decent price for them, and he probably had no intention of selling them to Hansen, wanting only to use them as security for a loan. Bloch had hoped to get them back, but hard luck and a premature death had defeated the plan. Elliott did not understand the nature of the Bloch loan and had never met Hansen, but he ventured that Hansen, a "cheap bargainer" with a "grasping nature," had "real-

ized their value, and with covetous eyes on the possibility of reaping profit scraped together the insignificant sum of $30 to loan to Bloch."

Sorensen in reply confessed: "the more I read about this matter the more
confused I get."[35] Elliott's letter had inspired him to call in Hansen, who insisted he had obtained the relics from John Bloch and had left them in the
basement of 33 Machar. "When I asked Hansen why he had not told me or
even [Roy] Ohlgren about getting these relics from Block, he said he had
promised Block not to tell anybody that he had them, he also stated that he
had offered to go to inspect them [at the ROM] as he had a right to claim
them, as having been stolen from him, if he recognizes them as the ones he
had in his possession." Sorensen agreed that, based on the expert advice from
A.W. Brøgger that Elliott had shared, the relics were from eastern Norway's
Ostfold District. "I have given this matter considerable thought and I have
come to the conclusion that most likely Hansens [sic] statement may be the
truth." Sorensen seemed to have taken entirely to heart Elliott's speculation
that Hansen was a grasping, cheap bargainer, and he lectured Hansen that,
while he had "the sneaking idea" he could claim the relics: "I informed him
that it was very evident that he had no right to them, and that he knew these
relics were not obtained honestly by the man he had received them from.
The result as I now see it, will be, that Dodds [sic] put one over, and that the
Vikings did not burry [sic] them at Beardmore." Sorensen provided two extra
copies of the letter that Elliott could share with Tanton and Stefansson.

It was an astonishing about-face for the man who had repeatedly and
publicly insisted that Hansen's story had no basis and that Bloch never
owned Norse relics. Sorensen's capitulation replaced one of the most crucial objections to Hansen's story with a cautious endorsement.

Teddy Elliott made one last try at getting something about the hoax into
print before Jim Curran's book was out. He appealed directly to Royd
Beamish, whose previous reporting efforts on the relics he admired.[36] Currelly, Elliott cautioned, "regards my story as silly because if true it places
him in an unenviable position. Therefore if you check with him he will
pooh-pooh the whole thing." Elliott stressed he was not seeking publicity
for himself. "I don't care if my name ever appears in connection with the
matter. On the other hand I am ready to back any statement personally
and with documents. In the interest of truth I am offering you full access
to all information in my possession which has been acquired since 1934."

Elliott also hoped that Stefansson, with his international reputation, could publicize the hoax case, and he sent him copies of the letters from Brøgger and Sorensen.[37] "Unfortunately," Elliott wrote, Currelly's CHR article "has lent an air of official sanction to Dodd's story, and consequently any attempt to publicize Hansen's story meets with little favour from the Doctor." Elliott shared that he had submitted a "rather lengthy criticism" of Currelly's article to CHR. Elliott feared that not being a recognized historian, his opinion "carrie[d] but little weight." He assured Stefansson he believed Hansen's story and had plenty of documentary evidence to support it.

On 9 August, four days after Elliott wrote Royd Beamish and Vilhjalmur Stefansson, *Here Was Vinland* arrived in Elliott's mail. Jim Curran had won the race to share with the public the truth about Eddy Dodd's relics.

War Declared

Jim Curran's *Here Was Vinland: A 1,000 Year Old Mystery Solved* is a peculiar book. The first part consists of twenty "documents," or articles, in which he places Lake Nipigon and the Beardmore relics at the heart of Vinland. Document 19 provides transcriptions of the affidavits Curran had gathered. Curran admits he was unable to contact John Drew Jacob (misidentified as John J. Jacob), and he paraphrases Jacob's evidence as presented by C.T. Currelly in the *Canadian Historical Review*. The second part consists of versions of his original twenty-six newspaper articles as well as a version of his November 1938 address to the Empire Club.[1]

Curran had consulted an array of experts, including the Norwegian archaeologist Theodor Petersen, who thought the Beardmore sword dated to the eighth or ninth century and was possibly from eastern Norway, which put its manufacture well before the voyages in the Vinland sagas and in a region from which those voyages did not originate. Curran proposed that the sword "may have been lost in Canada many years before Leif the Lucky came to Vinland."[2] He did not consider the problem of a very early sword from eastern Norway's being found in a grave near Lake Nipigon with a much later axe. Curran otherwise appealed to an anti-elitist sensibility that continues to define pseudohistory and pseudoarchaeology. "In the case of the white Indians some pooh-pooh yet, – no such thing as evidence of a Norse infiltration, etc. Well, who are we to contradict men who do a lot of reading and heavy thinking. But you and I who tramp the woods and have hob-nobbed for a lifetime with Indians and seen things nobody could give a reason for, we have our own notions. And after all isn't our education mostly just the things experience knocks into us even if it jars some old notions we have read somewhere."[3]

His 6 October 1938 article, retitled "How Doubt Was Cast on Dodd's Find," was extensively reworked. Curran had allowed in the original article that Eddy Dodd could be "exasperatingly uncertain" about dates, but the book version offered an extended discussion involving himself, Judge McComber, and Dodd in September 1938 over whether the discovery year was 1930 or 1931. Curran never explained how (or when) the date was shifted to 1930. In his article transcriptions, where the discovery date was concerned, he simply changed every original reference to 1931 to 1930.

Despite the revisions, errors went unaddressed. Foremost, Curran repeated the false assertion that C.T. Currelly conducted his typology research with Scandinavian experts before buying the relics. The Dodd affidavit Curran published even indicated that Currelly agreed to buy the relics before he had questioned Dodd on the discovery details. Curran also repeated the statements Carl Sorensen had made about Bloch's never having possessed relics. Curran could not know that only weeks before publication, in a letter to Elliott, Sorensen had dramatically changed his mind about James Hansen's story. Sorensen for some reason did not volunteer his new faith in Hansen to either Curran or Currelly.

In his introduction to the affidavits, Curran said he did not believe "there is any possible shade of doubt of the truth of Mr. Dodd's story. No small angle of it has been overlooked in the patient search."[4] He made no use either of Fletcher Gill's belated scenario of having heard from Dodd about the relics in the spring of 1930 or of the statement Hansen had provided to Judge McComber. He never acknowledged that Teddy Elliott, in trying to provide free advice in the autumn of 1938, had shared with him a "log" of events that indicated that Dodd had told the schoolteacher the discovery occurred in May 1933. Curran also did not know that the statement Dodd signed for the museum at the time of sale said that he had left the relics at the middle claim until 1933.

Not even Hjalmar Holand, who in May had dismissed Elliott's concerns over variances in the discovery date, could ignore the contradictions in Curran's book. "While most of the affidavits seem to point to the year 1930 as the year when Dodd found his relics, P.J. Bohan's affidavit is quite positive that the find was made in 1931," Holand wrote to Curran on 24 August. "What do you think?"[5] No reply is preserved. While extending some measure of congratulation, Holand scolded Curran for the book's title and central thesis: "You fail completely to prove that 'here' was Vinland. Many lay readers will pat you on the back and tell you that you have found the location of Vinland, but no experts on the discovery of America will agree with you." Holand was making final preparations for his own book, and on 7 October would tell Vilhjalmur Stefansson it would be called *Westward from Vinland* – a phrase from the original translation of the Kensington stone that likely also served as a retort to Curran's *Here Was Vinland*.[6]

Elliott was vacationing with family on the Niagara peninsula when, on 9 August, he received his copy of Curran's book. He saw at once the contradictory timing evidence in the affidavits. The next day, Elliott received a telephone call at his sister's house in Niagara Falls. It was Royd Beamish, and he wanted to meet. The *Globe and Mail* reporter arrived the next day, Friday, and they spent the afternoon reviewing the hoax evidence. Beamish envisioned a series of articles, and he returned to Toronto with documents to show his editors. Elliott visited with Beamish in Toronto on the following Tuesday to review details of the case. On Wednesday, Elliott learned that two editors had turned down Beamish's story pitch. If Hansen were brought to Toronto, they suggested, "the story would carry itself," according to Elliott, but otherwise they "feared the libellous nature of the information." Elliott's strongest opportunity to counter the Dodd discovery story had failed. He wondered if Currelly had been approached and had had the story killed.[7]

Elliott was not being paranoid. Canadian editors reflexively consulted the museum director before publishing anything that might involve him. On 14 September, Clifford P. Wilson, the director of the Hudson's Bay Company's Winnipeg museum and its magazine on Canadian history, *The Beaver*, sent Currelly the draft of his review of Curran's *Here Was Vinland*. "Please do not hesitate to criticize the enclosed review quite freely," Wilson instructed. Currelly did not hesitate to do so. "My general criticism is that you might rewrite the whole review not quite so harshly," he summarized. Wilson agreed his draft was "a bit severe. It was written just after I had put the book down, and such distortion of fact always makes me perhaps unreasonably indignant."[8] The review never ran.

Elliott was entitled to his bitterness as he recounted for Vilhjalmur Stefansson in late August how *Time*, *Maclean's*, the *Toronto Star*, and the *Globe and Mail* "rejected material on the hoax angle because they feared libel, respected Dr. Currelly's opinion, and distrusted a mere pedagogue who is neither archaeologist nor historian."[9] Elliott had felt a collegial bond with Currelly when he supported the authenticity of the Beardmore relics. Now, because of Currelly's machinations, he sensed he was regarded as an unlettered crank. The general press, to be fair, was deferring to an outsized authority who was gambling a lifetime of credibility on defending this single acquisition in the twilight of his stellar career. Currelly was sixty-three and had considered retiring that year, but he had chosen to stay on a while longer. Elliott told Stefansson he thought Currelly "is convinced of Dodd's duplicity but had committed himself to write *The Canadian Historical Review* article and hesitated to back down."

The hopelessness of Elliott's cause only seemed to deepen when the *Globe and Mail* published an effusive review of *Here Was Vinland* on its editorial page on 9 September.[10] It was scarcely surprising that the newspaper's editors had spiked Royd Beamish's proposal a few weeks earlier. The book, the product of the press of a fellow newspaperman: "represents the most notable contribution to Canadiana in some decades ... He has now placed Canada and the world in his debt for a serious study of early Canadian history." If Curran did not "prove beyond peradventure that Vinland was comprised of Ontario, Manitoba and North Dakota," he had produced "convincing evidence" that Norse colonists had used Hudson Strait to gain Hudson Bay and explore the Great Lakes region. Curran's evidence included an "imposing array of relics and other evidence," including the Beardmore materials now in the ROM, "the Curator of which established that they were genuine." Teddy Elliott had been fighting all summer to overcome Currelly's pronouncement of authenticity, and he had lost the battle, turned back in every effort to publish on it or to recruit a media ally.

The next day, Canada declared war on Germany.

When Canada declared war on Sunday, 10 September 1939, the nation prepared to send two divisions of troops to England. On the home front, life otherwise unfolded with a large degree of normalcy. Teddy Elliott resumed his teaching; T.L. Tanton returned from his fieldwork in northern Manitoba to his desk in Ottawa.

On 23 September, Elliott saw the new issue of *CHR* at the public library. His rebuttal to C.T. Currelly's Beardmore article had not run. It had been naive for him to think a submission of such length would materialize in print without any feedback from the editor. Instead, there was a brief mention of Thomas McIlwraith's address to the Ontario Historical Society in June on the Beardmore discovery.[11] Soon after came the October issue of *Canadian Geographical Journal*, in which journal co-founder Lawrence J. Burpee saluted Curran's *Here Was Vinland*.[12] He quoted Stewart Wallace's asking in *CHR* if there was any valid à priori reason the Beardmore relics should not be genuine. If the Kensington stone and the Beardmore relics are authentic, Burpee wrote, "one can hardly avoid the conclusion that Viking adventurers made their way into the heart of this continent long before the days of Columbus. Whatever the final conclusion may be, Mr. Curran is to be congratulated on a very comprehensive and suggestive piece of research."

"As a publicist I am sorry to report that I am a washout," Elliott told T.L. Tanton in mid-October in recounting his failed efforts to draw attention to the hoax case in the general press.[13] Scholarly ranks were hardly more receptive. In a recent encounter, Elliott reported, Reginald G. Trotter, Duncan McArthur's successor as the Douglas Professor of Canadian and Colonial History at Queen's University, who had served on CHR's board of editors in 1937–38, "scoffed at my suggestion that Dr. Currelly might be wrong." Vilhjalmur Stefansson was eager to make personal copies of Elliott's article drafts and to receive the letters that Elliott forwarded to him from A.W. Brøgger and Carl Sorensen, but he had made clear to Elliott in mid-September that he was unlikely to write anything about the Beardmore case in the next year.[14] When Stefansson wished to attract publicity for himself, he knew how to cultivate it. It would have been easy for him to write an article or a letter to the editor raising the typology problems posed by Brøgger and revealing Sorensen's change of heart about Hansen's story. Instead, Stefansson chose to write nothing and busied himself with helping Hjalmar Holand bring his new Kensington stone book to press.[15] Stefansson seemed unable to help himself when any opportunity arose to promote the idea of Norsemen venturing into North America via Hudson Strait and Hudson Bay. Stefansson submitted Holand's manuscript to his own publisher, Macmillan in New York. When Macmillan declined it, Stefansson quickly had the material at Duell, Sloan and Pearce, which to Holand's delight agreed to publish. *Westward from Vinland*, containing a stirring endorsement of the authenticity of the Beardmore relics, would be out in the summer of 1940.

"Lack of standing as an historian, or poor approach has yielded me no results," Elliott told Tanton, "but I'll keep at it."[16]

On Sunday, 22 October 1939, T.L. Tanton drove from Ottawa to visit with Teddy Elliott in Kingston. It was as much a social call as a strategic session – a genuine friendship had formed. The following Saturday, Tanton reported a potentially significant breakthrough.[17] He had been speaking with "an eminent archaeologist (whose name does not appear in this case)" who had agreed to edit an article addressing Currelly's CHR article "or otherwise explaining the presence of the Norse relics on this continent" that could be submitted as a paper to the Royal Society of Canada (RSC). The anonymous archaeologist was probably William Wintemberg of the DGS, who had the experience of presenting and publishing papers in the RSC's *Transactions* before being made a society fellow in 1934. Would Elliott allow Tanton to give the archaeologist a copy of the rejoinder to Currelly's article that Elliott had submitted (without result) to CHR?

Tanton's proposal raises the question of why no discussion was ever held about airing the hoax case through the Canadian Historical Association (CHA). Tanton's scheme, as it happened, came just as there was discussion of the possibility of the RSC absorbing the CHA, although nothing came of this.[18] The RSC had been organized in 1882 as a "national focus for scientific activity," but it was also a literary society.[19] It was organized into sections, with Section 2 the domain of literature, history, archaeology, sociology, and related disciplines. The Beardmore discovery fell substantially under the purview of archaeology, an interest of Section 2, whereas the CHA was the purview of historians working with documentary sources. The fact that Elliott's and Tanton's work was unlikely to receive a warm reception within the CHA was rendered moot by the fact that no CHA venue could accommodate a paper by Elliott. Since 1927, the CHA annual meeting had featured papers, but they were delivered (by invitation) by members, who were largely academic historians, and they adhered to an annual theme.

The RSC, as an institution with a diffuse national membership, was less likely to erect the sort of Toronto-centric obstacles Elliott was experiencing at CHR, which was a quasi-official publication of the CHA. CHA members received a subscription, the CHR advisory board gathered at the CHA annual meeting, and CHA president J.B. Brebner served on the CHR board in 1938–39. As a leading fellow of the RSC's Section 4 (geological sciences), Tanton enjoyed broad connections within the greater RSC and could arrange for a Section 2 fellow to sponsor a non-member's paper, as RSC protocol permitted. That neither Wintemberg nor Jenness, both Section 2 members, would step forward to sponsor the paper underscored the DGS's determination to remain discreetly supportive. Most important, once Elliott's paper was accepted for presentation at the RSC's annual meeting, it could be published in a leading scholarly forum, the society's annual *Transactions*. Tanton would still have to run a gauntlet of potential hostility to Elliott's paper within Section 2, which contained scholars loyal to Currelly, including Currelly himself and Stewart Wallace, who was Section 2 president in 1938–39 and, as the honorary editor, was responsible for the *Transactions*. The "honorary editor" was not a symbolic position. The society's bylaws stated that the honorary editor "shall have the direction of all printing authorized, under such regulations as may be made from time to time, by the Society or the Council."[20]

Elliott informed Tanton that the proposal for an RSC submission was a fine idea. He would update the CHR rejoinder to include the contradictions in affidavits in Curran's book.[21] He also wrote C.T. Currelly for the first time since April.[22] Elliott had come to the inspired conclusion that John Jacob had made more than one written statement for Currelly. Elliott had done remarkably well to pinpoint October 1938 as when Currelly secured an additional statement from Jacob and persuaded Curran (and Dodd) to backdate Dodd's discovery. Elliott was now a much more confident writer than he had been when he first tentatively raised his concerns with Currelly's CHR article in April. He made the barbed observation that, despite Jacob's being an "extremely accurate observer of birds" who had been in touch with the museum for years, he somehow could not get word of Dodd's discovery to Currelly and, upon giving an initial statement after the relics had been bought in December 1936, apparently waited another two years to provide a corrected one. (Elliott did not know there were three statements, with the second in June 1937.) "I can't quite make it out," Elliott dryly remarked. He further noted he had had no success in trying to contact Jacob, and that not even Curran had been able to reach him. "Yet the burden of proof of Mr. Dodd's story undoubtedly rests on Mr. Jacob's statement." He closed by requesting a copy of Jacob's statements and indicated he was willing to pay any associated cost. Elliott said nothing, however, about Carl Sorensen's change of heart on James Hansen's claim to the relics.

Currelly literally had nothing to say to Elliott. While Ethlyn Greenaway acknowledged receipt of Elliott's letter on 2 November, Currelly did not respond to the schoolteacher's shrewd deductions.[23] Elliott had shown he knew that, without Jacob's support, Currelly's authenticity case teetered precariously.

On 2 November, Teddy Elliott came up with a strategy for getting James Hansen to Toronto to inspect the relics. He wrote Peter Sandiford, a professor in the Department of Educational Research at the University of Toronto, reminding him that he had been one of his students in teacher's college.[24] Elliott wondered what Sandiford thought of his applying for a grant available to schoolteachers from the Canadian Council for Educa-

tional Research to bring Hansen to the ROM to help settle the provenance issue. He thought it would cost no more than one hundred dollars. Elliott waited, puzzled, as another letter went unanswered. "I can't understand Dr. Sandiford not even acknowledging my letter," he told Tanton.[25]

Elliott resumed his correspondence with Carl Sorensen. "There is no doubt about Hansen loaning Bloch money," given the documentation in hand, he assured the vice-consul. He wondered if Sorensen knew where Bloch's widow was now living.[26] Sorensen replied that he had heard the widow was in Vancouver, but he was writing contacts in Winnipeg first, and he confirmed that he believed Hansen most likely received the relics from Bloch: "It would seem that Mr. Dodd pulled a stunt netting him a sum of money." [27] Sorensen enclosed a photograph of the Viking float in the 1927 Dominion Day parade, in which he appeared in the company of Bloch and Roy Ohlgren. Sorensen explained that Bloch had designed the costumes for the crew, portrayed by local Norwegians, and that Ohlgren had painted the red and blue shields. Around the same time, Tanton received his own copy of the parade float photo from another source. The prominence of the shield bosses reinforced his suspicion that Eddy Dodd knew what one looked like long before selling the relics to the ROM in December 1936.[28]

The same day that Sorensen replied to Elliott, Tanton advised Elliott that his proposed RSC article had been vetted by an anonymous "authority" – as noted, likely Wintemberg. The article, "couched in language that avoids any possible charge of libel," would be submitted on Elliott's behalf for publication in *Transactions* after being presented at the RSC annual meeting at the University of Western Ontario in late May 1940. Tanton would take care of finding the sponsor. The article would have to be an original statement, which meant that Elliott had to agree not to publish anything substantially similar, including in CHR. "If this article is accepted and published by the R.S.C.," Tanton counselled, "it will make a much more valuable and permanent record than magazine and newspaper articles."[29] Elliott was reluctant not to share credit with Tanton, but went along with the plan.[30]

Elliott was frustrated that neither Currelly nor Sandiford replied to his letters, but otherwise November brought a flurry of progress. C.J. Bjorke, the Norwegian vice-consul in Vancouver, sent Elliott a copy of a death certificate for the man he presumed to be John Bloch – John Peter Blankenborg Block, who died on 20 October 1936, age forty-six, in Vancouver.[31] Bjorke did not know the whereabouts of his widow, but he recalled John

Block's telling him she had been a widow with one child when they married. While there were discrepancies in the death certificate and Bjorke's recollections, Elliott and Tanton provisionally concluded that Bjorke had found the right man. Now they needed to find the widow Bloch to see if she could provide any insight into her husband's relics.

On 1 December, Peter Sandiford finally replied to Elliott's letter of 2 November.[32] The Ontario Advisory Committee for grants had met that day, and the minutes recorded (as Sandiford shared) that the committee "feel it is not advisable to submit a formal request" for funding in support of Elliott's plan to bring Hansen to the ROM. Elliott could still submit a proposal himself, but it would be without the advisory committee's endorsement – an obvious waste of time. "Speaking privately and as a friend," Sandiford suggested Elliott try to secure evidence from Norway proving that Dodd's relics had been lost or stolen from a museum: "With such evidence in your possession the rest of your task should be easy." Elliott would take this advice to heart, but he was otherwise furious with Sandiford.[33] It would turn out that Elliott had cause for anger. Sandiford in truth had forwarded Elliott's grant proposal promptly to C.T. Currelly on 6 November. Long before the advisory committee met, the museum director had killed the idea, which Currelly as much as admitted to Elliott in the new year. "I definitely disapprove of spending a hundred dollars of terribly needed money to bring Hansen to Toronto," Currelly would inform Elliott. "I can't see anything that could be gained by it in any way whatever."[34] Hansen would not be coming to Toronto to confront the relics.

On 8 December, Eddy Dodd returned to the news for reasons that did not please him. The Fort William *Daily Times-Journal* reported he was in hospital with bruises and cuts to his right leg after slipping from the caboose of a westbound CNR train leaving the Port Arthur yard.[35] In Kingston and Ottawa, the plan to have Teddy Elliott present the case against Dodd's discovery to the RSC was gaining impressive traction. T.L. Tanton had found an eminent, if surprising, sponsor for the paper: Lawrence J. Burpee.

Burpee was not an academic historian: his training was limited to his undergraduate years at the University of Toronto. By avocation he was a civil servant, and he was the long-standing Canadian secretary on the International Joint Commission. But in a transitional period of the professionalization of historical scholarship, Burpee enjoyed considerable standing as a co-founder of the Canadian Historical Association and the *Canadian Geographical Journal*, and as a past president (1936–37) of the RSC.[36] Still, he was an unexpected recruit to the cause of exposing the Beardmore hoax, having just praised Jim Curran's *Here Was Vinland* in the *Canadian Geographical Journal*.

To be sure, Burpee's relationship with the Beardmore case was complex. Curran had written him in August 1938, enclosing one of his first articles in the *Here Was Vinland* series and asking him for help with Cree language sources.[37] Why Curran sought Burpee's help is unclear. Burpee had recommended that Curran contact Diamond Jenness or J.B. Tyrrell, but he also read Curran's enclosed article with "unusual interest."

Burpee enjoyed Curran's successive articles. As a leading figure in mainstream historical enterprises in English Canada, Burpee could still be charmed by Curran's speculative case for placing Vinland in the Great Lakes. As the newspaper series ended in February 1939, Burpee asked Curran to provide him with a copy of his forthcoming book so he could include it in the bibliography of a new edition of *The Discovery of Canada*.[38] Curran obliged Burpee, who told him *Here Was Vinland* was "an excellent piece of book-making." He promised Curran the *Canadian Geographical Journal* review that appeared in October, and he ventured *Here Was Vinland* could prove to be one of the three most important books published in Canada that year.[39]

It was odd that Burpee, as the editor of the Champlain Society's edition of the letters and journals of the Sieur de La Vérendrye and his sons, allowed Curran to escape unscathed from proposing that the Mandan people had been improved by interbreeding with Norsemen. Curran never employed Burpee's volume on the La Vérendryes, which left little doubt that the White Indians stories long attached to the Mandan had no basis in fact.[40] Burpee seemed more interested in encouraging vivid historical writing than in critiquing Curran's eccentric ideas. In the past, he had been resistant to the historical profession's revisionism and debunking. When A.S. Morton dared to portray La Vérendrye as a soldier of fortune in the pages of CHR in 1929, Burpee objected, saying Morton had joined "the ranks of the iconoclasts."[41]

When Curran initially wrote him for assistance, Burpee was willing to believe the Norse reached James Bay, but "whether or not any of them wandered as far afield as Beardmore or northern Minnesota is another matter. They liked to keep in touch with the sea."[42] By the time Burpee reviewed *Here Was Vinland*, he could entertain the possibility that the Beardmore relics were authentic. As Burpee's review noted, he had read Holand's *The Kensington Stone* and, "a year or two ago," had viewed the Beardmore relics at the ROM and discussed them with C.T. Currelly. The prominent doubters in Ottawa (Tanton among them) since the review's appearance must have persuaded Burpee that a persuasive counter-case for the find's being a hoax had not been aired and deserved to be heard before the RSC. According to Tanton, Burpee "some time ago" had discussed the discovery with Duncan McArthur as well as with Currelly. Burpee told Tanton that McArthur "was not convinced that the find was authentic and [that] this probably account[ed] for the delay in publication of the *Bulletin*."[43]

On 11 December, Tanton asked Burpee to review Elliott's draft and to consider presenting it to the RSC.[44] Burpee replied the next day, with recommended revisions, but (according to Tanton) felt the article was "good, and appropriate."[45] Burpee hoped that either Tanton or Elliott could be present at his presentation to Section 2 so that one of them could participate in discussions. Tanton had a paper of his own to present to Section 4, and he encouraged Elliott to consider attending.

Burpee's support was a considerable coup. One of the most respected members of the RSC and a leading figure in Canadian history was taking the hoax case seriously. And, having reviewed Curran's book so enthusiastically, Burpee could not be painted as a partisan ally of Tanton and Elliott who was hostile to any new idea about Norse adventuring.

The hoax investigation continued apace. The first Canadian troops had arrived in England on 17 December, but they had no immediate prospect of combat; Tanton and Elliott could still imagine a productive association with A.W. Brøgger in Oslo. Tanton provided Stefansson with a copy of the John Block death certificate and, after an exchange of letters, decided to send Brøgger a copy as well.[46] They were counting on Brøgger to find John Bloch's birth certificate and verify they had the right man. "That would be a fine finish," Elliott told Tanton.[47] It was impossible to know how deeply the war would affect their efforts to counter the momentum Currelly and Curran enjoyed in having the Beardmore find broadly accepted as a Norse burial, and Hjalmar Holand now had a supportive book headed to press – championed, in typically confounding fashion, by Stefansson. But if the war was not yet impeding their research, it was affecting Elliott's conscience. On 1 January 1940, Elliott, who had turned forty-one on 11 December, informed Tanton that he planned to enlist.[48]

"A Once Open Mind Is Closed"

T.L. Tanton reacted with "surprise and regret" on 3 January 1940 to Teddy Elliott's declaration of his intent to enlist. Accepting that Elliott's decision was "a very honourable one, based on a strong sense of duty," Tanton supplied Elliott with reference letters in support of a commission.[1] Elliott's sudden determination instilled an additional urgency in their efforts to expose the Beardmore hoax. On 9 January, Elliott submitted to Tanton his revised RSC article. At nine pages, it was a more focused and disciplined effort than his twenty-seven-page rebuttal to Currelly's CHR article. Currelly's theory for the relics, Elliott planned to assure the RSC audience in May, "seems most attractive on the surface, and makes a stirring appeal to the imagination. Unfortunately, a number of difficulties arise which make the acceptance of this theory well-nigh impossible."[2]

The shock waves from Lawrence Burpee's endorsement of Teddy Elliott's RSC paper, propagating through Canada's small circle of scholars since early December, must have been felt within the ROM and the University of Toronto. In early January, Elliott went from being completely ignored by C.T. Currelly at the ROM and George Brown at CHR to being earnestly engaged.

Currelly wrote Elliott on 8 January, apologizing for the delay in replying to his letter of 31 October.[3] He had been away from the office with unspecified illnesses, initially in the autumn and then for another spell since Christmas, and was under doctor's orders to take a month of rest from the museum. Currelly's battles with anxiety and mental exhaustion had apparently brought him down again. The stress of the Beardmore case was surely a factor. Currelly did not know of Carl Sorensen's change of heart about James Hansen: Tanton and Elliott were holding that revelation in strategic reserve, Sorensen himself was not sharing it widely, and Currelly had become estranged from Vilhjalmur Stefansson, who was aware. But Currelly knew that Elliott was homing in on John Jacob's central importance to the provenance case. Sheltering Jacob's statements from scrutiny was becoming indefensible for a public museum. As an RSC fellow and member of Section 2, Currelly also must have known that Burpee planned to sponsor and deliver Elliott's paper as the meeting agenda was finalized.

The paper could then appear in *Transactions* as a severe and widely readable rejoinder to Currelly's judgment. He needed to address this grave threat.

Currelly's tone was friendly, but he continued to insist on the unreliability of James Hansen and Eli Ragotte. He reiterated that Ragotte, on his visit to the museum, confessed he told his story of discovering the sword in the cellar "as a joke on Dodd; as a matter of fact, he had been kicked out of Dodd's house because Mrs. Dodd would not stand him any longer, and this was his revenge." (This would have been Ellen Dodd's version of events, not Ragotte's.) Currelly recounted questioning Ragotte "with the weapons lying in front of him on the table." Ragotte described the items he had found. "I then asked, 'For instance, they wouldn't be at all like these things?' and he said, 'Oh, no, not in the least,' and he then gave a more careful description of what he had found." Ragotte, however, had told Tanton that the sword was mounted as an intact weapon in a glass case when he saw it and that he only later realized the museum's sword had been in two pieces. "I am sorry my brain will not go against such evidence," Currelly wrote. "It's a very great misfortune that this drunk brakes-man threw a monkey wrench into the whole affair, because without his statement I do not believe Hansen's claim would ever have been imagined."

Currelly said that he had initially hoped to have Elliott visit the museum during the holidays to review the evidence. He now promised to "show you any papers" when he was back on duty at the museum. In the meantime, he provided Elliott with John Jacob's Toronto address. How useful Currelly knew this would be in reaching Jacob is open to question as he had had no success using it himself in early 1938, when he first tried to get hold of Jacob after the acquisition scandal erupted, but the letter held out hope that Currelly would share Jacob's statements. Currelly concluded with the admission that he had advised Peter Sandiford not to support Elliott's idea of securing a grant to bring Hansen to the museum to confront the relics.

As Elliott considered his response to Currelly's letter, George Brown at CHR wrote him on 16 January with sudden interest in his July 1939 riposte to Currelly's article.[4] Brown was about to turn forty-six. He had joined CHR as associate editor in 1928 and had been its editor since 1930, taking over from Stewart Wallace. Like every CHR editor, Brown was a history professor at the University of Toronto; he was also the first member of the department to earn a history PhD from an American institution (the University of Chicago, in 1924). "If Stewart Wallace (now busy enough as university librarian) was the founder of the quarterly," J.M.S. Careless has written, "George Brown was the builder who much enlarged its scope and profes-

sional appeal, paralleling the advancing professionalism of Canadian studies in the 1930s."[5] Brown is credited with making CHR less Toronto-centric,
expanding its board of editors beyond the ranks of University of Toronto
faculty, although its editorial focus continued to be central Canada.[6] For
the 1939 publishing year, when Currelly's article ran, Brown had been
joined by two associate editors from the University of Toronto's history department, Donald Creighton and George Glazebrook (Glazebrook's having just completed a term on the board of editors). The board of editors
was recast as the advisory board, which had twelve members, a reduction
from sixteen in 1938. In 1939, two members were affiliated with the University of Toronto – Thomas F. McIlwraith and Chester Martin, head of the
university's history department – and three additional members had been
educated there.[7] Since 1925, McIlwraith had provided CHR with an annual
review of publications in anthropology and, in 1930, when Brown was the
new editor, had written for it a major review of recent work in his field.[8]

George Brown was very much a product of, and participant in, the university world of Ned Burwash and C.T. Currelly – a world that was focused
on Victoria College, where Currelly regaled faculty with lunchtime tales
of his acquisitions and adventures. George Brown's father, Charles, had
been a star student at Victoria, graduating in philosophy in 1887, and then
in theology, becoming a Methodist (and, after amalgamation, a United
Church) minister. George Brown (who became an active lay figure in the
United Church) had been among the first students to live in Burwash
Hall, and he graduated from Victoria College in history in 1915. He married a classmate, Vera Beatrice Kenny; three of their four children would
graduate from Victoria.[9] In November 1936, as Currelly was poised to purchase Dodd's relics, Brown had delivered the annual Burwash Memorial
Lecture, titled "The Founding of Victoria," the subject of which was the
college itself. Donald Creighton, Brown's new associate editor of CHR,
shared his deep familial roots in Victoria College, where he earned his
bachelor's degree in 1925. His father, William, had attended Victoria University in Cobourg and had completed theology studies at Victoria after
the school moved to Toronto. As a former student and an assistant editor
of the Methodist Church's weekly newspaper in Toronto, William
Creighton was well known to Chancellor Burwash.[10]

Brown apologized to Elliott for the delay in responding to his criticism
of Currelly's CHR article, but assured him he had "given it a good deal of
thought and had it read by my editorial associates." It would turn out that
Brown had also shared it with Currelly, who possessed a copy. The world

of academic history in Canada was small and fraternal, even when extended beyond Victoria College. At CHR there was no such thing as a blind peer review of submitted articles. Currelly's Beardmore article had sailed straight onto the pages of the first available issue, on Currelly's command, and the publication once allowed W.P.M. Kennedy to hand-pick a reviewer of his book and then vet the draft.[11] It is not hard to believe that Brown had discussed Elliott's submission with Currelly and agreed that it was not worth printing (and, given its length, it was almost impossible to print) without bothering to respond to Elliott.

Brown now assured Elliott that Currelly, with his CHR article, "did not intend or attempt to make a detailed explanation of all the considerations connected with the finding and acquisition of the relics. He rather intended to tell merely how the museum had come into the situation and ended up by acquiring the weapons. It was recognized that there would probably be more careful examination later of the entire question by authoritative writers. There has never been any doubt that there were serious gaps and difficulties in the whole story, and I read with much interest your discussion of the details of the case and your criticisms of Dr. Currelly's statements." This was a generous interpretation of Currelly's view of the provenance question and of Brown's own interest in what Elliott submitted.

Whatever George Brown thought personally of the Beardmore case, he faced tremendous pressure, as a University of Toronto professor and the editor of a university journal, not to sully the reputations of Currelly, McIlwraith, the university, and the museum. As someone so deeply embedded in the milieu of Victoria College and the university overall, he also may have blanched at exposing his colleagues and their institutions to a Kingston vocational school teacher's criticisms. Brown thought Elliott's submission read like a "lawyer's brief," a perhaps inadvertent echo of Jim Curran's final article in his newspaper series, "Norse Case Summed Up for Jury" (*Sault Daily Star*, 20 February 1939). While Brown pleaded the lack of space in CHR for such commentary, he assured Elliott there was "no desire, however, to exclude from the *Review* suggestions that there are serious difficulties in connection with the story. If you care to write a letter pointing that out in a non-controversial way, I should be glad to have you do so." Brown had another idea: Elliott should review Jim Curran's book for him. This was a clever solution to the Beardmore dilemma. By turning Elliott loose on *Here Was Vinland*, Brown could allow him to criticize the Beardmore evidence at will, without assaulting Currelly's CHR article. It would be better for everyone if Curran, like Elliott an academic outsider, were the target.

On 18 January, T.L. Tanton confirmed with Elliott that his article would be presented in the Section 2 session at the May RSC meeting in Burpee's name.[12] "I can conceive of no way in which its presentation could now be side-tracked," Tanton advised. Elliott could: a CHR letter, which could transgress the RSC proviso that he would not publish anything substantially similar. Neither Elliott nor Tanton was paranoid enough to imagine that Brown had suggested Elliott write the letter as a way to kill the RSC paper, but Elliott abandoned the thought of attempting one. Brown's idea of reviewing Curran's *Here Was Vinland* was irresistible, and Elliott accepted the assignment. He must have been assured that a critique of Curran's book in CHR would be sufficiently different from his original RSC article not to violate the terms for the latter, which was aimed at Currelly's CHR article but would also address the affidavits in Curran's book. Elliott also accepted Currelly's "kind offer" to visit the museum and examine the Beardmore papers.[13] ("There can be no point in carrying on a controversial correspondence" with Currelly, Elliott advised Tanton.[14]) He could not, however, foresee a visit before the Easter break. As well, he used the address provided by Currelly to write John Jacob about his statements.[15] He never heard back.

T.L. Tanton located and borrowed a copy of Jan Petersen's *De Norske Vikingesverd* from Cornell University, thus becoming the first person in Canada concerned with the Beardmore find to gain access to the standard reference work on Norse weapons. Not having time to inspect it properly and make sense of its Norwegian text, he shipped it to Teddy Elliott. Elliott arranged for a Queen's engineering student whose mother was Norwegian to examine it with him and to provide translation on the fly.[16]

Identifying the heavily corroded Beardmore weapons, based on a single, small photograph, was not easy, even for a trained eye. C.T. Currelly had never made public the typology advice he had received, much of it based on Petersen's volume, and A.W. Brøgger and Sigurd Grieg had addressed only the sword for Tanton. The axe looked like a K type to Elliott, where Stefan Einarsson had told C.T. Currelly he thought the K type was not a good match and favoured the more recent M type. Brøgger and Grieg had identified the sword as a Q type, but to Elliott it looked more like the older M type, as (unknown to Elliott) several scholars consulted by Currelly had advised. To Elliott, it appeared Dodd's sword and axe could be from a single grave, albeit a grave in eastern Norway.[17]

Elliott found Petersen's information on shield bosses, but there was nothing about shield handles. Leafing through the rest of the volume, Elliott came upon a section devoted to items under the heading *Ranglene*.[18] "These peculiar instruments, whose use we are not to discuss here," Petersen began, in addressing the class of objects found only in male graves.[19] The text did not explain what they were, and Elliott's translator did not know the meaning of *ranglene*. They were wire-like contraptions on which metal rings were suspended. Elliott thought part of one of them, figure 46, looked similar to the Beardmore shield handle. He seems not to have turned to the next page, where he would have seen that Dodd's shield handle looked remarkably like the top part of the final example, in figure 50 (see illustrations).

Elliott assumed *ranglene* were some sort of sword harness. In truth, they were rangles, or rattles. These jangling contraptions are thought to have been attached to sleigh harnesses by pagan Norse to ward off malevolent spirits, and they were included exclusively in male burials to ensure the safe passage to Valhalla. The flat bar of the so-called shield handle matched the rattle base in figure 50; the "hooks" were all that was left of the wire-like configuration that held the rings as well as a bell. Petersen explained that rangles followed a clear chronology and that the later, figure 50 example was found only in burials with the more ornate (and comparatively rare) Z and Æ type swords.[20]

C.T. Currelly would have to explain why Beardmore's Norse adventurers, in addition to burying one of their number with a mid-tenth-century sword and a slightly later axe, first breaking the sword in the custom of pagan burials in the Ostfold region of eastern Norway, also had the foresight to bring along a winter sleigh rattle never associated with M or Q type swords, just in case someone needed a proper pagan sendoff. Without a handle, Dodd's scenario of trying to extract a crumbling shield from the ground by its handle would crumble. But as Elliott did not grasp the nature of *ranglene* and overlooked the example in figure 50, an extraordinary opportunity to overturn the discovery of a Viking grave went unrealized. Petersen's volume went back to Tanton. Tanton, who had no time to spend with it himself, accepted Elliott's notes, including the sword harness interpretation of the rangle, and returned the book to Cornell University. No one else in Canada concerned with the Beardmore controversy would examine *De Norske Vikingesverd*.

In early February, A.W. Brøgger sent to T.L. Tanton a copy of the christening certificate for Jens Petter Blanckenborg Bloch, dated 2 November 1890, in Oslo.²¹ There could be no doubt that this was the same person mentioned in the 1936 death certificate secured in Vancouver. Now that they had the beginning and end of John Bloch's life, they needed to fill the gap in between by locating his widow. In his accompanying letter, Brøgger shared his suspicion that Bloch's father acquired the relics between 1880 and 1890, when there was considerable private traffic in Viking grave goods in Norway involving dealers, "jobbers," and farmers who happened upon them. Several Viking graves were still found every year, and many examples of weapons similar to the Beardmore relics were known. As fifty years or more might have passed since the find was made, Brøgger said it was useless to try to determine the original finder or the owner of the land. He also advised that there was no possibility they had originated in a Norwegian museum as these institutions never disposed of or exchanged them.²²

Elliott changed his enlistment plans. His stepmother had recently died, and he now hoped to find a military role that would allow him to remain close to his aging father, which would make an overseas posting impossible. In addition to his teaching load, he was focused on completing his review of Jim Curran's *Here Was Vinland*. The DGS archaeologist William Wintemberg provided him with a lengthy critique of Curran's ideas. In April 1939, Diamond Jenness had forwarded to Wintemberg Curran's questions about an old axe in Ontario that he thought was Norse; Jenness thought it looked like a typical French trade axe, but whatever Wintemberg advised did not dissuade Curran from publishing his evidence of widespread Norse metalwork in Ontario.²³ Elliott was welcome to use Wintemberg's analysis, but he was not to attribute it to him. Foremost, Wintemberg demolished Curran's notion that Indigenous Copper Culture tools were actually Norse. "No archaeologist will agree with Mr. Curran that the copper implements he describes and illustrates were cast" or that they owed their appearance to "Norse influence," Wintemberg advised.²⁴ Curran had misidentified a longitudinal ridge on copper adzes and spear points as a Norse feature, when it was a natural result of the Indigenous manufacturing method of cold hammering and folding. On 18 February, Elliott submitted the draft to George Brown, and shared a copy with Tanton and Wintemberg, who both endorsed it immediately.²⁵

Teddy Elliott's continued delay in making good on C.T. Currelly's January invitation to inspect the Beardmore documents was costly but unavoidable. Currelly had entrenched, his confidence that he could carry the day in the scholarly world renewed. O.G.S. Crawford, editor of *Antiquity*, had written him on 30 December, having seen an item in the October issue of the *Geographical Journal* noting Currelly's March 1939 CHR article. Crawford had already reprinted Philip Godsell's notice in the *Geographical Journal* in his June 1938 issue, and he found the discovery credible. He now asked Currelly to send him a copy of the CHR article so that he could "write a few lines about it."[26] Currelly obliged with the original text and a museum photo of the relics on 17 January (nine days after inviting Elliott to the museum), and, as a bonus, he provided an unsolicited, two-page evisceration of the case against the Dodd discovery.[27] "I am asking you not to publish this letter, as the thing is really too silly to take seriously; and also Hansen, according to the reports I have had, is a man who would probably jump at the chance to enter legal proceedings if anything were published that he could consider libelous. He is poor, in difficulties, and a crooked lawyer might take on the case." Crawford pledged to respect the confidentiality of the letter and assured Currelly that the discovery "seems to be perfectly authentic." The rust stain on the rock, "the kind of thing that would be impossible to fake," was the most impressive detail.[28]

Crawford would reprint Currelly's text from the CHR article and the relics photo in the June 1940 issue.[29] As Currelly waited for Elliott's visit, he could look forward to this significant endorsement of his find from one of the world's leading publications for museum professionals, archaeologists, and collectors. But, on 8 March, a distressing telegram had arrived from a Stockholm newspaper, *Dagens Nyheter*: PLEASE SEND EXACT STATEMENT OF THE FINDCIRCUMSTANCES REGARDING THE VIKINGFIND FROM BEARDMORE PROFESSOR BROEGGER OSLO DECLARES IT IN AN INTERVIEW AS FALSIFICATION ARMS TAKEN OVER NOWTODAYS FROM NORWAY IS THE FIND DOUBTLESS GENUINE.[30]

Currelly did not reply.

Teddy Elliott was at last able to take advantage of the Easter week break to visit C.T. Currelly, but their meeting on 29 March was tense and unfriendly. As Elliott recorded in a memo for T.L. Tanton: "Dr. Currelly took up most of the time in repeating, practically word for word, without pause, the story of the Beardmore relics as he had given it in the *Canadian Historical Review*, March, 1939. During the relating he watched me intently, and at the conclusion abruptly asked me just what it was that I wanted."[31] Ethlyn Greenaway delivered "four or five files," and Currelly said, "I don't suppose you want to go over all this stuff." Elliott wanted to do precisely that, and they jousted over what Currelly had invited him to examine. As there would not be enough time to review everything with the hostile museum director, Elliott chose to begin with the John Jacob statement.

Currelly volunteered a new version of Jacob's visit to the museum in December 1936. A few days after Currelly purchased the relics, Jacob appeared and said, "I hear you bought the Beardmore weapons for $5,000." Currelly replied, "No, just $500." Jacob said it was rumoured in Port Arthur that the price was the higher figure. Currelly alleged to Elliott that the rumoured four-figure value was what had attracted James Hansen's interest. But when Elliott had met Currelly in December 1936 at the museum, Currelly told him that, when Jacob had dropped in a few weeks earlier, he had wanted to notify Currelly of the relics and was surprised to learn that the museum had just bought them. Currelly's new story was also the first mention of any rumour of a five-thousand-dollar sale in December 1936, and it hardly seemed to have inspired Hansen, as Hansen did not hear of the sale until the news broke about the purchase in January 1938.

Ethlyn Greenaway appeared with another folder, containing Jacob's statement. Currelly read it aloud and "continued in a rambling comment about Dodd having sold the relics to a Wisconsin tourist for $25, but as payment had not been completed he (Dodd) felt justified in selling them to the Museum." Elliott interrupted Currelly to ask to examine the statement himself. Currelly handed the material over "but kept up a running comment which made it very difficult to read and absorb details." Elliott recognized that there were actually three Jacob statements, not two as he had suspected: the original short note of 9 December 1936, the longer typed statement the museum dated to June 1937, and the undated, handwritten addendum to the second statement that fixed the discovery in 1930. Elliott absorbed as much of them as he could and questioned Currelly on how they had been prepared. He homed in on Jacob's reliance on the "memorandum notes" for setting the date of his visit to the middle claim to June 1930, as Jacob asserted in the handwritten amendment to his second statement. Currelly had told others that Jacob had recorded the visit in a government report; he now said that the memorandum notes were records kept by Jacob for his personal use and that Jacob had made no mention of visiting Dodd's claims in the official reports he made to the Department of Game and Fisheries. Elliott did not record whether he asked if Currelly had ever seen these memorandum notes.[32]

Currelly explained that the discovery date was changed to 1930 after Eddy and Ellen Dodd called on him at the museum and recalled the illness of their son. But the Dodds had never met with Currelly. Eddy Dodd had agreed to the 1930 date when he and Fletcher Gill met with Thomas McIlwraith in October; in November, Ellen Dodd and Eddy's brother Joseph had met with McIlwraith to cast aspersions on Eli Ragotte. "Dr. Currelly says that this was independent of Jacob's correction and that there was no collusion between Jacob and Dodd as far as he was aware." But Jacob's spring 1938 letters to Currelly (which may or may not have been in one of the folders Greenaway had produced) would have told Elliott that some five months before Dodd agreed with McIlwraith to the change in year, Jacob had informed Currelly he had just discussed changing the discovery year to 1930 with Dodd, on the alleged basis of Walter's illness.

Currelly reviewed Ned Burwash's role in bringing the relics to his attention. Elliott was dismayed to hear the museum director again tell a much different story than the one Elliott had heard during his museum visit in December 1936. Currelly then had said that Burwash admitted he had failed to notify him of the relics. Currelly now told a story of Burwash's involvement that agreed with the documentary record. Elliott found Currelly's complete change of account "a most unethical procedure." Among other elements of the case Currelly confidently reviewed was Eli Ragotte's visit to the museum on 30 September 1938 and the brakeman's declaration that the items he saw in Dodd's basement were nothing like the relics Currelly showed him.

As Elliott and Currelly continued to spar, "the files were piled to one side as if to indicate the interview was at an end, and I was given no further opportunity to examine anything else." Elliott decided to raise the issue of the Hansen-Bloch loan. Currelly allowed that he had heard of this loan from T.L. Tanton's daughter and advised that "it was easy to forge such a document." At that, Elliott produced his photostat of the loan document from the Port Arthur bank. Currelly agreed it was not a forgery but told Elliott: "in no way can it be construed as proof that Bloch passed the weapons over to Hansen as security for a loan. Besides the amount does not tally with that mentioned by Hansen." Currelly added that there could have been "a thousand such transactions between the two men. Why pick on one and say that it was proof?" Currelly assured him that, as evidence, it would be laughed out of court. Did Elliott really think it had any value? According to Elliott, when he tried to argue its weight as "strong, circumstantial evidence," Currelly "laughed in ridicule, and said that under no circumstances should I place myself in such a position by advancing the note as such flimsy evidence." In recounting the meeting for Duncan McArthur, Currelly would contend that Elliott "did not put forward one single fact until I was finished," and then he produced the photostat of the Bloch-Hansen loan document. "I asked Mr. Elliott how any sane person could associate the note and the [relics]."[33]

When Currelly turned to ridicule, Elliott decided there was no point in sharing any more information. Currelly mentioned Carl Sorensen's assurance that Hansen's story had no merit, and Elliott decided not to reveal that the vice-consul had concluded Hansen's story was likely correct. The meeting clearly was over. "I thanked him for his trouble and apologized for taking up so much of his time and withdrew."

"My interview was not particularly conducive of results," Elliott summarized for Tanton, "and I feel that little was gained beyond an impression that a once open mind is closed, that a man in authority is irritated by having his opinions questioned by some one of no standing."[34] Elliott's Toronto visit was a tour de force of disappointment. He had not been able to copy Jacob's statements, could not locate John Jacob as he had hoped, and an attempt to see Duncan McArthur about the long-promised government report on the Beardmore relics was equally fruitless.

Elliott returned home to a mail bag of good news. George Brown thought his review of Curran's *Here Was Vinland* was "very good indeed" and would run it in the June issue of CHR.[35] Manitoba's vital statistics office had found John Bloch's marriage certificate. C.J. Bjorke in Vancouver had advised that Bloch's wife was a widow of Icelandic descent, and the certificate for the marriage in Winnipeg on 5 March 1929 gave her name as Shana Lyons. To locate her, Tanton had already enlisted the help of a colleague, George McLeod Brownell, an assistant professor of geology and mineralogy at the University of Manitoba, who in turn gave a third-year student the unusual assignment of finding her. Vilhjalmur Stefansson was willing to assist in the investigations, if not to publicly challenge the Beardmore provenance. Tanton understood that Stefansson was arranging for something to be placed in an Icelandic community newspaper in

Manitoba in the hope that someone still knew Shana Lyons and where she could be reached.[36]

Elliott thought Currelly should have secured a statement from Aaron Lougheed to substantiate John Jacob's claim that they had seen the relics together at 296 Wilson.[37] Tanton agreed that it was time to resume his correspondence with Lougheed, and he wrote the retired surveyor around 10 April.[38] Tanton thought both Lougheed and Jacob were complicit in the hoax. Bloch had lived in the Ruttan Building, where Lougheed had long resided, and Tanton suspected Lougheed had known Bloch when he still owned the relics and had designed the Viking ship float for the 1927 parade. Lougheed either saw or knew about the relics, and he also knew what a shield boss looked like and how it would fit over a grip or handle from the parade float. "When the relics turned up in the possession of Dodd," Tanton proposed to Elliott, Lougheed "wouldn't need to go to a library in order to identify them – though in returning to his own residence to think things over he could very well say that he had gone to the library (in the Ruttan block)." John Jacob, as the brother of a well-known journalist, "may have appreciated and helped to develop the story or journalistic possibilities of the circumstances as he found them."[39]

Despite Tanton's suspicions about Lougheed and Jacob, it wasn't clear who had been – or still was – collaborating with Dodd. Lougheed outwardly appeared innocent, as in his note the previous spring he had encouraged Tanton to ask how the sword could have endured for centuries in such porous ground. But Lougheed was a loner, a notorious socialist, and Jacob, as Elliott and Tanton would learn, was also said to hold unorthodox political views. One could imagine Lougheed at least abetting a hoax, laughing at the sophisticated fools who fell for it, then teasing Tanton, whom he seemed to respect, with clues. All that appeared certain was that the relics had not emerged from beneath a dynamited tree stump on the middle claim and, instead, had probably been unearthed in a farmer's field in eastern Norway. Elliott and Tanton hoped to learn still more from Brøgger about their origin. Tanton's most recent letter to Brøgger included Elliott's notes on the weapons typology in Petersen.[40] Brøgger would be able to recognize the true significance of the *ranglene*, and the ROM's provenance case would all but collapse. But as Tanton observed to Elliott on 10 April, "It is fortunate we had correspondence with Dr. Brøgger before these serious complications." That day, on the front page of its international news section, a *Globe and Mail* headline announced: "Norway's Capital 'Goes Down Fighting' as Cities and Towns

Bombed, Occupied by Nazis." The German invasion of Norway was under way and Brøgger's Oslo had fallen.

Tanton would never hear back from Brøgger. Neither Tanton nor Elliott knew that Elliott had all but identified the shield handle as a pagan sleigh rattle. Elliott had submitted his RSC article without mentioning the *rang-lene* evidence, and he would never again note the similarity of the so-called handle to the strange items in Petersen. He had come within one obscure Norwegian word of securing the ammunition that would have devastated Dodd's discovery story.

22

"The Onus of Proof"

On 22 April 1940, Aaron Lougheed replied to T.L. Tanton with another short, enigmatic letter.[1] "I saw that relic & heard [Dodd's] story about 5 years ago – I did not know John Block but believe he was here [in the Ruttan Building] at the time you state, his present address seems to be unknown." Lougheed thus denied he was any part of the discovery scenario offered by John Jacob that Currelly had described in CHR and, further, stated that he had only learned of Dodd's find around 1935. "I have no personal knowledge of this matter – but will give you a sketch from memory of the relic it is in 2 pieces." Lougheed made a credible drawing of corroded sword parts, the hilt end marked as fifteen inches long, the blade as twelve inches (see illustrations). The museum's photos were so well known by this time, however, that it was impossible to be certain Lougheed's drawing was based entirely on memory. "The hilt part of about 15" was practically free from rust & the balance heavily rusted what condition would be necessary to give this result," Lougheed elaborated: "No inlays and no markings."

The fact that Lougheed knew to look for inlays and markings suggests he had more than a casual familiarity with Norse weapons, and so he may have done some library research after Dodd showed him the relics. He had otherwise written another teasing letter suggesting something was not right about Dodd's find. His previous letter had questioned how an iron relic could have survived some nine hundred years in the porous ground of Dodd's claim. Now Lougheed indicated that the pieces of the sword had been in completely different states of preservation. He was inviting Tanton to ask himself why. One possible explanation was that Dodd had shown him pieces from two different broken swords: Dodd had mismatched the parts when he showed a single sword to Lougheed. It was interesting that Lougheed specified the blade part was about twelve inches, when both the hilt and blade parts in the ROM purchase were about fifteen inches. Had Lougheed made a drawing and taken measurements before heading to the library?

If there were two swords, Eddy Dodd may have said he couldn't find the relics to show Elliott in August 1936 because he had sudden pangs about *which* sword his absent wife had shown Elliott a few days earlier. Had Dodd bought a broken sword from Bloch at the Mariaggi Hotel and then showed it to visitors to 296 Wilson around 1930, only to stumble on a set of Bloch relics, including another sword, in the basement of 33 Machar, which he then began showing off in 1933? If ever there was a second sword, it has long since disappeared. In summarizing Lougheed's short letter for Elliott, Tanton did not mention the sword's strange condition.[2] "I have written Mr. Lougheed inviting a further statement on points in the *Review* article," Tanton advised Elliott. Lougheed, perhaps exasperated by Tanton's failure to focus on the significance of the sword's peculiar condition, did not respond.

At the end of April, Teddy Elliott had an outstanding dollop of gossip to share with T.L. Tanton on Aaron Lougheed, John Jacob, and other Lakehead figures.[3] Elliott had been visited in Kingston by Robert Bell, the husband of Elliott's sister-in-law, Pearl. As a travelling salesman for a Port Arthur clothing store, Bell called on "every lumber, mining, and road camp in the district and knows most of the people." Lougheed, Elliott passed along from Bell, had lived in the Ruttan Building for almost twenty years. He "is getting old, and is rather abrupt and sparing with his words as we can see from the letters. Bell also said that Lougheed was checked up by the provincials for distributing leaflets that were Communistic, and warned to cease such operations."

Bell was a font of salacious material on John Jacob, "the slipperiest customer in the district," who reportedly went by the name Jacobson. "The provincials are trying to locate an outboard motor that Jacob obtained from an American tourist and hid in the bush in the hope of selling it." Bell was certain Jacob had lost his job as a provincial fish and game warden because the authorities had caught him trying to sell 124 beaver skins at Nipigon. He was "always up to some scheme" with William Feltham, who had provided Jim Curran with an affidavit asserting that he had seen the relics at Dodd's prospecting camp in the spring of 1930; Jacob had assured C.T. Currelly that Feltham was "a man whose word is good to all who know him and is accepted without reserve here." Bell didn't know Feltham well, "but says he has been mixed up in several shady deals having to do with bootlegging." Bell then reported that Jacob was staying at the Mariaggi Hotel and was "supposed to be working for a timber co. near

Capreol so you can't place much confidence in him."[4] Elliott further informed Tanton that Bell did not think much of Eddy Dodd or two of his affidavit writers, Patrick Bohan and George Hynes, "but says Gill is just a sucker for Dodd. Hansen he brands as a talkative soul."[5]

More intelligence trickled in from the Lakehead as Elliott's wife Kate encountered mining engineer Julian Cross, who was visiting his niece at Queen's University. Cross, laughing, allowed that Tanton "had written pages to him, but that he did not want to get mixed up in the affair. He added it was common knowledge in the north country that Dodd had planted the relics but did not suggest where proof could be obtained."[6]

Out west, there was a major break on the Bloch file. The Winnipeg geology professor George Brownell had tracked down Bloch's widow, Shana. Brownell had somehow learned that she was the daughter of Grimer and Isabella Grimson, in Red Deer, Alberta.[7] Records show that "Shana" was a nickname. Her proper name was Christina, or Kristana. She was born in Iceland in 1893 and adopted by her parents before they immigrated to Canada in 1902. Around 1914, Shana had married Irwin Lyons, a Manitoban employed as a CPR clerk. According to the 1916 Alberta census, the young couple had two children, a two-year-old daughter and a three-week-old son, when they were living next door to Shana's parents in Red Deer.[8] Shana was widowed when Irwin died in 1919.[9] After marrying John Bloch in Winnipeg in March 1929, Shana and her second husband had moved to Vancouver. City directories in the 1930s listed Bloch as a labourer with the Vancouver Harbour Commissioners.[10]

Brownell then learned that Shana, twice widowed, had recently remarried, to a carpenter named James Hastings, and was living in Vancouver on Pacific Street, near Sunset Beach. On 7 May, Brownell took the initiative of writing her.[11] He explained that Viking relics from Beardmore at the ROM were thought to have actually originated with her late husband. "If you have any recollection of having seen or heard about such relics in Mr. Bloch's possession and could tell us about them it would be of great assistance to us in attempting to straighten out this matter of history. We would like to know particularly if Mr. Bloch brought them out from Norway himself or where he obtained them. We would welcome your co-operation in this matter and I would especially appreciate hearing from you with as little delay as possible."

Shana Block Hastings replied to Brownell with the requested promptness, but with confounding information.[12] "I remember my late husband Mr. J. Block telling me of giving some articles to the Royal Ontario Mu-

seum, and I feel sure he did not bring them from Norway. He once told
me he had a dog team I believe for the Hudson['s] Bay [Company], on the
Lakes near Port Arthur, when he was investigating something for them, so
there may be some one there that could give you more information on it."
She had nothing more to add. Tanton and Elliott considered the letter
both encouraging and dismaying. Although Shana Block Hastings had
agreed that her late husband once possessed Norse relics, her story made
no sense and could hardly be considered supportive of their theory that
Bloch brought relics from Norway and surrendered them to Hansen.

Tanton decided Bloch's widow needed a more thorough briefing. He
wrote her on 13 May, with a personal touch that Brownell lacked.[13] He
thoroughly addressed Dodd's find, Hansen's claim, the loan involving her
late husband, Dodd's address changes, her late husband's father, and the
fact that Dodd had sold relics to the ROM for five hundred dollars. He
wondered if her late husband had any living relatives in Norway who
could be contacted as well as if she had ever seen artwork by Andreas
Bloch in which the relics might be identifiable. Tanton suspected that
Bloch's widow had avoided telling Brownell the truth because she knew
it had been illegal to remove the relics from Norway. "From those who
knew Mr. John Bloch I gather that he was a very fine, cultured gentleman,"
Tanton wrote, without directly mentioning the Norwegian law forbidding the export of cultural materials. "If he inherited the relics and wanted them as a personal keepsake I am sure that there was nothing wrong in
his having them. If there was any information available that would further
confirm the story by Mr. Hansen it would be much appreciated. The true
story of those Relics is a matter of very considerable historical importance.
While inviting you to recall Mr. Bloch, I wish to express my sympathy to
you, and hope that I am responsible for reviving only pleasant memories,
not the painful ones." It was a risky letter. Tanton may have mentioned the
price paid to Dodd to pique her interest in recovering the relics, but he
had provided so much information that anyone who simply wanted to get
at the money could manufacture a story based on what he had shared.

As Tanton waited to see if Mrs Block Hastings' memory improved, he
prepared for the RSC meeting, a week away. In addition to delivering his
own paper, on a new age for the granite at Saskatchewan's Amisk Lake,
Tanton was also presenting a paper on behalf of Ned Burwash, "Liquidus
and Solidus," on the nature of magma. Whether by accident or by design,
this arrangement had given Tanton the chance to question Burwash on
the Beardmore find.

Burwash did more to confuse than to clarify the record. He claimed he was the one to come up with the Norse provenance. Dodd "was apparently quite surprised … I do not know who if any one, thought of the Norse origin of the remains before myself, since no one much interested seems to have seen them before I did."[14] The assertion was not credible as Burwash had stated in his February 1934 letter to Currelly that Dodd, with a friend's help, had already determined a Norse provenance at the library.

Burwash revisited what Dodd had told him about the discovery, reaffirming the central role of the shield. It was "only about 9 inches by 18 if my memory is reliable. It was so completely rusted through that when he took hold of the handle to lift it out of its bed, it went completely to pieces leaving the handle only in his hand. The axe also puzzled him because of its pattern, and had something in the eye which looked like a piece of schist. He was sure it was not wood. (It may have been whalebone, which was sometimes used in making handles of war axes). He unfortunately lost it."

Burwash's recollection was another indication that Dodd had been trying to assert that the relics were so old that they had become fused with the ancient rock. This appeared not to bother Burwash the geologist, who considered Dodd's discovery credible, but he differed with his old friend Currelly on several points. Among them, Burwash had no time for John Jacob's story, as related by Currelly in CHR, of having investigated the provenance with Aaron Lougheed, and he believed that the Beardmore Vikings had approached via the St Lawrence as the route to Lake Nipigon from Hudson Bay "is, as you know, one of the poorest." He considered valueless Jim Curran's notion that the widespread Indigenous word for wooden boat arose from an encounter between James Bay Cree and Norsemen. When Tanton tried to shake Burwash's faith in Dodd's story, Burwash repeated Currelly's standard talking points about the poor case against Dodd. "Dodd's story bears examination much better than Hansen's. This also agrees with what responsible people in Port Arthur told me when I enquired as to the facts as near as my memory serves me now, and I remember deciding to let the matter stand at that."[15]

Tanton was making plans for a new summer of fieldwork at Steep Rock Lake, near Atikokan, west of Thunder Bay. He touched base with a Fort William lawyer, Harry Henault Beeman, to let him know he would be passing through town and hoped they could meet to discuss the Beardmore case. Tanton had learned the previous autumn that James Hansen was considering retaining Beeman if he decided to file suit against Dodd or the museum to retrieve the relics. Beeman, coincidentally, was an old classmate of Tanton's at the University of Toronto, and when the geologist initially contacted him, Beeman revealed that, as president of the local Canadian Club chapter, he had just hosted a talk by Jim Curran on his new book. Beeman put great faith in the opinion of C.T. Currelly, but he was intrigued by the possibility of a hoax.[16] However, he almost withdrew from further involvement after making his own enquiries. "I believe what Hansen says is the correct version of what occurred," Beeman had informed Tanton in late February. "The difficulty is, Hansen is such a discredited individual, in a personal sense, I do not believe anyone who knows him would believe him, under oath."[17] Tanton had been able to maintain Beeman's interest, even though the lawyer's time was severely limited by the demands of setting up a new practice with a young partner, James F.W. Ross. Beeman now felt that the impending visit by Tanton "may be a good opportunity for all interested parties to get together for an evening – I mean yourself, and probably Carl Sorensen, Judge McComber, Hansen and any other person interested. To speak very frankly I regard this matter as a serious one, and of such a nature that it is of no use whatever to merely brush the surface."[18] That Beeman thought Judge McComber might join a discussion of how to proceed was a promising sign.

Teddy Elliott was able to arrange one day away from school for the RSC meeting. The secretary of Section 2, James F. Kenney, director of historical research and publicity at the Public Archives of Canada, arranged to have the paper scheduled to accommodate him.[19] Elliott had hoped that Lawrence Burpee would present the paper and that he could limit himself to answering questions.[20] Kenney, however, informed him he would be expected to read it.[21]

On Monday, 21 May, Section 2 of the Royal Society of Canada assembled in the main building of the University of Western Ontario to hold one of its five sessions. Twenty-eight society fellows attended the sessions, along with "a considerable number of visitors."[22] T.L. Tanton, occupied elsewhere with his Section 4 obligations, was unable to join them in hearing Teddy Elliott present his Beardmore paper.

The war news that morning delivered false hope: "GERMAN DRIVE TO CHANNEL PORTS BOGS DOWN."[23] In truth, Allied forces were being crushed in Belgium; the Germans claimed to have taken 110,000 prisoners.[24] Canada pledged to raise a third division. The Battle of Britain had begun, and the desperate evacuation at Dunkirk was days away.

It was noon when Elliott's turn came to present, with the lunch break pressing. Before he could begin his delivery, he was met with a blindside assault by C.T. Currelly's loyal ranks. Stewart Wallace, the University of Toronto librarian and honorary editor of the RSC's *Transactions*, was going to read a statement from section member Currelly that presented the case *for* the authenticity of the Beardmore find. There was no mention of Wallace or Currelly in the program, and Elliott had received no forewarning.

On 13 May, Wallace had written Section 2's president, George Herbert Clarke, head of the English department at Queen's University.[25] "Currelly has called me up about the paper that is being presented before Section II by a Mr. Elliott on the Beardmore relics. He naturally regards the paper as an attack on the Royal Ontario Museum and its management, since the Museum has bought the relics and vouches for their authenticity." Currelly wanted to attend the meeting and "speak in answer to the paper," but a scheduling conflict with a museum board meeting would not allow it. Instead, Currelly wondered if Thomas McIlwraith could attend on his behalf "to reply to any criticism in the paper. I do not know whether Mr. Elliott is reading the paper in person, but if so, it would seem to be only proper to allow Professor McIlwraith to reply to him, especially when Currelly has requested it. Failing this, I would be glad myself to read a statement from Currelly; but McIlwraith is so much better acquainted with the background of the whole business that it would of course be much better for him to represent Currelly."

Clarke could see no reason why McIlwraith should not be allowed to reply to Elliott's paper, or, failing that, why Wallace (as Wallace suggested) could not read a statement from Currelly. "Our programme is pretty full, however, and I imagine it will be necessary to be a bit rigorous about the time limits."[26] Wallace let Clarke know he would inform Currelly that McIlwraith would be permitted to make a reply.[27] For reasons unknown, McIlwraith did not appear; instead, Wallace initiated the alternate plan of reading a Currelly statement. But rather than wait for Elliott to deliver his paper, Wallace insisted on going first, using a large dollop of Elliott's presentation time.

The Beardmore controversy surely resonated with Wallace's purported debunking of the myth of Laura Secord, the War of 1812 heroine who claimed to have crossed enemy lines and walked nineteen perilous miles to warn British troops of an impending American attack. (Coincidentally, another scholar who doubted Secord's story was Milo M. Quaife, one of Hjalmar Holand's chief irritants on the Kensington stone's authenticity.[28]) Wallace, in his Secord work, had intended to deliver "a lesson in the use of evidence," according to Donald Wright.[29] Cecilia Morgan argues that Wallace's "inveighing against unreliable memory highlights an important means by which professional historians attempted to distinguish themselves from the amateurish 'others': their preference for the solid, weighty documents found in the archives, as opposed to the supposedly ephemeral, insubstantial, and unverifiable reminiscences that many [historical] societies used (what present-day historians might call oral histories)."[30] As Elliott was an amateur relying substantially on oral recollections from James Hansen and others, his investigations were precisely the sort of thing Wallace sought to condemn. Mind you, the affidavits rounded up by Jim Curran in support of Dodd's find were no better. Their only difference was that personal recollections had been transformed into legal documents, which gave them a weight that historians preferred. Wallace may also have been put off by another similarity between the Secord and Beardmore cases. He suspected Secord of telling her story for financial gain – a ferry lease and a pension. Currelly was convinced Hansen was advancing a bogus claim to the relics to secure an underserved windfall.

Tanton had assured Elliott that, as a sponsored author, "you have in the section sessions the full privileges that go to Fellows."[31] That proved to be optimistic. Currelly's preemptive statement, delivered by Wallace, was an affront to scholarly protocol and professional courtesy. "When I think of it now," Elliott reflected around 1957, "there was a David and Goliath element in my naive presentation before such an August body."[32] The nature of Currelly's statement is unknown, but it was probably the bulk, if not the entirety, of his *CHR* article. Elliott's speaking time was curtailed, with lunch looming, much as Clarke had warned might happen. "Dr. Wallace, representing the Museum, gave his side, and I, urged by the Chairman to hurry because of the lagging agenda, sputtered and spoke so quickly that I doubt if any of the brainy ones knew what I was saying." The scholarly world was not a place where a vocational school teacher could necessarily engage in an unencumbered pursuit of the truth. Elliott was now well apprised of how Currelly could find new ways to hobble his efforts to expose a hoax, however genuinely Wallace might have felt that Elliott's evidence fell short of the evidentiary standards he set for professional historians.

Elliott chose to find something positive in the experience. "What is important is that Hansen's story was presented in quarters that will take some cognizance of it," he informed Tanton. "There was considerable personal satisfaction in the venture for me to be able to present our side of the story to those who were inclined to skepticism." He was particularly pleased to deliver the paper in the presence of Reginald Trotter of Queen's University, who had just been made a fellow of the society and previously "had derided any claim that ran counter to Currelly … Dr. Barbeau's comments did give the matter a filip [sic] in the right direction, I thought."[33] Tanton, too, was "quite pleased" with what he had heard of the "spontaneous contribution" of DSC anthropologist Marius Barbeau to the paper's discussion, especially as Barbeau had not been involved in discreet reaction to the Beardmore find at the DGS.[34] Barbeau had commented favourably on the unlikelihood of the Beardmore relics surviving for almost one thousand years where they were buried. Tanton also reported that Vilhjalmur Stefansson had asked him for a copy of Elliott's paper.[35] Elliott's work was being taken seriously.

From two other fronts came news of losses. Tanton's last letter to A.W. Brøgger had been returned, undelivered, for reasons that were scarcely surprising. All mail service to Norway was suspended now that it was under German occupation. There was no longer any possibility of drawing on the expertise of Brøgger or his colleagues. Brøgger would survive the war, but not without hardship. As a member of Norway's national theatre board, he was arrested and imprisoned for a few days in the summer of 1941, then rearrested in September and interred in the Grini concentration camp for more than a year.[36]

More shocking was the news that reached Elliott in the form of two clippings from the Lakehead, both dated 13 May. "Find Coat, Cap; Drowning Seen," read the Port Arthur *Daily News-Chronicle* headline. "Miner Believed Victim of Lake," was the Fort William *Daily Times-Journal* version. John Jacob had vanished.

Jacob's identity was elusive to the end. Both newspapers identified him as John Jacobs. The Port Arthur newspaper called him a former game warden in Quetico district; the Fort William newspaper said that he was a former overseer with the Department of Game and Fisheries. Both agreed he was from Toronto and was last seen on 9 May. That evening, he was "understood to have put out in a canoe" to cross an ice-strewn Eva Lake in the Kawene District, one hundred miles west of Thunder Bay. Jacob supposedly was planning to examine mining claims for a Toronto syndicate on the far side of the lake. On 11 May, his cap and coat were found on the shore, but there was no sign of him or, apparently, of the canoe. The Ontario Provincial Police had gone to the lake to begin a search. There was no mention of Robert Bell's rumour that the police were already looking for him regarding the matter of a missing outboard motor. Colonel L.S. Dear would recall in 1959 that he was with Jacob the night before he left for the Quetico area on a prospecting trip: "He was drowned in Eva Lake, but his body was never recovered."[37]

Tanton was deeply suspicious of Jacob's vanishing. It scarcely seemed possible that C.T. Currelly's troubled star witness to a Viking grave without a body had drowned without leaving a trace of his earthly remains and a cap and coat as his relics. Tanton wrote to Jacob at his Toronto address. The geologist could not have expected a reply, given how relentlessly Jacob had ignored him when he was unquestionably alive. But Tanton had served notice that he was watching and waiting for him back in the mortal realm.

Tanton's suspicions were well-founded. No death certificate was ever issued in Ontario for John Jacob in 1940, let alone for a drowning in Eva Lake in May. Jacob never resurfaced.

On 2 June Shana Block Hastings replied to T.L. Tanton with a story that differed entirely from the unlikely one she had offered to George Brownell.[38] "Mr. Dodd did not have any claim on those relics," she asserted. "Mr. Hansen's story is absolutely correct." She had not yet met John Bloch during the crucial period, but she remembered her husband's telling her he had borrowed thirty-five dollars from Hansen, using the relics, and "often said that when he was in better financial standing he was going to send him the money" as they were from his father's collection. "Mr. Bloch was very proud of his family and ancestors, and a very capable man, but through no fault of his own went through a lot of financial embarrassment, and I had hoped that it had not been brought up again." His father was "a noted artist and was a cartoonist for the largest Norwegian paper, also illustrated pictures for the schools, and portraits of nobility which is in possession of the Crown Prince of Norway."

To her credit, Shana Block Hastings did not show any interest in securing Eddy Dodd's five hundred dollars – or even the relics. Tanton immediately shared the letter with Elliott as well as with Stefansson, who was "ever so interested" in her statement. "It does seem to clear up the situation," Stefansson advised. He still had no specific plans to publish about the Beardmore relics, but he asked to continue to be kept apprised of the investigation.[39] In sharing Stefansson's comments, Tanton remarked to Elliott: "This seems to leave the field to you."[40]

About to leave for Steep Rock Lake, T.L. Tanton rushed to capitalize on the Block Hastings letter, working with Section 2 secretary James Kenney to draft a two-paragraph insert with excerpts at the end of Teddy Elliott's paper in the coming *Transactions*.[41] Tanton also had an important meeting scheduled en route, in Thunder Bay on 17 June: lawyer Harry Beeman had arranged the proposed conference with Judge McComber. Tanton stopped first in Hornepayne, where the local CNR superintendent told him that "local men along the line do not take the story of the find seriously." The superintendent promised to send him the employment record confirming when Patrick Bohan was stationed at Warneford.[42] But Tanton was never able to secure the record, which would have verified whether Bohan was indeed working at Warneford between May and July 1931 when he said he saw the relics at the middle claim.

Tanton's Monday in Thunder Bay was consumed by strategizing on how to challenge Dodd's find. He met with James Hansen and convened with Harry Beeman and his new law partner, James F.W. Ross; Judge McComber; and mining engineer Julian Cross, who was more willing to be involved in the Dodd affair than he had indicated to Elliott's wife in Kingston. Judge McComber's presence was a tribute to Teddy Elliott's persistence in challenging the discovery story championed by Jim Curran. Curran's ad hoc investigative committee, chaired by Judge McComber, apparently was no more. A new committee, dense with legal wisdom, was determined to extinguish the historical fiction of Dodd's discovery. Tanton informed the group of Elliott's RSC paper and shared a copy of Hjalmar Holand's new book, *Westward from Vinland*, which Vilhjalmur Stefansson had steered to its New York publisher.

Holand devoted a chapter to "The Viking Grave at Lake Nipigon." He made no effort to address the concerns Elliott had raised with him after Currelly's CHR article appeared. The investigations by Jim Curran and Judge McComber, Holand assured readers, "have been so thorough, with results so convincing, that there seems to be no doubt about the authenticity of the find."[43] That observation must have pained the judge.

Holand proposed that an exploration party from Greenland, hoping to circumnavigate the new lands to the west, had left the relics in Eddy

Dodd's mining claim. He crafted a romantic scene for the burial of the expedition's leader, beneath the wall of schist. "Down to the solid rock they
dug his grave, then placed him there beneath the monument that Nature
had provided. His head was to the west facing the dawn whence would
come the Lord of the Resurrection Morning. On his left side lay his trusty
sword, on his right his axe. His arms were folded over his breast and over
them lay his burnished shield. Then, perhaps, while his comrades in arms
stood bareheaded around the open grave, one of them repeated as much
of the liturgy for the dead as he could remember."[44] Holand was so swept
up in the moment he forgot to mention that the burial was a typical
pagan one and that there was not an actual body or any evidence for how
Holand had contrived to arrange the weapons.

As the Fort William conference attendees marvelled (or cringed) at
Holand's prose, Teddy Elliott was writing Holand.[45] Elliott had not been
in contact with him since the spring of 1939, and he brought him up to
date on his recent activities. He revealed not only that he had delivered a
paper to the RSC sponsored by Lawrence Burpee that cast doubt on the
discovery but also that John Bloch's widow had been found and had affirmed that Bloch had brought relics from Norway and given them to
Hansen as security for a loan. It is difficult to know how much (if at all)
Elliott still respected Holand's opinion. Tanton would write Holand an
overly aggressive letter on 29 June, all but accusing him of having forged
parts of the Kensington inscription.[46] Holand, in reply, was sceptical of Elliott's assurance that the Dodd provenance had been overturned, as one
would expect of someone who had just published an endorsement of it,
but Holand was genuinely confident that no counter-claim based on
Hansen's story was credible.[47] "I would suggest going slow before releasing any printed stuff about it," he cautioned. The only person who could
cast serious doubt on Dodd's find was Hansen: "and in a letter to me he
states definitely that he has no intention of doing so. He adds that he has
no knowledge that Mr. Dodd has made fraudulent claims." Holand did
not offer to share that letter with Elliott, but he asked for a copy of the
Block Hastings letter. Failing that, he wanted her address. "While you say
she has 'corroborated' your findings, that word is too elastic to depend
up[on]. Please let me know her exact words."

Elliott chose not to reply to Holand. It was enough that he had served
notice of what he was up to. Holand forwarded Elliott's letter to Jim Curran, assuming that Curran knew of Elliott's RSC presentation. "Judging by
former letters from Mr. Elliott he is motivated largely by disgruntlement

toward Mr. Currelly," Holand proposed.[48] Holand did not comment on the fact that Elliott had just reviewed Curran's book for CHR. For his part, Curran was unaware of Elliott's exercise in genteel demolition.

"This book presents the unusual views of an enthusiastic journalist regarding the location of Vinland of the Vikings," Elliott's review began.[49] He largely paraphrased William Wintemberg's (unattributed) criticisms of the archaeological evidence Curran presented in support of his "unorthodox views,"[50] then he addressed the discrepancies in the discovery date for Dodd's Beardmore find in the published affidavits. Elliott noted that Curran, in his original *Sault Daily Star* articles, mentioned the discovery date as 1931 twelve times but had offered no explanation for the change to 1930 in the book's version of the affidavits. "In fairness," Elliott concluded with transparent condemnation, "it must be pointed out that this book was not written as an historical treatise. Mr. Curran, undoubtedly, would be the first to admit that gaps in the logic of his arguments must be bridged by faith until time and research prove or disprove his contentions. There is no doubt that he has accumulated many interesting facts that stimulate the imagination."[51] Elliott had skewered Curran's fabulist historical interpretations for readers of Canada's leading historical journal while also airing doubts about the discovery of Dodd's relics.

Curran's scholarship may not have impressed a vocational school teacher, but it continued to enjoy support among leading academics. The Oxford geographer John Norman Lear Baker, author of the authoritative and oft-revised *A History of Geographical Discovery and Exploration*, reviewed the book favourably in the July 1940 *Geographical Journal*. Baker accepted the Beardmore relics as genuine, largely due to Currelly's authority. While he quibbled with Curran's scholarship, the book's contention that Vinland was around Lake Nipigon "certainly puts the onus of proof on those who are disposed to doubt it."[52] Teddy Elliott and T.L. Tanton were doing everything they could to produce that proof.

The Precedence of Fellows

On 2 July 1940, Teddy Elliott boxed up eight files containing 456 documents, all the evidence he had gathered on the Beardmore case, and entrusted them to the CNR to deliver to lawyer Harry Beeman in Fort William. A group consisting of Beeman, his partner James Ross, Judge McComber, T.L. Tanton, and Teddy Elliott had resolved to use the legal system to expose the truth about Eddy Dodd's find. Beeman and Ross hoped to launch an action against the ROM on behalf of Shana Block Hastings and James Hansen. Their objective was not to secure a financial windfall for their clients or even to recover the relics; rather, by establishing in court that the relics rightfully belonged to Block Hastings and/or to Hansen, they could correct a grave error of history as a successful suit would establish that the relics had originated in Norway with Andreas Bloch. If the relics remained on display at the ROM, they could no longer be used as proof of a Viking incursion into the Great Lakes.[1]

There is no record of Beeman's attempt to secure representation for Hansen, although Beeman would inform C.T. Currelly that Hansen was involved. The group may have concluded (as Beeman had already informed Tanton in February) that Hansen was too discredited for a court action. However much they were inclined to believe him now, his story had simply changed too many times; instead, they would act on behalf of Shana Block Hastings, who could then settle the outstanding debt with Hansen, should she want to recover the relics for herself or resell them.[2]

Harry Beeman had opened discussions with C.T. Currelly on 18 June, notifying the museum director that "certain parties" had located Bloch's widow.[3] (He was careful never to reveal to Currelly her name or location.) Beeman had evidence that tended to confirm the Beardmore relics were the property of either Bloch's widow or James Hansen, but any decision Beeman made to proceed with an action against the museum "will be entirely apart from any information given by Mr. Hansen in this connection." He invited Currelly to share his position on whether the relics "were ever rightfully owned by Dodd, and, of course, properly sold by Dodd to the Museum."

The two men sparred through the postal service for about six weeks, with Beeman's trying to get Currelly to confirm the museum had paid five hundred dollars for the relics and Currelly's doing his best to assure Beeman he didn't have a chance of making a case – and that even if he did it would not be worth Hansen's or Bloch's widow's (or Beeman's) time. Currelly would not say what the museum had paid, but he argued that the relics were worth far more as archaeological evidence for Vikings in the New World than they were as undocumented grave goods in Norway. If Beeman made his case, Currelly assured him, the relics might be worth about fifteen dollars, which surely was a bluff. Currelly further suggested the relics would be difficult to sell if a suit successfully recovered them as Norway's heritage export restrictions would have been violated.

Beeman made it clear that he was more interested in correcting the historical record than in securing a financial result for a client. His problem, as he circled with Currelly, was that he did not have an actual client. Discussions with Shana Block Hastings were proving to be protracted. She was unhappy with Hansen's behaviour. Hansen should have notified her when Dodd stole them, she informed Beeman, "as my late husband fully trusted him with them." [4] Bloch had left the relics with Hansen in a gentleman's agreement, she maintained. "Surely [Hansen] doesn't feel that he is the owner of said relics. I was the rightfull [sic] owner." But she admitted: "I don't suppose there were any written agreements concerning the relics." Before agreeing to representation, she wanted to know what would happen to Eddy Dodd, and who would benefit from a sale of the relics. She understood Dodd had sold them to the ROM for five hundred dollars "which was not half their value." Hastings concluded: "I would like this matter cleared up as soon as possible, as it keeps opening old sorrows."

Beeman explained that the group interested in the relics was concerned not so much with getting them back from the ROM as it was with "having wiped out entirely the assertion that these genuine Viking Relics (which they are) were found *in or near Beardmore*." As for their value, he understood that they had indeed been sold to the ROM for five hundred dollars. He enclosed a copy of a Currelly letter to him in which the museum director asserted they might be worth as little as fifteen dollars, which Beeman called "absurd and false."[5]

Beeman assured Hastings that he did not think anything very serious would happen to Dodd, in case that was a concern to her. He considered her the rightful owner of the relics and that, if she wanted them in the event of a satisfactory outcome, she could have them, subject to settling the outstanding debt payable to Hansen and meeting the legal costs of the recovery. The action was otherwise costing her nothing. Beeman ignored the considerable problem of Norway's export ban on cultural artefacts – prudently perhaps, as Norway had been seized by Hitler and an enemy-occupied country was unlikely to get them back. Beeman proposed the relics should be left at the museum, and be considered a gift from her, provided the ROM was prepared to remove any mention of their having been found at Beardmore in the display description.[6]

Beeman's best hope was that Currelly would simply acknowledge the provenance problems and change the display labelling. That was not going to happen. "I am as anxious as anyone can be about the Beardmore things," Currelly informed Beeman on 23 July, "but I cannot disbelieve the evidence that I have received and which I forwarded you" – a reference to his CHR article. "I don't see how Mr. Dodd could have stolen them from a house in which he was not living, and if he did how Mr. Jacobs could have seen the imprint on the rock, and the other men have seen them beside the trench."[7]

Beeman was back to Currelly at once.[8] Currelly's contention that the relics were discovered as stated in his CHR article appeared to rely on confirmations by two people. One was Dodd, "who is, in the opinion of the writer who is a lawyer and fairly critical, a wholly irresponsible person." The other was John Jacob. "I knew this man well in his lifetime," Beeman stated, presuming Currelly knew he was missing and considered dead. But Jacob's vanishing seemed to surprise Currelly – a penciled margin note on the letter read: "drowned last spring." Jacob, Beeman advised, "was a sort of dreamer, had most unusual views on many subjects, including politics and religion, and was generally regarded locally as a man who did not have a well-balanced mind." Beeman went on to raise doubts about the survival of these metal relics in a shallow burial at Beardmore for almost one thousand years. The next day, Beeman dangled the possibility Currelly could retain the relics if he would acknowledge the widow's rightful ownership and thus agree to remove any mention of Beardmore from their display.[9]

Currelly rejected any possibility the relics originated with John Bloch, continuing to uphold Jacob's testimony to the rust-stained rock and to defend the way the discovery date was changed. On the matter of the survival of metal relics, Currelly pointed out that "thousands of objects of the Viking period have survived (that is why we know them) buried in graves. More thousands of Roman things have survived, of steel."[10] He would not discuss the purchase price ("no museum is allowed to discuss its financial dealings") despite Dodd's having stated it in the affidavit published by Curran in *Here Was Vinland*. Currelly may have forgotten he had told Elliott the price on 29 March, but he was not about to commit it to paper for Beeman.

The suggestion Bloch's widow might relinquish ownership to the museum was irrelevant to Currelly. If the relics did belong to Bloch, then Hansen must have secured them the way he contended in a loan arrangement, in which case Bloch's widow "has nothing whatever to do with them."

Currelly faltered in recommending: "I think you might do well to have a chat with Judge McComber, who interviewed Mr. Hansen and could, I think, clear up quite a little bit." Currelly did not know McComber was involved in Beeman's actions, but he was gathering an impression from an unknown source of problems brewing at the Lakehead. The same day that Currelly suggested Beeman speak with Judge McComber, the museum director wrote Carl Sorensen.[11] "There seems to be a number of people who are trying to work up a case for Hansen's ownership of the Beardmore Viking weapons. One or two are stating that you are taking back completely what you said two years ago, and that you now believe that Hansen owned the things. How was it possible for Dodd to have possession of them months before he moved into Hansen's house is not explained. The thing looks positively silly, but I should like to be able to state that you have not contradicted what you wrote to me." Currelly also wanted to know if Bloch was married when Sorensen knew him in Port Arthur. Sorensen appears never to have replied.

Beeman assured Currelly he was "very glad indeed to discuss this matter with Judge McComber who is one of my closest personal friends and whose opinions in this matter I would regard very highly."[12] The letter was cc'd to Judge McComber as well as to T.L. Tanton, which formally made Currelly aware of Beeman's association with both men. Currelly replied on 6 August with a single paragraph recommending further reading on the survival of steel – and nothing else.[13] The correspondence between Beeman and Currelly ended, with Beeman still without a client.

T.L. Tanton meanwhile launched another strategy on 6 August by alleging to an unnamed member of the Ontario government, whose father Tanton had known, that a fraud had been committed in the relics' sale to the ROM.[14] Tanton notified the MLA of the hoax case that Elliott had made in his RSC paper and asked him to confirm that the museum (as an entity of the province) had paid five hundred dollars for them. He assured the MLA that Bloch's widow would donate the relics to the museum if she secured ownership.[15] Tanton waited as this torpedo ran to see if it would ever strike its intended target.

In mid-August, Teddy Elliott was in Thunder Bay. He had a lengthy meeting with Beeman, reviewing documents and hearing of a concern Beeman's partner James Ross had with the statute of limitations.[16] Elliott also finally met James Hansen. At times, it had been difficult for Elliott to maintain his faith in Hansen's story. But after Elliott was able to meet and question him, he was as certain as was Tanton that Hansen was telling the truth. Elliott "tried to shake him, or catch him on the horns of a dilemma but was unsuccessful," as he later told Tanton. Hansen "never wavered on the essentials of his original story, and ... I could not say the same staunchness was apparent in Dodd's various statements."[17]

Shana Block Hastings finally returned the retainer with her signature on 19 August.[18] She found Currelly's contention that such Viking relics were only worth a pittance "absolutely absurd. If what he says is right, why did they buy them?" She did not believe either her late husband or the elder Bloch would have bothered with items that could be bought for fifteen dollars. To her continuing credit, she was not pressing for any financial gain.

Having at last secured a retainer from Shana Block Hastings, Harry Beeman and James Ross paused to consider the next move. Summer turned to autumn, with no further steps taken. Ross informed his law partner on 10 October that he believed an action would fail under the statute of limitations.[19] Ross had also accepted Currelly's bluff and had concluded that, if they proved their case, the widow Bloch would be the owner of relics worth no more than twenty-five dollars: "there is, to all intents and purposes, nothing left to fight for." Ross may have sympathized with the idea of waging a legal battle on a matter of principle, to correct the historical record, but, as the pragmatic new law partner, he probably doubted their ability to undertake an action that would leave them out of pocket, even if the statute of limitations did not apply and they won. "I rather regret that the matter has turned out in this way because I was intrigued by the possibility of a lawsuit on such an interesting set of facts," Ross concluded. "That, however, is now beyond consideration."

The legal gambit was over. Teddy Elliott's considerable trove of documents was returned to him. C.T. Currelly had won an important round.

On 11 October, editor George Brown of CHR forwarded Teddy Elliott a letter from Jim Curran weakly contesting the schoolteacher's review of *Here Was Vinland*. Among other things, Curran absurdly attributed the change in the discovery date from 1931 in his original articles to 1930 in the book's versions to proofreading errors.[20] Curran had not requested that it be published, and Brown felt it would not be useful to do so, "as probably

other items pro and con will emerge. Some time, though, it would be very useful to have an objective appraisal of all the available evidence on both sides of the question. Whether such an appraisal would come within the limits of an article in *Canadian Historical Review* or whether it would be better to publish it independently would have to be decided later." Elliott liked the idea of an impartial investigation, whether it was conducted by CHR, the Ontario Historical Society, or some other such body. He had hoped his RSC presentation would lead to one, he told Brown. It would be the only way to remove doubt about the authenticity of the relics.[21]

Brown's suggestion that the CHR would take another look at the controversy, albeit an even-handed one that gave due space to both sides of the dispute, proved timely: Elliott's effort to raise doubts about Dodd's discovery through the RSC was about to come to a distressing end. On 4 November, T.L. Tanton jotted a short letter, asking Elliott if he had received the page galleys for his *Transactions* article as Tanton had just received the ones for his own and assumed they all went out at the same time.[22] Elliott had not.

A letter from Duncan McArthur to C.T. Currelly was suspiciously timed. McArthur had been promoted from deputy minister to the province's wartime cabinet as minister of education on 22 August 1940.[23] On 6 November, McArthur provided Currelly with a copy of Tanton's 6 August letter to the unnamed government MLA.[24] McArthur pointed out that he had not seen a copy of Elliott's RSC paper. McArthur, an RSC member, may have just learned (perhaps from Tanton) that Elliott's paper was missing from the galleys for the latest *Transactions*. McArthur also could have discussed the absence of Elliott's paper with Section 2 secretary James Kenney. Both men were born in 1884, and McArthur knew Kenney well from his years at the public archives after graduating from Queen's University, when McArthur began collaborating on papers on constitutional documents with his mentor at Queen's, social scientist Adam Shortt, and Dominion Archivist Arthur Doughty.[25] McArthur informed Currelly that the implication in Tanton's 6 August letter that Dodd had improperly acquired the relics was, as he put it, "news to me." The minister of education asked Currelly to provide "such information as may be in your possession relating to this purchase in order to be in a position to deal with them should any questions be raised in the Legislature."

On 11 November, Currelly composed a detailed report, covering most of six single-spaced pages, on the acquisition and subsequent events, including John Jacob's investigations for him in the spring of 1938.[26] He generally avoided hyperbole but said that James Hansen had a reputation of being "a liar, almost a mental case," and he continued to cling to Carl Sorensen's initial opinion that Hansen was lying and that John Bloch never owned relics, despite having become aware in July that Sorensen had changed his mind. He also belittled at length Elliott's efforts to overturn the Dodd provenance. Elliott "had seemed quite satisfied, even pleased, with my acknowledgment in the *Canadian Historical Review* of his part in bringing the weapons to my attention. But he seems to have gone on a crusade over the whole matter, why I cannot say." Currelly complained that Elliott, in his unpublished rejoinder to Currelly's CHR article, had treated Currelly's effort as if it were intended to be "an exhaustive scientific publication, and he proceeded to pull it to pieces line by line. The editors of the *Review* saw nothing to be gained" by publishing Elliott's critique. Currelly's letter at least revealed that the CHR's editors had forwarded Elliott's rejoinder to Currelly and had spiked it without consulting Elliott. Currelly reminded McArthur that the museum had hoped to complete its publishing on the relics by the fall of 1939 in a *Bulletin* – which suggested that McArthur's ministry had withheld the necessary funds. As well as giving his version of his meeting with Elliott the previous Easter break, Currelly noted Elliott's effort to secure one hundred dollars of public money to bring Hansen to the ROM to see the relics, but he did not explain his own role in killing the proposal or why he thought it was a bad idea.

Currelly also remarked that T.L. Tanton appeared connected with Harry Beeman, and he gave an account of his pas de deux that summer with the Fort William lawyer over a potential legal action. "If there should be any question of seriousness in this matter, I am quite prepared to pay for the things myself," Currelly advised in closing. "Personally I have never had the faintest doubt that they are all right and found at Beardmore. My judgment has been certainly severely trained, and suspicion of different kinds of trickery extremely well developed." McArthur's inquiry ended there, and the matter never did surface in the legislature.

Lawrence Burpee told T.L. Tanton on 20 November that he knew nothing of Elliott's paper being dropped from the *Transactions*: "he considered it worthy of publication and that he wasn't on [the] committee that decided such matters."[27] Tanton tried James Kenney; the secretary of Section 2 explained that funds did not permit the RSC to publish all the contributions and that, as Tanton reported to Elliott, "it had been left largely to Dr. W.S. Wallace to decide [the] method of elimination." Stewart Wallace, with Kenney and others concurring, had decided to give preference to papers by society fellows. Kenney suggested through Tanton that Elliott write Wallace for confirmation of whether the article would be printed and, if not, to request its return. There was no need: the 1940 *Transactions* was in Tanton's hands the next day, and he could confirm that the papers by non-fellows of Section 2 were not included.[28]

The fact that C.T. Currelly's champion Stewart Wallace was ultimately responsible for deciding how Section 2 articles would be eliminated raised suspicions that he had found a defensible way to keep Teddy Elliott's damaging paper out of print. Tanton reported that Burpee considered that the scheme of giving preference to RSC fellows for publication "was good, and he assured me [Tanton] that Wallace would not be biased against your [Elliott's] paper because of its contents or thesis."[29] James Kenney, however, had not been entirely forthcoming on what had transpired. He denied knowing whether the paper was running, when Elliott's paper had been excluded months earlier, with Kenney's meek approval.[30] Wallace evidently had used a budget problem as a pretext to ensure that Elliott's paper was eliminated.

Soon after the RSC's 1940 annual meeting in London, Stewart Wallace had learned that, because of a wartime tax, the forthcoming *Transactions* was facing a budget squeeze and that he would have to eliminate some papers.[31] Not all papers presented at an annual meeting were automatically included in a *Transactions* to begin with. They had to be considered publishable by the section secretary and then submitted as the section's choices to Wallace, the honorary editor. To stay within the revised budget, Wallace notified each section secretary on 11 June that their submissions could not exceed 150 pages.[32] On 22 June, Wallace further alerted paleontologist Walter A. Bell, the secretary of Section 4, to the budget problem and asked how he would prefer to eliminate some of the papers he had already submitted. "In Section II, for instance, we have had to eliminate all papers except those of Fellows."[33] Wallace left it to Bell to decide how to eliminate Section 4 papers, but for Section 2 he had made up his mind without consulting its secretary, James Kenney, who did not submit his list of papers until 5 July.[34]

Kenney was more than capable of judging which papers from the 1940 RSC meeting were worthy of inclusion. An undergraduate at the University of Toronto, Kenney earned a master's degree in history from the University of Wisconsin and a PhD from Columbia.[35] He had begun working at the Public Archives of Canada as a summer job in 1907, and he joined the staff full-time in 1912 after beginning doctoral studies at Columbia. The public archives were the locus of a "renaissance" in Canadian history, as A.L. Burt noted to his wife in 1926, remarking on visits by a parade of scholars, some of whom would figure in the Beardmore story – Harold Innis, Duncan McArthur, Reginald Trotter, and George Brown among them.[36] Both Wallace and Kenney believed in the importance of documents for objective history, but Kenney at least thought a history PhD was important enough for him to return to Columbia after a career delay to defend his dissertation in 1927, the year after he was made director of historical research and publicity at the archives. Kenney did so just as Wallace (who had a master's degree in library science) was publicly lamenting the lack of literary merit in doctoral dissertations. The 1929 publication by Columbia University Press of Kenney's dissertation, *The Sources for the Early History of Ireland*, which remains a seminal work, secured Kenney his RSC fellowship. He had already served as editor of the annual report of the Canadian Historical Association from 1922 to 1924 and had co-founded the Canadian Catholic Historical Association in 1933. From 1935 to 1937, Kenney served as acting Dominion archivist after the retirement of Arthur Doughty, and he was "bitterly disappointed" when a lobbying war secured the permanent position for his colleague, Gustave Lanctot.[37]

Heeding Wallace's directive to limit the section's submission to 150 pages, Kenney had determined that fifteen of the twenty-four papers presented in May were publishable. Among his choices were three by nonmembers, including Elliott's, on which Kenney had worked with Tanton to include an addendum for the Block Hastings letter. Missing from the list of Kenney's choices was a paper on Gabriel Sagard's dictionary of the Huron language by non-fellow Percy J. Robinson, which Wallace had sponsored.

If Kenney's choice of Elliott and not Robinson rankled, Wallace did not confront him. Robinson's paper had already been substantially published in 1939, by Wallace himself, as general editor of the Champlain Society, and Kenney was right to pass over it.[38] In reply, Wallace reminded Kenney of the budget problem. "I have always regarded it as axiomatic that papers of fellows should take precedence over papers by non-fellows, but I should be glad to know that you concur in this course."[39] Kenney had already offered to eliminate his own, lengthy paper, "The Public Records of the Old Province of Quebec, 1763–1791," and publish it privately if necessary.[40] Wallace, however, insisted on publishing Kenney's full paper (as well as his own, on Montreal fur trade merchants, which Kenney had included), even if it meant eliminating all papers by non-fellows.[41]

"I am in entire agreement with you as to the general rule that papers of Fellows ought to take precedence over papers by non-fellows in selection for publication," Kenney allowed. "It might, however, be better not to enunciate it in such a rigid form as to shackle us on some rare occasion when a paper of quite extraordinary merit might be offered by a non-fellow."[42] If this was Kenney's discreet way of attempting to save Elliott's Beardmore paper, Wallace rebuffed him on 1 August: "I am glad to know that you agree that as a general rule papers by fellows should precede papers by non-fellows. I quite agree that occasion might arise when exceptions might be made to this rule, but I do not think that any exceptions need to be made this time."[43]

On Wallace's decision, Kenney's paper would run in its entirety and none of the non-fellow papers in Section 2 would be included. Wallace's manoeuvrings to eliminate Section 2 papers had been more questionable than anyone realized.

"I cannot accuse anyone of improper discrimination," T.L. Tanton informed Teddy Elliott when the *Transactions* appeared with only an abstract of his paper.[44] Elliott accepted with good graces the RSC's decision to give preference to papers by fellows. "I regret not insisting that you accept authorship," he told Tanton, as Tanton had allowed that, had he been the one to author the RSC article, it probably would have been printed.[45] Lawrence Burpee thought Tanton could write an article for the *Canadian Geographical Journal*, but both Burpee and James Kenney advised Tanton that Elliott should submit his paper to George Brown at CHR.[46]

Tanton told Elliott to write Stewart Wallace, note the support of Tanton, Kenney, and Burpee for the article's appearance in CHR, and ask him to recommend it to Brown.[47] Wallace demurred; he agreed only to explain to Brown why Elliott's paper was not included in the *Transactions* and leave it to CHR's editor to decide whether to publish it.[48] On 10 December, Kenney wrote Brown with a forceful endorsement of Elliott's article.[49] Kenney explained that, due to limited funds, Wallace "quite rightly" had decided to omit Section 2 papers not authored by society fellows from the latest *Transactions*, but he found the nerve to argue for the importance of Elliott's paper – something that had eluded him when Wallace had manoeuvred him into agreeing to eliminate it. "The paper has a controversial character," Kenney advised, "and there might, therefore, be some objection to giving it space in the *Review*. But the subject is important – if the discovery (Beardmore) is authentic, I presume it is the most important discovery of archaeological remains of European origin ever made in Canada – and the matter presented by Mr. Elliott seems to have such a strong bearing on the question of authenticity, that I would think that this matter should be made available to Canadian historical students through the medium which will best serve that purpose, that is, the *Canadian Historical Review*. However, that is, of course, only my personal opinion." On Tanton's further recommendation, Elliott contacted Brown on 11 December, reminding him that Brown had indicated to him some months earlier "that at a later date further space might be permitted" in CHR on the Beardmore find.[50] His RSC paper, to his mind, fit the bill. It was now up to Brown to deal with a strongly worded assault on C.T. Currelly's judgment – something that he would have preferred never to consider for the pages of CHR.

Around seven in the evening on 11 December, Chief Constable H.B. Dickenson of the RCMP's detachment in Portage la Prairie, Manitoba, received a call informing him a body had been found in the snow by the CNR tracks. The man's head had been badly lacerated, he had an abrasion down his back, and one of his hands had been pulverized. It did not take long to determine that the dead man was Eli Ragotte. Somewhere down the tracks the previous day, between Oakville and Elie, a CNR freight train's crew had noticed that the conductor was missing. Ragotte had been adding cars as the locomotive rolled eastward for Winnipeg. He had apparently slipped and fallen in the winter weather and been run over by his own train, a fate Eddy Dodd had narrowly avoided the previous December departing the Port Arthur yard. Ragotte was fifty-three years old.[51]

"I was very sorry to hear of this," T.L. Tanton wrote Teddy Elliott on 16 December, two days after Ragotte's funeral in Winnipeg, "as I had expected that some further contribution might be made by him."[52] Elliott agreed: "It is unfortunate that Eli Ragotte passed on without contributing a definitive statement, which, in the present light, might have been corroborative. Is it not strange that Ragotte, Jacobs, Bloch, and now Dr. Burwash, have passed on before this thing is settled? And none of them in particularly advanced years."[53] Elliott was mistaken about Ned Burwash – it was his brother, Lachlan Taylor, who had died. But fate was proving to be unkind to the figures caught up in the Beardmore controversy. Elliott did not appear to know that Mary Black, the librarian who had made the first public announcement of the find in August 1936, had died as well, the previous winter, at age fifty-nine. The coming months would exact an additional toll.

24

The Judge's Survey

Canadian Historical Review editor George Brown began the new year of 1941 with the unhappy task of managing the Beardmore controversy. CHR was a University of Toronto publication, and the chief proponents for the relics' authenticity were leading university figures. Teddy Elliott, on the other hand, was neither an accredited historian nor an archaeologist, and he was arguing that the Royal Ontario Museum, a university institution, had failed to do its job in determining a defensible provenance for Dodd's relics. But Brown was also a history professor who had a scholarly duty not to leave Currelly's offhand article of March 1939 the publication's final word on a matter of such consequence. Elliott's unpublished Royal Society of Canada article raised enough serious questions that scholars like Lawrence Burpee and James Kenney believed that, in the name of historical integrity, they needed to be aired in CHR. The Beardmore controversy was becoming a litmus test on how Canada's professional historians managed a dissenting opinion, even when the dissent had support within scholarly ranks.

Brown wrote Elliott on 1 February 1941, having discussed his RSC paper with several faculty members of the University of Toronto: Chester Martin, head of the history department, Harold Innis, and Stewart Wallace, "and others here in Toronto."[1] He had shared the article with C.T. Currelly and Thomas McIlwraith, who were on the university faculty as well as the museum staff. He had also spoken with Kenney and Reginald Trotter of Queen's. Brown did not mention discussing the paper with any members of the CHR's current advisory board, although Martin and McIlwraith had been serving when Currelly's 1939 article ran and Trotter had served a term ending on 31 December 1938. The lack of consultation makes one wonder how effective and active the board was in providing editorial oversight.[2] Brown said everyone he had consulted agreed that the CHR "has a special obli[g]ation both in the way of bringing out relevant evidence and also of giving a lead to the whole discussion. I have felt the importance of this from the beginning, as it seems to me most desirable not to encourage an interminable argument such as has developed over the Minnesota Stone." This was an overly self-congratulatory interpretation of how CHR had treated the controversy as Brown had not responded to Elliott's objections to Currelly's statements for six months and, in fact, only did so after Lawrence Burpee had agreed to sponsor his RSC paper.

Brown assured Elliott he found "no disposition on the part of anyone to discourage or oppose the publication of the evidence which you have collected. The feeling is, rather, that we are all indebted to persons like yourself and Mr. Curran who have spent a great deal of time and effort in trying to get all the facts about this intriguing problem. There was general agreement that the *Review* should print a balanced survey of the available evidence up to date. My only query about your article is that it appears to take one side very positively. It is, if one may use the comparison, more like a lawyer's brief than a judge's survey and summing up of the entire evidence" – a criticism Brown had made of Elliott's spiked reply to Currelly's article the previous year.

Brown invited Elliott to write the judge's survey. "I can assure you of the assistance of Dr. Currelly and Mr. [sic] McIlwraith, and of others here whose views may be of some value." Brown had already secured written comments from McIlwraith on the RSC paper. "My feeling is that such a statement should not be forced to a dogmatic conclusion," Brown advised. "This, of course, does not necessitate that you leave a completely colourless impression." He wanted the reader, like a jury member, "left free to arrive at his own conclusion. Quite frankly my own feeling is that the question is still an open one, and that it may remain so for some time, if not permanently." Brown said he would publish such an article "without delay." The March issue was already in press, but he could include it in the June issue.

This letter contained abundant reasons for Elliott's dismay. The CHR did not have the confidence (or Brown the editorial independence) to accommodate the sort of no-holds-barred debate over the Kensington stone found in the *New England Quarterly* and *Minnesota History*. Brown expected Elliott to abandon his role as an investigator and critic of Currelly's and McIlwraith's scholarship and accept their advice – even their supervision – on the content of his article. Currelly especially (as Currelly's November letter to McArthur underscored) held Elliott's debunking efforts in complete contempt. T.L. Tanton saw no reason for Elliott to accede to Brown's request.[3] Currelly had published the initial story in CHR without adequately weighing evidence, he noted, and Elliott's article was intended to correct the imbalance. "Your article was written with full knowledge of all that had appeared in print," the geologist counselled. "It treated the salient facts of the case and is a complete statement. It should be published as it stands. You have the benefit of Dr. Burpee's opinion that your presentation of the case is sufficiently good to warrant his sponsor-ship for its reading before the Royal Soc. of Can. and his recommendation for publication ... The article that you have written is a really constructive contribution to knowledge regarding the Relics. To revise this in such a way as to accord with the view that the question is still an open one, and that it may remain so for a long time, would seem to involve a compro-mise with one's own intelligence and integrity."

Tanton allowed that his first reaction to Brown's letter was "to admit that the cards are stacked against you [Elliott] at Toronto" and to recom-mend that Elliott proceed with an alternate plan they had discussed, which involved working with the American historian of Swedish colonial history, Amandus Johnson, to make their investigations public, probably in an American journal. Instead, Tanton suggested that Elliott respond positively to Brown's proposal, asking him to edit the existing article and to indicate where points for the authenticity case should be addressed. Tanton drily suggested asking Brown to advise on how to present "well balanced evidence, with reference to Dr. Currelly's article as an example." Elliott could then decide on whether to proceed with CHR.

Elliott agreed to write the article. "It would be impossible to satisfy everyone," he informed Brown, "but I believe the incident could be pre-sented in such a way as to leave the reader free to form his own opinion."[4] He promised to produce a draft that could be discussed in person in March. He wrote McIlwraith, asking for the "interesting comments" he had provided Brown, along with "any other information regarding the Beard-more incident which you think should be considered in a comprehensive article on the topic."[5] McIlwraith, in reply, adopted a tone of collegial bon-homie that verged on obsequious.[6] "The whole matter is obviously one of intense historical importance. I fully agree with Professor Brown in think-ing that further publication is called for, and that it should be a scholarly, non-partisan appraisal. Without your interest in the first place it is doubt-ful if the relics would ever have got out of Dodds' [sic] wood-shed, and I am delighted that Brown is giving you the opportunity of writing what should be one of the most important documents in Canadian history."

For all its praise, McIlwraith's letter held out little promise of the muse-um's curator of ethnology shifting his opinion. He agreed with virtually none of Elliott's objections to the authenticity case. "Dodd obviously has a reputation as a raconteur," McIlwraith conceded, "and it goes without say-ing that one would feel much happier if the articles had been excavated by a scientist instead of a railway brakeman turned prospector. However, one can do nothing about that." McIlwraith's opinion of the find still came down to his gut sense that Dodd was telling the truth. "I spent a very full twenty-four hours with Dodds [sic] at Beardmore, and would have stayed much longer had I felt that there was anything to be gained by so doing, and came to the conclusion that his story was substantially correct." He acknowledged there might be discrepancies in dates and "embellishments" in Dodd's account, but the basic issue was whether the relics were found in the middle claim, "and it is my definite opinion that they were."

Elliott persuaded himself that writing the CHR article was worth the effort. "I would prefer to play ball and keep control than to have someone else try it and fail to make the proper points," he informed Tanton, but he was mindful of the possibility that the deck was indeed stacked against him in Toronto.[7] He had some cause to believe that scholarly momentum elsewhere was in his favour, having spoken with Reginald Trotter at Queen's. The history department chair, once so scornful of Elliott's efforts to challenge Currelly's professional authority, had been present for his RSC reading and appeared to be listening now. Trotter "suggested that the Museum people were having a difficult time to keep public support" for their Beardmore position. "I told him I wasn't interested in that angle of the story, but was concerned with the truth as I saw it." Elliott warned Tanton that he had heard from the RCAF and might be called to serve. Should he join up, he hoped Tanton would take over the article. "The one I had in mind would leave very little room for doubt as to what our conclusions are."

Teddy Elliott continued to chip away at evidence. A letter to the provincial Department of Game and Fisheries secured helpful information about William Feltham. Feltham had asserted in the affidavit published by Jim Curran that he normally fished in the spring but did not secure a fishing licence on Whitefish Lake in 1930 and so was at Eddy Dodd's camp that May or June and viewed the relics. The department's records showed that there was never an interruption in the licence.[8] Feltham's affidavit was worthless as proof that the relics had been discovered in 1930. Elliott still did not know that Feltham had been working at the middle claim for Dodd in the autumn of 1938, which disqualified him as an impartial eyewitness.

Letters were inadequate to discuss the details of the case, Elliott advised Thomas McIlwraith on 3 March, and he hoped they could meet in Toronto on some future Saturday.[9] Elliott strove to be cooperative while defending his right to question the evidence. "As you say, the matter is extremely in-volved and there have been misunderstandings," McIlwraith replied, and he agreed it would be best for Elliott to come to Toronto.[10] McIlwraith, how-ever, continued to resist evidence of fraud, and he questioned Elliott's con-viction that Dodd was a hoaxer. "I do not believe he is an angel, but I doubt he is a scheming crook. Only a clever and well-informed criminal would at-tempt such a thing, and I doubt if Dodd falls within that category."

George Brown proposed that Elliott submit a draft of no more than fif-teen pages and then come in "so that we could discuss it with anyone whose advice or information might be helpful."[11] At the minimum, the discussion would involve McIlwraith, but there could be no doubt the ar-ticle at some point would pass before Currelly's eyes.

"I have no desire to be wilfully malicious regarding Mr. Dodd," Elliott in-formed McIlwraith on 15 March, "but so many of his statements when checked prove to be erroneous that it is difficult to avoid extreme skepti-cism"[12] He now at least had John Jacob's original December 1936 state-ment, sent to him by McIlwraith, although he was still waiting to have a copy of Jacob's 1937 statement, which was amended around October 1938. On the war front, the air force had offered him a civil service position in Winnipeg, but he had declined it because of school board complications. Elliott suggested to McIlwraith that they meet during the Easter break, the week of 14 April, so he could examine the files Currelly had produced but had not allowed him to inspect the previous Easter. He also wrote Tanton with an update.[13] "If and when I get a chance to have a real discussion in Toronto I do not intend to hold back any longer but will definitely stand my ground. From the tone of McIlwraith's letters one would suppose that I was on trial." He wished that Tanton could join him for the Easter break conference. Tanton doubted he could do so but, on 17 March, wrote him with observations and support.[14] He shot down McIlwraith's various counter-arguments but did not discourage Elliott from pressing forward. Tanton also noted that he had written several letters to John Jacob at his Eglinton Avenue address since his reported drowning, enclosing stamped, self-addressed reply envelopes. No reply had been received, but evidently neither had his letters been returned as undeliverable.

On 7 April, Elliott sent Tanton a copy of his article draft and shared ter-rible news from Thunder Bay.[15] J.H. Bartlett, the wireless operator at Bar-riefield in Kingston, who had lived in Port Arthur, had dropped by his house. Bartlett was examining a group photograph from Port Arthur – probably the 1927 parade float photo – when he recognized Carl Sorensen.

Bartlett revealed Sorensen had died a few weeks earlier. "According to Mr. Bartlett the circumstances surrounding his death gave rise to the impression that it was not altogether an accident that Mr. Sorensen should be found dead while cleaning a revolver in his business office in Fort William." Elliott shared no information from Bartlett as to why the seventy-two-year-old Norwegian vice-consul would have taken his own life.

The truth was possibly more terrible than Bartlett understood. Sorensen had died on 4 February not of a self-inflicted gunshot wound in his office but, rather, from drinking a corrosive alkali in his home. The coroner, J.W. Cook, gave as the cause of death "accidental poisoning," but ingesting an alkali such as household bleach is a well-documented suicide strategy. There was another surprise in the death registration. When the coroner initially filed it on 5 February, he listed Sorensen as a widower, which was common knowledge. Sorensen had arrived from Minnesota with a wife, Nancy Stenersen, according to his 1916 consular registration, but identified himself as a widow in the 1921 Canadian census.[16] The coroner then learned from a second cousin of Sorensen's, Ove Ring, who had boarded with Sorensen when he arrived in Canada, that Sorensen was in fact married.[17] The coroner duly amended the certificate after Sorensen was buried in Minneapolis on 7 February. The coroner now listed a spouse, Karen, but evidently she was nowhere to be found, and Sorensen had no known children.[18]

Sorensen left no clues as to why he would have made his wife disappear, beyond the shame of a failed relationship, or why he would have ended his own life so horribly. He may have been mortified by his role in the Beardmore affair and found himself on the wrong side of opinions in the local Scandinavian community. His denouncements of James Hansen and the idea John Bloch could ever have possessed relics, both in public statements and sworn affidavits, had greatly buttressed C.T. Currelly's conviction that Dodd's find was authentic. After changing his mind about Hansen, Sorensen avoided admitting to Currelly that he now believed Hansen had been telling the truth and that the find was probably a hoax. For whatever reason, like John Jacob before him, Carl Sorensen had arranged his own vanishing; unlike Jacob, his end was as emphatic as Eli Ragotte's, if far less accidental.

For two days during Easter week Teddy Elliott engaged in meetings at the ROM over his CHR article draft. On Wednesday, he met with George Brown and Thomas McIlwraith, in McIlwraith's office. Elliott liked McIlwraith, even if they still disagreed on most everything. His impression of McIlwraith "as a man was good," he recounted for Tanton.[19] "At times there was a feeling of utmost frankness on both sides and despite sharp exchanges of opinion there was no hint of irritability." At one point their sparring ended with a bout of shared laughter. Elliott appreciated "the honest and sincere way in which he tried to see my viewpoints, or at least gave me ample opportunity to explain myself. If it wasn't for his official commitment as a Museum official I think he could be persuaded in time that the Museum story is not the watertight yarn it is supposed to be." But Elliott was disappointed in the CHR's editor. "I thought he would carry more weight than he does. Maybe I misjudge the man. He impressed me as an academic man, not too practical." Elliott foremost found Brown's flattery off-putting. Brown also tried to tell Elliott that no official publication by Duncan McArthur had yet appeared because the education minister "is by nature a procrastinator and means to do these things but never gets around to it." That explanation bore no resemblance to the intelligence from Lawrence Burpee, which indicated that McArthur refused to write about the find because he doubted the discovery.

Elliott and McIlwraith worked through the draft one paragraph at a time, finding almost no common ground. "I tried to hammer away on the unreliability of Dodd and Jacob as the fundamental supports of [the ROM] story," Elliott recounted for Tanton. "McIlwraith freely admits the ethical vagaries of Dodd but does not believe he is crafty enough to conceive of a planting scheme. He thinks such a scheme is too highly complicated for a man of Dodd's calibre." Elliott argued that the plan was, in fact, "exceedingly simple to Dodd." It was only in the minds of people like himself and McIlwraith that difficulties would exist. "I gave him many off-the-record instances of Dodd's unreliability which he could not deny." They sparred over Jacob's credibility and evidence, over the deterioration of iron objects, and over the pagan nature of the sword and burial. McIlwraith proposed that Christian Norse could have acquired pagan weapons through trade and that Dodd had broken the sword, as he had stated, in extracting it.

McIlwraith thought Bloch's widow was only hoping to cash in on the museum's purchase, and he ridiculed Hansen's evidence. When McIlwraith asked if he really thought Hansen's story was true, Elliott replied "there were elements of truth and circumstantial evidence which to my mind were more favorable to Hansen's claims than anything that Dodd could advance." He recounted his meeting with Hansen the previous August, when he was unable to shake him from his essential story.

They argued about the route the Vikings supposedly took to Beardmore. Elliott indicated the superiority of the Sturgeon River to the Blackwater River, but McIlwraith noted that "anything was a possibility if you were a lost group of Vikings wandering through the bush." Reviewing McIlwraith's visit to the site with Dodd, McIlwraith admitted it was Dodd who found the additional "boss" fragment, not him, but "he considered this was the natural act of a man who was not trying to plant anything, as a smart man would have let the investigator find them." It did not occur to McIlwraith that Dodd was forced to "find" the fragment because McIlwraith was digging in the wrong places with his trowel.

Elliott aired the idea that Dodd could have had access to Hansen's houses on Machar Avenue to inspect them as a prospective tenant and thus have helped himself to the relics from 33 Machar prior to any move from Wilson Street. "McIlwraith admitted he had not examined the factors in the time element very closely." When Elliott pointed out how Patrick Bohan's affidavit so authoritatively fixed the find in 1931, and raised Dodd's shifting statements about how long the relics had remained at his camp, Elliott commented: "I think he really suspected then that there was something more in the story than he had given it credit." Elliott, unfortunately, was unable to gain access to all the extant evidence that pointed to Dodd's only having begun to show off the relics in 1933, after he moved out of 33 Machar.

The meeting lasted until six in the evening and was resumed Thursday morning. They also visited C.T. Currelly's office that morning to examine the Beardmore files, some seven in all. Elliott was only able to leaf through them, but he was amused to see a copy of his criticism of Currelly's CHR article that he had sent to Brown the previous June. During the examination, Currelly appeared. "Frankly I am at a loss to know just what he was driving at," Elliott recalled for Tanton. "Much of what he said was a repetition of what he had said on former occasions" about the evidence. The museum director also insisted on the "suability" of people like himself and Elliott; their vulnerability to libel actions occupied much of his ad hoc lecture. Currelly suggested having lunch. "I had had enough of his parrying and declined with thanks."

As their two days of meetings concluded, Elliott moved to cut short a dollop of flattery from Brown and McIlwraith on his efforts "by telling them that regardless of their views and whether they used my article or not, I had spent much time, money and thought on the whole thing; that the article represented my honest presentation of all the facts, and that I was not prepared to change the facts as I saw them to suit them or anybody else, that I felt I had a right to stand on my ground as I felt I was competent to make a statement because of the laborious time spent in research." The meeting concluded with Brown's promising to return the article with comments that would shape it for publication.

On 19 April, McIlwraith sent Elliott the copies of Dodd's and Jacob's statements he had requested. "I enjoyed so much meeting you; discussion is always helpful and I thoroughly appreciated the cordial and cooperative way in which you put forward your views," McIlwraith shared in a handwritten note.[20] "I certainly found it most helpful. It is going to continue to be a tricky subject, I am afraid, but I am delighted that you are going to publish what will undoubtedly be the important pronouncement on the subject."

When Elliott recounted the meeting for Tanton on 26 April, he had still not heard back from Brown. "Frankly, I think that they were a little impatient with me because I had a better knowledge of the subject and could present their own facts in a different light from what they intended." Elliott had left Toronto unsure if anything further would happen with the article, and his hopes were waning. "Brown may so curb the article with requirements as to make the presentation of it from me an impossibility. He tried to tell me that it was decided I was the best 'neutral' to present the ca[s]e as anyone from the Museum would not be able to do so without risking the accusation of bias from the public."

While waiting for Brown to respond, Elliott received a letter from Currelly.[21] "May I ask you quite seriously to avoid any chance of litigation in anything you write?" Currelly began. The museum director then alleged a man had once telephoned him about "a statement regarding the Viking things" and asked him "if I didn't think that constituted a good case for action for defamation of character, as the implication, and in fact the statement, seemed to him clear that it said that Dodd was a cheat and a liar." Currelly did not reveal to Elliott who this caller was, only that Currelly had informed him that libel actions take money and that he doubted Dodd would file suit. "But if this were done for him, at no expense to himself, what then?" the caller countered. Currelly replied: "What would anyone get out of the man who made those remarks?"

"Now a man in your position is eminently suable," Currelly lectured, "just as I am; you can't put your salary in your wife's name, as far as I know. I have felt all through that the province owed you a deep dept [sic] of gratitude for having made those drawings and brought the things to the Museum's notice, and in my announcement of the find I took care to give you what I considered was the fullest credit for it. Therefore I would be very sorry to see any difficulty arise for you in the matter. I am naturally sorry that you do not agree with me as to what is evidence; but that is a private matter, and you have full right to your opinion, as I have to mine. As I told you the other day, my long experience here has made me terribly watchful of the man that you so aptly spoke of as the 'sheister lawyer.'"

If Elliott had spoken of Harry Beeman, perhaps he had made some vague, polite comment of agreement with Currelly during the latter's harangue about Beeman and threats of legal action. Elliott shared the letter with Tanton and wondered: "Is he trying to throw a smoke screen? Making a kindly gesture in looking after my welfare? Or is it a veiled hint to lay off?"[22]

"I am exceedingly grateful to you for your re-iterated warnings re the suable status of people in our positions," Elliott replied to Currelly.[23] His media experience, he continued, made him "well aware of the weird vagaries of the libel law, and [I] assure you that your warnings will be heeded. There is no intention on my part to cause anything to be published which might give cause for libellous or slanderous litigation." If Currelly's intention had been to warn Elliott that Currelly himself might file suit, Elliott was not flinching.

McIlwraith reported to Elliott on 28 April that the CHR editor was "working on the job" and that Elliot should hear from him soon.[24] "I am afraid you may be right in thinking that the Beardmore finds will never be proved or disproved to the satisfaction of everyone; I think the best way of avoiding this misfortune is the article you have written. So, more strength to your type-writer." McIlwraith had checked, as Elliott had requested, to see if an early letter from John Jacob to the museum about Dodd's find existed, as his statements alleged. McIlwraith had located nothing, and he wrongly asserted "the first word we had of the find (or, more accurately, the first word of a find to suggest its importance)" was Elliott's article draft and drawings in late 1936. McIlwraith was either overlooking or did not know about Ned Burwash's 1934 and 1935 letters to Currelly. The letters must not have been in the Beardmore files as Elliott had not noticed them in reviewing their contents, but Currelly had mentioned them in his long letter to McArthur the previous November. Their absence left at a serious disadvantage anyone trying to understand how the relics came to the museum's attention and what Dodd knew about their Norse nature (especially the alleged shield) more than two years before Currelly bought them.

Elliott had also asked McIlwraith about Currelly's lectures on his "suability." McIlwraith strove to put his mind at ease. Because of Currelly's long museum experience, especially his contact with "Levantine traders of all kinds," he was "very cautious about writing anything which could be picked up and used in litigation. Those of us who have had experience with him here can remember how often he has warned us about this danger. He obviously feels that the Beardmore remains might offer opportunity to someone; this may seem unlikely to those of us without his long museum background, but I judge that that is his belief." McIlwraith also stressed Currelly's kindness. "I have known Dr. Currelly for many years, and I can say I know few men who do more for their fellows. I don't know what he said to you on your first interview [in the spring of 1940], but I know he is grateful to you for bringing the Beardmore things to the attention of the Museum, and apparently he is afraid that you may write something which will expose you to litigation."

McIlwraith did not mention the personal agony the museum staff was enduring and how that might now be affecting Currelly's demeanor.

Time was running out on William Wintemberg's sixty-four years of defiance of a congenitally weak heart. T.L. Tanton had reported to Elliott the previous November that the DGS archaeologist who likely had vetted anonymously Elliott's unpublished riposte to C.T. Currelly's CHR article, with an eye to having it presented to the RSC, and had provided the expert opinion to back a demolition of Jim Curran's *Here Was Vinland*, was seriously unwell, having suffered a blood clot.[25] On 24 April, Wintemberg selected a Leonardo da Vinci quotation from some papers at home that concluded: "I thought I was learning how to live. I have been learning how to die."[26] He inserted the quotation into a book he was reading. It was found there when Wintemberg died the next day.

Tanton notified Elliott of Wintemberg's death on 28 April; the funeral was scheduled for that afternoon.[27] Two days later, C.T. Currelly and Thomas McIlwraith were among the pallbearers who carried a casket bearing the body of Ethlyn Greenaway to her grave in St John's cemetery.[28] The flag at the ROM flew at half-mast; the University of Toronto's president, H.J. Cody, and Bishop White, keeper of the ROM's magnificent Chinese collection, assisted at the funeral. Currelly's assistant had once secured a twelve-hundred-dollar judgment against the Toronto Transport Commission for injuries sustained while boarding a streetcar, but, in the end, she had been overwhelmed by several cancers.[29] She died in Toronto

Western Hospital (where Sigmund Samuel was a long-standing benefactor) on the day of Wintemberg's funeral, which was also the day McIlwraith had written Elliott to assure him of Currelly's essential kindness. Greenaway was forty-six and had never married. The ROM, where she had served Currelly for more than twenty years, was the hub of her life. Her absence was palpable in Elliott's account of his two days at the museum during Easter week. Had Greenaway been on hand, she could have told McIlwraith not to bother looking for the letter John Jacob allegedly wrote to the museum about the Beardmore relics when they were discovered as she had already attempted to find it the previous November.

Greenaway initially had been enthusiastic about the Beardmore relics, if harried by demands on her time after the controversy flared in January 1938. By the autumn of 1939, she had had enough of Dodd's find. In sending a copy of A.D. Fraser's *Dalhousie Review* article to Philip Ainsworth Means on 22 November 1939, she wrote with surprising bluntness: "Perhaps you are not as tired as I am of the question of the Vikings in North America."[30] Where Means could indulge a boyish enthusiasm for the idea of roving Norsemen, for Greenaway the relics were a source of escalating institutional anxiety, disruptions in her own duties, and lapses in the mental health of her superior. Jim Curran's book had appeared and "seemed only to make confusion worse confounded," she confessed to Means. A Kingston schoolteacher "is still working on the Beardmore things, and there will be some more controversy about them. Nothing has happened, however, to shake Dr. Currelly's belief in their having been found exactly as described." Eighteen months later, the schoolteacher was still working on the Beardmore things in the face of Currelly's unshaken belief, but Ethlyn Greenaway was no longer on hand to help keep the sixty-five-year-old director and the museum's archaeology division on an even keel, as she had since the end of the First World War.

With Ethlyn Greenaway's loss, the archaeology division had "suffered a well-nigh staggering blow," Currelly remarked in his annual report.[31] He would have to negotiate the remaining manoeuvres in the Beardmore controversy without her.

The Last Word

On 6 May 1941, George Brown notified T.L. Tanton that he had returned the Beardmore article draft to Teddy Elliott. As Tanton reported to Elliott, "He writes as if this might lead to a satisfactory conclusion."[1] The conclusion was anything but satisfactory, to Tanton or to Elliott.

The manuscript arrived with comments, some by Thomas McIlwraith, and a request by Brown for a new approach.[2] Brown had tossed aside his own request that Elliott write the judge's review on which the jury, the magazine's readers, could decide. He now wanted Elliott to evaluate first the Dodd evidence and then the Hansen case, plainly expecting the article to find Hansen's case wanting and to defend the museum's acquisition. "Dodd's story, while it has a number of gaps and uncertainties, is supported by a considerable body of evidence," he lectured Elliott. "Certainly it was so well supported when the Museum acquired the articles that I think the Museum would have been seriously open to criticism had they allowed the articles to go off to some museum in the United States. I think too that there did not appear to be any evidence of a hoax." Brown granted that the possibility of a hoax "cannot even yet be entirely ruled out … and I think perhaps that this point should be raised in your article." But Hansen's story, Brown continued, "seems to me to have extremely weak supporting evidence."

Tanton considered Brown's new concept unacceptable. He recommended Elliott retrieve the original RSC paper from Brown. "I think we can get that published," he advised on 14 May.[3] The RSC was holding its 1941 meeting in Kingston the following week, and Tanton would be on hand to deliver a paper. They could discuss a fresh strategy then.

Elliott notified Brown on 16 May that he had no time to revise the article.[4] In addition to his regular teaching load, he had at last secured war duties, instructing a class of army clerks three hours a day. Even if the additional time demand did not exist: "In all conscience, I cannot write an article upholding Dodd's story. My investigations strengthen my belief that Dodd's story and the interpretations are not justified in view of the unstable foundation upon which it rests." He had committed himself to a specific stand with his RSC paper and could not compromise it now. He intimated his suspicion that Brown was under pressure from C.T. Currelly and his allies when he noted: "I appreciate that you, of necessity, must take cognizance of other controlling factors."

On 22 May, Tanton and Brown spoke at the RSC meeting in Kingston.[5] Brown realized he had overstepped and was probably fearful that an article by Elliott critical of Currelly's 1939 CHR effort could instead appear in a leading American journal. Brown also met with Elliott. "He was greatly perturbed lest I drop the whole thing," Elliott informed Tanton, "and begged me not to do so as he considered that too much time and ground had been covered to date to throw away so lightly."[6] Elliott agreed, but he pointed out to Brown that, while dealing with the article was part of Brown's and McIlwraith's jobs, Elliott was not being compensated for his time. He was working twelve- to fourteen-hour days between his high school duties and war work, and could do as he pleased where the article was concerned. As Elliott had gathered he would not have difficulty placing his RSC article in another publication, he had no interest in cooperating any further with CHR "if I thought that the results of my work would be censored or curtailed in any way by anyone other than himself."

Brown offered to publish his original RSC article but reserved the right to include in the issue a counter-article by McIlwraith or someone else. Elliott would not accept someone from Currelly's side mounting a rejoinder in the same issue. "I preferred to present both stories in my own way." Brown relented. With Brown's "definitive assurance" that no one from the ROM would have a hand in editing his article, Elliott agreed to rewrite his submission in whatever way he saw fit and to submit it for the September issue.[7]

Tanton departed Ottawa for another summer of fieldwork at Steep Rock Lake. There was no stopping economic geology in wartime. On the other hand, with William Wintemberg's death, archaeology at the DGS contracted to the vanishing point during the war. The only employees left on the anthropology payroll at DGS were Diamond Jenness, Marius Barbeau, and Douglas Leechman. Jenness and Barbeau soon left for war duties, drawn into clerical work with the Dependents Allowance Board. Where Barbeau found a way to return to anthropology, Jenness moved on to serve as deputy director of special intelligence, a civilian position with the RCAF.[8]

Tanton stopped in Hornepayne en route, narrowly missing an encounter with Fletcher Gill, but a railway employee there assured Tanton that "no one really believed that the relics find was authentic. Dodd was well known to be windy."[9] In Port Arthur he checked with the tourist bureau to ensure it was not promoting the middle claim as a roadside attraction for the new highway. He met Dr George Eakins, the erstwhile member of Jim Curran's investigation committee, who "jovially accepts the matter is a probable hoax." An attempt to meet with Judge McComber brought unhappy news. He was "ill with a nervous or mental disorder" and could not be seen.

On 22 July, Elliott submitted his manuscript to Brown.[10] Elliott was wearying. He had not retyped a final draft and he told Brown to feel free to "delate or correct any minor errors or points that would not alter the main theme." He would be in Fort William from 1 August and could be reached there, and he closed by advising that he had not submitted the article to a lawyer to have it assessed for libel. He also sent a copy to Tanton, who did not think it read as smoothly or led to as clear a conclusion as had his RSC article, "but that could scarcely be expected in attempting to meet Dr. Brown's objective of a balanced presentation of both sides. You have done very well with a very difficult subject."[11]

On 11 August, Brown informed Elliott that the article had been sent for typesetting with minor edits and suggested one clarification that could be dealt with in the page proofs.[12] On 19 August, Brown shared not altogether surprising news: C.T. Currelly had "requested that the *Review* should take a statement of his conclusions and he has written a short article."[13] When Elliott agreed to write the "balanced statement" article, he had every expectation that it would stand alone. Although in his final agreement with Brown he secured the right to write the article in any way he saw fit, he had still striven to produce an even-handed assessment of the evidence. Nevertheless, Currelly had just wrested from Brown the right to a riposte in the September issue, which was at the printer. Brown scrambled to salvage his own credibility, arguing that where Elliott's article was "a kind of factual statement," Currelly's item "is an expression of opinion." It was nothing of the kind. Currelly's last-minute submission presented his own version of the evidence, addressing points in Elliott's article that Brown had run by him. Brown now strove to be fair in an impossible situation. He enclosed Currelly's statement and invited Elliott to submit a "short note" of his own to accompany what Currelly intended to be the final word. Brown, however, had written Elliott (in Fort William) on a Tuesday, and he needed a note, were it to be included, by early the following week in Toronto.

Elliott was remarkably restrained in not castigating Brown for accommodating a parallel statement from someone at the ROM, let alone a pointed rebuttal of his article by Currelly. "Apparently Dr. Currelly had requested that he be allowed to make comments, and in all fairness Dr. Brown extended me the same privilege," Elliott explained to Tanton.[14]

Still, Brown was asking a lot of him. "Frankly, I am under a handicap in that all of my Beardmore material is in Kingston," he told Brown.[15] He only had a day in which to compose the note and meet Brown's deadline.

Unbeknownst to Elliott, Brown immediately forwarded a copy of Elliott's comment to Currelly, along with the rest of the material that would form the article package, "so that if you wish to add anything to your statement or to change its wording you can do so."[16] Brown was anxious that Currelly approved of the way he had managed the controversy and, above all, that he had succeeded in blunting Elliott's assault on the acquisition. "I feel that we have reached on the whole a satisfactory result, and I hope you will agree. Elliott's article and statement are written in a much more desirable tone than the article he read at the Royal Society. He ends his statement with an expression of appreciation, and so far as I can tell from his letters he is happy about the whole thing. I was extremely anxious to do what I could to prevent feelings of annoyance which might easily create difficulty and would give the public the impression that a wrangle would develop. I trust I am right in feeling that these undesirable possibilities have been avoided."

The package of Beardmore materials appeared as scheduled in the September 1941 issue of CHR. Teddy Elliott's "A Survey of the Evidence" reviewed the Beardmore relics' provenance without any overt suggestion of a hoax or of incompetence on the part of C.T. Currelly, Thomas McIlwraith, and the ROM. Although the case Elliott presented to the RSC was greatly tempered, the article was a thorough tour of affidavits, correspondence gathered during Elliott's investigations with T.L. Tanton, A.W. Brøgger's opinion, and James Hansen's story. Elliott acknowledged discrepancies in his evidence and areas of doubt, and concluded: "Did Mr. Dodd discover a Norse grave containing a set of Viking weapons on May 24, 1930? Or did John Bloch bring a part of his father's collection with him when he emigrated from Norway to Canada in 1923? Is it possible that the issue is being confused by two sets of similar weapons? The full truth may never be revealed to the satisfaction of all."[17]

Currelly, in his rebuttal, sailed through Elliott's problematic details with trademark confidence. Projecting the assuring tone of an old hand in field archaeology and museum acquisitions, Currelly counselled that, as with many archaeological finds, in the Beardmore case the archaeologist "has had to rely on the memories of the unskilled, and often uninterested, men who dug out what have later proved to be important relics, and sometimes to sift laboriously evidence from conflicting statements."[18] Currelly argued that Dodd's unequivocal statements about the discovery were amply supported by affidavits, and he reiterated the support they gave for Dodd's having possessed the relics before moving to 33 Machar. He stressed the importance of Dodd's statement to him about the "bowl-shaped mass of rusted iron which fell to pieces" atop the shield handle. "This was where the boss should have been. Furthermore, the position is as it should have been if the shield were laid boss upright, as was customary in most burials."[19] While contradictions in the dates of discovery and the time the objects were seen by others were unfortunate, to Currelly they confirmed Dodd's statement "that he attached no importance to the relics when first found; this is further confirmed by his failure to take active steps to dispose of them to any scientific institution. It is obvious that, if unearthed at Beardmore, it is immaterial whether the date was 1930 or 1931."[20] Strangely, Currelly argued that dates were only important "in checking the possibility of a hoax," which was exactly what Elliott had been trying to do in exposing their inconsistencies and incongruities.[21]

Currelly dismissed T.L. Tanton's expert arguments that the relics would not have survived more than a few centuries. To accept the impossibility of such a survival in North America "is, in my opinion, untenable, as it upsets the whole archaeology of the iron age" in Europe.[22] He was willing to accept Tanton's opinion that the site of the find was not on a feasible portage route but argued "that the weapons can only tell us that a Viking was there, not why he was there, whence he had come, or whither he hoped to go."[23] Hansen's loan evidence was unpersuasive: the amount in the bank note did not match what Hansen recalled loaning Bloch, and there was no mention of relics as security. He insisted on retaining Sorensen's opinion that Bloch never owned such relics or that he would have lost them in a loan to Hansen. Currelly noted that, as John Bloch married after he moved away from Port Arthur, his widow "could have no direct knowledge of the facts and was drawn into the picture only after there had been considerable publicity about the finds," but he stopped short of accusing her of only being interested in the money paid to Dodd.[24] Eli Ragotte was dispensed with in a sentence.

Currelly dealt with much of the evidence against Dodd's find by declaring it did not matter. A.W. Brøgger's Ostfold weapons typology was swept aside. The sword could have been broken when being taken out of the ground, or it could have rusted into two pieces over the centuries. "The assumption of a heathen burial is unjustified."[25] Whether the weapons might have originated in eastern Norway "seems to me irrelevant. Weapons pass from hand to hand in war, trade, and travel, and I see nothing remarkable in the fact of an eastern type, rather than a western type, having reached the New World."[26] Whether there was a burial, as Currelly had claimed (despite the lack of a body), was "not material."[27] A careful excavation at the time of discovery might have confirmed one, but the ground was too extensively trenched to justify one after that. The weapons type and origin, and whether they were part of a burial or were simply left behind, had "nothing to do with the main question."[28] The date of Dodd's find "is also unimportant, except in its relation to where Mr. Dodd was living."[29] What mattered to Currelly was that the relics had been seen by eyewitnesses at the middle claim, near where they were found. They were seen in Dodd's house before he moved to 33 Machar. And John Jacob saw the rust imprint on the rock at the middle claim. The only evidence to the contrary was Hansen's claim that he had left them in his house, valued them at $150; but he only made this claim after Dodd had been trying for years to sell them "and [it] was not backed by a single statement that anybody had ever seen them in Mr. Hansen's possession. It seems to me that these are the essential facts and that they have not been disturbed by evidence which Mr. Elliott has presented."[30]

Currelly closed by thanking Elliott for his "continued and painstaking interest in the matter. I regret that I do not agree with all his inferences, and careful reading of his article only confirms the opinion I expressed in this journal two years ago that the weapons were found near Beardmore."[31]

With only a day to prepare his own rebuttal to Currelly's rebuttal, and without access to his personal archive, Elliott made an impressive effort. Currelly's intrusion into the publishing plan opened the door for Elliott to be more forceful than he had been in his balanced review of evidence. He reviewed the discrepancies in the circumstances and date of the find, the time that had elapsed between discovery and removal from the trench, their eventual removal to Port Arthur, and when the relics were seen, both at the claim and in Port Arthur. John Jacob's statements, none of which were made under oath, "confuse rather than clarify the situation."[32] Elliott stressed that only Jacob ever mentioned seeing rust stains from the sword. Jacob was also complicit in shifting the date from 1931 to 1930, yet this "unwittingly created a dilemma which casts doubt upon the value of the affidavits offered by the railroad employees who had rallied in support of the

Beardmore story."[33] Foremost was Patrick Bohan's use of railway records of his Warneford assignment to assert that he saw the sword at the middle claim between 15 May and 1 July 1931 and Fletcher Gill's affidavit attesting to a letter from Dodd in 1931. Elliott pointed out the inconsistencies in the various mentions of the shield boss, which ranged from a goose egg to a shallow bowl to an oval-shaped depression. Crucially, he noted that Dodd had described to him an oval-shaped depression with a strap of metal lying over it, rather than under it, which was the opposite orientation of what Currelly said Dodd told him and supposedly made the find consistent with a medieval warrior's burial. (Elliott was unable to note additional evidence that contradicted Currelly. Currelly himself had described to the *Toronto Star* in October 1938 that Dodd found a shallow metal bowl with the handle laying across it; Ned Burwash had related to Tanton how Dodd described grabbing the handle and having the shield beneath it crumble.) Elliott doubted a fragile metal bowl could have lain buried for nine hundred years and survived a detonation of "two charges of dynamite, not six feet distant."[34] McIlwraith and Curran, six and seven years later, respectively, recovered purported pieces of the boss, yet no one else "mentions the boss or admits seeing or owning pieces of it."[35] As for the idea that a Viking shield boss would be beyond the knowledge of ordinary men, "Any one of a number of Norwegians at the head of the lakes can give an accurate description of a shield boss."[36] It was of the greatest loss to the hoax case that Elliott was unable to address the nature of the so-called shield handle. He was not confident enough of what he had seen in Petersen's volume to propose that it was a sword harness, and the loss of A.W. Brøgger as an advisor meant that he had no way of realizing that it was a pagan sleigh rattle.

Regarding the dubious survival of the artefacts, Elliott emphasized Tanton's "intimate knowledge of numerous instances of rapid corrosion of iron objects at various silver locations in northern Ontario, and his personal knowledge of the moisture-laden overburden of the Beardmore area ... He is not alone in his scepticism regarding the survival of iron objects buried for nine hundred years at a spot which was so moisture-laden that water had to be bailed out before mining operations could be carried out."[37]

As for the discovery site's identity as a Viking grave, Elliott noted that plausible explanations had been offered for the lack of evidence in supporting the grave theory, "but not one piece of evidence has been offered in confirmation of the supposition that the site *was* a grave."[38] He repeated the evidence from A.W. Brøgger and his colleague Sigurd Grieg that the sword was a type from eastern Norway that had never been found in the areas that produced known Norse voyages to North America. "To say that such a weapon could have been traded to a member of an expedition to America is merely raising an academic possibility."[39] Elliott rejected the museum label's contention the relics were in a burial on a portage route from Hudson Bay to Lake Superior: "That the Blackwater River should be considered part of a recognized travel route is inconceivable." He recommended that the museum at the least should reword the label.[40]

Elliott defended Hansen's behaviour and testimony: "Interested in Norse lore, loyal to the wishes of his countrymen, Mr. Hansen has been cautious in his statements and slow to embroil himself in argument. In the main essentials he has not swerved from his original story and has always been willing to co-operate in the investigation of his claims." The fact that John Bloch's friends would not know about his relics was understandable, especially in the case of the vice-consul, Carl Sorensen, because the Norwegian law made relics the nominal property of the Crown and they could not be exported without the Crown's blessing. Bloch would have needed a visa from Sorensen if he were ever to return to Norway. "Was he to jeopardize his chances for such permission?"[41]

In conclusion, Elliott argued, the Hansen-Bloch story "has fewer bewildering and contradictory circumstances than the Dodd story and is easier to believe as a logical explanation of the presence of Viking weapons in America. I am inclined to accept it." Elliott thanked Currelly, Tanton, McIlwraith, Brown "and others" for the "full cooperation and encouragement" he had received over the past five years "in this interesting study."[42]

Elliott's comments were the closing argument of a skilled debater who had not only accepted a premise to defend but also had come to believe it, and to believe in the importance of being heard. Elliott had also managed to get in the last word on C.T. Currelly.

On 30 September, Teddy Elliott visited the library in Kingston and saw the September issue of CHR for the first time. "All the material is there just as written," he reported with relief to T.L. Tanton. "Our efforts to get the material in print have finally been successful. Many thanks to you for your continued help and advice."[43]

Tanton was still in the field at Steep Rock Lake when the issue appeared. On the way home on 2 October, he stopped at the University of Toronto and discussed the article with Thomas McIlwraith; John G.

Althouse, dean of the Faculty of Education at the University of Toronto;
and historian and essayist Frank Underhill, "all of whom were much interested and pleased at the way the subject had been presented." Tanton
congratulated Elliott on his "excellent presentation of the case." Elliott's
public acknowledgment of assistance was "ample reward for the time ex-
pended and I am very pleased to see the results of our research thus put
on record."[44] The day Tanton wrote Elliott, an even-handed news item appeared in the Toronto *Telegram* on the CHR material. The arguments presented by Elliott and Currelly were "well worth reading in full."[45] One of
the CHR readers who took Elliott's case to heart was its editor, George
Brown. He would make no mention of the Beardmore find in his discussion of Norse voyages in the new edition of his popular textbook, *Building the Canadian Nation* (1942).

In the aftermath of publication, T.L. Tanton pursued further insights from
John Bloch's widow. At his urging, Merton Yerwood (M.Y.) Williams, a former colleague at DGS who was now a professor of paleontology and
stratigraphy at the University of British Columbia, visited Shana Block
Hastings for an hour on 24 September. He was accompanied by R.L. Reid,
a prominent Vancouver lawyer, avocational historian, and RSC fellow, and
William Kaye Lamb, chief archivist and librarian of British Columbia and
the founder and editor of the *British Columbia Historical Quarterly*. Reid
had presented a paper to the RSC's Section 2 in 1940, the same year as Elliott (and had seen it published in *Transactions*), and was not impressed
with the hoax case. He is "rather critical, being quite convinced of the authenticity of the Beardmore find," Williams reported. "On the other hand,
Dr. Lamb is inclined to prefer your conclusions."[46]

Shana Block Hasting told her visitors that when she married John
Bloch in Winnipeg, "he had already parted with his Norse relics, but she
knew of them and frequently urged him to make arrangements to regain
them. He always stated that they were safe where they were and he could
get them at any time. She said that they had a very difficult time financially and it was embarrassing for him to discuss these relics as he was unable to pay his debts and so regain them." She also revealed that Bloch had
been previously married to a woman who had since remarried under the
name Hemmer and who worked for the CPR in Oslo.[47] Tanton and Elliott
realized that a statement from Bloch's previous wife could be key in es-

tablishing his ownership of the relics. Elliott suggested they try the International Red Cross, among other strategies, but the Nazi occupation of Norway made contacting her impossible. No one would ever verify John Bloch's possession of the Beardmore relics with Mrs Hemmer. A Professor Blessem (or Blesem), who was said by Shana Block Hastings to have known her late husband, was also never tracked down.

More information trickled in from the Lakehead. Colonel Henry A. Ruttan wrote Tanton on 20 October, thanking him for an offprint of the *CHR* article and informing him he had just left it with Aaron Lougheed.[48] "I know him quite well. He says, 'No, I won't write Dr. Tanton again. I have told him all I know about [the relics], but I would be glad to see him next time he is in the city and talk it over.' I asked him what his opinion was about them and he said 'a lot of bunkum.'" Lougheed also agreed that "there would have been nothing left of the iron relics if they had been in the ground so many years." Colonel Ruttan shared that he personally knew Bloch. "In fact he lived in the Ruttan Building. He was quite a gentleman." Colonel Ruttan could "quite understand [Hansen's] loaning Bloch money. The story Hansen tells does not seem unlikely to me, and I know friend Dodd's 'enough said.'"

On 13 November, A.D. Fraser thanked Elliott for an offprint of the *CHR* article, then largely dismissed the hoax case.[49] He recalled an exchange of letters with Eli Ragotte in 1938, after G.R.F. Prowse told Fraser he considered Ragotte "an honest man." Fraser said Ragotte "showed a definite bias against Dodd, whom he accused of being a thief of the first water [sic]. But when I saw his oath published in Curran's book, I realized that he was himself a profound liar. I am afraid that Hansen's honesty will not bear scrutiny either." Ragotte had told Fraser that Hansen said he had brought the relics himself from Norway, and Fraser had a copy of the letter from Hansen to Ragotte (made for him by Prowse) that differed in its statements from one Hansen wrote to Hjalmar Holand shortly afterward. "[Hansen] also told Holand that, if or when he saw the relics in the R.O.M.A., he was going to declare that they were not his – for certain reasons – whether he recognized them or not. So it seems to me that [Hansen] can be ruled out of the game along with the deceased Ragotte."

For Fraser, "speaking as a professional archaeologist," the case hinged on whether the pieces of metal recovered by McIlwraith in 1937 and Curran in 1938 were authentic examples of ancient iron and not a plant of modern iron: "If the iron conforms to the type, then the rest of the suspicions can go hang, for they must have arisen through misunderstanding, stupidity or malice." Fraser overlooked the possibility that the additional pieces might have been authentic *and* planted, just as the museum's relics evidently were. Fraser wanted to visit Beardmore "and spend a week prowling round the site. The professional archaeologist knows what to look for, in a case of this kind." He never would make that visit.

Tanton acknowledged to Elliott that Fraser's suggestion about investigating the bits of metal recovered in 1937 and 1938 "has some merit," but otherwise Diamond Jenness had remarked to him that, if he failed to acknowledge the typology evidence from Brøgger, Fraser "was probably not much of an archaeologist." Jenness tried to look Fraser up in a volume on leading archaeologists, and Tanton was amused to report he could not find him. Tanton conceded that, while it was difficult to defend Ragotte, "I think his statement to me was essentially correct." Hansen "has been very consistent in his statements to me. If I had copies of the conflicting letters from H[ansen] that F refers to, I might, at some time, get H's explanation of them." In a postscript, Tanton asked Elliott if he had G.R.F. Prowse's address. Further leads may have beckoned, but time and opportunity were running out on Tanton's and Elliott's investigations. This letter of 26 November 1941 from Tanton to Elliott is the last surviving communication between them on the Beardmore case.[50]

In December 1941, Teddy Elliott finally found the full-time war work he desired, as a veterans welfare officer in what was then the Department of Pensions and National Health. He relocated to Ottawa, and Kate followed in the new year. There, in July 1942, their first and only child after fourteen years of marriage, a daughter, Susan, was born.[51] Elliott never returned to teaching or to investigating the Beardmore case.

Teddy Elliott had accomplished something truly remarkable in scholarship. As a vocational school teacher working self-funded in his spare time, he had pursued the truth about the provenance of perhaps the most significant archaeological find in North America in the early twentieth century. Most important, he had done so publicly, treading where accredited historians and archaeologists dare not. To a large degree, with a government geologist's assistance, Teddy Elliott had done the scholarly world's dirty work for it, enduring its hostility and obstructionism along the way. As a writer, as a critical thinker, he had been transformed by the experience of challenging the Beardmore provenance. His CHR article was as fine as anything being published by accredited academics. It also contained the last words he would publish on any historical subject.

PART FOUR

Doctor Brøndsted Investigates

After the September 1941 issue of the *Canadian Historical Review* appeared, C.T. Currelly's faith in the Beardmore find was unwavering. As far as he was concerned, his arguments had carried the day. Currelly sent Philip Ainsworth Means the issue, confident Means would see how effectively he had quashed the hoax case mounted by Teddy Elliott. Means was preparing to publish his book *Newport Tower*, reviving the possibility the stone ruin was a Norse relic, and had been one of Currelly's most ardent supporters, contemptuous of the doubts A.W. Brøgger had expressed.[1] But after reading the CHR material, Means was troubled. "Apparently there is now considerable doubt as to the age in America of the Beardmore find," he replied in March 1942.[2] "There is no doubt as to the age of the things themselves, only doubt as to the date at which they were brought to the Continent. All this is very disturbing to the student and it must be especially so to you. Such disenchantments are extremely upsetting for all of us."

Means advised Currelly that he had decided to omit mention of the Beardmore relics from his forthcoming book for the dubious reason that "they are not pertinent to my subject," even though he had already secured a photograph of the relics from the museum and had intended to include it in his volume. "I do cite that unbelievable book by Curran as an example of how not to do it, and also Goodwin's almost equally absurd tome. In a later work, however, I hope to say a good deal about the Beardmore find, if I can only get it straight in my own mind."[3] Means died in 1944 before he could publish his long-envisioned work on pre-1494 voyages to North America.

Currelly did not share Means's despair. "This matter of the Beardmore things seems to be most extraordinary," he replied, and churned out two pages of well-worn, inflammatory arguments against the hoax case, including the familiar reference to the "drunk breaksman" [sic] Eli Ragotte.[4] Currelly continued to deploy Carl Sorensen's condemnation of James Hansen, ignoring the fact that Sorensen had changed his mind before he died, as Elliott had noted in CHR. "And yet people still say that there is serious doubt," Currelly summarized haughtily. It was the end of their discussions.

Despite losing Means's support, Currelly was still assured the hoax case had not prevailed. George Brown may have failed to mention the Beardmore relics in the 1942 edition of his textbook *Building the Canadian Nation*, but, in 1944, Donald G. Creighton included them in his own obligatory discussion of Vikings in the opening pages of his new history of Canada, *Dominion of the North*. The University of Toronto professor (and second-generation product of Victoria College) well knew the Beardmore controversy, having been an associate editor of CHR since 1938. Elliott's arguments plainly had not swayed him. The Vikings could have entered the continent through Hudson Bay, he advised, "and perhaps the deeply corroded Viking sword and axe which were discovered near Lake Nipigon in northern Ontario in 1930 belonged once to some members of a defiant expedition which struck out south-westward on an incredible overland journey from James Bay towards Lake Superior."[5] The mere entertainment of the relics' authenticity by "his generation's finest historian"[6] in a prominent and popular work would have assured Currelly that he had won the day.

For all the doubts that T.L. Tanton and Teddy Elliott raised, little to nothing changed in the public status of the Beardmore relics. C.T. Currelly had faced down his most serious challenge. The war suffocated any further investigation. The files were put away; the evidence trails that the war had made impossible to pursue remained unexplored as peace returned in 1945. Elliott made a permanent career change from teaching. Now with the new Ministry of Veterans Affairs, he moved to being the supervisor of counsellor training and the secretary to the cabinet committee on demobilization and rehabilitation and, in 1947, was named the administrator for North Bay District, which covered a vast swath of northern Ontario. In 1949, he transferred to St John's to serve as the first district administrator for the new Canadian province of Newfoundland. In 1954, Elliott would be named training chief of the entire department in Ottawa.[7] T.L. Tanton carried on with geology and would serve as president of the RSC's Section 4 in 1949–50. He stayed in touch with James Hansen, who sent him a box of stones and mineral samples for identification around 1950; Tanton favoured him with a reply.[8] But Tanton, too, was done with the Beardmore hoax.

After Currelly retired from the museum at age seventy on 1 July 1946, the Beardmore display's label was rendered less forthright regarding the items being the contents of a Viking grave on a portage to Lake Superior. Still, the label concluded: "Though the matter may never be settled to the complete satisfaction of everyone, our present evidence strongly supports the view that these objects really were unearthed near Lake Nipigon."[9]

On 21 September 1948, Lithgow Osborne, president of the American-Scandinavian Foundation in New York, informed Thomas McIlwraith, assistant director of the Royal Ontario Museum of Archaeology, of the foundation's investigation of evidence for the Norse in North America.[10] The foundation had secured a grant from the Viking Fund of New York (later the Wenner-Gren Foundation) to bring Johannes Brøndsted, an archaeology professor at the University of Copenhagen and a curator at the National Museum of Denmark, across the Atlantic to assess artefacts.[11] Brøndsted hoped to visit the ROM in October to examine the Beardmore find as part of a two-month tour of purported artefacts.

Brøndsted considered the Beardmore relics, the Kensington stone, and the Newport Tower the most significant purported evidence. Their authenticity was enjoying unprecedented support. The Beardmore relics were still offered by the ROM as proof of a circa 1000 Norse visit to northern Ontario. The Kensington stone had been on display in the Smithsonian in Washington since 17 February, where it would remain for a year, enjoying the institution's imprimatur of authenticity if not its official endorsement. The September 1948 issue of *National Geographic* featured a photograph of Neil M. Judd, the Smithsonian's curator of archaeology, examining the runes with a magnifying glass. The caption assured readers that the stone was "first believed to be a hoax. Later studies indicate that it was carved by white men who had traveled far into North America long before Columbus's first voyage."[12] Philip Ainsworth Means, in *The Newport Tower*, had somewhat revived the respectability of the tower as a Norse ruin. Means thought that if any archaeological evidence could be found, the most likely result would be that the tower was of Norse construction between 1121 and 1400; he also endorsed the authenticity of the Kensington stone and the scholarly wisdom of Hjalmar Holand. In 1946, Holand, in turn, reiterated his case for the Kensington stone in *America: 1355–1364*, in which he endorsed the late Means's scholarly wisdom on the Newport Tower.[13] Means at least argued for a proper archaeological investigation of the tower, and a doctoral student at the Peabody Museum, William S. Godfrey, Jr – a descendant of Rhode Island governor Benedict Arnold, who in the more conventional view built the structure in the mid-seventeenth century – was about to begin a dig.

Brøndsted planned to spend five or six days with Hjalmar Holand, evaluating his Knutson expedition evidence, before visiting the ROM to examine the Beardmore materials. On the morning of 13 October, Brøndsted and his wife arrived in Toronto by train from Chicago to be swept up in the hospitality of Thomas McIlwraith and the museum for two days.[14]

McIlwraith had been named assistant director of the archaeology division in 1942 and had fulfilled the acting director's role on Currelly's retirement. Although McIlwraith served on the search committee (along with Currelly) for Currelly's successor, he had hoped to succeed him. McIlwraith was "badly shaken" when he was passed over for Gerard Brett, a young British archaeologist from the Victoria and Albert Museum who had been a commando during the war and who had spent some time as a prisoner of the Germans.[15] Brett had started as the new director in January 1948, with McIlwraith back to being the assistant director.

Brett was doubtful about the Beardmore relics. In a letter in September 1948, Brett shared: "I myself incline to agree with Mr. Elliott's doubts of the genuineness of this story, but both sides are very fully written up in the [September 1941 *CHR*] article ... As the article makes clear, there is no question of its being a Viking sword, and others similar to it are exhibited in the same exhibition case. The only question that does arise is that of its origin."[16]

Brett was out of town when Brøndsted visited that October. We can never know how the Danish scholar would have responded to the relics had he not been exclusively in the care of McIlwraith, whose opinion of the Beardmore relics had not wavered. McIlwraith proposed to Brøndsted that Holand, in *Westward from Vinland*, "seems to have been very restrained in advancing the claims for their authenticity," when, in fact, Holand could not have been more supportive, offering the romantic scene of the burial of the dead Viking leader. "I wish the material had been found under other circumstances," McIlwraith wrote, "but I think the evidence is very strongly in favour of their authenticity."[17]

Brøndsted was disquieted by the fact that James Hansen had never been brought to the museum to view the relics. McIlwraith, to his credit, was not blinkered to the possibility Hansen might yet have something of value to say, and he encouraged Brøndsted to visit Port Arthur and interview him. "It might be that he would speak to you in a way that he would never do to one of us."[18] Brøndsted, however, was unable to visit Port Arthur because the Kensington stone, "which I am inclined to think is genuine," demanded more of his time at the Smithsonian before he departed for Denmark.[19] He would write Hansen instead. But he wondered: "Has Hansen seen the Nipigon find in your museum? I think he ought to." Brøndsted suggested the museum send Hansen a photograph of the relics and see if he recognized them. "I am not quite sure his statement would be honest," Brøndsted confided, "but I should like to hear it." McIlwraith's reply made it clear that Hansen had never seen the relics in person when they had been pur-

chased by the museum, and McIlwraith did not know if Hansen had visited the museum since they had gone on display. He regretted Brøndsted's
inability to meet Hansen: "An enquiry from a completely disinterested outsider might have produced good results."[20] McIlwraith suggested the museum would follow up with Hansen, were Brøndsted to hear from him.

As the ROM waited for Brøndsted to make his report, its internal opinion in
favour of the Beardmore relics' authenticity hardened. McIlwraith must
have assured his superior Brett that Brøndsted would rule in the relics'
favour. "There seems to be a general reaction going on now against the first
tendency to dismiss all these as fakes," Brett informed a German scholar in
May 1949. "Professor Brøndsted was here late last year, and gave his opinion
that both our sword and the other two main finds were all genuine ... I have
recently been rereading the Beardmore evidence myself, and my original
feeling that the balance of probability is very strongly in favour of the genuineness of the find has been confirmed." Brett had forgotten the scepticism
he had expressed in September 1948 but admitted: "I cannot, however, entirely silence a certain doubt in my mind about it, as the confusion and contradictions of the story told by the finder and his friends are so very great."[21]

On 1 March 1950, Brøndsted alerted McIlwraith to the findings he was
about to publish in Denmark.[22] Godfrey's dig was turning up only Colonial-era materials under the Newport Tower's foundations (the late Philip
Ainsworth Means had suggested there was a 5 percent chance of such a result), and Brøndsted suspected it was an English watch tower built about
1640. He had also changed his mind about the Kensington stone. There
was "too strong resistance among the Scandinavian linguistic experts. So
far useless as a document to American pre-Columbian history." That left
the Beardmore relics among the three major, purported proofs of a Norse
presence. It was Brøndsted's "pleasant duty" to inform McIlwraith that the
find was "no doubt a genuine Norwegian grave find from about 1000 AD."
Consulting Petersen's *De Norske Vikingesverd*, he concluded the sword was
an Eastern Norwegian M type, AD 850–950, while the axe was an L type
from AD 950–1025. "The combination: *this* sword together with *this* axe is
unusual, but not at all impossible. This Beardmore Viking has had his
own axe and his father's sword!" But the third item "cannot be a shield
handle, as such ones were not in use in Viking times – Norway (they never
appear in the Norwegian grave finds, nor in the Danish)." Brøndsted had

produced the identification that had barely eluded Teddy Elliott in 1940. He was certain that Dodd's "shield handle" was the upper part of a rangle found in eastern Norwegian graves in the company of weapons. "They were magic instruments to keep away evil from the n'de or sledge-man."

With the identification of the shield handle as a pagan sleigh rattle from eastern Norway, which never produced voyages to North America, Brøndsted had the archaeological ammunition to destroy Dodd's discovery story. Instead, he allowed the ROM to escape an embarrassing pronouncement of fraud. Brøndsted assured McIlwraith that he believed the relics represented a genuine grave discovery in Canada from the early eleventh century, but he admitted "that the doubt concerning the finding story, raised by Mr. Hansen, has not yet been removed. Therefore, I think it wise to wait and see, i.e., not to use this Beardmore find as a safe historic document yet. Let us wait for other corroborating finds; they will no doubt appear sooner or later." Brøndsted had given McIlwraith and the museum a collegial warning that he could not accept the Beardmore relics as unassailable proof of a Norse visit, and he had implied that the museum should reconsider making any forthright statements until evidence of other finds emerged.

As Johannes Brøndsted concluded his investigations, new theories and theorists emerged to argue for fresh evidence of the Norse in North America and to reiterate the authenticity of contested relics. In 1951, an Ohio civil engineer, Arlington H. Mallery, would publish an astonishing book, *Lost America*, in which he claims to have found remnants of a Norse iron-making furnace in Indigenous mounds south of Lake Erie. Mallery secured a supportive introduction for his book from Matthew W. Sterling, director of the bureau of American ethnology at the Smithsonian. Sterling (who specialized in Olmec archaeology) asserted: "the possible Norse connections with the Great Lakes copper culture seem more convincing in light of the present evidence."[23] Conflating medieval European metalworking methods with the folding/hammering production of Indigenous Copper Culture items (which predated Norse metallurgy by thousands of years) recall Jim Curran's ill-formed ideas in support of the Beardmore find and would have caused William Wintemberg to spin in his grave. Among the plethora of experts Mallery consulted was Thomas McIlwraith, although Beardmore never figured in his sprawling thesis.[24] The appearance of Mallery's book, with its endorsement by Sterling, soon after the Kensington stone was on display at the Smithsonian, suggested that mainstream North American archaeology was on the verge of going completely off the rails where pre-Columbian European visitors were concerned.

Another figure in revisionist history to emerge after the war was Frederick J. Pohl, a retired Brooklyn high school teacher with a master's degree in history from Columbia. Turning to exploration history in retirement, Pohl was fundamentally attracted by ideas of "firsts," or prior discoveries. Pohl published *Amerigo Vespucci: Pilot Major* with Columbia University Press in 1944.[25] Vespucci had made a disputed claim to a voyage to South America in 1497, which Pohl supported, hailing him as the first European to visit Brazil. By the early 1950s, Pohl would be convinced he had found archaeological proof of Leif Eiriksson's Leifsbooths at Follins Pond on Cape Cod.

Pohl had contacted C.T. Currelly about the Beardmore relics in May 1945. He had read the 1939 and 1941 CHR articles and wanted to clarify some points around Hansen and Ragotte.[26] Currelly in reply mentioned conclusive evidence he had received from an unnamed stranger: "The one thing that I hoped for turned up: Dodd told me that after he had thrown the things out on the edge of his digging a stranger came along, and they discussed the find before Dodd ever took the things home. Seeing the matter in the paper this stranger very kindly wrote the Museum, and I had him investigated and found he was well known as a thoroughly upright person. That fills up every link in the story."[27] The stranger was a figment of the director's imagination loosely based on William Feltham, possibly with a dash of John Jacob. One of Currelly's last acts as the purchaser of the Beardmore relics was to discredit Elliott based on testimony that did not exist.

Currelly left Pohl confident that Elliott was a crank, and Pohl shared with Currelly his dim view of Elliott's analysis.[28] Elliott, in his treatment of affidavits, "reveals his hand as a special pleader" – a condemnation Pohl probably absorbed from Stewart Wallace's categorization of Hjalmar Holand in CHR in 1939. Pohl's public critique of Elliott's analysis (and his support of the Beardmore find) waited until the appearance of *The Lost Discovery* in 1952. He dismissed Elliott as a "special pleader" in a book that also upheld the authenticity of the Kensington stone and the Newport Tower as a Norse relic.[29]

An English translation of Brøndsted's Danish report appeared in the 1953 *Annual Report of the Smithsonian's Board of Regents*, published in 1954, and was also issued as an offprint.[30] Brøndsted's forewarning to McIlwraith accurately reflected his assessment of the three main items of evidence for a Norse presence in North America. In arriving at his Beardmore conclusion, Brøndsted relied overwhelmingly on the materials in the September 1941 issue of CHR, and his rebuttals of Elliott's and Tanton's contentions echoed Currelly's comments. He did not consider significant either Brøgger's assessment of a typical Ostfold pagan burial or the peculiar presence of such weapons in North America. His identification of the "shield handle" as the remnant of a rangle was a significant breakthrough, but, as in his letter to McIlwraith, he made no attempt to explain what it was doing in a grave that was thousands of miles from eastern Norway. Brøndsted did not appreciate that, if the object absolutely was not a shield handle, then Dodd's discovery story, which appeared "trustworthy," lost considerable credibility.

The unlikelihood of the artefacts' survival in the sodden ground of the middle claim did not concern Brøndsted any more than it did Currelly, and he borrowed Currelly's reasoning. Brøndsted contributed the novel idea that the poor condition of the relics testified to their precarious survival in Dodd's trench because such relics would not have interested John Bloch. The theory took no account of what sentimental value Bloch might have attached to relics that had belonged to his late father; nor did Brøndsted consider that Bloch might have taken them to Canada as cheap mementoes because they were unlikely to fetch a decent price in Norway. Brøndsted did not go so far as to propose in print that the weapons belonged to a Norseman carrying his father's sword, but he said it was "quite possible" they were used by the same man around AD 1000.

Brøndsted granted that there were issues in the provenance case, and he reviewed the evidence relating to Ragotte and Hansen. Although sceptical of the counter-claim, he did not dismiss Hansen out of hand. Brøndsted may have discussed the case with Hansen by mail. "It would be helpful if Mr. Hansen could have an opportunity of seeing the Beardmore find, either at Toronto or at Port Arthur. Mr. Hansen has not seen the Beardmore find in the museum at Toronto; he knows of it only from photographs and on that basis he declines to say categorically that its iron objects are the same as those he received from Bloch; but he believes they are."[31] The museum made no attempt to have Hansen examine the relics, as Brøndsted urged.

In closing, Brøndsted noted that some investigators, himself included, accepted that a grave, or at least a deposit of Norwegian Viking weapons, was found near Beardmore. But even if this led to the conclusion that early eleventh-century Vikings penetrated deep into North America, perhaps via Hudson Bay and James Bay, to reach the Lake Nipigon area, "this does not conceal the fact that it has been impossible to produce *clear evidence* in support of it; we have merely a certain degree of probability. And in that case we lack justification for employing the Beardmore find as a reliable archaeological document for the present."[32]

The debate over Norse evidence in North America was diverging into two camps: on one side, the true believers like Pohl, Holand, Mallery, and their scholarly supporters; and on the other, the critics whose debunking efforts were rejuvenated after the Smithsonian's alarming display of the Kensington stone in 1949–50. But there were plenty of fence-sitters in scholarly circles who were willing to entertain some evidence, particularly the Beardmore relics, but not others. William S. Godfrey, Jr, published several updates on his Newport Tower dig in *Archaeology* and *American Antiquity*, which informed Brøndsted's report, and his findings ought to have erased any possibility that the structure predated the mid-seventeenth century.[33] In 1955, Godfrey (now an archaeology professor at Balliol College) published his own survey of the evidence for a Norse presence in North America in *American Anthropologist*. Like Brøndsted, he saw nothing that could be accepted without reservation, but he deferred to Brøndsted (and the ROM) in holding out some hope for the Beardmore relics. He repeated Brøndsted's speculation that "it is hardly likely that Bloch would have selected these miserable fragments" to bring to Canada. While the Beardmore relics could not be called "positive evidence of a Viking grave in Ontario … it is the only assemblage of objects that rises above the heirloom category in both nature of the material and circumstances of discovery. Likewise, the find was reported sufficiently quickly so that some scientific investigation of the site could be made. It is the best archaeological evidence for the Vikings in America, but it is none too good."[34] That Godfrey, who had made a painstaking, multi-season investigation of the Newport Tower, thought the Beardmore site had undergone a "scientific investigation" was testament to professional faith in the ROM that precluded any curiosity in McIlwraith's unpublished report of his one-day site visit in 1937.

The postwar years quickly swept away most of the remaining key figures in the Beardmore controversy. Already, Judge McComber had died in 1945. John Bloch's widow, Shana Block Hastings, died in 1946, at age fifty-two, after surgery for ulcerative colitis, ending a hard life in which she had lost two husbands to early deaths. The murmurings that she had only surfaced in the Beardmore story because of the chance to wring money out of the museum were baseless slanders. Jim Curran died in 1952, just short of his eighty-seventh birthday, his enthusiasms for a Vinland centred on Lake Nipigon more than a decade behind him. Aaron Lougheed was eighty-nine when he died in 1953, never having given a complete statement on what he knew about the Beardmore find. The following year took both partners in the middle claim. Eddy Dodd died on 15 April 1954, two months after his sixty-ninth birthday, having long defied the alarming, prematurely aged state in which the army medical officer had found him in October 1918. In July 1954, Fletcher Gill turned sixty-five and retired from the CNR. The widower had remarried, and had a son and a step-daughter and two grandchildren. His retirement was cruelly short: Gill died suddenly at home in Port Arthur that November.[35]

James Hansen was the only significant figure in the Beardmore contro-versy still alive. He made his first-ever visit to Toronto around the time of his seventy-second birthday on 14 June 1954 to see his daughter's family.[36] When James Hansen arrived, as his grandson John Garner recalls, "'seeing the relics' was the first thing he wanted to do." John Garner took his grand-father from his family's Mount Pleasant house on a short bus ride to the Eglinton station, the end of the Yonge line on the city's brand new sub-way system, to guide him to the ROM.

More than eighteen years after the Beardmore scandal had erupted, the ROM had still not invited Hansen to inspect the relics that he insisted Dodd had stolen from him. Entering the museum, Hansen asked where the famous objects were, and he was directed to the display, his grandson in tow. "His first reaction was that the sword he saw was intact, not bro-ken as his had been, and which of course he hadn't seen for several decades," John Garner recalls. Hansen looked for someone to speak with, and a young man appeared, whom Garner gathered was a curator. "The cu-rator explained how the two pieces were mounted and supported so as to appear as when originally made. That, I believe, convinced my grandfather that this was indeed his sword. There was also some discussion about the other item(s) displayed. In the course of this examination, he told the cu-rator his side of the story of the relics and how he had come to obtain them, and lose them ... this was all news to me, [which] is probably why I remember it as clearly as if I were standing there now." But whoever on staff had emerged to chat failed to appreciate the enormous significance of James Hansen's encounter with the relics he had long insisted were his. No notes were taken; and apparently no one in a senior position was ever alerted. John Garner's grandfather "seemed quite satisfied with the ROM visit ... I saw him as being, usually, a cool, calm and reflective person." James Hansen left without demanding to take the relics with him. He never returned to the museum or to the city.

Professor Carpenter Strikes Back

The collapse of the Beardmore relics as proof of a circa 1000 Viking incursion into the heart of North America would have been impossible without the determined investigations of Teddy Elliott and T.L. Tanton. But the relics' downfall required a final push. The scholarly assessments of Johannes Brøndsted and William S. Godfrey, Jr, in the early 1950s had left open the question of their authenticity and undermined Elliott's and Tanton's findings and arguments. Frederick J. Pohl, rising in prominence as an author specializing in pre-Columbian voyages, had dismissed Elliott's painstaking work in 1952 as the flawed analysis of a "special pleader." The push came from a surprising direction, one that could not have been imagined before the war, when C.T. Currelly was an unassailable force. The source was inside the University of Toronto and the ROM: a young anthropologist who paid little mind to the niceties of institutional hierarchies and allegiances.

Born in 1922, Edmund Snow Carpenter was an American from Rochester, New York, who had been interested in archaeology since childhood.[1] At thirteen he met archaeologist Arthur C. Parker and began excavating Iroquoian sites. He was just beginning his second year of anthropology studies under Frank Speck at the University of Pennsylvania when Japan bombed Pearl Harbor. Carpenter enlisted in the Marine Corps and fought with the 25th Regiment from New Guinea to Iwo Jima. While away fighting, seven of his papers on archaeology and ethnology were published. On demobilization, he was granted a bachelor's degree and resumed his education under Speck, working as an anthropology instructor as he pursued a doctorate on pre-Contact archaeology of the northeast. Before completing his doctorate, Carpenter accepted a teaching position from Thomas McIlwraith in the University of Toronto's anthropology department in 1948. Carpenter had to take on other jobs (including helping to dig the new Toronto subway) to make ends meet, which led him into freelance media work, some of it with the CBC in radio and television, as a new mass communications age arose. After completing his doctorate in 1950 and securing a professorship at the University of Toronto, Carpenter shifted his interest from pre-Contact archaeology to Arctic ethnography, making films and writing books. Around 1953, he became a close associate of Marshall McLuhan in a new University of Toronto venture, the Seminar on Culture and Communication. Carpenter launched "a series of controversial and stimulating seminars on the subjects of communication, mass media, and symbolism," which culminated in the journal *Explorations*, which he co-edited with McLuhan.[2]

A handsome, popular young professor, Carpenter's star was rising on multiple fronts. He worked in electronic and print media, while also creating film documentaries. He was a leading figure in the hot new academic field of media theory, as well as in ethnography, and had more experience as an archaeologist than anyone on the faculty of the University of Toronto or the staff of the ROM. (At the end of the war in the Pacific, when assigned to legal duties by the Marines, Carpenter had organized work parties of some five hundred Japanese prisoners to conduct a dig.) The university was striving to recover lost momentum in its archaeology program. J. Norman Emerson, who had switched from sociology to anthropology under the inspiring influence of Philleo Nash, had been hired in 1946 to teach and conduct archaeology. Emerson established an archaeological laboratory and founded the Ontario Archaeological Society in 1951, an effort to bridge the worlds of professionals and amateurs. Over at the ROM, archaeologist Kenneth E. Kidd had been hired as curator of ethnology, but the museum's field archaeology program was almost nonexistent. No work was performed from 1951 to 1955.[3] At the same time, a schism had developed between the museum and the university's archaeology efforts and its Faculty of Arts and Sciences. "Hard times contributed to sensitivity on both sides," according to Lovat Dickson. "The Museum curators complained that it was virtually impossible to persuade any member of the University staff to use the Museum."[4]

The ROM overall was struggling in the early 1950s. Attendance was languishing: visits by the general public collapsed from 296,500 in 1944 to 195,271 in 1953.[5] Funds were in short supply as the museum endured a series of institutional reforms. Under the Royal Ontario Museum Act, 1947, the ROM was completely absorbed by the University of Toronto in 1948 and, in the process, lost its annual provincial government funding, including grants for acquisitions. An unforeseen crisis of management arose with the rapid physical deterioration of the archaeology division's new director, Gerard Brett, from multiple sclerosis. In late 1953, the museum offered the director's position to Arlotte Douglas (A.D.) Tushingham, an Old Testament historian at Queen's University as well as an or-

dained United Church minister who had solid field experience in archaeology in the Middle East, where he served as director of the American
School of Oriental Research in Jerusalem.[6] The museum's trustees had
chosen the man that Nathanael Burwash had hoped C.T. Currelly would
become, someone who was both an ordained minister and an archaeologist of biblical lands.

The 1954 Glassco Report ushered in a major change in the museum's
operations.[7] It would continue to be answerable to the university, but it
would be guided by its own board of trustees as a distinct public institution. Beginning in July 1955, the ROM would be one museum under a single director, with three divisions: art and archaeology, geology and mineralogy, and zoology and paleontology. Theodore A. Heinrich, an assistant
curator of paintings at the Metropolitan Museum of New York, was hired
as the new director, and Tushingham, having committed to the art and archaeology division's directorship before the Glassco Report changed the
museum's management structure, agreed to report for work under him,
with Thomas McIlwraith serving as assistant director.

As the museum was reorganized and given fresh leadership, the authenticity case for the Beardmore relics was undermined from within. Because of a space shortage at the university, Edmund Carpenter was assigned an office in the museum, and he would walk past the Beardmore
relics case every day. "My children read about them in history texts," he
would recall.[8] Carpenter decided to probe the Beardmore acquisition
after a publisher, Macmillan, asked him to write a book about the prehistory of Ontario, which he never finished. Carpenter called on Mary
Campbell, the assistant to the archaeology division's director, who had
served Currelly after Ethlyn Greenaway's death, and asked to see the
Beardmore documents. "I still recall," Carpenter wrote in 2002, "in precise
detail, how she placed the file in front of me, silently. She knew."[9]

"I had no prejudices either way," Carpenter told archaeologist Birgitta
Wallace in 1965, "save a romantic interest in the Norse saga. But the file
chilled my blood."[10] Carpenter would later recall how the materials indicated that, initially, Currelly "got taken, innocently." But "when a local historian, a high-school teacher, sent the Director an accurate report on
Beardmore, he was told foolishness might cost him his job – a serious
threat during the Depression. To his credit, the historian published,
though he tempered his account."[11] In 1965, Carpenter told Wallace that
"Currelly rudely clobbered Elliott, about whom I knew little save from his
publications, which impressed me as the work of an honest, intelligent

gentleman." Carpenter believed that Eli Ragotte and James Hansen recanted their initial assertions of a hoax because members of the Scandinavian community in Thunder Bay had been infuriated.[12]

Carpenter made his first public criticism of the Beardmore acquisition
a few months before A.D. Tushingham reported as the head of the museum's new art and archaeology division. Carpenter was energized by the recent, spectacular collapse of England's "Piltdown Man" fossil find, which
consisted of portions of a skull and lower jaw that supposedly represented the missing link in the evolutionary divergence of humans from apes.
The fossil purportedly had been unearthed in East Sussex by British amateur archaeologist Charles Dawson, who announced the find of *Eoanthro-
pus dawsoni* (Dawson's Dawn Man) in 1912 and is generally thought to
have been the forger. In 1953, a scientific investigation proved that the
skull was from a medieval human, that the jaw portion was from a modern orangutan (which had been stained to simulate aging), and that the
teeth (which came from a chimpanzee) had been modified with a file.
Carpenter would become increasingly convinced that Canada was brimming with bad, even crooked, archaeology. In reviewing J.S. Weiner's *The
Piltdown Forgery* for the Toronto *Telegram* in April 1955, Carpenter declared that Canada had two bogus archaeological finds of its own: one was
a supposed prehistoric canal from Lake Superior to Hudson Bay; the
other was the Beardmore relics.[13]

It had taken more than forty years to expose the Piltdown hoax, and Carpenter wondered aloud in his book review why no one had sought to discredit either the fossil find or Dawson. He replied to his own question: "Because they felt that there was too much at stake – science, titled scholars,
upper class values, in fact, English society – that not even honest scientists
would listen to their amazing accusations. I suspect they were right."[14] The
parallels with the Beardmore case must have leapt out at Carpenter, who,
if not an outsider, was at least an outlier in the academic system that had
fostered the scandal and that continued to uphold the authenticity of the
relics. Carpenter was a young American who had none of C.T. Currelly's
enthusiasms for history rooted in British Imperialism, and he was not a
product of Victoria College or the greater University of Toronto. As events
would prove, Carpenter had a dim view of what little archaeology was
being performed in Ontario after the war. Another year passed before he
would launch a guerrilla campaign to finish the job Elliott and Tanton had
begun and destroy the Dodd provenance for the Beardmore relics.

Edmund Carpenter was never in contact with Teddy Elliott, who, in 1954, had left his regional manager's job in Newfoundland for veterans affairs to oversee the department's training operations in Ottawa. But Carpenter had access to the museum's Beardmore files, and at some point after his review of *The Piltdown Forgery* ran, *Maclean's* magazine asked him to write a reveal-all story about the Beardmore case.[15] In July 1956, the ROM's director of publicity, Duncan Cameron, learned from Carpenter that *Maclean's* was interested in the story, although it was not clear to him that Carpenter was planning to write it. "I was told that it would be an expose," Cameron would recount for A.D. Tushingham that November, "and the phrase, 'Canada's Piltdown Forgery,' was mentioned."[16]

Duncan Cameron was twenty-six years old. Born and raised in Toronto, he had just started work as the museum's publicity director after six years as a reporter at the Toronto *Telegram*. He would spend six years at the ROM before branching out as an advisor to various governments as a self-styled "museologist."[17] He was serving as national director of a lobby group, the Canadian Conference of the Arts, when he was hired in 1971 as director of the Brooklyn Museum, the seventh largest museum in the United States. His term there ended in shambles after thirty months, with Cameron's tendering his resignation amidst accusations by current and former curators of professional and social misconduct.[18] Cameron shrugged off the infamy and continued a career that included eleven years as director of Calgary's Glenbow Museum, burnishing a reputation as one of the museum world's more progressive if controversial thinkers.[19]

On the eve of Cameron's hiring as the ill-fated director of the Brooklyn Museum, he delivered an influential lecture on the challenges facing public museums.[20] He revealed himself as a McLuhanist in quoting McLuhan and (as a former print reporter) in embracing the importance of mass communications in public engagement. Like Edmund Carpenter, McLuhan's partner in media studies, Cameron was critical of elites, both in the collecting and curatorial classes, and was a proponent of democratizing the museum experience and the arts in general. Most important where the Beardmore scandal is concerned was Cameron's conception of the public museum as a "temple" of truth. With the rise of public museums, "the public generally accepted the idea that if [an object] was in the museum, it was not only real but represented a standard of excellence. If the museum said that this and that was so, then that was a statement of truth."[21] As he told the *New York Times* in 1971, a public museum was a place where "judgments of high standards have already been made" – whatever was on display had run a discerning gauntlet of curatorial evaluation.[22] He emphasized in his 1971 address: "The museum must be steadfast in its insistence on proved excellence, on the highest possible degree of objectivity in selection, organization, and interpretation. There must be a willingness to admit to the things that are not known, are not understood, as well as to argue with confidence for those things that are held to be true and for those things that are the considered judgments of time, if there is to be credibility."[23] As Shelley R. Butler would summarize Cameron's argument (in writing about the controversial *Into the Heart of Africa* exhibition at the ROM in 1989–90), "the museum visitor experiences the museum as a site of stability."[24] There could be no truth or stability in the public temple of historical truth if fakes were on display. Cameron never referenced the Beardmore crisis in his address, but it must have been a foundational experience in his convictions about the obligation of a public museum to maintain a high standard of truth. Having scarcely started his new career, the Beardmore case plunged Cameron into a rapidly evolving public-relations crisis that threatened to devastate the reputations of the ROM and its past and present staff.

Edmund Carpenter would recall that he offered to show the museum his *Maclean's* article draft, but he was too busy with a film project in the Canadian Arctic that summer to begin writing it.[25] In September, the museum learned that Carpenter instead was providing information to Elizabeth Trott for the *Maclean's* story.[26] Trott was close to Marshall McLuhan, Carpenter's partner in the university's Seminar on Culture and Communication, and to McLuhan's wife. She had attended the University of Manitoba a few years after McLuhan and was the godmother to his children.[27] In September 1956, Carpenter informed A.D. Tushingham that Trott's manuscript was in preparation for publication at *Maclean's*.

Scrambling to stay ahead of the *Maclean's* exposé, the museum considered forming a committee of independent scholars that would examine the museum's documents and produce "as final a decision as possible" on the authenticity of the Beardmore find, but Tushingham feared the expense.[28] Nothing further happened until the ROM learned on 8 November that the *Maclean's* article could be in print in January or February.[29] A plan arose, outlined by Duncan Cameron, to blunt the impact (if not discourage altogether) the *Maclean's* article. The museum would "carry out some sort of investigation of the case, and … have such an investigation responsibly reported, prior to any magazine article appearing."[30] Two years later, Tushingham would explain to Johannes Brøndsted that the museum had reopened the Beardmore case "in large part to forestall what could have been a most embarrassing expose in one of our national magazines. The article was intended to cry 'hoax' and to accuse the Museum of displaying material which it knew to be a hoax as genuine."[31] On 13 November, the museum arranged with the *Globe and Mail's* city editor, Bob Turnbull, "to have a reporter go through the museum files, interview those persons at the museum who were involved, and write [a] series of articles about the case."[32] Reporter Robert L. Gowe was assigned to the series. He was an experienced Canadian journalist who had spent the last eleven years based in New York and had returned to Toronto to join the staff of the *Globe and Mail* in September.[33]

Robert Gowe's first article, a preamble to the promised series, appeared Friday, 23 November 1956.[34] A photograph showed A.D. Tushingham examining, with calipers, the rangle as it was held by the museum's chief conservator, William Todd, who had treated the relics for Currelly in 1937. The article quoted from a statement the museum had released on the investigation on 21 November.[35] Tushingham announced that there had been sufficient evidence when the museum purchased the relics "to indicate the story of the find was not in itself improbable. However, over the twenty-five years there have been continuing claims that the whole story was a hoax. Because the Beardmore relics have constituted the chief evidence that Vikings penetrated to the centre of the North American continent some 1,000 years ago, and have been so used in the nation's textbooks, the museum feels it has a responsibility to bring to bear on the problem all the new scientific tools which were not available a quarter century ago." As well as arranging spectroscopic tests and x-rays on the relics, Tushingham promised the museum would dispatch "a party of experts to the Beardmore mine site as soon as the weather permits to take soil tests and excavate for bone fragments or any other scrap of evidence that might indicate a Norse warrior was buried at the spot with his weapons – in the old Norse custom."

The museum's initiative appeared to have the desired effect of at least delaying the *Maclean's* story. C.T. Currelly, meanwhile, was back in the public eye, with the appearance that fall of his memoir, *I Brought the Ages Home*, which the *Globe and Mail* reviewed glowingly.[36] Currelly could not resist devoting five of the last seven pages of his life story to the Beardmore acquisition, "one of the silliest things that ever came up in the museum's history."[37] In a reckless retelling, which included a defence of the Kensington stone, Hjalmar Holand became a man named Holland, and John Drew Jacob became a man named Mr. Deacon. Teddy Elliott and T.L. Tanton were never mentioned. Currelly took his usual care not to name Eli Ragotte (who had been dead for more than fifteen years) or James Hansen, instead rendering them as "a drunk brakes-man and a cellar-owner of more than doubtful honesty." He further demeaned Hansen by claiming Jim Curran had interviewed the "cellar-man" in the company of a "prominent lawyer," who told Curran "the man was obviously lying."[38] John Garner says that when his grandfather, Hansen, learned of Currelly's description, it "bothered him greatly," and he considered suing.[39]

Gowe's initial effort to unravel the Beardmore provenance appeared on Saturday, 24 November, labelled the first of a series.[40] He reviewed the essence of the controversy without demonstrating any special knowledge of materials within the ROM's files. He also killed off Johannes Brøndsted, declaring him dead when he was still very much alive and was now the director of the Danish National Museum. Gowe did interview Ellen Dodd, James Hansen, and T.L. Tanton. Teddy Elliott's debunking efforts were noted, but his role was largely limited to advancing metallurgy arguments against the relics' survival that were attributed to Tanton, who repeated for Gowe his conviction the relics could not have lasted so many centuries in the middle claim. Tanton was "convinced that the Beardmore find was a hoax." Dodd's widow Ellen stated that her husband "died believing he had got a rotten deal. At first he thought they were only Indian things but later he knew what they were. I have a book of affidavits which I will not release to anyone except responsible officials which prove everything we have said. I just wish my husband could have lived to see his story vindicated. He found them where he said he did, and that's all there is to it."

Hansen continued to confound. Gowe spoke with him by telephone and paraphrased his comments. "He said that he was in Toronto two years ago and went to see the museum exhibit. He said he was now convinced the pieces were not those he had received from Bloch. He said the Bloch relics had been in two sections and did not appear similar." Gowe allowed that "the experts crying hoax, point out the Beardmore sword is actually in two pieces but mounted to look like one and the cleaning up process would change their aspect considerably." Hansen's statement contradicted what his grandson recalls transpiring during their museum visit: his

grandfather already knew the sword was in two pieces and seemed satisfied the relics had belonged to him. Hansen does appear to have arrived
at two states of opinion about the relics, something that was already familiar from his statements between 1938 and 1940: a private one in which
he was convinced the museum's relics were once his and a more public
one that disavowed their similarity to the relics he had received from
Bloch so as not offend fellow members of the Scandinavian-Canadian
community (who remained proud of the Beardmore find). Edmund Carpenter would conclude that Hansen attempted "to ingratiate himself with
both sides by saying that there must have been two sets of relics."[41]

Gowe's series resumed on Monday, 26 November, with a story that
made it clear that he was not about to whitewash Currelly's acquisition.[42]
The article pitted Currelly and McIlwraith against a contemptuous Carpenter. Currelly was not interviewed, but McIlwraith made the case for authenticity in a series of paraphrased paragraphs. McIlwraith remained so
persuaded of the presence of Norsemen in the Great Lakes that, when he
investigated pits and cairns on the north shore of Lake Superior, he sent
photographs to Scandinavian authorities to make sure the Indigenous
sites were not Norse.[43]

McIlwraith "admitted he had doubts from the first. But he believes the
weight of evidence is on the side of the find, as Dodd told the story – even
though he may have embroidered it later." McIlwraith assured Gowe he
"got to know Dodd well and said that is unlikely he was the man to dream
up a story and carry it through so many years." If Dodd really knew what
the objects were worth, he would have tried to sell them earlier for much
more money to an American institution or the American-Scandinavian
Foundation. "If he was smart enough to plant the weapons and go
through with the scheme, Prof. McIlwraith thought he would have also
been smart enough to capitalize on it to the fullest extent."

Carpenter, a "noted debunker," was in "violent disagreement" with McIlwraith's defence. Carpenter "declares flatly no competent archaeologist
can support any claims that have been made to the finding of Norse relics
in the inner continent region." He also dismissed the Kensington stone
and the Newport Tower: archaeology "has not disclosed one vestige" of a
Norse presence in North America. Hjalmar Holand had just published a
fresh endorsement of the Beardmore find, relying in part on Johannes
Brøndsted's report, in *Explorations in America Before Columbus*.[44] Carpenter "scoffed" at Holand's acceptance of the Beardmore find. "Holand still
believes in the Kensington stone and the Newport Tower, which would

discredit his evidence. He wants to believe and refuses to consider all the evidence and discrepancies."

According to Carpenter, the evidence against the story of Dodd's find, as told by Dodd himself, "was devastating and proved beyond reasonable doubt that the Beardmore Find is a colossal hoax." Holand's defence of the Norse burial, with dynamiting as his explanation for the absence of a body, was "balderdash." The weapons "simply were not found at that spot. The complete absence of any bone fragments is one damning piece of evidence." Carpenter alluded to many cases of fraud (which Gowe did not itemize) that were perpetrated not for personal gain, "but simply from the joy of deceiving," and he was sure the Beardmore case was another one of them.

Carpenter's assault on the Beardmore artefacts was a remarkable, implied condemnation of Currelly and McIlwraith, unimaginable by anyone else, especially any other University of Toronto anthropologist who reported to McIlwraith. Carpenter would later confide to Birgitta Wallace that he could not write about what was in the museum's Beardmore file because McIlwraith was his superior and he personally retained respect for Currelly (whom he never met). "No matter what his misdeeds" in the Beardmore episode, Carpenter told Wallace, Currelly was "undoubtedly a great man."[45] Still, Carpenter spoke freely to Gowe as a popular, well-regarded professor with far more experience in North American field archaeology than anyone at the university or museum, McIlwraith included. And, like Philleo Nash before him, Carpenter was an American whose foremost employment prospects were not limited to the University of Toronto and the ROM. In another year, Carpenter would be gone – from the university and from Canada.

Gowe's article was billed as the "last of a series." The promised newspaper investigation was over after two articles, not counting the introductory item that announced the museum's investigation. Gowe had been filing his stories without any apparent idea that the Beardmore provenance case had taken a dramatic turn for the worse before his first official article in the series had even been published.

At eleven in the morning on Friday, 23 November, after Robert Gowe's article announcing the museum's plan to reinvestigate the Beardmore relics appeared in the *Globe and Mail*, the telephone rang at the ROM. A man identifying himself as Eddy Dodd's son, Walter, said he had information to share about his father's discovery. A.D. Tushingham made an appointment to see him at three that afternoon.[46] Into the rotunda strode "a slim man in a windbreaker, high rubber boots and a lumberjack shirt."[47] Walter Dodd, thirty-nine years old, had spent some time in the army and, for the past four years, had been surviving in Toronto on odd jobs and living in a rooming house. He was shown the Beardmore relics and identified them as the ones his father had owned. They were also the ones he had seen his father plant in the middle claim.

At some point Tushingham interviewed Walter Dodd for several hours as a tape recorder rolled. (Neither the recording nor a transcription survive.) Otherwise Dodd agreed to return and provide an affidavit. The museum, in the meantime, contacted Ellen Dodd. Whatever she said was not preserved, but she did not feel kindly towards her adopted son. With the affidavit session scheduled for eleven o'clock on Tuesday, 27 November, Duncan Cameron decided to visit Walter the night before, probably to get a better sense of his reliability and character after his mother had said her piece. Cameron and Dodd did not discuss the Beardmore case. Cameron reported to Tushingham the next morning: "Might say that Dodd lives in a good, clean rooming house, and that his own room was well kept. His mother had said, as you know, that 'poor Walter had just been drinkin' and drinkin' since he got out of the army.' Judging from his dress, manner and room last night, I'd say he was much closer to the commendable stereotype Scandinavian bush-worker than to the Toronto wine-hound. After talking to him last night he reminded me very much of the Swedes and Finns with whom I worked in the Kapuskasing pulp camps: drinkers, gamblers, but very honest and in their own way, exceptional citizens."[48]

Walter Dodd arrived as arranged at the ROM on 27 November to swear out his affidavit.[49] When he was twelve or thirteen years old, in 1930 or 1931, Eddy Dodd (whom Walter called his "stepfather") found in the basement of their home at 33 Machar "some rusty pieces of metal. I remember that there was a short bar that could be held in the hand, cigar-like in shape, a sword broken in two pieces, and an axe head much like a hatchet. I don't remember that there was anything else."

One weekend, Walter and Eddy Dodd visited the middle claim. They spent the night in the cabin, and in the morning Walter accompanied his father as he took the iron objects to the claim. "He laid them on the ground at a spot where he had been blasting some time before." Walter could not remember anything else about the day. They returned to Port Arthur without the relics, "and later on – I do not remember how long after, but it may have been months, certainly not years later – my stepfather made a trip to the claim by himself and brought back the weapons, and on his return told the story that he had found the weapons when blasting." He remembered the story being "spread about in the papers." Otherwise he recalled how his father kept the relics wrapped in brown paper in his bedroom and brought them out to show visitors. "He did not know what they were, just said they were old swords he found while blast-ing." Eddy Dodd's wont to call the relics his "old swords" was peculiar, an unrecognized clue that Dodd may have possessed more than one broken sword, as Aaron Lougheed's 1940 note to T.L. Tanton had implied.

"I was forced to sign an affidavit saying that I had been present when my stepfather discovered the weapons at his claim near Beardmore," Walter Dodd revealed. "I signed the affidavit, and have seen it since in a printed book." As for Eli Ragotte, "I remember only that he boarded in my stepfa-ther's house, that there was a dispute of some kind, and that he moved away."

Walter Dodd confessed: "I have never been easy in my mind about hav-ing signed an affidavit intended to prove what I knew was not the truth, and I hereby declare that I have now come to the Royal Ontario Museum of my own free will to revoke the statements contained in the affidavit made earlier by me under pressure, and that the above statement is a true statement of the facts as I know them concerning the Beardmore find." Tushingham provided Walter Dodd with a letter by which the museum "hereby resolves you from any legal or other action which may be taken as a result of the earlier affidavit you signed."[50]

Robert Gowe was in Port Arthur, following up with James Hansen, when he filed a fresh story on Walter Dodd's confession that ran on 30 November.[51] "Decades of historical research, the written records in histo-ry and school books, and archaeological documents, are washed out if the story told by Walter Dodd, 39, is proved true." Of the affidavit he had signed in 1939, Gowe quoted Dodd: "I hardly bothered to read it and be-sides I was afraid of my father. So I signed it. But my conscience has been bothering me about it – I have even seen my statement in a history book – and when I read those articles in *The Globe and Mail*, I decided it was time to tell the true story."[52] Walter didn't think his father "had any idea of their real worth and said he kept referring to them as 'old swords.'" Again, the possible significance of "old swords" went unrecognized, al-though Walter said he only ever saw the broken sword, axe head, and so-called shield handle that were in the museum's collection.

In Port Arthur, Gowe reviewed with Hansen his visit to the museum in 1954. Gowe told him the sword was broken in two, which was not apparent from the way it was mounted, and that considerable rust had been removed. Hansen said he had not realized that. "However, I would have thought that the two pieces put together would have made a shorter sword." Despite Walter Dodd's testimony all but affirming Hansen's story, Hansen declined to agree that the museum relics had once been in his basement. It is intriguing that, in 1940, Aaron Lougheed had drawn for T.L. Tanton a broken sword that was three inches shorter than the one in the museum's possession.

Tushingham stressed at the conclusion of Gowe's 30 November article that Walter Dodd's statement did not end the investigation. It was continuing "in hope that a really conclusive finding can eventually be made." Gowe would not return to the Beardmore story. He had never burrowed into the museum's documents; he probably never had the chance. The museum had made a rapid strategic change as another revelation reached it before Gowe published the final article.

After Walter Dodd swore out his affidavit on 27 November, Duncan Cameron drew up a recommended plan of action "on the basis of indications to date that the Beardmore relics may prove to be a hoax."[53] Walter Dodd's statement should be released to Gowe, and to the press generally, for publication on 30 November. The museum should take statements under oath from the museum's preparator, William Todd, from T.F. McIlwraith, and from the curator of ornithology, Leslie Snyder, presumably because of his knowledge of John Jacob. There was no mention of C.T. Currelly, who was long retired and unlikely to submit himself to questioning. Arrangements should be made immediately for spectrographic analysis of all the relics, including the fragments recovered in 1937 and 1938. A statement should be issued on 30 November announcing that, considering new evidence, the museum was classifying the relics as being of Norse origin that were "probably brought to Canada from Norway in recent times, and that this temporary classification will stand until further evidence of the authenticity of the Beardmore find is brought to light." Finally, that day the museum was to ask the Ontario government to appoint a Royal Commission to investigate the case.

Except for providing Walter Dodd's statement exclusively to Robert Gowe for his 30 November story, the rest of Cameron's recommendations were put on hold, as a letter shortly arrived (if it wasn't already in the building) that further damned Eddy Dodd's discovery story. On Sunday the twenty-fifth, a man named Carey M. Brooks, who lived in Fort William, had written a letter to the museum that was so compelling that Tushingham dispatched a team of representatives, including Duncan Cameron, to the Lakehead to question him.[54] Gowe, who had gone to Port Arthur to interview Hansen, does not appear to have been part of that team. It seems extraordinary that the museum had representatives in Fort William at the same time that Gowe was in Port Arthur, but the fact remains that Gowe never reported on what Brooks had to say.

Seventy-six years old, Carey Marshman Brooks was a retired prospector and miner. He was born in 1880, in Connecticut, to Canadian parents who had emigrated from New Brunswick. Brooks worked for a spell as a florist with his father but in 1901 headed to Canada. By 1911 he was working in the Temiskaming mining district, and when he enlisted in the Canadian army in Haileybury in February 1916, he gave his profession as mechanical engineer. At some point in the 1920s he relocated to Beardmore and secured a claim next to Dodd's three claims near Warneford Station. Brooks worked as a hoist man at the Northern Empire mine in the 1930s and became a leading Beardmore citizen.[55] In 1981, L.M. Lein shared his recollection of Brooks. "I think he was a member of the Board of Trustees of the Improvement District. But he was never called 'Carey' or 'Brooks' by anyone. When his name came up, it was always 'Mr. Brooks.' He was that kind of guy. Neatly dressed at all times, quiet and knowledgeable. He would never be part of a flim flam scheme to promote a phoney [sic] venture of any kind."[56]

In an "amplification" to the affidavit Brooks provided the museum on 30 November, he said he had been working for a man named Fox until 1926, then did odd jobs between 1926 and 1931, including, from time to time, some for Dodd on the middle claim.[57] In his affidavit, Brooks stated the middle claim "was actually trenched and dynamited by myself, and it was I who dug the trench in which Mr. Dodd claimed to have discovered the Relics." He thought the work was done in 1930–31. He was on Dodd's claim regularly, and "it would have been impossible for Mr. Dodd to discover any Relics on the said Claim without my knowledge. I did at no time see any evidence of the discovery, nor did I see the rust marks of a piece of buried iron on a rock at the Claim." Brooks's affidavit did not mean that *no one* could have seen the relics at the middle claim. It did mean that Dodd had artfully scattered the relics for anyone who genuinely saw them when Brooks was not around.

Brooks recalled visiting Dodd at his home on Wilson Street, which, on further questioning, appeared to be an error; he had meant Machar Avenue.[58] "At that time he mentioned to me that he had discovered some Norse Relics lying among some ashes in the basement of his house, and that he believed they had been left in his house by a Norwegian who had rented a room in the house when it was in the possession of a previous tenant. I did not ask to examine these Relics, as I did not attach a great deal of weight to statements made by Mr. Dodd." Several months later, when Brooks heard Dodd was spreading word he had found Norse relics on his middle claim, Brooks reminded Dodd that the latter had told him he had found them in the basement of his house. Dodd replied, "Oh well, they have been found at Beardmore now" and refused to discuss the matter further. When Brooks heard about the museum's purchase of the relics, "I wrote to the Parliament Buildings advising a [sic] investigation, but no reply was received." The letter is no longer extant, but it may explain why Duncan McArthur was dubious of the discovery.

The museum ended its relationship with the *Globe and Mail* as the evidence from Carey Brooks surfaced. The Brooks affidavit was not shared with the newspaper or otherwise reported. Duncan Cameron, however, showed no inclination to smother the truth. He was concerned with managing an escalating scandal while also getting to the bottom of the story. A.D. Tushingham, too, showed no inclination to defend the acquisition, although he did not publicly announce (as Cameron recommended) that the relics probably arrived in modern times from Norway – which was made even more certain by the Brooks affidavit – nor did he agree to Cameron's recommendation that the display label be changed. Tushingham wrote Ellen Dodd on the day Walter Dodd swore out his affidavit, obviously having read Brooks's letter. He gently reviewed the case in support of Hansen's claims (including her son's confession) in a way that made it plain he was inclined to believe them.[59] He assured her the museum was happy to have the relics, however Eddy Dodd found them. "If … there is any information you can give us, whether it substantiates or contradicts earlier statements made by yourself or others, we should be happy to have it. Please be assured that, as far as we are concerned, 'bye-gones are bye-gones,' and we will take no action which will bring discredit upon you or your family, nor try to recover the money we paid to your late husband."

He asked her to grant an interview with Duncan Cameron, the bearer of the letter, who was on his way to the Lakehead to oversee Brooks's affidavit.

Ellen Dodd wanted nothing to do with any revisionism that would cast her late husband as a liar and a cheat, and she lashed out at her son in the press. Walter's story was "spite" aimed at his father.[60] "She said he had quarreled with the family many years ago and had not been home for four years." As for her own knowledge of the relics, "she never heard of or saw them before the spring when her husband told her about finding them. She says she asked him why he didn't bring them home and 'he said they weren't worth carrying. He told me he thought they were Indian things.' Two or three months later he did return with them. 'They just looked like old scrap metal to me,' Mrs. Dodd said. 'He wrapped them in an old cloth and put them on top of the piano. I kept taking them off and got fed up with them. I threw them in a shack at the back where they stayed all winter. Finally, he brought them in again and he was going to find out what they were.'"

On 17 December 1956, the ROM began to implement some of the plan Duncan Cameron had proposed on 27 November. H.M. Turner, chairman of the museum's board of trustees, wrote Kelso Roberts, attorney general of Ontario, asking him to form a committee of inquiry that could "solve once and for all a problem of great importance to the history of this country and the education of its people."[61] The relics were sent to the Ontario Research Foundation for analysis. A card in the display case only said that they had been temporarily removed. On 21 December, A.D. Tushingham announced to the press the museum's request for a public inquiry.

In reporting the request, the *Globe and Mail* noted that "witnesses continued to come forward," without saying who they were.[62] One of them was Lewis E. Giles, who had written Tushingham with a recollection of an encounter with Eddy Dodd in a Port Arthur hotel beverage room in 1940 or 1941.[63] He was sharing a beer with Ed Dwyer, a prospector in Jellicoe, down the tracks from Beardmore, who was no longer alive.[64] Dodd appeared, and they were joined by several other men. "I knew Dwyer held a grievance against Dodd over some mining claims in the Beardmore Area ... Dwyer was getting pretty hot under the collar and proceeded to bawl Dodd out on the story of finding the Norse relics at Beardmore. Dodd said, 'I had to do something to get some publicity for Beardmore.' Dwyer expressed a strong opinion that such publicity was harmful to prospecting."

Tushingham had also heard from Hjalmar Holand, who evidently had read an AP wire service story that made it sound as although Walter Dodd had been compelled to sign an affidavit by his father in 1930 or 1931.[65] Holand had never heard of this early affidavit: "Is there any evidence that Walter Dodd ever signed such an affidavit; or is the whole thing a slander to injure the reputation of the stepfather with whom he had some embroilment?"

Tushingham, in reply, directed Holand to Walter Dodd's February 1939 affidavit in Jim Curran's *Here Was Vinland*.[66] He assured Holand that the museum had been "quite conscious" that Walter Dodd's latest statement "could have been a slander against his stepfather. However, several of us talked with Walter Dodd for several hours – the whole conversation recorded on tape – and there was at no time any indication that he was trying to injure his stepfather. He said quite simply that he did not get along with his stepfather, but did not say more. His whole bearing during our talks – we had several with him – was quiet. He did not hope to gain anything by coming forward of his own free will with his new statement, and he did not gain anything tangible. His reason for coming forward was to clear up something which weighed on his conscience – the earlier affidavit. At least, this is what he says." Tushingham assured Holand that Dodd's new affidavit did not settle the provenance case. "We are still carrying on our investigation and are not predicting the outcome. We all hope that sooner or later we may arrive at the truth of the matter. If we do, the Beardmore remains will either be strongly established as genuine evidence for the presence of the Vikings in interior America, or will be proved a hoax – in which case, the sooner we know it the better."

"I Am at Peace"

When the Beardmore scandal re-erupted in late 1956, Teddy Elliott was living in Ottawa, overseeing training for the federal Department of Veterans Affairs. On 27 November, he re-engaged with the controversy after a fifteen-year lapse by writing A.D. Tushingham. The articles by Robert Gowe in the *Globe and Mail* had prompted him, "reluctantly, to write you about the Beardmore relics. I did some research on this subject some years ago, and still have a volume of material on file which can be made available to any authorized person who may wish to examine it. I am not interested in any kudos or financial gain."[1] The puzzle of the hoax had remained with Elliott since his 1941 *Canadian Historical Review* article, and he suggested to Tushingham several unanswered questions that he should pursue.

Elliott wondered how the relics had managed to survive in Dodd's care before the museum acquired them. "Is it possible that these articles had already received electrolytic treatment prior to their possession by Dodd?" Elliott did not explain, but he was thinking of a suspicion he had never been able to follow up with A.W. Brøgger – that John Bloch might have possessed relics that had been liberated from a Norwegian museum. He wondered why no one "outside the Dodd family and J. Jacobs" had reported seeing the rust outline on the rock. Why had there been no effort to find the Ukrainian youth who supposedly witnessed Dodd's discovery? If James Hansen was declining to identify the relics owned by the ROM as the ones he claimed to have received from John Bloch, did a second set of artefacts exist? If so, where was it now? Dodd had told Elliott that he thought the relics were Indian or French armour. "Did he really know what they were, and therefore knew their potential value was greater than the seemingly generous offer of the American tourists?" He asked about the validity of the statements that had been made under oath by Dodd's friends. Finally: "What motive could Mr. Dodd have for 'planting' such relics?"

Tushingham recognized Elliott's name from the museum's Beardmore files and informed him of the ROM's latest actions on the day the museum announced its request for a provincial enquiry.[2] "I am sure that the evidence already published by Mr. Gow [sic] in his Globe and Mail columns will indicate that the case against the authenticity has been considerably strengthened," Tushingham allowed. He thanked Elliott for his "interesting questions. It may never be possible to answer some of the latter to our complete satisfaction, but it may not be necessary in order to establish whether the find was a true discovery or a 'plant.'"

Having offered Tushingham access to his files, Elliott admitted to his reluctance to surrender them, and he decided not to hand them over.[3] Elliott had only allowed his personal archive out of his control once, when he shipped the files to Harry Beeman in 1940 in support of a legal gambit that went nowhere. Elliott was not about to release them from his care again unless he could go with them to the government inquiry Tushingham had requested. The files had become relics as precious to Elliott as the Beardmore find had been to Dodd, who had refused to send his bits of metal to the ROM without accompanying them.

On 29 January 1957, Ontario's deputy attorney general informed Tushingham that the museum's request for an inquiry had been referred to Brian Cathcart, minister of travel and publicity. Perhaps because the museum's vision for an enquiry included an archaeological investigation of the so-called discovery site, the government had decided that the Beardmore issue fell under the purview of the Archaeological and Historic Sites Protection Act, which the province had passed in 1953. The Archaeological and Historic Sites Board, which the act created, had shifted from the Department of Education to Cathcart's ministry in 1956.[4]

As the museum's request wended its way through Queen's Park, Tushingham decided to cooperate with *Maclean's* to make possible the article he had initially hoped to blunt or discourage. On 22 February, Tushingham signed a form granting *Maclean's* permission for Beardmore-related photographs.[5] The form noted the images would probably appear in the 8 April issue in a feature story with the working title, "Is Canada's Most Historic Find Canada's Most Famous Hoax?" The article by then assuredly had a new writer. Elizabeth Trott was replaced by a veteran journalist, Robert Olson, who enjoyed the museum's cooperation. The materials to which he was given access included the recent Brooks affidavit, which Robert Gowe at the *Globe and Mail* had never seen.

Unfortunately, Elliott's considerable materials were not among the documents Olson examined. Whether Olson attempted to contact Elliott is unknown, but Olson's article, "Was Our Biggest Historical Find Our Biggest Hoax?" (13 April 1957), did a disservice to the Beardmore story by reducing Elliott to a nameless schoolteacher who had brought the relics to the attention of Currelly. No mention was made of his 1940 presentation to the Royal Society of Canada or his 1941 *CHR* article, let alone the years of work he and T.L. Tanton invested in striving to overturn the Dodd provenance, although the article's narrative would have been impossible without the evidence they presented. Not appreciating or acknowledging the enormous breadth and depth of sleuthing on the part of Elliott and Tanton caused Olson to wrongly assert that Hansen's inconsistent story led investigators into an "impasse" that diverted them from closely examining Dodd's story.[6]

Olson's article otherwise was a shrewd evaluation of the evidence and the case's many twists and turns. While addressing the history of inconsistencies in Hansen's story, Olson allowed that his statements "did follow a kind of eerie logic all their own."[7] Olson believed Hansen had tried to appease both sides of the controversy, especially the "fanatic" members of the local Scandinavian community who believed in the relics. Those attempts "seldom failed to outrage both."[8] From unknown sources Olson shared a story of how, at the Mariaggi Hotel, "Liar Dodd" showed off a nugget of gold that he had borrowed from another prospector, asserting that it was from his own claim. Olson expanded on the conflict between Walter Dodd and his mother. Ellen Dodd slapped a copy of his recent affidavit and declared: "This here is just a little bit of – I don't know what to say – spite." Walter Dodd allowed that relations with his family "started to go wrong when he realized he was adopted." He was adamant his father had planted the relics and, moreover, that his mother knew it. Olson was more charitable. Eddy Dodd "might have kept her innocent of the knowledge."[9] Perhaps Jim Curran got it right when he wrote of telling Dr George Eakins: "That woman is telling the truth as she knows it."

Nothing about C.T. Currelly's behaviour was directly questioned, although Olson stated: "The high reputation of the Royal Ontario Museum gave the Beardmore find a respectability it did not get from Dodd's testimony or the archaeological evidence."[10] Olson saluted Currelly's legendary dynamism as "creator and first curator of the Royal Ontario Museum," an accolade overreach that credited Currelly with the existence of the entire institution. "He begged, borrowed and browbeat for the funds that established the museum and spent them so cannily that it now contains a representation of natural history and human arts no longer obtainable at any price. He usually got what he went after. A man of decisions, who did not look back, but moved to new decisions. The same positive qualities that built the museum went into the Beardmore purchase – now, by an unkind fate, Currelly's most famous. Embarrassed museum officials today have no great love for the ironware. They are as ready to see it discredited as validated."[11]

Unless he was shown a manuscript version by the museum or a lawyer, C.T. Currelly never read Olson's evaluation, which hung the Beardmore albatross around his neck as his signature acquisition. The shocking disintegration of the Beardmore discovery story that Currelly had so long defended, coming as the octogenarian published his memoirs, may have been more than he could bear. He was in Florida when the news broke on 30 November that Walter Dodd swore that he had watched his father plant the relics in the middle claim. Currelly was admitted to hospital a few days later and stayed for an unknown period. In early March, the eighty-two-year-old Currelly was admitted to Johns Hopkins Hospital in Baltimore, where he died on 10 April, three days before the publication of Olson's article. The museum's announcement of his death the following day concluded by saying: "His aggressive and sometimes intuitive buying has given Toronto a storehouse of treasures that could not be purchased or replaced at any price today."[12]

Currelly's death spared him the parting condemnation of Edmund Carpenter, who left the University of Toronto to found an experimental program at California's San Fernando Valley State that combined art and anthropology. Carpenter had just begun his new job when his article on the Beardmore controversy appeared in the October 1957 issue of *American Anthropologist*. Carpenter (who signed himself as a member of the University of Toronto faculty) saluted Olson's article, "the most accurate and exhaustive of the many that have appeared. It is interesting that this journalist's study shows a judgment and integrity not always apparent in official reports on the relics. His often hilarious account indicates that for any informed person to have accepted this discovery subsequent to 1938 called for a naiveté beyond the capacity of ordinary minds."[13] Currelly may not have been alive to read the words, but Carpenter's former superior in the University of Toronto's anthropology department, T.L. McIlwraith, was.

The Royal Ontario Museum submitted the relics to the Ontario Research Foundation for testing, and archaeologist Walter Kenyon, who had joined the museum as its assistant curator of ethnology in 1956, attempted to re-examine the discovery site, but the rest of Tushingham's investigative plan died. No museum staff members were deposed, and the proposed public enquiry

sputtered out in its formative stages. A.D. Tushingham was asked for an enquiry budget by the Ministry of Travel and Publicity, only to be informed in
March 1957 that a committee of enquiry could not be formed because the
ministry's terms of reference did not permit the necessary financial aid.[14]

Without a public inquiry, Teddy Elliott was denied his opportunity to
testify to his efforts to expose Dodd's hoax. His files remained stored away
in his house. He wrote a short manuscript, "I Watched a Hoax Grow,"
around this time, revisiting the story of how he had encountered Dodd
and his relics and had tried to overturn the accepted provenance. If Elliott
tried to publish the article, there is no record of this. He would also leave
behind the last few pages of a manuscript written in longhand, perhaps
the working draft of the shorter version he typed up. In those pages, he
considered a fundamental question he had posed to Tushingham: Why
had Eddy Dodd perpetrated the hoax?

Elliott had almost twenty years to ponder what Eddy had been up to.
He suspected that Dodd always knew the relics were Norse and that the
story of a French or an Indian origin was part of the simple prospector
persona that he so carefully cultivated. Elliott wondered if Eddy had ever
truly tried to sell the relics before the museum bought them. Dodd had
told stories about *almost* having sold them to American tourists, sometimes for twenty-five dollars, sometimes for fifty, sometimes for one hundred. Sometimes the buyer was an engineer. Sometimes he was a vacationing fisherman. Teddy Elliott considered that perhaps these stories
were part of Eddy's bigger story and that he had never really had a buyer,
or had even wanted one. Perhaps Eddy only ever wanted to attract interest in his precious mining claims.

Was that all the Beardmore controversy amounted to – a quest for publicity and promotion for all involved? Lewis E. Giles had written A.D.
Tushingham in December 1956 with his story of Dodd's professing that
he had concocted the relics discovery to generate publicity. Dodd had
waylaid Ned Burwash with his custom-made case of relics in February
1934, two weeks after American monetary policy caused the price of gold
to spike 70 percent. Did Dodd tell the government geologist about
promising assays on his claim while he had his attention with the relics,
hoping he would spread the word? The Port Arthur grocer G.A. Simonsen
had told John Jacob that when he confronted Hansen about his relic
claims, Hansen replied that it had earned him publicity. C.T. Currelly excused Jim Curran's hyperbole in locating Vinland in the Great Lakes by
telling G.R.F. Prowse that the newspaperman was a great promoter of

northern Ontario. After the relics went on display in the ROM, Currelly intimated to the *Globe and Mail* that, as a story that promoted Canada's British heritage, the Beardmore scenario of Vikings on an epic journey to northern Ontario mattered more than the scientific fact of a find. For Scandinavian immigrants in North America, the relics were part of a home-making myth that promoted their ancestors, the Norsemen, as the original colonizers whose sacrifices presaged their own and who were the wellspring of culture, race, and governance that made their adoptive countries the envy of the world.

If Teddy Elliott's hunch was right, Eddy Dodd had only sold the relics because Elliott surprised him with a visit in August 1936 and then alerted C.T. Currelly to their existence. Perhaps Eddy had twice been reluctant to ship the relics to the museum because he could not bear to part with them. In the hardship of the Depression, he had finally relented because he had no other choice, agreeing to a price for his conversation starters that he could not refuse. Only then did the different stories Dodd had offered over the years to draw attention to his mining claims catch up with him. Or, rather, the different stories caught up with Currelly and everyone else who was determined to treat the relics as proof of a Viking grave and to promote their own agendas.

To Dodd, the middle claim was what mattered, far more than any scraps of old metal. The initial publicity that erupted around the find in January 1938 may not have been what he had hoped for, but he used the sensation of the Beardmore find to form the Norse-Beardmore syndicate. Long after the relics were sold and his rights to the middle claim had expired, Eddy was still visiting his treasured if worthless corner of the northern Ontario bush. According to Ellen Dodd (as paraphrased by Olson), when Eddy was in and out of hospital at the end of his life with heart problems "he always wanted to visit the claim. The last excursion was a drive of more than a hundred miles, followed by a laborious walk to the claim, just to look it over, to be on the special ground."[15]

Teddy Elliott left his final wonderings unused in the rough draft. "I am at peace," he wrote cryptically in concluding the short, typed manuscript. He may have known that more than his interest in the Beardmore relics was at an end. On 3 March 1958, Teddy Elliott died in hospital in Ottawa of an undisclosed illness.[16] In 1940, after the death of Eli Ragotte, he had remarked to T.L. Tanton that several people associated with the Beardmore mystery had now died before their time. At age fifty-nine, Teddy Elliott became one of them.

It would be nice to think Teddy Elliott was able to read Edmund Carpenter's assessment of the controversy in *American Anthropologist*. To the renowned professor, archaeologist, and debunker, Teddy Elliott the vocational school teacher was "a capable historian."[17]

For several years, A.D. Tushingham pursued the scientific investigation of the Beardmore relics at the Ontario Research Foundation (ORF). Small rectangular sections were cut from the sword blade as well as the three fragments for testing. Tushingham wobbled between resolving the authenticity dispute and resisting the overwhelming evidence of a hoax.

The museum's failure to forthrightly declare the acquisition a hoax proved too much for Edmund Carpenter. In 1961, in *Pennsylvania Archaeologist*, he published a devastating and sensational account of his experiences with the Beardmore find. The article, he promised, was to be the first in a series that would run for several years and expose frauds in Ontario archaeology. "Frauds – I used the word in the human sense, for an object cannot be other than itself – have seriously crippled archaeological research in Ontario."[18] In Carpenter's elastic definition, "fraud" seemed to apply more broadly to incompetence and poor practices in professional archaeology. Before turning to the Beardmore find for the bulk of the first article, Carpenter took extraordinary swipes at the fieldwork of two former colleagues, J. Norman Emerson and Kenneth E. Kidd. Carpenter's article was so scandalizing that the journal's editor, Vernon Leslie, was sacked. Carpenter's promised further articles on "frauds in Ontario archaeology" never ran.[19]

Carpenter addressed his involvement in exposing the Beardmore hoax and his experiences in the aftermath of its apparent collapse. He recounted debating the find's authenticity on television with Tushingham. "Before the show he informed me that what he thought privately, and what he said publicly about the relics, didn't necessarily coincide and that over television he felt obliged 'to represent the best interests of the Museum.' This he did by defending the relics."[20]

Carpenter argued that the fraud "was clearly Dodd's story, not the relics themselves, whose authenticity has never been doubted." He ventured that the museum, through the ORF investigation, "wanted to slip off the hook: they hoped some recently developed technique in science would toss out the relics, end the story, and allow them to say primly, 'Until this technique was developed, no scientist could possibly have known the truth.' However, such a technique was lacking, and, many felt, irrelevant."[21] Carpenter was implicitly linking the museum's Beardmore investigation to the exposure of the Piltdown hoax, where fluoroscopic investigation in 1953 revealed a fraud that predated the First World War.

As an anthropologist, Carpenter had raised issues of social class in his discussion of the Piltdown case in 1955. With the Beardmore case, he was more intrigued by how the fraud illuminated issues of institutional power. "It always seemed to me that Currelly, who was a great man, and who made an enormous contribution to Canadian life, was initially taken in by Dodd and then cut off from graceful retreat by his own publicity. He was said to be – I did not know him – extremely intolerant of contrary opinions and in this case he just brushed aside the Ragotte-Hansen-Bloch evidence. But what interested me most was the fact that after Currelly's retirement, even after his death, the Museum staff, not out of loyalty to Currelly but out of what I can only call 'identification with institutional power' (an attitude stronger in Ontario, in my opinion, than in any other part of America), defended these relics publicly, though they mocked them privately."[22]

In one aspect of his analysis, Carpenter was seriously misled. By 1965, he was convinced that Thomas McIlwraith, his old boss at the University of Toronto, was one of the scandal's victims. Carpenter assured Birgitta Wallace that McIlwraith "investigated & found [Dodd's] story fraudulent; Currelly silenced him (he later lectured widely on the subject, professing an open mind, but suppressing details he earlier had reported to Currelly)."[23] Nothing in the voluminous record of the Beardmore case would lead one to this conclusion as McIlwraith was a tireless supporter of the find. Perhaps after being stung by the broad hint at his incompetence in Carpenter's 1957 *American Anthropologist* article, McIlwraith persuaded Carpenter he had always doubted the find but had been under Currelly's thumb. If that were ever the case, it did not explain why McIlwraith failed to rally to the cause of exposing the hoax after Currelly died in April 1957. The "identification with institutional power" may have been too ingrained in McIlwraith to defy A.D. Tushingham's persistent belief that the relics might yet be proved authentic. Then again, Tushingham may have believed so because McIlwraith had stood by Dodd's find for so long.

At an unknown date in the late 1950s, the ORF turned in an eight-page draft report for Investigation No. 55236-10.[24] It was never made public. The

ORF examined the composition and structure of the sword, axe, and rangle (as the report accepted the so-called shield handle to be). A fragment
that was considered part of the rangle was later determined by the museum to have been part of the sword, and so only the sword and axe were
truly investigated. The museum provided their Viking swords from London and Paris for comparison.

"There is no metallurgical reason to doubt the age or authenticity of
pieces examined," the report concluded. But the tests produced some surprises. The axe head was effectively a piece of wrought iron. The ORF
found it "rather surprising" that it had not been hardened with carbon
after forging. The tests also indicated low levels of manganese for both the
axe head and the sword, whereas manganese levels were high for the Paris
and London swords. The low manganese content, the ORF advised, "is uncharacteristic of Scandinavian origin." Even the chief proponents of a hoax
had accepted that Eddy Dodd had pulled it off with authentic Norse
weapons that had made their way to Thunder Bay through Jens Bloch.
They still could have originated with Bloch, but might they have been
cheap replicas that had duped Bloch's father?

In July 1958, Tushingham wrote Johannes Brøndsted, now the director
of the Danish National Museum, with an update on the ROM's investigations. A copy of the letter was circulated by a museum staff member who
was outraged by the ROM's failure to publicly accept that the Beardmore
find was a hoax, and a copy found its way to Carpenter. Tushingham explained that the museum had reopened the Beardmore case about two
years earlier; the investigation "was as thorough as it could be under the
circumstances." Walter Kenyon, the museum's assistant curator of ethnology, had visited the alleged discovery site.[25] Nothing new was learned. The
net result, Tushingham explained to Brøndsted, "was as before: the evidence for and against the authenticity of the find were rather evenly balanced." Tushingham did allow, however, that metallurgy tests had suggested that the sword "was not made from Scandinavian ore and may, in fact,
be a forgery. If it were a forgery, of course, the whole story of the Beardmore discovery would collapse."[26]

The red flags raised by the ORF's metallurgy tests proved to be red herrings. Tushingham sought the advice of Brøndsted and other European experts in medieval weapons and could find no basis for the ORF's assertion
that a low manganese level indicated the sword and axe were not made in
Scandinavia.[27] Today, to the contrary, such a low level would favour a Scandinavian origin. Similarly, the lack of hardening in the axe head did not

disqualify it as a genuine artefact.[28] Tushingham reasonably concluded that the axe may have once had a hardened cutting edge fixed to it.[29]

Carpenter did not trust Tushingham to make an impartial assessment of the Beardmore case, which he thought Teddy Elliott had "exposed, fully and in documented detail" as a hoax in CHR in 1941.[30] Carpenter criticized Tushingham especially in *Pennsylvania Archaeologist* in 1961, and he quoted from Tushingham's letter to Brøndsted as part of his case that the museum had good reason to conclude Dodd's discovery was a hoax. He was brutal in his assessment of the ROM's overall performance in writing Birgitta Wallace in 1965. Carpenter was surprised Wallace was able to examine a Beardmore file at the ROM: he expected that staff would have at least partially destroyed it. "There isn't the slightest doubt in my mind that senior officials at the ROM knowingly misled the public for years about the Beardmore relics, in a pathetic effort to cover initial errors & later dishonesties," he told Wallace. "Tushingham became a partisan, & though an ordained clergyman, is, in my opinion, capable of suppressing evidence."[31] Carpenter was wrong to conclude that Tushingham or anyone else on the museum staff would go so far as to destroy internal evidence surrounding the acquisition. Still, Tushingham was about to demonstrate his interest in keeping the authenticity case alive.

The case was resurrected amidst excitement about fresh evidence for Vinland, and, as a young archaeologist, Birgitta Wallace was riding the wave of that excitement. Wallace was born and raised in Sweden and came to the United States to study at the University of Kansas. She landed a curating job at Pittsburgh's Carnegie Museum of Natural History and joined the archaeology team led by Anne Stine Ingstad, the Norwegian archaeologist who, with her husband, Helge, had discovered the only indisputable Norse site in North America, at L'Anse aux Meadows, in 1960. Wallace would later lead the Parks Canada excavations at the site. She had contacted Carpenter because her first assignment at the Carnegie, in the wake of the Ingstad discovery, was to assemble an exhibition on purported evidence for Norse visits. The evidence (on which she focused a sceptical gaze) included Hjalmar Holand's iron tools and weapons and the Beardmore relics. In addition to examining the ROM's files, she located a cousin of John Bloch, who filled in some of his family's history for her. The ROM agreed to loan castings as well as the original Beardmore objects for the Carnegie exhibition, which opened in 1968.

Excitement for all things Norse was further fuelled in October 1965 by Yale University Library's sensational announcement of its acquisition of a supposed circa 1440 depiction of the world that included Vinland on its left margin.[32] Today, the "Vinland Map" is widely accepted to be a forgery, but in the mid-1960s, interest in purported evidence for Norse voyages to North America was as great as it had ever been. Hjalmar Holand had published his last book, *A Pre-Columbian Crusade to America*, in 1962 and died the following year; Frederick Pohl published *Atlantic Crossings before Columbus* (1961) and *The Viking Explorers* (1966). In this heady atmosphere of finds and speculation, Tushingham could not resist reviving the Beardmore case. In 1966, the University of Toronto issued a twenty-page pamphlet by Tushingham as part of the ROM's "Who? What? When? Where? Why?" series. *The Beardmore Relics: Hoax or History?* revisited the controversy in an ostensibly scholarly manner, but there was no denying Tushingham's subtextual yearning to have the relics considered as a legitimate find. The museum had never officially declared the Beardmore relics a hoax, and Tushingham was selective in his analysis, his arguments compromised by omissions and elisions.

Tushingham asserted that when the ROM officially reopened the Beardmore case in November 1956, the museum had "opened all of its files" to Robert Gowe, who wrote five articles.[33] But apart from the fact that Gowe's series only amounted to two articles, with a third added on Walter Dodd's affidavit, Gowe clearly did not make use of the museum's files, and he did not see Carey Brooks's crucial affidavit.[34] Tushingham called Thomas McIlwraith (who had died in 1964) "an Indian archaeologist of much experience" when he investigated the site in 1937, at a time when McIlwraith had done no archaeology at all.[35] Johannes Brøndsted's determination that the so-called shield handle was a sleigh rangle was only an "alternate theory" that Tushingham did not accept: "It is hard to believe that our mystery object was one of these."[36] Tushingham proposed that it was a metal component of a wooden shield handle – without saying that such an object was unknown to Norse archaeology.[37] Tushingham wrongly asserted that Eddy Dodd had made no effort to profit from the relics before selling them to the ROM. He asked how Dodd could have reported a dome of rust if he had never seen it. (The simple answer: Dodd never saw it and was lying.) The museum's key discovery witness, John Jacob, was buffed in Currelly style as a "respectable man."[38] Tushingham also adopted Currelly's insistence that Carl Sorensen said his friend John Bloch never owned Norse relics, without acknowledging Sorensen's complete change of opinion about Hansen and Bloch, as Teddy Elliott had reported in *CHR* in 1941.[39]

As for Walter Dodd's 1956 affidavit, which stated that he had watched his father plant the relics, Tushingham assured readers that it did not settle the matter "at all," and he aired Ellen Dodd's charge that Walter Dodd changed his story out of spite to exact revenge on his father.[40] He said nothing about the fact that he had personally taken the affidavit, had interviewed Walter Dodd for hours, and had written the letter on behalf of the museum that assured Walter Dodd he would suffer no legal repercussions for having sworn his implicitly false affidavit of 3 February 1939.[41] Nor did Tushingham recall Duncan Cameron's memo to him that judged Walter to be honest and of good character, nor that he had informed Hjalmar Holand the museum had considered the possibility Dodd's son was acting out of malice but that, in the course of its lengthy conversations with him, "there was at no time any indication that he was trying to injure his stepfather."[42] Tushingham at least reproduced the Brooks affidavit in full.

"In the last analysis," Tushingham wrote, "it is impossible to explain all the discrepancies satisfactorily." Hjalmar Holand's theories had created an "atmosphere of belief, and [a] desire to believe" among Scandinavian immigrants that made the "tangled web of evidence surrounding Dodd's alleged discovery … very easy to understand." Tushingham did not address the intense desire to believe felt by scholars and museum professionals. The relics remained in storage, Tushingham reported, in that "uncertain limbo reserved for objects of uncertain history." He conceded that opinions leaned towards viewing them as a hoax. "This does not deny the possibility that Norsemen did reach the central area of North America. Perhaps some day unequivocal evidence will be uncovered to support that theory. At present, there is none."[43]

In 1972, a man walked into the domed rotunda of the Avenue Road entrance, just as had so many characters in the Beardmore story since Eddy Dodd had appeared with his case of relics in December 1936. He was carrying a different sort of Beardmore treasure to add to the museum's collection. Jim MacLatchie, the executive director of the John Howard Society of Canada, was the husband of Susan, daughter of Teddy Elliott. She had decided to donate her late father's papers from his years researching the Beardmore hoax to the ROM, and her husband had boarded a plane in Ottawa with the evidentiary trove.[44] Mounting the deeply worn limestone steps of the Avenue Road entrance, passing the chiselled promise of "The arts of man through all the ages," Jim MacLatchie manouevred the box of letters, clippings, story drafts, and notes into C.T. Currelly's beloved museum. A.D. Tushingham took charge of the materials that Teddy Elliott had offered and then had reconsidered loaning him some sixteen years earlier. An archivist placed the sorted contents in two boxes and entered them in the museum's inventory as SC 9. There the O.C. Elliott Fonds waited for the story within them to be unearthed.

The ROM abandoned the air of uncertainty (and hope) Tushingham had encouraged for the Beardmore relics in his 1966 publication (if most staff members had ever embraced it). When the relics returned from display at the Carnegie Museum, they went back into storage. In the 1970s, as Tushingham continued as director of art and archaeology, staff regularly rejected requests for photos of the relics for any publication that smacked of sensationalism, determined that, as a public institution devoted to education, the museum should not be complicit in spreading misinformation about the past.[45]

The notoriety of Dodd's relics was briefly revived that decade when the new Nipigon Historical Museum near Beardmore began a campaign to have the ROM essentially deaccession the relics and donate them so that they could be put back on public display. ROM staff, furious with the campaign's enlistment of political and media support, refused to grant the request, fearful that the small regional museum might try to revive the authenticity case. However, L.M. Lein, chair of the Nipigon museum board, had no doubt that Dodd had perpetrated a hoax. Perhaps to ward off the pressure to deaccession, without fanfare the ROM, in the late 1970s, returned the axe and sword to display as Norse weapons of no special significance. The ROM agreed to provide the Nipigon museum with replica castings of the sword, axe, and rangle (probably from the Carnegie exhibition), which went on display in 1982. The original rangle stayed in storage at the ROM, along with the other bits of metal that emerged from Eddy Dodd's middle claim in 1937 and 1938, where they remain today. When the Armour Court gave way to the Hall of Discovery in 1982, the Beardmore sword and axe moved with the rest of the weaponry to the third-floor display, where they can now be found, shorn of any reference to Eddy Dodd or a northern Ontario origin.

In 2017, the sword was removed from its display case for cleaning and treatment by conservator Susan Stock. She retrieved from storage the three small fragments and made a provisional reassembly of the broken sword that suggested they had once been part of its fracture area. The sword was about to go on display, at least temporarily, as Eddy Dodd's notorious find. *Vikings*, a touring exhibition of artefacts mounted by the Swedish History Museum and Austria's Museum Partners, opened on 4 November 2017. ROM curator Craig Cipolla added a coda of North American content, including items from L'Anse aux Meadows and artefacts thought to be Norse from Dorset culture sites in the Canadian Arctic.

The last item that exhibition visitors saw was the Beardmore sword, freshly restored. Under the heading "Vikings in Ontario?" the display label explained: "In 1931, the so-called 'Beardmore sword' (above) was reportedly discovered near Thunder Bay, Ontario, alongside several other Norse artifacts. James Edward Dodd claimed he found them while prospecting for gold in the area. The objects *appear* to be Norwegian in manufacture with estimated production dates ranging from 850 to 1025. It is now widely accepted that the relics, including this sword, are authentically Norse, but were planted there in the first quarter or so of the 20th century."

Some people believe that the ghost of C.T. Currelly tours the museum's galleries at night – shuffling in a bathrobe as he did while still alive and his duties so consumed him that he slept in a room next to his office on the second floor, above the rotunda entrance. One must wonder if he ever notices the DJs and dance parties on Friday nights in the former Armour Court, bewildered by the absence of all the weaponry he so painstakingly amassed. One must also wonder if he ever made his way to the museum's lower level during the *Vikings* exhibition to pause before the display case containing the Beardmore sword, read the label that pronounced the find a hoax, and sigh.

Conclusion

Our perception of hoaxes involving museums and art galleries tends to adhere to a standard script. A clever forger dupes the professional staff and nets a handsome windfall; an even cleverer detective exposes the fraud and brings the perpetrator to justice. Sometimes there is an intermediary, a dealer who may or may not be crooked, but the roles of perpetrator and victim are otherwise well defined. The motivation for the fraud is usually financial, but sometimes the fraudster wants to have one over on elite arbiters of taste and provenance – or at least says she/he does.

This standard script bears no resemblance to the Beardmore hoax. There was no clever perpetrator, nor was there a clear victim. Eddy Dodd was an itinerant prospector and con-man desperate for Depression cash who simply may have wanted to attract interest in his mining claim as he showed off the relics with an ever-changing story of how and when he found them. The impoverished Dodd probably never wanted to sell his precious relics, but when he finally responded to C.T. Currelly's eager desire to own them, he found himself in the presence of learned men who became intractably invested in keeping a crude scam alive for their own sakes, not Dodd's. Currelly, the outward victim, was as much a perpetrator of the fraud as was Dodd. From the moment Currelly laid his eyes on Dodd's relics – or even before that, when he saw Teddy Elliott's drawings – the museum director had an unwavering desire that the find be authentic. Sigmund Samuel, who provided the five hundred dollars for the ROM to purchase the relics from Eddy Dodd, managed never to be drawn into the controversy. If there was a victim, it was the historical record, and the schoolchildren who were taught on museum visits and in textbooks that Vikings came to Ontario.

If the Beardmore hoax does not satisfy the standard script, what should we make of it? Was it an unlikely, unrepeatable product of a particular time and place and cast of characters? Or does this hoax, more than eighty years after Currelly made the fateful purchase of Dodd's relics, deliver lessons that are more universal and timeless?

As unique (and as bewildering) in details as the Beardmore case may have been, it shares features with other hoaxes, before and after it, and speaks to us on several fronts. It delivers lessons about scholarship's vulnerability to distortions based on class when it comes to weighing evidence and credibility, as I discuss in the Introduction and hope have made clear in the narrative. It illuminates the way individual and institutional power can be exercised (and abused) across personal and professional networks. And it is part of a long and ongoing desire to produce physical proof of a Norse presence in North America that, time and again, has either overreached in its interpretation of evidence or fallen for frauds.

Many elements of the Beardmore hoax were peculiar to its time and circumstance. It would not have unfolded as it did without a myriad of contextual factors, including not only the Depression and the Second World War but also the state of scholarship in Canada, to which I will return. Foremost, the hoax could not have unfolded without Charles Trick Currelly.

There are reasons to empathize with Currelly. The hoax claims made by Eli Ragotte and James Hansen were, to put it mildly, problematic. Others, however, saw through and past those problems, and sensed the essential truths in their stories. The doubters also recognized the fundamental poverties of the authenticity case. Currelly's downfall lay in his hubris, his lack of due diligence, and his intransigence. Teddy Elliott (who changed his own mind dramatically about the discovery) remarked to T.L. Tanton after his hostile meeting with Currelly in April 1940: "I feel that little was gained beyond an impression that a once open mind is closed, that a man in authority is irritated by having his opinions questioned by some one of no standing."[1] Edmund Carpenter recalled that Currelly "was said to be – I did not know him – extremely intolerant of contrary opinions and in this case he just brushed aside the Ragotte-Hansen-Bloch evidence."[2] Hubris is a dangerous quality in a scholar, especially when it leads him or her not to pursue answers to basic questions. But Currelly was more than negligent of due diligence on matters like the weapons typology: he concealed and otherwise misrepresented evidence, and used his authority and connections to interfere with efforts to ask (and air publicly) hard, reasonable questions.

The academic and museum communities form a much different professional milieu today than they did in the 1930s or even the 1950s. Above all, those communities are so much larger, so much more specialized, so much more decentralized now than they were then. Anthropology and archaeology as academic disciplines scarcely existed in Canada when the Beardmore relics came to light. You can no longer count on the fingers of one hand the people in Canada with training to conduct an archaeological dig. Those days were beginning to pass in the 1950s, which made it

possible for an experienced archaeologist from within the University of
Toronto and the ROM, Edmund Carpenter, to aggressively deride the discovery and make possible the hoax's exposure. With anthropology and archaeology departments in universities across the country, we would not
have to venture beyond Canada's borders to find archaeologists who
would openly question a discovery like Beardmore and press for better evidence. Today, the ROM is unrecognizable when compared to its years
under Currelly's firm authority. In my research, I could not have asked for
more cooperative staff members: they shared their fascination with the
Beardmore case, permitted me access to files beyond those in the museum's archives, and enlisted my help in settling the weapons typology.

Currelly may not have consciously committed fraud on his own institution, but he was able to abet and perpetuate the Beardmore hoax in
large part because of his reputation. When a figure of considerable standing pronounces in favour of a controversial discovery, and defends it to the
extent that Currelly did, dissent requires courage that not everyone can
muster. The reputation factor is not limited to the Beardmore case. Piltdown Man was quickly pronounced authentic by the leading figures of
their age in anthropology – Grafton Eliot Smith, Sir Arthur Keith, and Sir
Arthur Smith Woodward (who attracted suspicion of having been complicit). The Vinland Map was acquired by a leading scholarly institution
and the book that was published in support of it by Yale University Press
in 1965 was co-authored by a formidable trio of leading experts: R.A. Skelton (superintendent of maps in the British Museum), Thomas E. Marston
(an assistant keeper in the British Museum's Department of Printed
Books), and George E. Painter (Yale's curator of medieval and Renaissance
manuscripts).[3] With the Beardmore case, C.T. Currelly and the ROM commanded tremendous respect from academics, the media, and the public.
C.T. Currelly's ability to dominate the debate surrounding the Beardmore
relics was due to his outsized status in Canada as a scholar who commanded the respect of people from all walks of life, including the general press. As he lectured Duncan McArthur in November 1940, his eye was
"severely trained." The Canadian media's deference to his opinion is plain
in the Beardmore record, and Teddy Elliott was not paranoid in suspecting that more than one of his own efforts to publicly question the Beardmore provenance was killed because editors deferred to Currelly's assurances that the hoax arguments were baseless. While some of Elliott's and
Tanton's arguments against the find might have raised legitimate questions of libel, newspapers were not shy about publishing materials in

favour of the provenance that cast aspersions on the characters of Hansen and Ragotte. I believe editors were far more concerned with the wrath they might face if airing the hoax case were to call Currelly's behaviour and judgment into question. Slandering a marginally employed railway worker like Dodd, or men like Ragotte and Hansen, was one thing: taking down an esteemed museum director was something else altogether.

Currelly had amassed a considerable amount of cultural and academic capital by the late 1930s. He gambled it all – even squandered it all – on one dubious acquisition. I am reminded of the sorry performance of Sir Hugh Trevor-Roper in the debacle of the Hitler diaries, a clumsy forgery that Trevor-Roper, the former Regis Professor of History at Oxford, rashly authenticated in 1983 at the height of his renown as a historian of Nazi Germany. Trevor-Roper, however, did not embark on an obstructive campaign to defend his opinion, as Currelly did, and he expressed grave doubts even as his authentication was being published.[4] R.A. Skelton, for his part, had hoped the Vinland Map and the volume in which it was bound would receive a scientific investigation, which did not happen until two years after his co-authored book was published.

Whenever a field is dominated by one or more like-minded individuals who have access to an array of levers of power, the potential exists for the suffocation, even suppression, of scholarship, if only for the sake of retaining the grip on those levers. In *Breaking the Maya Code*, Michael D. Coe writes of the decades of lost momentum in deciphering Mayan glyphs because of the overbearing authority of Sir Eric Thompson, who crushed any efforts to advance the idea that the glyphs contained a phonetic component, which proved key to unlocking their meaning in the 1980s.[5] Archaeologist Garret Fagan argues that "a case could be made that this much-honored figure crossed the line into pseudoarchaeology."[6] While the prevalence of the "Clovis-first" theory was not a case of one individual's dominating a profession, the long reign of this theory in archaeology, which held that no humans were in the Americas prior to about 12,000 BP, was due in part to a ruthless interrogation of evidence for older human occupations that verged on suppression. Questioning Clovis-first became a potential career-killer for professional archaeologists, as investigative journalist Elaine Dewar explores in *Bones*.[7]

Cases like the Mayan glyphs and Clovis-first give unfortunate fuel to the standard charge of pseudohistorians and pseudoarchaeologists that the academy is a closed shop that is hostile to new ideas, especially when they are posed by outsiders, the unaccredited possessors of more innovative minds who do not have institutional turfs and research funding to defend. Similar charges are flung at scientists by climate-change deniers. All professions are vulnerable to abuses of power and process, and it would be foolish not to allow that history and archaeology are among them. The Beardmore case had clear instances of abuse. Currelly, foremost, was deliberately misleading and unforthcoming, and Stewart Wallace behaved poorly in Currelly's defence, however much he sincerely believed the hoax case was baseless.

After the Second World War, Johannes Brøndsted and William S. Godfrey, Jr, were far too kind in their assessments of the Beardmore find as evidence of Norsemen in the Great Lakes region, especially considering Brøndsted recognized that the so-called shield handle was a pagan sleigh rattle. They had no difficulty dismissing other evidence (including Hjalmar Holand's various iron objects, the Kensington stone, and the Newport Tower), but the Beardmore find's association with the University of Toronto and the ROM induced a collegial indulgence the provenance case did not warrant.

The near-unanimous scholarly acceptance of Currelly's purchase as a Norse grave remains striking when compared with the Piltdown and Vinland Map cases. Although most scientists did embrace the sensational Piltdown find when it was announced, according to the renowned paleontologist Louis B. Leakey, "there were a few, at the very outset, who could not accept the evidence."[8] Granted, the initial dissent in the Piltdown case mainly surrounded whether the cranium and jaw belonged to a single individual (as opposed to declaring a fraud). Soon after it was revealed, the Vinland Map attracted informed criticism that suspected fakery – of course, by then, scholars concerned with things Norse in North America were well apprised of past controversies surrounding the Kensington stone (and innumerable other rune stones), the Newport Tower, and the Beardmore relics. The Beardmore hoax is not a rallying cry for disrespect and insolence within the academy, but it is a reminder that past achievements of individuals and institutions are not grounds for waiving the need for basic scepticism and standards of evidence.

While the documentary record shows that there was plenty of *private* demurring among associates of Currelly over the authenticity of the Beardmore find (G.R.F. Prowse and Vilhjalmur Stefansson foremost, and even Halmar Holand, at least initially), no one with acknowledged expertise, beyond A.W. Brøgger in the Scandinavian press, was willing to *publicly* challenge Dodd's discovery. Neither Diamond Jenness, the country's chief anthropologist, nor his esteemed archaeologist, William Wintemberg, would touch the controversy publicly, as much as they were willing to privately assist the hoax investigation. It was left to two scholarly outsiders – a high school teacher and a government geologist, working on their own time and at their own expense – to challenge the discovery narrative that Currelly and the ROM served up with a major assist from Jim Curran. Their lone public ally was Lawrence J. Burpee, an esteemed figure in Canadian historical circles who nevertheless was not an academic historian and had a secure day job as Canada's secretary on the International Joint Commission. The divide between scholarly insiders and outsiders was complex because Curran was no scholar, yet he was fundamental to advancing the authenticity case for the ROM, while Edmund Carpenter, who worked to expose the hoax in the 1950s, was a University of Toronto professor with an office in the museum. As I note, Carpenter was an academic outlier if not an outsider, an American without any ties to the university before his hiring. He was also something of a celebrity, a public intellectual active in a blossoming environment of print and electronic mass media. He was mindful of institutional authority but not beholden to the networks of power and influence that had surrounded and shielded Currelly. He disdained what he called the "identification with institutional power" that he contended led museum figures like director A.D. Tushingham to defend the museum's Beardmore acquisition in public while privately conceding to him that the find might be a hoax.

Like the two major scandals that came before and after it – Piltdown Man and the Yale Vinland Map – the Beardmore hoax was marked by the wider scholarly community's lack of access to evidence or documentation. Leakey recalled examining the Piltdown fossils in 1933 at the British Museum of Natural History. He was only allowed to view the original fossils briefly, and was not to handle them, before they were quickly removed and he was left with castings to examine. Leakey believed that all scientists who examined the material endured this restricted access until the fossils came under the care of Kenneth Oakley in 1953. Oakley drilled holes in the specimens to extract fluorine content and allowed colleagues to examine them closely. The hoax promptly collapsed. Leakey published his qualms about whether the cranium belonged with the jaw but confessed in his memoir: "I was foolish enough never to dream, even for a moment, that the true explanation lay in a deliberate forgery."[9] Leakey thought the Piltdown hoax succeeded and endured because the hoaxer created a fake that met expectations of what a "missing link" would be like. The Beardmore hoax succeeded, in part, because scholars with influential voices believed a Norse incursion into the Great Lakes was possible or even likely, especially via Hudson Bay and James Bay, whether or not they accepted the authenticity of the Kensington stone. The Beardmore and Piltdown hoaxes were also similar in that initial investigations were derailed by an intervening world war.

Yale University would be criticized for imposing confidentiality agreements and not engaging a larger community of experts before revealing a discovery as important as the Vinland Map in *The Vinland Map and the Tartar Relation*, published by Yale University Press in 1965. The earlier problems with C.T. Currelly's not adequately canvassing scholars before publishing on the Beardmore find should be so obvious as to not bear repeating; but, as Langdon Warner advised Currelly in 1937, "it is always well to have several minds mulling over the available material."[10] The Vinland Map was similarly bedeviled by an inadequate probing of its provenance.[11]

Today, as scientific disciplines have struggled with a rash of retractions, the Piltdown hoax is cited in arguments for wider access to evidence used to support published findings.[12] Beardmore is no less a reminder that, in the humanities and social sciences, evidence needs to be accessible and readily shared. The case of the Vinland Map was more a matter of inadequate initial scholarly engagement than of obfuscation and misleading behaviour, although disclosure agreements hindered a full and timely debate about the map's authenticity. Currelly's hoarding of evidence for the Beardmore find's provenance not only hobbled efforts to assess its authenticity but also allowed him to assert (and change) the facts as he pleased, as he told a selective, inconsistent, and at times inaccurate story about the acquisition. As I have argued, the efforts to prove or disprove the Beardmore find were hampered by the fact that no one had access to all the evidence. Eddy Dodd and John Jacob provided crucial statements that no public museum should have shielded from the public record. Currelly misrepresented Ned Burwash's role in bringing the relics to his attention, to the point that I do not believe Thomas McIlwraith ever saw Burwash's critical letters of 1934 and 1935. The experts Currelly canvassed on the weapons typology were given a grossly inadequate description of how the museum acquired them – none of them even knew the purported grave was in North America – and Currelly refused to respond when asked the basic detail of where the grave was located. Nor did he make public the specific opinions of these experts, or their identities, which allowed him to falsely assert in CHR that there was a broad consensus for a circa 950 grave. Although Currelly complained to Duncan McArthur that he was never able to publish the longer, scientific report that he repeatedly promised for the ROM *Bulletin*, it is difficult to imagine he would have been forthcoming about the expert opinions, as those who held them would have protested at not having been told that the "grave" was in northern Ontario when they were canvassed.

The arrogance that drove Currelly is as alive as ever in the world of museums and academia, but deference to reputation or status may be less widespread or at least less suffocating. Much had already changed in that world between Currelly's public display of the relics in 1938 and Carpenter's crusade against them in the mid-1950s. It is difficult to say how truly divided the spheres of academic insiders and outsiders were before the Second World War, with the balance of power resting with the insiders. When the ROM acquired the relics, academic history in Canada was still undergoing a process of professionalization, and a graduate degree in history was not considered a prerequisite to admission. T.L. Tanton, a respected government geologist with a PhD and a published interest in archaeology who was also a leading member of the Royal Society of Canada, qualified to some degree as an insider. Tanton had the ear and the respect of leading figures in the humanities and social sciences and the trust of Diamond Jenness. The Beardmore provenance debate might have unfolded much differently had Tanton chosen to be the lead agitator and not deferred to Elliott regarding the publishing role in their partnership.

The Beardmore case suggests that if you were someone like Elliott, you could be welcomed into the insider's fold (as he imagined he had been when he brought Dodd's relics to Currelly's attention), even found useful, if you did not disagree with or challenge the work of a scholarly insider. But once Elliott posed a threat, barriers to making his arguments public sprang up, even beyond the academic world. Still, the perception that such a profound divide, with its lopsided power relationship, existed may rest solely on the fact that the Beardmore case involved C.T. Currelly, whose authority and influence were outsized and whose inclination to flex them and mislead people who trusted and respected him went unchecked, in this increasingly desperate instance, by his own conscience. Regardless, the Beardmore case could not have unfolded without exploitable vulnerabilities in a system supposedly dedicated to the pursuit of knowledge. Tanton had ventured to Elliott in early 1941 that "the cards are stacked against you at Toronto." There was no problem with Elliott's scholarship (which, in large part, was Tanton's scholarship); the problem was with a system that could obstruct or compromise him behind a veneer of collegiality that was all but maddening.

When Stuart Wallace kept Elliott's RSC paper out of *Transactions*, George Brown was backed into an uncomfortable corner as CHR became the logical outlet. As editor, Brown was caught between a formal mandate to publish scholarship and an informal expectation not to offend fellow faculty at the University of Toronto and members of the network of powerful individuals loyal to Currelly (and Currelly himself) surrounding the journal's publisher, University of Toronto Press. To the very end of the process of preparing Elliott's article for press, Brown answered to Currelly's wishes. Elliott's article was subjected to a peer-review ordeal that was hardly blind or disinterested and that bore no resemblance to the way other articles were apparently prepared. Currelly's original, inadequate article had sailed onto the pages of CHR as a beyond-last-minute submission that Currelly all but ordered Brown to run in the coming issue.

The submission and editing processes followed by CHR from 1939 to 1941 for the Beardmore articles are a thing of the past in respected academic journals. Available avenues of communication also are much different today than they were in the late 1930s. Scholars have found a variety of strategies for communicating their work and ideas that did not exist in the era of the Beardmore scandal. That change has not been without problems as claims bypass peer review and are amplified in the popular media. Nevertheless, scholarly blogs and podcasts abound, as do online media that are either dedicated to certain disciplines or receptive to propagating their ideas, findings, and opinions.

While hoaxes and poor or rushed scholarship are still with us, new forms of media mean that the cycle from extraordinary claims to exposure is much shorter. Where the Beardmore hoax prevailed for almost twenty years, today controversial claims experience immediate blowback in the Twitterverse alone. As I completed this book in October 2017, Uppsala University made an extraordinary claim via press release that one of its scholars had found the word "Allah" embroidered in Viking funeral clothes. The announcement was carried widely by major global media outlets.[13] Within days, an American scholar of Islamic art and architecture, Stephennie Mulder, had shot down the claim (which had not been peer reviewed) in a blizzard of tweets, noting that the Arabic style of epigraphy supposedly found in tenth-century Scandinavian clothing did not come into use until the eleventh and twelfth centuries.[14]

For better or for worse, there are too many options in publishing and communications today for a powerful clique within the academy to stifle contrary views from within or from without, regardless of how fringe and even offensive some of these might be: if anything, in the public realm, fringe and offensive views now drown out the academy's sober voices. Were the Beardmore relics found tomorrow, Teddy Elliott and T.L. Tanton would have little problem airing their doubts, in one forum or another, or in securing a media ally to publicize their suspicions.

So long as there is broad interest in evidence of Vikings in North America, controversial finds will continue to be made. That interest is driven by a complex mélange of cultural desires and genuine scholarly curiosity. The cultural desires range from the home-making myths of Scandinavian immigrant communities described by Orm Øverland to darker, frankly racist impulses to celebrate the original White arrival in North America and champion the continent as a place of White destiny and entitlement. Between those extremes is a general fascination with Viking adventurers and culture, as evidenced by the popularity of the *Vikings* dramatic series produced for the History Channel.

There continues to be an overarching yearning for some physical proof of a Norse presence on the continent, beyond the small settlement at L'Anse aux Meadows. The will to believe in Eddy Dodd's find endures, as it does for the Kensington stone. For the better part of two centuries, that yearning has fuelled hoaxes, led researchers astray, and compelled true believers (not a few of them accredited professionals) to defend the so-called discoveries. The latest, much-hyped discovery was made at Point Rosee in southwestern Newfoundland by celebrated "space archaeologist" Sarah Parcak in 2015. By the spring of 2017, the initial assertions of promising evidence of turf walls and iron-processing at a site identified by satellite imaging had failed to withstand closer scrutiny by Parcak's own team. Nothing at the time of writing had been brought forward that would satisfy the archaeological community that Point Rosee represented any sort of occupation, let alone Norse. The important difference between Dr Parcak and earlier would-be discoverers of Norse sites was that her motivations were entirely scholarly and she allowed science to be the final arbiter. "Sarah Parcak is a true professional," archaeologist Birgitta Wallace, who visited the Point Rosee site in 2015, has assured me. "Although she was seriously disappointed, she fully accepted the conclusions."[15]

As Point Rosee fades from significance, and as Eddy Dodd's axe and sword rest in their third-floor display case in the Royal Ontario Museum, denuded of their notoriety, we must ask why people yearn for the presence of certain things in the historical and archaeological record. We also need to recognize how far some people are prepared to go to find and then keep them there.

Notes

INTRODUCTION

1 Molly McGown was able to identify twenty-one of the faces for ROM *Magazine*, Winter 2013/14, 8–9.

2 As is often noted, all Vikings were Norse, but not all Norse were Vikings. "Vikings" is a term applied to traders and sea-raiders active from about the eighth to the eleventh centuries. I have favoured the term "Norse" in referring to all the medieval peoples in Scandinavian Europe, Iceland, and Greenland as well as the figures in the Vinland sagas.

3 See Conn, *Museums and American Intellectual Life*, 4–9, 22–24.

4 Cameron, "Museum," 16.

5 Ibid., 17.

6 The accession file for the Beardmore relics notes that the items were mistakenly numbered 948.33.1-3. The accession was renumbered in 1966 to properly reflect the acquisition.

7 An accession year is not always necessarily the year an object was donated or otherwise acquired. It has taken several years to complete the accession process of some objects in the ROM collection.

8 W.S. Wallace to G.H. Clarke, 13 May 1940, WP, Royal Society (1940) A-H.

9 Carpenter, "Further Evidence," 876.

CHAPTER ONE

1 For O.C. Elliott's account of the meeting, see Elliott, "I Watched a Hoax Grow."

2 James Edward Dodd baptism at Portage du Fort from Quebec, Canada, Vital and Church Records (Drouin Collection), 1621–1968 (database online), Provo, Utah, USA, Ancestry.com Operations, Inc., 2008; Census of Canada, 1901, LAC, RG 31, Bristol, Pontiac, Quebec, p. 4, family 34; Dodd's military record, LAC, RG 150, acc. 1992–93/166, box 2556b–4. For the war diaries of the 28th Battalion, see LAC, RG 9, ser. III-D-3, vol. 4935, reel T-10739-10740, file 42.

3 For Walter Dodd's adoption, see Olson, "Was Our Biggest Historical Find Our Biggest Hoax?," 83; Census of Canada, 1921, LAC, RG 31, fol. 82, Port

Arthur City–Second Ward, Port Arthur and Kenora, Ontario, p. 11; Helena Dodd birth, Ancestry.com, Ontario, Canada, Catholic Church Records (Drouin Collection), 1802–1967 (database online), Provo, Utah, USA, Ancestry.com Operations, Inc., 2007.

4   "Rev. O.C. Elliott," *Colborne Express*, 25 July 1957.

5   For Elliott's father and family history, see "Rev. O.C. Elliott," *Colborne Express*, 25 July 1957. For Elliott's birth and family, see Census of Canada, 1901, LAC, RG 31, Peterborough (Town/Ville), Peterborough (west/ouest), Ontario, p. 20, family 185; Census of Canada, 1911, LAC, RG 31, St Thomas, Elgin West, Ontario, p. 17, family 212. For Elliott's military record, see LAC, RG 150, acc. 1992–93/166, box 2874-30. See Isitt, *From Victoria to Vladivostok*, 73, for composition of CSEF. Elliott is listed as Editor of Athletics in *McMaster University Monthly*, 31 October 1921 to May 1922. For the debating union, see "Intercollegiate Debating Union Executive, 1922–23," in *Torontonensis* 1923, 339. See also "New DVA Declares Vets Grade One Citizens," *North Bay Daily Nugget*, 23 August 1947.

6   Marriage information, Lillian Catharine Jarvis's education, courtesy Susan Maclatchie. Jarvis's birth and father, OA MS929, reel 176. Hamilton residence from Elliott letterhead on file, ROM, SC 9.

7   Elliott's prospecting at Longlac from Susan Maclatchie. For his prospecting relationship with Jack Gervais and the sale to Jowato Gold, see O.C. Elliott to Fletcher Gill, 17 June 1939, ROM, SC 9, box 1.

8   E.M. Burwash's biography, Edward Moore Burwash Fonds, United Church of Canada Archives. For his role in the Porcupine gold strike, see Burrows, "Porcupine Gold Area," 5.

9   Burwash, "Classes for Prospectors," 69–71.

10 For Dodd's mining activities, see A.J. McComber to J.W. Curran, 23 February 1939, CP; and Dodd affidavit in Curran, *Here Was Vinland*, 177.

11 See Federal Reserves History, "Roosevelt's Gold Program," http://www.federalreservehistory.org/Events/DetailView/24 (viewed 7 November 2017).

12 *Forty-Third Annual Report of the Ontario Department of Mines*, pt. 1, 1934 (Toronto: Legislative Assembly of Ontario, 1935), 95–6.

13 Teddy Elliott's brother-in-law, Jim "Bud" Jarvis, played 104 NHL games, including twenty-four games for the Toronto Maple Leafs in 1936–37. He joined the Geraldton Gold Minors of the Ontario Senior league for 1940–41.

14 Historical Atlas of Canada, "The Impact of the Great Depression, 1928–1940," http://www.historicalatlas.ca/website/hacolp/defining_episodes/social /UNIT_43/index.htm (viewed 7 November 2017).

15 E.M. Burwash to C.T. Currelly, 14 February 1934, ROM, RG 12.9.1.6.

16 E.M. Burwash to T.L. Tanton, 28 February 1940, ROM, SC 9, box 1.

17 Ontario Land Surveyors, "Aaron Lougheed, OLS," http://www.aols.org/sites
    /default/files/Lougheed-A.pdf (viewed 7 November 2017).

18 City of Thunder Bay, "Ruttan Building," http://www.thunderbay.ca/living
    /culture_and_heritage/heritage_properties/walking_tours/architectural_tour
    _of_thunder_bay_north/ruttan_building.htm (viewed 7 November 2017).

19 Leo Bolduc, Aaron Lougheed, and W.S. Ruttan are listed at 12½ Court Street
    South in the Census of Canada, 1921, LAC, RG 31, fol. 82, Port Arthur
    City–First Ward, Port Arthur and Kenora, Ontario, p. 11. In 1940, they were
    still closely associated with Walter S. Ruttan and Leo Bolduc (who died that
    year) sharing unit AB in the Ruttan Building, with Lougheed living next
    door in unit C and identifying himself as an engineer. See the voter list, Port
    Arthur electoral district, 1940, in LAC, Voters Lists, Federal Elections,
    1935–1980, R1003-6-3-E (RG113-B).

20 For Ruttan family members, see "Memorable Manitobans: Henry Norlande
    Ruttan (1848–1925)," Manitoba Historical Society, http://www.mhs.mb.ca
    /docs/people/ruttan_hn.shtml (viewed 28 August 2017); David R. Dyck,
    "Ruttan, Henry Norlande," Dictionary of Canadian Biography, http://www
    .biographi.ca/en/bio/ruttan_henry_norlande_15E.html (viewed 27 August
    2017). For Joseph Bolduc's profession as a mining recorder, see his entry at
    245 Court St N. for Port Arthur electoral district in the 1940, 1945, and 1949
    voter lists. For Adolphe Bolduc, see chapter 9.

21 Census of Canada, 1921, LAC, RG 31, fol. 82, Port Arthur City–First Ward,
    Port Arthur and Kenora, Ontario, p. 11.

22 Ellard, "From Moribund to Mobilized," 25, 29, 79.

23 George Alexander Drew, an Elora barrister who rose to a judgeship, married
    in 1856 Elizabeth Mary Jacob, the daughter of a merchant and shipowner in
    Conception Bay, Newfoundland. Elizabeth's brother, John Charles Jacob,
    came to Elora to study law and established himself as a local barrister. He
    married Augusta Fields, and John Drew Jacob was their first of five off-
    spring. John Drew Jacob's birth, OA, MS 929, reel 51; Jacob family, Census of
    Canada, 1891, LAC, RG 31, Elora, Wellington Centre, Ontario, roll T-6376,
    families 141, 270. See also Stephen Thorning, "Elora Native Fred Jacob's Sec-
    ond Book Was Published Posthumously," Wellington Advertiser, http://www
    .wellingtonadvertiser.com/comments/columns.cfm?articleID=1000001502
    (viewed 29 January 2017). Life and career of John Jacob, father of Elizabeth
    Mary, from Ancestry.com., Newfoundland, Canada, Index of Birth, Marriage
    and Death Notices from Newspapers, 1810–1890. For his ship ownership,
    see Ancestry.com, Canada, Seafarers of the Atlantic Provinces,
    1789–1935 (database online), Provo, Utah, USA, Ancestry.com Operations,

Inc., 2014. Census of Canada East, 1861, Wellington District, Elora Sub-District, roll C-1082.

24 The Chambers family was still in Elora in 1901. See Census of Canada, 1901, LAC, RG 31, Elora (Village), Wellington (Centre), Ontario, p. 10, family 108. For John Drew Jacob's 1907 marriage, see OA, MS 932, reel 131. John and Edith Jacob appear in the 1921 Census of Canada in O'Connor Township with four children, ages 3 to 11, LAC RG, 31, fol. 58, O'Connor (Township), Fort William and Rainy River, Ontario, p. 2, L.S. Dear, "John Drew Jacob."

25 For Dear's biography, see Ellard, "'From Moribund to Mobilized,'" 111; "Lt.-Col. L.S. Dear Dies in PA At 75," Times-Journal (Fort William), 22 May 1959. His obituary is in the journal of the Minnesota Ornithologists' Union, The Flicker 32 (Fall 1960), 28. (The journal is now The Loon.) For his military service, see LAC, RG 150, acc. 1992–93/166, box 2396–4.

26 Dear certificate of training, Port Arthur, October 1905, LAC, RG 9, II-K-6, vol. 172.

27 See Thunder Bay Field Naturalists, "Our History," http://www.tbfn.net/club-history (viewed 29 August 2017).

28 Dear, "John Drew Jacob." Dear's obituary in The Flicker (see above, n24) would note that Jacob ("a keen naturalist") "found southwest of the Lakehead a nest of the Northern Three-toed Woodpecker, May 27, 1904 and a nest of Wilson's Warbler on June 18, 1906, as well as nests of the Goshawk, Hooded Merganser, and Sharp-tailed Grouse."

29 Dear, "John Drew Jacob." Henry Jacob was a partner in the firm of H.G. Jacob and G.H. Dawson, consulting engineers.

30 Jacob first appears as a temporary overseer in District 6, hired for nine months at $93.75 per month, in Public Accounts of the Province of Ontario for the year ended 31 October 1930 (J16). (All public accounts published in Toronto by the Legislative Assembly of Ontario.) He is listed as a full-time overseer in the public accounts for the year ended 31 October 1931, at a salary of $1200 (J18), and is listed as such in the public accounts for the years ended 31 October 1932 (J17) and 1933 (J19). His travel expenses were $543.71 (YE1930), $633 (YE1931), $838.59 (YE1932), and $625.48 (YE1933). For the year ended 31 October 1934, the games and fisheries report no longer broke down enforcement expenses by district, but Jacob appears under travel expenses, with a much-reduced $472.73 (J9), which suggests he was not employed to year-end. The government changed to a year-end of 31 March, with the next report, a six-month period for 1934–35. District 6 no longer had salaried overseers, and Jacob does not appear among the men who received expenses as temporary or seasonal enforcement officers (J5).

31 Ancestry.com, Newfoundland, Canada, Index of Birth, Marriage and Death

Notices from Newspapers, 1810–1890. Married Hannah Bennett Garland 13 July 1830 [no source].

32 Thorning, "Elora Native Fred Jacob's second book."

33 OA, MS 935, reel 100.

34 H.H. Beeman to C.T. Currelly, 25 July 1940, ROM, RG 12.9.2.

35 J.H. Fleming to Gerald Wade, 19 February 1938, GP.

36 For Jacob's statements, see ROM, RG 12.9.1.17.

37 In November 1940, Currelly's assistant, Ethlyn Greenaway, asked the zoology division to search for the letter Jacob said he wrote in 1930, but it was not found. See ROM, RG 12.9.1, corr. 1935–40.

38 Snyder was an American hired as a technologist by the ROM's zoology division in 1917. Once hired he was unable to complete his bachelor's degree in museum studies at the State University of Iowa. He nevertheless was a respected bird scientist, publishing 183 papers in his career, and he served as the museum's curator of ornithology from 1935 until his retirement in 1963. See R. Charles Long and Jon C. Barlow, "In Memoriam: Lester L. Snyder," *Auk* 103 (October 1986): 809–11.

39 See Currelly, *I Brought the Ages Home*, 235–6; and ROM *Bulletin* no. 8 (January 1929), 9–12.

40 Currelly, "Viking Weapons Found," 4. See also J.H. Fleming to Gerald Wade, 19 February 1938, GP.

41 Conversion based on a Consumer Price Index value of 7.2 (1934) versus 100 (2014), Statistics Canada.

42 The 16 February 1934 letter does not survive, but a pencil annotation by Currelly to Burwash's 14 February 1934 letter reads "Wrote J.E. Dodd, Feb. 16—C.T.C." No reply from Dodd is on file.

43 Recounted by O.C. Elliott to T.L. Tanton, 15 October 1936, ROM, SC 9, box 1.

44 Currelly, "Viking Weapons Found," 5.

45 Lovat Dickson mentions Currelly's bouts of "nervous prostration, the effect of years of stress," in *Museum Makers*, 31.

46 Elliott, "I Watched a Hoax Grow," 3.

47 E.M. Burwash to C.T. Currelly, 25 January 1935, ROM, RG 12.9.1.6.

48 E.M. Burwash to T.L. Tanton, 28 February 1940, ROM, SC 9, box 1.

49 Dr. M.J. Haffey to C.T. Currelly, 13 October 1938, ROM, SC 12.9.1.13. Haffey did not give the brother's name, but of Eddy Dodd's four brothers, Joseph is the only one that records indicate lived in Toronto. He was living there when he married in Madoc in 1907 (OA, MS 932, reel 128) and gave his profession as "baggageman." In the 1921 Census of Canada, the couple was living in Toronto with four children and Joseph gave his profession as "foreman." See LAC, RG 31, fol. 79, Toronto, Parkdale, Ontario, p. 12.

50 See Aaron Lougheed to T.L. Tanton, 22 April 1940, ROM, SC 9, box 1.

51 "Denies Viking Relics Planted," *Daily News-Chronicle*, 26 January 1938.

52 O.C. Elliott, "Chats with a Teacher," *Globe and Mail*, 16 December 1933.

CHAPTER TWO

1 Elliott, "I Watched a Hoax Grow," 3.

2 Elliott would tell the story in two versions. In the first, related in October 1938 on Queen's University radio, one of Elliott's teenage daughters brought him the relics. See Elliott, "Some Sidelights on the Norse Relics of Beardmore," ROM, SC 9, box 2, file 6. The second, told around 1957, had Ellen Dodd bring him the relics. See Elliott, "I Watched a Hoax Grow," 3. I have opted for the version closer in time to the event.

3 ROM accession documents record the handle section as 38.1 cm and the blade section as 38.8 cm, for a total length of 76.9 cm, or about 30 inches. A.D. Tushingham estimated in 1966 that, originally, the sword was "slightly more than a yard long," owing to the loss of material at the tip and a presumption that several additional bits of metal "found" in the middle claim in 1937 and 1938 were from the break area. See Tushingham, *Beardmore Relics*, 1. A provisional reassembly by ROM conservator Susan Stock in 2017 supports Tushingham's suspicion that the additional bits are from the break area.

4 O.C. Elliott to T.L. Tanton, 15 October 1936, ROM, SC 9, box 1.

5 J.W. Curran, "Man Who Never Saw Dodd's Norse ..." *Sault Daily Star*, 6 October 1938.

6 Elliott, "Survey of the Evidence," 264.

7 Notebook, ROM, SC 9, box 2. It is not clear what Dodd meant by mile 180 on the Long Lac branch. Little Longlac was around mile 18 on the CNR's Kinghorn subdivision.

8 James Edward Dodd affidavit, in Curran, *Here Was Vinland*, 177. In the affidavit, Dodd also stated he staked sixteen claims in 1925. "Tom Halls" may have been a former railway colleague, Thomas Henry Hall, who arrived from England in 1920 and in the 1921 census was a thirty-eight-year-old railway section man on the National Transcontinental line at McIntosh Station in Kenora District. See LAC, RG 31, fol. 82, Port Arthur and Kenora, Ontario, p. 5.

9 O.C. Elliott to T.L. Tanton, 5 November 1936, ROM, SC 9, box 1; O.C. Elliott to Director, Royal Ontario Museum of Archaeology, 5 November 1936, ROM, RG 12.9.1.9.

10 Coleman had a long association with Ned Burwash and the Burwash family, stretching back to his own education at Victoria College and his first professorship there under Nathanael Burwash in 1882. As a geology professor at

the University of Toronto, Coleman was appointed director of the geology division of the new Royal Ontario Museum and retired from the university in 1922. See Emmanuel College Library, "Arthur P. Coleman, Biographical Sketch," http://library.vicu.utoronto.ca/collections/special_collections /f7_arthur_p_coleman (viewed 8 November 2017).

11 Canadian Press, "Former Lakehead Librarian is Dead," *Winnipeg Free Press*, 5 January 1939. City of Thunder Bay, "Mary J.L. Black," http://www.thunderbay .ca/City_Government/City_Records_and_Archives/Web_Exhibits/Women_s _History_Month/Mary_J__L__Black.htm (accessed 8 November 2017); Frederick Brent Scollie, "BLACK, MARY JOHANNA LOUISA," in EN:UNDEF :public_citation_publication, vol. 16, University of Toronto/Université Laval, 2003–, at http://www.biographi.ca/en/bio/black_mary_johanna_louisa _16E.html (viewed 6 December 2017).

12 Du Chaillu, *Viking Age*.

13 Elliott, "I Watched a Hoax Grow," 4.

14 "Early Viking Armor Found in Beardmore," *Daily Times-Journal* (Fort William), 19 August 1936.

15 Canadian Press, "Former Lakehead Librarian Is Dead."

16 "Early Viking Armor Found in Beardmore."

17 I discuss Rafn and *Antiquitates Americanae* at length in Hunter, *Place of Stone*, including Dighton Rock, the Newport Tower, the Fall River skeleton, and Longfellow's "Skeleton in Armor." See also Kolodny, *In Search of First Contact*.

18 I discuss Horsford in Hunter, *Place of Stone*, 200–1. See also Kolodny, *In Search of First Contact*, 231–41.

19 Notwithstanding Alice Beck Kehoe's radical proposal of its authenticity in *Kensington Runestone*, runic experts and archaeologists have consistently declared the Kensington stone a fake. For shorter overviews, see Williams, *Fantastic Archaeology*, 194–206; and Wallace and Fitzhugh, "Stumbles and Pitfalls in the Search for Viking America," in Fitzhugh and Ward, *Vikings*, 382, For a detailed assessment of the controversy, see Krueger, *Myths of the Rune Stone*, passim; Wahlgren, *Kensington Stone*, passim.

20 Hjalmar Holand would publish a slightly different reading. See Holand, *Westward from Vinland*, 101.

21 For Holand's basic biography, see "Biography/History," in Hjalmar and Harold Holand Papers, 1922–72, Wisconsin Historical Society, http://digital.library .wisc.edu/1711.dl/wiarchives.uw-whs-gb0060 (viewed 8 November 2017).

22 Seaver, *Maps, Myths, and Men*, 55. Wahlgren, *Kensington Stone*, discusses the Knutson document and Holand's application of it to the Kensington stone, 70–80. See also Krueger, *Myths of the Rune Stone*, 31–4.

23 Wahlgren, *Kensington Stone*, 9, 70.

24 Holand, *Kensington Rune Stone*.

25 Holand, *Kensington Stone*.

26 Larson, "Review," 184.

27 Cawley, "Review," 217.

28 Williams, "Review," 99–100.

29 For Hennig, see Wahlgren, *Kensington Stone*, 14.

30 "Obituary: Geoffrey Malcolm Gathorne-Hardy," *Polar Record* 16, 102 (1972): 447.

31 Gathorne-Hardy, in Holand, *Westward from Vinland*, 324–5.

32 Gathorne-Hardy inspected stone ruins in Labrador that the Inuit attributed to a people they called the Tunnit. He argued that the Tunnit may have been a mixed population of Greenland Norse and Inuit that could explain the fate of the so-called "lost" Greenland colony. Today the Tunnit are considered to have been a wholly Indigenous people – the Dorset, a Paleo-Eskimo group displaced by the Inuit's ancestors, the Thule. See Gathorne-Hardy, "Recent Journey to Northern Labrador."

33 Quaife, "Myth of the Kensington Rune Stone."

34 Holand, "'Myth' of the Kensington Stone"; Holand, "Concerning the Kensington Rune Stone."

CHAPTER THREE

1 In an article outline Elliott composed immediately after the Dodd meeting on 16 August, he wrote: "Get Coleman statement" (see ROM SC, 9, box 2). Composing a chronology of events in May 1938, Elliott would note that he wrote Coleman at the ROM on 21 August, with no additional note regarding trying to contact Burwash (see ROM, SC 9, box 2). Yet in a letter to T.L. Tanton on 15 October 1936, Elliott stated that, after being told by Dodd that Coleman or Burwash had suggested the Norse provenance: "I wrote to Mr. Burwash myself trying to get some opinion from him but received no answer" (see ROM, SC 9, box 1).

2 The letter and drawings are no longer extant.

3 Elliott, "I Watched a Hoax Grow." 5.

4 T.J. Wheeler to O.C. Elliott, 10 September 1936, ROM, SC 9, box 1.

5 O.C. Elliott to T.J. Wheeler, 12 September 1936, ROM, SC 9, box 1. "Were the Vikings in Northern Ontario? A Gold Prospector Blasts Out Historical Relics," manuscript, 11 September 1936, ROM, SC 9, box 2, file 6.

6 Main Johnson to O.C. Elliott, 18 September 1936, ROM, SC 9, box 1.

7 Øverland, *American Minds*, 8.

8 Ibid., 19.

9 Schuster, "Vikings Are Coming!" 27–8; Rygg, *Norwegians in New York*, 137–9.

10 Oslund, *Iceland Imagined*, 56. For the history of the Althing, see Helgi Thorláksson, "The Icelandic Commonwealth Period," 175–85, in Fitzhugh and Ward, *Vikings*.

11 Cadbury, "Norse-American Centennial," 21.

12 Leif Erikson Viking Ship Restoration Project, http://leiferiksonvikingship.com/index.htm (viewed 7 November 2017); Bob Kelleher, "The Landbound journey of Duluth's Viking longship," MPR News, 18 April 2006, http://www.mprnews.org/story/2006/04/17/vikingship (viewed 7 November 2017).

13 Southcott, "Ethnicity and Community in Thunder Bay," 13.

14 See tables 1–3, in Southcott, "Ethnicity and Community in Thunder Bay."

15 For Tanton's biography, see Gordon A. Gross, "Memorial to Thomas Leslie Tanton, 1890–1971," Geological Society of America, *Memorials*, vol. 3. ftp://rock.geosociety.org/pub/Memorials/v03/Tanton-TL.pdf.

16 For Tanton's publications, visit the Government of Canada GEOSCAN database, http://geoscan.nrcan.gc.ca/geoscan-index.html.

17 Gross, "Memorial."

18 For the history of the DGS and National Museum, see Richling, *In Twilight and in Dawn*, passim; Canadian Museum of Nature, "About Us: History and Buildings," http://nature.ca/en/about-us/history-buildings. See also Zaslow, *Reading the Rocks*.

19 For Wintemberg's biography, see Jenness, "William John Wintemberg."

20 T.L. Tanton to O.C. Elliott, 13 October 1936, ROM, SC 9, box 1.

21 O.C. Elliott to T.L. Tanton, 15 October 1936, ROM, SC 9, box 1.

22 T.L. Tanton to O.C. Elliott, 19 October 1936, ROM, SC 9, box 1.

23 See Richling, *In Twilight and in Dawn*, 120–1.

24 See Lovoll, *Norwegian Newspapers in America*, 280.

25 A.M. Fuhr to O.C. Elliott, 22 September 1936, ROM, SC 9, box 1; Elliott to Fuhr, 25 September 1936, ROM SC 9, box 1.

26 H.R. Holand to O.C. Elliott, 29 October 1936, ROM, SC 9, box 1.

27 John W. Maloney, "October 12 Revives Feuds over Who Discovered America," *Washington Post*, 27 September 1936.

28 See McKay and Bates, *In the Province of History*, 320, 321, 325–6.

29 Olof Strandwold to O.C. Elliott, 3 November 1936, ROM, SC 9, box 1.

30 O.C. Elliott to H.R. Holand, 5 November 1936, ROM, SC 9, box 1.

31 H.R. Holand to O.C. Elliott, 30 November 1936, ROM, SC 9, box 1.

32 O.C. Elliott to Director of Royal Ontario Museum of Archaeology, 5 November 1936, ROM, RG 12.9.1.3.

33 It is not clear if Elliott included the drawing in his 5 November letter or if he had sent it in the 21 August missive, which seems eventually to have worked its way to Currelly.

34 O.C. Elliott to Duncan McArthur, 24 May 1938, ROM, SC 9, box 1.

CHAPTER FOUR

1 Currelly birth, OA, MS 929, reel 23; John Currelly and Mary Ann Treble marriage, OA, MS 932, reel 6; Census of Canada, 1881, LAC, RG 31, Exeter, Huron South, roll C-13272, John and Susan Trick, p. 10, family 46; Census of Canada, 1881, LAC, RG 31, Exeter, Huron South, roll C-13272, John, Mary Ann, and Charles Currelly, p. 12, family 57. John Trick and John Currelly share an address in the 1881 and 1890 voters lists for Exeter, a property owned by Conrad Walper. See Ancestry.com, Ontario, Canada Voter Lists, 1867–1900 (database online), Provo, Utah, USA: Ancestry.com Operations Inc., 2008.

2 Currelly, *I Brought the Ages Home*, 5.

3 City of Toronto directories list John Currelly, salesman, at 95 Bloor Street West from 1892 to 1895. Charles Currelly is listed at the address as a student, 1893 to 1895.

4 Currelly, *I Brought the Ages Home*, 8.

5 For Nathanael Burwash's shorter biography, see Marguerite Van Die, "Burwash, Nathanael" in *Dictionary of Canadian Biography*, vol. 14, University of Toronto/Université Laval, 2003– , at http://www.biographi.ca/en/bio /burwash_nathanael_14E.html (viewed 4 February 2017). See also Van Die, *Evangelical Mind*; and Gauvreau, *Evangelical Century*, 167.

6 For this intellectual struggle, see Berger, *Science, God, and Nature*; Cook, *Regenerators*; Van Die, *Evangelical Mind*.

7 For Currelly's early life to his BA, see Currelly, *I Brought the Ages Home*, 3–14; Dickson, *Museum Makers*, 13–16; Teather, *Royal Ontario Museum*, 243–4.

8 For Sir Edmund Walker's life, see Marshall, "Sir Edmund Walker." For Walker's role in the founding of the ROM, see also Dickson, *Museum Makers*, 8–39; Needham, "Origins of the Royal Ontario Museum," chap. 7; Teather, *Royal Ontario Museum*, 247–66.

9 Currelly, *I Brought the Ages Home*, 13, 14, 32.

10 Ibid., 9.

11 Marshall, "Sir Edmund Walker," 81.

12 Toronto city directories list John Trick in a household at 40 Avenue Road, beginning in 1896, with Charles Currelly also living there, as a student. John Currelly appears in 1898 at the address as a "merchant," which changes to bankrupt stock" in 1899.

13 See David Roberts, "Massey, Lillian Frances," in *Dictionary of Canadian Biography*, vol. 14, University of Toronto/Université Laval, 2003–, at http://www.biographi.ca/en/bio/massey_lillian_frances_14E.html (viewed 30 November 2017).

14 For Currelly's missionary training years and doctoral project, see Currelly, *I Brought the Ages Home*, 12–30. For his relationship with Mavor, see pp. 14, 30, 35.

15 For Currelly's story of meeting Greuber and being introduced to Petrie, see *I Brought the Ages Home*, 35–6. Currelly addresses his initial years with Petrie in *I Brought the Ages Home*, 36–59.

16 Currelly addresses Holman Hunt throughout *I Brought the Ages Home*. For Hunt's biography, see Landow, "Shadows Cast."

17 C.T. Currelly to E.M. Burwash, 30 July 1906, BF, box 1, file 2.

18 For the Sandisons of Manitoba, see Currelly, *I Brought the Ages Home*, 25–7.

19 Currelly, *I Brought the Ages Home*, 3.

20 See Dickson, *Museum Makers*, 31–2. A nineteen-year-old "Mohamedean" male, born in an Egyptian desert and whose name the author cannot discern, appears as a lodger in the Currelly household in the 1911 Canadian census, taken 8 June. He was employed as an "attendant" and had worked twenty weeks in 1910, forty hours per week, and was paid a total of $360. Census of Canada, 1911, LAC, RG 31, Ward 3, Toronto North, Ontario, p. 14, family 133, microfilm T-20402.

21 Hunt, *Pre-Raphaelitism and the Pre-Raphaelite Brotherhood*, 1:14.

22 Currelly, *I Brought the Ages Home*, 38.

23 "Biblical Antiquities" had been part of Victoria University's curriculum when an 1878 report noted "a cabinet of Egyptian curiosities and a case of antiquities" at the university. Quoted in Needham, "Origins of the Royal Ontario Museum," 137. At the time, Nathanael Burwash was the modest museum's curator. See Needham, "Origins of the Royal Ontario Museum," 138.

24 Currelly, *I Brought the Ages Home*, 38.

25 See "Introduction," Petrie, *Abydos I*, 2. According to Currelly, Weigell's nerves had failed due to his working in underground tombs, and Petrie had found him a "small job" with Baron von Bissing (*I Brought the Ages Home*, 37). Weigell would shortly rise to chief inspector of antiquities for Upper Egypt in 1905 after another Petrie protégé, Howard Carter, was forced to resign.

26 Petrie, *Seventy Years in Archaeology*, 209.

27 C.T. Currelly to E.M. Burwash, 21 May 1903, BF, box 1, file 1.

28 Petrie, *Ehnasya 1904*, with chapters by C.T. Currelly. "Of the plates in this volume nearly half have been done by my wife, and the others by Mr. Ayrton, Mr. Currelly, and myself" (2).

29 Ayrton, Currelly, and Weigall, *Abydos, Part 3*.

30 C.T. Currelly, "Chapter VI, the Shrine of Teta-Shera," in Ayrton, Currelly, Weigall, *Abydos, Part 3*, 35.

31 C.T. Currelly to E.M. Burwash, 21 May 1903, BF, box 1, file 1.

32 Needham, "Origins," 13.

33 For a capsule history of early museums in Toronto, see Dickson, *Museum Makers*, 4–7. Teather, *Royal Ontario Museum*, more thoroughly addresses the Normal School Museum, David Boyle, and museums at the University of Toronto preceding the ROM. See also Needham, "Origins." Boyle is discussed extensively in Hamilton, *Collections and Objections*.

34 Naville and Hall, "Excavations at Deir el Bahari," 7.

35 Quoted in Dickson, *Museum Makers*, 20–1.

36 Ontario, *Report of the Royal Commission on the University of Toronto*, xl.

37 Marshall, "Sir Edmund Walker," 79.

38 For Edmund Murton Walker's biography, see Martin K. McNicholl, "Edmund Murton Walker," *Canadian Encyclopedia*, http://www.thecanadian encyclopedia.ca/en/article/edmund-murton-walker/ (viewed 10 February 2017).

39 See Dickson, *Museum Makers*, 35.

40 London Metropolitan Archives, Church of England Parish Registers, 1754–1931, ref. no. p87/js/045.

41 Dickson, *Museum Makers*, 33–4.

42 Ibid., 36.

43 Ibid.

44 C.T. Currelly to E.M. Burwash, 21 May 1903, BF, box 1, file 1.

45 Bennett, *Birth of the Museum*, 63, 47, 74.

46 Ibid., 8, 22–5, 63.

47 Ibid., 47, 73–4.

48 Marshall, "Sir Edmund Walker," 85.

49 Citizenship and Immigration Canada, "Forging Our Legacy: Canadian Citizenship and Immigration, 1900–1977. Chapter 5: Towards the Canadian Citizenship Act." https://web.archive.org/web/20110610200013/http://www .cic.gc.ca/english/resources/publications/legacy/chap-5.asp#chap5-1 (viewed 9 December 2017).

50 Fraser, *Canada As It Is*, 40.

51 John Herd Thompson, "Canada and the 'Third British Empire,' 1901–1939," in Buckner, *Canada and the British Empire*, 100. See Thompson for a discussion of British Imperial sentiment in Canada in the first decades of the twentieth century.

52 Robinson, *Toronto during the French Regime*, 219.

53 C.T. Currelly to Dr Pyne, 30 May 1913, quoted in Needham, "Origins," 153.

54 Clarkson, Gordon and Co., *Report on Survey of Royal Ontario Museum 1953–1954*, 14.

55 Cameron, "Museum," 16, 17.

56 Currelly, *I Brought the Ages Home*, 122.

57 C.T. Currelly to E.M. Burwash, June 1905, BF, box 1, file 1.

58 Dickson, *Museum Makers*, 26.

59 Margaret Tushingham, "Some Recollections of Dr C.T. Currelly," ROM, SC 3, box 1B.

60 Northrop Frye, "Editor's Introduction," in Currelly, *I Brought the Ages Home*, vii.

CHAPTER FIVE

1 Beardmore Scrapbook, ROM, RG 12.9.2.3.

2 C.T. Currelly to O.C. Elliott, 10 December 1936, ROM, SC 9, box 1.

3 C.T. Currelly to O.C. Elliott, 11 November 1936, ROM, SC 9, box 1. Currelly wondered aloud if the discovery Elliott related had anything to do with a sword he had been told about several months earlier. Currelly may have been recalling the press clipping he had been sent in September, or perhaps he had received Elliott's attempt to alert Ned Burwash or Arthur Coleman through the museum in August.

4 C.T. Currelly to J.E. Dodd, 12 November 1936, ROM, RG 12.9.1.7.

5 See Margaret S. Drower, "Petrie, Sir (William Matthew) Flinders (1853–1942)," *Oxford Dictionary of National Biography*, Oxford University Press, 2004, online edition, May 2012, at http://www.oxforddnb.com.proxy.lib.uwaterloo.ca/view/article/35496 (viewed 22 July 2016). See also Fargo, "Sir Flinders Petrie," 222.

6 Dickson, *Museum Makers*, 18.

7 Currelly, *I Brought the Ages Home*, 66.

8 For New World archaeological fakery, see Williams, *Fantastic Archaeology*, which addresses the Beardmore relics, 210–13. See also Fagan, *Archaeological Fantasies*; Feder, *Frauds, Myths, and Mysteries*; and Harrold and Eve, *Cult Archaeology and Creationism*.

9 Knute Haddeland to C.T. Currelly, 27 November 1935, and Currelly to Haddeland, 4 December 1935, ROM, RG 12.9.1, corr. 1935–40.

10 Currelly, *I Brought the Ages Home*, 236.

11 See Hunter, *Place of Stone*, for my discussions of Gothicism and Transatlantic Gothicism.

12 Royal Society of Northern Antiquaries, *Report*, vi–viii.

13 Anderson, *America Not Discovered by Columbus*, 40.

14 Schultz, "'Pride of the Race,'" 1273.

15 Ibid., 1290.

16 See Stern, *Eugenic Nation*, 67–8, for Scandinavian immigration and the Johnson-Reed Act (1924).

17 Falnes, "New England Interest in Scandinavian Culture and the Norsemen."

18 Thompson, "Canada and the 'Third British Empire,' 1901–1939," in Buckner, *Canada and the British Empire*, 93.

19 Currelly statement, 28 January 1938, ROM, RG 12.9.2.2, Beardmore Relics – Public Documents – press releases/public statements.

20 C.T. Currelly to J.E. Dodd, 12 November 1936, ROM, RG 12.9.1.7.

21 J.E. Dodd to C.T. Currelly, 19 November 1936, ROM, RG 12.9.1.7.

22 C.T. Currelly to J.E. Dodd, 24 November 1936, ROM, RG 12.9.1.7.

23 C.T. Currelly to J.E. Dodd, telegram, 23 November 1936, ROM, RG 12.9.1.7.

24 J.E. Dodd to C.T. Currelly, telegram, 23 November 1936, ROM, RG 12.9.1.7.

25 C.T. Currelly to J.E. Dodd, 24 November 1936, ROM, RG 12.9.1.7.

26 J.E. Dodd to C.T. Currelly, telegram, 1 December 1936; C.T. Currelly to Duncan McArthur, 1 December 1936, ROM, RG 12.9.1.7.

27 T.F. McIlwraith's presence was noted by McIlwraith in a letter to O.C. Elliott, 25 February 1941, ROM, SC 9, box 2, file 8.

28 "Is Confident Norse Relics Came from Mining Claim," *Toronto Star*, 6 October 1938.

29 Notes on Dodd statement and signed Dodd statement, ROM, RG 12.9.1.7.

30 James Edward Dodd affidavit, in Curran, *Here Was Vinland*, 177–8.

31 Clarkson, Gordon & Co., *Report on Survey of Royal Ontario Museum 1953–1954*, 6.

32 Dickson, *Museum Makers*, 26, 40. Sarah Warren was the only woman appointed to the museum's first board of trustees, an unusual honour for any major museum board at the time. Sir Robert Mond was a British chemist and philanthropist who was active in archaeology in Palestine and Egypt. See Thorpe, "Sir Robert Mond." His brother, Sir Alfred, was also an important ROM patron. The Mond Nickel Co. had a mine in Sudbury, and Sir Byron Edmund Walker was a member of its board. Walker recruited Samuel as well as the Monds as ROM patrons. See Adam, *Buying Respectability*, 168.

33 For Sigmund Samuel's life and patronage of the ROM, see Adam, *Buying Respectability*, 164–79.

34 Dickson, *Museum Makers*, 78–9; Adam, *Buying Respectability*, 173, 177.

35 Adam, *Buying Respectability*, 178.

36 Samuel, *Seven Years' War in Canada*.

37 J.W. Curran, "Man Who Never Saw Dodd's Norse..." *Sault Daily Star*, 6 October 1938.

38 Receipt for $500 purchase and $50.20 for Dodd's expenses, both dated 3 December 1936, in ROM, RG 12.9.3, Beardmore Relics – financial accounts.

39 C.T. Currelly to O.C. Elliott, 10 December 1936, ROM, SC 9, box 1.

40 For McArthur's career, see Christou, "Complexity of Intellectual Currents," 683. See also "McArthur, Duncan (1885–1943)," Queen's University Encyclopedia, http://www.queensu.ca/encyclopedia/m/mcarthur-duncan.

41 McArthur, "Some Problems of Canadian Historical Scholarship."

42 Nothing survives for McArthur's years of public service: "At the Archives of Ontario, not a single file or folder is devoted to the man who spent eight years engineering substantive changes in the province's system of schooling" (Christou, "Complexity of Intellectual Currents," 682).

43 C.T. Currelly to J.E. Dodd, 12 November 1936, ROM, RG 12.9.1.7.

44 O.C. Elliott to C.T. Currelly, 13 December 1936, ROM, RG 12.9.1.9.

45 O.C. Elliott to T.L. Tanton, 13 December 1936, ROM, SC 9, box 1.

46 O.C. Elliott to H.R. Holand, 13 December 1936, ROM, SC 9, box 1.

47 O.C. Elliott to Olof Strandwold, 13 December 1936, ROM, SC 9, box 1.

48 O.C. Elliott to T.L. Tanton, 9 March 1940, ROM, SC 9, box 1.

49 O.C. Elliott to T.L. Tanton, 1 April 1940, ROM, SC 9, box 1.

50 Jacob statement, 9 December 1936, ROM, RG 12.9.1.17.

CHAPTER SIX

1 See Rathgen, *Preservation of Antiquities*, 102–20, for iron preservation methods circa 1900.

2 Ibid., 109–10.

3 Currelly, *I Brought the Ages Home*, 200–1.

4 Gooding, "William Todd," 5. Sarah Stock, conversation with author, 6 November 2017.

5 Sarah Stock, conversation with author, 6 November 2017.

6 Vegard Vike, personal communication with author, 6 August 2017.

7 J.T. Fleming to Gerald Wade, 19 February 1938, GP.

8 C.T. Currelly to O.G.S. Crawford, 17 January 1940, ROM, RG 12.9.1.4.

9 Ontario, *Forty-Sixth Annual Report of the Ontario Department of Mines*, 246.

10 E. Ross MacKay, "Were Norsemen First to Reach Lake Superior?," *Sault Daily Star*, 20 January 1937.

11 Bovey, "Vinland Voyages."

12 Wilfrid Bovey to C.T. Currelly, 4 January 1937, ROM, RG 12.9.1, corr. 1935–40.

13 Chester Gould to J.D. Robins, 6 January 1937, ROM, RG 12.9.1, corr. 1935–40.

14 H.R. Holand to C.T. Currelly, 16 December 1936, ROM, RG 12.9.1, corr. 1935–40.

15 Graham Carey to H.R. Holand, 24 February 1937, HP.

16 Langdon Warner to C.T. Currelly, 23 February 1937, ROM, RG 12.9.1, corr. 1935-40.

17 C.T. Currelly to Langdon Warner, 1 March 1937, ROM, RG 12.9.1, corr. 1935-40.

18 Langdon Warner to C.T. Currelly, n.d., ROM, RG 12.9.1, corr. 1935–40.

19 Census of Canada, 1901, RG 31, Toronto, Ward 1, York East, Ontario, p. 1, family 3.

20 Fraser, "Catalogue of the Greek Vases in the Royal Ontario Museum of Archaeology."

21 Assistant to the Director to A.D. Fraser, 23 February 1937, ROM, RG 12.9.1, corr. 1935–40.

22 Fraser, "Norsemen in Canada," 179.

23 Ibid., 181.

24 Chester Gould to J.D. Robins, 6 January 1937, ROM, RG 12.9.1, corr. 1935–40.

25 Fraser, "Norsemen in Canada," 182.

26 Ibid., 186.

27 See chapter 8 and C.T. Currelly to H.G. Mann, 30 November 1937, ROM, RG 12.9.1, corr. 1935–40.

28 Jacob statement, June 1937, ROM, RG 12.9.1.17.

CHAPTER SEVEN

1 For the biography of Thomas McIlwraith III (1824–1903), see Thomas F. McIlwraith, "McIlwraith, Thomas," *Dictionary of Canadian Biography*, vol. 13, University of Toronto/Université Laval, 2003–, at http://www.biographi .ca/en/bio/mcilwraith_thomas_13E.html (viewed 12 August 2016).

2 Barker, "T.F. McIlwraith," 254. Barker provides the essential biographical details in this chapter.

3 LAC, RG 150, acc. 1992–93/166, box 6880-50.

4 Barker, "T.F. McIlwraith," 255.

5 Barker and Cole, *At Home with the Bella Coola Indians*, 3–4.

6 Ibid., 7.

7 Ibid., 8.

8 Barker, "T.F. McIlwraith," 255, 256.

9 Ibid., 256.

10 Ibid., 262.

11 For Smith's biography, see Leechman, "Harlan I. Smith," 114.

12 Barker, "T.F. McIlwraith," 256.

13 For Nash's biography, see Officer, "Philleo Nash."

14 Kelley and Williamson, "Positioning of Archaeology," 7. They date Nash's hiring to 1938, but in fact he began teaching in the autumn of 1937.

15 See Woolfrey et al., "Who Made the Pipes?" Nash returned to the United States in 1941 and would rise to the post of commissioner of Indian affairs in 1961. See Officer, "Philleo Nash." See also Canadian Archaeological Association, "J. Norman Emerson," at http://canadianarchaeology.com/caa/about/awards/recipients/smith-wintemberg-award/j-norman-emerson.

16 Dawson, "Archaeologists in the Continental Boreal Province," 25.

17 For communications planning McIlwraith's visit, see ROM, RG 12.9.1.7.

18 This spot may have been the Mount Regis flag stop at mile 23.5. Mileage on the Dorion subdivision was measured from Jellicoe.

19 All quotes from Thomas F. McIlwraith, "Report on Visit to Site of Viking Finds, Near Beardmore Ontario," 20 September 1937, ROM, RG 12.9.1.23.

20 While several small lakes appear to the east of the middle claim on modern topographic maps, none is named for Dodd.

21 L.M. Lein to Jack Stokes, 29 January 1981, ROM, acc. file 936.55.1-3.

22 See Quaife, "Myth of the Kensington Rune Stone," 636–8; and Wahlgren, *Kensington Stone*, 75–6.

23 Wallace, "Literature," 10.

24 For Lachlan Taylor Burwash's researches, see Potter, *Finding Franklin*.

CHAPTER EIGHT

1 Secretary, ROM Board of Trustees, to C.T. Currelly, 27 October 1937, ROM, RG 12.9.1.22.

2 T.L. Tanton to O.C. Elliott, 12 December 1939, ROM, SC 9, box 1.

3 H.R. Holand to C.T. Currelly, 20 August 1937, ROM, RG 12.9.1.16.

4 Quaife, "Footnote on Fire Steels." See Holand, "Climax Fire Steel"; and Armstrong, "Numerals on the Kensington Rune Stone."

5 C.T. Currelly to H.R. Holand, 24 August 1937, ROM, RG 12.9.1.16.

6 National Research Council, "Means, Philip Ainsworth," 98, in *International Directory of Anthropologists*, sec. 1, *Western Hemisphere*. Washington, DC: March 1940.

7 American Antiquarian Society, "Philip Ainsworth Means," *Proceedings of the American Antiquarian Society*, April 1945, 36–7.

8 P.A. Means to C.T. Currelly, 28 October 1937, ROM, RG 12.9.1, corr. 1941–55. Note: all Means correspondence is in this file, regardless of date.

9 Webb and Rafn, "Account of an Ancient Structure in Newport"; Brooks, *Controversy Touching the Old Stone Mill*.

10 Means, *Newport Tower*.

11 For Stefansson's biography, see Hunt, *Stef*; and Pálsson, *Travelling Passions*.

12 Hunt (*Stef*) treated sceptically the rumours that Stefansson had fathered an

Inuit child. Pálsson (*Travelling Passions*) made an indisputable case. See Pálsson, *Travelling Passions*, chap. 9 ("The Saga of Alex Stefansson").

13 "Generally, though, more often than not," Stefansson deadpanned, "truth is, in practice, bad – especially in the fields of aesthetics, ethics, morals, character-building, and business (which last we have not stopped to argue since it is so self-evident)." See Stefansson, *Adventures in Error*, 61.

14 Stefansson, *Standardization of Error*, 17.

15 P.A. Means to C.T. Currelly, 28 October 1937, ROM, RG 12.9.1, corr. 1941–55.

16 P.A. Means to C.T. Currelly, 7 November 1937, ROM, RG 12.9.1, corr. 1941–55.

17 H.R. Holand to C.T. Currelly, 3 March 1938, ROM, RG 12.9.1.16.

18 C.N. Gould to J.D. Robins, 6 January 1937, ROM, 12.9.1, corr. 1935–40.

19 H.R. Holand to J.W. Curran, 9 October 1938, CF, box 21.

20 Holand, *Explorations in America before Columbus*, 96.

21 Holand, *Westward from Vinland*, 66.

22 Recalled by H.R. Holand in letter to J.W. Curran, 9 October 1938, CF, box 21.

23 Prowse was the son of Daniel Woodley (D.W.) Prowse, a judge of Newfoundland's central district court, author of *A History of Newfoundland, from the English, Colonial, and Foreign Records*. In 1896, Prowse steered a second edition of his father's *A History of Newfoundland* through production (London: Eyre and Spottiswoode, 1896). He added, among other things, a photo of the statue of Leif Eiriksson installed in Boston in 1877. He moved to Manitoba in 1905, where he was a teacher and school principal from 1911 until his retirement in 1926, when he turned full-time to cartology. See Manitoba Historical Society, "Memorable Manitobans: George Robert Farrar Prowse (1860–1946)," at http://www.mhs.mb.ca/docs/people/prowse_grf.shtml (viewed 28 January 2017). University of Manitoba Libraries, G.R.F. Prowse Fonds, mss SC 91 (A.84-10); G.R.F. Prowse to Vilhjalmur Stefansson, 8 March 1939, SP, mss 196-45-14, 9 August 1940, SP, mss 196-50-34.

24 G.R.F. Prowse to Vilhjalmur Stefansson, 8 March 1939, SP, mss 196-45-14.

25 Vilhjalmur Stefansson to G.R.F. Prowse, 11 March 1935, SP, mss 196-37-15.

26 G.R.F. Prowse to C.T. Currelly, 24 November 1937, ROM, RG 12.9.1.25.

27 Currelly's letter to Prowse of 2 December 1937 does not survive. G.R.F. Prowse to Vilhjalmur Stefansson, 4 December 1937, SP, mss 196-41-31.

28 C.T. Currelly to P.A. Means, 1 December 1937, ROM, RG 12.9.1, corr. 1941–55.

29 C.T. Currelly to J.G. Mann, 30 November 1937, ROM, RG 12.9.1., corr. 1935–40.

30 Laking, *Record of European Armour and Arms*, 18, fig. 23.

31 "Agree Leif Erikson Discovered America," *Toronto Star*, 10 December 1937.

32 The newspaper story may have been inspired by a 1936 Kamban novel based on the Icelandic sagas, which was published in English translation as *I See a Wondrous Land* in 1938.

33 Wright, *Professionalization of History in English Canada*, 60–1. Wallace "was disturbed that trends in academic history that were resulting in dissertations that had all the required components in the form of copious citations and phalanxes of facts, but nothing that made them great books." See Shore, "'Remember the Future,'" 414.

34 Berger, *Writing of Canadian History*, 14.

35 Shore, "'Remember the Future,'" 414.

36 For Wallace's biography, see "William Stewart Wallace," *Canadian Encyclopedia*, at http://www.thecanadianencyclopedia.ca/en/article/william-stewart-wallace/ (viewed 16 February 2107). For his evaluation of Secord, see Colin Coates, in Coates and Morgan, *Heroines and History*.

37 "Agree Leif Erikson Discovered America," *Toronto Star*, 10 December 1937.

38 For the weapons typology correspondence, see ROM, RG 12.9.1, corr. 1935–40.

39 Vilhjalmur Stefansson to A.D. Fraser, 13 December 1937, SP, mss 196-40-35; Fraser to Stefansson, 16 December 1937, SP, mss 196-41-23.

40 Vilhjalmur Stefansson to C.T. Currelly, 14 December 1937, ROM, RG 12.9.1.32.

41 Thórdarson, *Vinland Voyages*, fig. 22, 23.

42 Hermannsson had rejected Holand's Kensington ideas in 1936. See Hermannsson, *Problem of Wineland*.

43 C.T. Currelly to Matthias Thórdarson, 18 November 1938, ROM, RG 12.9.1, corr. 1935–40.

44 For all the replies to Currelly's letter, see ROM, RG 12.9.1, corr. 1935–40.

45 See "Stefán Einarsson," America Pink, at http://america.pink/stefan-einarsson_4167895.html.

46 Einarsson, "Review, *The Kensington Stone*." Holand kept careful track of his critics and supporters. In a letter to Vilhjalmur Stefansson he listed twenty-eight reviews of *The Kensington Stone* and persuaded himself that most of them were positive. Of Einarsson's assessment, he wrote, "Favorable but points out some errors." H.R. Holand to Vilhjalmur Stefansson, 7 October 1939, SP, mss-196-46-20.

47 See "Anton Wilhelm Brøgger – 1, Arkeolog," Norsk Biografisk Leksikon, at https://nbl.snl.no/Anton_Wilhelm_Br%C3%B8gger_-_1.

48 C.T. Currelly to E.M. Burwash, 2 November 1904, BF, box 1, file 1.

49 Margaret Tushingham, "Some Recollections of Dr. C.T. Currelly," ROM, SC 3, box 1B.

50 Dickson, *Museum Makers*, 79.

51 In August 2017, ROM conservator Susan Stock shared with me detailed new photographs and x-rays of the sword for consultation with experts in hope of

clarifying their typology. I submitted them to Vegard A. Vike, an archaeological conservator at the University of Oslo's Museum of Cultural History who has dealt with and x-rayed hundreds of Viking-age swords and axes. Dr Vike informed me that the sword "is almost certainly a type M (ca 850-950)" and that the axe "is most definitely a type M (after ca 950), in the smaller size range (possibly a one-handed axe – the larger type M axes are for two-handed use." He further advised: "The axe and the sword could be from the same grave, they are both heavily corroded, and have touching date ranges. But I would not normally expect to find a type M sword together with a type M axe in the same grave. The M axe is probably 2–3 generations younger, and is often to be found with more refined swords with [a] precious metal decorated hilt. There is a possibility they are not from the same grave." Vegard Vike, personal communication with author, 6 August 2017.

CHAPTER NINE

1 For Godsell's biography, see the descriptive information for the Philip Godsell Fonds at the Glenbow Museum, at https://albertaonrecord.ca/philip-h-godsell-fonds. See also the biographical sheet for Godsell at the Hudson's Bay Company Archives, at https://www.gov.mb.ca/chc/archives/hbca/biographical/g/godsell_philip-henry.pdf.

2 Strange and Loo, *True Crime, True North*, 40.

3 P.H. Godsell to O.C. Elliott, 14 January 1938, ROM, SC 9, box 1.

4 In a list of clippings Godsell provided to the ROM on 21 December 1956, he stated that he provided the information to a *Winnipeg Free Press* reporter on Saturday, 22 January. "The reporter had called me anxious to obtain a story for his newspaper. Having spent many years in the Long Lake (Longuelac) and Nipigon country as inspector of Long Lake Post, I was in touch with J.E. Dodd's activities at Beardmore and gave him the following story." Godsell then listed the "Historian's Gold" story in the *Winnipeg Free Press*. Godsell's recollections, however, were not entirely truthful. Everything he knew about Dodd's discovery came from O.C. Elliott, and he had plainly provided the reporter with a prepared news item in advance of his talk. Godsell's list of clippings is also misleading in that many publication dates are wrong as he relied on the dateline rather than on the issue date. See ROM, RG 12.9.1, corr. 1956–58.

5 Canadian Press, "Writer Claims Vikings Penetrated Ontario During 11th Century," *Globe and Mail*, 25 January 1938; "Historian's Gold," *Winnipeg Free Press*, 26 January 1938.

6 Apparently, neither Godsell nor Elliott was aware of A.D. Fraser's article in the *Dalhousie Review* or of the *Toronto Star* article of 10 December 1937.

7 Godsell had similarly advised Elliott: "I never even heard of any tradition amongst the Indians that would point to Norse occupation. But then ... that would go back so far as to be lost in antiquity." See P.H. Godsell to O.C. Elliott, 14 January 1938, ROM, SC 9, box 1.

8 For Beamish's biography, see "'Two Die' or 'Not Two Die', Beamish Became Reporter," *News-Chronicle* (Port Arthur), 24 November 1953.

9 "Denies Viking Relics 'Planted' at Beardmore," *Daily News-Chronicle* (Port Arthur), 26 January 1938. The *Globe and Mail* carried much of the article as a "special" from Beamish (without a byline) on 27 January ("Miner Hotly Denies He Planted Weapons of Viking Warriors"), incorporating additional quotations. Quotations herewith are from both articles. Beamish's 26 January article for the *Daily News-Chronicle* identifies some of Dodd's interview as having occurred after the Godsell news broke; a subsequent interview Dodd gave, to respond to allegations by Eli Ragotte, was combined with the first interview and made into a single story. According to the *Winnipeg Free Press* ("Claims Relics Huge Hoax," 27 January), Dodd was interviewed in Port Arthur at noon on Wednesday, 26 January, about Ragotte's allegations; Beamish conducted the uncredited interview after receiving the *Free Press* telegram. It is difficult to know, with regard to every Dodd statement quoted by Beamish in the *Daily News-Chronicle* on 26 January, if it was made before or after the Ragotte allegations.

10 C.T. Currelly to H.R. Holand, 7 March 1938, ROM, RG 12.9.1.16.

11 "Claims Relics Huge Hoax," *Winnipeg Free Press*, 27 January 1938. The Wilson Street location was not reported by the *Free Press* but the latter provided it to the *Daily Chronicle Herald* for Beamish's questioning of Dodd on 26 January.

12 Private family genealogy composed by Michael Rashotte, "The First Rashotte Family in Tweed's French Settlement, Tweed, Ontario, 1855–1931," at https://www.scribd.com/doc/52206312/The-First-Rashotte-Family-in-Tweed-s-French-Settlement-Tweed-Ontario-1855-1931-by-Michael-Rashotte (viewed 30 November 2017). "Peeter Rashot," in Census of Canada, 1861, LAC, RG 31, Hastings, Canada West, roll C-1032.

13 Marriage of Charles Ragotte and Harriet Hott, OA, MS 932, reel 23; "Charles Rachott," US Federal Census, 1880, Pine River, Bay, Michigan, roll 572. Eli Ragotte's birth date varies in records. The 1900 US Federal Census gives his birth as June 1888 and is most likely correct. See US Federal Census, 1900, Dunbar, Marinette, Wisconsin, roll 1799, p. 1B.

14 LAC, Land Grants of Western Canada, 1870–1930, reel C-6160, Charles Ragotte, homestead 122414, Albert Ragotte, homestead 122415.

15 Gannon/Hott family tree, at Ancestry.com. https://www.ancestry.ca/family-tree/person/tree/38336780/person/220083295605/facts (viewed 10 November 2017).

16 US Bureau of Land Management, Wisconsin Pre-1908 Homestead and Cash Entry Patent and Cadastral Survey Plat Index, General Land Office Automated Records Project, doc. 4573.

17 Charles and Albert Ragotte residences in Idaho from US census databases at Ancestry.com. Charles Ragotte death, 28 November 1936, Potlatch, Idaho, Idaho Department of Health and Welfare, Bureau of Health Policy and Vital Statistics, Idaho Death Index, 1911–51.

18 LAC, Land Grants of Western Canada, 1870–1930, reel C-6160, homestead 214298.

19 Mitchell Ragotte was a farmer in Dauphin when drafted into the Canadian army. See LAC, RG 150, acc. 1992–93/166, box 8071–41. Edward Ragotte gave his profession as "farmer" when drafted. See LAC, RG 150, acc. 1992–93/166, box 8071–38.

20 George Ragotte enlisted in 1916. LAC RG 150, acc. 1992–93/166, box 4930–35; Eli Ragotte, LAC, RG 150, acc. 1992–93/166, box 8071–39.

21 Manitoba Vital Statistics: marriage, 1912-001318, birth of Violet, 1913-061603.

22 Ragotte's military record listed Violet's guardian as May Bolduc at 354 Bay Street in Port Arthur. The 1921 census lists Mary Bolduc, forty, as head of the household at that address. See LAC, RG 31, fol. 82, Port Arthur City – Second Ward, Port Arthur and Kenora, Ontario, p. 1.

23 Adolphe and Mary Bolduc. See Census of Canada, 1901, Port Arthur, Algoma, Ontario, p. 9, family 80; Adolphe Bolduc death, OA MS 935, reel 213.

24 LAC, RG 190-76-3-E, vol. 2.

25 Manitoba Vital Statistics, 1921-018201.

26 US Immigration and border agency records from Ancestry.com online databases.

27 1935 Winnipeg South voter list, LAC, Federal Elections, 1935–1980, R1003-6-3-E (RG113-B).

28 Ancestry.com, US, Social Security Applications and Claims Index, 1936–2007 (database online).

29 "Denies Viking Relics Planted," Daily News-Chronicle (Port Arthur), 26 January 1938.

30 Dodd may have said that he did not find the relics until 1931, three years after Ragotte claimed to have seen them at the Wilson Street address, and that Ragotte did not see the relics until 1934, three years after the discovery.

31 Marriage of Jens Hansen and Lise Irene Gunhelde, OA, MS 932, reel 131; Census of Canada, 1911, LAC, RG 31, Port Arthur, Thunder Bay, and Rainy River, Ontario, p. 17, family 181; John Garner, personal communications with author, 16 September 2016, 28 October 2017, and 30 October 2017.

32 Red Rock Township, "The Early Days," at http://www.redrocktownship.com
/article/the-early-days-127.asp (viewed 31 October 2017); John Garner, personal communication with author, 30 October 2017.

33 Hansen's business ledger in the possession of his grandson, John Garner, indicates that 37 Machar was the only property on Machar Avenue he still owned
in 1937 and that it was gone from his assets by 1940. (The 33 Machar property would burn down in 1998, 39 Machar in 2012.) The ledger also shows that
he purchased income properties at 18 Carrie Street (1926), 57 Hill Street
North (1926), and 119 Prospect Avenue (1927) and that he paid fire insurance on all of them in 1940. He also bought a lot at Loon Lake in McTavish
Township in 1931 and built a seasonal cottage there between 1933 and 1936.
He bought three more lots at Loon Lake in 1948 and built another cottage
between 1949 and 1956. The ledger makes references from 1925 to 1946 to a
farm property at Hurkett, Ontario, on Lake Superior. Insurance lists refer to
payments in 1937 and/or 1940 on more properties not otherwise mentioned
in the business ledger: a Lake Superior summer cottage at Green Point in
McGregor Township; a summer cottage on Lake Helen, north of Nipigon; a
miscellaneous Nipigon "summer dwelling"; and a general store with an Esso
gas station and a warehouse in McIntyre Township on the west side of Port
Arthur, which Hansen sold to its long-time tenant in 1959.

34 "Denies Viking Relics 'Planted' at Beardmore," *Daily News-Chronicle* (Port
Arthur), 26 January 1938.

35 "Affidavits over Relic Dispute Show Conflict," *Daily News-Chronicle* (Port
Arthur), 28 January 1938.

36 Consular Registration Certificates, compiled 1907–1918, ARC ID: 1244186,
General Records of the Department of State, 1763–2002, RG 59, National
Archives, Washington, DC; Ancestry.com, US, Evangelical Lutheran Church of
America, records, 1826–1940 (database online); Census of Canada, 1921, LAC,
RG 31, fol. 58, Fort William (City), Fort William and Rainy River, Ontario, p. 8.

37 "Affidavits," *Daily News-Chronicle* (Port Arthur), 28 January 1938.

38 Stephen Dodd appears in the 1921 Census of Canada as a thirty-four-year-
old railway conductor, married with two young children. See LAC, RG 31, fol.
58, Fort William (City), Fort William and Rainy River, Ontario, p. 16. He was
retired and living on Brodie Street North according to the 1957 voter list for
Fort William. See LAC, Federal Elections, 1935–1980, R1003-6-3-E (RG113-B).

39 "Affidavits," *Daily News-Chronicle* (Port Arthur), 28 January 1938.

40 "Man Hotly Denies He Planted Weapons of Viking Warriors," *Globe and
Mail*, 27 January 1938.

41 The telegram does not survive, but a note reviewing its contents, apparently
in Currelly's hand, is in ROM, RG 12.9.5, Beardmore Relics – Miscellaneous.

42 In addition to the Laking sword from London and the Paris sword, the museum had acquired a sword found in London, Danish in origin, and dated to circa 900–1050, acc. no. 925.49.32.

43 ROM, RG 12.9.2.2, Beardmore Relics – Public Documents – press releases/public statements.

44 Otto von Friesen to C.T. Currelly, 30 January 1938, ROM, RG 12.9.1, corr. 1935–40.

45 A.W. Brøgger to C.T. Currelly, 8 February 1938, ROM, RG 12.9.1, corr. 1935–40.

CHAPTER TEN

1 Eli Ragotte affidavit, 28 January 1938, ROM, RG 12.9.1.26.

2 James Hansen affidavit, 29 January 1938, ROM, RG 12.9.1.14.

3 One possible explanation is that the fragile sword was still in one piece when Dodd came upon it and that it only broke later, while in his possession. But, as Hansen would agree that the sword was broken when he owned it, this explanation can be dismissed.

4 James Hansen to Eli Ragotte, 31 January 1938 (copy), ROM, RG 12.9.1.14. G.R.F. Prowse made a copy of the original shown to him by Ragotte. The copy, in turn, was shared with A.D. Fraser, who shared it with H.R. Holand, who shared it with C.T. Currelly.

5 Census Returns of England and Wales, 1891, UK National Archives, RG 12, piece 1819, fol. 46, p. 14, GSU roll 6096929. Census Returns of England and Wales, 1901, UK National Archives, RG 13, piece 2206, fol. 72, p. 22; Great Western Railway Company Staff Records, UK National Archives, RAIL264, piece 181; Census Returns of England and Wales, 1911, UK National Archives, RG 14, piece 13730, schedule 52. Gill and his wife emigrated aboard the *Empress of Britain*, arriving in Canada 13 September 1912, LAC, RG 76–C, roll T-4791. Daughter Dorothy born/died 9 April 1913, OA, MS 935, reel 183. Deaths of Beatrice Gill, 31 January 1922, and infant, 30 January 1922, OA MS 935, reel 294. See also "Fletcher Gill Retired CNR Engineer Dies," *News-Chronicle* (Port Arthur), 10 November 1954.

6 Carl Sorensen affidavit, ROM, RG 12.9.1.31.

7 C.T. Currelly to E. Ross MacKay, 3 February 1939, ROM, RG 12.9.1.21.

8 For Fleming's biography, see L.L. Snyder, "In Memoriam: James Henry Fleming," *Auk* 58, 1 (1941): 1–12.

9 Wade passed along Fleming's correspondence to P.H. Godsell, who included them in a scrapbook, "Viking Footprints," m-433-326, in Godsell's papers in the Glenbow Museum.

10 Fleming, *On a New Genus and Species of Flightless Duck*.

11 "Fleming on a New Flightless Duck."

12 Fleming replied to criticisms in "[On] a New Genus and Species of Flightless Duck from Campbell Island." The specimen retained its legitimacy as a find at Campbell Island, but Fleming's new species would lose its new genus; *nesiotis* would be reassigned to *Anas*, Linnaeus's genus of "dabbling ducks."

13 Currelly, *I Brought the Ages Home*, 218–19.

14 Robinson and Harcum, *Catalogue of the Greek Vases*.

15 Technically, the Ontario government had already funded the Sturge Collection purchase when Samuel pledged the funds in 1920. He asked that his donation be applied to the collection and that the government's funds be reallocated to other acquisitions. See Adam, *Buying Respectability*, 172. Paul Denis, the ROM's curator of Greek and Roman materials, informed me: "I am not aware of any authenticity problems with our collection of vases we acquired in the Sturge Collection before or after 1938." Personal communication with author, 28 February 2017.

16 Harold Innis to C.T. Currelly, 24 February 1938, ROM, RG 12.9.1, corr. 1935–40.

17 Ontario, *Forty-Eighth Annual Report of the Ontario Department of Mines*, pt. 1, 48. "Norse-Beardmore Synd. Plans Diamond Drilling," *Globe and Mail*, 14 February 1938; "Drilling Contract Let for Norse-Beardmore," *Globe and Mail*, 11 March 1938; "Howey Takes Option on Norse-Beardmore, *Globe and Mail*, 15 March 1938. Percy Herron was probably Percival Washington Herron, born 6 February 1880 in Peterborough, Ontario (OA, MS 929, reel 45). He appears in the 1911 census as a contractor in New Liskeard (LAC, RG 31, New Liskeard, Nipissing, Ontario, p. 8, family 78). A Percival Herron, contractor, appears in the electoral rolls for York West in 1935 and in York South in 1940 (LAC, RG 113-B).

CHAPTER ELEVEN

1 Darby Coats to Gerald Wade, 2 February 1938, GF, m-433-326.

2 G.R.F. Prowse to Vilhjalmur Stefansson, 3 February 1938, SP, mss 196-44-19.

3 Vilhjalmur Stefansson to C.T. Currelly, 7 March 1938, ROM, RG 12.9.1.32.

4 The affidavits are on file in ROM, RG 12.9. Either Beamish provided them when he left Port Arthur to join the staff of the *Globe and Mail* or his editors did. C.T. Currelly to Vilhjalmur Stefansson, 11 March 1938, ROM, RG 12.9.1.32.

5 "Replies to Godsell on Finding Relics," *Winnipeg Free Press*, 23 March 1938.

6 G.R.F. Prowse to C.T. Currelly, 7 January 1939, ROM, RG 12.9.1.25.

7 A.D. Fraser to Eli Ragotte, 30 March 1938 [not extant]; quoted in Eli Ragotte to James Hansen, 4 April 1938, ROM, SC 9, box 1.

8 Eli Ragotte to A.D. Fraser, 4 April 1938, ROM, RG 12.9.1.26.

9 "Reported Find of Norse Relics in Ontario"; "Norse Relics in Ontario."

10 James Hansen to ROM, 8 April 1938, ROM, RG 12.9.1.14.

11 James Hansen to ROM, 11 May 1938, ROM, RG 12.9.1.14.

12 Census of Canada, 1881, LAC, RG 31, Silver Islet, Algoma, Ontario, roll C-13282, p. 14, family 52.

13 For all of Jacob's correspondence with Currelly on his fact-finding in the spring of 1938, see ROM, RG 12.9.1.17. T.F. McIlwraith may have made a trip to the Lakehead that spring to conduct his own reconnaissance. If he did, he must have returned empty-handed.

14 Nuttall was identified as a tug captain on the 1940 voter's list for Port Arthur (LAC, RG 113-B). He was a master mariner in the 1911 Census of Canada (LAC, RG 31), Port Arthur, Thunder Bay and Rainy River, Ontario, p. 4, family 33. Nuttall's birth date in the 1901 Census of Canada (LAC, RG 31) is given as 27 September 1878 (Port Arthur, Algoma, Ontario, p. 10, family 87).

15 Carl Sorensen to J.D. Jacob, 29 April 1938, ROM, RG 12.9.1.17.

16 G.A. Simonsen to J.D. Jacob, "Acting for the Royal Ontario Museum," 30 April 1938, ROM, RG 12.9.1.30.

17 See Chapter 9, note 33.

18 Os Hartvik emigrated from Norway on 28 December 1923 and arrived in early 1924. He gave his age as twenty-five and his profession as engineer. See LAC; Form 30A Ocean Arrivals (Individual Manifests), 1919–1924. He was listed as an engineer when naturalized in 1931. See http://data2.collections canada.gc.ca/cgc/nat/lowres/P31-32_764.pdf (viewed 24 October 2017).

19 Os Hartvik to J.D. Jacob, 6 May 1938, ROM, RG 12.91.15.

20 William Feltham to J.D. Jacob, 9 May 1938, ROM, RG 12.9.1.10.

21 Jacob also reported to Currelly that he found a "reliable" man named Tom Cornell who had encountered the relics. He may have been a janitor of that name who lived in Port Arthur. Cornell "did not give the relics much attention and placed no dependence in Dodds." Cornell also could not say with any certainty whether it was 1930, 1931, 1932 or 1933 when he saw the relics in Dodd's possession. Cornell never resurfaced in the investigations.

22 Bohan marriage licence, 18 June 1935, OA, RG 80-05-0-2322. He gave his occupation as "section foreman CNR."

23 John Patrick Bohan baptism, 17 June 1936, Orient Bay, Ancestry.com: Ontario, Canada, Catholic Church Records (Drouin Collection), 1802–1967 (database online).

24 "Howey Drops Option on Norse-Beardmore," *Globe and Mail*, 14 May 1938.

CHAPTER TWELVE

1 P.A. Means to C.T. Currelly, 20 April 1938, ROM, RG 12.9.1, corr. 1941–55. *Tidens Tegn* ceased publication in 1941. A copy of the original article does not survive in the ROM's Beardmore files. Holand's translation is in ROM, RG 12.9.1.2.1, Beardmore Relics – Public Documents – Articles.

2 P.A. Means to C.T. Currelly, 17 May 1938, ROM, RG 12.9.1, corr. 1941–55.

3 Assistant to the Director to P.A. Means, 21 May 1938, ROM, RG 12.9.1, corr. 1941–55.

4 P.A. Means to Ethlyn Greenaway, 25 May 1938, ROM, RG 12.9.1, corr. 1941–55.

5 Assistant to the Director to Harold Innis, 21 May 1938, ROM, RG 12.9.1, corr. 1935–40.

6 For the letters, see ROM, RG 12.9.1, corr. 1935–40.

7 C.T. Currelly to James Hansen, 30 May 1938, ROM, RG 12.9.1.14.

8 O.C. Elliott to Duncan McArthur, 24 May 1938, ROM, SC 9, box 1.

9 C.T. Currelly to O.C. Elliott, 30 May 1938, ROM, SC 9, box 1.

10 J.W. Curran, "Beardmore Norse Relics Tale Proven True," *Sault Daily Star*, 4 October 1938.

11 J.W. Curran, "Who Were the Wooden Boat Men?" *Sault Daily Star*, 13 August 1938.

12 For Curran's biography, see the finding aid for the James W. Curran Fonds, Trent University Archives.

13 A.J. McComber, "Some Early History of Thunder Bay and District," *Thunder Bay Historical Society, Fifteenth Annual Report, Papers of 1923–24*, 13–22.

14 J.W. Curran, "Beardmore Norse Relics Tale Proven True," *Sault Daily Star*, 4 October 1938.

15 Birth, see OA, Registrations of Deaths, RG 80-08-0-2408, cert. 040412; Marriage, OA MS932, reel 84; Lon Patterson, "PA Names Street for Judge McComber," *Times-Journal* (Fort William), 25 July 1966.

16 A.J. McComber to J.W. Curran, 22 December 1938, CF, box 30.

17 See, for example, Gabriel Sagard, in 1636: "Les Montagnais nous donnent le nom de Mistigoche, ou, Ouemichtigouchion, c'est à dire un homme qui est dans un canot de bois, ou batteau de bois, ou coffre de bois, selon l'interprétation d'aucun." *Histoire du Canada, et Voyages des Peres Recollects en La, Livre Second*, Chapitre IX, at http://www.gutenberg.ca/ebooks/sagard-histoire /sagard-histoire-00-h-dir/sagard-histoire-00-h.html (viewed 10 November 2017).

18 For my definition of the broad phenomenon I call "White Tribism," see Hunter, *Place of Stone*, 35–7.

19 Curran, "Beardmore Norse Relics Tale Proven True."
20 Ibid.
21 Curran, *Here Was Vinland*, 232–3.
22 Ibid., 233.
23 The fragment turned in by Curran was inventoried as 936.55.1d; the McIl-wraith piece is "e."
24 J.W. Curran, "Man Who Never Saw Dodd's Norse …," *Sault Daily Star*, 6 October 1938.
25 A.J. McComber to J.W. Curran, 28 September 1938, CF, box 30.
26 Eli Ragotte statements, 30 September 1938, ROM, RG 12.9.26.
27 "New Evidence Backs Truth of Norse Find," *Globe and Mail*, 5 October 1938.
28 Curran, "Beardmore Norse Relics Tale Proven True."
29 Curran, "Man Who Never Saw."
30 Ibid.
31 Ibid.
32 "Thinks Story Correct," *Toronto Star*, 6 October 1938.

CHAPTER THIRTEEN

1 Transcribed for T.L. Tanton and sent to O.C. Elliott, 17 November 1939, ROM, SC 9, box 1.
2 "Is Confident Norse Relics Came From Mining Claim," *Toronto Star*, 6 October 1938.
3 Ibid.
4 Ibid.
5 Ibid.
6 J.W. Curran, "Man Who Never Saw Dodd's Norse …," *Sault Daily Star*, 6 October 1938.
7 J.E. Dodd to J.W. Curran, 2 November 1938, CF, box 13.
8 Ellen Dodd for J.E. Dodd to C.T. Currelly, 16 November 1938, ROM, RG 12.9.1.7.
9 Curran also had the sequential roles of Burwash and O.C. Elliott (a nameless Kingston schoolteacher) backwards. In Curran's telling, Elliott alerted Currelly, who wrote to Dodd but received no reply. Next, Burwash saw them during his prospecting class duties and informed Currelly, who succeeded this time in getting Dodd to bring the relics to the museum. See J.W. Curran, "Beardmore Relics Tale Proven True," *Sault Daily Star*, 4 October 1938.
10 "Old Norse," *Time*, 24 October 1938, 52.
11 "Sault Writer Stirs Viking Relics Debate with New Evidence," *Globe and Mail*, 7 October 1938.

12 Royd E. Beamish, "Owner of House Claims He Obtained Norse Armor as Security for Debt and Left it in Cellar," *Globe and Mail*, 7 October 1938.

13 Royd E. Beamish, "'Two Die' or Not 'Two Die,' Beamish Became Reporter," *News-Chronicle* (Port Arthur), 24 November 1953.

14 "Mystery Hobo Witness to Norse Relics Discovery," *Toronto Star*, 7 October 1938.

15 "'Boss' of Norse Shield Collapsed…," *Sault Daily Star*, 8 October 1938; "Curran Quotes New Points to Back Early Norse Visit," *Toronto Star*, 8 October 1938.

16 "Ridicules Suggestion Norse Weapons Fakes," *Globe and Mail*, 12 October 1938.

17 "Curran Says Norse Record Referred to Great Lakes," *Toronto Star*, 11 October 1938.

18 "Viking Arms," *Globe and Mail*, 12 October 1938.

19 J.E. Dodd to J.W. Curran, 6 October 1938, CF, box 13.

20 Fletcher Gill to J.W. Curran, 30 October 1938, CF, box 18.

21 Fletcher Gill to J.W. Curran, 2 November 1938, CF, box 18.

22 J.E. Dodd to J.W. Curran, 2 November 1938, CF, box 13.

CHAPTER FOURTEEN

1 Reported in "North America's Aborigines," *Kingston Whig-Standard*, 5 October 1938.

2 Ellen Dodd for J.E. Dodd to J.W. Curran, 16 November 1938, CF, box 13.

3 Fred Landon to C.T. Currelly, 6 October 1938, ROM, RG 12.9.1.19. Landon was a member of the CHR board of editors until 31 December 1938.

4 C.T. Currelly to Fred Landon, 7 October 1938, ROM, RG 12.9.1.19.

5 C.T. Currelly to Fred Landon, 12 October 1938, ROM, RG 12.9.1.19.

6 Handwritten amendment to June 1937 Jacob statement, c. Oct. 1938, ROM, RG 12.9.1.17.

7 "A Famous Sword Found at 'The Fort,'" *Victoria Warder*, 5 October 1894. See Douglas Hunter, "Lost and Found in Ontario: The Case of Champlain's Sword(s)," *Findings/Trouvailles*, at http://www.champlainsociety.ca/lost-and-found-in-ontario-the-case-of-champlains-swords/.

8 A notation explained: "Above note given Prof McIlwraith by Mr. Dodd, Oct. 1938." ROM, RG 12.9.1.7.

9 Piece inventoried as 936.55.1c. See ROM, Beardmore acc. file 936.55.1-3. Donation form, ref. no. 1415, 17 October 1936; donation certificate, 10 November 1936, ROM, acc. file 936.55.1-3. See also ROM, RG 12.9.1, corr. 1956–58.

10 ROM, acc. file 936.55.1-3; Tushingham, *Beardmore Relics*, 1. In 2017, ROM conservator Susan Stock made a provisional reassembly of the sword with all three pieces in the break area.

11 "Is Confident Norse Relics Came from Mining Claim," *Toronto Star*, 6 October 1938.

12 See A.J. McComber to O.C. Elliott, 3 May 1939, ROM, SC 9, box 1.

13 Ibid.

14 Patrick Bohan affidavit, in Curran, *Here Was Vinland*, 184.

15 See McComber to Elliott, 3 May 1939.

16 McComber gathered his information from "Mr. Ruttan," probably Walter S. Ruttan. See A.J. McComber to J.W. Curran, 20 October 1938, CF, box 30.

17 Assistant to the Director to P.A. Means, 14 October 1938, ROM, RG 12.9.1, corr. 1941–55.

18 "Sault Writer Stirs Viking Relics Debate with New Evidence," *Globe and Mail*, 7 October 1938.

19 Vilhjalmur Stefansson to J.W. Curran, 24 October 1938, CF, box 39.

20 Assistant to the Director to P.A. Means, 14 October 1938, ROM, RG 12.9.1., corr. 1941–55.

21 J.W. Curran to C.T. Currelly, 3 November 1938, ROM, RG 12.9.1.5.

22 Thelma Craig, "Prof. Currelly Praises Spirit in Viking Saga," *Globe and Mail*, 8 November 1938.

23 Anne Merrill, "Pupils Find Norse Trail Intriguing," *Toronto Star Weekly*, 21 December 1940.

24 C.T. Currelly, "Statement Regarding the Museum of Archaeology," in University of Toronto, *President's Report for the Year Ending 30 June, 1940*, 130.

25 T.F. McIlwraith note of Ellen Dodd statement, 6 November 1938, ROM, RG 12.9.1.7.

26 H.R. Holand to J.W. Curran, 27 November 1938, CF, box 21. Clippings attached.

27 Curran, "Norseman Died," 97.

28 Ibid., 101.

29 Ibid., 108.

30 Ibid, 101.

CHAPTER FIFTEEN

1 P.A. Means to Ethlyn Greenaway, 17 October 1938, ROM, RG 12.9.1, corr. 1941–55.

2 Lechler correspondence, ROM, RG 12.9.1.20. "Lechler, George Th.," in *International Directory of Anthropologists*, section 1, *Western Hemisphere* (Washington, DC: National Research Council, March 1940), 83.

3 Frank Johnson to C.T. Currelly, 2 November 1938, ROM, RG 12.9.1.18.

4 "Stamp of Approval upon Viking Relics," *Toronto Star*, 5 November 1938.

5 Halfdan Hebo to C.T. Currelly, 28 October 1938; Currelly to Hebo, 22 November 1938, ROM, RG 12.9.1.27.

6 For "light war vessels," see Holand, *Westward from Vinland*, 144.

7 Holand argues in *Westward from Vinland* that the journey up the Nelson River was not as daunting as Milo M. Quaife had contended in the *New England Quarterly*. While Holand never inspected the river course himself, he believed the Hudson's Bay Company's use of York boats on the Nelson meant Knutson's expedition, employing perhaps two "light war vessels," would not have found the route as difficult as Quaife contended. See Holand, *Westward from Vinland*, 142.

8 H.R. Holand to J.W. Curran, 17 October 1938, CF, box 21.

9 H.R. Holand to C.T. Currelly, 30 October 1941, ROM, RG 12.9.1.16.

10 Ibid.

11 Ibid. Johannes Brøndsted would receive a copy of Hansen's letter from Holand and provide a translation to the ROM in 1948. In his version, Hansen had only said, "If I could see those that are in the Museum I would be able to say that they were not those I had if that be the case." But as Brøndsted struggled with pronouns – making Hansen say Dodd was Norwegian rather than acknowledging Holand was – Holand's version is presumably the more accurate one. See ROM, RG 12.9.1.3.

12 Robert Olsen essentially reached this conclusion in "Was Our Biggest Historical Find," 81.

13 J.E. Dodd to J.W. Curran, 2 November 1938, CF, box 13.

14 J.W. Curran to C.T. Currelly, 3 November 1938, ROM, RG 12.9.1.5.

15 H.R. Holand to J.W. Curran, 17 October 1938, "Your theory about the location of Vinland is no good," CF, box 21; H.R. Holand to J.W. Curran, 21 February 1939, "You fail completely to prove that 'here' was Vinland"; H.R. Holand to J.W. Curran, 24 August 1939, CF, box 21.

16 See Curran and Stefansson correspondence, CF, box 39.

17 Vilhjalmur Stefansson to J.W. Curran, 9 December 1938, CF, box 39.

18 C.T. Currelly to I. Van Meter, 11 November 1938, ROM, RG 12.9.1, corr. 1935–40.

19 Currelly initially proposed the article in a letter (no longer extant) of 15 November 1938, referenced by Brown's reply of 23 November. See ROM, RG 12.9.1, corr. 1935-40.

20 C.T. Currelly to Matthias Thórdarson, 18 November 1938, ROM, RG 12.9.1, corr. 1935–40.

21 C.T. Currelly to O.C. Elliott, 26 November 1938, ROM, SC 9, box 1.

22 H.R. Holand to Ethlyn Greenaway, 27 November 1938, ROM, RG 12.9.1.16.

23 C.T. Currelly to H.R. Holand, 30 November 1938, HP.

24 H.R. Holand to C.T. Currelly, 4 December 1938, ROM, RG 12.9.1.16.

25 C.T. Currelly to H.R. Holand, 7 December 1938, HP.

26 Port Arthur voter list (1935), LAC, RG 113-B.

27 McGugan affidavit, in Curran, *Here Was Vinland*, 182–3.

28 Hynes affidavit, in Curran, *Here Was Vinland*, 183.

29 Vilhjalmur Stefansson to C.T. Currelly, 29 November 1938, ROM, RG 12.9.1.32.

30 C.T. Currelly to Vilhjalmur Stefansson, 2 December 1938 (unsent), ROM, RG 12.9.1.32.

31 C.T. Currelly to George Lechler, 15 December 1938, ROM, RG 12.9.1.20. In a 30 December 1938 reply to a query from G.R.F. Prowse, the museum's librarian stated that the ROM hoped to publish a *Bulletin* on the Beardmore find "in the very near future." See Librarian to Prowse, [24 December 1938], ROM, RG 12.9.1.25.

32 G.R.F. Prowse to C.T. Currelly, 7 January 1939, ROM, RG 12.9.1.25.

33 C.T. Currelly to G.R.F. Prowse, 11 January 1939, ROM, RG 12.9.1.25.

34 George Brown to C.T. Currelly, 21 December 1938, ROM, RG 12.9.1, corr. 1935–40.

35 See ROM, RG 12.9.1.27.

36 Vilhjalmur Stefansson to Diamond Jenness, 28 November 1938, SP, mss 196-43-34.

37 "If she gets frozen in, she will be crushed," Jenness had written Henry Balfour. Quoted by Richling, *In Twilight and in Dawn*, 67. The *Karluk* episode is addressed by Richling, *In Twilight and in Dawn*, 66–70, 85; Palsson, *Travelling Passions*, 132–5; and Hunt, *Stef*, 71–88.

38 See Richling, *In Twilight and in Dawn*, 130–6. Hunt covers Stefansson's performance sympathetically in *Stef*, 186–94. Palsson mentions the controversy briefly in *Travelling Passions*, 167–8.

39 For Stefansson's initial claims, see, for example "Wants Eskimo Saved from Our Religion," *New York Times*, 30 September 1912. For Jenness's rebuttal, see Jenness, "'Blond' Eskimos." Stefansson's recounting of the "blond Eskimos" episode appears in *Adventurers in Error*. Palsson (*Travelling Passions*) and Hunt (*Stef*) devote chapters to the controversy.

40 Diamond Jenness to Vilhjalmur Stefansson, 29 November 1938, SP, mss 196-42-19.

41 Vilhjalmur Stefansson to Diamond Jenness, 28 December 1938, SP, mss 196-42-19.

42 Hansen showed Tanton's letter to Judge McComber on 6 February 1939. See A.J. McComber to J.W. Curran, 7 February 1939, CF, box 30.

43 Quoted by A.J. McComber to J.W. Curran, 7 February 1939, CF, box 30.

44 James Hansen to T.L. Tanton, 26 December 1938, ROM, SC 9, box 1.

45 The Jenness letter (not extant) is mentioned by James Hansen in a letter to T.L. Tanton, 10 January 1939, ROM, SC 9, box 1.

46 T.L. Tanton memo to Julian Cross, 7 February 1939, ROM, SC 9, box 1.

47 Letter not extant. Referenced in Vilhjalmur Stefansson to A.W. Brøgger, 8 December 1938, Brøgger to Stefansson, 3 January 1938, SP, mss 196-42-19. Stefansson and Brøgger had corresponded in the summer of 1938; a mutual friend had presented Brøgger with a copy of Stefansson's new book on Frobisher. In June, Brøgger had informed Stefansson he planned to visit the United States that September or October and hoped to see him. See Brøgger to Stefansson, 9 July 1938, SP, mss 196-42-25. Whether they met is not known, and to that point neither man seems to have breached the topic of Beardmore.

48 Vilhjalmur Stefansson to J.W. Curran, 9 December 1938, CF, box 39.

49 Vilhjalmur Stefansson to A.W. Brøgger, 8 December 1938, SP, mss 196-42-19.

50 Curran had written historian Lawrence J. Burpee in August 1938, enclosing one of his first articles in his series and asking him for help with Cree language sources. Burpee said he "was not in any sense an authority on the Cree or their language" and recommended that he contact Diamond Jenness or J.B. Tyrrell. Curran's letter is not extant; Burpee replied 24 August 1938, CF, box 5. Curran waited four months to write Jenness to ask him more generally about the Beardmore case, not about Cree language sources.

51 Diamond Jenness to J.W. Curran, 21 December 1938, CF, box 25. For Jenness's self-effacing view of his skills in archaeology, see Richling, *In Twilight and in Dawn*, 82–3.

52 A.W. Brøgger to Vilhjalmur Stefansson, 3 January 1938, SP, mss 196-42-19.

CHAPTER SIXTEEN

1 J.E. Dodd to J.W. Curran, n.d., received 2 November 1938, CF, box 13; Dodd to Curran, 24 November 1938, CF, box 13.

2 J.E. Dodd to J.W. Curran, 3 December 1938, CF, box 13.

3 J.E. Dodd to J.W. Curran, 18 December 1938, CF, box 13.

4 See J.E. Dodd to J.W. Curran, 30 December 1938, CF, box 13.

5 Fletcher Gill to J.W. Curran, 16 January 1939, CF, box 18.

6 "Ancient Relic at Rossport," *Daily News-Chronicle* (Port Arthur), 4 February 1938.

7 J.G. Molinski to J.E. Dodd, 16 January 1938 [sic; 1939], CF, box 13.

8 J.E. Dodd to J.W. Curran, 17 January 1939, CF, box 13.

9 J.E. Dodd to J.W. Curran, 24 January 1939, CF, box 13.

10 J.G. Molinski to J.W. Curran, 1 February 1939, CF, box 13.

11 J.W. Curran to C.T. Currelly, 3 February 1939, ROM, RG 12.9.1.5.

12 C.T. Currelly to J.G. Molinski, 14 February 1939, ROM, RG 12.9.1.5.

13 See, for example, Berger, *Writing of Canadian History*, 180–6, for a discussion of the cleavage between the English and French historical traditions in Canada.

14 Robinson, *Toronto during the French Regime*, 219.

15 Carl Sorensen to A.W. Brøgger, 5 January 1939, SP, mss 196-45-14.

16 A.W. Brøgger to Vilhjalmur Stefansson, 23 January 1939, SP, mss 196-45-14.

17 Vilhjalmur Stefansson to A.W. Brøgger, 3 February 1939, SP, mss 196-45-14.

18 George T. Flom, born in Wisconsin, was a renowned professor of Scandinavian languages at the University of Iowa and later at the University of Illinois. As noted in chapter 2, he had pronounced the Kensington stone a fake in 1910. He was president of the Linguistics Society of America in 1936, a member of the Norwegian Academy of Science and Letters, and, in 1939, received a knighthood in the Norwegian Order of St Olav.

19 Scott affidavit, in Curran, *Here Was Vinland*, 181–2.

20 Fletcher Gill to J.W. Curran, 4 February 1939, CF, box 18.

21 William Feltham affidavit, in Curran, *Here Was Vinland*, 181.

22 J.E. Dodd to J.W. Curran, 30 December 1938, CF, box 13.

23 A.J. McComber to J. W. Curran, 1 February 1939, CF, box 30.

24 James Edward Dodd affidavit, in Curran, *Here Was Vinland*, 177–8.

25 Dodd may have meant that Patrick Bohan was the senior man on the CNR's Dorion subdivision, which ran about 145 miles between Port Arthur and Jellicoe, through Beardmore.

26 Walter Dodd affidavit, in Curran, *Here Was Vinland*, 178–9.

27 Fletcher Gill affidavit, in Curran, *Here Was Vinland*, 180.

28 Patrick Bohan affidavit, in Curran, *Here was Vinland*, 184.

29 James Hansen to T.L. Tanton, 10 March 1939, ROM, SC 9, box 1.

30 James Hansen to T.L. Tanton, 10 January 1939, ROM, SC 9, box 1.

31 There were slight differences between Hansen's two accounts (and, since writing Tanton, Hansen had come up with the promissory notes), but the second account, gathered in a personal meeting, benefited from the judge's expert questioning on various points. See A.J. McComber to J.W. Curran, 7 February 1939, CF, box 30, which relates Hansen's statement.

32 Marriage announcement, *Daily News-Chronicle* (Port Arthur), 6 September 1927.

33 Hansen evidently was mistaken; John Bloch is believed to have been an only child.

34 According to John Garner, Hansen's business ledger indicates he bought the 240 St James property on 15 December 1928 for $3,500, with $250 down

and a note for the balance. Over the next year, he spent $2,585 remodelling the home and adding three garages. He spent a further $517 in 1930–31. Hansen's ledger does not include any information pertaining to Dodd or Bloch. Hansen maintained other records, now lost, as the ledger includes references to a Black Book and a Day Book as well as numbered files.

35 In a letter to Tanton (January 10), Hansen said he stored some items in the back porch and, in his in-person statement as related by McComber to Curran (7 February), in a shed. The discrepancy is minor and he probably had items in both locations. In both accounts, the relics were left in the basement.

36 A.J. McComber to J.W. Curran, 7 February 1939, CF, box 30.

37 A.J. McComber to J.W. Curran, 23 February 1939, CF, box 30.

CHAPTER SEVENTEEN

1 Assistant to the Director to George Brown, 27 January 1939, ROM, RG 12.9.1, corr. 1935–40.

2 C.T. Currelly to H.R. Holand, 3 February 1939, HP.

3 C.T. Currelly to Frank Johnson, 22 February 1939, ROM, RG 12.9.1.18.

4 G.R.F. Prowse to C.T. Currelly, 23 January 1939, ROM, RG 12.9.1.25. Prowse's friend may have been Knud Scheel, born in 1872, who had emigrated from Denmark in 1909. See 1916 Census of Canada, RG 31, Manitoba, Winnipeg Centre, roll T-21932, p. 50, family 575.

5 C.T. Currelly to G.R.F. Prowse, 13 February 1939, ROM, RG 12.9.1.25.

6 G.R.F. Prowse to C.T. Currelly, 21 February 1939, ROM, RG 12.9.1.25.

7 C.T. Currelly to G.R.F. Prowse, 27 February 1939, ROM, RG 12.9.1.25.

8 G.R.F. Prowse to C.T. Currelly, 21 February 1939, ROM, RG 12.9.1.25.

9 "Denies Viking Relics 'Planted' at Beardmore," *Daily News-Chronicle* (Port Arthur), 26 January 1938.

10 H.R. Holand to J.W. Curran, 13 February 1939, CF, box 21.

11 H.R. Holand to J.W. Curran, 21 February 1939, CF, box 21.

12 Jack Satterly was the son of John Satterly, an esteemed physicist at the University of Toronto and fellow of the Royal Society of Canada. Jack Satterly would join the staff of the province's Department of Mines around 1939 and be honoured with the Jack Satterly Geochronology Lab, initially housed in the ROM and subsequently moved to the University of Toronto. See Satterly note, 24 February 1939, ROM, RG 12.9.1.28.

13 C.T. Currelly to J.W. Curran, 28 February 1939, ROM, RG 12.9.1.5.

14 George Brown to C.T. Currelly, 6 March 1939, ROM, RG 12.9.1, corr. 1935–40.

15 Wallace, "Literature," 14.

16 Ibid.

17 Ibid., 15.

18 Ibid.

19 Ibid, 16.

20 Ibid.

21 Currelly, "Viking Weapons," 4.

22 Ibid.

23 Ibid.

24 Ibid.

25 Ibid.

26 Ibid.

27 Ibid., 5–6.

28 Ibid., 6.

29 "Is Confident Norse Relics Came from Mining Claim," *Toronto Star*, 6 October 1938.

30 E.M. Burwash to T.L. Tanton, February 28, 1940, ROM SC9, Box 1.

31 Currelly, "Viking Weapons," 6.

32 Ibid.

33 Ibid.

34 Ibid.

35 Ibid., 6–7.

36 Ibid., 7.

37 Ibid.

38 Ibid.

39 Ibid.

40 Ethlyn Greenaway to G.R.F. Prowse, 12 April 1940, ROM, RG 12.9.1.25.

41 J.W. Curran to C.T. Currelly, 1 March 1939, ROM, RG 12.9.1.5.

42 Eli Ragotte affidavit, in Curran, *Here Was Vinland*, 179–80.

43 Lechler, "Viking Finds," 128, 133.

44 G.R.F. Prowse to Vilhjalmur Stefansson, 8 March 1939, SP, mss 196-45-14.

45 Vilhjalmur Stefansson to G.R.F. Prowse, 10 March 1939, SP, mss 196-45-14; ROM RG 12.9.1.25.

46 James Hansen to T.L. Tanton, 10 March 1939 (two letters), ROM, SC 9, box 1.

47 T.L. Tanton to O.C. Elliott, 21 March 1939, ROM, SC 9, Box 1.

CHAPTER EIGHTEEN

1 "Some Sidelights on the Norse Relics of Beardmore," 21 October 1938, ROM, SC 9, box 1.

2 O.C. Elliott, "K.C.V.I. Teacher Suggests That American Indians Got Their Lacrosse Game from Norsemen," *Kingston Whig-Standard*, 28 November 1938.

3 See O.C. Elliott and J.W. Curran correspondence, October–November 1938, ROM, SC 9, box 1.

4 O.C. Elliott to *Toronto Star*, 12 November 1938; *Toronto Star* to O.C. Elliott, 16 November 1938, ROM, SC 9, box 1.

5 O.C. Elliott to Macmillan, 21 November 1938; Macmillan to O.C. Elliott, 24 November 1938, ROM, SC 9, box 1.

6 O.C. Elliott to C.T. Currelly, 24 November 1938, ROM, SC 9, box 1.

7 C.T. Currelly to O.C. Elliott, 26 November 1938, ROM, SC 9, box 1.

8 Lorne Pierce to O.C. Elliott, 17 February 1939, ROM, SC 9, box 1.

9 T.L. Tanton to O.C. Elliott, 21 March 1939, ROM, SC 9, box 1.

10 The list of comments does not survive, but his points are reviewed in his cover letter. See O.C. Elliott to T.L. Tanton, 1 April 1939, ROM, SC 9, box 1.

11 T.L. Tanton to O.C. Elliott, 5 April 1939, ROM, SC 9, box 1.

12 James Hansen to T.L. Tanton (two letters), 2 April 1939, ROM, SC 9, box 1.

13 The bank branch had already confirmed for Tanton the details of the Bloch loan. See H. Martin, "to whom it may concern," 24 March 1939 (copy), ROM, SC 9, box 1.

14 O.C. Elliott, "The Viking Relics of Beardmore," 6 April 1939, ROM, SC 9, box 2, file 6.

15 T.L. Tanton note, n.d., ROM, SC 9, box 1.

16 O.C. Elliott to T.L. Tanton, 6 April 1939, ROM, SC 9, box 1.

17 O.C. Elliott to Lorne Pierce, 8 April 1939, ROM, SC 9, box 1.

18 O.C. Elliott to H.R. Holand, 8 April 1939, ROM, SC 9, box 1.

19 H.R. Holand to O.C. Elliott, 10 December 1938, ROM, SC 9, box 1.

20 T.L. Tanton to O.C. Elliott, 9 April 1939, ROM, SC 9, box 1.

21 Lorne Pierce to O.C. Elliott, 24 April 1939, ROM, SC 9, box 1.

22 Currelly, "Viking Weapons," 5.

23 "The Vikings Were There," *Kingston Whig-Standard*, 15 April 1939.

24 O.C. Elliott to C.T. Currelly, 15 April 1939, ROM, RG 12.9.1.9.

25 O.C. Elliott to W.R. Davies, 18 April 1939, ROM, SC 9, box 1.

26 O.C. Elliott to George Brown, 18 April 1939, ROM, SC 9, box 1.

27 George Brown to O.C. Elliott, 24 April 1939, ROM, SC 9, box 1.

28 O.C. Elliott to George Brown, 28 April 1939, ROM, SC 9, box 1.

29 W. Thompson to C.T. Currelly, 10 April 1939, ROM, RG 12.9.1., corr. 1935–40.

30 C.T. Currelly to O.C. Elliott, 20 April 1939, ROM, SC 9, box 1.

31 C.T. Currelly to Vilhjalmur Stefansson, 24 April 1939, ROM, RG 12.9.1.32.

32 Stefansson's subsequent letter to Currelly does not survive but on 27 July

1939 Tanton reported to Elliott its existence, based on a letter to him from Stefansson (which is also not extant). See ROM, SC 9, box 1.

33 Fletcher Gill to O.C. Elliott, 30 April 1939, ROM, SC 9, box 1.

34 Fletcher Gill to J.W. Curran, n.d, CF, box 18.

35 The letter to Curran contained employment details found in Gill's subsequent letter to Elliott of 30 May 1939, ROM, SC 9, box 1.

36 O.C. Elliott to T.L. Tanton, 3 May 1939, ROM, SC 9, box 1.

37 A.J. McComber to O.C. Elliott, 3 May 1939, ROM, SC 9, box 1.

38 Eli Ragotte to T.L. Tanton, 9 May 1939, ROM, SC 9, box 1

39 O.C. Elliott to T.L. Tanton, 13 May 1939, ROM, SC 9, box 1.

40 T.L. Tanton to O.C. Elliott, 10 May 1939, ROM, SC 9, box 1

41 O.C. Elliott to T.L. Tanton, 3 May 1939, ROM, SC 9, box 1.

CHAPTER NINETEEN

1 H.R. Holand to O.C. Elliott, 8 May 1939, ROM, SC 9, box 1.

2 T.L. Tanton to A.W. Brøgger, 19 April 1939; Brøgger to Tanton, 6 May 1939; Tanton to O.C. Elliott, 18 May 1939. All in ROM, SC 9, box 1.

3 Vigard Vike suggested to me that "the dating discrepancy is probably the reason why Brøgger considered the type Q for the sword." As previously noted, Vike was confident the sword was an M type. Personal communication, 6 August 2017.

4 T.L. Tanton to O.C. Elliott, 16 May 1939, ROM, SC 9, box 1.

5 Aaron Lougheed to T.L. Tanton, 20 May 1939; copy made by Elliott, 23 May 1939, ROM, SC 9, box 1.

6 William Cross to T.L. Tanton, 24 May 1939, ROM SC 9, box 1.

7 O.C. Elliott to T.L. Tanton, 3 June 1939, ROM SC 9, box 1.

8 O.C. Elliott to A.J. McComber, 26 May 1939, ROM, SC 9, box 1.

9 Elliott's source for this information is unknown. Thomas Ernest Godson was Ontario's mining commissioner when he was appointed a judge through the Mining Court Act, 1924. See Marion Orr, "A Short History of the Ontario Mining and Lands Commissioner," at http://www.web2.mnr .gov.on.ca/mnr/omlc/MLC%20History.htm.

10 O.C. Elliott to Fletcher Gill, 23 May 1939, ROM, SC 9, box 1.

11 Fletcher Gill to O.C. Elliott, 30 May 1939, ROM, SC 9, box 1,

12 Fletcher Gill to J.W. Curran, 30 March 1939, CF, box 18.

13 The Dodd letter to Curran is dated 25 April, but Dodd refers to the article "Tracking Down the Vikings" by Martin J. Roberts, which appeared in the *Star Weekly*, 29 April 1939. See J.E. Dodd to J.W. Curran, 25[?] April 1939, CF, box 13.

14 O.C. Elliott to T.L. Tanton, 3 June 1939, ROM, SC 9, box 1.

15 O.C. Elliott to Mona Oliver, 15 July 1939, ROM, SC 9, box 1. The source of these rumours is unknown.

16 See the finding aid for the Clark Wissler Papers at Ball State University archives (http://www.bsu.edu/libraries/archives/findingaids/MSS304.pdf) for correspondence between Jenness and Wissler from 1927 to 1938.

17 Fletcher Gill to Diamond Jenness, 7 July 1939; Jenness to Gill, 17 July 1939, ROM, SC 9, box 1.

18 J.E. Dodd to Diamond Jenness, 31 July 1939, ROM, SC 9, box 1.

19 Oscar Gulin to Mona Oliver, 5 June 1939, ROM, SC 9, box 1; Oliver to O.C. Elliott, 6 June 1939, ROM, SC 9, box 1.

20 Mona Oliver to O.C. Elliott, 13 June 1939, ROM, SC 9, box 1.

21 Fletcher Gill to J.W. Curran, 30 May 1939, CP, box 18. The woman was not Mona Oliver. Dodd paid a more congenial return visit to Oliver and told her that "there were some books being published on the find and that two more relics had been discovered down there and they didn't want anyone digging on the property or any too much information until the books were out." The two additional relics would have been the additional bits of iron recovered in 1937 and 1938 that were not in the museum photograph. See Mona Oliver to O.C. Elliott, 13 June 1939, ROM, SC 9, box 1.

22 Canadian Press, "Expert Sure Norse Relics Are Authentic," *Globe and Mail*, 23 June 1939.

23 O.C. Elliott to George Brown, 29 June 1939, ROM, SC 9, box 1

24 *CHR* to O.C. Elliott, n.d., received 4 July 1939; O.C. Elliott to *CHR*, n.d [July], 1939, ROM, SC 9, box 1.

25 O.C. Elliott to *Time*, 27 May 1939, ROM, SC 9, box 1.

26 O.C. Elliott to *Maclean's*, 10 July 1939, ROM, SC 9, box 1; H. Napier Moore to Elliott, 14 July 1939, ROM, SC 9, box 1.

27 O.C. Elliott to *Globe and Mail*, 20 July 1939; A.L. MacIntyre, for E.G. Smith, to Elliott, 24 July 1939, ROM, SC 9, box 1.

28 O.C. Elliott to *Toronto Star*, 26 July 1939, ROM, SC 9, box 1.

29 See O.C. Elliott, "Summary of Efforts to Publicize the Hoax Angle of the Viking Relics of Beardmore," 17 October 1939, ROM, SC 9, box 1.

30 T.L. Tanton to O.C. Elliott, 27 July 1939, ROM, SC 9, box 1.

31 The Jenness letter was written to Stefansson on 17 July 1939 but not mailed until 3 August. See SP, mss 166-46-10.

32 Vilhjalmur Stefansson to Diamond Jenness, 5 August 1939, SP, mss 196-47-4.

33 O.C. Elliott to Carl Sorensen, 17 June 1939; Sorensen to Elliott, 23 June 1939, ROM, SC 9, box 1.

34 O.C. Elliott to Carl Sorensen, 15 July 1939, ROM, SC 9, box 1.

35 Carl Sorensen to O.C. Elliott, 24 July 1939, ROM, SC 9, box 1.

36 O.C. Elliott to Royd Beamish, 5 August 1939, ROM, SC 9, box 1.

37 O.C. Elliott to Vilhjalmur Stefansson, 5 August 1939, ROM, SC 9, box 1.

CHAPTER TWENTY

1 Curran allowed that "some of the articles are here expanded a little and some are just skeletons of the original, but all convey the ideas as first advanced" (*Here Was Vinland*, 189). Three original articles were compressed into a single article. Article 22, "Lake Michigan Gives Up a Sword," was discarded altogether for, as Curran explained, "later investigation did not bear out the statements in it" (189). Curran had misidentified a colonial-era sword as Norse. "I could have told you about the fort artillery sword found at Jacksonport," Hjalmar Holand had chided Curran after the article ran, "as I have photographs of several of them." See H.R. Holand to J.W. Curran, 13 February 1938, CF, box 21. Jacksonport was eleven miles from Holand's house in Door County, near Green Bay.

2 Curran, *Here Was Vinland*, 133.

3 Ibid., 252.

4 Ibid., 176.

5 H.R. Holand to J.W. Curran, 24 August 1939, CF, box 21.

6 H.R. Holand to Vilhjalmur Stefansson, 7 October 1939, SP, mss 196-46-20.

7 See Elliott, "Summary of Efforts to Publicize the Hoax Angle of the Viking Relics of Beardmore," 17 October 1939, ROM, SC 9, box 1, for details of his dealings with Royd Beamish.

8 C.P. Wilson to C.T. Currelly, 14 September 1939; Currelly to Wilson, 20 September 1939; Wilson to Currelly, 22 September 1939. All in ROM, RG 12.9.1., corr. 1935–40.

9 O.C. Elliott to Vilhjalmur Stefansson, 22 August 1939, ROM, SC 9, box 1.

10 "Canada as the Norse Vinland," *Globe and Mail*, 9 September 1939.

11 "Notes and Comments," *Canadian Historical Review* 20, 3 (1939): 366.

12 Lawrence J. Burpee, review of *Here Was Vinland*, in "Amongst the New Books," *Canadian Geographical Journal* 19, 4 (1939): v.

13 O.C. Elliott to T.L. Tanton, 17 October 1939, ROM, SC 9, box 1; "Summary of Efforts to Publicize the Hoax Angle of the Viking Relics of Beardmore," 17 October 1939, ROM, SC 9, box 1.

14 Vilhjalmur Stefansson to O.C. Elliott, 21 August 1939, ROM, SC 9, box 1; 13 September 1939, ROM, SC 9, box 1.

15 For the correspondence of H.R. Holand and Vilhjalmur Stefansson on publication of *Westward from Vinland*, see SP, mss 196-46-20.

16 O.C. Elliott to T.L. Tanton, 17 October 1939, ROM, SC 9, box 1.

17 T.L. Tanton to O.C. Elliott, 27 October 1939, ROM, SC 9, box 1; Tanton to El-liott, 28 October 1939, ROM, SC 9, box 1.

18 See Wright, *Professionalization of History*, 76; and Wright, *Canadian Historical Association*, 13.

19 Berger, *Science, God, and Nature*, 18.

20 The offices of treasurer, secretary, librarian, and editor were all called "hon-orary." See RSC By-Laws (Consolidated 1934), WP, Royal Society, box 34.

21 O.C. Elliott to T.L. Tanton, 31 October 1939, ROM, SC 9, box 1.

22 O.C. Elliott to C.T. Currelly, 31 October 1939, ROM, SC 9, box 1.

23 Assistant to the Director to O.C. Elliott, 2 November 1939, ROM, SC 9, box 1.

24 O.C. Elliott to Peter Sandiford, 2 November 1939, ROM, SC 9, box 1.

25 O.C. Elliott to T.L. Tanton, 25 November 1939, ROM, SC 9, box 1.

26 O.C. Elliott to Carl Sorensen, 3 November 1939, ROM, SC 9, box 1.

27 Carl Sorensen to O.C. Elliott, 13 November 1939, ROM, SC 9, box 1.

28 T.L. Tanton to O.C. Elliott, 13 November 1939, ROM, SC 9, box 1.

29 T.L. Tanton to O.C. Elliott, 3 November 1939, ROM, SC 9, box 1.

30 O.C. Elliott to T.L. Tanton, 16 November 1939, ROM, SC 9, box 1.

31 C.J. Bjorke to O.C. Elliott, 17 November 1939, ROM, SC 9, box 1; Elliott to T.L. Tanton, 21 November 1939, ROM, SC 9, box 1.

32 Peter Sandiford to O.C. Elliott, 1 December 1939, ROM, SC 9, box 1.

33 O.C. Elliott to Peter Sandiford (draft), 15 December 1939; Elliott to Sandi-ford, 18 December 1939; Elliott to T.L. Tanton, 10 December 1939; Tanton to Elliott, 12 December 1939; Elliott to Tanton, 18 December 1939. All in ROM SC 9, box 1.

34 C.T. Currelly to O.C. Elliott, 8 January 1940, ROM, SC 9, box 1.

35 "Finder of Norse Relics Injured," *Daily Times-Journal* (Fort William), 8 De-cember 1939.

36 See Wright, *Professionalization of History*, 65–7.

37 Curran's letter is not extant. Burpee replied 24 August 1938, CF, box 5.

38 L.J. Burpee to C.W. Curran, 20 February 1939, CF, box 5.

39 L.J. Burpee to C.W. Curran, 14 August 1939, CF, box 5.

40 Around 1733, La Vérendrye had heard stories from the Assiniboin and Cree that the Mandan were like Frenchmen, but when he finally met them in 1738 he could see there was no resemblance. The initial La Vérendrye story nevertheless became the foundation of interminable speculation that the Mandan were White Indians, with responsibility for their "improvement" usually assigned to a fabled expedition by the Welsh prince Madoc in 1170. See Hunter, *Place of Stone*, 122–3.

41 Shore, "'Remember the Future,'" 415. See Morton, "La Vérendrye"; "Corre-

spondence: Professor Morton and La Vérendrye," Lawrence J. Burpee to the editor, 15 January 1929, in *Canadian Historical Review* 10 (March 1929): 53–5.

42 L.J. Burpee to J.W. Curran, 24 August 1938, CF, box 5.

43 T.L. Tanton to O.C. Elliott, 12 December 1939, ROM, SC 9, box 1.

44 T.L. Tanton to L.J. Burpee, 11 December 1939, ROM, SC 9, box 1.

45 T.L. Tanton to O.C. Elliott, 12 December 1939, ROM, SC 9, box 1.

46 T.L. Tanton wrote A.W. Brøgger on 24 November 1939, enclosing a copy of the John Block death certificate. According to Brøgger's reply, 3 February 1940, Tanton's letter was not sent until 16 December, perhaps enclosed with later correspondence. For Tanton's exchange with Vilhjalmur Stefansson, see T.L. Tanton to O.C. Elliott, 26 December 1939, ROM, SC 9, box 1. The letters in the exchange do not survive, but Tanton had informed Elliott on 2 December 1939 that he would send a copy of the death certificate to Stefansson the next time he wrote him. See ROM, SC 9, box 1.

47 O.C. Elliott to T.L. Tanton, 29 December 1939, ROM, SC 9, box 1.

48 Elliott's letter to Tanton of 1 January 1940 does not survive. See T.L. Tanton to O.C. Elliott, 3 January 1940, ROM, SC 9, box 1.

CHAPTER TWENTY-ONE

1 Quotes, T.L. Tanton to O.C. Elliott, 3 January 1940; Tanton to Elliott, 10 January 1940, ROM, SC 9, box 1.

2 O.C. Elliott, "The Viking Relics of Beardmore," 2, ROM, SC 9, box 2, file 6.

3 C.T. Currelly to O.C. Elliott, 8 January 1940, ROM, SC 9, box 1.

4 George Brown to O.C. Elliott, 16 January 1940, ROM, SC 9, box 1.

5 Careless, "The *Review* Reviewed," 53–4.

6 Shore, "Remember the Future," 412.

7 T.F. McIlwraith served on the CHR board in 1938 and 1939. Chester Martin is listed as a member of the board of editors for vol. 19 (1938), with a retirement slated for 31 December 1939, but he does not appear in the board list for vol. 20 (1939). The other 1939 board members with connections to the University of Toronto were A.G. Bailey, W.N. Sage, and J.B. Brebner. Bailey, a pioneering ethnohistorian heading up the new history department at the University of New Brunswick, had just earned his PhD at the University of Toronto in 1937. Sage, head of the history department at the University of British Columbia, also earned his PhD there. Brebner, who was also the current president of the CHA, was a historian at Columbia University (where he earned his PhD); a University of Toronto graduate, Brebner had also taught there. The other advisory board members in 1939 were E.R. Adair, a history professor at McGill and past president of the CHA; D.C. Harvey, provincial

archivist of Nova Scotia; Percy J. Robinson, an artist and historian who taught Latin at Toronto's St Andrew's College and was best known for *Toronto during the French Regime, 1615–1793* (1933); G.S. Graham, a history professor at Queen's University; Gustave Lanctot, Dominion Archivist of Canada; A.R.M. Lower, a history professor at Winnipeg's Wesley College; and A.S. Morton, a historian and librarian at the University of Saskatchewan and the province's Keeper of Provincial Records.

8　Careless, "*Review* Reviewed," 53.

9　See "The Brown Family History at Victoria College," http://www.vicu .utoronto.ca/about/vic175/memories/Brown_Family_History_Victoria _College.htm

10　See Donald Wright, "Creighton, Donald Grant," in *Dictionary of Canadian Biography*, vol. 20, University of Toronto/Université Laval, 2003–, at http://www.biographi.ca/en/bio/creighton_donald_grant_20E.html (viewed 27 November 2017).

11　See Wright, *Professionalization of History*, 73–4.

12　T.L. Tanton to O.C. Elliott, 18 January 1940, ROM, SC 9, box 1.

13　O.C. Elliott to C.T. Currelly, 23 January 1940, ROM, RG 12.9.1.9.

14　O.C. Elliott to T.L. Tanton, 18 January 1940, ROM, SC 9, box 1.

15　O.C. Elliot to J.D. Jacob, 23 January 1940, ROM, SC 9, box 1.

16　See O.C. Elliott, "Comments on 'De Vikingesverd'/Petersen," 30 January 1939, ROM, SC 9, box 1.

17　Petersen noted that K type axes were found with (among other types) the Q type sword, less frequently with the M type; M type axes were found with Q type (but not M type) swords. As I have noted, Vegard Vike of Oslo's Museum of Cultural History, who examined for me a detailed set of photographs and x-rays of the sword as well as a photograph of the axe, said he was fairly certain both the sword and the axe were M types in the Petersen scheme.

18　See Petersen, *De Norske Vikingesverd*, 48–50.

19　Translated from Petersen, *De Norske Vikingesverd*, 48.

20　Petersen, *De Norske Vikingswerd*, 50.

21　A.W. Brøgger to T.L. Tanton, 6 February 1940, ROM, SC 9, box 1.

22　Brøgger's letter for some reason was in Norwegian. Tanton and Elliott experienced delays in having it translated, and its content was not shared with Tanton until the beginning of April. See O.C. Elliott to T.L. Tanton, 1 April 1940, ROM, SC 9, box 1.

23　Diamond Jenness to J.W. Curran, 5 April 1939, CF, box 25.

24　William Wintemberg to O.C. Elliott, 1 February 1940, ROM, SC 9, box 1.

25　O.C. Elliott to T.L. Tanton, 18 February 1940; Elliott to George Brown, 18 February 1940; Tanton to Elliott, 21 February 1940, ROM, SC 9, box 1.

26 O.G.S. Crawford to C.T. Currelly, 30 December 1939, ROM, RG 12.9.1.4.

27 C.T. Currelly to O.G.S. Crawford, 17 January 1940, ROM, RG 12.9.1.4.

28 O.G.S. Crawford to C.T. Currelly, 6 March 1940, ROM, RG 12.9.1.4.

29 "Viking Weapons Found Near Beardmore, Ontario," *Antiquity* 14, 4 (1940), 200–4.

30 *Dagens Nyheter* telegram, 8 March 1940, ROM, RG 12.9.1, corr. 1935–40.

31 "Visit to Dr. C.T. Currelly, Royal Ontario Museum of Archaeology. Made by O.C. Elliott, Kingston, on March 29, 1940," ROM, SC 9, box 1.

32 Elliott, in recounting his meeting with Currelly, referred to Jacob's alleged use of "memo books." Jacob used the term "memorandum notes."

33 C.T. Currelly to Duncan McArthur, 11 November 1940, ROM, 12.9.1.22.

34 O.C. Elliott to T.L. Tanton, 1 April 1940, ROM, SC 9, box 1.

35 George Brown to O.C. Elliott, 26 March 1940, ROM, SC 9, box 1.

36 T.L. Tanton to O.C. Elliott, 10 April 1940, ROM, SC 9, box 1.

37 O.C. Elliott to T.L. Tanton, 8 April 1940, ROM, SC 9, box 1. Elliott mentioned Curran, but plainly meant Currelly.

38 The letter is not extant, but Tanton reported writing to Lougheed in T.L. Tanton to O.C. Elliott, 10 April 1940, ROM, SC 9, box 1.

39 T.L. Tanton to O.C. Elliott, 10 April ROM, SC 9, box 1.

40 Tanton's letter to Brøgger is not extant. It is mentioned in T.L. Tanton to O.C. Elliott, 7 February 1940, ROM, SC 9, box 1.

CHAPTER TWENTY-TWO

1 Aaron Lougheed to T.L. Tanton, 22 April 1940, ROM, SC 9, box 1.

2 T.L. Tanton to O.C. Elliott, 27 April 1940, ROM, SC 9, box 1.

3 O.C. Elliott to T.L. Tanton, 30 April 1940, ROM, SC 9, box 1.

4 Robert Bell to O.C. Elliott, 29 April 1940, ROM, SC 9, box 1.

5 O.C. Elliott to T.L. Tanton, 5 May 1940, ROM, SC 9, box 1.

6 Ibid.

7 T.L. Tanton to O.C. Elliott, 27 April 1940, ROM, SC 9, box 1.

8 1906 Census of the Northwest Provinces, LAC, RG 31, Strathcona, Alberta, roll T-18363, p. 29, family 296; 1916 Canada Census, LAC, RG 31, Red Deer, Alberta, roll T-21953, p. 5, family 38.

9 See William Irwin Lyons burial in Red Deer, at https://www.findagrave.com /cgi-bin/fg.cgi?page=gr&GRid=132205562&ref=acom.

10 Archaeologist Birgitta Wallace located Bloch's cousin, Kristian, living in Oslo, in 1966. He thought Shana was a widow with three children, one daughter and two sons, who were 15, 13, and 11, respectively, when she married Bloch in Winnipeg in 1929. Wallace recounts Kristian advising: "They

moved to Vancouver in 1930 where he worked [in] 1931 for the Vancouver Harbour Commissioners' Terminal Railway [from] 1931 to his death in 1936 as 'anleggsinspektör,' Plant Inspector, if there is such a thing." Birgitta Wallace, personal communication to author, 1 September 2017. "John Block," however, was still listed as a labourer with Vancouver Harbour Commissioners, living at 2725 W37, in the 1935 BC and Yukon directory.

11 George Brownell to Shana Block Hastings, 7 May 1940, ROM, SC 9, box 1.

12 Shana Block Hastings to George Brownell, 9 May 1940, enclosed in Brownell to T.L. Tanton, 10 May 1940, ROM, SC 9, box 1.

13 T.L. Tanton to Shana Block Hastings, 13 May 1940, ROM, SC 9, box 1.

14 E.M. Burwash to T.L. Tanton, 28 February 1940, ROM, SC 9, box 1.

15 E.M. Burwash to T.L. Tanton, 20 March 1940, ROM, SC 9, box 1. Burwash wrongly asserted that Currelly had personally travelled to the Lakehead that spring to investigate the counter-claims.

16 T.L. Tanton to H.H. Beeman, 23 November 1939, ROM, SC 9, box 1; Beeman to Tanton, 25 November 1939, ROM, SC 9, box 1.

17 H.H. Beeman to T.L. Tanton, 28 February and 4 March 1940, ROM, SC 9, box 1.

18 H.H. Beeman to T.L. Tanton, 11 May 1940, ROM, SC 9, box 1.

19 For Kenney's biography, see Wright, "James Francis Kenney."

20 See O.C. Elliott to T.L. Tanton, 5 May 1940; quote, Tanton to Elliott, 9 May 1940; Elliott to Tanton, 12 May 1940; Elliott to James Kenney, 12 May 1940. All in ROM, SC 9, box 1.

21 James Kenney to O.C. Elliott, 14 May 1940, ROM, SC 9, box 1.

22 Report, RSC Transactions 1940, 54.

23 Globe and Mail headline, 21 May 1940.

24 "110,000 Allies Are Prisoners, Berlin Claims," Globe and Mail, 20 May 1940.

25 W.S. Wallace to G.H. Clarke, 13 May 1940, WP, Royal Society (1940) A-H.

26 G.H. Clarke to W.S. Wallace, 16 May 1940, WP, Royal Society (1940) A-H.

27 W.S. Wallace to G.H. Clarke, 17 May 1940, WP, Royal Society (1940) A-H.

28 Morgan, in Coates and Morgan, Heroines and History, 158.

29 Wright, Professionalization of History, 90.

30 Morgan, in Coates and Morgan, Heroines and History, 159.

31 T.L. Tanton to O.C. Elliott, 9 May 1940, ROM, SC 9, box 1.

32 O.C. Elliott, "I Watched a Hoax Grow."

33 O.C. Elliott to T.L. Tanton, 27 May 1940, ROM, SC 9, box 1.

34 T.L. Tanton to O.C. Elliott, 25 May 1940, ROM, SC 9, box 1. Barbeau's estrangement from the Beardmore discussions was understandable. He had been a close friend of Jenness's at Cambridge and in their early days together at DGS, but he had broken with him when he was passed over for the

head of anthropology in favour of Jenness when Edward Sapir retired to accept a teaching position at the University of Chicago in 1925. See Richling, *In Twilight and in Dawn*, 142–3.

35 Vilhjalmur Stefansson to T.L. Tanton, 17 May 1940, ROM, SC 9, box 1. Elliott sent Stefansson a copy on 27 May 1940, ROM, SC 9, box 1.

36 See "Anton Wilhelm Brøgger," at http://www.nsd.uib.no/polsys/index.cfm ?urlname=polsys&lan=&MenuItem=N1_1&ChildItem=&State=collapse &UttakNr=33&person=10458 (viewed 21 December 2016).

37 Dear, "John Drew Jacob."

38 Mrs J. Hastings to T.L. Tanton, 2 June 1940, ROM, SC 9, box 1

39 Vilhjalmur Stefansson, quoted in T.L. Tanton to O.C. Elliott, 12 June 1940, ROM, SC 9, box 1.

40 T.L. Tanton to O.C. Elliott, 12 June 1940, ROM, SC 9, box 1.

41 T.L. Tanton to O.C. Elliott, 12 June 1940; 14 June 1940, ROM, SC 9, box 1.

42 T.L. Tanton to O.C. Elliott, 18 June 1940, ROM, SC 9, box 1.

43 Holand, *Westward from Vinland*, 68.

44 Ibid., 72.

45 O.C. Elliott to H.R. Holand, 17 June 1940, ROM, SC 9, box 1.

46 T.L. Tanton to H.R. Holand, 29 June 1940, HP.

47 H.R. Holand to O.C. Elliott, 22 June 1940, ROM, SC 9, box 1.

48 H.R. Holand to J.W. Curran, 3 July 1940, CF, box 21. Curran replied, but the letter does not survive.

49 Elliott, Review of Curran, *Here Was Vinland*, 208.

50 Ibid., 208.

51 Ibid., 209.

52 Baker, Review of Curran, 50.

CHAPTER TWENTY-THREE

1 See T.L. Tanton to O.C. Elliott, 18 June 1940; Elliott to H.H. Beeman, 25 June 1940; Elliott to Tanton, 26 June 1940; Elliott to Beeman, 28 June 1940; Shipping receipt, 2 July 1940; Beeman to Elliott, 6 July 1940; Beeman to Shana Block Hastings, 15 July 1940. All in ROM, SC 9, box 1.

2 Retainer, addressed to Beeman and Ross, undated, ROM, SC 9, box 1.

3 H.H. Beeman to C.T. Currelly, 18 June 1940. For all correspondence between Beeman and Currelly, see ROM, RG 12.9.1.2.

4 Shana Block Hastings to H.H. Beeman, 12 July 1940, ROM, SC 9, box 1.

5 H.H. Beeman to Shana Block Hastings, 15 July 1940, ROM, SC 9, box 1.

6 Ibid.

7 C.T. Currelly to H.H. Beeman, 23 July 1940, ROM, RG 12.9.2.

8 H.H. Beeman to C.T. Currelly, 25 July 1940, ROM, RG 12.9.2.

9 H.H. Beeman to C.T. Currelly, 26 July 1940, ROM, RG 12.9.1.2.

10 C.T. Currelly to H.H. Beeman, 30 July 1940, ROM, RG 12.9.1.2.

11 C.T. Currelly to Carl Sorensen, 30 July 1940, ROM, RG 12.9.1.31.

12 H.H. Beeman to C.T. Currelly, 3 August 1940, ROM, RG 12.9.1.2.

13 C.T. Currelly to H.H. Beeman, 6 August 1940, ROM, RG 12.9.1.2.

14 A copy of T.L. Tanton's 6 August 1940 letter (ROM, RG 12.9.1.22) does not indicate the recipient.

15 See Duncan McArthur to C.T. Currelly, 5 November 1940, ROM, RG 12.9.1.22.

16 O.C. Elliott, Beeman memo, 15 August 1940, ROM, SC 9, box 1.

17 O.C. Elliott to T.L. Tanton, 26 April 1941, ROM, SC 9, box 1.

18 Shana Block Hastings to H.H. Beeman, 19 August 1940, ROM, SC 9, box 1.

19 J.F. Ross to H.H. Beeman, 10 October 1940, ROM, SC 9, box 1.

20 J.W. Curran to Editor of CHR, 3 October 1940, ROM, SC 9, box 1; George Brown to O.C. Elliott, 11 October 1940, ROM, SC 9, box 1. Curran wrote: "I am a thoroughly poor reviser of copy and proofreader. I still find mistakes even of names and dates in my book." Original copies of Curran's articles preserved in his papers at Trent University are marked up in pen, with the date changed from 1931 to 1930 in preparation for typesetting.

21 O.C. Elliott to George Brown, 14 October 1940, ROM, SC 9, box 1.

22 T.L. Tanton to O.C. Elliott, 4 November 1940, ROM, SC 9, box 1.

23 "Dr. McArthur Expected to Join Cabinet Today," Globe and Mail, 22 August 1940. W.S. Wallace sent McArthur a letter of congratulations on 23 August. See WP, Correspondence (1940).

24 Duncan McArthur to C.T. Currelly, 6 November 1940, ROM, 12.9.1.22.

25 Christou, "Complexity of Intellectual Currents," 683.

26 C.T. Currelly to Duncan McArthur, 11 November 1940, ROM, 12.9.1.22. Currelly appears to have made one significant factual error. He informed McArthur that McIlwraith had presented a paper on the Beardmore find to the CHA annual meeting in Montreal in May 1939. The report of the meeting, however, does not list such a paper. See Canadian Historical Association, Report of the Annual Meeting Held at Montreal, May 25–26, 1939 (Toronto: University of Toronto Press, 1939). Currelly was probably thinking of McIlwraith's presentation to the Ontario Historical Society in June 1939.

27 T.L. Tanton to O.C. Elliott, 20 November 1940, ROM, SC 9, box 1.

28 T.L. Tanton to O.C. Elliott, 21 November 1940, ROM, SC 9, box 1.

29 T.L. Tanton to O.C. Elliott, 20 November 1940, ROM, SC 9, box 1.

30 Ibid.

31 A.G. Burns to W.S. Wallace, 8 June 1940, WP, Royal Society (1940) A-H.

32 Wallace probably meant manuscript pages. See W.S. Wallace to A.G. Burns, 11 June 1940, ROM, SC 9, box 1.

33 W.S. Wallace to W.A. Bell, 22 June 1940, WP, Royal Society (1940) A-H.

34 James Kenney to W.S. Wallace, 5 July 1940, WP, Royal Society (1940), I-O.

35 For Kenney's biography, see Wright, "James Francis Kenney."

36 Quoted by Wright, *Professionalization of History*, 53.

37 Wright, "James Francis Kenney," 43.

38 Robinson, "Notes on Sagard's Dictionary," xiv–xlvii. Wallace nevertheless wrote Robinson to return his paper and to inform him of the decision to eliminate non-fellows' papers from the 1940 *Transactions* – not telling him that Kenney had not included his paper in the Section 2 selections in the first place. See W.S. Wallace to Percy Robinson, 1 August 1940, WP, Royal Society (1940), Q-Z.

39 W.S. Wallace to James Kenney, 8 July 1940, WP, Royal Society (1940), I-O.

40 James Kenney to W.S. Wallace, 5 July 1940, WP, Royal Society (1940), I-O.

41 The only paper by a fellow that Wallace was doubtful about printing was William Douw Lighthall's "The Law of Cosmic Evolutionary Adaptation: An Interpretation of Recent Thought." He did not feel the effort by this eighty-two-year-old member was up to RSC standards. In their exchange of letters, Kenney urged Wallace to publish the paper by Lighthall, who was a former RSC president and was anxious to see it in print, and repeated his offer to have his own paper eliminated, or at least cut significantly. If Wallace had agreed to include Lighthall but eliminate or reduce Kenney's paper, Elliott's paper probably could have been accommodated.

42 James Kenney to W.S. Wallace, 15 July 1940, WP, Royal Society (1940), I-O.

43 W.S. Wallace to James Kenney, 1 August 1940, WP, Royal Society (1940), I-O.

44 T.L. Tanton to O.C. Elliott, 21 November 1940, ROM, SC 9, Box 1.

45 T.L. Tanton to O.C. Elliott, 20 November 1940, ROM, SC 9, box 1; Elliott to Tanton, 24 November 1940, ROM, SC 9, box 1.

46 T.L. Tanton to O.C. Elliott, 20 November 1940, ROM, SC 9, box 1. Elliott also considered seeing if Lorne Pierce at Ryerson Press would agree to issue the article as a small booklet. There was also the possibility of allowing a writer for the *Kingston Whig-Standard* to produce an account of the article to re-open the question of Dodd's discovery.

47 T.L. Tanton to O.C. Elliott, 26 November 1940, ROM, SC 9, box 1.

48 O.C. Elliott to W.S. Wallace, 1 December 1940, ROM, SC 9, box 1; Wallace to Elliott, 4 December 1940, ROM, SC 9, box 1.

49 James Kenney to George Brown, 10 December 1940, ROM, SC 9, box 1.

50 O.C. Elliott to George Brown, 11 December 1940, ROM, SC 9, box 1.

51 "Winnipeg Train Conductor Killed," *Winnipeg Free Press*, 11 December 1940.

52 T.L. Tanton to O.C. Elliott, 16 December 1940, ROM, SC 9, box 1.
53 O.C. Elliott to T.L. Tanton, 23 December 1940, ROM, SC 9, box 1.

CHAPTER TWENTY-FOUR

1 George Brown to O.C. Elliott, 1 February 1941, ROM, SC 9, box 2, file 8.
2 It is possible Brown discussed Elliott's paper with board member R.M. Saunders, a history professor at the University of Toronto. The advisory board for vol. 22 (1941) otherwise consisted of J.S. Martell, a historian at the Archives of Nova Scotia; C.P. Stacey, a history professor at Princeton who had earned his bachelor's degree at the University of Toronto; Queen's University historian J.L Morison; A.R.M. Lower, a history professor at Winnipeg's Wesley College who was on the CHR board when C.T. Currelly's article ran in 1939; J.J. Talman, who had earned his PhD at the University of Toronto and was chief librarian at the University of Western Ontario; John Irwin Cooper, a history professor at McGill University; the Quebec historian, genealogist, and librarian, Gérard Malchelosse; Séraphin Marion, who taught French and French-Canadian literature at the University of Ottawa and was director of historical publications at the Public Archives of Canada; C.R. Sanderson, chief librarian of the Toronto Public Library; and W.M. Whitelaw, a history professor at the University of Saskatchewan.
3 T.L. Tanton to O.C. Elliott, 10 February 1941, ROM, SC 9, box 2, file 8.
4 O.C. Elliott to George Brown, 12 February 1941, ROM, SC 9, box 2, file 8.
5 O.C. Elliott to T.F. McIlwraith, 18 February 1941, ROM, SC 9, box 2, file 8.
6 T.F. McIlwraith to O.C. Elliott, 25 February 1941, ROM, SC 9, box 2, file 8.
7 O.C. Elliott to T.L. Tanton, 28 February 1941, ROM, SC 9, box 2, file 8.
8 Ontario Game and Fisheries Department to O.C. Elliott, 17 February 1941, ROM, SC 9, box 2, file 8.
9 O.C. Elliott to T.F. McIlwraith, 3 March 1941, ROM, SC 9, box 2, file 8.
10 T.F. McIlwraith to O.C. Elliott, 6 March 1941, ROM, SC 9, box 2, file 8.
11 George Brown to O.C. Elliott, 14 March 1941, ROM, SC 9, box 2, file 8.
12 O.C. Elliott to T.F. McIlwraith, 15 March 1941, ROM, SC 9, box 2, file 8.
13 O.C. Elliott to T.L. Tanton, 15 March 1941, ROM, SC 9, box 2, file 8.
14 T.L. Tanton to O.C. Elliott, 17 March 1941, ROM, SC 9, box 2, file 8.
15 O.C. Elliott to T.L. Tanton, 7 April 1941, ROM, SC 9, box 2, file 8.
16 See consular registration source, Chapter 9, n36; Census of Canada, 1921, RG 31, fol. 58, Fort William (City), Fort William and Rainy River, Ontario, p. 8.
17 Ring was boarding with Sorensen in Fort William and working as an accountant (possibly for Sorensen) when Sorensen indicated on the 1921 census form that he was a widower.

18 I am unable to confirm either the death of Nancy (Stenersen) Sorensen or any remarriage by Carl Sorensen to a woman named Karen.

19 The meetings are recounted in O.C. Elliott to T.L. Tanton, 26 April 1941, ROM, SC 9, box 2, file 8.

20 T.F. McIlwraith to O.C. Elliott, 19 April 1941, ROM, SC 9, box 2, file 8.

21 C.T. Currelly to O.C. Elliott, 19 April 1941, ROM, SC 9, box 2, file 8.

22 O.C. Elliott to T.L. Tanton, 26 April 1941, ROM, SC 9, box 2, file 8.

23 O.C. Elliott to C.T. Currelly, 25 April 1941, ROM, RG 12.9.1.9.

24 T.F. McIlwraith to O.C. Elliott, 28 April 1941, ROM, SC 9, box 2, file 8.

25 T.L. Tanton to O.C. Elliott, 4 November 1940, ROM, SC 9, box 2, file 8. For Wintemberg's life-long health problems, see Jenness, "William John Wintemberg."

26 Quoted by Jenness, "William John Wintemberg."

27 T.L. Tanton to O.C. Elliott, 28 April 1941, ROM, SC 9, box 2, file 8.

28 For Greenaway's death, see "Miss E.M. Greenaway Museum Worker, Dies," *Toronto Star*, 29 April 1941; "Lower Museum Flag to Mourn Secretary," *Toronto Star*, 30 April 1941; "Lower Flag at Museum as Miss Greenaway Buried, *Globe and Mail*, 1 May 1941.

29 "Osgood Hall: Court of Appeal." *Globe and Mail*, 4 December 1937. Province of Ontario, death registration no. 004026.

30 Ethlyn Greenaway to P.A. Means, 22 November 1939, ROM, RG 12.9.1, corr. 1935–40.

31 C.T. Currelly, "Report of the Director of the Royal Ontario Museum of Archaeology," in *University of Toronto President's Report for the Year Ending 30 June, 1941*, 54.

CHAPTER TWENTY-FIVE

1 T.L. Tanton to O.C. Elliott, 8 May 1941, ROM, SC 9, box 2, file 8. Brown's 6 May letter to Tanton is not extant.

2 George Brown to O.C. Elliott, 6 May 1941, ROM, SC 9, box 2, file 8.

3 T.L. Tanton to O.C. Elliott, 14 May 1941, ROM, SC 9, box 2, file 8.

4 O.C. Elliott to George Brown, 16 May 1941, ROM, SC 9, box 2, file 8.

5 T.L. Tanton to O.C. Elliott, 23 May 1941, ROM, SC 9, box 2, file 8.

6 O.C. Elliott to T.L. Tanton, 12 June 1941, ROM, SC 9, box 2, file 8.

7 Elliott recounted his negotiations with Brown in a letter to Tanton on 2 June 1941. See ROM, SC 9, box 2, file 8. Tanton had recalled for Elliott that, in his own meeting with Brown, the CHR editor offered two solutions. He could publish Elliott's submitted draft of the "balanced statement," with or without Elliott's consideration of the comments by himself and McIlwraith,

or he could run Elliott's original RSC paper and have McIlwraith or someone else present the opposing view. See T.L. Tanton to O.C. Elliott, 23 May
1941, ROM, SC 9, box 2, file 8.

8 Richling, *In Twilight and in Dawn*, 285–6.

9 T.L. Tanton to O.C. Elliott, 6 July 1941, ROM, SC 9, box 2, file 8.

10 O.C. Elliott to George Brown, 22 July 1941, ROM, SC 9, box 2, file 8.

11 T.L. Tanton to O.C. Elliott, 3 August 1941, ROM, SC 9, box 2, file 8.

12 George Brown to O.C. Elliott, 11 August 1941, ROM, SC 9, box 2, file 8.

13 George Brown to O.C. Elliott, 19 August 1941, ROM, SC 9, box 2, file 8.

14 O.C. Elliott to T.L. Tanton, 24 August 1941, ROM, SC 9, box 2, file 8.

15 O.C. Elliott to George Brown, 23 August 1941, ROM, SC 9, box 2, file 8.

16 George Brown to C.T. Currelly, 26 August 1941, ROM, RG 12.9.1, corr.
    1941–55.

17 Elliott, "Survey," 270–1.

18 Currelly, "Further Comments, I," 271.

19 Ibid., 272.

20 Ibid.

21 Ibid.

22 Ibid., 273.

23 Ibid., 274.

24 Ibid., 273.

25 Ibid., 274.

26 Ibid.

27 Ibid.

28 Ibid., 275.

29 Ibid.

30 Ibid.

31 Ibid.

32 Elliott, "Further Comments, II," 276.

33 Ibid.

34 Ibid., 277.

35 Ibid.

36 Ibid.

37 Ibid.

38 Ibid., 278.

39 Ibid.

40 Ibid.

41 Ibid., 279.

42 Ibid.

43 O.C. Elliott to T.L. Tanton, 1 October 1941, ROM, SC 9, box 2, file 8.

44 T.L. Tanton to O.C. Elliott, 4 October 1941, ROM, SC 9, box 2, file 8.

45 "Viking Relics Source Evidence is Surveyed," *Telegram* (Toronto), 4 October 1941.

46 M.Y. Williams to T.L. Tanton, 27 September 1941, ROM, SC 9, box 2, file 8.

47 John Bloch's cousin, Kristian Bloch, informed Birgitta Wallace in 1966 that Bloch's first marriage ended in divorce, without any children, before he immigrated to Canada. Birgitta Wallace, personal communication to author, 1 September 2017.

48 H.A. Ruttan to T.L. Tanton, n.d. (copy). Dated in letter from T.L. Tanton to O.C. Elliott, 22 October 1941, ROM, SC 9, box 2, file 8.

49 A.D. Fraser to O.C. Elliott, 13 November 1941, ROM, SC 9, box 2, file 8.

50 T.L. Tanton to O.C. Elliott, 26 November 1941, ROM, SC 9, box 2, file 8.

51 Information from Susan Maclatchie; "New DVA Declares Vets Grade One Citizens," *North Bay Daily Nugget*, 23 August 1947.

CHAPTER TWENTY-SIX

1 Means, *Newport Tower*.

2 P.A. Means to C.T. Currelly, 7 March 1942, ROM, RG 12.9.1, corr. 1941–55.

3 William Brownell Goodwin was a retired insurance executive in Hartford, Connecticut, who scoured New England in the 1930s for evidence in support of the Norse visit promised by *Antiquitates Americanae* (1837). He published *The Truth about Leif Ericsson* (Boston: Meador) in 1941. Then, in *The Ruins of Great Ireland in New England* (Boston: Meador, 1946), Goodwin contended that Irish Culdee monks had colonized New England.

4 C.T. Currelly to P.A. Means, 9 March 1942, ROM, RG 12.9.1, corr. 1941–55.

5 Creighton, *Dominion of the North*, 1–2.

6 Donald Wright, "Creighton, Donald Grant" in *Dictionary of Canadian Biography*, vol. 20, University of Toronto/Université Laval, 2003–, http://www.bio graphi.ca/en/bio/creighton_donald_grant_20E.html (viewed 7 January 2017).

7 "New DVA Declares Vets Grade One Citizens," *North Bay Daily Nugget*, 23 August 1947; Peter Neary, "How Newfoundland Veterans Became Canadian Veterans," in Hiller and Neary, *Twentieth-Century Newfoundland*, 217; "O.C. Elliott Named DVA Training Chief," *Ottawa Journal*, 8 March 1954.

8 Personal communication, John Garner to author, 20 October 2017.

9 Quoted by Carpenter, "Further Evidence on the Beardmore Relics," 878.

10 Lithgow Osborne to T.F. McIlwraith, 21 September 1948, ROM, RG 12.9.1.3. Brøndsted's coming research tour had already been publicized in the *New York Times*. See "Dane May Shed Light on Norse in America," *New York Times*, 19 July 1948.

11 Brøndsted would become director of the museum in 1951. The Viking Fund was founded by Swedish industrialist Axel Wenner-Gren in 1941. Initially, the fund operated broadly in support of scientific research, but it quickly shifted its focus to anthropology and established the prestigious Wenner-Gren Medal in 1946. The fund's name was changed to the Wenner-Gren Foundation in 1951. See http://www.wennergren.org/history/story-and-people-wenner-gren (viewed 22 February 2017).

12 "Norsemen Reached Minnesota 130 Years before 1492, This Inscription Says," *National Geographic* 94, 3 (1948): 343.

13 See Holand, *America.*

14 For correspondence relating to Brøndsted's visit, see ROM, RG 12.9.1.3.

15 Quotation, Barker, "T.F. McIlwraith," 258; Dickson, *Museum Makers*, 103–4.

16 Gerard Brett to John Matter, 10 September 1948, ROM, RG 12.9.1, corr. 1941–55.

17 T.F. McIlwraith to Johannes Brøndsted, 25 October 1948, ROM, RG 12.9.1.3.

18 Ibid.

19 Johannes Brøndsted to T.F. McIlwraith, 15 November 1948, ROM, RG 12.9.1.3.

20 T.F. McIlwraith to Johannes Brøndsted, 17 November 1948, ROM, RG 12.9.1.3.

21 Gerard Brett to H. Kühn, 23 May 1949, ROM, RG 12.9.1, corr. 1941–55.

22 Johannes Brøndsted to T.F. McIlwraith, 1 March 1950, ROM, RG 12.9.1.3. Johannes Brøndsted, "Problemet om Nordboer I Nordamerika før Columbus," *Aarbøger for Nordisk Oldkyndighed og Historie*, 1950.

23 Matthew W. Sterling, "Introduction," in Mallery, *Lost America*, x.

24 Mallery, *Lost America*, xiv.

25 See Pohl, *Amerigo Vespucci.* Pohl became devoted to cryptic accounts of pre-Columbian voyages to the New World as he produced a string of popular histories, beginning with a forty-six-page monograph in 1950, *The Sinclair Expedition to Nova Scotia in 1398*, that created the modern legend of a voyage by Henry Sinclair, Earl of Orkney, to Nova Scotia. His output included *The Lost Discovery* (1952), *Atlantic Crossings before Columbus* (1961), *The Viking Explorers* (1966), *Prince Henry Sinclair* (1967), and *The Viking Settlements of North America* (1971). Pohl also edited for publication the late Frederick A. Cook's *Return from the Pole* (1951), a manuscript written in the 1930s by the man who claimed to have beaten Peary to the North Pole in 1908.

26 F.J. Pohl to C.T. Currelly, 14 May 1945, ROM, RG 12.9.1.24.

27 Currelly's reply does not survive. Quoted by Pohl, in F.J. Pohl to C.T. Currelly, 31 May 1945, ROM, RG 12.9.1.24.

28 Ibid.

29 See Pohl, *Lost Discovery*, 283–9.

30 For his discussion of the Beardmore evidence, see Brøndsted, "Norsemen in North America Before Columbus," 377–82.

31 Brøndsted, "Norsemen in North America," 380.

32 Ibid., 382.

33 Godfrey, "Newport Puzzle"; Godfrey, "Newport Tower II," *Archaeology* 3, no. 2, 82–6; Godfrey, "Newport Tower, a reply"; Godfrey, "Archaeology of the Old Stone Mill."

34 Godfrey, "Vikings in America," 42.

35 "Fletcher Gill Retired CNR Engineer Dies," *Daily News-Journal* (Fort William), 10 November 1954.

36 John Garner, personal communication to author, 21 February 2017.

CHAPTER TWENTY-SEVEN

1 For Carpenter's biography, see Prins and Bishop, "Edmund Carpenter."

2 Barker, "T.F. McIlwraith and Anthropology," 261–2.

3 See "A Brief History of Anthropology at the University of Toronto," at http://www.chass.utoronto.ca/anthropology/history.htm.

4 Dickson, *Museum Makers*, 112.

5 See Clarkson, Gordon & Co., *Report on Survey of Royal Ontario Museum 1953–1954* (a.k.a. the Glassco Report, for J. Grant Glassco, the partner who oversaw it). Copy available at ROM.

6 See Dickson, *Museum Makers*, 106–19, for the museum's struggles in the immediate postwar years and Tushingham's hiring.

7 Clarkson, Gordon & Co., *Report on Survey of Royal Ontario Museum 1953–1954*.

8 Carpenter, "Frauds in Ontario Archaeology," 114.

9 Carpenter, *Norse Penny*, 17.

10 Edmund Carpenter to Birgitta Wallace, 27 September 1965. Personal letter in possession of Brigitta Wallace. Quoted with permission of Wallace.

11 Carpenter, *Norse Penny*, 17.

12 Carpenter, "Frauds in Ontario Archaeology," 115.

13 Carpenter, "A Scholar's Pleasure in a Swath of Lies," *Telegram* (Toronto), 11 April 1955.

14 Carpenter, "A Scholar's Pleasure," quoted in Carpenter, "Frauds in Ontario Archaeology," 116.

15 Carpenter, "Frauds in Ontario Archaeology," 116.

16 Memo, D. Cameron to A.D. Tushingham, re Beardmore relics, 27 November 1956, ROM, RG 12.9.1., corr. 1956–58.

17 For Cameron's biography, see "CAM Honours," CAM *Bulletin* no. 7, November 2001, at http://www.maltwood.uvic.ca/cam/publications/CAM_bulletins /007_cam_honours.html. See also his obituary in the *Calgary Herald*, at http://www.legacy.com/obituaries/calgaryherald/obituary.aspx?n=duncan-cameron&pid=17620988 (viewed 20 October 2017); and David L. Shirey, "Canadian Will Head Brooklyn Museum," *New York Times*, 18 February 1971.

18 Fred Ferretti, "Museum Board Hears Cameron Issue Today," *New York Times*, 11 December 1973; Fred Ferretti, "Duncan F. Cameron Resigns as Brooklyn Museum Director," *New York Times*, 19 December 1973.

19 Lois Irvine, "In Memoriam: Duncan Ferguson Cameron, 1930–2006," 29 April 2006, Commonwealth Association of Museums, at http://www.maltwood.uvic.ca/cam/archived_news/20060429_memoriam_ca meron.html (viewed 20 October 2017).

20 Cameron delivered his remarks at the 1971 University of Colorado Museum Lecture, "The Museum, a Temple, or the Forum." The lecture was reproduced in the *Journal of World History* special number, "Museums, Society, Knowledge" (1972), as well as in the *Curator* 14, 1 (1971), from which quotations are drawn.

21 Cameron, "Museum," 16.

22 David L. Shirey, "Canadian Will Head Brooklyn Museum," *New York Times*, 18 February 1971.

23 Cameron, "Museum," 16.

24 Butler, *Contested Representations*, 1.

25 Carpenter, "Frauds in Ontario Archaeology," 116.

26 Carpenter never mentioned Trott in his recollections of the *Maclean's* story.

27 Elizabeth Trott introduced Marshall McLuhan to the artist René Cera, and she would marry Cera in 1966. Her godson, Michael McLuhan, would remember her as an "aspiring journalist." See McLuhan, "Person Behind the Image," 24.

28 Cameron, memo, 27 November 1956, ROM, RG 12.9.1., corr. 1956–58.

29 Ibid.

30 Ibid.

31 A.D. Tushingham to Johannes Brøndsted, RG 12.9.1, corr. 1956–58.

32 Cameron, memo, 27 November 1956, ROM, RG 12.9.1., corr. 1956–58.

33 See Robert L. Gowe, "End of Exile in New York," *Globe and Mail*, 22 September 1956.

34 Robert L. Gowe, "Museum Opens Case: The Mystery of the Norse Sword," *Globe and Mail*, 23 November 1956.

35 "Announcement," 21 November 1956, ROM, RG 12.9.1, corr. 1956–58.

36 Peal McCarthy, "Conjured a Great Museum Out of Own Enthusiasm," *Globe and Mail*, 3 November 1956.

37 Currelly, *I Brought the Ages Home*, 300.

38 Ibid., 302.

39 John Garner, personal communication with author, 21 February 2016.

40 Robert L. Gowe, "How Dynamite Blast Uncovered Controversial Clues to Early Age," *Globe and Mail*, 24 November 1956.

41 Carpenter, "Frauds in Ontario Archaeology," 115.

42 Robert L. Gowe, "Viking Visitors" Beardmore Cache of Relics Resolves into Battle of Archaeologists," *Globe and Mail*, 26 November 1956.

43 See McIlwraith, "Archaeological Work."; McIlwraith, "Pukaskwa Pit Culture."

44 Holand, *Explorations in America before Columbus*, 94–102.

45 Edmund Carpenter to Birgittta Wallace, 27 September 1965.

46 See Cameron, memo, 27 November 1956, ROM, RG 12.9.1., corr. 1956–58.

47 Robert L. Gowe, "Viking Relics Myth Exploded? Adopted Son Swears Viking Relics Planted," *Globe and Mail*, 30 November 1956.

48 Cameron memo, 27 November 1956, ROM, RG 12.9.1., corr. 1956–58.

49 Walter Dodd affidavit, 27 November 1956, ROM, RG 12.9.1.8.

50 A.D. Tushingham to Walter Dodd, 28 November 1956, ROM, RG 12.9.1.8.

51 Gowe, "Viking Relics Myth."

52 Only Gowe's initial story announcing the investigation had run when Walter Dodd came forward, although Gowe's other articles had run by the time he swore out the affidavit.

53 Cameron, memo, 27 November 1956, ROM, RG 12.9.1., corr. 1956–58.

54 Tushingham wrote Brooks an undated letter, thanking him for his letter of 25 November 1956, which is no longer extant. "I wish to thank you for your subsequent courtesy in meeting with Museum representatives in Fort William a couple of weeks ago, and in giving them your statement of the facts." See A.D. Tushingham to C.M. Brooks, ROM, RG 12.9.1., corr. 1956–58.

55 Census of United States, 1900, Hartford, Connecticut, roll 137, p. 3B, FHL microfilm 1240137; Census of Canada, 1911, LAC, RG 31, James, Nipissing, Ontario, p. 13, family 101; Brooks military record, LAC, RG 150, acc. 1992-93/166, box 1102-7; Census of Canada, 1921, LAC, RG 31, fol. 87, Temiskaming, Ontario, p. 6. Voter rolls for 1935, Port Arthur District, rural polling division 79, Beardmore, in LAC, Voters Lists, Federal Elections, 1935–1980, R1003-6-3-E (RG113-B).

56 L.M. Lein to Jack Stokes, 29 January 1981, ROM, Beardmore acc. 936.55.1-3.

57 Brooks affidavit and "Amplification by Mr. Brooks of the Statement Made in Fort William on the 30th Day of November, 1956," ROM, RG 12.9.1., corr. 1956–58.

58 In supplemental questioning, Brooks wasn't sure if Dodd had been speaking

about finding relics in "the Wilson Street cellar or the Macker [sic] street cellar," and he added that he visited Dodd at his house just before he began working at the Northern Empire mine, "around '31 I think." Although the affidavit set his encounter with Dodd at 296 Wilson, its details make clear it must have occurred at 33 Machar.

59 A.D. Tushingham to Ellen Dodd, 28 November 1956, ROM, RG 12.9.1., corr. 1956–58.

60 Canadian Press, "Prospector's Widow Denies Report of Relics was Hoax," *Ottawa Citizen*, 3 December 1956.

61 H.M. Turner to Kelso Roberts, 17 December 1956, ROM, RG 12.9.1, corr. 1956–58.

62 "Inquiry Urged to Help Settle Beardmore Dispute, *Globe and Mail*, 21 December 1956.

63 L.E. Giles to A.D. Tushingham, 8 December 1956, ROM, RG 12.9.1, corr. 1956–58.

64 See Dyer in 1940 voter list for Ontario district, rural polling division 2, Pickering Township, in Voters Lists, Federal Elections, 1935–1980, LAC, R1003-6-3-E (RG113-B).

65 H.R. Holand to A.D. Tushingham, 17 December 1956, ROM, RG 12.9.1, corr. 1956–58. See Associated Press, "'Viking' Relics in Canada Are Pronounced a Hoax," *Washington Post*, 2 December 1956.

66 A.D. Tushingham to H.R. Holand, 23 January 1957, ROM, RG 12.9.1, corr. 1956–58.

CHAPTER TWENTY-EIGHT

1 O.C. Elliott to A.D. Tushingham, 27 November 1956, ROM, RG 12.9.1., corr. 1956–58.

2 A.D. Tushingham to O.C. Elliott, 21 December 1956, ROM, RG 12.9.1., corr. 1956–58.

3 O.C. Elliott to A.D. Tushingham, 14 January 1957, ROM, RG 12.9.1., corr. 1956–58.

4 See ROM, RG 12.9.1, corr. 1956–58, for correspondence on the proposed inquiry.

5 ROM, RG 12.9.1, corr. 1956–58.

6 Olson, "Was Our Biggest Historical Find," 81.

7 Ibid.

8 Ibid.

9 Ibid., 83.

10 Ibid.

11 Ibid., 84.

12 ROM, SC 3, box 1B.

13 Carpenter, "Further Evidence," 876.

14 See ROM, RG 12.9.1, corr. 1956–58, for communications on the inquiry.

15 Olson, "Was Our Biggest Historical Find," 84.

16 Obituary, O.C. Elliott, *Ottawa Journal*, 4 March 1958.

17 Carpenter, "Further Evidence," 876. Carpenter repeated the compliment in "Frauds in Ontario Archaeology," 114.

18 Carpenter, "Frauds in Ontario Archaeology," 113.

19 "As you may know, the reaction to my expose cost the editor of Penn. Arch. his position & split the Society for months." Edmund Carpenter to Birgitta Wallace, 27 September 1965 (private letter in possesion of Brigitta Wallace). A review of the *Pennsylvania Archaeologist* table of contents confirms that the issue in which Carpenter's article appeared was the last to feature work by Leslie.

20 Carpenter, "Frauds in Ontario Archaeology," 117.

21 Ibid., 118.

22 Ibid., 116.

23 Edmund Carpenter to Birgitta Wallace, 27 September 1965. Carpenter similarly wrote in *Norse Penny*: "The Director sent his assistant to Beardmore to check. The assistant did, accurately. But the Director silenced him" (17).

24 ORF report, undated, ROM, RG 12.9.1., corr. 1956–58.

25 See A.D. Tushingham to Walter Kenyon, "R.O.M. Expedition," 21 August 1957, ROM, RG 12.9.1, corr. 1956–58. Edmund Carpenter would write that Kenyon "failed to find the claim and made a public statement that there had never been such a claim. Later, after being assured that at least the claim was not in doubt, he said that it had probably been obliterated." See Carpenter, "Frauds in Ontario Archaeology," 116. Kenyon at least found and photographed Dodd's prospecting cabin. The photos are filed under Kenyon's name in the museum's New World Archaeology archives.

26 Quoted by Carpenter in "Frauds in Ontario Archaeology," 118. The carbon of the letter is on file in RG 12.9.1, corr. 1956–58.

27 See, for example, the letter from Dr H.J. Plenderleith, head of conservation, British Museum, to A.D. Tushingham, 1 April 1958, ROM, RG 12.9.1, corr. 1956–58. "We have not done any work on the metallurgy of the Viking period in this Museum and I can think of no Scandinavian Museum which has done analysis of the iron objects of the Viking period."

28 "Personally I would not think it unlikely that these two weapons originate in Scandinavia, based on weapon typology and similar finds … The lack of hardening of the axe does not weaken its authenticity. Not all Viking age weapons were properly hardened, and some had steel edges of lesser quality (low carbon level). Viking weapons were also frequently burnt on funeral pyres, and this

would remove the hardening and soften it. Also the steeling of the axe could be an inserted wedge, or it could have been a steel rod attached on one side of the axe edge. The [ORF] report lacks the detail of information necessary to deduce if the hardness test may have hit the wrong spot." Vegard Vike, personal communication to author, 6 August 2017. "Alan [Williams] tells me that a low manganese content is by no means unusual (rather the reverse) *and* in the light of the many more analyses of such artifacts carried out in more recent years, nowadays one would no longer sweepingly assert that low manganese 'ruled out' a Scandinavian origin." David Edge, Armourer/Head of Conservation, the Wallace Collection, personal communication to author, 2 August 2017.

29 In describing the sword and axe head in *The Beardmore Relics*, Tushingham made terse reference to "metallurgical analysis," without citing the specific ORF report. The sword had been tempered and "appears to be Norse, 900 to 1,000 years old." He admitted the absence of a hard cutting edge on the axe "is strange, but as it was probably welded to the wrought iron body of the axehead it may have corroded or broken away completely, leaving no trace." He said nothing about the low manganese levels in the sword and axe head. See Tushingham, *Beardmore Relics*, 2.

30 Carpenter, "Frauds in Ontario Archaeology," 114.

31 Edmund Carpenter to Birgitta Wallace, 27 September 1965.

32 See Seaver, *Maps, Myths, and Men*, for a thorough treatment of the map controversy. See also Douglas McNaughton's discussion in "Early Cartography of the North Atlantic," 267–69, in Fitzhugh and Ward, *Vikings*.

33 Tushingham, *Beardmore Relics*, 14.

34 The *Globe and Mail* published a preliminary article by Gowe on 23 November 1956, followed by two articles (24 and 26 November 1956) that were billed as a series, and, on 30 November, a fourth and final article that reported on Walter Dodd's affidavit.

35 Tushingham, *Beardmore Relics*, 9.

36 Ibid., 2.

37 Ibid., 5.

38 Ibid, 11.

39 Ibid., 12.

40 Ibid., 15.

41 A.D. Tushingham to Walter Dodd, 28 November 1956, ROM, RG 12.9.1.8.

42 A.D. Tushingham to H.R. Holand, 23 January 1957, ROM, RG 12.9.1, corr. 1956–58.

43 Tushingham, *Beardmore Relics*, 16.

44 For correspondence on the donation, see ROM, RG 12.9.1., corr. 1971–74. Donation details from Susan MacLatchie.

45 See correspondence RG 12.9.1, corr. 1971–74; and in the ROM Beardmore accession file.

CONCLUSION

1   Elliott to Tanton, 1 April 1940, ROM, SC 9, box 1.
2   Carpenter, "Frauds in Ontario Archaeology," 116.
3   Seaver, *Maps, Myths, and Men*, 3.
4   See Harris, *Selling Hitler*.
5   Coe, *Breaking the Maya Code*.
6   Garrett G. Fagan, "Diagnosing Pseudoarchaeology," in Fagan, *Archaeological Fantasies*, 29.
7   Dewar, *Bones*.
8   Leakey, *By the Evidence*, 23.
9   Leakey discusses the Piltdown forgery in *By the Evidence*, 22–4 (quote, 24).
10 Warner to Currelly, n.d., ROM, RG 12.9.1, corr. 1935–40.
11 Acquired by Yale from an antiquarian bookseller in Connecticut, the volume in which the map was bound was only said to have originated in a "private library." When challenged in 1966 on the volume's origin, the bookseller said that the provenance was a "blind alley" beyond the unnamed private library from which he had acquired it. See Seaver, *Maps, Myths, and Men*, 89–91.
12 See Samuel Redman, "Behind Closed Doors: What the Piltdown Man Hoax from 1912 can Teach Science Today," *The Conversation*, 4 May 2017, at http://theconversation.com/behind-closed-doors-what-the-piltdown-man-hoax-from-1912-can-teach-science-today-76967.
13 See, for example "Why Did Vikings Have 'Allah' Embroidered into Funeral Clothes?" BBC News Europe, 12 October 2017, at http://www.bbc.com/news/world-europe-41567391.
14 See the tweets of @stephenniem, beginning "Dear Entire World: #Viking 'Allah' textile actually doesn't have Allah on it. Vikings had rich contacts w/Arab world. This textile? No. 1/60." 7:06 a.m., 16 October 2017.
15 "She had assembled a remarkable team of archaeologists, soil, pollen, seed, and remote sensing experts from Scotland, Iceland, Canada, and the US to make sure that the investigation was as complete as possible." Birgitta Wallace, personal communication with author, 20 November 2017.

Bibliography

CITATION ABBREVIATIONS

BF	Edward Moore Burwash Fonds
CF	James W. Curran Fonds
GF	Philip H. Godsell Fonds
HP	Hjalmar and Harold Holand Papers
LAC	Library and Archives Canada
OA	Ontario Archives
ROM, RG 12.9	Beardmore Relics
ROM, SC 3	Collections about Charles Trick Currelly
ROM, SC 9	O.C. Elliott Fonds
SP	Vilhjalmur Stefansson Papers
WP	William Stewart Wallace Papers

PAPERS

Calgary, AB
  Glenbow Museum
    Philip H. Godsell Fonds, scrapbook, vol. 1, Viking Footprints M-433-326

Green Bay, WI
  Archives and Area Research Center, University of Wisconsin
    Hjalmar and Harold Holand Papers, mss 60

Hanover, NH
  Rauner Special Collections Library, Dartmouth College
    Vilhjalmur Stefansson Papers

Peterborough, ON
  Trent University Archives
    James W. Curran Fonds, 74-006

Toronto, ON
  Thomas Fisher Rare Book Library
    William Stewart Wallace Papers, MC 31
  Royal Ontario Museum
    Beardmore Relics, RG 12.9
    Beardmore Relics accession file, 936.55.1-3
    Collection about Charles Trick Currelly, SC 3
    O.C. Elliott Fonds, SC 9
  United Church of Canada Archives
    Edward Moore Burwash Fonds, 3049

PUBLISHED SOURCES

Adam, Thomas. *Buying Respectability: Philanthropy and Urban Society in Transnational Perspective, 1840s to 1930s.* Bloomington: University of Indiana Press, 2009.

Anderson, Rasmus B. *America Not Discovered by Columbus: An Historical Sketch of the Discovery of America by the Norsemen in the Tenth Century.* Chicago/London: S.C. Griggs & Co./ Trübner & Co., 1874.

Armstrong, John M. "The Numerals on the Kensington Rune Stone." *Minnesota History* 18, 2 (1937): 185–8.

Ayrton, E.R., C.T. Currelly, and A.E.P. Weigall. *Abydos.* Pt. 3: *1904.* London: Egypt Exploration Fund, 1904.

Baker, J.N.L. Review of Curran, *Here Was Vinland.* In *Geographical Journal* 96, 1 (1940): 48–50.

Barker, John. "T.F. McIlwraith and Anthropology at the University of Toronto, 1925–63." *Canadian Review of Sociology and Anthropology* 24, 2 (1987): 252–68.

Barker, John, and Douglas Cole. *At Home with the Bella Coola Indians: T.F. McIlwraith's Field Letters, 1922–4.* Toronto: University of Toronto Press, 2003.

Bennett, Tony. *The Birth of the Museum: History, Theory, Politics.* London: Routledge, 1995.

Berger, Carl. *Science, God, and Nature in Victorian Canada.* Toronto: University of Toronto Press, 1983.

– *The Writing of Canadian History: Aspects of English-Canadian Historical Writing: 1900 to 1970.* Toronto: Oxford University Press, 1976.

Bovey, Wilfrid. "The Vinland Voyages." *Transactions of the Royal Society of Canada,* ser. 3, vol. 30 (1936): sec. 2, 27–47.

Brøndsted, Johannes. "Norsemen in North America before Columbus." In *Annual Report of the Board of Regents of the Smithsonian Institution, 1953,* 367–406. Washington: Government Printing Office, 1954.

Brooks, Charles Timothy. *The Controversy Touching the Old Stone Mill, in the Town of Newport, Rhode Island*. Newport, RI: Charles E. Hammett, Jr, 1851.

Buckner, Phillip, ed. *Canada and the British Empire*. Oxford, UK: Oxford University Press, 2008 (paperback 2010).

Burrows, A.G. "The Porcupine Gold Area." In *Thirty-Third Annual Report of the Ontario Department of Mines*. Pt. 1: *1924*. Toronto: Legislative Assembly of Ontario, 1925.

Burwash, E.M. "Classes for Prospectors, 1927–28." In *Thirty-Seventh Annual Report of the Ontario Department of Mines*. Pt. 1: *1928*. Toronto: Legislative Assembly of Ontario, 1929.

Butler, Shelley Ruth. *Contested Representations: Revisiting* Into the Heart of Africa. London: Routledge, 1999.

Cadbury, Henry J. "The Norse-American Centennial." *Bulletin of Friends Historical Association* 15, 1 (1926): 21–5.

Cameron, Duncan F. "The Museum, a Temple or the Forum." *Curator* 14, 1 (1971): 10–24.

Careless, J.M.S. "The *Review* Reviewed, Or Fifty Years with the Beaver Patrol." *Canadian Historical Review* 51, 1 (1970): 48–71.

Carpenter, Edmund. "Frauds in Ontario Archaeology." *Pennsylvania Archaeologist* 31 (1961): 113–18.

– "Further Evidence on the Beardmore Relics." *American Anthropologist* 59, 5 (1957): 875–8.

– *Norse Penny*. New York: The Rock Foundation, 2002.

Cawley, F.S. "Review: *The Kensington Stone: A Study in Pre-Columbian American History* by Hjalmar R. Holand." *New England Quarterly* 6, 1 (1933), 210–17.

Christou, Theodore Michael. "The Complexity of Intellectual Currents: Duncan McArthur and Ontario's Progressivist Curriculum Reforms." *Paedagogica Historica* 49, 5 (2013): 677–97. http://dx.doi.org/10.1080/00309230.2012.739181.

Clarkson, Gordon and Co. *Report on Survey of Royal Ontario Museum 1953–1954*. Toronto: Clarkson, Gordon and Co., [1954].

Coates, Colin M., and Cecilia Morgan. *Heroines and History: Representations of Madeleine de Verchères and Laura Secord*. Toronto, University of Toronto Press, 2002.

Coe, Michael D. *Breaking the Maya Code*. New York: Thames and Hudson, 1992.

Conn, Steven. *Museums and American Intellectual Life, 1876–1926*. Chicago: University of Chicago Press, 1998.

Cook, Ramsay. *The Regenerators: Social Criticism in Late Victorian English Canada*. Toronto: University of Toronto Press, 1985.

Creighton, Donald Grant. *Dominion of the North: A History of Canada*. Boston: Houghton Mifflin, 1944.

Curran, James W. *Here Was Vinland: The Great Lakes Region of America*. Sault Ste Marie, ON: *Sault Daily Star*, 1939.

- "A Norseman Died in Ontario 900 Years Ago." In *Empire Club of Canada: Addresses Delivered to the Members During the Year 1938–39*, 96–109. Toronto: Maclean Publishing, 1939.

Currelly, C.T. *I Brought the Ages Home*. Toronto: Ryerson Press, 1956.

- "Further Comments Regarding the Beardmore Find, I." *Canadian Historical Review* 22, 3 (1941): 271–5.

- "Viking Weapons Found Near Beardmore, Ontario." *Canadian Historical Review* 20, 1 (1939), 4–7.

Dawson, Kenneth C.A. "Archaeologists in the Continental Boreal Province: A Personal Recollection." *Ontario Archaeology* 67 (1999): 23–39.

Dear, L.S. "John Drew Jacob." *News Letter of the Thunder Bay Naturalists Club*, 15 January 1959, 3.

Dewar, Elaine. *Bones: Discovering the First Americans*. Toronto: Random House, 2001.

Dickson, Lovat. *The Museum Makers: The History of the Royal Ontario Museum*. Toronto: Royal Ontario Museum, 1986.

Du Chaillu, Paul Belloni. *The Viking Age: The Early History, Manners, and Customs of the Ancestors of the English-Speaking Nations*, 2 vols. New York: Charles Scribners Sons, [1889] 1890.

Einarsson, Stefán. "Review, *The Kensington Stone: A Study in Pre-Columbia American History* by H.R. Holand." *Speculum* 8, 3 (1933): 400–8

Ellard, James. "'From Moribund to Mobilized': The Lake Superior Regiment 1920–1940." MA thesis, Lakehead University, 1999.

Elliott, O.C. "Further Comments Regarding the Beardmore Find, II." *Canadian Historical Review* 22, 3 (1941): 275–9.

- "I Watched a Hoax Grow." c. 1957 manuscript. ROM, SC 9, O.C. Elliott Fonds, box 2, file 6.

- Review of James W. Curran, *Here Was Vinland*. In *Canadian Historical Review* 21, 2 (1940): 208–9.

- "Some Sidelights on the Norse Relics of Beardmore." Queen's University Radio address, 21 October 1938 (ROM, SC 9, O.C. Elliott Fonds, box 2, file 6).

- "A Survey of the Evidence." *Canadian Historical Review* 22, 3 (1941): 254–71.

Fagan, Garrett G., ed. *Archaeological Fantasies*. New York: Routledge, 2006.

Falnes, Oscar J. "New England Interest in Scandinavian Culture and the Norsemen." *New England Quarterly* 10, 2 (1937): 211–42.

Fargo, Valerie M. "Sir Flinders Petrie." *Biblical Archaeologist* 47, 4 (1984): 220–3.

Feder, Kenneth L. *Frauds, Myths, and Mysteries: Science and Pseudoscience in Archaeology*, 9th ed. New York: Oxford University Press, 2017.

Fitzhugh, William W., and Elizabeth I. Ward, eds. *Vikings: The North Atlantic Saga*. Washington, DC: Smithsonian Institution Press, 2000.

"Fleming on a New Flightless Duck," *Ibis* 77, 4 (1935): 895.

Fleming, J.H. *On a New Genus and Species of Flightless Duck from Campbell Island off New Zealand*.

Occasional Papers, Royal Ontario Museum of Zoology, no. 1, 22 June 1935.

– "[On] a New Genus and Species of Flightless Duck from Campbell Island," letters, extracts, etc., *Ibis* 80, 3 (1938): 590–1

Fraser, A.D. "A Catalogue of the Greek Vases in the Royal Ontario Museum of Archaeology, Toronto [review of David M. Robinson and Cornelia G. Harcum]." *Art Bulletin* 14, 3 (1932): 278–80.

– "The Norsemen in Canada." *Dalhousie Review* 17, 2 (1937): 175–86.

Fraser, John Botsford. *Canada as It Is*. London: Cassell and Co., 1905.

Gathorne-Hardy, G.M. "A Recent Journey to Northern Labrador." *Geographical Journal* 59, 3 (1922): 153–67.

Gauvreau, Michael. *Evangelical Century: College and Creed in English Canada from the Great Revival to the Great Depression*. Montreal and Kingston: McGill-Queen's University Press, 1991.

Godfrey, William S., Jr. "The Archaeology of the Old Stone Mill in Newport, Rhode Island." *American Antiquity* 17, 2 (1951): 120–9.

– "The Newport Puzzle." *Archaeology* 2, 3 (1949): 146–9.

– "The Newport Tower, a reply to Mr. Pohl." *Archaeology* 4, 1 (1951): 54–6.

– "Vikings in America: Theories and Evidence." *American Anthropologist* n.s. 57, no. 1, pt. 1 (1955): 35–43.

Gooding, S. James. "William Todd, 1910–1963." *Bulletin of the American Group: International Institute for Conservation of Historic and Artistic Works* 4, 1 (1963): 5.

Hamilton, Michelle A. *Collections and Objections: Aboriginal Material Culture in Southern Ontario*. Montreal and Kingston: McGill-Queen's University Press, 2010.

Harris, Robert. *Selling Hitler: The Story of the Hitler Diaries*. London: Faber and Faber, 1986.

Harrold, Francis B., and Raymond E. Eve, ed. *Cult Archaeology and Creationism: Understanding Pseudoscientific Beliefs about the Past*. Iowa City: University of Iowa Press, 1995.

Hermannsson, Halldór. *The Problem of Wineland*. Ithaca, NY: Cornell University Press, 1936 [*Icelandica* no. 25].

Hiller, James, and Peter Neary, ed. *Twentieth-Century Newfoundland: Explorations*. St John's, NL: Breakwater, 1994.

Holand, Hjalmar R. *America: 1355–1364*. New York: Duell, Sloan and Pearce, 1946.

- "The Climax Fire Steel." *Minnesota History* 18, 2 (1937): 188–90.
- "Concerning the Kensington Rune Stone," *Minnesota History* 17, 2 (1936): 166–88.
- *Explorations in America before Columbus*. New York: Twayne, 1956.
- *The Kensington Rune Stone: The Oldest Native Document of American History*. Menasha WI: private printing, 1919.
- *The Kensington Stone: A Study in Pre-Columbian American History*. (Ephraim WI: private printing, 1932.
- "The 'Myth' of the Kensington Stone." *New England Quarterly* 8, 1 (1935): 42–62.
- *Westward from Vinland: The Story of Norse Discoveries and Exploration in America, Centuries before Columbus.* New York: Dull, Sloane and Pearce, 1940.

Hunt, William Holman. *Pre-Raphaelitism and the Pre-Raphaelite Brotherhood*, vol 1. New York and London: Macmillan, 1905.

Hunt, William R. *Stef: A Biography of Vilhjalmur Stefansson, Canadian Arctic Explorer.* Vancouver: UBC Press, 1986.

Hunter, Douglas. *The Place of Stone: Dighton Rock and the Erasure of America's Indigenous Past.* Chapel Hill: University of North Carolina Press, 2017.

Isitt, Benjamin. *From Victoria to Vladivostok: Canada's Siberian Expedition, 1917–19*. Vancouver: UBC Press, 2010.

Jenness, Diamond. "The 'Blond' Eskimos." *American Anthropologist* n.s. 23, 3 (1921): 257–67.

- "William John Wintemberg, 1876–1941." *American Antiquity* 7, 1 (1941), 64–6. Reprinted online by Canadian Archaeological Association, at http://canadian archaeology.com/caa/about/awards/smith-wintemberg-award/william-j-wintemberg.

Kehoe, Alice Beck. *The Kensington Runestone: Approaching a Research Question Holistically*. Long Grove, IL: Waveland Press, 2005.

Kelley, Jane H., and Ronald F. Williamson. "The Positioning of Archaeology within Anthropology: A Canadian Historical Perspective." *American Antiquity* 61, 1 (1996): 5–20.

Kolodny, Annette. *In Search of First Contact: The Vikings of Vinland, the Peoples of the Dawnland, and the Anglo-American Anxiety of Discovery*. Durham, NC: Duke University Press, 2012.

Krueger, David M. *Myths of the Rune Stone: Viking Martyrs and the Birthplace of America*. Minneapolis: University of Minnesota Press, 2015.

Laking, Sir Guy Francis. *A Record of European Armour and Arms through Seven Centuries*, vol. 1. London: Bell, 1920.

Landow, George P. "Shadows Cast by the Light of the World: William Holman Hunt's Religious Paintings, 1893–1905," *Art Bulletin* 65, 3 (1983): 471–84.

Larson, Laurence M. "Review: *The Kensington Stone*." *Minnesota History* 13, 2 (1932): 182–4.

Leakey, L.S.B. *By the Evidence: Memoirs, 1932–1951*. New York: Harcourt Brace Jovanovich, 1974.

Lechler, George. "The Viking Finds from Northern Ontario." *Art Quarterly* ser. 2, vol. 2 (1939): 128–33.

Leechman, Douglas. "Harlan I. Smith." *Canadian Field-Naturalist* 56 (October 1942): 114.

Lovoll, Odd S. *Norwegian Newspapers in America: Connecting Norway and the New Land.* St Paul: Minnesota Historical Society Press, 2010.

Mallery, Arlington H. *Lost America: The Story of Iron-Age Civilization Prior to Columbus.* Columbus and Washington: The Overlook Company, 1951.

Marshall, Barbara Ruth. "Sir Edmund Walker, Servant of Canada." MA thesis, University of British Columbia, 1971.

McArthur, D. "Some Problems of Canadian Historical Scholarship," *Canadian Historical Review* 8, 1 (1927): 3–8.

McIlwraith, Thomas, L. "Archaeological Work on the North Shore of Lake Superior." *Royal Society of Canada Transactions* 53, ser. 3, vol. 2 (1959): 37–42.

– "The Pukaskwa Pit Culture." *Ontario History* 50, 1 (1958): 41–3.

McKay, Ian, and Robin Bates. *In the Province of History: The Making of the Public Past in Twentieth-Century Nova Scotia.* Montreal and Kingston: McGill-Queen's University Press, 2010.

McLuhan, Michael. "The Person Behind the Image." *St. Michael's* 55, 2 (2016): 24.

Means, P.A. *Newport Tower*. New York: Henry Holt, 1942.

Morton, A.S. "La Vérendrye, Commandant, Fur-Trader, and Explorer." *Canadian Historical Reivew* 9 (December 1928): 283–4, 297.

Naville, Edouard, and H.R. Hall. "Excavations at Deir El Bahari." In *Archaeological Report (Egypt Exploration Fund), 1905–06*, 1–7.

Needham, Harold G. "The Origins of the Royal Ontario Museum." MA thesis, University of Toronto, 1970.

"Norse Relics in Ontario." *Antiquity* 12, 46 (1938): 232–3.

Officer, James. "Philleo Nash, 1909–1987." *American Anthropologist* n.s, 90, 4 (1988): 952–56.

Ontario. *Forty-Eighth Annual Report of the Ontario Department of Mines*. Pt. 1: *1939*. Toronto: Legislative Assembly of Ontario, 1940.

– *Forty-Sixth Annual Report of the Ontario Department of Mines*. Pt 1: 1937. Toronto: Legislative Assembly of Ontario, 1937.

– *Report of the Royal Commission on the University of Toronto.* Toronto: L.K. Cameron, King's Printer, 1906.

Olson, Robert. "Was Our Biggest Historical Find Our Biggest Hoax?" *Maclean's*, 13 April 1957, 30–1, 80–4.

Oslund, Karen. *Iceland Imagined: Nature, Culture, and Storytelling in the North Atlantic.* Seattle: University of Washington Press, 2013.

Øverland, Orm. *American Minds, American Identities: Making the United States Home, 1870–1930.* Urbana and Chicago: University of Illinois Press, 2000.

Pálsson, Gísli. *Travelling Passions: The Hidden Life of Vilhjalmur Stefansson.* Winnipeg: University of Manitoba Press, 2003.

Petersen, Jan. *De Norske Vikingesverd.* Kristiania (Oslo): Jacob Dybwad, 1919.

Petrie, W.M. Flinders. *Abydos I, 1902.* London: Egypt Exploration Fund, 1902.

– *Ehnasya 1904.* Memoir 26. London: Egypt Exploration Fund, 1905.

– *Seventy Years in Archaeology.* New York: Henry Holt, 1932.

Pohl, Frederick J. *Amerigo Vespucci, Pilot Major.* New York: Columbia University Press, 1944 (New York: Octogon Books, 1966).

– *The Lost Discovery: Uncovering the Track of Vikings in America.* New York: W. W. Norton, 1952.

Potter, Russell. *Finding Franklin: The Untold Story of the 165-Year Search.* Montreal and Kingston: McGill-Queen's University Press, 2016.

Prins, Harold E.L., and John Bishop. "Edmund Carpenter, Explorations in Media and Anthropology." *Visual Anthropology Review* 17, 2 (2001–02): 110–40.

Quaife, Milo M. "A Footnote on Fire Steels." *Minnesota History* 18, 1 (1937): 36–41.

– "The Myth of the Kensington Rune Stone: The Norse Discovery of Minnesota 1362." *New England Quarterly* 7, 4 (1934): 613–45.

Rathgen, Friedrich. *The Preservation of Antiquities: A Handbook for Curators.* Trans. George A. Auden and Harold A. Auden. Cambridge, UK: Cambridge University Press, 1905.

"Reported Find of Norse Relics in Ontario." *Geographical Journal* 91, 4 (1938): 395–6.

Richling, Barnett. *In Twilight and in Dawn: A Biography of Diamond Jenness.* Montreal and Kingston: McGill-Queen's University Press, 2012.

Robinson, David M., and Cornelia G. Harcum. *A Catalogue of the Greek Vases in the Royal Ontario Museum of Archaeology, Toronto,* 2 vols. Toronto: University of Toronto Press, 1930.

Robinson, Percy J. *Toronto during the French Regime: A History of the Toronto Region from Brulé to Simcoe, 1615–1793.* Toronto: Ryerson Press, 1933.

Robinson, Percy J. "Notes on Sagard's Dictionary." In Gabriel Sagard, *The Long Journey to the Country of the Hurons,* ed. George M. Wrong, trans. H.H. Langton. Toronto: Champlain Society: 1939.

Royal Society of Northern Antiquaries. *Report Addressed by the Royal Society of*

Northern Antiquaries to its British and American Members. Copenhagen: Royal Society of Northern Antiquaries, 1836.

– *Toronto during the French Regime: A History of the Toronto Region from Brulé to Simcoe, 1615–1793.* Toronto: Ryerson Press, 1933.

Rygg, A.N. *Norwegians in New York, 1825–1925.* Brooklyn, NY: Norwegian News Co., 1941.

Samuel, Sigmund. *The Seven Years' War in Canada, 1756–1763.* Toronto: Ryerson Press, 1934.

Schultz, April. "'The Pride of the Race Had Been Touched': The 1925 Norse-American Immigration Centennial and Ethnic Identity." *Journal of American History* 77, 4 (1991): 1265, 1287–8.

Schuster, Angela M.H. "The Vikings Are Coming!" *Archaeology* 44, 5 (1991): 27–8.

Seaver, Kirsten A. *Maps, Myths, and Men: The Story of the Vinland Map.* Stanford, CA: Stanford University Press, 2004.

Shore, Marlene. "'Remember the Future': The *Canadian Historical Review* and the Discipline of History, 1920–95." *Canadian Historical Review* 76, 3 (1995): 410–63.

Southcott, Chris. "Ethnicity and Community in Thunder Bay." *Polyphony: The Bulletin of the Multicultural History Society of Ontario* 9, 2 (1987), 10–20.

Stefansson, Vilhalmur. *Adventures in Error.* New York: McBride, 1936.

– *The Standardization of Error.* New York: W.W. Norton, 1927.

Stern, Alexandra Minna. *Eugenic Nation: Faults and Frontiers of Better Breeding in Modern America.* Berkeley: University of California Press, 2005.

Strange, Carolyn, and Tina Merrill Loo. *True Crime, True North: The Golden Age of Canadian Pulp Magazines.* Vancouver: Raincoast, 2004.

Teather, J. Lynne. *The Royal Ontario Museum: A Prehistory, 1830–1914.* Toronto: Canada University Press, 2005.

Thórdarson, Matthias. *The Vinland Voyages.* New York: American Geographical Society, 1930.

Thorpe, J.F. "Sir Robert Mond, 1867–1938," *Biographical Memoirs of Fellows of the Royal Society* 2, 7 (1939): 627–32.

Tushingham, A.D. *The Beardmore Relics: Hoax or History?* Toronto: University of Toronto Press, 1966.

University of Toronto. *President's Report for the Year Ending 30 June, 1940.* Toronto: University of Toronto, 1940.

Van Die, Marguerite. *An Evangelical Mind: Nathanael Burwash and the Methodist Tradition in Canada, 1839–1918.* Montreal and Kingston: McGill-Queen's University Press, 1989.

Wahlgren, Erik. *The Kensington Stone: A Mystery Solved*. Madison: University of Wisconsin Press, 1958.

Wallace, William. S. "The Literature Relating to the Norse Voyages to America." *Canadian Historical Review* 20, 1 (1939): 8–16.

Webb, Thomas H., and Carl C. Rafn. "Account of an Ancient Structure in Newport, Rhode-Island." In Royal Society of Northern Antiquaries, *Mémoires de la Societé royale des antiquaries du Nord, 1836–1839*, 361–85

Williams, Mary Wilhelmine. "Review: *The Kensington Stone*." *Mississippi Valley Historical Review* 19, 1 (1932): 99–100.

Williams, Stephen. *Fantastic Archaeology: The Wild Side of North American Prehistory*. Philadelphia: University of Pennsylvania Press, 1991.

Woolfrey, S., P. Chitwood, and N.E. Wagner. "Who Made the Pipes? A Study of Decorative Motifs on Middleport Pipe and Pottery Collections." *Ontario Archaeology* 27 (1976): 3–12.

Wright, Donald. *The Canadian Historical Association: A History*. Historical Booklet no. 62. Ottawa: Canadian Historical Association, 2003.

– *The Professionalization of History in English Canada*. Toronto: University of Toronto Press, 2005.

Wright, Glenn T. "James Francis Kenney, 1884–1946. Founder of the Canadian Catholic Historical Association." *CCHA Study Sessions* 50 (1983): 11–45.

Zaslow, Morris. *Reading the Rocks: The Story of the Geological Survey of Canada, 1842–1972*. Toronto: Macmillan of Canada, 1975.

Index

Literature
Reading Fiction, Poetry, and Drama

Literature
Reading Fiction, Poetry, and Drama

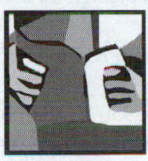

COMPACT EDITION

Robert DiYanni

ton   Burr Ridge, IL   Dubuque, IA   Madison, WI   New York   San Francisco
. Louis Bangkok Bogotá Caracas Lisbon   London   Madrid Mexico City
Milan   New Delhi   Seoul   Singapore   Sydney   Taipei   Toronto

McGraw-Hill Higher Education

A Division of The **McGraw-Hill** Companies

LITERATURE: READING FICTION, POETRY, AND DRAMA, COMPACT EDITION

This book is printed on acid-free paper.

1 2 3 4 5 6 7 8 9 0 KPH/KPH 9 0 4 3 2 1 0 9

ISBN 0-07-229507-4 (combined volume)
ISBN 0-07-229509-0 (fiction)
ISBN 0-07-229510-4 (poetry)
ISBN 0-07-229511-2 (drama)

Editorial director: *Phillip A. Butcher*
Sponsoring editor: *Sarah Touborg Moyers*
Developmental editor: *Alexis Walker*
Editorial assistant: *Bennett Morrison*
Project manager: *Margaret Rathke*
Manager, new book production: *Melonie Salvati*
Designer: *Kiera Cunningham*
Senior photo research coordinator: *Keri Johnson*
Supplement coordinator: *Marc Mattson*
Compositor: *GAC Indianapolis*
Typeface: *10.5/12 Bembo*
Printer: *Quebecor Printing Book Group/Hawkins*

Library of Congress Cataloging-in-Publication Data

DiYanni, Robert.
    Literature: reading fiction, poetry, and drama / Robert DiYanni.
    — Compact ed.
        p.   cm.
    Includes index.
        ISBN 0-07-229507-4 (combined). — ISBN 0-07-229509-0 (fiction). —
    ISBN 0-07-229510-4 (poetry). — ISBN 0-07-229511-2 (drama)
        1. Literature.   2. Literature—Collections.   I. Title.
PN49.D53   2000
808—dc21   99

About the Author

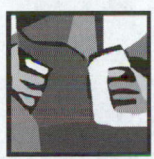

Robert DiYanni is Professor of English at Pace University, Pleasantville, New York, where he teaches courses in literature, writing, and humanities. He has also taught at Queens College of the City University of New York, at New York University in the Graduate Rhetoric Program, and most recently in the Expository Writing Program at Harvard University. He received his B.A. from Rutgers University (1968) and his Ph.D. from the City University of New York (1976).

Professor DiYanni has written articles and reviews on various aspects of literature, composition, and pedagogy. His books include *The McGraw-Hill Book of Poetry; Women's Voices; Like Season'd Timber: New Essays on George Herbert;* and *Modern American Poets: Their Voices and Visions* (a text to accompany the Public Broadcasting Television series that aired in 1988). With Kraft Rompf, he edited *The McGraw-Hill Book of Poetry* (1993) and *The McGraw-Hill Book of Fiction* (1995). With Janetta Benton he wrote *Arts & Culture: An Introduction to the Humanities* (1998).

In memory of
Palmer Turnheim

Brief Contents

PART THREE   DRAMA   721

PART FOUR   CRITICAL PERSPECTIVES AND RESEARCH   1345

Contents

xi

PART ONE   FICTION   19

PART TWO   POETRY 393

PART FOUR   CRITICAL PERSPECTIVES AND RESEARCH 1345

Preface

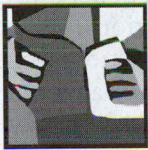

Literature the Compact Edition, presents an approach to literary works that emphasizes reading as an active enterprise involving thought and feeling. It encourages students to value their emotional reactions and their previous experience with life and with language. Students are introduced to interpretation through illustrated discussions of the elements of literature. They are invited to consider why they respond as they do and how their responses change during subsequent readings of a work; they are asked, in short, to relate their experience in reading literature to their experience in living. They are encouraged to see literature as a significant reflection of life and an imaginative extension of its possibilities.

From first page to last, *Literature* is designed to involve students in the twin acts of reading and analysis. Each of the genres fiction, poetry, and drama is introduced by a three-part explanatory overview of the reading process. The introductions are organized around the approach to texts outlined in Robert Scholes's *Textual Power* (Yale University Press, 1985), modified and adapted to my own approach to teaching literature. Scholes identifies three aspects of literary response: reading, interpretation, and criticism. The three-part structure of the introductions breaks down as follows:

the experience of literature
the interpretation of literature
the evaluation of literature

Our *experience* of literature concerns our impressions of a work, especially our subjective impressions and emotional responses. *Interpretation* involves intellectual and analytical thinking. And the *evaluation* of literature involves an assessment of aesthetic distinction along with a consideration of a work's social, moral, and cultural values.

Paralleling this schema for the introductory genre discussions is a similarly organized introduction to writing about literature. This chapter for each genre describes how to apply and adapt the approaches presented in the introductions. The writing chapters include examples of student writing, sample topics, documentation procedures, and a general review of the writing process.

For each of the genre introductions, I have also provided a separate illustration of "the act of reading." The fiction section includes an interpolated reading of Kate Chopin's "The Story of an Hour." The poetry section offers a set of annotations for Theodore Roethke's "My Papa's Waltz." The drama section provides a set of questions in response to the opening scene of Lady Gregory's *The Rising of the Moon.* Taken together, the three demonstrations suggest specific strategies for the critical reading of literary works.

In addition to emphasizing the subjective, analytical, and evaluative aspects of reading literature, *Literature* introduces the traditional elements such as plot, character, imagery, and dialogue, through discussions tied to works in each of the three genres. Throughout these discussions, students are asked to return to certain works and reconsider them from different perspectives. In Chapter Nine, Elements of Poetry, for example, students are encouraged to reread particular poems as they study a different element or technique. The repetition reinforces the recursive aspect of reading described in the opening Chapters on each genre and demonstrates the need to reread literary works for the fullest possible intellectual, emotional, and aesthetic enjoyment.

The poetry section of *Literature* broadens the study of the genre with two special features: a number of poems in translation and in Chapter Ten a special selection of poetic transformations: examples of ways in which poets have modified their own and other artists' work by means of revision, parody, and adaptation. Of particular interest are the poems inspired by paintings.

Finally, a word about the choice of works. The classic and contemporary selections of fiction, poetry, and drama reflect a wide range of styles, voices, subjects, and points of view. Complex and challenging works appear alongside more readily approachable and accessible ones. *Literature,* moreover, contains both in sufficient variety for instructors to assign the more accessible ones for students to read and write about on their own, while reserving the more ambitious selections for class discussion.

The compact edition of *Literature* parallels the fourth edition. Like its parent volume, this compact edition includes the following features:

- Writing instruction has been greatly amplified with new Chapters on Writing about Fiction, Poetry, and Drama. The final chapter, Writing with Sources, supplements the new genre-specific writing Chapters.
- Works are now provided with dates of publication, performance, or composition.
- For each genre the works of two or three writers are highlighted and contextualized. Multiple selections are included for D. H. Lawrence, Flannery O'Connor, Sandra Cisneros, Emily Dickinson, Robert Frost, Langston

Hughes, Sophocles, and Shakespeare. Each of these writers' works is accompanied by an extensive biocritical introduction and by critical perspectives written by the writers themselves and by literary scholars.

• Brief biographies of many of the writers included in *Literature,* the Compact Edition, are provided in an appendix.

• An extensive Chapter on Critical Approaches has been added in which the major schools of literary theory are described and illustrated. Guiding questions and brief bibliographies augment the application of ten critical approaches.

Acknowledgements

Literature represents the cooperative efforts of many people. Steve Pensinger—publisher, editor, and friend—encouraged me to develop the first edition of the book and supported my work generously and graciously. His associates initially at Random House and afterward at McGraw-Hill brought intelligence and enthusiasm to their work on the project.

For the compact edition I have had the pleasure of working with McGraw-Hill colleagues Sarah Moyers, English editor; Alexis Walker, developmental editor; and Peter de Lissovoy, copy editor. I have also benefited from the suggestions of many colleagues who responded to a survey about the third edition. In addition, the following reviewers provided thoughtful suggestions for revision:

Francis B. Hanify, Luzerne County Community College
Keith Higginbotham, Midlands Technical College
Sally P. Wheeler, DeKalb College
Elaine L. Horne, Manchester Community Technical College
Simone Gers, Pima County Community College
George Kanieski, Cuyahoga Community College
E. Suzanne Owens, Lorain County Community College
Richard Courage, Westchester Community College
Peter Cortland, Quinnipiac College

Reviewers of previous editions gave me much good advice. For their third edition suggestions thanks to the following:

Stephen Behrendt, Barbara Belson, Jon Burton, Cornelius Cronin, Charles Crow, Lois Cuddy, Robert Dell, Alan Ehmann, Ruth Eisenberg, Peter Evarts,

Chris Farris, Paula Feldman, Elizabeth Flynn, Robert Fraser, Susan Gannon, Frank Garratt, Harold Gleason, John Hanes, Jacqueline Hartwich, J. G. Janssen, Michael Johnson, Leonard Leff, Barry Maid, William McIntosh, George Miller, Hugh Ruppersburg, Robert Sayre, Thomas Watson, A. K. Weatherhead, Joseph Zavadil, and Karl Zender.

For the second edition I received lively and thoughtful advice from William McIntosh of the United States Military Academy, and also from: Bertha N. Booker, Virginia State University; Carl Brucker, Arkansas Tech University; Terre Burton, Laramie County Community College, Wyoming; James Bynum, Georgia Institute of Technology; Charles Dean, Middle Tennessee State University; William J. Everts, Jr., St. Michael's College, Vermont; John Hoey, SUNY—Genesee; Ted Johnston, El Paso Community College; Larry G. Mapp, Middle Tennessee State University; Sara M. Putzell, Georgia Institute of Technology; and Sharon Sellers, Clayton State College, Georgia.

Four reviewers of the first edition deserve acknowledgment for their perceptive comments on the entire manuscript: Richard F. Dietrich, University of South Florida; Kelley Griffith, University of North Carolina; Frank Hodgins, University of Illinois; and Richard Larson, Lehman College of the City University of New York. In addition, I benefited enormously on that edition from the expert assistance of Donald McQuade, University of California at Berkeley, and Robert B. Lyons, Queens College, City University of New York, who served as consultants.

In addition, many instructors who used the third edition of *Literature* responded to a questionnaire on the book. For their valuable comments and advice I am grateful to: Debbie A. Hanson (Augustana College); John Lux (Baruch College); Richard Stimac (Campbell University); Duncan McClinton (Central Washington University); Woodrow Holbein (The Citadel); Gary B. Cohen, Frederick Goldberg (Clayton State College); Laurie Temple (Clinton Community College); C. K. Farr (College of St. Catherine); Susan M. Marsala (Cuesta College); J. Steven Beauchamp, Rosemary D. Cox, L. A. Nardone, Mark Nunes (DeKalb College, Central Campus); Deborah Preston, Jack Riggs (DeKalb College, Gwinnett); Joanne Burgess, Marsha M. Harper, Barbara Nipp (DeKalb College, North Campus); Carole Creekmore (DeKalb College, Rochdale); Theodore Wadley, Sally Wheeler (DeKalb College, South Campus); Barbara Dodd Galloway (Draughons Junior College); Julienne Empric (Eckerd College); David Owens (Friends University); Colleen Richmond (George Fox College); Edith Blicksilver (Georgia Institute of Technology); James Zoller (Houghton College); Margaret Corgan (King's College); Peter A. Edmunds, Silvija Meija (Lansing Community College); James Childs (Middlesex Community Technical College); Ken Huggins (Monroe Community College); Ted Brown (Murray State University); Nelvin Jager (Muskegon Community College); Zorka Milich (Nassau Community College); William Foster, Sandra Newton, Lisa Schuchter (Naugatuck Valley Community Technical College); Elaine Brown, Diane Levy (New York Institute of Technology); Sheila Wood (North Idaho College); Jean Hodgin (North Shore Community College); J. P. Wysong (Northern Essex Community College); Martin R. Trapp (Northwestern Michigan College); Marie M. Garrett (Patrick Henry

Community College); Margaret Payne (Pierce Community College); David Zucker (Quinnipiac College); Emmett H. Carroll (Seattle University); Steven Beck, Robert Carter, Raymond Mize (Southeastern Community College); Michael C. White (Springfield College); Mark Jones (St. Louis University); Thomas M. Kitts, Joseph Marotta (St. Vincent's College–St. John's University); Mark W. Bourdeau, Elaine Preston (Suffolk County Community College); Rosemary Baker, Roxanna Pisiak (SUNY, Morrisville); Linda Ford, Tamara Kuzmenkov, Richard Wakefield (Tacoma Community College); Lea Williamson (Texas A & M University); Joseph Zaitchick (University of Massachusetts, Lowell); James E. Ford (University of Nebraska); Libby Bernardin University of South Carolina); Bruce G. Nims (University of South Carolina at Lancaster); Grace S. Kehrer (Valencia Community College); Marilyn Roberts (Waynesburg College); and Thomas L. Pier (Yakima Valley Community College).

I have had the additional pleasure of working with Professor Tom Kitts of St. John's University. Professor Kitts has written a practical and graceful instructor's manual, which serves as a rich and rewarding source of practical and provocative classroom applications.

Finally, I want to thank my wife, Mary, whose loving assistance enabled me to complete this revision on schedule.

ROBERT DiYANNI

Literature
Reading Fiction, Poetry, and Drama

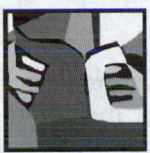

Reading (and Writing about) Literature

Many people read literature for pleasure. Many others read literary works to satisfy academic requirements in university general education programs. For them it is, initially at least, a duty. Duty and pleasure, however, are not mutually exclusive. If you are reading literature for a college course, largely as a duty, this does not prohibit you from enjoying what you read. One of the purposes of this chapter is to introduce you to some of the many pleasures literature offers.

Writing about literature is another matter. But not entirely. Most of those who write about literature typically do so for professional reasons—as book reviewers, as scholars and teachers. As a student in a university literature or writing course, you are one among many thousands around the country—indeed, around the world—who will write about literary works, partly to improve your writing ability, partly to increase your understanding of what you read. Another purpose of this chapter is to introduce you to some ways of writing about literature that you may find helpful.

The chapter is divided into two parts. First, we consider the pleasures of reading fiction, poetry, and drama—the three literary genres included in this book. Second, we consider some ways of writing about literary works. Both of these preliminary discussions are further developed in the chapters devoted to the specific genres and in the book's final part, "Critical Perspectives and Research."

READING LITERATURE

The Pleasures of Fiction

We read stories largely for the pleasures they bring us. These pleasures are emotional as well as intellectual. They include the pleasure of being surprised by a turn of events, being satisfied as our expectations are met, disturbed or confused as they are not. Well-told stories can involve us emotionally in the lives of their characters. They can also provide us with pleasures of recognition—in the worlds they portray and in the behavior of the characters who inhabit them.

But stories do more than entertain. They also instruct by showing us things about our world we had not known before reading them. Some stories make instruction, or teaching, their primary purpose, though we may enjoy other things about them besides their didactic intention. Consider this example of a fable by the ancient Greek storyteller, Aesop.

The Dog and the Shadow

One day a dog stole a piece of meat out of a butcher shop, and on his way to a safe place where he could eat it without interruption, he had to cross a footbridge over a clear stream. Looking down he saw his own reflection in the water.

Thinking that the reflection was another dog with another piece of meat, and being a greedy dog, he made up his mind to have that also. So he snarled and made a grab for the other dog's meat.

As he opened his mouth his meat dropped into the stream and was swept away.

Moral: Grasp at the shadow and lose the substance.

This story's didactic purpose is apparent in its explicit moral, though this moral invites us to put it into our own words. This, Aesop's fable says, is how you should—or rather should not—act. Don't be greedy. Don't grasp at the elusive false image of something, however attractive it appears. Be satisfied with what you have.

But why do we prefer the story to these morals? One reason is simply that stories are enjoyable in both the reading and the telling. Another reason is that stories are easy to remember. In remembering what happens to Aesop's dog, we remember the moral, or point, of the writer's fable.

Consider now another brief didactic story, this one a parable, a story with an implied moral teaching. This parable comes from the Asian tradition of religious teaching known as Zen.

Learning to Be Silent

The pupils of the Tendai school used to study meditation before Zen entered Japan. Four of them who were intimate friends promised one another to observe seven days of silence.

On the first day all were silent. Their meditation had begun auspiciously, but when night came and the oil lamps were growing dim one of the pupils could not help exclaiming to a servant: "Fix those lamps."

The second pupil was surprised to hear the first one talk: "We are not supposed to say a word," he remarked.

"You two are stupid. Why did you talk?" asked the third.

"I am the only one who has not talked," concluded the fourth pupil.

Unlike the moral of Aesop's fable, the point of "Learning to Be Silent" may not be clear right away. Perhaps you understood its point on first reading, perhaps after a second or third. Perhaps it made sense later, after you had time to think about it or talk about it with a classmate. Even then, you and your classmates may disagree about how to interpret the parable. Some may see it as being about the need for self-control; others may interpret it as being about the impossibility of achieving it. Others may understand it in still other ways—as being about pride or vanity, for example.

Although part of our pleasure in reading and hearing such stories comes from making sense of them, part derives from watching their unfolding action and their display of character. We may enjoy the crispness and directness of the dialogue. Each speaker in "Learning to be Silent" says something different. Each directs his comment to a different character, yet each does essentially the same thing. All break the rule of silence they had vowed to observe. Ironically, moreover, three of them break the rule because they try to show themselves worthier than the others, who have already broken the rule of silence. Part of our pleasure in "Learning to be Silent," thus, results from the skilled control of its telling.

In reading fiction we share the imaginative vision of another, adopting, however briefly, his or her way of perceiving the world. Through reading a wide variety of stories we can enter many different imaginative worlds, in the process enlarging and deepening our own perception of the world.

The Pleasures of Poetry

We read poetry for the many pleasures it offers—pleasures of sound and meaning, of image and symbol, of speech and feeling and thought. Some of the pleasures of poetry are intellectual, as when we enjoy a poet's witty wordplay or understand a poem's central idea. Others are emotional, as when a poem evokes sorrow or pity, fear or joy. Still others are physical, as when our skin tingles or we feel the impulse to tap our feet or nod in time to a poem's rhythmic beat. Emily Dickinson once suggested that she could tell she was reading poetry when she felt as if the top of her head was coming off. Although our own ways of acknowledging the power of poetry may not be as extravagant as Dickinson's, each of us experiences the pleasures of poetry in a meaningful way.

Poems may, at times, seem puzzling or mysterious. Yet mystery and confusion are not essential attributes of poetry. Nor is poetry simply dressed up prose, statements that have been made to look good (by being organized in stanzas) and sound good (by being arranged in patterns of rhythm and rhyme). And even though we can discuss the ideas in poems, poems can never be reduced to their intellectual content. Poems present experiences in language, experiences the poet creates for the reader to recreate. In reading poetry our experience involves more than considering the meanings of words. It includes our apprehension of a poem's form, our appreciation of its patterns of sound, and our understanding of its thought. The meaning of any poem involves our total experience of reading it, an experience that includes intellectual understanding but which is not restricted to it.

Poetry sharpens our perception of the world around us since it draws its energy from the fresh observation of life. Poetry can reveal to us things we didn't know or knew only vaguely. It can excite our capacity for wonder, and it can enlarge our appreciation of beauty. It can make us feel more acutely and deeply, and also make us more receptive to imaginative experience. Reading poetry also improves our ability to use and understand language since poems are made of words—at their best, the most carefully chosen words in the best order. Consider the following short poem.

ROBERT FROST

Dust of Snow

The way a crow
Shook down on me
The dust of snow
From a hemlock tree

Has given my heart
A change of mood
And saved some part
Of a day I had rued.

Part of our enjoyment of this poem comes from its brevity. It captures an experience and recreates it for us in just a few words. The poem's action may engage us, very likely sending us back almost immediately for a second look. We may be struck by the nature of the poem's action—a crow's jouncing a tree limb, which unloads its snow on a man beneath it. We may smile, considering that the crow's action may have been intentional. And we may reflect on the man's response—not anger or frustration, but a shift in his feelings, "a change of mood" (presumably from sorrow to something more joyous, elation perhaps).

Our pleasure in "Dust of Snow" may include a consideration of our own experience—whether or not that experience duplicates either the poem's external action or the speaker's internal change. We may find ourselves thinking about how our moods change and about what prompts those changes. We may enjoy the surprising reversal of our expectations in reading how Frost's speaker responds to the situation, perhaps comparing what our own imagined response might be.

These experiential or imaginative pleasures, moreover, might very well be supplemented by the pleasure we take in the poem's sounds—especially its rhythm and rhyme. And they may extend to other details we observe about its structure and language. We may enjoy noticing, for example, that though "Dust of Snow" is a single sentence, it is cast as two separate nearly symmetrical stanzas. And we might ask ourselves how it would differ if arranged as one stanza or constructed of two sentences. Furthermore, we might enjoy Frost's use of "rued," which stands out in a context of more common and familiar language.

Perhaps, "Dust of Snow" may lead us to speculate not only about the narrative incident it recounts, but about the event's larger significance. We might think about the relationship between human beings and the natural world that "Dust of Snow" implies—that nature can affect human beings in beneficial ways, that it can make people feel better about their experience. We may derive additional pleasure from considering other poems we have read by Frost or by other poets in relation to this one. We may find ourselves considering the larger implications of "Dust of Snow," along with a set of attitudes toward and values about the natural world and its relationship to the human world. This too may provide us with a kind of pleasure.

The Pleasures of Drama

Unlike the other literary genres, drama is meant to be performed on a stage. Much of the pleasure drama brings us comes in the way the language of the play's script comes alive in the speech of living actors who represent fictional or imaginary characters. We enjoy watching actors dramatically enact the "lives" of the characters they portray. We appreciate the way actors walk and talk, the way they interact with other characters, even their facial expressions and bodily gestures. The smallest gesture, such as the lowering of a hand, or the slightest facial movement, such as the raising of an eyebrow, contributes to our sense of the play's human experience.

When we read or view drama we are aware, if only implicitly, of its major characteristics or features. The first of these is its representational quality. Drama is a *mimetic* art, one that imitates or represents human life and experience. A large part of the pleasure drama brings us reflects its ability to show us aspects of human life meaningfully enacted. Drama is also an *active* art in which actors portraying characters say and do things to one another. Actors are agents, doers, who make things happen through speech and bodily action. In addition, drama is an *immediate* art, one that represents action that occurs in the play's present. This is so even when a play's subject is historical, that is, even when its dramatic action concerns the past. The important point about drama's immediacy is that plays bring the past into the present. Our experience of drama is thus one of watching events *as* they occur. We are first-hand witnesses of present-tense actions rather than auditors who simply hear about them later from a narrator at second hand.

One additional and critically important feature of drama derives from its mimetic, active, and immediate qualities: its *interactive nature.* The representation of human action displayed in drama is largely attributable to the interaction of its characters. The action of plays is based on *interaction,* for dramatic characters respond and relate to one another. They engage one another in dialogue and action, in speech and visual displays. Such character interaction is the heart of drama: it is the catalyst of plot, the source of meaning, and a central reason for our pleasure in dramatic experience.

Drama is interactive in still another way. Unlike fiction and poetry, which are largely verbal arts (though poetry is also allied with music or song) drama is a *composite* art—one that makes use of many of the other arts. Drama makes use of painting and architecture in the design and creation of stage sets and in the way stage and actors are lighted or kept in shadow. Drama may also use music and other sound effects to suggest feelings, to build tension, or to create mood and atmosphere. Sculpture and dance are suggested by the way characters are positioned on stage and by their movements around it. The point, however, is not so much that stationary characters can be compared with sculpture or moving ones with dancers, but rather that drama is a complex art that involves a dynamic interplay of visual and aural elements. In viewing drama and in reading it we need to be as alert as possible, keeping open our eyes, ears, and minds.

Our pleasure in drama arises from the cumulative impact of a multitude of impressions both visual and aural. Makeup and costume, lighting and sound, speech and action, posture and gesture, movement and expression—all work together to bring plays to life, to imbue them with meaning and feeling, and most importantly, to create a distinctive theatrical experience for the audience. It is this experience we attempt to capture when we read drama, knowing all the while that reading a play is not the same as sitting in a theater watching it enacted on a stage. To compensate for this fact we try to read drama *imaginatively,* as if we were watching it. We attempt to read drama *theatrically.*

But what does it mean to read a play theatrically? How do we imaginatively reconstruct a play in our minds? Essentially by translating the script we read into a mental performance that we imagine. By attending to the performative implications of the words on the page, we see imaginatively how they might be dramatized on the stage. We learn to look not only at what a play's words mean, but also at what they suggest about characters' behavior, movements, gestures, and feelings. We learn to listen for the effect their words have on one another. We try to imagine how those words might be uttered—gently or threateningly, sarcastically or sweetly, loudly or softly, swiftly or slowly—to suggest a few possibilities.

We also imagine where the characters are positioned relative to one another, how close or far apart. We imagine the manner of their walk, the style of their physical gestures, and the subtlest alteration of their voices and facial expressions. These details, coupled with changes in characters' body postures, their characteristic manner of delivering their lines, their costumes, the scenery of the play, the sounds of voices and of sound effects—all these things contribute to the richness of our imaginative reenactment of a play. The better we can imagine such elements, the better we will absorb the atmosphere and feeling of the play, and the more complete and theatrical will be our reading experience.

How do we learn to do this? By reading drama patiently and deliberately. By reading with care and attentiveness not only for the literal meanings of dialogue but for its implications and its sound and accent and rhythm as well. By reading aloud. By reading with other students in small groups. By talking with others about our mental reconstructions of scenes. In the process of learning to read plays theatrically we will also attend to the fullest expression of their literary meaning. Drama is literature as well as theater, for like poetry and fiction, drama is an art of language. While drama entertains us with its representation of life, it offers provocative ideas about the life it portrays, and it provides an imaginative extension of life's possibilities.

UNDERSTANDING LITERATURE: EXPERIENCE, INTERPRETATION, EVALUATION

This book's approach to reading, understanding, and appreciating literature is divided into three major parts: (1) experiencing and responding to literary works; (2) interpreting literary works; and (3) evaluating works of literature by considering the values they express. Since each genre discussion—fiction, poetry, and drama—employs this three-part approach in detail, we provide here a brief overview of what we mean by the experience, interpretation, and evaluation of literature.

When we read a literary work, something happens to us. We read the work subjectively—that is, according to our individual and subjective experience. A poem, for example, may provoke our thinking, evoke a memory, elicit a strong emotional response. A short story may arouse our curiosity about what will happen, engage our feelings for its characters, stimulate our thought about why things happen as they do. A play may move us to laughter or tears, may prompt us to link its dialogue and action with our lives.

In responding to literary works in these and other ways, we bring our personal and shared human experience to our reading of them. This kind of response—subjective, emotional, impressionistic—illustrates what we mean by the *experience* of literature. Our experience of literature, in this sense, however, is not enough for understanding and appreciating it, for which we need to move beyond our subjective impressions and emotional responses to literary works to other types of comprehension.

Our understanding of literary works results from our effort to interpret them, to make sense of their implied meanings. Our *interpretation* of literature provides an intellectual counterpart to our emotional experience. When we interpret literary works we concern ourselves less with how they affect us and more with what they mean. Interpretation, in short, aims at understanding; it relies on our intellectual comprehension and rational understanding rather than on our emotional response.

How do we come to understand works of literature? How do we develop an ability to interpret literature with competence and confidence? One way is to become familiar with its basic elements or characteristics. In reading fiction, for example, we rely on analysis of such elements as plot, character, setting, and point of view. In interpreting poems, we analyze their diction, imagery, syntax, and structure to get at meaning. In viewing or reading plays we focus on dialogue, setting, plot, and character. These and other literary elements are explained and illustrated in Chapter 3 (Elements of Fiction), Chapter 9 (Elements of Poetry), and Chapter 16 (Elements of Drama).

Our *evaluation* of literary works involves two kinds of judgments: (1) our assessment of their quality and value; and (2) our assessment of the cultural, social, and moral values they display. Evaluation of a literary work, which is a complex process, is closely related to our experience and interpretation of it. Grounded in interpretation, evaluation is also linked to our emotional response and subjective reactions regarding aspects of the work that please or shock us, that stimulate, frighten, repulse, amuse, or amaze us.

Consider the following brief fictional work, a sketch from *In Our Time,* by Ernest Hemingway, first published in 1925. This early modern work strongly embodies moral and cultural values.*

While the bombardment was knocking the trench to pieces at Fossalta, he lay very flat and sweated and prayed oh jesus christ get me out of here. Dear jesus please get me out. Christ please please please christ. If you'll only keep me from getting killed I'll do anything you say. I believe in you and I'll tell every one in the world that you are the only one that matters. Please please dear jesus. The shelling moved further up the line. We went to work on the trench and in the morning the sun came up and the day was hot and muggy, and cheerful and quiet. The next night back at Mestre he did not tell the girl he went upstairs with at the Villa Rossa about Jesus. And he never told anybody.

This text, though brief, is rich in cultural and moral implications. It assumes a modest knowledge of war as it was fought in the early twentieth century. It assumes, for example, that we know what trenches are, what shelling is, and also that we can make sense of the soldier's behavior. It also assumes some familiarity with a soldier going "upstairs" with a "girl" at a place like the "Villa Rossa."

The piece, however, is reticent about these and other matters. It says little directly. It's close-mouthed and tight-lipped about what it expects from us as readers—somewhat like the soldier who "never told anybody" about his

*For the Hemingway example and the approach taken to it I am indebted to Robert Scholes's discussion in *Textual Power* (New Haven: Yale University Press, 1985).

experience. But it makes a strong statement by implication, nonetheless, about its three central subjects, love, war, and religion, largely by playing off conventional expectations about these subjects. The soldier, for example, does not acquit himself heroically. Instead he cringes in the trenches to avoid being hit by enemy shells (though we may wonder what else he could do). And he prays to a God he probably ignores under normal circumstances. Moreover, his approach to prayer is to bargain with God: If you'll do this for me, I'll do something else for you. But it's a bargain he doesn't keep. Our response to this soldier's language and behavior is influenced by the cultural values we share and the moral dispositions we bring to both our reading and our lives.

Our evaluation of him turns on considerations such as whether he really believes in Jesus, and what such a belief may mean. It turns on whether you think the soldier's prayer is "answered" by God in a providential intervention to move the shelling "further up the line," or whether you see that as a coincidence, attributable purely to luck. It turns also on whether his going to a house of prostitution is something you can understand, sympathize with, and approve of—or not; and whether his not telling the girl or anybody else about Jesus is a serious violation of a solemn vow, or an excusable, perfectly understandable response.

Besides evaluating the behavior of the soldier, we also make a judgment about the values we think the text espouses. Does the author seem to display sympathy for the soldier? Does he judge him harshly? The narrative voice is noncommittal, concerned more with portraying a situation than with commenting on it. This stance of objectivity is itself a "value," an attitude or disposition we must eventually assess, as we must also respond to the fact that the world depicted is a man's world, a world of war and violence, in which women (or *girls* as the text stipulates them) figure only marginally, and then only as they can be used by men. (We know, for example, what the man feels and fears, but we are told nothing about the girl's thoughts and emotions.) Our sexual identity along with our religious disposition and our general cultural awareness and values will strongly influence what we make of and take from this text.

WRITING ABOUT LITERATURE

Reasons for Writing about Literature

Why write about literature? For many reasons. First, writing about a literary work encourages us to read it attentively and notice things we might miss during a more casual reading. Second, writing stimulates thinking, and enables us to discover what we think about literary works, how we feel about them, and why. Third, writing provides opportunities for us to state our views about the ideas and values expressed in literary works. Finally, through writing about literary works we enhance our enjoyment of the many pleasures they offer and deepen our appreciation of their artistic achievement.

Whatever our reasons for writing may be, a truly active engagement with literature intellectually and emotionally will broaden our understanding of life and language and will refine our aesthetic sensibilities. The literary works we read carefully will become a meaningful part of our lives, absorbed into our storehouse of knowledge and experience to become part of who we are, how we know, and what we feel.

Ways of Writing about Literature

Just as there are many reasons for writing about literature, there are many ways to write about it. In this section we will introduce a few common ways to write about literary works. Our approach is divided into three parts: Explicating, summarizing, and comparing and contrasting.

Explicating

A type of analysis frequently used to explain literary works is *explication,* a careful line-by-line or word-by-word examination of a passage in a poem, story, play, or essay. Explication involves a scrupulously close reading to unfold the layers of meaning in a text. It provides a close-up look at the language of a passage with a view to explaining its significance. Because explication involves such careful attention to detail, it is usually reserved for specific sections or parts of longer works, and sometimes even for parts of short works as well. As with any type of analysis, however, explication is most effective when it is used to illuminate the meaning of the work as a whole.

Explication is particularly useful for unraveling the meaning of a complex passage, something as long as a section, paragraph, stanza, or scene, or as brief as a bit of dialogue, a sentence, a line of poetry, or even a phrase. Our analysis of the ironic quality of the opening sentences of *Pride and Prejudice* (page 94) is one example. Others include the analysis of the final paragraph of Pirandello's "War" (page 249) and the final couplet of Hopkins's "Spring and Fall" (page 662). Beginnings and endings of literary works, whether they are as long as Jane Austen's novel or as short as a brief lyric poem, offer promising sections of text to explicate. These strategic locations afford opportunities for the writer to make a lasting impression on the reader.

Comparing and Contrasting

One of the most common approaches to writing interpretive papers is comparison and contrast, which can be applied in numerous ways. You might compare and contrast elements in a single work, or you might compare and contrast a particular aspect of two different works. You could compare and contrast, for example, the differing perspectives on knowledge and learning of the astronomer and the speaker in Whitman's "When I heard the learn'd astronomer" (page 476). Or you might compare the uses of irony in Crane's "War is Kind" (page 13) with Hardy's "Channel Firing" (page 659). You might compare and contrast the speech and actions of the two male characters in Boyle's "Astronomer's Wife" (page 57). Or you could compare the central character in Boyle's story with the protagonist of Silko's "Yellow Woman" (page 369) or

Gilman's "The Yellow Wallpaper" (page 239). Topics that reflect such a comparative approach would include these: "Active and Passive Learning in Whitman's 'When I heard the learn'd astronomer'"; "Two Uses of Irony: Satire and Humor in Poems by Stephen Crane and Thomas Hardy"; "Enchantment and Disenchantment: The Two Men in the Life of Kay Boyle's 'Astronomer's Wife'"; "Sanity or Madness: Women Protagonists in 'Astronomer's Wife' and 'The Yellow Wallpaper' (or 'Yellow Woman')."

Such comparative analyses can sharpen your perception of the works under consideration. By looking at two works together or at two aspects of a single work, you see their differences more clearly. In comparing two poems, you might notice, for example, that one includes rhyme and the other does not; that the action is external in one poem or story and internal in the other; that one story includes much dialogue and the other little; that the settings, tone, or points of the works differ in significant and interesting ways. Such comparative observations will lead you to ask why those differences exist and why the writers developed their works as they did.

When you write comparative papers, keep the following guidelines in mind:

1. Compare two things that seem worth the trouble, that will reward your effort. By attending carefully to a work's details you will often find significant parallels and contrasts. Follow the leads the work provides.
2. Compare works that have a significant feature in common, such as authorship, style, genre, historical period, subject, situation, or an aspect of technique like meter or point of view.
3. Make a point. Use comparison and contrast in the service of an idea, an argument, an interpretation. Your comparative analysis should lead you to a conclusion, perhaps to an evaluation, not merely to a set of parallels.
4. Decide whether to organize your comparative discussion according to the "block" method in which you discuss each subject separately; or according to the "alternating" method in which you discuss the two central subjects in point-by-point comparisons of specific characteristics. If you are comparing two characters, according to the block method, for example, you would devote the first half of your paper to one and the second half to the other character. If you followed the alternating structure, you would consider each side by side as you focused on such characteristics as their physical appearance, their interactions with other characters, their behavior at critical moments of the action, and so on.

Writing the Paper

Drafting

Once you have arrived at a tentative subject and an angle of approach, you are ready to write a rough draft of your paper. The purpose of this draft is simply to write down your ideas and to see how they can be developed and supported. Think of the rough draft as an opportunity to discover what you think about the subject and to test and refine your ideas. Don't worry about having a clearly defined thesis or main idea for your paper before beginning to write it. Instead, use your initial draft to discover an idea, to find a thesis and sharpen it so that your idea-thesis becomes clear, first to you and then to your readers.

In drafting your paper, consider your purpose. Are you writing to provide information and make observations about the work? Are you writing to argue for a particular way to interpret it? Ultimately, of course, all explanations of literary works are interpretations, and all interpretations are forms of argument. That is, they are persuasive attempts to see the literary text in one way rather than in other ways. When you write about a literary work you will often attempt to convince others that what you see and say about it makes sense. In doing so, you will be arguing for the validity of your way of seeing, not necessarily to the exclusion of all other ways, but to demonstrate that your understanding of the work is reasonable and valuable. Moreover, since your readers will respond as much to how you support your arguments as to your ideas themselves, you will need to concentrate on providing evidence for your ideas carefully and thoroughly. Most often this evidence will come in the form of textual support—details of action, dialogue, imagery, description, language, and structure. Additional evidence may come from secondary sources, from the comments of experienced readers whose observations and interpretations may influence and support your own thinking. In marshalling evidence for your ideas from the work itself and from secondary sources, however, keep the following guidelines in mind:

1. Be fair-minded. Avoid oversimplifying or distorting either the work or what others have written about it.
2. Be cautious. Qualify your claims. Limit your discussion to what you feel confident you can reasonably demonstrate.
3. Be logical. See that the various elements of your argument fit together and that one part of your approach doesn't contradict another.
4. Be accurate. If you present facts, details, or quotations, present them accurately.
5. Be confident. You should believe in your ideas and present them with conviction.

After writing the first draft, try to forget it for a while—for at least a day or two, longer if possible. When you return to it, assess whether what you are saying makes sense, whether you have provided enough examples to clarify your ideas and have presented sufficient evidence to make them persuasive. Read the draft critically, asking yourself what is convincing and what is not, what makes sense and what does not. Consider whether the draft centers on a single idea and stays on track. If the first draft accomplishes these things, you can begin thinking about how to tighten the paper's organization and polish its style. If, on the other hand, the draft contains frequent changes of direction and a number of different and unrelated ideas, then you will need to decide what to salvage and how to focus the paper more sharply. (This second scenario, by the way, is not uncommon in writing. It simply represents the way first efforts often begin: in some degree of confusion that eventually is dispelled with the emergence of a focus and the development of form.)

When you have written an acceptable draft, you are ready to view its organization more critically. A general organizational framework usually reveals an introductory section that clarifies your purpose and intention; a set of successive paragraphs that develop, explore, and explain your ideas; and a conclusion that rounds off the discussion. Within that framework, consider whether your ideas and examples have been arranged in a coherent and logical manner. Ask yourself whether the structure of your paper will be clear to readers. Consider also whether sufficient space (or perhaps too much space) has been allotted to clarifying and supporting your views. Ask someone to read your paper with an eye to its organization and structure.

Perhaps the most important aspect of organization is that you have a clear sense yourself of just how you are setting up the paper. You should be able to identify each part and explain how the parts are related. You should also be able to explain why you put them in the order you did. Consider the following example.

STEPHEN CRANE
[1871–1900]

War Is Kind

Do not weep, maiden, for war is kind.
Because your lover threw wild hands toward the sky
And the affrighted steed ran on alone,
Do not weep.
War is kind.   5

       Hoarse, booming drums of the regiment,
       Little souls who thirst for fight,
       These men were born to drill and die.
       The unexplained glory flies above them,
       Great is the battle god, great, and his kingdom   10
       A field where a thousand corpses lie.

Do not weep, babe, for war is kind.
Because your father tumbled in the yellow trenches,
Raged at his breast, gulped and died,
Do not weep.   15
War is kind.

       Swift blazing flag of the regiment,
       Eagle with crest of red and gold,

These men were born to drill and die.
Point for them the virtue of slaughter,   20
Make plain to them the excellence of killing
And a field where a thousand corpses lie.

Mother whose heart hung humble as a button
On the bright splendid shroud of your son,
Do not weep.   25
War is kind.

In discussing the ironic tone of "War Is Kind" you might focus on three or four details. You might decide to discuss first the ironic quality of the title. The word *kind* is not usually associated with war; war is associated instead with suffering, waste, death, and destruction. The title, then, cannot be taken literally. Next you might decide to include the speaker's advice to the lover, child, and mother of a slain soldier not to cry, since war is "kind." (These examples too will have to be arranged in a sequence that makes sense to you.) You will probably want to comment on how details such as the "field where a thousand corpses lie" and the soldier who "tumbled in the yellow trenches" can stand alongside the more seemingly patriotic images of regimental flag and thundering drums.

Whatever details you ultimately select, and however many you include, you will need to decide on a particular order in which to present them. Ask yourself how the ironic aspects of the poem can be related. Consider what these details contribute to the poem. Some details will seem more important than others; you may thus be able to subdivide and pair your examples, and perhaps contrast them. Or you may decide to consider them in order of increasing complexity, emotion, or importance. It is necessary, though, to devise an organizational plan that makes sense to you and that will seem sensible to your readers. If you write a comparative paper, your outline might look like this:

Ironic Contrasts in Crane's "War Is Kind"
  I. Advice to maiden
     A. Expectation: Sympathy for loss
     B. Reality: Command not to weep
        1. details horrible—not comforting
           a. "wild hands"
           b. "affrighted steed"
        2. repetition of "war is kind"
           a. emphasizes irony
           b. leads to stanza two, details of war
 II. Advice to babe
     A. Expectation: Commentary on sorrow
     B. Reality: Command not to weep
        1. details ugly—not noble
           a. "yellow trenches"
           b. "raged . . . gulped and died"

2. repetition of "war is kind"
   a. emphasizes irony
   b. leads to stanza three, details of war
III. Advice to mother
   A. Expectation: Empathy with bereavement
   B. Reality: Command not to weep
      1. details highlight ironic contrast
         a. mother's love is "humble as a button"
         b. son's shroud (furnished by military) is "bright" and "splendid"
      2. repetition of "war is kind"
         a. emphasizes irony
         b. ties together the three civilians who have suffered deep losses from "kind" war

On the other hand, you might want to examine the relationship of stanzas 1, 3, and 5 to stanzas 2 and 4. In that case, your outline might look like this:

War at Home and on the Battlefield
I. Repetition
   A. Stanzas 1, 3, 5 repeat "war is kind"
      1. represents the politic lies told to keep survivors quiet
      2. provides ironic contrast with details
   B. Stanzas 2, 4 repeat "A field where a thousand corpses lie"
      1. emphasizes the enormous losses of war
      2. contrasts with the "war is kind" lie told to those at home
      3. suggests that for everyone of the thousand corpses a "maiden," "babe," or "mother" mourns
II. Images: Effects of War
   A. Stanzas 1, 3, 5 show the sorrow of those left behind
      1. images suggest reality of death in war "threw wild hands"; "tumbled in the yellow trenches" which those at home must picture
      2. images suggest all that is left to those at home are empty symbols: "bright splendid shroud"
   B. Stanzas 2, 4 images show how the propaganda of war contrasts with its reality
      1. propaganda: "unexplained glory flies above them"; "Great is the battle god"; "Swift blazing flag of the regiment"
      2. reality: "drill and die"; "a thousand corpses lie"

Besides deciding on the order of ideas and examples in the paper and the amount of space allotted to each, you must consider how to move from one example to another. You will need to link the sections of your discussion so that the writing flows smoothly. Generally, you can create transitions with phrases and sentences at the beginnings of paragraphs. (Examples include such words and phrases as "first, . . . second, . . ."; "on the other hand, . . ."; "in addition to . . ."; "another way in which . . . .") Sometimes, however, such explicit marks of transition from one point to another will not be necessary: careful ordering of the details that support your argument will be evidence enough of how one paragraph follows from and is related to another.

Revising

Revision is not something that occurs only once, at the end of the writing process. Redrafting your paper to consider the ordering of paragraphs and the use of examples is itself a significant act of revision. So too is rereading the work and thinking about it a second or third time. Revision occurs throughout the entire span of reading and writing. It requires you to reconsider your writing and your thinking not once, but several times. This reconsideration is made on three levels: conceptual, organizational, and stylistic.

Conceptual revision involves reconsidering your ideas. As you write a first or second draft, your understanding of the work and what you plan to say about it may change. While accumulating textual evidence in support of one interpretation of the work, you may discover stronger evidence for a contrasting view. When this happens, you may need to go back to the note-taking stage to explore your revised vision of the work. You will then need to make major changes in the original draft. You may end up discarding much of it and beginning again with a stronger conviction about a different approach or a revised idea. In writing about Crane's "War Is Kind," for example, you may have started out with a literal interpretation, arguing that the poem is patriotic rather than ironic. Developing your idea, however, you may have become uneasy with certain details that run counter to your interpretation and that prompt you to change your mind about what the poem means. In that case, you revise your idea and begin again.

Organizational or structural revision involves asking yourself whether the arrangement best presents your line of thinking. Is the organizational framework readily discernible? Does it make sense? Have you written an introduction that clarifies your topic and intention? Have you organized your supporting details in a sensible and logical manner? Does your conclusion follow logically from your discussion and bring it to a satisfying close? Again, taking Crane's poem as an example, you might begin by identifying its general subject—war—and move toward suggesting that even though the poem contains some language that idealizes war, its details and its tone undermine a romanticized conception. From there you would move to the body of your argument, in which you would present details that appear supportive of war's glory and show how other details of incident and language contradict them. Capping your argument/interpretation would be a precise analysis of the poem's ironies. In your conclusion, you would repeat your main point, perhaps responding personally to the poem as you understand it. You could also relate the poem to some other work you've read (by Crane or by another writer), and perhaps include an apt quotation that sums up your sense of the work's significance.

However you choose to end your paper, remember that your conclusion should answer the question: "So what?" for your reader. Even though you have presented details, reasons, and examples to support your views, your reader will still expect you to explain their significance.

Stylistic revision concerns smaller-scale details, such as matters of syntax (word order), diction (word choice), tone, imagery, and rhythm. Even though you may think about these things in early drafts, it is better to defer critical attention to them until after writing a final draft, largely because such stylistic considerations may undergo significant alteration as you rethink and reorganize your paper.

To help you focus on aspects of style that may require revision, use the following questions as a guide.

1. Are your sentences concise and clear?
2. Can you eliminate words that are not doing their job?
3. Are your tone and voice consistent? (For example, you should eliminate shifts from a formal to an informal, or colloquial, style.)
4. Is your level of language appropriate for the subject of your paper?
5. Do your words and sentences say what you want them to? Do they say anything you don't want them to?
6. Are there any grammatical errors: inconsistencies in verb tenses, problems with subject-verb agreement, run-on sentences, fragments, and the like?
7. Are there any errors in spelling and punctuation?

As a final step, proofread the paper, and make sure it conforms to your instructor's guidelines on manuscript form.

Fiction

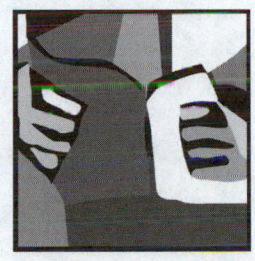

PART ONE

CHAPTER ONE

Reading Stories

We read stories for pleasure; they entertain us. And we read them for profit; they enlighten us. Stories draw us into their imaginative worlds and engage us with the power of their invention. They provide us with more than the immediate interest of narrative—of something happening—and more than the pleasures of imagination: they enlarge our understanding of ourselves and deepen our appreciation of life.

Consider this famous early story about a father and his two sons:

The Prodigal Son

A certain man had two sons: and the younger of them said to his father, "Father, give me the portion of goods that falleth to me." And he divided unto them his living. And not many days after, the younger son gathered all together, and took his journey into a far country, and there wasted his substance with riotous living. And when he had spent all, there arose a mighty famine in that land, and he began to be in want. And he went and joined himself to a citizen of that country, and he sent him into his fields to feed swine. And he would fain have filled his belly with the husks that the swine did eat: and no man gave unto him. And when he came to himself, he said, "How many hired servants of my father's have bread enough and to spare, and I perish with hunger? I will arise and go to my father, and will say unto him, 'Father, I have sinned against heaven, and before thee. And am no more worthy to be called thy son: make me as one of thy hired servants.'" And he arose, and came to his father. But when he was yet a great way off, his father saw him, and had compassion, and ran, and fell on his neck, and kissed him. And the son said unto him, "Father, I have sinned against heaven, and in thy sight, and am no more worthy to be called thy son." But the father said to his servants, "Bring forth the best robe, and put it on him, and put a ring on his hand, and shoes on his feet. And bring hither the fatted calf, and kill it, and let us eat, and be merry. For this my son was dead, and is alive again; he was lost, and is found." And they began to be merry. Now his elder son was in the field, and as he came and drew nigh to the house, he heard music and dancing. And he called one of the servants, and asked what these things meant. And he said unto him, "Thy brother is come, and thy father hath killed the fatted calf, because he hath received him safe and sound." And he was angry, and would not go in: therefore came his father out, and entreated him. And he answering said to his father, "Lo, these many years do I serve thee, neither transgressed I at any time thy commandment, and yet thou never gavest me a kid, that I might make merry with my friends: but as soon as this thy son was come, which hath de-voured thy living with harlots, thou hast killed for him the fatted calf." And he said unto him, "Son, thou art ever with me, and all that I have is thine. It was meet that we should make merry, and be glad: for this thy brother was dead, and is alive again: and was lost, and is found."

When we read the story of "The Prodigal Son," we do essentially three things: (1) we take in its surface features, and form impressions of character and action; (2) we observe details, make connections among them, and draw in-ferences and conclusions from those connections; (3) we evaluate the story, measuring its moral, political, and cultural values against our own. We can call these three aspects of the reading process: "experience," "interpretation," and "evaluation."

THE EXPERIENCE OF FICTION

Our "experience" of fiction concerns our feelings about the characters, our sense of involvement in the story's developing action, our pleasure or confusion in its language, our joy or sorrow at its outcome. We are concerned, in short, with what the story does to us, how it affects us—and why.

How did you react to "The Prodigal Son"? What feelings did the story evoke? Did you feel sorry for the prodigal son? Did you feel anger or re-sentment at his behavior? At his father's or brother's behavior? Did your feelings about any of the characters change during the course of your read-ing or afterward? How does the story relate to your experiences as a member of a family? How does it reflect what you have observed of family relations generally?

It is important to remember that readers respond to stories in different ways. When you compare the reactions of your classmates and teacher to "The Prodigal Son," you will discover different perceptions, attitudes, and feelings about it. Why is this so? Essentially, because we bring to our reading a wide range of personal experience, social attitudes, religious beliefs, and cultural dispositions that influence our responses. We do not read a story in a vacuum: our reading is always affected by who we are, what we believe, and how we think. Christians, for example, experience "The Prodigal Son" differently from Muslims, Buddhists, or atheists. Women experience the story differently from men. Practiced readers experience the story differently from inexperienced ones. But it is not only our religious beliefs, family background, and literary sophistication that create divergent reactions. We ourselves change: we grow older; we learn more. We shift our allegiances and develop new ideas, attitudes, and beliefs. We may become parents ourselves. And in making any or all of these changes, our ways of understanding life and literature change too.

In sorting out our thoughts and feelings about "The Prodigal Son," we have been emphasizing our subjective impressions of the story—how it affects us. But while we experience a story subjectively, we are also interpreting and evaluating it. This is inevitable, since the three parts of reading are interrelated.

THE INTERPRETATION OF FICTION

When we interpret a story we explain it to ourselves and try to make sense of it. We form subjective impressions as we experience fiction, but we have relatively objective considerations in mind when we interpret it. We say "relatively" objective because no reading of a story is entirely objective: every interpretation is one way of understanding the text among many; every interpretation is influenced by our particular language, culture, and experience. What then do we mean by *interpretation?* Understanding, essentially. An interpretation is an argument about a story's meaning as we understand it. It's our way of stating and supporting, with arguments based on analysis, what the story *means,* what it says or suggests, rather than how it affects us. Interpretation, in short, relies on our intellectual comprehension rather than on our emotional response to the literary work.

Interpretation involves four related intellectual acts: observing, connecting, inferring, and concluding. To understand a fictional work, we first observe its details. We notice, for example, descriptive details about the time and place of its action; we listen carefully to what the characters say and to their manner of saying it; we note how the characters interact. As we observe, we make connections among the details and begin to formulate a sense of the story's emphasis and point. On the basis of these connections we develop inferences or interpretive hypotheses about their significance. Finally, we come to some conclusion about the story's meaning based on our observations, connections, and inferences.

The four interpretive actions of observing, connecting, inferring, and concluding often occur simultaneously, and not in neatly segregated sequential stages. We don't delay making inferences, for example, until after we have registered and related all our observations. Instead, we develop tentative conclusions *as* we read and observe, *while* we relate our observations and develop our inferences. We may change and adjust our inferences and provisional conclusions both *during* our reading of a story and *afterward* as we think back over its details. This analytical process, however, is not something we keep separate from our subjective reactions and emotional responses as we read.

In "The Prodigal Son," for example, we notice that the father sees his younger son coming from far off, that he runs to him, falls on his neck, and kisses him. Such details imply that the father has been watching for his son and hoping for his return. The father's actions speak eloquently of his unreserved acceptance of his son and deep joy at his return. Reflecting on these actions, we may connect them with the father's behavior toward his elder son and wonder what is responsible for the difference. In the process of noticing and wondering, we may also respond emotionally, thinking perhaps of our own experience or of the situation of someone we know. And we may evaluate the father's behavior according to standards we adhere to either consciously or unconsciously. The point, then, is simply that even in performing the rational, analytical act of interpretation, we cannot entirely escape a tendency to respond emotionally or to evaluate.

But our approach to interpreting stories involves something else as well: that we see a story as a story, and even more important as a particular *kind* of story. We know, for example, that "The Prodigal Son" is not a factual account of the actions of a particular father and son. A journalistic account would have included their names, perhaps their ages and address, and details about the son's behavior in the foreign land, which would have been identified. But the story gives none of this information. In fact, the details included are not those we would typically expect to find in a newspaper. It's not just that "The Prodigal Son" is short on information, but that it goes out of its way to include the kind of repetitions, for example, that would be considered unnecessary in a factual account.

It is helpful to know that "The Prodigal Son" is *fiction,* an imagined story that is not based on historical fact, and to know the conventions or implicit rules of fiction. For this story is also more than fiction to be distinguished from fact; it is a particular kind of fiction—a *parable* or brief story that teaches a lesson, often religious or spiritual in nature. As someone once cleverly put it, a parable is "an earthly story with a heavenly meaning." Parables point toward spiritual beliefs or truths and should be read symbolically, with emphasis on their spiritual meaning.

But we must go further. "The Prodigal Son" is a Christian parable—not a Hebrew or Zen parable. It was spoken by Jesus roughly two thousand years ago and recorded by the evangelist Luke in his New Testament Gospel. Thus, we look to the parable for a religious idea consistent with Jesus's teaching. It has a religious meaning that may be paraphrased like this: God (the father) is willing to forgive man (the prodigal son) any sin man commits, no matter how grievous, if only he repents and asks God's forgiveness. Alternatively: God is eager to welcome the sinner back, and in fact is happier at his return than with the fidelity of those in no spiritual danger. We can read the parable, thus, as an example of God's love, as an illustration of man's need for repentance, as a description of the relationship between God and man—or as all three.

Whatever we decide about its religious meaning, we should realize that "The Prodigal Son" means more than any interpretive comments we can make about it. This is so because the full meaning of any literary work includes our experience in reading it as well as our understanding of it—our *emotional apprehension* as well as our *intellectual comprehension*. And it includes, further, our perceptions of what is valuable, important, significant about it, for these perceptions reflect our own social, political, moral, and cultural values.

THE EVALUATION OF FICTION

The third part of our approach to reading fiction is evaluation. When we evaluate a story we do two different things. First, we assess its literary quality; we make a judgment about how good it is, how successfully it realizes its intentions, how effectively it pleases us. Second, we consider the values the story endorses—or refutes.

An evaluation is essentially a judgment, an opinion about a work formulated as a conclusion. We may agree or disagree with the father's forgiveness or the elder brother's complaint in "The Prodigal Son." We may confirm or deny the models of behavior illustrated in this or any other story. However we evaluate them, though, we invariably measure the story's values against our own.

Although evaluation is partly an unconscious process, we can make it more deliberate and more fully conscious. We simply need to ask ourselves how we respond to the values a work supports, and why. In doing so we should be able to consider our own values more clearly and perhaps discuss more sensibly and fairly why we agree or disagree with the values a story displays.

When we evaluate a story, we appraise it according to our own special combination of cultural, moral, and aesthetic values. Our cultural values derive from our lives as members of families and societies. These values are affected by our race and gender and by the language we speak. Our moral values reflect our ethical norms—what we consider to be good and evil, right and wrong. These values are influenced by our religious beliefs and sometimes by our political convictions. Our aesthetic values determine what we see as beautiful or ugly, well or ill made. Over time, with education and experience, our values often change. Through contact with other languages and cultures, we may come to understand the limiting perspectives of our own. When we live with people other than our immediate families, we may be persuaded to different ways of seeing many things we previously took for granted. Some of our beliefs, assumptions, and attitudes about religion, family, marriage, sex, love, school, work, money, and other aspects of life are almost sure to change.

As our lives and outlooks change, we may change the way we view particular literary works. A story that we once admired for what it reveals about human behavior or one whose moral perspective impressed us may come to seem trivial or unimportant. Conversely, we may find that a work we once disliked later seems engaging. Just as individual tastes in literature change over time, so do collective literary tastes. Culture evolves; moral beliefs, aesthetic values, and social attitudes change. Literary works, like musical compositions and political ideas, go in and out of fashion.

Our evaluation of a story depends upon interpretation; our judgment of a story depends on how we understand it. Our evaluation may also be linked to our first experience of the story, to first impressions based on unconsidered reactions. If our initial reaction to a story or a character is unsympathetic, we may be reluctant to change our interpretation later, even if we discover convincing evidence to warrant such a change.

Of the kinds of evaluations we make in reading fiction, those about a story's aesthetic qualities are hardest to discuss. Aesthetic responses are difficult to describe because they involve our memories and sensations, our feelings and perceptions, our subjective impressions. They also involve our expectations, which are further affected by our prior experience of reading fiction. And they are additionally complicated by our tendency to react quickly and decisively to what we like and dislike, often without knowing why. Consider the aesthetic value of "The Prodigal Son." Is it a "beautiful" story? Does it seem to be a good example of its kind—the religious parable which teaches lessons about divine forgiveness? (Or should we emphasize its human dimension, especially the relationships between people?) As we mentioned in the discussion of interpretation, understanding what kind of work we are reading affects how we interpret it. Similarly, our perception of its genre or kind also affects our evaluation. Our preference for one kind of fiction over another complicates matters still further. (We may dislike ironic stories, for example, or we may love melodrama and adventure.) When we evaluate a story, we should judge it against what it attempts to do, what it is, rather than against something it is not.

How we arrive at an aesthetic evaluation is no easy matter. We develop our aesthetic responses to fiction by letting the informed responses of other experienced readers enrich our own perceptions, by determining the criteria for what makes a story "good," and by gradually developing our sense of literary tact—the kind of balanced judgment that comes with experience in reading and living coupled with thoughtful reflection on both. There are no shortcuts or simple formulas for this development; it comes only with practice and patience.

Admittedly, without a good deal of experience in reading fiction, judgments about the values supported in a story and about its aesthetic worth need to be made cautiously. But we must begin somewhere, since evaluation is inevitable. We cannot really avoid judging the stories we read any more than we can avoid judging the people we meet. The process is natural. What we should strive for in evaluating fiction is to understand the different kinds of values it presents, and to clarify our own attitudes, dispositions, and values in responding to them.

Consider the values in John Updike's "A & P." Evaluate the behavior of each of the major characters, particularly Sammy and Lengel. Consider their attitudes toward the three girls in the story and what those attitudes reveal about each of the males. Try to assess what part your experiences and personal values play in your assessment of the story, both as an embodiment of cultural values and as an object of aesthetic value.

JOHN UPDIKE
[*b. 1932*]

A & P

In walks these three girls in nothing but bathing suits. I'm in the third check-out slot, with my back to the door, so I don't see them until they're over by the bread. The one that caught my eye first was the one in the plaid green two-piece. She was a chunky kid, with a good tan and a sweet broad soft-looking can with those two crescents of white just under it, where the sun never seems to hit, at the top of the backs of her legs. I stood there with my hand on a box of HiHo crackers trying to remember if I rang it up or not. I ring it up again and the customer starts giving me hell. She's one of these cash-register-watchers, a witch about fifty with rouge on her cheekbones and no eyebrows, and I know it made her day to trip me up. She'd been watching cash registers for fifty years and probably never seen a mistake before.

By the time I got her feathers smoothed and her goodies into a bag—she gives me a little snort in passing, if she'd been born at the right time they would have burned her over in Salem—by the time I get her on her way the girls had circled around the bread and were coming back, without a pushcart, back my way along the counters, in the aisle between the check-outs and the Special bins. They didn't even have shoes on. There was this chunky one, with the two-piece—it was bright green and the seams on the bra were still sharp and her belly was still pretty pale so I guessed she just got it (the suit)—there was this one, with one of those chubby berry-faces, the lips all bunched together under her nose, this one, and a tall one, with black hair that hadn't quite frizzed right, and one of these sunburns right across under the eyes, and a chin that was too long—you know, the kind of girl other girls think is very "striking" and "attractive" but never quite makes it, as they very well know, which is why they like her so much—and then the third one, that wasn't quite so tall. She was the queen. She kind of led them, the other two peeking around and making their shoulders round. She didn't look around, not this queen, she just walked straight on slowly, on these long white prima donna legs. She came down a little hard on her heels, as if she didn't walk in her bare feet that much, putting down her heels and then letting the weight move along to her toes as if she was testing the floor with every step, putting a little deliberate extra action into it. You never know for sure how girls' minds work (do you really think it's a mind in there or just a little buzz like a bee in a glass jar?) but you got the idea she had talked the other two into coming in here with her, and now she was showing them how to do it, walk slow and hold yourself straight.

She had on a kind of dirty-pink—beige maybe, I don't know—bathing suit with a little nubble all over it and, what got me, the straps were down. They were off her shoulders looped loose around the cool tops of her arms, and I guess as a result the suit had slipped a little on her, so all around the top of the cloth there was this shining rim. If it hadn't been there you wouldn't have known there could have been anything whiter than those shoulders. With the straps pushed off, there was nothing between the top of the suit and the top of her head except just *her,* this clean bare plane of the top of her chest down from the shoulder bones like a dented sheet of metal tilted in the light. I mean, it was more than pretty.

She had sort of oaky hair that the sun and salt had bleached, done up in a bun that was unravelling, and a kind of prim face. Walking into the A & P with your straps down, I suppose it's the only kind of face you *can* have. She held her head so high her neck, coming up out of those white shoulders, looked kind of stretched, but I didn't mind. The longer her neck was, the more of her there was.

She must have felt in the corner of her eye me and over my shoulder Stokesie in the second slot watching, but she didn't tip. Not this queen. She kept her eyes moving across the racks, and stopped, and turned so slow it made my stomach rub the inside of my apron, and buzzed to the other two, who kind of huddled against her for relief, and they all three of them went up the cat-and-dog-food-breakfast-cereal-macaroni-rice-raisins-seasonings-spreads-spaghetti-soft-drinks-crackers-and-cookies aisle. From the third slot I look straight up this aisle to the meat counter, and I watched them all the way. The fat one with the tan sort of fumbled with the cookies, but on second thought she put the packages back. The sheep pushing their carts down the aisle—the girls were walking against the usual traffic (not that we have one-way signs or any-thing)—were pretty hilarious. You could see them, when Queenie's white shoulders dawned on them, kind of jerk, or hop, or hiccup, but their eyes snapped back to their own baskets and on they pushed. I bet you could set off dynamite in an A & P and the people would by and large keep reaching and checking oatmeal off their lists and mut-tering "Let me see, there was a third thing, began with A, asparagus, no, ah, yes, apple-sauce!" or whatever it is they do mutter. But there was no doubt, this jiggled them. A few houseslaves in pin curlers even looked around after pushing their carts past to make sure what they had seen was correct.

You know, it's one thing to have a girl in a bathing suit down on the beach, where what with the glare nobody can look at each other much anyway, and another thing in the cool of the A & P, under the fluorescent lights, against all those stacked pack-ages, with her feet paddling along naked over our checkerboard green-and-cream rubber-tile floor.

"Oh Daddy," Stokesie said beside me. "I feel so faint."

"Darling," I said. "Hold me tight." Stokesie's married, with two babies chalked up on his fuselage already, but as far as I can tell that's the only difference. He's twenty-two, and I was nineteen this April.

"Is it done?" he asks, the responsible married man finding his voice. I forgot to say he thinks he's going to be manager some sunny day, maybe in 1990 when it's called the Great Alexandrov and Petrooshki Tea Company or something.

What he meant was, our town is five miles from a beach, with a big summer colony out on the Point, but we're right in the middle of town, and the women generally put on a shirt or shorts or something before they get out of the car into the street. And anyway these are usually women with six children and varicose veins mapping their legs and nobody, including them, could care less. As I say, we're right in the middle of town, and if you stand at our front doors you can see two banks and the Congrega-tional church and the newspaper store and three real-estate offices and about twenty-seven old freeloaders tearing up Central Street because the sewer broke again. It's not as if we're on the Cape; we're north of Boston and there's people in this town haven't seen the ocean for twenty years.

The girls had reached the meat counter and were asking McMahon something. He pointed, they pointed, and they shuffled out of sight behind a pyramid of Diet Delight peaches. All that was left for us to see was old McMahon patting his mouth and looking after them sizing up their joints. Poor kids, I began to feel sorry for them, they couldn't help it.

Now here comes the sad part of the story, at least my family says it's sad but I don't think it's sad myself. The store's pretty empty, it being Thursday afternoon, so there was nothing much to do except lean on the register and wait for the girls to show up again. The whole store was like a pinball machine and I didn't know which tunnel they'd come out of. After a while they come around out of the far aisle, around the light bulbs, records at discount of the Caribbean Six or Tony Martin Sings or some such gunk you wonder they waste the wax on, sixpacks of candy bars, and plastic toys done up in cellophane that fall apart when a kid looks at them anyway. Around they come, Queenie still leading the way, and holding a little gray jar in her hand. Slots Three through Seven are unmanned and I could see her wondering between Stokes and me, but Stokesie with his usual luck draws an old party in baggy gray pants who stumbles up with four giant cans of pineapple juice (what do these bums *do* with all that pineapple juice? I've often asked myself) so the girls come to me. Queenie puts down the jar and I take it into my fingers icy cold. Kingfish Fancy Herring Snacks in Pure Sour Cream: 49¢. Now her hands are empty, not a ring or a bracelet, bare as God made them, and I wonder where the money's coming from. Still with that prim look she lifts a folded dollar bill out of the hollow at the center of her nubbled pink top. The jar went heavy in my hand. Really, I thought that was so cute.

Then everybody's luck begins to run out. Lengel comes in from haggling with a truck full of cabbages on the lot and is about to scuttle into that door marked MAN-AGER behind which he hides all day when the girls touch his eye. Lengel's pretty dreary, teaches Sunday school and the rest, but he doesn't miss that much. He comes over and says, "Girls, this isn't the beach."

Queenie blushes, though maybe it's just a brush of sunburn I was noticing for the first time, now that she was so close. "My mother asked me to pick up a jar of herring snacks." Her voice kind of startled me, the way voices do when you see the people first, coming out so flat and dumb yet kind of tony, too, the way it ticked over "pick up" and "snacks." All of a sudden I slid right down her voice into her living room. Her father and the other men were standing around in ice-cream coats and bow ties and the women were in sandals picking up herring snacks on toothpicks off a big plate and they were all holding drinks the color of water with olives and sprigs of mint in them. When my parents have somebody over they get lemonade and if it's a real racy affair Schlitz in tall glasses with "They'll Do It Every Time" cartoons stenciled on.

"That's all right," Lengel said. "But this isn't the beach." His repeating this struck me as funny, as if it had just occurred to him, and he had been thinking all these years the A & P was a great big dune and he was the head lifeguard. He didn't like my smiling— as I say he doesn't miss much—but he concentrates on giving the girls that sad Sunday-school-superintendent stare.

Queenie's blush is no sunburn now, and the plump one in plaid, that I liked better from the back—a really sweet can—pipes up, "We weren't doing any shopping. We just came in for the one thing."

"That makes no difference," Lengel tells her, and I could see from the way his eyes went that he hadn't noticed she was wearing a two-piece before. "We want you decently dressed when you come in here."

"We *are* decent," Queenie says suddenly, her lower lip pushing, getting sore now that she remembers her place, a place from which the crowd that runs the A & P must look pretty crummy. Fancy Herring Snacks flashed in her very blue eyes.

"Girls, I don't want to argue with you. After this come in here with your shoulders covered. It's our policy." He turns his back. That's policy for you. Policy is what the kingpins want. What the others want is juvenile delinquency.

All this while, the customers had been showing up with their carts but, you know, sheep, seeing a scene, they had all bunched up on Stokesie, who shook open a paper bag as gently as peeling a peach, not wanting to miss a word. I could feel in the silence everybody getting nervous, most of all Lengel, who asks me, "Sammy, have you rung up this purchase?"

I thought and said "No" but it wasn't about that I was thinking. I go through the punches, 4, 9, GROC, TOT—it's more complicated than you think, and after you do it often enough, it begins to make a little song, that you hear words to, in my case "Hello *(bing)* there, you *(gung)* hap-py *pee-pul (splat)!*"—the *splat* being the drawer flying out. I uncrease the bill, tenderly as you may imagine, it just having come from between the two smoothest scoops of vanilla I had ever known were there, and pass a half and a penny into her narrow pink palm, and nestle the herrings in a bag and twist its neck and hand it over, all the time thinking.

The girls, and who'd blame them, are in a hurry to get out, so I say "I quit" to Lengel quick enough for them to hear, hoping they'll stop and watch me, their unsuspected hero. They keep right on going, into the electric eye; the door flies open and they flicker across the lot to their car, Queenie and Plaid and Big Tall Goony-Goony (not that as raw material she was so bad), leaving me with Lengel and a kink in his eyebrow.

"Did you say something, Sammy?"

"I said I quit."

"I thought you did."

"You didn't have to embarrass them."

"It was they who were embarrassing us."

I started to say something that came out "Fiddle-de-doo." It's a saying of my grandmother's, and I know she would have been pleased.

"I don't think you know what you're saying," Lengel said.

"I know you don't," I said. "But I do." I pull the bow at the back of my apron and start shrugging it off my shoulders. A couple customers that had been heading for my slot begin to knock against each other, like scared pigs in a chute.

Lengel sighs and begins to look very patient and old and gray. He's been a friend of my parents for years. "Sammy, you don't want to do this to your Mom and Dad," he tells me. It's true, I don't. But it seems to me that once you begin a gesture it's fatal not to go through with it. I fold the apron, "Sammy" stitched in red on the pocket, and put it on the counter, and drop the bow tie on top of it. The bow tie is theirs, if you've ever wondered. "You'll feel this for the rest of your life," Lengel says, and I know that's true, too, but remembering how he made that pretty girl blush makes me so scrunchy inside I punch the No Sale tab and the machine whirs "pee-pul" and the drawer splats out. One advantage to this scene taking place in summer, I can follow this up with a clean exit, there's no fumbling around getting your coat and galoshes, I just saunter into the electric eye in my white shirt that my mother ironed the night before, and the door heaves itself open, and outside the sunshine is skating around on the asphalt.

I look around for my girls, but they're gone, of course. There wasn't anybody but some young married screaming with her children about some candy they didn't get by the door of a powder-blue Falcon station wagon. Looking back in the big windows, over the bags of peat moss and aluminum lawn furniture stacked on the pavement, I could see Lengel in my place in the slot, checking the sheep through. His face was dark gray and his back stiff, as if he'd just had an injection of iron, and my stomach kind of fell as I felt how hard the world was going to be to me hereafter.

(1961)

Use the following questions about "A & P" as a way of reviewing the three aspects of reading fiction we have discussed: experience, interpretation, and evaluation.

QUESTIONS FOR REFLECTION

Experience

1. Describe your experience in reading "A & P." Did the story surprise you, entertain you, annoy you? Why? Did the story engage you and hold your interest? Why or why not?
2. Consider the attitude expressed toward the girls by both Sammy and Lengel. Whose attitude do you find more appealing? Why? Do you object to Sammy's (and perhaps Updike's) language in describing Queenie—her name, her "white prima donna legs," her "two scoops of vanilla"?
3. Did your feelings about either Lengel or Sammy change in the course of reading? If so, explain where the shift occurred and why. Did they change later, on additional reflection?

Interpretation

4. Characterize Sammy's style of telling his story. What do you learn about him from the kind of language he uses? From the details he includes? From the comparisons he employs to describe the store, the girls, and the other shoppers?
5. Look back to the story's climactic point, in which Sammy says, "I quit." Are there other passages of description, dialogue, or action that you see as closely related to this one?
6. How do you interpret Sammy's own response to his action? What does he mean by saying that he "felt how hard the world was going to be" for him afterwards?

Evaluation

7. Whose values does the story seem to endorse? Whose values are criticized? How do you know? How do you see Sammy's decisive action? As heroic? As silly? Something else? Why?
8. Do you find the story meaningful? Can you relate it in any significant way to your own life?
9. Do you think it is a good story, a successful example of realistic fiction? Do you find anything in it to admire from the standpoint of its language or structure?
10. Compare "A & P" to another realistic short story you have read. Which is more valuable for you? Why? Which is the more artistically wrought work? Why?

THE ACT OF READING FICTION

When we move through a text we look forward and backward at the same time: we anticipate what is to come based on our memory of what has gone before. And even though we may read stories line by line, sentence by sentence, page by page, this linearity belies what happens mentally as we read. Our mental action is cyclical rather than linear. We project ahead and we glance back; we remember and we predict. By doing so, we are able to follow and understand a story in the first place, and to see more in it on subsequent readings.

To exemplify the actual process of reading a short work of fiction, we provide a stop-and-go reading of Kate Chopin's "The Story of an Hour." The story is "chunked," or broken up, into seven sections. Between these sections of the story are interpolated comments that make observations and raise questions about the story's details. These interpolated comments reflect the actual process of one reader's act of reading—his thinking about the story during his reading of it. The comments do not so much interpret the story as illustrate the act of reading; they represent the kinds of observations, inferences, and judgments we make as we move toward an understanding of the story—toward some ways of seeing and thinking about it.

KATE CHOPIN

[1851–1904]

The Story of an Hour

Knowing that Mrs. Mallard was afflicted with a heart trouble, great care was taken to break to her as gently as possible the news of her husband's death.

It was her sister Josephine who told her, in broken sentences, veiled hints that revealed in half concealing. Her husband's friend Richards was there, too, near her. It was he who had been in the newspaper office when intelligence of the railroad disaster was received, with Brently Mallard's name leading the list of "killed." He had only taken the time to assure himself of its truth by a second telegram, and had hastened to forestall any less careful, less tender friend in bearing the sad message.

She did not hear the story as many women have heard the same, with a paralyzed inability to accept its significance. She wept at once, with sudden, wild abandonment, in her sister's arms. When the storm of grief had spent itself she went away to her room alone. She would have no one follow her.

Comment   The opening action is presented quickly and economically. We are not given Mrs. Mallard's first name. And we might wonder if there is any significance in the name "Mallard." Do we hear something odd in the description of Mrs. Mallard's ailment as a "heart trouble"? More important than these details is the announcement of her husband's death. Mrs. Mallard is contrasted with other women who sit paralyzed by such news—women who refuse, initially at least, to accept the significance of such an announcement. Is there a difference between accepting the significance of a husband's death and accepting the simple fact of his death? We notice, finally, that Mrs. Mallard weeps with "sudden wild abandonment."

There stood, facing the open window, a comfortable, roomy armchair. Into this she sank, pressed down by a physical exhaustion that haunted her body and seemed to reach into her soul.

She could see in the open square before her house the tops of trees that were all aquiver with the new spring life. The delicious breath of rain was in the air. In the street below a peddler was crying his wares. The notes of a distant song which some one was singing reached her faintly, and countless sparrows were twittering in the eaves.

There were patches of blue sky showing here and there through the clouds that had met and piled above the other in the west facing her window.

She sat with her head thrown back upon the cushion of the chair quite motionless, except when a sob came up into her throat and shook her, as a child who has cried itself to sleep continues to sob in its dreams.

Comment   The setting for the middle section of the story is Mrs. Mallard's room. Is the open window through which she looks of any significance? Do the details that follow—trees, birds, rain, patches of blue sky, peddler, and song—have anything in common? We notice also that Mrs. Mallard is compared to a child who sobs in its dreams and may wonder about the implications of this comparison.

She was young, with a fair, calm face, whose lines bespoke repression and even a certain strength. But now there was a dull stare in her eyes, whose gaze was fixed away off yonder on one of those patches of blue sky. It was not a glance of reflection, but rather indicated a suspension of intelligent thought.

There was something coming to her and she was waiting for it, fearfully. What was it? She did not know; it was too subtle and elusive to name. But she felt it, creeping out of the sky, reaching toward her through the sounds, the scents, the color that filled the air.

Now her bosom rose and fell tumultuously. She was beginning to recognize this thing that was approaching to possess her, and she was striving to beat it back with her will—as powerless as her two white slender hands would have been.

Comment These paragraphs alter slightly the tone and pace of the story. We are not told what Mrs. Mallard is waiting for. Whatever it is, however, she *feels* it; she senses it coming as she looks out the window. And we see her resisting it—powerlessly. Do we perhaps also hear sexual overtones in the description of what is "approaching to possess" her? Or do we wish to assign religious or psychological significance to this imminent possession and her ambivalent feelings about it? We notice, in addition, that Mrs. Mallard is described as not conscious of what is happening to her. Chopin says that there is "a suspension of intelligent thought." She seems to *feel* rather than think.

When she abandoned herself a little whispered word escaped her slightly parted lips. She said it over and over under her breath: "Free, free, free!" The vacant stare and the look of terror that had followed it went from her eyes. They stayed keen and bright. Her pulse beat fast, and the coursing blood warmed and relaxed every inch of her body.

Comment In the first sentence the word "abandoned" echoes the earlier description of Mrs. Mallard's "wild abandonment." But she now seems in control of herself. Her repetition of "free" signals her excitement and perhaps convinces her of its truth. Her emotional excitement is rendered in physical imagery: her pulse beats fast, and her blood courses through her body—both signs of reawakened feeling.

She did not stop to ask if it were not a monstrous joy that held her. A clear and exalted perception enabled her to dismiss the suggestion as trivial.

She knew that she would weep again when she saw the kind, tender hands folded in death; the face that had never looked save with love upon her, fixed and gray and dead. But she saw beyond that bitter moment a long procession of years to come that would belong to her absolutely. And she opened and spread her arms out to them in welcome.

There would be no one to live for during those coming years; she would live for herself. There would be no powerful will bending her in that blind persistence with which men and women believe they have a right to impose a private will upon a fellow-creature. A kind intention or a cruel intention made the act seem no less a crime as she looked upon it in that brief moment of illumination.

And yet she had loved him—sometimes. Often she had not. What did it matter! What could love, the unsolved mystery, count for in face of this possession of self-assertion which she suddenly recognized as the strongest impulse of her being!

Comment We pause over the words "monstrous joy." Clearly Mrs. Mallard is overjoyed. And from one perspective her joy, however honestly felt, is monstrous. She is happy—exultantly happy—that her husband is dead. But the author makes clear that Mrs. Mallard does not think about what she is feeling.

The first paragraph underscores Mrs. Mallard's control and clear-sightedness. Her sense of confidence, anticipated earlier, becomes explicit and strong. We wonder if her husband treated her cruelly, but the text answers that he has been kind, which makes Mrs. Mallard's open-armed welcome of the coming years indeed monstrous. In the next paragraph Chopin does not exactly condemn Mr. Mallard but does suggest that Mrs. Mallard had to bend her will to his. Kind or not, he controlled her; loving wife or not, she resented it. Chopin here seems to move beyond the case of a particularly unhappy wife to the larger issue of the bonds of marriage, using language that strongly condemns the husband's dominance. We hear it in such words and phrases as "powerful will bending hers," "blind persistence," "impose," and "crime." This language is balanced by a lyrical evocation of Mrs. Mallard, in the years to come, living for herself rather than for her husband. The moment is described as "that brief moment of illumination." This description builds on the earlier description of her eyes as "keen and bright." Mrs. Mallard is possessed by a new sense of herself and a new self-confidence as she envisions her future life. This is the turning point of her life, a moment of recognition, insight, and enlightenment that makes her previous life with her husband pale into insignificance.

The next paragraphs could end the story:

"Free! Body and soul free!" she kept whispering.

Josephine was kneeling before the closed door with her lips to the keyhole, imploring for admission. "Louise, open the door! I beg; open the door—you will make yourself ill. What are you doing, Louise? For heaven's sake open the door."

"Go away. I am not making myself ill." No; she was drinking in a very elixir of life through that open window.

Her fancy was running riot along those days ahead of her. Spring days, and summer days, and all sorts of days that would be her own. She breathed a quick prayer that life might be long. It was only yesterday she had thought with a shudder that life might be long.

She arose at length and opened the door to her sister's importunities. There was a feverish triumph in her eyes, and she carried herself unwittingly like a goddess of Victory. She clasped her sister's waist, and together they descended the stairs. Richards stood waiting for them at the bottom.

Comment   The discrepancy between what Josephine thinks is Mrs. Mallard's reason for keeping herself locked in her room and our knowledge of the real reason is ironic.* There is irony, also, in Mrs. Mallard's praying for a long life, as only the day before she had shuddered at the thought of a long life with Brently Mallard. The language of these paragraphs is charged with feeling—somewhat overcharged perhaps—but it is in keeping with extending and intensifying Mrs. Mallard's emotion. She drinks in the "elixir of life," has a "feverish triumph in her eyes," and comports herself like a "goddess of Victory." These paragraphs could end the story, but they don't. Instead Chopin has a surprise:

*Irony involves some kind of opposition, usually between what appears to be and what is or between what is said and what is meant. See page 93.

Some one was opening the front door with a latchkey. It was Brently Mallard who entered, a little travel-stained, composedly carrying his grip-sack and umbrella. He had been far from the scene of accident, and did not even know there had been one. He stood amazed at Josephine's piercing cry; at Richards's quick motion to screen him from the view of his wife.

But Richards was too late.

When the doctors came they said she had died of heart disease—of joy that kills.

(1894)

Comment   The surprise, of course, is too much for Mrs. Mallard. Does she die of shock, of despair, of joy that kills? We are left with the impression that Josephine, Richards, and the doctor do not understand that Mrs. Mallard dies not of shock at seeing her husband alive, not out of joy, but out of something like despair. Why does the narrator suggest that none of them realize the truth?

Some interesting questions are left unresolved by this ending. Is Mrs. Mallard being punished for harboring a desire to be free of her husband? Or, is Mrs. Mallard a symbol of repressed womanhood yearning to be free of male bondage? Does the story transcend the sexual identity of its protagonist? Could we imagine a man in Mrs. Mallard's position?

Our emphasis in this interrupted reading of "The Story of an Hour" has been to illustrate the active process of thinking while you read. We have focused largely on issues of response and interpretation. But we should also consider a few additional questions about the story's values.

QUESTIONS FOR REFLECTION

Experience

1. Describe your experience in reading "The Story of an Hour." Did the story surprise you, annoy you, entertain you? Why? Did it hold your interest? Why or why not?

2. Consider the attitude expressed toward Brently Mallard by his wife. What was your reaction to her feelings about her husband? Why?

3. Did your response to Mrs. Mallard change at any point in the story? If so, where—and why? If not, what was your consistent response toward her? Why?

Interpretation

4. Characterize the two major actors in the story—Brently Mallard and his wife. Whom do we understand better? Why?

5. What role do the minor characters play in the story? Are any of those characters dispensable? Why or why not?

6. What is the narrator's attitude toward Mrs. Mallard? Where do you find this attitude most clearly suggested?

7. Why does Mrs. Mallard die? To what extent is her husband responsible for her death? For her unhappiness?
8. What general idea about marriage does the story convey?

Evaluation

9. What personal and social values influence your reading of the story?
10. What values animate Mrs. Mallard's behavior and feelings?
11. What values underlie her husband's treatment of her?
12. To what extent do their values reflect or depart from society's values at the time the story was written?
13. To what extent do their values reflect or depart from today's cultural values?
14. How are any or all of these values measured against your own?

CHAPTER TWO

Types of Short Fiction

In our discussion of reading stories in Chapter One, we considered three stories—a parable and two modern realistic short stories. But short fiction comes in more than these two varieties. Other popular forms we might know include fairy tales and mystery stories, science fiction stories, and popular romance. While we need not rehearse all of short fiction's various guises, it will nonetheless be useful to describe its more common and enduring types. We begin with some ancient forms.

EARLY FORMS: PARABLE, FABLE, AND TALE

In our discussion of "The Prodigal Son" (page 21), we defined a parable as a brief story that teaches a lesson, often of a religious or spiritual nature. Another early story form is the fable, a relative of the parable.

Like parables, *fables* are brief stories that point to a moral. The moral of the fable is stated explicitly, whereas the moral of the parable is implied. The two forms also differ in subject and tone. Fables highlight features of human nature and character, especially human failings. They frequently include animals as characters, and their tone is satirical. As we have stated, parables are stories about common life through which a religious or spiritual point is made. Their purpose is instructive, their tone serious. Although we can distinguish conveniently between fable and parable in these ways, there are stories in which such distinctions are blurred, as in George Orwell's *Animal Farm,* which includes characteristics of both. Here is a fable attributed to Aesop, whose name has become synonymous with the form.

AESOP
[c. 620–560 B.C.]

The Wolf and the Mastiff

A Wolf, who was almost skin and bone—so well did the dogs of the neighborhood keep guard—met, one moonshiny night, a sleek Mastiff, who was, moreover, as strong as he was fat. Bidding the Dog good-night very humbly, he praised his good looks. "It would be easy for you," replied the Mastiff, "to get as fat as I am if you liked.""What shall I have to do?" asked the Wolf. "Almost nothing," answered the Dog. They trotted off together, but, as they went along, the Wolf noticed a bare spot on the Dog's neck. "What is that mark?" said he. "Oh, the merest trifle," answered the Dog; "the collar which I wear when I am tied up is the cause of it." "Tied up!" exclaimed the Wolf, with a sudden stop; "tied up? Can you not always then run where you please?" "Well, not quite always," said the Mastiff; "but what can that matter?" "It matters much to me," rejoined the Wolf, and, leaping away, he ran once more to his native forest.

Moral: Better starve free, than be a fat slave.

Both the fable and the parable represent early forms of fiction. Another early form, one without the strong instructive intent of fable and parable, is the tale. A *tale* is a story that narrates strange or fabulous happenings in a direct manner, without detailed descriptions of character. A tale does not necessarily point to a moral as a fable or parable does, but it is almost as generalized in its depiction of character and setting. While we may read fable and parable to understand their meaning, to get the point so to speak, our interest in tales will generally incline more toward what happens. Our interest, that is, lies in action and its outcome. Additionally, it may reside in the emotions we experience in reading tales rather than in generalizations we can make about them. The following tale, written in the first century, is from the *Satyricon* of Petronius.

PETRONIUS
[d. A.D. 66?]

The Widow of Ephesus

Once upon a time there was a certain married woman in the city of Ephesus whose fidelity to her husband was so famous that the women from all the neighboring towns and villages used to troop into Ephesus merely to stare at this prodigy. It happened, however, that her husband one day died. Finding the normal custom of following the cortege with hair unbound and beating her breast in public quite inadequate to express her grief, the lady insisted on following the corpse right into the tomb, an underground vault of the Greek type, and there set herself to guard the body, weeping and wailing night and day. Although in her extremes of grief she was clearly courting death from starvation, her parents were utterly unable to persuade her to leave, and even the magistrates, after one last supreme attempt, were rebuffed and driven away. In short, all Ephesus had gone into mourning for this extraordinary woman, all the more since the lady was now passing her fifth consecutive day without once tasting food. Beside the failing woman sat her devoted maid, sharing her mistress's grief and relighting the lamp whenever it flickered out. The whole city could speak, in fact, of nothing else: here at last, all classes alike agreed, was the one true example of conjugal fidelity and love.

In the meantime, however, the governor of the province gave orders that several thieves should be crucified in a spot close by the vault where the lady was mourning her dead husband's corpse. So, on the following night, the soldier who had been assigned to keep watch on the crosses so that nobody could remove the thieves' bodies for burial suddenly noticed a light blazing among the tombs and heard the sounds of groaning. And prompted by a natural human curiosity to know who or what was making those sounds, he descended into the vault.

But at the sight of a strikingly beautiful woman, he stopped short in terror, thinking he must be seeing some ghostly apparition out of hell. Then, observing the corpse and seeing the tears on the lady's face and the scratches her fingernails had gashed in her cheeks, he realized what it was: a widow, in inconsolable grief. Promptly fetching his little supper back down to the tomb, he implored the lady not to persist in her sorrow or break her heart with useless mourning. All men alike, he reminded her, have the same end; the same resting place awaits us all. He used, in short, all those platitudes we use to comfort the suffering and bring them back to life. His consolations, being unwelcome, only exasperated the widow more; more violently than ever she beat her breast, and tearing out her hair by the roots, scattered it over the dead man's body. Undismayed, the soldier repeated his arguments and pressed her to take some food, until the little maid, quite overcome by the smell of the wine, succumbed and stretched out her hand to her tempter. Then, restored by the food and wine, she began herself to assail her mistress's obstinate refusal.

"How will it help you," she asked the lady, "if you faint from hunger? Why should you bury yourself alive, and go down to death before the Fates have called you? What does Vergil say?—

Do you suppose the shades and ashes of the dead are by such sorrow touched?

No, begin your life afresh. Shake off these woman's scruples; enjoy the light while you can. Look at that corpse of your poor husband: doesn't it tell you more eloquently than any words that you should live?"

None of us, of course, really dislikes being told that we must eat, that life is to be lived. And the lady was no exception. Weakened by her long days of fasting, her resistance crumbled at last, and she ate the food the soldier offered her as hungrily as the little maid had eaten earlier.

Well, you know what temptations are normally aroused in a man on a full stomach. So the soldier, mustering all those blandishments by means of which he had persuaded the lady to live, now laid determined siege to her virtue. And chaste though she was, the lady found him singularly attractive and his arguments persuasive. As for the maid, she did all she could to help the soldier's cause, repeating like a refrain the appropriate line of Vergil:

> If love is pleasing, lady, yield yourself to love.

To make the matter short, the lady's body soon gave up the struggle; she yielded and our happy warrior enjoyed a total triumph on both counts. That very night their marriage was consummated, and they slept together the second and the third night too, carefully shutting the door of the tomb so that any passing friend or stranger would have thought the lady of famous chastity had at last expired over her dead husband's body.

As you can perhaps imagine, our soldier was a very happy man, utterly delighted with his lady's ample beauty and that special charm that a secret love confers. Every night, as soon as the sun had set, he bought what few provisions his slender pay permitted and smuggled them down to the tomb. One night, however, the parents of one of the crucified thieves, noticing that the watch was being badly kept, took advantage of our hero's absence to remove their son's body and bury it. The next morning, of course, the soldier was horror-struck to discover one of the bodies missing from its cross, and ran to tell his mistress of the horrible punishment which awaited him for neglecting his duty. In the circumstances, he told her, he would not wait to be tried and sentenced, but would punish himself then and there with his own sword. All he asked of her was that she make room for another corpse and allow the same gloomy tomb to enclose husband and lover together.

Our lady's heart, however, was no less tender than pure. "God forbid," she cried, "that I should have to see at one and the same time the dead bodies of the only two men I have ever loved. No, better far, I say, to hang the dead than kill the living." With these words, she gave orders that her husband's body should be taken from its bier and strung up on the empty cross. The soldier followed this good advice, and the next morning the whole city wondered by what miracle the dead man had climbed up on the cross.

(1st century A.D.)

In responding to "The Widow of Ephesus" we look less to a moral than to its action. Much of the pleasure we take in a story like this resides in its series of surprises. We may be amazed at the way the lady expresses her sorrow, surprised at her capitulation to the soldier, and amused (or appalled) at where they make love. But before we can become absorbed in these events, Petronius surprises us with another series of actions culminating in the lady's still more amazing solution to the soldier's dilemma: putting the corpse of her dead husband up on the cross.

Our admiration for the inventiveness and economy of the tale's action, however, may not eliminate our desire to look for a moral of some sort. But in such a tale, we should search cautiously. Does the story's hypothetical moral have to do with the fickleness of women? Is the story told to illustrate that all women can be tempted and seduced? Does it suggest that life is to be lived and enjoyed? Or does it imply that people are credulous, that, rather than believe the widow capable of anything but unadulterated devotion to her dead husband, they believe in the miraculous ascent of a dead body onto the cross?

Whatever our sense of the tale's point and purpose, whatever meaning we finally take from it, "The Widow of Ephesus" is not as clear-cut as Aesop's fable or the parable of the Prodigal Son. And in that respect this tale more closely resembles the modern short story, whose meaning is often ambiguous or open to a variety of interpretations.

THE SHORT STORY

The *short story* as a form of short fiction developed and became popular in the nineteenth century. During this period, fiction was channeled in the direction of realism or a detailed representation of everyday life, typically the lives and experiences familiar to middle-class individuals. Besides its realistic impulse, the modern short story differs from the ancient forms of short fiction in still another way: in the ratio between summary and scene. Parables, fables, and tales tend to summarize action, to tell what happens in a general overview of the action. Short stories, on the other hand, typically reveal character in dramatic scenes, in moments of action, and in exchanges of dialogue detailed enough to represent the surface of life. In addition, the short story has traditionally been more concerned with the revelation of character through flashes of insight and shocks of recognition than the early fictional forms.

Typical features of the modern realistic short story include the following:

1. Its plot is based on probability, illustrating a sequence of causally related incidents.
2. Its characters are recognizably human, and they are motivated by identifiable social and psychological forces.
3. Its time and place are clearly established, with realistic rather than fantastic settings.
4. Its elements—plot, character, setting, style, point of view, irony, symbol and theme—work toward a single effect, unifying the story.

THE NONREALISTIC STORY

In an effort to break away from the prevailing conventions of the realistic short story, some modern storytellers have mixed features of the early story forms— elements of the supernatural, for example—with realistic conventions. I. B. Singer's "Gimpel the Fool" (page 300) includes supernatural elements, though they function in quite different ways. Such writers as Leslie Marmon Silko in "Yellow Woman" (page 369) and Gabriel Garcia Marquez in "A Very Old Man with Enormous Wings" (page 337) employ legendary materials in their stories. Shifting back and forth between the realistic and fantastic worlds, these modern storytellers have discovered and explored ways to represent human experience powerfully and incisively.

Occasionally modern writers of short fiction employ nonrealistic detail so heavily that readers are disoriented and unsettled. When we read a story like Jorge Luis Borges's "The Garden of the Forking Paths" (page 294), we may be uncertain about what exactly is happening. Part of the reason for our initial confusion is attributable to the author's use of surrealistic action or of mystery and riddle. Our confusion may also derive from our expectations: we expect the conventions of realism to operate, and when they do not we need to re-adjust our sense of what we are reading.

The important thing, however, about nonrealistic stories is to accept them on their own terms. In accepting their break from realistic fictional convention we increase our chances of responding fully to the pleasures they offer. We also enlarge our understanding of what a short story can be.

THE SHORT NOVEL

The short novel, sometimes called the *novella,* shares characteristics with both the novel and short story. Like the longer novel the *short novel* accumulates in-cidents and illustrates character over time in ways the short story cannot be-cause of its more limited scope. Yet like the short story, the short novel relies on glimpses of understanding, flashes of insight, quick turns of action to solidify theme or reveal character. And while in the short novel such moments are both more frequent and of longer duration than in the typical short story, they are rarely rendered with the leisure or richness of detail characteristic of most long novels.

Unlike the short story, which must make its mark quickly, the short novel can allow a slower unfolding of character, incident, idea. The short story's brevity demands a single snapshot of time rather than the collage or mosaic that can be created in a novel, long or short. What distinguishes the short novel from its longer counterpart in this respect is its greater efficiency and sharper focus. Lacking time and space to accumulate incident, develop character, and amplify theme, the short novel works within a narrow compass, disavowing the novel's panoramic sweep. The result is a consistency of style and focus and a concentration and compression of effect that are the hallmarks of the short novel form.

Henry James, an American master of the short novel, called it a "blessed" form. And the novelist Vladimir Nabokov suggested that "by diminishing large things and enlarging small ones," the short novel is "intrinsically artistic." Finally, Irving Howe, a contemporary critic and editor of a fine collection of modern short novels, has noted that "in masterpieces of the genre, the action forms a harmonious equivalent to the motivating idea." One short novel wor-thy of such high praise is James Joyce's "The Dead" (pp. 256–283).

CHAPTER THREE

Elements of Fiction

In learning to read fiction well, we must understand something about its techniques. One useful way to approach the techniques of fiction is to describe its basic elements or characteristics: plot and structure, character, setting, point of view, style and language, symbol, irony, and theme. We will discuss each element separately to highlight its special features. Be aware, however, that all the elements of a story work together to convey feeling and embody meaning. Thus, our analysis of any one fictional element—plot or character, for example—is related to the other elements and to the work as a whole.

PLOT AND STRUCTURE

Plot, the action element in fiction, is the arrangement of events that make up a story. A story's plot keeps us turning pages: we read to find out what will happen next. But for a plot to be effective, it must include a sequence of incidents that bear a significant causal relationship to each other. Causality is an important feature of realistic fictional plots: it simply means that one thing happens because of—as a result of—something else. An example from E. M. Forster's *Aspects of the Novel* clarifies this point. Forster notes that "The king died and then the queen died" promises a story, but not a plot. Why? Because there is no causal connection between the two deaths. But if the sentence read "The king died and then the queen died of grief," we have such a connection and hence a plot.★

Many fictional plots turn on a *conflict,* or struggle between opposing forces, that is usually resolved by the end of the story. Typical fictional plots begin with an *exposition* that provides background information we need to make sense of the action, describes the setting, and introduces the major characters; these

★E. M. Forster, *Aspects of the Novel* (New York: Harcourt, Brace and World, 1927), p. 130.

plots develop a series of *complications* or intensifications of the conflict that lead to a *crisis* or moment of great tension. The conflict may reach a *climax* or turning point, a moment of greatest tension that fixes the outcome; then, the action falls off as the plot's complications are sorted out and resolved (the *resolution* or *denouement*). The plot of a typical realistic short story can be diagrammed in the following manner:

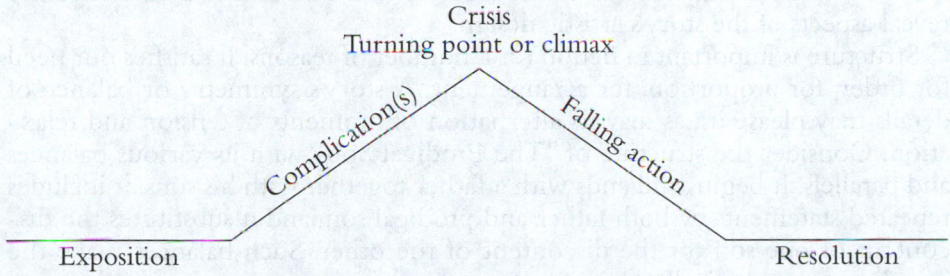

This diagram, however, is useful only as a point of departure for describing the plot of a particular story. Most stories do not exhibit such strict formality of design. A story's climactic moment, for example, may occur simultaneously with its ending, with little or no formal resolution. Or its action may rise and fall repeatedly in a jagged and uneven pattern rather than according to the neat symmetry of this diagram.

The action of a realistic story is usually composed of a sequence of causally related actions or events that are not necessarily presented in chronological order. For example, flashbacks that disrupt the linear movement of the plot to present an earlier action are employed in many stories. To distill the plot from William Faulkner's "A Rose for Emily" (later in the chapter), we must untangle a set of events that shift between past and present. In doing so we can clarify our sense of what happened, how it happened, and why.

Whatever the plot of a story may be, the writer has ordered the events with a view both to the overall meaning and to the responses of readers. To appreciate fictional plot, therefore, we should think about our experience in reading a story and remember what we thought and felt at different points. This subjective dimension of our reading experience should prompt us to investigate why the writer has chosen one arrangement of incidents over another. And it should lead us to see how writers control our emotional responses, how they vary the tempo of the action, and how they prepare for reversals and surprises.

Consider the plot of Chopin's "The Story of an Hour," with its surprises and dramatic reversals. It begins with a reference to the accident in which Brently Mallard is purportedly killed, then shows its effect on his wife. The tempo then slows down as we watch Mrs. Mallard's reactions, particularly her behavior in her room. The plot includes an ironic twist in this descriptive section as Mrs. Mallard's shock evolves into joyful self-assertion, and then produces a stronger and more abrupt and climactic ironic reversal with its final action: the arrival of a very much alive Brently Mallard and the collapse and death of Mrs. Mallard.

Returning to the beginning of the story, we can see how Chopin prepared for these shifts, how she shaped our expectations only to surprise us.

A story's structure can be examined in relation to its plot. If plot is the sequence of unfolding action, *structure* is the *design* or form of the completed action. In examining plot, we are concerned with causality, with how one action leads into or ties in with another. In examining structure, we look for patterns, for the shape of content that the story as a whole possesses. Plot directs us to the story in motion, structure to the story at rest. Plot and structure together reveal aspects of the story's artistic design.

Structure is important in fiction for a number of reasons. It satisfies our need for order, for proportion, for arrangement. A story's symmetry or balance of details may please us, as may its alternation of moments of tension and relaxation. Consider the structure of "The Prodigal Son" with its various balances and parallels. It begins and ends with a father together with his sons, it includes repeated statements by both father and prodigal son, and it substitutes the discontent of one son for the discontent of the other. Such balances make the story's form aesthetically pleasing. But structure is important for another reason: it provides a clue to a story's meaning.

We can be alert for a story's structure even as we read it for the first time, primarily by paying attention to repeated elements and recurrent details—of action and gesture, of dialogue and description—and to shifts in direction and changes of focus. Repetition signals important connections and relationships in the story, relationships between characters, connections between ideas. Shifts in direction are often signaled by such visual or aural clues as a change of scene, a new voice, blank space in the text. They may also include changes in the time and place of the action or alterations in characters' entrances and exits or in their behavior, or they may appear as changes in the pace of the story, and in its texture or language.

Keep these considerations about plot and structure in mind as you read Frank O'Connor's "Guests of the Nation," which follows. See how its plot, for example, both follows and deviates from the diagram on page 45. Note especially any shifts of emphasis and changes of tempo in the story's action. And once you have finished reading, look back and describe your expectations about the developing action.

FRANK O'CONNOR
[1903–1966]

Guests of the Nation

I

At dusk the big Englishman, Belcher, would shift his long legs out of the ashes and say "Well, chums, what about it?" and Noble or me would say "All right, chum" (for we had picked up some of their curious expressions), and the little Englishman, Hawkins, would light the lamp and bring out the cards. Sometimes Jeremiah Donovan would come up and supervise the game and get excited over Hawkins's cards, which he always played badly, and shout at him as if he was one of our own, "Ah, you divil, you, why didn't you play the tray?"

But ordinarily Jeremiah was a sober and contented poor devil like the big Englishman, Belcher, and was looked up to only because he was a fair hand at documents, though he was slow enough even with them. He wore a small cloth hat and big gaiters over his long pants, and you seldom saw him with his hands out of his pockets. He reddened when you talked to him, tilting from toe to heel and back, and looking down all the time at his big farmer's feet. Noble and me used to make fun of his broad accent, because we were from the town.

I couldn't at the time see the point of me and Noble guarding Belcher and Hawkins at all, for it was my belief that you could have planted that pair down anywhere from this to Claregalway and they'd have taken root there like a native weed. I never in my short experience seen two men to take to the country as they did.

They were handed on to us by the Second Battalion when the search for them became too hot, and Noble and myself, being young, took over with a natural feeling of responsibility, but Hawkins made us look like fools when he showed that he knew the country better than we did.

"You're the bloke they calls Bonaparte," he says to me. "Mary Brigid O'Connell told me to ask you what you done with the pair of her brother's socks you borrowed."

For it seemed, as they explained it, that the Second used to have little evenings, and some of the girls of the neighborhood turned in, and, seeing they were such decent chaps, our fellows couldn't leave the two Englishmen out of them. Hawkins learned to dance "The Walls of Limerick," "The Siege of Ennis," and "The Waves of Tory" as well as any of them, though, naturally, we couldn't return the compliment, because our lads at that time did not dance foreign dances on principle.

So whatever privileges Belcher and Hawkins had with the Second they just naturally took with us, and after the first day or two we gave up all pretense of keeping a close eye on them. Not that they could have got far, for they had accents you could cut with a knife and wore khaki tunics and overcoats with civilian pants and boots. But it's my belief that they never had any idea of escaping and were quite content to be where they were.

It was a treat to see how Belcher got off with the old woman of the house where we were staying. She was a great warrant to scold, and cranky even with us, but before ever she had a chance of giving our guests, as I may call them, a lick of her tongue, Belcher had made her his friend for life. She was breaking sticks, and Belcher, who hadn't been more than ten minutes in the house, jumped up from his seat and went over to her.

"Allow me, madam," he says, smiling his queer little smile, "please allow me"; and he takes the bloody hatchet. She was struck too paralytic to speak, and after that, Belcher would be at her heels, carrying a bucket, a basket, or a load of turf, as the case might be. As Noble said, he got into looking before she leapt, and hot water, or any little thing she wanted, Belcher would have it ready for her. For such a huge man (and though I am five foot ten myself I had to look up at him) he had an uncommon shortness—or should I say lack?—of speech. It took us some time to get used to him, walking in and out, like a ghost, without a word. Especially because Hawkins talked enough for a platoon, it was strange to hear big Belcher with his toes in the ashes come out with a solitary "Excuse me, chum," or "That's right, chum." His one and only passion was cards, and I will say for him that he was a good cardplayer. He could have fleeced myself and Noble, but whatever we lost to him Hawkins lost to us, and Hawkins played with the money Belcher gave him.

Hawkins lost to us because he had too much old gab, and we probably lost to Belcher for the same reason. Hawkins and Noble would spit at one another about religion into the early hours of the morning, and Hawkins worried the soul out of Noble, whose brother was a priest, with a string of questions that would puzzle a cardinal. To make it worse, even in treating of holy subjects, Hawkins had a deplorable tongue. I never in all my career met a man who could mix such a variety of cursing and bad language into an argument. He was a terrible man, and a fright to argue. He never did a stroke of work, and when he had no one else to talk to, he got stuck in the old woman.

He met his match in her, for one day when he tried to get her to complain profanely of the drought, she gave him a great come-down by blaming it entirely on Jupiter Pluvius (a deity neither Hawkins nor I had ever heard of, though Noble said that among the pagans it was believed that he had something to do with the rain). Another day he was swearing at the capitalists for starting the German war when the old lady laid down her iron, puckered up her little crab's mouth, and said: "Mr. Hawkins, you can say what you like about the war, and think you'll deceive me because I'm only a simple poor countrywoman, but I know what started the war. It was the Italian Count that stole the heathen divinity out of the temple in Japan. Believe me, Mr. Hawkins, nothing but sorrow and want can follow the people that disturb the hidden powers."

A queer old girl, all right.

2

We had our tea one evening, and Hawkins lit the lamp and we all sat into cards. Jeremiah Donovan came in too, and sat down and watched us for a while, and it suddenly struck me that he had no great love for the two Englishmen. It came as a great surprise to me, because I hadn't noticed anything about him before.

Late in the evening a really terrible argument blew up between Hawkins and Noble, about capitalists and priests and love of your country.

"The capitalists," says Hawkins with an angry gulp, "pays the priests to tell you about the next world so as you won't notice what the bastards are up to in this."

"Nonsense, man!" says Noble, losing his temper. "Before ever a capitalist was thought of, people believed in the next world."

Hawkins stood up as though he was preaching a sermon.

"Oh, they did, did they?" he says with a sneer. "They believed all the things you believe, isn't that what you mean? And you believe that God created Adam, and Adam created Shem, and Shem created Jehoshaphat. You believe all that silly old fairytale about Eve and Eden and the apple. Well, listen to me, chum. If you're entitled to hold a silly belief like that, I'm entitled to hold my silly belief—which is that the first thing your God created was a bleeding capitalist, with morality and Rolls-Royce complete. Am I right, chum?" he says to Belcher.

"You're right, chum," says Belcher with his amused smile, and got up from the table to stretch his long legs into the fire and stroke his moustache. So, seeing that Jeremiah Donovan was going, and that there was no knowing when the argument about religion would be over, I went out with him. We strolled down to the village together, and then he stopped and started blushing and mumbling and saying I ought to be behind, keeping guard on the prisoners. I didn't like the tone he took with me, and anyway I was bored with life in the cottage, so I replied by asking him what the hell we wanted guarding them at all for. I told him I'd talked it over with Noble, and that we'd both rather be out with a fighting column.

"What use are those fellows to us?" says I.

He looked at me in surprise and said: "I thought you knew we were keeping them as hostages."

"Hostages?" I said.

"The enemy have prisoners belonging to us," he says, "and now they're talking of shooting them. If they shoot our prisoners, we'll shoot theirs."

"Shoot them?" I said.

"What else did you think we were keeping them for?" he says.

"Wasn't it very unforeseen of you not to warn Noble and myself of that in the beginning?" I said.

"How was it?" says he. "You might have known it."

"We couldn't know it, Jeremiah Donovan," says I. "How could we when they were on our hands so long?"

"The enemy have our prisoners as long and longer," says he.

"That's not the same thing at all," says I.

"What difference is there?" says he.

I couldn't tell him, because I knew he wouldn't understand. If it was only an old dog that was going to the vet's, you'd try and not get too fond of him, but Jeremiah Donovan wasn't a man that would ever be in danger of that.

"And when is this thing going to be decided?" says I.

"We might hear tonight," he says. "Or tomorrow or the next day at latest. So if it's only hanging round here that's a trouble to you, you'll be free soon enough."

It wasn't the hanging round that was a trouble to me at all by this time. I had worse things to worry about. When I got back to the cottage the argument was still on. Hawkins was holding forth in his best style, maintaining that there was no next world, and Noble was maintaining that there was; but I could see that Hawkins had had the best of it.

"Do you know what, chum?" he was saying with a saucy smile. "I think you're just as big a bleeding unbeliever as I am. You say you believe in the next world, and you know just as much about the next world as I do, which is sweet damn-all. What's heaven? You don't know. Where's heaven? You don't know. You know sweet damn-all! I ask you again, do they wear wings?"

"Very well, then," says Noble, "they do. Is that enough for you? They do wear wings."

"Where do they get them, then? Who makes them? Have they a factory for wings? Have they a sort of store where you hands in your chit and takes your bleeding wings?"

"You're an impossible man to argue with," says Noble. "Now, listen to me—" And they were off again.

It was long after midnight when we locked up and went to bed. As I blew out the candle I told Noble what Jeremiah Donovan was after telling me. Noble took it very quietly. When we'd been in bed about an hour he asked me did I think we ought to tell the Englishmen. I didn't think we should, because it was more than likely that the English wouldn't shoot our men, and even if they did, the brigade officers, who were always up and down with the Second Battalion and knew the Englishmen well, wouldn't be likely to want them plugged. "I think so too," says Noble. "It would be great cruelty to put the wind up them now."

"It was very unforeseen of Jeremiah Donovan anyhow," says I.

It was next morning that we found it so hard to face Belcher and Hawkins. We went about the house all day scarcely saying a word. Belcher didn't seem to notice; he was stretched into the ashes as usual, with his usual look of waiting in quietness for something unforeseen to happen, but Hawkins noticed and put it down to Noble's being beaten in the argument of the night before.

"Why can't you take a discussion in the proper spirit?" he says severely. "You and your Adam and Eve! I'm a Communist, that's what I am. Communist or anarchist, it all comes to much the same thing." And for hours he went round the house, muttering when the fit took him. "Adam and Eve! Adam and Eve! Nothing better to do with their time than picking bleeding apples!"

3

I don't know how we got through that day, but I was very glad when it was over, the tea things were cleared away, and Belcher said in his peaceable way: "Well, chums, what about it?" We sat round the table and Hawkins took out the cards, and just then I heard Jeremiah Donovan's footstep on the path and a dark presentiment crossed my mind. I rose from the table and caught him before he reached the door.

"What do you want?" I asked.

"I want those two soldier friends of yours," he says, getting red.

"Is that the way, Jeremiah Donovan?" I asked.

"That's the way. There were four of our lads shot this morning, one of them a boy of sixteen."

"That's bad," I said.

At that moment Noble followed me out, and the three of us walked down the path together, talking in whispers. Feeney, the local intelligence officer, was standing by the gate.

"What are you going to do about it?" I asked Jeremiah Donovan.

"I want you and Noble to get them out; tell them they're being shifted again; that'll be the quietest way."

"Leave me out of that," says Noble under his breath.

Jeremiah Donovan looks at him hard.

"All right," he says. "You and Feeney get a few tools from the shed and dig a hole by the far end of the bog. Bonaparte and myself will be after you. Don't let anyone see you with the tools. I wouldn't like it to go beyond ourselves."

We saw Feeney and Noble go round to the shed and went in ourselves. I left Jeremiah Donovan to do the explanations. He told them that he had orders to send them back to the Second Battalion. Hawkins let out a mouthful of curses, and you could see that though Belcher didn't say anything, he was a bit upset too. The old woman was for having them stay in spite of us, and she didn't stop advising them until Jeremiah Donovan lost his temper and turned on her. He had a nasty temper, I noticed. It was pitch-dark in the cottage by this time, but no one thought of lighting the lamp, and in the darkness the two Englishmen fetched their topcoats and said good-bye to the old woman.

"Just as a man makes a home of a bleeding place, some bastard at headquarters thinks you're too cushy and shunts you off," says Hawkins, shaking her hand.

"A thousand thanks, madam," says Belcher. "A thousand thanks for everything"—as though he'd made it up.

We went round to the back of the house and down towards the bog. It was only then that Jeremiah Donovan told them. He was shaking with excitement.

"There were four of our fellows shot in Cork this morning and now you're to be shot as a reprisal."

"What are you talking about?" snaps Hawkins. "It's bad enough being mucked about as we are without having to put up with your funny jokes."

"It isn't a joke," says Donovan. "I'm sorry, Hawkins, but it's true," and begins on the usual rigmarole about duty and how unpleasant it is.

I never noticed that people who talk a lot about duty find it much of a trouble to them.

"Oh, cut it out!" says Hawkins.

"Ask Bonaparte," says Donovan, seeing that Hawkins isn't taking him seriously. "Isn't it true, Bonaparte?"

"It is," I say, and Hawkins stops.

"Ah, for Christ's sake, chum."

"I mean it, chum," I say.

"You don't sound as if you meant it."

"If he doesn't mean it, I do," says Donovan, working himself up.

"What have you against me, Jeremiah Donovan?"

"I never said I had anything against you. But why did your people take out four of our prisoners and shoot them in cold blood?"

He took Hawkins by the arm and dragged him on, but it was impossible to make him understand that we were in earnest. I had the Smith and Wesson° in my pocket and I kept fingering it and wondering what I'd do if they put up a fight for it or ran, and wishing to God they'd do one or the other. I knew if they did run for it, that I'd never fire on them. Hawkins wanted to know was Noble in it, and when we said yes, he asked us why Noble wanted to plug him. Why did any of us want to plug him? What had he done to us? Weren't we all chums? Didn't we understand him and didn't he understand us? Did we imagine for an instant that he'd shoot us for all the so-and-so officers in the so-and-so British Army?

By this time we'd reached the bog, and I was so sick I couldn't even answer him. We walked along the edge of it in the darkness, and every now and then Hawkins would call a halt and begin all over again, as if he was wound up, about our being chums, and I knew that nothing but the sight of the grave would convince him that we had to do it. And all the time I was hoping that something would happen; that they'd run for it

Smith and Wesson   pistol, like the Webley later

or that Noble would take over the responsibility from me. I had the feeling that it was worse on Noble than on me.

4

At last we saw the lantern in the distance and made towards it. Noble was carrying it, and Feeney was standing somewhere in the darkness behind him, and the picture of them so still and silent in the bogland brought it home to me that we were in earnest, and banished the last bit of hope I had.

Belcher, on recognizing Noble, said: "Hallo, chum," in his quiet way, but Hawkins flew at him at once, and the argument began all over again, only this time Noble had nothing to say for himself and stood with his head down, holding the lantern between his legs.

It was Jeremiah Donovan who did the answering. For the twentieth time, as though it was haunting his mind, Hawkins asked if anybody thought he'd shoot Noble.

"Yes, you would," says Jeremiah Donovan.

"No, I wouldn't, damn you!"

"You would, because you'd know you'd be shot for not doing it."

"I wouldn't, not if I was to be shot twenty times over. I wouldn't shoot a pal. And Belcher wouldn't—isn't that right, Belcher?"

"That's right, chum," Belcher said, but more by way of answering the question than of joining in the argument. Belcher sounded as though whatever unforeseen thing he'd always been waiting for had come at last.

"Anyway, who says Noble would be shot if I wasn't? What do you think I'd do if I was in his place, out in the middle of a blasted bog?"

"What would you do?" asks Donovan.

"I'd go with him wherever he was going, of course. Share my last bob with him and stick by him through thick and thin. No one can ever say of me that I let down a pal."

"We had enough of this," says Jeremiah Donovan, cocking his revolver. "Is there any message you want to send?"

"No, there isn't."

"Do you want to say your prayers?"

Hawkins came out with a cold-blooded remark that even shocked me and turned on Noble again.

"Listen to me, Noble," he says. "You and me are chums. You can't come over to my side, so I'll come over to your side. That show you I mean what I say? Give me a rifle and I'll go along with you and the other lads."

Nobody answered him. We knew that was no way out.

"Hear what I'm saying?" he says. "I'm through with it. I'm a deserter or anything else you like. I don't believe in your stuff, but it's no worse than mine. That satisfy you?"

Noble raised his head, but Donovan began to speak and he lowered it again without replying.

"For the last time, have you any messages to send?" says Donovan in a cold, excited sort of voice.

"Shut up, Donovan! You don't understand me, but these lads do. They're not the sort to make a pal and kill a pal. They're not the tools of any capitalist."

I alone of the crowd saw Donovan raise his Webley to the back of Hawkins's neck, and as he did so I shut my eyes and tried to pray. Hawkins had begun to say something else when Donovan fired, and as I opened my eyes at the bang, I saw Hawkins stagger at the knees and lie out flat at Noble's feet, slowly and as quiet as a kid falling asleep, with the lantern-light on his lean legs and bright farmer's boots. We all stood very still, watching him settle out in the last agony.

Then Belcher took out a handkerchief and began to tie it about his own eyes (in our excitement we'd forgotten to do the same for Hawkins), and, seeing it wasn't big enough, turned and asked for the loan of mine. I gave it to him and he knotted the two together and pointed with his foot at Hawkins.

"He's not quite dead," he says. "Better give him another."

Sure enough, Hawkins's left knee is beginning to rise. I bend down and put my gun to his head; then, recollecting myself, I get up again. Belcher understands what's in my mind.

"Give him his first," he says. "I don't mind. Poor bastard, we don't know what's happening to him now."

I knelt and fired. By this time I didn't seem to know what I was doing. Belcher, who was fumbling a bit awkwardly with the handkerchiefs, came out with a laugh as he heard the shot. It was the first time I heard him laugh and it sent a shudder down my back; it sounded so unnatural.

"Poor bugger!" he said quietly. "And last night he was so curious about it all. It's very queer, chums, I always think. Now he knows as much about it as they'll ever let him know, and last night he was all in the dark."

Donovan helped him to tie the handkerchiefs about his eyes. "Thanks, chum," he said. Donovan asked if there were any messages he wanted sent.

"No, chum," he says. "Not for me. If any of you would like to write to Hawkins's mother, you'll find a letter from her in his pocket. He and his mother were great chums. But my missus left me eight years ago. Went away with another fellow and took the kid with her. I like the feeling of a home, as you may have noticed, but I couldn't start again after that."

It was an extraordinary thing, but in those few minutes Belcher said more than in all the weeks before. It was just as if the sound of the shot had started a flood of talk in him and he could go on the whole night like that, quite happily, talking about himself. We stood round like fools now that he couldn't see us any longer. Donovan looked at Noble, and Noble shook his head. Then Donovan raised his Webley, and at that moment Belcher gives his queer laugh again. He may have thought we were talking about him, or perhaps he noticed the same thing I'd noticed and couldn't understand it.

"Excuse me, chums," he says. "I feel I'm talking the hell of a lot, and so silly, about my being so handy about a house and things like that. But this thing came on me suddenly. You'll forgive me, I'm sure."

"You don't want to say a prayer?" asked Donovan.

"No, chum," he says. "I don't think it would help. I'm ready, and you boys want to get it over."

"You understand that we're only doing our duty?" says Donovan.

Belcher's head was raised like a blind man's, so that you could only see his chin and the tip of his nose in the lantern-light.

"I never could make out what duty was myself," he said. "I think you're all good lads, if that's what you mean. I'm not complaining."

Noble, just as if he couldn't bear any more of it, raised his fist at Donovan, and in a flash Donovan raised his gun and fired. The big man went over like a sack of meal, and this time there was no need of a second shot.

I don't remember much about the burying, but that it was worse than all the rest because we had to carry them to the grave. It was all mad lonely with nothing but a patch of lantern-light between ourselves and the dark, and birds hooting and screeching all round, disturbed by the guns. Noble went through Hawkins's belongings to find the letter from his mother, and then joined his hands together. He did the same with Belcher. Then, when we'd filled in the grave, we separated from Jeremiah Donovan and Feeney and took our tools back to the shed. All the way we didn't speak a word. The kitchen was dark and cold as we'd left it, and the old woman was sitting over the hearth, saying her beads. We walked past her into the room, and Noble struck a match to light the lamp. She rose quietly and came to the doorway with all her cantankerousness gone.

"What did ye do with them?" she asked in a whisper, and Noble started so that the match went out in his hand.

"What's that?" he asked without turning round.

"I heard ye," she said.

"What did you hear?" asked Noble.

"I heard ye. Do ye think I didn't hear ye, putting the spade back in the houseen?"

Noble struck another match and this time the lamp lit for him.

"Was that what ye did to them?" she asked.

Then, by God, in the very doorway, she fell on her knees and began praying, and after looking at her for a minute or two Noble did the same by the fireplace. I pushed my way out past her and left them at it. I stood at the door, watching the stars and listening to the shrieking of the birds dying out over the bogs. It is so strange what you feel at times like that you can't describe it. Noble says he saw everything ten times the size, as though there were nothing in the whole world but that little patch of bog with the two Englishmen stiffening into it, but with me it was as if the patch of bog where the Englishmen were was a million miles away, and even Noble and the old woman, mumbling behind me, and the birds and the bloody stars were all far away, and I was somehow very small and very lost and lonely like a child astray in the snow. And anything that happened to me afterwards, I never felt the same about again.

(1931)

QUESTIONS FOR REFLECTION

1. "Guests of the Nation" is constructed in four parts. Identify the central action of each part, and explain how the parts are related.
2. Analyze the plot in terms of its exposition, complication, crisis, falling action, and denouement.

CHARACTER

As readers, we come to care about fictional *characters,* the imaginary people that writers create, sometimes identifying with them, sometimes judging them. Indeed, if one reason we read stories is to find out what happens (to see how the plot works out), an equally compelling reason is to follow the fortunes of the characters. Plot and character, in fact, are inseparable; we are often less concerned with "what happened" than with "what happened to him or her." We want to know not just "how did it work out," but "how did it work out for them?"

Well-wrought fictional characters come alive for us while we read. And they are real enough to live in our memories long after their stories have ended. We might say that fictional characters possess the kind of reality that dreams have, a reality no less intense for being imagined. Although fictional characters cannot step out of the pages of their stories, we grant them a kind of reality equivalent to if not identical with our own. In doing so we make an implied contract with the writer to suspend our belief that his or her story is "just a story," and instead take what happens as if it were real. When we grant fiction this kind of reality, we permit ourselves to be caught up in the life of the story and its characters, perhaps to the point of allowing our own lives to be affected by them.

In short, we approach fictional characters with the same concerns with which we approach people. We need to be alert for how we are to take them, for what we are to make of them, and we need to see how they may reflect our own experience. We need to observe their actions, to listen to *what* they say and *how* they say it, to notice how they relate to other characters and how other characters respond to them, especially to what they say about each other. To make inferences about characters, we look for connections, for links and clues to their function and significance in the story. In analyzing a character or characters' relationships (and fictional characters almost always exist in relation to one another) we relate one act, one speech, one physical detail to another until we understand the character.

Characters in fiction can be conveniently classified as major and minor, static and dynamic. A *major character* is an important figure at the center of the story's action or theme. Usually a character's status as major or minor is clear. On occasion, however, not one but two characters may dominate a story, their relationship being what matters most. In Luigi Pirandello's "War" (p. 249), for example, no single character dominates the story the way Emily Grierson dominates Faulkner's "A Rose for Emily" or (see later in the chapter) the narrator dominates James Joyce's story of "Araby."

The major character is sometimes called a *protagonist* whose conflict with an *antagonist* may spark the story's conflict. Supporting the major character are one or more secondary or *minor characters* whose function is partly to illuminate the major characters. Minor characters are often *static* or unchanging: they remain the same from the beginning of a work to the end. *Dynamic characters,* on the other hand, exhibit some kind of change—of attitude, of purpose, of behavior—as the story progresses. We should be careful not to automatically equate major characters with dynamic ones or minor characters with static ones. For example, Emily Grierson, the major character in "A Rose for Emily," is as static as the minor characters Richards and Brently Mallard in Chopin's "The Story of an Hour," whose major character, Mrs. Mallard, undergoes significant changes as the story unfolds.

Characterization is the means by which writers present and reveal character. We look first at the way James Joyce characterizes Mrs. Mooney, a major character, in "The Boarding House" (see page 252):

> Mrs. Mooney was a butcher's daughter. She was a woman who was quite able to keep things to herself: a determined woman. She had married her father's foreman and opened a butcher's shop near Spring Gardens.

The method of characterization is narrative description with explicit judgment. We are given facts (she was a butcher's daughter) and interpretive comment (she was a determined woman). From both fact and comment we derive an impression of a strong woman, one who can take care of herself. As a butcher's daughter, she does not stand high on the social ladder. This initial impression is confirmed when we later discover in the story that after her husband had become an alcoholic, had ruined his business, and had gone after Mrs. Mooney with a meat cleaver, she left him and opened a boarding house to support herself and her two children. When the narrator informs us that "she governed the house cunningly and firmly," and when he calls her "a shrewd judge," we come to share his respect for Mrs. Mooney's abilities.

The narrator's view of Mrs. Mooney, however, is not one of unqualified admiration. We learn, for example, that "all the resident young men spoke of her as *The Madam*"—a title suggestive of authority coupled with moral disrepute. And though Mrs. Mooney does not run a house of prostitution, we can't help but be aware of the moral dubiety that this title implies, for Mrs. Mooney allows her nineteen-year-old daughter, Polly, to flirt with the male residents of the boarding house. The following comment of the narrator clearly indicates that Mrs. Mooney was serious about finding Polly a husband: "Mrs. Mooney, who was a shrewd judge, knew that the young men were only passing the time away: none of them meant business." And for Mrs. Mooney, *business* means marriage to a serious and socially suitable man such as Bob Doran, a thirty-four-year-old clerk to a wine merchant.

Throughout "The Boarding House," Joyce characterizes Mrs. Mooney by means of narrative description with explicit judgment. In introducing Polly he varies the technique:

> Polly Mooney, the Madam's daughter, would also sing. She sang:
>
> *I'm a . . . naughty girl.*
> *You needn't sham.*
> *You know I am.*

Polly sings this seductive verse, presumably with her mother's approval. The implications of the song coupled with other descriptive details about Polly serve to characterize her. Unlike her mother, whose character is presented directly through narrative description with explicit judgment, Polly is characterized initially by means of narrative description with implied judgment: "Polly was a slim girl of nineteen; she had light soft hair and a small full mouth." The crucial detail is the full mouth, which suggests sensuality. Moreover, Joyce's narrator further embellishes Polly's description with the information that "her eyes . . . had a habit of glancing upwards when she spoke with anyone, which made her look like a little perverse "madonna." "Madonna," of course, is a word that sounds like *madam,* but is quite different in connotation. Polly is associated with innocence and holiness while also being called "perverse," a contradiction of the madonna image.

Joyce uses two additional devices of characterization in this story: he reveals a character's state of mind through surface details (the fogging of Bob Doran's glasses and the shaking of his hand while he attempts unsuccessfully to shave); he also reveals characters by letting us enter their consciousness, telling us what they think and feel.

We can generalize from these techniques to list the following major methods of revealing character in fiction:

1. Narrative summary without judgment.
2. Narrative description with implied or explicit judgment.
3. Surface details of dress and physical appearance.
4. Characters' actions—what they do.
5. Characters' speech—what they say (and how they say it).
6. Characters' consciousness—what they think and feel.

Keep the devices of characterization in mind as you read Kay Boyle's "Astronomer's Wife." Examine the relationships among the three characters—the astronomer, his wife, and the plumber—noting especially details of speech, gesture, and behavior that reveal the nature of each. Account for what you think and feel about each character.

KAY BOYLE
[b. 1903]

Astronomer's Wife

There is an evil moment on awakening when all things seem to pause. But for women, they only falter and may be set in action by a single move: a lifted hand and the pendulum will swing, or the voice raised and through every room the pulse takes up its beating. The astronomer's wife felt the interval gaping and at once filled it to the brim.

She fetched up her gentle voice and sent it warily down the stairs for coffee, swung her feet out upon the oval mat, and hailed the morning with her bare arms' quivering flesh drawn taut in rhythmic exercise: left, left, left my wife and fourteen children, right, right, right in the middle of the dusty road.

The day would proceed from this, beat by beat, without reflection, like every other day. The astronomer was still asleep, or feigning it, and she, once out of bed, had come into her own possession. Although scarcely ever out of sight of the impenetrable silence of his brow, she would be absent from him all the day in being clean, busy, kind. He was a man of other things, a dreamer. At times he lay still for hours, at others he sat upon the roof behind his telescope, or wandered down the pathway to the road and out across the mountains. This day, like any other, would go on from the removal of the spot left there from dinner on the astronomer's vest to the severe thrashing of the mayonnaise for lunch. That man might be each time the new arching wave, and woman the undertow that sucked him back, were things she had been told by his silence were so.

In spite of the earliness of the hour, the girl had heard her mistress's voice and was coming up the stairs. At the threshold of the bedroom she paused, and said: "Madame, the plumber is here."

The astronomer's wife put on her white and scarlet smock very quickly and buttoned it at the neck. Then she stepped carefully around the motionless spread of water in the hall.

"Tell him to come right up," she said. She laid her hands on the bannisters and stood looking down the wooden stairway. "Ah, I am Mrs. Ames," she said softly as she saw him mounting. "I am Mrs. Ames," she said softly, softly down the flight of stairs. "I am Mrs. Ames," spoken soft as a willow weeping. "The professor is still sleeping. Just step this way."

The plumber himself looked up and saw Mrs. Ames with her voice hushed, speaking to him. She was a youngish woman, but this she had forgotten. The mystery and silence of her husband's mind lay like a chiding finger on her lips. Her eyes were gray, for the light had been extinguished in them. The strange dim halo of her yellow hair was still uncombed and sideways on her head.

For all of his heavy boots, the plumber quieted the sound of his feet, and together they went down the hall, picking their way around the still lake of water that spread as far as the landing and lay docile there. The plumber was a tough, hardy man; but he took off his hat when he spoke to her and looked her fully, almost insolently in the eye.

"Does it come from the wash-basin," he said, "or from the other . . . ?"

"Oh, from the other," said Mrs. Ames without hesitation.

In this place the villas were scattered out few and primitive, and although beauty lay without there was no reflection of her face within. Here all was awkward and unfit; a sense of wrestling with uncouth forces gave everything an austere countenance. Even the plumber, dealing as does a woman with matters under hand, was grave and stately. The mountains round about seemed to have cast them into the shadow of great dignity.

Mrs. Ames began speaking of their arrival that summer in the little villa, mourning each event as it followed on the other.

"Then, just before going to bed last night," she said, "I noticed something was unusual."

The plumber cast down a folded square of sack-cloth on the brimming floor and laid his leather apron on it. Then he stepped boldly onto the heart of the island it shaped and looked long into the overflowing bowl.

"The water should be stopped from the meter in the garden," he said at last.

"Oh, I did that," said Mrs. Ames, "the very first thing last night. I turned it off at once, in my nightgown, as soon as I saw what was happening. But all this had already run in."

The plumber looked for a moment at her red kid slippers. She was standing just at the edge of the clear, pure-seeming tide.

"It's no doubt the soil lines," he said severely. "It may be that something has stopped them, but my opinion is that the water seals aren't working. That's the trouble often enough in such cases. If you had a valve you wouldn't be caught like this."

Mrs. Ames did not know how to meet this rebuke. She stood, swaying a little, looking into the plumber's blue relentless eye.

"I'm sorry—I'm sorry that my husband," she said, "is still—resting and cannot go into this with you. I'm sure it must be very interesting. . . ."

"You'll probably have to have the traps sealed," said the plumber grimly, and at the sound of this Mrs. Ames' hand flew in dismay to the side of her face. The plumber made no move, but the set of his mouth as he looked at her seemed to soften. "Anyway, I'll have a look from the garden end," he said.

"Oh, do," said the astronomer's wife in relief. Here was a man who spoke of action and object as simply as women did! But however hushed her voice had been, it carried clearly to Professor Ames who lay, dreaming and solitary, upon his bed. He heard their footsteps come down the hall, pause, and skip across the pool of overflow.

"Katherine!" said the astronomer in a ringing tone. "There's a problem worthy of your mettle!"

Mrs. Ames did not turn her head, but led the plumber swiftly down the stairs. When the sun in the garden struck her face, he saw there was a wave of color in it, but this may have been anything but shame.

"You see how it is," said the plumber, as if leading her mind away. "The drains run from these houses right down the hill, big enough for a man to stand upright in them, and clean as a whistle too." There they stood in the garden with the vegetation flowering in disorder all about. The plumber looked at the astronomer's wife. "They come out at the torrent on the other side of the forest beyond there," he said.

But the words the astronomer had spoken still sounded in her in despair. The mind of man, she knew, made steep and sprightly flights, pursued illusion, took foothold in the nameless things that cannot pass between the thumb and finger. But whenever the astronomer gave voice to the thoughts that soared within him, she returned in gratitude to the long expanses of his silence. Desert-like they stretched behind and before the articulation of his scorn.

Life, life is an open sea, she sought to explain it in sorrow, and to survive women cling to the floating debris on the tide. But the plumber had suddenly fallen upon his knees in the grass and had crooked his fingers through the ring of the drains' trap-door. When she looked down she saw that he was looking up into her face, and she saw too that his hair was as light as gold.

"Perhaps Mr. Ames," he said rather bitterly, "would like to come down with me and have a look around?"

"Down?" said Mrs. Ames in wonder.

"Into the drains," said the plumber brutally. "They're a study for a man who likes to know what's what."

"Oh, Mr. Ames," said Mrs. Ames in confusion. "He's still—still in bed, you see."

The plumber lifted his strong, weathered face and looked curiously at her. Surely it seemed to him strange for a man to linger in bed, with the sun pouring yellow as wine all over the place. The astronomer's wife saw his lean cheeks, his high, rugged bones, and the deep seams in his brow. His flesh was as firm and clean as wood, stained richly tan with the climate's rigor. His fingers were blunt, but comprehensible to her, gripped in the ring and holding the iron door wide. The backs of his hands were bound round and round with ripe blue veins of blood.

"At any rate," said the astronomer's wife, and the thought of it moved her lips to smile a little, "Mr. Ames would never go down there alive. He likes going up," she said. And she, in her turn, pointed, but impudently, towards the heavens. "On the roof. Or on the mountains. He's been up on the tops of them many times."

"It's a matter of habit," said the plumber, and suddenly he went down the trap. Mrs. Ames saw a bright little piece of his hair still shining, like a star, long after the rest of him had gone. Out of the depths, his voice, hollow and dark with foreboding, returned to her. "I think something has stopped the elbow," was what he said.

This was speech that touched her flesh and bone and made her wonder. When her husband spoke of height, having no sense of it, she could not picture it nor hear. Depth or magic passed her by unless a name were given. But madness in a daily shape, as elbow stopped, she saw clearly and well. She sat down on the grasses, bewildered that it should be a man who had spoken to her so.

She saw the weeds springing up, and she did not move to tear them up from life. She sat powerless, her senses veiled, with no action taking shape beneath her hands. In this way some men sat for hours on end, she knew, tracking a single thought back to its origin. The mind of man could balance and divide, weed out, destroy. She sat on the full, burdened grasses, seeking to think, and dimly waiting for the plumber to return.

Whereas her husband had always gone up, as the dead go, she knew now that there were others who went down, like the corporeal being of the dead. That men were then divided into two bodies now seemed clear to Mrs. Ames. This knowledge stunned her with its simplicity and took the uneasy motion from her limbs. She could not stir, but sat facing the mountains' rocky flanks, and harking in silence to lucidity. Her husband was the mind, this other man the meat, of all mankind.

After a little, the plumber emerged from the earth: first the light top of his head, then the burnt brow, and then the blue eyes fringed with whitest lash. He braced his thick hands flat on the pavings of the garden-path and swung himself completely from the pit.

"It's the soil lines," he said pleasantly. "The gases," he said as he looked down upon her lifted face, "are backing up the drains."

"What in the world are we going to do?" said the astronomer's wife softly. There was a young and strange delight in putting questions to which true answers would be given. Everything the astronomer had ever said to her was a continuous query to which there could be no response.

"Ah, come, now," said the plumber, looking down and smiling. "There's a remedy for every ill, you know. Sometimes it may be that," he said as if speaking to a child, "or sometimes the other thing. But there's always a help for everything amiss."

Things come out of herbs and make you young again, he might have been saying to her; or the first good rain will quench any drought; or time of itself will put a broken bone together.

"I'm going to follow the ground pipe out right to the torrent," the plumber was saying. "The trouble's between here and there and I'll find it on the way. There's nothing at all that can't be done over for the caring," he was saying, and his eyes were fastened on her face in insolence, or gentleness, or love.

The astronomer's wife stood up, fixed a pin in her hair, and turned around towards the kitchen. Even while she was calling the servant's name, the plumber began speaking again.

"I once had a cow that lost her cud," the plumber was saying. The girl came out on the kitchen-step and Mrs. Ames stood smiling at her in the sun.

"The trouble is very serious, very serious," she said across the garden. "When Mr. Ames gets up, please tell him I've gone down."

She pointed briefly to the open door in the pathway, and the plumber hoisted his kit on his arm and put out his hand to help her down.

"But I made her another in no time," he was saying, "out of flowers and things and what-not."

"Oh," said the astronomer's wife in wonder as she stepped into the heart of the earth. She took his arm, knowing that what he said was true.

(1936)

QUESTIONS FOR REFLECTION

1. "Astronomer's Wife" is built on two sets of character contrasts: wife versus husband; astronomer versus plumber. Explain how the characters differ. Consider physical descriptions as well as actions, words, and gestures.
2. Describe the wife's relationship with her husband.

SETTING

Writers describe the world they know, its sights and sounds, its colors, textures, and accents. Stories come to life, are imagined as occurring in a place, rooted in the soil of a writer's memories. This place or location of a story's action along with the time in which it occurs is its *setting*. For writers like James Joyce and William Faulkner, setting is essential to meaning. Functioning as more than a simple backdrop for action, it provides a historical and cultural context that enhances our understanding of the characters. In Joyce's "The Boarding House," for example, Bob Doran's Irish Catholicism powerfully influences his decision to marry Polly, to make "reparation" for his sexual sin. In Faulkner's

"A Rose for Emily," Emily Grierson's stubborn resistance to change is both a product of the decay of Jefferson (a fictional town in Mississippi) and the post–Civil War South and also a reflection of its shabby gentility. Moreover, Faulkner intensifies the images of decline of both Emily and the South by his careful description of the Grierson house:

> It was a big, squarish frame house that had once been white, dec-
> orated with cupolas and spires and scrolled balconies in the heav-
> ily lightsome style of the seventies, set on what had once been
> our most select street. But garages and cotton gins had en-
> croached and obliterated even the august names of that neigh-
> borhood; only Miss Emily's house was left, lifting its stubborn
> and coquettish decay above the cotton wagons and the gasoline
> pumps—an eyesore among eyesores.

Later we are taken inside the house, and finally inside one very unusual room. In each case, the physical details of setting are associated with the values, ideals, and attitudes of that place in different times. Setting in "A Rose for Emily" (and in fiction in general) is an important dimension of meaning since it reflects character and embodies theme.

Setting is important for an additional reason: it symbolizes the emotional state of the characters. In Chopin's "The Story of an Hour," for example, Mrs. Mallard looks out the window and observes life going on—birds singing, a peddler working, trees blooming. The contrast between the enclosed space of her room and the world outside implies a tension between Mrs. Mallard's sub-jugation and her desire for freedom. This contrast underscores a significant dif-ference between the natural and the human worlds: nature is free of social restrictions, of conventions, and of such obligations as marriage.

Writers know that they must root stories in a reality their readers can expe-rience, whether it is one readers actually know or one they must imagine. They realize further that the way to general truths is through concreteness and par-ticularity. Both Joyce's Dublin and Faulkner's Jefferson are highly specified places. Yet both cities transcend their particular locale to become symbolic, rep-resentative places. It is a stunning paradox that works of such imaginative splendor as Chekhov's "The Lady with the Dog" (page 228) and Faulkner's "A Rose for Emily" (page 74) also display careful representations of reality. Stories like these are both realistic and symbolic; they are concrete representations of actual life that illustrate general truths about human experience, applicable not just in Yalta or Dublin or Jefferson, but in many places human beings live.

One of our finest American storytellers, Eudora Welty, has spoken elo-quently about the importance of one aspect of setting—place in fiction. She suggests that "fiction depends for its life on place." Relating place to character and plot, Miss Welty writes that place is "the crossroads of circumstance, the proving ground of 'What happened? Who's here? Who's coming?'" But it is even more important than this. For as she suggests, place is the "conductor of all the currents of emotion and belief and moral conviction that charge out from the story." Moreover, when the world of experience is within reach of the world of appearance, place both makes and keeps the characters real; it animates them, so much so that, as Miss Welty observes, "every story would be another story, and unrecognizable as art, if it took up its characters and plot and happened somewhere else."[*]

In "Shiloh" by Bobbie Ann Mason you will read about a married couple who are trying to identify what they want from their lives both individually and together. Consider what the historical resonance of the title contributes to our view of character relationships in the story and how it relates to the setting.

BOBBIE ANN MASON
[b. 1940]

Shiloh

Leroy Moffitt's wife, Norma Jean, is working on her pectorals. She lifts three-pound dumbbells to warm up, then progresses to a twenty-pound barbell. Standing with her legs apart, she reminds Leroy of Wonder Woman.

"I'd give anything if I could just get these muscles to where they're real hard," says Norma Jean. "Feel this arm. It's not as hard as the other one."

"That's 'cause you're right-handed," says Leroy, dodging as she swings the barbell in an arc.

"Do you think so?"

"Sure."

Leroy is a truckdriver. He injured his leg in a highway accident four months ago, and his physical therapy, which involves weights and a pulley, prompted Norma Jean to try building herself up. Now she is attending a body-building class. Leroy has been collecting temporary disability since his tractor-trailer jackknifed in Missouri, badly twisting his left leg in its socket. He has a steel pin in his hip. He will probably not be able to drive his rig again. It sits in the backyard, like a gigantic bird that has flown home to roost. Leroy has been home in Kentucky for three months, and his leg is almost healed, but the accident frightened him and he does not want to drive any more long hauls. He is not sure what to do next. In the meantime, he makes things from craft kits. He started by building a miniature log cabin from notched Popsicle sticks. He varnished it and placed it on the TV set, where it remains. It reminds him of a rustic Nativity scene. Then he tried string art (sailing ships on black velvet), a macramé owl kit, a snap-together B-17 Flying Fortress, and a lamp made out of a model truck, with a light fixture screwed in the top of the cab. At first the kits were diversions, something to kill time, but now he is thinking about building a full-scale log house from a kit. It would be considerably cheaper than building a regular house, and besides, Leroy has grown to appreciate how things are put together. He has begun to realize that in all the years he was on the road he never took time to examine anything. He was always flying past scenery.

[*]See Miss Welty's essay "Place in Fiction" in her book *The Eye of the Story* (New York: Random House, 1979), pp. 116–33.

"They won't let you build a log cabin in any of the new subdivisions," Norma Jean tells him.

"They will if I tell them it's for you," he says, teasing her. Ever since they were married, he has promised Norma Jean he would build her a new home one day. They have always rented, and the house they live in is small and nondescript. It does not even feel like a home, Leroy realizes now.

Norma Jean works at the Rexall drugstore, and she has acquired an amazing amount of information about cosmetics. When she explains to Leroy the three stages of complexion care, involving creams, toners, and moisturizers, he thinks happily of other petroleum products—axle grease, diesel fuel. This is a connection between him and Norma Jean. Since he has been home, he has felt unusually tender about his wife and guilty over his long absences. But he can't tell what she feels about him. Norma Jean has never complained about his traveling; she has never made hurt remarks, like calling his truck a "widow-maker." He is reasonably certain she has been faithful to him, but he wishes she would celebrate his permanent homecoming more happily. Norma Jean is often startled to find Leroy at home, and he thinks she seems a little disappointed about it. Perhaps he reminds her too much of the early days of their marriage, before he went on the road. They had a child who died as an infant, years ago. They never speak about their memories of Randy, which have almost faded, but now that Leroy is home all the time, they sometimes feel awkward around each other, and Leroy wonders if one of them should mention the child. He has the feeling that they are waking up out of a dream together—that they must create a new marriage, start afresh. They are lucky they are still married. Leroy has read that for most people losing a child destroys the marriage—or else he heard this on *Donahue*. He can't always remember where he learns things anymore.

At Christmas, Leroy bought an electric organ for Norma Jean. She used to play the piano when she was in high school. "It don't leave you," she told him once. "It's like riding a bicycle."

The new instrument had so many keys and buttons that she was bewildered by it at first. She touched the keys tentatively, pushed some buttons, then pecked out "Chopsticks." It came out in an amplified fox-trot rhythm, with marimba sounds.

"It's an orchestra!" she cried.

The organ had a pecan-look finish and eighteen preset chords, with optional flute, violin, trumpet, clarinet, and banjo accompaniments. Norma Jean mastered the organ almost immediately. At first she played Christmas songs. Then she bought *The Sixties Songbook* and learned every tune in it, adding variations to each with the rows of brightly colored buttons.

"I didn't like these old songs back then," she said. "But I have this crazy feeling I missed something."

"You didn't miss a thing," said Leroy.

Leroy likes to lie on the couch and smoke a joint and listen to Norma Jean play "Can't Take My Eyes Off You" and "I'll Be Back." He is back again. After fifteen years on the road, he is finally settling down with the woman he loves. She is still pretty. Her skin is flawless. Her frosted curls resemble pencil trimmings.

Now that Leroy has come home to stay, he notices how much the town has changed. Subdivisions are spreading across western Kentucky like an oil slick. The sign at the edge of town says "Pop: 11,500"—only seven hundred more than it said twenty years before. Leroy can't figure out who is living in all the new houses. The farmers who used to gather around the courthouse square on Saturday afternoons to play checkers and spit tobacco juice have gone. It has been years since Leroy has thought about the farmers, and they have disappeared without his noticing.

Leroy meets a kid named Stevie Hamilton in the parking lot at the new shopping center. While they pretend to be strangers meeting over a stalled car, Stevie tosses an ounce of marijuana under the front seat of Leroy's car. Stevie is wearing orange jogging shoes and a T-shirt that says CHATTAHOOCHEE SUPER-RAT. His father is a prominent doctor who lives in one of the expensive subdivisions in a new white-columned brick house that looks like a funeral parlor. In the phone book under his name there is a separate number, with the listing "Teenagers."

"Where do you get this stuff?" asks Leroy. "From your pappy?"

"That's for me to know and you to find out," Stevie says. He is slit-eyed and skinny.

"What else you got?"

"What you interested in?"

"Nothing special. Just wondered."

Leroy used to take speed on the road. Now he has to go slowly. He needs to be mellow. He leans back against the car and says, "I'm aiming to build me a log house, soon as I get time. My wife, though, I don't think she likes the idea."

"Well, let me know when you want me again," Stevie says. He has a cigarette in his cupped palm, as though sheltering it from the wind. He takes a long drag, then stomps it on the asphalt and slouches away.

Stevie's father was two years ahead of Leroy in high school. Leroy is thirty-four. He married Norma Jean when they were both eighteen, and their child Randy was born a few months later, but he died at the age of four months and three days. He would be about Stevie's age now. Norma Jean and Leroy were at the drive-in, watching a double feature (*Dr. Strangelove* and *Lover Come Back*), and the baby was sleeping in the back seat. When the first movie ended, the baby was dead. It was the sudden infant death syndrome. Leroy remembers handing Randy to a nurse at the emergency room, as though he were offering her a large doll as a present. A dead baby feels like a sack of flour. "It just happens sometimes," said the doctor, in what Leroy always recalls as a nonchalant tone. Leroy can hardly remember the child anymore, but he still sees vividly a scene from *Dr. Strangelove* in which the President of the United States was talking in a folksy voice on the hot line to the Soviet premier about the bomber accidentally headed toward Russia. He was in the War Room, and the world map was lit up. Leroy remembers Norma Jean standing catatonically beside him in the hospital and himself thinking: Who is this strange girl? He had forgotten who she was. Now scientists are saying that crib death is caused by a virus. Nobody knows anything, Leroy thinks. The answers are always changing.

When Leroy gets home from the shopping center, Norma Jean's mother, Mabel Beasley, is there. Until this year, Leroy has not realized how much time she spends with Norma Jean. When she visits, she inspects the closets and then the plants, informing Norma Jean when a plant is droopy or yellow. Mabel calls the plants "flowers," although there are never any blooms. She always notices if Norma Jean's laundry is piling up. Mabel is a short, overweight woman whose tight, brown-dyed curls look more like a wig than the actual wig she sometimes wears. Today she has brought Norma

Jean an off-white dust ruffle she made for the bed; Mabel works in a custom-upholstery shop.

"This is the tenth one I made this year," Mabel says. "I got started and couldn't stop."

"It's real pretty," says Norma Jean.

"Now we can hide things under the bed," says Leroy, who gets along with his mother-in-law primarily by joking with her. Mabel has never really forgiven him for disgracing her by getting Norma Jean pregnant. When the baby died, she said that fate was mocking her.

"What's that thing?" Mabel says to Leroy in a loud voice, pointing to a tangle of yarn on a piece of canvas.

Leroy holds it up for Mabel to see. "It's my needlepoint," he explains. "This is a *Star Trek* pillow cover."

"That's what a woman would do," says Mabel. "Great day in the morning!"

"All the big football players on TV do it," he says.

"Why, Leroy, you're always trying to fool me. I don't believe you for one minute. You don't know what to do with yourself—that's the whole trouble. Sewing!"

"I'm aiming to build us a log house," says Leroy. "Soon as my plans come."

"Like *heck* you are," says Norma Jean. She takes Leroy's needlepoint and shoves it into a drawer. "You have to find a job first. Nobody can afford to build now anyway."

Mabel straightens her girdle and says, "I still think before you get tied down y'all ought to take a little run to Shiloh."

"One of these days, Mama," Norma Jean says impatiently.

Mabel is talking about Shiloh, Tennessee. For the past few years, she has been urging Leroy and Norma Jean to visit the Civil War battleground there. Mabel went there on her honeymoon—the only real trip she ever took. Her husband died of a perforated ulcer when Norma Jean was ten, but Mabel, who was accepted into the United Daughters of the Confederacy in 1975, is still preoccupied with going back to Shiloh.

"I've been to kingdom come and back in that truck out yonder," Leroy says to Mabel, "but we never yet set foot in that battleground. Ain't that something? How did I miss it?"

"It's not even that far," Mabel says.

After Mabel leaves, Norma Jean reads to Leroy from a list she has made. "Things you could do," she announces. "You could get a job as a guard at Union Carbide, where they'd let you set on a stool. You could get on at the lumberyard. You could do a little carpenter work, if you want to build so bad. You could—"

"I can't do something where I'd have to stand up all day."

"You ought to try standing up all day behind a cosmetics counter. It's amazing that I have strong feet, coming from two parents that never had strong feet at all." At the moment Norma Jean is holding on to the kitchen counter, raising her knees one at a time as she talks. She is wearing two-pound ankle weights.

"Don't worry," says Leroy. "I'll do something."

"You could truck calves to slaughter for somebody. You wouldn't have to drive any big old truck for that."

"I'm going to build you this house," says Leroy. "I want to make you a real home."

"I don't want to live in any log cabin."

"It's not a cabin. It's a house."

"I don't care. It looks like a cabin."

"You and me together could lift those logs. It's just like lifting weights."

Norma Jean doesn't answer. Under her breath, she is counting. Now she is marching through the kitchen. She is doing goose steps.

Before his accident, when Leroy came home he used to stay in the house with Norma Jean, watching TV in bed and playing cards. She would cook fried chicken, picnic ham, chocolate pie—all his favorites. Now he is home alone much of the time. In the mornings, Norma Jean disappears, leaving a cooling place in the bed. She eats a cereal called Body Buddies, and she leaves the bowl on the table, with the soggy tan balls floating in a milk puddle. He sees things about Norma Jean that he never realized before. When she chops onions, she stares off into a corner, as if she can't bear to look. She puts on her house slippers almost precisely at nine o'clock every evening and nudges her jogging shoes under the couch. She saves bread heels for the birds. Leroy watches the birds at the feeder. He notices the peculiar way goldfinches fly past the window. They close their wings, then fall, then spread their wings to catch and lift themselves. He wonders if they close their eyes when they fall. Norma Jean closes her eyes when they are in bed. She wants the lights turned out. Even then, he is sure she closes her eyes.

He goes for long drives around town. He tends to drive a car rather carelessly. Power steering and an automatic shift make a car feel so small and inconsequential that his body is hardly involved in the driving process. His injured leg stretches out comfortably. Once or twice he has almost hit something, but even the prospect of an accident seems minor in a car. He cruises the new subdivisions, feeling like a criminal rehearsing for a robbery. Norma Jean is probably right about a log house being inappropriate here in the new subdivisions. All the houses look grand and complicated. They depress him.

One day when Leroy comes home from a drive he finds Norma Jean in tears. She is in the kitchen making a potato and mushroom-soup casserole, with grated-cheese topping. She is crying because her mother caught her smoking.

"I didn't hear her coming. I was standing here puffing away pretty as you please," Norma Jean says, wiping her eyes.

"I knew it would happen sooner or later," says Leroy, putting his arm around her.

"She don't know the meaning of the word 'knock,'" says Norma Jean. "It's a wonder she hadn't caught me years ago."

"Think of it this way," Leroy says. "What if she caught me with a joint?"

"You better not let her!" Norma Jean shrieks. "I'm warning you, Leroy Moffitt!"

"I'm just kidding. Here, play me a tune. That'll help you relax."

Norma Jean puts the casserole in the oven and sets the timer. Then she plays a ragtime tune, with horns and banjo, as Leroy lights up a joint and lies on the couch, laughing to himself about Mabel's catching him at it. He thinks of Stevie Hamilton— a doctor's son pushing grass. Everything is funny. The whole town seems crazy and small. He is reminded of Virgil Mathis, a boastful policeman Leroy used to shoot pool with. Virgil recently led a drug bust in a back room at a bowling alley, where he seized ten thousand dollars' worth of marijuana. The newspaper had a picture of him holding up the bags of grass and grinning widely. Right now, Leroy can imagine Virgil breaking down the door and arresting him with a lungful of smoke. Virgil would probably have been alerted to the scene because of all the racket Norma Jean is making. Now she sounds like a hard-rock band. Norma Jean is terrific. When she switches to a Latin-rhythm version of "Sunshine Superman," Leroy hums along. Norma Jean's foot goes up and down, up and down.

"Well, what do you think?" Leroy says, when Norma Jean pauses to search through her music.

"What do I think about what?"

His mind has gone blank. Then he says, "I'll sell my rig and build us a house." That wasn't what he wanted to say. He wanted to know what she thought—what she *really* thought—about them.

"Don't start in on that again," says Norma Jean. She begins playing "Who'll Be the Next in Line?"

Leroy used to tell hitchhikers his whole life story—about his travels, his hometown, the baby. He would end with a question: "Well, what do you think?" It was just a rhetorical question. In time, he had the feeling that he'd been telling the same story over and over to the same hitchhikers. He quit talking to hitchhikers when he realized how his voice sounded—whining and self-pitying, like some teenage-tragedy song. Now Leroy has the sudden impulse to tell Norma Jean about himself, as if he had just met her. They have known each other so long they have forgotten a lot about each other. They could become reacquainted. But when the oven timer goes off and she runs to the kitchen, he forgets why he wants to do this.

The next day, Mabel drops by. It is Saturday and Norma Jean is cleaning. Leroy is studying the plans of his log house, which have finally come in the mail. He has them spread out on the table—big sheets of stiff blue paper, with diagrams and numbers printed in white. While Norma Jean runs the vacuum, Mabel drinks coffee. She sets her coffee cup on a blueprint.

"I'm just waiting for time to pass," she says to Leroy, drumming her fingers on the table.

As soon as Norma Jean switches off the vacuum, Mabel says in a loud voice, "Did you hear about the datsun dog that killed the baby?"

Norma Jean says, "The word is 'dachshund.'"

"They put the dog on trial. It chewed the baby's legs off. The mother was in the next room all the time." She raises her voice. "They thought it was neglect."

Norma Jean is holding her ears. Leroy manages to open the refrigerator and get some Diet Pepsi to offer Mabel. Mabel still has some coffee and she waves away the Pepsi.

"Datsuns are like that," Mabel says. "They're jealous dogs. They'll tear a place to pieces if you don't keep an eye on them."

"You better watch out what you're saying, Mabel," says Leroy.

"Well, facts is facts."

Leroy looks out the window at his rig. It is like a huge piece of furniture gathering dust in the backyard. Pretty soon it will be an antique. He hears the vacuum cleaner. Norma Jean seems to be cleaning the living room rug again.

Later, she says to Leroy, "She just said that about the baby because she caught me smoking. She's trying to pay me back."

"What are you talking about?" Leroy says, nervously shuffling blueprints.

"You know good and well," Norma Jean says. She is sitting in a kitchen chair with her feet up and her arms wrapped around her knees. She looks small and helpless. She says, "The very idea, her bringing up a subject like that! Saying it was neglect."

"She didn't mean that," Leroy says.

"She might not have *thought* she meant it. She always says things like that. You don't know how she goes on."

"But she didn't really mean it. She was just talking."

Leroy opens a king-sized bottle of beer and pours it into two glasses, dividing it carefully. He hands a glass to Norma Jean and she takes it from him mechanically. For a long time, they sit by the kitchen window watching the birds at the feeder.

Something is happening. Norma Jean is going to night school. She has graduated from her six-week body-building course and now she is taking an adult-education course in composition at Paducah Community College. She spends her evenings outlining paragraphs.

"First you have a topic sentence," she explains to Leroy. "Then you divide it up. Your secondary topic has to be connected to your primary topic."

To Leroy, this sounds intimidating. "I never was any good in English," he says.

"It makes a lot of sense."

"What are you doing this for, anyhow?"

She shrugs. "It's something to do." She stands up and lifts her dumbbells a few times.

"Driving a rig, nobody cared about my English."

"I'm not criticizing your English."

Norma Jean used to say, "If I lose ten minutes' sleep, I just drag all day." Now she stays up late, writing compositions. She got a B on her first paper—a how-to theme on soup-based casseroles. Recently Norma Jean has been cooking unusual foods— tacos, lasagna, Bombay chicken. She doesn't play the organ anymore, though her second paper was called "Why Music Is Important to Me." She sits at the kitchen table, concentrating on her outlines, while Leroy plays with his log house plans, practicing with a set of Lincoln Logs. The thought of getting a truckload of notched, numbered logs scares him, and he wants to be prepared. As he and Norma Jean work together at the kitchen table, Leroy has the hopeful thought that they are sharing something, but he knows he is a fool to think this. Norma Jean is miles away. He knows he is going to lose her. Like Mabel, he is just waiting for time to pass.

One day, Mabel is there before Norma Jean gets home from work, and Leroy finds himself confiding in her. Mabel, he realizes, must know Norma Jean better than he does.

"I don't know what's got into that girl," Mabel says. "She used to go to bed with the chickens. Now you say she's up all hours. Plus her a-smoking. I like to died."

"I want to make her this beautiful home," Leroy says, indicating the Lincoln Logs. "I don't think she even wants it. Maybe she was happier with me gone."

"She don't know what to make of you, coming home like this."

"Is that it?"

Mabel takes the roof off his Lincoln Log cabin. "You couldn't get *me* in a log cabin," she says. "I was raised in one. It's no picnic, let me tell you."

"They're different now," says Leroy.

"I tell you what," Mabel says, smiling oddly at Leroy.

"What?"

"Take her on down to Shiloh. Y'all need to get out together, stir a little. Her brain's all balled up over them books."

Leroy can see traces of Norma Jean's features in her mother's face. Mabel's worn face has the texture of crinkled cotton, but suddenly she looks pretty. It occurs to Leroy that Mabel has been hinting all along that she wants them to take her with them to Shiloh.

"Let's all go to Shiloh," he says. "You and me and her. Come Sunday."

Mabel throws up her hands in protest. "Oh, no, not me. Young folks want to be by theirselves."

When Norma Jean comes in with groceries, Leroy says excitedly, "Your mama here's been dying to go to Shiloh for thirty-five years. It's about time we went, don't you think?"

"I'm not going to butt in on anybody's second honeymoon," Mabel says.

"Who's going on a honeymoon, for Christ's sake?" Norma Jean says loudly.

"I never raised no daughter of mine to talk that-a-way," Mabel says.

"You ain't seen nothing yet," says Norma Jean. She starts putting away boxes and cans, slamming cabinet doors.

"There's a log cabin at Shiloh," Mabel says. "It was there during the battle. There's bullet holes in it."

"When are you going to *shut up* about Shiloh, Mama?" asks Norma Jean.

"I always thought Shiloh was the prettiest place, so full of history," Mabel goes on. "I just hoped y'all could see it once before I die, so you could tell me about it." Later, she whispers to Leroy, "You do what I said. A little change is what she needs."

"Your name means 'the king,'" Norma Jean says to Leroy that evening. He is trying to get her to go to Shiloh, and she is reading a book about another century.

"Well, I reckon I ought to be right proud."

"I guess so."

"Am I still king around here?"

Norma Jean flexes her biceps and feels them for hardness. "I'm not fooling around with anybody, if that's what you mean," she says.

"Would you tell me if you were?"

"I don't know."

"What does *your* name mean?"

"It was Marilyn Monroe's real name."

"No kidding!"

"Norma comes from the Normans. They were invaders," she says. She closes her book and looks hard at Leroy. "I'll go to Shiloh with you if you'll stop staring at me."

On Sunday, Norma Jean packs a picnic and they go to Shiloh. To Leroy's relief, Mabel says she does not want to come with them. Norma Jean drives, and Leroy, sitting beside her, feels like some boring hitchhiker she has picked up. He tries some conversation, but she answers him in monosyllables. At Shiloh, she drives aimlessly through the park, past bluffs and trails and steep ravines. Shiloh is an immense place, and Leroy cannot see it as a battleground. It is not what he expected. He thought it would look like a golf course. Monuments are everywhere, showing through the thick clusters of trees. Norma Jean passes the log cabin Mabel mentioned. It is surrounded by tourists looking for bullet holes.

"That's not the kind of log house I've got in mind," says Leroy apologetically.

"I know *that*."

"This is a pretty place. Your mama was right."

"It's O.K.," says Norma Jean. "Well, we've seen it. I hope she's satisfied."

They burst out laughing together.

At the park museum, a movie on Shiloh is shown every half hour, but they decide that they don't want to see it. They buy a souvenir Confederate flag for Mabel, and then they find a picnic spot near the cemetery. Norma Jean has brought a picnic cooler, with pimiento sandwiches, soft drinks, and Yodels. Leroy eats a sandwich and then smokes a joint, hiding it behind the picnic cooler. Norma Jean has quit smoking altogether. She is picking cake crumbs from the cellophane wrapper, like a fussy bird.

Leroy says, "So the boys in gray ended up in Corinth. The Union soldiers zapped 'em finally. April 7, 1862."

They both know that he doesn't know any history. He is just talking about some of the historical plaques they have read. He feels awkward, like a boy on a date with an older girl. They are still just making conversation.

"Corinth is where Mama eloped to," says Norma Jean.

They sit in silence and stare at the cemetery for the Union dead and, beyond, at a tall cluster of trees. Campers are parked nearby, bumper to bumper, and small children in bright clothing are cavorting and squealing. Norma Jean wads up the cake wrapper and squeezes it tightly in her hand. Without looking at Leroy, she says, "I want to leave you."

Leroy takes a bottle of Coke out of the cooler and flips off the cap. He holds the bottle poised near his mouth but cannot remember to take a drink. Finally he says, "No, you don't."

"Yes, I do."

"I won't let you."

"You can't stop me."

"Don't do me that way."

Leroy knows Norma Jean will have her own way. "Didn't I promise to be home from now on?" he says.

"In some ways, a woman prefers a man who wanders," says Norma Jean. "That sounds crazy, I know."

"You're not crazy."

Leroy remembers to drink from his Coke. Then he says, "Yes, you *are* crazy. You and me could start all over again. Right back at the beginning."

"We *have* started all over again," says Norma Jean. "And this is how it turned out."

"What did I do wrong?"

"Nothing."

"Is this one of those women's lib things?" Leroy asks.

"Don't be funny."

The cemetery, a green slope dotted with white markers, looks like a subdivision site. Leroy is trying to comprehend that his marriage is breaking up, but for some reason he is wondering about white slabs in a graveyard.

"Everything was fine till Mama caught me smoking," says Norma Jean, standing up. "That set something off."

"What are you talking about?"

"She won't leave me alone—*you* won't leave me alone." Norma Jean seems to be crying, but she is looking away from him. "I feel eighteen again. I can't face that all over again." She starts walking away. "No, it *wasn't* fine. I don't know what I'm saying. Forget it."

Leroy takes a lungful of smoke and closes his eyes as Norma Jean's words sink in. He tries to focus on the fact that thirty-five hundred soldiers died on the grounds around him. He can only think of that war as a board game with plastic soldiers. Leroy almost smiles, as he compares the Confederates' daring attack on the Union camps and Virgil Mathis's raid on the bowling alley. General Grant, drunk and furious, shoved the Southerners back to Corinth, where Mabel and Jet Beasley were married years later, when Mabel was still thin and good-looking. The next day, Mabel and Jet visited the battleground, and then Norma Jean was born, and then she married Leroy and they had a baby, which they lost, and now Leroy and Norma Jean are here at the same battleground. Leroy knows he is leaving out a lot. He is leaving out the insides of history. History was always just names and dates to him. It occurs to him that building a house out of logs is similarly empty—too simple. And the real inner workings of a marriage, like most of history, have escaped him. Now he sees that building a log house is the dumbest idea he could have had. It was clumsy of him to think Norma Jean would want a log house. It was a crazy idea: He'll have to think of something else, quickly. He will wad the blueprints into tight balls and fling them into the lake. Then he'll get moving again. He opens his eyes. Norma Jean has moved away and is walking through the cemetery, following a serpentine brick path.

Leroy gets up to follow his wife, but his good leg is asleep and his bad leg still hurts him. Norma Jean is far away, walking rapidly toward the bluff by the river, and he tries to hobble toward her. Some children run past him, screaming noisily. Norma Jean has reached the bluff, and she is looking out over the Tennessee River. Now she turns toward Leroy and waves her arms. Is she beckoning to him? She seems to be doing an exercise for her chest muscles. The sky is unusually pale—the color of the dust ruffle Mabel made for their bed.

(1982)

QUESTIONS FOR REFLECTION

1. What does the following information contribute to your understanding of the story? Shiloh was the location of a famous Civil War battle in which Union soldiers under the leadership of General Ulysses S. Grant soundly defeated the Confederate forces.
2. Look at the story's closing scene, which occurs at the famous battle site. How might that scene be related to what happened there during the Civil War? What other kinds of battlefields does the story describe?

POINT OF VIEW

An author's decisions about who is to tell the story and how it is to be told are among the most important he or she makes. In a story with an *objective point of view,* the writer shows what happens without directly stating more than can be inferred from its action and dialogue. The narrator, in short, does not tell us anything about what the characters think or feel. He remains a detached observer. The narrator of Chopin's "The Story of an Hour" does not participate in the action as a character. Kate Chopin employs a third-person point of view, letting us know directly what Mrs. Mallard feels. We learn about the characters from an outside source; in Chopin's case, it is an authority. Imagine the story told from a detached, objective point of view in which we were not let into Mrs. Mallard's consciousness. The tone and feel of the story would be radically altered.

Although third-person point of view may take us inside a character's consciousness or remain objective, it does not assume the perspective of any character. Stories with narrators who participate in the action are presented from a *first-person point of view.* Narrators of such fictions tell their stories in their own voices with their particular limitations of knowledge and vision. The limitations of a first-person narrator offer writers the opportunity to exploit the discrepancy between the writer's vision and the narrator's. In both Edgar Allan Poe's "The Black Cat" and Ralph Ellison's "Battle Royal," for example, we encounter narrators who perceive and present themselves one way, but whom we see in different ways. Reading stories narrated in the first person, we need to question the narrator's trustworthiness and remain alert for textual signals that either ensure or undermine it.

Whether a writer uses a first- or a third-person narrator, he or she must also decide how much to let the narrator know about the characters. Narrators who know everything about all the characters are "omniscient" (all-knowing) as is the narrator of Joyce's "The Boarding House," who enters the minds of each of the characters and reveals what they think and feel. Stories with such narrators are written from an *omniscient point of view.* If, however, the narrator's knowledge is limited to only one character, major or minor, rather than to all, the narrator possesses *limited omniscience,* as in Chopin's "The Story of an Hour." James Joyce imposes no limitations on his narrator in "The Boarding House." Here is the narrator revealing the thoughts of Mrs. Mooney:

> She was sure she would win. To begin with she had all the weight of social opinion on her side: she was an outraged mother. She had allowed him to live beneath her roof, assuming that he was a man of honour, and he had simply abused her hospitality. . . youth could not be pleaded as his excuse; nor could ignorance be his excuse. . . . He had simply taken advantage of Polly's youth and inexperience: that was evident. The question was: What reparation would he make?

And here is the same narrator granting us an inside view of Mr. Doran:

> He had a notion that he was being had. He could imagine his friends talking of the affair and laughing. She *was* a little vulgar; sometimes she said *I seen* and *If I had've known.* But what would grammar matter if he really loved her? He could not make up his mind whether to like her or despise her for what she had done.

> Of course, he had done it too. His instinct urged him to remain
> free, not to marry. Once you are married you are done for, it
> said.

Giving us an inside view of each character (Polly receives the same treatment),
Joyce's omniscient narrator makes us aware of multiple perspectives. That is, he
lets us see what each character experiences; he shows us their differing perceptions of the same situation. In doing so Joyce shifts our sympathies from
one character to another as we come to understand their different needs and
desires.

The omniscient point of view that Joyce employed in his twentieth-century
story "The Boarding House" was a popular choice of eighteenth- and
nineteenth-century novelists. But fashions in point of view change: the limited
omniscient and first-person points of view are currently popular with contemporary writers. We have described some of the narrative points of view available to writers, but there are others. As we read stories with point of view in
mind, we should remember:

1. That it is important to consider *how* point of view affects our responses to
   the characters and how it collaborates with the other elements of fiction to
   convey feeling and embody meaning.
2. That our response to a fictional narrator is influenced by the degree of the
   narrator's knowledge, the objectivity of a narrator's responses, and the degree
   of his or her participation in the action.
3. That a first-person narrator is not always a trustworthy guide; in fact, a large
   part of our work as readers is to determine a narrator's reliability, to estimate
   the truth of that narrator's disclosures.

With these considerations in mind, read the following story, William
Faulkner's "A Rose for Emily." How objective is the narrator's view of Miss
Emily? How does the perception we gain of her through observing her in dia-
logue and with other characters in action compare with the narrator's view?
Where and with what effect does the narrator's focus shift from presenting Miss
Emily objectively to presenting her subjectively?

WILLIAM FAULKNER
[1897–1962]

A Rose for Emily

I

When Miss Emily Grierson died, our whole town went to her funeral: the men
through a sort of respectful affection for a fallen monument, the women mostly out of
curiosity to see the inside of her house, which no one save an old manservant—a
combined gardener and cook—had seen in at least ten years.

It was a big, squarish frame house that had once been white, decorated with cupolas and spires and scrolled balconies in the heavily lightsome style of the seventies, set on what had once been our most select street. But garages and cotton gins had encroached and obliterated even the august names of that neighborhood; only Miss Emily's house was left, lifting its stubborn and coquettish decay above the cotton wagons and the gasoline pumps—an eyesore among eyesores. And now Miss Emily had gone to join the representatives of those august names where they lay in the cedar-bemused cemetery among the ranked and anonymous graves of Union and Confederate soldiers who fell at the battle of Jefferson.

Alive, Miss Emily had been a tradition, a duty, and a care; a sort of hereditary obligation upon the town, dating from that day in 1894 when Colonel Sartoris, the mayor—he who fathered the edict that no Negro woman should appear on the streets without an apron—remitted her taxes, the dispensation dating from the death of her father on into perpetuity. Not that Miss Emily would have accepted charity. Colonel Sartoris invented an involved tale to the effect that Miss Emily's father had loaned money to the town, which the town, as a matter of business, preferred this way of repaying. Only a man of Colonel Sartoris' generation and thought could have invented it, and only a woman could have believed it.

When the next generation, with its more modern ideas, became mayors and aldermen, this arrangement created some little dissatisfaction. On the first of the year they mailed her a tax notice. February came, and there was no reply. They wrote her a formal letter, asking her to call at the sheriff's office at her convenience. A week later the mayor wrote her himself, offering to call or to send his car for her, and received in reply a note on paper of an archaic shape, in a thin, flowing calligraphy in faded ink, to the effect that she no longer went out at all. The tax notice was also enclosed, without comment.

They called a special meeting of the Board of Aldermen. A deputation waited upon her, knocked at the door through which no visitor had passed since she ceased giving china-painting lessons eight or ten years earlier. They were admitted by the old Negro into a dim hall from which a stairway mounted into still more shadow. It smelled of dust and disuse—a close, dank smell. The Negro led them into the parlor. It was furnished in heavy, leather-covered furniture. When the Negro opened the blinds of one window, they could see that the leather was cracked; and when they sat down, a faint dust rose sluggishly about their thighs, spinning with slow motes in the single sun-ray. On a tarnished gilt easel before the fireplace stood a crayon portrait of Miss Emily's father.

They rose when she entered—a small, fat woman in black, with a thin gold chain descending to her waist and vanishing into her belt, leaning on an ebony cane with a tarnished gold head. Her skeleton was small and spare; perhaps that was why what would have been merely plumpness in another was obesity in her. She looked bloated, like a body long submerged in motionless water, and of that pallid hue. Her eyes, lost in the fatty ridges of her face, looked like two small pieces of coal pressed into a lump of dough as they moved from one face to another while the visitors stated their errand.

She did not ask them to sit. She just stood in the door and listened quietly until the spokesman came to a stumbling halt. Then they could hear the invisible watch ticking at the end of the gold chain.

Her voice was dry and cold. "I have no taxes in Jefferson. Colonel Sartoris explained it to me. Perhaps one of you can gain access to the city records and satisfy yourselves."

"But we have. We are the city authorities, Miss Emily. Didn't you get a notice from the sheriff, signed by him?"

"I received a paper, yes," Miss Emily said. "Perhaps he considers himself the sheriff. . . . I have no taxes in Jefferson."

"But there is nothing on the books to show that, you see. We must go by the—"

"See Colonel Sartoris. I have no taxes in Jefferson."

"But, Miss Emily—"

"See Colonel Sartoris." (Colonel Sartoris had been dead almost ten years.) "I have no taxes in Jefferson. Tobe!" The Negro appeared. "Show these gentlemen out."

2

So she vanquished them, horse and foot, just as she had vanquished their fathers thirty years before about the smell. That was two years after her father's death and a short time after her sweetheart—the one we believed would marry her—had deserted her. After her father's death she went out very little; after her sweetheart went away, people hardly saw her at all. A few of the ladies had the temerity to call, but were not received, and the only sign of life about the place was the Negro man—a young man then— going in and out with a market basket.

"Just as if a man—any man—could keep a kitchen properly," the ladies said; so they were not surprised when the smell developed. It was another link between the gross, teeming world and the high and mighty Griersons.

A neighbor, a woman, complained to the mayor, Judge Stevens, eighty years old.

"But what will you have me do about it, madam?" he said.

"Why, send her word to stop it," the woman said. "Isn't there a law?"

"I'm sure that won't be necessary," Judge Stevens said. "It's probably just a snake or a rat that nigger of hers killed in the yard. I'll speak to him about it."

The next day he received two more complaints, one from a man who came in diffident deprecation. "We really must do something about it, Judge. I'd be the last one in the world to bother Miss Emily, but we've got to do something." That night the Board of Aldermen met—three graybeards and one younger man, a member of the rising generation.

"It's simple enough," he said. "Send her word to have her place cleaned up. Give her a certain time to do it in, and if she don't. . . ."

"Dammit, sir," Judge Stevens said, "will you accuse a lady to her face of smelling bad?"

So the next night, after midnight, four men crossed Miss Emily's lawn and slunk about the house like burglars, sniffing along the base of the brickwork and at the cellar openings while one of them performed a regular sowing motion with his hand out of a sack slung from his shoulder. They broke open the cellar door and sprinkled lime there, and in all the outbuildings. As they recrossed the lawn, a window that had been dark was lighted and Miss Emily sat in it, the light behind her, and her upright torso motionless as that of an idol. They crept quietly across the lawn and into the shadow of the locusts that lined the street. After a week or two the smell went away.

That was when people had begun to feel really sorry for her. People in our town, remembering how old lady Wyatt, her great-aunt, had gone completely crazy at last, believed that the Griersons held themselves a little too high for what they really were. None of the young men were quite good enough for Miss Emily and such. We had long thought of them as a tableau, Miss Emily a slender figure in white in the background, her father a spraddled silhouette in the foreground, his back to her and clutching a horsewhip, the two of them framed by the backflung front door. So when she got to be thirty and was still single, we were not pleased exactly, but vindicated; even with insanity in the family she wouldn't have turned down all of her chances if they had really materialized.

When her father died, it got about that the house was all that was left to her; and in a way, people were glad. At last they could pity Miss Emily. Being left alone, and a pauper, she had become humanized. Now she too would know the old thrill and the old despair of a penny more or less.

The day after his death all the ladies prepared to call at the house and offer condolence and aid, as is our custom. Miss Emily met them at the door, dressed as usual and with no trace of grief on her face. She told them that her father was not dead. She did that for three days, with the ministers calling on her, and the doctors, trying to persuade her to let them dispose of the body. Just as they were about to resort to law and force, she broke down, and they buried her father quickly.

We did not say she was crazy then. We believed she had to do that. We remembered all the young men her father had driven away, and we knew that with nothing left, she would have to cling to that which had robbed her, as people will.

3

She was sick for a long time. When we saw her again, her hair was cut short, making her look like a girl, with a vague resemblance to those angels in colored church windows—sort of tragic and serene.

The town had just let the contracts for paving the sidewalks, and in the summer after her father's death they began the work. The construction company came with niggers and mules and machinery, and a foreman named Homer Barron, a Yankee—a big, dark, ready man, with a big voice and eyes lighter than his face. The little boys would follow in groups to hear him cuss the niggers, and the niggers singing in time to the rise and fall of picks. Pretty soon he knew everybody in town. Whenever you heard a lot of laughing anywhere about the square, Homer Barron would be in the center of the group. Presently, we began to see him and Miss Emily on Sunday afternoons driving in the yellow-wheeled buggy and the matched team of bays from the livery stable.

At first we were glad that Miss Emily would have an interest, because the ladies all said, "Of course a Grierson would not think seriously of a Northerner, a day laborer." But there were still others, older people, who said that even grief could not cause a real lady to forget *noblesse oblige*—without calling it *noblesse oblige*. They just said, "Poor Emily. Her kinsfolk should come to her." She had some kin in Alabama; but years ago her father had fallen out with them over the estate of old lady Wyatt, the crazy woman, and there was no communication between the two families. They had not even been represented at the funeral.

And as soon as the old people said, "Poor Emily," the whispering began. "Do you suppose it's really so?" they said to one another. "Of course it is. What else could. . . ." This behind their hands; rustling of craned silk and satin behind jalousies closed upon the sun of Sunday afternoon as the thin, swift clop-clop-clop of the matched team passed: "Poor Emily."

She carried her head high enough—even when we believed that she was fallen. It was as if she demanded more than ever the recognition of her dignity as the last Grierson; as if it had wanted that touch of earthiness to reaffirm her imperviousness. Like when she bought the rat poison, the arsenic. That was over a year after they had begun to say "Poor Emily," and while the two female cousins were visiting her.

"I want some poison," she said to the druggist. She was over thirty then, still a slight woman, though thinner than usual, with cold, haughty black eyes in a face the flesh of which was strained across the temples and about the eyesockets as you imagine a lighthouse-keeper's face ought to look. "I want some poison," she said.

"Yes, Miss Emily. What kind? For rats and such? I'd recom——"

"I want the best you have. I don't care what kind."

The druggist named several. "They'll kill anything up to an elephant. But what you want is——"

"Arsenic," Miss Emily said. "Is that a good one?"

"Is . . . arsenic? Yes, ma'am. But what you want——"

"I want arsenic."

The druggist looked down at her. She looked back at him, erect, her face like a strained flag. "Why, of course," the druggist said. "If that's what you want. But the law requires you to tell what you are going to use it for."

Miss Emily just stared at him, her head tilted back in order to look him eye for eye, until he looked away and went and got the arsenic and wrapped it up. The Negro delivery boy brought her the package; the druggist didn't come back. When she opened the package at home there was written on the box, under the skull and bones: "For rats."

4

So the next day we all said, "She will kill herself"; and we said it would be the best thing. When she had first begun to be seen with Homer Barron, we had said, "She will marry him." Then we said, "She will persuade him yet," because Homer himself had remarked—he liked men, and it was known that he drank with the younger men in the Elks' Club—that he was not a marrying man. Later we said, "Poor Emily" behind the jalousies as they passed on Sunday afternoon in the glittering buggy, Miss Emily with her head high and Homer Barron with his hat cocked and a cigar in his teeth, reins and whip in a yellow glove.

Then some of the ladies began to say that it was a disgrace to the town and a bad example to the young people. The men did not want to interfere, but at last the ladies forced the Baptist minister—Miss Emily's people were Episcopal—to call upon her. He would never divulge what happened during that interview, but he refused to go back again. The next Sunday they again drove about the streets, and the following day the minister's wife wrote to Miss Emily's relations in Alabama.

So she had blood-kin under her roof again and we sat back to watch developments. At first nothing happened. Then we were sure that they were to be married. We learned that Miss Emily had been to the jeweler's and ordered a man's toilet set in silver, with the letters H.B. on each piece. Two days later we learned that she had bought a complete outfit of men's clothing, including a nightshirt, and we said, "They are married." We were really glad. We were glad because the two female cousins were even more Grierson than Miss Emily had ever been.

So we were not surprised when Homer Barron—the streets had been finished some time since—was gone. We were a little disappointed that there was not a public blowing-off, but we believed that he had gone on to prepare for Miss Emily's coming, or to give her a chance to get rid of the cousins. (By that time it was a cabal, and we were all Miss Emily's allies to help circumvent the cousins.) Sure enough, after another week they departed. And, as we had expected all along, within three days Homer Barron was back in town. A neighbor saw the Negro man admit him at the kitchen door at dusk one evening.

And that was the last we saw of Homer Barron. And of Miss Emily for some time. The Negro man went in and out with the market basket, but the front door remained closed. Now and then we would see her at the window for a moment, as the men did that night when they sprinkled the lime, but for almost six months she did not appear on the streets. Then we knew that this was to be expected too; as if that quality of her father which had thwarted her woman's life so many times had been too virulent and too furious to die.

When we next saw Miss Emily, she had grown fat and her hair was turning gray. During the next few years it grew grayer and grayer until it attained an even pepper-and-salt iron-gray, when it ceased turning. Up to the day of her death at seventy-four it was still that vigorous iron-gray, like the hair of an active man.

From that time on her front door remained closed, save during a period of six or seven years, when she was about forty, during which she gave lessons in china-painting. She fitted up a studio in one of the downstairs rooms, where the daughters and granddaughters of Colonel Sartoris' contemporaries were sent to her with the same regularity and in the same spirit that they were sent to church on Sundays with a twenty-five-cent piece for the collection plate. Meanwhile her taxes had been remitted.

Then the newer generation became the backbone and the spirit of the town, and the painting pupils grew up and fell away and did not send their children to her with boxes of color and tedious brushes and pictures cut from the ladies' magazines. The front door closed upon the last one and remained closed for good. When the town got free postal delivery, Miss Emily alone refused to let them fasten the metal numbers above her door and attach a mailbox to it. She would not listen to them.

Daily, monthly, yearly we watched the Negro grow grayer and more stooped, going in and out with the market basket. Each December we sent her a tax notice, which would be returned by the post office a week later, unclaimed. Now and then we would see her in one of the downstairs windows—she had evidently shut up the top floor of the house—like the carven torso of an idol in a niche, looking or not looking at us, we could never tell which. Thus she passed from generation to generation— dear, inescapable, impervious, tranquil, and perverse.

And so she died. Fell ill in the house filled with dust and shadows, with only a doddering Negro man to wait on her. We did not even know she was sick; we had long since given up trying to get any information from the Negro. He talked to no one, probably not even to her, for his voice had grown harsh and rusty, as if from disuse.

She died in one of the downstairs rooms, in a heavy walnut bed with a curtain, her gray head propped on a pillow yellow and moldy with age and lack of sunlight.

5

The Negro met the first of the ladies at the front door and let them in, with their hushed, sibilant voices and their quick, curious glances, and then he disappeared. He walked right through the house and out the back and was not seen again.

The two female cousins came at once. They held the funeral on the second day, with the town coming to look at Miss Emily beneath a mass of bought flowers, with the crayon face of her father musing profoundly above the bier and the ladies sibilant and macabre; and the very old men—some in their brushed Confederate uniforms— on the porch and the lawn, talking of Miss Emily as if she had been a contemporary of theirs, believing that they had danced with her and courted her perhaps, confusing time with its mathematical progression, as the old do, to whom all the past is not a diminishing road but, instead, a huge meadow which no winter ever quite touches, divided from them now by the narrow bottleneck of the most recent decade of years.

Already we knew that there was one room in that region above stairs which no one had seen in forty years, and which would have to be forced. They waited until Miss Emily was decently in the ground before they opened it.

The violence of breaking down the door seemed to fill this room with pervading dust. A thin, acrid pall as of the tomb seemed to lie everywhere upon this room decked and furnished as for a bridal: upon the valance curtains of faded rose color, upon the rose-shaded lights, upon the dressing table, upon the delicate array of crystal and the man's toilet things backed with tarnished silver, silver so tarnished that the monogram was obscured. Among them lay a collar and tie, as if they had just been removed, which, lifted, left upon the surface a pale crescent in the dust. Upon a chair hung the suit, carefully folded; beneath it the two mute shoes and the discarded socks.

The man himself lay in the bed.

For a long while we just stood there, looking down at the profound and fleshless grin. The body had apparently once lain in the attitude of an embrace, but now the long sleep that outlasts love, that conquers even the grimace of love, had cuckolded him. What was left of him, rotted beneath what was left of the nightshirt, had become inextricable from the bed in which he lay; and upon him and upon the pillow beside him lay that even coating of the patient and biding dust.

Then we noticed that in the second pillow was the indentation of a head. One of us lifted something from it, and leaning forward, that faint and invisible dust dry and acrid in the nostrils, we saw a long strand of iron-gray hair.

(1930)

QUESTION FOR REFLECTION

Although "A Rose for Emily" is narrated in the first person, the narrator is not "I" but "we." The narrator thus represents a communal rather than an individual point of view.

How does the narrator (and the town) view Miss Emily? Find passages that represent more than one view of her, and explain their significance.

LANGUAGE AND STYLE

The way a writer chooses words, arranges them in sentences and longer units of discourse, and exploits their significance determines his or her *style.* Style is the verbal identity of a writer, as unmistakable as his or her face or voice. Reflecting their individuality, writers' styles convey their unique ways of seeing the world.

In the discussion of the language and style of fiction, we will concentrate on *diction,* the kinds of word choices a writer makes; *syntax,* the order those words assume in sentences; and the presence or absence of figurative language, especially figures of comparison (simile and metaphor).★

Here is a paragraph from William Faulkner's "A Rose for Emily."

> Alive, Miss Emily had been a tradition, a duty, and a care; a sort of hereditary obligation upon the town, dating from that day in 1894 when Colonel Sartoris, the mayor—he who fathered the edict that no Negro woman should appear on the streets without an apron—remitted her taxes, the dispensation dating from the death of her father on into perpetuity. Not that Miss Emily would have accepted charity. Colonel Sartoris invented an involved tale to the effect that Miss Emily's father had loaned money to the town, which the town, as a matter of business, preferred this way of repaying. Only a man of Colonel Sartoris' generation and thought could have invented it, and only a woman could have believed it.

In this passage from the beginning of the story, Faulkner introduces his central character, Miss Emily Grierson. He does so in a style both elegant and formal. This is equally apparent in the triple description of Miss Emily in the first sentence ("a tradition, a duty, and a care") and in the carefully balanced phrases of the final sentence ("only a man" . . . "only a woman"; and "could have invented it" . . . "could have believed it"). The sentences, with their artfully controlled rhythms, create an effect of eloquence. This eloquence is achieved partly by the balanced phrasing we have already noted, and partly by the studied formality of the long sentences, especially the first. Constructions like "he who fathered the edict" and "the dispensation dating from" create a tone more elevated than that of everyday speech. Also contributing to this tone is the repetition of words ("had loaned money to the town, which the town") and the heavy reliance on pauses within the first and third sentences. Finally, there is the play of sound, alliteration and assonance especially, in "*da*ting from that *day*" and "*di*spensation *da*ting from the *death*."

★For an extensive discussion of figurative language, see Chapter 9.

Faulkner's prose flows in a stately progression and expansion of phrases, gathering force as a sentence concludes. Faulkner's style seems more "written" rather than spoken—or if spoken, both eloquent and exalted.

The imagery and figures of comparison that Faulkner and other writers use enrich their prose and impart a unique and personal view of the world. They are simultaneously indelible stamps of each writer's style and keys to understanding their works. The language of the following story, "Araby" by James Joyce, reveals both the narrator's conception of himself as a boy and his adult understanding of his boyhood. Note carefully the descriptions of Mangan's sister, especially their mixture of erotic and religious details. Consider also the connotations of the first and last paragraphs and the implications of the religious imagery throughout.

J A M E S   J O Y C E
[1882–1941]

Araby

North Richmond Street, being blind, was a quiet street except at the hour when the Christian Brothers' School set the boys free. An uninhabited house of two storeys stood at the blind end, detached from its neighbours in a square ground. The other houses of the street, conscious of decent lives within them, gazed at one another with brown imperturbable faces.

The former tenant of our house, a priest, had died in the back drawing-room. Air, musty from having been long enclosed, hung in all the rooms, and the waste room behind the kitchen was littered with old useless papers. Among these I found a few paper-covered books, the pages of which were curled and damp: *The Abbot,* by Walter Scott, *The Devout Communicant* and *The Memoirs of Vidocq.* I liked the last best because its leaves were yellow. The wild garden behind the house contained a central apple-tree and a few straggling bushes under one of which I found the late tenant's rusty bicycle-pump. He had been a very charitable priest; in his will he had left all his money to institutions and the furniture of his house to his sister.

When the short days of winter came dusk fell before we had well eaten our dinners. When we met in the street the houses had grown sombre. The space of sky above us was the colour of ever-changing violet and towards it the lamps of the street lifted their feeble lanterns. The cold air stung us and we played till our bodies glowed. Our shouts echoed in the silent street. The career of our play brought us through the dark muddy lanes behind the houses where we ran the gantlet of the rough tribes from the cottages, to the back doors of the dark dripping gardens where odours arose from the ashpits, to the dark odorous stables where a coachman smoothed and combed the horse or shook music from the buckled harness. When we returned to the street light from the kitchen windows had filled the areas. If my uncle was seen turning the corner we hid in the shadow until we had seen him safely housed. Or if Mangan's sister came out on the doorstep to call her brother in to his tea we watched her from our shadow peer up and down the street. We waited to see whether she would remain or go in and, if she remained, we left our shadow and walked up to Mangan's steps resignedly. She was waiting for us, her figure defined by the light from the half-opened door. Her brother always teased her before he obeyed and I stood by the railings looking at her. Her dress swung as she moved her body and the soft rope of her hair tossed from side to side.

Every morning I lay on the floor in the front parlour watching her door. The blind was pulled down to within an inch of the sash so that I could not be seen. When she came out on the doorstep my heart leaped. I ran to the hall, seized my books and followed her. I kept her brown figure always in my eye and, when we came near the point at which our ways diverged, I quickened my pace and passed her. This happened morning after morning. I had never spoken to her, except for a few casual words, and yet her name was like a summons to all my foolish blood.

Her image accompanied me even in places the most hostile to romance. On Saturday evenings when my aunt went marketing I had to go to carry some of the parcels. We walked through the flaring streets, jostled by drunken men and bargaining women, amid the curses of labourers, the shrill litanies of shop-boys who stood on guard by the barrels of pigs' cheeks, the nasal chanting of street-singers, who sang a *come-all-you* about O'Donovan Rossa, or a ballad about the troubles in our native land. These noises converged in a single sensation of life for me: I imagined that I bore my chalice safely through a throng of foes. Her name sprang to my lips at moments in strange prayers and praises which I myself did not understand. My eyes were often full of tears (I could not tell why) and at times a flood from my heart seemed to pour itself out into my bosom. I thought little of the future. I did not know whether I would ever speak to her or not or, if I spoke to her, how I could tell her of my confused adoration. But my body was like a harp and her words and gestures were like fingers running upon the wires.

One evening I went into the back drawing-room in which the priest had died. It was a dark rainy evening and there was no sound in the house. Through one of the broken panes I heard the rain impinge upon the earth, the fine incessant needles of water playing in the sodden beds. Some distant lamp or lighted window gleamed below me. I was thankful that I could see so little. All my senses seemed to desire to veil themselves and, feeling that I was about to slip from them, I pressed the palms of my hands together until they trembled, murmuring: *O love! O love!* many times.

At last she spoke to me. When she addressed the first words to me I was so confused that I did not know what to answer. She asked me was I going to *Araby*. I forget whether I answered yes or no. It would be a splendid bazaar, she said; she would love to go.

—And why can't you? I asked.

While she spoke she turned a silver bracelet round and round her wrist. She could not go, she said, because there would be a retreat that week in her convent. Her brother and two other boys were fighting for their caps and I was alone at the railings. She held one of the spikes, bowing her head towards me. The light from the lamp opposite our door caught the white curve of her neck, lit up her hair that rested there and, falling, lit up the hand upon the railing. It fell over one side of her dress and caught the white border of a petticoat, just visible as she stood at ease.

—It's well for you, she said.

—If I go, I said, I will bring you something.

What innumerable follies laid waste my waking and sleeping thoughts after that evening! I wished to annihilate the tedious intervening days. I chafed against the work of school. At night in my bedroom and by day in the classroom her image came between me and the page I strove to read. The syllables of the word *Araby* were called to me through the silence in which my soul luxuriated and cast an Eastern enchantment over me. I asked for leave to go to the bazaar Saturday night. My aunt was surprised and hoped it was not some Freemason affair. I answered few questions in class. I watched my master's face pass from amiability to sternness; he hoped I was not beginning to idle. I could not call my wandering thoughts together. I had hardly any patience with the serious work of life which, now that it stood between me and my desire, seemed to me child's play, ugly monotonous child's play.

On Saturday morning I reminded my uncle that I wished to go to the bazaar in the evening. He was fussing at the hallstand, looking for the hat-brush, and answered me curtly:

—Yes, boy, I know.

As he was in the hall I could not go into the front parlour and lie at the window. I left the house in bad humour and walked slowly towards the school. The air was pitilessly raw and already my heart misgave me.

When I came home to dinner my uncle had not yet been home. Still it was early. I sat staring at the clock for some time and, when its ticking began to irritate me, I left the room. I mounted the staircase and gained the upper part of the house. The high cold empty gloomy rooms liberated me and I went from room to room singing. From the front window I saw my companions playing below in the street. Their cries reached me weakened and indistinct and, leaning my forehead against the cool glass, I looked over at the dark house where she lived. I may have stood there for an hour, seeing nothing but the brown-clad figure cast by my imagination, touched discreetly by the lamplight at the curved neck, at the hand upon the railings and at the border below the dress.

When I came downstairs again I found Mrs. Mercer sitting at the fire. She was an old garrulous woman, a pawnbroker's widow, who collected used stamps for some pious purpose. I had to endure the gossip of the tea-table. The meal was prolonged beyond an hour and still my uncle did not come. Mrs. Mercer stood up to go: she was sorry she couldn't wait any longer, but it was after eight o'clock and she did not like to be out late, as the night air was bad for her. When she had gone I began to walk up and down the room, clenching my fists. My aunt said:

—I'm afraid you may put off your bazaar for this night of Our Lord.

At nine o'clock I heard my uncle's latchkey in the halldoor. I heard him talking to himself and heard the hallstand rocking when it had received the weight of his overcoat. I could interpret these signs. When he was midway through his dinner I asked him to give me the money to go to the bazaar. He had forgotten.

—The people are in bed and after their first sleep now, he said.

I did not smile. My aunt said to him energetically:

—Can't you give him the money and let him go? You've kept him late enough as it is.

My uncle said he was very sorry he had forgotten. He said he believed in the old saying: *All work and no play makes Jack a dull boy.* He asked me where I was going and, when I had told him a second time he asked me did I know *The Arab's Farewell to his Steed*. When I left the kitchen he was about to recite the opening lines of the piece to my aunt.

I held a florin tightly in my hand as I strode down Buckingham Street towards the station. The sight of the streets thronged with buyers and glaring with gas recalled to me the purpose of my journey. I took my seat in a third-class carriage of a deserted train. After an intolerable delay the train moved out of the station slowly. It crept onward among ruinous houses and over the twinkling river. At Westland Row Station a crowd of people pressed to the carriage doors; but the porters moved them back, saying that it was a special train for the bazaar. I remained alone in the bare carriage. In a few minutes the train drew up beside an improvised wooden platform. I passed out on to the road and saw by the lighted dial of a clock that it was ten minutes to ten. In front of me was a large building which displayed the magical name.

I could not find any sixpenny entrance and, fearing that the bazaar would be closed, I passed in quickly through a turnstile, handing a shilling to a weary-looking man. I found myself in a big hall girdled at half its height by a gallery. Nearly all the stalls were closed and the greater part of the hall was in darkness. I recognised a silence like that which pervades a church after a service. I walked into the centre of the bazaar timidly. A few people were gathered about the stalls which were still open. Before a curtain, over which the words *Café Chantant* were written in coloured lamps, two men were counting money on a salver. I listened to the fall of the coins.

Remembering with difficulty why I had come I went over to one of the stalls and examined porcelain vases and flowered tea-sets. At the door of the stall a young lady was talking and laughing with two young gentlemen. I remarked their English accents and listened vaguely to their conversation.

—O, I never said such a thing!

—O, but you did!

—O, but I didn't!

—Didn't she say that?

—Yes. I heard her.

—O, there's a . . . fib!

Observing me the young lady came over and asked me did I wish to buy anything. The tone of her voice was not encouraging; she seemed to have spoken to me out of a sense of duty. I looked humbly at the great jars that stood like eastern guards at either side of the dark entrance to the stall and murmured:

—No, thank you.

The young lady changed the position of one of the vases and went back to the two young men. They began to talk of the same subject. Once or twice the young lady glanced at me over her shoulder.

I lingered before her stall, though I knew my stay was useless, to make my interest in her wares seem the more real. Then I turned away slowly and walked down the middle of the bazaar. I allowed the two pennies to fall against the sixpence in my pocket. I heard a voice call from one end of the gallery that the light was out. The upper part of the hall was now completely dark.

Gazing up into the darkness I saw myself as a creature driven and derided by vanity; and my eyes burned with anguish and anger.

(1914)

QUESTIONS FOR REFLECTION

1. Note the religious language of the fifth paragraph, especially the words "litanies," "chalice," "prayers and praises," and "confused adoration." What does this language reveal about the boy, about how he sees himself, about how he envisions what he is doing and thinking? Explain how the following sentence from this paragraph is related to the image invoked by his religious language: "But my body was like a harp and her words and gestures were like fingers running upon the wires."
2. Read the dialogue near the end of the story aloud, if possible with a friend. What do you hear? How can you characterize the conversation? What effect does it have on the boy? Why?
3. Reread the first and last paragraphs. Note repetitions and similarities in the language. Relate the use of the word "blind" for a dead-end street to the boy's situation as expressed at the end of the story. Why do the boy's "eyes" burn with "anguish" and "anger"?

THEME

In the Introduction, Reading (and Writing about) Literature, we noted that the meaning of a literary work is more than any statement that can be made about it, that its meaning consists of both our experience in reading it and the ideas we may extract from it. With that in mind, let us clarify what we mean by the theme of a story. Simply put, a story's *theme* is its idea or point formulated as a generalization. The theme of a fable is its moral; the theme of a parable is its teaching; the theme of a short story is its implied view of life and conduct. Unlike the fable and parable, however, most fiction is not designed primarily to teach or preach. Its theme, thus, is more obliquely presented. In fact theme in fiction is rarely *presented* at all; it is abstracted from the details of character and action that compose the story.

To be clear about theme, we should distinguish it from plot, the story's sequence of action, and from *subject,* what the story is generally about. In explaining a story's theme we do more than state its subject or summarize its plot. To say, for example, that Pirandello's "War" (p. 249) is about parents and children is more a statement of subject than of theme. To pinpoint its theme we would have to explain what the story implies about parents and children, what it suggests about parents' love for their children, and even more specifically, what it values in the attitudes toward the loss of children expressed by the two major characters.

Theme is related to the other elements of fiction more as consequence than as a parallel element that can be separately identified. A story's theme, that is, grows out of the relationship of the other elements. To formulate a story's theme, we try to explain what these elements collectively suggest. Since the theme of a story derives from its details of character, plot, setting, structure, language, and point of view, any statement of theme is valid and valuable to the extent that it accounts for these details. To explain the theme of "The Prodigal Son," for example, without accounting for the father's speech to the elder son would be to distort the meaning of the story.

Perhaps the most important thing to remember about theme is that it is an abstraction from a story's complex uses of language to describe and chart action, depict setting, and portray character. A statement of theme derives from the particulars embodied in language and action. The very concreteness and particularity of fiction should make us cautious in searching out theme. In fact, it would be more useful to avoid thinking of theme as hidden somehow beneath the surface of the story and instead to see theme as the implied significance of the story's details. There are a multiplicity of ways to state a story's theme, but any such statement involves a necessary simplification of the story. In clarifying our sense of a story's idea, we also inevitably exclude some dimensions of the story and include others. We should be aware that the themes we abstract from stories are provisional understandings that never completely explain the stories.

With these considerations in mind, read Eudora Welty's "A Worn Path," with an eye to explaining its theme.

EUDORA WELTY
[b. 1909]

A Worn Path

It was December—a bright frozen day in the early morning. Far out in the country there was an old Negro woman with her head tied in a red rag, coming along a path through the pinewoods. Her name was Phoenix Jackson. She was very old and small and she walked slowly in the dark pine shadows, moving a little from side to side in her steps, with the balanced heaviness and lightness of a pendulum in a grandfather clock. She carried a thin, small cane made from an umbrella, and with this she kept tapping the frozen earth in front of her. This made a grave and persistent noise in the still air, that seemed meditative like the chirping of a solitary little bird.

She wore a dark striped dress reaching down to her shoe tops, and an equally long apron of bleached sugar sacks, with a full pocket: all neat and tidy, but every time she took a step she might have fallen over her shoelaces, which dragged from her unlaced shoes. She looked straight ahead. Her eyes were blue with age. Her skin had a pattern all its own of numberless branching wrinkles and as though a whole little tree stood in the middle of her forehead, but a golden color ran underneath, and the two knobs of her cheeks were illumined by a yellow burning under the dark. Under the red rag her hair came down on her neck in the frailest of ringlets, still black, and with an odor like copper.

Now and then there was a quivering in the thicket. Old Phoenix said, "Out of my way, all you foxes, owls, beetles, jack rabbits, coons and wild animals! . . . Keep out from under these feet, little bob-whites. . . . Keep the big wild hogs out of my path. Don't let none of those come running my direction. I got a long way." Under her small black-freckled hand her cane, limber as a buggy whip, would switch at the brush as if to rouse up any hiding things.

On she went. The woods were deep and still. The sun made the pine needles almost too bright to look at, up where the wind rocked. The cones dropped as light as feathers. Down in the hollow was the mourning dove—it was not too late for him.

The path ran up a hill. "Seem like there is chains about my feet, time I get this far," she said, in the voice of argument old people keep to use with themselves. "Something always take a hold of me on this hill—pleads I should stay."

After she got to the top she turned and gave a full, severe look behind her where she had come. "Up through pines," she said at length. "Now down through oaks."

Her eyes opened their widest, and she started down gently. But before she got to the bottom of the hill a bush caught her dress.

Her fingers were busy and intent, but her skirts were full and long, so that before she could pull them free in one place they were caught in another. It was not possible to allow the dress to tear. "I in the thorny bush," she said. "Thorns, you doing your appointed work. Never want to let folks pass, no sir. Old eyes thought you was a pretty little *green* bush."

Finally, trembling all over, she stood free, and after a moment dared to stoop for her cane.

"Sun so high!" she cried, leaning back and looking, while the thick tears went over her eyes. "The time getting all gone here."

At the foot of this hill was a place where a log was laid across the creek.

"Now comes the trial," said Phoenix.

Putting her right foot out, she mounted the log and shut her eyes. Lifting her skirt, leveling her cane fiercely before her, like a festival figure in some parade, she began to march across. Then she opened her eyes and she was safe on the other side.

"I wasn't as old as I thought," she said.

But she sat down to rest. She spread her skirts on the bank around her and folded her hands over her knees. Up above her was a tree in a pearly cloud of mistletoe. She did not dare to close her eyes, and when a little boy brought her a plate with a slice of marble-cake on it she spoke to him. "That would be acceptable," she said. But when she went to take it there was just her own hand in the air.

So she left that tree, and had to go through a barbed-wire fence. There she had to creep and crawl, spreading her knees and stretching her fingers like a baby trying to climb the steps. But she talked loudly to herself: she could not let her dress be torn now, so late in the day, and she could not pay for having her arm or her leg sawed off if she got caught fast where she was.

At last she was safe through the fence and risen up out in the clearing. Big dead trees, like black men with one arm, were standing in the purple stalks of the withered cotton field. There sat a buzzard.

"Who you watching?"

In the furrow she made her way along.

"Glad this not the season for bulls," she said, looking sideways, "and the good Lord made his snakes to curl up and sleep in the winter. A pleasure I don't see no two-headed snake coming around that tree, where it come once. It took a while to get by him, back in the summer."

She passed through the old cotton and went into a field of dead corn. It whispered and shook and was taller than her head. "Through the maze now," she said, for there was no path.

Then there was something tall, black, and skinny there, moving before her.

At first she took it for a man. It could have been a man dancing in the field. But she stood still and listened, and it did not make a sound. It was as silent as a ghost.

"Ghost," she said sharply, "who be you the ghost of? For I have heard of nary death close by."

But there was no answer—only the ragged dancing in the wind.

She shut her eyes, reached out her hand, and touched a sleeve. She found a coat and inside that an emptiness, cold as ice.

"You scarecrow," she said. Her face lighted. "I ought to be shut up for good," she said with laughter. "My senses is gone. I too old. I the oldest people I ever know. Dance, old scarecrow," she said, "while I dancing with you."

She kicked her foot over the furrow, and with mouth drawn down, shook her head once or twice in a little strutting way. Some husks blew down and whirled in streamers about her skirts.

Then she went on, parting her way from side to side with the cane, through the whispering field. At last she came to the end, to a wagon track where the silver grass blew between the red ruts. The quail were walking around like pullets, seeming all dainty and unseen.

"Walk pretty," she said. "This the easy place. This the easy going."

She followed the track, swaying through the quiet bare fields, through the little strings of trees silver in their dead leaves, past cabins silver from weather, with the doors and windows boarded shut, all like old women under a spell sitting there. "I walking in their sleep," she said, nodding her head vigorously.

In a ravine she went where a spring was silently flowing through a hollow log. Old Phoenix bent and drank. "Sweet-gum makes the water sweet," she said, and drank more. "Nobody know who made this well, for it was here when I was born."

The track crossed a swampy part where the moss hung as white as lace from every limb. "Sleep on, alligators, and blow your bubbles." Then the track went into the road.

Deep, deep the road went down between the high green-colored banks. Overhead the live-oaks met, and it was as dark as a cave.

A black dog with a lolling tongue came up out of the weeds by the ditch. She was meditating, and not ready, and when he came at her she only hit him a little with her cane. Over she went in the ditch, like a little puff of milkweed.

Down there, her senses drifted away. A dream visited her, and she reached her hand up, but nothing reached down and gave her a pull. So she lay there and presently went to talking. "Old woman," she said to herself, "that black dog come up out of the weeds to stall you off, and now there he sitting on his fine tail, smiling at you."

A white man finally came along and found her—a hunter, a young man, with his dog on a chain.

"Well, Granny!" he laughed. "What are you doing there?"

"Lying on my back like a June-bug waiting to be turned over, mister," she said, reaching up her hand.

He lifted her up, gave her a swing in the air, and set her down. "Anything broken, Granny?"

"No, sir, them old dead weeds is springy enough," said Phoenix, when she had got her breath. "I thank you for your trouble."

"Where do you live, Granny?" he asked, while the two dogs were growling at each other.

"Away back yonder, sir, behind the ridge. You can't even see it from here."

"On your way home?"

"No sir, I going to town."

"Why, that's too far! That's as far as I walk when I come out myself, and I get something for my trouble." He patted the stuffed bag he carried, and there hung down a little closed claw. It was one of the bob-whites, with its beak hooked bitterly to show it was dead. "Now you go home, Granny!"

"I bound to go to town, mister," said Phoenix. "The time come around."

He gave another laugh, filling the whole landscape. "I know you old colored people! Wouldn't miss going to town to see Santa Claus!"

But something held old Phoenix very still. The deep lines in her face went into a fierce and different radiation. Without warning, she had seen with her own eyes a flashing nickel fall out of the man's pocket onto the ground.

"How old are you, Granny?" he was saying.

"There is no telling, mister," she said, "no telling."

Then she gave a little cry and clapped her hands and said, "Git on away from here, dog! Look! Look at that dog!" She laughed as if in admiration. "He ain't scared of nobody. He a big black dog." She whispered, "Sic him!"

"Watch me get rid of that cur," said the man. "Sic him, Pete! Sic him!"

Phoenix heard the dogs fighting, and heard the man running and throwing sticks. She even heard a gunshot. But she was slowly bending forward by that time, further and further forward, the lids stretched down over her eyes, as if she were doing this in her sleep. Her chin was lowered almost to her knees. The yellow palm of her hand came out from the fold of her apron. Her fingers slid down and along the ground under the piece of money with the grace and care they would have in lifting an egg from under a setting hen. Then she slowly straightened up, she stood erect, and the nickel was in her apron pocket. A bird flew by. Her lips moved. "God watching me the whole time. I come to stealing."

The man came back, and his own dog panted about them. "Well, I scared him off that time," he said, and then he laughed and lifted his gun and pointed it at Phoenix.

She stood straight and faced him.

"Doesn't the gun scare you?" he said, still pointing it.

"No, sir, I seen plenty go off closer by, in my day, and for less than what I done," she said, holding utterly still.

He smiled, and shouldered the gun. "Well, Granny," he said, "you must be a hundred years old, and scared of nothing. I'd give you a dime if I had any money with me. But you take my advice and stay home, and nothing will happen to you."

"I bound to go on my way, mister," said Phoenix. She inclined her head in the red rag. Then they went in different directions, but she could hear the gun shooting again and again over the hill.

She walked on. The shadows hung from the oak trees to the road like curtains. Then she smelled wood-smoke, and smelled the river, and she saw a steeple and the cabins on their steep steps. Dozens of little black children whirled around her. There ahead was Natchez shining. Bells were ringing. She walked on.

In the paved city it was Christmas time. There were red and green electric lights strung and criss-crossed everywhere, and all turned on in the daytime. Old Phoenix would have been lost if she had not distrusted her eyesight and depended on her feet to know where to take her.

She paused quietly on the sidewalk where people were passing by. A lady came along in the crowd, carrying an armful of red-, green- and silver-wrapped presents; she gave off perfume like the red roses in hot summer, and Phoenix stopped her.

"Please, missy, will you lace up my shoe?" She held up her foot.

"What do you want, Grandma?"

"See my shoe," said Phoenix. "Do all right for out in the country, but wouldn't look right to go in a big building."

"Stand still then, Grandma," said the lady. She put her packages down on the sidewalk beside her and laced and tied both shoes tightly.

"Can't lace 'em with a cane," said Phoenix. "Thank you, missy. I doesn't mind asking a nice lady to tie up my shoe, when I gets out on the street."

Moving slowly and from side to side, she went into the big building, and into a tower of steps, where she walked up and around and around until her feet knew to stop.

She entered a door, and there she saw nailed up on the wall the document that had been stamped with the gold seal and framed in the gold frame, which matched the dream that was hung up in her head.

"Here I be," she said. There was a fixed and ceremonial stiffness over her body.

"A charity case, I suppose," said an attendant who sat at the desk before her.

But Phoenix only looked above her head. There was sweat on her face, the wrinkles in her skin shone like a bright net.

"Speak up, Grandma," the woman said. "What's your name? We must have your history, you know. Have you been here before? What seems to be the trouble with you?"

Old Phoenix only gave a twitch to her face as if a fly were bothering her.

"Are you deaf?" cried the attendant.

But then the nurse came in.

"Oh, that's just old Aunt Phoenix," she said. "She doesn't come for herself—she has a little grandson. She makes these trips just as regular as clockwork. She lives away back off the Old Natchez Trace." She bent down. "Well, Aunt Phoenix, why don't you just take a seat? We won't keep you standing after your long trip." She pointed.

The old woman sat down, bolt upright in the chair.

"Now, how is the boy?" asked the nurse.

Old Phoenix did not speak.

"I said, how is the boy?"

But Phoenix only waited and stared straight ahead, her face very solemn and withdrawn into rigidity.

"Is his throat any better?" asked the nurse. "Aunt Phoenix, don't you hear me? Is your grandson's throat any better since the last time you came for the medicine?"

With her hands on her knees, the old woman waited, silent, erect and motionless, just as if she were in armor.

"You mustn't take up our time this way, Aunt Phoenix," the nurse said. "Tell us quickly about your grandson, and get it over. He isn't dead, is he?"

At last there came a flicker and then a flame of comprehension across her face, and she spoke.

"My grandson. It was my memory had left me. There I sat and forgot why I made my long trip."

"Forgot?" The nurse frowned. "After you came so far?"

Then Phoenix was like an old woman begging a dignified forgiveness for waking up frightened in the night. "I never did go to school, I was too old at the Surrender," she said in a soft voice. "I'm an old woman without an education. It was my memory fail me. My little grandson, he is just the same, and I forgot it in the coming."

"Throat never heals, does it?" said the nurse, speaking in a loud, sure voice to old Phoenix. By now she had a card with something written on it, a little list. "Yes. Swallowed lye. When was it? —January—two-three years ago—"

Phoenix spoke unasked now. "No, missy, he not dead, he just the same. Every little while his throat begin to close up again, and he not able to swallow. He not get his breath. He not able to help himself. So the time come around, and I go on another trip for the soothing medicine."

"All right. The doctor said as long as you came to get it, you could have it," said the nurse. "But it's an obstinate case."

"My little grandson, he sit up there in the house all wrapped up, waiting by himself," Phoenix went on. "We is the only two left in the world. He suffer and it don't seem to put him back at all. He got a sweet look. He going to last. He wear a little patch quilt and peep out holding his mouth open like a little bird. I remembers so plain now. I not going to forget him again, no, the whole enduring time. I could tell him from all the others in creation."

"All right." The nurse was trying to hush her now. She brought her a bottle of medicine. "Charity," she said, making a check mark in a book.

Old Phoenix held the bottle close to her eyes, and then carefully put it into her pocket.

"I thank you," she said.

"It's Christmas time, Grandma," said the attendant. "Could I give you a few pennies out of my purse?"

"Five pennies is a nickel," said Phoenix stiffly.

"Here's a nickel," said the attendant.

Phoenix rose carefully and held out her hand. She received the nickel and then fished the other nickel out of her pocket and laid it beside the new one. She stared at her palm closely, with her head on one side.

Then she gave a tap with her cane on the floor.

"This is what come to me to do," she said. "I going to the store and buy my child a little windmill they sells, made out of paper. He going to find it hard to believe there such a thing in the world. I'll march myself back where he waiting, holding it straight up in this hand."

She lifted her free hand, gave a little nod, turned around, and walked out of the doctor's office. Then her slow step began on the stairs, going down.

(1941)

QUESTIONS FOR REFLECTION

1. State in a sentence or two the idea of "A Worn Path." What point does the story seem to make?
2. Develop your understanding of the story's theme in a paragraph or a brief conversation. To support your views, cite details of plot, character, setting, and language.

IRONY AND SYMBOL

Two additional facets of fictional works are irony and symbol. While not as pervasive as elements such as plot and character, irony and symbol are tremendously important. Both aspects of fiction allow writers to compress a great deal of meaning into a brief space. Both require deliberation and tact if we are to appreciate and enjoy their full range of significance. And both require us to be alert to their existence if we are to understand the works in which they occur. If we do not perceive a writer's ironic intentions, we may not just misconstrue a particular story; we may interpret it as suggesting the opposite of what it actually is intended to mean. And if we overlook a story's symbols, we may underestimate its achievement and oversimplify its significance.

Irony

Irony is not so much an element of fiction as a pervasive quality in it. It may appear in fiction (and in the other literary genres as well) in three ways: in a work's language, in its incidents, or in its point of view. But in whatever forms it emerges, *irony* always involves a contrast or discrepancy between one thing and another. The contrast may be between what is said and what is meant or between what happens and what is expected to happen.

In *verbal irony,* for example, we say the opposite of what we mean. When someone says "That was a brilliant remark" and we know that it was anything but brilliant, we understand the speaker's ironic intention. In such relatively simple instances there is usually no problem in perceiving irony. In more complex instances, however, the designation of an action or a remark as ironic can be much more complicated. At the end of O'Connor's "Good Country People" (p. 171), Mrs. Freeman says: "Some can't be that simple." "I know I never could." Should we take her literally? Or do we detect irony?

Besides verbal irony—in which we understand the opposite of what a speaker says—fiction makes use of *irony of circumstance* (sometimes called *irony of situation*). Writers sometimes create discrepancies between what seems to be and what is. In Chopin's "The Story of an Hour," for example, Mrs. Mallard appears to be grieving over the news of her husband's death. At least that's how her action is perceived by other characters. But we soon realize that rather than grief, her tears celebrate the joy of her new-found freedom. Her tears are ironic because they indicate the opposite of what we expect them to. Another ironic situation prevails as Mrs. Mallard "prays" for long life, presumably so she can enjoy freedom from her husband: what she is praying for and why she prays for it are out of keeping with the expected reasons for prayer on such an occasion.

Irony of circumstance or situation also refers to occasions when an individual expects one thing to occur only to discover that the opposite happens. This indeed is what Mrs. Mallard experiences when she discovers her husband had not been killed in the train crash as she had thought. The final irony, of course, is that *she* dies when she sees him walk in the door.

Although verbal irony and irony of circumstance or situation are the prevalent forms irony assumes in fiction, two others deserve mention: dramatic irony and ironic vision. More typical of plays than stories, *dramatic irony* is the discrepancy between what characters know and what readers know. Writers sometimes direct our responses by letting us see things that their characters do not. At the conclusion of Flannery O'Connor's "Good Country People," for example, the reader has quite a different view of the Bible salesman's character than either Mrs. Freeman or Mrs. Hopewell does.

Some writers exploit the discrepancy between what readers and characters know to establish an ironic vision in a work. An *ironic vision* is established in a work as an overall tone that suggests how a writer views his or her characters and subject. It is more characteristic of longer fictional works such as the novels *Pride and Prejudice* by Jane Austen or *The Adventures of Huckleberry Finn* by Mark Twain than of short stories. We can find an ironic vision, nonetheless, in O'Connor's "Good Country People." For the moment, however, consider how an ironic vision informs the opening of Jane Austen's *Pride and Prejudice:*

> It is a truth universally acknowledged, that a single man in possession of a good fortune, must be in want of a wife.
>
> However little known the feelings or views of such a man may be on his first entering a neighborhood, this truth is so well fixed in the minds of the surrounding families, that he is considered as the rightful property of some one or other of their daughters.

Is it a truth—that is, do we accept as fact what the opening sentence seems to assert: that a single man of means must be looking for a wife? Do we believe that this search for a wife is a phenomenon universally acknowledged, that it is recognized around the world, not merely in nineteenth-century England or twentieth-century America? It is very likely that Jane Austen's sentence presents the opposite of what we believe: that single men of means more often than not are not in search of wives. The converse is probably closer to what we have seen: single women seek out single men of means as prospective husbands. This discrepancy between what the sentence says and what we know accounts in part for its ironic quality. We are not to take it literally; we do not accept it at face value.

We can feel more confident about the ironic quality of Austen's first sentence when we examine it in relation to the sentence that follows it. We are told there that the feelings or views of the eligible bachelor mean little. But they should mean much in such an important issue. That they do not is the opposite of what we expect and hence is ironic. An additional irony is that characteristics of marriageable eligibility are limited to bachelorhood and wealth. Nothing else is mentioned as important—not character, not intelligence, not wisdom or virtue.

Portraying characters whose view of marriage is so mercenary and limited, Austen distances herself from them and from their values. This ironic distance is enforced when Austen describes their misconceptions about single men. But there is a further irony in the fact that those misconceptions do not matter. All that matters is the final outcome: the single man's loss of his bachelorhood and his entrance into the ranks of the family. Moreover, their view represents a reversal of a traditional and familiar notion: that a wife is a man's property. This idea is given an additional twist when Austen indicates that it hardly matters which girl of which family captures the prize.

For these reasons and for others that emerge as the novel develops, Austen's tone can be described as ironic. When such an ironic tone is established strongly from the beginning of a work and when it is sustained consistently throughout, we say that it is informed by an ironic vision. The ironic vision of *Pride and Prejudice* infuses the novel: it informs the plot, it controls the dialogue, and it surfaces repeatedly in the tone of the narrator's comments.

Symbol

Symbols in fiction are simply objects, actions, or events that convey meaning. The meaning they convey extends beyond their literal significance, beyond their more obvious actual reason for being included in the story. In Kate Chopin's "The Story of an Hour," for example, the room in which Mrs. Mallard sits symbolizes her domestic, homebound life. She looks out a window into a world that has previously been closed to her. With the supposed death of her husband, she sees the outside world in a fresh and invigorating way. What she observes (the trees, for example) and how she now understands those things (in this case as emblems of life, hope, and possibility) signal, for us, that symbolism is at work in the story.

How do we know if a particular detail is symbolic? How do we decide whether we should look beyond the literal meaning of a dialogue or the literal value of an object or action? The simple answer to this question is that there is no way to be certain about the symbolic value of any particular details. But we can alert ourselves to the possible symbolic overtones of such details through the following questions.

QUESTIONS FOR REFLECTION

1. How important to the story is the object, action, gesture, or dialogue that we suspect is symbolic? Does it appear more than once? Does it occur at a climactic moment? Is it described in detail?
2. Does the story seem to warrant our granting its details more significance than their immediate literal value? Why?
3. Does a symbolic interpretation make sense? Does it fit in with a literal or commonsense explanation? Or does our symbolic reading contradict or otherwise distort the literal surface of the story?
4. What objections might be raised against our symbolic interpretation?

Even if we consider such questions carefully, we may still not be sure that a particular detail is symbolic. Sometimes we will be confident *that* such a detail is symbolic without being able to say just *what* it represents. This kind of uncertainty is natural, largely because symbols by their very nature resist easy and definitive explanation.

Read the following story, Edgar Allan Poe's "The Black Cat," with an eye to its ironies. Be alert for verbal irony, irony of situation, and dramatic irony. Consider whether the tone is sufficiently ironic to display an ironic vision. Identify and explain any symbols.

EDGAR ALLAN POE
[1809–1849]

The Black Cat

For the most wild yet most homely narrative which I am about to pen, I neither expect nor solicit belief. Mad indeed would I be to expect it, in a case where my very senses reject their own evidence. Yet, mad am I not—and very surely do I not dream. But to-morrow I die, and to-day I would unburden my soul. My immediate purpose is to place before the world, plainly, succinctly, and without comment, a series of mere household events. In their consequences, these events have terrified—have tortured—have destroyed me. Yet I will not attempt to expound them. To me, they have presented little but horror—to many they will seem less terrible than *baroques*. Hereafter, perhaps, some intellect may be found which will reduce my phantasm to the commonplace—some intellect more calm, more logical, and far less excitable than my own, which will perceive, in the circumstances I detail with awe, nothing more than an ordinary succession of very natural causes and effects.

From my infancy I was noted for the docility and humanity of my disposition. My tenderness of heart was even so conspicuous as to make me the jest of my companions. I was especially fond of animals, and was indulged by my parents with a great variety of pets. With these I spent most of my time, and never was so happy as when feeding and caressing them. This peculiarity of character grew with my growth, and, in my manhood, I derived from it one of my principal sources of pleasure. To those who have cherished an affection for a faithful and sagacious dog, I need hardly be at the trouble of explaining the nature or the intensity of the gratification thus derivable. There is something in the unselfish and self-sacrificing love of a brute, which goes directly to the heart of him who has had frequent occasion to test the paltry friendship and gossamer fidelity of mere *Man*.

I married early, and was happy to find in my wife a disposition not uncongenial with my own. Observing my partiality for domestic pets, she lost no opportunity of procuring those of the most agreeable kind. We had birds, gold-fish, a fine dog, rabbits, a small monkey, and a *cat*.

This latter was a remarkably large and beautiful animal, entirely black, and sagacious to an astonishing degree. In speaking of his intelligence, my wife, who at heart was not a little tinctured with superstition, made frequent allusion to the ancient popular notion, which regarded all black cats as witches in disguise. Not that she was ever *serious* upon this point—and I mention the matter at all for no better reason than that it happens, just now, to be remembered.

Pluto—this was the cat's name—was my favorite pet and playmate. I alone fed him, and he attended me wherever I went about the house. It was even with difficulty that I could prevent him from following me through the streets.

Our friendship lasted, in this manner, for several years, during which my general temperament and character—through the instrumentality of the Fiend Intemperance—had (I blush to confess it) experienced a radical alteration for the worse. I grew, day by day, more moody, more irritable, more regardless of the feelings of others. I suffered myself to use intemperate language to my wife. At length, I even offered her personal violence. My pets, of course, were made to feel the change in my disposition. I not only neglected, but ill-used them. For Pluto, however, I still retained sufficient regard to restrain me from maltreating him, as I made no scruple of maltreating the rabbits, the monkey, or even the dog, when, by accident, or through affection, they came in my way. But my disease grew upon me—for what disease is like Alcohol! —and at length even Pluto, who was now becoming old, and consequently somewhat peevish—even Pluto began to experience the effects of my ill temper.

One night, returning home, much intoxicated, from one of my haunts about town, I fancied that the cat avoided my presence. I seized him; when, in his fright at my violence, he inflicted a slight wound upon my hand with his teeth. The fury of a demon instantly possessed me. I knew myself no longer. My original soul seemed, at once, to take its flight from my body; and a more than fiendish malevolence, gin-nurtured, thrilled every fibre of my frame. I took from my waistcoat-pocket a penknife, opened it, grasped the poor beast by the throat, and deliberately cut one of its eyes from the socket! I blush, I burn, I shudder, while I pen the damnable atrocity.

When reason returned with the morning—when I had slept off the fumes of the night's debauch—I experienced a sentiment half of horror, half of remorse, for the crime of which I had been guilty; but it was, at best, a feeble and equivocal feeling, and the soul remained untouched. I again plunged into excess, and soon drowned in wine all memory of the deed.

In the meantime the cat slowly recovered. The socket of the lost eye presented, it is true, a frightful appearance, but he no longer appeared to suffer any pain. He went about the house as usual, but, as might be expected, fled in extreme terror at my approach. I had so much of my old heart left, as to be at first grieved by this evident dislike on the part of a creature which had once so loved me. But this feeling soon gave place to irritation. And then came, as if to my final and irrevocable overthrow, the spirit of Perverseness. Of this spirit philosophy takes no account. Yet I am not more sure that my soul lives, than I am that perverseness is one of the primitive impulses of the human heart—one of the indivisible primary faculties, or sentiments, which give direction to the character of Man. Who has not, a hundred times, found himself committing a vile or stupid action, for no other reason than because he knows he should *not*? Have we not a perpetual inclination, in the teeth of our best judgment, to violate that which is *Law*, merely because we understand it to be such? This spirit of perverseness, I say, came to my final overthrow. It was this unfathomable longing of the soul *to vex itself*—to offer violence to its own nature—to do wrong for the wrong's sake only—that urged me to continue and finally to consummate the injury I had inflicted upon the unoffending brute. One morning, in cold blood, I slipped a noose about its neck and hung it to the limb of a tree; —hung it with the tears streaming from my eyes, and with the bitterest remorse at my heart; —hung it *because* I knew that it had loved me, and *because* I felt it had given me no reason of offence; —hung it *because* I knew that in so doing I was committing a sin—a deadly sin that would so jeopardize my immortal soul as to place it—if such a thing were possible—even beyond the reach of the infinite mercy of the Most Merciful and Most Terrible God.

On the night of the day on which this most cruel deed was done, I was aroused from sleep by the cry of fire. The curtains of my bed were in flames. The whole house was blazing. It was with great difficulty that my wife, a servant, and myself, made our escape from the conflagration. The destruction was complete. My entire worldly wealth was swallowed up, and I resigned myself thenceforward to despair.

I am above the weakness of seeking to establish a sequence of cause and effect, between the disaster and the atrocity. But I am detailing a chain of facts—and wish not to leave even a possible link imperfect. On the day succeeding the fire, I visited the ruins. The walls, with one exception, had fallen in. This exception was found in a compartment wall, not very thick, which stood about the middle of the house, and against which had rested the head of my bed. The plastering had here, in great measure, resisted the action of the fire—a fact which I attributed to its having been recently spread. About this wall a dense crowd were collected, and many persons seemed to be examining a particular portion of it with very minute and eager attention. The words "strange!" "singular!" and other similar expressions, excited my curiosity. I approached and saw, as if graven in *bas-relief* upon the white surface, the figure of a gigantic *cat*. The impression was given with an accuracy truly marvelous. There was a rope about the animal's neck.

When I first beheld this apparition—for I could scarcely regard it as less—my wonder and my terror were extreme. But at length reflection came to my aid. The cat, I remembered, had been hung in a garden adjacent to the house. Upon the alarm of fire, this garden had been immediately filled by the crowd—by some one of whom the animal must have been cut from the tree and thrown, through an open window, into my chamber. This had probably been done with the view of arousing me from sleep. The falling of other walls had compressed the victim of my cruelty into the substance of the freshly-spread plaster, the lime of which, with the flames, and the *ammonia* from the carcass, had then accomplished the portraiture as I saw it.

Although I thus readily accounted to my reason, if not altogether to my conscience, for the startling fact just detailed, it did not the less fail to make a deep impression upon my fancy. For months I could not rid myself of the phantasm of the cat; and, during this period, there came back into my spirit a half-sentiment that seemed, but was not, remorse. I went so far as to regret the loss of the animal, and to look about me, among the vile haunts which I now habitually frequented, for another pet of the same species, and of somewhat similar appearance, with which to supply its place.

One night as I sat, half stupefied, in a den of more than infamy, my attention was suddenly drawn to some black object, reposing upon the head of one of the immense hogsheads of gin, or of rum, which constituted the chief furniture of the apartment. I had been looking steadily at the top of this hogshead for some minutes, and what now caused me surprise was the fact that I had not sooner perceived the object thereupon. I approached it, and touched it with my hand. It was a black cat—a very large one—fully as large as Pluto, and closely resembling him in every respect but one. Pluto had not a white hair upon any portion of his body; but this cat had a large, although indefinite splotch of white, covering nearly the whole region of the breast.

Upon my touching him, he immediately arose, purred loudly, rubbed against my hand, and appeared delighted with my notice. This, then, was the very creature of which I was in search. I at once offered to purchase it of the landlord; but this person made no claim to it—knew nothing of it—had never seen it before.

I continued my caresses, and when I prepared to go home, the animal evinced a disposition to accompany me. I permitted it to do so; occasionally stooping and patting it as I proceeded. When it reached the house it domesticated itself at once, and became immediately a great favorite with my wife.

For my own part, I soon found a dislike to it arising within me. This was just the reverse of what I had anticipated; but—I know not how or why it was—its evident fondness for myself rather disgusted and annoyed me. By slow degrees these feelings of disgust and annoyance rose into the bitterness of hatred. I avoided the creature; a certain sense of shame, and the remembrance of my former deed of cruelty, preventing me from physically abusing it. I did not, for some weeks, strike, or otherwise violently ill use it; but gradually—very gradually—I came to look upon it with unutterable loathing, and to flee silently from its odious presence, as from the breath of a pestilence.

What added, no doubt, to my hatred of the beast, was the discovery on the morning after I brought it home, that like Pluto, it also had been deprived of one of its eyes. This circumstance, however, only endeared it to my wife, who, as I have already said, possessed, in a high degree, that humanity of feeling which had once been my distinguishing trait, and the source of many of my simplest and purest pleasures.

With my aversion to this cat, however, its partiality for myself seemed to increase. It followed my footsteps with a pertinacity which it would be difficult to make the reader comprehend. Whenever I sat, it would crouch beneath my chair, or spring upon my knees, covering me with its loathsome caresses. If I arose to walk it would get between my feet and thus nearly throw me down, or, fastening its long and sharp claws in my dress, clamber, in this manner, to my breast. At such times, although I longed to destroy it with a blow, I was yet withheld from so doing, partly by a memory of my former crime, but chiefly—let me confess it at once—by absolute dread of the beast.

This dread was not exactly a dread of physical evil—and yet I should be at a loss how otherwise to define it. I am almost ashamed to own—yes, even in this felon's cell, I am almost ashamed to own—that the terror and horror with which the animal inspired me, had been heightened by one of the merest chimeras it would be possible to conceive. My wife had called my attention, more than once, to the character of the mark of white hair, of which I have spoken, and which constituted the sole visible difference between the strange beast and the one I had destroyed. The reader will remember that this mark, although large, had been originally very indefinite; but, by slow degrees—degrees nearly imperceptible, and which for a long time my reason struggled to reject as fanciful—it had, at length, assumed a rigorous distinctness of outline. It was now the representation of an object that I shudder to name—and for this, above all, I loathed, and dreaded, and would have rid myself of the monster *had I dared*—it was now, I say, the image of a hideous—of a ghastly thing—of the Gallows! —oh, mournful and terrible engine of Horror and of Crime—of Agony and of Death!

And now was I indeed wretched beyond the wretchedness of mere Humanity. And *a brute beast*—whose fellow I had contemptuously destroyed—*a brute beast* to work out for *me*—for me, a man fashioned in the image of the High God—so much of insufferable woe! Alas! neither by day nor by night knew I the blessing of rest any more! During the former the creature left me no moment alone, and in the latter I started hourly from dreams of unutterable fear to find the hot breath of *the thing* upon my face, and its vast weight—an incarnate nightmare that I had not power to shake off—incumbent eternally upon my *heart!*

Beneath the pressure of torments such as these the feeble remnant of the good within me succumbed. Evil thoughts became my sole intimates—the darkest and most evil of thoughts. The moodiness of my usual temper increased to hatred of all things and of all mankind; while from the sudden, frequent, and ungovernable outbursts of a fury to which I now blindly abandoned myself, my uncomplaining wife, alas, was the most usual and the most patient of sufferers.

One day she accompanied me, upon some household errand, into the cellar of the old building which our poverty compelled us to inhabit. The cat followed me down the steep stairs, and, nearly throwing me headlong, exasperated me to madness. Uplifting an axe, and forgetting in my wrath the childish dread which had hitherto stayed my hand, I aimed a blow at the animal, which, of course, would have proved instantly fatal had it descended as I wished. But this blow was arrested by the hand of my wife. Goaded by the interference into a rage more than demoniacal, I withdrew my arm from her grasp and buried the axe in her brain. She fell dead upon the spot without a groan.

This hideous murder accomplished, I set myself forthwith, and with entire deliberation, to the task of concealing the body. I knew that I could not remove it from the house, either by day or by night, without the risk of being observed by the neighbors. Many projects entered my mind. At one period I thought of cutting the corpse into minute fragments, and destroying them by fire. At another, I resolved to dig a grave for it in the floor of the cellar. Again, I deliberated about casting it in the well in the yard—about packing it in a box, as if merchandise, with the usual arrangements, and so getting a porter to take it from the house. Finally I hit upon what I considered a far better expedient than either of these. I determined to wall it up in the cellar, as the monks of the Middle Ages are recorded to have walled up their victims.

For a purpose such as this the cellar was well adapted. Its walls were loosely constructed, and had lately been plastered throughout with a rough plaster, which the dampness of the atmosphere had prevented from hardening. Moreover, in one of the walls was a projection, caused by a false chimney, or fireplace, that had been filled up and made to resemble the rest of the cellar. I made no doubt that I could readily displace the bricks at this point, insert the corpse, and wall the whole up as before, so that no eye could detect anything suspicious.

And in this calculation I was not deceived. By means of a crowbar I easily dislodged the bricks, and, having carefully deposited the body against the inner wall, I propped it in that position, while with little trouble I relaid the whole structure as it originally stood. Having procured mortar, sand, and hair, with every possible precaution, I prepared a plaster which could not be distinguished from the old, and with this, I very carefully went over the new brick-work. When I had finished, I felt satisfied that all was right. The wall did not present the slightest appearance of having been disturbed.

The rubbish on the floor was picked up with the minutest care. I looked around triumphantly, and said to myself: "Here at least, then, my labor has not been in vain."

My next step was to look for the beast which had been the cause of so much wretchedness; for I had, at length, firmly resolved to put it to death. Had I been able to meet with it at the moment, there could have been no doubt of its fate; but it appeared that the crafty animal had been alarmed at the violence of my previous anger, and forbore to present itself in my present mood. It is impossible to describe or to imagine the deep, blissful sense of relief which the absence of the detested creature occasioned in my bosom. It did not make its appearance during the night; and thus for one night, at least, since its introduction into the house, I soundly and tranquilly slept; aye, slept even with the burden of murder upon my soul.

The second and the third day passed, and still my tormentor came not. Once again I breathed as a freeman. The monster, in terror, had fled the premises for ever! I should behold it no more! My happiness was supreme! The guilt of my dark deed disturbed me but little. Some few inquiries had been made, but these had been readily answered. Even a search had been instituted—but of course nothing was to be discovered. I looked upon my future felicity as secured.

Upon the fourth day of the assassination, a party of the police came, very unexpectedly, into the house, and proceeded again to make a rigorous investigation of the premises. Secure, however, in the inscrutability of my place of concealment, I felt no embarrassment whatever. The officers bade me accompany them in their search. They left no nook or corner unexplored. At length, for the third or fourth time, they descended into the cellar. I quivered not in a muscle. My heart beat calmly as that of one who slumbers in innocence. I walked the cellar from end to end. I folded my arms upon my bosom, and roamed easily to and fro. The police were thoroughly satisfied and prepared to depart. The glee at my heart was too strong to be restrained. I burned to say if but one word, by way of triumph, and to render doubly sure their assurance of my guiltlessness.

"Gentlemen," I said at last, as the party ascended the steps, "I delight to have allayed your suspicions. I wish you all health and a little more courtesy. By the bye, gentlemen, this—this is a very well-constructed house," (in the rabid desire to say something easily, I scarcely knew what I uttered at all), —"I may say an excellently well-constructed house. These walls—are you going, gentlemen? —these walls are solidly put together"; and here, through the mere frenzy of bravado, I rapped heavily with a cane which I held in my hand, upon that very portion of the brick-work behind which stood the corpse of the wife of my bosom.

But may God shield and deliver me from the fangs of the Arch-Fiend! No sooner had the reverberation of my blows sunk into silence, than I was answered by a voice from within the tomb! —by a cry, at first muffled and broken, like the sobbing of a child, and then quickly swelling into one long, loud, and continuous scream, utterly anomalous and inhuman—a howl—a wailing shriek, half of horror and half of triumph, such as might have arisen only out of hell, conjointly from the throats of the damned in their agony and of the demons that exult in the damnation.

Of my own thoughts it is folly to speak. Swooning, I staggered to the opposite wall. For one instant the party on the stairs remained motionless, through extremity of terror and awe. In the next a dozen stout arms were toiling at the wall. It fell bodily. The corpse, already greatly decayed and clotted with gore, stood erect before the eyes of the spectators. Upon its head, with red extended mouth and solitary eye of fire, sat the hideous beast whose craft had seduced me into murder, and whose informing voice had consigned me to the hangman. I had walled the monster up within the tomb.

(1845)

QUESTIONS FOR REFLECTION

1. Identify the story's central and most important irony. Explain why it is important and how it affects our interpretation of the story and our evaluation of the narrator.
2. Consider whether the story may include other examples of irony besides that of its concluding action. Are there ironic aspects that include verbal, situational, or dramatic ironies? If so, identify a few of these and explain their significance.
3. Can the black cat be considered a symbol? Why or why not?

One of the most effective ways to improve your understanding of fiction is to read with a clear set of goals. Focus, for example, on the three aspects of the reading process explained in Chapter 1. Consider the various elements of fiction described in this chapter. And, where the opportunity arises, write about the works of fiction you read either formally or informally—to suit your own needs as a reader or to meet the requirements of a class assignment.

CHAPTER FOUR

Writing about Fiction

REASONS FOR WRITING ABOUT FICTION

Why write about fiction? One reason is to find out what you think about a story or novel. Another is to induce yourself to read it more carefully. You may write about a work of fiction because it engages you, and you may wish to celebrate it or to argue with its implied ideas and values. A fourth reason is that you may simply be required to do so as a course assignment.

Whatever your reasons for writing about fiction, a number of things happen when you do. First, in writing about a novel or story you tend to read it more attentively, noticing things you might overlook in a more casual reading. Second, since writing stimulates thinking, when you write about fiction you find yourself thinking more about what a particular work means and why you respond to it as you do. And third, you begin to acquire power over the works you write about, making them more meaningful to you.

INFORMAL WAYS OF WRITING ABOUT FICTION

When you write about a novel or short story, you may write for yourself or you may write for others. Writing for yourself, writing to discover what you think, often takes casual forms such as annotation and freewriting. These less formal kinds of writing are useful for helping you focus on your reading of fiction. They are helpful in studying for tests about fiction. They can serve also as preliminary forms of writing when you write more formal essays and papers about fiction.

Annotation

When you annotate a text, you make notes about it, usually in the margins or at the top and bottom of pages—or both. Annotations can also be made within the text, as underlined words, circled phrases, and bracketed sentences or paragraphs. Annotations may also assume the form of arrows, question marks, and various other marks.

Annotating a literary work offers a convenient and relatively painless way to begin writing about it. Annotating can get you started zeroing in on what you think interesting or important. You can also annotate to flag details that puzzle or disconcert you.

Your markings serve to focus your attention and clarify your understanding of a story or novel. Your annotations can save you time in rereading or studying a work. And they can also be used when you write a more formal paper.

Annotations for the following story illustrate the process.

KATHERINE ANNE PORTER
[1890–1980]

Magic

And, Madame Blanchard, believe that I am happy to be here with you and your family because it is so serene, everything, and before this I worked for a long time in a fancy house— maybe you don't know what is a fancy house? Naturally . . . everyone must have heard sometime or other. Well, Madame, I work always where there is work to be had, and so in this place I worked very hard all hours, and saw too many things, things you wouldn't believe, and I wouldn't think of telling you, only maybe it will rest you while I brush your hair. You'll excuse me too but I could not help hearing you say to the laundress maybe someone had bewitched your linens, they fall away so fast in the wash. Well, there was a girl there in that house, a poor thing, thin, but well-liked by all the men who called, and you understand she could not get along with the woman who ran the house. They quarreled, the madam cheated her on her checks: you know, the girl got a check, a brass one, every time, and at the week's end she gave those back to the madam, yes, that was the way, and got her percentage, a very small little of her earnings: it is a business, you see, like any other—and the madam used to pretend the girl had given back only so many checks, you see, and really she had given many more, but after they were out of her hands,

line 1: We enter into a monologue that has already begun.

line 8: Does she really not want to tell Madame B. what kind of work it is?

line 11: Bewitched linens? Magic?

what could she do? So she would say, I will get out of this place, and curse and cry. Then the madam would hit her over the head. She always hit people over the head with bottles, it was the way she fought. My good heavens, Madame Blanchard, what confusion there would be sometimes with a girl running raving downstairs, and the madam pulling her back by the hair and smashing a bottle on her forehead.

It was nearly always about the money, the girls got in debt so, and if they wished to go they could not without paying every sou marqué. The madam had full understanding with the police; the girls must come back with them or go to the jails. Well, they always came back with the policemen or with another kind of man friend of the madam: she could make men work for her too, but she paid them very well for all, let me tell you: and so the girls stayed on unless they were sick; if so, if they got too sick, she sent them away again.

Madame Blanchard said, 'You are pulling a little here,' and eased a strand of hair: 'and then what?'

Pardon—but this girl, there was a true hatred between her and the madam. She would say many times, I make more money than anybody else in the house, and every week were scenes. So at last she said one morning, Now I will leave this place, and she took out forty dollars from under her pillow and said, Here's your money! The madam began to shout, Where did you get all that, you—? and accused her of robbing the men who came to visit her. The girl said, Keep your hands off or I'll brain you: and at that the madam took hold of her shoulders, and began to lift her knee and kick this girl most terribly in the stomach, and even in her most secret place, Madame Blanchard, and then she beat her in the face with a bottle, and the girl fell back again into her room where I was making clean. I helped her to the bed, and she sat there holding her sides with her head hanging down, and when she got up again there was blood everywhere she had sat. So then the madam came in once more and screamed, Now you can get out, you are no good for me any more: I don't repeat all, you understand it is too much. But she took all the money she could find, and at the door she gave the girl a great push in the back with her knee, so that she fell again in the street, and then got up and went away with the dress barely on her.

After this the men who knew this girl kept saying, 'Where is Ninette? And they kept asking this in the next days, so that the madam could not say any longer, I put her out because she is a thief. No, she began to see she was wrong to send this Ninette away, and then she said, She will be back in a few days, don't trouble yourself.

And now, Madame Blanchard, if you wish to hear, I come to the strange part, the thing recalled to me when you said your linens were bewitched. For the cook in that place was a woman, colored like myself, like myself with much French blood just the same, like myself living always among people who worked spells. But she had a very hard heart, she helped the madam in everything, she liked to watch all that happened, and she gave away tales on the girls. The madam trusted her above everything, and she said, Well, where can I find that slut? because she had gone altogether out of Basin Street before the madam began to ask the police to bring her again. Well, the cook said, I know a charm that works here in New Orleans, colored women do it to bring back their men: in seven days they come again very happy to stay and they cannot say why: even your enemy will come back to you believing you are his friend. It is a New Orleans charm for sure, for certain, they say it does not work even across the river . . . And then they did it just as the cook said. They took the chamber pot of this girl from under her bed, and in it they mixed with water and milk all the relics of her they found there: the hair from her brush, and the face powder from the puff, and even little bits of her nails they found about the edges of the carpet where she sat by habit to cut her finger- and toe-nails; and they dipped the sheets with her blood into the water, and all the time the cook said something over it in a low voice; I could not hear all, but at last she said to the madam, Now spit in it: and the madam spat, the cook said, When she comes back she will be dirt under your feet.

Madame Blanchard closed her perfume bottle with a thin click: 'Yes, and then?'

Then in seven nights the girl came back and she looked very sick, the same clothes and all, but happy to be there. One of the men said, Welcome home, Ninette! and when she started to speak to the madam, the madam said, Shut up and get upstairs and dress yourself. So Ninette, this girl, she said, I'll be down in just a minute. And after that she lived there quietly.

(1930)

Freewriting

Freewriting is a kind of informal writing you do for yourself. In freewriting you explore a text to find out what you think about it and how you respond to it. When you freewrite you do not know ahead of time what your idea or your response to the work will be. Instead you write about the work to see where your thinking leads you.

[Handwritten margin notes:]

p 8: Magic again—this time the cook. Technique: Porter makes us curious.

Voodoo? Witchcraft? More magic?

It's the madam's psychological magic that brings her back. Why does it work?

Freewriting leads you to explore your memories and experience as well as aspects of the text itself. You sometimes wander from the details of the story or novel you are writing about. In the process you may discover thoughts and feelings you didn't know you had or were only dimly aware of. You can use freewriting to explore these responses. You can also use the technique to see where it leads you in thinking about the work itself.

Here is a group of responses written after students had read Kate Chopin's "The Story of an Hour" (pages 32–36). If you have not read the story, this will be a good time to do so. If you have read it, you can add your own freewriting response.

Before you read the interpolated comments printed between sections of the story, readjust the story itself. Then write down four or five sentences giving your reactions to it. Compare your response with the student responses that follow. Then read the story again, this time paying attention to the interpolated comments. What is your reaction to your own first response? To the student responses?

COLLEGE FRESHMAN   My first reaction was that Brently Mallard must have been an abusing husband. Maybe verbal or maybe physical abuse. But I noticed that Mrs. Mallard said his hands were "kind and tender" and she said his face "never looked on her save with love." Then I began to think that maybe Louise Mallard was an ungrateful wife who didn't appreciate what she had. Still, she obviously felt that she had to submit to everything he wanted. She talks about his "powerful will." So she really did feel abused in some ways and maybe that's what's important. I was confused and want to read the story again.

COLLEGE SOPHOMORE   Did Louise Mallard die at the end because she was shocked or because she was so upset at losing her freedom? I don't think she died of joy, even though she did have some love for her husband, so I think the doctor was wrong. She may have died of heart trouble, but maybe it was not a physical illness of the heart. Maybe what was wrong was that Louise had never had a chance to know her own heart. So when she did begin to feel some freedom and then lost it, she was sick in her spirit (what some people would call her heart). I think her death was finding a kind of freedom that she couldn't have in life. So maybe the whole incident came out for the best for Louise.

COLLEGE FRESHMAN   I thought maybe Brently's friend Richards had something going with Louise. That was why he rushed right over to tell her about his death. And at the end he tries to protect her. But on the other hand, I couldn't figure out why Louise wouldn't have some thoughts about Richards while she was imagining her freedom. If they really were having an affair. So maybe they weren't. But why would Louise be so glad to be free if she didn't have a reason?

COLLEGE FRESHMAN I liked all the metaphors and descriptions which really made you feel like you could understand how Louise's feelings changed. When she first heard the news she had a "storm of grief" but then she looks out the window and sees "patches of blue" so you get the idea that the storm is passing and that maybe Louise is not going to be so unhappy after all. When you read about her "two white slender hands" that are "powerless" they seem sort of like gentle swans, and you can imagine that Louise was sort of a household pet or a decoration for her husband. And that she did not have any way—or did not know any way—to oppose his "powerful will."

The focused freewriting on Kate Chopin's story and Robert Graves's poem (Chapter 11, pages 519–520) is very much like journal entries. In fact, keeping an informal log or journal of your responses to the literary works you read is a useful and fairly easy way to prepare for class discussion of them.

FORMAL WAYS OF WRITING ABOUT FICTION

Among the more common formal ways of writing about fiction is analysis. In writing an analytical essay about a short story or a novel, your goal is to explain how one or more particular aspects or issues in the work contribute to its overall meaning. You might analyze the dialogue in Boyle's "Astronomer's Wife" (page 57) or Pirandello's "War" (page 249), for example, in explaining what the verbal exchanges between characters contribute to the story's meaning. You might analyze the ironic qualities of Chopin's "The Story of an Hour" or O'-Connor's "Good Country People" (page 171). Or you might analyze the characters in Carver's "Cathedral" (page 347) or Lawrence's "The Blind Man" (page 128) to explain how the relationships between the characters reveal each story's theme.

In addition to analyzing these and other fictional elements in a single story, you might also compare two stories, perhaps by focusing on their symbolism, style, tone, setting, or point of view. Or, instead of focusing on literary elements per se, you might write to see how a particular critical perspective (see Chapter 22) illumines a story. For example, you might consider the feminist implications of Updike's "A & P" (page 27) or what a psychological approach to Hawthorne's "Young Goodman Brown" (page 219) contributes to your understanding.

The following brief analysis focuses on the characters in Pirandello's "War." The writer considers how the dialogue and descriptions of the characters lead to a metaphorical interpretation of the story's title.

Student Papers on Fiction

Carol Holt

DEFINING WAR

Luigi Pirandello calls his short story about grieving and
worried parents, "War." At first reading, the title seems a
bit misleading because the setting is a railroad car rather
than a battlefield, and the characters are people who have
sent their sons off to the front but who are not directly
involved themselves. Further reading, however, shows that each
mother and father is going through a personal struggle within
his or her mind. In addition, the characters fight among
themselves about what view they should take of their sons'
military service. In a sense, the railroad car becomes a
battlefield as the characters engage in war both within
themselves and with others.
    The dialogue between the bulky woman's husband and the man
who has two sons at the front seems like a war in several
ways. They engage in conflict and each tries to outdo the
other, bringing out more and more verbal weapons in an attempt
to be the victor. The arguments are as empty and meaningless
as are many real-life physical battles. One father argues that
losing an only son is the worst fate. The other counters that
the death of one son while the other lives prevents the
grieving parent from the "remedy" of suicide. This war is
certainly futile and cannot be resolved in a logical or
satisfactory way. Each side is convinced of the truth of its
own argument. Each looks only at its own point of view. Just
as with real warring factions, there seems to be no way to
bring the two sides together.
    When the fat, red-faced man speaks, he seems to be making a
statement with which all the passengers can agree. They all
shake their heads as if to approve when he speaks of love of
country and patriotism. Nevertheless, he too is involved in a
war. As he continues to speak and as the bulky woman starts to
listen, he becomes more and more emotional. For example, his
eyes are watery and he ends one of his speeches "with a shrill
laugh which might well have been a sob." The bulky woman tries
to resolve the conflict—the war—within herself, but as she
states the one fact most frightening to her, the red-faced man
reveals his own painful battle. When she says, "Then . . . is

your son really dead?" the red-faced man bursts into tears. He has not resolved the fight that is going on between his sense of patriotism and his love for his fallen son.

Pirandello has extended the definition of war. Conflicts, struggles, and exchange of ammunition occur not just on the actual battlefields but also in the lives of those connected to members of fighting forces. As the title of Pirandello's story suggests, wars may be fought on metaphoric battlefields and may produce casualties who never stop a bullet.

In the next sample paper, a student describes Mark Twain's use of satire in *The Adventures of Huckleberry Finn*. The writer's focus on Twain's use of satire to criticize greed, conformity, and slavery makes the paper's purpose clear. The use of specific examples with quotations from the novel illustrates Twain's satiric technique. And the choice of three objects of Twain's satire enables the writer to organize her essay clearly and effectively.

Karen Elizabeth
Professor Hogan
English 102
October 10, 1996

Mark Twain's Satire in
The Adventures of Huckleberry Finn

The Adventures of Huckleberry Finn, one of the great American
novels, tells a story of a young boy's journey down the
Mississippi River. The author, Mark Twain, uses many literary
techniques to enhance the mood and alert the reader to various
themes. One major literary technique he commonly uses in his
novel is satire. Satire is a method of taking a serious
subject and presenting it in a humorous way. The object of
satire is to ridicule the subject satirized. By using satire,
Twain can dramatize the weaknesses and failings of people and
society. In the novel, Twain's satire enables the reader to
view the flaws in American society while enjoying the exciting
adventures of Huckleberry Finn.

   While Huck journeys down the Mississippi River, he meets the
notorious "rapscallions" the king and the duke. They board
Huck's raft, hoping the river will be a channel to promote
their work. The king and duke represent people who honor money
and success above all things. Since they are both humorous
characters who are nothing "but just low down humbugs and
frauds," the reader laughs at their ridiculous behavior. But
they are more than just silly and harmless old men. They are
dangerous and destructive, causing many individuals to suffer.
What motivates them is greed. Through them Twain shows how
greed can lead to trouble and unhappiness.

   A second social fault Twain satirizes in *Huckleberry Finn* is
conformity. Twain demonstrates the psychological need of an
individual to conform to the ideas of a group rather than to
follow his own mind. The most important example of this
dangerous habit of conformity is the ridiculous feud between
the Grangerfords and the Shepherdsons. In his portrayal of the
feuding families, Twain creates a satire on the irrationality
of love and hate. Perhaps the best example of the
irrationality occurs during Huck's conversation with Buck
Grangerford. When Huck asks the young man what a feud is, he
replies:

         a feud is this way. A man has a quarrel
         with another man, and kills him; then that

> other man's brother kills *him;* then the
> other brothers, on both sides, goes for
> one another, then the *cousins* chip in—and
> by-and-by everybody's killed off, and
> there ain't no more feud. But it's kind of
> slow, and takes a long time.

As the conversation continues Twain shows that the two feuding families kill each other's members without even knowing why. Nobody seems to remember what started the feud or why the two families hate each other.

Throughout the chapters that describe the feud, Twain uses satire to show how nonsensical and irrational people can be. For example the Grangerfords and the Shepherdsons go to church on Sundays and listen to the minister preach "all about brotherly love and such like tiresomeness." Meanwhile their guns are lined up against the wall ready for use. The members of neither family ever stop to think about what they are doing and why they do it.

Finally and most importantly, the novel satirizes slavery, which Twain attacks as the greatest flaw in American society. Jim, the runaway slave, is a warm-hearted individual seeking freedom by escaping down the river with Huck. Twain shows how society's treatment of Jim is cruel, heartless, and irrational. Twain shows that Jim deserves a better fate than to be separated from the wife and children he loves and be forced to work for people who humiliate him.

Perhaps the most important way Twain reveals the absolute evil of slavery is to show how difficult it is for Huck not to turn Jim in even though Jim loves Huck dearly and has only done things to help him. Through his portrayal of Huck's crisis of conscience over what to do about Jim, Twain shows how society's values during that time were the opposite of what they should be.

Because Huck was taught at home and in school that slavery was right, it is difficult for him to go against that belief. Deep in his heart, however, he knows that Jim should be free, that he is a good man, and that to enslave and humiliate him is wrong. Society's values, however, affect Huck so strongly that he goes along with Tom Sawyer's ridiculous plans for Jim that result in Jim's further humiliation. Huck does, however, realize that Jim is not inferior to him, even though as he describes the time he apologized for his unkind treatment of Jim, he reveals that "it was fifteen minutes before I could work myself up to go and humble myself to a nigger." The important thing for Huck is that he does ask Jim's forgiveness. The important thing for Twain's readers is that

they realize that in doing what society has told Huck is
wrong, he ends up doing what is right and good.

Throughout the *Adventures of Huckleberry Finn*, Mark Twain
treats serious matters in a humorous way. By ridiculing the
weakness and faults in society, he entertains his readers
while at the same time instructing them in how they should
live. Through his use of satire, Twain illustrates the major
themes of the novel. He gives his readers a clear perspective
on the dangers of greed, the destructive consequences of
conformity, and the evils of slavery.

QUESTIONS FOR WRITING ABOUT FICTION

In writing about the elements of fiction, the following questions can help you focus
your thinking and prepare yourself for writing analytical essays and papers. Use the
questions as a checklist to guide you to important aspects of any story or novel you
read.

Plot and Structure

1. What incidents constitute the building blocks of the story's plot?
2. How are these incidents arranged? Chronologically? With flashbacks of action?
   With foreshadowing?
3. To what extent is the plot unified? How are its incidents related?
4. How is the story shaped, organized, or designed?
5. What patterns can you discern in the story's action? To what extent are repetition,
   balance, and contrast important? Why?

Character and Characterization

6. To what extent do you identify with any of the characters? To what extent do you
   sympathize with them or judge them harshly? Why?
7. To what extent does your response to the characters change? If your response does
   change, identify where that change occurs and why.
8. Are the characters dynamic or static? In the context of the story, are their actions
   believable? Why or why not? Do their names convey anything about them?
9. What is the function of any minor characters in the story?
10. How does the author characterize or reveal the characters? What do the charac-
    ters' speech and behavior reveal about them? What do the author's description and
    point of view contribute to your understanding of the characters?

Setting

11. Where and when is the action of the story set?
12. To what extent are aspects of the setting symbolic? How do you know?

13. Can you imagine the story set in another place or time? Why or why not?

Point of View

14. Who narrates the story's action? Is the point of view first person or third? Does the point of view shift during the course of the story? If so, where, why, and with what implications for meaning?
15. How much does the narrator know about the characters? Is the narrator completely omniscient? Does the narrator possess limited omniscience? Or does the narrator know only as much as the reader?
16. Is the narrator a participant in the story's action or merely an observer?
17. How trustworthy is the narrator? Is the narrator a reliable witness or commentator on the action and behavior of the story's characters? Why or why not?

Symbolism

18. Do you think any objects or events in the story are symbolic? Why or why not?
19. Are there other symbolic elements—elements of character, setting, language, for example?
20. What do the symbols contribute to the meaning of the story?

Language, Style, Tone

21. How would you characterize the style of the story? The style of the characters' dialogue? Does the style shift at any point?
22. How carefully do you have to read the text? Does the language seem particularly compelling or especially complicated at any point? If so, what makes it compelling or complicated?
23. What is the author's tone or attitude toward the story's characters and action? What aspects of language in particular—diction, imagery, syntax—create that tone?
24. Is the author's tone ironic? If so, how can you tell?

Theme

25. How would you characterize the theme of the story? Is there more than a single theme?
26. Does the author convey the theme(s) directly or indirectly? That is, can you identify a key passage in which the theme is made explicit? Or do you have to infer the theme from the story's action, dialogue, and details?
27. How does your analysis of the elements of fiction help you understand a story's theme(s)?

Critical Perspectives

28. Among the critical perspectives you might bring to bear on the story, which one(s) seem(s) particularly useful for interpreting it? Why?

29. To what extent can you base your interpretation of the story on its language and details alone? To what extent is outside information about historical and biographical context necessary or helpful in understanding it?
30. To what extent does the story mesh with your personal beliefs and values? To what extent is it antagonistic to your personal beliefs and values?

Suggestions for Writing
The Experience of Fiction

1. Write a paper in which you recount your experience of reading a particular story or series of stories by the same author. You may want to compare your initial experience with your experience when you reread the story or stories.
2. Compare the experience of reading a story with that of watching a film based on it.
3. Relate the action or situation of a story to your own experience. Explain how the story is relevant to your situation. Comment on how reading and thinking about it may have helped you view your own circumstances more clearly.

The Interpretation of Fiction

4. Describe a character who has an important decision to make. Identify the character's situation, explain the reasons for his or her decision, and speculate about the possible consequences.
5. Explicate the opening sentences or paragraph of any story. Explain the significance of the opening section in establishing the story's tone, announcing its theme, or otherwise preparing the reader for what follows.
6. Explicate the closing sentences or paragraph of any story. Explain the significance of the conclusion, commenting on its effectiveness as an ending.
7. Select two or three brief passages from a story and explain their significance. Consider how the passages may be related.
8. Analyze the plot of a story. Comment on its organization or structure. How is the plot designed to affect readers' responses? Notice whether the incidents are presented in chronological order or whether chronology is violated and, if so, for what purpose.
9. Analyze the setting of a story. Consider both the time and place of its action. Also consider small-scale aspects of setting such as whether the

action takes place indoors or out. If indoors, which room does the action occur in—and why? Notice any significant changes of setting.

10. Analyze a character from a story. Evaluate the character's behavior, offering reasons and evidence for your views. Consider what the character does, says, does not say or do—and why. Identify any significant changes the character undergoes. What do other characters say about him or her, and how do they respond in action?

11. Discuss the relationship of two characters. Consider how the characters affect each other, and explain the nature and significance of their relationship.

12. Analyze the symbolism of a story. Identify its major symbols and explain their significance. Some possibilities: Faulkner's "A Rose for Emily"; Hawthorne's forest in "Young Goodman Brown"; Gilman's "The Yellow Wallpaper"; Olsen's iron in "I Stand Here Ironing"; Walker's "Everyday Use"; Poe's "Black Cat."

13. Analyze the ironic dimensions of a story. Identify examples of irony, and explain their importance in the story. Some possibilities: Poe's "Black Cat"; Joyce's "Araby" and "The Boarding House"; Ellison's "Battle Royal"; Singer's "Gimpel the Fool"; O'Connor's "Guests of the Nation."

14. Analyze the point of view of a story. How would the story be different if it were narrated from a different point of view? Consider whether the narrator is believable or is somehow limited and/or perhaps unworthy of our trust.

15. Explain the theme of any story. Identify its overriding idea. Establish the grounds for your interpretation, and explain why the idea is important.

16. Analyze the use of figurative language in any story. Identify the major types of figurative language used and explain their function, effect, and significance. What would be gained or lost without them? Some possibilities: Faulkner's "A Rose for Emily"; O'Connor's "Good Country People"; Walker's "Everyday Use"; Atwood's "Rape Fantasies."

The Evaluation of Fiction

17. Discuss the values exemplified in any story. Identify those values, relate them to your own, and comment on their significance.

18. Do a comparative evaluation of the distinctive merits of any two stories. Explain what they have in common, how they differ, and why one is more interesting, impressive, or effective than the other.

19. Evaluate a story from the standpoint of its merit or literary excellence—or lack thereof. Explain why you consider it to be a successful or unsuccessful story.

To Research or Imagine

20. Develop an alternative ending for a story, changing the outcome in whatever way you like. Be prepared to defend your revised ending. Consider why the author chose to end the story as he or she did.
21. Read some letters or essays by a fiction writer you know and enjoy. Consider how they aid your understanding or increase your pleasure in reading the writer's stories.
22. Read a full-scale biography of a fiction writer. Write a paper explaining how the writer's life is or is not reflected in the work.
23. Read a novel by a writer whose short fiction you enjoy. Write a paper explaining how the novel is related to the shorter fiction.
24. Consider a writer of fiction in his or her historical context. Read a few of the writer's stories as reflections of or denunciations of the social, moral, and cultural dispositions of his or her time.
25. Read a critical study of a fiction writer. Explain how reading the book enhanced your understanding or appreciation of the writer's fiction.

CHAPTER FIVE

Three Fiction Writers in Context

READING D. H. LAWRENCE, FLANNERY O'CONNOR, AND SANDRA CISNEROS IN DEPTH

When you read a fiction writer in even moderate depth, it is useful to look for connections among the works you read. At the same time, however, you should also look for differences. You might read Lawrence's "The Horse Dealer's Daughter," for example, in light of what he himself says about fiction in his essays, "The Bright Book of Life" and "Morality and the Novel." You might also read this story in relation to others Lawrence has written. Although "The Blind Man" is not a love story in the same way as "The Horse Dealer's Daughter," you can nonetheless find shared emphases and values reflected in both stories.

In addition to looking for shared thematic preoccupations and common values espoused by different stories, you can also be alert for artistic links. At first glance, "The Rocking-Horse Winner" seems quite different from "The Blind Man" and "The Horse Dealer's Daughter." Yet each of the three stories shares stylistic traits with the others, and all three reflect characteristics of Lawrence's writerly temperament. (See these works reprinted later in this chapter.)

As you read for connections among a writer's works, be careful not to pour every story into the same mold. Recognize what links the stories, but remain alert for the distinctive and individual presence of each. Consider how each work manifests its individuality at the same time that it reveals shared thematic concerns and corresponding aesthetic qualities of other works by the writer.

What is said here of Lawrence's fiction applies with equal force to the works of Flannery O'Connor and Sandra Cisneros. O'Connor's fiction is often read in light of her religious faith. As a strong adherent of Roman Catholicism who has written about her faith, O'Connor seems to invite readers to bring a strong Christian perspective to their reading of her work. This invitation is strengthened by the explicit Christian references in the stories themselves. Nonetheless, when reading O'Connor's stories, readers need to maintain a balance between interpretations based on the stories' explicit use of Christian iconography and the quirky individuality of each particular fictional creation. The work of Sandra Cisneros explores the complex cultural identity of its author: born in Chicago, Cisneros grew up in a bilingual family and traveled frequently to Mexico to visit relatives. Her writing also profoundly addresses the experience of women, particularly those in urban settings.

In reading all of the following stories, enjoy the unique pleasures each story provides while constructing a sense of each writer's fictional world. Also, while attending to what both writers have said about their fiction, attend even more to the individual fictional works themselves. "Trust the tale," as Lawrence himself advises, not the teller. Or rather, trust the tale as the teller relates it rather than as the teller describes or otherwise explains it.

You can use the following questions as a general guide for in-depth reading of fiction, especially the three stories of Sandra Cisneros included in this chapter.

QUESTIONS FOR IN-DEPTH READING

1. What general or overall thematic connections can you make among different works?
2. What stylistic similarities do you notice between and among different works?
3. How do the works differ in emphasis, tone, and style?
4. Once you have identified a writer's major preoccupations, place each work on a spectrum or a grid that represents the range of the writer's concerns.
5. What connections and disjunctions do you find among the following literary elements as they are embodied in different stories by the same writer?
    (a) plot and structure
    (b) character and characterization
    (c) setting and symbolism
    (d) language, style, and tone
    (e) theme and thought
6. To what extent are your responses to and perceptions of different works by the same writer shared by others—by critics, by classmates, and by the writers themselves?
7. What relationships and differences do you see between the work of one writer and that of another who shares similar thematic interests, stylistic proclivities, or cultural, religious, or social values?
8. Which of the critical perspectives (Chapter 22) seem most useful as analytical tools for approaching the body of work of particular writers?

INTRODUCTION TO D. H. LAWRENCE

[1885–1930]

David Herbert Lawrence is best known for his novels, whose titles reveal their center of interest: *Sons and Lovers* (1913), *Women in Love* (1920), *Lady Chatterly's Lover* (1928), and *The Virgin and the Gypsy* (1930), among many others. Of these, *Lady Chatterly's Lover* achieved the greatest notoriety, if not the highest critical acclaim, when it became the occasion of a court obscenity battle. Like much of Lawrence's work, this novel explores the relations between the sexes, contrasting a debilitating relationship between Lady Chatterly and her impotent husband with a vital one between Lady Chatterly and the gamekeeper. The novel is also a compendium of Lawrence's major thematic preoccupations: the importance of instinctual life, the celebration of the natural world, the condemnation of the mechanical and the conventionally artificial, and the powerful effects of sexual surrender.

Lawrence derived a penchant for learning and an impulse to write partly from his mother, who was better educated than his father, an unschooled miner. She encouraged her son's intellectual pursuits, recognizing that his frail constitution made him unsuitable for the physical rigors of a miner's life. Affecting a somewhat self-conscious gentility, she was the intellectual superior of her husband, whose semiliteracy and working-class habits contrasted sharply with her sense of refinement. Lawrence himself, early in life, favored his mother but later came to see his father's virtues, especially his vitality, warmth, and love of the natural world.

D. H. Lawrence was born in Nottinghamshire, an English mining town. He was educated there, taking a teaching certificate from Nottingham College. He taught school from 1902 to 1912, with a one-year hiatus, before becoming a full-time writer. Between 1911, when he published his first novel, *The White Peacock*, and 1930, when he died of tuberculosis, Lawrence published more than sixty volumes, including novels, stories, poems, essays, plays, travel books, social criticism, and translations of Russian and Italian literature.

Lawrence's life was a tissue of unconventional choices. One of the most important was his love affair with Frieda von Richthofen, the German wife of a professor of French at Nottingham, whom Lawrence married after her divorce. With Frieda, Lawrence lived at various times in Germany, England, Italy, Australia, Mexico, and France, where he died. His unconventionality found its fiercest expression in his books, which repeatedly displayed the stultifying constraints and enervating hypocrisies that pervaded modern life, vestiges from Victorian pieties and the mindless conventionalism of an earlier time. Rebelling against constraints of all kinds—intellectual, emotional, sexual— Lawrence raised his voice in protest, most effectively in his art.

Lawrence waged his most intense battles against an overintellectual approach to living, especially against the exaggerated intellectualism about sexual experience he described as "sex in the head." In its place Lawrence celebrated the liberation of the body, arguing that human beings need to express their emotion with physical passion uncontaminated by puritanical attitudes and unrestrained by conventional moralistic tendencies. Lawrence saw sexuality as the source of a badly needed restoration of vitality and joy. He considered the primacy of erotic love an elemental force that was linked fundamentally with the physical energy of the natural world. In both his fiction and his poetry, Lawrence frequently employed elements of the natural world as emblems of human passions and impulses. Lawrence, moreover, was a careful and loving observer of nature, which he repeatedly demonstrated by his convincing depictions of animals and the natural landscape. Allied with his celebration of the natural world was his condemnation of the evils of industrialism, which he considered responsible for nearly destroying the English landscape and for its dehumanizing effects.

Lawrence was spiritual kin to the English Romantic poet William Blake and the American transcendentalist poet Walt Whitman. Like Blake, Lawrence was something of a visionary. Like Whitman, he was literarily unconventional, developing a style and voice to suit his unique vision of experience.

Lawrence's respect for instinct and his celebration of sexual love are eminently displayed in "The Horse Dealer's Daughter." This story offers a fine example of complex feelings and intense psychological drama in the developing erotic relationship between a young man and woman who, each very much alone, simultaneously desire and fear the sexual attraction that develops between them. Lawrence's patience in describing this encounter, his slowing of the narrative tempo to accommodate their conflicted feelings, and the insistence with which he describes its ultimately inevitable consequences vividly dramatize the power of sexual attraction.

The tensions in "The Blind Man" and "The Rocking-Horse Winner" are different though not unrelated to those displayed in "The Horse Dealer's Daughter." Like Dr. Fergusson in "The Horse Dealer's Daughter," the barrister Bertie in "The Blind Man" is afraid of physical contact. Lawrence sets him in opposition to the story's protagonist and places the blind man's wife squarely between the two men. She experiences a different kind of attraction toward each, the two men displaying an actual repulsion for one another. Part of our pleasure in reading this story derives from Lawrence's careful set of characterizations. Part comes also from the surprising sequence of developing action and the characters' varied understandings of its significance. Especially effective is the climactic scene in the dark barn where the blind man, alone with the barrister, attempts to breach the gulf that divides them.

"The Rocking-Horse Winner" takes us into another world—that of money and its power to affect our lives. The story can be read as an attack on materialist values, which Lawrence railed against throughout his life. But it also invites consideration of the relationship between a young boy and his mother, a subject Lawrence began exploring with his first important novel, *Sons and Lovers*, based largely on his experience.

Throughout his writing life Lawrence persisted in condemning societal attitudes that conflicted with his belief that human beings must become instinctive and intuitive, deeply in touch with their physical being and with the primal rhythms of nature. He repeatedly strove to depict not only the instinctually repressed and sexually inhibited world that he rejected, but also an alternative world in which men and women were in tune with their physical selves and could relate to one another passionately and openly. And all this would be in harmony with nature, at once source and sustenance, image and ideal of personal and social wholeness.

Lawrence rendered his romanticist vision with passionate intensity. Putting his passion in the service of art, Lawrence crafted stories at once wonderful and dangerous. Their language and incidents frequently surprise; their voice and vision repeatedly reveal Lawrence's astonishing energy and love of life.

CRITICAL COMMENTS BY LAWRENCE

from *The Bright Book of Life*

The novel is the one bright book of life. Books are not life. They are only tremulations on the ether. But the novel as a tremulation can make the whole man alive tremble. Which is more than poetry, philosophy, science, or any other book-tremulation can do.

The novel is the book of life. In this sense, the Bible is a great confused novel. You may say, it is about God. But it is really about man alive. Adam, Eve, Sarai, Abraham, Isaac, Jacob, Samuel, David, Bath-Sheba, Ruth, Esther, Solomon, Job, Isaiah, Jesus, Mark, Judas, Paul, Peter: what is it but man alive, from start to finish? Man alive, not mere bits. Even the Lord is another man alive, in a burning bush, throwing the tablets of stone at Moses's head.

I do hope you begin to get my idea, why the novel is supremely important, as a tremulation on the ether. Plato makes the perfect ideal being tremble in me. But that's only a bit of me. Perfection is only a bit, in the strange make-up of man alive. The Sermon on the Mount makes the selfless spirit of me quiver. But that, too, is only a bit of me. The Ten Commandments set the old Adam shivering in me, warning me that I am a thief and a murderer, unless I watch it. But even the old Adam is only a bit of me.

I very much like all these bits of me to be set trembling with life and the wisdom of life. But I do ask that the whole of me shall tremble in its wholeness, some time or other. . . .

To be alive, to be man alive, to be whole man alive: that is the point. And at its best, the novel, and the novel supremely, can help you. It can help you not to be dead man in life. So much of a man walks about dead and a carcass in the street and house, today: so much of women is merely dead. Like a pianoforte with half the notes mute.

But in the novel you can see, plainly, when the man goes dead, the woman goes inert. You can develop an instinct for life, if you will, instead of a theory of right and wrong, good and bad.

In life, there is right and wrong, good and bad, all the time. But what is right in one case is wrong in another. And in the novel you see one man becoming a corpse, because of his so-called goodness, another going dead because of his so-called wickedness. Right and wrong is an instinct: but an instinct of the whole consciousness in a man, bodily, mental, spiritual at once. And only in the novel are *all* things given full play, or at least, they may be given full play, when we realize that life itself, and not inert safety, is the reason for living. For out of the full play of all things emerges the only thing that is anything, the wholeness of a man, the wholeness of a woman, man alive, and live woman.

Man and Woman

from *Morality and the Novel*

The great relationship, for humanity, will always be the relation between man and woman. The relation between man and man, woman and woman, parent and child, will always be subsidiary.

And the relation between man and woman will change for ever, and will for ever be the new central clue to human life. It is the *relation itself* which is the quick and the central clue to life, not the man, nor the woman, nor the children that result from the relationship, as a contingency.

It is no use thinking you can put a stamp on the relation between man and woman, to keep it in the *status quo.* You can't. You might as well try to put a stamp on the rainbow or the rain.

As for the bond of love, better put it off when it galls. It is an absurdity, to say that men and women *must love.* Men and women will be for ever subtly and changingly related to one another; no need to yoke them with any "bond" at all. The only morality is to have man true to his manhood, woman to her womanhood, and let the relationship form of itself, in all honour. For it is, to each, *life itself.*

CRITICS ON LAWRENCE

MARK SPILKA

Ritual Form in "The Blind Man"

from *The Ethic of Love*

> . . . He lifted his hand, and laid the fingers on the scar, on the scarred eyes. Maurice suddenly covered them with his own hand, pressed the fingers of the other man upon his disfigured eye-sockets, trembling in every fibre, and rocking slightly, slowly, from side to side. He remained thus for a minute or more, whilst Bertie stood as if in a swoon, unconscious, imprisoned.

> Then suddenly Maurice removed the hand of the other man
> from his brow, and stood holding it in his own.
> "Oh, my God," he said, "we shall know each other now, shan't
> we? We shall know each other now."

A writer like James Joyce might see an "epiphany" in such an experience—a static, timeless manifestation of some spiritual essence; but Lawrence sees instead a kinetic transformation of being, in both Pervin and Reid: for when the two return to Isabel, Maurice stands "with his feet apart, like a strange colossus," while Bertie is now "like a mollusc whose shell is broken." Through the friendship rite, one man moves toward greater fullness of being; his blindness is transcended, his unresolved blood-intimacy released, and the limited circle of marriage itself is broken by "the new delicate fulfillment of mortal friendship"; but the other man is destroyed by the experience; his outer bulwark against life is smashed, his inner vacuum thoroughly exposed. Thus the ritual pattern of the story is complete. There are ironies, of course, and resonant implications, as in more static and symbolic forms. The path, the way out of darkness which opens for the Pervins is quickly closed by Bertie's fear of passionate friendship. Yet the change of being in Maurice, as in Bertie, is real and valid. The ritual form conveys a new life-possibility: a step beyond marriage which makes marriage possible, a breakthrough to that fuller life which Lawrence tried to project in all his work, in strongly dramatic terms, and with a strong *dramatic* sense of the odds against it.

W. D. SNODGRASS

A Rocking-Horse: Symbol, Pattern, Way to Live

from *The Hudson Review*

As several critics have noted, the story resembles many well-known fairy tales or magical stories in which the hero bargains with evil powers for personal advantages or forbidden knowledge. These bargains are always "rigged" so that the hero, after his apparent triumphs, will lose in the end—this being, in itself, the standard "moral." Gordon and Tate sum up their interpretation: "the boy, Paul, has invoked strange gods and pays the penalty with his death." Robert Gorham Davis goes on to point out that many witches supposedly rode hobby-horses of one sort or another (e.g., the witch's broom) to rock themselves into a magical and prophetic trance. When he rides, Paul's eyes glare blue and strange, he will speak to no one, his sisters fear him. He stares into the horse's wooden face: "Its red mouth was slightly open, its big eye was wide and glassy-bright." More and more engrossed in his doom as the story progresses, he becomes "wild-eyed and strange . . . his big blue eyes blazing with a sort of madness." We hear again and again of the uncanny blaze of his eyes until finally, at his collapse, they are "like blue stones." Clearly enough, he is held in some self-induced prophetic frenzy, a line of meaning carefully developed by the story. When Paul first asserts to his mother that he is "lucky," he claims that God told him so. This seems pure invention, yet may well be a kind of *hubris,* considering the conversation that had just passed with his mother:

> "Nobody ever knows why one person is lucky and another unlucky."
> "Don't they? Nobody at all? Does nobody know?"
> "Perhaps God. But He never tells."

Whether Paul really believes that God told him so, he certainly does become lucky. And others come to believe that superhuman powers are involved. Bassett thinks of "Master Paul" as a seer and takes an explicitly worshipful tone towards him. He grows "serious as a church" and twice tells Uncle Oscar in a "secret, religious voice. . . . 'It's as if he had it from heaven.'" These hints of occultism culminate in Uncle Oscar's benediction:

> "My God, Hester, you're eighty-odd thousand to the good, and a poor devil of a son to the bad. But poor devil, poor devil, he's best gone out of a life where he rides his rocking-horse to find a winner."

So, in some sense, Paul *is* demonic, yet a poor devil; though he has compacted with evil, his intentions were good and he has destroyed only himself. At first metaphorically, in the end literally, he has committed suicide. But that may be, finally, the essence of evil.

It is clear, then, that the story is talking about some sort of religious perversion. But *what* sort? Who are the strange gods: how does Paul serve them and receive their information? We must return here, I think, to the problem of knowledge and intellection. Paul is destroyed, we have said, by his desire to "know." It is not only that he has chosen wrong ways of knowing or wrong things to know. The evil is that he *has* chosen to know, to live by intellection. Lawrence wrote, in a letter to Ernest Collings:

> My great religion is a belief in the blood, the flesh, as being wiser than the intellect. We can go wrong in our minds. But what our blood feels and believes and says, is always true. *The intellect is only a bit and bridle.* What do I care about knowledge. . . . I conceive a man's body as a kind of flame . . . and the intellect is just the light that is shed on to the things around. . . . A flame isn't a flame because it lights up two, or twenty objects on a table. It's a flame because it is itself. And we have forgotten ourselves. . . . The real way of living is to answer to one's wants. Not "I want to light up with my intelligence as many things as possible" but ". . . I want that liberty, I want that woman, I want that pound of peaches, I want to go to sleep, I want to go to the pub and have a good time, I want to look a beastly swell today, I want to kiss that girl, I want to insult that man."

(I have italicized the bit and bridle metaphor to underscore an immediate relationship to the rocking-horse of the story.)

Not one member of this family really knows his wants. Like most idealists, they have ignored the most important part of the command *Know thyself,* and so cannot deal with their most important problem, their own needs. To know one's needs is really to know one's own limits, hence one's definition. Lawrence's notion of living by "feeling" or "blood" (as opposed to "knowledge," "mind" or "personality") may be most easily understood, perhaps, as living according to what you *are,* not what you think you should be made over into; knowing yourself, not external standards. Thus, what Lawrence calls "feeling" could well be glossed as "knowing one's wants." Paul's family, lacking true knowledge of themselves, have turned their light, their intellect, outward, hoping to control the external world. The mother, refusing to clarify what her emotions really *are,* hopes to control herself and her world by acting "gentle and anxious for her children." She tries to be or act what she thinks she should be, not taking adequate notice of what she is and needs. She acts from precepts about motherhood, not from recognition of her own will, self-respect for her own motherhood. Thus, the apparent contradiction between Hester's coldness, the "hard . . . center of her heart," and, on the other hand, "all her tormented motherhood flooding upon her" when Paul collapses near the end of the story. Some deep source of affection has apparently lain hidden (and so tormented) in her, all along; it was her business to find and release it sooner. Similarly, Paul has a need for affection which he does not, and perhaps cannot, understand or manage.

KINGSLEY WIDMER

On "The Horse Dealer's Daughter"

from *D. H. Lawrence: The Art of Perversity*

Originally entitled by Lawrence "The Miracle," *The Horse Dealer's Daughter* may be viewed as one of a series of Lawrence's tales turning about a moment of regenerative baptism. The young man, "spell-bound," "mesmerized," by something deeper than his consciousness, "felt delivered from his own fretted, daily self." The courageous breakthrough at the moment of despair and death brings out the new agony of desire. The man sees the "terrible shining joy in her eyes, which really terrified him, and yet which he wanted to see, because he feared the look of doubt still more." The necessary faith in life takes the form of erotic confrontation. Having been carried home, undressed, and warmed back to life by the doctor, Mabel regains consciousness to find herself on the desperate edge between life and death, love and despair. Lawrence has carefully created a figure of profound naiveté, and so, naked before the man, she simply draws the conclusion of need: either he loves her, or she is dead. By the very nakedness of her self and her need, she forces him to recognize desire—"he had crossed the gulf over to her." The story ends with the man's agonized assent to desire: " 'No, I want you, I want you,' " was all he answered to her question of love, "blindly, with that terrible intonation which frightened her almost more than her horror lest he should not *want* her."

Such elemental courtship is not only a choice of love over death but of love as itself a kind of death—the most characteristic mark of passion.

D. H. LAWRENCE: STORIES

The Blind Man

Isabel Pervin was listening for two sounds—for the sound of wheels on the drive outside and for the noise of her husband's footsteps in the hall. Her dearest and oldest friend, a man who seemed almost indispensable to her living, would drive up in the rainy dusk of the closing November day. The trap had gone to fetch him from the station. And her husband, who had been blinded in Flanders, and who had a disfiguring mark on his brow, would be coming in from the outhouses.

He had been home for a year now. He was totally blind. Yet they had been very happy. The Grange was Maurice's own place. The back was a farmstead, and the Wernhams, who occupied the rear premises, acted as farmers. Isabel lived with her husband in the handsome rooms in front. She and he had been almost entirely alone together since he was wounded. They talked and sang and read together in a wonderful and unspeakable intimacy. Then she reviewed books for a Scottish newspaper, carrying on her old interest, and he occupied himself a good deal with the farm. Sightless, he could still discuss everything with Wernham, and he could also do a good deal of work about the place—menial work, it is true, but it gave him satisfaction. He milked the cows, carried in the pails, turned the separator, attended to the pigs and horses. Life was still very full and strangely serene for the blind man, peaceful with the almost incomprehensible peace of immediate contact in darkness. With his wife he had a whole world, rich and real and invisible.

They were newly and remotely happy. He did not even regret the loss of his sight in these times of dark, palpable joy. A certain exultance swelled his soul.

But as time wore on, sometimes the rich glamour would leave them. Sometimes, after months of this intensity, a sense of burden overcame Isabel, a weariness, a terrible ennui, in that silent house approached between a colonnade of tall-shafted pines. Then she felt she would go mad, for she could not bear it. And sometimes he had devastating fits of depression, which seemed to lay waste his whole being. It was worse than depression—a black misery, when his own life was a torture to him, and when his presence was unbearable to his wife. The dread went down to the roots of her soul as these black days recurred. In a kind of panic she tried to wrap herself up still further in her husband. She forced the old spontaneous cheerfulness and joy to continue. But the effort it cost her was almost too much. She knew she could not keep it up. She felt she would scream with the strain, and would give anything, anything, to escape. She longed to possess her husband utterly; it gave her inordinate joy to have him entirely to herself. And yet, when again he was gone in a black and massive misery, she could not bear him, she could not bear herself; she wished she could be snatched away off the earth altogether, anything rather than live at this cost.

Dazed, she schemed for a way out. She invited friends, she tried to give him some further connection with the outer world. But it was no good. After all their joy and suffering, after their dark, great year of blindness and solitude and unspeakable nearness, other people seemed to them both shallow, rattling, rather impertinent. Shallow prattle seemed presumptuous. He became impatient and irritated, she was wearied. And so they lapsed into their solitude again. For they preferred it.

But now, in a few weeks' time, her second baby would be born. The first had died, an infant, when her husband first went out to France. She looked with joy and relief to the coming of the second. It would be her salvation. But also she felt some anxiety. She was thirty years old, her husband was a year younger. They both wanted the child very much. Yet she could not help feeling afraid. She had her husband on her hands, a terrible joy to her, and a terrifying burden. The child would occupy her love and attention. And then, what of Maurice? What would he do? If only she could feel that he, too, would be at peace and happy when the child came! She did so want to luxuriate in a rich, physical satisfaction of maternity. But the man, what would he do? How could she provide for him, how avert those shattering black moods of his, which destroyed them both?

She sighed with fear. But at this time Bertie Reid wrote to Isabel. He was her old friend, a second or third cousin, a Scotchman, as she was a Scotchwoman. They had been brought up near to one another, and all her life he had been her friend, like a brother, but better than her own brothers. She loved him—though not in the marrying sense. There was a sort of kinship between them, an affinity. They understood one another instinctively. But Isabel would never have thought of marrying Bertie. It would have seemed like marrying in her own family.

Bertie was a barrister and a man of letters, a Scotchman of the intellectual type, quick, ironical, sentimental, and on his knees before the woman he adored but did not want to marry. Maurice Pervin was different. He came of a good old country family— the Grange was not a very great distance from Oxford. He was passionate, sensitive, perhaps over-sensitive, wincing—a big fellow with heavy limbs and a forehead that flushed painfully. For his mind was slow, as if drugged by the strong provincial blood that beat in his veins. He was very sensitive to his own mental slowness, his feelings being quick and acute. So that he was just the opposite to Bertie, whose mind was much quicker than his emotions, which were not so very fine.

From the first the two men did not like each other. Isabel felt that they ought to get on together. But they did not. She felt that if only each could have the clue to the other there would be such a rare understanding between them. It did not come off, however. Bertie adopted a slightly ironical attitude, very offensive to Maurice, who returned the Scotch irony with English resentment, a resentment which deepened sometimes into stupid hatred.

This was a little puzzling to Isabel. However, she accepted it in the course of things. Men were made freakish and unreasonable. Therefore, when Maurice was going out to France for the second time, she felt that, for her husband's sake, she must discontinue her friendship with Bertie. She wrote to the barrister to this effect. Bertram Reid simply replied that in this, as in all other matters, he must obey her wishes, if these were indeed her wishes.

For nearly two years nothing had passed between the two friends. Isabel rather gloried in the fact; she had no compunction. She had one great article of faith, which was, that husband and wife should be so important to one another, that the rest of the world simply did not count. She and Maurice were husband and wife. They loved one another. They would have children. Then let everybody and everything else fade into insignificance outside this connubial felicity. She professed herself quite happy and ready to receive Maurice's friends. She was happy and ready: the happy wife, the ready woman in possession. Without knowing why, the friends retired abashed, and came no more. Maurice, of course, took as much satisfaction in this connubial absorption as Isabel did.

He shared in Isabel's literary activities, she cultivated a real interest in agriculture and cattle-raising. For she, being at heart perhaps an emotional enthusiast, always cultivated the practical side of life and prided herself on her mastery of practical affairs. Thus the husband and wife had spent the five years of their married life. The last had been one of blindness and unspeakable intimacy. And now Isabel felt a great indifference coming over her, a sort of lethargy. She wanted to be allowed to bear her child in peace, to nod by the fire and drift vaguely, physically, from day to day. Maurice was like an ominous thunder-cloud. She had to keep waking up to remember him.

When a little note came from Bertie, asking if he were to put up a tombstone to their dead friendship, and speaking of the real pain he felt on account of her husband's loss of sight, she felt a pang, a fluttering agitation of reawakening. And she read the letter to Maurice.

"Ask him to come down," he said.

"Ask Bertie to come here!" she re-echoed.

"Yes—if he wants to."

Isabel paused for a few moments.

"I know he wants to—he'd only be too glad," she replied. "But what about you, Maurice? How should you like it?"

"I should like it."

"Well—in that case—But I thought you didn't care for him—"

"Oh, I don't know. I might think differently of him now," the blind man replied. It was rather abstruse to Isabel.

"Well, dear," she said, "if you're quite sure—"

"I'm sure enough. Let him come," said Maurice.

So Bertie was coming, coming this evening, in the November rain and darkness. Isabel was agitated, racked with her old restlessness and indecision. She had always suffered from this pain of doubt, just an agonizing sense of uncertainty. It had begun to pass off, in the lethargy of maternity. Now it returned, and she resented it. She struggled as usual to maintain her calm, composed, friendly bearing, a sort of mask she wore over all her body.

A woman had lighted a tall lamp beside the table and spread the cloth. The long dining-room was dim, with its elegant but rather severe pieces of old furniture. Only the round table glowed softly under the light. It had a rich, beautiful effect. The white cloth glistened and dropped its heavy, pointed lace corners almost to the carpet, the china was old and handsome, creamy-yellow, with a blotched pattern of harsh red and deep blue, the cups large and bell-shaped, the teapot gallant. Isabel looked at it with superficial appreciation.

Her nerves were hurting her. She looked automatically again at the high, uncurtained windows. In the last dusk she could just perceive outside a huge fir-tree swaying its boughs: it was as if she thought it rather than saw it. The rain came flying on the window panes. Ah, why had she no peace? These two men, why did they tear at her? Why did they not come—why was there this suspense?

She sat in a lassitude that was really suspense and irritation. Maurice, at least, might come in—there was nothing to keep him out. She rose to her feet. Catching sight of her reflection in a mirror, she glanced at herself with a slight smile of recognition, as if she were an old friend to herself. Her face was oval and calm, her nose a little arched. Her neck made a beautiful line down to her shoulder. With hair knotted loosely behind, she had something of a warm, maternal look. Thinking this of herself, she arched her eyebrows and her rather heavy eyelids, with a little flicker of a smile, and for a moment her gray eyes looked amused and wicked, a little sardonic, out of her transfigured Madonna face.

Then, resuming her air of womanly patience—she was really fatally self-determined—she went with a little jerk towards the door. Her eyes were slightly reddened.

She passed down the wide hall and through a door at the end. Then she was in the farm premises. The scent of dairy, and of farm-kitchen, and of farm-yard and of leather almost overcame her: but particularly the scent of dairy. They had been scalding out the pans. The flagged passage in front of her was dark, puddled, and wet. Light came out from the open kitchen door. She went forward and stood in the doorway. The farm-people were at tea, seated at a little distance from her, round a long, narrow table, in the centre of which stood a white lamp. Ruddy faces, ruddy hands holding food, red mouths working, heads bent over the tea-cups: men, landgirls, boys: it was tea-time, feeding-time. Some faces caught sight of her. Mrs. Wernham, going round behind the chairs with a large black teapot, halting slightly in her walk, was not aware of her for a moment. Then she turned suddenly.

"Oh, it is Madam!" she exclaimed. "Come in, then, come in! We're at tea." And she dragged forward a chair.

"No, I won't come in," said Isabel. "I'm afraid I interrupt your meal."

"No—no—not likely, Madam, not likely."

"Hasn't Mr. Pervin come in, do you know?"

"I'm sure I couldn't say! Missed him, have you, Madam?"

"No, I only wanted him to come in," laughed Isabel, as if shyly.

"Wanted him, did ye? Get up, boy—get up, now—"

Mrs. Wernham knocked one of the boys on the shoulder. He began to scrape to his feet, chewing largely.

"I believe he's in top stable," said another face from the table.

"Ah! No, don't get up. I'm going myself," said Isabel.

"Don't you go out on a dirty night like this. Let the lad go. Get along wi' ye, boy," said Mrs. Wernham.

"No, no," said Isabel, with a decision that was always obeyed. "Go on with your tea, Tom. I'd like to go across to the stable, Mrs. Wernham."

"Did ever you hear tell!" exclaimed the woman.

"Isn't the trap late?" asked Isabel.

"Why, no," said Mrs. Wernham, peering into the distance at the tall, dim clock. "No, Madam—we can give it another quarter or twenty minutes yet, good—yes, every bit of a quarter."

"Ah! It seems late when darkness falls so early," said Isabel.

"It do, that it do. Bother the days, that they draw in so," answered Mrs. Wernham. "Proper miserable!"

"They are," said Isabel, withdrawing.

She pulled on her overshoes, wrapped a large tartan shawl around her, put on a man's felt hat, and ventured out along the causeways of the first yard. It was very dark. The wind was roaring in the great elms behind the outhouses. When she came to the second yard the darkness seemed deeper. She was unsure of her footing. She wished she had brought a lantern. Rain blew against her. Half she liked it, half she felt unwilling to battle.

She reached at last the just visible door of the stable. There was no sign of a light anywhere. Opening the upper half, she looked in: into a simple well of darkness. The smell of horses and ammonia, and of warmth was startling to her, in that full night. She listened with all her ears but could hear nothing save the night, and the stirring of a horse.

"Maurice!" she called, softly and musically, though she was afraid. "Maurice—are you there?"

Nothing came from the darkness. She knew the rain and wind blew in upon the horses, the hot animal life. Feeling it wrong, she entered the stable and drew the lower half of the door shut, holding the upper part close. She did not stir, because she was aware of the presence of the dark hind-quarters of the horses, though she could not see them, and she was afraid. Something wild stirred in her heart.

She listened intensely. Then she heard a small noise in the distance—far away, it seemed—the chink of a pan, and a man's voice speaking a brief word. It would be Maurice, in the other part of the stable. She stood motionless, waiting for him to come through the partition door. The horses were so terrifyingly near to her, in the invisible.

The loud jarring of the inner door-latch made her start; the door was opened. She could hear and feel her husband entering and invisibly passing among the horses near to her, darkness as they were, actively intermingled. The rather low sound of his voice as he spoke to the horses came velvety to her nerves. How near he was, and how invisible! The darkness seemed to be in a strange swirl of violent life, just upon her. She turned giddy.

Her presence of mind made her call quietly and musically:

"Maurice! Maurice—dear-ar!"

"Yes," he answered. "Isabel?"

She saw nothing, and the sound of his voice seemed to touch her.

"Hello!" she answered cheerfully, straining her eyes to see him. He was still busy, attending to the horses near her, but she saw only darkness. It made her almost desperate.

"Won't you come in, dear?" she said.

"Yes, I'm coming. Just half a minute. Stand over—now! Trap's not come, has it?"

"Not yet," said Isabel.

His voice was pleasant and ordinary, but it had a slight suggestion of the stable to her. She wished he would come away. Whilst he was so utterly invisible, she was afraid of him.

"How's the time?" he asked.

"Not yet six," she replied. She disliked to answer into the dark. Presently he came very near to her, and she retreated out of doors.

"The weather blows in here," he said, coming steadily forward, feeling for the doors. She shrank away. At last she could dimly see him.

"Bertie won't have much of a drive," he said, as he closed the doors.

"He won't indeed!" said Isabel calmly, watching the dark shape at the door.

"Give me your arm, dear," she said.

She pressed his arm close to her, as she went. But she longed to see him, to look at him. She was nervous. He walked erect, with face rather lifted, but with a curious tentative movement of his powerful, muscular legs. She could feel the clever, careful, strong contact of his feet with the earth, as she balanced against him. For a moment he was a tower of darkness to her, as if he rose out of the earth.

In the house-passage he wavered and went cautiously, with a curious look of silence about him as he felt for the bench. Then he sat down heavily. He was a man with rather sloping shoulders, but with heavy limbs, powerful legs that seemed to know the earth. His head was small, usually carried high and light. As he bent down to unfasten his gaiters and boots he did not look blind. His hair was brown and crisp, his hands were large, reddish, intelligent, the veins stood out in the wrists; and his thighs and knees seemed massive. When he stood up his face and neck were surcharged with blood, the veins stood out on his temples. She did not look at his blindness.

Isabel was always glad when they had passed through the dividing door into their own regions of repose and beauty. She was a little afraid of him, out there in the animal grossness of the back. His bearings also changed, as he smelt the familiar indefinable odour that pervaded his wife's surroundings, a delicate, refined scent, very faintly spicy. Perhaps it came from the potpourri bowls.

He stood at the foot of the stairs, arrested, listening. She watched him, and her heart sickened. He seemed to be listening to fate.

"He's not here yet," he said. "I'll go up and change."

"Maurice," she said, "you're not wishing he wouldn't come, are you?"

"I couldn't quite say," he answered. "I feel myself rather on the qui vive."

"I can see you are," she answered. And she reached up and kissed his cheek. She saw his mouth relax into a slow smile.

"What are you laughing at?" she said roguishly.

"You consoling me," he answered.

"Nay," she answered. "Why should I console you? You know we love each other— you know how married we are! What does anything else matter?"

"Nothing at all, my dear."

He felt for her face and touched it, smiling.

"You're all right, aren't you?" he asked anxiously.

"I'm wonderfully all right, love," she answered. "It's you I am a little troubled about, at times."

"Why me?" he said, touching her cheeks delicately with the tips of his fingers. The touch had an almost hypnotizing effect on her.

He went away upstairs. She saw him mount into the darkness, unseeing and unchanging. He did not know that the lamps on the upper corridor were unlighted. He went on into the darkness with unchanging step. She heard him in the bath-room.

Pervin moved about almost unconsciously in his familiar surroundings, dark though everything was. He seemed to know the presence of objects before he touched them. It was a pleasure to him to rock thus through a world of things, carried on the flood in a sort of blood-prescience. He did not think much or trouble much. So long as he kept this sheer immediacy of blood-contact with the substantial world he was happy, he wanted no intervention of visual consciousness. In this state there was a certain rich positivity, bordering sometimes on rapture. Life seemed to move in him like a tide lapping, lapping, and advancing, enveloping all things darkly. It was a pleasure to stretch forth the hand and meet the unseen object, clasp it, and possess it in pure contact. He did not try to remember, to visualize. He did not want to. The new way of consciousness substituted itself in him.

The rich suffusion of this state generally kept him happy, reaching its culmination in the consuming passion for his wife. But at times the flow would seem to be checked and thrown back. Then it would beat inside him like a tangled sea, and he was tortured in the shattered chaos of his own blood. He grew to dread this arrest, this throw-back, this chaos inside himself, when he seemed merely at the mercy of his own powerful and conflicting elements. How to get some measure of control or surety, this was the question. And when the question rose maddening in him, he would clench his fists as if he would compel the whole universe to submit to him. But it was in vain. He could not even compel himself.

Tonight, however, he was still serene, though little tremors of unreasonable exasperation ran through him. He had to handle the razor very carefully, as he shaved, for it was not at one with him, he was afraid of it. His hearing also was too much sharpened. He heard the woman lighting the lamps on the corridor, and attending to the fire in the visitors' room. And then, as he went to his room, he heard the trap arrive. Then came Isabel's voice, lifted and calling, like a bell ringing:

"Is it you, Bertie? Have you come?"

And a man's voice answered out of the wind:

"Hello, Isabel! There you are."

"Have you had a miserable drive? I'm so sorry we couldn't send a closed carriage. I can't see you at all, you know."

"I'm coming. No, I liked the drive—it was like Perthshire. Well, how are you? You're looking fit as ever, as far as I can see."

"Oh, yes," said Isabel. "I'm wonderfully well. How are you? Rather thin, I think—"

"Worked to death—everybody's old cry. But I'm all right, Ciss. How's Pervin?—isn't he here?"

"Oh, yes, he's upstairs changing. Yes, he's awfully well. Take off your wet things; I'll send them to be dried."

"And how are you both, in spirits? He doesn't fret?"

"No—no, not at all. No, on the contrary, really. We've been wonderfully happy, incredibly. It's more than I can understand—so wonderful: the nearness, and the peace—"

"Ah! Well, that's awfully good news—"

They moved away. Pervin heard no more. But a childish sense of desolation had come over him, as he heard their brisk voices. He seemed shut out—like a child that is left out. He was aimless and excluded, he did not know what to do with himself. The helpless desolation came over him. He fumbled nervously as he dressed himself, in a state almost of childishness. He disliked the Scotch accent in Bertie's speech, and the slight response it found on Isabel's tongue. He disliked the slight purr of complacency in the Scottish speech. He disliked intensely the glib way in which Isabel spoke of their happiness and nearness. It made him recoil. He was fretful and beside himself like a child, he had almost a childish nostalgia to be included in the life circle. And at the same time he was a man, dark and powerful and infuriated by his own weakness. By some fatal flaw, he could not be by himself, he had to depend on the support of another. And this very dependence enraged him. He hated Bertie Reid, and at the same time he knew the hatred was nonsense, he knew it was the outcome of his own weakness.

He went downstairs. Isabel was alone in the dining-room. She watched him enter, head erect, his feet tentative. He looked so strong-blooded and healthy and, at the same time, cancelled. Cancelled—that was the word that flew across her mind. Perhaps it was his scar suggested it.

"You heard Bertie come, Maurice?" she said.

"Yes—isn't he here?"

"He's in his room. He looks very thin and worn."

"I suppose he works himself to death."

A woman came in with a tray—and after a few minutes Bertie came down. He was a little dark man, with a very big forehead, thin, wispy hair, and sad, large eyes. His expression was inordinately sad—almost funny. He had odd, short legs.

Isabel watched him hesitate under the door, and glance nervously at her husband. Pervin heard him and turned.

"Here you are, now," said Isabel. "Come, let us eat."

Bertie went across to Maurice.

"How are you, Pervin?" he said, as he advanced.

The blind man stuck his hand out into space, and Bertie took it.

"Very fit. Glad you've come," said Maurice.

Isabel glanced at them, and glanced away, as if she could not bear to see them.

"Come," she said. "Come to table. Aren't you both awfully hungry? I am, tremendously."

"I'm afraid you waited for me," said Bertie, as they sat down.

Maurice had a curious monolithic way of sitting in a chair, erect and distant. Isabel's heart always beat when she caught sight of him thus.

"No," she replied to Bertie. "We're very little later than usual. We're having a sort of high tea, not dinner. Do you mind? It gives us such a nice long evening, uninterrupted."

"I like it," said Bertie.

Maurice was feeling, with curious little movements, almost like a cat kneading her bed, for his plate, his knife and fork, his napkin. He was getting the whole geography of his cover into his consciousness. He sat erect and inscrutable, remote-seeming. Bertie watched the static figure of the blind man, the delicate tactile discernment of the large, ruddy hands, and the curious mindless silence of the brow, above the scar. With difficulty he looked away, and without knowing what he did, picked up a little crystal bowl of violets from the table, and held them to his nose.

"They are sweet-scented," he said. "Where do they come from?"

"From the garden—under the windows," said Isabel.

"So late in the year—and so fragrant! Do you remember the violets under Aunt Bell's south wall?"

The two friends looked at each other and exchanged a smile, Isabel's eyes lighting up.

"Don't I?" she replied. "Wasn't she queer!"

"A curious old girl," laughed Bertie. "There's a streak of freakishness in the family, Isabel."

"Ah—but not in you and me, Bertie," said Isabel. "Give them to Maurice, will you?" she added, as Bertie was putting down the flowers. "Have you smelled the violets, dear? Do!—they are so scented."

Maurice held out his hand, and Bertie placed the tiny bowl against his large, warm-looking fingers. Maurice's hand closed over the thin white fingers of the barrister. Bertie carefully extricated himself. Then the two watched the blind man smelling the violets. He bent his head and seemed to be thinking. Isabel waited.

"Aren't they sweet, Maurice?" she said at last, anxiously.

"Very," he said. And he held out the bowl. Bertie took it. Both he and Isabel were a little afraid, and deeply disturbed.

The meal continued. Isabel and Bertie chatted spasmodically. The blind man was silent. He touched his food repeatedly, with quick, delicate touches of his knife-point, then cut irregular bits. He could not bear to be helped. Both Isabel and Bertie suffered: Isabel wondered why. She did not suffer when she was alone with Maurice. Bertie made her conscious of a strangeness.

After the meal the three drew their chairs to the fire, and sat down to talk. The decanters were put on a table near at hand. Isabel knocked the logs on the fire, and clouds of brilliant sparks went up the chimney. Bertie noticed a slight weariness in her bearing.

"You will be glad when your child comes now, Isabel?" he said.

She looked up to him with a quick wan smile.

"Yes, I shall be glad," she answered. "It begins to seem long. Yes, I shall be very glad. So will you, Maurice, won't you?" she added.

"Yes, I shall," replied her husband.

"We are both looking forward so much to having it," she said.

"Yes, of course," said Bertie.

He was a bachelor, three or four years older than Isabel. He lived in beautiful rooms overlooking the river, guarded by a faithful Scottish manservant. And he had his friends among the fair sex—not lovers, friends. So long as he could avoid any danger of courtship or marriage, he adored a few good women with constant and unfailing homage, and he was chivalrously fond of quite a number. But if they seemed to encroach on him, he withdrew and detested them.

Isabel knew him very well, knew his beautiful constancy, and kindness, also his incurable weakness, which made him unable ever to enter into close contact of any sort. He was ashamed of himself because he could not marry, could not approach women physically. He wanted to do so. But he could not. At the centre of him he was afraid, helplessly and even brutally afraid. He had given up hope, had ceased to expect any more that he could escape his own weakness. Hence he was a brilliant and successful barrister, also a litterateur of high repute, a rich man, and a great social success. At the centre he felt himself neuter, nothing.

Isabel knew him well. She despised him even while she admired him. She looked at his sad face, his little short legs, and felt contempt of him. She looked at his dark grey eyes, with their uncanny, almost childlike, intuition, and she loved him. He understood amazingly—but she had no fear of his understanding. As a man she patronized him.

And she turned to the impassive, silent figure of her husband. He sat leaning back, with folded arms, and face a little uptilted. His knees were straight and massive. She sighed, picked up the poker, and again began to prod the fire, to rouse the clouds of soft brilliant sparks.

"Isabel tells me," Bertie began suddenly, "that you have not suffered unbearably from the loss of sight."

Maurice straightened himself to attend but kept his arms folded.

"No," he said, "not unbearably. Now and again one struggles against it, you know. But there are compensations."

"They say it is much worse to be stone deaf," said Isabel.

"I believe it is," said Bertie. "Are there compensations?" he added to Maurice.

"Yes. You cease to bother about a great many things." Again Maurice stretched his figure, stretched the strong muscles of his back, and leaned backwards, with uplifted face.

"And that is a relief," said Bertie. "But what is there in place of the bothering? What replaces the activity?"

There was a pause. At length the blind man replied, as out of a negligent, unattentive thinking:

"Oh, I don't know. There's a good deal when you're not active."

"Is there?" said Bertie. "What exactly? It always seems to me that when there is no thought and no action, there is nothing."

Again Maurice was slow in replying.

"There is something," he replied. "I couldn't tell you what it is."

And the talk lapsed once more, Isabel and Bertie chatting gossip and reminiscence, the blind man silent.

At length Maurice rose restlessly, a big obtrusive figure. He felt tight and hampered. He wanted to go away.

"Do you mind," he said, "if I go and speak to Wernham?"

"No—go along, dear," said Isabel.

And he went out. A silence came over the two friends. At length Bertie said:

"Nevertheless, it is a great deprivation, Cissie."

"It is, Bertie. I know it is."

"Something lacking all the time," said Bertie.

"Yes, I know. And yet—and yet—Maurice is right. There is something else, something there, which you never knew was there, and which you can't express."

"What is there?" asked Bertie.

"I don't know—it's awfully hard to define it—but something strong and immediate. There's something strange in Maurice's presence—indefinable—but I couldn't do without it. I agree that it seems to put one's mind to sleep. But when we're alone I miss nothing; it seems awfully rich, almost splendid, you know."

"I'm afraid I don't follow," said Bertie.

They talked desultorily. The wind blew loudly outside, rain chattered on the window-panes, making a sharp drum-sound because of the closed, mellow-golden shutters inside. The logs burned slowly, with hot, almost invisible small flames. Bertie seemed uneasy, there were dark circles round his eyes. Isabel, rich with her approaching maternity, leaned looking into the fire. Her hair curled in odd, loose strands, very pleasing to the man. But she had a curious feeling of old woe in her heart, old timeless night-woe.

"I suppose we're all deficient somewhere," said Bertie.

"I suppose so," said Isabel wearily.

"Damned, sooner or later."

"I don't know," she said, rousing herself. "I feel quite all right, you know. The child coming seems to make me indifferent to everything, just placid. I can't feel that there's anything to trouble about, you know."

"A good thing, I should say," he replied slowly.

"Well, there it is. I suppose it's just Nature. If only I felt I needn't trouble about Maurice, I should be perfectly content—"

"But you feel you must trouble about him?"

"Well—I don't know—" She even resented this much effort.

The night passed slowly. Isabel looked at the clock. "I say," she said. "It's nearly ten o'clock. Where can Maurice be? I'm sure they're all in bed at the back. Excuse me a moment."

She went out, returning almost immediately.

"It's all shut up and in darkness," she said. "I wonder where he is. He must have gone out to the farm—"

Bertie looked at her.

"I suppose he'll come in," he said.

"I suppose so," she said. "But it's unusual for him to be out now."

"Would you like me to go out and see?"

"Well—if you wouldn't mind. I'd go, but—" She did not want to make the physical effort.

Bertie put on an old overcoat and took a lantern. He went out from the side door. He shrank from the wet and roaring night. Such weather had a nervous effect on him: too much moisture everywhere made him feel almost imbecile. Unwilling, he went through it all. A dog barked violently at him. He peered in all the buildings. At last, as he opened the upper door of a sort of intermediate barn, he heard a grinding noise, and looking in, holding up his lantern, saw Maurice, in his shirtsleeves, standing listening, holding the handle of a turnip-pulper. He had been pulping sweet roots, a pile of which lay dimly heaped in a corner behind him.

"That you, Wernham?" said Maurice, listening.

"No, it's me," said Bertie.

A large, half-wild grey cat was rubbing at Maurice's leg. The blind man stooped to rub its sides. Bertie watched the scene, then unconsciously entered and shut the door behind him. He was in a high sort of barn-place, from which, right and left, ran off the corridors in front of the stalled cattle. He watched the slow, stooping motion of the other man, as he caressed the great cat.

Maurice straightened himself.

"You came to look for me?" he said.

"Isabel was a little uneasy," said Bertie.

"I'll come in. I like messing about doing these jobs."

The cat had reared her sinister, feline length against his leg, clawing at his thigh affectionately. He lifted her claws out of his flesh.

"I hope I'm not in your way at all at the Grange here," said Bertie, rather shy and stiff.

"My way? No, not a bit. I'm glad Isabel has somebody to talk to. I'm afraid it's I who am in the way. I know I'm not very lively company. Isabel's all right, don't you think? She's not unhappy, is she?"

"I don't think so."

"What does she say?"

"She says she's very content—only a little troubled about you."

"Why me?"

"Perhaps afraid that you might brood," said Bertie, cautiously.

"She needn't be afraid of that." He continued to caress the flattened grey head of the cat with his fingers. "What I am a bit afraid of," he resumed, "is that she'll find me a dead weight, always alone with me down here."

"I don't think you need think that," said Bertie, though this was what he feared himself.

"I don't know," said Maurice. "Sometimes I feel it isn't fair that she's saddled with me." Then he dropped his voice curiously. "I say," he asked, secretly struggling, "is my face much disfigured? Do you mind telling me?"

"There is the scar," said Bertie, wondering. "Yes, it is a disfigurement. But more pitiable than shocking."

"A pretty bad scar, though," said Maurice.

"Oh, yes."

There was a pause.

"Sometimes I feel I am horrible," said Maurice, in a low voice, talking as if to himself. And Bertie actually felt a quiver of horror.

"That's nonsense," he said.

Maurice again straightened himself, leaving the cat.

"There's no telling," he said. Then again, in an odd tone, he added: "I don't really know you, do I?"

"Probably not," said Bertie.

"Do you mind if I touch you?"

The lawyer shrank away instinctively. And yet, out of very philanthropy, he said, in a small voice: "Not at all."

But he suffered as the blind man stretched out a strong, naked hand to him. Maurice accidentally knocked off Bertie's hat.

"I thought you were taller," he said, starting. Then he laid his hand on Bertie Reid's head, closing the dome of the skull in a soft, firm grasp, gathering it, as it were; then, shifting his grasp and softly closing again, with a fine, close pressure, till he had covered the skull and the face of the smaller man, tracing the brows, and touching the full, closed eyes, touching the small nose and the nostrils, the rough, short moustache, the mouth, the rather strong chin. The hand of the blind man grasped the shoulder, the arm, the hand of the other man. He seemed to take him, in the soft, travelling grasp.

"You seem young," he said quietly, at last.

The lawyer stood almost annihilated, unable to answer.

"Your head seems tender, as if you were young," Maurice repeated. "So do your hands. Touch my eyes, will you?—touch my scar."

Now Bertie quivered with revulsion. Yet he was under the power of the blind man, as if hypnotized. He lifted his hand, and laid the fingers on the scar, on the scarred eyes. Maurice suddenly covered them with his own hand, pressed the fingers of the other man upon his disfigured eye-sockets, trembling in every fibre, and rocking slightly, slowly, from side to side. He remained thus for a minute or more, whilst Bertie stood as if in a swoon, unconscious, imprisoned.

Then suddenly Maurice removed the hand of the other man from his brow, and stood holding it in his own.

"Oh, my God," he said, "we shall know each other now, shan't we? We shall know each other now."

Bertie could not answer. He gazed mute and terrorstruck, overcome by his own weakness. He knew he could not answer. He had an unreasonable fear lest the other man should suddenly destroy him. Whereas Maurice was actually filled with hot, poignant love, the passion of friendship. Perhaps it was this very passion of friendship which Bertie shrank from most.

"We're all right together now, aren't we?" said Maurice. "It's all right now, as long as we live, so far as we're concerned?"

"Yes," said Bertie, trying by any means to escape.

Maurice stood with head lifted, as if listening. The new delicate fulfilment of mortal friendship had come as a revelation and surprise to him, something exquisite and unhoped-for. He seemed to be listening to hear if it were real.

Then he turned for his coat.

"Come," he said, "we'll go to Isabel."

Bertie took the lantern and opened the door. The cat disappeared. The two men went in silence along the causeways. Isabel, as they came, thought their footsteps sounded strange. She looked up pathetically and anxiously for their entrance. There seemed a curious elation about Maurice. Bertie was haggard, with sunken eyes.

"What is it?" she asked.

"We've become friends," said Maurice, standing with his feet apart, like a strange colossus.

"Friends!" re-echoed Isabel. And she looked again at Bertie. He met her eyes with a furtive, haggard look; his eyes were as if glazed with misery.

"I'm so glad," she said, in sheer perplexity.

"Yes," said Maurice.

He was indeed so glad. Isabel took his hand with both hers, and held it fast.

"You'll be happier now, dear," she said.

But she was watching Bertie. She knew that he had one desire—to escape from this intimacy, this friendship, which had been thrust upon him. He could not bear it that he had been touched by the blind man, his insane reserve broken in. He was like a mollusc whose shell is broken.

(1922)

QUESTIONS FOR REFLECTION

Experience

1. How do you respond to the situation of Lawrence's blind man? Do you sympathize with him? Why or why not?
2. To what extent does the experience of Bertie reflect your own experience being around people who are blind?

Interpretation

3. What do you learn from the detailed descriptions of Maurice and Bertie early in the story?
4. How would you characterize the relationship between Maurice and his wife, Isabel? Between Isabel and her cousin Bertie? Between Bertie and Maurice?
5. What is the significance of the events that occur in the barn?

Evaluation

6. Whose values does the story seem to support?
7. Where do you find the strongest evidence for support of those values?

Connections

8. Compare the physical descriptions of Maurice with the detailed descriptions of the horses in Lawrence's "The Horse Dealer's Daughter."
9. Compare the scenes of touching in both stories—Maurice's touching of Bertie's face and Doctor Fergusson's touching of Mabel's shoulder.

The Horse Dealer's Daughter

"Well, Mabel, and what are you going to do with yourself?" asked Joe, with foolish flippancy. He felt quite safe himself. Without listening for an answer, he turned aside, worked a grain of tobacco to the tip of his tongue, and spat it out. He did not care about anything, since he felt safe himself.

The three brothers and the sister sat round the desolate breakfast-table, attempting some sort of desultory consultation. The morning's post had given the final tap to the family fortunes, and all was over. The dreary dining-room itself, with its heavy mahogany furniture, looked as if it were waiting to be done away with.

But the consultation amounted to nothing. There was a strange air of ineffectuality about the three men, as they sprawled at table, smoking and reflecting vaguely on their own condition. The girl was alone, a rather short, sullen-looking young woman of twenty-seven. She did not share the same life as her brothers. She would have been good-looking, save for the impressive fixity of her face, "bull-dog," as her brothers called it.

There was a confused tramping of horses' feet outside. The three men all sprawled round in their chairs to watch. Beyond the dark holly bushes that separated the strip of lawn from the high-road, they could see a cavalcade of shire horses swinging out of their own yard, being taken for exercise. This was the last time. These were the last horses that would go through their hands. The young men watched with critical, callous look. They were all frightened at the collapse of their lives, and the sense of disaster in which they were involved left them no inner freedom.

Yet they were three fine, well-set fellows enough. Joe, the eldest, was a man of thirty-three, broad and handsome in a hot, flushed way. His face was red, he twisted his black mustache over a thick finger, his eyes were shallow and restless. He had a sensual way of uncovering his teeth when he laughed, and his bearing was stupid. Now he watched the horses with a glazed look of helplessness in his eyes, a certain stupor of downfall.

The great draft-horses swung past. They were tied head to tail, four of them, and they heaved along to where a lane branched off from the high-road, planting their great hoofs floutingly in the fine black mud, swinging their great rounded haunches sumptuously, and trotting a few sudden steps as they were led into the lane, round the corner. Every movement showed a massive, slumbrous strength, and a stupidity which held them in subjection. The groom at the head looked back, jerking the leading rope. And the cavalcade moved out of sight up the lane, the tail of the last horse, bobbed up tight and stiff, held out taut from the swinging great haunches as they rocked behind the hedges in a motionlike sleep.

Joe watched with glazed hopeless eyes. The horses were almost like his own body to him. He felt he was done for now. Luckily he was engaged to a woman as old as himself, and therefore her father, who was steward of a neighboring estate, would provide him with a job. He would marry and go into harness. His life was over, he would be a subject animal now.

He turned uneasily aside, the retreating steps of the horses echoing in his ears. Then, with foolish restlessness, he reached for the scraps of bacon-rind from the plates, and making a faint whistling sound, flung them to the terrier that lay against the fender. He watched the dog swallow them, and waited till the creature looked into his eyes. Then a faint grin came on his face, and in a high, foolish voice he said:

"You won't get much more bacon, shall you, you little b———?"

The dog faintly and dismally wagged its tail, then lowered its haunches, circled round, and lay down again.

There was another helpless silence at the table. Joe sprawled uneasily in his seat, not willing to go till the family conclave was dissolved. Fred Henry, the second brother, was erect, clean-limbed, alert. He had watched the passing of the horses with more *sang-froid.*° If he was an animal, like Joe, he was an animal which controls, not one which is controlled. He was master of any horse, and he carried himself with a well-tempered air of mastery. But he was not master of the situations of life. He pushed his coarse brown mustache upwards, off his lip, and glanced irritably at his sister, who sat impassive and inscrutable.

sang-froid *coolness, composure*

"You'll go and stop with Lucy for a bit, shan't you?" he asked. The girl did not answer.

"I don't see what else you can do," persisted Fred Henry.

"Go as a skivvy,"° Joe interpolated laconically.

The girl did not move a muscle.

"If I was her, I should go in for training for a nurse," said Malcolm, the youngest of them all. He was the baby of the family, a young man of twenty-two, with a fresh, jaunty *museau*.°

But Mabel did not take any notice of him. They had talked at her and round her for so many years, that she hardly heard them at all.

The marble clock on the mantelpiece softly chimed the half-hour, the dog rose uneasily from the hearth-rug and looked at the party at the breakfast-table. But still they sat on in ineffectual conclave.

"Oh, all right," said Joe suddenly, apropos of nothing. "I'll get a move on."

He pushed back his chair, straddled his knees with a downward jerk, to get them free, in horsey fashion, and went to the fire. Still he did not go out of the room; he was curious to know what the others would do or say. He began to charge his pipe, looking down at the dog and saying in a high, affected voice:

"Going wi' me? Going wi' me are ter? Tha'rt goin' further than tha counts on just now, dost hear?"

The dog faintly wagged its tail, the man stuck out his jaw and covered his pipe with his hands, and puffed intently, losing himself in the tobacco, looking down all the while at the dog with an absent brown eye. The dog looked up at him in mournful distrust. Joe stood with his knees stuck out, in real horsey fashion.

"Have you had a letter from Lucy?" Fred Henry asked of his sister.

"Last week," came the neutral reply.

"And what does she say?"

There was no answer.

"Does she *ask* you to go and stop there?" persisted Fred Henry.

"She says I can if I like."

"Well, then, you'd better. Tell her you'll come on Monday."

This was received in silence.

"That's what you'll do then, is it?" said Fred Henry, in some exasperation.

But she made no answer. There was a silence of futility and irritation in the room. Malcolm grinned fatuously.

"You'll have to make up your mind between now and next Wednesday," said Joe loudly, "or else find yourself lodgings on the curbstone."

The face of the young woman darkened, but she sat on immutable.

"Here's Jack Fergusson!" exclaimed Malcolm, who was looking aimlessly out of the window.

"Where?" exclaimed Joe loudly.

"Just gone past."

"Coming in?"

Malcolm craned his neck to see the gate.

"Yes," he said.

---

skivvy　domestic worker　　*museau*　slang for face

There was a silence. Mabel sat on like one condemned, at the head of the table. Then a whistle was heard from the kitchen. The dog got up and barked sharply. Joe opened the door and shouted:

"Come on."

After a moment a young man entered. He was muffled up in overcoat and a purple woolen scarf, and his tweed cap, which he did not remove, was pulled down on his head. He was of medium height, his face was rather long and pale, his eyes looked tired.

"Hello, Jack! Well, Jack!" exclaimed Malcolm and Joe. Fred Henry merely said: "Jack."

"What's doing?" asked the newcomer, evidently addressing Fred Henry.

"Same. We've got to be out by Wednesday. Got a cold?"

"I have—got it bad, too."

"Why don't you stop in?"

"*Me* stop in? When I can't stand on my legs, perhaps I shall have a chance," the young man spoke huskily. He had a slight Scotch accent.

"It's a knock-out, isn't it," said Joe, boisterously, "if a doctor goes round croaking with a cold. Looks bad for the patients, doesn't it?"

The young doctor looked at him slowly.

"Anything the matter with *you,* then?" he asked sarcastically.

"Not as I know of. Damn your eyes, hope not. Why?"

"I thought you were very concerned about the patients, wondered if you might be one yourself."

"Damn it, no, I've never been patient to no flaming doctor, and hope I never shall be," returned Joe.

At this point Mabel rose from the table, and they all seemed to become aware of her existence. She began putting the dishes together. The young doctor looked at her, but did not address her. He had not greeted her. She went out of the room with the tray, her face impassive and unchanged.

"When are you off then, all of you?" asked the doctor.

"I'm catching the eleven-forty," replied Malcolm. "Are you goin' down wi' th' trap,° Joe?"

"Yes, I've told you I'm going down wi' th' trap, haven't I?"

"We'd better be getting her in then. So long, Jack, if I don't see you before I go," said Malcolm, shaking hands.

He went out, followed by Joe, who seemed to have his tail between his legs.

"Well, this is the devil's own," exclaimed the doctor, when he was left alone with Fred Henry. "Going before Wednesday, are you?"

"That's the orders," replied the other.

"Where, to Northampton?"

"That's it."

"The devil!" exclaimed Fergusson, with quiet chagrin.

And there was silence between the two.

"All settled up, are you?" asked Fergusson.

"About."

trap   *a light two-wheeled carriage*

There was another pause.

"Well, I shall miss yer, Freddy, boy," said the young doctor.

"And I shall miss thee, Jack," returned the other.

"Miss you like hell," mused the doctor.

Fred Henry turned aside. There was nothing to say. Mabel came in again, to finish clearing the table.

"What are *you* going to do, then, Miss Pervin?" asked Fergusson. "Going to your sister's, are you?"

Mabel looked at him with her steady, dangerous eyes, that always made him uncomfortable, unsettling his superficial ease.

"No," she said.

"Well, what in the name of fortune *are* you going to do? Say what you mean to do," cried Fred Henry, with futile intensity.

But she only averted her head, and continued her work. She folded the white tablecloth, and put on the chenille cloth.

"The sulkiest bitch that ever trod!" muttered her brother.

But she finished her task with perfectly impassive face, the young doctor watching her interestedly all the while. Then she went out.

Fred Henry stared after her, clenching his lips, his blue eyes fixing in sharp antagonism, as he made a grimace of sour exasperation.

"You could bray her into bits, and that's all you'd get out of her," he said, in a small, narrowed tone.

The doctor smiled faintly.

"What's she *going* to do, then?" he asked.

"Strike me if *I* know!" returned the other.

There was a pause. Then the doctor stirred.

"I'll be seeing you tonight, shall I?" he said to his friend.

"Ay—where's it to be? Are we going over to Jessdale?"

"I don't know. I've got such a cold on me. I'll come round to the 'Moon and Stars,' anyway."

"Let Lizzie and May miss their night for once, eh?"

"That's it—if I feel as I do now."

"All's one ——"

The two young men went through the passage and down to the back door together. The house was large, but it was servantless now, and desolate. At the back was a small bricked houseyard and beyond that a big square, graveled fine and red, and having stables on two sides. Sloping, dank, winter-dark fields stretched away on the open sides.

But the stables were empty. Joseph Pervin, the father of the family, had been a man of no education, who had become a fairly large horse dealer. The stables had been full of horses, there was a great turmoil and come-and-go of horses and of dealers and grooms. Then the kitchen was full of servants. But of late things had declined. The old man had married a second time, to retrieve his fortunes. Now he was dead and everything was gone to the dogs, there was nothing but debt and threatening.

For months, Mabel had been servantless in the big house, keeping the home together in penury for her ineffectual brothers. She had kept house for ten years. But previously it was with unstinted means. Then, however brutal and coarse everything was, the sense of money had kept her proud, confident. The men might be foul-mouthed, the women in the kitchen might have bad reputations, her brothers might have illegitimate children. But so long as there was money, the girl felt herself established, and brutally proud, reserved.

No company came to the house, save dealers and coarse men. Mabel had no associates of her own sex, after her sister went away. But she did not mind. She went regularly to church, she attended to her father. And she lived in the memory of her mother, who had died when she was fourteen, and whom she had loved. She had loved her father, too, in a different way, depending upon him, and feeling secure in him, until at the age of fifty-four he married again. And then she had set hard against him. Now he had died and left them all hopelessly in debt.

She had suffered badly during the period of poverty. Nothing, however, could shake the curious, sullen, animal pride that dominated each member of the family. Now, for Mabel, the end had come. Still she would not cast about her. She would follow her own way just the same. She would always hold the keys of her own situation. Mindless and persistent, she endured from day to day. Why should she think? Why should she answer anybody? It was enough that this was the end, and there was no way out. She need not pass any more darkly along the main street of the small town, avoiding every eye. She need not demean herself any more, going into the shops and buying the cheapest food. This was at an end. She thought of nobody, not even of herself. Mindless and persistent, she seemed in a sort of ecstasy to be coming nearer to her fulfillment, her own glorification, approaching her dead mother, who was glorified.

In the afternoon she took a little bag, with shears and sponge and a small scrubbing brush, and went out. It was a gray, wintry day, with saddened, dark green fields and an atmosphere blackened by the smoke of foundries not far off. She went quickly, darkly along the causeway, heeding nobody, through the town to the churchyard.

There she always felt secure, as if no one could see her, although as a matter of fact she was exposed to the stare of everyone who passed along under the churchyard wall. Nevertheless, once under the shadow of the great looming church, among the graves, she felt immune from the world, reserved within the thick churchyard wall as in another country.

Carefully she clipped the grass from the grave, and arranged the pinky white, small chrysanthemums in the tin cross. When this was done, she took an empty jar from a neighboring grave, brought water, and carefully, most scrupulously sponged the marble headstone and the coping-stone.

It gave her sincere satisfaction to do this. She felt in immediate contact with the world of her mother. She took minute pains, went through the park in a state bordering on pure happiness, as if in performing this task she came into a subtle, intimate connection with her mother. For the life she followed here in the world was far less real than the world of death she inherited from her mother.

The doctor's house was just by the church. Fergusson, being a mere hired assistant, was slave to the countryside. As he hurried now to attend to the outpatients in the surgery, glancing across the graveyard with his quick eye, he saw the girl at her task at the grave. She seemed so intent and remote, it was like looking into another world. Some mystical element was touching in him. He slowed down as he walked, watching her as if spellbound.

She lifted her eyes, feeling him looking. Their eyes met. And each looked again at once, each feeling, in some way, found out by the other. He lifted his cap and passed on down the road. There remained distinct in his consciousness, like a vision, the memory of her face, lifted from the tombstone in the churchyard, and looking at him with slow, large, portentous eyes. It *was* portentous, her face. It seemed to mesmerize him. There was a heavy power in her eyes which laid hold of his whole being, as if he had drunk some powerful drug. He had been feeling weak and done before. Now the life came back into him, he felt delivered from his own fretted, daily self.

He finished his duties at the surgery as quickly as might be, hastily filling up the bottles of the waiting people with cheap drugs. Then, in perpetual haste, he set off again to visit several cases in another part of his round, before teatime. At all times he preferred to walk if he could, but particularly when he was not well. He fancied the motion restored him.

The afternoon was falling. It was gray, deadened, and wintry, with a slow, moist, heavy coldness sinking in and deadening all the faculties. But why should he think or notice? He hastily climbed the hill and turned across the dark green fields, following the black cinder-track. In the distance, across a shallow dip in the country, the small town was clustered like smoldering ash, a tower, a spire, a heap of low, raw, extinct houses. And on the nearest fringe of the town, sloping into the dip, was Oldmeadow, the Pervins' house. He could see the stables and the outbuildings distinctly, as they lay towards him on the slope. Well, he would not go there many more times! Another resource would be lost to him, another place gone: the only company he cared for in the alien, ugly little town he was losing. Nothing but work, drudgery, constant hastening from dwelling to dwelling among the colliers and the iron-workers. It wore him out, but at the same time he had a craving for it. It was a stimulant to him to be in the homes of the working people, moving, as it were, through the innermost body of their life. His nerves were excited and gratified. He could come so near, into the very lives of the rough, inarticulate, powerful emotional men and women: He grumbled, he said he hated the hellish hole. But as a matter of fact it excited him, the contact with the rough, strongly-feeling people was a stimulant applied direct to his nerves.

Below Oldmeadow, in the green, shallow, soddened hollow of fields, lay a square, deep pond. Roving across the landscape, the doctor's quick eye detected a figure in black passing through the gate of the field, down towards the pond. He looked again. It would be Mabel Pervin. His mind suddenly became alive and attentive.

Why was she going down there? He pulled up on the path on the slope above, and stood staring. He could just make sure of the small black figure moving in the hollow of the failing day. He seemed to see her in the midst of such obscurity, that he was like a clairvoyant, seeing rather with the mind's eye than with ordinary sight. Yet he could see her positively enough, whilst he kept his eye attentive. He felt, if he looked away from her, in the thick, ugly falling dusk, he would lose her altogether.

He followed her minutely as she moved, direct and intent, like something transmitted rather than stirring in voluntary activity, straight down from the field towards the pond. There she stood on the bank for a moment. She never raised her head. Then she waded slowly into the water.

He stood motionless as the small black figure walked slowly and deliberately towards the center of the pond, very slowly, gradually moving deeper into the motionless water, and still moving forward as the water got up to her breast. Then he could see her no more in the dusk of the dead afternoon.

"There!" he exclaimed. "Would you believe it?"

And he hastened straight down, running over the wet, soddened fields, pushing through the hedges, down into the depression of callous wintry obscurity. It took him several minutes to come to the pond. He stood on the bank, breathing heavily. He could see nothing. His eyes seemed to penetrate the dead water. Yes, perhaps that was the dark shadow of her black clothing beneath the surface of the water.

He slowly ventured into the pond. The bottom was deep, soft clay, he sank in, and the water clasped dead cold round his legs. As he stirred he could smell the cold, rotten clay that fouled up into the water. It was objectionable in his lungs. Still, repelled and yet not heeding, he moved deeper into the pond. The cold water rose over his thighs, over his loins, upon his abdomen. The lower part of his body was all sunk in the hideous cold element. And the bottom was so deeply soft and uncertain, he was afraid of pitching with his mouth underneath. He could not swim, and was afraid.

He crouched a little, spreading his hands under the water and moving them round, trying to feel for her. The dead cold pond swayed upon his chest. He moved again, a little deeper, and again, with his hands underneath, he felt all around under the water. And he touched her clothing. But it evaded his fingers. He made a desperate effort to grasp it.

And so doing he lost his balance and went under, horribly, suffocating in the foul earthy water, struggling madly for a few moments. At last, after what seemed an eternity, he got his footing, rose again into the air, and looked around. He gasped, and knew he was in the world. Then he looked at the water. She had risen near him. He grasped her clothing, and drawing her nearer, turned to take his way to land again.

He went very slowly, carefully, absorbed in the slow progress. He rose higher, climbing out of the pond. The water was now only about his legs; he was thankful, full of relief to be out of the clutches of the pond. He lifted her and staggered on to the bank, out of the horror of wet, gray clay.

He laid her down on the bank. She was quite unconscious and running with water. He made the water come from her mouth, he worked to restore her. He did not have to work very long before he could feel the breathing begin again in her; she was breathing naturally. He worked a little longer. He could feel her live beneath his hands; she was coming back. He wiped her face, wrapped her in his overcoat, looked round into the dim, dark gray world, then lifted her and staggered down the bank and across the fields.

It seemed an unthinkably long way, and his burden so heavy he felt he would never get to the house. But at last he was in the stable-yard, and then in the house-yard. He opened the door and went into the house. In the kitchen he laid her down on the hearth-rug and called. The house was empty. But the fire was burning in the grate.

Then again he kneeled to attend to her. She was breathing regularly, her eyes were wide open and as if conscious, but there seemed something missing in her look. She was conscious in herself, but unconscious of her surroundings.

He ran upstairs, took blankets from a bed, and put them before the fire to warm. Then he removed her saturated, earthy-smelling clothing, rubbed her dry with a towel, and wrapped her naked in the blankets. Then he went into the dining-room, to look for spirits. There was a little whiskey. He drank a gulp himself, and put some into her mouth.

The effect was instantaneous. She looked full into his face, as if she had been seeing him for some time, and yet had only just become conscious of him.

"Dr. Fergusson?" she said.

"What?" he answered.

He was divesting himself of his coat, intending to find some dry clothing upstairs. He could not bear the smell of the dead, clayey water, and he was mortally afraid for his own health.

"What did I do?" she asked.

"Walked into the pond," he replied. He had begun to shudder like one sick, and could hardly attend to her. Her eyes remained full on him, he seemed to be going dark in his mind, looking back at her helplessly. The shuddering became quieter in him, his life came back to him, dark and unknowing, but strong again.

"Was I out of my mind?" she asked, while her eyes were fixed on him all the time.

"Maybe, for the moment," he replied. He felt quiet, because his strength had come back. The strange fretful strain had left him.

"Am I out of my mind now?" she asked.

"Are you?" he reflected a moment. "No," he answered truthfully, "I don't see that you are." He turned his face aside. He was afraid now, because he felt dazed, and felt dimly that her power was stronger than his, in this issue. And she continued to look at him fixedly all the time. "Can you tell me where I shall find some dry things to put on?" he asked.

"Did you dive into the pond for me?" she asked.

"No," he answered. "I walked in. But I went in overhead as well."

There was silence for a moment. He hesitated. He very much wanted to go upstairs to get into dry clothing. But there was another desire in him. And she seemed to hold him. His will seemed to have gone to sleep, and left him, standing there slack before her. But he felt warm inside himself. He did not shudder at all, though his clothes were sodden on him.

"Why did you?" she asked.

"Because I didn't want you to do such a foolish thing," he said.

"It wasn't foolish," she said, still gazing at him as she lay on the floor, with a sofa cushion under her head. "It was the right thing to do. *I* knew best, then."

"I'll go and shift these wet things," he said. But still he had not the power to move out of her presence, until she sent him. It was as if she had the life of his body in her hands, and he could not extricate himself. Or perhaps he did not want to.

Suddenly she sat up. Then she became aware of her own immediate condition. She felt the blankets about her, she knew her own limbs. For a moment it seemed as if her reason were going. She looked round, with wild eye, as if seeking something. He stood still with fear. She saw her clothing lying scattered.

"Who undressed me?" she asked, her eyes resting full and inevitable on his face.

"I did," he replied, "to bring you round."

For some moments she sat and gazed at him, awfully, her lips parted.

"Do you love me, then?" she asked.

He only stood and stared at her, fascinated. His soul seemed to melt.

She shuffled forward on her knees, and put her arms round him, round his legs, as he stood there, pressing her breasts against his knees and thighs, clutching him with strange, convulsive certainty, pressing his thighs against her, drawing him to her face, her throat, as she looked up at him with flaring, humble eyes of transfiguration, triumphant in first possession.

"You love me," she murmured, in strange transport, yearning and triumphant and confident. "You love me. I know you love me, I know."

And she was passionately kissing his knees, through the wet clothing, passionately and indiscriminately kissing his knees, his legs, as if unaware of everything.

He looked down at the tangled wet hair, the wild, bare, animal shoulders. He was amazed, bewildered, and afraid. He had never thought of loving her. He had never wanted to love her. When he rescued her and restored her, he was a doctor, and she was a patient. He had had no single personal thought of her. Nay, this introduction of the personal element was very distasteful to him, a violation of his professional honor. It was horrible to have her there embracing his knees. It was horrible. He revolted from it, violently. And yet—and yet—he had not the power to break away.

She looked at him again, with the same supplication of powerful love, and that same transcendent, frightening light of triumph. In view of the delicate flame which seemed to come from her face like a light, he was powerless. And yet he had never intended to love her. He had never intended. And something stubborn in him could not give way.

"You love me," she repeated, in a murmur of deep, rhapsodic assurance. "You love me."

Her hands were drawing him, drawing him down to her. He was afraid, even a little horrified. For he had, really, no intention of loving her. Yet her hands were drawing him towards her. He put out his hand quickly to steady himself, and grasped her bare shoulder. A flame seemed to burn the hand that grasped her soft shoulder. He had no intention of loving her: his whole will was against his yielding. It was horrible. And yet wonderful was the touch of her shoulders, beautiful the shining of her face. Was she perhaps mad? He had a horror of yielding to her. Yet something in him ached also.

He had been staring away at the door, away from her. But his hand remained on her shoulder. She had gone suddenly very still. He looked down at her. Her eyes were now wide with fear, with doubt, the light was dying from her face, a shadow of terrible grayness was returning. He could not bear the touch of her eyes' question upon him, and the look of death behind the question.

With an inward groan he gave way, and let his heart yield towards her. A sudden gentle smile came on his face. And her eyes, which never left his face, slowly, slowly filled with tears. He watched the strange water rise in her eyes, like some slow fountain coming up. And his heart seemed to burn and melt away in his breast.

He could not bear to look at her any more. He dropped on his knees and caught her head with his arms and pressed her face against his throat. She was very still. His heart, which seemed to have broken, was burning with a kind of agony in his breast. And he felt her slow, hot tears wetting his throat. But he could not move.

He felt the hot tears wet his neck and the hollows of his neck, and he remained motionless, suspended through one of man's eternities. Only now it had become indispensable to him to have her face pressed close to him; he could never let her go again. He could never let her head go away from the close clutch of his arm. He wanted to remain like that for ever, with his heart hurting him in a pain that was also life to him. Without knowing, he was looking down on her damp, soft brown hair.

Then, as it were suddenly, he smelt the horrid stagnant smell of that water. And at the same moment she drew away from him and looked at him. Her eyes were wistful and unfathomable. He was afraid of them, and he fell to kissing her, not knowing what he was doing. He wanted her eyes not to have that terrible, wistful, unfathomable look.

When she turned her face to him again, a faint delicate flush was glowing, and there was again dawning that terrible shining of joy in her eyes, which really terrified him, and yet which he now wanted to see, because he feared the look of doubt still more.

"You love me?" she said, rather faltering.

"Yes." The word cost him a painful effort. Not because it wasn't true. But because it was too newly true, the *saying* seemed to tear open again his newly-torn heart. And he hardly wanted it to be true, even now.

She lifted her face to him, and he bent forward and kissed her on the mouth, gently, with the one kiss that is an eternal pledge. And as he kissed her his heart strained again in his breast. He never intended to love her. But now it was over. He had crossed over the gulf to her, and all that he had left behind had shriveled and become void.

After the kiss, her eyes again slowly filled with tears. She sat still, away from him, with her face drooped aside, and her hands folded in her lap. The tears fell very slowly. There was complete silence. He too sat there motionless and silent on the hearth-rug. The strange pain of his heart that was broken seemed to consume him. That he should love her? That this was love! That he should be ripped open in this way! Him, a doctor! How they would all jeer if they knew! It was agony to him to think they might know.

In the curious naked pain of the thought he looked again to her. She was still sitting there drooped into a muse. He saw a tear fall, and his heart flared hot. He saw for the first time that one of her shoulders was quite uncovered, one arm bare, he could see one of her small breasts; dimly, because it had become almost dark in the room.

"Why are you crying?" he asked, in an altered voice.

She looked up at him, and behind her tears the consciousness of her situation for the first time brought a dark look of shame to her eyes.

"I'm not crying, really," she said, watching him, half frightened.

He reached his hand, and softly closed it on her bare arm.

"I love you! I love you!" he said in a soft, low vibrating voice, unlike himself.

She shrank, and dropped her head. The soft, penetrating grip of his hand on her arm distressed her. She looked up at him.

"I want to go," she said. "I want to go and get you some dry things."

"Why?" he said. "I'm all right."

"But I want to go," she said. "And I want you to change your things."

He released her arm, and she wrapped herself in the blanket, looking at him rather frightened. And still she did not rise.

"Kiss me," she said wistfully.

He kissed her, but briefly, half in anger.

Then, after a second, she rose nervously, all mixed up in the blanket. He watched her in her confusion as she tried to extricate herself and wrap herself up so that she could walk. He watched her relentlessly, as she knew. And as she went, the blanket trailing, and as he saw a glimpse of her feet and her white leg, he tried to remember her as she was when he had wrapped her in the blanket. But then he didn't want to remember, because she had been nothing to him then, and his nature revolted from remembering her as she was when she was nothing to him.

A tumbling, muffled noise from within the dark house startled him. Then he heard her voice: "There are clothes." He rose and went to the foot of the stairs, and gathered up the garments she had thrown down. Then he came back to the fire, to rub himself down and dress. He grinned at his own appearance when he had finished.

The fire was sinking, so he put on coal. The house was now quite dark, save for the light of a street-lamp that shone in faintly from beyond the holly trees. He lit the gas with matches he found on the mantelpiece. Then he emptied the pockets of his own clothes, and threw all his wet things in a heap into the scullery. After which he gathered up her sodden clothes, gently, and put them in a separate heap on the copper-top in the scullery.

It was six o'clock on the clock. His own watch had stopped. He ought to go back to the surgery. He waited, and still she did not come down. So he went to the foot of the stairs and called:

"I shall have to go."

Almost immediately he heard her coming down. She had on her best dress of black voile, and her hair was tidy, but still damp. She looked at him—and in spite of herself, smiled.

"I don't like you in those clothes," she said.

"Do I look a sight?" he answered.

They were shy of one another.

"I'll make you some tea," she said.

"No, I must go."

"Must you?" And she looked at him again with the wide, strained, doubtful eyes. And again, from the pain of his breast, he knew how he loved her. He went and bent to kiss her, gently, passionately, with his heart's painful kiss.

"And my hair smells so horrible," she murmured in distraction. "And I'm so awful, I'm so awful! Oh, no, I'm too awful." And she broke into bitter, heartbroken sobbing. "You can't want to love me, I'm horrible."

"Don't be silly, don't be silly," he said, trying to comfort her, kissing her, holding her in his arms. "I want you, I want to marry you, we're going to be married, quickly, quickly—tomorrow if I can."

But she only sobbed terribly, and cried:

"I feel awful. I feel awful. I feel I'm horrible to you."

"No, I want you, I want you," was all he answered, blindly, with that terrible intonation which frightened her almost more than her horror lest he should *not* want her.

(1922)

QUESTIONS FOR REFLECTION

Experience

1. How do you respond to Mabel's predicament? To the way her brothers treat her?
2. To what extent does your experience with love parallel that of Mabel or Jack?

Interpretation

3. Explain the symbolic significance of the horses by considering Lawrence's detailed descriptions of them.
4. Explain why Mabel attempts suicide and why the doctor thinks that he should save her and does save her.

5. What does Lawrence show through his detailed description of the doctor's hesitation in yielding to his feelings for Mabel? What is the significance of her response to him when she comes to her senses?

Evaluation

6. What values guide the life of the young doctor?
7. What value does Lawrence place on sexual love as evidenced by this story?

Connections

8. Compare the power Mabel has over Doctor Fergusson with that of Paul's mother over him in "The Rocking-Horse Winner."

The Rocking-Horse Winner

There was a woman who was beautiful, who started with all the advantages, yet she had no luck. She married for love, and the love turned to dust. She had bonny children, yet she felt they had been thrust upon her, and she could not love them. They looked at her coldly, as if they were finding fault with her. And hurriedly she felt she must cover up some fault in herself. Yet what it was that she must cover up she never knew. Nevertheless, when her children were present, she always felt the center of her heart go hard. This troubled her, and in her manner she was all the more gentle and anxious for her children, as if she loved them very much. Only she herself knew that at the center of her heart was a hard little place that could not feel love, no, not for anybody. Everybody else said of her: "She is such a good mother. She adores her children." Only she herself, and her children themselves, knew it was not so. They read it in each other's eyes.

There were a boy and two little girls. They lived in a pleasant house, with a garden, and they had discreet servants, and felt themselves superior to anyone in the neighborhood.

Although they lived in style, they felt always an anxiety in the house. There was never enough money. The mother had a small income, and the father had a small income, but not nearly enough for the social position which they had to keep up. The father went into town to some office. But though he had good prospects, these prospects never materialized. There was always the grinding sense of the shortage of money, though the style was always kept up.

At last the mother said: "I will see if *I* can't make something." But she did not know where to begin. She racked her brains, and tried this thing and the other, but could not find anything successful. The failure made deep lines come into her face. Her children were growing up, they would have to go to school. There must be more money, there must be more money. The father, who was always very handsome and expensive in his tastes, seemed as if he never *would* be able to do anything worth doing. And the mother, who had a great belief in herself, did not succeed any better, and her tastes were just as expensive.

And so the house came to be haunted by the unspoken phrase: *There must be more money! There must be more money!* The children could hear it all the time though nobody said it aloud. They heard it at Christmas, when the expensive and splendid toys filled the nursery. Behind the shining modern rocking horse, behind the smart doll's house, a voice would start whispering: "There *must* be more money! There *must* be more money!" And the children would stop playing, to listen for a moment. They would look into each other's eyes, to see if they had all heard. And each one saw in the eyes of the other two that they too had heard. "There *must* be more money! There *must* be more money!"

It came whispering from the springs of the still-swaying rocking horse, and even the horse, bending his wooden, champing head, heard it. The big doll, sitting so pink and smirking in her new pram, could hear it quite plainly, and seemed to be smirking all the more self-consciously because of it. The foolish puppy, too, that took the place of the teddy bear, he was looking so extraordinarily foolish for no other reason but that he heard the secret whisper all over the house: "There *must* be more money!"

Yet nobody ever said it aloud. The whisper was everywhere, and therefore no one spoke it. Just as no one ever says: "We are breathing!" in spite of the fact that breath is coming and going all the time.

"Mother," said the boy Paul one day, "why don't we keep a car of our own? Why do we always use Uncle's, or else a taxi?"

"Because we're the poor members of the family," said the mother.

"But why *are* we, Mother?"

"Well—I suppose," she said slowly and bitterly, "it's because your father has no luck."

The boy was silent for some time.

"Is luck money, Mother?" he asked rather timidly.

"No, Paul. Not quite. It's what causes you to have money."

"Oh!" said Paul vaguely. "I thought when Uncle Oscar said *filthy lucker,* it meant money."

"*Filthy lucre* does mean money," said the mother. "But it's lucre, not luck."

"Oh!" said the boy. "Then what *is* luck, Mother?"

"It's what causes you to have money. If you're lucky you have money. That's why it's better to be born lucky than rich. If you're rich, you may lose your money. But if you're lucky, you will always get more money."

"Oh! Will you? And is Father not lucky?"

"Very unlucky, I should say," she said bitterly.

The boy watched her with unsure eyes.

"Why?" he asked.

"I don't know. Nobody ever knows why one person is lucky and another unlucky."

"Don't they? Nobody at all? Does *nobody* know?"

"Perhaps God. But He never tells."

"He ought to, then. And aren't you lucky either, Mother?"

"I can't be, if I married an unlucky husband."

"But by yourself, aren't you?"

"I used to think I was, before I married. Now I think I am very unlucky indeed."

"Why?"

"Well—never mind! Perhaps I'm not really," she said.

The child looked at her, to see if she meant it. But he saw, by the lines of her mouth, that she was only trying to hide something from him.

"Well, anyhow," he said stoutly, "I'm a lucky person."

"Why?" said his mother, with a sudden laugh.

He stared at her. He didn't even know why he had said it.

"God told me," he asserted, brazening it out.

"I hope He did, dear!" she said, again with a laugh, but rather bitter.

"He did, Mother!"

"Excellent!" said the mother.

The boy saw she did not believe him; or, rather, that she paid no attention to his assertion. This angered him somewhat, and made him want to compel her attention.

He went off by himself, vaguely, in a childish way, seeking for the clue to "luck." Absorbed, taking no heed of other people, he went about with a sort of stealth, seeking inwardly for luck. He wanted luck, he wanted it, he wanted it. When the two girls were playing dolls in the nursery, he would sit on his big rocking horse, charging madly into space, with a frenzy that made the little girls peer at him uneasily. Wildly the horse careered, the waving dark hair of the boy tossed, his eyes had a strange glare in them. The little girls dared not speak to him.

When he had ridden to the end of his mad little journey, he climbed down and stood in front of his rocking horse, staring fixedly into its lowered face. Its red mouth was slightly open, its big eye was wide and glassy-bright.

Now! he could silently command the snorting steed. Now, take me to where there is luck! Now take me!

And he would slash the horse on the neck with the little whip he had asked Uncle Oscar for. He *knew* the horse could take him to where there was luck, if only he forced it. So he would mount again, and start on his furious ride, hoping at last to get there. He knew he could get there.

"You'll break your horse, Paul!" said the nurse.

"He's always riding like that! I wish he'd leave off!" said his elder sister Joan.

But he only glared down on them in silence. Nurse gave him up. She could make nothing of him. Anyhow he was growing beyond her.

One day his mother and his uncle Oscar came in when he was on one of his furious rides. He did not speak to them.

"Hallo, you young jockey! Riding a winner?" said his uncle.

"Aren't you growing too big for a rocking horse? You're not a very little boy any longer, you know," said his mother.

But Paul only gave a blue glare from his big, rather close-set eyes. He would speak to nobody when he was in full tilt. His mother watched him with an anxious expression on her face.

At last he suddenly stopped forcing his horse into the mechanical gallop, and slid down.

"Well, I got there!" he announced fiercely, his blue eyes still flaring, and his sturdy long legs straddling apart.

"Where did you get to?" asked his mother.

"Where I wanted to go," he flared back at her.

"That's right, son!" said Uncle Oscar. "Don't you stop till you get there. What's the horse's name?"

"He doesn't have a name," said the boy.

"Gets on without all right?" asked the uncle.

"Well, he has different names. He was called Sansovino last week."

"Sansovino, eh? Won the Ascot. How did you know his name?"

"He always talks about horse races with Bassett," said Joan.

The uncle was delighted to find that his small nephew was posted with all the racing news. Bassett, the young gardener, who had been wounded in the left foot in the war and had got his present job through Oscar Cresswell, whose batman he had been, was a perfect blade of the "turf." He lived in the racing events, and the small boy lived with him.

Oscar Cresswell got it all from Bassett.

"Master Paul comes and asks me, so I can't do more than tell him, sir," said Bassett, his face terribly serious, as if he were speaking of religious matters.

"And does he ever put anything on a horse he fancies?"

"Well—I don't want to give him away—he's a young sport, a fine sport, sir. Would you mind asking him himself? He sort of takes a pleasure in it, and perhaps he'd feel I was giving him away, sir, if you don't mind."

Bassett was serious as a church.

The uncle went back to his nephew and took him off for a ride in the car.

"Say, Paul, old man, do you ever put anything on a horse?" the uncle asked.

The boy watched the handsome man closely.

"Why, do you think I oughtn't to?" he parried.

"Not a bit of it! I thought perhaps you might give me a tip for the Lincoln."

The car sped on into the country, going down to Uncle Oscar's place in Hampshire.

"Honor bright?" said the nephew.

"Honor bright, son!" said the uncle.

"Well, then, Daffodil."

"Daffodil! I doubt it, sonny. What about Mirza?"

"I only know the winner," said the boy. "That's Daffodil."

"Daffodil, eh?"

There was a pause. Daffodil was an obscure horse comparatively.

"Uncle!"

"Yes, son?"

"You won't let it go any further, will you? I promised Bassett."

"Bassett be damned, old man! What's he got to do with it?"

"We're partners. We've been partners from the first. Uncle, he lent me my first five shillings, which I lost. I promised him, honor bright, it was only between me and him; only you gave me that ten-shilling note I started winning with, so I thought you were lucky. You won't let it go any further, will you?"

The boy gazed at his uncle from those big, hot, blue eyes, set rather close together. The uncle stirred and laughed uneasily.

"Right you are, son! I'll keep your tip private. Daffodil, eh? How much are you putting on him?"

"All except twenty pounds," said the boy. "I keep that in reserve."

The uncle thought it a good joke.

"You keep twenty pounds in reserve, do you, you young romancer? What are you betting, then?"

"I'm betting three hundred," said the boy gravely. "But it's between you and me, Uncle Oscar! Honor bright?"

The uncle burst into a roar of laughter.

"It's between you and me all right, you young Nat Gould," he said, laughing. "But where's your three hundred?"

"Bassett keeps it for me. We're partners."

"You are, are you! And what is Bassett putting on Daffodil?"

"He won't go quite as high as I do, I expect. Perhaps he'll go a hundred and fifty."

"What, pennies?" laughed the uncle.

"Pounds," said the child, with a surprised look at his uncle. "Bassett keeps a bigger reserve than I do."

Between wonder and amusement Uncle Oscar was silent. He pursued the matter no further, but he determined to take his nephew with him to the Lincoln races.

"Now, son," he said, "I'm putting twenty on Mirza, and I'll put five for you on any horse you fancy. What's your pick?"

"Daffodil, Uncle."

"No, not the fiver on Daffodil!"

"I should if it was my own fiver," said the child.

"Good! Good! Right you are! A fiver for me and a fiver for you on Daffodil."

The child had never been to a race meeting before, and his eyes were blue fire. He pursed his mouth tight, and watched. A Frenchman just in front had put his money on Lancelot. Wild with excitement, he flailed his arms up and down, yelling *"Lancelot! Lancelot!"* in his French accent.

Daffodil came in first, Lancelot second, Mirza third. The child, flushed and with eyes blazing, was curiously serene. His uncle brought him four five-pound notes, four to one.

"What am I to do with these?" he cried, waving them before the boy's eyes.

"I suppose we'll talk to Bassett," said the boy. "I expect I have fifteen hundred now; and twenty in reserve; and this twenty."

His uncle studied him for some moments.

"Look here, son!" he said. "You're not serious about Bassett and that fifteen hundred, are you?"

"Yes, I am. But it's between you and me, Uncle. Honor bright!"

"Honor bright all right, son! But I must talk to Bassett."

"If you'd like to be a partner, Uncle, with Bassett and me, we could all be partners. Only, you'd have to promise, honor bright, Uncle, not to let it go beyond us three. Bassett and I are lucky, and you must be lucky, because it was your ten shillings I started winning with. . . ."

Uncle Oscar took both Bassett and Paul into Richmond Park for an afternoon, and there they talked.

"It's like this, you see, sir," Bassett said. "Master Paul would get me talking about racing events, spinning yarns, you know, sir. And he was always keen on knowing if I'd made or if I'd lost. It's about a year since, now, that I put five shillings on Blush of Dawn for him—and we lost. Then the luck turned, with that ten shillings he had from you, that we put on Singhalese. And since then, it's been pretty steady, all things considering. What do you say, Master Paul?"

"We're all right when we're sure," said Paul. "It's when we're not quite sure that we go down."

"Oh, but we're careful then," said Bassett.

"But when are you *sure?*" Uncle Oscar smiled.

"It's Master Paul, sir," said Bassett, in a secret, religious voice. "It's as if he had it from heaven. Like Daffodil, now, for the Lincoln. That was as sure as eggs."

"Did you put anything on Daffodil?" asked Oscar Cresswell.

"Yes, sir. I made my bit."

"And my nephew?"

Bassett was obstinately silent, looking at Paul.

"I made twelve hundred, didn't I, Bassett? I told Uncle I was putting three hundred on Daffodil."

"That's right," said Bassett, nodding.

"But where's the money?" asked the uncle.

"I keep it safe locked up, sir. Master Paul he can have it any minute he likes to ask for it."

"What, fifteen hundred pounds?"

"And twenty! And *forty,* that is, with the twenty he made on the course."

"It's amazing!" said the uncle.

"If Master Paul offers you to be partners, sir, I would, if I were you; if you'll excuse me," said Bassett.

Oscar Cresswell thought about it.

"I'll see the money," he said.

They drove home again, and sure enough, Bassett came round to the garden house with fifteen hundred pounds in notes. The twenty pounds reserve was left with Joe Glee, in the Turf Commission deposit.

"You see, it's all right, Uncle, when I'm *sure!* Then we go strong, for all we're worth. Don't we, Bassett?"

"We do that, Master Paul."

"And when are you sure?" said the uncle, laughing.

"Oh, well, sometimes I'm *absolutely* sure, like about Daffodil," said the boy; "and sometimes I have an idea; and sometimes I haven't even an idea, have I, Bassett? Then we're careful, because we mostly go down."

"You do, do you! And when you're sure, like about Daffodil, what makes you sure, sonny?"

"Oh, well, I don't know," said the boy uneasily. "I'm sure, you know, Uncle; that's all."

"It's as if he had it from heaven, sir," Bassett reiterated.

"I should say so!" said the uncle.

But he became a partner. And when the Leger was coming on, Paul was "sure" about Lively Spark, which was a quite inconsiderable horse. The boy insisted on putting a thousand on the horse, Bassett went for five hundred, and Oscar Cresswell two hundred. Lively Spark came in first, and the betting had been ten to one against him. Paul had made ten thousand.

"You see," he said, "I was absolutely sure of him."

Even Oscar Cresswell had cleared two thousand.

"Look here, son," he said, "this sort of thing makes me nervous."

"It needn't, Uncle! Perhaps I shan't be sure again for a long time."

"But what are you going to do with your money?" asked the uncle.

"Of course," said the boy. "I started it for Mother. She said she had no luck, because Father is unlucky, so I thought if *I* was lucky, it might stop whispering."

"What might stop whispering?"

"Our house. I *hate* our house for whispering."

"What does it whisper?"

"Why—why"—the boy fidgeted—"why, I don't know. But it's always short of money, you know, Uncle."

"I know it, son, I know it."

"You know people send Mother writs, don't you, Uncle?"

"I'm afraid I do," said the uncle.

"And then the house whispers, like people laughing at you behind your back. It's awful, that is! I thought if I was lucky. . . ."

"You might stop it," added the uncle.

The boy watched him with big blue eyes, that had an uncanny cold fire in them, and he said never a word.

"Well, then!" said the uncle. "What are we doing?"

"I shouldn't like Mother to know I was lucky," said the boy.

"Why not, son?"

"She'd stop me."

"I don't think she would."

"Oh!"—and the boy writhed in an odd way—"I *don't* want her to know, Uncle."

"All right, son! We'll manage it without her knowing."

They managed it very easily. Paul, at the other's suggestion, handed over five thousand pounds to his uncle, who deposited it with the family lawyer, who was then to inform Paul's mother that a relative had put five thousand pounds into his hands, which sum was to be paid out a thousand pounds at a time, on the mother's birthday, for the next five years.

"So she'll have a birthday present of a thousand pounds for five successive years," said Uncle Oscar. "I hope it won't make it all the harder for her later."

Paul's mother had her birthday in November. The house had been "whispering" worse than ever lately, and, even in spite of his luck, Paul could not bear up against it. He was very anxious to see the effect of the birthday letter, telling his mother about the thousand pounds.

When there were no visitors, Paul now took his meals with his parents, as he was beyond the nursery control. His mother went into town nearly every day. She had discovered that she had an odd knack of sketching furs and dress materials, so she worked secretly in the studio of a friend who was the chief artist for the leading drapers. She drew the figures of ladies in furs and ladies in silk and sequins for the newspaper advertisements. This young woman artist earned several thousand pounds a year, but Paul's mother only made several hundreds, and she was again dissatisfied. She so wanted to be first in something, and she did not succeed, even in making sketches for drapery advertisements.

She was down to breakfast on the morning of her birthday. Paul watched her face as she read her letters. He knew the lawyer's letter. As his mother read it, her face hardened and became more expressionless. Then a cold, determined look came on her mouth. She hid the letter under the pile of others, and said not a word about it.

"Didn't you have anything nice in the post for your birthday, Mother?" said Paul.

"Quite moderately nice," she said, her voice cold and absent.

She went away to town without saying more.

But in the afternoon Uncle Oscar appeared. He said Paul's mother had had a long interview with the lawyer, asking if the whole five thousand could not be advanced at once, as she was in debt.

"What do you think, Uncle?" said the boy.

"I leave it to you, son."

"Oh, let her have it, then! We can get some more with the other," said the boy.

"A bird in the hand is worth two in the bush, laddie!" said Uncle Oscar.

"But I'm sure to *know* for the Grand National; or the Lincolnshire; or else the Derby. I'm sure to know for *one* of them," said Paul.

So Uncle Oscar signed the agreement, and Paul's mother touched the whole five thousand. Then something very curious happened. The voices in the house suddenly went mad, like a chorus of frogs on a spring evening. There were certain new furnishings, and Paul had a tutor. He was *really* going to Eton, his father's school, in the following autumn. There were flowers in the winter, and a blossoming of the luxury Paul's mother had been used to. And yet the voices in the house, behind the sprays of mimosa and almond blossom, and from under the piles of iridescent cushions, simply trilled and screamed in a sort of ecstasy: "There *must* be more money! Oh-h-h; there *must* be more money. Oh, now, now-w! Now-w-w—there *must* be more money!— more than ever! More than ever!"

It frightened Paul terribly. He studied away at his Latin and Greek. But his intense hours were spent with Bassett. The Grand National had gone by; he had not "known," and had lost a hundred pounds. Summer was at hand. He was in agony for the Lincoln. But even for the Lincoln he didn't "know," and he lost fifty pounds. He became wild-eyed and strange, as if something were going to explode in him.

"Let it alone, son! Don't you bother about it!" urged Uncle Oscar. But it was as if the boy couldn't really hear what his uncle was saying.

"I've got to know for the Derby! I've got to know for the Derby!" the child reiterated, his big blue eyes blazing with a sort of madness.

His mother noticed how overwrought he was.

"You'd better go to the seaside. Wouldn't you like to go now to the seaside, instead of waiting? I think you'd better," she said, looking down at him anxiously, her heart curiously heavy because of him.

But the child lifted his uncanny blue eyes. "I couldn't possibly go before the Derby, Mother!" he said. "I couldn't possibly!"

"Why not?" she said, her voice becoming heavy when she was opposed. "Why not? You can still go from the seaside to see the Derby with your uncle Oscar, if that's what you wish. No need for you to wait here. Besides, I think you care too much about these races. It's a bad sign. My family has been a gambling family, and you won't know till you grow up how much damage it has done. But it has done damage. I shall have to send Bassett away, and ask Uncle Oscar not to talk racing to you, unless you promise to be reasonable about it; go away to the seaside and forget it. You're all nerves!"

"I'll do what you like, Mother, so long as you don't send me away till after the Derby," the boy said.

"Send you away from where? Just from this house?"

"Yes," he said, gazing at her.

"Why, you curious child, what makes you care about this house so much, suddenly? I never knew you loved it."

He gazed at her without speaking. He had a secret within a secret, something he had not divulged, even to Bassett or to his uncle Oscar.

But his mother, after standing undecided and a little bit sullen for some moments, said:

"Very well, then! Don't go to the seaside till after the Derby, if you don't wish it. But promise me you won't let your nerves go to pieces. Promise you won't think so much about horse racing and *events,* as you call them!"

"Oh, no," said the boy casually. "I won't think much about them, Mother. You needn't worry. I wouldn't worry, Mother, if I were you."

"If you were me and I were you," said his mother, "I wonder what we *should* do!"

"But you know you needn't worry, Mother, don't you?" the boy repeated.

"I should be awfully glad to know it," she said wearily.

"Oh, well you *can,* you know. I mean, you *ought* to know you needn't worry," he insisted.

"Ought I? Then I'll see about it," she said.

Paul's secret of secrets was his wooden horse, that which had no name. Since he was emancipated from a nurse and a nursery governess, he had had his rocking horse removed to his own bedroom at the top of the house.

"Surely, you're too big for a rocking horse!" his mother had remonstrated.

"Well, you see, Mother, till I can have a *real* horse, I like to have *some* sort of animal about," had been his quaint answer.

"Do you feel he keeps you company?" She laughed.

"Oh, yes! He's very good, he always keeps me company, when I'm there," said Paul.

So the horse, rather shabby, stood in an arrested prance in the boy's bedroom.

The Derby was drawing near, and the boy grew more and more tense. He hardly heard what was spoken to him, he was very frail, and his eyes were really uncanny. His mother had sudden strange seizures of uneasiness about him. Sometimes, for half an hour, she would feel a sudden anxiety about him that was almost anguish. She wanted to rush to him at once, and know he was safe.

Two nights before the Derby, she was at a big party in town, when one of her rushes of anxiety about her boy, her firstborn, gripped her heart till she could hardly speak. She fought with the feeling, might and main, for she believed in common sense. But it was too strong. She had to leave the dance and go downstairs to telephone to the country. The children's nursery governess was terribly surprised and startled at being rung up in the night.

"Are the children all right, Miss Wilmot?"

"Oh, yes, they are quite all right."

"Master Paul? Is he all right?"

"He went to bed as right as a trivet. Shall I run up and look at him?"

"No," said Paul's mother reluctantly. "No! Don't trouble. It's all right. Don't sit up. We shall be home fairly soon." She did not want her son's privacy intruded upon.

"Very good," said the governess.

It was about one o'clock when Paul's mother and father drove up to their house. All was still. Paul's mother went to her room and slipped off her white fur cloak. She had told her maid not to wait up for her. She heard her husband downstairs, mixing a whisky and soda.

And then, because of the strange anxiety at her heart, she stole upstairs to her son's room. Noiselessly she went along the upper corridor. Was there a faint noise? What was it?

She stood, with arrested muscles, outside his door, listening. There was a strange, heavy, and yet not loud noise. Her heart stood still. It was a soundless noise, yet rushing and powerful. Something huge, in violent, hushed motion. What was it? What in God's name was it? She ought to know. She felt that she knew the noise. She knew what it was.

Yet she could not place it. She couldn't say what it was. And on and on it went, like a madness.

Softly, frozen with anxiety and fear, she turned the door handle.

The room was dark. Yet in the space near the window, she heard and saw something plunging to and fro. She gazed in fear and amazement.

Then suddenly she switched on the light, and saw her son, in his green pajamas, madly surging on the rocking horse. The blaze of light suddenly lit him up, as he urged the wooden horse, and lit her up, as she stood, blonde, in her dress of pale green and crystal, in the doorway.

"Paul!" she cried. "Whatever are you doing?"

"It's Malabar!" he screamed, in a powerful, strange voice. "It's Malabar!"

His eyes blazed at her for one strange and senseless second, as he ceased urging his wooden horse. Then he fell with a crash to the ground, and she, all her tormented motherhood flooding upon her, rushed to gather him up.

But he was unconscious, and unconscious he remained, with some brain fever. He talked and tossed, and his mother sat stonily by his side.

"Malabar! It's Malabar! Bassett, Bassett, I *know!* It's Malabar!"

So the child cried, trying to get up and urge the rocking horse that gave him his inspiration.

"What does he mean by Malabar?" asked the heart-frozen mother.

"I don't know," said the father stonily.

"What does he mean by Malabar?" she asked her brother Oscar.

"It's one of the horses running for the Derby," was the answer.

And, in spite of himself, Oscar Cresswell spoke to Bassett, and himself put a thousand on Malabar: at fourteen to one.

The third day of the illness was critical: they were waiting for a change. The boy, with his rather long, curly hair, was tossing ceaselessly on the pillow. He never slept nor regained consciousness, and his eyes were like blue stones. His mother sat, feeling her heart had gone, turned actually into a stone.

In the evening, Oscar Cresswell did not come, but Bassett sent a message, saying could he come up for one moment, just one moment? Paul's mother was very angry at the intrusion, but on second thought she agreed. The boy was the same. Perhaps Bassett might bring him to consciousness.

The gardener, a shortish fellow with a little brown mustache, and sharp little brown eyes, tiptoed into the room, touched his imaginary cap to Paul's mother, and stole to the bedside, staring with glittering, smallish eyes at the tossing, dying child.

"Master Paul!" he whispered. "Master Paul! Malabar came in first all right, a clean win. I did as you told me. You've made over seventy thousand pounds, you have; you've got over eighty thousand. Malabar came in all right, Master Paul."

"Malabar! Malabar! Did I say Malabar, Mother? Did I say Malabar? Do you think I'm lucky, Mother? I knew Malabar, didn't I? Over eighty thousand pounds! I call that lucky, don't you, Mother? Over eighty thousand pounds! I knew, didn't I know I knew? Malabar came in all right. If I ride my horse till I'm sure, then I tell you, Bassett, you can go as high as you like. Did you go for all you were worth, Bassett?"

"I went a thousand on it, Master Paul."

"I never told you, Mother, that if I can ride my horse, and *get there,* then I'm absolutely sure—oh, absolutely! Mother, did I ever tell you? I *am* lucky!"

"No, you never did," said the mother.

But the boy died in the night.

And even as he lay dead, his mother heard her brother's voice saying to her: "My God, Hester, you're eighty-odd thousand to the good, and a poor devil of a son to the bad. But, poor devil, poor devil, he's best gone out of a life where he rides his rocking horse to find a winner."

(1926)

QUESTIONS FOR REFLECTION

Experience

1. What were your initial impressions of Paul and of his mother? To what extent did these impressions about either or both characters change or remain the same?
2. How does your own experience relating to your own mother compare with that of Paul?

Interpretation

3. What does Paul try to do by riding his rocking horse?
4. What is the function of Paul's uncle, Oscar, in the story?
5. What is the significance of Paul's death? Of the repeated phrase in the house that "there must be more money"?

Evaluation

6. What values does Paul's mother live by? What is most important to her? Why?
7. Whose values does the story seem to endorse? Whose does it seem to condemn?

Connections

8. Compare the relationship between parent and child in this story with that in "The Prodigal Son."

INTRODUCTION TO FLANNERY O'CONNOR

[1925–1964]

Flannery O'Connor is considered one of the unique voices to emerge from the 1950s. Her widely anthologized short stories often employ humor, irony, and paradox within a system of Christian belief in evil and redemption. And because she is a social satirist as well as a religious thinker, O'Connor's images often highlight current American cultural challenges, as she delineates such timely issues as random violence, race relations, and class discrimination.

O'Connor's stories are also suggestive of the southern tradition of folktales and storytelling in which engaging, violent, and frequently grotesque characters are often treated with colloquial humor. Other writers identified with this tradition and often considered influential on O'Connor's fiction include Mark Twain, William Faulkner, and Katherine Anne Porter. Like O'Connor, these writers often point to the comic in calamity. O'Connor's forerunners would also have to include such American romance writers as Nathaniel Hawthorne, Herman Melville, Edgar Allan Poe, and Henry James, who explored questions of morality while presenting experience in highly imaginative and symbolic ways.

O'Connor herself suggested that there were two strong influences on her writing: her sense of herself as a southerner and her Roman Catholic roots. A southerner all her life, O'Connor was born in Savannah, Georgia, in 1925. In 1938 she moved to Milledgeville, Georgia, the city which had been Georgia's capital before the Civil War and where she would spend most of her life. She graduated from Women's College of Georgia in 1945 where she earned a reputation as a cartoonist, contributing weekly sketches to the campus newspaper. O'Connor then went on to earn an M.F.A. in writing from the State University of Iowa in 1947. At the age of twenty-five she was struck with a debilitating illness, disseminated lupus, which forced her to return to Milledgeville in 1950, where she lived and published her fiction until her death in 1964. O'Connor felt that her identity as a southerner provided her with many of the raw materials she needed to fabricate the settings and finely detailed characters of her stories. "The things we see, hear, smell, and touch," O'Connor wrote, "affect us long before we believe anything at all. The South impresses its image on the Southerner—be he Catholic or not—from the moment he is able to distinguish one sound from another."

Though the South served as the setting for O'Connor's fiction, Roman Catholicism allowed her to transcend the confines of regionalism to make a universal statement. "The woods are full of regional writers," she once stated, "and it is the great horror of every serious Southern writer that he will become one of them." Identifying her bearing as a fiction writer, O'Connor wrote: "I see from the standpoint of Christian orthodoxy. This means that for me the meaning of life is centered in our Redemption by Christ and what I see in the world I see in its relation to that." Understanding O'Connor's religious beliefs helps to interpret her fiction, but we need not share her faith to enjoy her work. Her genius as a writer eclipsed any religious devotion. Responding to a student who once queried her as to "just what enlightenment" a student might be expected to glean from an O'Connor narrative, the author suggested that the young reader "forget about the enlightenment" and just enjoy the story.

The typical O'Connor story often begins with a comic protagonist who indulges in fantasies of moral or social superiority or has a false sense of the certainty of things. The protagonist then has an ironic and traumatic (if not fatal) encounter with other characters or a situation that suggests the disturbing possibility of an incomprehensible and frequently terrifying universe. In "Everything That Rises Must Converge," for example, both Julian and his mother are ironic figures convinced of their personal superiority as well as the correctness of their respective world views. Julian's mother fortifies herself against disappointing circumstances by assuming aristocratic airs. Ironically, she proclaims that "if you know who you are you can go anywhere." When she climbs into the mass transit bus she enters the aisle "with a little smile, as if she were going into a drawing room where everyone had been waiting for her." From her perspective she and her son are the descendants of Godhighs and Chestnys, who count plantation owners and a former governor in their bloodline. Julian, on the other hand, insists that he has a truer sense of his mother's and his place in the changing world, and

> in spite of her, he had turned out so well . . . he had, on his own initiative, come out with a first-rate education; in spite of growing up dominated by a small mind, he had ended up with a large one; in spite of all her foolish views, he was free of prejudice and unafraid to face facts.

The narrator, however, implies that Julian is himself an ironic figure, as affected as his mother and only slightly more subtle in his racism. Rather than insist that black people ride in the back of the bus, he tries "to strike up an acquaintance . . . with some of the better types."

The title, "Everything That Rises Must Converge," is also ironic, alluding to the works of Teilhard de Chardin, who explains that the future will focus on an "omega point" where everything and everyone will be joined at the end of geologic time. As the story concludes, however, the characters do not so much converge as they collide, and from this collision the unimagined and terrifying universe is made apparent.

Though brief and tragically curtailed by illness, Flannery O'Connor's writing career was nevertheless recognized during her lifetime. She was awarded a *Kenyon Review* fellowship in fiction in 1953; a National Institute of Arts and Letters grant in literature in 1957; an O. Henry Award in 1957; a Ford Foundation grant in 1959; and an honorary doctor of literature from St. Mary's College in 1962 and another from Smith College in 1963. She was also awarded a Henry H. Bellaman Foundation special award in 1964. In 1971, her posthumous collection, *The Complete Stories of Flannery O'Connor,* won the National Book Award. In addition to her short-story collections [*A Good Man Is Hard to Find and Other Stories* (1955); *Everything That Rises Must Converge* (1965); *The Complete Stories of Flannery O'Connor* (1971)], Flannery

O'Connor published two novels, *Wise Blood* (1952) and *The Violent Bear It Away* (1960). Also significant are her essays and ideas on literature collected in *Mystery and Manners* (1969), *The Habit of Being: Selected Letters of Flannery O'Connor* (1979), and *The Correspondence of Flannery O'Connor and the Brainard Cheneys* (1986).

The novelist and critic V. S. Pritchett has suggested that the characters in O'Connor's stories are "plain human beings in whose fractured lives the writer has discovered an uncouth relationship with the lasting myths and the violent passions of human life." For O'Connor, truth was of the greatest importance—even when it revealed itself as fractured, uncouth, or violent.

CRITICAL COMMENTS BY O'CONNOR

On Symbol and Theme

from *"The Nature and Aim of Fiction"* (Mystery and Manners)

Now the word *symbol* scares a good many people off, just as the word *art* does. They seem to feel that a symbol is some mysterious thing put in arbitrarily by the writer to frighten the common reader—sort of a literary Masonic grip that is only for the initiated. They seem to think that it is a way of saying something that you aren't actually saying, and so if they can be got to read a reputedly symbolic work at all, they approach it as if it were a problem in algebra. Find *x*. And when they do find or think they find this abstraction, *x,* then they go off with an elaborate sense of satisfaction and the notion that they have "understood" the story. Many students confuse the *process* of understanding a thing with understanding it.

I think that for the fiction writer himself, symbols are something he uses simply as a matter of course. You might say that these are details that, while having their essential place in the literal level of the story, operate in depth as well as on the surface, increasing the story in every direction. . . .

People have a habit of saying, "What is the theme of your story?" and they expect you to give them a statement: "The theme of my story is the economic pressure of the machine on the middle class"—or some such absurdity. And when they've got a statement like that, they go off happy and feel it is no longer necessary to read the story.

Some people have the notion that you read the story and then climb out of it into the meaning, but for the fiction writer himself the whole story is the meaning, because it is an experience, not an abstraction. . . .

When you can state the theme of a story, when you can separate it from the story itself, then you can be sure the story is not a very good one. The meaning of a story has to be embodied in it, has to be made concrete in it. A story is a way to say something that can't be said any other way, and it takes every word in the story to say what the meaning is. You tell a story because a statement would be inadequate. When anybody asks what a story is about, the only proper thing is to tell him to read the story.

On "A Good Man Is Hard to Find"

from *The Habit of Being: Selected Letters of Flannery O'Connor*

Week before last I went to Wesleyan and read "A Good Man Is Hard to Find." After it I went to one of the classes where I was asked questions. There were a couple of young teachers there and one of them, an earnest type, started asking the questions. "Miss O'Connor," he said, "why was the Misfit's hat *black?*" I said most countrymen in Georgia wore black hats. He looked pretty disappointed. Then he said, "Miss O'Connor, the Misfit represents Christ, does he not?" "He does not," I said. He looked crushed. "Well, Miss O'Connor," he said, "what is the significance of the Misfit's hat?" I said it was to cover his head; and after that he left me alone. . . .

There is a change of tension from the first part of the story to the second where the Misfit enters, but this is no lessening of reality. This story is, of course, not meant to be realistic in the sense that it portrays the everyday doings of people in Georgia. It is stylized and its conventions are comic even though its meaning is serious.

Bailey's only importance is as the Grandmother's boy and the driver of the car. It is the Grandmother who first recognizes the Misfit and who is most concerned with him throughout. The story is a duel of sorts between the Grandmother and her superficial beliefs and the Misfit's more profoundly felt involvement with Christ's action which set the world off balance for him.

The meaning of a story should go on expanding for the reader the more he thinks about it, but meaning cannot be captured in an interpretation. If teachers are in the habit of approaching a story as if it were a research problem for which any answer is believable so long as it is not obvious, then I think students will never learn to enjoy fiction. Too much interpretation is certainly worse than too little, and where feeling for a story is absent, theory will not supply it.

On "Good Country People"

from "Writing Short Stories" (Mystery and Manners)

In good fiction, certain of the details will tend to accumulate meaning from the action of the story itself, and when this happens they become symbolic in the way they work. I once wrote a story called "Good Country People," in which a lady Ph.D. has her wooden leg stolen by a Bible salesman whom she has tried to seduce. Now I'll admit that, paraphrased in this way, the situation is simply a low joke. The average reader is pleased to observe anybody's wooden leg being stolen. But without ceasing to appeal to him and without making any statements of high intention, this story does manage to operate at another level of experience, by letting the wooden leg accumulate meaning. Early in the story, we're presented with the fact that the Ph.D. is spiritually as well as physically crippled. She believes in nothing but her own belief in nothing, and we perceive that there is a wooden part of her soul that corresponds to her wooden leg. Now of course this is never stated. The fiction writer states as little as possible. The reader makes this connection from things he is shown. He may not even know that he makes the connection, but the connection is there nevertheless and it has its effect on him. As the story goes on, the wooden leg continues to accumulate meaning. The reader learns how the girl feels about her leg, how her mother feels about it, and how the country woman on the place feels about it; and finally, by the time the Bible salesman comes along, the leg has accumulated so much meaning that it is, as the saying goes, loaded. And when the Bible salesman steals it, the reader realizes that he has taken away part of the girl's personality and has revealed her deeper affliction to her for the first time.

If you want to say that the wooden leg is a symbol, you can say that. But it is a wooden leg first, and as a wooden leg it is absolutely necessary to the story. It has its place on the literal level of the story, but it operates in depth as well as on the surface. It increases the story in every direction, and this is essentially the way a story escapes being short.

Now a little might be said about the way in which this happens. I wouldn't want you to think that in that story I sat down and said, "I am now going to write a story about a Ph.D. with a wooden leg, using the wooden leg as a symbol for another kind of affliction." I doubt myself if many writers know what they are going to do when they start out. When I started writing that story, I didn't know there was going to be a Ph.D. with a wooden leg in it. I merely found myself one morning writing a description of two women that I knew something about, and before I realized it, I had equipped one of them with a daughter with a wooden leg. As the story progressed, I brought in the Bible salesman, but I had no idea what I was going to do with him. I didn't know he was going to steal that wooden leg until ten or twelve lines before he did it, but when I found out that this was what was going to happen, I realized that it was inevitable. This is a story that produces a shock for the reader, and I think one reason for this is that it produced a shock for the writer.

CRITICS ON O'CONNOR

FREDERICK ASALS

On "A Good Man Is Hard to Find"

from *Flannery O'Connor: The Imagination of Extremity*

"A Good Man Is Hard to Find" continues to be O'Connor's best-known work, the story most often chosen to represent her in anthologies now as during her lifetime. Yet, fine as it is, it is not self-evidently her best story: something more than quality must account for its repeated selection by textbook editors. One reason for its popularity may well be precisely that "A Good Man Is Hard to Find" writes large the representative O'Connor themes and methods—comedy, violence, theological concern—and thus makes them quickly and unmistakably available. But another, surely, is the primordial appeal of the story, for "A Good Man Is Hard to Find" captures a very old truth, that in the midst of life we are in death, in its most compelling modern form. The characteristic contemporary nightmare of the sudden onslaught of violent death, a death that chooses its victims without warning, impersonally, apparently at random, without either motivation or remorse, the victims helpless either to escape or to defend themselves—this scenario for some of our deepest, most instinctual fears is the very basis of the story and the source of its immediate hold on our imaginations.

Interestingly enough, O'Connor's own public remarks on the story dismiss this level almost entirely. Stressing its spiritual implications, she emphasizes the grandmother's final action while brushing aside everything that leads up to it, saying, "If I took out this gesture and what she says with it, I would have no story. What was left would not be worth your attention." Her advice to readers of "A Good Man Is Hard to Find" is, "You should be on the lookout for such things as the action of grace in the Grandmother's soul, and not for the dead bodies" *(Mystery and Manners)*.

This is all very high-minded, but it would seem a little difficult for the unprejudiced reader of "A Good Man Is Hard to Find" to ignore the dead bodies; and while one may agree with O'Connor that the story is "something more than an account of a family murdered on the way to Florida" *(Mystery and Manners),* it surely is, most immediately, just that "account." Any full discussion of the story must deal with both the grandmother's soul and the dead bodies, and indeed with the tension between the two levels implied here, for that tension is at the very heart of the story.

KATHLEEN FEELEY

On "Good Country People"

from *Flannery O'Connor: Voice of the Peacock*

Perhaps it was her utter truthfulness which, paradoxically, allowed her to imagine and create characters who have destroyed their own integrity to pursue a false god. In a catalog of her freaks, characters who re-create themselves according to a chosen image would mark an extreme position. They are farthest away from grace because they lack the truthful appraisal of reality which grace demands. They have set up a false god—education, or art, or economic security, or comfort—and they falsify their very being in order to pay it homage. A number of Flannery O'Connor's short stories show her imagination working on the idea of falseness in a character. Some of the protagonists in these stories look perfectly normal; others have a physical deformity which is symbolic of a spiritual one. In the course of the action, all are given an opportunity to recognize their self-deception. In the author's vision, this recognition is the first step toward truth, which is, in turn, the necessary condition of Redemption. Conversion—a change of direction—is possible only after one recognizes his perversion.

Comic perversion is a key concept in "Good Country People." Both the girl Joy-Hulga and the Bible salesman have perverted their true selves, and each is revealed in his falsity after the word of God is perverted during a seduction scene—itself a perversion of love. Even the structure of the story appears to be a perversion of a traditional short-story form. Two-thirds of the story elapses before the initial meeting of Joy-Hulga and Manley Pointer, the Bible salesman, occurs. In the first section, Flannery O'Connor sets up a relationship between Mrs. Freeman, the hired man's wife, and Mrs. Hopewell, her employer, and between each of these women and the one-legged protagonist, Joy-Hulga. These relationships structure the story. The opening section also sketches Joy through the eyes of her mother: the hunting accident which destroyed her leg, her immersion in atheistic philosophy, and her attempt, at the age of twenty-one, to rename herself and to redirect her life. With relationships demonstrated, background sketched, and tone established, the first personal encounter of Hulga and her "saviour" takes place. From Manley Pointer's opening question ("You ever ate a chicken that was two days old?") to his final assertion ("I been believing in nothing since I was born") the story moves "like the advance of a heavy truck" to its moment of truth.

That the salesman is peddling Bibles is the central perversion of the story. Flannery O'Connor believed in the power of the word of God. The Bible was for her, as it is for Jews and for Scripture-oriented Christians, the power of God and the wisdom of God. God's scriptural word is not a dead letter; it is a living presence. Reading it does more than enlighten the intellect; it unleashes power that moves the spirit. As a perversion of Christianity has driven Joy to become Hulga, so a perversion of the meaning of Scripture jolts her into self-recognition.

DOROTHY TUCK MCFARLAND

On "Everything That Rises Must Converge"

from Flannery O'Connor

The stories in O'Connor's second collection reflect her concern with questions implicitly raised by the rather gnomic title "Everything That Rises Must Converge." The phrase comes from the work of Pierre Teilhard de Chardin, a Jesuit paleontologist-philosopher. Teilhard hypothesized that evolution, far from stopping with the emergence of *homo sapiens,* continues to progress toward higher levels of consciousness, and that its ultimate goal is pure consciousness, which is Being itself, or God.

Teilhard's concept of the progress of evolution, actual and predicted, can best be visualized as a globe. At the base of the globe—the beginning of the evolutionary process—lines radiate outward and upward, representing the diversification of many forms of life which are moving upward toward greater levels of biological complexity. At the mid-point of the globe the diversification stops and one species—man—comes to dominate the earth. Moving from the mid-point of the globe upward, the lines begin to converge as they approach the topmost pole, the evolutionary destination that Teilhard called the Omega point. The converging lines now represent individual human consciousnesses which, as they rise, grow closer and closer together.

One aspect of this convergence can be seen in the increased intercommunication and interdependence of men in modern mass society. The increasingly complex interaction of men, Teilhard believed, tends to generate fresh bursts of evolutionary energy that produce still higher levels of consciousness, and these increases in consciousness find material expression in new technological breakthroughs. Teilhard, however, did not equate rising in consciousness solely with social or intellectual or scientific advances; he saw these achievements as manifestations of an increase in consciousness that was primarily a growing toward the fullness of Being—God—that is the source of all life.

O'Connor certainly regarded an increase in consciousness—which in her stories is signified by an increase in vision—to be a growing toward Being. However, her characters typically resist this kind of rising and the spiritual convergence with others that accompanies it. This has led some commentators to conclude that O'Connor's use of the title "Everything That Rises Must Converge" is largely, if not completely, ironic. (According to one critic, nothing rises in the title story but Julian's mother's blood pressure.) It is true that O'Connor deliberately plays off the meaning of the title against numerous metaphors of non-convergent rising, and especially against her characters' desire to rise without convergence; for instance, the "rising" of Negroes is acceptable to Julian's mother only as long as there is no convergence: "they should rise, yes, but on their own side of the fence." The thrust of most of the stories, however, is to bring the protagonist to a vision of himself as he really is, and thus to make possible a true rising toward Being. That this rising is inevitably painful does not discredit its validity; rather, it emphasizes (as Teilhard's conception does not) the tension between the evolutionary thrust toward Being and the human warp that resists it—the warp which O'Connor would have called original sin.

FLANNERY O'CONNOR: STORIES

Good Country People

Besides the neutral expression that she wore when she was alone, Mrs. Freeman had two others, forward and reverse, that she used for all her human dealings. Her forward expression was steady and driving like the advance of a heavy truck. Her eyes never swerved to left or right but turned as the story turned as if they followed a yellow line down the center of it. She seldom used the other expression because it was not often necessary for her to retract a statement, but when she did, her face came to a complete stop, there was an almost imperceptible movement of her black eyes, during which they seemed to be receding, and then the observer would see that Mrs. Freeman, though she might stand there as real as several grain sacks thrown on top of each other, was no longer there in spirit. As for getting anything across to her when this was the case, Mrs. Hopewell had given it up. She might talk her head off. Mrs. Freeman could never be brought to admit herself wrong on any point. She would stand there and if she could be brought to say anything, it was something like, "Well, I wouldn't of said it was and I wouldn't of said it wasn't," or letting her gaze range over the top kitchen shelf where there was an assortment of dusty bottles, she might remark, "I see you ain't ate many of them figs you put up last summer."

They carried on their most important business in the kitchen at breakfast. Every morning Mrs. Hopewell got up at seven o'clock and lit her gas heater and Joy's. Joy was her daughter, a large blonde girl who had an artificial leg. Mrs. Hopewell thought of her as a child though she was thirty-two years old and highly educated. Joy would get up while her mother was eating and lumber into the bathroom and slam the door, and before long, Mrs. Freeman would arrive at the back door. Joy would hear her mother call, "Come on in," and then they would talk for a while in low voices that were indistinguishable in the bathroom. By the time Joy came in, they had usually finished the weather report and were on one or the other of Mrs. Freeman's daughters, Glynese or Carramae. Joy called them Glycerin and Caramel. Glynese, a redhead, was eighteen and had many admirers; Carramae, a blonde, was only fifteen but already married and pregnant. She could not keep anything on her stomach. Every morning Mrs. Freeman told Mrs. Hopewell how many times she had vomited since the last report.

Mrs. Hopewell liked to tell people that Glynese and Carramae were two of the finest girls she knew and that Mrs. Freeman was a *lady* and that she was never ashamed to take her anywhere or introduce her to anybody they might meet. Then she would tell how she had happened to hire the Freemans in the first place and how they were a godsend to her and how she had had them four years. The reason for her keeping them so long was that they were not trash. They were good country people. She had telephoned the man whose name they had given as a reference and he had told her that Mr. Freeman was a good farmer but that his wife was the nosiest woman ever to walk the earth. "She's got to be into everything," the man said. "If she don't get there before the dust settles, you can bet she's dead, that's all. She'll want to know all your business. I can stand him real good," he had said, "but me nor my wife neither could have stood that woman one more minute on this place." That had put Mrs. Hopewell off for a few days.

She had hired them in the end because there were no other applicants but she had made up her mind beforehand exactly how she would handle the woman. Since she was the type who had to be into everything, then, Mrs. Hopewell had decided, she would not only let her be into everything, she would *see to it* that she was into everything—she would give her the responsibility of everything, she would put her in charge. Mrs. Hopewell had no bad qualities of her own but she was able to use other people's in such a constructive way that she never felt the lack. She had hired the Freemans and she had kept them four years.

Nothing is perfect. This was one of Mrs. Hopewell's favorite sayings. Another was: that is life! And still another, the most important, was: well, other people have their opinions too. She would make these statements, usually at the table, in a tone of gentle insistence as if no one held them but her, and the large hulking Joy, whose constant outrage had obliterated every expression from her face, would stare just a little to the side of her, her eyes icy blue, with the look of someone who has achieved blindness by an act of will and means to keep it.

When Mrs. Hopewell said to Mrs. Freeman that life was like that, Mrs. Freeman would say, "I always said so myself." Nothing had been arrived at by anyone that had not first been arrived at by her. She was quicker than Mr. Freeman. When Mrs. Hopewell said to her after they had been on the place a while, "You know, you're the wheel behind the wheel," and winked, Mrs. Freeman had said, "I know it. I've always been quick. It's some that are quicker than others."

"Everybody is different," Mrs. Hopewell said.

"Yes, most people is," Mrs. Freeman said.

"It takes all kinds to make the world."

"I always said it did myself."

The girl was used to this kind of dialogue for breakfast and more of it for dinner; sometimes they had it for supper too. When they had no guest they ate in the kitchen because that was easier. Mrs. Freeman always managed to arrive at some point during the meal and to watch them finish it. She would stand in the doorway if it were summer but in the winter she would stand with one elbow on top of the refrigerator and look down on them, or she would stand by the gas heater, lifting the back of her skirt slightly. Occasionally she would stand against the wall and roll her head from side to side. At no time was she in any hurry to leave. All this was very trying on Mrs. Hopewell but she was a woman of great patience. She realized that nothing is perfect and that in the Freemans she had good country people and that if, in this day and age, you get good country people, you had better hang onto them.

She had had plenty of experience with trash. Before the Freemans she had averaged one tenant family a year. The wives of these farmers were not the kind you would want to be around you for very long. Mrs. Hopewell, who had divorced her husband long ago, needed someone to walk over the fields with her; and when Joy had to be impressed for these services, her remarks were usually so ugly and her face so glum that Mrs. Hopewell would say, "If you can't come pleasantly, I don't want you at all," to which the girl, standing square and rigid-shouldered with her neck thrust slightly forward, would reply, "If you want me, here I am—LIKE I AM."

Mrs. Hopewell excused this attitude because of the leg (which had been shot off in a hunting accident when Joy was ten). It was hard for Mrs. Hopewell to realize that her child was thirty-two now and that for more than twenty years she had had only one leg. She thought of her still as a child because it tore her heart to think instead of the poor stout girl in her thirties who had never danced a step or had any *normal* good times. Her name was really Joy but as soon as she was twenty-one and away from home, she had had it legally changed. Mrs. Hopewell was certain that she had thought and thought until she had hit upon the ugliest name in any language. Then she had gone and had the beautiful name, Joy, changed without telling her mother until after she had done it. Her legal name was Hulga.

When Mrs. Hopewell thought the name, Hulga, she thought of the broad blank hull of a battleship. She would not use it. She continued to call her Joy to which the girl responded but in a purely mechanical way.

Hulga had learned to tolerate Mrs. Freeman, who saved her from taking walks with her mother. Even Glynese and Carramae were useful when they occupied attention that might otherwise have been directed at her. At first she had thought she could not stand Mrs. Freeman for she had found that it was not possible to be rude to her. Mrs. Freeman would take on strange resentments and for days together she would be sullen but the source of her displeasure was always obscure; a direct attack, a positive leer, blatant ugliness to her face—these never touched her. And without warning one day, she began calling her Hulga.

She did not call her that in front of Mrs. Hopewell who would have been incensed but when she and the girl happened to be out of the house together, she would say something and add the name Hulga to the end of it, and the big spectacled Joy-Hulga would scowl and redden as if her privacy had been intruded upon. She considered the name her personal affair. She had arrived at it first purely on the basis of its ugly sound and then the full genius of its fitness had struck her. She had a vision of the name working like the ugly sweating Vulcan who stayed in the furnace and to whom, presumably, the goddess had to come when called. She saw it as the name of her highest creative act. One of her major triumphs was that her mother had not been able to turn her dust into Joy, but the greater one was that she had been able to turn it herself into Hulga. However, Mrs. Freeman's relish for using the name only irritated her. It was as if Mrs. Freeman's beady steel-pointed eyes had penetrated far enough behind her face to reach some secret fact. Something about her seemed to fascinate Mrs. Freeman and then one day Hulga realized that it was the artificial leg. Mrs. Freeman had a special fondness for the details of secret infections, hidden deformities, assaults upon children. Of diseases, she preferred the lingering or incurable. Hulga had heard Mrs. Hopewell give her the details of the hunting accident, how the leg had been literally blasted off, how she had never lost consciousness. Mrs. Freeman could listen to it any time as if it had happened an hour ago.

When Hulga stumped into the kitchen in the morning (she could walk without making the awful noise but she made it—Mrs. Hopewell was certain—because it was ugly sounding), she glanced at them and did not speak. Mrs. Hopewell would be in her red kimono with her hair tied around her head in rags. She would be sitting at the table, finishing her breakfast and Mrs. Freeman would be hanging by her elbow outward from the refrigerator, looking down at the table. Hulga always put her eggs on the stove to boil and then stood over them with her arms folded, and Mrs. Hopewell would look at her—a kind of indirect gaze divided between her and Mrs. Freeman—and would think that if she would only keep herself up a little, she wouldn't be so bad looking. There was nothing wrong with her face that a pleasant expression wouldn't help. Mrs. Hopewell said that people who looked on the bright side of things would be beautiful even if they were not.

Whenever she looked at Joy this way, she could not help but feel that it would have been better if the child had not taken the Ph.D. It had certainly not brought her out any and now that she had it, there was no more excuse for her to go to school again. Mrs. Hopewell thought it was nice for girls to go to school to have a good time but Joy had "gone through." Anyhow, she would not have been strong enough to go again. The doctors had told Mrs. Hopewell that with the best of care, Joy might see forty-five. She had a weak heart. Joy had made it plain that if it had not been for this condition, she would be far from these red hills and good country people. She would be in a university lecturing to people who knew what she was talking about. And Mrs. Hopewell could very well picture her there, looking like a scarecrow and lecturing to more of the same. Here she went about all day in a six-year-old skirt and a yellow sweat shirt with a faded cowboy on a horse embossed on it. She thought this was funny; Mrs. Hopewell thought it was idiotic and showed simply that she was still a child. She was brilliant but she didn't have a grain of sense. It seemed to Mrs. Hopewell that every year she grew less like other people and more like herself—bloated, rude, and squint-eyed. And she said such strange things! To her own mother she had said—without warning, without excuse, standing up in the middle of a meal with her face purple and her mouth half full—"Woman! do you ever look inside? Do you ever look inside and see what you are *not*? God!" she had cried sinking down again and staring at her plate, "Malebranche was right: we are not our own light. We are not our own light!" Mrs. Hopewell had no idea to this day what brought that on. She had only made the remark, hoping Joy would take it in, that a smile never hurt anyone.

The girl had taken the Ph.D. in philosophy and this left Mrs. Hopewell at a complete loss. You could say, "My daughter is a nurse," or "My daughter is a school teacher," or even, "My daughter is a chemical engineer." You could not say, "My daughter is a philosopher." That was something that had ended with the Greeks and Romans. All day Joy sat on her neck in a deep chair, reading. Sometimes she went for walks but she didn't like dogs or cats or birds or flowers or nature or nice young men. She looked at nice young men as if she could smell their stupidity.

One day Mrs. Hopewell had picked up one of the books the girl had just put down and opening it at random, she read, "Science, on the other hand, has to assert its soberness and seriousness afresh and declare that it is concerned solely with what–is. Nothing—how can it be for science anything but a horror and a phantasm? If science is right, then one thing stands firm: science wishes to know nothing of nothing. Such is after all the strictly scientific approach to Nothing. We know it by wishing to know nothing of Nothing." These words had been underlined with a blue pencil and they worked on Mrs. Hopewell like some evil incantation in gibberish. She shut the book quickly and went out of the room as if she were having a chill.

This morning when the girl came in, Mrs. Freeman was on Carramae. "She thrown up four times after supper," she said, "and was up twict in the night after three o'clock. Yesterday she didn't do nothing but ramble in the bureau drawer. All she did. Stand up there and see what she could run up on."

"She's got to eat," Mrs. Hopewell muttered, sipping her coffee, while she watched Joy's back at the stove. She was wondering what the child had said to the Bible salesman. She could not imagine what kind of a conversation she could possibly have had with him.

He was a tall gaunt hatless youth who had called yesterday to sell them a Bible. He had appeared at the door, carrying a large black suitcase that weighted him so heavily on one side that he had to brace himself against the door facing. He seemed on the point of collapse but he said in a cheerful voice, "Good morning, Mrs. Cedars!" and set the suitcase down on the mat. He was not a bad-looking young man though he had on a bright blue suit and yellow socks that were not pulled up far enough. He had prominent face bones and a streak of sticky-looking brown hair falling across his forehead.

"I'm Mrs. Hopewell," she said.

"Oh!" he said, pretending to look puzzled but with his eyes sparkling, "I saw it said 'The Cedars,' on the mailbox so I thought you was Mrs. Cedars!" and he burst out in a pleasant laugh. He picked up the satchel and under cover of a pant, he fell forward into her hall. It was rather as if the suitcase had moved first, jerking him after it. "Mrs. Hopewell!" he said and grabbed her hand. "I hope you are well!" and he laughed again and then all at once his face sobered completely. He paused and gave her a straight earnest look and said, "Lady, I've come to speak of serious things."

"Well, come in," she muttered, none too pleased because her dinner was almost ready. He came into the parlor and sat down on the edge of a straight chair and put the suitcase between his feet and glanced around the room as if he were sizing her up by it. Her silver gleamed on the two sideboards; she decided he had never been in a room as elegant as this.

"Mrs. Hopewell," he began, using her name in a way that sounded almost intimate, "I know you believe in Chrustian service."

"Well yes," she murmured.

"I know," he said and paused, looking very wise with his head cocked on one side, "that you're a good woman. Friends have told me."

Mrs. Hopewell never liked to be taken for a fool. "What are you selling?" she asked.

"Bibles," the young man said and his eye raced around the room before he added, "I see you have no family Bible in your parlor, I see that is the one lack you got!"

Mrs. Hopewell could not say, "My daughter is an atheist and won't let me keep the Bible in the parlor." She said, stiffening slightly, "I keep my Bible by my bedside." This was not the truth. It was in the attic somewhere.

"Lady," he said, "the word of God ought to be in the parlor."

"Well, I think that's a matter of taste," she began. "I think . . ."

"Lady," he said, "for a Chrustian, the word of God ought to be in every room in the house besides in his heart. I know you're a Chrustian because I can see it in every line of your face."

She stood up and said, "Well, young man, I don't want to buy a Bible and I smell my dinner burning."

He didn't get up. He began to twist his hands and looking down at them, he said softly, "Well lady, I'll tell you the truth—not many people want to buy one nowadays and besides, I know I'm real simple. I don't know how to say a thing but to say it. I'm just a country boy." He glanced up into her unfriendly face. "People like you don't like to fool with country people like me!"

"Why!" she cried, "good country people are the salt of the earth! Besides, we all have different ways of doing, it takes all kinds to make the world go 'round. That's life!"

"You said a mouthful," he said.

"Why, I think there aren't enough good country people in the world!" she said, stirred. "I think that's what's wrong with it!"

His face had brightened. "I didn't inraduce myself," he said. "I'm Manley Pointer from out in the country around Willohobie, not even from a place, just from near a place."

"You wait a minute," she said. "I have to see about my dinner." She went out to the kitchen and found Joy standing near the door where she had been listening.

"Get rid of the salt of the earth," she said, "and let's eat."

Mrs. Hopewell gave her a pained look and turned the heat down under the vegetables. "I can't be rude to anybody," she murmured and went back into the parlor.

He had opened the suitcase and was sitting with a Bible on each knee.

"You might as well put those up," she told him. "I don't want one."

"I appreciate your honesty," he said. "You don't see any more real honest people unless you go way out in the country."

"I know," she said, "real genuine folks!" Through the crack in the door she heard a groan.

"I guess a lot of boys come telling you they're working their way through college," he said, "but I'm not going to tell you that. Somehow," he said, "I don't want to go to college. I want to devote my life to Chrustian service. See," he said, lowering his voice, "I got this heart condition. I may not live long. When you know it's something wrong with you and you may not live long, well then, lady . . ." He paused, with his mouth open, and stared at her.

He and Joy had the same condition! She knew that her eyes were filling with tears but she collected herself quickly and murmured, "Won't you stay for dinner? We'd love to have you!" and was sorry the instant she heard herself say it.

"Yes mam," he said in an abashed voice, "I would sher love to do that!"

Joy had given him one look on being introduced to him and then throughout the meal had not glanced at him again. He had addressed several remarks to her, which she had pretended not to hear. Mrs. Hopewell could not understand deliberate rudeness, although she lived with it, and she felt she had always to overflow with hospitality to make up for Joy's lack of courtesy. She urged him to talk about himself and he did. He said he was the seventh child of twelve and that his father had been crushed under a tree when he himself was eight year old. He had been crushed very badly, in fact, almost cut in two and was practically not recognizable. His mother had got along the best she could by hard working and she had always seen that her children went to Sunday School and that they read the Bible every evening. He was now nineteen year old and he had been selling Bibles for four months. In that time he had sold seventy-seven Bibles and had the promise of two more sales. He wanted to become a missionary because he thought that was the way you could do most for people. "He who losest his life shall find it," he said simply and he was so sincere, so genuine and earnest that Mrs. Hopewell would not for the world have smiled. He prevented his peas from sliding onto the table by blocking them with a piece of bread which he later cleaned his plate with. She could see Joy observing sidewise how he handled his knife and fork and she saw too that every few minutes, the boy would dart a keen appraising glance at the girl as if he were trying to attract her attention.

After dinner Joy cleared the dishes off the table and disappeared and Mrs. Hopewell was left to talk with him. He told her again about his childhood and his father's accident and about various things that had happened to him. Every five minutes or so she would stifle a yawn. He sat for two hours until finally she told him she must go because she had an appointment in town. He packed his Bibles and thanked her and prepared to leave, but in the doorway he stopped and wrung her hand and said that not on any of his trips had he met a lady as nice as her and he asked if he could come again. She had said she would always be happy to see him.

Joy had been standing in the road, apparently looking at something in the distance, when he came down the steps toward her, bent to the side with his heavy valise. He stopped where she was standing and confronted her directly. Mrs. Hopewell could not hear what he said but she trembled to think what Joy would say to him. She could see that after a minute Joy said something and that then the boy began to speak again, making an excited gesture with his free hand. After a minute Joy said something else at which the boy began to speak once more. Then to her amazement, Mrs. Hopewell saw the two of them walk off together, toward the gate. Joy had walked all the way to the gate with him and Mrs. Hopewell could not imagine what they had said to each other, and she had not yet dared to ask.

Mrs. Freeman was insisting upon her attention. She had moved from the refrigerator to the heater so that Mrs. Hopewell had to turn and face her in order to seem to be listening. "Glynese gone out with Harvey Hill again last night," she said. "She had this sty."

"Hill," Mrs. Hopewell said absently, "is that the one who works in the garage?"

"Nome, he's the one that goes to chiropracter school," Mrs. Freeman said. "She had this sty. Been had it two days. So she says when he brought her in the other night he says, 'Lemme get rid of that sty for you,' and she says, 'How?' and he says, 'You just lay yourself down acrost the seat of that car and I'll show you.' So she done it and he popped her neck. Kept on a-popping it several times until she made him quit. This morning," Mrs. Freeman said, "she ain't got no sty. She ain't got no traces of a sty."

"I never heard of that before," Mrs. Hopewell said.

"He ast her to marry him before the Ordinary," Mrs. Freeman went on, "and she told him she wasn't going to be married in no *office*."

"Well, Glynese is a fine girl," Mrs. Hopewell said, "Glynese and Carramae are both fine girls."

"Carramae said when her and Lyman was married Lyman said it sure felt sacred to him. She said he said he wouldn't take five hundred dollars for being married by a preacher."

"How much would he take?" the girl asked from the stove.

"He said he wouldn't take five hundred dollars," Mrs. Freeman repeated.

"Well we all have work to do," Mrs. Hopewell said.

"Lyman said it just felt more sacred to him," Mrs. Freeman said. "The doctor wants Carramae to eat prunes. Says instead of medicine. Says them cramps is coming from pressure. You know where I think it is?"

"She'll be better in a few weeks," Mrs. Hopewell said.

"In the tube," Mrs. Freeman said. "Else she wouldn't be as sick as she is."

Hulga had cracked her two eggs into a saucer and was bringing them to the table along with a cup of coffee that she had filled too full. She sat down carefully and began to eat, meaning to keep Mrs. Freeman there by questions if for any reason she showed an inclination to leave. She could perceive her mother's eye on her. The first roundabout question would be about the Bible salesman and she did not wish to bring it on. "How did he pop her neck?" she asked.

Mrs. Freeman went into a description of how he had popped her neck. She said he owned a '55 Mercury but that Glynese said she would rather marry a man with only a '36 Plymouth who would be married by a preacher. The girl asked what if he had a '32 Plymouth and Mrs. Freeman said what Glynese had said was a '36 Plymouth.

Mrs. Hopewell said there were not many girls with Glynese's common sense. She said what she admired in those girls was their common sense. She said that reminded her that they had a nice visitor yesterday, a young man selling Bibles. "Lord," she said, "he bored me to death but he was so sincere and genuine I couldn't be rude to him. He was just good country people, you know," she said, "—just the salt of the earth."

"I seen him walk up," Mrs. Freeman said, "and then later—I seen him walk off," and Hulga could feel the slight shift in her voice, the slight insinuation, that he had not walked off alone, had he? Her face remained expressionless but the color rose into her neck and she seemed to swallow it down with the next spoonful of egg. Mrs. Freeman was looking at her as if they had a secret together.

"Well, it takes all kinds of people to make the world go 'round," Mrs. Hopewell said. "It's very good we aren't all alike."

"Some people are more alike than others," Mrs. Freeman said.

Hulga got up and stumped, with about twice the noise that was necessary, into her room and locked the door. She was to meet the Bible salesman at ten o'clock at the gate. She had thought about it half the night. She had started thinking of it as a great joke and then she had begun to see profound implications in it. She had lain in bed imagining dialogues for them that were insane on the surface but that reached below to depths that no Bible salesman would be aware of. Their conversation yesterday had been of this kind.

He had stopped in front of her and had simply stood there. His face was bony and sweaty and bright, with a little pointed nose in the center of it, and his look was different from what it had been at the dinner table. He was gazing at her with open curiosity, with fascination, like a child watching a new fantastic animal at the zoo, and he was breathing as if he had run a great distance to reach her. His gaze seemed somehow familiar but she could not think where she had been regarded with it before. For almost a minute he didn't say anything. Then on what seemed an insuck of breath, he whispered, "You ever ate a chicken that was two days old?"

The girl looked at him stonily. He might have just put this question up for consideration at the meeting of a philosophical association. "Yes," she presently replied as if she had considered it from all angles.

"It must have been mighty small!" he said triumphantly and shook all over with little nervous giggles, getting very red in the face, and subsiding finally into his gaze of complete admiration, while the girl's expression remained exactly the same.

"How old are you?" he asked softly.

She waited some time before she answered. Then in a flat voice she said, "Seventeen."

His smiles came in succession like waves breaking on the surface of a little lake. "I see you got a wooden leg," he said. "I think you're real brave. I think you're real sweet."

The girl stood blank and solid and silent.

"Walk to the gate with me," he said. "You're a brave sweet little thing and I liked you the minute I seen you walk in the door."

Hulga began to move forward.

"What's your name?" he asked, smiling down on the top of her head.

"Hulga," she said.

"Hulga," he murmured, "Hulga. Hulga. I never heard of anybody name Hulga before. You're shy, aren't you, Hulga?" he asked.

She nodded, watching his large red hand on the handle of the giant valise.

"I like girls that wear glasses," he said. "I think a lot. I'm not like these people that a serious thought don't ever enter their heads. It's because I may die."

"I may die too," she said suddenly and looked up at him. His eyes were very small and brown, glittering feverishly.

"Listen," he said, "don't you think some people was meant to meet on account of what all they got in common and all? Like they both think serious thoughts and all?" He shifted the valise to his other hand so that the hand nearest her was free. He caught hold of her elbow and shook it a little. "I don't work on Saturday," he said. "I like to walk in the woods and see what Mother Nature is wearing. O'er the hills and far away. Pic-nics and things. Couldn't we go on a pic-nic tomorrow? Say yes, Hulga," he said and gave her a dying look as if he felt his insides about to drop out of him. He had even seemed to sway slightly toward her.

During the night she had imagined that she seduced him. She imagined that the two of them walked on the place until they came to the storage barn beyond the two back fields and there, she imagined, that things came to such a pass that she very easily seduced him and that then, of course, she had to reckon with his remorse. True genius can get an idea across even to an inferior mind. She imagined that she took his remorse in hand and changed it into a deeper understanding of life. She took all his shame away and turned it into something useful.

She set off for the gate at exactly ten o'clock, escaping without drawing Mrs. Hopewell's attention. She didn't take anything to eat, forgetting that food is usually taken on a picnic. She wore a pair of slacks and a dirty white shirt, and as an afterthought, she had put some Vapex on the collar of it since she did not own any perfume. When she reached the gate no one was there.

She looked up and down the empty highway and had the furious feeling that she had been tricked, that he had only meant to make her walk to the gate after the idea of him. Then suddenly he stood up, very tall, from behind a bush on the opposite embankment. Smiling, he lifted his hat which was new and wide-brimmed. He had not worn it yesterday and she wondered if he had bought it for the occasion. It was toast-colored with a red and white band around it and was slightly too large for him. He stepped from behind the bush still carrying the black valise. He had on the same suit and the same yellow socks sucked down in his shoes from walking. He crossed the highway and said, "I knew you'd come!"

The girl wondered acidly how he had known this. She pointed to the valise and asked, "Why did you bring your Bibles?"

He took her elbow, smiling down on her as if he could not stop. "You can never tell when you'll need the word of God, Hulga," he said. She had a moment in which she doubted that this was actually happening and then they began to climb the embankment. They went down into the pasture toward the woods. The boy walked lightly by her side, bouncing on his toes. The valise did not seem to be heavy today; he even swung it. They crossed half the pasture without saying anything and then, putting his hand easily on the small of her back, he asked softly, "Where does your wooden leg join on?"

She turned an ugly red and glared at him and for an instant the boy looked abashed. "I didn't mean you no harm," he said. "I only meant you're so brave and all. I guess God takes care of you."

"No," she said, looking forward and walking fast, "I don't even believe in God."

At this he stopped and whistled. "No!" he exclaimed as if he were too astonished to say anything else.

She walked on and in a second he was bouncing at her side, fanning with his hat. "That's very unusual for a girl," he remarked, watching her out of the corner of his eye.

When they reached the edge of the wood, he put his hand on her back again and drew her against him without a word and kissed her heavily.

The kiss, which had more pressure than feeling behind it, produced that extra surge of adrenalin in the girl that enables one to carry a packed trunk out of a burning house, but in her, the power went at once to the brain. Even before he released her, her mind, clear and detached and ironic anyway, was regarding him from a great distance, with amusement but with pity. She had never been kissed before and she was pleased to discover that it was an unexceptional experience and all a matter of the mind's control. Some people might enjoy drain water if they were told it was vodka. When the boy, looking expectant but uncertain, pushed her gently away, she turned and walked on, saying nothing as if such business, for her, were common enough.

He came along panting at her side, trying to help her when he saw a root that she might trip over. He caught and held back the long swaying blades of thorn vine until she had passed beyond them. She led the way and he came breathing heavily behind her. Then they came out on a sunlit hillside, sloping softly into another one a little smaller. Beyond, they could see the rusted top of the old barn where the extra hay was stored.

The hill was sprinkled with small pink weeds. "Then you ain't saved?" he asked suddenly, stopping.

The girl smiled. It was the first time she had smiled at him at all. "In my economy," she said, "I'm saved and you are damned but I told you I didn't believe in God."

Nothing seemed to destroy the boy's look of admiration. He gazed at her now as if the fantastic animal at the zoo had put its paw through the bars and given him a loving poke. She thought he looked as if he wanted to kiss her again and she walked on before he had the chance.

"Ain't there somewhere we can sit down sometime?" he murmured, his voice softening toward the end of the sentence.

"In that barn," she said.

They made for it rapidly as if it might slide away like a train. It was a large two-story barn, cool and dark inside. The boy pointed up the ladder that led into the loft and said, "It's too bad we can't go up there."

"Why can't we?" she asked.

"Yer leg," he said reverently.

The girl gave him a contemptuous look and putting both hands on the ladder, she climbed it while he stood below, apparently awestruck. She pulled herself expertly through the opening and then looked down at him and said, "Well, come on if you're coming," and he began to climb the ladder, awkwardly bringing the suitcase with him.

"We won't need the Bible," she observed.

"You never can tell," he said, panting. After he had got into the loft, he was a few seconds catching his breath. She had sat down in a pile of straw. A wide sheath of sunlight, filled with dust particles, slanted over her. She lay back against a bale, her face turned away, looking out the front opening of the barn where hay was thrown from a wagon into the loft. The two pink-speckled hillsides lay back against a dark ridge of woods. The sky was cloudless and cold blue. The boy dropped down by her side and put one arm under her and the other over her and began methodically kissing her face, making little noises like a fish. He did not remove his hat but it was pushed far enough back not to interfere. When her glasses got in his way, he took them off of her and slipped them into his pocket.

The girl at first did not return any of the kisses but presently she began to and after she had put several on his cheek, she reached his lips and remained there, kissing him again and again as if she were trying to draw all the breath out of him. His breath was clear and sweet like a child's and the kisses were sticky like a child's. He mumbled about loving her and about knowing when he first seen her that he loved her, but the mumbling was like the sleepy fretting of a child being put to sleep by his mother. Her mind, throughout this, never stopped or lost itself for a second to her feelings. "You ain't said you love me none," he whispered finally, pulling back from her. "You got to say that."

She looked away from him off into the hollow sky and then down at a black ridge and then down farther into what appeared to be two green swelling lakes. She didn't realize he had taken her glasses but this landscape could not seem exceptional to her for she seldom paid any close attention to her surroundings.

"You got to say it," he repeated. "You got to say you love me."

She was always careful how she committed herself. "In a sense," she began, "if you use the word loosely, you might say that. But it's not a word I use. I don't have illusions. I'm one of those people who see *through* to nothing."

The boy was frowning. "You got to say it. I said it and you got to say it," he said.

The girl looked at him almost tenderly. "You poor baby," she murmured. "It's just as well you don't understand," and she pulled him by the neck, face-down, against her. "We are all damned," she said, "but some of us have taken off our blindfolds and see that there's nothing to see. It's a kind of salvation."

The boy's astonished eyes looked blankly through the ends of her hair. "Okay," he almost whined, "but do you love me or don'tcher?"

"Yes," she said and added, "in a sense. But I must tell you something. There mustn't be anything dishonest between us." She lifted his head and looked him in the eye. "I am thirty years old," she said. "I have a number of degrees."

The boy's look was irritated but dogged. "I don't care," he said. "I don't care a thing about what all you done. I just want to know if you love me or don'tcher?" and he caught her to him and wildly planted her face with kisses until she said, "Yes, yes."

"Okay then," he said, letting her go. "Prove it."

She smiled, looking dreamily out on the shifty landscape. She had seduced him without even making up her mind to try. "How?" she asked, feeling that he should be delayed a little.

He leaned over and put his lips to her ear. "Show me where your wooden leg joins on," he whispered.

The girl uttered a sharp little cry and her face instantly drained of color. The obscenity of the suggestion was not what shocked her. As a child she had sometimes been subject to feelings of shame but education had removed the last traces of that as a good surgeon scrapes for cancer; she would no more have felt it over what he was asking than she would have believed in his Bible. But she was as sensitive about the artificial leg as a peacock about his tail. No one ever touched it but her. She took care of it as someone else would his soul, in private and almost with her own eyes turned away. "No," she said.

"I known it," he muttered, sitting up. "You're just playing me for a sucker."

"Oh no no!" she cried. "It joins on at the knee. Only at the knee. Why do you want to see it?"

The boy gave her a long penetrating look. "Because," he said, "it's what makes you different. You ain't like anybody else."

She sat staring at him. There was nothing about her face or her round freezing-blue eyes to indicate that this had moved her; but she felt as if her heart had stopped and left her mind to pump her blood. She decided that for the first time in her life she was face to face with real innocence. This boy, with an instinct that came from beyond wisdom, had touched the truth about her. When after a minute, she said in a hoarse high voice, "All right," it was like surrendering to him completely. It was like losing her own life and finding it again, miraculously, in his.

Very gently he began to roll the slack leg up. The artificial limb, in a white sock and brown flat shoe, was bound in a heavy material like canvas and ended in an ugly jointure where it was attached to the stump. The boy's face and his voice were entirely reverent as he uncovered it and said, "Now show me how to take it off and on."

She took it off for him and put it back on again and then he took it off himself, handling it as tenderly as if it were a real one. "See!" he said with a delighted child's face. "Now I can do it myself!"

"Put it back on," she said. She was thinking that she would run away with him and that every night he would take the leg off and every morning put it back on again. "Put it back on," she said.

"Not yet," he murmured, setting it on its foot out of her reach. "Leave it off for a while. You got me instead."

She gave a little cry of alarm but he pushed her down and began to kiss her again. Without the leg she felt entirely dependent on him. Her brain seemed to have stopped thinking altogether and to be about some other function that it was not very good at. Different expressions raced back and forth over her face. Every now and then the boy, his eyes like two steel spikes, would glance behind him where the leg stood. Finally she pushed him off and said, "Put it back on me now."

"Wait," he said. He leaned the other way and pulled the valise toward him and opened it. It had a pale blue spotted lining and there were only two Bibles in it. He took one of these out and opened the cover of it. It was hollow and contained a pocket flask of whiskey, a pack of cards, and a small blue box with printing on it. He laid these out in front of her one at a time in an evenly spaced row, like one presenting offerings at the shrine of a goddess. He put the blue box in her hand. THIS PRODUCT TO BE USED ONLY FOR THE PREVENTION OF DISEASE, she read, and dropped it. The boy was unscrewing the top of the flask. He stopped and pointed, with a smile, to the deck of cards. It was not an ordinary deck but one with an obscene picture on the back of each card. "Take a swig," he said, offering her the bottle first. He held it in front of her, but like one mesmerized, she did not move.

Her voice when she spoke had an almost pleading sound. "Aren't you," she murmured, "aren't you just good country people?"

The boy cocked his head. He looked as if he were just beginning to understand that she might be trying to insult him. "Yeah," he said, curling his lip slightly, "but it ain't held me back none. I'm as good as you any day in the week."

"Give me my leg," she said.

He pushed it farther away with his foot. "Come on now, let's begin to have us a good time," he said coaxingly. "We ain't got to know one another good yet."

"Give me my leg!" she screamed and tried to lunge for it but he pushed her down easily.

"What's the matter with you all of a sudden?" he asked, frowning as he screwed the top on the flask and put it quickly back inside the Bible. "You just a while ago said you didn't believe in nothing. I thought you was some girl!"

Her face was almost purple. "You're a Christian!" she hissed. "You're a fine Christian! You're just like them all—say one thing and do another. You're a perfect Christian, you're . . ."

The boy's mouth was set angrily. "I hope you don't think," he said in a lofty indignant tone, "that I believe in that crap! I may sell Bibles but I know which end is up and I wasn't born yesterday and I know where I'm going!"

"Give me my leg!" she screeched. He jumped up so quickly that she barely saw him sweep the cards and the blue box back into the Bible and throw the Bible into the valise. She saw him grab the leg and then she saw it for an instant slanted forlornly across the inside of the suitcase with a Bible at either side of its opposite ends. He slammed the lid shut and snatched up the valise and swung it down the hole and then stepped through himself.

When all of him had passed but his head, he turned and regarded her with a look that no longer had any admiration in it. "I've gotten a lot of interesting things," he said. "One time I got a woman's glass eye this way. And you needn't to think you'll catch me because Pointer ain't really my name. I use a different name at every house I call at and don't stay nowhere long. And I'll tell you another thing, Hulga," he said, using the name as if he didn't think much of it, "you ain't so smart. I been believing in nothing ever since I was born!" and then the toast-colored hat disappeared down the hole and the girl was left, sitting on the straw in the dusty sunlight. When she turned her churning face toward the opening, she saw his blue figure struggling successfully over the green speckled lake.

Mrs. Hopewell and Mrs. Freeman, who were in the back pasture, digging up onions, saw him emerge a little later from the woods and head across the meadow toward the highway. "Why, that looks like that nice dull young man that tried to sell me a Bible yesterday," Mrs. Hopewell said, squinting. "He must have been selling them to the Negroes back in there. He was so simple," she said, "but I guess the world would be better off if we were all that simple."

Mrs. Freeman's gaze drove forward and just touched him before he disappeared under the hill. Then she returned her attention to the evil-smelling onion shoot she was lifting from the ground. "Some can't be that simple," she said. "I know I never could."

(1955)

QUESTIONS FOR REFLECTION

Experience

1. What was your initial response to the story's title? Did your impression of "good country people" change as you read it? Why or why not?

2. How did you respond to Hulga's loss of her artificial leg? Why?

Interpretation

3. What is the relationship between Mrs. Freeman and Mrs. Hopewell? To what extent are their names significant? What does the name change from Joy to Hulga suggest about Mrs. Hopewell's daughter?
4. What kinds of observations about life and people do Mrs. Freeman and Mrs. Hopewell make? How do the two women see themselves in relation to other people?
5. What does Hulga learn about herself and about other people through her encounter with the Bible salesman?

Evaluation

6. Which, if any, of the characters does O'Connor seem to admire, and whom does she satirize?
7. What religious values are evident in the story? What does O'Connor suggest about these values?

Connections

8. Compare O'Connor's humor in this story with her humor at the beginning of "A Good Man Is Hard to Find." Compare her use of irony in this story with that in one of her other stories.

A Good Man Is Hard to Find

The grandmother didn't want to go to Florida. She wanted to visit some of her connections in east Tennessee and she was seizing at every chance to change Bailey's mind. Bailey was the son she lived with, her only boy. He was sitting on the edge of his chair at the table, bent over the orange sports section of the *Journal*. "Now look here, Bailey," she said, "see here, read this," and she stood with one hand on her thin hip and the other rattling the newspaper at his bald head. "Here this fellow that calls himself The Misfit is aloose from the Federal Pen and headed toward Florida and you read here what it says he did to these people. Just you read it. I wouldn't take my children in any direction with a criminal like that aloose in it. I couldn't answer to my conscience if I did."

Bailey didn't look up from his reading so she wheeled around then and faced the children's mother, a young woman in slacks, whose face was as broad and innocent as a cabbage and was tied around with a green head-kerchief that had two points on the top like a rabbit's ears. She was sitting on the sofa, feeding the baby his apricots out of a jar. "The children have been to Florida before," the old lady said. "You all ought to take them somewhere else for a change so they would see different parts of the world and be broad. They never have been to east Tennessee."

The children's mother didn't seem to hear her but the eight-year-old boy, John Wesley, a stocky child with glasses, said, "If you don't want to go to Florida, why dontcha stay at home?" He and the little girl, June Star, were reading the funny papers on the floor.

"She wouldn't stay at home to be queen for a day," June Star said without raising her yellow head.

"Yes and what would you do if this fellow, The Misfit, caught you?" the grandmother asked.

"I'd smack his face," John Wesley said.

"She wouldn't stay at home for a million bucks," June Star said. "Afraid she'd miss something. She has to go everywhere we go."

"All right, Miss," the grandmother said. "Just remember that the next time you want me to curl your hair."

June Star said her hair was naturally curly.

The next morning the grandmother was the first one in the car, ready to go. She had her big black valise that looked like the head of a hippopotamus in one corner, and underneath it she was hiding a basket with Pity Sing, the cat, in it. She didn't intend for the cat to be left alone in the house for three days because he would miss her too much and she was afraid he might brush against one of the gas burners and accidentally asphyxiate himself. Her son, Bailey, didn't like to arrive at a motel with a cat.

She sat in the middle of the back seat with John Wesley and June Star on either side of her. Bailey and the children's mother and the baby sat in front and they left Atlanta at eight forty-five with the mileage on the car at 55890. The grandmother wrote this down because she thought it would be interesting to say how many miles they had been when they got back. It took them twenty minutes to reach the outskirts of the city.

The old lady settled herself comfortably, removing her white cotton gloves and putting them up with her purse on the shelf in front of the back window. The children's mother still had on slacks and still had her head tied up in a green kerchief, but the grandmother had on a navy blue straw sailor hat with a bunch of white violets on the brim and a navy blue dress with a small white dot in the print. Her collars and cuffs were white organdy trimmed with lace and at her neckline she had pinned a purple spray of cloth violets containing a sachet. In case of an accident, anyone seeing her dead on the highway would know at once that she was a lady.

She said she thought it was going to be a good day for driving, neither too hot nor too cold, and she cautioned Bailey that the speed limit was fifty-five miles an hour and that the patrolmen hid themselves behind billboards and small clumps of trees and sped out after you before you had a chance to slow down. She pointed out interesting details of the scenery: Stone Mountain; the blue granite that in some places came up to both sides of the highway; the brilliant red clay banks slightly streaked with purple; and the various crops that made rows of green lace-work on the ground. The trees were full of silver-white sunlight and the meanest of them sparkled. The children were reading comic magazines and their mother had gone back to sleep.

"Let's go through Georgia fast so we won't have to look at it much," John Wesley said.

"If I were a little boy," said the grandmother, "I wouldn't talk about my native state that way. Tennessee has the mountains and Georgia has the hills."

"Tennessee is just a hillbilly dumping ground," John Wesley said, "and Georgia is a lousy state too."

"You said it," June Star said.

"In my time," said the grandmother, folding her thin veined fingers, "children were more respectful of their native states and their parents and everything else. People did right then. Oh look at the cute little pickaninny!" she said and pointed to a Negro child standing in the door of a shack. "Wouldn't that make a picture, now?" she asked and they all turned and looked at the little Negro out of the back window. He waved.

"He didn't have any britches on," June Star said.

"He probably didn't have any," the grandmother explained. "Little niggers in the country don't have things like we do. If I could paint, I'd paint that picture," she said.

The children exchanged comic books.

The grandmother offered to hold the baby and the children's mother passed him over the front seat to her. She set him on her knee and bounced him and told him about the things they were passing. She rolled her eyes and screwed up her mouth and stuck her leathery thin face into his smooth bland one. Occasionally he gave her a far-away smile. They passed a large cotton field with five or six graves fenced in the middle of it, like a small island. "Look at the graveyard!" the grandmother said, pointing it out. "That was the old family burying ground. That belonged to the plantation."

"Where's the plantation?" John Wesley asked.

"Gone With the Wind," said the grandmother. "Ha. Ha."

When the children finished all the comic books they had brought, they opened the lunch and ate it. The grandmother ate a peanut butter sandwich and an olive and would not let the children throw the box and the paper napkins out the window. When there was nothing else to do they played a game by choosing a cloud and making the other two guess what shape it suggested. John Wesley took one of the shape of a cow and June Star guessed a cow and John Wesley said, no, an automobile, and June Star said he didn't play fair, and they began to slap each other over the grandmother.

The grandmother said she would tell them a story if they would keep quiet. When she told a story, she rolled her eyes and waved her head and was very dramatic. She said once when she was a maiden lady she had been courted by a Mr. Edgar Atkins Teagarden from Jasper, Georgia. She said he was a very good-looking man and a gentleman and that he brought her a watermelon every Saturday afternoon with his initials cut in it, E. A. T. Well, one Saturday, she said, Mr. Teagarden brought the watermelon and there was nobody at home and he left it on the front porch and returned in his buggy to Jasper, but she never got the watermelon, she said, because a nigger boy ate it when he saw the initials, E. A. T.! This story tickled John Wesley's funny bone and he giggled and giggled but June Star didn't think it was any good. She said she wouldn't marry a man that just brought her a watermelon on Saturday. The grandmother said she would have done well to marry Mr. Teagarden because he was a gentleman and had bought Coca-Cola stock when it first came out and that he had died only a few years ago, a very wealthy man.

They stopped at The Tower for barbecued sandwiches. The Tower was a part stucco and part wood filling station and dance hall set in a clearing outside of Timothy. A fat man named Red Sammy Butts ran it and there were signs stuck here and there on the building and for miles up and down the highway saying, TRY RED SAMMY'S FAMOUS BARBECUE. NONE LIKE FAMOUS RED SAMMY'S! RED SAM!

THE FAT BOY WITH THE HAPPY LAUGH! A VETERAN! RED SAMMY'S YOUR MAN!

Red Sammy was lying on the bare ground outside The Tower with his head under a truck while a gray monkey about a foot high, chained to a small chinaberry tree, chattered nearby. The monkey sprang back into the tree and got on the highest limb as soon as he saw the children jump out of the car and run toward him.

Inside, The Tower was a long dark room with a counter at one end and tables at the other and dancing space in the middle. They sat down at a board table next to the nickelodeon and Red Sam's wife, a tall burnt-brown woman with hair and eyes lighter than her skin, came and took their order. The children's mother put a dime in the machine and played "The Tennessee Waltz," and the grandmother said that tune always made her want to dance. She asked Bailey if he would like to dance but he only glared at her. He didn't have a naturally sunny disposition like she did and trips made him nervous. The grandmother's brown eyes were very bright. She swayed her head from side to side and pretended she was dancing in her chair. June Star said play something she could tap to so the children's mother put in another dime and played a fast number and June Star stepped out onto the dance floor and did her tap routine.

"Ain't she cute?" Red Sam's wife said, leaning over the counter. "Would you like to come be my little girl?"

"No I certainly wouldn't," June Star said. "I wouldn't live in a broken-down place like this for a million bucks!" and she ran back to the table.

"Ain't she cute?" the woman repeated, stretching her mouth politely.

"Aren't you ashamed?" hissed the grandmother.

Red Sam came in and told his wife to quit lounging on the counter and hurry up with these people's order. His khaki trousers reached just to his hip bones and his stomach hung over them like a sack of meal swaying under his shirt. He came over and sat down at a table nearby and let out a combination sigh and yodel. "You can't win," he said. "You can't win," and he wiped his sweating red face off with a gray handkerchief. "These days you don't know who to trust," he said. "Ain't that the truth?"

"People are certainly not nice like they used to be," said the grandmother.

"Two fellers come in here last week," Red Sammy said, "driving a Chrysler. It was a old beat-up car but it was a good one and these boys looked all right to me. Said they worked at the mill and you know I let them fellers charge the gas they bought? Now why did I do that?"

"Because you're a good man!" the grandmother said at once.

"Yes'm, I suppose so," Red Sam said as if he were struck with this answer.

His wife brought the orders, carrying the five plates all at once without a tray, two in each hand and one balanced on her arm. "It isn't a soul in this green world of God's that you can trust," she said. "And I don't count nobody out of that, not nobody," she repeated, looking at Red Sammy.

"Did you read about that criminal, The Misfit, that's escaped?" asked the grandmother.

"I wouldn't be a bit surprised if he didn't attact this place right here," said the woman. "If he hears about it being here, I wouldn't be none surprised to see him. If he hears it's two cent in the cash register, I wouldn't be a tall surprised if he . . ."

"That'll do," Red Sam said. "Go bring these people their Co'-Colas," and the woman went off to get the rest of the order.

"A good man is hard to find," Red Sammy said. "Everything is getting terrible. I remember the day you could go off and leave your screen door unlatched. Not no more."

He and the grandmother discussed better times. The old lady said that in her opinion Europe was entirely to blame for the way things were now. She said the way Europe acted you would think we were made of money and Red Sam said it was no use talking about it, she was exactly right. The children ran outside into the white sunlight and looked at the monkey in the lacy chinaberry tree. He was busy catching fleas on himself and biting each one carefully between his teeth as if it were a delicacy.

They drove off again into the hot afternoon. The grandmother took cat naps and woke up every few minutes with her own snoring. Outside of Toombsboro she woke up and recalled an old plantation that she had visited in this neighborhood once when she was a young lady. She said the house had six white columns across the front and that there was an avenue of oaks leading up to it and two little wooden trellis arbors on either side in front where you sat down with your suitor after a stroll in the garden. She recalled exactly which road to turn off to get to it. She knew that Bailey would not be willing to lose any time looking at an old house, but the more she talked about it, the more she wanted to see it once again and find out if the little twin arbors were still standing. "There was a secret panel in this house," she said craftily, not telling the truth but wishing that she were, "and the story went that all the family silver was hidden in it when Sherman came through but it was never found . . ."

"Hey!" John Wesley said. "Let's go see it! We'll find it! We'll poke all the woodwork and find it! Who lives there? Where do you turn off at? Hey Pop, can't we turn off there?"

"We never have seen a house with a secret panel!" June Star shrieked. "Let's go to the house with the secret panel! Hey Pop, can't we go see the house with the secret panel!"

"It's not far from here, I know," the grandmother said. "It wouldn't take over twenty minutes."

Bailey was looking straight ahead. His jaw was as rigid as a horseshoe. "No," he said.

The children began to yell and scream that they wanted to see the house with the secret panel. John Wesley kicked the back of the front seat and June Star hung over her mother's shoulder and whined desperately into her ear that they never had any fun even on their vacation, that they could never do what THEY wanted to do. The baby began to scream and John Wesley kicked the back of the seat so hard that his father could feel the blows in his kidney.

"All right!" he shouted and drew the car to a stop at the side of the road. "Will you all shut up? Will you all just shut up for one second? If you don't shut up, we won't go anywhere."

"It would be very educational for them," the grandmother murmured.

"All right," Bailey said, "but get this: this is the only time we're going to stop for anything like this. This is the one and only time."

"The dirt road that you have to turn down is about a mile back," the grandmother directed. "I marked it when we passed."

"A dirt road," Bailey groaned.

After they had turned around and were headed toward the dirt road, the grandmother recalled other points about the house, the beautiful glass over the front doorway and the candle-lamp in the hall. John Wesley said that the secret panel was probably in the fireplace.

"You can't go inside this house," Bailey said. "You don't know who lives there."

"While you all talk to the people in front, I'll run around behind and get in a window," John Wesley suggested.

"We'll all stay in the car," his mother said.

They turned onto the dirt road and the car raced roughly along in a swirl of pink dust. The grandmother recalled the times when there were no paved roads and thirty miles was a day's journey. The dirt road was hilly and there were sudden washes in it and sharp curves on dangerous embankments. All at once they would be on a hill, looking down over the blue tops of trees for miles around, then the next minute, they would be in a red depression with the dust-coated trees looking down on them.

"This place had better turn up in a minute," Bailey said, "or I'm going to turn around."

The road looked as if no one had traveled on it in months.

"It's not much farther," the grandmother said and just as she said it, a horrible thought came to her. The thought was so embarrassing that she turned red in the face and her eyes dilated and her feet jumped up, upsetting her valise in the corner. The instant the valise moved, the newspaper top she had over the basket under it rose with a snarl and Pitty Sing, the cat, sprang onto Bailey's shoulder.

The children were thrown to the floor and their mother, clutching the baby, was thrown out the door onto the ground; the old lady was thrown into the front seat. The car turned over once and landed right-side-up in a gulch off the side of the road. Bailey remained in the driver's seat with the cat—gray-striped with a broad white face and an orange nose—clinging to his neck like a caterpillar.

As soon as the children saw they could move their arms and legs, they scrambled out of the car, shouting, "We've had an ACCIDENT!" The grandmother was curled up under the dashboard, hoping she was injured so that Bailey's wrath would not come down on her all at once. The horrible thought she had had before the accident was that the house she had remembered so vividly was not in Georgia but in Tennessee.

Bailey removed the cat from his neck with both hands and flung it out the window against the side of a pine tree. Then he got out of the car and started looking for the children's mother. She was sitting against the side of the red gutted ditch, holding the screaming baby, but she only had a cut down her face and a broken shoulder. "We've had an ACCIDENT!" the children screamed in a frenzy of delight.

"But nobody's killed," June Star said with disappointment as the grandmother limped out of the car, her hat still pinned to her head but the broken front brim standing up at a jaunty angle and the violet spray hanging off the side. They all sat down in the ditch, except the children, to recover from the shock. They were all shaking.

"Maybe a car will come along," said the children's mother hoarsely.

"I believe I have injured an organ," said the grandmother, pressing her side, but no one answered her. Bailey's teeth were clattering. He had on a yellow sport shirt with bright blue parrots designed in it and his face was as yellow as the shirt. The grandmother decided that she would not mention that the house was in Tennessee.

The road was about ten feet above and they could see only the tops of the trees on the other side of it. Behind the ditch they were sitting in there were more woods, tall and dark and deep. In a few minutes they saw a car some distance away on top of a hill, coming slowly as if the occupants were watching them. The grandmother stood up and waved both arms dramatically to attract their attention. The car continued to come on slowly, disappeared around a bend and appeared again, moving even slower, on top of the hill they had gone over. It was a big black battered hearse-like automobile. There were three men in it.

It came to a stop just over them and for some minutes, the driver looked down with a steady expressionless gaze to where they were sitting, and didn't speak. Then he turned his head and muttered something to the other two and they got out. One was a fat boy in black trousers and a red sweat shirt with a silver stallion embossed on the front of it. He moved around on the right side of them and stood staring, his mouth partly open in a kind of loose grin. The other had on khaki pants and a blue striped coat and a gray hat pulled down very low, hiding most of his face. He came around slowly on the left side. Neither spoke.

The driver got out of the car and stood by the side of it, looking down at them. He was an older man than the other two. His hair was just beginning to gray and he wore silver-rimmed spectacles that gave him a scholarly look. He had a long creased face and didn't have on any shirt or undershirt. He had on blue jeans that were too tight for him and was holding a black hat and a gun. The two boys also had guns.

"We've had an ACCIDENT!" the children screamed.

The grandmother had the peculiar feeling that the bespectacled man was someone she knew. His face was as familiar to her as if she had known him all her life but she could not recall who he was. He moved away from the car and began to come down the embankment, placing his feet carefully so that he wouldn't slip. He had on tan and white shoes and no socks, and his ankles were red and thin. "Good afternoon," he said. "I see you all had you a little spill."

"We turned over twice!" said the grandmother.

"Oncet," he corrected. "We seen it happen. Try their car and see will it run, Hiram," he said quietly to the boy with the gray hat.

"What you got that gun for?" John Wesley asked. "Whatcha gonna do with that gun?"

"Lady," the man said to the children's mother, "would you mind calling them children to sit down by you? Children make me nervous. I want all you to sit down right together there where you're at."

"What are you telling US what to do for?" June Star asked.

Behind them the line of woods gaped like a dark open mouth. "Come here," said their mother.

"Look here now," Bailey began suddenly, "we're in a predicament! We're in . . ."

The grandmother shrieked. She scrambled to her feet and stood staring. "You're The Misfit!" she said. "I recognized you at once!"

"Yes'm," the man said, smiling slightly as if he were pleased in spite of himself to be known, "but it would have been better for all of you, lady, if you hadn't of reckernized me."

Bailey turned his head sharply and said something to his mother that shocked even the children. The old lady began to cry and The Misfit reddened.

"Lady," he said, "don't you get upset. Sometimes a man says things he don't mean. I don't reckon he meant to talk to you thataway."

"You wouldn't shoot a lady, would you?" the grandmother said and removed a clean handkerchief from her cuff and began to slap at her eyes with it.

The Misfit pointed the toe of his shoe into the ground and made a little hole and then covered it up again. "I would hate to have to," he said.

"Listen," the grandmother almost screamed, "I know you're a good man. You don't look a bit like you have common blood. I know you must come from nice people!"

"Yes mam," he said, "finest people in the world." When he smiled he showed a row of strong white teeth. "God never made a finer woman than my mother and my daddy's heart was pure gold," he said. The boy with the red sweat shirt had come around behind them and was standing with his gun at his hip. The Misfit squatted down on the ground. "Watch them children, Bobby Lee," he said. "You know they make me nervous." He looked at the six of them huddled together in front of him and he seemed to be embarrassed as if he couldn't think of anything to say. "Ain't a cloud in the sky," he remarked, looking up at it. "Don't see no sun but don't see no cloud neither."

"Yes, it's a beautiful day," said the grandmother. "Listen," she said, "you shouldn't call yourself The Misfit because I know you're a good man at heart. I can just look at you and tell."

"Hush!" Bailey yelled. "Hush! Everybody shut up and let me handle this!" He was squatting in the position of a runner about to sprint forward but he didn't move.

"I pre-chate that, lady," The Misfit said and drew a little circle in the ground with the butt of his gun.

"It'll take a half a hour to fix this here car," Hiram called, looking over the raised hood of it.

"Well, first you and Bobby Lee get him and that little boy to step over yonder with you," The Misfit said, pointing to Bailey and John Wesley. "The boys want to ast you something," he said to Bailey. "Would you mind stepping back in them woods there with them?"

"Listen," Bailey began, "we're in a terrible predicament! Nobody realizes what this is," his voice cracked. His eyes were as blue and intense as the parrots in his shirt and he remained perfectly still.

The grandmother reached up to adjust her hat brim as if she were going to the woods with him but it came off in her hand. She stood staring at it and after a second she let it fall on the ground. Hiram pulled Bailey up by the arm as if he were assisting an old man. John Wesley caught hold of his father's hand and Bobby Lee followed. They went off toward the woods and just as they reached the dark edge, Bailey turned and supporting himself against a gray naked pine trunk, he shouted, "I'll be back in a minute, Mamma, wait on me!"

"Come back this instant!" his mother shrilled but they all disappeared into the woods.

"Bailey Boy!" the grandmother called in a tragic voice but she found she was looking at The Misfit squatting on the ground in front of her. "I just know you're a good man," she said desperately. "You're not a bit common!"

"Nome, I ain't a good man," The Misfit said after a second as if he had considered her statement carefully, "but I ain't the worst in the world neither. My daddy said I was a different breed of dog from my brothers and sisters. 'You know,' Daddy said, 'it's some that can live their whole life out without asking about it and it's others has to know why it is, and this boy is one of the latters. He's going to be into everything!'" He put on his black hat and looked up suddenly and then away deep into the woods as if he were embarrassed again. "I'm sorry I don't have on a shirt before you ladies," he said, hunching his shoulders slightly. "We buried our clothes that we had on when we escaped and we're just making do until we can get better. We borrowed these from some folks we met," he explained.

"That's perfectly all right," the grandmother said. "Maybe Bailey has an extra shirt in his suitcase."

"I'll look and see terrectly," The Misfit said.

"Where are they taking him?" the children's mother screamed.

"Daddy was a card himself," The Misfit said. "You couldn't put anything over on him. He never got in trouble with the Authorities though. Just had the knack of handling them."

"You could be honest too if you'd only try," said the grandmother. "Think how wonderful it would be to settle down and live a comfortable life and not have to think about somebody chasing you all the time."

The Misfit kept scratching in the ground with the butt of his gun as if he were thinking about it. "Yes'm, somebody is always after you," he murmured.

The grandmother noticed how thin his shoulder blades were just behind his hat because she was standing up looking down on him. "Do you ever pray?" she asked.

He shook his head. All she saw was the black hat wiggle between his shoulder blades. "Nome," he said.

There was a pistol shot from the woods, followed closely by another. Then silence. The old lady's head jerked around. She could hear the wind move through the tree tops like a long satisfied insuck of breath. "Bailey Boy!" she called.

"I was a gospel singer for a while," The Misfit said. "I been most everything. Been in the arm service, both land and sea, at home and abroad, been twice married, been an undertaker, been with the railroads, plowed Mother Earth, been in a tornado, seen a man burnt alive oncet," and looked up at the children's mother and the little girl who were sitting close together, their faces white and their eyes glassy; "I even seen a woman flogged," he said.

"Pray, pray," the grandmother began, "pray, pray . . ."

"I never was a bad boy that I remember of," The Misfit said in an almost dreamy voice, "but somewheres along the line I done something wrong and got sent to the penitentiary. I was buried alive," and he looked up and held her attention to him by a steady stare.

"That's when you should have started to pray," she said. "What did you do to get sent to the penitentiary that first time?"

"Turn to the right, it was a wall," The Misfit said, looking up again at the cloudless sky. "Turn to the left, it was a wall. Look up it was a ceiling, look down it was a floor. I forget what I done, lady. I set there and set there, trying to remember what it was I done and I ain't recalled it to this day. Oncet in a while, I would think it was coming to me, but it never come."

"Maybe they put you in by mistake," the old lady said vaguely.

"Nome," he said. "It wasn't no mistake. They had the papers on me."

"You must have stolen something," she said.

The Misfit sneered slightly. "Nobody had nothing I wanted," he said. "It was a head-doctor at the penitentiary said what I had done was kill my daddy but I know that for a lie. My daddy died in nineteen ought nineteen of the epidemic flu and I never had a thing to do with it. He was buried in the Mount Hopewell Baptist churchyard and you can go there and see for yourself."

"If you would pray," the old lady said, "Jesus would help you."

"That's right," The Misfit said.

"Well then, why don't you pray?" she asked trembling with delight suddenly.

"I don't want no hep," he said. "I'm doing all right by myself."

Bobby Lee and Hiram came ambling back from the woods. Bobby Lee was dragging a yellow shirt with bright blue parrots in it.

"Throw me that shirt, Bobby Lee," The Misfit said. The shirt came flying at him and landed on his shoulder and he put it on. The grandmother couldn't name what the shirt reminded her of. "No, lady," The Misfit said while he was buttoning it up, "I found out the crime don't matter. You can do one thing or you can do another, kill a man or take a tire off his car, because sooner or later you're going to forget what it was you done and just be punished for it."

The children's mother had begun to make heaving noises as if she couldn't get her breath. "Lady," he asked, "would you and that little girl like to step off yonder with Bobby Lee and Hiram and join your husband?"

"Yes, thank you," the mother said faintly. Her left arm dangled helplessly and she was holding the baby, who had gone to sleep, in the other. "Hep that lady up, Hiram," The Misfit said as she struggled to climb out of the ditch, "and Bobby Lee, you hold onto that little girl's hand."

"I don't want to hold hands with him," June Star said. "He reminds me of a pig."

The fat boy blushed and laughed and caught her by the arm and pulled her off into the woods after Hiram and her mother.

Alone with The Misfit, the grandmother found that she had lost her voice. There was not a cloud in the sky nor any sun. There was nothing around her but woods. She wanted to tell him that he must pray. She opened and closed her mouth several times before anything came out. Finally she found herself saying, "Jesus, Jesus," meaning, Jesus will help you, but the way she was saying it, it sounded as if she might be cursing.

"Yes'm," The Misfit said as if he agreed. "Jesus thrown everything off balance. It was the same case with Him as with me except He hadn't committed any crime and they could prove I had committed one because they had the papers on me. Of course," he said, "they never shown me my papers. That's why I sign myself now. I said long ago, you get you a signature and sign everything you do and keep a copy of it. Then you'll know what you done and you can hold up the crime to the punishment and see do they match and in the end you'll have something to prove you ain't been treated right. I call myself The Misfit," he said, "because I can't make what all I done wrong fit what all I gone through in punishment."

There was a piercing scream from the woods, followed closely by a pistol report. "Does it seem right to you, lady, that one is punished a heap and another ain't punished at all?"

"Jesus!" the old lady cried. "You've got good blood! I know you wouldn't shoot a lady! I know you come from nice people! Pray! Jesus, you ought not to shoot a lady. I'll give you all the money I've got!"

"Lady," The Misfit said, looking beyond her far into the woods, "there never was a body that give the undertaker a tip."

There were two more pistol reports and the grandmother raised her head like a parched old turkey hen crying for water and called, "Bailey Boy, Bailey Boy!" as if her heart would break.

"Jesus was the only One that ever raised the dead." The Misfit continued, "and He shouldn't have done it. He thrown everything off balance. If He did what He said, then it's nothing for you to do but throw away everything and follow him, and if He didn't, then it's nothing for you to do but enjoy the few minutes you got left the best way you can—by killing somebody or burning down his house or doing some other meanness to him. No pleasure but meanness," he said and his voice had become almost a snarl.

"Maybe He didn't raise the dead," the old lady mumbled, not knowing what she was saying and feeling so dizzy that she sank down in the ditch with her legs twisted under her.

"I wasn't there so I can't say He didn't," The Misfit said. "I wisht I had of been there," he said, hitting the ground with his fist. "It ain't right I wasn't there because if I had of been there I would of known. Listen lady," he said in a high voice, "if I had of been there I would of known and I wouldn't be like I am now." His voice seemed about to crack and the grandmother's head cleared for an instant. She saw the man's face twisted close to her own as if he were going to cry and she murmured, "Why you're one of my babies. You're one of my own children!" She reached out and touched him on the shoulder. The Misfit sprang back as if a snake had bitten him and shot her three times through the chest. Then he put his gun down on the ground and took off his glasses and began to clean them.

Hiram and Bobby Lee returned from the woods and stood over the ditch, looking down at the grandmother who half sat and half lay in a puddle of blood with her legs crossed under her like a child's and her face smiling up at the cloudless sky.

Without his glasses, The Misfit's eyes were red-rimmed and pale and defenseless looking. "Take her off and throw her where you thrown the others," he said, picking up the cat that was rubbing itself against his leg.

"She was a talker, wasn't she?" Bobby Lee said, sliding down the ditch with a yodel.

"She would have been a good woman," The Misfit said, "if it had been somebody there to shoot her every minute of her life."

"Some fun!" Bobby Lee said.

"Shut up, Bobby Lee," The Misfit said. "It's no real pleasure in life."

(1955)

QUESTIONS FOR REFLECTION

Experience

1. Did you enjoy the opening section of the story? When did your perception of the kind of story you were reading change—if it did?
2. How did you respond to the Misfit's behavior? To his speech?

Interpretation

3. How does O'Connor characterize the grandmother? What do we learn about her from her conversation with the Misfit? What do we learn about him? What is his favorite saying, and what sense do you make of it?
4. How do you explain the story's title?

Evaluation

5. What religious qualities or elements emerge in this story? How, as the Misfit says, has Jesus "thrown everything off balance"?
6. In what sense could the grandmother have been a good woman if, as the Misfit says, there was "somebody there to shoot her every minute of her life"?

Connections

7. Compare this story's use of violence with that in Frank O'Connor's "Guests of the Nation" or Poe's "The Black Cat."

Everything That Rises Must Converge

Her doctor had told Julian's mother that she must lose twenty pounds on account of her blood pressure, so on Wednesday nights Julian had to take her downtown on the bus for a reducing class at the Y. The reducing class was designed for working girls over fifty, who weighed from 165 to 200 pounds. His mother was one of the slimmer ones, but she said ladies did not tell their age or weight. She would not ride the buses by herself at night since they had been integrated, and because the reducing class was one of her few pleasures, necessary for her health, and *free,* she said Julian could at least put himself out to take her, considering all she did for him. Julian did not like to consider all she did for him, but every Wednesday night he braced himself and took her.

She was almost ready to go, standing before the hall mirror, putting on her hat, while he, his hands behind him, appeared pinned to the door frame, waiting like Saint Sebastian for the arrows to begin piercing him. The hat was new and had cost her seven dollars and a half. She kept saying, "Maybe I shouldn't have paid that for it. No, I shouldn't have. I'll take it off and return it tomorrow. I shouldn't have bought it."

Julian raised his eyes to heaven. "Yes, you should have bought it," he said. "Put it on and let's go." It was a hideous hat. A purple velvet flap came down on one side of it and stood up on the other; the rest of it was green and looked like a cushion with the stuffing out. He decided it was less comical than jaunty and pathetic. Everything that gave her pleasure was small and depressed him.

She lifted the hat one more time and set it down slowly on top of her head. Two wings of gray hair protruded on either side of her florid face, but her eyes, sky-blue, were as innocent and untouched by experience as they must have been when she was ten. Were it not that she was a widow who had struggled fiercely to feed and clothe and put him through school and who was supporting him still, "until he got on his feet," she might have been a little girl that he had to take to town.

"It's all right, it's all right," he said. "Let's go." He opened the door himself and started down the walk to get her going. The sky was a dying violet and the houses stood out darkly against it, bulbous liver-colored monstrosities of a uniform ugliness though no two were alike. Since this had been a fashionable neighborhood forty years ago, his mother persisted in thinking they did well to have an apartment in it. Each house had a narrow collar of dirt around it in which sat, usually, a grubby child. Julian walked with his hands in his pockets, his head down and thrust forward and his eyes glazed with the determination to make himself completely numb during the time he would be sacrificed to her pleasure.

The door closed and he turned to find the dumpy figure, surmounted by the atrocious hat, coming toward him. "Well," she said, "you only live once and paying a little more for it, I at least won't meet myself coming and going."

"Some day I'll start making money," Julian said gloomily—he knew he never would—"and you can have one of those jokes whenever you take the fit." But first they would move. He visualized a place where the nearest neighbors would be three miles away on either side.

"I think you're doing fine," she said, drawing on her gloves. "You've only been out of school a year. Rome wasn't built in a day."

She was one of the few members of the Y reducing class who arrived in hat and gloves and who had a son who had been to college. "It takes time," she said, "and the world is in such a mess. This hat looked better on me than any of the others, though when she brought it out I said, 'Take that thing back. I wouldn't have it on my head,' and she said, 'Now wait till you see it on,' and when she put it on me, I said, 'we-ull,' and she said, 'If you ask me, that hat does something for you and you do something for that hat, and besides,' she said, 'with that hat, you won't meet yourself coming and going.'"

Julian thought he could have stood his lot better if she had been selfish, if she had been an old hag who drank and screamed at him. He walked along, saturated in depression, as if in the midst of his martyrdom he had lost his faith. Catching sight of his long, hopeless, irritated face, she stopped suddenly with a grief-stricken look, and pulled back on his arm. "Wait on me," she said. "I'm going back to the house and take this thing off and tomorrow I'm going to return it. I was out of my head. I can pay the gas bill with the seven-fifty."

He caught her arm in a vicious grip. "You are not going to take it back," he said. "I like it."

"Well," she said, "I don't think I ought . . ."

"Shut up and enjoy it," he muttered, more depressed than ever.

"With the world in the mess it's in," she said, "it's a wonder we can enjoy anything. I tell you, the bottom rail is on the top."

Julian sighed.

"Of course," she said, "if you know who you are, you can go anywhere." She said this every time he took her to the reducing class. "Most of them in it are not our kind of people," she said, "but I can be gracious to anybody. I know who I am."

"They don't give a damn for your graciousness," Julian said savagely. "Knowing who you are is good for one generation only. You haven't the foggiest idea where you stand now or who you are."

She stopped and allowed her eyes to flash at him. "I most certainly do know who I am," she said, "and if you don't know who you are, I'm ashamed of you."

"Oh hell," Julian said.

"Your great-grandfather was a former governor of this state," she said. "Your grandfather was a prosperous landowner. Your grandmother was a Godhigh."

"Will you look around you," he said tensely, "and see where you are now?" and he swept his arm jerkily out to indicate the neighborhood, which the growing darkness at least made less dingy.

"You remain what you are," she said. "Your great-grandfather had a plantation and two hundred slaves."

"There are no more slaves," he said irritably.

"They were better off when they were," she said. He groaned to see that she was off on that topic. She rolled onto it every few days like a train on an open track. He knew every stop, every junction, every swamp along the way, and knew the exact point at which her conclusion would roll majestically into the station: "It's ridiculous. It's simply not realistic. They should rise, yes, but on their own side of the fence."

"Let's skip it," Julian said.

"The ones I feel sorry for," she said, "are the ones that are half white. They're tragic."

"Will you skip it?"

"Suppose we were half white. We would certainly have mixed feelings."

"I have mixed feelings now," he groaned.

"Well let's talk about something pleasant," she said. "I remember going to Grandpa's when I was a little girl. Then the house had double stairways that went up to what was really the second floor—all the cooking was done on the first. I used to like to stay down in the kitchen on account of the way the walls smelled. I would sit with my nose pressed against the plaster and take deep breaths. Actually the place belonged to the Godhighs but your grandfather Chestny paid the mortgage and saved it for them. They were in reduced circumstances," she said, "but reduced or not, they never forgot who they were."

"Doubtless that decayed mansion reminded them," Julian muttered. He never spoke of it without contempt or thought of it without longing. He had seen it once when he was a child before it had been sold. The double stairways had rotted and been torn down. Negroes were living in it. But it remained in his mind as his mother had known it. It appeared in his dreams regularly. He would stand on the wide porch, listening to the rustle of oak leaves, then wander through the high-ceilinged hall into the parlor that opened onto it and gaze at the worn rugs and faded draperies. It occurred to him that it was he, not she, who could have appreciated it. He preferred its threadbare elegance to anything he could name and it was because of it that all the neighborhoods they had lived in had been a torment to him—whereas she had hardly known the difference. She called her insensitivity "being adjustable."

"And I remember the old darky who was my nurse, Caroline. There was no better person in the world. I've always had a great respect for my colored friends," she said. "I'd do anything in the world for them and they'd . . ."

"Will you for God's sake get off that subject?" Julian said. When he got on a bus by himself, he made it a point to sit down beside a Negro, in reparation as it were for his mother's sins.

"You're mighty touchy tonight," she said. "Do you feel all right?"

"Yes I feel all right," he said. "Now lay off."

She pursed her lips. "Well, you certainly are in a vile humor," she observed. "I just won't speak to you at all."

They had reached the bus stop. There was no bus in sight and Julian, his hands still jammed in his pockets and his head thrust forward, scowled down the empty street. The frustration of having to wait on the bus as well as ride on it began to creep up his neck like a hot hand. The presence of his mother was borne in upon him as she gave a pained sigh. He looked at her bleakly. She was holding herself very erect under the preposterous hat, wearing it like a banner of her imaginary dignity. There was in him an evil urge to break her spirit. He suddenly unloosened his tie and pulled it off and put it in his pocket.

She stiffened. "Why must you look like *that* when you take me to town?" she said. "Why must you deliberately embarrass me?"

"If you'll never learn where you are," he said, "you can at least learn where I am."

"You look like a—thug," she said.

"Then I must be one," he murmured.

"I'll just go home," she said. "I will not bother you. If you can't do a little thing like that for me . . ."

Rolling his eyes upward, he put his tie back on. "Restored to my class," he muttered. He thrust his face toward her and hissed, "True culture is in the mind, the *mind*," he said, and tapped his head, "the mind."

"It's in the heart," she said, "and in how you do things and how you do things is because of who you *are*."

"Nobody in the damn bus cares who you are."

"I care who I am," she said icily.

The lighted bus appeared on top of the next hill and as it approached, they moved out into the street to meet it. He put his hand under her elbow and hoisted her up on the creaking step. She entered with a little smile, as if she were going into a drawing room where everyone had been waiting for her. While he put in the tokens, she sat down on one of the broad front seats for three which faced the aisle. A thin woman with protruding teeth and long yellow hair was sitting on the end of it. His mother moved up beside her and left room for Julian beside herself. He sat down and looked at the floor across the aisle where a pair of thin feet in red and white canvas sandals were planted.

His mother immediately began a general conversation meant to attract anyone who felt like talking. "Can it get any hotter?" she said and removed from her purse a folding fan, black with a Japanese scene on it, which she began to flutter before her.

"I reckon it might could," the woman with the protruding teeth said, "but I know for a fact my apartment couldn't get no hotter."

"It must get the afternoon sun," his mother said. She sat forward and looked up and down the bus. It was half filled. Everybody was white. "I see we have the bus to ourselves," she said. Julian cringed.

"For a change," said the woman across the aisle, the owner of the red and white canvas sandals. "I come on one the other day and they were thick as fleas—up front and all through."

"The world is in a mess everywhere," his mother said. "I don't know how we've let it get in this fix."

"What gets my goat is all those boys from good families stealing automobile tires," the woman with the protruding teeth said. "I told my boy, I said you may not be rich but you been raised right and if I ever catch you in any such mess, they can send you on to the reformatory. Be exactly where you belong."

"Training tells," his mother said. "Is your boy in high school?"

"Ninth grade," the woman said.

"My son just finished college last year. He wants to write but he's selling typewriters until he gets started," his mother said.

The woman leaned forward and peered at Julian. He threw her such a malevolent look that she subsided against the seat. On the floor across the aisle there was an abandoned newspaper. He got up and got it and opened it out in front of him. His mother discreetly continued the conversation in a lower tone but the woman across the aisle said in a loud voice, "Well that's nice. Selling typewriters is close to writing. He can go right from one to the other."

"I tell him," his mother said, "that Rome wasn't built in a day."

Behind the newspaper Julian was withdrawing into the inner compartment of his mind where he spent most of his time. This was a kind of mental bubble in which he established himself when he could not bear to be a part of what was going on around him. From it he could see out and judge but in it he was safe from any kind of penetration from without. It was the only place where he felt free of the general idiocy of his fellows. His mother had never entered it but from it he could see her with absolute clarity.

The old lady was clever enough and he thought that if she had started from any of the right premises, more might have been expected of her. She lived according to the laws of her own fantasy world, outside of which he had never seen her set foot. The law of it was to sacrifice herself for him after she had first created the necessity to do so by making a mess of things. If he had permitted her sacrifices, it was only because her lack of foresight had made them necessary. All of her life had been a struggle to act like a Chestny without the Chestny goods, and to give him everything she thought a Chestny ought to have; but since, said she, it was fun to struggle, why complain? And when you had won, as she had won, what fun to look back on the hard times! He could not forgive her that she had enjoyed the struggle and that she thought *she* had won.

What she meant when she said she had won was that she had brought him up successfully and had sent him to college and that he had turned out so well—good looking (her teeth had gone unfilled so that his could be straightened), intelligent (he realized he was too intelligent to be a success), and with a future ahead of him (there was of course no future ahead of him). She excused his gloominess on the grounds that he was still growing up and his radical ideas on his lack of practical experience. She said he didn't yet know a thing about "life," that he hadn't even entered the real world—when already he was as disenchanted with it as a man of fifty.

The further irony of all this was that in spite of her, he had turned out so well. In spite of going to only a third-rate college, he had, on his own initiative, come out with a first-rate education; in spite of growing up dominated by a small mind, he had ended up with a large one; in spite of all her foolish views, he was free of prejudice and unafraid to face facts. Most miraculous of all, instead of being blinded by love for her as she was for him, he had cut himself emotionally free of her and could see her with complete objectivity. He was not dominated by his mother.

The bus stopped with a sudden jerk and shook him from his meditation. A woman from the back lurched forward with little steps and barely escaped falling in his newspaper as she righted herself. She got off and a large Negro got on. Julian kept his paper lowered to watch. It gave him a certain satisfaction to see injustice in daily operation. It confirmed his view that with a few exceptions there was no one worth knowing within a radius of three hundred miles. The Negro was well dressed and carried a briefcase. He looked around and then sat down on the other end of the seat where the woman with the red and white canvas sandals was sitting. He immediately unfolded a newspaper and obscured himself behind it. Julian's mother's elbow at once prodded insistently into his ribs. "Now you see why I won't ride on these buses by myself," she whispered.

The woman with the red and white canvas sandals had risen at the same time the Negro sat down and had gone further back in the bus and taken the seat of the woman who had got off. His mother leaned forward and cast her an approving look.

Julian rose, crossed the aisle, and sat down in the place of the woman with the canvas sandals. From this position, he looked serenely across at his mother. Her face had turned an angry red. He stared at her, making his eyes the eyes of a stranger. He felt his tension suddenly lift as if he had openly declared war on her.

He would have liked to get in conversation with the Negro and to talk with him about art or politics or any subject that would be above the comprehension of those around them, but the man remained entrenched behind his paper. He was either ignoring the change of seating or had never noticed it. There was no way for Julian to convey his sympathy.

His mother kept her eyes fixed reproachfully on his face. The woman with the protruding teeth was looking at him avidly as if he were a type of monster new to her.

"Do you have a light?" he asked the Negro.

Without looking away from his paper, the man reached in his pocket and handed him a packet of matches.

"Thanks," Julian said. For a moment he held the matches foolishly. A NO SMOKING sign looked down upon him from over the door. This alone would not have deterred him; he had no cigarettes. He had quit smoking some months before because he could not afford it. "Sorry," he muttered and handed back the matches. The Negro lowered the paper and gave him an annoyed look. He took the matches and raised the paper again.

His mother continued to gaze at him but she did not take advantage of his momentary discomfort. Her eyes retained their battered look. Her face seemed to be unnaturally red, as if her blood pressure had risen. Julian allowed no glimmer of sympathy to show on his face. Having got the advantage, he wanted desperately to keep it and carry it through. He would have liked to teach her a lesson that would last her a while, but there seemed no way to continue the point. The Negro refused to come out from behind his paper.

Julian folded his arms and looked stolidly before him, facing her but as if he did not see her, as if he had ceased to recognize her existence. He visualized a scene in which, the bus having reached their stop, he would remain in his seat and when she said, "Aren't you going to get off?" he would look at her as at a stranger who had rashly addressed him. The corner they got off on was usually deserted, but it was well lighted and it would not hurt her to walk by herself the four blocks to the Y. He decided to wait until the time came and then decide whether or not he would let her get off by herself. He would have to be at the Y at ten to bring her back, but he could leave her wondering if he was going to show up. There was no reason for her to think she could always depend on him.

He retired again into the high-ceilinged room sparsely settled with large pieces of antique furniture. His soul expanded momentarily but then he became aware of his mother across from him and the vision shriveled. He studied her coldly. Her feet in little pumps dangled like a child's and did not quite reach the floor. She was training on him an exaggerated look of reproach. He felt completely detached from her. At that moment he could with pleasure have slapped her as he would have slapped a particularly obnoxious child in his charge.

He began to imagine various unlikely ways by which he could teach her a lesson. He might make friends with some distinguished Negro professor or lawyer and bring him home to spend the evening. He would be entirely justified but her blood pressure would rise to 300. He could not push her to the extent of making her have a stroke, and moreover, he had never been successful at making any Negro friends. He had tried to strike up an acquaintance on the bus with some of the better types, with ones that looked like professors or ministers or lawyers. One morning he had sat down next to a distinguished-looking dark brown man who had answered his questions with a sonorous solemnity but who had turned out to be an undertaker. Another day he had sat down beside a cigar-smoking Negro with a diamond ring on his finger, but after a few stilted pleasantries, the Negro had rung the buzzer and risen, slipping two lottery tickets into Julian's hand as he climbed over him to leave.

He imagined his mother lying desperately ill and his being able to secure only a Negro doctor for her. He toyed with that idea for a few minutes and then dropped it for a momentary vision of himself participating as a sympathizer in a sit-in demonstration. This was possible but he did not linger with it. Instead, he approached the ultimate horror. He brought home a beautiful suspiciously Negroid woman. Prepare yourself, he said. There is nothing you can do about it. This is the woman I've chosen. She's intelligent, dignified, even good, and she's suffered and she hasn't thought it *fun*. Now persecute us, go ahead and persecute us. Drive her out of here, but remember, you're driving me too. His eyes were narrowed and through the indignation he had generated, he saw his mother across the aisle, purple-faced, shrunken to the dwarf-like proportions of her moral nature, sitting like a mummy beneath the ridiculous banner of her hat.

He was tilted out of his fantasy again as the bus stopped. The door opened with a sucking hiss and out of the dark a large, gaily dressed, sullen-looking colored woman got on with a little boy. The child, who might have been four, had on a short plaid suit and a Tyrolean hat with a blue feather in it. Julian hoped that he would sit down beside him and that the woman would push in beside his mother. He could think of no better arrangement.

As she waited for her tokens, the woman was surveying the seating possibilities— he hoped with the idea of sitting where she was least wanted. There was something familiar-looking about her but Julian could not place what it was. She was a giant of a woman. Her face was set not only to meet opposition but to seek it out. The downward tilt of her large lower lip was like a warning sign: DON'T TAMPER WITH ME. Her bulging figure was encased in a green crepe dress and her feet overflowed in red shoes. She had on a hideous hat. A purple velvet flap came down on one side of it and stood up on the other; the rest of it was green and looked like a cushion with the stuffing out. She carried a mammoth red pocketbook that bulged throughout as if it were stuffed with rocks.

To Julian's disappointment, the little boy climbed up on the empty seat beside his mother. His mother lumped all children, black and white, into the common category, "cute," and she thought little Negroes were on the whole cuter than little white children. She smiled at the little boy as he climbed on the seat.

Meanwhile the woman was bearing down upon the empty seat beside Julian. To his annoyance, she squeezed herself into it. He saw his mother's face change as the woman settled herself next to him and he realized with satisfaction that this was more objectionable to her than it was to him. Her face seemed almost gray and there was a look of dull recognition in her eyes, as if suddenly she had sickened at some awful confrontation. Julian saw that it was because she and the woman had, in a sense, swapped sons. Though his mother would not realize the symbolic significance of this, she would feel it. His amusement showed plainly on his face.

The woman next to him muttered something unintelligible to herself. He was conscious of a kind of bristling next to him, muted growling like that of an angry cat. He could not see anything but the red pocketbook upright on the bulging green thighs. He visualized the woman as she had stood waiting for her tokens—the ponderous figure, rising from the red shoes upward over the solid hips, the mammoth bosom, the haughty face, to the green and purple hat.

His eyes widened.

The vision of the two hats, identical, broke upon him with the radiance of a brilliant sunrise. His face was suddenly lit with joy. He could not believe that Fate had thrust upon his mother such a lesson. He gave a loud chuckle so that she would look at him and see that he saw. She turned her eyes on him slowly. The blue in them seemed to have turned a bruised purple. For a moment he had an uncomfortable sense of her innocence, but it lasted only a second before principle rescued him. Justice entitled him to laugh. His grin hardened until it said to her as plainly as if he were saying aloud: Your punishment exactly fits your pettiness. This should teach you a permanent lesson.

Her eyes shifted to the woman. She seemed unable to bear looking at him and to find the woman preferable. He became conscious again of the bristling presence at his side. The woman was rumbling like a volcano about to become active. His mother's mouth began to twitch slightly at one corner. With a sinking heart, he saw incipient signs of recovery on her face and realized that this was going to strike her suddenly as funny and was going to be no lesson at all. She kept her eyes on the woman and an amused smile came over her face as if the woman were a monkey that had stolen her hat. The little Negro was looking up at her with large fascinated eyes. He had been trying to attract her attention for some time.

"Carver!" the woman said suddenly. "Come heah!"

When he saw that the spotlight was on him at last, Carver drew his feet up and turned himself toward Julian's mother and giggled.

"Carver!" the woman said. "You heah me? Come heah!"

Carver slid down from the seat but remained squatting with his back against the base of it, his head turned slyly around toward Julian's mother, who was smiling at him. The woman reached a hand across the aisle and snatched him to her. He righted himself and hung backwards on her knees, grinning at Julian's mother. "Isn't he cute?" Julian's mother said to the woman with the protruding teeth.

"I reckon he is," the woman said without conviction.

The Negress yanked him upright but he eased out of her grip and shot across the aisle and scrambled, giggling wildly, onto the seat beside his love.

"I think he likes me," Julian's mother said, and smiled at the woman. It was the smile she used when she was being particularly gracious to an inferior. Julian saw everything lost. The lesson had rolled off her like rain on a roof.

The woman stood up and yanked the little boy off the seat as if she were snatching him from contagion. Julian could feel the rage in her at having no weapon like his mother's smile. She gave the child a sharp slap across his leg. He howled once and then thrust his head into her stomach and kicked his feet against her shins. "Behave," she said vehemently.

The bus stopped and the Negro who had been reading the newspaper got off. The woman moved over and set the little boy down with a thump between herself and Julian. She held him firmly by the knee. In a moment he put his hands in front of his face and peeped at Julian's mother through his fingers.

"I see yooooooooo!" she said and put her hand in front of her face and peeped at him.

The woman slapped his hand down. "Quit yo' foolishness," she said, "before I knock the living Jesus out of you!"

Julian was thankful that the next stop was theirs. He reached up and pulled the cord. The woman reached up and pulled it at the same time. Oh my God, he thought. He had the terrible intuition that when they got off the bus together, his mother would open her purse and give the little boy a nickel. The gesture would be as natural to her as breathing. The bus stopped and the woman got up and lunged to the front, dragging the child, who wished to stay on, after her. Julian and his mother got up and followed. As they neared the door, Julian tried to relieve her of her pocketbook.

"No," she murmured, "I want to give the little boy a nickel."

"No!" Julian hissed. "No!"

She smiled down at the child and opened her bag. The bus door opened and the woman picked him up by the arm and descended with him, hanging at her hip. Once in the street she set him down and shook him.

Julian's mother had to close her purse while she got down the bus step but as soon as her feet were on the ground, she opened it again and began to rummage inside. "I can't find but a penny," she whispered, "but it looks like a new one."

"Don't do it!" Julian said fiercely between his teeth. There was a streetlight on the corner and she hurried to get under it so that she could better see into her pocketbook. The woman was heading off rapidly down the street with the child still hanging backward on her hand.

"Oh little boy!" Julian's mother called and took a few quick steps and caught up with them just beyond the lamppost. "Here's a bright new penny for you," and she held out the coin, which shone bronze in the dim light.

The huge woman turned and for a moment stood, her shoulders lifted and her face frozen with frustrated rage, and stared at Julian's mother. Then all at once she seemed to explode like a piece of machinery that had been given one ounce of pressure too much. Julian saw the black fist swing out with the red pocketbook. He shut his eyes and cringed as he heard the woman shout, "He don't take nobody's pennies!" When he opened his eyes, the woman was disappearing down the street with the little boy staring wide-eyed over her shoulder. Julian's mother was sitting on the sidewalk.

"I told you not to do that," Julian said angrily. "I told you not to do that!"

He stood over her for a minute, gritting his teeth. Her legs were stretched out in front of her and her hat was on her lap. He squatted down and looked her in the face. It was totally expressionless. "You got exactly what you deserved," he said. "Now get up."

He picked up her pocketbook and put what had fallen out back in it. He picked the hat up off her lap. The penny caught his eye on the sidewalk and he picked that up and let it drop before her eyes into the purse. Then he stood up and leaned over and held his hands out to pull her up. She remained immobile. He sighed. Rising above them on either side were black apartment buildings, marked with irregular rectangles of light. At the end of the block a man came out of a door and walked off in the opposite direction. "All right," he said, "suppose somebody happens by and wants to know why you're sitting on the sidewalk?"

She took the hand and, breathing hard, pulled heavily up on it and then stood for a moment, swaying slightly as if the spots of light in the darkness were circling around her. Her eyes, shadowed and confused, finally settled on his face. He did not try to conceal his irritation. "I hope this teaches you a lesson," he said. She leaned forward and her eyes raked his face. She seemed trying to determine his identity. Then, as if she found nothing familiar about him, she started off with a headlong movement in the wrong direction.

"Aren't you going on to the Y?" he asked.

"Home," she muttered.

"Well, are we walking?"

For answer she kept going. Julian followed along, his hands behind him. He saw no reason to let the lesson she had had go without backing it up with an explanation of its meaning. She might as well be made to understand what had happened to her. "Don't think that was just an uppity Negro woman," he said. "That was the whole colored race which will no longer take your condescending pennies. That was your black double. She can wear the same hat as you, and to be sure," he added gratuitously (because he thought it was funny), "it looked better on her than it did on you. What all this means," he said, "is that the old world is gone. The old manners are obsolete and your graciousness is not worth a damn." He thought bitterly of the house that had been lost for him. "You aren't who you think you are," he said.

She continued to plow ahead, paying no attention to him. Her hair had come undone on one side. She dropped her pocketbook and took no notice. He stooped and picked it up and handed it to her but she did not take it.

"You needn't act as if the world had come to an end," he said, "because it hasn't. From now on you've got to live in a new world and face a few realities for a change. Buck up," he said, "it won't kill you."

She was breathing fast.

"Let's wait on the bus," he said.

"Home," she said thickly.

"I hate to see you behave like this," he said. "Just like a child. I should be able to expect more of you." He decided to stop where he was and make her stop and wait for a bus. "I'm not going any farther," he said, stopping. "We're going on the bus."

She continued to go on as if she had not heard him. He took a few steps and caught her arm and stopped her. He looked into her face and caught his breath. He was looking into a face he had never seen before. "Tell Grandpa to come get me," she said.

He stared, stricken.

"Tell Caroline to come get me," she said.

Stunned, he let her go and she lurched forward again, walking as if one leg were shorter than the other. A tide of darkness seemed to be sweeping her from him.

"Mother!" he cried. "Darling, sweetheart, wait!" Crumpling, she fell to the pavement. He dashed forward and fell at her side, crying, "Mamma, Mamma!" He turned her over. Her face was fiercely distorted. One eye, large and staring, moved slightly to the left as if it had become unmoored. The other remained fixed on him, raked his face again, found nothing and closed.

"Wait here, wait here!" he cried and jumped up and began to run for help toward a cluster of lights he saw in the distance ahead of him. "Help, help!" he shouted, but his voice was thin, scarcely a thread of sound. The lights drifted farther away the faster he ran and his feet moved numbly as if they carried him nowhere. The tide of darkness seemed to sweep him back to her, postponing from moment to moment his entry into the world of guilt and sorrow.

(1950)

QUESTIONS FOR REFLECTION

Experience

1. What were your initial impressions of Julian and his mother? Did these impressions remain consistent or did they change?
2. To what extent does your experience with racial prejudice parallel that depicted in the story? To what extent does it differ?

Interpretation

3. What is the significance of the name Godhigh? How does Julian's attitude toward his ancestors and toward the Godhigh family home reflect the central conflict of the story?
4. What is the significance of Julian's mother's response to the black woman's hat? What is the significance of Julian's response to his mother's behavior?
5. What is the meaning of the story's concluding action and dialogue?

Evaluation

6. What principles and beliefs guide Julian? What principles and beliefs does his mother live by?
7. Whose values, if anyone's, does the story seem to endorse? What values are satirized?

Connections

8. Compare the treatment of racial prejudice in O'Connor's story with that in Ellison's "Battle Royal."

INTRODUCTION TO SANDRA CISNEROS

[b. 1954]

Sandra Cisneros was born in Chicago to a Mexican father and a Mexican-American mother, the only daughter in a family with six sons. She was raised in Chicago, but often visited Mexico. She began writing at the age of ten, and as a young woman studied creative writing at the Iowa Writers' Workshop, where she earned a Master of Fine Arts degree in 1978. In addition to writing both poetry and fiction, Cisneros has taught creative writing in a variety of educational contexts, including high school and college. She has taught and been a visiting writer at the University of California at Irvine and at Berkeley and at the University of Michigan. She has also worked in educational and arts administration.

As a child she traveled frequently to Mexico to visit her father's family. Growing up in a bilingual family and shuttling back and forth between two cultures, Cisneros developed a cultural identity that blended American and Mexican qualities and perspectives. Nonetheless Cisneros saw herself in her early years not as a Chicana writer but as an American writer, one whose reading was in mainstream literature and who wrote in English, the mainstream language.

It was at the Iowa Workshop that Cisneros decided that her writing would be different from the mainstream. The Spanish that she had previously kept private in her life she injected into her writing, ironically after having been influenced by Vladimir Nabokov's memoirs. She began writing autobiographical sketches, experimenting with a child's voice and perspective.

Cisneros also explored her cultural identity in a series of poems, which served as her Master's thesis, and which, revised and enlarged, were later published under the title *My Wicked, Wicked Ways* (1987). The poems span a wide range of subjects, including identity, love, friendship, religion, and everyday life. Writing them prepared Cisneros for the more elaborate prose poems that would become her first work of fiction, *The House on Mango Street* (1989).

Dedicated to women, *The House on Mango Street* is composed of forty-four short narratives, which recount the experiences of a maturing adolescent girl discovering life around her in a Hispanic urban ghetto. The narrator's name is Esperanza, which in English means "hope," a quality she possesses all the while she develops a fuller, richer, more mature understanding of her own experience and of the life she witnesses all around her. *The House on Mango Street* brought Cisneros modest recognition, but it was the publication two years later of *Woman Hollering Creek* (1991) coupled with the reissue of *The House on Mango Street* that catapulted Cisneros to the attention of the academic and literary establishment. Contemporary novelist Ann Beattie has said of *Woman Hollering Creek:* "These stories about how and why we mythologize love are revelations about the constant, small sadnesses that erode our facades, as well as those unpredictably epiphanic moments that lift our hearts from despair."

Cisneros has received a number of grants that have given her the freedom to pursue her writing full time. She received a National Endowment for the Arts grant in 1982, and the following year she was an artist in residence in Vence, France. Most recently, in 1995, she was selected as a MacArthur Fellow. In addition she has won a number of prizes.

Like many of the stories in *Woman Hollering Creek*, "Eleven," "Barbie-Q," and "There Was a Man, There Was a Woman" touch on experiences in Cisneros's life, while resonating with sexual, social, and cultural significance.

CISNEROS ON HERSELF

from *"Conveying the Riches of the Latin American Culture . . ."*

Publisher's Weekly

Taped to her word processor is a prayer card to San Judas, a gift from a Mexico City cabdriver. Her two indispensable literary sources are mail order catalogues and the San Antonio (Tex.) phone book. She lights candles and reads the Popul Vuh before sitting down to write long into the night, becoming so immersed in her characters that she dreams their dialogue: once she awoke momentarily convinced she was Ines, bride of the Mexican revolutionary Emiliano Zapata.

Such identification with her characters and her culture is altogether natural for a writer who has always found her literary voice in the real voices of her people, her immediate family and the extended famiulis of Latino society.

"I'm trying to write the stories that haven't been written. I feel like a cartographer; I'm determined to fill a literary void," Cisneros says. With the . . . publication of her new collection of stories, *Woman Hollering Creek*, . . . and the simultaneous reissuing of her earlier collection of short fiction, *The House on Mango Street*, . . . Cisneros finds herself in a position to chart those barrio ditches and borderland arroyos that have not appeared on most copies of the American literary map but which, nonetheless, also flow into the "mainstream."

The 36-year-old daughter of a Mexican father and a Chicana mother, Cisneros is well aware of the additional pressure to succeed with this pair of books that represent the opportunity for a wider readership, not only for herself but for scores of other Latina and Latino writers right behind the door that she is cracking open.

"One of the most frightening pressures I faced as I wrote this book was the fear that I would blow it," Cisneros says, sweeping a lock of her closely cropped black hair from her forehead as she sips a midmorning cup of coffee. "I kept asking myself, What have I taken on here? That's why I was so obsessed with getting everybody's stories out. I didn't have the luxury of doing my own."

Coupled with that "responsibility to do a collective good job" is Cisneros's anxiety about how her work will be perceived by the general reading public. Universal as her themes are, Cisneros knows her characters live in an America very different from that of her potential readers. From her friend Lucy, "who smells like corn," to Salvador, whose essence resides "inside that wrinkled shirt, inside the throat that must clear itself and apologize each time it speaks," Cisneros's literary landscape teems with characters who live, love, and laugh in the flowing cadences of the Spanish language.

Yet, unlike her character Salvador, Cisneros offers no apologies when she speaks. Energetic and abounding with gusto—only the Spanish word will do to describe her engaging humor—Cisneros relishes the opportunity to startle the jaded reader and poetically unravel stereotypes, especially those that relate to Latinas.

"I'm the mouse who puts a thorn in the lion's paw," she says, with an arch smile reminiscent of the red-lipped *sonrisa* on the cover of *My Wicked, Wicked Ways*, . . . a collection of poetry celebrating the "bad girl" with her "lopsided symmetry of sin/and virtue."

"An unlucky fate is mine/to be born woman in a family of men," Cisneros writes in one of her "wicked" poems, yet it is that very "fate" that laid the groundwork for the literary career of this writer, whose name derives from the Spanish word for "swan."

Born in Chicago in 1954, Cisneros grew up in a family of six brothers and a father, or "seven fathers," as she puts it. She recalls spending much of her early childhood moving from place to place. Because her paternal grandmother was so attached to her favorite son, the Cisneros family returned to Mexico City "like the tides."

"The moving back and forth, the new schools, were very upsetting to me as a child. They caused me to be very introverted and shy. I do not remember making friends easily, and I was terribly self-conscious due to the cruelty of the nuns, who were majestic at making one feel little. Because we moved so much, and always in neighborhoods that appeared like France after World War II—empty lots and burned-out buildings—I retreated inside myself."

It was that "retreat" that transformed Cisneros into an observer, a role she feels she still plays today. "When I'm washing sheets at the laundromat, people still see me as just a girl. I take advantage of that idea. The little voice I used to hate I now see as an asset. It helps me get past the guards."

Among the first "guards" that Cisneros sneaked past were the literary sentinels at the University of Iowa's Writers' Workshop, which she attended in the late 70s. Her "breakthrough" occurred during a seminar discussion of archetypal memories in Bachelard's *Poetics of Space*. As her classmates spoke about the house of the imagination, the attics, stairways and cellars of childhood, Cisneros felt foreign and out of place.

"Everyone seemed to have some communal knowledge which I did not have—and then I realized that the metaphor of house was totally wrong for me. Suddenly I was homeless. There were no attics and cellars and crannies. I had no such house in my memories. As a child I had read of such things in books, and my family had promised such a house, but the best they could do was offer the miserable bungalow I was embarrassed with all my life. This caused me to question myself, to become defensive. What did I know? What could I know? My classmates were from the best schools in the country. They had been bred as fine hothouse flowers. I was a yellow weed among the city's cracks.

"It was not until this moment when I separated myself, when I considered myself truly distinct, that my writing acquired a voice. I knew I was a Mexican woman, but I didn't think it had anything to do with why I felt so much imbalance in my life, whereas it had everything to do with it! My race, my gender, my class! That's when I decided I would write about something my classmates couldn't write about."

from *"Straw into Gold"*

Texas Observer

I like to think that somehow my family, my Mexicanness, my poverty, all had something to do with shaping me into a writer. I like to think my parents were preparing me all along for my life as an artist even though they didn't know it. From my father I inherited a love of wandering. He was born in Mexico City but as a young man he traveled into the United States vagabonding. He eventually was drafted and thus became a citizen. Some of the stories he has told about his first months in the United States with little or no English surface in my stories in *The House on Mango Street* as well as others I have in mind to write in the future. From him I inherited a sappy heart. (He still cries when he watches Mexican soaps—especially if they deal with children who have forsaken their parents.)

My mother was born like me—in Chicago but of Mexican descent. It would be her tough streetwise voice that would haunt all my stories and poems. An amazing woman who loves to draw and read books and can sing an opera. A smart cookie. . . .

When I think of how I see myself it would have to be at age eleven. I know I'm thirty-two on the outside, but inside I'm eleven. I'm the girl in the picture with skinny arms and a crumpled skirt and crooked hair. I didn't like school because all they saw was the outside me. School was lots of rules and sitting with your hands folded and being very afraid all the time. I liked looking out the window and thinking. I liked staring at the girl across the way writing her name over and over again in red ink. I wondered why the boy with the dirty collar in front of me didn't have a mama who took better care of him.

I think my mama and papa did the best they could to keep us warm and clean and never hungry. We had birthday and graduation parties and things like that, but there was another hunger that had to be fed. There was a hunger I didn't even have a name for. Was this when I began writing?

In 1966 we moved into a house, a real one, our first real home. This meant we didn't have to change schools and be the new kids on the block every couple of years. We could make friends and not be afraid we'd have to say goodbye to them and start all over. My brothers and the flock of boys they brought home would become important characters eventually for my stories—Louis and his cousins, Meme Ortiz and his dog with two names, one in English and one in Spanish.

My mother flourished in her own home. She took books out of the library and taught herself to garden—to grow flowers so envied we had to put a lock on the gate to keep out the midnight flower thieves. My mother has never quit gardening. . . .

In the days when I would sit at my favorite people-watching spot, the snakey Woolworth's counter across the street from the Alamo (the Woolworth's which has since been torn down to make way for progress), I couldn't think of anything else I'd rather be than a writer. I've traveled and lectured from Cape Cod to San Francisco, to Spain, Yugoslavia, Greece, Mexico, France, Italy, and now today Texas. Along the way there has been straw for the taking. With a little imagination, it can be spun into gold.

CRITICS ON CISNEROS

JEFF THOMPSON

from *"What Is Called Heaven"*: Identity in Sandra Cisneros's *Woman Hollering Creek*

Studies in Short Fiction

This is a world without men, where the fathers are drunk or absent, the mothers are left to raise the children alone and the only possible salvation is a sisterhood that more often than not fails.

The stories continue in this vein, establishing aspects of an archetypal Chicana female identity. "Eleven" sets up a system of multiple selves like "little wooden dolls that fit one inside the other" and the difficulty of maintaining a unity of self in the face of authority. "Mexican Movies" and "Barbie-Q" are concerned with stereotypes and enforced identity. From her young girl's voice, Cisneros satirizes the portrayals of Mexicans in film by contrasting a Chicana family's daily life with the films of Pedro Infante (his name itself denotes a childlike, false identity) who "always sings riding a horse and wears a big sombrero and never tears the dresses off the ladies, and the ladies throw flowers from balconies and usually somebody dies, but not Pedro Infante because he has to sing the happy song at the end." Although the barrio life of Cisneros's families is usually far from wealthy, here at least she presents us with a world of safety and security, where the false happiness of women tossing flowers from balconies doesn't interfere with the games the sisters play in the aisles. And then

The movie ends. The Lights go on. Somebody picks us up . . . carries us in the cold to the car that smells like ashtrays. . . . [B]y now, we're awake but it's nice to go on pretending with our eyes shut because here's the best part. Mama and Papa carry us upstairs to the third-floor where we live, take off our shoes and cover us, so when we wake up it's Sunday already and we're in our beds and happy.

The satire is so subtle that one is led to believe the girls and perhaps even her parents do not see the films as stereotypes that limit their ability to be accepted in the white world, but the reader is obviously meant to.

Similarly, in "Barbie-Q" Cisneros attacks artificial feminine stereotypes that are epitomized in every Barbie doll. The narrator and her companion play Barbies with two basic dolls and an invisible Ken (again a comment on the absence of male figures in the culture) until there's a sale on smoke-damaged dolls. When the girls are able to buy an assortment of new dolls, Cisneros asks, in a bitingly satiric tone, "And if the prettiest doll, Barbie's MOD'ern cousin Francie . . . has a left foot that's melted a little—so? If you dress her in her new 'Prom Pinks' outfit, satin splendor with matching coat, gold belt, clutch and hair bow included, so long as you don't lift her dress, right—who's to know?" Cisneros is both attacking and acknowledging the depths our culture goes to in an attempt to hide women's assumed "faults"—not the least of which is the fact that her very sexuality is assumed to be based around the idea of the lack of a penis, as is winked at in Cisneros's linguistic raising of the dress. It is men whose theories and intellectual models have defined women as flawed, but it is also women who perpetuate that myth by buying Barbies for their daughters, in essence supporting male theory through their actions. The responsibility of both men and women for the system that keeps women confined in partial identity is a theme Cisneros will return to again and again. Ultimately, the female characters who escape this system are those who have assimilated characteristics of both sexes.

ROBIN GANZ

On "Woman Hollering Creek"

from "Sandra Cisneros: Border Crossings and Beyond," MELUS

About the experience of writing *Woman Hollering Creek* and giving voice to so many different characters, Cisneros said at the Santa Fe conference, "I felt like a ventriloquist." Her advice to the writers in attendance was to "transcribe voices of the people of a community you know," and confided that she keeps voluminous files of snippets of dialogue or monologue—records of conversations she hears wherever she goes. She emphasized that she'll mix and match to suit her purpose because, as she put it, "real life doesn't have shape. You have to snip and cut."

When Cisneros was at work on *Woman Hollering Creek,* she became so immersed in her characters that they began to penetrate her unconscious; once, while writing "Eyes of Zapata," she awakened in the middle of the night, convinced for the moment that she was Ines, the young bride of the Mexican revolutionary. Her dream conversation with Zapata then became those characters' dialogue in her story. The task of breaking the silence, of articulating the unpronounceable pain of the characters that populate *Woman Hollering Creek,* was a very serious undertaking for Cisneros. She said in a recent interview: "I'm trying to write the stories that haven't been written. I felt like a cartographer; I'm determined to fill a literary void." The pressure intensifies for her because of her bi-culturalism and bi-lingualism: She charts not only the big city barrio back alleyways, its mean streets and the dusty arroyos of the borderland, but also offers us a window into the experience of the educated, cosmopolitan Chicano/artist, writer and academic. While she revels in her bi-culturalism, enjoys her life in two worlds, and as a writer she's grateful to have "twice as many words to pick from . . . two ways of looking at the world," her wide range of experience is a double-edged sword. In the S . . . interview, she revealed another side of her motivation to tell many people's stories in their own voices—the responsibility and the anxiety which that task produces: "One of the most frightening pressures I faced as I wrote this book," she says, "was the fear that I would blow it. . . . I kept asking myself, What have I taken on here? That's why I was so obsessed with getting everybody's stories out." . . .

While it is undeniable that Sandra Cisneros has traversed the boundary dividing the small press market and the mainstream publishing establishment, a controversy continues about her writing among the critics over the issue of genre-crossing. In her review of *Woman Hollering Creek* in the *Los Angeles Times* titled "Poetic Fiction with a Tex-Mex Tilt," Barbara Kingsolver writes that "Sandra Cisneros has added length and dialogue and a hint of plot to her poems and published them in a stunning collection called *Woman Hollering Creek*." Later on in the review she elaborates:

"It's a practical thing for poets in the United States to turn to fiction. Elsewhere, poets have the cultural status of our rock stars and the income of our romance novelists. Here, a poet is something your mother probably didn't want you to grow up to be. . . . When you read this book, don't be fooled. It's poetry. Just don't tell your mother."

SANDRA CISNEROS: STORIES

Eleven

What they don't understand about birthdays and what they never tell you is that when you're eleven, you're also ten, and nine, and eight, and seven, and six, and five, and four, and three, and two, and one. And when you wake up on your eleventh birthday you expect to feel eleven, but you don't. You open your eyes and everything's just like yesterday, only it's today. And you don't feel eleven at all. You feel like you're still ten. And you are—underneath the year that makes you eleven.

Like some days you might say something stupid, and that's the part of you that's still ten. Or maybe some days you might need to sit on your mama's lap because you're scared, and that's the part of you that's five. And maybe one day when you're all grown up maybe you will need to cry like if you're three, and that's okay. That's what I tell Mama when she's sad and needs to cry. Maybe she's feeling three.

Because the way you grow old is kind of like an onion or like the rings inside a tree trunk or like my little wooden dolls that fit one inside the other, each year inside the next one. That's how being eleven years old is.

You don't feel eleven. Not right away. It takes a few days, weeks even, sometimes even months before you say Eleven when they ask you. And you don't feel smart eleven, not until you're almost twelve. That's the way it is.

Only today I wish I didn't have only eleven years rattling inside me like pennies in a tin Band-Aid box. Today I wish I was one hundred and two instead of eleven because if I was one hundred and two I'd have known what to say when Mrs. Price put the red sweater on my desk. I would've known how to tell her it wasn't mine instead of just sitting there with that look on my face and nothing coming out of my mouth.

"Whose is this?" Mrs. Price says, and she holds the red sweater up in the air for all the class to see. "Whose? It's been sitting in the coatroom for a month."

"Not mine," says everybody. "Not me."

"It has to belong to somebody," Mrs. Price keeps saying, but nobody can remember. It's an ugly sweater with red plastic buttons and a collar and sleeves all stretched out like you could use it for a jump rope. It's maybe a thousand years old and even if it belonged to me I wouldn't say so.

Maybe because I'm skinny, maybe because she doesn't like me, that stupid Sylvia Saldívar says, "I think it belongs to Rachel." An ugly sweater like that, all raggedy and old, but Mrs. Price believes her. Mrs. Price takes the sweater and puts it right on my desk, but when I open my mouth nothing comes out.

"That's not, I don't, you're not . . . Not mine," I finally say in a little voice that was maybe me when I was four.

"Of course it's yours," Mrs. Price says. "I remember you wearing it once." Because she's older and the teacher, she's right and I'm not.

Not mine, not mine, not mine, but Mrs. Price is already turning to page thirty-two, and math problem number four. I don't know why but all of a sudden I'm feeling sick inside, like the part of me that's three wants to come out of my eyes, only I squeeze them shut tight and bite down on my teeth real hard and try to remember today I am eleven, eleven. Mama is making a cake for me for tonight, and when Papa comes home everybody will sing Happy birthday, happy birthday to you.

But when the sick feeling goes away and I open my eyes, the red sweater's still sitting there like a big red mountain. I move the red sweater to the corner of my desk with my ruler. I move my pencil and books and eraser as far from it as possible. I even move my chair a little to the right. Not mine, not mine, not mine.

In my head I'm thinking how long till lunchtime, how long till I can take the red sweater and throw it over the schoolyard fence, or leave it hanging on a parking meter, or bunch it up into a little ball and toss it in the alley. Except when math period ends Mrs. Price says loud and in front of everybody, "Now, Rachel, that's enough," because she sees I've shoved the red sweater to the tippy tip corner of my desk and it's hanging all over the edge like a waterfall, but I don't care.

"Rachel," Mrs. Price says. She says it like she's getting mad. "You put that sweater on right now and no more nonsense."

"But it's not—"

"Now!" Mrs. Price says.

This is when I wish I wasn't eleven, because all the years inside of me—ten, nine, eight, seven, six, five, four, three, two, and one—are pushing at the back of my eyes when I put one arm through one sleeve of the sweater that smells like cottage cheese, and then the other arm through the other and stand there with my arms apart like if the sweater hurts me and it does, all itchy and full of germs that aren't even mine.

That's when everything I've been holding in since this morning, since when Mrs. Price put the sweater on my desk, finally lets go, and all of a sudden I'm crying in front of everybody. I wish I was invisible but I'm not. I'm eleven and it's my birthday today and I'm crying like I'm three in front of everybody. I put my head down on the desk and bury my face in the stupid clown-sweater arms. My face all hot and spit coming out of my mouth because I can't stop the little animal noises from coming out of me, until there aren't any more tears left in my eyes, and it's just my body shaking like when you have the hiccups, and my whole head hurts like when you drink milk too fast.

But the worst part is right before the bell rings for lunch. That stupid Phyllis Lopez, who is even dumber than Sylvia Saldívar, says she remembers the red sweater is hers! I take it off right away and give it to her, only Mrs. Price pretends like everything's okay.

Today I'm eleven. There's a cake Mama's making for tonight, and when Papa comes home from work we'll eat it. There'll be candles and presents and everybody will sing Happy birthday, happy birthday to you, Rachel, only it's too late.

I'm eleven today. I'm eleven, ten, nine, eight, seven, six, five, four, three, two, and one, but I wish I was one hundred and two. I wish I was anything but eleven, because I want today to be far away already, far away like a runaway balloon, like a tiny *o* in the sky, so tiny-tiny you have to close your eyes to see it.

(1991)

QUESTIONS FOR REFLECTION

Experience

1. To what extent does "Eleven" remind you of when you were eleven or so years old?
2. What is your impression of the narrator? How do you respond to her predicament?

Interpretation

3. What does the narrator mean by saying "when you're eleven, you're also ten, and nine, and eight, and seven, and six, and five, and four, and three, and two, and one"?
4. What are the function and effect of the comparisons the narrator makes in describing her experience?

Evaluation

5. What clash in values does the story dramatize?
6. What impression of the worlds of childhood and adulthood does it convey?

Connections

7. Compare the narrator of "Eleven" with the narrator of Updike's "A & P." What do these two narrators have in common? How are they different?

Barbie-Q

for Licha

Yours is the one with the mean eyes and a ponytail. Striped swimsuit, stilettos, sunglasses, and gold hoop earrings. Mine is the one with bubble hair. Red swimsuit, stilettos, pearl earrings, and a wire stand. But that's all we can afford, besides one extra outfit apiece. Yours, "Red Flair," sophisticated A-line coatdress with a Jackie Kennedy pillbox hat, white gloves, handbag, and heels included. Mine, "Solo in the Spotlight," evening elegance in black glitter strapless gown with a puffy skirt at the bottom like a mermaid tail, formal-length gloves, pink chiffon scarf, and mike included. From so much dressing and undressing, the black glitter wears off where her titties stick out. This and a dress invented from an old sock when we cut holes here and here and here, the cuff rolled over for the glamorous, fancy-free, off-the-shoulder look.

Every time the same story. Your Barbie is roommates with my Barbie, and my Barbie's boyfriend comes over and your Barbie steals him, okay? Kiss kiss kiss. Then the two Barbies fight, You dumbbell! He's mine. Oh no he's not, you stinky! Only Ken's invisible, right? Because we don't have money for a stupid-looking boy doll when we'd both rather ask for a new Barbie outfit next Christmas. We have to make do with your mean-eyed Barbie and my bubblehead Barbie and our one outfit apiece not including the sock dress.

Until next Sunday when we are walking through the flea market on Maxwell Street and *there!* Lying on the street next to some tool bits, and platform shoes with the heels all squashed, and a fluorescent green wicker wastebasket, and aluminum foil, and hubcaps, and a pink shag rug, and windshield wiper blades, and dusty mason jars, and a coffee can full of rusty nails. *There!* Where? Two Mattel boxes. One with the "Career Gal" ensemble, snappy black and white business suit, three-quarter-length sleeve jacket with kick-pleat skirt, red sleeveless shell, gloves, pumps, and matching hat included. The other, "Sweet Dreams," dreamy pink-and-white plaid nightgown and matching robe, lace-trimmed slippers, hair-brush and hand mirror included. How much? Please, please, please, please, please, please, please, until they say okay.

On the outside you and me skipping and humming but inside we are doing loopity-loops and pirouetting. Until at the next vendor's stand, next to boxed pies, and bright orange toilet brushes, and rubber gloves, and wrench sets, and bouquets of feather flowers, and glass towel racks, and steel wool, and Alvin and the Chipmunks records, *there!* And *there!* And *there!* And *there!* and *there!* and *there!* and *there!* Bendable Legs Barbie with her new page-boy hairdo. Midge, Barbie's best friend. Ken, Barbie's boyfriend. Skipper, Barbie's little sister. Tutti and Todd, Barbie and Skipper's tiny twin sister and brother. Skipper's friends, Scooter and Ricky. Alan, Ken's buddy. And Francie, Barbie's MOD'ern cousin.

Everybody today selling toys, all of them damaged with water and smelling of smoke. Because a big toy warehouse on Halsted Street burned down yesterday—see there?—the smoke still rising and drifting across the Dan Ryan expressway. And now there is a big fire sale at Maxwell Street, today only.

So what if we didn't get our new Bendable Legs Barbie and Midge and Ken and Skipper and Tutti and Todd and Scooter and Ricky and Alan and Francie in nice clean boxes and had to buy them on Maxwell Street, all water-soaked and sooty. So what if our Barbies smell like smoke when you hold them up to your nose even after you wash and wash and wash them. And if the prettiest doll, Barbie's MOD'ern cousin Francie with real eyelashes, eyelash brush included, has a left foot that's melted a little—so? If you dress her in her new "Prom Pinks" outfit, satin splendor with matching coat, gold belt, clutch, and hair bow included, so long as you don't lift her dress, right?—who's to know.

(1991)

QUESTIONS FOR REFLECTION

Experience

1. What is your impression of the girls described in the story?
2. How do you respond to the descriptions of their Barbie dolls? Why?

Interpretation

3. What are the purpose and effect of describing the dolls' clothes and accessories in detail?
4. What is the effect of the use of repetition: the repeated use of "please," and "And *there!*" Of "Barbie" and "Barbie's"?
5. What is the story's theme?

Evaluation

6. With what values are the Barbie dolls associated?

Connections

7. Compare the narrators of "Barbie-Q" and "Eleven." Which narrator do you like better, and why?

There Was a Man, There Was a Woman

There was a man and there was a woman. Every payday, every other Friday, the man went to the Friendly Spot Bar to drink and spend his money. Every payday, every other Friday, the woman went to the Friendly Spot Bar to drink and spend her money. The man was paid on the second and fourth Friday of the month. The woman was paid on the first and third Friday. Because of this the man and the woman did not know each other.

The man drank and drank with his friends and believed if he drank and drank, the words for what he was feeling would slip out more readily, but usually he simply drank and said nothing. The woman drank and drank with her friends and believed if she drank and drank, the words for what she was feeling would slip out more readily, but usually she simply drank and said nothing. Every other Friday the man drank his beer and laughed loudly. Every Friday in between the woman drank her beer and laughed loudly.

At home when the night came down and the moon appeared, the woman raised her pale eyes to the moon and cried. The man in his bed contemplated the same moon, and thought about the millions who had looked at the moon before him, those who had worshiped or loved or died before that same moon, mute and lovely. Now blue light streamed inside his window and tangled itself with the glow of the sheets. The moon, the same round O. The man looked and swallowed.

(1991)

QUESTIONS FOR REFLECTION

Experience

1. To what extent does this story remind you of a fairy tale? How did you respond to the story's repetitions of language and its parallel actions?

Interpretation

2. What is this story about?
3. What does it suggest about the central characters? What is the effect of their not being named?

Evaluation

4. What cultural values serve as context and backdrop for the story?

Connections

5. Compare this brief piece with Petronius' "The Widow of Ephesus" in Chapter Two or with "Learning to Be Silent" in the Introduction.

CHAPTER SIX

A Collection of Short Fiction

Fiction is not dream. Nor is it guess work. It is imagining based on facts. . . .
MARGARET BANNING

Fiction is like a spider's web, attached ever so slightly perhaps, but still attached to life at all four corners.

VIRGINIA WOOLF

NATHANIEL HAWTHORNE
[1804–1864]

Young Goodman Brown

Young Goodman Brown came forth at sunset, into the street of Salem village, but put his head back, after crossing the threshold, to exchange a parting kiss with his young wife. And Faith, as the wife was aptly named, thrust her own pretty head into the street, letting the wind play with the pink ribbons of her cap, while she called to Goodman Brown.

"Dearest heart," whispered she, softly and rather sadly, when her lips were close to his ear, "prithee, put off your journey until sunrise, and sleep in your own bed to-night. A lone woman is troubled with such dreams and such thoughts, that she's afeard of herself, sometimes. Pray, tarry with me this night, dear husband, of all nights in the year!"

"My love and my Faith," replied young Goodman Brown, "of all nights in the year, this one night must I tarry away from thee. My journey, as thou callest it, forth and back again, must needs be done 'twixt now and sunrise. What, my sweet, pretty wife, dost thou doubt me already, and we but three months married!"

"Then God bless you!" said Faith with the pink ribbons, "and may you find all well, when you come back."

"Amen!" cried Goodman Brown. "Say thy prayers, dear Faith, and go to bed at dusk, and no harm will come to thee."

So they parted; and the young man pursued his way, until, being about to turn the corner by the meeting-house, he looked back and saw the head of Faith still peeping after him, with a melancholy air, in spite of her pink ribbons.

"Poor little Faith!" thought he, for his heart smote him. "What a wretch am I, to leave her on such an errand! She talks of dreams, too. Methought, as she spoke, there was trouble in her face, as if a dream had warned her what work is to be done to-night. But no, no! 't would kill her to think it. Well; she's a blessed angel on earth; and after this one night, I'll cling to her skirts and follow her to Heaven."

With this excellent resolve for the future, Goodman Brown felt himself justified in making more haste on his present evil purpose. He had taken a dreary road, darkened by all the gloomiest trees of the forest, which barely stood aside to let the narrow path creep through, and closed immediately behind. It was as lonely as could be; and there is this peculiarity in such a solitude, that the traveller knows not who may be concealed by the innumerable trunks and the thick boughs overhead; so that, with lonely footsteps, he may yet be passing through an unseen multitude.

"There may be a devilish Indian behind every tree," said Goodman Brown to himself; and he glanced fearfully behind him, as he added, "What if the devil himself should be at my very elbow!"

His head being turned back, he passed a crook of the road, and looking forward again, beheld the figure of a man, in grave and decent attire, seated at the foot of an old tree. He arose at Goodman Brown's approach, and walked onward, side by side with him.

"You are late, Goodman Brown," said he. "The clock of the Old South was striking, as I came through Boston; and that is full fifteen minutes agone."

"Faith kept me back awhile," replied the young man, with a tremor in his voice, caused by the sudden appearance of his companion, though not wholly unexpected.

It was now deep dusk in the forest, and deepest in that part of it where these two were journeying. As nearly as could be discerned, the second traveller was about fifty years old, apparently in the same rank of life as Goodman Brown, and bearing a considerable resemblance to him, though perhaps more in expression than features. Still, they might have been taken for father and son. And yet, though the elder person was as simply clad as the younger, and as simple in manner too, he had an indescribable air of one who knew the world, and would not have felt abashed at the governor's dinner-table, or in King William's court, were it possible that his affairs should call him thither. But the only thing about him that could be fixed upon as remarkable, was his staff, which bore the likeness of a great black snake, so curiously wrought, that it might almost be seen to twist and wriggle itself like a living serpent. This, of course, must have been an ocular deception, assisted by the uncertain light.

"Come, Goodman Brown!" cried his fellow-traveller, "this is a dull pace for the beginning of a journey. Take my staff, if you are so soon weary."

"Friend," said the other, exchanging his slow pace for a full stop, "having kept covenant by meeting thee here, it is my purpose now to return whence I came. I have scruples, touching the matter thou wot'st of."

"Sayest thou so?" replied he of the serpent, smiling apart. "Let us walk on, nevertheless, reasoning as we go, and if I convince thee not, thou shalt turn back. We are but a little way in the forest, yet."

"Too far, too far!" exclaimed the goodman, unconsciously resuming his walk. "My father never went into the woods on such an errand, nor his father before him. We have been a race of honest men and good Christians, since the days of the martyrs. And shall I be the first of the name of Brown that ever took this path and kept—"

"Such company, thou wouldst say," observed the elder person, interrupting his pause. "Well said, Goodman Brown! I have been as well acquainted with your family as with ever a one among the Puritans; and that's no trifle to say. I helped your grandfather, the constable, when he lashed the Quaker woman so smartly through the streets of Salem. And it was I that brought your father a pitch-pine knot, kindled at my own hearth, to set fire to an Indian village, in King Philip's war. They were my good friends, both; and many a pleasant walk have we had along this path, and returned merrily after midnight. I would fain be friends with you, for their sake."

"If it be as thou sayest," replied Goodman Brown, "I marvel they never spoke of these matters. Or, verily, I marvel not, seeing that the least rumor of the sort would have driven them from New England. We are a people of prayer and good works to boot, and abide no such wickedness."

"Wickedness or not," said the traveller with the twisted staff, "I have a very general acquaintance here in New England. The deacons of many a church have drunk the communion wine with me; the selectmen, of divers towns, make me their chairman; and a majority of the Great and General Court are firm supporters of my interest. The governor and I, too—but these are state secrets."

"Can this be so!" cried Goodman Brown, with a stare of amazement at his undisturbed companion. "Howbeit, I have nothing to do with the governor and council; they have their own ways, and are no rule for a simple husbandman like me. But, were I to go on with thee, how should I meet the eye of that good old man, our minister, at Salem village? Oh, his voice would make me tremble, both Sabbath-day and lecture-day!"

Thus far, the elder traveller had listened with due gravity, but now burst into a fit of irrepressible mirth, shaking himself so violently, that his snakelike staff actually seemed to wriggle in sympathy.

"Ha, ha, ha!" shouted he, again and again; then composing himself, "Well, go on, Goodman Brown, go on; but, prithee, don't kill me with laughing!"

"Well, then, to end the matter at once," said Goodman Brown, considerably nettled, "there is my wife, Faith. It would break her dear little heart; and I'd rather break my own!"

"Nay, if that be the case," answered the other, "e'en go thy ways, Goodman Brown. I would not, for twenty old women like the one hobbling before us, that Faith should come to any harm."

As he spoke, he pointed his staff at a female figure on the path, in whom Goodman Brown recognized a very pious and exemplary dame, who had taught him his catechism in youth, and was still his moral and spiritual adviser, jointly with the minister and Deacon Gookin.

"A marvel, truly, that Goody Cloyse should be so far in the wilderness, at nightfall!" said he. "But, with your leave, friend, I shall take a cut through the woods, until we have left this Christian woman behind. Being a stranger to you, she might ask whom I was consorting with, and whither I was going."

"Be it so," said his fellow-traveller. "Betake you to the woods, and let me keep the path."

Accordingly, the young man turned aside, but took care to watch his companion, who advanced softly along the road, until he had come within a staff's length of the old dame. She, meanwhile, was making the best of her way, with singular speed for so aged a woman, and mumbling some indistinct words, a prayer, doubtless, as she went. The traveller put forth his staff, and touched her withered neck with what seemed the serpent's tail.

"The devil!" screamed the pious old lady.

"Then Goody Cloyse knows her old friend?" observed the traveller, confronting her, and leaning on his writhing stick.

"Ah, forsooth, and is it your worship, indeed?" cried the good dame. "Yea, truly is it, and in the very image of my old gossip, Goodman Brown, the grandfather of the silly fellow that now is. But, would your worship believe it? my broomstick hath strangely disappeared, stolen, as I suspect, by that unhanged witch, Goody Cory, and that, too, when I was all anointed with the juice of smallage and cinque-foil and wolf's-bane—"

"Mingled with fine wheat and the fat of a new-born babe," said the shape of old Goodman Brown.

"Ah, your worship knows the recipe," cried the old lady, cackling aloud. "So, as I was saying, being all ready for the meeting, and no horse to ride on, I made up my mind to foot it; for they tell me there is a nice young man to be taken into communion to-night. But now your good worship will lend me your arm, and we shall be there in a twinkling."

"That can hardly be," answered her friend. "I may not spare you my arm, Goody Cloyse, but here is my staff, if you will."

So saying, he threw it down at her feet, where, perhaps, it assumed life, being one of the rods which its owner had formerly lent to the Egyptian Magi. Of this fact, however, Goodman Brown could not take cognizance. He had cast his eyes in astonishment, and looking down again, beheld neither Goody Cloyse nor the serpentine staff, but his fellow-traveller alone, who waited for him as calmly as if nothing had happened.

"That old woman taught me my catechism!" said the young man; and there was a world of meaning in this simple comment.

They continued to walk onward, while the elder traveller exhorted his companion to make good speed and persevere in the path, discoursing so aptly, that his arguments seemed rather to spring up in the bosom of his auditor, than to be suggested by himself. As they went he plucked a branch of maple, to serve for a walking-stick, and began to strip it of the twigs and little boughs, which were wet with evening dew. The moment his fingers touched them, they became strangely withered and dried up, as with a week's sunshine. Thus the pair proceeded, at a good free pace, until suddenly, in a gloomy hollow of the road, Goodman Brown sat himself down on the stump of a tree, and refused to go any farther.

"Friend," said he, stubbornly, "my mind is made up. Not another step will I budge on this errand. What if a wretched old woman do choose to go to the devil, when I thought she was going to Heaven! Is that any reason why I should quit my dear Faith, and go after her?"

"You will think better of this by and by," said his acquaintance, composedly. "Sit here and rest yourself awhile; and when you feel like moving again, there is my staff to help you along."

Without more words, he threw his companion the maple stick, and was as speedily out of sight as if he had vanished into the deepening gloom. The young man sat a few moments by the roadside, applauding himself greatly, and thinking with how clear a conscience he should meet the minister, in his morning walk, nor shrink from the eye of good old Deacon Gookin. And what calm sleep would be his, that very night, which was to have been spent so wickedly, but purely and sweetly now, in the arms of Faith! Amidst these pleasant and praiseworthy meditations, Goodman Brown heard the tramp of horses along the road, and deemed it advisable to conceal himself within the verge of the forest, conscious of the guilty purpose that had brought him thither, though now so happily turned from it.

On came the hoof-tramps and the voices of the riders, two grave old voices, conversing soberly, as they drew near. These mingled sounds appeared to pass along the road, within a few yards of the young man's hiding-place; but owing, doubtless, to the depth of the gloom, at that particular spot, neither the travellers nor their steeds were visible. Though their figures brushed the small boughs by the wayside, it could not be seen that they intercepted, even for a moment, the faint gleam from the strip of bright sky, athwart which they must have passed. Goodman Brown alternately crouched and stood on tiptoe, pulling aside the branches, and thrusting forth his head as far as he durst, without discerning so much as a shadow. It vexed him the more, because he could have sworn, were such a thing possible, that he recognized the voices of the minister and Deacon Gookin, jogging along quietly, as they were wont to do, when bound to some ordination or ecclesiastical council. While yet within hearing, one of the riders stopped to pluck a switch.

"Of the two, reverend Sir," said the voice like the deacon's, "I had rather miss an ordination dinner than to-night's meeting. They tell me that some of our community are to be here from Falmouth and beyond, and others from Connecticut and Rhode Island; besides several of the Indian powwows, who, after their fashion, know almost as much deviltry as the best of us. Moreover, there is a goodly young woman to be taken into communion."

"Mighty well, Deacon Gookin!" replied the solemn old tones of the minister. "Spur up, or we shall be late. Nothing can be done, you know, until I get on the ground."

The hoofs clattered again, and the voices, talking so strangely in the empty air, passed on through the forest, where no church had ever been gathered, nor solitary Christian prayed. Whither, then, could these holy men be journeying, so deep into the heathen wilderness? Young Goodman Brown caught hold of a tree, for support, being ready to sink down on the ground, faint and over-burthened with the heavy sickness of his heart. He looked up to the sky, doubting whether there really was a Heaven above him. Yet, there was the blue arch, and the stars brightening in it.

"With Heaven above, and Faith below, I will yet stand firm against the devil!" cried Goodman Brown.

While he still gazed upward, into the deep arch of the firmament, and had lifted his hands to pray, a cloud, though no wind was stirring, hurried across the zenith, and hid the brightening stars. The blue sky was still visible, except directly overhead, where this black mass of cloud was sweeping swiftly northward. Aloft in the air, as if from the depths of the cloud, came a confused and doubtful sound of voices. Once, the listener fancied that he could distinguish the accents of townspeople of his own, men and women, both pious and ungodly, many of whom he had met at the communion-table, and had seen others rioting at the tavern. The next moment, so indistinct were the sounds, he doubted whether he had heard aught but the murmur of the old forest, whispering without a wind. Then came a stronger swell of those familiar tones, heard daily in the sunshine, at Salem village, but never, until now, from a cloud at night. There was one voice, of a young woman, tittering lamentations, yet with an uncertain sorrow, and entreating for some favor, which, perhaps, it would grieve her to obtain. And all the unseen multitude, both saints and sinners, seemed to encourage her onward.

"Faith!" shouted Goodman Brown, in a voice of agony and desperation; and the echoes of the forest mocked him, crying—"Faith! Faith!" as if bewildered wretches were seeking her, all through the wilderness.

The cry of grief, rage, and terror was yet piercing the night, when the unhappy husband held his breath for a response. There was a scream, drowned immediately in a louder murmur of voices fading into far-off laughter, as the dark cloud swept away, leaving the clear and silent sky above Goodman Brown. But something fluttered lightly down through the air, and caught on the branch of a tree. The young man seized it and beheld a pink ribbon.

"My Faith is gone!" cried he, after one stupefied moment. "There is no good on earth, and sin is but a name. Come, devil! for to thee is this world given."

And maddened with despair, so that he laughed loud and long, did Goodman Brown grasp his staff and set forth again, at such a rate, that he seemed to fly along the forest path, rather than to walk or run. The road grew wilder and drearier, and more faintly traced, and vanished at length, leaving him in the heart of the dark wilderness, still rushing onward, with the instinct that guides mortal man to evil. The whole forest was peopled with frightful sounds: the creaking of the trees, the howling of wild beasts, and the yell of Indians; while, sometimes, the wind tolled like a distant church bell, and sometimes gave a broad roar around the traveller, as if all Nature was laughing him to scorn. But he was himself the chief horror of the scene, and shrank not from its other horrors.

"Ha! ha! ha!" roared Goodman Brown, when the wind laughed at him. "Let us hear which will laugh loudest! Think not to frighten me with your deviltry! Come witch, come wizard, come Indian powwow, come devil himself! and here comes Goodman Brown. You may as well fear him as he fear you!"

In truth, all through the haunted forest, there could be nothing more frightful than the figure of Goodman Brown. On he flew, among the black pines, brandishing his staff with frenzied gestures, now giving vent to an inspiration of horrid blasphemy, and now shouting forth such laughter, as set all the echoes of the forest laughing like demons around him. The fiend in his own shape is less hideous, than when he rages in the breast of man. Thus sped the demoniac on his course, until, quivering among the trees, he saw a red light before him, as when the felled trunks and branches of a clearing have been set on fire, and throw up their lurid blaze against the sky, at the hour of midnight. He paused, in a lull of the tempest that had driven him onward, and heard the swell of what seemed a hymn, rolling solemnly from a distance, with the weight of many voices. He knew the tune. It was a familiar one in the choir of the village meeting-house. The verse died heavily away, and was lengthened by a chorus, not of human voices, but of all the sounds of the benighted wilderness, pealing in awful harmony together. Goodman Brown cried out; and his cry was lost to his own ear, by its unison with the cry of the desert.

In the interval of silence, he stole forward, until the light glared full upon his eyes. At one extremity of an open space, hemmed in by the dark wall of the forest, arose a rock, bearing some rude, natural resemblance either to an altar or a pulpit, and surrounded by four blazing pines, their tops aflame, their stems untouched, like candles at an evening meeting. The mass of foliage, that had overgrown the summit of the rock, was all on fire, blazing high into the night, and fitfully illuminating the whole field. Each pendent twig and leafy festoon was in a blaze. As the red light arose and fell, a numerous congregation alternately shone forth, then disappeared in shadow, and again grew, as it were, out of the darkness, peopling the heart of the solitary woods at once.

"A grave and dark-clad company!" quoth Goodman Brown.

In truth, they were such. Among them, quivering to-and-fro, between gloom and splendor, appeared faces that would be seen, next day, at the council-board of the province, and others which, Sabbath after Sabbath, looked devoutly heavenward, and benignantly over the crowded pews, from the holiest pulpits in the land. Some affirm, that the lady of the governor was there. At least, there were high dames well known to her, and wives of honored husbands, and widows a great multitude, and ancient maidens, all of excellent repute, and fair young girls, who trembled lest their mothers should espy them. Either the sudden gleams of light, flashing over the obscure field, bedazzled Goodman Brown, or he recognized a score of the church members of Salem village, famous for their especial sanctity. Good old Deacon Gookin had arrived, and waited at the skirts of that venerable saint, his reverend pastor. But, irreverently consorting with these grave, reputable, and pious people, these elders of the church, these chaste dames and dewy virgins, there were men of dissolute lives and women of spotted fame, wretches given over to all mean and filthy vice, and suspected even of horrid crimes. It was strange to see, that the good shrank not from the wicked, nor were the sinners abashed by the saints. Scattered, also, among their pale-faced enemies, were the Indian priests, or powwows, who had often scared their native forest with more hideous incantations than any known to English witchcraft.

"But, where is Faith?" thought Goodman Brown; and, as hope came into his heart, he trembled.

Another verse of the hymn arose, a slow and mournful strain, such as the pious love, but joined to words which expressed all that our nature can conceive of sin, and darkly hinted at far more. Unfathomable to mere mortals is the lore of fiends. Verse after verse was sung, and still the chorus of the desert swelled between, like the deepest tone of a mighty organ. And, with the final peal of that dreadful anthem, there came a sound, as if the roaring wind, the rushing streams, the howling beasts, and every other voice of the unconverted wilderness were mingling and according with the voice of guilty man, in homage to the prince of all. The four blazing pines threw up a loftier flame, and obscurely discovered shapes and visages of horror on the smoke-wreaths, above the impious assembly. At the same moment, the fire on the rock shot redly forth, and formed a glowing arch above its base, where now appeared a figure. With reverence be it spoken, the apparition bore no slight similitude, both in garb and manner, to some grave divine of the New England churches.

"Bring forth the converts!" cried a voice, that echoed through the field and rolled into the forest.

At the word, Goodman Brown stepped forth from the shadow of the trees, and approached the congregation, with whom he felt a loathful brotherhood, by the sympathy of all that was wicked in his heart. He could have well-nigh sworn, that the shape of his own dead father beckoned him to advance, looking downward from a smoke-wreath, while a woman, with dim features of despair, threw out her hand to warn him back. Was it his mother? But he had no power to retreat one step, nor to resist, even in thought, when the minister and good old Deacon Gookin seized his arms, and led him to the blazing rock. Thither came also the slender form of a veiled female, led between Goody Cloyse, that pious teacher of the catechism, and Martha Carrier, who had received the devil's promise to be queen of hell. A rampant hag was she! And there stood the proselytes, beneath the canopy of fire.

"Welcome, my children," said the dark figure, "to the communion of your race! Ye have found, thus young, your nature and your destiny. My children, look behind you!"

They turned; and flashing forth, as it were, in a sheet of flame, the fiend-worshippers were seen; the smile of welcome gleamed darkly on every visage.

"There," resumed the sable form, "are all whom ye have reverenced from youth. Ye deemed them holier than yourselves, and shrank from your own sin, contrasting it with their lives of righteousness and prayerful aspirations heavenward. Yet, here are they all, in my worshipping assembly! This night it shall be granted you to know their secret deeds; how hoary-bearded elders of the church have whispered wanton words to the young maids of their households; how many a woman, eager for widow's weeds, has given her husband a drink at bedtime, and let him sleep his last sleep in her bosom; how beardless youths have made haste to inherit their father's wealth; and how fair damsels—blush not, sweet ones!—have dug little graves in the garden, and bidden me, the sole guest, to an infant's funeral. By the sympathy of your human hearts for sin, ye shall scent out all the places—whether in church, bed-chamber, street, field, or forest—where crime has been committed, and shall exult to behold the whole earth one stain of guilt, one mighty blood-spot. Far more than this! It shall be yours to penetrate, in every bosom, the deep mystery of sin, the fountain of all wicked arts, and which inexhaustibly supplies more evil impulses than human power—than my power, at its utmost!—can make manifest in deeds. And now, my children, look upon each other."

They did so; and, by the blaze of the hell-kindled torches, the wretched man beheld his Faith, and the wife her husband, trembling before that unhallowed altar.

"Lo! there ye stand, my children," said the figure, in a deep and solemn tone, almost sad, with its despairing awfulness, as if his once angelic nature could yet mourn for our miserable race. "Depending upon one another's hearts, ye had still hoped that virtue were not all a dream! Now are ye undeceived!—Evil is the nature of mankind. Evil must be your only happiness. Welcome, again, my children, to the communion of your race!"

"Welcome!" repeated the fiend-worshippers, in one cry of despair and triumph.

And there they stood, the only pair, as it seemed, who were yet hesitating on the verge of wickedness, in this dark world. A basin was hollowed, naturally, in the rock. Did it contain water, reddened by the lurid light? or was it blood? or, perchance, a liquid flame? Herein did the Shape of Evil dip his hand, and prepare to lay the mark of baptism upon their foreheads, that they might be partakers of the mystery of sin, more conscious of the secret guilt of others, both in deed and thought, than they could now be of their own. The husband cast one look at his pale wife, and Faith at him. What polluted wretches would the next glance show them to each other, shuddering alike at what they disclosed and what they saw!

"Faith! Faith!" cried the husband. "Look up to Heaven, and resist the Wicked One!"

Whether Faith obeyed, he knew not. Hardly had he spoken, when he found himself amid calm night and solitude, listening to a roar of the wind, which died heavily away through the forest. He staggered against the rock, and felt it chill and damp, while a hanging twig, that had been all on fire, besprinkled his cheek with the coldest dew.

The next morning, young Goodman Brown came slowly into the street of Salem village staring around him like a bewildered man. The good old minister was taking a walk along the grave-yard, to get an appetite for breakfast and meditate his sermon, and bestowed a blessing, as he passed, on Goodman Brown. He shrank from the venerable saint, as if to avoid an anathema. Old Deacon Gookin was at domestic worship, and the holy words of his prayer were heard through the open window. "What God doth the wizard pray to?" quoth Goodman Brown. Goody Cloyse, that excellent old Christian, stood in the early sunshine, at her own lattice, catechizing a little girl, who had brought her a pint of morning's milk. Goodman Brown snatched away the child, as from the grasp of the fiend himself. Turning the corner by the meeting-house, he spied the head of Faith, with the pink ribbons, gazing anxiously forth, and bursting into such joy at sight of him that she skipt along the street, and almost kissed her husband before the whole village. But Goodman Brown looked sternly and sadly into her face, and passed on without a greeting.

Had Goodman Brown fallen asleep in the forest, and only dreamed a wild dream of a witch-meeting?

Be it so, if you will. But, alas! it was a dream of evil omen for young Goodman Brown. A stern, a sad, a darkly meditative, a distrustful, if not a desperate man did he become, from the night of that fearful dream. On the Sabbath day, when the congregation were singing a holy psalm, he could not listen, because an anthem of sin rushed loudly upon his ear, and drowned all the blessed strain. When the minister spoke from the pulpit, with power and fervid eloquence, and with his hand on the open Bible, of the sacred truths of our religion, and of saint-like lives and triumphant deaths, and of future bliss or misery unutterable, then did Goodman Brown turn pale, dreading lest the roof should thunder down upon the gray blasphemer and his hearers. Often, awaking suddenly at midnight, he shrank from the bosom of Faith, and at morning or eventide, when the family knelt down at prayer, he scowled, and muttered to himself, and gazed sternly at his wife, and turned away. And when he had lived long, and was borne to his grave, a hoary corpse, followed by Faith, an aged woman, and children and grand-children, a goodly procession, besides neighbors not a few, they carved no hopeful verse upon his tombstone; for his dying hour was gloom.

(1828)

ANTON CHEKHOV
[1860–1904]

The Lady with the Dog

TRANSLATED BY CONSTANCE GARNETT

I

It was said that a new person had appeared on the sea-front: a lady with a little dog. Dmitri Dmitritch Gurov, who had by then been a fortnight at Yalta, and so was fairly at home there, had begun to take an interest in new arrivals. Sitting in Verney's pavilion, he saw, walking on the sea-front, a fair-haired young lady of medium height, wearing a *béret;* a white Pomeranian dog was running behind her.

And afterwards he met her in the public gardens and in the square several times a day. She was walking alone, always wearing the same *béret,* and always with the same white dog; no one knew who she was, and every one called her simply "the lady with the dog."

"If she is here alone without a husband or friends, it wouldn't be amiss to make her acquaintance," Gurov reflected.

He was under forty, but he had a daughter already twelve years old, and two sons at school. He had been married young, when he was a student in his second year, and by now his wife seemed half as old again as he. She was a tall, erect woman with dark eyebrows, staid and dignified, and, as she said of herself, intellectual. She read a great deal, used phonetic spelling, called her husband, not Dmitri, but Dimitri, and he secretly considered her unintelligent, narrow, inelegant, was afraid of her, and did not like to be at home. He had begun being unfaithful to her long ago—had been unfaithful to her often, and, probably on that account, almost always spoke ill of women, and when they were talked about in his presence, used to call them "the lower race."

It seemed to him that he had been so schooled by bitter experience that he might call them what he liked, and yet he could not get on for two days together without "the lower race." In the society of men he was bored and not himself, with them he was cold and uncommunicative; but when he was in the company of women he felt free, and knew what to say to them and how to behave; and he was at ease with them even when he was silent. In his appearance, in his character, in his whole nature, there was something attractive and elusive which allured women and disposed them in his favour; he knew that, and some force seemed to draw him, too, to them.

Experience often repeated, truly bitter experience, had taught him long ago that with decent people, especially Moscow people—always slow to move and irresolute—every intimacy, which at first so agreeably diversifies life and appears a light and charming adventure, inevitably grows into a regular problem of extreme intricacy, and in the long run the situation becomes unbearable. But at every fresh meeting with an interesting woman this experience seemed to slip out of his memory, and he was eager for life, and everything seemed simple and amusing.

One evening he was dining in the gardens, and the lady in the *béret* came up slowly to take the next table. Her expression, her gait, her dress, and the way she did her hair told him that she was a lady, that she was married, that she was in Yalta for the first time and alone, and that she was dull there. . . . The stories told of the immorality in such places as Yalta are to a great extent untrue; he despised them, and knew that such stories were for the most part made up by persons who would themselves have been glad to sin if they had been able; but when the lady sat down at the next table three paces from him, he remembered these tales of easy conquests, of trips to the mountains, and the tempting thought of a swift, fleeting love affair, a romance with an unknown woman, whose name he did not know, suddenly took possession of him.

He beckoned coaxingly to the Pomeranian, and when the dog came up to him he shook his finger at it. The Pomeranian growled: Gurov shook his finger at it again.

The lady looked at him and at once dropped her eyes.

"He doesn't bite," she said, and blushed.

"May I give him a bone?" he asked; and when she nodded he asked courteously, "Have you been long in Yalta?"

"Five days."

"And I have already dragged out a fortnight here."

There was a brief silence.

"Time goes fast, and yet it is so dull here!" she said, not looking at him.

"That's only the fashion to say it is dull here. A provincial will live in Belyov or Zhidra and not be dull, and when he comes here it's 'Oh, the dullness! Oh, the dust!' One would think he came from Grenada."

She laughed. Then both continued eating in silence, like strangers, but after dinner they walked side by side; and there sprang up between them the light jesting conversation of people who are free and satisfied, to whom it does not matter where they go or what they talk about. They walked and talked of the strange light on the sea: the water was of a soft warm lilac hue, and there was a golden streak from the moon upon it. They talked of how sultry it was after a hot day. Gurov told her that he came from Moscow, that he had taken his degree in Arts, but had a post in a bank; that he had trained as an opera-singer, but had given it up, that he owned two houses in Moscow. . . . And from her he learnt that she had grown up in Petersburg, but had lived in S—— since her marriage two years before, that she was staying another month in Yalta, and that her husband, who needed a holiday too, might perhaps come and fetch her. She was not sure whether her husband had a post in a Crown Department or under the Provincial Council—and was amused by her own ignorance. And Gurov learnt, too, that she was called Anna Sergeyevna.

Afterwards he thought about her in his room at the hotel—thought she would certainly meet him next day; it would be sure to happen. As he got into bed he thought how lately she had been a girl at school, doing lessons like his own daughter; he recalled the diffidence, the angularity, that was still manifest in her laugh and her manner of talking with a stranger. This must have been the first time in her life she had been alone in surroundings in which she was followed, looked at, and spoken to merely from a secret motive which she could hardly fail to guess. He recalled her slender, delicate neck, her lovely grey eyes.

"There's something pathetic about her, anyway," he thought, and fell asleep.

2

A week had passed since they had made acquaintance. It was a holiday. It was sultry indoors, while in the street the wind whirled the dust round and round, and blew people's hats off. It was a thirsty day, and Gurov often went into the pavilion, and pressed Anna Sergeyevna to have syrup and water or an ice. One did not know what to do with oneself.

In the evening when the wind had dropped a little, they went out on the groyne to see the steamer come in. There were a great many people walking about the harbour; they had gathered to welcome some one, bringing bouquets. And two peculiarities of a well-dressed Yalta crowd were very conspicuous: the elderly ladies were dressed like young ones, and there were great numbers of generals.

Owing to the roughness of the sea, the steamer arrived late, after the sun had set, and it was a long time turning about before it reached the groyne. Anna Sergeyevna looked through her lorgnette at the steamer and the passengers as though looking for acquaintances, and when she turned to Gurov her eyes were shining. She talked a great deal and asked disconnected questions, forgetting next moment what she had asked; then she dropped her lorgnette in the crush.

The festive crowd began to disperse; it was too dark to see people's faces. The wind had completely dropped, but Gurov and Anna Sergeyevna still stood as though waiting to see some one else come from the steamer. Anna Sergeyevna was silent now, and sniffed the flowers without looking at Gurov.

"The weather is better this evening," he said. "Where shall we go now? Shall we drive somewhere?"

She made no answer.

Then he looked at her intently, and all at once put his arm round her and kissed her on the lips, and breathed in the moisture and the fragrance of the flowers; and he immediately looked round him, anxiously wondering whether any one had seen them.

"Let us go to your hotel," he said softly. And both walked quickly.

The room was close and smelt of the scent she had bought at the Japanese shop. Gurov looked at her and thought: "What different people one meets in the world!" From the past he preserved memories of careless, good-natured women, who loved cheerfully and were grateful to him for the happiness he gave them, however brief it might be; and of women like his wife who loved without any genuine feeling, with superfluous phrases, affectedly, hysterically, with an expression that suggested that it was not love nor passion, but something more significant; and of two or three others, very beautiful, cold women, on whose faces he had caught a glimpse of a rapacious expression—an obstinate desire to snatch from life more than it could give, and these were capricious, unreflecting, domineering, unintelligent women not in their first youth, and when Gurov grew cold to them their beauty excited his hatred, and the lace on their linen seemed to him like scales.

But in this case there was still the diffidence, the angularity of inexperienced youth, an awkward feeling; and there was a sense of consternation as though some one had suddenly knocked at the door. The attitude of Anna Sergeyevna—"the lady with the dog"—to what had happened was somehow peculiar, very grave, as though it were her fall—so it seemed, and it was strange and inappropriate. Her face dropped and faded, and on both sides of it her long hair hung down mournfully; she mused in a dejected attitude like "the woman who was a sinner" in an old-fashioned picture.

"It's wrong," she said. "You will be the first to despise me now."

There was a water-melon on the table. Gurov cut himself a slice and began eating it without haste. There followed at least half an hour of silence.

Anna Sergeyevna was touching; there was about her the purity of a good, simple woman who had seen little of life. The solitary candle burning on the table threw a faint light on her face, yet it was clear that she was very unhappy.

"How could I despise you?" asked Gurov. "You don't know what you are saying."

"God forgive me," she said, and her eyes filled with tears. "It's awful."

"You seem to feel you need to be forgiven."

"Forgiven? No. I am a bad, low woman; I despise myself and don't attempt to justify myself. It's not my husband but myself I have deceived. And not only just now; I have been deceiving myself for a long time. My husband may be a good, honest man, but he is a flunkey! I don't know what he does there, what his work is, but I know he is a flunkey! I was twenty when I was married to him. I have been tormented by curiosity; I wanted something better. 'There must be a different sort of life,' I said to myself. I wanted to live! To live, to live! . . . I was fired by curiosity . . . you don't understand it, but, I swear to God, I could not control myself; something happened to me: I could not be restrained. I told my husband I was ill, and came here. . . . And here I have been walking about as though I were dazed, like a mad creature; . . . and now I have become a vulgar, contemptible woman whom any one may despise."

Gurov felt bored already, listening to her. He was irritated by the naïve tone, by this remorse, so unexpected and inopportune; but for the tears in her eyes, he might have thought she was jesting or playing a part.

"I don't understand," he said softly. "What is it you want?"

She hid her face on his breast and pressed close to him.

"Believe me, believe me, I beseech you . . . " she said. "I love a pure, honest life, and sin is loathsome to me. I don't know what I am doing. Simple people say: 'The Evil One has beguiled me.' And I may say of myself now that the Evil One has beguiled me."

"Hush, hush! . . . " he muttered.

He looked at her fixed, scared eyes, kissed her, talked softly and affectionately, and by degrees she was comforted, and her gaiety returned; they both began laughing.

Afterwards when they went out there was not a soul on the sea-front. The town with its cypresses had quite a deathlike air, but the sea still broke noisily on the shore; a single barge was rocking on the waves, and a lantern was blinking sleepily on it.

They found a cab and drove to Oreanda.

"I found out your surname in the hall just now: it was written on the board—Von Diderits," said Gurov. "Is your husband a German?"

"No; I believe his grandfather was a German, but he is an Orthodox Russian himself."

At Oreanda they sat on a seat not far from the church, looked down at the sea, and were silent. Yalta was hardly visible through the morning mist; white clouds stood motionless on the mountain-tops. The leaves did not stir on the trees, grasshoppers chirruped, and the monotonous hollow sound of the sea rising up from below spoke of the peace, of the eternal sleep awaiting us. So it must have sounded when there was no Yalta, no Oreanda here; so it sounds now, and it will sound as indifferently and monotonously when we are all no more. And in this constancy, in this complete indifference to the life and death of each of us, there lies hid, perhaps, a pledge of our eternal salvation, of the unceasing movement of life upon earth, of unceasing progress towards perfection. Sitting beside a young woman who in the dawn seemed so lovely, soothed and spellbound in these magical surroundings—the sea, mountains, clouds, the open sky—Gurov thought how in reality everything is beautiful in this world when one reflects: everything except what we think or do ourselves when we forget our human dignity and the higher aims of our existence.

A man walked up to them—probably a keeper—looked at them and walked away. And this detail seemed mysterious and beautiful, too. They saw a steamer come from Theodosia, with its lights out in the glow of dawn.

"There is dew on the grass," said Anna Sergeyevna, after a silence.

"Yes. It's time to go home."

They went back to the town.

Then they met every day at twelve o'clock on the sea-front, lunched and dined together, went for walks, admired the sea. She complained that she slept badly, that her heart throbbed violently; asked the same questions, troubled now by jealousy and now by the fear that he did not respect her sufficiently. And often in the square or gardens, when there was no one near them, he suddenly drew her to him and kissed her passionately. Complete idleness, these kisses in broad daylight while he looked round in dread of some one's seeing them, the heat, the smell of the sea, and the continual passing to and fro before him of idle, well-dressed, well-fed people, made a new man of him; he told Anna Sergeyevna how beautiful she was, how fascinating. He was impatiently passionate, he would not move a step away from her, while she was often pensive and continually urged him to confess that he did not respect her, did not love her in the least, and thought of her as nothing but a common woman. Rather late almost every evening they drove somewhere out of town, to Oreanda or to the waterfall; and the expedition was always a success, the scenery invariably impressed them as grand and beautiful.

They were expecting her husband to come, but a letter came from him, saying that there was something wrong with his eyes, and he entreated his wife to come home as quickly as possible. Anna Sergeyevna made haste to go.

"It's a good thing I am going away," she said to Gurov. "It's the finger of destiny!"

She went by coach and he went with her. They were driving the whole day. When she had got into a compartment of the express, and when the second bell had rung, she said:

"Let me look at you once more . . . look at you once again. That's right."

She did not shed tears, but was so sad that she seemed ill, and her face was quivering.

"I shall remember you . . . think of you," she said. "God be with you; be happy. Don't remember evil against me. We are parting forever—it must be so, for we ought never to have met. Well, God be with you."

The train moved off rapidly, its lights soon vanished from sight, and a minute later there was no sound of it, as though everything had conspired together to end as quickly as possible that sweet delirium, that madness. Left alone on the platform, and gazing into the dark distance, Gurov listened to the chirrup of the grasshoppers and the hum of the telegraph wires, feeling as though he had only just waked up. And he thought, musing, that there had been another episode or adventure in his life, and it, too, was at an end, and nothing was left of it but a memory. . . . He was moved, sad, and conscious of a slight remorse. This young woman whom he would never meet again had not been happy with him; he was genuinely warm and affectionate with her, but yet in his manner, his tone, and his caresses there had been a shade of light irony, the coarse condescension of a happy man who was, besides, almost twice her age. All the time she had called him kind, exceptional, lofty; obviously he had seemed to her different from what he really was, so he had unintentionally deceived her. . . .

Here at the station was already a scent of autumn; it was a cold evening.

"It's time for me to go north," thought Gurov as he left the platform. "High time!"

3

At home in Moscow everything was in its winter routine; the stoves were heated, and in the morning it was still dark when the children were having breakfast and getting ready for school, and the nurse would light the lamp for a short time. The frost had begun already. When the first snow has fallen, on the first day of sledge-driving it is pleasant to see the white earth, the white roofs, to draw soft, delicious breath, and the season brings back the days of one's youth. The old limes and birches, white with hoar-frost, have a good-natured expression; they are nearer to one's heart than cypresses and palms, and near them one doesn't want to be thinking of the sea and the mountains.

Gurov was Moscow born; he arrived in Moscow on a fine frosty day, and when he put on his fur coat and warm gloves, and walked along Petrovka, and when on Saturday evening he heard the ringing of the bells, his recent trip and the places he had seen lost all charm for him. Little by little he became absorbed in Moscow life, greedily read three newspapers a day, and declared he did not read the Moscow papers on principle! He already felt a longing to go to restaurants, clubs, dinner-parties, anniversary celebrations and he felt flattered at entertaining distinguished lawyers and artists, and at playing cards with a professor at the doctors' club. He could already eat a whole plateful of salt fish and cabbage. . . .

In another month, he fancied, the image of Anna Sergeyevna would be shrouded in a mist in his memory, and only from time to time would visit him in his dreams with a touching smile as others did. But more than a month passed, real winter had come, and everything was still clear in his memory as though he had parted with Anna Sergeyevna only the day before. And his memories glowed more and more vividly. When in the evening stillness he heard from his study the voices of his children, preparing their lessons, or when he listened to a song or the organ at the restaurant, or the storm howled in the chimney, suddenly everything would rise up in his memory: what had happened on the groyne, and the early morning with the mist on the mountains, and the steamer coming from Theodosia and the kisses. He would pace a long time about his room, remembering it all and smiling; then his memories passed into dreams, and in his fancy the past was mingled with what was to come. Anna Sergeyevna did not visit him in dreams, but followed him about everywhere like a shadow and haunted him. When he shut his eyes he saw her as though she were living before him, and she seemed to him lovelier, younger, tenderer than she was; and he imagined himself finer than he had been in Yalta. In the evenings she peeped out at him from the bookcase, from the fireplace, from the corner—he heard her breathing, the caressing rustle of her dress. In the street he watched the women, looking for some one like her.

He was tormented by an intense desire to confide his memories to some one. But in his home it was impossible to talk of his love, and he had no one outside; he could not talk to his tenants nor to any one at the bank. And what had he to talk of? Had he been in love, then? Had there been anything beautiful, poetical, or edifying or simply interesting in his relations with Anna Sergeyevna? And there was nothing for him but to talk vaguely of love, of woman, and no one guessed what it meant; only his wife twitched her black eyebrows, and said: "The part of a lady-killer does not suit you at all, Dimitri."

One evening, coming out of the doctors' club with an official with whom he had been playing cards, he could not resist saying:

"If only you knew what a fascinating woman I made the acquaintance of in Yalta!"

The official got into his sledge and was driving away, but turned suddenly and shouted:

"Dmitri Dmitritch!"

"What?"

"You were right this evening: the sturgeon was a bit too strong!"

These words, so ordinary, for some reason moved Gurov to indignation, and struck him as degrading and unclean. What savage manners, what people! What senseless nights, what uninteresting, uneventful days! The rage for card-playing, the gluttony, the drunkenness, the continual talk always about the same thing. Useless pursuits and conversations always about the same things absorb the better part of one's time, the better part of one's strength, and in the end there is left a life grovelling and curtailed, worthless and trivial, and there is no escaping or getting away from it—just as though one were in a madhouse or a prison.

Gurov did not sleep all night, and was filled with indignation. And he had a headache all next day. And the next night he slept badly; he sat up in bed, thinking, or paced up and down his room. He was sick of his children, sick of the bank; he had no desire to go anywhere or to talk of anything.

In the holidays in December he prepared for a journey, and told his wife he was going to Petersburg to do something in the interests of a young friend—and he set off for S———. What for? He did not very well know himself. He wanted to see Anna Sergeyevna and to talk with her—to arrange a meeting, if possible.

He reached S——— in the morning, and took the best room at the hotel, in which the floor was covered with grey army cloth, and on the table was an inkstand, grey with dust and adorned with a figure on horseback, with its hat in its hand and its head broken off. The hotel porter gave him the necessary information; Von Diderits lived in a house of his own in Old Gontcharny Street—it was not far from the hotel: he was rich and lived in good style, and had his own horses; every one in the town knew him. The porter pronounced the name "Dridirits."

Gurov went without haste to Old Gontcharny Street and found the house. Just opposite the house stretched a long grey fence adorned with nails.

"One would run away from a fence like that," thought Gurov, looking from the fence to the windows of the house and back again.

He considered: to-day was a holiday, and the husband would probably be at home. And in any case it would be tactless to go into the house and upset her. If he were to send her a note it might fall into her husband's hands, and then it might ruin everything. The best thing was to trust to chance. And he kept walking up and down the street by the fence, waiting for the chance. He saw a beggar go in at the gate and dogs fly at him; then an hour later he heard a piano, and the sounds were faint and indistinct. Probably it was Anna Sergeyevna playing. The front door suddenly opened, and an old woman came out, followed by the familiar white Pomeranian. Gurov was on the point of calling to the dog, but his heart began beating violently, and in his excitement he could not remember the dog's name.

He walked up and down, and loathed the grey fence more and more, and by now he thought irritably that Anna Sergeyevna had forgotten him, and was perhaps already amusing herself with some one else, and that that was very natural in a young woman who had nothing to look at from morning till night but that confounded fence. He went back to his hotel room and sat for a long while on the sofa, not knowing what to do, then he had dinner and a long nap.

"How stupid and worrying it is!" he thought when he woke and looked at the dark windows: it was already evening. "Here I've had a good sleep for some reason. What shall I do in the night?"

He sat on the bed, which was covered by a cheap grey blanket, such as one sees in hospitals, and he taunted himself in his vexation:

"So much for the lady with the dog . . . so much for the adventure. . . . You're in a nice fix. . . ."

That morning at the station a poster in large letters had caught his eye. "The Geisha" was to be performed for the first time. He thought of this and went to the theatre.

"It's quite possible she may go to the first performance," he thought.

The theatre was full. As in all provincial theatres, there was a fog above the chandelier, the gallery was noisy and restless; in the front row the local dandies were standing up before the beginning of the performance, with their hands behind them; in the Governor's box the Governor's daughter, wearing a boa, was sitting in the front seat, while the Governor himself lurked modestly behind the curtain with only his hands visible; the orchestra was a long time tuning up; the stage curtain swayed. All the time the audience were coming in and taking their seats Gurov looked at them eagerly.

Anna Sergeyevna, too, came in. She sat down in the third row, and when Gurov looked at her his heart contracted, and he understood clearly that for him there was in the whole world no creature so near, so precious, and so important to him; she, this little woman, in no way remarkable, lost in a provincial crowd, with a vulgar lorgnette in her hand, filled his whole life now, was his sorrow and his joy, the one happiness that he now desired for himself, and to the sounds of the inferior orchestra, of the wretched provincial violins, he thought how lovely she was. He thought and dreamed.

A young man with small side-whiskers, tall and stooping, came in with Anna Sergeyevna, and sat down beside her; he bent his head at every step and seemed to be continually bowing. Most likely this was the husband whom at Yalta, in a rush of bitter feeling, she had called a flunkey. And there really was in his long figure, his side-whiskers, and the small bald patch on his head, something of the flunkey's obsequiousness; his smile was sugary, and in his buttonhole there was some badge of distinction like the number on a waiter.

During the first interval the husband went away to smoke; she remained alone in her stall. Gurov, who was sitting in the stalls, too, went up to her and said in a trembling voice, with a forced smile:

"Good-evening."

She glanced at him and turned pale, then glanced again with horror, unable to believe her eyes, and tightly gripped her fan and the lorgnette in her hands, evidently struggling with herself not to faint. Both were silent. She was sitting, he was standing, frightened by her confusion and not venturing to sit down beside her. The violins and the flute began tuning up. He felt suddenly frightened; it seemed as though all the people in the boxes were looking at them. She got up and went quickly to the door; he followed her, and both walked senselessly along passages, and up and down stairs, and figures in legal, scholastic, and civil service uniforms, all wearing badges, flitted before their eyes. They caught glimpses of ladies, of fur coats hanging on pegs; the draughts blew on them, bringing a smell of stale tobacco. And Gurov, whose heart was beating violently, thought:

"Oh, heavens! Why are these people here and this orchestra! . . . "

And at that instant he recalled how when he had seen Anna Sergeyevna off at the station he had thought that everything was over and they would never meet again. But how far they were still from the end!

On the narrow, gloomy staircase over which was written "To the Amphitheatre," she stopped.

"How you have frightened me!" she said, breathing hard, still pale and overwhelmed. "Oh, how you have frightened me! I am half dead. Why have you come? Why?"

"But do understand, Anna, do understand . . . " he said hastily in a low voice. "I entreat you to understand. . . . "

She looked at him with dread, with entreaty, with love; she looked at him intently, to keep his features more distinctly in her memory.

"I am so unhappy," she went on, not heeding him. "I have thought of nothing but you all the time; I live only in the thought of you. And I wanted to forget, to forget you; but why, oh, why, have you come?"

On the landing above them two schoolboys were smoking and looking down, but that was nothing to Gurov; he drew Anna Sergeyevna to him, and began kissing her face, her cheeks, and her hands.

"What are you doing, what are you doing!" she cried in horror, pushing him away. "We are mad. Go away to-day; go away at once. . . . I beseech you by all that is sacred, I implore you. . . . There are people coming this way!"

Some one was coming up the stairs.

"You must go away," Anna Sergeyevna went on in a whisper. "Do you hear, Dmitri Dmitritch? I will come and see you in Moscow. I have never been happy; I am miserable now, and I never, never shall be happy, never! Don't make me suffer still more! I swear I'll come to Moscow. But now let us part. My precious, good, dear one, we must part!"

She pressed his hand and began rapidly going downstairs, looking round at him, and from her eyes he could see that she really was unhappy. Gurov stood for a little while, listened, then, when all sound had died away, he found his coat and left the theatre.

4

And Anna Sergeyevna began coming to see him in Moscow. Once in two or three months she left S———, telling her husband that she was going to consult a doctor about an internal complaint—and her husband believed her, and did not believe her. In Moscow she stayed at the Slaviansky Bazaar hotel, and at once sent a man in a red cap to Gurov. Gurov went to see her, and no one in Moscow knew of it.

Once he was going to see her in this way on a winter morning (the messenger had come the evening before when he was out). With him walked his daughter, whom he wanted to take to school: it was on the way. Snow was falling in big wet flakes.

"It's three degrees above freezing-point, and yet it is snowing," said Gurov to his daughter. "The thaw is only on the surface of the earth; there is quite a different temperature at a greater height in the atmosphere."

"And why are there no thunderstorms in the winter, father?"

He explained that, too. He talked, thinking all the while that he was going to see *her,* and no living soul knew of it, and probably never would know. He had two lives: one, open, seen and known by all who cared to know, full of relative truth and of relative falsehood, exactly like the lives of his friends and acquaintances; and another life running its course in secret. And through some strange, perhaps accidental, conjunction of circumstances, everything that was essential, of interest and of value to him, everything in which he was sincere and did not deceive himself, everything that made the kernel of his life, was hidden from other people; and all that was false in him, the sheath in which he hid himself to conceal the truth—such, for instance, as his work in the bank, his discussions at the club, his "lower race," his presence with his wife at anniversary festivities—all that was open. And he judged of others by himself, not believing in what he saw, and always believing that every man had his real, most interesting life under the cover of secrecy and under the cover of night. All personal life rested on secrecy, and possibly it was partly on that account that civilised man was so nervously anxious that personal privacy should be respected.

After leaving his daughter at school, Gurov went on to the Slaviansky Bazaar. He took off his fur coat below, went upstairs, and softly knocked at the door. Anna Sergeyevna, wearing his favourite grey dress, exhausted by the journey and the suspense, had been expecting him since the evening before. She was pale; she looked at him, and did not smile, and he had hardly come in when she fell on his breast. Their kiss was slow and prolonged, as though they had not met for two years.

"Well, how are you getting on there?" he asked. "What news?"

"Wait; I'll tell you directly. . . . I can't talk."

She could not speak; she was crying. She turned away from him, and pressed her handkerchief to her eyes.

"Let her have her cry out. I'll sit down and wait," he thought, and he sat down in an arm-chair.

Then he rang and asked for tea to be brought him, and while he drank his tea she remained standing at the window with her back to him. She was crying from emotion, from the miserable consciousness that their life was so hard for them; they could only meet in secret, hiding themselves from people, like thieves! Was not their life shattered?

"Come, do stop!" he said.

It was evident to him that this love of theirs would not soon be over, that he could not see the end of it. Anna Sergeyevna grew more and more attached to him. She adored him, and it was unthinkable to say to her that it was bound to have an end some day; besides, she would not have believed it!

He went up to her and took her by the shoulders to say something affectionate and cheering, and at that moment he saw himself in the looking-glass.

His hair was already beginning to turn grey. And it seemed strange to him that he had grown so much older, so much plainer during the last few years. The shoulders on which his hands rested were warm and quivering. He felt compassion for this life, still so warm and lovely, but probably already not far from beginning to fade and wither like his own. Why did she love him so much? He always seemed to women different from what he was, and they loved in him not himself, but the man created by their imagination, whom they had been eagerly seeking all their lives; and afterwards, when they noticed their mistake, they loved him all the same. And not one of them had been happy with him. Time passed, he had made their acquaintance, got on with them, parted, but he had never once loved; it was anything you like, but not love.

And only now when his head was grey he had fallen properly, really in love—for the first time in his life.

Anna Sergeyevna and he loved each other like people very close and akin, like husband and wife, like tender friends; it seemed to them that fate itself had meant them for one another, and they could not understand why he had a wife and she a husband; and it was as though they were a pair of birds of passage, caught and forced to live in different cages. They forgave each other for what they were ashamed of in their past, they forgave everything in the present, and felt that this love of theirs had changed them both.

In moments of depression in the past he had comforted himself with any arguments that came into his mind, but now he no longer cared for arguments; he felt profound compassion, he wanted to be sincere and tender. . . .

"Don't cry, my darling," he said. "You've had your cry; that's enough. . . . Let us talk now, let us think of some plan."

Then they spent a long while taking counsel together, talked of how to avoid the necessity for secrecy, for deception, for living in different towns and not seeing each other for long at a time. How could they be free from this intolerable bondage?

"How? How?" he asked, clutching his head. "How?"

And it seemed as though in a little while the solution would be found, and then a new and splendid life would begin; and it was clear to both of them that they had still a long, long road before them, and that the most complicated and difficult part of it was only just beginning.

                                                                        (1899)

CHARLOTTE PERKINS GILMAN
[1860–1935]

The Yellow Wallpaper

It is very seldom that mere ordinary people like John and myself secure ancestral halls for the summer.

A colonial mansion, a hereditary estate, I would say a haunted house and reach the height of romantic felicity—but that would be asking too much of fate!

Still I will proudly declare that there is something queer about it.

Else, why should it be let so cheaply? And why have stood so long untenanted?

John laughs at me, of course, but one expects that.

John is practical in the extreme. He has no patience with faith, an intense horror of superstition, and he scoffs openly at any talk of things not to be felt and seen and put down in figures.

John is a physician, and *perhaps*—(I would not say it to a living soul, of course, but this is dead paper and a great relief to my mind)—*perhaps* that is one reason I do not get well faster.

You see, he does not believe I am sick! And what can one do?

If a physician of high standing, and one's own husband, assures friends and relatives that there is really nothing the matter with one but temporary nervous depression—a slight hysterical tendency—what is one to do?

My brother is also a physician, and also of high standing, and he says the same thing.

So I take phosphates or phosphites—whichever it is—and tonics, and air and exercise, and journeys, and am absolutely forbidden to "work" until I am well again.

Personally, I disagree with their ideas.

Personally, I believe that congenial work, with excitement and change, would do me good.

But what is one to do?

I did write for a while in spite of them; but it *does* exhaust me a good deal—having to be so sly about it, or else meet with heavy opposition.

I sometimes fancy that in my condition, if I had less opposition and more society and stimulus—but John says the very worst thing I can do is to think about my condition, and I confess it always makes me feel bad.

So I will let it alone and talk about the house.

The most beautiful place! It is quite alone, standing well back from the road, quite three miles from the village. It makes me think of English places that you read about, for there are hedges and walls and gates that lock, and lots of separate little houses for the gardeners and people.

There is a *delicious* garden! I never saw such a garden—large and shady, full of box-bordered paths, and lined with long grape-covered arbors with seats under them.

There were greenhouses, but they are all broken now.

There was some legal trouble, I believe, something about the heirs and co-heirs; anyhow, the place has been empty for years.

That spoils my ghostliness, I am afraid, but I don't care—there is something strange about the house—I can feel it.

I even said so to John one moonlight evening, but he said what I felt was a draught, and shut the window.

I get unreasonably angry with John sometimes. I'm sure I never used to be so sensitive. I think it is due to this nervous condition.

But John says if I feel so I shall neglect proper self-control; so I take pains to control myself—before him, at least, and that makes me very tired.

I don't like our room a bit. I wanted one downstairs that opened onto the piazza and had roses all over the window, and such pretty old-fashioned chintz hangings! But John would not hear of it.

He said there was only one window and not room for two beds, and no near room for him if he took another.

He is very careful and loving, and hardly lets me stir without special direction.

I have a schedule prescription for each hour in the day; he takes all care from me, and so I feel basely ungrateful not to value it more.

He said he came here solely on my account, that I was to have perfect rest and all the air I could get. "Your exercise depends on your strength, my dear," said he, "and your food somewhat on your appetite; but air you can absorb all the time." So we took the nursery at the top of the house.

It is a big, airy room, the whole floor nearly, with windows that look all ways, and air and sunshine galore. It was nursery first, and then playroom and gymnasium, I should judge, for the windows are barred for little children, and there are rings and things in the walls.

The paint and paper look as if a boys' school had used it. It is stripped off—the paper—in great patches all around the head of my bed, about as far as I can reach, and in a great place on the other side of the room low down. I never saw a worse paper in my life. One of those sprawling, flamboyant patterns committing every artistic sin.

It is dull enough to confuse the eye in following, pronounced enough constantly to irritate and provoke study, and when you follow the lame uncertain curves for a little distance they suddenly commit suicide—plunge off at outrageous angles, destroy themselves in unheard-of contradictions.

The color is repellent, almost revolting: a smouldering unclean yellow, strangely faded by the slow-turning sunlight. It is a dull yet lurid orange in some places, a sickly sulphur tint in others.

No wonder the children hated it! I should hate it myself if I had to live in this room long.

There comes John, and I must put this away—he hates to have me write a word.

We have been here two weeks, and I haven't felt like writing before, since that first day.

I am sitting by the window now, up in this atrocious nursery, and there is nothing to hinder my writing as much as I please, save lack of strength.

John is away all day, and even some nights when his cases are serious.

I am glad my case is not serious!

But these nervous troubles are dreadfully depressing.

John does not know how much I really suffer. He knows there is no reason to suffer, and that satisfies him.

Of course it is only nervousness. It does weigh on me so not to do my duty in any way!

I meant to be such a help to John, such a real rest and comfort, and here I am a comparative burden already!

Nobody would believe what an effort it is to do what little I am able—to dress and entertain, and order things.

It is fortunate Mary is so good with the baby. Such a dear baby!

And yet I *cannot* be with him, it makes me so nervous.

I suppose John never was nervous in his life. He laughs at me so about this wallpaper!

At first he meant to repaper the room, but afterward he said that I was letting it get the better of me, and that nothing was worse for a nervous patient than to give way to such fancies.

He said that after the wallpaper was changed it would be the heavy bedstead, and then the barred windows, and then that gate at the head of the stairs, and so on.

"You know the place is doing you good," he said, "and really, dear, I don't care to renovate the house just for a three months' rental."

"Then do let us go downstairs," I said. "There are such pretty rooms there."

Then he took me in his arms and called me a blessed little goose, and said he would go down cellar, if I wished, and have it whitewashed into the bargain.

But he is right enough about the beds and windows and things.

It is as airy and comfortable a room as anyone need wish, and, of course, I would not be so silly as to make him uncomfortable just for a whim.

I'm really getting quite fond of the big room, all but that horrid paper.

Out of one window I can see the garden—those mysterious deep-shaded arbors, the riotous old-fashioned flowers, and bushes and gnarly trees.

Out of another I get a lovely view of the bay and a little private wharf belonging to the estate. There is a beautiful shaded lane that runs down there from the house. I always fancy I see people walking in these numerous paths and arbors, but John has cautioned me not to give way to fancy in the least. He says that with my imaginative power and habit of story-making, a nervous weakness like mine is sure to lead to all manner of excited fancies, and that I ought to use my will and good sense to check the tendency. So I try.

I think sometimes that if I were only well enough to write a little it would relieve the press of ideas and rest me.

But I find I get pretty tired when I try.

It is so discouraging not to have any advice and companionship about my work. When I get really well, John says we will ask Cousin Henry and Julia down for a long visit; but he says he would as soon put fireworks in my pillow-case as to let me have those stimulating people about now.

I wish I could get well faster.

But I must not think about that. This paper looks to me as if it *knew* what a vicious influence it had!

There is a recurrent spot where the pattern lolls like a broken neck and two bulbous eyes stare at you upside down.

I get positively angry with the impertinence of it and the everlastingness. Up and down and sideways they crawl, and those absurd unblinking eyes are everywhere.

There is one place where two breadths didn't match, and the eyes go all up and down the line, one a little higher than the other.

I never saw so much expression in an inanimate thing before, and we all know how much expression they have! I used to lie awake as a child and get more entertainment and terror out of blank walls and plain furniture than most children could find in a toy-store.

I remember what a kindly wink the knobs of our big old bureau used to have, and there was one chair that always seemed like a strong friend.

I used to feel that if any of the other things looked too fierce I could always hop into that chair and be safe.

The furniture in this room is no worse than inharmonious, however, for we had to bring it all from downstairs. I suppose when this was used as a playroom they had to take the nursery things out, and no wonder! I never saw such ravages as the children have made here.

The wallpaper, as I said before, is torn off in spots, and it sticketh closer than a brother—they must have had perseverance as well as hatred.

Then the floor is scratched and gouged and splintered, the plaster itself is dug out here and there, and this great heavy bed, which is all we found in the room, looks as if it had been through the wars.

But I don't mind it a bit—only the paper.

There comes John's sister. Such a dear girl as she is, and so careful of me! I must not let her find me writing.

She is a perfect and enthusiastic housekeeper, and hopes for no better profession. I verily believe she thinks it is the writing which made me sick!

But I can write when she is out, and see her a long way off from these windows.

There is one that commands the road, a lovely shaded winding road, and one that just looks off over the country. A lovely country, too, full of great elms and velvet meadows.

This wallpaper has a kind of sub-pattern in a different shade, a particularly irritating one, for you can only see it in certain lights, and not clearly then.

But in the places where it isn't faded and where the sun is just so—I can see a strange, provoking, formless sort of figure that seems to skulk about behind that silly and conspicuous front design.

There's sister on the stairs!

Well, the Fourth of July is over! The people are all gone, and I am tired out. John thought it might do me good to see a little company, so we just had Mother and Nellie and the children down for a week.

Of course I didn't do a thing. Jennie sees to everything now.

But it tired me all the same.

John says if I don't pick up faster he shall send me to Weir Mitchell° in the fall.

But I don't want to go there at all. I had a friend who was in his hands once, and she says he is just like John and my brother, only more so!

Besides, it is such an undertaking to go so far.

I don't feel as if it was worthwhile to turn my hand over for anything, and I'm getting dreadfully fretful and querulous.

Weir Mitchell   Silas Weir Mitchell (1829–1914), neurologist who introduced the "rest cure" for psychoneurotics.

I cry at nothing, and cry most of the time.

Of course I don't when John is here, or anybody else, but when I am alone.

And I am alone a good deal just now. John is kept in town very often by serious cases, and Jennie is good and lets me alone when I want her to.

So I walk a little in the garden or down that lovely lane, sit on the porch under the roses, and lie down up here a good deal.

I'm getting really fond of the room in spite of the wallpaper. Perhaps *because* of the wallpaper.

It dwells in my mind so!

I lie here on this great immovable bed—it is nailed down, I believe—and follow that pattern about by the hour. It is as good as gymnastics, I assure you. I start, we'll say, at the bottom, down in the corner over there where it has not been touched, and I determine for the thousandth time that I *will* follow that pointless pattern to some sort of a conclusion.

I know a little of the principle of design, and I know this thing was not arranged on any laws of radiation, or alternation, or repetition, or symmetry, or anything else that I ever heard of.

It is repeated, of course, by the breadths, but not otherwise.

Looked at in one way, each breadth stands alone; the bloated curves and flourishes— a kind of "debased Romanesque" with delirium tremens—go waddling up and down in isolated columns of fatuity.

But, on the other hand, they connect diagonally, and the sprawling outlines run off in great slanting waves of optic horror, like a lot of wallowing sea-weeds in full chase.

The whole thing goes horizontally, too, at least it seems so, and I exhaust myself trying to distinguish the order of its going in that direction.

They have used a horizontal breadth for a frieze, and that adds wonderfully to the confusion.

There is one end of the room where it is almost intact, and there, when the crosslights fade and the low sun shines directly upon it, I can almost fancy radiation after all—the interminable grotesque seems to form around a common center and rush off in headlong plunges of equal distraction.

It makes me tired to follow it. I will take a nap, I guess.

I don't know why I should write this.

I don't want to.

I don't feel able.

And I know John would think it absurd. But I *must* say what I feel and think in some way—it is such a relief!

But the effort is getting to be greater than the relief.

Half the time now I am awfully lazy, and lie down ever so much. John says I mustn't lose my strength, and has me take cod liver oil and lots of tonics and things, to say nothing of ale and wine and rare meat.

Dear John! He loves me very dearly, and hates to have me sick. I tried to have a real earnest reasonable talk with him the other day, and tell him how I wish he would let me go and make a visit to Cousin Henry and Julia.

But he said I wasn't able to go, nor able to stand it after I got there; and I did not make out a very good case for myself, for I was crying before I had finished.

It is getting to be a great effort for me to think straight. Just this nervous weakness, I suppose.

And dear John gathered me up in his arms, and just carried me upstairs and laid me on the bed, and sat by me and read to me till it tired my head.

He said I was his darling and his comfort and all he had, and that I must take care of myself for his sake, and keep well.

He says no one but myself can help me out of it, that I must use my will and self-control and not let any silly fancies run away with me.

There's one comfort—the baby is well and happy, and does not have to occupy this nursery with the horrid wallpaper.

If we had not used it, that blessed child would have! What a fortunate escape! Why, I wouldn't have a child of mine, an impressionable little thing, live in such a room for worlds.

I never thought of it before, but it is lucky that John kept me here after all; I can stand it so much easier than a baby, you see.

Of course I never mention it to them any more—I am too wise—but I keep watch for it all the same.

There are things in that wallpaper that nobody knows about but me, or ever will.

Behind that outside pattern the dim shapes get clearer every day.

It is always the same shape, only very numerous.

And it is like a woman stooping down and creeping about behind that pattern. I don't like it a bit. I wonder—I begin to think—I wish John would take me away from here!

It is so hard to talk with John about my case, because he is so wise, and because he loves me so.

But I tried it last night.

It was moonlight. The moon shines in all around just as the sun does.

I hate to see it sometimes, it creeps so slowly, and always comes in by one window or another.

John was asleep and I hated to waken him, so I kept still and watched the moonlight on that undulating wallpaper till I felt creepy.

The faint figure behind seemed to shake the pattern, just as if she wanted to get out.

I got up softly and went to feel and see if the paper *did* move, and when I came back John was awake.

"What is it, little girl?" he said. "Don't go walking about like that—you'll get cold."

I thought it was a good time to talk, so I told him that I really was not gaining here, and that I wished he would take me away.

"Why, darling!" said he. "Our lease will be up in three weeks, and I can't see how to leave before.

"The repairs are not done at home, and I cannot possibly leave town just now. Of course, if you were in any danger, I could and would, but you really are better, dear, whether you can see it or not. I am a doctor, dear, and I know. You are gaining flesh and color, your appetite is better, I feel really much easier about you."

"I don't weigh a bit more," said I, "nor as much; and my appetite may be better in the evening when you are here but it is worse in the morning when you are away!"

"Bless her little heart!" said he with a big hug. "She shall be as sick as she pleases! But now let's improve the shining hours by going to sleep, and talk about it in the morning!"

"And you won't go away?" I asked gloomily.

"Why, how can I, dear? It is only three weeks more and then we will take a nice little trip of a few days while Jennie is getting the house ready. Really, dear, you are better!"

"Better in body perhaps—" I began, and stopped short, for he sat up straight and looked at me with such a stern, reproachful look that I could not say another word.

"My darling," said he, "I beg of you, for my sake and for our child's sake, as well as for your own, that you will never for one instant let that idea enter your mind! There is nothing so dangerous, so fascinating, to a temperament like yours. It is a false and foolish fancy. Can you not trust me as a physician when I tell you so?"

So of course I said no more on that score, and we went to sleep before long. He thought I was asleep first, but I wasn't, and lay there for hours trying to decide whether that front pattern and the back pattern really did move together or separately.

On a pattern like this, by daylight, there is a lack of sequence, a defiance of law, that is a constant irritant to a normal mind.

The color is hideous enough, and unreliable enough, and infuriating enough, but the pattern is torturing.

You think you have mastered it, but just as you get well under way in following, it turns a back-somersault and there you are. It slaps you in the face, knocks you down, and tramples upon you. It is like a bad dream.

The outside pattern is a florid arabesque, reminding one of a fungus. If you can imagine a toadstool in joints, an interminable string of toadstools, budding and sprouting in endless convolutions—why, that is something like it.

That is, sometimes!

There is one marked peculiarity about this paper, a thing nobody seems to notice but myself, and that is that it changes as the light changes.

When the sun shoots in through the east window—I always watch for that first long, straight ray—it changes so quickly that I never can quite believe it.

That is why I watch it always.

By moonlight—the moon shines in all night when there is a moon—I wouldn't know it was the same paper.

At night in any kind of light, in twilight, candlelight, lamplight, and worst of all by moonlight, it becomes bars! The outside pattern, I mean, and the woman behind it is as plain as can be.

I didn't realize for a long time what the thing was that showed behind, that dim sub-pattern, but now I am quite sure it is a woman.

By daylight she is subdued, quiet. I fancy it is the pattern that keeps her so still. It is so puzzling. It keeps me quiet by the hour.

I lie down ever so much now. John says it is good for me, and to sleep all I can.

Indeed he started the habit by making me lie down for an hour after each meal.

It is a very bad habit, I am convinced, for you see, I don't sleep.

And that cultivates deceit, for I don't tell them I'm awake—oh, no!

The fact is I am getting a little afraid of John.

He seems very queer sometimes, and even Jennie has an inexplicable look.

It strikes me occasionally, just as a scientific hypothesis, that perhaps it is the paper!

I have watched John when he did not know I was looking, and come into the room suddenly on the most innocent excuses, and I've caught him several times *looking at the paper!* And Jennie too. I caught Jennie with her hand on it once.

She didn't know I was in the room, and when I asked her in a quiet, a very quiet voice, with the most restrained manner possible, what she was doing with the paper, she turned around as if she had been caught stealing, and looked quite angry—asked me why I should frighten her so!

Then she said that the paper stained everything it touched, that she had found yellow smooches on all my clothes and John's and she wished we would be more careful!

Did not that sound innocent? But I know she was studying that pattern, and I am determined that nobody shall find it out but myself!

Life is very much more exciting now than it used to be. You see, I have something more to expect, to look forward to, to watch. I really do eat better, and am more quiet than I was.

John is so pleased to see me improve! He laughed a little the other day, and said I seemed to be flourishing in spite of my wallpaper.

I turned it off with a laugh. I had no intention of telling him it was *because* of the wallpaper—he would make fun of me. He might even want to take me away.

I don't want to leave now until I have found it out. There is a week more, and I think that will be enough.

I'm feeling so much better!

I don't sleep much at night, for it is so interesting to watch developments; but I sleep a good deal during the daytime.

In the daytime it is tiresome and perplexing.

There are always new shoots on the fungus, and new shades of yellow all over it. I cannot keep count of them, though I have tried conscientiously.

It is the strangest yellow, that wallpaper! It makes me think of all the yellow things I ever saw—not beautiful ones like buttercups, but old, foul, bad yellow things.

But there is something else about that paper—the smell! I noticed it the moment we came into the room, but with so much air and sun it was not bad. Now we have had a week of fog and rain, and whether the windows are open or not, the smell is here.

It creeps all over the house.

I find it hovering in the dining-room, skulking in the parlor, hiding in the hall, lying in wait for me on the stairs.

It gets into my hair.

Even when I go to ride, if I turn my head suddenly and surprise it—there is that smell!

Such a peculiar odor, too! I have spent hours in trying to analyze it, to find what it smelled like.

It is not bad—at first—and very gentle, but quite the subtlest, most enduring odor I ever met.

In this damp weather it is awful. I wake up in the night and find it hanging over me.

It used to disturb me at first. I thought seriously of burning the house—to reach the smell.

But now I am used to it. The only thing I can think of that it is like is the *color* of the paper! A yellow smell.

There is a very funny mark on this wall, low down, near the mopboard. A streak that runs round the room. It goes behind every piece of furniture, except the bed, a long, straight, even *smooch,* as if it had been rubbed over and over.

I wonder how it was done and who did it, and what they did it for. Round and round and round—round and round and round—it makes me dizzy!

I really have discovered something at last.

Through watching so much at night, when it changes so, I have finally found out.

The front pattern *does* move—and no wonder! The woman behind shakes it!

Sometimes I think there are a great many women behind, and sometimes only one, and she crawls around fast, and her crawling shakes it all over.

Then in the very bright spots she keeps still, and in the very shady spots she just takes hold of the bars and shakes them hard.

And she is all the time trying to climb through. But nobody could climb through that pattern—it strangles so; I think that is why it has so many heads.

They get through, and then the pattern strangles them off and turns them upside down, and makes their eyes white!

If those heads were covered or taken off it would not be half so bad.

I think that woman gets out in the daytime!

And I'll tell you why—privately—I've seen her!

I can see her out of every one of my windows!

It is the same woman, I know, for she is always creeping, and most women do not creep by daylight.

I see her in that long shaded lane, creeping up and down. I see her in those dark grape arbors, creeping all around the garden.

I see her on that long road under the trees, creeping along, and when a carriage comes she hides under the blackberry vines.

I don't blame her a bit. It must be very humiliating to be caught creeping by daylight!

I always lock the door when I creep by daylight. I can't do it at night, for I know John would suspect something at once.

And John is so queer now that I don't want to irritate him. I wish he would take another room! Besides, I don't want anybody to get that woman out at night but myself.

I often wonder if I could see her out of all the windows at once.

But, turn as fast as I can, I can only see out of one at one time.

And though I always see her, she *may* be able to creep faster than I can turn! I have watched her sometimes away off in the open country, creeping as fast as a cloud shadow in a wind.

If only that top pattern could be gotten off from the under one! I mean to try it, little by little.

I have found out another funny thing, but I shan't tell it this time! It does not do to trust people too much.

There are only two more days to get this paper off, and I believe John is beginning to notice. I don't like the look in his eyes.

And I heard him ask Jennie a lot of professional questions about me. She had a very good report to give.

She said I slept a good deal in the daytime.

John knows I don't sleep very well at night, for all I'm so quiet!

He asked me all sorts of questions, too, and pretended to be very loving and kind.

As if I couldn't see through him!

Still, I don't wonder he acts so, sleeping under this paper for three months.

It only interests me, but I feel sure John and Jennie are affected by it.

Hurrah! This is the last day, but it is enough. John is to stay in town over night, and won't be out until this evening.

Jennie wanted to sleep with me—the sly thing; but I told her I should undoubtedly rest better for a night all alone.

That was clever, for really I wasn't alone a bit! As soon as it was moonlight and that poor thing began to crawl and shake the pattern, I got up and ran to help her.

I pulled and she shook. I shook and she pulled, and before morning we had peeled off yards of that paper.

A strip about as high as my head and half around the room.

And then when the sun came and that awful pattern began to laugh at me, I declared I would finish it today!

We go away tomorrow, and they are moving all my furniture down again to leave things as they were before.

Jennie looked at the wall in amazement, but I told her merrily that I did it out of pure spite at the vicious thing.

She laughed and said she wouldn't mind doing it herself, but I must not get tired.

How she betrayed herself that time!

But I am here, and no person touches this paper but Me—not *alive!*

She tried to get me out of the room—it was too patent! But I said it was so quiet and empty and clean now that I believed I would lie down again and sleep all I could, and not to wake me even for dinner—I would call when I woke.

So now she is gone, and the servants are gone, and the things are gone, and there is nothing left but that great bedstead nailed down, with the canvas mattress we found on it.

We shall sleep downstairs tonight, and take the boat home tomorrow.

I quite enjoy the room, now it is bare again.

How those children did tear about here!

This bedstead is fairly gnawed!

But I must get to work.

I have locked the door and thrown the key down into the front path.

I don't want to go out, and I don't want to have anybody come in, till John comes.

I want to astonish him.

I've got a rope up here that even Jennie did not find. If that woman does get out, and tries to get away, I can tie her!

But I forgot I could not reach far without anything to stand on!

This bed will *not* move!

I tried to lift and push it until I was lame, and then I got so angry I bit off a little piece at one corner—but it hurt my teeth.

Then I peeled off all the paper I could reach standing on the floor. It sticks horribly and the pattern just enjoys it! All those strangled heads and bulbous eyes and waddling fungus growths just shriek with derision!

I am getting angry enough to do something desperate. To jump out of the window would be admirable exercise, but the bars are too strong even to try.

Besides I wouldn't do it. Of course not. I know well enough that a step like that is improper and might be misconstrued.

I don't like to *look* out of the windows even—there are so many of those creeping women, and they creep so fast.

I wonder if they all come out of that wallpaper as I did?

But I am securely fastened now by my well-hidden rope—you don't get *me* out in the road there!

I suppose I shall have to get back behind the pattern when it comes night, and that is hard!

It is so pleasant to be out in this great room and creep around as I please!

I don't want to go outside. I won't, even if Jennie asks me to.

For outside you have to creep on the ground, and everything is green instead of yellow.

But here I can creep smoothly on the floor, and my shoulder just fits in that long smooch around the wall, so I cannot lose my way.

Why, there's John at the door!

It is no use, young man, you can't open it!

How he does call and pound!

Now he's crying to Jennie for an axe.

It would be a shame to break down that beautiful door!

"John, dear!" said I in the gentlest voice. "The key is down by the front steps, under a plantain leaf!"

That silenced him for a few moments.

Then he said, very quietly indeed, "Open the door, my darling!"

"I can't," said I. "The key is down by the front door under a plantain leaf!" And then I said it again, several times, very gently and slowly, and said it so often that he had to go and see, and he got it of course, and came in. He stopped short by the door.

"What is the matter?" he cried. "For God's sake, what are you doing!"

I kept on creeping just the same, but I looked at him over my shoulder.

"I've got out at last," said I, "in spite of you and Jane. And I've pulled off most of the paper, so you can't put me back!"

Now why should that man have fainted? But he did, and right across my path by the wall, so that I had to creep over him every time!

(1892)

LUIGI PIRANDELLO
[1867–1936]

War

The passengers who had left Rome by the night express had to stop until dawn at the small station of Fabriano in order to continue their journey by the small old-fashioned local joining the main line with Sulmona.

At dawn, in a stuffy and smoky second-class carriage in which five people had already spent the night, a bulky woman in deep mourning was hoisted in—almost like a shapeless bundle. Behind her, puffing and moaning, followed her husband—a tiny man, thin and weakly, his face death-white, his eyes small and bright and looking shy and uneasy.

Having at last taken a seat he politely thanked the passengers who had helped his wife and who had made room for her; then he turn round to the woman trying to pull down the collar of her coat, and politely inquired:

"Are you all right, dear?"

The wife, instead of answering, pulled up her collar again to her eyes, so as to hide her face.

"Nasty world," muttered the husband with a sad smile.

And he felt it his duty to explain to his traveling companions that the poor woman was to be pitied, for the war was taking away from her her only son, a boy of twenty to whom both had devoted their entire life, even breaking up their home at Sulmona to follow him to Rome, where he had to go as a student, then allowing him to volunteer for war with an assurance, however, that at least for six months he would not be sent to the front and now, all of a sudden, receiving a wire saying that he was due to leave in three days' time and asking them to go and see him off.

The woman under the big coat was twisting and wriggling, at times growling like a wild animal, feeling certain that all those explanations would not have aroused even a shadow of sympathy from those people who—most likely—were in the same plight as herself. One of them, who had been listening with particular attention, said: "You should thank God that your son is only leaving now for the front. Mine has been sent there the first day of the war. He has already come back twice wounded and been sent back again to the front."

"What about me? I have two sons and three nephews at the front," said another passenger.

"Maybe, but in our case it is our *only* son," ventured the husband.

"What difference can it make? You may spoil your only son with excessive attentions, but you cannot love him more than you would all your other children if you had any. Paternal love is not like bread that can be broken into pieces and split amongst the children in equal shares. A father gives *all* his love to each one of his children without discrimination, whether it be one or ten, and if I am suffering now for my two sons, I am not suffering half for each of them but double . . . "

"True . . . true . . . " sighed the embarrassed husband, "but support (of course we all hope it will never be your case) a father has two sons at the front and he loses one of them, there is still one left to console him . . . while . . . "

"Yes," answered the other, getting cross, "a son left to console him but also a son left for whom he must survive, while in the case of the father of an only son if the son dies the father can die too and put an end to his distress. What of the two positions is the worse? Don't you see how my case would be worse than yours?"

"Nonsense," interrupted another traveler, a fat red-faced man with bloodshot eyes of the palest gray.

He was panting. From his bulging eyes seemed to spurt inner violence of an uncontrolled vitality which his weakened body could hardly contain.

"Nonsense," he repeated, trying to cover his mouth with his hand so as to hide the two missing front teeth. "Nonsense. Do we give life to our children for our own benefit?"

The other travelers stared at him in distress. The one who had his son at the front since the first day of the war sighed: "You are right. Our children do not belong to us, they belong to the Country. . . . "

"Bosh," retorted the fat traveler. "Do we think of the Country when we give life to our children? Our sons are born because . . . well, because they must be born and when they come to life they take our own life with them. This is the truth. We belong to them but they can never belong to us. And when they reach twenty they are exactly what we were at their age. We too had a father and mother, but there were so many other things as well . . . girls, cigarettes, illusions, new ties . . . and the Country, of course, whose call we would have answered—when we were twenty—even if father and mother had said no. Now at our age, the love of our Country is still great, of course, but stronger than it is the love for our children. Is there any one of us here who wouldn't gladly take his son's place at the front if he could?"

There was a silence all round, everybody nodding as to approve.

"Why then," continued the fat man, "shouldn't we consider the feelings of our children when they are twenty? Isn't it natural that at their age they should consider the love for their Country (I am speaking of decent boys, of course) even greater than the love for us? Isn't it natural that it should be so, as after all they must look upon us as upon old boys who cannot move any more and must stay at home? If Country exists, if Country is a natural necessity, like bread, of which each of us must eat in order not to die of hunger, somebody must go to defend it. And our sons go, when they are twenty, and they don't want tears, because if they die, they die inflamed and happy (I am speaking, of course, of decent boys). Now, if one dies young and happy, without having the ugly sides of life, the boredom of it, the pettiness, the bitterness of disillusion . . . what more can we ask for him? Everyone should stop crying, everyone should laugh as I do . . . or at least thank God—as I do—because my son, before dying sent me a message saying that he was dying satisfied at having ended his life in the best way he could have wished. That is why, as you see, I do not even wear mourning. . . . "

He shook his light fawn coat as to show it; his livid lip over his missing teeth was trembling, his eyes were watery and motionless, and soon after he ended with a shrill laugh which might well have been a sob.

"Quite so . . . quite so . . . " agreed the others.

The woman who, bundled in a corner under her coat, had been sitting and listening had—for the last three months—tried to find in the words of her husband and her friends something to console her in her deep sorrow, something that might show her how a mother should resign herself to send her son not even to death but to a probably dangerous life. Yet not a word had she found amongst the many which had been said . . . and her grief had been greater in seeing that nobody—as she thought—could share her feelings.

But now the words of the traveler amazed and almost stunned her. She suddenly realized that it wasn't the others who were wrong and could not understand her but herself who could not rise up to the same height of those fathers and mothers willing to resign themselves, without crying, not only to the departure of their sons but even to their death.

She lifted her head, she bent over from her corner trying to listen with great attention to the details which the fat man was giving to his companions about the way his son had fallen as a hero, for his King and his Country, happy and without regrets. It seemed to her that she had stumbled into a world she had never dreamt of, a world so far unknown to her and she was so pleased to hear everyone joining in congratulating that brave father who could so stoically speak of his child's death.

Then suddenly, just as if she had heard nothing of what had been said and almost as if waking up from a dream, she turned to the old man, asking him:

"Then . . . is your son really dead?"

Everybody stared at her. The old man, too, turned to look at her, fixing his great, bulging, horribly watery light gray eyes, deep in her face. For some little time he tried to answer, but words failed him. He looked at her, almost as if only then—at that silly, incongruous question—he had suddenly realized at last that his son was really dead—gone for ever—for ever. His face contracted, became horribly distorted, then he snatched in haste a handkerchief from his pocket and, to the amazement of everyone, broke into harrowing, heart-rending, uncontrollable sobs.

(1939)

JAMES JOYCE
[1882–1941]

The Boarding House

Mrs. Mooney was a butcher's daughter. She was a woman who was quite able to keep things to herself: a determined woman. She had married her father's foreman and opened a butcher's shop near Spring Gardens. But as soon as his father-in-law was dead Mr. Mooney began to go to the devil. He drank, plundered the till, ran headlong into debt. It was no use making him take the pledge: he was sure to break out again a few days after. By fighting his wife in the presence of customers and by buying bad meat he ruined his business. One night he went for his wife with the cleaver and she had to sleep in a neighbour's house.

After that they lived apart. She went to the priest and got a separation from him with care of the children. She would give him neither money nor food nor houseroom; and so he was obliged to enlist himself as a sheriff's man. He was a shabby stooped little drunkard with a white face and a white moustache and white eyebrows, pencilled above his little eyes, which were pink-veined and raw; and all day long he sat in the bailiff's room, waiting to be put on a job. Mrs. Mooney, who had taken what remained of her money out of the butcher business and set up a boarding house in Hardwicke Street, was a big imposing woman. Her house had a floating population made up of tourists from Liverpool and the Isle of Man and, occasionally, *artistes* from the music halls. Its resident population was made up of clerks from the city. She governed her house cunningly and firmly, knew when to give credit, when to be stern and when to let things pass. All the resident young men spoke of her as *The Madam*.

Mrs. Mooney's young men paid fifteen shillings a week for board and lodgings (beer or stout at dinner excluded). They shared in common tastes and occupations and for this reason they were very chummy with one another. They discussed with one another the chances of favourites and outsiders. Jack Mooney, the Madam's son, who was clerk to a commission agent in Fleet Street, had the reputation of being a hard case. He was fond of using soldiers' obscenities: usually he came home in the small hours. When he met his friends he had always a good one to tell them and he was always sure to be on to a good thing—that is to say, a likely horse or a likely *artiste*. He was also handy with the mitts and sang comic songs. On Sunday nights there would often be a re-union in Mrs. Mooney's front drawing room. The music-hall *artistes* would oblige; and Sheridan played waltzes and polkas and vamped accompaniments. Polly Mooney, the Madam's daughter, would also sing. She sang:

> *I'm a . . . naughty girl.*
> *You needn't sham:*
> *You know I am.*

Polly was a slim girl of nineteen, she had light soft hair and a small full mouth. Her eyes, which were grey with a shade of green through them, had a habit of glancing upwards when she spoke with anyone, which made her look like a little perverse madonna. Mrs. Mooney had first sent her daughter to be a typist in a corn-factor's office but, as a disreputable sheriff's man used to come every other day to the office, asking to be allowed to say a word to his daughter, she had taken her daughter home again and set her to do housework. As Polly was very lively the intention was to give her the run of the young men. Besides, young men like to feel that there is a young woman not very far away. Polly, of course, flirted with the young men but Mrs. Mooney, who was a shrewd judge, knew that the young men were only passing the time away: none of them meant business. Things went on so for a long time and Mrs. Mooney began to think of sending Polly back to typewriting when she noticed that something was going on between Polly and one of the young men. She watched the pair and kept her own counsel.

Polly knew that she was being watched, but still her mother's persistent silence could not be misunderstood. There had been no open complicity between mother and daughter, no open understanding but, though people in the house began to talk of the affair, still Mrs. Mooney did not intervene. Polly began to grow a little strange in her manner and the young man was evidently perturbed. At last, when she judged it to be the right moment, Mrs. Mooney intervened. She dealt with moral problems as a cleaver deals with meat: and in this case she had made up her mind.

It was a bright Sunday morning of early summer, promising heat, but with a fresh breeze blowing. All the windows of the boarding house were open and the lace curtains ballooned gently towards the street beneath the raised sashes. The belfry of George's Church sent out constant peals and worshippers, singly or in groups, traversed the little circus before the church, revealing their purpose by their self-contained demeanor no less than by the little volumes in their gloved hands. Breakfast was over in the boarding house and the table of the breakfast-room was covered with plates on which lay yellow streaks of eggs with morsels of bacon-fat and bacon-rind. Mrs. Mooney sat in the straw arm-chair and watched the servant Mary remove the breakfast things. She made Mary collect the crusts and pieces of broken bread to help to make Tuesday's bread-pudding. When the table was cleared, the broken bread collected, the sugar and butter safe under lock and key, she began to reconstruct the interview which she had had the night before with Polly. Things were as she had suspected: she had been frank in her questions and Polly had been frank in her answers. Both had been somewhat awkward, of course. She had been made awkward by her not wishing to receive the news in too cavalier a fashion or to seem to have connived and Polly had been made awkward not merely because allusions of that kind always made her awkward but also because she did not wish it to be thought that in her wise innocence she had divined the intention behind her mother's tolerance.

Mrs. Mooney glanced instinctively at the little gilt clock on the mantelpiece as soon as she had become aware through her revery that the bells of George's Church had stopped ringing. It was seventeen minutes past eleven: she would have lots of time to have the matter out with Mr. Doran and then catch short twelve at Marlborough Street. She was sure she would win. To begin with she had all the weight of social opinion on her side: she was an outraged mother. She had allowed him to live beneath her roof, assuming that he was a man of honour, and he had simply abused her hospitality. He was thirty-four or thirty-five years of age, so that youth could not be pleaded as his excuse; nor could ignorance be his excuse since he was a man who had seen something of the world. He had simply taken advantage of Polly's youth and inexperience: that was evident. The question was: What reparation would he make?

There must be reparation made in such cases. It is all very well for the man: he can go his ways as if nothing had happened, having had his moment of pleasure, but the girl has to bear the brunt. Some mothers would be content to patch up such an affair for a sum of money; she had known cases of it. But she would not do so. For her only one reparation could make up for the loss of her daughter's honour: marriage.

She counted all her cards again before sending Mary up to Mr. Doran's room to say that she wished to speak with him. She felt sure she would win. He was a serious young man, not rakish or loud-voiced like the others. If it had been Mr. Sheridan or Mr. Meade or Bantam Lyons her task would have been much harder. She did not think he would face publicity. All the lodgers in the house knew something of the affair; details had been invented by some. Besides, he had been employed for thirteen years in a great Catholic wine-merchant's office and publicity would mean for him, perhaps, the loss of his sit. Whereas if he agreed all might be well. She knew he had a good screw for one thing and she suspected he had a bit of stuff put by.

Nearly the half-hour! She stood up and surveyed herself in the pierglass. The decisive expression of her great florid face satisfied her and she thought of some mothers she knew who could not get their daughters off their hands.

Mr. Doran was very anxious indeed this Sunday morning. He had made two attempts to shave but his hand had been so unsteady that he had been obliged to desist. Three days' reddish beard fringed his jaws and every two or three minutes a mist gathered on his glasses so that he had to take them off and polish them with his pocket-handkerchief. The recollection of his confession of the night before was a cause of acute pain to him; the priest had drawn out every ridiculous detail of the affair and in the end had so magnified his sin that he was almost thankful at being afforded a loophole of reparation. The harm was done. What could he do now but marry her or run away? He could not brazen it out. The affair would be sure to be talked of and his employer would be certain to hear of it. Dublin is such a small city: everyone knows everyone else's business. He felt his heart leap warmly in his throat as he heard in his excited imagination old Mr. Leonard calling out in his rasping voice: *Send Mr Doran here, please.*

All his long years of service gone for nothing! All his industry and diligence thrown away! As a young man he had sown his wild oats, of course; he had boasted of his free-thinking and denied the existence of God to his companions in public-houses. But that was all passed and done with . . . nearly. He still bought a copy of *Reynold's News-paper* every week but he attended to his religious duties and for nine-tenths of the year lived a regular life. He had money enough to settle down on; it was not that. But the family would look down on her. First of all there was her disreputable father and then her mother's boarding house was beginning to get a certain fame. He had a notion that he was being had. He could imagine his friends talking of the affair and laughing. She *was* a little vulgar; sometimes she said *I seen* and *If I had've known.* But what would grammar matter if he really loved her? He could not make up his mind whether to like her or despise her for what she had done. Of course, he had done it too. His instinct urged him to remain free, not to marry. Once you are married you are done for, it said.

While he was sitting helplessly on the side of the bed in shirt and trousers she tapped lightly at his door and entered. She told him all, that she had made a clean breast of it to her mother and that her mother would speak with him that morning. She cried and threw her arms round his neck, saying:

—O, Bob! Bob! What am I to do! What am I to do at all?

She would put an end to herself, she said.

He comforted her feebly, telling her not to cry, that it would be all right, never fear. He felt against his shirt the agitation of her bosom.

It was not altogether his fault that it had happened. He remembered well, with the curious patient memory of the celibate, the first casual caresses her dress, her breath, her fingers had given him. Then late one night as he was undressing for bed she had tapped at his door, timidly. She wanted to relight her candle at his for hers had been blown out by a gust. It was her bath night. She wore a loose open combing-jacket of printed flannel. Her white instep shone in the opening of her furry slippers and the blood glowed warmly behind her perfumed skin. From her hands and wrists too as she lit and steadied her candle a faint perfume arose.

On nights when he came in very late it was she who warmed up his dinner. He scarcely knew what he was eating, feeling her beside him alone, at night, in the sleeping house. And her thoughtfulness! If the night was anyway cold or wet or windy there was sure to be a little tumbler of punch ready for him. Perhaps they could be happy together. . . .

They used to go upstairs together on tiptoe, each with a candle, and on the third landing exchange reluctant good-nights. They used to kiss. He remembered well her eyes, the touch of her hand and his delirium. . . .

But delirium passes. He echoed her phrase, applying it to himself: *What am I to do?* The instinct of the celibate warned him to hold back. But the sin was there; even his sense of honour told him that reparation must be made for such a sin.

While he was sitting with her on the side of the bed Mary came to the door and said that the missus wanted to see him in the parlour. He stood up to put on his coat and waistcoat, more helpless than ever. When he was dressed he went over to her to comfort her. It would be all right, never fear. He left her crying on the bed and moaning softly: *O my God!*

Going down the stairs his glasses became so dimmed with moisture that he had to take them off and polish them. He longed to ascend through the roof and fly away to another country where he would never hear again of his trouble, and yet a force pushed him downstairs step by step. The implacable faces of his employer and of the Madam stared upon his discomfiture. On the last flight of stairs he passed Jack Mooney who was coming up from the pantry nursing two bottles of *Bass.* They saluted coldly; and the lover's eyes rested for a second or two on a thick bulldog face and a pair of thick short arms. When he reached the foot of the staircase he glanced up and saw Jack regarding him from the door of the return room.

Suddenly he remembered the night when one of the music-hall *artistes,* a little blond Londoner, had made a rather free allusion to Polly. The reunion had been almost broken up on account of Jack's violence. Everyone tried to quiet him. The music-hall *artiste,* a little paler than usual, kept smiling and saying that there was no harm meant: but Jack kept shouting at him that if any fellow tried that sort of a game on with *his* sister he'd bloody well put his teeth down his throat, so he would.

Polly sat for a little time on the side of the bed, crying. Then she dried her eyes and went over to the looking-glass. She dipped the end of the towel in the water-jug and refreshed her eyes with the cool water. She looked at herself in profile and readjusted a hairpin above her ear. Then she went back to the bed again and sat at the foot. She regarded the pillows for a long time and the sight of them awakened in her mind secret amiable memories. She rested the nape of her neck against the cool iron bed-rail and fell into a revery. There was no longer any perturbation visible on her face.

She waited on patiently, almost cheerfully, without alarm, her memories gradually giving place to hopes and visions of the future. Her hopes and visions were so intricate that she no longer saw the white pillows on which her gaze was fixed or remembered that she was waiting for anything.

At last she heard her mother calling. She started to her feet and ran to the banisters.

—Polly! Polly!

—Yes, mamma?

Come down, dear. Mr. Doran wants to speak to you. Then she remembered what she had been waiting for.

                                                                              (1914)

JAMES JOYCE
[1882–1941]

The Dead

Lily, the caretaker's daughter, was literally run off her feet. Hardly had she brought one gentleman into the little pantry behind the office on the ground floor and helped him off with his overcoat than the wheezy hall-door bell clanged again and she had to scamper along the bare hallway to let in another guest. It was well for her she had not to attend to the ladies also. But Miss Kate and Miss Julia had thought of that and had converted the bathroom upstairs into a ladies' dressing-room. Miss Kate and Miss Julia were there, gossiping and laughing and fussing, walking after each other to the head of the stairs, peering down over the banisters and calling down to Lily to ask her who had come.

It was always a great affair, the Misses Morkan's annual dance. Everybody who knew them came to it, members of the family, old friends of the family, the members of Julia's choir, any of Kate's pupils that were grown up enough and even some of Mary Jane's pupils too. Never once had it fallen flat. For years and years it had gone off in splendid style as long as anyone could remember; ever since Kate and Julia, after the death of their brother Pat, had left the house in Stoney Batter and taken Mary Jane, their only niece, to live with them in the dark gaunt house on Usher's Island, the upper part of which they had rented from Mr. Fulham, the cornfactor on the ground floor. That was a good thirty years ago if it was a day. Mary Jane, who was then a little girl in short clothes, was now the main prop of the household for she had the organ in Haddington Road. She had been through the Academy and gave a pupils' concert every year in the upper room of the Antient Concert Rooms. Many of her pupils belonged to better-class families on the Kingstown and Dalkey line. Old as they were, her aunts also did their share. Julia, though she was quite grey, was still the leading soprano in Adam and Eve's, and Kate, being too feeble to go about much, gave music lessons to beginners on the old square piano in the back room. Lily, the caretaker's daughter, did housemaid's work for them. Though their life was modest they believed in eating well; the best of everything: diamond-bone sirloins, three-shilling tea and the best bottled stout. But Lily seldom made a mistake in the orders so that she got on well with her three mistresses. They were fussy, that was all. But the only thing they would not stand was back answers.

Of course they had good reason to be fussy on such a night. And then it was long after ten o'clock and yet there was no sign of Gabriel and his wife. Besides they were dreadfully afraid that Freddy Malins might turn up screwed. They would not wish for worlds that any of Mary Jane's pupils should see him under the influence; and when he was like that it was sometimes very hard to manage him. Freddy Malins always came late but they wondered what could be keeping Gabriel: and that was what brought them every two minutes to the banisters to ask Lily had Gabriel or Freddy come.

—O, Mr. Conroy, said Lily to Gabriel when she opened the door for him, Miss Kate and Miss Julia thought you were never coming. Good-night, Mrs. Conroy.

—I'll engage they did, said Gabriel, but they forgot that my wife here takes three mortal hours to dress herself.

He stood on the mat, scraping the snow from his goloshes, while Lily led his wife to the foot of the stairs and called out:

—Miss Kate, here's Mrs. Conroy.

Kate and Julia came toddling down the dark stairs at once. Both of them kissed Gabriel's wife, said she must be perished alive and asked was Gabriel with her.

—Here I am as right as the mail, Aunt Kate! Go on up. I'll follow, called out Gabriel from the dark.

He continued scraping his feet vigorously while the three women went upstairs, laughing, to the ladies' dressing-room. A light fringe of snow lay like a cape on the shoulders of his overcoat and like toecaps on the toes of his goloshes; and, as the buttons of his overcoat slipped with a squeaking noise through the snow-stiffened frieze, a cold fragrant air from out-of-doors escaped from crevices and folds.

—Is it snowing again, Mr. Conroy? asked Lily.

She had preceded him into the pantry to help him off with his overcoat. Gabriel smiled at the three syllables she had given his surname and glanced at her. She was a slim, growing girl, pale in complexion and with hay-coloured hair. The gas in the pantry made her look still paler. Gabriel had known her when she was a child and used to sit on the lowest step nursing a rag doll.

—Yes, Lily, he answered, and I think we're in for a night of it.

He looked up at the pantry ceiling, which was shaking with the stamping and shuffling of feet on the floor above, listened for a moment to the piano and then glanced at the girl, who was folding his overcoat carefully at the end of a shelf.

—Tell me, Lily, he said in a friendly tone, do you still go to school?

—O no, sir, she answered. I'm done schooling this year and more.

—O, then, said Gabriel gaily, I suppose we'll be going to your wedding one of these fine days with your young man, eh?

The girl glanced back at him over her shoulder and said with great bitterness:

—The men that is now is only all palaver and what they can get out of you.

Gabriel coloured as if he felt he had made a mistake and, without looking at her, kicked off his goloshes and flicked actively with his muffler at his patent-leather shoes.

He was a stout tallish young man. The high colour of his cheeks pushed upwards even to his forehead where it scattered itself in a few formless patches of pale red; and on his hairless face there scintillated restlessly the polished lenses and the bright gilt rims of the glasses which screened his delicate and restless eyes. His glossy black hair was parted in the middle and brushed in a long curve behind his ears where it curled slightly beneath the groove left by his hat.

When he had flicked lustre into his shoes he stood up and pulled his waistcoat down more tightly on his plump body. Then he took a coin rapidly from his pocket.

—O Lily, he said, thrusting it into her hands, it's Christmastime, isn't it? Just . . . here's a little. . . .

He walked rapidly towards the door.

—Oh no, sir! cried the girl, following him. Really, sir, I wouldn't take it.

—Christmas-time! Christmas-time! said Gabriel, almost trotting to the stairs and waving his hand to her in deprecation.

The girl, seeing that he had gained the stairs, called out after him:

—Well, thank you, sir.

He waited outside the drawing-room door until the waltz should finish, listening to the skirts that swept against it and to the shuffling of feet. He was still discomposed by the girl's bitter and sudden retort. It had cast a gloom over him which he tried to dispel by arranging his cuffs and the bows of his tie. Then he took from his waistcoat pocket a little paper and glanced at the headings he had made for his speech. He was undecided about the lines from Robert Browning for he feared they would be above the heads of his hearers. Some quotation that they could recognise from Shakespeare or from the Melodies would be better. The indelicate clacking of the men's heels and the shuffling of their soles reminded him that their grade of culture differed from his. He would only make himself ridiculous by quoting poetry to them which they could not understand. They would think that he was airing his superior education. He would fail with them just as he had failed with the girl in the pantry. He had taken up a wrong tone. His whole speech was a mistake from first to last, an utter failure.

Just then his aunts and his wife came out of the ladies' dressing-room. His aunts were two small plainly dressed old women. Aunt Julia was an inch or so the taller. Her hair, drawn low over the tops of her ears, was grey; and grey also, with darker shadows, was her large flaccid face. Though she was stout in build and stood erect her slow eyes and parted lips gave her the appearance of a woman who did not know where she was or where she was going. Aunt Kate was more vivacious. Her face, healthier than her sister's, was all puckers and creases, like a shrivelled red apple, and her hair, braided in the same old-fashioned way, had not lost its ripe nut colour.

They both kissed Gabriel frankly. He was their favorite nephew, the son of their dead elder sister, Ellen, who had married T. J. Conroy of the Port and Docks.

—Gretta tells me you're not going to take a cab back to Monkstown to-night, Gabriel, said Aunt Kate.

—No, said Gabriel, turning to his wife, we had quite enough of that last year, hadn't we? Don't you remember, Aunt Kate, what a cold Gretta got out of it? Cab windows rattling all the way, and the east wind blowing in after we passed Merrion. Very jolly it was. Gretta caught a dreadful cold.

Aunt Kate frowned severely and nodded her head at every word.

—Quite right, Gabriel, quite right, she said. You can't be too careful.

—But as for Gretta there, said Gabriel, she'd walk home in the snow if she were let.

Mrs. Conroy laughed.

—Don't mind him, Aunt Kate, she said. He's really an awful bother, what with green shades for Tom's eyes at night and making him do the dumb-bells, and forcing Eva to eat the stirabout. The poor child! And she simply hates the sight of it! . . . O, but you'll never guess what he makes me wear now!

She broke out into a peal of laughter and glanced at her husband, whose admiring and happy eyes had been wandering from her dress to her face and hair. The two aunts laughed heartily too, for Gabriel's solicitude was a standing joke with them.

—Goloshes! said Mrs. Conroy. That's the latest. Whenever it's wet underfoot I must put on my goloshes. To-night even he wanted me to put them on, but I wouldn't. The next thing he'll buy me will be a diving suit.

Gabriel laughed nervously and patted his tie reassuringly while Aunt Kate nearly doubled herself, so heartily did she enjoy the joke. The smile soon faded from Aunt Julia's face and her mirthless eyes were directed towards her nephew's face. After a pause she asked:

—And what are goloshes, Gabriel?

—Goloshes, Julia! exclaimed her sister. Goodness me, don't you know what goloshes are? You wear them over your . . . over your boots, Gretta, isn't it?

—Yes, said Mrs. Conroy. Guttapercha things. We both have a pair now. Gabriel says everyone wears them on the continent.

—O, on the continent, murmured Aunt Julia, nodding her head slowly.

Gabriel knitted his brows and said, as if he were slightly angered:

—It's nothing very wonderful but Gretta thinks it very funny because she says the world reminds her of Christy Minstrels.

—But tell me, Gabriel, said Aunt Kate, with brisk tact. Of course, you've seen about the room. Gretta was saying . . .

—O, the room is all right, replied Gabriel. I've taken one in the Gresham.

—To be sure, said Aunt Kate, by far the best thing to do. And the children, Gretta, you're not anxious about them?

—O, for one night, said Mrs. Conroy. Besides, Bessie will look after them.

—To be sure, said Aunt Kate again. What a comfort it is to have a girl like that, one you can depend on! There's that Lily, I'm sure I don't know what has come over her lately. She's not the girl she was at all.

Gabriel was about to ask his aunt some questions on this point but she broke off suddenly to gaze after her sister who had wandered down the stairs and was craning her neck over the banisters.

—Now, I ask you, she said, almost testily, where is Julia going? Julia! Julia! Where are you going?

Julia, who had gone halfway down one flight, came back and announced blandly:

—Here's Freddy.

At the same moment a clapping of hands and a final flourish of the pianist told that the waltz had ended. The drawing-room door was opened from within and some couples came out. Aunt Kate drew Gabriel aside hurriedly and whispered into his ear:

—Slip down, Gabriel, like a good fellow and see if he's all right, and don't let him up if he's screwed. I'm sure he's screwed. I'm sure he is.

Gabriel went to the stairs and listened over the banisters. He could hear two persons talking in the pantry. Then he recognized Freddy Malins' laugh. He went down the stairs noisily.

—It's such a relief, said Aunt Kate to Mrs. Conroy, that Gabriel is here. I always feel easier in my mind when he's here. . . . Julia, there's Miss Daly and Miss Power will take some refreshment. Thanks for your beautiful waltz, Miss Daly. It made lovely time.

A tall wizen-faced man, with a stiff grizzled moustache and swarthy skin, who was passing out with his partner said:

—And may we have some refreshment, too, Miss Morkan?

—Julia, said Aunt Kate summarily, and here's Mr. Browne and Miss Furlong. Take them in, Julia, with Miss Daly and Miss Power.

—I'm the man for the ladies, said Mr. Browne, pursing his lips until his moustache bristled and smiling in all his wrinkles. You know, Miss Morkan, the reason they are so fond of me is—

He did not finish his sentence, but, seeing that Aunt Kate was out of earshot, at once led the three young ladies into the back room. The middle of the room was occupied by two square tables placed end to end, and on these Aunt Julia and the caretaker were straightening and smoothing a large cloth. On the sideboard were arrayed dishes and plates, and glasses and bundles of knives and forks and spoons. The top of the closed square piano served also as a sideboard for viands and sweets. At a smaller sideboard in one corner two young men were standing, drinking hop-bitters.

Mr. Browne led his charges thither and invited them all, in jest, to some ladies' punch, hot, strong and sweet. As they said they never took anything strong he opened three bottles of lemonade for them. Then he asked one of the young men to move aside, and, taking hold of the decanter, filled out for himself a goodly measure of whisky. The young men eyed him respectfully while he took a trial sip.

—God help me, he said, smiling, it's the doctor's orders.

His wizened face broke into a broader smile, and the three young ladies laughed in musical echo to his pleasantry, swaying their bodies to and fro, with nervous jerks of their shoulders. The boldest said:

—O, now, Mr. Browne, I'm sure the doctor never ordered anything of the kind.

Mr. Browne took another sip of his whiskey and said, with sidling mimicry:

—Well, you see, I'm like the famous Mrs. Cassidy, who is reported to have said: *Now, Mary Grimes, if I don't take it, make me take it, for I feel I want it.*

His hot face had leaned forward a little too confidentially and he had assumed a very low Dublin accent so that the young ladies, with one instinct, received his speech in silence. Miss Furlong, who was one of Mary Jane's pupils, asked Miss Daly what was the name of the pretty waltz she had just played; and Mr. Browne, seeing that he was ignored, turned promptly to the two young men who were more appreciative.

A red-faced young woman, dressed in pansy, came into the room, excitedly clapping her hands and crying:

—Quadrilles! Quadrilles!

Close on her heels came Aunt Kate, crying:

—Two gentlemen and three ladies, Mary Jane!

—Oh, here's Mr. Bergin and Mr. Kerrigan, said Mary Jane. Mr. Kerrigan, will you take Miss Power? Miss Furlong, may I get you a partner, Mr. Bergin. O, that'll just do now.

—Three ladies, Mary Jane, said Aunt Kate.

The two young gentlemen asked the ladies if they might have the pleasure, and Mary Jane turned to Miss Daly.

—O, Miss Daly, you're really awfully good, after playing for the last two dances, but really we're so short of ladies to-night.

—I don't mind in the least, Miss Morkan.

—But I've a nice partner for you, Mr. Bartell D'Arcy, the tenor. I'll get him to sing later on. All Dublin is raving about him.

—Lovely voice, lovely voice! said Aunt Kate.

As the piano had twice begun the prelude to the first figure Mary Jane led her recruits quickly from the room. They had hardly gone when Aunt Julia wandered slowly into the room, looking behind her at something.

—What is the matter, Julia? asked Aunt Kate anxiously. Who is it?

Julia, who was carrying in a column of table-napkins turned to her sister and said, simply, as if the question had surprised her:

—It's only Freddy, Kate, and Gabriel with him.

In fact right behind her Gabriel could be seen piloting Freddy Malins across the landing. The latter, a young man of forty, was of Gabriel's size and build, with very round shoulders. His face was fleshy and pallid, touched with colour only at the thick hanging lobes of his ears and at the wide wings of his nose. He had coarse features, a blunt nose, a convex and receding brow, tumid and protruded lips. His heavy-lidded eyes and the disorder of his scanty hair made him look sleepy. He was laughing heartily in a high key at a story which he had been telling Gabriel on the stairs and at the same time rubbing the knuckles of his left fist backwards and forwards into his left eye.

—Good-evening, Freddy, said Aunt Julia.

Freddy Malins bade the Misses Morkan good-evening in what seemed an offhand fashion by reason of the habitual catch in his voice and then, seeing that Mr. Browne was grinning at him from the sideboard, crossed the room on rather shaky legs and began to repeat in an undertone the story he had just told to Gabriel.

—He's not so bad, is he? said Aunt Kate to Gabriel.

Gabriel's brows were dark but he raised them quickly and answered:

—O no, hardly noticeable.

—Now, isn't he a terrible fellow! she said. And his poor mother made him take the pledge on New Year's Eve. But come on, Gabriel, into the drawing-room.

Before leaving the room with Gabriel she signalled to Mr. Browne by frowning and shaking her forefinger in warning to and fro. Mr. Browne nodded in answer and, when she had gone, said to Freddy Malins:

—Now, then, Teddy, I'm going to fill you out a good glass of lemonade just to buck you up.

Freddy Malins, who was nearing the climax of his story, waved the offer aside impatiently but Mr. Browne, having first called Freddy Malins' attention to a disarray in his dress, filled out and handed him a full glass of lemonade. Freddy Malins' left hand accepted the glass mechanically, his right hand being engaged in the mechanical readjustment of his dress. Mr. Browne, whose face was once more wrinkling with mirth, poured out for himself a glass of whisky while Freddy Malins exploded, before he had well reached the climax of his story, in a kink of high-pitched bronchitic laughter and, setting down his untasted and overflowing glass, began to rub the knuckles of his left fist backwards and forwards into his left eye, repeating words of his last phrase as well as his fit of laughter would allow him.

Gabriel could not listen while Mary Jane was playing her Academy piece, full of runs and difficult passages, to the hushed drawing-room. He liked music but the piece she was playing had no melody for him and he doubted whether it had any melody for the other listeners, though they had begged Mary Jane to play something. Four young men, who had come from the refreshment-room to stand in the doorway at the sound of the piano, had gone away quietly in couples after a few minutes. The only persons who seemed to follow the music were Mary Jane herself, her hands racing along the key-board or lifted from it at the pauses like those of a priestess in momentary imprecation, and Aunt Kate standing at her elbow to turn the page.

Gabriel's eyes, irritated by the floor, which glittered with beeswax under the heavy chandelier, wandered to the wall above the piano. A picture of the balcony scene in *Romeo and Juliet* hung there and beside it was a picture of the two murdered princes in the Tower which Aunt Julia had worked in red, blue and brown wools when she was a girl. Probably in the school they had gone to as girls that kind of work had been taught, for one year his mother had worked for him as a birthday present a waistcoat of purple tabinet, with little foxes' heads upon it, lined with brown satin and having round mulberry buttons. It was strange that his mother had had no musical talent though Aunt Kate used to call her the brains carrier of the Morkan family. Both she and Julia had always seemed a little proud of their serious and matronly sister. Her photograph stood before the pierglass. She held an open book on her knees and was pointing out something in it to Constantine who, dressed in a man-o'-war suit, lay at her feet. It was she who had chosen the names for her sons for she was very sensible of the dignity of family life. Thanks to her, Constantine was now senior curate in Balbriggan and, thanks to her, Gabriel himself had taken his degree in the Royal University. A shadow passed over his face as he remembered her sullen opposition to his marriage. Some slighting phrases she had used still rankled in his memory; she had once spoken of Gretta as being country cute and that was not true of Gretta at all. It was Gretta who had nursed her during all her last long illness in their house at Monkstown.

He knew that Mary Jane must be near the end of her piece for she was playing again the opening melody with runs of scales after every bar and while he waited for the end the resentment died down in his heart. The piece ended with a trill of octaves in the treble and a final deep octave in the bass. Great applause greeted Mary Jane as, blushing and rolling up her music nervously, she escaped from the room. The most vigorous clapping came from the four young men in the doorway who had gone away to the refreshment-room at the beginning of the piece but had come back when the piano had stopped.

Lancers were arranged. Gabriel found himself partnered with Miss Ivors. She was a frank-mannered talkative young lady, with a freckled face and prominent brown eyes. She did not wear a low-cut bodice and the large brooch which was fixed in the front of her collar bore on it an Irish device.

When they had taken their places she said abruptly:

—I have a crow to pluck with you.

—With me? said Gabriel.

She nodded her head gravely.

—What is it? asked Gabriel, smiling at her solemn manner.

—Who is G. C.? answered Miss Ivors, turning her eyes upon him.

Gabriel coloured and was about to knit his brows, as if he did not understand, when she said bluntly:

—O, innocent Amy! I have found out that you write for *The Daily Express.* Now, aren't you ashamed of yourself?

—Why should I be ashamed of myself? asked Gabriel, blinking his eyes and trying to smile.

—Well, I'm ashamed of you, said Miss Ivors frankly. To say you'd write for a rag like that. I didn't think you were a West Briton.

A look of perplexity appeared on Gabriel's face. It was true that he wrote a literary column every Wednesday in *The Daily Express,* for which he was paid fifteen shillings. But that did not make him a West Briton surely. The books he received for review were almost more welcome than the paltry cheque. He loved to feel the covers and turn over the pages of newly printed books. Nearly every day when his teaching in the college was ended he used to wander down the quays to the second-hall book-sellers, to Hickey's on Bachelor's Walk, to Webb's or Massey's on Aston's Quay, or to O'Clohissey's in the by-street. He did not know how to meet her charge. He wanted to say that literature was above politics. But they were friends of many years' standing and their careers had been parallel, first at the University and then as teachers: he could not risk a grandiose phrase with her. He continued blinking his eyes and trying to smile and murmured lamely that he saw nothing political in writing reviews of books.

When their turn to cross had come he was still perplexed and inattentive. Miss Ivors promptly took his hand in a warm grasp and said in a soft friendly tone:

—Of course, I was only joking. Come, we cross now.

When they were together again she spoke of the University question, and Gabriel felt more at ease. A friend of hers had shown her his review of Browning's poems. That was how she had found out the secret: but she liked the review immensely. Then she said suddenly:

—O, Mr. Conroy, will you come for an excursion to the Aran Isles this summer? We're going to stay there a whole month. It will be splendid out in the Atlantic. You ought to come. Mr. Clancy is coming, and Mr. Kilkelly and Kathleen Kearney. It would be splendid for Gretta too if she'd come. She's from Connacht, isn't she?

—Her people are, said Gabriel shortly.

—But you will come, won't you? said Miss Ivors, laying her warm hand eagerly on his arm.

—The fact is, said Gabriel, I have already arranged to go—

—Go where? asked Miss Ivors.

—Well, you know, every year I go for a cycling tour with some fellows and so—

—But where? asked Miss Ivors.

—Well, we usually go to France or Belgium or perhaps Germany, said Gabriel awkwardly.

—And why do you go to France and Belgium, said Miss Ivors, instead of visiting your own land?

—Well, said Gabriel, it's partly to keep in touch with the languages and partly for a change.

—And haven't you your own language to keep in touch with—Irish? asked Miss Ivors.

—Well, said Gabriel, if it comes to that, you know, Irish is not my language.

Their neighbours had turned to listen to the cross-examination. Gabriel glanced right and left nervously and tried to keep his good humour under the ordeal which was making a blush invade his forehead.

—And haven't you your own land to visit, continued Miss Ivors, that you know nothing of, your own people, and your own country?

—O, to tell you the truth, retorted Gabriel suddenly, I'm sick of my own country, sick of it!

—Why? asked Miss Ivors.

Gabriel did not answer for his retort had heated him.

—Why? repeated Miss Ivors.

They had to go visiting together and, as he had not answered her, Miss Ivors said warmly:

—Of course, you've no answer.

Gabriel tried to cover his agitation by taking part in the dance with great energy. He avoided her eyes for he had seen a sour expression on her face. But when they met in the long chain he was surprised to feel his hand firmly pressed. She looked at him from under her brows for a moment quizzically until he smiled. Then, just as the chain was about to start again, she stood on tiptoe and whispered into his ear:

—West Briton!

When the lancers were over Gabriel went away to a remote corner of the room where Freddy Malins' mother was sitting. She was a stout feeble old woman with white hair. Her voice had a catch in it like her son's and she stuttered slightly. She had been told that Freddy had come and that he was nearly all right. Gabriel asked her whether she had had a good crossing. She lived with her married daughter in Glasgow and came to Dublin on a visit once a year. She answered placidly that she had had a beautiful crossing and that the captain had been most attentive to her. She spoke also of the beautiful house her daughter kept in Glasgow, and of all the nice friends they had there. While her tongue rambled on Gabriel tried to banish from his mind all memory of the unpleasant incident with Miss Ivors. Of course the girl or woman, or whatever she was, was an enthusiast but there was a time for all things. Perhaps he ought not to have answered her like that. But she had no right to call him a West Briton before people, even in joke. She had tried to make him ridiculous before people, heckling him and staring at him with her rabbit's eyes.

He saw his wife making her way towards him through the waltzing couples. When she reached him she said into his ear:

—Gabriel, Aunt Kate wants to know won't you carve the goose as usual. Miss Daly will carve the ham and I'll do the pudding.

—All right, said Gabriel.

—She's sending in the younger ones first as soon as this waltz is over so that we'll have the table to ourselves.

—Were you dancing? asked Gabriel.

—Of course I was. Didn't you see me? What words had you with Molly Ivors?

—No words. Why? Did she say so?

—Something like that. I'm trying to get that Mr. D'Arcy to sing. He's full of conceit, I think.

—There were no words, said Gabriel moodily, only she wanted me to go for a trip to the west of Ireland and I said I wouldn't.

His wife clasped her hands excitedly and gave a little jump.

—O, do go, Gabriel, she cried. I'd love to see Galway again.

—You can go if you like, said Gabriel coldly.

She looked at him for a moment, then turned to Mrs. Malins and said:

—There's a nice husband for you, Mrs. Malins.

While she was threading her way back across the room Mrs. Malins, without adverting to the interruption, went on to tell Gabriel what beautiful places there were in Scotland and beautiful scenery. Her son-in-law brought them every year to the lakes and they used to go fishing. Her son-in-law was a splendid fisher. One day he caught a fish, a beautiful big big fish, and the man in the hotel boiled it for their dinner.

Gabriel hardly heard what she said. Now that supper was coming near he began to think again about his speech and about the quotation. When he saw Freddy Malins coming across the room to visit his mother Gabriel left the chair free for him and retired into the embrasure of the window. The room had already cleared and from the back room came the clatter of plates and knives. Those who still remained in the drawing-room seemed tired of dancing and were conversing quietly in little groups. Gabriel's warm trembling fingers tapped the cold pane of the window. How cool it must be outside! How pleasant it would be to walk out alone, first along by the river and then through the park! The snow would be lying on the branches of the trees and forming a bright cap on the top of the Wellington Monument. How much more pleasant it would be there than at the supper-table!

He ran over the headings of his speech: Irish hospitality, sad memories, the Three Graces, Paris, the quotation from Browning. He repeated to himself a phrase he had written in his review: *One feels that one is listening to a thought-tormented music.* Miss Ivors had praised the review. Was she sincere? Had she really any life of her own behind all her propagandism? There had never been any ill-feeling between them until that night. It unnerved him to think that she would be at the supper-table, looking up at him while he spoke with her critical quizzing eyes. Perhaps she would not be sorry to see him fail in his speech. An idea came into his mind and gave him courage. He would say, alluding to Aunt Kate and Aunt Julia: *Ladies and Gentlemen, the generation which is now on the wane among us may have had its faults but for my part I think it had certain qualities of hospitality, of humour, of humanity, which the new and very serious and hyper-educated generation that is growing up around us seems to me to lack.* Very good: that was one for Miss Ivors. What did he care that his aunts were only two ignorant old women?

A murmur in the room attracted his attention. Mr. Browne was advancing from the door, gallantly escorting Aunt Julia, who leaned upon his arm, smiling and hanging her head. An irregular musketry of applause escorted her also as far as the piano and then, as Mary Jane seated herself on the stool, and Aunt Julia, no longer smiling, half turned so as to pitch her voice fairly into the room, gradually ceased. Gabriel recognized the prelude. It was that of an old song of Aunt Julia's—*Arrayed for the Bridal.* Her voice, strong and clear in tone, attacked with great spirit the runs which embellish the air and though she sang very rapidly she did not miss even the smallest of the grace notes. To follow the voice, without looking at the singer's face, was to feel and share the excitement of swift and secure flight. Gabriel applauded loudly with all the others at the close of the song and loud applause was borne in from the invisible supper-table. It sounded so genuine that a little colour struggled into Aunt Julia's face as she bent to replace in the music-stand the old leather-bound song-book that had her initials on the cover. Freddy Malins, who had listened with his head perched sideways to hear her better, was still applauding when everyone else had ceased and talking animatedly to his mother who nodded her head gravely and slowly in acquiescence. At last, when he could clap no more, he stood up suddenly and hurried across the room to Aunt Julia whose hand he seized and held in both his hands, shaking it when words failed him or the catch in his voice proved too much for him.

—I was just telling my mother, he said, I never heard you sing so well, never. No, I never heard your voice so good as it is to-night. Now! Would you believe that now? That's the truth. Upon my word and honour that's the truth. I never heard your voice sound so fresh and so . . . so clear and fresh, never.

Aunt Julia smiled broadly and murmured something about compliments as she released her hand from his grasp. Mr. Browne extended his open hand towards her and said to those who were near in the manner of a showman introducing a prodigy to an audience:

—Miss Julia Morkan, my latest discovery!

He was laughing very heartily at this himself when Freddy Malins turned to him and said:

—Well, Browne, if you're serious you might make a worse discovery. All I can say is I never heard her sing half so well as long as I am coming here. And that's the honest truth.

—Neither did I, said Mr. Browne. I think her voice has greatly improved.

Aunt Julia shrugged her shoulders and said with meek pride:

—Thirty years ago I hadn't a bad voice as voices go.

—I often told Julia, said Aunt Kate emphatically, that she was simply thrown away in that choir. But she never would be said by me.

She turned as if to appeal to the good sense of the others against a refractory child while Aunt Julia gazed in front of her, a vague smile of reminiscence playing on her face.

—No, continued Aunt Kate, she wouldn't be said or led by anyone, slaving there in that choir night and day, night and day. Six o'clock on Christmas morning! And all for what?

—Well, isn't it for the honour of God, Aunt Kate? asked Mary Jane, twisting round on the piano-stool and smiling.

Aunt Kate turned fiercely on her niece and said:

—I know all about the honour of God, Mary Jane, but I think it's not at all honourable for the pope to turn out the women out of the choirs that have slaved there all their lives and put little whipper-snappers of boys over their heads. I suppose it is for the good of the Church if the pope does it. But it's not just, Mary Jane, and it's not right.

She had worked herself into a passion and would have continued in defence of her sister for it was a sore subject with her but Mary Jane, seeing that all the dancers had come back, intervened pacifically:

—Now, Aunt Kate, you're giving scandal to Mr. Browne who is of the other persuasion.

Aunt Kate turned to Mr. Browne, who was grinning at this allusion to his religion, and said hastily:

—O, I don't question the pope's being right. I'm only a stupid old woman and I wouldn't presume to do such a thing. But there's such a thing as common everyday politeness and gratitude. And if I were in Julia's place I'd tell that Father Healy straight up to his face . . .

—And besides, Aunt Kate, said Mary Jane, we really are all hungry and when we are hungry we are all very quarrelsome.

—And when we are thirsty we are also quarrelsome, added Mr. Browne.

—So that we had better go to supper, said Mary Jane, and finish the discussion afterwards.

On the landing outside the drawing-room Gabriel found his wife and Mary Jane trying to persuade Miss Ivors to stay for supper. But Miss Ivors, who had put on her hat and was buttoning her cloak, would not stay. She did not feel in the least hungry and she had already overstayed her time.

—But only for ten minutes, Molly, said Mrs. Conroy. That won't delay you.

—To take a pick itself, said Mary Jane, after all your dancing.

—I really couldn't, said Miss Ivors.

—I am afraid you didn't enjoy yourself at all, said Mary Jane hopelessly.

—Ever so much, I assure you, said Miss Ivors, but you really must let me run off now.

—But how can you get home? asked Mrs. Conroy.

—O, it's only two steps up the quay.

Gabriel hesitated a moment and said:

—If you will allow me, Miss Ivors, I'll see you home if you really are obliged to go. But Miss Ivors broke away from them.

—I won't hear of it, she cried. For goodness sake go in to your suppers and don't mind me. I'm quite well able to take care of myself.

—Well, you're the comical girl, Molly, said Mrs. Conroy frankly.

—*Beannacht libh,* cried Miss Ivors, with a laugh, as she ran down the staircase.

Mary Jane gazed after her, a moody puzzled expression on her face, while Mrs. Conroy leaned over the banisters to listen for the hall-door. Gabriel asked himself was he the cause of her abrupt departure. But she did not seem to be in ill humour: she had gone away laughing. He stared blankly down the staircase.

At that moment Aunt Kate came toddling out of the supper-room, almost wringing her hands in despair.

—Where is Gabriel? she cried. Where on earth is Gabriel? There's everyone waiting in there, stage to let, and nobody to carve the goose!

—Here I am, Aunt Kate! cried Gabriel, with sudden animation, ready to carve a flock of geese, if necessary.

A fat brown goose lay at one end of the table and at the other end, on a bed of creased paper strewn with sprigs of parsley, lay a great ham, stripped of its outer skin and peppered over with crust crumbs, a neat paper frill round its shin and beside this was a round of spiced beef. Between these rival ends ran parallel lines of side-dishes: two little ministers of jelly, red and yellow; a shallow dish full of blocks of blancmange and red jam, a large green leaf-shaped dish with a stalk-shaped handle, on which lay bunches of purple raisins and peeled almonds, a companion dish on which lay a solid rectangle of Smyrna figs, a dish of custard topped with grated nutmeg, a small bowl full of chocolates and sweets wrapped in gold and silver papers and a glass vase in which stood some tall celery stalks. In the centre of the table there stood, as sentries to a fruit-stand which upheld a pyramid of oranges and American apples, two squat old-fashioned decanters of cut glass, one containing port and the other dark sherry. On the closed square piano a pudding in a huge yellow dish lay in waiting and behind it were three squads of bottles of stout and ale and minerals, drawn up according to the colours of their uniforms, the first two black, with brown and red labels, the third and smallest squad white, with transverse green sashes.

Gabriel took his seat boldly at the head of the table and, having looked to the edge of the carver, plunged his fork firmly into the goose. He felt quite at ease now for he was an expert carver and liked nothing better than to find himself at the head of a well-laden table.

—Miss Furlong, what shall I send you? he asked. A wing or a slice of the breast?

—Just a small slice of the breast.

—Miss Higgins, what for you?

—O, anything at all, Mr. Conroy.

While Gabriel and Miss Daly exchanged plates of goose and plates of ham and spiced beef Lily went from guest to guest with a dish of hot floury potatoes wrapped in a white napkin. This was Mary Jane's idea and she had also suggested apple sauce for the goose but Aunt Kate had said that plain roast goose without apple sauce had always been good enough for her and she hoped she might never eat worse. Mary Jane waited on her pupils and saw that they got the best slices and Aunt Kate and Aunt Julia opened and carried across from the piano bottles of stout and ale for the gentlemen and bottles of minerals for the ladies. There was a great deal of confusion and laughter and noise, the noise of orders and counter-orders, of knives and forks, of corks and glass-stoppers. Gabriel began to carve second helpings as soon as he had finished the first round without serving himself. Everyone protested loudly so that he compromised by taking a long draught of stout for he had found the carving hot work. Mary

Jane settled down quietly to her supper but Aunt Kate and Aunt Julia were still toddling round the table, walking on each other's heels, getting in each other's way and
giving each other unheeded orders. Mr. Browne begged of them to sit down and eat
their suppers and so did Gabriel but they said there was time enough so that, at last,
Freddy Malins stood up and, capturing Aunt Kate, plumped her down on her chair
amid general laughter.

When everyone had been well served Gabriel said, smiling:

—Now, if anyone wants a little more of what vulgar people call stuffing let him or
her speak.

A chorus of voices invited him to begin his own supper and Lily came forward with
three potatoes which she had reserved for him.

—Very well, said Gabriel amiably, as he took another preparatory draught, kindly
forget my existence, ladies and gentlemen, for a few minutes.

He set to his supper and took no part in the conversation with which the table covered Lily's removal of the plates. The subject of talk was the opera company which was
then at the Theatre Royal. Mr. Bartell D'Arcy, the tenor, a dark-complexioned young
man with a smart moustache, praised very highly the leading contralto of the company
but Miss Furlong thought she had a rather vulgar style of production. Freddy Malins
said there was a negro chieftain singing in the second part of the Gaiety pantomime
who had one of the finest tenor voices he had ever heard.

—Have you heard him? he asked Mr. Bartell D'Arcy across the table.

—No, answered Mr. Bartell D'Arcy carelessly.

—Because, Freddy Malins explained, now I'd be curious to hear your opinion of
him. I think he has a grand voice.

—It takes Teddy to find out the really good things, said Mr. Browne familiarly to
the table.

—And why couldn't he have a voice too? asked Freddy Malins sharply. Is it because
he's only a black?

Nobody answered this question and Mary Jane led the table back to the legitimate
opera. One of her pupils had given her a pass for *Mignon*. Of course it was very fine,
she said, but it made her think of poor Georgina Burns. Mr. Browne could go back
farther still, to the old Italian companies that used to come to Dublin—Tietjens, Ilma
de Murzka, Campanini, the great Trebelli, Giuglini, Ravelli, Aramburo. Those were
the days, he said, when there was something like singing to be heard in Dublin. He
told too of how the top gallery of the old Royal used to be packed night after night,
of how one night an Italian tenor had sung five encores to *Let Me Like a Soldier Fall*,
introducing a high C every time, and of how the gallery boys would sometimes in
their enthusiasm unyoke the horses from the carriage of some great *prima donna* and
pull her themselves through the streets to her hotel. Why did they never play the grand
old operas now, he asked, *Dinorah, Lucrezia Borgia*? Because they could not get the
voices to sing them: that was why.

—O, well, said Mr. Bartell D'Arcy, I presume there are as good singers to-day as
there were then.

—Where are they? asked Mr. Browne defiantly.

—In London, Paris, Milan, said Mr. Bartell D'Arcy warmly. I suppose Caruso, for
example, is quite as good, if not better than any of the men you have mentioned.

—Maybe so, said Mr. Browne. But I may tell you I doubt it strongly.

—O, I'd give anything to hear Caruso sing, said Mary Jane.

—For me, said Aunt Kate, who had been picking a bone, there was only one tenor. To please me, I mean. But I suppose none of you ever heard of him.

—Who was he, Miss Morkan? asked Mr. Bartell D'Arcy politely.

—His name, said Aunt Kate, was Parkinson. I heard him when he was in his prime and I think he had then the purest tenor voice that was ever put into a man's throat.

—Strange, said Mr. Bartell D'Arcy. I never even heard of him.

—Yes, yes, Miss Morkan is right, said Mr. Browne. I remember hearing of old Parkinson but he's too far back for me.

—A beautiful pure sweet mellow English tenor, said Aunt Kate with enthusiasm.

Gabriel having finished, the huge pudding was transferred to the table. The clatter of forks and spoons began again. Gabriel's wife served out spoonfuls of the pudding and passed the plates down the table. Midway down they were held up by Mary Jane, who replenished them with raspberry or orange jelly or with blancmange and jam. The pudding was of Aunt Julia's making and she received praises for it from all quarters. She herself said that it was not quite brown enough.

—Well, I hope, Miss Morkan, said Mr. Browne, that I'm brown enough for you because, you know, I'm all brown.

All the gentlemen, except Gabriel, ate some of the pudding out of compliment to Aunt Julia. As Gabriel never ate sweets the celery had been left for him. Freddy Malins also took a stalk of celery and ate it with his pudding. He had been told that celery was a capital thing for the blood and he was just then under doctor's care. Mrs. Malins, who had been silent all through the supper, said that her son was going down to Mount Melleray in a week or so. The table then spoke of Mount Melleray, how bracing the air was down there, how hospitable the monks were and how they never asked for a penny-piece from their guests.

—And do you mean to say, asked Mr. Browne incredulously, that a chap can go down there and put up there as if it were a hotel and live on the fat of the land and then come away without paying a farthing?

—O, most people give some donation to the monastery when they leave, said Mary Jane.

—I wish we had an institution like that in our Church, said Mr. Browne candidly.

He was astonished to hear that the monks never spoke, got up at two in the morning and slept in their coffins. He asked what they did it for.

—That's the rule of the order, said Aunt Kate firmly.

—Yes, but why? asked Mr. Browne.

Aunt Kate repeated that it was the rule, that was all. Mr. Browne still seemed not to understand. Freddy Malins explained to him, as best he could, that the monks were trying to make up for the sins committed by all the sinners in the outside world. The explanation was not very clear for Mr. Browne grinned and said:

—I like that idea very much but wouldn't a comfortable spring bed do them as well as a coffin?

—The coffin, said Mary Jane, is to remind them of their last end.

As the subject had grown lugubrious it was buried in a silence of the table during which Mrs. Malins could be heard saying to her neighbour in an indistinct undertone:

—They are very good men, the monks, very pious men.

The raisins and almonds and figs and apples and oranges and chocolates and sweets were now passed about the table and Aunt Julia invited all the guests to have either port or sherry. At first Mr. Bartell D'Arcy refused to take either but one of his neighbours nudged him and whispered something to him upon which he allowed his glass to be filled. Gradually as the last glasses were being filled the conversation ceased. A pause followed, broken only by the noise of the wine and by unsettlings of chairs. The Misses Morkan, all three, looked down at the tablecloth. Someone coughed once or twice and then a few gentlemen patted the table gently as a signal for silence. The silence came and Gabriel pushed back his chair and stood up.

The patting at once grew louder in encouragement and then ceased altogether. Gabriel leaned his ten trembling fingers on the tablecloth and smiled nervously at the company. Meeting a row of upturned faces he raised his eyes to the chandelier. The piano was playing a waltz tune and he could hear the skirts sweeping against the drawing-room door. People, perhaps, were standing in the snow on the quay outside, gazing up at the lighted windows and listening to the waltz music. The air was pure there. In the distance lay the park where the trees were weighted with snow. The Wellington Monument wore a gleaming cap of snow that flashed westward over the white field of Fifteen Acres.

He began:

—Ladies and Gentlemen.

—It has fallen to my lot this evening, as in years past, to perform a very pleasing task but a task for which I am afraid my poor powers as a speaker are all too inadequate.

—No, no! said Mr. Browne.

—But, however that may be, I can only ask you to-night to take the will for the deed and to lend me your attention for a few moments while I endeavour to express to you in words what my feelings are on this occasion.

—Ladies and Gentlemen. It is not the first time that we have gathered together under this hospitable roof, around this hospitable board. It is not the first time that we have been the recipients—or perhaps, I had better say, the victims—of the hospitality of certain good ladies.

He made a circle in the air with his arm and paused. Everyone laughed or smiled at Aunt Kate and Aunt Julia and Mary Jane who all turned crimson with pleasure. Gabriel went on more boldly:

—I feel more strongly with every recurring year that our country has no tradition which does it so much honour and which it should guard so jealously as that of its hospitality. It is a tradition that is unique as far as my experience goes (and I have visited not a few places abroad) among the modern nations. Some would say, perhaps, that with us it is rather a failing than anything to be boasted of. But granted even that, it is, to my mind, a princely failing, and one that I trust will long be cultivated among us. Of one thing, at least, I am sure. As long as this one roof shelters the good ladies aforesaid—and I wish from my heart it may do so for many and many a long year to come—the tradition of genuine warm-hearted courteous Irish hospitality, which our forefathers have handed down to us and which we in turn must hand down to our descendants, is still alive among us.

A hearty murmur of assent ran round the table. It shot through Gabriel's mind that Miss Ivors was not there and that she had gone away discourteously: and he said with confidence in himself:

—Ladies and Gentlemen.

—A new generation is growing up in our midst, a generation actuated by new ideas and new principles. It is serious and enthusiastic for these new ideas and its enthusiasm, even when it is misdirected, is, I believe, in the main sincere. But we are living in a sceptical and, if I may use the phrase, a thought-tormented age: and sometimes I fear that this new generation, educated or hypereducated as it is, will lack those qualities of humanity, of hospitality, of kindly humour which belonged to an older day. Listening to-night to the names of all those great singers of the past it seemed to me, I must confess, that we were living in a less spacious age. Those days might, without exaggeration, be called spacious days: and if they are gone beyond recall let us hope, at least, that in gatherings such as this we shall still speak of them with pride and affection, still cherish in our hearts the memory of those dead and gone great ones whose fame the world will not willingly let die.

—Hear, hear! said Mr. Browne loudly.

—But yet, continued Gabriel, his voice falling into a softer inflection, there are always in gatherings such as this sadder thoughts that will recur to our minds: thoughts of the past, of youth, of changes, of absent faces that we miss here tonight. Our path through life is strewn with many such sad memories: and were we to brood upon them always we could not find the heart to go on bravely with our work among the living. We have all of us living duties and living affections which claim, and rightly claim, our strenuous endeavours.

—Therefore, I will not linger on the past. I will not let any gloomy moralising intrude upon us here to-night. Here we are gathered together for a brief moment from the bustle and rush of our everyday routine. We are met here as friends, in the spirit of good-fellowship, as colleagues, also to a certain extent, in the true spirit of *camaraderie,* and as the guests of—what shall I call them?—the Three Graces of the Dublin musical world.

The table burst into applause and laughter at this sally. Aunt Julia vainly asked each of her neighbours in turn to tell her what Gabriel had said.

—He says we are the Three Graces, Aunt Julia, said Mary Jane.

Aunt Julia did not understand but she looked up, smiling, at Gabriel, who continued in the same vein:

—Ladies and Gentlemen.

—I will not attempt to play to-night the part that Paris played on another occasion. I will not attempt to choose between them. The task would be an invidious one and one beyond my poor powers. For when I view them in turn, whether it be our chief hostess herself, whose good heart, whose too good heart, has become a byword with all who know her, or her sister, who seems to be gifted with perennial youth and whose singing must have been a surprise and a revelation to us all to-night, or, last but not least, when I consider our youngest hostess, talented, cheerful, hard-working and the best of nieces, I confess, Ladies and Gentlemen, that I do not know to which of them I should award the prize.

Gabriel glanced down at his aunts and, seeing the large smile on Aunt Julia's face and the tears which had risen to Aunt Kate's eyes, hastened to his close. He raised his glass of port gallantly, while every member of the company fingered a glass expectantly, and said loudly:

—Let us toast them all three together. Let us drink to their health, wealth, long life, happiness and prosperity and may they long continue to hold the proud and self-won position which they hold in their profession and the position of honour and affection which they hold in our hearts.

All the guests stood up, glass in hand, and, turning towards the three seated ladies, sang in unison, with Mr. Browne as leader:

> For they are jolly gay fellows,
> For they are jolly gay fellows,
> For they are jolly gay fellows,
> Which nobody can deny.

Aunt Kate was making frank use of her handkerchief and even Aunt Julia seemed moved. Freddy Malins beat time with his pudding-fork and the singers turned towards one another, as if in melodious conference, while they sang, with emphasis:

> Unless he tells a lie,
> Unless he tells a lie.

Then, turning once more towards their hostesses, they sang:

> For they are jolly gay fellows,
> For they are jolly gay fellows,
> For they are jolly gay fellows,
> Which nobody can deny.

The acclamation which followed was taken up beyond the door of the supper-room by many of the other guests and renewed time after time, Freddy Malins acting as officer with his fork on high.

The piercing morning air came into the hall where they were standing so that Aunt Kate said:

—Close the door, somebody. Mrs. Malins will get her death of cold.

—Browne is out there, Aunt Kate, said Mary Jane.

—Browne is everywhere, said Aunt Kate, lowering her voice.

Mary Jane laughed at her tone.

—Really, she said archly, he is very attentive.

—He has been laid on here like the gas, said Aunt Kate in the same tone, all during the Christmas.

She laughed herself this time good-humouredly and then added quickly:

—But tell him to come in, Mary Jane, and close the door. I hope to goodness he didn't hear me.

At that moment the hall-door was opened and Mr. Browne came in from the doorstep, laughing as if his heart would break. He was dressed in a long green overcoat with mock astrakhan cuffs and collar and wore on his head an oval fur cap. He pointed down the snow-covered quay from where the sound of shrill prolonged whistling was borne in.

—Teddy will have all the cabs in Dublin out, he said.

Gabriel advanced from the little pantry behind the office, struggling into his overcoat and, looking round the hall, said:

—Gretta not down yet?

—She's getting on her things, Gabriel, said Aunt Kate.

—Who's playing up there? asked Gabriel.

—Nobody. They're all gone.

—O no, Aunt Kate, said Mary Jane. Bartell D'Arcy and Miss O'Callaghan aren't gone yet.

—Someone is strumming at the piano, anyhow, said Gabriel.

Mary Jane glanced at Gabriel and Mr. Browne and said with a shiver:

—It makes me feel cold to look at you two gentlemen muffled up like that. I wouldn't like to face your journey home at this hour.

—I'd like nothing better this minute, said Mr. Browne stoutly, than a rattling fine walk in the country or a fast drive with a good spanking goer between the shafts.

—We used to have a very good horse and trap at home, said Aunt Julia sadly.

—The never-to-be-forgotten Johnny, said Mary Jane, laughing.

Aunt Kate and Gabriel laughed too.

—Why, what was wonderful about Johnny? asked Mr. Browne.

—The late lamented Patrick Morkan, our grandfather, that is, explained Gabriel, commonly known in his later years as the old gentleman, was a glue-boiler.

—O, now, Gabriel, said Aunt Kate, laughing, he had a starch mill.

—Well, glue or starch, said Gabriel, the old gentleman had a horse by the name of Johnny. And Johnny used to work in the old gentleman's mill, walking round and round in order to drive the mill. That was all very well; but now comes the tragic part about Johnny. One fine day the old gentleman thought he'd like to drive out with the quality to a military review in the park.

—The Lord have mercy on his soul, said Aunt Kate compassionately.

—Amen, said Gabriel. So the old gentleman, as I said, harnessed Johnny and put on his very best tall hat and his very best stock collar and drove out in grand style from his ancestral mansion somewhere near Back Lane, I think.

Everyone laughed, even Mrs. Malins, at Gabriel's manner and Aunt Kate said:

—O now, Gabriel, he didn't live in Back Lane, really. Only the mill was there.

—Out from the mansion of his forefathers, continued Gabriel, he drove with Johnny. And everything went on beautifully until Johnny came in sight of King Billy's statue: and whether he fell in love with the horse King Billy sits on or whether he thought he was back again in the mill, anyhow he began to walk round the statue.

Gabriel paced in a circle round the hall in his goloshes amid the laughter of the others.

—Round and round he went, said Gabriel, and the old gentleman, who was a very pompous old gentleman, was highly indignant. *Go on, sir! What do you mean, sir? Johnny! Johnny! Most extraordinary conduct! Can't understand the horse!*

The peals of laughter which followed Gabriel's imitation of the incident were interrupted by a resounding knock at the hall-door. Mary Jane ran to open it and let in Freddy Malins. Freddy Malins, with his hat well back on his head and his shoulders humped with cold, was puffing and steaming after his exertions.

—I could only get one cab, he said.

—O, we'll find another along the quay, said Gabriel.

—Yes, said Aunt Kate. Better not keep Mrs. Malins standing in the draught.

Mrs. Malins was helped down the front steps by her son and Mr. Browne and, after many manœuvres, hoisted into the cab. Freddy Malins clambered in after her and spent a long time settling her on the seat, Mr. Browne helping him with advice. At last she was settled comfortably and Freddy Malins invited Mr. Browne into the cab. There was a good deal of confused talk, and then Mr. Browne got into the cab. The cabman settled his rug over his knees, and bent down for the address. The confusion grew greater and the cabman was directed differently by Freddy Malins and Mr. Browne, each of whom had his head out through a window of the cab. The difficulty was to know where to drop Mr. Browne along the route and Aunt Kate, Aunt Julia and Mary Jane helped the discussion from the doorstep with cross-directions and contradictions and abundance of laughter. As for Freddy Malins he was speechless with laughter. He popped his head in and out of the window every moment, to the great danger of his hat, and told his mother how the discussion was progressing till at last Mr. Browne shouted to the bewildered cabman above the din of everybody's laughter:

—Do you know Trinity College?

—Yes, sir, said the cabman.

—Well, drive bang up against Trinity College gates, said Mr. Browne, and then we'll tell you where to go. You understand now?

—Yes, sir, said the cabman.

—Make like a bird for Trinity College.

—Right, sir, cried the cabman.

The horse was whipped up and the cab rattled off along the quay amid a chorus of laughter and adieus.

Gabriel had not gone to the door with the others. He was in a dark part of the hall gazing up the staircase. A woman was standing near the top of the first flight, in the shadow also. He could not see her face but he could see the terracotta and salmonpink panels of her skirt which the shadow made appear black and white. It was his wife. She was leaning on the banisters, listening to something. Gabriel was surprised at her stillness and strained his ear to listen also. But he could hear little save the noise of laughter and dispute on the front steps, a few chords struck on the piano and a few notes of a man's voice singing.

He stood still in the gloom of the hall, trying to catch the air that the voice was singing and gazing up at his wife. There was grace and mystery in her attitude as if she were a symbol of something. He asked himself what is a woman standing on the stairs in the shadow, listening to distant music, a symbol of. If he were a painter he would paint her in that attitude. Her blue felt hat would show off the bronze of her hair against the darkness and the dark panels of her skirt would show off the light ones. *Distant Music* he would call the picture if he were a painter.

The hall-door was closed; and Aunt Kate, Aunt Julia and Mary Jane came down the hall, still laughing.

—Well, isn't Freddy terrible? said Mary Jane. He's really terrible.

Gabriel said nothing but pointed up the stairs towards where his wife was standing. Now that the hall-door was closed the voice and the piano could be heard more clearly. Gabriel held up his hand for them to be silent. The song seemed to be in the old Irish tonality and the singer seemed uncertain both of his words and of his voice. The voice, made plaintive by distance and by the singer's hoarseness, faintly illuminated the cadence of the air with words expressing grief:

> O, the rain falls on my heavy locks
> And the dew wets my skin,
> My babe lies cold . . .

—O, exclaimed Mary Jane. It's Bartell D'Arcy singing and he wouldn't sing all the night. O, I'll get him to sing a song before he goes.

—O do, Mary Jane, said Aunt Kate.

Mary Jane brushed past the others and ran to the staircase but before she reached it the singing stopped and the piano was closed abruptly.

—O, what a pity! she cried. Is he coming down, Gretta?

Gabriel heard his wife answer yes and saw her come down towards them. A few steps behind her were Mr. Bartell D'Arcy and Miss O'Callaghan.

—O, Mr. D'Arcy, cried Mary Jane, it's downright mean of you to break off like that when we were all in raptures listening to you.

—I have been at him all the evening, said Miss O'Callaghan, and Mrs. Conroy too and he told us he had a dreadful cold and couldn't sing.

—O, Mr. D'Arcy, said Aunt Kate, now that was a great fib to tell.

—Can't you see that I'm as hoarse as a crow? said Mr. D'Arcy roughly.

He went into the pantry hastily and put on his overcoat. The others, taken aback by his rude speech, could find nothing to say. Aunt Kate wrinkled her brows and made signs to the others to drop the subject. Mr. D'Arcy stood swathing his neck carefully and frowning.

—It's the weather, said Aunt Julia, after a pause.

—Yes, everybody has colds, said Aunt Kate readily, everybody.

—They say, said Mary Jane, we haven't had snow like it for thirty years; and I read this morning in the newspapers that the snow is general all over Ireland.

—I love the look of snow, said Aunt Julia sadly.

—So do I, said Miss O'Callaghan. I think Christmas is never really Christmas unless we have the snow on the ground.

—But poor Mr. D'Arcy doesn't like the snow, said Aunt Kate, smiling.

Mr. D'Arcy came from the pantry, fully swathed and buttoned, and in a repentant tone told them the history of his cold. Everyone gave him advice and said it was a great pity and urged him to be very careful of his throat in the night air. Gabriel watched his wife who did not join in the conversation. She was standing right under the dusty fanlight and the flame of the gas lit up the rich bronze of her hair which he had seen her drying at the fire a few days before. She was in the same attitude and seemed unaware of the talk about her. At last she turned towards them and Gabriel saw that there was colour on her cheeks and that her eyes were shining. A sudden tide of joy went leaping out of his heart.

—Mr. D'Arcy, she said, what is the name of that song you were singing?

—It's called *The Lass of Aughrim,* said Mr. D'Arcy, but I couldn't remember it properly. Why? Do you know it?

—*The Lass of Aughrim,* she repeated. I couldn't think of the name.

—It's a very nice air, said Mary Jane. I'm sorry you were not in voice to-night.

—Now, Mary Jane, said Aunt Kate, don't annoy Mr. D'Arcy. I won't have him annoyed.

Seeing that all were ready to start she shepherded them to the door where good-night was said:

—Well, good-night, Aunt Kate, and thanks for the pleasant evening.

—Good-night, Gabriel. Good-night, Gretta!

—Good-night, Aunt Kate, and thanks ever so much. Good-night, Aunt Julia.

—O, good-night, Gretta, I didn't see you.

—Good-night, Mr. D'Arcy. Good-night, Miss O'Callaghan.

—Good-night, Miss Morkan.

—Good-night, again.

—Good-night, all. Safe home.

—Good-night. Good-night.

The morning was still dark. A dull yellow light brooded over the houses and the river; and the sky seemed to be descending. It was slushy underfoot; and only streaks and patches of snow lay on the roofs, on the parapets of the quay and on the area railings. The lamps were still burning redly in the murky air and, across the river, the palace of the Four Courts stood out menacingly against the heavy sky.

She was walking on before him with Mr. Bartell D'Arcy, her shoes in a brown parcel tucked under one arm and her hands holding her skirt up from the slush. She had no longer any grace of attitude but Gabriel's eyes were still bright with happiness. The blood went bounding along his veins; and the thoughts went rioting through his brain, proud, joyful, tender, valorous.

She was walking on before him so lightly and so erect that he longed to run after her noiselessly, catch her by the shoulders and say something foolish and affectionate into her ear. She seemed to him so frail that he longed to defend her against something and then to be alone with her. Moments of their secret life together burst like stars upon his memory. A heliotrope envelope was lying beside his breakfast-cup and he was caressing it with his hand. Birds were twittering in the ivy and the sunny web of the curtain was shimmering along the floor: he could not eat for happiness. They were standing on the crowded platform and he was placing a ticket inside the warm palm of her glove. He was standing with her in the cold, looking in through a grated window at a man making bottles in a roaring furnace. It was very cold. Her face, fragrant in the cold air, was quite close to his; and suddenly she called out to the man at the furnace:

—Is the fire hot, sir?

But the man could not hear her with the noise of the furnace. It was just as well. He might have answered rudely.

A wave of yet more tender joy escaped from his heart and went coursing in warm flood along his arteries. Like the tender fires of stars moments of their life together, that no one knew of or would ever know of, broke upon and illumined his memory. He longed to recall to her those moments, to make her forget the years of their dull existence together and remember only their moments of ecstasy. For the years, he felt, had not quenched his soul or hers. Their children, his writing, her household cares had not quenched all their souls' tender fire. In one letter that he had written to her then he had said: *Why is it that words like these seem to me so dull and cold? Is it because there is no word tender enough to be your name?*

Like distant music these words that he had written years before were borne towards him from the past. He longed to be alone with her. When the others had gone away, when he and she were in their room in the hotel, then they would be alone together. He would call her softly:

—Gretta!

Perhaps she would not hear at once: she would be undressing. Then something in his voice would strike her. She would turn and look at him.

At the corner of Winetavern Street they met a cab. He was glad of its rattling noise as it saved him from conversation. She was looking out of the window and seemed tired. The others spoke only a few words, pointing out some building or street. The horse galloped along wearily under the murky morning sky, dragging his old rattling box after his heels, and Gabriel was again in a cab with her, galloping to catch the boat, galloping to their honeymoon.

As the cab drove across O'Connell Bridge Miss O'Callaghan said:

—They say you never cross O'Connell Bridge without seeing a white horse.

—I see a white man this time, said Gabriel.

—Where? asked Mr. Bartell D'Arcy.

Gabriel pointed to the statue, on which lay patches of snow. Then he nodded familiarly to it and waved his hand.

—Good-night, Dan, he said gaily.

When the cab drew up before the hotel Gabriel jumped out and, in spite of Mr. Bartell D'Arcy's protest, paid the driver. He gave the man a shilling over his fare. The man saluted and said:

—A prosperous New Year to you, sir.

—The same to you, said Gabriel cordially.

She leaned for a moment on his arm in getting out of the cab and while standing at the curbstone, bidding the others good-night. She leaned lightly on his arm, as lightly as when she had danced with him a few hours before. He had felt proud and happy then, happy that she was his, proud of her grace and wifely carriage. But now, after the kindling again of so many memories, the first touch of her body, musical and strange and perfumed, sent through him a keen pang of lust. Under cover of her silence he pressed her arm closely to his side; and, as they stood at the hotel door, he felt that they had escaped from their lives and duties, escaped from home and friends and run away together with wild and radiant hearts to a new adventure.

An old man was dozing in a great hooded chair in the hall. He lit a candle in the office and went before them to the stairs. They followed him in silence, their feet falling in soft thuds on the thickly carpeted stairs. She mounted the stairs behind the porter, her head bowed in the ascent, her frail shoulders curved as with a burden, her skirt girt tightly about her. He could have flung his arms about her hips and held her still for his arms were trembling with desire to seize her and only the stress of his nails against the palms of his hands held the wild impulse of his body in check. The porter halted on the stairs to settle his guttering candle. They halted too on the steps below him. In the silence Gabriel could hear the falling of the molten wax into the tray and the thumping of his own heart against his ribs.

The porter led them along a corridor and opened a door. Then he set his unstable candle down on a toilet-table and asked at what hour they were to be called in the morning.

—Eight, said Gabriel.

The porter pointed to the tap of the electric-light and began a muttered apology but Gabriel cut him short.

—We don't want any light. We have light enough from the street. And I say, he added, pointing to the candle, you might remove that handsome article, like a good man.

The porter took up his candle again, but slowly for he was surprised by such a novel idea. Then he mumbled good-night and went out. Gabriel shot the lock to.

A ghostly light from the street lamp lay in a long shaft from one window to the door. Gabriel threw his overcoat and hat on a couch and crossed the room towards the window. He looked down into the street in order that his emotion might calm a little. Then he turned and leaned against a chest of drawers with his back to the light. She had taken off her hat and cloak and was standing before a large swinging mirror, unhooking her waist. Gabriel paused for a few moments, watching her, and then said:

—Gretta!

She turned away from the mirror slowly and walked along the shaft of light towards him. Her face looked so serious and weary that the words would not pass Gabriel's lips. No, it was not the moment yet.

—You looked tired, he said.

—I am a little, she answered.

—You don't feel ill or weak?

—No, tired: that's all.

She went on to the window and stood there, looking out. Gabriel waited again and then, fearing that diffidence was about to conquer him, he said abruptly:

—By the way, Gretta!

—What is it?

—You know that poor fellow Malins? he said quickly.

—Yes. What about him?

—Well, poor fellow, he's a decent sort of chap after all, continued Gabriel in a false voice. He gave me back that sovereign I lent him and I didn't expect it really. It's a pity he wouldn't keep away from that Browne, because he's not a bad fellow at heart.

He was trembling now with annoyance. Why did she seem so abstracted? He did not know how he could begin. Was she annoyed, too, about something? If she would only turn to him or come to him of her own accord! To take her as she was would be brutal. No, he must see some ardour in her eyes first. He longed to be master of her strange mood.

—When did you lend him the pound? she asked, after a pause.

Gabriel strove to restrain himself from breaking out into brutal language about the sottish Malins and his pound. He longed to cry to her from his soul, to crush her body against his, to overmaster her. But he said:

—O, at Christmas, when he opened that little Christmas-card shop in Henry Street.

He was in such a fever of rage and desire that he did not hear her come from the window. She stood before him for an instant, looking at him strangely. Then, suddenly raising herself on tiptoe and resting her hands lightly on his shoulders, she kissed him.

—You are a very generous person, Gabriel, she said.

Gabriel, trembling with delight at her sudden kiss and at the quaintness of her phrase, put his hands on her hair and began smoothing it back, scarcely touching it with his fingers. The washing had made it fine and brilliant. His heart was brimming over with happiness. Just when he was wishing for it she had come to him of her own accord. Perhaps her thoughts had been running with his. Perhaps she had felt the impetuous desire that was in him and then the yielding mood had come upon her. Now that she had fallen to him so easily he wondered why he had been so diffident.

He stood, holding her head between his hands. Then, slipping one arm swiftly about her body and drawing her towards him, he said softly:

—Gretta dear, what are you thinking about?

She did not answer nor yield wholly to his arm. He said again, softly:

—Tell me what it is, Gretta. I think I know what is the matter. Do I know?

She did not answer at once. Then she said in an outburst of tears:

—O, I am thinking about that song, *The Lass of Aughrim*.

She broke loose from him and ran to the bed and, throwing her arms across the bed-rail, hid her face. Gabriel stood stock-still for a moment in astonishment and then followed her. As he passed in the way of the cheval-glass he caught sight of himself in full length, his broad, well-filled shirt-front, the face whose expression always puzzled him when he saw it in a mirror and his glimmering gilt-rimmed eyeglasses. He halted a few paces from her and said:

—What about the song? Why does that make you cry?

She raised her head from her arms and dried her eyes with the back of her hand like a child. A kinder note than he had intended went into his voice.

—Why, Gretta? he asked.

—I am thinking about a person long ago who used to sing that song.

—And who was the person long ago? asked Gabriel, smiling.

—It was a person I used to know in Galway when I was living with my grandmother, she said.

The smile passed away from Gabriel's face. A dull anger began to gather again at the back of his mind and the dull fires of his lust began to glow angrily in his veins.

—Someone you were in love with? he asked ironically.

—It was a young boy I used to know, she answered, named Michael Furey. He used to sing that song, *The Lass of Aughrim*. He was very delicate.

Gabriel was silent. He did not wish her to think that he was interested in this delicate boy.

—I can see him so plainly, she said after a moment. Such eyes as he had: big dark eyes! And such an expression in them—an expression!

—O then, you were in love with him? said Gabriel.

—I used to go out walking with him, she said, when I was in Galway.

A thought flew across Gabriel's mind.

—Perhaps that was why you wanted to go to Galway with that Ivors girl? he said coldly.

She looked at him and asked in surprise:

—What for?

Her eyes made Gabriel feel awkward. He shrugged his shoulders and said:

—How do I know? To see him perhaps.

She looked away from him along the shaft of light towards the window in silence.

—He is dead, she said at length. He died when he was only seventeen. Isn't it a terrible thing to die so young as that?

—What was he? asked Gabriel, still ironically.

—He was in the gasworks, she said.

Gabriel felt humiliated by the failure of his irony and by the evocation of this figure from the dead, a boy in the gasworks. While he had been full of memories of their secret life together, full of tenderness and joy and desire, she had been comparing him in her mind with another. A shameful consciousness of his own person assailed him. He saw himself as a ludicrous figure, acting as a pennyboy for his aunts, a nervous, well-meaning sentimentalist, orating to vulgarians and idealising his own clownish lusts, the pitiable fatuous fellow he had caught a glimpse of in the mirror. Instinctively he turned his back more to the light lest she might see the shame that burned upon his forehead.

He tried to keep up his tone of cold interrogation but his voice when he spoke was humble and indifferent.

—I suppose you were in love with this Michael Furey, Gretta, he said.

—I was great with him at that time, she said.

Her voice was veiled and sad. Gabriel, feeling now how vain it would be to try to lead her whither he had purposed, caressed one of her hands and said, also sadly:

—And what did he die of so young, Gretta? Consumption, was it?

—I think he died for me, she answered.

A vague terror seized Gabriel at this answer as if, at that hour when he had hoped to triumph, some impalpable and vindictive being was coming against him, gathering forces against him in its vague world. But he shook himself free of it with an effort of reason and continued to caress her hand. He did not question her again for he felt that she would tell him of herself. Her hand was warm and moist: it did not respond to his touch but he continued to caress it just as he had caressed her first letter to him that spring morning.

—It was in the winter, she said, about the beginning of the winter when I was going to leave my grandmother's and come up here to the convent. And he was ill at the time in his lodgings in Galway and wouldn't be let out and his people in Oughterard were written to. He was in decline, they said, or something like that. I never knew rightly.

She paused for a moment and sighed.

—Poor fellow, she said. He was very fond of me and he was such a gentle boy. We used to go out together, walking, you know, Gabriel, like the way they do in the country. He was going to study singing only for his health. He had a very good voice, poor Michael Furey.

—Well; and then? asked Gabriel.

—And then when it came to the time for me to leave Galway and come up to the convent he was much worse and I wouldn't be let see him so I wrote a letter saying I was going up to Dublin and would be back in the summer and hoping he would be better then.

She paused for a moment to get her voice under control and then went on:

—Then the night before I left I was in my grandmother's house in Nun's Island, packing up, and I heard gravel thrown up against the window. The window was so wet I couldn't see so I ran downstairs as I was and slipped out the back into the garden and there was the poor fellow at the end of the garden, shivering.

—And did you not tell him to go back? asked Gabriel.

—I implored of him to go home at once and told him he would get his death in the rain. But he said he did not want to live. I can see his eyes as well as well! He was standing at the end of the wall where there was a tree.

—And did he go home? asked Gabriel.

—Yes, he went home. And when I was only a week in the convent he died and he was buried in Oughterard where his people came from. O, the day I heard that, that he was dead!

She stopped, choking with sobs, and, overcome by emotion, flung herself face downward on the bed, sobbing in the quilt. Gabriel held her hand for a moment longer, irresolutely, and then, shy of intruding on her grief, let it fall gently and walked quietly to the window.

She was fast asleep.

Gabriel, leaning on his elbow, looked for a few moments unresentfully on her tangled hair and half-open mouth, listening to her deep-drawn breath. So she had had that romance in her life: a man had died for her sake. It hardly pained him now to think how poor a part he, her husband, had played in her life. He watched her while she slept as though he and she had never lived together as man and wife. His curious eyes rested long upon her face and on her hair: and, as he thought of what she must have been then, in that time of her first girlish beauty, a strange friendly pity for her entered his soul. He did not like to say even to himself that her face was no longer beautiful but he knew that it was no longer the face for which Michael Furey had braved death.

Perhaps she had not told him all the story. His eyes moved to the chair over which she had thrown some of her clothes. A petticoat string dangled to the floor. One boot stood upright, its limp upper fallen down: the fellow of it lay upon its side. He wondered at his riot of emotions of an hour before. From what had it proceeded? From his aunt's supper, from his own foolish speech, from the wine and dancing, the merry-making when saying good-night in the hall, the pleasure of the walk along the river in the snow. Poor Aunt Julia! She, too, would soon be a shade with the shade of Patrick Morkan and his horse. He had caught that haggard look upon her face for a moment when she was singing *Arrayed for the Bridal*. Soon, perhaps, he would be sitting in that same drawing-room, dressed in black, his silk hat on his knees. The blinds would be drawn down and Aunt Kate would be sitting beside him, crying and blowing her nose and telling him how Julia had died. He would cast about in his mind for some words that might console her, and would find only lame and useless ones. Yes, yes: that would happen very soon.

The air of the room chilled his shoulders. He stretched himself cautiously along under the sheets and lay down beside his wife. One by one they were all becoming shades. Better pass boldly into that other world, in the full glory of some passion, than fade and wither dismally with age. He thought of how she who lay beside him had locked in her heart for so many years that image of her lover's eyes when he had told her that he did not wish to live.

Generous tears filled Gabriel's eyes. He had never felt like that himself towards any woman but he knew that such a feeling must be love. The tears gathered more thickly in his eyes and in the partial darkness he imagined he saw the form of a young man standing under a dripping tree. Other forms were near. His soul had approached that region where dwell the vast hosts of the dead. He was conscious of, but could not apprehend, their wayward and flickering existence. His own identity was fading out into a grey impalpable world: the solid world itself which these dead had one time reared and lived in was dissolving and dwindling.

A few light taps upon the pane made him turn to the window. It had begun to snow again. He watched sleepily the flakes, silver and dark, falling obliquely against the lamplight. The time had come for him to set out on his journey westward. Yes, the newspapers were right: snow was general all over Ireland. It was falling on every part of the dark central plain, on the treeless hills, falling softly upon the Bog of Allen and, farther westward, softly falling into the dark mutinous Shannon waves. It was falling, too, upon every part of the lonely churchyard on the hill where Michael Furey lay buried. It lay thickly drifted on the crooked crosses and headstones, on the spears of the little gate, on the barren thorns. His soul swooned slowly as he heard the snow falling faintly through the universe and faintly falling, like the descent of their last end, upon all the living and the dead.

(1914)

KATHERINE ANNE PORTER
[1890–1980]

The Jilting of Granny Weatherall

She flicked her wrist neatly out of Doctor Harry's pudgy careful fingers and pulled the sheet up to her chin. The brat ought to be in knee breeches. Doctoring around the country with spectacles on his nose! "Get along now, take your schoolbooks and go. There's nothing wrong with me."

Doctor Harry spread a warm paw like a cushion on her forehead where the forked green vein danced and made her eyelids twitch. "Now, now, be a good girl, and we'll have you up in no time."

"That's no way to speak to a woman nearly eighty years old just because she's down. I'd have you respect your elders, young man."

"Well, Missy, excuse me." Doctor Harry patted her cheek. "But I've got to warn you, haven't I? You're a marvel, but you must be careful or you're going to be good and sorry."

"Don't tell me what I'm going to be. I'm on my feet now, morally speaking. It's Cornelia. I had to go to bed to get rid of her."

Her bones felt loose, and floated around in her skin, and Doctor Harry floated like a balloon around the foot of the bed. He floated and pulled down his waistcoat and swung his glasses on a cord. "Well, stay where you are, it certainly can't hurt you."

"Get along and doctor your sick," said Granny Weatherall. "Leave a well woman alone. I'll call for you when I want you. . . . Where were you forty years ago when

I pulled through milkleg and double pneumonia? You weren't even born. Don't let Cornelia lead you on," she shouted, because Doctor Harry appeared to float up to the ceiling and out. "I pay my own bills, and I don't throw my money away on nonsense!"

She meant to wave goodby, but it was too much trouble. Her eyes closed of themselves, it was like a dark curtain drawn around the bed. The pillow rose and floated under her, pleasant as a hammock in a light wind. She listened to the leaves rustling outside the window. No, somebody was swishing newspapers: no, Cornelia and Doctor Harry were whispering together. She leaped broad awake, thinking they whispered in her ear.

"She was never like this, *never* like this!" "Well, what can we expect?" "Yes, eighty years old. . . . "

Well, and what if she was? She still had ears. It was like Cornelia to whisper around doors. She always kept things secret in such a public way. She was always being tactful and kind. Cornelia was dutiful; that was the trouble with her. Dutiful and good: "So good and dutiful," said Granny, "that I'd like to spank her." She saw herself spanking Cornelia and making a fine job of it.

"What'd you say, Mother?"

Granny felt her face tying up in hard knots.

"Can't a body think, I'd like to know?"

"I thought you might want something."

"I do. I want a lot of things. First off, go away and don't whisper."

She lay and drowsed, hoping in her sleep that the children would keep out and let her rest a minute. It had been a long day. Not that she was tired. It was always pleasant to snatch a minute now and then. There was always so much to be done, let me see: tomorrow.

Tomorrow was far away and there was nothing to trouble about. Things were finished somehow when the time came; thank God there was always a little margin over for peace: then a person could spread out the plan of life and tuck in the edges orderly. It was good to have everything clean and folded away, with the hair brushes and tonic bottles sitting straight on the white embroidered linen: the day started without fuss and the pantry shelves laid out with rows of jelly glasses and brown jugs and white stone-china jars with blue whirligigs and words painted on them: coffee, tea, sugar, ginger, cinnamon, allspice: and the bronze clock with the lion on top nicely dusted off. The dust that lion could collect in twenty-four hours! The box in the attic with all those letters tied up, well, she'd have to go through that tomorrow. All those letters—George's letters and John's letters and her letters to them both—lying around for the children to find afterward made her uneasy. Yes, that would be tomorrow's business. No use to let them know how silly she had been once.

While she was rummaging around she found death in her mind and it felt clammy and unfamiliar. She had spent so much time preparing for death there was no need for bringing it up again. Let it take care of itself now. When she was sixty she had felt very old, finished, and went around making farewell trips to see her children and grandchildren, with a secret in her mind: This is the very last of your mother, children! Then she made her will and came down with a long fever. That was all just a notion like a lot of other things, but it was lucky too, for she had once and for all got over the idea of dying for a long time. Now she couldn't be worried. She hoped she had better sense now. Her father had lived to be one hundred and two years old and had drunk a noggin of strong hot toddy on his last birthday. He told the reporters it was his daily habit, and he owed his long life to that. He had made quite a scandal and was very pleased about it. She believed she'd just plague Cornelia a little.

"Cornelia! Cornelia!" No footsteps, but a sudden hand on her cheek. "Bless you, where have you been?"

"Here, Mother."

"Well, Cornelia, I want a noggin of hot toddy."

"Are you cold, darling?"

"I'm chilly, Cornelia. Lying in bed stops the circulation. I must have told you that a thousand times."

Well, she could just hear Cornelia telling her husband that Mother was getting a little childish and they'd have to humor her. The thing that most annoyed her was that Cornelia thought she was deaf, dumb, and blind. Little hasty glances and tiny gestures tossed around her and over her head saying, "Don't cross her, let her have her way, she's eighty years old," and she sitting there as if she lived in a thin glass cage. Sometimes Granny almost made up her mind to pack up and move back to her own house where nobody could remind her every minute that she was old. Wait, wait, Cornelia, till your own children whisper behind your back!

In her day she had kept a better house and had got more work done. She wasn't too old yet for Lydia to be driving eighty miles for advice when one of the children jumped the track, and Jimmy still dropped in and talked things over: "Now, Mammy, you've a good business head, I want to know what you think of this? . . ." Old. Cornelia couldn't change the furniture around without asking. Little things, little things! They had been so sweet when they were little. Granny wished the old days were back again with the children young and everything to be done over. It had been a hard pull, but not too much for her. When she thought of all the food she had cooked, and all the clothes she had cut and sewed, and all the gardens she had made—well, the children showed it. There they were, made out of her, and they couldn't get away from that. Sometimes she wanted to see John again and point to them and say, Well, I didn't do so badly, did I? But that would have to wait. That was for tomorrow. She used to think of him as a man, but now all the children were older than their father, and he would be a child beside her if she saw him now. It seemed strange and there was something wrong in the idea. Why, he couldn't possibly recognize her. She had fenced in a hundred acres once, digging the postholes herself and clamping the wires with just a Negro boy to help. That changed a woman. John would be looking for a young woman with the peaked Spanish comb in her hair and the painted fan. Digging postholes changed a woman. Riding country roads in the winter when women had their babies was another thing: sitting up nights with sick horses and sick Negroes and sick children and hardly ever losing one. John, I hardly ever lost one of them! John would see that in a minute, that would be something he could understand, she wouldn't have to explain anything!

It made her feel like rolling up her sleeves and putting the whole place to rights again. No matter if Cornelia was determined to be everywhere at once, there were a great many things left undone on this place. She would start tomorrow and do them. It was good to be strong enough for everything, even if all you made melted and changed and slipped under your hands, so that by the time you finished you almost forgot what you were working for. What was it I set out to do? she asked herself intently, but she could not remember. A fog rose over the valley, she saw it marching across the creek swallowing the trees and moving up the hill like an army of ghosts. Soon it would be at the near edge of the orchard, and then it was time to go in and light the lamps. Come in, children, don't stay out in the night air.

Lighting the lamps had been beautiful. The children huddled up to her and breathed like little calves waiting at the bars in the twilight. Their eyes followed the match and watched the flame rise and settle in a blue curve, then they moved away from her. The lamp was lit, they didn't have to be scared and hang on to mother any more. Never, never, never more. God, for all my life I thank Thee. Without Thee, my God, I could never have done it. Hail, Mary, full of grace.

I want you to pick all the fruit this year and see that nothing is wasted. There's always someone who can use it. Don't let good things rot for want of using. You waste life when you waste good food. Don't let things get lost. It's bitter to lose things. Now, don't let me get to thinking, not when I am tired and taking a little nap before supper. . . .

The pillow rose about her shoulders and pressed against her heart and the memory was being squeezed out of it: oh, push down the pillow, somebody: it would smother her if she tried to hold it. Such a fresh breeze blowing and such a green day with no threats in it. But he had not come, just the same. What does a woman do when she has put on the white veil and set out the white cake for a man and he doesn't come? She tried to remember. No, I swear he never harmed me but in that. He never harmed me but in that . . . and what if he did? There was the day, the day, but a whirl of dark smoke rose and covered it, crept up and over into the bright field where everything was planted so carefully in orderly rows. That was hell, she knew hell when she saw it. For sixty years she had prayed against remembering him and against losing her soul in the deep pit of hell, and now the two things were mingled in one and the thought of him was a smoky cloud from hell that moved and crept in her head when she had just got rid of Doctor Harry and was trying to rest a minute. Wounded vanity, Ellen, said a sharp voice in the top of her mind. Don't let your wounded vanity get the upper hand of you. Plenty of girls get jilted. You were jilted, weren't you? Then stand up to it. Her eyelids wavered and let in streamers of blue-gray light like tissue paper over her eyes. She must get up and pull the shades down or she'd never sleep. She was in bed again and the shades were not down. How could that happen? Better turn over, hide from the light, sleeping in the light gave you nightmares. "Mother, how do you feel now?" and a stinging wetness on her forehead. But I don't like having my face washed in cold water!

Hapsy? George? Lydia? Jimmy? No, Cornelia, and her features were swollen and full of little puddles. "They're coming, darling, they'll all be here soon." Go wash your face, child, you look funny.

Instead of obeying, Cornelia knelt down and put her head on the pillow. She seemed to be talking but there was no sound. "Well, are you tongue-tied? Whose birthday is it? Are you going to give a party?"

Cornelia's mouth moved urgently in strange shapes. "Don't do that, you bother me, daughter."

"Oh, no, Mother. Oh, no. . . ."

Nonsense. It was strange about children. They disputed your every word. "No what, Cornelia?"

"Here's Doctor Harry."

"I won't see that boy again. He just left five minutes ago."

"That was this morning, Mother. It's night now. Here's the nurse."

"This is Doctor Harry, Mrs. Weatherall. I never saw you look so young and happy!"

"Ah, I'll never be young again—but I'd be happy if they'd let me lie in peace and get rested."

She thought she spoke up loudly, but no one answered. A warm weight on her forehead, a warm bracelet on her wrist, and a breeze went on whispering, trying to tell her something. A shuffle of leaves in the everlasting hand of God, He blew on them and they danced and rattled. "Mother, don't mind, we're going to give you a little hypodermic." "Look here, daughter, how do ants get in this bed? I saw sugar ants yesterday." Did you send for Hapsy too?

It was Hapsy she really wanted. She had to go a long way back through a great many rooms to find Hapsy standing with a baby on her arm. She seemed to herself to be Hapsy also, and the baby on Hapsy's arm was Hapsy and himself and herself, all at once, and there was no surprise in the meeting. Then Hapsy melted from within and turned flimsy as gray gauze and the baby was a gauzy shadow, and Hapsy came up close and said, "I thought you'd never come," and looked at her very searchingly and said, "You haven't changed a bit!" They leaned forward to kiss, when Cornelia began whispering from a long way off, "Oh, is there anything you want to tell me? Is there anything I can do for you?"

Yes, she had changed her mind after sixty years and she would like to see George. I want you to find George. Find him and be sure to tell him I forgot him. I want him to know I had my husband just the same and my children and my house like any other woman. A good house too and a good husband that I loved and fine children out of him. Better than I hoped for even. Tell him I was given back everything he took away and more. Oh, no, oh, God, no, there was something else besides the house and the man and the children. Oh, surely they were not all? What was it? Something not given back. . . . Her breath crowded down under her ribs and grew into a monstrous frightening shape with cutting edges; it bored up into her head, and the agony was unbelievable: Yes, John, get the Doctor now, no more talk, my time has come.

When this one was born it should be the last. The last. It should have been born first, for it was the one she had truly wanted. Everything came in good time. Nothing left out, left over. She was strong, in three days she would be as well as ever. Better. A woman needed milk in her to have her full health.

"Mother, do you hear me?"

"I've been telling you—"

"Mother, Father Connolly's here."

"I went to Holy Communion only last week. Tell him I'm not so sinful as all that."

"Father just wants to speak to you."

He could speak as much as he pleased. It was like him to drop in and inquire about her soul as if it were a teething baby, and then stay on for a cup of tea and a round of cards and gossip. He always had a funny story of some sort, usually about an Irishman who made his little mistakes and confessed them, and the point lay in some absurd thing he would blurt out in the confessional showing his struggles between native piety and original sin. Granny felt easy about her soul. Cornelia, where are your manners? Give Father Connolly a chair. She had her secret comfortable understanding with a few favorite saints who cleared a straight road to God for her. All as surely signed and sealed as the papers for the new Forty Acres. Forever . . . heirs and assigns forever. Since the day the wedding cake was not cut, but thrown out and wasted. The whole bottom dropped out of the world, and there she was blind and sweating with nothing under her feet and the walls falling away. His hand had caught her under the breast, she had not fallen, there was the freshly polished floor with the green rug on it, just as before. He had cursed like a sailor's parrot and said, "I'll kill him for you." Don't lay a hand on him, for my sake leave something to God. "Now, Ellen, you must believe what I tell you. . . . "

So there was nothing, nothing to worry about any more, except sometimes in the night one of the children screamed in a nightmare, and they both hustled out shaking and hunting for the matches and calling, "There, wait a minute, here we are!" John, get the doctor now, Hapsy's time has come. But there was Hapsy standing by the bed in a white cap. "Cornelia, tell Hapsy to take off her cap. I can't see her plain."

Her eyes opened very wide and the room stood out like a picture she had seen somewhere. Dark colors with the shadows rising toward the ceiling in long angles. The tall black dresser gleamed with nothing on it but John's picture, enlarged from a little one, with John's eyes very black when they should have been blue. You never saw him, so how do you know how he looked? But the man insisted the copy was perfect, it was very rich and handsome. For a picture, yes, but it's not my husband. The table by the bed had a linen cover and a candle and a crucifix. The light was blue from Cornelia's silk lampshades. No sort of light at all, just frippery. You had to live forty years with kerosene lamps to appreciate honest electricity. She felt very strong and she saw Doctor Harry with a rosy nimbus around him.

"You look like a saint, Doctor Harry, and I vow that's as near as you'll ever come to it."

"She's saying something."

"I heard you, Cornelia. What's all this carrying-on?"

"Father Connolly's saying—"

Cornelia's voice staggered and bumped like a cart in a bad road. It rounded corners and turned back again and arrived nowhere. Granny stepped up in the cart very lightly and reached for the reins, but a man sat beside her and she knew him by his hands, driving the cart. She did not look in his face, for she knew without seeing, but looked instead down the road where the trees leaned over and bowed to each other and a thousand birds were singing a Mass. She felt like singing too, but she put her hand in the bosom of her dress and pulled out a rosary, and Father Connolly murmured Latin in a very solemn voice and tickled her feet. My God, will you stop that nonsense? I'm a married woman. What if he did run away and leave me to face the priest by myself? I found another a whole world better. I wouldn't have exchanged my husband for anybody except St. Michael himself, and you may tell him that for me with a thank you in the bargain.

Light flashed on her closed eyelids, and a deep roaring shook her. Cornelia, is that lightning? I hear thunder. There's going to be a storm. Close all the windows. Call the children in. . . . "Mother, here we are, all of us." "Is that you, Hapsy?" "Oh, no, I'm Lydia. We drove as fast as we could." Their faces drifted above her, drifted away. The rosary fell out of her hands and Lydia put it back. Jimmy tried to help, their hands fumbled together, and Granny closed two fingers around Jimmy's thumb. Beads wouldn't do; it must be something alive. She was so amazed her thoughts ran round and round. So, my dear Lord, this is my death and I wasn't even thinking about it. My children have come to see me die. But I can't, it's not time. Oh, I always hated surprises. I wanted to give Cornelia the amethyst set—Cornelia, you're to have the amethyst set, but Hapsy's to wear it when she wants, and, Doctor Harry, do shut up. Nobody sent for you. Oh, my dear Lord, do wait a minute. I meant to do something about the Forty Acres, Jimmy doesn't need it and Lydia will later on, with that worthless husband of hers. I meant to finish the altar cloth and send six bottles of wine to Sister Borgia for her dyspepsia. I want to send six bottles of wine to Sister Borgia, Father Connolly, now don't let me forget.

Cornelia's voice made short turns and tilted over and crashed. "Oh, Mother, oh, Mother, oh, Mother. . . . "

"I'm not going, Cornelia. I'm taken by surprise. I can't go."

You'll see Hapsy again. What about her? "I thought you'd never come." Granny made a long journey outward, looking for Hapsy. What if I don't find her? What then? Her heart sank down and down, there was no bottom to death, she couldn't come to the end of it. The blue light from Cornelia's lampshade drew into a tiny point in the center of her brain, it flickered and winked like an eye, quietly it fluttered and dwindled. Granny lay curled down within herself, amazed and watchful, staring at the point of light that was herself; her body was now only a deeper mass of shadow in an endless darkness and this darkness would curl around the light and swallow it up. God, give a sign!

For the second time there was no sign. Again no bridegroom and the priest in the house. She could not remember any other sorrow because this grief wiped them all away. Oh, no, there's nothing more cruel than this—I'll never forgive it. She stretched herself with a deep breath and blew out the light.

(1930)

ERNEST HEMINGWAY
[1898–1961]

Soldier's Home

Krebs went to the war from a Methodist college in Kansas. There is a picture which shows him among his fraternity brothers, all of them wearing exactly the same height and style collar. He enlisted in the Marines in 1917 and did not return to the United States until the second division returned from the Rhine in the summer of 1919.

There is a picture which shows him on the Rhine with two German girls and another corporal. Krebs and the corporal look too big for their uniforms. The German girls are not beautiful. The Rhine does not show in the picture.

By the time Krebs returned to his home town in Oklahoma the greeting of heroes was over. He came back much too late. The men from the town who had been drafted had all been welcomed elaborately on their return. There had been a great deal of hysteria. Now the reaction had set in. People seemed to think it was rather ridiculous for Krebs to be getting back so late, years after the war was over.

At first Krebs, who had been at Belleau Wood, Soissons, the Champagne, St. Mihiel and in the Argonne, did not want to talk about the war at all. Later he felt the need to talk but no one wanted to hear about it. His town had heard too many atrocity stories to be thrilled by actualities. Krebs found that to be listened to at all he had to lie, and after he had done this twice he, too, had a reaction against the war and against talking about it. A distaste for everything that had happened to him in the war set in because of the lies he had told. All of the times that had been able to make him feel cool and clean inside himself when he thought of them; the times so long back when he had done the one thing, the only thing for a man to do, easily and naturally, when he might have done something else, now lost their cool, valuable quality and then were lost themselves.

His lies were quite unimportant lies and consisted in attributing to himself things other men had seen, done or heard of, and stating as facts certain apocryphal incidents familiar to all soldiers. Even his lies were not sensational at the pool room. His acquaintances, who had heard detailed accounts of German women found chained to machine guns in the Argonne forest and who could not comprehend, or were barred by their patriotism from interest in, any German machine gunners who were not chained, were not thrilled by his stories.

Krebs acquired the nausea in regard to experience that is the result of untruth or exaggeration, and when he occasionally met another man who had really been a soldier and they talked a few minutes in the dressing room at a dance he fell into the easy pose of the old soldier among other soldiers: that he had been badly, sickeningly frightened all the time. In this way he lost everything.

During this time, it was late summer, he was sleeping late in bed, getting up to walk down town to the library to get a book, eating lunch at home, reading on the front porch until he became bored and then walking down through the town to spend the hottest hours of the day in the cool dark of the pool room. He loved to play pool.

In the evening he practised on his clarinet, strolled down town, read and went to bed. He was still a hero to his two young sisters. His mother would have given him breakfast in bed if he had wanted it. She often came in when he was in bed and asked him to tell her about the war, but her attention always wandered. His father was non-committal.

Before Krebs went away to the war he had never been allowed to drive the family motor car. His father was in the real estate business and always wanted the car to be at his command when he required it to take clients out into the country to show them a piece of farm property. The car always stood outside the First National Bank building where his father had an office on the second floor. Now, after the war, it was still the same car.

Nothing was changed in the town except that the young girls had grown up. But they lived in such a complicated world of already defined alliances and shifting feuds that Krebs did not feel the energy or the courage to break into it. He liked to look at them, though. There were so many good-looking young girls. Most of them had their hair cut short. When he went away only little girls wore their hair like that or girls that were fast. They all wore sweaters and shirt waists with round Dutch collars. It was a pattern. He liked to look at them from the front porch as they walked on the other side of the street. He liked to watch them walking under the shade of the trees. He liked the round Dutch collars above their sweaters. He liked their silk stockings and flat shoes. He liked their bobbed hair and the way they walked.

When he was in town their appeal to him was not very strong. He did not like them when he saw them in the Greek's ice cream parlor. He did not want them themselves really. They were too complicated. There was something else. Vaguely he wanted a girl but he did not want to have to work to get her. He would have liked to have a girl but he did not want to have to spend a long time getting her. He did not want to get into the intrigue and the politics. He did not want to have to do any courting. He did not want to tell any more lies. It wasn't worth it.

He did not want any consequences. He did not want any consequences ever again. He wanted to live along without consequences. Besides he did not really need a girl. The army had taught him that. It was all right to pose as though you had to have a girl. Nearly everybody did that. But it wasn't true. You did not need a girl. That was the funny thing. First a fellow boasted how girls mean nothing to him, that he never thought of them, that they could not touch him. Then a fellow boasted that he could not get along without girls, that he had to have them all the time, that he could not go to sleep without them.

That was all a lie. It was all a lie both ways. You did not need a girl unless you thought about them. He learned that in the army. Then sooner or later you always got one. When you were really ripe for a girl you always got one. You did not have to think about it. Sooner or later it would come. He had learned that in the army.

Now he would have liked a girl if she had come to him and not wanted to talk. But here at home it was all too complicated. He knew he could never get through it all again. It was not worth the trouble. That was the thing about French girls and German girls. There was not all this talking. You couldn't talk much and you did not need to talk. It was simple and you were friends. He thought about France and then he began to think about Germany. On the whole he had liked Germany better. He did not want to leave Germany. He did not want to come home. Still, he had come home. He sat on the front porch.

He liked the girls that were walking along the other side of the street. He liked the look of them much better than the French girls or the German girls. But the world they were in was not the world he was in. He would like to have one of them. But it was not worth it. They were such a nice pattern. He liked the pattern. It was exciting. But he would not go through all the talking. He did not want one badly enough. He liked to look at them all, though. It was not worth it. Not now when things were getting good again.

He sat there on the porch reading a book on the war. It was a history and he was reading about all the engagements he had been in. It was the most interesting reading he had ever done. He wished there were more maps. He looked forward with a good feeling to reading all the really good histories when they would come out with good detail maps. Now he was really learning about the war. He had been a good soldier. That made a difference.

One morning after he had been home about a month his mother came into his bedroom and sat on the bed. She smoothed her apron.

"I had a talk with your father last night, Harold," she said, "and he is willing for you to take the car out in the evenings."

"Yeah?" said Krebs, who was not fully awake. "Take the car out? Yeah?"

"Yes. Your father has felt for some time that you should be able to take the car out in the evenings whenever you wished but we only talked it over last night."

"I'll bet you made him," Krebs said.

"No. It was your father's suggestion that we talk the matter over."

"Yeah. I'll bet you made him," Krebs sat up in bed.

"Will you come down to breakfast, Harold?" his mother said.

"As soon as I get my clothes on," Krebs said.

His mother went out of the room and he could hear her frying something downstairs while he washed, shaved and dressed to go down into the dining-room for breakfast. While he was eating breakfast his sister brought in the mail.

"Well, Hare," she said. "You old sleepy-head. What do you ever get up for?"

Krebs looked at her. He liked her. She was his best sister.

"Have you got the paper?" he asked.

She handed him *The Kansas City Star* and he shucked off its brown wrapper and opened it to the sporting page. He folded *The Star* open and propped it against the water pitcher with his cereal dish to steady it, so he could read while he ate.

"Harold," his mother stood in the kitchen doorway, "Harold, please don't muss up the paper. Your father can't read his *Star* if it's been mussed."

"I won't muss it," Krebs said.

His sister sat down at the table and watched him while he read.

"We're playing indoor° over at school this afternoon," she said. "I'm going to pitch."

"Good," said Krebs. "How's the old wing?"

"I can pitch better than lots of the boys. I tell them all you taught me. The other girls aren't much good."

"Yeah?" said Krebs.

"I tell them all you're my beau. Aren't you my beau, Hare?"

"You bet."

"Couldn't your brother really be your beau just because he's your brother?"

"I don't know."

"Sure you know. Couldn't you be my beau, Hare, if I was old enough and if you wanted to?"

"Sure. You're my girl now."

"Am I really your girl?"

"Sure."

"Do you love me?"

"Uh, huh."

"Will you love me always?"

"Sure."

"Will you come over and watch me play indoor?"

"Maybe."

"Aw, Hare, you don't love me. If you loved me, you'd want to come over and watch me play indoor."

Krebs's mother came into the dining-room from the kitchen. She carried a plate with two fried eggs and some crisp bacon on it and a plate of buckwheat cakes.

"You run along, Helen," she said. "I want to talk to Harold."

She put eggs and bacon down in front of him and brought in a jug of maple syrup for the buckwheat cakes. Then she sat down across the table from Krebs.

"I wish you'd put down the paper a minute, Harold," she said.

indoor   *that is, a softball game*

Krebs took down the paper and folded it.

"Have you decided what you are going to do yet, Harold?" his mother said, taking off her glasses.

"No," said Krebs.

"Don't you think it's about time?" His mother did not say this in a mean way. She seemed worried.

"I hadn't thought about it," Krebs said.

"God has some work for every one to do," his mother said. "There can be no idle hands in His Kingdom."

"I'm not in His Kingdom," Krebs said.

"We are all of us in His Kingdom."

Krebs felt embarrassed and resentful as always.

"I've worried about you so much, Harold," his mother went on. "I know the temptations you must have been exposed to. I know how weak men are. I know what your own dear grandfather, my own father, told us about the Civil War and I have prayed for you. I pray for you all day long, Harold."

Krebs looked at the bacon fat hardening on his plate.

"Your father is worried, too," his mother went on. "He thinks you have lost your ambition, that you haven't got a definite aim in life. Charley Simmons, who is just your age, has a good job and is going to be married. The boys are all settling down; they're all determined to get somewhere; you can see that boys like Charley Simmons are on their way to being really a credit to the community."

Krebs said nothing.

"Don't look that way, Harold," his mother said. "You know we love you and I want to tell you for your own good how matters stand. Your father does not want to hamper your freedom. He thinks you should be allowed to drive the car. If you want to take some of the nice girls out riding with you, we are only too pleased. We want you to enjoy yourself. But you are going to have to settle down to work, Harold. Your father doesn't care what you start in at. All work is honorable as he says. But you've got to make a start at something. He asked me to speak to you this morning and then you can stop in and see him at his office."

"Is that all?" Krebs said.

"Yes. Don't you love your mother, dear boy?"

"No," Krebs said.

His mother looked at him across the table. Her eyes were shiny. She started crying.

"I don't love anybody," Krebs said.

It wasn't any good. He couldn't tell her, he couldn't make her see it. It was silly to have said it. He had only hurt her. He went over and took hold of her arm. She was crying with her head in her hands.

"I didn't mean it," he said. "I was just angry at something. I didn't mean I didn't love you."

His mother went on crying. Krebs put his arm on her shoulder.

"Can't you believe me, mother?"

His mother shook her head.

"Please, please, mother. Please believe me."

"All right," his mother said chokily. She looked up at him. "I believe you, Harold."

Krebs kissed her hair. She put her face up to him.

"I'm your mother," she said. "I held you next to my heart when you were a tiny baby."

Krebs felt sick and vaguely nauseated.

"I know, Mummy," he said. "I'll try and be a good boy for you."

"Would you kneel and pray with me, Harold?" his mother asked.

They knelt down beside the dining-room table and Krebs's mother prayed.

"Now, you pray, Harold," she said.

"I can't," Krebs said.

"Try, Harold."

"I can't."

"Do you want me to pray for you?"

"Yes."

So his mother prayed for him and then they stood up and Krebs kissed his mother and went out of the house. He had tried so to keep his life from being complicated. Still, none of it had touched him. He had felt sorry for his mother and she had made him lie. He would go to Kansas City and get a job and she would feel all right about it. There would be one more scene maybe before he got away. He would not go down to his father's office. He would miss that one. He wanted his life to go smoothly. It had just gotten going that way. Well, that was all over now, anyway. He would go over to the schoolyard and watch Helen play indoor baseball.

(1925)

JORGE LUIS BORGES
· [1899–1986]

The Garden of Forking Paths

TRANSLATED BY DONALD YATES

On page 22 of Liddell Hart's *History of World War I* you will read that an attack against the Serre-Montauban line by thirteen British divisions (supported by 1,400 artillery pieces), planned for the 24th of July, 1916, had to be postponed until the morning of the 29th. The torrential rains, Captain Liddell Hart comments, caused this delay, an insignificant one, to be sure.

The following statement, dictated, reread and signed by Dr. Yu Tsun, former professor of English at the *Hochschule* at Tsingtao, throws an unsuspected light over the whole affair. The first two pages of the document are missing.

". . . and I hung up the receiver. Immediately afterwards, I recognized the voice that had answered in German. It was that of Captain Richard Madden. Madden's presence in Viktor Runeberg's apartment meant the end of our anxieties and—but this seemed, *or should have seemed,* very secondary to me—also the end of our lives. It meant that Runeberg had been arrested or murdered. Before the sun set on that day, I would encounter the same fate. Madden was implacable. Or rather, he was obliged to be so. An

Irishman at the service of England, a man accused of laxity and perhaps of treason, how could he fail to seize and be thankful for such a miraculous opportunity: the discovery, capture, maybe even the death of two agents of the German Reich? I went up to my room; absurdly I locked the door and threw myself on my back on the narrow iron cot. Through the window I saw the familiar roofs and the cloud-shaded six o'clock sun. It seemed incredible to me that that day without premonitions or symbols should be the one of my inexorable death. In spite of my dead father, in spite of having been a child in a symmetrical garden of Hai Feng, was I—now—going to die? Then I reflected that everything happens to a man precisely, precisely *now.* Centuries of centuries and only in the present do things happen; countless men in the air, on the face of the earth and the sea, and all that really is happening is happening to me . . . The almost intolerable recollection of Madden's horselike face banished these wanderings. In the midst of my hatred and terror (it means nothing to me now to speak of terror, now that I have mocked Richard Madden, now that my throat yearns for the noose) it occurred to me that the tumultuous and doubtless happy warrior did not suspect that I possessed the Secret. The name of the exact location of the new British artillery park on the River Ancre. A bird streaked across the gray sky and blindly I translated it into an airplane and that airplane into many (against the French sky) annihilating the artillery station with vertical bombs. If only my mouth, before a bullet shattered it, could cry out that secret name so it could be heard in Germany . . . My human voice was very weak. How might I make it carry to the ear of the Chief? To the ear of that sick and hateful man who knew nothing of Runeberg and me save that we were in Staffordshire and who was waiting in vain for our report in his arid office in Berlin, endlessly examining newspapers . . . I said out loud: *I must flee.* I sat up noiselessly, in a useless perfection of silence, as if Madden were already lying in wait for me. Something—perhaps the mere vain ostentation of proving my resources were nil—made me look through my pockets. I found what I knew I would find. The American watch, the nickel chain and the square coin, the key ring with the incriminating useless keys to Runeberg's apartment, the notebook, a letter which I resolved to destroy immediately (and which I did not destroy), a crown, two shillings and a few pence, the red and blue pencil, the handkerchief, the revolver with one bullet. Absurdly, I took it in my hand and weighed it in order to inspire courage within myself. Vaguely I thought that a pistol report can be heard at a great distance. In ten minutes my plan was perfected. The telephone book listed the name of the only person capable of transmitting the message; he lived in a suburb of Fenton, less than a half hour's train ride away.

I am a cowardly man. I say it now, now that I have carried to its end a plan whose perilous nature no one can deny. I know its execution was terrible. I didn't do it for Germany, no. I care nothing for a barbarous country which imposed upon me the abjection of being a spy. Besides, I know of a man from England—a modest man—who for me is no less great than Goethe. I talked with him for scarcely an hour, but during that hour he was Goethe . . . I did it because I sensed that the Chief somehow feared people of my race—for the innumerable ancestors who merge within me. I wanted to prove to him that a yellow man could save his armies. Besides, I had to flee from Captain Madden. His hands and his voice could call at my door at any moment. I dressed silently, bade farewell to myself in the mirror, went downstairs, scrutinized the peaceful street and went out. The station was not far from my home, but I judged it wise to take a cab. I argued that in this way I ran less risk of being recognized; the fact is that in the deserted street I felt myself visible and vulnerable, infinitely so. I remember that I told the cab driver to stop a short distance before the main entrance. I got out with voluntary, almost painful slowness; I was going to the village of Ashgrove but I bought a ticket for a more distant station. The train left within a very few minutes, at eight-fifty. I hurried; the next one would leave at nine-thirty. There was hardly a soul on the platform. I went through the coaches; I remember a few farmers, a woman dressed in mourning, a young boy who was reading with fervor the *Annals* of Tacitus, a wounded and happy soldier. The coaches jerked forward at last. A man whom I recognized ran in vain to the end of the platform. It was Captain Richard Madden. Shattered, trembling, I shrank into the far corner of the seat, away from the dreaded window.

From this broken state I passed into an almost abject felicity. I told myself that the duel had already begun and that I had won the first encounter by frustrating, even if for forty minutes, even if by a stroke of fate, the attack of my adversary. I argued that this slightest of victories foreshadowed a total victory. I argued (no less fallaciously) that my cowardly felicity proved that I was a man capable of carrying out the adventure successfully. From this weakness I took strength that did not abandon me. I foresee that man will resign himself each day to more atrocious undertakings; soon there will be no one but warriors and brigands; I give them this counsel: *The author of an atrocious undertaking ought to imagine that he has already accomplished it, ought to impose upon himself a future as irrevocable as the past.* Thus I proceeded as my eyes of a man already dead registered the elapsing of that day, which was perhaps the last, and the diffusion of the night. The train ran gently along, amid ash trees. It stopped, almost in the middle of the fields. No one announced the name of the station. "Ashgrove?" I asked a few lads on the platform. "Ashgrove," they replied. I got off.

A lamp enlightened the platform but the faces of the boys were in shadow. One questioned me, "Are you going to Dr. Stephen Albert's house?" Without waiting for my answer, another said, "The house is a long way from here, but you won't get lost if you take this road to the left and at every crossroads turn again to your left." I tossed them a coin (my last), descended a few stone steps and started down the solitary road. It went downhill, slowly. It was of elemental earth; overhead the branches were tangled; the low, full moon seemed to accompany me.

For an instant, I thought that Richard Madden in some way had penetrated my desperate plan. Very quickly, I understood that that was impossible. The instructions to turn always to the left reminded me that such was the common procedure for discovering the central point of certain labyrinths. I have some understanding of labyrinths: not for nothing am I the great grandson of that Ts'ui Pên who was governor of Yunnan and who renounced worldly power in order to write a novel that might be even more populous than the *Hung Lu Meng* and to construct a labyrinth in which all men would become lost. Thirteen years he dedicated to these heterogeneous tasks, but the hand of a stranger murdered him—and his novel was incoherent and no one found the labyrinth. Beneath English trees I meditated on that lost maze; I imagined it inviolate and perfect at the secret crest of a mountain; I imagined it erased by rice fields or beneath the water; I imagined it infinite, no longer composed of octagonal kiosks and returning paths, but of rivers and provinces and kingdoms . . . I thought of a labyrinth of labyrinths, of one sinuous spreading labyrinth that would encompass the past and the future and in some way involve the stars. Absorbed in these illusory images, I forgot my destiny of one pursued. I felt myself to be, for an unknown period of time, an abstract perceiver of the world. The vague, living countryside, the moon, the remains of the day worked on me, as well as the slope of the road which eliminated any possibility of weariness. The afternoon was intimate, infinite. The road descended and forked among the now confused meadows. A high-pitched, almost syllabic music approached and receded in the shifting of the wind, dimmed by leaves and distance. I thought that a man can be an enemy of other men, of the moments of other men, but not of a country: not of fireflies, woods, gardens, streams of water, sunsets. Thus I arrived before a tall, rusty gate. Between the iron bars I made out a poplar grove and a pavilion. I understood suddenly two things, the first trivial, the second almost unbelievable: the music came from the pavilion, and the music was Chinese. For precisely that reason I had openly accepted it without paying it any heed. I do not remember whether there was a bell or whether I knocked with my hand. The sparkling of the music continued.

From the rear of the house within a lantern approached: a lantern that the trees sometimes striped and sometimes eclipsed, a paper lantern that had the form of a drum and the color of the moon. A tall man bore it. I didn't see his face for the light blinded me. He opened the door and said slowly, in my own language: "I see that the pious Hsi P'êng persists in correcting my solitude. You no doubt wish to see the garden?"

I recognized the name of one of our consuls and I replied, disconcerted, "The garden?"

"The garden of forking paths."

Something stirred in my memory and I uttered with incomprehensible certainty, "The garden of my ancestor Ts'ui Pên."

"Your ancestor? Your illustrious ancestor? Come in."

The damp path zigzagged like those of my childhood. We came to a library of Eastern and Western books. I recognized bound in yellow silk several volumes of the Lost Encyclopedia, edited by the Third Emperor of the Luminous Dynasty but never printed. The record on the phonograph revolved next to a bronze phoenix. I also recall a *famille rose* vase and another, many centuries older, of that shade of blue which our craftsmen copied from the potters of Persia . . .

Stephen Albert observed me with a smile. He was, as I have said, very tall, sharp featured, with gray eyes and a gray beard. He told me that he had been a missionary in Tientsin "before aspiring to become a Sinologist."

We sat down—I on a long, low divan, he with his back to the window and a tall circular clock. I calculated that my pursuer, Richard Madden, could not arrive for at least an hour. My irrevocable determination could wait.

"An astounding fate, that of Ts'ui Pên," Stephen Albert said. "Governor of his native province, learned in astronomy, in astrology and in the tireless interpretation of the canonical books, chess player, famous poet and calligrapher—he abandoned all this in order to compose a book and a maze. He renounced the pleasures of both tyranny and justice, of his populous couch, of his banquets and even of erudition—all to close himself up for thirteen years in the Pavilion of the Limpid Solitude. When he died, his heirs found nothing save chaotic manuscripts. His family, as you may be aware, wished to condemn them to the fire; but his executor—a Taoist or Buddhist monk—insisted on their publication."

"We descendants of Ts'ui Pên," I replied, "continue to curse that monk. Their publication was senseless. The book is an indeterminate heap of contradictory drafts. I examined it once: in the third chapter the hero dies, in the fourth he is alive. As for the other undertaking of Ts'ui Pên, his labyrinth . . . "

"Here is Ts'ui Pên's labyrinth," he said, indicating a tall lacquered desk.

"An ivory labyrinth!" I exclaimed. "A minimum labyrinth."

"A labyrinth of symbols," he corrected. "An invisible labyrinth of time. To me, a barbarous Englishman, has been entrusted the revelation of this diaphanous mystery. After more than a hundred years, the details are irretrievable; but it is not hard to conjecture what happened. Ts'ui Pên must have said once: *I am withdrawing to write a book.* And another time: *I am withdrawing to construct a labyrinth.* Every one imagined two works; to no one did it occur that the book and the maze were one and the same thing. The Pavilion of the Limpid Solitude stood in the center of a garden that was perhaps intricate; that circumstance could have suggested to the heirs a physical labyrinth. Ts'ui Pên died; no one in the vast territories that were his came upon the labyrinth; the confusion of the novel suggested to me that *it* was the maze. Two circumstances gave me the correct solution of the problem. One: the curious legend that Ts'ui Pên had planned to create a labyrinth which would be strictly infinite. The other: a fragment of a letter I discovered."

Albert rose. He turned his back on me for a moment; he opened a drawer of the black and gold desk. He faced me and in his hands he held a sheet of paper that had once been crimson, but was now pink and tenuous and cross-sectioned. The fame of Ts'ui Pên as a calligrapher had been justly won. I read, uncomprehendingly and with fervor, these words written with a minute brush by a man of my blood: *I leave to the various futures (not to all) my garden of forking paths.* Wordlessly, I returned the sheet. Albert continued:

"Before unearthing this letter, I had questioned myself about the ways in which a book can be infinite. I could think of nothing other than a cyclic volume, a circular one. A book whose last page was identical with the first, a book which had the possibility of continuing indefinitely. I remembered too that night which is at the middle of the Thousand and One Nights when Scheherazade (through a magical oversight of the copyist) begins to relate word for word the story of the Thousand and One Nights, establishing the risk of coming once again to the night when she must repeat it, and thus on to infinity. I imagined as well a Platonic, hereditary work, transmitted from father to son, in which each new individual adds a chapter or corrects with pious care the pages of his elders. These conjectures diverted me; but none seemed to correspond, not even remotely, to the contradictory chapters of Ts'ui Pên. In the midst of this perplexity, I received from Oxford the manuscript you have examined. I lingered, naturally, on the sentence: *I leave to the various futures (not to all) my garden of forking paths.* Almost instantly, I understood: 'the garden of forking paths' was the chaotic novel; the phrase 'the various futures (not to all)' suggested to me the forking in time, not in space. A broad rereading of the work confirmed the theory. In all fictional works, each time a man is confronted with several alternatives, he chooses one and eliminates the others; in the fiction of Ts'ui Pên, he chooses—simultaneously—all of them. *He creates,* in this way, diverse futures, diverse times which themselves also proliferate and fork. Here, then, is the explanation of the novel's contradictions. Fang, let us say, has a secret; a stranger calls at his door; Fang resolves to kill him. Naturally, there are several possible outcomes: Fang can kill the intruder, the intruder can kill Fang, they both can escape, they both can die, and so forth. In the work of Ts'ui Pên, all possible outcomes occur; each one is the point of departure for other forkings. Sometimes, the paths of this labyrinth converge: for example, you arrive at this house, but in one of the possible pasts you are my enemy, in another, my friend. If you will resign yourself to my incurable pronunciation, we shall read a few pages."

His face, within the vivid circle of the lamplight, was unquestionably that of an old man, but with something unalterable about it, even immortal. He read with slow precision two versions of the same epic chapter. In the first, an army marches to a battle across a lonely mountain; the horror of the rocks and shadows makes the men undervalue their lives and they gain an easy victory. In the second, the same army traverses a palace where a great festival is taking place; the resplendent battle seems to them a continuation of the celebration and they win the victory. I listened with proper veneration to these ancient narratives, perhaps less admirable in themselves than the fact that they had been created by my blood and were being restored to me by a man of a remote empire, in the course of a desperate adventure, on a Western isle. I remember the last words, repeated in each version like a secret commandment: *Thus fought the heroes, tranquil their admirable hearts, violent their swords, resigned to kill and to die.*

From that moment on, I felt about me and within my dark body an invisible, intangible swarming. Not the swarming of the divergent, parallel and finally coalescent armies, but a more inaccessible, more intimate agitation that they in some manner prefigured. Stephen Albert continued:

"I don't believe that your illustrious ancestor played idly with these variations. I don't consider it credible that he would sacrifice thirteen years to the infinite execution of a rhetorical experiment. In your country, the novel is a subsidiary form of literature; in Ts'ui Pên's time it was a despicable form. Ts'ui Pên was a brilliant novelist, but he was also a man of letters who doubtless did not consider himself a mere novelist. The testimony of his contemporaries proclaims—and his life fully confirms—his metaphysical and mystical interests. Philosophic controversy usurps a good part of the novel. I know that of all problems, none disturbed him so greatly nor worked upon him so much as the abysmal problem of time. Now then, the latter is the only problem that does not figure in the pages of the *Garden*. He does not even use the word that signifies *time*. How do you explain this voluntary omission?"

I proposed several solutions—all unsatisfactory. We discussed them. Finally, Stephen Albert said to me:

"In a riddle whose answer is chess, what is the only prohibited word?"

I thought a moment and replied, "The word *chess*."

"Precisely," said Albert. "*The Garden of Forking Paths* is an enormous riddle, or parable, whose theme is time; this recondite cause prohibits its mention. To omit a word always, to resort to inept metaphors and obvious periphrases, is perhaps the most emphatic way of stressing it. That is the tortuous method preferred, in each of the meanderings of his indefatigable novel, by the oblique Ts'ui Pên. I have compared hundreds of manuscripts, I have corrected the errors that the negligence of the copyists has introduced. I have guessed the plan of this chaos, I have re-established—I believe I have re-established—the primordial organization, I have translated the entire work: it is clear to me that not once does he employ the word 'time.' The explanation is obvious: *The Garden of Forking Paths* is an incomplete, but not false, image of the universe as Ts'ui Pên conceived it. In contrast to Newton and Schopenhauer, your ancestor did not believe in a uniform, absolute time. He believed in an infinite series of times, in a growing, dizzying net of divergent, convergent and parallel times. This network of times which approached one another, forked, broke off, or were unaware of one another for centuries, embraces *all* possibilities of time. We do not exist in the majority of these times; in some you exist, and not I; in others I, and not you; in others, both of us. In the present one, which a favorable fate has granted me, you have arrived at my house; in another, while crossing the garden, you found me dead; in still another, I utter these same words, but I am a mistake, a ghost."

"In every one," I pronounced, not without a tremble to my voice, "I am grateful to you and revere you for your re-creation of the garden of Ts'ui Pên."

"Not in all," he murmured with a smile. "Time forks perpetually toward innumerable futures. In one of them I am your enemy."

Once again I felt the swarming sensation of which I have spoken. It seemed to me that the humid garden that surrounded the house was infinitely saturated with invisible persons. Those persons were Albert and I, secret, busy and multiform in other dimensions of time. I raised my eyes and the tenuous nightmare dissolved. In the yellow and black garden there was only one man; but this man was as strong as a statue . . . this man was approaching along the path and he was Captain Richard Madden.

"The future already exists," I replied, "but I am your friend. Could I see the letter again?"

Albert rose. Standing tall, he opened the drawer of the tall desk; for the moment his back was to me. I had readied the revolver. I fired with extreme caution. Albert fell uncomplainingly, immediately. I swear his death was instantaneous—a lightning stroke.

The rest is unreal, insignificant. Madden broke in, arrested me. I have been condemned to the gallows. I have won out abominably; I have communicated to Berlin the secret name of the city they must attack. They bombed it yesterday; I read it in the same papers that offered to England the mystery of the learned Sinologist Stephen Albert who was murdered by a stranger, one Yu Tsun. The Chief had deciphered this mystery. He knew my problem was to indicate (through the uproar of the war) the city called Albert, and that I had found no other means to do so than to kill a man of that name. He does not know (no one can know) my innumerable contrition and weariness."

(1941)

ISAAC BASHEVIS SINGER
[1904–1991]

Gimpel the Fool

TRANSLATED BY SAUL BELLOW

I

I am Gimpel the fool. I don't think myself a fool. On the contrary. But that's what folks call me. They gave me the name while I was still in school. I had seven names in all: imbecile, donkey, flax-head, dope, glump, ninny, and fool. The last name stuck. What did my foolishness consist of? I was easy to take in. They said, "Gimpel, you know the rabbi's wife has been brought to childbed?" So I skipped school. Well, it turned out to be a lie. How was I supposed to know? She hadn't had a big belly. But I never looked at her belly. Was that really so foolish? The gang laughed and hee-hawed, stomped and danced and chanted a good-night prayer. And instead of the raisins they give when a woman's lying in, they stuffed my hand full of goat turds. I was no weakling. If I slapped someone he'd see all the way to Cracow. But I'm really not a slugger by nature. I think to myself: Let it pass. So they take advantage of me.

I was coming home from school and heard a dog barking. I'm not afraid of dogs, but of course I never want to start up with them. One of them may be mad, and if he bites there's not a Tartar in the world who can help you. So I made tracks. Then I looked around and saw the whole market place wild with laughter. It was no dog at all but Wolf-Leib the Thief. How was I supposed to know it was he? It sounded like a howling bitch.

When the pranksters and leg-pullers found that I was easy to fool, every one of them tried his luck with me. "Gimpel, the Czar is coming to Frampol; Gimpel, the moon fell down in Turbeen; Gimpel, little Hodel Furpiece found a treasure behind the bathhouse." And I like a golem° believed everyone. In the first place, everything is possible, as it is written in the Wisdom of the Fathers. I've forgotten just how. Second, I had to believe when the whole town came down on me! If I ever dared to say, "Ah, you're kidding!" there was trouble. People got angry. "What do you mean! You want to call everyone a liar?" What was I to do? I believed them, and I hope at least that did them some good.

I was an orphan. My grandfather who brought me up was already bent toward the grave. So they turned me over to a baker, and what a time they gave me there! Every woman or girl who came to bake a batch of noodles had to fool me at least once. "Gimpel, there's a fair in heaven; Gimpel, the rabbi gave birth to a calf in the seventh month; Gimpel, a cow flew over the roof and laid brass eggs." A student from the yeshiva came once to buy a roll, and he said, "You, Gimpel, while you stand here scraping with your baker's shovel the Messiah has come. The dead have arisen." "What do you mean?" I said. "I heard no one blowing the ram's horn!" He said, "Are you deaf?" And all began to cry, "We heard it, we heard!" Then in came Rietze the Candle-dipper and called out in her hoarse voice, "Gimpel, your father and mother have stood up from the grave. They're looking for you."

To tell the truth, I knew very well that nothing of the sort had happened, but all the same, as folks were talking, I threw on my wool vest and went out. Maybe something had happened. What did I stand to lose by looking? Well, what a cat music went up! And then I took a vow to believe nothing more. But that was no go either. They confused me so that I didn't know the big end from the small.

I went to the rabbi to get some advice. He said, "It is written, better to be a fool all your days than for one hour to be evil. You are not a fool. They are the fools. For he who causes his neighbor to feel shame loses Paradise himself." Nevertheless the rabbi's daughter took me in. As I left the rabbinical court she said, "Have you kissed the wall yet?" I said, "No; what for?" She answered, "It's the law; you've got to do it after every visit." Well, there didn't seem to be any harm in it. And she burst out laughing. It was a fine trick. She put one over on me, all right.

golem simpleton

I wanted to go off to another town, but then everyone got busy matchmaking, and they were after me so they nearly tore my coat tails off. They talked at me and talked until I got water on the ear. She was no chaste maiden, but they told me she was virgin pure. She had a limp, and they said it was deliberate, from coyness. She had a bastard, and they told me the child was her little brother. I cried, "You're wasting your time. I'll never marry that whore." But they said indignantly, "What a way to talk! Aren't you ashamed of yourself? We can take you to the rabbi and have you fined for giving her a bad name." I saw then that I wouldn't escape them so easily and I thought: They're set on making me their butt. But when you're married the husband's the master, and if that's all right with her it's agreeable to me too. Besides, you can't pass through life unscathed, nor expect to.

I went to her clay house, which was built on the sand, and the whole gang, hollering and chorusing, came after me. They acted like bear-baiters. When we came to the well they stopped all the same. They were afraid to start anything with Elka. Her mouth would open as if it were on a hinge, and she had a fierce tongue. I entered the house. Lines were strung from wall to wall and clothes were drying. Barefoot she stood by the tub, doing the wash. She was dressed in a worn hand-me-down gown of plush. She had her hair put up in braids and pinned across her head. It took my breath away, almost, the reek of it all.

Evidently she knew who I was. She took a look at me and said, "Look who's here! He's come, the drip. Grab a seat."

I told her all; I denied nothing. "Tell me the truth," I said, "are you really a virgin, and is that mischievous Yechiel actually your little brother? Don't be deceitful with me, for I'm an orphan."

"I'm an orphan myself," she answered, "and whoever tries to twist you up, may the end of his nose take a twist. But don't let them think they can take advantage of me. I want a dowry of fifty guilders, and let them take up a collection besides. Otherwise they can kiss my you-know-what." She was very plainspoken. I said, "It's the bride and not the groom who gives a dowry." Then she said, "Don't bargain with me. Either a flat 'yes' or a flat 'no'—Go back where you came from."

I thought: No bread will ever be baked from *this* dough. But ours is not a poor town. They consented to everything and proceeded with the wedding. It so happened that there was a dysentery epidemic at the time. The ceremony was held at the cemetery gates, near the little corpse-washing hut. The fellows got drunk. While the marriage contract was being drawn up I heard the most pious high rabbi ask, "Is the bride a widow or a divorced woman?" And the sexton's wife answered for her, "Both a widow and divorced." It was a black moment for me. But what was I to do, run away from under the marriage canopy?

There was singing and dancing. An old granny danced opposite me, hugging a braided white *chalah*. The master of revels made a "God 'a mercy" in memory of the bride's parents. The schoolboys threw burrs, as on Tishe b'Av fast day. There were a lot of gifts after the sermon: a noodle board, a kneading trough, a bucket, brooms, ladles, household articles galore. Then I took a look and saw two strapping young men carrying a crib. "What do we need this for?" I asked. So they said, "Don't rack your brains about it. It's all right, it'll come in handy." I realized I was going to be rooked. Take it another way though, what did I stand to lose? I reflected: I'll see what comes of it. A whole town can't go altogether crazy.

2

At night I came where my wife lay, but she wouldn't let me in. "Say, look here, is this what they married us for?" I said. And she said, "My monthly has come." "But yesterday they took you to the ritual bath, and that's afterward, isn't it supposed to be?" "Today isn't yesterday," said she, "and yesterday's not today. You can beat it if you don't like it." In short, I waited.

Not four months later she was in childbed. The townsfolk hid their laughter with their knuckles. But what could I do? She suffered intolerable pains and clawed at the walls. "Gimpel," she cried, "I'm going. Forgive me!" The house filled with women. They were boiling pans of water. The screams rose to the welkin.°

The thing to do was to go to the House of Prayer to repeat Psalms, and that was what I did.

The townsfolk liked that, all right. I stood in a corner saying Psalms and prayers, and they shook their heads at me. "Pray, pray!" they told me. "Prayer never made any woman pregnant." One of the congregation put a straw to my mouth and said, "Hay for the cows." There was something to that too, by God!

She gave birth to a boy. Friday at the synagogue the sexton stood up before the Ark, pounded on the reading table, and announced, "The wealthy Reb Gimpel invites the congregation to a feast in honor of the birth of a son." The whole House of Prayer rang with laughter. My face was flaming. But there was nothing I could do. After all, I *was* the one responsible for the circumcision honors and rituals.

Half the town came running. You couldn't wedge another soul in. Women brought peppered chick-peas, and there was a keg of beer from the tavern. I ate and drank as much as anyone, and they all congratulated me. Then there was a circumcision, and I named the boy after my father, may he rest in peace. When all were gone and I was left with my wife alone, she thrust her head through the bed-curtain and called me to her.

"Gimpel," said she, "why are you silent? Has your ship gone and sunk?"

"What shall I say?" I answered. "A fine thing you've done to me! If my mother had known of it she'd have died a second time."

She said, "Are you crazy, or what?"

"How can you make such a fool," I said, "of one who should be the lord and master?"

"What's the matter with you?" she said. "What have you taken it into your head to imagine?"

I saw that I must speak bluntly and openly. "Do you think this is the way to use an orphan?" I said. "You have borne a bastard."

She answered, "Drive this foolishness out of your head. The child is yours."

"How can he be mine?" I argued. "He was born seventeen weeks after the wedding."

She told me then that he was premature. I said, "Isn't he a little too premature?" She said, she had had a grandmother who carried just as short a time and she resembled this grandmother of hers as one drop of water does another. She swore to it with such oaths that you would have believed a peasant at the fair if he had used them. To tell the plain truth, I didn't believe her; but when I talked it over next day with the

---

welkin   the sky

schoolmaster he told me that the very same thing had happened to Adam and Eve. Two they went up to bed, and four they descended.

"There isn't a woman in the world who is not the granddaughter of Eve," he said.

That was how it was; they argued me dumb. But then, who really knows how such things are?

I began to forget my sorrow. I loved the child madly, and he loved me too. As soon as he saw me he'd wave his little hands and want me to pick him up, and when he was colicky I was the only one who could pacify him. I bought him a little bone teething ring and a little gilded cap. He was forever catching the evil eye from someone, and then I had to run to get one of those abracadabras for him that would get him out of it. I worked like an ox. You know how expenses go up when there's an infant in the house. I don't want to lie about it; I didn't dislike Elka either, for that matter. She swore at me and cursed, and I couldn't get enough of her. What strength she had! One of her looks could rob you of the power of speech. And her orations! Pitch and sulphur, that's what they were full of, and yet somehow also full of charm. I adored her every word. She gave me bloody wounds though.

In the evening I brought her a white loaf as well as a dark one, and also poppyseed rolls I baked myself. I thieved because of her and swiped everything I could lay my hands on: macaroons, raisins, almonds, cakes. I hope I may be forgiven for stealing from the Saturday pots the women left to warm in the baker's oven. I would take out scraps of meat, a chunk of pudding, a chicken leg or head, a piece of tripe, whatever I could nip quickly. She ate and became fat and handsome.

I had to sleep away from home all during the week, at the bakery. On Friday nights when I got home she always made an excuse of some sort. Either she had heartburn, or a stitch in the side, or hiccups, or headaches. You know what women's excuses are. I had a bitter time of it. It was rough. To add to it, this little brother of hers, the bastard, was growing bigger. He'd put lumps on me, and when I wanted to hit back she'd open her mouth and curse so powerfully I saw a green haze floating before my eyes. Ten times a day she threatened to divorce me. Another man in my place would have taken French leave and disappeared. But I'm the type that bears it and says nothing. What's one to do? Shoulders are from God, and burdens too.

One night there was a calamity in the bakery; the oven burst, and we almost had a fire. There was nothing to do but go home, so I went home. Let me, I thought, also taste the joy of sleeping in bed in mid-week. I didn't want to wake the sleeping mite and tiptoed into the house. Coming in, it seemed to me that I heard not the snoring of one but, as it were, a double snore, one a thin enough snore and the other like the snoring of a slaughtered ox. Oh, I didn't like that! I didn't like it at all. I went up to the bed, and things suddenly turned black. Next to Elka lay a man's form. Another in my place would have made an uproar, and enough noise to rouse the whole town, but the thought occurred to me that I might wake the child. A little thing like that—why frighten a little swallow, I thought. All right then, I went back to the bakery and stretched out on a sack of flour and till morning I never shut an eye. I shivered as if I had had malaria. "Enough of being a donkey," I said to myself. "Gimpel isn't going to be a sucker all his life. There's a limit even to the foolishness of a fool like Gimpel."

In the morning I went to the rabbi to get advice, and it made a great commotion in the town. They sent the beadle for Elka right away. She came, carrying the child. And what do you think she did? She denied it, denied everything, bone and stone! "He's out of his head," she said. "I know nothing of dreams or divinations." They yelled at her, warned her, hammered on the table, but she stuck to her guns: it was a false accusation, she said.

The butchers and the horse-traders took her part. One of the lads from the slaughterhouse came by and said to me, "We've got our eye on you, you're a marked man." Meanwhile the child started to bear down and soiled itself. In the rabbinical court there was an Ark of the Covenant, and they couldn't allow that, so they sent Elka away.

I said to the rabbi, "What shall I do?"

"You must divorce her at once," said he.

"And what if she refuses?" I asked.

He said, "You must serve the divorce. That's all you'll have to do."

I said, "Well, all right, Rabbi. Let me think about it."

"There's nothing to think about," said he. "You mustn't remain under the same roof with her."

"And if I want to see the child?" I asked.

"Let her go, the harlot," said he, "and her brood of bastards with her."

The verdict he gave was that I mustn't even cross her threshold—never again, as long as I should live.

During the day it didn't bother me so much. I thought: It was bound to happen, the abscess had to burst. But at night when I stretched out upon the sacks I felt it all very bitterly. A longing took me, for her and for the child. I wanted to be angry, but that's my misfortune exactly, I don't have it in me to be really angry. In the first place—this was how my thoughts went—there's bound to be a slip sometimes. You can't live without errors. Probably that lad who was with her led her on and gave her presents and what not, and women are often long on hair and short on sense, and so he got around her. And then since she denies it so, maybe I was only seeing things? Hallucinations do happen. You see a figure or a mannikin or something, but when you come up closer it's nothing, there's not a thing there. And if that's so, I'm doing her an injustice. And when I got so far in my thoughts I started to weep. I sobbed so that I wet the flour where I lay. In the morning I went to the rabbi and told him that I had made a mistake. The rabbi wrote on with his quill, and he said that if that were so he would have to reconsider the whole case. Until he had finished I wasn't to go near my wife, but I might send her bread and money by messenger.

3

Nine months passed before all the rabbis could come to an agreement. Letters went back and forth. I hadn't realized that there could be so much erudition about a matter like this.

Meanwhile Elka gave birth to still another child, a girl this time. On the Sabbath I went to the synagogue and invoked a blessing on her. They called me up to the Torah, and I named the child for my mother-in-law—may she rest in peace. The louts and loudmouths of the town who came into the bakery gave me a going over. All Frampol refreshed its spirits because of my trouble and grief. However, I resolved that I would always believe what I was told. What's the good of *not* believing? Today it's your wife you don't believe; tomorrow it's God Himself you won't take stock in.

By an apprentice who was her neighbor I sent her daily a corn or a wheat loaf, or a piece of pastry, rolls or bagels, or, when I got the chance, a slab of pudding, a slice of honeycake, or wedding strudel—whatever came my way. The apprentice was a goodhearted lad, and more than once he added something on his own. He had formerly annoyed me a lot, plucking my nose and digging me in the ribs, but when he started to be a visitor to my house he became kind and friendly. "Hey, you, Gimpel," he said to me, "you have a very decent little wife and two fine kids. You don't deserve them."

"But the things people say about her," I said.

"Well, they have long tongues," he said, "and nothing to do with them but babble. Ignore it as you ignore the cold of last winter."

One day the rabbi sent for me and said, "Are you certain, Gimpel, that you were wrong about your wife?"

I said, "I'm certain."

"Why, but look here! You yourself saw it."

"It must have been a shadow," I said.

"The shadow of what?"

"Just one of the beams, I think."

"You can go home then. You owe thanks to the Yanover rabbi. He found an obscure reference in Maimonides that favored you."

I seized the rabbi's hand and kissed it.

I wanted to run home immediately. It's no small thing to be separated for so long a time from wife and child. Then I reflected: I'd better go back to work now, and go home in the evening. I said nothing to anyone, although as far as my heart was concerned it was like one of the Holy Days. The women teased and twitted me as they did every day, but my thought was: Go on, with your loose talk. The truth is out, like the oil upon the water. Maimonides says it's right, and therefore it is right!

At night, when I had covered the dough to let it rise, I took my share of bread and a little sack of flour and started homeward. The moon was full and the stars were glistening, something to terrify the soul. I hurried onward, and before me darted a long shadow. It was winter, and a fresh snow had fallen. I had a mind to sing, but it was growing late and I didn't want to wake the householders. Then I felt like whistling, but I remembered that you don't whistle at night because it brings the demons out. So I was silent and walked as fast as I could.

Dogs in the Christian yards barked at me when I passed, but I thought: Bark your teeth out! What are you but mere dogs? Whereas I am a man, the husband of a fine wife, the father of promising children.

As I approached the house my heart started to pound as though it were the heart of a criminal. I felt no fear, but my heart went thump! thump! Well, no drawing back. I quietly lifted the latch and went in. Elka was asleep. I looked at the infant's cradle. The shutter was closed, but the moon forced its way through the cracks. I saw the newborn child's face and loved it as soon as I saw it—immediately—each tiny bone.

Then I came nearer to the bed. And what did I see but the apprentice lying there beside Elka. The moon went out all at once. It was utterly black, and I trembled. My teeth chattered. The bread fell from my hands, and my wife waked and said, "Who is that, ah?"

I muttered, "It's me."

"Gimpel?" she asked. "How come you're here? I thought it was forbidden."

"The rabbi said," I answered and shook as with a fever.

"Listen to me, Gimpel," she said, "go out to the shed and see if the goat's all right. It seems she's been sick." I have forgotten to say that we had a goat. When I heard she was unwell I went into the yard. The nannygoat was a good little creature. I had a nearly human feeling for her.

With hesitant steps I went up to the shed and opened the door. The goat stood there on her four feet. I felt her everywhere, drew her by the horns, examined her udders, and found nothing wrong. She had probably eaten too much bark. "Good night, little goat," I said. "Keep well." And the little beast answered with a "Maa" as though to thank me for the good will.

I went back. The apprentice had vanished.

"Where," I asked, "is the lad?"

"What lad?" my wife answered.

"What do you mean?" I said. "The apprentice. You were sleeping with him."

"The things I have dreamed this night and the night before," she said, "may they come true and lay you low, body and soul! An evil spirit has taken root in you and dazzles your sight." She screamed out, "You hateful creature! You moon calf! You spook! You uncouth man! Get out, or I'll scream all Frampol out of bed!"

Before I could move, her brother sprang out from behind the oven and struck me a blow on the back of the head. I thought he had broken my neck. I felt that something about me was deeply wrong, and I said, "Don't make a scandal. All that's needed now is that people should accuse me of raising spooks and *dybbuks*."° For that was what she had meant. "No one will touch bread of my baking."

In short, I somehow calmed her.

"Well," she said, "that's enough. Lie down, and be shattered by wheels."

Next morning I called the apprentice aside. "Listen here, brother!" I said. And so on and so forth. "What do you say?" He stared at me as though I had dropped from the roof or something.

"I swear," he said, "you'd better go to an herb doctor or some healer. I'm afraid you have a screw loose, but I'll hush it up for you." And that's how the thing stood.

To make a long story short, I lived twenty years with my wife. She bore me six children, four daughters and two sons. All kinds of things happened, but I neither saw nor heard. I believed, and that's all. The rabbi recently said to me, "Belief in itself is beneficial. It is written that a good man lives by his faith."

Suddenly my wife took sick. It began with a trifle, a little growth upon the breast. But she evidently was not destined to live long; she had no years. I spent a fortune on her. I have forgotten to say that by this time I had a bakery of my own and in Frampol was considered to be something of a rich man. Daily the healer came, and every witch doctor in the neighborhood was brought. They decided to use leeches, and after that to try cupping. They even called a doctor from Lublin, but it was too late. Before she died she called me to her bed and said, "Forgive me, Gimpel."

I said, "What is there to forgive? You have been a good and faithful wife."

"Woe, Gimpel!" she said. "It was ugly how I deceived you all these years. I want to go clean to my Maker, and so I have to tell you that the children are not yours."

If I had been clouted on the head with a piece of wood it couldn't have bewildered me more.

---

dybbuks   demons or souls of the dead that enter the bodies of the living to take possession of them

"Whose are they?" I asked.

"I don't know," she said. "There were a lot — but they're not yours." And as she spoke she tossed her head to the side, her eyes turned glassy, and it was all up with Elka. On her whitened lips there remained a smile.

I imagined that, dead as she was, she was saying, "I deceived Gimpel. That was the meaning of my brief life."

4

One night, when the period of mourning was done, as I lay dreaming on the flour sacks, there came the Spirit of Evil himself and said to me, "Gimpel, why do you sleep?"

I said, "What should I be doing? Eating *kreplach*?"

"The whole world deceives you," he said, "and you ought to deceive the world in your turn."

"How can I deceive the world?" I asked him.

He answered, "You might accumulate a bucket of urine every day and at night pour it into the dough. Let the sages of Frampol eat filth."

"What about the judgment in the world to come?" I said.

"There is no world to come," he said. "They've sold you a bill of goods and talked you into believing you carried a cat in your belly. What nonsense!"

"Well, then," I said, "and is there a God?"

He answered, "There is no God either."

"What," I said, "*is* there, then?"

"A thick mire."

He stood before my eyes with a goatish beard and horn, long-toothed, and with a tail. Hearing such words, I wanted to snatch him by the tail, but I tumbled from the flour sacks and nearly broke a rib. Then it happened that I had to answer the call of nature, and, passing, I saw the risen dough, which seemed to say to me, "Do it!" In brief, I let myself be persuaded.

At dawn the apprentice came. We kneaded the bread, scattered caraway seeds on it, and set it to bake. Then the apprentice went away, and I was left sitting in the little trench by the oven, on a pile of rags. Well, Gimpel, I thought, you've revenged yourself on them for all the shame they've put on you. Outside the frost glittered, but it was warm beside the oven. The flames heated my face. I bent my head and fell into a doze.

I saw in a dream, at once, Elka in her shroud. She called to me, "What have you done, Gimpel?"

I said to her, "It's all your fault," and started to cry.

"You fool!" she said. "You fool! Because I was false is everything false too? I never deceived anyone but myself. I'm paying for it all, Gimpel. They spare you nothing here."

I looked at her face. It was black; I was startled and waked, and remained sitting dumb. I sensed that everything hung in the balance. A false step now and I'd lose Eternal Life. But God gave me His help. I seized the long shovel and took out the loaves, carried them into the yard, and started to dig a hole in the frozen earth.

My apprentice came back as I was doing it. "What are you doing, boss?" he said, and grew pale as a corpse.

"I know what I'm doing," I said, and I buried it all before his very eyes.

Then I went home, took my hoard from its hiding place, and divided it among the children. "I saw your mother tonight," I said. "She's turning black, poor thing."

They were so astounded they couldn't speak a word.

"Be well," I said, "and forget that such a one as Gimpel ever existed." I put on my short coat, a pair of boots, took the bag that held my prayer shawl in one hand, my stock in the other, and kissed the *mezzuzah*. When people saw me in the street they were greatly surprised.

"Where are you going?" they said.

I answered, "Into the world." And so I departed from Frampol.

I wandered over the land, and good people did not neglect me. After many years I became old and white; I heard a great deal, many lies and falsehoods, but the longer I lived the more I understood that there were really no lies. Whatever doesn't really happen is dreamed at night. It happens to one if it doesn't happen to another, tomorrow if not today, or a century hence if not next year. What difference can it make? Often I heard tales of which I said, "Now this is a thing that cannot happen." But before a year had elapsed I heard that it actually had come to pass somewhere.

Going from place to place, eating at strange tables, it often happens that I spin yarns—improbable things that could never have happened—about devils, magicians, windmills, and the like. The children run after me, calling, "Grandfather, tell us a story." Sometimes they ask for particular stories, and I try to please them. A fat young boy once said to me, "Grandfather, it's the same story you told us before." The little rogue, he was right.

So it is with dreams too. It is many years since I left Frampol, but as soon as I shut my eyes I am there again. And whom do you think I see? Elka. She is standing by the washtub, as at our first encounter, but her face is shining and her eyes are as radiant as the eyes of a saint, and she speaks outlandish words to me, strange things. When I wake I have forgotten it all. But while the dream lasts I am comforted. She answers all my queries, and what comes out is that all is right. I weep and implore, "Let me be with you." And she consoles me and tells me to be patient. The time is nearer than it is far. Sometimes she strokes and kisses me and weeps upon my face. When I awaken I feel her lips and taste the salt of her tears.

No doubt the world is entirely an imaginary world, but it is only once removed from the true world. At the door of the hovel where I lie, there stands the plank on which the dead are taken away. The gravedigger Jew has his spade ready. The grave waits and the worms are hungry; the shrouds are prepared—I carry them in my beggar's sack. Another *shnorrer*° is waiting to inherit my bed of straw. When the time comes I will go joyfully. Whatever may be there, it will be real, without complication, without ridicule, without deception. God be praised: there even Gimpel cannot be deceived.

(1953)

shnorrer *a beggar; sponger*

TILLIE OLSEN

[b. 1913]

I Stand Here Ironing

I stand here ironing, and what you asked me moves tormented back and forth with the iron.

"I wish you would manage the time to come in and talk with me about your daughter. I'm sure you can help me understand her. She's a youngster who needs help and whom I'm deeply interested in helping."

"Who needs help." . . . Even if I came, what good would it do? You think because I am her mother I have a key, or that in some way you could use me as a key? She has lived for nineteen years. There is all that life that has happened outside of me, beyond me.

And when is there time to remember, to sift, to weigh, to estimate, to total? I will start and there will be an interruption and I will have to gather it all together again. Or I will become engulfed with all I did or did not do, with what should have been and what cannot be helped.

She was a beautiful baby. The first and only one of our five that was beautiful at birth. You do not guess how new and uneasy her tenancy in her now-loveliness. You did not know her all those years she was thought homely, or see her poring over her baby pictures, making me tell her over and over how beautiful she had been—and would be, I would tell her—and was now, to the seeing eye. But the seeing eyes were few or non-existent. Including mine.

I nursed her. They feel that's important nowadays. I nursed all the children, but with her, with all the fierce rigidity of first motherhood, I did like the books then said. Though her cries battered me to trembling and my breasts ached with swollenness, I waited till the clock decreed.

Why do I put that first? I do not even know if it matters, or if it explains anything.

She was a beautiful baby. She blew shining bubbles of sound. She loved motion, loved light, loved color and music and textures. She would lie on the floor in her blue overalls patting the surface so hard in ecstasy her hands and feet would blur. She was a miracle to me, but when she was eight months old I had to leave her daytimes with the woman downstairs to whom she was no miracle at all, for I worked or looked for work and for Emily's father, who "could no longer endure" (he wrote in his good-bye note) "sharing want with us."

I was nineteen. It was the pre-relief, pre-WPA world of the depression. I would start running as soon as I got off the streetcar, running up the stairs, the place smelling sour, and awake or asleep to startle awake, when she saw me she would break into a clogged weeping that could not be comforted, a weeping I can hear yet.

After a while I found a job hashing at night so I could be with her days, and it was better. But it came to where I had to bring her to his family and leave her.

It took a long time to raise the money for her fare back. Then she got chicken pox and I had to wait longer. When she finally came, I hardly knew her, walking quick and nervous like her father, looking like her father, thin, and dressed in a shoddy red that yellowed her skin and glared at the pockmarks. All the baby loveliness gone.

She was two. Old enough for nursery school they said, and I did not know then what I know now—the fatigue of the long day, and the lacerations of group life in the kinds of nurseries that are only parking places for children.

Except that it would have made no difference if I had known. It was the only place there was. It was the only way we could be together, the only way I could hold a job.

And even without knowing, I knew. I knew the teacher that was evil because all these years it has curdled into my memory, the little boy hunched in the corner, her rasp, "why aren't you outside, because Alvin hits you? that's no reason, go out, scaredy." I knew Emily hated it even if she did not clutch and implore "don't go Mommy" like the other children, mornings.

She always had a reason why we should stay home. Momma, you look sick, Momma. I feel sick. Momma, the teachers aren't there today, they're sick. Momma, we can't go, there was a fire there last night. Momma, it's a holiday today, no school, they told me.

But never a direct protest, never rebellion. I think of our others in their three-, four-year-oldness—the explosions, the tempers, the denunciations, the demands—and I feel suddenly ill. I put the iron down. What in me demanded that goodness in her? And what was the cost, the cost to her of such goodness?

The old man living in the back once said in his gentle way: "You should smile at Emily more when you look at her." What *was* in my face when I looked at her? I loved her. There were all the acts of love.

It was only with the others I remembered what he said, and it was the face of joy, and not of care or tightness or worry I turned to them—too late for Emily. She does not smile easily, let alone almost always as her brothers and sisters do. Her face is closed and sombre, but when she wants, how fluid. You must have seen it in her pantomimes, you spoke of her rare gift for comedy on the stage that rouses a laughter out of the audience so dear they applaud and applaud and do not want to let her go.

Where does it come from, that comedy? There was none of it in her when she came back to me that second time, after I had had to send her away again. She had a new daddy now to learn to love, and I think perhaps it was a better time.

Except when we left her alone nights, telling ourselves she was old enough.

"Can't you go some other time, Mommy, like tomorrow?" she would ask. "Will it be just a little while you'll be gone? Do you promise?"

The time we came back, the front door open, the clock on the floor in the hall. She rigid awake. "It wasn't just a little while. I didn't cry. Three times I called you, just three times, and then I ran downstairs to open the door so you could come faster. The clock talked loud. I threw it away, it scared me what it talked."

She said the clock talked loud again that night I went to the hospital to have Susan. She was delirious with the fever that comes before red measles, but she was fully conscious all the week I was gone and the week after we were home when she could not come near the new baby or me.

She did not get well. She stayed skeleton thin, not wanting to eat, and night after night she had nightmares. She would call for me, and I would rouse from exhaustion to sleepily call back: "You're all right, darling, go to sleep, it's just a dream," and if she still called, in a sterner voice, "now go to sleep, Emily, there's nothing to hurt you." Twice, only twice, when I had to get up for Susan anyhow, I went in to sit with her.

Now when it is too late (as if she would let me hold and comfort her like I do the others) I get up and go to her at once at her moan or restless stirring. "Are you awake, Emily? Can I get you something?" And the answer is always the same: "No, I'm all right, go back to sleep, Mother."

They persuaded me at the clinic to send her away to a convalescent home in the country where "she can have the kind of food and care you can't manage for her, and you'll be free to concentrate on the new baby." They still send children to that place. I see pictures on the society page of sleek young women planning affairs to raise money for it, or dancing at the affairs, or decorating Easter eggs or filling Christmas stockings for the children.

They never have a picture of the children so I do not know if the girls still wear those gigantic red bows and the ravaged looks on the every other Sunday when parents can come to visit "unless otherwise notified"—as we were notified the first six weeks.

Oh it is a handsome place, green lawns and tall trees and fluted flower beds. High up on the balconies of each cottage the children stand, the girls in their red bows and white dresses, the boys in white suits and giant red ties. The parents stand below shrieking up to be heard and the children shriek down to be heard, and between them the invisible wall "Not To Be Contaminated by Parental Germs or Physical Affection."

There was a tiny girl who always stood hand in hand with Emily. Her parents never came. One visit she was gone. "They moved her to Rose Cottage," Emily shouted in explanation. "They don't like you to love anybody here."

She wrote once a week, the labored writing of a seven-year-old. "I am fine. How is the baby. If I write my letter nicly I will have a star. Love." There never was a star. We wrote every other day, letters she could never hold or keep but only hear read—once. "We simply do not have room for children to keep any personal possessions," they patiently explained when we pieced one Sunday's shrieking together to plead how much it would mean to Emily, who loved so to keep things, to be allowed to keep her letters and cards.

Each visit she looked frailer. "She isn't eating," they told us.

(They had runny eggs for breakfast or mush with lumps, Emily said later, I'd hold it in my mouth and not swallow. Nothing ever tasted good, just when they had chicken.)

It took us eight months to get her released home, and only the fact that she gained back so little of her seven lost pounds convinced the social worker.

I used to try to hold and love her after she came back, but her body would stay stiff, and after a while she'd push away. She ate little. Food sickened her, and I think much of life too. Oh she had physical lightness and brightness, twinkling by on skates, bouncing like a ball up and down up and down over the jump rope, skimming over the hill; but these were momentary.

She fretted about her appearance, thin and dark and foreign-looking at a time when every little girl was supposed to look or thought she should look a chubby blonde replica of Shirley Temple. The doorbell sometimes rang for her, but no one seemed to come and play in the house or be a best friend. Maybe because we moved so much.

There was a boy she loved painfully through two school semesters. Months later she told me how she had taken pennies from my purse to buy him candy. "Licorice was his favorite and I brought him some every day, but he still liked Jennifer better'n me. Why, Mommy?" The kind of question for which there is no answer.

School was a worry to her. She was not glib or quick in a world where glibness and quickness were easily confused with ability to learn. To her overworked and exasperated teachers she was an overconscientious "slow learner" who kept trying to catch up and was absent entirely too often.

I let her be absent, though sometimes the illness was imaginary. How different from my now-strictness about attendance with the others. I wasn't working. We had a new baby, I was home anyhow. Sometimes, after Susan grew old enough, I would keep her home from school, too, to have them all together.

Mostly Emily had asthma, and her breathing, harsh and labored, would fill the house with a curiously tranquil sound. I would bring the two old dresser mirrors and her boxes of collections to her bed. She would select beads and single earrings, bottle tops and shells, dried flowers and pebbles, old postcards and scraps, all sorts of oddments; then she and Susan would play Kingdom, setting up landscapes and furniture, peopling them with action.

Those were the only times of peaceful companionship between her and Susan. I have edged away from it, that poisonous feeling between them, that terrible balancing of hurts and needs I had to do between the two, and did so badly, those earlier years.

Oh there are conflicts between the others too, each one human, needing, demanding, hurting, taking—but only between Emily and Susan, no, Emily toward Susan that corroding resentment. It seems so obvious on the surface, yet it is not obvious. Susan, the second child, Susan, golden- and curly-haired and chubby, quick and articulate and assured, everything in appearance and manner Emily was not; Susan, not able to resist Emily's precious things, losing or sometimes clumsily breaking them; Susan telling jokes and riddles to company for applause while Emily sat silent (to say to me later: that was *my* riddle, Mother, I told it to Susan); Susan, who for all the five years' difference in age was just a year behind Emily in developing physically.

I am glad for that slow physical development that widened the difference between her and her contemporaries, though she suffered over it. She was too vulnerable for that terrible world of youthful competition, of preening and parading, of constant measuring of yourself against every other, of envy, "If I had that copper hair," "If I had that skin. . . ." She tormented herself enough about not looking like the others, there was enough of the unsureness, the having to be conscious of words before you speak, the constant caring—what are they thinking of me? without having it all magnified by the merciless physical drives.

Ronnie is calling. He is wet and I change him. It is rare there is such a cry now. That time of motherhood is almost behind me when the ear is not one's own but must always be racked and listening for the child cry, the child call. We sit for a while and I hold him, looking out over the city spread in charcoal with its soft aisles of light. "*Shoogily*," he breathes and curls closer. I carry him back to bed, asleep. *Shoogily*. A funny word, a family word, inherited from Emily, invented by her to say: *comfort*.

In this and other ways she leaves her seal, I say aloud. And startle at my saying it. What do I mean? What did I start to gather together, to try and make coherent? I was at the terrible, growing years. War years. I do not remember them well. I was working, there were four smaller ones now, there was not time for her. She had to help be a mother, and housekeeper, and shopper. She had to set her seal. Mornings of crisis and near hysteria trying to get lunches packed, hair combed, coats and shoes found, everyone to school or Child Care on time, the baby ready for transportation. And always the paper scribbled on by a smaller one, the book looked at by Susan then mislaid, the homework not done. Running out to that huge school where she was one, she was lost, she was a drop; suffering over the unpreparedness, stammering and unsure in her classes.

There was so little time left at night after the kids were bedded down. She would struggle over books, always eating (it was in those years she developed her enormous appetite that is legendary in our family) and I would be ironing, or preparing food for the next day, or writing V-mail to Bill, or tending the baby. Sometimes, to make me laugh, or out of her despair, she would imitate happenings or types at school.

I think I said once: "Why don't you do something like this in the school amateur show?" One morning she phoned me at work, hardly understandable through the weeping: "Mother, I did it. I won, I won; they gave me first prize; they clapped and clapped and wouldn't let me go."

Now suddenly she was Somebody, and as imprisoned in her difference as she had been in anonymity.

She began to be asked to perform at other high schools, even in colleges, then at city and statewide affairs. The first one we went to, I only recognized her that first moment when thin, shy, she almost drowned herself into the curtains. Then: Was this Emily? The control, the command, the convulsing and deadly clowning, the spell, then the roaring, stamping audience, unwilling to let this rare and precious laughter out of their lives.

Afterwards: You ought to do something about her with a gift like that—but without money or knowing how, what does one do? We have left it all to her, and the gift has as often eddied inside, clogged and clotted, as been used and growing.

She is coming. She runs up the stairs two at a time with her light graceful step, and I know she is happy tonight. Whatever it was that occasioned your call did not happen today.

"Aren't you ever going to finish the ironing, Mother? Whistler painted his mother in a rocker. I'd have to paint mine standing over an ironing board." This is one of her communicative nights and she tells me everything and nothing as she fixes herself a plate of food out of the icebox.

She is so lovely. Why did you want me to come in at all? Why were you concerned? She will find her way.

She starts up the stairs to bed. "Don't get me up with the rest in the morning." "But I thought you were having midterms." "Oh, those," she comes back in, kisses me, and says lightly, "in a couple of years when we'll all be atom-dead they won't matter a bit."

She has said it before. She *believes* it. But because I have been dredging the past, and all that compounds a human being is so heavy and meaningful in me, I cannot endure it tonight.

I will never total it all. I will never come in to say: She was a child seldom smiled at.
Her father left me before she was a year old. I had to work her first six years when
there was work, or I sent her home and to his relatives. There were years she had care
she hated. She was dark and thin and foreign-looking in a world where the prestige
went to blondeness and curly hair and dimples, she was slow where glibness was
prized. She was a child of anxious, not proud, love. We were poor and could not afford for her the soil of easy growth. I was a young mother, I was a distracted mother.
There were the other children pushing up, demanding. Her younger sister seemed all
that she was not. There were years she did not want me to touch her. She kept too
much in herself, her life was such she had to keep too much in herself. My wisdom
came too late. She has much to her and probably little will come of it. She is a child of
her age, of depression, of war, of fear.

   Let her be. So all that is in her will not bloom—but in how many does it? There
is still enough left to live by. Only help her to know—help make it so there is cause
for her to know—that she is more than this dress on the ironing board, helpless before
the iron.

                                                                          (1961)

RALPH ELLISON
[1914–1994]

Battle Royal

It goes a long way back, some twenty years. All my life I had been looking for something, and everywhere I turned someone tried to tell me what it was. I accepted their
answers too, though they were often in contradiction and even self-contradictory. I was
naïve. I was looking for myself and asking everyone except myself questions which I,
and only I, could answer. It took me a long time and much painful boomeranging of
my expectations to achieve a realization everyone else appears to have been born with:
That I am nobody but myself. But first I had to discover that I am an invisible man!

   And yet I am no freak of nature, nor of history. I was in the cards, other things having been equal (or unequal) eighty-five years ago. I am not ashamed of my grandparents for having been slaves. I am only ashamed of myself for having at one time been
ashamed. About eighty-five years ago they were told that they were free, united with
others of our country in everything pertaining to the common good, and, in everything social, separate like the fingers of the hand. And they believed it. They exulted
in it. They stayed in their place, worked hard, and brought up my father to do the
same. But my grandfather is the one. He was an odd old guy, my grandfather, and I
am told I take after him. It was he who caused the trouble. On his deathbed he called
my father to him and said, "Son, after I'm gone I want you to keep up the good fight.
I never told you, but our life is a war and I have been a traitor all my born days, a
spy in the enemy's country ever since I give up my gun back in the Reconstruction.
Live with your head in the lion's mouth. I want you to overcome 'em with yeses,

undermine 'em with grins, agree 'em to death and destruction, let 'em swoller you till they vomit or bust wide open." They thought the old man had gone out of his mind. He had been the meekest of men. The younger children were rushed from the room, the shades drawn and the flame of the lamp turned so low that it sputtered on the wick like the old man's breathing. "Learn it to the younguns," he whispered fiercely; then he died.

But my folks were more alarmed over his last words than over his dying. It was as though he had not died at all, his words caused so much anxiety. I was warned emphatically to forget what he had said and, indeed, this is the first time it has been mentioned outside the family circle. It had a tremendous effect upon me, however. I could never be sure of what he meant. Grandfather had been a quiet old man who never made any trouble, yet on his deathbed he had called himself a traitor and a spy, and he had spoken of his meekness as a dangerous activity. It became a constant puzzle which lay unanswered in the back of my mind. And whenever things went well for me I remembered my grandfather and felt guilty and uncomfortable. It was as though I was carrying out his advice in spite of myself. And to make it worse, everyone loved me for it. I was praised by the most lily-white men of the town. I was considered an example of desirable conduct—just as my grandfather had been. And what puzzled me was that the old man had defined it as *treachery*. When I was praised for my conduct I felt a guilt that in some way I was doing something that was really against the wishes of the white folks, that if they had understood they would have desired me to act just the opposite, that I should have been sulky and mean, and that that really would have been what they wanted, even though they were fooled and thought they wanted me to act as I did. It made me afraid that some day they would look upon me as a traitor and I would be lost. Still I was more afraid to act any other way because they didn't like that at all. The old man's words were like a curse. On my graduation day I delivered an oration in which I showed that humility was the secret, indeed, the very essence of progress. (Not that I believed this—how could I, remembering my grandfather?—I only believed that it worked.) It was a great success. Everyone praised me and I was invited to give the speech at a gathering of the town's leading white citizens. It was a triumph for our whole community.

It was in the main ballroom of the leading hotel. When I got there I discovered that it was on the occasion of a smoker, and I was told that since I was to be there anyway I might as well take part in the battle royal to be fought by some of my schoolmates as part of the entertainment. The battle royal came first.

All of the town's big shots were there in their tuxedoes, wolfing down the buffet foods, drinking beer and whiskey and smoking black cigars. It was a large room with a high ceiling. Chairs were arranged in neat rows around three sides of a portable boxing ring. The fourth side was clear, revealing a gleaming space of polished floor. I had some misgivings over the battle royal, by the way. Not from a distaste for fighting, but because I didn't care too much for the other fellows who were to take part. They were tough guys who seemed to have no grandfather's curse worrying their minds. No one could mistake their toughness. And besides, I suspected that fighting a battle royal might detract from the dignity of my speech. In those pre-invisible days I visualized myself as a potential Booker T. Washington. But the other fellows didn't care too much for me either, and there were nine of them. I felt superior to them in my way, and I didn't like the manner in which we were all crowded together into the servants' elevator. Nor did they like my being there. In fact, as the warmly lighted floors flashed past the elevator we had words over the fact that I, by taking part in the fight, had knocked one of their friends out of a night's work.

We were led out of the elevator through a rococo hall into an anteroom and told to get into our fighting togs. Each of us was issued a pair of boxing gloves and ushered out into the big mirrored hall, which we entered looking cautiously about us and whispering, lest we might accidentally be heard above the noise of the room. It was foggy with cigar smoke. And already the whiskey was taking effect. I was shocked to see some of the most important men of the town quite tipsy. They were all there—bankers, lawyers, judges, doctors, fire chiefs, teachers, merchants. Even one of the more fashionable pastors. Something we could not see was going on up front. A clarinet was vibrating sensuously and the men were standing up and moving eagerly forward. We were a small tight group, clustered together, our bare upper bodies touching and shining with anticipatory sweat; while up front the big shots were becoming increasingly excited over something we still could not see. Suddenly I heard the school superintendent, who had told me to come, yell, "Bring up the shines gentlemen! Bring up the little shines!"

We were rushed up to the front of the ballroom, where it smelled even more strongly of tobacco and whiskey. Then we were pushed into place. I almost wet my pants. A sea of faces, some hostile, some amused, ringed around us, and in the center, facing us, stood a magnificent blonde—stark naked. There was dead silence. I felt a blast of cold air chill me. I tried to back away, but they were behind me and around me. Some of the boys stood with lowered heads, trembling. I felt a wave of irrational guilt and fear. My teeth chattered, my skin turned to goose flesh, my knees knocked. Yet I was strongly attracted and looked in spite of myself. Had the price of looking been blindness, I would have looked. The hair was yellow like that of a circus kewpie doll, the face heavily powdered and rouged, as though to form an abstract mask, the eyes hollow and smeared a cool blue, the color of a baboon's butt. I felt a desire to spit upon her as my eyes brushed slowly over her body. Her breasts were firm and round as the domes of East Indian temples, and I stood so close as to see the fine skin texture and beads of pearly perspiration glistening like dew around the pink and erected buds of her nipples. I wanted at one and the same time to run from the room, to sink through the floor, or go to her and cover her from my eyes and the eyes of the others with my body; to feel the soft thighs, to caress her and destroy her, to love her and murder her, to hide from her, and yet to stroke where below the small American flag tattooed upon her belly her thighs formed a capital V. I had a notion that of all in the room she saw only me with her impersonal eyes.

And then she began to dance, a slow sensuous movement; the smoke of a hundred cigars clinging to her like the thinnest of veils. She seemed like a fair bird-girl girdled in veils calling to me from the angry surface of some gray and threatening sea. I was transported. Then I became aware of the clarinet playing and the big shots yelling at us. Some threatened us if we looked and others if we did not. On my right I saw one boy faint. And now a man grabbed a silver pitcher from a table and stepped close as he dashed ice water upon him and stood him up and forced two of us to support him as his head hung and moans issued from his thick bluish lips. Another boy began to plead to go home. He was the largest of the group, wearing dark red fighting trunks much too small to conceal the erection which projected from him as though in answer to the insinuating low-registered moaning of the clarinet. He tried to hide himself with his boxing gloves.

And all the while the blonde continued dancing, smiling faintly at the big shots who watched her with fascination, and faintly smiling at our fear. I noticed a certain merchant who followed her hungrily, his lips loose and drooling. He was a large man who wore diamond studs in a shirtfront which swelled with the ample paunch underneath, and each time the blonde swayed her undulating hips he ran his hand through the thin hair of his bald head and, with his arms upheld, his posture clumsy like that of an intoxicated panda, wound his belly in a slow and obscene grind. This creature was completely hypnotized. The music had quickened. As the dancer flung herself about with a detached expression on her face, the men began reaching out to touch her. I could see their beefy fingers sink into her soft flesh. Some of the others tried to stop them and she began to move around the floor in graceful circles, as they gave chase, slipping and sliding over the polished floor. It was mad. Chairs went crashing, drinks were spilt, as they ran laughing and howling after her. They caught her just as she reached a door, raised her from the floor, and tossed her as college boys are tossed at a hazing, and above her red, fixed-smiling lips I saw the terror and disgust in her eyes, almost like my own terror and that which I saw in some of the other boys. As I watched, they tossed her twice and her soft breasts seemed to flatten against the air and her legs flung wildly as she spun. Some of the more sober ones helped her to escape. And I started off the floor, heading for the anteroom with the rest of the boys.

Some were still crying and in hysteria. But as we tried to leave we were stopped and ordered to get into the ring. There was nothing to do but what we were told. All ten of us climbed under the ropes and allowed ourselves to be blindfolded with broad bands of white cloth. One of the men seemed to feel a bit sympathetic and tried to cheer us up as we stood with our backs against the ropes. Some of us tried to grin. "See that boy over there?" one of the men said. "I want you to run across at the bell and give it to him right in the belly. If you don't get him, I'm going to get you. I don't like his looks." Each of us was told the same. The blindfolds were put on. Yet even then I had been going over my speech. In my mind each word was as bright as flame. I felt the cloth pressed into place, and frowned so that it would be loosened when I relaxed.

But now I felt a sudden fit of blind terror. I was unused to darkness. It was as though I had suddenly found myself in a dark room filled with poisonous cottonmouths. I could hear the bleary voices yelling insistently for the battle royal to begin.

"Get going in there!"

"Let me at that big nigger!"

I strained to pick up the school superintendent's voice, as though to squeeze some security out of that slightly more familiar sound.

"Let me at those black sonsabitches!" someone yelled.

"No, Jackson, no!" another voice yelled. "Here, somebody, help me hold Jack."

"I want to get at that ginger-colored nigger. Tear him limb from limb," the first voice yelled.

I stood against the ropes trembling. For in those days I was what they called ginger-colored, and he sounded as though he might crunch me between his teeth like a crisp ginger cookie.

Quite a struggle was going on. Chairs were being kicked about and I could hear voices grunting as with a terrific effort. I wanted to see, to see more desperately than ever before. But the blindfold was as tight as a thick skin-puckering scab and when I raised my gloved hands to push the layers of white aside a voice yelled, "Oh, no you don't, black bastard! Leave that alone!"

"Ring the bell before Jackson kills him a coon!" someone boomed in the sudden silence. And I heard the bell clang and the sound of the feet scuffling forward.

A glove smacked against my head. I pivoted, striking out stiffly as someone went past, and felt the jar ripple along the length of my arm to my shoulder. Then it seemed as though all nine of the boys had turned upon me at once. Blows pounded me from all sides while I struck out as best I could. So many blows landed upon me that I wondered if I were not the only blindfolded fighter in the ring, or if the man called Jackson hadn't succeeded in getting me after all.

Blindfolded, I could no longer control my motions. I had no dignity. I stumbled about like a baby or a drunken man. The smoke had become thicker and with each new blow it seemed to sear and further restrict my lungs. My saliva became like hot bitter glue. A glove connected with my head, filling my mouth with warm blood. It was everywhere. I could not tell if the moisture I felt upon my body was sweat or blood. A blow landed hard against the nape of my neck. I felt myself going over, my head hitting the floor. Streaks of blue light filled the black world behind the blindfold. I lay prone, pretending that I was knocked out, but felt myself seized by hands and yanked to my feet. "Get going, black boy! Mix it up!" My arms were like lead, my head smarting from blows. I managed to feel my way to the ropes and held on, trying to catch my breath. A glove landed in my midsection and I went over again, feeling as though the smoke had become a knife jabbed into my guts. Pushed this way and that by the legs milling around me, I finally pulled erect and discovered that I could see the black, sweat-washed forms weaving in the smoky-blue atmosphere like drunken dancers weaving to the rapid drum-like thuds of blows.

Everyone fought hysterically. It was complete anarchy. Everybody fought everybody else. No group fought together for long. Two, three, four, fought one, then turned to fight each other, were themselves attacked. Blows landed below the belt and in the kidney, with the gloves open as well as closed, and with my eye partly opened now there was not so much terror. I moved carefully, avoiding blows, although not too many to attract attention, fighting from group to group. The boys groped about like blind, cautious crabs crouching to protect their mid-sections, their heads pulled in short against their shoulders, their arms stretched nervously before them, with their fists testing the smoke-filled air like the knobbed feelers of hypersensitive snails. In one corner I glimpsed a boy violently punching the air and heard him scream in pain as he smashed his hand against a ring post. For a second I saw him bent over holding his hand, then going down as a blow caught his unprotected head. I played one group against the other, slipping in and throwing a punch then stepping out of range while pushing the others into the melee to take the blows blindly aimed at me. The smoke was agonizing and there were no rounds, no bells at three minute intervals to relieve our exhaustion. The room spun round me, a swirl of lights, smoke, sweating bodies surrounded by tense white faces. I bled from both nose and mouth, the blood spattering upon my chest.

The men kept yelling, "Slug him, black boy! Knock his guts out!"

"Uppercut him! Kill him! Kill that big boy!"

Taking a fake fall, I saw a boy going down heavily beside me as though we were felled by a single blow, saw a sneaker-clad foot shoot into his groin as the two who had knocked him down stumbled upon him. I rolled out of range, feeling a twinge of nausea.

The harder we fought the more threatening the men became. And yet, I had begun to worry about my speech again. How would it go? Would they recognize my ability? What would they give me?

I was fighting automatically and suddenly I noticed that one after another of the boys was leaving the ring. I was surprised, filled with panic, as though I had been left alone with an unknown danger. Then I understood. The boys had arranged it among themselves. It was the custom for the two men left in the ring to slug it out for the winner's prize. I discovered this too late. When the bell sounded two men in tuxedoes leaped into the ring and removed the blindfold. I found myself facing Tatlock, the biggest of the gang. I felt sick at my stomach. Hardly had the bell stopped ringing in my ears than it clanged again and I saw him moving swiftly toward me. Thinking of nothing else to do I hit him smash on the nose. He kept coming, bringing the rank sharp violence of stale sweat. His face was a black blank of a face, only his eyes alive— with hate of me and aglow with a feverish terror from what had happened to us all. I became anxious. I wanted to deliver my speech and he came at me as though he meant to beat it out of me. I smashed him again and again, taking his blows as they came. Then on a sudden impulse I struck him lightly and as we clinched, I whispered, "Fake like I knocked you out, you can have the prize."

"I'll break your behind," he whispered hoarsely.

"For *them?*"

"For *me,* sonofabitch!"

They were yelling for us to break it up and Tatlock spun me half around with a blow, and as a joggled camera sweeps in a reeling scene, I saw the howling red faces crouching tense beneath the cloud of blue-gray smoke. For a moment the world wavered, unraveled, flowed, then my head cleared and Tatlock bounced before me. That fluttering shadow before my eyes was his jabbing left hand. Then falling forward, my head against his damp shoulder, I whispered, "I'll make it five dollars more."

"Go to hell!"

But his muscles relaxed a trifle beneath my pressure and I breathed, "Seven!"

"Give it to your ma," he said, ripping me beneath the heart.

And while I still held him I butted him and moved away. I felt myself bombarded with punches. I fought back with hopeless desperation. I wanted to deliver my speech more than anything else in the world, because I felt that only these men could judge truly my ability, and now this stupid clown was ruining my chances. I began fighting carefully now, moving in to punch him and out again with my greater speed. A lucky blow to his chin and I had him going too—until I heard a loud voice yell, "I got my money on the big boy."

Hearing this, I almost dropped my guard. I was confused: Should I try to win against the voice out there? Would not this go against my speech, and was not this a moment for humility, for nonresistance? A blow to my head as I danced about sent my right eye popping like a jack-in-the-box and settled my dilemma. The room went red as I fell. It was a dream fall, my body languid and fastidious as to where to land, until the floor became impatient and smashed up to meet me. A moment later I came to. An hypnotic voice said FIVE emphatically. And I lay there, hazily watching a dark red spot of my own blood shaping itself into a butterfly, glistening and soaking into the soiled gray world of the canvas.

When the voice drawled TEN I was lifted up and dragged to a chair. I sat dazed. My eye pained and swelled with each throb of my pounding heart and I wondered if now I would be allowed to speak. I was wringing wet, my mouth still bleeding. We were grouped along the wall now. The other boys ignored me as they congratulated Tatlock and speculated as to how much they would be paid. One boy whimpered over his smashed hand. Looking up front, I saw attendants in white jackets rolling the portable ring away and placing a small square rug in the vacant space surrounded by chairs. Perhaps, I thought, I will stand on the rug to deliver my speech.

Then the M.C. called to us, "Come on up here boys and get your money."

We ran forward to where the men laughed and talked in their chairs, waiting. Everyone seemed friendly now.

"There it is on the rug," the man said. I saw the rug covered with coins of all dimensions and a few crumpled bills. But what excited me, scattered here and there, were the gold pieces.

"Boys, it's all yours," the man said. "You get all you grab."

"That's right, Sambo," a blond man said, winking at me confidentially.

I trembled with excitement, forgetting my pain. I would get the gold and the bills, I thought. I would use both hands. I would throw my body against the boys nearest me to block them from the gold.

"Get down around the rug now," the man commanded, "and don't anyone touch it until I give the signal."

"This ought to be good," I heard.

As told, we got around the square rug on our knees. Slowly the man raised his freckled hand as we followed it upward with our eyes.

I heard, "These niggers look like they're about to pray!"

Then, "Ready," the man said. "Go!"

I lunged for a yellow coin lying on the blue design of the carpet, touching it and sending a surprised shriek to join those rising around me. I tried frantically to remove my hand but could not let go. A hot, violent force tore through my body, shaking me like a wet rat. The rug was electrified. The hair bristled up on my head as I shook myself free. My muscles jumped, my nerves jangled, writhed. But I saw that this was not stopping the other boys. Laughing in fear and embarrassment, some were holding back and scooping up the coins knocked off by the painful contortions of the others. The men roared above us as we struggled.

"Pick it up, goddamnit, pick it up!" someone called like a bass-voiced parrot. "Go on, get it!"

I crawled rapidly around the floor, picking up the coins, trying to avoid the coppers and to get greenbacks and the gold. Ignoring the shock by laughing, as I brushed the coins off quickly, I discovered that I could contain the electricity—a contradiction, but it works. Then the men began to push us onto the rug. Laughing embarrassedly, we struggled out of their hands and kept after the coins. We were all wet and slippery and hard to hold. Suddenly I saw a boy lifted into the air, glistening with sweat like a circus seal, and dropped, his wet back landing flush upon the charged rug, heard him yell and saw him literally dance upon his back, his elbows beating a frenzied tattoo upon the floor, his muscles twitching like the flesh of a horse stung by many flies. When he finally rolled off, his face was gray and no one stopped him when he ran from the floor amid booming laughter.

"Get the money," the M.C. called. "That's good hard American cash!"

And we snatched and grabbed, snatched and grabbed. I was careful not to come too close to the rug now, and when I felt the hot whiskey breath descend upon me like a cloud of foul air I reached out and grabbed the leg of a chair. It was occupied and I held on desperately.

"Leggo, nigger! Leggo!"

The huge face wavered down to mine as he tried to push me free. But my body was slippery and he was too drunk. It was Mr. Colcord, who owned a chain of movie houses and "entertainment palaces." Each time he grabbed me I slipped out of his hands. It became a real struggle. I feared the rug more than I did the drunk, so I held on, surprising myself for a moment by trying to topple *him* upon the rug. It was such an enormous idea that I found myself actually carrying it out. I tried not to be obvious, yet when I grabbed his leg, trying to tumble him out of the chair, he raised up roaring with laughter, and, looking at me with soberness dead in the eye, kicked me viciously in the chest. The chair leg flew out of my hand. I felt myself going and rolled. It was as though I had rolled through a bed of hot coals. It seemed a whole century would pass before I would roll free, a century in which I was seared through the deepest levels of my body to the fearful breath within me and the breath seared and heated to the point of explosion. It'll all be over in a flash, I thought as I rolled clear. It'll all be over in a flash.

But not yet, the men on the other side were waiting, red faces swollen as though from apoplexy as they bent forward in their chairs. Seeing their fingers coming toward me I rolled away as a fumbled football rolls off the receiver's fingertips, back into the coals. That time I luckily sent the rug sliding out of place and heard the coins ringing against the floor and the boys scuffling to pick them up and the M.C. calling, "All right, boys, that's all. Go get dressed and get your money."

I was limp as a dish rag. My back felt as though it had been beaten with wires.

When we had dressed the M.C. came in and gave us each five dollars, except Tatlock, who got ten for being last in the ring. Then he told us to leave. I was not to get a chance to deliver my speech, I thought. I was going out into the dim alley in despair when I was stopped and told to go back. I returned to the ballroom, where the men were pushing back their chairs and gathering in groups to talk.

The M.C. knocked on a table for quiet. "Gentlemen," he said, "we almost forgot an important part of the program. A most serious part, gentlemen. This boy was brought here to deliver a speech which he made at his graduation yesterday. . . . "

"Bravo!"

"I'm told that he is the smartest boy we've got out there in Greenwood. I'm told that he knows more big words than a pocket-sized dictionary."

Much applause and laughter.

"So now, gentlemen, I want you to give him your attention."

There was still laughter as I faced them, my mouth dry, my eye throbbing. I began slowly, but evidently my throat was tense, because they began shouting, "Louder! Louder!"

"We of the younger generation extol the wisdom of that great leader and educator," I shouted, "who first spoke these flaming words of wisdom: 'A ship lost at sea for many days suddenly sighted a friendly vessel. From the mast of the unfortunate vessel was seen a signal: "Water, water; we die of thirst!" The answer from the friendly vessel came back: "Cast down your bucket where you are." The captain of the distressed vessel, at last heeding the injunction, cast down his bucket, and it came up full of fresh sparkling water from the mouth of the Amazon River.' And like him I say, and in his words, 'To those of my race who depend upon bettering their condition in a foreign land, or who underestimate the importance of cultivating friendly relations with the Southern white man, who is his next-door neighbor, I would say: "Cast down your bucket where you are"—cast it down in making friends in every manly way of the people of all races by whom we are surrounded. . . .' "

I spoke automatically and with such fervor that I did not realize that the men were still talking and laughing until my dry mouth, filling up with blood from the cut, almost strangled me. I coughed, wanting to stop and go to one of the tall brass, sand filled spittoons to relieve myself, but a few of the men, especially the superintendent, were listening and I was afraid. So I gulped it down, blood, saliva and all, and continued. (What powers of endurance I had during those days! What enthusiasm! What a belief in the rightness of things!) I spoke even louder in spite of the pain. But still they talked and still they laughed, as though deaf with cotton in dirty ears. So I spoke with greater emotional emphasis. I closed my ears and swallowed blood until I was nauseated. The speech seemed a hundred times as long as before, but I could not leave out a single word. All had to be said, each memorized nuance considered, rendered. Nor was that all. Whenever I uttered a word of three or more syllables a group of voices would yell for me to repeat it. I used the phrase "social responsibility" and they yelled:

"What's the word you say, boy?"

"Social responsibility," I said.

"What?"

"Social . . . "

"Louder."

" . . . responsibility."

"More!"

"Respon—"

"Repeat!"

"—sibility."

The room filled with the uproar of laughter until, no doubt, distracted by having to gulp down my blood, I made a mistake and yelled a phrase I had often seen denounced in newspaper editorials, heard debated in private.

"Social . . . "

"What?" they yelled.

" . . . equality—"

The laughter hung smokelike in the sudden stillness. I opened my eyes, puzzled. Sounds of displeasure filled the room. The M.C. rushed forward. They shouted hostile phrases at me. But I did not understand.

A small dry mustached man in the front row blared out, "Say that slowly, son!"

"What sir?"

"What you just said!"

"Social responsibility, sir," I said.

"You weren't being smart, were you, boy?" he said, not unkindly.

"No, sir!"

"You sure that about 'equality' was a mistake?"

"Oh, yes, sir," I said. "I was swallowing blood."

"Well, you had better speak more slowly so we can understand. We mean to do right by you, but you've got to know your place at all times. All right, now, go on with your speech."

I was afraid. I wanted to leave but I wanted also to speak and I was afraid they'd snatch me down.

"Thank you, sir," I said, beginning where I had left off, and having them ignore me as before.

Yet when I finished there was a thunderous applause. I was surprised to see the superintendent come forth with a package wrapped in white tissue paper, and, gesturing for quiet, address the men.

"Gentlemen, you see that I did not overpraise this boy. He makes a good speech and some day he'll lead his people in the proper paths. And I don't have to tell you that that is important in these days and times. This is a good, smart boy, and so to encourage him in the right direction, in the name of the Board of Education I wish to present him a prize in the form of this . . . "

He paused, removing the tissue paper and revealing a gleaming calfskin brief case.

" . . . in the form of this first-class article from Shad Whitmore's shop."

"Boy," he said, addressing me, "take this prize and keep it well. Consider it a badge of office. Prize it. Keep developing as you are and some day it will be filled with important papers that will help shape the destiny of your people."

I was so moved that I could hardly express my thanks. A rope of bloody saliva forming a shape like an undiscovered continent drooled upon the leather and I wiped it quickly away. I felt an importance that I had never dreamed.

"Open it and see what's inside," I was told.

My fingers a-tremble, I complied, smelling the fresh leather and finding an official-looking document inside. It was a scholarship to the state college for Negroes. My eyes filled with tears and I ran awkwardly off the floor.

I was overjoyed; I did not even mind when I discovered that the gold pieces I had scrambled for were brass pocket tokens advertising a certain make of automobile.

When I reached home everyone was excited. Next day the neighbors came to congratulate me. I even felt safe from grandfather, whose deathbed curse usually spoiled my triumphs. I stood beneath his photograph with my brief case in hand and smiled triumphantly into his stolid black peasant's face. It was a face that fascinated me. The eyes seemed to follow everywhere I went.

That night I dreamed I was at a circus with him and that he refused to laugh at the clowns no matter what they did. Then later he told me to open my brief case and read what was inside and I did, finding an official envelope stamped with the state seal; and inside the envelope I found another and another, endlessly, and I thought I would fall of weariness. "Them's years," he said. "Now open that one." And I did and in it I found an engraved document containing a short message in letters of gold. "Read it," my grandfather said. "Out loud."

"To Whom It May Concern," I intoned. "Keep This Nigger-Boy Running."

I awoke with the old man's laughter ringing in my ears.

(It was a dream I was to remember and dream again for many years after. But at the time I had no insight into its meaning. First I had to attend college.)

(1952)

JEAN STAFFORD
[*b. 1915*]

Bad Characters

Up until I learned my lesson in a very bitter way, I never had more than one friend at a time, and my friendships, though ardent, were short. When they ended and I was sent packing in unforgetting indignation, it was always my fault; I would swear vilely in front of a girl I knew to be pious and prim (by the time I was eight, the most grandiloquent gangster could have added nothing to my vocabulary—I had an awful tongue), or I would call a Tenderfoot Scout a sissy or make fun of athletics to the daughter of the high-school coach. These outbursts came without plan; I would simply one day, in the middle of a game of Russian bank or a hike or a conversation, be possessed with a passion to be by myself, and my lips instantly and without warning would accommodate me. My friend was never more surprised than I was when this irrevocable slander, this terrible, talented invective, came boiling out of my mouth.

Afterward, when I had got the solitude I had wanted, I was dismayed, for I did not like it. Then I would sadly finish the game of cards as if someone were still across the table from me; I would sit down on the mesa and through a glaze of tears would watch my friend departing with outraged strides; mournfully, I would talk to myself. Because I had already alienated everyone I knew, I then had nowhere to turn, so a famine set in and I would have no companion but Muff, the cat, who loathed all human beings except, significantly, me—truly. She bit and scratched the hands that fed her, she arched her back like a Halloween cat if someone kindly tried to pet her, she hissed, laid her ears flat to her skull, growled, fluffed up her tail into a great bush and flailed it like a bullwhack. But she purred for me, she patted me with her paws, keeping her claws in their velvet scabbards. She was not only an ill-natured cat, she was also badly dressed. She was a calico, and the distribution of her colors was a mess; she looked as if she had been left out in the rain and her paint had run. She had a Roman nose as the result of some early injury, her tail was skinny, she had a perfectly venomous look in her eye. My family said—my family discriminated against me—that I was much closer kin to Muff than I was to any of them. To tease me into a tantrum, my brother Jack and my sister Stella often called me Kitty instead of Emily. Little Tess did not dare, because she knew I'd chloroform her if she did. Jack, the meanest boy I have ever known in my life, called me Polecat and talked about my mania for fish, which, it so happened, I despised. The name would have been far more appropriate for *him*, since he trapped skunks up in the foothills—we lived in Adams, Colorado—and quite often, because he was careless and foolhardy, his clothes had to be buried, and even when that was done, he sometimes was sent home from school on the complaint of girls sitting next to him.

Along about Christmastime when I was eleven, I was making a snowman with Virgil Meade in his backyard, and all of a sudden, just as we had got around to the right arm, I had to be alone. So I called him a son of a sea cook, said it was common knowledge that his mother had bedbugs and that his father, a dentist and the deputy marshal, was a bootlegger on the side. For a moment, Virgil was too aghast to speak—a little earlier we had agreed to marry someday and become millionaires—and then, with a bellow of fury, he knocked me down and washed my face in snow. I saw stars, and black balls bounced before my eyes. When finally he let me up, we were both crying, and he hollered that if I didn't get off his property that instant, his father would arrest me and send me to Canon City. I trudged slowly home, half frozen, critically sick at heart. So it was old Muff again for me for quite some time. Old Muff, that is, until I met Lottie Jump, although "met" is a euphemism for the way I first encountered her.

I saw Lottie for the first time one afternoon in our own kitchen, stealing a chocolate cake. Stella and Jack had not come home from school yet—not having my difficult disposition, they were popular, and they were at their friends' houses, pulling taffy, I suppose, making popcorn balls, playing casino, having fun—and my mother had taken Tess with her to visit a friend in one of the T. B. sanitariums. I was alone in the house, and making a funny-looking Christmas card, although I had no one to send it to. When I heard someone in the kitchen, I thought it was Mother home early, and I went out to ask her why the green pine tree I had pasted on a square of red paper looked as if it were falling down. And there, instead of Mother and my baby sister, was this pale, conspicuous child in the act of lifting the glass cover from the devil's-food my mother had taken out of the oven an hour before and set on the plant shelf by the window. The child had her back to me, and when she heard my footfall, she wheeled with an amazing look of fear and hatred on her pinched and pasty face. Simultaneously, she put the cover over the cake again, and then she stood motionless as if she were under a spell.

I was scared, for I was not sure what was happening, and anyhow it gives you a turn to find a stranger in the kitchen in the middle of the afternoon, even if the stranger is only a skinny child in a moldy coat and sopping-wet basketball shoes. Between us there was a lengthy silence, but there was a great deal of noise in the room: the alarm clock ticked smugly; the teakettle simmered patiently on the back of the stove; Muff, cross at having been waked up, thumped her tail against the side of the terrarium on the window where she had been sleeping—contrary to orders—among the geraniums. This went on, it seemed to me, for hours and hours while that tall, sickly girl and I confronted each other. When, after a long time, she did open her mouth, it was to tell a prodigious lie. "I came to see if you'd like to play with me," she said. I think she sighed and stole a sidelong and regretful glance at the cake.

Beggars cannot be choosers, and I had been missing Virgil so sorely, as well as all those other dear friends forever lost to me, that in spite of her flagrance (she had never clapped eyes on me before, she had had no way of knowing there was a creature of my age in the house—she had come in like a hobo to steal my mother's cake), I was flattered and consoled. I asked her name and, learning it, believed my ears no better than my eyes: Lottie Jump. What on earth! What on earth—you surely will agree with me—and yet when I told her mine, Emily Vanderpool, she laughed until she coughed and gasped. "Beg pardon," she said. "Names like them always hit my funny bone. There was this towhead boy in school named Delbert Saxonfield." I saw no connection and I was insulted (what's so funny about Vanderpool, I'd like to know), but Lottie Jump was, technically, my guest and I *was* lonesome, so I asked her, since she had spoken of playing with me, if she knew how to play Andy-I-Over. She said "Naw." It turned out that she did not know how to play any games at all; she couldn't do anything and didn't want to do anything; her only recreation and her only gift was, and always had been, stealing. But this I did not know at the time.

As it happened, it was too cold and snowy to play outdoors that day anyhow, and after I had run through my list of indoor games and Lottie had shaken her head at all of them (when I spoke of Parcheesi, she went, "Ugh!" and pretended to be sick), she suggested that we look through my mother's bureau drawers. This did not strike me as strange at all, for it was one of my favorite things to do, and I led the way to Mother's bedroom without a moment's hesitation. I loved the smell of the lavender she kept in gauze bags among her chamois gloves and linen handkerchiefs and filmy scarves; there was a pink fascinator knitted of something as fine as spider's thread, and it made me go quite soft—I wasn't soft as a rule, I was as hard as nails and I gave my mother a rough time—to think of her wearing it around her head as she waltzed on the ice in the by-gone days. We examined stockings, nightgowns, camisoles, strings of beads, and mosaic pins, keepsake buttons from dresses worn on memorial occasions, tortoiseshell combs, and a transformation made from Aunt Joey's hair when she had racily had it bobbed. Lottie admired particularly a blue cloisonné perfume flask with ferns and peacocks on it. "Hey," she said, "this sure is cute. I like thing-daddies like this here." But very abruptly she got bored and said, "Let's talk instead. In the front room." I agreed, a little perplexed this time, because I had been about to show her a remarkable powder box that played *The Blue Danube.* We went into the parlor, where Lottie looked at her image in the pier glass for quite a while and with great absorption, as if she had never seen herself before. Then she moved over to the window seat and knelt on it, looking out at the front walk. She kept her hands in the pockets of her thin dark-red coat; once she took out one of her dirty paws to rub her nose for a minute and I saw a bulge in that pocket, like a bunch of jackstones. I know now that it wasn't jackstones, it was my mother's perfume flask; I thought at the time her hands were cold and that was why she kept them put away, for I had noticed that she had no mittens.

Lottie did most of the talking, and while she talked, she never once looked at me but kept her eyes fixed on the approach to our house. She told me that her family had come to Adams a month before from Muskogee, Oklahoma, where her father, before he got tuberculosis, had been a brakeman on the Frisco. Now they lived down by Arapahoe Creek, on the west side of town, in one of the cottages of a wretched settlement made up of people so poor and so sick—for in nearly every ramshackle house someone was coughing himself to death—that each time I went past I blushed with guilt because my shoes were sound and my coat was warm and I was well. I wished that Lottie had not told me where she lived, but she was not aware of any pathos in her family's situation, and, indeed, it was with a certain boastfulness that she told me her mother was the short-order cook at the Comanche Café (she pronounced this word in one syllable), which I knew was the dirtiest, darkest, smelliest place in town, patronized by coal miners who never washed their faces and sometimes had such dangerous fights after drinking dago red that the sheriff had to come. Laughing, Lottie told me that her mother was half Indian, and, laughing even harder, she said that her brother didn't have any brains and had never been to school. She herself was eleven years old, but she was only in the third grade, because teachers had always had it in for her—making her go to the blackboard and all like that when she was tired. She hated school—she went to Ashton, on North Hill, and that was why I had never seen her, for I went to Carlyle Hill—and she especially hated the teacher, Miss Cudahy, who had a head shaped like a pine cone and who had killed several people with her ruler.

Lottie loved the movies ("Not them Western ones or the ones with apes in," she said. "Ones about hugging and kissing. I love it when they die in that big old soft bed with the curtains up top, and he comes in and says, 'Don't leave me, Marguerite de la Mar'"), and she loved to ride in cars. She loved Mr. Goodbars, and if there was one thing she despised worse than another it was tapioca. ("Pa calls it fish eyes. He calls floating island horse spit. He's a big piece of cheese. I hate him.") She did not like cats (Muff was now sitting on the mantelpiece, glaring like an owl); she kind of liked snakes—except cottonmouths and rattlers—because she found them kind of funny; she had once seen a goat eat a tin can. She said that one of these days she would take me downtown—it was a slowpoke town, she said, a one-horse burg (I had never heard such gaudy, cynical talk and was trying to memorize it all)—if I would get some money for the trolley fare; she hated to walk, and I ought to be proud that she had walked all the way from Arapahoe Creek today for the sole solitary purpose of seeing me.

Seeing our freshly baked dessert in the window was a more likely story, but I did not care, for I was deeply impressed by this bold, sassy girl from Oklahoma and greatly admired the poise with which she aired her prejudices. Lottie Jump was certainly nothing to look at. She was tall and made of skin and bones; she was evilly ugly, and her clothes were a disgrace, not just ill-fitting and old and ragged but dirty, unmentionably so; clearly she did not wash much or brush her teeth, which were notched like a saw, and small and brown (it crossed my mind that perhaps she chewed tobacco); her long, lank hair looked as if it might have nits. But she had personality. She made me think of one of those self-contained dogs whose home is where his handout is and who travels alone but, if it suits him to, will become the leader of a pack. She was aloof, never looking at me, but amiable in the way she kept calling me "kid." I liked her enormously, and presently I told her so.

At this, she turned around and smiled at me. Her smile was the smile of a jack-o'-lantern—high, wide, and handsome. When it was over, no trace of it remained. "Well, that's keen, kid, and I like you, too," she said in her downright Muskogee accent. She gave me a long, appraising look. Her eyes were the color of mud. "Listen, kid, how much do you like me?"

"I like you loads, Lottie," I said. "Better than anybody else, and I'm not kidding."

"You want to be pals?"

"Do I?" I cried. So *there*, Virgil Meade, you big fat hootnanny, I thought.

"All right, kid, we'll be pals." And she held out her hand for me to shake. I had to go and get it, for she did not alter her position on the window seat. It was a dry, cold hand, and the grip was severe, with more a feeling of bones in it than friendliness.

Lottie turned and scanned our path and scanned the sidewalk beyond, and then she said, in a lower voice, "Do you know how to lift?"

"Lift?" I wondered if she meant to lift *her*. I was sure I could do it, since she was so skinny, but I couldn't imagine why she would want me to.

"Shoplift, I mean. Like in the five-and-dime."

"*Steal*, for crying in the beer!" she said impatiently. This she said so loudly that Muff jumped down from the mantel and left the room in contempt.

I was thrilled to death and shocked to pieces. "Stealing is a sin," I said. "You get put in jail for it."

"Ish ka bibble! I should worry if it's a sin or not," said Lottie, with a shrug. "And they'll never put a smart old whatsis like *me* in jail. It's fun, stealing is—it's a picnic. I'll teach you if you want to learn, kid." Shamelessly she winked at me and grinned again. (That grin! She could have taken it off her face and put it on the table.) And she added, "If you don't, we can't be pals, because lifting is the only kind of playing I like. I hate those dumb games like Statues. Kick-the-Can—phooey!"

I was torn between agitation (I went to Sunday school and knew already about morality; Judge Bay, a crabby old man who loved to punish sinners, was a friend of my father's and once had given Jack a lecture on the criminal mind when he came to call and found Jack looking up an answer in his arithmetic book) and excitement over the daring invitation to misconduct myself in so perilous a way. My life, on reflection, looked deadly prim; all I'd ever done to vary the monotony of it was to swear. I knew that Lottie Jump meant what she said—that I could have her friendship only on her terms (plainly, she had gone it alone for a long time and could go it alone for the rest of her life)—and although I trembled like an aspen and my heart went pitapat, I said, "I want to be pals with you, Lottie."

"All right, Vanderpool," said Lottie, and got off the window seat. "I wouldn't go braggin' about it if I was you. I wouldn't go telling my ma and pa and the next door neighbor that you and Lottie Jump are going down to the five-and-dime next Saturday aft and lift us some nice rings and garters and things like that. I mean it, kid." And she drew the back of her forefinger across her throat and made a dire face.

"I won't. I promise I won't. My *gosh*, why would I?"

"That's the ticket," said Lottie, with a grin. "I'll meet you at the trolley shelter at two o'clock. You have the money. For both down and up. I ain't going to climb up that ornery hill after I've had my fun."

"Yes, Lottie," I said. Where was I going to get twenty cents? I was going to have to start stealing before she even taught me how. Lottie was facing the center of the room, but she had eyes in the back of her head, and she whirled around back to the window; my mother and Tess were turning in our front path.

"Back way," I whispered, and in a moment Lottie was gone; the swinging door that usually squeaked did not make a sound as she vanished through it. I listened and I never heard the back door open and close. Nor did I hear her, in a split second, lift the glass cover and remove that cake designed to feed six people.

I was restless and snappish between Wednesday afternoon and Saturday. When Mother found the cake was gone, she scolded me for not keeping my ears cocked. She assumed, naturally, that a tramp had taken it, for she knew I hadn't eaten it; I never ate anything if I could help it (except for raw potatoes, which I loved) and had been known as a problem feeder from the beginning of my life. At first it occurred to me to have a tantrum and bring her around to my point of view: my tantrums scared the living daylights out of her because my veins stood out and I turned blue and couldn't get my breath. But I rejected this for a more sensible plan. I said, "It just so happens I didn't hear anything. But if I had, I suppose you wish I had gone out in the kitchen and let the robber cut me up into a million little tiny pieces with his sword. You wouldn't even bury me. You'd just put me on the dump. *I* know who's wanted in this family and who isn't." Tears of sorrow, not anger, came in powerful tides and I groped blindly to the bedroom I shared with Stella, where I lay on my bed and shook with big, silent *weltschmerzlich* sobs. Mother followed me immediately, and so did Tess, and both of them comforted me and told me how much they loved me. I said they didn't; they said they did. Presently, I got a headache, as I always did when I cried, so I got to have an aspirin and a cold cloth on my head, and when Jack and Stella came home, they had to be quiet. I heard Jack say, "Emily Vanderpool is the biggest polecat in the U.S.A. Whyn't she go in the kitchen and say, 'Hands up'? He would lit out." And Mother said, "Sh-h-h! You don't want your sister to be sick, do you?" Muff, not realizing that Lottie had replaced her, came in and curled up at my thigh, purring lustily; I found myself glad that she had left the room before Lottie Jump made her proposition to me, and in gratitude I stroked her unattractive head.

Other things happened. Mother discovered the loss of her perfume flask and talked about nothing else at meals for two whole days. Luckily, it did not occur to her that it had been stolen—she simply thought she had mislaid it—but her monomania got on my father's nerves and he lashed out at her and at the rest of us. And because I was the cause of it all and my conscience was after me with red-hot pokers, I finally *had* to have a tantrum. I slammed my fork down in the middle of supper on the second day and yelled, "If you don't stop fighting, I'm going to kill myself. Yammer, yammer, nag, nag!" And I put my fingers in my ears and squeezed my eyes tight shut and screamed so the whole country could hear, "Shut *up!*" And then I lost my breath and began to turn blue. Daddy hastily apologized to everyone, and Mother said she was sorry for carrying on so about a trinket that had nothing but sentimental value—she was just vexed with herself for being careless, that was all, and she wasn't going to say another word about it.

I never heard so many references to stealing and cake, and even to Oklahoma (ordinarily no one mentioned Oklahoma once in a month of Sundays) and the ten-cent store as I did throughout those next days. I myself once made a ghastly slip and said something to Stella about "the five-and-dime." "The five-and-*dime!*" she exclaimed. "Where'd you get *that* kind of talk? Do you by any chance have reference to the *ten-cent store?*"

The worst of all was Friday night—the very night before I was to meet Lottie Jump—when Judge Bay came to play two-handed pinochle with Daddy. The Judge, a giant in intimidating haberdashery—for some reason, the white piping on his vest bespoke, for me, handcuffs and prison bars—and with an aura of disapproval for almost everything on earth except what pertained directly to himself, was telling Daddy, before they began their game, about the infamous vandalism that had been going on among the college students. "I have reason to believe that there are girls in this gang as well as boys," he said. "They ransack vacant houses and take everything. In one house on Pleasant Street, up there by the Catholic Church, there wasn't anything to take, so they took the kitchen sink. Wasn't a question of taking everything *but*—they took the kitchen sink."

"What ever would they want with a kitchen sink?" asked my mother.

"Mischief," replied the Judge. "If we ever catch them and if they come within my jurisdiction, I can tell you I will give them no quarter. A thief, in my opinion, is the lowest of the low."

Mother told about the chocolate cake. By now, the fiction was so factual in my mind that each time I thought of it I saw a funny-paper bum in baggy pants held up by rope, a hat with holes through which tufts of hair stuck up, shoes from which his toes protruded, a disreputable stubble on his face; he came up beneath the open window where the devil's food was cooling and he stole it and hotfooted it for the woods, where his companion was frying a small fish in a beat-up skillet. It never crossed my mind any longer that Lottie Jump had hooked that delicious cake.

Judge Bay was properly impressed. "If you will steal a chocolate cake, if you will steal a kitchen sink, you will steal diamonds and money. The small child who pilfers a penny from his mother's pocketbook has started down a path that may lead him to holding up a bank."

It was a good thing I had no homework that night, for I could not possibly have concentrated. We were all sent to our rooms, because the pinochle players had to have absolute quiet. I spent the evening doing cross-stitch. I was making a bureau runner for a Christmas present; as in the case of the Christmas card, I had no one to give it to, but now I decided to give it to Lottie Jump's mother. Stella was reading *Black Beauty*, crying. It was an interminable evening. Stella went to bed first; I saw to that, because I didn't want her lying there awake listening to me talking in my sleep. Besides, I didn't want her to see me tearing open the cardboard box—the one in the shape of a church, which held my Christmas Sunday-school offering. Over the door of the church was this shaming legend: "My mite for the poor widow." When Stella had begun to grind her teeth in her first deep sleep, I took twenty cents away from the poor widow, whoever she was (the owner of the kitchen sink, no doubt), for the trolley fare, and secreted it and the remaining three pennies in the pocket of my middy. I wrapped the money well in a handkerchief and buttoned the pocket and hung my skirt over the middy. And then I tore the paper church into bits—the heavens opened and Judge Bay came toward me with a double-barrelled shotgun—and hid the bits under a pile of pajamas. I did not sleep one wink. Except that I must have, because of the stupendous nightmares that kept wrenching the flesh off my skeleton and caused me to come close to perishing of thirst; once I fell out of bed and hit my head on Stella's ice skates. I would have waked her up and given her a piece of my mind for leaving them in such a lousy place, but then I remembered: I wanted *no* commotion of any kind.

I couldn't eat breakfast and I couldn't eat lunch. Old Johnny-on-the-spot Jack kept saying, "*Poor* Polecat. Polecat wants her fish for dinner." Mother made an abortive attempt to take my temperature. And when all that hullabaloo subsided, I was nearly in the soup because Mother asked me to mind Tess while she went to the sanitarium to see Mrs. Rogers, who, all of a sudden, was too sick to have anyone but grownups near her. Stella couldn't stay with the baby, because she had to go to ballet, and Jack couldn't, because he had to go up to the mesa and empty his traps. ("No, they *can't* wait. You want my skins to rot in this hot-one-day-cold-the-next weather?") I was arguing and whining when the telephone rang. Mother went to answer it and came back with a look of great sadness; Mrs. Rogers, she had learned, had had another hemorrhage. So Mother would not be going to the sanitarium after all and I needn't stay with Tess.

By the time I left the house, I was as cross as a bear. I felt awful about the widow's mite and I felt awful for being mean about staying with Tess, for Mrs. Rogers was a kind old lady, in a cozy blue hug-me-tight and an old-fangled boudoir cap, dying here all alone; she was a friend of Grandma's and had lived just down the street from her in Missouri, and all in the world Mrs. Rogers wanted to do was go back home and lie down in her own big bedroom in her own big, high-ceilinged house and have Grandma and other members of the Eastern Star come in from time to time to say hello. But they wouldn't let her go home; they were going to kill or cure her. I could not help feeling that my hardness of heart and evil of intention had had a good deal to do with her new crisis; right at the very same minute I had been saying "Does that old Mrs. Methuselah *always* have to spoil my fun?" the poor wasted thing was probably coughing up her blood and saying to the nurse, "Tell Emily Vanderpool not to mind me, she can run and play."

I had a bad character. I know that, but my badness never gave me half the enjoyment Jack and Stella thought it did. A good deal of the time I wanted to eat lye. I was certainly having no fun now, thinking of Mrs. Rogers and of depriving that poor widow of bread and milk; what if this penniless woman without a husband had a dog to feed, too? Or a baby? And besides, I didn't want to go downtown to steal anything from the ten-cent store; I didn't want to see Lottie Jump again—not really, for I knew in my bones that that girl was trouble with a capital "T." And still, in our short meeting she had mesmerized me; I would think about her style of talking and the expert way she had made off with the perfume flask and the cake (how had she carried the cake through the streets without being noticed?) and be bowled over, for the part of me that did not love God was a black-hearted villain. And apart from these considerations, I had some sort of idea that if I did not keep my appointment with Lottie Jump, she would somehow get revenge; she had seemed a girl of purpose. So, revolted and fascinated, brave and lily-livered, I plodded along through the snow in my flopping galoshes up toward the Chautauqua, where the trolley stop was. On my way, I passed Virgil Meade's house; there was not just a snowman, there was a whole snow family in the back yard, and Virgil himself was throwing a stick for his dog. I was delighted to see that he was alone.

Lottie, who was sitting on a bench in the shelter eating a Mr. Goodbar, looked the same as she had the other time except that she was wearing an amazing hat. I think I had expected her to have a black handkerchief over the lower part of her face or to be wearing a Jesse James waistcoat. But I had never thought of a hat. It was felt; it was the color of cooked meat; it had some flowers appliquéd on the front of it; it had no brim, but rose straight up to a very considerable height, like a monument. It sat so low on her forehead and it was so tight that it looked, in a way, like part of her.

"How's every little thing, bub?" she said, licking her candy wrapper.

"Fine, Lottie," I said, freshly awed.

A silence fell. I drank some water from the drinking fountain, sat down, fastened my galoshes, and unfastened them again.

"My mother's teeth grow wrong way too," said Lottie, and showed me what she meant: the lower teeth were in front of the upper ones. "That so-called trolley car takes its own sweet time. This town is blah."

To save the honor of my home town, the trolley came scraping and groaning up the hill just then, its bell clanging with an idiotic frenzy, and ground to a stop, Its broad, proud cowcatcher was filled with dirty snow, in the middle of which rested a tomato can, put there, probably, by somebody who was bored to death and couldn't think of anything else to do—I did a lot of pointless things like that on lonesome Saturday afternoons. It was the custom of this trolley car, a rather mysterious one, to pause at the shelter for five minutes while the conductor, who was either Mr. Jansen or Mr. Peck, depending on whether it was the A.M. run or the P.M., got out and stretched and smoked and spit. Sometimes the passengers got out, too, acting like sightseers whose destination was this sturdy stucco gazebo instead of, as it really was, the Piggly Wiggly or the Nelson Dry. You expected them to take snapshots of the drinking fountain or of the Chautauqua meeting house up on the hill. And when they all got back in the car, you expected them to exchange intelligent observations on the aborigines and the ruins they had seen.

Today there were no passengers, and as soon as Mr. Peck got out and began staring at the mountains as if he had never seen them before while he made himself a cigarette, Lottie, in her tall hat (was it something like the Inspector's hat in the Katzenjammer Kids?), got into the car, motioning me to follow. I put our nickels in the empty box and joined her on the very last double seat. It was only then that she mapped out the plan for the afternoon, in a low but still insouciant voice. The hat—she did not apologize for it, she simply referred to it as "my hat"—was to be the repository of whatever we stole. In the future, it would be advisable for me to have one like it. (How? Surely it was unique. The flowers, I saw on closer examination, were tulips, but they were blue, and a very unsettling shade of blue.) I was to engage a clerk on one side of the counter, asking her the price of, let's say, a tube of Daggett & Ramsdell vanishing cream, while Lottie would lift a round comb or a barrette or a hair net or whatever on the other side. Then, at a signal, I would decide against the vanishing cream and would move on to the next counter that she indicated. The signal was interesting; it was to be the raising of her hat from the rear—"like I've got the itch and gotta scratch," she said. I was relieved that I was to have no part in the actual stealing, and I was touched that Lottie, who was going to do all the work, said we would "go halvers" on the take. She asked me if there was anything in particular I wanted—she herself had nothing special in mind and was going to shop around first—and I said I would like some rubber gloves. This request was entirely spontaneous; I had never before in my life thought of rubber gloves in one way or another, but a psychologist—or Judge Bay—might have said that this was most significant and that I was planning at that moment to go on from petty larceny to bigger game, armed with a weapon on which I wished to leave no fingerprints.

On the way downtown, quite a few people got on the trolley, and they all gave us such peculiar looks that I was chickenhearted until I realized it must be Lottie's hat they were looking at. No wonder. I kept looking at it myself out of the corner of my eye; it was like a watermelon standing on end. No, it was like a tremendous test tube. On this trip—a slow one, for the trolley pottered through that part of town in a desultory, neighborly way, even going into areas where no one lived—Lottie told me some of the things she had stolen in Muskogee and here in Adams. They included a white satin prayer book (think of it!), Mr. Goodbars by the thousands (she had probably never paid for a Mr. Goodbar in her life), a dinner ring valued at two dollars, a strawberry emery, several cans of corn, some shoelaces, a set of poker chips, countless pencils, four spark plugs ("Pa had this old car, see, and it was broke, so we took 'er to get fixed; I'll build me a radio with 'em sometime—you know? Listen in on them ear muffs to Tulsa?"), a Boy Scout knife, and a Girl Scout folding cup. She made a regular practice of going through the pockets of the coats in the cloakroom every day at recess, but she had never found anything there worth a red cent and was about to give that up. Once, she had taken a gold pencil from a teacher's desk and had got caught— she was sure that this was one of the reasons she was only in the third grade. Of this unjust experience, she said, "The old hoot owl! If I was drivin' in a car on a lonesome stretch and she was settin' beside me, I'd wait till we got to a pile of gravel and then I'd stop and say, 'Git out, Miss Priss.' She'd git out, all right."

Since Lottie was so frank, I was emboldened at last to ask her what she had done with the cake. She faced me with her grin; this grin, in combination with the hat, gave me a surprise from which I have never recovered. "I ate it up," she said. "I went in your garage and sat on your daddy's old tires and ate it. It was pretty good."

There were two ten-cent stores side by side in our town, Kresge's and Woolworth's, and as we walked down the main street toward them, Lottie played with a Yo-Yo. Since the street was thronged with Christmas shoppers and farmers in for Saturday, this was no ordinary accomplishment; all in all, Lottie Jump was someone to be reckoned with. I cannot say that I was proud to be seen with her; the fact is that I hoped I would not meet anyone I knew, and I thanked my lucky stars that Jack was up in the hills with his dead skunks because if he had seen her with that lid and that Yo-Yo, I would never have heard the last of it. But in another way I *was* proud to be with her; in a smaller hemisphere, in one that included only her and me, I was swaggering—I felt like Somebody, marching along beside this lofty Somebody from Oklahoma who was going to hold up the dime store.

There is nothing like Woolworth's at Christmastime. It smells of peanut brittle and terrible chocolate candy, Djer-Kiss talcum powder and Ben Hur Perfume—smells sourly of tinsel and waxily of artificial poinsettias. The crowds are made up largely of children and women, with here and there a deliberative old man; the women are buying ribbons and wrappings and Christmas cards, and the children are buying asbestos pot holders for their mothers and, for their fathers, suède bookmarks with a burnt-in design that says "A good book is a good friend" or "Souvenir from the Garden of the Gods." It is very noisy. The salesgirls are forever ringing their bells and asking the floorwalker to bring them change for a five; babies in go-carts are screaming as parcels fall on their heads; the women, waving rolls of red tissue paper, try to attract the attention of the harried girl behind the counter. ("Miss! All I want is this one batch of the red. Can't I just give you the dime?" And the girl, beside herself, mottled with vexation, cries back, "Has to be rung up, Moddom, that's the rule.") There is pandemonium at the toy counter, where things are being tested by the customers—wound up, set off, tooted, pounded, made to say "Maaaah-Maaaah!" There is very little gaiety in the scene and, in fact, those baffled old men look as if they were walking over their own dead bodies, but there is an atmosphere of carnival, nevertheless, and as soon as Lottie and I entered the doors of Woolworth's golden-and-vermilion bedlam, I grew giddy and hot—not pleasantly so. The feeling, indeed, was distinctly disagreeable, like the beginning of a stomach upset.

Lottie gave me a nudge and said softly, "Go look at the envelopes. I want some rubber bands."

This counter was relatively uncrowded (the seasonal stationery supplies—the Christmas cards and wrapping paper and stickers—were at a separate counter), and I went around to examine some very beautiful letter paper; it was pale pink and it had a border of roses all around it. The clerk here was a cheerful middle-aged woman wearing an apron, and she was giving all her attention to a seedy old man who could not make up his mind between mucilage and paste. "Take your time, Dad," she said. "Compared to the rest of the girls, I'm on my vacation." The old man, holding a tube in one hand and a bottle in the other, looked at her vaguely and said, "I want it for stamps. Sometimes I write a letter and stamp it and then don't mail it and steam the stamp off. Must have ninety cents' worth of stamps like that." The woman laughed. "I know what you mean," she said. "I get mad and write a letter and then I tear it up."

The old man gave her a condescending look and said, "That so? But I don't suppose yours are of a political nature." He bent his gaze again to the choice of adhesives.

This first undertaking was duck soup for Lottie. I did not even have to exchange a word with the woman; I saw Miss Fagin lift up *that hat* and give me the high sign, and we moved away, she down one aisle and I down the other, now and again catching a glimpse of each other through the throngs. We met at the foot of the second counter, where notions were sold.

"Fun, huh?" said Lottie, and I nodded, although I felt wholly dreary. "I want some crochet hooks," she said. "Price the rickrack."

This time the clerk was adding up her receipts and did not even look at me or at a woman who was angrily and in vain trying to buy a paper of pins. Out went Lottie's scrawny hand, up went her domed chimney. In this way for some time she bagged sitting birds: a tea strainer (there was no one at all at that counter), a box of Mrs. Carpenter's All Purpose Nails, the rubber gloves I had said I wanted, and four packages of mixed seeds. Now you have some idea of the size of Lottie Jump's hat.

I was nervous, not from being her accomplice but from being in this crowd on an empty stomach, and I was getting tired—we had been in the store for at least an hour—and the whole enterprise seemed pointless. There wasn't a thing in her hat I wanted—not even the rubber gloves. But in exact proportion as my spirits descended, Lottie's rose; clearly she had only been target-practicing and now she was moving in for the kill.

We met beside the books of paper dolls, for reconnaissance, "I'm gonna get me a pair of pearl beads," said Lottie. "You go fuss with the hairpins, hear?"

Luck, combined with her skill, would have stayed with Lottie, and her hat would have been a cornucopia by the end of the afternoon if, at the very moment her hand went out for the string of beads, that idiosyncrasy of mine had not struck me full force. I had never known it to come with so few preliminaries; probably this was so because I was oppressed by all the masses of bodies poking and pushing me, and all the open mouths breathing in my face. Anyhow, right then, at the crucial time, I *had to be alone*.

I stood staring down at the bone hairpins for a moment, and when the girl behind the counter said, "What kind does Mother want, hon? What color is Mother's hair?" I looked past her and across at Lottie and I said, "Your brother isn't the only one in your family that doesn't have any brains." The clerk, astonished, turn to look where I was looking and caught Lottie in the act of lifting up her hat to put the pearls inside. She had unwisely chosen a long strand and was having a little trouble; I had the nasty thought that it looked as if her brains were leaking out.

The clerk, not able to deal with this emergency herself, frantically punched her bell and cried, "Floorwalker! Mr. Bellamy! I've caught a thief!"

Momentarily there was a violent hush—then such a clamor as you have never heard. Bells rang, babies howled, crockery crashed to the floor as people stumbled in their rush to the arena.

Mr. Bellamy, nineteen years old but broad of shoulder and jaw, was instantly standing beside Lottie, holding her arm with one hand while with the other he removed her hat to reveal to the overjoyed audience that incredible array of merchandise. Her hair all wild, her face a mask of innocent bewilderment, Lottie Jump, the scurvy thing, pretended to be deaf and dumb. She pointed at the rubber gloves and then she pointed at me, and Mr. Bellamy, able at last to prove his mettle, said "Aha!" and, still holding

Lottie, moved around the counter to me and grabbed *my* arm. He gave the hat to the clerk and asked her kindly to accompany him and his redhanded catch to the manager's office.

I don't know where Lottie is now—whether she is on the stage or in jail. If her performance after our arrest meant anything, the first is quite as likely as the second. (I never saw her again, and for all I know she lit out of town that night on a freight train. Or perhaps her whole family decamped as suddenly as they had arrived; ours was a most transient population. You can be sure I made no attempt to find her again, and for months I avoided going anywhere near Arapahoe Creek or North Hill.) She never said a word but kept making signs with her fingers, adlibbing the whole thing. They tested her hearing by shooting off a popgun right in her ear and she never batted an eyelid.

They called up my father, and he came over from the Safeway on the double. I heard very little of what he said because I was crying so hard, but one thing I did hear him say was "Well young lady, I guess you've seen to it that I'll have to part company with my good friend Judge Bay." I tried to defend myself, but it was useless. The manager, Mr. Bellamy, the clerk, and my father patted Lottie on the shoulder, and the clerk said, "Poor, afflicted child." For being a poor, afflicted child, they gave her a bag of hard candy, and she gave them the most fraudulent smile of gratitude, and slobbered a little, and shuffled out, holding her empty hat in front of her like a beggar-man. I hate Lottie Jump to this day, but I have to hand it to her—she was a genius.

The floorwalker would have liked to see me sentenced to the reform school for life, I am sure, but the manager said that considering this was my first offense, he would let my father attend to my punishment. The old-mail clerk, who looked precisely like Emmy Schmalz, clucked her tongue and shook her head at me. My father hustled me out of the office and out of the store and into the car and home, muttering the entire time; now and again I'd hear the words "morals" and "nowadays."

What's the use of telling the rest? You know what happened. Daddy on second thoughts decided not to hang his head in front of Judge Bay but to make use of his friendship in this time of need, and he took me to see the scary old curmudgeon at his house. All I remember of that long declamation, during which the Judge sat behind his desk never taking his eyes off me, was the warning "I want you to give this a great deal of thought, Miss. I want you to search and seek in the innermost corners of your conscience and root out every bit of badness." Oh, *him!* Why, listen, if I'd rooted out all the badness in me, there wouldn't have been anything left of me. My mother cried for days because she had nurtured an outlaw and was ashamed to show her face at the neighborhood store; my father was silent, and he often looked at me. Stella, who was a prig, said, "And to think you did it at *Christmas* time!" As for Jack—well, Jack a couple of times did not know how close he came to seeing glory when I had a butcher knife in my hand. It was Polecat this and Polecat that until I nearly went off my rocker. Tess, of course, didn't know what was going on, and asked so many questions that finally I told her to go to Helen Hunt Jackson in a savage tone of voice.

Good old Muff.

It is not true that you don't learn by experience. At any rate, I did that time. I began immediately to have two or three friends at a time—to be sure, because of the stigma on me, they were by no means the élite of Carlyle Hill Grade—and never again when that terrible need to be alone arose did I let fly. I would say, instead, "I've got a headache. I'll have to go home and take an aspirin," or "Gosh all hemlocks, I forgot—I've got to go to the dentist."

After the scandal died down, I got into the Campfire Girls. It was through pull, of course, since Stella had been a respected member for two years and my mother was a friend of the leader. But it turned out all right. Even Muff did not miss our periods of companionship, because about that time she grew up and started having literally millions of kittens.

GABRIEL GARCIA MARQUEZ
[b. 1928]

A Very Old Man with Enormous Wings

A TALE FOR CHILDREN

TRANSLATED BY GREGORY RABASSA

On the third day of rain they had killed so many crabs inside the house that Pelayo had to cross his drenched courtyard and throw them into the sea, because the newborn child had a temperature all night and they thought it was due to the stench. The world had been sad since Tuesday. Sea and sky were a single ash-gray thing and the sands of the beach, which on March nights glimmered like powdered light, had become a stew of mud and rotten shellfish. The light was so weak at noon that when Pelayo was coming back to the house after throwing away the crabs, it was hard for him to see what it was that was moving and groaning in the rear of the courtyard. He had to go very close to see that it was an old man, a very old man, lying face down in the mud, who, in spite of his tremendous efforts, couldn't get up, impeded by his enormous wings.

Frightened by that nightmare, Pelayo ran to get Elisenda, his wife, who was putting compresses on the sick child, and he took her to the rear of the courtyard. They both looked at the fallen body with mute stupor. He was dressed like a ragpicker. There were only a few faded hairs left on his bald skull and very few teeth in his mouth, and his pitiful condition of a drenched great-grandfather had taken away any sense of grandeur he might have had. His huge buzzard wings, dirty and half-plucked, were forever entangled in the mud. They looked at him so long and so closely that Pelayo and Elisenda very soon overcame their surprise and in the end found him familiar. Then they dared speak to him, and he answered in an incomprehensible dialect with a strong sailor's voice. That was how they skipped over the inconvenience of the wings and quite intelligently concluded that he was a lonely castaway from some foreign ship wrecked by the storm. And yet, they called in a neighbor woman who knew everything about life and death to see him, and all she needed was one look to show them their mistake.

"He's an angel," she told them. "He must have been coming for the child, but the poor fellow is so old that the rain knocked him down."

On the following day everyone knew that a flesh-and-blood angel was held captive in Pelayo's house. Against the judgment of the wise neighbor woman, for whom angels in those times were the fugitive survivors of a celestial conspiracy, they did not have the heart to club him to death. Pelayo watched over him all afternoon from the kitchen, armed with his bailiff's club, and before going to bed he dragged him out of the mud and locked him up with the hens in the wire chicken coop. In the middle of the night, when the rain stopped, Pelayo and Elisenda were still killing crabs. A short time afterward the child woke up without a fever and with a desire to eat. Then they felt magnanimous and decided to put the angel on a raft with fresh water and provisions for three days and leave him to his fate on the high seas. But when they went out into the courtyard with the first light of dawn, they found the whole neighborhood in front of the chicken coop having fun with the angel, without the slightest reverence, tossing him things to eat through the openings in the wire as if he weren't a supernatural creature but a circus animal.

Father Gonzaga arrived before seven o'clock, alarmed at the strange news. By that time onlookers less frivolous than those at dawn had already arrived and they were making all kinds of conjectures concerning the captive's future. The simplest among them thought that he should be named mayor of the world. Others of sterner mind felt that he should be promoted to the rank of five-star general in order to win all wars. Some visionaries hoped that he could be put to stud in order to implant on earth a race of winged wise men who could take charge of the universe. But Father Gonzaga, before becoming a priest, had been a robust woodcutter. Standing by the wire, he reviewed his catechism in an instant and asked them to open the door so that he could take a close look at that pitiful man who looked more like a huge decrepit hen among the fascinated chickens. He was lying in a corner drying his open wings in the sunlight among the fruit peels and breakfast leftovers that the early risers had thrown him. Alien to the impertinences of the world, he only lifted his antiquarian eyes and murmured something in his dialect when Father Gonzaga went into the chicken coop and said good morning to him in Latin. The parish priest had his first suspicion of an imposter when he saw that he did not understand the language of God or know how to greet His ministers. Then he noticed that seen close up he was much too human: he had an unbearable smell of the outdoors, the back side of his wings was strewn with parasites and his main feathers had been mistreated by terrestrial winds, and nothing about him measured up to the proud dignity of angels. Then he came out of the chicken coop and in a brief sermon warned the curious against the risks of being ingenuous. He reminded them that the devil had the bad habit of making use of carnival tricks in order to confuse the unwary. He argued that if wings were not the essential element in determining the difference between a hawk and an airplane, they were even less so in the recognition of angels. Nevertheless, he promised to write a letter to his bishop so that the latter would write to his primate so that the latter would write to the Supreme Pontiff in order to get the final verdict from the highest courts.

His prudence fell on sterile hearts. The news of the captive angel spread with such rapidity that after a few hours the courtyard had the bustle of a marketplace and they had to call in troops with fixed bayonets to disperse the mob that was about to knock the house down. Elisenda, her spine all twisted from sweeping up so much marketplace trash, then got the idea of fencing in the yard and charging five cents admission to see the angel.

The curious came from far away. A traveling carnival arrived with a flying acrobat who buzzed over the crowd several times, but no one paid any attention to him because his wings were not those of an angel but, rather, those of a sidereal bat. The most unfortunate invalids on earth came in search of health: a poor woman who since childhood had been counting her heartbeats and had run out of numbers; a Portuguese man who couldn't sleep because the noise of the stars disturbed him; a sleepwalker who got up at night to undo the things he had done while awake; and many others with less serious ailments. In the midst of that shipwreck disorder that made the earth tremble, Pelayo and Elisenda were happy with fatigue, for in less than a week they had crammed their rooms with money and the line of pilgrims waiting their turn to enter still reached beyond the horizon.

The angel was the only one who took no part in his own act. He spent his time trying to get comfortable in his borrowed nest, befuddled by the hellish heat of the oil lamps and sacramental candles that had been placed along the wire. At first they tried to make him eat some mothballs, which, according to the wisdom of the wise neighbor woman, were the food prescribed for angels. But he turned them down, just as he turned down the papal lunches that the penitents brought him, and they never found out whether it was because he was an angel or because he was an old man that in the end he ate nothing but eggplant mush. His only supernatural virtue seemed to be patience. Especially during the first days, when the hens pecked at him, searching for the stellar parasites that proliferated in his wings, and the cripples pulled out feathers to touch their defective parts with, and even the most merciful threw stones at him, trying to get him to rise so they could see him standing. The only time they succeeded in arousing him was when they burned his side with an iron for branding steers, for he had been motionless for so many hours that they thought he was dead. He awoke with a start, ranting in his hermetic language and with tears in his eyes, and he flapped his wings a couple of times, which brought on a whirlwind of chicken dung and lunar dust and a gale of panic that did not seem to be of this world. Although many thought that his reaction had been one not of rage but of pain, from then on they were careful not to annoy him, because the majority understood that his passivity was not that of a hero taking his ease but that of a cataclysm in repose.

Father Gonzaga held back the crowd's frivolity with formulas of maidservant inspiration while awaiting the arrival of a final judgment on the nature of the captive. But the mail from Rome showed no sense of urgency. They spent their time finding out if the prisoner had a navel, if his dialect had any connection with Aramaic, how many times he could fit on the head of a pin, or whether he wasn't just a Norwegian with wings. Those meager letters might have come and gone until the end of time if a providential event had not put an end to the priest's tribulations.

It so happened that during those days, among so many other carnival attractions, there arrived in town the traveling show of the woman who had been changed into a spider for having disobeyed her parents. The admission to see her was not only less than the admission to see the angel, but people were permitted to ask her all manner of questions about her absurd state and to examine her up and down so that no one would ever doubt the truth of her horror. She was a frightful tarantula the size of a ram and with the head of a sad maiden. What was most heart-rending, however, was not her outlandish shape but the sincere affliction with which she recounted the details of her misfortune. While still practically a child she had sneaked out of her parents' house to go to a dance, and while she was coming back through the woods after having danced all night without permission, a fearful thunderclap rent the sky in two and through the crack came the lightning bolt of brimstone that changed her into a spider. Her only nourishment came from the meatballs that charitable souls chose to toss into her mouth. A spectacle like that, full of so much human truth and with such a fearful lesson, was bound to defeat without even trying that of a haughty angel who scarcely deigned to look at mortals. Besides, the few miracles attributed to the angel showed a certain mental disorder, like the blind man who didn't recover his sight but grew three new teeth, or the paralytic who didn't get to walk but almost won the lottery, and the leper whose sores sprouted sunflowers. Those consolation miracles, which were more like mocking fun, had already ruined the angel's reputation when the woman who had been changed into a spider finally crushed him completely. That was how Father Gonzaga was cured forever of his insomnia and Pelayo's courtyard went back to being as empty as during the time it had rained for three days and crabs walked through the bedrooms.

The owners of the house had no reason to lament. With the money they saved they built a two-story mansion with balconies and gardens and high netting so that crabs wouldn't get in during the winter, and with iron bars on the windows so that angels wouldn't get in. Pelayo also set up a rabbit warren close to town and gave up his job as bailiff for good, and Elisenda bought some satin pumps with high heels and many dresses of iridescent silk, the kind worn on Sunday by the most desirable women in those times. The chicken coop was the only thing that didn't receive any attention. If they washed it down with creolin and burned tears of myrrh inside it every so often, it was not in homage to the angel but to drive away the dungheap stench that still hung everywhere like a ghost and was turning the new house into old one. At first, when the child learned to walk, they were careful that he not get too close to the chicken coop. But then they began to lose their fears and got used to the smell, and before the child got his second teeth he'd gone inside the chicken coop to play, where the wires were falling apart. The angel was no less standoffish with him than with other mortals, but he tolerated the most ingenious infamies with the patience of a dog who had no illusions. They both came down with chicken pox at the same time. The doctor who took care of the child couldn't resist the temptation to listen to the angel's heart, and he found so much whistling in the heart and so many sounds in his kidneys that it seemed impossible for him to be alive. What surprised him most, however, was the logic of his wings. They seemed so natural on that completely human organism that he couldn't understand why other men didn't have them too.

When the child began school it had been some time since the sun and rain had caused the collapse of the chicken coop. The angel went dragging himself about here and there like a stray dying man. They would drive him out of the bedroom with a broom and a moment later find him in the kitchen. He seemed to be in so many places at the same time that they grew to think that he'd been duplicated, that he was reproducing himself all through the house, and the exasperated and unhinged Elisenda shouted that it was awful living in that hell full of angels. He could scarcely eat and his antiquarian eyes had also become so foggy that he went about bumping into posts. All he had left were the bare cannulae of his last feathers. Pelayo threw a blanket over him and extended him the charity of letting him sleep in the shed, and only then did they notice that he had a temperature at night, and was delirious with the tongue twisters of an old Norwegian. That was one of the few times they became alarmed, for they thought he was going to die and not even the wise neighbor woman had been able to tell them what to do with dead angels.

And yet he not only survived his worst winter, but seemed improved with the first sunny days. He remained motionless for several days in the farthest corner of the courtyard, where no one would see him, and at the beginning of December some large, stiff feathers began to grow on his wings, the feathers of a scarecrow, which looked more like another misfortune of decrepitude. But he must have known the reason for those changes, for he was quite careful that no one should notice them, that no one should hear the sea chanteys that he sometimes sang under the stars. One morning Elisenda was cutting some bunches of onions for lunch when a wind that seemed to come from the high seas blew into the kitchen. Then she went to the window and caught the angel in his first attempts at flight. They were so clumsy that his fingernails opened a furrow in the vegetable patch and he was on the point of knocking the shed down with the ungainly flapping that slipped on the light and couldn't get a grip on the air. But he did manage to gain altitude. Elisenda let out a sigh of relief, for herself and for him, when she saw him pass over the last houses, holding himself up in some way with the risky flapping of a senile vulture. She kept watching him even when she was through cutting the onions and she kept on watching until it was no longer possible for her to see him, because then he was no longer an annoyance in her life but an imaginary dot on the horizon of the sea.

(1955)

MARGARET ATWOOD

[*b. 1939*]

Rape Fantasies

The way they're going on about it in the magazines you'd think it was just invented, and not only that but it's something terrific, like a vaccine for cancer. They put it in capital letters on the front cover, and inside they have these questionnaires like the ones they used to have about whether you were a good enough wife or an endomorph or an ectomorph, remember that? with the scoring upside down on page 73, and then these numbered do-it-yourself dealies, you know? RAPE, TEN THINGS TO DO ABOUT IT, like it was ten new hairdos or something. I mean, what's so new about it?

So at work they all have to talk about it because no matter what magazine you open, there it is, staring you right between the eyes, and they're beginning to have it on the television, too. Personally I'd prefer a June Allyson movie anytime but they don't make them anymore and they don't even have them that much on the Late Show. For instance, day before yesterday, that would be Wednesday, thank god it's Friday as they say, we were sitting around in the women's lunch room—the *lunch* room, I mean you'd think you could get some peace and quiet in there—and Chrissy closes up the magazine she's been reading and says, "How about it, girls, do you have rape fantasies?"

The four of us were having our game of bridge the way we always do, and I had a bare twelve points counting the singleton with not that much of a bid in anything. So I said one club, hoping Sondra would remember about the one club convention, because the time before when I used that she thought I really meant clubs and she bid us up to three, and all I had was four little ones with nothing higher than a six, and we went down two and on top of that we were vulnerable. She is not the world's best bridge player. I mean, neither am I but there's a limit.

Darlene passed but the damage was done, Sondra's head went round like it was on ball bearings and she said, "*What* fantasies?"

"Rape fantasies," Chrissy said. She's a receptionist and she looks like one; she's pretty but cool as a cucumber, like she's been painted all over with nail polish, if you know what I mean. Varnished. "It says here all women have rape fantasies."

"For Chrissake, I'm eating an egg sandwich," I said, "and I bid one club and Darlene passed."

"You mean, like some guy jumping you in an alley or something," Sondra said. She was eating her lunch, we all eat our lunches during the game, and she bit into a piece of that celery she always brings and started to chew away on it with this thoughtful expression in her eyes and I knew we might as well pack it in as far as the game was concerned.

"Yeah, sort of like that," Chrissy said. She was blushing a little, you could see it even under her makeup.

"I don't think you should go out alone at night," Darlene said, "you put yourself in a position," and I may have been mistaken but she was looking at me. She's the oldest, she's forty-one though you wouldn't know it and neither does she, but I looked it up in the employees' file. I like to guess a person's age and then look it up to see if I'm right. I let myself have an extra pack of cigarettes if I am, though I'm trying to cut down. I figure it's harmless as long as you don't tell. I mean, not everyone has access to that file, it's more or less confidential. But it's all right if I tell you, I don't expect you'll ever meet her, though you never know, it's a small world. Anyway.

"For *heaven's* sake, it's only *Toronto*," Greta said. She worked in Detroit for three years and she never lets you forget it, it's like she thinks she's a war hero or something, we should all admire her just for the fact that she's still walking this earth, though she was really living in Windsor the whole time, she just worked in Detroit. Which for me doesn't really count. It's where you sleep, right?

"Well, do you?" Chrissy said. She was obviously trying to tell us about hers but she wasn't about to go first, she's cautious, that one.

"I certainly don't," Darlene said, and she wrinkled up her nose, like this, and I had to laugh. "I think it's disgusting." She's divorced, I read that in the file too, she never talks about it. It must've been years ago anyway. She got up and went over to the coffee machine and turned her back on us as though she wasn't going to have anything more to do with it.

"Well," Greta said. I could see it was going to be between her and Chrissy. They're both blondes, I don't mean that in a bitchy way but they do try to outdress each other. Greta would like to get out of Filing, she'd like to be a receptionist too so she could meet more people. You don't meet much of anyone in Filing except other people in Filing. Me, I don't mind it so much, I have outside interests.

"Well," Greta said, "I sometimes think about, you know my apartment? It's got this little balcony, I like to sit out there in the summer and I have a few plants out there. I never bother that much about locking the door to the balcony, it's one of those sliding glass ones, I'm on the eighteenth floor for heaven's sake, I've got a good view of the lake and the CN Tower and all. But I'm sitting around one night in my housecoat, watching TV with my shoes off, you know how you do, and I see this guy's feet, coming down past the window, and the next thing you know he's standing on the balcony, he's let himself down by a rope with a hook on the end of it from the floor above, that's the nineteenth, and before I can even get up off the chesterfield he's inside the apartment. He's all dressed in black with black gloves on"—I knew right away what show she got the black gloves off because I saw the same one—"and then he, well, you know."

"You know what?" Chrissy said, but Greta said, "And afterwards he tells me that he goes all over the outside of the apartment building like that, from one floor to another, with his rope and his hook . . . and then he goes out to the balcony and tosses his rope, and he climbs up it and disappears."

"Just like Tarzan," I said, but nobody laughed.

"Is that all?" Chrissy said. "Don't you ever think about, well, I think about being in the bathtub, with no clothes on . . . "

"So who takes a bath in their clothes?" I said, you have to admit it's stupid when you come to think of it, but she just went on, " . . . with lots of bubbles, what I use is Vitabath, it's more expensive but it's so relaxing, and my hair pinned up, and the door opens and this fellow's standing there . . . "

"How'd he get in?" Greta said.

"Oh, I don't know, through a window or something. Well, I can't very well get out of the bathtub, the bathroom's too small and besides he's blocking the doorway, so I just lie there, and he starts to very slowly take his own clothes off, and then he gets into the bathtub with me."

"Don't you scream or anything?" said Darlene. She'd come back with her cup of coffee, she was getting really interested. "I'd scream like bloody murder."

"Who'd hear me?" Chrissy said. "Besides, all the articles say it's better not to resist, that way you don't get hurt."

"Anyway you might get bubbles up your nose," I said, "from the deep breathing," and I swear all four of them looked at me like I was in bad taste, like I'd insulted the Virgin Mary or something. I mean, I don't see what's wrong with a little joke now and then. Life's too short, right?

"Listen," I said, "those aren't *rape* fantasies. I mean, you aren't getting *raped,* it's just some guy you haven't met formally who happens to be more attractive than Derek Cummins"—he's the Assistant Manager, he wears elevator shoes or at any rate they have these thick soles and he has this funny way of talking, we call him Derek Duck—"and you have a good time. Rape is when they've got a knife or something and you don't want to."

"So what about you, Estelle," Chrissy said, she was miffed because I laughed at her fantasy, she thought I was putting her down. Sondra was miffed too, by this time she'd finished her celery and she wanted to tell about hers, but she hadn't got in fast enough.

"All right, let me tell you one," I said. "I'm walking down this dark street at night and this fellow comes up and grabs my arm. Now it so happens that I have a plastic lemon in my purse, you know how it always says you should carry a plastic lemon in your purse? I don't really do it, I tried it once but the darn thing leaked all over my checkbook, but in this fantasy I have one, and I say to him, 'You're intending to rape me, right?' and he nods, so I open my purse to get the plastic lemon, and I can't find it! My purse is full of all this junk, Kleenex and cigarettes and my change purse and my lipstick and my driver's license, you know the kind of stuff; so I ask him to hold out his hands, like this, and I pile all this junk into them and down at the bottom there's the plastic lemon, and I can't get the top off. So I hand it to him and he's very obliging, he twists the top off and hands it back to me, and I squirt him in the eye."

I hope you don't think that's too vicious. Come to think of it, it is a bit mean, especially when he was so polite and all.

"*That's* your rape fantasy?" Chrissy says. "I don't believe it."

"She's a card," Darlene says, she and I are the ones that've been here the longest and she never will forget the time I got drunk at the office party and insisted I was going to dance under the table instead of on top of it, I did a sort of Cossack number but then I hit my head on the bottom of the table—actually it was a desk—when I went to get up, and I knocked myself out cold. She's decided that's the mark of an original mind and she tells everyone new about it and I'm not sure that's fair. Though I did do it.

"I'm being totally honest," I say. I always am and they know it. There's no point in being anything else, is the way I look at it, and sooner or later the truth will come out so you might as well not waste the time, right? "You should hear the one about the Easy-Off Oven Cleaner."

But that was the end of the lunch hour, with one bridge game shot to hell, and the next day we spent most of the time arguing over whether to start a new game or play out the hands we had left over from the day before, so Sondra never did get a chance to tell about her rape fantasy.

It started me thinking though, about my own rape fantasies. Maybe I'm abnormal or something, I mean I have fantasies about handsome strangers coming in through the window too, like Mr. Clean, I wish one would, please god somebody without flat feet and big sweat marks on his shirt, and over five feet five, believe me being tall is a handicap though it's getting better, tall guys are starting to like someone whose nose reaches higher than their belly button. But if you're being totally honest you can't count those as rape fantasies. In a real rape fantasy, what you should feel is this anxiety, like when you think about your apartment building catching on fire and whether you should use the elevator or the stairs or maybe just stick your head under a wet towel, and you try to remember everything you've read about what to do but you can't decide.

For instance, I'm walking along this dark street at night and this short, ugly fellow comes up and grabs my arm, and not only is he ugly, you know, with a sort of puffy nothing face, like those fellows you have to talk to in the bank when your account's overdrawn—of course I don't mean they're all like that—but he's absolutely covered in pimples. So he gets me pinned against the wall, he's short but he's heavy, and he starts to undo himself and the zipper gets stuck. I mean, one of the most significant moments in a girl's life, it's almost like getting married or having a baby or something, and he sticks the zipper.

So I say, kind of disgusted, "Oh for Chrissake," and he starts to cry. He tells me he's never been able to get anything right in his entire life, and this is the last straw, he's going to go jump off a bridge.

"Look," I say, I feel so sorry for him, in my rape fantasies I always end up feeling sorry for the guy, I mean there has to be something *wrong* with them, if it was Clint

Eastwood it'd be different but worse luck it never is. I was the kind of little girl who buried dead robins, know what I mean? It used to drive my mother nuts, she didn't like me touching them, because of the germs I guess. So I say, "Listen, I know how you feel. You really should do something about those pimples, if you got rid of them you'd be quite good looking, honest; then you wouldn't have to go around doing stuff like this. I had them myself once," I say, to comfort him, but in fact I did, and it ends up I give him the name of my old dermatologist, the one I had in high school, that was back in Leamington, except I used to go to St. Catharines for the dermatologist. I'm telling you, I was really lonely when I first came here; I thought it was going to be such a big adventure and all, but it's a lot harder to meet people in a city. But I guess it's different for a guy.

Or I'm lying in bed with this terrible cold, my face is all swollen up, my eyes are red and my nose is dripping like a leaky tap, and this fellow comes in through the window and *he* has a terrible cold too, it's a new kind of flu that's been going around. So he says, "I'b goig do rabe you"—I hope you don't mind me holding my nose like this but that's the way I imagine it—and he lets out this terrific sneeze, which slows him down a bit, also I'm no object of beauty myself, you'd have to be some kind of pervert to want to rape someone with a cold like mine, it'd be like raping a bottle of LePages mucilage the way my nose is running. He's looking wildly around the room, and I realize it's because he doesn't have a piece of Kleenex! "Id's ride here," I say, and I pass him the Kleenex, god knows why he even bothered to get out of bed, you'd think if you were going to go around climbing in windows you'd wait till you were healthier, right? I mean, that takes a certain amount of energy. So I ask him why doesn't he let me fix him a Neo-Citran and scotch, that's what I always take, you still have the cold but you don't feel it, so I do and we end up watching the Late Show together. I mean, they aren't all sex maniacs, the rest of the time they must lead a normal life. I figure they enjoy watching the Late Show just like anybody else.

I do have a scarier one though . . . where the fellow says he's hearing angel voices that're telling him he's got to kill me, you know, you read about things like that all the time in the papers. In this one I'm not in the apartment where I live now, I'm back in my mother's house in Leamington and the fellow's been hiding in the cellar, he grabs my arm when I go downstairs to get a jar of jam and he's got hold of the axe too, out of the garage, that one is really scary. I mean, what do you say to a nut like that?

So I start to shake but after a minute I get control of myself and I say, is he sure the angel voices have got the right person, because I hear the same angel voices and they've been telling me for some time that I'm going to give birth to the reincarnation of St. Anne who in turn has the Virgin Mary and right after that comes Jesus Christ and the end of the world, and he wouldn't want to interfere with that, would he? So he gets confused and listens some more, and then he asks for a sign and I show him my vaccination mark, you can see it's sort of an odd-shaped one, it got infected because I scratched the top off, and that does it, he apologizes and climbs out the coal chute again, which is how he got in in the first place, and I say to myself there's some advantage in having been brought up a Catholic even though I haven't been to church since they changed the service into English, it just isn't the same, you might as well be a Protestant. I must write to Mother and tell her to nail up that coal chute, it always has bothered me. Funny, I couldn't tell you at all what this man looks like but I know exactly what kind of shoes he's wearing, because that's the last I see of him, his shoes going up the coal chute, and they're the old-fashioned kind that lace up the ankles, even though he's a young fellow. That's strange, isn't it?

Let me tell you though I really sweat until I see him safely out of there and I go upstairs right away and make myself a cup of tea. I don't think about that one much. My mother always said you shouldn't dwell on unpleasant things and I generally agree with that, I mean, dwelling on them doesn't make them go away. Though not dwelling on them doesn't make them go away either, when you come to think of it.

Sometimes I have these short ones where the fellow grabs my arm but I'm really a Kung-Fu expert, can you believe it, in real life I'm sure it would just be a conk on the head and that's that, like getting your tonsils out, you'd wake up and it would be all over except for the sore places, and you'd be lucky if your neck wasn't broken or something, I could never even hit the volleyball in gym and a volleyball is fairly large, you know?—and I just go *zap* with my fingers into his eyes and that's it, he falls over, or I flip him against a wall or something. But I could never really stick my fingers in anyone's eyes, could you? It would feel like hot jello and I don't even like cold jello, just thinking about it gives me the creeps. I feel a bit guilty about that one, I mean how would you like walking around knowing someone's been blinded for life because of you?

But maybe it's different for a guy.

The most touching one I have is when the fellow grabs my arm and I say, sad and kind of dignified, "You'd be raping a corpse." That pulls him up short and I explain that I've just found out I have leukemia and the doctors have only given me a few months to live. That's why I'm out pacing the streets alone at night, I need to think, you know, come to terms with myself. I don't really have leukemia but in the fantasy I do, I guess I chose that particular disease because a girl in my grade four class died of it, the whole class sent her flowers when she was in the hospital. I didn't understand then that she was going to die and I wanted to have leukemia too so I could get flowers. Kids are funny, aren't they? Well, it turns out that he has leukemia himself, and *he* only has a few months to live, that's why he's going around raping people, he's very bitter because he's so young and his life is being taken from him before he's really lived it. So we walk along gently under the street lights, it's spring and sort of misty, and we end up going for coffee, we're happy we've found the only other person in the world who can understand what we're going through, it's almost like fate, and after a while we just sort of look at each other and our hands touch, and he comes back with me and moves into my apartment and we spend our last months together before we die, we just sort of don't wake up in the morning, though I've never decided which one of us gets to die first. If it's him I have to go on and fantasize about the funeral, if it's me I don't have to worry about that, so it just about depends on how tired I am at the time. You may not believe this but sometimes I even start crying. I cry at the ends of movies, even the ones that aren't all that sad, so I guess it's the same thing. My mother's like that too.

The funny thing about these fantasies is that the man is always someone I don't know, and the statistics in the magazines, well, most of them anyway, they say it's often someone you do know, at least a little bit, like your boss or something—I mean, it wouldn't be *my* boss, he's over sixty and I'm sure he couldn't rape his way out of a paper bag, poor old thing, but it might be someone like Derek Duck, in his elevator shoes, perish the thought—or someone you just met, who invites you up for a drink, it's getting so you can hardly be sociable anymore, and how are you supposed to meet people if you can't trust them even that basic amount? You can't spend your whole life in the Filing Department or cooped up in your own apartment with all the doors and windows locked and the shades down. I'm not what you would call a drinker but I like to go out now and then for a drink or two in a nice place, even if I am by myself, I'm with Women's Lib on that even though I can't agree with a lot of other things they say. Like here for instance, the waiters all know me and if anyone, you know, bothers me. . . . I don't know why I'm telling you all this, except I think it helps you get to know a person, especially at first, hearing some of the things they think about. At work they call me the office worry wart, but it isn't so much like worrying, it's more like figuring out what you should do in an emergency, like I said before.

Anyway, another thing about it is that there's a lot of conversation, in fact I spend most of my time, in the fantasy that is, wondering what I'm going to say and what he's going to say, I think it would be better if you could get a conversation going. Like, how could a fellow do that to a person he's just had a long conversation with, once you let them know you're human, you have a life too, I don't see how they could go ahead with it, right? I mean, I know it happens but I just don't understand it, that's the part I really don't understand.

(1977)

RAYMOND CARVER
[1939–1989]

Cathedral

This blind man, an old friend of my wife's, he was on his way to spend the night. His wife had died. So he was visiting the dead wife's relatives in Connecticut. He called my wife from his in-laws'. Arrangements were made. He would come by train, a five-hour trip, and my wife would meet him at the station. She hadn't seen him since she worked for him one summer in Seattle ten years ago. But she and the blind man had kept in touch. They made tapes and mailed them back and forth. I wasn't enthusiastic about his visit. He was no one I knew. And his being blind bothered me. My idea of blindness came from the movies. In the movies, the blind moved slowly and never laughed. Sometimes they were led by seeing-eye dogs. A blind man in my house was not something I looked forward to.

That summer in Seattle she had needed a job. She didn't have any money. The man she was going to marry at the end of the summer was in officers' training school. He didn't have any money, either. But she was in love with the guy, and he was in love with her, etc. She'd seen something in the paper: HELP WANTED—*Reading to Blind Man,* and a telephone number. She phoned and went over, was hired on the spot. She'd worked with this blind man all summer. She read stuff to him, case studies, reports, that sort of thing. She helped him organize his little office in the county social-service department. They'd become good friends, my wife and the blind man. How do I know these things? She told me. And she told me something else. On her last day in the office, the blind man asked if he could touch her face. She agreed to this. She told me he touched his fingers to every part of her face, her nose—even her neck! She never forgot it. She even tried to write a poem about it. She was always trying to write a poem. She wrote a poem or two every year, usually after something really important had happened to her.

When we first started going out together, she showed me the poem. In the poem, she recalled his fingers and the way they had moved around over her face. In the poem, she talked about what she had felt at the time, about what went through her mind when the blind man touched her nose and lips. I can remember I didn't think much of the poem. Of course, I didn't tell her that. Maybe I just don't understand poetry. I admit it's not the first thing I reach for when I pick up something to read.

Anyway, this man who'd first enjoyed her favors, the officer-to-be, he'd been her childhood sweetheart. So okay. I'm saying that at the end of the summer she let the blind man run his hands over her face, said goodbye to him, married her childhood etc., who was now a commissioned officer, and she moved away from Seattle. But they'd kept in touch, she and the blind man. She made the first contact after a year or so. She called him up one night from an Air Force base in Alabama. She wanted to talk. They talked. He asked her to send him a tape and tell him about her life. She did this. She sent the tape. On the tape, she told the blind man about her husband and about their life together in the military. She told the blind man she loved her husband but she didn't like it where they lived and she didn't like it that he was a part of the military-industrial thing. She told the blind man she'd written a poem and he was in it. She told him that she was writing a poem about what it was like to be an Air Force officer's wife. The poem wasn't finished yet. She was still writing it. The blind man made a tape. He sent her the tape. She made a tape. This went on for years. My wife's officer was posted to one base and then another. She sent tapes from Moody AFB, McGuire, McConnell, and finally Travis, near Sacramento, where one night she got to feeling lonely and cut off from people she kept losing in that moving-around life. She got to feeling she couldn't go it another step. She went in and swallowed all the pills and capsules in the medicine chest and washed them down with a bottle of gin. Then she got into a hot bath and passed out.

But instead of dying, she got sick. She threw up. Her officer—why should he have a name? he was the childhood sweetheart, and what more does he want?—came home from somewhere, found her, and called the ambulance. In time, she put it all on a tape and sent the tape to the blind man. Over the years, she put all kinds of stuff on tapes and sent the tapes off lickety-split. Next to writing a poem every year, I think it was her chief means of recreation. On one tape, she told the blind man she'd decided to live away from her officer for a time. On another tape, she told him about her divorce. She and I began going out, and of course she told her blind man about it. She told him everything, or so it seemed to me. Once she asked me if I'd like to hear the latest tape from the blind man. This was a year ago. I was on the tape, she said. So I said okay, I'd listen to it. I got us drinks and we settled down in the living room. We made ready to listen. First she inserted the tape into the player and adjusted a couple of dials. Then she pushed a lever. The tape squeaked and someone began to talk in this loud voice. She lowered the volume. After a few minutes of harmless chitchat, I heard my own name in the mouth of this stranger, this blind man I didn't even know! And then this:

"From all you've said about him, I can only conclude—" But we were interrupted, a knock at the door, something, and we didn't ever get back to the tape. Maybe it was just as well. I'd heard all I wanted to.

Now this same blind man was coming to sleep in my house.

"Maybe I could take him bowling," I said to my wife. She was at the draining board doing scalloped potatoes. She put down the knife she was using and turned around.

"If you love me," she said, "you can do this for me. If you don't love me, okay. But if you had a friend, any friend, and the friend came to visit, I'd make him feel comfortable." She wiped her hands with the dish towel.

"I don't have any blind friends," I said.

"You don't have *any* friends," she said. "Period. Besides," she said, "goddamn it, his wife's just died! Don't you understand that? The man's lost his wife!"

I didn't answer. She'd told me a little about the blind man's wife. Her name was Beulah. Beulah! That's a name for a colored woman.

"Was his wife a Negro?" I asked.

"Are you crazy?" my wife said. "Have you just flipped or something?" She picked up a potato. I saw it hit the floor, then roll under the stove. "What's wrong with you?" she said. "Are you drunk?"

"I'm just asking," I said.

Right then my wife filled me in with more detail than I cared to know. I made a drink and sat at the kitchen table to listen. Pieces of the story began to fall into place.

Beulah had gone to work for the blind man the summer after my wife had stopped working for him. Pretty soon Beulah and the blind man had themselves a church wedding. It was a little wedding—who'd want to go to such a wedding in the first place?—just the two of them, plus the minister and the minister's wife. But it was a church wedding just the same. It was what Beulah had wanted, he'd said. But even then Beulah must have been carrying the cancer in her glands. After they had been inseparable for eight years—my wife's word, *inseparable*—Beulah's health went into a rapid decline. She died in a Seattle hospital room, the blind man sitting beside the bed and holding on to her hand. They'd married, lived and worked together, slept together—had sex, sure—and then the blind man had to bury her. All this without his having ever seen what the goddamned woman looked like. It was beyond my understanding. Hearing this, I felt sorry for the blind man for a little bit. And then I found myself thinking what a pitiful life this woman must have led. Imagine a woman who could never see herself as she was seen in the eyes of her loved one. A woman who could go on day after day and never receive the smallest compliment from her beloved. A woman whose husband could never read the expression on her face, be it misery or something better. Someone who could wear makeup or not—what difference to him? She could, if she wanted, wear green eye-shadow around one eye, a straight pin in her nostril, yellow slacks and purple shoes, no matter. And then to slip off into death, the blind man's hand on her hand, his blind eyes streaming tears—I'm imagining now— her last thought maybe this: that he never even knew what she looked like, and she on an express to the grave. Robert was left with a small insurance policy and half of a twenty-peso Mexican coin. The other half of the coin went into the box with her. Pathetic.

So when the time rolled around, my wife went to the depot to pick him up. With nothing to do but wait—sure, I blamed him for that—I was having a drink and watching the TV when I heard the car pull into the drive. I got up from the sofa with my drink and went to the window to have a look.

I saw my wife laughing as she parked the car. I saw her get out of the car and shut the door. She was still wearing a smile. Just amazing. She went around to the other side of the car to where the blind man was already starting to get out. This blind man, feature this, he was wearing a full beard! A beard on a blind man! Too much, I say. The blind man reached into the back seat and dragged out a suitcase. My wife took his arm, shut the car door, and, talking all the way, moved him down the drive and then up the steps to the front porch. I turned off the TV. I finished my drink, rinsed the glass, dried my hands. Then I went to the door.

My wife said, "I want you to meet Robert. Robert, this is my husband. I've told you all about him." She was beaming. She had this blind man by his coat sleeve.

The blind man let go of his suitcase and up came his hand.

I took it. He squeezed hard, held my hand, and then he let it go.

"I feel like we've already met," he boomed.

"Likewise," I said. I didn't know what else to say. Then I said, "Welcome. I've heard a lot about you." We began to move then, a little group, from the porch into the living room, my wife guiding him by the arm. The blind man was carrying his suitcase in his other hand. My wife said things like, "To your left here, Robert. That's right. Now watch it, there's a chair. That's it. Sit down right here. This is the sofa. We just bought this sofa two weeks ago."

I started to say something about the old sofa. I'd liked that old sofa. But I didn't say anything. Then I wanted to say something else, small-talk, about the scenic ride along the Hudson. How going *to* New York, you should sit on the right-hand side of the train, and coming *from* New York, the left-hand side.

"Did you have a good train ride?" I said. "Which side of the train did you sit on, by the way?"

"What a question, which side!" my wife said. "What's it matter which side?" she said.

"I just asked," I said.

"Right side," the blind man said. "I hadn't been on a train in nearly forty years. Not since I was a kid. With my folks. That's been a long time. I'd nearly forgotten the sensation. I have winter in my beard now," he said. "So I've been told, anyway. Do I look distinguished, my dear?" the blind man said to my wife.

"You look distinguished, Robert," she said. "Robert," she said. "Robert, it's just so good to see you."

My wife finally took her eyes off the blind man and looked at me. I had the feeling she didn't like what she saw. I shrugged.

I've never met, or personally known, anyone who was blind. This blind man was late forties, a heavy-set, balding man with stooped shoulders, as if he carried a great weight there. He wore brown slacks, brown shoes, a light-brown shirt, a tie, a sports coat. Spiffy. He also had this full beard. But he didn't use a cane and he didn't wear dark glasses. I'd always thought dark glasses were a must for the blind. Fact was, I wished he had a pair. At first glance, his eyes looked like anyone else's eyes. But if you looked close, there was something different about them. Too much white in the iris, for one thing, and the pupils seemed to move around in the sockets without his knowing it or being able to stop it. Creepy. As I stared at his face, I saw the left pupil turn in toward his nose while the other made an effort to keep in one place. But it was only an effort, for that eye was on the roam without his knowing it or wanting it to be.

I said, "Let me get you a drink. What's your pleasure? We have a little of everything. It's one of our pastimes."

"Bub, I'm a Scotch man myself," he said fast enough in this big voice.

"Right," I said. Bub! "Sure you are. I knew it."

He let his fingers touch his suitcase, which was sitting alongside the sofa. He was taking his bearings. I didn't blame him for that.

"I'll move that up to your room," my wife said.

"No, that's fine," the blind man said loudly. "It can go up when I go up."

"A little water with the Scotch?" I said.

"Very little," he said.

"I knew it," I said.

He said, "Just a tad. The Irish actor, Barry Fitzgerald? I'm like that fellow. When I drink water, Fitzgerald said, I drink water. When I drink whiskey, I drink whiskey." My wife laughed. The blind man brought his hand up under his beard. He lifted his beard slowly and let it drop.

I did the drinks, three big glasses of Scotch with a splash of water in each. Then we made ourselves comfortable and talked about Robert's travels. First the long flight from the West Coast to Connecticut, we covered that. Then from Connecticut up here by train. We had another drink concerning that leg of the trip.

I remembered having read somewhere that the blind didn't smoke because, as speculation had it, they couldn't see the smoke they exhaled. I thought I knew that much and that much only about blind people. But this blind man smoked his cigarette down to the nubbin and then lit another one. This blind man filled his ashtray and my wife emptied it.

When we sat down at the table for dinner, we had another drink. My wife heaped Robert's plate with cube steak, scalloped potatoes, green beans. I buttered him up two slices of bread. I said, "Here's bread and butter for you." I swallowed some of my drink. "Now let us pray," I said, and the blind man lowered his head. My wife looked at me, her mouth agape. "Pray the phone won't ring and the food doesn't get cold," I said.

We dug in. We ate everything there was to eat on the table. We ate like there was no tomorrow. We didn't talk. We ate. We scarfed. We grazed that table. We were into serious eating. The blind man had right away located his foods, he knew just where everything was on his plate. I watched with admiration as he used his knife and fork on the meat. He'd cut two pieces of meat, fork the meat into his mouth, and then go all out for the scalloped potatoes, the beans next, and then he'd tear off a hunk of buttered bread and eat that. He'd follow this up with a big drink of milk. It didn't seem to bother him to use his fingers once in a while, either.

We finished everything, including half a strawberry pie. For a few moments, we sat as if stunned. Sweat beaded on our faces. Finally, we got up from the table and left the dirty plates. We didn't look back. We took ourselves into the living room and sank into our places again. Robert and my wife sat on the sofa. I took the big chair. We had us two or three more drinks while they talked about the major things that had come to pass for them in the past ten years. For the most part, I just listened. Now and then I joined in. I didn't want him to think I'd left the room, and I didn't want her to think I was feeling left out. They talked of things that had happened to them—to them!—these past ten years. I waited in vain to hear my name on my wife's sweet lips: "And then my dear husband came into my life"—something like that. But I heard nothing of the sort. More talk of Robert. Robert had done a little of everything, it seemed, a regular blind jack-of-all-trades. But most recently he and his wife had had an Amway distributorship, from which, I gathered, they'd earned their living, such as it was. The blind man was also a ham radio operator. He talked in his loud voice about conversations he'd had with fellow operators in Guam, in the Philippines, in Alaska, and even in Tahiti. He said he'd have a lot of friends there if he ever wanted to go visit those places. From time to time, he'd turn his blind face toward me, put his hand under his beard, ask me something. How long had I been in my present position? (Three years.) Did I like my work? (I didn't.) Was I going to stay with it? (What were the options?) Finally, when I thought he was beginning to run down, I got up and turned on the TV.

My wife looked at me with irritation. She was heading toward a boil. Then she looked at the blind man and said, "Robert, do you have a TV?"

The blind man said, "My dear, I have two TVs. I have a color set and a black-and-white thing, an old relic. It's funny, but if I turn the TV on, and I'm always turning it on, I turn on the color set. It's funny, don't you think?"

I didn't know what to say to that. I had absolutely nothing to say to that. No opinion. So I watched the news program and tried to listen to what the announcer was saying.

"This is a color TV," the blind man said. "Don't ask me how, but I can tell."

"We traded up a while ago," I said.

The blind man had another taste of his drink. He lifted his beard, sniffed it, and let it fall. He leaned forward on the sofa. He positioned his ashtray on the coffee table, then put the lighter to his cigarette. He leaned back on the sofa and crossed his legs at the ankles.

My wife covered her mouth, and then she yawned. She stretched. She said, "I think I'll go upstairs and put on my robe. I think I'll change into something else. Robert, you make yourself comfortable," she said.

"I'm comfortable," the blind man said.

"I want you to feel comfortable in this house," she said.

"I am comfortable," the blind man said.

After she'd left the room, he and I listened to the weather report and then to the sports roundup. By that time, she'd been gone so long I didn't know if she was going to come back. I thought she might have gone to bed. I wished she'd come back downstairs. I didn't want to be left alone with a blind man. I asked him if he wanted another drink, and he said sure. Then I asked if he wanted to smoke some dope with me. I said I'd just rolled a number. I hadn't, but I planned to do so in about two shakes.

"I'll try some with you," he said.

"Damn right," I said. "That's the stuff."

I got our drinks and sat down on the sofa with him. Then I rolled us two fat numbers. I lit one and passed it. I brought it to his fingers. He took it and inhaled.

"Hold it as long as you can," I said. I could tell he didn't know the first thing.

My wife came back downstairs wearing her pink robe and her pink slippers.

"What do I smell?" she said.

"We thought we'd have us some cannabis," I said.

My wife gave me a savage look. Then she looked at the blind man and said, "Robert, I didn't know you smoked."

He said, "I do now, my dear. There's a first time for everything. But I don't feel anything yet."

"This stuff is pretty mellow," I said. "This stuff is mild. It's dope you can reason with," I said. "It doesn't mess you up."

"Not much it doesn't, bub," he said, and laughed.

My wife sat on the sofa between the blind man and me. I passed her the number. She took it and toked and then passed it back to me. "Which way is this going?" she said. Then she said, "I shouldn't be smoking this. I can hardly keep my eyes open as it is. That dinner did me in. I shouldn't have eaten so much."

"It was the strawberry pie," the blind man said. "That's what did it," he said, and he laughed his big laugh. Then he shook his head.

"There's more strawberry pie," I said.

"Do you want some more, Robert?" my wife said.

"Maybe in a little while," he said.

We gave our attention to the TV. My wife yawned again. She said, "Your bed is made up when you feel like going to bed, Robert. I know you must have had a long day. When you're ready to go to bed, say so." She pulled his arm. "Robert?"

He came to and said, "I've had a real nice time. This beats tapes, doesn't it?"

I said, "Coming at you," and I put the number between his fingers. He inhaled, held the smoke, and then let it go. It was like he'd been doing it since he was nine years old.

"Thanks, bub," he said. "But I think this is all for me. I think I'm beginning to feel it," he said. He held the burning roach out for my wife.

"Same here," she said. "Ditto. Me, too." She took the roach and passed it to me. "I may just sit here for a while between you two guys with my eyes closed. But don't let me bother you, okay? Either one of you. If it bothers you, say so. Otherwise, I may just sit here with my eyes closed until you're ready to go to bed," she said. "Your bed's made up, Robert, when you're ready. It's right next to our room at the top of the stairs. We'll show you up when you're ready. You wake me up now, you guys, if I fall asleep." She said that and then she closed her eyes and went to sleep.

The news program ended. I got up and changed the channel. I sat back down on the sofa. I wished my wife hadn't pooped out. Her head lay across the back of the sofa, her mouth open. She'd turned so that her robe had slipped away from her legs, exposing a juicy thigh. I reached to draw her robe back over her, and it was then that I glanced at the blind man. What the hell! I flipped the robe open again.

"You say when you want some strawberry pie," I said.

"I will," he said.

I said, "Are you tired? Do you want me to take you up to your bed? Are you ready to hit the hay?"

"Not yet," he said. "No, I'll stay up with you, bub. If that's all right. I'll stay up until you're ready to turn in. We haven't had a chance to talk. Know what I mean? I feel like me and her monopolized the evening." He lifted his beard and he let it fall. He picked up his cigarettes and his lighter.

"That's all right," I said. Then I said, "I'm glad for the company."

And I guess I was. Every night I smoked dope and stayed up as long as I could before I fell asleep. My wife and I hardly ever went to bed at the same time. When I did go to sleep, I had these dreams. Sometimes I'd wake up from one of them, my heart going crazy.

Something about the church and the Middle Ages was on the TV. Not your run-of-the-mill TV fare. I wanted to watch something else. I turned to the other channels. But there was nothing on them, either. So I turned back to the first channel and apologized.

"Bub, it's all right," the blind man said. "It's fine with me. Whatever you want to watch is okay. I'm always learning something. Learning never ends. It won't hurt me to learn something tonight. I got ears," he said.

We didn't say anything for a time. He was leaning forward with his head turned at me, his right ear aimed in the direction of the set. Very disconcerting. Now and then his eyelids drooped and then they snapped open again. Now and then he put his fingers into his beard and tugged, like he was thinking about something he was hearing on the television.

On the screen, a group of men wearing cowls was being set upon and tormented by men dressed in skeleton costumes and men dressed as devils. The men dressed as devils wore devil masks, horns, and long tails. This pageant was part of a procession. The Englishman who was narrating the thing said it took place in Spain once a year. I tried to explain to the blind man what was happening.

"Skeletons," he said. "I know about skeletons," he said, and he nodded.

The TV showed this one cathedral. Then there was a long, slow look at another one. Finally, the picture switched to the famous one in Paris, with its flying buttresses and its spires reaching up to the clouds. The camera pulled away to show the whole of the cathedral rising above the skyline.

There were times when the Englishman who was telling the thing would shut up, would simply let the camera move around over the cathedrals. Or else the camera would tour the countryside, men in fields walking behind oxen. I waited as long as I could. Then I felt I had to say something. I said, "They're showing the outside of this cathedral now. Gargoyles. Little statues carved to look like monsters. Now I guess they're in Italy. Yeah, they're in Italy. There's paintings on the walls of this one church."

"Are those fresco paintings, bub?" he asked, and he sipped from his drink.

I reached for my glass. But it was empty. I tried to remember what I could remember. "You're asking me are those frescoes?" I said. "That's a good question. I don't know."

The camera moved to a cathedral outside Lisbon. The differences in the Portuguese cathedral compared with the French and Italian were not that great. But they were there. Mostly the interior stuff. Then something occurred to me, and I said, "Something has occurred to me. Do you have any idea what a cathedral is? What they look like, that is? Do you follow me? If somebody says cathedral to you, do you have any notion what they're talking about? Do you know the difference between that and a Baptist church, say?"

He let the smoke dribble from his mouth. "I know they took hundreds of workers fifty or a hundred years to build," he said. "I just heard the man say that, of course. I know generations of the same families worked on a cathedral. I heard him say that, too. The men who began their life's work on them, they never lived to see the completion of their work. In that wise, bub, they're no different from the rest of us, right?" He laughed. Then his eyelids drooped again. His head nodded. He seemed to be snoozing. Maybe he was imagining himself in Portugal. The TV was showing another cathedral now. This one was in Germany. The Englishman's voice droned on. "Cathedrals," the blind man said. He sat up and rolled his head back and forth. "If you want the truth, bub, that's about all I know. What I just said. What I heard him say. But maybe you could describe one to me? I wish you'd do it. I'd like that. If you want to know, I really don't have a good idea."

I stared hard at the shot of the cathedral on the TV. How could I even begin to describe it? But say my life depended on it. Say my life was being threatened by an insane guy who said I had to do it or else.

I stared some more at the cathedral before the picture flipped off into the countryside. There was no use. I turned to the blind man and said, "To begin with, they're very tall." I was looking around the room for clues. "They reach way up. Up and up. Toward the sky. They're so big, some of them, they have to have these supports. To help hold them up, so to speak. These supports are called buttresses. They remind me of viaducts, for some reason. But maybe you don't know viaducts, either? Sometimes the cathedrals have devils and such carved into the front. Sometimes lords and ladies. Don't ask me why this is," I said.

He was nodding. The whole upper part of his body seemed to be moving back and forth.

"I'm not doing so good, am I?" I said.

He stopped nodding and leaned forward on the edge of the sofa. As he listened to me, he was running his fingers through his beard. I wasn't getting through to him, I could see that. But he waited for me to go on just the same. He nodded, like he was trying to encourage me. I tried to think what else to say. "They're really big," I said. "They're massive. They're built of stone. Marble, too, sometimes. In those olden days, when they built cathedrals, men wanted to be close to God. In those olden days, God was an important part of everyone's life. You could tell this from their cathedral-building. I'm sorry," I said, "but it looks like that's the best I can do for you. I'm just no good at it."

"That's all right, bub," the blind man said. "Hey, listen. I hope you don't mind my asking you. Can I ask you something? Let me ask you a simple question, yes or no. I'm just curious and there's no offense. You're my host. But let me ask if you are in any way religious? You don't mind my asking?"

I shook my head. He couldn't see that, though. A wink is the same as a nod to a blind man. "I guess I don't believe in it. In anything. Sometimes it's hard. You know what I'm saying?"

"Sure, I do," he said.

"Right," I said.

The Englishman was still holding forth. My wife sighed in her sleep. She drew a long breath and went on with her sleeping.

"You'll have to forgive me," I said. "But I can't tell you what a cathedral looks like. It just isn't in me to do it. I can't do any more than I've done."

The blind man sat very still, his head down, as he listened to me.

I said, "The truth is, cathedrals don't mean anything special to me. Nothing. Cathedrals. They're something to look at on late-night TV. That's all they are."

It was then that the blind man cleared his throat. He brought something up. He took a handkerchief from his back pocket. Then he said, "I get it, bub. It's okay. It happens. Don't worry about it," he said. "Hey, listen to me. Will you do me a favor? I got an idea. Why don't you find us some heavy paper? And a pen. We'll do something. We'll draw one together. Get us a pen and some heavy paper. Go on, bub, get the stuff," he said.

So I went upstairs. My legs felt like they didn't have any strength in them. They felt like they did after I'd done some running. In my wife's room, I looked around. I found some ballpoints in a little basket on her table. And then I tried to think where to look for the kind of paper he was talking about.

Downstairs, in the kitchen, I found a shopping bag with onion skins in the bottom of the bag. I emptied the bag and shook it. I brought it into the living room and sat down with it near his legs. I moved some things, smoothed the wrinkles from the bag, spread it out on the coffee table.

The blind man got down from the sofa and sat next to me on the carpet. He ran his fingers over the paper. He went up and down the sides of the paper. The edges, even the edges. He fingered the corners.

"All right," he said. "All right, let's do her."

He found my hand, the hand with the pen. He closed his hand over my hand. "Go ahead, bub, draw," he said. "Draw. You'll see. I'll follow along with you. It'll be okay. Just begin now like I'm telling you. You'll see. Draw," the blind man said.

So I began. First I drew a box that looked like a house. It could have been the house I lived in. Then I put a roof on it. At either end of the roof, I drew spires. Crazy.

"Swell," he said. "Terrific. You're doing fine," he said. "Never thought anything like this could happen in your lifetime, did you, bub? Well, it's a strange life, we all know that. Go on now. Keep it up."

I put in windows with arches. I drew flying buttresses. I hung great doors. I couldn't stop. The TV station went off the air. I put down the pen and closed and opened my fingers. The blind man felt around over the paper. He moved the tips of his fingers over the paper, all over what I had drawn, and he nodded.

"Doing fine," the blind man said.

I took up the pen again, and he found my hand. I kept at it. I'm no artist. But I kept drawing just the same.

My wife opened up her eyes and gazed at us. She sat up on the sofa, her robe hanging open. She said, "What are you doing? Tell me, I want to know."

I didn't answer her.

The blind man said, "We're drawing a cathedral. Me and him are working on it. Press hard," he said to me. "That's right. That's good," he said. "Sure. You got it, bub. I can tell. You didn't think you could. But you can, can't you? You're cooking with gas now. You know what I'm saying? We're going to really have us something here in a minute. How's the old arm?" he said. "Put some people in there now. What's a cathedral without people?"

My wife said, "What's going on? Robert, what are you doing? What's going on?"

"It's all right," he said to her. "Close your eyes now," the blind man said to me.

I did it. I closed them just like he said.

"Are they closed?" he said. "Don't fudge."

"They're closed," I said.

"Keep them that way," he said. He said, "Don't stop now. Draw."

So we kept on with it. His fingers rode my fingers as my hand went over the paper. It was like nothing else in my life up to now.

Then he said, "I think that's it. I think you got it," he said. "Take a look. What do you think?"

But I had my eyes closed. I thought I'd keep them that way for a little longer. I thought it was something I ought to do.

"Well?" he said. "Are you looking?"

My eyes were still closed. I was in my house. I knew that. But I didn't feel like I was inside anything.

"It's really something," I said.

(1983)

ALICE WALKER
[b. 1944]

Everyday Use

for your grandmama

I will wait for her in the yard that Maggie and I made so clean and wavy yesterday afternoon. A yard like this is more comfortable than most people know. It is not just a yard. It is like an extended living room. When the hard clay is swept clean as a floor and the fine sand around the edges lined with tiny, irregular grooves anyone can come and sit and look up into the elm tree and wait for the breezes that never come inside the house.

Maggie will be nervous until after her sister goes: she will stand hopelessly in corners, homely and ashamed of the burn scars down her arms and legs, eyeing her sister with a mixture of envy and awe. She thinks her sister has held life always in the palm of one hand, that "no" is a word the world never learned to say to her.

You've no doubt seen those TV shows° where the child who has "made it" is confronted, as a surprise, by her own mother and father, tottering in weakly from backstage. (A pleasant surprise, of course: What would they do if parent and child came on the show only to curse out and insult each other?) On TV mother and child embrace and smile into each other's faces. Sometimes the mother and father weep, the child wraps them in her arms and leans across the table to tell how she would not have made it without their help. I have seen these programs.

Sometimes I dream a dream in which Dee and I are suddenly brought together on a TV program of this sort. Out of a dark and soft-seated limousine I am ushered into a bright room filled with many people. There I meet a smiling, gray, sporty man like

TV shows   *in the early days of television, a popular show was "This Is Your Life," which the narrator describes exactly here.*

Johnny Carson who shakes my hand and tells me what a fine girl I have. Then we are on the stage and Dee is embracing me with tears in her eyes. She pins on my dress a large orchid, even though she has told me once that she thinks orchids are tacky flowers.

In real life I am a large, big-boned woman with rough, man-working hands. In the winter I wear flannel nightgowns to bed and overalls during the day. I can kill and clean a hog as mercilessly as a man. My fat keeps me hot in zero weather. I can work outside all day, breaking ice to get water for washing; I can eat pork liver cooked over the open fire minutes after it comes steaming from the hog. One winter I knocked a bull calf straight in the brain between the eyes with a sledge hammer and had the meat hung up to chill before nightfall. But of course all this does not show on television. I am the way my daughter would want me to be: a hundred pounds lighter, my skin like an uncooked barley pancake. My hair glistens in the hot bright lights. Johnny Carson has much to do to keep up with my quick and witty tongue.

But that is a mistake. I know even before I wake up. Who ever knew a Johnson with a quick tongue? Who can even imagine me looking a strange white man in the eye? It seems to me I have talked to them always with one foot raised in flight, with my head turned in whichever way is farthest from them. Dee, though. She would always look anyone in the eye. Hesitation was no part of her nature.

"How do I look, Mama?" Maggie says, showing just enough of her thin body enveloped in pink skirt and red blouse for me to know she's there, almost hidden by the door.

"Come out into the yard," I say.

Have you ever seen a lame animal, perhaps a dog run over by some careless person rich enough to own a car, sidle up to someone who is ignorant enough to be kind to him? That is the way my Maggie walks. She has been like this, chin on chest, eyes on ground, feet in shuffle, ever since the fire that burned the other house to the ground.

Dee is lighter than Maggie, with nicer hair and a fuller figure. She's a woman now, though sometimes I forget. How long ago was it that the other house burned? Ten, twelve years? Sometimes I can still hear the flames and feel Maggie's arms sticking to me, her hair smoking and her dress falling off her in little black papery flakes. Her eyes seemed stretched open, blazed open by the flames reflected in them. And Dee. I see her standing off under the sweet gum tree she used to dig gum out of; a look of concentration on her face as she watched the last dingy gray board of the house fall in toward the red-hot brick chimney. Why don't you do a dance around the ashes? I'd wanted to ask her. She had hated the house that much.

I used to think she hated Maggie, too. But that was before we raised the money, the church and me, to send her to Augusta° to school. She used to read to us without pity; forcing words, lies, other folks' habits, whole lives upon us two, sitting trapped and ignorant underneath her voice. She washed us in a river of make-believe, burned us with a lot of knowledge we didn't necessarily need to know. Pressed us to her with the serious way she read, to shove us away at just the moment, like dimwits, we seemed about to understand.

Dee wanted nice things. A yellow organdy dress to wear to her graduation from high school; black pumps to match a green suit she'd made from an old suit somebody

Augusta *city in eastern Georgia, the location of Paine College.*

gave me. She was determined to stare down any disaster in her efforts. Her eyelids would not flicker for minutes at a time. Often I fought off the temptation to shake her. At sixteen she had a style of her own: and knew what style was.

I never had an education myself. After second grade the school was closed down. Don't ask me why: in 1927 colored asked fewer questions than they do now. Sometimes Maggie reads to me. She stumbles along good-naturedly but can't see well. She knows she is not bright. Like good looks and money, quickness passed her by. She will marry John Thomas (who has mossy teeth in an earnest face) and then I'll be free to sit here and I guess just sing church songs to myself. Although I never was a good singer. Never could carry a tune. I was always better at a man's job. I used to love to milk till I was hooked in the side° in '49. Cows are soothing and slow and don't bother you, unless you try to milk them the wrong way.

I have deliberately turned my back on the house. It is three rooms, just like the one that burned, except the roof is tin; they don't make shingle roofs any more. There are no real windows, just some holes cut in the sides, like the portholes in a ship, but not round and not square, with rawhide holding the shutters up on the outside. This house is in a pasture, too, like the other one. No doubt when Dee sees it she will want to tear it down. She wrote me once that no matter where we "choose" to live, she will manage to come see us. But she will never bring her friends. Maggie and I thought about this and Maggie asked me, "Mama, when did Dee ever *have* any friends?"

She had a few. Furtive boys in pink shirts hanging about on washday after school. Nervous girls who never laughed. Impressed with her they worshiped the well-turned phrase, the cute shape, the scalding humor that erupted like bubbles in lye. She read to them.

When she was courting Jimmy T she didn't have much time to pay to us, but turned all her faultfinding power on him. He *flew* to marry a cheap city gal from a family of ignorant flashy people. She hardly had time to recompose herself.

When she comes I will meet—but there they are!

Maggie attempts to make a dash for the house, in her shuffling way, but I stay her with my hand. "Come back here," I say. And she stops and tries to dig a well in the sand with her toe.

It is hard to see them clearly through the strong sun. But even the first glimpse of leg out of the car tells me it is Dee. Her feet were always neat-looking, as if God himself had shaped them with a certain style. From the other side of the car comes a short, stocky man. Hair is all over his head a foot long and hanging from his chin like a kinky mule tail. I hear Maggie suck in her breath. "Uhnnnh," is what it sounds like. Like when you see the wriggling end of a snake just in front of your foot on the road. "Uhnnnh."

Dee next. A dress down to the ground, in this hot weather. A dress so loud it hurts my eyes. There are yellows and oranges enough to throw back the light of the sun. I feel my whole face warming from the heat waves it throws out. Earrings gold, too, and hanging down to her shoulders. Bracelets dangling and making noises when she moves her arm up to shake the folds of the dress out of her armpits. The dress is loose and flows, and as she walks closer, I like it. I hear Maggie go "Uhnnnh" again. It is her

hooked in the side   *kicked by a cow.*

sister's hair. It stands straight up like the wool on a sheep. It is black as night and around the edges are two long pigtails that rope about like small lizards disappearing behind her ears.

"Wa-su-zo-Tean-o!"° she says, coming on in that gliding way the dress makes her move. The short stocky fellow with the hair to his navel is all grinning and he follows up with "Asalamalakim,° my mother and sister!" He moves to hug Maggie but she falls back, right up against the back of my chair. I feel her trembling there and when I look up I see the perspiration falling off her chin.

"Don't get up," says Dee. Since I am stout it takes something of a push. You can see me trying to move a second or two before I make it. She turns, showing white heels through her sandals, and goes back to the car. Out she peeks next with a Polaroid. She stoops down quickly and lines up picture after picture of me sitting there in front of the house with Maggie cowering behind me. She never takes a shot without making sure the house is included. When a cow comes nibbling around the edge of the yard she snaps it and me and Maggie *and* the house. Then she puts the Polaroid in the back seat of the car, and comes up and kisses me on the forehead.

Meanwhile Asalamalakim is going through motions with Maggie's hand. Maggie's hand is as limp as a fish, and probably as cold, despite the sweat, and she keeps trying to pull it back. It looks like Asalamalakim wants to shake hands but wants to do it fancy. Or maybe he don't know how people shake hands. Anyhow, he soon gives up on Maggie.

"Well," I say. "Dee."

"No, Mama," she says. "Not 'Dee,' Wangero Leewanika Kemanjo!"

"What happened to 'Dee'?" I wanted to know.

"She's dead," Wangero said. "I couldn't bear it any longer being named after the people who oppress me."

"You know as well as me you was named after your aunt Dicie," I said. Dicie is my sister. She named Dee. We called her "Big Dee" after Dee was born.

"But who was *she* named after?" asked Wangero.

"I guess after Grandma Dee," I said.

"And who was she named after?" asked Wangero.

"Her mother," I said, and saw Wangero was getting tired. "That's about as far back as I can trace it," I said. Though, in fact, I probably could have carried it back beyond the Civil War through the branches.

"Well," said Asalamalakim, "there you are."

"Uhnnnh," I heard Maggie say.

"There I was not," I said, "before 'Dicie' cropped up in our family, so why should I try to trace it that far back?"

He just stood there grinning, looking down on me like somebody inspecting a Model A car.° Every once in a while he and Wangero sent eye signals over my head.

"How do you pronounce this name?" I asked.

"You don't have to call me by it if you don't want to," said Wangero.

"Why shouldn't I?" I asked. "If that's what you want us to call you, we'll call you."

"I know it might sound awkward at first," said Wangero.

Wa-su-zo-Tean-o *greeting used by black Muslims.* **Asalamalakim** *Muslim salutation meaning "Peace be with you."* **Model A car** *the Ford car that replaced the Model T in the late 1920s. The Model A was proverbial for its quality and durability.*

"I'll get used to it," I said. "Ream it out again."

Well, soon we got the name out of the way. Asalamalakim had a name twice as long and three times as hard. After I tripped over it two or three times he told me to just call him Hakim-a-barber. I wanted to ask him was he a barber, but I didn't really think he was, so I didn't ask.

"You must belong to those beef-cattle peoples down the road," I said. They said "Asalamalakim" when they met you, too, but they didn't shake hands. Always too busy: feeding the cattle, fixing the fences, putting up salt-lick shelters,° throwing down hay. When the white folks poisoned some of the herd the men stayed up all night with rifles in their hands. I walked a mile and a half just to see the sight.

Hakim-a-barber said, "I accept some of their doctrines, but farming and raising cat-tle is not my style." (They didn't tell me, and I didn't ask, whether Wangero [Dee] had really gone and married him.)

We sat down to eat and right away he said he didn't eat collards and pork was un-clean. Wangero, though, went on through the chitlins and corn bread, the greens and everything else. She talked a blue streak over the sweet potatoes. Everything delighted her. Even the fact that we still used the benches her daddy made for the table when we couldn't afford to buy chairs.

"Oh, Mama!" she cried. Then turned to Hakim-a-barber. "I never knew how lovely these benches are. You can feel the rump prints," she said, running her hands under-neath her and along the bench. Then she gave a sigh and her hand closed over Grandma Dee's butter dish. "That's it!" she said. "I knew there was something I wanted to ask you if I could have." She jumped up from the table and went over in the corner where the churn stood, the milk in it clabber° by now. She looked at the churn and looked at it.

"This churn top is what I need," she said. "Didn't Uncle Buddy whittle it out of a tree you all used to have?"

"Yes," I said.

"Uh huh," she said happily. "And I want the dasher, too."

"Uncle Buddy whittle that, too?" asked the barber.

Dee (Wangero) looked up at me.

"Aunt Dee's first husband whittled the dash," said Maggie so low you almost couldn't hear her. "His name was Henry, but they called him Stash."

"Maggie's brain is like an elephant's," Wangero said, laughing. "I can use the churn top as a centerpiece for the alcove table," she said, sliding a plate over the churn, "and I'll think of something artistic to do with the dasher."

When she finished wrapping the dasher the handle stuck out. I took it for a mo-ment in my hands. You didn't even have to look close to see where hands pushing the dasher up and down to make butter had left a kind of sink in the wood. In fact, there were a lot of small sinks; you could see where thumbs and fingers had sunk into the wood. It was beautiful light yellow wood, from a tree that grew in the yard where Big Dee and Stash had lived.

After dinner Dee (Wangero) went to the trunk at the foot of my bed and started rifling through it. Maggie hung back in the kitchen over the dishpan. Out came Wangero with two quilts. They had been pieced by Grandma Dee and then Big Dee

---

salt-lick shelters *shelters built to prevent rain from dissolving large blocks of rock salt set up on poles for cattle.*
clabber *curdled, turned sour.*

and me had hung them on the quilt frames on the front porch and quilted them. One was in the Lone Star pattern. The other was Walk Around the Mountain. In both of them were scraps of dresses Grandma Dee had worn fifty and more years ago. Bits and pieces of Grandpa Jarrell's Paisley shirts. And one teeny faded blue piece, about the size of a penny matchbox, that was from Great Grandpa Ezra's uniform that he wore in the Civil War.

"Mama," Wangero said sweet as a bird. "Can I have these old quilts?"

I heard something fall in the kitchen, and a minute later the kitchen door slammed.

"Why don't you take one or two of the others?" I asked. "These old things was just done by me and Big Dee from some tops your grandma pieced before she died."

"No," said Wangero. "I don't want those. They are stitched around the borders by machine."

"That'll make them last better," I said.

"That's not the point," said Wangero. "These are all pieces of dresses Grandma used to wear. She did all this stitching by hand. Imagine!" She held the quilts securely in her arms, stroking them.

"Some of the pieces, like those lavender ones, come from old clothes her mother handed down to her," I said, moving up to touch the quilts. Dee (Wangero) moved back just enough so that I couldn't reach the quilts. They already belonged to her.

"Imagine!" she breathed again, clutching them closely to her bosom.

"The truth is," I said, "I promised to give them quilts to Maggie, for when she marries John Thomas."

She gasped like a bee had stung her.

"Maggie can't appreciate these quilts!" she said. "She'd probably be backward enough to put them to everyday use."

"I reckon she would," I said. "God knows I been saving 'em for long enough with nobody using 'em. I hope she will!" I didn't want to bring up how I had offered Dee (Wangero) a quilt when she went away to college. Then she had told me they were old-fashioned, out of style.

"But they're *priceless!*" she was saying now, furiously; for she has a temper. "Maggie would put them on the bed and in five years they'd be in rags. Less than that!"

"She can always make some more," I said. "Maggie knows how to quilt."

Dee (Wangero) looked at me with hatred. "You just will not understand. The point is these quilts, *these* quilts!"

"Well," I said, stumped. "What would *you* do with them?"

"Hang them," she said. As if that was the only thing you *could* do with quilts.

Maggie by now was standing in the door. I could almost hear the sound her feet made as they scraped over each other.

"She can have them, Mama," she said, like somebody used to never winning anything, or having anything reserved for her. "I can 'member Grandma Dee without the quilts."

I looked at her hard. She had filled her bottom lip with checkerberry snuff and it gave her face a kind of dopey, hangdog look. It was Grandma Dee and Big Dee who taught her how to quilt herself. She stood there with her scarred hands hidden in the folds of her skirt. She looked at her sister with something like fear but she wasn't mad at her. This was Maggie's portion. This was the way she knew God to work.

When I looked at her like that something hit me in the top of my head and ran down to the soles of my feet. Just like when I'm in church and the spirit of God touches me and I get happy and shout. I did something I never had done before: hugged Maggie to me, then dragged her on into the room, snatched the quilts out of Miss Wangero's hands and dumped them into Maggie's lap. Maggie just sat there on my bed with her mouth open.

"Take one or two of the others," I said to Dee.

But she turned without a word and went out to Hakim-a-barber.

"You just don't understand," she said, as Maggie and I came out to the car.

"What don't I understand?" I wanted to know.

"Your heritage," she said. And then she turned to Maggie, kissed her, and said, "You ought to try to make something of yourself, too, Maggie. It's really a new day for us. But from the way you and Mama still live you'd never know it."

She put on some sunglasses that hid everything above the tip of her nose and her chin.

Maggie smiled; maybe at the sunglasses. But a real smile, not scared. After we watched the car dust settle I asked Maggie to bring me a dip of snuff. And then the two of us sat there just enjoying, until it was time to go in the house and go to bed.

(1973)

LEE K. ABBOTT
[b. 1947]

The View of Me from Mars

A week before I became a father, which now seems like the long ago and far away fairy tales happen in, I read a father-child story that went straight at the surprise one truth between children and parents is. It was called "Mirrors," and had an end, to the twenty-three-year-old would-be know-it-all I was, that literally threw me back in my chair—an end, sad somehow and wise, which held that it is now and then necessary for the child, in ways mysterious with love, to forgive the parent.

In "Mirrors" the child was a girl, though it could have been a boy just as easily, whose father—a decent man, we have to believe—takes her to the sideshow tent at a one-horse and one-elephant circus in the flatlands of Iowa or Nebraska or Kansas. She's seven or eight at this time, and—as we have all begged for toys or experiences it can be, I see now, our misfortune to receive—she begs and begs to see the snake charmer and the tattooed lady, the giant and the dwarf. He gives in, the girl decides much later, because of his decency; or he gives in, as my own father might say, because he's too much a milk-and-cookies sort of fool to understand that in that smelly, ill-lit tent is knowledge it is a parent's duty often to deny or to avoid. It is a good moment, I tell you, this moment when they pay their quarters and go in, one person full of pride, the other sucking on cotton candy, the sad end of them still pages and pages away.

In that tent—a whole hour, I think—walking from little stage to little stage, the girl is awestruck and puzzled and, well, breath-taken, full of questions about where these people, these creatures, live and what they do when they're not standing in front of a bunch of hayseeds and would it be possible to get a face, a tattoo, printed on her knee. "Can I touch?" she asks. "Do they talk?" A spotlight comes on, blue and harsh, and nearby, in a swirl of cigarette smoke and field dust, are two little people, Mr. and Mrs. Tiny, gussied up like a commodore and his society bride; another light snaps on, yellow this time and ten paces away, and there stands a man—"A boy," the barker tells us, "only eighteen and still growing!"—who's already nine feet tall, his arms long as shovels, nothing in his face about his own parents or what he wants to be at twenty-five. These are clichés, my smart wife, Ellen Kay, tells me ("Sounds too artsy-fartsy," her exact words were when I read the thing to her), but in the story I remember, these are the exhibitions girl and man pass by—the girl Christmas Eve impatient, the man nervous—before they come to the main display, which is, in "Mirrors," a young woman, beautiful and smooth as china, who has no arms and no legs.

The father, complaining that he's grubby-feeling and hot, wants to get out, but his daughter, her heart hammering in her ears, can't move. As never before, she's conscious of her own hands and feet, the wonders they are. She's aware of smells—breath and oil and two-dollar cologne—and of sounds—a gasp here, a whisper there, exclamations that have in them ache and horror and fear. "C'mon," the father says, taking her elbow. But onstage, businesslike as a banker, the woman—"The Human Torso," the barker announces, "smart like the dickens"—is drinking water, the glass clamped against her neck by her shoulder; is putting on lipstick; is writing her name with a brush between her teeth; is, Lordy, about to type—with her chin maybe—a letter to a Spec 4 with the Army in Korea, her boyfriend.

Outside, the midway glittering and crowded with Iowans going crosswise, the girl, more fascinated than frightened (though the fright is coming), asks how that was done. The father has a Lucky Strike out now, and the narrator—seven or eight but on the verge of learning what will stay with her until seventy or eighty—realizes he's stalling. He's embarrassed, maybe sick. He says "Howdy" to a deadbeat he'd never otherwise talk to. He says he's hungry, how about a hot dog, some buttered popcorn? He's cold, he says, too cold for September. "How?" she says again, pulling at his sleeve a little and watching his face go stiff and loose in a way that has her saying to herself, "I am not scared. No, I am not." And then he says what the narrator realizes will be his answer—sometimes comic, often not—for all thereafter that astounds or baffles and will not be known: "Mirrors, it's done with mirrors."

There's a pause here, I remember, six sentences that tell what the weather is like and how, here and there, light bulbs are missing and what the girl's favorite subjects are in school. "What?" she thinks to ask, but doesn't. "It's an illusion," he says, his voice squeaky the way it gets when he talks about money they don't have much of. "A trick, like magic." Part of her—the part that can say the sum of two plus two, and that A is for Apple, B is for Boy—knows that mirrors have nothing to do with what she's seen; another part—this the half of her that will remember this incident forever and ever—knows that her father, now as strange to her as the giant and the dwarf, is lying.

His hand is working up and down, and his expression says, as lips and eyes and cheeks will, that he's sorry, he didn't mean for her to see that, she's so young. Something is trembling inside her, a muscle or a bone. One-Mississippi, she says to herself. Two-Mississippi. Over there sits a hound dog wearing a hat and somewhere a shout is going up that says somebody won a Kewpie doll or a stuffed monkey, and up ahead, creaking and clanking, the Tilt-A-Whirl is full of people spinning round and round goggle-eyed. Her father has a smile not connected to his eyes—another lie—and his hand out to be held, and going by them is a fat lady who lives on Jefferson Street and a man with a limp who lives on Spruce. Her father seems too hairy to her now, and maybe not sharp-minded enough, with a nose too long and knobby. She tells herself what she is, which is a good dancer and smart about which side the fork goes on and who gets introduced first when strangers meet; and what she is not, which is strong enough to do pull-ups and watchful about who goes where and why. She is learning something, she thinks. There is being good, she thinks. And there is not. There is the truth, she thinks. And there is not.

And so, in the climax of what I read years and years ago, she says, her hands sticky and her dress white as Hollywood daylight, "Yes, mirrors, I thought so"—words that, years and years ago, said all I thought possible about lies and love and how forgiveness works.

In this story, which is true and only two days old and also about forgiveness, I am the father to be read about and the child is my son, Stuart Eliot Polk, Jr. (called "Pudge" in and out of the family); he's a semifat golfer—"linksman," he insists the proper term is—and honor student who will at the end of this summer go off to college and so cease to be a citizen in the sideshow tent my big house here in El Paso now clearly is. Yes, forgiveness—particularly ironic in that, since my graduation years ago from Perkins Seminary at SMU, it has been my job to say, day after day after day, the noises that are "It will get better" and "We all make mistakes" to a thousand Methodists who aim to be themselves forgiven and sent home happy. There is no "freak" here, except the ordinary one I am, and no storybook midway, except my modern kitchen and its odd come and go.

I am an adulterer—an old-fashioned word, sure, but the only one appropriate to the ancient sin it names; and my lover—a modern word not so full of terror and guilt and judgment as another—was, until two days ago, Terri Ann Mackey, a rich, three-times-married former Zeta Tau Alpha Texas girl who might one day make headlines for the dramatic hair she has or the way she can sing Conway Twitty tunes. In every way likable and loud and free-minded, she has, in the last four years, met me anywhere and everywhere—in the Marriott and Hilton hotels, in the Cavern of Music in Juarez, even at a preachers' retreat at the Inn of the Mountain Gods near Ruidoso in southern New Mexico's piney forests. Dressed up in this or that outfit she sent away for or got on a trip to Dallas, she has, to my delight and education, pretended to be naughty as what we imagine the Swedish are or nice as Snow White; she has pretended, in a hundred rented rooms, to be everything I thought my wife was not—daring and wicked, heedless as a tyrant. Shameful to say, it seems we have always been here, in this bright desert cowtown, now far-flung and fifty percent ticky-tacky, drinking wine and fornicating and then hustling home to deceive people we were wed to. Shameful to say, it seems we have always been playing the eyes' version of footsy—her in pink and cactus yellow in a pew in the middle of St. Paul's, me in the pulpit sermonizing about parables and Jesus and what welfare we owe the lost and poor and beaten down.

"Yes," my wife, Ellen Kay, would answer when I told her I was at the Stanton Street Racquet Club playing handball with a UTEP management professor named Red Walker. "Go change," she'd say, herself lovely and schoolgirl trim as that woman I'd collapsed atop a half-hour before. "I phoned," she'd say, "Mrs. Denbo said you were out." Yes, I'd tell her. I was in the choir room, hunting organ music that would inspire and not be hokey; I was in the library, looking up what the Puritan Mathers had written about witchcraft and gobbledygook we are better off without; I was taking a drive in my Volvo, the better to clear my head so I could get to the drafting of a speech for the Rotarians, or the LULAC Club of Ysleta, or the Downtown Optimists. "You work too hard," she'd say, "let's go to Acapulco this year." And I'd head to my big bedroom, the men I am, the public one amazed by his private self—the first absolutely in love with a blonde continental-history major he'd courted at the University of Texas in 1967; the second still frazzled by what, in the afternoon, is made from deceit and bednoise and indecency. And until two days ago, it was possible to believe that I knew which was which, what what.

"Where were you?" Ellen Kay said, making (though too violently, I think now) the tuna casserole I like enough to eat twice a year. "I called everywhere," she said. "It was as if you didn't exist." Upset, her hair spilling out of the French roll she prefers, she said more, two or three paragraphs whose theme was my peculiar behavior and the sly way I had lately and what time I was supposed to be somewhere and was not; and suddenly, taking note of the thump-thump my heart made and how one cloud in the east looked like a bell, I stood at the sink, steadily drinking glass after glass of water, trying to put some miles between me and her suspicions. Terri Ann Mackey Cruz Robinson Cross was all over me, my hands and my thighs and my face; and, a giant step away, my wife was asking where I'd been. "You were going to call," Ellen Kay said. "You had an appointment, a meeting." I had one thought, which was about the bricked-up middle of me, and another, which was about how like TV this situation was. "I talked to Bill Watson at the bank," she said. "He hasn't seen you for a week, ten days. I called—" And her wayward husband had a moment then, familiar to all cheaters and sorry folks, when he thought he'd tell the truth; a moment, before fear hit him and he got a 3-D vision of the cheap world he'd have to live in, when he thought to make plain the creature he was and the no-account stage he stood upon.

"I was at the golf course," I said, "watching Pudge. They have a match tomorrow." The oven was closed, the refrigerator opened. "Which course?" she said. Forks and knives had been brought out, made a pile of. "Coronado Hills," I said. "Pudge is hitting the ball pretty good." She went past me a dozen times, carrying the plates and the bread and the fruit bowl, and I tried to meet her eyes and so not give away the corrupt inside of me. I thought of several Latin words—*bellum* and *verus* and *fatum*—and the Highland Park classroom I learned them in. "All right," she said, though by the dark notes in her voice it was clear she was going to ask Pudge if he'd seen me there, by the green I'd claimed to have stood next to, applauding the expert wedge shot I'd seen with my very own eyes.

As in the former story of illusions and the mess they make crashing down, there is a pause here, one of two; and you are to imagine now how herky-jerky time moved in our house when Pudge drove up and came in and said howdy and washed his hands as he'd been a million times told. You are to imagine, too, the dinner we picked at and our small talk about school and American government and what money does. While time went up and down, I thought about Pudge the way evil comic-book Martians are said to think about us: I was curious to know how I'd be affected by what, in a minute or an hour, would come from the mouth of an earthling who, so far as I knew, had never looked much beyond himself to see the insignificant dust ball he stood upon. I saw him as his own girlfriend, Traci Dixon, must: polite, fussy as a nun, soft-spoken about everything except golf and how it is, truly, a full-fledged sport.

Part of me—that eye and ear which would make an excellent witness at an auto wreck or similar calamity—flew up to one high corner of the room, like a ghost or an angel, and wondered what could be said about these three people who sat there and there and there. They were Democrats who, in a blue moon, liked what Reagan did; they had Allstate insurance and bank books and stacks of paper that said where they were in the world and what business they conducted with it; they played Scrabble and Clue and chose to watch the news Dan Rather read. The wife, who once upon a time could run fast enough to be useful in flag football, now used all her energy to keep mostly white-collar rednecks from using the words "nigger" and "spic" in her company; the son, who had once wanted to be an astronaut or a Houston brain surgeon, now aimed to be the only Ph.D. in computer science to win the Masters at Augusta, Georgia; and the father—well, what was there to say about a supposedly learned man for whom the spitting image of God, Who was up and yonder and everywhere, was his own father, a bent-over and gin-soaked cattle rancher in Midland, Texas? I hovered in that corner, distant and disinterested, and then Ellen Kay spoke to Pudge, and I came rushing back, dumb and helpless as anything human that falls from a great height.

"Daddy says you had a good round this afternoon," Ellen Kay began. "You had an especially nice wedge shot, he says." She was being sneaky, which my own sneaky self admired; and Pudge quit the work his chewing was, a little confusion in his round, smart face. He was processing, that machine between his ears crunching data that in no way could ever be, and for the fifteen seconds we made eye contact I wanted him to put aside reason and logic and algebra and see me with his guts and heart. On his lip he had a crumb that, if you didn't tell him, would stay until kingdom come; I wanted him to stop blinking and wrinkling his forehead like a first-year theater student. The air was heavy in that room, the light coming from eight directions at once, and I wanted to remind him of our trip last January to the Phoenix Open and that too-scholarly talk we'd had about the often mixed-up relations between men and women. I had a picture of me throwing a ball to him, and of him catching it. I had a picture of him learning to drive a stick shift, and of him so carefully mowing our lawn. Oddly, I thought about fishing, which I hate, and bowling, which I am silly at, and then Ellen Kay, putting detergent in the dishwasher, asked him again about events that never happened, and I took a deep breath I expected to hold until the horror stopped.

Here is that second pause I spoke of—that moment, before time lurches forward again, when the eye needs to look elsewhere to see what is ruined, what not. Pudge now knew I was lying. His eyes went here and there, to the clock above my shoulder, to his mother's overwatered geranium on the windowsill, to his mostly empty plate. He was learning something about me—and about himself too. Like his made-up counterpart in "Mirrors," he was seeing that I, his father, was afraid and weak and damaged; and like the invented daddy in that story I read, a daddy whose interior life we were not permitted to see, I wanted my own child, however numbed or shocked, to forgive me for the tilt the world now stood at, to say I was not responsible for the sad magic trick our common back-and-forth really is. "Tell her," I said. I had in mind a story he could confirm—the Coke we shared in the clubhouse, a corny joke that was heard, and the help I tried to be with his short game—a story that had nowhere in it, two days ago, a father cold and alone and small.

(1991)

JAMAICA KINCAID
[b. 1949]

Girl

Wash the white clothes on Monday and put them on the stone heap; wash the color clothes on Tuesday and put them on the clothesline to dry; don't walk barehead in the hot sun; cook pumpkin fritters in very hot sweet oil; soak your little cloths right after you take them off; when buying cotton to make yourself a nice blouse, be sure that it doesn't have gum on it, because that way it won't hold up well after a wash; soak salt fish overnight before you cook it; is it true that you sing benna in Sunday school?; always eat your food in such a way that it won't turn someone else's stomach; on Sundays try to walk like a lady and not like the slut you are so bent on becoming; don't sing benna in Sunday school; you mustn't speak to wharf-rat boys, not even to give directions; don't eat fruits on the street—flies will follow you; *but I don't sing benna on Sundays at all and never in Sunday school;* this is how to sew on a button; this is how to make a buttonhole for the button you have just sewed on; this is how to hem a dress when you see the hem coming down and so to prevent yourself from looking like the slut I know you are so bent on becoming; this is how you iron your father's khaki shirt so that it doesn't have a crease; this is how you iron your father's khaki pants so that they don't have a crease; this is how you grow okra—far from the house, because okra tree harbors red ants; when you are growing dasheen, make sure it gets plenty of water or else it makes your throat itch when you are eating it; this is how you sweep a corner; this is how you sweep a whole house; this is how you sweep a yard; this is how you smile to someone you don't like too much; this is how you smile to someone you don't like at all; this is how you smile to someone you like completely; this is how you set a table for tea; this is how you set a table for dinner; this is how you set a table for dinner with an important guest; this is how you set a table for lunch; this is how you set a table for breakfast; this is how to behave in the presence of men who don't know you very well, and this way they won't recognize immediately the slut I have warned you against becoming; be sure to wash every day, even if it is with your own spit; don't squat down to play marbles—you are not a boy, you know; don't pick people's flowers—you might catch something; don't throw stones at blackbirds, because it might not be a blackbird at all; this is how to make a bread pudding; this is how to make doukona; this is how to make pepper pot; this is how to make a good medicine for a cold; this is how to make a good medicine to throw away a child before it even becomes a child; this is how to catch a fish; this is how to throw back a fish you don't like, and that way something bad won't fall on you; this is how to bully a man; this is how a man bullies you; this is how to love a man, and if this doesn't work there are other ways, and if they don't work don't feel too bad about giving up; this is how to spit up in the air if you feel like it, and this is how to move quick so that it doesn't fall on you; this is how to make ends meet; always squeeze bread to make sure it's fresh; *but what if the baker won't let me feel the bread?;* you mean to say that after all you are really going to be the kind of woman who the baker won't let near the bread?

(1984)

LESLIE SILKO
[b. 1948]

Yellow Woman

I

My thigh clung to his with dampness, and I watched the sun rising up through the tamaracks and willows. The small brown water birds came to the river and hopped across the mud, leaving brown scratches in the alkali-white crust. They bathed in the river silently. I could hear the water, almost at our feet where the narrow fast channel bubbled and washed green ragged moss and fern leaves. I looked at him beside me, rolled in the red blanket on the white river sand. I cleaned the sand out of the cracks between my toes, squinting because the sun was above the willow trees. I looked at him for the last time, sleeping on the white river sand.

I felt hungry and followed the river south the way we had come the afternoon before, following our footprints that were already blurred by lizard tracks and bug trails. The horses were still lying down, and the black one whinnied when he saw me but he did not get up—maybe it was because the corral was made out of thick cedar branches and the horses had not yet felt the sun like I had. I tried to look beyond the pale red mesas to the pueblo. I knew it was there, even if I could not see it, on the sandrock hill above the river, the same river that moved past me now and had reflected the moon last night.

The horse felt warm underneath me. He shook his head and pawed the sand. The bay whinnied and leaned against the gate trying to follow, and I remembered him asleep in the red blanket beside the river. I slid off the horse and tied him close to the other horse. I walked north with the river again, and the white sand broke loose in footprints over footprints.

"Wake up."

He moved in the blanket and turned his face to me with his eyes still closed. I knelt down to touch him.

"I'm leaving."

He smiled now, eyes still closed. "You are coming with me, remember?" He sat up now with his bare dark chest and belly in the sun.

"Where?"

"To my place."

"And will I come back?"

He pulled his pants on. I walked away from him, feeling him behind me and smelling the willows.

"Yellow Woman," he said.

I turned to face him. "Who are you?" I asked.

He laughed and knelt on the low, sandy bank, washing his face in the river. "Last night you guessed my name, and you knew why I had come."

I stared past him at the shallow moving water and tried to remember the night, but I could only see the moon in the water and remember his warmth around me.

"But I only said that you were him and that I was Yellow Woman—I'm not really her—I have my own name and I come from the pueblo on the other side of the mesa. Your name is Silva and you are a stranger I met by the river yesterday afternoon."

He laughed softly. "What happened yesterday has nothing to do with what you will do today, Yellow Woman."

"I know—that's what I'm saying—the old stories about the ka'tsina spirit and Yellow Woman can't mean us."

My old grandpa liked to tell those stories best. There is one about Badger and Coyote who went hunting and were gone all day, and when the sun was going down they found a house. There was a girl living there alone, and she had light hair and eyes and she told them that they could sleep with her. Coyote wanted to be with her all night so he sent Badger into a prairie-dog hole, telling him he thought he saw something in it. As soon as Badger crawled in, Coyote blocked up the entrance with rocks and hurried back to Yellow Woman.

"Come here," he said gently.

He touched my neck and I moved close to him to feel his breathing and to hear his heart. I was wondering if Yellow Woman had known who she was—if she knew that she would become part of the stories. Maybe she'd had another name that her husband and relatives called her so that only the ka'tsina from the north and the storytellers would know her as Yellow Woman. But I didn't go on; I felt him all around me, pushing me down into the white river sand.

Yellow Woman went away with the spirit from the north and lived with him and his relatives. She was gone for a long time, but then one day she came back and she brought twin boys.

"Do you know the story?"

"What story?" He smiled and pulled me close to him as he said this. I was afraid lying there on the red blanket. All I could know was the way he felt, warm, damp, his body beside me. This is the way it happens in the stories, I was thinking, with no thought beyond the moment she meets the ka'tsina spirit and they go.

"I don't have to go. What they tell in stories was real only then, back in time immemorial, like they say."

He stood up and pointed at my clothes tangled in the blanket. "Let's go," he said.

I walked beside him, breathing hard because he walked fast, his hand around my wrist. I had stopped trying to pull away from him, because his hand felt cool and the sun was high, drying the river bed into alkali. I will see someone, eventually I will see someone, and then I will be certain that he is only a man—some man from nearby—and I will be sure that I am not Yellow Woman. Because she is from out of time past and I live now and I've been to school and there are highways and pickup trucks that Yellow Woman never saw.

It was an easy ride north on horseback. I watched the change from the cottonwood trees along the river to the junipers that brushed past us in the foothills, and finally there were only piñons, and when I looked up at the rim of the mountain plateau I could see pine trees growing on the edge. Once I stopped to look down, but the pale sandstone had disappeared and the river was gone and the dark lava hills were all around. He touched my hand, not speaking, but always singing softly a mountain song and looking into my eyes.

I felt hungry and wondered what they were doing at home now—my mother, my grandmother, my husband, and the baby. Cooking breakfast, saying, "Where did she go?—maybe kidnapped," and Al going to the tribal police with the details: "She went walking along the river."

The house was made with black lava rock and red mud. It was high above the spreading miles of arroyos and long mesas. I smelled a mountain smell of pitch and buck brush. I stood there beside the black horse, looking down on the small, dim country we had passed, and I shivered.

"Yellow Woman, come inside where it's warm."

2

He lit a fire in the stove. It was an old stove with a round belly and an enamel coffeepot on top. There was only the stove, some faded Navajo blankets, and a bedroll and cardboard box. The floor was made of smooth adobe plaster, and there was one small window facing east. He pointed at the box.

"There's some potatoes and the frying pan." He sat on the floor with his arms around his knees pulling them close to his chest and he watched me fry the potatoes. I didn't mind him watching me because he was always watching me—he had been watching me since I came upon him sitting on the river bank trimming leaves from a willow twig with his knife. We ate from the pan and he wiped the grease from his fingers on his Levis.

"Have you brought women here before?" He smiled and kept chewing, so I said, "Do you always use the same tricks?"

"What tricks?" He looked at me like he didn't understand.

"The story about being a ka'tsina from the mountains. The story about Yellow Woman."

Silva was silent; his face was calm.

"I don't believe it. Those stories couldn't happen now," I said.

He shook his head and said softly, "But someday they will talk about us, and they will say, 'Those two lived long ago when things like that happened.'"

He stood up and went out. I ate the rest of the potatoes and thought about things—about the noise the stove was making and the sound of the mountain wind outside. I remembered yesterday and the day before, and then I went outside.

I walked past the corral to the edge where the narrow trail cut through the black rim rock. I was standing in the sky with nothing around me but the wind that came down from the blue mountain peak behind me. I could see faint mountain images in the distance, miles across the vast spread of mesas and valleys and plains. I wondered who was over there to feel the mountain wind on those sheer blue edges—who walks on the pine needles in those blue mountains.

"Can you see the pueblo?" Silva was standing behind me.

I shook my head. "We're too far away."

"From here I can see the world." He stepped out on the edge. "The Navajo reservation begins over there." He pointed to the east. "The Pueblo boundaries are over here." He looked below us to the south, where the narrow trail seemed to come from. "The Texans have their ranches over there, starting with that valley, the Concho Valley. The Mexicans run some cattle over there too."

"Do you ever work for them?"

"I steal from them," Silva answered. The sun was dropping behind us and shadows were filling the land below. I turned away from the edge that dropped forever into the valleys below.

"I'm cold," I said; "I'm going inside." I started wondering about this man who could speak the Pueblo language so well but who lived on a mountain and rustled cattle. I decided that this man Silva must be Navajo, because Pueblo men didn't do things like that.

"You must be a Navajo."

Silva shook his head gently. "Little Yellow Woman," he said, "you never give up, do you? I have told you who I am. The Navajo people know me, too." He knelt down and unrolled the bedroll and spread the extra blankets out on a piece of canvas. The sun was down, and the only light in the house came from outside—the dim orange light from sundown.

I stood there and waited for him to crawl under the blankets.

"What are you waiting for?" he said, and I lay down beside him. He undressed me slowly like the night before beside the river—kissing my face gently and running his hands up and down my belly and legs. He took off my pants and then he laughed.

"Why are you laughing?"

"You are breathing so hard."

I pulled away from him and turned my back to him.

He pulled me around and pinned me down with his arms and chest. "You don't understand, do you, little Yellow Woman? You will do what I want."

And again he was all around me with his skin slippery against mine, and I was afraid because I understood that his strength could hurt me. I lay underneath him and I knew that he could destroy me. But later, while he slept beside me, I touched his face and I had a feeling—the kind of feeling for him that overcame me that morning along the river. I kissed him on the forehead and he reached out for me.

When I woke up in the morning he was gone. It gave me a strange feeling because for a long time I sat there on the blankets and looked around the little house for some object of his—some proof that he had been there or maybe that he was coming back. Only the blankets and the cardboard box remained. The .30–30 that had been leaning in the corner was gone, and so was the knife I had used the night before. He was gone, and I had my chance to go now. But first I had to eat, because I knew it would be a long walk home.

I found some dried apricots in the cardboard box, and I sat down on a rock at the edge of the plateau rim. There was no wind and the sun warmed me. I was surrounded by silence. I drowsed with apricots in my mouth, and I didn't believe that there were highways or railroads or cattle to steal.

When I woke up, I stared down at my feet in the black mountain dirt. Little black ants were swarming over the pine needles around my foot. They must have smelled the apricots. I thought about my family far below me. They would be wondering about me, because this had never happened to me before. The tribal police would file a report. But if old Grandpa weren't dead he would tell them what happened—he would laugh and say, "Stolen by a ka'tsina, a mountain spirit. She'll come home—they usually do." There are enough of them to handle things. My mother and grandmother will raise the baby like they raised me. Al will find someone else, and they will go on like before, except that there will be a story about the day I disappeared while I was walking along the river. Silva had come for me, he said he had. I did not decide to go. I just went. Moonflowers blossom in the sand hills before dawn, just as I followed him. That's what I was thinking as I wandered along the trail through the pine trees.

It was noon when I got back. When I saw the stone house I remembered that I had meant to go home. But that didn't seem important any more, maybe because there were little blue flowers growing in the meadow behind the stone house and the gray squirrels were playing in the pines next to the house. The horses were standing in the corral, and there was a beef carcass hanging on the shady side of a big pine in front of the house. Flies buzzed around the clotted blood that hung from the carcass. Silva was washing his hands in a bucket full of water. He must have heard me coming because he spoke to me without turning to face me.

"I've been waiting for you."

"I went walking in the big pine trees."

I looked into the bucket full of bloody water with brown-and-white animal hairs floating in it. Silva stood there letting his hands drip, examining me intently.

"Are you coming with me?"

"Where?" I asked him.

"To sell the meat in Marquez."

"If you're sure it's O.K."

"I wouldn't ask you if it wasn't," he answered.

He sloshed the water around in the bucket before he dumped it out and set the bucket upside down near the door. I followed him to the corral and watched him saddle the horses. Even beside the horses he looked tall, and I asked him again if he wasn't Navajo. He didn't say anything; he just shook his head and kept cinching up the saddle.

"But Navajos are tall."

"Get on the horse," he said, "and let's go."

The last thing he did before we started down the steep trail was to grab the .30–30 from the corner. He slid the rifle into the scabbard that hung from his saddle.

"Do they ever try to catch you?" I asked.

"They don't know who I am."

"Then why did you bring the rifle?"

"Because we are going to Marquez where the Mexicans live."

3

The trail leveled out on a narrow ridge that was steep on both sides like an animal spine. On one side I could see where the trail went around the rocky gray hills and disappeared into the southeast where the pale sandrock mesas stood in the distance near my home. On the other side was a trail that went west, and as I looked far into the distance I thought I saw the little town. But Silva said no, that I was looking in the wrong place, that I just thought I saw houses. After that I quit looking off into the distance; it was hot and the wildflowers were closing up their deep-yellow petals. Only the waxy cactus flowers bloomed in the bright sun, and I saw every color that a cactus blossom can be; the white ones and the red ones were still buds, but the purple and the yellow were blossoms, open full and the most beautiful of all.

Silva saw him before I did. The white man was riding a big gray horse, coming up the trail toward us. He was traveling fast and the gray horse's feet sent rocks rolling off the trail into the dry tumbleweeds. Silva motioned for me to stop and we watched the white man. He didn't see us right away, but finally his horse whinnied at our horses and he stopped. He looked at us briefly before he loped the gray horse across the three hundred yards that separated us. He stopped his horse in front of Silva, and his young fat face was shadowed by the brim of his hat. He didn't look mad, but his small, pale eyes moved from the blood-soaked gunny sacks hanging from my saddle to Silva's face and then back to my face.

"Where did you get the fresh meat?" the white man asked.

"I've been hunting," Silva said, and when he shifted his weight in the saddle the leather creaked.

"The hell you have, Indian. You've been rustling cattle. We've been looking for the thief for a long time."

The rancher was fat, and sweat began to soak through his white cowboy shirt and the wet cloth stuck to the thick rolls of belly fat. He almost seemed to be panting from the exertion of talking, and he smelled rancid, maybe because Silva scared him.

Silva turned to me and smiled. "Go back up the mountain, Yellow Woman."

The white man got angry when he heard Silva speak in a language he couldn't understand. "Don't try anything, Indian. Just keep riding to Marquez. We'll call the state police from there."

The rancher must have been unarmed because he was very frightened and if he had a gun he would have pulled it out then. I turned my horse around and the rancher yelled, "Stop!" I looked at Silva for an instant and there was something ancient and dark—something I could feel in my stomach—in his eyes, and when I glanced at his hand I saw his finger on the trigger of the .30–30 that was still in the saddle scabbard. I slapped my horse across the flank and the sacks of raw meat swung against my knees as the horse leaped up the trail. It was hard to keep my balance, and once I thought I felt the saddle slipping backward; it was because of this that I could not look back.

I didn't stop until I reached the ridge where the trail forked. The horse was breathing deep gasps and there was a dark film of sweat on its neck. I looked down in the direction I had come from, but I couldn't see the place. I waited. The wind came up and pushed warm air past me. I looked up at the sky, pale blue and full of thin clouds and fading vapor trails left by jets.

I think four shots were fired—I remember hearing four hollow explosions that reminded me of deer hunting. There could have been more shots after that, but I couldn't have heard them because my horse was running again and the loose rocks were making too much noise as they scattered around his feet.

Horses have a hard time running downhill, but I went that way instead of uphill to the mountain because I thought it was safer. I felt better with the horse running southeast past the round gray hills that were covered with cedar trees and black lava rock. When I got to the plain in the distance I could see the dark green patches of tamaracks that grew along the river; and beyond the river I could see the beginning of the pale sandrock mesas. I stopped the horse and looked back to see if anyone was coming; then I got off the horse and turned the horse around, wondering if it would go back to its corral under the pines on the mountain. It looked back at me for a moment and then plucked a mouthful of green tumbleweeds before it trotted back up the trail with its ears pointed forward, carrying its head daintily to one side to avoid stepping on the dragging reins. When the horse disappeared over the last hill, the gunny sacks full of meat were still swinging and bouncing.

4

I walked toward the river on a wood-hauler's road that I knew would eventually lead to the paved road. I was thinking about waiting beside the road for someone to drive by, but by the time I got to the pavement I had decided it wasn't very far to walk if I followed the river back the way Silva and I had come.

The river water tasted good, and I sat in the shade under a cluster of silvery willows. I thought about Silva, and I felt sad at leaving him; still, there was something strange about him, and I tried to figure it out all the way back home.

I came back to the place on the river bank where he had been sitting the first time I saw him. The green willow leaves that he had trimmed from the branch were still lying there, wilted in the sand. I saw the leaves and I wanted to go back to him—to kiss him and to touch him—but the mountains were too far away now. And I told myself, because I believe it, he will come back sometime and be waiting again by the river.

I followed the path up from the river into the village. The sun was getting low, and I could smell supper cooking when I got to the screen door of my house. I could hear their voices inside—my mother was telling my grandmother how to fix the Jell-O and my husband, Al, was playing with the baby. I decided to tell them that some Navajo had kidnapped me, but I was sorry that old Grandpa wasn't alive to hear my story because it was the Yellow Woman stories he liked to tell best.

(1973)

AMY TAN

[*b. 1952*]

Rules of the Game

I was six when my mother taught me the art of invisible strength. It was a strategy for winning arguments, respect from others, and eventually, though neither of us knew it at the time, chess games.

"Bite back your tongue," scolded my mother when I cried loudly, yanking her hand toward the store that sold bags of salted plums. At home, she said, "Wise guy, he not go

against wind. In Chinese we say, Come from South, blow with wind—poom!—
North will follow. Strongest wind cannot be seen."

The next week I bit back my tongue as we entered the store with the forbidden
candies. When my mother finished her shopping, she quietly plucked a small bag of
plums from the rack and put it on the counter with the rest of the items.

My mother imparted her daily truths so she could help my older brothers and me rise
above our circumstances. We lived in San Francisco's Chinatown. Like most of the
other Chinese children who played in the back alleys of restaurants and curio shops, I
didn't think we were poor. My bowl was always full, three five-course meals every day,
beginning with a soup full of mysterious things I didn't want to know the names of.

We lived on Waverly Place, in a warm, clean, two-bedroom flat that sat above a
small Chinese bakery specializing in steamed pastries and dim sum. In the early morning, when the alley was still quiet, I could smell fragrant red beans as they were cooked
down to a pasty sweetness. By daybreak, our flat was heavy with the odor of fried
sesame balls and sweet curried chicken crescents. From my bed, I would listen as my
father got ready for work, then locked the door behind him, one-two-three clicks.

At the end of our two-block alley was a small sandlot playground with swings and
slides well-shined down the middle with use. The play area was bordered by wood-
slat benches where old-country people sat cracking roasted watermelon seeds with
their golden teeth and scattering the husks to an impatient gathering of gurgling
pigeons. The best playground, however, was the dark alley itself. It was crammed with
daily mysteries and adventures. My brothers and I would peer into the medicinal herb
shop, watching old Li dole out onto a stiff sheet of white paper the right amount of in-
sect shells, saffron-colored seeds, and pungent leaves for his ailing customers. It was said
that he once cured a woman dying of an ancestral curse that had eluded the best of
American doctors. Next to the pharmacy was a printer who specialized in gold-
embossed wedding invitations and festive red banners.

Farther down the street was Ping Yuen Fish Market. The front window displayed a
tank crowded with doomed fish and turtles struggling to gain footing on the slimy
green-tiled sides. A hand-written sign informed tourists, "Within this store, is all for
food, not for pet." Inside, the butchers with their bloodstained white smocks deftly
gutted the fish while customers cried out their orders and shouted, "Give me your
freshest," to which the butchers always protested, "All are freshest." On less crowded
market days, we would inspect the crates of live frogs and crabs which we were warned
not to poke, boxes of dried cuttlefish, and row upon row of iced prawns, squid, and
slippery fish. The sanddabs made me shiver each time; their eyes lay on one flattened
side and reminded me of my mother's story of a careless girl who ran into a crowded
street and was crushed by a cab. "Was smash flat," reported my mother.

At the corner of the alley was Hong Sing's, a four-table café with a recessed stair-
well in front that led to a door marked "Tradesmen." My brothers and I believed the
bad people emerged from this door at night. Tourists never went to Hong Sing's, since
the menu was printed only in Chinese. A Caucasian man with a big camera once
posed me and my playmates in front of the restaurant. He had us move to the side of
the picture window so the photo would capture the roasted duck with its head dangling from a juice-covered rope. After he took the picture, I told him he should go
into Hong Sing's and eat dinner. When he smiled and asked me what they served, I

shouted, "Guts and duck's feet and octopus gizzards!" Then I ran off with my friends, shrieking with laughter as we scampered across the alley and hid in the entryway grotto of the China Gem Company, my heart pounding with hope that he would chase us.

My mother named me after the street that we lived on: Waverly Place Jong, my official name for important American documents. But my family called me Meimei, "Little Sister." I was the youngest, the only daughter. Each morning before school, my mother would twist and yank on my thick black hair until she had formed two tightly wound pigtails. One day, as she struggled to weave a hard-toothed comb through my disobedient hair, I had a sly thought.

I asked her, "Ma, what is Chinese torture?" My mother shook her head. A bobby pin was wedged between her lips. She wetted her palm and smoothed the hair above my ear, then pushed the pin in so that it nicked sharply against my scalp.

"Who say this word?" she asked without a trace of knowing how wicked I was being. I shrugged my shoulders and said, "Some boy in my class said Chinese people do Chinese torture."

"Chinese people do many things," she said simply. "Chinese people do business, do medicine, do painting. Not lazy like American people. We do torture. Best torture."

My older brother Vincent was the one who actually got the chess set. We had gone to the annual Christmas party held at the First Chinese Baptist Church at the end of the alley. The missionary ladies had put together a Santa bag of gifts donated by members of another church. None of the gifts had names on them. There were separate sacks for boys and girls of different ages.

One of the Chinese parishioners had donned a Santa Claus costume and a stiff paper beard with cotton balls glued to it. I think the only children who thought he was the real thing were too young to know that Santa Claus was not Chinese. When my turn came up, the Santa man asked me how old I was. I thought it was a trick question; I was seven according to the American formula and eight by the Chinese calendar. I said I was born on March 17, 1951. That seemed to satisfy him. He then solemnly asked if I had been a very, very good girl this year and did I believe in Jesus Christ and obey my parents. I knew the only answer to that. I nodded back with equal solemnity.

Having watched the other children opening their gifts, I already knew that the big gifts were not necessarily the nicest ones. One girl my age got a large coloring book of biblical characters, while a less greedy girl who selected a smaller box received a glass vial of lavender toilet water. The sound of the box was also important. A ten-year-old boy had chosen a box that jangled when he shook it. It was a tin globe of the world with a slit for inserting money. He must have thought it was full of dimes and nickels, because when he saw that it had just ten pennies, his face fell with such undisguised disappointment that his mother slapped the side of his head and led him out of the church hall, apologizing to the crowd for her son who had such bad manners he couldn't appreciate such a fine gift.

As I peered into the sack, I quickly fingered the remaining presents, testing their weight, imagining what they contained. I chose a heavy, compact one that was wrapped in shiny silver foil and a red satin ribbon. It was a twelve-pack of Life Savers and I spent the rest of the party arranging and rearranging the candy tubes in the order of my favorites. My brother Winston chose wisely as well. His present turned out to be a box of intricate plastic parts; the instructions on the box proclaimed that when they were properly assembled he would have an authentic miniature replica of a World War II submarine.

Vincent got the chess set, which would have been a very decent present to get at a church Christmas party, except it was obviously used and, as we discovered later, it was missing a black pawn and a white knight. My mother graciously thanked the unknown benefactor, saying, "Too good. Cost too much." At which point, an old lady with fine white, wispy hair nodded toward our family and said with a whistling whisper, "Merry, merry Christmas."

When we got home, my mother told Vincent to throw the chess set away. "She not want it. We not want it," she said, tossing her head stiffly to the side with a tight, proud smile. My brothers had deaf ears. They were already lining up the chess pieces and reading from the dog-eared instruction book.

I watched Vincent and Winston play during Christmas week. The chessboard seemed to hold elaborate secrets waiting to be untangled. The chessmen were more powerful than old Li's magic herbs that cured ancestral curses. And my brothers wore such serious faces that I was sure something was at stake that was greater than avoiding the tradesmen's door to Hong Sing's.

"Let me! Let me!" I begged between games when one brother or the other would sit back with a deep sigh of relief and victory, the other annoyed, unable to let go of the outcome. Vincent at first refused to let me play, but when I offered my Life Savers as replacements for the buttons that filled in for the missing pieces, he relented. He chose the flavors: wild cherry for the black pawn and peppermint for the white knight. Winner could eat both.

As our mother sprinkled flour and rolled out small doughy circles for the steamed dumplings that would be our dinner that night, Vincent explained the rules, pointing to each piece. "You have sixteen pieces and so do I. One king and queen, two bishops, two knights, two castles, and eight pawns. The pawns can only move forward one step, except on the first move. Then they can move two. But they can only take men by moving crossways like this, except in the beginning, when you can move ahead and take another pawn."

"Why?" I asked as I moved my pawn. "Why can't they move more steps?"

"Because they're pawns," he said.

"But why do they go crossways to take other men? Why aren't there any women and children?"

"Why is the sky blue? Why must you always ask stupid questions?" asked Vincent. "This is a game. These are the rules. I didn't make them up. See. Here. In the book." He jabbed a page with a pawn in his hand. "Pawn. P-A-W-N. Pawn. Read it yourself."

My mother patted the flour off her hands. "Let me see book," she said quietly. She scanned the pages quickly, not reading the foreign English symbols, seeming to search deliberately for nothing in particular.

"This American rules," she concluded at last. "Every time people come out from foreign country, must know rules. You not know, judge say, Too bad, go back. They not telling you why so you can use their way go forward. They say, Don't know why, you find out yourself. But they knowing all the time. Better you take it, find out why yourself." She tossed her head back with a satisfied smile.

I found out about all the whys later. I read the rules and looked up all the big words in a dictionary. I borrowed books from the Chinatown library. I studied each chess piece, trying to absorb the power each contained.

I learned about opening moves and why it's important to control the center early on; the shortest distance between two points is straight down the middle. I learned about the middle game and why tactics between two adversaries are like clashing ideas; the one who plays better has the clearest plans for both attacking and getting out of traps. I learned why it is essential in the endgame to have foresight, a mathematical understanding of all possible moves, and patience; all weaknesses and advantages become evident to a strong adversary and are obscured to a tiring opponent. I discovered that for the whole game one must gather invisible strengths and see the endgame before the game begins.

I also found out why I should never reveal "why" to others. A little knowledge withheld is a great advantage one should store for future use. That is the power of chess. It is a game of secrets in which one must show and never tell.

I loved the secrets I found within the sixty-four black and white squares. I carefully drew a handmade chessboard and pinned it to the wall next to my bed, where at night I would stare for hours at imaginary battles. Soon I no longer lost any games or Life Savers, but I lost my adversaries. Winston and Vincent decided they were more interested in roaming the streets after school in their Hopalong Cassidy cowboy hats.

On a cold spring afternoon, while walking home from school, I detoured through the playground at the end of our alley. I saw a group of old men, two seated across a folding table playing a game of chess, others smoking pipes, eating peanuts, and watching. I ran home and grabbed Vincent's chess set, which was bound in a cardboard box with rubber bands. I also carefully selected two prized rolls of Life Savers. I came back to the park and approached a man who was observing the game.

"Want to play?" I asked him. His face widened with surprise and he grinned as he looked at the box under my arm.

"Little sister, been a long time since I play with dolls," he said, smiling benevolently. I quickly put the box down next to him on the bench and displayed my retort.

Lau Po, as he allowed me to call him, turned out to be a much better player than my brothers. I lost many games and many Life Savers. But over the weeks, with each diminishing roll of candies, I added new secrets. Lau Po gave me the names. The Double Attack from the East and West Shores. Throwing Stones on the Drowning Man. The Sudden Meeting of the Clan. The Surprise from the Sleeping Guard. The Humble Servant Who Kills the King. Sand in the Eyes of Advancing Forces. A Double Killing Without Blood.

There were also the fine points of chess etiquette. Keep captured men in neat rows, as well-tended prisoners. Never announce "Check" with vanity, lest someone with an unseen sword slit your throat. Never hurl pieces into the sandbox after you have lost a game, because then you must find them again, by yourself, after apologizing to all around you. By the end of the summer, Lau Po had taught me all he knew, and I had become a better chess player.

A small weekend crowd of Chinese people and tourists would gather as I played and defeated my opponents one by one. My mother would join the crowds during these outdoor exhibition games. She sat proudly on the bench, telling my admirers with proper Chinese humility, "Is luck."

A man who watched me play in the park suggested that my mother allow me to play in local chess tournaments. My mother smiled graciously, an answer that meant nothing. I desperately wanted to go, but I bit back my tongue. I knew she would not let me play among strangers. So as we walked home I said in a small voice that I didn't want to play in the local tournament. They would have American rules. If I lost, I would bring shame on my family.

"Is shame you fall down nobody push you," said my mother.

During my first tournament, my mother sat with me in the front row as I waited for my turn. I frequently bounced my legs to unstick them from the cold metal seat of the folding chair. When my name was called, I leapt up. My mother unwrapped something in her lap. It was her *chang,* a small tablet of red jade which held the sun's fire. "Is luck," she whispered, and tucked it into my dress pocket. I turned to my opponent, a fifteen-year-old boy from Oakland. He looked at me, wrinkling his nose.

As I began to play, the boy disappeared, the color ran out of the room, and I saw only my white pieces and his black ones waiting on the other side. A light wind began blowing past my ears. It whispered secrets only I could hear.

"Blow from the South," it murmured. "The wind leaves no trail." I saw a clear path, the traps to avoid. The crowd rustled. "Shhh! Shhh!" said the corners of the room. The wind blew stronger. "Throw sand from the East to distract him." The knight came forward ready for the sacrifice. The wind hissed, louder and louder. "Blow, blow, blow. He cannot see. He is blind now. Make him lean away from the wind so he is easier to knock down."

"Check," I said, as the wind roared with laughter. The wind died down to little puffs, my own breath.

My mother placed my first trophy next to a new plastic chess set that the neighborhood Tao society had given to me. As she wiped each piece with a soft cloth, she said, "Next time win more, lose less."

"Ma, it's not how many pieces you lose," I said. "Sometimes you need to lose pieces to get ahead."

"Better to lose less, see if you really need."

At the next tournament, I won again, but it was my mother who wore the triumphant grin.

"Lost eight piece this time. Last time was eleven. What I tell you? Better off lose less!" I was annoyed, but I couldn't say anything.

I attended more tournaments, each one farther away from home. I won all games, in all divisions. The Chinese bakery downstairs from our flat displayed my growing collection of trophies in its window, amidst the dust-covered cakes that were never picked up. The day after I won an important regional tournament, the window encased a fresh sheet cake with whipped-cream frosting and red script saying "Congratulations, Waverly Jong, Chinatown Chess Champion." Soon after that, a flower shop, headstone engraver, and funeral parlor offered to sponsor me in national tournaments. That's when my mother decided I no longer had to do the dishes. Winston and Vincent had to do my chores.

"Why does she get to play and we do all the work," complained Vincent.

"Is new American rules," said my mother. "Meimei play, squeeze all her brains out for win chess. You play, worth squeeze towel."

By my ninth birthday, I was a national chess champion. I was still some 429 points away from grand-master status, but I was touted as the Great American Hope, a child prodigy and a girl to boot. They ran a photo of me in *Life* magazine next to a quote in which Bobby Fischer said, "There will never be a woman grand master." "Your move, Bobby," said the caption.

The day they took the magazine picture I wore neatly plaited braids clipped with plastic barrettes trimmed with rhinestones. I was playing in a large high school auditorium that echoed with phlegmy coughs and the squeaky rubber knobs of chair legs sliding across freshly waxed wooden floors. Seated across from me was an American man, about the same age as Lau Po, maybe fifty. I remember that his sweaty brow seemed to weep at my every move. He wore a dark, malodorous suit. One of his pockets was stuffed with a great white kerchief on which he wiped his palm before sweeping his hand over the chosen chess piece with great flourish.

In my crisp pink-and-white dress with scratchy lace at the neck, one of two my mother had sewn for these special occasions, I would clasp my hands under my chin, the delicate points of my elbows poised lightly on the table in the manner my mother had shown me for posing for the press. I would swing my patent leather shoes back and forth like an impatient child riding on a school bus. Then I would pause, suck in my lips, twirl my chosen piece in midair as if undecided, and then firmly plant it in its new threatening place, with a triumphant smile thrown back at my opponent for good measure.

I no longer played in the alley of Waverly Place. I never visited the playground where the pigeons and old men gathered. I went to school, then directly home to learn new chess secrets, cleverly concealed advantages, more escape routes.

But I found it difficult to concentrate at home. My mother had a habit of standing over me while I plotted out my games. I think she thought of herself as my protective ally. Her lips would be sealed tight, and after each move I made, a soft "Hmmmmph" would escape from her nose.

"Ma, I can't practice when you stand there like that," I said one day. She retreated to the kitchen and made loud noises with the pots and pans. When the crashing stopped, I could see out of the corner of my eye that she was standing in the doorway. "Hmmmmph!" Only this one came out of her tight throat.

My parents made many concessions to allow me to practice. One time I complained that the bedroom I shared was so noisy that I couldn't think. Thereafter, my brothers slept in a bed in the living room facing the street. I said I couldn't finish my rice; my head didn't work right when my stomach was too full. I left the table with half-finished bowls and nobody complained. But there was one duty I couldn't avoid. I had to accompany my mother on Saturday market days when I had no tournament to play. My mother would proudly walk with me, visiting many shops, buying very little. "This my daughter Wave-ly Jong," she said to whoever looked her way.

One day after we left a shop I said under my breath, "I wish you wouldn't do that, telling everybody I'm your daughter." My mother stopped walking. Crowds of people with heavy bags pushed past us on the sidewalk, bumping into first one shoulder, then another.

"Aiii-ya. So shame be with mother?" She grasped my hand even tighter as she glared at me.

I looked down. "It's not that, it's just so obvious. It's just so embarrassing."

"Embarrass you be my daughter?" Her voice was cracking with anger.

"That's not what I meant. That's not what I said."

"What you say?"

I knew it was a mistake to say anything more, but I heard my voice speaking, "Why do you have to use me to show off? If you want to show off, then why don't you learn to play chess."

My mother's eyes turned into dangerous black slits. She had no words for me, just sharp silence.

I felt the wind rushing around my hot ears. I jerked my hand out of my mother's tight grasp and spun around, knocking into an old woman. Her bag of groceries spilled to the ground.

"Aii-ya! Stupid girl!" my mother and the woman cried. Oranges and tin cans careened down the sidewalk. As my mother stooped to help the old woman pick up the escaping food, I took off.

I raced down the street, dashing between people, not looking back as my mother screamed shrilly, "Meimei! Meimei!" I fled down an alley, past dark curtained shops and merchants washing the grime off their windows. I sped into the sunlight, into a large street crowded with tourists examining trinkets and souvenirs. I ducked into another dark alley, down another street, up another alley. I ran until it hurt and I realized I had nowhere to go, that I was not running from anything. The alleys contained no escape routes.

My breath came out like angry smoke. It was cold. I sat down on an upturned plastic pail next to a stack of empty boxes, cupping my chin with my hands, thinking hard. I imagined my mother, first walking briskly down one street or another looking for me, then giving up and returning home to await my arrival. After two hours, I stood up on creaking legs and slowly walked home.

The alley was quiet and I could see the yellow lights shining from our flat like two tiger's eyes in the night. I climbed the sixteen steps to the door, advancing quietly up each so as not to make any warning sounds. I turned the knob; the door was locked. I heard a chair moving, quick steps, the locks turning—click! click! click!—and then the door opened.

"About time you got home," said Vincent. "Boy, are you in trouble."

He slid back to the dinner table. On a platter were the remains of a large fish, its fleshy head still connected to bones swimming upstream in vain escape. Standing there waiting for my punishment, I heard my mother speak in a dry voice.

"We not concerning this girl. This girl not have concerning for us."

Nobody looked at me. Bone chopsticks clinked against the inside of bowls being emptied into hungry mouths.

I walked into my room, closed the door, and lay down on my bed. The room was dark, the ceiling filled with shadows from the dinnertime lights of neighboring flats.

In my head, I saw a chessboard with sixty-four black and white squares. Opposite me was my opponent, two angry black slits. She wore a triumphant smile. "Strongest wind cannot be seen," she said.

Her black men advanced across the plane, slowly marching to each successive level as a single unit. My white pieces screamed as they scurried and fell off the board one by one. As her men drew closer to my edge, I felt myself growing light. I rose up into the air and flew out the window. Higher and higher, above the alley, over the tops of tiled roofs, where I was gathered up by the wind and pushed up toward the night sky until everything below me disappeared and I was alone.

I closed my eyes and pondered my next move.

(1989)

LOUISE ERDRICH
[*b. 1954*]

American Horse

The woman sleeping on the cot in the woodshed was Albertine American Horse. The name was left over from her mother's short marriage. The boy was the son of the man she had loved and let go. Buddy was on the cot too, sitting on the edge because he'd been awake three hours watching out for his mother and besides, she took up the whole cot. Her feet hung over the edge, limp and brown as two trout. Her long arms reached out and slapped at things she saw in her dreams.

Buddy had been knocked awake out of hiding in a washing machine while herds of policemen with dogs searched through a large building with many tiny rooms. When the arm came down, Buddy screamed because it had a blue cuff and sharp silver buttons. "Tss," his mother mumbled, half awake, "wasn't nothing." But Buddy sat up after her breathing went deep again, and he watched.

There was something coming and he knew it.

It was coming from very far off but he had a picture of it in his mind. It was a large thing made of metal with many barbed hooks, points, and drag chains on it, something like a giant potato peeler that rolled out of the sky, scraping clouds down with it and jabbing or crushing everything that lay in its path on the ground.

Buddy watched his mother. If he woke her up, she would know what to do about the thing, but he thought he'd wait until he saw it for sure before he shook her. She was pretty, sleeping, and he liked knowing he could look at her as long and close up as he wanted. He took a strand of her hair and held it in his hands as if it was the rein to a delicate beast. She was strong enough and could pull him along like the horse their name was.

Buddy had his mother's and his grandmother's name because his father had been a big mistake.

"They're all mistakes, even your father. But *you* are the best thing that ever happened to me."

That was what she said when he asked.

Even Kadie, the boyfriend crippled from being in a car wreck, was not as good a thing that had happened to his mother as Buddy was. "He was a medium-sized mistake," she said. "He's hurt and I shouldn't even say that, but it's the truth." At the moment, Buddy knew that being the best thing in his mother's life, he was also the reason they were hiding from the cops.

He wanted to touch the satin roses sewed on her pink T-shirt, but he knew he shouldn't do that even in her sleep. If she woke up and found him touching the roses, she would say, "Quit that, Buddy." Sometimes she told him to stop hugging her like a gorilla. She never said that in the mean voice she used when he oppressed her, but when she said that he loosened up anyway.

There were times he felt like hugging her so hard and in such a special way that she would say to him, "Let's get married." There were also times he closed his eyes and wished that she would die, only a few times, but still it haunted him that his wish might come true. He and Uncle Lawrence would be left alone. Buddy wasn't worried, though, about his mother getting married to somebody else. She had said to her friend, Madonna, "All men suck," when she thought Buddy wasn't listening. He had made an uncertain sound, and when they heard him they took him in their arms.

"Except for you, Buddy," his mother said. "All except for you and maybe Uncle Lawrence, although he's pushing it."

"The cops suck the worst, though," Buddy whispered to his mother's sleeping face, "because they're after us." He felt tired again, slumped down, and put his legs beneath the blanket. He closed his eyes and got the feeling that the cot was lifting up beneath him, that it was arching its canvas back and then traveling, traveling very fast and in the wrong direction for when he looked up he saw the three of them were advancing to meet the great metal thing with hooks and barbs and all sorts of sharp equipment to catch their bodies and draw their blood. He heard its insides as it rushed toward them, purring softly like a powerful motor and then they were right in its shadow. He pulled the reins as hard as he could and the beast reared, lifting him. His mother clapped her hand across his mouth.

"Okay," she said. "Lay low. They're outside and they're gonna hunt."

She touched his shoulder and Buddy leaned over with her to look through a crack in the boards.

They were out there all right, Albertine saw them. Two officers and that social worker woman. Vicki Koob. There had been no whistle, no dream, no voice to warn her that they were coming. There was only the crunching sound of cinders in the yard, the engine purring, the dust sifting off their car in a fine light brownish cloud and settling around them.

The three people came to a halt in their husk of metal—the car emblazoned with the North Dakota State Highway Patrol emblem which is the glowing profile of the Sioux policeman, Red Tomahawk, the one who killed Sitting Bull. Albertine gave Buddy the blanket and told him that he might have to wrap it around him and hide underneath the cot.

"We're gonna wait and see what they do." She took him in her lap and hunched her arms around him. "Don't you worry," she whispered against his ear. "Lawrence knows how to fool them."

Buddy didn't want to look at the car and the people. He felt his mother's heart beating beneath his ear so fast it seemed to push the satin roses in and out. He put his face to them carefully and breathed the deep, soft powdery woman smell of her. That smell was also in her little face cream bottles, in her brushes, and around the washbowl after she used it. The satin felt so unbearably smooth against his cheek that he had to press closer. She didn't push him away, like he expected, but hugged him still tighter until he felt as close as he had ever been to back inside her again where she said he came from. Within the smells of her things, her soft skin, and the satin of her roses, he closed his eyes then, and took his breaths softly and quickly with her heart.

They were out there, but they didn't dare get out of the car yet because of Lawrence's big, ragged dogs. Three of these dogs had loped up the dirt driveway with the car. They were rangy, alert, and bounced up and down on their cushioned paws like wolves. They didn't waste their energy barking, but positioned themselves quietly, one at either car door and the third in front of the bellied-out screen door to Uncle Lawrence's house. It was six in the morning but the wind was up already, blowing dust, ruffling their short moth-eaten coats. The big brown one on Vicki Koob's side had unusual black and white markings, stripes almost, like a hyena and he grinned at her, tongue out and teeth showing.

"Shoo!" Miss Koob opened her door with a quick jerk.

The brown dog sidestepped the door and jumped before her, tiptoeing. Its dirty white muzzle curled and its eyes crossed suddenly as if it was zeroing its cross-hair sights in on the exact place it would bite her. She ducked back and slammed the door.

"It's mean," she told Officer Brackett. He was printing out some type of form. The other officer, Harmony, a slow man, had not yet reacted to the car's halt. He had been sitting quietly in the back seat, but now he rolled down his window and with no change in expression unsnapped his holster and drew his pistol out and pointed it at the dog on his side. The dog smacked down on its belly, wiggled under the car and was out and around the back of the house before Harmony drew his gun back. The other dogs vanished with him. From wherever they had disappeared to they began to yap and howl, and the door to the low shoebox-style house fell open.

"Heya, what's going on?"

Uncle Lawrence put his head out the door and opened wide the one eye he had in working order. The eye bulged impossibly wider in outrage when he saw the police car. But the eyes of the two officers and Miss Vicki Koob were wide open too because they had never seen Uncle Lawrence in his sleeping get-up or, indeed, witnessed anything like it. For his ribs, which were cracked from a bad fall and still mending, Uncle Lawrence wore a thick white corset laced up the front with a striped sneakers' lace. His glass eye and his set of dentures were still out for the night so his face puckered here and there, around its absences and scars, like a damaged but fierce little cake. Although he had a few gray streaks now, Uncle Lawrence's hair was still thick, and because he wore a special contraption of elastic straps around his head every night, two oiled waves always crested on either side of his middle part. All of this would have been sufficient to astonish, even without the most striking part of his outfit—the smoking jacket. It was made of black satin and hung open around his corset, dragging a tasseled belt. Gold thread dragons struggled up the lapels and blasted their furry red breath around his neck. As Lawrence walked down the steps, he put his arms up in surrender and the gold tassels in the inner seams of his sleeves dropped into view.

"My heavens, what a sight." Vicki Koob was impressed.

"A character," apologized Officer Harmony.

As a tribal police officer who could be counted on to help out the State Patrol, Harmony thought he always had to explain about Indians or get twice as tough to show he did not favor them. He was slow-moving and shy but two jumps ahead of other people all the same, and now, as he watched Uncle Lawrence's splendid approach, he gazed speculatively at the torn and bulging pocket of the smoking jacket. Harmony had been inside Uncle Lawrence's house before and knew that above his draped orange-crate shelf of war medals a blue-black German luger was hung carefully in a net of flat-headed nails and fishing line. Thinking of this deadly exhibition, he got out of the car and shambled toward Lawrence with a dreamy little smile of welcome on his face. But when he searched Lawrence, he found that the bulging pocket held only the lonesome-looking dentures from Lawrence's empty jaw. They were still dripping denture polish.

"I had been cleaning them when you arrived," Uncle Lawrence explained with acid dignity.

He took the toothbrush from his other pocket and aimed it like a rifle.

"Quit that, you old idiot." Harmony tossed the toothbrush away. "For once you ain't done nothing. We came for your nephew."

Lawrence looked at Harmony with a faint air of puzzlement.

"Ma Frere, listen," threatened Harmony amiably, "those two white people in the car came to get him for the welfare. They got papers on your nephew that give them the right to take him."

"Papers?" Uncle Lawrence puffed out his deeply pitted cheeks. "Let me see them papers."

The two of them walked over to Vicki's side of the car and she pulled a copy of the court order from her purse. Lawrence put his teeth back in and adjusted them with busy workings of his jaw.

"Just a minute," he reached into his breast pocket as he bent close to Miss Vicki Koob. "I can't read these without I have in my eye."

He took the eye from his breast pocket delicately, and as he popped it into his face the social worker's mouth fell open in a consternated O.

"What is this," she cried in a little voice.

Uncle Lawrence looked at her mildly. The white glass of the eye was cold as lard. The black iris was strangely charged and menacing.

"He's nuts," Brackett huffed along the side of Vicki's neck. "Never mind him."

Vicki's hair had sweated down her nape in tiny corkscrews and some of the hairs were so long and dangly now that they disappeared into the zippered back of her dress. Brackett noticed this as he spoke into her ear. His face grew red and the backs of his hands prickled. He slid under the steering wheel and got out of the car. He walked around the hood to stand with Leo Harmony.

"We could take you in too," said Brackett roughly. Lawrence eyed the officers in what was taken as defiance. "If you don't cooperate, we'll get out the handcuffs," they warned.

One of Lawrence's arms was stiff and would not move until he'd rubbed it with witch hazel in the morning. His other arm worked fine though, and he stuck it out in front of Brackett.

"Get them handcuffs," he urged them. "Put me in a welfare home."

Brackett snapped one side of the handcuffs on Lawrence's good arm and the other to the handle of the police car.

"That's to hold you," he said. "We're wasting our time. Harmony, you search that little shed over by the tall grass and Miss Koob and myself will search the house."

"My rights is violated!" Lawrence shrieked suddenly. They ignored him. He tugged at the handcuff and thought of the good heavy file he kept in his tool box and the German luger oiled and ready but never loaded, because of Buddy, over his shelf. He should have used it on these bad ones, even Harmony in his big-time white man job. He wouldn't last long in that job anyway before somebody gave him what for.

"It's a damn scheme," said Uncle Lawrence, rattling his chains against the car. He looked over at the shed and thought maybe Albertine and Buddy had sneaked away before the car pulled into the yard. But he sagged, seeing Albertine move like a shadow within the boards. "Oh, it's all a damn scheme," he muttered again.

"I want to find that boy and salvage him," Vicki Koob explained to Officer Brackett as they walked into the house. "Look at his family life—the old man crazy as a bedbug, the mother intoxicated somewhere."

Brackett nodded, energetic, eager. He was a short hopeful redhead who failed consistently to win the hearts of women. Vicki Koob intrigued him. Now, as he watched, she pulled a tiny pen out of an ornamental clip on her blouse. It was attached to a retractable line that would suck the pen back, like a child eating one strand of spaghetti. Something about the pen on its line excited Brackett to the point of discomfort. His hand shook as he opened the screendoor and stepped in, beckoning Miss Koob to follow.

They could see the house was empty at first glance. It was only one rectangular room with whitewashed walls and a little gas stove in the middle. They had already come through the cooking lean-to with the other stove and washstand and rusty old refrigerator. That refrigerator had nothing in it but some wrinkled potatoes and a package of turkey necks. Vicki Koob noted that in her perfect-bound notebook. The beds along the walls of the big room were covered with quilts that Albertine's mother, Sophie, had made from bits of old wool coats and pants that the Sisters sold in bundles at the mission. There was no one hiding beneath the beds. No one was under the little aluminum dinette table covered with a green oilcloth, or the soft brown wood chairs tucked up to it. One wall of the big room was filled with neatly stacked crates of things—old tools and springs and small half-dismantled appliances. Five or six television sets were stacked against the wall. Their control panels spewed colored wires and at least one was cracked all the way across. Only the topmost set, with coathanger antenna angled sensitively to catch the bounding signals around Little Shell, looked like it could possibly work.

Not one thing escaped Vicki Koob's trained and cataloguing gaze. She made note of the cupboard that held only commodity flour and coffee. The unsanitary tin oil drum beneath the kitchen window, full of empty surplus pork cans and beer bottles, caught her eye as did Uncle Lawrence's physical and mental deteriorations. She quickly described these "benchmarks of alcoholic dependency within the extended family of Woodrow (Buddy) American Horse" as she walked around the room with the little notebook open, pushed against her belly to steady it. Although Vicki had been there before, Albertine's presence had always made it difficult for her to take notes.

"Twice the maximum allowable space between door and threshold," she wrote now. "Probably no insulation. Two three-inch cracks in walls inadequately sealed with whitewashed mud." She made a mental note but could see no point in describing Lawrence's stuffed reclining chair that only reclined, the shadeless lamp with its plastic orchid in the bubble glass base, or the three-dimensional picture of Jesus that Lawrence had once demonstrated to her. When plugged in, lights rolled behind the water the Lord stood on so that he seemed to be strolling although he never actually went forward, of course, but only pushed the glowing waves behind him forever like a poor tame rat in a treadmill.

Brackett cleared his throat with a nervous rasp and touched Vicki's shoulder.

"What are you writing?"

She moved away and continued to scribble as if thoroughly absorbed in her work. "Officer Brackett displays an undue amount of interest in my person," she wrote. "Perhaps?"

He snatched playfully at the book, but she hugged it to her chest and moved off smiling. More curls had fallen, wetted to the base of her neck. Looking out the window, she sighed long and loud.

"All night on brush rollers for this. What a joke."

Brackett shoved his hands in his pockets. His mouth opened slightly, then shut with a small throttled cluck.

When Albertine saw Harmony ambling across the yard with his big brown thumbs in his belt, his placid smile, and his tiny black eyes moving back and forth, she put Buddy under the cot. Harmony stopped at the shed and stood quietly. He spread his arms to show her he hadn't drawn his big police gun.

"Ma Cousin," he said in the Michif dialect that people used if they were relatives or sometimes if they needed gas or a couple of dollars, "why don't you come out here and stop this foolishness?"

"I ain't your cousin," Albertine said. Anger boiled up in her suddenly. "I ain't related to no pigs."

She bit her lip and watched him through the cracks, circling, a big tan punching dummy with his boots full of sand so he never stayed down once he fell. He was empty inside, all stale air. But he knew how to get to her so much better than a white cop could. And now he was circling because he wasn't sure she didn't have a weapon, maybe a knife or the German luger that was the only thing that her father, Albert American Horse, had left his wife and daughter besides his name. Harmony knew that Albertine was a tall strong woman who took two big men to subdue when she didn't want to go in the drunk tank. She had hard hips, broad shoulders, and stood tall like her Sioux father, the American Horse who was killed threshing in Belle Prairie.

"I feel bad to have to do this," Harmony said to Albertine. "But for godsakes, let's nobody get hurt. Come on out with the boy, why don't you? I know you got him in there."

Albertine did not give herself away this time. She let him wonder. Slowly and quietly she pulled her belt through its loops and wrapped it around and around her hand until only the big oval buckle with turquoise chunks shaped into a butterfly stuck out over her knuckles. Harmony was talking but she wasn't listening to what he said. She was listening to the pitch of his voice, the tone of it that would tighten or tremble at a certain moment when he decided to rush the shed. He kept talking slowly and reasonably, flexing the dialect from time to time, even mentioning her father.

"He was a damn good man. I don't care what they say, Albertine, I knew him."

Albertine looked at the stone butterfly that spread its wings across her fist. The wings looked light and cool, not heavy. It almost looked like it was ready to fly. Harmony wanted to get to Albertine through her father but she would not think about American Horse. She concentrated on the sky blue stone.

Yet the shape of the stone, the color, betrayed her.

She saw her father suddenly, bending at the grille of their old gray car. She was small then. The memory came from so long ago it seemed like a dream—narrowly focused, snapshot-clear. He was bending by the grille in the sun. It was hot summer. Wings of sweat, dark blue, spread across the back of his work shirt. He always wore soft blue shirts, the color of shade cloudier than this stone. His stiff hair had grown out of its short haircut and flopped over his forehead. When he stood up and turned away from the car, Albertine saw that he had a butterfly.

"It's dead," he told her. "Broke its wings and died on the grille."

She must have been five, maybe six, wearing one of the boy's T-shirts Mama bleached in Hilex-water. American Horse took the butterfly, a black and yellow one, and rubbed it on Albertine's collarbone and chest and arms until the color and the powder of it were blended into her skin.

"For grace," he said.

And Albertine had felt a strange lightening in her arms, in her chest, when he did this and said, "For grace." The way he said it, grace meant everything the butterfly was. The sharp delicate wings. The way it floated over grass. The way its wings seemed to breathe fanning in the sun. The wisdom of the way it blended into flowers or changed into a leaf. In herself she felt the same kind of possibilities and closed her eyes almost in shock or pain, she felt so light and powerful at that moment.

Then her father had caught her and thrown her high into the air. She could not remember landing in his arms or landing at all. She only remembered the sun filling her eyes and the world tipping crazily behind her, out of sight.

"He was a damn good man," Harmony said again.

Albertine heard his starched uniform gathering before his boots hit the ground. Once, twice, three times. It took him four solid jumps to get right where she wanted him. She kicked the plank door open when he reached for the handle and the corner caught him on the jaw. He faltered, and Albertine hit him flat on the chin with the butterfly. She hit him so hard the shock of it went up her arm like a string pulled taut. Her fist opened, numb, and she let the belt unloop before she closed her hand on the tip end of it and sent the stone butterfly swooping out in a wide circle around her as if it was on the end of a leash. Harmony reeled backward as she walked toward him swinging the belt. She expected him to fall but he just stumbled. And then he took the gun from his hip.

Albertine let the belt go limp. She and Harmony stood within feet of each other, breathing. Each heard the human sound of air going in and out of the other person's lungs. Each read the face of the other as if deciphering letters carved into softly eroding veins of stone. Albertine saw the pattern of tiny arteries that age, drink, and hard living had blown to the surface of the man's face. She saw the spoked wheels of his iris and the arteries like tangled threads that sewed him up. She saw the living net of springs and tissue that held him together, and trapped him. She saw the random, intimate plan of his person.

She took a quick shallow breath and her face went strange and tight. She saw the black veins in the wings of the butterfly, roads burnt into a map, and then she was located somewhere in the net of veins and sinew that was the tragic complexity of the world so she did not see Officer Brackett and Vicki Koob rushing toward her, but felt them instead like flies caught in the same web, rocking it.

"Albertine!" Vicki Koob had stopped in the grass. Her voice was shrill and tight. "It's better this way, Albertine. We're going to help you."

Albertine straightened, threw her shoulders back. Her father's hand was on her chest and shoulders lightening her wonderfully. Then on wings of her father's hands, on dead butterfly wings, Albertine lifted into the air and flew toward the others. The light powerful feeling swept her up the way she had floated higher, seeing the grass below. It was her father throwing her up into the air and out of danger. Her arms opened for bullets but no bullets came. Harmony did not shoot. Instead, he raised his fist and brought it down hard on her head.

Albertine did not fall immediately, but stood in his arms a moment. Perhaps she gazed still farther back behind the covering of his face. Perhaps she was completely stunned and did not think as she sagged and fell. Her face rolled forward and hair covered her features, so it was impossible for Harmony to see with just what particular expression she gazed into the head-splitting wheel of light, or blackness, that overcame her.

Harmony turned the vehicle onto the gravel road that led back to town. He had convinced the other two that Albertine was more trouble than she was worth, and so they left her behind, and Lawrence too. He stood swearing in his cinder driveway as the car rolled out of sight. Buddy sat between the social worker and Officer Brackett. Vicki tried to hold Buddy fast and keep her arm down at the same time, for the words she'd screamed at Albertine had broken the seal of antiperspirant beneath her arms. She was sweating now as though she'd stored up an ocean inside of her. Sweat rolled down her back in a shallow river and pooled at her waist and between her breasts. A thin sheen of water came out on her forearms, her face. Vicki gave an irritated moan but Brackett seemed not to take notice, or take offense at least. Air-conditioned breezes were sweeping over the seat anyway, and very soon they would be comfortable. She smiled at Brackett over Buddy's head. The man grinned back. Buddy stirred. Vicki remembered the emergency chocolate bar she kept in her purse, fished it out, and offered it to Buddy. He did not react, so she closed his fingers over the package and peeled the paper off one end.

The car accelerated. Buddy felt the road and wheels pummeling each other and the rush of the heavy motor purring in high gear. Buddy knew that what he'd seen in his mind that morning, the thing coming out of the sky with barbs and chains, had hooked him. Somehow he was caught and held in the sour tin smell of the pale woman's armpit. Somehow he was pinned between their pounds of breathless flesh. He looked at the chocolate in his hand. He was squeezing the bar so hard that a thin brown trickle had melted down his arm. Automatically he put the bar in his mouth.

As he bit down he saw his mother very clearly, just as she had been when she carried him from the shed. She was stretched flat on the ground, on her stomach, and her arms were curled around her head as if in sleep. One leg was drawn up and it looked for all the world like she was running full tilt into the ground, as though she had been trying to pass into the earth, to bury herself, but at the last moment something had stopped her.

There was no blood on Albertine, but Buddy tasted blood now at the sight of her, for he bit down hard and cut his own lip. He ate the chocolate, every bit of it, tasting his mother's blood. And when he had the chocolate down inside him and all licked off his hands, he opened his mouth to say thank you to the woman, as his mother had taught him. But instead of a thank you coming out he was astonished to hear a great rattling scream, and then another, rip out of him like pieces of his own body and whirl onto the sharp things all around him.

(1983)

Poetry

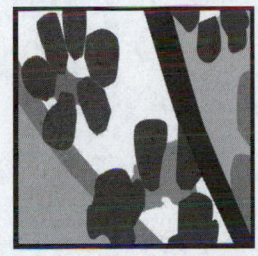

PART TWO

Poetry

PART TWO

Reading Poems

In some ways reading poetry is much like reading fiction and drama: we observe details of action and language, make connections and inferences, and draw conclusions. We also bring to poetry the same intellectual and emotional dispositions, the same general experience with life and literature that we draw on in reading drama and fiction. And yet there is something different about reading poems. The difference, admittedly more one of degree than of kind, involves our being more attentive to the connotations of words, more receptive to the expressive qualities of sound and rhythm in line and stanza, more discerning about details of syntax and punctuation. This increased attention to linguistic detail is necessary because of the density and compression characteristic of poetry. More than fiction or drama, poetry is an art of condensation and implication; poems concentrate meaning and distill feeling.

Learning to read poetry well and to savor its pleasures involves learning to ask questions about how we experience poems, how we interpret them, and how we evaluate them. Such questions include the following:

1. What feelings does the poem evoke? What sensations, associations, and memories does it give rise to?
2. What ideas does the poem express, either directly or indirectly? What sense does it make? What do we understand it to say and suggest?
3. What view of the world does the poet present? Does it agree with your view? What do you think of the poet's view? What value does the poem hold for you as a work of art and as an influence on your way of understanding yourself and others?

Our discussion is divided into three parts: the experience of poetry, the interpretation of poetry, and the evaluation of poetry. In the experience section we will be concerned primarily with subjective responses, with personal reactions. We will reflect on how the poem may be related to our lives. In the interpretation section our concern will be the intellectual processes that we engage in as we develop an understanding of poetry. Here the focus will be analytical rather than impressionistic, rational rather than emotional. And in the evaluation of poetry, we will be concerned with the ways we bring our sense of who we are and what we believe into our consideration of any poem's significance, and with how poems are evaluated aesthetically.

THE EXPERIENCE OF POETRY

We begin by considering the following poem, first from the standpoint of our experience.

ROBERT HAYDEN
[1913–1980]

Those Winter Sundays

Sundays too my father got up early
and put his clothes on in the blueblack cold,
then with cracked hands that ached
from labor in the weekday weather made
banked fires blaze. No one ever thanked him.   5

I'd wake and hear the cold splintering, breaking.
When the rooms were warm, he'd call,
and slowly I would rise and dress,
fearing the chronic angers of that house,

Speaking indifferently to him,   10
who had driven out the cold
and polished my good shoes as well.
What did I know, what did I know
of love's austere and lonely offices?

Even from a single reading we see that the speaker of "Those Winter Sundays," now an adult, is remembering how his father used to get up on cold Sunday mornings and light the fires that would warm the house for his sleeping family. We sense that he regrets how unappreciative of his father he was as a child. We may wonder what prompts these memories and feelings. Our initial reading may also call up a memory much like the one described in Hayden's poem. But even if our experience does not echo the speaker's or if our feelings differ from his, we may respond to the description of waking up on a cold day in a warm house. Such personal responses, whatever their precise nature, are important to our reading of poetry, for in arriving at a sense of a poem's meaning and value, we often begin with them.

Here is a sampling of one reader's responses to the poem: a set of notes that describe both memories and feelings. Notice how the responses, subjective and impressionistic as they are, nonetheless reveal the reader beginning to reflect on the poem's meaning and values.

I remember how my father used to wake up at five A.M. to light the furnace so the house would be warm when the rest of the family got up. My strongest memories of this come from my early adolescence, perhaps because it was then that I began to assume this responsibility. I would never have thought to describe the cold as "blue-black" but I like how that makes me remember what the cold felt like at that merciless hour. I also remember the way my father would come and wake us up around 6:30 to get ready for school. By then the floor was warm and the radiators crackled with steam.

Like the rest of my brothers and sisters, I took my father's early morning efforts for granted. We never thought of thanking him. Perhaps we should have. He always knew that we loved him. That wasn't a problem. But as I think back, I don't remember thanking him for much of anything. I guess we were all guilty of speaking indifferently to him, or of not speaking much at all.

A couple of other things about the poem strike me. One is the shoes the father polished for his son. A nice touch, those shoes. I wonder when a boy begins to be responsible for polishing his own shoes. I can't remember when I started polishing mine—high school perhaps—but I do remember often polishing my father's as well—especially on Sundays when he would rush around to get ready for church. A more confusing item is the line about "fearing the chronic angers" of the house. How can a house be angry? Perhaps the writer is referring to the father's anger? I remember my own father becoming angry. He blew his top, as he used to say, pretty regularly, one time punching a hole in the dining room wall, another time ripping the phone off the kitchen wall. I wasn't the target of his anger often, but it was unsettling to see him lose his temper.

The last couple of lines with the repeated question, "What did I know, what did I know," hit me the hardest. I hear regret in them, regret for lost opportunities, regret for understanding too late the motive behind the attentions of the speaker's father. Perhaps there is also regret for the distance that separated father and son. I know a little about that. But I also hear in these lines how love involves sacrifice and that such quiet expressions of love don't always or even often receive the recognition they deserve. For people whose fathers are still alive there is time perhaps to compensate. For me, it's too late.

THE INTERPRETATION OF POETRY

When we interpret a poem, we explain it to ourselves in order to understand it. We makes sense of it, in short. If one of our initial acts is to somehow appropriate the poem personally by relating it to our experience, another is to consider its meaning. When we interpret a poem, we concern ourselves less with how it affects us than with what it means or suggests. Interpretation relies on our intellectual comprehension and rational understanding rather than on our emotional apprehension and response.

The act of interpretation involves essentially four things: observing, connecting, inferring, and concluding. We observe details of description and action, of language and form. We look for connections among these details and begin to establish a sense of the poem's coherence (the way its details fit together in meaningful relationships). On the basis of these connections we make inferences or interpretive guesses about their significance. And finally, we come to a provisional conclusion about the poem's meaning based on our observations, connections, and inferences.

As we continue our discussion of "Those Winter Sundays," we will offer additional observations, inferences, and conclusions, pretty much in that order. This description of the interpretive process makes it seem as if we perform each of these analytical acts in succession. That's not the way it happens. Just as our personal responses and subjective impressions, our memories, sensations, and associations are stirred up *while* we read and *after,* so too all four aspects of interpretation occur simultaneously.

To see what Hayden's poem implies, let's give it a second look. We might notice, for example, that the first words, "Sundays too," indicate that the speaker's father performed his housewarming chores every day, including Sundays. We might notice also that the poem contrasts cold and warmth, with the cold dissipated as the warmth of the fires the father has started suffuses the house. And we might note further that the poem shifts from father to son, from "him" to "I." The first stanza, for example, describes the father's act, the second the boy's awakening to a warm house, while the third records a different kind of awakening—the speaker's realization of his earlier indifference and of his father's love. It is in this third and final stanza that we feel most strongly the contrast between the speaker's past and present, between the then and the now of the poem, between the love that the speaker neither noticed nor acknowledged and the love he later acknowledges and understands.

So far we have centered on the poem's speaker and its subject. (The *speaker* refers to the voice of the character we hear in the poem; the *subject* indicates what the poem is about.) Our first readings of a poem will usually focus on who is speaking about what, and why. In considering speaker and subject, we solidify our sense of what the poem implies, whether its implications concern, primarily, ideas or feelings. When the speaker notes that he feared "the chronic angers of that house," we may sense that he points toward something important. Presumably he feared his father's anger, which on occasion may have been directed at him. But by using the plural form of the word rather than the singular ("angers" rather than "anger") the speaker may be suggesting that there was discord between the father and other members of the family as well. Whatever the specific nature of his fear, the speaker intimates that his fear was the source of his own wariness and indifference toward his father.

The lines that convey the speaker's feeling most intensely, however, are those that end the poem:

> What did I know, what did I know
> of love's austere and lonely offices?

In these lines we sense the speaker's remorse and regret for not being aware of all his father did for him; we sense further that even though he didn't understand and feel the extent of his father's devotion, he certainly does later. Moreover, we sense the intensity of his feelings both in his repetition of the phrase "what did I know," and in the words that describe his father's actions: "love's austere and lonely offices." "Austere" suggests both the rigor and self-discipline of the father's acts and perhaps the stern severity with which he may have performed them. "Lonely" indicates that the father performed his early morning labors alone, without help from the other members of the family. It also suggests that the father was emotionally isolated from the speaker and perhaps from other members of the family.

But the word "offices" conveys other ideas as well. It implies both the duties the father fulfills and the corresponding authority he possesses. In addition, it suggests something done for another, as in the good offices of a friend. Beyond these related meanings, "offices" also refers to the daily prayers recited by clerics. Thus, the words "austere" and "offices" convey the speaker's understanding of his father's sacrifices for him. Moreover, the highly abstract language of the conclusion—so different from the concrete details of the preceding stanzas—may also indicate the speaker's inability to express affection directly (an inadequacy he intimates his father suffered from as well).

To read poetry well we need to slow down enough to observe details of language, form, and sound. By reading slowly and deliberately, we give ourselves a chance to form connections among the poem's details. Read the following poem twice, once straight through without stopping, then again with the interpolated commentary.

ROBERT FROST

[1874–1963]

Stopping by Woods on a Snowy Evening

Whose woods these are I think I know.
His house is in the village though;
He will not see me stopping here
To watch his woods fill up with snow.

My little horse must think it queer   5
To stop without a farmhouse near
Between the woods and frozen lake
The darkest evening of the year.

He gives his harness bells a shake
To ask if there is some mistake.   10
The only other sound's the sweep
Of easy wind and downy flake.

The woods are lovely, dark and deep,
But I have promises to keep,
And miles to go before I sleep,   15
And miles to go before I sleep.

Read the poem once more, this time along with the comments that follow each stanza. Attend to the way you make sense of the poem during this reading, particularly in light of the suggestions made in the commentary.

Whose woods these are I think I know.
His house is in the village though;
He will not see me stopping here
To watch his woods fill up with snow.

Comment   Frost's poem opens with a speaker who seems concerned momentarily about who owns the woods. The speaker seems reassured that the owner can't see him. We might wonder why the speaker should be concerned and why he bothers to mention it. Does he feel that he is doing something wrong? The poem doesn't say; instead it paints a picture of man, of woods and snow. And it raises questions: Why does he stop? What attracts him? Again, the poem doesn't provide explicit answers.

My little horse must think it queer
To stop without a farmhouse near
Between the woods and frozen lake
The darkest evening of the year.

Comment   In the first stanza the speaker describes the scene and his own action. In this stanza, although he further describes this scene and action, he begins by mentioning that his horse is unaccustomed to stopping without a reason. The first line says that the horse "must" think it queer to stop this way, indicating that the horse can't really look at the man's action any other way. Accustomed to stops for food and rest, the horse couldn't possibly understand the man's impractical reason for stopping. And though the horse is said to "think," we realize that the horse's thoughts are really the speaker's—that the speaker projects his thoughts onto the horse because a part of him sees the impracticality of his action.

> He gives his harness bells a shake
> To ask if there is some mistake.
> The only other sound's the sweep
> Of easy wind and downy flake.

Comment The third stanza continues the emphasis of the second. The speaker interprets the horse's shaking of his harness bells as a signal to move on, as a sign that stopping there serves no useful purpose. We might notice that the poet here emphasizes the stillness of the night, the isolation and privacy of the moment, which is broken only by the sound of the horse's bell. Tension builds in the mind of the speaker: even though he seems to enjoy the stillness of the night and takes pleasure in the "easy wind" and the "downy flake," he also experiences some doubt about what he is doing.

Stanza four:

> The woods are lovely, dark and deep,
> But I have promises to keep,
> And miles to go before I sleep,
> And miles to go before I sleep.

Comment The opening line summarizes the implications of the details in the preceding stanzas. It's as if the speaker here answers the question why he stopped by the woods. He stopped because he was attracted by their dark beauty. He nevertheless feels a pressure to move on, to return to his responsibilities and obligations.

The final stanza is solemn and serious: Frost slows its pace by including pauses (indicated by punctuation) and by repeating the third line, "And miles to go before I sleep," which he uses to end the poem. In repeating this line, the poet lifts it beyond its literal meaning, inviting us to read "sleep" as the final sleep of death. Once we make this interpretive leap, we can consider "Miles to go" as perhaps the time the speaker has left to live, and "promises" as the obligations and responsibilities he must fulfill before he dies. His stopping to look at the falling snow can be seen as a temporary reprieve from such responsibilities; it might also be seen as a desire to escape them. The essential point, however, seems to be the tug of war going on in the speaker's mind between the two possibilities—stopping to contemplate the beauty of nature, and moving on to return to the active world of work and responsibility.

We have been reading and interpreting the poem one stanza at a time to suggest the way interpretation builds cumulatively as we move through a poem. The process, however, is not simply linear or sequential. For although we interpret later details in light of earlier ones, we also make sense of earlier ones after having interpreted later ones. The act of interpretation, like the experience of reading generally, is recursive. We move back and forth through a text, remembering what we read and anticipating what is to come. The process of interpretation does not end with reading the poem; it continues as we reflect on it afterward. New ideas may come to us, particularly after we have discussed the work with a teacher and classmates or after we have read other works that we can relate to it.

One final point about the interpretation of poetry (and of literature generally): interpretation never really ends. When we interpret a work, we should be concerned less with finding the single right way of understanding it than with arriving at a satisfying explanation, one that makes sense to us, and one whose logic and good sense will appeal to others. Some interpretations, nonetheless, will be more satisfying than others. They will be more convincing, largely because they take into account more of the poem's details, more of its language and form and action. Other interpretations, while perhaps not as convincing, may be valuable for the intellectual stimulation they provide and for the pleasure they afford. Because we invariably bring different experiences of life and of literature to our reading of poems, we will see different things in them and will make different kinds of sense of them. The varying interpretations we make of poems depend largely on what matters to us, what *we* consider vital. It is to this subject, values in poetry, that we turn now.

THE EVALUATION OF POETRY

When we evaluate a poem, we do two different kinds of things. First, we assess its literary quality and make a judgment about how good it is and how successfully it realizes its poetic intentions. We examine its language and structure, for example, and consider how well they work together to embody meaning and convey feeling. Second, we consider how much significance the poem has for us personally, and what significance it may have for other readers—both those who are like us and those who differ in age, race, gender, culture, and ideology. We also consider the significance the poem may have had for the poet, both its general value as part of a body of writing and its particular expression of feelings, attitudes, ideas, and values—its perspective on experience.

Our consideration of a poem's value is a measure of its involvement with our lives, with our way of thinking and being in the actual world. Some poems "speak" to us more than others; some poems mean more to us on some days than on others; and some poems mean both more and less to us at different periods of our lives. In evaluating poems, we explore the how and why of such differences. In doing so, we turn inevitably to a consideration of the various cultural assumptions, moral attitudes, and political convictions that animate particular poems. We consider the perspective from which they were written. Our consideration may involve an investigation into the circumstances of its composition, the external facts and internal experiences of the poet's life, the attitudes and beliefs he or she may have expressed in letters or other comments, the audience and occasion for which a particular poem was written, its publication history and reception by readers past and present.

From even this brief list, we can see how complex literary evaluation can be. Complicating matters even further is how we encounter the poems we evaluate. We come to the poems in this book after many preliminary acts of evaluation by others. The poets who wrote them decided they were valuable enough to preserve. The publishers who put them in print valued them, perhaps more for their potential profit than for the feelings, attitudes, or ideas they express. The editor/author of this book values them, some for how they affect him as a reader, others for their use as illustrations of particular aspects or elements of poetry. Other readers, including the teachers who use them in their courses, also value these poems. But not all readers and teachers value them the same way, and not all for the same reasons.

Does this mean then that we cannot make definitive, final, and absolute evaluations of poems? Probably, since change and variety are the hallmarks of literary evaluation. Our valuing of any poem is therefore subject to change (though not necessarily a radical reevaluation) because the way we see and understand any poem changes as we change. We will find merit in poems whose meaning we understand and whose values are like our own. We will come to value poems whose content we have lived. And we will appreciate poems in relation to other literary works that have had an impact on our lives and our thinking. To put this another way: we can't *not* evaluate the poems we read because we inevitably and automatically measure them against other works we already value. Our evaluation of any poem, moreover, depends not only upon how we understand it (that is, upon how we interpret its meaning), but also upon how we see its relation to our lives at the time we read it.

With these considerations in mind, we can suggest a few general principles upon which to ground preliminary evaluations. First is the realization that an evaluation is essentially a judgment, a set of opinions about a literary work based on a thoughtful consideration of it. We may agree or disagree with the speaker's response to the woods in Frost's "Stopping by Woods." We may confirm or deny the models of experience illustrated in Hayden's "Those Winter Sundays." Invariably, however, we measure the sentiments of a poem against our own. We may or may not appreciate responsibility as much as Frost's speaker seems to. We may or may not cherish our memories of our fathers as Hayden's speaker seems to. And depending on these and other factors, we may arrive at very different assessments of either poem's worth for us as individual readers.

It is important to realize that in evaluating any poem, we appraise it according to our own special combination of cultural, moral, and aesthetic values which derive from our place in family and society. These values are affected by race, gender, and language. Our moral values reflect our ethical norms—what we consider good and evil, right and wrong. They are influenced by our religious beliefs and perhaps by our political convictions as well. Our aesthetic values concern what we see as beautiful or ugly, well or poorly made.

Our response to any poem's outlook (and our opinion of it) is closely related to our interpretation of it. Evaluation depends upon interpretation, for our judgment of a poem depends on how we understand it. That evaluation may be linked to our initial experience of the work, with first impressions conditioning a later response. This is not always the case, fortunately. In fact, one of the benefits of interpretation is its ability to free us from enslavement to our initial responses by enabling us to move beyond them. By bringing our intellect to bear on a work, we may discover meanings in it that were not apparent on initial reading. And while making such interpretive discoveries we may come to feel differently about a poem and derive considerable pleasure from it.

Of the kinds of evaluations we make in reading poetry, those about a poem's aesthetic merit are hardest to discuss. Aesthetic responses are difficult to describe because they involve subjective reactions about what is beautiful or not, what is pleasing or not, what is well-made or not. Our occasional unwillingness to move beyond our initial impressions, our tendency to settle into comfortable judgments and well-worn opinions, further complicates our responses. We may think that as long as we know what we like, that's enough. It's not enough if we are truly interested in developing our capacity for aesthetic appreciation.

Is Frost's "Stopping by Woods" or Hayden's "Those Winter Sundays" a beautiful poem? Does either seem to be a good example of its type—in this case, the lyric poem? What criteria will you use to make a judgment? To answer these questions, you will need to know more about poetry than you are likely to at this point. It would be helpful to have read and absorbed much of the material in Chapter 9, Elements of Poetry. Measuring a poem's achievement requires some knowledge of how poets exploit diction, imagery, syntax, and sound; how they establish form and control tone; how they work within or against a literary tradition.

Admittedly, without a good deal of knowledge about poetry and without considerable practice in reading it, judgments about the aesthetic worth of particular poems need to be made with caution. But we cannot really avoid judging the poems we read any more than we avoid judging the people we meet; the process is natural. What we should strive for in evaluating poems is to understand the merits of different kinds of poems, to judge them fairly against what they were meant to be rather than something we think they should be. Our goal should be, ultimately, to develop a sense of literary tact, the kind of informed and balanced judgment that comes with experience in reading and living, coupled with continued thoughtful reflection on both.

Your evaluation of poetry may very well change as you change. What you consider important criteria now (narrative action, perhaps, or rhymed stanzas) may not be important after you have read many more poems. Poems you dismiss now as irrelevant or uninteresting may mean much more to you if your life changes so that the concerns of those poems become your concerns. As with literary interpretation, so with literary evaluation; it does not remain constant. In the same way that our understanding of literature changes, and in the same way we acknowledge more than one absolute, definitive, and correct interpretation of literary works, so too do we recognize the many ways they may be evaluated.

We can put these ideas to the test by reading Adrienne Rich's "Aunt Jennifer's Tigers" from the standpoint of evaluation. The questions that follow the poem invite you to consider your experience and interpretation, as well as your evaluation of it. To get started, keep these questions in mind during your first couple of readings: What do each of the characters stand for? How would you describe the relationship between the uncle and his wife, Jennifer? Between the men and the tigers? Between Aunt Jennifer and the speaker? And between Aunt Jennifer and the tigers?

ADRIENNE RICH
[*b. 1929*]

Aunt Jennifer's Tigers

Aunt Jennifer's tigers prance across a screen,
Bright topaz denizens of a world of green.
They do not fear the men beneath the tree;
They pace in sleek chivalric certainty.

Aunt Jennifer's fingers fluttering through her wool   5
Find even the ivory needle hard to pull.
The massive weight of Uncle's wedding band
Sits heavily upon Aunt Jennifer's hand.

When Aunt is dead, her terrified hands will lie
Still ringed with ordeals she was mastered by.   10
The tigers in the panel that she made
Will go on prancing, proud and unafraid.

QUESTIONS FOR REFLECTION

Experience

1. What feelings surfaced as you read this poem?
2. What words, phrases, and details triggered your strongest responses?
3. What associations about your own aunts and uncles do you bring to the poem?
4. Can the situation described here apply to your parents rather than to your aunts and uncles? To both? To neither? Why or why not?

Interpretation

5. What words, phrases, lines, and details may have confused or baffled you? Why?
6. What observations can you make about the poem's details?
7. What words and phrases recur? How? Where? Why?
8. What connections can you establish among the details of action and language?
9. What inferences can you draw from these connections?
10. How, for now at least, do you understand "Aunt Jennifer's Tigers"?

Evaluation

11. What values are associated with Aunt Jennifer? With her husband, the speaker's
    uncle? With the tigers? With the men who hunt them?
12. What is the relationship among the values associated with these figures?
13. What is the speaker's attitude toward her aunt, her uncle, and the tigers? To what
    extent do you think the speaker's attitudes are those of the author? On what do
    you base your view?
14. How do your own ideas and standards influence your experience, interpretation,
    and evaluation of the poem? Describe how the poem affects you as a reader. Do
    you like it? Comment on the poem's aesthetic accomplishment.
15. Return to this poem later in the term, after you have had the opportunity to read
    many more poems, or after you have discussed the poem with teacher(s) and class-
    mates. (Perhaps you can learn something about the life and work of the poet by
    reading her own poetry and prose or by reading critical studies of her work—or
    both.) Discuss your initial evaluation and your later evaluation, how they may have
    changed, and why.

THE ACT OF READING POETRY

Thus far we have read two poems, each followed by comments and questions
emphasizing the experience and interpretation of poetry. Next we illustrate active reading—what we actually do when we read and reread a poem. Some of
the marginal annotations record observations, others raise questions; all are abbreviated notes that reflect a reading that embodies both thought and feeling.
In making notes about a poem in this manner, we become actively engaged in
seeing and thinking. Our observations lead us to notice details of language and
to think about the poem's implications. As we formulate answers to our questions, however provisional, we find ourselves exploring both the poem's meaning and its value.

   The annotations for Theodore Roethke's "My Papa's Waltz" are not concerned with technical matters such as form, rhyme scheme, and meter, or with
what such technical features contribute to meaning and feeling. Another set of
annotations could be made highlighting these features. In fact, some technical
consideration of Roethke's poem appears on page 422. For now, however, we
focus on the poem's situation and subject. Here is the poem without annotation:

THEODORE ROETHKE
[1908–1963]

My Papa's Waltz

The whiskey on your breath
Could make a small boy dizzy;

> But I hung on like death:
> Such waltzing was not easy.
>
> We romped until the pans   5
> Slid from the kitchen shelf;
> My mother's countenance
> Could not unfrown itself.
>
> The hand that held my wrist
> Was battered on one knuckle;   10
> At every step you missed
> My right ear scraped a buckle.
>
> You beat time on my head
> With a palm caked hard by dirt,
> Then waltzed me off to bed   15
> Still clinging to your shirt.

And here it is again with annotations:

My Papa's Waltz

	An affectionate term for his father—papa
The whiskey on your breath	
Could make a small boy dizzy;	
But I hung on like death:	
Such waltzing was not easy.	What kind of waltzing and who instigated it?
We romped until the pans	"Waltzed" or "danced" for "romped"?
Slid from the kitchen shelf;	
My mother's countenance	"Face" or "expression" for "countenance"?
Could not unfrown itself.	The mother—angry? disapproving? mother as audience—as non-participant—
The hand that held my wrist	
Was battered on one knuckle;	
At every step you missed	
My right ear scraped a buckle.	The father misses steps but he can dance—not drunk.
You beat time on my head	
With a palm caked hard by dirt,	
Then waltzed me off to bed	Clinging—how?
Still clinging to your shirt.	Fearfully? Joyfully? Both?

The boy's father, a manual laborer, is clearly not literally "waltzing" with his son. His "dance" is more a romp through the house with a stop in the kitchen and another at the boy's bedroom, where presumably he is unceremoniously dumped into bed. The mother watches, her frown indicating disapproval, perhaps even anger.

The dance is somewhat rough because the boy's father has been drinking. It is also rough because he scrapes the child's ear on his belt buckle as he keeps a steady rhythm by beating time on the boy's head. The boy is described as "clinging" to his father's shirt, but the language doesn't clarify whether that clinging is purely out of terror—or whether it is part of the game father and son enjoy together. Presumably this bedtime romp is a regular ritual rather than a one-time occurrence.

The tone of the poem seems nostalgic, though not sentimentally so. The boy, now a man, remembers his father as "papa," clearly an affectionate term. The high-spirited bouncing rhythm of the poem seems to counter any indication that the father's drinking or the son's fear are its central concerns.

CHAPTER EIGHT

Types of Poetry

Poetry can be classified as narrative or lyric. Narrative poems stress action, and lyrics song. Each of these types has numerous subdivisions: narrative poetry includes the epic, romance, and ballad; lyric poetry includes the elegy and epigraph, sonnet and sestina, aubade and villanelle. Moreover, each major type of poetry adheres to different conventions. *Narrative poems,* for example, tell stories and describe actions; *lyric poems* combine speech and song to express feeling in varying degrees of verbal music.

NARRATIVE POETRY

The grandest of narratives is the epic. *Epics* are long narrative poems that record the adventures of a hero whose exploits are important to the history of a nation. Typically they chronicle the origins of a civilization and embody its central beliefs and values. Epics tend to be larger than life as they recount valorous deeds enacted in vast landscapes. The epic style is as grand as the action; the conventions require that the epic be formal, complex, and serious—suitable to its important subjects.

Among the more famous epics in Western literature are Homer's *Iliad* (about the Greek and Trojan war), Virgil's *Aeneid* (about the founding of Rome), Dante's *Divine Comedy* (a journey through hell, purgatory, and heaven), and Milton's *Paradise Lost* (about the revolt of the angels, and man's creation and fall). For a hint of the epic's subjects and language listen to these opening lines from *The Aeneid* and from *Paradise Lost*. First Virgil:

> I sing of warfare and a man at war.
> From the sea-coast of Troy in early days
> He came to Italy by destiny,
> To our Lavinian western shore,

A fugitive, this captain, buffeted   5
Cruelly on land as on the sea
By blows from powers of the air—behind them
Baleful Juno in her sleepless rage.
And cruel losses were his lot in war,
Till he could found a city and bring home   10
His gods to Latium, land of the Latin race,
The Alban lords, and the high walls of Rome.
Tell me the causes now, O Muse, how galled
In her divine pride, and how sore at heart
From her old wound, the queen of gods compelled him—   15
A man apart, devoted to his mission—
To undergo so many perilous days
And enter on so many trials.

And now Milton:

Of man's first disobedience, and the fruit
Of that forbidden tree whose mortal taste
Brought death into the world, and all our woe,
With loss of Eden, till one greater Man
Restore us, and regain the blissful seat,   5
Sing, Heavenly Muse, that, on the secret top
Of Oreb, or of Sinai, didst inspire
That shepherd who first taught the chosen seed
In the beginning how the Heavens and Earth
Rose out of Chaos: or, if Sion hill   10
Delight thee more, and Siloa's brook that flowed
Fast by the oracle of God, I thence
Invoke thy aid to my adventurous song,
That with no middle flight intends to soar
Above th' Aonian mount, while it pursues   15
Things unattempted yet in prose or rhyme.
And chiefly thou, O Spirit, that dost prefer
Before all temples th' upright heart and pure,
Instruct me, for thou know'st; thou from the first
Wast present, and, with mighty wings outspread,   20
Dovelike sat'st brooding on the vast abyss,
And mad'st it pregnant: what in me is dark
Illumine; what is low, raise and support;
That, to the height of this great argument,
I may assert Eternal Providence,   25
And justify the ways of God to men.

Far less ambitious than epics, *ballads* are perhaps the most popular form of narrative poetry. Originally ballads were meant to be sung or recited. Folk ballads (or popular ballads as they are sometimes called) were passed on orally, only to be written down much later. This accounts for the different versions of many ballads such as "Barbara Allan" and "Edward, Edward" (pages 604 and 606).

In addition to folk ballads of unknown (and sometimes multiple) authorship, there are also literary ballads (of known authorship). One example is "La Belle Dame sans Merci" by John Keats (page 637). Literary ballads imitate the folk ballad by adhering to its basic conventions—repeated lines and stanzas in a refrain, swift action with occasional surprise endings, extraordinary events evoked in direct, simple language, and scant characterization—but are more polished stylistically and more self-conscious in their use of poetic techniques.

Another type of narrative poem is the *romance,* in which adventure is a central feature. The plots of romances tend to be complex, with surprising and even magical actions common. The chief characters are human beings, though they often confront monsters, dragons, and disguised animals in a world that does not adhere consistently to the laws of nature as we know them. Romance in short deals with the marvelous—with, for example, St. George slaying a dragon in a magical forest. Popular during the Middle Ages and Renaissance, the romance as a poetic genre has fallen from favor. Nevertheless, some of its chief characteristics have found expression in popular fictional types such as the western, the adventure story, and the romantic love story.

LYRIC POETRY

Although narrative poems, especially literary ballads, combine story with song, action with emotion, story and action predominate. In lyric poetry, however, story is subordinated to song, and action to emotion. We can define *lyrics* as subjective poems, often brief, that express the feelings and thoughts of a single speaker (who may or may not represent the poet). The lyric is more a poetic manner than a form; it is more variable and less subject to strict convention than narrative poetry.

Lyric poetry is typically characterized by brevity, melody, and emotional intensity. The music of lyrics makes them memorable, and their brevity contributes to the intensity of their emotional expression. Originally designed to be sung to a musical accompaniment (the word *lyric* derives from the Greek *lyre*), lyrics have been the predominant type of poetry in the West for several hundred years.

Forms of lyric poetry range from the *epigram,* a brief witty poem that is often satirical, such as Alexander Pope's "On the Collar of a Dog" to the *elegy,* a lament for the dead, such as Seamus Heaney's "Mid-Term Break" (page 707). Lyric forms also include the *ode,* a long stately poem in stanzas of varied length, meter, and form; and the *aubade,* a love lyric expressing complaint that dawn means the speaker must part from his lover. An example of the ode is John Keats's "Ode to a Nightingale" (page 639); the aubade is represented by John Donne's "The Sun Rising" (page 450).

The tones, moods, and voices of lyric poems are as variable and as complexly intertwined as human feeling, thought, and imagination allow. Generally considered the most compressed poetic type, the lyric poem typically expresses much in little. The *sonnet,* for example, condenses into fourteen lines an expression of emotion or an articulation of idea according to one of two basic patterns: the *Italian* (or *Petrarchan*) and the *English* (or *Shakespearean*). An Italian sonnet is composed of an eight-line octave and a six-line sestet. A Shakespearean sonnet is composed of three four-line quatrains and a concluding two-line couplet (see pages 474–475). The thought and feeling expressed in each sonnet form typically follow the divisions suggested by their structural patterns. Thus an Italian sonnet may state a problem in the octave and present a solution in its sestet. A Shakespearean sonnet will usually introduce a subject in the first quatrain, expand and develop it in the second and third quatrains, and conclude something about it in its final couplet.

Although sonnets reached the height of their popularity during the Renaissance, later writers have continued to be attracted to the form. Some sonnet writers, in fact, like Gerard Manley Hopkins, William Butler Yeats, Robert Frost, and E. E. Cummings have combined the two basic patterns to suit their poetic needs. Occasionally these and other poets have modified the form itself. Robert Frost's "Acquainted with the Night" (page 578), for example, is composed of four tercets and a couplet rather than the familiar three quatrains and a couplet. Frost, moreover, has been known to write fifteen-line sonnets as well.

Less important historically than the sonnet but no less intricate and musical are two other lyric forms, sestina and villanelle, both deriving from French poetry. The *sestina* consists of six stanzas of six lines each followed by a three-line conclusion or *envoy*. The sestina requires a strict pattern of repetition of six key words that end the lines of the first stanza. Elizabeth Bishop's "Sestina" (page 687) is an example.

The *villanelle,* which also relies heavily on repetition, is composed of five three-line tercets and a final four-line quatrain. Its singular feature is the way its first and third lines repeat throughout the poem. The entire first line reappears as the final line of the second and fourth tercets, and again as the third line of the third and fifth tercets and as the concluding line of the poem. Examples include Theodore Roethke's "The Waking" (page 481) and Dylan Thomas's "Do Not Go Gentle into That Good Night" (page 691).

C H A P T E R   N I N E

Elements of Poetry

We can learn to interpret and appreciate poems by understanding their basic elements. The elements of a poem include a *speaker* whose voice we hear in it; its *diction* or selection of words; its *syntax* or the order of those words; its *imagery* or details of sight, sound, taste, smell, and touch; its *figures of speech* or nonliteral ways of expressing one thing in terms of another, such as symbol and metaphor; its *sound effects,* especially rhyme, assonance, and alliteration; its *rhythm and meter* or the pattern of accents we hear in the poem's words, phrases, lines, and sentences; and its *structure* or formal pattern of organization. All the elements of a poem work together harmoniously to convey feeling and embody meaning.

VOICE: SPEAKER AND TONE

When we read or hear a poem, we hear a speaker's voice. It is this voice that conveys the poem's *tone,* its implied attitude toward its subject. Tone is an abstraction we make from the details of a poem's language: the use of meter and rhyme (or lack of them); the inclusion of certain kinds of details and exclusion of other kinds; particular choices of words and sentence pattern, of imagery and figurative language. When we listen to a poem's language and hear the voice of its speaker, we catch its tone and feeling and ultimately its meaning.

In listening to the speaker's voice, for example, in Roethke's "My Papa's Waltz" (in Chapter Seven), we hear a tone different from that of the speaker in Hayden's "Those Winter Sundays" (Chapter Seven). Roethke's speaker remembers his father fondly and addresses him ("your breath," "you missed"). He remembers and celebrates their spirited cavorting as a "romp" and a "waltz" and includes such comic details as the mother frowning while pans slide off the kitchen shelves and the father keeping time by steadily patting the boy's head. The poem's complex tone comes from its contrasted details: the boy's hanging on "like death," his ear scraping his father's belt buckle, and his "clinging" to his father's shirt.

The speaker of Hayden's "Those Winter Sundays" admires his father and perhaps feared him as a child. His attitude is suggested by the details he remembers and by the way he meticulously describes his father's attentive labors. But his tone conveys more than admiration; it conveys also a sense of regret, disappointment, and perhaps anguish at having been indifferent toward him as a child. The tone of Hayden's poem has none of the ease and playfulness of Roethke's; it is serious in its portrayal of the speaker's father and solemn in its account of the speaker's subsequent feelings.

The range of tones we find in poems is as various and complex as the range of voices and attitudes we discern in everyday experience. One of the more important and persistent is the *ironic tone* of voice. We have previously defined irony as a way of speaking that implies a discrepancy or opposition between what is said and what is meant (see pages 93–95). We repeat the following poem by Stephen Crane that illustrates this ironic tone of voice.

STEPHEN CRANE
[1871–1900]

War Is Kind

Do not weep, maiden, for war is kind.
Because your lover threw wild hands toward the sky
And the affrighted steed ran on alone,
Do not weep.
War is kind.   5

    Hoarse, booming drums of the regiment,
    Little souls who thirst for fight,
    These men were born to drill and die.
    The unexplained glory flies above them,
    Great is the battle god, great, and his kingdom   10
    A field where a thousand corpses lie.

    Do not weep, babe, for war is kind.
    Because your father tumbled in the yellow trenches,
    Raged at his breast, gulped and died,
    Do not weep.   15
    War is kind.

    Swift blazing flag of the regiment,
    Eagle with crest of red and gold,
    These men were born to drill and die.

Point for them the virtue of slaughter,   20
Make plain to them the excellence of killing
And a field where a thousand corpses lie.

Mother whose heart hung humble as a button
On the bright splendid shroud of your son,
Do not weep.   25
War is kind.

How do we know that the speaker's attitude towards war is not what his words indicate, that his words are ironic? We know because the details of death in battle are antithetical to the consoling refrain of stanzas one, three, and five: "Do not weep. War is kind." Moreover the details of stanzas two and four also work toward the same ironic end, but in a different way. Instead of the ironic consoling voice of stanzas one, three, and five (which of course offers no real consolation given the brutality described), stanzas two and four sound more supportive of military glory: Crane uses a march-like rhythm along with words connoting military glory in a context that makes them sound hollow and false. The view that war is glorious and that death in battle is honorable is countered with images of slaughter. Compare Crane's poem to another treating the glory of dying for one's country ironically, Wilfred Owen's "Dulce et Decorum Est" (page 13).

   Unlike the poems we have been considering in which the speaker is alone, the next poem we will examine contains a speaker who is addressing someone present. A poem in which a speaker addresses a silent listener is called a *dramatic monologue*. As we listen to the speaker's monologue, we usually gain a vivid sense of his character and personality. The following poem, Robert Browning's "My Last Duchess," is a striking example of this form.

ROBERT BROWNING
[1812–1889]

My Last Duchess

FERRARA

That's my last Duchess painted on the wall,
Looking as if she were alive. I call
That piece a wonder, now; Frà Pandolf's hands
Worked busily a day, and there she stands.
Will 't please you sit and look at her? I said   5
"Frà Pandolf" by design, for never read
Strangers like you that pictured countenance,
The depth and passion of its earnest glance,

But to myself they turned (since none puts by
The curtain I have drawn for you, but I)   10
And seemed as they would ask me, if they durst,
How such a glance came there; so, not the first
Are you to turn and ask thus. Sir, 'twas not
Her husband's presence only, called that spot
Of joy into the Duchess' cheek; perhaps   15
Frá Pandolf chanced to say, "Her mantle laps
Over my lady's wrist too much," or "Paint
Must never hope to reproduce the faint
Half-flush that dies along her throat." Such stuff
Was courtesy, she thought, and cause enough   20
For calling up that spot of joy. She had
A heart—how shall I say?—too soon made glad,
Too easily impressed; she liked whate'er
She looked on, and her looks went everywhere.
Sir, 'twas all one! My favor at her breast,   25
The dropping of the daylight in the West,
The bough of cherries some officious fool
Broke in the orchard for her, the white mule
She rode with round the terrace—all and each
Would draw from her alike the approving speech,   30
Or blush, at least. She thanked men,—good! but thanked
Somehow—I know not how—as if she ranked
My gift of a nine-hundred-years-old name
With anybody's gift. Who'd stoop to blame
This sort of trifling? Even had you skill   35
In speech—which I have not—to make your will
Quite clear to such an one, and say "Just this
Or that in you disgusts me; here you miss,
Or there exceed the mark"—and if she let
Herself be lessoned so, nor plainly set   40
Her wits to yours, forsooth, and made excuse—
E'en then would be some stooping; and I choose
Never to stoop. Oh sir, she smiled, no doubt,
Whene'er I passed her; but who passed without
Much the same smile? This grew; I gave commands;   45
Then all smiles stopped together. There she stands
As if alive. Will 't please you rise? We'll meet
The company below, then. I repeat,
The Count your master's known munificence
Is ample warrant that no just pretense   50
Of mine for dowry will be disallowed;
Though his fair daughter's self, as I avowed
At starting, is my object. Nay, we'll go
Together down, sir. Notice Neptune, though,
Taming a sea-horse, thought a rarity,   55
Which Claus of Innsbruck cast in bronze for me!

The situation of the poem is this: the Duke of Ferrara, a city-state in Renaissance Italy, is addressing an ambassador who represents a count, the father of a marriageable aristocratic daughter. Although we hear only the duke's voice, we are aware of the ambassador's presence. We probably wonder how the ambassador reacts to what the duke tells him—especially to what he says in lines 45–46. But while the poet hints at the ambassador's actions (lines 12–13; 47–48, for instance) he doesn't reveal his thoughts. Instead he centers our attention on the duke, whose manner, language, gestures, and concerns all reveal the kind of man he is and how he conducted himself in his relations with his last duchess.

The duke reveals himself as a monumental egotist—proud, shrewd, arrogant, and murderous. He shows himself to be a man who will not allow his will to be thwarted or his honor ignored. Intolerant of his former duchess's joy in things other than those he provided, and unwilling to "stoop" to telling her how her behavior insulted him, the duke has had her killed: "I gave commands," he says. "Then all smiles stopped together."

But what has the duchess done to deserve her fate? She expressed joy in compliments given her; she took pleasure in simple things—riding her white mule, watching the sun set, accepting a gift of fruit. Her crime in the duke's eyes was in not recognizing the value of his aristocratic heritage: his name, rank, and pride did not mean enough to her.

Part of our shock in realizing what the duke has done comes from his certainty that he has behaved properly. What else could I do, he seems to say. And part derives perhaps also from the matter-of-fact manner in which the duke turns the conversation from his last duchess to the business at hand, the negotiations about the impending marriage and the dowry. But revealing as these things are, an even stronger index of the duke's egoistic pride is the way he refers to his last duchess as an object, as a possession that has been appropriately added to his prized collection. As a portrait on the wall, the duchess is fully and finally under the duke's control. (He even keeps her portrait behind a curtain so no one can see her without his authority.) The duke's pride in his wife's portrait is equal to his pride in his prized statue of Neptune taming a sea horse.

A few poems notable for their speakers and tones of voice follow. For each identify the speaker and situation. Describe the tone(s) of voice you hear, and consider what the speaker's tone contributes to the ideas and feelings that the poems convey.

MURIEL STUART
[b. 1889–?]

In the Orchard

'I thought you loved me.' 'No, it was only fun.'
'When we stood there, closer than all?' 'Well, the harvest moon
Was shining and queer in your hair, and it turned my head.'
'That made you?' 'Yes.' 'Just the moon and the light it made
Under the tree?' 'Well, your mouth, too.' 'Yes, my mouth?'   5

'And the quiet there that sang like the drum in the booth.
You shouldn't have danced like that.' 'Like what?' 'So close,
With your head turned up, and the flower in your hair, a rose
That smelt all warm.' 'I loved you. I thought you knew
I wouldn't have danced like that with any but you.'   10
'I didn't know. I thought you knew it was fun.'
'I thought it was love you meant.' 'Well, it's done.' 'Yes, it's done.
I've seen boys stone a blackbird, and watched them drown
A kitten . . . it clawed at the reeds, and they pushed it down
Into the pool while it screamed. Is that fun, too?'   15
'Well, boys are like that . . . Your brothers . . .' 'Yes, I know.
But you, so lovely and strong! Not you! Not you!'
'They don't understand it's cruel. It's only a game.'
'And are girls fun, too?' 'No, still in a way it's the same.
It's queer and lovely to have a girl . . .' 'Go on.'   20
'It makes you mad for a bit to feel she's your own,
And you laugh and kiss her, and maybe you give her a ring,
But it's only in fun.' 'But I gave you everything.'
'Well, you shouldn't have done it. You know what a fellow thinks
When a girl does that.' 'Yes, he talks of her over his drinks   25
And calls her a—' 'Stop that now. I thought you knew.'
'But it wasn't with anyone else. It was only you.'
'How did I know? I thought you wanted it too.
I thought you were like the rest. Well, what's to be done?'
'To be done?' 'Is it all right?' 'Yes.' 'Sure?' 'Yes, but why?'   30
'I don't know. I thought you were going to cry.
You said you had something to tell me.' 'Yes, I know.
It wasn't anything really . . . I think I'll go.'
'Yes, it's late. There's thunder about, a drop of rain
Fell on my hand in the dark. I'll see you again   35
At the dance next week. You're sure that everything's right?'
'Yes.' 'Well, I'll be going.' 'Kiss me . . .' 'Good night.' . . . 'Good night.'

QUESTIONS FOR REFLECTION

1. What differences exist in the dialogue of the two speakers? How do those differences characterize the tone of each speaker's voice?
2. What do the questions, ellipses, and repeated words contribute to the poem's tone?

GERARD MANLEY HOPKINS
[1844–1889]

Thou art indeed just, Lord

*Justus quidem tu es, Domine, si disputem tecum: verumtamen
justa loquar ad te: Quare via impiorum prosperatur?°*

Thou art indeed just, Lord, if I contend
With thee; but, sir, so what I plead is just.
Why do sinners' ways prosper? and why must
Disappointment all I endeavour end?
Wert thou my enemy, O thou my friend,   5
How wouldst thou worse, I wonder, than thou dost
Defeat, thwart me? Oh, the sots and thralls of lust
Do in spare hours more thrive than I that spend,

Sir, life upon thy cause. See, banks and brakes
Now, leavèd how thick! lacèd they are again   10
With fretty chervil, look, and fresh wind shakes

Them; birds build—but not I build; no, but strain,
Time's eunuch, and not breed one work that wakes.
Mine, O thou lord of life, send my roots rain.

QUESTIONS FOR REFLECTION

1. How do the words the speaker uses to address God help establish the tone of the first four lines? What is his attitude toward God here?
2. Lines 5–7 might be paraphrased according to the familiar saying: "with friends like you, who needs enemies." What tone of voice do you hear in those lines? In lines 9–13? In the final line?

ANONYMOUS

Western Wind

Western wind, when will thou blow,
    The small rain down can rain?
Christ, if my love were in my arms
    And I in my bed again!

QUESTION FOR REFLECTION

What tone bursts through the final couplet? What feeling does the speaker convey? How does the tone of the following alteration compare with the poem's final two lines as written?

Oh God I wish I were in bed
With my lover again.

"Thou art indeed just, Lord" **Justus quidem tu es, Domine, si disputem tecum: verumtamen justa loquar ad te: Quare via impiorum prosperatur?** *the first three lines of the poem (up to prosper) translate the Latin epigraph.*

HENRY REED

[b. 1914]

Naming of Parts

Today we have naming of parts. Yesterday,
We had daily cleaning. And tomorrow morning,
We shall have what to do after firing. But today,
Today we have naming of parts. Japonica
Glistens like coral in all of the neighboring gardens,   5
     And today we have naming of parts.

This is the lower sling swivel. And this
Is the upper sling swivel, whose use you will see,
When you are given your slings. And this is the piling swivel,
Which in your case you have not got. The branches   10
Hold in the gardens their silent, eloquent gestures,
     Which in our case we have not got.

This is the safety-catch, which is always released
With an easy flick of the thumb. And please do not let me
See anyone using his finger. You can do it quite easy   15
If you have any strength in your thumb. The blossoms
Are fragile and motionless, never letting anyone see
     Any of them using their finger.

And this you can see is the bolt. The purpose of this
Is to open the breech, as you see. We can slide it   20
Rapidly backwards and forwards: we call this
Easing the spring. And rapidly backwards and forwards
The early bees are assaulting and fumbling the flowers:
     They call it easing the Spring.

They call it easing the Spring: it is perfectly easy   25
If you have any strength in your thumb: like the bolt,
And the breech, and the cocking-piece, and the point of balance,
Which in our case we have not got; and the almond-blossom
Silent in all of the gardens and the bees going backwards and forwards,
     For today we have naming of parts.   30

QUESTIONS FOR REFLECTION

1. Each stanza of "Naming of Parts" contains two distinct voices. Where does the first voice end and the second begin? Describe and characterize each voice.
2. Pinpoint the place where the two voices converge. What is the effect of their convergence?

JACQUES PRÉVERT
[1900–1977]

Family Portrait

The mother knits
The son goes to war
She finds it all perfectly natural, Mama
And the father, what is he doing? Papa?
He is making little deals   5
His wife knits
His son goes to war
He is making little deals
He finds it all perfectly natural, Papa
And the son, the son   10
What does the son find?
The son finds absolutely nothing, the son
For the son the war his Mama the knitting his Papa little deals for him the war
When it is all over, that war
He will make little deals, he and his Papa   15
The war continues Mama continues she knits
Papa continues he carries on his activity
The son is killed he no longer carries on
Papa and Mama go to the cemetery
They find it all perfectly natural, Papa and Mama   20
Life continues life with knitting war little deals
Deals war knitting war
Deals deals activity
Life along with the cemetery.

TRANSLATED BY HARRIET ZINNES

QUESTION FOR REFLECTION

Characterize the tone of the first three lines. How is this tone reinforced or altered as the poem develops? What do the repeated words and phrases contribute to the tone?

DICTION

At their most successful, poems include "the best words in the best order," as Samuel Taylor Coleridge has said. In reading any poem it is necessary to know what the words mean, but it is equally important to understand what the words imply or suggest. The *denotation* or dictionary meaning of *dictator,* for example, is "a person exercising absolute power, especially one who assumes absolute control without the free consent of the people." But *dictator* also carries additional *connotations* or associations both personal and public. Beyond its dictionary meaning, *dictator* may suggest repressive force and tyrannical oppression; it may call up images of bloodbaths, purges, executions; it may trigger associations that prompt us to think of Hitler, for example, or Mussolini. The same kind of associative resonance occurs with a word like *vacation,* the connotations of which far outstrip its dictionary definition: "a period of suspension of work, study, or other activity."

Because poets often hint indirectly at more than their words directly state, it is necessary to develop the habit of considering the connotations of words as well as their denotations. Often for both poets and readers the "best words" are those that do the most work; they convey feelings and indirectly imply ideas rather than state them outright. Poets choose a particular word because it suggests what they want to suggest. Its appropriateness is a function of both its denotation and its connotation. Consider, for example, the second stanza of Roethke's "My Papa's Waltz":

> We romped until the pans
> Slid from the kitchen shelf;
> My mother's countenance
> Could not unfrown itself.

"Romped" could be replaced by *danced* since the poet is describing a dance, specifically a waltz. Why "romped" then? For one thing, it means something different from *danced.* That is, its denotation provides a different meaning, indicating play or frolic of a boisterous nature. Although "romped" is not really a dance word at all, here it suggests a kind of rough, crude dancing, far less elegant and systematic than waltzing. But it also connotes the kind of vigorous roughhousing that fathers and sons occasionally engage in and from which many mothers are excluded—though here, of course, the romp is occasioned by the father's having had too much to drink. "Romped" then both describes more precisely the kind of dance and suggests the speaker's attitude toward the experience.

Perhaps the most unusual words in the stanza, however, are "countenance" and "unfrown." "Countenance" is less familiar and more surprising than face. This is also true of "unfrown," a word you won't find in the dictionary. What makes these words noticeable is not just their uncommonness but their strangeness in the context of the stanza. "Countenance," a formal word, contrasts with the informal language of the two lines before it, lines that describe the informal romp of a dance; it suggests the mother's formality as she watches the informal play of her husband and son. Although her frown indicates disapproval, perhaps annoyance that her pans are falling, the disapproval and annoyance may be put on, part of an act. It is possible that she is responding as she is expected to respond.

If we look up *countenance* in the *Random House College Dictionary,* here is what we find:

noun   1. appearance, esp. the expression of the face . . .

         2. the face; visage

         3. calm facial expression; composure

         4. (obsolete) bearing; behavior

trans. verb   6. to permit or tolerate

         7. to approve, support, or encourage . . .

Let's consider briefly the implications of these multiple denotations. The second meaning is more general than the first. It is this first meaning to which we gave priority in the discussion above. We determined our sense of the kind of expression on the mother's face from the line, "Could not unfrown itself." But in looking at definitions 3 and 4, we encounter a problem, or at least a complication. Isn't the mother's "frown" a sign of *discomposure* rather than one of the "composure" suggested by a "calm facial expression"? Or is it possible that Roethke has used *countenance* with two meanings in mind: the meaning of "facial expression" on one hand; the meanings of "tolerate and permit, approve and encourage" on the other? This double sense of *countenance* thus parallels the double sense of the experience for the child as both pleasurable and frightening.

Let us look closely at the language of the following poem.

WILLIAM WORDSWORTH
[1770–1850]

I wandered lonely as a cloud

I wandered lonely as a cloud
That floats on high o'er vales and hills,
When all at once I saw a crowd,
A host, of golden daffodils;
Beside the lake, beneath the trees,   5
Fluttering and dancing in the breeze.

Continuous as the stars that shine
And twinkle on the milky way,
They stretched in never-ending line
Along the margin of a bay: 10
Ten thousand saw I at a glance,
Tossing their heads in sprightly dance.

The waves beside them danced; but they
Outdid the sparkling waves in glee:
A poet could not but be gay,   15
In such a jocund company:
I gazed—and gazed—but little thought
What wealth the show to me had brought:

For oft, when on my couch I lie
In vacant or in pensive mood,   20
They flash upon that inward eye
Which is the bliss of solitude;
And then my heart with pleasure fills,
And dances with the daffodils.

The words of the poem are familiar; their meanings should pose no problems. We might mention that "o'er" in line 2 is an *elision,* the omission of an
unstressed vowel or syllable to preserve the meter, of *over,* and that "oft" in
line 19 is an abbreviated form of *often.* The language, overall, is simple, direct,
and clear.

We can assure ourselves of the rightness or appropriateness of the poem's
diction by considering the connotations of a few words. We can take lines 3
and 4 as examples.

> When all at once I saw a crowd,
> A host, of golden daffodils;

Suppose they had been written this way:

> When all at once I spied a bunch,
> A group of yellow daffodils;

Consider the connotations of each version. "Spied" may indicate something secretive or even prying about the speaker's looking. It may also suggest that he
was looking for them. In contrast, "saw" carries less intense and fewer connotations; it merely indicates that the speaker noticed the daffodils, and its tone is
more matter-of-fact. The alternate version's "bunch" and "group" suggest, on
the one hand, a smaller number than Wordsworth's corresponding "crowd"
and, on the other, a less communal sense. "Crowd" and "host," moreover, carry
connotations of a social gathering, of people congregated to share an experience or simply enjoy one another's company. This implicit humanizing or per-
sonifying of the daffodils (identifying them with human actions and feelings)
brings the daffodils to life: they are described as dancing and as "tossing their
heads" (line 12), and they are called a "jocund company" (line 16). "Company"
underscores the sociality of the daffodils and "jocund" indicates the human
quality of being joyful.

This emphasis on the happiness of the daffodils and their large number
serves to point up sharply the isolation and disspiritedness of the speaker. Their

vast number is emphasized in the second stanza where they are described as "continuous" and as stretching in a "never-ending line." (And, of course, in the count: "ten thousand.") But this important contrast between the isolation of the speaker and the solidarity of the daffodils, though continued into the second stanza, gives way in stanzas three and four as the speaker imagines himself among the daffodils rather than simply looking at them from a distance. More important, when he remembers them later, he thinks about being "with" them, not literally but imaginatively.

But before we look at words describing the speaker from later stanzas, we should return to the first adjective that describes the flowers: "golden" (line 4). Wordsworth uses "golden," not "yellow," or "amber," or "tawny" because "golden" suggests more than a color; it connotes light (it shines and glitters) and wealth (money and fortune). In fact the speaker uses the word "wealth" in line 18 to indicate how important the experience of seeing the daffodils has been. And in the last two stanzas, we notice that the speaker uses in succession five words denoting *joy* ("glee," "gay," "jocund," "bliss," and "pleasure") in a crescendo that suggests the intensity of the speaker's happiness.

Although Wordsworth uses various words to indicate joy, he occasionally repeats rather than varies his diction. The repetitions of the words for seeing ("saw," "gazed") inaugurate and sustain the imagery of vision that is central to the poem's meaning; the forms of the verb *to dance* ("dancing," "danced," "dance," and "dances") suggest both that the various elements of nature are in harmony with one another and that nature is also in harmony with man. The poet conveys this by bringing the elements of nature together in pairs: daffodils and wind (stanza one); daffodils and flowers, daffodils and stars (stanza two); water and wind (stanza three). Nature and man come together explicitly in stanza four when the speaker says that his heart dances with the daffodils.

A different kind of repetition appears in the movement from the loneliness of line one to the solitude of line 22. Both words denote an alone-ness, but they suggest a radical difference in the solitary person's attitude to his state of being alone. The poem moves from the sadly alienated separation felt by the speaker in the beginning to his joy in reimagining the natural scene, a movement framed by the words "loneliness" and "solitude." An analogous movement is suggested within the final stanza by the words "vacant" and "fills." The emptiness of the speaker's spirit is transformed into a fullness of feeling as he remembers the daffodils.

To gain practice in discerning and appreciating diction in poetry, read the following poems with special attention to their words.

EDWIN ARLINGTON ROBINSON
[1869–1935]

Miniver Cheevy

Miniver Cheevy, child of scorn,
    Grew lean while he assailed the seasons;
He wept that he was ever born,
    And he had reasons.

Miniver loved the days of old   5
    When swords were bright and steeds were prancing;
The vision of a warrior bold
    Would set him dancing.

Miniver sighed for what was not,
    And dreamed, and rested from his labors;   10
He dreamed of Thebes° and Camelot,°
    And Priam's neighbors.°

Miniver mourned the ripe renown
    That made so many a name so fragrant;
He mourned Romance, now on the town,   15
    And Art, a vagrant.

Miniver loved the Medici,°
    Albeit he had never seen one;
He would have sinned incessantly
    Could he have been one.   20

Miniver cursed the commonplace
    And eyed a khaki suit with loathing;
He missed the mediæval grace
    Of iron clothing.

Miniver scorned the gold he sought,   25
    But sore annoyed was he without it;
Miniver thought, and thought, and thought,
    And thought about it.

"Miniver Cheevy" [11]**Thebes** *Greek city famous in history and legend.* [11]**Camelot** *the seat of King Arthur's court.* [12]**Priam** *king of Troy during the Trojan war.* [17]**The Medici** *family of powerful merchants and bankers, rulers of Florence in the fourteenth, fifteenth, and sixteenth centuries who were known for their patronage of the arts.*

Miniver Cheevy, born too late,
    Scratched his head and kept on thinking;   30
Miniver coughed, and called it fate,
    And kept on drinking.

QUESTIONS FOR REFLECTION

1. List the words in the poem that illustrate what is said in line 5: that "Miniver loved the days of old." List all the verbs that describe Miniver's action or inaction. What do they reveal about him?
2. What are the connotations of "ripe"? (line 13) and "fragrant" (line 14)? What does the combination of each respectively with ideas of fame and nobility suggest about these ideas? And how do the connotations of "on the town" (to describe Romance) and "a vagrant" (to characterize Art) suggest what has happened to Art and Romance?

WILLIAM WORDSWORTH
[1770–1850]

It is a beauteous evening

It is a beauteous evening, calm and free,
The holy time is quiet as a Nun
Breathless with adoration; the broad sun
Is sinking down in its tranquility;
The gentleness of heaven broods o'er the Sea: 5
Listen! the mighty Being is awake,
And doth with his eternal motion make
A sound like thunder—everlastingly.
Dear Child! dear Girl! that walkest with me here,
If thou appear untouched by solemn thought,   10
Thy nature is not therefore less divine:
Thou liest in Abraham's bosom all the year,
And worship'st at the Temple's inner shrine,
God being with thee when we know it not.

QUESTION FOR REFLECTION

What do the following words have in common: *holy, eternal, solemn, divine, nun, adoration, heaven, God?* Which words in the last four lines are congruent with these? And how does this diction reinforce the idea and feeling of the poem?

ROBERT HERRICK
[1591–1667]

Delight in Disorder

A sweet disorder in the dress
Kindles in clothes a wantonness.
A lawn° about the shoulders thrown   fine linen
Into a fine distractiön;
An erring lace, which here and there   5
Enthralls the crimson stomacher;°
A cuff neglectful, and thereby
Ribbons to flow confusedly;
A winning wave, deserving note,
In the tempestuous petticoat;   10
A careless shoestring, in whose tie
I see a wild civility;
Do more bewitch me than when art
Is too precise in every part.

QUESTIONS FOR REFLECTION

1. Examine the connotations of the words suggesting disorder: *thrown, distraction, neg-lectful, confusedly, careless.* Consider especially the connotations and etymology (word origin) of "erring" (line 5) and "tempestuous" (line 10).
2. Consider the words that describe the speaker's reaction to the disordered dress he describes: *sweet, kindles, wantonness, fine, wild, bewitch.* What do the connotations of these words suggest about the speaker?

ADRIENNE RICH
[b. 1929]

Rape

There is a cop who is both prowler and father:
he comes from your block, grew up with your brothers,
had certain ideals.
You hardly know him in his boots and silver badge,
on horseback, one hand touching his gun.   5

"Delight in Disorder" [6]**stomacher** *a garment worn under the laces of the bodice.*

You hardly know him but you have to get to know him:
he has access to machinery that could kill you.
He and his stallion clop like warlords among the trash,
his ideals stand in the air, a frozen cloud
from between his unsmiling lips.   10

And so, when the time comes, you have to turn to him,
the maniac's sperm still greasing your thighs,
your mind whirling like crazy. You have to confess
to him, you are guilty of the crime
of having been forced.   15

And you see his blue eyes, the blue eyes of all the family
whom you used to know, grow narrow and glisten,
his hand types out the details
and he wants them all
but the hysteria in your voice pleases him best.   20

You hardly know him but now he thinks he knows you:
he has taken down your worst moment
on a machine and filed it in a file.
He knows, or thinks he knows, how much you imagined;
he knows, or thinks he knows, what you secretly wanted.   25

He has access to machinery that could get you put away;
and if, in the sickening light of the precinct,
and if, in the sickening light of the precinct,
your details sound like a portrait of your confessor,
will you swallow, will you deny them, will you lie your way home?   30

QUESTION FOR REFLECTION

The man referred to in the poem is described in line 1 as a "prowler and father," and
in line 29 as a "confessor." What are the implications of each? Explain also the implications of line 8: "He and his stallion clop like warlords among the trash."

IMAGERY

Poems are grounded in the concrete and the specific—in details that stimulate
our senses—for it is through our senses that we perceive the world. We see daylight break and fade; we hear dogs bark and children laugh; we feel the sting of
a bitterly cold wind; we smell the heavy aroma of perfume; we taste the tartness
of lemon and the sweetness of chocolate. Poems include such details which trigger our memories, stimulate our feelings, and command our response.

When such specific details appear in poems they are called images. An *image* is a concrete representation of a sense impression, feeling, or idea. Images appeal to one or more of our senses—or, more precisely, they trigger our imaginative reenactment of sensory experience by rendering feeling and thought in concrete details related directly to our physical perception of the world. Images may be visual (something seen), aural (something heard), tactile (something felt), olfactory (something smelled), or gustatory (something tasted).

Tactile images of heat and cold inform Hayden's "Those Winter Sundays" (page 396), in which the speaker's father wakes up early "in the blueblack cold" to make "banked fires blaze." Visual and tactile images appear in Frost's "Stopping by Woods" (page 399), in which the speaker has stopped "between the woods and frozen lake" to listen to "the sweep of easy wind" and watch the fall of "downy" flakes of snow.

We sometimes use the word *imagery* to refer to a pattern of related details in a poem. Shakespeare's sonnet "That time of year thou may'st in me behold," for example (page 437), includes images of darkness and light, cold and warmth, day and night. The images cluster together to describe the passing of time. When images form patterns of related details that convey an idea or feeling beyond what the images literally describe, we call them *metaphorical* or *symbolic*. Such imagistic details suggest a meaning, attitude, or idea—they suggest one thing in terms of another—as for example when images of light are indicative of knowledge or of life and images of darkness are suggestive of ignorance or death.

Poetry describes specific things—daffodils, fires, and finches' wings, for example. And it describes such things in specific terms: the color of the daffodils, the glare of the fire, the beating of the finches' wings. From these and other specific details we derive both meaning and feeling.

For an indication of how images work together to convey feelings and ideas, consider the images in the following poem.

ELIZABETH BISHOP
[1911–1979]

First Death in Nova Scotia

In the cold, cold parlor
my mother laid out Arthur
beneath the chromographs:
Edward, Prince of Wales,
with Princess Alexandra,   5
and King George with Queen Mary.
Below them on the table
stood a stuffed loon
shot and stuffed by Uncle
Arthur, Arthur's father.   10

Since Uncle Arthur fired
a bullet into him,
he hadn't said a word.
He kept his own counsel
on his white, frozen lake,   15
the marble-topped table.
His breast was deep and white,
cold and caressable;
his eyes were red glass,
much to be desired.   20

"Come," said my mother,
"Come and say good-bye
to your little cousin Arthur."
I was lifted up and given
one lily of the valley   25
to put in Arthur's hand.
Arthur's coffin was
a little frosted cake,
and the red-eyed loon eyed it
from his white, frozen lake.   30

Arthur was very small.
He was all white, like a doll
that hadn't been painted yet.
Jack Frost had started to paint him
the way he always painted   35
the Maple Leaf (Forever).
He had just begun on his hair,
a few red strokes, and then
Jack Frost had dropped the brush
and left him white, forever.   40

The gracious royal couples
were warm in red and ermine;
their feet were well wrapped up
in the ladies' ermine trains.
They invited Arthur to be   45
the smallest page at court.
But how could Arthur go,
clutching his tiny lily,
with his eyes shut up so tight
and the roads deep in snow?   50

The poem describes a child's view of death. Through images of what the little girl sees and hears, it renders her incomprehension and confused feelings about her cousin Arthur's death. Bishop does this by filtering the child's perceptions through an adult sensibility. In a similar way, the poet presents a voice childlike in its syntactic constructions and adult in its vocabulary. Through the double perspective of the adult/the child we gain a complex inner view of the speaker's impressions and understanding of her experience, vividly rendered in the poem's images.

Our first sense impression is tactile: we imagine "the cold, cold parlor." Immediately after, we see two things: a picture of the British royal family and a stuffed loon, which had been shot by the dead boy's father, also named Arthur. The second stanza describes the loon in more detail. It sits on a marble-topped table, a detail that conveys two tactile impressions, hardness and coldness. This imagery is emphasized in the description of the marble table as the loon's "white, frozen lake."

These visual images are continued in the third stanza in which the speaker sees her dead cousin in his coffin. She holds a long-stemmed white flower which she puts in the dead boy's hand. The images of whiteness and cold (the frozen lake, marble table top, and the dead, stuffed white loon of the previous stanzas) are continued: the speaker describes Arthur's coffin as a "frosted cake." The birthday cake image also indicates the limited extent of the speaker's comprehension of the reality and finality of death.

With the repeated details about the loon's red eyes and its frozen posture and base, the child unconsciously (and the poet consciously) associate the dead boy and the dead loon. This connection is further established by the imagery of the fourth stanza in which Arthur is described as "all white," with "a few red strokes" for his hair. Unlike the maple leaf with its complete and thorough redness, little Arthur is left "unpainted" by Jack Frost (another image of the cold) and is thus left white "forever." On the one hand, such a description clearly indicates the child's fantastic incomprehension of Arthur's death; on the other, it suggests that she intuitively senses that Arthur has been drained of color and of life. A similar combination of intuitive understanding and conscious ignorance is echoed in the speaker's comparison of Arthur with the doll. She sees how similar they look on the surface, but she does not consciously register their similar lifelessness.

The images of the final stanzas recall those of stanza 1. The royal couples of the chromograph are described as dressed in red clothes with white fur trim, details that connect directly with the dead loon. Moreover, the lily of the third stanza (white and short-lived like the boy) reappears clutched in Arthur's hand. The final image is one of whiteness and coldness: deep snow covers the cold ground where Arthur will soon lie.

The poem's concrete details, mostly visual and tactile images, strongly evoke the coldness and lifelessness of the dead child. But they suggest other things as well. The portrait of the royal family and the stuffed loon suggest something of the family's social identity—especially its conservatism and propriety. More importantly, however, these details, along with the others noted above, reveal the limitation of the speaker's understanding. She sees the loon, for example, as quiet: "he hadn't said a word," and "he kept his own counsel." In addition, she fantasizes that the royal family (which she sees as very much alive in their warm furs) have invited little Arthur to serve as "the smallest page at court." Even though this may be the speaker's way of coping with death, the final two images of white lily and cold snow, and the tone in which she asks her final question all point toward her near acknowledgment of the truth.

It should prove useful to return at this point to a few of the poems considered in earlier sections of this introduction and examine their imagery. For further practice in responding to poetic images, read the following poems.

WILLIAM BUTLER YEATS
[1865–1939]

The Lake Isle of Innisfree

I will arise and go now, and go to Innisfree,
And a small cabin build there, of clay and wattles° made: interwoven twigs
Nine bean-rows will I have there, a hive for the honey-bee,
And live alone in the bee-loud glade.

And I shall have some peace there, for peace comes dropping slow,   5
Dropping from the veils of the morning to where the cricket sings;
There midnight's all a glimmer, and noon a purple glow,
And evening full of the linnet's wings.

I will arise and go now, for always night and day
I hear lake water lapping with low sounds by the shore;   10
While I stand on the roadway, or on the pavements gray,
I hear it in the deep heart's core.

QUESTION FOR REFLECTION

Identify the images of sound and sight and explain what they contribute to the idea and feeling of the poem.

ROBERT BROWNING
[1812–1889]

Meeting at Night

The gray sea and the long black land;
And the yellow half-moon large and low;
And the startled little waves that leap
In fiery ringlets from their sleep,
As I gain the cove with pushing prow,   5
And quench its speed i' the slushy sand.

Then a mile of warm sea-scented beach;
Three fields to cross till a farm appears;
A tap at the pane, the quick sharp scratch
And blue spurt of a lighted match,   10
And a voice less loud, through its joys and fears,
Than the two hearts beating each to each!

QUESTION FOR REFLECTION

In a series of images averaging one per line, the poet describes a lover traveling to meet his beloved. Identify each image, the specific sense it stimulates, and the feelings the images evoke.

H. D. (HILDA DOOLITTLE)
[1886–1961]

Heat

O wind, rend open the heat,
cut apart the heat,
rend it to tatters.

Fruit cannot drop
through this thick air—   5
that presses up and blunts
the points of pears
and rounds the grapes.

Cut the heat—
plow through it,   10
turning it on either side
of your path.

QUESTION FOR REFLECTION

By asking the wind to "rend open," "cut apart," and "plow through" the heat, the poet creates an image of it. Identify this image and explain what stanza two contributes to it.

THOMAS HARDY
[1840–1929]

Neutral Tones

We stood by a pond that winter day,
And the sun was white, as though chidden of God,
And a few leaves lay on the starving sod;
    —They had fallen from an ash, and were gray.

Your eyes on me were as eyes that rove   5
Over tedious riddles of years ago;
And some words played between us to and fro
    On which lost the more by our love.

The smile on your mouth was the deadest thing
Alive enough to have strength to die;   10
And a grin of bitterness swept thereby
    Like an ominous bird a-wing. . . .

Since then, keen lessons that love deceives,
And wrings with wrong, have shaped to me
Your face, and the God-curst sun, and a tree,   15
    And a pond edged with grayish leaves.

QUESTIONS FOR REFLECTION

1. Examine the images of stanza one. What mood do they create? How do the images of stanzas two and three develop and expand those of the opening stanza?
2. What do you notice about the images of the final stanza in relation to those that come before?

FIGURES OF SPEECH: SIMILE AND METAPHOR

Language can be conveniently classified as either literal or figurative. When we speak literally, we mean exactly what each word conveys; when we use *figurative language* we mean something other than the actual meaning of the words. "Go jump in the lake," for example, if meant literally would be intended as a command to leave (go) and jump (not dive or wade) into a lake (not a pond or stream). Usually, however, such an expression is not literally meant. In telling someone to go jump in the lake we are telling them something, to be sure, but what we mean is different from the literal meaning of the words. To get lost, perhaps, which is itself a figurative expression.

Rhetoricians have catalogued more than 250 different *figures of speech,* expressions or ways of using words in a nonliteral sense. They include *hyperbole* or exaggeration ("I'll die if I miss that game"); *litotes* or understatement ("Being flayed alive is somewhat painful"); *synecdoche* or using a part to signify the whole ("Lend me a hand"); *metonymy* or substituting an attribute of a thing for the thing itself ("step on the gas"); *personification,* endowing inanimate objects or abstract concepts with animate characteristics or qualities ("the lettuce was lonely without tomatoes and cucumbers for company"). We will not go on to name and illustrate the others but instead will concentrate on two specially important for poetry (and for the other literary genres as well): simile and metaphor.

The heart of both these figures is comparison—the making of connections between normally unrelated things, seeing one thing in terms of another. More than 2,300 years ago Aristotle defined *metaphor* as "an intuitive perception of the similarity in dissimilars." And he suggested further that to be a "master of metaphor" is the greatest of a poet's achievements. In our century, Robert Frost has echoed Aristotle by suggesting that metaphor is central to poetry, and that, essentially, poetry is a way of "saying one thing and meaning another, saying one thing in terms of another."

Although both figures involve comparisons between unlike things, *simile* establishes the comparison explicitly with the words *like* or *as. Metaphor,* on the other hand, employs no such explicit verbal clue. The comparison is *implied* in such a way that the figurative term is substituted for or identified with the literal one. "My daughter dances like an angel" is a simile; "my daughter is an angel" is a metaphor. In this example the difference involves more than the word *like:* the simile is more restricted in its comparative suggestion than is the metaphor. That is, the daughter's angelic attributes are more extensive in the unspecified and unrestricted metaphor. In the simile, however, she only dances like an angel. (There's no suggestion that she possesses other angelic qualities.)

Consider the opening line of Wordsworth's poem about the daffodils: "I wandered lonely as a cloud" (page 423). The simile suggests the speaker's isolation and his aimless wandering. But it doesn't indicate other ways in which cloud and speaker are related. Later the speaker uses another simile to compare the daffodils with stars. This simile specifically highlights one aspect of the connection between stars and flowers: number. It also contains an example of hyperbole in its suggestion that the daffodils stretch in "a never-ending line."

In these examples the poet provides explicit clues that direct us to the comparative connection. He also restricts their application, as we have noted. In a metaphor, Wordsworth writes that the daffodils "flash" upon the "inward eye" of the speaker. The "flash" (an image of light) implies that he sees the flowers in his mind's eye, the inward eye of memory. Moreover, when he "sees" the daffodils in his "inward eye," he realizes the "wealth" they have brought him. This "wealth" is also figurative—Wordsworth uses "wealth" as a metaphor for joy.

These examples of simile and metaphor from Wordsworth's poem are fairly straightforward and uncomplicated. For a more complex example, consider the use of metaphor in the following sonnet by William Shakespeare.

WILLIAM SHAKESPEARE
[1564–1616]

That time of year thou may'st in me behold

That time of year thou may'st in me behold
When yellow leaves, or none, or few, do hang
Upon those boughs which shake against the cold,
Bare ruined choirs where late the sweet birds sang.
In me thou see'st the twilight of such day   5
As after sunset fadeth in the west,
Which by-and-by black night doth take away,
Death's second self that seals up all in rest.
In me thou see'st the glowing of such fire
That on the ashes of his youth doth lie,   10
As the deathbed whereon it must expire,
Consumed with that which it was nourished by.
   This thou perceiv'st, which makes thy love more strong,
   To love that well which thou must leave ere long.

Perhaps the first thing to mention about the poem's metaphorical language is that its images appeal to three senses: sight, hearing, and touch. The images of the first four lines include appeals to each of these senses: we *see* the yellow leaves and bare branches; we *feel* the cold that shakes the boughs; we *hear* (in memory) the singing birds of summer.

But these concrete representations of sensory experience become more than images with emotional reverberations. They become metaphors, ways of talking about one thing in terms of something else. The first image extended into a metaphor is that of autumn, "that time of year" when leaves turn yellow and branches become bare. The fourth line extends the image by describing the tree branches as a choir loft that the birds have recently vacated. Because Shakespeare's speaker says that "you" (we) can behold autumn *in him* ("In me thou see'st the twilight of such day," line 5), we know that he is speaking of more than autumn. We realize that he is talking about one thing in terms of another—about aging in terms of the seasons.

In the next four lines the metaphor of autumn gives way to another: that of twilight ending the day. The sun has set; night is coming on. The "black" night is described as taking away the sun's light (line 7); the sun's setting is seen as a dying of its light. The implied comparison of night with death is directly stated in line 8, where night is called "death's second self"; like death, night "seals up all in rest." Night's rest is, of course, temporary; death's, however, is final. The metaphor is both consoling (death is a kind of restful sleep) and frightening (death "seals up" life in a way that suggests there will be no unsealing).

So far we have noted two extended metaphors of autumn and of evening. Each comparison highlights the way death begins with a prelude: twilight precedes night; autumn precedes winter; illness precedes death. The speaker knows that he is in the autumn of his life, the twilight of his time. This metaphor is continued in a third image: the dying of the fire, which represents the dying out of the speaker's life. This third image emphasizes the extinguishing of light and of heat. The speaker's youth is "ashes," which serve as the "deathbed" on which he will "expire" (line 11). Literally, the lines say that the fire will expire as it burns up the fuel that feeds it. As it does so, it glows with light and heat. The glowing fire is a metaphor for the speaker's life, which is presently still "glowing" but which is beginning to die out as it consumes itself. We might notice that the fire will "expire," a word which means literally to "breathe out . . . to emit the last breath," an image that suggests the termination of breathing in the dying.

The final element of this image of the dying fire is given in line 12: "Consumed with that which it was nourished by." Literally the fire consumes itself by using up its fuel, burning up logs. In its very glowing it burns toward its own extinction. Analogously, the speaker's youthful vitality consumes itself in living. His very living has been and continues to be a dying.

For a few additional examples of how poets employ figurative language, read the following poems. Attend particularly to their figures of comparison and especially to how those comparisons aid your understanding.

JOHN DONNE
[1572–1631]

Hymn to God the Father

1

Wilt thou forgive that sin where I begun,
Which was my sin though it were done before?
Wilt thou forgive that sin through which I run,

And do run still, though still I do deplore?
　　When thou hast done, thou hast not done,　　　　5
　　　For I have more.

2

Wilt thou forgive that sin by which I've won
　Others to sin, and made my sin their door?
Wilt thou forgive that sin which I did shun
　A year or two, but wallowed in a score?　　　　10
　　When thou hast done, thou hast not done,
　　　For I have more.

3

I have a sin of fear, that when I've spun
　My last thread, I shall perish on the shore;
But swear by thyself that at my death thy son　　15
　Shall shine as he shines now, and heretofore;
　　And having done that, Thou hast done;
　　　I fear no more.

QUESTIONS FOR REFLECTION

1. Explain the images in stanza two: the door of sin and wallowing in sin. Relate these two images from stanza three: spinning the last thread and perishing on the shore.
2. The final stanza contains two puns or plays on words. Identify and explain each. What do they contribute to the meaning and tone of the poem?

R O B E R T　W A L L A C E

[b. 1932]

The Double Play

In his sea-lit
distance, the pitcher winding
like a clock about to chime comes down with

the ball, hit
sharply, under the artificial　　　　　5
banks of arc lights, bounds like a vanishing string

over the green
to the shortstop magically
scoops to his right whirling above his invisible

shadows   10
in the dust redirects
its flight to the running poised second baseman

pirouettes
leaping, above the slide, to throw
from mid-air, across the colored tightened interval,   15

to the leaning-
out first baseman ends the dance
drawing it disappearing into his long brown glove

stretches. What
is too swift for deception   20
is final, lost, among the loosened figures

jogging off the field
(the pitcher walks), casual
in the space where the poem has happened.

QUESTIONS FOR REFLECTION

1. As its title suggests the poem describes a double play in baseball—getting two offensive players out on a single play. Throughout the poem the double play is compared to a dance. Pinpoint the words and phrases that establish this metaphorical
   connection, and explain what precisely about the double play makes it like a dance.
2. Besides the central metaphor that controls the poem, the poet has introduced other
   comparisons to illuminate and describe aspects or details of the double play. Identify and explain these comparisons.
3. In what way has the double play occurred "in the space where the poem has happened" (line 24)? How has a double play occurred both on the page and in the poem?

LOUIS SIMPSON
[*b. 1923*]

The Battle

Helmet and rifle, pack and overcoat
Marched through a forest. Somewhere up ahead
Guns thudded. Like the circle of a throat
The night on every side was turning red.

They halted and they dug. They sank like moles   5
Into the clammy earth between the trees.
And soon the sentries, standing in their holes,
Felt the first snow. Their feet began to freeze.

At dawn the first shell landed with a crack.
Then shells and bullets swept the icy woods.   10
This lasted many days. The snow was black.
The corpses stiffened in their scarlet hoods.

Most clearly of that battle I remember
The tiredness in eyes, how hands looked thin
Around a cigarette, and the bright ember   15
Would pulse with all the life there was within.

QUESTION FOR REFLECTION

Identify and explain the figures of speech in the first two stanzas. What impression
does each create? How is the mood they establish enforced by the rest of the poem?

JUDITH WRIGHT
[*b. 1915*]

Woman to Child

You who were darkness warmed my flesh
where out of darkness rose the seed.
Then all a world I made in me;
all the world you hear and see
hung upon my dreaming blood.   5

There moved the multitudinous stars,
and coloured birds and fishes moved.
There swam the sliding continents.
All time lay rolled in me, and sense,
and love that knew not its beloved.   10

O node and focus of the world;
I hold you deep within that well
you shall escape and not escape—
that mirrors still your sleeping shape;
that nurtures still your crescent cell.   15

I wither and you break from me;
yet though you dance in living light
I am the earth, I am the root,
I am the stem that fed the fruit,
the link that joins you to the night.   20

QUESTION FOR REFLECTION

Explain the following figurative expressions:

"All a world I made in me" (line 3)
"All time lay rolled in me" (line 9)
"I hold you deep within that well" (line 12)
"I am the earth, I am the root,
I am the stem that fed the fruit" (lines 18–19)

SYMBOLISM AND ALLEGORY

A *symbol* is any object or action that means more than itself, any object or action that represents something beyond itself. A rose, for example, can represent beauty or love or transience. A tree may represent a family's roots and branches. A soaring bird might stand for freedom. Light might symbolize hope or knowledge or life. These and other familiar symbols may represent different, even opposite things, depending on how they are deployed in a particular poem. Natural symbols like light and darkness, fire and water can stand for contradictory things. Water, for example, which typically symbolizes life (rain, fertility, food, life) can also stand for death (tempests, hurricanes, floods). And fire, which often indicates destruction, can represent purgation or purification. The meaning of any symbol, whether an object, an action, or a gesture, is controlled by its context.

How then do we know if a poetic detail is symbolic? How do we decide whether to leap beyond the poem's literal detail into a symbolic interpretation?

There are no simple answers to these questions. Like any interpretive connections we make in reading, the decision to view something as symbolic depends partly on our skill in reading and partly on whether the poetic context invites and rewards a symbolic reading. The following questions can guide our thinking about interpreting symbols:

1. Is the object, action, gesture, or event important to the poem? Is it described in detail? Does it occur repeatedly? Does it appear at a climactic moment in the poem?
2. Does the poem seem to warrant our granting its details more significance than their immediate literal meaning?
3. Does our symbolic reading make sense? Does it account for the literal details without either ignoring or distorting them?

Even in following such guidelines, there will be occasions when we are not certain that a poem is symbolic. And there will be times when, though we are fairly confident *that* certain details are symbolic, we are not confident about *what* they symbolize. Such uncertainty is due largely to the nature of interpretation, which is an art rather than a science. But these interpretive complications are also due to the differences in complexity and variability with which poets use symbols. The most complex symbols resist definitive and final explanation. We can circle around them, but we neither exhaust their significance nor define their meaning.

As an example of how literal details assume symbolic significance observe their use in the following poem.

PETER MEINKE

[b. 1932]

Advice to My Son

The trick is, to live your days
as if each one may be your last
(for they go fast, and young men lose their lives
in strange and unimaginable ways)
but at the same time, plan long range   5
(for they go slow: if you survive
the shattered windshield and the bursting shell
you will arrive
at our approximation here below
of heaven or hell).   10

To be specific, between the peony and the rose
plant squash and spinach, turnips and tomatoes;

beauty is nectar
and nectar, in a desert, saves—
but the stomach craves stronger sustenance   15
than the honied vine.
Therefore, marry a pretty girl
after seeing her mother;
speak truth to one man,
work with another;   20
and always serve bread with your wine.

But, son,
always serve wine.

The concrete details that invite symbolic reading are these: peony and rose; squash, spinach, turnips and tomatoes; bread and wine. If we read the poem literally and assume the advice is meant that way, we learn something about the need to plant and enjoy these flowers and foods. But if we suspect that the speaker is advising his son about more than food and flowers, we will look toward their symbolic implications.

What then do the various plants and the bread and wine symbolize? How is the speaker's advice about them related to the more general advice about living? In the first stanza the general advice implies two contradictory courses of action: (1) live each day to the fullest as if it will be the last; (2) look to the future and plan wisely so your future will not be marred by unwise decisions. By advising his son to plant peonies and roses, the speaker urges him to see the need for beauty and luxury, implying that he needs food for the spirit as well as sustenance for the body.

The symbols of bread and wine suggest a related point. The speaker urges his son to serve both bread and wine as bread is a dietary staple, something basic and common, but wine enhances the bread, making it seem more than mere common fare. Wine symbolizes something festive; it provides a touch of celebration. Thus the speaker's advice about bread and wine parallels his earlier suggestions. In each case, he urges his son to balance and blend, to fulfill both his basic and his spiritual needs. By making his advice concrete the speaker does indeed advocate literally what he says: plant roses and peonies with your vegetables; drink wine with your bread. But by including such specific instructions in a poem that contains other more serious advice about living (live for today, live for the future) the poet invites us to see bread and wine, vegetables and flowers more than literally. If our interpretation of their symbolic dimension is congruent with other parts of the poem, and if it makes sense, then we should feel confident that we are not imposing a symbolic reading where it is not warranted.

Related to symbolism, *allegory* is a form of narrative in which people, places, and happenings have hidden or symbolic meaning; allegory is especially suitable as a vehicle for teaching. In an allegorical work there are most often two levels of meaning, the literal and the symbolic. To understand an allegorical work we must make sense of its details by interpreting their symbolic meaning.

Allegory is thus a type of symbolism. It differs from symbolism in establishing a strict system of correspondences between details of action and a pattern of meaning. Symbolic works that are not allegorical are less systematic and more open-ended in what their symbols mean.

The following allegorical poem describes a journey along an uphill road that ends with the traveler arriving at an inn. We can readily see that the uphill road represents a struggling journey through life, that day and night stand for a life span ending in death. The question-and-answer structure of the poem and its reassuring tone suggest that it can be read as a religious allegory, specifically a Christian one.

CHRISTINA ROSSETTI
[1830–1894]

Up-Hill

Does the road wind up-hill all the way?
    Yes, to the very end.
Will the day's journey take the whole long day?
    From morn to night, my friend.

But is there for the night a resting-place?   5
    A roof for when the slow dark hours begin.
May not the darkness hide it from my face?
    You cannot miss that inn.

Shall I meet other wayfarers at night?
    Those who have gone before.   10
Then must I knock, or call when just in sight?
    They will not keep you standing at that door.

Shall I find comfort, travel-sore and weak?
    Of labor you shall find the sum.
Will there be beds for me and all who seek?   15
    Yea, beds for all who come.

For more exercise in interpreting symbol and allegory, read the following poems with attention to their symbolic and allegorical details. All the poems are symbolic, but not in the same way.

WILLIAM BLAKE
[1757–1827]

A Poison Tree

I was angry with my friend:
I told my wrath, my wrath did end.
I was angry with my foe:
I told it not, my wrath did grow.

And I waterd it in fears,   5
Night & morning with my tears;
And I sunnéd it with smiles,
And with soft deceitful wiles.

And it grew both day and night,
Till it bore an apple bright.   10
And my foe beheld it shine,
And he knew that it was mine,

And into my garden stole,
When the night had veild the pole;
In the morning glad I see   15
My foe outstretchd beneath the tree.

QUESTIONS FOR REFLECTION

1. "A Poison Tree" describes a series of events—it tells a story. Explain your under-standing of the story's significance.
2. What does the apple in a garden represent? What difference would it make if it were a peach in an orchard?

ROBERT FROST
[1874–1963]

The Road Not Taken

Two roads diverged in a yellow wood,
And sorry I could not travel both
And be one traveler, long I stood
And looked down one as far as I could
To where it bent in the undergrowth;   5

Then took the other, as just as fair,
And having perhaps the better claim,
Because it was grassy and wanted wear;
Though as for that, the passing there
Had worn them really about the same,   10

And both that morning equally lay
In leaves no step had trodden black.
Oh, I kept the first for another day!
Yet knowing how way leads on to way,
I doubted if I should ever come back.   15

I shall be telling this with a sigh
Somewhere ages and ages hence:
Two roads diverged in a wood, and I—
I took the one less traveled by,
And that has made all the difference.   20

QUESTIONS FOR REFLECTION

1. On one level this is a poem about walking in the woods and choosing one of two
   paths to follow. What invites us to see the poem as something more? What is this
   something more?
2. Frost is careful not to specify what the two roads represent: he does not limit their
   possible symbolic meanings. And yet the nature of the experience he describes does
   pivot the poem on a central human problem: the inescapable necessity to make
   choices. Specify some of the choices we all must make that could be represented by
   the two roads of the poem.

GEORGE HERBERT
[1593–1633]

Virtue

Sweet day, so cool, so calm, so bright,
   The bridal of the earth and sky:
The dew shall weep thy fall tonight;
   For thou must die.

Sweet rose, whose hue, angry and brave,   5
   Bids the rash gazer wipe his eye:
Thy root is ever in its grave,
   And thou must die.

Sweet spring, full of sweet days and roses,
   A box where sweets° compacted lie;   perfumes 10
My music shows ye have your closes,°   musical cadences
   And all must die.

Only a sweet and virtuous soul,
   Like seasoned timber, never gives;
But though the whole world turn to coal,   15
   Then chiefly lives.

QUESTION FOR REFLECTION

The major contrast in the poem is between things that die and the one thing that does not. Identify and comment on the aptness of Herbert's symbols for transience and mortality.

EMILY DICKINSON
[1830–1886]

Because I could not stop for Death

Because I could not stop for Death—
He kindly stopped for me—
The Carriage held but just Ourselves—
And Immortality.

We slowly drove—He knew no haste   5
And I had put away
My labor and my leisure too,
For His Civility—

We passed the School, where Children strove
At Recess—in the Ring—   10
We passed the Fields of Gazing Grain—
We passed the Setting Sun—

Or rather—He passed Us—
The Dews drew quivering and chill—
For only Gossamer, my Gown—   15
My Tippet°—only Tulle—   scarf or stole

We paused before a House that seemed
A Swelling of the Ground—
The Roof was scarcely visible—
The Cornice—in the Ground—   20

Since then—'tis Centuries—and yet
Feels shorter than the Day
I first surmised the Horses' Heads
Were toward Eternity—

QUESTION FOR REFLECTION

Is this poem generally symbolic or is it allegorical? Explain the significance of the details in lines 9–13 and lines 17–20.

SYNTAX

We have previously defined *syntax* as the order of words in sentence, phrase, or clause. From a Greek word meaning "to arrange together," *syntax* refers to the grammatical structure of words in sentences and the deployment of sentences in longer units throughout the poem. Poets use syntax as they use imagery, diction, structure, sound, and rhythm—to express meaning and convey feeling. A poem's syntax is an important element of its tone and a guide to a speaker's state of mind. Speakers who repeat themselves or who break off abruptly in the midst of a thought, for example, reveal something about how they feel.

Let us briefly consider what syntax contributes to the meaning and feeling of a few poems discussed earlier. In "Those Winter Sundays" (page 396), Robert Hayden uses normal word order for each of the poem's four sentences, but he varies their lengths radically. In the first stanza, for example, Hayden follows a long sentence with a short one. The effect is to increase the emphasis on the short sentence: "No one ever thanked him." In the last stanza, Hayden uses a question rather than a statement for the speaker's remembrance of his father's acts of love. Both the question and the repetition of the phrase "What did I know" reveal the intensity of the speaker's regret at his belated understanding.

In "Stopping by Woods on a Snowy Evening" (page 399), Robert Frost achieves emphasis differently through *inversion* or the reversal of the standard order of words in a line or sentence. The word order of the first line of the poem is inverted:

Whose woods these are I think I know.

Normal word order would be:

I think I know whose woods these are.

In the more conversational alternative, emphasis falls on what the speaker knows or thinks he knows. In Frost's line emphasis falls on "the woods," which are more important than what the speaker thinks he knows as he looks at them. Perhaps more important still is the difference in tone between the two versions. Frost's inverted syntax lifts the line, giving it a more even rhythm, slowing it down slightly. The alternate version lacks the rhythmic regularity of Frost's original and reads like a casual statement.

Another aspect of syntax worth noting in Frost's poem is the variations in tempo among the four stanzas. The sentences of the first and last stanzas are the most heavily stopped with punctuation and pauses. The opening stanza contains three pauses before it ends; stanza four includes three in its first line alone and five altogether. In contrast stanza three contains only one stop, halfway through. And stanza two is one long sentence without a single pause or break. Frost carefully controls the movement and speed, the pace and pause of his poem by using punctuation and grammatical form to heighten its expressiveness and to control its tone.

Unlike the inverted and varied syntax of Frost's "Stopping by Woods on a Snowy Evening," William Wordsworth's syntax in "I wandered lonely as a cloud" (page 423) is simple and direct; it does not call attention to itself. The two little syntactic twists that it does contain highlight an important dimension of the poem—visual imagery. One is an inversion: "saw I" (line 11); the other is a repetition: "I gazed—and gazed" (line 17). And consider Walt Whitman's "When I heard the learn'd astronomer" (page 476), which is cast as a single expansive subordinate sentence that sweeps over the first four lines like a wave and then ebbs in the next four. The action of the last four lines is suspended over the first four: we are made to wait for the final simple and important act that Whitman renders in the most direct syntax of any line in the poem: the speaker "look'd up in perfect silence at the stars."

Consider how syntax orders thought and highlights feeling in "The Sun Rising," by John Donne.

JOHN DONNE
[1572–1631]

The Sun Rising

Busy old fool, unruly sun,
    Why dost thou thus,
Through windows, and through curtains call on us?
Must to thy motions lovers' seasons run?
    Saucy pedantic wretch, go chide   5
    Late schoolboys, and sour prentices,
  Go tell court-huntsmen that the King will ride,
  Call country ants to harvest offices;
Love, all alike, no season knows, nor clime,
Nor hours, days, months, which are the rags of time.   10

> Thy beams, so reverend and strong
> Why shouldst thou think?
> I could eclipse and cloud them with a wink,
> But that I would not lose her sight so long;
> If her eyes have not blinded thine,   15
> Look, and tomorrow late, tell me
> Whether both the Indias of spice and mine
> Be where thou left'st them, or lie here with me.
> Ask for those kings whom thou saw'st yesterday,
> And thou shalt hear, All here in one bed lay.   20

> She's all states, and all princes, I,
> Nothing else is.
> Princes do but play us; compared to this,
> All's honor's mimic, all wealth alchemy.
> Thou, sun, art half as happy as we,   25
> In that the world's contracted thus;
> Thine age asks ease, and since thy duties be
> To warm the world, that's done in warming us.
> Shine here to us, and thou art everywhere;
> This bed thy center is, these walls, thy sphere.   30

Perhaps the first thing we notice is the dislocation of syntax in the two opening questions. The first question could be rewritten so as to approximate more conventional discourse:

> Unruly sun, busy old fool,
> Why dost thou thus call on us
> Through windows, and through curtains?

Besides an alteration of rhythm, we notice a different emphasis in Donne's lines. The alternate version puts the emphasis on "windows" and "curtains," far less important words than "us," the word Donne's lines emphasize, as the poem is about a pair of lovers.

After another inverted sentence ("Must to thy motions lovers' seasons run") and a short one following the longer opening sentence, we hear a series of tonal shifts. The speed and abruptness of Donne's second question convey the speaker's tone of impatient defiance. The two questions with their emphatic dislocations prepare the way for the series of imperatives that increase our sense of the speaker's authority. This tone gives way abruptly in the last two lines of the stanza to a more leisurely verse movement ("Love, all alike, no season knows, nor clime, / Nor hours, days, months, which are the rags of time"). The dignified and stately tone of these lines derives partly from the simple declarative sentences, partly from the monosyllabic diction, and partly from the frequent pauses marked by punctuation. The overall effect is a slower line and a more exalted tone.

In stanza two the tone shifts back to the playful exaggeration of the beginning of the poem, with similar dislocations of syntax in its opening question. The second sentence (lines 13–18), neither question, statement, nor command, is a statement of possibility. The tone remains playfully defiant ("tell me / Whether both the Indias of spice and mine / Be where thou left'st them"); the speaker continues to exaggerate. The syntax is more convoluted, the sentences more complex than in the first stanza. Again, however, as in the opening stanza, the final line of stanza two resolves into a direct authoritative assertion:

> . . . All here in one bed lay.

Unlike the first two stanzas, the last begins with the declarative syntax and simple, direct assertiveness with which the other two stanzas end. The entire stanza is composed of a series of balanced statements, some parallel, some antithetical. (Not completely, however, since there is something of the complex argument of stanza two midway through this last stanza. And there is also a brief return to the imperative voice in line 29, "Shine here to us.") But from these deviations the speaker quickly returns to the authority of direct declaration, an authority enhanced by the parallel form of the final line, by its slight dislocation of the verbs, and by the tightness of its structure (eliminating a conjunction between the clauses and omitting the implied verb of the second half of the line):

> This bed thy center is, these walls thy sphere.

There are many syntactical possibilities available to poets. For some interesting syntactical forms and their effects see T. S. Eliot's "The Love Song of J. Alfred Prufrock" for its associative syntax (syntax that reflects the mental associations of the speaker [page 673]); Gerard Manley Hopkins's "Thou art indeed just, Lord" (page 418) for its use of fractured or broken syntax; John Milton's "On the Late Massacre in Piedmont" (page 620) for its Latinate syntax; and Alexander Pope's "An Essay on Man," (page 623) for its tightly formal, balanced, and antithetical syntax.

In the poems that follow Thomas Hardy uses broken syntax in "The Man He Killed"; William Butler Yeats uses balanced syntax in "An Irish Airman Foresees His Death"; Robert Frost uses ambiguous syntax so that multiple meanings coexist and coincide in "The Silken Tent"; and E. E. Cummings uses mimetic syntax, which imitates what it describes, in "Me up at does."

THOMAS HARDY
[1840–1928]

The Man He Killed

"Had he and I but met
By some old ancient inn,
We should have sat us down to wet
Right many a nipperkin!

"But ranged as infantry,   5
And staring face to face,
I shot at him as he at me,
And killed him in his place.

"I shot him dead because—
Because he was my foe,   10
Just so: my foe of course he was;
That's clear enough; although

"He thought he'd 'list, perhaps,
Off-hand-like—just as I—
Was out of work—had sold his traps—   15
No other reason why.

"Yes; quaint and curious war is!
You shoot a fellow down
You'd treat if met where any bar is,
Or help to half-a-crown."   20

QUESTIONS FOR REFLECTION

1. The first two stanzas are each a single sentence. Explain their logical and syntactic relationship.
2. Unlike the smooth unbroken sentences of the first two stanzas, we find breaks in the syntax (indicated by dashes) in the next two stanzas. After reading the stanzas aloud, explain what the breaks suggest about the speaker's state of mind.
3. Does the speaker's fluent syntax in the last stanza suggest that he has worked through the state of mind you found evident in stanzas three and four? Explain.

WILLIAM BUTLER YEATS
[*1865–1939*]

An Irish Airman Foresees His Death

I know that I shall meet my fate
Somewhere among the clouds above;
Those that I fight I do not hate,
Those that I guard I do not love;°
My country is Kiltartan Cross   5
My countrymen Kiltartan's poor,
No likely end could bring them loss
Or leave them happier than before.
Nor law, nor duty bade me fight,
Nor public men, nor cheering crowds,   10
A lonely impulse of delight
Drove to this tumult in the clouds;
I balanced all, brought all to mind,
The years to come seemed waste of breath,
A waste of breath the years behind   15
In balance with this life, this death.

QUESTIONS FOR REFLECTION

1. Point out the ways the syntax of this poem is balanced and controlled. How does the poem's balanced syntax reinforce its meaning?
2. Explain the connection between its syntax and its central idea: the pilot's attitude toward his country, his enemy, his fate.

ROBERT FROST
[*1874–1963*]

The Silken Tent

She is as in a field a silken tent
At midday when a sunny summer breeze
Has dried the dew and all its ropes relent,

"An Irish Airman Foresees His Death"   ³⁻⁴*Those that I fight . . . I do not love;*   Yeats is referring to the Germans and the English respectively; the war is World War I.

So that in guys it gently sways at ease,
And its supporting central cedar pole,   5
That is its pinnacle to heavenward
And signifies the sureness of the soul,
Seems to owe naught to any single cord,
But strictly held by none, is loosely bound
By countless silken ties of love and thought   10
To everything on earth the compass round,
And only by one's going slightly taut
In the capriciousness of summer air
Is of the slightest bondage made aware.

QUESTION FOR REFLECTION

Perhaps the most astonishing thing about this sonnet is that it is only a single sentence.
Go through the poem again attending to the way the sentence develops. Account for
all the conjunctions: *so* (line 4), *and* (line 5), *And* (line 7), *But* (line 9), *And* (line 12).
How do those conjunctions help us follow the sentence?

E. E. CUMMINGS
[1894–1962]

"Me up at does"

Me up at does

out of the floor
quietly Stare

a poisoned mouse

still who alive

is asking What
have i done that

You wouldn't have

QUESTIONS FOR REFLECTION

1. Rearrange the syntax of this poem to approximate the normal word order of an English sentence. Where do you have to make the heaviest adjustment?
2. How is Cummings's word order related to the situation the poem describes? What does Cummings gain by ordering his words as he does?

STEVIE SMITH
[1902–1971]

Mother, Among the Dustbins

Mother, among the dustbins and the manure
I feel the measure of my humanity, an allure
As of the presence of God. I am sure

In the dustbins, in the manure, in the cat at play,
Is the presence of God, in a sure way   5
He moves there. Mother, what do you say?

I too have felt the presence of God in the broom
I hold, in the cobwebs in the room,
But most of all in the silence of the tomb.

Ah! but that thought that informs the hope of our kind   10
Is but an empty thing, what lies behind?—
Naught but the vanity of a protesting mind

That would not die. This is the thought that bounces
Within a conceited head and trounces
Inquiry. Man is most frivolous when he pronounces.   15

Well Mother, I shall continue to think as I do,
And I think you would be wise to do so too,
Can you question the folly of man in the creation of God?
    Who are you?

QUESTION FOR REFLECTION

Examine the way the poet uses balanced phrasing, primarily repeated phrases throughout the poem. Notice the play of long sentence against short, of question against statement. What do these syntactic elements contribute to the tone and attitude of the poem?

SOUND: RHYME, ALLITERATION, ASSONANCE

The most familiar element of poetry is *rhyme,* which can be defined as the matching of final vowel and consonant sounds in two or more words. When the corresponding sounds occur at the ends of lines we have *end rhyme;* when they occur within lines we have *internal rhyme.* The opening stanza of Edgar Allan Poe's "The Raven" illustrates both:

> Once upon a midnight dreary, while I pondered weak and weary,
> Over many a quaint and curious volume of forgotten lore—
> While I nodded nearly napping, suddenly there came a tapping,
> As of some one gently rapping, rapping at my chamber door.
> "'Tis some visitor," I muttered, "tapping at my chamber door—
> Only this and nothing more."

For the reader rhyme is a pleasure, for the poet a challenge. Part of its pleasure for the reader is in anticipating and hearing a poem's echoing song. Part of its challenge for the poet is in rhyming naturally, without forcing the rhythm, the syntax, or the sense. When the challenge is met successfully, the poem is a pleasure to listen to; it sounds natural to the ear, and its rhyme makes it easier to remember.

Robert Frost's "Stopping by Woods on a Snowy Evening" is one such rhyming success. Reread it once more, preferably aloud, and listen to its music.

> Whose woods these are I think I know.
> His house is in the village, though;
> He will not see me stopping here
> To watch his woods fill up with snow.
>
> My little horse must think it queer
> To stop without a farmhouse near
> Between the woods and frozen lake
> The darkest evening of the year.
>
> He gives his harness bells a shake
> To ask if there is some mistake.
> The only other sound's the sweep
> Of easy wind and downy flake.
>
> The woods are lovely, dark and deep,
> But I have promises to keep,
> And miles to go before I sleep,
> And miles to go before I sleep.

Notice how in each of the first three stanzas, three of the four lines rhyme (lines 1, 2, and 4), and Frost picks up the nonrhymed sound of each stanza (the third line) and links it with the rhyming sound of the stanza that follows it, until the fourth stanza when he closes with four matching rhymes. Part of our pleasure in Frost's rhyming may derive from the pattern of departure and return it voices. Part may stem also from the way the rhyme pattern supports the poem's meaning. The speaker is caught between his desire to remain still, peacefully held by the serene beauty of the woods, and his contrasting need to leave, to return to his responsibilities. In a similar way, the poem's rhyme is caught between a surge forward toward a new sound and a return to a sound repeated earlier. The pull and counterpull of the rhyme reflect the speaker's ambivalence.

The rhymes in Frost's poem are *exact* or *perfect rhymes:* that is, the rhyming words share corresponding sounds and stresses and a similar number of syllables. While Frost's poem contains perfect rhymes ("know," "though," and "snow," for example), we sometimes hear in poems a less exact, *imperfect, approximate,* or *slant rhyme.* Emily Dickinson's "Crumbling is not an instant's Act" (page 483) includes both exact rhyme ("dust"-"rust") and slant rhyme ("slow"-"law"). Theodore Roethke's "My Papa's Waltz" (page 406) contains a slant rhyme on (*"dizzy"-"easy"*), which also exemplifies *feminine rhyme.* In feminine rhyme the final syllable of a rhymed word is unstressed; in *masculine rhyme* the final syllable is stressed—or the words rhymed are each only one syllable.

Besides rhyme, two other forms of sound play prevail in poetry: *alliteration* or the repetition of consonant sounds, especially at the beginning of words, and *assonance* or the repetition of vowel sounds. In his witty guide to poetic technique, *Rhyme's Reason,* John Hollander describes alliteration and assonance like this:

> Assonance is the spirit of a rhyme,
> A common vowel, hovering like a sigh
> After its consonantal body dies. . . .
>
> . . .
>
> Alliteration lightly links
> Stressed syllables with common consonants.

Walt Whitman's "When I Heard the Learn'd Astronomer" (page 476) though lacking in end rhyme, possesses a high degree of assonance. The long *i*'s in lines 1, 3, and 4 accumulate and gather force as the poem glides into its last four lines: *"I," "tired," "rising," "gliding," "I," "myself," "night," "time to time,"* and *"silence."* This assonance sweetens the sound of the second part of the poem, highlighting its radical shift of action and feeling.

Both alliteration and assonance are clearly audible in "Stopping by Woods," particularly in the third stanza:

> He gives his harness bells a shake
> To ask if there is some mistake.
> The only other sound's the sweep
> Of easy wind and downy flake.

Notice that the long *e* of "sweep" is echoed in *"ea*-sy" and "down-*y*," and that the *ow* of "downy" echoes the same sound in "sound's." These repetitions of sound accentuate the images the words embody, aural images (wind-blow and snow-fall), tactile images (the soft fluff of down and the feel of the gently blowing wind), and visual images (the white flakes of snow).

The alliterative *s*'s in "*some*," "*sound*," and "*sweep*" are supported by the internal and terminal *s*'s: "Gives," "his," "harness bells," and "is," and also by midword *s*'s: "ask," "mistake," and "easy." Some of these sounds are heavier than others—the two similar heavy *s*'s of "easy" and "his" contrast the lighter softer "*s*" in "harness" and "mistake."

Listen to the sound effects of rhyme, alliteration, and assonance, in the following poem. Try to determine what *sound* contributes to the poem's meaning.

GERARD MANLEY HOPKINS
[1844–1889]

In the Valley of the Elwy

I remember a house where all were good
  To me, God knows, deserving no such thing:
  Comforting smell breathed at very entering,
Fetched fresh, as I suppose, off some sweet wood.
That cordial air made those kind people a hood   5
  All over, as a bevy of eggs the mothering wing
  Will, or mild nights the new morsels of Spring:
Why, it seemed of course; seemed of right it should.

Lovely the woods, waters, meadows, combes, vales,
All the air things wear that build this world of Wales;   10
  Only the inmate does not correspond:

God, lover of souls, swaying considerate scales,
Complete thy creature dear O where it fails,
  Being mighty a master, being a father and fond.

We note first that the rhyme scheme reveals a Petrarchan sonnet: *abba, abba, ccd, ccd* (see page 474). Also we might note that its rhyme pattern corresponds to its sentence structure: the octave splits into two sentences, lines 1–4 and 5–8; the sestet, though only one sentence, splits into two equal parts, lines 9–11 and 12–14. Hopkins's use of the Italian rhyme scheme keeps similar sounds repeating throughout: *good, wood, hood, should; thing, entering, wing, Spring; vales, Wales, scales, fails; correspond, fond.* (The rhyme pattern of the Shakespearean or English sonnet, by contrast, as heard in "That time of year," [page 437] contains fewer rhyming repetitions, as it uses a greater number of different sounds.)

Besides extensive rhyme, Hopkins uses alliteration and assonance—lightly in the octave and more heavily in the sestet. Lines 3–6, for example, collect short *e*'s in "sm*e*ll," "v*e*ry," "*e*ntering," "f*e*tched" and "fr*e*sh," "b*e*vy" and "*e*ggs." Lines 4–8 begin an alliterative use of *w,* which is more elaborately sounded in lines 9–10 of the sestet; in lines 4–8 we hear: "*sw*eet *w*ood," "*w*ing *W*ill," and "*w*hy." In addition, in line 7 "m*i*ld n*i*ghts" picks up the long *i* of "Wh*y*," which finds an echo in the rhyme on "r*i*ght." This seventh line also contains what we might call a reversed or crisscrossed alliteration in *"m*ild *n*ights" and *"n*ew *m*orsels."

But these sound effects are only a pale indication of what we hear in the sestet. Perhaps the most musical lines of the entire poem are the opening lines of the sestet (lines 9–10). *L*'s frame both of these lines: *"L*ovely . . . va*l*es" and "A*ll* . . . Wa*l*es." *L*'s are further sounded in "bui*l*d this wor*l*d." The *w,* which as we noted ended the octave, is carried into the sestet in *"w*oods," *"w*aters," "mead-o*w*s," *"w*ear," *"w*orld," and *"W*ales." The sestet also includes a variety of vowels: lovely, woods, water, meadows, combes, vales, all, air, wear, that, build, this, world, Wales.

Hopkins sounds a similarly varied vowel music in the last line, where he also uses alliteration and repetition to call attention to important attributes of God:

> Being mighty a master, being a father and fond.

One line, however, especially lacks music: line 11. Coming amidst such splendid sounds, it stands out even more sharply:

> Only the inmate does not correspond.

This expressive use of sound variation supports the idea that the line conveys: that in this beautiful natural world, the "inmate," the speaker in the guise of prisoner, does not fit. He feels out of place, out of harmony with his environment. In the lines that follow (12–14), he asks God to "complete" him, to make him whole, to integrate him into the world. And he prays in language that immediately picks up the sound play of assonance and alliteration that had been momentarily suspended in line 11. The speaker's harmony and wholeness are thus restored in the poem's beauty of sound.

To further develop your ear for sound in poetry, listen to the poems that follow:

THOMAS HARDY
[1840–1928]

During Wind and Rain

They sing their dearest songs—
He, she, all of them—yea,
Treble and tenor and bass,
   And one to play;
With the candles mooning each face. . . .   5
   Ah, no; the years O!
How the sick leaves reel down in throngs!

They clear the creeping moss—
Elders and juniors—aye,
Making the pathway neat   10
   And the garden gay;
And they build a shady seat. . . .
   Ah, no; the years, the years;
See, the white stormbirds wing across!

They are blithely breakfasting all—   15
Men and maidens—yea,
Under the summer tree,
   With a glimpse of the bay,
While pet fowl come to the knee. . . .
   Ah, no; the years O!   20
And the rotten rose is ripped from the wall.

They change to a high new house,
He, she, all of them—aye,
Clocks and carpets, and chairs
   On the lawn all day,   25
And brightest things that are theirs. . . .
   Ah, no; the years, the years;
Down their carved names the rain drop ploughs.

QUESTIONS FOR REFLECTION

1. Chart the poem's rhyme scheme. Note the repetitions of lines ("Ah no: the years") and of words ("O," "aye," and "yea"). What do these repetitions contribute to the idea and feeling of the poem?
2. Identify examples of alliteration and comment on their effect.

ALEXANDER POPE
[1688–1744]

Sound and Sense

True ease in writing comes from art, not chance,
As those move easiest who have learned to dance.
'Tis not enough no harshness gives offense,
The sound must seem an echo to the sense:
Soft is the strain when Zephyr° gently blows,   5
And the smooth stream in smoother numbers flows;
But when loud surges lash the sounding shore,
The hoarse, rough verse should like the torrent roar.
When Ajax° strives, some rock's vast weight to throw,
The line too labors, and the words move slow;   10
Not so, when swift Camilla° scours the plain,
Flies o'er th' unbending corn, and skims along the main.
Hear how Timotheus'° varied lays surprise,
And bid alternate passions fall and rise!
While, at each change, the son of Libyan Jove,°   15
Now burns with glory, and then melts with love;
Now his fierce eyes with sparkling fury glow,
Now sighs steal out, and tears begin to flow;
Persians and Greeks like turns of nature found,
And the world's victor stood subdued by sound!   20
The pow'r of music all our hearts allow,
And what Timotheus was, is DRYDEN now.

QUESTIONS FOR REFLECTION

1. How does the poet enact verbally what he asserts in line 4, that "the sound must seem an echo to the sense"?
2. What contrast is described and imitated in sound effects in lines 5–6 and 7–8? Between lines 9–10 and lines 11–12?

"Sound And Sense" ⁵**Zephyr** *the west wind.* ⁹**Ajax** *a strong Greek warrior in the Trojan War.* ¹¹**Camilla** *an ancient Volcian queen noted for her speed and lightness of step.*
"Sound And Sense" ¹³**Timotheus** *a musician in John Dryden's poem "Alexander's Feast."* ¹⁵**the son of Libyan Jove** *Alexander the Great (356–323 B.C.), king of Macedonia and military conqueror who spread Greek culture throughout the ancient world.*

MAY SWENSON
[1919–1989]

The Universe

What
　　　is it about,
　　　　the universe,
　　　　　the universe about us stretching out?
We, within our brains,　　　　　　　　　　　　　5
　　within it,
　　　　think
we must unspin
the laws that spin it.
　　　　We think *why*　　　　　　　　　　　　10
because we think
because.
Because we think,
　　　we think
　　　　the universe about us.　　　　　　　　15

But does it think,
　　　the universe?
　　　　Then what about?
　　　　　About us?
　　　　　　If not,　　　　　　　　　　　　20
must there be cause
　　　　in the universe?
Must it have laws?
　　　　And what
　　　if the universe　　　　　　　　　　　　25
　　　　　is not about us?
　　　Then what?
　　　　What
　　　　　is it about?
　　　And what　　　　　　　　　　　　　　30
　　　　　　about *us?*

QUESTION FOR REFLECTION

Is this poem merely a witty game of repeating words or does it employ sound effects
to sound effect? Consider especially lines 10–15 and 24–31.

BOB MCKENTY
[b. 1935]

Adam's Song

Come live with me and be my love.
Come romp with me in Eden's grove
In unabated joy, not shy
But unabashed by nudity,
Where you can bare—sans shame—your breast   5
Until the fell Forbidden Feast.
Thereafter I shall toil and sweat
To earn whatever bread we eat
And you, in bearing children, shall
Know pain and suffering. The Fall   10
Will bring us sickness, death, and fear,
Embarrassment and underwear
(For which the Fig donates its leaf)
And poets who are surely deaf.

QUESTION FOR REFLECTION

Identify the sound effects at play in "Adam's Song." Consider especially the poem's rhymes.

HELEN CHASIN
[b. 1938]

The Word *Plum*

The word *plum* is delicious

pout and push, luxury of
self-love, and savoring murmur

full in the mouth and falling
like fruit   5

taut skin
pierced, bitten, provoked into
juice, and tart flesh

> question
> and reply, lip and tongue   10
> of pleasure.

QUESTIONS FOR REFLECTION

1. How is the word *p-l-u-m* sounded and resounded in the poem? Look at and listen to lines 2–3 in particular.
2. Map out the poem's patterns of alliteration and vowel repetition.

RHYTHM AND METER

Rhythm refers to the regular recurrence of the accent or stress in poem or song. It is the pulse or beat we feel in a phrase of music or a line of poetry. We derive our sense of rhythm from everyday life and from our experience with language and music. We experience the rhythm of day and night, the seasonal rhythms of the year, the beat of our hearts, and the rise and fall of our chests as we breathe in and out.

Perhaps our earliest memories of rhythm in language are associated with nursery rhymes like

> JACK and JILL went UP the HILL★
> to FETCH a PAIL of WAter.

Later we probably learned songs like "America," whose rhythm we might indicate like this:

> MY COUN-TRY 'tis of THEE
> SWEET LAND of LIberTY
> Of THEE i SING.

Since then we have developed an ear for the rhythm of language in everyday speech:

> I THINK I'll HIT the HAY
> Did you SEE that?
> Or: Did you see THAT?
> or: GO and DON'T come BACK.

★Capitalization indicates stressed syllables, lowercase letters unstressed ones.

Poets rely heavily on rhythm to express meaning and convey feeling. In "The Sun Rising" John Donne puts words together in a pattern of stressed and unstressed syllables:

> BUsy old FOOL, unRULy SUN
> WHY DOST THOU THUS
> Through WINdows, and through CURtains, CALL on US?

Donne uses four accents per line—even in the second more slowly paced short line. Later in the stanza, he retards the tempo further. Listen to the accents in the following lines:

> LOVE, all aLIKE, no SEAson knows, nor CLIME,
> Nor HOURS, DAYS, MONTHS, which ARE the RAGS of TIME.

The accents result partly from Donne's use of monosyllabic words and partly from pauses within the line (indicated by commas). Such pauses are called *caesuras* and are represented by a double slash (//). The final couplet of Donne's poem illustrates a common use of caesura—to split a line near its midpoint:

> Shine here to us, // and thou art everywhere;
> This bed thy center is, // these walls thy sphere.

Marking the accents as well, we get this:

> SHINE HERE to US, // and THOU art EVeryWHERE;
> THIS BED thy CENter IS, // THESE WALLS thy SPHERE.

Notice again how the monosyllabic diction and the balanced phrasing combine with the caesuras to slow the lines down. The stately rhythm enforces the speaker's dignified tone and serious point: "Here is everywhere; this room is a world in itself; it is all that matters to us."

In the following brief poem by Robert Frost, you can readily hear and feel the contrasting pace and rhythms of its two lines:

The Span of Life

> The OLD DOG BARKS BACKward withOUT GETting UP.
> I can reMEMber when HE was a PUP.

The first line is slower than the second. It is harder to pronounce and takes longer to say because Frost clusters the hard consonants, *d, k,* and *g* sounds, in the first line, and because the first line contains seven stresses to the four accents of the second. Three of the seven stresses fall at the beginning of the line, which gets it off to a slow start, whereas the accents of the second line are evenly spaced. The contrasting rhythms of the lines reinforce their contrasting images and sound effects. More importantly, however, the differences in the sounds and rhythms in the two lines echo their contrast of youth and age.

But we cannot proceed any further in this discussion of rhythm without introducing more precise terms to refer to the patterns of accents we hear in a poem. If rhythm is the pulse or beat we hear in the line, then we can define *meter* as the measure or patterned count of a poetic line. Meter is a count of the stresses we feel in the poem's rhythm. By convention the unit of poetic meter in English is the *foot*, a unit of measure consisting of stressed and unstressed syllables. A poetic foot may be either *iambic* or *trochaic, anapestic* or *dactylic.* An iambic line is composed primarily of *iambs*, an *iamb* being defined as an unaccented syllable followed by an accented one as in the word "preVENT" or "conTAIN." Reversing the order of accented and unaccented syllables we get a *trochee,* which is an accented syllable followed by an unaccented one, as in "FOOTball" or "LIquor." We can represent an accented syllable by a ' and an unaccented syllable by a ˘: thus, prĕve'nt(˘ '), an iamb, and li'quŏr (' ˘), a trochee. Because both iambic and trochaic feet contain two syllables per foot, they are called *duple* (or double) meters. These duple meters can be distinguished from *triple* meters (three-syllable meters) like anapestic and dactylic meters. An *anapest* (˘˘ ') consists of two unaccented syllables followed by an accented one as in cŏmprĕHE'ND or ĭntĕrVE'NE. A *dactyl* reverses the anapest, beginning with an accented syllable followed by two unaccented ones. DA'Ngĕroŭs and CHE'ERfŭllў are examples. So is the word AN'ăpĕst.

Three additional points must be noted about poetic meter. First, anapestic (˘˘ ') and iambic (˘ ') meters move from an unstressed syllable to a stressed one. For this reason they are called *rising* meters. (They "rise" to the stressed syllable.) Lines in anapestic or iambic meter frequently end with a stressed syllable. Trochaic (' ˘) and dactylic ('˘˘) meters, on the other hand, are said to be *falling* meters because they begin with a stressed syllable and decline in pitch and emphasis. (Syllables at the ends of trochaic and dactylic lines are generally unstressed.)

Second, the regularity of a poem's meter is not inflexible. In a predominantly iambic poem (Shakespeare's sonnet "That time of year thou may'st in me behold," for example, or Frost's "Stopping by Woods"), every line will not usually conform exactly to the strict metrical pattern. Frost's poem is much more regular in its iambic meter than is Shakespeare's, but Frost avoids metrical monotony by subtly altering his rhythm. And in one important instance Frost departs from the pattern slightly. We can divide the last stanza of Frost's poem into metrical feet and mark the accents in this manner, separating the feet with slashes.

The woo'ds / ăre lo've / lў da'rk / ănd de'ep. /
Bŭt I' / ha've pr'o / mĭsĕs / tŏ ke'ep,
Ănd mil'es / tŏ g'o /bĕfo're / Ĭ sle'ep,
Ănd mil'es / tŏ g'o /bĕfo're / Ĭ sle'ep,

If we regard the pattern of this stanza and the pattern of the poem as a whole as regularly, even insistently, iambic, then the second line of this final stanza marks a slight deviation from that norm. The second and third feet of the line can be read as two accented syllables followed by two unaccented syllables, a spondaic foot followed by a pyrrhic. That's the way I've marked them. Two accented syllables together is called a *spondee* (KNI'CK-KNA'CK); two unaccented ones, a *pyrrhic* (ŏf thĕ). Both spondaic and pyrrhic feet serve as substitute feet for iambic and trochaic feet. Neither can serve as the metrical norm of an English poem.

Third, we give names to lines of poetry based on the number of feet they contain. You may have noticed in looking back at "Stopping by Woods on a Snowy Evening" that it consists of eight-syllable or *octosyllabic* lines. Since the meter is iambic (˘ ´) with two syllables per foot, the line contains four iambic feet and is hence called a *tetrameter* line (from the Greek word for *four*). Thus Frost's poem is written in *iambic tetrameter,* unlike Shakespeare's sonnet "That time of year thou may'st in me behold," for example, which contains ten-syllable lines, also predominantly iambic. Such five-foot lines are named *pentameters* (from the Greek "penta" for five), making the sonnet a poem in *iambic pentameter.*

Here is a chart of the various meters and poetic feet.

	Foot	Meter	Example
Rising or Ascending Feet	iamb	iambic	prevent
	anapest	anapestic	comprehend
Falling or Descending Feet	trochee	trochaic	football
	dactyl	dactylic	cheerfully
Substitute Feet	spondee	spondaic	knick-knack
	pyrrhic	pyrrhic	(light) of the (world)

Duple Meters: two syllables per foot: iambic and trochaic
Triple Meters: three syllables per foot: anapestic and dactylic

Number of feet per line

one foot	monometer
two feet	dimeter
three feet	trimeter
four feet	tetrameter
five feet	pentameter
six feet	hexameter
seven feet	heptameter
eight feet	octameter

You should now be better able to discern the meter and rhythm of a poem. You can make an instructive comparison for yourself by taking the measure of two poems in the same meter: Shakespeare's sonnet "That time of year thou may'st in me behold" (page 437) and Hopkins's "In the Valley of the Elwy," (page 459) both written in iambic pentameter. In Hopkins's sonnet, see if you can account for the speed of the octave and the slower pace of the sestet: look to changes in the basic iambic pattern; look for caesuras; and watch for *enjambed* or run-on lines, whose sense and grammar runs over and into the next line. You should be alert in both poems for how parallel sentence structure and the sound play of alliteration and assonance collaborate with rhythm and meter to support each poem's feeling and meaning. Listen carefully, especially to the last line of the octave and sestet of Hopkins's sonnet and to Shakespeare's concluding couplet.

Metrical Variation

We noted earlier that Frost's "Stopping by Woods" is written in strict iambic pentameter with only one slight variation in line 14. How then does Frost manage to avoid the monotony of fifteen lines of ta TUM / ta TUM / ta TUM / ta TUM / ? One way is by varying the reader's focus on different details: woods, snow, and speaker (stanza one); horse and darkness (stanza two); horse and snow (stanza three); woods and darkness and speaker (stanza four). Another is to vary the syntax, as he does with the inversion of the opening line. A third is simply to use a familiar diction in a normal speaking voice. Fourth and perhaps most important is Frost's masterful control of tempo. Of the four stanzas none carry the same pattern of end stopping. Stanza one is end-stopped at the first, second, and fourth lines, with line 3 enjambed. Stanza three is the closest to the second stanza, with two end-stopped lines and two enjambed lines. Stanza four is heavily stopped with two caesuras in its initial line and with end stops at every line. (It is here that we are slowed down to feel the seductive beauty of the woods; it is here that the symbolic weight of the poem is heaviest.) But we should not overlook the contrasting second stanza, which is cast as a single flowing sentence. The iambic pattern inhabits this stanza as it beats in the others. But as a result of the variety of technical resources Frost displays in the poem, we hear the iambic beat but are not overwhelmed by it.

Frost's rhythmical variations can be compared with Whitman's expressive use of metrical variation in "When I heard the learn'd astronomer" (page 476), a poem in *free verse,* verse without a fixed metrical pattern. Whitman's poem is characteristic of much free verse in its varying line lengths and accents per line, and in its imitation of the cadences of speech. The poem's final line ("Look'd up in perfect silence at the stars"), however, differs from the others, as Paul Fussell has pointed out in *Poetic Meter and Poetic Form.** It is written in strict iambic pentameter, a variation which carries considerable expressive power, coming after the seemingly casual metrical organization of the previous lines. Because Whitman's line must be read in the context of the whole poem for its expressive impact to be felt, you should turn to it, preferably to read it aloud. Consider whether, as some readers have suggested, the poem is not really in free verse at all, but rather in *blank verse,* unrhymed iambic pentameter.

Besides this expressive use of metrical variation, Whitman's poem exhibits additional elements of rhythmic control: in its consistency of end-stopped lines; in its flexible use of caesura (lines 2, 3, and 7); in its absence of caesura from the shorter lines (1, and 4–8). We can perhaps gain a greater appreciation of Whitman's rhythmical accomplishment by recasting his lines like this:

---

*Paul Fussell, *Poetic Meter and Poetic Form* (New York: Random House, 1979), p. 85.

> When I heard the learn'd astronomer,
> When the proofs, the figures
> Were ranged in columns before me,
> When I was shown the charts and diagrams
> To add, divide, and measure them,
> When I sitting heard the astronomer
> Where he lectured to much applause
> In the lecture-room. . . .

Or like this:

> When I heard
> The learn'd astronomer,
> When the proofs,
> The figures were ranged
> In columns
> Before me,
> When I was shown
> The charts and diagrams
> To add, divide and
> Measure them. . . .

Both versions destroy the poem: they eliminate the sweep of its long lines, destroying its cadences and rhythm, and ultimately inhibiting its expressiveness.

Before leaving the poem, we should note that Whitman's rhythmic effects work together with other devices of sound, structure, and diction. In the same way, for example, that the strict iambic pentameter of the last line varies the prevailing meter expressively, so too does its assonance (the long *i*'s) deviate expressively from the poem's previously established avoidance of vowel music. In addition, the meter of the final line stresses *si'lence* and *sta'rs,* both of which the speaker values. Finally, the iambic rhythm of the line has us looking U'P and A'T the stars, an unusual metrical effect since prepositions are almost always unstressed.

Throughout these comments on the rhythm and meter of the poems by Whitman and Frost, we have been engaged in the act of *scansion,* measuring verse, identifying its prevailing meter and rhythm, and accounting for deviations from the metrical pattern. In scanning a poem, we try to determine its dominant rhythm and meter, and to account for variations from the norm. The pattern we hear as dominant will influence how we read lines that do not conform metrically, and also how we interpret and respond to those lines. Consider, for example, the words "at a glance" abstracted from their place in a line of Wordsworth's "I wandered lonely as a cloud." Do you hear them as anapestic: ăt ă gla'nce? This is a likely way to hear the words outside the context of the poem. But when we return them to the poem, we may hear them another way:

Tĕn thousănd sa'w Ĭ at ă gla'nce.

In such a case we will probably hear both the rhythmic pattern of the normal speaking voice (aᵗ ă glánce) and the metrical pattern of iambic pentameter (aᵗ ă glánce). Our experience of rhythm thus will often involve a tension between the two patterns as we hear one superimposed on the other.

One last note about rhythm and meter. Without the turn of the poetic line, without the division of words into lines, we have no poem. For what distinguishes poetry from prose is the line; it is the line that makes verse what it is (from the Latin *versus*, to turn). And as the poet Wendell Berry has pointed out, it is the line of verse that "checks the merely impulsive flow of speech, subjects it to another pulse, to measure."* Without the measure of meter, without the turn of the line, there is no music and no poem. Meter and rhythm are not merely technical elements, no more than diction and imagery, syntax and structure and sound. All of these interrelated elements of poetry have effects on readers, do things to readers. We sense them and feel them and thereby understand a poem, not just with our minds, but also with our eyes and ears.

Here are a few additional poems for rhythmic and metrical consideration.

GEORGE GORDON, LORD BYRON
[1788–1824]

The Destruction of Sennacherib°

The Assyrian came down like the wolf on the fold,
And his cohorts were gleaming in purple and gold;
And the sheen of their spears was like stars on the sea,
When the blue wave rolls nightly on deep Galilee.

Like the leaves of the forest when summer is green,   5
That host with their banners at sunset were seen:
Like the leaves of the forest when autumn hath blown,
That host on the morrow lay withered and strown.

For the Angel of Death spread his wings on the blast,
And breathed in the face of the foe as he passed;   10
And the eyes of the sleepers waxed deadly and chill,
And their hearts but once heaved—and for ever grew still!

And there lay the steed with his nostril all wide,
But through it there rolled not the breath of his pride;
And the foam of his gasping lay white on the turf,   15
And cold as the spray of the rock-beating surf.

---

*Wendell Berry, *Standing By Words* (San Francisco: North Point Press, 1983), p. 28.

And there lay the rider distorted and pale,
With the dew on his brow, and the rust on his mail;
And the tents were all silent, the banners alone,
The lances unlifted, the trumpet unblown.   20

And the widows of Ashur are loud in their wail,
And the idols are broke in the temple of Baal;
And the might of the Gentile, unsmote by the sword,
Hath melted like snow in the glance of the Lord!

QUESTIONS FOR REFLECTION

1. Identify the poem's meter. What kind of movement and rhythm does the meter create?
2. How is it appropriate to the action and idea of the poem?

ANNE SEXTON
[1928–1974]

Her Kind

I have gone out, a possessed witch,
haunting the black air, braver at night;
dreaming evil, I have done my hitch
over the plain houses, light by light:
lonely thing, twelve-fingered, out of mind.   5
A woman like that is not a woman, quite.
I have been her kind.
I have found the warm caves in the woods,
filled them with skillets, carvings, shelves,
closets, silks, innumerable goods;   10
fixed the suppers for the worms and the elves:
whining, rearranging the disaligned.
A woman like that is misunderstood.
I have been her kind.

I have ridden in your cart, driver,   15
waved my nude arms at villages going by,
learning the last bright routes, survivor
where your flames still bite my thigh
and my ribs crack where your wheels wind.
A woman like that is not ashamed to die.   20
I have been her kind.

"*The Destruction of Sennacherib*" **The Destruction of Sennacherib**   *the poem is based on the biblical account (II Kings 19:35) of the Assyrian king, Sennacherib, whose army was destroyed by the angel of the Lord in an invasion of Jerusalem.*

QUESTIONS FOR REFLECTION

1. Identify the prevailing meter of the poem. How does Sexton keep the poem moving?
2. Examine her uses of caesura and enjambment, and comment on their effect on the poem's rhythm.

W I L L I A M   C A R L O S   W I L L I A M S
[1883–1963]

The Red Wheelbarrow

so much depends
upon

a red wheel
barrow

glazed with rain   5
water

beside the white
chickens

QUESTIONS FOR REFLECTION

1. Mark the poem's meter. Which lines match each other metrically?
2. What is the effect of the breaks between lines 3 and 4 and between lines 5 and 6?

STRUCTURE: CLOSED FORM AND OPEN FORM

When we analyze a poem's structure, we focus on its patterns of organization. *Form* exists in poems on many levels from patterns of sound and image to structures of syntax and of thought; it is as much a matter of phrase and line as of stanza and whole poem.

Among the most popular forms of poetry has been the *sonnet,* a fourteen-line poem usually written in iambic pentameter (see pp. 467–469). Because the form of the sonnet is strictly constrained, it is considered a *closed* or *fixed form.* We can recognize poems in fixed forms such as the sonnet, sestina, and villanelle by their patterns of rhyme, meter, and repetition; they reveal their structural patterns both aurally and visually. We see the shapes of their stanzas and the patterns of their line lengths; we feel their metrical beat, and we hear their play of sound.

The *Shakespearean* or *English sonnet* falls into three *quatrains* or four-line sections with the rhyme pattern *abab cdcd efef* followed by a *couplet* or pair of rhymed lines with the pattern *gg.* Let us reread Shakespeare's sonnet, "That time of year thou may'st in me behold."

That time of year thou may'st in me behold	*a*
When yellow leaves, or none, or few, do hang	*b*
Upon those boughs which shake against the cold,	*a*
Bare ruined choirs, where late the sweet birds sang.	*b*
In me thou see'st the twilight of such day	*c* 5
As after sunset fadeth in the west;	*d*
Which by-and-by black night doth take away,	*c*
Death's second self that seals up all in rest.	*d*
In me thou see'st the glowing of such fire	*e*
That on the ashes of his youth doth lie,	*f* 10
As the deathbed whereon it must expire,	*e*
Consumed with that which it was nourished by.	*f*
This thou perceiv'st, which makes thy love more strong,	*g*
To love that well which thou must leave ere long.	*g*

Each of the three quatrains of the poem is a single sentence, as is the couplet. This organization of the poem's sentences corresponds to its rhyme and images, which are also arranged in three quatrains and a final couplet. The pattern is reinforced, moreover, by the use of repeated words in the three quatrains: "In me behold"; "In me thou see'st"; "In me thou see'st."

There is a progression in the imagery in the sonnet: daylight becomes twilight; twilight turns into night. And there is a countermovement from images of longer duration to those of shorter: from the dying of a season to the dying of a day to the dying of a fire. In addition, within each image there is a movement from optimism to pessimism. Each image begins more hopefully than it ends: the yellow leaves become "bare ruined choirs" (lines 1–4); the twilight gives way to "Death's second self" (lines 5–8); the "glowing . . . fire" becomes "ashes" on a "deathbed" (lines 9–12).

The couplet is both a logical and an emotional response to the three quatrains that precede it. In the couplet is an implied *therefore* or *because* that can be heard by reversing the word order of its first line: Since you perceive this, it makes your love more strong. The last line is both a plea and a command to "love that well which thou must leave ere long," with "which" carrying the force of *because.*

Not every sonnet Shakespeare wrote is structured as tightly as this one. Look at the sonnets on pages 610–612 to see how Shakespeare varies this pattern, how, for example, he uses the couplet not only to respond to the quatrains, but to summarize their point or extend their implications as well.

An alternative to the Shakespearean sonnet is the *Petrarchan* or *Italian sonnet,* which falls into two parts: an *octave* of eight lines and a *sestet* of six. The octave rhyme pattern is *abba abba* (two sets of four lines); the sestet's lines are more variable: *cde cde;* or *ced ced;* or *cd cd cd.* The following is an example of the Italian form:

JOHN KEATS
[1795–1821]

On First Looking into Chapman's Homer°

Much have I traveled in the realms of gold	*a*
And many goodly states and kingdoms seen;	*b*
Round many western islands have I been	*b*
Which bards in fealty° to Apollo° hold.	*a* allegiance
Oft of one wide expanse had I been told	*a* 5
That deep-browed Homer ruled as his demesne;°	*b* domain
Yet never did I breathe its pure serene°	*b* atmosphere
Till I heard Chapman speak out loud and bold:	*a*
Then felt I like some watcher of the skies	*c*
When a new planet swims into his ken;	*d* 10
Or like stout Cortez° when with eagle eyes	*c*
He stared at the Pacific—and all his men	*d*
Looked at each other with a wild surmise—	*c*
Silent, upon a peak in Darien.	*d*

Perhaps the most notable structural feature of the Italian sonnet is the way it turns on the ninth line. The first eight lines of Keats's sonnet describe the speaker's wide reading and compare reading with traveling. Lines 9–14 dramatically convey the speaker's feelings upon first reading Chapman's translation of Homer's great epic poems, *The Iliad* and *The Odyssey.* The speaker's excitement appears in lines 12 and 13, whose broken syntax contrasts with the smooth fluency of the first part of the sonnet. In addition, the octave and sestet differ in diction as well. The diction of the octave is elevated and formal, employing archaic words like "goodly" and "bards," and roundabout expressions like "realms of gold." Such words and phrases create an impression of the remoteness of the past, of its grandeur and dignity. In the sestet the diction is simpler and more direct. Keats's use of figures of comparison in the sestet contributes to the striking change in diction. The two major comparisons, both similes, convey the excitement of discovery. By means of descriptions of action (they "looked" and "stared") and reaction (their "wild surmise" and stunned silence) Keats conveys vividly the speaker's feeling of elation and excitement. Keats capitalizes on the structural possibilities of the Italian sonnet by reserving this elation for the sestet and by varying the diction of octave and sestet.

But not all poems are written in fixed forms. Many poets have resisted the limitations inherent in using a consistent and specific metrical pattern or in

---

"On First Looking into Chapman's Homer" **Chapman's Homer** *translation of Homer's Odyssey by George Chapman, a contemporary of Shakespeare.*   [4]**Apollo** *god of the sun and poetic inspiration.*   [11-14]**Cortez . . . Darien Cortez,** *Spanish conqueror of Mexico. Balboa, not Cortez, however, was the first European to see the Pacific from Darien in Panama.*

rhyming lines in a prescribed manner. As an alternative to the strictness of fixed form, they developed and discovered looser, more *open* and *free forms. Open* or *free form* does not imply formlessness. It suggests, instead, that poets capitalize on the freedom either to create their own forms or to use the traditional fixed forms in more flexible ways. An example of a poem in open form by Walt Whitman follows.

WALT WHITMAN
[1819–1892]

When I heard the learn'd astronomer

When I heard the learn'd astronomer,
When the proofs, the figures, were ranged in columns before me,
When I was shown the charts and diagrams, to add, divide, and measure them,
When I sitting heard the astronomer where he lectured with much applause in the
    lecture-room,
How soon unaccountable I became tired and sick,   5
Till rising and gliding out I wander'd off by myself,
In the mystical moist night-air, and from time to time,
Look'd up in perfect silence at the stars.

Although Whitman's poem is arranged as a single sentence, it can be divided into two parts, each of four lines. The two-part division accumulates a set of contrasts: the speaker with other people and the speaker alone; the speaker sitting inside and the speaker standing outside looking at the stars; the noise inside and the silence outside; the lecturer's activity and the speaker's passivity; the clutter of details in lines 1–4 and the spareness of details in lines 5–8.

These contrasts reflect the poem's movement from one kind of learning about nature to another: from passive listening to active observation; from indirect factual knowledge to direct mystical apprehension. Whether the poet rejects the first form of knowledge for the second, or whether he suggests that both are needed is not directly stated. The emphasis, nevertheless, is on the speaker's need to be alone and to experience nature directly.

More elaborate departures from fixed form include poems such as this unusual configuration of E. E. Cummings:

E. E. CUMMINGS
[1894–1962]

l (a

l(a

le
af
fa

ll

s)
one
l

iness

Perhaps the first things to notice are the lack of capital letters and the absence of punctuation (except for the parentheses). What we don't see is as important as what we do. We don't see any recognizable words or sentences, to say nothing of traditional stanzas or lines of poetry. The poem strikes the eye as a series of letters that stream down the page, for the most part two to a line. Rearranging the letters horizontally we find these words: *(a leaf falls) loneliness.* (The first *l* of *loneliness* appears before the parenthesis, like this: *l (a leaf falls) oneliness;* to get *loneliness* you have to move the *l* in front of *oneliness.*

A single falling leaf is a traditional symbol of loneliness; this image is not new. What is new, however, is the way Cummings has coupled the concept with the image, the way he has formed and shaped them into a nontraditional poem. But what has the poet gained by arranging his poem this way? By breaking the horizontal line of verse into a series of fragments (from the horizontal viewpoint), Cummings illustrates visually the separation that is the primary cause of loneliness. Both the word *loneliness* and the image described in *a leaf falls* are broken apart, separated in this way. In addition, by splitting the initial letter from *loneliness,* the poet has revealed the hidden *one* in the word. It's as if he is saying: loneliness is *one*-liness. This idea is further corroborated in the visual ambiguity of "l." Initially we are not sure whether this symbol "l" is a number—*one*—or the letter *l.* By shaping and arranging his poem this way, Cummings unites form and content, structure and idea. He also invites us to play the poetry game with him by remaking the poem as we put its pieces together. In doing so we step back and see in the design of the poem a leaf falling

d
o
w
n

the page. By positioning the letters as he does; Cummings pictures a
leaf fall:

le
af
fa
ll
s.

If "l(a" is a poem for the eye, the following poem, also by Cummings, is
arranged for voice. From the standpoint of traditional poetic form, it too exhibits peculiarities of sound and structure, line and stanza.

E. E. CUMMINGS
[1894–1962]

[Buffalo Bill's]

Buffalo Bill's
defunct
      who used to
        ride a watersmooth-silver
               stallion   5
and break onetwothreefourfive pigeons justlikethat
                      Jesus
he was a handsome man
              and what i want to know is
how do you like your blueeyed boy   10
Mister Death

Before we listen closely to the voice of the poem, let's glance at how it hits
the eye. "Buffalo Bill's," "stallion," "defunct," "Jesus," and "Mister Death" are all
set on separate lines *as* complete lines. "Buffalo Bill's," "Mister Death," and "Jesus" are the only words capitalized. "Buffalo Bill's and "Mister Death" frame
the poem; "Jesus" is set off on its own as far to the right as the line will go.
Other words also receive a visual stress. At two points in line 6, Cummings
buncheswordstogetherlikethis. Both of these visual effects are translated from
eye to voice to ear so that we read the poem acknowledging the stress in each
case. Cummings has used typography as a formal way of laying out language
on the page to direct our reading. To see and hear what he has accomplished
in this respect, read aloud the following rearranged version, which deliberately
flattens the special effects Cummings highlights.

Buffalo Bill's defunct,
Who used to ride
a water-smooth silver stallion
and break one, two, three, four, five
pigeons just like that
Jesus he was a handsome man
And what I would like to know is
how do you like your
blueeyed boy, Mister Death?

Let us, finally, summarize our remarks about structure and form. By discerning a poem's structure, we gain a clue to its meaning. We can increase our ability to apprehend a poem's organization by doing the following:

1. Looking and listening for changes of diction and imagery, tone and mood, rhythm and rhyme, time and place and circumstance.
2. Watching for repeated elements: words, images, patterns of syntax, rhythm and rhyme.
3. Remembering that structure is an aspect of meaning. It is not something independent of meaning, but works with other poetic elements to embody meaning, to formulate it. A poem's structure, its form, is part of what the poem says, part of how it means what it does.

Test out these ideas by analyzing the form of the following poems.

WILLIAM CARLOS WILLIAMS
[1883–1963]

The Dance

In Breughel's° great picture, The Kermess,
the dancers go round, they go round and
around, the squeal and the blare and the
tweedle of bagpipes, a bugle and fiddles
tipping their bellies (round as the thick-   5
sided glasses whose wash they impound)
their hips and their bellies off balance
to turn them. Kicking and rolling about
the Fair Grounds, swinging their butts, those
shanks must be sound to bear up under such   10
rollicking measures, prance as they dance
in Breughel's great picture, The Kermess.

"The Dance" [1]**Breughel** *Pieter Breughel the Elder (1525–1569), Flemish painter of peasant life. The Kermess is a painting of a peasant wedding dance. See pp. 505–507 for reproductions of two of Breughel's paintings and the poems they inspired.*

QUESTIONS FOR REFLECTION

1. What kind of dance does the poem describe? What kind of action does the first long sentence imitate (lines 1–8)?
2. Comment on the relationship between the first and last lines.

DENISE LEVERTOV
[b. 1923]

O Taste and See

The world is
not with us enough.
O taste and see

the subway Bible poster said,
meaning The Lord, meaning   5
if anything all that lives
to the imagination's tongue,

grief, mercy, language,
tangerine, weather, to
breathe them, bite,   10
savor, chew, swallow, transform

into our flesh our
deaths, crossing the street, plum, quince,
living in the orchard and being

hungry, and plucking   15
the fruit.

QUESTION FOR REFLECTION

Imagine this poem written as a single stanza. What is the advantage of the poet's having structured it as she has?

THEODORE ROETHKE
[1908–1963]

The Waking

I wake to sleep, and take my waking slow.
I feel my fate in what I cannot fear.
I learn by going where I have to go.

We think by feeling. What is there to know?
I hear my being dance from ear to ear.   5
I wake to sleep, and take my waking slow.

Of those so close beside me, which are you?
God bless the Ground! I shall walk softly there,
And learn by going where I have to go.

Light takes the Tree; but who can tell us how?   10
The lowly worm climbs up a winding stair;
I wake to sleep, and take my waking slow.

Great Nature has another thing to do
To you and me; so take the lively air,
And, lovely, learn by going where to go.   15

This shaking keeps me steady. I should know.
What falls away is always. And is near.
I wake to sleep, and take my waking slow.
I learn by going where I have to go.

QUESTION FOR REFLECTION

Describe the patterns of repetition that prevail in the poem. Consider repeated rhyme and repeated lines. What is their effect on the poem's tone and feeling?

C. P. CAVAFY
[1863–1933]

The City

You said: "I'll go to another country, go to another shore,
find another city better than this one.
Whatever I try to do is fated to turn out wrong
and my heart lies buried as though it were something dead.
How long can I let my mind moulder in this place?   5
Wherever I turn, wherever I happen to look,
I see the black ruins of my life, here,
where I've spent so many years, wasted them, destroyed
     them totally."

You won't find a new country, won't find another shore.   10
This city will always pursue you. You will walk
the same streets, grow old in the same neighborhoods,
will turn gray in these same houses.
You will always end up in this city. Don't hope for things
     elsewhere: 15
there is no ship for you, there is no road.
As you've wasted your life here, in this small corner,
you've destroyed it everywhere else in the world.

TRANSLATED BY EDMUND KEELEY AND PHILIP SHERRARD

QUESTION FOR REFLECTION

Why is the poem divided the way it is?

THEME

We have previously defined theme as an abstraction or generalization drawn
from the details of a literary work and stated that theme refers to an idea or intellectually apprehensible meaning inherent and implicit in a work (see pp.
86–87). In determining a poem's theme we should be careful neither to oversimplify the poem nor to distort its meaning. To suggest that the theme of
Hayden's "Those Winter Sundays," for example, is a father's loving concern for
his family is to highlight only part of the poem's meaning, for it does not take
into account the speaker's remorse about his indifference to his father. Analogously, if we see Roethke's "My Papa's Waltz" as a statement about a child's ter-

ror at his father's horseplay, we misrepresent the complexity of the speaker's response to his memories of his father and their bedtime ritual.

We should also recognize that poems can have multiple themes: poems can be interpreted from more than one perspective and there is more than one way to state or explain a poem's meaning. Let us briefly reconsider Frost's "Stopping by Woods on a Snowy Evening" (page 399).

We can say, for example, that the theme of Frost's poem is the necessity to face the responsibilities inherent in adult life. We can go on to say that the poem centers on a tension in our lives between our desire for rest and peace and our need to fulfill responsibilities and meet obligations. But we shouldn't remain satisfied with this explanation. For, as we have previously stated, the speaker's "miles to go" before he "sleeps" metaphorically describes all he must accomplish before he dies. The final stanza reveals a tension between the speaker's desire to continue and an impulse to stay at rest, to ease himself into the peace of death. We might further interpret the seductiveness of death as an attractive way of escaping the pressures of circumstance and the weight of responsibility.

We can abstract yet another theme: the ability of man to appreciate beauty, particularly the beauty of nature. We might argue, for example, that Frost contrasts man's capacity for taking pleasure in watching the snow fall in a dark wood with an animal's inability to enjoy either the spectacular beauty of the scene or its serenity. Presumably, animals, unlike men, do not possess an aesthetic faculty, the ability to appreciate beauty.

Consider the subject and theme of the following poem.

EMILY DICKINSON
[1830–1886]

Crumbling is not an instant's Act

> Crumbling is not an instant's Act,
> A fundamental pause
> Dilapidation's processes
> Are organized Decays.
>
> 'Tis first a Cobweb on the Soul,   5
> A Cuticle of Dust,
> A Borer in the Axis,
> An Elemental Rust—
>
> Ruin is formal—Devil's work,
> Consecutive and slow—   10
> Fail in an instant, no man did
> Slipping—is Crash's law.

The central idea of the poem is expressed in its opening line. We might paraphrase it this way: crumbling does not happen instantaneously; it is a gradual
process, occurring slowly, cumulatively over time. The remainder of the first
stanza further establishes this idea by accenting how "crumbling" is a consequence of dilapidation, which is a result of "decay." The deterioration that results is progressive; it is an organized, systematic process: one stage of decay
leads to the next until destruction inevitably follows.

The gradual nature of decay is emphasized in the final stanza with the statement that no one ever failed in an "instant," that the catastrophe occurs after,
and as a consequence of, a series of failures. We can thus read the poem as a
statement about the process of ruin (personal, emotional, financial) as well as a
description of the process of decay. And we can summarize its theme thus: failure and destruction can be traced to small-scale elements that precede and
cause them in the sense of natural law ("Crash's law").

The theme is illustrated in the second stanza's four images of decay: cobweb,
rust, dust, and the borer in the axis. These images are all accompanied by bits
of specifying detail. The dust is a "cuticle," an image with suggestions of something at the edges, of something on the outside and also of something human;
the "Cobweb on the Soul" suggests *spiritual* deterioration ("cobwebs" suggest
neglect); the "elemental" rust puts decay at the heart of things, at the center and
vital core where the "borer" is operating. The poet applies each of these images
of decay to a person, particularly to his or her soul: the dust encircling it, the
cobweb netting it, the borer eating into it, and the rust corrupting it. Such an
interpretation of spiritual decay seems further warranted by the first line of the
third stanza: "Ruin is formal—devil's work." *Ruin* is perhaps the word most
strongly suggestive of human and spiritual collapse; "Devil's work" is a grand,
"old-fashioned" image of active evil. Thus, a statement of the poem's theme
must accommodate the idea of spiritual decay.

Centering on a poem's theme then, we work toward understanding a poem's
significance—what it says, what it implies, what it means.

Transformations

REVISIONS

Unlike the goddess Athena, who sprang full-grown from the head of Zeus, poems rarely emerge fully formed from poets' heads. When they do, however, it is often because the poet worked on them both consciously and subconsciously before putting a word on paper. The product of labor as well as inspiration, good poems are the result of considerable care, of repeated efforts to find the right words and put them in the right order.

And yet for all the effort involved, the words and lines of a poem should seem natural, even inevitable. The great modern Irish poet William Butler Yeats put it this way:

> . . . A line will take us hours maybe;
> Yet if it does not seem a moment's thought,
> Our stitching and unstitching has been nought.

We suspect that these lines and the complete poem from which they are taken, "Adam's Curse," took more than a few moments to compose. So too did the following lines in which John Keats describes a woman preparing for bed. Keats's notebook reveals his struggle to bring them to the point where he felt satisfied with them. Here are the lines as published in his "The Eve of St. Agnes":

> . . . her vespers done,
> Of all its wreathed pearls her hair she frees
> Unclasps her warmed jewels one by one;
> Loosens her fragrant bodice; by degrees
> Her rich attire creeps rustling to her knees . . .

Other less successful renderings, however, preceded this final version of the description. Previously, for example, Keats had written "her praying done" rather than "her vespers done." And before that he had written: "her prayers said." Both of these versions are less precise and less musical than the final one. "Vespers," which means evening prayers, is more precise than "prayers"; it is also more musical, echoing the *e* of "her." For "frees" Keats had previously written "strips," a word with quite different connotations and sound. For "warmed" he had written "bosom," and for "rich," "sweet." Of her dress he had also written that it "falls light" instead of "creeps rustling" to her knees. In each case Keats worked toward phrases that possess greater sensuousness and that are richer in sound and imagistic effects. But it is in the fourth line that we can see Keats struggle hardest before he settles on "Loosens her fragrant bodice; by degrees." Here are his earlier attempts:

1. Loosens her bursting, her bodice from her
2. Loosens her bodice lace string
3. Loosens her bodice and her bosom bare
4. Loosens her fragrant bodice and doth bare/Her
5. Loosens her fragrant bodice: and down slips

We have only to consider the images and connotations of "bursting bodice" and "bosom bare" to see how different an effect is achieved with "fragrant bodice." Keats deliberately avoids the stronger sexual overtones of the earlier versions, replacing words suggesting physical sensuality with others of a sensuous rather than a sensual nature.

We can see the process of revision at work more fully in the following poem by William Blake, reprinted in two versions.

WILLIAM BLAKE
[1757–1827]

London

I wander thro' each dirty street,
Near where the dirty Thames does flow,
And [see] mark in every face I meet
Marks of weakness, marks of woe.

In every cry of every man   5
In [every voice of every child] every infant's cry of fear
In every voice, in every ban
The [german] mind forg'd [links I hear] manacles I hear.

[But most] How the chimney sweeper's cry
[Blackens o'er the churches' walls]
Every black'ning church appalls,   10
And the hapless soldier's sigh
Runs in blood down palace walls.

[But most the midnight harlot's curse
From every dismal street I hear,
Weaves around the marriage hearse   15
And blasts the new born infant's tear.]

[Alternate fourth stanza]
But most [from every] thro' wintry streets I hear
How the midnight harlot's curse
Blasts the new born infant's tear,   20
And [hangs] smites with plagues the marriage hearse.

London

I wander thro' each charter'd street,
Near where the charter'd Thames does flow,
And mark in every face I meet
Marks of weakness, marks of woe.

In every cry of every Man,   5
In every Infant's cry of fear,
In every voice, in every ban,
The mind-forg'd manacles I hear.

How the Chimney-sweeper's cry
Every black'ning Church appalls;   10
And the hapless Soldier's sigh
Runs in blood down Palace walls.

But most thro' midnight streets I hear
How the youthful Harlot's curse
Blasts the new born Infant's tear,   15
And blights with plagues the Marriage hearse.

Let's consider the changes in "London" stanza by stanza to determine the implications of each alteration and to estimate how the accumulated changes affect the tone and meaning of the poem as Blake published it.

Stanza One In line 1 "charter'd" replaces "dirty." Although both words are trochaic, the sound of "charter'd" echoes "wander." More important than this use of assonance are the meanings of "charter'd." It denotes something for lease or hire, something established by a charter (a written certificate defining the legal conditions under which a corporate body is organized). The applicable meaning seems to be "hired out." The word's connotations include something defined, planned, laid out, bounded, limited by law, perhaps fixed or determined by decree. Both the street and the river Thames are described as "charter'd," as hired out and bound.

The second alteration in this stanza is Blake's substitution of "mark" for "see." "Mark" means "to take notice of; to give attention; to consider." But it also suggests a more emotionally moving seeing, a more intense noticing than "see." This use of *mark* as a verb in line 3 is further intensified with its appearance as a noun in the next line. Two denotations of the word there seem applicable: "something appearing distinctly on a surface, as a line, spot, scar, or dent" and "something indicative of one's condition, feelings."

Stanza Two   "Man" replaces "man" and "Infant's" replaces "infant's." How important, in each case, is the difference? The early version of the second line has "voice" of a "child." Why do you think Blake changed these words to the "cry" of an infant, and a "cry of fear" at that? "German" in the fourth line means "germane," suggesting something closely related or akin. This word gives way in the later version to "mind-forg'd." "Links" is replaced by "manacles." Consider the denotations and connotations of the words of the later version. How does the meaning of "manacles" support the meanings of "charter'd" and "marks"? How can "manacles" be "mind-forg'd"? And why "forg'd" and not some other word like "made"?

Stanza Three   Consider the implications of the second line in both versions. In the early version the blackening is attributed to the chimney sweeper's cry. In the revised version Blake makes "black'ning" an adjective modifying Church. How can the church's walls be blackened by the cry of a chimney sweeper? And, why does Blake use the adjective "black'ning" to modify "Church"? Reflect on the connotations of "black," "blacken," and "black'ning," and consider the denotations and connotations of "appalls."

Stanza Four   Here we have more than revisions of words or lines. Though many details from the early version are carried over to the later one, they are rearranged, recombined, and rethought. In addition, some details disappear and others emerge. The rhymes, though the same, are reversed, with "hear-tear" ending the early version and "curse-hearse" concluding the final one. In the later version "the midnight harlot" has become "the youthful Harlot"—the word *youthful* a detail that intensifies our emotional response. The "curse" of the second line is both the curse that the harlot passes on to her infant, blinding it at birth with the effects of venereal disease, and the curse of the harlot's own life. Her position echoes the implications of "charter'd" and "wandered" of stanza one. She wanders the streets, but she is hardly free. She is bound, fixed, a body for hire. The final line of the stanza is the most heavily altered. "Blights" and "plagues" suggest not only the ruin of the harlot and her child, but also the destruction of the social order: marriage is cursed, innocent children suffer, soldiers die senselessly, and in general the London populace exhibits signs of desperate suffering.

Blake's revisions intensify his indictment of the institutions—moral, military, and legal—responsible for the human squalor and the misery suffered by innocent people. His revisions increase the emotional intensity of the poem as they darken its view of the lives of the people of London and, by extension, the lives of other urban inhabitants.

Below you will find two versions of three different poems. For each pair examine changes in diction, imagery, syntax, structure, sound, rhythm, meter, and meaning. Explain the significance of the changes and indicate which version of each pair you prefer and why.

WILLIAM BUTLER YEATS
[1865–1939]

A Dream of Death

I dreamed that one had died in a strange place
Near no accustomed hand,
And they had nailed the boards above her face
The peasants of that land,

And wondering planted by her solitude   5
A cypress and a yew.
I came and wrote upon a cross of wood—
Man had no more to do—

'She was more beautiful than thy first love,
This lady by the trees';   10
And gazed upon the mournful stars above,
And heard the mournful breeze.

A Dream of Death

I dreamed that one had died in a strange place
Near no accustomed hand;
And they had nailed the boards above her face,
The peasants of that land,
Wondering to lay her in that solitude,   5
And raised above her mound
A cross they had made out of two bits of wood,
And planted cypress round;

And left her to the indifferent stars above
Until I carved these words: 10
She was more beautiful than thy first love,
But now lies under boards.

QUESTIONS FOR REFLECTION

1. Compare the tone of the last four lines of each version. Consider especially the difference between "mournful stars" and "indifferent stars."
2. What details have disappeared in the second version and what has been added? To what effect?

EMILY DICKINSON
[1830–1886]

The Wind begun to knead the Grass

The Wind begun to knead the Grass—
As Women do a Dough—
He flung a Hand full at the Plain—
A Hand full at the Sky—
The Leaves unhooked themselves from Trees— 5
And started all abroad—
The Dust did scoop itself like Hands—
And throw away the Road—
The Wagons quickened on the Street—
The Thunders gossiped low— 10
The Lightning showed a Yellow Head—
And then a livid Toe—
The Birds put up the Bars to Nests—
The Cattle flung to Barns—
Then came one drop of Giant Rain— 15
And then, as if the Hands
That held the Dams—had parted hold—
The Waters Wrecked the Sky—
But overlooked my Father's House—
Just Quartering a Tree— 20

The Wind begun to rock the Grass

The Wind begun to rock the Grass
With threatening Tunes and low—
He threw a Menace at the Earth—
A Menace at the Sky.

The Leaves unhooked themselves from Trees—   5
And started all abroad
The Dust did scoop itself like Hands
And threw away the Road.

The Wagons quickened on the Streets
The Thunder hurried slow—   10
The Lightning showed a Yellow Beak
And then a livid Claw.

The Birds put up the Bars to Nests—
The Cattle fled to Barns—
There came one drop of Giant Rain   15
And then as if the Hands

That held the Dams had parted hold
The Waters Wrecked the Sky,
But overlooked my Father's House—
Just quartering a Tree—   20

QUESTIONS FOR REFLECTION

1. Comment on the change in the organization. Does the poem's appearance in stanzas make it easier or more difficult to read?
2. Compare the tone of the first four lines of each version.
3. In lines 11–12 of each version, which image is more consistent and more vivid?

D. H. LAWRENCE
[1885–1930]

The Piano

Somewhere beneath that piano's superb sleek black
Must hide my mother's piano, little and brown, with the back
That stood close to the wall, and the front's faded silk both torn,
And the keys with little hollows, that my mother's fingers had worn.

Softly, in the shadows, a woman is singing to me   5
Quietly, through the years I have crept back to see
A child sitting under the piano, in the boom of the shaking strings
Pressing the little poised feet of the mother who smiles as she sings.

The full throated woman has chosen a winning, living song
And surely the heart that is in me must belong   10
To the old Sunday evenings, when darkness wandered outside
And hymns gleamed on our warm lips, as we watched mother's fingers glide.

Or this is my sister at home in the old front room
Singing love's first surprised gladness, alone in the gloom.
She will start when she sees me, and blushing, spread out her hands   15
To cover my mouth's raillery, till I'm bound in her shame's heart-spun bands

A woman is singing me a wild Hungarian air
And her arms, and her bosom, and the whole of her soul is bare,
And the great black piano is clamouring as my mother's never could clamour
And my mother's tunes are devoured of this music's ravaging glamour.   20

Piano

Softly, in the dusk, a woman is singing to me;
Taking me back down the vista of years, till I see
A child sitting under the piano, in the boom of the tingling strings
And pressing the small, poised feet of a mother who smiles as she sings.

In spite of myself, the insidious mastery of song   5
Betrays me back, till the heart of me weeps to belong
To the old Sunday evenings at home, with winter outside
And hymns in the cosy parlour, the tinkling piano our guide.

So now it is vain for the singer to burst into clamour
With the great black piano appassionato. The glamour   10
Of childish days is upon me, my manhood is cast
Down in the flood of remembrance, I weep like a child for the past.

QUESTIONS FOR REFLECTION

1. Which details have been eliminated from the second version? Which have been added?
2. Discuss the difference in tone and idea between the two versions of the poem.

PARODIES

A *parody* is a humorous, mocking imitation of another work. A parodic poem ridicules by distorting and exaggerating aspects of the poem it imitates. There may be distortions of the tone and purpose of the original poem or exaggerations of its stylistic mannerisms. The best parodists respect the works they parody, for to write parody well writers must understand and appreciate what they poke fun at. Good parodies catch the special manner and flavor of the originals. In them we hear echoes of the voice of the earlier poem. By extending the original beyond its limits, a parodist can point to the virtues of the poem he or she parodies. The following parody of William Carlos Williams's "This Is Just to Say" seems to do this. First, Williams's poem.

WILLIAM CARLOS WILLIAMS
[1883–1963]

This Is Just to Say

I have eaten
the plums
that were in
the icebox

and which   5
you were probably
saving
for breakfast

Forgive me
they were delicious   10
so sweet
and so cold

Now Kenneth Koch's parody:

KENNETH KOCH
[b. 1925]

Variations on a Theme by William Carlos Williams

1

I chopped down the house that you had been saving to live in next summer.
I am sorry, but it was morning, and I had nothing to do
and its wooden beams were so inviting.

2

We laughed at the hollyhocks together
And then I sprayed them with lye.   5
Forgive me. I simply do not know what I am doing.

3

I gave away the money that you had been saving to live on for the next ten years.
The man who asked for it was shabby
and the firm March wind on the porch was so juicy and cold.

4

Last evening we went dancing and I broke your leg.   10
Forgive me. I was clumsy, and
I wanted you here in the wards, where I am the doctor!

QUESTIONS FOR REFLECTION

1. Explain Koch's title.
2. Would his parody be as effective if he cut it down to one or two stanzas? If the four
   stanzas were rearranged? How long, in comparison, is Williams's poem, and why do
   you think Koch made his parody four times as long?
3. What do the four "variations" have in common?
4. Does the parody seem fair to Williams? Is it a coherent and engaging poem in its
   own right?

The following poem and its parodic counterpart are sonnets. Gary Hatch
follows G. M. Hopkins closely as he parodies "Carrion Comfort," imitating the
earlier poet's syntax strictly in some lines and more loosely in others.

GERARD MANLEY HOPKINS
[*1844–1889*]

Carrion Comfort

Not, I'll not, carrion comfort, Despair, not feast on thee;
Not untwist—slack they may be—these last strands of man
In me ór, most weary, cry *I can no more*. I can;
Can something, hope, wish day come, not choose not to be.

But ah, but O thou terrible, why wouldst thou rude on me   5
Thy wring-world right foot rock? lay a lionlimb against me? scan
With darksome devouring eyes my bruisèd bones? and fan,
O in turns of tempest, me heaped there; me frantic to avoid thee and flee?

Why? That my chaff might fly; my grain lie, sheer and clear.
Nay in all that toil, that coil, since (seems) I kissed the rod,   10
Hand rather, my heart lo! lapped strength, stole joy, would laugh, chéer.
Cheer whom though? The hero whose heaven-handling flung me, fóot tród
Me? or me that fought him? O which one? is it each one? That night, that year
Of now done darkness I wretch lay wrestling with (my God!) my God.

GARY LAYNE HATCH
[*b. 1964*]

Terrier Torment; or, Mr. Hopkins and his Dog
(FROM THE LESSER-KNOWN TERRIER SONNETS)

Put, stay put, Terrier Torment, Heel! I'll put on thee—
Quick though thou be—this leash. And,
Most wary, try to hold you still. I can;
Plan something—hold, wash dog, (come!) not choose to let you flee.

But ow! but oh thou terrier, why wouldst thou, wet on me,   5
Thy bark-loud-mutt-mouth munch? put a puppy paw against me? You plan
With funsome, frolicking eyes to dodge my dives and land
(Ow!) in squalls of squiggling—dog-piled there—wiggling to get free.

Why? That thy hair might dry, thy fur lie sheen and clean.
In all that toil, that soil, since (seems) I washed the dog,　　　　　　10
(Dried rather) his hide (oh!) gobbed grime, caked crud.
I could wash, clean. Clean whom though? Him whose water-wiggling soused me, sud
Soaked me? or me that caught him? O which one? is it each one? That hour, that day
That soap-sick Saturday when I (drench) lay wrestling with my doggone dog.

(1995)

In the next pair of poems you hear two very different voices. Account for the difference in tone between them. Explain how Howard Moss's poem parodies Shakespeare's sonnet. Consider, finally, the sense the later poem makes on its own, unrelated to the sonnet.

WILLIAM SHAKESPEARE
[1564–1616]

Shall I compare thee to a summer's day

Shall I compare thee to a summer's day?
Thou art more lovely and more temperate:
Rough winds do shake the darling buds of May,
And summer's lease hath all too short a date;
Sometime too hot the eye of heaven shines,　　　　　　5
And often is his gold complexion dimm'd;
And every fair from fair sometime declines,
By chance or nature's changing course untrimm'd:
But thy eternal summer shall not fade
Nor lose possession of that fair thou ow'st;　　　　　　10
Nor shall Death brag thou wand'rest in his shade,
When in eternal lines to time thou grow'st;
So long as men can breathe or eyes can see,
So long lives this, and this gives life to thee.

HOWARD MOSS
[*b. 1922*]

Shall I Compare Thee to a Summer's Day?

Who says you're like one of the dog days?
You're nicer. And better.
Even in May, the weather can be gray,
And a summer sub-let doesn't last forever.
Sometimes the sun's too hot;   5
Sometimes it is not.
Who can stay young forever?
People break their necks or just drop dead!
But you? Never!
If there's just one condensed reader left   10
Who can figure out the abridged alphabet
    After you're dead and gone,
    In this poem you'll live on!

Finally, consider again the following brief poem by Robert Frost (see Introduction for discussion) and an equally brief parody by Bob McKenty.

ROBERT FROST
[*1874–1963*]

Dust of Snow

The way a crow
Shook down on me
The dust of snow
From a hemlock tree

Has given my heart   5
A change of mood
And saved some part
Of a day I had rued.

BOB MCKENTY
[b. 1935]

Snow on Frost

A wayward crow
Shook down on him
The dust of snow
From a hemlock limb.

Amused (I recall)　　　　　　　　　　　　　　　　5
The poet stopped,
Delighted that's all
The black bird dropped.

QUESTION FOR REFLECTION

In what ways does McKenty's parody mimic Frost's poem? In what ways does the parody depart from the original?

POEMS AND PAINTINGS

In Roman times and again during the Renaissance, poems were characterized as speaking pictures and painting as silent poetry. A poem, that is, was seen as a visual image given speech, a painting as a silent visual poem. Earlier, in our discussion of structure, we noted that the shape of a poem, its arrangement on the page, is an important dimension of its effect.

Here, however, we will consider another dimension of the relationship between words and visual images. On the pages that follow you will find poems paired with the paintings that inspired them. Three of the paintings are accompanied by more than one poem so you will have a chance to compare different interpretations and "translations" of a painting into a poem. As you consider each pair, spend some time looking carefully at the painting. Take an inventory of its details; observe its color and texture, its organization and perspective, its line, and its form. Think about the implications of its title; examine the action or scene it depicts. Then read the poem(s) as interpretation(s) and translation(s) of the painting. Notice what the poets include, what they omit, what they alter.

Even though you will be comparing poem with painting and poem with poem, remember that each poem is a separate and individual work. Read each the way you would read any other poem, giving careful attention to its formal elements. Consider whether the poems can stand alone without their corresponding paintings. And finally, observe how each poet has transformed the painting to create a new work, one which conveys its own feelings and bears its own implications.

QUESTIONS FOR REFLECTION

Vincent Van Gogh, *The Starry Night*

1. About the series of poems he wrote based on Van Gogh's paintings, Robert Fagles has written: "I wanted to try my hand at a kind of translation I hadn't done before, not from a foreign language, but from a group of paintings." What has Fagles translated from the painting into the poem?
2. Does either Fagles's poem or Sexton's help you to see things in the painting that you had overlooked? Why or why not?
3. Does either poem seem to emphasize the painting more than the painter? Does it present a neutral description of the work? Does it imply or state a judgment about either the artist or his painting?
4. Compare Fagles's poem with Anne Sexton's "The Starry Night." Consider tone, imagery, structure, and feeling.

Francesco de Goya, *The Third of May, 1808*

1. Compare Gewanter's use of Goya with Fagles's use of Van Gogh. How does each poet convey the sense of the art he describes? How does each use that art for his own purposes?
2. Is Gewanter's poem comprehensible without the *painting*? Why or why not? How does the poem help you to see and understand Goya's art better?

Pieter Breughel the Elder, *Landscape with the Fall of Icarus*

1. Where is Icarus mentioned in Auden's poem? What does Auden end with and what does that ending imply?
2. How does Auden's poem offer us a clue to its intentions from the beginning? Would it matter if Auden's stanzas were reversed? Why or why not?
3. "Museé des Beaux Arts" can be divided into two parts. What is their relationship?
4. How does the title of Auden's poem reflect its author's preoccupations with the painting?

Pieter Breughel the Elder, *Hunters in the Snow*

1. How does Langland's poem better help you to see the details of the painting? How does the poem help you to better understand its symbolic implications?

2. Where does the poem depart from the details of the painting? In what ways and for what purposes?
3. What is emphasized in the opening stanza and the ending?
4. Langland's poem neither rhymes nor uses a consistent metrical pattern, yet it does exhibit formal organization. What devices of form, sound, and rhythm does it include? What do they contribute to the meaning and feeling of the work?

Edward Hopper, *Sunday*

1. How would you characterize the mood of Hopper's painting? What details contribute to or help establish that mood?
2. What does the poet E. Ward Herlands do with Hopper's painting? How does her treatment differ from that of the other poets inspired by paintings?
3. What is different about the form of Herlands's piece, a "prose poem"? What qualities make it poetic, and what qualities make it prosaic?

William Blake, *The Sick Rose*

1. How does Blake's art help you to understand his poem? How does it enable you to see something about the poem you may have overlooked, or to make connections you may have missed?
2. To what extent, if any, does Blake's illustration channel your reading of the poem, limiting the way you interpret it? Is it possible that the poem was written to illustrate the painting, or do you think the painting was designed to parallel the poem?

Sandro Botticelli, Giotto di Bondone, *Adoration of the Magi*

1. Compare the two paintings as stories. What does Botticelli emphasize? What does Giotto focus on? Identify figures common to both paintings and explain their significance.
2. Compare Eliot's and Yeats's poems as treatments of the general subject of the Magi. What is Yeats's concern and what is Eliot's? Do you think either poem was inspired by a painting? Why or why not?
3. Consider the poetic styles of Eliot and Yeats. Characterize each by focusing on the poet's uses of language and detail, rhythm and structure.
4. Who is the speaker in Eliot's poem? In Yeats's? Which line or lines in each poem best reveal the speaker's attitude toward what he describes?

Henri Matisse, *Dance*

1. How would you characterize the mood and spirit of the painting? What elements contribute most to these?
2. What is the significance of the ring of dancers and of the space between two of them?

3. Describe the relationship between Matisse's painting and Natalie Safir's poem. To what extent do the two works share a common theme and tone?
4. Why do you think Matisse used large patches of bold simple colors against which to set his human figures? How detailed is his rendering of the human figures? What is the effect of that rendering?

Pablo Picasso, *Girl with Mandolin*

1. What do you see when you look at Picasso's painting? What is the effect of the painter's transforming and combining objects in the manner he has done here?
2. What is the relation of Vinnie D'Ambrosio's poem to Picasso's painting?
3. Consider the language D'Ambrosio employs, especially the sounds of the words she uses. Why does she choose the sounds she does?
4. Do you prefer this painting of Picasso or the next one? Why?

Pablo Picasso, *Still Life with Pitcher, Bowl, & Fruit*

1. What elements of Picasso's painting are echoed in the poem?
2. To what extent does D'Ambrosio's poem suggest Picasso's style of painting?
3. If you could devise an alternative title for this painting, what would it be? Why?
4. Identify elements of sound play in Vinnie D'Ambrosio's poem. What do they contribute to the tone of the poem? What feeling do you come away with from reading "If I Were a Maker I'd"?

Gustav Klimt, *The Kiss*

1. What is your initial impression upon looking at Klimt's painting? How would you characterize the painting's style? its emphasis?
2. What effect does Ferlinghetti's poem have on your subsequent viewing of the painting? Why?
3. To what extent is Ferlinghetti's poem a description of Klimt's painting? To what extent is his poem an interpretation of the painting? Where is this interpretive inclination strongest?
4. Do you think the title of the poem and that of the painting are aptly chosen? Why or why not?

Vincent van Gogh, The Starry Night (1889). OIL ON CANVAS, 29 × 36¼″.
COLLECTION, THE MUSEUM OF MODERN ART, NEW YORK.
ACQUIRED THROUGH THE LILLIE P. BLISS BEQUEST.

ANNE SEXTON
[1928–1975]

The Starry Night

That does not keep me from having a terrible need of—shall I say the word—religion.
Then I go out at night to paint the stars.

VINCENT VAN GOGH in a letter to his brother

The town does not exist
except where one black-haired tree slips
up like a drowned woman into the hot sky.
The town is silent. The night boils with eleven stars
Oh starry starry night! This is how   5
I want to die.

It moves. They are all alive.
Even the moon bulges in its orange irons
to push children, like a god, from its eye.
The old unseen serpent swallows up the stars.   10
Oh starry starry night! This is how
I want to die:

into that rushing beast of the night,
sucked up by that great dragon, to split
from my life with no flag,   15
no belly,
no cry.

ROBERT FAGLES
[b. 1933]

The Starry Night

Long as I paint
I feel myself
less mad
the brush in my hand
a lightning rod to madness   5

But never ground that madness
execute it ride the lightning up
from these benighted streets and steeple up
with the cypress look its black is burning green

I am that I am it cries   10
it lifts me up the nightfall up
the cloudrack coiling like a dragon's flanks
a third of the stars of heaven wheeling in its wake
wheels in wheels around the moon that cradles round the sun

and if I can only trail these whirling eternal stars   15
with one sweep of the brush like Michael's sword if I can
cut the life out of the beast—safeguard the mother and the son
all heaven will hymn in conflagration blazing down
              the night the mountain ranges down
the claustrophobic valleys of the mad   20

          Madness
is what I have instead of heaven
God deliver me—help me now deliver
all this frenzy back into your hands
our brushstrokes burning clearer into dawn   25

Francesco de Goya, The Third of May, 1808: The Execution of the Defenders of Madrid (1814). PRADO MUSEUM, MADRID. SCALA/ART RESOURCE.

DAVID GEWANTER

[b. 1954]

Goya's "The Third of May, 1808"

I'll show you:
onto the dirt-grey
canvas he's smeared—
jam on bread—
a sticky red for blood   5
oozed from the broken
heads and shot-up bodies
heaped near the cowering group
agape at soldiers hunched above
their knived rifles.   10
The air is oil-black,
smokeless, the whole scene
painted right before the guns
report, and more killed;
see the soldiers bend   15
in careful aim, bent
like mothers nursing—
one geometry of care:
exact angle for Madonna,
for men aiming murder—   20
and yet suspended,
the crisis held up for us

to observe at leisure—
in "The Resurrection" by
Grünewald, think how Christ   25
has bolted from his tomb,
rising, splendid,
while blinded soldiers
hurl themselves down,
never landing—   30
all are trapped in place:
one can't reach heaven,
the others never fall—
and here, before the dull wedge
representing *hill,*   35
one of Goya's victims
raises his arms up,
waiting always—
you know him, his shirt
blank as a page—   40
here, hand me a butterknife
to scrape with, I'll show you how
he painted bullets
inside the painted guns.

Pieter Breughel the Elder, Landscape with the Fall of Icarus (c. 1558). MUSÉES ROYAUX DES BEAUX-ARTS, BRUSSELS. SCALA/ART RESOURCE, NY.

W . H . A U D E N

[1907—1973]

Musée des Beaux Arts

About suffering they were never wrong,
The old Masters: how well they understood
Its human position: how it takes place
While someone else is eating or opening a window or just walking dully along;
How, when the aged are reverently, passionately waiting   5
For the miraculous birth, there always must be
Children who did not specially want it to happen, skating
On a pond at the edge of the wood:
They never forgot
That even the dreadful martyrdom must run its course   10
Anyhow in a corner, some untidy spot
Where the dogs go on with their doggy life and the torturer's horse
Scratches its innocent behind on a tree.

In Breughel's *Icarus,* for instance: how everything turns away
Quite leisurely from the disaster; the ploughman may   15
Have heard the splash, the forsaken cry,
But for him it was not an important failure; the sun shone
As it had to on the white legs disappearing into the green
Water, and the expensive delicate ship that must have seen
Something amazing, a boy falling out of the sky,   20
Had somewhere to get to and sailed calmly on.

JOSEPH LANGLAND
[b. 1917]

Hunters in the Snow: Breughel

Quail and rabbit hunters with tawny hounds,
Shadowless, out of late afternoon
Trudge toward the neutral evening of indeterminate form.
Done with their blood-annunciated day
Public dogs and all the passionless mongrels   5
Through deep snow
Trail their deliberate masters
Descending from the upper village home in lowering light.
Sooty lamps
Glow in the stone-carved kitchens.   10

This is the fabulous hour of shape and form
When Flemish children are gray-black-olive
And green-dark-brown
Scattered and skating informal figures
On the mill ice pond.   15
Moving in stillness
A hunched dame struggles with her bundled sticks,
Letting her evening's comfort cudgel her
While she, like jug or wheel, like a wagon cart
Walked by lazy oxen along the old snowlanes,   20
Creeps and crunches down the dusky street.
High in the fire-red dooryard
Half unhitched the sign of the Inn
Hangs in wind
Tipped to the pitch of the roof.   25
Near it anonymous parents and peasant girl,
Living like proverbs carved in the alehouse walls,
Gather the country evening into their arms
And lean to the glowing flames.

Now in the dimming distance fades   30
The other village; across the valley
Imperturbable Flemish cliffs and crags
Vaguely advance, close in loom
Lost in nearness. Now
The night-black raven perched in branching boughs   35
Opens its early wing and slipping out
Above the gray-green valley
Weaves a net of slumber over the snow-capped homes.
And now the church, and then the walls and roofs
Of all the little houses are become   40

506

Close kin to shadow with small lantern eyes.
And now the bird of evening
With shadows streaming down from its gliding wings
Circles the neighboring hills
Of Hertogenbosch, Brabant.   45

Darkness stalks the hunters,
Slowly sliding down,
Falling in beating rings and soft diagonals.
Lodged in the vague vast valley the village sleeps.

Pieter Breughel the Elder, Hunters in the Snow (1565). KUNSTHISTORISCHES MUSEUM, VIENNA. ART RESOURCE, NY.

Edward Hopper, Sunday, (1926). OIL ON CANVAS, 29 × 34. THE PHILLIPS COLLECTION, WASHINGTON, D.C.

E. WARD HERLANDS
[*b. 1925*]

When Edward Hopper Was Painting

I like to think that on a Sunday afternoon when Edward Hopper was painting his lone man seated on a street curb, with shaft of light warming that man's right arm & right cheek, I like to think that on that very same day I was there, somewhere round that corner, dressed in a Wedgewood-blue velvet-collared English wool coat, (incongruous elegance for a workingman's child) offspring of a proud Austro-Hungarian immigrant & a first generation American. I like to believe that in the minutes just after the seated man arose from his head-bowed position, that my father came strolling down the very same street pushing me in my gray straw perambulator & when his path & ours were parallel & as that man approached, I like to think that the lone man in the Hopper painting looked down at me, smiled & said, Nice kid you've got there, Dad.

WILLIAM BLAKE
[1757–1827]

The Sick Rose

O Rose, thou art sick!
The invisible worm
That flies in the night,
In the howling storm,

Has found out thy bed
Of crimson joy,
And his dark secret love
Does thy life destroy.

Sandro Botticelli, Adoration of the Magi *(c. 1475).*
UFFIZI GALLERY, FLORENCE. SCALA/ART RESOURCE, NY.

T. S. ELIOT

[1888–1965]

Journey of the Magi

'A cold coming we had of it,
Just the worst time of the year
For a journey, and such a long journey:
The ways deep and the weather sharp,
The very dead of winter.'   5
And the camels galled, sore-footed, refractory,
Lying down in the melting snow.
There were times we regretted
The summer palaces on slopes, the terraces,
And the silken girls bringing sherbet.   10
Then the camel men cursing and grumbling
And running away, and wanting their liquor and women,
And the night-fires going out, and the lack of shelters,
And the cities hostile and the towns unfriendly
And the villages dirty and charging high prices: 15
A hard time we had of it.
At the end we preferred to travel all night,
Sleeping in snatches,
With the voices singing in our ears, saying
That this was all folly.   20

Then at dawn we came down to a temperate valley,
Wet, below the snow line, smelling of vegetation;
With a running stream and a water-mill beating the darkness,
And three trees on the low sky,

And an old white horse galloped away in the meadow. 25
Then we came to a tavern with vine-leaves over the lintel,
Six hands at an open door dicing for pieces of silver,
And feet kicking the empty wine-skins.
But there was no information, and so we continued
And arrived at evening, not a moment too soon 30
Finding the place; it was (you may say) satisfactory.

All this was a long time ago, I remember,
And I would do it again, but set down
This set down
This: were we led all that way for 35
Birth or Death? There was a Birth, certainly,
We had evidence and no doubt. I had seen birth and death,
But had thought they were different; this Birth was
Hard and bitter agony for us, like Death, our death.
We returned to our places, these Kingdoms, 40
But no longer at ease here, in the old dispensation,
With an alien people clutching their gods.
I should be glad of another death.

Giotto di Bondone, Adoration of the Magi (1313).
SCROVEGNI CHAPEL, PADUA. SCALA/ART RESOURCE.

WILLIAM BUTLER YEATS
[1865–1939]

The Magi

Now as at all times I can see in the mind's eye,
In their stiff, painted clothes, the pale unsatisfied ones
Appear and disappear in the blue depth of the sky
With all their ancient faces like rain-beaten stones,
And all their helms of silver hovering side by side, 5
And all their eyes still fixed, hoping to find once more,
Being by Calvary's turbulence unsatisfied,
The uncontrollable mystery on the bestial floor.

Henri Matisse, Dance (first version). Paris. (March 1909). OIL ON CANVAS, 8′ 6½″ × 12′ 9½″. MUSEUM OF MODERN ART, NEW YORK. GIFT OF NELSON A. ROCKEFELLER IN HONOR OF ALFRED H. BARR, JR.

NATALIE SAFIR
[b. 1935]

Matisse's Dance

A break in the circle dance of naked women,
dropped stitch between the hands
of the slender figure stretching too hard
to reach her joyful sisters.

Spirals of glee sail from the arms   5
of the tallest woman. She pulls the circle
around with her fire. What has she found
that she doesn't keep losing,
her torso a green-burning torch?

Grass mounds curve ripely beneath   10
two others who dance beyond the blue.
Breasts swell and multiply and
rhythms rise to a gallop.

Hurry, frightened one, and grab on—before
the stitch is forever lost, before the dance   15
unravels and a black sun swirls from that space.

Pablo Picasso, Girl with a Mandolin (Fanny Tellier). Paris (late spring 1910). OIL ON CANVAS 39½″ × 29″. THE MUSEUM OF MODERN ART, NEW YORK. NELSON A. ROCKEFELLER BEQUEST.

VINNIE-MARIE D'AMBROSIO
[b. 1928]

If I Were a Maker I'd

make a melon
          orange in yellow
add a rod
fret it   and string it

and trim a pick   5
from a suppleplump pit.

My tools would burgeon
bunches of grapes and

then ghosts in motley
no–shaped and graced   10
would pin the grapes

to their pointed shoes   ' and ring–a–ling them.

One shade would dandle my banjo gently—
and soon

you'd see a melon roll through air!   15
you'd see grapes leaping and lighting!

and you'd hear my mooncurled song!

Pablo Picasso, Still Life with Pitcher, Bowl, & Fruit (1931). PRIVATE COLLECTION.
GIRAUDON/ART RESOURCE, NY.

Gustav Klimt, The Kiss (1907–1908). KUNSTHISTORICHES
MUSEUM, VIENNA. ERICK LESSING/ART RESOURCE, NY.

LAWRENCE FERLINGHETTI
[b. 1919]

Short Story on a Painting of Gustav Klimt

They are kneeling upright on a flowered bed
    He
        has just caught her there
                and holds her still
    Her gown   5
        has slipped down
                off her shoulder
    He has an urgent hunger
        His dark head
            bends to hers   10
                hungrily
And the woman the woman
    turns her tangerine lips from his
        one hand like the head of a dead swan
           draped down over   15
                his heavy neck
        the fingers
           strangely crimped
              tightly together
her other arm doubled up   20
    against her tight breast

                    her hand a languid claw
                                clutching his hand
                    which would turn her mouth
                                            to his   25
            her long dress made
                            of multicolored blossoms
                                quilted on gold
            her Titian hair
                    with blue stars in it   30
        And his gold
                    harlequin robe
                                checkered with
                                    dark squares
            Gold garlands   35
                    stream down over
                                her bare calves &
                                tensed feet
        Nearby there must be
                a jeweled tree   40
                    with glass leaves aglitter
                        in the gold air
        It must be
                    morning
                        in a faraway place somewhere   45
        They
            are silent together
                                as in a flowered field
                upon the summer couch
                            which must be hers   50
            And he holds her still
                            so passionately
                holds her head to his
                            so gently so insistently
                to make her turn   55
                        her lips to his
        Her eyes are closed
                        like folded petals
        She
            will not open   60
                    He
                        is not the One

Writing about Poetry

REASONS FOR WRITING ABOUT POETRY

Why write about poetry? One reason is to find out what you think about a poem. Another is to induce yourself to read a poem more carefully. You may write about a work of poetry because it engages you, and you may wish to celebrate it or to argue with its implied ideas and values. Still another reason is that you may simply be required to do so as a course assignment.

Whatever your reasons for writing about poetry, a number of things happen when you do. First, in writing about a poem you tend to read it more attentively, noticing things you might overlook in a more casual reading. Second, since writing stimulates thinking, when you write about poetry you find yourself thinking more about what a particular work means and why you respond to it as you do. And third, you begin to acquire power over the works you write about, making them more meaningful to you.

INFORMAL WAYS OF WRITING ABOUT POETRY

When you write about a poem, you may write for yourself or you may write for others. Writing for yourself, writing to discover what you think, often takes casual forms such as annotation and freewriting. These less formal kinds of writing are useful for helping you focus on your reading of fiction. They are helpful in studying for tests about poetry. They can also serve as preliminary forms of writing when you write more formal essays and papers about poetry.

Annotation

When you annotate a text, you make notes about it, usually in the margins or at the top and bottom of pages—or both. Annotations can also be made within the text, as underlined words, circled phrases, and bracketed sentences or paragraphs. Annotations may also assume the form of arrows, question marks, and various other marks.

Annotating a literary work offers a convenient and relatively painless way to begin writing about it. Annotating can get you started zeroing in on what you think interesting or important. You can also annotate to signal details that puzzle or disconcert you.

Your markings serve to focus your attention and clarify your understanding of a poem. Your annotations can save you time in rereading or studying a work. And they can also be used when you write a more formal paper.

Annotations for the following poem illustrate the process.

ROBERT HAYDEN

Those Winter Sundays

Sundays <u>too my father</u> got up early
and put <u>his</u> clothes on in the <u>blueblack</u>
   cold,
then with cracked hands that ached
from labor in the weekday weather made
banked fires blaze. <u>No one ever thanked</u>
   him.

<u>I'd</u> wake and hear the cold splintering,
   breaking,
When the rooms were warm, <u>he'd</u> call,
and slowly <u>I</u> would rise and dress,
<u>fearing</u> the chronic angers of that house,

Speaking <u>indifferently</u> to him,
who had driven out the <u>cold</u>
and polished my good shoes as well.
<u>What did I know, what did I know</u> of
   love's austere and <u>lonely</u> offices?

This father gets up early every *day—*even *on Sundays.*

How can cold be "blueblack"?

No one? Not other family members? Not the speaker?

Stanza one emphasizes the speaker's father; stanza two shifts emphasis to the speaker himself.

Speaker remembers his *fear.* Fear of what? His father's anger? Was it directed at him?

Father drives out the cold—warms the house, literally. Is the father himself a "warm" person, or "cold"?

Repeats the question. Tone? Feeling? Speaker knows *now* what he did not know then.

Father's loneliness/father's love.

Freewriting

Freewriting is a kind of informal writing you do for yourself. In freewriting you explore a text to find out what you think about it and how you respond to it. When you freewrite, you do not know ahead of time what your ideas about the work will be. Freewriting leads you to explore your memories and experience as well as aspects of the text itself. You sometimes wander from the details of the poem you are writing about. In the process you may discover thoughts and feelings you didn't know you had or were only dimly aware of. You can use freewriting to explore all your responses to a work. You can also use the technique to see where it leads you in thinking about the work itself.

First read Robert Graves's "Symptoms of Love," then look at some sample responses written by students who had heard Graves's poem read aloud and then read it once to themselves.

ROBERT GRAVES
[1895–1985]

Symptoms of Love

Love is a universal migraine,
A bright stain on the vision
Blotting out reason.

Symptoms of true love
Are leanness, jealousy,   5
Laggard dawns;

Are omens and nightmares—
Listening for a knock,
Waiting for a sign:

For a touch of her fingers   10
In a darkened room,
For a searching look.

Take courage, lover!
Could you endure such pain
At any hand but hers?   15

COLLEGE FRESHMAN: This lover is really bitter. He thinks love is a headache (migraine) and sees love mainly as negative and frightening. I noticed he talked about "omens and nightmares." He could have said "promises and dreams" or something like that, but he didn't. So as far as I am concerned, this speaker is a person who does not see any hope or possibility of growing better because of love. This is all pessimistic.

COLLEGE SOPHOMORE: Not that I haven't seen many failed relationships, but as a "thirty-something" male, I think the speaker in this poem (who also seems to be male) is very young. He sees "true love" as something that "blots out reason" and is always jealously waiting for a sign that the lady returns his feelings. I think as most people get older, they do not spend so much time thinking about "how is she (or he, in the case of a woman) going to react to me?" Instead they are looking for someone who will not cause them pain, someone who will be on the same wavelength.

COLLEGE JUNIOR: The first thing I thought when I was listening to the poem being read was that it was a terrible way to look at love. Like a migraine headache. Then when I read it myself, it made me smile some at the end. It was a sad smile—or maybe an ironic smile is what I mean. Because at the end, the speaker advises other lovers to "Take courage," so I thought that showed that he was at least willing to try again. He seemed to be saying that, yes, love is painful but it is a pain that can be worth it if you get rewarded with that "searching look" while the two of you are "in a darkened room." What he is talking about is that "chemistry" between two people who are really attracted to each other, but maybe they aren't meant for each other because of their opposing personalities. But the physical attraction is something that you just can't always push away.

COLLEGE FRESHMAN: A man wrote this poem and the character in the poem is a man, but the feelings are something I can really understand. I think more of women or girls being the ones who wait around for signs or who stay up all night or lose weight because they are in love with someone who isn't responding. I can certainly understand watching for every look and trying to figure out what it might mean and whether it might be saying that this person likes you. I've had plenty of headaches waiting for the phone to ring. Graves is right on target when he says "Love is a universal migraine."

The responses show the wide variety of reactions readers have when they encounter the same text. Note that the second reader and the fourth reader, particularly, include thoughts and feelings related to their own circumstances.

FORMAL WAYS OF WRITING ABOUT POETRY

Among the more common formal ways of writing about poetry is analysis. In writing an analytical essay about a poem, your goal is to explain how one or more particular aspects or issues in the work contribute to its overall meaning. You might analyze the dialogue in Stuart's "In the Orchard" or the voices in Reed's "Naming of Parts," for example, in explaining what the verbal exchanges between characters or the difference in voices contributes to each poem's meaning. You might analyze the imagery of H. D.'s "Heat" or Hardy's "Neutral Tones" to see what that imagery suggests about the speaker's perspective or the author's attitude. Or you might analyze the syntax of Frost's "The

Silken Tent" or Cummings's "Me up at does" for what that syntax reveals about each poem's theme.

In addition to analyzing these and other poetic elements in a single poem, you might also write to compare two poems, perhaps by focusing on their symbolism, sound effects, rhythm and meter, structure, or figures of speech. Or, instead of focusing on literary elements per se, you might write to see how a particular critical perspective (see our discussion in Chapter Twenty-Two) illuminates a poem. For example, you might consider the ways reader response criticism contributes to your understanding of Piercy's "A Work of Artifice" (page 705) or new historicism contributes to your understanding of Poe's "To Helen" (page 643).

The following brief analysis of Plath's "Mirror" (page 703) focuses on the poem's imagery and its structure. The writer considers how Plath's language and organization convey an implied idea about women.

Student Papers on Poetry

Jennifer Stepkowski
Professor O'Leary

Reflections on Sylvia Plath's "Mirror"

Sylvia Plath's poem, "Mirror," presents a portrayal of
womanhood that is both accurate and upsetting. The mirror in
Plath's poem reflects honestly both inanimate objects and the
faces of those who peer into it. To convey the mirror's
uncompromising accuracy in reflecting what shows in its glass
surface, Plath uses such words as "exact," "truthful,"
"really," and "faithfully." Plath personifies her mirror and
makes it the poem's speaker. "I am silver and exact," the
speaker begins. "I have no preconceptions" (1.1). This
exactness of the mirror's reflection of reality coupled with
Plath's precise diction present a harsh reality in which women
grow old inexorably. Women have old age to look forward to,
and old age in which the young girls they once were have been
"drowned" (1.17).

The image of drowning follows logically from the opening of
the poem's second stanza in which the mirror is compared to a
lake. It is in this lake (or mirror as lake) that a woman
searches for her self, reaching, as Plath writes, "for what
she really is" (1.11). What the woman finds, however, so
disconcerts her that she responds with "an agitation of hands"
(1.14), which calls up a vision of the woman's hands in
flurried motion around her face. Yet even though she is upset
by what she sees in the mirror, the woman returns repeatedly,
for as the mirror says, "I am important to her" (1.15).

Plath is uncompromising in portraying women's need to see
themselves, a need fed by a powerful concern with their
appearance. She also conveys without compromise the inevitable
process of aging, rendered powerfully in the simile that
concludes the poem. Plath conveys a sense of the woman at
three stages of life: as she is now, growing older in the
poem's present; as she was once as a young girl; and as she
will be as an old woman who "rises toward her day after day,
like a terrible fish" (1.18).

The images of the second stanza—of lake and tears and
agitated hands of a drowning girl and old woman rising like a
fish—reflect concretely the first stanza's general

statements. There Plath describes the mirror as having "no preconceptions" (1.1), as "swallow[ing] immediately just as it is," whatever it sees, "unmisted by love or dislike." Soon the woman will be swallowed by the mirror as it has swallowed the young girl she once was. Only the old woman remains, coming and going from the mirror, staring into it and looking for the middle-aged woman and the young girl who will have long since vanished.

A Paper That Compares Two Versions of a Poem

In the following paper Amanda Ackerman compares an early version of Blake's "London" with the published version (pages 486–487). The writer carefully analyzes Blake's diction and selection of detail to arrive at an interpretation of the later version. Seeing what words Blake rejected and changed helped her understand what Blake's published poem emphasizes.

Ackerman, Amanda
DiYanni
8/3/92
Third Essay

                    The Sad World of "London"

In William Blake's "London," the speaker takes a midnight walk
through London's dismal streets. As the speaker travels, he
remarks on the depravity, the weakness, and the sad
restrictions which abound in the London society. However,
because of Blake's affinity for perfection in his poetry, the
speaker's footsteps are thoughtfully planned. In fact, it was
necessary for Blake to make several revisions within his first
draft of "London" before he was satisfied with the final
version. Each change that Blake makes bears significance,
whether it is as subtle as the capitalization of one letter,
or as dramatic as the complete revision of an entire stanza.
With each change, the poem becomes richer with connotations of
restraint, with imagery far more vivid and alarming, and with
an expression of a devastation ultimately more heart-felt.
   The majority of the changes that Blake makes within the
first three stanzas of the poem are deceptively minute, yet
their impact is anything but insignificant. For example, by
simply replacing three words within the first stanza of the
original version, Blake allows the second version of "London"
to immediately take on an altogether different feeling. In the
earlier version of the poem, Blake expresses his discontent by
describing the Thames and the London streets as "dirty." By
sharp contrast, in the later version Blake describes the same
scene as "charter'd," a word that denotes boundaries and
restrictions: "I wander through each charter'd street, Near
where the charter'd Thames does flow . . ." (lines 1–2).
Instead of providing the reader with a vague and somewhat
cryptic idea of London's decay, Blake instantly alerts the
reader to the sad reality of London's restrictions. London is
a world so devastated by repression that even the "free
flowing" Thames and the city streets themselves are weakened.
Nothing and no one is left untouched by London's all-consuming
restrictions, for the reader "sees in every face [he] meets,
Marks of weakness, marks of woe." This image, although
disturbing, cannot compare to the deeper despair expressed in
the second version, for in this version the speaker "marks in
every face [he] meets, Marks of weakness, marks of woe . . ."
The grief of those that the speaker sees becomes much more
terrifying, for their faces are so miserable and weak that
they are able to leave a permanent impression on those who see

them. This is a much more powerful image than that of a person despondently "seeing" the sad faces of those around him. Also, by changing "see" to "mark," Blake creates a haunting repetition which not only enhances the fluidity of the poem, but more importantly "marks" the reader himself by echoing the dismal truth.

Again, Blake makes revisions in the second stanza which appear small, but nonetheless which add tremendously to the impact of the poem. To begin with, Blake makes what appears to be a simple grammatical change; he capitalizes words such as "Man" and "Infant" in the second version. By doing this, Blake makes those unknown people that he describes seem much more frighteningly human, for he capitalizes their names just as we would capitalize the name of an individual person. Also, the striking image of a grown man crying becomes much more devastating when that "man" becomes "Man"—a universal representation for all mankind. In addition, the capitalized letters of these words allow them to stand out, and thus magnify their impact. Blake also makes another significantly effective change within the second stanza; he changes "In every voice of every child" to "In every Infant's cry of fear," a line much richer in impact and feeling. The first line gives a somewhat vague picture of the sadness in the lives of many faceless children, whereas the second line evokes a much more specific and alarming image, for it is the purest and most innocent of all human beings—the newborn baby—which even in its naivete feels the pain of repression so intensely that it "cries out."

As frightening as that image is, Blake affects the reader even more deeply by revealing the two terrifying sources of London's restricted freedom—one being the human mind. The already unnerving image of the human mind being its own means of imprisonment is made much more vivid when Blake changes the "mind forg'd links" described in the first version, to the "mind-forg'd manacles" of the second. The word "manacles" is a word so rich with connotations of restraint and imprisonment that the reader is given a both alarming and sickening image of the mind itself—the only possession of man thought to be truly incapable of being barred or restricted—eating away at its own freedom. Blake also reveals the other source of London's grief and repressed freedom in a bold protest against the leadership of his time—Blake identifies the leaders themselves as the source of London's anguish. Again, by capitalizing certain words and by changing one line in the third stanza, Blake makes his attack on the leadership of his time all the more forceful and justifiable. In the second version, Blake capitalizes words such as "Chimney-sweeper's,"

"Church," "Soldier's," and "Palace" in order to display his
discontent much more emphatically. The reader ultimately takes
much more notice of the young Chimney-sweeper's cry, and of
the unfortunate Soldier whose own lifeblood is "running down
the walls" of the buildings where the incompetent leaders
reside. Blake further stresses the heartlessness of London's
leaders through another significant revision; he changes the
line "Blacken's o'er the church walls" to "Every black'ning
Church appalls." In the second version, the Church of England—
thought to be a sacred place of sanctuary and of
guidance—instead of providing its people with any kind of
relief, is actively "appalling" or denunciating the efforts of
its impoverished people, particularly the poor child-laborers
who must sweep chimneys in order to survive. This is a much
more horrifying image than that of the first.

However, in the last stanza Blake provides the reader with
perhaps the most alarming imagery of all, as London has been
reduced to a state where nothing at all is sacred. In the last
stanza, Blake brings about a marked difference in the impact
of the poem through several dramatic changes. The earlier
version of the poem uses imagery which vaguely connotes the
sadness and the depravity found in the London society.
However, Blake expresses this detestable human condition much
more forcefully in the final version. Instead of the "midnight
harlot," "dismal street," and "curses weaving and blasting,"
Blake uses much more powerful words and imagery. A strong
image such as a "midnight street" brings a much darker and
ominous feeling to the poem. Also, in an astonishing paradox,
Blake refers to the harlot as "youthful." By doing this, Blake
brings about a much more alarming image of the corrupted and
devastated innocence of a child. Also, the "curses" of the
harlot appear to be much more cruel and hurtful as they
"blight with plagues" rather than "weave" around a marriage
hearse. In this second image a youthful mother is trying to
destroy her own infant's tears—no sooner has the infant
experienced its first moments of life in the world, than it
is feeling the sickness of repression. Nothing is sacred any
longer in the dismal world of London, certainly not the bond
between mother and child, and not even marriage. Blake ends
the final version of his poem with the lasting impression of
a "Marriage Hearse." This last image leaves the reader
devastated, as it is marriage—probably considered the most
sacred and beautiful institution of man—which itself is dead
and on its way to being buried.

Although the reader encounters feelings of deep sadness,
corruption, and repression within the lines of Blake's first
version of "London," the walk that the reader takes through

London's dreary streets in the final version of the poem provides the reader with a much more heart-felt insight into London's miserable reality. Regardless of the size of each revision, each change that Blake makes within his poem produces a more powerful understanding and a more profound idea: specifically, the idea of restriction, the idea that man himself has created a world in which he has stifled his own expression and put boundaries on his growth—in the sad world of London.

QUESTIONS FOR WRITING ABOUT POETRY

In writing about the elements of poetry, the following questions can help you focus your thinking and prepare yourself for writing analytical essays and papers. Use the questions as a checklist to guide you to important aspects of any poem you read.

Voice: Speaker and Situation

1. Who is the speaker of the poem? How would you characterize this speaker?
2. Where does the speaker reveal his or her attitude toward the poem's subject? Do the speaker's attitude or feelings change at any point? If so, where and with what implications?
3. What is the speaker's situation? What is happening in the poem?

Diction and Imagery

4. Do you understand the denotations of all the words used in the poem? Look up any words you are not completely sure of.
5. Which words convey the richest connotations? What do these connotations contribute to your understanding of the poem?
6. What kinds of imagery does the poem include? Do you detect any patterns among the images? What do the images collectively suggest?

Figures of Speech

7. What kinds of figures of speech occur in the poem? How important are figures of comparison—simile and metaphor?
8. How do the poem's figures of speech contribute to the poem's vividness and concreteness? What do they contribute to its feeling and meaning?

Symbolism and Allegory

9. What details of language and action carry symbolic implications? How do you know?
10. Does the poem exhibit a pattern of linked allegorical details?

Syntax and Structure

11. What kinds of sentences does the poet use? What kinds of structure and pattern do the poem's sentences exhibit?
12. What does the poem's syntax reveal about the state of mind of its speaker?
13. How is the poem organized? How do its stanzas or major sections develop?
14. How are the stanzas or major sections of the poem related?

Sound, Rhythm, and Meter

15. Does the poem rhyme? Does it employ assonance, alliteration, onomatopoeia, or other forms of sound play? With what effects?
16. What kinds of rhythm and meter does the poem include? Does the rhythm change or is the meter varied at any point? With what effects?

Theme

17. How do the poetic elements create and convey the poem's meaning(s)?
18. Do you think there is more than one theme? Why or why not?
19. Is the theme of the poem explicit or implicit? Is it conveyed more clearly in one part of the poem than another?

Critical Perspectives

20. Which of the critical perspectives (Chapter 22) best helps you make sense of the poem? Why?
21. To what extent do the poem's language and details convey its meaning? To what extent do you need to go outside the poem for an understanding of its allusions, its historical or biographical implications, or other kinds of information?
22. To what extent does the poem confirm or support, confute or contradict your personal values, beliefs, attitudes, or dispositions? Why?

Suggestions for Writing

The Experience of Poetry

1. Write a paper in which you recount your experience of reading a particular poem or a series of poems by the same author. You may want to compare your initial experience of reading the poem(s) with your subsequent experience.
2. Relate the action or situation of a poem to your experience. Explain how the poem is relevant to your situation, and comment on how

reading and thinking about it may have helped you view your own situation and experience more clearly.

The Interpretation of Poetry

3. Characterize the speaker of any poem. Present a sketch of the speaker's character by referring to the language of the poem. Consider not only what the speaker says but the manner in which it is said and what it reveals about the speaker.

4. Describe the narrative element in any poem. Consider how important its "story" or narrative material is, and what would be gained or lost without it. Consider also how the narrative dimension of the poem would work as a story, play, or essay.

5. Explicate the opening lines of a poem. Explain the significance of the lines in the context of the poem overall.

6. Explicate the closing lines of a poem. Consider how they can be related to earlier lines.

7. Select two or more key lines from a short poem (or groups of lines from longer ones). Explain their significance and consider their relationship to one another.

8. Read five or more poems by the same poet and discuss the features they have in common.

9. Analyze a single poem that is representative of a poet's work. Explain what makes the poem representative.

10. Analyze the diction or word choices of a poem. Consider other words the poet could have chosen. Examine the denotations and connotations of the words the poet chose. Use your analysis of the diction to develop an interpretation of the poem.

11. Analyze the imagery of a poem. List the poem's significant details (if a long poem) or all the details if it's short. Discuss what the images contribute to the poem's tone, feeling, and/or meaning.

12. Analyze the figurative language of a poem. Identify and explain each figure of speech and discuss its function in the poem overall.

13. Discuss the ironic dimensions of a poem. Identify examples of irony, and explain their significance and effect.

14. Identify the allusions in a poem and explain what they contribute to your understanding of it.

15. Analyze the structure of a poem. Consider both its overall structure and its small-scale structure—how the individual parts themselves are organized. Identify the main parts of the poem and comment on their relationship to each other.

16. Analyze the sound effects of a poem. Explain how sound contributes to its sense and spirit.

17. Analyze the rhythm and meter of a poem. Identify its prevailing metrical pattern. Acknowledge any deviations from this meter and

comment on the significance of these deviations. Consider what the poem's rhythm and meter contribute to its overall meaning and feeling.

The Evaluation of Poetry

18. Discuss the values exemplified in one or more poems. Consider, that is, the cultural, moral, social, or ethical norms that either appear explicitly in the poem(s) or are implied by it. Identify those values, relate them to your own, and comment on their significance.

19. Compare two poems, evaluating their literary and linguistic merit. Explain what the two poems have in common, how they differ, and why one is superior to the other.

20. Evaluate a poem from the standpoint of its literary excellence. Explain why you consider it to be an effective or ineffective poem.

To Research or Imagine

21. Develop an alternative ending for a poem, changing the outcome of its action, altering its pattern of rhythm or rhyme, or making other changes. Be prepared to defend your alternative version as a reasonable possibility. Consider why the poet chose to end the poem as he or she did.

22. Read some letters or essays by a poet whose poetry you know and enjoy. Consider how your reading of the poet's prose aids your understanding or increases your enjoyment.

23. Read a full-scale biography of a poet whose work you admire. Write a paper explaining how the poet's life is or is not reflected in the poetic work.

24. Write a paper in which you examine how a particular poet worked within and/or against the prevailing social attitudes, moral beliefs, or cultural dispositions of his or her time.

25. Read a critical study of any poet you would like to learn more about. Write a paper explaining how reading the book has increased your understanding and/or appreciation of the poetry.

CHAPTER TWELVE

Three Poets in Context

READING EMILY DICKINSON, ROBERT FROST, AND LANGSTON HUGHES IN DEPTH

The primary context for reading any single poem is other poems by the same poet. Additional contexts include other poems by contemporary poets and by poets with similar thematic preoccupations or stylistic inclinations. Emily Dickinson's poems, for example, can be read in relation to those of her contemporary Walt Whitman. Dickinson's poems can also be read in relation to seventeenth-century metaphysical poetry, especially the poems of George Herbert and John Donne, with whom Dickinson shared religious interests and some stylistic traits.

Additional contexts for reading Dickinson's poetry include her letters and her life. To some extent at least, a poet's work reflects his or her life. Knowing at least the broad outlines of poets' lives can be helpful in gaining additional perspectives on their poetry.

The context of poets' lives is naturally extended by their culture and environment. Knowing something of nineteenth-century New England culture enhances a reader's understanding of Dickinson's poetry. Knowing something about the development of literary modernism and about Robert Frost's and Langston Hughes' relationship to that movement situates their poetry in the context of their time and delineates it sharply against that backdrop.

Moreover, what is true for the life of Dickinson is also true for the life of Frost and Hughes. Knowing the facts of their lives enhances our reading of their poetry. This having been said, however, it is the inner lives of these poets rather than their external lives that are of interest in their poems. Thus, primary emphasis in reading Dickinson, Frost, and Hughes should be on their artistry, on how they deploy language to create art, rather than on how their poems manifest aspects of their lives.

Still another context for reading Dickinson, Frost, and Hughes is provided by their comments on the art and craft of poetry. Dickinson discusses poetry in her letters, Frost in both letters and essays. Neither poet provides interpretations of their poems. Frost, in fact, often had fun with audiences who asked about the meanings of particular poems, frequently teasing them with irrelevant information (only occasionally accurate) about how his poems were composed. Nonetheless poets' comments on the art of poetry generally and on their particular poetic intentions can be helpful in approaching their work. Frost's interest in how a poem can convey the intonational qualities of the spoken voice is a case in point. For Langston Hughes' poems, readers should attend both to their speech and to their song, particularly to the feeling of the blues they so often invoke

Dickinson, Frost, and Hughes have attracted a wide range of critical interpretation, providing still another context for their work. A sample of that criticism is included in this chapter.

QUESTIONS FOR IN-DEPTH READING

1. What general or overall thematic connections can you make between different works?
2. What stylistic similarities do you notice between and among different works?
3. How do the works differ in emphasis, tone, and style?
4. Once you have identified a writer's major preoccupations, place each work on a spectrum or a grid that represents the range of the writer's concerns.
5. What connections and disjunctions do you find among the following literary elements as they are embodied in different poems by the same writer?
   a. speaker and situation
   b. diction and imagery
   c. figures of speech
   d. symbolism and allegory
   e. syntax and structure
   f. sound and sense
   g. rhythm and meter
   h. theme and thought
6. To what extent are your responses to and perceptions of different works by the same writer shared by others—by critics, by classmates, and by the writers themselves?
7. What relationships and differences do you see between the work of one writer and that of another who shares similar thematic interests, stylistic proclivities, or cultural, religious, or social values?
8. Which of the critical perspectives seem most useful as analytical tools for approaching the body of work of particular writers?

INTRODUCTION TO EMILY DICKINSON

[1830–1886]

Emily Dickinson's external life was remarkably circumscribed. Born in 1830 in Amherst, Massachusetts, and educated at Amherst Academy, she lived there her entire life, except for a brief stay at what was later to become Mount Holyoke College. She lived a life of seclusion, leaving Massachusetts only once and rarely leaving her father's house during the last fifteen years of her life. She died in the house where she was born.

If Dickinson's external life was unadventurous, her interior life was not. Her mind was anything but provincial. She read widely in English literature and thought deeply about what she read. She expressed a particular fondness for the poetry of John Keats and Robert Browning, the prose of John Ruskin and Sir Thomas Browne, and the novels of George Eliot and Charlotte and Emily Brontë. And although she disclaimed knowledge of Whitman's work, she treasured a book that significantly influenced both Whitman's poetry and her own: the King James translation of the Bible. She especially liked the Book of Revelation.

Dickinson is often bracketed with Whitman as a cofounder of modern American poetry. Each brought to poetry something new, fresh, and strikingly original. But their poems, however prototypically modern, could not be more different. A mere glance at the page reveals a significant visual difference. Whitman's poems are large and expansive. The lines are long and the poems are typically ample and open. Dickinson's poems, by contrast, are highly compressed. They squeeze moments of intensely felt life and thought into tight four-line stanzas that compress feeling and condense thought.

The openness of Whitman's form is paralleled by the openness of his stance, his public outgoing manner. Dickinson's poetry is much more private, tending toward inwardness. Hers is a more meditative poetry than Whitman's, a poetry rooted partly in the metaphysical poetry of such seventeenth-century writers as John Donne and George Herbert. More directly influential on Dickinson's poetry than the metaphysical poets, however, was the tradition of Protestant hymnology. Her poems frequently employ the meter of hymns and follow their typical stanzaic pattern. Here, for example, is the opening verse of "Our God, Our Help in Ages Past," its accented syllables marked with ´.

> Oŭr Go´d, oŭr he´lp iň a´gĕs pa´st,
> Oŭr ho´pe fŏr ye´ars tŏ co´me,
> Oŭr she´ltĕr fro´m thĕ sto´rmў bla´st,
> Aňd ou´r ĕte´rnăl ho´me.

The hymn's meter and formal structure are highly regular. The first and third lines are in iambic tetrameter, the second and fourth in iambic trimeter. The lack of metrical variation results in a steady, predictable rhythm, essential for singing. Dickinson varies this standard pattern to suit her poetic purpose. Her numerous variations amply testify to the ingenious and stunning uses to which she put this familiar meter. Consider, for example, "I felt a Funeral, in my Brain," "I like a look of Agony," "I died for Beauty—but was scarce," and "I heard a Fly buzz—when I died."

Dickinson's adaptation of hymn meter accords with her adaptation of the traditional religious doctrines of orthodox Christianity. For although her poems reflect a Calvinist heritage—particularly in their probing self-analysis, in which an intensely religious disposition intersects with profound psychological experience—she was not an orthodox Christian. Her religious ideas, like her life and poetry, were distinctive and individual. And even when her views tend toward orthodox teaching, as in her attitude toward immortality, her literary expression of such a belief is strikingly original. In addition, Dickinson's mischievous wit contrasts sharply with the brooding solemnity characteristic of much Calvinist-inspired religious writing. Finally, her love for nature separates her from her Puritan precursors, allying her instead with such transcendentalist contemporaries as Emerson, Whitman, and Thoreau, though her vision of life is starker than theirs.

Dickinson's poetry requires repeated and careful readings. Her diction is frequently surprising. Her elliptical syntax occasionally departs from the normal pattern. Readers must consequently fill in the gaps her language creates. Her taut lines need to be loosened; her tight poems need to be opened up. Words, phrases, lines cry out for the expansion of interpretive paraphrase.

Though a dictionary is necessary to identify the meanings of many of the words in Dickinson's poems, we need to attend to their richness of connotation as well. In "A narrow Fellow in the Grass," for example, we can explore the connotations of "Fellow," "transport," "cordiality," and "Zero at the Bone," considering how they fuse thought and feeling. In "The Bustle in a House," we can be alert for the fresh treatment of metaphor in the second stanza and attentive to the connotations of "industries," "Morning," and "Enacted" from the opening lines. And in "Tell all the Truth but tell it slant," we can discover the general idea implied by the poem and then apply it to specific areas of our experience. In doing so we will discover how Dickinson treats both nature and human experience obliquely and indirectly. To read her poems requires, in addition, a willingness to wait for the poem's possibilities of meaning to reveal themselves. Since many of her poems are cast as riddles, we must be willing to accept uncertainty, ambiguity, and partial understanding in interpreting them.

We also have to extend our notion of what constitutes acceptable poetic technique—something her contemporaries found nearly impossible. Dickinson was criticized for using inexact rhymes, rough rhythms, and colloquial diction, and for taking liberties with grammar. Her odd punctuation—heavy on dashes—and her peculiar use of capitalization were also unappreciated. But Dickinson exploited these and other poetic resources to convey complex states of mind and feeling. She employed these and other poetic idiosyncrasies not for their own sake, but for emotional and psychological impact.

In his extensive biography of Dickinson, Richard B. Sewall describes her resolve to portray the state of her mind and being in all their unorthodox complexity. He also describes Dickinson's early and futile hopes for publication and appreciation as well as her resignation to what she termed her "barefoot rank: of anonymity." Sewall also reveals her determination to pursue truth and to make poems her way. When Thomas Wentworth Higginson, an influential contemporary critic, advised her to write a more polite poetry, less indirect and metaphoric, smoother in rhythm and rhyme, simpler in thought, and less colloquial in idiom, she replied with a poem. Her answer is that although she could have written otherwise, she chose to write as she did.

I cannot dance upon my Toes

I cannot dance upon my Toes—
No Man instructed me—
But oftentimes, among my mind,
A Glee possesseth me,

That had I Ballet knowledge—   5
Would put itself abroad
In Pirouette to blanch a Troupe—
Or lay a Prima, mad,

And though I had no Gown of Gauze—
No ringlet, to my Hair,   10
Nor hopped to Audiences—like Birds,
One claw upon the Air,

Nor tossed my shape in Eider Balls,
Nor rolled on wheels of snow
Till I was out of sight, in sound,   15
The House encore me so—

Nor any know I know the Art
I mention—easy—Here—
Nor any Placard boast me—
It's full as Opera   20

(#326)

Sewall describes how Dickinson's poems reflect her poetic vocation. He demonstrates how basic religious texts such as the Bible and Thomas à Kempis's *The Imitation of Christ* sustained her both spiritually and poetically. Though allowing that Dickinson's decision to cloister herself in her chamber could have had its roots in neurosis, he argues that her firm resolve was motivated by a commitment to the art of poetry akin to the ascetic discipline of religious devotion. In fact, he suggests that one of her more famous poems—one usually interpreted as a love poem—can be read as a dedication to the spiritual or poetic life. It can also be read as a celebration of individual choice.

The Soul selects her own Society

The Soul selects her own Society—
Then—shuts the Door—
To her divine Majority—
Present no more—

Unmoved—she notes the Chariots—pausing—   5
At her low Gate—
Unmoved—an Emperor be kneeling
Upon her Mat—

I've known her—from an ample nation—
Choose One—   10
Then—close the Valves of her attention—
Like Stone—

                                                      (#303)

Sewall's central point about the relationship between Dickinson's life and art is that although we may not be certain which interpretation to favor when considering this and many other poems, we can remain satisfied with our uncertainty because such ambiguity is central to her art. She writes metaphorically, concealing as much as she reveals. As readers we share in apprehending the nature of the experience she describes—in the poem above, the experience of making a decisive choice involving commitment and renunciation. In doing so, however, we also supply specific details from our own lives to render the decision specific and significant. Dickinson's poetry, in other words, conveys the essence of an experience, its heart and core. Her poems, as Sewall aptly notes, do not tell us so much how to live as what it feels like to be alive.

Emily Dickinson's poems do not encompass a wide range of experience; instead they probe deeply into a few of life's major experiences—love, death, doubt, and faith. In examining her experience, Dickinson makes a scrupulous effort to tell the truth, but she tells it "slant." Part of her originality and artistry includes the way she invites us to share in her search for truth. The qualified assertions we frequently find in her poems, their riddles and uncertainties, and their questioning stance demand our participation and response. In considering her representation of intensely felt moments of consciousness, we experience for ourselves her explosive power. And in learning to share Dickinson's acute perceptions and feelings, we also come to understand our own.

EMILY DICKINSON ON HERSELF AND HER FIRST POEMS

Letter to Thomas Higginson

Mr Higginson,

Your kindness claimed earlier gratitude—but I was ill—and write today, from my pillow.

Thank you for the surgery—it was not so painful as I supposed. I bring you others—as you ask—though they might not differ—

While my thought is undressed—I can make the distinction, but when I put them in the Gown—they look alike, and numb.

You asked how old I was? I made no verse—but one or two—until this winter—Sir—

I had a terror—since September—I could tell to none—and so I sing, as the Boy does by the Burying Ground—because I am afraid—You inquire my Books—For Poets—I have Keats—and Mr and Mrs Browning. For Prose—Mr Ruskin—Sir Thomas Browne—and the Revelations. I went to school—but in your manner of the phrase—had no education. When a little Girl, I had a friend, who taught me Immortality—but venturing too near, himself—he never returned—Soon after, my Tutor, died—and for several years, my Lexicon—was my only companion—Then I found one more—but he was not contented I be his scholar—so he left the Land.

You ask of my Companions Hills—Sir—and the Sundown—and a Dog—large as myself, that my Father bought me—They are better than Beings—because they know—but do not tell—and the noise in the Pool, at Noon—excels my Piano. I have a Brother and Sister—My Mother does not care for thought—and Father, too busy with his Briefs—to notice what we do—He buys me many Books—but begs me not to read them—because he fears they joggle the Mind. They are religious—except me—and address an Eclipse, every morning—whom they call their "Father." But I fear my story fatigues you—I would like to learn—Could you tell me how to grow—or is it unconveyed—like Melody—or Witchcraft?

(from a letter to Thomas Wentworth Higginson, April 25, 1862)

CRITICS ON DICKINSON

ALLEN TATE

Dickinson and Knowledge

from *"Emily Dickinson,"* in *Collected Essays*

Dickinson pursues that knowledge wherever it is to be found, no matter how it makes her feel. She reports her pursuit, seemingly as it occurs, with such profound attention that her poems offer exhilaration, no matter how sombre their topic.

To see Dickinson as an epistemological poet, a poet who advances a theory of knowledge in her work, doesn't mean that she is exclusively, or even primarily, an intellectual poet. She was brilliant, well educated, and confident in her use of conceptual, scientific, legal and linguistic terminology, but the truly remarkable quality of mind in her poetry comes from her refusal to separate this mind from the body and emotions which temper it. Dickinson writes close to the traditions of post-Romantic poetry and women's poetry in that her poetry expresses strong emotion. She stands to the side of it to the extent that the drive for knowledge dominates, and the affairs of the heart are seen as part of that knowledge, not separate. Hers is an epistemology of feeling. It is actually quite difficult to locate Dickinson's refusal to sublimate in literary-historical terms, because it is so alien to our usual structuring of dualism. Dickinson has the direct access to emotion which is thought to be—and is—a characteristic of much women's poetry. She doesn't, however, soften those emotions into acceptability or use poetry as an escape, either for herself or for her reader. Perhaps her knowledge has gone unrecognized for just this reason: she doesn't present it as a solution to human loss and pain. Rather, it is a way of experiencing fully and with utmost clarity whatever must be experienced.

Emily Dickinson's poetry runs the full emotive range from ecstatic celebration to numb despair. Huge shifts of perspective, imagery of thresholds, gems, open and closed space, stars, planets and firmaments mark Dickinson's sublime. In a few, very striking, poems she sees both human and writerly desires as capable of fulfilment. Imagery of plentitude—wine, feasting, nectar, flood and luxury—accompanies Dickinson's joyous knowledge. In these poems, her tone is often highly erotic:

> Wild Nights—Wild Nights!
> Were I with thee
> Wild Nights should be
> Our luxury!

As Dickinson would have known, the Latin word *luxus,* from which 'luxury' stems, means sensual excess or debauchery. Her declaration is actually redundant, further emphasizing its ecstatic triumph by the repetition of 'Wild Nights'. It is as if sensuous bliss is a state in which everything means the same thing, which is itself. The second stanza of 'Wild Nights—Wild Nights!' develops this oceanic emotion into a nautical metaphor as Dickinson, somewhat more conventionally, declares that 'Winds' are 'futile' 'To a Heart in port—'. Nor will this mariner need 'Compass' or 'Chart' to guide herself.

The poem's last stanza takes off from this hint of exultant freedom. The sexual beat of the rower's oars gives way to sheer exclamation:

> Rowing in Eden—
> Ah, the Sea!
> Might I but moor—Tonight—
> In Thee!

The last image may look like gender reversal, with the speaker seeing herself as the active partner, but Dickinson isn't concerned with whether or not her ecstasy fits

Victorian convention. The image is one of choosing to be contained by the lover. Mooring tonight is a way of remaining eternally in the oceanic paradise of Eros.

J U D I T H   F A R R

On "Wild Nights"

from *The Passion of Emily Dickinson*

"Wild Nights," its theatrical opening spondees worthy of turbulence and storm, justifies Dickinson's heritage as an admirer of Emily Brontë and *Wuthering Heights.* The seas that separate or unite Charlotte Brontë's heroines and their "masters" also come to mind. Here is a scene reminiscent not only of the intensity of the Brontës' world but also of hundreds of dark canvases by the Hudson River and Luminist painters. Cole's *Tornado in an American Forest* (1835), like his *Expulsion from Eden,* had made the frenzy of storm synonymous with *passio*—distress or love—while seascapes like Fitz Hugh Lane's *Ships and an Approaching Storm off Owl's Head, Maine* (1860) or Heade's *Approaching Storm: Beach Near Newport* (1860) made angry seas expressive of the sea of feeling. Furthermore, Dickinson's image of the rowboat was conceived during the 1860s, when the idea of the lone boat in contest with high seas was particularly popular. There were many studies like Church's *An Old Boat* (1850), in which failure and loss were described by an abandoned rowboat at the edge of brimming, light-filled waters. Whistler expressed *The Sea* (1865) of defeat by picturing a rowboat stranded at the edge of sullen tides. Dickinson's lyrics about the "Edifice of Ocean" with its "tumultuous Rooms" (1217) would find analogues in the vehement seascapes of Winslow Homer, for whom the ocean could also be a metaphor of grandeur and grief. As a favorite nineteenth-century sport, however, rowing on smooth water was described by Thomas Eakins' Luminist paintings: for example, the famous *Max Schmitt in a Single Scull* (1871), which has a serene if rather triste formality.

Having said all this, it is equally important to say that "Wild Nights" is among the most Dickinsonian of the lyrics: ironic, paradoxical, voluptuous, and terse all at once. At first it projects a tumultuous nocturnal seascape, the wildness Nature's. But the next three lines of the first quatrain propose this as a luxury: that is, a rare experience to be enjoyed. Thus the imagined wildness is also human, internal, joyous. The next quatrain, spoken from the vantage point of one who has felt winds, declares how futile they would be in port, at rest, where neither they nor a compass or chart—the scientific instruments of explorers—are needed. By the closing quatrain, the speaker is "Rowing in Eden," her visionary desire having triumphed over the course of a life's voyage. Dickinson may have been remembering Bowles's rowing in Eden and all those betrothed nineteenth-century lovers so often depicted rowing together as one stroke in the same boat. (Thus in chapter 41 of *Little Women,* to give a popular example, Amy and Laurie row their boat "smoothly through the water" opposite Chillon, then decide to marry.) In Eden Dickinson finds a sea of love that is pleasurable, not frightening, and a Thee in which she might safely moor or harbor. Dickinson's inclusion of a sea in Eden, a garden, reminds us that the book of Genesis provides a river in Eden that waters the garden (2:10). (Other poems, such as "My River runs to thee" [162], may be related to her imagery of primal—sexual—waters. That poem was sent in a letter to Mary Bowles in August 1861; but like most of her words to Mary, it was probably intended for her husband.) In *Expulsion from Eden* Cole included a placid lake and a gentle waterfall in his Eden. When Dickinson's first quatrain is taken together with the last in poem 249, however, the reader realizes that she means to "moor" in passion, to luxuriate in wildness. For though hers is a boat that rows rather than rides the waters, her satisfaction in "Wild Nights" comes from strong delight. Even in Eden, she hears the sea. To moor is still to be wild for this prohibited voice that prays "Might I . . ."

ALLEN TATE

On "Because I Could Not Stop for Death"

from "Emily Dickinson" in Collected Essays

If the word "great" means anything in poetry, this poem is one of the greatest in the English language. The rhythm charges with movement the pattern of suspended action back of the poem. Every image is precise and, moreover, not merely beautiful, but fused with the central idea. Every image extends and intensifies every other. The third stanza especially shows Miss Dickinson's power to fuse, into a single order of perception, a heterogeneous series: the children, the grain, and the setting sun (time) have the same degree of credibility; the first subtly preparing for the last. The sharp *gazing* before *grain* instills into nature a cold vitality of which the qualitative richness has infinite depth. The content of death in the poem eludes explicit definition. He is a gentleman taking a lady out for a drive. But note the restraint that keeps the poet from carrying this so far that it becomes ludicrous and incredible; and note the subtly interfused erotic motive, which the idea of death has presented to most romantic poets, love being a symbol interchangeable with death. The terror of death is objectified through this figure of the genteel driver, who is made ironically to serve the end of Immortality. This is the heart of the poem: she has presented a typical Christian theme in its final irresolution, without making any final statements about it. There is no solution to the problem; there can be only a presentation of it in the full context of intellect and feeling. A construction of the human will, elaborated with all the abstracting powers of the mind, is put to the concrete test of experience: the idea of immortality is confronted with the fact of physical disintegration. We are not told what to think; we are told to look at the situation.

The framework of the poem is, in fact, the two abstractions, mortality and eternity, which are made to associate in equality with the images: she sees the ideas, and thinks the perceptions. She did, of course, nothing of the sort; but we must use the logical distinctions, even to the extent of paradox, if we are to form any notion of this rare quality of mind. She could not in the proper sense think at all, and unless we prefer the feeble poetry of moral ideas that flourished in New England in the eighties, we must conclude that her intellectual deficiency contributed at least negatively to her great distinction. Miss Dickinson is probably the only Anglo-American poet of her century whose work exhibits the perfect literary situation—in which is possible the fusion of sensibility and thought. Unlike her contemporaries, she never succumbed to her ideas, to easy solutions, to her private desires. . . .

Neither the feeling nor the style of Miss Dickinson belongs to the seventeenth century; yet between her and Donne there are remarkable ties. Their religious ideas, their abstractions, are momently toppling from the rational plane to the level of perception. The ideas, in fact, are no longer the impersonal religious symbols created anew in the heat of emotion, that we find in poets like Herbert and Vaughan. They have become, for Donne, the terms of personality; they are mingled with the miscellany of sensation. In Miss Dickinson, as in Donne, we may detect a singularly morbid concern, not for religious truth, but for personal revelation. The modern word is self-exploitation. It is egoism grown irresponsible in religion and decadent in morals. In religion it is blasphemy; in society it means usually that culture is not self-contained and sufficient, that the spiritual community is breaking up. This is, along with some other features that do not concern us here, the perfect literary situation.

HELEN MCNEIL

Dickinson's Method

from *Emily Dickinson*

Many Victorian poems describe unexamined abstractions, as if society agreed about what constituted sorrow or love. These could be personified, and their attributes could be listed and elaborated metaphorically. Dickinson takes on a frightening abstraction and evolves its attributes from experience, not tradition. In poetry and philosophy, the subject—the experiencing person—may wonder about the existence of other minds. Dickinson wrote many poems on this problem. In 'Pain—has an Element of Blank,' she contemplates the possibility that there may be circumstances in which the perceiving consciousness also does not exist, erased by its own emotion. 'The Soul has

Bandaged moments—' she begins another poem; the abstract soul is a bandaged body, in a metaphor which denies dualism. Time is also represented physically, bound up by pain. As Dickinson concludes at the end of 'The Soul has Bandaged moments—,' such recognitions 'are not brayed of Tongue—' in the public discourse of her society, or, for that matter, our society either.

Dickinson wrote about feeling, but out of feeling she constructed a theory of knowledge—not *beyond* feeling, or free from it, or in any way separate, but using it as a kind of knowing. In effect—though not in conventional terms—she is an epistemological poet, a poet who advances a theory of knowledge. Dickinson made this concern explicit. After the forms of the verb 'to be,' 'know' is the most frequently used verb in Dickinson's poetry, appearing 230 times, more even than any noun except 'day.'

Dickinson's constant pressure towards knowing means that she can treat even the most tormented situations with great calm. She can begin by writing 'I felt a Funeral, in my Brain,' or 'Pain—has an Element of Blank—' or 'I felt my life with both my hands—' and then proceed to delineate that state with a commanding accuracy. In a manner more resembling the Metaphysical poets than her Victorian contemporaries, male or female, she uses emotionally heightened states as occasions for clarity.

American poetry characteristically embodies acts of process: the Dickinsonian 'process' is passionate investigation. Her investigative process often implies narrative by taking speaker and reader through a sequence of rapidly changing images, even when all the action is interior. These investigations structure Dickinson's poetry; I suspect that the flexibility of her investigative movement is the major reason why Dickinson generally was contented with common metre. She may even have enjoyed the way her condensed discoveries press against the limits of a small form.

THREE POEMS BY EMILY DICKINSON WITH ALTERED PUNCTUATION

After her death, Emily Dickinson's poems were published with their punctuation changed to conform to the conventional usage of the time. Compare these versions with Dickinson's originals in the next section of this chapter.

650

Pain has an element of blank;
It cannot recollect
When it began, or if there were
A day when it was not.

It has no future but itself,
Its infinite realms contain
Its past, enlightened to perceive
New periods of pain.

632

The brain is wider than the sky,
For, put them side by side,
The one the other will include
With ease, and you beside.

The brain is deeper than the sea
For, hold them, blue to blue,
The one the other will absorb,
As sponges, buckets do.

The brain is just the weight of God,
For, lift them, pound for pound,
And they will differ, if they do,
As syllable from sound.

303

The soul selects her own society,
Then shuts the door;
On her divine majority
Obtrude no more.

Unmoved, she notes the chariot's pausing
At her low gate;
Unmoved, an emperor is kneeling
Upon her mat.

I've known her from an ample nation
Choose one;
Then close the valves of her attention
Like stone.

EMILY DICKINSON: POEMS

I'm "wife"—I've finished that

I'm "wife"—I've finished that
That other state—
I'm Czar—I'm "Woman" now—
It's safer so—

How odd the Girl's life looks
Behind this soft Eclipse—
I think that Earth feels so
To folks in Heaven—now—

5

This being comfort—then
That other kind—was pain—
But why compare?
I'm "Wife"! Stop there!

10

(#199, 1860, 1890)

I taste a liquor never brewed

I taste a liquor never brewed—
From Tankards scooped in Pearl—
Not all the Vats upon the Rhine
Yield such an Alcohol!

Inebriate of Air—am I—
And Debauchee of Dew—
Reeling—thro endless summer days—
From inns of Molten Blue—

5

When "Landlords" turn the drunken Bee
Out of the Foxglove's door—
When Butterflies—renounce their "drams"—
I shall but drink the more!

10

Till Seraphs swing their snowy Hats—
And Saints—to windows run—
To see the little Tippler
Leaning against the—Sun—

15

(#214, 1860, 1861)

I like a look of Agony

I like a look of Agony,
Because I know it's true—
Men do not sham Convulsion,
Nor simulate, a Throe—

The Eyes glaze once—and that is Death—
Impossible to feign
The Beads upon the Forehead
By homely Anguish strung.

5

(#241, 1861, 1890)

Wild Nights—Wild Nights!

Wild Nights—Wild Nights!
Were I with thee
Wild Nights should be
Our luxury!

Futile—the Winds— 5
To a Heart in port—
Done with the Compass—
Done with the Chart!

Rowing in Eden—
Ah, the Sea! 10
Might I but moor—Tonight—
In Thee!

(#249, 1861, 1891)

There's a certain Slant of light

There's a certain Slant of light,
Winter Afternoons—
That oppresses, like the Heft
Of Cathedral Tunes—

Heavenly Hurt, it gives us— 5
We can find no scar,
But internal difference,
Where the Meanings, are—

None may teach it—Any—
'Tis the Sea Despair— 10
An imperial affliction
Sent us of the Air—

When it comes, the Landscape listens—
Shadows—hold their breath—
When it goes, 'tis like the Distance 15
On the look of Death—

(#258, 1861, 1890)

I felt a Funeral, in my Brain

I felt a Funeral, in my Brain,
And Mourners to and fro
Kept treading—treading—till it seemed
That Sense was breaking through—

And when they all were seated,   5
A Service, like a Drum—
Kept beating—beating—till I thought
My Mind was going numb—

And I heard them lift a Box
And creak across my Soul   10
With those same Boots of Lead, again,
Then Space—began to toll,

As all the Heavens were a Bell,
And Being, but an Ear,
And I, and Silence, some strange Race   15
Wrecked, solitary, here—

And then a Plank in Reason, broke,
And I dropped down, and down—
And hit a World, at every plunge,
And Finished knowing—then—   20

(#280, 1861, 1896)

Some keep the Sabbath going to Church

Some keep the Sabbath going to Church—
I keep it, staying at Home—
With a Bobolink for a Chorister—
And an Orchard, for a Dome—

Some keep the Sabbath in Surplice—   5
I just wear my Wings—
And instead of tolling the Bell, for Church,
Our little Sexton—sings.

God preaches, a noted Clergyman—
And the sermon is never long,   10
So instead of getting to Heaven, at last—
I'm going, all along.

(#328, 1862, 1891)

After great pain, a formal feeling comes

After great pain, a formal feeling comes—
The Nerves sit ceremonious, like Tombs—
The stiff Heart questions was it He, that bore,
And Yesterday, or Centuries before?

The Feet, mechanical, go round—   5
Of Ground, or Air, or Ought—
A Wooden way
Regardless grown,
A Quartz contentment, like a stone—

This is the Hour of Lead—   10
Remembered, if outlived,
As Freezing persons, recollect the Snow—
First—Chill—then Stupor—then the letting go—

(#341, 1862, 1929)

I dreaded that first Robin, so

I dreaded that first Robin, so,
But He is mastered, now,
I'm some accustomed to Him grown,
He hurts a little, though—

I thought if I could only live   5
Till that first Shout got by—
Not all Pianos in the Woods
Had power to mangle me—

I dared not meet the Daffodils—
For fear their Yellow Gown   10
Would pierce me with a fashion
So foreign to my own—

I wished the Grass would hurry—
So—when 'twas time to see—
He'd be too tall, the tallest one   15
Could stretch—to look at me—

I could not bear the Bees should come,
I wished they'd stay away
In those dim countries where they go,
What word had they, for me?   20

They're here, though; not a creature failed—
No Blossom stayed away
In gentle deference to me—
The Queen of Calvary—

Each one salutes me, as he goes,　　　　　　　　　　　　25
And I, my childish Plumes,
Lift, in bereaved acknowledgment
Of their unthinking Drums—

(#348, 1862, 1891)

We grow accustomed to the Dark

We grow accustomed to the Dark—
When Light is put away—
As when the Neighbor holds the Lamp
To witness her Goodbye—

A Moment—We uncertain step　　　　　　　　　　　　　5
For newness of the night—
Then—fit our Vision to the Dark—
And meet the Road—erect—

And so of larger—Darknesses—
Those Evenings of the Brain—　　　　　　　　　　　　10
When not a Moon disclose a sign—
Or Star—come out—within—

The Bravest—grope a little—
And sometimes hit a Tree
Directly in the Forehead—　　　　　　　　　　　　　　15
But as they learn to see—

Either the Darkness alters—
Or something in the sight
Adjusts itself to Midnight—
And Life steps almost straight.　　　　　　　　　　　20

(#419, 1862, 1935)

Much Madness is divinest Sense

Much Madness is divinest Sense—
To a discerning Eye—
Much Sense—the starkest Madness—

'Tis the Majority
In this, as All, prevail— 5
Assent—and you are sane—
Demur—you're straightway dangerous—
And handled with a Chain—

(#435, 1862, 1935)

I died for Beauty—but was scarce

I died for Beauty—but was scarce
Adjusted in the Tomb
When One who died for Truth, was lain
In an adjoining Room—

He questioned softly "Why I failed?" 5
"For Beauty," I replied—
"And I—for Truth—Themself are One—
We Brethren, are," He said—

And so, as Kinsmen, met a Night—
We talked between the Rooms— 10
Until the Moss had reached our lips—
And covered up—our names—

(#449, 1862, 1890)

I heard a Fly buzz—when I died

I heard a Fly buzz—when I died—
The Stillness in the Room
Was like the Stillness in the Air—
Between the Heaves of Storm—

The Eyes around—had wrung them dry— 5
And Breaths were gathering firm
For that last Onset—when the King
Be witnessed—in the Room—

I willed my Keepsakes—Signed away
What portion of me be 10
Assignable—and then it was
There interposed a Fly—

With Blue—uncertain stumbling Buzz—
Between the light—and me—
And then the Windows failed—and then   15
I could not see to see—

(#465, 1862, 1896)

The Heart asks Pleasure—first

The Heart asks Pleasure—first—
And then—Excuse from Pain—
And then—those little Anodynes
That deaden suffering—

And then—to go to sleep—   5
And then—if it should be
The will of its Inquisition
The privilege to die—

(#536, 1862, 1890)

I like to see it lap the Miles

I like to see it lap the Miles—
And lick the Valleys up—
And stop to feed itself at Tanks—
And then—prodigious step

Around a Pile of Mountains—   5
And supercilious peer
In Shanties—by the sides of Roads—
And then a Quarry pare

To fit its Ribs
And crawl between   10
Complaining all the while
In horrid—hooting stanza—
Then chase itself down Hill—

And neigh like Boanerges—
Then—punctual as a Star   15
Stop—docile and omnipotent
At its own stable door—

(#585, 1862, 1891)

There is a pain—so utter

There is a pain—so utter—
It swallows substance up—
Then covers the Abyss with Trance—
So Memory can step
Around—across—upon it—   5
As one within a Swoon—
Goes safely—where an open eye—
Would drop Him—Bone by Bone.

(#599, 1862, 1929)

632

The Brain—is wider than the Sky—
For—put them side by side—
The one the other will contain
With ease—and You—beside—

The Brain is deeper than the sea—
For—hold them—Blue to Blue—
The one the other will absorb—
As Sponges—Buckets—do—

The Brain is just the weight of God—
For—Heft them—Pound for Pound—
And they will differ—if they do—
As Syllable from Sound—

Pain—has an Element of Blank

Pain—has an Element of Blank—
It cannot recollect
When it begun—or if there were
A time when it was not—

It has no Future—but itself—   5
Its Infinite contain
Its Past—enlightened to perceive
New Periods—of Pain.

(#650, 1862, 1890)

Remorse—is Memory—awake

Remorse—is Memory—awake—
Her Parties all astir—
A Presence of Departed Acts—
At window—and at Door—

Its Past—set down before the Soul   5
And lighted with a Match—
Perusal—to facilitate—
And help Belief to stretch—

Remorse is cureless—the Disease
Not even God—can heal—   10
For 'tis His institution—and
The Adequate of Hell—

(#744, 1863, 1891)

My Life had stood—a Loaded Gun

My Life had stood—a Loaded Gun—
In Corners—till a Day
The Owner passed—identified—
And carried Me away—

And now We roam in Sovereign Woods—   5
And now We hunt the Doe—
And every time I speak for Him—
The Mountains straight reply—

And do I smile, such cordial light
Upon the Valley glow—   10
It is as a Vesuvian face
Had let its pleasure through—

And when at Night—Our good Day done—
I guard My Master's Head—
'Tis better than the Eider-Duck's   15
Deep Pillow—to have shared—

To foe of His—I'm deadly foe—
None stir the second time—
On whom I lay a Yellow Eye—
Or an emphatic Thumb—   20

Though I than He—may longer live
He longer must—than I—
For I have but the power to kill,
Without—the power to die—

(#754, 1863, 1929)

A narrow Fellow in the Grass

A narrow Fellow in the Grass
Occasionally rides—
You may have met Him—did you not
His notice sudden is—

The Grass divides as with a Comb—   5
A spotted shaft is seen—
And then it closes at your feet
And opens further on—

He likes a Boggy Acre
A floor too cool for Corn—   10
Yet when a Boy, and Barefoot—
I more than once at Noon
Have passed, I thought, a Whip lash
Unbraiding in the Sun
When stooping to secure it   15
It wrinkled, and was gone—

Several of Nature's People
I know, and they know me—
I feel for them a transport
Of cordiality—   20

But never met this Fellow
Attended, or alone
Without a tighter breathing
And Zero at the Bone—

(#986, 1865, 1866)

Further in Summer than the Birds

Further in Summer than the Birds
Pathetic from the Grass
A minor Nation celebrates
Its unobtrusive Mass.

No Ordinance be seen   5
So gradual the Grace
A pensive Custom it becomes
Enlarging Loneliness.

Antiquest felt at Noon
When August burning low   10
Arise this spectral Canticle
Repose to typify

Remit as yet no Grace
No Furrow on the Glow
Yet a Druidic Difference   15
Enhances Nature now

                                        (#1068, 1866, 1891)

The Bustle in a House

The Bustle in a House
The Morning after Death
Is solemnest of industries
Enacted upon Earth—

The Sweeping up the Heart   5
And putting Love away
We shall not want to use again
Until Eternity.

                                        (#1078, 1866, 1890)

The last Night that She lived

The last Night that She lived
It was a Common Night
Except the Dying—this to Us
Made Nature different

We noticed smallest things—   5
Things overlooked before
By this great light upon our Minds
Italicized—as 'twere.

As We went out and in
Between Her final Room   10
And Rooms where Those to be alive
Tomorrow were, a Blame

That Others could exist
While She must finish quite
A Jealousy for Her arose   15
So nearly infinite—

We waited while She passed—
It was a narrow time—
Too jostled were Our Souls to speak
At length the notice came.   20

She mentioned, and forgot—
Then lightly as a Reed
Bent to the Water, struggled scarce—
Consented, and was dead—

And We—We placed the Hair—   25
And drew the Head erect—
And then an awful leisure was
Belief to regulate—

                                        (#1100, 1866, 1890)

Tell all the Truth but tell it slant

Tell all the Truth but tell it slant—
Success in Circuit lies
Too bright for our infirm Delight
The Truth's superb surprise

As Lightning to the Children eased   5
With explanation kind
The Truth must dazzle gradually
Or every man be blind—

                                        (#1129, 1868, 1945)

A Route of Evanescence

A Route of Evanescence
With a revolving Wheel—
A Resonance of Emerald—
A Rush of Cochineal—
And every Blossom on the Bush   5
Adjusts its tumbled Head—
The mail from Tunis, probably,
An easy Morning's Ride—

(#1463, 1879, 1891)

Apparently with no surprise

Apparently with no surprise
To any happy Flower
The Frost beheads it at its play—
In accidental power—
The blonde Assassin passes on—   5
The Sun proceeds unmoved
To measure off another Day
For an Approving God.

(#1624, 1884, 1890)

My life closed twice before its close

My life closed twice before its close—
It yet remains to see
If Immortality unveil
A third event to me

So huge, so hopeless to conceive   5
As these that twice befell.
Parting is all we know of heaven,
And all we need of hell.

(#1732, 1896)

INTRODUCTION TO ROBERT FROST

[1874–1963]

Like Walt Whitman before him, Robert Frost yearned to become America's foremost poet. Aiming for both critical and popular acclaim, Frost hoped to achieve recognition as a major poet and to reach the widest possible audience. And although he did succeed in becoming a popular poet (perhaps the most popular in America's history), in the minds of some readers his very popularity diminished his critical stature. Frost himself, however, was partly responsible for this. The image he projected—folksy, lovable, homespun—undercut his reputation as a major poet. Even today, with Frost's poetic stature widely acknowledged, he is occasionally seen as a less serious, less impressive, less demanding, and hence less important poet than his contemporaries Ezra Pound, T. S. Eliot, and Wallace Stevens.

There is a measure of truth in this assessment, perhaps, but only a small measure. Frost's poems are easier to read than those of Pound, Eliot, or Stevens: his familiar vocabulary and traditional forms enhance their accessibility. But his poems are neither simple nor easy to understand. Their diction is more richly allusive and connotative than at first may appear. Their paraphrasable thought is subtler and more profound than an initial reading might suggest. Moreover, their form, though traditional, is more intricately wrought and more decisively experimental than is generally recognized. Before turning to consider these claims, we should be aware of the course of Frost's poetic career, particularly of his popularity as an honored national poet, who, ironically, was first recognized abroad rather than at home.

Although Robert Frost is considered a New England farmer-poet who captures in his verse the tang of Yankee speech, he was born in San Francisco and lived there until the age of eleven, when his family moved to Lawrence, Massachusetts. He attended high school in Lawrence and was covaledictorian of his graduating class with Elinor White, whom he later married. Frost continued his education at Dartmouth College, where he remained for only one term, and later at Harvard University, where he studied for two years without taking a degree. After working at a succession of odd jobs including farming and factory work, Frost taught at Pinkerton Academy, where from 1906 to 1910 he reformed the English syllabus, directed theatrical productions, and wrote many of the poems later included in his first book, *A Boy's Will.*

In 1911, in an attempt to attract the attention of prominent and influential members in the literary world, he sold his farm in Derry, New Hampshire, and moved with his family to England. There he met and received the support of Ezra Pound, who helped secure publication of his first two volumes of poems, and of Edward Thomas, who reviewed them perceptively. Having launched his career, Frost returned to America in 1915 and quickly secured an American publisher—Henry Holt and Co.—for the two books published in England, *A Boy's Will* (1913) and *North of Boston* (1914), and for subsequent volumes as well. With the publication in 1916 of *Mountain Interval,* Frost's fame grew. In 1917, and periodically thereafter, he was poet in residence at Amherst College and served in a similar capacity at various other colleges and universities including Dartmouth, Wesleyan, Michigan, Harvard, and Yale. Frost received awards and prizes, among them the Bollingen Poetry Prize (1963) and four Pulitzer Prizes (1924, 1931, 1937, and 1943). In addition many honorary degrees, including ones from Oxford and Cambridge universities, were conferred on him. Although Frost was fond of joking that he could make a blanket of the many academic hoods he had acquired, he valued them, particularly those from the British institutions. Later in his life Frost was appointed goodwill emissary to South America and the Soviet Union. At the time he was also the only American poet honored with an invitation to read his work at a presidential inauguration. In January 1961, at the inauguration of John F. Kennedy, Frost read "The Gift Outright" and another poem he had composed for the occasion.

This brief summary of Frost's career, however, oversimplifies what was in reality a more complex and arduous process. Initially an obscure writer, Frost experienced difficulty in breaking into print in a significant way. He later struggled with the decline of his poetic powers, most of his best work having been produced when he was younger. And more tragically, he suffered the deaths of his wife and three of his children, one of whom committed suicide. He also saw his sister and one of his daughters succumb to mental illness. And finally, despite his many prizes and awards, Frost was bitter that he never won a Nobel Prize. He died in 1963, two weeks short of his eighty-ninth birthday.

What accounts for Frost's fame and popularity? Three things, at least: his shrewd management of his career, including the cultivation of his poetic image; his use of familiar subjects, especially the natural world and people engaged in recognizable activities; and his accessible language and apparent simplicity of thought. From the beginning, Frost skillfully managed his poetic career, going abroad to England to win the approval of the prominent poets and critics of his day. Frost, of course, did not plan every step of his rise to fame; rather he trusted to his highly developed instinct for sizing up opportunities and capitalizing on them. As William Pritchard explains in *Robert Frost: A Literary Life Reconsidered,* Frost retrospectively structured his literary life as one of adversity overcome. The most important aspect of this biographical semifictionalizing was Frost's portrayal of himself as a literary exile unappreciated in his home country. Allied with this biographical mythmaking was Frost's control over his public image. He refused, for example, to read his darker, more skeptical poems in public, preferring instead to reveal his more congenial, folksy side. And he carefully masked from public exposure his hunger for fame and an occasional nasty denigration of those poets he considered his strongest rivals.

More important to his popularity than his masterly manipulation of his public persona, however, is the readability of his poetry. Frost avoids obscure language, preferring the familiar word and the idiomatic phrase. He also shuns foreign words and shies away from all but the scantiest of references to economic, literary, and political history. And instead of the structural openness, fragmentation, and discontinuity favored by some of his contemporaries, Frost used traditional poetic forms characterized by coherence and continuity.

That Frost's poems are relatively easy to read does not mean that they are necessarily easy to understand. Frost is a master of concealment, of saying one thing in terms of another, and especially of saying two or more things simultaneously. Even his most accessible poems such as "Birches," "Mending Wall," and "The Road Not Taken" contain clear invitations to consider their symbolic ramifications. The symbolic nature of these poems doesn't manifest itself immediately. To appreciate the fullness of Frost's achievement, we need to read with attention to their symbolic detail, whether we are reading the meditative blank verse of "Birches" or "Mending Wall" or the lyrical descriptions of "Desert Places" or "Stopping by Woods on a Snowy Evening."

It is also a mistake to assume, on the basis of a familiarity with a few of Frost's more famous lyrics, that his poetry lacks either drama or humor. "Departmental" reveals Frost's humorous side, while "Home Burial" shows him at work in a longer, more dramatic form. Though his poems are certainly serious, they are not solemn. This is as true of "Stopping by Woods" and "The Road Not Taken" as it is for "The Silken Tent," a witty extended comparison between a woman and a pitched tent; "Provide, Provide," a pragmatic set of admonitions about how to get on in the world; and "A Considerable Speck," a satirical jab at human limitations, particularly the performances of writers. Moreover, Frost himself warned us against taking him too seriously. Although we cannot completely trust him in such matters since he enjoyed teasing his audiences, we can at least regard his work as a mixture of playfulness and seriousness. "If it is with outer seriousness," he once remarked, "it must with inner humor; if with inner seriousness, then with outer humor."

Complicating matters further is Frost's view of nature. More often than not, nature appears as a powerful, dangerous, and cruel force, its purpose and design not immediately apparent. Frost avoids a simple representation of the relationship between the natural and human worlds. He does not share Emerson's belief in nature as a moral teacher. He does not believe, for example, that in reading nature we discover moral and spiritual truths. That romantic view is questioned in poems like "Desert Places" and "The Most of It," where nature seems to express "nothing" to the human observer. Yet other poems, such as "The Tuft of Flowers" and "Two Look at Two," are entirely compatible with Emersonian and Whitmanesque transcendentalist ideas, in which nature and man form part of a harmonious whole.

Frost's response to nature is, essentially, to wonder skeptically just how much "meaning" in nature there really is for human beings. A poem like "Tree at My Window" explores this issue. In the first part of the poem, there seems to be a definite connection between nature (trees) and people; the human and the natural worlds intersect. But the last stanza suggests that there are radical differences between the two worlds, differences that separate them more than their similarities bind them.

The complexity and richness of Frost's vision of nature are paralleled by the subtlety of his technical achievement. Though he worked in traditional forms—sonnet, heroic couplet, blank verse, four-line stanza—the effects he wrought in them are remarkable for their range and versatility. To take just one example, consider his sonnets, which include poems in both of the traditional forms,

Shakespearean and Petrarchan. "Putting in the Seed" is constructed according to the Shakespearean, or English, pattern with three quatrains and a concluding couplet (though Frost alters the rhyme pattern slightly). "Design" follows the Petrarchan model: an octave of eight lines followed by a sestet of six. The octave of "Design" describes a natural scene (a white spider finding on a white flower a white moth that it kills and devours). The sestet explores the significance of the event. Though conventional in logical organization, "Design" exhibits a variation from the Petrarchan rhyme scheme: *abba abba cde cde* (or *cd cd cd*). Frost's poem uses only three rhymes throughout both octave and sestet: *abba abba acc caa*.

Frost's sonnets often diverge in some way from the traditional sonnet and thus make something new and fresh of the form. "Mowing," for example, while composed according to the Petrarchan structure, contains a strong concluding couplet more characteristic of the Shakespearean sonnet. It also varies from the rhyme scheme of both traditional patterns, though using the same number of different sounds as the Shakespearean form: *abca bdec dfeg fg*. The poem displays a curious use of overlapping sound effects that Frost worked out more elaborately and systematically in other lyrics. Other sonnet variations appear in "The Silken Tent," which is constructed as a single sentence spun out over the fourteen lines in a Shakespearean pattern. Working against that rhyme scheme, however, is a logical structure more characteristic of the Petrarchan division into two major sections, with a turn at the ninth line. Such hybrid sonnets are accompanied by other sonnet experiments such as "Once by the Pacific," in seven couplets rhyming *aa bb cc dd ee ff gg,* and "Acquainted with the Night," composed in the interlocking rhymes of *terza rima: aba bcb cdc ded ee.*

Frost was a skilled wordsmith who cared about the sounds of his sentences. He noted more than once how "the sentence sound says more than the words"; how "tones of voice" can "mean more than words." In such voice tones Frost heard the sounds of sense and captured them in his verse, heightening their expressiveness by combining the inflections of ordinary speech with the measured regularity of meter. Because Frost's achievement in this regard surpasses that of most other modern American poets, we should be particularly attentive to the way he makes poetry out of the spoken word. His poems often mask the most elegant and subtle of his technical accomplishments. Perhaps the best way to read Frost's poems is to approach them as performances, as poetic acts of skillful daring, of risks taken, of technical dangers overcome. In doing so we may share the pleasure Frost took in poetic performance. In addition, we can see how Frost's poetry often "begins in delight and ends in wisdom," offering along the way what he called "a momentary stay against confusion."

CRITICAL COMMENTS BY FROST

from *The Figure a Poem Makes*

The figure a poem makes. It begins in delight and ends in wisdom. The figure is the same as for love. No one can really hold that the ecstasy should be static and stand still in one place. It begins in delight, it inclines to the impulse, it assumes direction with the first line laid down, it runs a course of lucky events, and ends in a clarification of life—not necessarily a great clarification, such as sects and cults are founded on, but in a momentary stay against confusion. It has denouement. It has an outcome that though unforeseen was predestined from the first image of the original mood—and indeed from the very mood. It is but a trick poem and no poem at all if the best of it was thought of first and saved for the last. It finds its own name as it goes and discovers the best waiting for it in some final phrase at once wise and sad—the happy-sad blend of the drinking song.

No tears in the writer, no tears in the reader. No surprise for the writer, no surprise for the reader. For me the initial delight is in the surprise of remembering something I didn't know I knew. I am in a place, in a situation, as if I had materialized from cloud or risen out of the ground. There is a glad recognition of the long lost and the rest follows. Step by step the wonder of unexpected supply keeps growing. The impressions most useful to my purpose seem always those I was unaware of and so made no note of at the time when taken, and the conclusion is come to that like giants we are always hurling experience ahead of us to pave the future with against the day when we may want to strike a line of purpose across it for somewhere. The line will have the more charm for not being mechanically straight. We enjoy the straight crookedness of a good walking stick. Modern instruments of precision are being used to make things crooked as if by eye and hand in the old days. . . .

More than once I should have lost my soul to radicalism if it had been the originality it was mistaken for by its young converts. Originality and initiative are what I ask for my country. For myself the originality need be no more than the freshness of a poem run in the way I have described: from delight to wisdom. The figure is the same as for love. Like a piece of ice on a hot stove the poem must ride on its own melting. A poem may be worked over once it is in being, but may not be worried into being. Its most previous quality will remain its having run itself and carried away the poet with it. Read it a hundred times: it will forever keep its freshness as a metal keeps its fragrance. It can never lose its sense of a meaning that once unfolded by surprise as it went.

from *"The Constant Symbol"*

I give you a new definition of a sentence:

A sentence is a sound in itself on which other sounds called words may be strung.

You may string words together without a sentence-sound to string them on just as you may tie clothes together by the sleeves and stretch them without a clothes line between two trees, but—it is bad for the clothes.

The number of words you may string on one sentence-sound is not fixed but there is always danger of overloading.

The sentence-sounds are very definite entities. (This is no literary mysticism I am preaching.) They are as definite as words. It is not impossible that they could be collected in a book though I don't at present see on what system they would be catalogued.

They are apprehended by the ear. They are gathered by the ear from the vernacular and brought into books. Many of them are already familiar to us in books. I think no writer invents them. The most original writer only catches them fresh from talk, where they grow spontaneously.

A man is all a writer if *all* his words are strung on definite recognizable sentence sounds. The voice of the imagination, the speaking voice must know certainly how to behave how to posture in every sentence he offers.

A man is a marked writer if his words are largely strung on the more striking sentence sounds.

A word about recognition: In literature it is our business to give people the thing that will make them say, "Oh yes I know what you mean." It is never to tell them something they don't know, but something they know and hadn't thought of saying. It must be something they recognize. . . .

The sentence as a sound in itself apart from the word sounds is no mere figure of speech. I shall show the sentence sound saying all that the sentence conveys with little or no help from the meaning of the words. I shall show the sentence sound opposing the sense of the words as in irony. And so till I establish the distinction between the grammatical sentence and the vital sentence. The grammatical sentence is merely accessory to the other and chiefly valuable as furnishing a clue to the other. You recognize the sentence sound in this: *You,* you—! It is so strong that if you hear it as I do you have to pronounce the two you's differently. Just so many sentence sounds belong to man as just so many vocal runs belong to one kind of bird. We come into the world with them and create none of them.

There are many other things I have found myself saying about poetry, but the chiefest of these is that it is metaphor, saying one thing and meaning another, saying one thing in terms of another, the pleasure of ulteriority. Poetry is simply made of metaphor. So also is philosophy—and science, too, for that matter, if it will take the soft impeachment from a friend. Every poem is a new metaphor inside or it is nothing. And there is a sense in which all poems are the same old metaphor always.

from *"The Unmade Word, Or Fetching and Far-Fetching"*

There are two kinds of language: the spoken language and the written language—our everyday speech which we call the vernacular; and a more literary, sophisticated, artificial, elegant language that belongs to books. We often hear it said that a man talks like a book in this second way. We object to anybody's talking in this literary, artificial English; we don't object to anybody's writing in it; we rather expect people to write in a literary, somewhat artificial style. I, myself, could get along very well without this bookish language altogether. I agree with the poet who visited this country not long ago when he said that all our literature has got to come down, sooner or later, to the talk of everyday life. William Butler Yeats says that all our words, phrases, and idioms to be effective must be in the manner of everyday speech.

We've got to come down to this speech of everyday, to begin with—the hard everyday word of the street, business, trades, work in summer—to begin with; but there is some sort of obligation laid on us, to lift the words of every day, to give them a metaphorical turn. No, you don't want to use that term—give the words a poetic touch. I'll show you what I mean by an example: take for example the word "lemon," that's a good practical word with no literary associations—a word that you use with the grocer and in the kitchen; it has no literary associations at all; "Peach" is another one; but you boys have taken these two words and given them a poetic twist.

CRITICS ON FROST

NORMAN HOLLAND

Reading Frost

from *The Brain of Robert Frost*

We can explore the workings of Frost's brain—or mind—through one of his better-known poems, "Once by the Pacific" [see page 578 of this text]. I think this poem had at the core of its creation a widespread and well-known childhood fear. I find it of particular interest therefore, because it allows us to see how Frost defended himself against fears we may well have experienced ourselves. As I put the poem together for myself, I respond most immediately to its violence, to words like "rage," "din," or the menacing phrase, "dark intent." The first substantial word I hear is "shattered" and the final rhyme is "broken," although, to be sure, it is only "water" that is shattered and broken, a water that is (ironically) "Pacific"—peaceful.

This night is unique: the waves "thought of doing something to the shore/That water never did to land before." And immense. I imagine huge dimensions from phrases like "great waves," "ocean-water," or words like "land," "continent," or (in time) "an age." I find these sizes made still bigger by a pattern of buttressing, doubling, and increasing. The shore is backed by cliff, and the cliff is backed by continent. "There would be *more* than ocean-water broken." Waves looked over *other* waves. This was not just a night, but an age. And finally, the poem, having begun with the storm, ends with God and the Last Judgment, a final doubling, a bigness bigger than even waves and continent, an immensity of words called forth by words. In reciting this poem, one of the critics recalls, Frost would drop into a deep voice for God's words at the end.

I hear about a "misty din," and waves think of "doing something." "Someone had better be prepared." I get a feeling of indefiniteness from these phrases. "You could not tell" exactly, but you surmise a "dark intent." "More than ocean-water" would be broken—but what? "Something," Stanley Burnshaw points out, is "the most significant single word in the poems." It occurs 137 times in the Frost canon, "someone" 77 times, and "somehow" 8 times. They are all part of what Frost called in an essay of his, "Extravagance," the going beyond domestic boundaries to find something wild and, here, ominous.

"Someone" is going to be a victim, and in "some*one*," I find yet another tendency, one that works along with the vagueness, namely, personification. Frost gives the whole scene human attributes. The sea "looked" and "thought." The night has an "intent," and the land is "lucky" because it is backed by other land. One critic, Judith P. Saunders, is "amused to see waves and clouds endowed with the motives and appearance of stock villains in a Grade B movie." Most see it as beginning ominously and becoming still more ominous.

One would think that personification would counter the sense of indefiniteness, but somehow, in my mind, at any rate, it makes it still more ominous: the people are huge and vague and therefore all the more menacing. Intimations of warring personalities reach a height for me in lines 6 and 7, when the poem pivots from "the gleam of eyes" associated with the skies to a direct "you." It is as if the interpersonal conflict comes about precisely because *you looked*. Finally, at the end of the poem, there is God who seems to be both the instigator of violence and the one who puts an end to it. Possibly, C. Hines Edwards suggests, Blake's picture of God inspired Frost's imagining here. . . .

Here, it seems to me, we are coming very close to the nature of Frost's creativity as a poet, perhaps the creativity of all poets. Language occupies a special, pivotal place in Frost's psychic economy. He can use words two ways: to call up the kind of thing he most fears (being overpowered, unmanned, unselved, fused into another) and to manage that same fantasy. He can use words both to evoke a fantasy that feels particularly dangerous to him and to limit that same fantasy. To the extent we can re-create in our own terms our equivalent for that fearful fantasy and manage it using *his* words (because we share Frost's language), we say his poem succeeds. We award its author the accolade of "creativity."

In effect, language serves Frost as an agent both of fantasy and of mastery. In "Once by the Pacific," he uses a poetic form that resembles a familiar defense mechanism: projection. He starts with a storm, but it turns out to be more than a storm. In this poem, he starts with a wall but it turns out not to be "just a wall." In both instances, his language enables him and us to build a process of projection: "something" doesn't like the wall; its gaps have a mysterious quality ("No one has seen them made or heard them made"); it seems to be engaged in a struggle between human beings (as the high waves by the Pacific were). In effect, Frost's language projects (in a paranoid way that probably accounts for the faint *frisson* I feel at this poem) human attributes onto the inanimate world. His words put the dangerous wishes and fears within himself out into the world around him. Then his poem explores those mental states in the guise of physically dealing with the actualities of a New England farm or the San Francisco coast.

WILLIAM PRITCHARD

On "Stopping by Woods"

from *Robert Frost: A Literary Life Reconsidered*

With respect to his most anthologized poem, "Stopping by Woods . . ." which he called "my best bid for remembrance," such "feats" are seen in its rhyme scheme, with the third unrhyming line in each of the first three stanzas becoming the rhyme word of each succeeding stanza until the last one, all of whose end words rhyme and whose final couplet consists of a repeated "And miles to go before I sleep." Or they can be heard in the movement of the last two lines of stanza three:

> He gives his harness bells a shake
> To ask if there is some mistake.
> The only other sound's the sweep
> Of easy wind and downy flake.

As with "Her early leaf's a flower," the contraction effortlessly carries us along into "the sweep/Of easy wind" so that we arrive at the end almost without knowing it.

Discussion of this poem has usually concerned itself with matters of "content" or meaning (What do the woods represent? Is this a poem in which suicide is contemplated?). Frost, accordingly, as he continued to read it in public made fun of efforts to draw out or fix its meaning as something large and impressive, something to do with man's existential loneliness or other ultimate matters. Perhaps because of these efforts, and on at least one occasion—his last appearance in 1962 at the Ford Forum in Boston—he told his audience that the thing which had given him most pleasure in composing the poem was the effortless sound of that couplet about the horse and what it does when stopped by the woods: "He gives his harness bells a shake / To ask if there is some mistake." We might guess that he held these lines up for admiration because they are probably the hardest ones in the poem out of which to make anything significant: regular in their iambic rhythm and suggesting nothing more than they assert, they establish a sound against which the "other sound" of the following lines can, by contrast, make itself heard. Frost's fondness for this couplet suggests that however much he cared about the "larger" issues or questions which "Stopping by Woods . . ." raises and provokes, he wanted to direct his readers away from solemnly debating them; instead he invited them simply to be pleased with how he had put it. He was to say later on about Edwin Arlington Robinson something which could more naturally have been said about himself—that his life as a poet was "a revel in the felicities of labguage." "Stopping by Woods . . . " can be appreciated only by removing it from its pedestal and noting how it is a miniature revel in such felicities.

RICHARD POIRIER

On "Stopping by Woods on a Snowy Evening"

from *Robert Frost: The Work of Knowing*

As its opening words suggest—"Whose woods these are I think I know"—["Stopping by Woods on a Snowy Evening"] is a poem concerned with ownership and also with someone who cannot be or does not choose to be very emphatic even about owning himself. He does not want or expect to be seen. And his reason, aside from being on someone else's property, is that it would apparently be out of character for him to be there, communing alone with a woods fast filling up with snow. He is, after all, a man of business who has promised his time, his future to other people. It would appear that he is not only a scheduled man but a fairly convivial one. He knows who owns which parcels of land, or thinks he does, and his language has a sort of pleasant neighborliness, as in the phrase "stopping by." It is no wonder that his little horse would think his actions "queer" or that he would let the horse, instead of himself, take responsibility for the judgment. He is in danger of losing himself; and his language by the end of the third stanza begins to carry hints of a seductive luxuriousness unlike anything preceding it—"Easy wind and downy flake . . . lovely, dark and deep." Even before the somnolent repetition of the last two lines, he is ready to drop off. His opening question about who owns the woods becomes, because of the very absence from the poem of any man "too exactly himself," a question of whether the woods are to "own" him. With the drowsy repetitiousness of rhymes in the last stanza, four in a row, it takes some optimism to be sure that (thanks mostly to his little horse, who makes the only assertive sound in the poem) he will be able to keep his promises. At issue, of course, is really whether or not he will be able to "keep" his life.

RICHARD POIRIER

On "Mending Wall"

from *Robert Frost: The Work of Knowing*

The limits, boundaries, or customs which define a "home," a personal property, are often taken, that is, as an occasion for freedom rather than for confinement. The real significance of the famous poem "Mending Wall" is that it suggests how much for Frost freedom is contingent upon some degree of restriction. More specifically, it can be said that restrictions, or forms, are a precondition for expression. Without them, even nature ceases to offer itself up for a reading. Forms of any sort have been so overwhelmed in "Desert Places," for example, that the prospect is for "a blanker whiteness of benighted snow / With no expression, nothing to express," the world as a blank sheet of paper enveloped in darkness.

Natural forces in "Mending Wall," having each year to encounter the human imposition of a freshly repaired wall, tend to become expressive in a quite selective way. Whatever it is "that doesn't love a wall," "*sends* the frozen-ground-swell under it/And *spills* the upper boulders in the sun, / And *makes* gaps even two can pass abreast" (my italics). More important, this active response to human structurings prompts a counterresponse and activity from people who are committed to the making and remaking of those structures. And who are such people? The point usually missed, along with most other things importantly at work in this poem, is that it is not the neighbor, described as "an old-stone savage armed," a man who can only dully repeat, "Good fences make good neighbors"—that it is not he who initiates the fence-making. Rather it is the far more spirited, lively, and "mischievous" speaker of the poem. While admitting that they do not need the wall, it is he who each year "lets my neighbor know beyond the hill" that it is time to do the job anyway, and who will go out alone to fill the gaps made in the wall by hunters: "I have come after them and made repairs / When they have left not one stone on a stone." Though the speaker may or may not think that good neighbors are made by good fences, it is abundantly clear that he likes the yearly ritual, the yearly "outdoor game" by which fences are made. Because if fences do not "make good neighbors" the *"making"* of fences can. More is "made" in this "outdoor game" than fences. The two men also "make" talk, or at least that is what the speaker tries to do as against the reiterated assertions of his companion, which are as heavy and limited as the wall itself. So hopeless is this speaker of any response, that all his talk may be only to himself. He is looking for some acknowledgment of those forces at work which are impatient of convention and of merely repeated forms; but he is looking in vain.

YVOR WINTERS

Robert Frost: Or, the Spiritual Drifter as Poet

from *The Function of Criticism*

Frost writes of rural subjects, and the American reader of our time has an affection for rural subjects which is partly the product of the Romantic sentimentalization of "nature," but which is partly also a nostalgic looking back to the rural life which predominated in this nation a generation or two ago; the rural life is somehow regarded as the truly American life. I have no objection to the poet's employing rural settings; but we should remember that it is the poet's business to evaluate human experience, and the rural setting is no more valuable for this purpose than any other or than no particular setting, and one could argue with some plausibility that an exclusive concentration on it may be limiting.

Frost early began his endeavor to make his style approximate as closely as possible the style of conversation, and this endeavor has added to his reputation: it has helped to make him seem "natural." But poetry is not conversation, and I see no reason why poetry should be called upon to imitate conversation. Conversation is the most careless and formless of human utterance; it is spontaneous and unrevised, and its vocabulary is commonly limited. Poetry is the most difficult form of human utterance; we revise poems carefully in order to make them more nearly perfect. The two forms of expression are extremes, they are not close to each other. We do not praise a violinist for playing as if he were improvising; we praise him for playing well. And when a man plays well or writes well, his audience must have intelligence, training, and patience in order to appreciate him. We do not understand difficult matters "naturally." . . .

Frost, as far as we have examined him, then, is a poet who holds the following views: he believes that impulse is trustworthy and reason contemptible, that formative decisions should be made casually and passively, that the individual should retreat from cooperative action with his kind, should retreat not to engage in intellectual activity but in order to protect himself from the contamination of outside influence, that affairs manage themselves for the best if left alone, that ideas of good and evil need not be taken very seriously. These views are sure to be a hindrance to self-development, and they effectually cut Frost off from any really profound understanding of human experience, whether political, moral, metaphysical, or religious. The result in the didactic poems is the perversity and incoherence of thought; the result in the narrative poems is either slightness of subject or a flat and uninteresting apprehension of the subject; the result in the symbolic lyrics is a disturbing dislocation between the descriptive surface, which is frequently lovely, and the ultimate meaning, which is usually sentimental and unacceptable. The result in nearly all the poems is a measure of carelessness in the style, sometimes small and sometimes great, but usually evident: the conversational manner will naturally suit a poet who takes all experience so casually, and it is only natural that the conversational manner should often become very conversational indeed.

ROBERT FROST: POEMS

Mowing

There was never a sound beside the wood but one,
And that was my long scythe whispering to the ground.
What was it it whispered? I knew not well myself;
Perhaps it was something about the heat of the sun,
Something, perhaps, about the lack of sound—   5
And that was why it whispered and did not speak.
It was no dream of the gift of idle hours,
Or easy gold at the hand of fay or elf:
Anything more than the truth would have seemed too weak
To the earnest love that laid the swale in rows,   10
Not without feeble-pointed spikes of flowers
(Pale orchises), and scared a bright green snake.
The fact is the sweetest dream that labor knows.
My long scythe whispered and left the hay to make.

                                                                    (1913)

The Tuft of Flowers

I went to turn the grass once after one
Who mowed it in the dew before the sun.

The dew was gone that made his blade so keen
Before I came to view the leveled scene.

I looked for him behind an isle of trees;   5
I listened for his whetstone in the breeze.

But he had gone his way, the grass all mown,
And I must be, as he had been,—alone,

"As all must be," I said within my heart,
"Whether they work together or apart."   10

But as I said it, swift there passed me by
On noiseless wing a bewildered butterfly,

Seeking with memories grown dim o'er night
Some resting flower of yesterday's delight.

And once I marked his flight go round and round,   15
As where some flower lay withering on the ground.

And then he flew as far as eye could see,
And then on tremulous wing came back to me.

I thought of questions that have no reply,
And would have turned to toss the grass to dry;   20

But he turned first, and led my eye to look
At a tall tuft of flowers beside a brook,

A leaping tongue of bloom the scythe had spared
Beside a reedy brook the scythe had bared.

The mower in the dew had loved them thus,   25
By leaving them to flourish, not for us,

Nor yet to draw one thought of ours to him,
But from sheer morning gladness at the brim.

The butterfly and I had lit upon,
Nevertheless, a message from the dawn,   30

That made me hear the wakening birds around,
And hear his long scythe whispering to the ground,

And feel a spirit kindred to my own;
So that henceforth I worked no more alone;

But glad with him, I worked as with his aid,   35
And weary, sought at noon with him the shade;

And dreaming, as it were, held brotherly speech
With one whose thought I had not hoped to reach.

"Men work together," I told him from the heart,
"Whether they work together or apart."   40

(1913)

Mending Wall

Something there is that doesn't love a wall,
That sends the frozen-ground-swell under it,
And spills the upper boulders in the sun;
And makes gaps even two can pass abreast.
The work of hunters is another thing: 5
I have come after them and made repair
Where they have left not one stone on a stone,
But they would have the rabbit out of hiding,
To please the yelping dogs. The gaps I mean,
No one has seen them made or heard them made,   10
But at spring mending-time we find them there.
I let my neighbor know beyond the hill;
And on a day we meet to walk the line
And set the wall between us once again.
We keep the wall between us as we go.   15
To each the boulders that have fallen to each.
And some are loaves and some so nearly balls
We have to use a spell to make them balance:
"Stay where you are until our backs are turned!"
We wear our fingers rough with handling them.   20
Oh, just another kind of outdoor game,
One on a side. It comes to little more:
There where it is we do not need the wall:
He is all pine and I am apple orchard.
My apple trees will never get across   25
And eat the cones under his pines, I tell him.
He only says, "Good fences make good neighbors."
Spring is the mischief in me, and I wonder
If I could put a notion in his head:
"*Why* do they make good neighbors? Isn't it   30
Where there are cows? But here there are no cows.
Before I built a wall I'd ask to know
What I was walling in or walling out,
And to whom I was like to give offense.
Something there is that doesn't love a wall,   35
That wants it down." I could say "Elves" to him,
But it's not elves exactly, and I'd rather
He said it for himself. I see him there
Bringing a stone grasped firmly by the top
In each hand, like an old-stone savage armed.   40
He moves in darkness as it seems to me,
Not of woods only and the shade of trees.
He will not go behind his father's saying,
And he likes having thought of it so well
He says again, "Good fences make good neighbors."   45

(1914)

Birches

When I see birches bend to left and right
Across the lines of straighter darker trees,
I like to think some boy's been swinging them.
But swinging doesn't bend them down to stay
As ice-storms do. Often you must have seen them   5
Loaded with ice a sunny winter morning
After a rain. They click upon themselves
As the breeze rises, and turn many-colored
As the stir cracks and crazes their enamel.
Soon the sun's warmth makes them shed crystal shells   10
Shattering and avalanching on the snow-crust—
Such heaps of broken glass to sweep away
You'd think the inner dome of heaven had fallen.
They are dragged to the withered bracken by the load,
And they seem not to break; though once they are bowed   15
So low for long, they never right themselves:
You may see their trunks arching in the woods
Years afterwards, trailing their leaves on the ground
Like girls on hands and knees that throw their hair
Before them over their heads to dry in the sun.   20
But I was going to say when Truth broke in
With all her matter-of-fact about the ice-storm,
I should prefer to have some boy bend them
As he went out and in to fetch the cows—
Some boy too far from town to learn baseball,   25
Whose only play was what he found himself,
Summer or winter, and could play alone.
One by one he subdued his father's trees
By riding them down over and over again
Until he took the stiffness out of them,   30
And not one but hung limp, not one was left
For him to conquer. He learned all there was
To learn about not launching out too soon
And so not carrying the tree away
Clear to the ground. He always kept his poise   35
To the top branches, climbing carefully
With the same pains you use to fill a cup
Up to the brim, and even above the brim.
Then he flung outward, feet first, with a swish,
Kicking his way down through the air to the ground.   40
So was I once myself a swinger of birches.
And so I dream of going back to be.
It's when I'm weary of considerations,
And life is too much like a pathless wood

Where your face burns and tickles with the cobwebs   45
Broken across it, and one eye is weeping
From a twig's having lashed across it open.
I'd like to get away from earth awhile
And then come back to it and begin over.
May no fate willfully misunderstand me   50
And half grant what I wish and snatch me away
Not to return. Earth's the right place for love:
I don't know where it's likely to go better.
I'd like to go by climbing a birch tree,
And climb black branches up a snow-white trunk   55
Toward heaven, till the tree could bear no more,
But dipped its top and set me down again.
That would be good both going and coming back.
One could do worse than be a swinger of birches.

(1916)

Home Burial

He saw her from the bottom of the stairs
Before she saw him. She was starting down,
Looking back over her shoulder at some fear.
She took a doubtful step and then undid it
To raise herself and look again. He spoke   5
Advancing toward her: "What is it you see
From up there always—for I want to know."
She turned and sank upon her skirts at that,
And her face changed from terrified to dull.
He said to gain time: "What is it you see"   10
Mounting until she cowered under him.
"I will find out now—you must tell me, dear."
She, in her place, refused him any help
With the least stiffening of her neck and silence.
She let him look, sure that he wouldn't see,   15
Blind creature; and awhile he didn't see.
But at last he murmured, "Oh," and again, "Oh."

"What is it—what?" she said.
        "Just that I see."

"You don't," she challenged. "Tell me what it is."

"The wonder is I didn't see at once.   20
I never noticed it from here before.
I must be wonted to it—that's the reason.

The little graveyard where my people are!
So small the window frames the whole of it.
Not so much larger than a bedroom, is it?   25
There are three stones of slate and one of marble,
Broad-shouldered little slabs there in the sunlight
On the sidehill. We haven't to mind *those*.
But I understand: it is not the stones,
But the child's mound—"

      "Don't, don't, don't, don't," she cried.   30

She withdrew shrinking from beneath his arm
That rested on the banister, and slid downstairs;
And turned on him with such a daunting look,
He said twice over before he knew himself:
"Can't a man speak of his own child he's lost?"   35

"Not you! Oh, where's my hat? Oh, I don't need it!
I must get out of here. I must get air.
I don't know rightly whether any man can."

"Amy! Don't go to someone else this time.
Listen to me. I won't come down the stairs."   40
He sat and fixed his chin between his fists.
"There's something I should like to ask you, dear."
"You don't know how to ask it."
     "Help me, then."

Her fingers moved the latch for all reply.

"My words are nearly always an offense.   45
I don't know how to speak of anything
So as to please you. But I might be taught
I should suppose. I can't say I see how.
A man must partly give up being a man
With women-folk. We could have some arrangement   50
By which I'd bind myself to keep hands off
Anything special you're a-mind to name.
Though I don't like such things 'twixt those that love.
Two that don't love can't live together without them.
But two that do can't live together with them."   55
She moved the latch a little. "Don't—don't go.
Don't carry it to someone else this time.
Tell me about it if it's something human.
Let me into your grief. I'm not so much
Unlike other folks as your standing there   60
Apart would make me out. Give me my chance.
I do think, though, you overdo it a little.

What was it brought you up to think it the thing
To take your mother-loss of a first child
So inconsolably—in the face of love.   65
You'd think his memory might be satisfied—"

"There you go sneering now!"
        "I'm not, I'm not!
You make me angry. I'll come down to you.
God, what a woman! And it's come to this,
A man can't speak of his own child that's dead."   70

"You can't because you don't know how to speak.
If you had any feelings, you that dug
With your own hand—how could you?—his little grave;
I saw you from that very window there,
Making the gravel leap and leap in air,   75
Leap up, like that, like that, and land so lightly
And roll back down the mound beside the hole.
I thought, Who is that man? I didn't know you.
And I crept down the stairs and up the stairs
To look again, and still your spade kept lifting.   80
Then you came in. I heard your rumbling voice
Out in the kitchen, and I don't know why,
But I went near to see with my own eyes.
You could sit there with the stains on your shoes
Of the fresh earth from your own baby's grave   85
And talk about your everyday concerns.
You had stood the spade up against the wall
Outside there in the entry, for I saw it."

"I shall laugh the worst laugh I ever laughed.
I'm cursed. God, if I don't believe I'm cursed."   90

"I can repeat the very words you were saying.
'Three foggy mornings and one rainy day
Will rot the best birch fence a man can build.'
Think of it, talk like that at such a time!
What had how long it takes a birch to rot   95
To do with what was in the darkened parlor?
You *couldn't* care! The nearest friends can go
With anyone to death, comes so far short
They might as well not try to go at all.
No, from the time when one is sick to death,   100
One is alone, and he dies more alone.
Friends make pretense of following to the grave,
But before one is in it, their minds are turned
And making the best of their way back to life

And living people, and things they understand.   105
But the world's evil. I won't have grief so
If I can change it. Oh, I won't, I won't!"

"There, you have said it all and you feel better.
You won't go now. You're crying. Close the door.
The heart's gone out of it: why keep it up.   110
Amy! There's someone coming down the road!"

"You—oh, you think the talk is all. I must go—
Somewhere out of this house. How can I make you—"

"If—you—do!" She was opening the door wider.
"Where do you mean to go? First tell me that.   115
I'll follow and bring you back by force. I *will!*—"

                                                   (1914)

Hyla Brook

By June our brook's run out of song and speed.
Sought for much after that, it will be found
Either to have gone groping underground
(And taken with it all the Hyla breed
That shouted in the mist a month ago,   5
Like ghost of sleigh bells in a ghost of snow)—
Or flourished and come up in jewelweed,
Weak foliage that is blown upon and bent
Even against the way its waters went.
Its bed is left a faded paper sheet   10
Of dead leaves stuck together by the heat—
A brook to none but who remember long.
This as it will be seen is other far
Than with brooks taken otherwise in song.
We love the things we love for what they are.   15

                                                   (1916)

Putting in the Seed

You come to fetch me from my work tonight
When supper's on the table, and we'll see
If I can leave off burying the white
Soft petals fallen from the apple tree
(Soft petals, yes, but not so barren quite,   5
Mingled with these, smooth bean and wrinkled pea),

And go along with you ere you lose sight
Of what you came for and become like me,
Slave to a springtime passion for the earth.
How Love burns through the Putting in the Seed   10
On through the watching for that early birth
When, just as the soil tarnishes with weed,
The sturdy seedling with arched body comes
Shouldering its way and shedding the earth crumbs.

(1916)

Fire and Ice

Some say the world will end in fire,
Some say in ice.
From what I've tasted of desire
I hold with those who favor fire.
But if it had to perish twice,   5
I think I know enough of hate
To say that for destruction ice
Is also great
And would suffice.

(1923)

For Once, Then, Something

Others taunt me with having knelt at well-curbs
Always wrong to the light, so never seeing
Deeper down in the well than where the water
Gives me back in a shining surface picture
Me myself in the summer heaven godlike   5
Looking out of a wreath of fern and cloud puffs.
Once, when trying with chin against a well-curb,
I discerned, as I thought, beyond the picture,
Through the picture, a something white, uncertain,
Something more of the depths—and then I lost it.   10
Water came to rebuke the too clear water.
One drop fell from a fern, and lo, a ripple
Shook whatever it was lay there at bottom,
Blurred it, blotted it out. What was that whiteness?
Truth? A pebble of quartz? For once, then, something.   15

(1923)

Two Look at Two

Love and forgetting might have carried them
A little further up the mountainside
With night so near, but not much further up.
They must have halted soon in any case
With thoughts of the path back, how rough it was   5
With rock and washout, and unsafe in darkness;
When they were halted by a tumbled wall
With barbed-wire binding. They stood facing this,
Spending what onward impulse they still had
In one last look the way they must not go,   10
On up the failing path, where, if a stone
On earthside moved at night, it moved itself;
No footstep moved it. "This is all," they sighed,
"Good-night to woods." But not so; there was more.
A doe from round a spruce stood looking at them   15
Across the wall, as near the wall as they.
She saw them in their field, they her in hers.
The difficulty of seeing what stood still,
Like some up-ended boulder split in two,
Was in her clouded eyes: they saw no fear there.   20
She seemed to think that two thus they were safe.
Then, as if they were something that, though strange,
She could not trouble her mind with too long,
She sighed and passed unscared along the wall.
"This, then, is all. What more is there to ask?"   25
But no, not yet. A snort to bid them wait.
A buck from round the spruce stood looking at them
Across the wall, as near the wall as they.
This was an antlered buck of lusty nostril,
Not the same doe come back into her place.   30
He viewed them quizzically with jerks of head,
As if to ask, "Why don't you make some motion?
Or give some sign of life? Because you can't.
I doubt if you're as living as you look."
Thus till he had them almost feeling dared   35
To stretch a proffering hand—and a spell-breaking.
Then he too passed unscared along the wall.
Two had seen two, whichever side you spoke from.
"This *must* be all." It was all. Still they stood,
A great wave from it going over them,   40
As if the earth in one unlooked-for favor
Had made them certain earth returned their love.

(1923)

Once by the Pacific

The shattered water made a misty din.
Great waves looked over others coming in,
And thought of doing something to the shore
That water never did to land before.
The clouds were low and hairy in the skies,   5
Like locks blown forward in the gleam of eyes.
You could not tell, and yet it looked as if
The shore was lucky in being backed by cliff,
The cliff in being backed by continent;
It looked as if a night of dark intent   10
Was coming, and not only a night, an age.
Someone had better be prepared for rage.
There would be more than ocean-water broken
Before God's last *Put out the Light* was spoken.

(1928)

Acquainted with the Night

I have been one acquainted with the night.
I have walked out in rain—and back in rain.
I have outwalked the furthest city light.

I have looked down the saddest city lane.
I have passed by the watchman on his beat   5
And dropped my eyes, unwilling to explain.

I have stood still and stopped the sound of feet
When far away an interrupted cry
Came over houses from another street,

But not to call me back or say good-by;   10
And further still at an unearthly height
One luminary clock against the sky

Proclaimed the time was neither wrong nor right.
I have been one acquainted with the night.

(1928)

Tree at my Window

Tree at my window, window tree,
My sash is lowered when night comes on;
But let there never be curtain drawn
Between you and me.

Vague dream-head lifted out of the ground,   5
And thing next most diffuse to cloud,
Not all your light tongues talking aloud
Could be profound.

But, tree, I have seen you taken and tossed,
And if you have seen me when I slept,   10
You have seen me when I was taken and swept
And all but lost.

That day she put our heads together,
Fate had her imagination about her,
Your head so much concerned with outer,   15
Mine with inner, weather.

(1928)

Departimental

An ant on the tablecloth
Ran into a dormant moth
Of many times his size.
He showed not the least surprise.
His business wasn't with such.   5
He gave it scarcely a touch,
And was off on his duty run.
Yet if he encountered one
Of the hive's enquiry squad
Whose work is to find out God   10
And the nature of time and space,
He would put him onto the case.
Ants are a curious race;
One crossing with hurried tread
The body of one of their dead   15
Isn't given a moment's arrest—
Seems not even impressed.
But he no doubt reports to any
With whom he crosses antennae,
And they no doubt report   20
To the higher up at court.
Then word goes forth in Formic:
"Death's come to Jerry McCormic,
Our selfless forager Jerry.
Will the special Janizary   25
Whose office it is to bury
The dead of the commissary

Go bring him home to his people.
Lay him in state on a sepal.
Wrap him for shroud in a petal.   0
Embalm him with ichor of nettle.
This is the word of your Queen."
And presently on the scene
Appears a solemn mortician:
And taking formal position   35
With feelers calmly atwiddle,
Seizes the dead by the middle,
And heaving him high in the air,
Carries him out of there.
No one stands round to stare.   40
It is nobody else's affair.

It couldn't be called ungentle.
But how thoroughly departmental.

(1936)

Desert Places

Snow falling and night falling fast, oh, fast
In a field I looked into going past,
And the ground almost covered smooth in snow,
But a few weeds and stubble showing last.

The woods around it have it—it is theirs.   5
All animals are smothered in their lairs.
I am too absent-spirited to count;
The loneliness includes me unawares.

And lonely as it is, that loneliness
Will be more lonely ere it will be less—   10
A blanker whiteness of benighted snow
With no expression, nothing to express.

They cannot scare me with their empty spaces
Between stars—on stars where no human race is.
I have it in me so much nearer home   15
To scare myself with my own desert places.

(1936)

Design

I found a dimpled spider, fat and white,
On a white heal-all, holding up a moth
Like a white piece of rigid satin cloth—
Assorted characters of death and blight
Mixed ready to begin the morning right,   5
Like the ingredients of a witches' broth—
A snow-drop spider, a flower like a froth,
And dead wings carried like a paper kite.

What had that flower to do with being white,
The wayside blue and innocent heal-all?   10
What brought the kindred spider to that height,
Then steered the white moth thither in the night?
What but design of darkness to appall?—
If design govern in a thing so small.

                                                        (1936)

Provide, Provide

The witch that came (the withered hag)
To wash the steps with pail and rag,
Was once the beauty Abishag,

The picture pride of Hollywood.
Too many fall from great and good   5
For you to doubt the likelihood.

Die early and avoid the fate.
Or if predestined to die late,
Make up your mind to die in state.

Make the whole stock exchange your own!   10
If need be occupy a throne,
Where nobody can call *you* crone.

Some have relied on what they knew;
Others on being simply true.
What worked for them might work for you.   15

No memory of having starred
Atones for later disregard
Or keeps the end from being hard.

Better to go down dignified
With boughten friendship at your side   20
Than none at all. Provide, provide!

                                                        (1936)

The Most of It

He thought he kept the universe alone;
For all the voice in answer he could wake
Was but the mocking echo of his own
From some tree-hidden cliff across the lake.
Some morning from the boulder-broken beach   5
He would cry out on life, that what it wants
Is not its own love back in copy speech,
But counter-love, original response.
And nothing ever came of what he cried
Unless it was the embodiment that crashed   10
In the cliff's talus on the other side,
And then in the far-distant water splashed,
But after a time allowed for it to swim,
Instead of proving human when it neared
And someone else additional to him,   15
As a great buck it powerfully appeared,
Pushing the crumpled water up ahead,
And landed pouring like a waterfall,
And stumbled through the rocks with horny tread,
And forced the underbrush—and that was all.   20

(1942)

INTRODUCTION TO LANGSTON HUGHES

[1902–1967]

"Poetry," Langston Hughes once remarked, "should be direct, comprehensible, and the epitome of simplicity." His poems illustrate these guidelines with remarkable consistency. Avoiding the obscure and the difficult, Hughes wrote poems that could be understood by readers and listeners who had little prior experience with poetry. He sought to write poems that were immediately understandable, poems that express concretely the concerns of daily life.

Hughes's poetry offers a transcription of urban life through a portrayal of the speech, habits, attitudes, and feelings of an oppressed people. The poems do more, however, than reveal the pain of poverty. They also illustrate racial pride and dignity. Hughes's poems cling, moreover, to the spoken language. They derive from an oral tradition in which folk poetry is recited and performed, rather than published in written form. In the oral tradition poems are passed down from one generation to the next through performance and recitation. As a result Hughes's poems, more than most, need to be read aloud to be fully appreciated. Hughes himself became famous for his public readings, which were sometimes accompanied by a glee club or jazz combo.

Music, in fact, is a central feature of Hughes's poetry. And the kind of music most evident in his work is the blues, an important influence in the work of many modern black writers, especially those associated with the Harlem Renaissance, a flowering of artistic activity among black artists and writers of Harlem in the 1920s. Hughes once described the blues as "sad funny songs— too sad to be funny and too funny to be sad," songs that contain "laughter and pain, hunger and heartache." The bittersweet tone and view of life reflected in Hughes's perspective on the blues is consistently mirrored in his poems, which sometimes adapt the stanza form of the typical blues song. This stanza includes two nearly identical lines followed by a third that contrasts with the first two. "Same in Blues" exhibits this characteristic with only slight modifications. In this and other poems, Hughes succeeds in grafting the inflections of the urban black dialect onto the rhythms of the blues.

But the blues is not the only musical influence on Hughes's poetry; his work also makes use of jazz as both subject and style, though Hughes's jazz poems are freer and looser in form than his blues poems. This difference reflects the improvisatory nature of jazz as well as its energy and vitality, which contrast with the more controlled idiom of the blues. The aggressive exuberance of jazz, its relaxed but vigorous informality is evident in poems like "Trumpet Player."

Hughes was a prolific writer whose published books span forty years (1926–1967). His output includes sixteen volumes of poems; two novels; three collections of short stories; four documentary works; three historical works; twenty dramatic pieces, including plays, musicals, and operettas; two volumes of autobiography; eight children's books; and twelve radio and television scripts. In addition, Hughes edited seven books—mostly collections of poems by black writers—and translated four others, including the poems of the renowned modern Spanish poet Federico García Lorca. Such versatility established Hughes as an important man of letters, contributing to his stature as a leading figure in the arts, especially the theater, whose audience Hughes was instrumental in enlarging.

The writers who influenced Hughes included Paul Dunbar, whose poems re-created the black vernacular, and W. E. B. DuBois, whose collection of essays on Afro-American life, *The Souls of Black Folk,* exerted a lasting influence on many writers, including novelists Richard Wright and James Baldwin. Hughes was also strongly influenced by the democratic idealism of Walt Whitman and the populism of Carl Sandburg, whom Hughes designated his "guiding star." From Sandburg, Hughes learned to write free verse. From Dunbar, he learned a method of incorporating local dialect into poems. And from DuBois, he derived what later came to be called black pride. These influences were combined and amalgamated in myriad ways, resulting in poems that provided insight into urban life.

Hughes's life was as varied as his writing. Born in Joplin, Missouri, in 1902, Hughes lived in Kansas and Ohio before studying at Columbia University in New York and later and more fully at Lincoln University in Pennsylvania. He worked as a seaman and as a newspaper correspondent and columnist for the *Chicago Defender,* the *Baltimore Afro-American,* and the *New York Post.* He also worked briefly as a cook at a fashionable restaurant in

France and as a busboy in a Washington, D.C., hotel. It was there that Hughes left three of his poems beside the plate of a hotel dinner guest, the poet Vachel Lindsay, who recognized their merit and helped Hughes to secure their publication.

Hughes also founded theaters on both coasts—the Harlem Suitcase Theatre (New York, 1938) and, in the Midwest, the Skyloft Players (Chicago, 1941). He traveled extensively, visiting and at various times living in Africa and Europe, especially Italy and France, as well as in Cuba, Haiti, Russia, Korea, and Japan. His life and travels are richly and engagingly chronicled in his two volumes of autobiography, *The Big Sea* (1940) and *I Wonder As I Wander* (1956).

As a writer who believed it was his vocation to "explain and illuminate the Negro condition in America," Hughes captured the experience as "the hurt of their lives, the monotony of their jobs, and the veiled weariness of their songs." He accomplished this in poems remarkable not only for their directness and simplicity but for their economy, lucidity, and wit. Whether he was writing poems of racial protest like "Dream Deferred" and "Ballad of the Landlord" or poems of racial affirmation like "Mother to Son" and "The Negro Speaks of Rivers," Hughes was able to find language and forms to express not only the pain of urban life but also its splendid vitality.

LANGSTON HUGHES ON HARLEM

A Toast to Harlem

Quiet can seem unduly loud at times. Since nobody at the bar was saying a word during a lull in the bright blues-blare of the Wishing Well's usually overworked juke box, I addressed my friend Simple.

"Since you told me last night you are an Indian, explain to me how it is you find yourself living in a furnished room in Harlem, my brave buck, instead of on a reservation?"

"I am a colored Indian," said Simple.

"In other words, a Negro."

"A Black Foot Indian, daddy-o, not a red one. Anyhow, Harlem is the place I always did want to be. And if it wasn't for landladies, I would be happy. That's a fact! I love Harlem."

"What is it you love about Harlem?"

"It's so full of Negroes," said Simple. "I feel like I got protection."

"From what?"

"From white folks," said Simple. "Furthermore, I like Harlem because it belongs to me."

"Harlem does not belong to you. You don't own the houses in Harlem. They belong to white folks."

"I might not own 'em," said Simple, "but I live in 'em. It would take an atom bomb to get me out."

"Or a depression," I said.

"I would not move for no depression. No, I would not go back down South, not even to Baltimore. I am in Harlem to stay! You say the houses ain't mine. Well, the sidewalk is—and don't nobody push me off. The cops don't even say, 'Move on,' hardly no more. They learned something from them Harlem riots. They used to beat your head right in public, but now they only beat it after they get you down to the station-house. And they don't beat it then if they think you know a colored congressman."

"Harlem has few Negro leaders," I said.

"Elected by my *own* vote," said Simple. "Here I ain't scared to vote—that's another thing I like about Harlem. I also like it because we've got subways and it does not take all day to get downtown, neither are you Crowed on the way. Why, Negroes is running some of these subway trains. This morning I rode the A Train down to 34th street. There were a Negro driving it, making ninety miles a hour. That cat *were really driving* that train! Every time he flew by one of them local stations looks like he was saying, 'Look at me! This train is mine!' That cat were gone, ole man. Which is another reason why I like Harlem! Sometimes I run into Duke Ellington on 125th Street and I say, 'What you know there, Duke?' Duke says, 'Solid, ole man.' He does not know me from Adam, but he speaks. One day I saw Lena Horne coming out of the Hotel Theresa and I said, 'Huba! Huba!' Lena smiled. Folks is friendly in Harlem. I feel like I got the world in a jug and the stopper in my hand! So drink a toast to Harlem!"

Simple lifted his glass of beer:

> *"Here's to Harlem!*
> *They say Heaven is Paradise.*
> *If Harlem ain't Heaven,*
> *Then a mouse ain't mice!"*

(1950)

CRITICS ON HUGHES

ARNOLD RAMPERSAD

Langston Hughes as Folk Poet

from *Langston Hughes*

Hughes was often called and sometimes called himself, a folk poet. To some people this means that his work is almost artless and thus possibly beneath criticism. The truth indeed is that Hughes published many poems that are doggerel. To reach his primary audience—the black masses—he was prepared to write "down" to them. Some of the pieces in this volume were intended for public recitation mainly; some started as song lyrics. Like many democratic poets, such as William Carlos Williams, he believed that the full range of his poetry should reach print as soon as possible; poetry is a form of social action. However, for Hughes, as for all serious poets, the writing of poetry was

virtually a sacred commitment. And while he wished to write no verse that was beyond the ability of the masses of people to understand, his poetry, in common with
that of other committed writers, is replete with allusions that must be respected and
understood if it is to be properly appreciated. To respect Hughes's work, above all one
must respect the African American people and their culture, as well as the American
people in general and their national culture.

If Hughes kept at the center of his art the hopes and dreams, as well as the actual
lived conditions, of African Americans, he almost always saw these factors in the context of the eternally embattled but eternally inspiring American democratic tradition,
even as changes in the world order, notably the collapse of colonialism in Africa, re-
defined experiences of African peoples around the world. Almost always, too, Hughes
attempted to preserve a sense of himself as a poet beyond race and other corrosive social pressures. By his absolute dedication to his art and to his social vision, as well as
to his central audience, he fused his unique vision of himself as a poet to his production of art.

"What is poetry?" Langston Hughes was asked near his death. He answered, "It is
the human soul entire, squeezed like a lemon or a lime, drop by drop, into atomic
words." He wanted no definition of the poet that divorced his art from the immediacy of life. "A poet is a human being," he declared. "Each human being must live
within his time, with and for his people, and within the boundaries of his country."
Hughes constantly called upon himself for the courage and the endurance necessary
to write according to these beliefs. "Hang yourself, poet, in your own words," he
urged all those who would take up the mantle of the poet and dare to speak to the
world. "Otherwise, you are dead."

ONWUCHEKWA JEMIE

Hughes and the Evolution of Consciousness in Black Poetry

from *Langston Hughes: An Introduction to the Poetry*

W. E. B. DuBois's formulation of the dilemma of the black artist was one of the earliest and is still, perhaps, the most lucid. As he stated it, the black artist's problem was in
deciding whether to reflect "the beauty revealed to him . . . the soul-beauty of a race
which his larger audience despised," or to "articulate the message of another people."
As Afro-American history is in part the history of a people caught between two conflicting worlds, and of their efforts to reconcile those worlds, to bring an end their
"double-consciousness" by merging their African and American selves into a single,
undivided whole, so is Afro-American literary history in part a record of the black
writer's choices between revealing the soul-beauty of his own people and articulating
the message of another people; so is it the history of his efforts to bring to an end the
very need for choice by somehow bringing the two things together.

The literary beauty revealed to the black writer is contained in his oral folk tradition with its vast universe of themes and images and its smooth and complex strategies of delivery. The "message of another people," on the other hand, is carried in the forms and attitudes, themes and styles and sensibilities of white American and European culture and literature. In another sense, the black writers' problem is as much one of medium as of ethos: his problem is how to actualize the oral tradition in written form, how to recreate the vital force, the sights and sounds and smells of the performance-event on dumb, flat, one-dimensional paper. This problem of *media transfer* is one which the black musician, for instance, does not have, for his art operates within the continuum of the oral medium. The black writer's problem is further complicated by the fact that he has no long written tradition of his own to emulate; and for him to abandon the effort to translate into written form that oral medium which is the full reservoir of his culture would be to annihilate his identity and become a zombie, a programmed vehicle for "the message of another people."

Hardly any black writer of any generation has found it easy, or even possible, to avoid making a choice. And as might be expected, the choices have been neither uniform nor consistent in any era. In every generation, some writers have chosen to reveal the soul-beauty of their own people, some to carry the message of another people. Sometimes the writer vacillates, yielding to the one imperative at one time or in one work, to the other in another, or attempting to answer to both imperatives at the same time and in the same works. Or the writer may undercut the self-acceptance evident in his works with actions and pronouncements indicating reservations and self-doubt.

R I C H A R D   K .   B A R K S D A L E

On Hughes's "Ballad of the Landlord"

from *Langston Hughes: The Poet and His Critics*

An interesting prelude to the social, economic, and political concerns expressed in his poems about Harlem in the 1940s was Hughes's *Ballad of the Landlord,* first published in *Opportunity* (Dec. 1940) and then included as one of the poems in *Jim Crow's Last Stand* (1943) and later in *Montage of a Dream Deferred.* In 1940, the poem was a rather innocuous rendering of an imaginary dialogue between a disgruntled tenant and a tight-fisted landlord. In creating a poem about two such social archetypes, the poet was by no means taking any new steps in dramatic poetry. The literature of most capitalist and noncapitalist societies often pits the haves against the have-nots, and not infrequently the haves are wealthy men of property who "lord" it over improvident men who own nothing. So the confrontation between tenant and landlord was in 1940 just another instance of the social malevolence of a system that punished the powerless and excused the powerful. In fact, Hughes's tone of dry irony throughout the poem leads one to suspect that the poet deliberately overstated a situation and that some sardonic humor was supposed to be squeezed out of the incident. Says the Tenant in furious high dudgeon:

> What? You gonna get eviction orders?
> You gonna cut off my heat?
> You gonna take my furniture and
> Throw it in the street?
>
> Um-huh! You talking high and mighty.
> Talk on—till you get through.
> You ain't gonna be able to say a word
> If I land my fist on you.

The Man of Property, in fear and trembling, invokes the symbols of law and order:

> *Police! Police!*
> *Come and get this man!*
> *He's trying to ruin the government*
> *And overturn the land!*

Ironically, this poem, which in 1940 depicted a highly probable incident in American urban life and was certainly not written to incite an economic revolt or promote social unrest, became, by the mid-1960s, a verboten assignment in a literature class in a Boston high school. In his Langston Hughes headnote in *Black Voices* (1967), Abraham Chapman reported that a Boston high school English teacher named Jonathan Kozol was fired for assigning it to his students. By the mid-sixties, Boston and many other American cities had become riot-torn, racial tinderboxes, and their ghettos seethed with tenant anger and discontent. So the poem gathered new meanings reflecting the times, and the word of its tenant persona bespoke the collective anger of thousands of black have-nots. In his review of Gwendolyn Brooks's "Street in Bronzeville" in *Opportunity* (Fall 1945), Hughes praised that young poet's initial volume of poems for its incisive social and political statements and for its "picture-power." His conclusion was that "Poets often say these things better than politicians." Such a comment aptly fits "Ballad of the Landlord." At least, someone on the Boston School Committee evidently thought so.

ONWUCHEKWA JEMIE

On "The Negro Speaks of Rivers"

from *Langston Hughes: An Introduction to the Poetry*

"The Negro Speaks of Rivers" is perhaps the most profound of these poems of heritage and strength. Composed when Hughes was a mere 17 years old, and dedicated to W. E. B. DuBois, it is a sonorous evocation of transcendent essences so ancient as to appear timeless, predating human existence, longer than human memory. The rivers are part of God's body, and participate in his immortality. They are the earthly analogues of eternity: deep, continuous, mysterious. They are named in the order of their association with black history. The black man has drunk of their life-giving essences, and thereby borrowed their immortality. He and the rivers have become one. The magical transformation of the Mississippi from mud to gold by the sun's radiance is mirrored in the transformation of slaves into free men by Lincoln's Proclamation (and, in Hughes's poems, the transformation of shabby cabarets into gorgeous palaces, dancing girls into queens and priestesses by the spell of black music). As the rivers deepen with time, so does the black man's soul; as their waters ceaselessly flow, so will the black soul endure. The black man has seen the rise and fall of civilizations from the earliest times, seen the beauty and death-changes of the world over the thousands of years, and will survive even this America. The poem's meaning is related to Zora Neale Hurston's judgment of the mythic High John de Conquer, whom she held as a symbol of the triumphant spirit of black America: that John was of the "Be" class. "*Be* here when the ruthless man comes, and *be* here when he is gone." In a time and place where black life is held cheap and the days of black men appear to be numbered, the poem is a majestic reminder of the strength and fullness of history, of the source of that life which transcends even ceaseless labor and burning crosses.

JAMES A. EMANUEL

On "Trumpet Player"

from *Langston Hughes*

The meaning of jazz to the musician is combined with racial background in "Trumpet Player" in *Fields of Wonder*. Jazz is "honey/Mixed with liquid fire"; and the trumpet player, says the poet at the end, never knows "upon what riff the music slips/Its hypodermic needle/To his soul." Finally, to the musician, trouble "Mellows to a golden note." The first third of the poem outlines the Negro musician, tired eyes smoldering with memories of slavery, hair "tamed down." The weakest stanza shows the Negro's longing for the moon and sea as "old desire" distilled into rhythm. The quoted lines and a few others reveal the true distillation, jazz made precious by its long and sacrificial birth.

While writing "Trumpet Player," Hughes was fully abreast of the new be-bop music emerging from Minton's Playhouse in Harlem. Among the poems inspired by be-bop— a rhythmically complex and experimental kind of jazz characterized by dissonance, improvisation, and unusual lyrics—the best is the leadoff "Dream Boogie" in *Montage of a Dream Deferred* (1951):

> Good morning, daddy!
> Ain't you heard
> The boogie-woogie rumble
> Of a dream deferred?

Listen closely:
You'll hear their feet
Beating out and beating out a —

You think
It's a happy beat?

Listen to it closely:
Ain't you heard
something underneath
like a —

What did I say?

Sure,
I'm happy!
Take it away!

Hey, pop!
Re-bop!
Mop!

Y-e-a-h!

Keeping up with a changing Harlem, Hughes is alert to the "hip" insider's elastic jargon as well as the generations-old truth of Negro life—the dream deferred. "Dream Boogie" perfectly fulfills its purpose, wasting no word. It has variations in mood: ease, irony, sarcasm, and terse joviality. It mixes old devices of the dramatic monologue with a contemporary boogiewoogie beat. Its rough-hewn grace adds power to its clarity.

LANGSTON HUGHES: POEMS

Dream Deferred

What happens to a dream deferred?

Does it dry up
like a raisin in the sun?
Or fester like a sore—
And then run?
Does it stink like rotten meat?
Or crust and sugar over—
like a syrupy sweet?

Maybe it just sags
like a heavy load.

Or does it explode?

Same in Blues

I said to my baby,
Baby, take it slow
I can't, she said, I can't!
I got to go!

    There's a certain   5
    amount of traveling
    in a dream deferred.

Lulu said to Leonard,
I want a diamond ring.
Leonard said to Lulu,   10
You won't get a goddamn thing!

    A certain
    amount of nothing
    in a dream deferred.

Daddy, daddy, daddy,   15
All I want is you.
You can have me, baby—
but my lovin' days is through.

    A certain
    amount of impotence
    in a dream deferred.   20

Three parties
On my party line—
But that third party,
Lord, ain't mine!   25

    There's liable
    to be confusion
    in a dream deferred.

From river to river
Uptown and down,   30
There's liable to be confusion
when a dream gets kicked around.

You talk like
they don't kick
dreams around   35
Downtown.

I expect they do—
But I'm talking about
Harlem to you!
Harlem to you!   40
Harlem to you!
Harlem to you!

The Negro Speaks of Rivers

I've known rivers:
I've known rivers ancient as the world and older than the flow
   of human blood in human veins.
My soul has grown deep like the rivers.

I bathed in the Euphrates when dawns were young.
I built my hut near the Congo and it lulled me to sleep.   5
I looked upon the Nile and raised the pyramids above it.
I heard the singing of the Mississippi when Abe Lincoln
       went down to New Orleans, and I've seen its muddy
       bosom turn all golden in the sunset.

I've known rivers:
Ancient, dusky rivers.

My soul has grown deep like the rivers.   10

Mother to Son

Well, son, I'll tell you:
Life for me ain't been no crystal stair.
It's had tacks in it,
And splinters,
And boards torn up,   5
And places with no carpet on the floor—
Bare.
But all the time
I'se been a-climbin' on,
And reachin' landin's,   10
And turnin' corners,
And sometimes goin' in the dark

Where there ain't been no light.
So boy, don't you turn back.
Don't you set down on the steps   15
'Cause you finds it's kinder hard.
Don't you fall now—
For I'se still goin', honey,
I'se still climbin',
And life for me ain't been no crystal stair.   20

I, Too

I, too, sing America.

I am the darker brother.
They send me to eat in the kitchen.
When company comes,
But I laugh,   5
And eat well,
And grow strong.

Tomorrow,
I'll be at the table
When company comes.   10
Nobody'll dare
Say to me,
"Eat in the kitchen,"
Then.

Besides,   15
They'll see how beautiful I am
And be ashamed—
I, too, am America.

My People

The night is beautiful,
So the faces of my people.

The stars are beautiful,
So the eyes of my people.

Beautiful, also, is the sun.   5
Beautiful, also, are the souls of my people.

The Weary Blues

Droning a drowsy syncopated tune,
Rocking back and forth to a mellow croon,
    I heard a Negro play.
Down on Lenox Avenue the other night
By the pale dull pallor of an old gas light   5
    He did a lazy sway. . . .
    He did a lazy sway. . . .
To the tune o' those Weary Blues.
With his ebony hands on each ivory key
He made that poor piano moan with melody.   10
    O Blues!
Swaying to and fro on his rickety stool
He played that sad raggy tune like a musical fool.
    Sweet Blues!   15
Coming from a black man's soul.
    O Blues!
In a deep song voice with a melancholy tone
I heard that Negro sing, that old piano moan—
    "Ain't got nobody in all this world,
    Ain't got nobody but ma self.   20
    I's gwine to quit ma frownin'
    And put ma troubles on the shelf."
Thump, thump, thump, went his foot on the floor.
He played a few chords then he sang some more—
    "I got the Weary Blues   25
    And I can't be satisfied.
    Got the Weary Blues
    And can't be satisfied—
    I ain't happy no mo'
    And I wish that I had died."   30
And far into the night he crooned that tune.
The stars went out and so did the moon.
The singer stopped playing and went to bed
While the Weary Blues echoed through his head
He slept like a rock or a man that's dead.

Young Gal's Blues

I'm gonna walk to the graveyard
'Hind ma friend Miss Cora Lee.
Gonna walk to the graveyard
'Hind ma dear friend Cora Lee.
Cause when I'm dead some   5
Body'll have to walk behind me.

I'm goin' to the po' house
To see ma old Aunt Clew.
Goin' to the po' house
To see ma old Aunt Clew.   10
When I'm old an' ugly
I'll want to see somebody, too.

The po' house is lonely
An' the grave is cold.
O, the po' house is lonely,   15
The graveyard grave is cold.
But I'd rather be dead than
To be ugly an' old.

When love is gone what
Can a young gal do?
When love is gone, O,   20
What can a young gal do?
Keep on a-lovin' me, daddy,
Cause I don't want to be blue.

Morning After

I was so sick last night I
Didn't hardly know my mind.
So sick last night I
Didn't know my mind.
I drunk some bad licker that   5
Almost made me blind.
Had a dream last night I
Thought I was in hell.
I drempt last night I
Thought I was in hell.   10
Woke up and looked around me—
Babe, your mouth was open like a well.
I said, Baby! Baby!
Please don't snore so loud.
Baby! Please!   15
Please don't snore so loud.
You jest a little bit o' woman but you
Sound like a great big crowd.

Trumpet Player

The Negro
With the trumpet at his lips
Has dark moons of weariness
Beneath his eyes
Where the smoldering memory   5
Of slave ships
Blazed to the crack of whips
About his thighs.

The Negro
With the trumpet at his lips   10
Has a head of vibrant hair
Tamed down,
Patent-leathered now
Until it gleams
Like jet—   15
Were jet a crown.

The music
From the trumpet at his lips
Is honey
Mixed with liquid fire.   20
The rhythm
From the trumpet at his lips
Is ecstasy
Distilled from old desire—

Desire   25
That is longing for the moon
Where the moonlight's but a spotlight
In his eyes,
Desire
That is longing for the sea   30
Where the sea's a bar-glass
Sucker size.

The Negro
With the trumpet at his lips
Whose jacket   35
Has a *fine* one-button roll,
Does not know
Upon what riff the music slips
Its hypodermic needle
To his soul—   40

But softly
As the tune comes from his throat
Trouble
Mellows to a golden note.

Dream Boogie

Good morning, daddy!
Ain't you heard
The boogie-woogie rumble
Of a dream deferred?

Listen closely: 5
You'll hear their feet
Beating out and beating out a—

    You think
    It's a happy beat?

Listen to it closely: 10
Ain't you heard
something underneath
like a—

    What did I say?

Sure,   15
I'm happy!
Take it away!

    Hey, pop!
    Re-bop!
    Mop!   20

    Y-e-a-h!

    What don't bug
    them white kids
    sure bugs me:
    We knows everybody   25
    ain't free!

Some of these young ones is cert'ly bad—
One batted a hard ball right through my window
and my gold fish et the glass.

What's written down   30
for white folks
ain't for us a-tall:
"Liberty And Justice—
Huh—For All."

Oop-pop-a-da!   35
Skee! Daddle-de-do!
Be-bop!

Salt'peanuts!

De-dop!

Madam and the Rent Man

The rent man knocked.
He said, Howdy-do?
I said, What
Can I do for you?
He said, You know   5
Your rent is due.

I said, Listen,
Before I'd pay
I'd go to Hades
And rot away!   10

The sink is broke,
The water don't run,
And you ain't done a thing
You promised to've done.

Back window's cracked,   15
Kitchen floor squeaks,
There's rats in the cellar,
And the attic leaks.

He said, Madam,
It's not up to me.   20
I'm just the agent,
Don't you see?

I said, Naturally,
You pass the buck.
If it's money you want   25
You're out of luck.

He said, Madam,
I ain't pleased!
I said, Neither am I.

So we agrees!   30

Theme for English B

The instructor said,

> Go home and write
> a page tonight.
> And let that page come out of you—
> Then, it will be true.   5

I wonder if it's that simple?

I am twenty-two, colored, born in Winston-Salem.
I went to school there, then Durham, then here
to this college on the hill above Harlem.
I am the only colored student in my class.   10
The steps from the hill lead down into Harlem,
through a park, then I cross St. Nicholas,
Eighth Avenue, Seventh, and I come to the Y,
the Harlem Branch Y, where I take the elevator
up to my room, sit down, and write this page: 15

It's not easy to know what is true for you or me
at twenty-two, my age. But I guess I'm what
I feel and see and hear. Harlem, I hear you:
hear you, hear me—we two—you, me, talk on this page.
(I hear New York, too.) Me—who?   20

Well, I like to eat, sleep, drink, and be in love.
I like to work, read, learn, and understand life.
I like a pipe for a Christmas present,
or records—Bessie, bop, or Bach.
I guess being colored doesn't make me *not* like   25
the same things other folks like who are other races.

So will my page be colored that I write?
Being me, it will not be white.
But it will be
a part of you, instructor.   30
You are white—
yet a part of me, as I am a part of you.

That's American.
Sometimes perhaps you don't want to be a part of me.
Nor do I often want to be a part of you.   35
But we are, that's true!
As I learn from you,
I guess you learn from me—
although you're older—and white—
and somewhat more free.   40

This is my page for English B.

Aunt Sue's Stories

Aunt Sue has a head full of stories.
Aunt Sue has a whole heart full of stories.
Summer nights on the front porch
Aunt Sue cuddles a brown-faced child to her bosom
And tells him stories.   5

Black slaves
Working in the hot sun,
And black slaves
Walking in the dewy night,
And black slaves   10
Singing sorrow songs on the banks of a mighty river
Mingle themselves softly
In the flow of old Aunt Sue's voice,
Mingle themselves softly
In the dark shadows that cross and recross   15
Aunt Sue's stories.

And the dark-faced child, listening,
Knows that Aunt Sue's stories are real stories.
He knows that Aunt Sue never got her stories
Out of any book at all,   20
But that they came
Right out of her own life.

The dark-faced child is quiet
Of a summer night
Listening to Aunt Sue's stories.   25

Ballad of the Landlord

Landlord, landlord,
My roof has sprung a leak.
Don't you 'member I told you about it
Way last week?

Landlord, landlord,   5
These steps is broken down.
When you come up yourself
It's a wonder you don't fall down.

Ten Bucks you say I owe you?
Ten Bucks you say is due?   10
Well, that's Ten Bucks more'n I'll pay you.
Till you fix this house up new.

What? You gonna get eviction orders?
You gonna cut off my heat?
You gonna take my furniture and   15
Throw it in the street?

Um-huh! You talking high and mighty.
Talk on—till you get through.
You ain't gonna be able to say a word
If I land my fist on you.   20

> *Police! Police!*
> *Come and get this man!*
> *He's trying to ruin the government*
> *And overturn the land!*

Copper's whistle!   25
Patrol bell!
Arrest.

Precinct Station.
Iron cell.
Headlines in press:

MAN THREATENS LANDLORD

TENANT HELD NO BAIL

JUDGE GIVES NEGRO 90 DAYS IN COUNTY JAIL

[1949]

Let America Be America Again

Let America be America again.
Let it be the dream it used to be.
Let it be the pioneer on the plain
Seeking the home where he himself is free.

(America never was America to me.)   5

Let America be the dream the dreamers dreamed—
Let it be that great strong land of love
Where never kings connive nor tyrants scheme
That any man be crushed by one above.

(It never was America to me.)   10

CHAPTER THIRTEEN

A Collection of Poems

The forms of things unknown, the poet's pen / Turns them to shapes, and gives to airy nothing / A local habitation and a name.

WILLIAM SHAKESPEARE

A good poem is a contribution to reality. The world is never the same once a good poem has been added to it.

DYLAN THOMAS

SAPPHO

[*7th–6th century* B.C.]

To me he seems like a god

To me he seems like a god
as he sits facing you and
hears you near as you speak
softly and laugh
in a sweet echo that jolts
the heart in my ribs. For now
as I look at you my voice
is empty and

5

603

can say nothing as my tongue
cracks and slender fire is quick   10
under my skin. My eyes are dead
to light, my ears

pound, and sweat pours over me.
I convulse, paler than grass,
and feel my mind slip as I   15
go close to death

[but must suffer all, being poor.]

TRANSLATED BY WILLIS BARNSTONE

(c. 6th century B.C.)

ANONYMOUS

Barbara Allan

1

It was in and about the Martinmas time,°
    When the green leaves were a falling,
That Sir John Græme, in the West Country,
    Fell in love with Barbara Allan.

2

He sent his man down through the town,   5
    To the place where she was dwelling:
"O haste and come to my master dear,
    Gin° ye be Barbara Allan."   if

3

O hooly,° hooly rose she up,   gently
    To the place where he was lying,   10
And when she drew the curtain by:
    "Young man, I think you're dying."

4

"O it's I'm sick, and very, very sick,
    And 'tis a' for Barbara Allan."
"O the better for me ye s'° never be,   shall   15
    Though your heart's blood were a-spilling."

"Barbara Allan"   [1]**Martinmas**   *Mass (or feast) of St. Martin (d. 655) on November 11.*

5

"O dinna ye mind,° young man," said she,
  "When ye was in the tavern a drinking,
That ye made the healths gae° round and round,   go
  And slighted Barbara Allan?"   20

6

He turned his face unto the wall,
  And death was with him dealing:
"Adieu, adieu, my dear friends all,
  And be kind to Barbara Allan."

7

And slowly, slowly raise she up,   25
  And slowly, slowly left him,
And sighing said, she could not stay,
  Since death of life had reft° him.   deprived

8

She had not gane° a milé but twa,°   gone/two
  When she heard the dead-bell ringing,   30
And every jow° that the dead-bell geid,°   beat/gave
  It cried, "Woe to Barbara Allan!"

9

"O mother, mother, make my bed!
  O make it saft and narrow!
Since my love died for me to-day,   35
  I'll die for him to-morrow."

(c. 14th century)

---

[17] **dinna ye mind**   *don't you remember.*

ANONYMOUS

Edward, Edward

1

"Why does your brand° sae° drap wi' bluid,   *sword/so*
     Edward, Edward,
Why does your brand sae drap wi' bluid,
     And why sae sad gang° ye, O?"   *go*
"O I ha'e killed my hawk sae guid,   5
     Mither, mither,
O I ha'e killed my hawk sae guid,
     And I had nae mair but he, O."

2

"Your hawk's bluid was never sae reid,°   *red*
     Edward, Edward,   10
Your hawk's bluid was never sae reid,
     My dear son, I tell thee, O."
"O I ha'e killed my reid-roan steed,
     Mither, mither,
O I ha'e killed my reid-roan steed,   15
     That erst was sae fair and free, O."

3

"Your steed was auld, and ye ha'e gat mair,
     Edward, Edward,
Your steed was auld, and ye ha'e gat mair,
     Some other dule° ye drie°, O."   *grief/suffer*   20
"O I ha'e killed my fader dear,
     Mither, mither,
O I ha'e killed my fader dear,
     Alas, and wae° is me, O!"   *woe*

4

"And whatten° penance wul ye dree for that,   *what kind of*   25
     Edward, Edward?
And whatten penance wul ye dree for that,
     My dear son, now tell me O?"
"I'll set my feet in yonder boat,
     Mither, mither,   30
I'll set my feet in yonder boat,
     And I'll fare over the sea, O."

5

"And what wul ye do wi' your towers and your ha',
    Edward, Edward?
And what wul ye do wi' your towers and your ha',   35
    That were sae fair to see, O?"
"I'll let them stand tul they down fa',
    Mither, mither,
I'll let them stand tul they down fa',
    For here never mair maun° I be, O."   must 40

6

"And what wul ye leave to your bairns° and your wife,   children
    Edward, Edward?
And what wul ye leave to your bairns and your wife,
    Whan ye gang over the sea, O?"
"The warlde's room, let them beg thrae° life,   through 45
    Mither, mither,
The warlde's room, let them beg thrae life,
    For them never mair wul I see, O."

7

"And what wul ye leave to your ain mither dear,
    Edward, Edward?   50
And what wul ye leave to your ain mither dear,
    My dear son, now tell me, O?"
"The curse of hell frae° me sall° ye bear,   from/shall
    Mither, mither,
The curse of hell frae me sall ye bear,   55
    Sic° counsels ye gave to me, O."   such

(c. 14th century)

THOMAS WYATT
[1503–1542]

They flee from me

They flee from me, that sometime did me seek,
With naked foot stalking in my chamber.
I have seen them, gentle, tame, and meek,
That now are wild, and do not remember
That sometime they put themselves in danger   5
To take bread at my hand; and now they range,
Busily seeking with a continual change.

Thanked be Fortune it hath been otherwise,
Twenty times better; but once in special,
In thin array, after a pleasant guise,   10
When her loose gown from her shoulders did fall,
And she me caught in her arms long and small,°   thin
And therewith all sweetly did me kiss
And softly said, "Dear heart, how like you this?"

It was no dream, I lay broad waking.   15
But all is turned, thorough° my gentleness,   through
Into a strange fashion of forsaking;
And I have leave to go, of her goodness,
And she also to use newfangleness.
But since that I so kindely am served,   20
I fain would know what she hath deserved.

                                                        (1557)

EDMUND SPENSER
[1552–1599]

One day I wrote her name upon the strand

One day I wrote her name upon the strand,°   beach
But came the waves and washéd it away:
Agayne I wrote it with a second hand,
But came the tyde, and made my paynes his pray.
"Vayne man," sayd she, "that doest in vaine assay,   5
A mortall thing so to immortalize,
For I my selve shall lyke to this decay,
And eek° my name bee wypéd out lykewize."   also
"Not so," quod° I, "let baser things devize°   said/devise
To dy in dust, but you shall live by fame: 10
My verse your vertues rare shall eternize,
And in the hevens wryte your glorious name.
Where whenas death shall all the world subdew,
Our love shall live, and later life renew."

                                                        (1595)

SIR WALTER RALEIGH
[*c. 1552–1618*]

The Nymph's Reply to the Shepherd

If all the world and love were young,
And truth in every shepherd's tongue,
These pretty pleasures might me move
To live with thee and be thy love.

Time drives the flocks from field to fold   5
When rivers rage and rocks grow cold,
And Philomel° becometh dumb;
The rest complains of cares to come.

The flowers do fade, and wanton fields
To wayward winter reckoning yields;   10
A honey tongue, a heart of gall,
Is fancy's spring, but sorrow's fall.

Thy gowns, thy shoes, thy beds of roses,
Thy cap, thy kirtle,° and thy posies   *long dress*
Soon break, soon wither, soon forgotten—   15
In folly ripe, in reason rotten.

Thy belt of straw and ivy buds,
Thy coral clasps and amber studs,
All these in me no means can move
To come to thee and be thy love.   20

But could youth last and love still breed,
Had joys no date° nor age no need,   *end*
Then these delights my mind might move
To live with thee and be thy love.

"The Nymph's Reply to the Shepherd" [7]**Philomel** *the nightingale. According to Ovid's* Metamorphoses,
Philomel's brother-in-law Tereus had her tongue cut out to prevent her from revealing that he had raped her. See also
Bob McKenty's "Adam's Song," page 463.

CHRISTOPHER MARLOWE
[1564–1593]

The Passionate Shepherd to His Love

Come live with me and be my love,
And we will all the pleasures prove°   try
That valleys, groves, hills, and fields,
Woods, or steepy mountain yields.

And we will sit upon the rocks,   5
Seeing the shepherds feed their flocks,
By shallow rivers to whose falls
Melodious birds sing madrigals.

And I will make thee beds of roses
And a thousand fragrant posies,   10
A cap of flowers, and a kirtle°   a long dress
Embroidered all with leaves of myrtle;

A gown made of the finest wool
Which from our pretty lambs we pull;
Fair lined slippers for the cold,   15
With buckles of the purest gold;

A belt of straw and ivy buds,
With coral clasps and amber studs:
And if these pleasures may thee move,   20
Come live with me, and be my love.

The shepherds' swains shall dance and sing
For they delight each May morning:
If these delights thy mind may move,
Then live with me and be my love.

WILLIAM SHAKESPEARE
[1564–1616]

When in disgrace with fortune and men's eyes

When, in disgrace with fortune and men's eyes,
I all alone beweep my outcast state,
And trouble deaf heaven with my bootless° cries,   useless

And look upon myself, and curse my fate,
Wishing me like to one more rich in hope,   5
Featured like him, like him with friends possessed,
Desiring this man's art and that man's scope,
With what I most enjoy contented least;
Yet in these thoughts myself almost despising,
Haply I think on thee—and then my state,   10
Like to the lark at break of day arising
From sullen earth, sings hymns at heaven's gate;
For thy sweet love remembered such wealth brings
That then I scorn to change my state with kings.

(1609)

Let me not to the marriage of true minds

Let me not to the marriage of true minds
Admit impediments.° Love is not love   hindrances
Which alters when it alteration finds,
Or bends with the remover to remove:
Oh, no! it is an ever-fixéd mark,   5
That looks on tempests and is never shaken;
It is the star to every wandering bark,°   ship
Whose worth's unknown, although his height be taken.°
Love's not Time's fool, though rosy lips and cheeks
Within his bending sickle's compass come;   10
Love alters not with his brief hours and weeks,
But bears° it out even to the edge of doom.°   lasts/judgment day
If this be error and upon me proved,
I never writ, nor no man ever loved.

(1609)

Th' expense of spirit in a waste of shame

Th' expense of spirit in a waste of shame
Is lust in action; and till action, lust
Is perjured, murderous, bloody, full of blame,
Savage, extreme, rude, cruel, not to trust;
Enjoyed no sooner but despiséd straight: 5
Past reason hunted; and no sooner had,
Past reason hated, as a swallowed bait,
On purpose laid to make the taker mad:
Mad in pursuit, and in possession so;

"Let me not to the marriage of true minds"   [8]*height be taken*   *its elevation be measured.*

Had, having, and in quest to have, extreme;   10
A bliss in proof,° and proved, a very woe;   in the experience
Before, a joy proposed; behind, a dream.
All this the world well knows; yet none knows well
To shun the heaven that leads men to this hell.

(1609)

My mistress' eyes are nothing like the sun

My mistress' eyes are nothing like the sun;
Coral is far more red than her lips' red;
If snow be white, why then her breasts are dun;
If hairs be wires, black wires grow on her head.
I have seen roses damasked,° red and white,   variegated   5
But no such roses see I in her cheeks;
And in some perfumes is there more delight
Than in the breath that from my mistress reeks.
I love to hear her speak, yet well I know
That music hath a far more pleasing sound;   10
I grant I never saw a goddess go;°   walk
My mistress, when she walks, treads on the ground.
And yet, by heaven, I think my love as rare
As any she belied with false compare.

(1609)

JOHN DONNE
[1572–1631]

Song

Go, and catch a falling star,
    Get with child a mandrake root,°
Tell me, where all past years are,
    Or who cleft the devil's foot,
Teach me to hear mermaids singing   5
Or to keep off envy's stinging,
        And find
        What wind
Serves to advance an honest mind.

"Song" ²**mandrake root** *Resembling a human body, the forked root of the mandrake was used as a medicine to induce conception.*

If thou beest born to strange sights,   10
  Things invisible to see,
Ride ten thousand days and nights,
  Till age snow white hairs on thee;
Thou, when thou return'st, wilt tell me
All strange wonders that befell thee,   15
    And swear,
    No where
Lives a woman true, and fair.

If thou find'st one, let me know:
  Such a pilgrimage were sweet.   20
Yet do not, I would not go,
  Though at next door we might meet:
Though she were true when you met her,
And last till you write your letter,
    Yet she   25
    Will be
False, ere I come, to two, or three.

                              (1633)

The Canonization

For God's sake hold your tongue, and let me love,
  Or chide my palsy, or my gout,
My five gray hairs, or ruined fortune, flout,
  With wealth your state, your mind with arts improve,
    Take you a course,° get you a place,°   direction/appointment   5
    Observe His Honor, or His Grace,
Or the King's real, or his stampéd face°   on a coin
    Contémplate; what you will, approve,°   try
    So you will let me love.

Alas, alas, who's injured by my love?   10
  What merchant's ships have my sighs drowned?
Who says my tears have overflowed his ground?
  When did my colds a forward spring remove?
    When did the heats which my veins fill
    Add one more to the plaguy bill?°   list of victims   15
Soldiers find wars, and lawyers find out still
  Litigious men, which quarrels move,
  Though she and I do love.

Call us what you will, we're made such by love;
  Call her one, me another fly,   20

We're tapers too, and at our own cost die,°
    And we in us find th' eagle and the dove
        The phoenix riddle° hath more wit°   sense
        By us: we two being one, are it.
So, to one neutral thing both sexes fit.   25
    We die and rise the same, and prove
    Mysterious by this love.

We can die by it, if not live by love,
    And if unfit for tombs and hearse
Our legend be, it will be fit for verse;   30
    And if no piece of chronicle we prove,
        We'll build in sonnets pretty rooms;
        As well a well-wrought urn becomes
The greatest ashes, as half-acre tombs;
    And by these hymns, all shall approve   35
    Us canonized for love:

And thus invoke us: You whom reverend love
    Made one another's hermitage;
You, to whom love was peace, that now is rage;
    Who did the whole world's soul contract, and drove   40
        Into the glasses of your eyes
        (So made such mirrors, and such spies,
That they did all to you epitomize)
    Countries, towns, courts: Beg from above
    A pattern of your love!

                                                  (1633)

A Valediction: Forbidding Mourning

As virtuous men pass mildly away,
    And whisper to their souls to go,
Whilst some of their sad friends do say,
    "The breath goes now," and some say, "No,"

So let us melt, and make no noise,   5
    No tear-floods, nor sigh-tempests move;
'Twere profanation of our joys
    To tell the laity our love.

"The Canonization"   **21 at our own cost die**   *Death was a metaphor for sexual intercourse; each act of sexual congress supposedly shortened one's life by a day.*   **23 the phoenix riddle**   *a legendary, mythological bird, the only one of its kind. It is consumed in fire and then resurrected from the ashes to begin life anew.*

Moving of the earth° brings harms and fears,   earthquakes
   Men reckon what it did and meant;   10
But trepidation of the spheres,°
   Though greater far, is innocent.

Dull sublunary° lovers' love   earthly
   (Whose soul is sense) cannot admit
Absence, because it doth remove   15
   Those things which elemented° it.   composed

But we, by a love so much refined
   That our selves know not what it is,
Inter-assured of the mind,
   Care less, eyes, lips, and hands to miss.   20

Our two souls therefore, which are one,
   Though I must go, endure not yet
A breach, but an expansion,
   Like gold to airy thinness beat.

If they be two, they are two so   25
   As stiff twin compasses° are two:
Thy soul, the fixed foot, makes no show
   To move, but doth, if the other do;

And though it in the center sit,
   Yet when the other far doth roam,   30
It leans, and hearkens after it,
   And grows erect, as that comes home.

Such wilt thou be to me, who must,
   Like the other foot, obliquely run;
Thy firmness makes my circle just,   35
   And makes me end where I begun.

                                           (1633)

The Flea

Mark but this flea, and mark in this
How little that which thou deny'st me is;
It sucked me first, and now sucks thee,
And in this flea our two bloods mingled be;

"A Valediction"   [11] **trepidation of the spheres**   *movement in the outermost of the heavenly spheres. In Ptolemy's astronomy these outer spheres caused others to vary from their orbits.*   [26] **twin compasses**   *the two feet of a mathematical compass used for drawing circles.*

Thou know'st that this cannot be said   5
A sin, nor shame, nor loss of maidenhead;
    Yet this enjoys before it woo,
    And pampered swells with one blood made of two,
    And this, alas, is more than we would do.

Oh stay, three lives in one flea spare,   10
Where we almost, yea, more than married are.
This flea is you and I, and this
Our marriage bed and marriage temple is;
Though parents grudge, and you, we are met
And cloistered in these living walls of jet.   15
    Though use° make you apt to kill me,   custom
    Let not to that, self-murder added be,
    And sacrilege, three sins in killing three.

Cruel and sudden, hast thou since
Purpled thy nail in blood of innocence?   20
Wherein could this flea guilty be,
Except in that drop which it sucked from thee?
Yet thou triumph'st and say'st that thou
Find'st not thyself, nor me the weaker now.
    'Tis true. Then learn how false fears be: 25
    Just so much honor, when thou yield'st to me,
    Will waste, as this flea's death took life from thee.

                                        (1633)

Death, be not proud

Death, be not proud, though some have calléd thee
Mighty and dreadful, for thou are not so;
For those whom thou think'st thou dost overthrow
Die not, poor Death, nor yet canst thou kill me.
From rest and sleep, which but thy pictures be,   5
Much pleasure; then from thee much more must flow,
And soonest our best men with thee do go,
Rest of their bones, and soul's delivery.
Thou art slave to fate, chance, kings, and desperate men,
And dost with poison, war, and sickness dwell,   10
And poppy or charms can make us sleep as well
And better than thy stroke; why swell'st thou then?
One short sleep past, we wake eternally
And death shall be no more; Death, thou shalt die.

                                        (1633)

Batter my heart, three-personed God

Batter my heart, three-personed God; for You
As yet but knock, breathe, shine, and seek to mend;
That I may rise and stand, o'erthrow me, and bend
Your force to break, blow, burn, and make me new.
I, like an usurped town, to another due,   5
Labor to admit You, but O, to no end;
Reason, Your viceroy in me, me should defend,
But is captíved, and proves weak or untrue.
Yet dearly I love You, and would be lovéd fain,°   gladly
But am betrothed unto Your enemy.   10
Divorce me, untie or break that knot again;
Take me to You, imprison me, for I,
Except You enthrall me, never shall be free,
Nor ever chaste, except You ravish me.

(1633)

BEN JONSON
[1573?–1637]

On My First Son

Farewell, thou child of my right hand,° and joy;
My sin was too much hope of thee, loved boy:
Seven years thou wert lent to me, and I thee pay,
Exacted by thy fate, on the just day.°
O could I lose all father now! for why   5
Will man lament the state he should envý,
To have so soon 'scaped world's and flesh's rage,
And, if no other misery, yet age?
Rest in soft peace, and asked, say, "Here doth lie
Ben Jonson his best piece of poetry."   10
For whose sake henceforth all his vows be such
As what he loves may never like too much.

(1616)

"On My First Son"   [1]**child of my right hand**   *the literal meaning, in Hebrew, of Benjamin, the boy's name.*
[4]**the just day**   *Jonson's son died on his seventh birthday.*

Song: To Celia

Drink to me only with thine eyes,
And I will pledge with mine;
Or leave a kiss but in the cup,
And I'll not look for wine.
The thirst that from the soul doth rise,   5
Doth ask a drink divine:
But might I of Jove's nectar sup,
I would not change for thine.

I sent thee late a rosy wreath,
Not so much honoring thee,   10
As giving it a hope, that there
It could not withered be.
But thou thereon did'st only breathe,
And sent'st it back to me;
Since when it grows and smells, I swear,   15
Not of itself, but thee.

                                        (1606)

ROBERT HERRICK
[1591–1667]

Upon Julia's Clothes

Whenas in silks my Julia goes,
Then, then, methinks, how sweetly flows
That liquefaction of her clothes.

Next, when I cast mine eyes and see
That brave vibration each way free,   5
O how that glittering taketh me!

                                        (1648)

To the Virgins, to Make Much of Time

Gather ye rosebuds while ye may:
    Old Time is still a-flying;
And this same flower that smiles today,
    Tomorrow will be dying.

The glorious lamp of heaven, the sun,   5
   The higher he's a-getting,
The sooner will his race be run,
   And nearer he's to setting.

That age is best which is the first,
   When youth and blood are warmer;   10
But being spent, the worse, and worst
   Times, still succeed the former.

Then be not coy, but use your time;
   And while ye may, go marry:
For, having lost but once your prime,   15
   You may for ever tarry.

(1648)

GEORGE HERBERT
[1593–1633]

The Altar

A broken ALTAR, Lord, Thy servant rears,
Made of a heart and cemented with tears;
  Whose parts are as Thy hand did frame;
  No workman's tool hath touched the same.
     A HEART alone   5
     Is   such   a   stone,
     As   nothing   but
     Thy power doth cut.
     Wherefore each part
     Of my hard heart   10
     Meets in this frame
     To praise Thy name,
  That if I chance to hold my peace,
  These stones to praise Thee may not cease.
Oh, let Thy blessed SACRIFICE be mine,
And sanctify this ALTAR to be Thine.   15

(1633)

JOHN MILTON
[1608–1674]

When I consider how my light is spent°

When I consider how my light is spent
   Ere half my days, in this dark world and wide,
   And that one talent° which is death to hide
   Lodged with me useless, though my soul more bent
To serve therewith my Maker, and present   5
   My true account, lest he returning chide;
   "Doth God exact day-labor, light denied?"
   I fondly° ask; but Patience to prevent   foolishly
That murmur, soon replies, "God doth not need
   Either man's work or his own gifts; who best   10
   Bear his mild yoke, they serve him best. His state
Is kingly. Thousands at his bidding speed
   And post o'er land and ocean without rest:
   They also serve who only stand and wait."

                                                   (1673)

On the Late Massacre in Piedmont°

Avenge, O Lord, thy slaughtered saints, whose bones
   Lie scattered on the Alpine mountains cold,
   Even them who kept thy truth so pure of old
   When all our fathers worshiped stocks° and stones   idols
Forget not: in thy book record their groans   5
   Who were thy sheep and in their ancient fold
   Slain by the bloody Piedmontese that rolled
   Mother with infant down the rocks. Their moans
The vales redoubled to the hills, and they
   To Heaven. Their martyred blood and ashes sow   10
   O'er all th' Italian fields where still doth sway
The triple tyrant:° that from these may grow
   A hundredfold, who having learnt thy way
   Early may fly the Babylonian woe.

                                                   (1673)

"When I consider how my light is spent"   *Milton went blind in 1651.*   [3]**one talent** *an allusion to Jesus's parable of the talents, in which the servant who buried the talent given him by his master was cast into the darkness (Matthew 25:14–30).*   "On the Late Massacre" *The Duke of Savoy in 1655 massacred 1,700 Waldensians, members of a Protestant sect.* [12]**The triple tyrant** *the pope, whose tiara contains three crowns.*

ANNE BRADSTREET
[1612–1672]

To My Dear and Loving Husband

If ever two were one, then surely we.
If ever man were loved by wife, then thee;
If ever wife was happy in a man,
Compare with me, ye women, if you can.
I prize thy love more than whole mines of gold   5
Or all the riches that the East doth hold.
My love is such that rivers cannot quench,
Nor aught but love from thee give recompense.
Thy love is such I can no way repay,
The heavens reward thee manifold, I pray.   10
Then while we live, in love let's so perséver
That when we live no more, we may live ever.

          (1678)

ANDREW MARVELL
[1621–1678]

To His Coy Mistress

Had we but world enough, and time,
This coyness, lady, were no crime.
We would sit down, and think which way
To walk, and pass our long love's day.
Thou by the Indian Ganges' side   5
Shoudst rubies° find; I by the tide
Of Humber° would complain. I would
Love you ten years before the flood,
And you should, if you please, refuse
Till the conversion of the Jews.°   10
My vegetable love° should grow
Vaster than empires and more slow;
An hundred years should go to praise
Thine eyes, and on thy forehead gaze;

"To His Coy Mistress" °rubies associated with virginity. °Humber the river that runs through Marvell's native town, Hull. °the conversion of the Jews supposedly to occur at the end of time. °vegetable love a reference to the idea that vegetables have the power to grow but lack consciousness.

Two hundred to adore each breast,   15
But thirty thousand to the rest;
An age at least to every part,
And the last age should show your heart.
For, lady, you deserve this state,
Nor would I love at lower rate.   20
   But at my back I always hear
Time's wingéd chariot hurrying near;
And yonder all before us lie
Deserts of vast eternity.
Thy beauty shall no more be found;   25
Nor, in thy marble vault, shall sound
My echoing song; then worms shall try
That long-preserved virginity,
And your quaint° honor turn to dust,   overscrupulous
And into ashes all my lust: 30
The grave's a fine and private place,
But none, I think, do there embrace.
   Now therefore, while the youthful hue
Sits on thy skin like morning dew
And while thy willing soul transpires°   breathes forth   35
At every pore with instant fires,
Now let us sport us while we may,
And now, like amorous birds of prey,
Rather at once our time devour
Than languish in his slow-chapped° power.   slow-jawed   40
Let us roll all our strength and all
Our sweetness up into one ball,
And tear our pleasures with rough strife
Through the iron gates of life:
Thus, though we cannot make our sun   45
Stand still, yet we will make him run.

                                                                 (1681)

ALEXANDER POPE
[1688–1744]

from *An Essay on Man*

FROM *EPISTLE II*

I. Know then thyself, presume not God to scan;°   scrutinize
The proper study of mankind is Man.
Placed on this isthmus of a middle state,
A being darkly wise, and rudely° great;   crudely
With too much knowledge for the Sceptic side,   5
With too much weakness for the Stoic's pride,
He hangs between; in doubt to act, or rest,
In doubt to deem himself a god, or beast;
In doubt his mind or body to prefer,
Born but to die, and reasoning but to err;   10
Alike in ignorance, his reason such,
Whether he thinks too little, or too much:
Chaos of thought and passion, all confused;
Still by himself abused, or disabused;
Created half to rise, and half to fall;   15
Great lord of all things, yet a prey to all;
Sole judge of truth, in endless error hurled:
The glory, jest, and riddle of the world!

(1711)

WILLIAM BLAKE
[1757–1827]

The Clod & the Pebble

"Love seeketh not Itself to please,
Nor for itself hath any care;
But for another gives its ease,
And builds a Heaven in Hell's despair."

    So sang a little Clod of Clay,   5
    Trodden with the cattle's feet;
    But a Pebble of the brook,
    Warbled out these metres meet:

"Love seeketh only Self to please,
To bind another to its delight,   10
Joys in another's loss of ease,
And builds a Hell in Heaven's despite."

(1794)

The Lamb

Little Lamb, who made thee?
  Dost thou know who made thee?
Gave thee life & bid thee feed,
By the stream & o'er the mead;
Gave thee clothing of delight,   5
Softest clothing wooly bright;
Gave thee such a tender voice,
Making all the vales rejoice!
  Little Lamb who made thee?
  Dost thou know who made thee?   10

  Little Lamb I'll tell thee,
  Little Lamb I'll tell thee!
He is calléd by thy name,
For he calls himself a Lamb:
He is meek & he is mild,   15
He became a little child:
I a child & thou a lamb,
We are calléd by his name.
  Little Lamb God bless thee.
  Little Lamb God bless thee.   20

(1789)

The Tyger

Tyger! Tyger! burning bright
In the forests of the night,
What immortal hand or eye
Could frame thy fearful symmetry?

In what distant deeps or skies   5
Burnt the fire of thine eyes?
On what wings dare he aspire?
What the hand, dare seize the fire?

And what shoulder, & what art,
Could twist the sinews of thy heart?   10
And when thy heart began to beat,
What dread hand? & what dread feet?

What the hammer? what the chain?
In what furnace was thy brain?
What the anvil? what dread grasp   15
Dare its deadly terrors clasp?

When the stars threw down their spears,
And water'd heaven with their tears,
Did he smile his work to see?
Did he who made the Lamb make thee?   20

Tyger! Tyger! burning bright
In the forests of the night,
What immortal hand or eye
Dare frame thy fearful symmetry?

(1794)

The Garden of Love

I went to the Garden of Love,
And saw what I never had seen:
A Chapel was built in the midst,
Where I used to play on the green.

And the gates of this Chapel were shut,   5
And "Thou shalt not" writ over the door;
So I turn'd to the Garden of Love,
That so many sweet flowers bore,

And I saw it was filled with graves,
And tomb-stones where flowers should be: 10
And Priests in black gowns were walking their rounds,
And binding with briars my joys & desires.

(1794)

ROBERT BURNS
[1759–1796]

A Red, Red Rose

O my luve's like a red, red rose,
    That's newly sprung in June;
O my luve's like the melodie
    That's sweetly played in tune.

As fair art thou, my bonnie lass,   5
    So deep in luve am I;
And I will luve thee still, my dear,
    Till a' the seas gang dry.

Till a' the seas gang dry, my dear,
    And the rocks melt wi' the sun: 10
O I will love thee still, my dear,
    While the sands o' life shall run.

And fare thee weel, my only luve,
    And fare thee weel awhile!
And I will come again, my luve,   15
    Though it were ten thousand mile.

(1796)

WILLIAM WORDSWORTH
[1770–1850]

The world is too much with us

The world is too much with us; late and soon,
Getting and spending, we lay waste our powers;
Little we see in Nature that is ours;
We have given our hearts away, a sordid boon!°   gift
This Sea that bares her bosom to the moon,   5
The winds that will be howling at all hours,
And are up-gathered now like sleeping flowers,
For this, for everything, we are out of tune;
It moves us not.—Great God! I'd rather be
A Pagan suckled in a creed outworn;   10

So might I, standing on this pleasant lea,
Have glimpses that would make me less forlorn;
Have sight of Proteus rising from the sea;
Or hear old Triton° blow his wreathéd horn.

(1807)

The Solitary Reaper

Behold her, single in the field,
Yon solitary Highland Lass!
Reaping and singing by herself;
Stop here, or gently pass!
Alone she cuts and binds the grain,   5
And sings a melancholy strain;
O listen! for the Vale profound
Is overflowing with the sound.

No Nightingale did ever chaunt
More welcome notes to weary bands   10
Of travelers in some shady haunt,
Among Arabian sands;
A voice so thrilling ne'er was heard
In springtime from the Cuckoo bird,
Breaking the silence of the seas   15
Among the farthest Hebrides.

Will no one tell me what she sings?—
Perhaps the plaintive numbers flow
For old, unhappy, far-off things,
And battles long ago;   20
Or is it some more humble lay,
Familiar matter of today?
Some natural sorrow, loss, or pain,
That has been, and may be again?

Whate'er the theme, the Maiden sang   25
As if her song could have no ending;
I saw her singing at her work,
And o'er the sickle bending—
I listened, motionless and still;
And, as I mounted up the hill,   30
The music in my heart I bore,
Long after it was heard no more.

(1807)

"The world is too much with us" 13–14 **Proteus ... Triton** *classical sea gods. Triton's conch-shell horn calmed the waves.*

Composed upon Westminster Bridge, September 3, 1802

Earth has not anything to show more fair:
Dull would he be of soul who could pass by
A sight so touching in its majesty;
This City now doth, like a garment, wear
The beauty of the morning; silent, bare,   5
Ships, towers, domes, theaters, and temples lie
Open unto the fields, and to the sky;
All bright and glittering in the smokeless air.
Never did sun more beautifully steep
In his first splendor, valley, rock, or hill;   10
Ne'er saw I, never felt, a calm so deep!
The river glideth at his own sweet will:
Dear God! the very houses seem asleep;
And all that mighty heart is lying still!

(1807)

Lines

COMPOSED A FEW MILES ABOVE TINTERN ABBEY ON REVISITING THE BANKS OF THE
WYE DURING A TOUR, JULY 13, 1798

Five years have passed; five summers, with the length
Of five long winters! and again I hear
These waters, rolling from their mountain-springs
With a soft inland murmur. Once again
Do I behold these steep and lofty cliffs,   5
That on a wild secluded scene impress
Thoughts of more deep seclusion; and connect
The landscape with the quiet of the sky.
The day is come when I again repose
Here, under this dark sycamore, and view   10
These plots of cottage ground, these orchard tufts,
Which at this season, with their unripe fruits,
Are clad in one green hue, and lose themselves
Mid groves and copses.° Once again I see   thickets
These hedgerows, hardly hedgerows, little lines   15
Of sportive wood run wild; these pastoral farms,
Green to the very door; and wreaths of smoke
Sent up, in silence, from among the trees!
With some uncertain notice, as might seem
Of vagrant dwellers in the houseless woods,   20
Or of some Hermit's cave, where by his fire
The Hermit sits alone.
                         These beauteous forms,
Through a long absence, have not been to me

As is a landscape to a blind man's eye;
But oft, in lonely rooms, and 'mid the din   25
Of towns and cities, I have owed to them,
In hours of weariness, sensations sweet,
Felt in the blood, and felt along the heart;
And passing even into my purer mind
With tranquil restoration—feelings too   30
Of unremembered pleasure; such, perhaps,
As have no slight or trivial influence
On that best portion of a good man's life,
His little, nameless, unremembered, acts
Of kindness and of love. Nor less, I trust,   35
To them I may have owed another gift,
Of aspect more sublime; that blessed mood,
In which the burthen of the mystery,
In which the heavy and the weary weight
Of all this unintelligible world,   40
Is lightened—that serene and blessed mood,
In which the affections gently lead us on—
Until, the breath of this corporeal frame
And even the motion of our human blood
Almost suspended, we are laid asleep   45
In body, and become a living soul;
While with an eye made quiet by the power
Of harmony, and the deep power of joy,
We see into the life of things.

          If this
Be but a vain belief, yet, oh! how oft—   50
In darkness and amid the many shapes
Of joyless daylight; when the fretful stir
Unprofitable, and the fever of the world,
Have hung upon the beatings of my heart—
How oft, in spirit, have I turned to thee,   55
O sylvan Wye! thou wanderer through the woods,
How often has my spirit turned to thee!

    And now, with gleams of half-extinguished thought,
With many recognitions dim and faint,
And somewhat of a sad perplexity,   60
The picture of the mind revives again;
While here I stand, not only with the sense
Of present pleasure, but with pleasing thoughts
That in this moment there is life and food
For future years. And so I dare to hope,   65
Though changed, no doubt, from what I was when first
I came among these hills; when like a roe

I bounded o'er the mountains, by the sides
Of the deep rivers, and the lonely streams,
Wherever nature led—more like a man   70
Flying from something that he dreads than one
Who sought the thing he loved. For nature then
(The coarser pleasures of my boyish days,
And their glad animal movements all gone by)
To me was all in all.—I cannot paint   75
What then I was. The sounding cataract
Haunted me like a passion; the tall rock,
The mountain, and the deep and gloomy wood,
Their colors and their forms, were then to me
An appetite; a feeling and a love,   80
That had no need of a remoter charm,
By thought supplied, nor any interest
Unborrowed from the eye.—That time is past,
And all its aching joys are now no more,
And all its dizzy raptures. Not for this   85
Faint I, nor mourn nor murmur; other gifts
Have followed; for such loss, I would believe,
Abundant recompense. For I have learned
To look on nature, not as in the hour
Of thoughtless youth, but hearing oftentimes   90
The still, sad music of humanity,
Nor harsh nor grating, though of ample power
To chasten and subdue. And I have felt
A presence that disturbs me with the joy
Of elevated thoughts; a sense sublime   95
Of something far more deeply interfused,
Whose dwelling is the light of setting suns,
And the round ocean and the living air,
And the blue sky, and in the mind of man:
A motion and a spirit, that impels   100
All thinking things, all objects of all thought,
And rolls through all things. Therefore am I still
A lover of the meadows and the woods,
And mountains; and of all that we behold
From this green earth; of all the mighty world   105
Of eye, and ear—both what they half create,
And what perceive; well pleased to recognize
In nature and the language of the sense
The anchor of my purest thoughts, the nurse,
The guide, the guardian of my heart, and soul   110
Of all my moral being.

                              Nor perchance,
If I were not thus taught, should I the more
Suffer my genial spirits° to decay: powers

For thou art with me here upon the banks
Of this fair river; thou my dearest Friend,° 115
My dear, dear Friend; and in thy voice I catch
The language of my former heart, and read
My former pleasures in the shooting lights
Of thy wild eyes. Oh! yet a little while
May I behold in thee what I was once, 120
My dear, dear Sister! and this prayer I make,
Knowing that Nature never did betray
The heart that loved her; 'tis her privilege,
Through all the years of this our life, to lead
From joy to joy: for she can so inform°   give form to 125
The mind that is within us, so impress
With quietness and beauty, and so feed
With lofty thoughts, that neither evil tongues,
Rash judgments, nor the sneers of selfish men,
Nor greetings where no kindness is, nor all 130
The dreary intercourse of daily life,
Shall e'er prevail against us, or disturb
Our cheerful faith, that all which we behold
Is full of blessings. Therefore let the moon
Shine on thee in thy solitary walk; 135
And let the misty mountain winds be free
To blow against thee: and, in after years,
When these wild ecstasies shall be matured
Into a sober pleasure; when thy mind
Shall be a mansion for all lovely forms, 140
Thy memory be as a dwelling place
For all sweet sounds and harmonies; oh! then,
If solitude, or fear, or pain, or grief
Should be thy portion, with what healing thoughts
Of tender joy wilt thou remember me, 145
And these my exhortations! Nor, perchance—
If I should be where I no more can hear
Thy voice, nor catch from thy wild eyes these gleams
Of past existence—wilt thou then forget
That on the banks of this delightful stream 150
We stood together; and that I, so long
A worshiper of Nature, hither came
Unwearied in that service; rather say
With warmer love—oh! with far deeper zeal
Of holier love. Nor wilt thou then forget, 155
That after many wanderings, many years
Of absence, these steep woods and lofty cliffs,
And this green pastoral landscape, were to me
More dear, both for themselves and for thy sake!

(1798)

"Lines Composed a Few Miles above Tintern Abbey"   [115]**Friend**   *Wordsworth's sister, Dorothy.*

SAMUEL TAYLOR COLERIDGE
[1772–1834]

Kubla Khan°

OR A VISION IN A DREAM. A FRAGMENT

In Xanadu did Kubla Khan
A stately pleasure dome decree:
Where Alph, the sacred river, ran
Through caverns measureless to man
    Down to a sunless sea.   5

So twice five miles of fertile ground
With walls and towers were girdled round:
And there were gardens bright with sinuous rills,
Where blossomed many an incense-bearing tree;
And here were forests ancient as the hills,   10
Enfolding sunny spots of greenery.

But oh! that deep romantic chasm which slanted
Down the green hill athwart a cedarn cover!
A savage place! as holy and enchanted
As e'er beneath a waning moon was haunted   15
By woman wailing for her demon lover!
And from this chasm, with ceaseless turmoil seething,
As if this earth in fast thick pants were breathing,
A mighty fountain momently was forced:
Amid whose swift half-intermitted burst   20
Huge fragments vaulted like rebounding hail,
Or chaffy grain beneath the thresher's flail:
And 'mid these dancing rocks at once and ever
It flung up momently the sacred river.
Five miles meandering with a mazy motion   25
Through wood and dale the sacred river ran,
Then reached the caverns measureless to man,
And sank in tumult to a lifeless ocean:
And 'mid this tumult Kubla heard from far
Ancestral voices prophesying war!   30

    The shadow of the dome of pleasure
    Floated midway on the waves;

"Kubla Khan"   *the first ruler of the Mongol dynasty in thirteenth-century China. Coleridge's topography and place names are imaginary.*

Where was heard the mingled measure
From the fountain and the caves.
It was a miracle of rare device,   35
A sunny pleasure dome with caves of ice!

A damsel with a dulcimer
In a vision once I saw:
It was an Abyssinian maid,
And on her dulcimer she played,   40
Singing of Mount Abora.
Could I revive within me
Her symphony and song,
To such a deep delight 'twould win me,
That with music loud and long,   45
I would build that dome in air,
That sunny dome! those caves of ice!
And all who heard should see them there,
And all should cry, Beware! Beware!
His flashing eyes, his floating hair!   50
Weave a circle round him thrice,
And close your eyes with holy dread,
For he on honey-dew hath fed,
And drunk the milk of Paradise.

                                                      (1798)

GEORGE GORDON, LORD BYRON
[1788–1824]

She walks in beauty

1

She walks in beauty, like the night
   Of cloudless climes and starry skies;
And all that's best of dark and bright
   Meet in her aspect and her eyes:
Thus mellowed to that tender light   5
   Which heaven to gaudy day denies.

2

One shade the more, one ray the less,
   Had half impaired the nameless grace
Which waves in every raven tress,
   Or softly lightens o'er her face;   10
Where thoughts serenely sweet express
   How pure, how dear their dwelling place.

3

And on that cheek, and o'er that brow,
   So soft, so calm, yet eloquent,
The smiles that win, the tints that glow,   15
   But tell of days in goodness spent,
A mind at peace with all below,
   A heart whose love is innocent!

(1815)

PERCY BYSSHE SHELLEY
[1792–1822]

Ozymandias°

I met a traveler from an antique land
Who said: Two vast and trunkless legs of stone
Stand in the desert . . . Near them, on the sand,
Half sunk, a shattered visage lies, whose frown,
And wrinkled lip, and sneer of cold command,   5
Tell that its sculptor well those passions read
Which yet survive, stamped on these lifeless things,
The hand that mocked them, and the heart that fed:
And on the pedestal these words appear:
"My name is Ozymandias, king of kings: 10
Look on my works, ye Mighty, and despair!"
Nothing beside remains. Round the decay
Of that colossal wreck, boundless and bare
The lone and level sands stretch far away.

(1818)

Ode to the West Wind

1

O wild West Wind, thou breath of Autumn's being,
Thou, from whose unseen presence the leaves dead
Are driven, like ghosts from an enchanter fleeing,

Yellow, and black, and pale, and hectic red,
Pestilence-stricken multitudes: O thou,   5
Who chariotest to their dark wintry bed

"Ozymandias"   *Greek name for the Egyptian ruler Rameses II, who erected a huge statue in his own likeness, among numerous other monuments.*

The wingéd seeds, where they lie cold and low,
Each like a corpse within its grave, until
Thine azure sister of the Spring shall blow

Her clarion° o'er the dreaming earth, and fill   trumpet call   10
(Driving sweet buds like flocks to feed in air)
With living hues and odors plain and hill:

Wild Spirit, which art moving everywhere;
Destroyer and preserver; hear, oh, hear!

2

Thou on whose stream, mid the steep sky's commotion,   15
Loose clouds like earth's decaying leaves are shed,
Shook from the tangled boughs of Heaven and Ocean,

Angels° of rain and lightning: there are spread   messengers
On the blue surface of thine aëry surge,
Like the bright hair uplifted from the head   20

Of some fierce Maenad,° even from the dim verge
Of the horizon to the zenith's height,
The locks of the approaching storm. Thou dirge

Of the dying year, to which this closing night
Will be the dome of a vast sepulcher,   25
Vaulted with all thy congregated might

Of vapors, from whose solid atmosphere
Black rain, and fire, and hail will burst: oh, hear!

3

Thou who didst waken from his summer dreams
The blue Mediterranean, where he lay,   30
Lulled by the coil of his crystálline streams,

Beside a pumice isle in Baiae's bay,
And saw in sleep old palaces and towers
Quivering within the wave's intenser day,

All overgrown with azure moss and flowers   35
So sweet, the sense faints picturing them! Thou
For whose path the Atlantic's level powers

"Ode to the West Wind"   21**Maenad**   *frenzied female worshipper of Dionysus, god of wine and fertility.*

Cleave themselves into chasms, while far below
The sea-blooms and the oozy woods which wear
The sapless foliage of the ocean, know   40

Thy voice, and suddenly grow gray with fear,
And tremble and despoil themselves: oh, hear!

4

If I were a dead leaf thou mightest bear;
If I were a swift cloud to fly with thee;
A wave to pant beneath thy power, and share   45

The impulse of thy strength, only less free
Than thou, O uncontrollable! If even
I were as in my boyhood, and could be

The comrade of thy wanderings over Heaven,
As then, when to outstrip thy skyey speed   50
Scarce seemed a vision; I would ne'er have striven

As thus with thee in prayer in my sore need.
Oh, lift me as a wave, a leaf, a cloud!
I fall upon the thorns of life! I bleed!

A heavy weight of hours has chained and bowed   55
One too like thee: tameless, and swift, and proud.

5

Make me thy lyre,° even as the forest is: small harp
What if my leaves are falling like its own!
The tumult of thy mighty harmonies

Will take from both a deep, autumnal tone,   60
Sweet though in sadness. Be thou, Spirit fierce,
My spirit! Be thou me, impetuous one!

Drive my dead thoughts over the universe
Like withered leaves to quicken a new birth!
And, by the incantation of this verse,   65

Scatter, as from an unextinguished hearth
Ashes and sparks, my words among mankind!
Be through my lips to unawakened earth

The trumpet of a prophecy! O Wind,
If Winter comes, can Spring be far behind?   70

(1820)

JOHN KEATS
[1795–1821]

When I have fears that I may cease to be

When I have fears that I may cease to be
  Before my pen has gleaned my teeming brain,
Before high-piléd books, in charact'ry,°   written symbols
  Hold like rich garners the full-ripened grain;
When I behold, upon the night's starred face,   5
  Huge cloudy symbols of a high romance,
And think that I may never live to trace
  Their shadows, with the magic hand of chance;
And when I feel, fair creature of an hour,
  That I shall never look upon thee more,   10
Never have relish in the faery° power   magical
  Of unreflecting love!—then on the shore
Of the wide world I stand alone, and think
Till Love and Fame to nothingness do sink.

                        (1818, 1848)

La Belle Dame sans Merci°

O what can ail thee, Knight at arms,
  Alone and palely loitering?
The sedge has withered from the Lake
  And no birds sing!

O what can ail thee, Knight at arms,   5
  So haggard, and so woebegone?
The squirrel's granary is full
  And the harvest's done.

I see a lily on thy brow
  With anguish moist and fever dew,   10
And on thy cheeks a fading rose
  Fast withereth too.

"I met a Lady in the Meads,°   meadows
  Full beautiful, a faery's child,
Her hair was long, her foot was light   15
  And her eyes were wild.

"I made a Garland for her head,
    And bracelets too, and fragrant Zone;°   girdle
She looked at me as she did love
    And made sweet moan.   20

"I set her on my pacing steed
    And nothing else saw all day long,
For sidelong would she bend and sing
    A faery's song.

"She found me roots of relish sweet,   25
    And honey wild, and manna dew,
And sure in language strange she said
    'I love thee true.'

"She took me to her elfin grot
    And there she wept and sighed full sore,   30
And there I shut her wild wild eyes
    With kisses four.

"And there she lulléd me asleep,
    And there I dreamed, Ah Woe betide!
The latest dream I ever dreamt   35
    On the cold hill side.

"I saw pale Kings, and Princes too,
    Pale warriors, death-pale were they all;
They cried, 'La belle dame sans merci
    Hath thee in thrall!'   40

"I saw their starved lips in the gloam
    With horrid warning gapéd wide,
And I awoke, and found me here
    On the cold hill's side.

"And this is why I sojourn here,   45
    Alone and palely loitering;
Though the sedge is withered from the Lake
    And no birds sing."

                                                  (1819, 1888)

"La Belle Dame sans Merci"   *the beautiful lady without mercy.*

Ode to a Nightingale

1

My heart aches, and a drowsy numbness pains
  My sense, as though of hemlock° I had drunk,
Or emptied some dull opiate to the drains°   dregs
  One minute past, and Lethe-wards° had sunk:
'Tis not through envy of thy happy lot,   5
  But being too happy in thine happiness—
    That thou, light-wingéd Dryad° of the trees,   tree nymph
      In some melodious plot
Of beechen green, and shadows numberless,
    Singest of summer in full-throated ease.   10

2

O, for a draught of vintage! that hath been
  Cooled a long age in the deep-delvéd earth,
Tasting of Flora° and the country green,
  Dance, and Provençal song,° and sunburnt mirth!
O for a beaker full of the warm South,   15
  Full of the true, the blushful Hippocrene,°
    With beaded bubbles winking at the brim,
      And purple-stainéd mouth;
That I might drink, and leave the world unseen,
  And with thee fade away into the forest dim: 20

3

Fade far away, dissolve, and quite forget
  What thou among the leaves hast never known,
The weariness, the fever, and the fret
  Here, where men sit and hear each other groan;
Where palsy shakes a few, sad, last gray hairs,   25
  Where youth grows pale, and specter-thin, and dies,
    Where but to think is to be full of sorrow
      And leaden-eyed despairs,
Where Beauty cannot keep her lustrous eyes,
  Or new Love pine at them beyond tomorrow.   30

"Ode to a Nightingale"   ²**hemlock**   opiate; poisonous in large quantities.   ⁴**Lethe-wards**   towards Lethe, the river of forgetfulness.   ¹³**Flora**   goddess of the flowers.   ¹⁴**Provençal song**   Provence, in southern France, home of the troubadours.   ¹⁶**true . . . Hippocrene**   wine. A fountain on Mount Helicon in Greece, whose waters reputedly stimulated poetic imagination.

4

Away! away! for I will fly to thee,
   Not charioted by Bacchus and his pards,°
But on the viewless° wings of Poesy,   invisible
   Though the dull brain perplexes and retards:
Already with thee! tender is the night,   35
   And haply° the Queen-Moon is on her throne,   perhaps
      Clustered around by all her starry Fays;°   fairies
        But here there is no light,
Save what from heaven is with the breezes blown
   Through verdurous glooms and winding mossy ways.   40

5

I cannot see what flowers are at my feet,
   Nor what soft incense hangs upon the boughs,
But, in embalméd° darkness, guess each sweet   scented
   Wherewith the seasonable month endows
The grass, the thicket, and the fruit tree wild;   45
   White hawthorn, and the pastoral eglantine;°   sweetbriar
      Fast fading violets covered up in leaves;
        And mid-May's eldest child,
The coming musk-rose, full of dewy wine,
   The murmurous haunt of flies on summer eves.   50

6

Darkling° I listen; and for many a time   in darkness
I have been half in love with easeful Death,
Called him soft names in many a muséd rhyme,
   To take into the air my quiet breath;
Now more than ever seems it rich to die,   55
   To cease upon the midnight with no pain,
      While thou art pouring forth thy soul abroad
        In such an ecstasy!
Still wouldst thou sing, and I have ears in vain—
   To thy high requiem become a sod.   60

7

Thou wast not born for death, immortal Bird!
   No hungry generations tread thee down;
The voice I hear this passing night was heard
   In ancient days by emperor and clown:
Perhaps the selfsame song that found a path   65
   Through the sad heart of Ruth, when, sick for home,
      She stood in tears amid the alien corn;°

---

³²**Bacchus . . . pards**   *the god of wine and revelry and the leopards who drew his chariot.*

The same that ofttimes hath
Charmed magic casements, opening on the foam
Of perilous seas, in faery lands forlorn.   70

8

Forlorn! the very word is like a bell
To toll me back from thee to my sole self!
Adieu! the fancy cannot cheat so well
As she is famed to do, deceiving elf.
Adieu! adieu! thy plaintive anthem fades   75
Past the near meadows, over the still stream,
Up the hill side; and now 'tis buried deep
In the next valley-glades:
Was it a vision, or a waking dream?
Fled is that music:—Do I wake or sleep?   80

(1819, 1820)

Ode on a Grecian Urn

1

Thou still unravished bride of quietness,
Thou foster child of silence and slow time,
Sylvan° historian, who canst thus express   woodland
A flowery tale more sweetly than our rhyme:
What leaf-fringed legend haunts about thy shape   5
Of deities or mortals, or of both,
In Tempe or the dales of Arcady?°
What men or gods are these? What maidens loath?
What mad pursuit? What struggle to escape?
What pipes and timbrels? What wild ecstasy?   10

2

Heard melodies are sweet, but those unheard
Are sweeter; therefore, ye soft pipes, play on;
Not to the sensual ear, but, more endeared,
Pipe to the spirit ditties of no tone:
Fair youth, beneath the trees, thou canst not leave   15
Thy song, nor ever can those trees be bare;
Bold Lover, never, never canst thou kiss,
Though winning near the goal—yet, do not grieve;
She cannot fade, though thou hast not thy bliss,
Forever wilt thou love, and she be fair!   20

"Ode on a Grecian Urn" ⁷*Tempe . . . Arcady* in Greece, beautiful rural regions.   ⁶⁶⁻⁶⁷*Ruth . . . corn*
a Biblical heroine who worked in the harvest fields in a foreign land.

3

Ah, happy, happy boughs! that cannot shed
　　Your leaves, nor ever bid the Spring adieu;
And, happy melodist, unweariéd,
　　Forever piping songs forever new;
More happy love! more happy, happy love!　　　　　　　25
　　Forever warm and still to be enjoyed,
　　　　Forever panting, and forever young;
All breathing human passion far above,
　　That leaves a heart high-sorrowful and cloyed,
　　　　A burning forehead, and a parching tongue.　　　30

4

Who are these coming to the sacrifice?
　　To what green altar, O mysterious priest,
Lead'st thou that heifer lowing at the skies,
　　And all her silken flanks with garlands dressed?
What little town by river or sea shore,　　　　　　35
　　Or mountain-built with peaceful citadel,
　　　　Is emptied of this folk, this pious morn?
And, little town, thy streets forevermore
　　Will silent be; and not a soul to tell
　　　　Why thou art desolate, can e'er return.　　　　40

5

O Attic shape! Fair attitude! with brede°　　　　　woven pattern
　　Of marble men and maidens overwrought,°　　　ornamented
With forest branches and the trodden weed;
　　Thou, silent form, dost tease us out of thought
As doth eternity: Cold Pastoral!　　　　　　　　　45
　　When old age shall this generation waste,
　　　　Thou shalt remain, in midst of other woe
Than ours, a friend to man, to whom thou say'st,
"Beauty is truth, truth beauty,"—that is all
　　Ye know on earth, and all ye need to know.

(1819, 1820)

ELIZABETH BARRETT BROWNING
[1806–1861]

How do I love thee? Let me count the ways

How do I love thee? Let me count the ways.
I love thee to the depth and breadth and height
My soul can reach, when feeling out of sight
For the ends of Being and ideal Grace.
I love thee to the level of everyday's   5
Most quiet need, by sun and candle-light.
I love thee freely, as men strive for Right;
I love thee purely, as they turn from Praise.
I love thee with the passion put to use
In my old griefs, and with my childhood's faith.   10
I love thee with a love I seemed to lose
With my lost saints—I love thee with the breath,
Smiles, tears, of all my life!—and, if God choose,
I shall but love thee better after death.

(1850)

EDGAR ALLAN POE
[1809–1849]

To Helen

Helen, thy beauty is to me
  Like those Nicean barks° of yore,   ships
That gently, o'er a perfumed sea,
  The weary, way-worn wanderer bore
    To his own native shore.   5

On desperate seas long wont to roam,
  Thy hyacinth hair,° thy classic face,
Thy Naiad° airs have brought me home
  To the glory that was Greece
    And the grandeur that was Rome.   10

Lo! in yon brilliant window-niche
  How statue-like I see thee stand!
  The agate lamp within thy hand,
Ah! Psyche from the regions which
    Are Holy Land!   15

(1831, 1845)

"To Helen" [7]*hyacinth hair* allusion to the curled hair of the slain youth Hyacinthus, beloved of Apollo.
[8]*Naiad* water nymph.

The Raven

Once upon a midnight dreary, while I pondered, weak and weary,
Over many a quaint and curious volume of forgotten lore—
While I nodded, nearly napping, suddenly there came a tapping,
As of some one gently rapping, rapping at my chamber door—
" 'Tis some visiter," I muttered, "tapping at my chamber door—   5
    Only this and nothing more."

Ah, distinctly I remember it was in the bleak December;
And each separate dying ember wrought its ghost upon the floor.
Eagerly I wished the morrow;—vainly I had sought to borrow
From my books surcease of sorrow—sorrow for the lost Lenore—   10
For the rare and radiant maiden whom the angels name Lenore—
    Nameless *here* for evermore.

And the silken, sad, uncertain rustling of each purple curtain
Thrilled me—filled me with fantastic terrors never felt before;
So that now, to still the beating of my heart, I stood repeating   15
" 'Tis some visiter entreating entrance at my chamber door—
Some late visiter entreating entrance at my chamber door;—
    This it is and nothing more."

Presently my soul grew stronger; hesitating then no longer,
"Sir," said I, "or Madam, truly your forgiveness I implore;   20
But the fact is I was napping, and so gently you came rapping,
And so faintly you came tapping, tapping at my chamber door,
  That I scarce was sure I heard you"—here I opened wide the door;—
    Darkness there and nothing more.

Deep into that darkness peering, long I stood there wondering,
    fearing,   25
Doubting, dreaming dreams no mortal ever dared to dream before;
But the silence was unbroken, and the stillness gave no token,
And the only word there spoken was the whispered word, "Lenore!"
This I whispered, and an echo murmured back the word, "Lenore!"
    Merely this and nothing more.   30

Back into the chamber turning, all my soul within me burning,
Soon again I heard a tapping somewhat louder than before.
"Surely," said I, "surely that is something at my window lattice;
Let me see, then, what thereat is, and this mystery explore—
Let my heart be still a moment and this mystery explore;—   35
    'Tis the wind and nothing more!"

Open here I flung the shutter, when, with many a flirt and flutter,
In there stepped a stately Raven of the saintly days of yore;

Not the least obeisance made he; not a minute stopped or stayed he;
But, with mien of lord or lady, perched above my chamber door—   40
Perched upon a bust of Pallas° just above my chamber door—
    Perched, and sat, and nothing more.

Then this ebony bird beguiling my sad fancy into smiling,
By the grave and stern decorum of the countenance it wore,
"Though thy crest be shorn and shaven, thou," I said, "art sure no craven,   45
Ghastly grim and ancient Raven wandering from the Nightly shore—
Tell me what thy lordly name is on the Night's Plutonian° shore!"
    Quoth the Raven "Nevermore."

Much I marvelled this ungainly fowl to hear discourse so plainly,
Though its answer little meaning—little relevancy bore;   50
For we cannot help agreeing that no living human being
Ever yet was blessed with seeing bird above his chamber door—
Bird or beast upon the sculptured bust above his chamber door,
    With such name as "Nevermore."

But the Raven, sitting lonely on the placid bust, spoke only   55
That one word, as if his soul in that one word he did outpour.
Nothing farther then he uttered—not a feather then he fluttered—
Till I scarcely more than muttered "Other friends have flown before—
On the morrow *he* will leave me, as my Hopes have flown before."
    Then the bird said "Nevermore."   60

Startled at the stillness broken by reply so aptly spoken,
"Doubtless," said I, "what it utters is its only stock and store
Caught from some unhappy master whom unmerciful Disaster
Followed fast and followed faster till his songs one burden bore—
Till the dirges of his Hope that melancholy burden bore   65
    Of 'Never—nevermore.'"

But the Raven still beguiling my sad fancy into smiling,
Straight I wheeled a cushioned seat in front of bird, and bust and door;
Then, upon the velvet sinking, I betook myself to linking
Fancy unto fancy, thinking what this ominous bird of yore—   70
What this grim, ungainly, ghastly, gaunt, and ominous bird of yore
    Meant in croaking "Nevermore."

Thus I sat engaged in guessing, but no syllable expressing
To the fowl whose fiery eyes now burned into my bosom's core;
This and more I sat divining, with my head at ease reclining   75
On the cushion's velvet lining that the lamp-light gloated o'er,
But whose velvet-violet lining with the lamp-light gloating o'er,
    She shall press, ah, nevermore!

"The Raven"   [41] **Pallas**   *Pallas Athene, patron goddess of Athens.*   [47] **Plutonian**   *Pluto, god of the underworld.*

Then, methought, the air grew denser, perfumed from an unseen censer
Swung by seraphim whose foot-falls tinkled on the tufted floor.　　　　80
"Wretch," I cried, "thy God hath lent thee—by these angels he hath sent thee
Respite—respite and nepenthe from thy memories of Lenore;
Quaff, oh quaff this kind nepenthe and forget this lost Lenore!"
　　　　Quoth the Raven "Nevermore."

"Prophet!" said I, "thing of evil!—prophet still, if bird or devil!—　　　　85
Whether Tempter sent, or whether tempest tossed thee here ashore,
Desolate yet all undaunted, on this desert land enchanted—
Oh this home by Horror haunted—tell me truly, I implore—
Is there—is there balm in Gilead?—tell me—tell me, I implore!"
　　　　Quoth the Raven "Nevermore."　　　　90

"Prophet!" said I, "thing of evil!—prophet still, if bird or devil!
By that Heaven that bends above us—by that God we both adore—
Tell this soul with sorrow laden if, within the distant Aidenn,
It shall clasp a sainted maiden whom the angels name Lenore—
Clasp a rare and radiant maiden whom the angels name Lenore."　　　　95
　　　　Quoth the Raven "Nevermore."

"Be that word our sign of parting, bird or fiend!" I shrieked, upstarting—
"Get thee back into the tempest and the Night's Plutonian shore!
Leave no black plume as a token of that lie thy soul hath spoken!
Leave my loneliness unbroken!—quit the bust above my door!　　　　100
Take thy beak from out my heart, and take thy form from off my door!"
　　　　Quoth the Raven "Nevermore."

And the Raven, never flitting, still is sitting, still is sitting
On the pallid bust of Pallas just above my chamber door;
And his eyes have all the seeming of a demon's that is dreaming,　　　　105
And the lamp-light o'er him streaming throws his shadow on the floor;
And my soul from out that shadow that lies floating on the floor
　　　　Shall be lifted—nevermore!

(1845)

ALFRED, LORD TENNYSON
[1809–1892]

Ulysses°

It little profits that an idle king,
By this still hearth, among these barren crags,
Matched with an aged wife, I mete and dole
Unequal laws unto a savage race,
That hoard, and sleep, and feed, and know not me.   5
I cannot rest from travel; I will drink
Life to the lees. All times I have enjoyed
Greatly, have suffered greatly, both with those
That loved me, and alone; on shore, and when
Through scudding drifts the rainy Hyades°   10
Vext the dim sea. I am become a name;
For always roaming with a hungry heart
Much have I seen and known—cities of men
And manners,° climates, councils, governments,   *customs*
Myself not least, but honored of them all,—   15
And drunk delight of battle with my peers,
Far on the ringing plains of windy Troy.
I am a part of all that I have met;
Yet all experience is an arch wherethrough
Gleams that untraveled world whose margin fades   20
For ever and for ever when I move.
How dull it is to pause, to make an end,
To rust unburnished, not to shine in use!
As though to breathe were life! Life piled on life
Were all too little, and of one to me   25
Little remains; but every hour is saved
From that eternal silence, something more,
A bringer of new things; and vile it were
For some three suns to store and hoard myself,
And this gray spirit yearning in desire   30
To follow knowledge like a sinking star,
Beyond the utmost bound of human thought.
   This is my son, mine own Telemachus,
To whom I leave the scepter and the isle,
Well-loved of me, discerning to fulfill   35
This labor, by slow prudence to make mild
A rugged people, and through soft degrees

"Ulysses"   *according to Dante (in* The Inferno, *Canto 26) Ulysses, having been away for ten years during the Trojan War, is restless upon returning to his island kingdom of Ithaca, and he persuades a band of followers to accompany him on a journey.*   10**Hyades**   *a constellation of stars whose rising with the sun forecasts rain.*

Subdue them to the useful and the good.
Most blameless is he, centered in the sphere
Of common duties, decent° not to fail   proper   40
In offices° of tenderness, and pay   duties
Meet° adoration to my household gods,   appropriate
When I am gone. He works his work, I mine.
    There lies the port; the vessel puffs her sail;
There gloom the dark, broad seas. My mariners,   45
Souls that have toiled, and wrought, and thought with me,
That ever with a frolic welcome took
The thunder and the sunshine, and opposed
Free hearts, free foreheads—you and I are old;
Old age hath yet his honor and his toil.   50
Death closes all; but something ere the end,
Some work of noble note, may yet be done,
Not unbecoming men that strove with gods.
The lights begin to twinkle from the rocks;
The long day wanes; the slow moon climbs; the deep   55
Moans round with many voices. Come, my friends,
'Tis not too late to seek a newer world.
Push off, and sitting well in order smite
The sounding furrows; for my purpose holds
To sail beyond the sunset, and the baths   60
Of all the western stars, until I die.
It may be that the gulfs will wash us down;
It may be we shall touch the Happy Isles,°
And see the great Achilles, whom we knew.
Though much is taken, much abides; and though   65
We are not now that strength which in old days
Moved earth and heaven, that which we are, we are,
One equal temper of heroic hearts,
Made weak by time and fate, but strong in will
To strive, to seek, to find, and not to yield.   70

                                                                      (1842)

The Eagle

FRAGMENT

He clasps the crag with crooked hands;
Close to the sun in lonely lands,
Ringed with the azure world, he stands.

The wrinkled sea beneath him crawls;
He watches from his mountain walls,   5
And like a thunderbolt he falls.

                                                                      (1851)

---

63 **Happy Isles**   *the abode after death of those favored by the gods.*

ROBERT BROWNING
[*1812–1889*]

Soliloquy of the Spanish Cloister

1

Gr-r-r—there go, my heart's abhorrence!
    Water your damned flower-pots, do!
If hate killed men, Brother Lawrence,
    God's blood,° would not mine kill you!
What? your myrtle-bush wants trimming?   5
    Oh, that rose has prior claims—
Needs its leaden vase filled brimming?
    Hell dry you up with its flames!

2

At the meal we sit together:
    Salve tibi!° I must hear   10
Wise talk of the kind of weather,
    Sort of season, time of year:
Not a plenteous cork-crop: scarcely
    Dare we hope oak-galls,° *I doubt:*
What's the Latin name for "parsley"?   15
    What's the Greek name for Swine's Snout?

3

Whew! We'll have our platter burnished,
    Laid with care on our own shelf!
With a fire-new spoon we're furnished,
    And a goblet for ourself,   20
Rinsed like something sacrificial
    Ere 'tis fit to touch our chaps—
Marked with L for our initial!
    (He-he! There his lily snaps!)

4

Saint, forsooth! While brown Dolores   25
    Squats outside the Convent bank
With Sanchicha, telling stories,
    Steeping tresses in the tank,
Blue-black, lustrous, thick like horsehairs,

"Soliloquy of the Spanish Cloister"   **4God's blood** *an oath.*   **10Salve tibi** Hail to thee!   **14oak-**
galls *growths produced on oak leaves by gallflies.*

—Can't I see his dead eye glow,   30
Bright as 'twere a Barbary corsair's?°
(That is, if he'd let it show!)

                                    5

When he finishes refection,°   dinner
    Knife and fork he never lays
Cross-wise, to my recollection,   35
    As do I, in Jesu's praise.
I the Trinity illustrate,
    Drinking watered orange-pulp—
In three sips the Arian° frustrate;
    While he drains his at one gulp.   40

                                    6

Oh, those melons? If he's able
    We're to have a feast! so nice!
One goes to the Abbot's table,
    All of us get each a slice.
How go on your flowers? None double?   45
    Not one fruit-sort can you spy?
Strange! And I, too, at such trouble,
    Keep them close-nipped on the sly!

                                    7

There's a great text in Galatians,°
    Once you trip on it, entails   50
Twenty-nine distinct damnations,
    One sure, if another fails:
If I trip him just a-dying,
    Sure of heaven as sure can be,
Spin him around and send him flying   55
    Off to hell, a Manichee?°

                                    8

Or, my scrofulous French novel
    On grey paper with blunt type!
Simply glance at it, you grovel
    Hand and foot in Belial's gripe:°
If I double down its pages   60

"Soliloquy of the Spanish Cloister"   [31] **Barbary corsair's** *pirate's.*   [39] **Arian** *Arius, a fourth-century heretic, denied the doctrine of the Trinity.*   [49] **Galatians** *a New Testament epistle of St. Paul; see chapter 5, 14–15 and 16–24.*   [56] **Manichee** *the Manichean heresy divided the world into two equally powerful forces of darkness (evil) and light (good).*   [60] **Belial's gripe** *in the devil's grip.*

> At the woeful sixteenth print,
> When he gathers his greengages,
> Ope a sieve and slip it in't?

9

> Or, there's Satan! one might venture   65
> Pledge one's soul to him, yet leave
> Such a flaw in the indenture
> As he'd miss till, past retrieve,
> Blasted lay that rose-acacia
> We're so proud of! *Hy, Zy, Hine*° . . .   70
> 'St, there's vespers! *Plena gratiâ*°
> *Ave, Virgo!*° Gr-r-r—you swine!

                                    (1842)

WALT WHITMAN
[1819–1892]

A noiseless patient spider

A noiseless patient spider,
I mark'd where on a little promontory it stood isolated,
Mark'd how to explore the vacant vast surrounding,
It launch'd forth filament, filament, filament, out of itself,
Ever unreeling them, ever tirelessly speeding them.   5

And you O my soul where you stand,
Surrounded, detached, in measureless oceans of space,
Ceaselessly musing, venturing, throwing, seeking the spheres to connect them,
Till the bridge you will need be form'd, till the ductile anchor hold,
Till the gossamer thread you fling catch somewhere, O my soul.   10

                                      (1881)

Crossing Brooklyn Ferry

1

Flood-tide below me! I see you face to face!
Clouds of the west—sun there half an hour high—I see you also face to face.
Crowds of men and women attired in the usual costumes, how curious you are to me!

---

⁷⁰**Hy, Zy, Hine**   *an incantation.*   ⁷¹**Plena gratiâ**   *Full of grace.*   ⁷²**Ave, Virgo**   *Hail Virgin (reverses the opening words of the Ave Maria).*

On the ferry-boats the hundreds and hundreds that cross, returning home, are more
    curious to me than you suppose,
And you that shall cross from shore to shore years hence are more to me, and more
    in my meditations, than you might suppose.   5

2

The impalpable sustenance of me from all things at all hours of the day,
The simple, compact, well-join'd scheme, myself disintegrated, every one
    disintegrated yet part of the scheme,
The similitudes of the past and those of the future,
The glories strung like beads on my smallest sights and hearings, on the walk in the
    street and the passage over the river,
The current rushing so swiftly and swimming with me far away,   10
The others that are to follow me, the ties between me and them,
The certainty of others, the life, love, sight, hearing of others.
Others will enter the gates of the ferry and cross from shore to shore,
Others will watch the run of the flood-tide,
Others will see the shipping of Manhattan north and west, and the heights of
    Brooklyn to the south and east,   15
Others will see the islands large and small;
Fifty years hence, others will see them as they cross, the sun half an hour high,
A hundred years hence, or ever so many hundred years hence, others will see them,
Will enjoy the sunset, the pouring-in of the flood-tide, the falling-back to the sea of
    the ebb-tide.

3

It avails not, time nor place—distance avails not,   20
I am with you, you men and women of a generation, or ever so many generations
    hence,
Just as you feel when you look on the river and sky, so I felt,
Just as any of you is one of a living crowd, I was one of a crowd,
Just as you are refresh'd by the gladness of the river and the bright flow, I was
    refresh'd,
Just as you stand and lean on the rail, yet hurry with the swift current, I stood yet
    was hurried,   25
Just as you look on the numberless masts of ships and the thick-stemm'd pipes of
    steamboats, I look'd.

I too many and many a time cross'd the river of old,
Watched the Twelfth-month° sea-gulls, saw them high in the air floating   December
    with motionless wings, oscillating their bodies,
Saw how the glistening yellow lit up parts of their bodies and left the rest in strong
    shadow,
Saw the slow-wheeling circles and the gradual edging toward the south,   30
Saw the reflection of the summer sky in the water,

Had my eyes dazzled by the shimmering track of beams,
Look'd at the fine centrifugal spokes of light round the shape of my head in the
    sunlit water,
Look'd on the haze on the hills southward and south-westward,
Look'd on the vapor as it flew in fleeces tinged with violet,   35
Look'd toward the lower bay to notice the vessels arriving,
Saw their approach, saw aboard those that were near me,
Saw the white sails of schooners and sloops, saw the ships at anchor,
The sailors at work in the rigging or out astride the spars,
The round masts, the swinging motion of the hulls, the slender serpentine   40
    pennants,
The large and small steamers in motion, the pilots in their pilot-houses,
The white wake left by the passage, the quick tremulous whirl of the wheels,
The flags of all nations, the falling of them at sunset,
The scallop-edged waves in the twilight, the ladled cups, the frolicsome crests and
    glistening,
The stretch afar growing dimmer and dimmer, the gray walls of the granite
    storehouses by the docks,   45
On the river the shadowy group, the big steam-tug closely flank'd on each side by
    the barges, the hay-boat, the belated lighter,
On the neighboring shore the fires from the foundry chimneys burning high and
    glaringly into the night,
Casting their flicker of black contrasted with wild red and yellow light over the tops
    of houses, and down into the clefts of streets.

4

These and all else were to me the same as they are to you,
I loved well those cities, loved well the stately and rapid river,   50
The men and women I saw were all near to me,
Others the same—others who look back on me because I look'd forward to them,
(The time will come, though I stop° here to-day and to-night.)   stay

5

What is it then between us?
What is the count of the scores or hundreds of years between us?   55

Whatever it is, it avails not—distance avails not, and place avails not,
I too lived, Brooklyn of ample hills was mine,
I too walk'd the streets of Manhattan island, and bathed in the waters around it,
I too felt the curious abrupt questionings stir within me,
In the day among crowds of people sometimes they came upon me,   60
In my walks home late at night or as I lay in my bed they came upon me,
I too had been struck from the float forever held in solution,
I too had receiv'd identity by my body,
That I was I knew was of my body, and what I should be I knew I should be of my
    body.

6

It is not upon you alone the dark patches fall, 65
The dark threw its patches down upon me also,
The best I had done seem'd to me blank and suspicious,
My great thoughts as I supposed them, were they not in reality meager?
Nor is it you alone who know what it is to be evil,
I am he who knew what it was to be evil, 70
I too knitted the old knot of contrariety,
Blabb'd, blush'd, resented, lied, stole, grudg'd,
Had guile, anger, lust, hot wishes I dared not speak,
Was wayward, vain, greedy, shallow, sly, cowardly, malignant,
The wolf, the snake, the hog, not wanting in me, 75
The cheating look, the frivolous word, the adulterous wish, not wanting,
Refusals, hates, postponements, meanness, laziness, none of these wanting,
Was one with the rest, the days and haps of the rest,
Was call'd by my nighest name by clear loud voices of young men as they saw me
    approaching or passing,
Felt their arms on my neck as I stood, or the negligent leaning of their flesh against
    me as I sat, 80
Saw many I loved in the street or ferry-boat or public assembly, yet never told them
    a word,
Lived the same life with the rest, the same old laughing, gnawing, sleeping,
Play'd the part that still looks back on the actor or actress,
The same old role, the role that is what we make it, as great as we like,
Or as small as we like, or both great and small. 85

7

Closer yet I approach you,
What thought you have of me now, I had as much of you—I laid in my stores in
    advance,
I consider'd long and seriously of you before you were born.

Who was to know what should come home to me?
Who knows but I am enjoying this? 90
Who knows, for all the distance, but I am as good as looking at you now, for all you
    cannot see me?

8

Ah, what can ever be more stately and admirable to me than mast-hemm'd
    Manhattan?
River and sunset and scallop-edg'd waves of flood-tide?
The sea-gulls oscillating their bodies, the hay-boat in the twilight, and the belated
    lighter?
What gods can exceed these that clasp me by the hand, and with voices I love call
    me promptly and loudly by my nighest name as I approach? 95

What is more subtle than this which ties me to the woman or man that looks in my
     face?
Which fuses me into you now, and pours my meaning into you?

We understand then do we not?
What I promis'd without mentioning it, have you not accepted?
What the study could not teach—what the preaching could not accomplish is
     accomplish'd, is it not?   100

9

Flow on, river! flow with the flood-tide, and ebb with the ebb-tide!
Frolic on, crested and scallop-edg'd waves!
Gorgeous clouds of the sunset! drench with your splendor me, or the men and
     women generations after me!
Cross from shore to shore, countless crowds of passengers!
Stand up, tall masts of Manhattan! stand up, beautiful hills of Brooklyn!   105
Throb, baffled and curious brain! throw out questions and answers!
Suspend here and everywhere, eternal float of solution!
Gaze, loving and thirsting eyes, in the house or street or public assembly!
Sound out, voices of young men! loudly and musically call me by my nighest name!
Live, old life! play the part that looks back on the actor or actress!   110
Play the old role, the role that is great or small according as one makes it!
Consider, you who peruse me, whether I may not in unknown ways be looking
     upon you;
Be firm, rail over the river, to support those who lean idly, yet haste with the hasting
     current;
Fly on, sea birds! fly sideways, or wheel in large circles high in the air;
Receive the summer sky, you water, and faithfully hold it till all downcast eyes have
     time to take it from you!   115
Diverge, fine spokes of light, from the shape of my head, or any one's head, in the
     sunlit water!
Come on, ships from the lower bay! pass up or down, white-sail'd schooners, sloops,
     lighters!
Flaunt away, flags of all nations! be duly lower'd at sunset!
Burn high your fires, foundry chimneys! cast black shadows at nightfall! cast red and
     yellow light over the tops of the houses!
Appearances, now or henceforth, indicate what you are,   120
You necessary film, continue to envelop the soul,
About my body for me, and your body for you, be hung our divinest aromas,
Thrive, cities—bring your freight, bring your shows, ample and sufficient rivers,
Expand, being than which none else is perhaps more spiritual,
Keep your places, objects than which none else is more lasting.   125

You have waited, you always wait, you dumb, beautiful ministers,
We receive you with free sense at last, and are insatiate henceforward,
Not you any more shall be able to foil us, or withhold yourselves from us,

We use you, and do not cast you aside—we plant you permanently within us,
We fathom you not—we love you—there is perfection in you also, 130
You furnish your parts toward eternity,
Great or small, you furnish your parts toward the soul.

(1856)

MATTHEW ARNOLD
[1822–1888]

Dover Beach

The sea is calm tonight.
The tide is full, the moon lies fair
Upon the straits; on the French coast the light
Gleams and is gone; the cliffs of England stand,
Glimmering and vast, out in the tranquil bay. 5
Come to the window, sweet is the night-air!
Only, from the long line of spray
Where the sea meets the moon-blanched land,
Listen! you hear the grating roar
Of pebbles which the waves draw back, and fling, 10
At their return, up the high strand,
Begin, and cease, and then again begin,
With tremulous cadence slow, and bring
The eternal note of sadness in.

Sophocles long ago 15
Heard it on the Aegean,° and it brought
Into his mind the turbid ebb and flow
Of human misery; we
Find also in the sound a thought,
Hearing it by this distant northern sea. 20

The Sea of Faith
Was once, too, at the full, and round earth's shore
Lay like the folds of a bright girdle furled.
But now I only hear
Its melancholy, long, withdrawing roar, 25
Retreating, to the breath
Of the night-wind, down the vast edges drear
And naked shingles of the world.

"Dover Beach" ¹⁶*Aegean* See Sophocles, *Antigone, ll. 732–736* (chapter fourteen in this text).

Ah, love, let us be true
To one another! for the world, which seems   30
To lie before us like a land of dreams,
So various, so beautiful, so new,
Hath really neither joy, nor love, nor light,
Nor certitude, nor peace, nor help for pain;
And we are here as on a darkling plain   35
Swept with confused alarms of struggle and flight,
Where ignorant armies clash by night.

LEWIS CARROLL (CHARLES LUTWIDGE DODGSON)
[1832–1898]

Jabberwocky

'Twas brillig, and the slithy toves
    Did gyre and gimble in the wabe:
All mimsy were the borogoves,
    And the mome raths outgrabe.

"Beware the Jabberwock, my son!   5
    The jaws that bite, the claws that catch!
Beware the Jubjub bird, and shun
    The frumious Bandersnatch!"

He took his vorpal sword in hand:
    Long time the manxome foe he sought—   10
So rested he by the Tumtum tree,
    And stood awhile in thought.

And, as in uffish thought he stood,
    The Jabberwock, with eyes of flame,
Came whiffling through the tulgey wood,   15
    And burbled as it came!

One, two! One, two! And through and through
    The vorpal blade went snicker-snack!
He left it dead, and with its head
    He went galumphing back.   20

"And hast thou slain the Jabberwock?
    Come to my arms, my beamish boy!
O frabjous day! Callooh! Callay!"
    He chortled in his joy.

'Twas brillig, and the slithy toves   25
   Did gyre and gimble in the wabe:
All mimsy were the borogoves,
   And the mome raths outgrabe.

                                                                                                          (1871)

THOMAS HARDY
[1840–1928]

The Ruined Maid

"O'Melia, my dear, this does everything crown!
Who could have supposed I should meet you in Town?
And whence such fair garments, such prosperi-ty?"
"O didn't you know I'd been ruined?" said she.

"You left us in tatters, without shoes or socks,   5
Tired of digging potatoes, and spudding up docks;
And now you've gay bracelets and bright feathers three!"
"Yes: that's how we dress when we're ruined," said she.

"At home in the barton° you said 'thee' and 'thou,'   farm
And 'thik oon,' and 'theäs oon,' and 't'other'; but now   10
Your talking quite fits 'ee for high compa-ny!"
"Some polish is gained with one's ruin," said she.

"Your hands were like paws then, your face blue and bleak
But now I'm bewitched by your delicate cheek,
And your little gloves fit as on any la-dy!"   15
"We never do work when we're ruined," said she.

"You used to call home-life a hag-ridden dream,
And you'd sigh, and you'd sock; but at present you seem
To know not of megrims° or melancho-ly!"   low spirits
"True. One's pretty lively when ruined," said she.   20

"I wish I had feathers, a fine sweeping gown,
And a delicate face, and could strut about Town!"
"My dear—a raw country girl, such as you be,
Cannot quite expect that. You ain't ruined," said she.

                                                                                                          (1898)

Channel Firing

That night your great guns, unawares,
Shook all our coffins as we lay,
And broke the chancel window-squares,
We thought it was the Judgment-day

And sat upright. While drearisome   5
Arose the howl of wakened hounds:
The mouse let fall the altar-crumb,
The worms drew back into the mounds,

The glebe° cow drooled. Till God called, "No;   small field
It's gunnery practice out at sea   10
Just as before you went below;
The world is as it used to be:

"All nations striving strong to make
Red war yet redder. Mad as hatters
They do no more for Christés sake   15
Than you who are helpless in such matters.

"That this is not the judgment-hour
For some of them's a blessed thing,
For if it were they'd have to scour
Hell's floor for so much threatening. . . .   20

"Ha, ha. It will be warmer when
I blow the trumpet (if indeed
I ever do; for you are men,
And rest eternal sorely need)."

So down we lay again. "I wonder,   25
Will the world ever saner be,"
Said one, "than when He sent us under
In our indifferent century!"

And many a skeleton shook his head.
"Instead of preaching forty year,"   30
My neighbor Parson Thirdly said,
"I wish I had stuck to pipes and beer."

Again the guns disturbed the hour,
Roaring their readiness to avenge,
As far inland as Stourton Tower,   35
And Camelot, and starlit Stonehenge.°

(1914)

"Channel Firing" ³⁶**Stonehenge** *a circular grouping of stone monuments near Salisbury, England, dating back to the Bronze Age.*

Afterwards

When the Present has latched its postern° behind my tremulous stay,
   And the May month flaps its glad green leaves like wings,
Delicate-filmed as new-spun silk, will the neighbours say,
   "He was a man who used to notice such things"?

If it be in the dusk when, like an eyelid's soundless blink,   5
   The dewfall-hawk comes crossing the shades to alight
Upon the wind-warped upland thorn, a gazer may think,
   "To him this must have been a familiar sight."

If I pass during some nocturnal blackness, mothy, and warm,
   When the hedgehog travels furtively over the lawn,   10
One may say, "He strove that such innocent creatures should come to no harm,
   But he could do little for them; and now he is gone."

If, when hearing that I have been stilled at last, they stand at the door,
   Watching the full-starred heavens that winter sees,
Will this thought rise on those who will meet my face no more,   15
   "He was one who had an eye for such mysteries"?

And will any say when my bell of quittance° is heard in the gloom
   And a crossing breeze cuts a pause in its outrollings,
Till they rise again, as they were a new bell's boom,
   "He hears it not now, but used to notice such things"?   20

                 (1928)

GERARD MANLEY HOPKINS
[*1844–1889*]

God's Grandeur

The world is charged with the grandeur of God.
   It will flame out, like shining from shook foil;°
   It gathers to a greatness, like the ooze of oil
Crushed.° Why do men then now not reck his rod?
Generations have trod, have trod, have trod;   5
   And all is seared with trade; bleared, smeared with toil;
   And wears man's smudge and shares man's smell: the soil
Is bare now, nor can foot feel, being shod.

"Afterwards" ¹**postern** *gate.* ¹⁷**bell of quittance** *death bell.* "God's Grandeur" ²*foil* *gold or tinsel foil* ⁴**Crushed** *as when olives are crushed for their oil.*

And for all this, nature is never spent;
  There lives the dearest freshness deep down things; 10
And though the last lights off the black West went
  Oh, morning, at the brown brink eastward, springs—
Because the Holy Ghost over the bent
  World broods with warm breast and with ah! bright wings.

(1877, 1895)

The Windhover°

TO CHRIST OUR LORD

I caught this morning morning's minion,° king-   darling
  dom of daylight's dauphin,° dapple-dawn-drawn Falcon, in his   prince
    riding
  Of the rolling level underneath him steady air, and striding
High there, how he rung upon the rein of a wimpling° wing   rippling
In his ecstasy! then off, off forth on swing,   5
  As a skate's heel sweeps smooth on a bow-bend: the hurl and gliding
  Rebuffed the big wind. My heart in hiding
Stirred for a bird,—the achieve of, the mastery of the thing!

Brute beauty and valour and act, oh, air, pride, plume, here
  Buckle! AND the fire that breaks from thee then, a billion
Times told lovelier, more dangerous, O my chevalier!°   knight 10

No wonder of it: shéer plód makes plough down sillion°   furrow
Shine, and blue-bleak embers, ah my dear,
  Fall, gall themselves, and gash gold-vermilion.

(1877, 1918)

Pied° Beauty   variegated

Glory be to God for dappled things—
  For skies of couple-colour as a brinded° cow;   brindled, streaked
    For rose-moles all in stipple upon trout that swim;
Fresh-firecoal chestnut-falls°; finches' wings;
  Landscape plotted and pieced—fold, fallow, and plough;   5
    And áll trádes, their gear and tackle and trim.°   equipment
All things counter, original, spare,° strange;   unusual
  Whatever is fickle, freckled (who knows how?)
    With swift, slow; sweet, sour; adazzle, dim;
He fathers-forth whose beauty is past change: 10
              Praise him.

(1877, 1918)

"The Windhover" *a kestrel, a kind of falcon.* "Pied Beauty" [4]**chestnut-falls** *roasted chestnuts stripped of their husks.*

Spring and Fall:
to a Young Child

Márgarét, áre you grieving
Over Goldengrove unleaving?
Leáves, like the things of man, you
With your fresh thoughts care for, can you?
Áh! ás the heart grows older   5
It will come to such sights colder
By and by, nor spare a sigh
Though worlds of wanwood leafmeal lie;
And yet you *will* weep and know why
Now no matter, child, the name: 10
Sórrow's spríngs áre the same.
Nor mouth had, no nor mind, expressed
What heart heard of, ghost guessed:
It ís the blight man was born for,
It is Márgarét you mourn for.   15

A. E. HOUSMAN
[1859–1936]

When I was one-and-twenty

When I was one-and-twenty
  I heard a wise man say,
'Give crowns and pounds and guineas
  But not your heart away;
Give pearls away and rubies   5
  But keep your fancy free.'
But I was one-and-twenty,
  No use to talk to me.

When I was one-and-twenty
  I heard him say again,   10
'The heart out of the bosom
  Was never given in vain;
'Tis paid with sighs a plenty
  And sold for endless rue.'
And I am two-and-twenty,   15
  And oh, 'tis true, 'tis true.

(1896)

To an Athlete Dying Young

The time you won your town the race
We chaired you through the market-place;
Man and boy stood cheering by,
And home we brought you shoulder-high.

To-day, the road all runners come,   5
Shoulder-high we bring you home,
And set you at your threshold down,
Townsman of a stiller town.

Smart lad, to slip betimes away
From fields where glory does not stay   10
And early though the laurel grows
It withers quicker than the rose.

Eyes the shady night has shut
Cannot see the record cut,
And silence sounds no worse than cheers   15
After earth has stopped the ears:

Now you will not swell the rout
Of lads that wore their honours out,
Runners whom renown outran
And the name died before the man.   20

So set, before its echoes fade,
The fleet foot on the sill of shade,
And hold to the low lintel up
The still-defended challenge-cup.

And round that early-laurelled head   25
Will flock to gaze the strengthless dead
And find unwithered on its curls
The garland briefer than a girl's.

(1896)

WILLIAM BUTLER YEATS
[1865–1939]

The Second Coming°

Turning and turning in the widening gyre°   *spiral*
The falcon cannot hear the falconer;
Things fall apart; the center cannot hold;
Mere anarchy is loosed upon the world,
The blood-dimmed tide is loosed, and everywhere   5
The ceremony of innocence is drowned;
The best lack all conviction, while the worst
Are full of passionate intensity.

Surely some revelation is at hand;
Surely the Second Coming is at hand;   10
The Second Coming! Hardly are those words out
When a vast image out of *Spiritus Mundi*°
Troubles my sight: somewhere in sands of the desert
A shape with lion body and the head of a man,
A gaze blank and pitiless as the sun,   15
Is moving its slow thighs, while all about it
Reel shadows of the indignant desert birds.
The darkness drops again; but now I know
That twenty centuries of stony sleep
Were vexed to nightmare by a rocking cradle,   20
And what rough beast, its hour come round at last,
Slouches towards Bethlehem to be born?

(1921)

The Wild Swans at Coole

The trees are in their autumn beauty,
The woodland paths are dry,
Under the October twilight the water
Mirrors a still sky;
Upon the brimming water among the stones   5
Are nine-and-fifty swans.

The nineteenth autumn has come upon me
Since I first made my count;
I saw, before I had well finished,
All suddenly mount   10

"The Second Coming" *the title alludes to the prophesied return of Jesus Christ and also to the beast of the Apocalypse. See Matthew 24 and Revelation.* [12] **Spiritus Mundi** *for Yeats, a common storehouse of images, a communal human memory.*

And scatter wheeling in great broken rings
Upon their clamorous wings.

I have looked upon those brilliant creatures,
And now my heart is sore.
All's changed since I, hearing at twilight,   15
The first time on this shore,
The bell-beat of their wings above my head,
Trod with a lighter tread.

Unwearied still, lover by lover,
They paddle in the cold   20
Companionable streams or climb the air;
Their hearts have not grown old;
Passion or conquest, wander where they will,
Attend upon them still.

But now they drift on the still water,   25
Mysterious, beautiful;
Among what rushes will they build,
By what lake's edge or pool
Delight men's eyes when I awake some day
To find they have flown away?   30

(1917)

Leda and the Swan°

A sudden blow: the great wings beating still
Above the staggering girl, her thighs caressed
By the dark webs, her nape caught in his bill,
He holds her helpless breast upon his breast.

How can those terrified vague fingers push   5
The feathered glory from her loosening thighs?
And how can body, laid in that white rush,
But feel the strange heart beating where it lies?

A shudder in the loins engenders there
The broken wall, the burning roof and tower   10
And Agamemnon dead.
                    Being so caught up,
So mastered by the brute blood of the air,
Did she put on his knowledge with his power
Before the indifferent beak could let her drop?   15

(1928)

"Leda and the Swan"   *Zeus, in the guise of a swan, raped Leda, Queen of Sparta. Helen, their daughter, married Menelaus, King of Sparta, but ran off with Paris, son of Priam, King of Troy. A ten-year siege of Troy by the Greeks ensued to bring Helen back.*

Sailing to Byzantium°

1

That is no country for old men. The young
In one another's arms, birds in the trees
—Those dying generations—at their song,
The salmon-falls, the mackerel-crowded seas,
Fish, flesh, or fowl, commend all summer long   5
Whatever is begotten, born, and dies.
Caught in that sensual music all neglect
Monuments of unaging intellect.

2

An aged man is but a paltry thing,
A tattered coat upon a stick, unless   10
Soul clap its hands and sing, and louder sing
For every tatter in its mortal dress,
Nor is there singing school but studying
Monuments of its own magnificence;
And therefore I have sailed the seas and come   15
To the holy city of Byzantium.

3

O sages standing in God's holy fire
As in the gold mosaic of a wall,
Come from the holy fire, perne° in a gyre,°   descend/spiral
And be the singing-masters of my soul.   20
Consume my heart away; sick with desire
And fastened to a dying animal
It knows not what it is; and gather me
Into the artifice of eternity.

4

Once out of nature I shall never take   25
My bodily form from any natural thing,
But such a form as Grecian goldsmiths make
Of hammered gold and gold enameling
To keep a drowsy Emperor awake;
Or set upon a golden bough to sing   30
To lords and ladies of Byzantium
Of what is past, or passing, or to come.

                                        (1927)

"Sailing to Byzantium" *Byzantium was the capital of the eastern Roman Empire and an important center of art and architecture.*

EDWIN ARLINGTON ROBINSON
[1869–1935]

Richard Cory

Whenever Richard Cory went down town,
We people on the pavement looked at him:
He was a gentleman from sole to crown,
Clean favored and imperially slim.

And he was always quietly arrayed,   5
And he was always human when he talked;
But still he fluttered pulses when he said,
"Good-morning," and he glittered when he walked.

And he was rich—yes, richer than a king—
And admirably schooled in every grace: 10
In fine, we thought that he was everything
To make us wish that we were in his place.

So on we worked, and waited for the light,
And went without the meat and cursed the bread;
And Richard Cory, one calm summer night,   15
Went home and put a bullet through his head.

PAUL LAURENCE DUNBAR
[1872–1906]

We wear the mask

We wear the mask that grins and lies,
It hides our cheeks and shades our eyes—
This debt we pay to human guile;
With torn and bleeding hearts we smile,
And mouth with myriad subtleties.   5

Why should the world be over-wise,
In counting all our tears and sighs?
Nay, let them only see us, while
    We wear the mask.

We smile, but, O great Christ, our cries
To thee from tortured souls arise.   10
We sing, but oh the clay is vile
Beneath our feet, and long the mile;
But let the world dream otherwise,
    We wear the mask!

                                                    (1896)

WALLACE STEVENS
[1879–1955]

Thirteen Ways of Looking at a Blackbird

1

Among twenty snowy mountains,
The only moving thing
Was the eye of the blackbird.

2

I was of three minds,
Like a tree   5
In which there are three blackbirds.

3

The blackbird whirled in the autumn winds.
It was a small part of the pantomime.

4

A man and a woman
Are one.
A man and a woman and a blackbird   10
Are one.

5

I do not know which to prefer,
The beauty of inflections
Or the beauty of innuendoes,
The blackbird whistling   15
Or just after.

6

Icicles filled the long window
With barbaric glass.
The shadow of the blackbird   20
Crossed it to and fro.
The mood
Traced in the shadow
An indecipherable cause.

7

O thin men of Haddam,   25
Why do you imagine golden birds?
Do you not see how the blackbird
Walks around the feet
Of the women about you?

8

I know noble accents   30
And lucid, inescapable rhythms;
But I know, too,
That the blackbird is involved
In what I know.

9

When the blackbird flew out of sight,   35
It marked the edge
Of one of many circles.

10

At the sight of blackbirds
Flying in a green light,
Even the bawds of euphony   40
Would cry out sharply.

11

He rode over Connecticut
In a glass coach.
Once, a fear pierced him,
In that he mistook   45
The shadow of his equipage
For blackbirds.

12

The river is moving.
The blackbird must be flying.

13

It was evening all afternoon.   50
It was snowing
And it was going to snow.
The blackbird sat
In the cedar-limbs.

                 (1923)

WILLIAM CARLOS WILLIAMS
[*1883–1963*]

Spring and All

By the road to the contagious hospital
under the surge of the blue
mottled clouds driven from the
northeast—a cold wind. Beyond, the
waste of broad, muddy fields   5
brown with dried weeds, standing and fallen

patches of standing water
the scattering of tall trees

All along the road the reddish
purplish, forked, upstanding, twiggy   10
stuff of bushes and small trees
with dead, brown leaves under them
leafless vines—

Lifeless in appearance, sluggish
dazed spring approaches—   15

They enter the new world naked,
cold, uncertain of all
save that they enter. All about them
the cold, familiar wind—

Now the grass, tomorrow   20
the stiff curl of wildcarrot leaf
One by one objects are defined—
It quickens: clarity, outline of leaf

But now the stark dignity of
entrance—Still, the profound change   25
has come upon them: rooted, they
grip down and begin to awaken

(1923)

Danse Russe

If when my wife is sleeping
and the baby and Kathleen
are sleeping
and the sun is a flame-white disc
in silken mists   5
above shining trees,—
if I in my north room
dance naked, grotesquely
before my mirror
waving my shirt round my head   10
and singing softly to myself:
"I am lonely, lonely.
I was born to be lonely,
I am best so!"
If I admire my arms, my face,   15
my shoulders, flanks, buttocks
against the yellow drawn shades,—

Who shall say I am not
the happy genius of my household?

(1917)

EZRA POUND
[1885–1972]

The River-Merchant's Wife: A Letter°

While my hair was still cut straight across my forehead
Played I about the front gate, pulling flowers.
You came by on bamboo stilts, playing horse,
You walked about my seat, playing with blue plums.
And we went on living in the village of Chōkan: 5
Two small people, without dislike or suspicion.

"The River-Merchant's Wife"   *Pound translated and adapted this poem from the Chinese. Rihaku is the Japanese name for the Chinese poet, Li T'ai Po, who wrote the poem that Pound adapted.*

At fourteen I married My Lord you.
I never laughed, being bashful.
Lowering my head, I looked at the wall.
Called to, a thousand times, I never looked back.   10

At fifteen I stopped scowling,
I desired my dust to be mingled with yours
Forever and forever and forever.
Why should I climb the look out?

At sixteen you departed,   15
You went into far Ku-tō-en, by the river of swirling eddies,
And you have been gone five months.
The monkeys make sorrowful noise overhead.

You dragged your feet when you went out.
By the gate now, the moss is grown, the different mosses,   20
Too deep to clear them away!
The leaves fall early this autumn, in wind.
The paired butterflies are already yellow with August

Over the grass in the West garden;
They hurt me. I grow older.   25
If you are coming down through the narrows of the river Kiang,
Please let me know before hand,
And I will come out to meet you
        As far as Chō-fū-Sa.

by Rihaku

(1916)

MARIANNE MOORE
[1887–1972]

Poetry

I, too, dislike it: there are things that are important beyond all this fiddle.
  Reading it, however, with a perfect contempt for it, one discovers in
  it after all, a place for the genuine.
    Hands that can grasp, eyes
    that can dilate, hair that can rise   5
      if it must, these things are important not because a

high-sounding interpretation can be put upon them but because they are
   useful. When they become so derivative as to become unintelligible,
    the same thing may be said for all of us, that we
       do not admire what   10
       we cannot understand: the bat
         holding on upside down or in quest of something to

eat, elephants pushing, a wild horse taking a roll, a tireless wolf under
   a tree, the immovable critic twitching his skin like a horse that feels
    a flea, the base-
   ball fan, the statistician—   15
       nor is it valid
        to discriminate against "business documents and

school-books"; all these phenomena are important. One must make a distinction
   however: when dragged into prominence by half poets, the result is not poetry,
   nor till the poets among us can be   20
       "literalists of
     the imagination"—above
        insolence and triviality and can present

for inspection, "imaginary gardens with real toads in them," shall we have
   it. In the meantime, if you demand on the one hand,   25
   the raw material of poetry in
     all its rawness and
     that which is on the other hand
       genuine, you are interested in poetry.

                                (1921)

T. S. ELIOT
[1888–1965]

The Love Song of J. Alfred Prufrock

S'io credesse che mia risposta fosse
A persona che mai tornasse al mondo,
Questa fiamma staria senza più scosse.
Ma perciocche giammai di questo fondo
Non tornò vivo alcun, s'i'odo il vero,
Senza tema d'infamia ti rispondo.°

"The Love Song of J. Alfred Prufrock"   *epigraph from Dante's Inferno, canto XXVII, 61–66. The words are spoken by Guido da Montefeltro when asked to identify himself: "If I thought my answer were given to anyone who could ever return to the world, this flame would shake no more; but since none ever did return above from this depth, if what I hear is true, without fear of infamy I answer thee."*

Let us go then, you and I,
When the evening is spread out against the sky
Like a patient etherized upon a table;
Let us go, through certain half-deserted streets,
The muttering retreats   5
Of restless nights in one-night cheap hotels
And sawdust restaurants with oyster-shells:
Streets that follow like a tedious argument
Of insidious intent
To lead you to an overwhelming question . . .   10
Oh, do not ask, "What is it?"
Let us go and make our visit.

In the room the women come and go
Talking of Michelangelo.

The yellow fog that rubs its back upon the window-panes   15
The yellow smoke that rubs its muzzle on the window-panes
Licked its tongue into the corners of the evening,
Lingered upon the pools that stand in drains,
Let fall upon its back the soot that falls from chimneys,
Slipped by the terrace, made a sudden leap,   20
And seeing that it was a soft October night,
Curled once about the house, and fell asleep.

And indeed there will be time
For the yellow smoke that slides along the street,
Rubbing its back upon the window-panes;   25
There will be time, there will be time
To prepare a face to meet the faces that you meet;
There will be time to murder and create,
And time for all the works and days of hands
That lift and drop a question on your plate;   30
Time for you and time for me,
And time yet for a hundred indecisions,
And for a hundred visions and revisions,
Before the taking of a toast and tea.

In the room the women come and go   35
Talking of Michelangelo.

And indeed there will be time
To wonder, "Do I dare?" and, "Do I dare?"
Time to turn back and descend the stair,
With a bald spot in the middle of my hair—   40
(They will say: "How his hair is growing thin!")
My morning coat, my collar mounting firmly to the chin,
My necktie rich and modest, but asserted by a simple pin—

(They will say: "But how his arms and legs are thin!")
Do I dare   45
Disturb the universe?
In a minute there is time
For decisions and revisions which a minute will reverse.

For I have known them all already, known them all:
Have known the evenings, mornings, afternoons,   50
I have measured out my life with coffee spoons;
I know the voices dying with a dying fall
Beneath the music from a farther room.
     So how should I presume?

And I have known the eyes already, known them all—   55
The eyes that fix you in a formulated phrase,
And when I am formulated, sprawling on a pin,
When I am pinned and wriggling on the wall,
Then how should I begin
To spit out all the butt-ends of my days and ways?   60
     And how should I presume?

And I have known the arms already, known them all—
Arms that are braceleted and white and bare
(But in the lamplight, downed with light brown hair!)
Is it perfume from a dress   65
That makes me so digress?
Arms that lie along a table, or wrap about a shawl.
     And should I then presume?
     And how should I begin?

Shall I say, I have gone at dusk through narrow streets   70
And watched the smoke that rises from the pipes
Of lonely men in shirt-sleeves, leaning out of windows? . . .

I should have been a pair of ragged claws
Scuttling across the floors of silent seas.

     . . . . .

And the afternoon, the evening, sleeps so peacefully!   75
Smoothed by long fingers,
Asleep . . . tired . . . or it malingers,
Stretched on the floor, here beside you and me.
Should I, after tea and cakes and ices,
Have the strength to force the moment to its crisis?   80
But though I have wept and fasted, wept and prayed,
Though I have seen my head (grown slightly bald) brought in upon a platter,°

---

[82]**head . . . platter** *John the Baptist was beheaded at the order of King Herod to please his wife and daughter. See Matthew 14:1–11.*

I am no prophet—and here's no great matter;
I have seen the moment of my greatness flicker,
And I have seen the eternal Footman hold my coat, and snicker,   85
And in short, I was afraid.

And would it have been worth it, after all,
After the cups, the marmalade, the tea,
Among the porcelain, among some talk of you and me,
Would it have been worth while,   90
To have bitten off the matter with a smile,
To have squeezed the universe into a ball
To roll it toward some overwhelming question,
To say: "I am Lazarus,° come from the dead,
Come back to tell you all, I shall tell you all"—   95
If one, settling a pillow by her head,
     Should say: "That is not what I meant at all.
     That is not it, at all."

And would it have been worth it, after all,
Would it have been worth while,   100
After the sunsets and the dooryards and the sprinkled streets,
After the novels, after the teacups, after the skirts that trail along the floor—
And this, and so much more?—
It is impossible to say just what I mean!
But as if a magic lantern threw the nerves in patterns on a screen: 105
Would it have been worth while
If one, settling a pillow or throwing off a shawl,
And turning toward the window, should say:
     "That is not it at all,
     That is not what I meant, at all."   110

No! I am not Prince Hamlet, nor was meant to be;
Am an attendant lord, one that will do
To swell a progress, start a scene or two,
Advise the prince; no doubt, an easy tool,
Deferential, glad to be of use,   115
Politic, cautious, and meticulous;
Full of high sentence,° but a bit obtuse;   sententiousness
At times, indeed, almost ridiculous—
Almost, at times, the Fool.

I grow old . . . I grow old . . .   120
I shall wear the bottoms of my trousers rolled.

Shall I part my hair behind? Do I dare to eat a peach?

94**Lazarus**   *Jesus raised him from the dead. See John 11:1–44.*

I shall wear white flannel trousers, and walk upon the beach.
I have heard the mermaids singing, each to each.

I do not think that they will sing to me.   125

I have seen them riding seaward on the waves
Combing the white hair of the waves blown back
When the wind blows the water white and black.
We have lingered in the chambers of the sea
By sea-girls wreathed with seaweed red and brown   130
Till human voices wake us, and we drown.

                                                        (1917)

JOHN CROWE RANSOM
[1888–1974]

Piazza Piece

—I am a gentleman in a dustcoat trying
To make you hear. Your ears are soft and small
And listen to an old man not at all,
They want the young men's whispering and sighing.
But see the roses on your trellis dying   5
And hear the spectral singing of the moon;
For I must have my lovely lady soon,
I am a gentleman in a dustcoat trying.

—I am a lady young in beauty waiting
Until my truelove comes, and then we kiss.   10
But what grey man among the vines is this
Whose words are dry and faint as in a dream?
Back from my trellis, Sir, before I scream!
I am a lady young in beauty waiting.

                                                        (1927)

VICENTE HUIDOBRO
[1892–1948]

Ars Poetica°   The art of poetry

        Let poetry be like a key
        Opening a thousand doors.
        A leaf falls; something flies by;

Let all the eye sees be created
And the soul of the listener tremble.   5

Invent new worlds and watch your word;
The adjective, when it doesn't give life, kills it.
We are in the age of nerves.
The muscle hangs,
Like a memory, in museums;   10
But we are not the weaker for it:
True vigor
Resides in the head.

Oh Poets, why sing of roses!
Let them flower in your poems;   15

For us alone
Do all things live beneath the Sun.

The poet is a little God.

TRANSLATED BY DAVID M. GUSS

(1932)

ARCHIBALD MACLEISH
[1892–1982]

Ars Poetica

A poem should be palpable and mute
As a globed fruit,

Dumb
As old medallions to the thumb,

Silent as the sleeve-worn stone   5
Of casement ledges where the moss has grown—

A poem should be wordless
As the flight of birds.

A poem should be motionless in time
As the moon climbs,   10

Leaving, as the moon releases
Twig by twig the night-entangled trees,

Leaving, as the moon behind the winter leaves,
Memory by memory the mind—

A poem should be motionless in time   15
As the moon climbs.

A poem should be equal to:
Not true.

For all the history of grief
An empty doorway and a maple leaf.   20

For love
The leaning grasses and two lights above the sea—

A poem should not mean
But be.

                                                                  (1926)

WILFRED OWEN
[1893–1918]

Dulce et Decorum Est°

Bent double, like old beggars under sacks,
Knock-kneed, coughing like hags, we cursed through sludge,
Till on the haunting flares we turned our backs
And towards our distant rest began to trudge.
Men marched asleep. Many had lost their boots   5
But limped on, blood-shod. All went lame; all blind;
Drunk with fatigue; deaf even to the hoots
Of tired, outstripped Five-Nines that dropped behind.

Gas! GAS! Quick, boys!—An ecstasy of fumbling,
Fitting the clumsy helmets just in time;   10
But someone still was yelling out and stumbling
And flound'ring like a man in fire or lime . . .
Dim, through the misty panes and thick green light,
As under a green sea, I saw him drowning.

"Dulce et Decorum Est"   *"It is sweet and fitting to die for one's country."* See the last two lines, which are from
Horace, Odes, *III, ii. 13.*

In all my dreams, before my helpless sight,   15
He plunges at me, guttering, choking, drowning.
If in some smothering dreams you too could pace
Behind the wagon that we flung him in,
And watch the white eyes writhing in his face,
His hanging face, like a devil's sick of sin;   20
If you could hear, at every jolt, the blood
Come gargling from the froth-corrupted lungs,
Obscene as cancer, bitter as the cud
Of vile, incurable sores on innocent tongues,—
My friend, you would not tell with such high zest   25
To children ardent for some desperate glory,
The old Lie: *Dulce et decorum est
Pro patria mori.*

(1920)

E. E. CUMMINGS
[1894–1962]

anyone lived in a pretty how town

anyone lived in a pretty how town
(with up so floating many bells down)
spring summer autumn winter
he sang his didn't he danced his did.

Women and men(both little and small)   5
cared for anyone not at all
they sowed their isn't they reaped their same
sun moon stars rain

children guessed(but only a few
and down they forgot as up they grew   10
autumn winter spring summer)
that noone loved him more by more

when by now and tree by leaf
she laughed his joy she cried his grief
bird by snow and stir by still   15
anyone's any was all to her

someones married their everyones
laughed their cryings and did their dance

(sleep wake hope and then)they
said their nevers they slept their dream   20

stars rain sun moon
(and only the snow can begin to explain
how children are apt to forget to remember
with up so floating many bells down)

one day anyone died i guess   25
(and noone stooped to kiss his face)
busy folk buried them side by side
little by little and was by was

all by all and deep by deep
and more by more they dream their sleep   30
noone and anyone earth by april
wish by spirit and if by yes.

Women and men(both dong and ding)
summer autumn winter spring
reaped their sowing and went their came   35
sun moon stars rain

                                                        (1940)

i thank You God for most this amazing

i thank You God for most this amazing
day:for the leaping greenly spirits of trees
and a blue true dream of sky; and for everything
which is natural which is infinite which is yes

(i who have died am alive again today,   5
and this is the sun's birthday; this is the birth
day of life and of love and wings:and of the gay
great happening illimitably earth)

how should tasting touching hearing seeing
breathing any—lifted from the no   10
of all nothing—human merely being
doubt unimaginable You?

(now the ears of my ears awake and
now the eyes of my eyes are opened)

                                                        (1950)

JEAN TOOMER
[1894–1967]

Song of the Son

Pour, O pour, that parting soul in song,
O pour it in the saw-dust glow of night,
Into the velvet pine-smoke air tonight,
And let the valley carry it along,
And let the valley carry it along.   5

O land and soil, red soil and sweet-gum tree
So scant of grass, so profligate of pines,
Now just before an epoch's sun declines
Thy son, in time, I have returned to thee,
Thy son, I have in time returned to thee.   10

In time, for though the sun is setting on
A song-lit race of slaves, it has not set;
Though late, O soil it is not too late yet
To catch thy plaintive soul, leaving, soon gone,
Leaving, to catch thy plaintive soul soon gone.   15

O Negro slaves, dark-purple ripened plums,
Squeezed, and bursting in the pine-wood air,
Passing, before they stripped the old tree bare
One plum was saved for me, one seed becomes

An everlasting song, a singing tree,   20
Carolling softly souls of slavery,
All that they were, and that they are to me,—
Carolling softly souls of slavery.

                                                       (1922)

Reapers

Black reapers with the sound of steel on stones
Arc sharpening scythes. I see them place the hones
In their hip-pockets as a thing that's done,
And start their silent swinging, one by one.
Black horses drive a mower through the weeds,   5
And there, a field rat, startled, squealing bleeds,
His belly close to ground. I see the blade,
Blood-stained, continue cutting weeds and shade.

                                                       (1923)

W. H. AUDEN
[1907–1973]

The Unknown Citizen

(To JS/07/M/378 This Marble Monument Is Erected by the State)

He was found by the Bureau of Statistics to be
One against whom there was no official complaint,
And all the reports on his conduct agree
That, in the modern sense of an old-fashioned word, he was a saint,
For in everything he did he served the Greater Community.   5
Except for the War till the day he retired
He worked in a factory and never got fired
But satisfied his employers, Fudge Motors Inc.
Yet he wasn't a scab or odd in his views,
For his Union reports that he paid his dues,   10
(Our report on his Union shows it was sound)
And our Social Psychology workers found
That he was popular with his mates and liked a drink.
The Press are convinced that he bought a paper every day
And that his reactions to advertisements were normal in every way.   15
Policies taken out in his name prove that he was fully insured,
And his Health-card shows he was once in hospital but left it cured.
Both Producers Research and High-Grade Living declare
He was fully sensible to the advantages of the Installment Plan
And had everything necessary to the Modern Man,   20
A phonograph, a radio, a car and a frigidaire.
Our researchers into Public Opinion are content
That he held the proper opinions for the time of year;
When there was peace, he was for peace; when there was war, he went.
He was married and added five children to the population,   25
Which our Eugenist says was the right number for a parent of his generation.
And our teachers report that he never interfered with their education.

Was he free? Was he happy? The question is absurd:
Had anything been wrong, we should certainly have heard.

(1940)

In Memory of W. B. Yeats

[d. January 1939]

1

He disappeared in the dead of winter:
The brooks were frozen, the air-ports almost deserted,
And snow disfigured the public statues;
The mercury sank in the mouth of the dying day.
O all the instruments agree   5
The day of his death was a dark cold day.

Far from his illness
The wolves ran on through the evergreen forests,
The peasant river was untempted by the fashionable quays;
By mourning tongues   10
The death of the poet was kept from his poems.

But for him it was his last afternoon as himself,
An afternoon of nurses and rumours;
The provinces of his body revolted,
The squares of his mind were empty,   15
Silence invaded the suburbs,
The current of his feeling failed: he became his admirers.

Now he is scattered among a hundred cities
And wholly given over to unfamiliar affections;
To find his happiness in another kind of wood   20
And be punished under a foreign code of conscience.
The words of a dead man
Are modified in the guts of the living.

But in the importance and noise of to-morrow
When the brokers are roaring like beasts on the floor of
    the Bourse,°   stock exchange 25
And the poor have the sufferings to which they are fairly accustomed,
And each in the cell of himself is almost convinced of his freedom;
A few thousand will think of this day
As one thinks of a day when one did something slightly unusual.

O all the instruments agree   30
The day of his death was a dark cold day.

2

You were silly like us: your gift survived it all;
The parish of rich women, physical decay,

Yourself; mad Ireland hurt you into poetry.
Now Ireland has her madness and her weather still, 35
For poetry makes nothing happen: it survives
In the valley of its saying where executives
Would never want to tamper; it flows south
From ranches of isolation and the busy griefs,
Raw towns that we believe and die in; it survives, 40
A way of happening, a mouth.

3

Earth, receive an honoured guest;
William Yeats is laid to rest:
Let the Irish vessel lie
Emptied of its poetry. 45

Time that is intolerant
Of the brave and innocent,
And indifferent in a week
To a beautiful physique,

Worships language and forgives 50
Everyone by whom it lives;
Pardons cowardice, conceit,
Lays its honours at their feet.

Time that with this strange excuse
Pardoned Kipling° and his views, 55
And will pardon Paul Claudel,°
Pardons him for writing well.

In the nightmare of the dark°
All the dogs of Europe bark,
And the living nations wait, 60
Each sequestered in its hate;

Intellectual disgrace
Stares from every human face,
And the seas of pity lie
Locked and frozen in each eye. 65

Follow, poet, follow right
To the bottom of the night,
With your unconstraining Voice
Still persuade us to rejoice;

"In Memory of W. B. Yeats" [55]**Kipling** *Rudyard Kipling (1865–1936), English writer with imperialistic views.* [56]**Paul Claudel** *French Catholic writer (1868–1955) of extreme political conservatism.* [58]**the dark** *World War II broke out a few months after Auden wrote this poem.*

With the farming of a verse   70
Make a vineyard of the curse,
Sing of human unsuccess
In a rapture of distress;

In the deserts of the heart
Let the healing fountain start,   75
In the prison of his days
Teach the free man how to praise.

(1940)

THEODORE ROETHKE
[1908–1963]

Elegy for Jane

MY STUDENT, THROWN BY A HORSE

I remember the neckcurls, limp and damp as tendrils;
And her quick look, a sidelong pickerel smile;
And how, once startled into talk, the light syllables leaped for her,
And she balanced in the delight of her thought,
A wren, happy, tail into the wind,   5
Her song trembling the twigs and small branches.
The shade sang with her;
The leaves, their whispers turned to kissing;
And the mold sang in the bleached valleys under the rose.

Oh, when she was sad, she cast herself down into such a pure depth,   10
Even a father could not find her:
Scraping her cheek against straw;
Stirring the clearest water.

My sparrow, you are not here,
Waiting like a fern, making a spiny shadow   15
The sides of wet stones cannot console me,
Nor the moss, wound with the last light.

If only I could nudge you from this sleep,
My maimed darling, my skittery pigeon.
Over this damp grave I speak the words of my love: 20
I, with no rights in this matter,
Neither father nor lover.

(1953)

ELIZABETH BISHOP
[1911–1979]

Sestina

September rain falls on the house.
In the failing light, the old grandmother
sits in the kitchen with the child
beside the Little Marvel Stove,
reading the jokes from the almanac,   5
laughing and talking to hide her tears.

She thinks that her equinoctial tears
and the rain that beats on the roof of the house
were both foretold by the almanac,
but only known to a grandmother.   10
The iron kettle sings on the stove.
She cuts some bread and says to the child,

It's time for tea now; but the child
is watching the teakettle's small hard tears
dance like mad on the hot black stove,   15
the way the rain must dance on the house.
Tidying up, the old grandmother
hangs up the clever almanac

on its string. Birdlike, the almanac
hovers half open above the child,   20
hovers above the old grandmother
and her teacup full of dark brown tears.
She shivers and says she thinks the house
feels chilly, and puts more wood in the stove.

It was to be, says the Marvel Stove.   25
I know what I know, says the almanac.
With crayons the child draws a rigid house
and a winding pathway. Then the child
puts in a man with buttons like tears
and shows it proudly to the grandmother.   30

But secretly, while the grandmother
busies herself about the stove,
the little moons fall down like tears
from between the pages of the almanac

into the flower bed the child
has carefully placed in the front of the house.

35

Time to plant tears, says the almanac.
The grandmother sings to the marvelous stove
and the child draws another inscrutable house.

(1965)

MAY SWENSON
[1913–1989]

Women

Women   Or they
should be   should be
pedestals   little horses
moving   those wooden
pedestals   sweet
moving   oldfashioned
to the   painted
motions   rocking
of men   horses

the gladdest things in the toyroom.

The   feelingly
pegs   and then
of their   unfeelingly
ears   To be
so familiar   joyfully
and dear   ridden
to the trusting   rockingly
fists   ridden until
To be chafed   the restored

egos dismount and the legs stride away

Immobile   willing
sweetlipped   to be set
sturdy   into motion
and smiling   Women
women   should be
should always   pedestals
be waiting   to men

(1970)

WILLIAM STAFFORD
[b. 1914]

Traveling through the dark

Traveling through the dark I found a deer
dead on the edge of the Wilson River road.
It is usually best to roll them into the canyon:
that road is narrow; to swerve might make more dead.

By glow of the tail-light I stumbled back of the car   5
and stood by the heap, a doe, a recent killing;
she had stiffened already, almost cold.
I dragged her off; she was large in the belly.

My fingers touching her side brought me the reason—
her side was warm; her fawn lay there waiting,   10
alive, still, never to be born.
Beside that mountain road I hesitated.

The car aimed ahead its lowered parking lights;
under the hood purred the steady engine.
I stood in the glare of the warm exhaust turning red;   15
around our group I could hear the wilderness listen.

I thought hard for us all—my only swerving—,
then pushed her over the edge into the river.

(1957)

DYLAN THOMAS
[1914–1953]

Fern Hill

Now as I was young and easy under the apple boughs
About the lilting house and happy as the grass was green,
     The night above the dingle starry,
          Time let me hail and climb
     Golden in the heydays of his eyes,   5
And honored among wagons I was prince of the apple towns
And once below a time I lordly had the trees and leaves
          Trail with daisies and barley
     Down the rivers of the windfall light.

And as I was green and carefree, famous among the barns   10
About the happy yard and singing as the farm was home,
    In the sun that is young once only,
       Time let me play and be
     Golden in the mercy of his means,
And green and golden I was huntsman and herdsman, the calves   15
Sang to my horn, the foxes on the hills barked clear and cold,
       And the sabbath rang slowly
     In the pebbles of the holy streams.

All the sun long it was running, it was lovely, the hay
Fields high as the house, the tunes from the chimneys, it was air   20
    And playing, lovely and watery
       And fire green as grass.
     And nightly under the simple stars
As I rode to sleep the owls were bearing the farm away,
All the moon long I heard, blessed among stables, the night-jars   25
    Flying with the ricks, and the horses
      Flashing into the dark.

And then to awake, and the farm, like a wanderer white
With the dew, come back, the cock on his shoulder: it was all
    Shining, it was Adam and maiden,   30
      The sky gathered again
     And the sun grew round that very day.
So it must have been after the birth of the simple light
In the first, spinning place, the spellbound horses walking warm
    Out of the whinnying green stable   35
      On to the fields of praise.

And honored among foxes and pheasants by the gay house
Under the new made clouds and happy as the heart was long,
    In the sun born over and over,
      I ran my heedless ways,   40
     My wishes raced through the house high hay
And nothing I cared, at my sky blue trades, that time allows
In all his tuneful turning so few and such morning songs
    Before the children green and golden
      Follow him out of grace,   45

Nothing I cared, in the lamb white days, that time would take me
Up to the swallow thronged loft by the shadow of my hand,
    In the moon that is always rising,
      Nor that riding to sleep
     I should hear him fly with the high fields   50
And wake to the farm forever fled from the childless land.
Oh as I was young and easy in the mercy of his means,

Time held me green and dying
Though I sang in my chains like the sea.

(1946)

Do not go gentle into that good night

Do not go gentle into that good night,
Old age should burn and rave at close of day;
Rage, rage against the dying of the light.

Though wise men at their end know dark is right,
Because their words had forked no lightning they   5
Do not go gentle into that good night.

Good men, the last wave by, crying how bright
Their frail deeds might have danced in a green bay,
Rage, rage against the dying of the light.

Wild men who caught and sang the sun in flight,   10
And learn, too late, they grieved it on its way,
Do not go gentle into that good night.

Grave men, near death, who see with blinding sight
Blind eyes could blaze like meteors and be gay,
Rage, rage against the dying of the light.   15

And you, my father, there on the sad height,
Curse, bless, me now with your fierce tears, I pray.
Do not go gentle into that good night.
Rage, rage against the dying of the light.

(1952)

GWENDOLYN BROOKS

[b. 1917]

the mother

Abortions will not let you forget.
You remember the children you got that you did not get,
The damp small pulps with a little or with no hair,
The singers and workers that never handled the air.
You will never neglect or beat   5

Them, or silence or buy with a sweet.
You will never wind up the sucking-thumb
Or scuttle off ghosts that come.
You will never leave them, controlling your luscious sigh,
Return for a snack of them, with gobbling mother-eye.   10

I have heard in the voices of the wind the voices of my dim killed children.
I have contracted. I have eased
My dim dears at the breasts they could never suck.
I have said, Sweets, if I sinned, if I seized
Your luck   15
And your lives from your unfinished reach,
If I stole your births and your names,
Your straight baby tears and your games,
Your stilted or lovely loves, your tumults, your marriages, aches, and your deaths,
If I poisoned the beginnings of your breaths,
Believe that even in my deliberateness I was not deliberate.   20
Though why should I whine,
Whine that the crime was other than mine?—
Since anyhow you are dead.
Or rather, or instead,
You were never made.   25

But that too, I am afraid,
Is faulty: oh, what shall I say, how is the truth to be said?
You were born, you had body, you died.
It is just that you never giggled or planned or cried.
Believe me, I loved you all.   30
Believe me, I knew you, though faintly, and I loved, I loved you
All.

                                                                    (1945)

First fight. Then fiddle

First fight. Then fiddle. Ply the slipping string
With feathery sorcery; muzzle the note
With hurting love; the music that they wrote
Bewitch, bewilder. Qualify to sing
Threadwise. Devise no salt, no hempen thing   5
For the dear instrument to bear. Devote
The bow to silks and honey. Be remote
A while from malice and from murdering.
But first to arms, to armor. Carry hate
In front of you and harmony behind.   10
Be deaf to music and to beauty blind.

Win war. Rise bloody, maybe not too late
For having first to civilize a space
Wherein to play your violin with grace.

(1945)

LAWRENCE FERLINGHETTI
[b. 1919]

Constantly Risking Absurdity

Constantly risking absurdity
                              and death
            whenever he performs
                        above the heads
                                    of his audience   5

        the poet like an acrobat
                        climbs on rime
                    to a high wire of his own making
and balancing on eyebeams
                        above a sea of faces   10
            paces his way
                        to the other side of day
        performing entrechats

                        and sleight-of-foot tricks
and other high theatrics   15

                        and all without mistaking
            any thing
                        for what it may not be
        For he's the super realist
                        who must perforce perceive   20
            taut truth
                        before the taking of each stance or step
in his supposed advance
                        toward that still higher perch
where Beauty stands and waits   25
                        with gravity
                              to start her death-defying leap

        And he
            a little charleychaplin man

who may or may not catch   30
her fair eternal form
                    spreadeagled in the empty air
of existence

                                                    (1958)

RICHARD WILBUR
[*b. 1921*]

The Death of a Toad

    A toad the power mower caught,
Chewed and clipped off a leg, with a hobbling hop has got
    To the garden verge, and sanctuaried him
    Under the cineraria leaves, in the shade
        Of the ashen heartshaped leaves, in a dim,   5
            Low, and a final glade.

    The rare original heartsblood goes,
Spends on the earthen hide, in the folds and wizenings, flows
    In the gutters of the banked and staring eyes. He lies
    As still as if he would return to stone,   10
        And soundlessly attending, dies
            Toward some deep monotone,

    Toward misted and ebullient seas
And cooling shores, toward lost Amphibia's emperies.
    Day dwindles, drowning, and at length is gone   15
    In the wide and antique eyes, which still appear
        To watch, across the castrate lawn,
            The haggard daylight steer.

                                                    (1956)

PHILIP LARKIN
[*b. 1922*]

A Study of Reading Habits

    When getting my nose in a book
    Cured most things short of school,
    It was worth ruining my eyes

To know I could still keep cool,
And deal out the old right hook   5
To dirty dogs twice my size.

Later, with inch-thick specs,
Evil was just my lark:
Me and my cloak and fangs
Had ripping times in the dark.   10
The women I clubbed with sex!
I broke them up like meringues.

Don't read much now: the dude
Who lets the girl down before
The hero arrives, the chap   15
Who's yellow and keeps the store,
Seem far too familiar. Get stewed:
Books are a load of crap.

                                                                (1964)

ROSARIO CASTELLANOS
[1925–1974]

Chess

Because we were friends and sometimes loved each other,
perhaps to add one more tie
to the many that already bound us,
we decided to play games of the mind.

We set up a board between us;   5
equally divided into pieces, values,
and possible moves.
We learned the rules, we swore to respect them,
and the match began.

We've been sitting here for centuries, meditating   10
ferociously
how to deal the one last blow that will finally
annihilate the other one forever.

TRANSLATED BY MAUREEN AHERN

                                                                (1988)

GALWAY KINNELL
[*b. 1927*]

Saint Francis and the Sow

The bud
stands for all things,
even for those things that don't flower,
for everything flowers, from within, of self-blessing;
though sometimes it is necessary   5
to reteach a thing its loveliness,
to put a hand on its brow
of the flower
and retell it in words and in touch
it is lovely   10
until it flowers again from within, of self-blessing;
as Saint Francis°
put his hand on the creased forehead
of the sow, and told her in words and in touch
blessings of earth on the sow, and the sow   15
began remembering all down her thick length,
from the earthen snout all the way
through the fodder and slops to the spiritual curl of the tail,
from the hard spininess spiked out from the spine
down through the great broken heart   20
to the sheer blue milken dreaminess spurting and shuddering
from the fourteen teats into the fourteen mouths sucking and
    blowing beneath them:
the long, perfect loveliness of sow.

                                                              (1980)

JAMES WRIGHT
[*b. 1927*]

Lying in a Hammock at William Duffy's
Farm in Pine Island, Minnesota

Over my head, I see the bronze butterfly,
Asleep on the black trunk,

"Saint Francis and the Sow"   ¹²**Saint Francis**   *Saint Francis of Assisi (1182–1226) was famed for his love of
all creation, especially animals.*

Blowing like a leaf in green shadow.
Down the ravine behind the empty house,
The cowbells follow one another   5
Into the distances of the afternoon.
To my right,
In a field of sunlight between two pines,
The droppings of last year's horses
Blaze up into golden stones.   10
I lean back, as the evening darkens and comes on.
A chicken hawk floats over, looking for home.
I have wasted my life.

         (1963)

A Blessing

Just off the highway to Rochester, Minnesota,
Twilight bounds softly forth on the grass.
And the eyes of those two Indian ponies
Darken with kindness.
They have come gladly out of the willows 5
To welcome my friend and me.
We step over the barbed wire into the pasture
Where they have been grazing all day, alone.
They ripple tensely, they can hardly contain their happiness
That we have come.   10
They bow shyly as wet swans. They love each other.
There is no loneliness like theirs.
At home once more,
They begin munching the young tufts of spring in the darkness.
I would like to hold the slenderer one in my arms, 15
For she has walked over to me
And nuzzled my left hand.
She is black and white,
Her mane falls wild on her forehead,
And the light breeze moves me to caress her long ear 20
That is delicate as the skin over a girl's wrist.
Suddenly I realize
That if I stepped out of my body I would break
Into blossom.

         (1963)

ANNE SEXTON
[1928–1975]

Two Hands

From the sea came a hand,
ignorant as a penny,
troubled with the salt of its mother,
mute with the silence of the fishes,
quick with the altars of the tides,   5
and God reached out of His mouth
and called it man.
Up came the other hand
and God called it woman.
The hands applauded.   10
And this was no sin.
It was as it was meant to be.

I see them roaming the streets:
Levi complaining about his mattress,
Sarah studying a beetle,   15
Mandrake holding his coffee mug,
Sally playing the drum at a football game,
John closing the eyes of the dying woman,
and some who are in prison,
even the prison of their bodies,   20
as Christ was prisoned in His body
until the triumph came.

Unwind, hands,
you angel webs,
unwind like the coil of a jumping jack,   25
cup together and let yourselves fill up with sun
and applaud, world,
applaud.

(1969)

A SELECTION OF CONTEMPORARY POEMS

DONALD HALL
[b. 1928]

My son, my executioner

My son, my executioner,
 I take you in my arms,
Quiet and small and just astir,
 And whom my body warms.

Sweet death, small son, our instrument   5
 Of immortality,
Your cries and hungers document
 Our bodily decay.

We twenty-five and twenty-two,
 Who seemed to live forever,   10
Observe enduring life in you
 And start to die together.

(1955)

GREGORY CORSO
[b. 1930]

Marriage

Should I get married? Should I be good?
Astound the girl next door with my velvet suit and faustus hood?°
Don't take her to movies but to cemeteries
tell all about werewolf bathtubs and forked clarinets
then desire her and kiss her and all the preliminaries   5
and she going just so far and I understanding why
not getting angry saying You must feel! It's beautiful to feel!
Instead take her in my arms lean against an old crooked tombstone
and woo her the entire night the constellations in the sky—

"Marriage" ²*faustus hood* *Dr. Faustus, German magician and astrologer (ca. 1480–1538) was reputed to have sold his soul to the Devil in exchange for knowledge and power.*

When she introduces me to her parents   10
back straightened, hair finally combed, strangled by a tie,
should I sit knees together on their 3rd degree sofa
and not ask Where's the bathroom?
How else to feel other than I am,
often thinking Flash Gordon soap—   15
O how terrible it must be for a young man
seated before a family and the family thinking
We never saw him before! He wants our Mary Lou!
After tea and homemade cookies they ask What do you do for a living?

Should I tell them? Would they like me then?   20
Say All right get married, we're losing a daughter
but we're gaining a son—
And should I then ask Where's the bathroom?

O God, and the wedding! All her family and her friends
and only a handful of mine all scroungy and bearded   25
just wait to get at the drinks and food—
And the priest! he looking at me as if I masturbated
asking me Do you take this woman for your lawful wedded wife?
And I trembling what to say say Pie Glue!
I kiss the bride all those corny men slapping me on the back   30
She's all yours, boy! Ha-ha-ha!
And in their eyes you could see some obscene honeymoon going on—
Then all that absurd rice and clanky cans and shoes
Niagara Falls! Hordes of us! Husbands! Wives! Flowers! Chocolates!
All streaming into cozy hotels   35
All going to do the same thing tonight

The indifferent clerk he knowing what was going to happen
The lobby zombies they knowing what
The whistling elevator man he knowing
The winking bellboy knowing   40
Everybody knowing! I'd be almost inclined not to do anything!
Stay up all night! Stare that hotel clerk in the eye!
Screaming: I deny honeymoon! I deny honeymoon!
running rampant into those almost climactic suites
yelling Radio belly! Cat shovel!   45
O I'd live in Niagara forever! in a dark cave beneath the Falls
I'd sit there the Mad Honeymooner
devising ways to break marriages, a scourge of bigamy
a saint of divorce—

But I should get married I should be good   50
How nice it'd be to come home to her
and sit by the fireplace and she in the kitchen

aproned young and lovely wanting my baby
and so happy about me she burns the roast beef
and comes crying to me and I get up from my big papa chair   55
saying Christmas teeth! Radiant brains! Apple deaf!
God what a husband I'd make! Yes, I should get married!
So much to do! like sneaking into Mr Jones' house late at night
and cover his golf clubs with 1920 Norwegian books
Like hanging a picture of Rimbaud° on the lawnmower   60
like pasting Tannu Tuva° postage stamps all over the picket fence
like when Mrs Kindhead comes to collect for the Community Chest
grab her and tell her There are unfavorable omens in the sky!
And when the mayor comes to get my vote tell him
When are you going to stop people killing whales!   65
And when the milkman comes leave him a note in the bottle
Penguin dust, bring me penguin dust, I want penguin dust—

Yet if I should get married and it's Connecticut and snow
and she gives birth to a child and I am sleepless, worn,
up for nights, head bowed against a quiet window, the past behind me,   70
finding myself in the most common of situations a trembling man
knowledged with responsibility not twig-smear nor Roman coin soup—
O what would that be like!
Surely I'd give it for a nipple a rubber Tacitus°
For a rattle a bag of broken Bach records   75
Tack Della Francesca° all over its crib
Sew the Greek alphabet on its bib
And build for its playpen a roofless Parthenon

No, I doubt I'd be that kind of father
Not rural not snow no quiet window   80
but hot smelly tight New York City
seven flights up, roaches and rats in the walls
a fat Reichian° wife screeching over potatoes Get a job!
And five nose running brats in love with Batman
And the neighbors all toothless and dry haired   85
like those hag masses of the 18th century
all wanting to come in and watch TV

The landlord wants his rent
Grocery store Blue Cross Gas & Electric Knights of Columbus
Impossible to lie back and dream Telephone snow, ghost parking—   90
No! I should not get married I should never get married!
But—imagine if I were married to a beautiful sophisticated woman

---

[60]**Rimbaud**   *Arthur Rimbaud (1854–1891), French poet.*   [61]**Tannu Tuva**   *a republic in Siberia, part of the USSR.*   [74]**Tacitus**   *Roman historian (A.D. 55–117).*   [76]**Della Francesca**   *Italian Renaissance painter (1420–1492).*   [83]**Reichian**   *follower of psychoanalyst Wilhelm Reich (1897–1957).*

tall and pale wearing an elegant black dress and long black gloves
holding a cigarette holder in one hand and a highball in the other
and we lived high up in a penthouse with a huge window   95
from which we could see all of New York and ever farther on clearer days
No, can't imagine myself married to that pleasant prison dream—
O but what about love? I forget love
not that I am incapable of love
it's just that I see love as odd as wearing shoes—   100
I never wanted to marry a girl who was like my mother
And Ingrid Bergman was always impossible
And there's maybe a girl now but she's already married
And I don't like men and—
but there's got to be somebody!   105
Because what if I'm 60 years old and not married,
all alone in a furnished room with pee stains on my underwear
and everybody else is married! All the universe married but me!

Ah, yet well I know that were a woman possible as I am possible
then marriage would be possible—   110
Like SHE° in her lonely alien gaud waiting her Egyptian lover
so I wait—bereft of 2,000 years and the bath of life.

                                                              (1960)

LINDA PASTAN
[b. 1932]

Ethics

In ethics class so many years ago
our teacher asked this question every fall:
if there were a fire in a museum
which would you save, a Rembrandt painting
or an old woman who hadn't many   5
years left anyhow? Restless on hard chairs
caring little for pictures or old age
we'd opt one year for life, the next for art
and always half-heartedly. Sometimes
the woman borrowed my grandmother's face   10
leaving her usual kitchen to wander
some drafty, half imagined museum.

---

[111] **SHE**   *the heroine of H. Rider Haggard's novel* She *(1887) who gains eternal youth by bathing in fire and who waits thousands of years for her lover's return.*

One year, feeling clever, I replied
why not let the woman decide herself?
Linda, the teacher would report, eschews   15
the burdens of responsibility.
This fall in a real museum I stand
before a real Rembrandt, old woman,
or nearly so, myself. The colors
within this frame are darker than autumn,   20
darker even than winter—the browns of earth,
though earth's most radiant elements burn
through the canvas. I know now that woman
and painting and season are almost one
and all beyond saving by children.   25

(1981)

SYLVIA PLATH
[1932–1963]

Mirror

I am silver and exact. I have no preconceptions.
Whatever I see I swallow immediately
Just as it is, unmisted by love or dislike.
I am not cruel, only truthful—
The eye of a little god, four-cornered.   5
Most of the time I meditate on the opposite wall.
It is pink, with speckles. I have looked at it so long
I think it is a part of my heart. But it flickers.
Faces and darkness separate us over and over.

Now I am a lake. A woman bends over me,   10
Searching my reaches for what she really is.
Then she turns to those liars, the candles or the moon.
I see her back, and reflect it faithfully.
She rewards me with tears and an agitation of hands.
I am important to her. She comes and goes.   15
Each morning it is her face that replaces the darkness.
In me she has drowned a young girl, and in me an old woman
Rises toward her day after day, like a terrible fish.

AUDRE LORDE
[1934–1992]

Hanging Fire

I am fourteen
and my skin has betrayed me
the boy I cannot live without
still sucks his thumb
in secret   5
how come my knees are
always so ashy
what if I die
before morning
and mamma's in the bedroom   10
with the door closed.

I have to learn how to dance
in time for the next party
my room is too small for me
suppose I die before graduation   15
they will sing sad melodies
but finally
tell the truth about me
There is nothing I want to do
and too much   20
that has to be done
and momma's in the bedroom
with the door closed.

Nobody even stops to think
about my side of it   25
I should have been on Math Team
my marks were better than his
why do I have to be
the one
wearing braces   30
I have nothing to wear tomorrow
will I live long enough
to grow up
and momma's in the bedroom
with the door closed.   35

(1978)

LUCILLE CLIFTON
[*b. 1936*]

Homage to My Hips

these hips are big hips.
they need space to
move around in.
they don't fit into little
petty places. these hips   5
are free hips.
they don't like to be held back.
these hips have never been enslaved,
they go where they want to go
they do what they want to do.   10
these hips are mighty hips.
these hips are magic hips.
i have known them
to put a spell on a man and
spin him like a top!   15

(1972)

MARGE PIERCY
[*b. 1936*]

A Work of Artifice

The bonsai tree
in the attractive pot
could have grown eighty feet tall
on the side of a mountain
till split by lightning.   5
But a gardener
carefully pruned it.
It is nine inches high.
Every day as he
whittles back the branches   10
the gardener croons,
It is your nature
to be small and cozy,
domestic and weak;
how lucky, little tree,   15

to have a pot to grow in.
With living creatures
one must begin very early
to dwarf their growth:
the bound feet,   20
the crippled brain,
the hair in curlers,
the hands you
love to touch.

(1973)

MARGARET ATWOOD
[b. 1939]

This Is a Photograph of Me

It was taken some time ago.
At first it seems to be
a smeared
print: blurred lines and grey flecks
blended with the paper;   5
then, as you scan
it, you see in the left-hand corner
a thing that is like a branch: part of a tree
(balsam or spruce) emerging
and, to the right, halfway up   10
what ought to be a gentle
slope, a small frame house.

In the background there is a lake,
and beyond that, some low hills.

(The photograph was taken   15
the day after I drowned.

I am in the lake, in the center
of the picture, just under the surface.

It is difficult to say where
precisely, or to say   20
how large or small I am:
the effect of water
on light is a distortion

but if you look long enough,
eventually 25
you will be able to see me.)

(1966)

RAYMOND CARVER
[1939–1988]

Photograph of My Father in His Twenty-second Year

October. Here in this dank, unfamiliar kitchen
I study my father's embarrassed young man's face.
Sheepish grin, he holds in one hand a string
of spiny yellow perch, in the other
a bottle of Carlsbad beer. 5

In jeans and denim shirt, he leans
against the front fender of a 1934 Ford.
He would like to pose bluff and hearty for his posterity,
wear his old hat cocked over his ear.
All his life my father wanted to be bold. 10

But the eyes give him away, and the hands
that limply offer the string of dead perch
and the bottle of beer. Father, I love you,
yet how can I say thank you, I who can't hold my liquor either,
and don't even know the places to fish? 15

(1988)

SEAMUS HEANEY
[b. 1939]

Mid-Term Break

I sat all morning in the college sick bay
Counting bells knelling classes to a close.
At two o'clock our neighbors drove me home.

In the porch I met my father crying—
He had always taken funerals in his stride— 5
And Big Jim Evans saying it was a hard blow.

The baby cooed and laughed and rocked the pram
When I came in, and I was embarrassed
By old men standing up to shake my hand

And tell me they were "sorry for my trouble,"   10
Whispers informed strangers I was the eldest,
Away at school, as my mother held my hand

In hers and coughed out angry tearless sighs.
At ten o'clock the ambulance arrived
With the corpse, stanched and bandaged by the nurses.   15

Next morning I went up into the room. Snowdrops
And candles soothed the bedside; I saw him
For the first time in six weeks. Paler now,

Wearing a poppy bruise on his left temple,
He lay in the four foot box as in his cot.   20
No gaudy scars, the bumper knocked him clear.

A four foot box, a foot for every year.

                                                        (1966)

Digging

Between my finger and my thumb
The squat pen rests; snug as a gun.

Under my window, a clean rasping sound
When the spade sinks into gravelly ground:
My father, digging. I look down   5

Till his straining rump among the flowerbeds
Bends low, comes up twenty years away
Stooping in rhythm through potato drills
Where he was digging.

The coarse boot nestled on the lug, the shaft   10
Against the inside knee was levered firmly.
He rooted out tall tops, buried the bright edge deep
To scatter new potatoes that we picked
Loving their cool hardness in our hands.

By God, the old man could handle a spade.   15
Just like his old man.

My grandfather cut more turf in a day
Than any other man on Toner's bog.
Once I carried him milk in a bottle
Corked sloppily with paper. He straightened up　　20
To drink it, then fell to right away

Nicking and slicing neatly, heaving sods
Over his shoulder, going down and down
For the good turf. Digging.

The cold smell of potato mould, the squelch and slap　　25
Of soggy peat, the curt cuts of an edge
Through living roots awaken in my head.
But I've no spade to follow men like them.

Between my finger and my thumb
The squat pen rests.　　30
I'll dig with it.

　　　　　　　　　　　　　　　　(1966)

NIKKI GIOVANNI
[b. 1943]

Ego Tripping
(THERE MAY BE A REASON WHY)

I was born in the congo
I walked to the fertile crescent and built
　　the sphinx
I designed a pyramid so tough that a star
　　that only glows every one hundred years falls　　5
　　into the center giving divine perfect light
I am bad

I sat on the throne
　　drinking nectar with allah
I got hot and sent an ice age to europe　　10
　　to cool my thirst
My oldest daughter is nefertiti
　　the tears from my birth pains
　　created the nile
I am a beautiful woman　　15

I gazed on the forest and burned
    out the sahara desert
    with a packet of goat's meat
    and a change of clothes
I crossed it in two hours   20
I am a gazelle so swift
    so swift you can't catch me

    For a birthday present when he was three
I gave my son hannibal an elephant
    He gave me rome for mother's day   25
My strength flows ever on

My son noah built new/ark and
I stood proudly at the helm
    as we sailed on a soft summer day
I turned myself into myself and was   30
    jesus
    men intone my loving name
    All praises All praises
I am the one who would save

I sowed diamonds in my back yard   35
My bowels deliver uranium
    the filings from my fingernails are
    semi-precious jewels
    On a trip north
I caught a cold and blew   40
My nose giving oil to the arab world
I am so hip even my errors are correct
I sailed west to reach east and had to round off
    the earth as I went
    The hair from my head thinned and gold was laid   45
    across three continents
I am so perfect so divine so ethereal so surreal
I cannot be comprehended
    except by my permission

I mean . . . I . . . can fly   50
    like a bird in the sky . . .

                    (1970)

SHARON OLDS
[b. 1942]

Size and Sheer Will

The fine, green pajama cotton,
washed so often it is paper-thin and
iridescent, has split like a sheath
and the glossy white naked bulbs of
Gabriel's toes thrust forth like crocus   5
this early Spring. The boy is growing
as fast as he can, elongated
wrists dangling, lean meat
showing between the shirt and the belt.
If there were a rack to stretch himself, he would   10
strap his slight body to it.
If there were a machine to enter,
skip the next ten years and be
sixteen immediately, this boy would
do it. All day long he cranes his   15
neck, like a plant in the dark with a single
light above it, or a sailor under
tons of green water, longing
for the surface, for his rightful life.

(1975)

TOM MOLITO
[b. 1944]

Cosmic Simplicities

We basically don't know where we
came from before birth—

We basically don't know where we go
after death—

Now, tell me how to live my life if you   5
dare—

The truth probably lies somewhere
between Plato and Pluto.

(1998)

JANE KENYON
[1947–1995]

Notes from the Other Side

I divested myself of despair
and fear when I came here.

Now there is no more catching
one's own eye in the mirror,

there are no bad books, no plastic,   5
no insurance premiums, and of course

no illness. Contrition
does not exist, nor gnashing

of teeth. No one howls as the first
clod of earth hits the casket.   10

The poor we no longer have with us.
Our calm hearts strike only the hour,

and God, as promised, proves
to be mercy clothed in light.

(1990)

YUSEF KOMUNYAKAA
[b. 1947]

Facing It

My black face fades,
hiding inside the black granite.
I said I wouldn't,
dammit: No tears.
I'm stone. I'm flesh.   5
My clouded reflection eyes me
like a bird of prey, the profile of night
slanted against morning. I turn
this way—the stone lets me go.

I turn that way—I'm inside   10
the Vietnam Veterans Memorial
again, depending on the light
to make a difference.
I go down the 58,022 names,
half-expecting to find   15
my own in letters like smoke.
I touch the name Andrew Johnson;
I see the booby trap's white flash.
Names shimmer on a woman's blouse
but when she walks away   20
the names stay on the wall.
Brushstrokes flash, a red bird's
wings cutting across my stare.
The sky. A plane in the sky.
A white vet's image floats   25
closer to me, then his pale eyes
look through mine. I'm a window.
He's lost his right arm
inside the stone. In the black mirror
a woman's trying to erase names: 30
No, she's brushing a boy's hair.

    (1988)

NEAL BOWERS
[b. 1948]

Driving Lessons

I learned to drive in a parking lot
on Sundays, when the stores were closed—
slow maneuvers out beyond the light-poles,
no destination, just the ritual of clutch and gas,
my father clenching with the grinding gears,   5
finally giving up and leaving my mother
to buck and plunge with me and say,
repeatedly, "Once more. Try just once more."

She walked out on him once
when I was six or seven, my father   10
driving beside her, slow as a beginner,
pleading, my baby brother and I
crying out the windows, "Mama, don't go!"
It was a scene to break your heart

or make you laugh—those wailing kids,   15
a woman walking briskly with a suitcase,
the slow car following like a faithful dog.

I don't know why she finally got in
and let us take her back
to whatever she had made up her mind to leave;   20
but the old world swallowed her up
as soon as she opened that door,
and the other life she might have lived
lay down forever in its dark infancy.

Sometimes, when I'm home, driving   25
through the old neighborhoods, stopping
in front of each little house we rented,
my stillborn other life gets in,
the boy I would have been if
my mother had kept on walking.   30
He wants to be just like her,
far away and gone forever, wants
me to press down on the gas;
but however fast I squeal away,
the shaggy past keeps loping behind,   35
sniffing every turn.

When I stop in the weedy parking lot,
the failed stores of the old mall
make a dark wall straight ahead;
and I'm alone again, until my parents get in,   40
unchanged after all these years,
my father, impatient, my mother
trying hard to smile, waiting for me
to steer my way across this emptiness.

(1992)

KRAFT ROMPF
[*b. 1948*]

Waiting Table

To serve, I wait and pluck
the rose, brush crumbs, carry

madly trays of oysters and
Bloody Marys. Swinging through

doors, I hear them: mouths   5
open, eyes bugging, choking;

they beat a white clothed
table for caffeine piping

hot and sweet, sweet sugar.
Oh, I should pour it in   10

their eyes! And set their
tongues afire. How the chef

understands when I order
tartare and shout, "Let them

eat it raw!" Oh I would stuff   15
their noses with garlic

and the house pianist
could play the Hammer March

on their toes. But for a
tip—for a tip, for a tip   20

I would work so very, very
hard, and so gladly let

them shine into my soul,
and bow to them and laugh

with them and sing. I would   25
gladly give them everything.

(1978)

JIMMY SANTIAGO BACA
[b. 1952]

from *Meditations on the South Valley*

XVII

I love the wind
when it blows through my barrio.
It hisses its snake love
down calles de polvo,
and cracks egg-shell skins   5
of abandoned homes.
Stray dogs find shelter
along the river,
where great cottonwoods rattle
like old covered wagons,   10
stuck in stagnant waterholes.
Days when the wind blows
full of sand and grit,
men and women make decisions
that change their whole lives.   15
Windy days in the barrio
give birth to divorce papers
and squalling separation. The wind tells us
what others refuse to tell us,
informing men and women of a secret,   20
that they move away to hide from.

(1979)

RITA DOVE
[b. 1952]

Canary

FOR MICHAEL S. HARPER

Billie Holiday's burned voice
had as many shadows as lights,
a mournful candelabra against a sleek piano,
the gardenia her signature under that ruined face.

(Now you're cooking, drummer to bass,   5
magic spoon, magic needle.

Take all day if you have to
with your mirror and your bracelet of song.)

Fact is, the invention of women under siege
has been to sharpen love in the service of myth.   10

If you can't be free, be a mystery.

     (1989)

JUDITH ORTIZ COFER
[*b. 1952*]

The Idea of Islands

The place where I was born,
that mote in a cartographer's eye,
interests you?
Today Atlanta is like a port city
enveloped in mist. The temperature   5
is plunging with the abandon
of a woman rushing to a rendezvous.
Since you ask, things were simpler
on the island. Food and shelter
were never the problem. Most days,   10
a hat and a watchful eye were all
one needed for protection, the climate being
rarely inclement. Fruit could be plucked
from trees languishing under the weight
of their own fecundity. The thick sea   15
spewed out fish that crawled into the pots
of women whose main occupation was to dress
each other's manes with scarlet hibiscus,
which as you may know, blooms
without restraint in the tropics.   20
I was always the ambitious one, overdressed
by my neighbors' standards, and unwilling
to eat mangoes three times a day.
In truth, I confess to spending my youth
guarding the fire by the beach, waiting   25
to be rescued from the futile round
of paradisial life.
How do I like the big city?
City lights are just as bright
as the stars that enticed me then;   30

the traffic ebbs and rises like the tides
and in a crowd,
    everyone is an island.

(1989)

ALBERTO RIOS
[b. 1952]

A Dream of Husbands

Though we thought it, Doña Carolina did not die.
She was too old for that nonsense, and too set.
That morning she walked off just a little farther
into her favorite dream, favorite but not nice
so much, not nice and not bad, so it was not death.   5
She dreamed the dream of husbands
and over there she found him after all the years.
Cabrón, she called him, *animal,* very loud
so we could hear it, for us it was a loud truck
passing, or thunder, or too many cats, very loud   10
for having left her for so long and so far. Days now
her voice is the squeak of the rocking chair
as she complains, we hear it, it will not go
not with oils or sanding or shouts back at her.
But it becomes too the sound a spoon makes, her old   15
very large wooden spoon as it stirs a pot of soup.
Dinnertimes, we think of her, the good parts, of her
cooking, we like her best then, even the smell of her.
But then, *cabrones* she calls us, *animales,* irritated,
from over there, from the dream, they come, her words   20
they are the worst sounds of the street in the night
so that we will not get so comfortable about her,
so comfortable with her having left us
we thinking that her husband and her long dream
are so perfect, because no, they are not, not so much,   25
she is not so happy this way, not in this dream,
this is not heaven, don't think it. She tells us this,
sadness too is hers, a half measure, sadness at having
no time for the old things, for rice, for chairs.

(1985)

GERTRUDE SCHNACKENBERG
[b. 1952]

Signs

Threading the palm, a web of little lines
Spells out the lost money, the heart, the head,
The wagging tongues, the sudden deaths, in signs
We would smooth out, like imprints on a bed,

In signs that can't be helped, geese heading south,   5
In signs read anxiously, like breath that clouds
A mirror held to a barely open mouth,
Like telegrams, the gathering of crowds—

The plane's X in the sky, spelling disaster:
Before the whistle and hit, a tracer flare;   10
Before rubble, a hairline crack in plaster
And a housefly's panicked scribbling on the air.

(1982)

GARY SOTO
[b. 1952]

Behind Grandma's House

At ten I wanted fame. I had a comb
And two Coke bottles, a tube of Bryl-creem.
I borrowed a dog, one with
Mismatched eyes and a happy tongue,
And wanted to prove I was tough   5
In the alley, kicking over trash cans,
A dull chime of tuna cans falling.
I hurled light bulbs like grenades
And men teachers held their heads,
Fingers of blood lengthening   10
On the ground. I flicked rocks at cats,
Their goofy faces spurred with foxtails.
I kicked fences. I shooed pigeons.
I broke a branch from a flowering peach

And frightened ants with a stream of spit.   15
I said *"Chale,"* "In your face," and "No way
Daddy-O" to an imaginary priest
Until grandma came into the alley,
Her apron flapping in a breeze,
Her hair mussed, and said, "Let me help you,"   20
And punched me between the eyes.

(1985)

LOUISE ERDRICH
[b. 1954]

Indian Boarding School: The Runaways

Home's the place we head for in our sleep.
Boxcars stumbling north in dreams
don't wait for us. We catch them on the run.
The rails, old lacerations that we love,
shoot parallel across the face and break   5
just under Turtle Mountains. Riding scars
you can't get lost. Home is the place they cross.

The lame guard strikes a match and makes the dark
less tolerant. We watch through cracks in boards
as the land starts rolling, rolling till it hurts   10
to be here, cold in regulation clothes.
We know the sheriff's waiting at midrun
to take us back. His car is dumb and warm.
The highway doesn't rock, it only hums
like a wing of long insults. The worn-down welts   15
of ancient punishments lead back and forth.

All runaways wear dresses, long green ones,
the color you would think shame was. We scrub
the sidewalks down because it's shameful work.
Our brushes cut the stone in watered arcs   20
and in the soak frail outlines shiver clear
a moment, things us kids pressed on the dark
face before it hardened, place, remembering
delicate old injuries, the spines of names and leaves.

(1984)

Drama

PART THREE

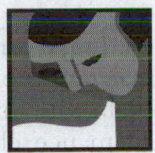

Reading Plays

Drama, unlike the other literary genres, is a staged art. Plays are written to be performed by actors before an audience. But the plays we wish to see are not always performed. We might have to wait years, for example, to see a production of Sophocles' *Oedipus Rex* or Arthur Miller's *Death of a Salesman*. We simply might never have an opportunity to see certain plays. A reasonable alternative is to read them with attention to both their theatrical and literary dimensions.

THE EXPERIENCE OF DRAMA

As a literary genre, drama has affinities with fiction and poetry. Like fiction, drama possesses a narrative dimension: a play often narrates a story in the form of a plot. Like fiction, drama relies on dialogue and description, which takes the form of *stage directions,* lines describing characters, scenes, or actions with clues to production. Unlike fiction, however, in which a narrator often mediates between us and the story, there is no such authorial presence in drama. Instead, we hear the words of the characters directly.

Although drama is most like fiction, it shares features with poetry as well. Plays may, in fact, be written in verse: Shakespeare wrote in *blank verse* (unrhymed iambic pentameter), Molière in rhymed couplets. Plays, like lyric poems, are also overheard: we listen to characters expressing their concerns as if there were no audience present. Poems also contain dramatic elements. The dramatic lyrics and monologues of Robert Browning and some of the poems of John Donne portray characters speaking and listening to one another.

Plays may be vehicles of persuasion. Henrik Ibsen and Bernard Shaw frequently used the stage to dramatize ideas and issues. For most of his plays Shaw wrote prefaces in which he discussed the plays' dominant ideas. In drama, ideas possess more primacy than they do in poetry and fiction, something to which critics of the genre testify. Aristotle, for example, made *thought* one of his six elements of drama; Eric Bentley, a modern critic, entitled one of his books *The Playwright as Thinker.*

But if we look exclusively to the literary aspects of drama, to its poetic and fictional elements, and to its dramatization of ideas, we may fail to appreciate its uniquely theatrical idiom. To gain this appreciation we should read drama with special attention to its performance elements. We can try to hear the voices of characters, and imagine tones and inflections. We can try to see mentally how characters look, where they stand in relation to one another, how they move and gesture. We can read, in short, as armchair directors and as aspiring actors and actresses considering the physical and practical realities of performance.

In doing so we will enrich our experience of the plays we read. Our experience of drama includes more than an intellectual understanding of the ideas particular plays may dramatize. It also includes our emotional reactions to plots and our responses to the interaction of the characters. It encompasses our vision of their dramatic worlds, and it is affected by our changing perceptions and feelings as we read. Our experience of reading drama involves more than a rational and analytic understanding of the text. More inclusive, more integrated, and more imaginative, that experience includes feelings as well as thought, emotional apprehension as well as intellectual comprehension.

As active readers of drama we will bring a special awareness of the ways the written text of a play (its *script*) suggests possibilities for performance. To suggest how we might do this, we include excerpts from three plays, each accompanied by notes and comments. As you read the first excerpt, the opening scene of Henrik Ibsen's *A Doll House,* consider what the stage directions and cast of characters reveal about the world of the play.

CHARACTERS

TORVALD HELMER, *A LAWYER*

NORA, *HIS WIFE*

DR. RANK

MRS. LINDE

NILS KROGSTAD, *A BANK CLERK*

THE HELMERS' THREE SMALL CHILDREN

ANNE-MARIE, *THEIR NURSE*

HELENE, *A MAID*

A DELIVERY BOY

The action takes place in HELMER'S *residence.*

ACT I

A comfortable room, tastefully but not expensively furnished. A door to the right in the back wall leads to the entryway, another to the left leads to HELMER'S *study. Between these doors, a piano. Midway in the left-hand wall a door, and further back a window. Near the window a round table with an armchair and a small sofa. In the right-hand wall, toward the rear a door, and nearer the foreground a porcelain stove with two armchairs and a rocking chair beside it. Between the stove and the side door, a small table. Engravings on the walls. An* etagére *with china figures and other small art objects; a small bookcase with richly bound books; the floor carpeted; a fire burning in the stove. It is a winter day.*

A bell rings in the entryway; shortly after we hear the door being unlocked. NORA *comes into the room, humming happily to herself; she is wearing street clothes and carries an armload of packages, which she puts down on the table to the right. She has left the hall door open; and through it a* DELIVERY BOY *is seen, holding a Christmas tree and a basket which he gives to the* MAID *who let them in.*

NORA: Hide the tree well, Helene. The children mustn't get a glimpse of it till this evening, after it's trimmed. (*To the* DELIVERY BOY, *taking out her purse*) How much?

DELIVERY BOY: Fifty, ma'am.

NORA: There's a crown. No, keep the change. (*The* BOY *thanks her and leaves.* NORA *shuts the door. She laughs softly to herself while taking off her street things. Drawing a bag of macaroons from her pocket, she eats a couple, then steals over and listens at her husband's study door.*) Yes, he's home. (*Hums again as she moves to the table, right.*)

HELMER (*from the study*): Is that my little lark twittering out there?

NORA (*busy opening some packages*): Yes, it is.

HELMER: Is that my squirrel rummaging around?

NORA: Yes!

HELMER: When did my squirrel get in?

NORA: Just now. (*Putting the macaroon bag in her pocket and wiping her mouth*) Do come in, Torvald, and see what I've bought.

HELMER: Can't be disturbed. (*After a moment he opens the door and peers in, pen in hand.*) Bought, you say? All that there? Has the little spendthrift been out throwing money around again?

NORA: Oh, but Torvald, this year we really should let ourselves go a bit. It's the first Christmas we haven't had to economize.

HELMER: But you know we can't go squandering.

NORA: Oh yes, Torvald, we can squander a little now. Can't we? Just a tiny, wee bit. Now that you've got a big salary and are going to make piles and piles of money.

HELMER: Yes—starting New Year's. But then it's a full three months till the raise comes through.

NORA: Pooh! We can borrow that long.

HELMER: Nora! (*Goes over and playfully takes her by the ear*) Are your scatterbrains off again? What if today I borrowed a thousand crowns, and you squandered them over Christmas week, and then on New Year's Eve a roof tile fell on my head, and I lay there—

NORA (*putting her hand on his mouth*): Oh! Don't say such things!

HELMER: Yes, but what if it happened—then what?

NORA: If anything so awful happened, then it just wouldn't matter if I had debts or not.

HELMER: Well, but the people I'd borrowed from?

NORA: Them? Who cares about them! They're strangers.

HELMER: Nora, Nora, how like a woman! No, but seriously, Nora, you know what I think about that. No debts! Never borrow! Something of freedom's lost—and something of beauty, too—from a home that's founded on borrowing and debt. We've made a brave stand up to now, the two of us; and we'll go right on like that the little while we have to.

NORA (*going toward the stove*): Yes, whatever you say, Torvald.

HELMER (*following her*): Now, now, the little lark's wings mustn't droop. Come on, don't be a sulky squirrel. (*Taking out his wallet*) Nora, guess what I have here.

NORA (*turning quickly*): Money!

HELMER: There, see. (*Hands her some notes*) Good grief, I know how costs go up in a house at Christmastime.

NORA: Ten—twenty—thirty—forty. Oh, thank you, Torvald; I can manage no end on this.

HELMER: You really will have to.

NORA: Oh yes, I promise I will! But come here so I can show you everything I bought. And so cheap! Look, new clothes for Ivar here—and a sword. Here a horse and a trumpet for Bob. And a doll and a doll's bed here for Emmy; they're nothing much, but she'll tear them to bits in no time anyway. And here I have dress material and handkerchiefs for the maids. Old Anne-Marie really deserves something more.

HELMER: And what's in that package there?

NORA (*with a cry*): Torvald, no! You can't see that till tonight!

HELMER: I see. But tell me now, you little prodigal, what have you thought of for yourself?

NORA: For myself? Oh, I don't want anything at all.

HELMER: Of course you do. Tell me just what—within reason—you'd most like to have.

NORA: I honestly don't know. Oh, listen, Torvald—

HELMER: Well?

NORA (*fumbling at his coat buttons, without looking at him*): If you want to give me something, then maybe you could—you could—

HELMER: Come on, out with it.

NORA (*hurriedly*): You could give me money, Torvald. No more than you think you can spare, then one of these days I'll buy something with it.

HELMER: But Nora—

NORA: Oh, please, Torvald darling, do that! I beg you, please. Then I could hang the bills in pretty gilt paper on the Christmas tree. Wouldn't that be fun?

HELMER: What are those little birds called that always fly through their fortunes?

NORA: Oh yes, spendthrifts; I know all that. But let's do as I say, Torvald; then I'll have time to decide what I really need most. That's very sensible, isn't it?

HELMER (*smiling*): Yes, very—that is, if you actually hung onto the money I give you, and you actually used it to buy yourself something. But it goes for the house and for all sorts of foolish things, and then I only have to lay out some more.

NORA: Oh, but Torvald—

HELMER: Don't deny it, my dear little Nora. (*Putting his arm around her waist*) Spendthrifts are sweet, but they use up a frightful amount of money. It's incredible what it costs a man to feed such birds.

NORA: Oh, how can you say that! Really, I save everything I can.

HELMER (*laughing*):   Yes, that's the truth. Everything you can. But that's nothing at all.

NORA (*humming, with a smile of quiet satisfaction*):   Hm, if you only knew what expenses we larks and squirrels have, Torvald.

HELMER: You're an odd little one. Exactly the way your father was. You're never at a loss for scaring up money; but the moment you have it, it runs right out through your fingers; you never know what you've done with it. Well, one takes you as you are. It's deep in your blood. Yes, these things are hereditary, Nora.

NORA: Ah, I could wish I'd inherited many of Papa's qualities.

HELMER: And I couldn't wish you anything but just what you are, my sweet little lark. But wait; it seems to me you have a very—what should I call it?—a very suspicious look today—

NORA: I do?

HELMER: You certainly do. Look me straight in the eye.

NORA (*looking at him*):   Well?

HELMER (*shaking an admonitory finger*):   Surely my sweet tooth hasn't been running riot in town today, has she?

NORA: No. Why do you imagine that?

HELMER: My sweet tooth really didn't make a little detour through the confectioner's?

NORA: No, I assure you, Torvald—

HELMER: Hasn't nibbled some pastry?

NORA: No, not at all.

HELMER: Not even munched a macaroon or two?

NORA: No, Torvald, I assure you, really—

HELMER: There, there now. Of course I'm only joking.

NORA (*going to the table, right*):   You know I could never think of going against you.

HELMER: No, I understand that; and you *have* given me your word. (*Going over to her*) Well, you keep your little Christmas secrets to yourself, Nora darling. I expect they'll come to light this evening, when the tree is lit.

NORA: Did you remember to ask Dr. Rank?

HELMER: No. But there's no need for that; it's assumed he'll be dining with us. All the same, I'll ask him when he stops by here this morning. I've ordered some fine wine. Nora, you can't imagine how I'm looking forward to this evening.

NORA: So am I. And what fun for the children, Torvald!

HELMER: Ah, it's so gratifying to know that one's gotten a safe, secure job, and with a comfortable salary. It's a great satisfaction, isn't it?

NORA: Oh, it's wonderful!

HELMER: Remember last Christmas? Three whole weeks before, you shut yourself in every evening till long after midnight, making flowers for the Christmas tree, and all the other decorations to surprise us. Ugh, that was the dullest time I've ever lived through.

NORA: It wasn't at all dull for me.

HELMER (*smiling*):   But the outcome *was* pretty sorry, Nora.

NORA: Oh, don't tease me with that again. How could I help it that the cat came in and tore everything to shreds.

HELMER: No, poor thing, you certainly couldn't. You wanted so much to please us all, and that's what counts. But it's just as well that the hard times are past.

NORA: Yes, it's really wonderful.

HELMER: Now I don't have to sit here alone, boring myself, and you don't have to tire your precious eyes and your fair little delicate hands—

NORA (*clapping her hands*):   No, is it really true, Torvald, I don't have to? Oh, how wonderfully lovely to hear! (*Taking his arm*) Now I'll tell you just how I've thought we should plan things. Right after Christmas—(*The doorbell rings.*) Oh, the bell. (*Straightening the room up a bit*) Somebody would have to come. What a bore!

HELMER: I'm not at home to visitors, don't forget.

MAID (*from the hall doorway*):   Ma'am, a lady to see you—

NORA: All right, let her come in.

MAID (*to* HELMER):   And the doctor's just come too.

HELMER: Did he go right to my study?

MAID: Yes, he did.

The first thing we notice is the title: *A Doll House.* Does Ibsen alert us to a central concern of the play with this provocative title? Is it literal or symbolic? As we read the opening scene we test our preliminary sense of the title's implications. As we watch the relationship between Nora and Torvald unfold, we consider what the title suggests about their marriage.

Beneath the title is a list of characters. It's worth pausing over, for a playwright may signal important relationships there. Although only the husband-and-wife relationship of Torvald and Nora is signaled in Ibsen's list, we gain a sense of the play's social milieu from it. We notice that Torvald Helmer is a lawyer and Nils Krogstad a bank clerk, and that another woman and a doctor appear (in addition to minor figures such as a nurse and delivery boy).

We may pass quickly over these details before getting to the script. The first sentences set the scene we must keep in our mind's eye. The italicized words are stage directions (notes to the reader that establish the play's social context). Ibsen's opening stage directions describe the living room of a middle-class family with its piano, books, and pictures. The room represents a familiar world for many readers both in its realistic detail and its bourgeois domesticity.

The manner of Nora's arrival with her packages, the Christmas tree, and basket create an impression of the gaiety typically associated with the Christmas season. The playful quality of Nora's first words—about hiding the Christmas tree—reinforce our sense of this lightheartedness.

As we watch the initial incidents unfold, we begin making inferences and drawing tentative conclusions about the characters. We may wonder, for example, about the large tip Nora gives the delivery boy. Is it a sign of generosity or of extravagance? Does it reflect her state of mind? Does it reveal an inadequate attentiveness to money? Such questions occur almost unconsciously as we read, and the provisional answers we arrive at will be modified, strengthened, or abandoned as we read further.

After the exchange with the delivery boy, Nora hums softly to herself. Eating a few macaroons, she tiptoes stealthily to the closed door of her husband's study. Whatever our sense of these opening moments, the brief series of actions forms a prologue to the first major action of the play, Nora's conversation with Torvald. It is here that we gain our sense of Torvald, particularly of his concern for Nora's spending habits, which may unsettle our previous expectations about Nora's tip as an instance of generosity. We become alert.

Perhaps even stronger is our response to Torvald's pet names for Nora. He calls her "little lark" and "my squirrel," and repeatedly uses diminutives and possessives in addressing her. He also teases her, calling her "the little spendthrift," then gives her the money she wants. In a few swift strokes of dialogue and action, Ibsen shows us how seriously Torvald takes himself and how patronizingly he treats his wife.

Nora seems to accept the role Torvald assigns her. She submits to his teasing, accepts his explanations, and responds with childlike enthusiasm. Their gestures bear out the implications of the dialogue: Torvald pulls her ear, Nora clamps her hand over his mouth, plays flirtatiously with Torvald's coat buttons, claps her hands, and twice walks away from him—presumably knowing that he will follow. Torvald seems to enjoy the game as much as Nora. He follows her, probably not realizing that she is leading him and that he is responding as she wants him to.

When we see Torvald wag his finger at Nora and accuse her of eating sweets, we may sense that he doesn't really believe his accusation; he says as much almost immediately. But we, of course, know something that he does not: that Nora has indeed been eating macaroons. And we may suspect that there are other things about her that Torvald does not know from her previous remark, "Hm. If you only knew what expenses we larks and squirrels have, Torvald."

This dialogue is worth considering a bit further. Essentially, Ibsen has Torvald repeat his suspicious question and Nora deny that she has eaten sweets four times. The game that they make of this suggests that it is a familiar ritual. The action seems humorous partly because Torvald's accusations become increasingly accurate while he seems to remain unaware of their truth. Ibsen treats him ironically; there is a discrepancy between his view of himself and our view of him. How do we respond to his presumption and complacency? How do we evaluate his position as master of his house? And how might we sum up Torvald's attitude toward women?

THE INTERPRETATION OF DRAMA

In our discussion of the opening scene of *A Doll House,* we have focused on our experience of the developing action, on our impression of its two central characters, and on our attitudes toward them. Implicit in this discussion, however, was also an inevitable movement in the direction of interpretation. The questions we raised, the details we observed, and the hypotheses we entertained are all aspects of interpretation.

As we read the opening scene of *A Doll House,* observing the action and listening in on the dialogue, we have been drawing tentative conclusions about the characters and their relationship. Our curiosity has been aroused by dialogue, by action, and by the arrival of additional characters. Subsequent dialogue and action will either confirm our initial impressions or dispel them. We are left at the end of this first scene with a sense of uncertainty. While we don't know that this is not a happy household, neither do we know that it is. We have become alerted to possible problems involving matters of money and of secrecy. And we have been prepared to attend to the developing action as the scene changes and new characters appear. When we read the entire play later in this book, we will discover if our inferences are accurate and our suspicions justified.

Interpretation is a series of intellectual and analytical mental acts that lead to a conclusion about the play's meaning and significance. We can isolate four aspects of interpretation that we perform almost automatically. First, we observe details of speech, setting, and action. Second, we connect these details into patterns; we relate them so they begin to make sense to us. Third, we draw inferences—educated guesses or hypotheses—based on these connections. Finally, we formulate from our inferences a consistent and coherent interpretation of the play.

In reading (or viewing) any play, it is important to distinguish between our experience of a play and our interpretation of it. Our experience concerns our direct apprehension of the ongoing performance either on stage or in our mind's eye; interpretation concerns our comprehension of the work after we have finished reading or seeing it performed. Our experience of a play involves our emotions and subjective impressions of the play's dramatic action. Our interpretation of a play involves our ideas and thoughts about the meaning of that action. Our experience of a play is private, personal, and subjective: we discover how it entertains, moves, pleases, frustrates, or otherwise affects us. Our interpretation, though based on our experience, moves outward from it toward a set of more public and objective considerations. In interpreting a play, we try to discover what it might mean for others as well. We ask ourselves not so much: "How do I respond to the speech and actions of the characters?" but instead "What do their speech and actions signify; what do they mean?"

In answering the last question about Ibsen's *A Doll House,* we move beyond our personal response to consider what the play and its characters "say" or suggest more generally. Although it is not possible to understand a play's meaning without viewing or reading it in its entirety, we can nonetheless offer some interpretive possibilities from reading its opening scene alone. We might say, for example, that Ibsen's play appears to be about the relations between the sexes, especially the marital relationship. What *A Doll House* suggests, finally, about that relationship remains best determined by considering the play's final act.

From the opening scene we might surmise that the play is about more than marriage, however. There are hints in the first scene that *A Doll House* will have something to say about moral issues, particularly concerning money and secrecy. There are also hints that the play will concern itself with issues of character, not so much about how people behave, but why they behave as they do, and about who they really are and what they might become.

THE EVALUATION OF DRAMA

Our discussion of the scene from *A Doll House* focused explicitly on our experience of the play and on our acts of interpretation. And although we separated these discussions to identify more precisely each aspect of reading drama, our experience and interpretation of plays actually occur simultaneously; the two aspects of reading reinforce each other. But there is a third dimension to our reading of drama—evaluation—which was implicit in our previous discussions. Our comments about *A Doll House* raised questions about the values displayed in the characters' speech and actions.

What do we mean by the values displayed in a play? Generally speaking, we mean such things as cultural attitudes, moral dispositions, religious beliefs, and social norms. In considering such values as they emerge from our reading of any play, we should be careful to distinguish between the attitudes and dispositions of individual characters and those of the play (those of the author). We should also be aware of how our social and cultural perspectives may differ in important ways from the social norms and cultural attitudes of earlier times. To acknowledge how our individual way of responding to a play is influenced by gender, race, and ethnicity, as well as religious and cultural identity, is important in assessing its worth both for ourselves and for others. Since the values a play's characters display typically constitute an important focus of dramatic interest, our perception of the characters' values will affect to a considerable degree our own experience, interpretation, and evaluation of the overall work.

Further complicating our evaluation of a play is the extent to which we appreciate and enjoy its literary and theatrical artistry. For example, we may admire the way playwrights structure plots, largely by dangling before us a series of temporarily unanswered questions. We may find merit in portrayals of characters or the symbolic use of costume and setting. We may be affected by the language of the play, both in long speeches and in briefer exchanges of dialogue. We may derive aesthetic pleasure from these and many other exhibitions of stagecraft. And the enjoyment we derive, coupled with our assessment of what we understand as the playwright's central values or controlling idea, constitute the basis for our evaluation.

So the evaluation of any play is tied to our interpretation of it. But our interpretation is affected by our perception of the moral and cultural values it exhibits. In identifying the play's central concerns and in deciding which values are endorsed by the playwright, we shift back and forth between interpretation and evaluation. We do not first interpret the play and then evaluate it; we perform the two acts together. We evaluate and interpret a play, moreover, in conjunction with a subjective and immediate response to our experience of it. We can say, then, that each aspect of reading (experience, interpretation, evaluation) affects the other, and that the three aspects of reading drama taken together define our "reading" of any play.

Consider for a moment the way our values shape our interpretation and evaluation. If we see Ibsen's Torvald as an admirable figure, one whose treatment of his wife is appropriate and commendable, we will regard his behavior differently than if we see him as a fool who is manipulated by his wife. Our perspective on Torvald's character and on Nora's will be influenced partly by our gender. Women may be even more affected by Nora's game playing than by Torvald's male chauvinism. Additional influences on our perceptions of *A Doll House* include our cultural background, our experiences as a member of a family, our religious beliefs, and our ethnic traditions as they relate to marriage and the norms governing the relationship between husbands and wives.

Our aesthetic evaluation of *A Doll House* will be based on these and similar observations about the characters and our understanding of the author's view of them. Our evaluation will be affected by how relevant we find the central concerns of the play. (And what we find relevant at one time we may find irrelevant at another—and vice versa.) Our evaluation will also be influenced by our experience in reading and seeing other plays. Aesthetic evaluation thus involves comparing the literary and theatrical artistry of one play with the stagecraft of others. Without considerable experience with drama, judgments about a play's aesthetic merit need to be made with caution. But we must begin somewhere. Evaluation is inevitable, and we cannot avoid judging the plays we read, any more than we can avoid judging the people we meet.

The scene from Sophocles' *Antigonê* that follows provides an immediate opportunity to test these ideas. In reading the entire play later, we can consider how the characters' competing values, as evidenced in the excerpt, serve as the central conflict in the play. Scene II begins at the point where Antigonê, the daughter of Oedipus, has been taken into custody for violating an edict of Creon, King of Thebes. The edict concerns Antigonê's brother, Polyneicês, who was killed in a battle while fighting against Thebes. Creon has forbidden Polyneicês' burial; Antigonê has buried him.

SCENE II

(*Reenter* SENTRY *leading* ANTIGONÊ)

CHORAGOS: What does this mean? Surely this captive woman
  Is the Princess, Antigonê. Why should she be taken?
SENTRY: Here is the one who did it! We caught her
  In the very act of burying him.—Where is Creon?
CHORAGOS: Just coming from the house.

(*Enter* CREON, *center.*)

CREON: What has happened?   5
  Why have you come back so soon?
SENTRY (*expansively*):   O King,
  A man should never be too sure of anything:
  I would have sworn
  That you'd not see me here again: your anger

Frightened me so, and the things you threatened me with;   10
But how could I tell then
That I'd be able to solve the case so soon?
No dice-throwing this time: I was only too glad to come!
Here is this woman. She is the guilty one:
We found her trying to bury him.   15
Take her, then; question her; judge her as you will.
I am through with the whole thing now, and glad of it.

CREON: But this is Antigonê! Why have you brought her here?

SENTRY: She was burying him, I tell you!

CREON (*severely*):   Is this the truth?

SENTRY: I saw her with my own eyes. Can I say more?   20

CREON: The details: come, tell me quickly!

SENTRY: It was like this:
After those terrible threats of yours, King,
We went back and brushed the dust away from the body.
The flesh was soft by now, and stinking,
So we sat on a hill to windward and kept guard.   25
No napping this time! We kept each other awake.
But nothing happened until the white round sun
Whirled in the center of the round sky over us:
Then, suddenly,
A storm of dust roared up from the earth, and the sky   30
Went out, the plain vanished with all its trees
In the stinging dark. We closed our eyes and endured it.
The whirlwind lasted a long time, but it passed;
And then we looked, and there was Antigonê!
I have seen   35
A mother bird come back to a stripped nest, heard
Her crying bitterly a broken note or two
For the young ones stolen. Just so, when this girl
Found the bare corpse, and all her love's work wasted,
She wept, and cried on heaven to damn the hands   40
That had done this thing.
                 And then she brought more dust
And sprinkled wine three times for her brother's ghost.
We ran and took her at once. She was not afraid,
Not even when we charged her with what she had done.
She denied nothing.
              And this was a comfort to me,   45
And some uneasiness: for it is a good thing
To escape from death, but it is no great pleasure
To bring death to a friend.
              Yet I always say
There is nothing so comfortable as your own safe skin!

CREON (*slowly, dangerously*):   And you, Antigonê,   50
You with your head hanging,—do you confess this thing?

ANTIGONÊ: I do. I deny nothing.

CREON (*to* SENTRY):   You may go.

(*Exit* SENTRY.)

(*To* ANTIGONÊ.) Tell me, tell me briefly:
Had you heard my proclamation touching this matter?

ANTIGONÊ: It was public. Could I help hearing it?   55

CREON: And yet you dared defy the law.

ANTIGONÊ: I dared.
It was not God's proclamation. That final Justice
That rules the world below makes no such laws.

Your edict, King, was strong,
But all your strength is weakness itself against   60
The immortal unrecorded laws of God.
They are not merely now: they were, and shall be,
Operative for ever, beyond man utterly.

I knew I must die, even without your decree:
I am only mortal. And if I must die   65
Now, before it is my time to die,
Surely this is no hardship: can anyone
Living, as I live, with evil all about me,
Think Death less than a friend? This death of mine
Is of no importance; but if I had left my brother   70
Lying in death unburied, I should have suffered.
Now I do not.

                You smile at me. Ah Creon,
Think me a fool, if you like; but it may well be
That a fool convicts me of folly.

CHORAGOS: Like father, like daughter: both headstrong, deaf to reason!   75
She has never learned to yield:

CREON: She has much to learn.
The inflexible heart breaks first, the toughest iron
Cracks first, and the wildest horses bend their necks
At the pull of the smallest curb.

                           Pride? In a slave?
This girl is guilty of a double insolence,   80
Breaking the given laws and boasting of it.
Who is the man here,
She or I, if this crime goes unpunished?
Sister's child, or more than sister's child,
Or closer yet in blood—she and her sister   85
Win bitter death for this!

(*To* SERVANTS.)

Go, some of you,
Arrest Ismenê. I accuse her equally.
Bring her: you will find her sniffling in the house there.
Her mind's a traitor: crimes kept in the dark
Cry for light, and the guardian brain shudders;   90
But how much worse than this
Is brazen boasting of barefaced anarchy!

ANTIGONÊ: Creon, what more do you want than my death?

CREON: Nothing.
That gives me everything.

ANTIGONÊ: Then I beg you: kill me.
This talking is a great weariness: your words   95
Are distasteful to me, and I am sure that mine
Seem so to you. And yet they should not seem so:
I should have praise and honor for what I have done.
All these men here would praise me
Were their lips not frozen shut with fear of you.   100
(*Bitterly.*) Ah the good fortune of kings,
Licensed to say and do whatever they please!

CREON: You are alone here in that opinion.

ANTIGONÊ: No, they are with me. But they keep their tongues in leash.

CREON: Maybe. But you are guilty, and they are not.   105

ANTIGONÊ: There is no guilt in reverence for the dead.

CREON: But Eteoclês—was he not your brother too?

ANTIGONÊ: My brother too.

CREON: And you insult his memory?

ANTIGONÊ (*softly*):   The dead man would not say that I insult it.

CREON: He would: for you honor a traitor as much as him.   110

ANTIGONÊ: His own brother, traitor or not, and equal in blood.

CREON: He made war on his country. Eteoclês defended it.

ANTIGONÊ: Nevertheless, there are honors due all the dead.

CREON: But not the same for the wicked as for the just.

ANTIGONÊ: Ah Creon, Creon,   115
Which of us can say what the gods hold wicked?

CREON: An enemy is an enemy, even dead.

ANTIGONÊ: It is my nature to join in love, not hate.

CREON (*finally losing patience*):   Go join them then; if you must have your
    love, Find it in hell!   120

CHORAGOS: But see, Ismenê comes:

(*Enter* ISMENÊ, *guarded.*)

Those tears are sisterly, the cloud
That shadows her eyes rains down gentle sorrow.

CREON: You too, Ismenê,
Snake in my ordered house, sucking my blood   125
Stealthily—and all the time I never knew
That these two sisters were aiming at my throne!

                                                              Ismenê,
Do you confess your share in this crime, or deny it?
Answer me.

ISMENÊ: Yes, if she will let me say so. I am guilty.   130

ANTIGONÊ (*coldly*):   No, Ismenê. You have no right to say so.
You would not help me, and I will not have you help me.

ISMENÊ: But now I know what you meant; and I am here
To join you, to take my share of punishment.

ANTIGONÊ: The dead man and the gods who rule the dead   135
Know whose act this was. Words are not friends.

ISMENÊ: Do you refuse me, Antigonê? I want to die with you:
I too have a duty that I must discharge to the dead.

ANTIGONÊ: You shall not lessen my death by sharing it.

ISMENÊ: What do I care for life when you are dead?   140

ANTIGONÊ: Ask Creon. You're always hanging on his opinions.

ISMENÊ: You are laughing at me. Why, Antigonê?

ANTIGONÊ: It's a joyless laughter, Ismenê.

ISMENÊ: But can I do nothing?

ANTIGONÊ: Yes. Save yourself. I shall not envy you.
There are those who will praise you; I shall have honor, too.   145

ISMENÊ: But we are equally guilty!

ANTIGONÊ: No more, Ismenê.
You are alive, but I belong to Death.

CREON (*to the* CHORUS):   Gentlemen, I beg you to observe these girls:
One has just now lost her mind; the other,
It seems, has never had a mind at all.   150

ISMENÊ: Grief teaches the steadiest minds to waver, King.

CREON: Yours certainly did, when you assumed guilt with the guilty!

ISMENÊ: But how could I go on living without her?

CREON: You are.
She is already dead.

ISMENÊ: But your own son's bride!

CREON: There are places enough for him to push his plow.   155
I want no wicked women for my sons!

ISMENÊ: O dearest Haimon, how your father wrongs you!

CREON: I've had enough of your childish talk of marriage!

CHORAGOS: Do you really intend to steal this girl from your son?

CREON: No; Death will do that for me.

CHORAGOS: Then she must die?   160

CREON (*ironically*):   You dazzle me.

                    —But enough of this talk!
(*To* GUARDS.) You, there, take them away and guard them well:
For they are but women, and even brave men run
When they see Death coming.

                    (*Exeunt* ISMENÊ, ANTIGONÊ, *and* GUARDS.)

In this scene we witness a developing conflict between Creon and Antigonê,
one that is more than a clash of two stubborn wills. Opposing views of propriety

emerge, along with competing moral values and contrasting attitudes toward political authority. What are we to make of these attitudes and these arguments? How does our sense of their tone and manner affect our perception and evaluation of the substance of their speech and action? Whose values do you think should take precedence, and why? And finally, how highly do we rate the literary and theatrical qualities of the text? As a portion of a work of art, how successfully does it achieve its artistic and dramatic aims?

THE ACT OF READING DRAMA

To read drama actively, it is helpful to read with a pen in hand and to make notes in the margins. Here we illustrate a variation on that approach to active reading: asking questions of the play as we read it. Our questions will range over various concerns we have in reading, including evaluation, interpretation, and our experience of the text, as well as how to bring its theatrical and performance qualities to life in our minds.

To this end, we consider the opening scene of Isabella Augusta Persse, Lady Gregory's *The Rising of the Moon*.

Scene: Side of a quay in a seaport town. Some posts and chains. A large barrel. Enter three policemen. Moonlight.

SERGEANT, *who is older than the others, crosses the stage to right and looks down steps. The others put down a pastepot and unroll a bundle of placards.*

POLICEMAN B: I think this would be a good place to put up a notice. (*He points to barrel.*)

POLICEMAN X: Better ask him. (*Calls to* SERGEANT) Will this be a good place for a placard? (*No answer.*)

POLICEMAN B: Will we put up a notice here on the barrel? (*No answer.*)

SERGEANT: There's a flight of steps here that leads to the water. This is a place that should be minded well. If he got down here, his friends might have a boat to meet him; they might send it in here from outside.

POLICEMAN B: Would the barrel be a good place to put a notice up?

SERGEANT: It might; you can put it there.

(*They paste the notice up.*)

SERGEANT (*reading it*):   Dark hair—dark eyes, smooth face, height five feet five—there's not much to take hold of in that—It's a pity I had no chance of seeing him before he broke out of gaol. They say he's a wonder, that it's he makes all the plans for the whole organization. There isn't another man in Ireland would have broken gaol the way he did. He must have some friends among the gaolers.

POLICEMAN B: A hundred pounds is little enough for the Government to offer for him. You may be sure any man in the force that takes him will get promotion.

SERGEANT: I'll mind this place myself. I wouldn't wonder at all if he came this way. He might come slipping along there (*points to side of quay*), and his friends might be waiting for him there (*points down steps*), and once he got away it's little chance we'd have of finding him; it's maybe under a load of kelp he'd be in a fishing boat, and not one to help a married man that wants it to the reward.

POLICEMAN X: And if we get him itself, nothing but abuse on our heads for it from the people, and maybe from our own relations.

SERGEANT: Well, we have to do our duty in the force. Haven't we the whole country depending on us to keep law and order? It's those that are down would be up and those that are up would be down, if it wasn't for us. Well, hurry on, you have plenty of other places to placard yet, and come back here then to me. You can take the lantern. Don't be too long now. It's very lonesome here with nothing but the moon.

POLICEMAN B: It's a pity we can't stop with you. The Government should have brought more police into the town, with *him* in gaol, and at assize time too. Well, good luck to your watch. (*They go out.*)

SERGEANT (*walks up and down once or twice and looks at placard*):   A hundred pounds and promotion sure. There must be a great deal of spending in a hundred pounds. It's a pity some honest man not to be the better of that.

(*A ragged man appears at left and tries to slip past.* SERGEANT *suddenly turns.*)

Here is a list of questions we might generate during an active interrogation of the text.

1. What are the implications of the title, "The Rising of the Moon"? How is the title related to the suggested lighting? How important will the moon and the moonlight become?
2. Why don't the policemen have names? Of what importance are their repeated questions and the sergeant's distracted answer?
3. Why does the sergeant say that "it's a pity" he didn't see the criminal before his escape from jail? Is it simply that the sergeant would know what the man looked like and thus could recognize him more easily?
4. How does Lady Gregory draw us into the play? How does she engage our interest in these characters and their situation?
5. How important will the theme of duty become? Is it significant that the sergeant introduces this topic?
6. How effective theatrically is the sergeant's pointing to the quay and steps as he imagines the escaped man coming past where he stands?
7. Where in fact do the sergeant and his men stand on stage? How are they dressed? And where is the barrel placed?
8. As each character speaks, how does he gesture? At whom does he look? Where is he positioned in relation to the others?
9. How important to the play's action and idea are the props—the barrel, placards, and lantern? What other props will become important?
10. Of what significance is policeman X's comment about getting abuse from the people and his relatives for capturing the escaped convict?
11. How important are the sergeant's references to a reward and promotion? His references to the escaped man's friends? Might these references be significant beyond their function in the play's action?
12. Why are certain words and phrases repeated?
13. How helpful are the italicized stage directions in letting us imagine the scene and the action?

14. What do we expect to happen next? How well has the playwright prepared readers/viewers for the sergeant's encounter with the "ragged man"?
15. With whom do our sympathies lie? Why? How do our attitudes about police officers and the concept of the "law" affect our response?

Asking questions such as these involves us actively in reading the play. Some of these questions can be asked during an initial reading; others may arise during subsequent readings. Writing out a series of questions enables us to focus on aspects of the text we may have overlooked or perhaps noticed only vaguely. Also, interrogating the text can lead us to an interpretation that is thoroughly grounded in careful observation. The answers to our questions provide the authoritative basis for an interpretation worthy of consideration by other readers.

CHAPTER FIFTEEN

Types of Drama

Some plays elicit laughter, others evoke tears. Some are comic, others tragic, still others a mixture of both. The two major dramatic modes, *tragedy* and *comedy,* have been represented traditionally by contrasting masks, one sorrowful, the other joyful. The masks represent more than different types of plays: they also stand for contrasting ways of looking at the world, aptly summarized in Horace Walpole's remark, "the world is a comedy to those who think and a tragedy to those who feel."

The comic view celebrates life and affirms it; it is typically joyous and festive. The tragic view highlights life's sorrows; it is typically brooding and solemn. Tragic plays end unhappily, often with the death of the hero; comedies usually end happily, often with a celebration such as a marriage. Both comedy and tragedy contain changes of fortune, with the fortunes of comic characters turning from bad to good and those of tragic characters from good to bad.

TRAGEDY

In the *Poetics,* Aristotle described *tragedy* as "an imitation of an action that is serious, complete in itself, and of a certain magnitude." This definition suggests that tragedies are solemn plays concerned with grave human actions and their consequences. The action of a tragedy is complete—it possesses a beginning, a middle, and an end. Elsewhere in the *Poetics,* Aristotle notes that the incidents of a tragedy must be causally connected. The events have to be logically related, one growing naturally out of another, each leading to the inevitable catastrophe, usually the downfall of the hero.

Some readers of tragedy have suggested that, according to Aristotle, the catastrophe results from a flaw in the character of the hero. Others have contended that the hero's tragic flaw results from fate or coincidence, from circumstances beyond the hero's control. A third view proposes that tragedy results from an error of judgment committed by the hero, one that may or may not have as its source a weakness in character. Typically, tragic protagonists make mistakes: they misjudge other characters, they misinterpret events, and they confuse appearance with reality. Shakespeare's Othello, for example, mistakes Iago for an honest, loving friend; and he mistakes his faithful wife, Desdemona, for an adulteress. Sophocles' Oedipus mistakes his own identity and misconstrues his destiny. The misfortune and catastrophes of tragedy are frequently precipitated by errors of judgment; mistaken perceptions lead to misdirected actions that eventually result in catastrophe.

Tragic heroes such as Oedipus and Othello are grand, noble characters. They are men, as Aristotle says, "of high estate," who enjoy "great reputation and prosperity." Tragic heroes, in short, are privileged, exalted personages who have earned their high repute and status by heroic exploit (Othello), by intelligence (Oedipus), or by their inherent nobility (Othello and Oedipus). Their tragedy resides in a fall from glory that crushes not only the tragic hero himself but other related characters as well. Othello's tragedy includes his wife and his faithful lieutenant, Cassio. Oedipus' tragedy extends to his entire family, including his wife-mother, his two sons, his daughters, and his brother-in-law, Creon, and his family. Greek tragedy, typically, involves the destruction and downfall of an entire house or family, reaching across generations. The catastrophe of Shakespearean tragedy is usually not as extensive.

An essential element of the tragic hero's experience is a *recognition* of what has happened to him. Frequently this takes the form of the hero discovering something previously unknown or something he knew but misconstrued. According to Aristotle, the tragic hero's recognition (or discovery) is often allied with a reversal of his expectations. Such an ironic reversal occurs in *Oedipus Rex* when the messenger's speech unsettles rather than reassures Oedipus about who he is and what he has done. Once the reversal and discovery occur, tragic plots move swiftly to their conclusions.

We may consider why, amid such suffering and catastrophe, tragedies are not depressing. Aristotle suggested that the pity and fear aroused in the audience are purged or released and the audience experiences a cleansing of those emotions and a sense of relief that the action is over. Perhaps tragedy represents for us the ultimate downfall we will all experience in death: we watch in fascination and awe a dramatic reminder of our own inevitable mortality. Or perhaps we are somehow exalted in witnessing the high human aspiration and the noble conception of human character embodied in tragic heroes like Oedipus and Othello.

COMEDY

Some of the same dramatic elements we find in tragedy occur in comedy as well. Discovery scenes and consequent reversals of fortune, for example, occur in both. So too do misperceptions and errors of judgment, exhibitions of human weakness and failure. But in comedy the reversals and errors lead not to calamity as they do in tragedy, but to prosperity and happiness. Comic heroes

are usually ordinary people; they are less grand, less noble than tragic protagonists. Moreover, comic characters are frequently one-dimensional to the extent
that many are stereotypes: the braggart, for example, or the hypocrite, the unfaithful wife, the cuckold, the ardent young lovers.

If comic characters are frequently predictable in their behavior, comic plots
are not: they thrive on the surprise of the unexpected and on improbability.
Cinderella stories like these are the staples of comedy: an impoverished student
inherits a fortune; a beggar turns out to be a prince; a wife (or husband or
child) presumed dead turns up alive and well; the war (between nations, classes,
families, the sexes) ends, the two sides are reconciled and everybody lives happily ever after. But whether the incongruities of comedy exist between a character's speech and actions, between what we expect the characters to be and
what they show themselves to be, or between how they think of themselves
and how we see them, things work out in the end.

The happy endings of comedies are not always happy for all the characters
involved. This marks one of the significant differences between the two major
types of comedy: *satiric* and *romantic* comedy. Though much of what we have
said so far about comedy applies to both types, it applies more extensively to
romantic than to satiric comedy, or satire. *Satire* exposes human folly, criticizes
human conduct, and aims to correct it. Ridiculing the weaknesses of human
nature, satiric comedy shows us the low level to which human behavior can
sink. Molière's *Tartuffe* is such a satiric comedy; it exposes religious hypocrisy,
castigates folly, and ultimately celebrates virtue. Although things may work out
well in the end for most of the characters, the play contains some harsh moments and a bitter ending for at least one character.

Romantic comedy, on the other hand, portrays characters gently, even generously; its spirit is more tolerant and its tone more genial. Whatever adversities the heroes and heroines of romantic comedy must overcome, the tone is
typically devoid of rancor and bitterness. The humor of romantic comedy is
more sympathetic than corrective, and it intends more to entertain than instruct, to delight than ridicule.

Because of such differences, our approaches to reading satire and romance
should be different. When we read satiric comedies such as Shaw's *Arms and the
Man,* we should identify the object of the dramatist's criticism and determine
why the behavior of certain characters is objectionable. In reading romantic
comedies, such as Shakespeare's *A Midsummer Night's Dream,* we are invited
simply to enjoy the raveling and unraveling of plot as the protagonists are led
to the inevitable happy ending.

These distinctions, however, are useful only as they help us gauge a play's
prevailing characteristics. They should serve as guidelines to prevailing tendencies rather than as rigid descriptions of dramatic types. Frequently romantic
comedies may contain elements of satire and satiric comedies elements of
romance.

CHAPTER SIXTEEN

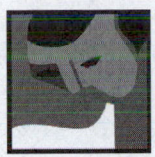

Elements of Drama

The elements of drama include plot, character, dialogue, staging, and theme. Our discussions of each of these elements individually allows us to highlight the characteristic features of drama in a convenient way. We should remember, however, that analysis of any single element of drama (plot, for example) should not blind us to its function in conjunction with such other elements as character. Ultimately any analysis we engage in must be followed by an act of synthesis in which we bring a number of elements of the play into relationship with one another.

PLOT

Plot is the structure of a play's action. Although it encompasses what happens in a play, plot is more than the sum of its incidents. Plot is the order of the incidents, their arrangement and form. Following Aristotle, we can distinguish between all the little actions or incidents that make up a play and the single *action* that unifies them. It is this unified structure of incidents (or little actions) Aristotle calls *action* and we call *plot*.

Traditional plot structure consists of an *exposition,* presentation of background information necessary for the development of the plot; *rising action,* a set of conflicts and crises; *climax,* the play's most decisive crisis; *falling action,* a follow-up that moves toward the play's resolution or *denouement* (French for the untying of a knot).

The plot of a realistic drama can be diagrammed in the following manner:

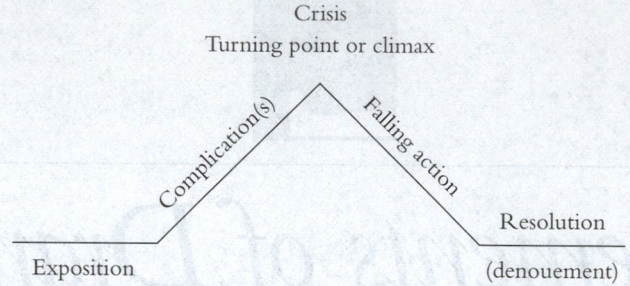

Crisis
Turning point or climax

Complication(s)

Falling action

Resolution
(denouement)

Exposition

Whether playwrights use a traditional plot structure or vary the formula, they control our expectations about what is happening through plot. They decide when to present action and information, what to reveal and what to conceal. By the arrangement of incidents, a dramatist may create suspense, evoke laughter, cause anxiety, or elicit surprise. One of our main sources of pleasure in plot is surprise, whether we are shown something we didn't expect or whether we see *how* something will happen even when we may know *what* will happen. Frequently surprise follows suspense—fulfilling our need to find out what will happen as we wait for a resolution of a play's action.

Suspense is created by conflict. Drama is essentially the development and resolution of conflicts. Each of the scenes excerpted in Chapter Fourteen, Reading Plays, contains conflict. The conflict in Sophocles' *Antigonê* is overt and explicit. It occurs relentlessly in the play's dialogue and action. In the opening scene of Ibsen's *A Doll House* the conflict is implicit, at least initially. As the play develops, we see that Nora's conflict is less an opposition to Torvald than a conflict within herself.

Besides looking at how instances of conflict are structured into plot in these scenes, we must also consider what each contributes to the plot of the play overall. What, for example, in Sophocles' *Oedipus Rex* does Oedipus's debate with Teiresias lead up to? How is the opening scene of *A Doll House* related to its developing action, its concluding scene, its themes?

When we examine the plot of any play, we should be concerned with its developing action, the play in motion, and its completed action, the play at rest. By remaining attentive to what happens to us as we read and by highlighting the arrangement of scenes, we alert ourselves to the play as a performance. When we detach ourselves from the play to study its construction, the relationship among its parts, we study and appreciate the play as literature. Drama is both theater and literature. Study of plot can enrich our experience of each.

CHARACTER

If plot is the skeletal framework of a play, character is its vital center. Characters bring plays to life. First and last we become absorbed in the characters: how they look and what their appearance tells us about them; what they say and what their manner of saying expresses; what they do and how their actions reveal who they are and what they represent. We may come to know them and respond to them in ways we come to know and respond to actual people, all the while realizing that characters are literary imitations of human beings.

But even though the characters in plays are not real people, their human dimension is impossible to ignore since actors portray them, and their human qualities are perhaps their most engaging feature. It is, indeed, their *human* aspect that attracts us to the characters of drama, not their symbolic significance. When we see characters engaged in significant human action, we examine their words and deeds. We make sense of them by relying on models of human behavior and by applying standards of conduct derived from our everyday experience; we assess their motives and evaluate their behavior in accordance with psychological probability. It is nearly impossible not to.

Nonetheless, it is helpful to remain mindful of the distinction between dramatic characters and actual people so that we do not always expect them to behave realistically. Nor should we expect playwrights to tell us everything about them. They will tell us only what we need to know. If it is not important for us to know Nora's age or Torvald's height, the playwrights won't bother us with such information. Dramatists reveal only what is relevant to their dramatic purposes.

Drama lives in the encounter of characters, for its action is interaction. Its essence is human relationships, the things men and women say and do to each other. Dramatic characters come together and affect each other, making things happen by coming into conflict. It is in conflict that characters reveal themselves and advance the plot.

DIALOGUE

Ezra Pound, the modern American poet, once described drama as "persons moving about on a stage using words"—in short, people talking. Listening to their talk we hear identifiable, individual voices. In their presence we encounter persons, for dialogue inevitably brings us back to character, drama's human center. And though dialogue in plays typically has three major functions—to advance the plot, to establish setting (the time and place of the action), and to reveal character, its most important and consistent function is the revelation of character.

Our examples come from Act IV, Scene III of Shakespeare's *Othello*. Consider first the following conversation between Desdemona (wife of the military hero Othello) and Emilia (maid to Desdemona and wife of Othello's lieutenant, Iago). They are talking about adultery:

DESDEMONA: Dost thou in conscience think, tell me, Emilia,
That there be women do abuse their husbands
In such gross kind?

EMILIA: There be some such, no question.

DESDEMONA: Wouldst thou do such a deed for all the world?

EMILIA: Why, would not you?

DESDEMONA: No, by this heavenly light!

EMILIA: Nor I either by this heavenly light.
I might do't as well i'the dark.

DESDEMONA: Wouldst thou do such a deed for all the world?

EMILIA: The world's a huge thing; it is a great price for a small vice.

DESDEMONA: In troth, I think thou wouldst not.

EMILIA: In troth, I think I should; and undo't when I had done. Marry, I would not do such a thing for a joint-ring, nor for measures of lawn, nor gowns, petticoats, nor caps, nor any petty exhibition, but for all the whole world? Why, who would not make her husband a cuckold to make a monarch? I should venture purgatory for't.

DESDEMONA: Beshrew me if I would do such a wrong for the whole world.

EMILIA: Why, the wrong is but a wrong i' th'world; and having the world for your labor, 'tis a wrong in your own world, and you might quickly make it right.

DESDEMONA: I do not think there is any such woman.

In this dialogue we not only see and hear evidence of a radical difference of values, but we also observe a striking difference of character. Desdemona's innocence is underscored by her unwillingness to be unfaithful to her husband; her naiveté, by her inability to believe in any woman's infidelity. Emilia is willing to compromise her virtue and finds enough practical reasons to assure herself of its correctness. Her joking tone and bluntness also contrast with Desdemona's solemnity and inability to name directly what she is referring to: adultery.

And now listen to Iago working on Desdemona's father, Brabantio, to tell him about his daughter's elopement with Othello (Act I, Scene I):

> Zounds, sir y'are robbed! For shame. Put on your gown!
> Your heart is burst, you have lost half your soul.
> Even now, now, very now, an old black ram
> Is tupping your white ewe. Arise, arise!
> Awake the snorting citizens with the bell,
> Or else the devil will make a grandsire of you.
> . . .
> I am one sir, that comes to tell you your daughter
> and the Moor are making the beast with two backs.

Iago's language reveals his coarseness; he crudely reduces sexual love to animal copulation. It also shows his ability to make things happen: he has infuriated Brabantio. The remainder of the scene shows the consequences of his speech, its power to inspire action. Iago is thus revealed as both an instigator and a man of crude sensibilities.

His language is cast in a similar mold in Act II, Scene I, when he tries to convince Roderigo, a rejected suitor of Desdemona, that Desdemona will tire of Othello and turn to someone else for sexual satisfaction. Notice how Iago's words stress the carnality of sex and reveal his violent imagination:

> Her eye must be fed. And what delight
> shall she have to look on the devil? When the
> blood is made dull with the act of sport, there
> should be a game to inflame it and to give
> satiety a fresh appetite, loveliness in favor,
> sympathy in years, manners, and beauties; all
> which the Moor is defective in. Now for want of
> these required conveniences, her delicate tenderness will find
> itself abused, begin to heave the gorge, disrelish and
> abhor the Moor. Very nature will instruct her in it
> and compel her to some second choice. . . .

Othello's language, like Iago's, reveals his character and his decline from a courageous and confident leader to a jealous lover distracted to madness by Iago's insinuations about his wife's infidelity. The elegance and control, even the exaltation of his early speeches, give way to the crude degradation of his later remarks. Here is Othello in Act I, Scene II, responding to a search party out to find him:

> Hold your hands,
> Both you of my inclining and the rest,
> Were it my cue to fight, I should have known it
> Without a prompter. Whither will you that I go
> To answer this your charge?

The language of this speech is formal, stately, and controlled. It bespeaks a man in command of himself, one who assumes authority naturally and easily.

In Act I, Scene III, Othello speaks to the political authorities and to Brabantio, Desdemona's enraged father:

> Most potent, grave, and reverend signiors,
> My very noble and approved good masters,
> That I have ta'en away this old man's daughter,
> It is most true; true I have married her.
> The very head and front of my offending
> Hath this extent, no more. . . .

From these few lines alone we can sense Othello's stature, his dignity, his self-confidence, and his courtesy. Coupled with other passages from the first two acts of the play, we come away impressed with Othello's gravity and grandeur. His language in large part accounts for our sympathetic response to him, for our admiration, not only for his military exploits, but for his measure of control, poise, and equanimity.

By the middle of Act III, however, this view of Othello is no longer tenable. Othello is reduced by Iago to an incoherent babbler, to a man at odds with himself, one who has lost his equilibrium. In Act IV, Scene I, we see the Othello Iago has created by suggesting that Desdemona has been unchaste with Othello's lieutenant, Michael Cassio:

OTHELLO: Lie with her? Lie on her?—We say lie on her when they belie her—Lie with her!
Zounds, that's fulsome. Handkerchief—confession—handkerchief—To confess, and be
hanged for his labor—first to be hanged, and then to confess! I tremble at it. . . . It is not
words that shake me thus.—Pish! Noses, ears, and lips? Is't possible?—Confess?—
Handkerchief?—O devil.

In the language of both Iago and Othello we see meaning enacted as well as
expressed. The verbal dimension of their dialogue is reinforced by action, gesture, movement. We can observe in these brief excerpts and throughout the
play not only how language reveals character, advances the action, and establishes the setting, but how it also makes things happen and in effect itself becomes action.

STAGING

By *staging* we have in mind the spectacle a play presents in performance, its visual detail. This includes such things as the positions of actors onstage (sometimes referred to as *blocking*), their nonverbal gestures and movements (also
called *stage business*), the scenic background, the props and costumes, lighting,
and sound effects.

Though often taken for granted, costumes can reveal the characters beneath
them. Ibsen's Nora changes costumes more than once. She appears by turns in
ordinary clothing, in a multicolored shawl, in a dancing costume, and in a black
shawl. Each costume change expresses a change in Nora's feelings.

Besides costume, any physical object that appears in a play has the potential
to become an important dramatic symbol. The Christmas tree, which stands
throughout Ibsen's *A Doll House,* is an ironic visual counterpart to the play's
unfolding action. More dramatic perhaps and more central to plot is the handkerchief in *Othello.* Having its own history, which we learn when Desdemona
wipes Othello's brow, the handkerchief becomes a crucial dramatic object, one
that offers Othello the "ocular proof" he requires to condemn Desdemona as
an adulterer.

From costumes and objects, we turn to sound. Ibsen uses sound effectively
in *A Doll House* when he asks for music to accompany Nora's frenzied dancing
as she attempts to delay Torvald's discovery of Krogstad's letter. In this same
scene Ibsen also uses sound to heighten suspense as he has Torvald open the
mailbox off-stage: we hear but don't see the mailbox click open.

A playwright's stage directions will sometimes help us see and hear things
like these as we read. But with or without stage directions, we have to use our
aural as well as our visual imagination. An increased imaginative alertness to the
sights and sounds of a play, while no substitute for direct physical apprehension,
can nonetheless help us approximate the experience of a dramatic performance. It can also enhance our appreciation of the dramatist's craftsmanship and
increase our understanding of the play.

THEME

From plot, character, dialogue, and staging we derive a sense of the play's meaning or significance. An abstraction of this meaning is its central idea or *theme*. It is often helpful to try to express the theme of a play in a carefully worded sentence or two, but we should be aware, however, that any summary statement of a complex work of art is bound to be limited and limiting.

Nonetheless as readers we reach for theme as a way of organizing our responses to a play. At the same time we also let the work modify and alter our notion of its theme. We work back and forth between its details (of dialogue, gesture, and movement, for example) and our conception of their significance. As we notice details and connect them, as we discover and remember, our sense of the play's theme changes. It may change in such a way that we end up, provisionally at least, seeing the play's theme as ambiguous (suggesting contradictory or opposite ideas simultaneously with a resulting uncertainty and indefiniteness about its meaning). And of course there is the very good chance that a play will include more than one theme.

Perhaps we can best approach consideration of a play's theme by noting the dialogue of its characters, who frequently represent conflicting ideals and viewpoints. Some plays, for example, Sophocles' *Antigonê,* can certainly be approached this way. Antigonê herself, for example, represents a commitment to a religious ideal ineluctably in conflict with the political idea that Creon stands for. In her debate with Creon, Antigonê appeals to higher laws, religious and spiritual principles that require burial of the dead, especially if the dead are relatives. Because Antigonê acts in violation of Creon's edict, and since Creon as king represents the supreme authority of the state, she can be seen to pit God's law against man's. Another way of saying this is to note that she values a religious obligation more than a legal code. Still another is to see it as a conflict between two kinds of duty: duty to the state and duty to one's family. Legal obligation conflicts with moral responsibility; public duty collides with private conscience.

We have stated that Antigonê and Creon represent two different positions, two conflicting ideals. We make such a generalization, confident that we are not violating the play because the speeches of both characters refer directly to the ideals that motivate them. If we elaborate, however, we will have to qualify the view of their conflict suggested so far for two reasons. This paradigm is too neat: it ignores aspects of Antigonê's and Creon's motivation and character, and it also reduces the play as a whole to this conflict of values.

Because Greek tragedy typically enacts a reconciliation of the human and divine orders, Antigonê's appeal must be seen as an attempt to make that reconciliation and Creon's refusal as a denial of it. Thus, her appeal is not only personal—based on family honor—but is much more inclusive, far more so than Creon's reasons of state. To express this as a theme we might say that in the conflict between two goods, one divinely based (Antigonê's) and one humanly based (Creon's) the higher good should prevail.

We have been using Sophocles' drama to suggest that it is both natural and necessary to generalize from a play's action and dialogue to an idea it embodies. But we have also noted that to reduce the play's thought to a satisfactorily inclusive statement of theme is no easy matter. At best such a statement offers an approximation of a play's meaning, one that clarifies and illuminates our experience. At worst it oversimplifies the play, distorting its significance and impoverishing our experience of it.

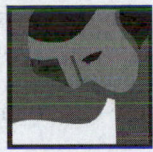

CHAPTER SEVENTEEN

Writing about Drama

REASONS FOR WRITING ABOUT DRAMA

Why write about drama? One reason is to find out what you think about a play that interests you. Another is to induce yourself to read a play you have heard about or that you like more carefully. You may write about a work of drama because it engages you, and you may wish to celebrate it or to argue with its implied ideas and values. Still another reason is that you may simply be required to do so as a course assignment.

Whatever your reasons for writing about drama, a number of things happen when you do. First, in writing about a play you tend to read it more attentively, noticing things you might overlook in a more casual reading. Second, since writing stimulates thinking, when you write about drama you find yourself thinking more about what a particular work means and why you respond to it as you do. And third, you begin to acquire power over the works you write about, making them part of your experience and more meaningful to you.

INFORMAL WAYS OF WRITING ABOUT DRAMA

When you write about a play, you may write for yourself or you may write for others. Writing for yourself, to discover what you think, often takes casual forms such as annotation and freewriting. These less formal kinds of writing are useful for helping you focus on your reading of plays. They are helpful in studying for tests about drama. They can also serve as preliminary forms of writing when you write more formal essays and papers.

Annotation

When you annotate a text, you make notes about it, usually in the margins or at the top and bottom of pages—or both. Annotations can also be made within the text, as underlined words, circled phrases, or bracketed sentences or paragraphs. Annotations may also assume the form of arrows, question marks, and various other marks.

Annotating a literary work offers a convenient and relatively painless way to begin writing about it. Annotating can get you started zeroing in on what you think interesting or important. You can also annotate to signal details that puzzle or disconcert you.

Your markings serve to focus your attention and clarify your understanding of a story or novel. Your annotations can save you time in rereading or studying a work. And they can also be used when you write a more formal paper.

Annotations for the following scene illustrate the process.

The following excerpt from *Antigonê* begins at the point where Antigonê has been taken into custody for violating an edict of Creon, king of Thebes. Creon's edict concerns Antigonê's brother, Polyneicês, who was killed in a battle while fighting against Thebes. Creon has forbidden Polyneicês' burial, but in violation of the edict Antigonê has buried him.

CREON (*to* SENTRY):   You may go.

                 (*Exit* SENTRY.)

(*To* ANTIGONÊ):   Tell me, tell me briefly:
   Had you heard my proclamation touching this matter?   *Creon can't believe that she would disobey—hence his question.*
ANTIGONÊ: It was public. Could I help hearing it?
CREON: And yet you dared defy the law.   *He sees himself as "the law."*
ANTIGONÊ: I dared.
   It was not God's proclamation. That final Justice
   That rules the world below makes no such laws.

   Your edict, King, was strong,
   But all your strength is weakness itself against   *Antigonê identifies conflict: God/man divine/human*
   The immortal unrecorded laws of God.
   They are not merely now: they were, and shall be,
   Operative for ever, beyond man utterly.

   I knew I must die, even without your decree:
   I am only mortal. And if I must die   *Is she a bit too eager to die?*
   Now, before it is my time to die,
   Surely this is no hardship: can anyone
   Living, as I live, with evil all about me,
   Think Death less than a friend? This death of mine
   is of no importance; but if I had left my brother
   lying in death unburied, I should have suffered.
   Now I do not.
           You smile at me. Ah Creon,
   Think me a fool, if you like; but it may well be   *implicit stage direction: "You smile . . ."*

That a fool convicts me of folly.

CHORAGOS: Like father, like daughter:
both headstrong, deaf to reason!
She has never learned to yield:

How important is this
choral comment?

CREON: She has much to learn.
The inflexible heart breaks first, the toughest iron
Cracks first, and the wildest horses bend their necks
At the pull of the smallest curb.

images: iron, horses

                         Pride? In a slave?
This girl is guilty of a double insolence.
Breaking the given laws and boasting of it.
Who is the man here,
She or I, if this crime goes unpunished?
Sister's child, or more than sister's child,
Or closer yet in blood—she and her sister
Win bitter death for this!

conflict: man/woman
age/youth

                    (*To* SERVANTS)

                Go, some of you.
Arrest Ismenê. I accuse her equally.
Bring her: you will find her sniffling in the house there.
Her mind's a traitor: crimes kept in the dark
Cry for light, and the guardian brain shudders;
But how much worse than this
Is brazen boasting of barefaced anarchy!

Why does Creon accuse
Ismenê?

Anarchy? Is Creon a bit
paranoid?

ANTIGONÊ: Creon, what more do you want than my death?

CREON: Nothing.
That gives me everything.

ANTIGONÊ: Then I beg you: kill me.
This talking is a great weariness: your words
Are distasteful to me, and I am sure that mine
Seem so to you. And yet they should not seem so:
I should have praise and honor for what I have done.
All these men here would praise me
Were their lips not frozen shut with fear of you.
(*Bitterly*) Ah the good fortune of kings.
Licensed to say and do whatever they please!

She knows how to fight
back.

CREON: You are alone here in that opinion.

ANTIGONÊ: No, they are with me. But they
keep their tongues in leash.

image: dogs on a leash
held in check by fear

CREON: Maybe. But you are guilty, and they are not.

ANTIGONÊ: There is no guilt in reverence for the dead.

CREON: But Eteoclês—was he not your brother too?

a complication: the other
brother, Eteoclês

ANTIGONÊ: My brother too.

CREON: And you insult his memory?

ANTIGONÊ (*softly*):   The dead man would not say that I insult it.

CREON: He would: for you honor a traitor as much as him.

tempo: pace picks up here
with rapid-fire dialogue
exchange

ANTIGONÊ: His own brother, traitor or not, and equal in blood.

CREON: He made war on his country. Eteoclês defended it.

ANTIGONÊ: Nevertheless, there are honors due all the dead.

CREON: But not the same for the wicked as for the just.

buildup of intensity

ANTIGONÊ: Ah Creon, Creon,
    Which of us can say what the gods hold wicked?
CREON: An enemy is an enemy, even dead.
ANTIGONÊ: It is my nature to join in love, not hate.
CREON (*finally losing patience*):   Go join them then;
    if you must have your love. Find it in hell!

Double-Column Notebook

Another way of writing for yourself, informally, is to use the double-column notebook. To create a double-column notebook, divide a page in half vertically (or open a notebook so that you face two blank pages side by side). On one side *take* notes, summarizing the scene's situation, action, and ideas. On the other side, the responding side, *make* notes, recording your thinking about what you summarized on the opposite side. On the responding side, ask questions; speculate; make connections.

Here is an example of a double-column notebook for the excerpt from *Antigonê* annotated above. Notice how the entries in the double-column notebook are more detailed, and written in a more formal style, than the annotations shown with the excerpt.

Summary and Observations	Responses and Reactions
Creon's language is formal, even self-important. He sounds like, or tries to sound like, a king.	Creon is unpalatable here. He's pompous and arrogant. Yet to some extent he seems justified in being angry. What's interesting here is why Creon reacts so strongly to the violation of his edict. It probably has something to do with his recent acquisition of power. He is very likely more than a little insecure in his new position. He must feel the need to assert himself and establish his authority. Suppose he ignores Antigonê's action. What will people think of him? Won't they see him as weak?
Part of Creon's anger stems from Antigonê's rebellion against *him,* against *his* law. Part derives from her seeming disregard for the law of the land more generally.	
Antigonê's view seems to be that since Creon's law was a bad one, she shouldn't obey it. And even further, that she has a responsibility to disobey it since the gods require that family members honor their dead. She points out that her burial of her brother was necessary for her own peace of mind.	Antigonê's point has merit. She has to do what she has to do.
	Antigonê seems the more likeable of the two.
Antigonê at one point angers Creon by reminding him that he is not almighty. She attempts to put him in his place, to remind him that his rule has limits. He doesn't like that. Nor does he like her suggestion that it is better to die than to obey an unjust law or live in a corrupt society.	Antigonê enjoys pulling Creon down a peg. Her tone does sound insulting. She almost seems to enjoy thinking of herself as a martyr for a cause. Isn't she a bit theatrical here, relishing her role and the image she projects as much as, or even more than, the idea and point of view she stands up for?
Creon, of course, sees her act of rebellion and her disrespectful attitude toward him as king as the cause of societal corruption.	Doesn't Creon overreact here in seeing Antigonê's action as an example of "anarchy"? And doesn't he also overreact in assuming

that Ismenê is also guilty? He assumes things without testing them.

During the course of their dialogue (more a confrontation or debate than a conversation), they insult each other. Creon calls Antigonê stubborn; Antigonê calls Creon a fool.

As in any good fight, the antagonists really do try to hurt each other.

It's an enjoyable verbal battle—for us readers.

Creon's long speech parallels and answers Antigonê's. Once the two positions have been established, we watch and listen as the dialogue speeds up as Antigonê and Creon trade arguments and insults.

Even though the dialogue is somewhat stylized and conventional, it is beautifully arranged for maximum punch and counter-punch.

Throughout this taut scene both characters seem tense and angry. They neither like nor respect each other.

The effect overall is of tension building to the point of explosion.

FORMAL WAYS OF WRITING ABOUT DRAMA

Among the more common formal ways of writing about drama is analysis. In writing an analytical essay about a play or a scene from a play, your goal is to explain how one or more particular aspects or issues in the work or the scene contributes to its overall meaning. You might analyze the dialogue in a scene from Ibsen's *A Doll House* or Lady Gregory's *The Rising of the Moon*. Your goal would be to explain what the verbal exchanges between characters contribute to the play's meaning and to its effect on the audience. You might analyze the imagery of Sophocles' *Oedipus the King* or Shakespeare's *Othello* to see what that imagery suggests about a character's perspective or the author's attitude toward the characters or the action. Or you might analyze the plot or staging of Glaspell's *Trifles* to see how the playwright's manipulation of action creates tension and conflict, humor and irony. (See these plays and others that we discuss reproduced in the chapters that follow.)

In addition to analyzing these and other dramatic elements in a play, you might also compare two plays or scenes, perhaps by focusing on their use of stage directions, lighting, or other theatrical effects. Or, instead of focusing on literary elements per se, you might write to see how a particular critical perspective (see Chapter Twenty-Two) illuminates a play. For example, you might consider the ways reader response criticism or new historicism contributes to your understanding of Hansberry's *A Raisin in the Sun*.

The following student papers analyze significant aspects of *Hamlet* and *Antigonê* respectively. In the first paper, the writer examines the character Hamlet's internal conflicts and then explains how they are resolved in the play. In the second paper, the writer analyzes the character Antigonê's conflict between her duty to the law of the state and her obligation to honor her dead brother by burying him.

Student Papers on Drama

Carolyn Kaparini
Prof. Eisenstadt

Hamlet's Conflict Resolved

In Shakespearean tragedies, characters often are confronted
with problems they must resolve. *The Tragedy of Hamlet, Prince
of Denmark* is one tragedy that reveals a tormented hero who
suffers greatly during the course of the play. Hamlet, the
tragic hero, must resolve many conflicts, which include
confusion and anger at his mother's hasty remarriage, horror
at the ghost's request to avenge the murder of his father, and
a general disgust with life as he contemplates suicide. Before
he can accept the responsibility of setting his world aright,
Hamlet must resolve his internal conflicts.

The first dilemma Hamlet must resolve results from the loss
of his father. Hamlet is first seen dressed in black as he
mourns the death of King Hamlet, his father. Hamlet cannot
understand why no one besides himself and Horatio continues to
grieve for Hamlet's father. What is even more upsetting to
Hamlet is that the court is celebrating the coronation of
Claudius and his royal marriage to Hamlet's mother, Queen
Gertrude. Hamlet is especially infuriated with his mother, who
he thinks has not mourned her husband's death sufficiently. In
an important soliloquy in Act I, scene ii, Hamlet complains
that even a beast "would have mourned longer" than his mother
did. And he reveals his disgust with both her and Claudius
when he calls their hasty marriage both "wicked" and
"incestuous." Throughout the play, Hamlet will continue to
find their marriage itself and its hasty occurrence after his
father's death consistently painful to think about.

A second internal conflict with which Hamlet deals is the
problem presented by the ghost. When Hamlet first encounters
the ghost he asks whether the ghost is "a spirit of health or
goblin damned." Before anything else, Hamlet has to resolve
the problem of the ghost's good or evil nature, of whether he
can trust the ghost to be honest and truthful. Once he decides
that the ghost really is the spirit of his dead father, Hamlet
faces an even greater problem: to act on the command the ghost
gives him to avenge the foul murder committed by Claudius.
Hamlet is appalled by the story the ghost of his father tells
about how Claudius murdered him to acquire first his crown and

then his queen. The absolute evil of Claudius's actions and
Hamlet's disgust with his mother's behavior lead him to
recognize that "something's rotten in the state of Denmark."
Hamlet describes his predicament in the following lines:

> The time is out of joint. O cursed spite,
> That ever I was born to set it right.

Before Hamlet can set things right, however, he has to come to
terms with the world of destructive evil that Claudius's act
typifies.

   Hamlet's greatest conflict occurs as a result of his
indecision over what to do about his mother and how to avenge
his father's murder. Even though these both distress him
greatly, he suffers from a deeper and more pervasive disgust
with life. Because of Claudius's crime, he sees evil all
around him, especially at court. Because of his mother's
actions, he thinks of all women as sinful, even the innocent
Ophelia. He expresses his general dissatisfaction with life
many times. On one occasion right after describing man as
"noble" and a "paragon," after comparing him with angels and
gods, Hamlet says "and yet to me, what is this quintessence of
dust? Man delights not me." Later, he considers the question
of whether it is better to live or to die:

> To be, or not to be: that is the question:
> Whether 'tis nobler in the mind to suffer
> The slings and arrows of outrageous fortune,
> Or to take arms against a sea of troubles,
> And by opposing end them.

These and many other lines in the play reveal Hamlet
disappointed with the injustice and cruelty of life. His anger
and frustration lead him to think constantly about death and
to make plans to avenge his father's death. But he does not
act. Instead he thinks and delays acting.

   Hamlet perceives how difficult his task really is. Perhaps
that is why it takes him so long to act. He is also seriously
depressed by the state of affairs in Denmark. One turning
point comes when Hamlet decides to confront his mother. He
unleashes his anger and criticizes her severely for marrying
Claudius. He also urges her not to sleep with the king.
Another turning point occurs, when upon discovering Claudius's
plot to have him murdered, Hamlet substitutes another letter
ensuring the deaths of Rosencrantz and Guildenstern. In
addition, during Hamlet's time away from the court when he is
captured by pirates and then released to make his way home, he

seems to have changed. When he reappears in Act V, Hamlet is more accepting of what fate or God has in store for him. Even though he does not yet know of the treachery that Laertes and Claudius have planned for him, he is determined to do what is necessary and to accept the consequences.

One important indication of this change of attitude occurs when he holds the skull of Yorick and he talks about the inevitability of death. He describes how death comes to all people, the great and important as well as the common people. All are equal when their bodies have decayed and their souls have departed. In addition, Hamlet recognizes that, as he tells Horatio, "there's a divinity that shapes our ends," regardless of what we prepare for ourselves. This recognition of a divine power governing the lives of men is acknowledged in another speech that reveals that Hamlet has learned from his suffering. It suggests that he has mentally resolved his internal conflicts. He says to Horatio:

> There is special providence in the fall of a
> sparrow. If it be now, 'tis not to come; if it
> be not to come, it will be now; if it be not
> now, yet it will come. The readiness is all.
> Since no man of aught he leaves knows, what is't
> to leave betimes? Let be.

In the play's final scene, Hamlet settles the score with Claudius by stabbing him with his sword. He has already resolved his argument with his mother, and the treacherous drink Claudius had prepared for Hamlet does the rest. After Hamlet and Laertes, Gertrude and Claudius die, Horatio is left to explain what really happened and what Hamlet himself was really like. It is left to Fortinbras to restore order to the disorder of Denmark. Even though Hamlet alone could not set his world aright, he had found his own peace and resolved his internal conflicts.

Alayna Phieffer
Dr. Kitts
12/10/96

Antigonê: A Struggle between Human and Divine Powers

In *Antigonê* by Sophocles there are several ways to interpret the conflict between Creon and Antigonê. Perhaps the most widely accepted interpretation is that their conflict represents a struggle between state and individual. This reading is valid but it is also shallow; if looked into deeper, we can see that the struggle in this play lies between earthly and divine powers.

Creon represents a tyrannical rule that makes no allowances for the unwritten laws, spiritual in nature, which so often guide humans to act. He is so consumed with ruling the state and so intoxicated with the power he possesses that he is unable to comprehend the motives behind Antigonê's burial of her brother Polyneicês. This can be seen in the first encounter between Antigonê and Creon.

> *Creon:* And yet you dared defy the law.
> *Antigonê:*   I dared.
>   It was not God's proclamation. That final Justice
>   That rules the world below makes no such law.
>
>   Your edict, King, was strong,
>   But all your strength is weakness itself against
>   The immortal unrecorded laws of God.
>   They are not merely now: they were, and shall be,
>   Operative for ever, beyond man utterly.
>
>   . . . but if I had left my brother
>   Lying in death unburied, I should have suffered.
>   Now I do not.   (II, 56-70)

This conversation immediately establishes Antigonê's ideal; to her, divine law is more powerful and right than any law decreed by the state. Creon, to save face and maintain order, sticks to his decree and sentences her to death.

This conflict of harsh state laws with one's inner duty goes still deeper, and it is clear that the gods are on Antigonê's side. It seems best to look at what Antigonê and others say about divine intervention and their actions concerning it. The first evidence that the gods are involved

can be seen in the double burial. Antigonê is apprehended
when she goes to her brother's body, but just before this we
are told by the Sentry that someone has buried the body of
Polyneicês. He states that there are no signs of human
involvement, no wheel tracks or any sign of animals present;
the body is covered with a light dusting. We can perceive
this statement to be true; otherwise why would Sophocles have
included it? Why did Antigonê then go back to her brother for
a second time? Perhaps the answer lies in a statement made by
the chorus-leader: "I have been wondering, King: can it be
that the gods have done this?" (I, 99).

The watchman's actions, upon entering the palace, are
revealing. He twists and turns as though he is afraid that
Creon will not believe him; after all, he cannot understand it
himself. If the body had been buried deep in the ground, one
could argue that this is evidence that it was done by man, but
the light dusting of the body implies something more.

Another piece of evidence to support God's involvement in
this play's action is apparent in the first conversation
between Antigonê and Ismenê. Antigonê says "Creon is not
strong enough to stand in my way" (Prologue, 35). And later
after Ismenê says how dangerous it is to go against authority,
Antigonê responds:

<blockquote>

                    If that is what you think,
I should not want you, even if you asked to come.
You have made your choice, you can be what you want to be.
But I will bury him; and if I must die,
I say that this crime is holy: I shall lie down
With him in death, and I shall be as dear
To him as he is to me.
                                It is the dead,
Not the living, who make the longest demands:
We die for ever . . .
                        You may do as you like,
Since apparently the laws of the gods mean nothing to you.

                                        (Prologue, 52-61)

</blockquote>

Antigonê is saying that she is acting in accordance with the
will of the gods; divine law will always surpass any human
laws.

Later, she tells Creon that it was not the words of the gods
that she disobeyed, but it was their word that led her to act.
This idea is common in Greek tragedy. When characters like
Antigonê act in ways fundamentally necessary in human life, or
out of a place deep within themselves, they are said to be
working with the gods, and this becomes so sacred that not
even written law could stop them.

As Antigonê is about to be buried alive, she realizes that no one understands her. Still she feels that she was obeying a divine law, even though now the gods seem to have nothing to do with her and have made no attempt to save her. But still she maintains her deep belief that she had to do it, and says that she had no choice:

> Thebes, and you my fathers' gods,
> And rulers of Thebes, you see me now, the last
> Unhappy daughter of a line of kings,
> Your kings, led away to death. You will remember
> What things I suffer, and at what men's hands,
> Because I would not transgress the laws of heaven.
>
> (IV, 75–80)

To her, the laws of heaven must guide our lives and they must always be obeyed no matter the consequence.

Finally we see the divine hand in prophecy, most obviously in the tragic destiny of Oedipus. His tragedy is sorrowfully left behind to his descendants. Tragedy must fall upon Antigonê as it fell upon her brothers. When she decides to bury Polyneicês, it is indeed an act of freewill, but one cannot disclaim the necessity of this action by fate—a tragic, inherited curse.

Teiresias may help Creon decide to amend his law, but he also serves a deeper purpose. Prophecy delivered by the gods implies law. Creon, by refusing to bury Polyneicês, has gone against the gods. Teiresias makes Creon's offense to the gods clear. He tells of evil omens that he has witnessed, like the fighting birds and the fat not catching on fire. These incidents portend Creon's tragic destiny. His conflicts are now with both upper and nether gods.

Creon's actions lead him into a world of suffering; for although he recognizes his mistakes and tries to correct them, he is too late. After taking care of Polyneicês's remains, he hurries to Antigonê's tomb only to find his son and Antigonê dead. Upon hearing the news of her son, his wife kills herself. This leaves Creon in a world full of despair. With his son and wife dead he is left to suffer and remember that universal laws are more powerful than any he may ever decree.

The idea that runs throughout this play is that there will always be certain forces and absolutes in life that must be respected, and essentially will be because they are divine in nature. When individuals do not look past the apparent causes and fail to see the divine implications, they may work against these laws. If the laws are offended, the wrath will be felt, not necessarily from supernatural powers, but in the actions and reactions of people who are strong enough or desperate

enough to follow their own hearts and live by their ideals.
Life on earth produces no human laws that are unbreakable. The
only way to be sure of not wreaking this havoc upon oneself is
to understand and respect the gods. By doing so one
demonstrates respect for humanity as well.

QUESTIONS FOR WRITING ABOUT DRAMA

In writing about the elements of drama, the following questions can help you
focus your thinking and prepare yourself for writing analytical essays and papers. Use the questions as a checklist to guide you to important aspects of any
play you read.

Plot

1. How does the playwright order the incidents of the play? What is the effect of this
   arrangement of incidents?
2. What is the central conflict of the play? What subsidiary conflicts are related to it?
3. Where is the play's climax? How is that climax prepared for dramatically? With
   what effects?

Character

4. To what extent are the play's characters—its *dramatis personae*—similar to actual
   people? In what ways are the play's characters different from actual people?
5. Using the characters' actions and speech, how would you evaluate their behavior?
   How are the characters related to one another dramatically and in other ways?
6. What function does each of the minor characters serve? If there is a chorus, what
   are its functions?

Dialogue

7. How would you characterize the voices of the various characters? How do you
   imagine them sounding in each of their major soliloquies or exchanges with other
   characters?
8. How does the dialogue advance the plot of the play? How does the dialogue establish setting?
9. How does the dialogue reveal character and motivation? Which particular
   speeches or other verbal exchanges are especially important for revealing character? Why?

Staging

10. What information is explicitly provided or implicitly suggested about how the play's characters are costumed? Do they change costumes at any point? Why? To what extent might such costume changes signal changes in attitude, behavior, or state of mind?

11. What objects or props in the play are emphasized? Which carry symbolic weight? How do you know?

12. What kinds of stage directions are provided? How do they help you understand the action? What do they contribute to your understanding of the characters?

13. How does the setting of the play contribute to its mood and theme? What do lighting and the use of sound contribute to the play's overall effects?

Theme

14. What is the central theme of the play? What subsidiary or ancillary themes support or accompany it?

15. How does your analysis of the elements of drama help you understand a play's theme?

16. Does the playwright convey the theme directly or indirectly? Can you identify one or more key passages in which the theme is made explicit? Or do you have to infer the theme from the implications of the play's dialogue and action, setting, staging, and character relationships?

Critical Perspectives

17. Among the critical perspectives you might bring to bear on the play, which one(s) seem(s) particularly useful for interpreting it? Why?

18. To what extent can you base your interpretation of the play on its language and details alone? To what extent is outside information about historical and biographical context necessary or helpful in understanding it?

19. To what extent does the play confirm or support your personal beliefs and values? To what extent is it in conflict with those beliefs and values? To what extent do your values and personal dispositions affect or influence your interpretation?

20. How do you imagine seeing the play staged would enhance your understanding, increase your emotional response, or otherwise alter your perception of the play?

QUESTIONS FOR IN-DEPTH READING

1. What general or overall thematic connections can you make between different works?

2. What stylistic similarities do you notice between and among different works?

3. How do the works differ in emphasis, tone, and style?

4. Once you have identified a writer's major preoccupations, place each work on a spectrum or a grid that represents the range of the writer's concerns.

5. What connections and disjunctions do you find among the following literary elements as they are embodied in different plays by the same writer?
    (a) plot and structure
    (b) character and characterization
    (c) dialogue and monologue
    (d) staging and setting
    (e) theme and thought

6. To what extent are your responses to and perceptions of different works by the same writer shared by others—by critics, by classmates, and by the writers themselves?

7. What relationships and differences do you see between the work of one writer and that of another who shares similar thematic interests, stylistic proclivities, or cultural, religious, or social values?

8. Which of the critical perspectives (see Chapter Twenty-Two) seem most useful as analytical tools for approaching the body of work of particular writers?

Suggestions for Writing
The Experience of Drama

1. Write a paper in which you recount your experience of reading a particular play or series of plays by the same author. You may want to compare your initial experience with your experience in later readings.

2. Write a paper comparing your experience reading a play with your experience witnessing a performance of it.

3. Discuss your changing perception or understanding of a particular play. Indicate how you felt about the play initially and what made you change your way of responding to it.

4. Relate the action or situation of a play to your own experience. Explain how the play is relevant to your situation, and comment on how reading and thinking about it may have helped you see your own life and experience more clearly.

5. Compare reading a play with watching a film of a performance or a film based on a play. For a filmed performance of a play, consider watching the videocassette of Arthur Miller's *Death of a Salesman,* starring Dustin Hoffman. For a film based on a play, consider viewing the movie version of Hansberry's *A Raisin in the Sun,* starring Sidney Poitier.

The Interpretation of Drama

6. Describe and characterize a single character from any play. Present a sketch of the character by referring to the language of his or her speeches and to the playwright's use of costume and stage directions.

7. Analyze a character at the moment he or she is making an important decision. Identify the situation, explain the reasons for the character's decision, and speculate about the possible consequences. Some possibilities: Nora in *A Doll House,* Antigonê in *Antigonê,* Othello in *Othello,* the Sergeant in *The Rising of the Moon.*

8. Explicate the opening dialogue of any play. Explain the significance of the opening section in setting the tone, establishing thematic preoccupations, and preparing us for what follows.

9. Select two or three brief passages that appear to be significant in their implications. They may be descriptive passages or dialogue. Establish the connections between one passage and the others, and explain their cumulative significance.

10. Analyze the closing dialogue of any play. Explain the significance of the ending and comment on its appropriateness.

11. Analyze the imagery of a play. Consider how particular kinds of language serve to advance the play's theme(s) or to reveal its characters. Some possibilities: political and natural images in Sophocles' *Antigonê;* animal imagery in *Othello;* images of dream and illusion in Arthur Miller's *Death of a Salesman.*

12. Analyze the ironic dimensions of any play. Consider how the playwright uses irony in the plot, dialogue, and/or setting. Some possibilities: *Oedipus Rex, Antigonê, Trifles.*

13. Explain the symbolic implications of any props used in the play. Consider the dramatic functions of the objects and their resonance as symbols. Some possibilities: the handkerchief in *Othello;* the Christmas tree in *A Doll House;* the balloons in *Andre's Mother.*

14. Analyze the structure of any play. Consider its major parts or sections—its acts and scenes. Explain what each contributes to the whole and how the parts fit together into a unified whole.

15. Analyze the plot of a play. Comment on the way it illustrates or deviates from the classic plot structure.

16. Analyze the setting of a play. Consider both time and place. Also consider small-scale aspects of setting, such as whether the action occurs indoors or out. Notice the descriptive details about the setting, whether the setting changes, and whether the action occurs in one time or place.

17. Analyze a character from any play. Evaluate the character, offering reasons and evidence for your views. Consider what the character does, says, does not do or say—and why. Note also what other characters say about him or her, and how they respond in action. Consider whether the character changes during the course of the play and what that possible change (or lack thereof) may signify.

18. Discuss any character relationship. Consider how the characters affect each other. Explain the nature of their relationship and speculate on its probable future.

The Evaluation of Drama

19. Evaluate a play from the point of view of its merit or excellence—or lack thereof. Explain why you consider it to be a successful or unsuccessful play.
20. Do a comparative evaluation of the merit of any two plays. Explain what they share, how they differ, and why one is more impressive or effective than the other.
21. Discuss the values exemplified by the characters in any play. Identify those values, relate them to your own, and comment on their significance. You may also wish to discuss the author's point of view as you see it reflected in the play.
22. Write a review of the performance of a play. Consider the staging and lighting of the performance, the costumes, the set design, and the sound effects.
23. Write a review of a play's performance concentrating on the acting. Consider how well the actors and actresses delivered their lines, how well they worked together and how well they communicated emotions and ideas.
24. Write a review of a film, concentrating on its theatrical characteristics and qualities.

To Research or Imagine

25. Develop an alternative ending for any play, changing the outcome in whatever way you deem appropriate. Be prepared to defend your alternative ending as a reasonable possibility. Consider why the author chose to end the play as he or she did.
26. Try your hand at writing a scene from a play. Invent a scenario, create a couple of characters, and start them talking and acting.
27. Read a few letters or essays written by a dramatist. Consider what light they shed on your reading of the play(s).
28. Read a full-scale biography of a dramatist. Write a paper explaining how the author's life is or is not reflected in his work.
29. Discuss how a particular playwright reflects or rebels against important social, political, moral, or cultural issues of his or her time.
30. Read a critical study of a writer's plays. Write a paper explaining how the book aids your understanding or enhances your enjoyment of the play(s).

CHAPTER EIGHTEEN

The Greek Theater: Sophocles in Context

Greek drama developed from celebrations honoring Dionysus, the Greek god of wine and fertility. These celebrations included choric dancing as part of the religious ritual. It is possible that the leader of the chorus (the *choragos*) may have engaged the rest of the chorus in responsive chanting. Legend suggests that the poet Thespis introduced a speaker who, detached from the chorus, engaged in dialogue with it. At that point drama was born. A second actor was added by Aeschylus (524–456 B.C.) and a third by Sophocles (496?–406 B.C.). In Greek drama no more than three characters appeared onstage together at one time, although it was common for actors to double and triple parts, changing masks for their multiple roles.

Greek plays were performed in huge outdoor amphitheaters capable of seating upwards of fourteen thousand people. Members of the audience were seated in tiers that sloped up hillsides where the theaters were built; the hills echoed the sound of the actors' voices. The actors wore masks that amplified their voices in the manner of megaphones. The masks were large, and with the elevated shoes sometimes worn by the actors, they projected the characters as larger-than-life figures. The masks and elevated shoes restricted what the actors could do and what the dramatist could expect of them. Subtle nuances of voice, of facial expression, and of gesture were impossible. The playwright's language rather than his stage business conveyed nuances of meaning and feeling.

The plays were performed on an elevated platform. Behind the acting area was a scene building *(skene)* that functioned both as dressing room and as scenic background, and below the stage was the *orchestra* or dancing place for the chorus. Standing between the actors and the audience, the chorus represented the common or communal viewpoint. Its leader, the choragos, sometimes engaged the chorus in dialogue with the other characters, and sometimes the choragos engaged in dialogue with the chorus itself.

An important function of the chorus was to mark the divisions between the scenes of a play, when the chorus would dance and chant poetry. Lyric rather than dramatic in form, these choral interludes sometimes commented on the action, sometimes generalized from it. They remained in Greek drama as vestiges of its origins in religious ritual. For modern readers these choric interludes pace the play, affording respite from the gradually intensifying action, and allowing time to ponder its implications.

The scenes of Greek plays usually consist of two, sometimes three characters with the third usually acting as an observer who occasionally comments on the debate occurring between the other two characters. Sometimes most of a scene is given over to a debate between two characters, as, for example, in Scene III of *Antigonê* with Haimon challenging Creon, his father, or Scene I of *Oedipus Rex* in which Oedipus argues with Teiresias. Some scenes, such as Scene II of *Antigonê,* include debates between Creon-Antigonê, Antigonê-Ismenê, Ismenê-Creon, and Creon-Choragos. The debates typically begin with leisurely speeches in which each character sets forth a position. The speeches are followed by rapid-fire dialogue *(stichomythia)* that brings the characters' antagonisms to a climax. This pattern is repeated throughout the play in something like a theme with variations, each scene usually developing a conflict. The accumulation of conflicts advances the action, leading to the inevitable tragic catastrophe.

Brevity is a characteristic of Greek tragedy: the plays are short with most having a playing time of roughly ninety minutes. Greek dramatists based their plays on myths that were familiar to the audience, which reduced the amount of time allotted for exposition. The plays also have a musical dimension, which, combined with the dancing and chanting of the chorus, increased the emotional impact of the ancient performances.

Of the three great Greek tragic dramatists, Sophocles is perhaps the most widely read today. Unlike his forebear Aeschylus, Sophocles focused his plays on human rather than religious concerns. As theater historian Peter Arnott has noted, he wrote "for a generation whose religious faith was waning."★ His most famous plays center on a crisis and portray characters under duress. *Antigonê,* which takes place in Thebes, a city prostrated by war, turns on the difficult decisions both Antigonê and Creon must make. In *Oedipus Rex,* set against a background of the plague-stricken city of Thebes, Sophocles examines the behavior of Oedipus, who has been destined to murder his father and marry his mother. Though the two tragedies differ in the way their calamities ensue, both raise questions about inescapable human problems and portray characters confronting them with dignity and courage.

The following chart clarifies the relationships among the Theban royal families:

★Peter Arnott, *The Theatre in Its Time* (Boston: Little, Brown, 1981), page 51.

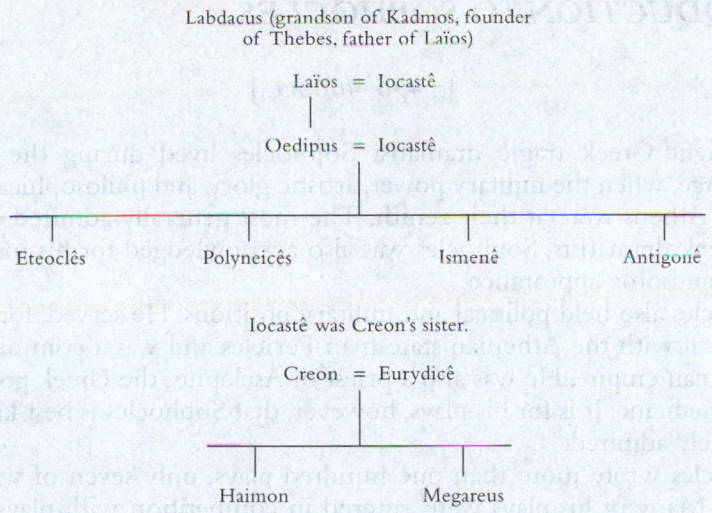

Labdacus (grandson of Kadmos, founder
of Thebes, father of Laïos)

Laïos = Iocastê

Oedipus = Iocastê

Eteoclês   Polyneicês   Ismenê   Antigonê

Iocastê was Creon's sister.

Creon = Eurydicê

Haimon   Megareus

The Athenian audience that watched performances of *Oedipus Tyrannus* (the original Greek title of the play) would have been familiar with Oedipus's story from sources as early as Homer's *Odyssey*. They would have known, for example, that Oedipus was fated to kill his father and marry his mother, and that to prevent this from happening, the infant Oedipus was given up by his parents, King Laius and Queen Jocasta, and left in the wilderness to die. This plan went awry when Oedipus was taken by a shepherd to Corinth, where he was adopted by a childless couple, King Polybus and Queen Merope. The Athenian audience would also have been aware of the reason for Oedipus's clubfoot (his feet had been pinned together as an infant). They would have known too of how upon hearing the oracle pronounce his grisly fate, Oedipus had left Corinth, where he had been raised as a prince, thinking that he had to get as far away as he could from Polybus and Merope, who he assumed were his biological parents. For the Athenian audience, then, and for later audiences who know the Oedipus story, the play's power resides less in the surprising twists and turns of its plot than in its relentless tragic action.

Oedipus Rex begins at the point when Thebes is undergoing a series of catastrophes, most important of which is a devastating plague. Prior to this series of events, Oedipus had saved Thebes from the Sphinx, a winged creature with the body of a lion and the head of a woman. The Sphinx had terrorized the city by devouring anyone who crossed its path and who was unable to answer its riddle correctly: What goes on four legs in the morning, two legs in the afternoon, and three legs in the evening? Oedipus solved the riddle by answering "Man." After he slew the Sphinx, he was given in reward the kingship of Thebes and the hand of its recently widowed queen, Jocasta. Unknown to Oedipus, but known to the Athenian audience, was the fact that Jocasta was his mother and that her recently slain husband, Laius, had been killed by Oedipus himself (who of course did not know who Laius really was). All this and more Oedipus soon discovers.

INTRODUCTION TO SOPHOCLES

[*c. 496–406 B.C.*]

The ancient Greek tragic dramatist Sophocles lived during the Athenian Golden Age, when the military power, artistic glory, and philosophical achievements of Athens were at their zenith. The most generally admired of the ancient Greek dramatists, Sophocles was also acknowledged for his musical skill and his handsome appearance.

Sophocles also held political and military positions. He served, for example, as a general with the Athenian statesman Pericles and was a commissioner of the Athenian empire. He was also a priest of Asclepius, the Greek god of healing and medicine. It is for his plays, however, that Sophocles is best known and most widely admired.

Sophocles wrote more than one hundred plays, only seven of which have survived. Many of his plays were entered in competition with plays by other Greek tragic dramatists, including Aeschylus and Euripides, whose work Sophocles surpassed on at least twenty occasions. More conservative than the other Greek dramatists who were his contemporaries, Sophocles emphasized the individual's uncompromising search for truth, which is evident in both his plays *Oedipus Rex* and *Antigonê*.

Oedipus Rex

AN ENGLISH VERSION BY DUDLEY FITTS AND ROBERT FITZGERALD

CHARACTERS

OEDIPUS
A PRIEST
CREON
TEIRESIAS
IOCASTÊ
MESSENGER
SHEPHERD OF LAÏOS
SECOND MESSENGER
CHORUS OF THEBAN ELDERS

Scene. *Before the palace of* OEDIPUS, *King of Thebes. A central door and two lateral doors open onto a platform which runs the length of the façade. On the platform, right and left, are altars; and three steps lead down into the "orchestra," or chorus-ground. At the beginning of the action these steps are crowded by* SUPPLIANTS *who have brought branches and chaplets of olive leaves and who lie in various attitudes of despair.* OEDIPUS *enters.*

PROLOGUE

OEDIPUS: My children, generations of the living
   In the line of Kadmos,° nursed at his ancient hearth:
   Why have you strewn yourselves before these altars
   In supplication, with your boughs and garlands?
   The breath of incense rises from the city   5
   With a sound of prayer and lamentation.

                       Children,
   I would not have you speak through messengers,
   And therefore I have come myself to hear you—
   I, Oedipus, who bear the famous name.
   (*To a* PRIEST.) You, there, since you are eldest in the company,   10
   Speak for them all, tell me what preys upon you,
   Whether you come in dread, or crave some blessing:
   Tell me, and never doubt that I will help you
   In every way I can; I should be heartless
   Were I not moved to find you suppliant here.   15

PRIEST: Great Oedipus, O powerful King of Thebes!
   You see how all the ages of our people
   Cling to your altar steps: here are boys
   Who can barely stand alone, and here are priests
   By weight of age, as I am a priest of God,   20
   And young men chosen from those yet unmarried;
   As for the others, all that multitude,
   They wait with olive chaplets in the squares,
   At the two shrines of Pallas,° and where Apollo°
   Speaks in the glowing embers.

                 Your own eyes   25
   Must tell you: Thebes is in her extremity
   And cannot lift her head from the surge of death.
   A rust consumes the buds and fruits of the earth;
   The herds are sick; children die unborn,
   And labor is vain. The god of plague and pyre   30
   Raids like detestable lightning through the city,
   And all the house of Kadmos is laid waste,
   All emptied, and all darkened: Death alone
   Battens upon the misery of Thebes.
   You are not one of the immortal gods, we know;   35
   Yet we have come to you to make our prayer
   As to the man of all men best in adversity
   And wisest in the ways of God. You saved us
   From the Sphinx,° that flinty singer, and the tribute

---

²**Kadmos** *legendary founder of Thebes.*   ²⁴**Pallas** *Athena, goddess of wisdom.*   ²⁴**Apollo** *god of poetry and prophecy.*   ³⁹**the Sphinx** *a monster with a lion's body, birds' wings, and woman's face.*

We paid to her so long; yet you were never   40
Better informed than we, nor could we teach you:
It was some god breathed in you to set us free.

Therefore, O mighty King, we turn to you:
Find us our safety, find us a remedy,
Whether by counsel of the gods or the men.   45
A king of wisdom tested in the past
Can act in a time of troubles, and act well.
Noblest of men, restore
Life to your city! Think how all men call you
Liberator for your triumph long ago;   50
Ah, when your years of kingship are remembered,
Let them not say *We rose, but later fell*—
Keep the State from going down in the storm!
Once, years ago, with happy augury,
You brought us fortune; be the same again!   55
No man questions your power to rule the land:
But rule over men, not over a dead city!
Ships are only hulls, citadels are nothing,
When no life moves in the empty passageways.

OEDIPUS: Poor children! You may be sure I know   60
All that you longed for in your coming here.
I know that you are deathly sick; and yet,
Sick as you are, not one is as sick as I.
Each of you suffers in himself alone
His anguish, not another's; but my spirit   65
Groans for the city, for myself, for you.

I was not sleeping, you are not waking me.
No, I have been in tears for a long while
And in my restless thought walked many ways.
In all my search, I found one helpful course,   70
And that I have taken: I have sent Creon,
Son of Menoikeus, brother of the Queen,
To Delphi, Apollo's place of revelation,
To learn there, if he can,
What act or pledge of mine may save the city.   75
I have counted the days, and now, this very day,
I am troubled, for he has overstayed his time.
What is he doing? He has been gone too long.
Yet whenever he comes back, I should do ill
To scant whatever hint the god may give.   80

PRIEST: It is a timely promise. At this instant
They tell me Creon is here.

OEDIPUS: O Lord Apollo!
May his news be fair as his face is radiant!

PRIEST: It could not be otherwise: he is crowned with bay,

The chaplet is thick with berries.

OEDIPUS: We shall soon know;   85
He is near enough to hear us now.

Enter CREON.

O Prince:

Brother: son of Menoikeus:
What answer do you bring us from the god?

CREON: It is favorable. I can tell you, great afflictions
Will turn out well, if they are taken well.   90

OEDIPUS: What was the oracle? These vague words
Leave me still hanging between hope and fear.

CREON: Is it your pleasure to hear me with all these
Gathered around us? I am prepared to speak,
But should we not go in?

OEDIPUS: Let them all hear it.   95
It is for them I suffer, more than myself.

CREON: Then I will tell you what I heard at Delphi.

In plain words
The god commands us to expel from the land of Thebes
An old defilement that it seems we shelter.   100
It is a deathly thing, beyond expiation.
We must not let it feed upon us longer.

OEDIPUS: What defilement? How shall we rid ourselves of it?

CREON: By exile or death, blood for blood. It was
Murder that brought the plague-wind on the city.   105

OEDIPUS: Murder of whom? Surely the god has named him?

CREON: My lord: long ago Laïos was our king,
Before you came to govern us.

OEDIPUS: I know;
I learned of him from others; I never saw him.

CREON: He was murdered; and Apollo commands us now   110
To take revenge upon whoever killed him.

OEDIPUS: Upon whom? Where are they? Where shall we find a clue
To solve that crime, after so many years?

CREON: Here in this land, he said.

If we make enquiry,
We may touch things that otherwise escape us.   115

OEDIPUS: Tell me: Was Laïos murdered in his house,
Or in the fields, or in some foreign country?

CREON: He said he planned to make a pilgrimage.
He did not come home again.

OEDIPUS: And was there no one,
No witness, no companion, to tell what happened?   120

CREON: They were all killed but one, and he got away
So frightened that he could remember one thing only.

OEDIPUS: What was that one thing? One may be the key

To everything, if we resolve to use it.
CREON: He said that a band of highwaymen attacked them,   125
  Outnumbered them, and overwhelmed the King.
OEDIPUS: Strange, that a highwayman should be so daring—
  Unless some faction here bribed him to do it.
CREON: We thought of that. But after Laïos' death
  New troubles arose and we had no avenger.   130
OEDIPUS: What troubles could prevent your hunting down the killers?
CREON: The riddling Sphinx's song
  Made us deaf to all mysteries but her own.
OEDIPUS: Then once more I must bring what is dark to light.
  It is most fitting that Apollo shows,   135
  As you do, this compunction for the dead.
  You shall see how I stand by you, as I should,
  To avenge the city and the city's god,
  And not as though it were for some distant friend,
  But for my own sake, to be rid of evil.   140
  Whoever killed King Laïos might—who knows?—
  Decide at any moment to kill me as well.
  By avenging the murdered king I protect myself.
  Come, then, my children: leave the altar steps,
  Lift up your olive boughs!
          One of you go   145
  And summon the people of Kadmos to gather here.
  I will do all that I can; you may tell them that.

                    (*Exit a* PAGE.)

So, with the help of God,
We shall be saved—or else indeed we are lost.
PRIEST: Let us rise, children. It was for this we came,   150
  And now the King has promised it himself.
  Phoibos° has sent us an oracle; may he descend
  Himself to save us and drive out the plague.

  Exeunt OEDIPUS *and* CREON *into the palace by the central door. The* PRIEST *and the*
  SUPPLIANTS *disperse right and left. After a short pause the* CHORUS *enters the orchestra.*

                    PÁRODOS°

Strophe 1

CHORUS: What is God singing in his profound
  Delphi of gold and shadow?

---

¹⁵²**Phoibos** *Phoebus Apollo, the sun god.*   **Párodos**   *sung as the chorus enters the stage area. Presumably they*
sang the strophe *while dancing from right to left and the* antistrophe *as they reversed direction.*

What oracle for Thebes, the sunwhipped city?
Fear unjoints me, the roots of my heart tremble.
Now I remember, O Healer, your power, and wonder; 5
Will you send doom like a sudden cloud, or weave it
Like nightfall of the past?
Speak, speak to us, issue of holy sound:
Dearest to our expectancy: be tender!

Antistrophe 1

Let me pray to Athenê, the immortal daughter of Zeus, 10
And to Artemis her sister
Who keeps her famous throne in the market ring,
And to Apollo, bowman at the far butts of heaven—

O gods, descend! Like three streams leap against
The fires of our grief, the fires of darkness; 15
Be swift to bring us rest!

As in the old time from the brilliant house
Of air you stepped to save us, come again!

Strophe 2

Now our afflictions have no end,
Now all our stricken host lies down 20
And no man fights off death with his mind;

The noble plowland bears no grain,
And groaning mothers cannot bear—

See, how our lives like birds take wing.
Like sparks that fly when a fire soars, 25
To the shore of the god of evening.

Antistrophe 2

The plague burns on, it is pitiless,
Though pallid children laden with death
Lie unwept in the stony ways,
And old gray women by every path 30

Flock to the strand about the altars
There to strike their breasts and cry
Worship of Phoibos in wailing prayers:
Be kind, God's golden child!

Strophe 3

> There are no swords in this attack by fire,   35
> No shields, but we are ringed with cries.
> Send the besieger plunging from our homes
> Into the vast sea-room of the Atlantic
> Or into the waves that foam eastward of Thrace—
> For the day ravages what the night spares—   40
>
> Destroy our enemy, lord of the thunder!
> Let him be riven by lightning from heaven!

Antistrophe 3

> Phoibos Apollo, stretch the sun's bowstring,
> That golden cord, until it sing for us,
> Flashing arrows in heaven!
>   Artemis,° Huntress,   45
> Race with flaring lights upon our mountains!
> O scarlet god, O golden-banded brow,
> O Theban Bacchos° in a storm of Maenads,°

                        Enter OEDIPUS, *center.*

> Whirl upon Death, that all the Undying hate!
> Come with blinding cressets, come in joy!   50

SCENE I

OEDIPUS: Is this your prayer? It may be answered. Come,
  Listen to me, act as the crisis demands,
  And you shall have relief from all these evils.

  Until now I was a stranger to this tale,
  As I had been a stranger to the crime.   5
  Could I track down the murderer without a clue?
  But now, friends,
  As one who became a citizen after the murder,
  I make this proclamation to all Thebans:
  If any man knows by whose hand Laïos, son of Labdakos,   10
  Met his death, I direct that man to tell me everything,
  No matter what he fears for having so long withheld it.
  Let it stand as promised that no further trouble

---

45 **Artemis**   *goddess of hunting and chastity.*   48 **Bacchos . . . Maenads**   *god of wine and revelry with his attendants.*

Will come to him, but he may leave the land in safety.
Moreover: If anyone knows the murderer to be foreign, 15
Let him not keep silent: he shall have his reward from me.
However, if he does conceal it; if any man
Fearing for his friend or for himself disobeys this edict,
Hear what I propose to do:

I solemnly forbid the people of this country, 20
Where power and throne are mine, ever to receive that man
Or speak to him, no matter who he is, or let him
Join in sacrifice, lustration, or in prayer.
I decree that he be driven from every house,

Being, as he is, corruption itself to us: the Delphic 25
Voice of Zeus has pronounced this revelation.
Thus I associate myself with the oracle
And take the side of the murdered king.

As for the criminal, I pray to God—
Whether it be a lurking thief, or one of a number— 30
I pray that that man's life be consumed in evil and
   wretchedness.
And as for me, this curse applies no less
If it should turn out that the culprit is my guest here,
Sharing my hearth.
          You have heard the penalty.
I lay it on you now to attend to this 35
For my sake, for Apollo's, for the sick
Sterile city that heaven has abandoned.
Suppose the oracle had given you no command:
Should this defilement go uncleansed for ever?
You should have found the murderer: your king, 40
A noble king, had been destroyed!
        Now I,
Having the power that he held before me,
Having his bed, begetting children there
Upon his wife, as he would have, had he lived—
Their son would have been my children's brother, 45
If Laïos had had luck in fatherhood!
(But surely ill luck rushed upon his reign)—
I say I take the son's part, just as though
I were his son, to press the fight for him
And see it won! I'll find the hand that brought 50
Death to Labdakos' and Polydoros' child,
Heir of Kadmos' and Agenor's line.
And as for those who fail me,
May the gods deny them the fruit of the earth,

Fruit of the womb, and may they rot utterly!   55
Let them be wretched as we are wretched, and worse!
For you, for loyal Thebans, and for all
Who find my actions right, I pray the favor
Of justice, and of all the immortal gods.
CHORAGOS: Since I am under oath, my lord, I swear   60
I did not do the murder, I cannot name
The murderer. Might not the oracle
That has ordained the search tell where to find him?
OEDIPUS: An honest question. But no man in the world
Can make the gods do more than the gods will.   65
CHORAGOS: There is one last expedient—
OEDIPUS: Tell me what it is.
Though it seem slight, you must not hold it back.
CHORAGOS: A lord clairvoyant to the lord Apollo,
As we all know, is the skilled Teiresias.
One might learn much about this from him, Oedipus.   70
OEDIPUS: I am not wasting time:
Creon spoke of this, and I have sent for him—
Twice, in fact; it is strange that he is not here.
CHORAGOS: The other matter—that old report—seems useless.
OEDIPUS: Tell me. I am interested in all reports.   75
CHORAGOS: The King was said to have been killed by highwaymen.
OEDIPUS: I know. But we have no witnesses to that.
CHORAGOS: If the killer can feel a particle of dread,
Your curse will bring him out of hiding!
OEDIPUS: No.
The man who dared that act will fear no curse.   80

Enter the blind seer TEIRESIAS, *led by a* PAGE.

CHORAGOS: But there is one man who may detect the criminal.
This is Teiresias, this is the holy prophet
In whom, alone of all men, truth was born.
OEDIPUS: Teiresias: seer: student of mysteries,
Of all that's taught and all that no man tells,   85
Secrets of Heaven and secrets of the earth:
Blind though you are, you know the city lies
Sick with plague; and from this plague, my lord,
We find that you alone can guard or save us.

Possibly you did not hear the messengers?   90
Apollo, when we sent to him,
Sent us back word that this great pestilence
Would lift, but only if we established clearly
The identity of those who murdered Laïos.
They must be killed or exiled.
                           Can you use   95

Birdflight or any art of divination
To purify yourself, and Thebes, and me
From this contagion? We are in your hands.
There is no fairer duty
Than that of helping others in distress.   100

TEIRESIAS: How dreadful knowledge of the truth can be
When there's no help in truth! I knew this well,
But did not act on it: else I should not have come.

OEDIPUS: What is troubling you? Why are your eyes so cold?

TEIRESIAS: Let me go home. Bear your own fate, and I'll   105
Bear mine. It is better so: trust what I say.

OEDIPUS: What you say is ungracious and unhelpful
To your native country. Do not refuse to speak.

TEIRESIAS: When it comes to speech, your own is neither temperate
Nor opportune. I wish to be more prudent.   110

OEDIPUS: In God's name, we all beg you—

TEIRESIAS: You are all ignorant.
No; I will never tell you what I know.
Now it is my misery; then, it would be yours.

OEDIPUS: What! You do know something, and will not tell us?
You would betray us all and wreck the State?   115

TEIRESIAS: I do not intend to torture myself, or you.
Why persist in asking? You will not persuade me.

OEDIPUS: What a wicked old man you are! You'd try a stone's
Patience! Out with it! Have you no feeling at all?

TEIRESIAS: You call me unfeeling. If you could only see   120
The nature of your own feelings . . .

OEDIPUS: Why,
Who would not feel as I do? Who could endure
Your arrogance toward the city?

TEIRESIAS: What does it matter!
Whether I speak or not, it is bound to come.

OEDIPUS: Then, if "it" is bound to come, you are bound
to tell me.   125

TEIRESIAS: No, I will not go on. Rage as you please.

OEDIPUS: Rage? Why not!
                          And I'll tell you what I think:
You planned it, you had it done, you all but
Killed him with your own hands: if you had eyes,
I'd say the crime was yours, and yours alone.   130

TEIRESIAS: So? I charge you, then,
Abide by the proclamation you have made:
From this day forth
Never speak again to these men or to me;
You yourself are the pollution of this country.   135

OEDIPUS: You dare say that! Can you possibly think you have
Some way of going free, after such insolence?

TEIRESIAS: I have gone free. It is the truth sustains me.

OEDIPUS: Who taught you shamelessness? It was not your craft.

TEIRESIAS: You did. You made me speak. I did not want to.　　　　140

OEDIPUS: Speak what? Let me hear it again more clearly.

TEIRESIAS: Was it not clear before? Are you tempting me?

OEDIPUS: I did not understand it. Say it again.

TEIRESIAS: I say that you are the murderer whom you seek.

OEDIPUS: Now twice you have spat out infamy. You'll
　　　pay for it!　　　　145

TEIRESIAS: Would you care for more? Do you wish to be really angry?

OEDIPUS: Say what you will. Whatever you say is worthless.

TEIRESIAS: I say you live in hideous shame with those
　　　Most dear to you. You cannot see the evil.

OEDIPUS: It seems you can go on mouthing like this for ever.　　　　150

TEIRESIAS: I can, if there is power in truth.

OEDIPUS:　　　　　　　　　　　　There is:
　　　But not for you, not for you,
　　　You sightless, witless, senseless, mad old man!

TEIRESIAS: You are the madman. There is no one here
　　　Who will not curse you soon, as you curse me.　　　　155

OEDIPUS: You child of endless night! You cannot hurt me
　　　Or any other man who sees the sun.

TEIRESIAS: True: it is not from me your fate will come.
　　　That lies within Apollo's competence,
　　　As it is his concern.

OEDIPUS:　　　　　　　　Tell me:　　　　160
　　　Are you speaking for Creon, or for yourself?

TEIRESIAS: Creon is no threat. You weave your own doom.

OEDIPUS: Wealth, power, craft of statesmanship!
　　　Kingly position, everywhere admired!
　　　What savage envy is stored up against these,　　　　165
　　　If Creon, whom I trusted, Creon my friend,
　　　For this great office which the city once
　　　Put in my hands unsought—if for this power
　　　Creon desires in secret to destroy me!
　　　He has brought this decrepit fortune-teller, this　　　　170
　　　Collector of dirty pennies, this prophet fraud—
　　　Why, he is no more clairvoyant than I am!

　　　　　　　　　　　　　Tell us:
　　　Has your mystic mummery ever approached the truth?
　　　When that hellcat the Sphinx was performing here,
　　　What help were you to these people?　　　　175
　　　Her magic was not for the first man who came along:
　　　It demanded a real exorcist. Your birds—
　　　What good were they? or the gods, for the matter of that?
　　　But I came by,
　　　Oedipus, the simple man, who knows nothing—　　　　180

I thought it out for myself, no birds helped me!
And this is the man you think you can destroy,
That you may be close to Creon when he's king!
Well, you and your friend Creon, it seems to me,
Will suffer most. If you were not an old man, 185
You would have paid already for your plot.

CHORAGOS: We cannot see that his words or yours
Have been spoken except in anger, Oedipus,
And of anger we have no need. How can God's will
Be accomplished best? That is what most concerns us. 190

TEIRESIAS: You are a king. But where argument's concerned
I am your man, as much a king as you.
I am not your servant, but Apollo's.
I have no need of Creon to speak for me.

Listen to me. You mock my blindness, do you? 195
But I say that you, with both your eyes, are blind:
You cannot see the wretchedness of your life,
Nor in whose house you live, no, nor with whom.
Who are your father and mother? Can you tell me?
You do not even know the blind wrongs 200
That you have done them, on earth and in the world below.
But the double lash of your parents' curse will whip you
Out of this land some day, with only night
Upon your precious eyes.
Your cries then—where will they not be heard? 205
What fastness of Kithairon will not echo them?
And that bridal-descant of yours—you'll know it then,
The song they sang when you came here to Thebes
And found your misguided berthing.
All this, and more, that you cannot guess at now, 210
Will bring you to yourself among your children.
Be angry, then. Curse Creon. Curse my words.
I tell you, no man that walks upon the earth
Shall be rooted out more horribly than you.

OEDIPUS: Am I to bear this from him?—Damnation 215
Take you! Out of this place! Out of my sight!

TEIRESIAS: I would not have come at all if you had not asked me.

OEDIPUS: Could I have told that you'd talk nonsense, that
You'd come here to make a fool of yourself, and of me?

TEIRESIAS: A fool? Your parents thought me sane enough. 220

OEDIPUS: My parents again!—Wait: who were my parents?

TEIRESIAS: This day will give you a father, and break your heart.

OEDIPUS: Your infantile riddles! Your damned abracadabra!

TEIRESIAS: You were a great man once at solving riddles.

OEDIPUS: Mock me with that if you like; you will find it true. 225

TEIRESIAS: It was true enough. It brought about your ruin.

OEDIPUS: But if it saved this town?

TEIRESIAS (*to the* PAGE): Boy, give me your hand.

OEDIPUS: Yes, boy; lead him away.

—While you are here

    We can do nothing. Go; leave us in peace.

TEIRESIAS: I will go when I have said what I have to say.   230

    How can you hurt me? And I tell you again:

    The man you have been looking for all this time,

    The damned man, the murderer of Laïos,

    That man is in Thebes. To your mind he is foreignborn,

    But it will soon be shown that he is a Theban,   235

    A revelation that will fail to please.

                         A blind man,

    Who has his eyes now; a penniless man, who is rich now;

    And he will go tapping the strange earth with his staff;

    To the children with whom he lives now he will be

    Brother and father—the very same; to her   240

    Who bore him, son and husband—the very same

    Who came to his father's bed, wet with his father's blood.

    Enough. Go think that over.

    If later you find error in what I have said,

    You may say that I have no skill in prophecy.   245

    Exit TEIRESIAS, *led by his* PAGE. OEDIPUS *goes into the palace.*

ODE I°

Strophe 1

CHORUS: The Delphic stone of prophecies

    Remembers ancient regicide

    And a still bloody hand.

    That killer's hour of flight has come.

    He must be stronger than riderless   5

    Coursers of untiring wind,

    For the son of Zeus° armed with his father's thunder

    Leaps in lightning after him;

    And the Furies° follow him, the sad Furies.

Antistrophe 1

    Holy Parnossos' peak of snow   10

    Flashes and blinds that secret man,

    That all shall hunt him down:

    Though he may roam the forest shade

---

ode   *a poetic song sung by the chorus.*   [7]*son of Zeus*   *Apollo.*   [9]*the Furies*   *three women spirits who punished evildoers.*

Like a bull gone wild from pasture
To rage through glooms of stone.   15
Doom comes down on him; flight will not avail him;
For the world's heart calls him desolate,
And the immortal Furies follow, for ever follow.

Strophe 2

But now a wilder thing is heard
From the old man skilled at hearing Fate in the
    wingbeat of a bird.   20
Bewildered as a blown bird, my soul hovers and cannot find
Foothold in this debate, or any reason or rest of mind.
But no man ever brought—none can bring
Proof of strife between Thebes' royal house,
Labdakos' line,° and the son of Polybos;°   25
And never until now has any man brought word
Of Laïos' dark death staining Oedipus the King.

Antistrophe 2

Divine Zeus and Apollo hold
Perfect intelligence alone of all tales ever told;
And well though this diviner works, he works in his own night;   30
No man can judge that rough unknown or trust in second sight,
For wisdom changes hands among the wise.
Shall I believe my great lord criminal
At a raging word that a blind old man let fall?
I saw him, when the carrion woman faced him of old,   35
Prove his heroic mind! These evil words are lies.

SCENE II

CREON: Men of Thebes:
I am told that heavy accusations
Have been brought against me by King Oedipus.
I am not the kind of man to bear this tamely.

If in these present difficulties   5
He holds me accountable for any harm to him
Through anything I have said or done—why, then,
I do not value life in this dishonor.
It is not as though this rumor touched upon
Some private indiscretion. The matter is grave.   10
The fact is that I am being called disloyal
To the State, to my fellow citizens, to my friends.

---

²⁵**Labdakos' line** *his descendants.*   ²⁵**Polybos** *King of Corinth who adopted Oedipus as an infant.*

CHORAGOS: He may have spoken in anger, not from his mind.
CREON: But did you not hear him say I was the one
   Who seduced the old prophet into lying?   15
CHORAGOS: The thing was said; I do not know how seriously.
CREON: But you were watching him! Were his eyes steady?
   Did he look like a man in his right mind?
CHORAGOS: I do not know.
   I cannot judge the behavior of great men.
   But here is the King himself.

Enter OEDIPUS.

OEDIPUS: So you dared come back.   20
   Why? How brazen of you to come to my house,
   You murderer!
              Do you think I do not know
   That you plotted to kill me, plotted to steal my throne?
   Tell me, in God's name: am I coward, a fool,
   That you should dream you could accomplish this?   25
   A fool who could not see your slippery game?
   A coward, not to fight back when I saw it?
   You are the fool, Creon, are you not? hoping
   Without support or friends to get a throne?
   Thrones may be won or bought: you could do neither.   30
CREON: Now listen to me. You have talked; let me talk, too.
   You cannot judge unless you know the facts.
OEDIPUS: You speak well: there is one fact; but I find it hard
   To learn from the deadliest enemy I have.
CREON: That above all I must dispute with you.   35
OEDIPUS: That above all I will not hear you deny.
CREON: If you think there is anything good in being stubborn
   Against all reason, then I say you are wrong.
OEDIPUS: If you think a man can sin against his own kind
   And not be punished for it, I say you are mad.   40
CREON: I agree. But tell me: what have I done to you?
OEDIPUS: You advised me to send for that wizard, did you not?
CREON: I did. I should do it again.
OEDIPUS: Very well. Now tell me:
   How long has it been since Laïos—
CREON: What of Laïos?
OEDIPUS: Since he vanished in that onset by the road?   45
CREON: It was long ago, a long time.
OEDIPUS: .   And this prophet,
   Was he practicing here then?
CREON: He was; and with honor, as now.
OEDIPUS: Did he speak of me at that time?
CREON: He never did;
   At least, not when I was present.

OEDIPUS: But . . . the enquiry?
   I suppose you held one?
CREON: We did, but we learned nothing.   50
OEDIPUS: Why did the prophet not speak against me then?
CREON: I do not know; and I am the kind of man
   Who holds his tongue when he has no facts to go on.
OEDIPUS: There's one fact that you know, and you could tell it.
CREON: What fact is that? If I know it, you shall have it.   55
OEDIPUS: If he were not involved with you, he could not say
   That it was I who murdered Laïos.
CREON: If he says that, you are the one that knows it!—
   But now it is my turn to question you.
OEDIPUS: Put your questions. I am no murderer.   60
CREON: First, then: You married my sister?
OEDIPUS: I married your sister.
CREON: And you rule the kingdom equally with her?
OEDIPUS: Everything that she wants she has from me.
CREON: And I am the third, equal to both of you?
OEDIPUS: That is why I call you a bad friend.   65
CREON: No. Reason it out, as I have done.
   Think of this first. Would any sane man prefer
   Power, with all a king's anxieties,
   To that same power and the grace of sleep?
   Certainly not I.   70
   I have never longed for the king's power—only his rights.
   Would any wise man differ from me in this?
   As matters stand, I have my way in everything
   With your consent, and no responsibilities.
   If I were king, I should be a slave to policy.   75
   How could I desire a scepter more
   Than what is now mine—untroubled influence?
   No, I have not gone mad; I need no honors,
   Except those with the perquisites I have now.
   I am welcome everywhere; every man salutes me,   80
   And those who want your favor seek my ear,
   Since I know how to manage what they ask.
   Should I exchange this ease for that anxiety?
   Besides, no sober mind is treasonable.
   I hate anarchy   85
   And never would deal with any man who likes it.

   Test what I have said. Go to the priestess
   At Delphi, ask if I quoted her correctly.
   And as for this other thing: if I am found
   Guilty of treason with Teiresias,   90
   Then sentence me to death! You have my word
   It is a sentence I should cast my vote for—

But not without evidence!

                  You do wrong

When you take good men for bad, bad men for good.

A true friend thrown aside—why, life itself   95

Is not more precious!

                  In time you will know this well:

For time, and time alone, will show the just man,

Though scoundrels are discovered in a day.

CHORAGOS: This is well said, and a prudent man would ponder it.

    Judgments too quickly formed are dangerous.   100

OEDIPUS: But is he not quick in his duplicity?

    And shall I not be quick to parry him?

    Would you have me stand still, hold my peace, and let

    This man win everything, through my inaction?

CREON: And you want—what is it, then? To banish me?   105

OEDIPUS: No, not exile. It is your death I want,

    So that all the world may see what treason means.

CREON: You will persist, then? You will not believe me?

OEDIPUS: How can I believe you?

CREON: Then you are a fool.

OEDIPUS: To save myself?

CREON: In justice, think of me.   110

OEDIPUS: You are evil incarnate.

CREON: But suppose that you are wrong?

OEDIPUS: Still I must rule.

CREON: But not if you rule badly.

OEDIPUS: O city, city!

CREON: It is my city, too!

CHORAGOS: Now, my lords, be still. I see the Queen,

    Iocastê, coming from her palace chambers;

    And it is time she came, for the sake of you both.   115

    This dreadful quarrel can be resolved through her.

Enter IOCASTÊ.

IOCASTÊ: Poor foolish men, what wicked din is this?

    With Thebes sick to death, is it not shameful

    That you should rake some private quarrel up?   120

              (*To* OEDIPUS.)

Come into the house.

              —And you, Creon, go now:

Let us have no more of this tumult over nothing.

CREON: Nothing? No, sister: what your husband plans for me

    Is one of two great evils: exile or death.

OEDIPUS: He is right.

            Why, woman, I have caught him squarely   125

    Plotting against my life.

CREON: No! Let me die
   Accurst if ever I have wished you harm!
IOCASTÊ: Ah, believe it, Oedipus!
   In the name of the gods, respect this oath of his
   For my sake, for the sake of these people here!   130

Strophe 1

CHORAGOS: Open your mind to her, my lord. Be ruled by her, I beg you!
OEDIPUS: What would you have me do?
CHORAGOS: Respect Creon's word. He has never spoken like a fool,
   And now he has sworn an oath.
OEDIPUS: You know what you ask?
CHORAGOS: I do.
OEDIPUS: Speak on, then.
CHORAGOS: A friend so sworn should not be baited so,   135
   In blind malice, and without final proof.
OEDIPUS: You are aware, I hope, that what you say
   Means death for me, or exile at the least.

Strophe 2

CHORAGOS: No, I swear by Helios, first in Heaven!
   May I die friendless and accurst,   140
   The worst of deaths, if ever I meant that!
        It is the withering fields
           That hurt my sick heart:
      Must we bear all these ills,
              And now your bad blood as well?   145
OEDIPUS: Then let him go. And let me die, if I must,
   Or be driven by him in shame from the land of Thebes.
   It is your unhappiness, and not his talk,
   That touches me.
                   As for him—
   Wherever he is, I will hate him as long as I live.   150
CREON: Ugly in yielding, as you were ugly in rage!
   Natures like yours chiefly torment themselves.
OEDIPUS: Can you not go? Can you not leave me?
CREON: I can.
   You do not know me; but the city knows me,
   And in its eyes I am just, if not in yours.   155

                   (*Exit* CREON.)

Antistrophe 1

CHORAGOS: Lady Iocastê, did you not ask the King
   to go to his chambers?

IOCASTÊ: First tell me what has happened.

CHORAGOS: There was suspicion without evidence; yet it rankled
　As even false charges will.

IOCASTÊ:　　　　　　　　　On both sides?

CHORAGOS:　　　　　　　　　　　　On both.

IOCASTÊ:　　　　　　　　　　　　But what was said?

CHORAGOS: Oh let it rest, let it be done with!　　　　　　　　　　160
　Have we not suffered enough?

OEDIPUS: You see to what your decency has brought you:
　You have made difficulties where my heart saw none.

Antistrophe 2

CHORAGOS: Oedipus, it is not once only I have told you—
　You must know I should count myself unwise　　　　　　　　　165
　To the point of madness, should I now forsake you—
　　　You, under whose hand,
　　　　In the storm of another time,
　　　Our dear land sailed out free.
　　　　But now stand fast at the helm!　　　　　　　　　　170

IOCASTÊ: In God's name, Oedipus, inform your wife as well:
　Why are you so set in this hard anger?

OEDIPUS: I will tell you, for none of these men deserves
　My confidence as you do. It is Creon's work,
　His treachery, his plotting against me.　　　　　　　　　175

IOCASTÊ: Go on, if you can make this clear to me.

OEDIPUS: He charges me with the murder of Laïos.

IOCASTÊ: Has he some knowledge? Or does he speak from hearsay?

OEDIPUS: He would not commit himself to such a charge,
　But he has brought in that damnable soothsayer　　　　　　　180
　To tell his story.

IOCASTÊ:　　　　　Set your mind at rest.
　If it is a question of soothsayers, I tell you
　That you will find no man whose craft gives knowledge
　Of the unknowable.

　　　　　　　　　Here is my proof:

An oracle was reported to Laïos once　　　　　　　　　185
(I will not say from Phoibos himself, but from
His appointed ministers, at any rate)
That his doom would be death at the hands of his own son—
His son, born of his flesh and of mine!

Now, you remember the story: Laïos was killed　　　　　　　190
By marauding strangers where three highways meet;
But his child had not been three days in this world

Before the King had pierced the baby's ankles
And left him to die on a lonely mountainside.

Thus, Apollo never caused that child   195
To kill his father, and it was not Laïos' fate
To die at the hands of his son, as he had feared.
This is what prophets and prophecies are worth!
Have no dread of them.
                              It is God himself
Who can show us what he wills, in his own way.   200
OEDIPUS: How strange a shadowy memory crossed my mind,
  Just now while you were speaking; it chilled my heart.
IOCASTÊ: What do you mean? What memory do you speak of?
OEDIPUS: If I understand you, Laïos was killed
  At a place where three roads meet.
IOCASTÊ: So it was said;   205
  We have no later story.
OEDIPUS: Where did it happen?
IOCASTÊ: Phokis, it is called: at a place where the Theban Way
  Divides into the roads towards Delphi and Daulia.
OEDIPUS: When?
IOCASTÊ: We had the news not long before you came
  And proved the right to your succession here.   210
OEDIPUS: Ah, what net has God been weaving for me?
IOCASTÊ: Oedipus! Why does this trouble you?
OEDIPUS: Do not ask me yet.
  First, tell me how Laïos looked, and tell me
  How old he was.
IOCASTÊ: He was tall, his hair just touched
  With white; his form was not unlike your own.   215
OEDIPUS: I think that I myself may be accurst
  By my own ignorant edict.
IOCASTÊ: You speak strangely.
  It makes me tremble to look at you, my King.
OEDIPUS: I am not sure that the blind man cannot see.
  But I should know better if you were to tell me—   220
IOCASTÊ: Anything—though I dread to hear you ask it.
OEDIPUS: Was the King lightly escorted, or did he ride
  With a large company, as a ruler should?
IOCASTÊ: There were five men with him in all: one was a herald;
  And a single chariot, which he was driving.   225
OEDIPUS: Alas, that makes it plain enough!
                                  But who—
  Who told you how it happened?
IOCASTÊ: A household servant,
  The only one to escape.
OEDIPUS: And is he still

A servant of ours?

IOCASTÊ: No; for when he came back at last
  And found you enthroned in the place of the dead king,   230
  He came to me, touched my hand with his, and begged
  That I would send him away to the frontier district
  Where only the shepherds go—
  As far away from the city as I could send him.
  I granted his prayer; for although the man was a slave,   235
  He had earned more than this favor at my hands.

OEDIPUS: Can he be called back quickly?

IOCASTÊ: Easily.
  But why?

OEDIPUS: I have taken too much upon myself
  Without enquiry; therefore I wish to consult him.

IOCASTÊ: Then he shall come.

                              But am I not one also   240
  To whom you might confide these fears of yours!

OEDIPUS: That is your right; it will not be denied you,
  Now least of all; for I have reached a pitch
  Of wild foreboding. Is there anyone
  To whom I should sooner speak?   245
  Polybos of Corinth is my father.
  My mother is a Dorian: Meropê.
  I grew up chief among the men of Corinth
  Until a strange thing happened—
  Not worth my passion, it may be, but strange.   250

  At a feast, a drunken man maundering in his cups
  Cries out that I am not my father's son!
  I contained myself that night, though I felt anger
  And a sinking heart. The next day I visited
  My father and mother, and questioned them. They stormed,   255
  Calling it all the slanderous rant of a fool;
  And this relieved me. Yet the suspicion
  Remained always aching in my mind;
  I knew there was talk; I could not rest;
  And finally, saying nothing to my parents,   260
  I went to the shrine at Delphi.
  The god dismissed my question without reply;
  He spoke of other things.

                              Some were clear,
  Full of wretchedness, dreadful, unbearable:
  As, that I should lie with my own mother, breed   265
  Children from whom all men would turn their eyes;
  And that I should be my father's murderer.

  I heard all this, and fled. And from that day
  Corinth to me was only in the stars

Descending in that quarter of the sky,   270
As I wandered farther and farther on my way
To a land where I should never see the evil
Sung by the oracle. And I came to this country
Where, so you say, King Laïos was killed.
I will tell you all that happened there, my lady.   275

There were three highways
Coming together at a place I passed;
And there a herald came towards me, and a chariot
Drawn by horses, with a man such as you describe
Seated in it. The groom leading the horses   280
Forced me off the road at his lord's command;
But as this charioteer lurched over towards me
I struck him in my rage. The old man saw me
And brought his double goad down upon my head
As I came abreast.
                    He was paid back, and more!   285
Swinging my club in this right hand I knocked him
Out of his car, and he rolled on the ground.
                              I killed him.

I killed them all.
Now if that stranger and Laïos were—kin,
Where is a man more miserable than I?   290
More hated by the gods? Citizen and alien alike
Must never shelter me or speak to me—
I must be shunned by all.
                        And I myself
Pronounced this malediction upon myself!

Think of it: I have touched you with these hands,   295
These hands that killed your husband. What defilement!

Am I all evil, then? It must be so,
Since I must flee from Thebes, yet never again
See my own countrymen, my own country,
For fear of joining my mother in marriage   300
And killing Polybos, my father.
                              Ah,
If I was created so, born to this fate,
Who could deny the savagery of God?

O holy majesty of heavenly powers!
May I never see that day! Never!   305
Rather let me vanish from the race of men
Than know the abomination destined me!
CHORAGOS: We too, my lord, have felt dismay at this.

But there is hope: you have yet to hear the shepherd.
OEDIPUS: Indeed, I fear no other hope is left me.   310
IOCASTÊ: What do you hope from him when he comes?
OEDIPUS: This much:
   If his account of the murder tallies with yours,
   Then I am cleared.
IOCASTÊ: What was it that I said
   Of such importance?
OEDIPUS: Why, "marauders," you said,
   Killed the King, according to this man's story.   315
   If he maintains that still, if there were several,
   Clearly the guilt is not mine: I was alone.
   But if he says one man, singlehanded, did it,
   Then the evidence all points to me.
IOCASTÊ: You may be sure that he said there were several;   320
   And can he call back that story now? He cannot.
   The whole city heard it as plainly as I.
   But suppose he alters some detail of it:
   He cannot ever show that Laïos' death
   Fulfilled the oracle: for Apollo said   325
   My child was doomed to kill him; and my child—
   Poor baby!—it was my child that died first.

   No. From now on, where oracles are concerned,
   I would not waste a second thought on any.
OEDIPUS: You may be right.
                              But come: let someone go   330
   For the shepherd at once. This matter must be settled.
IOCASTÊ: I will send for him.
   I would not wish to cross you in anything,
   And surely not in this.—Let us go in.

                    Exeunt into the palace.

                         ODE II

Strophe 1

CHORUS: Let me be reverent in the ways of right,
   Lowly the paths I journey on;
   Let all my words and actions keep
   The laws of the pure universe
   From highest Heaven handed down.   5
   For Heaven is their bright nurse,
   Those generations of the realms of light;
   Ah, never of mortal kind were they begot,

Nor are they slaves of memory, lost in sleep:
Their Father is greater than Time, and ages not.   10

Antistrophe 1

The tyrant is a child of Pride
Who drinks from his great sickening cup
Recklessness and vanity,
Until from his high crest headlong
He plummets to the dust of hope.   15
That strong man is not strong.
But let no fair ambition be denied;
May God protect the wrestler for the State
In government, in comely policy,
Who will fear God, and on His ordinance wait.   20

Strophe 2

Haughtiness and the high hand of disdain
Tempt and outrage God's holy law;
And any mortal who dares hold
No immortal Power in awe
Will be caught up in a net of pain: 25
The price for which his levity is sold.
Let each man take due earnings, then,
And keep his hands from holy things,
And from blasphemy stand apart—
Else the crackling blast of heaven   30
Blows on his head, and on his desperate heart;
Though fools will honor impious men,
In their cities no tragic poet sings.

Antistrophe 2

Shall we lose faith in Delphi's obscurities,
We who have heard the world's core   35
Discredited, and the sacred wood
Of Zeus at Elis praised no more?
The deeds and the strange prophecies
Must make a pattern yet to be understood.
Zeus, if indeed you are lord of all,   40
Throned in light over night and day,
Mirror this in your endless mind:
Our masters call the oracle
Words on the wind, and the Delphic vision blind!
Their hearts no longer know Apollo,   45
And reverence for the gods has died away.

SCENE III

Enter IOCASTÊ.

IOCASTÊ: Princes of Thebes, it has occurred to me
  To visit the altars of the gods, bearing
  These branches as a suppliant, and this incense.
  Our King is not himself: his noble soul
  Is overwrought with fantasies of dread,   5
  Else he would consider
  The new prophecies in the light of the old.
  He will listen to any voice that speaks disaster,
  And my advice goes for nothing.

She approaches the altar, right.

                         To you, then, Apollo,
  Lycean lord, since you are nearest, I turn in prayer.   10
  Receive these offerings, and grant us deliverance
  From defilement. Our hearts are heavy with fear
  When we see our leader distracted, as helpless sailors
  Are terrified by the confusion of their helmsman.

Enter MESSENGER.

MESSENGER: Friends, no doubt you can direct me: 15
  Where shall I find the house of Oedipus,
  Or, better still, where is the King himself?
CHORAGOS: It is this very place, stranger; he is inside.
  This is his wife and mother of his children.
MESSENGER: I wish her happiness in a happy house,   20
  Blest in all the fulfillment of her marriage.
IOCASTÊ: I wish as much for you: your courtesy
  Deserves a like good fortune. But now, tell me:
  Why have you come? What have you to say to us?
MESSENGER: Good news, my lady, for your house and your husband.   25
IOCASTÊ: What news? Who sent you here?
MESSENGER: I am from Corinth.
  The news I bring ought to mean joy for you,
  Though it may be you will find some grief in it.
IOCASTÊ: What is it? How can it touch us in both ways?
MESSENGER: The people of Corinth, they say,   30
  Intend to call Oedipus to be their king.
IOCASTÊ: But old Polybos—is he not reigning still?
MESSENGER: No. Death holds him in his sepulchre.
IOCASTÊ: What are you saying? Polybos is dead?
MESSENGER: If I am not telling the truth, may I die myself.   35
IOCASTÊ (*to a* MAIDSERVANT): Go in, go quickly; tell this to your master.

O riddlers of God's will, where are you now!
This was the man whom Oedipus, long ago,
Feared so, fled so, in dread of destroying him—
But it was another fate by which he died.   40

Enter OEDIPUS, *center.*

OEDIPUS: Dearest Iocastê, why have you sent for me?

IOCASTÊ: Listen to what this man says, and then tell me
What has become of the solemn prophecies.

OEDIPUS: Who is this man? What is his news for me?

IOCASTÊ: He has come from Corinth to announce your father's death!   45

OEDIPUS: Is it true, stranger? Tell me in your own words.

MESSENGER: I cannot say it more clearly: the King is dead.

OEDIPUS: Was it by treason? Or by an attack of illness?

MESSENGER: A little thing brings old men to their rest.

OEDIPUS: It was sickness, then?

MESSENGER: Yes, and his many years.   50

OEDIPUS: Ah!
Why should a man respect the Pythian hearth,° or
Give heed to the birds that jangle above his head?
They prophesied that I should kill Polybos,
Kill my own father; but he is dead and buried,   55
And I am here—I never touched him, never,
Unless he died in grief for my departure,
And thus, in a sense, through me. No. Polybos
Has packed the oracles off with him underground.
They are empty words.

IOCASTÊ: Had I not told you so?   60

OEDIPUS: You had; it was my faint heart that betrayed me.

IOCASTÊ: From now on never think of those things again.

OEDIPUS: And yet—must I not fear my mother's bed?

IOCASTÊ: Why should anyone in this world be afraid,
Since Fate rules us and nothing can be foreseen?   65
A man should live only for the present day.
Have no more fear of sleeping with your mother:
How many men, in dreams, have lain with their mothers!
No reasonable man is troubled by such things.

OEDIPUS: That is true; only—   70
If only my mother were not still alive!
But she is alive. I cannot help my dread.

IOCASTÊ: Yet this news of your father's death is wonderful.

OEDIPUS: Wonderful. But I fear the living woman.

MESSENGER: Tell me, who is this woman that you fear?   75

OEDIPUS: It is Meropê, man; the wife of King Polybos.

MESSENGER: Meropê? Why should you be afraid of her?

---

[52] **Pythian hearth**   *Delphi, also called Pytho because a large dragon, the Python, had guarded the chasm at Delphi until Apollo killed it and established his oracle on the site.*

OEDIPUS: An oracle of the gods, a dreadful saying.

MESSENGER: Can you tell me about it or are you sworn to silence?

OEDIPUS: I can tell you, and I will.   80

    Apollo said through his prophet that I was the man

    Who should marry his own mother, shed his father's blood

    With his own hands. And so, for all these years

    I have kept clear of Corinth, and no harm has come—

    Though it would have been sweet to see my parents again.   85

MESSENGER: And is this the fear that drove you out of Corinth?

OEDIPUS: Would you have me kill my father?

MESSENGER: As for that

    You must be reassured by the news I gave you.

OEDIPUS: If you could reassure me, I would reward you.

MESSENGER: I had that in mind, I will confess: I thought   90

    I could count on you when you returned to Corinth.

OEDIPUS: No: I will never go near my parents again.

MESSENGER: Ah, son, you still do not know what you are doing—

OEDIPUS: What do you mean? In the name of God tell me!

MESSENGER: —If these are your reasons for not going home.   95

OEDIPUS: I tell you, I fear the oracle may come true.

MESSENGER: And guilt may come upon you through your parents?

OEDIPUS: That is the dread that is always in my heart.

MESSENGER: Can you not see that all your fears are groundless?

OEDIPUS: How can you say that? They are my parents, surely?   100

MESSENGER: Polybos was not your father.

OEDIPUS: Not my father?

MESSENGER: No more your father than the man speaking to you.

OEDIPUS: But you are nothing to me!

MESSENGER: Neither was he.

OEDIPUS: Then why did he call me son?

MESSENGER: I will tell you:

    Long ago he had you from my hands, as a gift.   105

OEDIPUS: Then how could he love me so, if I was not his?

MESSENGER: He had no children, and his heart turned to you.

OEDIPUS: What of you? Did you buy me? Did you find me by chance?

MESSENGER: I came upon you in the crooked pass of Kithairon.

OEDIPUS: And what were you doing there?

MESSENGER: Tending my flocks.   110

OEDIPUS: A wandering shepherd?

MESSENGER: But your savior, son, that day.

OEDIPUS: From what did you save me?

MESSENGER: Your ankles should tell you that.

OEDIPUS: Ah, stranger, why do you speak of that childhood pain?

MESSENGER: I cut the bonds that tied your ankles together.

OEDIPUS: I have had the mark as long as I can remember.   115

MESSENGER: That was why you were given the name you bear.°

116**name you bear**   *"Oedipus" means "swollen-foot."*

OEDIPUS: God! Was it my father or my mother who did it?
　Tell me!

MESSENGER: I do not know. The man who gave you to me
　Can tell you better than I.   120

OEDIPUS: It was not you that found me, but another?

MESSENGER: It was another shepherd gave you to me.

OEDIPUS: Who was he? Can you tell me who he was?

MESSENGER: I think he was said to be one of Laïos' people.

OEDIPUS: You mean the Laïos who was king here years ago?   125

MESSENGER: Yes; King Laïos; and the man was one of his herdsmen.

OEDIPUS: Is he still alive? Can I see him?

MESSENGER:　　　　　　　　　　　These men here
　Know best about such things.

OEDIPUS:　　　　　　　　　　Does anyone here
　Know this shepherd that he is talking about?
　Have you seen him in the fields, or in the town?
　If you have, tell me. It is time things were made plain.   130

CHORAGOS: I think the man he means is that same shepherd
　You have already asked to see. Iocastê perhaps
　Could tell you something.

OEDIPUS:　　　　　　　　　　Do you know anything
　About him, Lady? Is he the man we have summoned?   135
　Is that the man this shepherd means?

IOCASTÊ:　　　　　　　　　　Why think of him?
　Forget this herdsman. Forget it all.
　This talk is a waste of time.

OEDIPUS:　　　　　　　　　　How can you say that,
　When the clues to my true birth are in my hands?

IOCASTÊ: For God's love, let us have no more questioning!   140
　Is your life nothing to you?
　My own is pain enough for me to bear.

OEDIPUS: You need not worry. Suppose my mother a slave,
　And born of slaves: no baseness can touch you.

IOCASTÊ: Listen to me, I beg you: do not do this thing!   145

OEDIPUS: I will not listen; the truth must be made known.

IOCASTÊ: Everything that I say is for your own good!

OEDIPUS:　　　　　　　　　　　　My own good
　Snaps my patience, then: I want none of it.

IOCASTÊ: You are fatally wrong! May you never learn who you are!

OEDIPUS: Go, one of you, and bring the shepherd here.   150
　Let us leave this woman to brag of her royal name.

IOCASTÊ: Ah, miserable!
　That is the only word I have for you now.
　That is the only word I can ever have.

Exit into the palace.

CHORAGOS: Why has she left us, Oedipus? Why has she gone   155
　In such a passion of sorrow? I fear this silence:

Something dreadful may come of it.

OEDIPUS: Let it come!
  However base my birth, I must know about it.
  The Queen, like a woman, is perhaps ashamed
  To think of my low origin. But I   160
  Am a child of luck; I cannot be dishonored.
  Luck is my mother; the passing months, my brothers,
  Have seen me rich and poor.
                              If this is so,
  How could I wish that I were someone else?
  How could I not be glad to know my birth?   165

ODE III

Strophe

CHORUS: If ever the coming time were known
  To my heart's pondering,
  Kithairon, now by Heaven I see the torches
  At the festival of the next full moon,
  And see the dance, and hear the choir sing   5
  A grace to your gentle shade:
  Mountain where Oedipus was found,
  O mountain guard of a noble race!
  May the god who heals us lend his aid,
  And let that glory come to pass   10
  For our king's cradling-ground.

Antistrophe

  Of the nymphs that flower beyond the years,
  Who bore you, royal child,
  To Pan of the hills or the timberline Apollo,
  Cold in delight where the upland clears,   15
  Or Hermês for whom Kyllenê's heights° are piled?
  Or flushed as evening cloud,
  Great Dionysos, roamer of mountains,
  He—was it he who found you there,
  And caught you up in his own proud   20
  Arms from the sweet god-ravisher
  Who laughed by the Muses' fountains?

SCENE IV

OEDIPUS: Sirs: though I do not know the man,
  I think I see him coming, this shepherd we want:

---

[16] **Kyllenê's heights**   *holy mountain, birthplace of Hermes, messenger of the gods.*

He is old, like our friend here, and the men
Bringing him seem to be servants of my house.
But you can tell, if you have ever seen him.   5

Enter SHEPHERD *escorted by servants.*

CHORAGOS: I know him, he was Laïos' man. You can trust him.

OEDIPUS: Tell me first, you from Corinth: is this the shepherd
  We were discussing?

MESSENGER: This is the very man.

OEDIPUS (*to* SHEPHERD): Come here. No, look at me. You must answer
  Everything I ask.—You belonged to Laïos?   10

SHEPHERD: Yes: born his slave, brought up in his house.

OEDIPUS: Tell me: what kind of work did you do for him?

SHEPHERD: I was a shepherd of his, most of my life.

OEDIPUS: Where mainly did you go for pasturage?

SHEPHERD: Sometimes Kithairon, sometimes the hills near-by.   15

OEDIPUS: Do you remember ever seeing this man out there?

SHEPHERD: What would he be doing there? This man?

OEDIPUS: This man standing here. Have you ever seen him before?

SHEPHERD: No. At least, not to my recollection.

MESSENGER: And that is not strange, my lord. But I'll refresh   20
  His memory: he must remember when we two
  Spent three whole seasons together, March to September,
  On Kithairon or thereabouts. He had two flocks;
  I had one. Each autumn I'd drive mine home
  And he would go back with his to Laïos' sheepfold.—   25
  Is this not true, just as I have described it?

SHEPHERD: True, yes; but it was all so long ago.

MESSENGER: Well, then: do you remember, back in those days
  That you gave me a baby boy to bring up as my own?

SHEPHERD: What if I did? What are you trying to say?   30

MESSENGER: King Oedipus was once that little child.

SHEPHERD: Damn you, hold your tongue!

OEDIPUS: No more of that!
  It is your tongue needs watching, not this man's.

SHEPHERD: My King, my Master, what is it I have done wrong?

OEDIPUS: You have not answered his question about the boy.   35

SHEPHERD: He does not know . . . He is only making trouble . . .

OEDIPUS: Come, speak plainly, or it will go hard with you.

SHEPHERD: In God's name, do not torture an old man!

OEDIPUS: Come here, one of you; bind his arms behind him.

SHEPHERD: Unhappy king! What more do you wish to learn?   40

OEDIPUS: Did you give this man the child he speaks of?

SHEPHERD: I did.
  And I would to God I had died that very day.

OEDIPUS: You will die now unless you speak the truth.

SHEPHERD: Yet if I speak the truth, I am worse than dead.

OEDIPUS: Very well; since you insist upon delaying—   45

SHEPHERD: No! I have told you already that I gave him the boy.

OEDIPUS: Where did you get him? From your house?
    From somewhere else?

SHEPHERD: Not from mine, no. A man gave him to me.

OEDIPUS: Is that man here? Do you know whose slave he was?

SHEPHERD: For God's love, my King, do not ask me any more!   50

OEDIPUS: You are a dead man if I have to ask you again.

SHEPHERD: Then . . . Then the child was from the palace of Laïos.

OEDIPUS: A slave child? or a child of his own line?

SHEPHERD: Ah, I am on the brink of dreadful speech!

OEDIPUS: And I of dreadful hearing. Yet I must hear.   55

SHEPHERD: If you must be told, then . . .
                              They said it was Laïos' child,
    But it is your wife who can tell you about that.

OEDIPUS: My wife!—Did she give it to you?

SHEPHERD: My lord, she did.

OEDIPUS: Do you know why?

SHEPHERD: I was told to get rid of it.

OEDIPUS: An unspeakable mother!

SHEPHERD: There had been prophecies . . .   60

OEDIPUS: Tell me.

SHEPHERD: It was said that the boy would kill his own father.

OEDIPUS: Then why did you give him over to this old man?

SHEPHERD: I pitied the baby, my King.
    And I thought that this man would take him far away
    To his own country.
                    He saved him—but for what a fate!   65
    For if you are what this man says you are,
    No man living is more wretched than Oedipus.

OEDIPUS: Ah God!
    It was true!
              All the prophecies!
                    —Now,
    O Light, may I look on you for the last time!   70
    I, Oedipus,
    Oedipus, damned in his birth, in his marriage damned,
    Damned in the blood he shed with his own hand!

                    He rushes into the palace.

                              ODE IV

Strophe 1

CHORUS: Alas for the seed of men.
    What measure shall I give these generations

That breathe on the void and are void
And exist and do not exist?

Who bears more weight of joy 5
Than mass of sunlight shifting in images,
Or who shall make his thought stay on
That down time drifts away?

Your splendor is all fallen.

O naked brow of wrath and tears, 10
O change of Oedipus!
I who saw your days call no man blest—
Your great days like ghósts góne.

Antistrophe 1

That mind was a strong bow.
Deep, how deep you drew it then, hard archer, 15
At a dim fearful range,
And brought dear glory down!

You overcame the stranger—
The virgin with her hooking lion claws—
And though death sang, stood like a tower 20
To make pale Thebes take heart.

Fortress against our sorrow!

Divine king, giver of laws,
Majestic Oedipus!
No prince in Thebes had ever such renown, 25
No prince won such grace of power.

Strophe 2

And now of all men ever known
Most pitiful is this man's story:
His fortunes are most changed, his state
Fallen to a low slave's 30
Ground under bitter fate.

O Oedipus, most royal one!
The great door that expelled you to the light
Gave at night—ah, gave night to your glory:
As to the father, to the fathering son. 35

All understood too late.

How could that queen whom Laïos won,
The garden that he harrowed at his height,
Be silent when that act was done?

Antistrophe 2

But all eyes fail before time's eye,   40
All actions come to justice there.
Though never willed, though far down the deep past,
Your bed, your dread sirings,
Are brought to book at last.
Child by Laïos doomed to die,   45
Then doomed to lose that fortunate little death,
Would God you never took breath in this air
That with my wailing lips I take to cry:

For I weep the world's outcast.

I was blind, and now I can tell why: 50
Asleep, for you had given ease of breath
To Thebes, while the false years went by.

EXODOS

Enter, from the palace, SECOND MESSENGER.

SECOND MESSENGER: Elders of Thebes, most honored in this land,
    What horrors are yours to see and hear, what weight
    Of sorrow to be endured, if, true to your birth,
    You venerate the line of Labdakos!
    I think neither Istros nor Phasis, those great rivers,   5
    Could purify this place of the corruption
    It shelters now, or soon must bring to light—
    Evil not done unconsciously, but willed.

    The greatest griefs are those we cause ourselves.
CHORAGOS: Surely, friend, we have grief enough already;   10
    What new sorrow do you mean?
SECOND MESSENGER: The Queen is dead.
CHORAGOS: Iocastê? Dead? But at whose hand?
SECOND MESSENGER: Her own.
    The full horror of what happened you cannot know,
    For you did not see it; but I, who did, will tell you
    As clearly as I can how she met her death.   15

When she had left us,
In passionate silence, passing through the court,
She ran to her apartment in the house,
Her hair clutched by the fingers of both hands.
She closed the doors behind her; then, by that bed   20
Where long ago the fatal son was conceived—
That son who should bring about his father's death—
We heard her call upon Laïos, dead so many years,
And heard her wail for the double fruit of her marriage,
A husband by her husband, children by her child.   25

Exactly how she died I do not know:
For Oedipus burst in moaning and would not let us
Keep vigil to the end: it was by him
As he stormed about the room that our eyes were caught.
From one to another of us he went, begging a sword,   30
Cursing the wife who was not his wife, the mother
Whose womb had carried his own children and himself.
I do not know: it was none of us aided him,
But surely one of the gods was in control!
For with a dreadful cry   35
He hurled his weight, as though wrenched out of himself,
At the twin doors: the bolts gave, and he rushed in.
And there we saw her hanging, her body swaying
From the cruel cord she had noosed about her neck.
A great sob broke from him heartbreaking to hear,   40
As he loosed the rope and lowered her to the ground.

I would blot out from my mind what happened next!
For the King ripped from her gown the golden brooches
That were her ornament, and raised them, and plunged them down
Straight into his own eyeballs, crying, "No more,   45
No more shall you look on the misery about me,
The horrors of my own doing! Too long you have known
The faces of those whom I should never have seen,
Too long been blind to those for whom I was searching!
From this hour, go in darkness!" And as he spoke,   50
He struck at his eyes—not once, but many times;
And the blood spattered his beard,
Bursting from his ruined sockets like red hail.

So from the unhappiness of two this evil has sprung,
A curse on the man and woman alike. The old   55
Happiness of the house of Labdakos
Was happiness enough: where is it today?
It is all wailing and ruin, disgrace, death—all
The misery of mankind that has a name—

And it is wholly and for ever theirs.   60

CHORAGOS: Is he in agony still? Is there no rest for him?

SECOND MESSENGER: He is calling for someone to lead him to the gates
So that all the children of Kadmos may look upon
His father's murderer, his mother's—no,
I cannot say it!
             And then he will leave Thebes,   65
Self-exiled, in order that the curse
Which he himself pronounced may depart from the house.
He is weak, and there is none to lead him,
So terrible is his suffering.
      But you will see:
Look, the doors are opening; in a moment   70
You will see a thing that would crush a heart of stone.

        The central door is opened; OEDIPUS, *blinded, is led in.*

CHORAGOS: Dreadful indeed for men to see.
    Never have my own eyes
    Looked on a sight so full of fear.

    Oedipus!   75
    What madness came upon you, what daemon
    Leaped on your life with heavier
    Punishment than a mortal man can bear?
    No: I cannot even
    Look at you, poor ruined one.   80
    And I would speak, question, ponder,
    If I were able. No.
    You make me shudder.

OEDIPUS: God. God.
    Is there a sorrow greater?   85
    Where shall I find harbor in this world?
    My voice is hurled far on a dark wind.
    What has God done to me?

CHORAGOS: Too terrible to think of, or to see.

Strophe 1

OEDIPUS: O cloud of night,   90
    Never to be turned away: night coming on,
    I cannot tell how: night like a shroud!
    My fair winds brought me here.
                Oh God. Again
    The pain of the spikes where I had sight,
    The flooding pain   95
    Of memory, never to be gouged out.

CHORAGOS: This is not strange.

You suffer it all twice over, remorse in pain,
Pain in remorse.

Antistrophe 1

OEDIPUS: Ah dear friend   100
  Are you faithful even yet, you alone?
  Are you still standing near me, will you stay here,
  Patient, to care for the blind?
                              The blind man!
  Yet even blind I know who it is attends me,
  By the voice's tone—   105
  Though my new darkness hide the comforter.
CHORAGOS: Oh fearful act!
  What god was it drove you to rake black
  Night across your eyes?

Strophe 2

OEDIPUS: Apollo. Apollo. Dear   110
  Children, the god was Apollo.
  He brought my sick, sick fate upon me.
  But the blinding hand was my own!
  How could I bear to see
  When all my sight was horror everywhere?   115
CHORAGOS: Everywhere; that is true.
OEDIPUS: And now what is left?
  Images? Love? A greeting even,
  Sweet to the senses? Is there anything?
  Ah, no, friends: lead me away.   120
  Lead me away from Thebes.
                              Lead the great wreck
  And hell of Oedipus, whom the gods hate.
CHORAGOS: Your fate is clear, you are not blind to that.
  Would God you had never found it out!

Antistrophe 2

OEDIPUS: Death take the man who unbound   125
  My feet on that hillside
  And delivered me from death to life! What life?
  If only I had died,
  This weight of monstrous doom
  Could not have dragged me and my darlings down.   130
CHORAGOS: I would have wished the same.
OEDIPUS: Oh never to have come here
  With my father's blood upon me! Never

To have been the man they call his mother's husband!
Oh accurst! Oh child of evil,
To have entered that wretched bed—   135
        the selfsame one!
More primal than sin itself, this fell to me.
CHORAGOS: I do not know how I can answer you.
 You were better dead than alive and blind.
OEDIPUS: Do not counsel me any more. This punishment   140
 That I have laid upon myself is just.
 If I had eyes,
 I do not know how I could bear the sight
 Of my father, when I came to the house of Death,
 Or my mother: for I have sinned against them both   145
 So vilely that I could not make my peace
 By strangling my own life.
      Or do you think my children,
 Born as they were born, would be sweet to my eyes?
 Ah never, never! Nor this town with its high walls,
 Nor the holy images of the gods.
       For I,   150
 Thrice miserable—Oedipus, noblest of all the line
 Of Kadmos, have condemned myself to enjoy
 These things no more, by my own malediction
 Expelling that man whom the gods declared
 To be a defilement in the house of Laïos.   155
 After exposing the rankness of my own guilt,
 How could I look men frankly in the eyes?
 No, I swear it,
 If I could have stifled my hearing at its source,
 I would have done it and made all this body   160
 A tight cell of misery, blank to light and sound:
 So I should have been safe in a dark agony
 Beyond all recollection.
     Ah Kithairon!
 Why did you shelter me? When I was cast upon you,
 Why did I not die? Then I should never   165
 Have shown the world my execrable birth.

 Ah Polybos! Corinth, city that I believed
 The ancient seat of my ancestors: how fair
 I seemed, your child! And all the while this evil
 Was cancerous within me!
      For I am sick   170
 In my daily life, sick in my origin.

 O three roads, dark ravine, woodland and way
 Where three roads met you, drinking my father's blood,

My own blood, spilled by my own hand: can you remember
The unspeakable things I did there, and the things 175
I went on from there to do?

O marriage, marriage!

The act that engendered me, and again the act
Performed by the son in the same bed—

Ah, the net

Of incest, mingling fathers, brothers, sons,
With brides, wives, mothers: the last evil 180
That can be known by men: no tongue can say
How evil!

No. For the love of God, conceal me

Somewhere far from Thebes; or kill me; or hurl me
Into the sea, away from men's eyes for ever.
Come, lead me. You need not fear to touch me. 185
Of all men, I alone can bear this guilt.

Enter CREON.

CHORAGOS: We are not the ones to decide; but Creon here
    May fitly judge of what you ask. He only
    Is left to protect the city in your place.
OEDIPUS: Alas, how can I speak to him? What right have I 190
    To beg his courtesy whom I have deeply wronged?
CREON: I have not come to mock you, Oedipus,
    Or to reproach you, either.

(*To* ATTENDANTS.)

—You, standing there:

If you have lost all respect for man's dignity,
At least respect the flame of Lord Helios: 195
Do not allow this pollution to show itself
Openly here, an affront to the earth
And Heaven's rain and the light of day. No, take him
Into the house as quickly as you can.
For it is proper 200
That only the close kindred see his grief.
OEDIPUS: I pray you in God's name, since your courtesy
    Ignores my dark expectation, visiting
    With mercy this man of all men most execrable:
    Give me what I ask—for your good, not for mine. 205
CREON: And what is it that you would have me do?
OEDIPUS: Drive me out of this country as quickly as may be
    To a place where no human voice can ever greet me.
CREON: I should have done that before now—only,
    God's will had not been wholly revealed to me. 210
OEDIPUS: But his command is plain: the parricide
    Must be destroyed. I am that evil man.

CREON: That is the sense of it, yes; but as things are,
  We had best discover clearly what is to be done.
OEDIPUS: You would learn more about a man like me?   215
CREON: You are ready now to listen to the god.
OEDIPUS: I will listen. But it is to you
  That I must turn for help. I beg you, hear me.

The woman in there—
Give her whatever funeral you think proper: 220
She is your sister.
               —But let me go, Creon!
Let me purge my father's Thebes of the pollution
Of my living here, and go out to the wild hills,
To Kithairon, that has won such fame with me,
The tomb my mother and father appointed for me,   225
And let me die there, as they willed I should.
And yet I know
Death will not ever come to me through sickness
Or in any natural way: I have been preserved
For some unthinkable fate. But let that be.   230
As for my sons, you need not care for them.
They are men, they will find some way to live.
But my poor daughters, who have shared my table,
Who never before have been parted from their father—
Take care of them, Creon; do this for me.   235
And will you let me touch them with my hands
A last time, and let us weep together?
Be kind, my lord,
Great prince, be kind!
              Could I but touch them,
They would be mine again, as when I had my eyes.   240

        Enter ANTIGONÊ *and* ISMENÊ, *attended.*

Ah, God!
Is it my dearest children I hear weeping?
Has Creon pitied me and sent my daughters?
CREON: Yes, Oedipus: I knew that they were dear to you
  In the old days, and know you must love them still.   245
OEDIPUS: May God bless you for this—and be a friendlier
  Guardian to you than he has been to me!

Children, where are you?
Come quickly to my hands: they are your brother's—
Hands that have brought your father's once clear eyes   250
To this way of seeing—
             Ah dearest ones,
I had neither sight nor knowledge then, your father

By the woman who was the source of his own life!
And I weep for you—having no strength to see you—,
I weep for you when I think of the bitterness   255
That men will visit upon you all your lives.
What homes, what festivals can you attend
Without being forced to depart again in tears?
And when you come to marriageable age,
Where is the man, my daughters, who would dare   260
Risk the bane that lies on all my children?
Is there any evil wanting? Your father killed
His father; sowed the womb of her who bore him;
Engendered you at the fount of his own existence!
That is what they will say of you.

                            Then, whom   265
Can you ever marry? There are no bridegrooms for you,
And your lives must wither away in sterile dreaming.
O Creon, son of Menoikeus!
You are the only father my daughters have,
Since we, their parents, are both of us gone for ever.   270
They are your own blood: you will not let them
Fall into beggary and loneliness;
You will keep them from the miseries that are mine!
Take pity on them; see, they are only children,
Friendless except for you. Promise me this,   275
Great Prince, and give me your hand in token of it.

           CREON *clasps his right hand.*

Children:
I could say much, if you could understand me,
But as it is, I have only this prayer for you:
Live where you can, be as happy as you can—   280
Happier, please God, than God has made your father!

CREON: Enough. You have wept enough. Now go within.

OEDIPUS: I must; but it is hard.

CREON: Time eases all things.

OEDIPUS: But you must promise—

CREON: Say what you desire.

OEDIPUS: Send me from Thebes!

CREON: God grant that I may!   285

OEDIPUS: But since God hates me . . .

CREON: No, he will grant your wish.

OEDIPUS: You promise?

CREON: I cannot speak beyond my knowledge.

OEDIPUS: Then lead me in.

CREON: Come now, and leave your children.

OEDIPUS: No! Do not take them from me!

CREON: Think no longer

That you are in command here, but rather think   290
How, when you were, you served your own destruction.

Exeunt into the house all but the CHORUS; *the* CHORAGOS *chants directly to the audience.*

CHORAGOS: Men of Thebes: look upon Oedipus.
This is the king who solved the famous riddle
And towered up, most powerful of men
No mortal eyes but looked on him with envy.   295
Yet in the end ruin swept over him.

Let every man in mankind's frailty
Consider his last day; and let none
Presume on his good fortune until he find
Life, at his death, a memory without pain.   300

(*c. 430 B.C.*)

QUESTIONS FOR REFLECTION

Experience

1. Describe your experience of reading *Oedipus Rex*. Were you surprised? Baffled? Horrified—at any point? If so, where and why?

Interpretation

2. What makes Oedipus a tragic hero? What makes his predicament fascinating rather than merely horrifying? Account for the continued appeal of the play.
3. Identify and explain the different types of irony in *Oedipus Rex*. (For a discussion of irony see pages 93–95.)
4. How is the imagery of light and darkness employed throughout the play? How is it related to Oedipus' blindness?
5. What roles do the chorus and choragos assume? Compare their functions in the beginning, middle, and end of the play.
6. Rather than dramatize on stage the shocking and horrible events in which the play culminates, Sophocles has them occur offstage, and we learn about them through a messenger's report. What are the limitations and advantages of such a method?
7. Iocastê appears a number of times, but she has little to say. What is she like? How much do we know about her—especially her thoughts and feelings?

Evaluation

8. Evaluate Oedipus's actions. Is he to blame for what happens? Account for his change of attitude and manner by comparing his speech and behavior in the opening and closing scenes.

Readers will be able to understand *Antigonê* more fully if they understand the background of Polyneicês' death. After Oedipus exiled himself from

Thebes (see the conclusion of *Oedipus Rex*), his two sons, Eteoclês and Polyneicês, shared the rule of Thebes. Although they originally agreed to reign in alternate years, Eteoclês refused to step down when his allotted time had passed. Polyneicês, with the help of the king of Argos, attempted to remove Eteoclês from the throne. In the attack on Thebes, the brothers killed one another. Creon assumed the throne and declared that Eteoclês should be buried with full honors. Because Polyneicês had attacked his native city, his body was to be shamefully left lying where he fell.

The stage directions for *Antigonê* are simple, stating that the play begins at dawn in front of the palace in Thebes. Antigonê and Ismenê enter from the palace, engaged in a conversation that clearly establishes their relationship and the conflicts between them. Tension builds slowly; Antigonê and Creon do not come face to face until Scene II, with the clash between law (represented by Creon) and justice (represented by Antigonê) constituting one of the play's primary themes.

Antigonê

AN ENGLISH VERSION BY DUDLEY FITTS AND ROBERT FITZGERALD

CHARACTERS

ANTIGONÊ
ISMENÊ
EURYDICÊ
CREON
HAIMON
TEIRESIAS
A SENTRY
A MESSENGER
CHORUS

Scene. *Before the palace of* CREON, *King of Thebes. A central double door, and two lateral doors. A platform extends the length of the façade, and from this platform three steps lead down into the "orchestra," or chorus-ground.*
Time. *Dawn of the day after the repulse of the Argive army from the assault on Thebes.*

PROLOGUE

ANTIGONÊ *and* ISMENÊ *enter from the central door of the palace.*

ANTIGONÊ: Ismenê, dear sister,
  You would think that we had already suffered enough

For the curse on Oedipus.°
I cannot imagine any grief
That you and I have not gone through. And now—   5
Have they told you of the new decree of our King Creon?
ISMENÊ: I have heard nothing: I know
That two sisters lost two brothers, a double death
In a single hour; and I know that the Argive army
Fled in the night; but beyond this, nothing.   10
ANTIGONÊ: I thought so. And that is why I wanted you
To come out here with me. There is something we must do.
ISMENÊ: Why do you speak so strangely?
ANTIGONÊ: Listen, Ismenê:
Creon buried our brother Eteoclês   15
With military honors, gave him a soldier's funeral,
And it was right that he should; but Polyneicês,
Who fought as bravely and died as miserably—
They say that Creon has sworn
No one shall bury him, no one mourn for him,   20
But his body must lie in the fields, a sweet treasure
For carrion birds to find as they search for food.
That is what they say, and our good Creon is coming here
To announce it publicly; and the penalty—
Stoning to death in the public square!
                                        There it is,   25
And now you can prove what you are:
A true sister, or a traitor to your family.
ISMENÊ: Antigonê, you are mad! What could I possibly do?
ANTIGONÊ: You must decide whether you will help me or not.
ISMENÊ: I do not understand you. Help you in what?   30
ANTIGONÊ: Ismenê, I am going to bury him. Will you come?
ISMENÊ: Bury him! You have just said the new law forbids it.
ANTIGONÊ: He is my brother. And he is your brother, too.
ISMENÊ: But think of the danger! Think what Creon will do!
ANTIGONÊ: Creon is not strong enough to stand in my way.   35
ISMENÊ: Ah sister!
Oedipus died, everyone hating him
For what his own search brought to light, his eyes
Ripped out by his own hand; and Iocastê died,
His mother and wife at once: she twisted the cords   40
That strangled her life; and our two brothers died,
Each killed by the other's sword. And we are left:
But oh, Antigonê,
Think how much more terrible than these

---

[3] **Oedipus**   *former King of Thebes, father of Antigonê and Ismenê, and of Polyneicês and Eteoclês, their brothers. Oedipus unwittingly killed his father, Laïos, and married his mother, Iocastê. When he learned what he had done, he blinded himself and left Thebes. Eteoclês and Polyneicês quarreled; Polyneicês was defeated but returned to assault Thebes. Both brothers were killed in the battle; Creon ordered that Polyneicês remain unburied.*

Our own death would be if we should go against Creon   45
And do what he has forbidden! We are only women,
We cannot fight with men, Antigonê!
The law is strong, we must give in to the law
In this thing, and in worse. I beg the Dead
To forgive me, but I am helpless: I must yield   50
To those in authority. And I think it is dangerous business
To be always meddling.

ANTIGONÊ: If that is what you think,
   I should not want you, even if you asked to come.
   You have made your choice, you can be what you want to be.
   But I will bury him; and if I must die,   55
   I say that this crime is holy: I shall lie down
   With him in death, and I shall be as dear
   To him as he to me.
                          It is the dead,
   Not the living, who make the longest demands:
   We die for ever . . .
                          You may do as you like,   60
   Since apparently the laws of the gods mean nothing to you.

ISMENÊ: They mean a great deal to me; but I have no strength
   To break laws that were made for the public good.

ANTIGONÊ: That must be your excuse, I suppose. But as for me,
   I will bury the brother I love.

ISMENÊ: Antigonê,   65
   I am so afraid for you!

ANTIGONÊ: You need not be:
   You have yourself to consider, after all.

ISMENÊ: But no one must hear of this, you must tell no one!
   I will keep it a secret, I promise!

ANTIGONÊ: O tell it! Tell everyone!
   Think how they'll hate you when it all comes out   70
   If they learn that you knew about it all the time!

ISMENÊ: So fiery! You should be cold with fear.

ANTIGONÊ: Perhaps. But I am doing only what I must.

ISMENÊ: But can you do it? I say that you cannot.

ANTIGONÊ: Very well: when my strength gives out,
   I shall do no more.   75

ISMENÊ: Impossible things should not be tried at all.

ANTIGONÊ: Go away, Ismenê:
   I shall be hating you soon, and the dead will too,
   For your words are hateful. Leave me my foolish plan:
   I am not afraid of the danger; if it means death,   80
   It will not be the worst of deaths—death without honor.

ISMENÊ: Go then, if you feel that you must.
   You are unwise,
   But a loyal friend indeed to those who love you.

Exit into the palace. ANTIGONÊ *goes off, left. Enter the* CHORUS.

PÁRODOS

Strophe 1

CHORUS: Now the long blade of the sun, lying
    Level east to west, touches with glory
    Thebes of the Seven Gates. Open, unlidded
    Eye of golden day! O marching light
    Across the eddy and rush of Dircê's stream,°   5
    Striking the white shields of the enemy
    Thrown headlong backward from the blaze of morning!
CHORAGOS:°   Polyneicês their commander
    Roused them with windy phrases,
    He the wild eagle screaming
    Insults above our land,   10
    His wings their shields of snow,
    His crest their marshalled helms.

Antistrophe 1

CHORUS: Against our seven gates in a yawning ring
    The famished spears came onward in the night;
    But before his jaws were sated with our blood,   15
    Or pinefire took the garland of our towers,
    He was thrown back; and as he turned, great Thebes—
    No tender victim for his noisy power—
    Rose like a dragon behind him, shouting war.   20
CHORAGOS: For God hates utterly
    The bray of bragging tongues;
    And when he beheld their smiling,
    Their swagger of golden helms,
    The frown of his thunder blasted   25
    Their first man from our walls.

Strophe 2

CHORUS: We heard his shout of triumph high in the air
    Turn to a scream; far out in a flaming arc
    He fell with his windy torch, and the earth struck him.
    And others storming in fury no less than his   30
    Found shock of death in the dusty joy of battle.
CHORAGOS: Seven captains at seven gates

---

⁵**Dircê's stream** *river near Thebes.*   ⁸**Choragos** *leader of the chorus.*

Yielded their clanging arms to the god
That bends the battle-line and breaks it.
These two only, brothers in blood,   35
Face to face in matchless rage,
Mirroring each the other's death,
Clashed in long combat.

Antistrophe 2

CHORUS: But now in the beautiful morning of victory
Let Thebes of the many chariots sing for joy!   40
With hearts for dancing we'll take leave of war:
Our temples shall be sweet with hymns of praise,
And the long nights shall echo with our chorus.

SCENE I

CHORAGOS: But now at last our new King is coming:
Creon of Thebes, Menoikeus' son.
In this auspicious dawn of his reign
What are the new complexities
That shifting Fate has woven for him?   5
What is his counsel? Why has he summoned
The old men to hear him?

Enter CREON *from the palace, center. He addresses the* CHORUS *from the top step.*

CREON: Gentlemen: I have the honor to inform you that our Ship of State, which
recent storms have threatened to destroy, has come safely to harbor at last, guided   10
by the merciful wisdom of Heaven. I have summoned you here this morning
because I know that I can depend upon you: your devotion to King Laïos was
absolute; you never hesitated in your duty to our late ruler Oedipus; and when
Oedipus died, your loyalty was transferred to his children. Unfortunately, as you
know, his two sons, the princes Eteoclês and Polyneicês, have killed each other   15
in battle; and I, as the next in blood, have succeeded to the full power of the
throne.

I am aware, of course, that no Ruler can expect complete loyalty from his
subjects until he has been tested in office. Nevertheless, I say to you at the very
outset that I have nothing but contempt for the kind of Governor who is afraid,   20
for whatever reason, to follow the course that he knows is best for the State; and
as for the man who sets private friendship above the public welfare,—I have no
use for him, either. I call God to witness that if I saw my country headed for
ruin, I should not be afraid to speak out plainly; and I need hardly remind you
that I would never have any dealings with an enemy of the people. No one   25
values friendship more highly than I; but we must remember that friends made
at the risk of wrecking our Ship are not real friends at all.

These are my principles, at any rate, and that is why I have made the following
decision concerning the sons of Oedipus: Eteoclês, who died as a man should die,   30
fighting for his country, is to be buried with full military honors, with all the
ceremony that is usual when the greatest heroes die; but his brother Polyneicês,
who broke his exile to come back with fire and sword against his native city and
the shrines of his fathers' gods, whose one idea was to spill the blood of his blood
and sell his own people into slavery—Polyneicês, I say, is to have no burial: no man   35
is to touch him or say the least prayer for him; he shall lie on the plain, unburied;
and the birds and the scavenging dogs can do with him whatever they like.

This is my command, and you can see the wisdom behind it. As long as I am   40
King, no traitor is going to be honored with the loyal man. But whoever shows
by word and deed that he is on the side of the State,—he shall have my respect
while he is living and my reverence when he is dead.

CHORAGOS: If that is your will, Creon son of Menoikeus,
You have the right to enforce it: we are yours.   45
CREON: That is my will. Take care that you do your part.
CHORAGOS: We are old men: let the younger ones carry it out.
CREON: I do not mean that: the sentries have been appointed.
CHORAGOS: Then what is it that you would have us do?
CREON: You will give no support to whoever breaks this law.   50
CHORAGOS: Only a crazy man is in love with death!
CREON: And death it is; yet money talks, and the wisest
Have sometimes been known to count a few coins too many.

Enter SENTRY *from left.*

SENTRY: I'll not say that I'm out of breath from running, King, because every time
I stopped to think about what I have to tell you, I felt like going back. And all   55
the time a voice kept saying, "You fool, don't you know you're walking straight
into trouble?"; and then another voice: "Yes, but if you let somebody else get the
news to Creon first, it will be even worse than that for you!" But good sense
won out, at least I hope it was good sense, and here I am with a story that makes
no sense at all; but I'll tell it anyhow, because, as they say, what's going to
happen's going to happen and—
CREON: Come to the point. What have you to say?
SENTRY: I did not do it. I did not see who did it. You must not punish me for
what someone else has done.   65
CREON: A comprehensive defense! More effective, perhaps,
If I knew its purpose. Come: what is it?
SENTRY: A dreadful thing . . . I don't know how to put it—
CREON: Out with it!
SENTRY: Well, then;
The dead man—
Polyneicês—

Pause. The SENTRY *is overcome, fumbles for words.* CREON *waits impassively.*

out there—
someone,—   70

New dust on the slimy flesh!

Pause. No sign from CREON.

Someone has given it burial that way, and
Gone . . .

Long pause. CREON *finally speaks with deadly control.*

CREON: And the man who dared do this?
SENTRY: I swear I
  Do not know! You must believe me!   75
    Listen:
  The ground was dry, not a sign of digging, no,
  Not a wheeltrack in the dust, no trace of anyone.
  It was when they relieved us this morning: and one of them,
  The corporal, pointed to it.
                  There it was,
  The strangest—
          Look: 80
  The body, just mounded over with light dust: you see?
  Not buried really, but as if they'd covered it
  Just enough for the ghost's peace. And no sign
  Of dogs or any wild animal that had been there.
  And then what a scene there was! Every man of us   85
  Accusing the other: we all proved the other man did it,
  We all had proof that we could not have done it.
  We were ready to take hot iron in our hands,
  Walk through fire, swear by all the gods,
  It was not I!   90
  I do not know who it was, but it was not I!

CREON's *rage has been mounting steadily, but the* SENTRY *is too intent upon his story to notice it.*

  And then, when this came to nothing, someone said
  A thing that silenced us and made us stare
  Down at the ground: you had to be told the news,
  And one of us had to do it! We threw the dice,   95
  And the bad luck fell to me. So here I am,
  No happier to be here than you are to have me:
  Nobody likes the man who brings bad news.
CHORAGOS: I have been wondering, King: can it be that the gods have
  done this?
CREON (*furiously*): Stop!   100
  Must you doddering wrecks
  Go out of your heads entirely? "The gods"!
  Intolerable!
  The gods favor this corpse? Why? How had he served them?
  Tried to loot their temples, burn their images,   105

Yes, and the whole State, and its laws with it!
Is it your senile opinion that the gods love to honor bad men?
A pious thought!—

                   No, from the very beginning
There have been those who have whispered together,
Stiff-necked anarchists, putting their heads together,   110
Scheming against me in alleys. These are the men,
And they have bribed my own guard to do this thing.
(*Sententiously.*) Money!
There's nothing in the world so demoralizing as money.
Down go your cities,   115
Homes gone, men gone, honest hearts corrupted,
Crookedness of all kinds, and all for money!

                        (*To* SENTRY.)

                              But you—!
I swear by God and by the throne of God,
The man who has done this thing shall pay for it!
Find that man, bring him here to me, or your death   120
Will be the least of your problems: I'll string you up
Alive, and there will be certain ways to make you
Discover your employer before you die;
And the process may teach you a lesson you seem to have missed:
The dearest profit is sometimes all too dear: 125
That depends on the source. Do you understand me?
A fortune won is often misfortune.
SENTRY: King, may I speak?
CREON: Your very voice distresses me.
SENTRY: Are you sure that it is my voice, and not your conscience?
CREON: By God, he wants to analyze me now!   130
SENTRY: It is not what I say, but what has been done, that hurts you.
CREON: You talk too much.
SENTRY: Maybe; but I've done nothing.
CREON: Sold your soul for some silver: that's all you've done.
SENTRY: How dreadful it is when the right judge judges wrong!
CREON: Your figures of speech   135
May entertain you now; but unless you bring me the man,
You will get little profit from them in the end.

              Exit CREON *into the palace.*

SENTRY: "Bring me the man"—!
I'd like nothing better than bringing him the man!
But bring him or not, you have seen the last of me here.   140
At any rate, I am safe!

(*Exit* SENTRY.)

ODE I

Strophe 1

CHORUS: Numberless are the world's wonders, but none
   More wonderful than man; the stormgray sea
   Yields to his prows, the huge crests bear him high;
   Earth, holy and inexhaustible, is graven
   With shining furrows where his plows have gone   5
   Year after year, the timeless labor of stallions.

Antistrophe 1

   The lightboned birds and beasts that cling to cover,
   The lithe fish lighting their reaches of dim water,
   All are taken, tamed in the net of his mind;
   The lion on the hill, the wild horse windy-maned,   10
   Resign to him; and his blunt yoke has broken
   The sultry shoulders of the mountain bull.

Strophe 2

   Words also, and thought as rapid as air,
   He fashions to his good use; statecraft is his,
   And his the skill that deflects the arrows of snow,   15
   The spears of winter rain: from every wind
   He has made himself secure—from all but one:
   In the late wind of death he cannot stand.

Antistrophe 2

   O clear intelligence, force beyond all measure!
   O fate of man, working both good and evil!   20
   When the laws are kept, how proudly his city stands!
   When the laws are broken, what of his city then?
   Never may the anárchic man find rest at my hearth,
   Never be it said that my thoughts are his thoughts.

SCENE II

Reenter SENTRY *leading* ANTIGONÊ.

CHORAGOS: What does this mean? Surely this captive woman
    Is the Princess, Antigonê. Why should she be taken?
SENTRY: Here is the one who did it! We caught her
    In the very act of burying him.—Where is Creon?
CHORAGOS: Just coming from the house.

Enter CREON, *center.*

CREON: What has happened?   5
    Why have you come back so soon?
SENTRY (*expansively*):   O King,
    A man should never be too sure of anything:
    I would have sworn
    That you'd not see me here again: your anger
    Frightened me so, and the things you threatened me with;   10
    But how could I tell then
    That I'd be able to solve the case so soon?
    No dice-throwing this time: I was only too glad to come!
    Here is this woman. She is the guilty one:
    We found her trying to bury him.   15
    Take her, then; question her; judge her as you will.
    I am through with the whole thing now, and glad of it.
CREON: But this is Antigonê! Why have you brought her here?
SENTRY: She was burying him, I tell you!
CREON (*severely*):   Is this the truth?
SENTRY: I saw her with my own eyes. Can I say more?   20
CREON: The details: come, tell me quickly!
SENTRY: It was like this:
    After those terrible threats of yours, King,
    We went back and brushed the dust away from the body.
    The flesh was soft by now, and stinking,
    So we sat on a hill to windward and kept guard.   25
    No napping this time! We kept each other awake.
    But nothing happened until the white round sun
    Whirled in the center of the round sky over us:
    Then, suddenly,
    A storm of dust roared up from the earth, and the sky   30
    Went out, the plain vanished with all its trees
    In the stinging dark. We closed our eyes and endured it.
    The whirlwind lasted a long time, but it passed;
    And then we looked, and there was Antigonê!
    I have seen   35
    A mother bird come back to a stripped nest, heard

Her crying bitterly a broken note or two
For the young ones stolen. Just so, when this girl
Found the bare corpse, and all her love's work wasted,
She wept, and cried on heaven to damn the hands   40
That had done this thing.
     And then she brought more dust
And sprinkled wine three times for her brother's ghost.

We ran and took her at once. She was not afraid,
Not even when we charged her with what she had done.
She denied nothing.
     And this was a comfort to me,   45
And some uneasiness: for it is a good thing
To escape from death, but it is no great pleasure
To bring death to a friend.
     Yet I always say
There is nothing so comfortable as your own safe skin!
CREON (*slowly, dangerously*): And you, Antigonê,   50
 You with your head hanging,—do you confess this thing?
ANTIGONÊ: I do. I deny nothing.
CREON (*to* SENTRY):   You may go.

     (*Exit* SENTRY.)

(*To* ANTIGONÊ.) Tell me, tell me briefly:
 Had you heard my proclamation touching this matter?
ANTIGONÊ: It was public. Could I help hearing it?   55
CREON: And yet you dared defy the law.
ANTIGONÊ: I dared.
 It was not God's proclamation. That final Justice
That rules the world below makes no such laws.

Your edict, King, was strong,
But all your strength is weakness itself against   60
The immortal unrecorded laws of God.
They are not merely now: they were, and shall be,
Operative for ever, beyond man utterly.

I knew I must die, even without your decree:
I am only mortal. And if I must die   65
Now, before it is my time to die,
Surely this is no hardship: can anyone
Living, as I live, with evil all about me,
Think Death less than a friend? This death of mine
Is of no importance; but if I had left my brother   70
Lying in death unburied, I should have suffered.
Now I do not.
   You smile at me. Ah Creon,

Think me a fool, if you like; but it may well be
That a fool convicts me of folly.

CHORAGOS: Like father, like daughter: both headstrong, deaf to reason!   75
    She has never learned to yield:

CREON: She has much to learn.
    The inflexible heart breaks first, the toughest iron
    Cracks first, and the wildest horses bend their necks
    At the pull of the smallest curb.

                                    Pride? In a slave?
    This girl is guilty of a double insolence,   80
    Breaking the given laws and boasting of it.
    Who is the man here,
    She or I, if this crime goes unpunished?
    Sister's child, or more than sister's child,
    Or closer yet in blood—she and her sister   85
    Win bitter death for this!

                        (*To* SERVANTS.)

                        Go, some of you,
    Arrest Ismenê. I accuse her equally.
    Bring her: you will find her sniffling in the house there.

    Her mind's a traitor: crimes kept in the dark
    Cry for light, and the guardian brain shudders;   90
    But how much worse than this
    Is brazen boasting of barefaced anarchy!

ANTIGONÊ: Creon, what more do you want than my death?

CREON: Nothing.
    That gives me everything.

ANTIGONÊ: Then I beg you: kill me.
    This talking is a great weariness: your words   95
    Are distasteful to me, and I am sure that mine
    Seem so to you. And yet they should not seem so:
    I should have praise and honor for what I have done.
    All these men here would praise me
    Were their lips not frozen shut with fear of you.   100
    (*Bitterly.*) Ah the good fortune of kings,
    Licensed to say and do whatever they please!

CREON: You are alone here in that opinion.

ANTIGONÊ: No, they are with me. But they keep their tongues in leash.

CREON: Maybe. But you are guilty, and they are not.   105

ANTIGONÊ: There is no guilt in reverence for the dead.

CREON: But Eteoclês—was he not your brother too?

ANTIGONÊ: My brother too.

CREON: And you insult his memory?

ANTIGONÊ (*softly*): The dead man would not say that I insult it.

CREON: He would: for you honor a traitor as much as him.   110

ANTIGONÊ: His own brother, traitor or not, and equal in blood.

CREON: He made war on his country. Eteoclês defended it.

ANTIGONÊ: Nevertheless, there are honors due all the dead.

CREON: But not the same for the wicked as for the just.

ANTIGONÊ: Ah Creon, Creon,   115

Which of us can say what the gods hold wicked?

CREON: An enemy is an enemy, even dead.

ANTIGONÊ: It is my nature to join in love, not hate.

CREON (*finally losing patience*): Go join them then; if you must have your love,

Find it in hell!   120

CHORAGOS: But see, Ismenê comes:

Enter ISMENÊ, *guarded*.

Those tears are sisterly, the cloud

That shadows her eyes rains down gentle sorrow.

CREON: You too, Ismenê,

Snake in my ordered house, sucking my blood   125

Stealthily—and all the time I never knew

That these two sisters were aiming at my throne!

                                    Ismenê,

Do you confess your share in this crime, or deny it?

Answer me.

ISMENÊ: Yes, if she will let me say so. I am guilty.   130

ANTIGONE (*coldly*): No, Ismenê. You have no right to say so.

You would not help me, and I will not have you help me.

ISMENÊ: But now I know what you meant; and I am here

To join you, to take my share of punishment.

ANTIGONÊ: The dead man and the gods who rule the dead   135

Know whose act this was. Words are not friends.

ISMENÊ: Do you refuse me, Antigonê? I want to die with you:

I too have a duty that I must discharge to the dead.

ANTIGONÊ: You shall not lessen my death by sharing it.

ISMENÊ: What do I care for life when you are dead?   140

ANTIGONÊ: Ask Creon. You're always hanging on his opinions.

ISMENÊ: You are laughing at me. Why, Antigonê?

ANTIGONÊ: It's a joyless laughter, Ismenê.

ISMENÊ: But can I do nothing?

ANTIGONÊ: Yes. Save yourself. I shall not envy you.

There are those who will praise you; I shall have honor, too. 145

ISMENÊ: But we are equally guilty!

ANTIGONÊ: No more, Ismenê.

You are alive, but I belong to Death.

CREON (*to the* CHORUS): Gentlemen, I beg you to observe these girls:

One has just now lost her mind; the other,

It seems, has never had a mind at all.   150

ISMENÊ: Grief teaches the steadiest minds to waver, King.

CREON: Yours certainly did, when you assumed guilt with the guilty!

ISMENÊ: But how could I go on living without her?
CREON: You are.
   She is already dead.
ISMENÊ: But your own son's bride!
CREON: There are places enough for him to push his plow.   155
   I want no wicked women for my sons!
ISMENÊ: O dearest Haimon, how your father wrongs you!
CREON: I've had enough of your childish talk of marriage!
CHORAGOS: Do you really intend to steal this girl from your son?
CREON: No; Death will do that for me.
CHORAGOS: Then she must die?   160
CREON (ironically): You dazzle me.
                       —But enough of this talk!
   (To GUARDS.) You, there, take them away and guard them well:
   For they are but women, and even brave men run
   When they see Death coming.

                    Exeunt ISMENÊ, ANTIGONÊ, and GUARDS.

                              ODE II

Strophe 1

CHORUS: Fortunate is the man who has never tasted God's vengeance!
   Where once the anger of heaven has struck, that house is shaken
   For ever: damnation rises behind each child
   Like a wave cresting out of the black northeast,
   When the long darkness under sea roars up   5
   And bursts drumming death upon the windwhipped sand.

Antistrophe 1

   I have seen this gathering sorrow from time long past
   Loom upon Oedipus' children: generation from generation
   Takes the compulsive rage of the enemy god.
   So lately this last flower of Oedipus' line   10
   Drank the sunlight! but now a passionate word
   And a handful of dust have closed up all its beauty.

Strophe 2

      What mortal arrogance
      Transcends the wrath of Zeus?
   Sleep cannot lull him nor the effortless long months   15
   Of the timeless gods: but he is young for ever,

And his house is the shining day of high Olympos.
>   All that is and shall be,
>   And all the past, is his.
No pride on earth is free of the curse of heaven.   20

Antistrophe 2

The straying dreams of men
>   May bring them ghosts of joy:
But as they drowse, the waking embers burn them;
Or they walk with fixed eyes, as blind men walk.
But the ancient wisdom speaks for our own time: 25
>   *Fate works most for woe*
>   *With Folly's fairest show.*
Man's little pleasure is the spring of sorrow.

SCENE III

CHORAGOS: But here is Haimon, King, the last of all your sons.
>   Is it grief for Antigonê that brings him here,
>   And bitterness at being robbed of his bride?

Enter HAIMON.

CREON: We shall soon see, and no need of diviners.
>   —Son,
>   You have heard my final judgment on that girl: 5
>   Have you come here hating me, or have you come
>   With deference and with love, whatever I do?
HAIMON: I am your son, father. You are my guide.
>   You make things clear for me, and I obey you.
>   No marriage means more to me than your continuing wisdom.   10
CREON: Good. That is the way to behave: subordinate
>   Everything else, my son, to your father's will.
>   This is what a man prays for, that he may get
>   Sons attentive and dutiful in his house,
>   Each one hating his father's enemies,   15
>   Honoring his father's friends. But if his sons
>   Fail him, if they turn out unprofitably,
>   What has he fathered but trouble for himself
>   And amusement for the malicious?
>   So you are right
>   Not to lose your head over this woman.   20
>   Your pleasure with her would soon grow cold, Haimon,
>   And then you'd have a hellcat in bed and elsewhere.

Let her find her husband in Hell!
Of all the people in this city, only she
Has had contempt for my law and broken it.   25

Do you want me to show myself weak before the people?
Or to break my sworn word? No, and I will not.
The woman dies.
I suppose she'll plead "family ties." Well, let her.
If I permit my own family to rebel,   30
How shall I earn the world's obedience?
Show me the man who keeps his house in hand,
He's fit for public authority.
                              I'll have no dealings
With lawbreakers, critics of the government:
Whoever is chosen to govern should be obeyed—   35
Must be obeyed, in all things, great and small,
Just and unjust! O Haimon,
The man who knows how to obey, and that man only,
Knows how to give commands when the time comes.
You can depend on him, no matter how fast   40
The spears come: he's a good soldier, he'll stick it out.

Anarchy, anarchy! Show me a greater evil!
This is why cities tumble and the great houses rain down,
This is what scatters armies!
No, no: good lives are made so by discipline.   45
We keep the laws then, and the lawmakers,
And no woman shall seduce us. If we must lose,
Let's lose to a man, at least! Is a woman stronger than we?
CHORAGOS: Unless time has rusted my wits,
What you say, King, is said with point and dignity.   50
HAIMON (*boyishly earnest*): Father:
Reason is God's crowning gift to man, and you are right
To warn me against losing mine. I cannot say—
I hope that I shall never want to say!—that you
Have reasoned badly. Yet there are other men   55
Who can reason, too; and their opinions might be helpful.
You are not in a position to know everything
That people say or do, or what they feel:
Your temper terrifies—everyone
Will tell you only what you like to hear.   60
But I, at any rate, can listen; and I have heard them
Muttering and whispering in the dark about this girl.
They say no woman has ever, so unreasonably,
Died so shameful a death for a generous act:
"She covered her brother's body. Is this indecent?   65
She kept him from dogs and vultures. Is this a crime?

Death?—She should have all the honor that we can give her!"

This is the way they talk out there in the city.

You must believe me:
Nothing is closer to me than your happiness.   70
What could be closer? Must not any son
Value his father's fortune as his father does his?
I beg you, do not be unchangeable:
Do not believe that you alone can be right.
The man who thinks that,   75
The man who maintains that only he has the power
To reason correctly, the gift to speak, the soul—
A man like that, when you know him, turns out empty.

It is not reason never to yield to reason!

In flood time you can see how some trees bend,   80
And because they bend, even their twigs are safe,
While stubborn trees are torn up, roots and all.
And the same thing happens in sailing:
Make your sheet fast, never slacken,—and over you go,
Head over heels and under: and there's your voyage.   85
Forget you are angry! Let yourself be moved!
I know I am young; but please let me say this:
The ideal condition
Would be, I admit, that men should be right by instinct;
But since we are all too likely to go astray,   90
The reasonable thing is to learn from those who can teach.
CHORAGOS: You will do well to listen to him, King,
    If what he says is sensible. And you, Haimon,
    Must listen to your father.—Both speak well.
CREON: You consider it right for a man of my years and experience   95
    To go to school to a boy?
HAIMON: It is not right
    If I am wrong. But if I am young, and right,
    What does my age matter?
CREON: You think it right to stand up for an anarchist?
HAIMON: Not at all. I pay no respect to criminals.   100
CREON: Then she is not a criminal?
HAIMON: The City would deny it, to a man.
CREON: And the City proposes to teach me how to rule?
HAIMON: Ah. Who is it that's talking like a boy now?
CREON: My voice is the one voice giving orders in this City!   105
HAIMON: It is no City if it takes orders from one voice.
CREON: The State is the King!
HAIMON: Yes, if the State is a desert.

Pause.

CREON: This boy, it seems, has sold out to a woman.

HAIMON: If you are a woman: my concern is only for you.

CREON: So? Your "concern"! In a public brawl with your father!   110

HAIMON: How about you, in a public brawl with justice?

CREON: With justice, when all that I do is within my rights?

HAIMON: You have no right to trample on God's right.

CREON (*completely out of control*): Fool, adolescent fool! Taken in
    by a woman!

HAIMON: You'll never see me taken in by anything vile.   115

CREON: Every word you say is for her!

HAIMON (*quietly, darkly*):   And for you.
    And for me. And for the gods under the earth.

CREON: You'll never marry her while she lives.

HAIMON: Then she must die.—But her death will cause another.

CREON: Another?   120
    Have you lost your senses? Is this an open threat?

HAIMON: There is no threat in speaking to emptiness.

CREON: I swear you'll regret this superior tone of yours!
    You are the empty one!

HAIMON: If you were not my father, I'd say you were
    perverse.   125

CREON: You girlstruck fool, don't play at words with me!

HAIMON: I am sorry. You prefer silence.

CREON: Now, by God—!
    I swear, by all the gods in heaven above us,
    You'll watch it, I swear you shall!

(*To the* SERVANTS.)

             Bring her out!
    Bring the woman out! Let her die before his eyes!   130
    Here, this instant, with her bridegroom beside her!

HAIMON: Not here, no; she will not die here, King.
    And you will never see my face again.
    Go on raving as long as you've a friend to endure you.

(*Exit* HAIMON.)

CHORAGOS: Gone, gone.
    Creon, a young man in a rage is dangerous!   135

CREON: Let him do, or dream to do, more than a man can.
    He shall not save these girls from death.

CHORAGOS: These girls?
    You have sentenced them both?

CREON: No, you are right.
    I will not kill the one whose hands are clean.   140

CHORAGOS: But Antigonê?

CREON (*somberly*):   I will carry her far away
    Out there in the wilderness, and lock her
    Living in a vault of stone. She shall have food,
    As the custom is, to absolve the State of her death.
    And there let her pray to the gods of hell: 145
    They are her only gods:
    Perhaps they will show her an escape from death,
    Or she may learn,
              though late,
    That piety shown the dead is pity in vain.

                (*Exit* CREON.)

ODE III

Strophe

CHORUS: Love, unconquerable
    Waster of rich men, keeper
    Of warm lights and all-night vigil
    In the soft face of a girl:
    Sea-wanderer, forest-visitor!   5
    Even the pure Immortals cannot escape you,
    And mortal man, in his one day's dusk,
    Trembles before your glory.

Antistrophe

    Surely you swerve upon ruin
    The just man's consenting heart,   10
    As here you have made bright anger
    Strike between father and son—
    And none has conquered but Love!
    A girl's glánce wórking the will of heaven:
    Pleasure to her alone who mocks us,   15
    Merciless Aphroditê.°

SCENE IV

CHORAGOS (*as* ANTIGONÊ *enters guarded*): But I can no longer stand
    in awe of this,
    Nor, seeing what I see, keep back my tears.

16 **Aphroditê**   *goddess of love.*

Here is Antigonê, passing to that chamber
Where all find sleep at last.

Strophe 1

ANTIGONÊ: Look upon me, friends, and pity me   5
  Turning back at the night's edge to say
  Good-by to the sun that shines for me no longer;
  Now sleepy Death
  Summons me down to Acheron,° that cold shore:
  There is no bridesong there, nor any music.   10
CHORUS: Yet not unpraised, not without a kind of honor,
  You walk at last into the underworld;
  Untouched by sickness, broken by no sword.
  What woman has ever found your way to death?

Antistrophe 1

ANTIGONÊ: How often I have heard the story of Niobê,   15
  Tantalos' wretched daughter, how the stone
  Clung fast about her, ivy-close: and they say
  The rain falls endlessly
  And sifting soft snow; her tears are never done.
  I feel the loneliness of her death in mine.   20
CHORUS: But she was born of heaven, and you
  Are woman, woman-born. If her death is yours,
  A mortal woman's, is this not for you
  Glory in our world and in the world beyond?

Strophe 2

ANTIGONÊ: You laugh at me. Ah, friends, friends,   25
  Can you not wait until I am dead? O Thebes,
  O men many-charioted, in love with Fortune,
  Dear springs of Dircê, sacred Theban grove,
  Be witnesses for me, denied all pity,
  Unjustly judged! and think a word of love   30
  For her whose path turns
  Under dark earth, where there are no more tears.
CHORUS: You have passed beyond human daring and come at last
  Into a place of stone where Justice sits.
  I cannot tell   35
  What shape of your father's guilt appears in this.

---

[9]*Acheron*   *a river of the underworld.*

Antistrophe 2

ANTIGONÊ: You have touched it at last: that bridal bed
    Unspeakable, horror of son and mother mingling:
    Their crime, infection of all our family!
    O Oedipus, father and brother!   40
    Your marriage strikes from the grave to murder mine.
    I have been a stranger here in my own land:
    All my life
    The blasphemy of my birth has followed me.
CHORUS: Reverence is a virtue, but strength   45
    Lives in established law: that must prevail.
    You have made your choice,
    Your death is the doing of your conscious hand.

Epode

ANTIGONÊ: Then let me go, since all your words are bitter,
    And the very light of the sun is cold to me.   50
    Lead me to my vigil, where I must have
    Neither love nor lamentation; no song, but silence.

        CREON *interrupts impatiently.*

CREON: If dirges and planned lamentations could put off death,
    Men would be singing for ever.

        (*To the* SERVANTS.)

        Take her, go!
    You know your orders: take her to the vault   55
    And leave her alone there. And if she lives or dies,
    That's her affair, not ours: our hands are clean.
ANTIGONÊ: O tomb, vaulted bride-bed in eternal rock,
    Soon I shall be with my own again
    Where Persephonê° welcomes the thin ghosts underground: 60
    And I shall see my father again, and you, mother,
    And dearest Polyneicês—
        dearest indeed
    To me, since it was my hand
    That washed him clean and poured the ritual wine:
    And my reward is death before my time!   65

    And yet, as men's hearts know, I have done no wrong,
    I have not sinned before God. Or if I have,
    I shall know the truth in death. But if the guilt
    Lies upon Creon who judged me, then, I pray,

---

60 **Persephonê**   *queen of the underworld.*

May his punishment equal my own.

CHORAGOS: O passionate heart,   70
   Unyielding, tormented still by the same winds!

CREON: Her guards shall have good cause to regret their delaying.

ANTIGONÊ: Ah! That voice is like the voice of death!

CREON: I can give you no reason to think you are mistaken.

ANTIGONÊ: Thebes, and you my fathers' gods,   75
   And rulers of Thebes, you see me now, the last
   Unhappy daughter of a line of kings,
   Your kings, led away to death. You will remember
   What things I suffer, and at what men's hands,
   Because I would not transgress the laws of heaven.   80
   (*To the* GUARDS, *simply.*) Come: let us wait no longer.

(*Exit* ANTIGONÊ, *left, guarded.*)

ODE IV

Strophe 1

CHORUS: All Danaê's beauty was locked away
   In a brazen cell where the sunlight could not come:
   A small room still as any grave, enclosed her.
   Yet she was a princess too,
   And Zeus in a rain of gold poured love upon her.   5
   O child, child,
   No power in wealth or war
   Or tough sea-blackened ships
   Can prevail against untiring Destiny!

Antistrophe 1

   And Dryas' son° also, that furious king,   10
   Bore the god's prisoning anger for his pride:
   Sealed up by Dionysos in deaf stone,
   His madness died among echoes.
   So at the last he learned what dreadful power
   His tongue had mocked: 15
   For he had profaned the revels,
   And fired the wrath of the nine
   Implacable Sisters° that love the sound of the flute.

Strophe 2

   And old men tell a half-remembered tale
   Of horror where a dark ledge splits the sea   20

---

[10] **Dryas' son**   *Lycurgus, King of Thrace.*   [18] **Implacable Sisters**   *the Muses.*

And a double surf beats on the gráy shóres:
How a king's new woman,° sick
With hatred for the queen he had imprisoned,
Ripped out his two sons' eyes with her bloody hands
While grinning Arês° watched the shuttle plunge   25
Four times: four blind wounds crying for revenge,

Antistrophe 2

Crying, tears and blood mingled.—Piteously born,
Those sons whose mother was of heavenly birth!
Her father was the god of the North Wind
And she was cradled by gales,   30
She raced with young colts on the glittering hills
And walked untrammeled in the open light:
But in her marriage deathless Fate found means
To build a tomb like yours for all her joy.

SCENE V

Enter blind TEIRESIAS, *led by a boy. The opening speeches of* TEIRESIAS *should be in singsong contrast to the realistic lines of* CREON.

TEIRESIAS: This is the way the blind man comes, Princes, Princes,
   Lock-step, two heads lit by the eyes of one.
CREON: What new thing have you to tell us, old Teiresias?
TEIRESIAS: I have much to tell you: listen to the prophet, Creon.
CREON: I am not aware that I have ever failed to listen.   5
TEIRESIAS: Then you have done wisely, King, and ruled well.
CREON: I admit my debt to you. But what have you to say?
TEIRESIAS: This, Creon: you stand once more on the edge of fate.
CREON: What do you mean? Your words are a kind of dread.
TEIRESIAS: Listen, Creon: 10
   I was sitting in my chair of augury, at the place
   Where the birds gather about me. They were all a-chatter,
   As is their habit, when suddenly I heard
   A strange note in their jangling, a scream, a
   Whirring fury; I knew that they were fighting,   15
   Tearing each other, dying
   In a whirlwind of wings clashing. And I was afraid.
   I began the rites of burnt-offering at the altar,
   But Hephaistos° failed me: instead of bright flame,
   There was only the sputtering slime of the fat thigh-flesh   20

---

²²**King's new woman** *Eidothea, second wife of King Phineas, blinded her stepsons after the King had imprisoned their mother in a cave.* ²⁵**Arês** *god of war.* ¹⁹**Hephaistos** *god of fire.*

Melting: the entrails dissolved in gray smoke,
The bare bone burst from the welter. And no blaze!
This was a sign from heaven. My boy described it,
Seeing for me as I see for others.

I tell you, Creon, yourself have brought   25
This new calamity upon us. Our hearths and altars
Are stained with the corruption of dogs and carrion birds
That glut themselves on the corpse of Oedipus' son.
The gods are deaf when we pray to them, their fire
Recoils from our offering, their birds of omen   30
Have no cry of comfort, for they are gorged
With the thick blood of the dead.
                            O my son,
These are no trifles! Think: all men make mistakes,
But a good man yields when he knows his course is wrong,
And repairs the evil. The only crime is pride.   35

Give in to the dead man, then: do not fight with a corpse—
What glory is it to kill a man who is dead?
Think, I beg you:
It is for your own good that I speak as I do.
You should be able to yield for your own good.   40
CREON: It seems that prophets have made me their especial province.
All my life long
I have been a kind of butt for the dull arrows
Of doddering fortune-tellers!
                    No, Teiresias:
If your birds—if the great eagles of God himself   45
Should carry him stinking bit by bit to heaven,
I would not yield. I am not afraid of pollution:
No man can defile the gods.
                  Do what you will,
Go into business, make money, speculate
In India gold or that synthetic gold from Sardis,   50
Get rich otherwise than by my consent to bury him.
Teiresias, it is a sorry thing when a wise man
Sells his wisdom, lets out his words for hire!
TEIRESIAS: Ah Creon! Is there no man left in the world—
CREON: To do what?—Come, let's have the aphorism!   55
TEIRESIAS: No man who knows that wisdom outweighs any wealth?
CREON: As surely as bribes are baser than any baseness.
TEIRESIAS: You are sick, Creon! You are deathly sick!
CREON: As you say: it is not my place to challenge a prophet.
TEIRESIAS: Yet you have said my prophecy is for sale.
CREON: The generation of prophets has always loved gold.   60
TEIRESIAS: The generation of kings has always loved brass.

CREON: You forget yourself! You are speaking to your King.

TEIRESIAS: I know it. You are a king because of me.

CREON: You have a certain skill; but you have sold out.   65

TEIRESIAS: King, you will drive me to words that—

CREON: Say them, say them!
    Only remember: I will not pay you for them.

TEIRESIAS: No, you will find them too costly.

CREON: No doubt. Speak:
    Whatever you say, you will not change my will.

TEIRESIAS: Then take this, and take it to heart!   70
    The time is not far off when you shall pay back
    Corpse for corpse, flesh of your own flesh.
    You have thrust the child of this world into living night,
    You have kept from the gods below the child that is theirs:
    The one in a grave before her death, the other,   75
    Dead, denied the grave. This is your crime:
    And the Furies and the dark gods of Hell
    Are swift with terrible punishment for you.

    Do you want to buy me now, Creon?
    Not many days,
    And your house will be full of men and women weeping,   80
    And curses will be hurled at you from far
    Cities grieving for sons unburied, left to rot
    Before the walls of Thebes.

    These are my arrows, Creon: they are all for you.

    (*To* BOY.) But come, child: lead me home.   85
    Let him waste his fine anger upon younger men.
    Maybe he will learn at last
    To control a wiser tongue in a better head.

                    (*Exit* TEIRESIAS.)

CHORAGOS: The old man has gone, King, but his words
    Remain to plague us. I am old, too,   90
    But I cannot remember that he was ever false.

CREON: That is true. . . . It troubles me.
    Oh it is hard to give in! but it is worse
    To risk everything for stubborn pride.

CHORAGOS: Creon: take my advice.

CREON: What shall I do?   95

CHORAGOS: Go quickly: free Antigonê from her vault
    And build a tomb for the body of Polyneicês.

CREON: You would have me do this!

CHORAGOS: Creon, yes!
    And it must be done at once: God moves

Swiftly to cancel the folly of stubborn men.   100
CREON: It is hard to deny the heart! But I
    Will do it: I will not fight with destiny.
CHORAGOS: You must go yourself, you cannot leave it to others.
CREON: I will go.
                —Bring axes, servants:
    Come with me to the tomb. I buried her. I   105
    Will set her free.
                    Oh quickly!
    My mind misgives—
    The laws of the gods are mighty, and a man must serve them
    To the last day of his life!

                    (*Exit* CREON.)

                    PAEAN°

Strophe 1

CHORAGOS: God of many names
CHORUS: O Iacchos°
                                son
    of Kadmeian Sémelê°
                    O born of the Thunder!
    Guardian of the West
                        Regent
    of Eleusis' plain
                O Prince of maenad° Thebes
    and the Dragon Field by rippling Ismenós.°   5

Antistrophe 1

CHORAGOS: God of many names
CHORUS: the flame of torches
    flares on our hills
                    the nymphs of Iacchos
    dance at the spring of Castalia.°
    from the vine-close mountain
                            come ah come in ivy:
    Evohé evohé! sings through the streets of Thebes   10

Paean *a hymn.*   [1]**Iacchos** *Bacchos or Dionysos, god of wine and revelry.*   [2]**Sémelê** *mother of Iacchos, consort of Zeus.*   [4]**maenad** *female worshipper, attendant of Iacchos.*   [5]**Ismenós** *a river near Thebes where, according to legend, dragon's teeth were sown from which sprang the ancestors of Thebes.*   [8]**Castalia** *a spring on Mount Parnasos.*

Strophe 2

CHORAGOS: God of many names
CHORUS: Iacchos of Thebes
   heavenly Child
               of Sémelê bride of the Thunderer!
   The shadow of plague is upon us:
                        come
   with clement feet
                oh come from Parnasos
   down the long slopes
              across the lamenting water   15

Antistrophe 2

CHORAGOS: Iô Fire! Chorister of the throbbing stars!
   O purest among the voices of the night!
   Thou son of God, blaze for us!
CHORUS: Come with choric rapture of circling Maenads
   Who cry *Iô Iacche!*
                 God of many names!   20

EXODOS

Enter MESSENGER *from left.*

MESSENGER: Men of the line of Kadmos,° you who live
   Near Amphion's citadel,°
                  I cannot say
Of any condition of human life "This is fixed,
This is clearly good, or bad." Fate raises up,
And Fate casts down the happy and unhappy alike: 5
No man can foretell his Fate.
                    Take the case of Creon:
Creon was happy once, as I count happiness:
Victorious in battle, sole governor of the land,
Fortunate father of children nobly born.
And now it has all gone from him! Who can say   10
That a man is still alive when his life's joy fails?
He is a walking dead man. Grant him rich,
Let him live like a king in his great house:
If his pleasure is gone, I would not give

---

¹**Kadmos**   *sowed the dragon's teeth; founded Thebes.*   ²**Amphion's citadel**   *Amphion's lyre playing charmed stones to form a wall around Thebes.*

So much as the shadow of smoke for all he owns.   15
CHORAGOS: Your words hint at sorrow: what is your news for us?
MESSENGER: They are dead. The living are guilty of their death.
CHORAGOS: Who is guilty? Who is dead? Speak!
MESSENGER: Haimon.
   Haimon is dead; and the hand that killed him
   Is his own hand.
CHORAGOS: His father's? or his own?   20
MESSENGER: His own, driven mad by the murder his father had done.
CHORAGOS: Teiresias, Teiresias, how clearly you saw it all!
MESSENGER: This is my news: you must draw what conclusions you can
   from it.
CHORAGOS: But look: Eurydicê, our Queen:
   Has she overheard us?   25

Enter EURYDICÊ *from the palace, center.*

EURYDICÊ: I have heard something, friends:
   As I was unlocking the gate of Pallas' shrine,
   For I needed her help today, I heard a voice
   Telling of some new sorrow. And I fainted
   There at the temple with all my maidens about me.   30
   But speak again: whatever it is, I can bear it:
   Grief and I are no strangers.
MESSENGER: Dearest Lady,
   I will tell you plainly all that I have seen.
   I shall not try to comfort you: what is the use,
   Since comfort could lie only in what is not true?   35
   The truth is always best.
               I went with Creon
   To the outer plain where Polyneicês was lying,
   No friend to pity him, his body shredded by dogs.
   We made our prayers in that place to Hecatê
   And Pluto, that they would be merciful. And we bathed   40
   The corpse with holy water, and we brought
   Fresh-broken branches to burn what was left of it,
   And upon the urn we heaped up a towering barrow
   Of the earth of his own land.
              When we were done, we ran
   To the vault where Antigonê lay on her couch of stone.   45
   One of the servants had gone ahead,
   And while he was yet far off he heard a voice
   Grieving within the chamber, and he came back
   And told Creon. And as the King went closer,
   The air was full of wailing, the words lost,   50
   And he begged us to make all haste. "Am I a prophet?"
   He said, weeping, "And must I walk this road,
   The saddest of all that I have gone before?

My son's voice calls me on. Oh quickly, quickly!
Look through the crevice there, and tell me   55
If it is Haimon, or some deception of the gods!"

We obeyed; and in the cavern's farthest corner
We saw her lying:
She had made a noose of her fine linen veil
And hanged herself. Haimon lay beside her,   60
His arms about her waist, lamenting her,
His love lost under ground, crying out
That his father had stolen her away from him.

When Creon saw him the tears rushed to his eyes
And he called to him: "What have you done, child?
     Speak to me.   65
What are you thinking that makes your eyes so strange?
O my son, my son, I come to you on my knees!"
But Haimon spat in his face. He said not a word,
Staring—
               And suddenly drew his sword
And lunged. Creon shrank back, the blade missed; and the boy, 70
Desperate against himself, drove it half its length
Into his own side, and fell. And as he died
He gathered Antigonê close in his arms again,
Choking, his blood bright red on her white cheek.
And now he lies dead with the dead, and she is his   75
At last, his bride in the house of the dead.

Exit EURYDICÈ *into the palace.*

CHORAGOS: She has left us without a word. What can this mean?
MESSENGER: It troubles me, too; yet she knows what is best,
     Her grief is too great for public lamentation,
     And doubtless she has gone to her chamber to weep   80
     For her dead son, leading her maidens in his dirge.

Pause.

CHORAGOS: It may be so: but I fear this deep silence.
MESSENGER: I will see what she is doing. I will go in.

Exit MESSENGER *into the palace.*

Enter CREON *with attendants, bearing* HAIMON'S *body.*

CHORAGOS: But here is the king himself: oh look at him,
     Bearing his own damnation in his arms.   85
CREON: Nothing you say can touch me any more.
     My own blind heart has brought me
     From darkness to final darkness. Here you see

The father murdering, the murdered son—
And all my civic wisdom!   90
Haimon my son, so young, so young to die,
I was the fool, not you; and you died for me.

CHORAGOS: That is the truth; but you were late in learning it.

CREON: This truth is hard to bear. Surely a god
Has crushed me beneath the hugest weight of heaven,   95
And driven me headlong a barbaric way
To trample out the thing I held most dear.
The pains that men will take to come to pain!

Enter MESSENGER *from the palace.*

MESSENGER: The burden you carry in your hands is heavy,
But it is not all: you will find more in your house.   100

CREON: What burden worse than this shall I find there?

MESSENGER: The Queen is dead.

CREON: O port of death, deaf world,
Is there no pity for me? And you, Angel of evil,
I was dead, and your words are death again.   105
Is it true, boy? Can it be true?
Is my wife dead? Has death bred death?

MESSENGER: You can see for yourself.

The doors are opened and the body of EURYDICÊ *is disclosed within.*

CREON: Oh pity!
All true, all true, and more than I can bear!   110
O my wife, my son!

MESSENGER: She stood before the altar, and her heart
Welcomed the knife her own hand guided,
And a great cry burst from her lips for Megareus dead,
And for Haimon dead, her sons; and her last breath   115
Was a curse for their father, the murderer of her sons.
And she fell, and the dark flowed in through her closing eyes.

CREON: O God, I am sick with fear.
Are there no swords here? Has no one a blow for me?

MESSENGER: Her curse is upon you for the deaths of both.   120

CREON: It is right that it should be. I alone am guilty.
I know it, and I say it. Lead me in,
Quickly, friends.
I have neither life nor substance. Lead me in.

CHORAGOS: You are right, if there can be right in so much wrong.   125
The briefest way is best in a world of sorrow.

CREON: Let it come,
Let death come quickly, and be kind to me.
I would not ever see the sun again.

CHORAGOS: All that will come when it will; but we, meanwhile,   130
Have much to do. Leave the future to itself.

CREON: All my heart was in that prayer!

CHORAGOS: Then do not pray any more: the sky is deaf.
CREON: Lead me away. I have been rash and foolish.
  I have killed my son and my wife. 135
  I look for comfort; my comfort lies here dead.
  Whatever my hands have touched has come to nothing.
  Fate has brought all my pride to a thought of dust.

As CREON *is being led into the house, the* CHORAGOS *advances and speaks directly to the audience.*

CHORAGOS: There is no happiness where there is no wisdom;
  No wisdom but in submission to the gods. 140
  Big words are always punished,
  And proud men in old age learn to be wise.

                        (*c. 441 B.C.*)

QUESTIONS FOR REFLECTION

Experience

1. To what extent can you relate to the dilemma faced by Antigonê? Why?

Interpretation

2. Describe the central problem of the play. Whose rights should assume priority—Creon's to legislate and punish, or Antigonê's to bury her brother? Is there any way to resolve the competing claims of Creon and Antigonê?
3. How does Sophocles characterize Creon and Antigonê? Consider their speeches, actions, and gestures.
4. What is Haimon's role in the play? What does Haimon's dialogue with his father reveal about the two characters?
5. What do Ismenê and Euridycê contribute to the play? How would *Antigonê* differ if either or both were absent?
6. Describe the structure of the play. How is its plot constructed and developed? Explain the focus of each scene. What is the purpose of the poetic odes that punctuate the dramatic action of the play?
7. What is the chorus's role? Single out two important comments made by the chorus and explain their significance.
8. Compare Antigonê's tragedy with Creon's suffering. Which character do you sympathize with most? Why?
9. Compare Creon's actions at the beginning and end of the play. How does he change?

Evaluation

10. Whose values does the play finally seem to endorse? Antigonê's? Creon's? Both? Neither? Explain.

CRITICS ON SOPHOCLES

ARISTOTLE
[384–322 B.C.]

The Six Elements of Tragedy

TRANSLATED BY GERALD F. ELSE

from *Poetics: Tragedy*

At present let us deal with tragedy, recovering from what has been said so far the definition of its essential nature, as it was in development. Tragedy, then, is a process of imitating an action which has serious implications, is complete, and possesses magnitude; by means of language which has been made sensuously attractive, with each of its varieties found separately in the parts; enacted by the persons themselves and not presented through narrative; through a course of pity and fear completing the purification of tragic acts which have those emotional characteristics. By "language made sensuously attractive" I mean language that has rhythm and melody, and by "its varieties found separately" I mean the fact that certain parts of the play are carried on through spoken verses alone and others the other way around, through song.

Now first of all, since they perform the imitation through action (by acting it), the adornment of their visual appearance will perforce constitute some part of the making of tragedy; and song-composition and verbal expression also, for those are the media in which they perform the imitation. By "verbal expression" I mean the actual composition of the verses, and by "song-composition" something whose meaning is entirely clear.

Next, since it is an imitation of an action and is enacted by certain people who are performing the action, and since those people must necessarily have certain traits both of character and thought (for it is thanks to these two factors that we speak of people's actions also as having a defined character, and it is in accordance with their actions that all either succeed or fail); and since the imitation of the action is the plot, for by "plot" I mean here the structuring of the events, and by the "characters" that in accordance with which we say that the persons who are acting have a defined moral character, and by "thought" all the passages in which they attempt to prove some thesis or set forth an opinion—it follows of necessity, then, that tragedy as a whole has just six constituent elements, in relation to the essence that makes it a distinct species; and they are plot, characters, verbal expression, thought, visual adornment, and song-composition. For the elements by which they imitate are two (i.e., verbal expression and song-composition), the manner in which they imitate is one (visual adornment), the things they imitate are three (plot, characters, thought), and there is nothing more beyond these. These then are the constituent forms they use.

Simple and Complex Plots

from *Poetics: Tragedy*

Among simple plots and actions the episodic are the worst. By "episodic" plot I mean one in which there is no probability or necessity for the order in which the episodes follow one another. Such structures are composed by the bad poets because they are bad poets, but by the good poets because of the actors: in composing contest pieces for them, and stretching out the plot beyond its capacity, they are forced frequently to dislocate the sequence.

Furthermore, since the tragic imitation is not only of a complete action but also of events that are fearful and pathetic, and these come about best when they come about contrary to one's expectation yet logically, one following from the other; that way they will be more productive of wonder than if they happen merely at random, by chance—because even among chance occurrences the ones people consider most marvelous are those that seem to have come about as if on purpose: for example the way the statue of Mitys at Argos killed the man who had been the cause of Mitys's death, by falling on him while he was attending the festival; it stands to reason, people think, that such things don't happen by chance—so plots of that sort cannot fail to be artistically superior.

Some plots are simple, others are complex; indeed the actions of which the plots are imitations already fall into these two categories. By "simple" action I mean one the development of which being continuous and unified in the manner stated above, the reversal comes without peripety or recognition, and by "complex" action one in which the reversal is continuous but with recognition or peripety or both. And these developments must grow out of the very structure of the plot itself, in such a way that on the basis of what has happened previously this particular outcome follows either by necessity or in accordance with probability; for there is a great difference in whether these events happen because of those or merely after them.

"Peripety" is a shift of what is being undertaken to the opposite in the way previously stated, and that in accordance with probability or necessity as we have just been saying; as for example in the *Oedipus* the man who has come, thinking that he will reassure Oedipus, that is, relieve him of his fear with respect to his mother, by revealing who he once was, brings about the opposite; and in the *Lynceus,* as he (Lynceus) is being led away with every prospect of being executed, and Danaus pursuing him with every prospect of doing the executing, it comes about as a result of the other things that have happened in the play that *he* is executed and Lynceus is saved. And "recognition" is, as indeed the name indicates, a shift from ignorance to awareness, pointing in the direction either of close blood ties or of hostility, of people who have previously been in a clearly marked state of happiness or unhappiness.

The finest recognition is one that happens at the same time as a peripety, as is the case with the one in the *Oedipus*. Naturally, there are also other kinds of recognition: it is possible for one to take place in the prescribed manner in relation to inanimate objects and chance occurrences, and it is possible to recognize whether a person has acted or not acted. But the form that is most integrally a part of the plot, the action, is the one aforesaid; for that kind of recognition combined with peripety will excite either pity or fear (and these are the kinds of action of which tragedy is an imitation according to our definition), because both good and bad fortune will also be most likely to follow that kind of event. Since, further, the recognition is a recognition of persons, some are of one person by the other one only (when it is already known who the "other one" is), but sometimes it is necessary for both persons to go through a recognition, as for example, Iphigenia is recognized by her brother through the sending of the letter, but of him by Iphigenia another recognition is required.

These then are two elements of plot: peripety and recognition; third is the *pathos*. Of these, peripety and recognition have been discussed; a *pathos* is a destructive or painful act, such as deaths on stage, paroxysms of pain, woundings, and all that sort of thing.

SIGMUND FREUD
[1856–1939]

The Oedipus Complex
from The Interpretation of Dreams

The action of the play consists in nothing other than the process of revealing, with cunning delays and ever-mounting excitement—a process that can be likened to the work of a psychoanalysis—that Oedipus himself is the murderer of Laïus, but further that he is the son of the murdered man and of Jocasta. Appalled at the abomination which he has unwittingly perpetrated, Oedipus blinds himself and forsakes his home. The oracle has been fulfilled.

Oedipus Rex is what is known as a tragedy of destiny. Its tragic effect is said to lie in the contrast between the supreme will of the gods and the vain attempts of mankind to escape the evil that threatens them. The lesson which, it is said, the deeply moved spectator should learn from the tragedy is submission to the divine will and realization of his own impotence. Modern dramatists have accordingly tried to achieve a similar tragic effect by weaving the same contrast into a plot invented by themselves. But the spectators have looked on unmoved while a curse or an oracle was fulfilled in spite of all the efforts of some innocent man: later tragedies of destiny have failed in their effect.

If *Oedipus Rex* moves a modern audience no less than it did the contemporary Greek one, the explanation can only be that its effect does not lie in the contrast between destiny and human will, but is to be looked for in the particular nature of the material on which that contrast is exemplified. There must be something which makes a voice within us ready to recognize the compelling force of destiny in the *Oedipus,* while we can dismiss as merely arbitrary such dispositions as are laid down in [Grillparzer's] *Die Ahnfrau* or other modern tragedies of destiny. And a factor of this kind is in fact involved in the story of King Oedipus. His destiny moves us only because it might have been ours—because the oracle laid the same curse upon us before our birth as upon him. It is the fate of all of us, perhaps, to direct our first sexual impulse toward our mother and our first hatred and our first murderous wish against our father. Our dreams convince us that that is so. King Oedipus, who slew his father Laïus and married his mother Jocasta, merely shows us the fulfillment of our own childhood wishes. But, more fortunate than he, we have meanwhile succeeded, in so far as we have not become psychoneurotics, in detaching our sexual impulses from our mothers and in forgetting our jealousy of our fathers. Here is one in whom these primeval wishes of our childhood have been fulfilled, and we shrink back from him with the whole force of the repression by which those wishes have since that time been held down within us. While the poet, as he unravels the past, brings to light the guilt of Oedipus, he is at the same time compelling us to recognize our own inner minds, in which those same impulses, though suppressed, are still to be found. The contrast with which the closing Chorus leaves us confronted—

> . . . Fix on Oedipus your eyes,
> Who resolved the dark enigma, noblest champion and most wise.
> Like a star his envied fortune mounted beaming far and wide:
> Now he sinks in seas of anguish, whelmed beneath a raging tide . . .

—strikes as a warning at ourselves and our pride, at us who since our childhood have grown so wise and so mighty in our own eyes. Like Oedipus, we live in ignorance of these wishes, repugnant to morality, which have been forced upon us by Nature, and after their revelation we may all of us well seek to close our eyes to the scenes of our childhood.

There is an unmistakable indication in the text of Sophocles' tragedy itself that the legend of Oedipus sprang from some primeval dream material which had as its content the distressing disturbance of a child's relation to his parents owing to the first stirrings of sexuality. At a point when Oedipus, though he is not yet enlightened, has begun to feel troubled by his recollection of the oracle, Jocasta consoles him by referring to a dream which many people dream, though, as she thinks, it has no meaning:

> Many a man ere now in dreams hath lain
> With her who bare him. He hath least annoy
> Who with such omens troubleth not his mind.

Today, just as then, many men dream of having sexual relations with their mothers, and speak of the fact with indignation and astonishment. It is clearly the key to the tragedy and the complement to the dream of the dreamer's father being dead. The story of Oedipus is the reaction of the imagination to these two typical dreams. And just as these dreams, when dreamt by adults, are accompanied by feelings of repulsion, so too the legend must include horror and self-punishment. Its further modification originates once again in a misconceived secondary revision of the material, which has sought to exploit it for theological purposes. . . . The attempt to harmonize divine omnipotence with human responsibility must naturally fail in connection with this subject matter just as with any other.

BERNARD KNOX

Sophocles' Oedipus

from Word and Action

In an earlier Sophoclean play, *Antigonê,* the chorus sings a hymn to this man the conqueror. "Many are the wonders and terrors, and nothing more wonderful and terrible than man." He has conquered the sea, "this creature goes beyond the white sea pressing forward as the swell crashes about him"; and he has conquered the land, "earth, highest of the gods . . . he wears away with the turning plough." He has mastered not only the elements, sea, and land, but the birds, beasts, and fishes; "through knowledge and technique," sings the chorus, he is yoker of the horse, tamer of the bull. "And he has taught himself speech and thought swift as the wind and attitudes which enable him to live in communities and means to shelter himself from the frost and rain. Full of resources he faces the future, nothing will find him at a loss. Death, it is true, he will not avoid, yet he has thought out ways of escape from desperate diseases. His knowledge, ingenuity and technique are beyond anything that could have been foreseen." These lyrics describe the rise to power of *anthropos tyrannos;* self-taught, he seizes control of his environment, he is master of the elements, the animals, the arts and sciences of civilization. "Full of resources he faces the future"—an apt description of Oedipus at the beginning of our play.

And it is not the only phrase of this ode which is relevant; for Oedipus is connected by the terms he uses, and which are used to and about him, with the whole range of human achievement which has raised man to his present level. All the items of this triumphant catalog recur in the *Oedipus Tyrannos* [*Oedipus Rex*]; the images of the play define him as helmsman, conqueror of the sea, and ploughman, conqueror of the land, as hunter, master of speech and thought, inventor, legislator, physician. Oedipus is faced in the play with an intellectual problem, and as he marshals his intellectual resources to solve it, the language of the play suggests a comparison between Oedipus' methods in the play and the whole range of sciences and techniques which have brought man to mastery, made him *tyrannos* of the world.

Oedipus' problem is apparently simple: "Who is the murderer of Laius?" But as he pursues the answer, the question changes shape. It becomes a different problem: "Who am I?" And the answer to this problem involves the gods as well as man. The answer to the question is not what he expected, it is in fact a reversal, that *peripeteia* which Aristotle speaks of in connection with this play. The state of Oedipus is reversed from "first of men" to "most accursed of men"; his attitude from the proud ἀρκτέον, "I must rule," to the humble πειστέον, "I must obey." "Reversal," says Aristotle, "is a change of the action into the opposite," and one meaning of this much disputed phrase is that the action produces the opposite of the actor's intentions. So Oedipus curses the murderer of Laius and it turns out that he has cursed himself. But this reversal is not confined to the action; it is also the process of all the great images of the play which identify Oedipus as the inventive, critical spirit of his century. As the images unfold, the inquirer turns into the object of inquiry, the hunter into the prey, the doctor into the patient, the investigator into the criminal, the revealer into the thing revealed, the finder into the thing found, the savior into the thing saved ("I was saved, for some dreadful destiny"), the liberator into the thing released ("I released your feet from the bonds which pierced your ankles," says the Corinthian messenger). The accuser becomes the defendant, the ruler the subject, the teacher not only the pupil but also the object lesson, the example—a change of the action into its opposite, from active to passive.

And the two opening images of the *Antigonê* ode recur with hideous effect. Oedipus the helmsman, who steers the ship of state, is seen, in Tiresias' words, as one who "steers his ship into a nameless anchorage," who, in the chorus's words, "shared the same great harbour with his father." And Oedipus the ploughman—"How," asks the chorus, "how could the furrows which your father ploughed bear you in silence for so long?"

This reversal is the movement of the play, parallel in the imagery and the action: it is the overthrow of the *tyrannos,* of man who seized power and thought himself "equated to the gods." The bold metaphor of the priest introduces another of the images which parallel in their development the reversal of the hero and suggest that Oedipus is a figure symbolic of human intelligence and achievement in general. He is not only helmsman, ploughman, inventor, legislator, liberator, revealer, doctor—he is also equator, mathematician, calculator; "equated" is a mathematical term, and it is only one of a whole complex of such terms which present Oedipus in yet a fresh aspect of man *tyrannos.* One of Oedipus' favorite words is "measure," and this is of course a significant metaphor: measure, mensuration, number, calculation—these are among the most important inventions which have brought man to power. Aeschylus' Prometheus, the mythical civilizer of human life, counts number among the foremost of his gifts to man. "And number, too, I invented, outstanding among clever devices." In the river valleys of the East, generations of mensuration and calculation had brought man to an understanding of the movements of the stars and of time: in the histories of his friend Herodotus, Sophocles had read of the calculation and mensuration which had gone into the building of the pyramids. "Measure"—it is Protagoras' word: "Man is the measure of all things." In this play man's measure is taken, his true equation found. The play is full of equations, some of them incomplete, some false; the final equation shows man equated not to the gods but to himself, as Oedipus is finally equated to himself. For there are in the play not one Oedipus but two.

One is the magnificent figure set before us in the opening scenes, *tyrannos,* the man of wealth and power, first of men, the intellect and energy which drive on the search. The other is the object of the search, a shadowy figure who has violated the most fundamental human taboos, an incestuous parricide, "most accursed of men." And even before the one Oedipus finds the other, they are connected and equated in the name which they both bear, Oedipus. Oedipus—Swollen-foot; it emphasizes the physical blemish which scars the body of the splendid *tyrannos,* a defect which he tries to forget but which reminds us of the outcast child this *tyrannos* once was and the outcast man he is soon to be. The second half of the name πους, "foot," recurs throughout the play, as a mocking phrase which recalls this other Oedipus. "The Sphinx forced us to look at what was at our feet," says Creon. Tiresias invokes "the dread-footed curse of your father and mother." And the choral odes echo and re-echo with this word. "Let the murderer of Laius set his foot in motion in flight." "The murderer is a man alone with forlorn foot." "The laws of Zeus are high-footed." "The man of pride plunges down into doom where he cannot use his foot."

These mocking repetitions of one-half the name invoke the unknown Oedipus who will be revealed: the equally emphatic repetition of the first half emphasizes the dominant attitude of the man before us.

ADRIAN POOLE

Oedipus and Athens

from *Tragedy: Shakespeare and the Greek Example*

Oedipus is quick to decide and to act; he anticipates advice and suggestion. When the priest hints that he should send to Delphi for help, he has already done so; when the chorus suggests sending for Tiresias, the prophet has already been summoned and is on the way. This swiftness in action is a well-known Athenian quality, one their enemies are well aware of. "They are the only people," say the Corinthians, "who simultaneously hope for and have what they plan, because of their quick fulfillment of decisions." But this action is not rash, it is based on reflection; Oedipus reached the decision to apply to Delphi "groping, laboring over many paths of thought." This too is typically Athenian. "We are unique," says Pericles, "in our combination of the most courageous action and rational discussion of our plans." The Athenians also spoke with pride of the intelligence that informed such discussion: Pericles attributes the Athenian victories over the Persians "not to luck, but to intelligence." And this is the claim of Oedipus, too. "The flight of my own intelligence hit the mark," he says, as he recalls his solution of the riddle of the Sphinx. The riddle has sinister verbal connections with his fate (his name in Greek is *Oidipous,* and *dipous* is the Greek word for "two-footed" in the riddle, not to mention the later prophecy of Tiresias that he would leave Thebes as a blind man, "a stick tapping before him step by step"), but the answer he proposed to the riddle—"Man"—is appropriate for the optimistic picture of man's achievement and potential that the figure of Oedipus represents.

Above all, as we see from the priest's speech in the prologue and the prompt, energetic action Oedipus takes to rescue his subjects from the plague, he is a man dedicated to the interests and the needs of the city. It is this public spirit that drives him on to the discovery of the truth—to reject Creon's hint that the matter should be kept under wraps, to send for Tiresias, to pronounce the curse and sentence of banishment on the murderer of Laius. This spirit was the great civic virtue that Pericles preached—"I would have you fix your eyes every day on the greatness of Athens until you fall in love with her"—and that the enemies of Athens knew they had to reckon with. "In the city's service," say the Corinthians, "they use their bodies as if they did not belong to them."

All this does not necessarily mean that Sophocles' audience drew a conscious parallel between Oedipus and Athens (or even that Sophocles himself did); what is important is that they could have seen in Oedipus a man endowed with the temperament and talents they prized most highly in their own democratic leaders and in their ideal vision of themselves. Oedipus the King is a dramatic embodiment of the creative vigor and intellectual daring of the fifth-century Athenian spirit.

But there is an even greater dimension to this extraordinary dramatic figure. The fifth century in Athens saw the birth of the historical spirit. The past came to be seen no longer as a golden age from which there had been a decline if not a fall, but as a steady progress from primitive barbarism to the high civilization of the city-state. . . .

The figure of Oedipus represents not only the techniques of the transition from savagery to civilization and the political achievements of the newly settled society, but also the temper and methods of the fifth-century intellectual revolution. His speeches are full of words, phrases, and attitudes that link him with the "enlightenment" of Sophocles' own Athens. "I'll bring it all to light," he says; he is like some Protagoras or Democritus dispelling the darkness of ignorance and superstition. He is a questioner, a researcher, a discoverer—the Greek words are those of the sophistic vocabulary. Above all Oedipus is presented to the audience as a symbol of two of the greatest scientific achievements of the age—mathematics and medicine. Mathematical language recurs incessantly in the imagery of the play—such terms as "measure" (*metrein*), "equate" (*isoun*), "define" (*diorizein*)—and at one climactic moment Oedipus expresses as a mathematical axiom his hope that a discrepancy in the evidence will clear him of the charge of Laius's murder: "One can't equal many." This obsessive image, Oedipus the calculator, is one more means of investing the mythical figure with the salient characteristics of the fifth-century achievement, but it is also magnificently functional. For, in his search for truth, he is engaged in a great calculation to determine the measure of man, whom Protagoras called "the measure of all things."

GEORGE STEINER
[b. 1929]

Principal Constants of Conflict in Antigonê

from *Antigonê*

It has, I believe, been given to only one literary text to express all the principal constants of conflict in the condition of man. These constants are fivefold: the confrontation of men and of women; of age and of youth; of society and of the individual; of the living and the dead; of men and of god(s). The conflicts which come of these five orders of confrontation are not negotiable. Men and women, old and young, the individual and the community or state, the quick and the dead, mortals and immortals, define themselves in the conflictual process of defining each other. Self-definition and the agonistic recognition of "otherness" (of *l'autre*) across the threatened boundaries of self are indissociable. The polarities of masculinity and of femininity, of aging and of youth, of private autonomy and of social collectivity, of existence and mortality, of the human and the divine, can be crystallized only in adversative terms (whatever the many shades of accommodation between them). To arrive at oneself—the primordial journey—is to come up, polemically, against "the other." The boundary-conditions of the human person are those set by gender, by age, by community, by the cut between life and death, and by the potentials of accepted or denied encounter between the existential and the transcendent.

But "collision" is, of course, a monistic and, therefore, inadequate term. Equally decisive are those categories of reciprocal perception, of grappling with "otherness," that can be defined as erotic, filial, social, ritual, and metaphysical. Men and women, old and young, individual and *communitas,* living and deceased, mortals and gods, meet and mesh in contiguities of love, of kinship, of commonality and group-communion, of caring remembrance, of worship. Sex, the honeycomb of generations and of kinship, the social unit, the presentness of the departed in the weave of the living, the practices of religion, are the modes of enactment of ultimate ontological dualities. In essence, the constants of conflict and of positive intimacy are the same. When man and woman meet, they stand against each other as they stand close. Old and young seek in each other the pain of remembrance and the matching solace of futurity. Anarchic individuation seeks interaction with the compulsions of law, of collective cohesion in the body politic. The dead inhabit the living and, in turn, await their visit. The duel between men and god(s) is the most aggressively amorous known to experience. In the physics of man's being, fission is also fusion. . . .

Creon and Antigonê clash as man and as woman. Creon is a mature, indeed an aging, man; Antigonê's is the virginity of youth. Their fatal debate turns on the nature of the coexistence between private vision and public need, between ego and community. The imperatives of immanence, of the living in the [*polis*], πόλισ, press on Creon; in Antigonê, these imperatives encounter the no less exigent night-throng of the dead. No syllable spoken, no gesture made, in the dialogue of Antigone and Creon but has within it the manifold, perhaps duplicitous, nearness of the gods.

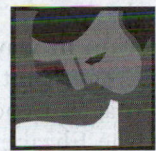

CHAPTER NINETEEN

The Elizabethan Theater: Shakespeare in Context

STAGECRAFT IN THE ELIZABETHAN AGE

The drama of Shakespeare's time, the Elizabethan Age (1558–1603), shares some features with Greek drama. Like the Greek dramatists, Elizabethan playwrights wrote both comedies and tragedies, but the Elizabethans extended the possibilities of each genre. They wrote domestic tragedies, tragedies of character, and revenge tragedies; they contributed comedies of manners and comedies of humors to the earlier romantic and satiric comedies. In Greek and Elizabethan theater, props were few, scenery was simple, and dialogue often indicated changes of locale and time. Elizabethan plays were also written in verse rather than prose.

An Elizabethan playhouse such as the Globe, where many of Shakespeare's plays were staged, had a much smaller seating capacity than the large Greek amphitheaters, which could seat thousands (fifteen thousand at Epidaurus). The Globe could accommodate about twenty-three hundred people, including roughly eight hundred groundlings who, exposed to the elements, stood around the stage. The stage itself projected from an inside wall into their midst. More prosperous spectators sat in one of the three stories that nearly encircled the stage. The vastly smaller size and seating capacity of the Elizabethan theater and the projection of its stage made for a greater intimacy between actors and audience. Though actors still had to project their voices and exaggerate their gestures, they could be heard and seen without the aid of large megaphonic masks and elevated shoes. Elizabethan actors could modulate their voices and vary their pitch, stress, and intonation in ways not suited to the Greek stage. They could also make greater and more subtle use of facial expression and of gesture to enforce their greater verbal and vocal flexibility.

In addition to greater intimacy, the Elizabethan stage also offered more versatility than its Greek counterpart. Although the Greek *skene* building could be used for scenes occuring above the ground, such as a god descending in a machine (*deus ex machina*),* the Greek stage was really a single-level acting area. Not so the Elizabethan stage, which contained a second-level balcony (from which Brabantio looks out in Act I, scene ii of *Othello*). Besides its balcony, Shakespeare's stage had doors at the back for entrances and exits, a curtained alcove (useful for scenes of intrigue), and a stage floor trapdoor, from which the Ghost ascends in Shakespeare's *Hamlet*. Such a stage was suitable for rapidly shifting scenes and continuous action. Thus, Elizabethan stage conventions did not include divisions between scenes as in Greek drama. The act and scene divisions that appear in *Othello* and *Hamlet* were devised by modern editors.

INTRODUCTION TO SHAKESPEARE

[1564–1616]

William Shakespeare, the most famous English writer, is also among the most popular. His fame and popularity rest on his plays more than on his nondramatic poetry—though his sonnets remain perennially in fashion. What makes Shakespeare such a literary phenomenon? Why are readers so drawn to his work? Here are two simple explanations: (1) his revelation of human character, especially his exploration of complex states of mind and feeling; (2) his explosive and exuberant language, particularly the richness and variety of his metaphors. Both of these literary virtues abound in the sequence of 154 sonnets Shakespeare wrote in the 1590s. Both also consistently appear in his thirty-seven plays, particularly in the soliloquies, those inward meditative speeches of the major characters. The richness of Shakespeare's language is also apparent in the songs he wrote for the plays, especially the songs in the comedies.

Another source of Shakespeare's popularity is his immense quotability. Shakespeare's plays and poems provide a repository of familiar sayings and recognizable quotations. From *Hamlet* alone we glean the following:

> In my mind's eye
>
> To the manner born
>
> There are more things in heaven and earth

---

*A god who resolves the entanglements of a play by his supernatural intervention (literally, a god from the machine) or any artificial device used to resolve a plot.

Hold the mirror up to nature

I must be cruel only to be kind.

Brevity is the soul of wit.

To be or not to be, that is the question.

Neither a borrower nor a lender be.

Something's rotten in the state of Denmark.

What a piece of work is a man.

To reduce Shakespeare's appeal to the fact that he is eminently quotable, however, is to ignore other important dimensions of his popularity. It is, moreover, to get things backward—to put the cart before the horse. Shakespeare is not a great writer because he is quotable; he is quotable because he is a great writer. It is his manipulation of language and his revelation of character that have made him both widely read and deeply revered.

Very little is known with certainty about Shakespeare's life. Scholars, however, have determined the following basic facts. He was born in Stratford-on-Avon in April of 1564. He attended the local grammar school, where he would have studied Latin and perhaps a little Greek. His formal education did not include attendance at the university—in his day either Oxford or Cambridge. Instead, at eighteen, he married Anne Hathaway, who bore three children in as many years, a daughter in 1583 and twins, a boy and girl, in 1585. Shakespeare wrote and acted in plays, for by 1592 he was known in London as both actor and playwright.

Many tributes have been paid to Shakespeare. One, however, stands above the rest: his contemporary Ben Jonson's judgment that "he is not for an age, but for all time."

Othello

Shakespeare's plays generally, and *Othello* in particular, appealed to an audience ranging from the illiterate to the educated: bawdy jokes exist alongside sublime poetry; subtle introspective moments coexist with violence and passion. Shakespeare's language is among the richest and most resourceful ever written (and spoken), and *Othello* testifies to its vitality and exuberance. Written predominantly in blank verse, *Othello* also includes prose passages (many spoken by Iago) and rhymed couplets (which punctuate the ends of some scenes). The play's language is rich in metaphor and images, puns, and other forms of wordplay.

Deriving the story of Othello from a sixteenth-century tale by Giraldi Cinthio, Shakespeare improved the plot, enriched the language, and deepened the characters. *Othello* has been among the most admired of Shakespeare's plays. Part of its attraction is its language, but its characters are perhaps even more immediately compelling: the noble Othello; his gentle and naive Venetian wife, Desdemona; the brilliant, magnetic, and inexplicable Iago; his crude and manipulated wife, Emilia. The play's central concerns—love and trust, good and evil, nobility and debasement—are also universal.

The Tragedy of Othello

THE MOOR OF VENICE

EDITED BY ALVIN KERNAN

CHARACTERS

OTHELLO, *the Moor*

BRABANTIO, *father to Desdemona*

CASSIO, *an honorable lieutenant*

IAGO, *a villain*

RODERIGO, *a gulled gentleman*

DUKE OF VENICE

SENATORS

MONTANO, *Governor of Cyprus*

GENTLEMEN OF CYPRUS

LODOVICO AND GRATIANO, *two noble Venetians*

SAILORS

CLOWN

DESDEMONA, *wife to Othello*

EMILIA, *wife to Iago*

BIANCA, *a courtesan*

(MESSENGER, HERALD, OFFICERS, GENTLEMEN, MUSICIANS, ATTENDANTS)

Scene. *Venice and Cyprus.*

ACT I

Scene I [*Venice. A street.*]

RODERIGO: Tush! Never tell me? I take it much unkindly
  That thou, Iago, who hast had my purse
  As if the strings were thine, shouldst know of this.

IAGO: 'Sblood,° but you'll not hear me! If ever I did dream
  Of such a matter, abhor me.

RODERIGO: Thou told'st me   5
  Thou didst hold him in thy hate.

IAGO: Despise me

I.i. ⁴*Sblood* *by God's blood.*

If I do not. Three great ones of the city,
In personal suit to make me his lieutenant,
Off-capped° to him; and, by the faith of man,
I know my price; I am worth no worse a place.   10
But he, as loving his own pride and purposes,
Evades them with a bombast circumstance,°
Horribly stuffed with epithets of war;
Nonsuits° my mediators. For, "Certes," says he,
"I have already chose my officer." And what was he?   15
Forsooth, a great arithmetician,°
One Michael Cassio, a Florentine,
(A fellow almost damned in a fair wife)°
That never set a squadron in the field,
Nor the division of a battle knows   20
More than a spinster; unless the bookish theoric,
Wherein the tonguèd° consuls can propose
As masterly as he. Mere prattle without practice
Is all his soldiership. But he, sir, had th' election;
And I, of whom his eyes had seen the proof   25
At Rhodes, at Cyprus, and on other grounds
Christian and heathen, must be belee'd and calmed
By debitor and creditor. This counter-caster,°
He, in good time, must his lieutenant be,
And I—God bless the mark!—his Moorship's ancient.°   30
RODERIGO: By heaven, I rather would have been his hangman.
IAGO: Why, there's no remedy. 'Tis the curse of service:
Preferment goes by letter and affection,°
And not by old gradation,° where each second
Stood heir to th' first. Now, sir, be judge yourself,   35
Whether I in any just term am affined°
To love the Moor.
RODERIGO: I would not follow him then.
IAGO: O, sir, content you.
I follow him to serve my turn upon him.
We cannot all be masters, nor all masters   40
Cannot be truly followed. You shall mark
Many a duteous and knee-crooking° knave
That, doting on his own obsequious bondage,
Wears out his time, much like his master's ass,

---

⁹**Off-capped** _doffed their caps—as a mark of respect._   ¹²**bombast circumstance** _stuffed, roundabout speech._
¹⁴**Nonsuits** _rejects._   ¹⁶**arithmetician** _theorist (rather than practical)._   ¹⁸(_A . . . wife_) _a much-disputed
passage, probably best taken as a general sneer at Cassio as a dandy and a ladies' man. But in the story from which
Shakespeare took his plot the counterpart of Cassio is married, and it may be that at the beginning of the play, Shakespeare had decided to keep him married but later changed his mind._   ²²**tonguèd** _eloquent._   ²⁸**counter-caster**
i.e., a bookkeeper who casts (reckons up) figures on a counter (abacus).   ³⁰**ancient** _standard-bearer; an under-
officer._   ³³**letter and affection** _recommendations (from men of power) and personal preference._   ³⁴**old gradation** _seniority._   ³⁶**affined** _bound._   ⁴²**knee-crooking** _bowing._

For naught but provender; and when he's old, cashiered.   45
Whip me such honest knaves! Others there are
Who, trimmed in forms and visages of duty,
Keep yet their hearts attending on themselves,
And, throwing but shows of service on their lords,
Do well thrive by them, and when they have lined their coats,   50
Do themselves homage. These fellows have some soul;
And such a one do I profess myself. For, sir,
It is as sure as you are Roderigo,
Were I the Moor, I would not be Iago.
In following him, I follow but myself.   55
Heaven is my judge, not I for love and duty,
But seeming so, for my peculiar° end;
For when my outward action doth demonstrate
The native° act and figure of my heart
In complement extern,° 'tis not long after   60
But I will wear my heart upon my sleeve
For daws to peck at; I am not what I am.

RODERIGO: What a full fortune does the thick-lips owe°
     If he can carry't thus!

IAGO: Call up her father,
     Rouse him. Make after him, poison his delight,   65
     Proclaim him in the streets, incense her kinsmen,
     And though he in a fertile climate dwell,
     Plague him with flies; though that his joy be joy,
     Yet throw such chances of vexation on't
     As it may lose some color.   70

RODERIGO: Here is her father's house. I'll call aloud.

IAGO: Do, with like timorous° accent and dire yell
     As when, by night and negligence, the fire
     Is spied in populous cities.

RODERIGO: What, ho, Brabantio! Signior Brabantio, ho!   75

IAGO: Awake! What, ho, Brabantio! Thieves! Thieves!
     Look to your house, your daughter, and your bags!
     Thieves! Thieves!

                 BRABANTIO *above°* [*at a window*].

BRABANTIO: What is the reason of this terrible summons?
     What is the matter there?   80

RODERIGO: Signior, is all your family within?

IAGO: Are your doors locked?

BRABANTIO: Why, wherefore ask you this?

IAGO: Zounds, sir, y'are robbed! For shame. Put on your gown!

---

⁵⁷**peculiar** *personal.*   ⁵⁹**native** *natural, innate.*   ⁶⁰**complement extern** *outward appearance.*   ⁶³**owe**
own.   ⁷²**timorous** *frightening.*   ⁷⁸**s.d. above** *(i.e., on the small upper stage above and to the rear of the*
main platform stage, which resembled the projecting upper story of an Elizabethan house).

Your heart is burst, you have lost half your soul.
Even now, now, very now, an old black ram 85
Is tupping your white ewe. Arise, arise!
Awake the snorting citizens with the bell,
Or else the devil will make a grandsire of you.
Arise, I say!

BRABANTIO: What, have you lost your wits?

RODERIGO: Most reverend signior, do you know my voice? 90

BRABANTIO: Not I. What are you?

RODERIGO: My name is Roderigo.

BRABANTIO: The worser welcome!
I have charged thee not to haunt about my doors.
In honest plainness thou hast heard me say
My daughter is not for thee; and now, in madness, 95
Being full of supper and distemp'ring draughts,°
Upon malicious knavery dost thou come
To start° my quiet.

RODERIGO: Sir, sir, sir—

BRABANTIO: But thou must needs be sure
My spirits and my place° have in their power 100
To make this bitter to thee.

RODERIGO: Patience, good sir.

BRABANTIO: What tell'st thou me of robbing? This is Venice,
My house is not a grange.°

RODERIGO: Most grave Brabantio,
In simple and pure soul I come to you.

IAGO: Zounds, sir, you are one of those that will not serve God if the devil bid you.
Because we come to do you service and you think we are ruffians, you'll have
your daughter covered with a Barbary° horse, you'll have your nephews° neigh
to you, you'll have coursers for cousins,° and gennets for germans.°

BRABANTIO: What profane wretch art thou? 110

IAGO: I am one, sir, that comes to tell you your daughter and the Moor are making
the beast with two backs.

BRABANTIO: Thou art a villain.

IAGO: You are—a senator.

BRABANTIO: This thou shalt answer. I know thee, Roderigo.

RODERIGO: Sir, I will answer anything. But I beseech you, 115
If't be your pleasure and most wise consent,
As partly I find it is, that your fair daughter,
At this odd-even° and dull watch o' th' night,
Transported, with no worse nor better guard

---

⁹⁶**distemp'ring draughts** *unsettling drinks.* ⁹⁸**start** *disrupt.* ¹⁰⁰**place** *rank, i.e., of senator.* ¹⁰³**grange**
isolated house. ¹⁰⁷**Barbary** *Arabian, i.e., Moorish.* ¹⁰⁸**nephews** *i.e., grandsons.* ¹⁰⁸**cousins** *relations.* ¹⁰⁹**gennets for germans** *Spanish horses for blood relatives.* ¹¹⁸**odd-even** *between night and
morning.*

But with a knave of common hire, a gondolier,   120
To the gross clasps of a lascivious Moor—
If this be known to you, and your allowance,
We then have done you bold and saucy wrongs;
But if you know not this, my manners tell me
We have your wrong rebuke. Do not believe   125
That from the sense of all civility°
I thus would play and trifle with your reverence.
Your daughter, if you have not given her leave,
I say again, hath made a gross revolt,
Tying her duty, beauty, wit, and fortunes   130
In an extravagant° and wheeling stranger
Of here and everywhere. Straight satisfy yourself.
If she be in her chamber, or your house,
Let loose on me the justice of the state
For thus deluding you.
BRABANTIO: Strike on the tinder, ho!   135
Give me a taper! Call up all my people!
This accident° is not unlike my dream.
Belief of it oppresses me already.
Light, I say! Light!   *Exit [above].*
IAGO: Farewell, for I must leave you.
It seems not meet, nor wholesome to my place,   140
To be produced—as, if I stay, I shall—
Against the Moor. For I do know the State,
However this may gall him with some check,°
Cannot with safety cast° him; for he's embarked
With such loud reason to the Cyprus wars,   145
Which even now stands in act,° that for their souls
Another of his fathom° they have none
To lead their business; in which regard,
Though I do hate him as I do hell-pains,
Yet, for necessity of present life,   150
I must show out a flag and sign of love,
Which is indeed but sign. That you shall surely find him,
Lead to the Sagittary° that raisèd search:
And there will I be with him. So farewell.   *[Exit.]*

Enter BRABANTIO *[in his nightgown], with* SERVANTS *and torches.*

BRABANTIO: It is too true an evil. Gone she is;   155
And what's to come of my despisèd time
Is naught but bitterness. Now, Roderigo,

---

¹²⁶**sense of all civility** *feeling of what is proper.*   ¹³¹**extravagant** *vagrant, wandering (Othello is not Vene-*
tian and thus may be considered a wandering soldier of fortune).   ¹³⁷**accident** *happening.*   ¹⁴³**check** *re-*
straint.   ¹⁴⁴**cast** *dismiss.*   ¹⁴⁶**stands in act** *takes place.*   ¹⁴⁷**fathom** *ability.*   ¹⁵³**Sagittary**
probably the name of an inn.

Where didst thou see her?—O unhappy girl!—
With the Moor, say'st thou?—Who would be a father?—
How didst thou know 'twas she?—O, she deceives me   160
Past thought!—What said she to you? Get moe° tapers!
Raise all my kindred!—Are they married, think you?

RODERIGO: Truly I think they are.

BRABANTIO: O heaven! How got she out? O treason of the blood!
Fathers, from hence trust not your daughters' minds   165
By what you see them act.° Is there not charms
By which the property° of youth and maidhood
May be abused? Have you not read, Roderigo,
Of some such thing?

RODERIGO: Yes, sir, I have indeed.

BRABANTIO: Call up my brother.—O, would you had had her!—   170
Some one way, some another.—Do you know
Where we may apprehend her and the Moor?

RODERIGO: I think I can discover him, if you please
To get good guard and go along with me.

BRABANTIO: Pray you lead on. At every house I'll call;   175
I may command at most.—Get weapons, ho!
And raise some special officers of night.—
On, good Roderigo; I will deserve your pains.°   [Exeunt.]

Scene II [A street.]

Enter OTHELLO, IAGO, ATTENDANTS *with torches.*

IAGO: Though in the trade of war I have slain men,
Yet do I hold it very stuff° o' th' conscience
To do no contrived murder. I lack iniquity
Sometime to do me service. Nine or ten times
I had thought t' have yerked° him here, under the ribs.   5

OTHELLO: 'Tis better as it is.

IAGO: Nay, but he prated,
And spoke such scurvy and provoking terms
Against your honor, that with the little godliness I have
I did full hard forbear him. But I pray you, sir,
Are you fast married? Be assured of this,   10
That the magnifico° is much beloved,
And hath in his effect a voice potential
As double as the Duke's.° He will divorce you,
Or put upon you what restraint or grievance
The law, with all his might to enforce it on,   15

161**moe** *more.*   166**act** *do.*   167**property** *true nature.*   178**deserve your pains** *be worthy of (and reward) your efforts.*   **I.ii.** ²**stuff** *essence.* ⁵**yerked** *stabbed.* ¹¹**magnifico** *nobleman.* 12–13**hath . . . Duke's** *i.e., can be as effective as the Duke.*

Will give him cable.°

OTHELLO: Let him do his spite.
My services which I have done the Signiory°
Shall out-tongue his complaints. 'Tis yet to know°—
Which when I know that boasting is an honor
I shall promulgate—I fetch my life and being   20
From men of royal siege,° and my demerits°
May speak unbonneted to as proud a fortune
As this that I have reached.° For know, Iago,
But that I love the gentle Desdemona,
I would not my unhousèd° free condition   25
Put into circumscription and confine
For the seas' worth. But look, what lights come yond?

Enter CASSIO, *with* [OFFICERS *and*] *torches.*

IAGO: Those are the raisèd father and his friends.
    You were best go in.

OTHELLO: Not I. I must be found.
My parts, my title, and my perfect soul°   30
Shall manifest me rightly. Is it they?

IAGO: By Janus, I think no.

OTHELLO: The servants of the Duke? And my lieutenant?
The goodness of the night upon you, friends.
What is the news?

CASSIO: The Duke does greet you, general;   35
And he requires your haste-posthaste appearance
Even on the instant.

OTHELLO: What is the matter, think you?

CASSIO: Something from Cyprus, as I may divine.
It is a business of some heat. The galleys
Have sent a dozen sequent° messengers   40
This very night at one another's heels,
And many of the consuls, raised and met,
Are at the Duke's already. You have been hotly called for.
When, being not at your lodging to be found,
The Senate hath sent about three several° quests   45
To search you out.

OTHELLO: 'Tis well I am found by you.
I will but spend a word here in the house,
And go with you.   [*Exit.*]

CASSIO: Ancient, what makes he here?

IAGO: Faith, he tonight hath boarded a land carack.°

---

¹⁶**cable**   *range, scope.*   ¹⁷**Signiory**   *the rulers of Venice.*   ¹⁸**yet to know**   *unknown as yet.*   ²¹**siege**
rank.   ²¹**demerits**   *deserts.*   ²²⁻²³**May . . . reached**   *i.e., are the equal of the family I have married into.*
²⁵**unhousèd**   *unconfined.*   ³⁰**perfect soul**   *clear, unflawed conscience.*   ⁴⁰**sequent**   *successive.*   ⁴⁵**several**
separate.   ⁴⁹**carack**   *treasure ship.*

If it prove lawful prize, he's made forever.   50
CASSIO: I do not understand.
IAGO: He's married.
CASSIO: To who?

[*Enter* OTHELLO.]

IAGO: Marry,° to—Come captain, will you go?
OTHELLO: Have with you.
CASSIO: Here comes another troop to seek for you.

Enter BRABANTIO, RODERIGO, *with* OFFICERS *and torches.*

IAGO: It is Brabantio. General, be advised.
  He comes to bad intent.
OTHELLO: Holla! Stand there!   55
RODERIGO: Signior, it is the Moor.
BRABANTIO: Down with him, thief!   [*They draw swords.*]
IAGO: You, Roderigo? Come, sir, I am for you.
OTHELLO: Keep up your bright swords, for the dew will rust them.
  Good signior, you shall more command with years
  Than with your weapons.   60
BRABANTIO: O thou foul thief, where hast thou stowed my daughter?
  Damned as thou art, thou hast enchanted her!
  For I'll refer me to all things of sense,°
  If she in chains of magic were not bound,
  Whether a maid so tender, fair, and happy,   65
  So opposite to marriage that she shunned
  The wealthy, curlèd darlings of our nation,
  Would ever have, t'incur a general mock,°
  Run from her guardage to the sooty bosom
  Of such a thing as thou—to fear, not to delight.   70
  Judge me the world if 'tis not gross in sense°
  That thou hast practiced° on her with foul charms,
  Abused her delicate youth with drugs or minerals
  That weaken motion.° I'll have't disputed on;
  'Tis probable, and palpable to thinking.   75
  I therefore apprehend and do attach° thee
  For an abuser of the world, a practicer
  Of arts inhibited and out of warrant.°
  Lay hold upon him. If he do resist,
  Subdue him at his peril.
OTHELLO: Hold your hands,   80
  Both you of my inclining and the rest.

Were it my cue to fight, I should have known it
Without a prompter. Whither will you that I go
To answer this your charge?
BRABANTIO: To prison, till fit time
Of law and course of direct session   85
Call thee to answer.
OTHELLO: What if I do obey?
How may the Duke be therewith satisfied,
Whose messengers are here about my side
Upon some present° business of the state
To bring me to him?
OFFICER: 'Tis true, most worthy signior.   90
The Duke's in council, and your noble self
I am sure is sent for.
BRABANTIO: How? The Duke in council?
In this time of the night? Bring him away.
Mine's not an idle cause. The Duke himself,
Or any of my brothers° of the state,   95
Cannot but feel this wrong as 'twere their own;
For if such actions may have passage free,
Bondslaves and pagans shall our statesmen be.   *Exeunt.*

Scene III [*A council chamber.*]

   Enter DUKE, SENATORS, *and* OFFICERS [*set at a table, with lights and* ATTENDANTS].

DUKE: There's no composition° in this news
   That gives them credit.°
FIRST SENATOR: Indeed, they are disproportioned.
   My letters say a hundred and seven galleys.
DUKE: And mine a hundred forty.
SECOND SENATOR: And mine two hundred.
   But though they jump° not on a just accompt°—   5
   As in these cases where the aim° reports
   'Tis oft with difference—yet do they all confirm
   A Turkish fleet, and bearing up to Cyprus.
DUKE: Nay, it is possible enough to judgment.°
   I do not so secure me in the error,   10
   But the main article I do approve
   In fearful sense.°
SAILOR [*Within*]:   What, ho! What, ho! What, ho!

                        Enter SAILOR.

---

⁸⁹*present* *immediate.*   ⁹⁵*brothers* *i.e., the other senators.*   **I.iii.** ¹*composition* *agreement.* ²*gives*
them credit *makes them believable.*   ⁵*jump* *agree.* ⁵*just accompt* *exact counting.* ⁶*aim* *ap-*
proximation. ⁹*to judgment* *when carefully considered.* ¹⁰⁻¹²*I do . . . sense* *i.e., just because the num-*
bers disagree in the reports, I do not doubt that the principal information (that the Turkish fleet is out) is fearfully true.

OFFICER: A messenger from the galleys.

DUKE: Now? What's the business?

SAILOR: The Turkish preparation makes for Rhodes.
So was I bid report here to the State   15
By Signior Angelo.

DUKE: How say you by this change?

FIRST SENATOR: This cannot be
By no assay of reason. 'Tis a pageant°
To keep us in false gaze.° When we consider
Th' importancy of Cyprus to the Turk,   20
And let ourselves again but understand
That, as it more concerns the Turk than Rhodes,
So may he with more facile question° bear it,
For that it stands not in such warlike brace,°
But altogether lacks th' abilities   25
That Rhodes is dressed in. If we make thought of this,
We must not think the Turk is so unskillful
To leave that latest which concerns him first,
Neglecting an attempt of ease and gain
To wake and wage a danger profitless.   30

DUKE: Nay, in all confidence he's not for Rhodes.

OFFICER: Here is more news.

Enter a MESSENGER.

MESSENGER: The Ottomites, reverend and gracious,
Steering with due course toward the isle of Rhodes,
Have there injointed them with an after° fleet.   35

FIRST SENATOR: Ay, so I thought. How many, as you guess?

MESSENGER: Of thirty sail; and now they do restem
Their backward course, bearing with frank appearance
Their purposes toward Cyprus. Signior Montano,
Your trusty and most valiant servitor,   40
With his free duty° recommends° you thus,
And prays you to believe him.

DUKE: 'Tis certain then for Cyprus.
Marcus Luccicos, is not he in town?

FIRST SENATOR: He's now in Florence.   45

DUKE: Write from us to him; post-posthaste dispatch.

FIRST SENATOR: Here comes Brabantio and the valiant Moor.

Enter BRABANTIO, OTHELLO, CASSIO, IAGO, RODERIGO, *and* OFFICERS.

DUKE: Valiant Othello, we must straight° employ you
Against the general° enemy Ottoman.

---

[18] **pageant** *show, pretense.*   [19] **in false gaze** *looking the wrong way.*   [23] **facile question** *easy struggle.*
[24] **warlike brace** *"military posture."*   [35] **after** *following.*   [41] **free duty** *unlimited respect.*   [41] **recom-**
mends *informs.*   [48] **straight** *at once.*   [49] **general** *universal.*

[*To* BRABANTIO] I did not see you. Welcome, gentle signior.   50
We lacked your counsel and your help tonight.

BRABANTIO: So did I yours. Good your grace, pardon me.
Neither my place, nor aught I heard of business,
Hath raised me from my bed; nor doth the general care
Take hold on me; for my particular grief   55
Is of so floodgate and o'erbearing nature
That it engluts and swallows other sorrows,
And it is still itself.

DUKE: Why, what's the matter?

BRABANTIO: My daughter! O, my daughter!

SENATORS: Dead?

BRABANTIO: Ay, to me.
She is abused, stol'n from me, and corrupted   60
By spells and medicines bought of mountebanks;
For nature so prepost'rously to err,
Being not deficient, blind, or lame of sense,
Sans° witchcraft could not.

DUKE: Whoe'er he be that in this foul proceeding   65
Hath thus beguiled your daughter of herself,
And you of her, the bloody book of law
You shall yourself read in the bitter letter
After your own sense; yea, though our proper° son
Stood in your action.°

BRABANTIO: Humbly I thank your Grace.   70
Here is the man—this Moor, whom now, it seems,
Your special mandate for the state affairs
Hath hither brought.

ALL: We are very sorry for't.

DUKE [*To* OTHELLO]: What in your own part can you say to this?

BRABANTIO: Nothing, but this is so.   75

OTHELLO: Most potent, grave, and reverend signiors,
My very noble and approved° good masters,
That I have ta'en away this old man's daughter,
It is most true; true I have married her.
The very head and front° of my offending   80
Hath this extent, no more. Rude am I in my speech,
And little blessed with the soft phrase of peace.
For since these arms of mine had seven years' pith°
Till now some nine moons wasted,° they have used
Their dearest° action in the tented field;   85
And little of this great world can I speak
More than pertains to feats of broils and battle;

---

⁶⁴**Sans** *without.*   ⁶⁹**proper** *own.*   ⁷⁰**Stood in your action** *were the accused in your suit.*   ⁷⁷**ap-**
proved *tested, proven by past performance.*   ⁸⁰**head and front** *extreme form (front = forehead).*   ⁸³**pith**
strength.   ⁸⁴**wasted** *past.*   ⁸⁵**dearest** *most important.*

And therefore little shall I grace my cause
In speaking for myself. Yet, by your gracious patience,
I will a round° unvarnished tale deliver   90
Of my whole course of love—what drugs, what charms,
What conjuration, and what mighty magic,
For such proceeding I am charged withal,
I won his daughter—

BRABANTIO: A maiden never bold,
Of spirit so still and quiet that her motion   95
Blushed at herself,° and she, in spite of nature,
Of years, of country, credit, everything,
To fall in love with what she feared to look on!
It is a judgment maimed and most imperfect
That will confess perfection so could err   100
Against all rules of nature, and must be driven
To find out practices of cunning hell
Why this should be. I therefore vouch again
That with some mixtures pow'rful o'er the blood,
Or with some dram, conjured to this effect,   105
He wrought upon her.

DUKE: To vouch this is no proof,
Without more wider and more overt test
Than these thin habits° and poor likelihoods
Of modern° seeming do prefer against him.

FIRST SENATOR: But, Othello, speak.   110
Did you by indirect and forcèd courses
Subdue and poison this young maid's affections?
Or came it by request, and such fair question°
As soul to soul affordeth?

OTHELLO: I do beseech you,
Send for the lady to the Sagittary   115
And let her speak of me before her father.
If you do find me foul in her report,
The trust, the office, I do hold of you
Not only take away, but let your sentence
Even fall upon my life.

DUKE: Fetch Desdemona hither.   120

OTHELLO: Ancient, conduct them; you best know the place.

[*Exit* IAGO, *with two or three* ATTENDANTS.]

And till she come, as truly as to heaven
I do confess the vices of my blood,
So justly to your grave ears I'll present
How I did thrive in this fair lady's love,   125

---

⁹⁰**round** blunt.   ⁹⁵⁻⁹⁶**her motion/Blushed at herself** *i.e., she was so modest that she blushed at every thought (and movement).*   ¹⁰⁸**habits** clothing.   ¹⁰⁹**modern** trivial.   ¹¹³**question** discussion.

And she in mine.

DUKE:　　　　　　　Say it, Othello.

OTHELLO: Her father loved me; oft invited me;
　　Still° questioned me the story of my life
　　From year to year, the battle, sieges, fortune
　　That I have passed.
　　I ran it through, even from my boyish days
　　To th' very moment that he bade me tell it.
　　Wherein I spoke of most disastrous chances,
　　Of moving accidents by flood and field,
　　Of hairbreadth scapes i' th' imminent° deadly breach,
　　Of being taken by the insolent foe
　　And sold to slavery, of my redemption thence
　　And portance° in my travel's history,
　　Wherein of anters° vast and deserts idle,°
　　Rough quarries, rocks, and hills whose heads touch heaven,
　　It was my hint to speak. Such was my process.
　　And of the Cannibals that each other eat,
　　The Anthropophagi,° and men whose heads
　　Grew beneath their shoulders. These things to hear
　　Would Desdemona seriously incline;
　　But still the house affairs would draw her thence;
　　Which ever as she could with haste dispatch,
　　She'd come again, and with a greedy ear
　　Devour up my discourse. Which I observing,
　　Took once a pliant hour, and found good means
　　To draw from her a prayer of earnest heart
　　That I would all my pilgrimage dilate,°
　　Whereof by parcels she had something heard,
　　But not intentively.° I did consent,
　　And often did beguile her of her tears
　　When I did speak of some distressful stroke
　　That my youth suffered. My story being done,
　　She gave me for my pains a world of kisses.
　　She swore in faith 'twas strange, 'twas passing° strange;
　　'Twas pitiful, 'twas wondrous pitiful.
　　She wished she had not heard it; yet she wished
　　That heaven had made her such a man. She thanked me,
　　And bade me, if I had a friend that loved her,
　　I should but teach him how to tell my story,
　　And that would woo her. Upon this hint I spake.
　　She loved me for the dangers I had passed,
　　And I loved her that she did pity them.

130

135

140

145

150

155

160

165

128**Still**　*regularly.*　135**imminent**　*threatening.*　138**portance**　*manner of acting.*　139**anters**　*caves.*
139**idle**　*empty, sterile.*　143**Anthropophagi**　*maneaters.*　152**dilate**　*relate in full.*　154**intentively**
at length and in sequence.　159**passing**　*surpassing.*

This only is the witchcraft I have used.
Here comes the lady. Let her witness it.

Enter DESDEMONA, IAGO, ATTENDANTS.

DUKE: I think this tale would win my daughter too. 170
    Good Brabantio, take up this mangled matter at the best.°
    Men do their broken weapons rather use
    Than their bare hands.
BRABANTIO: I pray you hear her speak.
    If she confess that she was half the wooer,
    Destruction on my head if my bad blame 175
    Light on the man. Come hither, gentle mistress.
    Do you perceive in all this noble company
    Where most you owe obedience?
DESDEMONA: My noble father,
    I do perceive here a divided duty.
    To you I am bound for life and education; 180
    My life and education both do learn me
    How to respect you. You are the lord of duty,
    I am hitherto your daughter. But here's my husband,
    And so much duty as my mother showed
    To you, preferring you before her father, 185
    So much I challenge° that I may profess
    Due to the Moor my lord.
BRABANTIO: God be with you. I have done.
    Please it your Grace, on to the state affairs.
    I had rather to adopt a child than get° it.
    Come hither, Moor. 190
    I here do give thee that with all my heart
    Which, but thou hast already, with all my heart
    I would keep from thee. For your sake,° jewel,
    I am glad at soul I have no other child,
    For thy escape would teach me tyranny, 195
    To hang clogs on them. I have done, my lord.
DUKE: Let me speak like yourself and lay a sentence°
    Which, as a grise° or step, may help these lovers.
    When remedies are past, the griefs are ended
    By seeing the worst, which late on hopes depended.° 200
    To mourn a mischief that is past and gone
    Is the next° way to draw new mischief on.
    What cannot be preserved when fortune takes,
    Patience her injury a mock'ry makes.
    The robbed that smiles, steals something from the thief; 205

171**take . . . best** *i.e., make the best of this disaster.*   186**challenge** *claim as right.*   189**get** *beget.*
193**For your sake** *because of you.*   197**lay a sentence** *provide a maxim.*   198**grise** *step.*   200**late on hopes depended** *was supported by hope (of a better outcome) until lately.*   202**next** *closest, surest.*

He robs himself that spends a bootless° grief.
BRABANTIO: So let the Turk of Cyprus us beguile:
We lose it not so long as we can smile.
He bears the sentence well that nothing bears
But the free comfort which from thence he hears;   210
But he bears both the sentence and the sorrow
That to pay grief must of poor patience borrow.
These sentences, to sugar, or to gall,
Being strong on both sides, are equivocal.
But words are words. I never yet did hear   215
That the bruisèd heart was piercèd° through the ear.
I humbly beseech you, proceed to th' affairs of state.
DUKE: The Turk with a most mighty preparation makes for Cyprus. Othello, the
fortitude° of the place is best known to you; and though we have there a
substitute° of most allowed sufficiency,° yet opinion, a more sovereign mistress 220
of effects, throws a more safer voice on you.° You must therefore be content to
slubber° the gloss of your new fortunes with this more stubborn and
boisterous° expedition.
OTHELLO: The tyrant Custom, most grave senators,
Hath made the flinty and steel couch of war   225
My thrice-driven° bed of down. I do agnize°
A natural and prompt alacrity
I find in hardness and do undertake
These present wars against the Ottomites.
Most humbly, therefore, bending to your state,   230
I crave fit disposition for my wife,
Due reference of place, and exhibition,°
With such accommodation and besort
As levels with° her breeding.
DUKE: Why, at her father's.
BRABANTIO: I will not have it so.
OTHELLO: Nor I.   235
DESDEMONA: Nor would I there reside,
To put my father in impatient thoughts
By being in his eye. Most gracious Duke,
To my unfolding° lend your prosperous° ear,
And let me find a charter° in your voice,   240
T' assist my simpleness.

206**bootless** valueless.   216**piercèd** (some editors emend to piecèd, i.e., "healed." But piercèd makes good sense: Brabantio is saying in effect that his heart cannot be further hurt [pierced] by the indignity of the useless, conventional advice the Duke offers him. Piercèd can also mean, however, "lanced" in the medical sense, and would then mean "treated").   219**fortitude** fortification.   220**substitute** viceroy.   220**most allowed sufficiency** generally acknowledged capability.   220-221**opinion. . . you** i.e., the general opinion, which finally controls affairs, is that you would be the best man in this situation.   222**slubber** besmear.   223**stubborn and boisterous** rough and violent.   226**thrice-driven** i.e., softest.   226**agnize** known in myself.   232**exhibition** grant of funds.   234**levels with** is suitable to.   239**unfolding** explanation.   239**prosperous** favoring. 240**charter** permission.

DUKE: What would you, Desdemona?
DESDEMONA: That I love the Moor to live with him,
  My downright violence, and storm of fortunes,
  May trumpet to the world. My heart's subdued
  Even to the very quality of my lord.°   245
  I saw Othello's visage in his mind,
  And to his honors and his valiant parts
  Did I my soul and fortunes consecrate.
  So that, dear lords, if I be left behind,
  A moth of peace, and he go to the war,   250
  The rites° for why I love him are bereft me,
  And I a heavy interim shall support
  By his dear absence. Let me go with him.
OTHELLO: Let her have your voice.°
  Vouch with me, heaven, I therefore beg it not   255
  To please the palate of my appetite,
  Nor to comply with heat°—the young affects°
  In me defunct—and proper satisfaction;°
  But to be free and bounteous to her mind;
  And heaven defend° your good souls that you think   260
  I will your serious and great business scant
  When she is with me. No, when light-winged toys
  Of feathered Cupid seel° with wanton° dullness
  My speculative and officed instrument,°
  That my disports corrupt and taint my business,   265
  Let housewives make a skillet of my helm,
  And all indign° and base adversities
  Make head° against my estimation!°—
DUKE: Be it as you shall privately determine,
  Either for her stay or going. Th' affair cries haste,   270
  And speed must answer it.
FIRST SENATOR: You must away tonight.
OTHELLO: With all my heart.
DUKE: At nine i' th' morning here we'll meet again.
Othello, leave some officer behind,
  And he shall our commission bring to you,   275
  And such things else of quality and respect
  As doth import you.
OTHELLO: So please your grace, my ancient;
  A man he is of honesty and trust.

244-245**My . . . lord** *i.e., I have become one in nature and being with the man I married (therefore, I too would go
to the wars like a soldier).*   251**rites** *(may refer either to the marriage rites or to the rites, formalities, of war).*
254**voice** *consent.*   257**heat** *lust.*   257**affects** *passions.*   258**proper satisfaction** *i.e., consummation of the marriage.*   260**defend** *forbid.*   263**seel** *sew up.*   263**wanton** *lascivious.*   264**speculative . . . instrument** *i.e., sight (and, by extension, the mind).*   267**indign** *unworthy.*   268**Make head**
form an army, i.e., attack.   268**estimation** *reputation.*

To his conveyance I assign my wife,
With what else needful your good grace shall think   280
to be sent after me.

DUKE: Let it be so.
Good night to every one. [*To* BRABANTIO] And, noble signior,
If virtue no delighted° beauty lack,
Your son-in-law is far more fair than black.

FIRST SENATOR: Adieu, brave Moor. Use Desdemona well.   285

BRABANTIO: Look to her, Moor, if thou hast eyes to see:
She has deceived her father, and may thee.

[*Exeunt* DUKE, SENATORS, OFFICERS, & *c.*]

OTHELLO: My life upon her faith! Honest Iago,
My Desdemona must I leave to thee.
I prithee let thy wife attend on her,
And bring them after in the best advantage.°   290
Come, Desdemona. I have but an hour
Of love, of worldly matter, and direction
To spend with thee. We must obey the time.

Exit [MOOR *with* DESDEMONA].

RODERIGO: Iago?   295

IAGO: What say'st thou, noble heart?

RODERIGO: What will I do, think'st thou?

IAGO: Why, go to bed and sleep.

RODERIGO: I will incontinently° drown myself.

IAGO: If thou dost, I shall never love thee after. Why, thou silly gentleman?   300

RODERIGO: It is silliness to live when to live is torment; and then have we a
prescription to die when death is our physician.

IAGO: O villainous! I have looked upon the world for four times seven years, and
since I could distinguish betwixt a benefit and an injury, I never found man that
knew how to love himself. Ere I would say I would drown myself for the love   305
of a guinea hen, I would change my humanity with a baboon.

RODERIGO: What should I do? I confess it is my shame to be so fond, but it is not
in my virtue° to amend it.

IAGO: Virtue? A fig! 'Tis in ourselves that we are thus, or thus. Our bodies are   310
our gardens, to the which our wills are gardeners; so that if we will plant nettles
or sow lettuce, set hyssop and weed up thyme, supply it with one gender of
herbs or distract° it with many—either to have it sterile with idleness or
manured with industry—why, the power and corrigible° authority of this lies
in our wills. If the balance of our lives had not one scale of reason to poise   315
another of sensuality, the blood and baseness of our natures would conduct us
to most prepost'rous conclusions.° But we have reason to cool our raging

---

²⁸³**delighted** *delightful.*   ²⁹¹**advantage** *opportunity.*   ²⁹⁹**incontinently** *at once.*   ³⁰⁹**virtue**
strength (Roderigo is saying that his nature controls him).   ³¹³**distract** *vary.*   ³¹⁴**corrigible** *corrective.*
³¹⁷**conclusions** *ends.*

motions, our carnal sting or unbitted° lusts, whereof I take this that you call
love to be a sect or scion.°

RODERIGO: It cannot be.   320

IAGO: It is merely a lust of the blood and a permission of the will. Come, be a
   man! Drown thyself? Drown cats and blind puppies! I have professed me thy
   friend, and I confess me knit to thy deserving with cables of perdurable
   toughness. I could never better stead° thee than now. Put money in thy purse.
   Follow thou the wars; defeat thy favor° with an usurped° beard. I say, put   325
   money in thy purse. It cannot be long that Desdemona should continue her
   love to the Moor. Put money in thy purse. Nor he his to her. It was a violent
   commencement in her and thou shalt see an answerable° sequestration—put
   but money in thy purse. These Moors are changeable in their wills—fill thy   330
   purse with money. The food that to him now is as luscious as locusts° shall be
   to him shortly as bitter as coloquintida.° She must change for youth; when she
   is sated with his body, she will find the errors of her choice. Therefore, put
   money in thy purse. If thou wilt needs damn thyself, do it a more delicate way
   than drowning. Make all the money thou canst. If sanctimony° and a frail vow   335
   betwixt an erring° barbarian and supersubtle Venetian be not too hard for my
   wits, and all the tribe of hell, thou shalt enjoy her. Therefore, make money. A
   pox of drowning thyself, it is clean out of the way. Seek thou rather to be
   hanged in compassing° thy joy than to be drowned and go without her.   340

RODERIGO: Wilt thou be fast to my hopes, if I depend on the issue?

IAGO: Thou art sure of me. Go, make money. I have told thee often, and I retell
   thee again and again, I hate the Moor. My cause is hearted;° thine hath no less
   reason. Let us be conjunctive° in our revenge against him. If thou canst cuckold
   him, thou dost thyself a pleasure, me a sport. There are many events in the   345
   womb of time, which will be delivered. Traverse, go, provide thy money! We
   will have more of this tomorrow. Adieu.

RODERIGO: Where shall we meet i' th' morning?

IAGO: At my lodging.

RODERIGO: I'll be with thee betimes.   350

IAGO: Go to, farewell. Do you hear, Roderigo?

RODERIGO: I'll sell all my land.   *Exit.*

IAGO: Thus do I ever make my fool my purse;
   For I mine own gained knowledge° should profane
   If I would time expend with such snipe   355
   But for my sport and profit. I hate the Moor,
   And it is thought abroad that 'twixt my sheets
   H'as done my office. I know not if't be true,
   But I, for mere suspicion in that kind,
   Will do, as if for surety.° He holds me well;   360

---

³¹⁸**unbitted** *i.e., uncontrolled.*   ³¹⁹**sect or scion** *off-shoot.*   ³²⁴**stead** *serve.*   ³²⁵**defeat thy favor**
disguise your face.   ³²⁵**usurped** *assumed.*   ³²⁹**answerable** *similar.*   ³³¹**locusts** *(a sweet fruit).*
³³²**coloquintida** *a purgative derived from a bitter apple.*   ³³⁵**sanctimony** *sacred bond (of marriage).*
³³⁶**erring** *wandering.*   ³³⁹**compassing** *encompassing, achieving.*   ³⁴³**hearted** *deepseated in the heart.*
³⁴⁴**conjunctive** *joined.*   ³⁵⁴**gained knowledge** *i.e., practical, worldly wisdom.*   ³⁶⁰**surety** *certainty.*

The better shall my purpose work on him.
Cassio's a proper° man. Let me see now:
To get his place, and to plume up my will°
In double knavery. How? How? Let's see.
After some time, to abuse Othello's ears   365
That he is too familiar with his wife.
He hath a person and a smooth dispose°
To be suspected—framed° to make women false.
The Moor is of a free and open nature
That thinks men honest that but seem to be so;   370
And will as tenderly be led by th' nose
As asses are.
I have't! It is engendered! Hell and night
Must bring this monstrous birth to the world's light. *[Exit.]*

ACT II

Scene I [Cyprus.]

> *Enter* MONTANO *and two* GENTLEMEN [*one above*]°.

MONTANO: What from the cape can you discern at sea?
FIRST GENTLEMAN: Nothing at all, it is a high-wrought flood.
 I cannot 'twixt the heaven and the main
 Descry a sail.
MONTANO: Methinks the wind hath spoke aloud at land;   5
 A fuller blast ne'er shook our battlements.
 If it hath ruffianed so upon the sea,
 What ribs of oak, when mountains melt on them,
 Can hold the mortise? What shall we hear of this?
SECOND GENTLEMAN: A segregation° of the Turkish fleet. 10
 For do but stand upon the foaming shore,
 The chidden billow seems to pelt the clouds;
 The wind-shaked surge, with high and monstrous main,°
 Seems to cast water on the burning Bear
 And quench the guards of th' ever-fixèd pole.°   15
 I never did like molestation view
 On the enchafèd flood.

362**proper** *handsome.* 363**plume up my will** *(many explanations have been offered for this crucial line, which in Q1, reads "make up my will." The general sense is something like "to make more proud and gratify my ego").* 367**dispose** *manner.* 368**framed** *designed.* **II.i. s.d. above** *(the Folio arrangement of this scene requires that the First Gentleman stand above—on the upper stage—and act as a lookout reporting sights which cannot be seen by Montano standing below on the main stage).* 10**segregation** *separation.* 13**main** *(both "ocean" and "strength").* 14–15**Seems . . . pole** *(the constellation Ursa Minor contains two stars which are the guards, or companions, of the pole, or North Star).*

MONTANO: If that the Turkish fleet
  Be not ensheltered and embayed, they are drowned;
  It is impossible to bear it out.

Enter a [third] GENTLEMAN.

THIRD GENTLEMAN: News, lads! Our wars are done.   20
  The desperate tempest hath so banged the Turks
  That their designment halts. A noble ship of Venice
  Hath seen a grievous wrack and sufferance°
  On most part of their fleet.
MONTANO: How? Is this true?
THIRD GENTLEMAN: The ship is here put in,   25
  A Veronesa; Michael Cassio,
  Lieutenant to the warlike Moor Othello,
  Is come on shore; the Moor himself at sea,
  And is in full commission here for Cyprus.
MONTANO: I am glad on't. 'Tis a worthy governor.   30
THIRD GENTLEMAN: But this same Cassio, though he speak of comfort
  Touching the Turkish loss, yet he looks sadly
  And prays the Moor be safe, for they were parted
  With foul and violent tempest.
MONTANO: Pray heavens he be;
  For I have served him, and the man commands   35
  Like a full soldier. Let's to the seaside, ho!
  As well to see the vessel that's come in
  As to throw out our eyes for brave Othello,
  Even till we make the main and th' aerial blue
  An indistinct regard.°
THIRD GENTLEMAN: Come, let's do so;   40
  For every minute is expectancy
  Of more arrivancie.°

Enter CASSIO.

CASSIO: Thanks, you the valiant of the warlike isle,
  That so approve° the Moor. O, let the heavens
  Give him defense against the elements,   45
  For I have lost him on a dangerous sea.
MONTANO: Is he well shipped?
CASSIO: His bark is stoutly timbered, and his pilot
  Of very expert and approved allowance;°
  Therefore my hopes, not surfeited to death,°   50
  Stand in bold cure.° (*Within:* A sail, a sail, a sail!)

---

²³**sufferance** *damage.*   ^{39–40}**the main . . . regard** *i.e., the sea and sky become indistinguishable.*   ⁴²**ar-**
rivancie *arrivals.*   ⁴⁴**approve** *("honor" or, perhaps, "are as warlike and valiant as your governor").*   ⁴⁹**ap-**
proved allowance *known and tested.*   ⁵⁰**not surfeited to death** *i.e., not so great as to be in danger.*
⁵¹**Stand in bold cure** *i.e., are likely to be restored.*

CASSIO: What noise?

FIRST GENTLEMAN: The town is empty; on the brow o' th' sea
   Stand ranks of people, and they cry, "A sail!"

CASSIO: My hopes do shape him for the governor.   [A shot.] 55

SECOND GENTLEMAN: They do discharge their shot of courtesy:
   Our friends at least.

CASSIO: I pray you, sir, go forth
   And give us truth who 'tis that is arrived.

SECOND GENTLEMAN: I shall.   [Exit.]

MONTANO: But, good lieutenant, is your general wived?   60

CASSIO: Most fortunately. He hath achieved a maid
   That paragons° description and wild fame;°
   One that excels the quirks of blazoning pens,°
   And in th' essential vesture of creation°
   Does tire the ingener.°

Enter [Second] GENTLEMAN.

            How now? Who has put in?   65

SECOND GENTLEMAN: 'Tis one Iago, ancient to the general.

CASSIO: H'as had most favorable and happy speed:
   Tempests themselves, high seas, and howling winds,
   The guttered° rocks and congregated° sands,
   Traitors ensteeped° to enclog the guiltless keel,   70
   As having sense° of beauty, do omit
   Their mortal° natures, letting go safely by
   The divine Desdemona.

MONTANO: What is she?

CASSIO: She that I spake of, our great captain's captain,
   Left in the conduct of the bold Iago,   75
   Whose footing° here anticipates our thoughts
   A se'nnight's° speed. Great Jove, Othello guard,
   And swell his sail with thine own pow'rful breath,
   That he may bless this bay with his tall° ship,
   Make love's quick pants in Desdemona's arms,   80
   Give renewed fire to our extinct spirits,
   And bring all Cyprus comfort!

Enter DESDEMONA, IAGO, RODERIGO, and EMILIA.

   O, behold! The riches of the ship is come on shore!
   You men of Cyprus, let her have your knees.   [Kneeling.]
   Hail to thee, lady! and the grace of heaven,
   Before, behind thee, and on every hand,   85

62**paragons** exceeds.   62**wild fame** extravagant report.   63**quirks of blazoning pens** ingenuities of praising pens.   64**essential vesture of creation** essential human nature as given by the Creator.   65**tire the ingener** a difficult line that probably means something like "outdo the human ability to imagine and picture." 69**guttered** jagged.   69**congregated** gathered.   70**ensteeped** submerged.   71**sense** awareness. 72**mortal** deadly.   76**footing** landing.   77**se'n-night's** week's.   79**tall** brave.

Enwheel thee round.

DESDEMONA: I thank you, valiant Cassio.

What tidings can you tell of my lord?

CASSIO: He is not yet arrived, nor know I aught

But that he's well and will be shortly here.

DESDEMONA: O but I fear. How lost you company? 90

CASSIO: The great contention of sea and skies

Parted our fellowship. (*Within:* A sail, a sail!) [*A shot.*]

But hark. A sail!

SECOND GENTLEMAN: They give this greeting to the citadel;

This likewise is a friend.

CASSIO: See for the news. [*Exit* GENTLEMAN.] 95

Good ancient, you are welcome. [*To* EMILIA] Welcome, mistress.

Let it not gall your patience, good Iago,

That I extend° my manners. 'Tis my breeding°

That gives me this bold show of courtesy. [*Kisses* EMILIA.]

IAGO: Sir, would she give you so much of her lips 100

As of her tongue she oft bestows on me,

You would have enough.

DESDEMONA: Alas, she has no speech.

IAGO: In faith, too much.

I find it still when I have leave to sleep.°

Marry, before your ladyship,° I grant, 105

She puts her tongue a little in her heart

And chides with thinking.

EMILIA: You have little cause to say so.

IAGO: Come on, come on! You are pictures° out of door,

Bells in your parlors, wildcats in your kitchens,

Saints in your injuries,° devils being offended, 110

Players in your housewifery,° and housewives in your beds.

DESDEMONA: O, fie upon thee, slanderer!

IAGO: Nay, it is true, or else I am a Turk:

You rise to play, and go to bed to work.

EMILIA: You shall not write my praise.

IAGO: No, let me not. 115

DESDEMONA: What wouldst write of me, if thou shouldst praise me?

IAGO: O gentle lady, do not put me to't.

For I am nothing if not critical.

DESDEMONA: Come on, assay. There's one gone to the harbor?

IAGO: Ay, madam.

---

⁹⁸**extend** *stretch.*   ⁹⁸**breeding** *careful training in manners (Cassio is considerably more the polished gentleman than Iago, and aware of it).*   ¹⁰⁴**still . . . sleep** *i.e., even when she allows me to sleep she continues to scold.* ¹⁰⁵**before your ladyship** *in your presence.*   ¹⁰⁸**pictures** *models (of virtue).*   ¹¹⁰**in your injuries** *when you injure others.*   ¹¹¹**housewifery** *this word can mean "careful, economical household management," and Iago would then be accusing women of only pretending to be good housekeepers, while in bed they are either [1] economical of their favors, or more likely [2] serious and dedicated workers.*

DESDEMONA [*Aside*]: I am not merry; but I do beguile   120
    The thing I am by seeming otherwise.—
    Come, how wouldst thou praise me?
IAGO: I am about it; but indeed my invention
    Comes from my pate as birdlime° does from frieze°—
    It plucks out brains and all. But my Muse labors,   125
    And thus she is delivered:
    If she be fair° and wise: fairness and wit,
    The one's for use, the other useth it.
DESDEMONA: Well praised. How if she be black° and witty?
IAGO: If she be black, and thereto have a wit,   130
    She'll find a white that shall her blackness fit.
DESDEMONA: Worse and worse!
EMILIA: How if fair and foolish?
IAGO: She never yet was foolish that was fair,
    For even her folly helped her to an heir.   135
DESDEMONA: Those are old fond° paradoxes to make fools laugh i' th' alehouse.
    What miserable praise hast thou for her that's foul and foolish?
IAGO: There's none so foul, and foolish thereunto,
    But does foul pranks which fair and wise ones do.
DESDEMONA: O heavy ignorance. Thou praisest the worst best. But what praise
    couldst thou bestow on a deserving woman indeed—one that in the authority   140
    of her merit did justly put on the vouch of very malice itself?°
IAGO: She that was ever fair, and never proud;
    Had tongue at will, and yet was never loud;
    Never lacked gold, and yet went never gay;   145
    Fled from her wish, and yet said "Now I may";
    She that being angered, her revenge being nigh,
    Bade her wrong stay, and her displeasure fly;
    She that in wisdom never was so frail   150
    To change the cod's head for the salmon's tail;°
    She that could think, and nev'r disclose her mind;
    See suitors following, and not look behind:
    She was a wight° (if ever such wights were)—
DESDEMONA: To do what?   155
IAGO: To suckle fools and chronicle small beer.°
DESDEMONA: O most lame and impotent conclusion. Do not learn of him, Emilia,
    though he be thy husband. How say you, Cassio? Is he not a most profane and
    liberal° counselor?
CASSIO: He speaks home,° madam. You may relish him more in° the soldier than   160
    in the scholar. [*Takes* DESDEMONA'S *hand.*]

---

¹²⁴*birdlime*   *a sticky substance put on branches to catch birds.*   ¹²⁴*frieze*   *rough cloth.*   ¹²⁷*fair*   *light-complexioned.*   ¹²⁹*black*   *brunette.*   ¹³⁶*fond*   *foolish.*   ¹⁴¹⁻¹⁴³*one . . . itself*   *i.e., a woman so honest and deserving that even malice would be forced to approve of her.*   ¹⁵¹*To . . . tail*   *i.e., to exchange something valuable for something useless.*   ¹⁵⁴*wight*   *person.*   ¹⁵⁶*chronicle small beer*   *i.e., keep household accounts (the most trivial of occupations in Iago's opinion).*   ¹⁵⁹*liberal*   *licentious.*   ¹⁶⁰*speaks home*   *thrusts deeply with his speech.*   ⁶⁰*relish him more in*   *enjoy him more as.*

IAGO [*Aside*]: He takes her by the palm. Ay, well said, whisper! With as little a web
as this will I ensnare as great a fly as Cassio. Ay, smile upon her, do! I will gyve°
thee in thine own courtship.—You say true; 'tis so, indeed!—If such tricks as
these strip you out of your lieutenantry, it had been better you had not kissed   165
your three fingers so oft—which now again you are most apt to play the sir° in.
Very good! Well kissed! An excellent curtsy!° 'Tis so, indeed. Yet again your
fingers to your lips? Would they were clyster pipes° for your sake! [*Trumpets
within.*] The Moor! I know his trumpet.°   170

CASSIO: 'Tis truly so.

DESDEMONA: Let's meet him and receive him.

CASSIO: Lo, where he comes.

Enter OTHELLO *and* ATTENDANTS.

OTHELLO: O my fair warrior!

DESDEMONA: My dear Othello.

OTHELLO: It gives me wonder great as my content   175
　　To see you here before me. O my soul's joy!
　　If after every tempest come such calms,
　　May the winds blow till they have wakened death.
　　And let the laboring bark climb hills of seas
　　Olympus-high, and duck again as low   180
　　As hell's from heaven. If it were now to die,
　　'Twere now to be most happy; for I fear
　　My soul hath her content so absolute
　　That not another comfort like to this
　　Succeeds in unknown fate.

DESDEMONA: The heavens forbid   185
　　But that our loves and comforts should increase
　　Even as our days do grow.

OTHELLO: Amen to that, sweet powers!
　　I cannot speak enough of this content:
　　It stops me here [*touches his heart*]; it is too much of joy.
　　And this, and this, the greatest discords be   [*They kiss.*] 190
　　That e'er our hearts shall make!

IAGO [*Aside*]:   O, you are well tuned now!
　　But I'll set down the pegs° that make this music,
　　As honest as I am.

OTHELLO: Come, let us to the castle.
　　News, friends! Our wars are done; the Turks are drowned.
　　How does my old acquaintance of this isle?   195
　　Honey, you shall be well desired in Cyprus;
　　I have found great love amongst them. O my sweet,
　　I prattle out of fashion, and I dote

---

¹⁶⁴**gyve** bind.　　¹⁶⁷**the sir** the fashionable gentleman.　　¹⁶⁸**curtsy** courtesy, i.e., bow.　　¹⁶⁹**clyster
pipes** enema tubes.　　¹⁷⁰**his trumpet** (great men had their own distinctive calls).　　¹⁹²**set down the pegs**
loosen the strings (to produce discord).

In mine own comforts. I prithee, good Iago,
Go to the bay and disembark my coffers.   200
Bring thou the master to the citadel;
He is a good one and his worthiness
Does challenge° much respect. Come, Desdemona,
Once more well met at Cyprus.

Exit OTHELLO *and* DESDEMONA [*and all but* IAGO *and* RODERIGO].

IAGO [*To an Attendant*]: Do thou meet me presently at the harbor. [*To* RODERIGO]   205
Come hither. If thou be'st valiant (as they say base men being in love have then
a nobility in their natures more than is native to them), list me. The lieutenant
tonight watches on the court of guard.° First, I must tell thee this: Desdemona
is directly in love with him.

RODERIGO: With him? Why, 'tis not possible.   210

IAGO: Lay thy finger thus [*puts his finger to his lips*], and let thy soul be instructed.
Mark me with what violence she first loved the Moor but for bragging and
telling her fantastical lies. To love him still for prating? Let not thy discreet heart
think it. Her eye must be fed. And what delight shall she have to look on the
devil? When the blood is made dull with the act of sport, there should be a   215
game° to inflame it and to give satiety a fresh appetite, loveliness in favor,°
sympathy in years,° manners, and beauties; all which the Moor is defective in.
Now for want of these required conveniences,° her delicate tenderness will find
itself abused, begin to heave the gorge,° disrelish and abhor the Moor. Very
nature will instruct her in it and compel her to some second choice. Now sir,   220
this granted—as it is a most pregnant° and unforced position—who stands so
eminent in the degree of this fortune as Cassio does? A knave very voluble; no
further conscionable° than in putting on the mere form of civil and humane°
seeming for the better compass of his salt° and most hidden loose° affection.
Why, none! Why, none! A slipper° and subtle knave, a finder of occasion, that   225
has an eye can stamp and counterfeit advantages, though true advantage never
present itself. A devilish knave. Besides, the knave is handsome, young, and hath
all those requisites in him that folly and green minds look after. A pestilent
complete knave, and the woman hath found him already.   230

RODERIGO: I cannot believe that in her; she's full of most blessed condition.

IAGO: Blessed fig's-end! The wine she drinks is made of grapes. If she had been
blessed, she would never have loved the Moor. Blessed pudding! Didst thou not
see her paddle with the palm of his hand? Didst not mark that?   235

RODERIGO: Yes, that I did; but that was but courtesy.

IAGO: Lechery, by this hand! [*Extends his index finger.*] An index° and obscure
prologue to the history of lust and foul thoughts. They met so near with their
lips that their breaths embraced together. Villainous thoughts, Roderigo. When

---

²⁰³**challenge** *require, exact.*   ²⁰⁸**court of guard** *guardhouse.*   ²¹⁶**game** *sport (with the added sense of
"gamey," "rank").*   ²¹⁷**favor** *countenance, appearance.*   ²¹⁷**sympathy in years** *sameness of age.*
²¹⁹**conveniences** *advantages.*   ²²⁰**heave the gorge** *vomit.*   ²²²**pregnant** *likely.*   223–224**no further conscionable** *having no more conscience.*   ²²⁴**humane** *polite.*   ²²⁵**salt** *lecherous.*   ²²⁵**loose**
immoral.   ²²⁶**slipper** *slippery.*   ²³⁷**index** *pointer.*

these mutualities so marshal the way, hard at hand comes the master and main 240
exercise, th' incorporate° conclusion: Pish! But, sir, be you ruled by me. I have
brought you from Venice. Watch you tonight; for the command, I'll lay't upon
you. Cassio knows you not. I'll not be far from you. Do you find some occasion
to anger Cassio, either by speaking too loud, or tainting° his discipline, or from 245
what other course you please which the time shall more favorably minister.

RODERIGO: Well.

IAGO: Sir, he's rash and very sudden in choler,° and haply may strike at you.
Provoke him that he may; for even out of that will I cause these of Cyprus to
mutiny, whose qualification shall come into no true taste° again but by the 250
displanting of Cassio. So shall you have a shorter journey to your desires by the
means I shall then have to prefer them; and the impediment most profitably
removed without the which there were no expectation of our prosperity.

RODERIGO: I will do this if you can bring it to any opportunity. 255

IAGO: I warrant thee. Meet me by and by at the citadel. I must fetch his
necessaries ashore. Farewell.

RODERIGO: Adieu.   *Exit.*

IAGO: That Cassio loves her, I do well believe't;
That she loves him, 'tis apt and of great credit. 260
The Moor, howbeit that I endure him not,
Is of a constant, loving, noble nature,
And I dare think he'll prove to Desdemona
A most dear° husband. Now I do love her too;
Not out of absolute° lust, though peradventure° 265
I stand accountant for as great a sin,
But partly led to diet° my revenge,
For that I do suspect the lusty Moor
Hath leaped into my seat; the thought whereof
Doth, like a poisonous mineral, gnaw my inwards; 270
And nothing can or shall content my soul
Till I am evened with him, wife for wife.
Or failing so, yet that I put the Moor
At least into a jealousy so strong
That judgment cannot cure. Which thing to do, 275
If this poor trash of Venice, whom I trace°
For his quick hunting, stand the putting on,
I'll have our Michael Cassio on the hip,
Abuse him to the Moor in the right garb°
(For I fear Cassio with my nightcap too), 280
Make the Moor thank me, love me, and reward me
For making him egregiously an ass

---

²⁴¹**incorporate** *carnal.*   ²⁴⁵**tainting** *discrediting.*   ²⁴⁸**choler** *anger.*   ²⁵⁰**qualification . . . taste**
i.e., appeasement will not be brought about (wine was "qualified" by adding water).   ²⁶⁴**dear** *expensive*
²⁶⁵**out of absolute** *absolutely out of.*   ²⁶⁵**peradventure** *perchance.*   ²⁶⁷**diet** *feed.*   ²⁷⁶**trace** *(most
editors emend to "trash," meaning to hang weights on a dog to slow his hunting: but "trace" clearly means something
like "put on the trace" or "set on the track").*   ²⁷⁹**right garb** *i.e., "proper fashion."*

And practicing upon° his peace and quiet,
Even to madness. 'Tis here, but yet confused:
Knavery's plain face is never seen till used.   *Exit.* 285

Scene II [*A street.*]

Enter OTHELLO'S HERALD, *with a proclamation.*

HERALD: It is Othello's pleasure, our noble and valiant general, that upon certain
tidings now arrived importing the mere perdition° of the Turkish fleet, every
man put himself into triumph. Some to dance, some to make bonfires, each
man to what sport and revels his addition° leads him. For, besides these
beneficial news, it is the celebration of his nuptial. So much was his pleasure   5
should be proclaimed. All offices° are open, and there is full liberty of feasting
from this present hour of five till the bell have told eleven. Bless the isle of
Cyprus and our noble general Othello!   *Exit.*

Scene III [*The citadel of Cyprus.*]

Enter OTHELLO, DESDEMONA, CASSIO, *and* ATTENDANTS.

OTHELLO: Good Michael, look you to the guard tonight.
Let's teach ourselves that honorable stop,
Not to outsport discretion.
CASSIO: Iago hath direction what to do;
But notwithstanding, with my personal eye
Will I look to't.   5
OTHELLO: Iago is most honest.
Michael, good night. Tomorrow with your earliest
Let me have speech with you. [*To* DESDEMONA] Come, my dear love,
The purchase made, the fruits are to ensue.
That profit's yet to come 'tween me and you.
Good night.   *Exit* [OTHELLO *with* DESDEMONA *and* ATTENDANTS].   10

Enter IAGO.

CASSIO: Welcome, Iago. We must to the watch.
IAGO: Not this hour, lieutenant; 'tis not yet ten o' th' clock. Our general cast° us
thus early for the love of his Desdemona; who let us not therefore blame. He
hath not yet made wanton the night with her, and she is sport for Jove.   15
CASSIO: She's a most exquisite lady.
IAGO: And, I'll warrant her, full of game.
CASSIO: Indeed, she's a most fresh and delicate creature.
IAGO: What an eye she has! Methinks it sounds a parley to provocation.
CASSIO: An inviting eye; and yet methinks right modest.   20

283*practicing upon* *scheming to destroy.*   **II.ii.** 2*mere perdition* *absolute destruction.*   4*addition*
rank.   6*offices* *kitchens and storerooms of food.*   **II.iii.** 13*cast* *dismissed.*

IAGO: And when she speaks, is it not an alarum° to love?

CASSIO: She is indeed perfection.

IAGO: Well, happiness to their sheets! Come, lieutenant, I have a stoup° of wine,
and here without are a brace of Cyprus gallants that would fain have a measure   25
to the health of black Othello.

CASSIO: Not tonight, good Iago. I have very poor and unhappy brains for
drinking; I could well wish courtesy would invent some other custom of
entertainment.

IAGO: O, they are our friends. But one cup! I'll drink for you.   30

CASSIO: I have drunk but one tonight, and that was craftily qualified° too; and
behold what innovation it makes here. I am unfortunate in the infirmity and
dare not task my weakness with any more.

IAGO: What, man! 'Tis a night of revels, the gallants desire it.

CASSIO: Where are they?   35

IAGO: Here, at the door. I pray you call them in.

CASSIO: I'll do't, but it dislikes me.   *Exit.*

IAGO: If I can fasten but one cup upon him
    With that which he hath drunk tonight already,
    He'll be as full of quarrel and offense   40
    As my young mistress' dog. Now, my sick fool Roderigo,
    Whom love hath turned almost the wrong side out,
    To Desdemona hath tonight caroused
    Potations pottle-deep;° and he's to watch.
    Three else° of Cyprus, noble swelling spirits,   45
    That hold their honors in a wary distance,°
    The very elements of this warlike isle,
    Have I tonight flustered with flowing cups,
    And they watch too. Now, 'mongst this flock of drunkards
    Am I to put our Cassio in some action   50
    That may offend the isle. But here they come.

Enter CASSIO, MONTANO, *and* GENTLEMEN.

    If consequence do but approve my dream,
    My boat sails freely, both with wind and stream.

CASSIO: 'Fore God, they have given me a rouse° already.

MONTANO: Good faith, a little one; not past a pint, as I am a soldier.   55

IAGO: Some wine, ho!

    [*Sings*] And let me the canakin clink, clink;
                And let me the canakin clink.
                    A soldier's a man;
                    O man's life's but a span.   60
                Why then, let a soldier drink.
    Some wine, boys!

---

²²**alarum**   *the call to action, "general quarters."*   ²⁴**stoup**   *two-quart tankard.*   ³¹**qualified**   *diluted.*
⁴⁴**pottle-deep**   *to the bottom of the cup.*   ⁴⁵**else**   *others.*   ⁴⁶**hold . . . distance**   *are scrupulous in main-*
taining their honor.   ⁵⁴**rouse**   *drink.*

CASSIO: 'Fore God, an excellent song!

IAGO: I learned it in England, where indeed they are most potent in potting. Your
    Dane, your German, and your swag-bellied° Hollander—Drink, ho!—are   65
    nothing to your English.

CASSIO: Is your Englishman so exquisite° in his drinking?

IAGO: Why, he drinks you with facility your Dane dead drunk; he sweats not to
    overthrow your Almain; he gives your Hollander a vomit ere the next pottle
    can be filled.   70

CASSIO: To the health of our general!

MONTANO: I am for it, lieutenant, and I'll do you justice.

IAGO: O sweet England!

    [Sings]   King Stephen was and a worthy peer;
          His breeches cost him but a crown;   75
          He held them sixpence all too dear,
          With that he called the tailor lown.°
          He was a wight of high renown,
          And thou art but of low degree:
          'Tis pride that pulls the country down;   80
          And take thine auld cloak about thee.
    Some wine, ho!

CASSIO: 'Fore God, this is a more exquisite song than the other.

IAGO: Will you hear't again?

CASSIO: No, for I hold him to be unworthy of his place that does those things.   85
    Well, God's above all; and there be souls must be saved, and there be souls must
    not be saved.

IAGO: It's true, good lieutenant.

CASSIO: For mine own part—no offense to the general, nor any man of quality—I
    hope to be saved.   90

IAGO: And so do I too, lieutenant.

CASSIO: Ay, but, by your leave, not before me. The lieutenant is to be saved before
    the ancient. Let's have no more of this; let's to our affairs.—God forgive us our
    sins!—Gentlemen, let's look to our business. Do not think, gentlemen, I am
    drunk. This is my ancient; this is my right hand, and this is my left. I am not   95
    drunk now. I can stand well enough, and I speak well enough.

GENTLEMEN: Excellent well!

CASSIO: Why, very well then. You must not think then that I am drunk.

                                                    Exit.

MONTANO: To th' platform, masters. Come, let's set the watch.   100

IAGO: You see this fellow that is gone before.
    He's a soldier fit to stand by Caesar
    And give direction; and do but see his vice.
    'Tis to his virtue a just equinox,°
    The one as long as th' other. 'Tis pity of him.   105
    I fear the trust Othello puts him in,
    On some odd time of his infirmity,

---

⁶⁵*swag-bellied* pendulous-bellied.   ⁶⁷*exquisite* superb.   ⁷⁷*lown* lout.   ¹⁰⁴*just equinox* exact balance (of dark and light).

Will shake this island.

MONTANO: But is he often thus?

IAGO: 'Tis evermore his prologue to his sleep:

   He'll watch the horologe a double set°   110

   If drink rock not his cradle.

MONTANO: It were well

   The general were put in mind of it.

   Perhaps he sees it not, or his good nature

   Prizes the virtue that appears in Cassio

   And looks not on his evils. Is not this true?   115

Enter RODERIGO.

IAGO [*Aside*]: How now, Roderigo?

   I pray you after the lieutenant, go!   [*Exit* RODERIGO.]

MONTANO: And 'tis great pity that the noble Moor

   Should hazard such a place as his own second

   With one of an ingraft° infirmity.   120

   It were an honest action to say so

   To the Moor.

IAGO: Not I, for this fair island!

   I do love Cassio well and would do much

   To cure him of this evil.   (Help! Help! *Within*.)

   But hark! What noise?   125

Enter CASSIO, *pursuing* RODERIGO.

CASSIO: Zounds, you rogue! You rascal!

MONTANO: What's the matter, lieutenant?

CASSIO: A knave teach me my duty? I'll beat the knave into a twiggen°

   bottle.

RODERIGO: Beat me?   130

CASSIO: Dost thou prate, rogue?   [*Strikes him.*]

MONTANO: Nay, good lieutenant! I pray you, sir, hold your hand.

[*Stays him.*]

CASSIO: Let me go, sir, or I'll knock you o'er the mazzard.°

MONTANO: Come, come, you're drunk!

CASSIO: Drunk?   [*They fight.*] 135

IAGO [*Aside to* RODERIGO]: Away, I say! Go out and cry a mutiny!

[*Exit* RODERIGO.]

Nay, good lieutenant. God's will, gentlemen!

Help, ho! Lieutenant. Sir. Montano.

Help, masters! Here's a goodly watch indeed!   [*A bell rung.*]

Who's that which rings the bell? Diablo, ho!   140

---

¹¹⁰**watch . . . set**   *stay awake twice around the clock.*   ¹²⁰**ingraft**   *ingrained.*   ¹²⁸**twiggen**   *wicker-covered.*   ¹³³**mazzard**   *head.*

The two will rise. God's will, lieutenant,
You'll be ashamed forever.

Enter OTHELLO *and* ATTENDANTS.

OTHELLO: What is the matter here?
MONTANO: Zounds, I bleed still. I am hurt to the death.
He dies.   [*He and* CASSIO *fight again.*]
OTHELLO: Hold for your lives!   145
IAGO: Hold, ho! Lieutenant. Sir. Montano. Gentlemen!
Have you forgot all place of sense and duty?
Hold! The general speaks to you. Hold, for shame!
OTHELLO: Why, how now, ho? From whence ariseth this?
Are we turned Turks, and to ourselves do that   150
Which heaven hath forbid the Ottomites?°
For Christian shame put by this barbarous brawl!
He that stirs next to carve for his own rage
Holds his soul light;° he dies upon his motion.
Silence that dreadful bell! It frights the isle   155
From her propriety.° What is the matter, masters?
Honest Iago, that looks dead with grieving,
Speak. Who began this? On thy love, I charge thee.
IAGO: I do not know. Friends all, but now, even now,
In quarter° and in terms like bride and groom   160
Devesting them for bed; and then, but now—
As if some planet had unwitted men—
Swords out, and tilting one at other's breasts
In opposition bloody. I cannot speak
Any beginning to this peevish odds,°   165
And would in action glorious I had lost
Those legs that brought me to a part of it!
OTHELLO: How comes it, Michael, you are thus forgot?
CASSIO: I pray you pardon me; I cannot speak.
OTHELLO: Worthy Montano, you were wont to be civil;   170
Thy gravity and stillness of your youth
The world hath noted, and your name is great
In mouths of wisest censure.° What's the matter
That you unlace° your reputation thus
And spend your rich opinion° for the name   175
Of a night-brawler? Give me answer to it.
MONTANO: Worthy Othello, I am hurt to danger.
Your officer, Iago, can inform you.
While I spare speech, which something now offends° me,

---

¹⁵¹**heaven . . . Ottomites**   *i.e., by sending the storm which dispersed the Turks.*   ¹⁵⁴**Holds his soul light**   *values his soul lightly.*   ¹⁵⁶**propriety**   *proper order.*   ¹⁶⁰**In quarter**   *on duty.*   ¹⁶⁵**odds**   *quarrel.*   ¹⁷³**censure**   *judgment.*   ¹⁷⁴**unlace**   *undo (the term refers specifically to the dressing of a wild boar killed in the hunt).*   ¹⁷⁵**opinion**   *reputation.*   ¹⁷⁹**offends**   *harms, hurts.*

Of all that I do know; nor know I aught 180
By me that's said or done amiss this night,
Unless self-charity be sometimes a vice,
And to defend ourselves it be a sin
When violence assails us.

OTHELLO: Now, by heaven,
My blood begins my safer guides to rule, 185
And passion, having my best judgment collied,°
Assays to lead the way. If I once stir
Or do but lift this arm, the best of you
Shall sink in my rebuke. Give me to know
How this foul rout began, who set it on; 190
And he that is approved in this offense,
Though he had twinned with me, both at a birth,
Shall lose me. What? In a town of war
Yet wild, the people's hearts brimful of fear,
To manage° private and domestic quarrel? 195
In night, and on the court and guard of safety?
'Tis monstrous. Iago, who began't?

MONTANO: If partially affined, or leagued in office,°
Thou dost deliver more or less than truth,
Thou art no soldier.

IAGO: Touch me not so near. 200
I had rather have this tongue cut from my mouth
Than it should do offense to Michael Cassio.
Yet I persuade myself to speak the truth
Shall nothing wrong him. This it is, general.
Montano and myself being in speech, 205
There comes a fellow crying out for help,
And Cassio following him with determined sword
To execute upon him. Sir, this gentleman
Steps in to Cassio and entreats his pause.
Myself the crying fellow did pursue, 210
Lest by his clamor—as it so fell out—
The town might fall in fright. He, swift of foot,
Outran my purpose; and I returned then rather
For that I heard the clink and fall of swords,
And Cassio high in oath; which till tonight 215
I ne'er might say before. When I came back—
For this was brief—I found them close together
At blow and thrust, even as again they were
When you yourself did part them.
More of this matter cannot I report; 220
But men are men; the best sometimes forget.

186**collied** *darkened.* 195**manage** *conduct.* 198**If . . . office** *if you are partial because you are related*
("affined") *or the brother officer (of Cassio).*

Though Cassio did some little wrong to him,
As men in rage strike those that wish them best,
Yet surely Cassio I believe received
From him that fled some strange indignity,   225
Which patience could not pass.°

OTHELLO: I know, Iago,
Thy honesty and love doth mince° this matter,
Making it light to Cassio. Cassio, I love thee;
But never more be officer of mine.

Enter DESDEMONA, *attended.*

Look if my gentle love be not raised up.   230
I'll make thee an example.

DESDEMONA: What is the matter, dear?

OTHELLO: All's well, sweeting; come away to bed.
[*To* MONTANO] Sir, for your hurts, myself will be your surgeon.
Lead him off.   [MONTANO *led off.*]
Iago, look with care about the town   235
And silence those whom this vile brawl distracted.
Come, Desdemona: 'tis the soldiers' life
To have their balmy slumbers waked with strife.

Exit [with all but IAGO *and* CASSIO].

IAGO: What, are you hurt, lieutenant?

CASSIO: Ay, past all surgery.   240

IAGO: Marry, God forbid!

CASSIO: Reputation, reputation, reputation! O, I have lost my reputation! I have
lost the immortal part of myself, and what remains is bestial. My reputation,
Iago, my reputation.

IAGO: As I am an honest man, I had thought you had received some bodily   245
wound. There is more sense° in that than in reputation. Reputation is an idle
and most false imposition,° oft got without merit and lost without deserving.
You have lost no reputation at all unless you repute yourself such a loser. What,
man, there are more ways to recover the general again. You are but now cast in
his mood°—a punishment more in policy° than in malice—even so as one   250
would beat his offenseless dog to affright an imperious lion. Sue to him again,
and he's yours.

CASSIO: I will rather sue to be despised than to deceive so good a commander with
so slight, so drunken, and so indiscreet an officer. Drunk! And speak parrot!°
And squabble! Swagger! Swear! and discourse fustian° with one's own shadow!   255
O thou invisible spirit of wine, if thou hast no name to be known by, let us call
thee devil!

---

²²⁶**pass**   *allow to pass.*   ²²⁷**mince**   *cut up (i.e., tell only part of).*   ²⁴⁶**sense**   *physical feeling.*   ²⁴⁷**imposition**   *external thing.*   ²⁵⁰**cast in his mood**   *dismissed because of his anger.*   ²⁵⁰**in policy**   *politically
necessary.*   ²⁵⁴⁻⁵⁵**speak parrot**   *gabble without sense.*   ²⁵⁵**discourse fustian**   *speak nonsense ("fustian"
was a coarse cotton cloth used for stuffing).*

IAGO: What was he that you followed with your sword? What had he done to you?

CASSIO: I know not.   260

IAGO: Is't possible?

CASSIO: I remember a mass of things, but nothing distinctly: a quarrel, but nothing wherefore. O God, that men should put an enemy in their mouths to steal away their brains! that we should with joy, pleasance, revel, and applause transform ourselves into beasts!   265

IAGO: Why, but you are now well enough. How came you thus recovered?

CASSIO: It hath pleased the devil drunkenness to give place to the devil wrath. One unperfectness shows me another, to make me frankly despise myself.

IAGO: Come, you are too severe a moraler. As the time, the place, and the condition of this country stands, I could heartily wish this had not befall'n; but   270 since it is as it is, mend it for your own good.

CASSIO: I will ask him for my place again: he shall tell me I am a drunkard. Had I as many mouths as Hydra, such an answer would stop them all. To be now a sensible man, by and by a fool, and presently a beast! O strange! Every inordinate cup is unblest, and the ingredient is a devil.   275

IAGO: Come, come, good wine is a good familiar creature if it be well used. Exclaim no more against it. And, good lieutenant, I think you think I love you.

CASSIO: I have well approved it, sir. I drunk?

IAGO: You or any man living may be drunk at a time, man. I tell you what you   280 shall do. Our general's wife is now the general. I may say so in this respect, for all he hath devoted and given up himself to the contemplation, mark, and devotement of her parts° and graces. Confess yourself freely to her; importune her help to put you in your place again. She is of so free, so kind, so apt, so blessed a disposition she holds it a vice in her goodness not to do more than she   285 is requested. This broken joint between you and her husband entreat her to splinter;° and my fortunes against any lay° worth naming, this crack of your love shall grow stronger than it was before.

CASSIO: You advise me well.

IAGO: I protest, in the sincerity of love and honest kindness.   290

CASSIO: I think it freely; and betimes in the morning I will beseech the virtuous Desdemona to undertake for me. I am desperate of my fortunes if they check° me.

IAGO: You are in the right. Good night, lieutenant; I must to the watch.

CASSIO: Good night, honest Iago.   *Exit* CASSIO. 295

IAGO: And what's he then that says I play the villain,
  When this advice is free° I give, and honest,
  Probal to° thinking, and indeed the course
  To win the Moor again? For 'tis most easy
  Th' inclining° Desdemona to subdue   300
  In any honest suit; she's framed as fruitful°

283**devotement of her parts** *devotion to her qualities.*   287**splinter** *splint.*   287**lay** *wager.*
293**check** *repulse.*   297**free** *generous and open.*   298**Probal to** *provable by.*   300**inclining** *inclined*
(to be helpful).   301**framed as fruitful** *made as generous.*

As the free elements.° And then for her
To win the Moor—were't to renounce his baptism,
All seals and symbols of redeemèd sin—
His soul is so enfettered to her love   305
That she may make, unmake, do what she list,
Even as her appetite° shall play the god
With his weak function.° How am I then a villain
To counsel Cassio to this parallel course,
Directly to his good? Divinity of hell!   310
When devils will the blackest sins put on,°
They do suggest at first with heavenly shows,°
As I do now. For whiles this honest fool
Plies Desdemona to repair his fortune,
And she for him pleads strongly to the Moor,   315
I'll pour this pestilence into his ear:
That she repeals him° for her body's lust;
And by how much she strives to do him good,
She shall undo her credit with the Moor.
So will I turn her virtue into pitch,   320
And out of her own goodness make the net
That shall enmesh them all. How now, Roderigo?

                                                                    Enter RODERIGO.

RODERIGO: I do not follow here in the chase, not like a hound that hunts, but one
that fills up the cry.° My money is almost spent; I have been tonight
exceedingly well cudgeled; and I think the issue will be, I shall have so much   325
experience for my pains; and so, with no money at all, and a little more wit,
return again to Venice.
IAGO: How poor are they that have not patience!
What wound did ever heal but by degrees?
Thou know'st we work by wit, and not by witchcraft;   330
And wit depends on dilatory time.
Does't not go well? Cassio hath beaten thee,
And thou by that small hurt hath cashiered Cassio.
Though other things grow fair against the sun,
Yet fruits that blossom first will first be ripe.   335
Content thyself awhile. By the mass, 'tis morning!
Pleasure and action make the hours seem short.
Retire thee, go where thou art billeted.
Away, I say! Thou shalt know more hereafter.
Nay, get thee gone!   *Exit* RODERIGO.
            Two things are to be done: 340

302*elements*   *i.e., basic nature.*   307*appetite*   *liking.*   308***function***   *thought.*   311***put on***   *advance,*
further.   312***shows***   *appearances.*   317***repeals him***   *asks for (Cassio's reinstatement).*   324***fills up the***
cry   *makes up one of the hunting pack, adding to the noise but not actually tracking.*

My wife must move° for Cassio to her mistress;
I'll set her on;
Myself awhile° to draw the Moor apart
And bring him jump° when he may Cassio find
Soliciting his wife. Ay, that's the way!   345
Dull not device by coldness and delay.   *Exit.*

ACT III

Scene I [A street.]

Enter CASSIO [*and*] MUSICIANS.

CASSIO: Masters, play here. I will content your pains.°
   Something that's brief; and bid "Good morrow, general." [*They play.*]

[*Enter* CLOWN.°]

CLOWN: Why, masters, have your instruments been in Naples° that they speak i' th'
nose thus?
MUSICIAN: How, sir, how?   5
CLOWN: Are these, I pray you, wind instruments?
MUSICIAN: Ay, marry, are they, sir.
CLOWN: O, thereby hangs a tale.
MUSICIAN: Whereby hangs a tale, sir?
CLOWN: Marry, sir, by many a wind instrument that I know. But, masters, here's   10
   money for you; and the general so likes your music that he desires you, for
   love's sake, to make no more noise with it.
MUSICIAN: Well, sir, we will not.
CLOWN: If you have any music that may not be heard, to't again. But, as they say,
to hear music the general does not greatly care.   15
MUSICIAN: We have none such, sir.
CLOWN: Then put up your pipes in your bag, for I'll away. Go, vanish into air,
away!   *Exit* MUSICIANS.
CASSIO: Dost thou hear me, mine honest friend?
CLOWN: No. I hear not your honest friend. I hear you.   20
CASSIO: Prithee keep up thy quillets.° There's a poor piece of gold for
thee. If the gentlewoman that attends the general's wife be stirring, tell her there's
one Cassio entreats her a little favor of speech. Wilt thou do this?
CLOWN: She is stirring, sir. If she will stir hither, I shall seem to notify unto her.° 25

Exit CLOWN.

---

³⁴¹**move** *petition.*   ³⁴³**awhile** *at the same time.*   ³⁴⁴**jump** *at the precise moment and place.*   **III.i.**
¹**content your pains** *reward your efforts.*   **s.d. Clown** *fool.*   ³**Naples** *this may refer either to the
Neapolitan nasal tone, or to syphilis—rife in Naples—which breaks down the nose.*   ²¹**quillets** *puns.*
²⁵⁻²⁶**seem . . . her** *(the Clown is mocking Cassio's overly elegant manner of speaking).*

Enter IAGO.

CASSIO: In happy time, Iago.

IAGO: You have not been abed then?

CASSIO: Why no, the day had broke before we parted.
    I have made bold, Iago, to send in to your wife;
    My suit to her is that she will to virtuous Desdemona   30
    Procure me some access.

IAGO: I'll send her to you presently,
    And I'll devise a mean to draw the Moor
    Out of the way, that your converse and business
    May be more free.

CASSIO: I humbly thank you for't.   *Exit* [IAGO]. 35
                          I never knew
    A Florentine° more kind and honest.

Enter EMILIA.

EMILIA: Good morrow, good lieutenant. I am sorry
    For your displeasure;° but all will sure be well.
    The general and his wife are talking of it,   40
    And she speaks for you stoutly. The Moor replies
    That he you hurt is of great fame in Cyprus
    And great affinity,° and that in wholesome wisdom
    He might not but refuse you. But he protests he loves you.
    And needs no other suitor but his likings   45
    To bring you in again.

CASSIO: Yet I beseech you,
    If you think fit, or that it may be done,
    Give me advantage of some brief discourse
    With Desdemona alone.

EMILIA: Pray you come in.
    I will bestow you where you shall have time   50
    To speak your bosom° freely.

CASSIO: I am much bound to you. [*Exeunt.*]

Scene II [*The citadel.*]

Enter OTHELLO, IAGO, *and* GENTLEMEN.

OTHELLO: These letters give, Iago, to the pilot
    And by him do my duties to the Senate.
    That done, I will be walking on the works;
    Repair° there to me.

IAGO: Well, my good lord, I'll do't.

OTHELLO: This fortification, gentlemen, shall we see't?   5

---

³⁷**Florentine** *i.e., Iago is as kind as if he were from Cassio's home town, Florence.*   ³⁹**displeasure** *discom-*
forting.   ⁴³**affinity** *family.*   ⁵¹**bosom** *inmost thoughts.*   **III.ii.**   ⁴**Repair** *go.*

GENTLEMEN: We'll wait upon your lordship.   [*Exeunt.*]

Scene III [*The citadel.*]

Enter DESDEMONA, CASSIO, *and* EMILIA.

DESDEMONA: Be thou assured, good Cassio, I will do
   All my abilities in thy behalf.
EMILIA: Good madam, do. I warrant it grieves my husband
   As if the cause were his.
DESDEMONA: O, that's an honest fellow. Do not doubt, Cassio,   5
   But I will have my lord and you again
   As friendly as you were.
CASSIO: Bounteous madam,
   Whatever shall become of Michael Cassio,
   He's never anything but your true servant.
DESDEMONA: I know't; I thank you. You do love my lord.   10
   You have known him long, and be you well assured
   He shall in strangeness stand no farther off
   Than in a politic distance.°
CASSIO: Ay, but, lady,
   That policy may either last so long,
   Or feed upon such nice° and waterish diet,   15
   Or breed itself so out of circumstances,°
   That, I being absent, and my place supplied,°
   My general will forget my love and service.
DESDEMONA: Do not doubt° that; before Emilia here
   I give thee warrant of thy place. Assure thee,   20
   If I do vow a friendship, I'll perform it
   To the last article. My lord shall never rest;
   I'll watch him tame° and talk him out of patience;
   His bed shall seem a school, his board a shrift;°
   I'll intermingle everything he does   25
   With Cassio's suit. Therefore be merry, Cassio,
   For thy solicitor shall rather die
   Than give thy cause away.

Enter OTHELLO *and* IAGO [*at a distance*].

EMILIA: Madam, here comes my lord.
CASSIO: Madam, I'll take my leave.   30
DESDEMONA: Why, stay, and hear me speak.
CASSIO: Madam, not now. I am very ill at ease,

III.iii.   12–13**He . . . distance**   *i.e., he shall act no more distant to you than is necessary for political reasons.*
15**nice**   *trivial.*   16**Or . . . circumstances**   *i.e., or grow so on the basis of accidental happenings and political*
needs.   17**supplied**   *filled.*   19**doubt**   *imagine.*   23**watch him tame**   *(animals were tamed by being*
kept awake).   24**board a shrift**   *table (seem) a confessional.*

Unfit for mine own purposes.

DESDEMONA: Well, do your discretion.   *Exit* CASSIO.

IAGO: Ha! I like not that.

OTHELLO: What dost thou say?   35

IAGO: Nothing, my lord; or if—I know not what.

OTHELLO: Was not that Cassio parted from my wife?

IAGO: Cassio, my lord? No, sure, I cannot think it

   That he would steal away so guilty-like,

   Seeing you coming.

OTHELLO: I do believe 'twas he.   40

DESDEMONA [*Coming to them*]: How now, my lord?

   I have been talking with a suitor here,

   A man that languishes in your displeasure.

OTHELLO: Who is't you mean?

DESDEMONA: Why, your lieutenant, Cassio. Good my lord,   45

   If I have any grace or power to move you,

   His present° reconciliation take.

   For if he be not one that truly loves you,

   That errs in ignorance, and not in cunning,

   I have no judgment in an honest face.   50

   I prithee call him back.

OTHELLO: Went he hence now?

DESDEMONA: I' sooth so humbled

   That he hath left part of his grief with me

   To suffer with him. Good love, call him back.

OTHELLO: Not now, sweet Desdemon; some other time.   55

DESDEMONA: But shall't be shortly?

OTHELLO: The sooner, sweet, for you.

DESDEMONA: Shall't be tonight at supper?

OTHELLO: No, not tonight.

DESDEMONA: Tomorrow dinner then?

OTHELLO: I shall not dine at home;

   I meet the captains at the citadel.

DESDEMONA: Why then, tomorrow night, on Tuesday morn,   60

   On Tuesday noon, or night, on Wednesday morn.

   I prithee name the time, but let it not

   Exceed three days. In faith, he's penitent;

   And yet his trespass, in our common reason

   (Save that, they say, the wars must make example   65

   Out of her best), is not almost a fault

   T' incur a private check.° When shall he come?

   Tell me, Othello. I wonder in my soul

   What you would ask me that I should deny

   Or stand so mamm'ring° on. What? Michael Cassio,   70

---

⁴⁷**present**   *immediate.*   ⁶⁶⁻⁶⁷**is . . . check**   *is almost not serious enough for a private rebuke (let alone a public disgrace).*   ⁷⁰**mamm'ring**   *hesitating.*

That came awooing with you, and so many a time,
When I have spoke of you dispraisingly,
Hath ta'en your part—to have so much to do
To bring him in? By'r Lady, I could do much—

OTHELLO: Prithee no more. Let him come when he will!   75
  I will deny thee nothing.

DESDEMONA: Why, this is not a boon;
  'Tis as I should entreat you wear your gloves,
  Or feed on nourishing dishes, or keep you warm,
  Or sue to you to do a peculiar profit°
  To your own person. Nay, when I have a suit   80
  Wherein I mean to touch your love indeed,
  It shall be full of poise° and difficult weight,
  And fearful to be granted.

OTHELLO: I will deny thee nothing!
  Whereon I do beseech thee grant me this,
  To leave me but a little to myself.   85

DESDEMONA: Shall I deny you? No. Farewell, my lord.

OTHELLO: Farewell, my Desdemona: I'll come to thee straight.°

DESDEMONA: Emilia, come. Be as your fancies teach you;
  Whate'er you be, I am obedient.   *Exit [with* EMILIA].

OTHELLO: Excellent wretch! Perdition catch my soul   90
  But I do love thee! And when I love thee not,
  Chaos is come again.

IAGO: My noble lord—

OTHELLO: What dost thou say, Iago?

IAGO: Did Michael Cassio, when you wooed my lady,
  Know of your love?   95

OTHELLO: He did, from first to last. Why dost thou ask?

IAGO: But for a satisfaction of my thought,
  No further harm.

OTHELLO: Why of thy thought, Iago?

IAGO: I did not think he had been acquainted with her.

OTHELLO: O, yes, and went between us° very oft.   100

IAGO: Indeed?

OTHELLO: Indeed? Ay, indeed! Discern'st thou aught in that?
  Is he not honest?

IAGO: Honest, my lord?

OTHELLO: Honest? Ay, honest.

IAGO: My lord, for aught I know.

OTHELLO: What dost thou think?

IAGO: Think, my lord?

OTHELLO: Think, my lord?   105
  By heaven, thou echoest me,

---

⁷⁹**peculiar profit**   *particularly personal good.*   ⁸²**poise**   *weight.*   ⁸⁷**straight**   *at once.*   ¹⁰⁰**between us**
i.e., as messenger.

As if there were some monster in thy thought
Too hideous to be shown. Thou dost mean something.
I heard thee say even now, thou lik'st not that,
When Cassio left my wife. What didst not like?   110
And when I told thee he was of my counsel°
Of my whole course of wooing, thou cried'st "Indeed?"
And didst contract and purse thy brow together,
As if thou then hadst shut up in thy brain
Some horrible conceit.° If thou dost love me,   115
Show me thy thought.

IAGO: My lord, you know I love you.

OTHELLO: I think thou dost;
And, for I know thou'rt full of love and honesty
And weigh'st thy words before thou giv'st them breath,
Therefore these stops° of thine fright me the more;   120
For such things in a false disloyal knave
Are tricks of custom;° but in a man that's just
They're close dilations,° working from the heart
That passion cannot rule.

IAGO: For Michael Cassio,
I dare be sworn, I think that he is honest.   125

OTHELLO: I think so too.

IAGO: Men should be what they seem;
Or those that be not, would they might seem none!

OTHELLO: Certain, men should be what they seem.

IAGO: Why then, I think Cassio's an honest man.

OTHELLO: Nay, yet there's more in this?   130
I prithee speak to me as to thy thinkings,
As thou dost ruminate, and give thy worst of thoughts
The worst of words.

IAGO: Good my lord, pardon me:
Though I am bound to every act of duty,
I am not bound to that all slaves are free to.   135
Utter my thoughts? Why, say they are vile and false,
As where's that palace whereinto foul things
Sometimes intrude not? Who has that breast so pure
But some uncleanly apprehensions
Keep leets and law days,° and in sessions sit   140
With meditations lawful?

OTHELLO: Thou dost conspire against thy friend, Iago,
If thou but think'st him wronged, and mak'st his ear
A stranger to thy thoughts.

IAGO: I do beseech you—

---

¹¹¹*of my counsel* *in my confidence.*   ¹¹⁵*conceit* *thought.*   ¹²⁰*stops* *interruptions.*   ¹²²*of custom*
customary.   ¹²³*close dilations* *expressions of hidden thoughts.*   ¹⁴⁰*leets and law days* *meetings of local*
courts.

Though I perchance am vicious in my guess 145
(As I confess it is my nature's plague
To spy into abuses, and of my jealousy
Shape faults that are not), that your wisdom
From one that so imperfectly conceits
Would take no notice, nor build yourself a trouble 150
Out of his scattering and unsure observance.
It were not for your quiet nor your good,
Nor for my manhood, honesty, and wisdom,
To let you know my thoughts.

OTHELLO: What dost thou mean?

IAGO: Good name in man and woman, dear my lord, 155
Is the immediate jewel of their souls.
Who steals my purse steals trash; 'tis something, nothing;
'Twas mine, 'tis his, and has been slave to thousands;
But he that filches from me my good name
Robs me of that which not enriches him 160
And makes me poor indeed.

OTHELLO: By heaven, I'll know thy thoughts!

IAGO: You cannot, if my heart were in your hand;
Nor shall not whilst 'tis in my custody.

OTHELLO: Ha!

IAGO: O, beware, my lord, of jealousy! 165
It is the green-eyed monster, which doth mock
The meat it feeds on. That cuckold lives in bliss
Who, certain of his fate, loves not his wronger;
But O, what damnèd minutes tells° he o'er
Who dotes, yet doubts—suspects, yet fondly° loves! 170

OTHELLO: O misery.

IAGO: Poor and content is rich, and rich enough;
But riches fineless° is as poor as winter
To him that ever fears he shall be poor.
Good God the souls of all my tribe defend 175
From jealousy!

OTHELLO: Why? Why is this?
Think'st thou I'd make a life of jealousy,
To follow still° the changes of the moon
With fresh suspicions? No! To be once in doubt
Is to be resolved. Exchange me for a goat 180
When I shall turn the business of my soul
To such exsufflicate and blown° surmises,
Matching thy inference. 'Tis not to make me jealous
To say my wife is fair, feeds well, loves company,
Is free of speech, sings, plays, and dances; 185

---

¹⁶⁹**tells** counts.   ¹⁷⁰**fondly** foolishly.   ¹⁷³**fineless** infinite.   ¹⁷⁸**To follow still** to change always
(as the phases of the moon).   ¹⁸²**exsufflicate and blown** inflated and flyblown.

Where virtue is, these are more virtuous.
Nor from mine own weak merits will I draw
The smallest fear or doubt of her revolt,
For she had eyes, and chose me. No, Iago;
I'll see before I doubt; when I doubt, prove;   190
And on the proof there is no more but this:
Away at once with love or jealousy!

IAGO: I am glad of this; for now I shall have reason
To show the love and duty that I bear you
With franker spirit. Therefore, as I am bound,   195
Receive it from me. I speak not yet of proof.
Look to your wife; observe her well with Cassio;
Wear your eyes thus: not jealous nor secure.
I would not have your free and noble nature
Out of self-bounty° be abused. Look to't.   200
I know our country disposition well:
In Venice they do let heaven see the pranks
They dare not show their husbands; their best conscience
Is not to leave't undone, but kept unknown.°

OTHELLO: Dost thou say so?   205

IAGO: She did deceive her father, marrying you;
And when she seemed to shake and fear your looks,
She loved them most.

OTHELLO: And so she did.

IAGO: Why, go to then!
She that so young could give out such a seeming
To seel° her father's eyes up close as oak°—   210
He thought 'twas witchcraft. But I am much to blame.
I humbly do beseech you of your pardon
For too much loving you.

OTHELLO: I am bound to thee forever.

IAGO: I see this hath a little dashed your spirits.

OTHELLO: Not a jot, not a jot.

IAGO: Trust me, I fear it has.   215
I hope you will consider what is spoke
Comes from my love. But I do see y' are moved.
I am to pray you not to strain° my speech
To grosser issues nor to larger reach°
Than to suspicion.   220

OTHELLO: I will not.

IAGO: Should you do so, my lord,
My speech should fall into such vile success
Which my thoughts aimed not. Cassio's my worthy friend—
My lord, I see y' are moved.

---

²⁰⁰*self-bounty*   innate kindness (which attributes his own motives to others).   ²⁰³⁻⁴*their … unknown*   i.e.,
their morality does not forbid adultery, but it does forbid being found out.   ²¹⁰*seel*   hoodwink.   ²¹⁰*oak*   (a
close-grained wood).   ²¹⁸*strain*   enlarge the meaning.   ²¹⁹*reach*   meaning.

OTHELLO: No, not much moved.
  I do not think but Desdemona's honest.   225
IAGO: Long live she so. And long live you to think so.
OTHELLO: And yet, how nature erring from itself—
IAGO: Ay, there's the point, as (to be bold with you)
  Not to affect many proposèd matches
  Of her own clime, complexion, and degree,°   230
  Whereto we see in all things nature tends°—
  Foh! one may smell in such a will most rank,
  Foul disproportions, thoughts unnatural.
  But, pardon me, I do not in position°
  Distinctly° speak of her; though I may fear   235
  Her will, recoiling to her better judgment,
  May fall to match° you with her country forms,°
  And happily° repent.
OTHELLO: Farewell, farewell!
  If more thou dost perceive, let me know more.
  Set on thy wife to observe. Leave me, Iago.   240
IAGO: My lord, I take my leave.   [*Going.*]
OTHELLO: Why did I marry? This honest creature doubtless
  Sees and knows more, much more, than he unfolds.
IAGO [*Returns*]: My lord, I would I might entreat your honor
  To scan this thing no farther. Leave it to time.   245
  Although 'tis fit that Cassio have his place,
  For sure he fills it up with great ability,
  Yet, if you please to hold him off awhile,
  You shall by that perceive him and his means.
  Note if your lady strains his entertainment°   250
  With any strong or vehement importunity;
  Much will be seen in that. In the meantime
  Let me be thought too busy in my fears
  (As worthy cause I have to fear I am)
  And hold her free, I do beseech your honor.   255
OTHELLO: Fear not my government.°
IAGO: I once more take my leave.   *Exit.*
OTHELLO: This fellow's of exceeding honesty,
  And knows all qualities,° with a learnèd spirit
  Of human dealings. If I do prove her haggard,°
  Though that her jesses° were my dear heartstrings,   260
  I'd whistle her off and let her down the wind°
  To prey at fortune. Haply for° I am black

---

²³⁰**degree** *social station*   ²³¹**in . . . tends**   *i.e., all things in nature seek out their own kind.*   ²³⁴**position**
general argument.   ²³⁵**Distinctly** *specifically*   ²³⁷**fall to match** *happen to compare.*   ²³⁷**country forms**
i.e., the familiar appearance of her countrymen.   ²³⁸**happily** *by chance.*   ²⁵⁰**strains his entertainment** *urge*
strongly that he be reinstated.   ²⁵⁶**government** *self-control.*   ²⁵⁸**qualities** *natures, types of people.*
²⁵⁹**haggard** *a partly trained hawk which has gone wild again.*   ²⁶⁰**jesses** *straps which held the hawk's legs to*
the trainer's wrist.   ²⁶¹**I'd . . . wind** *I would release her (like an untamable hawk and let her fly free.*
²⁶²**Haply for** *it may be because.*

And have not those soft parts° of conversation
That chamberers° have, or for I am declined
Into the vale of years—yet that's not much—   265
She's gone. I am abused, and my relief
Must be to loathe her. O curse of marriage,
That we can call these delicate creatures ours,
And not their appetites! I had rather be a toad
And live upon the vapor of a dungeon   270
Than keep a corner in the thing I love
For others' uses. Yet 'tis the plague to great ones;
Prerogatived are they less than the base.
'Tis destiny unshunnable, like death.
Even then this forkèd° plague is fated to us   275
When we do quicken.° Look where she comes.

Enter DESDEMONA *and* EMILIA.

If she be false, heaven mocked itself!
I'll not believe't.
DESDEMONA: How now, my dear Othello?
Your dinner, and the generous islanders
By you invited, do attend° your presence.   280
OTHELLO: I am to blame.
DESDEMONA: Why do you speak so faintly?
Are you not well?
OTHELLO: I have a pain upon my forehead, here.°
DESDEMONA: Why, that's with watching; 'twill away again,
Let me but bind it hard, within this hour   285
It will be well.
OTHELLO: Your napkin° is too little;

[*He pushes the handkerchief away, and it falls.*]

Let it° alone. Come, I'll go in with you.
DESDEMONA: I am very sorry that you are not well.   *Exit* [*with* OTHELLO].
EMILIA: I am glad I have found this napkin;
This was her first remembrance from the Moor.   290
My wayward husband hath a hundred times
Wooed me to steal it; but she so loves the token
(For he conjured her she should ever keep it)
That she reserves it evermore about her
To kiss and talk to. I'll have the work ta'en out°   295
And give't Iago. What he will do with it,

---

²⁶³**soft parts** *gentle qualities and manners.*   ²⁶⁴**chamberers** *courtiers—or, perhaps, accomplished seducers.*
²⁷⁵**forkèd** *horned (the sign of the cuckold was horns).*   ²⁷⁶**do quicken** *are born.*   ²⁸³**here** *(he points to his imaginary horns).*   ²⁸⁶**napkin** *elaborately worked handkerchief.*   ²⁸⁷**it** *(it makes a considerable differ-ence in the interpretation of later events whether this "it" refers to Othello's forehead or to the handkerchief; nothing in the text makes the reference clear).*   ²⁹⁵**work ta'en out** *needlework copied.*

Heaven knows, not I; I nothing° but to please his fantasy.°

Enter IAGO.

IAGO: How now? What do you here alone?

EMILIA: Do not you chide; I have a thing for you.

IAGO: You have a thing for me? It is a common thing—   300

EMILIA: Ha?

IAGO: To have a foolish wife.

EMILIA: O, is that all? What will you give me now
    For that same handkerchief?

IAGO: What handkerchief?

EMILIA: What handkerchief!   305
    Why, that the Moor first gave to Desdemona,
    That which so often you did bid me steal.

IAGO: Hast stol'n it from her?

EMILIA: No, but she let it drop by negligence,
    And to th' advantage,° I, being here, took't up.   310
    Look, here 't is.

IAGO: A good wench. Give it me.

EMILIA: What will you do with't, that you have been so earnest
    To have me filch it?

IAGO: Why, what is that to you?   *[Takes it.]*

EMILIA: If it be not for some purpose of import,°
    Give't me again. Poor lady, she'll run mad   315
    When she shall lack° it.

IAGO: Be not acknown on't.°
I have use for it. Go, leave me.   *Exit* EMILIA.
I will in Cassio's lodging lose this napkin
And let him find it. Trifles light as air
Are to the jealous confirmations strong   320
As proofs of Holy Writ. This may do something.
The Moor already changes with my poison:
Dangerous conceits are in their natures poisons,
Which at the first are scarce found to distaste,°
But with a little,° act upon the blood,   325
Burn like the mines of sulfur. I did say so.

Enter OTHELLO.

Look where he comes! Not poppy nor mandragora,°
Nor all the drowsy syrups of the world,
Shall ever medicine thee to that sweet sleep
Which thou owedst° yesterday.

---

²⁹⁷**I nothing** *I wish nothing.*   ²⁹⁷**fantasy** *fancy, whim.*   ³¹⁰**to th' advantage** *being lucky.*   ³¹⁴**im-**
port *importance.*   ³¹⁶**lack** *miss.*   ³¹⁶**Be not acknown on't.** *forget you ever saw it.*   ³²⁴**are scarce**
found to distaste *scarcely can be tasted.*   ³²⁵**with a little** *in a short time.*   ³²⁷**poppy nor mandragora**
soporifics.   ³³⁰**owedst** *possessed.*

OTHELLO: Ha! ha! False to me?   330

IAGO: Why, how now, general? No more of that.

OTHELLO: Avaunt! be gone! Thou hast set me on the rack.
  I swear 'tis better to be much abused
  Than but to know't a little.

IAGO: How now, my lord?

OTHELLO: What sense had I of her stol'n hours of lust?   335
  I saw't not, thought it not, it harmed not me;
  I slept the next night well, fed well, was free and merry;
  I found not Cassio's kisses on her lips.
  He that is robbed, not wanting° what is stol'n,
  Let him not know't, and he's not robbed at all.   340

IAGO: I am sorry to hear this.

OTHELLO: I had been happy if the general camp,
  Pioners° and all, had tasted her sweet body,
  So I had nothing known. O now, forever
  Farewell the tranquil mind! Farewell content!   345
  Farewell the plumèd troops, and the big wars
  That make ambition virtue! O, farewell!
  Farewell the neighing steed and the shrill trump,
  The spirit-stirring drum, th' ear-piercing fife,
  The royal banner, and all quality,   350
  Pride, pomp, and circumstance° of glorious war!
  And O you mortal engines° whose rude throats
  Th' immortal Jove's dread clamors° counterfeit,
  Farewell! Othello's occupation's gone!

IAGO: Is't possible, my lord?   355

OTHELLO: Villain, be sure thou prove my love a whore!
  Be sure of it; give me the ocular proof;
  Or, by the worth of mine eternal soul,
  Thou hadst been better have been born a dog
  Than answer my waked wrath!

IAGO: Is't come to this?   360

OTHELLO: Make me to see't; or at the least so prove it
  That the probation° bear no hinge nor loop
  To hang a doubt on—or woe upon thy life!

IAGO: My noble lord—

OTHELLO: If thou dost slander her and torture me,   365
  Never pray more; abandon all remorse;
  On horror's head horrors accumulate;
  Do deeds to make heaven weep, all earth amazed;
  For nothing canst thou to damnation add
  Greater than that.

---

³³⁹**wanting** *missing.*   ³⁴³**Pioners** *the basest manual laborers in the army, who dug trenches and mines.*
³⁵¹**circumstance** *pageantry.*   ³⁵²**mortal engines** *lethal weapons, i.e., cannon.*   ³⁵³**clamors** *i.e., thunder.*   ³⁶²**probation** *proof.*

IAGO: O grace! O heaven forgive me!   370
  Are you a man? Have you a soul or sense?
  God b' wi' you! Take mine office. O wretched fool,
  That lov'st to make thine honesty a vice!
  O monstrous world! Take note, take note, O world,
  To be direct and honest is not safe.   375
  I thank you for this profit, and from hence
  I'll love no friend, sith° love breeds such offense.
OTHELLO: Nay, stay. Thou shouldst be honest.
IAGO: I should be wise; for honesty's a fool
  And loses that it works for.
OTHELLO: By the world,   380
  I think my wife be honest, and think she is not;
  I think that thou art just, and think thou are not.
  I'll have some proof. My name, that was as fresh
  As Dian's° visage, is now begrimed and black
  As mine own face. If there be cords, or knives,   385
  Poison, or fire, or suffocating streams,
  I'll not endure it. Would I were satisfied!
IAGO: I see you are eaten up with passion.
  I do repent me that I put it to you.
  You would be satisfied?
OTHELLO: Would? Nay, and I will.   390
IAGO: And may; but how? How satisfied, my lord?
  Would you, the supervisor,° grossly gape on?
  Behold her topped?
OTHELLO: Death and damnation! O!
IAGO: It were a tedious° difficulty, I think,
  To bring them to that prospect.° Damn them then,   395
  If ever mortal eyes do see them bolster°
  More than their own! What then? How then?
  What shall I say? Where's satisfaction?
  It is impossible you should see this,
  Were they as prime° as goats, as hot as monkeys,   400
  As salt as wolves in pride,° and fools as gross
  As ignorance made drunk. But yet, I say,
  If imputation and strong circumstances
  Which lead directly to the door of truth
  Will give you satisfaction, you might hav't.   405
OTHELLO: Give me a living reason she's disloyal.
IAGO: I do not like the office.°
  But sith I am entered in this cause so far,
  Pricked° to't by foolish honesty and love,

---

³⁷⁷**sith**   *since.*   ³⁸⁴**Dian's**   *Diana's (goddess of the moon and of chastity).*   ³⁹²**supervisor**   *onlooker.*
³⁹⁴**tedious**   *hard to arrange.*   ³⁹⁵**prospect**   *sight (where they can be seen).*   ³⁹⁶**bolster**   *go to bed with*
⁴⁰⁰–⁰¹**prime, salt**   *lustful.*   ⁴⁰¹**pride**   *heat.*   ⁴⁰⁷**office**   *duty.*   ⁴⁰⁹**Pricked**   *spurred.*

I will go on. I lay with Cassio lately,   410
And being troubled with a raging tooth,
I could not sleep.
There are a kind of men so loose of soul
That in their sleeps will mutter their affairs.
One of this kind is Cassio.   415
In sleep I heard him say, "Sweet Desdemona,
Let us be wary, let us hide our loves!"
And then, sir, would he gripe° and wring my hand,
Cry "O sweet creature!" Then kiss me hard,
As if he plucked up kisses by the roots   420
That grew upon my lips; laid his leg o'er my thigh,
And sigh, and kiss, and then cry, "Cursèd fate
That gave thee to the Moor!"

OTHELLO: O monstrous! monstrous!

IAGO: Nay, this was but his dream.

OTHELLO: But this denoted a foregone conclusion,°   425
'Tis a shrewd doubt,° though it be but a dream.

IAGO: And this may help to thicken other proofs
That do demonstrate° thinly.

OTHELLO: I'll tear her all to pieces!

IAGO: Nay, yet be wise. Yet we see nothing done;
She may be honest yet. Tell me but this: 430
Have you not sometimes seen a handkerchief
Spotted with strawberries in your wife's hand?

OTHELLO: I gave her such a one; 'twas my first gift.

IAGO: I know not that; but such a handkerchief—
I am sure it was your wife's—did I today   435
See Cassio wipe his beard with.

OTHELLO: If it be that—

IAGO: If it be that or any that was hers,
It speaks against her with the other proofs.

OTHELLO: O, that the slave had forty thousand lives!
One is too poor, too weak for my revenge.   440
Now do I see 'tis true. Look here, Iago:
All my fond love thus do I blow to heaven.
'Tis gone.
Arise, black vengeance, from the hollow hell!
Yield up, O love, thy crown and hearted° throne   445
To tyrannous hate! Swell, bosom, with thy fraught,°
For 'tis of aspics'° tongues.

IAGO: Yet be content.°

OTHELLO: O, blood, blood, blood!

---

^{418}**gripe** *seize.* ^{425}**foregone conclusion** *consummated fact.* ^{426}**shrewd doubt** *penetrating guess.*
^{428}**demonstrate** *show, appear.* ^{445}**hearted** *seated in the heart.* ^{446}**fraught** *burden.* ^{447}**aspics'**
asps'. ^{447}**content** *patient, quiet.*

IAGO: Patience, I say. Your mind may change.

OTHELLO: Never, Iago. Like to the Pontic Sea,°   450
Whose icy current and compulsive course
Nev'r keeps retiring ebb, but keeps due on
To the Propontic and the Hellespont,
Even so my bloody thoughts, with violent pace,
Shall nev'r look back, nev'r ebb to humble love,   455
Till that a capable and wide° revenge
Swallow them up. [*He kneels.*] Now, by yond marble heaven,
In the due reverence of a sacred vow
I here engage my words.

IAGO: Do not rise yet.   [IAGO *kneels.*]
Witness, you ever-burning lights above,   460
You elements that clip° us round about,
Witness that here Iago doth give up
The execution° of his wit, hands, heart
To wronged Othello's service! Let him command,
And to obey shall be in me remorse,°   465
What bloody business ever.°   [*They rise.*]

OTHELLO: I greet thy love,
Not with vain thanks but with acceptance bounteous,°
And will upon the instant put thee to 't°
Within these three days let me hear thee say
That Cassio's not alive.   470

IAGO: My friend is dead. 'Tis done at your request.
But let her live.

OTHELLO: Damn her, lewd minx! O, damn her! Damn her!
Come, go with me apart. I will withdraw
To furnish me with some swift means of death
For the fair devil. Now art thou my lieutenant.   475

IAGO: I am your own forever.   *Exeunt.*

Scene IV [*A street.*]

Enter DESDEMONA, EMILIA, *and* CLOWN.

DESDEMONA: Do you know, sirrah, where Lieutenant Cassio lies?°

CLOWN: I dare not say he lies anywhere.

DESDEMONA: Why, man?

CLOWN: He's a soldier, and for me to say a soldier lies, 'tis stabbing.

DESDEMONA: Go to. Where lodges he?   5

450**Pontic Sea** *the Black Sea (famous for the strong and constant current with which it flows through the Bosporus into the Mediterranean, where the water level is lower).* 456**capable and wide** *sufficient and far-reaching.* 461**clip** *enfold.* 463**execution** *workings, action.* 465**remorse** *pity.* 466**ever** *soever.* 467**bounteous** *absolute.* 468**to't** *i.e., to the work you have said you are prepared to do.* **III.iv.** 1**lies** *lodges.*

CLOWN: To tell you where he lodges is to tell you where I lie.

DESDEMONA: Can anything be made of this?

CLOWN: I know not where he lodges, and for me to devise a lodging, and say he lies here or he lies there, were to lie in mine own throat.°

DESDEMONA: Can you enquire him out, and be edified° by report?   10

CLOWN: I will catechize the world for him; that is, make questions, and by them answer.

DESDEMONA: Seek him, bid him come hither. Tell him I have moved° my lord on his behalf and hope all will be well.

CLOWN: To do this is within the compass° of man's wit, and therefore I will attempt   15
the doing it.   *Exit* CLOWN.

DESDEMONA: Where should° I lose the handkerchief, Emilia?

EMILIA: I know not, madam.

DESDEMONA: Believe me, I had rather have lost my purse
Full of crusadoes.° And but my noble Moor   20
Is true of mind, and made of no such baseness
As jealous creatures are, it were enough
To put him to ill thinking.

EMILIA: Is he not jealous?

DESDEMONA: Who? He? I think the sun where he was born
Drew all such humors° from him.

EMILIA: Look where he comes.   25

Enter OTHELLO.

DESDEMONA: I will not leave him now till Cassio
Be called to him. How is't with you, my lord?

OTHELLO: Well, my good lady. [*Aside*] O, hardness to dissemble!°—
How do you, Desdemona?

DESDEMONA: Well, my good lord.

OTHELLO: Give me your hand. This hand is moist,° my lady.   30

DESDEMONA: It hath felt no age nor known no sorrow.

OTHELLO: This argues° fruitfulness and liberal° heart.
Hot, hot, and moist. This hand of yours requires
A sequester° from liberty; fasting and prayer;
Much castigation; exercise devout;   35
For here's a young and sweating devil here
That commonly rebels. 'Tis a good hand,
A frank one.

DESDEMONA: You may, indeed, say so;

---

⁹**lie in mine own throat**   (to lie in the throat is to lie absolutely and completely).   ¹⁰**edified**   enlightened (Desdemona mocks the Clown's overly elaborate diction).   ¹³**moved**   pleaded with.   ¹⁵**compass**   reach.
¹⁷**should**   might.   ²⁰**crusadoes**   Portuguese gold coins.   ²⁵**humors**   characteristics.   ²⁸**hardness to**
dissemble   (Othello may refer here either to the difficulty he has in maintaining his appearance of composure, or to
what he believes to be Desdemona's hardened hypocrisy).   ³⁰**moist**   (a moist, hot hand was taken as a sign of a
lustful nature).   ³²**argues**   suggests.   ³²**liberal**   free, open (but also with a suggestion of "licentious"; from
here on in this scene Othello's words bear a double meaning, seeming to be normal but accusing Desdemona of being unfaithful).   ³⁴**sequester**   separation.

For 'twas that hand that gave away my heart.

OTHELLO: A liberal hand! The hearts of old gave hands,   40
  But our new heraldry° is hands, not hearts.

DESDEMONA: I cannot speak of this. Come now, your promise!

OTHELLO: What promise, chuck?

DESDEMONA: I have sent to bid Cassio come speak with you.

OTHELLO: I have a salt and sorry rheum° offends me.   45
  Lend me thy handkerchief.

DESDEMONA: Here, my lord.

OTHELLO: That which I gave you.

DESDEMONA: I have it not about me.

OTHELLO: Not?

DESDEMONA: No, indeed, my lord.

OTHELLO: That's a fault.
  That handkerchief   50
  Did an Egyptian to my mother give.
  She was a charmer,° and could almost read
  The thoughts of people. She told her, while she kept it
  'Twould make her amiable° and subdue my father
  Entirely to her love; but if she lost it   55
  Or made a gift of it, my father's eye
  Should hold her loathèd, and his spirits should hunt
  After new fancies. She, dying, gave it me,
  And bid me, when my fate would have me wived,
  To give it her. I did so; and take heed on't;   60
  Make it a darling like your precious eye.
  To lose't or give't away were such perdition
  As nothing else could match.

DESDEMONA: Is't possible?

OTHELLO: 'Tis true. There's magic in the web° of it.
  A sibyl that had numbered in the world   65
  The sun to course two hundred compasses,
  In her prophetic fury° sewed the work;
  The worms were hallowed that did breed the silk,
  And it was dyed in mummy° which the skillful
  Conserved of maidens' hearts.

DESDEMONA: Indeed? Is't true?   70

OTHELLO: Most veritable. Therefore look to't well.

DESDEMONA: Then would to God that I had never seen't!

OTHELLO: Ha! Wherefore?

DESDEMONA: Why do you speak so startingly and rash?

OTHELLO: Is't lost? Is't gone? Speak, is it out o' th' way?   75

DESDEMONA: Heaven bless us!

---

⁴¹**heraldry** *heraldic symbolism.*   ⁴⁵**a salt and sorry rheum** *a heavy, running head cold.*   ⁵²**charmer** *magician.*   ⁵⁴**amiable** *desirable.*   ⁶⁴**web** *weaving.*   ⁶⁷**prophetic fury** *seized by the spirit and able to prophesy.*   ⁶⁹**mummy** *liquid drained from embalmed bodies.*

OTHELLO: Say you?

DESDEMONA: It is not lost. But what an if it were?

OTHELLO: How?

DESDEMONA: I say it is not lost.   80

OTHELLO: Fetch't, let me see't!

DESDEMONA: Why, so I can; but I will not now.
  This is a trick to put me from my suit:
  Pray you let Cassio be received again.

OTHELLO: Fetch me the handkerchief! My mind misgives.   85

DESDEMONA: Come, come!
  You'll never meet a more sufficient° man—

OTHELLO: The handkerchief!

DESDEMONA: A man that all his time
  Hath founded his good fortunes on your love,
  Shared dangers with you—   90

OTHELLO: The handkerchief!

DESDEMONA: I'faith, you are to blame.

OTHELLO: Away!   *Exit* OTHELLO.

EMILIA: Is not this man jealous?

DESDEMONA: I nev'r saw this before.   95
  Sure there's some wonder in this handkerchief;
  I am most unhappy in the loss of it.

EMILIA: 'Tis not a year or two shows us a man.
  They are all but stomachs, and we all but food;
  They eat us hungerly, and when they are full,   100
  They belch us.

                    Enter IAGO *and* CASSIO.

          Look you, Cassio and my husband.

IAGO: There is no other way; 'tis she must do't.
  And lo the happiness! Go and importune her.

DESDEMONA: How now, good Cassio? What's the news with you?

CASSIO: Madam, my former suit. I do beseech you   105
  That by your virtuous means I may again
  Exist, and be a member of his love
  Whom I with all the office° of my heart
  Entirely honor. I would not be delayed.
  If my offense be of such mortal kind   110
  That nor my service past, nor present sorrows,
  Nor purposed merit in futurity,
  Can ransom me into his love again,
  But to know so must be my benefit.°
  So shall I clothe me in a forced content,   115
  And shut myself up in some other course
  To fortune's alms.

---

⁸⁷*sufficient*   *complete, with all proper qualities.*   ¹⁰⁸*office*   *duty.*   ¹¹⁴*benefit*   *good.*

DESDEMONA: Alas, thrice-gentle Cassio,
  My advocation° is not now in tune.
  My lord is not my lord; nor should I know him
  Were he in favor° as in humor altered.   120
  So help me every spirit sanctified
  As I have spoken for you all my best
  And stood within the blank° of his displeasure
  For my free speech. You must awhile be patient.
  What I can do I will; and more I will   125
  Than for myself I dare. Let that suffice you.
IAGO: Is my lord angry?
EMILIA: He went hence but now,
  And certainly in strange unquietness.
IAGO: Can he be angry? I have seen the cannon
  When it hath blown his ranks into the air   130
  And, like the devil, from his very arm
  Puffed his own brother. And is he angry?
  Something of moment° then. I will go meet him.
  There's matter in't indeed if he be angry.
DESDEMONA: I prithee do so.   *Exit* [IAGO.]
               Something sure of state,°   135
  Either from Venice or some unhatched practice°
  Made demonstrable here in Cyprus to him,
  Hath puddled° his clear spirit; and in such cases
  Men's natures wrangle with inferior things,
  Though great ones are their object. 'Tis even so.   140
  For let our finger ache, and it endues°
  Our other, healthful members even to a sense
  Of pain. Nay, we must think men are not gods,
  Nor of them look for such observancy
  As fits the bridal. Beshrew me much, Emilia,   145
  I was, unhandsome warrior as I am,
  Arraigning his unkindness with my soul;
  But now I find I had suborned the witness,
  And he's indicted falsely.
EMILIA: Pray heaven it be
  State matters, as you think, and no conception   150
  Nor no jealous toy° concerning you.
DESDEMONA: Alas the day! I never gave him cause.
EMILIA: But jealous souls will not be answered so;
  They are not ever jealous for the cause,
  But jealous for they're jealous. It is a monster   155
  Begot upon itself, born on itself.

---

¹¹⁸**advocation** *advocacy.*   ¹²⁰**favor** *countenance.*   ¹²³**blank** *bull's-eye of a target.*   ¹³³**moment** *im-portance.*   ¹³⁵**of state** *state affairs.*   ¹³⁶**unhatched practice** *undisclosed plot.*   ¹³⁸**puddled** *muddied.*   ¹⁴¹**endues** *leads.*   ¹⁵¹**toy** *trifle.*

DESDEMONA: Heaven keep the monster from Othello's mind!

EMILIA: Lady, amen.

DESDEMONA: I will go seek him. Cassio, walk here about.

    If I do find him fit,° I'll move your suit   160

    And seek to effect it to my uttermost.

CASSIO: I humbly thank your ladyship.   *Exit* [DESDEMONA *with* EMILIA].

Enter BIANCA.

BIANCA: Save you, friend Cassio!

CASSIO: What make you from home?

    How is't with you, my most fair Bianca?

    I' faith, sweet love, I was coming to your house.   165

BIANCA: And I was going to your lodging, Cassio.

    What, keep a week away? Seven days and nights?

    Eightscore eight hours? And lovers' absent hours

    More tedious than the dial eightscore times?

    O weary reck'ning.°

CASSIO: Pardon me, Bianca.   170

    I have this while with leaden thoughts been pressed,

    But I shall in a more continuate° time

    Strike off this score° of absence. Sweet Bianca,

[*Gives her* DESDEMONA'S *handkerchief.*]

    Take me this work out.

BIANCA: O Cassio, whence came this?

    This is some token from a newer friend.   175

    To the felt absence now I feel a cause.

    Is't come to this? Well, well.

CASSIO: Go to, woman!

    Throw your vile guesses in the devil's teeth,

    From whence you have them. You are jealous now

    That this is from some mistress, some remembrance.   180

    No, by my faith, Bianca.

BIANCA: Why, whose is it?

CASSIO: I know not neither; I found it in my chamber.

    I like the work well; ere it be demanded,°

    As like enough it will, I would have it copied.

    Take it and do't, and leave me for this time.   185

BIANCA: Leave you? Wherefore?

CASSIO: I do attend here on the general

    And think it no addition, nor my wish,

    To have him see me womaned.

BIANCA: Why, I pray you?

160**fit** *receptive.*   170**reck'ning** *addition.*   172**continuate** *uninterrupted.*   173**Strike off this score** *i.e., pay this bill (the score being the account of drinks kept in a tavern).*   183**demanded** *asked for (by the person who lost it).*

CASSIO: Not that I love you not.

BIANCA: But that you do not love me!   190
  I pray you bring° me on the way a little,
  And say if I shall see you soon at night.

CASSIO: 'Tis but a little way that I can bring you,
  For I attend here; but I'll see you soon.

BIANCA: 'Tis very good. I must be circumstanced.°   *Exeunt omnes.* 195

ACT IV

Scene I [A street.]

Enter OTHELLO *and* IAGO.

IAGO: Will you think so?

OTHELLO: Think so, Iago?

IAGO: What,
  To kiss in private?

OTHELLO: An unauthorized° kiss?

IAGO: Or to be naked with her friend in bed
  An hour or more, not meaning any harm?

OTHELLO: Naked in bed, Iago, and not mean harm?   5
  It is hypocrisy against the devil.
  They that mean virtuously, and yet do so,
  The devil their virtue tempts, and they tempt heaven.

IAGO: If they do nothing, 'tis a venial slip.
  But if I give my wife a handkerchief—   10

OTHELLO: What then?

IAGO: Why, then 'tis hers, my lord; and being hers,
  She may, I think, bestow't on any man.

OTHELLO: She is protectress of her honor too.
  May she give that?   15

IAGO: Her honor is an essence that's not seen;
  They have it very oft that have it not.
  But for the handkerchief—

OTHELLO: By heaven, I would most gladly have forgot it!
  Thou said'st—O, it comes o'er my memory   20
  As doth the raven° o'er the infected house,
  Boding to all—he had my handkerchief.

IAGO: Ay, what of that?

OTHELLO: That's not so good now.

IAGO: What if I had said I had seen him do you wrong?

---

¹⁹¹**bring**   *accompany.*   ¹⁹⁵**be circumstanced**   *accept things as they are.*   **IV.i.**   ²**unauthorized**   *illicit.*
²¹**raven**   *(a harbinger of death).*

Or heard him say—as knaves be such abroad°   25
Who having, by their own importunate suit,
Or voluntary dotage° of some mistress,
Convincèd or supplied° them, cannot choose
But they must blab—

OTHELLO: Hath he said anything?

IAGO: He hath, my lord; but be you well assured,   30
No more than he'll unswear.

OTHELLO: What hath he said?

IAGO: Why, that he did—I know not what he did.

OTHELLO: What? what?

IAGO: Lie—

OTHELLO: With her?

IAGO: With her, on her; what you will.   35

OTHELLO: Lie with her? Lie on her?—We say lie on her when they belie her.—
Lie with her! Zounds, that's fulsome.°—Handkerchief—confessions—   40
handkerchief!—To confess, and be hanged for his labor—first to be hanged,
and then to confess! I tremble at it. Nature would not invest herself in such
shadowing passion without some instruction.° It is not words that shakes me
thus.—Pish! Noses, ears, and lips? Is't possible?—Confess?—Handkerchief?—
O devil!   *Falls in a trance.*

IAGO: Work on.
My med'cine works! Thus credulous fools are caught,
And many worthy and chaste dames even thus,   45
All guiltless, meet reproach.° What, ho! My lord!
My lord, I say! Othello!

Enter CASSIO.

How now, Cassio?

CASSIO: What's the matter?

IAGO: My lord is fall'n into an epilepsy.
This is his second fit; he had one yesterday.   50

CASSIO: Rub him about the temples.

IAGO: The lethargy° must have his quiet course.
If not, he foams at mouth, and by and by
Breaks out to savage madness. Look, he stirs.
Do you withdraw yourself a little while.   55
He will recover straight. When he is gone,
I would on great occasion° speak with you.   [*Exit* CASSIO.]
How is it, general? Have you not hurt your head?

OTHELLO: Dost thou mock° me?

---

²⁵*abroad*   i.e., in the world.   ²⁷*voluntary dotage*   weakness of the will.   ²⁸*Convincèd or supplied*   persuaded or gratified (the mistress).   ³⁷*fulsome*   foul, repulsive.   ³⁹⁻⁴⁰*Nature . . . instruction*   i.e., my
mind would not become so darkened (with anger) unless there were something in this (accusation); (it should be remembered that Othello believes in the workings of magic and supernatural forces).   ⁴⁶*reproach*   shame.
⁵²*lethargy*   coma.   ⁵⁷*great occasion*   very important matter.   ⁵⁹*mock*   (Othello takes Iago's comment as
a reference to his horns—which it is).

IAGO: I mock you not, by heaven.
  Would you would bear your fortune like a man.   60
OTHELLO: A hornèd man's a monster and a beast.
IAGO: There's many a beast then in a populous city,
  And many a civil° monster.
OTHELLO: Did he confess it?
IAGO: Good, sir, be a man.   65
  Think every bearded fellow that's but yoked
  May draw° with you. There's millions now alive
  That nightly lie in those unproper° beds
  Which they dare swear peculiar.° Your case is better.
  O, 'tis the spite of hell, the fiend's arch-mock,
  To lip a wanton in a secure couch,   70
  And to suppose her chaste. No, let me know;
  And knowing what I am, I know what she shall be.
OTHELLO: O, thou art wise! 'Tis certain.
IAGO: Stand you awhile apart;
  Confine yourself but in a patient list.°
  Whilst you were here, o'erwhelmèd with your grief—   75
  A passion most unsuiting such a man—
  Cassio came hither. I shifted him away°
  And laid good 'scuses upon your ecstasy,°
  Bade him anon return, and here speak with me;
  The which he promised. Do but encave° yourself   80
  And mark the fleers,° the gibes, and notable° scorns
  That dwell in every region of his face.
  For I will make him tell the tale anew:
  Where, how, how oft, how long ago, and when
  He hath, and is again to cope your wife.   85
  I say, but mark his gesture. Marry patience,
  Or I shall say you're all in all in spleen,°
  And nothing of a man.
OTHELLO: Dost thou hear, Iago?
  I will be found most cunning in my patience;
  But—dost thou hear?—most bloody.
IAGO: That's not amiss;   90
  But yet keep time in all. Will you withdraw?

[OTHELLO *moves to one side, where his remarks are not audible to* CASSIO *and* IAGO.]

  Now will I question Cassio of Bianca,
  A huswife° that by selling her desires

°⁶³**civil** *city-dwelling.*   °⁶⁶**draw** *i.e., like the horned ox.*   °⁶⁷**unproper** *i.e., not exclusively the husband's.*
°⁶⁸**peculiar** *their own alone.*   ⁷⁴**a patient list** *the bounds of patience.*   ⁷⁷**shifted him away** *got rid of
him by a strategem.*   ⁷⁸**ecstasy** *trance (the literal meaning, "outside oneself," bears on the meaning of the change
Othello is undergoing).*   ⁸⁰**encave** *hide.*   ⁸¹**fleers** *mocking looks or speeches.*   ⁸¹**notable** *obvious.*
⁸⁷**spleen** *passion, particularly anger.*   ⁹³**huswife** *housewife (but with the special meaning here of "prostitute").*

Buys herself bread and cloth. It is a creature
That dotes on Cassio, as 'tis the strumpet's plague   95
To beguile many and be beguiled by one.
He, when he hears of her, cannot restrain
From the excess of laughter. Here he comes.

Enter CASSIO.

As he shall smile, Othello shall go mad:
And his unbookish° jealousy must conster°   100
Poor Cassio's smiles, gestures, and light behaviors
Quite in the wrong. How do you, lieutenant?
CASSIO: The worser that you give me the addition°
Whose want even kills me.
IAGO: Ply Desdemona well, and you are sure on't.   105
Now, if this suit lay in Bianca's power,
How quickly should you speed!
CASSIO: Alas, poor caitiff!°
OTHELLO: Look how he laughs already!
IAGO: I never knew woman love man so.
CASSIO: Alas, poor rogue! I think, i' faith, she loves me.   110
OTHELLO: Now he denies it faintly, and laughs it out.
IAGO: Do you hear, Cassio?
OTHELLO: Now he importunes him
To tell it o'er. Go to! Well said, well said!
IAGO: She gives it out that you shall marry her.
Do you intend it?   115
CASSIO: Ha, ha, ha!
OTHELLO: Do ye triumph, Roman? Do you triumph?
CASSIO: I marry? What, a customer?° Prithee bear some charity to my wit; do not
think it so unwholesome. Ha, ha, ha!
OTHELLO: So, so, so, so. They laugh that win.   120
IAGO: Why, the cry goes that you marry her.
CASSIO: Prithee, say true.
IAGO: I am a very villain else.
OTHELLO: Have you scored° me? Well.   125
CASSIO: This is the monkey's own giving out. She is persuaded I will marry her
out of her own love and flattery, not out of my promise.
OTHELLO: Iago beckons me; now he begins the story.

[OTHELLO *moves close enough to hear.*]

CASSIO: She was here even now; she haunts me in every place. I was the other day
talking on the sea bank with certain Venetians, and thither comes the bauble,°   130
and falls me thus about my neck—

---

¹⁰⁰**unbookish** *ignorant.*   ¹⁰⁰**conster** *construe.*   ¹⁰³**addition** *title.*   ¹⁰⁷**caitiff** *wretch.*
¹¹⁸**customer** *one who sells, a merchant (here, a prostitute).*   ¹²⁴**scored** *marked, defaced.*   ¹³⁰**bauble**
plaything.

OTHELLO: Crying "O dear Cassio!" as it were. His gesture imports it.

CASSIO: So hangs, and lolls, and weeps upon me; so shakes and pulls me! Ha, ha, ha!

OTHELLO: Now he tells how she plucked him to my chamber. O, I see that nose 135
of yours, but not that dog I shall throw it to.

CASSIO: Well, I must leave her company.

IAGO: Before me!° Look where she comes.

Enter BIANCA.

CASSIO: 'Tis such another fitchew!° Marry a perfumed one? What do you mean
by this haunting of me?   140

BIANCA: Let the devil and his dam haunt you! What did you mean by that same
handkerchief you gave me even now? I was a fine fool to take it. I must take out
the work? A likely piece of work that you should find it in your chamber and
know not who left it there! This is some minx's token, and I must take out the
work? There! [*She throws down the handkerchief.*] Give it your hobbyhorse.° 145
Wheresoever you had it, I'll take out no work on't.

CASSIO: How now, my sweet Bianca? How now? how now?

OTHELLO: By heaven, that should be my handkerchief!

BIANCA: If you'll come to supper tonight, you may; if you will not, come when 150
you are next prepared for.°   *Exit.*

IAGO: After her, after her!

CASSIO: Faith, I must; she'll rail in the streets else.

IAGO: Will you sup there?

CASSIO: Yes, I intend so.   155

IAGO: Well, I may chance to see you, for I would very fain speak with you.

CASSIO: Prithee come. Will you?

IAGO: Go to, say no more.   [*Exit* CASSIO.]

OTHELLO [*Comes forward*]: How shall I murder him, Iago?

IAGO: Did you perceive how he laughed at his vice?   160

OTHELLO: O Iago!

IAGO: And did you see the handkerchief?

OTHELLO: Was that mine?

IAGO: Yours, by this hand! And to see how he prizes the foolish woman your wife!
She gave it him, and he hath giv'n it his whore.   165

OTHELLO: I would have him nine years a-killing!—A fine woman, a fair woman,
a sweet woman?

IAGO: Nay, you must forget that.

OTHELLO: Ay, let her rot, and perish, and be damned tonight; for she shall not live.
No, my heart is turned to stone; I strike it, and it hurts my hand. O, the world 170
hath not a sweeter creature! She might lie by an emperor's side and command
him tasks.

IAGO: Nay, that's not your way.°

137*Before me!* (an exclamation of surprise).   138*fitchew* polecat, i.e, strong-smelling creature.   145*hobbyhorse* prostitute.   150*next prepared for* next expected—i.e., never.   172*way* proper course.

OTHELLO: Hang her! I do but say what she is. So delicate with her needle. An ad-
    mirable musician. O, she will sing the savageness out of a bear! Of so high and
    plenteous wit and invention°—   175
IAGO: She's the worse for all this.
OTHELLO: O, a thousand, a thousand times. And then, of so gentle a condition?°
IAGO: Ay, too gentle.
OTHELLO: Nay, that's certain. But yet the pity of it, Iago. O Iago, the pity of it,
    Iago.   180
IAGO: If you are so fond over her iniquity, give her patent to offend; for if it touch°
    not you, it comes near nobody.
OTHELLO: I will chop her into messes!° Cuckold me!
IAGO: O, 'tis foul in her.   185
OTHELLO: With mine officer!
IAGO: That's fouler.
OTHELLO: Get me some poison, Iago, this night. I'll not expostulate with her, lest
    her body and beauty unprovide my mind° again. This night, Iago!
IAGO: Do it not with poison. Strangle her in her bed, even the bed she hath   190
    contaminated.
OTHELLO: Good, good! The justice of it pleases. Very good!
IAGO: And for Cassio, let me be his undertaker.° You shall hear more by midnight.
OTHELLO: Excellent good!   [A trumpet.]
                    What trumpet is that same?   195
IAGO: I warrant something from Venice.

               Enter LODOVICO, DESDEMONA, *and* ATTENDANTS.

                            'Tis Lodovico.
    This comes from the Duke. See, your wife's with him.
LODOVICO: God save you, worthy general.
OTHELLO: With° all my heart, sir.
LODOVICO: The Duke and the senators of Venice greet you.

                                             [*Gives him a letter.*]

OTHELLO: I kiss the instrument of their pleasures.   200

                                             [*Opens the letter and reads.*]

DESDEMONA: And what's the news, good cousin Lodovico?
IAGO: I am very glad to see you, signior.
    Welcome to Cyprus.
LODOVICO: I thank you. How does Lieutenant Cassio?
IAGO: Lives, sir.
DESDEMONA: Cousin, there's fall'n between him and my lord   205
    An unkind° breach; but you shall make all well.
OTHELLO: Are you sure of that?
DESDEMONA: My lord?

---

¹⁷⁵**invention** *imagination.*   ¹⁷⁷⁻⁷⁸**gentle a condition** *(1) well born (2) of a gentle nature.*   ¹⁸³**touch** *affects.*   ¹⁸⁴**messes** *bits.*   ¹⁸⁹**unprovide my mind** *undo my resolution.*   ¹⁹³**undertaker** *(not "burier"
but "one who undertakes to do something").*   ¹⁹⁸**With** *i.e., I greet you with.*   ²⁰⁶**unkind** *unnatural.*

OTHELLO [*Reads*]: "This fail you not to do, as you will—"

LODOVICO: He did not call; he's busy in the paper.   210

  Is there division 'twixt my lord and Cassio?

DESDEMONA: A most unhappy one. I would do much

  T' atone° them, for the love I bear to Cassio.

OTHELLO: Fire and brimstone!

DESDEMONA: My lord?

OTHELLO: Are you wise?

DESDEMONA: What, is he angry?

LODOVICO: May be th' letter moved him;   215

  For, as I think, they do command him home,

  Deputing Cassio in his government.°

DESDEMONA: Trust me, I am glad on't.

OTHELLO: Indeed?

DESDEMONA: My lord?

OTHELLO: I am glad to see you mad.

DESDEMONA: Why, sweet Othello—

OTHELLO: Devil!   [*Strikes her.*] 220

DESDEMONA: I have not deserved this.

LODOVICO: My lord, this would not be believed in Venice,

  Though I should swear I saw't. 'Tis very much.

  Make her amends; she weeps.

OTHELLO: O devil, devil!

  If that the earth could teem° with woman's tears,   225

  Each drop she falls° would prove a crocodile.°

  Out of my sight!

DESDEMONA: I will not stay to offend you.   [*Going.*]

LODOVICO: Truly, an obedient lady.

  I do beseech your lordship call her back.

OTHELLO: Mistress!

DESDEMONA: My lord?

OTHELLO: What would you with her, sir?   230

LODOVICO: Who? I, my lord?

OTHELLO: Ay! You did wish that I would make her turn.

  Sir, she can turn, and turn, and yet go on

  And turn again; and she can weep, sir, weep;

  And she's obedient; as you say, obedient.   235

  Very obedient. Proceed you in your tears.

  Concerning this, sir—O well-painted passion!

  I am commanded home.—Get you away;

  I'll send for you anon.—Sir, I obey the mandate

  And will return to Venice.—Hence, avaunt!   [*Exit* DESDEMONA.] 240

  Cassio shall have my place. And, sir, tonight

  I do entreat that we may sup together.

213*atone* reconcile.   217*government* office.   225*teem* conceive.   226*falls* drops.   226*crocodile*
(*the crocodile was supposed to shed false tears to lure its victims*).

You are welcome, sir, to Cyprus.—Goats and monkeys!   *Exit.*
LODOVICO: Is this the noble Moor whom our full Senate
    Call all in all sufficient? Is this the nature   245
    Whom passion could not shake? whose solid virtue
    The shot of accident nor dart of chance
    Could neither graze nor pierce?
IAGO: He is much changed.
LODOVICO: Are his wits safe? Is he not light of brain?
IAGO: He's that he is; I may not breathe my censure.   250
    What he might be (if, what he might, he is not)
    I would to heaven he were!
LODOVICO: What, strike his wife?
IAGO: Faith, that was not so well; yet would I knew
    That stroke would prove the worst.
LODOVICO: Is it his use?°
    Or did the letters work upon his blood°   255
    And new-create his fault?
IAGO: Alas, alas!
    It is not honesty in me to speak
    What I have seen and known. You shall observe him,
    And his own courses° will denote him so
    That I may save my speech. Do but go after   260
    And mark how he continues.
LODOVICO: I am sorry that I am deceived in him.   *Exeunt.*

Scene II [The citadel.]

Enter OTHELLO *and* EMILIA.

OTHELLO: You have seen nothing then?
EMILIA: Nor ever heard, nor ever did suspect.
OTHELLO: Yes, you have seen Cassio and she together.
EMILIA: But then I saw no harm, and then I heard
    Each syllable that breath made up° between them.   5
OTHELLO: What, did they never whisper?
EMILIA: Never, my lord.
OTHELLO: Nor send you out o' th' way?
EMILIA: Never.
OTHELLO: To fetch her fan, her gloves, her mask, nor nothing?
EMILIA: Never, my lord.   10
OTHELLO: That's strange.
EMILIA: I durst, my lord, to wager she is honest,
    Lay down my soul at stake.° If you think other,
    Remove your thought. It doth abuse your bosom.

---

²⁵⁴**use** habit   ²⁵⁵**blood** passion.   ²⁵⁹**courses** actions.   **IV.ii.**   ⁵**that breath made up** spoken.
¹³**at stake** as the wager.

If any wretch have put this in your head, 15
Let heaven requite it with the serpent's curse,°
For if she be not honest,° chaste, and true,
There's no man happy. The purest of their wives
Is foul as slander.
OTHELLO: Bid her come hither. Go.   *Exit* EMILIA.
She says enough; yet she's a simple bawd° 20
That cannot say as much. This is a subtle whore,
A closet lock and key of villainous secrets,
And yet she'll kneel and pray; I have seen her do't.

Enter DESDEMONA *and* EMILIA.

DESDEMONA: My lord, what is your will?
OTHELLO: Pray you, chuck, come hither.
DESDEMONA: What is your pleasure?
OTHELLO: Let me see your eyes. 25
Look in my face.
DESDEMONA: What horrible fancy's this?
OTHELLO [*To* EMILIA]: Some of your function°, mistress:
Leave procreants alone and shut the door;
Cough or cry hem if anybody come.
Your mystery°, your mystery! Nay, dispatch!   *Exit* EMILIA. 30
DESDEMONA: Upon my knee, what doth your speech import?
I understand a fury in your words.°
OTHELLO: Why, what art thou?
DESDEMONA: Your wife, my lord; your true
And loyal wife.
OTHELLO: Come, swear it, damn thyself;
Lest, being like one of heaven, the devils themselves 35
Should fear to seize thee. Therefore be doubledamned:
Swear thou art honest.
DESDEMONA: Heaven doth truly know it.
OTHELLO: Heaven truly knows that thou art false as hell.
DESDEMONA: To whom, my lord? With whom? How am I false?
OTHELLO: Ah, Desdemon! Away! Away! Away! 40
DESDEMONA: Alas the heavy day! Why do you weep?
Am I the motive° of these tears, my lord?
If haply° you my father do suspect
An instrument of this your calling back,
Lay not your blame on me. If you have lost him, 45
I have lost him too.
OTHELLO: Had it pleased heaven
To try me with affliction, had they rained

16**serpent's curse** (*God's curse on the serpent after the fall of Eden*).   17**honest** chaste.   20**bawd** pro-
curess.   27**Some of your function** *do your proper work (as the operator of a brothel).*   30**mystery** trade.
32**words** words (*Q1 adds to this line, "But not the words"*).   42**motive** cause.   43**haply** by chance.

All kinds of sores and shames on my bare head,
Steeped° me in poverty to the very lips,
Given to captivity me and my utmost hopes,   50
I should have found in some place of my soul
A drop of patience. But alas, to make me
The fixèd figure for the time of scorn°
To point his slow and moving finger at.
Yet could I bear that too, well, very well.   55
But there where I have garnered up my heart,
Where either I must live or bear no life,
The fountain from the which my current runs
Or else dries up—to be discarded thence,
Or keep it as a cistern for foul toads   60
To knot and gender° in—turn thy complexion there,
Patience, thou young and rose-lipped cherubin!
I here look grim as hell!°

DESDEMONA: I hope my noble lord esteems me honest.

OTHELLO: O, ay, as summer flies are in the shambles,°   65
That quicken even with blowing.° O thou weed,
Who art so lovely fair, and smell'st so sweet,
That the sense aches at thee, would thou hadst never been born!

DESDEMONA: Alas, what ignorant° sin have I committed?

OTHELLO: Was this fair paper, this most goodly book,   70
Made to write "whore" upon? What committed?
Committed? O thou public commoner,°
I should make very forges of my cheeks
That would to cinders burn up modesty,
Did I but speak thy deeds. What committed?   75
Heaven stops the nose at it, and the moon winks;°
The bawdy wind that kisses all it meets
Is hushed within the hollow mine of earth
And will not hear't. What committed?

DESDEMONA: By heaven, you do me wrong!   80

OTHELLO: Are not you a strumpet?

DESDEMONA: No, as I am a Christian!
If to preserve this vessel for my lord
From any other foul unlawful touch
Be not to be a strumpet, I am none.

OTHELLO: What, not a whore?

DESDEMONA: No, as I shall be saved!   85

OTHELLO: Is't possible?

---

⁴⁹**Steeped** _submerged._   ⁵³**The . . . scorn** _the very image of scorn in our time._   ⁶¹**knot and gender**
twist in bunches and procreate.   ⁶¹⁻⁶³**turn . . . hell** _(the rough sense would seem to be "even Patience would
grow pale, turn complexion, at Desdemona's perfidy, but that Othello looks grimly on")._   ⁶⁵**shambles** _abattoirs._
⁶⁶**quicken even with blowing** _become impregnated as soon as they lay their eggs._   ⁶⁹**ignorant** _unknowing._
⁷²**commonor** _prostitute._   ⁷⁶**winks** _closes its eyes (the moon was the symbol of chastity)._

DESDEMONA: O, heaven forgive us!

OTHELLO: I cry you mercy° then.

  I took you for that cunning whore of Venice

  That married with Othello. [*Calling*] You, mistress,

Enter EMILIA.

  That have the office opposite to Saint Peter   90

  And keep the gate of hell! You, you, ay, you!

  We have done our course; there's money for your pains.

[*Throws her some coins.*]

  I pray you turn the key and keep our counsel.   *Exit.*

EMILIA: Alas, what does this gentleman conceive?

  How do you, madam? How do you, my good lady?   95

DESDEMONA: Faith, half asleep.

EMILIA: Good madam, what's the matter with my lord?

DESDEMONA: With who?

EMILIA: Why, with my lord, madam.

DESDEMONA: Who is thy lord?

EMILIA: He that is yours, sweet lady.   100

DESDEMONA: I have none. Do not talk to me, Emilia.

  I cannot weep, nor answers have I none

  But what should go by water.° Prithee tonight

  Lay on my bed my wedding sheets, remember;

  And call thy husband hither.

EMILIA: Here's a change indeed!   *Exit.* 105

DESDEMONA: 'Tis meet I should be used so, very meet.

  How have I been behaved, that he might stick

  The small'st opinion on my least misuse?°

Enter IAGO *and* EMILIA.

IAGO: What is your pleasure, madam? How is't with you?

DESDEMONA: I cannot tell. Those that do teach young babes   110

  Do it with gentle means and easy tasks.

  He might have chid me so; for, in good faith,

  I am a child to chiding.

IAGO: What is the matter, lady?

EMILIA: Alas, Iago, my lord hath so bewhored her,

  Thrown such despite° and heavy terms upon her   115

  That true hearts cannot bear it.

DESDEMONA: Am I that name, Iago?

IAGO: What name, fair lady?

DESDEMONA: Such as she said my lord did say I was.

EMILIA: He called her whore. A beggar in his drink

87**cry you mercy** *ask your pardon.*   103**water** *tears.*   107–8**stick ... misuse** *base any doubt on my smallest fault.*   115**despite** *abuse.*

  Could not have laid such terms upon his callet.°   120
IAGO: Why did he so?
DESDEMONA: I do not know; I am sure I am none such.
IAGO: Do not weep, do not weep. Alas the day.
EMILIA: Hath she forsook so many noble matches,
  Her father and her country, and her friends,   125
  To be called whore? Would it not make one weep?
DESDEMONA: It is my wretched fortune.
IAGO: Beshrew° him for't!
  How comes this trick upon him?
DESDEMONA: Nay, heaven doth know.
EMILIA: I will be hanged if some eternal villain,
  Some busy and insinuating rogue,   130
  Some cogging,° cozening slave, to get some office,
  Have not devised this slander. I will be hanged else.
IAGO: Fie, there is no such man! It is impossible.
DESDEMONA: If any such there be, heaven pardon him.
EMILIA: A halter pardon him! And hell gnaw his bones!   135
  Why should he call her whore? Who keeps her company?
  What place? What time? What form? What likelihood?
  The Moor's abused by some most villainous knave,
  Some base notorious knave, some scurvy fellow.
  O heavens, that such companions° thou'dst unfold,°   140
  And put in every honest hand a whip
  To lash the rascals naked through the world
  Even from the east to th' west!
IAGO: Speak within door.°
EMILIA: O, fie upon them! Some such squire° he was
  That turned your wit the seamy side without   145
  And made you to suspect me with the Moor.
IAGO: You are a fool. Go to.
DESDEMONA: Alas, Iago,
  What shall I do to win my lord again?
  Good friend, go to him, for, by this light of heaven,
  I know not how I lost him. Here I kneel: 150
  If e'er my will did trespass 'gainst his love
  Either in discourse of thought° or actual deed,
  Or that mine eyes, mine ears, or any sense
  Delighted them in any other form;
  Or that I do not yet, and ever did,   155
  And ever will (though he do shake me off
  To beggarly divorcement) love him dearly,
  Comfort forswear me. Unkindness may do much,

---

¹²⁰**callet** *slut.* ¹²⁷**Beshrew** *curse.* ¹³¹**cogging** *cheating.* ¹⁴⁰**companions** *fellows, rogues.*
¹⁴⁰**unfold** *disclose.* ¹⁴³**within door** *more quietly and moderately.* ¹⁴⁴**squire** *(a term of contempt).*
¹⁵²**discourse of thought** *thinking.*

And his unkindness may defeat° my life,
But never taint my love. I cannot say "whore." 160
It does abhor me now I speak the word;
To do the act that might the addition earn
Not the world's mass of vanity could make me.

IAGO: I pray you be content. 'Tis but his humor.° 165
The business of the state does him offense.

DESDEMONA: If 'twere no other.

IAGO: It is but so, I warrant. [*Trumpets within.*]
Hark how these instruments summon to supper.
The messengers of Venice stay the meat.°
Go in, and weep not. All things shall be well.

[*Exeunt* DESDEMONA *and* EMILIA. *Enter* RODERIGO.]

How now, Roderigo? 170

RODERIGO: I do not find that thou deal'st justly with me.

IAGO: What in the contrary?

RODERIGO: Every day thou daff'st° me with some device,° Iago, and rather, as it
    seems to me now, keep'st from me all conveniency° than suppliest me with the
    least advantage of hope. I will indeed no longer endure it; nor am I yet 175
    persuaded to put up° in peace what already I have foolishly suffered.

IAGO: Will you hear me, Roderigo?

RODERIGO: I have heard too much, and your words and performances are no kin
    together. 180

IAGO: You charge me most unjustly.

RODERIGO: With naught but truth. I have wasted myself out of my means. The
    jewels you have had from me to deliver Desdemona would half have corrupted
    a votarist.° You have told me she hath received them, and returned me
    expectations and comforts of sudden respect° and acquaintance; but I find none. 185

IAGO: Well, go to; very well.

RODERIGO: Very well? Go to? I cannot go to, man; nor 'tis not very well. Nay, I
    think it is scurvy, and begin to find myself fopped° in it.

IAGO: Very well.

RODERIGO: I tell you 'tis not very well. I will make myself known to Desdemona. 190
    If she will return me my jewels, I will give over my suit and repent my unlawful
    solicitation. If not, assure yourself I will seek satisfaction of you.

IAGO: You have said now?

RODERIGO: Ay, and said nothing but what I protest° intendment of doing. 195

IAGO: Why, now I see there's mettle° in thee, and even from this instant do build
    on thee a better opinion than ever before. Give me thy hand, Roderigo. Thou
    hast taken against me a most just exception,° but yet I protest I have dealt most
    directly° in thy affair.

159**defeat** *destroy.*   164**humor** *mood.*   168**stay the meat** *await the meal.*   173**daff'st** *put off.*
173**device** *scheme.*   174**conveniency** *what is needful.*   176**put up** *accept.*   185**sudden respect** *im-*
mediate *consideration.*   189**fopped** *duped.*   184**votarist** *nun.*   196**protest** *aver.*   197**mettle**
spirit.   199**exception** *objection.*   200**directly** *straight-forwardly.*

RODERIGO: It hath not appeared.

IAGO: I grant indeed it hath not appeared, and your suspicion is not without wit and judgment. But, Roderigo, if thou hast that in thee indeed which I have greater reason to believe now than ever—I mean purpose, courage, and valor—this night show it. If thou the next night following enjoy not Desdemona, take 205 me from this world with treachery and devise engines for° my life.

RODERIGO: Well, what is it? Is it within reason and compass?°

IAGO: Sir, there is especial commission come from Venice to depute Cassio in Othello's place. 210

RODERIGO: Is that true? Why, then Othello and Desdemona return again to Venice.

IAGO: O, no; he goes into Mauritania and taketh away with him the fair Desdemona, unless his abode be lingered here by some accident; wherein none can be so determinate° as the removing of Cassio. 215

RODERIGO: How do you mean, removing him?

IAGO: Why, by making him uncapable of Othello's place—knocking out his brains.

RODERIGO: And that you would have me to do?

IAGO: Ay, if you dare do yourself a profit and a right. He sups tonight with a 220 harlotry,° and thither will I go to him. He knows not yet of his honorable fortune. If you will watch his going thence, which I will fashion to fall out° between twelve and one, you may take him at your pleasure. I will be near to second° your attempt, and he shall fall between us. Come, stand not amazed at it, but go along with me. I will show you such a necessity in his death that 225 you shall think yourself bound to put it on him. It is now high supper time, and the night grows to waste. About it.

RODERIGO: I will hear further reason for this.

IAGO: And you shall be satisfied.   *Exeunt.*

Scene III [*The citadel.*]

Enter OTHELLO, LODOVICO, DESDEMONA, EMILIA, *and* ATTENDANTS.

LODOVICO: I do beseech you, sir, trouble yourself no further.

OTHELLO: O, pardon me; 'twill do me good to walk.

LODOVICO: Madam, good night. I humbly thank your ladyship.

DESDEMONA: Your honor is most welcome.

OTHELLO: Will you walk, sir? O, Desdemona. 5

DESDEMONA: My lord?

OTHELLO: Get you to bed on th' instant; I will be returned forthwith. Dismiss your attendant there. Look't be done.

DESDEMONA: I will, my lord.   *Exit* [OTHELLO, *with* LODOVICO *and* ATTENDANTS].

EMILIA: How goes it now? He looks gentler than he did. 10

DESDEMONA: He says he will return incontinent,°
    And hath commanded me to go to bed.

206–207*engines for* schemes against.   208*compass* possibility.   215*determinate* effective.   221*har-lotry* female.   222–23*fall out* occur.   224*second* support.   **IV.iii.** 11*incontinent* at once.

And bade me to dismiss you.
EMILIA: Dismiss me?
DESDEMONA: It was his bidding; therefore, good Emilia,
　Give me my nightly wearing, and adieu.   15
　We must not now displease him.
EMILIA: I would you had never seen him!
DESDEMONA: So would not I. My love doth so approve him
　That even his stubbornness, his checks,° his frowns—
　Prithee unpin me—have grace and favor.   20
EMILIA: I have laid these sheets you bade me on the bed.
DESDEMONA: All's one.° Good Father, how foolish are our minds!
　If I do die before, prithee shroud me
　In one of these same sheets.
EMILIA: Come, come! You talk.
DESDEMONA: My mother had a maid called Barbary.   25
　She was in love; and he she loved proved mad
　And did forsake her. She had a song of "Willow";
　An old thing 'twas, but it expressed her fortune,
　And she died singing it. That song tonight
　Will not go from my mind; I have much to do   30
　But to go hang my head all at one side
　And sing it like poor Barbary. Prithee dispatch.
EMILIA: Shall I go fetch your nightgown?
DESDEMONA: No, unpin me here.
　This Lodovico is a proper man.   35
EMILIA: A very handsome man.
DESDEMONA: He speaks well.
EMILIA: I know a lady in Venice would have walked barefoot to Palestine for a
　touch of his nether lip.
DESDEMONA [*Sings*]:
　"The poor soul sat singing by a sycamore tree,   40
　　Sing all a green willow;
　Her hand on her bosom, her head on her knee,
　　Sing willow, willow, willow.
　The fresh streams ran by her and murmured her moans;
　　Sing willow, willow, willow;   45
　Her salt tears fell from her, and soft'ned the stones—
　　Sing willow, willow, willow—"
　Lay by these.   [*Gives* EMILIA *her clothes.*]
　　"Willow, Willow"—
　Prithee hie° thee; he'll come anon.°   50
　　"Sing all a green willow must be my garland
　　Let nobody blame him; his scorn I approve"—
　Nay, that's not next. Hark! Who is't that knocks?
EMILIA: It is the wind.

19**checks**　*rebukes.*　　22***All's one***　*no matter.*　　50**hie**　*hurry.*　　50***anon***　*at once.*

DESDEMONA [*Sings*]:
   "I called my love false love; but what said he then?   55
   Sing willow, willow, willow:
   If I court moe° women, you'll couch with moe men."
   So, get thee gone; good night. Mine eyes do itch.
   Doth that bode weeping?
EMILIA: 'Tis neither here nor there.
DESDEMONA: I have heard it said so. O, these men, these men.   60
   Dost thou in conscience think, tell me, Emilia,
   That there be women do abuse their husbands
   In such gross kind?
EMILIA: There be some such, no question.
DESDEMONA: Wouldst thou do such a deed for all the world?
EMILIA: Why, would not you?
DESDEMONA: No, by this heavenly light!   65
EMILIA: Nor I neither by this heavenly light.
   I might do't as well i' th' dark.
DESDEMONA: Wouldst thou do such a deed for all the world?
EMILIA: The world's a huge thing; it is a great price for a small vice.
DESDEMONA: In troth, I think thou wouldst not.   70
EMILIA: In troth, I think I should; and undo't when I had done. Marry, I would not
   do such a thing for a joint-ring,° nor for measures of lawn,° nor for gowns,
   petticoats, nor caps, nor any petty exhibition,° but for all the whole world?
   Why, who would not make her husband a cuckold to make him a monarch? I
   should venture purgatory for't.
DESDEMONA: Beshrew me if I would do such a wrong for the whole world.   75
EMILIA: Why, the wrong is but a wrong i' th' world; and having the world for your
   labor, 'tis a wrong in your own world, and you might quickly make it right.
DESDEMONA: I do not think there is any such woman.
EMILIA: Yes, a dozen; and as many to th' vantage as would store° the world they   80
   played for.
   But I do think it is their husbands' faults
   If wives do fall. Say that they slack their duties
   And pour our treasures into foreign° laps;   85
   Or else break out in peevish jealousies,
   Throwing restraint upon us; or say they strike us,
   Or scant our former having in despite°—
   Why, we have galls; and though we have some grace,
   Yet have we some revenge. Let husbands know   90
   Their wives have sense like them. They see, and smell,
   And have their palates both for sweet and sour,
   As husbands have. What is it that they do
   When they change° us for others? Is it sport?

---

[57]**moe** more.   [72]**joint-ring** *(a ring with two interlocking halves)*.   [72]**lawn** *fine linen.*   [73]**exhibi-**
tion *payment.*   [81]**to . . . store** *in addition as would fill.*   [85]**foreign** *alien, i.e., other than the wife.*
[88]**scant . . . despite** *reduce, in spite, our household allowance (?).*   [94]**change** *exchange.*

I think it is. And doth affection° breed it?   95
I think it doth. Is't frailty that thus errs?
It is so too. And have not we affections?
Desires for sport? and frailty? as men have?
Then let them use us well; else let them know,
The ills we do, their ills instruct us so.°   100
DESDEMONA: Good night, good night. Heaven me such uses° send,
Not to pick bad from bad, but by bad mend.   *Exeunt.*

ACT V

Scene I [A street.]

Enter IAGO *and* RODERIGO.

IAGO: Here, stand behind this bulk;° straight will he come.
Wear thy good rapier bare, and put it home.
Quick, quick! Fear nothing; I'll be at thy elbow.
It makes us, or it mars us, think on that,
And fix most firm thy resolution.   5
RODERIGO: Be near at hand; I may miscarry in't.
IAGO: Here, at thy hand. Be bold, and take thy stand.   *[Moves to one side.]*
RODERIGO: I have no great devotion to the deed,
And yet he hath given me satisfying reasons.
'Tis but a man gone. Forth my sword! He dies!   10
IAGO: I have rubbed this young quat° almost to the sense,°
And he grows angry. Now, whether he kill Cassio,
Or Cassio him, or each do kill the other,
Every way makes my gain. Live Roderigo,
He calls me to a restitution large   15
Of gold and jewels that I bobbed° from him
As gifts to Desdemona.
It must not be. If Cassio do remain,
He hath a daily beauty in his life
That makes me ugly; and besides, the Moor   20
May unfold me to him; there stand I in much peril.
No, he must die. But so, I hear him coming.

Enter CASSIO.

RODERIGO: I know his gait. 'Tis he. Villain, thou diest!   *[Thrusts at* CASSIO.]
CASSIO: That thrust had been mine enemy indeed
But that my coat° is better than thou know'st.   25

95**affection** *strong feeling, desire.*   100**instruct us so** *teach us to do likewise.*   101**uses** *practices.*
V.i.   1**bulk** *projecting stall of a shop.*   11**quat** *pimple.*   11**to the sense** *raw.*   16**bobbed** *swindled.*
25**coat** *i.e., a mail shirt or bullet-proof vest.*

I will make proof of thine.   [*Fights with* RODERIGO.]
RODERIGO: O, I am slain!°
CASSIO: I am maimed forever. Help, ho! Murder! Murder!

Enter OTHELLO [*to one side*].

OTHELLO: The voice of Cassio. Iago keeps his word.
RODERIGO: O, villain that I am!
OTHELLO: It is even so.
CASSIO: O help, ho! Light! A surgeon!   30
OTHELLO: 'Tis he. O brave Iago, honest and just,
   That hast such noble sense of thy friend's wrong!
   Thou teachest me. Minion,° your dear lies dead,
   And your unblest° fate hies.° Strumpet, I come.
   Forth of my heart those charms, thine eyes, are blotted.   35
   Thy bed, lust-stained, shall with lust's blood be spotted.

Exit OTHELLO. *Enter* LODOVICO *and* GRATIANO.

CASSIO: What, ho? No watch? No passage?° Murder! Murder!
GRATIANO: 'Tis some mischance. The voice is very direful.
CASSIO: O, help!
LODOVICO: Hark!   40
RODERIGO: O wretched villain!
LODOVICO: Two or three groan. 'Tis heavy night.
   These may be counterfeits. Let's think't unsafe
   To come into the cry without more help.
RODERIGO: Nobody come? Then shall I bleed to death.   45
LODOVICO: Hark!

Enter IAGO [*with a light*].

GRATIANO: Here's one comes in his shirt, with light and weapons.
IAGO: Who's there? Whose noise is this that cries on murder?
LODOVICO: We do not know.
IAGO: Do not you hear a cry?
CASSIO: Here, here! For heaven's sake, help me!
IAGO: What's the matter?   50
GRATIANO: This is Othello's ancient, as I take it.
LODOVICO: The same indeed, a very valiant fellow.
IAGO: What are you here that cry so grievously?
CASSIO: Iago? O, I am spoiled, undone by villains.
   Give me some help.   55

---

²⁶**slain**   *most editors add here a stage direction that has Iago wounding Cassio in the leg from behind, but remaining*
unseen. However, nothing in the text requires this, and Cassio's wound can be given him in the fight with Roderigo, for
presumably when Cassio attacks Roderigo the latter would not simply accept the thrust but would parry. Since Iago en-
ters again at line 46, he must exit at some point after line 22.   ³³**Minion**   *hussy, i.e., Desdemona.*   ³⁴**un-**
blest   *unsanctified.*   ³⁴**hies**   *approaches swiftly.*   ³⁷**passage**   *passers-by.*

IAGO: O me, lieutenant! What villains have done this?

CASSIO: I think that one of them is hereabout

And cannot make away.

IAGO: O treacherous villains!

  [*To* LODOVICO *and* GRATIANO] What are you there?

  Come in, and give some help.   60

RODERIGO: O, help me here!

CASSIO: That's one of them.

IAGO: O murd'rous slave! O villain!   [*Stabs* RODERIGO.]

RODERIGO: O damned Iago! O inhuman dog!

IAGO: Kill men i' th' dark?—Where be these bloody thieves?—

  How silent is this town!—Ho! Murder! Murder!—   65

  What may you be? Are you of good or evil?

LODOVICO: As you shall prove us, praise us.

IAGO: Signior Lodovico?

LODOVICO: He, sir.

IAGO: I cry you mercy. Here's Cassio hurt by villains.   70

GRATIANO: Cassio?

IAGO: How is't, brother?

CASSIO: My leg is cut in two.

IAGO: Marry, heaven forbid!

  Light, gentlemen. I'll bind it with my shirt.

Enter BIANCA.

BIANCA: What is the matter, ho? Who is't that cried?   75

IAGO: Who is't that cried?

BIANCA: O my dear Cassio! My sweet Cassio!

  O Cassio, Cassio, Cassio!

IAGO: O notable strumpet!—Cassio, may you suspect

  Who they should be that have thus mangled you?   80

CASSIO: No.

GRATIANO: I am sorry to find you thus. I have been to seek you.

IAGO: Lend me a garter. So. O for a chair

  To bear him easily hence.

BIANCA: Alas, he faints! O Cassio, Cassio, Cassio!   85

IAGO: Gentlemen all, I do suspect this trash

  To be a party in this injury.—

  Patience awhile, good Cassio.—Come, come.

  Lend me a light. Know we this face or no?

  Alas, my friend and my dear countryman   90

  Roderigo? No.—Yes, sure.—Yes, 'tis Roderigo!

GRATIANO: What, of Venice?

IAGO: Even he, sir. Did you know him?

GRATIANO: Know him? Ay.

IAGO: Signior Gratiano? I cry your gentle pardon.

  These bloody accidents must excuse my manners   95

  That so neglected you.

GRATIANO: I am glad to see you.
IAGO: How do you, Cassio?—O, a chair, a chair!
GRATIANO: Roderigo?
IAGO: He, he, 'tis he! [*A chair brought in.*] O, that's well said;° the chair.
  Some good man bear him carefully from hence.   100
  I'll fetch the general's surgeon. [*To* BIANCA] For you, mistress,
  Save you your labor. [*To* CASSIO] He that lies slain here, Cassio,
  Was my dear friend. What malice was between you?
CASSIO: None in the world; nor do I know the man.
IAGO: What, look you pale?—O, bear him out o' th' air.   105

                    [CASSIO *is carried off.*]

  Stay you, good gentlemen.—Look you pale, mistress?
  Do you perceive the gastness° of her eye?
  Nay, if you stare, we shall hear more anon.
  Behold her well; I pray you look upon her.
  Do you see, gentlemen? Nay, guiltiness will speak,   110
  Though tongues were out of use.°

                    [*Enter* EMILIA.]

EMILIA: Alas, what is the matter? What is the matter, husband?
IAGO: Cassio hath here been set on in the dark
  By Roderigo and fellows that are scaped.
  He's almost slain, and Roderigo quite dead.   115
EMILIA: Alas, good gentleman! Alas, good Cassio!
IAGO: This is the fruits of whoring. Prithee, Emilia,
  Go know of Cassio where he supped tonight.
  [*To* BIANCA] What, do you shake at that?
BIANCA: He supped at my house; but I therefore shake not.   120
IAGO: O, did he so? I charge° you go with me.
EMILIA: Oh fie upon thee, strumpet!
BIANCA: I am no strumpet, but of life as honest
  As you that thus abuse me.
EMILIA: As I? Fie upon thee!
IAGO: Kind gentlemen, let's go see poor Cassio dressed.°   125
  [*To* BIANCA] Come, mistress, you must tell's another tale.
  Emilia, run you to the citadel
  And tell my lord and lady what hath happed   [*Exit* EMILIA.]
  Will you go on afore?   *Exeunt* [*all but* IAGO].
                    This is the night
  That either makes me or fordoes me quite.°   [*Exit.*] 130

---

⁹⁹*well said*   well done   ¹⁰⁷*gastness*   terror.   ¹¹¹*tongues out of use*   men no longer spoke.
¹²¹*charge*   command.   ¹²⁵*dressed*   bandaged.   ¹³⁰*fordoes me quite*   completely ruins me.

Scene II. [DESDEMONA'S *chamber.*]

Enter OTHELLO [*with a light*]; *and* DESDEMONA *in her bed.*

OTHELLO: It is the cause, it is the cause, my soul.
  Let me not name it to you, you chaste stars.
  It is the cause. Yet I'll not shed her blood,
  Nor scar that whiter skin of hers than snow
  And smooth as monumental alabaster.   5
  Yet she must die, else she'll betray more men.
  Put out the light, and then put out the light.
  If I quench thee, thou flaming minister,°
  I can again thy former light restore,
  Should I repent me; but once put out thy light,   10
  Thou cunning'st° pattern of excelling nature,
  I know not where is that Promethean heat°
  That can thy light relume.° When I have plucked the rose,
  I cannot give it vital° growth again;
  It needs must wither. I'll smell thee on the tree.   [*He kisses her.*] 15
  O balmy breath, that dost almost persuade
  Justice to break her sword. One more, one more!
  Be thus when thou art dead, and I will kill thee,
  And love thee after. One more, and that's the last!
  So sweet was ne'er so fatal. I must weep,   20
  But they are cruel tears. This sorrow's heavenly;
  It strikes where it doth love. She wakes.
DESDEMONA: Who's there? Othello?
OTHELLO: Ay, Desdemona.
DESDEMONA: Will you come to bed, my lord?
OTHELLO: Have you prayed tonight, Desdemon?
DESDEMONA: Ay, my lord.   25
OTHELLO: If you bethink yourself of any crime
  Unreconciled as yet to heaven and grace,
  Solicit for it straight.
DESDEMONA: Alack, my lord, what may you mean by that?
OTHELLO: Well, do it, and be brief; I will walk by.°   30
  I would not kill thy unprepared spirit.
  No, heavens forfend! I would not kill thy soul.
DESDEMONA: Talk you of killing?
OTHELLO: Ay, I do.
DESDEMONA: Then heaven
  Have mercy on me!
OTHELLO: Amen, with all my heart.

V.ii. ⁸**minister** *worker, servant.* ¹¹**cunning'st** *most intricate and skilfully wrought (by nature excelling it-*
self). ¹²**Promethean heat** *divine fire (Prometheus is the Titan who stole fire from heaven and gave it to man).*
¹³**relume** *relight.* ¹⁴**vital** *living.* ³⁰**by** *nearby.*

DESDEMONA: If you say so, I hope you will not kill me.   35
OTHELLO: Humh.
DESDEMONA: And yet I fear you; for you're fatal then
    When your eyes roll so. Why I should fear I know not,
    Since guiltiness I know not; but yet I feel I fear.
OTHELLO: Think on thy sins.
DESDEMONA: They are loves I bear to you.   40
OTHELLO: Ay, and for that thou diest.
DESDEMONA: That death's unnatural that kills for loving.
    Alas, why gnaw you so your nether lip?
    Some bloody passion shakes your very frame.
    These are portents; but yet I hope, I hope,   45
    They do not point on me.
OTHELLO: Peace and be still.
DESDEMONA: I will so. What's the matter?
OTHELLO: That handkerchief which I so loved and gave thee,
    Thou gav'st to Cassio.
DESDEMONA: No, by my life and soul!
    Send for the man and ask him.
OTHELLO: Sweet soul, take heed,   50
    Take heed of perjury; thou art on thy deathbed.
DESDEMONA: Ay, but not yet to die.
OTHELLO: Presently.°
    Therefore confess thee freely of thy sin,
    For to deny each article° with oath
    Cannot remove nor choke the strong conception   55
    That I do groan withal. Thou art to die.
DESDEMONA: Then Lord have mercy on me.
OTHELLO: I say, amen.
DESDEMONA: And have you mercy too. I never did
    Offend you in my life; never loved Cassio
    But with such general warranty° of heaven   60
    As I might love. I never gave him token.
OTHELLO: By heaven, I saw my handkerchief in's hand!
    O perjured woman! thou dost stone° my heart,
    And mak'st me call what I intend to do
    A murder, which I thought a sacrifice.   65
    I saw the handkerchief.
DESDEMONA: He found it then.
    I never gave it him. Send for him hither.
    Let him confess a truth.
OTHELLO: He hath confessed.
DESDEMONA: What, my lord?
OTHELLO: That he hath used thee.
DESDEMONA: How? Unlawfully?

52**Presently** *immediately.*   54**article** *item (of the charge of adultery. Othello makes heavy use of legal terms in this scene).*   60**warranty** *allowance.*   63**stone** *turn to stone.*

OTHELLO: Ay.   70
DESDEMONA: He will not say so.
OTHELLO: No, his mouth is stopped.
  Honest Iago hath ta'en order for't.°
DESDEMONA: O, my fear interprets. What, is he dead?
OTHELLO: Had all his hairs been lives, my great revenge
  Had stomach° for them all.   75
DESDEMONA: Alas, he is betrayed, and I undone!
OTHELLO: Out, strumpet! Weep'st thou for him to my face?
DESDEMONA: O, banish me, my lord, but kill me not!
OTHELLO: Down, strumpet!
DESDEMONA: Kill me tomorrow; let me live tonight!   80
OTHELLO: Nay, if you strive—
DESDEMONA: But half an hour!
OTHELLO: Being done, there is no pause.
DESDEMONA: But while I say one prayer!
OTHELLO: It is too late.   *Smothers her.*

                      EMILIA *at the door.*

EMILIA [*Calls within*]: My lord, my lord! What, ho, my lord, my lord!
OTHELLO: What noise is this? Not dead? Not yet quite dead?   85
  I that am cruel am yet merciful;
  I would not have thee linger in thy pain.
EMILIA [*Within*]: What, ho! My lord, my lord!
OTHELLO: So, so. Who's there?
EMILIA [*Within*]: O, good my lord, I would speak a word with you.
OTHELLO: Yes, 'tis Emilia.—By and by.—She's dead.—   90
  'Tis like she comes to speak of Cassio's death.
  The noise was high.° Ha! No more moving?
  Still as the grave.—Shall she come in? Were't good?—
  I think she stirs again. No.—What's best to do?
  If she come in, she'll sure speak to my wife.   95
  My wife! My wife! What wife? I have no wife.
  O, insupportable! O heavy hour!
  Methinks° it should be now a huge eclipse
  Of sun and moon, and that th' affrighted globe
  Should yawn° at alteration.
EMILIA [*Within*]:   I do beseech you   100
  That I may speak with you, O good my lord!
OTHELLO: I had forgot thee. O, come in, Emilia.
  Soft, by and by.—Let me the curtains draw.—

                 [*Draws the bed hangings and then opens the door.*]

  Where art thou?

---

⁷²*ta'en order for't* made sure of it.   ⁷⁵*stomach* appetite.   ⁹²*high* loud (Q1 reads "here").
^{98–100}*Methinks . . . alteration* (the Elizabethans believed that great changes in human affairs were reflected by disorders in nature).   ¹⁰⁰*yawn* gape open (as in an earthquake).

Enter EMILIA.

                     What's the matter with thee now?

EMILIA: O my good lord, yonder's foul murders done!   105

OTHELLO: What? Now?

EMILIA: But now, my lord.

OTHELLO: It is the very error° of the moon.

   She comes more nearer earth than she was wont

   And makes men mad.   110

EMILIA: Cassio, my lord, hath killed a young Venetian

   Called Roderigo.

OTHELLO: Roderigo killed?

   And Cassio killed?

EMILIA: No, Cassio is not killed.

OTHELLO: Not Cassio killed? Then murder's out of tune,

   And sweet revenge grows harsh.   115

DESDEMONA: O, falsely, falsely murdered!

EMILIA: O Lord! What cry is that?

OTHELLO: That? What?

EMILIA: Out and alas! that was my lady's voice.

   Help! Help, ho! Help! O lady, speak again!

   Sweet Desdemona! O sweet mistress, speak!   120

DESDEMONA: A guiltless death I die.

EMILIA: O, who hath done this deed?

DESDEMONA: Nobody—I myself. Farewell.

   Commend me to my kind lord. O, farewell!   [*She dies.*]

OTHELLO: Why, how should she be murd'red?

EMILIA: Alas, who knows?   125

OTHELLO: You heard her say herself, it was not I.

EMILIA: She said so. I must needs report the truth.

OTHELLO: She's like a liar gone to burning hell!

   'Twas I that killed her.

EMILIA: O, the more angel she,

   And you the blacker devil!   130

OTHELLO: She turned to folly, and she was a whore.

EMILIA: Thou dost belie her, and thou art a devil.

OTHELLO: She was false as water.

EMILIA: Thou art rash as fire to say

   That she was false. O, she was heavenly true!

OTHELLO: Cassio did top her. Ask thy husband else.   135

   O, I were damned beneath all depth in hell

   But that I did proceed upon just grounds

   To this extremity. Thy husband knew it all.

EMILIA: My husband?

---

¹⁰⁸**error**   *wandering out of regular course (disorders in the heavens were believed by some to cause disorders on earth, as well as vice versa).*

OTHELLO: Thy husband.

EMILIA: That she was false to wedlock?

OTHELLO: Ay, with Cassio. Had she been true,   140

  If heaven would make me such another world

  Of one entire and perfect chrysolite,°

  I'd not have sold her for it.

EMILIA: My husband?

OTHELLO: Ay, 'twas he that told me on her first.

  An honest man he is, and hates the slime   145

  That sticks on filthy deeds.

EMILIA: My husband?

OTHELLO: What needs this iterance? Woman, I say thy husband.

EMILIA: O mistress, villainy hath made mocks with love!

  My husband say she was false?

OTHELLO: He, woman.

  I say, thy husband. Dost understand the word?   150

  My friend, thy husband; honest, honest Iago.

EMILIA: If he say so, may his pernicious soul

  Rot half a grain a day! He lies to th' heart.

  She was too fond of her most filthy bargain.

OTHELLO: Hah?   155

EMILIA: Do thy worst.

  This deed of thine is no more worthy heaven

  Than thou wast worthy her.

OTHELLO: Peace, you were best.°

EMILIA: Thou hast not half that pow'r to do me harm

  As I have to be hurt. O gull! O dolt!   160

  As ignorant as dirt! Thou hast done a deed—

[OTHELLO *moves to draw his sword.*]

  I care not for thy sword; I'll make thee known,

  Though I lost twenty lives. Help! Help! Ho! Help!

  The Moor hath killed my mistress! Murder! murder!

Enter MONTANO, GRATIANO, *and* IAGO [*and Others*].

MONTANO: What is the matter? How now, general?   165

EMILIA: O, are you come, Iago? You have done well,

  That men must lay their murders on your neck.

GRATIANO: What is the matter?

EMILIA: Disprove this villain, if thou be'st a man.

  He says thou told'st him that his wife was false.   170

  I know thou didst not; thou'rt not such a villain.

  Speak, for my heart is full.

IAGO: I told him what I thought, and told no more

  Than what he found himself was apt and true.

---

¹⁴²*chrysolite* topaz.   ¹⁵⁸**Peace, you were best** *i.e., you had better be silent.*

EMILIA: But did you ever tell him she was false?   175
IAGO: I did.
EMILIA: You told a lie, an odious damnèd lie!
  Upon my soul, a lie! A wicked lie!
  She false with Cassio? Did you say with Cassio?
IAGO: With Cassio, mistress. Go to, charm° your tongue.   180
EMILIA: I will not charm my tongue; I am bound to speak:
  My mistress here lies murdered in her bed.
  ALL: O heavens forfend!
EMILIA: And your reports have set the murder on.
OTHELLO: Nay, stare not, masters. It is true indeed.   185
GRATIANO: 'Tis a strange truth.
MONTANO: O monstrous act!
EMILIA: Villainy, villainy, villainy!
  I think upon't—I think I smell't!—O villainy!
  I thought so then.—I'll kill myself for grief.—
  O villainy, villainy!   190
IAGO: What, are you mad? I charge you get you home.
EMILIA: Good gentlemen, let me have leave to speak.
  'Tis proper I obey him, but not now.
  Perchance, Iago, I will ne'er go home.
OTHELLO: O! O! O!   [Falls on the bed.]
EMILIA: Nay, lay thee down and roar,   195
  For thou hast killed the sweetest innocent
  That e'er did lift up eye.
OTHELLO: O, she was foul!   [Rises.]
  I scarce did know you, uncle. There lies your niece,
  Whose breath, indeed, these hands have newly stopped.
  I know this act shows horrible and grim.   200
GRATIANO: Poor Desdemona! I am glad thy father's dead.
  Thy match was mortal to him, and pure grief
  Shore his old thread in twain. Did he live now,
  This sight would make him do a desperate turn;
  Yea, curse his better angel from his side,   205
  And fall to reprobation.°
OTHELLO: 'Tis pitiful; but yet Iago knows
  That she with Cassio hath the act of shame
  A thousand times committed. Cassio confessed it;
  And she did gratify his amorous works   210
  With that recognizance and pledge of love,
  Which I first gave her. I saw it in his hand.
  It was a handkerchief, an antique token
  My father gave my mother.
EMILIA: O God! O heavenly God!   215
IAGO: Zounds, hold your peace!

180**charm** *control.*   206**reprobation** *damnation.*

EMILIA: 'Twill out, ''twill out! I peace?
  No, I will speak as liberal as the north.°
  Let heaven and men and devils, let them all,
  All, all, cry shame against me, yet I'll speak.
IAGO: Be wise, and get you home.
EMILIA: I will not.   220

> [IAGO *draws and threatens* EMILIA.]

GRATIANO: Fie! Your sword upon a woman?
EMILIA: O thou dull Moor, that handkerchief thou speak'st of
  I found by fortune, and did give my husband;
  For often with a solemn earnestness—
  More than indeed belonged to such a trifle—   225
  He begged of me to steal't.
IAGO: Villainous whore!
EMILIA: She give it Cassio? No, alas, I found it,
  And I did give't my husband.
IAGO: Filth, thou liest!
EMILIA: By heaven, I do not, I do not, gentlemen.
  O murd'rous coxcomb! What should such a fool   230
  Do with so good a wife?
OTHELLO: Are there no stones° in heaven
  But what serves for the thunder? Precious villain!

> [The MOOR *runs at* IAGO, *but is disarmed by* MONTANO. IAGO *kills his wife.*]

GRATIANO: The woman falls. Sure he hath killed his wife.
EMILIA: Ay, ay. O, lay me by my mistress' side.   [Exit IAGO.]
GRATIANO: He's gone, but his wife's killed.   235
MONTANO: 'Tis a notorious° villain. Take you this weapon,
  Which I have recovered from the Moor.
  Come, guard the door without. Let him not pass,
  But kill him rather. I'll after that same villain,
  For 'tis a damnèd slave.   Exit [with all but OTHELLO and EMILIA].
OTHELLO: I am not valiant neither;   240
  But every puny whipster° gets my sword.
  But why should honor outlive honesty?
  Let it go all.
EMILIA: What did thy song bode, lady?
  Hark, canst thou hear me? I will play the swan,
  And die in music. [Sings] "Willow, willow, willow."   245
  Moor, she was chaste. She loved thee, cruel Moor,
  So come my soul to bliss as I speak true.
  So speaking as I think, alas, I die.   [She dies.]
OTHELLO: I have another weapon in this chamber;

<hr>

²¹⁷**liberal as the north** *freely (and bitingly) as the north wind blows.* ²³¹**stones** *thunderbolts.* ²³⁶**notorious** *out-and-out.* ²⁴¹**puny whipster** *small top-whipping boy (?).*

It was a sword of Spain, the ice-brook's temper. 250
Ｏ, here it is.—Uncle, I must come forth.
GRATIANO [*Within*]: If thou attempt it, it will cost thee dear.
Thou hast no weapon, and perforce must suffer.
OTHELLO: Look in upon me then and speak with me,
Or, naked as I am, I will assault thee. 255

[*Enter* GRATIANO.]

GRATIANO: What is the matter?
OTHELLO: Behold, I have a weapon;
A better never did itself sustain
Upon a soldier's thigh. I have seen the day
That with this little arm and this good sword
I have made my way through more impediments 260
Than twenty times your stop. But O vain boast!
Who can control his fate? 'Tis not so now.
Be not afraid, though you do see me weaponed.
Here is my journey's end, here is my butt,°
And very seamark of my utmost sail.° 265
Do you go back dismayed? 'Tis a lost fear.
Man but a rush° against Othello's breast.
And he retires. Where should Othello go?
Now, how dost thou look now? O ill-starred wench!
Pale as thy smock! When we shall meet at compt,° 270
This look of thine will hurl my soul from heaven,
And fiends will snatch at it. Cold, cold, my girl?
Even like thy chastity.
Ｏ cursèd, cursèd slave! Whip me, ye devils,
From the possession of ° this heavenly sight! 275
Blow me about in winds! roast me in sulfur!
Wash me in steep-down gulfs of liquid fire!
Ｏ Desdemon! Dead Desdemon; dead. O! O!

Enter LODOVICO, CASSIO, MONTANO, *and* IAGO [*as prisoner,*] *with* OFFICERS.

LODOVICO: Where is this rash and most unfortunate man?
OTHELLO: That's he that was Othello? Here I am. 280
LODOVICO: Where is that viper? Bring the villain forth.
OTHELLO: I look down towards his feet°—but that's a fable.
If that thou be'st a devil, I cannot kill thee.   [*Wounds* IAGO.]
LODOVICO: Wrench his sword from him.   [OTHELLO *is disarmed.*]
IAGO: I bleed, sir, but not killed.
OTHELLO: I am not sorry neither. I'd have thee live; 285
For in my sense, 'tis happiness to die.

264**butt**   *target, stopping place.*   265**seamark of my utmost sail**   *maker of my furthest journey.*   267**Man but a rush**   *attack with only a reed.*   270**compt**   *Judgment Day.*   275**the possession of**   *being possessed by.*   282**towards his feet**   *i.e., for his cloven hoofs.*

LODOVICO: O thou Othello that was once so good,
    Fall'n in the practice° of a cursèd slave,
    What shall be said to thee?
OTHELLO: Why, anything:
    An honorable murderer, if you will;   290
    For naught I did in hate, but all in honor.
LODOVICO: This wretch hath part confessed his villainy.
    Did you and he consent in Cassio's death?
OTHELLO: Ay.
CASSIO: Dear general, I never gave you cause.   295
OTHELLO: I do believe it, and I ask your pardon.
    Will you, I pray, demand that demi-devil
    Why he hath thus ensnared my soul and body?
IAGO: Demand me nothing. What you know, you know.
    From this time forth I never will speak word.   300
LODOVICO: What, not to pray?
GRATIANO: Torments will ope your lips.
OTHELLO: Well, thou dost best.
LODOVICO: Sir, you shall understand what hath befall'n,
    Which, as I think, you know not. Here is a letter
    Found in the pocket of the slain Roderigo;   305
    And here another. The one of them imports
    The death of Cassio to be undertook
    By Roderigo.
OTHELLO: O villain!
CASSIO: Most heathenish and most gross!
LODOVICO: Now here's another discontented paper   310
    Found in his pocket too; and this, it seems,
    Roderigo meant t' have sent this damnèd villain;
    But that, belike, Iago in the interim
    Came in and satisfied him.
OTHELLO: O thou pernicious caitiff!
    How came you, Cassio, by that handkerchief   315
    That was my wife's?
CASSIO: I found it in my chamber;
    And he himself confessed it but even now
    That there he dropped it for a special purpose
    Which wrought to his desire.
OTHELLO: O fool! Fool! Fool!
CASSIO: There is besides in Roderigo's letter,   320
    How he upbraids Iago that he made him
    Brave me upon the watch; whereon it came
    That I was cast; and even but now he spake,
    After long seeming dead—Iago hurt him,
    Iago set him on.   325

288*practice* plotting.

LODOVICO: You must forsake this room and go with us.
    Your power and your command is taken off,
    And Cassio rules in Cyprus. For this slave,
    If there be any cunning cruelty
    That can torment him much and hold him long,   330
    It shall be his. You shall close prisoner rest
    Till that the nature of your fault be known
    To the Venetian state. Come, bring away.
OTHELLO: Soft you, a word or two before you go.
    I have done the state some service and they know't.   335
    No more of that. I pray you, in your letters,
    When you shall these unlucky deeds relate,
    Speak of me as I am. Nothing extenuate,
    Nor set down aught in malice. Then must you speak
    Of one that loved not wisely, but too well;   340
    Of one not easily jealous, but, being wrought,
    Perplexed in the extreme; of one whose hand,
    Like the base Judean,° threw a pearl away
    Richer than all his tribe; of one whose subdued eyes,
    Albeit unusèd to the melting mood,   345
    Drops tears as fast as the Arabian trees
    Their med'cinable gum. Set you down this.
    And say besides that in Aleppo once,
    Where a malignant and a turbaned Turk
    Beat a Venetian and traduced the state,   350
    I took by th' throat the circumcisèd dog
    And smote him—thus.   [He stabs himself.]
LODOVICO: O bloody period!°
GRATIANO: All that is spoke is marred.
OTHELLO: I kissed thee ere I killed thee. No way but this,
    Killing myself, to die upon a kiss.   [He falls over DESDEMONA and dies.] 355
CASSIO: This did I fear, but thought he had no weapon;
    For he was great of heart.
LODOVICO [To IAGO]:   O Spartan dog,
    More fell° than anguish, hunger, or the sea!
    Look on the tragic loading of this bed.
    This is thy work. The object poisons sight;   360
    Let it be hid.   [Bed curtains drawn.]
          Gratiano, keep° the house,
    And seize upon the fortunes of the Moor,
    For they succeed on you. To you, lord governor,
    Remains the censure of this hellish villain,
    The time, the place, the torture. O, enforce it!   365
    Myself will straight aboard, and to the state
    This heavy act with heavy heart relate.
                                            Exeunt.

---

³⁴³**Judean** *(most editors use the Q1 reading, "Indian," here, but F is clear: both readings point toward the infidel, the unbeliever).* ³⁵³**period** *end.* ³⁵⁸**fell** *cruel.* ³⁶¹**keep** *remain in.*

QUESTIONS FOR REFLECTION

Experience

1. Describe your experience in reading *Othello*. To what extent can you identify with any one of the play's characters?

Interpretation

2. What makes Othello a tragic figure? Is his tragedy self-inflicted or is it beyond his control? What is his tragic flaw?
3. Compare Othello's speeches from the beginning, middle, and end of the play (Acts I, III, and V). Explain the significance of their differences in style and tone.
4. Iago is a resourceful and clever character who knows how to manipulate people. Explain how he manipulates Roderigo, Cassio, and Othello.
5. What reason does Iago give for seeking Othello's destruction? Does this seem an adequate or a credible motive?
6. How does Emilia's role help us to better understand Iago? In what ways is she a *foil* (a contrasting character) to Desdemona? What other characters serve to balance each other?
7. Of what significance is Bianca's role in the play? Brabantio's?
8. *Othello* has a dual setting—Venice and Cyprus. With what values and ideas is each place associated, and how are these related to the action and themes of the play?
9. What ideas about love are expressed by Othello and Desdemona? What images of the sexual bond emerge in the speech and actions of Roderigo, Iago, and Emilia?
10. How does Shakespeare use Desdemona's handkerchief dramatically and symbolically? In which scenes is it most important? With what is it associated?
11. Examine the scene in which Othello kills Desdemona (Act V, Scene II). Read his speech beginning, "It is the cause" (lines 1–22). Explain how Othello sees himself at this point, and describe his state of mind.
12. Examine the scene in which Othello secretly watches Cassio talking to Bianca (Act IV, Scene I). Explain how Iago controls Othello's perception, leading him to misinterpret what he sees. In what other scenes does Iago direct other characters to misinterpret one another's actions and speech?
13. Any staging of Othello requires careful attention to lighting. Single out two scenes in which lighting is especially important, and explain how you would stage them.
14. Look carefully at the beginning and ending of any two acts. Consider how Shakespeare guides the audience's responses at these points. Consider also the effectiveness of each beginning and ending in relation to the development of the plot.
15. Locate two scenes in which characters' speeches shift between prose and verse. Explain the significance of these shifts.

Evaluation

16. What judgment does Shakespeare's *Othello* make about jealousy? About the power of evil over goodness?
17. How effectively do you think Shakespeare dramatizes Iago's power over others?

Hamlet

Hamlet, the most famous play in English literature, continues to fascinate and challenge both readers and audiences. Interpretations of Hamlet's character and actions abound, because the play has produced so many intense and varied responses. No small indication of the tragedy's power is that actors long to play its title role.

A brief summary can suggest the movement of the plot but not the depth of Hamlet's character. After learning of his father's death, Prince Hamlet returns to the Danish court from his university studies to find Claudius, the dead king's brother, ruling Denmark and married to Hamlet's mother, Gertrude. Her remarriage within two months of his father's death has left Hamlet disillusioned, confused, and suspicious of Claudius. When his father's ghost appears before Hamlet to reveal that Claudius murdered the king, Hamlet is confronted with having to avenge his father's death.

Hamlet's efforts to carry out this obligation would have been a familiar kind of plot to Elizabethan audiences. *Revenge tragedy* was a well-established type of drama that traced its antecedents to Greek and Roman plays, particularly through the Roman playwright Seneca (c. 3 B.C.–A.D. 65), whose plays were translated and produced in English in the late sixteenth century. Shakespeare's audiences knew its conventions, particularly from Thomas Kyd's popular *Spanish Tragedy* (c. 1587). Basically, this type of play consists of a murder that has to be avenged by a relative of the victim. Typically, the victim's ghost appears to demand revenge, and invariably madness of some sort is worked into subsequent events, which ultimately result in the deaths of the murderer, the avenger, and a number of other characters. Crime, madness, ghostly anguish, poison, overheard conversations, conspiracies, and a final scene littered with corpses: *Hamlet* subscribes to the basic ingredients of the formula, but it also transcends the conventions of revenge tragedy because Hamlet contemplates not merely revenge but suicide and the meaning of life itself.

Hamlet must face not only a diseased social order but also conflicts within himself when his indecisiveness becomes as agonizing as the corruption surrounding him. However, Hamlet is also a forceful and attractive character. His intelligence is repeatedly revealed in his penetrating use of language; through images and metaphors he creates a perspective on his world that is at once satiric and profoundly painful. His astonishing and sometimes shocking wit is leveled at his mother, his beloved Ophelia, and Claudius as well as at himself. Nothing escapes his critical eye and divided imagination. Hamlet, no less than the people around him, is perplexed by his alienation from life.

Hamlet's limitations as well as his virtues make him one of Shakespeare's most complex characters. His keen self-awareness is both agonizing and liberating. Although he struggles throughout the play with painful issues ranging from family loyalties to matters of state, he retains his dignity as a tragic hero, whom generations of audiences have found compelling.

Hamlet, Prince of Denmark

CHARACTERS

CLAUDIUS, *King of Denmark*
HAMLET, *son to the late and nephew to the present king*
POLONIUS, *lord chamberlain*
HORATIO, *friend to Hamlet*
LAERTES, *son to Polonius*
VOLTIMAND
CORNELIUS
ROSENCRANTZ } *courtiers*
GUILDENSTERN
OSRIC
A GENTLEMAN
A PRIEST
MARCELLUS } *officers*
BERNARDO
FRANCISCO, *a soldier*
REYNALDO, *servant to Polonius*
PLAYERS
TWO CLOWNS, *grave-diggers*
FORTINBRAS, *Prince of Norway*
A CAPTAIN
ENGLISH AMBASSADORS
GERTRUDE, *Queen of Denmark, and mother to Hamlet*
OPHELIA, *daughter to Polonius*
GHOST *of Hamlet's father*
(LORDS, LADIES, OFFICERS, SOLDIERS, SAILORS, MESSENGERS, AND OTHER ATTENDANTS)

Scene. Denmark.

ACT I

Scene I [*Elsinore. A platform° before the castle.*]

Enter BERNARDO *and* FRANCISCO, *two sentinels.*

BERNARDO: Who's there?

I.i.   **s.d. platform**   *a level space on the battlements of the royal castle at Elsinore, a Danish seaport; now Helsingör.*

FRANCISCO: Nay, answer me:° stand, and unfold yourself.
BERNARDO: Long live the king°!
FRANCISCO: Bernardo?
BERNARDO: He.
FRANCISCO: You come most carefully upon your hour.   5
BERNARDO: 'Tis now struck twelve; get thee to bed, Francisco.
FRANCISCO: For this relief much thanks: 'tis bitter cold,
   And I am sick at heart.
BERNARDO: Have you had quiet guard?
FRANCISCO: Not a mouse stirring.   10
BERNARDO: Well, good night.
   If you do meet Horatio and Marcellus,
   The rivals° of my watch, bid them make haste.

Enter HORATIO *and* MARCELLUS.

FRANCISCO: I think I hear them. Stand, ho! Who is there?
HORATIO: Friends to this ground.
MARCELLUS: And liegemen to the Dane.   15
FRANCISCO: Give you° good night.
MARCELLUS: O, farewell, honest soldier:
   Who hath reliev'd you?
FRANCISCO: Bernardo hath my place.
   Give you good night.   *Exit* FRANCISCO.
MARCELLUS: Holla! Bernardo!
BERNARDO: Say,
   What, is Horatio there?
HORATIO: A piece of him.
BERNARDO: Welcome, Horatio: welcome, good Marcellus.   20
MARCELLUS: What, has this thing appear'd again to-night?
BERNARDO: I have seen nothing.
MARCELLUS: Horatio says 'tis but our fantasy,
   And will not let belief take hold of him.
   Touching this dreaded sight, twice seen of us: 25
   Therefore I have entreated him along
   With us to watch the minutes of this night;
   That if again this apparition come,
   He may approve° our eyes and speak to it.
HORATIO: Tush, tush, 'twill not appear.
BERNARDO: Sit down awhile;   30
   And let us once again assail your ears,
   That are so fortified against our story
   What we have two nights seen.
HORATIO: Well, sit we down,

---

²**me** *this is emphatic, since Francisco is the sentry.*   ³**Long live the king!** *either a password or greeting; Hora-*
tio and Marcellus use a different one in line 15.   ¹³**rivals** *partners.*   ¹⁶**Give you** *God give you.*
²⁹**approve** *corroborate.*

And let us hear Bernardo speak of this.

BERNARDO: Last night of all,   35

When yond same star that's westward from the pole°

Had made his course t' illume that part of heaven

Where now it burns, Marcellus and myself,

The bell then beating one,—

Enter GHOST.

MARCELLUS: Peace, break thee off; look, where it comes again!   40

BERNARDO: In the same figure, like the king that's dead.

MARCELLUS: Thou art a scholar;° speak to it, Horatio.

BERNARDO: Looks 'a not like the king? mark it, Horatio.

HORATIO: Most like: it harrows° me with fear and wonder.

BERNARDO: It would be spoke to.°

MARCELLUS: Speak to it, Horatio.   45

HORATIO: What art thou that usurp'st this time of night,

Together with that fair and warlike form

In which the majesty of buried Denmark°

Did sometimes march? by heaven I charge thee, speak!

MARCELLUS: It is offended.

BERNARDO: See it stalks away!   50

HORATIO: Stay! speak, speak! I charge thee, speak!   *Exit* GHOST.

MARCELLUS: 'Tis gone, and will not answer.

BERNARDO: How now, Horatio! you tremble and look pale:

Is not this something more than fantasy?

What think you on 't?   55

HORATIO: Before my God, I might not this believe

Without the sensible and true avouch

Of mine own eyes.

MARCELLUS: Is it not like the king?

HORATIO: As thou art to thyself:

Such was the very armour he had on   60

When he the ambitious Norway combated;

So frown'd he once, when, in an angry parle,

He smote° the sledded Polacks° on the ice.

'Tis strange.

MARCELLUS: Thus twice before, and jump° at this dead hour,   65

With martial stalk hath he gone by our watch.

HORATIO: In what particular thought to work I know not;

But in the gross and scope° of my opinion,

This bodes some strange eruption to our state.

MARCELLUS: Good now,° sit down, and tell me, he that knows,   70

---

³⁶**pole** *polestar.*   ⁴²**scholar** *exorcisms were performed in Latin, which Horatio as an educated man would be able to speak.*   ⁴⁴**harrows** *lacerates the feelings.*   ⁴⁵**It . . . to** *a ghost could not speak until spoken to.* ⁴⁸**buried Denmark** *the buried king of Denmark.*   ⁶³**smote** *defeated.*   ⁶³**sledded Polacks** *Polanders using sledges.*   ⁶⁵**jump** *exactly.*   ⁶⁸**gross and scope** *general drift.*⁷⁰**Good now** *an expression denoting entreaty or expostulation.*

Why this same strict and most observant watch
So nightly toils° the subject° of the land,
And why such daily cast° of brazen cannon,
And foreign mart° for implements of war;
Why such impress° of shipwrights, whose sore task   75
Does not divide the Sunday from the week;
What might be toward, that this sweaty haste
Doth make the night joint-labourer with the day:
Who is't that can inform me?

HORATIO: That can I;
   At least, the whisper goes so. Our last king,   80
Whose image even but now appear'd to us,
Was, as you know, by Fortinbras of Norway,
Thereto prick'd on° by a most emulate° pride,
Dar'd to the combat; in which our valiant Hamlet—
For so this side of our known world esteem'd him—   85
Did slay this Fortinbras; who, by a seal'd compact,
Well ratified by law and heraldry,°
Did forfeit, with his life, all those his lands
Which he stood seiz'd° of, to the conqueror:
Against the which, a moiety competent°   90
Was gaged by our king; which had return'd
To the inheritance of Fortinbras,
Had he been vanquisher; as, by the same comart,°
And carriage° of the article design'd,
His fell to Hamlet. Now, sir, young Fortinbras,   95
Of unimproved° mettle hot and full,°
Hath in the skirts of Norway here and there
Shark'd up° a list of lawless resolutes,°
For food and diet,° to some enterprise
That hath a stomach in't; which is no other—   100
As it doth well appear unto our state—
But to recover of us, by strong hand
And terms compulsatory, those foresaid lands
So by his father lost: and this, I take it,
Is the main motive of our preparations,   105
The source of this our watch and the chief head
Of this post-haste and romage° in the land.

BERNARDO: I think it be no other but e'en so:
   Well may it sort° that this portentous figure

---

⁷²**toils** *causes or makes to toil.* ⁷²**subject** *people, subjects.* ⁷³**cast** *casting, founding.* ⁷⁴**mart** *buying and selling, traffic.* ⁷⁵**impress** *impressment.* ⁸³**prick'd on** *incited.* ⁸³**emulate** *rivaling.* ⁸⁷**law and heraldry** *heraldic law, governing combat.* ⁸⁹**seiz'd** *possessed.* ⁹⁰**moiety competent** *adequate or sufficient portion.* ⁹³**comart** *joint bargain.* ⁹⁴**carriage** *import, bearing.* ⁹⁶**unimproved** *not turned to account.* ⁹⁶**hot and full** *full of fight.* ⁹⁸**Shark'd up** *got together in haphazard fashion.* ⁹⁸**resolutes** *desperadoes.* ⁹⁹**food and diet** *no pay but their keep.* ¹⁰⁷**romage** *bustle, commotion.* ¹⁰⁹**sort** *suit.*

Comes armed through our watch; so like the king   110
That was and is the question of these wars.
HORATIO: A mote° it is to trouble the mind's eye.
In the most high and palmy state° of Rome,
A little ere the mightiest Julius fell,
The graves stood tenantless and the sheeted dead   115
Did squeak and gibber in the Roman streets:
As stars with trains of fire° and dews of blood,
Disasters° in the sun; and the moist star°
Upon whose influence Neptune's empire° stands
Was sick almost to doomsday with eclipse: 120
And even the like precurse° of fear'd events,
As harbingers preceding still the fates
And prologue to the omen coming on,
Have heaven and earth together demonstrated
Unto our climatures and countrymen.—   125

Enter GHOST.

But soft, behold! lo, where it comes again!
I'll cross° it, though it blast me. Stay, illusion!
If thou hast any sound, or use of voice,
Speak to me!   *It° spreads his arms.*
If there be any good thing to be done,   130
That may to thee do ease and grace to me,
Speak to me!
If ° thou art privy to thy country's fate,
Which, happily, foreknowing may avoid,
O, speak!   135
Or if thou hast uphoarded in thy life
Extorted treasure in the womb of earth,
For which, they say, you spirits oft walk in death,   *The cock crows.*
Speak of it: stay, and speak! Stop it, Marcellus.
MARCELLUS: Shall I strike at it with my partisan?°   140
HORATIO: Do, if it will not stand.
BERNARDO: 'Tis here!
HORATIO: 'Tis here!
MARCELLUS: 'Tis gone!   [*Exit* GHOST.]
We do it wrong, being so majestical,
To offer it the show of violence;
For it is, as the air, invulnerable,   145

112**mote** *speck of dust.*   113**palmy state** *triumphant sovereignty.*   117**stars . . . fire** *i.e., comets.*
118**Disasters** *unfavorable aspects.*   118**moist star** *the moon, governing tides.*   119**Neptune's empire** *the
sea.*   121**precurse** *heralding.*   127**cross** *meet, face, thus bringing down the evil influence on the person who
crosses it.*   129**It** *the Ghost, or perhaps Horatio.*   133-139**If . . .** *in the following seven lines, Horatio recites
the traditional reasons why ghosts might walk.*   140**partisan** *long-handled spear with a blade having lateral pro-
jections.*

And our vain blows malicious mockery.

BERNARDO: It was about to speak, when the cock crew.°

HORATIO: And then it started like a guilty thing
Upon a fearful summons. I have heard,
The cock, that is the trumpet to the morn,   150
Doth with his lofty and shrill-sounding throat
Awake the god of day; and, at his warning,
Whether in sea or fire, in earth or air,
Th' extravagant and erring° spirit hies
To his confine:° and of the truth herein   155
This present object made probation.°

MARCELLUS: It faded on the crowing of the cock.
Some say that ever 'gainst° that season comes
Wherein our Saviour's birth is celebrated,
The bird of dawning singeth all night long: 160
And then, they say, no spirit dare stir abroad;
The nights are wholesome; then no planets strike,°
No fairy takes, nor witch hath power to charm,
So hallow'd and so gracious° is that time.

HORATIO: So have I heard and do in part believe it.   165
But, look, the morn, in russet mantle clad,
Walks o'er the dew of yon high eastward hill:
Break we our watch up; and by my advice,
Let us impart what we have seen to-night
Unto young Hamlet; for, upon my life,   170
This spirit, dumb to us, will speak to him.
Do you consent we shall acquaint him with it,
As needful in our loves, fitting our duty?

MARCELLUS: Let's do 't, I pray; and I this morning know
Where we shall find him most conveniently.   *Exeunt.*   175

Scene II [A room of state in the castle.]

Flourish. Enter CLAUDIUS, *King of Denmark,* GERTRUDE *the Queen,* COUNCILORS, POLO-
NIUS *and his Son* LAERTES, HAMLET, *cum aliis°* [*including* VOLTIMAND *and* CORNELIUS].

KING: Though yet of Hamlet our dear brother's death
The memory be green, and that it us befitted
To bear our hearts in grief and our whole kingdom
To be contracted in one brow of woe,
Yet so far hath discretion fought with nature   5
That we with wisest sorrow think on him,

147**cock crew** *according to traditional ghost lore, spirits returned to their confines at cockcrow.*   154**extravagant**
and erring *wandering. Both words mean the same thing.*   155**confine** *place of confinement.*   156**proba-**
tion *proof, trial.*   158**'gainst** *just before.*   162**planets strike** *it was thought that planets were malignant*
and might strike travelers by night.   164**gracious** *full of goodness.*   **I.ii. s.d. cum aliis** *with others.*

Together with remembrance of ourselves.
Therefore our sometime sister, now our queen,
Th' imperial jointress° to this warlike state,
Have we, as 'twere with a defeated joy,—   10
With an auspicious and a dropping eye,
With mirth in funeral and with dirge in marriage,
In equal scale weighing delight and dole,—
Taken to wife: nor have we herein barr'd
Your better wisdoms, which have freely gone   15
With this affair along. For all, our thanks.
Now follows, that° you know, young Fortinbras,
Holding a weak supposal° of our worth,
Or thinking by our late dear brother's death
Our state to be disjoint° and out of frame,°   20
Colleagued° with this dream of his advantage,°
He hath not fail'd to pester us with message,
Importing° the surrender of those lands
Lost by his father, with all bands of law,
To our most valiant brother. So much for him.   25
Now for ourself and for this time of meeting:
Thus much the business is: we have here writ
To Norway, uncle of young Fortinbras,—
Who, impotent and bed-rid, scarcely hears
Of this his nephew's purpose,—to suppress   30
His further gait° herein; in that the levies,
The lists and full proportions, are all made
Out of his subject:° and we here dispatch
You, good Cornelius, and you, Voltimand,
For bearers of this greeting to old Norway;   35
Giving to you no further personal power
To business with the king, more than the scope
Of these delated° articles allow.
Farewell, and let your haste commend your duty.

CORNELIUS: }
VOLTIMAND: } In that and all things will we show our duty.   40

KING: We doubt it nothing: heartily farewell.

[*Exeunt* VOLTIMAND *and* CORNELIUS.]

And now, Laertes, what's the news with you?
You told us of some suit; what is't, Laertes?
You cannot speak of reason to the Dane,°

---

⁹**jointress** *woman possessed of a jointure, or, joint tenancy of an estate.*   ¹⁷**that** *that which.*   ¹⁸**weak supposal** *low estimate.*   ²⁰**disjoint** *distracted, out of joint.*   ²⁰**frame** *order.*   ²¹**Colleagued** *added to.*   ²¹**dream . . . advantage** *visionary hope of success.*   ²³**Importing** *purporting, pertaining to.*   ³¹**gait** *proceeding.*   ³³**Out of his subject** *at the expense of Norway's subjects (collectively).*   ³⁸**delated** *expressly stated.*   ⁴⁴**the Dane** *Danish king.*

And lose your voice:° what wouldst thou beg, Laertes,   45
That shall not be my offer, not thy asking?
The head is not more native° to the heart,
The hand more instrumental° to the mouth,
Than is the throne of Denmark to thy father.
What wouldst thou have, Laertes?

LAERTES: My dread lord,   50
Your leave and favour to return to France;
From whence though willingly I came to Denmark,
To show my duty in your coronation,
Yet now, I must confess, that duty done,
My thoughts and wishes bend again toward France   55
And bow them to your gracious leave and pardon.°

KING: Have you your father's leave? What says Polonius?

POLONIUS: He hath, my lord, wrung from me my slow leave
By laboursome petition, and at last
Upon his will I seal'd my hard consent: 60
I do beseech you, give him leave to go.

KING: Take thy fair hour, Laertes; time be thine,
And thy best graces spend it at thy will!
But now, my cousin° Hamlet, and my son,—

HAMLET [aside]: A little more than kin, and less than kind!°   65

KING: How is it that the clouds still hang on you?

HAMLET: Not so, my lord; I am too much in the sun.°

QUEEN: Good Hamlet, cast thy nighted colour off,
And let thine eye look like a friend on Denmark.
Do not for ever with thy vailed lids   70
Seek for thy noble father in the dust:
Thou know'st 'tis common; all that lives must die,
Passing through nature to eternity.

HAMLET: Ay, madam, it is common.°

QUEEN: If it be,
Why seems it so particular with thee?   75

HAMLET: Seems, madam! nay, it is; I know not "seems."
'Tis not alone my inky cloak, good mother,
Nor customary suits° of solemn black,
Nor windy suspiration° of forc'd breath,
No, nor the fruitful river in the eye,   80
Nor the dejected 'haviour of the visage,

---

⁴⁵*lose your voice*   *speak in vain.*   ⁴⁷*native*   *closely connected, related.*   ⁴⁸*instrumental*   *serviceable.*
⁵⁶*leave and pardon*   *permission to depart.*   ⁶⁴*cousin*   *any kin not of the immediate family.*   ⁶⁵*A little*
... kind   *i.e., my relation to you has become more than kinship warrants; it has also become unnatural.*   ⁶⁷*I am*
... sun   *the senses seem to be: I am too much out of doors, I am too much in the sun of your grace (ironical), I am
too much of a son to you. Possibly an allusion to the proverb "Out of heaven's blessing into the warm sun"; i.e., Hamlet is out of house and home in being deprived of the kingship.*   ⁷⁴*Ay ... common*   *i.e., it is common, but it
hurts nevertheless; possibly a reference to the commonplace quality of the queen's remark.*   ⁷⁸*customary suits*   *suits
prescribed by custom for mourning.*   ⁷⁹*windy suspiration*   *heavy sighing.*

Together with all forms, moods, shapes of grief,
That can denote me truly: these indeed seem,
For they are actions that a man might play:
But I have that within which passeth show; 85
These but the trappings and the suits of woe.
KING: 'Tis sweet and commendable in your nature, Hamlet,
To give these mourning duties to your father:
But, you must know, your father lost a father;
That father lost, lost his, and the survivor bound 90
In filial obligation for some term
To do obsequious° sorrow: but to persever
In obstinate condolement° is a course
Of impious stubbornness; 'tis unmanly grief;
It shows a will most incorrect° to heaven, 95
A heart unfortified, a mind impatient,
An understanding simple and unschool'd:
For what we know must be and is as common
As any the most vulgar thing° to sense,
Why should we in our peevish opposition 100
Take it to heart? Fie! 'tis a fault to heaven,
A fault against the dead, a fault to nature,
To reason most absurd; whose common theme
Is death of fathers, and who still hath cried,
From the first corse till he that died to-day, 105
"This must be so." We pray you, throw to earth
This unprevailing° woe, and think of us
As of a father: for let the world take note,
You are the most immediate° to our throne;
And with no less nobility° of love 110
Than that which dearest father bears his son,
Do I impart° toward you. For your intent
In going back to school in Wittenberg,°
It is most retrograde° to our desire:
And we beseech you, bend you° to remain 115
Here, in the cheer and comfort of our eye,
Our chiefest courtier, cousin, and our son.
QUEEN: Let not thy mother lose her prayers, Hamlet:
I pray thee, stay with us; go not to Wittenberg.
HAMLET: I shall in all my best obey you, madam. 120
KING: Why, 'tis a loving and a fair reply:
Be as ourself in Denmark. Madam, come;
This gentle and unforc'd accord of Hamlet

92**obsequious** *dutiful.*   93**condolement** *sorrowing.*   95**incorrect** *Untrained, uncorrected.*   99**vulgar thing** *common experience.*   107**unprevailing** *unavailing.*   109**most immediate** *next in succession.*   110**nobility** *high degree.*   112**impart** *the object is apparently love (1.110).*   113**Wittenberg** *famous German university founded in 1502.*   114**retrograde** *contrary.*   115**bend you** *incline yourself; imperative.*

Sits smiling to my heart: in grace whereof,
No jocund health that Denmark drinks to-day,   125
But the great cannon to the clouds shall tell,
And the king's rouse° the heaven shall bruit again,°
Re-speaking earthly thunder. Come away.

Flourish. Exeunt all but HAMLET.

HAMLET: O, that this too too sullied flesh would melt,
Thaw and resolve itself into a dew!   130
Or that the Everlasting had not fix'd
His canon 'gainst self-slaughter! O God! God!
How weary, stale, flat and unprofitable,
Seem to me all the uses of this world!
Fie on't! ah fie! 'tis an unweeded garden,   135
That grows to seed; things rank and gross in nature
Possess it merely.° That it should come to this!
But two months dead: nay, not so much, not two:
So excellent a king; that was, to this,
Hyperion° to a satyr; so loving to my mother   140
That he might not beteem° the winds of heaven
Visit her face too roughly. Heaven and earth!
Must I remember? why, she would hang on him,
As if increase of appetite had grown
By what it fed on: and yet, within a month—   145
Let me not think on't—Frailty, thy name is woman!—
A little month, or ere those shoes were old
With which she followed my poor father's body,
Like Niobe,° all tears: —why she, even she—
O God! a beast, that wants discourse of reason,°   150
Would have mourn'd longer—married with my uncle,
My father's brother, but no more like my father
Than I to Hercules: within a month:
Ere yet the salt of most unrighteous tears
Had left the flushing in her galled° eyes,   155
She married. O, most wicked speed, to post
With such dexterity° to incestuous sheets!
It is not nor it cannot come to good:
But break, my heart; for I must hold my tongue.

Enter HORATIO, MARCELLUS, *and* BERNARDO.

HORATIO: Hail to your lordship!

---

¹²⁷**rouse**   *draft of liquor.*   ¹²⁷**bruit again**   *echo.*   ¹³⁷**merely**   *completely, entirely.*   ¹⁴⁰**Hyperion**
God of the sun in the older regime of ancient gods.   ¹⁴¹**beteem**   *allow.*   ¹⁴⁹**Niobe**   *Tantalus's daughter, who*
boasted that she had more sons and daughters than Leto; for this Apollo and Artemis slew her children. She was turned
into stone by Zeus on Mount Sipylus.   ¹⁵⁰**discourse of reason**   *process or faculty of reason.*   ¹⁵⁵**galled**
irritated.   ¹⁵⁷**dexterity**   *facility.*

HAMLET: I am glad to see you well: 160
    Horatio!—or I do forget myself.

HORATIO: The same, my lord, and your poor servant ever.

HAMLET: Sir, my good friend; I'll change that name with you:°
    And what make you from Wittenberg, Horatio?
    Marcellus? 165

MARCELLUS: My good lord—

HAMLET: I am very glad to see you. Good even, sir.
    But what, in faith, make you from Wittenberg?

HORATIO: A truant disposition, good my lord.

HAMLET: I would not hear your enemy say so, 170
    Nor shall you do my ear that violence,
    To make it truster of your own report
    Against yourself: I know you are no truant.
    But what is your affair in Elsinore?
    We'll teach you to drink deep ere you depart. 175

HORATIO: My lord, I came to see your father's funeral.

HAMLET: I prithee, do not mock me, fellow-student;
    I think it was to see my mother's wedding.

HORATIO: Indeed, my lord, it follow'd hard° upon.

HAMLET: Thrift, thrift, Horatio! the funeral bak'd meats° 180
    Did coldly furnish forth the marriage tables.
    Would I had met my dearest° foe in heaven
    Or ever I had seen that day, Horatio!
    My father!—methinks I see my father.

HORATIO: Where, my lord!

HAMLET: In my mind's eye, Horatio. 185

HORATIO: I saw him once; 'a° was a goodly king.

HAMLET: 'A was a man, take him for all in all,
    I shall not look upon his like again.

HORATIO: My lord, I think I saw him yesternight.

HAMLET: Saw? who? 190

HORATIO: My lord, the king your father.

HAMLET: The king my father!

HORATIO: Season your admiration° for a while
    With an attent ear, till I may deliver,
    Upon the witness of these gentlemen,
    This marvel to you.

HAMLET: For God's love, let me hear. 195

HORATIO: Two nights together had these gentlemen,
    Marcellus and Bernardo, on their watch,
    In the dead waste and middle of the night,

163*I'll ... you*   *I'll be your servant, you shall be my friend; also explained as "I;ll exchange the name of friend with you."*   179*hard* *close.*   180*bak'd meats* *meat pies.*   182*dearest* *direst; the adjective dear in Shakespeare has two different origins: O.E. deore, "beloved," and O.E. deor, "fierce." Dearest is the superlative of the second*   186*'a* *he.*   192*Season your admiration* *restrain your astonishment.*

Been thus encount'red. A figure like your father,
Armed at point exactly, cap-a-pe,°   200
Appears before them, and with solemn march
Goes slow and stately by them: thrice he walk'd
By their oppress'd° and fear-surprised eyes,
Within his truncheon's° length; whilst they, distill'd°
Almost to jelly with the act° of fear,   205
Stand dumb and speak not to him. This to me
In dreadful secrecy impart they did;
And I with them the third night kept the watch:
Where, as they had deliver'd, both in time,
Form of the thing, each word made true and good,   210
The apparition comes: I knew your father;
These hands are not more like.

HAMLET: But where was this?
MARCELLUS: My lord, upon the platform where we watch'd.
HAMLET: Did you not speak to it?
HORATIO: My lord, I did;
But answer made it none: yet once methought   215
It lifted up it° head and did address
Itself to motion, like as it would speak;
But even then the morning cock crew loud,
And at the sound it shrunk in haste away,
And vanish'd from our sight.

HAMLET: 'Tis very strange.   220
HORATIO: As I do live, my honour'd lord, 'tis true;
And we did think it writ down in our duty
To let you know of it.

HAMLET: Indeed, indeed, sirs, but this troubles me.
Hold you the watch to-night?

MARCELLUS: }
BERNARDO: }   We do, my lord.   225

HAMLET: Arm'd, say you?

MARCELLUS: }
BERNARDO: } Arm'd, my lord.

HAMLET: From top to toe?

MARCELLUS: }
BERNARDO: }   My lord, from head to foot.

HAMLET: Then saw you not his face?
HORATIO: O, yes, my lord; he wore his beaver° up.   230
HAMLET: What, look'd he frowningly?
HORATIO: A countenance more
In sorrow than in anger.

HAMLET: Pale or red?
HORATIO: Nay, very pale.

HAMLET: And fix'd his eyes upon you?

HORATIO: Most constantly.

HAMLET: I would I had been there.

HORATIO: It would have much amaz'd you.   235

HAMLET: Very like, very like. Stay'd it long?

HORATIO: While one with moderate haste might tell a hundred.

MARCELLUS: ⎫
BERNARDO: ⎬ Longer, longer.

HORATIO: Not when I saw't.

HAMLET: His beard was grizzled,—no?

HORATIO: It was, as I have seen it in his life,   240
    A sable° silver'd.

HAMLET: I will watch to-night;
    Perchance 'twill walk again.

HORATIO: I warr'nt it will.

HAMLET: If it assume my noble father's person,
    I'll speak to it, though hell itself should gape
    And bid me hold my peace. I pray you all,   245
    If you have hitherto conceal'd this sight,
    Let it be tenable in your silence still;
    And whatsoever else shall hap to-night,
    Give it an understanding, but no tongue:
    I will requite your loves. So, fare you well: 250
    Upon the platform, 'twixt eleven and twelve,
    I'll visit you.

ALL: Our duty to your honour.

HAMLET: Your loves, as mine to you: farewell.   *Exeunt* [*all but* HAMLET].
    My father's spirit in arms! all is not well;
    I doubt° some foul play: would the night were come!   255
    Till then sit still, my soul: foul deeds will rise,
    Though all the earth o'erwhelm them, to men's eyes.   *Exit.*

Scene III [*A room in Polonius's house.*]

Enter LAERTES *and* OPHELIA, *his Sister.*

LAERTES: My necessaries are embark'd: farewell:
    And, sister, as the winds give benefit
    And convoy is assistant,° do not sleep,
    But let me hear from you.

OPHELIA: Do you doubt that?

LAERTES: For Hamlet and the trifling of his favour,   5
    Hold it a fashion° and a toy in blood,°
    A violet in the youth of primy° nature,
    Forward,° not permanent, sweet, not lasting,

---

²⁴¹**sable**   *black color.*   ²⁵⁵**doubt**   *fear.*   **I.iii.**   ³**convoy is assistant** *means of conveyance are available.*
⁶**fashion**   *custom, prevailing usage.*   ⁶**toy in blood**   *passing amorous fancy.*   ⁷**primy**   *in its prime.*
⁸**Forward**   *precocious.*

The perfume and suppliance of a minute;°
No more.

OPHELIA: No more but so?

LAERTES: Think it no more: 10
For nature, crescent,° does not grow alone
In thews° and bulk, but, as this temple° waxes,
The inward service of the mind and soul
Grows wide withal. Perhaps he loves you now,
And now no soil° nor cautel° doth besmirch   15
The virtue of his will: but you must fear,
His greatness weigh'd,° his will is not his own;
For he himself is subject to his birth:
He may not, as unvalued persons do,
Carve for himself; for on his choice depends   20
The safety and health of this whole state;
And therefore must his choice be circumscrib'd
Unto the voice and yielding° of that body
Whereof he is the head. Then if he says he loves you,
It fits your wisdom so far to believe it   25
As he in his particular act and place
May give his saying deed;° which is no further
Than the main voice of Denmark goes withal.
Then weigh what loss your honour may sustain,
If with too credent° ear you list his songs,   30
Or lose your heart, or your chaste treasure open
To his unmast'red° importunity.
Fear it, Ophelia, fear it, my dear sister,
And keep you in the rear of your affection,
Out of the shot and danger of desire.   35
The chariest° maid is prodigal enough,
If she unmask her beauty to the moon:
Virtue itself 'scapes not calumnious strokes:
The canker galls the infants of the spring,°
Too oft before their buttons° be disclos'd,°   40
And in the morn and liquid dew° of youth
Contagious blastments° are most imminent.
Be wary then; best safety lies in fear:
Youth to itself rebels, though none else near.

OPHELIA: I shall the effect of this good lesson keep,   45
As watchman to my heart. But, good my brother,

---

⁹**suppliance of a minute** *diversion to fill up a minute.* ¹¹**crescent** *growing, waxing.* ¹²**thews** *bodily strength.* ¹²**temple** *body.* ¹⁵**soil** *blemish.* ¹⁵**cautel** *crafty device.* ¹⁷**greatness weigh'd** *high position considered.* ²³**voice and yielding** *assent, approval.* ²⁷**deed** *effect.* ³⁰**credent** *credulous.* ³²**unmast'red** *unrestrained.* ³⁶**chariest** *most scrupulously modest.* ³⁹**The canker ... spring** *the cankerworm destroys the young plants of spring.* ⁴⁰**buttons** *buds.* ⁴⁰**disclos'd** *opened.* ⁴¹**liquid dew** *i.e., time when dew is fresh.* ⁴²**blastments** *blights.*

Do not, as some ungracious° pastors do,
Show me the steep and thorny way to heaven;
Whiles, like a puff'd° and reckless libertine,
Himself the primrose path of dalliance treads,
And recks° not his own rede.°   50

Enter POLONIUS.

LAERTES: O, fear me not.
  I stay too long: but here my father comes.
  A double° blessing is a double grace;
  Occasion° smiles upon a second leave.
POLONIUS: Yet here, Laertes? aboard, aboard, for shame!   55
  The wind sits in the shoulder of your sail,
  And you are stay'd for. There; my blessing with thee!
  And these few precepts° in thy memory
  Look thou character.° Give thy thoughts no tongue,
  Nor any unproportion'd° thought his act.   60
  Be thou familiar, but by no means vulgar.°
  Those friends thou hast, and their adoption tried,
  Grapple them to thy soul with hoops of steel;
  But do not dull thy palm with entertainment
  Of each new-hatch'd, unfledg'd° comrade. Beware   65
  Of entrance to a quarrel, but being in,
  Bear't that th' opposed may beware of thee.
  Give every man thy ear, but few thy voice;
  Take each man's censure, but reserve thy judgement.
  Costly thy habit as thy purse can buy,   70
  But not express'd in fancy;° rich, not gaudy;
  For the apparel oft proclaims the man,
  And they in France of the best rank and station
  Are of a most select and generous chief in that.°
  Neither a borrower nor a lender be;   75
  For loan oft loses both itself and friend,
  And borrowing dulleth edge of husbandry.°
  This above all: to thine own self be true,
  And it must follow, as the night the day,
  Thou canst not then be false to any man.   80
  Farewell: my blessing season° this in thee!
LAERTES: Most humbly do I take my leave, my lord.
POLONIUS: The time invites you; go; your servants tend.

---

⁴⁷**ungracious** *graceless.*   ⁴⁹**puff'd** *bloated.*   ⁵¹**recks** *heeds.*   ⁵¹**rede** *counsel.*   ⁵³**double** *i.e.,*
Laertes has already bade his father good-by.   ⁵⁴**Occasion** *opportunity.*   ⁵⁸**precepts** *many parallels have*
been found to the series of maxims which follows, one of the closer being that in Lyly's Euphues.   ⁵⁹**character** *in-*
scribe.   ⁶⁰**unproportion'd** *inordinate.*   ⁶¹**vulgar** *common.*   ⁶⁵**unfledg'd** *immature.*   ⁷¹**ex-**
press'd in fancy *fantastical in design.*   ⁷⁴**Are ... that** *chief is usually taken as a substantive meaning*
"head," "eminence."   ⁷⁷**husbandry** *thrift.*   ⁸¹**season** *mature.*

LAERTES: Farewell, Ophelia; and remember well
  What I have said to you.
OPHELIA: 'Tis in my memory lock'd,   85
  And you yourself shall keep the key of it.
LAERTES: Farewell.   *Exit* LAERTES.
POLONIUS: What is 't, Ophelia, he hath said to you?
OPHELIA: So please you, something touching the Lord Hamlet.
POLONIUS: Marry, well bethought: 90
  'Tis told me, he hath very oft of late
  Given private time to you; and you yourself
  Have of your audience been most free and bounteous:
  If it be so, as so't is put on° me,
  And that in way of caution, I must tell you,   95
  You do not understand yourself so clearly
  As it behooves my daughter and your honour.
  What is between you? give me up the truth.
OPHELIA: He hath, my lord, of late made many tenders°
  Of his affection to me.   100
POLONIUS: Affection! pooh! you speak like a green girl,
  Unsifted° in such perilous circumstance.
  Do you believe his tenders, as you call them?
OPHELIA: I do not know, my lord, what I should think.
POLONIUS: Marry, I will teach you: think yourself a baby;   105
  That you have ta'en these tenders° for true pay,
  Which are not sterling.° Tender° yourself more dearly;
  Or—not to crack the wind° of the poor phrase,
  Running it thus—you'll tender me a fool.°
OPHELIA: My lord, he hath importun'd me with love   110
  In honourable fashion.
POLONIUS: Ay, fashion° you may call it; go to, go to.
OPHELIA: And hath given countenance° to his speech, my lord,
  With almost all the holy vows of heaven.
POLONIUS: Ay, springes° to catch woodcocks.° I do know,   115
  When the blood burns, how prodigal the soul
  Lends the tongue vows: these blazes, daughter,
  Giving more light than heat, extinct in both,
  Even in their promise, as it is a-making,
  You must not take for fire. From this time   120
  Be somewhat scanter of your maiden presence;
  Set your entreatments° at a higher rate
  Than a command to parley.° For Lord Hamlet,

---

[94]**put on** *impressed on.* [99, 103]***tenders*** *offers.* [102]***Unsifted*** *untried.* [106]***tenders*** *promises to pay* [107]***sterling*** *legal currency.* [107]**Tender** *hold.* [108]**crack the wind** *i.e., run it until it is broken-winded.* [109]***tender . . . fool*** *show me a fool (for a daughter).* [112]***fashion*** *mere form, pretense.* [113]***countenance*** *credit, support.* [115]***springes*** *snares.* [115]***woodcocks*** *birds easily caught, type of stupidity.* [122]***entreatments*** *conversations, interviews.* [123]***command to parley*** *mere invitation to talk.*

Believe so much in him,° that he is young,
And with a larger tether may he walk   125
Than may be given you: in few,° Ophelia,
Do not believe his vows; for they are brokers;°
Not of that dye° which their investments° show,
But mere implorators of ° unholy suits,
Breathing° like sanctified and pious bawds,   130
The better to beguile. This is for all:
I would not, in plain terms, from this time forth,
Have you so slander° any moment leisure,
As to give words or talk with the Lord Hamlet.
Look to 't, I charge you: come your ways.   135
OPHELIA: I shall obey, my lord.   *Exeunt.*

Scene IV [*The platform.*]

Enter HAMLET, HORATIO, *and* MARCELLUS.

HAMLET: The air bites shrewdly; it is very cold.
HORATIO: It is a nipping and an eager air.
HAMLET: What hour now?
HORATIO: I think it lacks of twelve.
MARCELLUS: No, it is struck.
HORATIO: Indeed? I heard it not: then it draws near the season   5
    Wherein the spirit held his wont to walk.

A flourish of trumpets, and two pieces go off.

    What does this mean, my lord?
HAMLET: The king doth wake° to-night and takes his rouse,°
    Keeps wassail,° and the swagg'ring up-spring° reels;°
    And, as he drains his draughts of Rhenish° down,   10
    The kettle-drum and trumpet thus bray out
    The triumph of his pledge.°
HORATIO: Is it a custom?
HAMLET: Ay, marry, is 't:
    But to my mind, though I am native here
    And to the manner born,° it is a custom   15
    More honour'd in the breach than the observance.
    This heavy-headed revel east and west
    Makes us traduc'd and tax'd of other nations:

---

¹²⁴**so . . . him** *this much concerning him.*   ¹²⁶**in few** *briefly.*   ¹²⁷**brokers** *go-betweens, procurers.*
¹²⁸**dye** *color or sort.*   ¹²⁸**investments** *clothes.*   ¹²⁹**implorators of** *solicitors of.*   ¹³⁰**Breathing**
speaking.   ¹³³**slander** *bring disgrace or reproach upon.*   **I.iv.**   ⁸**wake** *stay awake, hold revel.*   ⁸**rouse**
carouse, drinking bout.   ⁹**wassail** *carousal.*   ⁹**up-spring** *last and wildest dance at German merry-makings.*
⁹**reels** *reels through.*   ¹⁰**Rhenish** *rhine wine.*   ¹²**triumph . . . pledge** *his glorious achievement as a
drinker.*   ¹⁵**to . . . born** *destined by birth to be subject to the custom in question.*

They clepe° us drunkards, and with swinish phrase°
Soil our addition;° and indeed it takes   20
From our achievements, though perform'd at height,
The pith and marrow of our attribute.°
So, oft it chances in particular men,
That for some vicious mole of nature° in them,
As, in their birth—wherein they are not guilty,   25
Since nature cannot choose his origin—
By the o'ergrowth of some complexion,
Oft breaking down the pales° and forts of reason,
Or by some habit that too much o'er-leavens°
The form of plausive° manners, that these men,   30
Carrying, I say, the stamp of one defect,
Being nature's livery,° or fortune's star,°—
Their virtues else—be they as pure as grace,
As infinite as man may undergo—
Shall in the general censure take corruption   35
From that particular fault: the dram of eale°
Doth all the noble substance of a doubt
To his own scandal.°

Enter GHOST.

HORATIO: Look, my lord, it comes!
HAMLET: Angels and ministers of grace° defend us!
Be thou a spirit of health or goblin damn'd,   40
Bring with thee airs from heaven or blasts from hell,
Be thy intents wicked or charitable,
Thou com'st in such a questionable° shape
That I will speak to thee: I'll call thee Hamlet,
King, father, royal Dane: O, answer me!   45
Let me not burst in ignorance; but tell
Why thy canoniz'd° bones, hearsed° in death,
Have burst their cerements;° why the sepulchre,
Wherein we saw thee quietly interr'd,
Hath op'd his ponderous and marble jaws,   50
To cast thee up again. What may this mean,
That thou, dead corse, again in complete steel
Revisits thus the glimpses of the moon,°
Making night hideous; and we fools of nature°

---

¹⁹**clepe** *call.*   ¹⁹**with swinish phrase** *by calling us swine.*   ²⁰**addition** *reputation*   ²²**attribute** *reputation*   ²⁴**mole of nature** *natural blemish in one's constitution.*   ²⁸**pales** *palings (as of a fortification).*   ²⁹**o'er-leavens** *induces a change throughout (as yeast works in bread).*   ³⁰**plausive** *pleasing.*   ³²**nature's livery** *endowment from nature.*   ³²**fortune's star** *the position in which one is placed by fortune, a reference to astrology. The two phrases are aspects of the same thing.*   ³⁶**dram of eale** *has had various interpretations, the preferred one being probably, "a dram of evil."*   ³⁶⁻³⁸**the dram . . . scandal** *a famous crux.*   ³⁹**ministers of grace** *messengers of God.*   ⁴³**questionable** *inviting question or conversation.*   ⁴⁷**canoniz'd** *buried according to the canons of the church.*   ⁴⁷**hearsed** *coffined.*   ⁴⁸**cerements** *grave-clothes.*   ⁵³**glimpses of the moon** *the earth by night.*   ⁵⁴**fools of nature** *mere men, limited to natural knowledge.*

So horridly to shake our disposition   55
With thoughts beyond the reaches of our souls?
Say, why is this? wherefore? what should we do?

[GHOST] *beckons* [HAMLET].

HORATIO: It beckons you to go away with it,
  As if it some impartment° did desire
  To you alone.
MARCELLUS: Look, with what courteous action   60
  It waves you to a more removed° ground:
  But do not go with it.
HORATIO: No, by no means.
HAMLET: It will not speak; then I will follow it.
HORATIO: Do not, my lord!
HAMLET: Why, what should be the fear?
  I do not set my life at a pin's fee;   65
  And for my soul, what can it do to that,
  Being a thing immortal as itself?
  It waves me forth again: I'll follow it.
HORATIO: What if it tempt you toward the flood, my lord,
  Or to the dreadful summit of the cliff   70
  That beetles o'er° his base into the sea,
  And there assume some other horrible form,
  Which might deprive your sovereignty of reason°
  And draw you into madness? think of it:
  The very place puts toys of desperation,°   75
  Without more motive, into every brain
  That looks so many fathoms to the sea
  And hears it roar beneath.
HAMLET: It waves me still.
  Go on; I'll follow thee.
MARCELLUS: You shall not go, my lord.
HAMLET: Hold off your hands!   80
HORATIO: Be rul'd; you shall not go.
HAMLET: My fate cries out,
  And makes each petty artere° in this body
  As hardy as the Nemean lion's° nerve.°
  Still am I call'd. Unhand me, gentlemen.
  By heaven, I'll make a ghost of him that lets° me!   85
  I say, away! Go on; I'll follow thee.   *Exeunt* GHOST *and* HAMLET.

---

⁵⁹**impartment** *communication.*   ⁶¹**removed** *remote.*   ⁷¹**beetles   o'er** *overhangs   threateningly.*
⁷³**deprive . . . reason** *take away the sovereignty of your reason. It was thought that evil spirits would sometimes as-*
sume the form of departed spirits in order to work madness in a human creature.   ⁷⁵**toys of desperation** *freakish*
notions of suicide. ⁸²**artere** *artery.*   ⁸³**Nemean lion's** *Nemean lion was one of the monsters slain by Her-*
cules.   ⁸³**nerve** *sinew, tendon. The point is that the arteries which were carrying the spirits out into the body were*
functioning and were as stiff and hard as the sinews of the lion.   ⁸⁵**lets** *hinders.*

HORATIO: He waxes desperate with imagination.
MARCELLUS: Let's follow; 'tis not fit thus to obey him.
HORATIO: Have after. To what issue° will this come?
MARCELLUS: Something is rotten in the state of Denmark.   90
HORATIO: Heaven will direct it.°
MARCELLUS: Nay, let's follow him.   *Exeunt.*

Scene V [*Another part of the platform.*]

Enter GHOST *and* HAMLET.

HAMLET: Whither wilt thou lead me? speak; I'll go no further.
GHOST: Mark me.
HAMLET: I will.
GHOST: My hour is almost come,
  When I to sulphurous and tormenting flames
  Must render up myself.
HAMLET: Alas, poor ghost!
GHOST: Pity me not, but lend thy serious hearing   5
  To what I shall unfold.
HAMLET: Speak; I am bound to hear.
GHOST: So art thou to revenge, when thou shalt hear.
HAMLET: What?
GHOST: I am thy father's spirit,
  Doom'd for a certain term to walk the night,   10
  And for the day confin'd to fast° in fires,
  Till the foul crimes done in my days of nature
  Are burnt and purg'd away. But that I am forbid
  To tell the secrets of my prison-house,
  I could a tale unfold whose lightest word   15
  Would harrow up thy soul, freeze thy young blood,
  Make thy two eyes, like stars, start from their spheres,°
  Thy knotted° and combined° locks to part
  And each particular hair to stand an end,
  Like quills upon the fretful porpentine: °   20
  But this eternal blazon° must not be
  To ears of flesh and blood. List, list, O, list!
  If thou didst ever thy dear father love—
HAMLET: O God!
GHOST: Revenge his foul and most unnatural° murder.   25
HAMLET: Murder!

89*issue* outcome.   91*it* i.e., the outcome.   **I.v.** 11*fast* probably, do without food. It has been sometimes taken in the sense of doing general penance.   17*spheres* orbits.   18*knotted* perhaps intricately arranged. 18*combined* tied, bound.   20*porpentine* porcupine.   21*eternal blazon* promulgation or proclamation of eternity, revelation of the hereafter.   25*unnatural* i.e., pertaining to fratricide.

GHOST: Murder most foul, as in the best it is;
   But this most foul, strange and unnatural.
HAMLET: Haste me to know't, that I, with wings as swift
   As meditation or the thoughts of love, 30
   May sweep to my revenge.
GHOST: I find thee apt;
   And duller shouldst thou be than the fat weed°
   That roots itself in ease on Lethe wharf,°
   Wouldst thou not stir in this. Now, Hamlet, hear:
   'Tis given out that, sleeping in my orchard, 35
   A serpent stung me; so the whole ear of Denmark
   Is by a forged process of my death
   Rankly abus'd: but know, thou noble youth,
   The serpent that did sting thy father's life
   Now wears his crown.
HAMLET: O my prophetic soul! 40
   My uncle!
GHOST: Ay, that incestuous, that adulterate° beast,
   With witchcraft of his wit, with traitorous gifts,—
   O wicked wit and gifts, that have the power
   So to seduce!—won to his shameful lust 45
   The will of my most seeming-virtuous queen:
   O Hamlet, what a falling-off was there!
   From me, whose love was of that dignity
   That it went hand in hand even with the vow
   I made to her in marriage, and to decline 50
   Upon a wretch whose natural gifts were poor
   To those of mine!
   But virtue, as it never will be moved,
   Though lewdness court it in a shape of heaven,
   So lust, though to a radiant angel link'd, 55
   Will sate itself in a celestial bed,
   And prey on garbage.
   But, soft! methinks I scent the morning air;
   Brief let me be. Sleeping within my orchard,
   My custom always of the afternoon, 60
   Upon my secure° hour thy uncle stole,
   With juice of cursed hebona° in a vial,
   And in the porches of my ears did pour
   The leperous° distilment; whose effect
   Holds such an enmity with blood of man 65
   That swift as quicksilver it courses through

---

³²**fat weed** *many suggestions have been offered as to the particular plant intended, including asphodel; probably a general figure for plants growing along rotting wharves and piles.* ³³**Lethe wharf** *bank of the river of forgetfulness in Hades.* ⁴²**adulterate** *adulterous.* ⁶¹**secure** *confident, unsuspicious.* ⁶²**hebona** *generally supposed to mean henbane, conjectured hemlock; ebenus, meaning "yew."* ⁶⁴**leperous** *causing leprosy.*

The natural gates and alleys of the body,
And with a sudden vigour it doth posset°
And curd, like eager° droppings into milk,
The thin and wholesome blood: so did it mine;   70
And a most instant tetter bark'd about,
Most lazar-like,° with vile and loathsome crust,
All my smooth body.
Thus was I, sleeping, by a brother's hand
Of life, of crown, of queen, at once dispatch'd:°   75
Cut off even in the blossoms of my sin,
Unhous'led,° disappointed,° unanel'd,°
No reck'ning made, but sent to my account
With all my imperfections on my head:
O, horrible! O, horrible! most horrible!°   80
If thou hast nature in thee, bear it not;
Let not the royal bed of Denmark be
A couch for luxury° and damned incest.
But, howsomever thou pursues this act,
Taint not thy mind,° nor let thy soul contrive   85
Against thy mother aught: leave her to heaven
And to those thorns that in her bosom lodge,
To prick and sting her. Fare thee well at once!
The glow-worm shows the matin° to be near,
And 'gins to pale his uneffectual fire:°   90
Adieu, adieu, adieu! remember me.   [*Exit.*]
HAMLET: O all you host of heaven! O earth! what else?
And shall I couple° hell? O, fie! Hold, hold, my heart;
And you, my sinews, grow not instant old,
But bear me stiffly up. Remember thee!   95
Ay, thou poor ghost, whiles memory holds a seat
In this distracted globe.° Remember thee!
Yea, from the table of my memory
I'll wipe away all trivial fond records,
All saws° of books, all forms, all pressures° past,   100
That youth and observation copied there;
And thy commandment all alone shall live
Within the book and volume of my brain,
Unmix'd with baser matter: yes, by heaven!
O most pernicious woman!   105
O villain, villain, smiling, damned villain!

---

⁶⁸**posset** *coagulate, curdle.*   ⁶⁹**eager** *sour, acid.*   ⁷²**lazar-like** *leperlike.*   ⁷⁵**dispatch'd** *suddenly
bereft.*   ⁷⁷**Unhous'led** *without having received the sacrament.*   ⁷⁷**disappointed** *unready, without equipment for the last journey.*   ⁷⁷**unanel'd** *without having received extreme unction.*   ⁸⁰**O . . . horrible** *many
editors give this line to Hamlet; Garrick and Sir Henry Irving spoke it in that part.*   ⁸³**luxury** *lechery.*
⁸⁵**Taint . . . mind** *probably, deprave not thy character, do nothing except in the pursuit of a natural revenge.*
⁸⁹**matin** *morning.*   ⁹⁰**uneffectual fire** *cold light.*   ⁹³**couple** *add.*   ⁹⁷**distracted globe** *confused head.*
¹⁰⁰**saws** *wise sayings.*   ¹⁰⁰**pressures** *impressions stamped.*

My tables,°—meet it is I set it down,
That one may smile, and smile, and be a villain;
At least I am sure it may be so in Denmark: [*Writing.*]
So, uncle, there you are. Now to my word;°   110
It is "Adieu, adieu! remember me,"
I have sworn't.

Enter HORATIO *and* MARCELLUS.

HORATIO: My lord, my lord—
MARCELLUS: Lord Hamlet,—
HORATIO: Heavens secure him!
HAMLET: So be it!
MARCELLUS: Hillo, ho, ho,° my lord!   115
HAMLET: Hillo, ho, ho, boy! come, bird, come.
MARCELLUS: How is't, my noble lord?
HORATIO: What news, my lord?
HAMLET: O, wonderful!
HORATIO: Good my lord, tell it.
HAMLET: No; you will reveal it.
HORATIO: Not I, my lord, by heaven.
MARCELLUS: Nor I, my lord.   120
HAMLET: How say you, then; would heart of man once think it?
   But you'll be secret?
HORATIO: }
MARCELLUS: }   Ay, by heaven, my lord.
HAMLET: There's ne'er a villain dwelling in all Denmark
   But he's an arrant° knave.
HORATIO: There needs no ghost, my lord, come from the grave   125
   To tell us this.
HAMLET: Why, right; you are in the right;
   And so, without more circumstance at all,
   I hold it fit that we shake hands and part:
   You, as your business and desire shall point you;
   For every man has business and desire,   130
   Such as it is; and for my own poor part,
   Look you, I'll go pray.
HORATIO: These are but wild and whirling words, my lord.
HAMLET: I am sorry they offend you, heartily;
   Yes, 'faith, heartily.
HORATIO: There's no offence, my lord.   135
HAMLET: Yes, by Saint Patrick,° but there is, Horatio,
   And much offence too. Touching this vision here,
   It is an honest° ghost, that let me tell you:

---

¹⁰⁷**tables**   *probably a small portable writing-tablet carried at the belt.*   ¹¹⁰**word**   *watchword.*   ¹¹⁵**Hillo,
ho, ho**   *a falconer's call to a hawk in air.*   ¹²⁴**arrant**   *thoroughgoing.*   ¹³⁶**Saint Patrick**   *St. Patrick was
keeper of Purgatory and patron saint of all blunders and confusion.*   ¹³⁸**honest**   *i.e., a real ghost and not an evil
spirit.*

For your desire to know what is between us,
O'ermaster 't as you may. And now, good friends,   140
As you are friends, scholars and soldiers,
Give me one poor request.

HORATIO: What is 't, my lord? we will.

HAMLET: Never make known what you have seen to-night.

HORATIO: }
MARCELLUS: }   My lord, we will not.

HAMLET: Nay, but swear 't.

HORATIO: In faith,   145
My lord, not I.

MARCELLUS: Nor I, my lord, in faith.

HAMLET: Upon my sword.°

MARCELLUS: We have sworn, my lord, already.

HAMLET: Indeed, upon my sword, indeed.   GHOST cries under the stage.

GHOST: Swear.

HAMLET: Ah, ha, boy! say'st thou so? art thou there, truepenny?°   150
Come on—you hear this fellow in the cellarage—
Consent to swear.

HORATIO: Propose the oath, my lord.

HAMLET: Never to speak of this that you have seen,
Swear by my sword.

GHOST [beneath]: Swear.   155

HAMLET: Hic et ubique?° then we'll shift our ground.
Come hither, gentlemen,
And lay your hands again upon my sword:
Swear by my sword,
Never to speak of this that you have heard.   160

GHOST [beneath]: Swear by his sword.

HAMLET: Well said, old mole! canst work i' th' earth so fast?
A worthy pioner!° Once more remove, good friends.

HORATIO: O day and night, but this is wondrous strange!

HAMLET: And therefore as a stranger give it welcome.   165
There are more things in heaven and earth, Horatio,
Than are dreamt of in your philosophy.
But come;
Here, as before, never, so help you mercy,
How strange or odd soe'er I bear myself,   170
As I perchance hereafter shall think meet
To put an antic° disposition on,
That you, at such times seeing me, never shall,
With arms encumb'red° thus, or this head-shake,

147**sword** *i.e., the hilt in the form of a cross.*   150**truepenny** *good old boy, or the like.*   156**Hic et ubique?**
here and everywhere?   163**pioner** *digger, miner.*   172**antic** *fantastic.*   174**encumb'red** *folded or en-*
twined.

Or by pronouncing of some doubtful phrase,   175
As "Well, well, we know," or "We could, an if we would,"
Or "If we list to speak," or "There be, an if they might,"
Or such ambiguous giving out,° to note°
That you know aught of me: this not to do,
So grace and mercy at your most need help you,   180
Swear.
GHOST [*beneath*]: Swear.
HAMLET: Rest, rest, perturbed spirit! [*They swear.*] So, gentlemen,
With all my love I do commend me to you:
And what so poor a man as Hamlet is   185
May do, t' express his love and friending° to you,
God willing, shall not lack. Let us go in together;
And still your fingers on your lips, I pray.
The time is out of joint: O cursed spite,
That ever I was born to set it right!   190
Nay, come, let's go together.   *Exeunt.*

ACT II

Scene I [A room in Polonius's house.]

Enter old POLONIUS *with his man* [REYNALDO].

POLONIUS: Give him this money and these notes, Reynaldo.
REYNALDO: I will, my lord.
POLONIUS: You shall do marvellous wisely, good Reynaldo,
Before you visit him, to make inquire
Of his behaviour.
REYNALDO: My lord, I did intend it.   5
POLONIUS: Marry, well said; very well said. Look you, sir,
Inquire me first what Danskers° are in Paris;
And how, and who, what means, and where they keep,°
What company, at what expense; and finding
By this encompassment° and drift° of question   10
That they do know my son, come you more nearer
Than your particular demands will touch it:°
Take° you as 'twere, some distant knowledge of him;
As thus, "I know his father and his friends;
And in part him": do you mark this, Reynaldo?   15

---

¹⁷⁸**giving out** *profession of knowledge.*   ¹⁷⁸**to note** *to give a sign.*   ¹⁸⁶**friending** *friendliness.*   **II.i.**
⁷**Danskers** *Danke was a common variant for "Denmark"; hence "Dane."*   ⁸**keep** *dwell.*   ¹⁰**encompass-**
ment *roundabout talking.*   ¹⁰**drift** *gradual approach or course.*   ^{11–12}**come ... it** *i.e., you will find*
out more this way than by asking pointed questions.   ¹³**Take** *assume, pretend.*

REYNALDO: Ay, very well, my lord.
POLONIUS: "And in part him; but" you may say "not well:
  But, if 't be he I mean, he's very wild;
  Addicted so and so": and there put on° him
  What forgeries° you please; marry, none so rank   20
  As may dishonour him; take heed of that;
  But, sir, such wanton,° wild and usual slips
  As are companions noted and most known
  To youth and liberty.
REYNALDO: As gaming, my lord.
POLONIUS: Ay, or drinking, fencing,° swearing, quarrelling,   25
  Drabbing;° you may go so far.
REYNALDO: My lord, that would dishonour him.
POLONIUS: 'Faith, no; as you may season it in the charge.
  You must not put another scandal on him,
  That he is open to incontinency;°   30
  That's not my meaning: but breathe his faults so quaintly°
  That they may seem the taints of liberty,°
  The flash and outbreak of a fiery mind,
  A savageness in unreclaimed° blood,
  Of general assault.°
REYNALDO: But, my good lord,—   35
POLONIUS: Wherefore should you do this?
REYNALDO: Ay, my lord,
  I would know that.
POLONIUS: Marry, sir, here's my drift;
  And, I believe, it is a fetch of wit:°
  You laying these slight sullies on my son,
  As 'twere a thing a little soil'd i' th' working,   40
  Mark you,
  Your party in converse, him you would sound,
  Having ever° seen in the prenominate° crimes
  The youth you breathe of guilty, be assur'd
  He closes with you in this consequence;°   45
  "Good sir," or so, or "friend," or "gentleman,"
  According to the phrase or the addition
  Of man and country.
REYNALDO: Very good, my lord.
POLONIUS: And then, sir, does 'a this—'a does—what was I about to say?
  By the mass, I was about to say something: where did I leave?   50

---

[19]**put on** _impute to._   [20]**forgeries** _invented tales._   [22]**wanton** _sportive, unrestrained._   [25]**fencing** _indicative of the ill repute of professional fencers and fencing schools in Elizabethan times._   [26]**Drabbing** _associated with immoral women._   [30]**incontinency** _habitual loose behavior._   [31]**quaintly** _delicately, ingeniously._   [32]**taints of liberty** _blemishes due to freedom._   [34]**unreclaimed** _untamed._   [36]**general assault** _tendency that assails all untrained youth._   [38]**fetch of wit** _clever trick._   [43]**ever** _at any time._   [43]**prenominate** _before-mentioned._   [45]**closes . . . consequence** _agrees with you in this conclusion._

REYNALDO: At "closes in the consequence," at "friend or so," and "gentleman."

POLONIUS: At "closes in the consequence," ay, marry;

 He closes thus: "I know the gentleman;

 I saw him yesterday, or t' other day,   55

 Or then, or then; with such, or such; and, as you say,

 There was 'a gaming; there o'ertook in's rouse;°

 There falling out at tennis": or perchance,

 "I saw him enter such a house of sale,"

 Videlicet,° a brothel, or so forth.   60

 See you now;

 Your bait of falsehood takes this carp of truth:

 And thus do we of wisdom and of reach,°

 With windlasses° and with assays of bias,°

 By indirections° find directions° out: 65

 So by my former lecture° and advice,

 Shall you my son. You have me, have you not?

REYNALDO: My lord, I have.

POLONIUS: God bye ye;° fare ye well.

REYNALDO: Good my lord!

POLONIUS: Observe his inclination in yourself.°   70

REYNALDO: I shall, my lord.

POLONIUS: And let him ply his music.°

REYNALDO: Well, my lord.

POLONIUS: Farewell!   *Exit* REYNALDO.

     Enter OPHELIA.

   How now, Ophelia! what's the matter?

OPHELIA: O, my lord, my lord, I have been so affrighted!

POLONIUS: With what, i' th' name of God?   75

OPHELIA: My lord, as I was sewing in my closet,°

 Lord Hamlet, with his doublet° all unbrac'd;°

 No hat upon his head; his stockings foul'd,

 Ungart'red, and down-gyved° to his ankle;

 Pale as his shirt; his knees knocking each other;   80

 And with a look so piteous in purport

 As if he had been loosed out of hell

 To speak of horrors,—he comes before me.

POLONIUS: Mad for thy love?

OPHELIA: My lord, I do not know;

 But truly, I do fear it.

---

⁵⁷**o'ertook in's rouse** *overcome by drink.* ⁶⁰**Videlicet** *namely.* ⁶³**reach** *capacity, ability.* ⁶⁴**wind-lasses** *i.e., circuitous paths.* ⁶⁴**assays of bias** *attempts that resemble the course of the bowl, which, being weighted on one side, has a curving motion.* ⁶⁵**indirections** *devious courses.* ⁶⁵**directions** *straight courses, i.e., the truth.* ⁶⁶**lecture** *admonition.* ⁶⁸**bye ye** *be with you.* ⁷⁰**Observe ... yourself** *in your own person, not by spies; or conform your own conduct to his inclination; or test him by studying yourself.* ⁷²**ply his music** *probably to be taken literally.* ⁷⁶**closet** *private chamber.* ⁷⁷**doublet** *close-fitting coat.* ⁷⁷**unbrac'd** *unfastened.* ⁷⁹**down-gyved** *fallen to the ankles (like gyves or fetters).*

POLONIUS: What said he?   85
OPHELIA: He took me by the wrist and held me hard;
   Then goes he to the length of all his arm;
   And, with his other hand thus o'er his brow,
   He falls to such perusal of my face
   As 'a would draw it. Long stay'd he so;   90
   At last, a little shaking of mine arm
   And thrice his head thus waving up and down,
   He rais'd a sigh so piteous and profound
   As it did seem to shatter all his bulk°
   And end his being: that done, he lets me go: 95
   And, with his head over his shoulder turn'd,
   He seem'd to find his way without his eyes;
   For out o'doors he went without their helps,
   And, to the last, bended their light on me.
POLONIUS: Come, go with me: I will go seek the king.   100
   This is the very ecstasy of love,
   Whose violent property° fordoes° itself
   And leads the will to desperate undertakings
   As oft as any passion under heaven
   That does afflict our natures. I am sorry.   105
   What, have you given him any hard words of late?
OPHELIA: No, my good lord, but, as you did command,
   I did repel his letters and denied
   His access to me.
POLONIUS: That hath made him mad.
   I am sorry that with better heed and judgement   110
   I had not quoted° him: I fear'd he did but trifle,
   And meant to wrack thee; but, beshrew my jealousy!°
   By heaven, it is as proper to our age
   To cast beyond° ourselves in our opinions
   As it is common for the younger sort   115
   To lack discretion. Come, go we to the king:
   This must be known; which, being kept close, might move
   More grief to hide than hate to utter love.°
   Come.   Exeunt.

Scene II [*A room in the castle.*]

Flourish. Enter KING *and* QUEEN, ROSENCRANTZ, *and* GUILDENSTERN [*with others*].

KING: Welcome, dear Rosencrantz and Guildenstern!

---

⁹⁴**bulk** *body.*   ¹⁰²**property** *nature.*   ¹⁰²**fordoes** *destroys.*   ¹¹¹**quoted** *observed.*   ¹¹²**beshrew**
my jealousy *curse my suspicions.*   ¹¹⁴**cast beyond** *overshoot, miscalculate.*   ¹¹⁷⁻¹¹⁸**might . . . love**
i.e., I might cause more grief to others by hiding the knowledge of Hamlet's love to Ophelia than hatred to me and mine
by telling of it.

Moreover that° we much did long to see you,
The need we have to use you did provoke
Our hasty sending. Something have you heard
Of Hamlet's transformation; so call it, 5
Sith° nor th' exterior nor the inward man
Resembles that it was. What it should be,
More than his father's death, that thus hath put him
So much from th' understanding of himself,
I cannot dream of: I entreat you both, 10
That, being of so young days° brought up with him,
And sith so neighbour'd to his youth and haviour,
That you vouchsafe your rest° here in our court
Some little time: so by your companies
To draw him on to pleasures, and to gather, 15
So much as from occasion you may glean,
Whether aught, to us unknown, afflicts him thus,
That, open'd, lies within our remedy.

QUEEN: Good gentlemen, he hath much talk'd of you;
And sure I am two men there are not living 20
To whom he more adheres. If it will please you
To show us so much gentry° and good will
As to expend your time with us awhile,
For the supply and profit° of our hope,
Your visitation shall receive such thanks 25
As fits a king's remembrance.

ROSENCRANTZ: Both your majesties
Might, by the sovereign power you have of us,
Put your dread pleasures more into command
Than to entreaty.

GUILDENSTERN: But we both obey,
And here give up ourselves, in the full bent° 30
To lay our service freely at your feet,
To be commanded.

KING: Thanks, Rosencrantz and gentle Guildenstern.

QUEEN: Thanks, Guildenstern and gentle Rosencrantz:
And I beseech you instantly to visit 35
My too much changed son. Go, some of you,
And bring these gentlemen where Hamlet is.

GUILDENSTERN: Heavens make our presence and our practices
Pleasant and helpful to him!

QUEEN: Ay, amen!

Exeunt ROSENCRANTZ *and* GUILDENSTERN [*with some* ATTENDANTS].

II.ii. ²**Moreover that** *besides the fact that.* ⁶**Sith** *since.* ¹¹*of . . . days* *from such early youth.*
¹³**vouchsafe your rest** *please to stay.* ²²**gentry** *courtesy.* ²⁴**supply and profit** *aid and successful out-*
come. ³⁰**in . . . bent** *to the utmost degree of our mental capacity.*

Enter POLONIUS.

POLONIUS: Th' ambassadors from Norway, my good lord,   40
    Are joyfully return'd.
KING: Thou still hast been the father of good news.
POLONIUS: Have I, my lord? I assure my good liege,
    I hold my duty, as I hold my soul,
    Both to my God and to my gracious king: 45
    And I do think, or else this brain of mine
    Hunts not the trail of policy so sure
    As it hath us'd to do, that I have found
    The very cause of Hamlet's lunacy.
KING: O, speak of that; that do I long to hear.   50
POLONIUS: Give first admittance to th' ambassadors;
    My news shall be the fruit to that great feast.
KING: Thyself do grace to them, and bring them in.   [*Exit* POLONIUS.]
    He tells me, my dear Gertrude, he hath found
    The head and source of all your son's distemper.   55
QUEEN: I doubt° it is no other but the main;°
    His father's death, and our o'erhasty marriage.
KING: Well, we shall sift him.

Enter AMBASSADORS [VOLTIMAND *and* CORNELIUS, *with* POLONIUS].

                Welcome, my good friends!
    Say, Voltimand, what from our brother Norway?
VOLTIMAND: Most fair return of greetings and desires.   60
    Upon our first, he sent out to suppress
    His nephew's levies; which to him appear'd
    To be a preparation 'gainst the Polack;
    But, better look'd into, he truly found
    It was against your highness: whereat griev'd,   65
    That so his sickness, age and impotence
    Was falsely borne in hand,° sends out arrests
    On Fortinbras; which he, in brief, obeys;
    Receives rebuke from Norway, and in fine°
    Makes vow before his uncle never more   70
    To give th' assay° of arms against your majesty.
    Whereon old Norway, overcome with joy,
    Gives him three score thousand crowns in annual fee,
    And his commission to employ those soldiers,
    So levied as before, against the Polack: 75
    With an entreaty, herein further shown, [*giving a paper.*]
    That it might please you to give quiet pass
    Through your dominions for this enterprise,

56**doubt** *fear.*   56**main** *chief point, principal concern.*   67**borne in hand** *deluded.*   69**in fine** *in the end.*   71**assay** *assault, trial (of arms).*

On such regards of safety and allowance°
As therein are set down.

KING: It likes° us well;   80

And at our more consider'd° time we'll read,
Answer, and think upon this business.
Meantime we thank you for your well-took labour:
Go to your rest; at night we'll feast together:
Most welcome home!   *Exeunt* AMBASSADORS.

POLONIUS: This business is well ended.   85

My liege, and madam, to expostulate
What majesty should be, what duty is,
Why day is day, night night, and time is time,
Were nothing but to waste night, day and time.
Therefore, since brevity is the soul of wit,°   90
And tediousness the limbs and outward flourishes,°
I will be brief: your noble son is mad:
Mad call I it; for, to define true madness
What is 't but to be nothing else but mad?
But let that go.

QUEEN: More matter, with less art.   95

POLONIUS: Madam, I swear I use no art at all.
That he is mad, 'tis true: 'tis true 'tis pity;
And pity 'tis 'tis true: a foolish figure;°
But farewell it, for I will use no art.
Mad let us grant him, then: and now remains   100
That we find out the cause of this effect,
Or rather say, the cause of this defect,
For this effect defective comes by cause:
Thus it remains, and the remainder thus.
Perpend.°   105
I have a daughter—have while she is mine—
Who, in her duty and obedience, mark,
Hath given me this: now gather, and surmise.   *[Reads the letter]*
"To the celestial and my soul's idol, the most beautified Ophelia,"—   110
That's an ill phrase, a vile phrase; "beautified" is a vile phrase: but you shall hear.
Thus: *[Reads.]*
"In her excellent white bosom, these, & c."

QUEEN: Came this from Hamlet to her?

POLONIUS: Good madam, stay awhile; I will be faithful.   *[Reads.]* 115

           "Doubt thou the stars are fire;
              Doubt that the sun doth move;
            Doubt truth to be a liar;
            But never doubt I love.

---

[79] **safety and allowance** *pledges of safety to the country and terms of permission for the troops to pass.*
[80] **likes** *pleases.*   [81] **consider'd** *suitable for deliberation.*   [90] **wit** *sound sense or judgment.*
[91] **flourishes** *ostentation, embellishments.*   [98] **figure** *figure of speech.*   [105] **Perpend** *consider.*

"O dear Ophelia, I am ill at these numbers;° I have not art to reckon° my 120
groans: but that I love thee best, O most best, believe it. Adieu.
"Thine evermore, most dear lady, whilst this machine° is to him,

HAMLET."

This, in obedience, hath my daughter shown me,
And more above,° hath his solicitings,   125
As they fell out° by time, by means° and place,
All given to mine ear.

KING: But how hath she
   Receiv'd his love?

POLONIUS: What do you think of me?

KING: As of a man faithful and honourable.

POLONIUS: I would fain prove so. But what might you think,   130
   When I had seen this hot love on the wing—
   As I perceiv'd it, I must tell you that,
   Before my daughter told me—what might you,
   Or my dear majesty your queen here, think,
   If I had play'd the desk or table-book,°   135
   Or given my heart a winking,° mute and dumb,
   Or look'd upon this love with idle sight;
   What might you think? No, I went round to work,
   And my young mistress thus I did bespeak: °
   "Lord Hamlet is a prince, out of thy star;°   140
   This must not be": and then I prescripts gave her,
   That she should lock herself from his resort,
   Admit no messengers, receive no tokens.
   Which done, she took the fruits of my advice;
   And he, repelled—a short tale to make—   145
   Fell into a sadness, then into a fast,
   Thence to a watch,° thence into a weakness,
   Thence to a lightness,° and, by this declension,°
   Into the madness wherein now he raves,
   And all we mourn for.

KING: Do you think 'tis this?   150

QUEEN: It may be, very like.

POLONIUS: Hath there been such a time—I would fain know that—
   That I have positively said "'Tis so,"
   When it prov'd otherwise?

KING: Not that I know.

POLONIUS [pointing to his head and shoulder]: Take this from this, if this be
   otherwise:

120*ill ... numbers* *unskilled at writing verses.*   120*reckon* *number metrically, scan.*   122*machine* *bodily frame.*   125*more above* *moreover.*   126*fill out* *occurred.*   126*means* *opportunities (of access).*
135*play'd ... table-book* *i.e., remained shut up, concealed this information.*   136*given ... winking* *given my heart a signal to keep silent.*   139*bespeak* *address.*   140*out ... star* *above thee in position.*
147*watch* *state of sleeplessness.*   148*lightness* *lightheartedness.*   148*declension* *decline, deterioration.*

If circumstances lead me, I will find
Where truth is hid, though it were hid indeed
Within the centre.°
KING: How may we try it further?
POLONIUS: You know, sometimes he walks four hours together
Here in the lobby.
QUEEN: So he does indeed.   160
POLONIUS: At such a time I'll loose my daughter to him:
Be you and I behind an arras° then;
Mark the encounter: if he love her not
And be not from his reason fall'n thereon,°
Let me be no assistant for a state,   165
But keep a farm and carters.
KING: We will try it.

Enter HAMLET [*reading on a book*].

QUEEN: But, look, where sadly the poor wretch comes reading.
POLONIUS: Away, I do beseech you both, away:

Exeunt KING *and* QUEEN [*with* ATTENDANTS].

I'll board° him presently. O, give me leave.
How does my good Lord Hamlet?   170
HAMLET: Well, God-a-mercy.
POLONIUS: Do you know me, my lord?
HAMLET: Excellent well; you are a fishmonger.°
POLONIUS: Not I, my lord.
HAMLET: Then I would you were so honest a man.   175
POLONIUS: Honest, my lord!
HAMLET: Ay, sir; to be honest, as this world goes, is to be one man picked out of
ten thousand.
POLONIUS: That's very true, my lord.
HAMLET: For if the sun breed maggots in a dead dog, being a good kissing   180
carrion,°—Have you a daughter?
POLONIUS: I have, my lord.
HAMLET: Let her not walk i' the sun:° conception° is a blessing: but as your
daughter may conceive—Friend, look to 't.
POLONIUS [*aside*]: How say you by° that? Still harping on my daughter: yet he   185
knew me not at first; 'a said I was a fishmonger: 'a is far gone, far gone: and
truly in my youth I suffered much extremity for love; very near this. I'll speak
to him again. What do you read, my lord?
HAMLET: Words, words, words.

---

¹⁵⁸*centre* *middle point of the earth.*   ¹⁶²*arras* *hanging, tapestry.*   ¹⁶⁴*thereon* *on that account.*
¹⁶⁹*board* *accost.*   ¹⁷³*fishmonger* *an opprobrious expression meaning "bawd," "procurer."*
^{180–181}*good kissing carrion* *i.e., a good piece of flesh for kissing (?).*   ¹⁸³*i' the sun* *in the sunshine of*
princely favors.   ¹⁸³*conception* *quibble on "understanding" and "pregnancy."*   ¹⁸⁵*by* *concerning.*

POLONIUS: What is the matter,° my lord?   190

HAMLET: Between who?°

POLONIUS: I mean, the matter that you read, my lord.

HAMLET: Slanders, sir: for the satirical rogue says here that old men have grey
beards, that their faces are wrinkled, their eyes purging° thick amber and plum-   195
tree gum and that they have a plentiful lack of wit, together with most weak
hams: all which, sir, though I most powerfully and potently believe, yet I hold
it not honesty° to have it thus set down, for yourself, sir, should be old as I am,
if like a crab you could go backward.

POLONIUS [aside]: Though this be madness, yet there is method in 't.—Will you   200
walk out of the air, my lord?

HAMLET: Into my grave.

POLONIUS: Indeed, that's out of the air. [Aside.] How pregnant sometimes his
replies are! a happiness° that often madness hits on, which reason and sanity
could not so prosperously° be delivered of. I will leave him, and suddenly con-   205
trive the means of meeting between him and my daughter.—My honourable
lord, I will most humbly take my leave of you.

HAMLET: You cannot, sir, take from me any thing that I will more willingly part
withal: except my life, except my life, except my life.

Enter GUILDENSTERN and ROSENCRANTZ.

POLONIUS: Fare you well, my lord.   210

HAMLET: These tedious old fools!

POLONIUS: You go to seek the Lord Hamlet; there he is.

ROSENCRANTZ [to POLONIUS]: God save you, sir!   [Exit POLONIUS.]

GUILDENSTERN: My honoured lord!

ROSENCRANTZ: My most dear lord!   215

HAMLET: My excellent good friends! How dost thou, Guildenstern? Ah, Rosencrantz! Good lads, how do ye both?

ROSENCRANTZ: As the indifferent° children of the earth.

GUILDENSTERN: Happy, in that we are not over-happy;
On Fortune's cap we are not the very button.   220

HAMLET: Nor the soles of her shoe?

ROSENCRANTZ: Neither, my lord.

HAMLET: Then you live about her waist, or in the middle of her favours?

GUILDENSTERN: 'Faith, her privates° we.

HAMLET: In the secret parts of Fortune? O, most true; she is a strumpet. What's the   225
news?

ROSENCRANTZ: None, my lord, but that the world's grown honest.

HAMLET: Then is doomsday near: but your news is not true. Let me question more
in particular: what have you, my good friends, deserved at the hands of Fortune, that she sends you to prison hither?   230

---

¹⁹⁰**matter** substance.   ¹⁹¹**Between who?** Hamlet deliberately takes matter as meaning "basis of dispute."
¹⁹⁴**purging** discharging.   ¹⁹⁷**honesty** decency.   ²⁰³**happiness** felicity of expression.   ²⁰⁴**prosper-**
ously successfully.   ²¹⁷**indifferent** ordinary.   ²²³**privates** i.e., ordinary men (sexual pun on private
parts).

GUILDENSTERN: Prison, my lord!

HAMLET: Denmark's a prison.

ROSENCRANTZ: Then is the world one.

HAMLET: A goodly one; in which there are many confines,° wards and dungeons, Denmark being one o' the worst. 235

ROSENCRANTZ: We think not so, my lord.

HAMLET: Why, then, 'tis none to you; for there is nothing either good or bad, but thinking makes it so: to me it is a prison.

ROSENCRANTZ: Why then, your ambition makes it one; 'tis too narrow for your mind. 240

HAMLET: O God, I could be bounded in a nutshell and count myself a king of infinite space, were it not that I have bad dreams.

GUILDENSTERN: Which dreams indeed are ambition, for the very substance of the ambitious° is merely the shadow of a dream.

HAMLET: A dream itself is but a shadow. 245

ROSENCRANTZ: Truly, and I hold ambition of so airy and light a quality that it is but a shadow's shadow.

HAMLET: Then are our beggars bodies, and our monarchs and outstretched heroes the beggars' shadows. Shall we to the court? for, by my fay,° I cannot reason.°

ROSENCRANTZ: ⎫ 250
GUILDENSTERN: ⎬ We'll wait upon° you.

HAMLET: No such matter: I will not sort° you with the rest of my servants, for, to speak to you like an honest man, I am most dreadfully attended.° But, in the beaten way of friendship,° what make you at Elsinore?

ROSENCRANTZ: To visit you, my lord: no other occasion. 255

HAMLET: Beggar that I am, I am ever poor in thanks; but I thank you: and sure, dear friends, my thanks are too dear a° halfpenny. Were you not sent for? Is it your own inclining? Is it a free visitation? Come, come, deal justly with me: come, come; nay, speak.

GUILDENSTERN: What should we say, my lord? 260

HAMLET: Why, any thing, but to the purpose. You were sent for; and there is a kind of confession in your looks which your modesties have not craft enough to colour: I know the good king and queen have sent for you.

ROSENCRANTZ: To what end, my lord?

HAMLET: That you must teach me. But let me conjure° you, by the rights of our 265 fellowship, by the consonancy of our youth,° by the obligation of our ever-preserved love, and by what more dear a better proposer° could charge you withal, be even and direct with me, whether you were sent for, or no?

ROSENCRANTZ [*aside to* GUILDENSTERN]: What say you? 270

HAMLET [*aside*]: Nay, then, I have an eye of you.—If you love me, hold not off.

GUILDENSTERN: My lord, we were sent for.

233**confines** *places of confinement.*   243**very … ambitious** *that seemingly most substantial thing which the ambitious pursue.*   248**fay** *faith.*   249**reason** *argue.*   250**wait upon** *accompany.*   251**sort** *class.*   252**dreadfully attended** *poorly provided with servants.*   253**in the … friendship** *as a matter of course among friends.*   256**a** *i.e., at a.*   264**conjure** *adjure, entreat.*   265**consonancy of our youth** *the fact that we are of the same age.*   266**better proposer** *one more skillful in finding proposals.*

HAMLET: I will tell you why; so shall my anticipation prevent your discovery,° and your secrecy to the king and queen moult no feather. I have of late—but wherefore I know not—lost all my mirth, forgone all custom of exercises; and 275 indeed it goes so heavily with my disposition that this goodly frame, the earth, seems to me a sterile promontory, this most excellent canopy, the air, look you, this brave o'erhanging firmament, this majestical roof fretted° with golden fire, why, it appeareth nothing to me but a foul and pestilent congregation of vapours. What a piece of work is a man! how noble in reason! how infinite in 280 faculties!° in form and moving how express° and admirable! in action how like an angel! in apprehension° how like a god! the beauty of the world! the paragon of animals! And yet, to me, what is this quintessence° of dust? man delights not me: no, nor woman neither, though by your smiling you seem to say so. 285

ROSENCRANTZ: My lord, there was no such stuff in my thoughts.

HAMLET: Why did you laugh then, when I said "man delights not me"?

ROSENCRANTZ: To think, my lord, if you delight not in man, what lenten° entertainment the players shall receive from you: we coted° them on the way; and hither are they coming, to offer you service. 290

HAMLET: He that plays the king shall be welcome; his majesty shall have tribute of me; the adventurous knight shall use his foil and target;° the lover shall not sigh gratis; the humorous man° shall end his part in peace; the clown shall make those laugh whose lungs are tickle o' the sere;° and the lady shall say her mind freely, or the blank verse shall halt for 't.° What players are they? 295

ROSENCRANTZ: Even those you were wont to take delight in, the tragedians of the city.

HAMLET: How chances it they travel? their residence,° both in reputation and profit, was better both ways.

ROSENCRANTZ: I think their inhibition° comes by the means of the late 300 innovation.°

HAMLET: Do they hold the same estimation they did when I was in the city? are they so followed?

ROSENCRANTZ: No, indeed, are they not.

HAMLET: How° comes it? do they grow rusty? 305

ROSENCRANTZ: Nay, their endeavour keeps in the wonted pace: but there is, sir, an aery° of children, little eyases,° that cry out on the top of question,° and are

---

²⁷³**prevent your discovery**   *forestall your disclosure.*   ²⁷⁸**fretted**   *adorned.*   ²⁸¹**faculties**   *capacity.* ²⁸¹**express**   *well-framed (?), exact (?).*   ²⁸³**apprehension**   *understanding.*   ²⁸³**quintessence**   *the fifth essence of ancient philosophy, supposed to be the substance of the heavenly bodies and to be latent in all things.*   ²⁸⁹**lenten**   *meager.*   ²⁸⁹**coted**   *overtook and passed beyond.*   ²⁸⁹**foil and target**   *sword and shield.*   ²⁹⁸**humorous man**   *actor who takes the part of the humor characters.*   ²⁹³**tickle o' the sere**   *easy on the trigger.*   ²⁹⁶**the lady . . . for 't**   *the lady (fond of talking) shall have opportunity to talk, blank verse or no blank verse.*   ²⁹⁸**residence**   *remaining in one place.*   ³⁰⁰**inhibition**   *formal prohibition (from acting plays in the city or, possibly, at court).*   ³⁰⁰**innovation**   *the new fashion in satirical plays performed by boy actors in the "private" theaters.*   ³⁰⁵⁻³²³**How . . . load too**   *the passage is the famous one dealing with the War of the Theatres (1599–1602); namely, the rivalry between the children's companies and the adult actors.*   ³⁰⁷**aery**   *nest.*   ³⁰⁷**eyases**   *young hawks.*   ³⁰⁷**cry . . . question**   *speak in a high key dominating conversation; clamor forth the height of controversy; probably "excel" (cf. line 459); perhaps intended to decry leaders of the dramatic profession.*

most tyrannically° clapped for 't: these are now the fashion, and so berattle° the
common stages°—so they call them—that many wearing rapiers° are afraid of
goose-quills° and dare scarce come thither.   310
HAMLET: What, are they children? who maintains 'em? how are they escoted?°
Will they pursue the quality° no longer than they can sing?° will they not say
afterwards, if they should grow themselves to common° players—as it is most
like, if their means are no better—their writers do them wrong, to make them
exclaim against their own succession?°   315
ROSENCRANTZ: 'Faith, there has been much to do on both sides; and the nation
holds it no sin to tarre° them to controversy: there was, for a while, no money
bid for argument,° unless the poet and the players went to cuffs° in the
question.°
HAMLET: Is't possible?   320
GUILDENSTERN: O, there has been much throwing about of brains.
HAMLET: Do the boys carry it away?°
ROSENCRANTZ: Ay, that they do, my lord; Hercules and his load° too.
HAMLET: It is not very strange; for my uncle is king of Denmark, and those that
would make mows° at him while my father lived, give twenty, forty, fifty, a 325
hundred ducats° a-piece for his picture in little.° 'Sblood, there is something in
this more than natural, if philosophy could find it out.

A flourish [of trumpets within].

GUILDENSTERN: There are the players.   330
HAMLET: Gentlemen, you are welcome to Elsinore. Your hands, come then: the
appurtenance of welcome is fashion and ceremony: let me comply° with you
in this garb,° lest my extent° to the players, which, I tell you, must show fairly
outwards, should more appear like entertainment than yours. You are welcome:
but my uncle-father and aunt-mother are deceived.   335
GUILDENSTERN: In what, my dear lord?
HAMLET: I am but mad north-north-west:° when the wind is southerly I know a
hawk from a handsaw.°

Enter POLONIUS.

POLONIUS: Well be with you, gentlemen!   340

308*tyrannically* outrageously.   308*berattle* berate.   309*common stages* public theaters.   309*many
wearing rapiers* many men of fashion, who were afraid to patronize the common players for fear of being satirized by the
poets who wrote for the children.   310*goose-quills* i.e., pens of satirists.   311*escoted* maintained.   32*quality* acting profession.   312*no longer ... sing* i.e., until their voices change.   313*common* regular, adult.
315*succession* future careers.   319*tarre* set on (as dogs).   318*argument* probably, plot for a play.
320*went to cuffs* came to blows.   319*question* controversy.   322*carry it away* win the day.   323*Hercules ... load* regarded as an allusion to the sign of the Globe Theatre, which was Hercules bearing the world on his
shoulder.   325*mows* grimaces.   326*ducats* gold coins worth 9s. 4d.   326*in little* in miniature.
332*comply* observe the formalities of courtesy.   333*garb* manner.   333*extent* showing of kindness.   338*I
am ... north-north-west* I am only partly mad, i.e., in only one point of the compass.   339*handsaw* a proposed reading of hernshaw would mean "heron"; handsaw may be an early corruption of hernshaw. Another view regards
hawk as the variant of hack, a tool of the pickax type, and handsaw as a saw operated by hand.

HAMLET: Hark you, Guildenstern; and you too: at each ear a hearer: that great baby you see there is not yet out of his swaddling-clouts.°

ROSENCRANTZ: Happily he is the second time come to them; for they say an old man is twice a child.

HAMLET: I will prophesy he comes to tell me of the players; mark it.—You say   345
right, sir: o' Monday morning;° 'twas then indeed.

POLONIUS: My lord, I have news to tell you.

HAMLET: My lord, I have news to tell you. When Roscius° was an actor in Rome,—

POLONIUS: The actors are come hither, my lord.   350

HAMLET: Buz, buz!°

POLONIUS: Upon my honour,—

HAMLET: Then came each actor on his ass,—

POLONIUS: The best actors in the world, either for tragedy, comedy, history, pastoral, pastoral-comical, historical-pastoral, tragical-historical, tragical-   355
comical-historical-pastoral, scene individable,° or poem unlimited:° Seneca° cannot be too heavy, nor Plautus° too light. For the law of writ and the liberty,° these are the only men.

HAMLET: O Jephthah, judge of Israel,° what a treasure hadst thou!

POLONIUS: What a treasure had he, my lord?   360

HAMLET: Why,

> "One fair daughter, and no more,
> The which he loved passing well."

POLONIUS [aside]:Still on my daughter.

HAMLET: Am I not i' the right, old Jephthah?   365

POLONIUS: If you call me Jephthah, my lord, I have a daughter that I love passing° well.

HAMLET: Nay, that follows not.

POLONIUS: What follows, then, my lord?

HAMLET: Why,   370

> "As by lot, God wot,"

and then, you know,

> "It came to pass, as most like° it was,"—

the first row° of the pious chanson° will show you more; for look, where my abridgement comes.°   375

Enter the PLAYERS.

You are welcome, masters; welcome, all. I am glad to see thee well. Welcome, good friends. O, old friend! why, thy face is valanced° since I saw thee last:

---

³⁴²**swaddling-clouts** *clothes in which to wrap a newborn baby.*   ³⁴⁶**o' Monday morning** *said to mislead Polonius.*   ³⁴⁸**Roscius** *a famous Roman actor.*   ³⁵¹**Buz, buz** *an interjection used at Oxford to denote stale news.*   ³⁵⁶**scene individable** *a play observing the unity of place.*   ³⁵⁶**poem unlimited** *a play disregarding the unities of time and place.*   ³⁵⁷**Seneca** *writer of Latin tragedies, model of early Elizabethan writers of tragedy.*   ³⁵⁷**Plautus** *writer of Latin comedy.*   ³⁵⁷**law ... liberty** *pieces written according to rules and without rules, i.e., "classical" and "romantic" dramas.*   ³⁵⁹**Jephthah ... Israel** *Jephthah had to sacrifice his daughter; see Judges 11.*   ³⁶⁷**passing** *surpassingly.*   ³⁷³**like** *probable.*   ³⁷⁴**row** *stanza.*   ³⁷⁴**chanson** *ballad.*   ³⁷⁵**abridgement comes** *opportunity comes for cutting short the conversation.*   ³⁷⁷**valanced** *fringed (with a beard).*

comest thou to beard me in Denmark? What, my young lady and mistress! By'r lady, your ladyship is nearer to heaven than when I saw you last, by the altitude of a chopine.° Pray God, your voice, like a piece of uncurrent° gold, be not 380 cracked within the ring.° Masters, you are all welcome. We'll e'en to 't like French falconers, fly at any thing we see: we'll have a speech straight: come, give us a taste of your quality; come, a passionate speech.

FIRST PLAYER: What speech, my good lord?

HAMLET: I heard thee speak me a speech once, but it was never acted; or, if it was, 385 not above once; for the play, I remember, pleased not the million; 'twas caviary to the general:° but it was—as I received it, and others, whose judgements in such matters cried in the top of° mine—an excellent play, well digested in the scenes, set down with as much modesty as cunning.° I remember, one said there were no sallets° in the lines to make the matter savoury, nor no matter in 390 the phrase that might indict° the author of affectation; but called it an honest method, as wholesome as sweet, and by very much more handsome than fine.° One speech in 't I chiefly loved: 'twas Æneas' tale to Dido;° and thereabout of it especially, where he speaks of Priam's slaughter: if it live in your memory, begin at this line: let me see, let me see— 395 "The rugged Pyrrhus,° like th' Hyrcanian beast,"°— 'tis not so:—it begins with Pyrrhus:—

"The rugged Pyrrhus, he whose sable arms,
Black as his purpose, did the night resemble
When he lay couched in the ominous horse,° 400
Hath now this dread and black complexion smear'd
With heraldry more dismal; head to foot
Now is he total gules;° horridly trick'd°
With blood of fathers, mothers, daughters, sons,
Bak'd and impasted° with the parching streets, 405
That lend a tyrannous and a damned light
To their lord's murder: roasted in wrath and fire,
And thus o'er-sized° with coagulate gore,
With eyes like carbuncles, the hellish Pyrrhus
Old grandsire Priam seeks." 410
So, proceed you.

POLONIUS: 'Fore God, my lord, well spoken, with good accent and good discretion.

380**chopine**   *kind of shoe raised by the thickness of the heel; worn in Italy, particularly at Venice.*   381**un-current**   *not passable as lawful coinage.*   381**cracked within the ring**   *in the center of coins were rings enclosing the sovereign's head; if the coin was cracked within this ring, it was unfit for currency.*   388**caviary to the general**   *not relished by the multitude.*   389**cried in the top of**   *spoke with greater authority than.*   391**cunning**   *skill.*   391**sallets**   *salads: here, spicy improprieties.*   392**indict**   *convict.*   394**as wholesome . . . fine**   *its beauty was not that of elaborate ornament, but that of order and proportion.*   395**Æneas' tale to Dido**   *the lines recited by the player are imitated from Marlowe and Nashe's Dido Queen of Carthage (II.i.214 ff.). They are written in such a way that the conventionality of the play within a play is raised above that of ordinary drama.*   398**Pyrrhus**   *a Greek hero in the Trojan War.*   398**Hyrcanian beast** *the tiger; see Virgil, Aeneid, IV.266.*   402**ominous horse**   *Trojan horse.*   405**gules**   *red, a heraldic term.*   405**trick'd**   *spotted, smeared.*   407**impasted**   *made into a paste.*   410**o'er-sized**   *covered as with size or glue.*

FIRST PLAYER: "Anon he finds him
   Striking too short at Greeks; his antique sword,
   Rebellious to his arm, lies where it falls,
   Repugnant° to command: unequal match'd,
   Pyrrhus at Priam drives; in rage strikes wide;
   But with the whiff and wind of his fell sword
   Th' unnerved father falls. Then senseless Ilium,°
   Seeming to feel this blow, with flaming top
   Stoops to his base, and with a hideous crash
   Takes prisoner Pyrrhus' ear: for, lo! his sword   425
   Which was declining on the milky head
   Of reverend Priam, seem'd i' th' air to stick:
   So, as a painted tyrant,° Pyrrhus stood,
   And like a neutral to his will and matter,°
   Did nothing.   430
   But, as we often see, against° some storm,
   A silence in the heavens, the rack° stand still,
   The bold winds speechless and the orb below
   As hush as death, anon the dreadful thunder
   Doth rend the region,° so, after Pyrrhus' pause,   435
   Aroused vengeance sets him new a-work;
   And never did the Cyclops' hammers fall
   On Mars's armour forg'd for proof eterne°
   With less remorse than Pyrrhus' bleeding sword
   Now falls on Priam.   440
   Out, out, thou strumpet, Fortune! All you gods,
   In general synod,° take away her power;
   Break all the spokes and fellies° from her wheel,
   And bowl the round nave° down the hill of heaven,
   As low as to the fiends!"   445
POLONIUS: This is too long.
HAMLET: It shall to the barber's, with your beard. Prithee, say on: he's for a jig° or
   a tale of bawdry,° or he sleeps: say on: come to Hecuba.°
FIRST PLAYER: "But who, ah woe! had seen the mobled° queen—"
HAMLET: "The mobled queen?"   450
POLONIUS: That's good; "mobled queen" is good.
FIRST PLAYER: "Run barefoot up and down, threat'ning the flames
   With bisson rheum;° a clout° upon that head
   Where late the diadem stood, and for a robe,
   About her lank and all o'er-teemed° loins,   455
   A blanket, in the alarm of fear caught up;

419**Repugnant** disobedient.   422**Then senseless Ilium** insensate Troy.   428**painted tyrant** tyrant in a picture.   429**matter** task.   431**against** before.   432**rack** mass of clouds.   435**region** assembly. 438**proof eterne** external resistance to assault.   442**synod** assembly.   443**fellies** pieces of wood forming the rim of a wheel.   444**nave** hub.   448**jig** comic performance given at the end or in an interval of a play. 448**bawdry** indecency.   448**Hecuba** wife of Priam, king of Troy.   449**mobled** muffled.   453**bisson rheum** blinding tears.   453**clout** piece of cloth.   455**o'er-teemed** worn out with bearing children.

Who this had seen, with tongue in venom steep'd,
'Gainst Fortune's state would treason have pronounc'd:°
But if the gods themselves did see her then
When she saw Pyrrhus make malicious sport   460
In mincing with his sword her husband's limbs,
The instant burst of clamour that she made,
Unless things mortal move them not at all,
Would have made milch° the burning eyes of heaven,
And passion in the gods."   465

POLONIUS: Look, whe'r he has not turned° his colour and has tears in 's eyes.
  Prithee, no more.

HAMLET: 'Tis well; I'll have thee speak out the rest soon. Good my lord, will you
  see the players well bestowed? Do you hear, let them be well used; for they are
  the abstract° and brief chronicles of the time: after your death you were better 470
  have a bad epitaph than their ill report while you live.

POLONIUS: My lord, I will use them according to their desert.

HAMLET: God's bodykins,° man, much better: use every man after his desert, and
  who shall 'scape whipping? Use them after your own honour and dignity: the
  less they deserve, the more merit is in your bounty. Take them in.   475

POLONIUS: Come, sirs.

HAMLET: Follow him, friends: we'll hear a play tomorrow. [*Aside to* FIRST PLAYER.]
  Dost thou hear me, old friend; can you play the Murder of Gonzago?

FIRST PLAYER: Ay, my lord.

HAMLET: We'll ha 't to-morrow night. You could, for a need, study a speech of 480
  some dozen or sixteen lines,° which I would set down and insert in 't, could
  you not?

FIRST PLAYER: Ay, my lord.

HAMLET: Very well. Follow that lord; and look you mock him not.—My good
  friends, I'll leave you till night: you are welcome to Elsinore.   485

Exeunt POLONIUS *and* PLAYERS.

ROSENCRANTZ: Good my lord!   *Exeunt* [ROSENCRANTZ *and* GUILDENSTERN.]

HAMLET: Ay, so, God bye to you.—Now I am alone.
  O, what a rogue and peasant° slave am I!   490
  Is it not monstrous that this player here,
  But in a fiction, in a dream of passion,
  Could force his soul so to his own conceit
  That from her working all his visage wann'd,°
  Tears in his eyes, distraction in 's aspect,   495
  A broken voice, and his whole function suiting
  With forms to his conceit?° and all for nothing!
  For Hecuba!

What's Hecuba to him, or he to Hecuba,
That he should weep for her? What would he do,   500
Had he the motive and the cue for passion
That I have? He would drown the stage with tears
And cleave the general ear with horrid speech,
Make mad the guilty and appall the free,
Confound the ignorant, and amaze indeed   505
The very faculties of eyes and ears.
Yet I,
A dull and muddy-mettled° rascal, peak,°
Like John-a-dreams,° unpregnant of° my cause,
And can say nothing; no, not for a king.   510
Upon whose property° and most dear life
A damn'd defeat was made. Am I a coward?
Who calls me villain? breaks my pate across?
Plucks off my beard, and blows it in my face?
Tweaks me by the nose? gives me the lie i' th' throat,   515
As deep as to the lungs? who does me this?
Ha!
'Swounds, I should take it: for it cannot be
But I am pigeon-liver'd° and lack gall
To make oppression bitter, or ere this   520
I should have fatted all the region kites°
With this slave's offal: bloody, bawdy villain!
Remorseless, treacherous, lecherous, kindless° villain!
O, vengeance!
Why, what an ass am I! This is most brave,   525
That I, the son of a dear father murder'd,
Prompted to my revenge by heaven and hell,
Must, like a whore, unpack my heart with words,
And fall a-cursing, like a very drab,°
A stallion!°   530
Fie upon 't! foh! About,° my brains! Hum, I have heard
That guilty creatures sitting at a play
Have by the very cunning of the scene
Been struck so to the soul that presently
They have proclaim'd their malefactions;   535
For murder, though it have no tongue, will speak
With most miraculous organ. I'll have these players
Play something like the murder of my father

---

[508]**muddy-mettled** dull-spirited.   [508]**peak** mope, pine.   [509]**John-a-dreams** an expression occurring
elsewhere in Elizabethan literature to indicate a dreamer.   [509]**unpregnant of** not quickened by.   [511]**property** proprietorship (of crown and life).   [519]**pigeon-liver'd** the pigeon was supposed to secrete no gall; if Hamlet, so he says, had had gall, he would have felt the bitterness of oppression, and avenged it.   [521]**region kites** kites
of the air.   [523]**kindless** unnatural.   [529]**drab** prostitute.   [530]**stallion** prostitute (male or female).
[531]**About** about it, or turn thou right about.

Before mine uncle: I'll observe his looks:
I'll tent° him to the quick: if 'a do blench,°   540
I know my course. The spirit that I have seen
May be the devil:° and the devil hath power
T' assume a pleasing shape; yea, and perhaps
Out of my weakness and my melancholy,
As he is very potent with such spirits,°   545
Abuses me to damn me: I'll have grounds
More relative° than this:° the play's the thing
Wherein I'll catch the conscience of the king.   *Exit.*

ACT III

Scene I [A room in the castle.]

Enter KING, QUEEN, POLONIUS, OPHELIA, ROSENCRANTZ, GUILDENSTERN, LORDS.

KING: And can you, by no drift of conference,°
  Get from him why he puts on this confusion,
  Grating so harshly all his days of quiet
  With turbulent and dangerous lunacy?
ROSENCRANTZ: He does confess he feels himself distracted;   5
  But from what cause 'a will by no means speak.
GUILDENSTERN: Nor do we find him forward° to be sounded,
  But, with a crafty madness, keeps aloof,
  When we would bring him on to some confession
  Of his true state.
QUEEN: Did he receive you well?   10
ROSENCRANTZ: Most like a gentleman.
GUILDENSTERN: But with much forcing of his disposition.°
ROSENCRANTZ: Niggard of question;° but, of our demands,
  Most free in his reply.
QUEEN: Did you assay° him
  To any pastime?   15
ROSENCRANTZ: Madam, it so fell out, that certain players
  We o'er-raught° on the way: of these we told him;
  And there did seem in him a kind of joy
  To hear of it: they are here about the court,
  And, as I think, they have already order   20

°540**tent** *probe.*   °540**blench**   *quail, flinch.*   °542**May be the devil**   *Hamlet's suspicion is properly grounded in the belief of the time.*   °545**spirits**   *humors.*   °547**relative**   *closely related, definite.*   °547**this**   *i.e., the ghost's story.*   **III.i.**   ¹**drift of conference**   *device of conversation.*   ⁷**forward**   *willing.*   ¹²**forcing of his disposition**   *i.e., against his will.*   ¹³**Niggard of question**   *sparing of conversation.*   ¹⁴**assay**   *try to win.*   ¹⁷**o'er-raught**   *overtook.*

This night to play before him.

POLONIUS: 'Tis most true:
And he beseech'd me to entreat your majesties
To hear and see the matter.

KING: With all my heart; and it doth much content me
To hear him so inclin'd.   25
Good gentlemen, give him a further edge,°
And drive his purpose into these delights.

ROSENCRANTZ: We shall, my lord.   *Exeunt* ROSENCRANTZ *and* GUILDENSTERN.

KING: Sweet Gertrude, leave us too;
For we have closely° sent for Hamlet hither,
That he, as 'twere by accident, may here   30
Affront° Ophelia:
Her father and myself, lawful espials,°
Will so bestow ourselves that, seeing, unseen,
We may of their encounter frankly judge,
And gather by him, as he is behav'd,   35
If 't be th' affliction of his love or no
That thus he suffers for.

QUEEN: I shall obey you.
And for your part, Ophelia, I do wish
That your good beauties be the happy cause
Of Hamlet's wildness:° so shall I hope your virtues   40
Will bring him to his wonted way again,
To both your honours.

OPHELIA: Madam, I wish it may.   [*Exit* QUEEN.]

POLONIUS: Ophelia, walk you here. Gracious,° so please you,
We will bestow ourselves. [*To* OPHELIA.] Read on this book;
That show of such an exercise° may colour°   45
Your loneliness. We are oft to blame in this,—
'Tis too much prov'd—that with devotion's visage
And pious action we do sugar o'er
The devil himself.

KING: [*Aside*] O, 'tis too true!
How smart a lash that speech doth give my conscience!   50
The harlot's cheek, beautied with plast'ring art,
Is not more ugly to° the thing° that helps it
Than is my deed to my most painted word:
O heavy burthen!

POLONIUS: I hear him coming: let's withdraw, my lord.   55

[*Exeunt* KING *and* POLONIUS.]

Enter HAMLET.

---

²⁶*edge*   incitement.   ²⁹*closely*   secretly.   ³¹*Affront*   confront.   ³²*lawful espials*   legitimate spies.
⁴⁰*wildness*   madness.   ⁴³*Gracious*   your grace (addressed to the king).   ⁴⁵*exercise*   act of devotion (the
book she reads is one of devotion).   ⁴⁵*colour*   give a plausible appearance to.   ⁵²*to*   compared to.
⁵²*thing*   i.e., the cosmetic.

HAMLET: To be, or not to be: that is the question:
　　　Whether 'tis nobler in the mind to suffer
　　　The slings and arrows of outrageous fortune,
　　　Or to take arms against a sea° of troubles,
　　　And by opposing end them? To die: to sleep; 　　　　　60
　　　No more; and by a sleep to say we end
　　　The heart-ache and the thousand natural shocks
　　　That flesh is heir to, 'tis a consummation
　　　Devoutly to be wish'd. To die, to sleep;
　　　To sleep: perchance to dream: ay, there's the rub; 　　65
　　　For in that sleep of death what dreams may come
　　　When we have shuffled° off this mortal coil,°
　　　Must give us pause: there's the respect°
　　　That makes calamity of so long life;°
　　　For who would bear the whips and scorns of time,° 　70
　　　Th' oppressor's wrong, the proud man's contumely,
　　　The pangs of despis'd° love, the law's delay,
　　　The insolence of office° and the spurns°
　　　That patient merit of th' unworthy takes,
　　　When he himself might his quietus° make 　　　　　75
　　　With a bare bodkin?° who would fardels° bear,
　　　To grunt and sweat under a weary life,
　　　But that the dread of something after death,
　　　The undiscover'd country from whose bourn°
　　　No traveller returns, puzzles the will 　　　　　　80
　　　And makes us rather bear those ills we have
　　　Than fly to others that we know not of?
　　　Thus conscience° does make cowards of us all;
　　　And thus the native hue° of resolution
　　　Is sicklied o'er° with the pale cast° of thought, 　　85
　　　And enterprises of great pitch° and moment°
　　　With this regard° their currents° turn awry,
　　　And lose the name of action—Soft you now!
　　　The fair Ophelia! Nymph, in thy orisons°
　　　Be all my sins rememb'red.
OPHELIA: 　　　　　　　　Good my lord, 　　　　　　90
　　　How does your honour for this many a day?

59*sea*　*the mixed metaphor of this speech has often been commented on; a later emendation siege has sometimes been spoken on the stage.*　67*shuffled*　*sloughed, cast.*　67*coil*　*usually means "turmoil"; here, possibly "body" (conceived of as wound about the soul like rope); clay, soil, veil, have been suggested as emendations.*　68*respect consideration.*　69*of . . . life*　*so long-lived.*　70*time*　*the world.*　72*despis'd*　*rejected.*　73*office office-holders.*　73*spurns*　*insults.*　75*quietus*　*acquittance; here, death.*　76*bare bodkin*　*mere dagger; bare is sometimes understood as "unsheathed."*　76*fardels*　*burdens.*　79*bourn*　*boundary.*　83*conscience probably, inhibition by the faculty of reason restraining the will from doing wrong.*　84*native hue*　*natural color; metaphor derived from the color of the face.*　85*sicklied o'er*　*given a sickly tinge.*　85*cast*　*shade of color.*　86*pitch*　*height (as of falcon's flight).*　86*moment*　*importance.*　87*regard*　*respect, consideration.*　87*currents*　*courses.*　89*orisons*　*prayers.*

HAMLET: I humbly thank you; well, well, well.

OPHELIA: My lord, I have remembrances of yours,
   That I have longed long to re-deliver;
   I pray you, now receive them.

HAMLET: No, not I;   95
   I never gave you aught.

OPHELIA: My honour'd lord, you know right well you did;
   And, with them, words of so sweet breath compos'd
   As made the things more rich: their perfume lost,
   Take these again; for to the noble mind   100
   Rich gifts wax poor when givers prove unkind.
   There, my lord.

HAMLET: Ha, ha! are you honest?°

OPHELIA: My lord?

HAMLET: Are you fair?   105

OPHELIA: What means your lordship?

HAMLET: That if you be honest and fair, your honesty° should admit no discourse
   to° your beauty.

OPHELIA: Could beauty, my lord, have better commerce° than with honesty?

HAMLET: Ay, truly; for the power of beauty will sooner transform honesty from   110
   what it is to a bawd than the force of honesty can translate beauty into his
   likeness: this was sometime a paradox, but now the time° gives it proof. I did
   love you once.

OPHELIA: Indeed, my lord, you made me believe so.

HAMLET: You should not have believed me; for virtue cannot so inoculate° our old   115
   stock but we shall relish of it:° I loved you not.

OPHELIA: I was the more deceived.

HAMLET: Get thee to a nunnery: why wouldst thou be a breeder of sinners? I am
   myself indifferent honest;° but yet I could accuse me of such things that it were
   better my mother had not borne me: I am very proud, revengeful, ambitious,   120
   with more offences at my beck° than I have thoughts to put them in,
   imagination to give them shape, or time to act them in. What should such
   fellows as I do crawling between earth and heaven? We are arrant knaves, all;
   believe none of us. Go thy ways to a nunnery. Where's your father?

OPHELIA: At home, my lord.   125

HAMLET: Let the doors be shut upon him, that he may play the fool no where but
   in 's own house. Farewell.

OPHELIA: O, help him, you sweet heavens!

HAMLET: If thou dost marry, I'll give thee this plague for thy dowry: be thou as
   chaste as ice, as pure as snow, thou shalt not escape calumny. Get thee to a   130

103–8**are you honest … beauty** *honest meaning "truthful" and "chaste" and fair meaning "just, honorable" (line 105) and "beautiful" (line 107) are not mere quibbles; the speech has the irony of a double entendre.*   107**your honesty** *your chastity.*   108**discourse to** *familiar intercourse with.*   109**commerce** *intercourse.* 112**the time** *the present age.*   115**inoculate** *graft (metaphorical).*   116**but … it** *i.e., that we do not still have about us a taste of the old stock, i.e., retain our sinfulness.*   119**indifferent honest** *moderately virtuous.* 121**beck** *command.*

nunnery, go: farewell. Or, if thou wilt needs marry, marry a fool; for wise men
know well enough what monsters° you make of them. To a nunnery, go, and
quickly too. Farewell.

OPHELIA: O heavenly powers, restore him! 135

HAMLET: I have heard of your° paintings too, well enough; God hath given you
one face, and you make yourselves another: you jig,° you amble, and you lisp;
you nick-name God's creatures, and make your wantonness your ignorance.°
Go to, I'll no more on 't; it hath made me mad. I say, we will have no more
marriage: those that are married already, all but one,° shall live; the rest shall 140
keep as they are. To a nunnery, go.   *Exit.*

OPHELIA: O, what a noble mind is here o'er-thrown!
  The courtier's, soldier's, scholar's, eye, tongue, sword;
  Th' expectancy and róse° of the fair state,
  The glass of fashion and the mould of form,° 145
  Th' observ'd of all observers,° quite, quite down!
  And I, of ladies most deject and wretched,
  That suck'd the honey of his music vows,
  Now see that noble and most sovereign reason,
  Like sweet bells jangled, out of time and harsh; 150
  That unmatch'd form and feature of blown° youth
  Blasted with ecstasy:° O, woe is me,
  T' have seen what I have seen, see what I see!

Enter KING *and* POLONIUS.

KING: Love! his affections do not that way tend;
  Nor what he spake, though it lack'd form a little, 155
  Was not like madness. There's something in his soul,
  O'er which his melancholy sits on brood;
  And I do doubt° the hatch and the disclose°
  Will be some danger: which for to prevent,
  I have in quick determination 160
  Thus set it down: he shall with speed to England,
  For the demand of our neglected tribute:
  Haply the seas and countries different
  With variable° objects shall expel
  This something-settled° matter in his heart, 165
  Whereon his brains still beating puts him thus
  From fashion of himself.° What think you on 't?

POLONIUS: It shall do well: but yet do I believe
  The origin and commencement of his grief

---

¹³³**monsters** *an allusion to the horns of a cuckold* ¹³⁶**your** *indefinite use.* ¹³⁷**jig** *move with jerky motion; probably allusion to the jig, or song and dance, of the current stage.* ¹³⁸⁻¹³⁹**make ... ignorance** *i.e., excuse your wantonness on the ground of your ignorance.* ¹⁴⁰**one** *i.e., the king.* ¹⁴⁴**expectancy and rose** *source of hope.* ¹⁴⁵**The glass ... form** *the mirror of fashion and the pattern of courtly behavior.* ¹⁴⁶**observ'd ... observers** *i.e., the center of attention in the court.* ¹⁵¹**blown** *blooming.* ¹⁵²**ecstasy** *madness.* ¹⁵⁸**doubt** *fear.* ¹⁵⁸**disclose** *disclosure or revelation (by chipping of the shell).* ¹⁶⁴**variable** *various.* ¹⁶⁵**something-settled** *somewhat settled.* ¹⁶⁷**From ... himself** *out of his natural manner.*

Sprung from neglected love. How now, Ophelia!   170
You need not tell us what Lord Hamlet said;
We heard it all. My lord, do as you please;
But, if you hold it fit, after the play
Let his queen mother all alone entreat him
To show his grief: let her be round° with him;   175
And I'll be plac'd, so please you, in the ear
Of all their conference. If she find him not,
To England send him, or confine him where
Your wisdom best shall think.
KING: It shall be so:
Madness in great ones must not unwatch'd go.   *Exeunt.*   180

Scene II [*A hall in the castle.*]

Enter HAMLET *and three of the* PLAYERS.

HAMLET: Speak the speech, I pray you, as I pronounced it to you, trippingly on the
tongue: but if you mouth it, as many of your° players do, I had as lief the town-
crier spoke my lines. Nor do not saw the air too much with your hand, thus,
but use all gently; for in the very torrent, tempest, and, as I may say, whirlwind
of your passion, you must acquire and beget a temperance that may give it   5
smoothness. O, it offends me to the soul to hear a robustious° periwig-pated°
fellow tear a passion to tatters, to very rags, to split the ears of the groundlings,°
who for the most part are capable of° nothing but inexplicable° dumb-shows
and noise: I would have such a fellow whipped for o'er-doing Termagant;° it
out-herods Herod:° pray you, avoid it.   10
FIRST PLAYER: I warrant your honour.
HAMLET: Be not too tame neither, but let your own discretion be your tutor: suit
the action to the word, the word to the action; with this special observance, that
you o'er-step not the modesty of nature: for any thing so overdone is from the
purpose of playing, whose end, both at the first and now, was and is, to hold, as 15
't were, the mirror up to nature; to show virtue her own feature, scorn her own
image, and the very age and body of the time his form and pressure.° Now this
overdone, or come tardy off,° though it make the unskilful laugh, cannot but
make the judicious grieve; the censure of the which one° must in your
allowance o'erweigh a whole theatre of others. O, there be players that I have   20
seen play, and heard others praise, and that highly, not to speak it profanely, that,
neither having the accent of Christians nor the gait of Christian, pagan, nor

---

¹⁷⁵*round* blunt.   **III.ii.** ²*your* indefinite use.   ⁶*robustious* violent, boisterous.   ⁶*periwig-pated*
⁷*groundlings* those who stood in the yard of the theater.   ⁸*capable of* susceptible of being influenced by.
⁸*inexplicable* of no significance worth explaining.   ⁹*Termagant* a god of the Saracens; a character in the St.
Nicholas play, where one of his worshipers, leaving him in charge of goods, returns to find them stolen; whereupon he
beats the god (or idol), which howls vociferously.   ¹⁰*Herod* Herod of Jewry; a character in The Slaughter of the
Innocents and other cycle plays. The part was played with great noise and fury.   ¹⁷*pressure* stamp, impressed character.   ¹⁸*come tardy off* inadequately done.   ¹⁹*the censure ... one* the judgment of even one of whom.

man, have so strutted and bellowed that I have thought some of nature's
journeymen° had made men and not made them well, they imitated humanity
so abominably.   25

FIRST PLAYER: I hope we have reformed that indifferently° with us, sir.

HAMLET: O, reform it altogether. And let those that play your clowns speak no
more than is set down for them; for there be of ° them that will themselves
laugh, to set on some quantity of barren° spectators to laugh too; though, in the
mean time, some necessary question of the play be then to be considered: that's   30
villanous, and shows a most pitiful ambition in the fool that uses it. Go, make
you ready.

[*Exeunt* PLAYERS.]

Enter POLONIUS, GUILDENSTERN, *and* ROSENCRANTZ.

How now, my lord! will the king hear this piece of work?   35

POLONIUS: And the queen too, and that presently.

HAMLET: Bid the players make haste.   [*Exit* POLONIUS.]

   Will you two help to hasten them?

ROSENCRANTZ: ⎫   *Exeunt they two.*
                   ⎬ We will, my lord.
GUILDENSTERN: ⎭

HAMLET: What ho! Horatio!

Enter HORATIO.

HORATIO: Here, sweet lord, at your service.   40

HAMLET: Horatio, thou art e'en as just° a man
   As e'er my conversation cop'd withal.

HORATIO: O, my dear lord,—

HAMLET: Nay, do not think I flatter;
   For what advancement may I hope from thee
   That no revenue hast but thy good spirits,   45
   To feed and clothe thee? Why should the poor be flatter'd?
   No, let the candied tongue lick absurd pomp,
   And crook the pregnant° hinges of the knee
   Where thrift° may follow fawning. Dost thou hear?
   Since my dear soul was mistress of her choice   50
   And could of men distinguish her election,
   S' hath seal'd thee for herself; for thou hast been
   As one, in suff'ring all, that suffers nothing,
   A man that fortune's buffets and rewards
   Hast ta'en with equal thanks: and blest are those   55
   Whose blood and judgement are so well commeddled,
   That they are not a pipe for fortune's finger
   To sound what stop° she please. Give me that man

---

²⁴**journeymen**   *laborers not yet masters in their trade.*   ²⁶**indifferently**   *fairly, tolerably.*   ²⁸**of**   *i.e., some*
among them.   ²⁹**barren**   *i.e., of wit.*   ⁴¹**just**   *honest, honorable.*   ⁴⁸**pregnant**   *pliant.*   ⁴⁹**thrift**
profit.   ⁵⁸**stop**   *hole in a wind instrument for controlling the sound.*

That is not passion's slave, and I will wear him
In my heart's core, ay, in my heart of heart,   60
As I do thee.—Something too much of this.—
There is a play to-night before the king;
One scene of it comes near the circumstance
Which I have told thee of my father's death:
I prithee, when thou seest that act afoot,   65
Even with the very comment of thy soul°
Observe my uncle: if his occulted° guilt
Do not itself unkennel in one speech,
It is a damned° ghost that we have seen,
And my imaginations are as foul   70
As Vulcan's stithy.° Give him heedful note;
For I mine eyes will rivet to his face,
And after we will both our judgements join
In censure of his seeming.°
HORATIO: Well, my lord:
    If 'a steal aught the whilst this play is playing,   75
    And 'scape detecting, I will pay the theft.

Enter trumpets and kettledrums, KING, QUEEN, POLONIUS, OPHELIA, [ROSENCRANTZ, GUILDENSTERN, *and* OTHERS].

HAMLET: They are coming to the play; I must be idle:° Get you a place.
KING: How fares our cousin Hamlet?
HAMLET: Excellent, i' faith; of the chameleon's dish:° I eat the air, promise-
    crammed: you cannot feed capons so.   80
KING: I have nothing with° this answer, Hamlet; these words are not mine.°
HAMLET: No, nor mine now. [*To* POLONIUS.] My lord, you played once i' the
    university, you say?
POLONIUS: That did I, my lord; and was accounted a good actor.
HAMLET: What did you enact?   85
POLONIUS: I did enact Julius Cæsar: I was killed i' the Capitol; Brutus killed me.
HAMLET: It was a brute part of him to kill so capital a calf there. Be the players
    ready?
ROSENCRANTZ: Ay, my lord; they stay upon your patience.
QUEEN: Come hither, my dear Hamlet, sit by me.   90
HAMLET: No, good mother, here's metal more attractive.
POLONIUS [*to the king*]: O, ho! do you mark that?
HAMLET: Lady, shall I lie in your lap?   [*Lying down at* OPHELIA'S *feet.*]
OPHELIA: No, my lord.
HAMLET: I mean, my head upon your lap?   95

---

[66]**very . . . soul** *inward and sagacious criticism.*   [67]**occulted** *hidden.*   [69]**damned** *in league with Satan.*   [71]**stithy** *smithy, place of stiths (anvils).*   [74]**censure . . . seeming** *judgment of his appearance or behavior.*   [77]**idle** *crazy, or not attending to anything serious.*   [79]**chameleon's dish** *chameleons were supposed to feed on air. (Hamlet deliberately misinterprets the king's "fares" as "feeds.")*   [81]**have . . . with** *make nothing of.*   [81]**are not mine** *do not respond to what I ask.*

OPHELIA: Ay, my lord.

HAMLET: Do you think I meant country° matters?

OPHELIA: I think nothing, my lord.

HAMLET: That's a fair thought to lie between maids' legs.　　　　　100

OPHELIA: What is, my lord?

HAMLET: Nothing.

OPHELIA: You are merry, my lord.

HAMLET: Who, I?

OPHELIA: Ay, my lord.　　　　　105

HAMLET: O God, your only° jig-maker.° What should a man do but be merry? for, look you, how cheerfully my mother looks, and my father died within's two hours.

OPHELIA: Nay, 'tis twice two months, my lord.

HAMLET: So long? Nay then, let the devil wear black, for I'll have a suit of sables.°　110 O heavens! die two months ago, and not forgotten yet? Then there's hope a great man's memory may outlive his life half a year: but, by 'r lady, 'a must build churches, then; or else shall 'a suffer not thinking on,° with the hobbyhorse, whose epitaph is "For, O, for, O, the hobbyhorse is forgot."°　　　115

The trumpets sound. Dumb show follows.

Enter a KING *and a* QUEEN [*very lovingly*]; *the* QUEEN *embracing him, and he her.* [*She kneels, and makes show of protestation unto him.*] *He takes her up, and declines his head upon her neck: he lies him down upon a bank of flowers: she, seeing him asleep, leaves him. Anon comes in another man, takes off his crown, kisses it, pours poison in the sleeper's ears, and leaves him. The* QUEEN *returns; finds the* KING *dead, makes passionate action. The* POISONER, *with some three or four come in again, seem to condole with her. The dead body is carried away. The* POISONER *woos the* QUEEN *with gifts: she seems harsh awhile, but in the end accepts love.* [*Exeunt.*]

OPHELIA: What means this, my lord?

HAMLET: Marry, this is miching mallecho;° it means mischief.

OPHELIA: Belike this show imports the argument of the play.

Enter PROLOGUE.

HAMLET: We shall know by this fellow: the players cannot keep counsel; they'll tell all.　　　　　120

OPHELIA: Will 'a tell us what this show meant?

HAMLET: Ay, or any show that you'll show him: be not you ashamed to show, he'll not shame to tell you what it means.

OPHELIA: You are naught, you are naught:° I'll mark the play.

PROLOGUE: For us, and for our tragedy,　　　　　125
　　Here stooping° to your clemency,
　　We beg your hearing patiently.　　　　　[*Exit.*]

---

⁹⁸**country** *with a bawdy pun.* 　¹⁰⁶**your only** *only your.*　¹⁰⁶**jig-maker** *composer of jigs (song and dance).*　¹¹⁰**suit of sables** *garments trimmed with the fur of the sable, with a quibble on sable meaning "black."*　¹¹⁴**suffer ... on** *undergo oblivion.*　¹¹⁵**"For ... forgot"** *verse of a song occurring also in Love's Labour's Lost, III.i.30; the hobbyhorse was a character in the Morris Dance.*　¹¹⁷**miching mallecho** *sneaking mischief.*　¹²⁴**naught** *indecent.*　¹²⁶**stooping** *bowing.*

HAMLET: Is this a prologue, or the posy° of a ring?
OPHELIA: 'Tis brief, my lord.
HAMLET: As woman's love.   130

Enter [two Players as] KING *and* QUEEN.

PLAYER KING: Full thirty times hath Phoebus' cart gone round
　　Neptune's salt wash° and Tellus'° orbed ground,
　　And thirty dozen moons with borrowed° sheen
　　About the world have times twelve thirties been,
　　Since love our hearts and Hymen° did our hands   135
　　Unite commutual° in most sacred bands.
PLAYER QUEEN: So many journeys may the sun and moon
　　Make us again count o'er ere love be done!
　　But, woe is me, you are so sick of late,
　　So far from cheer and from your former state,   140
　　That I distrust° you. Yet, though I distrust,
　　Discomfort you, my lord, it nothing must:
　　For women's fear and love holds quantity;°
　　In neither aught, or in extremity.
　　Now, what my love is, proof hath made you know;   145
　　And as my love is siz'd, my fear is so:
　　Where love is great, the littlest doubts are fear;
　　Where little fears grow great, great love grows there.
PLAYER KING: 'Faith, I must leave thee, love, and shortly too;
　　My operant° powers their functions leave° to do: 150
　　And thou shalt live in this fair world behind,
　　Honour'd, belov'd; and haply one as kind
　　For husband shalt thou—
PLAYER QUEEN:　　　　　　　　O, confound the rest!
　　Such love must needs be treason in my breast:
　　In second husband let me be accurst!   155
　　None wed the second but who kill'd the first.
HAMLET (*aside*): Wormwood, wormwood.
PLAYER QUEEN: The instances that second marriage move
　　Are base respects of thrift, but none of love:
　　A second time I kill my husband dead,   160
　　When second husband kisses me in bed.
PLAYER KING: I do believe you think what now you speak;
　　But what we do determine oft we break.
　　Purpose is but the slave to memory,
　　Of violent birth, but poor validity: 165
　　Which now, like fruit unripe, sticks on the tree;
　　But fall, unshaken, when they mellow be.

128**posy** *motto.*   132**salt wash** *the sea.*   132**Tellus** *goddess of the earth (orbed ground).*   133**bor-**
rowed *i.e., reflected.*   135**Hymen** *god of matrimony.*   136**commutual** *mutually.*   141**distrust** *an*
anxious about.   143**holds quantity** *keeps proportion between.*   150**operant** *active.*   150**leave** *cease.*

Most necessary 'tis that we forget
To pay ourselves what to ourselves is debt:
What to ourselves in passion we propose, 170
The passion ending, doth the purpose lose.
The violence of either grief or joy
Their own enactures° with themselves destroy:
Where joy most revels, grief doth most lament;
Grief joys, joy grieves, on slender accident. 175
This world is not for aye,° nor 'tis not strange
That even our loves should with our fortunes change;
For 'tis a question left us yet to prove,
Whether love lead fortune, or else fortune love.
The great man down, you mark his favourite flies; 180
The poor advanc'd makes friends of enemies.
And hitherto doth love on fortune tend;
For who° not needs shall never lack a friend,
And who in want a hollow friend doth try,
Directly seasons° him his enemy. 185
But, orderly to end where I begun,
Our wills and fates do so contrary run
That our devices still are overthrown;
Our thoughts are ours, their ends° none of our own:
So think thou wilt no second husband wed; 190
But die thy thoughts when thy first lord is dead.
PLAYER QUEEN: Nor earth to me give food, nor heaven light!
Sport and repose lock from me day and night!
To desperation turn my trust and hope!
An anchor's° cheer° in prison be my scope! 195
Each opposite° that blanks° the face of joy
Meet what I would have well and it destroy!
Both here and hence pursue me lasting strife,
If, once a widow, ever I be wife!
HAMLET: If she should break it now! 200
PLAYER KING: 'Tis deeply sworn. Sweet, leave me here awhile;
My spirits grow dull, and fain I would beguile
The tedious day with sleep.   [*Sleeps.*]
PLAYER QUEEN: Sleep rock thy brain;
And never come mischance between us twain!   *Exit.*
HAMLET: Madam, how like you this play? 205
QUEEN: The lady doth protest too much, methinks.
HAMLET: O, but she'll keep her word.
KING: Have you heard the argument? Is there no offence in 't?
HAMLET: No, no, they do but jest, poison in jest; no offence i' the world.

---

¹⁷³**enactures** *fulfillments.*   ¹⁷⁶**aye** *ever.*   ¹⁸³**who** *whoever.*   ¹⁸⁵**seasons** *matures,   ripens.*
¹⁸⁹**ends** *results.*   ¹⁹⁵**An anchor's** *an anchorite's.*   ¹⁹⁵**cheer** *fare; sometimes printed as* chair.
¹⁹⁶**opposite** *adverse thing.*   ¹⁹⁶**blanks** *causes to blanch or grow pale.*

KING: What do you call the play?   210

HAMLET: The Mouse-trap. Marry, how? Tropically.° This play is the image of a
murder done in Vienna: Gonzago° is the duke's name; his wife, Baptista: you
shall see anon; 't is a knavish piece of work: but what o' that? your majesty and
we that have free souls, it touches us not: let the galled jade° winch,° our
withers° are unwrung.°

Enter LUCIANUS.

This is one Lucianus, nephew to the king.

OPHELIA: You are as good as a chorus,° my lord.

HAMLET: I could interpret between you and your love, if I could see the puppets
dallying.°

OPHELIA: You are keen, my lord, you are keen.   220

HAMLET: It would cost you a groaning to take off my edge.

OPHELIA: Still better, and worse.°

HAMLET: So you mistake° your husbands. Begin, murderer; pox,° leave thy
damnable faces, and begin. Come: the croaking raven doth bellow for revenge.

LUCIANUS: Thoughts black, hands apt, drugs fit, and time agreeing;   225
Confederate° season, else no creature seeing;
Thou mixture rank, of midnight weeds collected,
With Hecate's° ban° thrice blasted, thrice infected,
Thy natural magic and dire property,   230
On wholesome life usurp immediately.

[*Pours the poison into the sleeper's ears.*]

HAMLET: 'A poisons him i' the garden for his estate. His name's Gonzago: the story
is extant, and written in very choice Italian: you shall see anon how the
murderer gets the love of Gonzago's wife.

OPHELIA: The king rises.   235

HAMLET: What, frighted with false fire!°

QUEEN: How fares my lord?

POLONIUS: Give o'er the play.

KING: Give me some light away!

POLONIUS: Lights, lights, lights!   *Exeunt all but* HAMLET *and* HORATIO.   240

HAMLET: Why, let the strucken deer go weep,
     The hart ungalled play;

211**Tropically** *figuratively,* tropically *suggests a pun on* trap *in* Mouse-trap *(1.211).*   212**Gonzago** *in
1538 Luigi Gonzago murdered the Duke of Urbano by pouring poisoned lotion in his ears.*   214**galled jade**
horse whose hide is rubbed by saddle or harness.   215**winch** *wince.*   215**withers** *the part between the horse's
shoulder blades.*   215**unwrung** *not wrung or twisted.*   217**chorus** *in many Elizabethan plays the action
was explained by an actor known as the "chorus"; at a puppet show the actor who explained the action was known as
an "interpreter," as indicated by the lines following.*   219–21**dallying** *with sexual suggestion, continued in* **keen**
(sexually aroused), **groaning** *(i.e., in pregnancy)), and* **edge** *(i.e., sexual desire or impetuosity).*   222**Still . . .
worse** *more keen, less decorous.*   223**mistake** *err in taking.*   223**pox** *an imprecation.*   227**Confederate** *conspiring (to assist the murderer).*   229**Hecate** *the goddess of witchcraft.*   229**ban** *curse.*
236**false fire** *fireworks, or a blank discharge.*   241–44**Why . . . away** *probably from an old ballad, with allusion to the popular belief that a wounded deer retires to weep and die. Cf.* As You Like It, *II,i.66.*

For some must watch, while some must sleep:
   Thus runs the world away.°
Would not this,° sir, and a forest of feathers°—if the rest of my fortunes turn
Turk with° me—with two Provincial roses° on my razed° shoes, get me a
fellowship in a cry° of players,° sir?

HORATIO: Half a share.°

HAMLET: A whole one, I.
   For thou dost know, O Damon dear,   250
     This realm dismantled° was
   Of Jove himself; and now reigns here
     A very, very°—pajock.°

HORATIO: You might have rhymed.

HAMLET: O good Horatio, I'll take the ghost's word for a thousand pound.   255
   Didst perceive?

HORATIO: Very well, my lord.

HAMLET: Upon the talk of the poisoning?

HORATIO: I did very well note him.

HAMLET: Ah, ha! Come, some music! come, the recorders!°   260
   For if the king like not the comedy,
   Why then, belike, he likes it not, perdy.°
   Come, some music!

        Enter ROSENCRANTZ *and* GUILDENSTERN.

GUILDENSTERN: Good my lord, vouchsafe me a word with you.

HAMLET: Sir, a whole history.   265

GUILDENSTERN: The king, sir,—

HAMLET: Ay, sir, what of him?

GUILDENSTERN: Is in his retirement marvellous distempered.

HAMLET: With drink, sir?

GUILDENSTERN: No, my lord, rather with choler.°   270

HAMLET: Your wisdom should show itself more richer to signify this to his doctor;
   for, for me to put him to his purgation would perhaps plunge him into far
   more choler.

GUILDENSTERN: Good my lord, put your discourse into some frame° and start not
   so wildly from my affair.   275

HAMLET: I am tame, sir: pronounce.

GUILDENSTERN: The queen, your mother, in most great affliction of spirit, hath
   sent me to you.

---

²⁴⁵*this* i.e., the play.   ²⁴⁵*feathers* allusion to the plumes which Elizabethan actors were fond of wearing.
²⁴⁶*turn Turk with* go back on.   ²⁴⁶*two Provincial roses* rosettes of ribbon like the roses of Provins near Paris,
or else the roses of Provence.   ²⁴⁶*razed* cut, slashed (by way of ornament).   ²⁴⁷*cry* pack (as of hounds).
²⁴⁷*fellowship . . . players* partnership in a theatrical company.   ²⁴⁸*Half a share* allusion to the custom in
dramatic companies of dividing the ownership into a number of shares among the householders.   ²⁵¹*dismantled*
stripped, divested.   ²⁵⁰⁻⁵³*For . . . very* probably from an old ballad having to do with Damon and Pythias.
²⁵³*pajock* peacock (a bird with a bad reputation). Possibly the word was patchock, diminutive of patch, clown.
²⁶⁰*recorders* wind instruments of the flute kind.   ²⁶²*perdy* corruption of par dieu.   ²⁷⁰*choler* bilious disorder, with quibble on the sense "anger."   ²⁷⁴*frame* order.

HAMLET: You are welcome.

GUILDENSTERN: Nay, good my lord, this courtesy is not of the right breed. If it 280
shall please you to make me a wholesome° answer, I will do your mother's
commandment; if not, your pardon and my return shall be the end of my
business.

HAMLET: Sir, I cannot.

GUILDENSTERN: What, my lord? 285

HAMLET: Make you a wholesome answer; my wit's diseased: but, sir, such answer as
I can make, you shall command; or, rather, as you say, my mother: therefore no
more, but to the matter:° my mother, you say,—

ROSENCRANTZ: Then thus she says; your behaviour hath struck her into
amazement and admiration. 290

HAMLET: O wonderful son, that can so 'stonish a mother! But is there no sequel at
the heels of this mother's admiration? Impart.

ROSENCRANTZ: She desires to speak with you in her closet, ere you go to bed.

HAMLET: We shall obey, were she ten times our mother. Have you any further
trade with us? 295

ROSENCRANTZ: My lord, you once did love me.

HAMLET: And do still, by these pickers and stealers.°

ROSENCRANTZ: Good my lord, what is your cause of distemper? you do, surely, bar
the door upon your own liberty, if you deny your griefs to your friend.

HAMLET: Sir, I lack advancement. 300

ROSENCRANTZ: How can that be, when you have the voice° of the king himself
for your succession in Denmark?

HAMLET: Ay, sir, but "While the grass grows,"°—the proverb is something musty.

Enter the PLAYERS *with recorders.*

O, the recorders! let me see one. To withdraw° with you:—why do you go 305
about to recover the wind° of me, as if you would drive me into a toil?°

GUILDENSTERN: O, my lord, if my duty be too bold, my love is too unmannerly.°

HAMLET: I do not well understand that. Will you play upon this pipe?

GUILDENSTERN: My lord, I cannot.

HAMLET: I pray you. 310

GUILDENSTERN: Believe me, I cannot.

HAMLET: I beseech you.

GUILDENSTERN: I know no touch of it, my lord.

HAMLET: 'Tis as easy as lying: govern these ventages° with your fingers and thumb,
give it breath with your mouth, and it will discourse most eloquent music. 315
Look you, these are the stops.

GUILDENSTERN: But these cannot I command to any utterance of harmony; I have
not the skill.

281**wholesome** *sensible.*   288**matter** *matter in hand.*   297**pickers and stealers** *hands, so called from the catechism "to keep my hands from picking and stealing."*   301**voice** *support.*   303**While ... grows"** *the rest of the proverb is "the silly horse starves." Hamlet may be destroyed while he is waiting for the succession to the kingdom.*   305**withdraw** *speak in private.*   306**recover the wind** *get to the windward side.*   306**toil** snare.   307**if ... unmannerly** *if I am using an unmannerly boldness, it is my love which occasions it.* 314**ventages** *stops of the recorders.*

HAMLET: Why, look you now, how unworthy a thing you make of me! You would
play upon me; you would seem to know my stops; you would pluck out the
heart of my mystery; you would sound me from my lowest note to the top of
my compass:° and there is much music, excellent voice, in this little organ;° yet
cannot you make it speak. 'Sblood, do you think I am easier to be played on
than a pipe? Call me what instrument you will, though you can fret° me, you
cannot play upon me.

Enter POLONIUS.

God bless you, sir!

POLONIUS: My lord, the queen would speak with you, and presently.   330
HAMLET: Do you see yonder cloud that 's almost in shape of a camel?
POLONIUS: By the mass, and 'tis like a camel, indeed.
HAMLET: Methinks it is like a weasel.
POLONIUS: It is backed like a weasel.
HAMLET: Or like a whale?   335
POLONIUS: Very like a whale.
HAMLET: Then I will come to my mother by and by. [*Aside.*] They fool me to the
    top of my bent.°—I will come by and by.°
POLONIUS: I will say so.   [*Exit.*]
HAMLET: By and by is easily said.   340
    Leave me, friends.   [*Exeunt all but* HAMLET.]
    'Tis now the very witching time° of night,
    When churchyards yawn and hell itself breathes out
    Contagion to this world: now could I drink hot blood,
    And do such bitter business as the day   345
    Would quake to look on. Soft! now to my mother.
    O heart, lose not thy nature; let not ever
    The soul of Nero° enter this firm bosom:
    Let me be cruel, not unnatural:
    I will speak daggers to her, but use none;   350
    My tongue and soul in this be hypocrites;
    How in my words somever she be shent,°
    To give them seals° never, my soul, consent!   *Exit.*

Scene III [*A room in the castle.*]

Enter KING, ROSENCRANTZ, *and* GUILDENSTERN.

KING: I like him not, nor stands it safe with us
    To let his madness range. Therefore prepare you;

---

³²²*compass* *range of voice.*   ³²²*organ* *musical instrument, i.e., the pipe.*   ³²⁴*fret* *quibble on meaning*
"irritate" and the piece of wood, gut, or metal which regulates the fingering. ³³⁵*top of my bent* *limit of en-*
durance, i.e., extent to which a bow may be bent. ³³⁵*by and by* *immediately.* ³³⁹*witching time* *i.e.,*
time when spells are cast. ³⁴⁵*Nero* *murderer of his mother, Agrippina.* ³⁴⁹*shent* *rebuked.* ³⁵⁰*give*
them seals *confirm with deeds.*

I your commission will forthwith dispatch,°
And he to England shall along with you:
The terms° of our estate° may not endure   5
Hazard so near us as doth hourly grow
Out of his brows.°

GUILDENSTERN: We will ourselves provide:
Most holy and religious fear it is
To keep those many many bodies safe
That live and feed upon your majesty.   10

ROSENCRANTZ: The single and peculiar° life is bound,
With all the strength and armour of the mind,
To keep itself from noyance;° but much more
That spirit upon whose weal depend and rest
The lives of many. The cess° of majesty   15
Dies not alone; but, like a gulf,° doth draw
What's near it with it: it is a massy wheel,
Fix'd on the summit of the highest mount,
To whose huge spokes ten thousand lesser things
Are mortis'd and adjoin'd; which, when it falls,   20
Each small annexment, petty consequence,
Attends° the boist'rous ruin. Never alone
Did the king sigh, but with a general groan.

KING: Arm° you, I pray you, to this speedy voyage;
For we will fetters put about this fear,   25
Which now goes too free-footed.

ROSENCRANTZ: We will haste us.

Exeunt GENTLEMEN [ROSENCRANTZ *and* GUILDENSTERN].

Enter POLONIUS.

POLONIUS: My lord, he's going to his mother's closet:
Behind the arras° I'll convey° myself,
To hear the process;° I'll warrant she'll tax him home:°
And, as you said, and wisely was it said,   30
'Tis meet that some more audience than a mother,
Since nature makes them partial, should o'erhear
The speech, of vantage.° Fare you well, my liege:
I'll call upon you ere you go to bed,
And tell you what I know.

KING: Thanks, dear my lord.   *Exit* [POLONIUS]. 35

III.iii. ³*dispatch* prepare.   ⁵*terms* condition, circumstances.   ⁵*estate* state.   ⁷*brows* effronteries.
¹¹*single and peculiar* individual and private.   ¹³*noyance* harm.   ¹⁵*cess* decease.   ¹⁶*gulf*
whirlpool.   ²²*Attends* participates in.   ²⁴*Arm* prepare.   ²⁸*arras* screen of tapestry placed around
the walls of household apartments.   ²⁸*convey* implication of secrecy; convey was often used to mean "steal."
²⁹*process* proceedings.   ²⁹*tax him home* reprove him severely.   ³³*of vantage* from an advantageous
place.

O, my offence is rank, it smells to heaven;
It hath the primal eldest curse° upon't,
A brother's murder. Pray can I not,
Though inclination be as sharp as will:°
My stronger guilt defeats my strong intent;   40
And, like a man to double business bound,
I stand in pause where I shall first begin,
And both neglect. What if this cursed hand
Were thicker than itself with brother's blood,
Is there not rain enough in the sweet heavens   45
To wash it white as snow? Whereto serves mercy
But to confront° the visage of offence?
And what's in prayer but this two-fold force,
To be forestalled° ere we come to fall,
Or pardon'd being down? Then I'll look up;   50
My fault is past. But, O, what form of prayer
Can serve my turn? "Forgive me my foul murder"?
That cannot be: since I am still possess'd
Of those effects for which I did the murder,
My crown, mine own ambition° and my queen.   55
May one be pardon'd and retain th' offence?°
In the corrupted currents° of this world
Offence's gilded hand° may shove by justice,
And oft 'tis seen the wicked prize° itself
Buys out the law: but 'tis not so above;   60
There is no shuffling,° there the action lies°
In his true nature; and we ourselves compell'd,
Even to the teeth and forehead° of our faults,
To give in evidence. What then? what rests?°
Try what repentance can: what can it not?   65
Yet what can it when one can not repent?
O wretched state! O bosom black as death!
O limed° soul, that, struggling to be free,
Art more engag'd!° Help, angels! Make assay!°
Bow, stubborn knees; and, heart with strings of steel,   70
Be soft as sinews of the new-born babe!
All may be well.   [He kneels.]

Enter HAMLET.

HAMLET: Now might I do it pat,° now he is praying;
    And now I'll do't. And so 'a goes to heaven;

---

³⁷**primal eldest curse**   *the curse of Cain, the first to kill his brother.*   ³⁹**sharp as will**   *i.e., his desire is as strong as his determination.*   ⁴⁷**confront**   *oppose directly.*   ⁴⁹**forestalled**   *prevented.*   ⁵⁵**ambition**   *i.e., realization of ambition.*   ⁵⁶**offence**   *benefit accruing from offense.*   ⁵⁷**currents**   *courses.*   ⁵⁸**gilded hand** *hand offering gold as a bribe.*   ⁵⁹**wicked prize**   *prize won by wickedness.*   ⁶¹**shuffling**   *escape by trickery.* ⁶¹**lies**   *is sustainable.*   ⁶³**teeth and forehead**   *very face.*   ⁶⁴**rests**   *remains.*   ⁶⁸**limed**   *caught as with birdlime.*   ⁶⁹**engag'd**   *embedded.*   ⁶⁹**assay**   *trial.*   ⁷³**pat**   *opportunely.*

And so am I reveng'd. That would be scann'd:°   75
A villain kills my father; and for that,
I, his sole son, do this same villain send
To heaven.
Why, this is hire and salary, not revenge.
'A took my father grossly, full of bread;°   80
With all his crimes broad blown,° as flush° as May;
And how his audit stands who knows save heaven?
But in our circumstance and course° of thought,
'Tis heavy with him: and am I then reveng'd,
To take him in the purging of his soul,   85
When he is fit and season'd for his passage?°
No!
Up, sword; and know thou a more horrid hent:°
When he is drunk asleep,° or in his rage,
Or in th' incestuous pleasure of his bed;   90
At game, a-swearing, or about some act
That has no relish of salvation in't;
Then trip him, that his heels may kick at heaven,
And that his soul may be as damn'd and black
As hell, whereto it goes. My mother stays: 95
This physic° but prolongs thy sickly days.   *Exit.*
KING [*Rising*]: My words fly up, my thoughts remain below:
     Words without thoughts never to heaven go.   *Exit.*

Scene IV [*The Queen's closet.*]

Enter [QUEEN] GERTRUDE *and* POLONIUS.

POLONIUS: 'A will come straight. Look you lay° home to him:
     Tell him his pranks have been too broad° to bear with,
     And that your grace hath screen'd and stood between
     Much heat° and him. I'll sconce° me even here.
     Pray you, be round° with him.   5
HAMLET (*within*): Mother, mother, mother!
QUEEN: I'll warrant you,
     Fear me not: withdraw, I hear him coming.

                                   [POLONIUS *hides behind the arras.*]

Enter HAMLET.

HAMLET: Now, mother, what's the matter?

75**would be scann'd**   needs to be looked into.   80**full of bread**   enjoying his worldly pleasures (see Ezekiel
16:49).   81**broad blown**   in full bloom.   81**flush**   lusty.   83**in ... course**   as we see it in our mortal situation.   86**fit ... passage**   i.e., reconciled to heaven by forgiveness of his sins.   88**hent**   seizing; or
more probably, occasion of seizure.   89**drunk asleep**   in a drunken sleep.   96**physic**   purging (by prayer).
III.iv. 1**lay**   thrust.   2**broad**   unrestrained.   4**Much heat**   i.e., the king's anger.   4**sconce**   hide.
5**round**   blunt.

QUEEN: Hamlet, thou hast thy father much offended.

HAMLET: Mother, you have my father° much offended.   10

QUEEN: Come, come, you answer with an idle tongue.

HAMLET: Go, go, you question with a wicked tongue.

QUEEN: Why, how now, Hamlet!

HAMLET: What's the matter now?

QUEEN: Have you forgot me?

HAMLET: No, by the rood,° not so:

  You are the queen, your husband's brother's wife;   15

  And—would it were not so!—you are my mother.

QUEEN: Nay, then, I'll set those to you that can speak.

HAMLET: Come, come, and sit you down; you shall not budge;

  You go not till I set you up a glass

  Where you may see the inmost part of you.   20

QUEEN: What wilt thou do? thou wilt not murder me?

  Help, help, ho!

POLONIUS [*behind*]: What, ho! help, help; help!

HAMLET [*drawing*]: How now! a rat? Dead, for a ducat, dead!

                                        [*Makes a pass through the arras.*]

POLONIUS [*behind*]: O, I am slain!   [*Falls and dies.*] 25

QUEEN: O me, what hast thou done?

HAMLET: Nay, I know not:

  Is it the king?

QUEEN: O, what a rash and bloody deed is this!

HAMLET: A bloody deed! almost as bad, good mother,

  As kill a king, and marry with his brother.   30

QUEEN: As kill a king!

HAMLET: Ay, lady, it was my word.

                [*Lifts up the arras and discovers* POLONIUS.]

  Thou wretched, rash, intruding fool, farewell!

  I took thee for thy better: take thy fortune;

  Thou find'st to be too busy is some danger.

  Leave wringing of your hands: peace! sit you down,   35

  And let me wring your heart; for so I shall,

  If it be made of penetrable stuff,

  If damned custom have not braz'd° it so

  That it be proof and bulwark against sense.

QUEEN: What have I done, that thou dar'st wag thy tongue   40

  In noise so rude against me?

HAMLET: Such an act

  That blurs the grace and blush of modesty,

  Calls virtue hypocrite, takes off the rose

  From the fair forehead of an innocent love

  And sets a blister° there, makes marriage-vows   45

9–10**thy father . . . my father** *i.e., Claudius, the elder Hamlet.*   14**rood** *cross.*   38**braz'd** *brazened,* hardened.   45**sets a blister** *brands as a harlot.*

As false as dicers' oaths: O, such a deed
As from the body of contraction° plucks
The very soul, and sweet religion° makes
A rhapsody° of words: heaven's face does glow
O'er this solidity and compound mass   50
With heated visage, as against the doom
Is thought-sick at the act.°

QUEEN: Ay me, what act,
That roars so loud, and thunders in the index?°

HAMLET: Look here, upon this picture, and on this.
The counterfeit presentment° of two brothers.   55
See, what a grace was seated on this brow;
Hyperion's° curls; the front° of Jove himself;
An eye Mars, to threaten and command;
A station° like the herald Mercury
New-lightned on a heaven-kissing hill;   60
A combination and form indeed,
Where every god did seem to set his seal,
To give the world assurance° of a man:
This was your husband. Look you now, what follows: 65
Here is your husband; like a mildew'd ear,°
Blasting his wholesome brother. Have you eyes?
Could you on this fair mountain leave to feed,
And batten° on this moor?° Ha! have you eyes?
You cannot call it love; for at your age
The hey-day° in the blood is tame, it's humble,   70
And waits upon the judgement: and what judgement
Would step from this to this? Sense, sure, you have,
Else could you not have motion,° but sure, that sense
Is apoplex'd° for madness would not err.
Nor sense to ecstasy was ne'er so thrall'd°   75
But it reserv'd some quality of choice,°
To serve in such a difference. What devil was't
Tha thus hath cozen'd° you ar hoodman-blind?°
Eyes without feeling, feeling without sight,
Ears without hands or eyes, smelling sans° all,   80

47**contraction** the marriage contract.   48**religion** religious vows.   49**rhapsody** senseless string.
49–52**heaven's . . . act** heaven's face blushes to look down upon this world, compounded of the four elements,
with hot face as though the day of doom were near, and thought-sick at the deed (i.e., Gertrude's marriage).
53**index** prelude or preface.   55**counterfeit presentment** portrayed representation.   57**Hyperion's**
the sun god's.   57**front** brow.   59**station** manner of standing.   63**assurance** pledge, guarantee.
65**mildew'd ear** see Genesis 41:5–7 .68**batten** grow fat.   68**moor** barren upland.   70**hey-day**
state of excitement.   72–73**Sense . . . motion** sense and motion are functions of the middle or sensible soul,
the possession of sense being the basis of motion.   74**apoplex'd** paralyzed; mental derangement was thus of
three sorts: apoplexy, ecstasy, and diabolic possession.   75**thrall'd** enslaved.   76**quantity of choice** fragment of the power to choose.   78**cozen'd** tricked, cheated.   78**hoodman-blind** blindman's buff.
80**sans** without.

Or but a sickly part of one true sense
Could not so mope.°
O shame! where is thy blush? Rebellious hell,
If thou canst mutine° in a matron's bones,
To flaming youth let virtue be as wax,   85
And melt in her own fire: proclaim no shame
When the compulsive ardour gives the charge,°
Since frost itself as actively doth burn
And reason panders will°

QUEEN: O Hamlet, speak no more:
Thou turn'st mine eyes into my very soul;   90
And there I see such black and grained° spots
As will not leave their tinct.

HAMLET: Nay, but to live
In the rank sweat of an enseamed° bed,
Stew'd in corruption, honeying and making love
Over the nasty sty,—

QUEEN: O, speak to me no more;   95
These words, like daggers, enter in mine ears;
No more, sweet Hamlet!

HAMLET: A murderer and a villain;
A slave that is not twentieth part the tithe
Of your precedent lord;° a vice of kings;°
A cutpurse of the empire and the rule,   100
That from a shelf the precious diadem stole,
And put it in his pocket!

QUEEN: No more!

Enter GHOST.

HAMLET: A king of shreds and patches,°—
Save me, and hover o'er me with your wings,
You heavenly guards! What would your gracious figure?   105

QUEEN: Alas, he's mad!

HAMLET: Do you not come your tardy son to chide,
That, laps'd in time and passion,° lets go by
Th' important° acting of your dread command?
O, say!   110

GHOST: Do not forget: this visitation
Is but to whet thy almost blunted purpose.

---

⁸²**mope**   *be in a depressed, spiritless state, act aimlessly.*   ⁸⁴**mutine**   *mutiny, rebel.*   ⁸⁷**gives the charge** *delivers the attack.*   ⁸⁹**reason pandars will**   *the normal and proper situation was one in which reason guided the will in the direction of good; here, reason is perverted and leads in the direction of evil.*   ⁹¹**grained**   *dyed in grain.*   ⁹³**enseamed**   *loaded with grease, greased.*   ⁹⁹**precedent lord**   *i.e., the elder Hamlet.*   ⁹⁹**vice of kings**   *buffoon of kings; a referenced to the Vice, or clown, of the morality plays and interludes.*   ¹⁰³**shreds and patches**   *i.e., motley, the traditional costume of the Vice.*   ¹⁰⁸**laps'd ... passion**   *having suffered time to slip and passion to cool; also explained as "engrossed in casual events and lapsed into mere fruitless passion, so that he no longer entertains a rational purpose."*   ¹⁰⁹**important**   *urgent.*

But, look, amazement° on thy mother sits:
O, step between her and her fighting soul:
Conceit in weakest bodies strongest works: 115
Speak to her, Hamlet.
HAMLET: How is it with you, lady?
QUEEN: Alas, how is 't with you,
That you do bend your eye on vacancy
And with th' incorporal° air do hold discourse?
Forth at your eyes your spirits wildly peep;   120
And, as the sleeping soldiers in th' alarm,
Your bedded° hair, like life in excrements,°
Start up, and stand an° end. O gentle son,
Upon the heat and flame of thy distemper
Sprinkle cool patience. Whereon do you look?   125
HAMLET: On him, on him! Look you, how pale he glares!
His form and cause conjoin'd,° preaching to stones,
Would make them capable.—Do not look upon me;
Lest with this piteous action you convert
My stern effects:° then what I have to do   130
Will want true colour;° tears perchance for blood.
QUEEN: To whom do you speak this?
HAMLET: Do you see nothing there?
QUEEN: Nothing at all; yet all that is I see.
HAMLET: Nor did you nothing hear?
QUEEN: No, nothing but ourselves.
HAMLET: Why, look you there! look, how it steals away!   135
My father, in his habit as he liv'd!
Look, where he goes, even now, out at the portal!   *Exit* GHOST.
QUEEN: This is the very coinage of your brain:
This bodiless creation ecstasy
Is very cunning in.
HAMLET: Ecstasy!   140
My pulse, as yours, doth temperately keep time,
And makes as healthful music: it is not madness
That I have utt'red: bring me to the test,
And I the matter will re-word,° which madness
Would gambol° from. Mother, for love of grace,   145
Lay not that flattering unction° to your soul,
That not your trespass, but my madness speaks:
It will but skin and film the ulcerous place,

113*amazement* *frenzy, distraction.*   119*incorporal* *immaterial.*   122*bedded* *laid in smooth layers.*
122*excrements*   *the hair was considered an excrement or voided part of the body.*   123*an* *on.*   127*con-*
join'd *united.*   129–30*convert ... effects* *divert me from my stern duty. For effects, possibly affects (affec-*
tions of the mind).   131*want true colour* *lack good reason so that (with a play on the normal sense of*
colour) I shall shed tears instead of blood.   144*re-word* *repeat in words.*   145*gambol* *skip away.*
146*unction* *ointment used medicinally or as a rite; suggestion that forgiveness for sin may not be so easily achieved.*

Whiles rank corruption, mining° all within,
Infects unseen. Confess yourself to heaven;   150
Repent what's past; avoid what is to come;°
And do not spread the compost° on the weeds,
To make them ranker. Forgive me this my virtue;°
For in the fatness° of these pursy° times
Virtue itself of vice must pardon beg,   155
Yea, curb° and woo for leave to do him good.

QUEEN: O Hamlet, thou hast cleft my heart in twain.

HAMLET: O, throw away the worser part of it,
And live the purer with the other half.
Good night: but go not to my uncle's bed;   160
Assume a virtue, if you have it not.
That monster, custom, who all sense doth eat,
Of habits devil, is angel yet in this,
That to the use of actions fair and good
He likewise gives a frock or livery,   165
That aptly is put on. Refrain to-night,
And that shall lend a kind of easiness
To the next abstinence: the next more easy;
For use almost can change the stamp of nature,
And either ... the devil, or throw him out°   170
With wondrous potency. Once more, good night:
And when you are desirous to be bless'd,°
I'll blessing beg of you. For this same lord,   [*Pointing to* POLONIUS.]
I do repent: but heaven hath pleas'd it so,
To punish me with this and this with me,   175
That I must be their scourge and minister.
I will bestow him, and will answer well
The death I gave him. So, again, good night.
I must be cruel, only to be kind:
Thus bad begins and worse remains behind.   180
One word more, good lady.

QUEEN: What shall I do?

HAMLET: Not this, by no means, that I bid you do:
Let the bloat° king tempt you again to bed;
Pinch wanton on your cheek; call you his mouse;
And let him, for a pair of reechy° kisses,   185
Or paddling in your neck with his damn'd fingers,
Make you to ravel all this matter out,
That I essentially° am not in madness,
But mad in craft. 'Twere good you let him know;

---

¹⁴⁹**mining** *working under the surface.*   ¹⁵¹**what is to come** *i.e., the sins of the future.*   ¹⁵²**compost**
manure.   ¹⁵³**this my virtue** *my virtuous talk in reproving you.*   ¹⁵⁴**fatness** *grossness.*   ¹⁵⁴**pursy**
short-winded, corpulent.   ¹⁵⁶**curb** *bow, bend the knee.*   ¹⁷⁰*defective line usually emended by inserting mas-*
ter after either.   ¹⁷²**be bless'd** *become blessed, i.e., repentant.*   ¹⁸³**bloat** *bloated.*   ¹⁸⁵**reechy** *dirty,*
filthy   ¹⁸⁸**essentially** *in my essential nature.*

For who, that's but a queen, fair, sober, wise,   190
Would from a paddock,° from a bat, a gib,°
Such dear concernings° hide? who would do so?
No, in despite of sense and secrecy,
Unpeg the basket on the house's top,
Let the birds fly, and, like the famous ape,°   195
To try conclusions,° in the basket creep,
And break your own neck down.
QUEEN: Be thou assur'd, if words be made of breath,
  And breath of life, I have no life to breathe
  What thou hast said to me.   200
HAMLET: I must to England; you know that?
QUEEN: Alack,
  I had forgot: 'tis so concluded on.
HAMLET: There's letters seal'd: and my two schoolfellows,
  Whom I will trust as I will adders fang'd,
  They bear the mandate; they must sweep my way,°   205
  And marshal me to knavery. Let it work;
  For 'tis the sport to have the enginer°
  Hoist° with his own petar:° and 't shall go hard
  But I will delve one yard below their mines,
  And blow them at the moon: O, 'tis most sweet,   210
  When in one line two crafts° directly meet.
  This man shall set me packing:°
  I'll lug the guts into the neighbour room.
  Mother, good night. Indeed this counsellor
  Is now most still, most secret and most grave,   215
  Who was in life a foolish prating knave.
  Come, sir, to draw° toward an end with you.
  Good night, mother.

                    Exeunt [severally; HAMLET *dragging in* POLONIUS.]

191**paddock** *toad.*   191**gib** *tomcat.*   192**dear concernings** *important affairs.*   195**the famous ape**
a letter from Sir John Suckling seems to supply other details of the story, otherwise not identified: "It is the story of the
jackanapes and the partridges; thou starest after a beauty till it be lost to thee, then let'st out another, and starest after
that till it is gone too."   196**conclusions** *experiments.*   205**sweep my way** *clear my path.*   207**en-**
giner *constructor of military works, or possibly, artilleryman.*   208**Hoist** *blown up.*   208**petar** *defined*
as a small enginer of war used to blow in a door or make a breach, and as a case filled with explosive materials.
211**two crafts** *two acts of guile, with quibble on the sense of "two ships."*   212**set me packing** *set me to mak-*
ing schemes, and set me to lugging (him), and, also, send me off in a hurry.   217**draw** *come, with quibble on lit-*
eral sense.

ACT IV

Scene I [A room in the castle.]

Enter KING *and* QUEEN, *with* ROSENCRANTZ *and* GUILDENSTERN.

KING: There's matter in these sighs, these profound heaves:
You must translate: 'tis fit we understand them.
Where is your son?
QUEEN: Bestow this place on us a little while.

[*Exeunt* ROSENCRANTZ *and* GUILDENSTERN.]

Ah, mine own lord, what have I seen to-night!   5
KING: What, Gertrude? How does Hamlet?
QUEEN: Mad as the sea and wind, when both contend
Which is the mightier: in his lawless fit,
Behind the arras hearing something stir,
Whips out his rapier, cries, "A rat, a rat!"   10
And, in this brainish° apprehension,° kills
The unseen good old man.
KING: O heavy deed!
It had been so with us, had we been there:
His liberty is full of threats to all;
To you yourself, to us, to every one.   15
Alas, how shall this bloody deed be answer'd?
It will be laid to us, whose providence°
Should have kept short,° restrain'd and out of haunt,°
This mad young man: but so much was our love,
We would not understand what was most fit;   20
But, like the owner of a foul disease,
To keep it from divulging,° let it feed
Even on the pith of life. Where is he gone?
QUEEN: To draw apart the body he hath kill'd:
O'er whom his very madness, like some ore   25
Among a mineral° of metals base,
Shows itself pure; 'a weeps for what is done.
KING: O Gertrude, come away!
The sun no sooner shall the mountains touch,
But we will ship him hence: and this vile deed   30
We must, with all our majesty and skill,
Both countenance and excuse. Ho, Guildenstern!

Enter ROSENCRANTZ *and* GUILDENSTERN.

Friends both, go join you with some further aid:

IV.i. ¹¹**brainish** *headstrong, passionate.* ¹¹**apprehension** *conception, imagination.* ¹⁷**providence**
foresight. ¹⁸**short** *i.e., on a short tether.* ¹⁸**out of haunt** *secluded.* ²²**divulging** *becoming evident.*
²⁶**mineral** *mine.*

Hamlet in madness hath Polonius slain,
And from his mother's closet hath he dragg'd him: 35
Go seek him out; speak fair, and bring the body
Into the chapel. I pray you, haste in this.

                    [*Exeunt* ROSENCRANTZ *and* GUILDENSTERN.]

Come, Gertrude, we'll call up our wisest friends;
And let them know, both what we mean to do,
And what's untimely done . . .°   40
Whose whisper o'er the world's diameter,°
As level° as the cannon to his blank,°
Transports his pois'ned shot, may miss our name,
And hit the woundless° air. O, come away!
My soul is full of discord and dismay.   *Exeunt.* 45

Scene II [*Another room in the castle.*]

                    Enter HAMLET.

HAMLET: Safely stowed.
ROSENCRANTZ:
GUILDENSTERN: }   (*WITHIN*) Hamlet! Lord Hamlet!
HAMLET: But soft, what noise? Who calls on Hamlet? O, here they come.

           Enter ROSENCRANTZ *and* GUILDENSTERN.

ROSENCRANTZ: What have you done, my lord, with the dead body?
HAMLET: Compounded it with dust, whereto 'tis kin.
ROSENCRANTZ: Tell us where 'tis, that we may take it thence   5
    And bear it to the chapel.
HAMLET: Do not believe it.
ROSENCRANTZ: Believe what?
HAMLET: That I can keep your counsel° and not mine own. Besides, to be de-
    manded of a sponge! What replication° should be made by the son of a king?   10
ROSENCRANTZ: Take you me for a sponge, my lord?
HAMLET: Ay, sir, that soaks up the king's countenance, his rewards, his authorities.°
    But such officers do the king best service in the end: he keeps them, like an ape
    an apple, in the corner of his jaw; first mouthed, to be last swallowed: when he
    needs what you have gleaned, it is but squeezing you, and, sponge, you shall be
    dry again.   15
ROSENCRANTZ: I understand you not, my lord.
HAMLET: I am glad of it: a knavish speech sleeps in a foolish ear.
ROSENCRANTZ: My lord, you must tell us where the body is, and go with us to the
    king.

---

⁴⁰*defective line; some editors add:* so haply, slander; *others add:* for, haply, slander; *other conjectures.*   ⁴¹**diameter** *extent from side to side.*   ⁴²**level** *straight.*   ⁴²**blank** *white spot in the center of a target.*
⁴⁴**woundless** *invulnerable.*   **IV.ii.** ⁹**keep your counsel** *Hamlet is aware of their treachery but says nothing
about it.*   ¹⁰**replication** *reply.*   ¹²**authorities** *authoritative backing.*

HAMLET: The body is with the king, but the king is not with the body.° The king   20
    is a thing—
GUILDENSTERN: A thing, my lord!
HAMLET: Of nothing: bring me to him. Hide fox, and all after.°   *Exeunt*

Scene III [Another room in the castle.]

Enter KING, *and two or three.*

KING: I have sent to seek him, and to find the body.
    How dangerous is it that this man goes loose!
    Yet must not we put the strong law on him:
    He's lov'd of the distracted° multitude,
    Who like not in their judgement, but their eyes;   5
    And where 'tis so, th' offender's scourge° is weigh'd,°
    But never the offence. To bear all smooth and even,
    This sudden sending him away must seem
    Deliberate pause:° diseases desperate grown
    By desperate appliance are reliev'd,   10
    Or not at all.

Enter ROSENCRANTZ, [GUILDENSTERN,] *and all the rest.*

    How now! what hath befall'n?
ROSENCRANTZ: Where the dead body is bestow'd, my lord,
    We cannot get from him.
KING: But where is he?
ROSENCRANTZ: Without, my lord; guarded, to know your pleasure.
KING: Bring him before us.   15
ROSENCRANTZ: Ho! bring in the lord.

They enter [with HAMLET].

KING: Now, Hamlet, where's Polonius?
HAMLET: At supper.
KING: At supper! where?
HAMLET: Not where he eats, but where 'a is eaten: a certain convocation of   20
    politic° worms° are e'en at him. Your worm is your only emperor for diet: we fat
    all creatures else to fat us, and we fat ourselves for maggots: your fat king and your
    lean beggar is but variable service,° two dishes, but to one table: that's the end.
KING: Alas, alas!   25
HAMLET: A man may fish with the worm that hath eat of a king, and eat of the fish
    that hath fed of that worm.

---

²⁰**The body ... body**   *there are many interpretations; possibly, "The body lies in death with the king, my father;
but my father walks disembodied"; or "Claudius has the bodily possession of kingship, but kingliness, or justice of
inheritance, is not with him."*   ²⁴**Hide ... after**   *an old signal cry in the game of hide-and-seek.*   **IV.iii.**
⁴**distracted**   *i.e., without power of forming logical judgments.*   ⁶**scourge**   *punishment.*   ⁶**weigh'd**   *taken
into consideration.*   ⁹**Deliberate pause**   *considered action.*   ^{20–21}**convocation ... worms**   *allusion to the
Diet of Worms (1521).*   ²¹**politic**   *crafty.*   ²³**variable service**   *a variety of dishes.*

KING: What dost thou mean by this?

HAMLET: Nothing but to show you how a king may go a progress° through the guts 30
of a beggar.

KING: Where is Polonius?

HAMLET: In heaven; send thither to see: if your messenger find him not there, seek
him i' the other place yourself. But if indeed you find him not within this
month, you shall nose him as you go up the stairs into the lobby.

KING [to some ATTENDANTS]: Go seek him there.   35

HAMLET: 'A will stay till you come.   [Exeunt ATTENDANTS.]

KING: Hamlet, this deed, for thine especial safety,—
    Which we do tender,° as we dearly grieve
    For that which thou hast done,—must send thee hence
    With fiery quickness: therefore prepare thyself;   40
    The bark is ready, and the wind at help,
    Th' associates tend, and everything is bent
    For England.

HAMLET: For England!

KING: Ay, Hamlet.

HAMLET: Good.

KING: So is it, if thou knew'st our purposes.

HAMLET: I see a cherub° that sees them. But, come; for England! Farewell, 45
dear mother.

KING: Thy loving father, Hamlet.

HAMLET: My mother: father and mother is man and wife; man and wife is one flesh;
and so, my mother. Come, for England!   Exit.

KING: Follow him at foot;° tempt him with speed aboard;   50
    Delay it not; I'll have him hence to-night:
    Away! for every thing is seal'd and done
    That else leans on th' affair: pray you, make haste.

                                        [Exeunt all but the KING.]

    And, England, if my love thou hold'st at aught—
    As my great power thereof may give thee sense,   55
    Since yet thy cicatrice° looks raw and red
    After the Danish sword, and thy free awe°
    Pays homage to us—thou mayst not coldly set
    Our sovereign process; which imports at full,
    By letters congruing to that effect,   60
    The present death of Hamlet. Do it, England;
    For like the hectic° in my blood he rages,
    And thou must cure me: till I know 'tis done,
    Howe'er my haps,° my joys were ne'er begun.   Exit.

---

³⁰**progress** *royal journey of state.*   ³⁸**tender** *regard, hold dear.*   ⁴⁵**cherub** *cherubim are angels of knowl-*
edge.   ⁵⁰**at foot** *close behind, at heel.*   ⁵⁶**cicatrice** *scar.*   ⁵⁷**free awe** *voluntary show of respect.*
⁶²**hectic** *fever.*   ⁶⁴**haps** *fortunes.*

Scene IV [*A plain in Denmark.*]

Enter FORTINBRAS *with his Army over the stage.*

FORTINBRAS: Go, captain, from me greet the Danish king;
　Tell him that, by his license,° Fortinbras
　Craves the conveyance° of a promis'd march
　Over his kingdom. You know the rendezvous.
　If that his majesty would aught with us,　　　　　　　　　5
　We shall express our duty in his eye;°
　And let him know so.
CAPTAIN: I will do't, my lord.
FORTINBRAS: 　　Go softly° on.　　　　　　[*Exeunt all but* CAPTAIN.]

Enter HAMLET, ROSENCRANTZ, [GUILDENSTERN,] *&c.*

HAMLET: Good sir, whose powers are these?
CAPTAIN: They are of Norway, sir.　　　　　　　　　　　　10
HAMLET: How purpos'd, sir, I pray you?
CAPTAIN: Against some part of Poland.
HAMLET: Who commands them, sir?
CAPTAIN: The nephew to old Norway, Fortinbras.
HAMLET: Goes it against the main° of Poland, sir,　　　　　15
　Or for some frontier?
CAPTAIN: Truly to speak, and with no addition,
　We go to gain a little patch of ground
　That hath in it no profit but the name.
　To pay five ducats, five, I would not farm it;°　　　　　20
　Nor will it yield to Norway or the Pole
　A ranker rate, should it be sold in fee.°
HAMLET: Why, then the Polack never will defend it.
CAPTAIN: Yes, it is already garrison'd.
HAMLET: Two thousand souls and twenty thousand ducats　25
　Will not debate the question of this straw;°
　This is th' imposthume° of much wealth and peace,
　That inward breaks, and shows no cause without
　Why the man dies. I humbly thank you, sir.
CAPTAIN: God be wi' you, sir.　　　　　　　　　　[*Exit.*]
ROSENCRANTZ: 　　　　　Will 't please you go, my lord?　30
HAMLET: I'll be with you straight. Go a little before.
　　　　　　　　　　　　　[*Exeunt all except* HAMLET.]
　How all occasions° do inform against° me,
　And spur my dull revenge! What is a man,

IV.iv. ²*license* leave. ³*conveyance* escort, convey. ⁶*in his eye* in his presence. ⁸*softly* slowly.
¹⁵*main* country itself. ²⁰*farm it* take a lease of it. ²²*fee* fee simple. ²⁶*debate ... straw* settle this
trifling matter. ²⁷*imposthume* purulent abscess or swelling. ³²*occasions* incidents, events. ³²*inform against*
generally defined as "show," "betray" (i.e., his tardiness); more probably inform means "take shape," as in Macbeth, II.i.48.

If his chief good and market of his time°
Be but to sleep and feed? a beast, no more.   35
Sure, he that made us with such large discourse,
Looking before and after, gave us not
That capability and god-like reason
To fust° in us unus'd. Now, whether it be
Bestial oblivion, or some craven scruple   40
Of thinking too precisely on th' event,
A thought which, quarter'd, hath but one part wisdom
And ever three parts coward, I do not know
Why yet I live to say "This thing 's to do";
Sith I have cause and will and strength and means   45
To do 't. Examples gross as earth exhort me:
Witness this army of such mass and charge
Led by a delicate and tender prince,
Whose spirit with divine ambition puff'd
Makes mouths at the invisible event,   50
Exposing what is mortal and unsure
To all that fortune, death and danger dare,
Even for an egg-shell. Rightly to be great
Is not to stir without great argument,
But greatly to find quarrel in a straw   55
When honour's at the stake. How stand I then,
That have a father kill'd, a mother stain'd,
Excitements of ° my reason and my blood,
And let all sleep? while, to my shame, I see
The imminent death of twenty thousand men,   60
That, for a fantasy and trick° of fame,
Go to their graves like beds, fight for a plot°
Whereon the numbers cannot try the cause,
Which is not tomb enough and continent
To hide the slain? O, from this time forth,   65
My thoughts be bloody, or be nothing worth!   *Exit.*

Scene V [*Elsinore. A room in the castle.*]

Enter HORATIO, [QUEEN] GERTRUDE, *and a* GENTLEMAN.

QUEEN: I will not speak with her.
GENTLEMAN: She is importunate, indeed distract:
    Her mood will needs be pitied.
QUEEN: What would she have?
GENTLEMAN: She speaks much of her father; says she hears
    There's tricks° i' th' world; and hems, and beats her heart;°   5

---

³⁴**market of his time**   *the best use he makes of his time, or, that for which he sells his time.*   ³⁹**fust**   *grow moldy.*
⁵⁸**Excitements of**   *incentives to.*   ⁶¹**trick** *toy, trifle.*   ⁶²**plot** *i.e., of ground.*   **IV.v.**⁵**tricks**   *deceptions.*
⁵**heart**   *i.e., breast.*

Spurns enviously at straws;° speaks things in doubt,
That carry but half sense: her speech is nothing,
Yet the unshaped° use of it doth move
The hearers to collection;° they yawn° at it,
And botch° the words up fit to their own thoughts; 10
Which, as her winks, and nods, and gestures yield° them,
Indeed would make one think there might be thought,
Though nothing sure, yet much unhappily.°
HORATIO: 'Twere good she were spoken with: for she may strew
Dangerous conjectures in ill-breeding minds.° 15
QUEEN: Let her come in. [*Exit* GENTLEMAN.]
[*Aside.*] To my sick soul, as sin's true nature is,
Each toy seems prologue to some great amiss:°
So full of artless jealousy is guilt,
It spills itself in fearing to be spilt.° 20

Enter OPHELIA [*distracted*].

OPHELIA: Where is the beauteous majesty of Denmark?
QUEEN: How now, Ophelia!
OPHELIA (*she sings*): How should I your true love know
    From another one?
By his cockle hat° and staff, 25
    And his sandal shoon.°
QUEEN: Alas, sweet lady, what imports this song?
OPHELIA: Say you? nay, pray you mark.
    (*Song*) He is dead and gone, lady,
    He is dead and gone; 30
At his head a grass-green turf,
    At his heels a stone.
O, ho!
QUEEN: Nay, but, Ophelia—
OPHELIA: Pray you, mark 35
    [*Sings.*] White his shroud as the mountain snow,—

Enter KING.

QUEEN: Alas, look here, my lord.
OPHELIA (*Song*): Larded° all with flowers;
    Which bewept to the grave did not go
    With true-love showers. 40
KING: How do you, pretty lady?

---

[6]**Spurns . . . straws** *kicks spitefully at small objects in her path.* [8]**unshaped** *unformed, artless.* [9]**collection** *inference, a guess at some sort of meaning.* [9]**yawn** *wonder.* [10]**botch** *patch.* [11]**yield** *deliver, bring forth (her words).* [13]**much unhappily** *expressive of much unhappiness.* [15]**ill-breeding minds** *minds bent on mischief.* [18]**great amiss** *calamity, disaster.* [19-20]**So . . . split** *guilt is so full of suspicion that it unskillfully betrays itself in fearing to be betrayed.* [25]**cockle hat** *hat with cockleshell stuck in it as a sign that the wearer has been a pilgrim to the shrine of St. James of Compostella; the pilgrim's garb was a conventional disguise for lovers.* [26]**schoon** *shoes.* [38]**Larded** *decorated.*

OPHELIA: Well, God 'ild° you! They say the owl° was a baker's daughter. Lord, we
    know what we are, but know not what we may be. God be at your table!

KING: Conceit upon her father.

OPHELIA: Pray let's have no words of this; but when they ask you what it   45
    means, say you this:

  (Song) To-morrow is Saint Valentine's day,
    All in the morning betime,
  And I a maid at your window,
    To be your Valentine.°   50
  Then up he rose, and donn'd his clothes,
    And dupp'd° the chamber-door;
  Let in the maid, that out a maid
    Never departed more.

KING: Pretty Ophelia!   55

OPHELIA: Indeed, la, without an oath, I'll make an end on 't:

  [Sings.] By Gis° and by Saint Charity,
    Alack, and fie for shame!
  Young men will do 't, if they come to 't;
    By cock,° they are to blame.   60
  Quoth she, before you tumbled me,
    You promis'd me to wed.
  So would I ha' done, by yonder sun,
    An thou hadst not come to my bed.

KING: How long hath she been thus?   65

OPHELIA: I hope all will be well. We must be patient: but I cannot choose but weep,
    to think they would lay him i' the cold ground. My brother shall know of it: and
    so I thank you for your good counsel. Come, my coach! Good night, ladies; good
    night, sweet ladies; good night, good night.   [Exit.]

KING: Follow her close; give her good watch, I pray you.   [Exit HORATIO.]
  O, this is the poison of deep grief; it springs
  All from her father's death. O Gertrude, Gertrude,
  When sorrows come, they come not single spies,
  But in battalions. First, her father slain: 75
  Next your son gone; and he most violent author
  Of his own just remove: the people muddied,
  Thick and unwholesome in their thoughts and whispers,
  For good Polonius' death; and we have done but greenly,°
  In hugger-mugger° to inter him: poor Ophelia   80
  Divided from herself and her fair judgement,
  Without the which we are pictures, or mere beasts:
  Last, and as much containing as all these,
  Her brother is in secret come from France;

42**God 'ild** *god yield or reward.* 42**owl** *reference to a monkish legend that a baker's daughter was turned into an owl for refusing bread to the Savior.* 50**Valentine** *this song alludes to the belief that the first girl seen by a man on the morning of this day was his valentine or true love.* 52**dupp'd** *opened.* 57**Gis** *Jesus.* 60**cock** *perversion of "God" in oaths.* 79**greenly** *foolishly.* 80**hugger-mugger** *secret haste.*

Feeds on his wonder, keeps himself in clouds,° 85
And wants not buzzers° to infect his ear
With pestilent speeches of his father's death;
Wherein necessity, of matter beggar'd,°
Will nothing stick° our person to arraign
In ear and ear.° O my dear Gertrude, this, 90
Like to a murd'ring-piece,° in many places
Gives me superfluous death.   *A noise within.*

QUEEN: Alack, what noise is this?
KING: Where are my Switzers?° Let them guard the door.

Enter a MESSENGER.

What is the matter?
MESSENGER: Save yourself, my lord:
The ocean, overpeering° of his list,° 95
Eats not the flats with more impiteous haste
Than young Laertes, in a riotous head,
O'erbears your officers. The rabble call him lord;
And, as the world were now but to begin,
Antiquity forgot, custom not known, 100
The ratifiers and props of every word,°
They cry "Choose we: Laertes shall be king":
Caps, hands, and tongues, applaud it to the clouds:
"Laertes shall be king, Laertes king!"   *A noise within.*

QUEEN:: How cheerfully on the false trail they cry! 105
O, this is counter,° you false Danish dogs!
KING: The doors are broke.

Enter LAERTES *with others.*

LAERTES: Where is this king? Sirs, stand you all without.
DANES: No, let's come in.
LAERTES: I pray you, give me leave.
DANES: We will, we will.   [*They retire without the door.*] 110
LAERTES: I thank you: keep the door. O thou vile king,
Give me my father!
QUEEN: Calmly, good Laertes.
LAERTES: That drop of blood that's calm proclaims me bastard,
Cries cuckold to my father, brands the harlot
Even here, between the chaste unsmirched brow 115
Of my true mother.
KING: What is the cause, Laertes,

That thy rebellion looks so giant-like?
Let him go, Gertrude; do not fear our person:
There's such divinity doth hedge a king,
That treason can but peep to° what it would,°   120
Acts little of his will. Tell me, Laertes,
Why thou art thus incens'd. Let him go, Gertrude.
Speak, man.

LAERTES: Where is my father?

KING: Dead.

QUEEN: But not by him.

KING: Let him demand his fill.   125

LAERTES: How came he dead? I'll not be juggled with:
To hell, allegiance! vows, to the blackest devil!
Conscience and grace, to the profoundest pit!
I dare damnation. To this point I stand,
That both the worlds I give to negligence,°   130
Let come what comes; only I'll be reveng'd
Most thoroughly° for my father.

KING: Who shall stay you?

LAERTES: My will,° not all the world's:
And for my means, I'll husband them so well,
They shall go far with little.

KING: Good Laertes,   135
If you desire to know the certainty
Of your dear father, is 't writ in your revenge,
That, swoopstake,° you will draw both friend and foe,
Winner and loser?

LAERTES: None but his enemies.

KING: Will you know them then?   140

LAERTES: To his good friends thus wide I'll ope my arms;
And like the kind life-rend'ring pelican,°
Repast° them with my blood.

KING: Why, now you speak
Like a good child and a true gentleman.
That I am guiltless of your father's death,   145
And am most sensibly in grief for it,
It shall as level to your judgement 'pear
As day does to your eye.

                    A noise within: "Let her come in."

LAERTES: How now! what noise is that?

---

¹²⁰**peep to**   *i.e., look at from afar off.*   ¹²⁰**would**   *wishes to do.*   ¹³⁰**give to negligence**   *he despises both the here and the hereafter.*   ¹³²**throughly**   *thoroughly.*   ¹³³**My will**   *he will not be stopped except by his own will.*   ¹³⁸**swoopstake**   *literally, drawing the whole stake at once, i.e., indiscriminately.*   ¹⁴²**pelican**   *reference to the belief that the pelican feeds its young with its own blood.*   ¹⁴³**Repast**   *feed.*

Enter OPHELIA.

O heat,° dry up my brains! tears seven times salt,   150
Burn out the sense and virtue of mine eye!
By heaven, thy madness shall be paid with weight,
Till our scale turn the beam. O rose of May!
Dear maid, kind sister, sweet Ophelia!
O heavens! is 't possible, a young maid's wits   155
Should be as mortal as an old man's life?
Nature is fine in love, and where 'tis fine,
It sends some precious instance of itself
After the thing it loves.
OPHELIA (*Song*): They bore him barefac'd on the bier,   160
  Hey non nonny, nonny, hey nonny;
  And in his grave rain'd many a tear:—
Fare you well, my dove!
LAERTES: Hadst thou thy wits, and didst persuade revenge,
  It could not move thus.   165
OPHELIA [*sings*]: You must sing a-down a-down,
   An you call him a-down-a.
  O, how the wheel° becomes it! It is the false steward,° that stole his
  master's daughter.
LAERTES: This nothing's more than matter.   170
OPHELIA: There's rosemary,° that's for remembrance; pray you, love, remember:
  and there is pansies,° that's for thoughts.
LAERTES: A document° in madness, thoughts and remembrance fitted.
OPHELIA: There's fennel° for you, and columbines:° there's rue° for you; and here's   175
  some for me: we may call it herb of grace o' Sundays: O, you must wear your
  rue with a difference. There's a daisy:° I would give you some violets,° but they
  withered all when my father died: they say 'a made a good end,—
  [*Sings.*] For bonny sweet Robin is all my joy.°
LAERTES: Thought° and affliction, passion, hell itself,   180
  She turns to favour and to prettiness.
OPHELIA (*Song*): And will 'a not come again?°
  And will 'a not come again?
   No, no, he is dead:
   Go to thy death-bed: 185
  He never will come again.

---

¹⁵⁰**heat**   *probably the heat generated by the passion of grief.*   ¹⁶⁸**wheel**   *spinning wheel as accompaniment to the song refrain.*   ¹⁶⁸⁻⁶⁹**false steward . . . daughter**   *the story is unknown.*   ¹⁷¹**rosemary**   *used as a symbol of remembrance both at weddings and at funerals.*   ¹⁷²**pansies**   *emblems of love and courtship. Cf. French pensées.*   ¹⁷³**document**   *piece of instruction or lesson.*   ¹⁷⁴**fennel**   *emblem of flattery.*   ¹⁷⁴**columbines**   *emblem of unchastity (?) or ingratitude (?).*   ¹⁷⁴**rue**   *emblem of repentance. It was usually mingled with holy water and then known as herb of grace. Ophelia is probably playing on the two meanings of rue "repentant" and "even for Ruth (pity)"; the former signification is for the queen, the latter for herself.*   ¹⁷⁶**daisy**   *emblem of dissembling, faithlessness.*   ¹⁷⁷**violets**   *emblems of faithfulness.*   ¹⁷⁹**For . . . joy**   *probably a line from a Robin Hood ballad.*   ¹⁸⁰**Thought**   *melancholy thought.*   ¹⁸²**And . . . again**   *this song appeared in the songbooks as "The Merry Milkmaids' Dumps."*

His beard was as white as snow,
All flaxen was his poll:°
  He is gone, he is gone,
    And we cast away° moan: 190
God ha' mercy on his soul!
And of all Christian souls, I pray God. God be wi' you.   [*Exit.*]
LAERTES: Do you see this, O God?
KING: Laertes, I must commune with your grief,
  Or you deny me right.° Go but apart,   195
  Make choice of whom your wisest friends you will,
  And they shall hear and judge 'twixt you and me:
  If by direct or by collateral° hand
  They find us touch'd,° we will our kingdom give,
  Our crown, our life, and all that we call ours,   200
  To you in satisfaction; but if not,
  Be you content to lend your patience to us,
  And we shall jointly labour with your soul
  To give it due content.
LAERTES: Let this be so;
  His means of death, his obscure funeral—   205
  No trophy, sword, nor hatchment° o'er his bones,
  No noble rite nor formal ostentation—
  Cry to be heard, as 'twere from heaven to earth,
  That I must call 't in question.
KING: So you shall;
  And where th' offence is let the great axe fall.   210
  I pray you, go with me.   *Exeunt.*

Scene VI [*Another room in the castle.*]

Enter HORATIO *and others.*

HORATIO: What are they that would speak with me?
GENTLEMAN: Sea-faring men, sir: they say they have letters for you.
HORATIO: Let them come in.   [*Exit* GENTLEMAN.]
  I do not know from what part of the world
  I should be greeted, if not from lord Hamlet.   5

Enter SAILORS.

FIRST SAILOR: God bless you, sir.
HORATIO: Let him bless thee too.
FIRST SAILOR: 'A shall sir, an 't please him. There's a letter for you, sir; it comes
  from the ambassador that was bound for England; if your name be Horatio, as I
  am let to know it is.   10

---

¹⁸⁸**poll** *head.*   ¹⁹⁰**cast away** *shipwrecked.*   ¹⁹⁵**right** *my rights.*   ¹⁹⁸**collateral** *indirect.*
¹⁹⁹**touch'd** *implicated.*   ²⁰⁶**hatchment** *tablet displaying the armorial bearings of a deceased person.*

HORATIO [reads]:"Horatio, when thou shalt have overlooked this, give these fellows
some means° to the king: they have letters for him. Ere we were two days old at
sea, a pirate of very warlike appointment gave us chase. Finding ourselves too
slow of sail, we put on a compelled valour, and in the grapple I boarded them:
on the instant they got clear of our ship; so I alone became their prisoner. They   15
have dealt with me like thieves of mercy:° but they knew what they did; I am to
do a good turn for them. Let the king have the letters I have sent; and repair
thou to me with as much speed as thou wouldst fly death. I have words to speak
in thine ear will make thee dumb; yet are they much too light for the bore° of
the matter. These good fellows will bring thee where I am. Rosencrantz and   20
Guildenstern hold their course for England: of them I have much to tell thee.
Farewell.

                                          "He that thou knowest thine, HAMLET."

Come, I will give you way for these your letters;   25
And do 't the speedier, that you may direct me
To him from whom you brought them.   *Exeunt.*

Scene VII [*Another room in the castle.*]

                    Enter KING *and* LAERTES.

KING: Now must your conscience° my acquittance seal,
    And you must put me in your heart for friend,
    Sith you have heard, and with a knowing ear,
    That he which hath your noble father slain
    Pursued my life.
LAERTES: It well appears: but tell me   5
    Why you proceeded not against these feats,
    So criminal and so capital° in nature,
    As by your safety, wisdom, all things else,
    You mainly° were stirr'd up.
KING: O, for two special reasons;
    Which may to you, perhaps, seem much unsinew'd,°   10
    But yet to me th' are strong. The queen his mother
    Lives almost by his looks; and for myself—
    My virtue or my plague, be it either which—
    She's so conjunctive° to my life and soul,
    That, as the star moves not but in his sphere,°   15
    I could not but by her. The other motive,
    Why to a public count° I might not go,

IV.vi. ¹²*means* *means of access.*   ¹⁶⁻¹⁷*thieves of mercy* *merciful thieves.*   ²⁰*bore* *caliber, importance.*
IV.vii. ¹*conscience* *knowledge that this is true.*   ⁷*capital* *punishable by death.*   ⁹*mainly* *greatly.*
¹⁰*Unsinew'd* *weak.*   ¹⁴*conjunctive* *conformable (the next line suggesting planetary conjunction).*
¹⁵*sphere* *the hollow sphere in which, according to Ptolemaic astronomy, the planets were supposed to move.*
¹⁷*count* *account, reckoning.*

Is the great love the general gender° bear him;
Who, dipping all his faults in their affection,
Would, like the spring° that turneth wood to stone,   20
Convert his gyves° to graces; so that my arrows,
Too slightly timber'd° for so loud° a wind,
Would have reverted to my bow again,
And not where I had aim'd them.

LAERTES: And so have I a noble father lost;   25
A sister driven into desp'rate terms,°
Whose worth, if praises may go back° again,
Stood challenger on mount° of all the age°
For her perfections: but my revenge will come.

KING: Break not your sleeps for that: you must not think   30
That we are made of stuff so flat and dull
That we can let our beard be shook with danger
And think it pastime. You shortly shall hear more:
I lov'd your father, and we love ourself;
And that, I hope, will teach you to imagine—   35

Enter a MESSENGER *with letters.*

How now! what news?
MESSENGER: Letters, my lord, from Hamlet:
These to your majesty; this to the queen.°
KING: From Hamlet! who brought them?
MESSENGER: Sailors, my lord, they say; I saw them not:
They were given me by Claudio;° he receiv'd them   40
Of him that brought them.
KING: Laertes, you shall hear them.
Leave us.   [*Exit* MESSENGER.]
[*Reads.*] "High and mighty, You shall know I am set naked° on your king-
dom. To-morrow shall I beg leave to see your kingly eyes: when I shall,
first asking your pardon thereunto, recount the occasion of my sudden and   45
more strange return.   "HAMLET."
What should this mean? Are all the rest come back?
Or is it some abuse, and no such thing?
LAERTES: Know you the hand?
KING: 'Tis Hamlet's character. "Naked!"
And in a postscript here, he says "alone."   50
Can you devise° me?
LAERTES: I'm lost in it, my lord. But let him come;
It warms the very sickness in my heart,

---

¹⁸**general gender** *common people.*   ²⁰**spring** *i.e., one heavily charged with lime.*   ²¹**gyves** *fetters; here,*
faults, or possibly, punishments inflicted (on him).   ²²**slightly timber'd** *light.*   ²²**loud** *strong.*
²⁶**terms** *state, condition.*   ²⁷**go back** *i.e., to Ophelia's former virtues.*   ²⁸**on mount** *set up on high,*
mounted (on horseback).   ²⁸**of all the age** *qualifies* challenger *and not* mount.   ³⁷**to the queen** *one*
hears no more of the letter to the queen.   ⁴⁰**Claudio** *this character does not appear in the play.*   ⁴³**naked**
unprovided (with retinue).   ⁵¹**devise** *explain to.*

That I shall live and tell him to his teeth,
"Thus didst thou."
KING: If it be so, Laertes—   55
   As how should it be so? how otherwise?°—
   Will you be rul'd by me?
LAERTES: Ay, my lord;
   So you will not o'errule me to a peace.
KING: To thine own peace. If he be now return'd,
   As checking at° his voyage, and that he means   60
   No more to undertake it, I will work him
   To an exploit, now ripe in my device,
   Under the which he shall not choose but fall:
   And for his death no wind of blame shall breathe,
   But even his mother shall uncharge the practice°   65
   And call it accident.
LAERTES: My lord, I will be rul'd;
   The rather, if you could devise it so
   That I might be the organ.°
KING: It falls right.
   You have been talk'd of since your travel much,
   And that in Hamlet's hearing, for a quality   70
   Wherein, they say, you shine: your sum of parts
   Did not together pluck such envy from him
   As did that one, and that, in my regard,
   Of the unworthiest siege.°
LAERTES: What part is that, my lord?
KING: A very riband in the cap of youth,   75
   Yet needful too; for youth no less becomes
   The light and careless livery that it wears
   Than settled age his sables° and his weeds,
   Importing health and graveness. Two months since,
   Here was a gentleman of Normandy:—   80
   I have seen myself, and serv'd against, the French,
   And they can well° on horseback: but this gallant
   Had witchcraft in 't; he grew unto his seat;
   And to such wondrous doing brought his horse,
   As had he been incorps'd and demi-natur'd°   85
   With the brave beast: so far he topp'd° my thought,
   That I, in forgery° of shapes and tricks,
   Come short of what he did.
LAERTES: A Norman was 't?

56*As ... otherwise?* *how can this (Hamlet's return) be true? (yet) how otherwise than true (since we have the*
evidence of his letter)? Some editors read "How should it not be so," etc., making the words refer to Laertes's desire to
meet with Hamlet.   60*checking at* *used in falconry of a hawk's leaving the quarry to fly at a chance bird, turn*
aside.   65*uncharge the practice* *acquit the stratagem of being a plot.*   68*organ* *agent, instrument.*
74*siege* *rank.*   78*sables* *rich garments.*   82*can well* *are skilled.*   85*incorps'd and demi-natur'd*
of one body and nearly of one nature (like the centaur).   86*topp'd* *surpassed.*   87*forgery* *invention.*

KING: A Norman.

LAERTES: Upon my life, Lamord.°

KING: The very same.

LAERTES: I know him well: he is the brooch indeed   90

And gem of all the nation.

KING: He made confession° of you,

And gave you such a masterly report

For art and exercise° in your defence°

And for your rapier most especial,   95

That he cried out, 'twould be a sight indeed,

If one could match you: the scrimers° of their nation,

He swore, had neither motion, guard, nor eye,

If you oppos'd them. Sir, this report of his

Did Hamlet so envenom with his envy   100

That he could nothing do but wish and beg

Your sudden coming o'er, to play° with you.

Now, out of this,—

LAERTES: What out of this, my lord?

KING: Laertes, was your father dear to you?   105

Or are you like the painting of a sorrow,

A face without a heart?

LAERTES: Why ask you this?

KING: Not that I think you did not love your father;

But that I know love is begun by time;

And that I see, in passages of proof,°   110

Time qualifies the spark and fire of it.

There lives within the very flame of love

A kind of wick or snuff that will abate it;

And nothing is at a like goodness still;

For goodness, growing to a plurisy,°   115

Dies in his own too much:° that we would do,

We should do when we would; for this "would" changes

And hath abatements° and delays as many

As there are tongues, are hands, are accidents;°

And then this "should" is like a spendthrift° sigh,   120

That hurts by easing. But, to the quick o' th' ulcer:°—

Hamlet comes back: what would you undertake,

To show yourself your father's son in deed

More than in words?

LAERTES: To cut his throat i' th' church.

---

⁹⁰**Lamord**   this refers possibly to Pietro Monte, instructor to Louis XII's master of the horse.   ⁹³**confession** grudging admission of superiority.   ⁹⁵**art and exercise** skillful exercise.   ⁹⁵**defence**   science of defense in sword practice.   ⁹⁸**scrimers** fencers.   ¹⁰³**play**   fence.   ¹¹⁰**passages of proof**   proved instances.   ¹¹⁵**plurisy**   excess, plethora.   ¹¹⁶**in his own too much**   of its own excess.   ¹¹⁸**abatements**   diminutions.   ¹¹⁹**accidents**   occurrences, incidents.   ¹²⁰**spendthrift**   an allusion to the belief that each sigh cost the heart a drop of blood.   ¹²¹**quick o' th' ulcer**   heart of the difficulty.

KING: No place, indeed, should murder sanctuarize;° 125
    Revenge should have no bounds. But, good Laertes,
    Will you do this, keep close within your chamber.
    Hamlet return'd shall know you are come home:
    We'll put on those shall praise your excellence
    And set a double varnish on the fame 130
    The Frenchman gave you, bring you in fine together
    And wager on your heads: he, being remiss,
    Most generous and free from all contriving,
    Will not peruse the foils; so that, with ease,
    Or with a little shuffling, you may choose 135
    A sword unbated,° and in a pass of practice°
    Requite him for your father.
LAERTES: I will do 't:
    And, for that purpose, I'll anoint my sword.
    I bought an unction of a mountebank,°
    So mortal that, but dip a knife in it, 140
    Where it draws blood no cataplasm° so rare,
    Collected from all simples° that have virtue
    Under the moon,° can save the thing from death
    That is but scratch'd withal: I'll touch my point
    With this contagion, that, if I gall° him slightly, 145
    It may be death.
KING: Let's further think of this;
    Weigh what convenience both of time and means
    May fit us to our shape:° if this should fail,
    And that our drift look through our bad performance,°
    'Twere better not assay'd: therefore this project 150
    Should have a back or second, that might hold,
    If this should blast in proof.° Soft! let me see:
    We'll make a solemn wager on your cunnings:°
    I ha 't:
    When in your motion you are hot and dry— 155
    As make your bouts more violent to that end—
    And that he calls for drink, I'll have prepar'd him
    A chalice° for the nonce, whereon but sipping,
    If he by chance escape your venom'd stuck,°
    Our purpose may hold there. But stay, what noise? 160

---

[125]**sanctuarize** *protect from punishment; allusion to the right of sanctuary with which certain religious places were invested.* [136]**unbated** *not blunted, having no button.* [136]**pass of practice** *treacherous thrust.* [139]**mountebank** *quack doctor.* [141]**cataplasm** *plaster or poultice.* [142]**simples** *herbs.* [143]**Under the moon** *i.e., when collected by moonlight to add to their medicinal value.* [145]**gall** *graze, wound.* [148]**shape** *part we propose to act.* [149]**drift . . . performance** *intention be disclosed by our bungling.* [152]**blast in proof** *burst in the test (like a cannon).* [153]**cunnings** *skills.* [158]**chalice** *cup.* [159]**stuck** *thrust (from stoccado).*

Enter QUEEN.

QUEEN: One woe doth tread upon another's heel,
  So fast they follow: your sister's drown'd, Laertes.
LAERTES: Drown'd! O, where?
QUEEN: There is a willow° grows askant° the brook,
  That shows his hoar° leaves in the glassy stream;   165
  There with fantastic garlands did she make
  Of crow-flowers,° nettles, daisies, and long purples°
  That liberal° shepherds give a grosser name,
  But our cold maids do dead men's fingers call them:
  There, on the pendent boughs her crownet° weeds   170
  Clamb'ring to hang, an envious sliver° broke;
  When down her weedy° trophies and herself
  Fell in the weeping brook. Her clothes spread wide;
  And, mermaid-like, awhile they bore her up:
  Which time she chanted snatches of old lauds;°   175
  As one incapable° of her own distress,
  Or like a creature native and indued°
  Upon that element: but long it could not be
  Till that her garments, heavy with their drink,
  Pull'd the poor wretch from her melodious lay   180
  To muddy death.
LAERTES: Alas, then, she is drown'd?
QUEEN: Drown'd, drown'd.
LAERTES: Too much of water hast thou, poor Ophelia,
  And therefore I forbid my tears: but yet
  It is our trick;° nature her custom holds,   185
  Let shame say what it will: when these are gone,
  The woman will be out.° Adieu, my lord:
  I have a speech of fire, that fain would blaze,
  But that this folly drowns it.   *Exit.*
KING: Let's follow, Gertrude: 190
  How much I had to do to calm his rage!
  Now fear I this will give it start again;
  Therefore let 's follow.   *Exeunt.*

164*willow*   *for its significance of forsaken love.*   164*askant*   *aslant.*   165*hoar*   *white (i.e., on the under-side).*   167*crow-flowers*   *buttercups.*   167*long purples*   *early purple orchids.*   168*liberal*   *probably, free-spoken.*   170*crownet*   *coronet; made into a chaplet.*   171*sliver*   *branch.*   172*weedy*   *i.e., of plants.*   175*lauds*   *hymns.*   176*incapable*   *lacking capacity to apprehend.*   177*indued*   *endowed with qualities fitting her for living in water.*   185*trick*   *way.*   186-187*when . . . out*   *when my tears are all shed, the woman in me will be satisfied.*

ACT V

Scene I [A churchyard.]

Enter two CLOWNS° [*with spades, &c.*].

FIRST CLOWN: Is she to be buried in Christian burial when she wilfully seeks her own salvation?

SECOND CLOWN: I tell thee she is; therefore make her grave straight:° the crowner° hath sat on her, and finds it Christian burial.

FIRST CLOWN: How can that be, unless she drowned herself in her own defence? 5

SECOND CLOWN: Why, 'tis found so.

FIRST CLOWN: It must be "se offendendo";° it cannot be else. For here lies the point: if I drown myself wittingly,° it argues an act: and an act hath three branches;° it is, to act, to do, and to perform: argal,° she drowned herself 10 wittingly.

SECOND CLOWN: Nay, but hear you, goodman delver,°—

FIRST CLOWN: Give me leave. Here lies the water; good: here stands the man; good: if the man go to this water, and drown himself, it is, will he, nill he, he goes,—mark you that; but if the water come to him and drown him, he 15 drowns not himself: argal, he that is not guilty of his own death shortens not his own life.

SECOND CLOWN: But is this law?

FIRST CLOWN: Ay, marry, is 't; crowner's quest° law.

SECOND CLOWN: Will you ha' the truth on 't? If this had not been a gentle- 20 woman, she should have been buried out o' Christian burial.

FIRST CLOWN: Why, there thou say'st:° and the more pity that great folk should have countenance° in this world to drown or hang themselves, more than their even° Christian. Come, my spade. There is no ancient gentlemen but gardeners, ditchers, and grave-makers: they hold up° Adam's profession. 25

SECOND CLOWN: Was he a gentleman?

FIRST CLOWN: 'A was the first that ever bore arms.

SECOND CLOWN: Why, he had none.

FIRST CLOWN: What, art a heathen? How dost thou understand the Scripture? 30 The Scripture says "Adam digged": could he dig without arms? I'll put another question to thee: if thou answerest me not to the purpose, confess thyself °—

SECOND CLOWN: Go to.°

V.i. **clowns** *the word clown was used to denote peasants as well as humorous characters; here applied to the rus-tic type of clown.* ³**straight** *straightway, immediately; some interpret "from east to west in a direct line, parallel with the church."* ⁴**crowner** *coroner.* ⁷**"se offendendo"** *for se defendendo, term used in verdicts of jus-tifiable homicide.* ⁸**wittingly** *intentionally.* ⁸⁻⁹**three branches** *parody of legal phraseology.* ¹⁰**argal** *corruption of ergo, therefore* ¹²**delver** *digger.* ¹⁹**quest** *inquest.* ²²**there thou say'st** *that's right.* ²³**countenance** *privilege.* ²⁴**even** *fellow.* ²⁵**hold up** *maintain, continue.* ³²⁻³³**confess thyself** *"and be hanged" completes the proverb.* ³⁴**Go to** *perhaps, "begin," or some other form of concession.*

FIRST CLOWN: What is he that builds stronger than either the mason, the ship-   35
wright, or the carpenter?

SECOND CLOWN: The gallows-maker; for that frame outlives a thousand tenants.

FIRST CLOWN: I like thy wit well, in good faith: the gallows does well; but how
does it well? it does well to those that do ill: now thou dost ill to say the gallows is built stronger than the church: argal, the gallows may do well to thee.   40
To 't again, come.

SECOND CLOWN: Who builds stronger than a mason, a shipwright, or a
carpenter?

FIRST CLOWN: Ay, tell me that, and unyoke.°

SECOND CLOWN: Marry, now I can tell.   45

FIRST CLOWN: To 't.

SECOND CLOWN: Mass,° I cannot tell.

Enter HAMLET *and* HORATIO [*at a distance*].

FIRST CLOWN: Cudgel thy brains no more about it, for your dull ass will not
mend his pace with beating; and, when you are asked this question next, say   50
"a grave-maker": the houses he makes lasts till doomsday. Go, get thee in, and
fetch me a stoup° of liquor.

[*Exit* SECOND CLOWN.] *Song.* [*He digs.*]

In youth, when I did love, did love,
    Methought it was very sweet,
To contract—O—the time, for—a—my behove,°
O, methought, there—a—was nothing—a—meet.   55

HAMLET: Has this fellow no feeling of his business, that 'a sings at gravemaking?

HORATIO: Custom hath made it in him a property of easiness.°

HAMLET: 'Tis e'en so: the hand of little employment hath the daintier sense.

FIRST CLOWN: (*Song.*) But age, with his stealing steps,   60
    Hath claw'd me in his clutch,
And hath shipped me into the land
    As if I had never been such.   [*Throws up a skull.*]

HAMLET: That skull had a tongue in it, and could sing once: how the knave
jowls° it to the ground, as if 'twere Cain's jaw-bone,° that did the first   65
murder! This might be the pate of a politician,° which this ass now o'er-
reaches;° one that would circumvent God, might it not?

HORATIO: It might, my lord.

HAMLET: Or of a courtier; which could say "Good morrow, sweet lord! How dost
thou, sweet lord?" This might be my lord such-a-one, that praised my lord   70
such-a-one's horse, when he meant to beg it; might it not?

45**unyoke**   *after this great effort you may unharness the team of your wits.*   48**Mass**   *by the Mass.*   52**stoup**
two-quart measure.   55**behove**   *benefit.*   59**property of easiness**   *a peculiarity that now is easy.*
66**jowls**   *dashes.*   66**Cain's jaw-bone**   *allusion to the old tradition that Cain slew Abel with the jawbone of
an ass.*   67**politician**   *schemer, plotter.*   67–68**o'er-reaches**   *quibble on the literal sense and the sense
"circumvent."*

HORATIO: Ay, my lord.

HAMLET: Why, e'en so: and now my Lady Worm's; chapless,° and knocked about
the mazzard° with a sexton's spade: here's fine revolution, an we had the trick 75
to see 't. Did these bones cost no more the breeding, but to play at loggats°
with 'em? mine ache to think on 't.

FIRST CLOWN: (*Song.*) A pick-axe, and a spade, a spade,
    For and° a shrouding sheet:
    O, a pit of clay for to be made 80
    For such a guest is meet.   [*Throws up another skull.*]

HAMLET: There's another: why may not that be the skull of a lawyer? Where be
his quiddities° now, his quillities,° his cases, his tenures,° and his tricks? why
does he suffer this mad knave now to knock him about the sconce° with a
dirty shovel, and will not tell him of his action of battery? Hum! This fellow 85
might be in 's time a great buyer of land, with his statutes, his recognizances,°
his fines, his double vouchers,° his recoveries:° is this the fine° of his fines, and
the recovery of his recoveries, to have his fine pate full of fine dirt? will his
vouchers vouch him no more of his purchases, and double ones too, than the
length and breadth of a pair of indentures?° The very conveyances of his lands 90
will scarcely lie in this box; and must the inheritor° himself have no more, ha?

HORATIO: Not a jot more, my lord.

HAMLET: Is not parchment made of sheep-skins?

HORATIO: Ay, my lord, and of calf-skins° too. 95

HAMLET: They are sheep and calves which seek out assurance in that.° I will
speak to this fellow. Whose grave's this, sirrah?

FIRST CLOWN: Mine, sir.
    [*Sings.*] O, a pit of clay for to be made 100
    For such a guest is meet.

HAMLET: I think it be thine, indeed; for thou liest in 't.

FIRST CLOWN: You lie out on 't, sir, and therefore 't is not yours: for my part, I do
not lie in 't, yet it is mine.

HAMLET: Thou dost lie in 't, to be in 't and say it is thine: 'tis for the dead, not for
the quick; therefore thou liest. 105

FIRST CLOWN: 'Tis a quick lie, sir; 'twill away again, from me to you.

HAMLET: What man dost thou dig it for?

FIRST CLOWN: For no man, sir.

HAMLET: What woman, then?

FIRST CLOWN: For none, neither. 110

HAMLET: Who is to be buried in 't?

FIRST CLOWN: One that was a woman, sir; but, rest her soul, she's dead.

74**chapless** *having no lower jaw.*   75**mazzard** *head.*   76**loggats** *a game in which six sticks are thrown
to lie as near as possible to a stake fixed in the ground, or block of wood on a floor.*   79**For and** *and moreover.*
83**quiddities** *subtleties, quibbles.*   83**quillities** *verbal niceties, subtle distinctions.*   83**tenures** *the holding
of a piece of property or office or the conditions or period of such holding.*   84**sconce** *head.*   86**statutes,
recognizances** *legal terms connected with the transfer of land.*   87**vouchers** *persons called on to warrant a tenant's title.*   87**recoveries** *process for transfer of entailed estate.*   87**fine** *the four uses of this word are as follows: (1) end, (2) legal process, (3) elegant, (4) small.*   90**indentures** *conveyances or contracts.*   91**inheritor**
possessor, owner.   95**calf-skins** *parchments.*   96**assurance in that** *safety in legal parchments.*

HAMLET: How absolute° the knave is! we must speak by the card,° or equivoca-
tion° will undo us. By the Lord, Horatio, these three years I have taken note
of it; the age is grown so picked° that the toe of the peasant comes so near the   115
heel of the courtier, he galls° his kibe.° How long hast thou been a grave-
maker?

FIRST CLOWN: Of all the day i' the year, I came to 't that day that our last king
Hamlet overcame Fortinbras.

HAMLET: How long is that since?   120

FIRST CLOWN: Cannot you tell that? every fool can tell that: it was the very day
that young Hamlet was born; he that is mad, and sent into England.

HAMLET: Ay, marry, why was he sent into England?

FIRST CLOWN: Why, because 'a was mad: 'a shall recover his wits there; or, if 'a do
not, 'tis no great matter there.   125

HAMLET: Why?

FIRST CLOWN: 'Twill not be seen in him there; there the men are as mad as he.

HAMLET: How came he mad?

FIRST CLOWN: Very strangely, they say.   130

HAMLET: How strangely?

FIRST CLOWN: Faith, e'en with losing his wits.

HAMLET: Upon what ground?

FIRST CLOWN: Why, here in Denmark: I have been sexton here, man and boy,
thirty years.°

HAMLET: How long will a man lie i' the earth ere he rot?   135

FIRST CLOWN: Faith, if 'a be not rotten before 'a die—as we have many pocky°
corses now-a-days, that will scarce hold the laying in—'a will last you some
eight year or nine year: a tanner will last you nine year.

HAMLET: Why he more than another?

FIRST CLOWN: Why, sir, his hide is so tanned with his trade, that 'a will keep out   140
water a great while; and your water is a sore decayer of your whoreson dead
body. Here's a skull now hath lain you i' th' earth three and twenty years.

HAMLET: Whose was it?

FIRST CLOWN: A whoreson mad fellow's it was: whose do you think it was?   145

HAMLET: Nay, I know not.

FIRST CLOWN: A pestilence on him for a mad rogue! 'a poured a flagon of
Rhenish on my head once. This same skull, sir, was Yorick's skull, the king's
jester.

HAMLET: This?   150

FIRST CLOWN: E'en that.

HAMLET: Let me see. [*Takes the skull.*] Alas, poor Yorick! I knew him, Horatio: a
fellow of infinite jest, of most excellent fancy: he hath borne me on his back
a thousand times; and now, how abhorred in my imagination it is! my gorge
rises at it. Here hung those lips that I have kissed I know not how oft. Where   155

113**absolute**   positive, decided.   113**by the card**   with precision, i.e., by the mariner's card on which the points of
the compass were marked.   113–14**equivocation**   ambiguity in the use of terms.   115**picked**   refined, fastidious .   116**galls**   chafes.   116**kibe**   chilblain.   134**thirty years**   this statement with that in line 122
shows Hamlet's age to be thirty years.   136**pocky**   rotton, diseased.

be your gibes now? your gambols? your songs? your flashes of merriment, that
were wont to set the table on a roar? Not one now, to mock your own grinning? quite chap-fallen? Now get you to my lady's chamber, and tell her, let
her paint an inch thick, to this favour she must come; make her laugh at that.
Prithee, Horatio, tell me one thing.   160

HORATIO: What's that, my lord?

HAMLET: Dost thou think Alexander looked o' this fashion i' the earth?

HORATIO: E'en so.

HAMLET: And smelt so? pah!   [*Puts down the skull.*]

HORATIO: E'en so, my lord.   165

HAMLET: To what base uses we may return, Horatio! Why may not imagination
trace the noble dust of Alexander, till'a find it stopping a bunghole?

HORATIO: 'Twere to consider too curiously,° to consider so.

HAMLET: No, faith, not a jot; but to follow him thither with modesty enough, and   170
likelihood to lead it: as thus: Alexander died, Alexander was buried, Alexander
returneth into dust; the dust is earth; of earth we make loam;° and why of that
loam, whereto he was converted, might they not stop a beer-barrel?

> Imperious° Cæsar, dead and turn'd to clay,   175
> Might stop a hole to keep the wind away:
> O, that that earth, which kept the world in awe,
> Should patch a wall t'expel the winter's flaw!°

But soft! but soft awhile! here comes the king,

Enter KING, QUEEN, LAERTES, *and the Corse of*
[OPHELIA, *in procession, with* PRIEST, LORDS, *etc.*].

The queen, the courtiers: who is this they follow?   180
And with such maimed rites? This doth betoken
The corse they follow did with desp'rate hand
Fordo° it° own life: 'twas of some estate.
Couch° we awhile, and mark.   [*Retiring with* HORATIO.]

LAERTES: What ceremony else?

HAMLET: That is Laertes,   185
A very noble youth: mark.

LAERTES: What ceremony else?

FIRST PRIEST: Her obsequies have been as far enlarg'd°
As we have warranty: her death was doubtful;
And, but that great command o'ersways the order,   190
She should in ground unsanctified have lodg'd
Till the last trumpet; for charitable prayers,
Shards,° flints and pebbles should be thrown on her:
Yet here she is allow'd her virgin crants,°

---

¹⁶⁸**curiously** *minutely.*   ¹⁷²**loam** *clay paste for brickmaking.*   ¹⁷⁵**Imperious** *imperial.*   ¹⁷⁸**flaw**
gust of wind.   ¹⁸³**Fordo** *destroy.*   ¹⁸³**it** *its.*   ¹⁸⁴**Couch** *hide, lurk.*   ¹⁸⁸**enlarg'd** *extended,*
referring to the fact that suicides are not given full burial rites.   ¹⁹³**Shards** *broken bits of pottery.*   ¹⁹⁴**crants**
garlands customarily hung upon the biers of unmarried women.

Her maiden strewments° and the bringing home   195
Of bell and burial.°

LAERTES: Must there no more be done?

FIRST PRIEST: No more be done:
We should profane the service of the dead
To sing a requiem and such rest to her
As to peace-parted° souls.

LAERTES: Lay her i' th' earth: 200
And from her fair and unpolluted flesh
May violets spring! I tell thee, churlish priest,
A minist'ring angel shall my sister be,
When thou liest howling.°

HAMLET: What, the fair Ophelia!

QUEEN: Sweets to the sweet: farewell!   [*Scattering flowers.*] 205
I hop'd thou shouldst have been my Hamlet's wife;
I thought thy bride-bed to have deck'd, sweet maid,
And not have strew'd thy grave.

LAERTES: O, treble woe
Fall ten times treble on that cursed head,
Whose wicked deed thy most ingenious sense°   210
Depriv'd thee of! Hold off the earth awhile,
Till I have caught her once more in mine arms: [*Leaps into the grave.*]
Now pile your dust upon the quick and dead,
Till of this flat a mountain you have made,
T' o'ertop old Pelion,° or the skyish head   215
Of blue Olympus.

HAMLET: [*Advancing*] What is he whose grief
Bears such an emphasis? whose phrase of sorrow
Conjures the wand'ring stars,° and makes them stand
Like wonder-wounded hearers? This is I,
Hamlet the Dane.   [*Leaps into the grave.*]

LAERTES: The devil take thy soul!   [*Grappling with him.*] 220

HAMLET: Thou pray'st not well.
I prithee, take thy fingers from my throat;
For, though I am not splenitive° and rash,
Yet have I in me something dangerous,
Which let thy wisdom fear: hold off thy hand.   225

KING: Pluck them asunder.

QUEEN: Hamlet, Hamlet!

ALL: Gentlemen,—

HORATIO: Good my lord, be quiet.

---

¹⁹⁵**strewments** *traditional strewing of flowers.*   ¹⁹⁵⁻⁹⁶**bring ... burial** *the laying to rest of the body, to the sound of the bell.*   ²⁰⁰**peace-parted** *allusion to the text "Lord, now lettest thy servant depart in peace."* ²⁰⁴**howling** *i.e, in hell.*   ²¹⁰**ingenious sense** *mind endowed with finest qualities.*   ²¹⁵**Pelion** *Olympus, Pelion, and Ossa are mountains in the north of Thessaly.*   ²¹⁸**wand'ring stars** *planets..*   ²²³**splenitive** *quick-tempered.*

[*The* ATTENDANTS *part them, and they come out of the grave.*]

HAMLET: Why, I will fight with him upon this theme
    Until my eyelids will no longer wag.°

QUEEN: O my son, what theme?   230

HAMLET: I lov'd Ophelia: forty thousand brothers
    Could not, with all their quantity° of love,
    Make up my sum. What wilt thou do for her?

KING: O, he is mad, Laertes.

QUEEN: For love of God, forbear° him.   235

HAMLET: 'Swounds,° show me what thou 'lt do:
    Woo 't° weep? woo 't fight? woo 't fast? woo 't tear thyself?
    Woo 't drink up eisel?° eat a crocodile?
    I'll do 't. Dost thou come here to whine?
    To outface me with leaping in her grave?   240
    Be buried quick with her, and so will I:
    And, if thou prate of mountains, let them throw
    Millions of acres on us, till our ground,
    Singeing his pate against the burning zone,°
    Make Ossa like a wart! Nay, an thou 'lt mouth,   245
    I'll rant as well as thou.

QUEEN: This is mere madness:
    And thus awhile the fit will work on him;
    Anon, as patient as the female dove.
    When that her golden couplets° are disclos'd,
    His silence will sit drooping.

HAMLET: Hear you, sir;   250
    What is the reason that you use me thus?
    I lov'd you ever: but it is no matter;
    Let Hercules himself do what he may,
    The cat will mew and dog will have his day.

KING: I pray thee, good Horatio, wait upon him.   *Exit* HAMLET *and* HORATIO. 255
    [*To* LAERTES.] Strengthen your patience in° our last night's speech;
    We'll put the matter to the present push.°
    Good Gertrude, set some watch over your son.
    This grave shall have a living° monument:
    An hour of quiet shortly shall we see;   260
    Till then, in patience our proceeding be.   *Exeunt.*

---

²²⁹**wag** *move (not used ludicrously).*   ²³²**quantity** *some suggest that the word is used in a deprecatory sense*
(little bits, fragments).   ²³⁵**forbear** *leave alone.*   ²³⁶**'Swounds** *oath, "God's wounds."*   ²³⁷**Woo 't**
wilt thou.   ²³⁸**eisel** *vinegar. Some editors have taken this to be the name of a river, such as the Yssel, the Weissel,*
and the Nile.   ²⁴⁴**burning zone** *sun's orbit.*   ²⁴⁹**golden couplets** *the pigeon lays two eggs; the young*
when hatched are covered with golden down.   ²⁵⁶**in** *by recalling.*   ²⁵⁷**present push** *immediate test.*
²⁵⁹**living** *lasting; also refers (for Laertes' benefit) to the plot against Hamlet.*

Scene II [*A hall in the castle.*]

Enter HAMLET *and* HORATIO.

HAMLET: So much for this, sir: now shall you see the other;
  You do remember all the circumstance?
HORATIO: Remember it, my lord!
HAMLET: Sir, in my heart there was a kind of fighting,
  That would not let me sleep: methought I lay   5
  Worse than the mutines° in the bilboes.° Rashly,°
  And prais'd be rashness for it, let us know,
  Our indiscretion sometime serves us well,
  When our deep plots do pall:° and that should learn us
  There's a divinity that shapes our ends,   10
  Rough-hew° them how we will,—
HORATIO: That is most certain.
HAMLET: Up from my cabin,
  My sea-gown° scarf'd about me, in the dark
  Grop'd I to find out them; had my desire,
  Finger'd° their packet, and in fine° withdrew   15
  To mine own room again; making so bold,
  My fears forgetting manners, to unseal
  Their grand commission; where I found, Horatio,—
  O royal knavery!—an exact command,
  Larded° with many several sorts of reasons   20
  Importing Denmark's health and England's too,
  With, ho! such bugs° and goblins in my life,°
  That, on the supervise,° no leisure bated,°
  No, not to stay the grinding of the axe,
  My head should be struck off.
HORATIO: Is 't possible?   25
HAMLET: Here's the commission: read it at more leisure.
  But wilt thou hear me how I did proceed?
HORATIO: I beseech you.
HAMLET: Being thus be-netted round with villanies,—
  Ere I could make a prologue to my brains,   30
  They had begun the play°—I sat me down,
  Devis'd a new commission, wrote it fair:
  I once did hold it, as our statists° do,
  A baseness to write fair° and labour'd much

V.ii. **⁶mutines** *mutineers.*   **⁶bilboes** *shackels.*   **⁶Rashly** *goes with line 12.*   **⁹pall** *fail.*
¹¹Rough-hew *shape roughly; it may mean "bungle."*   **¹³sea-gown** *"A sea-gown, or a corase, high-collered,*
and short-sleeved gowne, reaching down to the mid-leg, and used most by seamen and saylors" (Cotgrave, quoted by
Singer).   **¹⁵finger'd** *pilfered, filched.*   **¹⁵in fine** *finally.*   **²⁰Larded** *enriched.*   **²²bugs** *bug-bears.*
²²such ... life *such imaginary dangers if I were allowed to live.*   **²³supervise** *perusal.*   **²³leisure bated**
delay allowed.   **²⁰⁻³¹prologue ... play** *i.e., before I could begin to think, my mind had made its decision.*
³³statists *statesmen.*   **³⁴fair** *in a clear hand.*

How to forget that learning, but, sir, now　35
It did me yeoman's° service: wilt thou know
Th' effect of what I wrote?

HORATIO:　　　　　　　　Ay, good my lord.

HAMLET: An earnest conjuration from the king,
 As England was his faithful tributary,
 As love between them like the palm might flourish,　40
 As peace should still her wheaten garland° wear
 And stand a comma° 'tween their amities,
 And many such-like 'As'es° of great charge,°
 That, on the view and knowing of these contents,
 Without debatement further, more or less,　45
 He should the bearers put to sudden death,
 Not shriving-time° allow'd.

HORATIO:　　　　　　　How was this seal'd?

HAMLET: Why, even in that was heaven ordinant.°
 I had my father's signet in my purse,
 Which was the model of that Danish seal;　50
 Folded the writ up in the form of th' other,
 Subscrib'd it, gave 't th' impression, plac'd it safely,
 The changeling never known. Now, the next day
 Was our sea-fight; and what to this was sequent°
 Thou know'st already.　55

HORATIO: So Guildenstern and Rosencrantz go to 't.

HAMLET: Why, man, they did make love to this employment;
 They are not near my conscience; their defeat
 Does by their own insinuation° grow:
 'Tis dangerous when the baser nature comes　60
 Between the pass° and fell incensed° points
 Of mighty opposites.

HORATIO:　　　　　　　Why, what a king is this!

HAMLET: Does it not, think thee, stand° me now upon—
 He that hath kill'd my king and whor'd my mother,
 Popp'd in between th' election° and my hopes,　65
 Thrown out his angle° for my proper life,
 And with such coz'nage°—is 't not perfect conscience,
 To quit° him with this arm? and is 't not to be damn'd,
 To let this canker° of our nature come
 In further evil?　70

---

³⁶**yeoman's** *i.e., faithful.*　⁴¹**wheaten garland** *symbol of peace.*　⁴²**comma** *smallest break or separation. Here amity begins and amity ends the period, and peace stands between like a dependent clause. The comma indicates continuity, link.*　⁴³**'As'es** *the "whereases" of a formal document, with play on the word ass.*　⁴³**charge** *import, and burden.*　⁴⁷**shriving-time** *time for absolution.*　⁴⁸**ordinant** *directing.*　⁵⁴**sequent** *subsequent.*　⁵⁹**insinuation** *interference.*　⁶¹**pass** *thrust.*　⁶¹**fell incensed** *fiercely angered.*　⁶³**stand** *become incumbent.*　⁶⁵**election** *the Danish throne was filled by election.*　⁶⁶**angle** *fishing line.*　⁶⁷**coz'nage** *trickery.*　⁶⁸**quit** *repay.*　⁶⁹**canker** *ulcer, or possibly the worm which destroys buds and leaves.*

HORATIO: It must be shortly known to him from England
  What is the issue of the business there.
HAMLET: It will be short: the interim is mine;
  And a man's life's no more than to say "One."
  But I am very sorry, good Horatio,   75
  That to Laertes I forgot myself;
  For, by the image of my cause, I see
  The portraiture of his: I'll court his favours:
  But, sure, the bravery° of his grief did put me
  Into a tow'ring passion.
HORATIO: Peace! who comes here?   80

Enter a COURTIER [OSRIC].

OSRIC: Your lordship is right welcome back to Denmark.
HAMLET: I humbly thank you, sir. [*To* HORATIO.] Dost know this water-fly?°
HORATIO: No, my good lord.
HAMLET: Thy state is the more gracious; for 'tis a vice to know him. He hath
  much land, and fertile: let a beast be lord of beasts,° and his crib shall stand at   85
  the king's mess:° 'tis a chough;° but, as I say, spacious in the possession of dirt.
OSRIC: Sweet lord, if your lordship were at leisure, I should impart a thing to you
  from his majesty.
HAMLET: I will receive it, sir, with all diligence of spirit. Put your bonnet to his   90
  right use; 'tis for the head.
OSRIC: I thank you lordship, it is very hot.
HAMLET: No, believe me, 'tis very cold; the wind is northerly.
OSRIC: It is indifferent° cold, my lord, indeed.
HAMLET: But yet methinks it is very sultry and hot for my complexion.   95
OSRIC: Exceedingly, my lord; it is very sultry,—as 'twere,—I cannot tell how.
  But, my lord, his majesty bade me signify to you that 'a has laid a great wager
  on your head: sir, this is the matter,—
HAMLET: I beseech you, remember°—

                    [HAMLET *moves him to put on his hat.*]
OSRIC: Nay, good my lord; for mine ease,° in good faith. Sir, here is newly come   100
  to court Laertes; believe me, an absolute gentleman, full of most excellent differences, of very soft° society and great showing:° indeed, to speak feelingly°
  of him, he is the card° or calendar of gentry,° for you shall find in him the
  continent of what part a gentleman would see.
HAMLET: Sir, his definement° suffers no perdition° in you; though, I know, to   105
  divide him inventorially° would dozy° the arithmetic of memory, and yet but

---

yaw° neither, in respect of his quick sail. But, in the verity of extolment, I take him to be a soul of great article;° and his infusion° of such dearth and rareness,° as, to make true diction of him, his semblable° is his mirror; and who else would trace° him, his umbrage,° nothing more.   110

OSRIC: Your lordship speaks most infallibly of him.

HAMLET: The concernancy,° sir? why do we wrap the gentleman in our more rawer breath?°

OSRIC: Sir?   115

HORATIO [*aside to* HAMLET]: Is 't not possible to understand in another tongue?° You will do 't, sir, really.

HAMLET: What imports the nomination° of this gentleman?

OSRIC: Of Laertes?

HORATIO [*aside to* HAMLET]: His purse is empty already; all 's golden words are   120 spent.

HAMLET: Of him, sir.

OSRIC: I know you are not ignorant—

HAMLET: I would you did, sir; yet, in faith, if you did, it would not much approve° me. Well, sir?   125

OSRIC: You are not ignorant of what excellence Laertes is—

HAMLET: I dare not confess that, lest I should compare with him in excellence; but, to know a man well, were to know himself.°

OSRIC: I mean, sir, for his weapon; but in the imputation° laid on him by them, in his meed° he's unfellowed.   130

HAMLET: What's his weapon?

OSRIC: Rapier and dagger.

HAMLET: That's two of his weapons: but, well.

OSRIC: The king, sir, hath wagered with him six Barbary horses: against the which he has impawned,° as I take it, six French rapiers and poniards, with their assigns,   135 as girdle, hangers,° and so: three of the carriages, in faith, are very dear to fancy,° very responsive° to the hilts, most delicate° carriages, and of very liberal conceit.°

HAMLET: What call you the carriages?

HORATIO [*aside to* HAMLET]:   I knew you must be edified by the margent° ere   140 you had done.

OSRIC: The carriages, sir, are the hangers.

HAMLET: The phrase would be more german° to the matter, if we could carry cannon by our sides: I would it might be hangers till then. But, on: six Barbary horses against six French swords, their assigns, and three liberal-conceited   145

107*yaw*   to move unsteadily (of a ship).   108*article*   moment or importance.   108*infusion*   infused temperament, character imparted by nature.   109*dearth and rareness*   rarity   109*semblable*   true likeness.   110*trace*   follow.   110*umbrage*   shadow.   113*concernancy*   import.   114*breath*   speech.   116–17*Is 't ... tongue?*   i.e., can one converse with Osric only in this outlandish jargon?   118*nomination*   naming.   125*approve*   command.   128*but ... himself*   but to know a man as excellent were to know Laertes.   129*imputation*   reputation.   130*meed*   merit.   135*he has impawned*   he has wagered.   136*hangers*   straps on the sword belt from which the sword hung.   137*dear to fancy*   fancifully made.   137*responsive*   probably, well balanced, corresponding closely.   137*delicate*   i.e., in workmanship.   138*liberal conceit*   elaborate design.   140*margent*   margin of a book, place for explanatory notes.   143*german*   germane, appropriate.

carriages; that's the French bet against the Danish. Why is this "impawned," as you call it?

OSRIC: The king, sir, hath laid, that in a dozen passes between yourself and him, he shall not exceed you three hits: he hath laid on twelve for nine; and it would come to immediate trial, if your lordship would vouchsafe the answer. 150

HAMLET: How if I answer "no"?

OSRIC: I mean, my lord, the opposition of your person in trial.

HAMLET: Sir, I will walk here in the hall: if it please his majesty, it is the breathing time° of day with me; let the foils be brought, the gentleman willing, and the king hold his purpose, I will win for him as I can; if not, I will gain nothing but my shame and the odd hits. 155

OSRIC: Shall I re-deliver you e'en so?

HAMLET: To this effect, sir; after what flourish your nature will. 160

OSRIC: I commend my duty to your lordship.

HAMLET: Yours, yours. [*Exit* OSRIC.] He does well to commend it himself; there are no tongues else for 's turn.

HORATIO: This lapwing° runs away with the shell on his head.

HAMLET: 'A did comply, sir, with his dug,° before 'a sucked it. Thus has hey—and many more of the same breed that I know the drossy° age dotes on—only got the tune° of the time and out of an habit of encounter;° a kind of yesty° collection, which carries them through and through the most fann'd and winnowed° opinions; and do but blow them to their trial, the bubbles are out.° 165

Enter a LORD.

LORD: My lord, his majesty commended him to you by young Osric, who brings back to him, that you attend him in the hall: he sends to know if your pleasure hold to play with Laertes, or that you will take longer time. 170

HAMLET: I am constant to my purposes; they follow the king's pleasure: if his fitness speaks, mine is ready; now or whensoever, provided I be so able as now. 175

LORD: The king and queen and all are coming down.

HAMLET: In happy time.°

LORD: The queen desires you to use some gentle entertainment to Laertes before you fall to play.

HAMLET: She well instructs me.   [*Exit* LORD.] 180

HORATIO: You will lose this wager, my lord.

HAMLET: I do not think so; since he went into France, I have been in continual practice; I shall win at the odds. But thou wouldst not think how ill all 's here about my heart: but it is no matter.

HORATIO: Nay, good my lord,— 185

HAMLET: It is but foolery; but it is such a kind of gain-giving,° as would perhaps trouble a woman.

---

¹⁵⁵**breathing time** *exercise period.*   ¹⁶³**lapwing** *peewit; noted for its wiliness in drawing a visitor away from its nest and its supposed habit of running about when newly hatched with its head in the shell; possibly an allusion to Osric's hat.*   ¹⁶⁴**did comply . . . dug** *paid compliments to his mother's breast.*   ¹⁶⁵**drossy** *frivolous.* ¹⁶⁶**tune** *temper, mood.*   ¹⁶⁶**habit of encounter** *demeanor of social intercourse.*   ¹⁶⁷**yesty** *frothy.* ¹⁶⁸**fann'd and winnowed** *select and refined.*   ^{168–69}**blow . . . out** *i.e., put them to the test, and their ignorance is exposed.*   ¹⁷⁷**in happy time** *a phrase of courtesy.* ¹⁸⁶**gain-giving** *misgiving.*

HORATIO: If your mind dislike any thing, obey it: I will forestall their repair hither, and say you are not fit.

HAMLET: Not a whit, we defy augury: there's a special providence in the fall of a   190
sparrow. If it be now, 'tis not to come; if it be not to come, it will be now; if it
be not now, yet it will come: the readiness is all:° since no man of aught he
leaves knows, what is 't to leave betimes? Let be.

A table prepared. [Enter] Trumpets, Drums, and Officers with cushions; KING, QUEEN, [OSRIC,]
and all the State; foils, daggers, [and wine borne in;] and LAERTES.

KING: Come, Hamlet, come, and take this hand from me.

> [*The* KING *puts* LAERTES'S *hand into* HAMLET'S.]

HAMLET: Give me your pardon, sir: I have done you wrong;   195
But pardon 't as you are a gentleman.
This presence° knows,
And you must needs have heard, how I am punish'd
With a sore distraction. What I have done,
That might your nature, honour and exception°   200
Roughly awake, I here proclaim was madness.
Was 't Hamlet wrong'd Laertes? Never Hamlet:
If Hamlet from himself be ta'en away,
And when he's not himself does wrong Laertes,
Then Hamlet does it not, Hamlet denies it.   205
Who does it, then? His madness: if 't be so,
Hamlet is of the faction that is wrong'd;
His madness is poor Hamlet's enemy.
Sir, in this audience,
Let my disclaiming from a purpos'd evil   210
Free me so far in your most generous thoughts,
That I have shot mine arrow o'er the house,
And hurt my brother.

LAERTES: I am satisfied in nature,°
Whose motive, in this case, should stir me most
To my revenge: but in my terms of honour   215
I stand aloof; and will no reconcilement,
Till by some elder masters, of known honour,
I have a voice° and precedent of peace,
To keep my name ungor'd. But till that time,
I do receive your offer'd love like love,   220
And will not wrong it.

HAMLET: I embrace it freely;
And will this brother's wager frankly play.
Give us the foils. Come on.

192**all** *all that matters.*   197**presence** *royal assembly.*   200**exception** *disapproval.*   213**nature** *i.e.,*
he is personally satisfied, but his honor must be satisfied by the rules of the code of honor.   218**voice** *authoritative*
pronouncement.

LAERTES: Come, one for me.
HAMLET: I'll be your foil,° Laertes: in mine ignorance
  Your skill shall, like a star i' th' darkest night,   225
  Stick fiery off ° indeed.
LAERTES: You mock me, sir.
HAMLET: No, by this hand.
KING: Give them the foils, young Osric. Cousin Hamlet,
  You know the wager?
HAMLET: Very well, my lord;
  Your grace has laid the odds o' th' weaker side.   230
KING: I do not fear it; I have seen you both:
  But since he is better'd, we have therefore odds.
LAERTES: This is too heavy, let me see another.
HAMLET: This likes me well. These foils have all a length?

                [They prepare to play.]

OSRIC: Ay, my good lord.   235
KING: Set me the stoups of wine upon that table.
  If Hamlet give the first or second hit,
  Or quit in answer of the third exchange,
  Let all the battlements their ordnance fire;
  The king shall drink to Hamlet's better breath;   240
  And in the cup an union° shall he throw,
  Richer than that which four successive kings
  In Denmark's crown have worn. Give me the cups;
  And let the kettle° to the trumpet speak,
  The trumpet to the cannoneer without,   245
  The cannons to the heavens, the heavens to earth,
  "Now the king drinks to Hamlet." Come begin: *Trumpets the while.*
  And you, the judges, bear a wary eye.
HAMLET: Come on, sir.
LAERTES: Come, my lord.   *[They play.]*
HAMLET: One.
LAERTES: No.
HAMLET: Judgement.
OSRIC: A hit, a very palpable hit.

    Drums, trumpets, and shot. Flourish. A piece goes off.

LAERTES: Well; again.   250
KING: Stay; give me drink. Hamlet, this pearl° is thine;
  Here's to thy health. Give him the cup.
HAMLET: I'll play this bout first; set it by awhile.
  Come. *[They play.]* Another hit; what say you?

---

²²⁴**foil**   *quibble on the two senses: "background which sets something off," and "blunted rapier for fencing."*
²²⁶**Stick fiery off**   *stand out brilliantly.*   ²⁴³**union** *pearl.*   ²⁴⁴**kettle** *kettledrum.*   ²⁵¹**pearl** *i.e.,*
the poison.

LAERTES: A touch, a touch, I do confess 't.   255

KING: Our son shall win.

QUEEN: He's fat,° and scant of breath.

  Here, Hamlet, take my napkin, rub thy brows:

  The queen carouses° to thy fortune, Hamlet.

HAMLET: Good madam!

KING: Gertrude, do not drink.

QUEEN: I will, my lord; I pray you, pardon me.   [*Drinks.*]   260

KING [*aside*]: It is the poison'd cup: it is too late.

HAMLET: I dare not drink yet, madam; by and by.

QUEEN: Come, let me wipe thy face.

LAERTES: My lord, I'll hit him now.

KING: I do not think 't.

LAERTES [*aside*]:   And yet 'tis almost 'gainst my conscience.   265

HAMLET: Come, for the third, Laertes: you but dally;

  I pray you, pass with your best violence;

  I am afeard you make a wanton° of me.

LAERTES: Say you so? come on.   [*They play.*]

OSRIC: Nothing, neither way.   270

LAERTES: Have at you now!

[LAERTES *wounds* HAMLET; *then, in scuffling, they change rapiers,°* and HAMLET *wounds* LAERTES.*]

KING: Part them; they are incens'd.

HAMLET: Nay, come again.   [*The* QUEEN *falls.*]

OSRIC: Look to the queen there, ho!

HORATIO: They bleed on both sides. How is it, my lord?

OSRIC: How is 't, Laertes?

LAERTES: Why, as a woodcock° to mine own springe,° Osric;   275

  I am justly kill'd with mine own treachery.

HAMLET: How does the queen?

KING: She swounds° to see them bleed.

QUEEN: No, no, the drink, the drink,—O my dear Hamlet,—

  The drink, the drink! I am poison'd.   [*Dies.*]

HAMLET: O villany! Ho! let the door be lock'd: 280

  Treachery! Seek it out.   [LAERTES *falls.*]

LAERTES: It is here, Hamlet: Hamlet, thou art slain;

  No med'cine in the world can do thee good;

  In thee there is not half an hour of life;

  The treacherous instrument is in thy hand,   285

256**fat**   *not physically fit, out of training. Some earlier editors speculated that the term applied to the corpulence of Richard Burbage, who originally played the part, but the allusion now appears unlikely. "Fat" may also suggest "sweaty."*   258**carouses**   *drinks a toast.*   268**wanton**   *spoiled child.*   271**in scuffling, they change rapiers** *according to a widespread stage tradition, Hamlet receives a scratch, realizes that Laertes's sword is unbated (not blunted), and accordingly forces an exchange.*   275**woodcock**   *as type of stupidity or as decoy.*   275**springe**   *trap, snare.*   277**swounds**   *swoons.*

Unbated° and envenom'd: the foul practice
Hath turn'd itself on me; lo, here I lie,
Never to rise again: thy mother's poison'd:
I can no more: the king, the king's to blame.

HAMLET: The point envenom'd too!   290
Then, venom, to thy work.   [*Stabs the* KING.]

ALL: Treason! treason!

KING: O, yet defend me, friends; I am but hurt.

HAMLET: Here, thou incestuous, murd'rous, damned Dane.
Drink off this potion. Is thy union here?   295
Follow my mother.   [KING *dies.*]

LAERTES: He is justly serv'd;
It is a poison temper'd° by himself.
Exchange forgiveness with me, noble Hamlet:
Mine and my father's death come not upon thee,
Nor thine on me!   [*Dies.*] 300

HAMLET: Heaven make thee free of it! I follow thee.
I am dead, Horatio. Wretched queen, adieu!
You that look pale and tremble at this chance,
That are but mutes° or audience to this act,
Had I but time—as this fell sergeant,° Death,   305
Is strict in his arrest—O, I could tell you—
But let it be. Horatio, I am dead;
Thou livest; report me and my cause aright
To the unsatisfied.

HORATIO: Never believe it:
I am more an antique Roman° than a Dane: 310
Here's yet some liquor left.

HAMLET: As th' art a man,
Give me the cup: let go, by heaven, I'll ha 't.
O God! Horatio, what a wounded name,
Things standing thus unknown, shall live behind me!
If thou didst ever hold me in thy heart,   315
Absent thee from felicity awhile,
And in this harsh world draw thy breath in pain,
To tell my story.   *A march afar off.*
                What warlike noise is this?

OSRIC: Young Fortinbras, with conquest come from Poland,
To the ambassadors of England gives   320
This warlike volley.

HAMLET: O, I die, Horatio;
The potent poison quite o'er-crows° my spirit:
I cannot live to hear the news from England;
But I do prophesy th' election lights

---

²⁸⁶**Unbated** *Not blunted with a button.*   ²⁹⁷**temper'd** *mixed.*   ³⁰⁴**mutes** *performers in a play who speak no words.*   ³⁰⁵**sergeant** *sheriff's officer.*   ³¹⁰**Roman** *it was the Roman custom to follow masters in death.*   ³²²**o'er-crows** *triumphs over.*

On Fortinbras: he has my dying voice; 325
So tell him, with th' occurrents,° more and less,
Which have solicited.° The rest is silence. [*Dies.*]
HORATIO: Now cracks a noble heart. Good night, sweet prince;
And flights of angels sing thee to thy rest!
Why does the drum come hither? [*March within.*] 330

Enter FORTINBRAS, *with the* [English] AMBASSADORS [*and others*].

FORTINBRAS: Where is this sight?
HORATIO: What is it you would see?
If aught of woe or wonder, cease your search.
FORTINBRAS: This quarry° cries on havoc.° O proud Death,
What feast is toward in thine eternal cell,
That thou so many princes at a shot 335
So bloodily hast struck?
FIRST AMBASSADOR: The sight is dismal;
And our affairs from England come too late:
The ears are senseless that should give us hearing,
To tell him his commandment is fulfill'd,
That Rosencrantz and Guildenstern are dead: 340
Where should we have our thanks?
HORATIO: Not from his mouth,°
Had it th' ability of life to thank you:
He never gave commandment for their death.
But since, so jump° upon this bloody question,°
You from the Polack wars, and you from England, 345
Are here arriv'd, give order that these bodies
High on a stage° be placed to the view;
And let me speak to th' yet unknowing world
How these things came about: so shall you hear
Of carnal, bloody, and unnatural acts, 350
Of accidental judgements, casual slaughters,
Of deaths put on by cunning and forc'd cause,
And, in this upshot, purposes mistook
Fall'n on th' inventors' heads: all this can I
Truly deliver.
FORTINBRAS: Let us haste to hear it, 355
And call the noblest to the audience.
For me, with sorrow I embrace my fortune:
I have some rights of memory° in this kingdom,
Which now to claim my vantage doth invite me.
HORATIO: Of that I shall have also cause to speak, 360
And from his mouth whose voice will draw on more:°

---

³²⁶*occurrents* *events, incidents.* ³²⁷*solicited* *moved, urged.* ³³³*quarry* *heap of dead.* ³³³*cries on havoc* *proclaims a general slaughter.* ³⁴¹*his mouth* *i.e., the king's.* ³⁴⁴*jump* *precisely.* ³⁴⁴*question* *dispute.* ³⁴⁷*stage* *platform.* ³⁵⁸*of memory* *traditional, remembered.* ³⁶¹*voice ... more* *vote will influence still others.*

But let this same be presently perform'd,
Even while men's minds are wild; lest more mischance,
On° plots and errors, happen.
FORTINBRAS: Let four captains
Bear Hamlet, like a soldier, to the stage;   365
For he was likely, had he been put on,
To have prov'd most royal: and, for his passage,°
The soldiers' music and the rites of war
Speak loudly for him.
Take up the bodies: such a sight as this   370
Becomes the field,° but here shows much amiss.
Go, bid the soldiers shoot.

Exeunt [marching, bearing off the dead bodies; after which a peal of ordnance is shot off].

(1600)

QUESTIONS FOR REFLECTION

Experience

1. Describe your experience of reading *Hamlet*. If this is your second or later reading of the play, compare this reading experience with earlier ones.
2. If you have seen the play performed, compare your experience of seeing it with your experience of reading it.

Interpretation

3. What makes Hamlet a tragic figure? To what extent is he responsible for the tragic events of the play?
4. Compare Hamlet's speeches from the beginning and end of the play. Select one of his speeches from Act I or II and compare its tone, attitude, and feeling with a speech from the last act.
5. Explain the roles of Laertes and Fortinbras in the play.
6. What reasons are suggested for Hamlet's delay in exacting revenge for his father's death? Do you find these reasons plausible? Why or why not?
7. Identify the various settings in the play. Explain how each setting contributes to the play's dramatic mood and action. Compare, for example, the settings in Act I, scene i, and Act I, scene ii.
8. What images of women are found in the play? How are Ophelia and Gertrude characterized?
9. Discuss the character of Claudius. Can he be considered a tragic figure? Why or why not?

364**On** *on account of, or possibly, on top of, in addition to.*   367**passage** *death.*   371**field** *i.e., of battle.*

10. Characterize Horatio. What functions does Horatio serve in the play? Which of his personal qualities does Hamlet most admire? Why?

11. Rosencrantz and Guildenstern appear briefly and then disappear from the play. Explain their purpose for the plot of the play.

12. Explain how you would direct the actor playing Polonius. How, for example, would you advise the actor to deliver Polonius's counsel? How much self-knowledge and understanding do you think Polonius possesses?

13. Compare Hamlet and Othello as tragic heroes. What qualities of character distinguish them?

14. Compare Claudius and Iago as villains who precipitate tragedy in the lives of others.

15. What does the gravedigger scene in Act V, scene i, contribute to the play's tone and themes?

16. Any staging of *Hamlet* requires careful attention to lighting. Single out any two scenes in which lighting seems important and explain how you would stage these scenes.

17. Identify two scenes in which the characters' speeches shift between verse and prose. Explain the significance of these shifts.

18. One of the highlights of *Hamlet* is its language. Single out two places where you find the language especially rich, complex, and suggestive. You may choose soliloquies, dialogue exchanges, or both.

Evaluation

19. Whose values does the play most seriously question? Most rigorously criticize? Most generously support?

20. According to some critics, *Hamlet* is Shakespeare's greatest play. What are some of its most accomplished aspects?

CRITICS ON SHAKESPEARE

ADRIAN POOLE

Hamlet and Oedipus

FROM *TRAGEDY: SHAKESPEARE AND THE GREEK EXAMPLE*

For Freud, Hamlet was always closely associated with Oedipus. Again Freud finds a likeness solely in what the two fictional characters suffer from, the desires with which they are supposedly cursed. But Hamlet too has a side to him that Freud ignores. What Hamlet has in common with Oedipus and Freud is that he asks a lot of questions. Freud sees only half of each character, the half that could play the part of patient to his own analyst. And in extricating them from their own dramas and recasting them in his own, Freud seizes the role of analyst for himself, displacing the Oedipus and the Hamlet who make such courageous efforts to understand the story of their lives in the very act of its composition.

The most significant thing that Freud has to say about Sophocles' Oedipus is to do with the form and structure of the play rather than its hidden content: "The action of the play consists in nothing other than the process of revelation, with cunning delays and ever mounting excitement—a process that can be likened to the work of a psychoanalysis—that Oedipus himself is the murderer of Laius." "The work of a psychoanalysis": that is, the specific confrontation and intercourse between analyst and patient. This suggests that a psychoanalysis is constructed like a tragedy, or at least like this tragedy, and that what a psychoanalysis and a tragedy have in common is something to do with their work of discovery. In each case we are moved by the products of revelation only in so far as we are moved by the process of revelation.

When we consider the importance of Oedipus for Freud, we should therefore recall not only the image of a man who acts out our (supposedly) deepest fantasies, but also the action of the play through which Oedipus must discover the truth. If there is a "compulsion" in Sophocles' play, it is much less obviously the compulsion to act out infantile fantasies than the compulsion to know the truth. Sophocles' Oedipus and Shakespeare's Hamlet are the two characters in tragic drama most actively engaged in analysis and interpretation. Their importance for Freud is more to do with a passion for knowledge than with an occult or repressed guilt. Or rather, it is with their exploration of the mysterious relations between knowledge and guilt, a mystery which Freud radically simplifies by attributing guilt solely to the object of interpretation.

Oedipus and Hamlet are on their own within their worlds. Watching their efforts to interpret and understand from within the flow of their own lives, we recognize a universal predicament. Both Oedipus and Hamlet possess great powers of mind, but the questions to which they address themselves involve their whole being. The riddles they attempt to solve, the guilts discovered and incurred in the process of trying to solve them, these are written in flesh and blood, their own and others'.

JOHN ASHWORTH

Olivier, Freud, and Hamlet

FROM *THE ATLANTIC MONTHLY*

Following the fashion in movies and books, Sir Laurence Olivier has acted and directed a *Hamlet* with a simplified Freudian interpretation. The mad Ophelia makes caressing motions over a phallic ornament on the back of a chair, the camera focuses with heavy significance on the labial drapes over the Queen's bed, and why Hamlet doesn't kill the King in the first reel can be explained only in Hamlet's unconscious. In brief, the drama of Hamlet's life is replaced by the drama of what Hamlet might reveal from a couch.

At the beginning of the movie, a narrator intones through the fogs of Elsinore: "This is the tragedy of a man who couldn't make up his mind." Then Sir Laurence appears as the ineffective dreamer, the hysteric, the oversensitive "scholar." Hamlet's alleged procrastination, which for over a century was considered a literary enigma, is attributed—by Freudian trappings, by the neurasthenic quality of the acting, and by cutting significant parts of the play—to the Oedipus complex.

After writing that Shakespeare's play "does not give the cause or motive" of Hamlet's "hesitation," Freud himself explained it as follows: Hamlet can't take vengeance upon the man who takes his father's place with his mother, because Hamlet as a child has repressed the desire to do the same thing. So Hamlet's unconscious tells him that "he himself is no better than the murderer whom he is required to punish," and the "loathing" which should have driven him to revenge is replaced by "self-reproach" and "conscientious scruples." Thus Freud found an explanation for what most intellectuals of his generation, following Goethe and other nineteenth century critics, already believed in—Hamlet's "hesitation."

The main trouble with this "interpretation" is that Hamlet does not hesitate. He does in fact kill the King with remarkable dispatch, as a whole generation of Shakespearians since George Lyman Kittredge have pointed out. So Freud's description of Hamlet's character was based on a wrong premise. Because he couldn't perceive Hamlet's motives, he swallowed the nonsense that a workmanlike dramatist like Shakespeare had written a play without showing the motives of the central character. In consequence he was able to exchange for Hamlet's real motives the prevalent "interpretation" of his day that Hamlet was a procrastinator, and then to deal clinically with the alleged procrastination. . . .

Let's look at the play as Shakespeare intended it to be looked at—from the point of view of an Elizabethan audience. To them, Hamlet's "hesitation" is no occult problem because the play is half over before Hamlet can be sure that the King really did the murder. All that Hamlet has to go on is the word of a ghost, and he isn't sure of the Ghost's identity. For Hamlet, like nearly all Elizabethans, not only believes in ghosts, but also believes that demons can masquerade as ghosts. The apparition may be the ghost of his father or it may be a demon disguised as the ghost of his father, trying to trick him into killing an innocent man. This doubt about the Ghost was perfectly clear to an Elizabethan audience, if not to Freud; and because it is of first importance in understanding the plot, Shakespeare takes the trouble, as any competent dramatist might, to explain it three times: when Hamlet first speaks to the Ghost ("Be thou a spirit of health or goblin damn'd . . . ?"); in Horatio's warning not to follow the Ghost ("What is it tempt you toward the flood, my lord, . . . And there assume some other, horrible form . . . ?"); and in Hamlet's explanation that he will use the players to trick the King into revealing his guilt, if he is guilty.

When Freud ignores Hamlet's sensible precaution not to kill a man who might be innocent and assumes that Hamlet is hesitating to kill a man with whom he unconsciously identifies himself, he simply annihilates the Elizabethan audience for whom Shakespeare wrote, to whom Hamlet's scheme in the players' scene was obvious.

MAYNARD MACK

The Readiness Is All: Hamlet

FROM *EVERYBODY'S SHAKESPEARE*

Hamlet's world is preeminently in the interrogative mood. It reverberates with questions, anguished, meditative, alarmed. There are questions that in this play, to an extent I think unparalleled in any other, mark the phases and even the nuances of the action, helping to establish its peculiar baffled tone. There are other questions whose interrogations, innocent at first glance, are subsequently seen to have reached beyond their contexts and to point toward some pervasive inscrutability in Hamlet's world as a whole. Such is that tense series of challenges with which the tragedy begins: Bernardo's of Francisco, "Who's there?" Francisco's of Horatio and Marcellus, "Who is there?" Horatio's of the ghost, "What art thou . . . ?"

And then there are the famous questions. In them the interrogations seem to point not only beyond the context but beyond the play, out of Hamlet's predicaments into everyone's: "What a piece of work is a man! . . . And yet to me what is this quintessence of dust?" (Act 2. Scene 2). "To be, or not to be—that is the question" (3.1.). "Get thee to a nunnery. Why wouldst thou be a breeder of sinners?" (3.1.). "I am very proud, revengeful, ambitious, with more offenses at my beck than I have thoughts to put them in, imagination to give them shape, or time to act them in. What should such fellows as I do crawling between earth and heaven?" (3.1.). "Dost thou think Alexander looked o' this fashion i' th' earth? . . . And smelt so?" (5.1.).

Further, Hamlet's world is a world of riddles. The hero's own language is often riddling, as the critics have pointed out. When he puns, his puns have receding depths in them, like the one which constitutes his first speech: "A little more than kin, and less than kind!" (1.2.). His utterances in madness, even if wild and whirling, are simultaneously, as Polonius discovers, pregnant: "Do you know me, my lord?" "Excellent well. You are a fishmonger" (2.2.). Even the madness itself is riddling: How much is real? How much is feigned? What does it mean?

Sane or mad, Hamlet's mind plays restlessly about his world, turning up one riddle upon another. The riddle of character, for example, and how it is that in a man whose virtues else are "pure as grace," some vicious mole of nature, some "dram of evil," can "all the noble substance [oft adulter]" (1.4.). Or the riddle of the player's art, and how a man can so project himself into a fiction, a dream of passion, that he can weep for Hecuba (2.2.). Or the riddle of action: how we may think too little—"What to ourselves in passion we propose," says the player-king. "The passion ending, doth the purpose lose" (3.2.); and again, how we may think too much: "Thus conscience does make cowards of us all, And thus the native hue of resolution Is sicklied o'er with the pale cast of thought" (3.1.).

There are also more immediate riddles. His mother—how could she "on this fair mountain leave to feed, And batten on this moor" (3.4.)? The ghost—which may be a devil, for "the devil hath power T' assume a pleasing shape" (2.2.). Ophelia—what does her behavior to him mean? Surprising her in her closet, he falls to such perusal of her face as he would draw it (2.1.). Even the king at his prayers is a riddle. Will a revenge that takes him in the purging of his soul be vengeance, or hire and salary (3.3.)? As for himself, Hamlet realizes, he is the greatest riddle of all—a mystery, he warns Rosencrantz and Guildenstern, from which he will not have the heart plucked out. He cannot tell why he has of late lost all his mirth, forgone all custom of exercises. Still less can he tell why he delays: "I do not know Why yet I live to say, 'This thing's to do,' Sith I have cause, and will, and strength, and means To do't" (4.4.).

Thus the mysteriousness of Hamlet's world is of a piece. It is not simply a matter of missing motivations, to be expunged if only we could find the perfect clue. It is built in. It is evidently an important part of what the play wishes to say to us. And it is certainly an element that the play thrusts upon us from the opening word. Everyone, I think, recalls the mysteriousness of that first scene. The cold middle of the night on the castle platform, the muffled sentries, the uneasy atmosphere of apprehension, the challenges leaping out of the dark, the questions that follow the challenges, feeling out the darkness, searching for identities, for relations, for assurance. "Bernardo?" "Have you had quiet guard?" "Who hath relieved you?" "What, is Horatio there?" "What, has this thing appeared again tonight?" "Looks 'a not like the king?" "How now, Horatio! ... Is not this something more than fantasy? What think you on 't?" "Is it not like the King?" "Why this same strict and most observant watch ... ?" "Shall I strike at it with my partisan?" "Do you consent we shall acquaint [young Hamlet] with it?"

We need not be surprised that critics and playgoers alike have been tempted to see in this an evocation not simply of Hamlet's world but of their own. Human beings in their aspect of bafflement, moving in darkness on a rampart between two worlds, unable to reject, or quite accept, the one that, when they face it, "to-shakes" their dispositions with thoughts beyond the reaches of their souls—comforting themselves with hints and guesses. We hear these hints and guesses whispering through the darkness as the several watchers speak. "At least, the whisper goes so" (1.1.), says one. "I think it be no other but e'en so," says another. "I have heard" that on the crowing of the cock "Th' extravagant and erring spirit hies To his confine," says a third. "Some say" at Christmas time "This bird of dawning" sings all night, "And then, they say, no spirit dare stir abroad." "So have I heard," says the first, "and do in part believe it." However we choose to take the scene, it is clear that it creates a world where uncertainties are of the essence.

CAROLYN HEILBRUN

The Character of Hamlet's Mother

FROM *HAMLET'S MOTHER AND OTHER WOMEN*

To understand Gertrude properly, it is only necessary to examine the lines Shakespeare has chosen for her to say. She is, except for her description of Ophelia's death, concise and pithy in speech, with a talent for seeing the essence of every situation presented before her eyes. If she is not profound, she is certainly never silly. We first hear her asking

Hamlet to stop wearing black, to stop walking about with his eyes downcast, and to realize that death is an inevitable part of life. She is, in short, asking him not to give way to the passion of grief, a passion of whose force and dangers the Elizabethans were aware, as Miss Campbell has shown. Claudius echoes her with a well-reasoned argument against grief which was, in its philosophy if not in its language, a piece of commonplace Elizabethan lore. After Claudius' speech, Gertrude asks Hamlet to remain in Denmark, where he is rightly loved. Her speeches have been short, however warm and loving, and conciseness of statement is not the mark of a dull and shallow woman.

We next hear her, as Queen and gracious hostess, welcoming Rosencrantz and Guildenstern to the court, hoping, with the King, that they may cheer Hamlet and discover what is depressing him. Claudius then tells Gertrude, when they are alone, that Polonius believes he knows what is upsetting Hamlet. The Queen answers:

> I doubt it is no other than the main,
> His father's death and our o'er-hasty marriage.
>
> (II.ii. 56–57)

This statement is concise, remarkably to the point, and not a little courageous. It is not the statement of a dull, slothful woman who can only echo her husband's words. Next, Polonius enters with his most unbrief apotheosis to brevity. The Queen interrupts him with five words: "More matter, with less art" (II. ii. 95). It would be difficult to find a phrase more applicable to Polonius. When this gentleman, in no way deterred from his loquacity, after purveying the startling news that he has a daughter, begins to read a letter, the Queen asks pointedly "Came this from Hamlet to her?" (II. ii. 114).

We see Gertrude next in Act III, asking Rosencrantz and Guildenstern, with her usual directness, if Hamlet received them well, and if they were able to tempt him to any pastime. But before leaving the room, she stops for a word of kindness to Ophelia. It is a humane gesture, for she is unwilling to leave Ophelia, the unhappy tool of the King and Polonius, without some kindly and intelligent appreciation of her help:

> And for your part, Ophelia, I do wish
> That your good beauties be the happy cause
> Of Hamlet's wildness. So shall I hope your virtues
> Will bring him to his wonted way again,
> To both your honors.   (III. i. 38–42)

[S]he dies. But before she dies she does not waste time on vituperation; she warns Hamlet that the drink is poisoned to prevent his drinking it. They are her last words. Those critics who have thought her stupid admire her death; they call it uncharacteristic.

In Act III, when Hamlet goes to his mother in her closet his nerves are pitched at the very height of tension; he is on the edge of hysteria. The possibility of murdering his mother has in fact entered his mind, and he has just met and refused an opportunity to kill Claudius. His mother, meanwhile, waiting for him, has told Polonius not to fear for her, but she knows when she sees Hamlet that he may be violently mad. Hamlet quips with her, insults her, tells her he wishes she were not his mother, and when she, still retaining dignity, attempts to end the interview, Hamlet seizes her and she cries for help. The important thing to note is that the Queen's cry "Thou wilt not murder me?" (III. iv. 21) is not foolish. She has seen from Hamlet's demeanor that he is capable of murder, as indeed in the next instant he proves himself to be.

We next learn from the Queen's startled "As kill a king?" (III. iv. 31) that she has no knowledge of the murder, though of course this is only confirmation here of what we already know. Then the Queen asks Hamlet why he is so hysterical:

> What have I done, that thou dar'st wag thy tongue
> In noise so rude against me?　　(III. iv. 40–41)

Hamlet tells her: it is her lust, the need of sexual passion, which has driven her from the arms and memory of her husband to the incomparably cruder charms of his brother.

A. D. NUTTAL

Othello

FROM *A NEW MIMESIS*

Othello's tragedy indeed is strangely—and formally—introverted; it consists in the fact that he left the arena proper to tragedy, the battlefield, and entered a subtragic world for which he was not fitted. *Othello* is the story of a hero who went into a house.

Long ago A. C. Bradley observed that, if the heroes of *Hamlet* and *Othello* change places, each play ends very quickly. Hamlet would see through Iago in the first five minutes and be parodying him in the next. Othello, receiving clear instructions like "Kill that usurper" from a ghost, would simply have gone to work. Thus, as the classic problem of *Hamlet* is the hero's delay, so the classic problem of *Othello* is the hero's gullibility. The stronger our sense of Othello's incongruity in the domestic world, the less puzzling this becomes. Certainly, *Othello* is about a man who, having come from a strange and remote place, found his feet in the world of Venetian professional soldier-ship—and then exchanged that spacious world for a little, dim world of unimaginable horror. "War is no strife/To the dark house and the detested wife" comes not from Othello but from a comedy, but it will serve here. Its note of peculiarly masculine pain and hatred can still score the nerves. It is therefore not surprising that Shakespeare avails himself of the metaphor of the caged hawk. Desdemona says, "I'll watch him tame," at III. iii. 23. The real process of taming a hawk by keeping it awake and so breaking its spirit is described at length in T. H. White's *The Goshawk* [1953]. Othello turns the image round when he says of Desdemona,

> If I do prove her haggard,
> Though that her jesses were my dear heart-strings,
> I'd whistle her off and let her down the wind

To prey at fortune.   (III. iii. 259–62)

He speaks formally of Desdemona, but it is hard not to feel that in the last words it is his own dream of liberty which speaks.

Othello is also about insiders and outsiders. The exotic Moor finds when he leaves the public, martial sphere that he is not accepted, is not understood and cannot understand. The Venetian colour bar is sexual, not professional. Iago plays on this with his "old black ram . . . tupping your white ewe" (I. i. 85–86) and the same note is struck by Roderigo with his "gross clasps of a lascivious Moor" (I. i. 121). Othello's gullibility is not really so very strange. Coal-black among the glittering Venetians, he is visibly the outsider, and in his bewilderment he naturally looks for the man who is visibly the insider, the man who knows the ropes, the sort of man who is always around in the bar, the "good chap" or (as they said then) the "honest" man. And he finds him.

There are two schools of thought on the sort of actor who should play Iago. School A chooses a dark, waspish fellow. School B chooses a bluff, straw-haired, pink-faced sort of man, solid-looking with no nonsense about him. In production School B triumphs, for the role, cast in this way, becomes both credible and terrifying. Although Iago is everywhere spoken of as a "good chap," he has no friends, no loves, no positive desires. He, and not Othello, proves to be the true outsider of the play, for he is foreign to humanity itself. Othello comes from a remote clime, but Iago, in his simpler darkness, comes from the far side of chaos—hence the pathos of Shakespeare's best departure from his source. In Cinthio's *novella* the Ensign (that is, the Iago-figure) with a cunning affectation of reluctance, suggests that Desdemona is false and then seeing his chance, adds, "Your blackness already displeases her." In Shakespeare's play we have instead a note of bar-room masculine intimacy, in assumed complicity of sentiment. Iago says, in effect "Well, she went with black man, so what is one to think?" (III. iii. 228–33). Othello's need to be accepted and guided makes him an easy victim of this style. The hero is set for his sexual humiliation.

MAURICE CHARNEY

Shakespeare's Villains

FROM *HOW TO READ SHAKESPEARE*

The malevolence of Shakespeare's villains is difficult to account for either by their past history or by their present grievances. Shakespeare wants to avoid giving them a believable background that would justify or explain their evil. The villains are generally not motivated at all—at least not by detective-story standards—but are presented to us already securely entrenched in their moral condition. Their evil is a positive and active force, and its unquestioned energy makes the villains seem diabolic. We need to accept them as they appear without probing the origins of their conduct. This requires forbearance from the audience, whose love of scandalous explanation is deliberately frustrated.

What are we to make of the reasons Iago offers for his savage revenge on Othello? Is he acting from thwarted ambition, because Cassio has the promotion Iago thinks he himself deserves? Or are the reasons more subtle and more personal? As Iago tells us,

> I hate the Moor;
> And it is thought abroad that 'twixt my
>   sheets
> 'Has done my office. I know not if 't be true;
> Yet I, for mere suspicion in that kind,
> Will do as if for surety.   (1.3.356–60)

There is a cynical coldness in "I know not if 't be true," and Iago never troubles himself to find out. Personal honor means nothing to him, since in his view all women are whores and all human activity is base, coarse, gross, and disgusting. What is important is that Iago hates the Moor. That is enough, and reasons are alleged merely to satisfy public opinion.

In a much-quoted phrase, Coleridge spoke of this aspect of Iago's morality as the "motive-hunting of motiveless malignity." In other words, there are no motives and there is no cause that can account for Iago's evil. Othello never understands this, because even at the very end of the play he still wants to learn from that "demi-devil" "Why he hath thus ensnar'd my soul and body" (5.2.298). But Iago refuses any final comforts for Othello's tragic rationalism: "Demand me nothing. What you know, you know./ From this time forth I never will speak word" (299–300). Ultimately, there can be no answer to Othello's question. We have only a hint of explanation when Iago justifies the murder of Cassio: "He hath a daily beauty in his life/ That makes me ugly" (5.1.19–20). This judgment has the true satanic ring. Like Lucifer, Iago is irresistibly attracted to the beauty from which he has been excluded for all eternity, and this sense of damnation makes his revenge so monomaniacal.

Iago is Shakespeare's most brilliant villain, who dominates his play in a way no other villain can (except perhaps Macbeth, a villain-hero). He forces us to consider one of the most difficult paradoxes of tragedy: Why is the villain usually so much more intelligent, insightful, sensitive, and imaginative than his victim? The villain seems to be the surrogate for the diabolic-creative powers of the dramatist. Iago is wonderfully complex in his manipulation of the dramatic action; his plots and Shakespeare's seem to come together, so that one could speak of the stagecraft of villainy and its aesthetics. But in his moral nature Iago is wonderfully simple, if not actually simplified. The presence of both Iago and Desdemona in a single play assumes that good and evil exist as warring postulates. This is the morality play aspect of Shakespearean tragedy.

CHAPTER TWENTY

The Modern Realistic Theater: Ibsen

Realism can be defined as the representation of everyday life in literature. Concerned with the average, the commonplace, the ordinary, realism employs theatrical conventions to create the illusion of everyday life. With realistic drama came the depiction of subjects close to the lives of middle-class people: work, marriage, and family life. From this standpoint, Arthur Miller's *Death of a Salesman* and Henrik Ibsen's *A Doll House* are more realistic than Shakespeare's *Othello,* which in turn, is more realistic than Sophocles' *Oedipus Rex*. Though each of these plays possesses a true-to-life quality, each operates according to different theatrical conventions. Royal personages, gods, military heroes, and exalted language are absent from Miller's and Ibsen's plays, as modern dramatists turned to an approximation of the daily life of the lower and middle classes.

One means by which realistic drama creates the illusion of everyday life is through setting. Whereas settings consist primarily of painted backdrops in Molière's plays and are often established by dialogue in Shakespeare's plays, the settings of modern realistic plays are designed to look authentic. Moreover, setting in plays such as Ibsen's *A Doll House* often functions symbolically. In *Elements of Literature 3*, Robert Scholes has noted that the elaborately detailed setting of *A Doll House* symbolizes both "the impact of the Helmers' environment on their marriage" and the "very nature of their marriage"; it also embodies "the profound pressures placed on Helmer and Nora by the material and social conditions of their world."★

Other conventions designed to create and sustain the illusion that the audience was watching a slice of domestic life include the following: the use of a three-walled room with an open fourth wall into which the audience peers to view and overhear the action; dialogue that approximates the idiom of everyday discourse, polished to be sure, but designed especially to sound like speech rather than poetry; plots that, though highly contrived, seem to turn on a series of causally related actions; subjects not from mythology or history, but from the concerns of ordinary life.

INTRODUCTION TO HENRIK IBSEN

[1828–1906]

Besides accommodating himself to the conventions of realism in *A Doll House*, Ibsen also made the play a *cause célèbre* by raising questions in it about the rights of women, a subject that was beginning to receive attention in the late nineteenth century. *A Doll House,* written in 1879, performed in London (1889) and Paris (1894), attracted attention wherever it played. Nonetheless, Ibsen insisted that the play was less about the rights of women than about human rights generally, less about the particular social conditions responsible for the position of women in nineteenth-century Norway than about the need for individuals of both sexes to treat each other with mutual respect.

A Doll House

TRANSLATED BY ROLF FJELDE

CHARACTERS

TORVALD HELMER, *a lawyer*
NORA, *his wife*
DR. RANK
MRS. LINDE
NILS KROGSTAD, *a bank clerk*
THE HELMERS' THREE SMALL CHILDREN
ANNE-MARIE, *their nurse*
HELENE, *a maid*
A DELIVERY BOY

The action takes place in HELMER's *residence.*

★Robert Scholes et al., *Elements of Literature 3* (New York: Oxford University Press, 1982), p. 966.

ACT I

A comfortable room, tastefully but not expensively furnished. A door to the right in the back wall leads to the entryway, another to the left leads to HELMER's *study. Between these doors, a piano. Midway in the left-hand wall a door, and further back a window. Near the window a round table with an armchair and a small sofa. In the right-hand wall, toward the rear a door, and nearer the foreground a porcelain stove with two armchairs and a rocking chair beside it. Between the stove and the side door, a small table. Engravings on the walls. An etagére with china figures and other small art objects; a small bookcase with richly bound books; the floor carpeted; a fire burning in the stove. It is a winter day.*

A bell rings in the entryway; shortly after we hear the door being unlocked. NORA *comes into the room, humming happily to herself; she is wearing street clothes and carries an armload of packages, which she puts down on the table to the right. She has left the hall door open; and through it a* DELIVERY BOY *is seen, holding a Christmas tree and a basket which he gives to the* MAID *who let them in.*

NORA: Hide the tree well, Helene. The children mustn't get a glimpse of it till this evening, after it's trimmed. (*To the* DELIVERY BOY, *taking out her purse*) How much?

DELIVERY BOY: Fifty, ma'am.

NORA: There's a crown. No, keep the change. (*The* BOY *thanks her and leaves.* NORA *shuts the door. She laughs softly to herself while taking off her street things. Drawing a bag of macaroons from her pocket, she eats a couple, then steals over and listens at her husband's study door.*) Yes, he's home. (*Hums again as she moves to the table, right.*)

HELMER (*from the study*):   Is that my little lark twittering out there?

NORA (*busy opening some packages*):   Yes, it is.

HELMER: Is that my squirrel rummaging around?

NORA: Yes!

HELMER: When did my squirrel get in?

NORA: Just now. (*Putting the macaroon bag in her pocket and wiping her mouth*) Do come in, Torvald, and see what I've bought.

HELMER: Can't be disturbed. (*After a moment he opens the door and peers in, pen in hand.*) Bought, you say? All that there? Has the little spendthrift been out throwing money around again?

NORA: Oh, but Torvald, this year we really should let ourselves go a bit. It's the first Christmas we haven't had to economize.

HELMER: But you know we can't go squandering.

NORA: Oh yes, Torvald, we can squander a little now. Can't we? Just a tiny, wee bit. Now that you've got a big salary and are going to make piles and piles of money.

HELMER: Yes—starting New Year's. But then it's a full three months till the raise comes through.

NORA: Pooh! We can borrow that long.

HELMER: Nora! (*Goes over and playfully takes her by the ear*) Are your scatterbrains off again? What if today I borrowed a thousand crowns, and you squandered them over Christmas week, and then on New Year's Eve a roof tile fell on my head, and I lay there—

NORA (*putting her hand on his mouth*):   Oh! Don't say such things!

HELMER: Yes, but what if it happened—then what?

NORA: If anything so awful happened, then it just wouldn't matter if I had debts or not.

HELMER: Well, but the people I'd borrowed from?

NORA: Them? Who cares about them! They're strangers.

HELMER: Nora, Nora, how like a woman! No, but seriously, Nora, you know what I think about that. No debts! Never borrow! Something of freedom's lost—and something of beauty, too—from a home that's founded on borrowing and debt. We've made a brave stand up to now, the two of us; and we'll go right on like that the little while we have to.

NORA (*going toward the stove*): Yes, whatever you say, Torvald.

HELMER (*following her*): Now, now, the little lark's wings mustn't droop. Come on, don't be a sulky squirrel. (*Taking out his wallet*) Nora, guess what I have here.

NORA (*turning quickly*): Money!

HELMER: There, see. (*Hands her some notes*) Good grief, I know how costs go up in a house at Christmastime.

NORA: Ten—twenty—thirty—forty. Oh, thank you. Torvald; I can manage no end on this.

HELMER: You really will have to.

NORA: Oh yes, I promise I will! But come here so I can show you everything I bought. And so cheap! Look, new clothes for Ivar here—and a sword. Here a horse and a trumpet for Bob. And a doll and a doll's bed here for Emmy; they're nothing much, but she'll tear them to bits in no time anyway. And here I have dress material and handkerchiefs for the maids. Old Anne-Marie really deserves something more.

HELMER: And what's in that package there?

NORA (*with a cry*): Torvald, no! You can't see that till tonight!

HELMER: I see. But tell me now, you little prodigal, what have you thought of for yourself?

NORA: For myself? Oh, I don't want anything at all.

HELMER: Of course you do. Tell me just what—within reason—you'd most like to have.

NORA: I honestly don't know. Oh, listen, Torvald—

HELMER: Well?

NORA (*fumbling at his coat buttons, without looking at him*): If you want to give me something, then maybe you could—you could—

HELMER: Come on, out with it.

NORA (*hurriedly*): You could give me money, Torvald. No more than you think you can spare, then one of these days I'll buy something with it.

HELMER: But Nora—

NORA: Oh, please, Torvald darling, do that! I beg you, please. Then I could hang the bills in pretty gilt paper on the Christmas tree. Wouldn't that be fun?

HELMER: What are those little birds called that always fly through their fortunes?

NORA: Oh yes, spendthrifts; I know all that. But let's do as I say, Torvald; then I'll have time to decide what I really need most. That's very sensible, isn't it?

HELMER (*smiling*): Yes, very—that is, if you actually hung onto the money I give you, and you actually used it to buy yourself something. But it goes for the house and for all sorts of foolish things, and then I only have to lay out some more.

NORA: Oh, but Torvald—

HELMER: Don't deny it, my dear little Nora. (*Putting his arm around her waist*) Spendthrifts are sweet, but they use up a frightful amount of money. It's incredible what it costs a man to feed such birds.

NORA: Oh, how can you say that! Really, I save everything I can.

HELMER (*laughing*):   Yes, that's the truth. Everything you can. But that's nothing at all.

NORA (*humming, with a smile of quiet satisfaction*):   Hm, if you only knew what expenses we larks and squirrels have, Torvald.

HELMER: You're an odd little one. Exactly the way your father was. You're never at a loss for scaring up money; but the moment you have it, it runs right out through your fingers; you never know what you've done with it. Well, one takes you as you are. It's deep in your blood. Yes, these things are hereditary, Nora.

NORA: Ah, I could wish I'd inherited many of Papa's qualities.

HELMER: And I couldn't wish you anything but just what you are, my sweet little lark. But wait; it seems to me you have a very—what should I call it?—a very suspicious look today—

NORA: I do?

HELMER: You certainly do. Look me straight in the eye.

NORA (*looking at him*):   Well?

HELMER (*shaking an admonitory finger*):   Surely my sweet tooth hasn't been running riot in town today, has she?

NORA: No. Why do you imagine that?

HELMER: My sweet tooth really didn't make a little detour through the confectioner's?

NORA: No, I assure you, Torvald—

HELMER: Hasn't nibbled some pastry?

NORA: No, not at all.

HELMER: Nor even munched a macaroon or two?

NORA: No, Torvald, I assure you, really—

HELMER: There, there now. Of course I'm only joking.

NORA (*going to the table, right*):   You know I could never think of going against you.

HELMER: No, I understand that; and you *have* given me your word. (*Going over to her.*) Well, you keep your little Christmas secrets to yourself, Nora darling. I expect they'll come to light this evening, when the tree is lit.

NORA: Did you remember to ask Dr. Rank?

HELMER: No. But there's no need for that; it's assumed he'll be dining with us. All the same, I'll ask him when he stops by here this morning. I've ordered some fine wine. Nora, you can't imagine how I'm looking forward to this evening.

NORA: So am I. And what fun for the children, Torvald!

HELMER: Ah, it's so gratifying to know that one's gotten a safe, secure job, and with a comfortable salary. It's a great satisfaction, isn't it?

NORA: Oh, it's wonderful!

HELMER: Remember last Christmas? Three whole weeks before, you shut yourself in every evening till long after midnight, making flowers for the Christmas tree, and all the other decorations to surprise us. Ugh, that was the dullest time I've ever lived through.

NORA: It wasn't at all dull for me.

HELMER (*smiling*):   But the outcome *was* pretty sorry, Nora.

NORA: Oh, don't tease me with that again. How could I help it that the cat came in and tore everything to shreds.

HELMER: No, poor thing, you certainly couldn't. You wanted so much to please us all, and that's what counts. But it's just as well that the hard times are past.

NORA: Yes, it's really wonderful.

HELMER: Now I don't have to sit here alone, boring myself, and you don't have to tire your precious eyes and your fair little delicate hands—

NORA (*clapping her hands*):   No, is it really true, Torvald, I don't have to? Oh, how wonderfully lovely to hear! (*Taking his arm.*) Now I'll tell you just how I've thought we should plan things. Right after Christmas—(*The doorbell rings.*) Oh, the bell. (*Straightening the room up a bit.*) Somebody would have to come. What a bore!

HELMER: I'm not at home to visitors, don't forget.

MAID (*from the hall doorway*):   Ma'am, a lady to see you—

NORA: All right, let her come in.

MAID (*to Helmer*):   And the doctor's just come too.

HELMER: Did he go right to my study?

MAID: Yes, he did.

HELMER *goes into his room. The* MAID *shows in* MRS. LINDE, *dressed in traveling clothes, and shuts the door after her.*

MRS. LINDE (*in a dispirited and somewhat hesitant voice*):   Hello, Nora.

NORA (*uncertain*):   Hello—

MRS. LINDE: You don't recognize me.

NORA: No, I don't know—but wait, I think—(*Exclaiming.*) What! Kristine! Is it really you?

MRS. LINDE: Yes, it's me.

NORA: Kristine! To think I didn't recognize you. But then, how could I? (*More quietly.*) How you've changed, Kristine!

MRS. LINDE: Yes, no doubt I have. In nine—ten long years.

NORA: Is it so long since we met! Yes, it's all of that. Oh, these last eight years have been a happy time, believe me. And so now you've come in to town, too. Made the long trip in the winter. That took courage.

MRS. LINDE: I just got here by ship this morning.

NORA: To enjoy yourself over Christmas, of course. Oh, how lovely! Yes, enjoy ourselves, we'll do that. But take your coat off. You're not still cold? (*Helping her.*) There now, let's get cozy here by the stove. No, the easy chair there! I'll take the rocker here. (*Seizing her hands.*) Yes, now you have your old look again; it was only in that first moment. You're a bit more pale, Kristine—and maybe a bit thinner.

MRS. LINDE: And much, much older, Nora.

NORA: Yes, perhaps, a bit older; a tiny, tiny bit; not much at all. (*Stopping short; suddenly serious*) Oh, but thoughtless me, to sit here, chattering away. Sweet, good Kristine, can you forgive me?

MRS. LINDE: What do you mean, Nora?

NORA (*softly*):   Poor Kristine, you've become a widow.

MRS. LINDE: Yes, three years ago.

NORA: Oh, I knew it, of course; I read it in the papers. Oh Kristine, you must believe me; I often thought of writing you then, but I kept postponing it, and something always interfered.

MRS. LINDE: Nora dear, I understand completely.

NORA: No, it was awful of me, Kristine. You poor thing, how much you must have gone through. And he left you nothing?

MRS. LINDE: No.

NORA: And no children?

MRS. LINDE: No.

NORA: Nothing at all, then?

MRS. LINDE: Not even a sense of loss to feed on.

NORA (looking incredulously at her): But Kristine, how could that be?

MRS. LINDE (smiling wearily and smoothing her hair): Oh, sometimes it happens, Nora.

NORA: So completely alone. How terribly hard that must be for you. I have three lovely children. You can't see them now; they're out with the maid. But now you must tell me everything—

MRS. LINDE: No, no, no, tell me about yourself.

NORA: No, you begin. Today I don't want to be selfish. I want to think only of you today. But there is something I must tell you. Did you hear of the wonderful luck we had recently?

MRS. LINDE: No, what's that?

NORA: My husband's been made manager in the bank, just think!

MRS. LINDE: Your husband? How marvelous!

NORA: Isn't it? Being a lawyer is such an uncertain living, you know, especially if one won't touch any cases that aren't clean and decent. And of course Torvald would never do that, and I'm with him completely there. Oh, we're simply delighted, believe me! He'll join the bank right after New Year's and start getting a huge salary and lots of commissions. From now on we can live quite differently—just as we want. Oh, Kristine, I feel so light and happy! Won't it be lovely to have stacks of money and not a care in the world?

MRS. LINDE: Well, anyway, it would be lovely to have enough for necessities.

NORA: No, not just for necessities, but stacks and stacks of money!

MRS. LINDE (smiling): Nora, Nora, aren't you sensible yet? Back in school you were such a free spender.

NORA (with a quiet laugh): Yes, that's what Torvald still says. (Shaking her finger) But "Nora, Nora" isn't as silly as you all think. Really, we've been in no position for me to go squandering. We've had to work, both of us.

MRS. LINDE: You too?

NORA: Yes, at odd jobs—needlework, crocheting, embroidery, and such—(Casually) and other things too. You remember that Torvald left the department when we were married? There was no chance of promotion in his office, and of course he needed to earn more money. But that first year he drove himself terribly. He took on all kinds of extra work that kept him going morning and night. It wore him down, and then he fell deathly ill. The doctors said it was essential for him to travel south.

MRS. LINDE: Yes, didn't you spend a whole year in Italy?

NORA: That's right. It wasn't easy to get away, you know. Ivar had just been born. But of course we had to go. Oh, that was a beautiful trip, and it saved Torvald's life. But it cost a frightful sum, Kristine.

MRS. LINDE: I can well imagine.

NORA: Four thousand, eight hundred crowns it cost. That's really a lot of money.

MRS. LINDE: But it's lucky you had it when you needed it.

NORA: Well, as it was, we got it from Papa.

MRS. LINDE: I see. It was just about the time your father died.

NORA: Yes, just about then. And, you know, I couldn't make the trip out to nurse him. I had to stay here, expecting Ivar any moment, and with my poor sick Torvald to care for. Dearest Papa, I never saw him again, Kristine. Oh, that was the worst time I've known in all my marriage.

MRS. LINDE: I know how you loved him. And then you went off to Italy?

NORA: Yes. We had the means now, and the doctors urged us. So we left a month after.

MRS. LINDE: And your husband came back completely cured?

NORA: Sound as a drum!

MRS. LINDE: But—the doctor?

NORA: Who?

MRS. LINDE: I thought the maid said he was a doctor, the man who came in with me.

NORA: Yes, that was Dr. Rank—but he's not making a sick call. He's our closest friend, and he stops by at least once a day. No, Torvald hasn't had a sick moment since, and the children are fit and strong, and I am, too. (*Jumping up and clapping her hands*) Oh, dear God, Kristine, what a lovely thing to live and be happy! But how disgusting of me—I'm talking of nothing but my own affairs. (*Sits on a stool close by* KRISTINE, *arms resting across her knees*) Oh, don't be angry with me! Tell me, is it really true that you weren't in love with your husband? Why did you marry him, then?

MRS. LINDE: My mother was still alive, but bedridden and helpless—and I had two younger brothers to look after. In all conscience, I didn't think I could turn him down.

NORA: No, you were right there. But was he rich at the time?

MRS. LINDE: He was very well off, I'd say. But the business was shaky, Nora. When he died, it all fell apart, and nothing was left.

NORA: And then—?

MRS. LINDE: Yes, so I had to scrape up a living with a little shop and a little teaching and whatever else I could find. The last three years have been like one endless workday without a rest for me. Now it's over, Nora. My poor mother doesn't need me, for she's passed on. Nor the boys, either; they're working now and can take care of themselves.

NORA: How free you must feel—

MRS. LINDE: No—only unspeakably empty. Nothing to live for now. (*Standing up anxiously*) That's why I couldn't take it any longer out in that desolate hole. Maybe here it'll be easier to find something to do and keep my mind occupied. If I could only be lucky enough to get a steady job, some office work—

NORA: Oh, but Kristine, that's so dreadfully tiring, and you already look so tired. It would be much better for you if you could go off to a bathing resort.

MRS. LINDE (*going toward the window*): I have no father to give me travel money, Nora.

NORA (*rising*): Oh, don't be angry with me.

MRS. LINDE (*going to her*): Nora dear, don't you be angry with me. The worst of my kind of situation is all the bitterness that's stored away. No one to work for, and yet you're always having to snap up your opportunities. You have to live; and so you grow selfish. When you told me the happy change in your lot, do you know I was delighted less for your sakes than for mine?

NORA: How so? Oh, I see. You think maybe Torvald could do something for you.

MRS. LINDE: Yes, that's what I thought.

NORA: And he will, Kristine! Just leave it to me; I'll bring it up so delicately—find something attractive to humor him with. Oh, I'm so eager to help you.

MRS. LINDE: How very kind of you, Nora, to be so concerned over me—doubly kind, considering you really know so little of life's burdens yourself.

NORA: I—? I know so little—?

MRS. LINDE (smiling):   Well, my heavens—a little needlework and such—Nora, you're just a child.

NORA (tossing her head and pacing the floor):   You don't have to act so superior.

MRS. LINDE: Oh?

NORA: You're just like the others. You all think I'm incapable of anything serious—

MRS. LINDE: Come now—

NORA: That I've never had to face the raw world.

MRS. LINDE: Nora dear, you've just been telling me all your troubles.

NORA: Hm! Trivia! (Quietly) I haven't told you the big thing.

MRS. LINDE: Big thing? What do you mean?

NORA: You look down on me so, Kristine, but you shouldn't. You're proud that you worked so long and hard for your mother.

MRS. LINDE: I don't look down on a soul. But it is true; I'm proud—and happy, too—to think it was given to me to make my mother's last days almost free of care.

NORA: And you're also proud thinking of what you've done for your brothers.

MRS. LINDE: I feel I've a right to be.

NORA: I agree. But listen to this, Kristine—I've also got something to be proud and happy for.

MRS. LINDE: I don't doubt it. But whatever do you mean?

NORA: Not so loud. What if Torvald heard! He mustn't, not for anything in the world. Nobody must know, Kristine. No one but you.

MRS. LINDE: But what is it, then?

NORA: Come here. (Drawing her down beside her on the sofa) It's true—I've also got something to be proud and happy for. I'm the one who saved Torvald's life.

MRS. LINDE: Saved—? Saved how?

NORA: I told you about the trip to Italy. Torvald never would have lived if he hadn't gone south—

MRS. LINDE: Of course, your father gave you the means—

NORA (smiling):   That's what Torvald and all the rest think, but—

MRS. LINDE: But—?

NORA: Papa didn't give us a pin. I was the one who raised the money.

MRS. LINDE: You? The whole amount?

NORA: Four thousand, eight hundred crowns. What do you say to that?

MRS. LINDE: But Nora, how was it possible? Did you win the lottery?

NORA (disdainfully):   The lottery? Pooh! No art to that.

MRS. LINDE: But where did you get it from then?

NORA (humming, with a mysterious smile):   Hmm, tra-la-la-la.

MRS. LINDE: Because you couldn't have borrowed it.

NORA: No? Why not?

MRS. LINDE: A wife can't borrow without her husband's consent.

NORA (*tossing her head*):   Oh, but a wife with a little business sense, a wife who knows how to manage—

MRS. LINDE: Nora, I simply don't understand—

NORA: You don't have to. Whoever said I *borrowed* the money? I could have gotten it other ways. (*Throwing herself back on the sofa*) I could have gotten it from some admirer or other. After all, a girl with my ravishing appeal—

MRS. LINDE: You lunatic.

NORA: I'll bet you're eaten up with curiosity, Kristine.

MRS. LINDE: Now listen here, Nora—you haven't done something indiscreet?

NORA (*sitting up again*):   Is it indiscreet to save your husband's life?

MRS. LINDE: I think it's indiscreet that without his knowledge you—

NORA: But that's the point: he mustn't know! My Lord, can't you understand? He mustn't ever know the close call he had. It was to *me* the doctors came to say his life was in danger—that nothing could save him but a stay in the south. Didn't I try strategy then! I began talking about how lovely it would be for me to travel abroad like other young wives; I begged and I cried; I told him please to remember my condition, to be kind and indulge me; and then I dropped a hint that he could easily take out a loan. But at that, Kristine, he nearly exploded. He said I was frivolous, and it was his duty as man of the house not to indulge me in whims and fancies—as I think he called them. Aha, I thought, now you'll just have to be saved—and that's when I saw my chance.

MRS. LINDE: And your father never told Torvald the money wasn't from him?

NORA: No, never. Papa died right about then. I'd considered bringing him into my secret and begging him never to tell. But he was too sick at the time—and then, sadly, it didn't matter.

MRS. LINDE: And you've never confided in your husband since?

NORA: For heaven's sake, no! Are you serious? He's so strict on that subject. Besides—Torvald, with all his masculine pride—how painfully humiliating for him if he ever found out he was in debt to me. That would just ruin our relationship. Our beautiful happy home would never be the same.

MRS. LINDE: Won't you ever tell him?

NORA (*thoughtfully, half smiling*):   Yes—maybe sometime, years from now, when I'm no longer so attractive. Don't laugh! I only mean when Torvald loves me less than now, when he stops enjoying my dancing and dressing up and reciting for him. Then it might be wise to have something in reserve—(*Breaking off*) How ridiculous! That'll never happen—Well, Kristine, what do you think of my big secret? I'm capable of something too, hm? You can imagine, of course, how this thing hangs over me. It really hasn't been easy meeting the payments on time. In the business world there's what they call quarterly interest and what they call amortization, and these are always so terribly hard to manage. I've had to skimp a little here and there, wherever I could, you know. I could hardly spare anything from my house allowance, because Torvald has to live well. I couldn't let the children go poorly dressed; whatever I got for them, I felt I had to use up completely—the darlings!

MRS. LINDE: Poor Nora, so it had to come out of your own budget, then?

NORA: Yes, of course. But I was the one most responsible, too. Every time Torvald gave me money for new clothes and such, I never used more than half; always bought the simplest, cheapest outfits. It was a godsend that everything looks so well on me that Torvald never noticed. But it did weigh me down at times, Kristine. It *is* such a joy to wear fine things. You understand.

MRS. LINDE: Oh, of course.

NORA: And then I found other ways of making money. Last winter I was lucky enough to get a lot of copying to do. I locked myself in and sat writing every evening till late in the night. Ah, I was tired so often, dead tired. But still it was wonderful fun, sitting and working like that, earning money. It was almost like being a man.

MRS. LINDE: But how much have you paid off this way so far?

NORA: That's hard to say, exactly. These accounts, you know, aren't easy to figure. I only know that I've paid out all I could scrape together. Time and again I haven't known where to turn. (*Smiling*) Then I'd sit here dreaming of a rich old gentleman who had fallen in love with me—

MRS. LINDE: What! Who is he?

NORA: Oh, really! And that he'd died, and when his will was opened, there in big letters it said, "All my fortune shall be paid over in cash, immediately, to that enchanting Mrs. Nora Helmer."

MRS. LINDE: But Nora dear—who *was* this gentleman?

NORA: Good grief, can't you understand? The old man never existed; that was only something I'd dream up time and again whenever I was at my wits' end for money. But it makes no difference now; the old fossil can go where he pleases for all I care; I don't need him or his will—because now I'm free. (*Jumping up*) Oh, how lovely to think of that, Kristine! Carefree! To know you're carefree, utterly carefree, to be able to romp and play with the children, and to keep up a beautiful, charming home— everything just the way Torvald likes it! And think, spring is coming, with big blue skies. Maybe we can travel a little then. Maybe I'll see the ocean again. Oh yes, it *is* so marvelous to live and be happy!

(*The front doorbell rings.*)

MRS. LINDE (*rising*):   There's the bell. It's probably best that I go.

NORA: No, stay. No one's expected. It must be for Torvald.

MAID (*from the hall doorway*):   Excuse me, ma'am—there's a gentleman here to see Mr. Helmer, but I didn't know—since the doctor's with him—

NORA: Who is the gentleman?

KROGSTAD (*from the doorway*):   It's me, Mrs. Helmer.

(MRS. LINDE *starts and turns away toward the window.*)

NORA (*stepping toward him, tense, her voice a whisper*):   You? What is it? Why do you want to speak to my husband?

KROGSTAD: Bank business—after a fashion. I have a small job in the investment bank, and I hear now your husband is going to be our chief—

NORA: In other words, it's—

KROGSTAD: Just dry business, Mrs. Helmer. Nothing but that.

NORA: Yes, then please be good enough to step into the study. (*She nods indifferently, as she sees him out by the hall door, then returns and begins stirring up the stove.*)

MRS. LINDE: Nora—who was that man?

NORA: That was a Mr. Krogstad—a lawyer.

MRS. LINDE: Then it really was him.

NORA: Do you know that person?

MRS. LINDE: I did once—many years ago. For a time he was a law clerk in our town.

NORA: Yes, he's been that.

MRS. LINDE: How he's changed.

NORA: I understand he had a very unhappy marriage.

MRS. LINDE: He's a widower now.

NORA: With a number of children. There now, it's burning. (*She closes the stove door and moves the rocker a bit to one side.*)

MRS. LINDE: They say he has a hand in all kinds of business.

NORA: Oh? That may be true; I wouldn't know. But let's not think about business. It's so dull.

(DR. RANK *enters from* HELMER'S *study.*)

RANK (*still in the doorway*):   No, no, really—I don't want to intrude, I'd just as soon talk a little while with your wife. (*Shuts the door, then notices* MRS. LINDE) Oh, beg pardon, I'm intruding here too.

NORA: No, not at all. (*Introducing him*) Dr. Rank, Mrs. Linde.

RANK: Well now, that's a name much heard in this house. I believe I passed the lady on the stairs as I came.

MRS. LINDE: Yes, I take the stairs very slowly. They're rather hard on me.

RANK: Uh-hm, some touch of internal weakness?

MRS. LINDE: More overexertion, I'd say.

RANK: Nothing else? Then you're probably here in town to rest up in a round of parties?

MRS. LINDE: I'm here to look for work.

RANK: Is that the best cure for overexertion?

MRS. LINDE: One has to live, Doctor.

RANK: Yes, there's a common prejudice to that effect.

NORA: Oh, come on, Dr. Rank—you really do want to live yourself.

RANK: Yes, I really do. Wretched as I am, I'll gladly prolong my torment indefinitely. All my patients feel like that. And it's quite the same, too, with the morally sick. Right at this moment there's one of those moral invalids in there with Helmer—

MRS. LINDE (*softly*):   Ah!

NORA: Who do you mean?

RANK: Oh, it's a lawyer, Krogstad, a type you wouldn't know. His character is rotten to the root—but even he began chattering all-importantly about how he had to *live.*

NORA: Oh? What did he want to talk to Torvald about?

RANK: I really don't know. I only heard something about the bank.

NORA: I didn't know that Krog—that this man Krogstad had anything to do with the bank.

RANK: Yes, he's gotten some kind of berth down there. (*To* MRS. LINDE) I don't know if you also have, in your neck of the woods, a type of person who scuttles about breathlessly, sniffing out hints of moral corruption, and then maneuvers his victim into some sort of key position where he can keep an eye on him. It's the healthy these days that are out in the cold.

MRS. LINDE: All the same, it's the sick who most need to be taken in.

RANK (*with a shrug*):   Yes, there we have it. That's the concept that's turning society into a sanatorium.

(NORA, *lost in her thoughts, breaks out into quiet laughter and claps her hands.*)

RANK: Why do you laugh at that? Do you have any real idea of what society is?

NORA: What do I care about dreary old society? I was laughing at something quite different—something terribly funny. Tell me, Doctor—is everyone who works in the bank dependent now on Torvald?

RANK: Is that what you find so terribly funny?

NORA (*smiling and humming*):   Never mind, never mind! (*Pacing the floor*) Yes, that's really immensely amusing: that we—that Torvald has so much power now over all those people. (*Taking the bag out of her pocket*) Dr. Rank, a little macaroon on that?

RANK: See here, macaroons! I thought they were contraband here.

NORA: Yes, but these are some that Kristine gave me.

MRS. LINDE: What? I—?

NORA: Now, now, don't be afraid. You couldn't possibly know that Torvald had forbidden them. You see, he's worried they'll ruin my teeth. But hmp! Just this once! Isn't that so, Dr. Rank? Help yourself! (*Puts a macaroon in his mouth*) And you too, Kristine. And I'll also have one, only a little one—or two, at the most. (*Walking about again*) Now I'm really tremendously happy. Now there's just one last thing in the world that I have an enormous desire to do.

RANK: Well! And what's that?

NORA: It's something I have such a consuming desire to say so Torvald could hear.

RANK: And why can't you say it?

NORA: I don't dare. It's quite shocking.

MRS. LINDE: Shocking?

RANK: Well, then it isn't advisable. But in front of us you certainly can. What do you have such a desire to say so Torvald could hear?

NORA: I have such a huge desire to say—to hell and be damned!

RANK: Are you crazy?

MRS. LINDE: My goodness, Nora!

RANK: Go on, say it. Here he is.

NORA (*hiding the macaroon bag*):   Shh, shh, shh!

(HELMER *comes in from his study, hat in hand, overcoat over his arm.*)

NORA (*going toward him*):   Well, Torvald dear, are you through with him?

HELMER: Yes, he just left.

NORA: Let me introduce you—this is Kristine, who's arrived here in town.

HELMER: Kristine—? I'm sorry, but I don't know—

NORA: Mrs. Linde, Torvald dear. Mrs. Kristine Linde.

HELMER: Of course. A childhood friend of my wife's, no doubt?

MRS. LINDE: Yes, we knew each other in those days.

NORA: And just think, she made the long trip down here in order to talk with you.

HELMER: What's this?

MRS. LINDE: Well, not exactly—

NORA: You see, Kristine is remarkably clever in office work, and so she's terribly eager to come under a capable man's supervision and add more to what she already knows—

HELMER: Very wise, Mrs. Linde.

NORA: And then when she heard that you'd become a bank manager—the story was wired out to the papers—then she came in as fast as she could and—Really, Torvald, for my sake you can do a little something for Kristine, can't you?

HELMER: Yes, it's not at all impossible. Mrs. Linde, I suppose you're a widow?

MRS. LINDE: Yes.

HELMER: Any experience in office work?

MRS. LINDE: Yes, a good deal.

HELMER: Well, it's quite likely that I can make an opening for you—

NORA (*clapping her hands*): You see, you see!

HELMER: You've come at a lucky moment, Mrs. Linde.

MRS. LINDE: Oh, how can I thank you?

HELMER: Not necessary. (*Putting his overcoat on*) But today you'll have to excuse me—

RANK: Wait, I'll go with you. (*He fetches his coat from the hall and warms it at the stove.*)

NORA: Don't stay out long, dear.

HELMER: An hour; no more.

NORA: Are you going too, Kristine?

MRS. LINDE (*putting on her winter garments*): Yes, I have to see about a room now.

HELMER: Then perhaps we can all walk together.

NORA (*helping her*): What a shame we're so cramped here, but it's quite impossible for us to—

MRS. LINDE: Oh, don't even think of it! Good-bye, Nora dear, and thanks for everything.

NORA: Good-bye for now. Of course you'll be back again this evening. And you too, Dr. Rank. What? If you're well enough? Oh, you've got to be! Wrap up tight now.

(*In a ripple of small talk the company moves out into the hall; children's voices are heard outside on the steps.*)

NORA: There they are! There they are! (*She runs to open the door. The children come in with their nurse,* ANNE-MARIE.) Come in, come in! (*Bends down and kisses them*) Oh, you darlings—! Look at them, Kristine. Aren't they lovely!

RANK: No loitering in the draft here.

HELMER: Come, Mrs. Linde—this place is unbearable now for anyone but mothers.

(DR. RANK, HELMER, *and* MRS. LINDE *go down the stairs.* ANNE-MARIE *goes into the living room with the children.* NORA *follows, after closing the hall door.*)

NORA: How fresh and strong you look. Oh, such red cheeks you have! Like apples and roses. (*The children interrupt her throughout the following.*) And it was so much fun? That's wonderful. Really? You pulled both Emmy and Bob on the sled? Imagine, all together! Yes, you're a clever boy, Ivar. Oh, let me hold her a bit, Anne-Marie. My sweet little doll baby! (*Takes the smallest from the nurse and dances with her*) Yes, yes, Mama will dance with Bob as well. What? Did you throw snowballs? Oh, if I'd only been there! No, don't bother, Anne-Marie—I'll undress them myself. Oh yes, let me.

It's such fun. Go in and rest; you look half frozen. There's hot coffee waiting for you on the stove. (*The nurse goes into the room to the left. Nora takes the children's winter things off, throwing them about, while the children talk to her all at once.*) Is that so? A big dog chased you? But it didn't bite? No, dogs never bite little, lovely doll babies. Don't peek in the packages, Ivar! What is it? Yes, wouldn't you like to know. No, no, it's an ugly something. Well? Shall we play? What shall we play? Hide-and-seek? Yes, let's play hide-and-seek. Bob must hide first. I must? Yes, let me hide first. (*Laughing and shouting, she and the children play in and out of the living room and the adjoining room to the right. At last* NORA *hides under the table. The children come storming in, search, but cannot find her, then hear her muffled laughter, dash over to the table, lift the cloth and find her. Wild shouting. She creeps forward as if to scare them. More shouts. Meanwhile, a knock at the hall door; no one has noticed it. Now the door half opens, and* KROGSTAD *appears. He waits a moment; the game goes on.*)

KROGSTAD: Beg pardon, Mrs. Helmer—

NORA (*with a strangled cry, turning and scrambling to her knees*): Oh! what do you want?

KROGSTAD: Excuse me. The outer door was ajar; it must be someone forgot to shut it—

NORA (*rising*): My husband isn't home, Mr. Krogstad.

KROGSTAD: I know that.

NORA: Yes—then what do you want here?

KROGSTAD: A word with you.

NORA: With—? (*To the children, quietly*) Go in to Anne-Marie. What? No, the strange man won't hurt Mama. When he's gone, we'll play some more. (*She leads the children into the room to the left and shuts the door after them. Then, tense and nervous*) You want to speak to me?

KROGSTAD: Yes, I want to.

NORA: Today? But it's not yet the first of the month—

KROGSTAD: No, it's Christmas Eve. It's going to be up to you how merry a Christmas you have.

NORA: What is it you want? Today I absolutely can't—

KROGSTAD: We won't talk about that till later. This is something else. You do have a moment to spare, I suppose?

NORA: Oh yes, of course—I do, except—

KROGSTAD: Good. I was sitting over at Olsen's Restaurant when I saw your husband go down the street—

NORA: Yes?

KROGSTAD: With a lady.

NORA: Yes. So?

KROGSTAD: If you'll pardon my asking: wasn't that lady a Mrs. Linde?

NORA: Yes.

KROGSTAD: Just now come into town?

NORA: Yes, today.

KROGSTAD: She's a good friend of yours?

NORA: Yes, she is. But I don't see—

KROGSTAD: I also knew her once.

NORA: I'm aware of that.

KROGSTAD: Oh? You know all about it. I thought so, Well, then let me ask you short and sweet: is Mrs. Linde getting a job in the bank?

NORA: What makes you think you can cross-examine me, Mr. Krogstad—you, one of my husband's employees? But since you ask, you might as well know—yes, Mrs. Linde's going to be taken on at the bank. And I'm the one who spoke for her, Mr. Krogstad. Now you know.

KROGSTAD: So I guessed right.

NORA (*pacing up and down*): Oh, one does have a tiny bit of influence, I should hope. Just because I am a woman, don't think it means that—When one has a subordinate position, Mr. Krogstad, one really ought to be careful about pushing somebody who—hm—

KROGSTAD: Who has influence?

NORA: That's right.

KROGSTAD (*in a different tone*): Mrs. Helmer, would you be good enough to use your influence on my behalf?

NORA: What? What do you mean?

KROGSTAD: Would you please make sure that I keep my subordinate position in the bank?

NORA: What does that mean? Who's thinking of taking away your position?

KROGSTAD: Oh, don't play the innocent with me. I'm quite aware that your friend would hardly relish the chance of running into me again; and I'm also aware now whom I can thank for being turned out.

NORA: But I promise you—

KROGSTAD: Yes, yes, yes, to the point: there's still time, and I'm advising you to use your influence to prevent it.

NORA: But Mr. Krogstad, I have absolutely no influence.

KROGSTAD: You haven't? I thought you were just saying—

NORA: You shouldn't take me so literally. I! How can you believe that I have any such influence over my husband?

KROGSTAD: Oh, I've known your husband from our student days. I don't think the great bank manager's more steadfast than any other married man.

NORA: You speak insolently about my husband, and I'll show you the door.

KROGSTAD: The lady has spirit.

NORA: I'm not afraid of you any longer. After New Year's, I'll soon be done with the whole business.

KROGSTAD (*restraining himself*): Now listen to me, Mrs. Helmer. If necessary, I'll fight for my little job in the bank as if it were life itself.

NORA: Yes, so it seems.

KROGSTAD: It's not just a matter of income; that's the least of it. It's something else—All right, out with it! Look, this is the thing. You know, just like all the others, of course, that once, a good many years ago, I did something rather rash.

NORA: I've heard rumors to that effect.

KROGSTAD: The case never got into court; but all the same, every door was closed in my face from then on. So I took up those various activities you know about. I had to grab hold somewhere; and I dare say I haven't been among the worst. But now I want to drop all that. My boys are growing up. For their sakes, I'll have to win back as much respect as possible here in town. That job in the bank was like the first rung in my ladder. And now your husband wants to kick me right back down in the mud again.

NORA: But for heaven's sake, Mr. Krogstad, it's simply not in my power to help you.

KROGSTAD: That's because you haven't the will to—but I have the means to make you.

NORA: You certainly won't tell my husband that I owe you money?

KROGSTAD: Hm—what if I told him that?

NORA: That would be shameful of you. (*Nearly in tears*) This secret—my joy and my pride—that he should learn it in such a crude and disgusting way—learn it from you. You'd expose me to the most horrible unpleasantness—

KROGSTAD: Only unpleasantness?

NORA (*vehemently*):   But go on and try. It'll turn out the worst for you, because then my husband will really see what a crook you are, and then you'll *never* be able to hold your job.

KROGSTAD: I asked if it was just domestic unpleasantness you were afraid of?

NORA: If my husband finds out, then of course he'll pay what I owe at once, and then we'd be through with you for good.

KROGSTAD (*a step closer*):   Listen, Mrs. Helmer—you've either got a very bad memory, or else no head at all for business. I'd better put you a little more in touch with the facts.

NORA: What do you mean?

KROGSTAD: When your husband was sick, you came to me for a loan of four thousand, eight hundred crowns.

NORA: Where else could I go?

KROGSTAD: I promised to get you that sum—

NORA: And you got it.

KROGSTAD: I promised to get you that sum, on certain conditions. You were so involved in your husband's illness, and so eager to finance your trip, that I guess you didn't think out all the details. It might just be a good idea to remind you. I promised you the money on the strength of a note I drew up.

NORA: Yes, and that I signed.

KROGSTAD: Right. But at the bottom I added some lines for your father to guarantee the loan. He was supposed to sign down there.

NORA: Supposed to? He did sign.

KROGSTAD: I left the date blank. In other words, your father would have dated his signature himself. Do you remember that?

NORA: Yes, I think—

KROGSTAD: Then I gave you the note for you to mail to your father. Isn't that so?

NORA: Yes.

KROGSTAD: And naturally you sent it at once—because only some five, six days later you brought me the note, properly signed. And with that, the money was yours.

NORA: Well, then; I've made my payments regularly, haven't I?

KROGSTAD: More or less. But—getting back to the point—those were hard times for you then, Mrs. Helmer.

NORA: Yes, they were.

KROGSTAD: Your father was very ill, I believe.

NORA: He was near the end.

KROGSTAD: He died soon after?

NORA: Yes.

KROGSTAD: Tell me, Mrs. Helmer, do you happen to recall the date of your father's death? The day of the month, I mean.

NORA: Papa died the twenty-ninth of September.

KROGSTAD: That's quite correct; I've already looked into that. And now we come to a curious thing—(*Taking out a paper*) which I simply cannot comprehend.

NORA: Curious thing? I don't know—

KROGSTAD: This is the curious thing: that your father co-signed the note for your loan three days after his death.

NORA: How—? I don't understand.

KROGSTAD: Your father died the twenty-ninth of September. But look. Here your father dated his signature October second. Isn't that curious, Mrs. Helmer? (NORA *is silent.*) Can you explain it to me? (NORA *remains silent.*) It's also remarkable that the words "October second" and the year aren't written in your father's hand, but rather in one that I think I know. Well, it's easy to understand. Your father forgot perhaps to date his signature, and then someone or other added it, a bit sloppily, before anyone knew of his death. There's nothing wrong in that. It all comes down to the signature. And there's no question about *that,* Mrs. Helmer. It really *was* your father who signed his own name here, wasn't it?

NORA (*after a short silence, throwing her head back and looking squarely at him*): No, it wasn't. I signed Papa's name.

KROGSTAD: Wait, now—are you fully aware that this is a dangerous confession?

NORA: Why? You'll soon get your money.

KROGSTAD: Let me ask you a question—why didn't you send the paper to your father?

NORA: That was impossible. Papa was so sick. If I'd asked him for his signature, I also would have had to tell him what the money was for. But I couldn't tell him, sick as he was, that my husband's life was in danger. That was just impossible.

KROGSTAD: Then it would have been better if you'd given up the trip abroad.

NORA: I couldn't possibly. The trip was to save my husband's life. I couldn't give that up.

KROGSTAD: But didn't you ever consider that this was a fraud against me?

NORA: I couldn't let myself be bothered by that. You weren't any concern of mine. I couldn't stand you, with all those cold complications you made, even though you knew how badly off my husband was.

KROGSTAD: Mrs. Helmer, obviously you haven't the vaguest idea of what you've involved yourself in. But I can tell you this: it was nothing more and nothing worse than I once did—and it wrecked my whole reputation.

NORA: You? Do you expect me to believe that you ever acted bravely to save your wife's life?

KROGSTAD: Laws don't inquire into motives.

NORA: Then they must be very poor laws.

KROGSTAD: Poor or not—if I introduce this paper in court, you'll be judged according to law.

NORA: This I refuse to believe. A daughter hasn't a right to protect her dying father from anxiety and care? A wife hasn't a right to save her husband's life? I don't know much about laws, but I'm sure that somewhere in the books these things are allowed. And you don't know anything about it—you who practice the law? You must be an awful lawyer, Mr. Krogstad.

KROGSTAD: Could be. But business—the kind of business we two are mixed up in—don't you think I know about that? All right. Do what you want now. But I'm telling you *this:* if I get shoved down a second time, you're going to keep me company.

(He bows and goes out through the hall.)

NORA (*pensive for a moment, then tossing her head*):   Oh, really! Trying to frighten me! I'm not so silly as all that. (*Begins gathering up the children's clothes, but soon stops*) But—? No, but that's impossible! I did it out of love.

THE CHILDREN (*in the doorway, left*):   Mama, that strange man's gone out the door.

NORA: Yes, yes, I know it. But don't tell anyone about the strange man. Do you hear. Not even Papa!

THE CHILDREN: No, Mama. But now will you play again?

NORA: No, not now.

THE CHILDREN: Oh, but Mama, you promised.

NORA: Yes, but I can't now. Go inside; I have too much to do. Go in, go in, my sweet darlings. (*She herds them gently back in the room and shuts the door after them. Settling on the sofa, she takes up a piece of embroidery and makes some stitches, but soon stops abruptly.*) No! (*Throws the work aside, rises, goes to the hall door and calls out*) Helene! Let me have the tree in here. (*Goes to the table, left, opens the table drawer, and stops again*) No, but that's utterly impossible!

MAID (*with the Christmas tree*):   Where should I put it, Ma'am?

NORA: There. The middle of the floor.

MAID: Should I bring anything else?

NORA: No, thanks. I have what I need.

(The MAID, who has set the tree down, goes out.)

NORA (*absorbed in trimming the tree*):   Candles here—and flowers here. That terrible creature! Talk, talk, talk! There's nothing to it at all. The tree's going to be lovely. I'll do anything to please you, Torvald. I'll sing for you, dance for you—

(HELMER *comes in from the hall, with a sheaf of papers under his arm.*)

NORA: Oh! You're back so soon?

HELMER: Yes. Has anyone been here?

NORA: Here? No.

HELMER: That's odd. I saw Krogstad leaving the front door.

NORA: So? Oh yes, that's true. Krogstad was here a moment.

HELMER: Nora, I can see by your face that he's been here, begging you to put in a good word for him.

NORA: Yes.

HELMER: And it was supposed to seem like your own idea? You were to hide it from me that he'd been here. He asked you that, too, didn't he?

NORA: Yes, Torvald, but—

HELMER: Nora, Nora, and you could fall for that? Talk with that sort of person and promise him anything? And then in the bargain, tell me an untruth.

NORA: An untruth—?

HELMER: Didn't you say that no one had been here? (*Wagging his finger*) My little songbird must never do that again. A songbird needs a clean beak to warble with. No false notes. (*Putting his arm about her waist*) That's the way it should be, isn't it? Yes, I'm sure of it. (*Releasing her*) And so, enough of that. (*Sitting by the stove*) Ah, how snug and cozy it is here. (*Leafing among his papers*)

NORA (*busy with the tree, after a short pause*):   Torvald!

HELMER: Yes.

NORA: I'm so much looking forward to the Stenborg's costume party, day after tomorrow.

HELMER: And I can't wait to see what you'll surprise me with.

NORA: Oh, that stupid business.

HELMER: What?

NORA: I can't find anything that's right. Everything seems so ridiculous, so inane.

HELMER: So my little Nora's come to *that* recognition?

NORA (*going behind his chair, her arms resting on its back*):   Are you very busy, Torvald?

HELMER: Oh—

NORA: What papers are those?

HELMER: Bank matters.

NORA: Already?

HELMER: I've gotten full authority from the retiring management to make all necessary changes in personnel and procedure. I'll need Christmas week for that. I want to have everything in order by New Year's.

NORA: So that was the reason this poor Krogstad—

HELMER: Hm.

NORA (*still leaning on the chair and slowly stroking the nape of his neck*):   If you weren't so very busy, I would have asked you an enormous favor, Torvald.

HELMER: Let's hear. What is it?

NORA: You know, there isn't anyone who has your good taste—and I want so much to look well at the costume party. Torvald, couldn't you take over and decide what I should be and plan my costume?

HELMER: Ah, is my stubborn little creature calling for a lifeguard?

NORA: Yes, Torvald, I can't get anywhere without your help.

HELMER: All right—I'll think it over. We'll hit on something.

NORA: Oh, how sweet of you. (*Goes to the tree again. Pause.*) Aren't the red flowers pretty—? But tell me, was it really such a crime that this Krogstad committed?

HELMER: Forgery. Do you have any idea what that means?

NORA: Couldn't he have done it out of need?

HELMER: Yes, or thoughtlessness, like so many others. I'm not so heartless that I'd condemn a man categorically for just one mistake.

NORA: No, of course not, Torvald!

HELMER: Plenty of men have redeemed themselves by openly confessing their crimes and taking their punishments.

NORA: Punishment—?

HELMER: But now Krogstad didn't go that way. He got himself out by sharp practices, and that's the real cause of his moral breakdown.

NORA: Do you really think that would—?

HELMER: Just imagine how a man with that sort of guilt in him has to lie and cheat and deceive on all sides, has to wear a mask even with the nearest and dearest he has, even with his own wife and children. And with the children, Nora—that's where it's most horrible.

NORA: Why?

HELMER: Because that kind of atmosphere of lies infects the whole life of a home. Every breath the children take in is filled with the terms of something degenerate.

NORA (*coming closer behind him*):   Are you sure of that?

HELMER: Oh, I've seen it often enough as a lawyer. Almost everyone who goes bad early in life has a mother who's a chronic liar.

NORA: Why just—the mother?

HELMER: It's usually the mother's influence that's dominant, but the father's works in the same way, of course. Every lawyer is quite familiar with it. And still this Krogstad's been going home year in, year out, poisoning his own children with lies and pretense; that's why I call him morally lost. (*Reaching his hands out toward her*) So my sweet little Nora must promise me never to plead his cause. Your hand on it. Come, come, what's this? Give me your hand. There, now. All settled. I can tell you it'd be impossible for me to work alongside of him. I literally feel physically revolted when I'm anywhere near such a person.

NORA (*withdraws her hand and goes to the other side of the Christmas tree*):   How hot it is here! And I've got so much to do.

HELMER (*getting up and gathering his papers*):   Yes, and I have to think about getting some of these read through before dinner. I'll think about your costume, too. And something to hang on the tree in gilt paper, I may even see about that. (*Putting his hand on her head*) Oh you, my darling little songbird.

(*He goes into his study and closes the door after him.*)

NORA (*softly, after a silence*):   Oh, really! it isn't so. It's impossible. It must be impossible.

ANNE-MARIE (*in the doorway, left*):   The children are begging so hard to come in to Mama.

NORA: No, no, no, don't let them in to me! You stay with them, Anne-Marie.

ANNE-MARIE: Of course, Ma'am. (*Closes the door*)

NORA (*pale with terror*):   Hurt my children—! Poison my home? (*A moment's pause; then she tosses her head.*) That's not true. Never. Never in all the world.

ACT II

Same room. Beside the piano the Christmas tree now stands stripped of ornament, burned-down candle stubs on its ragged branches. NORA's *street clothes lie on the sofa.* NORA, *alone in the room, moves restlessly about; at last she stops at the sofa and picks up her coat.*

NORA (*dropping the coat again*):   Someone's coming! (*Goes toward the door, listens*) No—there's no one. Of course—nobody's coming today, Christmas Day—or tomorrow, either. But maybe—(*Opens the door and looks out*) No, nothing in the mailbox. Quite empty. (*Coming forward*) What nonsense! He won't do anything serious. Nothing terrible could happen. It's impossible. Why, I have three small children.

(ANNE-MARIE, *with a large carton, comes in from the room to the left.*)

ANNE-MARIE: Well, at last I found the box with the masquerade clothes.

NORA: Thanks. Put it on the table.

ANNE-MARIE (*does so*):   But they're all pretty much of a mess.

NORA: Ahh! I'd love to rip them in a million pieces!

ANNE-MARIE: Oh, mercy, they can be fixed right up. Just a little patience.

NORA: Yes, I'll go get Mrs. Linde to help me.

ANNE-MARIE: Out again now? In this nasty weather? Miss Nora will catch cold—get sick.

NORA: Oh, worse things could happen—How are the children?

ANNE-MARIE: The poor mites are playing with their Christmas presents, but—

NORA: Do they ask for me much?

ANNE-MARIE: They're so used to having Mama around, you know.

NORA: Yes, but Anne-Marie, I *can't* be together with them as much as I was.

ANNE-MARIE: Well, small children get used to anything.

NORA: You think so? Do you think they'd forget their mother if she was gone for good?

ANNE-MARIE: Oh, mercy—gone for good!

NORA: Wait, tell me, Anne-Marie—I've wondered so often—how could you ever have the heart to give your child over to strangers?

ANNE-MARIE: But I had to, you know, to become little Nora's nurse.

NORA: Yes, but how could you *do* it?

ANNE-MARIE: When I could get such a good place? A girl who's poor and who's gotten in trouble is glad enough for that. Because that slippery fish, he didn't do a thing for me, you know.

NORA: But your daughter's surely forgotten you.

ANNE-MARIE: Oh, she certainly has not. She's written to me, both when she was confirmed and when she was married.

NORA (*clasping her about the neck*):   You old Anne-Marie, you were a good mother for me when I was little.

ANNE-MARIE: Poor little Nora, with no other mother but me.

NORA: And if the babies didn't have one, then I know that you'd—What silly talk! (*Opening the carton*) Go in to them. Now I'll have to—Tomorrow you can see how lovely I'll look.

ANNE-MARIE: Oh, there won't be anyone at the party as lovely as Miss Nora.

(*She goes off into the room, left.*)

NORA (*begins unpacking the box, but soon throws it aside*):   Oh, if I dared to go out. If only nobody would come. If only nothing would happen here while I'm out. What craziness—nobody's coming. Just don't think. This muff—needs a brushing. Beautiful gloves, beautiful gloves. Let it go. Let it go! One, two, three, four, five, six—(*With a cry*) Oh, there they are! (*Poises to move toward the door, but remains irresolutely standing.* MRS. LINDE *enters from the hall, where she has removed her street clothes.*)

NORA: Oh, it's you, Kristine. There's no one else out there? How good that you've come.

MRS. LINDE: I hear you were up asking for me.

NORA: Yes, I just stopped by. There's something you really can help me with. Let's get settled on the sofa. Look, there's going to be a costume party tomorrow evening at the Stenborgs' right above us, and now Torvald wants me to go as a Neapolitan peasant girl and dance the tarantella that I learned in Capri.

MRS. LINDE: Really, you are giving a whole performance?

NORA: Torvald says yes, I should. See, here's the dress. Torvald had it made for me down there; but now it's all so tattered that I just don't know—

MRS. LINDE: Oh, we'll fix that up in no time. It's nothing more than the trimmings—they're a bit loose here and there. Needle and thread? Good, now we have what we need.

NORA: Oh, how sweet of you!

MRS. LINDE (*sewing*):   So you'll be in disguise tomorrow, Nora. You know what? I'll stop by then for a moment and have a look at you all dressed up. But listen, I've absolutely forgotten to thank you for that pleasant evening yesterday.

NORA (*getting up and walking about*):   I don't think it was as pleasant as usual yesterday. You should have come to town a bit sooner, Kristine—Yes, Torvald really knows how to give a home elegance and charm.

MRS. LINDE: And you do, too, if you ask me. You're not your father's daughter for nothing. But tell me, is Dr. Rank always so down in the mouth as yesterday?

NORA: No, that was quite an exception. But he goes around critically ill all the time—tuberculosis of the spine, poor man. You know, his father was a disgusting thing who kept mistresses and so on—and that's why the son's been sickly from birth.

MRS. LINDE (*lets her sewing fall to her lap*):   But my dearest Nora, how do you know about such things?

NORA (*walking more jauntily*):   Hmp! When you've had three children, then you've had a few visits from—women who know something of medicine, and they tell you this and that.

MRS. LINDE (*resumes sewing; a short pause*):   Does Dr. Rank come here every day?

NORA: Every blessed day. He's Torvald's best friend from childhood, and *my* good friend, too. Dr. Rank almost belongs to this house.

MRS. LINDE: But tell me—is he quite sincere? I mean, doesn't he rather enjoy flattering people?

NORA: Just the opposite. Why do you think that?

MRS. LINDE: When you introduced us yesterday, he was proclaiming that he'd often heard my name in this house; but later I noticed that your husband hadn't the slightest idea who I really was. So how could Dr. Rank—?

NORA: But it's all true, Kristine. You see, Torvald loves me beyond words, and, as he puts it, he'd like to keep me all to himself. For a long time he'd almost be jealous if I even mentioned any of my old friends back home. So of course I dropped that. But with Dr. Rank I talk a lot about such things, because he likes hearing about them.

MRS. LINDE: Now listen, Nora; in many ways you're still like a child. I'm a good deal older than you, with a little more experience. I'll tell you something; you ought to put an end to all this with Dr. Rank.

NORA: What should I put an end to?

MRS. LINDE: Both parts of it, I think. Yesterday you said something about a rich admirer who'd provide you with money—

NORA: Yes, one who doesn't exist—worse luck. So?

MRS. LINDE: Is Dr. Rank well off?

NORA: Yes, he is.

MRS. LINDE: With no dependents?

NORA: No, no one. But—

MRS. LINDE: And he's over here every day?

NORA: Yes, I told you that.

MRS. LINDE: How can a man of such refinement be so grasping?

NORA: I don't follow you at all.

MRS. LINDE: Now don't try to hide it, Nora. You think I can't guess who loaned you the forty-eight hundred crowns?

NORA: Are you out of your mind? How could you think of such a thing! A friend of ours, who comes here every single day. What an intolerable situation that would have been!

MRS. LINDE: Then it really wasn't him.

NORA: No, absolutely not. It never even crossed my mind for a moment—And he had nothing to lend in those days; his inheritance came later.

MRS. LINDE: Well, I think that was a stroke of luck for you, Nora dear.

NORA: No, it never would have occurred to me to ask Dr. Rank—Still, I'm quite sure that if I had asked him—

MRS. LINDE: Which you won't, of course.

NORA: No, of course not. I can't see that I'd ever need to. But I'm quite positive that if I talked to Dr. Rank—

MRS. LINDE: Behind your husband's back?

NORA: I've got to clear up this other thing; *that's* also behind his back. I've *got* to clear it all up.

MRS. LINDE: Yes, I was saying that yesterday, but—

NORA (*pacing up and down*): A man handles these problems so much better than a woman—

MRS. LINDE: One's husband does, yes.

NORA: Nonsense. (*Stopping*) When you pay everything you owe, then you get your note back, right?

MRS. LINDE: Yes, naturally.

NORA: And can rip it into a million pieces and burn it up—that filthy scrap of paper!

MRS. LINDE (*looking hard at her, laying her sewing aside, and rising slowly*): Nora, you're hiding something from me.

NORA: You can see it in my face?

MRS. LINDE: Something's happened to you since yesterday morning. Nora, what is it?

NORA (*hurrying toward her*): Kristine! (*Listening*) Shh! Torvald's home. Look, go in with the children a while. Torvald can't bear all this snipping and stitching. Let Anne-Marie help you.

MRS. LINDE (*gathering up some of the things*): All right, but I'm not leaving here until we've talked this out. (*She disappears into the room, left, as* TORVALD *enters from the hall.*)

NORA: Oh, how I've been waiting for you, Torvald dear.

HELMER: Was that the dressmaker?

NORA: No, that was Kristine. She's helping me fix up my costume. You know, it's going to be quite attractive.

HELMER: Yes, wasn't that a bright idea I had?

NORA: Brilliant! But then wasn't I good as well to give in to you?

HELMER: Good—because you give in to your husband's judgment? All right, you little goose, I know you didn't mean it like that. But I won't disturb you. You'll want to have a fitting, I suppose.

NORA: And you'll be working?

HELMER: Yes. (*Indicating a bundle of papers*) See. I've been down to the bank. (*Starts toward his study*)

NORA: Torvald.

HELMER (*stops*):   Yes.

NORA: If your little squirrel begged you, with all her heart and soul, for something—?

HELMER: What's that?

NORA: Then would you do it?

HELMER: First, naturally, I'd have to know what it was.

NORA: Your squirrel would scamper about and do tricks, if you'd only be sweet and give in.

HELMER: Out with it.

NORA: Your lark would be singing high and low in every room—

HELMER: Come on, she does that anyway.

NORA: I'd be a wood nymph and dance for you in the moonlight.

HELMER: Nora—don't tell me it's that same business from this morning?

NORA (*coming closer*):   Yes, Torvald, I beg you, please!

HELMER: And you actually have the nerve to drag that up again?

NORA: Yes, yes, you've got to give in to me; you have to let Krogstad keep his job in the bank.

HELMER: My dear Nora, I've slated his job for Mrs. Linde.

NORA: That's awfully kind of you. But you could just fire another clerk instead of Krogstad.

HELMER: This is the most incredible stubbornness! Because you go and give an impulsive promise to speak up for him, I'm expected to—

NORA: That's not the reason, Torvald. It's for your own sake. That man does writing for the worst papers; you said it yourself. He could do you any amount of harm. I'm scared to death of him—

HELMER: Ah, I understand. It's the old memories haunting you.

NORA: What do you mean by that?

HELMER: Of course, you're thinking about your father.

NORA: Yes, all right. Just remember how those nasty gossips wrote in the papers about Papa and slandered him so cruelly. I think they'd have had him dismissed if the department hadn't sent you up to investigate, and if you hadn't been so kind and openminded toward him.

HELMER: My dear Nora, there's a notable difference between your father and me. Your father's official career was hardly above reproach. But mine is; and I hope it'll stay that way as long as I hold my position.

NORA: Oh, who can ever tell what vicious minds can invent? We could be so snug and happy now in our quiet, carefree home—you and I and the children, Torvald! That's why I'm pleading with you so—

HELMER: And just by pleading for him you make it impossible for me to keep him on. It's already known at the bank that I'm firing Krogstad. What if it's rumored around now that the new bank manager was vetoed by his wife—

NORA: Yes, what then—?

HELMER: Oh yes—as long as your little bundle of stubbornness gets her way—! I should go and make myself ridiculous in front of the whole office—whole office—

give people the idea I can be swayed by all kinds of outside pressure. Oh, you can bet I'd feel the effects of that soon enough! Besides—there's something that rules Krogstad right out at the bank as long as I'm the manager.

NORA: What's that?

HELMER: His moral failings I could maybe overlook if I had to—

NORA: Yes, Torvald, why not?

HELMER: And I hear he's quite efficient on the job. But he was a crony of mine back in my teens—one of those rash friendships that crop up again and again to embarrass you later in life. Well, I might as well say it straight out: we're on a first-name basis. And that tactless fool makes no effort at all to hide it in front of others. Quite the contrary—he thinks that entitles him to take a familiar air around me, and so every other second he comes booming out with his "Yes, Torvald!" and "Sure thing, Torvald!" I tell you, it's been excruciating for me. He's out to make my place in the bank unbearable.

NORA: Torvald, you can't be serious about all this.

HELMER: Oh no? Why not?

NORA: Because these are such petty considerations.

HELMER: What are you saying? Petty? You think I'm petty!

NORA: No, just the opposite, Torvald dear. That's exactly why—

HELMER: Never mind. You call my motives petty; then I might as well be just that. Petty! All right! We'll put a stop to this for good. (*Goes to the hall door and calls*) Helene!

NORA: What do you want?

HELMER (*searching among his papers*):   A decision. (*The* MAID *comes in.*) Look here; take this letter; go out with it at once. Get hold of a messenger and have him deliver it. Quick now. It's already addressed. Wait, here's some money.

MAID: Yes, sir. (*She leaves with the letter.*)

HELMER (*straightening his papers*):   There, now, little Miss Willful.

NORA (*breathlessly*):   Torvald, what was that letter?

HELMER: Krogstad's notice.

NORA: Call it back, Torvald! There's still time. Oh, Torvald, call it back! Do it for my sake—for your sake, for the children's sake! Do you hear, Torvald; do it! You don't know how this can harm us.

HELMER: Too late.

NORA: Yes, too late.

HELMER: Nora dear, I can forgive you this panic, even though basically you're insulting me. Yes, you are! Or isn't it an insult to think that I should be afraid of a courtroom hack's revenge? But I forgive you anyway, because this shows so beautifully how much you love me. (*Takes her in his arms*) This is the way it should be, my darling Nora. Whatever comes, you'll see: when it really counts, I have strength and courage enough as a man to take on the whole weight myself.

NORA (*terrified*):   What do you mean by that?

HELMER: The whole weight, I said.

NORA (*resolutely*):   No, never in all the world.

HELMER: Good. So we'll share it, Nora, as man and wife. That's as it should be. (*Fondling her*) Are you happy now? There, there, there—not these frightened dove's eyes. It's nothing at all but empty fantasies—Now you should run through your tarantella and practice your tambourine. I'll go to the inner office and shut both doors, so I won't hear a thing; you can make all the noise you like. (*Turning in the doorway*) And when Rank comes, just tell him where he can find me. (*He nods to her and goes with his papers into the study, closing the door.*)

NORA (*standing as though rooted, dazed with fright, in a whisper*):   He really could do it. He will do it. He'll do it in spite of everything. No, not that, never, never! Anything but that! Escape! A way out—(*The doorbell rings.*) Dr. Rank! Anything but that! Anything, whatever it is! (*Her hands pass over her face, smoothing it; she pulls herself together, goes over and opens the hall door.* DR. RANK *stands outside, hanging his fur coat up. During the following scene, it begins getting dark.*)

NORA: Hello, Dr. Rank. I recognized your ring. But you mustn't go in to Torvald yet; I believe he's working.

RANK: And you?

NORA: For you, I always have an hour to spare—you know that. (*He has entered, and she shuts the door after him.*)

RANK: Many thanks. I'll make use of these hours while I can.

NORA: What do you mean by that? While you can?

RANK: Does that disturb you?

NORA: Well, it's such an odd phrase. Is anything going to happen?

RANK: What's going to happen is what I've been expecting so long—but I honestly didn't think it would come so soon.

NORA (*gripping his arm*):   What is it you've found out? Dr. Rank, you have to tell me!

RANK (*sitting by the stove*):   It's all over with me. There's nothing to be done about it.

NORA (*breathing easier*):   Is it you—then—?

RANK: Who else? There's no point in lying to one's self. I'm the most miserable of all my patients, Mrs. Helmer. These past few days I've been auditing my internal accounts. Bankrupt! Within a month I'll probably be laid out and rotting in the churchyard.

NORA: Oh, what a horrible thing to say.

RANK: The thing itself is horrible. But the worst of it is all the other horror before it's over. There's only one final examination left; when I'm finished with that, I'll know about when my disintegration will begin. There's something I want to say. Helmer with his sensitivity has such a sharp distaste for anything ugly. I don't want him near my sickroom.

NORA: Oh, but Dr. Rank—

RANK: I won't have him in there. Under no condition. I'll lock my door to him— As soon as I'm completely sure of the worst, I'll send you my calling card marked with a black cross, and you'll know then the wreck has started to come apart.

NORA: No, today you're completely unreasonable. And I wanted you so much to be in a really good humor.

RANK: With death up my sleeve? And then to suffer this way for somebody else's sins. Is there any justice in that? And in every single family, in some way or another, this inevitable retribution of nature goes on—

NORA (*her hands pressed over her ears*):   Oh, stuff! Cheer up! Please—be gay!

RANK: Yes, I'd just as soon laugh at it all. My poor, innocent spine, serving time for my father's gay army days.

NORA (*by the table, left*):   He was so infatuated with asparagus tips and *pâté de foie gras,* wasn't that it?

RANK: Yes—and with truffles.

NORA: Truffles, yes. And then with oysters, I suppose?

RANK: Yes, tons of oysters, naturally.

NORA: And then the port and champagne to go with it. It's so sad that all these delectable things have to strike at our bones.

RANK: Especially when they strike at the unhappy bones that never shared in the fun.

NORA: Ah, that's the saddest of all.

RANK (*looks searchingly at her*):   Hm.

NORA (*after a moment*):   Why did you smile?

RANK: No, it was you who laughed.

NORA: No, it was you who smiled, Dr. Rank!

RANK (*getting up*):   You're even a bigger tease than I'd thought.

NORA: I'm full of wild ideas today.

RANK: That's obvious.

NORA (*putting both hands on his shoulders*):   Dear, dear Dr. Rank, you'll never die for Torvald and me.

RANK: Oh, that loss you'll easily get over. Those who go away are soon forgotten.

NORA (*looks fearfully at him*):   You believe that?

RANK: One makes new connections, and then—

NORA: Who makes new connections?

RANK: Both you and Torvald will when I'm gone. I'd say you're well under way already. What was that Mrs. Linde doing here last evening?

NORA: Oh, come—you can't be jealous of poor Kristine?

RANK: Oh yes, I am. She'll be my successor here in the house. When I'm down under, that woman will probably—

NORA: Shh! Not so loud. She's right in there.

RANK: Today as well. So you see.

NORA: Only to sew on my dress. Good gracious, how unreasonable you are. (*Sitting on the sofa*) Be nice now, Dr. Rank. Tomorrow you'll see how beautifully I'll dance, and you can imagine then that I'm dancing only for you—yes, and of course for Torvald, too—that's understood. (*Takes various items out of the carton*) Dr. Rank, sit over here and I'll show you something.

RANK (*sitting*):   What's that?

NORA: Look here. Look.

RANK: Silk stockings.

NORA: Flesh-colored. Aren't they lovely? Now it's so dark here, but tomorrow— No, no, no, just look at the feet. Oh well, you might as well look at the rest.

RANK: Hm—

NORA: Why do you look so critical? Don't you believe they'll fit?

RANK: I've never had any chance to form an opinion on that.

NORA (*glancing at him a moment*):   Shame on you. (*Hits him lightly on the ear with the stockings*) That's for you. (*Puts them away again*)

RANK: And what other splendors am I going to see now?

NORA: Not the least bit more, because you've been naughty. (*She hums a little and rummages among her things.*)

RANK (*after a short silence*):   When I sit here together with you like this, completely easy and open, then I don't know—I simply can't imagine—whatever would have become of me if I'd never come into this house.

NORA (*smiling*):   Yes, I really think you feel completely at ease with us.

RANK (*more quietly, staring straight ahead*):   And then to have to go away from it all—

NORA: Nonsense, you're not going away.

RANK (*his voice unchanged*):   —and not even be able to leave some poor show of gratitude behind, scarcely a fleeting regret—no more than a vacant place that anyone can fill.

NORA: And if I asked you now for—? No—

RANK: For what?

NORA: For a great proof of your friendship—

RANK: Yes, yes?

NORA: No, I mean—for an exceptionally big favor—

RANK: Would you really, for once, make me so happy?

NORA: Oh, you haven't the vaguest idea what it is.

RANK: All right, then tell me.

NORA: No, but I can't, Dr. Rank—it's all out of reason. It's advice and help, too—and a favor—

RANK: So much the better. I can't fathom what you're hinting at. Just speak out. Don't you trust me?

NORA: Of course. More than anyone else. You're my best and truest friend, I'm sure. That's why I want to talk to you. All right, then, Dr. Rank: there's something you can help me prevent. You know how deeply, how inexpressibly dearly Torvald loves me; he'd never hesitate a second to give up his life for me.

RANK (*leaning close to her*):   Nora—do you think he's the only one—

NORA (*with a slight start*):   Who—?

RANK: Who'd gladly give up his life for you.

NORA (*heavily*):   I see.

RANK: I swore to myself you should know this before I'm gone. I'll never find a better chance. Yes, Nora, now you know. And also you know now that you can trust me beyond anyone else.

NORA (*rising, natural and calm*):   Let me by.

RANK (*making room for her, but still sitting*):   Nora—

NORA (*in the hall doorway*):   Helene, bring the lamp in. (*Goes over to the stove*) Ah, dear Dr. Rank, that was really mean of you.

RANK (*getting up*):   That I've loved you just as deeply as somebody else? Was *that* mean?

NORA: No, but that you came out and told me. That was quite unnecessary—

RANK: What do you mean? Have you known—?

(*The* MAID *comes in with the lamp, sets it on the table, and goes out again.*)

RANK: Nora—Mrs. Helmer—I'm asking you: have you known about it?

NORA: Oh, how can I tell what I know or don't know? Really, I don't know what to say.—Why did you have to be so clumsy, Dr. Rank! Everything was so good.

RANK: Well, in any case, you now have the knowledge that my body and soul are at your command. So won't you speak out?

NORA (*Looking at him*):   After that?

RANK: Please, just let me know what it is.

NORA: You can't know anything now.

RANK: I have to. You mustn't punish me like this. Give me the chance to do whatever is humanly possible for you.

NORA: Now there's nothing you can do for me. Besides, actually, I don't need any help. You'll see—it's only my fantasies. That's what it is. Of course! (*Sits in the rocker, looks at him, and smiles*) What a nice one you are, Dr. Rank. Aren't you a little bit ashamed, now that the lamp is here?

RANK: No, not exactly. But perhaps I'd better go—for good?

NORA: No, you certainly can't do that. You must come here just as you always have. You know Torvald can't do without you.

RANK: Yes, but *you?*

NORA: You know how much I enjoy it when you're here.

RANK: That's precisely what threw me off. You're a mystery to me. So many times I've felt you'd almost rather be with me than with Helmer.

NORA: Yes—you see, there are some people that one loves most and other people that one would almost prefer being with.

RANK: Yes, there's something to that.

NORA: When I was back home, of course I loved Papa most. But I always thought it was so much fun when I could sneak down to the maids' quarters, because they never tried to improve me, and it was always so amusing, the way they talked to each other.

RANK: Aha, so it's *their* place that I've filled.

NORA (*jumping up and going to him*):   Oh, dear sweet Dr. Rank, that's not what I meant at all. But you can understand that with Torvald it's just the same as with Papa—

(*The* MAID *enters from the hall.*)

MAID: Ma'am—please! (*She whispers to* NORA *and hands her a calling card.*)

NORA (*glancing at the card*):   Ah! (*Slips it into her pocket*)

RANK: Anything wrong?

NORA: No, no, not at all. It's only some—it's my new dress—

RANK: Really? But—there's your dress.

NORA: Oh, that. But this is another one—I ordered it—Torvald mustn't know—

RANK: Ah, now we have the big secret.

NORA: That's right. Just go in with him—he's back in the inner study. Keep him there as long as—

RANK: Don't worry. He won't get away. (*Goes into the study.*)

NORA (*to the* MAID):   And he's standing waiting in the kitchen.

MAID: Yes, he came up by the back stairs.

NORA: But didn't you tell him somebody was here?

MAID: Yes, but that didn't do any good.

NORA: He won't leave?

MAID: No, he won't go till he's talked with you, ma'am.

NORA: Let him come in, then—but quietly. Helene, don't breathe a word about this. It's a surprise for my husband.

MAID: Yes, yes, I understand— (*Goes out.*)

NORA: This horror—it's going to happen. No, no, no, it can't happen, it mustn't. (*She goes and bolts* HELMER'*s door. The* MAID *opens the hall door for* KROGSTAD *and shuts it behind him. He is dressed for travel in a fur coat, boots and a fur cap.*)

NORA (*going toward him*):   Talk softly. My husband's home.

KROGSTAD: Well, good for him.

NORA: What do you want?

KROGSTAD: Some information.

NORA: Hurry up, then. What is it?

KROGSTAD: You know, of course, that I got my notice.

NORA: I couldn't prevent it, Mr. Krogstad. I fought for you to the bitter end, but nothing worked.

KROGSTAD: Does your husband's love for you run so thin? He knows everything I can expose you too, and all the same he dares to—

NORA: How can you imagine he knows anything about this?

KROGSTAD: Ah, no—I can't imagine it either, now. It's not at all like my fine Torvald Helmer to have so much guts—

NORA: Mr. Krogstad, I demand respect for my husband!

KROGSTAD: Why, of course—all due respect. But since the lady's keeping it so carefully hidden, may I presume to ask if you're also a bit better informed than yesterday about what you've actually done?

NORA: More than you ever could teach me.

KROGSTAD: Yes, I *am* such an awful lawyer.

NORA: What is it you want from me?

KROGSTAD: Just a glimpse of how you are, Mrs. Helmer. I've been thinking about you all day long. A cashier, a night-court scribbler, a—well, a type like me also has a little of what they call a heart, you know.

NORA: Then show it. Think of my children.

KROGSTAD: Did you or your husband ever think of mine? But never mind. I simply wanted to tell you that you don't need to take this thing too seriously. For the present, I'm not proceeding with any action.

NORA: Oh no, really! Well—I knew that.

KROGSTAD: Everything can be settled in a friendly spirit. It doesn't have to get around town at all; it can stay just among us three.

NORA: My husband may never know anything of this.

KROGSTAD: How can you manage that? Perhaps you can pay me the balance?

NORA: No, not right now.

KROGSTAD: Or you know some way of raising the money in a day or two?

NORA: No way that I'm willing to use.

KROGSTAD: Well, it wouldn't have done you any good, anyway. If you stood in front of me with a fistful of bills, you still couldn't buy your signature back.

NORA: Then tell me what you're going to do with it.

KROGSTAD: I'll just hold onto it—keep it on file. There's no outsider who'll even get wind of it. So if you've been thinking of taking some desperate step—

NORA: I have.

KROGSTAD: Been thinking of running away from home—

NORA: I have!

KROGSTAD: Or even of something worse—

NORA: How could you guess that?

KROGSTAD: You can drop those thoughts.

NORA: How could you guess I was thinking of *that*?

KROGSTAD: Most of us think about *that* at first. I thought about it too, but I discovered I hadn't the courage—

NORA (*lifelessly*):   I don't either.

KROGSTAD (*relieved*):   That's true, you haven't the courage? You too?

NORA: I don't have it—I don't have it.

KROGSTAD: It would be terribly stupid, anyway. After that first storm at home blows out, why, then—I have here in my pocket a letter for your husband—

NORA: Telling everything?

KROGSTAD: As charitably as possible.

NORA (*quickly*):   He mustn't ever get that letter. Tear it up. I'll find some way to get money.

KROGSTAD: Beg pardon, Mrs. Helmer, but I think I just told you—

NORA: Oh, I don't mean the money I owe you. Let me know how much you want from my husband, and I'll manage it.

KROGSTAD: I don't want any money from your husband.

NORA: What do you want, then?

KROGSTAD: I'll tell you what. I want to recoup, Mrs. Helmer; I want to get on in the world—and there's where your husband can help me. For a year and a half I've kept myself clean of anything disreputable—all that time struggling with the worst conditions; but I was satisfied, working my way up step by step. Now I've been written right off, and I'm just not in the mood to come crawling back. I tell you, I want to move on. I want to get back in the bank—in a better position. Your husband can set up a job for me—

NORA: He'll never do that!

KROGSTAD: He'll do it. I know him. He won't dare breathe a word of protest. And once I'm in there together with him, you just wait and see! Inside of a year, I'll be the manager's right-hand man. It'll be Nils Krogstad, not Torvald Helmer, who runs the bank.

NORA: You'll never see the day!

KROGSTAD: Maybe you think you can—

NORA: I have the courage now—for *that*.

KROGSTAD: Oh, you don't scare me. A smart, spoiled lady like you—

NORA: You'll see; you'll see!

KROGSTAD: Under the ice, maybe? Down in the freezing, coal-black water? There, till you float up in the spring, ugly, unrecognizable, with your hair falling out—

NORA: You don't frighten me.

KROGSTAD: Nor do you frighten me. One doesn't do these things, Mrs. Helmer. Besides, what good would it be? I'd still have him safe in my pocket.

NORA: Afterwards? When I'm no longer—?

KROGSTAD: Are you forgetting that *I'll* be in control then over your final reputation? (NORA *stands speechless, staring at him.*) Good; now I've warned you. Don't do anything stupid. When Helmer's read my letter, I'll be waiting for his reply. And bear in mind that it's your husband himself who's forced me back to my old ways. I'll never forgive him for that. Good-bye, Mrs. Helmer.   (*He goes out through the hall.*)

NORA (*goes to the hall door, opens it a crack, and listens*):   He's gone. Didn't leave the letter. Oh no, no, that's impossible too! (*Opening the door more and more*) What's that?

He's standing outside—not going downstairs. He's thinking it over? Maybe he'll—? (*A letter falls in the mailbox; then* KROGSTAD's *footsteps are heard, dying away down a flight of stairs.* NORA *gives a muffled cry and runs over toward the sofa table. A short pause.*) In the mailbox. (*Slips warily over to the hall door*) It's lying there. Torvald, Torvald—now we're lost!

MRS. LINDE (*entering with the costume from the room, left*):   There now, I can't see anything else to mend. Perhaps you'd like to try—

NORA (*in a hoarse whisper*):   Kristine, come here.

MRS. LINDE (*tossing the dress on the sofa*):   What's wrong? You look upset.

NORA: Come here. See that letter? *There!* Look—through the glass in the mailbox.

MRS. LINDE: Yes, yes, I see it.

NORA: That letter's from Krogstad—

MRS. LINDE: Nora—it's Krogstad who loaned you the money!

NORA: Yes, and now Torvald will find out everything.

MRS. LINDE: Believe me, Nora, it's best for both of you.

NORA: There's more you don't know. I forged a name.

MRS. LINDE: But for heaven's sake—?

NORA: I only want to tell you that, Kristine, so that you can be my witness.

MRS. LINDE: Witness? Why should I—?

NORA: If I should go out of my mind—it could easily happen—

MRS. LINDE: Nora!

NORA: Or anything else occurred—so I couldn't be present here—

MRS. LINDE: Nora, Nora, you aren't yourself at all!

NORA: And someone should try to take on the whole weight, all of the guilt, you follow me—

MRS. LINDE: Yes, of course, but why do you think—?

NORA: Then you're the witness that it isn't true, Kristine. I'm very much myself; my mind right now is perfectly clear; and I'm telling you: nobody else has known about this; I alone did everything. Remember that.

MRS. LINDE: I will. But I don't understand all this.

NORA: Oh, how could you ever understand it? It's the miracle now that's going to take place.

MRS. LINDE: The miracle?

NORA: Yes, the miracle. But it's so awful, Kristine. It mustn't take place, not for anything in the world.

MRS. LINDE: I'm going right over and talk with Krogstad.

NORA: Don't go near him; he'll do you some terrible harm!

MRS. LINDE: There was a time once when he'd gladly have done anything for me.

NORA: He?

MRS. LINDE: Where does he live?

NORA: Oh, how do I know? Yes. (*Searches in her pocket*) Here's his card. But the letter, the letter—!

HELMER (*from the study, knocking on the door*):   Nora!

NORA (*with a cry of fear*):   Oh! What is it? What do you want?

HELMER: Now, now, don't be so frightened. We're not coming in. You locked the door—are you trying on the dress?

NORA: Yes, I'm trying it. I'll look just beautiful, Torvald.

MRS. LINDE (*who has read the card*):   He's living right around the corner.

NORA: Yes, but what's the use? We're lost. The letter's in the box.

MRS. LINDE: And your husband has the key?

NORA: Yes, always.

MRS. LINDE: Krogstad can ask for his letter back unread; he can find some excuse—

NORA: But it's just this time that Torvald usually—

MRS. LINDE: Stall him. Keep him in there. I'll be back as quick as I can. (*She hurries out through the hall entrance.*)

NORA (*goes to* HELMER*'s door, opens it, and peers in*): Torvald!

HELMER (*from the inner study*): Well—does one dare set foot in one's own living room at last? Come on, Rank, now we'll get a look—(*In the doorway*) But what's this?

NORA: What, Torvald dear?

HELMER: Rank had me expecting some grand masquerade.

RANK (*in the doorway*): That was my impression, but I must have been wrong.

NORA: No one can admire me in my splendor—not until tomorrow.

HELMER: But Nora dear, you look so exhausted. Have you practiced too hard?

NORA: No, I haven't practiced at all yet.

HELMER: You know, it's necessary—

NORA: Oh, it's absolutely necessary, Torvald. But I can't get anywhere without your help. I've forgotten the whole thing completely.

HELMER: Ah, we'll soon take care of that.

NORA: Yes, take care of me, Torvald, please! Promise me that? Oh, I'm so nervous. That big party—You must give up everything this evening for me. No business—don't even touch your pen. Yes? Dear Torvald, promise?

HELMER: It's a promise. Tonight I'm totally at your service—you little helpless thing. Hm—but first there's one thing I want to—(*Goes toward the hall door*)

NORA: What are you looking for?

HELMER: Just to see if there's any mail.

NORA: No, no, don't do that, Torvald!

HELMER: Now what?

NORA: Torvald, please. There isn't any.

HELMER: Let me look, though. (*Starts out.* NORA, *at the piano, strikes the first notes of the tarantella.* HELMER, *at the door, stops.*) Aha!

NORA: I can't dance tomorrow if I don't practice with you.

HELMER (*going over to her*): Nora dear, are you really so frightened?

NORA: Yes, so terribly frightened. Let me practice right now; there's still time before dinner. Oh, sit down and play for me, Torvald. Direct me. Teach me, the way you always have.

HELMER: Gladly, if it's what you want. (*Sits at the piano*)

NORA (*snatches the tambourine up from the box, then a long, varicolored shawl, which she throws around herself, whereupon she springs forward and cries out*): Play for me now! Now I'll dance!

(HELMER *plays and* NORA *dances.* RANK *stands behind* HELMER *at the piano and looks on.*)

HELMER (*as he plays*): Slower. Slow down.

NORA: Can't change it.

HELMER: Not so violent, Nora!

NORA: Has to be just like this.

HELMER (*stopping*):   No, no, that won't do at all.

NORA (*laughing and swinging her tambourine*):   Isn't that what I told you?

RANK: Let me play for her.

HELMER (*getting up*):   Yes, go on. I can teach her more easily then.

(RANK *sits at the piano and plays;* NORA *dances more and more wildly.* HELMER *has stationed himself by the stove and repeatedly gives her directions; she seems not to hear them; her hair loosens and falls over her shoulders; she does not notice, but goes on dancing.* MRS. LINDE *enters.*)

MRS. LINDE (*standing dumbfounded at the door*):   Ah——!

NORA (*still dancing*):   See what fun, Kristine!

HELMER: But Nora darling, you dance as if your life were at stake.

NORA: And it is.

HELMER: Rank, stop! This is pure madness. Stop it, I say!

(RANK *breaks off playing, and* NORA *halts abruptly.*)

HELMER (*going over to her*):   I never would have believed it. You've forgotten everything I taught you.

NORA (*throwing away the tambourine*):   You see for yourself.

HELMER: Well, there's certainly room for instruction here.

NORA: Yes, you see how important it is. You've got to teach me to the very last minute. Promise me that, Torvald?

HELMER: You can bet on it.

NORA: You mustn't, either today or tomorrow, think about anything else but me; you mustn't open any letters—or the mailbox—

HELMER: Ah, it's still the fear of that man—

NORA: Oh yes, yes, that too.

HELMER: Nora, it's written all over you—there's already a letter from him out there.

NORA: I don't know. I guess so. But you mustn't read such things now; there mustn't be anything ugly between us before it's all over.

RANK (*quietly to* HELMER):   You shouldn't deny her.

HELMER (*putting his arm around her*):   The child can have her way. But tomorrow night, after you've danced—

NORA: Then you'll be free.

MAID (*in the doorway, right*):   Ma'am, dinner is served.

NORA: We'll be wanting champagne, Helene.

MAID: Very good, ma'am.   (*Goes out*)

HELMER: So—a regular banquet, hm?

NORA: Yes, a banquet—champagne till daybreak! (*Calling out*) And some macaroons, Helene. Heaps of them—just this once.

HELMER (*taking her hands*):   Now, now, now—no hysterics. Be my own little lark again.

NORA: Oh, I will soon enough. But go on in—and you, Dr. Rank. Kristine, help me put up my hair.

RANK (*whispering, as they go*):   There's nothing wrong—really wrong, is there?

HELMER: Oh, of course not. It's nothing more than this childish anxiety I was telling you about.   (*They go out, right.*)

NORA: Well?

MRS. LINDE: Left town.

NORA: I could see by your face.

MRS. LINDE: He'll be home tomorrow evening. I wrote him a note.

NORA: You shouldn't have. Don't try to stop anything now. After all, it's a wonderful joy, this waiting here for the miracle.

MRS. LINDE: What is it you're waiting for?

NORA: Oh, you can't understand that. Go in to them, I'll be along in a moment.

(MRS. LINDE *goes into the dining room.* NORA *stands a short while as if composing herself; then she looks at her watch.*)

NORA: Five. Seven hours to midnight. Twenty-four hours to the midnight after, and then the tarantella's done. Seven and twenty-four? Thirty-one hours to live.

HELMER (*in the doorway, right*): What's become of the little lark?

NORA (*going toward him with open arms*): Here's your lark!

ACT III

Same scene. The table, with chairs around it, has been moved to the center of the room. A lamp on the table is lit. The hall door stands open. Dance music drifts down from the floor above. MRS. LINDE *sits at the table, absently paging through a book, trying to read, but apparently unable to focus her thoughts. Once or twice she pauses, tensely listening for a sound at the outer entrance.*

MRS. LINDE (*glancing at her watch*): Not yet—and there's hardly any time left. If only he's not—(*Listening again*) Ah, there he is. (*She goes out in the hall and cautiously opens the outer door. Quiet footsteps are heard on the stairs. She whispers.*) Come in. Nobody's here.

KROGSTAD (*in the doorway*): I found a note from you at home. What's back of all this?

MRS. LINDE: I just *had* to talk to you.

KROGSTAD: Oh? And it just *had* to be here in this house?

MRS. LINDE: At my place it was impossible; my room hasn't a private entrance. Come in; we're all alone. The maid's asleep, and the Helmers are at the dance upstairs.

KROGSTAD (*entering the room*): Well, well, the Helmers are dancing tonight? Really?

MRS. LINDE: Yes, why not?

KROGSTAD: How true—why not?

MRS. LINDE: All right, Krogstad, let's talk.

KROGSTAD: Do we two have anything more to talk about?

MRS. LINDE: We have a great deal to talk about.

KROGSTAD: I wouldn't have thought so.

MRS. LINDE: No, because you've never understood me, really.

KROGSTAD: Was there anything more to understand—except what's all too common in life? A calculating woman throws over a man the moment a better catch comes by.

MRS. LINDE: You think I'm so thoroughly calculating? You think I broke it off lightly?

KROGSTAD: Didn't you?

MRS. LINDE: Nils—is that what you really thought?

KROGSTAD: If you cared, then why did you write me the way you did?

MRS. LINDE: What else could I do? If I had to break off with you, then it was my job as well to root out everything you felt for me.

KROGSTAD (*wringing his hands*):   So that was it. And this—all this, simply for money!

MRS. LINDE: Don't forget I had a helpless mother and two small brothers. We couldn't wait for you, Nils; you had such a long road ahead of you then.

KROGSTAD: That may be; but you still hadn't the right to abandon me for somebody else's sake.

MRS. LINDE: Yes—I don't know. So many, many times I've asked myself if I did have that right.

KROGSTAD (*more softly*):   When I lost you, it was as if all the solid ground dissolved from under my feet. Look at me; I'm a half-drowned man now, hanging onto a wreck.

MRS. LINDE: Help may be near.

KROGSTAD: It was near—but then you came and blocked it off.

MRS. LINDE: Without my knowing it, Nils. Today for the first time I learned that it's you I'm replacing at the bank.

KROGSTAD: All right—I believe you. But now that you know, will you step aside?

MRS. LINDE: No, because that wouldn't benefit you in the slightest.

KROGSTAD: Not "benefit" me, hm! I'd step aside anyway.

MRS. LINDE: I've learned to be realistic. Life and hard, bitter necessity have taught me that.

KROGSTAD: And life's taught me never to trust fine phrases.

MRS. LINDE: Then life's taught you a very sound thing. But you do have to trust in actions, don't you?

KROGSTAD: What does that mean?

MRS. LINDE: You said you were hanging on like a half-drowned man to a wreck.

KROGSTAD: I've good reason to say that.

MRS. LINDE: I'm also like a half-drowned woman on a wreck. No one to suffer with; no one to care for.

KROGSTAD: You made your choice.

MRS. LINDE: There wasn't any choice then.

KROGSTAD: So—what of it?

MRS. LINDE: Nils, if only we two shipwrecked people could reach across to each other.

KROGSTAD: What are you saying?

MRS. LINDE: Two on one wreck are at least better off than each on his own.

KROGSTAD: Kristine!

MRS. LINDE: Why do you think I came into town?

KROGSTAD: Did you really have some thought of me?

MRS. LINDE: I have to work to go on living. All my born days, as long as I can remember, I've worked, and it's been my best and my only joy. But now I'm completely alone in the world; it frightens me to be so empty and lost. To work for yourself—there's no joy in that. Nils, give me something—someone to work for.

KROGSTAD: I don't believe all this. It's just some hysterical feminine urge to go out and make a noble sacrifice.

MRS. LINDE: Have you ever found me to be hysterical?

KROGSTAD: Can you honestly mean this? Tell me—do you know everything about my past?

MRS. LINDE: Yes.

KROGSTAD: And you know what they think I'm worth around here.

MRS. LINDE: From what you were saying before, it would seem that with me you could have been another person.

KROGSTAD: I'm positive of that.

MRS. LINDE: Couldn't it happen still?

KROGSTAD: Kristine—you're saying this in all seriousness? Yes, you are! I can see it in you. And do you really have the courage, then—?

MRS. LINDE: I need to have someone to care for; and your children need a mother. We both need each other. Nils, I have faith that you're good at heart—I'll risk everything together with you.

KROGSTAD (*gripping her hands*):   Kristine, thank you, thank you—Now I know I can win back a place in their eyes. Yes—but I forgot—

MRS. LINDE (*listening*):   Shh! The tarantella. Go now! Go on!

KROGSTAD: Why? What is it?

MRS. LINDE: Hear the dance up there? When that's over, they'll be coming down.

KROGSTAD: Oh, then I'll go. But—it's all pointless. Of course, you don't know the move I made against the Helmers.

MRS. LINDE: Yes, Nils, I know.

KROGSTAD: And all the same, you have the courage to—?

MRS. LINDE: I know how far despair can drive a man like you.

KROGSTAD: Oh, if I only could take it all back.

MRS. LINDE: You easily could—your letter's still lying in the mailbox.

KROGSTAD: Are you sure of that?

MRS. LINDE: Positive. But—

KROGSTAD (*looks at her searchingly*):   Is that the meaning of it, then? You'll have your friend at any price. Tell me straight out. Is that it?

MRS. LINDE: Nils—anyone who's sold herself for somebody else once isn't going to do it again.

KROGSTAD: I'll demand my letter back.

MRS. LINDE: No, no.

KROGSTAD: Yes, of course. I'll stay here till Helmer comes down; I'll tell him to give me my letter again—that it only involves my dismissal—that he shouldn't read it—

MRS. LINDE: No, Nils, don't call the letter back.

KROGSTAD: But wasn't that exactly why you wrote me to come here?

MRS. LINDE: Yes, in that first panic. But it's been a whole day and night since then, and in that time I've seen such incredible things in this house. Helmer's got to learn everything; this dreadful secret has to be aired; those two have to come to a full understanding; all these lies and evasions can't go on.

KROGSTAD: Well, then, if you want to chance it. But at least there's one thing I can do, and do right away—

MRS. LINDE (*listening*):   Go now, go quick! The dance is over. We're not safe another second.

KROGSTAD: I'll wait for you downstairs.

MRS. LINDE: Yes, please do; take me home.

KROGSTAD: I can't believe it; I've never been so happy. (*He leaves by way of the outer door; the door between the room and the hall stays open.*)

MRS. LINDE (*straightening up a bit and getting together her street clothes*):   How different now! How different! Someone to work for, to live for—a home to build. Well, it is worth the try! Oh, if they'd only come! (*Listening*) Ah, there they are. Bundle up. (*She picks up her hat and coat.* NORA's *and* HELMER's *voices can be heard outside; a key turns in the lock, and* HELMER *brings* NORA *into the hall almost by force. She is wearing the Italian costume with a large black shawl about her; he has on evening dress, with a black domino open over it.*)

NORA (*struggling in the doorway*):   No, no, no, not inside! I'm going up again. I don't want to leave so soon.

HELMER: But Nora dear—

NORA: Oh, I beg you, please, Torvald. From the bottom of my heart, *please*—only an hour more!

HELMER: Not a single minute, Nora darling. You know our agreement. Come on, in we go; you'll catch cold out here. (*In spite of her resistance, he gently draws her into the room.*)

MRS. LINDE: Good evening.

NORA: Kristine!

HELMER: Why, Mrs. Linde—are you here so late?

MRS. LINDE: Yes, I'm sorry, but I did want to see Nora in costume.

NORA: Have you been sitting here, waiting for me?

MRS. LINDE: Yes. I didn't come early enough; you were all upstairs; and then I thought I really couldn't leave without seeing you.

HELMER (*removing* NORA's *shawl*):   Yes, take a good look. She's worth looking at, I can tell you that, Mrs. Linde. Isn't she lovely?

MRS. LINDE: Yes, I should say—

HELMER: A dream of loveliness, isn't she? That's what everyone thought at the party, too. But she's horribly stubborn—this sweet little thing. What's to be done with her? Can you imagine, I almost had to use force to pry her away.

NORA: Oh, Torvald, you're going to regret you didn't indulge me, even for just a half hour more.

HELMER: There, you see. She danced her tarantella and got a tumultuous hand—which was well earned, although the performance may have been a bit too naturalistic—I mean it rather overstepped the proprieties of art. But never mind—what's important is, she made a success, an overwhelming success. You think I could let her stay on after that and spoil the effect? Oh no; I took my lovely little Capri girl—my capricious little Capri girl, I should say—took her under my arm; one quick tour of the ballroom, a curtsy to every side, and then—as they say in novels—the beautiful vision disappeared. An exit should always be effective, Mrs. Linde, but that's what I can't get Nora to grasp. Phew, it's hot in here. (*Flings the domino on a chair and opens the door to his room*) Why's it dark in here? Oh yes, of course. Excuse me. (*He goes in and lights a couple of candles.*)

NORA (*in a sharp, breathless whisper*):   So?

MRS. LINDE (*quietly*):   I talked with him.

NORA: And—?

MRS. LINDE: Nora—you must tell your husband everything.

NORA (*dully*):   I knew it.

MRS. LINDE: You've got nothing to fear from Krogstad, but you have to speak out.

NORA: I won't tell.

MRS. LINDE: Then the letter will.

NORA: Thanks, Kristine. I know now what's to be done. Shh!

HELMER (*reentering*):   Well, then, Mrs. Linde—have you admired her?

MRS. LINDE: Yes, and now I'll say good night.

HELMER: Oh, come, so soon? Is this yours, this knitting?

MRS. LINDE: Yes, thanks. I nearly forgot it.

HELMER: Do you knit, then?

MRS. LINDE: Oh yes.

HELMER: You know what? You should embroider instead.

MRS. LINDE: Really? Why?

HELMER: Yes, because it's a lot prettier. See here, one holds the embroidery so, in the left hand, and then one guides the needle with the right—so—in an easy, sweeping curve—right?

MRS. LINDE: Yes, I guess that's—

HELMER: But, on the other hand, knitting—it can never be anything but ugly. Look, see here, the arms tucked in, the knitting needles going up and down—there's something Chinese about it. Ah, that was really a glorious champagne they served.

MRS. LINDE: Yes, good night, Nora, and don't be stubborn anymore.

HELMER: Well put, Mrs. Linde!

MRS. LINDE: Good night, Mr. Helmer.

HELMER (*accompanying her to the door*):   Good night, good night. I hope you get home all right. I'd be very happy to—but you don't have far to go. Good night, good night. (*She leaves. He shuts the door after her and returns.*) There, now, at last we got her out the door. She's a deadly bore, that creature.

NORA: Aren't you pretty tired, Torvald?

HELMER: No, not a bit.

NORA: You're not sleepy?

HELMER: Not at all. On the contrary, I'm feeling quite exhilarated. But you? Yes, you really look tired and sleepy.

NORA: Yes, I'm very tired. Soon now I'll sleep.

HELMER: See! You see! I was right all along that we shouldn't stay longer.

NORA: Whatever you do is always right.

HELMER (*kissing her brow*):   Now my little lark talks sense. Say, did you notice what a time Rank was having tonight?

NORA: Oh, was he? I didn't get to speak with him.

HELMER: I scarcely did either, but it's a long time since I've seen him in such high spirits. (*Gazes at her a moment, then comes nearer her*) Hm—it's marvelous, though, to be back home again—to be completely alone with you. Oh, you bewitchingly lovely young woman!

NORA: Torvald, don't look at me like that!

HELMER: Can't I look at my richest treasure? At all that beauty that's mine, mine alone—completely and utterly.

NORA (*moving around to the other side of the table*):   You mustn't talk to me that way tonight.

HELMER (*following her*):   The tarantella is still in your blood, I can see—and it makes you even more enticing. Listen. The guests are beginning to go. (*Dropping his voice*) Nora—it'll soon be quiet through this whole house.

NORA: Yes, I hope so.

HELMER: You do, don't you, my love? Do you realize—when I'm out at a party like this with you—do you know why I talk to you so little, and keep such a distance away; just send you a stolen look now and then—you know why I do it? It's because I'm imagining then that you're my secret darling, my secret young bride-to-be, and that no one suspects there's anything between us.

NORA: Yes, yes; oh, yes, I know you're always thinking of me.

HELMER: And then when we leave and I place the shawl over those fine young rounded shoulders—over that wonderful curving neck—then I pretend that you're my young bride, that we're just coming from the wedding, that for the first time I'm bringing you into my house—that for the first time I'm alone with you—completely alone with you, your trembling young beauty! All this evening I've longed for nothing but you. When I saw you turn and sway in the tarantella—my blood was pounding till I couldn't stand it—that's why I brought you down here so early—

NORA: Go away, Torvald! Leave me alone. I don't want all this.

HELMER: What do you mean? Nora, you're teasing me. You will, won't you? Aren't I your husband—?

(A knock at the outside door)

NORA (*startled*):   What's that?

HELMER (*going toward the hall*):   Who is it?

RANK (*outside*):   It's me. May I come in a moment?

HELMER (*with quiet irritation*):   Oh, what does he want now? (*Aloud*) Hold on. (*Goes and opens the door*) Oh, how nice that you didn't just pass us by!

RANK: I thought I heard your voice, and then I wanted so badly to have a look in. (*Lightly glancing about*) Ah, me, these old familiar haunts. You have it snug and cozy in here, you two.

HELMER: You seemed to be having it pretty cozy upstairs, too.

RANK: Absolutely. Why shouldn't I? Why not take in everything in life? As much as you can, anyway, and as long as you can. The wine was superb—

HELMER: The champagne especially.

RANK: You noticed that too? It's amazing how much I could guzzle down.

NORA: Torvald also drank a lot of champagne this evening.

RANK: Oh?

NORA: Yes, and that always makes him so entertaining.

RANK: Well, why shouldn't one have a pleasant evening after a well-spent day?

HELMER: Well spent? I'm afraid I can't claim that.

RANK (*slapping him on the back*):   But I can, you see!

NORA: Dr. Rank, you must have done some scientific research today.

RANK: Quite so.

HELMER: Come now—little Nora talking about scientific research!

NORA: And can I congratulate you on the results?

RANK: Indeed you may.

NORA: Then they were good?

RANK: The best possible for both doctor and patient—certainty.

NORA (*quickly and searchingly*):   Certainty?

RANK: Complete certainty. So don't I owe myself a gay evening afterwards?

NORA: Yes, you're right, Dr. Rank.

HELMER: I'm with you—just so long as you don't have to suffer for it in the morning.

RANK: Well, one never gets something for nothing in life.

NORA: Dr. Rank—are you very fond of masquerade parties?

RANK: Yes, if there's a good array of odd disguises—

NORA: Tell me, what should we two go as at the next masquerade?

HELMER: You little feather head—already thinking of the next!

RANK: We two? I'll tell you what: you must go as Charmed Life—

HELMER: Yes, but find a costume for *that!*

RANK: Your wife can appear just as she looks every day.

HELMER: That was nicely put. But don't you know what you're going to be?

RANK: Yes, Helmer, I've made up my mind.

HELMER: Well?

RANK: At the next masquerade I'm going to be invisible.

HELMER: That's a funny idea.

RANK: They say there's a hat—black, huge—have you never heard of the hat that makes you invisible? You put it on, and then no one on earth can see you.

HELMER (*suppressing a smile*):   Ah, of course.

RANK: But I'm quite forgetting what I came for. Helmer, give me a cigar, one of the dark Havanas.

HELMER: With the greatest pleasure. (*Holds out his case*)

RANK: Thanks. (*Takes one and cuts off the tip*)

NORA (*striking a match*):   Let me give you a light.

RANK: Thank you. (*She holds the match for him; he lights the cigar.*) And now good-bye.

HELMER: Good-bye, good-bye, old friend.

NORA: Sleep well, Doctor.

RANK: Thanks for that wish.

NORA: Wish me the same.

RANK: You? All right, if you like—Sleep well. And thanks for the light.

(*He nods to them both and leaves.*)

HELMER (*his voice subdued*):   He's been drinking heavily.

NORA (*absently*):   Could be. (HELMER *takes his keys from his pocket and goes out in the hall.*) Torvald—what are you after?

HELMER: Got to empty the mailbox; it's nearly full. There won't be room for the morning papers.

NORA: Are you working tonight?

HELMER: You know I'm not. Why—what's this? Someone's been at the lock.

NORA: At the lock—?

HELMER: Yes, I'm positive. What do you suppose—? I can't imagine one of the maids—? Here's a broken hairpin. Nora, it's yours—

NORA (*quickly*):   Then it must be the children—

HELMER: You'd better break them of that. Hm, hm—well, opened it after all. (*Takes the contents out and calls into the kitchen*) Helene! Helene, would you put out the lamp in the hall. (*He returns to the room, shutting the hall door, then displays the handful of mail.*) Look how it's piled up. (*Sorting through them*) Now what's this?

NORA (*at the window*):   The letter! Oh, Torvald, no!

HELMER: Two calling cards—from Rank.

NORA: From Dr. Rank?

HELMER (*examining them*):   "Dr. Rank, Consulting Physician." They were on top. He must have dropped them in as he left.

NORA: Is there anything on them?

HELMER: There's a black cross over the name. See? That's a gruesome notion. He could almost be announcing his own death.

NORA: That's just what he's doing.

HELMER: What! You've heard something? Something he's told you?

NORA: Yes. That when those cards came, he'd be taking his leave of us. He'll shut himself in now and die.

HELMER: Ah, my poor friend! Of course I knew he wouldn't be here much longer. But so soon—And then to hide himself away like a wounded animal.

NORA: If it has to happen, then it's best it happens in silence—don't you think so, Torvald?

HELMER (*pacing up and down*):   He's grown right into our lives. I simply can't imagine him gone. He with his suffering and loneliness—like a dark cloud setting off our sunlit happiness. Well, maybe it's best this way. For him, at least. (*Standing still*) And maybe for us too, Nora. Now we're thrown back on each other, completely. (*Embracing her*) Oh you, my darling wife, how can I hold you close enough? You know what, Nora—time and again I've wished you were in some terrible danger, just so I could stake my life and soul and everything, for your sake.

NORA (*tearing herself away, her voice firm and decisive*):   Now you must read your mail, Torvald.

HELMER: No, no, not tonight. I want to stay with you, dearest.

NORA: With a dying friend on your mind?

HELMER: You're right. We've both had a shock. There's ugliness between us— these thoughts of death and corruption. We'll have to get free of them first. Until then—we'll stay apart.

NORA *clinging about his neck*):   Torvald—good night! Good night!

HELMER (*kissing her on the cheek*):   Good night, little songbird. Sleep well, Nora. I'll be reading my mail now.

(*He takes the letters into his room and shuts the door after him.*)

NORA (*with bewildered glances, groping about, seizing* HELMER*'s domino, throwing it around her, and speaking in short, hoarse, broken whispers*):   Never see him again. Never, never. (*Putting her shawl over her head*) Never see the children either—them, too. Never, never. Oh, the freezing black water! The depths—down—Oh, I wish it were over—He has it now; he's reading it—now. Oh no, no, not yet. Torvald, good-bye, you and the children— (*She starts for the hall; as she does,* HELMER *throws open his door and stands with an open letter in his hand.*)

HELMER: Nora!

NORA (*screams*):   Oh—!

HELMER: What is this? You know what's in this letter?

NORA: Yes, I know. Let me go! Let me out!

HELMER (*holding her back*):   Where are you going?

NORA (*struggling to break loose*):   You can't save me, Torvald!

HELMER (*slumping back*):   True! Then it's true what he writes? How horrible! No, no, it's impossible—it can't be true.

NORA: It *is* true. I've loved you more than all this world.

HELMER: Ah, none of your slippery tricks.

NORA (*taking one step toward him*): Torvald—!

HELMER: What *is* this you've blundered into!

NORA: Just let me loose. You're not going to suffer for my sake. You're not going to take on my guilt.

HELMER: No more playacting. (*Locks the hall door*) You stay right here and give me a reckoning. You understand what you've done? Answer! You understand?

NORA (*looking squarely at him, her face hardening*): Yes. I'm beginning to understand everything now.

HELMER (*striding about*): Oh, what an awful awakening! In all these eight years— she who was my pride and joy—a hypocrite, a liar—worse, worse—a criminal! How infinitely disgusting it all is! The shame! (NORA *says nothing and goes on looking straight at him. He stops in front of her.*) I should have suspected something of the kind. I should have known. All your father's flimsy values—Be still! All your father's flimsy values have come out in you. No religion, no morals, no sense of duty—Oh, how I'm punished for letting him off! I did it for your sake, and you repay me like this.

NORA: Yes, like this.

HELMER: Now you've wrecked all my happiness—ruined my whole future. Oh, it's awful to think of. I'm in a cheap little grafter's hands; he can do anything he wants with me, ask for anything, play with me like a puppet—and I can't breathe a word. I'll be swept down miserably into the depths on account of a featherbrained woman.

NORA: When I'm gone from this world, you'll be free.

HELMER: Oh, quit posing. Your father had a mess of those speeches too. What good would that ever do me if you were gone from this world, as you say? Not the slightest. He can still make the whole thing known; and if he does, I could be falsely suspected as your accomplice. They might even think that I was behind it—that I put you up to it. And all that I can thank you for—you that I've coddled the whole of our marriage. Can you see now what you've done to me?

NORA (*icily calm*): Yes.

HELMER: It's so incredible, I just can't grasp it. But we'll have to patch up whatever we can. Take off the shawl. I said, take it off! I've got to appease him somehow or other. The thing has to be hushed up at any cost. And as for you and me, it's got to seem like everything between us is just as it was—to the outside world, that is. You'll go right on living in this house, of course. But you can't be allowed to bring up the children; I don't dare trust you with them.—Oh, to have to say this to someone I've loved so much! Well, that's done with. From now on happiness doesn't matter; all that matters is saving the bits and pieces, the appearance—(*The doorbell rings.* HELMER *starts.*) What's that? And so late. Maybe the worst—? You think he'd—? Hide, Nora! Say you're sick. (NORA *remains standing motionless.* HELMER *goes and opens the door.*)

MAID (*half dressed, in the hall*): A letter for Mrs. Helmer.

HELMER: I'll take it. (*Snatches the letter and shuts the door*) Yes, it's from him. You don't get it; I'm reading it myself.

NORA: Then read it.

HELMER (*by the lamp*): I hardly dare. We may be ruined, you and I. But—I've got to know. (*Rips open the letter, skims through a few lines, glances at an enclosure, then cries out joyfully*) Nora! (NORA *looks inquiringly at him.*) Nora! Wait—better check it again—Yes, yes, it's true. I'm saved. Nora, I'm saved!

NORA: And I?

HELMER: You too, of course. We're both saved, both of us. Look. He's sent back your note. He says he's sorry and ashamed—that a happy development in his life—oh, who cares what he says! Nora, we're saved! No one can hurt you. Oh, Nora, Nora— but first, this ugliness all has to go. Let me see—(*Takes a look at the note*) No, I don't want to see it; I want the whole thing to fade like a dream. (*Tears the note and both letters to pieces, throws them into the stove and watches them burn*) There—now there's nothing left.—He wrote that since Christmas Eve you—oh, they must have been three terrible days for you, Nora.

NORA: I fought a hard fight.

HELMER: And suffered pain and saw no escape but—no, we're not going to dwell on anything unpleasant. We'll just be grateful and keep on repeating; it's over now, it's over! You hear me, Nora? You don't seem to realize—it's over. What's it mean—that frozen look? Oh, poor little Nora, I understand. You can't believe I've forgiven you. But I have, Nora; I swear I have. I know that what you did, you did out of love for me.

NORA: That's true.

HELMER: You loved me the way a wife ought to love her husband. It's simply the means that you couldn't judge. But you think I love you any the less for not knowing how to handle your affairs? No, no—just lean on me: I'll guide you and teach you. I wouldn't be a man if this feminine helplessness didn't make you twice as attractive to me. You mustn't mind those sharp words I said—that was all in the first confusion of thinking my world had collapsed. I've forgiven you, Nora; I swear I've forgiven you.

NORA: My thanks for your forgiveness.   (*She goes out through the door, right.*)

HELMER: No, wait—(*Peers in*) What are you doing in there?

NORA (*inside*): Getting out of my costume.

HELMER (*by the open door*): Yes, do that. Try to calm yourself and collect your thoughts again, my frightened little songbird. You can rest easy now; I've got wide wings to shelter you with. (*Walking about close by the door*) How snug and nice our home is, Nora. You're safe here; I'll keep you like a hunted dove I've rescued out of a hawk's claws. I'll bring peace to your poor, shuddering heart. Gradually it'll happen, Nora; you'll see. Tomorrow all this will look different to you; then everything will be as it was. I won't have to go on repeating I forgive you; you'll feel it for yourself. How can you imagine I'd ever conceivably want to disown you—or even blame you in any way? Ah, you don't know a man's heart, Nora. For a man there's something indescribably sweet and satisfying in knowing he's forgiven his wife—and forgiven her out of a full and open heart. It's as if she belongs to him in two ways now: in a sense he's given her fresh into the world again, and she's become his wife and his child as well. From now on that's what you'll be to me—you little, bewildered, helpless thing. Don't be afraid of anything, Nora; just open your heart to me, and I'll be conscience and will to you both—(NORA *enters in her regular clothes.*) What's this? Not in bed? You've changed your dress?

NORA: Yes, Torvald, I've changed my dress.

HELMER: But why now, so late?

NORA: Tonight I'm not sleeping.

HELMER: But Nora dear—

NORA (*looking at her watch*): It's still not so very late. Sit down, Torvald; we have a lot to talk over. (*She sits at one side of the table.*)

HELMER: Nora—what is this? That hard expression—

NORA: Sit down. This'll take some time. I have a lot to say.

HELMER (*sitting at the table directly opposite her*):   You worry me, Nora. And I don't understand you.

NORA: No, that's exactly it. You don't understand me. And I've never understood you either—until tonight. No, don't interrupt. You can just listen to what I say. We're closing out accounts, Torvald.

HELMER: How do you mean that?

NORA (*after a short pause*):   Doesn't anything strike you about our sitting here like this?

HELMER: What's that?

NORA: We've been married now eight years. Doesn't it occur to you that this is the first time we two, you and I, man and wife, have ever talked seriously together?

HELMER: What do you mean—seriously?

NORA: In eight whole years—longer even—right from our first acquaintance, we've never exchanged a serious word on any serious thing.

HELMER: You mean I should constantly go and involve you in problems you couldn't possibly help me with?

NORA: I'm not talking of problems. I'm saying that we've never sat down seriously together and tried to get to the bottom of anything.

HELMER: But dearest, what good would that ever do you?

NORA: That's the point right there: you've never understood me. I've been wronged greatly, Torvald—first by Papa, and then by you.

HELMER: What! By us—the two people who've loved you more than anyone else?

NORA (*shaking her head*):   You never loved me. You've thought it fun to be in love with me, that's all.

HELMER: Nora, what a thing to say!

NORA: Yes, it's true now, Torvald. When I lived at home with Papa, he told me all his opinions, so I had the same ones too; or if they were different I hid them, since he wouldn't have cared for that. He used to call me his doll-child, and he played with me the way I played with my dolls. Then I came into your house—

HELMER: How can you speak of our marriage like that?

NORA (*unperturbed*):   I mean, then I went from Papa's hands into yours. You arranged everything to your own taste, and so I got the same taste as you—or I pretended to; I can't remember. I guess a little of both, first one, then the other. Now when I look back, it seems as if I'd lived here like a beggar—just from hand to mouth. I've lived by doing tricks for you, Torvald. But that's the way you wanted it. It's a great sin what you and Papa did to me. You're to blame that nothing's become of me.

HELMER: Nora, how unfair and ungrateful you are! Haven't you been happy here?

NORA: No, never. I thought so—but I never have.

HELMER: Not—not happy!

NORA: No, only lighthearted. And you've always been so kind to me. But our home's been nothing but a playpen. I've been your doll-wife here, just as at home I was Papa's doll-child. And in turn the children have been my dolls. I thought it was fun when you played with me, just as they thought it fun when I played with them. That's been our marriage, Torvald.

HELMER: There's some truth in what you're saying—under all the raving exaggeration. But it'll all be different after this. Playtime's over; now for the schooling.

NORA: Whose schooling—mine or the children's?

HELMER: Both yours and the children's, dearest.

NORA: Oh, Torvald, you're not the man to teach me to be a good wife to you.

HELMER: And you can say that?

NORA: And I—how am I equipped to bring up children?

HELMER: Nora!

NORA: Didn't you say a moment ago that that was no job to trust me with?

HELMER: In a flare of temper! Why fasten on that?

NORA: Yes, but you were so very right. I'm not up to the job. There's another job I have to do first. I have to try to educate myself. You can't help me with that. I've got to do it alone. And that's why I'm leaving you now.

HELMER (*jumping up*): What's that?

NORA: I have to stand completely alone, if I'm ever going to discover myself and the world out there. So I can't go on living with you.

HELMER: Nora, Nora!

NORA: I want to leave right away. Kristine should put me up for the night—

HELMER: You're insane! You've no right! I forbid you!

NORA: From here on, there's no use forbidding me anything. I'll take with me whatever is mine. I don't want a thing from you, either now or later.

HELMER: What kind of madness is this!

NORA: Tomorrow I'm going home—I mean, home where I came from. It'll be easier up there to find something to do.

HELMER: Oh, you blind, incompetent child!

NORA: I must learn to be competent, Torvald.

HELMER: Abandon your home, your husband, your children! And you're not even thinking what people will say.

NORA: I can't be concerned about that. I only know how essential this is.

HELMER: Oh, it's outrageous. So you'll run out like this on your most sacred vows.

NORA: What do you think are my most sacred vows?

HELMER: And I have to tell you that! Aren't they your duties to your husband and children?

NORA: I have other duties equally sacred.

HELMER: That isn't true. What duties are they?

NORA: Duties to myself.

HELMER: Before all else, you're a wife and a mother.

NORA: I don't believe in that anymore. I believe that, before all else, I'm a human being, no less than you—or anyway, I ought to try to become one. I know the majority thinks you're right, Torvald, and plenty of books agree with you, too. But I can't go on believing what the majority says, or what's written in books. I have to think over these things myself and try to understand them.

HELMER: Why can't you understand your place in your own home? On a point like that, isn't there one everlasting guide you can turn to? Where's your religion?

NORA: Oh, Torvald, I'm really not sure what religion is.

HELMER: What—?

NORA: I only know what the minister said when I was confirmed. He told me religion was this thing and that. When I get clear and away by myself, I'll go into that problem too. I'll see if what the minister said was right, or, in any case, if it's right for me.

HELMER: A young woman your age shouldn't talk like that. If religion can't move you, I can try to rouse your conscience. You do have some moral feeling? Or, tell me—has that gone too?

NORA: It's not easy to answer that, Torvald. I simply don't know. I'm all confused about these things. I just know I see them so differently from you. I find out, for one thing, that the law's not at all what I'd thought—but I can't get it through my head that the law is fair. A woman hasn't a right to protect her dying father or save her husband's life! I can't believe that.

HELMER: You talk like a child. You don't know anything of the world you live in.

NORA: No, I don't. But now I'll begin to learn for myself. I'll try to discover who's right, the world or I.

HELMER: Nora, you're sick; you've got a fever. I almost think you're out of your head.

NORA: I've never felt more clearheaded and sure in my life.

HELMER: And—clearheaded and sure—you're leaving your husband and children?

NORA: Yes.

HELMER: Then there's only one possible reason.

NORA: What?

HELMER: You no longer love me.

NORA: No. That's exactly it.

HELMER: Nora! You can't be serious!

NORA: Oh, this is so hard, Torvald—you've been so kind to me always. But I can't help it. I don't love you anymore.

HELMER (*struggling for composure*):   Are you also clearheaded and sure about that?

NORA: Yes, completely. That's why I can't go on staying here.

HELMER: Can you tell me what I did to lose your love?

NORA: Yes, I can tell you. It was this evening when the miraculous thing didn't come—then I knew you weren't the man I'd imagined.

HELMER: Be more explicit; I don't follow you.

NORA: I've waited now so patiently eight long years—for, my Lord, I know miracles don't come every day. Then this crisis broke over me, and such a certainty filled me: *now* the miraculous event would occur. While Krogstad's letter was lying out there, I never for an instant dreamed that you could give in to his terms. I was so utterly sure you'd say to him: go on, tell your tale to the whole wide world. And when he'd done that—

HELMER: Yes, what then? When I'd delivered my own wife into shame and disgrace—!

NORA: When he'd done that, I was so utterly sure that you'd step forward, take the blame on yourself and say: I am the guilty one.

HELMER: Nora—!

NORA: You're thinking I'd never accept such a sacrifice from you? No, of course not. But what good would my protests be against you? That was the miracle I was waiting for, in terror and hope. And to stave that off, I would have taken my life.

HELMER: I'd gladly work for you day and night, Nora—and take on pain and deprivation. But there's no one who gives up honor for love.

NORA: Millions of women have done just that.

HELMER: Oh, you think and talk like a silly child.

NORA: Perhaps. But you neither think nor talk like the man I could join myself to. When your big fright was over—and it wasn't from any threat against me, only for what might damage you—when all the danger was past, for you it was just as if nothing had happened. I was exactly the same, your little lark, your doll, that you'd have to handle with double care now that I'd turned out so brittle and frail. (*Gets up*) Torvald—in that instant it dawned on me that for eight years I've been living here with a stranger, and that I'd even conceived three children—oh, I can't stand the thought of it! I could tear myself to bits.

HELMER (*heavily*):   I see. There's a gulf that's opened between us—that's clear. Oh, but Nora, can't we bridge it somehow?

NORA: The way I am now, I'm no wife for you.

HELMER: I have the strength to make myself over.

NORA: Maybe—if your doll gets taken away.

HELMER: But to part! To part from you! No, Nora, no—I can't imagine it.

NORA (*going out, right*):   All the more reason why it has to be. (*She reenters with her coat and a small overnight bag, which she puts on a chair by the table.*)

HELMER: Nora, Nora, not now! Wait till tomorrow.

NORA: I can't spend the night in a strange man's room.

HELMER: But couldn't we live here like brother and sister—

NORA: You know very well how long that would last. (*Throws her shawl about her*) Good-bye, Torvald. I won't look in on the children. I know they're in better hands than mine. The way I am now, I'm no use to them.

HELMER: But someday, Nora—someday—?

NORA: How can I tell? I haven't the least idea what'll become of me.

HELMER: But you're my wife, now and wherever you go.

NORA: Listen, Torvald—I've heard that when a wife deserts her husband's house just as I'm doing, then the law frees him from all responsibility. In any case, I'm freeing you from being responsible. Don't feel yourself bound, any more than I will. There has to be absolute freedom for us both. Here, take your ring back. Give me mine.

HELMER: That too?

NORA: That too.

HELMER: There it is.

NORA: Good. Well, now it's all over. I'm putting the keys here. The maids know all about keeping up the house—better than I do. Tomorrow, after I've left town, Kristine will stop by to pack up everything that's mine from home. I'd like those things shipped to me.

HELMER: Over! All over! Nora, won't you ever think about me?

NORA: I'm sure I'll think of you often, and about the children and the house here.

HELMER: May I write you?

NORA: No—never. You're not to do that.

HELMER: Oh, but let me send you—

NORA: Nothing. Nothing.

HELMER: Or help you if you need it.

NORA: No. I accept nothing from strangers.

HELMER: Nora—can I never be more than a stranger to you?

NORA (*picking up the overnight bag*):   Ah, Torvald—it would take the greatest miracle of all—

HELMER: Tell me the greatest miracle!

NORA: You and I both would have to transform ourselves to the point that—oh, Torvald, I've stopped believing in miracles.

HELMER: But I'll believe. Tell me! Transform ourselves to the point that—?

NORA: That our living together could be a true marriage.

(*She goes out down the hall.*)

HELMER (*sinks down on a chair by the door, face buried in his hands*):   Nora! Nora! (*Looking about and rising*) Empty. She's gone. (*A sudden hope leaps in him*) The greatest miracle—?

(*From below, the sound of a door slamming shut*)

(*1879*)

QUESTIONS FOR REFLECTION

Experience

1. Describe your experience of reading (or viewing) *A Doll House*. How do you respond to Torvald Helmer's treatment of his wife, Nora? How do you respond to Nora's behavior? Why?
2. Describe Torvald Helmer. What aspects of his character are most evident in the early scenes? Does he give any evidence of having changed by the end of the play? Do you think he is capable of sharing the kind of marriage Nora describes at the end of the play?

Interpretation

3. Consider the function of the following characters: Nils Krogstad, Dr. Rank, and Kristine Linde.
4. Examine the play's plot. How does Ibsen control our responses and arouse our curiosity? Point out places where the tempo or pace of the play changes. What effects do these changes have?
5. Identify two or three visual details or objects that function as symbols, and explain their significance.
6. Choose one scene important for its revelation of character and explain how you would dramatize it.

Evaluation

7. Evaluate Nora's behavior. Does she make the right decision in leaving her family? Why or why not?
8. Ibsen has remarked that *A Doll House* is more about human rights than women's rights. What kind of rights do you think he had in mind?
9. *A Doll House* has been performed with an alternative ending in which Nora and Torvald are reconciled, and Nora remains with her family. Is this an artistically appropriate and theatrically effective ending? Why or why not?

CHAPTER TWENTY-ONE

A Collection of Modern and Contemporary Plays

All the world's a stage,
And all the men and women merely players:
They have their exits and their entrances,
And one man in his time plays many parts. . . .

WILLIAM SHAKESPEARE, *As You Like It*, II, VII

ISABELLA AUGUSTA PERSSE, LADY GREGORY

[1859–1932]

Born to a wealthy landowning family in Galway, in western Ireland, Isabella Augusta Persse, who married Sir William Gregory, a former governor of Ceylon, was a patroness of the Irish poet William Butler Yeats before she became a writer. Although she edited legendary Irish tales and translated Gaelic epics, she is best known as a writer of witty nationalistic plays like *The Rising of the Moon*. With Yeats, she founded the Irish Literary Theatre, an institution central to the rise of the Irish nationalist movement at the beginning of the twentieth century.

ISABELLA AUGUSTA PERSSE, LADY GREGORY

The Rising of the Moon

Scene: *Side of a quay in a seaport town. Some posts and chains. A large barrel. Enter three policemen. Moonlight.*

SERGEANT, *who is older than the others, crosses the stage to right and looks down steps. The others put down a pastepot and unroll a bundle of placards.*

POLICEMAN B: I think this would be a good place to put up a notice. (*He points to a barrel.*)

POLICEMAN X: Better ask him. (*Calls to* SERGEANT) Will this be a good place for a placard? (*No answer.*)

POLICEMAN B: Will we put up a notice here on the barrel? (*No answer.*)

SERGEANT: There's a flight of steps here that leads down to the water. This is a place that should be minded well. If he got down here, his friends might have a boat to meet him; they might send it in here from outside.

POLICEMAN B: Would the barrel be a good place to put a notice up?

SERGEANT: It might; you can put it there.

(*They paste the notice up.*)

SERGEANT (*reading it*):   Dark hair—dark eyes, smooth face, height over five feet five—there's not much to take hold of in that—It's a pity I had no chance of seeing him before he broke out of gaol. They say he's a wonder, that it's he makes all the plans for the whole organization. There isn't another man in Ireland would have broken gaol the way he did. He must have some friends among the gaolers.

POLICEMAN B: A hundred pounds is little enough for the Government to offer for him. You may be sure any man in the force that takes him will get promotion.

SERGEANT: I'll mind this place myself. I wouldn't wonder at all if he came this way. He might come slipping along there (*points to side of quay*), and his friends might be waiting for him there (*points down steps*), and once he got away it's little chance we'd have of finding him; it's maybe under a load of kelp he'd be in a fishing boat, and not one to help a married man that wants it to the reward.

POLICEMAN X: And if we get him itself, nothing but abuse on our heads for it from the people, and maybe from our own relations.

SERGEANT: Well, we have to do our duty in the force. Haven't we the whole country depending on us to keep law and order? It's those that are down would be up and those that are up would be down, if it wasn't for us. Well, hurry on, you have plenty of other places to placard yet, and come back here then to me. You can take the lantern. Don't be too long now. It's very lonesome here with nothing but the moon.

POLICEMAN B: It's a pity we can't stop with you. The Government should have brought more police into the town, with *him* in gaol, and at assize time too. Well, good luck to your watch. (*They go out.*)

SERGEANT (*walks up and down once or twice and looks at placard*):   A hundred pounds and promotion sure. There must be a great deal of spending in a hundred pounds. It's a pity some honest man not to be the better of that.

(*A ragged man appears at left and tries to slip past.* SERGEANT *suddenly turns.*)

SERGEANT: Where are you going?

MAN: I'm a poor ballad-singer, your honor. I thought to sell some of these (*holds out bundle of ballads*) to the sailors. (*He goes on.*)

SERGEANT: Stop! Didn't I tell you to stop? You can't go on there.

MAN: Oh, very well. It's a hard thing to be poor. All the world's against the poor!

SERGEANT: Who are you?

MAN: You'd be as wise as myself if I told you, but I don't mind. I'm one Jimmy Walsh, a ballad-singer.

SERGEANT: Jimmy Walsh? I don't know that name.

MAN: Ah, sure, they know it well enough in Ennis. Were you ever in Ennis, Sergeant?

SERGEANT: What brought you here?

MAN: Sure, it's to the assizes I came, thinking I might make a few shillings here or there. It's in the one train with the judges I came.

SERGEANT: Well, if you came so far, you may as well go farther, for you'll walk out of this.

MAN: I will, I will; I'll just go on where I was going. (*Goes toward steps.*)

SERGEANT: Come back from those steps; no one has leave to pass down them tonight.

MAN: I'll just sit on the top of the steps till I see will some sailor buy a ballad off me that would give me my supper. They do be late going back to the ship. It's often I saw them in Cork carried down the quay in a hand-cart.

SERGEANT: Move on, I tell you. I won't have any one lingering about the quay tonight.

MAN: Well, I'll go. It's the poor have the hard life! Maybe yourself might like one, Sergeant. Here's a good sheet now. (*Turns one over*) "Content and a pipe"—that's not much. "The Peeler and the Goat"—you wouldn't like that. "Johnny Hart"—that's a lovely song.

SERGEANT: Move on.

MAN: Ah, wait till you hear it.

(*Sings.*)

> There was a rich farmer's daughter lived near the town of Ross;
> She courted a Highland soldier, his name was Johnny Hart;
> Says the mother to her daughter, "I'll go distracted mad
> If you marry that Highland soldier dressed up in Highland plaid."

SERGEANT: Stop that noise.

(*MAN wraps up his ballads and shuffles toward the steps.*)

SERGEANT: Where are you going?

MAN: Sure you told me to be going, and I am going.

SERGEANT: Don't be a fool. I didn't tell you to go that way; I told you to go back to the town.

MAN: Back to the town, is it?

SERGEANT (*taking him by the shoulder and shoving him before him*):   Here, I'll show you the way. Be off with you. What are you stopping for?

MAN (*who has been keeping his eye on the notice, points to it*):   I think I know what you're waiting for, Sergeant.

SERGEANT: What's that to you?

MAN: And I know well the man you're waiting for—I know him well—I'll be going. (*He shuffles on.*)

SERGEANT: You know him? Come back here. What sort is he?

MAN: Come back is it, Sergeant? Do you want to have me killed?

SERGEANT: Why do you say that?

MAN: Never mind. I'm going. I wouldn't be in your shoes if the reward was ten times as much. (*Goes on off stage to left*) Not if it was ten times as much.

SERGEANT (*rushing after him*):   Come back here, come back. (*Drags him back*) What sort is he? Where did you see him?

MAN: I saw him in my own place, in the County Clare. I tell you you wouldn't like to be looking at him. You'd be afraid to be in the one place with him. There isn't a weapon he doesn't know the use of, and as to strength, his muscles are as hard as that board. (*Slaps barrel.*)

SERGEANT: Is he as bad as that?

MAN: He is then.

SERGEANT: Do you tell me so?

MAN: There was a poor man in our place, a sergeant from Ballyvaughan.—It was with a lump of stone he did it.

SERGEANT: I never heard of that.

MAN: And you wouldn't, Sergeant. It's not everything that happens gets into the papers. And there was a policeman in plain clothes, too . . . It is in Limerick he was. . . . It was after the time of the attack on the police barrack at Kilmallock. . . . Moonlight . . . just like this . . . waterside. . . . Nothing was known for certain.

SERGEANT: Do you say so? It's a terrible county to belong to.

MAN: That's so, indeed! You might be standing there, looking out that way, thinking you saw him coming up this side of the quay (*points*) and he might be coming up this other side (*points*), and he'd be on you before you knew where you were.

SERGEANT: It's a whole troop of police they ought to put here to stop a man like that.

MAN: But if you'd like me to stop with you, I could be looking down this side. I could be sitting up here on this barrel.

SERGEANT: And you know him well, too?

MAN: I'd know him a mile off, Sergeant.

SERGEANT: But you wouldn't want to share the reward?

MAN: Is it a poor man like me, that has to be going the roads and singing in fairs, to have the name on him that he took a reward? But you don't want me. I'll be safer in the town.

SERGEANT: Well, you can stop.

MAN (*getting up on barrel*):   All right, Sergeant. I wonder, now, you're not tired out, Sergeant, walking up and down the way you are.

SERGEANT: If I'm tired I'm used to it.

MAN: You might have hard work before you tonight yet. Take it easy while you can. There's plenty of room up here on the barrel, and you see farther when you're higher up.

SERGEANT: Maybe so. (*Gets up beside him on barrel, facing right. They sit back to back, looking different ways*) You made me feel a bit queer with the way you talked.

MAN: Give me a match, Sergeant (*he gives it and* MAN *lights pipe*); take a draw yourself? It'll quiet you. Wait now till I give you a light, but you needn't turn round. Don't take your eye off the quay for the life of you.

SERGEANT: Never fear, I won't. (*Lights pipe. They both smoke*) Indeed it's a hard thing to be in the force, out at night and no thanks for it, for all the danger we're in. And it's little we get but abuse from the people, and no choice but to obey our orders, and never asked when a man is sent into danger, if you are a married man with a family.

MAN (*sings*):

> As through the hills I walked to view the hills and shamrock plain,
> I stood awhile where nature smiles to view the rocks and streams,
> On a matron fair I fixed my eyes beneath a fertile vale,
> As she sang her song it was on the wrong of poor old Granuaile.

SERGEANT: Stop that; that's no song to be singing in these times.

MAN: Ah, Sergeant, I was only singing to keep my heart up. It sinks when I think of him. To think of us two sitting here, and he creeping up the quay, maybe, to get to us.

SERGEANT: Are you keeping a good lookout?

MAN: I am; and for no reward too. Amn't I the foolish man? But when I saw a man in trouble, I never could help trying to get him out of it. What's that? Did something hit me? (*Rubs his heart.*)

SERGEANT (*patting him on the shoulder*):   You will get your reward in heaven.

MAN: I know that, I know that, Sergeant, but life is precious.

SERGEANT: Well, you can sing if it gives you more courage.

MAN (*sings*):

> Her head was bare, her hands and feet with iron bands were bound,
> Her pensive strain and plaintive wail mingles with the evening gale,
> And the song she sang with mournful air, I am old Granuaile.
> Her lips so sweet that monarchs kissed . . .

SERGEANT: That's not it. . . . "Her gown she wore was stained with gore." . . . That's it—you missed that.

MAN: You're right, Sergeant, so it is; I missed it. (*Repeats line*) But to think of a man like you knowing a song like that.

SERGEANT: There's many a thing a man might know and might not have any wish for.

MAN: Now, I daresay, Sergeant, in your youth, you used to be sitting up on a wall, the way you are sitting up on this barrel now, and the other lads beside you, and you singing "Granuaile"? . . .

SERGEANT: I did then.

MAN: And the "Shan Bhean Bhocht"? . . .

SERGEANT: I did then.

MAN: And the "Green on the Cape"?

SERGEANT: That was one of them.

MAN: And maybe the man you are watching for tonight used to be sitting on the wall, when he was young, and singing those same songs. . . . It's a queer world.

SERGEANT: Whisht! . . . I think I see something coming. . . . It's only a dog.

MAN: And isn't it a queer world? . . . Maybe it's one of the boys you used to be singing with that time you will be arresting today or tomorrow, and sending into the dock.

SERGEANT: That's true indeed.

MAN: And maybe one night, after you had been singing, if the other boys had told you some plan they had, some plan to free the country, you might have joined with them . . . and maybe it is you might be in trouble now.

SERGEANT: Well, who knows but I might? I had a great spirit in those days.

MAN: It's a queer world, Sergeant, and it's little any mother knows when she sees her child creeping on the floor what might happen to it before it has gone through its life, or who will be who in the end.

SERGEANT: That's a queer thought now, and a true thought. Wait now till I think it out. . . . If it wasn't for the sense I have, and for my wife and family, and for me joining the force the time I did, it might be myself now would be after breaking gaol and hiding in the dark, and it might be him that's hiding in the dark and that got out of gaol would be sitting up where I am on this barrel. . . . And it might be myself would be creeping up trying to make my escape from himself, and it might be himself would be keeping the law, and myself would be breaking it, and myself would be trying maybe to put a bullet in his head, or to take up a lump of a stone the way you said he did . . . no, that myself did. . . . Oh! (*Gasps. After a pause*) What's that? (*Grasps* MAN's *arm.*)

MAN (*jumps off barrel and listens, looking out over water*):   It's nothing, Sergeant.

SERGEANT: I thought it might be a boat. I had a notion there might be friends of his coming about the quays with a boat.

MAN: Sergeant, I am thinking it was with the people you were, and not with the law you were, when you were a young man.

SERGEANT: Well, if I was foolish then, that time's gone.

MAN: Maybe, Sergeant, it comes into your head sometimes, in spite of your belt and your tunic, that it might have been as well for you to have followed Granuaile.

SERGEANT: It's no business of yours what I think.

MAN: Maybe, Sergeant, you'll be on the side of the country yet.

SERGEANT (*gets off barrel*):   Don't talk to me like that. I have my duties and I know them. (*Looks round*) That was a boat; I hear the oars. (*Goes to the steps and looks down.*)

MAN (*sings*):

> O, then, tell me, Shawn O'Farrell,
>   Where the gathering is to be.
> In the old spot by the river
>   Right well known to you and me!

SERGEANT: Stop that! Stop that, I tell you!

MAN (*sings louder*):

> One word more, for signal token,
>   Whistle up the marching tune,
> with your pike upon your shoulder,
>   At the Rising of the Moon.

SERGEANT: If you don't stop that, I'll arrest you.
(*A whistle from below answers, repeating the air.*)

SERGEANT: That's a signal. (*Stands between him and steps*) You must not pass this way. . . . Step farther back. . . . Who are you? You are no ballad-singer.

MAN: You needn't ask who I am; that placard will tell you. (*Points to placard.*)

SERGEANT: You are the man I am looking for.

MAN (*takes off hat and wig.* SERGEANT *seizes them*):   I am. There's a hundred pounds on my head. There is a friend of mine below in a boat. He knows a safe place to bring me to.

SERGEANT (*looking still at hat and wig*):   It's a pity! It's a pity. You deceived me. You deceived me well.

MAN: I am a friend of Granuaile. There is a hundred pounds on my head.

SERGEANT: It's a pity, it's a pity!

MAN: Will you let me pass, or must I make you let me?

SERGEANT: I am in the force. I will not let you pass.

MAN: I thought to do it with my tongue. (*Puts hand in breast*) What is that?
(*Voice of* POLICEMAN X *outside.*) Here, this is where we left him.

SERGEANT: It's my comrades coming.

MAN: You won't betray me . . . the friend of Granuaile. (*Slips behind barrel.*)
(*Voice of* POLICEMAN B.) That was the last of the placards.

POLICEMAN X (*as they come in*):   If he makes his escape it won't be unknown he'll make it.
(SERGEANT *puts hat and wig behind his back.*)

POLICEMAN B: Did any one come this way?

SERGEANT (*after a pause*):   No one.

POLICEMAN B: No one at all?

SERGEANT: No one at all.

POLICEMAN B: We had no orders to go back to the station; we can stop along with you.

SERGEANT: I don't want you. There is nothing for you to do here.

POLICEMAN B: You bade us to come back here and keep watch with you.

SERGEANT: I'd sooner be alone. Would any man come this way and you making all that talk? It is better the place be quiet.

POLICEMAN B: Well, we'll leave you the lantern anyhow. (*Hands it to him.*)

SERGEANT: I don't want it. Bring it with you.

POLICEMAN B: You might want it. There are clouds coming up and you have the darkness of the night before you yet. I'll leave it over here on the barrel. (*Goes to barrel.*)

SERGEANT: Bring it with you I tell you. No more talk.

POLICEMAN B: Well, I thought it might be a comfort to you. I often think when I have it in my hand and can be flashing it about into every dark corner (*doing so*) that it's the same as being beside the fire at home, and the bits of bogwood blazing up now and again. (*Flashes it about, now on the barrel, now on* SERGEANT.)

SERGEANT (*furious*):   Be off the two of you, yourselves and your lantern!
(*They go out.* MAN *comes from behind barrel. He and* SERGEANT *stand looking at one another.*)

SERGEANT: What are you waiting for?

MAN: For my hat, of course, and my wig. You wouldn't wish me to get my death of cold?

(SERGEANT *gives them.*)

MAN (*going toward steps*):   Well, good night, comrade, and thank you. You did me a good turn tonight, and I'm obliged to you. Maybe I'll be able to do as much for you when the small rise up and the big fall down . . . when we all change places at the Rising (*waves his hand and disappears*) of the Moon.

SERGEANT (*turning his back to audience and reading placard*):   A hundred pounds reward! A hundred pounds! (*Turns toward audience*) I wonder, now, am I as great a fool as I think I am?

(1907)

QUESTIONS FOR REFLECTION

Experience

1. As you read *The Rising of the Moon,* at what point did you realize the Sergeant's divided loyalties? How do you respond to the Sergeant's predicament? To what extent do you sympathize with him? To what extent have you experienced an analogous division of loyalties? With what consequences?

Interpretation

2. What are the central issues of the play?
3. Which side do you think the playwright takes on the issues? Why?
4. What is ironic about the situations of the Sergeant and the hunted man?

Evaluation

5. Lady Gregory's play turns on a conflict of values, with the Sergeant caught between his sympathy for the hunted man and his desire to earn a substantial reward for turning him in. What do you think the Sergeant should do? Why?

Connections

6. Compare the decision the Sergeant must make with that made by Antigonê to bury her brother and with Nora Helmer's decision to forge her husband's signature. In each case a character goes against a law or decree. What is at stake in each case?

JOHN MILLINGTON SYNGE

[1871–1909]

Like Lady Gregory and William Butler Yeats, John Millington Synge was an Irish dramatist intensely involved in the Irish literary renaissance. With Yeats and Lady Gregory, Synge served as codirector of the Abbey Theatre in Dublin. At Yeats's suggestion, Synge brought his knowledge and experience of the Irish peasantry, especially from his visits to the Aran Islands, into the language and dramatic situations of his plays. Yeats convinced Synge to abandon writing criticism and to write plays about simple people whose language reflected an intimate contact with earth, sea, and sky. In addition to *Riders to the Sea* (1904), which shows the extent to which he took Yeats's advice, Synge is best known for his masterful comedy, *The Playboy of the Western World* (1907). His journal of impressions (*The Aran Islands*) provides important information about the life of the island people and a helpful glimpse into the raw material Synge shaped into dramatic art.

JOHN MILLINGTON SYNGE

Riders to the Sea

CHARACTERS

MAURYA, *an old woman*
BARTLEY, *her son*
CATHLEEN, *her daughter*
NORA, *a younger daughter*
MEN AND WOMEN

Scene. *An island off the West of Ireland.*

Cottage kitchen, with nets, oilskins, spinning-wheel, some new boards standing by the wall, etc. CATHLEEN, *a girl of about twenty, finishes kneading cake, and puts it down in the pot-oven by the fire; then wipes her hands, and begins to spin at the wheel.* NORA, *a young girl, puts her head in at the door.*

NORA (*in a low voice*):   Where is she?
CATHLEEN: She's lying down, God help her, and maybe sleeping, if she's able.

NORA *comes in softly, and takes a bundle from under her shawl.*

CATHLEEN (*spinning the wheel rapidly*):   What is it you have?

NORA: The young priest is after bringing them. It's a shirt and a plain stocking were got off a drowned man in Donegal.

CATHLEEN *stops her wheel with a sudden movement, and leans out to listen.*

NORA: We're to find out if it's Michael's they are, some time herself will be down looking by the sea.

CATHLEEN: How would they be Michael's, Nora? How would he go the length of that way to the far north?

NORA: The young priest says he's known the like of it. 'If it's Michael's they are,' says he, 'you can tell herself he's got a clean burial, by the grace of God; and if they're not his, let no one say a word about them, for she'll be getting her death,' says he, 'with crying and lamenting.'

The door which NORA *half closed is blown open by a gust of wind.*

CATHLEEN (*looking out anxiously*): Did you ask him would he stop Bartley going this day with the horses to the Galway fair?

NORA: 'I won't stop him,' says he; 'but let you not be afraid. Herself does be saying prayers half through the night, and the Almighty God won't leave her destitute,' says he, 'with no son living.'

CATHLEEN: Is the sea bad by the white rocks, Nora?

NORA: Middling bad, God help us. There's a great roaring in the west, and it's worse it'll be getting when the tide's turned to the wind. (*She goes over to the table with the bundle.*) Shall I open it now?

CATHLEEN: Maybe she'd wake up on us, and come in before we'd done (*coming to the table*). It's a long time we'll be, and the two of us crying.

NORA (*goes to the inner door and listens*): She's moving about on the bed. She'll be coming in a minute.

CATHLEEN: Give me the ladder, and I'll put them up in the turf-loft, the way she won't know of them at all, and maybe when the tide turns she'll be going down to see would he be floating from the east.

They put the ladder against the gable of the chimney; CATHLEEN *goes up a few steps and hides the bundle in the turf-loft.* MAURYA *comes from the inner room.*

MAURYA (*looking up at* CATHLEEN *and speaking querulously*): Isn't it turf enough you have for this day and evening?

CATHLEEN: There's a cake baking at the fire for a short space (*throwing down the turf*), and Bartley will want it when the tide turns if he goes to Connemara.

NORA *picks up the turf and puts it round the pot-oven.*

MAURYA (*sitting down on a stool at the fire*): He won't go this day with the wind rising from the south and west. He won't go this day, for the young priest will stop him surely.

NORA: He'll not stop him, mother; and I heard Eamon Simon and Stephen Pheety and Colum Shawn saying he would go.

MAURYA: Where is he itself?

NORA: He went down to see would there be another boat sailing in the week, and I'm thinking it won't be long till he's here now, for the tide's turning at the green head, and the hooker's tacking from the east.

CATHLEEN: I hear some one passing the big stones.

NORA (*looking out*):   He's coming now, and he in a hurry.

BARTLEY (*comes in and looks round the room. Speaking sadly and quietly*):   Where is the bit of new rope, Cathleen, was bought in Connemara?

CATHLEEN (*coming down*):   Give it to him, Nora; it's on a nail by the white boards. I hung it up this morning, for the pig with the black feet was eating it.

NORA (*giving him a rope*):   Is that it, Bartley?

MAURYA: You'd do right to leave that rope, Bartley, hanging by the boards (BARTLEY *takes the rope*). It will be wanting in this place, I'm telling you, if Michael is washed up tomorrow morning or the next morning, or any morning in the week; for it's a deep grave we'll make him, by the grace of God.

BARTLEY (*beginning to work with the rope*):   I've no halter the way I can ride down on the mare, and I must go now quickly. This is the one boat going for two weeks or beyond it, and the fair will be a good fair for horses, I heard them saying below.

MAURYA: It's a hard thing they'll be saying below if the body is washed up and there's no man in it to make the coffin, and I after giving a big price for the finest white boards you'd find in Connemara.

She looks round at the boards.

BARTLEY: How would it be washed up, and we after looking each day for nine days, and a strong wind blowing a while back from the west and south?

MAURYA: If it isn't found itself, that wind is raising the sea, and there was a star up against the moon, and it rising in the night. If it was a hundred horses, or a thousand horses, you had itself, what is the price of a thousand horses against a son where there is one son only?

BARTLEY (*working at the halter, to* CATHLEEN):   Let you go down each day, and see the sheep aren't jumping in on the rye, and if the jobber comes you can sell the pig with the black feet if there is a good price going.

MAURYA: How would the like of her get a good price for a pig?

BARTLEY (*to* CATHLEEN):   If the west wind holds with the last bit of the moon let you and Nora get up weed enough for another cock for the kelp. It's hard set we'll be from this day with no one in it but one man to work.

MAURYA: It's hard set we'll be surely the day you're drowned with the rest. What way will I live and the girls with me, and I an old woman looking for the grave?

BARTLEY *lays down the halter, takes off his old coat, and puts on a newer one of the same flannel.*

BARTLEY (*to* NORA):   Is she coming to the pier?

NORA (*looking out*):   She's passing the green head and letting fall her sails.

BARTLEY (*getting his purse and tobacco*):   I'll have half an hour to go down, and you'll see me coming again in two days, or in three days, or maybe in four days if the wind is bad.

MAURYA (*turning round to the fire, and putting her shawl over her head*):   Isn't it a hard and cruel man won't hear a word from an old woman, and she holding him from the sea?

CATHLEEN: It's the life of a young man to be going on the sea, and who would listen to an old woman with one thing and she saying it over?

BARTLEY (*taking the halter*): I must go now quickly. I'll ride down on the red mare, and the grey pony 'ill run behind me. . . . The blessing of God on you.

He goes out.

MAURYA (*crying out as he is in the door*): He's gone now, God spare us, and we'll not see him again. He's gone now, and when the black night is falling I'll have no son left me in the world.

CATHLEEN: Why wouldn't you give him your blessing and he looking round in the door? Isn't it sorrow enough is on every one in this house without you sending him out with an unlucky word behind him, and a hard word in his ear?

MAURYA *takes up the tongs and begins raking the fire aimlessly without looking round.*

NORA (*turning towards her*): You're taking away the turf from the cake.

CATHLEEN (*crying out*): The Son of God forgive us, Nora, we're after forgetting his bit of bread. (*She comes over to the fire.*)

NORA: And it's destroyed he'll be going till dark night, and he after eating nothing since the sun went up.

CATHLEEN (*turning the cake out of the oven*): It's destroyed he'll be, surely. There's no sense left on any person in a house where an old woman will be talking for ever.

MAURYA *sways herself on her stool.*

CATHLEEN (*cutting off some of the bread and rolling it in a cloth; to* MAURYA): Let you go down now to the spring well and give him this and he passing. You'll see him then and the dark word will be broken, and you can say 'God speed you,' the way he'll be easy in his mind.

MAURYA (*taking the bread*): Will I be in it as soon as himself?

CATHLEEN: If you go now quickly.

MAURYA (*standing up unsteadily*): It's hard set I am to walk.

CATHLEEN (*looking at her anxiously*): Give her the stick, Nora, or maybe she'll slip on the big stones.

NORA: What stick?

CATHLEEN: The stick Michael brought from Connemara.

MAURYA (*taking a stick* NORA *gives her*). In the big world the old people do be leaving things after them for their sons and children, but in this place it is the young men do be leaving things behind for them that do be old.

She goes out slowly. NORA *goes over to the ladder.*

CATHLEEN: Wait, Nora, maybe she'd turn back quickly. She's that sorry, God help her, you wouldn't know the thing she'd do.

NORA: Is she gone round by the bush?

CATHLEEN (*looking out*): She's gone now. Throw it down quickly, for the Lord knows when she'll be out of it again.

NORA (*getting the bundle from the loft*): The young priest said he'd be passing to-morrow, and we might go down and speak to him below if it's Michael's they are surely.

CATHLEEN (*taking the bundle*): Did he say what way they were found?

NORA (*coming down*): 'There were two men,' says he, 'and they rowing round with poteen before the cocks crowed, and the oar of one of them caught the body, and they passing the black cliffs of the north.'

CATHLEEN (*trying to open the bundle*):   Give me a knife, Nora; the string's perished with salt water, and there's a black knot on it you wouldn't loosen in a week.

NORA (*giving her a knife*):   I've heard tell it was a long way to Donegal.

CATHLEEN (*cutting the string*):   It is surely. There was a man in here a while ago—the man sold us that knife—and he said if you set off walking from the rocks beyond, it would be in seven days you'd be in Donegal.

NORA: And what time would a man take, and he floating?

CATHLEEN *opens the bundle and takes out a bit of a shirt and a stocking. They look at them eagerly.*

CATHLEEN (*in a low voice*):   The Lord spare us, Nora! isn't it a queer hard thing to say if it's his they are surely?

NORA: I'll get his shirt off the hook the way we can put the one flannel on the other. (*She looks through some clothes hanging in the corner.*) It's not with them, Cathleen, and where will it be?

CATHLEEN: I'm thinking Bartley put it on him in the morning, for his own shirt was heavy with the salt in it. (*Pointing to the corner.*) There's a bit of a sleeve was of the same stuff. Give me that and it will do.

NORA *brings it to her and they compare the flannel.*

CATHLEEN: It's the same stuff, Nora; but if it is itself, aren't there great rolls of it in the shops of Galway, and isn't it many another man may have a shirt of it as well as Michael himself?

NORA (*who has taken up the stocking and counted the stitches, crying out*):   It's Michael, Cathleen, it's Michael; God spare his soul, and what will herself say when she hears this story, and Bartley on the sea?

CATHLEEN (*taking the stocking*):   It's a plain stocking.

NORA: It's the second one of the third pair I knitted, and I put up three-score stitches, and I dropped four of them.

CATHLEEN (*counts the stitches*):   It's that number is in it (*crying out*). Ah, Nora, isn't it a bitter thing to think of him floating that way to the far north, and no one to keen him but the black hags that do be flying on the sea?

NORA (*swinging herself half round, and throwing out her arms on the clothes*):   And isn't it a pitiful thing when there is nothing left of a man who was a great rower and fisher but a bit of an old shirt and a plain stocking?

CATHLEEN (*after an instant*):   Tell me is herself coming, Nora? I hear a little sound on the path.

NORA (*looking out*):   She is, Cathleen. She's coming up to the door.

CATHLEEN: Put these things away before she'll come in. Maybe it's easier she'll be after giving her blessing to Bartley, and we won't let on we've heard anything the time he's on the sea.

NORA (*helping* CATHLEEN *to close the bundle*):   We'll put them here in the corner.

They put them into a hole in the chimney corner. CATHLEEN *goes back to the spinning-wheel.*

NORA: Will she see it was crying I was?

CATHLEEN:　Keep your back to the door the way the light'll not be on you.

NORA *sits down at the chimney corner, with her back to the door.* MAURYA *comes in very slowly, without looking at the girls, and goes over to her stool at the other side of the fire. The cloth with the bread is still in her hand. The girls look at each other, and* NORA *points to the bundle of bread.*

CATHLEEN (*after spinning for a moment*):　You didn't give him his bit of bread?

MAURYA *begins to keen softly, without turning round.*

CATHLEEN:　Did you see him riding down?

MAURYA *goes on keening.*

CATHLEEN (*a little impatiently*):　God forgive you; isn't it a better thing to raise your voice and tell what you seen, than to be making lamentation for a thing that's done? Did you see Bartley, I'm saying to you?

MAURYA (*with a weak voice*):　My heart's broken from this day.

CATHLEEN (*as before*):　Did you see Bartley?

MAURYA:　I seen the fearfulest thing.

CATHLEEN (*leaves her wheel and looks out*):　God forgive you; he's riding the mare now over the green head, and the grey pony behind him.

MAURYA (*Starts, so that her shawl falls back from her head and shows her white tossed hair. With a frightened voice*):　The grey pony behind him. . . .

CATHLEEN (*coming to the fire*):　What is it ails you at all?

MAURYA (*speaking very slowly*):　I've seen the fearfulest thing any person has seen since the day Bride Dara seen the dead man with the child in his arms.

CATHLEEN *and* NORA:　Uah.

They crouch down in front of the old woman at the fire.

NORA:　Tell us what it is you seen.

MAURYA:　I went down to the spring well, and I stood there saying a prayer to myself. Then Bartley came along, and he riding on the red mare with the grey pony behind him (*she puts up her hands, as if to hide something from her eyes*). The Son of God spare us, Nora!

CATHLEEN:　What is it you seen?

MAURYA:　I seen Michael himself.

CATHLEEN (*speaking softly*):　You did not, mother. It wasn't Michael you seen, for his body is after being found in the far north, and he's got a clean burial, by the grace of God.

MAURYA (*a little defiantly*):　I'm after seeing him this day, and he riding and galloping. Bartley came first on the red mare, and I tried to say 'God speed you,' but something choked the words in my throat. He went by quickly; and 'the blessing of God on you,' says he, and I could say nothing. I looked up then, and I crying, at the grey pony, and there was Michael upon it—with fine clothes on him, and new shoes on his feet.

CATHLEEN (*begins to keen*):　It's destroyed we are from this day. It's destroyed, surely.

NORA:　Didn't the young priest say the Almighty God won't leave her destitute with no son living?

MAURYA (*in a low voice, but clearly*):　It's little the like of him knows of the sea. . . . Bartley will be lost now, and let you call in Eamon and make me a good coffin out of the white boards, for I won't live after them. I've had a husband, and a husband's father, and six sons in this house—six fine men, though it was a hard birth I had with every one of them and they coming to the world—and some of them were found and some of them were not found, but they're gone now the lot of them. . . . There were Stephan and Shawn were lost in the great wind, and found after in the Bay of Gregory of the Golden Mouth, and carried up the two of them on one plank, and in by that door.

She pauses for a moment, the girls start as if they heard something through the door that is half open behind them.

NORA (*in a whisper*):   Did you hear that, Cathleen? Did you hear a noise in the north-east?

CATHLEEN (*in a whisper*):   There's someone after crying out by the seashore.

MAURYA (*continues without hearing anything*):   There was Sheamus and his father, and his own father again, were lost in a dark night, and not a stick or sign was seen of them when the sun went up. There was Patch after was drowned out of a curagh that turned over. I was sitting here with Bartley, and he a baby lying on my two knees, and I seen two women, and three women, and four women coming in, and they crossing themselves and not saying a word. I looked out then, and there were men coming after them, and they holding a thing in the half of a red sail, and water dripping out of it— it was a dry day, Nora—and leaving a track to the door.

She pauses again with her hand stretched out towards the door. It opens softly and old women begin to come in, crossing themselves on the threshold, and kneeling down in front of the stage with red petticoats over their heads.

MAURYA (*half in a dream, to* CATHLEEN):   Is it Patch, or Michael, or what is it at all?

CATHLEEN: Michael is after being found in the far north, and when he is found there how could he be here in this place?

MAURYA: There does be a power of young men floating round in the sea, and what way would they know if it was Michael they had, or another man like him, for when a man is nine days in the sea, and the wind blowing, it's hard set his own mother would be to say what man was in it.

CATHLEEN: It's Michael, God spare him, for they're after sending us a bit of his clothes from the far north.

She reaches out and hands MAURYA *the clothes that belonged to Michael.* MAURYA *stands up slowly, and takes them in her hands.* NORA *looks out.*

NORA: They're carrying a thing among them, and there's water dripping out of it and leaving a track by the big stones.

CATHLEEN (*in a whisper to the women who have come in*):   Is it Bartley it is?

ONE OF THE WOMEN: It is, surely, God rest his soul.

Two younger women come in and pull out the table. Then men carry in the body of BARTLEY, *laid on a plank, with a bit of a sail over it, and lay it on the table.*

CATHLEEN (*to the women as they are doing so*):   What way was he drowned?

ONE OF THE WOMEN: The grey pony knocked him over into the sea, and he was washed out where there is a great surf on the white rocks.

MAURYA *has gone over and knelt down at the head of the table. The women are keening softly and swaying themselves with a slow movement.* CATHLEEN *and* NORA *kneel at the other end of the table. The men kneel near the door.*

MAURYA (*raising her head and speaking as if she did not see the people around her*): They're all gone now, and there isn't anything more the sea can do to me. . . . I'll have no call now to be up crying and praying when the wind breaks from the south, and you can hear the surf is in the east, and the surf is in the west, making a great stir with the two noises, and they hitting one on the other. I'll have no call now to be going down and getting Holy Water in the dark nights after Samhain, and I won't care what way the sea is when the other women will be keening. (*To* NORA.) Give me the Holy Water, Nora; there's a small sup still on the dresser.

NORA *gives it to her.*

MAURYA (*drops Michael's clothes across* BARTLEY*'s feet, and sprinkles the Holy Water over him*): It isn't that I haven't prayed for you, Bartley, to the Almighty God. It isn't that I haven't said prayers in the dark night till you wouldn't know what I'd be saying; but it's a great rest I'll have now, and it's time, surely. It's a great rest I'll have now, and great sleeping in the long nights after Samhain, if it's only a bit of wet flour we do have to eat, and maybe a fish that would be stinking.

She kneels down again, crossing herself, and saying prayers under her breath.

CATHLEEN (*to an old man*): Maybe yourself and Eamon would make a coffin when the sun rises. We have fine white boards herself bought, God help her, thinking Michael would be found, and I have a new cake you can eat while you'll be working.
THE OLD MAN (*looking at the boards*): Are there nails with them?
CATHLEEN: There are not, Colum; we didn't think of the nails.
ANOTHER MAN: It's a great wonder she wouldn't think of the nails, and all the coffins she's seen made already.
CATHLEEN: It's getting old she is, and broken.

MAURYA *stands up again very slowly and spreads out the pieces of Michael's clothes beside the body, sprinkling them with the last of the Holy Water.*

NORA (*in a whisper to* CATHLEEN): She's quiet now and easy; but the day Michael was drowned you could hear her crying out from this to the spring well. It's fonder she was of Michael, and would anyone have thought that?
CATHLEEN (*slowly and clearly*): An old woman will be soon tired with anything she will do, and isn't it nine days herself is after crying and keening, and making great sorrow in the house?
MAURYA (*puts the empty cup mouth downwards on the table, and lays her hands together on* BARTLEY*'s feet*): They're all together this time, and the end is come. May the Almighty God have mercy on Bartley's soul, and on Michael's soul, and on the souls of Sheamus and Patch, and Stephen and Shawn (*bending her head*); and may He have mercy on my soul, Nora, and on the soul of every one is left living in the world.

She pauses, and the keen rises a little more loudly from the women, then sinks away.

MAURYA (*continuing*):   Michael has a clean burial in the far north, by the grace of Almighty God. Bartley will have a fine coffin out of the white boards, and a deep grave surely. What more can we want than that? No man at all can be living for ever, and we must be satisfied.

She kneels down again and the curtain falls slowly.

(*1904*)

QUESTIONS FOR REFLECTION

Experience

1. To what extent can you appreciate the characters' tragic situation? How has your experience prepared you to understand their predicament?

Interpretation

2. To what extent can *Riders to the Sea* be described as a tragedy?
3. Characterize the play's language, especially the speech style of the central characters. Of what importance is its religious dimension?
4. Distinguish between the rank and roles of Nora and Cathleen.
5. What is Maurya's role? Describe in general terms the kind of actress you imagine would be well suited to her role.
6. Identify the props used, and comment on their dramatic and symbolic significance.
7. Explain the significance of the title. How does Synge make the presence and the power of the sea felt?

Evaluation

8. Do you think this is a successful drama? Do you find it a tragic play? Why or why not?

SUSAN GLASPELL

[1882–1948]

Susan Glaspell, an American novelist and playwright, was one of the co-founders of the Provincetown Players, an influential theatrical company. With her husband, George Cram Cook, she collaborated on a number of plays, including her one-act satire on Freudian psychoanalysis, *Suppressed Desires,* published in 1916. In the same year Glaspell produced another fine one-act play, *Trifles,* which has continued to be her most frequently performed play.

SUSAN GLASPELL

Trifles

CHARACTERS

GEORGE HENDERSON, *County Attorney*
HENRY PETERS, *Sheriff*
LEWIS HALE, *A Neighboring Farmer*
MRS. PETERS
MRS. HALE

Scene. *The kitchen in the now abandoned farmhouse of* JOHN WRIGHT, *a gloomy kitchen, and left without having been put in order—unwashed pans under the sink, a loaf of bread outside the breadbox, a dish towel on the table—other signs of incompleted work. At the rear the outer door opens and the* SHERIFF *comes in followed by the* COUNTY ATTORNEY *and* HALE. *The* SHER-IFF *and* HALE *are men in middle life, the* COUNTY ATTORNEY *is a young man; all are much bundled up and go at once to the stove. They are followed by two women—the* SHERIFF's *wife first; she is a slight wiry woman, a thin* nervous *face.* MRS. HALE *is larger and would ordinarily be called more comfortable looking, but she is disturbed now and looks fearfully about as she enters. The women have come in slowly, and stand close together near the door.*

COUNTY ATTORNEY [*rubbing his hands*]:   This feels good. Come up to the fire, ladies.

MRS. PETERS [*after taking a step forward*]:   I'm not—cold.

SHERIFF [*unbuttoning his overcoat and stepping away from the stove as if to mark the beginning of official business*]:   Now, Mr. Hale, before we move things about, you explain to Mr. Henderson just what you saw when you came here yesterday morning.

COUNTY ATTORNEY: By the way, has anything been moved? Are things just as you left them yesterday?

SHERIFF [*looking about*]:   It's just the same. When it dropped below zero last night I thought I'd better send Frank out this morning to make a fire for us—no use getting pneumonia with a big case on, but I told him not to touch anything except the stove—and you know Frank.

COUNTY ATTORNEY: Somebody should have been left here yesterday.

SHERIFF: Oh—yesterday. When I had to send Frank to Morris Center for that man who went crazy—I want you to know I had my hands full yesterday, I knew you could get back from Omaha by today and as long as I went over everything here myself—

COUNTY ATTORNEY: Well, Mr. Hale, tell just what happened when you came here yesterday morning.

HALE: Harry and I had started to town with a load of potatoes. We came along the road from my place and as I got here I said, "I'm going to see if I can't get John Wright to go in with me on a party telephone." I spoke to Wright about it once before and he put me off, saying folks talked too much anyway, and all he asked was peace and quiet—I guess you know about how much he talked himself; but I thought maybe if I went to the house and talked about it before his wife, though I said to Harry that I didn't know as what his wife wanted made much difference to John—

COUNTY ATTORNEY: Let's talk about that later, Mr. Hale. I do want to talk about that, but tell now just what happened when you got to the house.

HALE: I didn't hear or see anything; I knocked at the door, and still it was all quiet inside. I knew they must be up, it was past eight o'clock. So I knocked again, and I thought I heard somebody say, "Come in." I wasn't sure, I'm not sure yet, but I opened the door—this door [*Indicating the door by which the two women are still standing*] and there in that rocker—[*Pointing to it*] sat Mrs. Wright.

[*They all look at the rocker.*]

COUNTY ATTORNEY: What—was she doing?

HALE: She was rockin' back and forth. She had her apron in her hand and was kind of—pleating it.

COUNTY ATTORNEY: And how did she—look?

HALE: Well, she looked queer.

COUNTY ATTORNEY: How do you mean—queer?

HALE: Well, as if she didn't know what she was going to do next. And kind of done up.

COUNTY ATTORNEY: How did she seem to feel about your coming?

HALE: Why, I don't think she minded—one way or other. She didn't pay much attention. I said, "How do, Mrs. Wright, it's cold, ain't it?" And she said, "Is it?"—and went on kind of pleating at her apron. Well, I was surprised; she didn't ask me to come up to the stove, or to set down, but just sat there, not even looking at me, so I said, "I want to see John." And then she—laughed. I guess you would call it a laugh. I thought of Harry and the team outside, so I said a little sharp: "Can't I see John?" "No," she says, kind o' dull like. "Ain't he home?" says I. "Yes," says she, "he's home." "Then why can't I see him?" I asked her, out of patience. "'Cause he's dead," says she. *"Dead?"* says I. She just nodded her head, not getting a bit excited, but rockin' back and forth. "Why—where is he?" says I, not knowing what to say. She just pointed upstairs—like that [*Himself pointing to the room above*]. I got up, with the idea of going up there. I walked from there to here—then I says, "Why, what did he die of?" "He died of a rope round his neck," says she, and just went on pleatin' at her apron. Well, I went out and called Harry. I thought I might—need help. We went upstairs and there he was lyin'—

COUNTY ATTORNEY: I think I'd rather have you go into that upstairs, where you can point it all out. Just go on now with the rest of the story.

HALE: Well, my first thought was to get that rope off. It looked . . . [*Stops, his face twitches.*] . . . but Harry, he went up to him, and he said, "No, he's dead all right, and we'd better not touch anything." So we went back down stairs. She was still sitting that same way. "Has anybody been notified?" I asked. "No," says she, unconcerned. "Who did this, Mrs. Wright?" said Harry. He said it businesslike—and she stopped pleatin' of her apron. "I don't know," she says. "You don't *know?*" says Harry. "No," says she. "Weren't you sleepin' in the bed with him?" says Harry. "Yes," says she, "but I was on the inside." "Somebody slipped a rope round his neck and strangled him and you didn't wake up?" says Harry. "I didn't wake up," she said after him. We must 'a looked as if we didn't see how that could be, for after a minute she said, "I sleep sound." Harry was going to ask her more questions but I said maybe we ought to let her tell her story first to the coroner, or the sheriff, so Harry went fast as he could to Rivers' place, where there's a telephone.

COUNTY ATTORNEY: And what did Mrs. Wright do when she knew that you had gone for the coroner?

HALE: She moved from that chair to this one over here [*Pointing to a small chair in the corner*] and just sat there with her hands held together and looking down. I got a feeling that I ought to make some conversation, so I said I had come in to see if John wanted to put in a telephone, and at that she started to laugh, and then she stopped and looked at me—scared. [*The* COUNTY ATTORNEY, *who has had his notebook out, makes a note.*] I dunno, maybe it wasn't scared. I wouldn't like to say it was. Soon Harry got back, and then Dr. Lloyd came, and you, Mr. Peters, and so I guess that's all I know that you don't.

COUNTY ATTORNEY [*looking around*]:   I guess we'll go upstairs first—and then out to the barn and around there. [*to the* SHERIFF] You're convinced that there was nothing important here—nothing that would point to any motive.

SHERIFF: Nothing here but kitchen things.

[*The* COUNTY ATTORNEY, *after again looking around the kitchen, opens the door of a cupboard closet. He gets up on a chair and looks on a shelf. Pulls his hand away, sticky.*]

COUNTY ATTORNEY: Here's a nice mess.

[*The women draw nearer.*]

MRS. PETERS [*to the other woman*]:   Oh, her fruit; it did freeze. [*To the* COUNTY ATTORNEY] She worried about that when it turned so cold. She said the fire'd go out and her jars would break.

SHERIFF: Well, can you beat the women! Held for murder and worryin' about her preserves.

COUNTY ATTORNEY: I guess before we're through she may have something more serious than preserves to worry about.

HALE: Well, women are used to worrying over trifles.

[*The two women move a little closer together.*]

COUNTY ATTORNEY [*with the gallantry of a young politician*]:   And yet, for all their worries, what would we do without the ladies? [*The women do not unbend. He goes to the sink, takes a dipperful of water from the pail and pouring it into a basin, washes his hands. Starts to wipe them on the roller towel, turns it for a cleaner place.*] Dirty towels! [*Kicks his foot against the pans under the sink.*] Not much of a housekeeper, would you say, ladies?

MRS. HALE [*stiffly*]:   There's a great deal of work to be done on a farm.

COUNTY ATTORNEY: To be sure. And yet [*With a little bow to her*] I know there are some Dickson county farmhouses which do not have such roller towels.

[*He gives it a pull to expose its full length again.*]

MRS. HALE: Those towels get dirty awful quick. Men's hands aren't always as clean as they might be.

COUNTY ATTORNEY: Ah, loyal to your sex, I see. But you and Mrs. Wright were neighbors. I suppose you were friends, too.

MRS. HALE [*shaking her head*]:   I've not seen much of her of late years. I've not been in this house—it's more than a year.

COUNTY ATTORNEY: And why was that? You didn't like her?

MRS. HALE: I liked her all well enough. Farmers' wives have their hands full, Mr. Henderson. And then—

COUNTY ATTORNEY: Yes—?

MRS. HALE [*looking about*]:   It never seemed a very cheerful place.

COUNTY ATTORNEY: No—it's not cheerful. I shouldn't say she had the homemaking instinct.

MRS. HALE: Well, I don't know as Wright had, either.

COUNTY ATTORNEY: You mean that they didn't get on very well?

MRS. HALE: No, I don't mean anything. But I don't think a place'd be any cheerfuller for John Wright's being in it.

COUNTY ATTORNEY: I'd like to talk more of that a little later. I want to get the lay of things upstairs now.

[*He goes to the left, where three steps lead to a stair door.*]

SHERIFF: I suppose anything Mrs. Peters does'll be all right. She was to take in some clothes for her, you know, and a few little things. We left in such a hurry yesterday.

COUNTY ATTORNEY: Yes, but I would like to see what you take, Mrs. Peters, and keep an eye out for anything that might be of use to us.

MRS. PETERS: Yes, Mr. Henderson.

[*The women listen to the men's steps on the stairs, then look about the kitchen.*]

MRS. HALE: I'd hate to have men coming into my kitchen, snooping around and criticising.

[*She arranges the pans under sink which the* COUNTY ATTORNEY *had shoved out of place.*]

MRS. PETERS: Of course it's no more than their duty.

MRS. HALE: Duty's all right, but I guess that deputy sheriff that came out to make the fire might have got a little of this on. [*Gives the roller towel a pull.*] Wish I'd thought of that sooner. Seems mean to talk about her for not having things slicked up when she had to come away in such a hurry.

MRS. PETERS [*Who has gone to a small table in the left rear corner of the room, and lifted one end of a towel that covers a pan*]:   She had bread set.

[*Stands still.*]

MRS. HALE [*eyes fixed on a loaf of bread beside the breadbox, which is on a low shelf at the other side of the room. Moves slowly toward it*]:   She was going to put this in there. [*Picks up loaf, then abruptly drops it. In a manner of returning to familiar things.*] It's a shame about her fruit. I wonder if it's all gone. [*Gets up on the chair and looks.*] I think there's some here that's all right, Mrs. Peters. Yes—here; [*Holding it toward the window.*] this is cherries, too. [*Looking again.*] I declare I believe that's the only one. [*Gets down, bottle in her hand. Goes to the sink and wipes it off on the outside.*] She'll feel awful bad after all her hard work in the hot weather. I remember the afternoon I put up my cherries last summer.

[*She puts the bottle on the big kitchen table, center of the room. With a sigh, is about to sit down in the rocking-chair. Before she is seated realizes what chair it is; with a slow look at it, steps back. The chair which she has touched rocks back and forth.*]

MRS. PETERS: Well, I must get those things from the front room closet. [*She goes to the door at the right, but after looking into the other room, steps back.*] You coming with me, Mrs. Hale? You could help me carry them.

[*They go in the other room; reappear,* MRS. PETERS *carrying a dress and skirt,* MRS. HALE *following with a pair of shoes.*]

MRS. PETERS: My, it's cold in there.

[*She puts the clothes on the big table, and hurries to the stove.*]

MRS. HALE [*examining her skirt*]:   Wright was close. I think maybe that's why she kept so much to herself. She didn't even belong to the Ladies Aid. I suppose she felt she couldn't do her part, and then you don't enjoy things when you feel shabby. She used to wear pretty clothes and be lively, when she was Minnie Foster, one of the town girls singing in the choir. But that—oh, that was thirty years ago. This all you was to take in?

MRS. PETERS: She said she wanted an apron. Funny thing to want, for there isn't much to get you dirty in jail, goodness knows. But I suppose just to make her feel more natural. She said they was in the top drawer in this cupboard. Yes, here. And then her little shawl that always hung behind the door. [*Opens stair door and looks.*] Yes, here it is.

[*Quickly shuts door leading upstairs.*]

MRS. HALE [*abruptly moving toward her*]:   Mrs. Peters?

MRS. PETERS: Yes, Mrs. Hale?

MRS. HALE: Do you think she did it?

MRS. PETERS [*in a frightened voice*]:   Oh, I don't know.

MRS. HALE: Well, I don't think she did. Asking for an apron and her little shawl. Worrying about her fruit.

MRS. PETERS [*starts to speak, glances up, where footsteps are heard in the room above. In a low voice*]:   Mr. Peters says it looks bad for her. Mr. Henderson is awful sarcastic in a speech and he'll make fun of her sayin' she didn't wake up.

MRS. HALE: Well, I guess John Wright didn't wake when they was slipping that rope under his neck.

MRS. PETERS: No, it's strange. It must have been done awful crafty and still. They say it was such a—funny way to kill a man, rigging it all up like that.

MRS. HALE: That's just what Mr. Hale said. There was a gun in the house. He says that's what he can't understand.

MRS. PETERS: Mr. Henderson said coming out that what was needed for the case was a motive; something to show anger, or—sudden feeling.

MRS. HALE [*who is standing by the table*]:   Well, I don't see any signs of anger around here. [*She puts her hand on the dish towel which lies on the table, stands looking down at table, one half of which is clean, the other half messy.*] It's wiped to here. [*Makes a move as if to finish work, then turns and looks at loaf of bread outside the breadbox. Drops towel. In that voice of coming back to familiar things.*] Wonder how they are finding things upstairs. I hope she had it a little more red-up up there. You know, it seems kind of *sneaking*. Locking her up in town and then coming out here and trying to get her own house to turn against her!

MRS. PETERS: But Mrs. Hale, the law is the law.

MRS. HALE: I s'pose 'tis. [*Unbuttoning her coat.*] Better loosen up your things, Mrs. Peters. You won't feel them when you go out.

[MRS. PETERS *takes off her fur tippet, goes to hang it on hook at back of room, stands looking at the under part of the small corner table.*]

MRS. PETERS: She was piecing a quilt.

[*She brings the large sewing basket and they look at the bright pieces.*]

MRS. HALE: It's log cabin pattern. Pretty, isn't it? I wonder if she was goin' to quilt it or just knot it?

[*Footsteps have been heard coming down the stairs. The* SHERIFF *enters followed by* HALE *and the* COUNTY ATTORNEY.]

SHERIFF: They wonder if she was going to quilt it or just knot it!

[*The men laugh; the women look abashed.*]

COUNTY ATTORNEY [*rubbing his hands over the stove*]:   Frank's fire didn't do much up there, did it? Well, let's go out to the barn and get that cleared up.

[*The men go outside.*]

MRS. HALE [*resentfully*]:   I don't know as there's anything so strange, our takin' up our time with little things while we're waiting for them to get the evidence. [*She sits down at the big table smoothing out a block with decision.*] I don't see as it's anything to laugh about.

MRS. PETERS [*apologetically*]:   Of course they've got awful important things on their minds.

[*Pulls up a chair and joins* MRS. HALE *at the table.*]

MRS. HALE [*examining another block*]:   Mrs. Peters, look at this one. Here, this is the one she was working on, and look at the sewing! All the rest of it has been so nice and even. And look at this! It's all over the place! Why, it looks as if she didn't know what she was about!

[*After she has said this they look at each other, then start to glance back at the door. After an instant* MRS. HALE *has pulled at a knot and ripped the sewing.*]

MRS. PETERS: Oh, what are you doing, Mrs. Hale?

MRS. HALE [*mildly*]:   Just pulling out a stitch or two that's not sewed very good. [*Threading a needle.*] Bad sewing always made me fidgety.

MRS. PETERS [*nervously*]:   I don't think we ought to touch things.

MRS. HALE: I'll just finish up this end. [*Suddenly stopping and leaning forward.*] Mrs. Peters?

MRS. PETERS: Yes, Mrs. Hale?

MRS. HALE: What do you suppose she was so nervous about?

MRS. PETERS: Oh—I don't know. I don't know as she was nervous. I sometimes sew awful queer when I'm just tired. [MRS. HALE *starts to say something, looks at* MRS. PETERS, *then goes on sewing.*] Well, I must get these things wrapped up. They may be through sooner than we think. [*Putting apron and other things together.*] I wonder where I can find a piece of paper, and string.

MRS. HALE: In that cupboard, maybe.

MRS. PETERS [*looking in cupboard*]:   Why, here's a birdcage. [*Holds it up.*] Did she have a bird, Mrs. Hale?

MRS. HALE: Why, I don't know whether she did or not—I've not been here for so long. There was a man around last year selling canaries cheap, but I don't know as she took one; maybe she did. She used to sing real pretty herself.

MRS. PETERS [*glancing around*]:   Seems funny to think of a bird here. But she must have had one, or why would she have a cage? I wonder what happened to it.

MRS. HALE: I s'pose maybe the cat got it.

MRS. PETERS: No, she didn't have a cat. She's got that feeling some people have about cats—being afraid of them. My cat got in her room and she was real upset and asked me to take it out.

MRS. HALE: My sister Bessie was like that. Queer, ain't it?

MRS. PETERS [*examining the cage*]:   Why, look at this door. It's broke. One hinge is pulled apart.

MRS. HALE [*looking too*]:   Looks as if someone must have been rough with it.

MRS. PETERS: Why, yes.

[*She brings the cage forward and puts it on the table.*]

MRS. HALE: I wish if they're going to find any evidence they'd be about it. I don't like this place.

MRS. PETERS: But I'm awful glad you came with me, Mrs. Hale. It would be lonesome for me sitting here alone.

MRS. HALE: It would, wouldn't it? [*Dropping her sewing.*] But I tell you what I do wish, Mrs. Peters. I wish I had come over sometimes when *she* was here. I—[*Looking around the room.*]—wish I had.

MRS. PETERS: But of course you were awful busy, Mrs. Hale—your house and your children.

MRS. HALE: I could've come. I stayed away because it weren't cheerful—and that's why I ought to have come. I—I've never liked this place. Maybe because it's down in a hollow and you don't see the road. I dunno what it is but it's a lonesome place and always was. I wish I had come over to see Minnie Foster sometimes. I can see now—

[*Shakes her head.*]

MRS. PETERS: Well, you mustn't reproach yourself, Mrs. Hale. Somehow we just don't see how it is with other folks until—something comes up.

MRS. HALE: Not having children makes less work—but it makes a quiet house, and Wright out to work all day, and no company when he did come in. Did you know John Wright, Mrs. Peters?

MRS. PETERS: Not to know him; I've seen him in town. They say he was a good man.

MRS. HALE: Yes—good; he didn't drink, and kept his word as well as most, I guess, and paid his debts. But he was a hard man, Mrs. Peters. Just to pass the time of day with him—[*Shivers.*] Like a raw wind that gets to the bone. [*Pauses, her eye falling on the cage.*] I should think she would 'a wanted a bird. But what do you suppose went with it?

MRS. PETERS: I don't know, unless it got sick and died.

[*She reaches over and swings the broken door, swings it again. Both women watch it.*]

MRS. HALE: You weren't raised round here, were you? [MRS. PETERS *shakes her head.*] You didn't know—her?

MRS. PETERS: Not till they brought her yesterday.

MRS. HALE: She—come to think of it, she was kind of like a bird herself—real sweet and pretty, but kind of timid and—fluttery. How—she—did—change. [*Silence; then as if struck by a happy thought and relieved to get back to every day things.*] Tell you what, Mrs. Peters, why don't you take the quilt in with you? It might take up her mind.

MRS. PETERS: Why, I think that's a real nice idea, Mrs. Hale. There couldn't possibly be any objection to it, could there? Now, just what would I take? I wonder if her patches are in here—and her things.

[*They look in the sewing basket.*]

MRS. HALE: Here's some red. I expect this has got sewing things in it. [*Brings out a fancy box.*] What a pretty box. Looks like something somebody would give you. Maybe her scissors are in here. [*Opens box. Suddenly puts her hand to her nose.*] Why—[MRS. PETERS *bends nearer, then turns her face away.*] There's something wrapped up in this piece of silk.

MRS. PETERS: Why, this isn't her scissors.

MRS. HALE [*lifting the silk*]:   Oh, Mrs. Peters—it's—

[MRS. PETERS *bends closer.*]

MRS. PETERS: It's the bird.

MRS. HALE [*jumping up*]:   But, Mrs. Peters—look at it! Its neck! Look at its neck! It's all—other side *to.*

MRS. PETERS: Somebody—wrung—its—neck.

[*Their eyes meet. A look of growing comprehension, of horror. Steps are heard outside.* MRS. HALE *slips box under quilt pieces, and sinks into her chair. Enter* SHERIFF *and* COUNTY ATTORNEY. MRS. PETERS *rises.*]

COUNTY ATTORNEY [*as one turning from serious things to little pleasantries*]:   Well, ladies have you decided whether she was going to quilt it or knot it?

MRS. PETERS: We think she was going to—knot it.

COUNTY ATTORNEY: Well, that's interesting, I'm sure. [*Seeing the birdcage.*] Has the bird flown?

MRS. HALE [*putting more quilt pieces over the box*]:   We think the—cat got it.

COUNTY ATTORNEY [*Preoccupied*]: Is there a cat?

[MRS. HALE *glances in a quick covert way at* MRS. PETERS.]

MRS. PETERS: Well, not *now.* They're superstitious, you know. They leave.

COUNTY ATTORNEY [*to* SHERIFF PETERS, *continuing an interrupted conversation*]: No sign at all of anyone having come from the outside. Their own rope. Now let's go up again and go over it piece by piece. [*They start upstairs.*] It would have to have been someone who knew just the—

[MRS. PETERS *sits down. The two women sit there not looking at one another, but as if peering into something and at the same time holding back. When they talk now it is in the manner of feeling their way over strange ground, as if afraid of what they are saying, but as if they can not help saying it.*]

MRS. HALE: She liked the bird. She was going to bury it in that pretty box.

MRS. PETERS [*in a whisper*]: When I was a girl—my kitten—there was a boy took a hatchet, and before my eyes—and before I could get there—[*Covers her face an instant.*] If they hadn't held me back I would have—[*Catches herself, looks upstairs where steps are heard, falters weakly.*]—hurt him.

MRS. HALE [*with a slow look around her*]: I wonder how it would seem never to have had any children around. [*Pause.*] No, Wright wouldn't like the bird—a thing that sang. She used to sing. He killed that, too.

MRS. PETERS [*moving uneasily*]: We don't know who killed the bird.

MRS. HALE: I knew John Wright.

MRS. PETERS: It was an awful thing was done in this house that night, Mrs. Hale. Killing a man while he slept, slipping a rope around his neck that choked the life out of him.

MRS. HALE: His neck. Choked the life out of him.

[*Her hand goes out and rests on the birdcage.*]

MRS. PETERS [*with rising voice*]: We don't know who killed him. We don't *know.*

MRS. HALE [*her own feeling not interrupted*]: If there'd been years and years of nothing, then a bird to sing to you, it would be awful—still, after the bird was still.

MRS. PETERS [*something within her speaking*]: I know what stillness is. When we homesteaded in Dakota, and my first baby died—after he was two years old, and me with no other then—

MRS. HALE [*moving*]: How soon do you suppose they'll be through, looking for the evidence?

MRS. PETERS: I know what stillness is. [*Pulling herself back.*] The law has got to punish crime, Mrs. Hale.

MRS. HALE [*not as if answering that*]: I wish you'd seen Minnie Foster when she wore a white dress with blue ribbons and stood up there in the choir and sang. [*A look around the room.*] Oh, I *wish* I'd come over here once in a while! That was a crime! That was a crime! Who's going to punish that?

MRS. PETERS [*looking upstairs*]: We mustn't—take on.

MRS. HALE: I might have known she needed help! I know how things can be—for women. I tell you, it's queer, Mrs. Peters. We live close together and we live far apart. We all go through the same things—it's all just a different kind of the same thing.

[*Brushes her eyes; noticing the bottle of fruit, reaches out for it.*] If I was you I wouldn't tell her her fruit was gone. Tell her it *ain't.* Tell her it's all right. Take this in to prove it to her. She—she may never know whether it was broke or not.

MRS. PETERS [*takes the bottle, looks about for something to wrap it in; takes petticoat from the clothes brought from the other room, very nervously begins winding this around the bottle. In a false voice*]: My, it's a good thing the men couldn't hear us. Wouldn't they just laugh! Getting all stirred up over a little thing like a—dead canary. As if that could have anything to do with—with—wouldn't they *laugh!*

[*The men are heard coming down stairs.*]

MRS. HALE [*under her breath*]: Maybe they would—maybe they wouldn't.

COUNTY ATTORNEY: No, Peters, it's all perfectly clear except a reason for doing it. But you know juries when it comes to women. If there was some definite thing. Something to show—something to make a story about—a thing that would connect up with this strange way of doing it—

[*The women's eyes meet for an instant. Enter* HALE *from outer door.*]

HALE: Well, I've got the team around. Pretty cold out there.

COUNTY ATTORNEY: I'm going to stay here a while by myself. [*To the* SHERIFF.] You can send Frank out for me, can't you? I want to go over everything. I'm not satisfied that we can't do better.

SHERIFF: Do you want to see what Mrs. Peters is going to take in?

[*The* COUNTY ATTORNEY *goes to the table, picks up the apron, laughs.*]

COUNTY ATTORNEY: Oh, I guess they're not very dangerous things the ladies have picked out. [*Moves a few things about, disturbing the quilt pieces which cover the box. Steps back.*] No, Mrs. Peters doesn't need supervising. For that matter, a sheriff's wife is married to the law. Ever think of it that way, Mrs. Peters?

MRS. PETERS: Not—just that way.

SHERIFF [*Chuckling*]: Married to the law. [*Moves toward the other room.*] I just want you to come in here a minute, George. We ought to take a look at these windows.

COUNTY ATTORNEY [*scoffingly*]: Oh, windows!

SHERIFF: We'll be right out, Mr. Hale.

[HALE *goes outside. The* SHERIFF *follows the* COUNTY ATTORNEY *into the other room. Then* MRS. HALE *rises, hands tight together, looking intensely at* MRS. PETERS, *whose eyes make a slow turn, finally meeting* MRS. HALE'S. *A moment* MRS. HALE *holds her, then her own eyes point the way to where the box is concealed. Suddenly* MRS. PETERS *throws back quilt pieces and tries to put the box in the bag she is wearing. It is too big. She opens box, starts to take bird out, cannot touch it, goes to pieces, stands there helpless. Sound of a knob turning in the other room.* MRS. HALE *snatches the box and puts it in the pocket of her big coat. Enter* COUNTY ATTORNEY *and* SHERIFF.]

COUNTY ATTORNEY [*facetiously*]: Well, Henry, at least we found out that she was not going to quilt it. She was going to—what is it you call it, ladies?

MRS. HALE [*her hand against her pocket*]: We call it—knot it, Mr. Henderson.

Curtain

(1916)

QUESTIONS FOR REFLECTION

Experience

1. At what point in reading *Trifles* did you realize that Mrs. Wright had murdered her husband?
2. What is your response to the women's behavior? To the behavior of the men? Why?

Interpretation

3. Explain the significance of the title. Do you prefer this title or the one Glaspell gave her rewriting of the play as a short story, "A Jury of Her Peers"? Why?
4. How does Glaspell characterize the men in the play? The sheriff? The attorney? The neighboring farmer? What attitudes toward women do the men display?
5. How does Glaspell enlist our sympathy for the women? How do Mrs. Hale and Mrs. Peters get along with the men?
6. Which of the stage props are most important for the play's dramatic action? For its theme? Why?
7. Explain the significance of the final line of dialogue.

Evaluation

8. What does Glaspell's play suggest about the relative merits of men's and women's perspectives? What implications might we derive about men's and women's ways of seeing things after reading or viewing this play? Why?

ARTHUR MILLER

[b. 1915]

Death of a Salesman is Arthur Miller's most famous and notable play. Produced and published in 1949, it had a long original Broadway run and has been frequently revived, most recently in 1984 with noted film actor Dustin Hoffman as the salesman Willy Loman. The play is in the tradition of social realism inaugurated by Ibsen and continued by Chekhov, Strindberg, and Shaw. The dialogue of the characters, their financial and emotional problems, and their behavior are all indicative of a typically realistic drama. Like Ibsen's *A Doll House,* Miller's *Salesman* raises questions about social values and attitudes—in this case, the pursuit of success and the American dream. Like Chekhov's tone in *The Cherry Orchard,* Miller's tone mixes sympathy and judgment, criticism and compassion. Miller provides extensive and detailed stage directions. Miller furnishes information about the lives his characters lead, giving us a better sense of their past.

These realistic touches blend, however, with other dramatic elements that are less realistic and that we will call *expressionistic.* Expressionistic playwrights attempt to dramatize a subjective picture of reality as seen by an individual consciousness. They attempt to show the inner life of a character, portraying external reality as he or she sees it. *Death of a Salesman* is expressionistic in that it dramatizes Willy Loman's subjective sense of things, rather than exhibiting a concern for a strict and exact representation of external detail. The play is particularly expressionistic in its memory scenes, in which Willy recalls events from the past in such a way that he reenacts rather than merely remembers them. In these scenes different times, places, and states of mind fluctuate and merge as Miller reveals Willy's thoughts, attitudes, and beliefs, his inflated hopes and deflated dreams. The expressionistic quality of the play is enhanced by lighting and music that signal flashbacks and contribute to its mood.

One issue readers, audiences, and critics have consistently raised about *Death of a Salesman* concerns its status as tragedy. The main question turns on whether Willy Loman is a tragic figure. Is he grand and noble enough to be a tragic hero? Is his failure tragic or merely pathetic? Over the years Miller has written about these and related questions in essays such as "On Social Drama" and "Tragedy and the Common Man." He has suggested that "the common man is as apt a subject for tragedy as kings"; and also that "the tragic feeling is evoked in us when we are in the presence of a character who is ready to lay down his life" to secure his dignity. How far these observations apply to Willy Loman is a matter for discussion.

ARTHUR MILLER

Death of a Salesman

CERTAIN PRIVATE CONVERSATIONS IN TWO ACTS AND A REQUIEM

CHARACTERS

WILLY LOMAN
LINDA
BIFF
HAPPY
BERNARD
THE WOMAN
CHARLEY
UNCLE BEN
HOWARD WAGNER
JENNY
STANLEY
MISS FORSYTHE
LETTA

The action takes place in WILLY LOMAN*'s house and yard and in various places he visits in the New York and Boston of today.*

Throughout the play, in the stage directions, left and right mean stage left and stage right.

ACT I

A melody is heard, played upon a flute. It is small and fine, telling of grass and trees and the horizon. The curtain rises.

Before us is the Salesman's house. We are aware of towering, angular shapes behind it, surrounding it on all sides. Only the blue light of the sky falls upon the house and forestage; the surrounding area shows an angry glow of orange. As more light appears, we see a solid vault of apartment houses around the small, fragile-seeming home. An air of the dream clings to the place, a dream rising out of reality. The kitchen at center seems actual enough, for there is a kitchen table with three chairs, and a refrigerator. But no other fixtures are seen. At the back of the kitchen there is a draped entrance, which leads to the livingroom. To the right of the kitchen, on a level raised two feet, is a bedroom furnished only with a brass bedstead and a straight chair. On a shelf over the bed a silver athletic trophy stands. A window opens onto the apartment house at the side.

Behind the kitchen, on a level raised six and a half feet, is the boys' bedroom, at present barely visible. Two beds are dimly seen, and at the back of the room a dormer window. (This bedroom is above the unseen livingroom.) At the left a stairway curves up to it from the kitchen.

The entire setting is wholly or, in some places, partially transparent. The roof-line of the house is one-dimensional; under and over it we see the apartment buildings. Before the house lies an apron, curving beyond the forestage into the orchestra. This forward area serves as the back yard as well as the locale of all WILLY*'s imaginings and of his city scenes. Whenever the action is in the present the actors observe the imaginary wall-lines, entering the house only through the door at the left. But in the scenes of the past these boundaries are broken, and characters enter or leave a room by stepping "through" a wall onto the forestage.*

From the right, WILLY LOMAN, *the Salesman, enters, carrying two large sample cases. The flute plays on. He hears but is not aware of it. He is past sixty years of age, dressed quietly. Even as he crosses the stage to the doorway of the house, his exhaustion is apparent. He unlocks the door, comes into the kitchen, and thankfully lets his burden down, feeling the soreness of his palms. A word-sigh escapes his lips—it might be "Oh, boy, oh, boy." He closes the door, then carries his cases out into the livingroom, through the draped kitchen doorway.*

LINDA, *his wife, has stirred in her bed at the right. She gets out and puts on a robe, listening. Most often jovial, she has developed an iron repression of her exceptions to* WILLY*'s behavior— she more than loves him, she admires him, as though his mercurial nature, his temper, his massive dreams and little cruelties, served her only as sharp reminders of the turbulent longings within him, longings which she shares but lacks the temperament to utter and follow to their end.*

LINDA (*hearing* WILLY *outside the bedroom, calls with some trepidation*): Willy!

WILLY: It's all right. I came back.

LINDA: Why? What happened? (*Slight pause.*) Did something happen, Willy?

WILLY: No, nothing happened.

LINDA: You didn't smash the car, did you?

WILLY (*with casual irritation*): I said nothing happened. Didn't you hear me?

LINDA: Don't you feel well?

WILLY: I am tired to the death. (*The flute has faded away. He sits on the bed beside her, a little numb.*) I couldn't make it. I just couldn't make it, Linda.

LINDA (*very carefully, delicately*):   Where were you all day? You look terrible.

WILLY: I got as far as a little above Yonkers. I stopped for a cup of coffee. Maybe it was the coffee.

LINDA: What?

WILLY (*after a pause*):   I suddenly couldn't drive any more. The car kept going onto the shoulder, y'know?

LINDA (*helpfully*):   Oh. Maybe it was the steering again. I don't think Angelo knows the Studebaker.

WILLY: No, it's me, it's me. Suddenly I realize I'm goin' sixty miles an hour and I don't remember the last five minutes. I'm—I can't seem to—keep my mind to it.

LINDA: Maybe it's your glasses. You never went for your new glasses.

WILLY: No, I see everything. I came back ten miles an hour. It took me nearly four hours from Yonkers.

LINDA (*resigned*):   Well, you'll just have to take a rest, Willy, you can't continue this way.

WILLY: I just got back from Florida.

LINDA: But you didn't rest your mind. Your mind is overactive, and the mind is what counts, dear.

WILLY: I'll start out in the morning. Maybe I'll feel better in the morning. (*She is taking off his shoes.*) These goddam arch supports are killing me.

LINDA: Take an aspirin. Should I get you an aspirin? It'll soothe you.

WILLY (*with wonder*):   I was driving along, you understand? And I was fine. I was even observing the scenery. You can imagine, me looking at scenery, on the road every week of my life. But it's so beautiful up there, Linda, the trees are so thick, and the sun is warm. I opened the windshield and just let the warm air bathe over me. And then all of a sudden I'm goin' off the road! I'm tellin' ya, I absolutely forgot I was driving. If I'd've gone the other way over the white line I might've killed somebody. So I went on again—and five minutes later I'm dreamin' again, and I nearly—(*He presses two fingers against his eyes.*) I have such thoughts, I have such strange thoughts.

LINDA: Willy, dear. Talk to them again. There's no reason why you can't work in New York.

WILLY: They don't need me in New York. I'm the New England man. I'm vital in New England.

LINDA: But you're sixty years old. They can't expect you to keep traveling every week.

WILLY: I'll have to send a wire to Portland. I'm supposed to see Brown and Morrison tomorrow morning at ten o'clock to show the line. Goddammit, I could sell them! (*He starts putting on his jacket.*)

LINDA (*taking the jacket from him*):   Why don't you go down to the place tomorrow and tell Howard you've simply got to work in New York? You're too accommodating, dear.

WILLY: If old man Wagner was alive I'd a been in charge of New York now! That man was a prince, he was a masterful man. But that boy of his, that Howard, he don't appreciate. When I went north the first time, the Wagner Company didn't know where New England was!

LINDA: Why don't you tell those things to Howard, dear?

WILLY (*encouraged*):   I will, I definitely will. Is there any cheese?

LINDA: I'll make you a sandwich.

WILLY: No, go to sleep. I'll take some milk. I'll be up right away. The boys in?

LINDA: They're sleeping. Happy took Biff on a date tonight.

WILLY (*interested*):   That so?

LINDA: It was so nice to see them shaving together, one behind the other, in the bathroom. And going out together. You notice? The whole house smells of shaving lotion.

WILLY: Figure it out. Work a lifetime to pay off a house. You finally own it, and there's nobody to live in it.

LINDA: Well, dear, life is a casting off. It's always that way.

WILLY: No, no, some people—some people accomplish something. Did Biff say anything after I went this morning?

LINDA: You shouldn't have criticized him, Willy, especially after he just got off the train. You mustn't lose your temper with him.

WILLY: When the hell did I lose my temper? I simply asked him if he was making any money. Is that a criticism?

LINDA: But, dear, how could he make any money?

WILLY (*worried and angered*):   There's such an undercurrent in him. He became a moody man. Did he apologize when I left this morning?

LINDA: He was crestfallen, Willy. You know how he admires you. I think if he finds himself, then you'll both be happier and not fight any more.

WILLY: How can he find himself on a farm? Is that a life? A farmhand? In the beginning, when he was young, I thought, well, a young man, it's good for him to tramp around, take a lot of different jobs. But it's more than ten years now and he has yet to make thirty-five dollars a week!

LINDA: He's finding himself, Willy.

WILLY: Not finding yourself at the age of thirty-four is a disgrace!

LINDA: Shh!

WILLY: The trouble is he's lazy, goddammit!

LINDA: Willy, please!

WILLY: Biff is a lazy bum!

LINDA: They're sleeping. Get something to eat. Go on down.

WILLY: Why did he come home? I would like to know what brought him home.

LINDA: I don't know. I think he's still lost, Willy. I think he's very lost.

WILLY: Biff Loman is lost. In the greatest country in the world a young man with such—personal attractiveness, gets lost. And such a hard worker. There's one thing about Biff—he's not lazy.

LINDA: Never.

WILLY (*with pity and resolve*):   I'll see him in the morning; I'll have a nice talk with him. I'll get him a job selling. He could be big in no time. My God! Remember how they used to follow him around in high school? When he smiled at one of them their faces lit up. When he walked down the street . . . (*He loses himself in reminiscences.*)

LINDA (*trying to bring him out of it*):   Willy, dear, I got a new kind of American-type cheese today. It's whipped.

WILLY: Why do you get American when I like Swiss?

LINDA: I just thought you'd like a change—

WILLY: I don't want a change! I want Swiss cheese. Why am I always being contradicted?

LINDA (*with a covering laugh*):   I thought it would be a surprise.

WILLY: Why don't you open a window in here, for God's sake?

LINDA (*with infinite patience*):   They're all open, dear.

WILLY: The way they boxed us in here. Bricks and windows, windows and bricks.

LINDA: We should've bought the land next door.

WILLY: The street is lined with cars. There's not a breath of fresh air in the neighborhood. The grass don't grow any more, you can't raise a carrot in the back yard. They should've had a law against apartment houses. Remember those two beautiful elm trees out there? When I and Biff hung the swing between them?

LINDA: Yeah, like being a million miles from the city.

WILLY: They should've arrested the builder for cutting those down. They massacred the neighborhood. (*Lost.*) More and more I think of those days, Linda. This time of year it was lilac and wisteria. And then the peonies would come out, and the daffodils. What fragrance in this room!

LINDA: Well, after all, people had to move somewhere.

WILLY: No, there's more people now.

LINDA: I don't think there's more people. I think—

WILLY: There's more people! That's what's ruining this country! Population is getting out of control. The competition is maddening! Smell the stink from that apartment house! And another on the other side . . . How can they whip cheese?

On WILLY's *last line,* BIFF *and* HAPPY *raise themselves up in their beds, listening.*

LINDA: Go down, try it. And be quiet.

WILLY (*turning to* LINDA, *guiltily*):   You're not worried about me, are you, sweetheart?

BIFF: What's the matter?

HAPPY: Listen!

LINDA: You've got too much on the ball to worry about.

WILLY: You're my foundation and my support, Linda.

LINDA: Just try to relax, dear. You make mountains out of molehills.

WILLY: I won't fight with him any more. If he wants to go back to Texas, let him go.

LINDA: He'll find his way.

WILLY: Sure. Certain men just don't get started till later in life. Like Thomas Edison, I think. Or B. F. Goodrich. One of them was deaf. (*He starts for the bedroom doorway.*) I'll put my money on Biff.

LINDA: And Willy—if it's warm Sunday we'll drive in the country. And we'll open the windshield, and take lunch.

WILLY: No, the windshields don't open on the new cars.

LINDA: But you opened it today.

WILLY: Me? I didn't. (*He stops.*) Now isn't that peculiar! Isn't that a remarkable— (*He breaks off in amazement and fright as the flute is heard distantly.*)

LINDA: What, darling?

WILLY: That is the most remarkable thing.

LINDA: What, dear?

WILLY: I was thinking of the Chevvy. (*Slight pause.*) Nineteen twenty-eight . . . when I had that red Chevvy—(*Breaks off.*) That funny? I coulda sworn I was driving that Chevvy today.

LINDA: Well, that's nothing. Something must've reminded you.

WILLY: Remarkable. Ts. Remember those days? The way Biff used to simonize that car? The dealer refused to believe there was eighty thousand miles on it. (*He shakes his head.*) Heh! (*To* LINDA.) Close your eyes, I'll be right up. (*He walks out of the bedroom.*)

HAPPY (*to Biff*): Jesus, maybe he smashed up the car again!

LINDA (*calling after* WILLY): Be careful on the stairs, dear! The cheese is on the middle shelf! (*She turns, goes over to the bed, takes his jacket, and goes out of the bedroom.*)

Light has risen on the boys' room. Unseen, WILLY *is heard talking to himself, "Eighty thousand miles," and a little laugh.* BIFF *gets out of bed, comes downstage a bit, and stands attentively.* BIFF *is two years older than his brother* HAPPY, *well built, but in these days bears a worn air and seems less self-assured. He has succeeded less, and his dreams are stronger and less acceptable than* HAPPY's. HAPPY *is tall, powerfully made. Sexuality is like a visible color on him, or a scent that many women have discovered. He, like his brother, is lost, but in a different way, for he has never allowed himself to turn his face toward defeat and is thus more confused and hard-skinned, although seemingly more content.*

HAPPY (*getting out of bed*): He's going to get his license taken away if he keeps that up. I'm getting nervous about him, y'know, Biff?

BIFF: His eyes are going.

HAPPY: No, I've driven with him. He sees all right. He just doesn't keep his mind on it. I drove into the city with him last week. He stops at a green light and then it turns red and he goes. (*He laughs.*)

BIFF: Maybe he's color-blind.

HAPPY: Pop? Why he's got the finest eye for color in the business. You know that.

BIFF (*sitting down on his bed*): I'm going to sleep.

HAPPY: You're not still sour on Dad, are you, Biff?

BIFF: He's all right, I guess.

WILLY (*underneath them, in the livingroom*): Yes, sir, eighty thousand miles—eighty-two thousand!

BIFF: You smoking?

HAPPY (*holding out a pack of cigarettes*): Want one?

BIFF (*taking a cigarette*): I can never sleep when I smell it.

WILLY: What a simonizing job, heh!

HAPPY (*with deep sentiment*): Funny, Biff, y'know? Us sleeping in here again? The old beds. (*He pats his bed affectionately.*) All the talk that went across those two beds, huh? Our whole lives.

BIFF: Yeah. Lotta dreams and plans.

HAPPY (*with a deep and masculine laugh*): About five hundred women would like to know what was said in this room.

They share a soft laugh.

BIFF: Remember that big Betsy something—what the hell was her name—over on Bushwick Avenue?

HAPPY (*combing his hair*):   With the collie dog!

BIFF: That's the one. I got you in there, remember?

HAPPY: Yeah, that was my first time—I think. Boy, there was a pig! (*They laugh, almost crudely.*) You taught me everything I know about women. Don't forget that.

BIFF: I bet you forgot how bashful you used to be. Especially with girls.

HAPPY: Oh, I still am, Biff.

BIFF: Oh, go on.

HAPPY: I just control it, that's all. I think I got less bashful and you got more so. What happened, Biff? Where's the old humor, the old confidence? (*He shakes* BIFF's *knee.* BIFF *gets up and moves restlessly about the room.*) What's the matter?

BIFF: Why does Dad mock me all the time?

HAPPY: He's not mocking you, he—

BIFF: Everything I say there's a twist of mockery on his face. I can't get near him.

HAPPY: He just wants you to make good, that's all. I wanted to talk to you about Dad for a long time, Biff. Something's—happening to him. He—talks to himself.

BIFF: I noticed that this morning. But he always mumbled.

HAPPY: But not so noticeable. It got so embarrassing I sent him to Florida. And you know something? Most of the time he's talking to you.

BIFF: What's he say about me?

HAPPY: I can't make it out.

BIFF: What's he say about me?

HAPPY: I think the fact that you're not settled, that you're still kind of up in the air . . .

BIFF: There's one or two other things depressing him, Happy.

HAPPY: What do you mean?

BIFF: Never mind. Just don't lay it all to me.

HAPPY: But I think if you just got started—I mean—is there any future for you out there?

BIFF: I tell ya, Hap, I don't know what the future is. I don't know—what I'm supposed to want.

HAPPY: What do you mean?

BIFF: Well, I spent six or seven years after high school trying to work myself up. Shipping clerk, salesman, business of one kind or another. And it's a measly manner of existence. To get on that subway on the hot mornings in summer. To devote your whole life to keeping stock, or making phone calls, or selling or buying. To suffer fifty weeks of the year for the sake of a two-week vacation, when all you really desire is to be outdoors, with your shirt off. And always to have to get ahead of the next fella. And still—that's how you build a future.

HAPPY: Well, you really enjoy it on a farm? Are you content out there?

BIFF (*with rising agitation*):   Hap, I've had twenty or thirty different kinds of jobs since I left home before the war, and it always turns out the same. I just realized it lately. In Nebraska when I herded cattle, and the Dakotas, and Arizona, and now in Texas. It's why I came home now, I guess, because I realized it. This farm I work on, it's spring there now, see? And they've got about fifteen new colts. There's nothing more inspiring or—beautiful than the sight of a mare and a new colt. And it's cool there now, see? Texas is cool now, and it's spring. And whenever spring comes to where I am, I suddenly get the feeling, my God, I'm not gettin' anywhere! What the hell am I doing, playing around with horses, twenty-eight dollars a week! I'm thirty-four years old, I oughta be makin' my future. That's when I come running home. And now, I get here, and I don't know what to do with myself. (*After a pause.*) I've always made a point of not wasting my life, and everytime I come back here I know that all I've done is to waste my life.

HAPPY: You're a poet, you know that, Biff? You're a—you're an idealist!

BIFF: No, I'm mixed up very bad. Maybe I oughta get married. Maybe I oughta get stuck into something. Maybe that's my trouble. I'm like a boy. I'm not married, I'm not in business, I just—I'm like a boy. Are you content, Hap? You're a success, aren't you? Are you content?

HAPPY: Hell, no!

BIFF: Why? You're making money, aren't you?

HAPPY (*moving about with energy, expressiveness*):   All I can do now is wait for the merchandise manager to die. And suppose I get to be merchandise manager? He's a good friend of mine, and he just built a terrific estate on Long Island. And he lived there about two months and sold it, and now he's building another one. He can't enjoy it once it's finished. And I know that's just what I would do. I don't know what the hell I'm workin' for. Sometimes I sit in my apartment—all alone. And I think of the rent I'm paying. And it's crazy. But then, it's what I always wanted. My own apartment, a car, and plenty of women. And still, goddammit, I'm lonely.

BIFF (*with enthusiasm*):   Listen, why don't you come out West with me?

HAPPY: You and I, heh?

BIFF: Sure, maybe we could buy a ranch. Raise cattle, use our muscles. Men built like we are should be working out in the open.

HAPPY (*avidly*):   The Loman Brothers, heh?

BIFF (*with vast affection*):   Sure, we'd be known all over the counties!

HAPPY (*enthralled*):   That's what I dream about, Biff. Sometimes I want to just rip my clothes off in the middle of the store and outbox that goddam merchandise manager. I mean I can outbox, outrun, and outlift anybody in that store, and I have to take orders from those common, petty, sons-of-bitches till I can't stand it any more.

BIFF: I'm tellin' you, kid, if you were with me I'd be happy out there.

HAPPY (*enthused*):   See, Biff, everybody around me is so false that I'm constantly lowering my ideals . . .

BIFF: Baby, together we'd stand up for one another, we'd have someone to trust.

HAPPY: If I were around you—

BIFF: Hap, the trouble is we weren't brought up to grub for money. I don't know how to do it.

HAPPY: Neither can I!

BIFF: Then let's go!

HAPPY: The only thing is—what can you make out there?

BIFF: But look at your friend. Builds an estate and then hasn't the peace of mind to live in it.

HAPPY: Yeah, but when he walks into the store the waves part in front of him. That's fifty-two thousand dollars a year coming through the revolving door, and I got more in my pinky finger than he's got in his head.

BIFF: Yeah, but you just said—

HAPPY: I gotta show some of those pompous, self-important executives over there that Hap Loman can make the grade. I want to walk into the store the way he walks in. Then I'll go with you, Biff. We'll be together yet, I swear. But take those two we had tonight. Now weren't they gorgeous creatures?

BIFF: Yeah, yeah, most gorgeous I've had in years.

HAPPY: I get that any time I want, Biff. Whenever I feel disgusted. The only trouble is, it gets like bowling or something. I just keep knockin' them over and it doesn't mean anything. You still run around a lot?

BIFF: Naa. I'd like to find a girl—steady, somebody with substance.

HAPPY: That's what I long for.

BIFF: Go on! You'd never come home.

HAPPY: I would! Somebody with character, with resistance! Like Mom, y'know? You're gonna call me a bastard when I tell you this. That girl Charlotte I was with tonight is engaged to be married in five weeks. (*He tries on his new hat.*)

BIFF: No kiddin'!

HAPPY: Sure, the guy's in line for the vice-presidency of the store. I don't know what gets into me, maybe I just have an overdeveloped sense of competition or something, but I went and ruined her, and furthermore I can't get rid of her. And he's the third executive I've done that to. Isn't that a crummy characteristic? And to top it all, I go to their weddings! (*Indignantly, but laughing.*) Like I'm not supposed to take bribes. Manufacturers offer me a hundred-dollar bill now and then to throw an order their way. You know how honest I am, but it's like this girl, see. I hate myself for it. Because I don't want the girl, and, still, I take it and—I love it!

BIFF: Let's go to sleep.

HAPPY: I guess we didn't settle anything, heh?

BIFF: I just got one idea that I think I'm going to try.

HAPPY: What's that?

BIFF: Remember Bill Oliver?

HAPPY: Sure, Oliver is very big now. You want to work for him again?

BIFF: No, but when I quit he said something to me. He put his arm on my shoulder, and he said, "Biff, if you ever need anything, come to me."

HAPPY: I remember that. That sounds good.

BIFF: I think I'll go to see him. If I could get ten thousand or even seven or eight thousand dollars I could buy a beautiful ranch.

HAPPY: I bet he'd back you. 'Cause he thought highly of you, Biff, I mean, they all do. You're well liked, Biff. That's why I say to come back here, and we both have the apartment. And I'm tellin' you, Biff, any babe you want . . .

BIFF: No, with a ranch I could do the work I like and still be something. I just wonder though. I wonder if Oliver still thinks I stole that carton of basketballs.

HAPPY: Oh, he probably forgot that long ago. It's almost ten years. You're too sensitive. Anyway, he didn't really fire you.

BIFF: Well, I think he was going to. I think that's why I quit. I was never sure whether he knew or not. I know he thought the world of me, though. I was the only one he'd let lock up the place.

WILLY (*below*):   You gonna wash the engine, Biff?

HAPPY: Shh!

BIFF *looks at* HAPPY, *who is gazing down, listening.* WILLY *is mumbling in the parlor.*

HAPPY: You hear that?

They listen. WILLY *laughs warmly.*

BIFF (*growing angry*):   Doesn't he know Mom can hear that?
WILLY: Don't get your sweater dirty, Biff!

A look of pain crosses BIFF's *face.*

HAPPY: Isn't that terrible? Don't leave again, will you? You'll find a job here. You gotta stick around. I don't know what to do about him, it's getting embarrassing.
WILLY: What a simonizing job!
BIFF: Mom's hearing that!
WILLY: No kiddin', Biff, you got a date? Wonderful!
HAPPY: Go on to sleep. But talk to him in the morning, will you?
BIFF (*reluctantly getting into bed*):   With her in the house. Brother!
HAPPY (*getting into bed*):   I wish you'd have a good talk with him.

The light on their room begins to fade.

BIFF (*to himself in bed*):   That selfish, stupid . . .
HAPPY: Sh . . . Sleep, Biff.

Their light is out. Well before they have finished speaking, WILLY's *form is dimly seen below in the darkened kitchen. He opens the refrigerator, searches in there, and takes out a bottle of milk. The apartment houses are fading out, and the entire house and surroundings become covered with leaves. Music insinuates itself as the leaves appear.*

WILLY: Just wanna be careful with those girls, Biff, that's all. Don't make any promises. No promises of any kind. Because a girl, y'know, they always believe what you tell 'em, and you're very young, Biff, you're too young to be talking seriously to girls.

Light rises on the kitchen. WILLY, *talking, shuts the refrigerator door and comes downstage to the kitchen table. He pours milk into a glass. He is totally immersed in himself, smiling faintly.*

WILLY: Too young entirely, Biff. You want to watch your schooling first. Then when you're all set, there'll be plenty of girls for a boy like you. (*He smiles broadly at a kitchen chair.*) That so? The girls pay for you? (*He laughs.*) Boy, you must really be makin' a hit.

WILLY *is gradually addressing—physically—a point offstage, speaking through the wall of the kitchen, and his voice has been rising in volume to that of a normal conversation.*

WILLY: I been wondering why you polish the car so careful. Ha! Don't leave the hubcaps, boys. Get the chamois to the hubcaps. Happy, use newspaper on the windows, it's the easiest thing. Show him how to do it, Biff! You see, Happy? Pad it up, use it like a pad. That's it, that's it, good work. You're doin' all right, Hap. (*He pauses, then nods in approbation for a few seconds, then looks upward.*) Biff, first thing we gotta do when we get time is clip that big branch over the house. Afraid it's gonna fall in a storm and hit the roof. Tell you what. We get a rope and sling her around, and then we climb up there with a couple of saws and take her down. Soon as you finish the car, boys, I wanna see ya. I got a surprise for you, boys.

BIFF (*offstage*): Whatta ya got, Dad?

WILLY: No, you finish first. Never leave a job till you're finished—remember that. (*Looking toward the "big trees."*) Biff, up in Albany I saw a beautiful hammock. I think I'll buy it next trip, and we'll hang it right between those two elms. Wouldn't that be something? Just swingin' there under those branches. Boy, that would be . . .

YOUNG BIFF *and* YOUNG HAPPY *appear from the direction* WILLY *was addressing.* HAPPY *carries rags and a pail of water.* BIFF, *wearing a sweater with a block "S," carries a football.*

BIFF (*pointing in the direction of the car offstage*): How's that, Pop, professional?

WILLY: Terrific. Terrific job, boys. Good work, Biff.

HAPPY: Where's the surprise, Pop?

WILLY: In the back seat of the car.

HAPPY: Boy! (*He runs off.*)

BIFF: What is it, Dad? Tell me, what'd you buy?

WILLY (*laughing, cuffs him*): Never mind, something I want you to have.

BIFF (*turns and starts off*): What is it, Hap?

HAPPY (*offstage*): It's a punching bag!

BIFF: Oh, Pop!

WILLY: It's got Gene Tunney's signature on it!

HAPPY *runs onstage with a punching bag.*

BIFF: Gee, how'd you know we wanted a punching bag?

WILLY: Well, it's the finest thing for the timing.

HAPPY (*lies down on his back and pedals with his feet*): I'm losing weight, you notice, Pop?

WILLY (*to* HAPPY): Jumping rope is good too.

BIFF: Did you see the new football I got?

WILLY (*examining the ball*): Where'd you get a new ball?

BIFF: The coach told me to practice my passing.

WILLY: That so? And he gave you the ball, heh?

BIFF: Well, I borrowed it from the locker room. (*He laughs confidentially.*)

WILLY (*laughing with him at the theft*): I want you to return that.

HAPPY: I told you he wouldn't like it!

BIFF (*angrily*): Well, I'm bringing it back!

WILLY (*stopping the incipient argument, to* HAPPY): Sure, he's gotta practice with a regulation ball, doesn't he? (*To* BIFF.) Coach'll probably congratulate you on your initiative!

BIFF: Oh, he keeps congratulating my initiative all the time, Pop.

WILLY: That's because he likes you. If somebody else took that ball there'd be an uproar. So what's the report, boys, what's the report?

BIFF: Where'd you go this time, Dad? Gee we were lonesome for you.

WILLY (*pleased, puts an arm around each boy and they come down to the apron*): Lonesome, heh?

BIFF: Missed you every minute.

WILLY: Don't say? Tell you a secret, boys. Don't breathe it to a soul. Someday I'll have my own business, and I'll never have to leave home any more.

HAPPY: Like Uncle Charley, heh?

WILLY: Bigger than Uncle Charley! Because Charley is not—liked. He's liked, but he's not—well liked.

BIFF: Where'd you go this time, Dad?

WILLY: Well, I got on the road, and I went north to Providence. Met the Mayor.

BIFF: The Mayor of Providence!

WILLY: He was sitting in the hotel lobby.

BIFF: What'd he say?

WILLY: He said, "Morning!" And I said, "You've got a fine city here, Mayor." And then he had coffee with me. And then I went to Waterbury. Waterbury is a fine city. Big clock city, the famous Waterbury clock. Sold a nice bill there. And then Boston— Boston is the cradle of the Revolution. A fine city. And a couple of other towns in Mass., and on to Portland and Bangor and straight home!

BIFF: Gee, I'd love to go with you sometime, Dad.

WILLY: Soon as summer comes.

HAPPY: Promise?

WILLY: You and Hap and I, and I'll show you all the towns. America is full of beautiful towns and fine, upstanding people. And they know me, boys, they know me up and down New England. The finest people. And when I bring you fellas up, there'll be open sesame for all of us, 'cause one thing, boys: I have friends. I can park my car in any street in New England, and the cops protect it like their own. This summer, heh?

BIFF *and* HAPPY (*together*):   Yeah! You bet!

WILLY: We'll take our bathing suits.

HAPPY: We'll carry your bags, Pop!

WILLY: Oh, won't that be something! Me comin' into the Boston stores with you boys carryin' my bags. What a sensation!

BIFF *is prancing around, practicing passing the ball.*

WILLY: You nervous, Biff, about the game?

BIFF: Not if you're gonna be there.

WILLY: What do they say about you in school, now that they made you captain?

HAPPY: There's a crowd of girls behind him everytime the classes change.

BIFF (*taking* WILLY'*s hand*):   This Saturday, Pop, this Saturday—just for you, I'm going to break through for a touchdown.

HAPPY: You're supposed to pass.

BIFF: I'm takin' one play for Pop. You watch me, Pop, and when I take off my helmet, that means I'm breakin' out. Then you watch me crash through that line!

WILLY (*kisses* BIFF):   Oh, wait'll I tell this in Boston!

BERNARD *enters in knickers. He is younger than* BIFF, *earnest and loyal, a worried boy.*

BERNARD: Biff, where are you? You're supposed to study with me today.

WILLY: Hey, looka Bernard. What're you lookin' so anemic about, Bernard?

BERNARD: He's gotta study, Uncle Willy. He's got Regents next week.

HAPPY (*tauntingly, spinning* BERNARD *around*):   Let's box, Bernard!

BERNARD: Biff! (*He gets away from* HAPPY.) Listen, Biff, I heard Mr. Birnbaum say that if you don't start studyin' math he's gonna flunk you, and you won't graduate. I heard him!

WILLY: You better study with him, Biff. Go ahead now.

BERNARD: I heard him!

BIFF: Oh, Pop, you didn't see my sneakers! (*He holds up a foot for* WILLY *to look at.*)

WILLY: Hey, that's a beautiful job of printing!

BERNARD (*wiping his glasses*):   Just because he printed University of Virginia on his sneakers doesn't mean they've got to graduate him, Uncle Willy!

WILLY (*angrily*):   What're you talking about? With scholarships to three universities they're gonna flunk him?

BERNARD: But I heard Mr. Birnbaum say—

WILLY: Don't be a pest, Bernard! (*To his boys.*) What an anemic!

BERNARD: Okay, I'm waiting for you in my house, Biff.

BERNARD *goes off. The* LOMANS *laugh.*

WILLY: Bernard is not well liked, is he?

BIFF: He's liked, but he's not well liked.

HAPPY: That's right, Pop.

WILLY: That's just what I mean. Bernard can get the best marks in school, y'understand, but when he gets out in the business world, y'understand, you are going to be five times ahead of him. That's why I thank Almighty God you're both built like Adonises. Because the man who makes an appearance in the business world, the man who creates personal interest, is the man who gets ahead. Be liked and you will never want. You take me, for instance. I never have to wait in line to see a buyer. "Willy Loman is here!" That's all they have to know, and I go right through.

BIFF: Did you knock them dead, Pop?

WILLY: Knocked 'em cold in Providence, slaughtered 'em in Boston.

HAPPY (*on his back, pedaling again*):   I'm losing weight, you notice, Pop?

LINDA *enters, as of old, a ribbon in her hair, carrying a basket of washing.*

LINDA (*with youthful energy*):   Hello, dear!

WILLY: Sweetheart!

LINDA: How'd the Chevvy run?

WILLY: Chevrolet, Linda, is the greatest car ever built. (*To the boys.*) Since when do you let your mother carry wash up the stairs?

BIFF: Grab hold there, boy!

HAPPY: Where to, Mom?

LINDA: Hang them up on the line. And you better go down to your friends, Biff. The cellar is full of boys. They don't know what to do with themselves.

BIFF: Ah, when Pop comes home they can wait!

WILLY (*laughs appreciatively*):   You better go down and tell them what to do, Biff.

BIFF: I think I'll have them sweep out the furnace room.

WILLY: Good work, Biff.

BIFF (*goes through wall-line of kitchen to doorway at back and calls down*):   Fellas! Everybody sweep out the furnace room! I'll be right down!

VOICES: All right! Okay, Biff.

BIFF: George and Sam and Frank, come out back! We're hangin' up the wash! Come on, Hap, on the double! (*He and* HAPPY *carry out the basket.*)

LINDA: The way they obey him!

WILLY: Well, that's training, the training. I'm tellin' you, I was sellin' thousands and thousands, but I had to come home.

LINDA: Oh, the whole block'll be at that game, Did you sell anything?

WILLY: I did five hundred gross in Providence and seven hundred gross in Boston.

LINDA: No! Wait a minute, I've got a pencil. (*She pulls pencil and paper out of her apron pocket.*) That makes your commission . . . Two hundred—my God! Two hundred and twelve dollars!

WILLY: Well, I didn't figure it yet, but . . .

LINDA: How much did you do?

WILLY: Well, I—I did—about a hundred and eighty gross in Providence. Well, no—it came to—roughly two hundred gross on the whole trip.

LINDA(*without hesitation*):   Two hundred gross. That's . . . (*She figures.*)

WILLY: The trouble was that three of the stores were half closed for inventory in Boston. Otherwise I woulda broke records.

LINDA: Well, it makes seventy dollars and some pennies. That's very good.

WILLY: What do we owe?

LINDA: Well, on the first there's sixteen dollars on the refrigerator—

WILLY: Why sixteen?

LINDA: Well, the fan belt broke, so it was a dollar eighty.

WILLY: But it's brand new.

LINDA: Well, the man said that's the way it is. Till they work themselves in, y'know.

They move through the wall-line into the kitchen.

WILLY: I hope we didn't get stuck on that machine.

LINDA: They got the biggest ads of any of them!

WILLY: I know, it's a fine machine. What else?

LINDA: Well, there's nine-sixty for the washing machine. And for the vacuum cleaner there's three and a half due on the fifteenth. Then the roof, you got twenty-one dollars remaining.

WILLY: It don't leak, does it?

LINDA: No, they did a wonderful job. Then you owe Frank for the carburetor.

WILLY: I'm not going to pay that man! That goddam Chevrolet, they ought to prohibit the manufacture of that car!

LINDA: Well, you owe him three and a half. And odds and ends, comes to around a hundred and twenty dollars by the fifteenth.

WILLY: A hundred and twenty dollars! My God, if business don't pick up I don't know what I'm gonna do!

LINDA: Well, next week you'll do better.

WILLY: Oh, I'll knock them dead next week. I'll go to Hartford. I'm very well liked in Hartford. You know, the trouble is, Linda, people don't seem to take to me.

They move onto the forestage.

LINDA: Oh, don't be foolish.

WILLY: I know it when I walk in. They seem to laugh at me.

LINDA: Why? Why would they laugh at you? Don't talk that way, Willy.

WILLY *moves to the edge of the stage.* LINDA *goes into the kitchen and starts to darn stockings.*

WILLY: I don't know the reason for it, but they just pass me by. I'm not noticed.

LINDA: But you're doing wonderful, dear. You're making seventy to a hundred dollars a week.

WILLY: But I gotta be at it ten, twelve hours a day. Other men—I don't know—they do it easier. I don't know why—I can't stop myself—I talk too much. A man oughta come in with a few words. One thing about Charley. He's a man of few words, and they respect him.

LINDA: You don't talk too much, you're just lively.

WILLY (*smiling*):   Well, I figure, what the hell, life is short, a couple of jokes. (*To himself.*) I joke too much! (*The smile goes.*)

LINDA: Why? You're—

WILLY: I'm fat. I'm very—foolish to look at, Linda. I didn't tell you, but Christmas time I happened to be calling on F. H. Stewarts, and a salesman I know, as I was going in to see the buyer I heard him say something about—walrus. And I—I cracked him right across the face. I won't take that. I simply will not take that. But they do laugh at me. I know that.

LINDA: Darling . . .

WILLY: I gotta overcome it. I know I gotta overcome it. I'm not dressing to advantage, maybe.

LINDA: Willy, darling, you're the handsomest man in the world—

WILLY: Oh, no, Linda.

LINDA: To me you are. (*Slight pause.*) The handsomest.

From the darkness is heard the laughter of a woman. WILLY *doesn't turn to it, but it continues through* LINDA'S *lines.*

LINDA: And the boys, Willy. Few men are idolized by their children the way you are.

Music is heard as behind a scrim, to the left of the house, THE WOMAN, *dimly seen, is dressing.*

WILLY (*with great feeling*):   You're the best there is, Linda, you're a pal, you know that? On the road—on the road I want to grab you sometimes and just kiss the life outa you.

The laughter is loud now, and he moves into a brightening area at the left, where THE WOMAN *has come from behind the scrim and is standing, putting on her hat, looking into a "mirror" and laughing.*

WILLY: 'Cause I get so lonely—especially when business is bad and there's nobody to talk to. I get the feeling that I'll never sell anything again, that I won't make a living for you, or a business, a business for the boys. (*He talks through* THE WOMAN'S *subsiding laughter;* THE WOMAN *primps at the "mirror."*) There's so much I want to make for—

THE WOMAN: Me? You didn't make me, Willy. I picked you.

WILLY (*pleased*):   You picked me?

THE WOMAN (*who is quite proper-looking,* WILLY'S *age*):   I did. I've been sitting at that desk watching all the salesmen go by, day in, day out. But you've got such a sense of humor, and we do have such a good time together, don't we?

WILLY: Sure, sure. (*He takes her in his arms.*) Why do you have to go now?

THE WOMAN: It's two o'clock . . .

WILLY: No, come on 'in! (*He pulls her.*)

THE WOMAN: . . . my sisters'll be scandalized. When'll you be back?

WILLY: Oh, two weeks about. Will you come up again?

THE WOMAN: Sure thing. You do make me laugh. It's good for me. (*She squeezes his arm, kisses him.*) And I think you're a wonderful man.

WILLY: You picked me, heh?

THE WOMAN: Sure. Because you're so sweet. And such a kidder.

WILLY: Well, I'll see you next time I'm in Boston.

THE WOMAN: I'll put you right through to the buyers.

WILLY (*slapping her bottom*):   Right. Well, bottoms up!

THE WOMAN (*slaps him gently and laughs*):   You just kill me, Willy. (*He suddenly grabs her and kisses her roughly.*) You kill me. And thanks for the stockings. I love a lot of stockings. Well, good night.

WILLY: Good night. And keep your pores open!

THE WOMAN: Oh, Willy!

THE WOMAN *bursts out laughing, and* LINDA*'s laughter blends in.* THE WOMAN *disappears into the dark. Now the area at the kitchen table brightens.* LINDA *is sitting where she was at the kitchen table, but now is mending a pair of silk stockings.*

LINDA: You are, Willy. The handsomest man. You've got no reason to feel that—

WILLY (*coming out of* THE WOMAN'S *dimming area and going over to* LINDA):   I'll make it all up to you, Linda, I'll—

LINDA: There's nothing to make up, dear. You're doing fine, better than—

WILLY (*noticing her mending*):   What's that?

LINDA: Just mending my stockings. They're so expensive—

WILLY (*angrily, taking them from her*):   I won't have you mending stockings in this house! Now throw them out!

LINDA *puts the stockings in her pocket.*

BERNARD (*entering on the run*):   Where is he? If he doesn't study!

WILLY (*moving to the forestage, with great agitation*):   You'll give him the answers!

BERNARD: I do, but I can't on a Regents! That's a state exam! They're liable to arrest me!

WILLY: Where is he? I'll whip him, I'll whip him!

LINDA: And he'd better give back that football, Willy, it's not nice.

WILLY: Biff! Where is he? Why is he taking everything?

LINDA: He's too tough with the girls, Willy. All the mothers are afraid of him!

WILLY: I'll whip him!

BERNARD: He's driving the car without a license!

THE WOMAN'*s laugh is heard.*

WILLY: Shut up!

LINDA: All the mothers—

WILLY: Shut up!

BERNARD (*backing quietly away and out*):   Mr. Birnbaum says he's stuck up.

WILLY: Get outa here!

BERNARD: If he doesn't buckle down he'll flunk math! (*He goes off.*)

LINDA: He's right, Willy, you've gotta—

WILLY (*exploding at her*):   There's nothing the matter with him! You want him to be a worm like Bernard? He's got spirit, personality . . .

As he speaks, LINDA, *almost in tears, exits into the livingroom.* WILLY *is alone in the kitchen, wilting and staring. The leaves are gone. It is night again, and the apartment houses look down from behind.*

WILLY: Loaded with it. Loaded! What is he stealing? He's giving it back, isn't he? Why is he stealing? What did I tell him? I never in my life told him anything but decent things.

HAPPY *in pajamas has come down the stairs;* WILLY *suddenly becomes aware of* HAPPY'*s presence.*

HAPPY: Let's go now, come on.

WILLY (*sitting down at the kitchen table*):   Huh! Why did she have to wax the floors herself? Everytime she waxes the floors she keels over. She knows that!

HAPPY: Shh! Take it easy. What brought you back tonight?

WILLY: I got an awful scare. Nearly hit a kid in Yonkers. God! Why didn't I go to Alaska with my brother Ben that time! Ben! That man was a genius, that man was success incarnate! What a mistake! He begged me to go.

HAPPY: Well, there's no use in—

WILLY: You guys! There was a man started with the clothes on his back and ended up with diamond mines!

HAPPY: Boy, someday I'd like to know how he did it.

WILLY: What's the mystery? The man knew what he wanted and went out and got it! Walked into a jungle, and comes out, the age of twenty-one, and he's rich! The world is an oyster, but you don't crack it open on a mattress!

HAPPY: Pop, I told you I'm gonna retire you for life.

WILLY: You'll retire me for life on seventy goddam dollars a week? And your women and your car and your apartment, and you'll retire me for life! Christ's sake, I couldn't get past Yonkers today! Where are you guys, where are you? The woods are burning! I can't drive a car!

CHARLEY *has appeared in the doorway. He is a large man, slow of speech, laconic, immovable. In all he says, despite what he says, there is pity, and, now, trepidation. He has a robe over his pajamas, slippers on his feet. He enters the kitchen.*

CHARLEY: Everything all right?

HAPPY: Yeah, Charley, everything's . . .

WILLY: What's the matter?

CHARLEY: I heard some noise. I thought something happened. Can't we do something about the walls? You sneeze in here, and in my house hats blow off.

HAPPY: Let's go to bed, Dad. Come on.

CHARLEY *signals to* HAPPY *to go.*

WILLY: You go ahead, I'm not tired at the moment.

HAPPY (*to* WILLY):   Take it easy, huh? (*He exits.*)

WILLY: What're you doin' up?

CHARLEY (*sitting down at the kitchen table opposite* WILLY):   Couldn't sleep good. I had a heartburn.

WILLY: Well, you don't know how to eat.

CHARLEY: I eat with my mouth.

WILLY: No, you're ignorant. You gotta know about vitamins and things like that.

CHARLEY: Come on, let's shoot. Tire you out a little.

WILLY (*hesitantly*):   All right. You got cards?

CHARLEY (*taking a deck from his pocket*):   Yeah, I got them. Someplace. What is it with those vitamins?

WILLY (*dealing*):   They build up your bones. Chemistry.

CHARLEY: Yeah, but there's no bones in a heartburn.

WILLY: What are you talkin' about? Do you know the first thing about it?

CHARLEY: Don't get insulted.

WILLY: Don't talk about something you don't know anything about.

They are playing. Pause.

CHARLEY: What're you doin' home?

WILLY: A little trouble with the car.

CHARLEY: Oh. (*Pause.*) I'd like to take a trip to California.

WILLY: Don't say.

CHARLEY: You want a job?

WILLY: I got a job, I told you that. (*After a slight pause.*) What the hell are you offering me a job for?

CHARLEY: Don't get insulted.

WILLY: Don't insult me.

CHARLEY: I don't see no sense in it. You don't have to go on this way.

WILLY: I got a good job. (*Slight pause.*) What do you keep comin' in here for?

CHARLEY: You want me to go?

WILLY (*after a pause, withering*):   I can't understand it. He's going back to Texas again. What the hell is that?

CHARLEY: Let him go.

WILLY: I got nothin' to give him, Charley, I'm clean, I'm clean.

CHARLEY: He won't starve. None a them starve. Forget about him.

WILLY: Then what have I got to remember?

CHARLEY: You take it too hard. To hell with it. When a deposit bottle is broken you don't get your nickel back.

WILLY: That's easy enough for you to say.

CHARLEY: That ain't easy for me to say.

WILLY: Did you see the ceiling I put up in the livingroom?

CHARLEY: Yeah, that's a piece of work. To put up a ceiling is a mystery to me. How do you do it?

WILLY: What's the difference?

CHARLEY: Well, talk about it.

WILLY: You gonna put up a ceiling?

CHARLEY: How could I put up a ceiling?

WILLY: Then what the hell are you bothering me for?

CHARLEY: You're insulted again.

WILLY: A man who can't handle tools is not a man. You're disgusting.

CHARLEY: Don't call me disgusting, Willy.

UNCLE BEN, *carrying a valise and an umbrella, enters the forestage from around the right corner of the house. He is a stolid man, in his sixties, with a mustache and an authoritative air. He is utterly certain of his destiny, and there is an aura of far places about him. He enters exactly as* WILLY *speaks.*

WILLY: I'm getting awfully tired, Ben.

BEN's *music is heard.* BEN *looks around at everything.*

CHARLEY: Good, keep playing; you'll sleep better. Did you call me Ben?

BEN *looks at his watch.*

WILLY: That's funny. For a second there you reminded me of my brother Ben.

BEN: I have only a few minutes. (*He strolls, inspecting the place.* WILLY *and* CHARLEY *continue playing.*)

CHARLEY: You never heard from him again, heh? Since that time?

WILLY: Didn't Linda tell you? Couple of weeks ago we got a letter from his wife in Africa. He died.

CHARLEY: That so.

BEN (*chuckling*): So this is Brooklyn, eh?

CHARLEY: Maybe you're in for some of his money.

WILLY: Naa, he had seven sons. There's just one opportunity I had with that man . . .

BEN: I must make a train, William. There are several properties I'm looking at in Alaska.

WILLY: Sure, sure! If I'd gone with him to Alaska that time, everything would've been totally different.

CHARLEY: Go on, you'd froze to death up there.

WILLY: What're you talking about?

BEN: Opportunity is tremendous in Alaska, William. Surprised you're not up there.

WILLY: Sure, tremendous.

CHARLEY: Heh?

WILLY: There was the only man I ever met who knew the answers.

CHARLEY: Who?

BEN: How are you all?

WILLY (*taking a pot, smiling*): Fine, fine.

CHARLEY: Pretty sharp tonight.

BEN: Is Mother living with you?

WILLY: No, she died a long time ago.

CHARLEY: Who?

BEN: That's too bad. Fine specimen of a lady, Mother.

WILLY (*to* CHARLEY): Heh?

BEN: I'd hoped to see the old girl.

CHARLEY: Who died?

BEN: Heard anything from Father, have you?

WILLY (*unnerved*): What do you mean, who died?

CHARLEY (*taking a pot*):   What're you talkin' about?

BEN (*looking at his watch*):   William, it's half-past eight!

WILLY (*as though to dispel his confusion he angrily stops* CHARLEY*'s hand*):   That's my build!

CHARLEY: I put the ace—

WILLY: If you don't know how to play the game I'm not gonna throw my money away on you!

CHARLEY (*rising*):   It was my ace, for God's sake!

WILLY: I'm through, I'm through!

BEN: When did Mother die?

WILLY: Long ago. Since the beginning you never knew how to play cards.

CHARLEY (*picks up the cards and goes to the door*):   All right! Next time I'll bring a deck with five aces.

WILLY: I don't play that kind of game!

CHARLEY (*turning to him*):   You should be ashamed of yourself!

WILLY: Yeah?

CHARLEY: Yeah! (*He goes out.*)

WILLY (*slamming the door after him*):   Ignoramus!

BEN (*as* WILLY *comes toward him through the wall-line of the kitchen*):   So you're William.

WILLY (*shaking* BEN*'S hand*):   Ben! I've been waiting for you so long! What's the answer? How did you do it?

BEN: Oh, there's a story in that.

> LINDA *enters the forestage, as of old, carrying the wash basket.*

LINDA: Is this Ben?

BEN (*gallantly*):   How do you do, my dear.

LINDA: Where've you been all these years? Willy's always wondered why you—

WILLY (*pulling* BEN *away from her impatiently*):   Where is Dad? Didn't you follow him? How did you get started?

BEN: Well, I don't know how much you remember.

WILLY: Well, I was just a baby, of course, only three or four years old—

BEN: Three years and eleven months.

WILLY: What a memory, Ben!

BEN: I have many enterprises, William, and I have never kept books.

WILLY: I remember I was sitting under the wagon in—was it Nebraska?

BEN: It was South Dakota, and I gave you a bunch of wild flowers.

WILLY: I remember you walking away down some open road.

BEN (*laughing*):   I was going to find Father in Alaska.

WILLY: Where is he?

BEN: At that age I had a very faulty view of geography, William. I discovered after a few days that I was heading due south, so instead of Alaska, I ended up in Africa.

LINDA: Africa!

WILLY: The Gold Coast!

BEN: Principally, diamond mines.

LINDA: Diamond mines!

BEN: Yes, my dear. But I've only a few minutes—

WILLY: No! Boys! Boys! (YOUNG BIFF *and* HAPPY *appear.*) Listen to this. This is your Uncle Ben, a great man! Tell my boys, Ben!

BEN: Why, boys, when I was seventeen I walked into the jungle, and when I was twenty-one I walked out. (*He laughs.*) And by God I was rich.

WILLY (*to the boys*):   You see what I been talking about? The greatest things can happen!

BEN (*glancing at his watch*):   I have an appointment in Ketchikan Tuesday week.

WILLY: No, Ben! Please tell about Dad. I want my boys to hear. I want them to know the kind of stock they spring from. All I remember is a man with a big beard, and I was in Mamma's lap, sitting around a fire, and some kind of high music.

BEN: His flute. He played the flute.

WILLY: Sure, the flute, that's right!

New music is heard, a high, rollicking tune.

BEN: Father was a very great and a very wild-hearted man. We would start in Boston, and he'd toss the whole family into the wagon, and then he'd drive the team right across the country; through Ohio, and Indiana, Michigan, Illinois, and all the Western states. And we'd stop in the towns and sell the flutes that he'd made on the way. Great inventor, Father. With one gadget he made more in a week than a man like you could make in a lifetime.

WILLY: That's just the way I'm bringing them up, Ben—rugged, well liked, all-around.

BEN: Yeah? (*To* BIFF.) Hit that, boy—hard as you can. (*He pounds his stomach.*)

BIFF: Oh, no, sir!

BEN (*taking boxing stance*):   Come on, get to me! (*He laughs.*)

WILLY: Go to it, Biff! Go ahead, show him!

BIFF: Okay! (*He cocks his fist and starts in.*)

LINDA (*to* WILLY):   Why must he fight, dear?

BEN (*sparring with* BIFF):   Good boy! Good boy!

WILLY: How's that, Ben, heh?

HAPPY: Give him the left, Biff!

LINDA: Why are you fighting?

BEN: Good boy! (*Suddenly comes in, trips* BIFF, *and stands over him, the point of his umbrella poised over* BIFF'S *eye.*)

LINDA: Look out, Biff!

BIFF: Gee!

BEN (*patting* BIFF'S *knee*):   Never fight fair with a stranger, boy. You'll never get out of the jungle that way. (*Taking* LINDA'S *hand and bowing.*) It was an honor and a pleasure to meet you, Linda.

LINDA (*withdrawing her hand coldly, frightened*):   Have a nice—trip.

BEN (*to* WILLY):   And good luck with your—what do you do?

WILLY: Selling.

BEN: Yes. Well . . . (*He raises his hand in farewell to all.*)

WILLY: No, Ben, I don't want you to think . . . (*He takes* BEN'S *arm to show him.*) It's Brooklyn, I know, but we hunt too.

BEN: Really, now.

WILLY: Oh, sure, there's snakes and rabbits and—that's why I moved out here. Why, Biff can fell any one of these trees in no time! Boys! Go right over to where they're building the apartment house and get some sand. We're gonna rebuild the entire front stoop right now! Watch this, Ben!

BIFF: Yes, sir! On the double, Hap!

HAPPY (*as he and* BIFF *run off*):   I lost weight, Pop, you notice?

CHARLEY *enters in knickers, even before the boys are gone.*

CHARLEY: Listen, if they steal any more from that building the watchman'll put the cops on them!

LINDA (*to* WILLY):   Don't let Biff . . .

BEN *laughs lustily.*

WILLY: You shoulda seen the lumber they brought home last week. At least a dozen six-by-tens worth all kinds a money.

CHARLEY: Listen, if that watchman—

WILLY: I gave them hell, understand. But I got a couple of fearless characters there.

CHARLEY: Willy, the jails are full of fearless characters.

BEN (*clapping* WILLY *on the back, with a laugh at* CHARLEY):   And the stock exchange, friend!

WILLY (*joining in* BEN'S *laughter*):   Where are the rest of your pants?

CHARLEY: My wife bought them.

WILLY: Now all you need is a golf club and you can go upstairs and go to sleep. (*To* BEN.) Great athlete! Between him and his son Bernard they can't hammer a nail!

BERNARD (*rushing in*):   The watchman's chasing Biff!

WILLY (*angrily*):   Shut up! He's not stealing anything!

LINDA (*alarmed, hurrying off left*):   Where is he? Biff, dear! (*She exits.*)

WILLY (*moving toward the left, away from* BEN):   There's nothing wrong. What's the matter with you?

BEN: Nervy boy. Good!

WILLY (*laughing*):   Oh, nerves of iron, that Biff!

CHARLEY: Don't know what it is. My New England man comes back and he's bleedin', they murdered him up there.

WILLY: It's contacts, Charley, I got important contacts!

CHARLEY (*sarcastically*):   Glad to hear it, Willy. Come in later, we'll shoot a little casino. I'll take some of your Portland money. (*He laughs at* WILLY *and exits.*)

WILLY (*turning to* BEN):   Business is bad, it's murderous. But not for me, of course.

BEN: I'll stop by on my way back to Africa.

WILLY (*longingly*):   Can't you stay a few days? You're just what I need, Ben, because I—I have a fine position here, but I—well, Dad left when I was such a baby and I never had a chance to talk to him and I still feel—kind of temporary about myself.

BEN: I'll be late for my train.

They are at opposite ends of the stage.

WILLY: Ben, my boys—can't we talk? They'd go into the jaws of hell for me, see, but I—

BEN: William, you're being first-rate with your boys. Outstanding, manly chaps!

WILLY (*hanging on to his words*):   Oh, Ben, that's good to hear! Because sometimes I'm afraid that I'm not teaching them the right kind of—Ben, how should I teach them?

BEN (*giving great weight to each word, and with a certain vicious audacity*):   William, when I walked into the jungle, I was seventeen. When I walked out I was twenty-one. And, by God, I was rich! (*He goes off into darkness around the right corner of the house.*)

WILLY: . . . was rich! That's just the spirit I want to imbue them with! To walk into a jungle! I was right! I was right! I was right!

BEN *is gone, but* WILLY *is still speaking to him as* LINDA, *in nightgown and robe, enters the kitchen, glances around for* WILLY, *then goes to the door of the house, looks out and sees him. Comes down to his left. He looks at her.*

LINDA: Willy, dear? Willy?

WILLY: I was right!

LINDA: Did you have some cheese? (*He can't answer.*) It's very late, darling. Come to bed, heh?

WILLY (*looking straight up*):   Gotta break your neck to see a star in this yard.

LINDA: You coming in?

WILLY: What ever happened to that diamond watch fob? Remember? When Ben came from Africa that time? Didn't he give me a watch fob with a diamond in it?

LINDA: You pawned it, dear. Twelve, thirteen years ago. For Biff's radio correspondence course.

WILLY: Gee, that was a beautiful thing. I'll take a walk.

LINDA: But you're in your slippers.

WILLY (*starting to go around the house at the left*):   I was right! I was! (*Half to* LINDA, *as he goes, shaking his head.*) What a man! There was a man worth talking to. I was right!

LINDA (*calling after* WILLY):   But in your slippers, Willy!

WILLY *is almost gone when* BIFF, *in his pajamas, comes down the stairs and enters the kitchen.*

BIFF: What is he doing out there?

LINDA: Sh!

BIFF: God Almighty, Mom, how long has he been doing this?

LINDA: Don't, he'll hear you.

BIFF: What the hell is the matter with him?

LINDA: It'll pass by morning.

BIFF: Shouldn't we do anything?

LINDA: Oh, my dear, you should do a lot of things, but there's nothing to do, so go to sleep.

HAPPY *comes down the stairs and sits on the steps.*

HAPPY: I never heard him so loud, Mom.

LINDA: Well, come around more often; you'll hear him. (*She sits down at the table and mends the lining of* WILLY'S *jacket.*)

BIFF: Why didn't you ever write me about this, Mom?

LINDA: How would I write to you? For over three months you had no address.

BIFF: I was on the move. But you know I thought of you all the time. You know that, don't you, pal?

LINDA: I know, dear, I know. But he likes to have a letter. Just to know that there's still a possibility for better things.

BIFF: He's not like this all the time, is he?

LINDA: It's when you come home he's always the worst.

BIFF: When I come home?

LINDA: When you write you're coming, he's all smiles, and talks about the future, and—he's just wonderful. And then the closer you seem to come, the more shaky he gets, and then, by the time you get here, he's arguing, and he seems angry at you. I think it's just that maybe he can't bring himself to—to open up to you. Why are you so hateful to each other? Why is that?

BIFF (*evasively*): I'm not hateful, Mom.

LINDA: But you no sooner come in the door than you're fighting!

BIFF: I don't know why. I mean to change. I'm tryin', Mom, you understand?

LINDA: Are you home to stay now?

BIFF: I don't know. I want to look around, see what's doin'.

LINDA: Biff, you can't look around all your life, can you?

BIFF: I just can't take hold, Mom. I can't take hold of some kind of a life.

LINDA: Biff, a man is not a bird, to come and go with the springtime.

BIFF: Your hair . . . (*He touches her hair.*) Your hair got so gray.

LINDA: Oh, it's been gray since you were in high school. I just stopped dyeing it, that's all.

BIFF: Dye it again, will ya? I don't want my pal looking old. (*He smiles.*)

LINDA: You're such a boy! You think you can go away for a year and . . . You've got to get it into your head now that one day you'll knock on this door and there'll be strange people here—

BIFF: What are you talking about? You're not even sixty, Mom.

LINDA: But what about your father?

BIFF (*lamely*): Well, I meant him too.

HAPPY: He admires Pop.

LINDA: Biff, dear, if you don't have any feeling for him, then you can't have any feeling for me.

BIFF: Sure I can, Mom.

LINDA: No. You can't just come to see me, because I love him. (*With a threat, but only a threat, of tears.*) He's the dearest man in the world to me, and I won't have anyone making him feel unwanted and low and blue. You've got to make up your mind now, darling, there's no leeway any more. Either he's your father and you pay him that respect, or else you're not to come here. I know he's not easy to get along with—nobody knows that better than me—but . . .

WILLY (*from the left, with a laugh*): Hey, hey, Biffo!

BIFF (*starting to go out after* WILLY): What the hell is the matter with him? (HAPPY *stops him.*)

LINDA: Don't—don't go near him!

BIFF: Stop making excuses for him! He always, always wiped the floor with you. Never had an ounce of respect for you.

HAPPY: He's always had respect for—

BIFF: What the hell do you know about it?

HAPPY (*surlily*): Just don't call him crazy!

BIFF: He's got no character—Charley wouldn't do this. Not in his own house—spewing out that vomit from his mind.

HAPPY: Charley never had to cope with what he's got to.

BIFF: People are worse off than Willy Loman. Believe me, I've seen them!

LINDA: Then make Charley your father, Biff. You can't do that, can you? I don't say he's a great man. Willy Loman never made a lot of money. His name was never in the paper. He's not the finest character that ever lived. But he's a human being, and a terrible thing is happening to him. So attention must be paid. He's not to be allowed to fall into his grave like an old dog. Attention, attention must be finally paid to such a person. You called him crazy—

BIFF: I didn't mean—

LINDA: No, a lot of people think he's lost his—balance. But you don't have to be very smart to know what his trouble is. The man is exhausted.

HAPPY: Sure!

LINDA: A small man can be just as exhausted as a great man. He works for a company thirty-six years this March, opens up unheard-of territories to their trademark, and now in his old age they take his salary away.

HAPPY (indignantly): I didn't know that, Mom.

LINDA: You never asked, my dear! Now that you get your spending money someplace else you don't trouble your mind with him.

HAPPY: But I gave you money last—

LINDA: Christmas time, fifty dollars! To fix the hot water it cost ninety-seven fifty! For five weeks he's been on straight commission, like a beginner, an unknown!

BIFF: Those ungrateful bastards!

LINDA: Are they any worse than his sons? When he brought them business, when he was young, they were glad to see him. But now his old friends, the old buyers that loved him so and always found some order to hand him in a pinch—they're all dead, retired. He used to be able to make six, seven calls a day in Boston. Now he takes his valises out of the car and puts them back and takes them out again and he's exhausted. Instead of walking he talks now. He drives seven hundred miles, and when he gets there no one knows him any more, no one welcomes him. And what goes through a man's mind, driving seven hundred miles home without having earned a cent? Why shouldn't he talk to himself? Why? When he has to go to Charley and borrow fifty dollars a week and pretend to me that it's his pay? How long can that go on? How long? You see what I'm sitting here and waiting for? And you tell me he has no character? The man who never worked a day but for your benefit? When does he get the medal for that? Is this his reward—to turn around at the age of sixty-three and find his sons, who he loved better than his life, one a philandering bum—

HAPPY: Mom!

LINDA: That's all you are, my baby! (To BIFF.) And you! What happened to the love you had for him? You were such pals! How you used to talk to him on the phone every night! How lonely he was till he could come home to you!

BIFF: All right, Mom. I'll live here in my room, and I'll get a job. I'll keep away from him, that's all.

LINDA: No, Biff. You can't stay here and fight all the time.

BIFF: He threw me out of this house, remember that.

LINDA: Why did he do that? I never knew why.

BIFF: Because I know he's a fake and he doesn't like anybody around who knows!

LINDA: Why a fake? In what way? What do you mean?

BIFF: Just don't lay it all at my feet. It's between me and him—that's all I have to say. I'll chip in from now on. He'll settle for half my pay check. He'll be all right. I'm going to bed. (*He starts for the stairs.*)

LINDA: He won't be all right.

BIFF (*turning on the stairs, furiously*): I hate this city and I'll stay here. Now what do you want?

LINDA: He's dying, Biff.

HAPPY *turns quickly to her, shocked.*

BIFF (*after a pause.*): Why is he dying?

LINDA: He's been trying to kill himself.

BIFF (*with great horror*): How?

LINDA: I live from day to day.

BIFF: What're you talking about?

LINDA: Remember I wrote you that he smashed up the car again? In February?

BIFF: Well?

LINDA: The insurance inspector came. He said that they have evidence. That all these accidents in the last year—weren't—weren't—accidents.

HAPPY: How can they tell that? That's a lie.

LINDA: It seems there's a woman . . . (*She takes a breath as—*)

BIFF (*sharply but contained*): What woman?

LINDA (*simultaneously*): . . . and this woman . . .

LINDA: What?

BIFF: Nothing. Go ahead.

LINDA: What did you say?

BIFF: Nothing. I just said what woman?

HAPPY: What about her?

LINDA: Well, it seems she was walking down the road and saw his car. She says that he wasn't driving fast at all, and that he didn't skid. She says he came to that little bridge, and then deliberately smashed into the railing, and it was only the shallowness of the water that saved him.

BIFF: Oh, no, he probably just fell asleep again.

LINDA: I don't think he fell asleep.

BIFF: Why not?

LINDA: Last month . . . (*With great difficulty.*) Oh, boys, it's so hard to say a thing like this! He's just a big stupid man to you, but I tell you there's more good in him than in many other people. (*She chokes, wipes her eyes.*) I was looking for a fuse. The lights blew out, and I went down the cellar. And behind the fuse box—it happened to fall out— was a length of rubber pipe—just short.

HAPPY: No kidding?

LINDA: There's a little attachment on the end of it. I knew right away. And sure enough, on the bottom of the water heater there's a new little nipple on the gas pipe.

HAPPY (*angrily*): That—jerk.

BIFF: Did you have it taken off?

LINDA: I'm—I'm ashamed to. How can I mention it to him? Every day I go down and take away that little rubber pipe. But, when he comes home, I put it back where it was. How can I insult him that way? I don't know what to do. I live from day to day, boys. I tell you, I know every thought in his mind. It sounds so old-fashioned and silly, but I tell you he put his whole life into you and you've turned your backs on him. (*She is bent over in the chair, weeping, her face in her hands.*) Biff, I swear to God! Biff, his life is in your hands!

HAPPY (*to* BIFF):   How do you like that damned fool!

BIFF (*kissing her*):   All right, pal, all right. It's all settled now. I've been remiss. I know that, Mom. But now I'll stay, and I swear to you, I'll apply myself. (*Kneeling in front of her, in a fever of self-reproach.*) It's just—you see, Mom, I don't fit in business. Not that I won't try. I'll try, and I'll make good.

HAPPY: Sure you will. The trouble with you in business was you never tried to please people.

BIFF: I know, I—

HAPPY: Like when you worked for Harrison's. Bob Harrison said you were tops, and then you go and do some damn fool thing like whistling whole songs in the elevator like a comedian.

BIFF (*against* HAPPY):   So what? I like to whistle sometimes.

HAPPY: You don't raise a guy to a responsible job who whistles in the elevator!

LINDA: Well, don't argue about it now.

HAPPY: Like when you'd go off and swim in the middle of the day instead of taking the line around.

BIFF (*his resentment rising*):   Well, don't you run off? You take off sometimes, don't you? On a nice summer day?

HAPPY: Yeah, but I cover myself!

LINDA: Boys!

HAPPY: If I'm going to take a fade the boss can call any number where I'm supposed to be and they'll swear to him that I just left. I'll tell you something that I hate to say, Biff, but in the business world some of them think you're crazy.

BIFF (*angered*):   Screw the business world!

HAPPY: All right, screw it! Great, but cover yourself!

LINDA: Hap, Hap!

BIFF: I don't care what they think! They've laughed at Dad for years, and you know why? Because we don't belong in this nut-house of a city! We should be mixing cement on some open plain, or—or carpenters. A carpenter is allowed to whistle!

WILLY *walks in from the entrance of the house, at left.*

WILLY: Even your grandfather was better than a carpenter. (*Pause. They watch him.*) You never grew up. Bernard does not whistle in the elevator, I assure you.

BIFF (*as though to laugh* WILLY *out of it*):   Yeah, but you do, Pop.

WILLY: I never in my life whistled in an elevator! And who in the business world thinks I'm crazy?

BIFF: I didn't mean it like that, Pop. Now don't make a whole thing out of it, will ya?

WILLY: Go back to the West! Be a carpenter, a cowboy, enjoy yourself!

LINDA: Willy, he was just saying—

WILLY: I heard what he said!

HAPPY (*trying to quiet* WILLY):   Hey, Pop, come on now . . .

WILLY (*continuing over* HAPPY's *line*):   They laugh at me, heh? Go to Filene's, go to the Hub, go to Slattery's, Boston. Call out the name Willy Loman and see what happens! Big shot!

BIFF: All right, Pop.

WILLY: Big!

BIFF: All right!

WILLY: Why do you always insult me?

BIFF: I didn't say a word. (*To* LINDA.) Did I say a word?

LINDA: He didn't say anything, Willy.

WILLY (*going to the doorway of the livingroom*):   All right, good night, good night.

LINDA: Willy, dear, he just decided . . .

WILLY (*to* BIFF):   If you get tired hanging around tomorrow, paint the ceiling I put up in the livingroom.

BIFF: I'm leaving early tomorrow.

HAPPY: He's going to see Bill Oliver, Pop.

WILLY (*interestedly*):   Oliver? For what?

BIFF (*with reserve, but trying, trying*):   He always said he'd stake me. I'd like to go into business, so maybe I can take him up on it.

LINDA: Isn't that wonderful?

WILLY: Don't interrupt. What's wonderful about it? There's fifty men in the City of New York who'd stake him. (*To* BIFF.) Sporting goods?

BIFF: I guess so. I know something about it and—

WILLY: He knows something about it! You know sporting goods better than Spalding, for God's sake! How much is he giving you?

BIFF: I don't know, I didn't even see him yet, but—

WILLY: Then what're you talkin' about?

BIFF (*getting angry*):   Well, all I said was I'm gonna see him, that's all!

WILLY (*turning away*):   Ah, you're counting your chickens again.

BIFF (*starting left for the stairs*):   Oh, Jesus, I'm going to sleep!

WILLY (*calling after him*):   Don't curse in this house!

BIFF (*turning*):   Since when did you get so clean?

HAPPY (*trying to stop them*):   Wait a . . .

WILLY: Don't use that language to me! I won't have it!

HAPPY (*grabbing* BIFF, *shouts*):   Wait a minute! I got an idea. I got a feasible idea. Come here, Biff, let's talk this over now, let's talk some sense here. When I was down in Florida last time, I thought of a great idea to sell sporting goods. It just came back to me. You and I, Biff—we have a line, the Loman Line. We train a couple of weeks, and put on a couple of exhibitions, see?

WILLY: That's an idea!

HAPPY: Wait! We form two basketball teams, see? Two water-polo teams. We play each other. It's a million dollars' worth of publicity. Two brothers, see? The Loman Brothers. Displays in the Royal Palms—all the hotels. And banners over the ring and the basketball court: "Loman Brothers." Baby, we could sell sporting goods!

WILLY: That is a one-million-dollar idea.

LINDA: Marvelous!

BIFF: I'm in great shape as far as that's concerned.

HAPPY: And the beauty of it is, Biff, it wouldn't be like a business. We'd be out playin' ball again . . .

BIFF (*enthused*):   Yeah, that's . . .

WILLY: Million-dollar . . .

HAPPY: And you wouldn't get fed up with it, Biff. It'd be the family again. There'd be the old honor, and comradeship, and if you wanted to go off for a swim or some-thin'—well, you'd do it! Without some smart cooky gettin' up ahead of you!

WILLY: Lick the world! You guys together could absolutely lick the civilized world.

BIFF: I'll see Oliver tomorrow. Hap, if we could work that out . . .

LINDA: Maybe things are beginning to—

WILLY (*wildly enthused, to* LINDA):   Stop interrupting! (*To* BIFF.) But don't wear sport jacket and slacks when you see Oliver.

BIFF: No, I'll—

WILLY: A business suit, and talk as little as possible, and don't crack any jokes.

BIFF: He did like me. Always liked me.

LINDA: He loved you!

WILLY (*to* LINDA):   Will you stop! (*To* BIFF.) Walk in very serious. You are not ap-plying for a boy's job. Money is to pass. Be quiet, fine, and serious. Everybody likes a kidder, but nobody lends him money.

HAPPY: I'll try to get some myself, Biff. I'm sure I can.

WILLY: I can see great things for you, kids, I think your troubles are over. But re-member, start big and you'll end big. Ask for fifteen. How much you gonna ask for?

BIFF: Gee, I don't know—

WILLY: And don't say "Gee." "Gee" is a boy's word. A man walking in for fifteen thousand dollars does not say "Gee!"

BIFF: Ten, I think, would be top though.

WILLY: Don't be so modest. You always started too low. Walk in with a big laugh. Don't look worried. Start off with a couple of your good stories to lighten things up. It's not what you say, it's how you say it—because personality always wins the day.

LINDA: Oliver always thought the highest of him—

WILLY: Will you let me talk?

BIFF: Don't yell at her, Pop, will ya?

WILLY (*angrily*):   I was talking, wasn't I?

BIFF: I don't like you yelling at her all the time, and I'm tellin' you, that's all.

WILLY: What're you, takin' over this house?

LINDA: Willy—

WILLY (*turning on her*):   Don't take his side all the time, goddammit!

BIFF (*furiously*):   Stop yelling at her!

WILLY (*suddenly pulling on his cheek, beaten down, guilt ridden*):   Give my best to Bill Oliver—he may remember me. (*He exits through the livingroom doorway.*)

LINDA (*her voice subdued*):   What'd you have to start that for? (BIFF *turns away.*) You see how sweet he was as soon as you talked hopefully? (*She goes over to* BIFF.) Come up and say good night to him. Don't let him go to bed that way.

HAPPY: Come on, Biff, let's buck him up.

LINDA: Please, dear. Just say good night. It takes so little to make him happy. Come. (*She goes through the livingroom doorway, calling upstairs from within the livingroom.*) Your pa-jamas are hanging in the bathroom. Willy!

HAPPY (*looking toward where* LINDA *went out*):   What a woman! They broke the mold when they made her. You know that, Biff?

BIFF: He's off salary. My God, working on commission!

HAPPY: Well, let's face it: he's no hot-shot selling man. Except that sometimes, you have to admit, he's a sweet personality.

BIFF (*deciding*):   Lend me ten bucks, will ya? I want to buy some new ties.

HAPPY: I'll take you to a place I know. Beautiful stuff. Wear one of my striped shirts tomorrow.

BIFF: She got gray. Mom got awful old. Gee, I'm gonna go in to Oliver tomorrow and knock him for a—

HAPPY: Come on up. Tell that to Dad. Let's give him a whirl. Come on.

BIFF (*steamed up*):   You know, with ten thousand bucks, boy!

HAPPY (*as they go into the livingroom*):   That's the talk, Biff, that's the first time I've heard the old confidence out of you! (*From within the livingroom, fading off.*) You're gonna live with me, kid, and any babe you want just say the word . . . (*The last lines are hardly heard. They are mounting the stairs to their parents' bedroom.*)

LINDA (*entering her bedroom and addressing* WILLY, *who is in the bathroom. She is straightening the bed for him*):   Can you do anything about the shower? It drips.

WILLY (*from the bathroom*):   All of a sudden everything falls to pieces! Goddam plumbing, oughta be sued, those people. I hardly finished putting it in and the thing . . . (*His words rumble off.*)

LINDA: I'm just wondering if Oliver will remember him. You think he might?

WILLY (*coming out of the bathroom in his pajamas*):   Remember him? What's the matter with you, you crazy? If he'd've stayed with Oliver he'd be on top by now! Wait'll Oliver gets a look at him. You don't know the average caliber any more. The average young man today—(*he is getting into bed*)—is got a caliber of zero. Greatest thing in the world for him was to bum around.

BIFF *and* HAPPY *enter the bedroom. Slight pause.*

WILLY (*stops short, looking at* BIFF):   Glad to hear it, boy.

HAPPY: He wanted to say good night to you, sport.

WILLY (*to* BIFF):   Yeah. Knock him dead, boy. What'd you want to tell me?

BIFF: Just take it easy, Pop. Good night. (*He turns to go.*)

WILLY (*unable to resist*):   And if anything falls off the desk while you're talking to him—like a package or something—don't you pick it up. They have office boys for that.

LINDA: I'll make a big breakfast—

WILLY: Will you let me finish? (*To* BIFF.) Tell him you were in the business in the West. Not farm work.

BIFF: All right, Dad.

LINDA: I think everything—

WILLY (*going right through her speech*):   And don't undersell yourself. No less than fifteen thousand dollars.

BIFF (*unable to bear him*):   Okay. Good night, Mom. (*He starts moving.*)

WILLY: Because you got a greatness in you, Biff, remember that. You got all kinds a greatness . . . (*He lies back, exhausted.* BIFF *walks out.*)

LINDA (*calling after* BIFF):   Sleep well, darling!

HAPPY: I'm gonna get married, Mom. I wanted to tell you.

LINDA: Go to sleep, dear.

HAPPY (*going*):   I just wanted to tell you.

WILLY: Keep up the good work. (HAPPY *exits.*) God . . . remember that Ebbets Field game? The championship of the city?

LINDA: Just rest. Should I sing to you?

WILLY: Yeah. Sing to me. (LINDA *hums a soft lullaby.*) When that team came out—he was the tallest, remember?

LINDA: Oh, yes. And in gold.

BIFF *enters the darkened kitchen, takes a cigarette, and leaves the house. He comes downstage into a golden pool of light. He smokes, staring at the night.*

WILLY: Like a young god. Hercules—something like that. And the sun, the sun all around him. Remember how he waved to me? Right up from the field, with the representatives of three colleges standing by? And the buyers I brought, and the cheers when he came out—Loman, Loman, Loman! God Almighty, he'll be great yet. A star like that, magnificent, can never really fade away!

The light on WILLY *is fading. The gas heater begins to glow through the kitchen wall, near the stairs, a blue flame beneath red coils.*

LINDA (*timidly*):   Willy, dear, what has he got against you?

WILLY: I'm so tired. Don't talk any more.

BIFF *slowly returns to the kitchen. He stops, stares toward the heater.*

LINDA: Will you ask Howard to let you work in New York?

WILLY: First thing in the morning. Everything'll be all right.

BIFF *reaches behind the heater and draws out a length of rubber tubing. He is horrified and turns his head toward* WILLY*'s room, still dimly lit, from which the strains of* LINDA*'s desperate but monotonous humming rise.*

WILLY (*staring through the window into the moonlight*):   Gee, look at the moon moving between the buildings!

BIFF *wraps the tubing around his hand and quickly goes up the stairs. Curtain.*

ACT II

Music is heard, gay and bright. The curtain rises as the music fades away. WILLY, *in shirt sleeves, is sitting at the kitchen table, sipping coffee, his hat in his lap.* LINDA *is filling his cup when she can.*

WILLY: Wonderful coffee. Meal in itself.

LINDA: Can I make you some eggs?

WILLY: No. Take a breath.

LINDA: You look so rested, dear.

WILLY: I slept like a dead one. First time in months. Imagine, sleeping till ten on a Tuesday morning. Boys left nice and early, heh?

LINDA: They were out of here by eight o'clock.

WILLY: Good work!

LINDA: It was so thrilling to see them leaving together. I can't get over the shaving lotion in this house.

WILLY (*smiling*):   Mmm—

LINDA: Biff was very changed this morning. His whole attitude seemed to be hopeful. He couldn't wait to get downtown to see Oliver.

WILLY: He's heading for a change. There's no question, there simply are certain men that take longer to get—solidified. How did he dress?

LINDA: His blue suit. He's so handsome in that suit. He could be a—anything in that suit!

WILLY *gets up from the table.* LINDA *holds his jacket for him.*

WILLY: There's no question, no question at all. Gee, on the way home tonight I'd like to buy some seeds.

LINDA (*laughing*):   That'd be wonderful. But not enough sun gets back there. Nothing'll grow any more.

WILLY: You wait, kid, before it's all over we're gonna get a little place out in the country, and I'll raise some vegetables, a couple of chickens . . .

LINDA: You'll do it yet, dear.

WILLY *walks out of his jacket.* LINDA *follows him.*

WILLY: And they'll get married, and come for a weekend. I'd build a little guest house. 'Cause I got so many fine tools, all I'd need would be a little lumber and some peace of mind.

LINDA (*joyfully*):   I sewed the lining . . .

WILLY: I could build two guest houses, so they'd both come. Did he decide how much he's going to ask Oliver for?

LINDA (*getting him into the jacket*):   He didn't mention it, but I imagine ten or fifteen thousand. You going to talk to Howard today?

WILLY: Yeah. I'll put it to him straight and simple. He'll just have to take me off the road.

LINDA: And Willy, don't forget to ask for a little advance, because we've got the insurance premium. It's the grace period now.

WILLY: That's a hundred . . . ?

LINDA: A hundred and eight, sixty-eight. Because we're a little short again.

WILLY: Why are we short?

LINDA: Well, you had the motor job on the car . . .

WILLY: That goddam Studebaker!

LINDA: And you got one more payment on the refrigerator . . .

WILLY: But it just broke again!

LINDA: Well, it's old, dear.

WILLY: I told you we should've bought a well-advertised machine. Charley bought a General Electric and it's twenty years old and it's still good, that son-of-a-bitch.

LINDA: But, Willy—

WILLY: Whoever heard of a Hastings refrigerator? Once in my life I would like to own something outright before it's broken! I'm always in a race with the junkyard! I just finished paying for the car and it's on its last legs. The refrigerator consumes belts like a goddam maniac. They time those things. They time them so when you finally paid for them, they're used up.

LINDA (*buttoning up his jacket as he unbuttons it*):   All told, about two hundred dollars would carry us, dear. But that includes the last payment on the mortgage. After this payment, Willy, the house belongs to us.

WILLY: It's twenty-five years!

LINDA: Biff was nine years old when we bought it.

WILLY: Well, that's a great thing. To weather a twenty-five year mortgage is—

LINDA: It's an accomplishment.

WILLY: All the cement, the lumber, the reconstruction I put in this house! There ain't a crack to be found in it any more.

LINDA: Well, it served its purpose.

WILLY: What purpose? Some stranger'll come along, move in, and that's that. If only Biff would take this house, and raise a family . . . (*He starts to go.*) Good-by, I'm late.

LINDA (*suddenly remembering*):   Oh, I forgot! You're supposed to meet them for dinner.

WILLY: Me?

LINDA: At Frank's Chop House on Forty-eighth near Sixth Avenue.

WILLY: Is that so! How about you?

LINDA: No, just the three of you. They're gonna blow you to a big meal!

WILLY: Don't say! Who thought of that?

LINDA: Biff came to me this morning, Willy, and he said, "Tell Dad, we want to blow him to a big meal." Be there six o'clock. You and your two boys are going to have dinner.

WILLY: Gee whiz! That's really somethin'. I'm gonna knock Howard for a loop, kid. I'll get an advance, and I'll come home with a New York job. Goddammit, now I'm gonna do it!

LINDA: Oh, that's the spirit, Willy!

WILLY: I will never get behind a wheel the rest of my life!

LINDA: It's changing, Willy, I can feel it changing!

WILLY: Beyond a question. G'by, I'm late. (*He starts to go again.*)

LINDA (*calling after him as she runs to the kitchen table for a handkerchief*):   You got your glasses?

WILLY (*feels for them, then comes back in*):   Yeah, yeah, got my glasses.

LINDA (*giving him the handkerchief*):   And a handkerchief.

WILLY: Yeah, handkerchief.

LINDA: And your saccharine?

WILLY: Yeah, my saccharine.

LINDA: Be careful on the subway stairs.

She kisses him, and a silk stocking is seen hanging from her hand. WILLY *notices it.*

WILLY: Will you stop mending stockings? At least while I'm in the house. It gets me nervous. I can't tell you. Please.

LINDA *hides the stocking in her hand as she follows* WILLY *across the forestage in front of the house.*

LINDA: Remember, Frank's Chop House.

WILLY (*passing the apron*):   Maybe beets would grow out there.

LINDA (*laughing*):   But you tried so many times.

WILLY: Yeah. Well, don't work hard today. (*He disappears around the right corner of the house.*)

LINDA: Be careful!

As WILLY *vanishes,* LINDA *waves to him. Suddenly the phone rings. She runs across the stage and into the kitchen and lifts it.*

LINDA: Hello? Oh, Biff! I'm so glad you called, I just . . . Yes, sure, I just told him. Yes, he'll be there for dinner at six o'clock, I didn't forget. Listen, I was just dying to tell you. You know that little rubber pipe I told you about? That he connected to the gas heater? I finally decided to go down the cellar this morning and take it away and destroy it. But it's gone! Imagine? He took it away himself, it isn't there! (*She listens.*) When? Oh, then you took it. Oh—nothing, it's just that I'd hoped he'd taken it away himself. Oh, I'm not worried, darling, because this morning he left in such high spirits, it was like the old days! I'm not afraid any more. Did Mr. Oliver see you? . . . Well, you wait there then. And make a nice impression on him, darling. Just don't perspire too much before you see him. And have a nice time with Dad. He may have big news too! . . . That's right, a New York job. And be sweet to him tonight, dear. Be loving to him. Because he's only a little boat looking for a harbor. (*She is trembling with sorrow and joy.*) Oh, that's wonderful, Biff, you'll save his life. Thanks, darling. Just put your arm around him when he comes into the restaurant. Give him a smile. That's the boy . . . Good-by, dear. . . . You got your comb? . . . That's fine. Good-by, Biff dear.

In the middle of her speech, HOWARD WAGNER, *thirty-six, wheels in a small typewriter table on which is a wire-recording machine and proceeds to plug it in. This is on the left forestage. Light slowly fades on* LINDA *as it rises on* HOWARD. HOWARD *is intent on threading the machine and only glances over his shoulder as* WILLY *appears.*

WILLY: Pst! Pst!

HOWARD: Hello, Willy, come in.

WILLY: Like to have a little talk with you, Howard.

HOWARD: Sorry to keep you waiting. I'll be with you in a minute.

WILLY: What's that, Howard?

HOWARD: Didn't you ever see one of these? Wire recorder.

WILLY: Oh. Can we talk a minute?

HOWARD: Records things. Just got delivery yesterday. Been driving me crazy, the most terrific machine I ever saw in my life. I was up all night with it.

WILLY: What do you do with it?

HOWARD: I bought it for dictation, but you can do anything with it. Listen to this. I had it home last night. Listen to what I picked up. The first one is my daughter. Get this. (*He flicks the switch and "Roll out the Barrel" is heard being whistled.*) Listen to that kid whistle.

WILLY: That is lifelike, isn't it?

HOWARD: Seven years old. Get that tone.

WILLY: Ts, ts. Like to ask a little favor if you . . .

The whistling breaks off, and the voice of HOWARD'S DAUGHTER *is heard.*

HIS DAUGHTER: "Now you, Daddy."

HOWARD: She's crazy for me! (*Again the same song is whistled.*) That's me! Ha! (*He winks.*)

WILLY: You're very good!

The whistling breaks off again. The machine runs silent for a moment.

HOWARD: Sh! Get this now, this is my son.

HIS SON: "The capital of Alabama is Montgomery; the capital of Arizona is Phoenix; the capital of Arkansas is Little Rock; the capital of California is Sacramento . . ." (*And on, and on.*)

HOWARD (*holding up five fingers*):   Five years old, Willy!

WILLY: He'll make an announcer some day!

HIS SON (*continuing*):   "The capital . . ."

HOWARD: Get that—alphabetical order! (*The machine breaks off suddenly.*) Wait a minute. The maid kicked the plug out.

WILLY: It certainly is a—

HOWARD: Sh, for God's sake!

HIS SON: "It's nine o'clock, Bulova watch time. So I have to go to sleep."

WILLY: That really is—

HOWARD: Wait a minute! The next is my wife.

They wait.

HOWARD'S VOICE: "Go on, say something." (*Pause.*) "Well, you gonna talk?"

HIS WIFE: "I can't think of anything."

HOWARD'S VOICE: "Well, talk—it's turning."

HIS WIFE (*shyly, beaten*):   "Hello." (*Silence.*) "Oh, Howard, I can't talk into this . . ."

HOWARD (*snapping the machine off*):   That was my wife.

WILLY: That is a wonderful machine. Can we—

HOWARD: I tell you, Willy, I'm gonna take my camera, and my bandsaw, and all my hobbies, and out they go. This is the most fascinating relaxation I ever found.

WILLY: I think I'll get one myself.

HOWARD: Sure, they're only a hundred and a half. You can't do without it. Supposing you wanna hear Jack Benny, see? But you can't be at home at that hour. So you tell the maid to turn the radio on when Jack Benny comes on, and this automatically goes on with the radio . . .

WILLY: And when you come home you . . .

HOWARD: You can come home twelve o'clock, one o'clock, any time you like, and you get yourself a Coke and sit yourself down, throw the switch, and there's Jack Benny's program in the middle of the night!

WILLY: I'm definitely going to get one. Because lots of time I'm on the road, and I think to myself, what I must be missing on the radio!

HOWARD: Don't you have a radio in the car?

WILLY: Well, yeah, but who ever thinks of turning it on?

HOWARD: Say, aren't you supposed to be in Boston?

WILLY: That's what I want to talk to you about, Howard. You got a minute?

He draws a chair in from the wing.

HOWARD: What happened? What're you doing here?

WILLY: Well . . .

HOWARD: You didn't crack up again, did you?

WILLY: Oh, no. No . . .

HOWARD: Geez, you had me worried there for a minute. What's the trouble?

WILLY: Well, to tell you the truth, Howard, I've come to the decision that I'd rather not travel any more.

HOWARD: Not travel! Well, what'll you do?

WILLY: Remember, Christmas time, when you had the party here? You said you'd try to think of some spot for me here in town.

HOWARD: With us?

WILLY: Well, sure.

HOWARD: Oh, yeah, yeah. I remember. Well, I couldn't think of anything for you, Willy.

WILLY: I tell ya, Howard. The kids are all grown up, y'know. I don't need much any more. If I could take home—well, sixty-five dollars a week, I could swing it.

HOWARD: Yeah, but Willy, see I—

WILLY: I tell ya why, Howard. Speaking frankly and between the two of us, y'know—I'm just a little tired.

HOWARD: Oh, I could understand that, Willy. But you're a road man, Willy, and we do a road business. We've only got a half-dozen salesmen on the floor here.

WILLY: God knows, Howard, I never asked a favor of any man. But I was with the firm when your father used to carry you in here in his arms.

HOWARD: I know that, Willy, but—

WILLY: Your father came to me the day you were born and asked me what I thought of the name of Howard, may he rest in peace.

HOWARD: I appreciate that, Willy, but there just is no spot here for you. If I had a spot I'd slam you right in, but I just don't have a single, solitary spot.

He looks for his lighter. WILLY *has picked it up and gives it to him. Pause.*

WILLY (*with increasing anger*): Howard, all I need to set my table is fifty dollars a week.

HOWARD: But where am I going to put you, kid?

WILLY: Look, it isn't a question of whether I can sell merchandise, is it?

HOWARD: No, but it's a business, kid, and everybody's gotta pull his own weight.

WILLY (*desperately*): Just let me tell you a story, Howard—

HOWARD: 'Cause you gotta admit, business is business.

WILLY (*angrily*): Business is definitely business, but just listen for a minute. You don't understand this. When I was a boy—eighteen, nineteen—I was already on the road. And there was a question in my mind as to whether selling had a future for me. Because in those days I had a yearning to go to Alaska. See, there were three gold strikes in one month in Alaska, and I felt like going out. Just for the ride, you might say.

HOWARD (*barely interested*): Don't say.

WILLY: Oh, yeah, my father lived many years in Alaska. He was an adventurous man. We've got quite a little streak of self-reliance in our family. I thought I'd go out with my older brother and try to locate him, and maybe settle in the North with the old man. And I was almost decided to go, when I met a salesman in the Parker House. His name was Dave Singleman. And he was eighty-four years old, and he'd drummed merchandise in thirty-one states. And old Dave, he'd go up to his room, y'understand, put on his green velvet slippers—I'll never forget—and pick up his phone and call the buyers, and without ever leaving his room, at the age of eighty-four, he made his living. And when I saw that, I realized that selling was the greatest career a man could want. 'Cause what could be more satisfying than to be able to go, at the age of eighty-four, into twenty or thirty different cities, and pick up a phone, and be remembered and loved and helped by so many different people? Do you know? when he died—and by the way he died the death of a salesman, in his green velvet slippers in the smoker of the New York, New Haven and Hartford, going into Boston—when he died, hundreds of salesmen and buyers were at his funeral. Things were sad on a lotta trains for months after that. (*He stands up.* HOWARD *has not looked at him.*) In those days there was personality in it, Howard. There was respect, and comradeship, and gratitude in it. To-day, it's all cut and dried, and there's no chance for bringing friendship to bear—or personality. You see what I mean? They don't know me any more.

HOWARD (*moving away, to the right*):   That's just the thing, Willy.

WILLY: If I had forty dollars a week—that's all I'd need. Forty dollars, Howard.

HOWARD: Kid, I can't take blood from a stone, I—

WILLY (*desperation is on him now*):   Howard, the year Al Smith was nominated, your father came to me and—

HOWARD (*starting to go off*):   I've got to see some people, kid.

WILLY (*stopping him*):   I'm talking about your father! There were promises made across this desk! You mustn't tell me you've got people to see—I put thirty-four years into this firm, Howard, and now I can't pay my insurance! You can't eat the orange and throw the peel away—a man is not a piece of fruit! (*After a pause.*) Now pay attention. Your father—in 1928 I had a big year. I averaged a hundred and seventy dollars a week in commissions.

HOWARD (*impatiently*):   Now, Willy, you never averaged—

WILLY (*banging his hand on the desk*):   I averaged a hundred and seventy dollars a week in the year of 1928! And your father came to me—or rather, I was in the office here—it was right over this desk—and he put his hand on my shoulder—

HOWARD (*getting up*):   You'll have to excuse me, Willy, I gotta see some people. Pull yourself together. (*Going out.*) I'll be back in a little while.

On HOWARD's *exit, the light on his chair grows very bright and strange.*

WILLY: Pull myself together! What the hell did I say to him? My God, I was yelling at him! How could I! (WILLY *breaks off, staring at the light, which occupies the chair, animating it. He approaches this chair, standing across the desk from it.*) Frank, Frank, don't you remember what you told me that time? How you put your hand on my shoulder, and Frank . . . (*He leans on the desk and as he speaks the dead man's name he accidentally switches on the recorder, and instantly—*)

HOWARD'S SON: " . . . of New York is Albany. The capital of Ohio is Cincinnati, the capital of Rhode Island is . . ." (*The recitation continues.*)

WILLY (*leaping away with fright, shouting*):   Ha! Howard! Howard! Howard!

HOWARD (*rushing in*):   What happened?

WILLY (*pointing at the machine, which continues nasally, childishly, with the capital cities*): Shut it off! Shut it off!

HOWARD (*pulling the plug out*):   Look, Willy . . .

WILLY (*pressing his hands to his eyes*):   I gotta get myself some coffee. I'll get some coffee . . .

> WILLY *starts to walk out.* HOWARD *stops him.*

HOWARD (*rolling up the cord*):   Willy, look . . .

WILLY: I'll go to Boston.

HOWARD: Willy, you can't go to Boston for us.

WILLY: Why can't I go?

HOWARD: I don't want you to represent us. I've been meaning to tell you for a long time now.

WILLY: Howard, are you firing me?

HOWARD: I think you need a good long rest, Willy.

WILLY: Howard—

HOWARD: And when you feel better, come back, and we'll see if we can work something out.

WILLY: But I gotta earn money, Howard. I'm in no position—

HOWARD: Where are your sons? Why don't your sons give you a hand?

WILLY: They're working on a very big deal.

HOWARD: This is no time for false pride, Willy. You go to your sons and tell them that you're tired. You've got two great boys, haven't you?

WILLY: Oh, no question, no question, but in the meantime . . .

HOWARD: Then that's that, heh?

WILLY: All right, I'll go to Boston tomorrow.

HOWARD: No, no.

WILLY: I can't throw myself on my sons. I'm not a cripple!

HOWARD: Look, kid, I'm busy this morning.

WILLY (*grasping* HOWARD'S *arm*):   Howard, you've got to let me go to Boston!

HOWARD (*hard, keeping himself under control*):   I've got a line of people to see this morning. Sit down, take five minutes, and pull yourself together, and then go home, will ya? I need the office, Willy. (*He starts to go, turns, remembering the recorder, starts to push off the table holding the recorder.*) Oh, yeah. Whenever you can this week, stop by and drop off the samples. You'll feel better, Willy, and then come back and we'll talk. Pull yourself together, kid, there's people outside.

HOWARD *exits, pushing the table off left.* WILLY *stares into space, exhausted. Now the music is heard—*BEN'S *music—first distantly, then closer, closer. As* WILLY *speaks,* BEN *enters from the right. He carries valise and umbrella.*

WILLY: Oh, Ben, how did you do it? What is the answer? Did you wind up the Alaska deal already?

BEN: Doesn't take much time if you know what you're doing. Just a short business trip. Boarding ship in an hour. Wanted to say good-by.

WILLY: Ben, I've got to talk to you.

BEN (*glancing at his watch*):   Haven't the time, William.

WILLY (*crossing the apron to* BEN):   Ben, nothing's working out. I don't know what to do.

BEN: Now, look here, William. I've bought timberland in Alaska and I need a man to look after things for me.

WILLY: God, timberland! Me and my boys in those grand outdoors!

BEN: You've a new continent at your doorstep, William. Get out of these cities, they're full of talk and time payments and courts of law. Screw on your fists and you can fight for a fortune up there.

WILLY: Yes, yes! Linda! Linda!

LINDA *enters as of old, with the wash.*

LINDA: Oh, you're back?

BEN: I haven't much time.

WILLY: No, wait! Linda, he's got a proposition for me in Alaska.

LINDA: But you've got—(*To* BEN.) He's got a beautiful job here.

WILLY: But in Alaska, kid, I could—

LINDA: You're doing well enough, Willy!

BEN (*to* LINDA):   Enough for what, my dear?

LINDA (*frightened of* BEN *and angry at him*):   Don't say those things to him! Enough to be happy right here, right now. (*To* WILLY, *while* BEN *laughs.*) Why must everybody conquer the world? You're well liked, and the boys love you, and someday—(*to* BEN)— why, old man Wagner told him just the other day that if he keeps it up he'll be a member of the firm, didn't he, Willy?

WILLY: Sure, sure. I am building something with this firm, Ben, and if a man is building something he must be on the right track, mustn't he?

BEN: What are you building? Lay your hand on it. Where is it?

WILLY (*hesitantly*):   That's true, Linda, there's nothing.

LINDA: Why? (*To* BEN.) There's a man eighty-four years old—

WILLY: That's right, Ben, that's right. When I look at that man I say, what is there to worry about?

BEN: Bah!

WILLY: It's true, Ben. All he has to do is go into any city, pick up the phone, and he's making his living and you know why?

BEN (*picking up his valise*):   I've got to go.

WILLY (*holding* BEN *back*):   Look at this boy!

BIFF, *in his high school sweater, enters carrying suitcase.* HAPPY *carries* BIFF'*s shoulder guards, gold helmet, and football pants.*

WILLY: Without a penny to his name, three great universities are begging for him, and from there the sky's the limit, because it's not what you do, Ben. It's who you know and the smile on your face! It's contacts, Ben, contacts! The whole wealth of Alaska passes over the lunch table at the Commodore Hotel, and that's the wonder, the wonder of this country, that a man can end with diamonds here on the basis of being liked! (*He turns to* BIFF.) And that's why when you get out on that field today it's important. Because thousands of people will be rooting for you and loving you. (*To* BEN, *who has again begun to leave.*) And Ben! when he walks into a business office his name will sound out like a bell and all the doors will open to him! I've seen it, Ben, I've seen it a thousand times! You can't feel it with your hand like timber, but it's there!

BEN: Good-by, William.

WILLY: Ben, am I right? Don't you think I'm right? I value your advice.

BEN: There's a new continent at your doorstep, William. You could walk out rich. Rich. (*He is gone.*)

WILLY: We'll do it here, Ben! You hear me? We're gonna do it here!

Young BERNARD *rushes in. The gay music of the boys is heard.*

BERNARD: Oh, gee, I was afraid you left already!

WILLY: Why? What time is it?

BERNARD: It's half-past one!

WILLY: Well, come on, everybody! Ebbets Field next stop! Where's the pennants? (*He rushes through the wall-line of the kitchen and out into the livingroom.*)

LINDA (*to* BIFF):   Did you pack fresh underwear?

BIFF (*who has been limbering up*):   I want to go!

BERNARD: Biff, I'm carrying your helmet, ain't I?

HAPPY: No, I'm carrying the helmet.

BERNARD: Oh, Biff, you promised me.

HAPPY: I'm carrying the helmet.

BERNARD: How am I going to get in the locker room?

LINDA: Let him carry the shoulder guards. (*She puts her coat and hat on in the kitchen.*)

BERNARD: Can I, Biff? 'Cause I told everybody I'm going to be in the locker room.

HAPPY: In Ebbets Field it's the clubhouse.

BERNARD: I meant the clubhouse. Biff!

HAPPY: Biff!

BIFF (*grandly, after a slight pause*):   Let him carry the shoulder guards.

HAPPY (*as he gives* BERNARD *the shoulder guards*):   Stay close to us now.

WILLY *rushes in with the pennants.*

WILLY (*handing them out*):   Everybody wave when Biff comes out on the field. (HAPPY *and* BERNARD *run off.*) You set now, boy?

The music has died away.

BIFF: Ready to go, Pop. Every muscle is ready.

WILLY (*at the edge of the apron*):   You realize what this means?

BIFF: That's right, Pop.

WILLY (*feeling* BIFF's *muscles*):   You're comin' home this afternoon captain of the All-Scholastic Championship Team of the City of New York.

BIFF: I got it, Pop. And remember, pal, when I take off my helmet, that touchdown is for you.

WILLY: Let's go! (*He is starting out, with his arm around* BIFF, *when* CHARLEY *enters, as of old, in knickers.*) I got no room for you, Charley.

CHARLEY: Room? For what?

WILLY: In the car.

CHARLEY: You goin' for a ride? I wanted to shoot some casino.

WILLY (*furiously*):   Casino! (*Incredulously*): Don't you realize what today is?

LINDA: Oh, he knows, Willy. He's just kidding you.

WILLY: That's nothing to kid about!

CHARLEY: No, Linda, what's goin' on?

LINDA: He's playing in Ebbets Field.

CHARLEY: Baseball in this weather?

WILLY: Don't talk to him. Come on, come on! (*He is pushing them out.*)

CHARLEY: Wait a minute, didn't you hear the news?

WILLY: What?

CHARLEY: Don't you listen to the radio? Ebbets Field just blew up.

WILLY: You go to hell! (CHARLEY *laughs. Pushing them out.*) Come on, come on! We're late.

CHARLEY (*as they go*):   Knock a homer, Biff, knock a homer!

WILLY (*the last to leave, turning to* CHARLEY):   I don't think that was funny, Charley. This is the greatest day of his life.

CHARLEY: Willy, when are you going to grow up?

WILLY: Yeah, heh? When this game is over, Charley, you'll be laughing out of the other side of your face. They'll be calling him another Red Grange. Twenty-five thousand a year.

CHARLEY (*kidding*):   Is that so?

WILLY: Yeah, that's so.

CHARLEY: Well, then, I'm sorry, Willy. But tell me something.

WILLY: What?

CHARLEY: Who is Red Grange?

WILLY: Put up your hands. Goddam you, put up your hands!

CHARLEY, *chuckling, shakes his head and walks away, around the left corner of the stage.* WILLY *follows him. The music rises to a mocking frenzy.*

WILLY: Who the hell do you think you are, better than everybody else? You don't know everything, you big, ignorant, stupid . . . Put up your hands!

Light rises, on the right side of the forestage, on a small table in the reception room of CHARLEY's *office. Traffic sounds are heard.* BERNARD, *now mature, sits whistling to himself. A pair of tennis rackets and an overnight bag are on the floor beside him.*

WILLY (*offstage*):   What are you walking away for? Don't walk away! If you're going to say something say it to my face! I know you laugh at me behind my back. You'll laugh out of the other side of your goddam face after this game. Touchdown! Touchdown! Eighty thousand people! Touchdown! Right between the goal posts.

BERNARD *is a quiet, earnest, but self-assured young man.* WILLY's *voice is coming from right upstage now.* BERNARD *lowers his feet off the table and listens.* JENNY, *his father's secretary, enters.*

JENNY (distressed):   Say, Bernard, will you go out in the hall?

BERNARD: What is that noise? Who is it?

JENNY: Mr. Loman. He just got off the elevator.

BERNARD (*getting up*):   Who's he arguing with?

JENNY: Nobody. There's nobody with him. I can't deal with him any more, and your father gets all upset everytime he comes. I've got a lot of typing to do, and your father's waiting to sign it. Will you see him?

WILLY (*entering*):   Touchdown! Touch—(*He sees* JENNY.) Jenny, Jenny, good to see you. How're ya? Workin'? Or still honest?

JENNY: Fine. How've you been feeling?

WILLY: Not much any more, Jenny. Ha, ha! (*He is surprised to see the rackets.*)

BERNARD: Hello, Uncle Willy.

WILLY (*almost shocked*):   Bernard! Well, look who's here! (*He comes quickly, guiltily, to* BERNARD *and warmly shakes his hand.*)

BERNARD: How are you? Good to see you.

WILLY: What are you doing here?

BERNARD: Oh, just stopped by to see Pop. Get off my feet till my train leaves. I'm going to Washington in a few minutes.

WILLY: Is he in?

BERNARD: Yes, he's in his office with the accountant. Sit down.

WILLY (*sitting down*):   What're you going to do in Washington?

BERNARD: Oh, just a case I've got there, Willy.

WILLY: That so? (*indicating the rackets.*) You going to play tennis there?

BERNARD: I'm staying with a friend who's got a court.

WILLY: Don't say. His own tennis court. Must be fine people, I bet.

BERNARD: They are, very nice. Dad tells me Biff's in town.

WILLY (*with a big smile*):   Yeah, Biff's in. Working on a very big deal, Bernard.

BERNARD: What's Biff doing?

WILLY: Well, he's been doing very big things in the West. But he decided to establish himself here. Very big. We're having dinner. Did I hear your wife had a boy?

BERNARD: That's right. Our second.

WILLY: Two boys! What do you know!

BERNARD: What kind of a deal has Biff got?

WILLY: Well, Bill Oliver—very big sporting-goods man—he wants Biff very badly. Called him in from the West. Long distance, carte blanche, special deliveries. Your friends have their own private tennis court?

BERNARD: You still with the old firm, Willy?

WILLY (*after a pause*):   I'm—I'm overjoyed to see how you made the grade, Bernard, overjoyed. It's an encouraging thing to see a young man really—really—Looks very good for Biff—very—(*He breaks off, then.*) Bernard—(*He is so full of emotion, he breaks off again.*)

BERNARD: What is it, Willy?

WILLY (*small and alone*):   What—what's the secret?

BERNARD: What secret?

WILLY: How—how did you? Why didn't he ever catch on?

BERNARD: I wouldn't know that, Willy.

WILLY (*confidentially, desperately*):   You were his friend, his boyhood friend. There's something I don't understand about it. His life ended after that Ebbets Field game. From the age of seventeen nothing good ever happened to him.

BERNARD: He never trained himself for anything.

WILLY: But he did, he did. After high school he took so many correspondence courses. Radio mechanics; television; God knows what, and never made the slightest mark.

BERNARD (*taking off his glasses*):   Willy, do you want to talk candidly?

WILLY (*rising, faces* BERNARD):   I regard you as a very brilliant man, Bernard. I value your advice.

BERNARD: Oh, the hell with the advice, Willy. I couldn't advise you. There's just one thing I've always wanted to ask you. When he was supposed to graduate, and the math teacher flunked him—

WILLY: Oh, that son-of-a-bitch ruined his life.

BERNARD: Yeah, but, Willy, all he had to do was go to summer school and make up that subject.

WILLY: That's right, that's right.

BERNARD: Did you tell him not to go to summer school?

WILLY: Me? I begged him to go. I ordered him to go!

BERNARD: Then why wouldn't he go?

WILLY: Why? Why! Bernard, that question has been trailing me like a ghost for the last fifteen years. He flunked the subject, and laid down and died like a hammer hit him!

BERNARD: Take it easy, kid.

WILLY: Let me talk to you—I got nobody to talk to. Bernard, Bernard, was it my fault? Y'see? It keeps going around in my mind, maybe I did something to him. I got nothing to give him.

BERNARD: Don't take it so hard.

WILLY: Why did he lay down? What is the story there? You were his friend!

BERNARD: Willy, I remember, it was June, and our grades came out. And he'd flunked math.

WILLY: That son-of-a-bitch!

BERNARD: No, it wasn't right then. Biff just got very angry, I remember, and he was ready to enroll in summer school.

WILLY (*surprised*):   He was?

BERNARD: He wasn't beaten by it at all. But then, Willy, he disappeared from the block for almost a month. And I got the idea that he'd gone up to New England to see you. Did he have a talk with you then?

WILLY *stares in silence.*

BERNARD: Willy?

WILLY (*with a strong edge of resentment in his voice*):   Yeah, he came to Boston. What about it?

BERNARD: Well, just that when he came back—I'll never forget this, it always mystifies me. Because I'd thought so well of Biff, even though he'd always taken advantage of me. I loved him, Willy, y'know? And he came back after that month and took his sneakers—remember those sneakers with "University of Virginia" printed on them? He was so proud of those, wore them every day. And he took them down in the cellar, and burned them up in the furnace. We had a fist fight. It lasted at least half an hour. Just the two of us, punching each other down the cellar, and crying right through it. I've often thought of how strange it was that I knew he'd given up his life. What happened in Boston, Willy?

WILLY *looks at him as at an intruder.*

BERNARD: I just bring it up because you asked me.

WILLY (*angrily*):   Nothing. What do you mean, "What happened?" What's that got to do with anything?

BERNARD: Well, don't get sore.

WILLY: What are you trying to do, blame it on me? If a boy lays down is that my fault?

BERNARD: Now, Willy, don't get—

WILLY: Well, don't—don't talk to me that way! What does that mean, "What happened?"

CHARLEY *enters. He is in his vest, and he carries a bottle of bourbon.*

CHARLEY: Hey, you're going to miss that train. (*He waves the bottle.*)

BERNARD: Yeah, I'm going. (*He takes the bottle.*) Thanks, Pop. (*He picks up his rackets and bag.*) Good-by, Willy, and don't worry about it. You know, "If at first you don't succeed . . ."

WILLY: Yes, I believe in that.

BERNARD: But sometimes, Willy, it's better for a man just to walk away.

WILLY: Walk away?

BERNARD: That's right.

WILLY: But if you can't walk away?

BERNARD (*after a slight pause*):   I guess that's when it's tough. (*Extending his hand.*) Good-by, Willy.

WILLY (*shaking* BERNARD'*s hand*):   Good-by, boy.

CHARLEY (*an arm on* BERNARD'*s shoulder*):   How do you like this kid? Gonna argue a case in front of the Supreme Court.

BERNARD (*protesting*):   Pop!

WILLY (*genuinely shocked, pained, and happy*):   No! The Supreme Court!

BERNARD: I gotta run. 'By, Dad!

CHARLEY: Knock 'em dead, Bernard!

BERNARD *goes off.*

WILLY (*as* CHARLEY *takes out his wallet*):   The Supreme Court! And he didn't even mention it!

CHARLEY (*counting out money on the desk*):   He don't have to—he's gonna do it.

WILLY: And you never told him what to do, did you? You never took any interest in him.

CHARLEY: My salvation is that I never took any interest in anything. There's some money—fifty dollars. I got an accountant inside.

WILLY: Charley, look . . . (*With difficulty.*) I got my insurance to pay. If you can manage it—I need a hundred and ten dollars.

CHARLEY *doesn't reply for a moment; merely stops moving.*

WILLY: I'd draw it from my bank but Linda would know, and I . . .

CHARLEY: Sit down, Willy.

WILLY (*moving toward the chair*):   I'm keeping an account of everything, remember. I'll pay every penny back. (*He sits.*)

CHARLEY: Now listen to me, Willy.

WILLY: I want you to know I appreciate . . .

CHARLEY (*sitting down on the table*):   Willy, what're you doin'? What the hell is goin' on in your head?

WILLY: Why? I'm simply . . .

CHARLEY: I offered you a job. You can make fifty dollars a week. And I won't send you on the road.

WILLY: I've got a job.

CHARLEY: Without pay? What kind of a job is a job without pay? (*He rises.*) Now, look, kid, enough is enough. I'm no genius but I know when I'm being insulted.

WILLY: Insulted!

CHARLEY: Why don't you want to work for me?

WILLY: What's the matter with you? I've got a job.

CHARLEY: Then what're you walkin' in here every week for?

WILLY (*getting up*):   Well, if you don't want me to walk in here—

CHARLEY: I am offering you a job.

WILLY: I don't want your goddam job!

CHARLEY: When the hell are you going to grow up?

WILLY (*furiously*):   You big ignoramus, if you say that to me again I'll rap you one! I don't care how big you are! (*He's ready to fight.*)

Pause.

CHARLEY (*kindly, going to him*):   How much do you need, Willy?

WILLY: Charley, I'm strapped. I'm strapped. I don't know what to do. I was just fired.

CHARLEY: Howard fired you?

WILLY: That snotnose. Imagine that? I named him. I named him Howard.

CHARLEY: Willy, when're you gonna realize that them things don't mean anything? You named him Howard, but you can't sell that. The only thing you got in this world is what you can sell. And the funny thing is that you're a salesman, and you don't know that.

WILLY: I've always tried to think otherwise, I guess. I always felt that if a man was impressive, and well liked, that nothing—

CHARLEY: Why must everybody like you? Who liked J. P. Morgan? Was he impressive? In a Turkish bath he'd look like a butcher. But with his pockets on he was very well liked. Now listen, Willy, I know you don't like me, and nobody can say I'm in love with you, but I'll give you a job because—just for the hell of it, put it that way. Now what do you say?

WILLY: I—I just can't work for you, Charley.

CHARLEY: What're you, jealous of me?

WILLY: I can't work for you, that's all, don't ask me why.

CHARLEY (*angered, takes out more bills*):   You been jealous of me all your life, you damned fool! Here, pay your insurance. (*He puts the money in* WILLY'S *hand.*)

WILLY: I'm keeping strict accounts.

CHARLEY: I've got some work to do. Take care of yourself. And pay your insurance.

WILLY (*moving to the right*):   Funny, y'know? After all the highways, and the trains, and the appointments, and the years, you end up worth more dead than alive.

CHARLEY: Willy, nobody's worth nothin' dead. (*After a slight pause.*) Did you hear what I said?

WILLY *stands still, dreaming.*

CHARLEY: Willy!

WILLY: Apologize to Bernard for me when you see him. I didn't mean to argue with him. He's a fine boy. They're all fine boys, and they'll end up big—all of them. Someday they'll all play tennis together. Wish me luck, Charley. He saw Bill Oliver today.

CHARLEY: Good luck.

WILLY (*on the verge of tears*):   Charley, you're the only friend I got. Isn't that a remarkable thing? (*He goes out.*)

CHARLEY: Jesus!

CHARLEY *stares after him a moment and follows. All light blacks out. Suddenly raucous music is heard, and a red glow rises behind the screen at right.* STANLEY, *a young waiter, appears, carrying a table, followed by* HAPPY, *who is carrying two chairs.*

STANLEY (*putting the table down*):   That's all right, Mr. Loman, I can handle it myself. (*He turns and takes the chairs from* HAPPY *and places them at the table.*)

HAPPY (*glancing around*):   Oh, this is better.

STANLEY: Sure, in the front there you're in the middle of all kinds a noise. Whenever you got a party, Mr. Loman, you just tell me and I'll put you back here. Y'know, there's a lotta people they don't like it private, because when they go out they like to see a lotta action around them because they're sick and tired to stay in the house by theirself. But I know you, you ain't from Hackensack. You know what I mean?

HAPPY (*sitting down*):   So how's it coming, Stanley?

STANLEY: Ah, it's a dog's life. I only wish during the war they'd a took me in the Army. I coulda been dead by now.

HAPPY: My brother's back, Stanley.

STANLEY: Oh, he come back, heh? From the Far West.

HAPPY: Yeah, big cattle man, my brother, so treat him right. And my father's coming too.

STANLEY: Oh, your father too!

HAPPY: You got a couple of nice lobsters?

STANLEY: Hundred per cent, big.

HAPPY: I want them with the claws.

STANLEY: Don't worry, I don't give you no mice. (HAPPY *laughs.*) How about some wine? It'll put a head on the meal.

HAPPY: No. You remember, Stanley, that recipe I brought you from overseas? With the champagne in it?

STANLEY: Oh, yeah, sure. I still got it tacked up yet in the kitchen. But that'll have to cost a buck apiece anyways.

HAPPY: That's all right.

STANLEY: What'd you, hit a number or somethin'?

HAPPY: No, it's a little celebration. My brother is—I think he pulled off a big deal today. I think we're going into business together.

STANLEY: Great! That's the best for you. Because a family business, you know what I mean?—that's the best.

HAPPY: That's what I think.

STANLEY: 'Cause what's the difference? Somebody steals? It's in the family. Know what I mean? (*Sotto voce.*) Like this bartender here. The boss is goin' crazy what kinda leak he's got in the cash register. You put it in but it don't come out.

HAPPY (*raising his head*):   Sh!

STANLEY: What?

HAPPY: You notice I wasn't lookin' right or left, was I!

STANLEY: No.

HAPPY: And my eyes are closed.

STANLEY: So what's the—?

HAPPY: Strudel's comin'.

STANLEY (*catching on, looks around*):   Ah, no, there's no—

He breaks off as a furred, lavishly dressed GIRL *enters and sits at the next table. Both follow her with their eyes.*

STANLEY: Geez, how'd ya know?

HAPPY: I got radar or something. (*Staring directly at her profile.*) Oooooooo . . . Stanley.

STANLEY: I think that's for you, Mr. Loman.

HAPPY: Look at that mouth. Oh, God. And the binoculars.

STANLEY: Geez, you got a life, Mr. Loman.

HAPPY: Wait on her.

STANLEY (*going to* THE GIRL'*s table*):   Would you like a menu, ma'am?

GIRL: I'm expecting someone, but I'd like a—

HAPPY: Why don't you bring her—excuse me, miss, do you mind? I sell champagne, and I'd like you to try my brand. Bring her a champagne, Stanley.

GIRL: That's awfully nice of you.

HAPPY: Don't mention it. It's all company money. (*He laughs.*)

GIRL: That's a charming product to be selling, isn't it?

HAPPY: Oh, gets to be like everything else. Selling is selling, y'know.

GIRL: I suppose.

HAPPY: You don't happen to sell, do you?

GIRL: No, I don't sell.

HAPPY: Would you object to a compliment from a stranger? You ought to be on a magazine cover.

GIRL (*looking at him a little archly*):   I have been.

STANLEY *comes in with a glass of champagne.*

HAPPY: What'd I say before, Stanley? You see? She's a cover girl.

STANLEY: Oh, I could see, I could see.

HAPPY (*to* THE GIRL):   What magazine?

GIRL: Oh, a lot of them. (*She takes the drink.*) Thank you.

HAPPY: You know what they say in France, don't you? "Champagne is the drink of the complexion"—Hya, Biff!

BIFF *has entered and sits with* HAPPY.

BIFF: Hello, kid. Sorry I'm late.

HAPPY: I just got here. Uh, Miss—?

GIRL: Forsythe.

HAPPY: Miss Forsythe, this is my brother.

BIFF: Is Dad here?

HAPPY: His name is Biff. You might've heard of him. Great football player.

GIRL: Really? What team?

HAPPY: Are you familiar with football?

GIRL: No, I'm afraid I'm not.

HAPPY: Biff is quarterback with the New York Giants.

GIRL: Well, that is nice, isn't it? (*She drinks.*)

HAPPY: Good health.

GIRL: I'm happy to meet you.

HAPPY: That's my name. Hap. It's really Harold, but at West Point they called me Happy.

GIRL (*now really impressed*): Oh, I see. How do you do? (*She turns her profile.*)

BIFF: Isn't Dad coming?

HAPPY: You want her?

BIFF: Oh, I could never make that.

HAPPY: I remember the time that idea would never come into your head. Where's the old confidence, Biff?

BIFF: I just saw Oliver—

HAPPY: Wait a minute. I've got to see that old confidence again. Do you want her? She's on call.

BIFF: Oh, no. (*He turns to look at* THE GIRL.)

HAPPY: I'm telling you. Watch this. (*Turning to* THE GIRL.) Honey? (*She turns to him.*) Are you busy?

GIRL: Well, I am . . . but I could make a phone call.

HAPPY: Do that, will you, honey? And see if you can get a friend. We'll be here for a while. Biff is one of the greatest football players in the country.

GIRL (*standing up*): Well, I'm certainly happy to meet you.

HAPPY: Come back soon.

GIRL: I'll try.

HAPPY: Don't try, honey, try hard.

THE GIRL *exits.* STANLEY *follows, shaking his head in bewildered admiration.*

HAPPY: Isn't that a shame now? A beautiful girl like that? That's why I can't get married. There's not a good woman in a thousand. New York is loaded with them, kid!

BIFF: Hap, look—

HAPPY: I told you she was on call!

BIFF (*strangely unnerved*): Cut it out, will ya? I want to say something to you.

HAPPY: Did you see Oliver?

BIFF: I saw him all right. Now look, I want to tell Dad a couple of things and I want you to help me.

HAPPY: What? Is he going to back you?

BIFF: Are you crazy? You're out of your goddam head, you know that?

HAPPY: Why? What happened?

BIFF (*breathlessly*): I did a terrible thing today, Hap. It's been the strangest day I ever went through. I'm all numb, I swear.

HAPPY: You mean he wouldn't see you?

BIFF: Well, I waited six hours for him, see? All day. Kept sending my name in. Even tried to date his secretary so she'd get me to him, but no soap.

HAPPY: Because you're not showin' the old confidence, Biff. He remembered you, didn't he?

BIFF (*stopping* HAPPY *with a gesture*):   Finally, about five o'clock, he comes out. Didn't remember who I was or anything. I felt like such an idiot, Hap.

HAPPY: Did you tell him my Florida idea?

BIFF: He walked away. I saw him for one minute. I got so mad I could've torn the walls down! How the hell did I ever get the idea I was a salesman there? I even believed myself that I'd been a salesman for him! And then he gave me one look and—I realized what a ridiculous lie my whole life has been! We've been talking in a dream for fifteen years. I was a shipping clerk.

HAPPY: What'd you do?

BIFF (*with great tension and wonder*):   Well, he left, see. And the secretary went out. I was all alone in the waiting-room. I don't know what came over me, Hap. The next thing I know I'm in his office—paneled walls, everything. I can't explain it. I—Hap, I took his fountain pen.

HAPPY: Geez, did he catch you?

BIFF: I ran out. I ran down all eleven flights. I ran and ran and ran.

HAPPY: That was an awful dumb—what'd you do that for?

BIFF (*agonized*):   I don't know, I just—wanted to take something, I don't know. You gotta help me, Hap. I'm gonna tell Pop.

HAPPY: You crazy? What for?

BIFF: Hap, he's got to understand that I'm not the man somebody lends that kind of money to. He thinks I've been spiting him all these years and it's eating him up.

HAPPY: That's just it. You tell him something nice.

BIFF: I can't.

HAPPY: Say you got a lunch date with Oliver tomorrow.

BIFF: So what do I do tomorrow?

HAPPY: You leave the house tomorrow and come back at night and say Oliver is thinking it over. And he thinks it over for a couple of weeks, and gradually it fades away and nobody's the worse.

BIFF: But it'll go on forever!

HAPPY: Dad is never so happy as when he's looking forward to something!

WILLY enters.

HAPPY: Hello, scout!

WILLY: Gee, I haven't been here in years!

STANLEY *has followed* WILLY *in and sets a chair for him.* STANLEY *starts off but* HAPPY *stops him.*

HAPPY: Stanley!

STANLEY stands by, waiting for an order.

BIFF (*going to* WILLY *with guilt, as to an invalid*):   Sit down, Pop. You want a drink?

WILLY: Sure, I don't mind.

BIFF: Let's get a load on.

WILLY: You look worried.

BIFF: N-no. (*To* STANLEY.) Scotch all around. Make it doubles.

STANLEY: Doubles, right. (*He goes.*)

WILLY: You had a couple already, didn't you?

BIFF: Just a couple, yeah.

WILLY: Well, what happened, boy? (*Nodding affirmatively, with a smile.*) Everything go all right?

BIFF (*takes a breath, then reaches out and grasps* WILLY's *hand*):   Pal . . . (*He is smiling bravely, and* WILLY *is smiling too.*) I had an experience today.

HAPPY: Terrific, Pop.

WILLY: That so? What happened?

BIFF (*high, slightly alcoholic, above the earth*):   I'm going to tell you everything from first to last. It's been a strange day. (*Silence. He looks around, composes himself as best he can, but his breath keeps breaking the rhythm of his voice.*) I had to wait quite a while for him, and—

WILLY: Oliver?

BIFF: Yeah, Oliver. All day, as a matter of cold fact. And a lot of—instances—facts, Pop, facts about my life came back to me. Who was it, Pop? Who ever said I was a salesman with Oliver?

WILLY: Well, you were.

BIFF: No, Dad, I was a shipping clerk.

WILLY: But you were practically—

BIFF (*with determination*):   Dad, I don't know who said it first, but I was never a salesman for Bill Oliver.

WILLY: What're you talking about?

BIFF: Let's hold on to the facts tonight, Pop. We're not going to get anywhere bullin' around. I was a shipping clerk.

WILLY (*angrily*):   All right, now listen to me—

BIFF: Why don't you let me finish?

WILLY: I'm not interested in stories about the past or any crap of that kind because the woods are burning, boys, you understand? There's a big blaze going on all around. I was fired today.

BIFF (*shocked*):   How could you be?

WILLY: I was fired, and I'm looking for a little good news to tell your mother, be-cause the woman has waited and the woman has suffered. The gist of it is that I haven't got a story left in my head, Biff. So don't give me a lecture about facts and aspects. I am not interested. Now what've you got to say to me?

STANLEY *enters with three drinks. They wait until he leaves.*

WILLY: Did you see Oliver?

BIFF: Jesus, Dad!

WILLY: You mean you didn't go up there?

HAPPY: Sure he went up there.

BIFF: I did. I—saw him. How could they fire you?

WILLY (*on the edge of his chair*):   What kind of a welcome did he give you?

BIFF: He won't even let you work on commission?

WILLY: I'm out! (*Driving.*) So tell me, he gave you a warm welcome?

HAPPY: Sure, Pop, sure!

BIFF (*driven*):   Well, it was kind of—

WILLY: I was wondering if he'd remember you. (*To* HAPPY.) Imagine, man doesn't see him for ten, twelve years and gives him that kind of a welcome!

HAPPY: Damn right!

BIFF (*trying to return to the offensive*):   Pop, look—

WILLY: You know why he remembered you, don't you? Because you impressed him in those days.

BIFF: Let's talk quietly and get this down to the facts, huh?

WILLY (*as though* BIFF *had been interrupting*):   Well, what happened? It's great news, Biff. Did he take you into his office or'd you talk in the waiting room?

BIFF: Well, he came in, see, and—

WILLY: (*with a big smile*):   What'd he say? Betcha he threw his arm around you.

BIFF: Well, he kinda—

WILLY: He's a fine man. (*To* HAPPY.) Very hard man to see, y'know.

HAPPY (*agreeing*):   Oh, I know.

WILLY (*to* BIFF):   Is that where you had the drinks?

BIFF: Yeah, he gave me a couple of—no, no!

HAPPY (*cutting in*):   He told him my Florida idea.

WILLY: Don't interrupt. (*To* BIFF.) How'd he react to the Florida idea?

BIFF: Dad, will you give me a minute to explain?

WILLY: I've been waiting for you to explain since I sat down here! What happened? He took you into his office and what?

BIFF: Well—I talked. And—and he listened, see.

WILLY: Famous for the way he listens, y'know. What was his answer?

BIFF: His answer was—(*He breaks off, suddenly angry.*) Dad, you're not letting me tell you what I want to tell you!

WILLY (*accusing, angered*):   You didn't see him, did you?

BIFF: I did see him!

WILLY: What'd you insult him or something? You insulted him, didn't you?

BIFF: Listen, will you let me out of it, will you just let me out of it!

HAPPY: What the hell!

WILLY: Tell me what happened!

BIFF (*to* HAPPY):   I can't talk to him!

A single trumpet note jars the ear. The light of green leaves stains the house, which holds the air of night and a dream. YOUNG BERNARD *enters and knocks on the door of the house.*

YOUNG BERNARD (*frantically*):   Mrs. Loman, Mrs. Loman!

HAPPY: Tell him what happened!

BIFF (*to* HAPPY):   Shut up and leave me alone!

WILLY: No, no! You had to go and flunk math!

BIFF: What math? What're you talking about?

YOUNG BERNARD: Mrs. Loman, Mrs. Loman!

LINDA *appears in the house, as of old.*

WILLY (*wildly*):   Math, math, math!

BIFF: Take it easy, Pop!

YOUNG BERNARD: Mrs. Loman!

WILLY (*furiously*):   If you hadn't flunked you'd've been set by now!

BIFF: Now, look, I'm gonna tell you what happened, and you're going to listen to me.

YOUNG BERNARD: Mrs. Loman!

BIFF: I waited six hours—

HAPPY: What the hell are you saying?

BIFF: I kept sending in my name but he wouldn't see me. So finally he . . . (*He continues unheard as light fades low on the restaurant.*)

YOUNG BERNARD: Biff flunked math!

LINDA: No!

YOUNG BERNARD: Birnbaum flunked him! They won't graduate him!

LINDA: But they have to. He's gotta go to the university. Where is he? Biff! Biff!

YOUNG BERNARD: No, he left. He went to Grand Central.

LINDA: Grand—You mean he went to Boston!

YOUNG BERNARD: Is Uncle Willy in Boston?

LINDA: Oh, maybe Willy can talk to the teacher. Oh, the poor, poor boy!

Light on house area snaps out.

BIFF (*at the table, now audible, holding up a gold fountain pen*):   . . . so I'm washed up with Oliver, you understand? Are you listening to me?

WILLY (*at a loss*):   Yeah, sure. If you hadn't flunked—

BIFF: Flunked what? What're you talking about?

WILLY: Don't blame everything on me! I didn't flunk math—you did! What pen?

HAPPY: That was awful dumb, Biff, a pen like that is worth—

WILLY (*seeing the pen for the first time*):   You took Oliver's pen?

BIFF (*weakening*):   Dad, I just explained it to you.

WILLY: You stole Bill Oliver's fountain pen!

BIFF: I didn't exactly steal it! That's just what I've been explaining to you!

HAPPY: He had it in his hand and just then Oliver walked in, so he got nervous and stuck it in his pocket!

WILLY: My God, Biff!

BIFF: I never intended to do it, Dad!

OPERATOR'S VOICE: Standish Arms, good evening!

WILLY (*shouting*):   I'm not in my room!

BIFF (*frightened*):   Dad, what's the matter? (*He and* HAPPY *stand up.*)

OPERATOR: Ringing Mr. Loman for you!

WILLY: I'm not there, stop it!

BIFF (*horrified, gets down on one knee before* WILLY):   Dad, I'll make good, I'll make good. (WILLY *tries to get to his feet.* BIFF *holds him down.*) Sit down now.

WILLY: No, you're no good, you're no good for anything.

BIFF: I am, Dad, I'll find something else, you understand? Now don't worry about anything. (*He holds up* WILLY's *face.*) Talk to me, Dad.

OPERATOR: Mr. Loman does not answer. Shall I page him?

WILLY (*attempting to stand, as though to rush and silence the* OPERATOR):   No, no, no!

HAPPY: He'll strike something, Pop.

WILLY: No, no . . .

BIFF (*desperately, standing over* WILLY):   Pop, listen! Listen to me! I'm telling you something good. Oliver talked to his partner about the Florida idea. You listening? He—he talked to his partner, and he came to me . . . I'm going to be all right, you hear? Dad, listen to me, he said it was just a question of the amount!

WILLY: Then you . . . got it?

HAPPY: He's gonna be terrific, Pop!

WILLY (*trying to stand*):   Then you got it, haven't you? You got it! You got it!

BIFF (*agonized, holds* WILLY *down*):   No, no. Look, Pop. I'm supposed to have lunch with them tomorrow. I'm just telling you this so you'll know that I can still make an impression, Pop. And I'll make good somewhere, but I can't go tomorrow, see?

WILLY: Why not? You simply—

BIFF: But the pen, Pop!

WILLY: You give it to him and tell him it was an oversight!

HAPPY: Sure, have lunch tomorrow!

BIFF: I can't say that—

WILLY: You were doing a crossword puzzle and accidentally used his pen!

BIFF: Listen, kid, I took those balls years ago, now I walk in with his fountain pen? That clinches it, don't you see? I can't face him like that! I'll try elsewhere.

PAGE'S VOICE: Paging Mr. Loman!

WILLY: Don't you want to be anything?

BIFF: Pop, how can I go back?

WILLY: You don't want to be anything, is that what's behind it?

BIFF (*now angry at* WILLY *for not crediting his sympathy*):   Don't take it that way! You think it was easy walking into that office after what I'd done to him? A team of horses couldn't have dragged me back to Bill Oliver!

WILLY: Then why'd you go?

BIFF: Why did I go? Why did I go? Look at you! Look at what's become of you!

Off left, THE WOMAN *laughs.*

WILLY: Biff, you're going to go to that lunch tomorrow, or—

BIFF: I can't go. I've got no appointment!

HAPPY: Biff, for . . . !

WILLY: Are you spiting me?

BIFF: Don't take it that way! Goddammit!

WILLY (*strikes* BIFF *and falters away from the table*):   You rotten little louse! Are you spiting me?

THE WOMAN: Someone's at the door, Willy!

BIFF: I'm no good, can't you see what I am?

HAPPY (*separating them*):   Hey, you're in a restaurant! Now cut it out, both of you! (THE GIRLS *enter.*) Hello, girls, sit down.

THE WOMAN *laughs, off left.*

MISS FORSYTHE: I guess we might as well. This is Letta.

THE WOMAN: Willy, are you going to wake up?

BIFF (*ignoring* WILLY):   How're ya, miss, sit down. What do you drink?

MISS FORSYTHE: Letta might not be able to stay long.

LETTA: I gotta get up very early tomorrow. I got jury duty. I'm so excited! Were you fellows ever on a jury?

BIFF: No, but I been in front of them! (THE GIRLS *laugh*.) This is my father.

LETTA: Isn't he cute? Sit down with us, Pop.

HAPPY: Sit him down, Biff!

BIFF (*going to him*):   Come on, slugger, drink us under the table. To hell with it! Come on, sit down, pal.

On BIFF's *last insistence,* WILLY *is about to sit.*

THE WOMAN (*now urgently*):   Willy, are you going to answer the door!

THE WOMAN's *call pulls* WILLY *back. He starts right, befuddled.*

BIFF: Hey, where are you going?

WILLY: Open the door.

BIFF: The door?

WILLY: The washroom . . . the door . . . where's the door?

BIFF (*leading* WILLY *to the left*):   Just go straight down.

WILLY *moves left.*

THE WOMAN: Willy, Willy, are you going to get up, get up, get up, get up?

WILLY *exits left.*

LETTA: I think it's sweet you bring your daddy along.

MISS FORSYTHE: Oh, he isn't really your father!

BIFF (*at left, turning to her resentfully*):   Miss Forsythe, you've just seen a prince walk by. A fine, troubled prince. A hard-working, unappreciated prince. A pal, you understand? A good companion. Always for his boys.

LETTA: That's so sweet.

HAPPY: Well, girls, what's the program? We're wasting time. Come on, Biff. Gather round. Where would you like to go?

BIFF: Why don't you do something for him?

HAPPY: Me!

BIFF: Don't you give a damn for him, Hap?

HAPPY: What're you talking about? I'm the one who—

BIFF: I sense it, you don't give a good goddam about him. (*He takes the rolled-up hose from his pocket and puts it on the table in front of* HAPPY.) Look what I found in the cellar, for Christ's sake. How can you bear to let it go on?

HAPPY: Me? Who goes away? Who runs off and—

BIFF: Yeah, but he doesn't mean anything to you. You could help him—I can't! Don't you understand what I'm talking about? He's going to kill himself, don't you know that?

HAPPY: Don't I know it! Me!

BIFF: Hap, help him! Jesus . . . help him . . . Help me, help me, I can't bear to look at his face! (*Ready to weep, he hurries out, up right.*)

HAPPY (*starting after him*):   Where are you going?

MISS FORSYTHE: What's he so mad about?

HAPPY: Come on, girls, we'll catch up with him.

MISS FORSYTHE (*as* HAPPY *pushes her out*):   Say, I don't like that temper of his!

HAPPY: He's just a little overstrung, he'll be all right!

WILLY (*off left, as* THE WOMAN *laughs*):   Don't answer! Don't answer!

LETTA: Don't you want to tell your father—

HAPPY: No, that's not my father. He's just a guy. Come on, we'll catch Biff, and, honey, we're going to paint this town! Stanley, where's the check! Hey, Stanley!

They exit. STANLEY *looks toward left.*

STANLEY (*calling to* HAPPY *indignantly*):   Mr. Loman! Mr. Loman!

STANLEY *picks up a chair and follows them off. Knocking is heard off left.* THE WOMAN *enters, laughing.* WILLY *follows her. She is in a black slip; he is buttoning his shirt. Raw, sensuous music accompanies their speech.*

WILLY: Will you stop laughing? Will you stop?

THE WOMAN: Aren't you going to answer the door? He'll wake the whole hotel.

WILLY: I'm not expecting anybody.

THE WOMAN: Whyn't you have another drink, honey, and stop being so damn self-centered?

WILLY: I'm so lonely.

THE WOMAN: You know you ruined me, Willy? From now on, whenever you come to the office, I'll see that you go right through to the buyers. No waiting at my desk any more, Willy. You ruined me.

WILLY: That's nice of you to say that.

THE WOMAN: Gee, you are self-centered! Why so sad? You are the saddest self-centeredest soul I ever did see-saw. (*She laughs. He kisses her.*) Come on inside, drummer boy. It's silly to be dressing in the middle of the night. (*As knocking is heard.*) Aren't you going to answer the door?

WILLY: They're knocking on the wrong door.

THE WOMAN: But I felt the knocking. And he heard us talking in here. Maybe the hotel's on fire!

WILLY (*his terror rising*):   It's a mistake.

THE WOMAN: Then tell him to go away!

WILLY: There's nobody there.

THE WOMAN: It's getting on my nerves, Willy. There's somebody standing out there and it's getting on my nerves!

WILLY (*pushing her away from him*):   All right, stay in the bathroom here, and don't come out. I think there's a law in Massachusetts about it, so don't come out. It may be that new room clerk. He looked very mean. So don't come out. It's a mistake, there's no fire.

The knocking is heard again. He takes a few steps away from her, and she vanishes into the wing. The light follows him, and now he is facing YOUNG BIFF, *who carries a suitcase.* BIFF *steps toward him. The music is gone.*

BIFF: Why didn't you answer?

WILLY: Biff! What are you doing in Boston?

BIFF: Why didn't you answer? I've been knocking for five minutes, I called you on the phone—

WILLY: I just heard you. I was in the bathroom and had the door shut. Did anything happen home?

BIFF: Dad—I let you down.

WILLY: What do you mean?

BIFF: Dad . . .

WILLY: Biffo, what's this about? (*Putting his arm around* BIFF.) Come on, let's go downstairs and get you a malted.

BIFF: Dad, I flunked math.

WILLY: Not for the term?

BIFF: The term. I haven't got enough credits to graduate.

WILLY: You mean to say Bernard wouldn't give you the answers?

BIFF: He did, he tried, but I only got a sixty-one.

WILLY: And they wouldn't give you four points?

BIFF: Birnbaum refused absolutely. I begged him, Pop, but he won't give me those points. You gotta talk to him before they close the school. Because if he saw the kind of man you are, and you just talked to him in your way, I'm sure he'd come through for me. The class came right before practice, see, and I didn't go enough. Would you talk to him? He'd like you, Pop. You know the way you could talk.

WILLY: You're on. We'll drive right back.

BIFF: Oh, Dad, good work! I'm sure he'll change it for you!

WILLY: Go downstairs and tell the clerk I'm checkin' out. Go right down.

BIFF: Yes, Sir! See, the reason he hates me, Pop—one day he was late for class so I got up at the blackboard and imitated him. I crossed my eyes and talked with a lithp.

WILLY (*laughing*):   You did? The kids like it?

BIFF: They nearly died laughing!

WILLY: Yeah? What'd you do?

BIFF: The thquare root of thixty twee is . . . (WILLY *bursts out laughing;* BIFF *joins him.*) And in the middle of it he walked in!

WILLY *laughs and* THE WOMAN *joins in offstage.*

WILLY (*without hesitating*):   Hurry downstairs and—

BIFF: Somebody in there?

WILLY: No, that was next door.

THE WOMAN *laughs offstage.*

BIFF: Somebody got in your bathroom!

WILLY: No, it's the next room, there's a party—

THE WOMAN (*enters, laughing. She lisps this*):   Can I come in? There's something in the bathtub, Willy, and it's moving!

WILLY *looks at* BIFF, *who is staring open-mouthed and horrified at* THE WOMAN.

WILLY: Ah—you better go back to your room. They must be finished painting by now. They're painting her room so I let her take a shower here. Go back, go back . . . (*He pushes her.*)

THE WOMAN (*resisting*):   But I've got to get dressed, Willy, I can't—

WILLY: Get out of here! Go back, go back . . . (*Suddenly striving for the ordinary.*) This is Miss Francis, Biff, she's a buyer. They're painting her room. Go back, Miss Francis, go back . . .

THE WOMAN: But my clothes, I can't go out naked in the hall!

WILLY (*pushing her offstage*):   Get outa here! Go back, go back!

BIFF *slowly sits down on his suitcase as the argument continues offstage.*

THE WOMAN: Where's my stockings? You promised me stockings, Willy!

WILLY: I have no stockings here!

THE WOMAN: You had two boxes of size nine sheers for me, and I want them!

WILLY: Here, for God's sake, will you get outa here!

THE WOMAN (*enters holding a box of stockings*):   I just hope there's nobody in the hall. That's all I hope. (*To* BIFF.) Are you football or baseball?

BIFF: Football.

THE WOMAN (*angry, humiliated*):   That's me too. G'night. (*She snatches her clothes from* WILLY, *and walks out.*)

WILLY (*after a pause*):   Well, better get going. I want to get to the school first thing in the morning. Get my suits out of the closet. I'll get my valise. (BIFF *doesn't move.*) What's the matter? (BIFF *remains motionless, tears falling.*) She's a buyer. Buys for J. H. Simmons. She lives down the hall—they're painting. You don't imagine—(*He breaks off. After a pause.*) Now listen, pal, she's just a buyer. She sees merchandise in her room and they have to keep it looking just so . . . (*Pause. Assuming command.*) All right, get my suits. (BIFF *doesn't move.*) Now stop crying and do as I say. I gave you an order. Biff, I gave you an order! Is that what you do when I give you an order? How dare you cry! (*Putting his arm around* BIFF.) Now look, Biff, when you grow up you'll understand about these things. You mustn't—you mustn't overemphasize a thing like this. I'll see Birnbaum first thing in the morning.

BIFF: Never mind.

WILLY (*getting down beside* BIFF):   Never mind! He's going to give you those points. I'll see to it.

BIFF: He wouldn't listen to you.

WILLY: He certainly will listen to me. You need those points for the U. of Virginia.

BIFF: I'm not going there.

WILLY: Heh? If I can't get him to change that mark you'll make it up in summer school. You've got all summer to—

BIFF (*his weeping breaking from him*):   Dad . . .

WILLY (*infected by it*):   Oh, my boy . . .

BIFF: Dad . . .

WILLY: She's nothing to me, Biff. I was lonely, I was terribly lonely.

BIFF: You—you gave her Mama's stockings! (*His tears break through and he rises to go.*)

WILLY (*grabbing for* BIFF):   I gave you an order!

BIFF: Don't touch me, you—liar!

WILLY: Apologize for that!

BIFF: You fake! You phony little fake! You fake! (*Overcome, he turns quickly and weeping fully goes out with his suitcase.* WILLY *is left on the floor on his knees.*)

WILLY: I gave you an order! Biff, come back here or I'll beat you! Come back here! I'll whip you!

STANLEY *comes quickly in from the right and stands in front of* WILLY.

WILLY (*shouts at* STANLEY):   I gave you an order . . .

STANLEY: Hey, let's pick it up, pick it up, Mr. Loman. (*He helps* WILLY *to his feet.*) Your boys left with the chippies. They said they'll see you home.

A second waiter watches some distance away.

WILLY: But we were supposed to have dinner together.

Music is heard, WILLY's *theme.*

STANLEY: Can you make it?

WILLY: I'll—sure, I can make it. (*Suddenly concerned about his clothes.*) Do I—I look all right?

STANLEY: Sure, you look all right. (*He flicks a speck off* WILLY's *lapel.*)

WILLY: Here—here's a dollar.

STANLEY: Oh, your son paid me. It's all right.

WILLY (*putting it in* STANLEY's *hand*): No, take it. You're a good boy.

STANLEY: Oh, no, you don't have to . . .

WILLY: Here—here's some more, I don't need it any more. (*After a slight pause.*) Tell me—is there a seed store in the neighborhood?

STANLEY: Seeds? You mean like to plant?

As WILLY *turns,* STANLEY *slips the money back into his jacket pocket.*

WILLY: Yes. Carrots, peas . . .

STANLEY: Well, there's hardware stores on Sixth Avenue, but it may be too late now.

WILLY (*anxiously*): Oh, I'd better hurry. I've got to get some seeds. (*He starts off to the right.*) I've got to get some seeds, right away. Nothing's planted. I don't have a thing in the ground.

WILLY *hurries out as the light goes down.* STANLEY *moves over to the right after him, watches him off. The other waiter has been staring at* WILLY.

STANLEY (*to the waiter*): Well, whatta you looking at?

The waiter picks up the chairs and moves off right. STANLEY *takes the table and follows him. The light fades on this area. There is a long pause, the sound of the flute coming over. The light gradually rises on the kitchen, which is empty.* HAPPY *appears at the door of the house, followed by* BIFF. HAPPY *is carrying a large bunch of long-stemmed roses. He enters the kitchen, looks around for* LINDA. *Not seeing her, he turns to* BIFF, *who is just outside the house door, and makes a gesture with his hands, indicating "Not here, I guess." He looks into the livingroom and freezes. Inside,* LINDA, *unseen, is seated,* WILLY's *coat on her lap. She rises ominously and quietly and moves toward* HAPPY, *who backs up into the kitchen, afraid.*

HAPPY: Hey, what're you doing up? (LINDA *says nothing but moves toward him implacably.*) Where's Pop? (*He keeps backing to the right, and now* LINDA *is in full view in the doorway to the livingroom.*) Is he sleeping?

LINDA: Where were you?

HAPPY (*trying to laugh it off*): We met two girls, Mom, very fine types. Here, we brought you some flowers. (*Offering them to her.*) Put them in your room, Ma.

She knocks them to the floor at BIFF's *feet. He has now come inside and closed the door behind him. She stares at* BIFF, *silent.*

HAPPY: Now what'd you do that for? Mom, I want you to have some flowers—

LINDA (*cutting* HAPPY *off, violently to* BIFF): Don't you care whether he lives or dies?

HAPPY (*going to the stairs*):   Come upstairs, Biff.

BIFF (*with a flare of disgust, to* HAPPY):   Go away from me! (*To* LINDA.) What do you mean, lives or dies? Nobody's dying around here, pal.

LINDA: Get out of my sight! Get out of here!

BIFF: I wanna see the boss.

LINDA: You're not going near him!

BIFF: Where is he? (*He moves into the livingroom and* LINDA *follows.*)

LINDA (*shouting after* BIFF):   You invite him for dinner. He looks forward to it all day—(BIFF *appears in his parents' bedroom, looks around, and exits*)—and then you desert him there. There's no stranger you'd do that to!

HAPPY: Why? He had a swell time with us. Listen, when I—(LINDA *comes back into the kitchen*)—desert him I hope I don't outlive the day!

LINDA: Get out of here!

HAPPY: Now look, Mom . . .

LINDA: Did you have to go to women tonight? You and your lousy rotten whores!

BIFF *re-enters the kitchen.*

HAPPY: Mom, all we did was follow Biff around trying to cheer him up! (*To* BIFF.) Boy, what a night you gave me!

LINDA: Get out of here, both of you, and don't come back! I don't want you tormenting him any more. Go on now, get your things together! (*To* BIFF.) You can sleep in his apartment. (*She starts to pick up the flowers and stops herself.*) Pick up this stuff, I'm not your maid any more. Pick it up, you bum, you!

HAPPY *turns his back to her in refusal.* BIFF *slowly moves over and gets down on his knees, picking up the flowers.*

LINDA: You're a pair of animals! Not one, not another living soul would have had the cruelty to walk out on that man in a restaurant!

BIFF (*not looking at her*):   Is that what he said?

LINDA: He didn't have to say anything. He was so humiliated he nearly limped when he came in.

HAPPY: But, Mom, he had a great time with us—

BIFF (*cutting him off violently*):   Shut up!

Without another word, HAPPY *goes upstairs.*

LINDA: You! You didn't even go in to see if he was all right!

BIFF (*still on the floor in front of* LINDA, *the flowers in his hand; with self-loathing*):   No. Didn't. Didn't do a damned thing. How do you like that, heh? Left him babbling in a toilet.

LINDA: You louse. You . . .

BIFF: Now you hit it on the nose! (*He gets up, throws the flowers in the wastebasket.*) The scum of the earth, and you're looking at him!

LINDA: Get out of here!

BIFF: I gotta talk to the boss, Mom. Where is he?

LINDA: You're not going near him. Get out of this house!

BIFF (*with absolute assurance, determination*):   No. We're gonna have an abrupt conversation, him and me.

LINDA: You're not talking to him!

Hammering is heard from outside the house, off right. BIFF *turns toward the noise.*

LINDA (*suddenly pleading*):   Will you please leave him alone?
BIFF: What's he doing out there?
LINDA: He's planting the garden!
BIFF (*quietly*):   Now? Oh, my God!

BIFF *moves outside,* LINDA *following. The light dies down on them and comes up on the center of the apron as* WILLY *walks into it. He is carrying a flashlight, a hoe and a handful of seed packets. He raps the top of the hoe sharply to fix it firmly, and then moves to the left, measuring off the distance with his foot. He holds the flashlight to look at the seed packets, reading off the instructions. He is in the blue of night.*

WILLY: Carrots . . . quarter-inch apart. Rows . . . one-foot rows. (*He measures it off.*) One foot. (*He puts down a package and measures off.*) Beets. (*He puts down another package and measures again.*) Lettuce. (*He reads the package, puts it down.*) One foot—(*He breaks off as* BEN *appears at the right and moves slowly down to him.*) What a proposition, ts, ts. Terrific, terrific. 'Cause she's suffered, Ben, the woman has suffered. You understand me? A man can't go out the way he came in, Ben, a man has got to add up to something. You can't, you can't—(BEN *moves toward him as though to interrupt.*) You gotta consider, now. Don't answer so quick. Remember, it's a guaranteed twenty-thousand-dollar proposition. Now look, Ben, I want you to go through the ins and outs of this thing with me. I've got nobody to talk to, Ben, and the woman has suffered, you hear me?
BEN (*standing still, considering*):   What's the proposition?
WILLY: It's twenty thousand dollars on the barrelhead. Guaranteed, gilt-edged, you understand?
BEN: You don't want to make a fool of yourself. They might not honor the policy.
WILLY: How can they dare refuse? Didn't I work like a coolie to meet every premium on the nose? And now they don't pay off? Impossible!
BEN: It's called a cowardly thing, William.
WILLY: Why? Does it take more guts to stand here the rest of my life ringing up a zero?
BEN (*yielding*):   That's a point, William. (*He moves, thinking, turns.*) And twenty thousand—that is something one can feel with the hand, it is there.
WILLY (*now assured, with rising power*):   Oh, Ben, that's the whole beauty of it! I see it like a diamond, shining in the dark, hard and rough, that I can pick up and touch in my hand. Not like—like an appointment! This would not be another damned-fool appointment, Ben, and it changes all the aspects. Because he thinks I'm nothing, see, and so he spites me. But the funeral—(*Straightening up.*) Ben, that funeral will be massive! They'll come from Maine, Massachusetts, Vermont, New Hampshire! All the old-timers with the strange license plates—that boy will be thunder-struck, Ben, because he never realized—I am known! Rhode Island, New York, New Jersey—I am known, Ben, and he'll see it with his eyes once and for all. He'll see what I am, Ben! He's in for a shock, that boy!
BEN (*coming down to the edge of the garden*):   He'll call you a coward.
WILLY (*suddenly fearful*):   No, that would be terrible.
BEN: Yes. And a damned fool.

WILLY: No, no, he mustn't, I won't have that! (*He is broken and desperate.*)

BEN: He'll hate you, William.

The gay music of the boys is heard.

WILLY: Oh, Ben, how do we get back to all the great times? Used to be so full of light, and comradeship, the sleigh-riding in winter, and the ruddiness on his cheeks. And always some kind of good news coming up, always something nice coming up ahead. And never even let me carry the valises in the house, and simonizing, simonizing that little red car! Why, why can't I give him something and not have him hate me?

BEN: Let me think about it. (*He glances at his watch.*) I still have a little time. Remarkable proposition, but you've got to be sure you're not making a fool of yourself.

BEN *drifts off upstage and goes out of sight.* BIFF *comes down from the left.*

WILLY (*suddenly conscious of* BIFF, *turns and looks up at him, then begins picking up the packages of seeds in confusion*):   Where the hell is that seed? (*Indignantly.*) You can't see nothing out here! They boxed in the whole goddam neighborhood!

BIFF: There are people all around here. Don't you realize that?

WILLY: I'm busy. Don't bother me.

BIFF (*taking the hoe from* WILLY):   I'm saying good-by to you, Pop. (WILLY *looks at him, silent, unable to move.*) I'm not coming back any more.

WILLY: You're not going to see Oliver tomorrow?

BIFF: I've got no appointment, Dad.

WILLY: He put his arm around you, and you've got no appointment?

BIFF: Pop, get this now, will you? Everytime I've left it's been a fight that sent me out of here. Today I realized something about myself and I tried to explain it to you and I—I think I'm just not smart enough to make any sense out of it for you. To hell with whose fault it is or anything like that. (*He takes* WILLY's *arm.*) Let's just wrap it up, heh? Come on in, we'll tell Mom. (*He gently tries to pull* WILLY *to the left.*)

WILLY (*frozen, immobile, with guilt in his voice*):   No, I don't want to see her.

BIFF: Come on! (*He pulls again, and* WILLY *tries to pull away.*)

WILLY (*highly nervous*):   No, no, I don't want to see her.

BIFF (*tries to look into* WILLY's *face, as if to find the answer there*):   Why don't you want to see her?

WILLY (*more harshly now*):   Don't bother me, will you?

BIFF: What do you mean, you don't want to see her? You don't want them calling you yellow, do you? This isn't your fault; it's me, I'm a bum. Now come inside! (WILLY *strains to get away.*) Did you hear what I said to you?

WILLY *pulls away and quickly goes by himself into the house.* BIFF *follows.*

LINDA (*to* WILLY):   Did you plant, dear?

BIFF (*at the door, to* LINDA):   All right, we had it out. I'm going and I'm not writing any more.

LINDA (*going to* WILLY *in the kitchen*):   I think that's the best way, dear. 'Cause there's no use drawing it out, you'll just never get along.

WILLY *doesn't respond.*

BIFF: People ask where I am and what I'm doing, you don't know, and you don't care. That way it'll be off your mind and you can start brightening up again. All right? That clears it, doesn't it? (WILLY *is silent, and* BIFF *goes to him.*) You gonna wish me luck, scout? (*He extends his hand.*) What do you say?

LINDA: Shake his hand, Willy.

WILLY (*turning to her, seething with hurt*):   There's no necessity to mention the pen at all, y'know.

BIFF (*gently*):   I've got no appointment, Dad.

WILLY (*erupting fiercely*):   He put his arm around . . . ?

BIFF: Dad, you're never going to see what I am, so what's the use of arguing? If I strike oil I'll send you a check. Meantime forget I'm alive.

WILLY (*to* LINDA):   Spite, see?

BIFF: Shake hands, Dad.

WILLY: Not my hand.

BIFF: I was hoping not to go this way.

WILLY: Well, this is the way you're going. Good-by.

BIFF *looks at him a moment, then turns sharply and goes to the stairs.*

WILLY (*stops him with*):   May you rot in hell if you leave this house!

BIFF (*turning*):   Exactly what is it that you want from me?

WILLY: I want you to know, on the train, in the mountains, in the valleys, wherever you go, that you cut down your life for spite!

BIFF: No, no.

WILLY: Spite, spite, is the word of your undoing! And when you're down and out, remember what did it. When you're rotting somewhere beside the railroad tracks, remember, and don't you dare blame it on me!

BIFF: I'm not blaming it on you!

WILLY: I won't take the rap for this, you hear?

HAPPY *comes down the stairs and stands on the bottom step, watching.*

BIFF: That's just what I'm telling you!

WILLY (*sinking into a chair at the table, with full accusation*):   You're trying to put a knife in me—don't think I don't know what you're doing!

BIFF: All right, phony! Then let's lay it on the line. (*He whips the rubber tube out of his pocket and puts it on the table.*)

HAPPY: You crazy—

LINDA: Biff! (*She moves to grab the hose, but* BIFF *holds it down with his hand.*)

BIFF: Leave it there! Don't move it!

WILLY (*not looking at it*):   What is that?

BIFF: You know goddam well what that is.

WILLY (*caged, wanting to escape*):   I never saw that.

BIFF: You saw it. The mice didn't bring it into the cellar! What is this supposed to do, make a hero out of you? This supposed to make me sorry for you?

WILLY: Never heard of it.

BIFF: There'll be no pity for you, you hear it? No pity!

WILLY (*to* LINDA):   You hear the spite!

BIFF: No, you're going to hear the truth—what you are and what I am!

LINDA: Stop it!

WILLY: Spite!

HAPPY (*coming down toward* BIFF):   You cut it now!

BIFF (*to* HAPPY):   The man don't know who we are! The man is gonna know! (*To* WILLY.) We never told the truth for ten minutes in this house!

HAPPY: We always told the truth!

BIFF (*turning on him*):   You big blow, are you the assistant buyer? You're one of the two assistants to the assistant, aren't you?

HAPPY: Well, I'm practically—

BIFF: You're practically full of it! We all are! And I'm through with it. (*To* WILLY.) Now hear this, Willy, this is me.

WILLY: I know you!

BIFF: You know why I had no address for three months? I stole a suit in Kansas City and I was in jail. (*To* LINDA, *who is sobbing.*) Stop crying. I'm through with it.

> LINDA *turns away from them, her hands covering her face.*

WILLY: I suppose that's my fault!

BIFF: I stole myself out of every good job since high school!

WILLY: And whose fault is that?

BIFF: And I never got anywhere because you blew me so full of hot air I could never stand taking orders from anybody! That's whose fault it is!

WILLY: I hear that!

LINDA: Don't, Biff!

BIFF: It's goddam time you heard that! I had to be boss big shot in two weeks, and I'm through with it!

WILLY: Then hang yourself! For spite, hang yourself!

BIFF: No! Nobody's hanging himself, Willy! I ran down eleven flights with a pen in my hand today. And suddenly I stopped, you hear me? And in the middle of that office building, do you hear this? I stopped in the middle of that building and I saw—the sky. I saw the things that I love in this world. The work and the food and time to sit and smoke. And I looked at the pen and said to myself, what the hell am I grabbing this for? Why am I trying to become what I don't want to be? What am I doing in an office, making a contemptuous, begging fool of myself, when all I want is out there, waiting for me the minute I say I know who I am! Why can't I say that, Willy? (*He tries to make* WILLY *face him, but* WILLY *pulls away and moves to the left.*)

WILLY (*with hatred, threateningly*):   The door of your life is wide open!

BIFF: Pop! I'm a dime a dozen, and so are you!

WILLY (*turning on him now in an uncontrolled outburst*):   I am not a dime a dozen! I am Willy Loman, and you are Biff Loman!

> BIFF *starts for* WILLY, *but is blocked by* HAPPY. *In his fury,* BIFF *seems on the verge of attacking his father.*

BIFF: I am not a leader of men, Willy, and neither are you. You were never anything but a hard-working drummer who landed in the ash can like all the rest of them!

I'm one dollar an hour, Willy! I tried seven states and couldn't raise it. A buck an hour! Do you gather my meaning? I'm not bringing home any prizes any more, and you're going to stop waiting for me to bring them home!

WILLY (*directly to* BIFF): You vengeful, spiteful mutt!

> BIFF *breaks from* HAPPY. WILLY, *in fright, starts up the stairs.* BIFF *grabs him.*

BIFF (*at the peak of his fury*): Pop, I'm nothing! I'm nothing, Pop. Can't you understand that? There's no spite in it any more. I'm just what I am, that's all.

BIFF's *fury has spent itself, and he breaks down, sobbing, holding on to* WILLY, *who dumbly fumbles for* BIFF's *face.*

WILLY (*astonished*): What're you doing? What're you doing? (*To* LINDA.) Why is he crying?

BIFF (*crying, broken*): Will you let me go, for Christ's sake? Will you take that phony dream and burn it before something happens? (*Struggling to contain himself, he pulls away and moves to the stairs.*) I'll go in the morning. Put him—put him to bed. (*Exhausted,* BIFF *moves up the stairs to his room.*)

WILLY (*after a long pause, astonished, elevated*): Isn't that remarkable? Biff—he likes me!

LINDA: He loves you, Willy!

HAPPY (*deeply moved*): Always did, Pop.

WILLY: Oh, Biff! (*Staring wildly.*) He cried! Cried to me. (*He is choking with his love, and now cries out his promise.*) That boy—that boy is going to be magnificent!

> BEN *appears in the light just outside the kitchen.*

BEN: Yes, outstanding, with twenty thousand behind him.

LINDA (*sensing the racing of his mind, fearfully, carefully*): Now come to bed, Willy. It's all settled now.

WILLY (*finding it difficult not to rush out of the house*): Yes, we'll sleep. Come on. Go to sleep, Hap.

BEN: And it does take a great kind of man to crack the jungle.

> In accents of dread, BEN's *idyllic music starts up.*

HAPPY (*his arm around* LINDA): I'm getting married, Pop, don't forget it. I'm changing everything. I'm gonna run that department before the year is up. You'll see, Mom. (*He kisses her.*)

BEN: The jungle is dark but full of diamonds, Willy.

> WILLY *turns, moves, listening to* BEN.

LINDA: Be good. You're both good boys, just act that way, that's all.

HAPPY: 'Night, Pop. (*He goes upstairs.*)

LINDA (*to* WILLY): Come, dear.

BEN (*with greater force*): One must go in to fetch a diamond out.

WILLY (*to* LINDA, *as he moves slowly along the edge of the kitchen, toward the door*): I just want to get settled down, Linda. Let me sit alone for a little.

LINDA (*almost uttering her fear*): I want you upstairs.

WILLY (*taking her in his arms*): In a few minutes, Linda. I couldn't sleep right now. Go on, you look awful tired. (*He kisses her.*)

BEN: Not like an appointment at all. A diamond is rough and hard to the touch.

WILLY: Go on now. I'll be right up.

LINDA: I think this is the only way, Willy.

WILLY: Sure, it's the best thing.

BEN: Best thing!

WILLY: The only way. Everything is gonna be—go on, kid, get to bed. You look so tired.

LINDA: Come right up.

WILLY: Two minutes.

LINDA *goes into the livingroom, then reappears in her bedroom.* WILLY *moves just outside the kitchen door.*

WILLY: Loves me. (*Wonderingly.*) Always loved me. Isn't that a remarkable thing? Ben, he'll worship me for it!

BEN (*with promise*):   It's dark there, but full of diamonds.

WILLY: Can you imagine that magnificence with twenty thousand dollars in his pocket?

LINDA (*calling from her room*):   Willy! Come up!

WILLY (*calling from the kitchen*):   Yes! Yes. Coming! It's very smart, you realize that, don't you, sweetheart? Even Ben sees it. I gotta go, baby. 'By! By! (*Going over to* BEN, *almost dancing.*) Imagine? When the mail comes he'll be ahead of Bernard again!

BEN: A perfect proposition all around.

WILLY: Did you see how he cried to me? Oh, if I could kiss him, Ben!

BEN: Time, William, time!

WILLY: Oh, Ben, I always knew one way or another we were gonna make it, Biff and I!

BEN (*looking at his watch*):   The boat. We'll be late. (*He moves slowly off into the darkness.*)

WILLY (*elegiacally, turning to the house*):   Now when you kick off, boy, I want a seventy-yard boot, and get right down the field under the ball, and when you hit, hit low and hit hard, because it's important, boy. (*He swings around and faces the audience.*) There's all kinds of important people in the stands, and the first thing you know . . . (*Suddenly realizing he is alone.*) Ben! Ben, where do I . . . ? (*He makes a sudden movement of search.*) Ben, how do I . . . ?

LINDA (*calling*):   Willy, you coming up?

WILLY (*uttering a gasp of fear, whirling about as if to quiet her*):   Sh! (*He turns around as if to find his way; sounds, faces, voices, seem to be swarming in upon him and he flicks at them, crying.*) Sh! Sh! (*Suddenly music, faint and high, stops him. It rises in intensity, almost to an unbearable scream. He goes up and down on his toes, and rushes off around the house.*) Shhh!

LINDA: Willy?

There is no answer. LINDA *waits.* BIFF *gets up off his bed. He is still in his clothes.* HAPPY *sits up.* BIFF *stands listening.*

LINDA (*with real fear*):   Willy, answer me! Willy!

There is the sound of a car starting and moving away at full speed.

LINDA: No!

BIFF (*rushing down the stairs*):   Pop!

As the car speeds off, the music crashes down in a frenzy of sound, which becomes the soft pulsation of a single cello string. BIFF *slowly returns to his bedroom. He and* HAPPY *gravely don their jackets.* LINDA *slowly walks out of her room. The music has developed into a dead march. The leaves of day are appearing over everything.* CHARLEY *and* BERNARD, *somberly dressed, appear and knock on the kitchen door.* BIFF *and* HAPPY *slowly descend the stairs to the kitchen as* CHARLEY *and* BERNARD *enter. All stop a moment when* LINDA, *in clothes of mourning, bearing a little bunch of roses, comes through the draped doorway into the kitchen. She goes to* CHARLEY *and takes his arm. Now all move toward the audience, through the wall-line of the kitchen. At the limit of the apron,* LINDA *lays down the flowers, kneels, and sits back on her heels. All stare down at the grave.*

REQUIEM

CHARLEY: It's getting dark, Linda.

LINDA *doesn't react. She stares at the grave.*

BIFF: How about it, Mom? Better get some rest, heh? They'll be closing the gate soon.

LINDA *makes no move. Pause.*

HAPPY (*deeply angered*):   He had no right to do that! There was no necessity for it. We would've helped him.
CHARLEY (*grunting*):   Hmmm.
BIFF: Come along, Mom.
LINDA: Why didn't anybody come?
CHARLEY: It was a very nice funeral.
LINDA: But where are all the people he knew? Maybe they blame him.
CHARLEY: Naa. It's a rough world, Linda. They wouldn't blame him.
LINDA: I can't understand it. At this time especially. First time in thirty-five years we were just about free and clear. He only needed a little salary. He was even finished with the dentist.
CHARLEY: No man only needs a little salary.
LINDA: I can't understand it.
BIFF: There were a lot of nice days. When he'd come home from a trip; or on Sundays, making the stoop; finishing the cellar; putting on the new porch; when he built the extra bathroom; and put up the garage. You know something, Charley, there's more of him in that front stoop than in all the sales he ever made.
CHARLEY: Yeah. He was a happy man with a batch of cement.
LINDA: He was so wonderful with his hands.
BIFF: He had the wrong dreams. All, all, wrong.
HAPPY (*almost ready to fight* BIFF):   Don't say that!
BIFF: He never knew who he was.
CHARLEY (*stopping* HAPPY's *movement and reply. To* BIFF.)   Nobody dast blame this man. You don't understand: Willy was a salesman. And for a salesman, there is no rock

bottom to the life. He don't put a bolt to a nut, he don't tell you the law or give you medicine. He's a man out there in the blue, riding on a smile and a shoeshine. And when they start not smiling back—that's an earthquake. And then you get yourself a couple of spots on your hat, and you're finished. Nobody dast blame this man. A salesman is got to dream, boy. It comes with the territory.

BIFF: Charley, the man didn't know who he was.

HAPPY (*infuriated*):   Don't say that!

BIFF: Why don't you come with me, Happy?

HAPPY: I'm not licked that easily. I'm staying right in this city, and I'm gonna beat this racket! (*He looks at* BIFF, *his chin set.*) The Loman Brothers!

BIFF: I know who I am, kid.

HAPPY: All right, boy. I'm gonna show you and everybody else that Willy Loman did not die in vain. He had a good dream. It's the only dream you can have— to come out number-one man. He fought it out here, and this is where I'm gonna win it for him.

BIFF (*with a hopeless glance at* HAPPY, *bends toward his mother*):   Let's go, Mom.

LINDA: I'll be with you in a minute. Go on, Charley. (*He hesitates.*) I want to, just for a minute. I never had a chance to say good-by.

CHARLEY *moves away, followed by* HAPPY. BIFF *remains a slight distance up and left of* LINDA. *She sits there, summoning herself. The flute begins, not far away, playing behind her speech.*

LINDA: Forgive me, dear. I can't cry. I don't know what it is, but I can't cry. I don't understand it. Why did you ever do that? Help me, Willy, I can't cry. It seems to me that you're just on another trip. I keep expecting you. Willy, dear, I can't cry. Why did you do it? I search and search and I search, and I can't understand it, Willy. I made the last payment on the house today. Today, dear. And there'll be nobody home. (*A sob rises in her throat.*) We're free and clear. (*Sobbing more fully, released.*) We're free. (BIFF *comes slowly toward her.*) We're free . . . We're free . . .

BIFF *lifts her to her feet and moves out up right with her in his arms.* LINDA *sobs quietly.* BERNARD *and* CHARLEY *come together and follow them, followed by* HAPPY. *Only the music of the flute is left on the darkening stage as over the house the hard towers of the apartment buildings rise into sharp focus, and—*

Curtain

(*1949*)

QUESTIONS FOR REFLECTION

Experience

1. Identify the places in the play, if any, where you were confused. What may have accounted for your confusion?
2. To what extent do you identify with the dreams of the play's characters? Why?

Interpretation

3. Comment on the significance of the title. What kinds of deaths might be referred to? Explain.
4. What significance do you attach to the names of the characters?
5. Describe Biff's relationship with his father and with his brother, Happy.
6. How does Miller characterize Willy? Which of his characteristics are highlighted? What kind of man is he? To what extent and by what means is he considered a failure? Does anyone consider him a success? Why or why not?
7. What roles do women have in this play? Comment on Willy's relationships with them. Consider Biff's relationship with women as well.
8. Identify two minor characters and explain their significance for the play's action and theme(s).
9. Describe Miller's staging of the play. Consider his use of lighting and music, and the way he dramatizes dreams and memories.

Evaluation

10. What is typically "American" about Miller's play? What cultural attitudes and values displayed by the characters provide it with an American tone?
11. Published in 1947, *Death of a Salesman* has been among the most popular plays of the American theater. What accounts for the play's perennial appeal?
12. Read Miller's essay "Tragedy and the Common Man" and comment on the degree to which his remarks illuminate his intentions and define his achievement in the play.

LORRAINE HANSBERRY

[1930–1965]

Lorraine Hansberry was born and raised in Chicago. She studied painting at the Chicago Art Institute and the University of Wisconsin before turning to writing following a move to New York. *A Raisin in the Sun* (1959), her first Broadway play, was quickly made into a movie, starring Sidney Poitier and Claudia McNeil. Although the play reflects Hansberry's deep concern with civil rights, it transcends its racial and urban focus. Like Arthur Miller's *Death of a Salesman*, *A Raisin in the Sun* dramatizes the powerful attractions of the American dream of success. Like Miller's play also, Hansberry's is largely concerned with family life.

LORRAINE HANSBERRY

A Raisin in the Sun

What happens to a dream deferred?
Does it dry up
Like a raisin in the sun?
Or fester like a sore—
And then run?
Does it stink like rotten meat?
Or crust and sugar over—
Like a syrupy sweet?

Maybe it just sags
Like a heavy load.

Or does it explode?

LANGSTON HUGHES

CHARACTERS

(In order of appearance)
RUTH YOUNGER
TRAVIS YOUNGER
WALTER LEE YOUNGER (BROTHER)
BENEATHA YOUNGER
LENA YOUNGER (MAMA)
JOSEPH ASAGAI
GEORGE MURCHISON
KARL LINDNER
BOBO
MOVING MEN

The action of the play is set in Chicago's Southside, sometime between World War II and the present.

Act I
Scene One: Friday morning.
Scene Two: The following morning.
Act II
Scene One: Later, the same day.
Scene Two: Friday night, a few weeks later.
Scene Three: Moving day, one week later.
Act III
An hour later.

ACT I

Scene I

The YOUNGER *living room would be a comfortable and well-ordered room if it were not for a number of indestructible contradictions to this state of being. Its furnishings are typical and undistinguished and their primary feature now is that they have clearly had to accommodate the living of too many people for too many years—and they are tired. Still, we can see that at some time, a time probably no longer remembered by the family (except perhaps for* MAMA*), the furnishings of this room were actually selected with care and love and even hope—and brought to this apartment and arranged with taste and pride.*

That was a long time ago. Now the once loved pattern of the couch upholstery has to fight to show itself from under acres of crocheted doilies and couch covers which have themselves finally come to be more important than the upholstery. And here a table or a chair has been moved to disguise the worn places in the carpet; but the carpet has fought back by showing its weariness, with depressing uniformity, elsewhere on its surface.

Weariness has, in fact, won in this room. Everything has been polished, washed, sat on, used, scrubbed too often. All pretenses but living itself have long since vanished from the very atmosphere of this room.

Moreover, a section of this room, for it is not really a room unto itself, though the landlord's lease would make it seem so, slopes backward to provide a small kitchen area, where the family prepares the meals that are eaten in the living room proper, which must also serve as dining room. The single window that has been provided for these "two" rooms is located in this kitchen area. The sole natural light the family may enjoy in the course of a day is only that which fights its way through this little window.

At left, a door leads to a bedroom which is shared by MAMA *and her daughter,* BENEATHA. *At right, opposite, is a second room (which in the beginning of the life of this apartment was probably a breakfast room) which serves as a bedroom for* WALTER *and his wife,* RUTH.

Time: Sometime between World War II and the present.

Place: Chicago's Southside.

At Rise: It is morning dark in the living room. TRAVIS *is asleep on the make-down bed at center. An alarm clock sounds from within the bedroom at right, and presently* RUTH *enters from that room and closes the door behind her. She crosses sleepily toward the window. As she passes her sleeping son she reaches down and shakes him a little. At the window she raises the shade and a dusky Southside morning light comes in feebly. She fills a pot with water and puts it on to boil. She calls to the boy, between yawns, in a slightly muffled voice.*

RUTH *is about thirty. We can see that she was a pretty girl, even exceptionally so, but now it is apparent that life has been little that she expected, and disappointment has already begun to hang in her face. In a few years, before thirty-five even, she will be known among her people as a "settled woman."*

She crosses to her son and gives him a good, final, rousing shake.

RUTH: Come on now, boy, it's seven thirty! (*Her son sits up at last, in a stupor of sleepiness*) I say hurry up, Travis! You ain't the only person in the world got to use a bathroom! (*The child, a sturdy, handsome little boy of ten or eleven, drags himself out of the bed and almost blindly takes his towels and "today's clothes" from drawers and a closet and goes out to the bathroom, which is in an outside hall and which is shared by another family or families on the same floor.* RUTH *crosses to the bedroom door at right and opens it and calls in to her husband)* Walter Lee! . . . It's after seven thirty! Lemme see you do some waking up in there now! (*She waits*) You better get up from there, man! It's after seven thirty I tell you. (*She waits again*) All right, you just go ahead and lay there and next thing you know Travis be finished and Mr. Johnson'll be in there and you'll be fussing and cussing round here like a madman! And be late too! (*She waits, at the end of patience*) Walter Lee—it's time for you to GET UP!

(*She waits another second and then starts to go into the bedroom, but is apparently satisfied that her husband has begun to get up. She stops, pulls the door to, and returns to the kitchen area. She wipes her face with a moist cloth and runs her fingers through her sleep-disheveled hair in a vain effort and ties an apron around her housecoat. The bedroom door at right opens and her husband stands in the doorway in his pajamas, which are rumpled and mismated. He is a lean, intense young man in his middle thirties, inclined to quick nervous movements and erratic speech habits—and always in his voice there is a quality of indictment.*)

WALTER: Is he out yet?

RUTH: What you mean *out?* He ain't hardly got in there good yet.

WALTER (*wandering in, still more oriented to sleep than to a new day*):   Well, what was you doing all that yelling for if I can't even get in there yet? (*Stopping and thinking*) Check coming today?

RUTH: They *said* Saturday and this is just Friday and I hopes to God you ain't going to get up here first thing this morning and start talking to me 'bout no money— 'cause I 'bout don't want to hear it.

WALTER: Something the matter with you this morning?

RUTH: No—I'm just sleepy as the devil. What kind of eggs you want?

WALTER: Not scrambled. (RUTH *starts to scramble eggs*) Paper come? (RUTH *points impatiently to the rolled up* Tribune *on the table, and he gets it and spreads it out and vaguely reads the front page*) Set off another bomb yesterday.

RUTH (*maximum indifference*):   Did they?

WALTER (*looking up*):   What's the matter with you?

RUTH: Ain't nothing the matter with me. And don't keep asking me that this morning.

WALTER: Ain't nobody bothering you. (*Reading the news of the day absently again*) Say Colonel McCormick is sick.

RUTH (*affecting tea-party interest*):   Is he now? Poor thing.

WALTER (*sighing and looking at his watch*):   Oh, me. (*He waits*) Now what is that boy doing in that bathroom all this time? He just going to have to start getting up earlier. I can't be being late to work on account of him fooling around in there.

RUTH (*turning on him*):   Oh, no he ain't going to be getting up no earlier no such thing! It ain't his fault that he can't get to bed no earlier nights 'cause he got a bunch of crazy good-for-nothing clowns sitting up running their mouths in what is supposed to be his bedroom after ten o'clock at night . . .

WALTER: That's what you mad about, ain't it? The things I want to talk about with my friends just couldn't be important in your mind, could they?

(*He rises and finds a cigarette in her handbag on the table and crosses to the little window and looks out, smoking and deeply enjoying this first one*)

RUTH (*almost matter of factly, a complaint too automatic to deserve emphasis*):   Why you always got to smoke before you eat in the morning?

WALTER (*at the window*):   Just look at 'em down there . . . Running and racing to work . . . (*He turns and faces his wife and watches her a moment at the stove, and then, suddenly*) You look young this morning, baby.

RUTH (*indifferently*):   Yeah?

WALTER: Just for a second—stirring them eggs. Just for a second it was—you looked real young again. (*He reaches for her; she crosses away. Then, drily*) It's gone now—you look like yourself again!

RUTH: Man, if you don't shut up and leave me alone.

WALTER (*looking out to the street again*):   First thing a man ought to learn in life is not to make love to no colored woman first thing in the morning. You all some eeeevil people at eight o'clock in the morning.

(TRAVIS *appears in the hall doorway, almost fully dressed and quite wide awake now, his towels and pajamas across his shoulders. He opens the door and signals for his father to make the bathroom in a hurry*)

TRAVIS (*watching the bathroom*):   Daddy, come on!

(WALTER *gets his bathroom utensils and flies out to the bathroom*)

RUTH: Sit down and have your breakfast, Travis.

TRAVIS: Mama, this is Friday. (*Gleefully*) Check coming tomorrow, huh?

RUTH: You get your mind off money and eat your breakfast.

TRAVIS (*eating*):   This is the morning we supposed to bring the fifty cents to school.

RUTH: Well, I ain't got no fifty cents this morning.

TRAVIS: Teacher say we have to.

RUTH: I don't care what teacher say. I ain't got it. Eat your breakfast, Travis.

TRAVIS: I *am* eating.

RUTH: Hush up now and just eat!

(*The boy gives her an exasperated look for her lack of understanding, and eats grudgingly*)

TRAVIS: You think Grandmama would have it?

RUTH: No! And I want you to stop asking your grandmother for money, you hear me?

TRAVIS (*outraged*):   Gaaaleee! I don't ask her, she just gimme it sometimes!

RUTH: Travis Willard Younger—I got too much on me this morning to be—

TRAVIS: Maybe Daddy—

RUTH: *Travis!*

(*The boy hushes abruptly. They are both quiet and tense for several seconds*)

TRAVIS (*presently*):   Could I maybe go carry some groceries in front of the supermarket for a little while after school then?

RUTH: Just hush, I said. (TRAVIS *jabs his spoon into his cereal bowl viciously, and rests his head in anger upon his fists*) If you through eating, you can get over there and make up your bed.

(*The boy obeys stiffly and crosses the room, almost mechanically, to the bed and more or less folds the bedding into a heap, then angrily gets his books and cap*)

TRAVIS (*sulking and standing apart from her unnaturally*):   I'm gone.

RUTH (*looking up from the stove to inspect him automatically*):   Come here. (*He crosses to her and she studies his head*) If you don't take this comb and fix this here head, you better! (TRAVIS *puts down his books with a great sigh of oppression, and crosses to the mirror. His mother mutters under her breath about his "slubbornness"*) 'Bout to march out of here with that head looking just like chickens slept in it! I just don't know where you get your slubborn ways . . . And get your jacket, too. Looks chilly out this morning.

TRAVIS (*with conspicuously brushed hair and jacket*):   I'm gone.

RUTH: Get carfare and milk money—(*Waving one finger*)—and not a single penny for no caps, you hear me?

TRAVIS (*with sullen politeness*):   Yes'm.

(*He turns in outrage to leave. His mother watches after him as in his frustration he approaches the door almost comically. When she speaks to him, her voice has become a very gentle tease*)

RUTH (*mocking; as she thinks he would say it*):   Oh, Mama makes me so mad sometimes, I don't know what to do! (*She waits and continues to his back as he stands stock-still in front of the door*) I wouldn't kiss that woman good-bye for nothing in this world this morning! (*The boy finally turns around and rolls his eyes at her, knowing the mood has changed and he is vindicated; he does not, however, move toward her yet*) Not for nothing in this world! (*She finally laughs aloud at him and holds out her arms to him and we see that it is a way between them, very old and practiced. He crosses to her and allows her to embrace him warmly but keeps his face fixed with masculine rigidity. She holds him back from her presently and looks at him and runs her fingers over the features of his face. With utter gentleness—*) Now—whose little old angry man are you?

TRAVIS (*the masculinity and gruffness start to fade at last*):   Aw gaalee—Mama . . .

RUTH (*Mimicking*):   Aw—gaaaaalleeeee, Mama! (*She pushes him, with rough playfulness and finality, toward the door*) Get on out of here or you going to be late.

TRAVIS (*in the face of love, new aggressiveness*):   Mama, could I *please* go carry groceries?

RUTH: Honey, it's starting to get so cold evenings.

WALTER (*coming in from the bathroom and drawing a make-believe gun from a make-believe holster and shooting at his son*):   What is it he wants to do?

RUTH: Go carry groceries after school at the supermarket.

WALTER: Well, let him go . . .

TRAVIS (*quickly, to the ally*):   I *have* to—she won't gimme the fifty cents . . .

WALTER (*to his wife only*):   Why not?

RUTH (*simply, and with flavor*):   'Cause we don't have it.

WALTER (*to RUTH only*):   What you tell the boy things like that for? (*Reaching down into his pants with a rather important gesture*) Here, son—

(*He hands the boy the coin, but his eyes are directed to his wife's.* TRAVIS *takes the money happily*)

TRAVIS: Thanks, Daddy.

(*He starts out.* RUTH *watches both of them with murder in her eyes.* WALTER *stands and stares back at her with defiance, and suddenly reaches into his pocket again on an afterthought*)

WALTER (*without even looking at his son, still staring hard at his wife*):   In fact, here's another fifty cents . . . Buy yourself some fruit today—or take a taxicab to school or something!

TRAVIS: Whoopee—

(*He leaps up and clasps his father around the middle with his legs, and they face each other in mutual appreciation; slowly* WALTER LEE *peeks around the boy to catch the violent rays from his wife's eyes and draws his head back as if shot*)

WALTER: You better get down now—and get to school, man.

TRAVIS (*at the door*):   O.K. Good-bye.

(*He exits*)

WALTER (*after him, pointing with pride*):   That's my boy. (*She looks at him in disgust and turns back to her work*) You know what I was thinking 'bout in the bathroom this morning?

RUTH: No.

WALTER: How come you always try to be so pleasant!

RUTH: What is there to be pleasant 'bout!

WALTER: You want to know what I was thinking 'bout in the bathroom or not!

RUTH: I know what you thinking 'bout.

WALTER (*ignoring her*):   'Bout what me and Willy Harris was talking about last night.

RUTH (*immediately—a refrain*):   Willy Harris is a good-for-nothing loudmouth.

WALTER: Anybody who talks to me has got to be a good-for-nothing loudmouth, ain't he? And what you know about who is just a good-for-nothing loudmouth? Charlie Atkins was just a "good-for-nothing loudmouth" too, wasn't he! When he wanted me to go in the dry-cleaning business with him. And now—he's grossing a hundred thousand a year. A hundred thousand dollars a year! You still call *him* a loudmouth!

RUTH (*bitterly*):   Oh, Walter Lee . . .

(*She folds her head on her arms over the table*)

WALTER (*rising and coming to her and standing over her*):   You tired, ain't you? Tired of everything. Me, the boy, the way we live—this beat-up hole—everything. Ain't you? (*She doesn't look up, doesn't answer*) So tired—moaning and groaning all the time, but you wouldn't do nothing to help, would you? You couldn't be on my side that long for nothing, could you?

RUTH: Walter, please leave me alone.

WALTER: A man needs for a woman to back him up . . .

RUTH: Walter—

WALTER: Mama would listen to you. You know she listen to you more than she do me and Bennie. She think more of you. All you have to do is just sit down with her when you drinking your coffee one morning and talking 'bout things like you do and—(*He sits down beside her and demonstrates graphically what he thinks her methods and tone should be*)—you just sip your coffee, see, and say easy like that you been thinking 'bout that deal Walter Lee is so interested in, 'bout the store and all, and sip some more coffee, like what you saying ain't really that important to you—And the next thing you know, she be listening good and asking you questions and when I come home—I can tell her the details. This ain't no fly-by-night proposition, baby. I mean we figured it out, me and Willy and Bobo.

RUTH (*with a frown*):   Bobo?

WALTER: Yeah. You see, this little liquor store we got in mind cost seventy-five thousand and we figured the initial investment on the place be 'bout thirty thousand, see. That be ten thousand each. Course, there's a couple of hundred you got to pay so's you don't spend your life just waiting for them clowns to let your license get approved—

RUTH: You mean graft?

WALTER (*frowning impatiently*):   Don't call it that. See there, that just goes to show you what women understand about the world. Baby, don't *nothing* happen for you in this world 'less you pay *somebody* off!

RUTH: Walter, leave me alone! (*She raises her head and stares at him vigorously—then says, more quietly*) Eat your eggs, they gonna be cold.

WALTER (*straightening up from her and looking off*):   That's it. There you are. Man say to his woman: I got me a dream. His woman say: Eat your eggs. (*Sadly, but gaining in power*) Man say: I got to take hold of this here world, baby! And a woman will say: Eat your eggs and go to work. (*Passionately now*) Man say: I got to change my life, I'm choking to death, baby! And his woman say—(*In utter anguish as he brings his fists down on his thighs*)—Your eggs is getting cold!

RUTH (*softly*):   Walter, that ain't none of our money.

WALTER (*not listening at all or even looking at her*):   This morning, I was lookin' in the mirror and thinking about it . . . I'm thirty-five years old; I been married eleven years and I got a boy who sleeps in the living room—(*Very, very quietly*)—and all I got to give him is stories about how rich white people live . . .

RUTH: Eat your eggs, Walter.

WALTER (*slams the table and jumps up*):   —DAMN MY EGGS—DAMN ALL THE EGGS THAT EVER WAS!

RUTH: Then go to work.

WALTER (*looking up at her*):   See—I'm trying to talk to you 'bout myself—(*Shaking his head with the repetition*)—and all you can say is eat them eggs and go to work.

RUTH (*wearily*):   Honey, you never say nothing new. I listen to you every day, every night and every morning, and you never say nothing new. (*Shrugging*) So you would rather *be* Mr. Arnold than be his chauffeur. So—I would *rather* be living in Buckingham Palace.

WALTER: That is just what is wrong with the colored woman in this world . . . Don't understand about building their men up and making 'em feel like they somebody. Like they can do something.

RUTH (*drily, but to hurt*):   There *are* colored men who do things.

WALTER: No thanks to the colored woman.

RUTH: Well, being a colored woman, I guess I can't help myself none.

(*She rises and gets the ironing board and sets it up and attacks a huge pile of rough-dried clothes, sprinkling them in preparation for the ironing and then rolling them into tight fat balls*)

WALTER (*mumbling*):   We one group of men tied to a race of women with small minds!

(*His sister* BENEATHA *enters. She is about twenty, as slim and intense as her brother. She is not as pretty as her sister-in-law, but her lean, almost intellectual face has a handsomeness of its own.*

She wears a bright-red flannel nightie, and her thick hair stands wildly about her head. Her speech is a mixture of many things; it is different from the rest of the family's insofar as education has permeated her sense of English—and perhaps the Midwest rather than the South has finally—at last—won out in her inflection; but not altogether, because over all of it is a soft slurring and transformed use of vowels which is the decided influence of the Southside. She passes through the room without looking at either RUTH or WALTER and goes to the outside door and looks, a little blindly, out to the bathroom. She sees that it has been lost to the Johnsons. She closes the door with a sleepy vengeance and crosses to the table and sits down a little defeated)

BENEATHA: I am going to start timing those people.

WALTER: You should get up earlier.

BENEATHA (*her face in her hands. She is still fighting the urge to go back to bed*):   Really— would you suggest dawn? Where's the paper?

WALTER (*pushing the paper across the table to her as he studies her almost clinically, as though he has never seen her before*):   You a horrible-looking chick at this hour.

BENEATHA (*drily*):   Good morning, everybody.

WALTER (*senselessly*):   How is school coming?

BENEATHA (*in the same spirit*):   Lovely. Lovely. And you know, biology is the greatest. (*Looking up at him*) I dissected something that looked just like you yesterday.

WALTER: I just wondered if you've made up your mind and everything.

BENEATHA (*gaining in sharpness and impatience*):   And what did I answer yesterday morning—and the day before that?

RUTH (*from the ironing board, like someone disinterested and old*):   Don't be so nasty, Bennie.

BENEATHA (*still to her brother*):   And the day before that and the day before that!

WALTER (*defensively*):   I'm interested in you. Something wrong with that? Ain't many girls who decide—

WALTER *and* BENEATHA (*in unison*):   —"to be a doctor."

(*Silence*)

WALTER: Have we figured out yet just exactly how much medical school is going to cost?

RUTH: Walter Lee, why don't you leave that girl alone and get out of here to work?

BENEATHA (*exits to the bathroom and bangs on the door*):   Come on out of there, please!

(*She comes back into the room*)

WALTER (*looking at his sister intently*):   You know the check is coming tomorrow.

BENEATHA (*turning on him with a sharpness all her own*):   That money belongs to Mama, Walter, and it's for her to decide how she wants to use it. I don't care if she wants to buy a house or a rocket ship or just nail it up somewhere and look at it. It's hers. Not ours—*hers*.

WALTER (*bitterly*):   Now ain't that fine! You just got your mother's interest at heart, ain't you, girl? You such a nice girl—but if Mama got that money she can always take a few thousand and help you through school too—can't she?

BENEATHA: I have never asked anyone around here to do anything for me!

WALTER: No! And the line between asking and just accepting when the time comes is big and wide—ain't it!

BENEATHA (*with fury*):   What do you want from me, Brother—that I quit school or just drop dead, which!

WALTER: I don't want nothing but for you to stop acting holy 'round here. Me and Ruth done made some sacrifices for you—why can't you do something for the family?

RUTH: Walter, don't be dragging me in it.

WALTER: You are in it—Don't you get up and go work in somebody's kitchen for the last three years to help put clothes on her back?

RUTH: Oh, Walter—that's not fair . . .

WALTER: It ain't that nobody expects you to get on your knees and say thank you, Brother; thank you, Ruth; thank you, Mama—and thank you, Travis, for wearing the same pair of shoes for two semesters—

BENEATHA (*dropping to her knees*):   Well—I *do*—all right?—thank everybody! And forgive me for ever wanting to be anything at all! (*Pursuing him on her knees across the floor*) FORGIVE ME, FORGIVE ME, FORGIVE ME!

RUTH: Please stop it! Your mama'll hear you.

WALTER: Who the hell told you you had to be a doctor? If you so crazy 'bout messing 'round with sick people—then go be a nurse like other women—or just get married and be quiet . . .

BENEATHA: Well—you finally got it said . . . It took you three years but you finally got it said. Walter, give up; leave me alone—it's Mama's money.

WALTER: *He was my father, too!*

BENEATHA: So what? He was mine, too—and Travis' grandfather—but the insurance money belongs to Mama. Picking on me is not going to make her give it to you to invest in any liquor stores—(*Underbreath, dropping into a chair*)—and I for one say, God bless Mama for that!

WALTER (*to* RUTH):   See—did you hear? Did you hear!

RUTH: Honey, please go to work.

WALTER: Nobody in this house is ever going to understand me.

BENEATHA: Because you're a nut.

WALTER: Who's a nut?

BENEATHA: You—you are a nut. Thee is mad, boy.

WALTER (*looking at his wife and his sister from the door, very sadly*):   The world's most backward race of people, and that's a fact.

BENEATHA (*turning slowly in her chair*):   And then there are all those prophets who would lead us out of the wilderness—(WALTER *slams out of the house*)—into the swamps!

RUTH: Bennie, why you always gotta be pickin' on your brother? Can't you be a little sweeter sometimes? (*Door opens.* WALTER *walks in. He fumbles with his cap, starts to speak, clears throat, looks everywhere but at* RUTH. *Finally:*)

WALTER (*to* RUTH):   I need some money for carfare.

RUTH (*looks at him, then warms; teasing, but tenderly*):   Fifty cents? (*She goes to her bag and gets money*) Here—take a taxi!

(WALTER *exits.* MAMA *enters. She is a woman in her early sixties, full-bodied and strong. She is one of those women of a certain grace and beauty who wear it so unobtrusively that it takes a while to notice. Her dark-brown face is surrounded by the total whiteness of her hair, and, being a woman who has adjusted to many things in life and overcome many more, her face is full of strength. She has, we can see, wit and faith of a kind that keep her eyes lit and full of interest and expectancy. She is, in a word, a beautiful woman. Her bearing is perhaps most like the noble bearing of the women of the Hereros of Southwest Africa—rather as if she imagines that as she walks she still bears a basket or a vessel upon her head. Her speech, on the other hand, is as careless as her carriage is precise—she is inclined to slur everything—but her voice is perhaps not so much quiet as simply soft)*

MAMA: Who that 'round here slamming doors at this hour?

(She crosses through the room, goes to the window, opens it, and brings in a feeble little plant growing doggedly in a small pot on the window sill. She feels the dirt and puts it back out)

RUTH: That was Walter Lee. He and Bennie was at it again.

MAMA: My children and they tempers. Lord, if this little old plant don't get more sun than it's been getting it ain't never going to see spring again. (*She turns from the window*) What's the matter with you this morning, Ruth? You looks right peaked. You aiming to iron all them things? Leave some for me. I'll get to 'em this afternoon. Bennie honey, it's too drafty for you to be sitting 'round half dressed. Where's your robe?

BENEATHA: In the cleaners.

MAMA: Well, go get mine and put it on.

BENEATHA: I'm not cold, Mama, honest.

MAMA: I know—but you so thin . . .

BENEATHA (*irritably*):   Mama, I'm not cold.

MAMA (*seeing the make-down bed as* TRAVIS *has left it*):   Lord have mercy, look at that poor bed. Bless his heart—he tries, don't he?

(She moves to the bed TRAVIS *has sloppily made up)*

RUTH: No—he don't half try at all 'cause he knows you going to come along behind him and fix everything. That's just how come he don't know how to do nothing right now—you done spoiled that boy so.

MAMA (*folding bedding*):   Well—he's a little boy. Ain't supposed to know 'bout housekeeping. My baby, that's what he is. What you fix for his breakfast this morning?

RUTH (*angrily*):   I feed my son, Lena!

MAMA: I ain't meddling—(*Underbreath; busy-bodyish*) I just noticed all last week he had cold cereal, and when it starts getting this chilly in the fall a child ought to have some hot grits or something when he goes out in the cold—

RUTH (*furious*):   I gave him hot oats—is that all right!

MAMA: I ain't meddling. (*Pause*) Put a lot of nice butter on it? (RUTH *shoots her an angry look and does not reply*) He likes lots of butter.

RUTH (*exasperated*):   Lena—

MAMA (*to* BENEATHA. MAMA *is inclined to wander conversationally sometimes*):   What was you and your brother fussing 'bout this morning?

BENEATHA: It's not important, Mama.

(She gets up and goes to look out at the bathroom, which is apparently free, and she picks up her towels and rushes out)

MAMA: What was they fighting about?

RUTH: Now you know as well as I do.

MAMA (*shaking her head*):   Brother still worrying hisself sick about that money?

RUTH: You know he is.

MAMA: You had breakfast?

RUTH: Some coffee.

MAMA: Girl, you better start eating and looking after yourself better. You almost thin as Travis.

RUTH: Lena—

MAMA: Uh-hunh?

RUTH: What are you going to do with it?

MAMA: Now don't you start, child. It's too early in the morning to be talking about money. It ain't Christian.

RUTH: It's just that he got his heart set on that store—

MAMA: You mean that liquor store that Willy Harris want him to invest in?

RUTH: Yes—

MAMA: We ain't no business people, Ruth. We just plain working folks.

RUTH: Ain't nobody business people till they go into business. Walter Lee say colored people ain't never going to start getting ahead till they start gambling on some different kinds of things in the world—investments and things.

MAMA: What done got into you, girl? Walter Lee done finally sold you on investing.

RUTH: No. Mama, something is happening between Walter and me. I don't know what it is—but he needs something—something I can't give him any more. He needs this chance, Lena.

MAMA (*frowning deeply*):   But liquor, honey—

RUTH: Well—like Walter say—I spec people going to always be drinking themselves some liquor.

RUTH: Well—whether they drinks it or not ain't none of my business. But whether I go into business selling it to 'em *is,* and I don't want that on my ledger this late in life. (*Stopping suddenly and studying her daughter-in-law*) Ruth Younger, what's the matter with you today? You look like you could fall over right there.

RUTH: I'm tired.

MAMA: Then you better stay home from work today.

RUTH: I can't stay home. She'd be calling up the agency and screaming at them, "My girl didn't come in today—send me somebody! My girl didn't come in!" Oh, she just have a fit . . .

MAMA: Well, let her have it. I'll just call her up and say you got the flu—

RUTH (*laughing*):   Why the flu?

MAMA: 'Cause it sounds respectable to 'em. Something white people get, too. They know 'bout the flu. Otherwise they think you been cut up or something when you tell 'em you sick.

RUTH: I got to go in. We need the money.

MAMA: Somebody would of thought my children done all but starved to death the way they talk about money here late. Child, we got a great big old check coming tomorrow.

RUTH (*sincerely, but also self-righteously*):   Now that's your money. It ain't got nothing to do with me. We all feel like that—Walter and Bennie and me—even Travis.

MAMA (*thoughtfully, and suddenly very far away*):   Ten thousand dollars—

RUTH: Sure is wonderful.

MAMA: Ten thousand dollars.

RUTH: You know what you should do, Miss Lena? You should take yourself a trip somewhere. To Europe or South America or someplace—

MAMA (*throwing up her hands at the thought*): Oh, child!

RUTH: I'm serious. Just pack up and leave! Go on away and enjoy yourself some. Forget about the family and have yourself a ball for once in your life—

MAMA (*drily*): You should like I'm just about ready to die. Who'd go with me? What I look like wandering 'round Europe by myself?

RUTH: Shoot—these here rich white women do it all the time. They don't think nothing of packing up they suitcases and piling on one of them big steamships and—swoosh!—they gone, child.

MAMA: Something always told me I wasn't no rich white woman.

RUTH: Well—what are you going to do with it then?

MAMA: I ain't rightly decided. (*Thinking. She speaks now with emphasis*) Some of it got to be put away for Beneatha and her schoolin'—and ain't nothing going to touch that part of it. Nothing. (*She waits several seconds, trying to make up her mind about something, and looks at* RUTH *a little tentatively before going on*) Been thinking that we maybe could meet the notes on a little old two-story somewhere, with a yard where Travis could play in the summertime, if we use part of the insurance for a down payment and everybody kind of pitch in. I could maybe take on a little day work again, few days a week—

RUTH (*studying her mother-in-law furtively and concentrating on her ironing, anxious to encourage without seeming to*): Well, Lord knows, we've put enough rent into this here rat trap to pay for four houses by now . . .

MAMA (*looking up at the words "rat trap" and then looking around and leaning back and sighing—in a suddenly reflective mood—*): "Rat trap"—yes, that's all it is. (*Smiling*) I remember just as well the day me and Big Walter moved in here. Hadn't been married but two weeks and wasn't planning on living here no more than a year. (*She shakes her head at the dissolved dream*) We was going to set away, little by little, don't you know, and buy a little place out in Morgan Park. We had even picked out the house. (*Chuckling a little*) Looks right dumpy today. But Lord, child, you should know all the dreams I had 'bout buying that house and fixing it up and making me a little garden in the back—(*She waits and stops smiling*) And didn't none of it happen.

(*Dropping her hands in a futile gesture*)

RUTH (*keeps her head down, ironing*): Yes, life can be a barrel of disappointments, sometimes.

MAMA: Honey, Big Walter would come in here some nights back then and slump down on that couch there and just look at the rug, and look at me and look at the rug and then back at me—and I'd know he was down then . . . really down. (*After a second very long and thoughtful pause; she is seeing back to times that only she can see*) And then, Lord, when I lost that baby—little Claude—I almost thought I was going to lose Big Walter too. Oh, that man grieved hisself! He was one man to love his children.

RUTH: Ain't nothin' can tear at you like losin' your baby.

MAMA: I guess that's how come that man finally worked hisself to death like he done. Like he was fighting his own war with this here world that took his baby from him.

RUTH: He sure was a fine man, all right. I always liked Mr. Younger.

MAMA: Crazy 'bout his children! God knows there was plenty wrong with Walter Younger—hard-headed, mean, kind of wild with women—plenty wrong with him. But he sure loved his children. Always wanted them to have something—be something. That's where Brother gets all these notions, I reckon. Big Walter used to say, he'd get right wet in the eyes sometimes, lean his head back with the water standing in his eyes and say, "Seem like God didn't see fit to give the black man nothing but dreams—but He did give us children to make them dreams seem worth while." (*She smiles*) He could talk like that, don't you know.

RUTH: Yes, he sure could. He was a good man, Mr. Younger.

MAMA: Yes, a fine man—just couldn't never catch up with his dreams, that's all.

(BENEATHA *comes in, brushing her hair and looking up to the ceiling, where the sound of a vacuum cleaner has started up*)

BENEATHA: What could be so dirty on that woman's rugs that she has to vacuum them every single day?

RUTH: I wish certain young women 'round here who I could name would take inspiration about certain rugs in a certain apartment I could also mention.

BENEATHA (*shrugging*):   How much cleaning can a house need, for Christ's sakes.

MAMA (*not liking the Lord's name used thus*):   Bennie!

RUTH: Just listen to her—just listen!

BENEATHA: Oh, God!

MAMA: If you use the Lord's name just one more time—

BENEATHA (*a bit of a whine*):   Oh, Mama—

RUTH: Fresh—just fresh as salt, this girl!

BENEATHA (*drily*):   Well—if the salt loses its savor—

MAMA: Now that will do. I just ain't going to have you 'round here reciting the scriptures in vain—you hear me?

BENEATHA: How did I manage to get on everybody's wrong side by just walking into a room?

RUTH: If you weren't so fresh—

BENEATHA: Ruth, I'm twenty years old.

MAMA: What time you be home from school today?

BENEATHA: Kind of late. (*With enthusiasm*) Madeline is going to start my guitar lessons today.

(MAMA *and* RUTH *look up with the same expression*)

MAMA: Your *what* kind of lessons?

BENEATHA: Guitar.

RUTH: Oh, Father!

MAMA: How come you done taken it in your mind to learn to play the guitar?

BENEATHA: I just want to, that's all.

MAMA (*smiling*):   Lord, child, don't you know what to do with yourself? How long it going to be before you get tired of this now—like you got tired of that little play-acting group you joined last year? (*Looking at* RUTH) And what was it the year before that?

RUTH: The horseback-riding club for which she bought that fifty-five-dollar riding habit that's been hanging in the closet ever since!

MAMA (*to* BENEATHA):   Why you got to flit so from one thing to another, baby?

BENEATHA (*sharply*): I just want to learn to play the guitar. Is there anything wrong with that?

MAMA: Ain't nobody trying to stop you. I just wonders sometimes why you has to flit so from one thing to another all the time. You ain't never done nothing with all that camera equipment you brought home—

BENEATHA: I don't flit! I—I experiment with different forms of expression—

RUTH: Like riding a horse?

BENEATHA: —People have to express themselves one way or another.

MAMA: What is it you want to express?

BENEATHA (*angrily*): Me! (MAMA *and* RUTH *look at each other and burst into raucous laughter*) Don't worry—I don't expect you to understand.

MAMA (*to change the subject*): Who you going out with tomorrow night?

BENEATHA (*with displeasure*): George Murchison again.

MAMA (*pleased*): Oh—you getting a little sweet on him?

RUTH: You ask me, this child ain't sweet on nobody but herself—(*Underbreath*) Express herself!

(*They laugh*)

BENEATHA: Oh—I like George all right, Mama. I mean I like him enough to go out with him and stuff, but—

RUTH (*for devilment*): What does *and stuff* mean?

BENEATHA: Mind your own business.

MAMA: Stop picking at her now, Ruth. (*She chuckles—then a suspicious sudden look at her daughter as she turns in her chair for emphasis*) What DOES it mean?

BENEATHA (*wearily*): Oh, I just mean I couldn't ever really be serious about George. He's—he's so shallow.

RUTH: Shallow—what do you mean he's shallow? He's *Rich*!

MAMA: Hush, Ruth.

BENEATHA: I know he's rich. He knows he's rich, too.

RUTH: Well—what other qualities a man got to have to satisfy you, little girl?

BENEATHA: You wouldn't even begin to understand. Anybody who married Walter could not possibly understand.

MAMA (*outraged*): What kind of way is that to talk about your brother?

BENEATHA: Brother is a flip—let's face it.

MAMA (*to* RUTH, *helplessly*): What's a flip?

RUTH (*glad to add kindling*): She's saying he's crazy.

BENEATHA: Not crazy. Brother isn't really crazy yet—he—he's an elaborate neurotic.

MAMA: Hush your mouth!

BENEATHA: As for George. Well. George looks good—he's got a beautiful car and he takes me to nice places and, as my sister-in-law says, he is probably the richest boy I will ever get to know and I even like him sometimes—but if the Youngers are sitting around waiting to see if their little Bennie is going to tie up the family with the Murchisons, they are wasting their time.

RUTH: You mean you wouldn't marry George Murchison if he asked you someday? That pretty, rich thing? Honey, I knew you was odd—

BENEATHA: No I would not marry him if all I felt for him was what I feel now. Besides, George's family wouldn't really like it.

MAMA: Why not?

BENEATHA: Oh, Mama—The Murchisons are honest-to-God-real-*live*-rich colored people, and the only people in the world who are more snobbish than rich white people are rich colored people. I thought everybody knew that. I've met Mrs. Murchison. She's a scene!

MAMA: You must not dislike people 'cause they well off, honey.

BENEATHA: Why not? It makes just as much sense as disliking people 'cause they are poor, and lots of people do that.

RUTH (*a wisdom-of-the-ages manner. To* MAMA):   Well, she'll get over some of this—

BENEATHA: Get over it? What are you talking about, Ruth? Listen, I'm going to be a doctor. I'm not worried about who I'm going to marry yet—if I ever get married.

MAMA *and* RUTH: *If!*

MAMA: Now, Bennie—

BENEATHA: Oh, I probably will . . . but first I'm going to be a doctor, and George, for one, still thinks that's pretty funny. I couldn't be bothered with that. I am going to be a doctor and everybody around here better understand that!

MAMA (*kindly*):   'Course you going to be a doctor, honey, God willing.

BENEATHA (*drily*):   God hasn't got a thing to do with it.

MAMA: Beneatha—that just wasn't necessary.

BENEATHA: Well—neither is God. I get sick of hearing about God.

MAMA: Beneatha!

BENEATHA: I mean it! I'm just tired of hearing about God all the time. What has He got to do with anything? Does he pay tuition?

MAMA: You 'bout to get your fresh little jaw slapped!

RUTH: That's just what she needs, all right!

BENEATHA: Why? Why can't I say what I want to around here, like everybody else?

MAMA: It don't sound nice for a young girl to say things like that—you wasn't brought up that way. Me and your father went to trouble to get you and Brother to church every Sunday.

BENEATHA: Mama, you don't understand. It's all a matter of ideas, and God is just one idea I don't accept. It's not important. I am not going out and be immoral or commit crimes because I don't believe in God. I don't even think about it. It's just that I get tired of Him getting credit for all the things the human race achieves through its own stubborn effort. There simply is no blasted God—there is only man and it is *he* who makes miracles!

(MAMA *absorbs this speech, studies her daughter and rises slowly and crosses to* BENEATHA *and slaps her powerfully across the face. After, there is only silence and the daughter drops her eyes from her mother's face, and* MAMA *is very tall before her*)

MAMA: Now—you say after me, in my mother's house there is still God. (*There is a long pause and* BENEATHA *stares at the floor wordlessly.* MAMA *repeats the phrase with precision and cool emotion*) In my mother's house there is still God.

BENEATHA: In my mother's house there is still God.

(*A long pause*)

MAMA (*walking away from* BENEATHA, *too disturbed for triumphant posture. Stopping and turning back to her daughter*):   There are some ideas we ain't going to have in this house. Not long as I am at the head of this family.

BENEATHA: Yes, ma'am.

(MAMA *walks out of the room*)

RUTH (*almost gently, with profound understanding*): You think you a woman, Bennie—but you still a little girl. What you did was childish—so you got treated like a child.

BENEATHA: I see. (*Quietly*) I also see that everybody thinks it's all right for Mama to be a tyrant. But all the tyranny in the world will never put a God in the heavens!

(*She picks up her books and goes out. Pause*)

RUTH (*goes to* MAMA's *door*): She said she was sorry.

MAMA (*coming out, going to her plant*): They frightens me, Ruth. My children.

RUTH: You got good children, Lena. They just a little off sometimes—but they're good.

MAMA: No—there's something come down between me and them that don't let us understand each other and I don't know what it is. One done almost lost his mind thinking 'bout money all the time and the other done commence to talk about things I can't seem to understand in no form or fashion. What is it that's changing, Ruth.

RUTH (*soothingly, older than her years*): Now . . . you taking it all too seriously. You just got strong-willed children and it takes a strong woman like you to keep 'em in hand.

MAMA (*looking at her plant and sprinkling a little water on it*): They spirited all right, my children. Got to admit they got spirit—Bennie and Walter. Like this little old plant that ain't never had enough sunshine or nothing—and look at it . . .

(*She has her back to* RUTH, *who has had to stop ironing and lean against something and put the back of her hand to her forehead*)

RUTH (*trying to keep* MAMA *from noticing*): You . . . sure . . . loves that little old thing, don't you? . . .

MAMA: Well, I always wanted me a garden like I used to see sometimes at the back of the houses down home. This plant is close as I ever got to having one. (*She looks out of the window as she replaces the plant*) Lord, ain't nothing as dreary as the view from this window on a dreary day, is there? Why ain't you singing this morning, Ruth? Sing that "No Ways Tired." That song always lifts me up so—(*She turns at last to see that* RUTH *has slipped quietly to the floor, in a state of semiconsciousness*) Ruth! Ruth honey—what's the matter with you . . . Ruth!

Curtain

Scene II

It is the following morning; a Saturday morning, and house cleaning is in progress at the YOUNGERS. *Furniture has been shoved hither and yon and* MAMA *is giving the kitchen-area walls a washing down.* BENEATHA, *in dungarees, with a handkerchief tied around her face, is spraying insecticide into the cracks in the walls. As they work, the radio is on and a Southside disk-jockey program is inappropriately filling the house with a rather exotic saxophone blues.* TRAVIS, *the sole idle one, is leaning on his arms, looking out of the window.*

TRAVIS: Grandmama, that stuff Bennie is using smells awful. Can I go downstairs, please?

MAMA: Did you get all them chores done already? I ain't seen you doing much.

TRAVIS: Yes'm—finished early. Where did Mama go this morning?

MAMA (*looking at* BENEATHA):   She had to go on a little errand.

(*The phone rings.* BENEATHA *runs to answer it and reaches it before* WALTER, *who has entered from bedroom*)

TRAVIS: Where?

MAMA: To tend to her business.

BENEATHA: Haylo . . . (*Disappointed*) Yes, he is. (*She tosses the phone to* WALTER, *who barely catches it*) It's Willie Harris again.

WALTER (*as privately as possible under* MAMA'S *gaze*):   Hello, Willie. Did you get the papers from the lawyer? . . . No, not yet. I told you the mailman doesn't get here till ten-thirty . . . No, I'll come there . . . Yeah! Right away. (*He hangs up and goes for his coat*)

BENEATHA: Brother, where did Ruth go?

WALTER (*as he exits*):   How should I know!

TRAVIS: Aw come on, Grandma. Can I go outside?

MAMA: Oh, I guess so. You stay right in front of the house, though, and keep a good lookout for the postman.

TRAVIS: Yes'm. (*He darts into bedroom for stickball and bat, reenters, and sees* BENEATHA *on her knees spraying under sofa with behind upraised. He edges closer to the target, takes aim, and lets her have it. She screams*) Leave them poor little cockroaches alone, they ain't bothering you none! (*He runs as she swings the spray-gun at him viciously and playfully*) Grandma! Grandma!

MAMA: Look out there, girl, before you be spilling some of that stuff on that child!

TRAVIS (*safely behind the bastion of* MAMA):   That's right—look out, now! (*He exits*)

BENEATHA (*drily*):   I can't imagine that it would hurt him—it has never hurt the roaches.

MAMA: Well, little boys' hides ain't as tough as Southside roaches. You better get over there behind the bureau. I seen one marching out of there like Napoleon yesterday.

BENEATHA: There's really only one way to get rid of them, Mama—

MAMA: How?

BENEATHA: Set fire to this building! Mama, where did Ruth go?

MAMA (*looking at her with meaning*):   To the doctor, I think.

BENEATHA: The doctor? What's the matter? (*They exchange glances*) You don't think—

MAMA (*with her sense of drama*):   Now I ain't saying what I think. But I ain't never been wrong 'bout a woman neither.

(*The phone rings*)

BENEATHA (*at the phone*):   Hay-lo . . . (*Pause, and a moment of recognition*) Well—when did you get back! . . . And how was it? . . . Of course I've missed you—in my way . . . This morning? No . . . house cleaning and all that and Mama hates it if I let people come over when the house is like this . . . You *have*? Well, that's different . . . What is it—Oh, what the hell, come on over . . . Right, see you then. *Arrivederci.*

(*She hangs up*)

MAMA (*who has listened vigorously, as is her habit*):   Who is that you inviting over here with this house looking like this? You ain't got the pride you was born with!

BENEATHA: Asagai doesn't care how houses look, Mama—he's an intellectual.

MAMA: *Who?*

BENEATHA: Asagai—Joseph Asagai. He's an African boy I met on campus. He's been studying in Canada all summer.

MAMA: What's his name?

BENEATHA: Asagai, Joseph. Ah-sah-guy . . . He's from Nigeria.

MAMA: Oh, that's the little country that was founded by slaves way back . . .

BENEATHA: No, Mama—that's Liberia.

MAMA: I don't think I never met no African before.

BENEATHA: Well, do me a favor and don't ask him a whole lot of ignorant questions about Africans. I mean, do they wear clothes and all that—

MAMA: Well, now, I guess if you think we so ignorant 'round here maybe you shouldn't bring your friends here—

BENEATHA: It's just that people ask such crazy things. All anyone seems to know about when it comes to Africa is Tarzan—

MAMA (*indignantly*):   Why should I know anything about Africa?

BENEATHA: Why do you give money at church for the missionary work?

MAMA: Well, that's to help save people.

BENEATHA: You mean save them from *heathenism*—

MAMA (*innocently*):   Yes.

BENEATHA: I'm afraid they need more salvation from the British and the French.

(RUTH *comes in forlornly and pulls off her coat with dejection. They both turn to look at her*)

RUTH (*dispiritedly*):   Well, I guess from all the happy faces—everybody knows.

BENEATHA: You pregnant?

MAMA: Lord have mercy, I sure hope it's a little old girl. Travis ought to have a sister.

(BENEATHA *and* RUTH *give her a hopeless look for this grandmotherly enthusiasm*)

BENEATHA: How far along are you?

RUTH: Two months.

BENEATHA: Did you mean to? I mean did you plan it or was it an accident?

MAMA: What do you know about planning or not planning?

BENEATHA: Oh, Mama.

RUTH (*wearily*):   She's twenty years old, Lena.

BENEATHA: Did you plan it, Ruth?

RUTH: Mind your own business.

BENEATHA: It is my business—where is he going to live, on the *roof*? (*There is silence following the remark as the three women react to the sense of it*) Gee—I didn't mean that, Ruth, honest. Gee, I don't feel like that at all. I—I think it is wonderful.

RUTH (*dully*):   Wonderful.

BENEATHA: Yes—really.

MAMA (*looking at* RUTH, *worried*):   Doctor say everything going to be all right?

RUTH (*far away*):   Yes—she says everything is going to be fine . . .

MAMA (*immediately suspicious*):   "She"—What doctor you went to?

(RUTH *folds over, near hysteria*)

MAMA (*worriedly hovering over* RUTH):   Ruth honey—what's the matter with you—you sick?

(RUTH *has her fists clenched on her thighs and is fighting hard to suppress a scream that seems to be rising in her*)

BENEATHA: What's the matter with her, Mama?

MAMA (*working her fingers in* RUTH's *shoulders to relax her*):   She be all right. Women gets right depressed sometimes when they get her way. (*Speaking softly, expertly, rapidly*) Now you just relax. That's right . . . just lean back, don't think 'bout nothing at all . . . nothing at all—

RUTH: I'm all right . . .

(*The glassy-eyed look melts and then she collapses into a fit of heavy sobbing. The bell rings*)

BENEATHA: Oh, my God—that must be Asagai.

MAMA (*to* RUTH):   Come on now, honey. You need to lie down and rest awhile . . . then have some nice hot food.

(*They exit,* RUTH's *weight on her mother-in-law.* BENEATHA, *herself profoundly disturbed, opens the door to admit a rather dramatic-looking young man with a large package*)

ASAGAI: Hello, Alaiyo—

BENEATHA (*holding the door open and regarding him with pleasure*):   Hello . . . (*Long pause*) Well—come in. And please excuse everything. My mother was very upset about my letting anyone come here with the place like this.

ASAGAI (*coming into the room*):   You look disturbed too . . . Is something wrong?

BENEATHA (*still at the door, absently*):   Yes . . . we've all got acute ghetto-itus. (*She smiles and comes toward him, finding a cigarette and sitting*) So—sit down! No! Wait! (*She whips the spraygun off sofa where she had left it and puts the cushions back. At last perches on arm of sofa. He sits*) So, how was Canada?

ASAGAI (*a sophisticate*):   Canadian.

BENEATHA (*looking at him*):   Asagai, I'm very glad you are back.

ASAGAI (*looking back at her in turn*):   Are you really?

BENEATHA: Yes—very.

ASAGAI: Why?—you were quite glad when I went away. What happened?

BENEATHA: You went away.

ASAGAI: Ahhhhhhhh.

BENEATHA: Before—you wanted to be so serious before there was time.

ASAGAI: How much time must there be before one knows what one feels?

BENEATHA (*stalling this particular conversation. Her hands pressed together, in a deliberately childish gesture*):   What did you bring me?

ASAGAI (*handing her the package*):   Open it and see.

BENEATHA (*eagerly opening the package and drawing out some records and the colorful robes of a Nigerian woman*):   Oh, Asagai! . . . You got them for me! . . . How beautiful . . . and the records too! (*She lifts out the robes and runs to the mirror with them and holds the drapery up in front of herself*)

ASAGAI (*coming to her at the mirror*):   I shall have to teach you how to drape it properly. (*He flings the material about her for the moment and stands back to look at her*) Ah—Oh-pay-gay-day, oh-gbah-mu-shay. (*A Yoruba exclamation for admiration*) You wear it well . . . very well . . . mutilated hair and all.

BENEATHA (*turning suddenly*):   My hair—what's wrong with my hair?

ASAGAI (*shrugging*):   Were you born with it like that?

BENEATHA (*reaching up to touch it*):   No . . . of course not.

(*She looks back to the mirror, disturbed*)

ASAGAI (*smiling*):   How then?

BENEATHA: You know perfectly well how . . . as crinkly as yours . . . that's how.

ASAGAI: And it is ugly to you that way?

BENEATHA (*quickly*):   Oh, no—not ugly . . . (*More slowly, apologetically*) But it's so hard to manage when it's, well—raw.

ASAGAI: And so to accommodate that—you mutilate it every week?

BENEATHA: It's not mutilation!

ASAGAI (*laughing aloud at her seriousness*):   Oh . . . please! I am only teasing you because you are so very serious about these things. (*He stands back from her and folds his arms across his chest as he watches her pulling at her hair and frowning in the mirror*) Do you remember the first time you met me at school? . . . (*He laughs*) You came up to me and you said—and I thought you were the most serious little thing I had ever seen—you said: (*He imitates her*) "Mr. Asagai—I want very much to talk with you. About Africa. You see, Mr. Asagai, I am looking for my *identity!*"

(*He laughs*)

BENEATHA (*turning to him, not laughing*):   Yes—

(*Her face is quizzical, profoundly disturbed*)

ASAGAI (*still teasing and reaching out and taking her face in his hands and turning her profile to him*):   Well . . . it is true that this is not so much a profile of a Hollywood queen as perhaps a queen of the Nile—(*A mock dismissal of the importance of the question*) But what does it matter? Assimilationism is so popular in your country.

BENEATHA (*wheeling, passionately, sharply*):   I am not an assimilationist!

ASAGAI (*the protest hangs in the room for a moment and* ASAGAI *studies her, his laughter fading*):   Such a serious one. (*There is a pause*) So—you like the robes? You must take excellent care of them—they are from my sister's personal wardrobe.

BENEATHA (*with incredulity*):   You—you sent all the way home—for me?

ASAGAI (*with charm*):   For you—I would do much more . . . Well, that is what I came for. I must go.

BENEATHA: Will you call me Monday?

ASAGAI: Yes . . . We have a great deal to talk about. I mean about identity and time and all that.

BENEATHA: Time?

ASAGAI: Yes. About how much time one needs to know what one feels.

BENEATHA: You see! You never understood that there is more than one kind of feeling which can exist between a man and a woman—or, at least, there should be.

ASAGAI (*shaking his head negatively but gently*):   No. Between a man and a woman there need be only one kind of feeling. I have that for you . . . Now even . . . right this moment . . .

BENEATHA: I know—and by itself—it won't do. I can find that anywhere.

ASAGAI: For a woman it should be enough.

BENEATHA: I know—because that's what it says in all the novels that men write. But it isn't. Go ahead and laugh—but I'm not interested in being someone's little episode in America or—(*With feminine vengeance*)—one of them! (ASAGAI *has burst into laughter again*) That's funny as hell, huh!

ASAGAI: It's just that every American girl I have known has said that to me. White—black—in this you are all the same. And the same speech, too!

BENEATHA (*angrily*):   Yuk, yuk, yuk!

ASAGAI: It's how you can be sure that the world's most liberated women are not liberated at all. You all talk about it too much!

(MAMA *enters and is immediately all social charm because of the presence of a guest*)

BENEATHA: Oh—Mama—this is Mr. Asagai.

MAMA: How do you do?

ASAGAI (*total politeness to an elder*):   How do you do, Mrs. Younger. Please forgive me for coming at such an outrageous hour on a Saturday.

MAMA: Well, you are quite welcome. I just hope you understand that our house don't always look like this. (*Chatterish*) You must come again. I would love to hear all about—(*Not sure of the name*)—your country. I think it's so sad the way our American Negroes don't know nothing about Africa 'cept Tarzan and all that. And all that money they pour into these churches when they ought to be helping you people over there drive out them French and Englishmen done taken away your land.

(*The mother flashes a slightly superior look at her daughter upon completion of the recitation*)

ASAGAI (*taken aback by this sudden and acutely unrelated expression of sympathy*):   Yes . . . yes . . .

MAMA (*smiling at him suddenly and relaxing and looking him over*):   How many miles is it from here to where you come from?

ASAGAI: Many thousands.

MAMA (*looking at him as she would* WALTER):   I bet you don't half look after yourself, being away from your mama either. I spec you better come 'round here from time to time to get yourself some decent home-cooked meals . . .

ASAGAI (*moved*):   Thank you. Thank you very much. (*They are all quiet, then—*) Well . . . I must go. I will call you Monday, Alaiyo.

MAMA: What's that he call you?

ASAGAI: Oh—"Alaiyo." I hope you don't mind. It is what you would call a nick-name, I think. It is a Yoruba word. I am a Yoruba.

MAMA (*looking at* BENEATHA):   I—I thought he was from—(*Uncertain*)

ASAGAI (*understanding*):   Nigeria is my country. Yoruba is my tribal origin—

BENEATHA: You didn't tell us what Alaiyo means . . . for all I know, you might be calling me Little Idiot or something . . .

ASAGAI: Well . . . let me see . . . I do not know how just to explain it . . . The sense of a thing can be so different when it changes languages.

BENEATHA: You're evading.

ASAGAI: No—really it is difficult . . . (*Thinking*) It means . . . it means One for Whom Bread—Food—Is Not Enough. (*He looks at her*) Is that all right?

BENEATHA (*understanding, softly*):   Thank you.

MAMA (*looking from one to the other and not understanding any of it*):   Well . . . that's nice . . . You must come see us again—Mr.——

ASAGAI: Ah-sah-guy . . .

MAMA: Yes . . . Do come again.

ASAGAI: Good-bye.

(*He exits*)

MAMA (*after him*):   Lord, that's a pretty thing just went out here! (*Insinuatingly, to her daughter*) Yes, I guess I see why we done commence to get so interested in Africa 'round here. Missionaries my aunt Jenny!

(*She exits*)

BENEATHA: Oh, Mama! . . .

(*She picks up the Nigerian dress and holds it up to her in front of the mirror again. She sets the headdress on haphazardly and then notices her hair again and clutches at it and then replaces the headdress and frowns at herself. Then she starts to wriggle in front of the mirror as she thinks a Nigerian woman might.* TRAVIS *enters and stands regarding her*)

TRAVIS: What's the matter, girl, you cracking up?

BENEATHA: Shut up.

(*She pulls the headdress off and looks at herself in the mirror and clutches at her hair again and squinches her eyes as if trying to imagine something. Then, suddenly, she gets her raincoat and kerchief and hurriedly prepares for going out*)

MAMA (*coming back into the room*):   She's resting now. Travis, baby, run next door and ask Miss Johnson to please let me have a little kitchen cleanser. This here can is empty as Jacob's kettle.

TRAVIS: I just came in.

MAMA: Do as you told. (*He exits and she looks at her daughter*) Where you going?

BENEATHA (*halting at the door*):   To become a queen of the Nile!

(*She exits in a breathless blaze of glory.* RUTH *appears in the bedroom doorway*)

MAMA: Who told you to get up?

RUTH: Ain't nothing wrong with me to be lying in no bed for. Where did Bennie go?

MAMA (*drumming her fingers*):   Far as I could make out—to Egypt. (RUTH *just looks at her*) What time is it getting to?

RUTH: Ten twenty. And the mailman going to ring that bell this morning just like he done every morning for the last umpteen years.

(TRAVIS *comes in with the cleanser can*)

TRAVIS: She say to tell you that she don't have much.

MAMA (*angrily*):   Lord, some people I could name sure is tight-fisted! (*Directing her grandson*) Mark two cans of cleanser down on the list there. If she that hard up for kitchen cleanser, I sure don't want to forget to get her none!

RUTH: Lena—maybe the woman is just short on cleanser—

MAMA (*not listening*):   —Much baking powder as she done borrowed from me all these years, she could of done gone into the baking business!

(*The bell sounds suddenly and sharply and all three are stunned—serious and silent—mid-speech. In spite of all the other conversations and distractions of the morning, this is what they have been waiting for, even* TRAVIS, *who looks helplessly from his mother to his grandmother.* RUTH *is the first to come to life again*)

RUTH (*to* TRAVIS):   Get down them steps, boy!

(TRAVIS *snaps to life and flies out to get the mail*)

MAMA (*her eyes wide, her hand to her breast*):   You mean it done really come?

RUTH (*excited*):   Oh, Miss Lena!

MAMA (*collecting herself*):   Well . . . I don't know what we all so excited about 'round here for. We known it was coming for months.

RUTH: That's a whole lot different from having it come and being able to hold it in your hands . . . a piece of paper worth ten thousand dollars . . . (TRAVIS *bursts back into the room. He holds the envelope high above his head, like a little dancer, his face is radiant and he is breathless. He moves to his grandmother with sudden slow ceremony and puts the envelope into her hands. She accepts it, and then merely holds it and looks at it*) Come on! Open it . . . Lord have mercy, I wish Walter Lee was here!

TRAVIS: Open it, Grandmama!

MAMA (*staring at it*):   Now you all be quiet. It's just a check.

RUTH: Open it . . .

MAMA (*still staring at it*):   Now don't act silly . . . We ain't never been no people to act silly 'bout no money—

RUTH (*swiftly*):   We ain't never had none before—OPEN IT!

(MAMA *finally makes a good strong tear and pulls out the thin blue slice of paper and inspects it closely. The boy and his mother study it raptly over* MAMA's *shoulders*)

MAMA: *Travis!* (*She is counting off with doubt*) Is that the right number of zeros?

TRAVIS: Yes'm . . . ten thousand dollars. Gaalee, Grandmama, you rich.

MAMA (*she holds the check away from her, still looking at it. Slowly her face sobers into a mask of unhappiness*):   Ten thousand dollars. (*She hands it to* RUTH) Put it away somewhere, Ruth. (*She does not look at* RUTH; *her eyes seem to be seeing something somewhere very far off*) Ten thousand dollars they give you. Ten thousand dollars.

TRAVIS (*to his mother, sincerely*):   What's the matter with Grandmama—don't she want to be rich?

RUTH (*distractedly*):   You go on out and play now, baby. (TRAVIS *exits.* MAMA *starts wiping dishes absently, humming intently to herself.* RUTH *turns to her, with kind exasperation*) You've gone and got yourself upset.

MAMA (*not looking at her*):   I spec if it wasn't for you all . . . I would just put that money away or give it to the church or something.

RUTH: Now what kind of talk is that. Mr. Younger would just be plain mad if he could hear you talking foolish like that.

MAMA (*stopping and staring off*):   Yes . . . he sure would. (*Sighing*) We got enough to do with that money, all right. (*She halts then, and turns and looks at her daughter-in-law hard;* RUTH *avoids her eyes and* MAMA *wipes her hands with finality and starts to speak firmly to* RUTH) Where did you go today, girl?

RUTH: To the doctor.

MAMA (*impatiently*): Now, Ruth . . . you know better than that. Old Doctor Jones is strange enough in his way but there ain't nothing 'bout him make somebody slip and call him "she"—like you done this morning.

RUTH: Well, that's what happened—my tongue slipped.

MAMA: You went to see that woman, didn't you?

RUTH (*defensively, giving herself away*): What woman you talking about?

MAMA (*angrily*): That woman who—

(WALTER *enters in great excitement*)

WALTER: Did it come?

MAMA (*quietly*): Can't you give people a Christian greeting before you start asking about money?

WALTER (*to* RUTH): Did it come? (RUTH *unfolds the check and lays it quietly before him, watching him intently with thoughts of her own.* WALTER *sits down and grasps it close and counts off the zeros*) Ten thousand dollars—(*He turns suddenly, frantically to his mother and draws some papers out of his breast pocket*) Mama—look. Old Willy Harris put everything on paper—

MAMA: Son—I think you ought to talk to your wife . . . I'll go on out and leave you alone if you want—

WALTER: I can talk to her later—Mama, look—

MAMA: Son—

WALTER: WILL SOMEBODY PLEASE LISTEN TO ME TODAY!

MAMA (*quietly*): I don't 'low no yellin' in this house, Walter Lee, and you know it—(WALTER *stares at them in frustration and starts to speak several times*) And there ain't going to be no investing in no liquor stores.

WALTER: But, Mama, you ain't even looked at it.

MAMA: I don't aim to have to speak on that again.

(*A long pause*)

WALTER: You ain't looked at it and you don't aim to have to speak on that again? You ain't even looked at it and *you* have decided—(*Crumpling his papers*) Well, *you* tell that to my boy tonight when you put him to sleep on the living-room couch . . . (*Turning to* MAMA *and speaking directly to her*) Yeah—and tell it to my wife, Mama, to-morrow when she has to go out of here to look after somebody else's kids. And tell it to *me*, Mama, every time we need a new pair of curtains and I have to watch *you* go out and work in somebody's kitchen. Yeah, you tell me then!

(WALTER *starts out*)

RUTH: Where you going?

WALTER: I'm going out!

RUTH: Where?

WALTER: Just out of this house somewhere—

RUTH (*getting her coat*): I'll come too.

WALTER: I don't want you to come!

RUTH: I got something to talk to you about, Walter.

WALTER: That's too bad.

MAMA (*still quietly*):   Walter Lee—(*She waits and he finally turns and looks at her*) Sit down.

WALTER: I'm a grown man, Mama.

MAMA: Ain't nobody said you wasn't grown. But you still in my house and my presence. And as long as you are—you'll talk to your wife civil. Now sit down.

RUTH (*suddenly*):   Oh, let him go on out and drink himself to death! He makes me sick to my stomach! (*She flings her coat against him and exits to bedroom*)

WALTER (*violently flinging the coat after her*):   And you turn mine too, baby! (*The door slams behind her*) That was my biggest mistake—

MAMA (*still quietly*):   Walter, what is the matter with you?

WALTER: Matter with me? Ain't nothing the matter with *me!*

MAMA: Yes there is. Something eating you up like a crazy man. Something more than me not giving you this money. The past few years I been watching it happen to you. You get all nervous acting and kind of wild in the eyes—(WALTER *jumps up impatiently at her words*) I said sit there now, I'm talking to you!

WALTER: Mama—I don't need no nagging at me today.

MAMA: Seem like you getting to a place where you always tied up in some kind of knot about something. But if anybody ask you 'bout it you just yell at 'em and bust out the house and go out and drink somewheres. Walter Lee, people can't live with that. Ruth's a good, patient girl in her way—but you getting to be too much. Boy, don't make the mistake of driving that girl away from you.

WALTER: Why—what she do for me?

MAMA: She loves you.

WALTER: Mama—I'm going out. I want to go off somewhere and be by myself for a while.

MAMA: I'm sorry 'bout your liquor store, son. It just wasn't the thing for us to do. That's what I want to tell you about—

WALTER: I got to go out, Mama—

(*He rises*)

MAMA: It's dangerous, son.

WALTER: What's dangerous?

MAMA: When a man goes outside his home to look for peace.

WALTER (*beseechingly*):   Then why can't there never be no peace in this house then?

MAMA: You done found it in some other house?

WALTER: No—there ain't no woman! Why do women always think there's a woman somewhere when a man gets restless. (*Picks up the check*) Do you know what this money means to me? Do you know what this money can do for us? (*Puts it back*) Mama—Mama—I want so many things . . .

MAMA: Yes, son—

WALTER: I want so many things that they are driving me kind of crazy . . . Mama—look at me.

MAMA: I'm looking at you. You a good-looking boy. You got a job, a nice wife, a fine boy and—

WALTER: A job. (*Looks at her*) Mama, a job? I open and close car doors all day long. I drive a man around in his limousine and I say, "Yes, sir; no, sir; very good, sir; shall I take the Drive, sir?" Mama, that ain't no kind of job . . . that ain't nothing at all. (*Very quietly*) Mama, I don't know if I can make you understand.

MAMA: Understand what, baby?

WALTER (*quietly*): Sometimes it's like I can see the future stretched out in front of me—just plain as day. The future, Mama. Hanging over there at the edge of my days. Just waiting for me—a big, looming blank space—full of *nothing*. Just waiting for *me*. But it don't have to be. (*Pause. Kneeling beside her chair*) Mama—sometimes when I'm downtown and I pass them cool, quiet-looking restaurants where them white boys are sitting back and talking 'bout things . . . sitting there turning deals worth millions of dollars . . . sometimes I see guys don't look much older than me—

MAMA: Son—how come you talk so much 'bout money?

WALTER (*with immense passion*): Because it is life, Mama!

MAMA (*quietly*): Oh—(*Very quietly*) So now it's life. Money is life. Once upon a time freedom used to be life—now it's money. I guess the world really do change . . .

WALTER: No—it was always money, Mama. We just didn't know about it.

MAMA: No . . . something has changed. (*She looks at him*) You something new, boy. In my time we was worried about not being lynched and getting to the North if we could and how to stay alive and still have a pinch of dignity too . . . Now here come you and Beneatha—talking 'bout things we ain't never even thought about hardly, me and your daddy. You ain't satisfied or proud of nothing we done. I mean that you had a home; that we kept you out of trouble till you was grown; that you don't have to ride to work on the back of nobody's streetcar—You my children—but how different we done become.

WALTER (*a long beat. He pats her hand and gets up*): You just don't understand, Mama, you just don't understand.

MAMA: Son—do you know your wife is expecting another baby? (WALTER *stands, stunned, and absorbs what his mother has said*) That's what she wanted to talk to you about. (WALTER *sinks down into a chair*) This ain't for me to be telling—but you ought to know. (*She waits*) I think Ruth is thinking 'bout getting rid of that child.

WALTER (*slowly understanding*): —No—no—Ruth wouldn't do that.

MAMA: When the world gets ugly enough—a woman will do anything for her family. *The part that's already living.*

WALTER: You don't know Ruth, Mama, if you think she would do that.

(RUTH *opens the bedroom door and stands there a little limp*)

RUTH (*beaten*): Yes I would too, Walter. (*Pause*) I gave her a five-dollar down payment.

(*There is total silence as the man stares at his wife and the mother stares at her son*)

MAMA (*presently*): Well—(*Tightly*) Well—son, I'm waiting to hear you say something . . . (*She waits*) I'm waiting to hear how you be your father's son. Be the man he was . . . (*Pause. The silence shouts*) Your wife say she going to destroy your child. And I'm waiting to hear you talk like him and say we a people who give children life, not who destroys them—(*She rises*) I'm waiting to see you stand up and look like your daddy and say we done give up one baby to poverty and that we ain't going to give up nary another one . . . I'm waiting.

WALTER: Ruth—(*He can say nothing*)

MAMA: If you a son of mine, tell her! (WALTER *picks up his keys and his coat and walks out. She continues, bitterly*) You . . . you are a disgrace to your father's memory. Somebody get me my hat!

Curtain

ACT II

Scene I

Time: Later the same day.

At rise: RUTH *is ironing again. She has the radio going. Presently* BENEATHA's *bedroom door opens and* RUTH's *mouth falls and she puts down the iron in fascination.*

RUTH: What have we got on tonight!

BENEATHA (*emerging grandly from the doorway so that we can see her thoroughly robed in the costume Asagai brought*):   You are looking at what a well-dressed Nigerian woman wears—(*She parades for* RUTH, *her hair completely hidden by the headdress; she is coquettishly fanning herself with an ornate oriental fan, mistakenly more like Butterfly than any Nigerian that ever was*) Isn't it beautiful? (*She promenades to the radio and, with an arrogant flourish, turns off the good loud blues that is playing*) Enough of this assimilationist junk! (RUTH *follows her with her eyes as she goes to the phonograph and puts on a record and turns and waits ceremoniously for the music to come up. Then, with a shout—*) OCOMOGOSIAY!

(RUTH *jumps. The music comes up, a lovely Nigerian melody.* BENEATHA *listens, enraptured, her eyes far away—"back to the past." She begins to dance.* RUTH *is dumbfounded*)

RUTH: What kind of dance is that?

BENEATHA: A folk dance.

RUTH (*Pearl Bailey*):   What kind of folks do that, honey?

BENEATHA: It's from Nigeria. It's a dance of welcome.

RUTH: Who you welcoming?

BENEATHA: The men back to the village.

RUTH: Where they been?

BENEATHA: How should I know—out hunting or something. Anyway, they are coming back now . . .

RUTH: Well, that's good.

BENEATHA (*with the record*):

Alundi, alundi

Alundi alunya

Jop pu à jeepua

Ang gu soooooooooo

Ai yai yae . . .

Ayehaye—alundi . . .

(WALTER *comes in during this performance; he has obviously been drinking. He leans against the door heavily and watches his sister, at first with distaste. Then his eyes look off—"back to the past"—as he lifts both his fists to the roof, screaming*)

WALTER: YEAH . . . AND ETHIOPIA STRETCH FORTH HER HANDS AGAIN! . . .

RUTH (*drily, looking at him*): Yes—and Africa sure is claiming her own tonight. (*She gives them both up and starts ironing again*)

WALTER (*all in a drunken, dramatic shout*): Shut up! . . . I'm digging them drums . . . them drums move me! . . . (*He makes his weaving way to his wife's face and leans in close to her*) In my *heart of hearts*—(*He thumps his chest*)—I am much warrior!

RUTH (*without even looking up*): In your heart of hearts you are much drunkard.

WALTER (*coming away from her and starting to wander around the room, shouting*): Me and Jomo . . . (*Intently, in his sister's face. She has stopped dancing to watch him in this unknown mood*) That's my man, Kenyatta. (*Shouting and thumping his chest*) FLAMING SPEAR! HOT DAMN! (*He is suddenly in possession of an imaginary spear and actively spearing enemies all over the room*) OCOMOGOSIAY . . .

BENEATHA (*to encourage* WALTER, *thoroughly caught up with this side of him*): OCO-MOGOSIAY, FLAMING SPEAR!

WALTER: THE LION IS WAKING . . . OWIMOWEH!

(*He pulls his shirt open and leaps up on the table and gestures with his spear*)

BENEATHA: OWIMOWEH!

WALTER (*on the table, very far gone, his eyes pure glass sheets. He sees what we cannot, that he is a leader of his people, a great chief, a descendant of Chaka, and that the hour to march has come*): Listen, my black brothers—

BENEATHA: OCOMOGOSIAY!

WALTER: —Do you hear the waters rushing against the shores of the coastlands—

BENEATHA: OCOMOGOSIAY!

WALTER: —Do you hear the screeching of the cocks in yonder hills beyond where the chiefs meet in council for the coming of the mighty war—

BENEATHA: OCOMOGOSIAY!

(*And now the lighting shifts subtly to suggest the world of* WALTER*'s imagination, and the mood shifts from pure comedy. It is the inner* WALTER *speaking: the Southside chauffeur has assumed an unexpected majesty*)

WALTER: —Do you hear the beating of the wings of the birds flying low over the mountains and the low places of our land—

BENEATHA: OCOMOGOSIAY!

WALTER: —Do you hear the singing of the women, singing the war songs of our fathers to the babies in the great houses? Singing the sweet war songs! (*The doorbell rings*) OH, DO YOU HEAR, MY *BLACK* BROTHERS!

BENEATHA (*completely gone*): We hear you, Flaming Spear—

(RUTH *shuts off the phonograph and opens the door.* GEORGE MURCHISON *enters*)

WALTER: Telling us to prepare for the GREATNESS OF THE TIME! (*Lights back to normal. He turns and sees* GEORGE) Black Brother!

(*He extends his hand for the fraternal clasp*)

GEORGE: Black Brother, hell!

RUTH (*having had enough, and embarrassed for the family*): Beneatha, you got company—what's the matter with you? Walter Lee Younger, get down off that table and stop acting like a fool . . .

(WALTER *comes down off the table suddenly and makes a quick exit to the bathroom*)

RUTH: He's had a little to drink . . . I don't know what her excuse is.

GEORGE (*to* BENEATHA):   Look honey, we're going *to* the theatre—we're not going to be *in* it . . . so go change, huh?

(BENEATHA *looks at him and slowly, ceremoniously, lifts her hands and pulls off the headdress. Her hair is close-cropped and unstraightened.* GEORGE *freezes mid-sentence and* RUTH's *eyes all but fall out of her head*)

GEORGE: What in the name of—

RUTH (*touching* BENEATHA's *hair*):   Girl, you done lost your natural mind!? Look at your head!

GEORGE: What have you done to your head—I mean your hair!

BENEATHA: Nothing—except cut it off.

RUTH: Now that's the truth—it's what ain't been done to it! You expect this boy to go out with you with your head all nappy like that?

BENEATHA (*looking at* GEORGE):   That's up to George. If he's ashamed of his heritage—

GEORGE: Oh, don't be so proud of yourself, Bennie—just because you look eccentric.

BENEATHA: How can something that's natural be eccentric?

GEORGE: That's what being eccentric means—being natural. Get dressed.

BENEATHA: I don't like that, George.

RUTH: Why must you and your brother make an argument out of everything people say?

BENEATHA: Because I hate assimilationist Negroes!

RUTH: Will somebody please tell me what assimila-who-ever means!

GEORGE: Oh, it's just a college girl's way of calling people Uncle Toms—but that isn't what it means at all.

RUTH: Well, what does it mean?

BENEATHA (*cutting* GEORGE *off and staring at him as she replies to* RUTH):   It means someone who is willing to give up his own culture and submerge himself completely in the dominant, and in this case *oppressive* culture!

GEORGE: Oh, dear, dear, dear! Here we go! A lecture on the African past! On our Great West African Heritage! In one second we will hear all about the great Ashanti empires; the great Songhay civilizations; and the great sculpture of Bénin—and then some poetry in the Bantu—and the whole monologue will end with the word *heritage!* (*Nastily*) Let's face it, baby, your heritage is nothing but a bunch of raggedy-assed spirituals and some grass huts!

BENEATHA: GRASS HUTS! (RUTH *crosses to her and forcibly pushes her toward the bedroom*) See there . . . you are standing there in your splendid ignorance talking about people who were the first to smelt iron on the face of the earth! (RUTH *is pushing her through the door*) The Ashanti were performing surgical operations when the English— (RUTH *pulls the door to, with* BENEATHA *on the other side, and smiles graciously at* GEORGE. BENEATHA *opens the door and shouts the end of the sentence defiantly at* GEORGE)—were still tatooing themselves with blue dragons! (*She goes back inside*)

RUTH: Have a seat, George (*They both sit.* RUTH *folds her hands rather primly on her lap, determined to demonstrate the civilization of the family*) Warm, ain't it? I mean for September. (*Pause*) Just like they always say about Chicago weather: If it's too hot or cold for you, just wait a minute and it'll change. (*She smiles happily at this cliché of clichés*) Everybody say it's got to do with them bombs and things they keep setting off. (*Pause*) Would you like a nice cold beer?

GEORGE: No, thank you. I don't care for beer. (*He looks at his watch*) I hope she hurries up.

RUTH: What time is the show?

GEORGE: It's an eight-thirty curtain. That's just Chicago, though. In New York standard curtain time is eight forty.

(*He is rather proud of this knowledge*)

RUTH (*properly appreciating it*): You get to New York a lot?

GEORGE (*offhand*): Few times a year.

RUTH: Oh—that's nice. I've never been to New York.

(WALTER *enters. We feel he has relieved himself, but the edge of unreality is still with him*)

WALTER: New York ain't got nothing Chicago ain't. Just a bunch of hustling people all squeezed up together—being "Eastern."

(*He turns his face into a screw of displeasure*)

GEORGE: Oh—you've been?

WALTER: *Plenty* of times.

RUTH (*shocked at the lie*): Walter Lee Younger!

WALTER (*staring her down*): Plenty! (*Pause*) What we got to drink in this house? Why don't you offer this man some refreshment. (*To* GEORGE) They don't know how to entertain people in this house, man.

GEORGE: Thank you—I don't really care for anything.

WALTER (*feeling his head; sobriety coming*): Where's Mama?

RUTH: She ain't come back yet.

WALTER (*looking* MURCHISON *over from head to toe, scrutinizing his carefully casual tweed sports jacket over cashmere V-neck sweater over soft eyelet shirt and tie, and soft slacks, finished off with white buckskin shoes*): Why all you college boys wear them faggoty-looking white shoes?

RUTH: Walter Lee!

(GEORGE MURCHISON *ignores the remark*)

WALTER (*to* RUTH): Well, they look crazy as hell—white shoes, cold as it is.

RUTH (*crushed*): You have to excuse him—

WALTER: No he don't! Excuse me for what? What you always excusing me for! I'll excuse myself when I needs to be excused! (*A pause*) They look as funny as them black knee socks Beneatha wears out of here all the time.

RUTH: It's the college *style*, Walter.

WALTER: Style, hell. She looks like she got burnt legs or something!

RUTH: Oh, Walter—

WALTER (*an irritable mimic*): Oh, Walter! Oh, Walter! (*To* MURCHISON) How's your old man making out? I understand you all going to buy that big hotel on the Drive? (*He finds a beer in the refrigerator, wanders over to* MURCHISON, *sipping and wiping his lips with the back of his hand, and straddling a chair backwards to talk to the other man)* Shrewd move. Your old man is all right, man. (*Tapping his head and half winking for emphasis*) I mean he knows how to operate. I mean he thinks *big,* you know what I mean, I mean for a *home,* you know? But I think he's kind of running out of ideas now. I'd like to talk to him. Listen, man, I got some plans that could turn this city upside down. I mean think like he does. *Big.* Invest big, gamble big, hell, lose *big* if you have to, you know what I mean. It's hard to find a man on this whole Southside who understands my kind of thinking—you dig? (*He scrutinizes* MURCHISON *again, drinks his beer, squints his eyes and leans in close, confidential, man to man*) Me and you ought to sit down and talk sometimes, man. Man, I got me some ideas . . .

MURCHISON (*with boredom*):   Yeah—sometimes we'll have to do that, Walter.

WALTER (*understanding the indifference, and offended*):   Yeah—well, when you get the time, man. I know you a busy little boy.

RUTH: Walter, please—

WALTER (*bitterly, hurt*):   I know ain't nothing in this world as busy as you colored college boys with your fraternity pins and white shoes . . .

RUTH (*covering her face with humiliation*):   Oh, Walter Lee—

WALTER: I see you all all the time—with the books tucked under your arms—going to your (*British A—a mimic*) "clahsses." And for what! What the hell you learning over there? Filling up your heads—(*Counting off on his fingers*)—with the sociology and the psychology—but they teaching you how to be a man? How to take over and run the world? They teaching you how to run a rubber plantation or a steel mill? Naw—just to talk proper and read books and wear them faggoty-looking white shoes . . .

GEORGE (*looking at him with distaste, a little above it all*):   You're all wacked up with bitterness, man.

WALTER (*intently, almost quietly, between the teeth, glaring at the boy*):   And you—ain't you bitter, man? Ain't you just about had it yet? Don't you see no stars gleaming that you can't reach out and grab? You happy?—You contented son-of-a-bitch—you happy? You got it made? Bitter? Man, I'm a volcano. Bitter? Here I am a giant—surrounded by ants! Ants who can't even understand what it is the giant is talking about.

RUTH (*passionately and suddenly*):   Oh, Walter—ain't you with nobody!

WALTER (*violently*):   No! 'Cause ain't nobody with me! Not even my own mother!

RUTH: Walter, that's a terrible thing to say!

(BENEATHA *enters, dressed for the evening in a cocktail dress and earrings, hair natural*)

GEORGE: Well—hey—(*Crosses to* BENEATHA; *thoughtful, with emphasis, since this is a reversal*) You look great!

WALTER (*seeing his sister's hair for the first time*):   What's the matter with your head?

BENEATHA (*tired of the jokes now*):   I cut it off, Brother.

WALTER (*coming close to inspect it and walking around her*):   Well, I'll be damned. So that's what they mean by the African bush . . .

BENEATHA: Ha ha. Let's go, George.

GEORGE (*looking at her*):   You know something? I like it. It's sharp. I mean it really is. (*Helps her into her wrap*)

RUTH: Yes—I think so, too. (*She goes to the mirror and starts to clutch at her hair*)

WALTER: Oh no! You leave yours alone, baby. You might turn out to have a pin-shaped head or something!

BENEATHA: See you all later.

RUTH: Have a nice time.

GEORGE: Thanks. Good night. (*Half out the door, he reopens it. To* WALTER) Good night, Prometheus!

(BENEATHA *and* GEORGE *exit*)

WALTER (*to* RUTH): Who is Prometheus?

RUTH: I don't know. Don't worry about it.

WALTER (*in fury, pointing after* GEORGE): See there—they get to a point where they can't insult you man to man—they got to go talk about something ain't nobody never heard of!

RUTH: How do you know it was an insult? (*To humor him*) Maybe Prometheus is a nice fellow.

WALTER: Prometheus! I bet there ain't even no such thing! I bet that simple-minded clown—

RUTH: Walter—

(*She stops what she is doing and looks at him*)

WALTER (*yelling*): Don't start!

RUTH: Start what?

WALTER: Your nagging! Where was I? Who was I with? How much money did I spend?

RUTH (*plaintively*): Walter Lee—why don't we just try to talk about it . . .

WALTER (*not listening*): I been out talking with people who understand me. People who care about the things I got on my mind.

RUTH (*wearily*): I guess that means people like Willy Harris.

WALTER: Yes, people like Willy Harris.

RUTH (*with a sudden flash of impatience*): Why don't you all just hurry up and go into the banking business and stop talking about it!

WALTER: Why? You want to know why? 'Cause we all tied up in a race of people that don't know how to do nothing but moan, pray and have babies!

(*The line is too bitter even for him and he looks at her and sits down*)

RUTH: Oh, Walter . . . (*Softly*) Honey, why can't you stop fighting me?

WALTER (*without thinking*): Who's fighting you? Who even cares about you?

(*This line begins the retardation of his mood*)

RUTH: Well—(*She waits a long time, and then with resignation starts to put away her things*) I guess I might as well go on to bed . . . (*More or less to herself*) I don't know where we lost it . . . but we have . . . (*Then, to him*) I—I'm sorry about this new baby, Walter. I guess maybe I better go on and do what I started . . . I guess I just didn't realize how bad things was with us . . . I guess I just didn't really realize—(*She starts out to the bedroom and stops*) You want some hot milk?

WALTER: Hot milk?

RUTH: Yes—hot milk.

WALTER: Why hot milk?

RUTH: 'Cause after all that liquor you come home with you ought to have something hot in your stomach.

WALTER: I don't want no milk.

RUTH: You want some coffee then?

WALTER: No, I don't want no coffee. I don't want nothing hot to drink. (*Almost plaintively*) Why you always trying to give me something to eat?

RUTH (*standing and looking at him helplessly*):   What *else* can I give you, Walter Lee Younger?

(*She stands and looks at him and presently turns to go out again. He lifts his head and watches her going away from him in a new mood which began to emerge when he asked her "Who cares about you?"*)

WALTER: It's been rough, ain't it, baby? (*She hears and stops but does not turn around and he continues to her back*) I guess between two people there ain't never as much understood as folks generally thinks there is. I mean like between me and you—(*She turns to face him*) How we gets to the place where we scared to talk softness to each other. (*He waits, thinking hard himself*) Why you think it got to be like that? (*He is thoughtful, almost as a child would be*) Ruth, what is it gets into people ought to be close?

RUTH: I don't know, honey. I think about it a lot.

WALTER: On account of you and me, you mean? The way things are with us. The way something done come down between us.

RUTH: There ain't so much between us, Walter . . . Not when you come to me and try to talk to me. Try to be with me . . . a little even.

WALTER (*total honesty*):   Sometimes . . . sometimes . . . I don't even know how to try.

RUTH: Walter—

WALTER: Yes?

RUTH (*coming to him, gently and with misgiving, but coming to him*):   Honey . . . life don't have to be like this. I mean sometimes people can do things so that things are better . . . You remember how we used to talk when Travis was born . . . about the way we were going to live . . . the kind of house . . . (*She is stroking his head*) Well, it's all starting to slip away from us . . .

(*He turns her to him and they look at each other and kiss, tenderly and hungrily. The door opens and MAMA enters—WALTER breaks away and jumps up. A beat*)

WALTER: Mama, where have you been?

MAMA: My—them steps is longer than they used to be. Whew! (*She sits down and ignores him*) How you feeling this evening, Ruth?

(*RUTH shrugs, disturbed at having been interrupted and watching her husband knowingly*)

WALTER: Mama, where have you been all day?

MAMA (*still ignoring him and leaning on the table and changing to more comfortable shoes*): Where's Travis?

RUTH: I let him go out earlier and he ain't come back yet. Boy, is he going to get it!

WALTER: Mama!

MAMA (*as if she has heard him for the first time*):   Yes, son?

WALTER: Where did you go this afternoon?

MAMA: I went downtown to tend to some business that I had to tend to.

WALTER: What kind of business?

MAMA: You know better than to question me like a child, Brother.

WALTER (*rising and bending over the table*):   Where were you, Mama? (*Bringing his fists down and shouting*) Mama, you didn't go do something with that insurance money, something crazy?

(*The front door opens slowly, interrupting him, and* TRAVIS *peeks his head in, less than hopefully*)

TRAVIS (*to his mother*):   Mama, I—

RUTH: "Mama I" nothing! You're going to get it, boy! Get on in that bedroom and get yourself ready!

TRAVIS: But I—

MAMA: Why don't you all never let the child explain hisself.

RUTH: Keep out of it now, Lena.

(MAMA *clamps her lips together, and* RUTH *advances toward her son menacingly*)

RUTH: A thousand times I have told you not to go off like that—

MAMA (*holding out her arms to her grandson*):   Well—at least let me tell him something. I want him to be the first one to hear . . . Come here, Travis. (*The boy obeys, gladly*) Travis—(*She takes him by the shoulder and looks into his face*)—you know that money we got in the mail this morning?

TRAVIS: Yes'm—

MAMA: Well—what you think your grandmama gone and done with that money?

TRAVIS: I don't know, Grandmama.

MAMA (*putting her finger on his nose for emphasis*):   She went out and she bought you a house! (*The explosion comes from* WALTER *at the end of the revelation and he jumps up and turns away from all of them in a fury.* MAMA *continues, to* TRAVIS) You glad about the house? It's going to be yours when you get to be a man.

TRAVIS: Yeah—I always wanted to live in a house.

MAMA: All right, gimme some sugar then—(TRAVIS *puts his arms around her neck as she watches her son over the boy's shoulder. Then, to* TRAVIS, *after the embrace*) Now when you say your prayers tonight, you thank God and your grandfather—'cause it was him who give you the house—in his way.

RUTH (*taking the boy from* MAMA *and pushing him toward the bedroom*):   Now you get out of here and get ready for your beating.

TRAVIS: Aw, Mama—

RUTH: Get on in there—(*Closing the door behind him and turning radiantly to her mother-in-law*) So you went and did it!

MAMA (*quietly, looking at her son with pain*):   Yes, I did.

RUTH (*raising both arms classically*):   PRAISE GOD! (*Looks at* WALTER *a moment, who says nothing. She crosses rapidly to her husband*) Please, honey—let me be glad . . . you be glad too. (*She has laid her hands on his shoulders, but he shakes himself free of her roughly, without turning to face her*) Oh, Walter . . . a home . . . a home. (*She comes back to* MAMA) Well—where is it? How big is it? How much it going to cost?

MAMA: Well—

RUTH: When we moving?

MAMA (*smiling at her*):   First of the month.

RUTH (*throwing back her head with jubilance*):   *Praise God!*

MAMA (*tentatively, still looking at her son's back turned against her and* RUTH):   It's—it's a nice house too . . . (*She cannot help speaking directly to him. An imploring quality in her voice, her manner, makes her almost like a girl now*) Three bedrooms—nice big one for you and Ruth. . . . Me and Beneatha still have to share our room, but Travis have one of his own—and (*With difficulty*) I figure if the—new baby—is a boy, we could get one of them double-decker outfits . . . And there's a yard with a little patch of dirt where I could maybe get to grow me a few flowers . . . And a nice big basement . . .

RUTH: Walter honey, be glad—

MAMA (*still to his back, fingering things on the table*):   'Course I don't want to make it sound fancier than it is . . . It's just a plain little old house—but it's made good and solid—and it will be *ours*. Walter Lee—it makes a difference in a man when he can walk on floors that belong to *him* . . .

RUTH: Where is it?

MAMA (*frightened at this telling*):   Well—well—it's out there in Clybourne Park—

(RUTH's *radiance fades abruptly, and* WALTER *finally turns slowly to face his mother with incredulity and hostility*)

RUTH: Where?

MAMA (*matter-of-factly*):   Four o six Clybourne Street, Clybourne Park.

RUTH: Clybourne Park? Mama, there ain't no colored people living in Clybourne Park.

MAMA (*almost idiotically*):   Well, I guess there's going to be some now.

WALTER (*bitterly*):   So that's the peace and comfort you went out and bought for us today!

MAMA (*raising her eyes to meet his finally*):   Son—I just tried to find the nicest place for the least amount of money for my family.

RUTH (*trying to recover from the shock*):   Well—well—'course I ain't one never been 'fraid of no crackers, mind you—but—well, wasn't there no other houses nowhere?

MAMA: Them houses they put up for colored in them areas way out all seem to cost twice as much as other houses. I did the best I could.

RUTH (*struck senseless with the news, in its various degrees of goodness and trouble, she sits a moment, her fists propping her chin in thought, and then she starts to rise, bringing her fists down with vigor, the radiance spreading from cheek to cheek again*):   Well—well!—All I can say is—if this is my time in life—MY TIME—to say good-bye—(*And she builds with momentum as she starts to circle the room with an exuberant, almost tearfully happy release*)—to these Goddamned cracking walls!—(*She pounds the walls*)—and these marching roaches!—(*She wipes at an imaginary army of marching roaches*)—and this cramped little closet which ain't now or never was no kitchen! . . . then I say it loud and good, HALLELUJAH! AND GOOD-BYE MISERY . . . I DON'T NEVER WANT TO SEE YOUR UGLY FACE AGAIN! (*She laughs joyously, having practically destroyed the apartment, and flings her arms up and lets them come down happily, slowly, reflectively, over her abdomen, aware for the first time perhaps that the life therein pulses with happiness and not despair*) Lena?

MAMA (*moved, watching her happiness*):   Yes, honey?

RUTH (*looking off*):   Is there—is there a whole lot of sunlight?

MAMA (*understanding*):   Yes, child, there's a whole lot of sunlight.

(*Long pause*)

RUTH (*collecting herself and going to the door of the room* TRAVIS *is in*):   Well—I guess I better see 'bout Travis. (*To* MAMA) Lord, I sure don't feel like whipping nobody today!

(*She exits*)

MAMA (*the mother and son are left alone now and the mother waits a long time, considering deeply, before she speaks*):   Son—you—you understand what I done, don't you? (WALTER *is silent and sullen*) I—I just seen my family falling apart today ... just falling to pieces in front of my eyes ... We couldn't of gone on like we was today. We was going backwards 'stead of forwards—talking 'bout killing babies and wishing each other was dead ... When it gets like that in life—you just got to do something different, push on out and do something bigger ... (*She waits*) I wish you say something, son ... I wish you'd say how deep inside you you think I done the right thing—

WALTER (*crossing slowly to his bedroom door and finally turning there and speaking measuredly*):   What you need me to say you done right for? *You* the head of this family. You run our lives like you want to. It was your money and you did what you wanted with it. So what you need for me to say it was all right for? (*Bitterly, to hurt her as deeply as he knows is possible*) So you butchered up a dream of mine—you—who always talking 'bout your children's dreams ...

MAMA: Walter Lee—

(*He just closes the door behind him.* MAMA *sits alone, thinking heavily*)

Curtain

Scene II

Time: Friday night. A few weeks later.

At rise: Packing crates mark the intention of the family to move. BENEATHA *and* GEORGE *come in, presumably from an evening out again.*

GEORGE: O.K. . . . O.K., whatever you say . . . (*They both sit on the couch. He tries to kiss her. She moves away*) Look, we've had a nice evening; let's not spoil it, huh? . . .

(*He again turns her head and tries to nuzzle in and she turns away from him, not with distaste but with momentary lack of interest; in a mood to pursue what they were talking about*)

BENEATHA: I'm *trying* to talk to you.

GEORGE: We always talk.

BENEATHA: Yes—and I love to talk.

GEORGE (*exasperated; rising*):   I know it and I don't mind it sometimes . . . I want you to cut it out, see—The moody stuff, I mean. I don't like it. You're a nice-looking girl . . . all over. That's all you need, honey, forget the atmosphere. Guys aren't going to go for the atmosphere—they're going to go for what they see. Be glad for that. Drop the Garbo routine. It doesn't go with you. As for myself, I want a nice—(*Groping*)—simple (*Thoughtfully*)—sophisticated girl . . . not a poet—O.K.?

(*He starts to kiss her, she rebuffs him again and he jumps up*)

BENEATHA: Why are you angry, George?

GEORGE: Because this is stupid! I don't go out with you to discuss the nature of "quiet desperation" or to hear all about your thoughts—because the world will go on thinking what it thinks regardless—

BENEATHA: Then why read books? Why go to school?

GEORGE (*with artificial patience, counting on his fingers*):   It's simple. You read books—to learn facts—to get grades—to pass the course—to get a degree. That's all—it has nothing to do with thoughts.

(*A long pause*)

BENEATHA: I see. (*He starts to sit*) Good night, George.

(GEORGE *looks at her a little oddly, and starts to exit. He meets* MAMA *coming in*)

GEORGE: Oh—hello, Mrs. Younger.

MAMA: Hello, George, how you feeling?

GEORGE: Fine—fine, how are you?

MAMA: Oh, a little tired. You know them steps can get you after a day's work. You all have a nice time tonight?

GEORGE: Yes—a fine time. A fine time.

MAMA: Well, good night.

GEORGE: Good night. (*He exits.* MAMA *closes the door behind her*) Hello, honey. What you sitting like that for?

BENEATHA: I'm just sitting.

MAMA: Didn't you have a nice time?

BENEATHA: No.

MAMA: No? What's the matter?

BENEATHA: Mama, George is a fool—honest. (*She rises*)

MAMA (*hustling around unloading the packages she has entered with. She stops*):   Is he, baby?

BENEATHA: Yes.

(BENEATHA *makes up* TRAVIS' *bed as she talks*)

MAMA: You sure?

BENEATHA: Yes.

MAMA: Well—I guess you better not waste your time with no fools.

(BENEATHA *looks up at her mother, watching her put groceries in the refrigerator. Finally she gathers up her things and starts into the bedroom. At the door she stops and looks back at her mother*)

BENEATHA: Mama—

MAMA: Yes, baby—

BENEATHA: Thank you.

MAMA: For what?

BENEATHA: For understanding me this time.

(*She exits quickly and the mother stands, smiling a little, looking at the place where* BENEATHA *just stood.* RUTH *enters*)

RUTH: Now don't you fool with any of this stuff, Lena—

MAMA: Oh, I just thought I'd sort a few things out. Is Brother here?

RUTH: Yes.

MAMA (*with concern*): Is he—

RUTH (*reading her eyes*): Yes.

(MAMA *is silent and someone knocks on the door.* MAMA *and* RUTH *exchange weary and knowing glances and* RUTH *opens it to admit the neighbor,* MRS. JOHNSON, * *who is a rather squeaky wide-eyed lady of no particular age, with a newspaper under her arm*)

*This character and the scene of her visit were cut from the original production and early editions of the play.

MAMA (*changing her expression to acute delight and a ringing cheerful greeting*): Oh—hello there, Johnson.

JOHNSON (*This is a woman who decided long ago to be enthusiastic about EVERYTHING in life and she is inclined to wave her wrist vigorously at the height of her exclamatory comments*): Hello there, yourself! H'you this evening, Ruth?

RUTH (*not much of a deceptive type*): Fine, Mis' Johnson, h'you?

JOHNSON: Fine. (*Reaching out quickly, playfully, and patting* RUTH'S *stomach*) Ain't you starting to poke out none yet! (*She mugs with delight at the over-familiar remark and her eyes dart around looking at the crates and packing preparation;* MAMA'S *face is a cold sheet of endurance*) Oh, ain't we getting ready round here, though! Yessir! Lookathere! I'm telling you the Youngers is really getting ready to "move on up a little higher!"—Bless God!

MAMA (*a little drily, doubting the total sincerity of the Blesser*): Bless God.

JOHNSON: He's good, ain't He?

MAMA: Oh yes, He's good.

JOHNSON: I mean sometimes He works in mysterious ways . . . but He works, don't He!

MAMA (*the same*): Yes, he does.

JOHNSON: I'm just soooooo happy for y'all. And this here child—(*About* RUTH) looks like she could just pop open with happiness, don't she. Where's all the rest of the family?

MAMA: Bennie's gone to bed—

JOHNSON: Ain't no . . . (*The implication is pregnancy*) sickness done hit you—I hope . . . ?

MAMA: No—she just tired. She was out this evening.

JOHNSON (*all is a coo, an emphatic coo*): Aw—ain't that lovely. She still going out with the little Murchison boy?

MAMA (*drily*): Ummmm huh.

JOHNSON: That's lovely. You sure got lovely children, Younger. Me and Isaiah talks all the time 'bout what fine children you was blessed with. We sure do.

MAMA: Ruth, give Mis' Johnson a piece of sweet potato pie and some milk.

JOHNSON: Oh honey, I can't stay hardly a minute—I just dropped in to see if there was anything I could do. (*Accepting the food easily*) I guess y'all seen the news what's all over the colored paper this week . . .

MAMA: No—didn't get mine yet this week.

JOHNSON (*lifting her head and blinking with the spirit of catastrophe*): You mean you ain't read 'bout them colored people that was bombed out their place out there?

(RUTH *straightens with concern and takes the paper and reads it.* JOHNSON *notices her and feeds commentary*)

JOHNSON: Ain't it something how bad these here white folks is getting here in Chicago! Lord, getting so you think you right down in Mississippi! (*With a tremendous and rather insincere sense of melodrama*) 'Course I thinks it's wonderful how our folks keeps on pushing out. You hear some of these Negroes round here talking 'bout how they don't go where they ain't wanted and all that—but not me, honey! (*This is a lie*) Wilhemenia Othella Johnson goes anywhere, any time she feels like it! (*With head movement for emphasis*) Yes I do! Why if we left it up to these here crackers, the poor niggers wouldn't have nothing—(*She clasps her hand over her mouth*) Oh, I always forgets you don't 'low that word in your house.

MAMA (*quietly, looking at her*):   No—I don't 'low it.

JOHNSON (*vigorously again*):   Me neither! I was just telling Isaiah yesterday when he come using it in front of me—I said, "Isaiah, it's just like Mis' Younger says all the time—"

MAMA: Don't you want some more pie?

JOHNSON: No—no thank you; this was lovely. I got to get on over home and have my midnight coffee. I hear some people say it don't let them sleep but I finds I can't close my eyes right lessen I done had that laaaast cup of coffee . . . (*She waits. A beat. Undaunted*) My Goodnight coffee, I calls it!

MAMA (*with much eye-rolling and communication between herself and* RUTH):   Ruth, why don't you give Mis' Johnson some coffee.

(RUTH *gives* MAMA *an unpleasant look for her kindness*)

JOHNSON (*accepting the coffee*):   Where's Brother tonight?

MAMA: He's lying down.

JOHNSON: MMmmmmm, he sure gets his beauty rest, don't he? Good-looking man. Sure is a good-looking man! (*Reaching out to pat* RUTH'S *stomach again*) I guess that's how come we keep on having babies around here. (*She winks at* MAMA) One thing 'bout Brother, he always know how to have a *good* time. And soooooo ambitious! I bet it was his idea y'all moving out to Clybourne Park. Lord—I bet this time next month y'all's names will have been in the papers plenty—(*Holding up her hands to mark off each word of the headline she can see in front of her*) "NEGROES INVADE CLYBOURNE PARK—BOMBED!"

MAMA (*she and* RUTH *look at the woman in amazement*):   We ain't exactly moving out there to get bombed.

JOHNSON: Oh, honey—you know I'm praying to God every day that don't nothing like that happen! But you have to think of life like it is—and these here Chicago peckerwoods is some baaaad peckerwoods.

MAMA (*wearily*):   We done thought about all that Mis' Johnson.

(BENEATHA *comes out of the bedroom in her robe and passes through to the bathroom.* MRS. JOHNSON *turns*)

JOHNSON: Hello there, Bennie!

BENEATHA (*crisply*):   Hello, Mrs. Johnson.

JOHNSON: How is school?

BENEATHA (*crisply*):   Fine, thank you. (*She goes out.*)

JOHNSON (*insulted*):   Getting so she don't have much to say to nobody.

MAMA: The child was on her way to the bathroom.

JOHNSON: I know—but sometimes she act like ain't got time to pass the time of day with nobody ain't been to college. Oh—I ain't criticizing her none. It's just—you know how some of our young people gets when they get a little education. (MAMA *and* RUTH *say nothing, just look at her*) Yes—well. Well, I guess I better get on home. (*Unmoving*) 'Course I can understand how she must be proud and everything—being the only one in the family to make something of herself. I know just being a chauffeur ain't never satisfied Brother none. He shouldn't feel like that, though. Ain't nothing wrong with being a chauffeur.

MAMA: There's plenty wrong with it.

JOHNSON: What?

MAMA: Plenty. My husband always said being any kind of a servant wasn't a fit thing for a man to have to be. He always said a man's hands was made to make things, or to turn the earth with—not to drive nobody's car for 'em—or—(*She looks at her own hands*) carry they slop jars. And my boy is just like him—he wasn't meant to wait on nobody.

JOHNSON (*rising, somewhat offended*):   Mmmmmmmmm. The Youngers is too much for me! (*She looks around*) You sure one proud-acting bunch of colored folks. Well—I always thinks like Booker T. Washington said that time—"Education has spoiled many a good plow hand"—

MAMA: Is that what old Booker T. said?

JOHNSON: He sure did.

MAMA: Well, it sounds just like him. The fool.

JOHNSON (*indignantly*):   Well—he was one of our great men.

MAMA: Who said so?

JOHNSON (*nonplussed*):   You know, me and you ain't never agreed about some things, Lena Younger. I guess I better be going—

RUTH (*quickly*):   Good night.

JOHNSON: Good night. Oh—(*Thrusting it at her*) You can keep the paper! (*With a trill*) 'Night.

MAMA: Good night, Mis' Johnson.

(MRS. JOHNSON *exits*)

RUTH: If ignorance was gold . . .

MAMA: Shush. Don't talk about folks behind their backs.

RUTH: You do.

MAMA: I'm old and corrupted. (BENEATHA *enters*) You was rude to Mis' Johnson, Beneatha, and I don't like it at all.

BENEATHA (*at her door*):   Mama, if there are two things we, as a people, have got to overcome, one is the Klu Klux Klan—and the other is Mrs. Johnson. (*She exits*)

MAMA: Smart aleck.

(*The phone rings*)

RUTH: I'll get it.

MAMA: Lord, ain't this a popular place tonight.

RUTH (*at the phone*):   Hello—Just a minute. (*Goes to door*) Walter, it's Mrs. Arnold. (*Waits. Goes back to the phone. Tense*) Hello. Yes, this is his wife speaking . . . He's lying down now. Yes . . . well, he'll be in tomorrow. He's been very sick. Yes—I know we should have called, but we were so sure he'd be able to come in today. Yes—yes, I'm very sorry. Yes . . . Thank you very much. (*She hangs up.* WALTER *is standing in the doorway of the bedroom behind her*) That was Mrs. Arnold.

WALTER (*indifferently*):   Was it?

RUTH: She said if you don't come in tomorrow that they are getting a new man . . .

WALTER: Ain't that sad—ain't that crying sad.

RUTH: She said Mr. Arnold has had to take a cab for three days . . . Walter, you ain't been to work for three days! (*This is a revelation to her*) Where you been, Walter Lee Younger? (WALTER *looks at her and starts to laugh*) You're going to lose your job.

WALTER: That's right . . . (*He turns on the radio*)

RUTH: Oh, Walter, and with your mother working like a dog every day—

(*A steamy, deep blues pours into the room*)

WALTER: That's sad too—Everything is sad.

MAMA: What you been doing for these three days, son?

WALTER: Mama—you don't know all the things a man what got leisure can find to do in this city . . . What's this—Friday night? Well—Wednesday I borrowed Willy Harris' car and I went for a drive . . . just me and myself and I drove and drove . . . Way out . . . way past South Chicago, and I parked the car and I sat and looked at the steel mills all day long. I just sat in the car and looked at them big black chimneys for hours. Then I drove back and I went to the Green Hat. (*Pause*) And Thursday—Thursday I borrowed the car again and I got in it and I pointed it the other way and I drove the other way—for hours—way, way up to Wisconsin, and I looked at the farms. I just drove and looked at the farms. Then I drove back and I went to the Green Hat. (*Pause*) And today—today I didn't get the car. Today I just walked. All over the Southside. And I looked at the Negroes and they looked at me and finally I just sat down on the curb at Thirty-ninth and South Parkway and I just sat there and watched the Negroes go by. And then I went to the Green Hat. You all sad? You all depressed? And you know where I am going right now—

(RUTH *goes out quietly*)

MAMA: Oh, Big Walter, is this the harvest of our days?

WALTER: You know what I like about the Green Hat? I like this little cat they got there who blows a sax . . . He blows. He talks to me. He ain't but 'bout five feet tall and he's got a conked head and his eyes is always closed and he's all music—

MAMA (*rising and getting some papers out of her handbag*):   Walter—

WALTER: And there's this other guy who plays the piano . . . and they got a sound. I mean they can work on some music . . . They got the best little combo in the world in the Green Hat . . . You can just sit there and drink and listen to them three men play and you realize that don't nothing matter worth a damn, but just being there—

MAMA: I've helped do it to you, haven't I, son? Walter I been wrong.

WALTER: Naw—you ain't never been wrong about nothing, Mama.

MAMA: Listen to me, now. I say I been wrong, son. That I been doing to you what the rest of the world been doing to you. (*She turns off the radio*) Walter—(*She stops and he looks up slowly at her and she meets his eyes pleadingly*) What you ain't never understood is that I ain't got nothing, don't own nothing, ain't never really wanted nothing that wasn't for you. There ain't nothing as precious to me . . . There ain't nothing worth holding on to, money, dreams, nothing else—if it means—if it means it's going to destroy my boy. (*She takes an envelope out of her handbag and puts it in front of him and he watches her without speaking or moving*) I paid the man thirty-five hundred dollars down on the house. That leaves sixty-five hundred dollars. Monday morning I want you to take this money and take three thousand dollars and put it in a savings account for Beneatha's medical schooling. The rest you put in a checking account—with your name on it. And from now on any penny that come out of it or that go in it is for you to look after. For you to decide. (*She drops her hands a little helplessly*) It ain't much, but it's all I got in the world and I'm putting it in your hands. I'm telling you to be the head of this family from now on like you supposed to be.

WALTER (*stares at the money*):   You trust me like that, Mama?

MAMA: I ain't never stop trusting you. Like I ain't never stop loving you.

(*She goes out, and* WALTER *sits looking at the money on the table. Finally, in a decisive gesture, he gets up, and, in mingled joy and desperation, picks up the money. At the same moment,* TRAVIS *enters for bed*)

TRAVIS: What's the matter, Daddy? You drunk?

WALTER (*sweetly, more sweetly than we have ever known him*):   No, Daddy ain't drunk. Daddy ain't going to never be drunk again. . . .

TRAVIS: Well, good night, Daddy.

(*The* FATHER *has come from behind the couch and leans over, embracing his son*)

WALTER: Son, I feel like talking to you tonight.

TRAVIS: About what?

WALTER: Oh, about a lot of things. About you and what kind of man you going to be when you grow up. . . . Son—son, what do you want to be when you grow up?

TRAVIS: A bus driver.

WALTER (*laughing a little*):   A what? Man, that ain't nothing to want to be!

TRAVIS: Why not?

WALTER: 'Cause, man—it ain't big enough—you know what I mean.

TRAVIS: I don't know then. I can't make up my mind. Sometimes Mama asks me that too. And sometimes when I tell her I just want to be like you—she says she don't want me to be like that and sometimes she says she does. . . .

WALTER (*gathering him up in his arms*):   You know what, Travis? In seven years you going to be seventeen years old. And things is going to be very different with us in seven years, Travis. . . . One day when you are seventeen I'll come home—home from my office downtown somewhere—

TRAVIS: You don't work in no office, Daddy.

WALTER: No—but after tonight. After what your daddy gonna do tonight, there's going to be offices—a whole lot of offices. . . .

TRAVIS: What you gonna do tonight, Daddy?

WALTER: You wouldn't understand yet, son, but your daddy's gonna make a transaction . . . a business transaction that's going to change our lives. . . . That's how come one day when you 'bout seventeen years old I'll come home and I'll be pretty tired, you know what I mean, after a day of conferences and secretaries getting things wrong the way they do . . . 'cause an executive's life is hell, man—(*The more he talks the farther away he gets*) And I'll pull the car up on the driveway . . . just a plain black Chrysler, I think, with white walls—no—black tires. More elegant. Rich people don't have to be flashy . . . though I'll have to get something a little sportier for Ruth—maybe a Cadillac convertible to do her shopping in. . . . And I'll come up the steps to the house and the gardener will be clipping away at the hedges and he'll say, "Good evening, Mr. Younger." And I'll say, "Hello, Jefferson, how are you this evening?" And I'll go inside and Ruth will come downstairs and meet me at the door and we'll kiss each other and she'll take my arm and we'll go up to your room to see you sitting on the floor with the catalogues of all the great schools in America around you. . . . All the great schools in the world! And—and I'll say, all right son—it's your seventeenth birthday, what is it you've decided? . . . Just tell me where you want to go to school and you'll *go.* Just tell me, what it is you want to be—and you'll *be* it. . . . Whatever you want to be—Yessir! (*He holds his arms open for* TRAVIS) You just name it, son . . . (TRAVIS *leaps into them*) and I hand you the world!

(WALTER'*s voice has risen in pitch and hysterical promise and on the last line he lifts* TRAVIS *high*)

(*Blackout*)

Scene III

Time: Saturday, moving day, one week later.
    Before the curtain rises, RUTH'*s voice, a strident, dramatic church alto, cuts through the silence.*
    It is, in the darkness, a triumphant surge, a penetrating statement of expectation: "Oh, Lord, I don't feel no ways tired! Children, oh, glory hallelujah!"
    As the curtain rises we see that RUTH *is alone in the living room, finishing up the family's packing. It is moving day. She is nailing crates and tying cartons.* BENEATHA *enters, carrying a guitar case, and watches her exuberant sister-in-law.*

RUTH: Hey!
BENEATHA (*putting away the case*):   Hi.
RUTH (*pointing at a package*):   Honey—look in that package there and see what I found on sale this morning at the South Center. (RUTH *gets up and moves to the package and draws out some curtains*) Lookahere—hand-turned hems!
BENEATHA: How do you know the window size out there?
RUTH (*who hadn't thought of that*):   Oh—Well, they bound to fit something in the whole house. Anyhow, they was too good a bargain to pass up. (RUTH *slaps her head, suddenly remembering something*) Oh, Bennie—I meant to put a special note on that carton over there. That's your mama's good china and she wants 'em to be very careful with it.
BENEATHA: I'll do it.

(BENEATHA *finds a piece of paper and starts to draw large letters on it*)

RUTH: You know what I'm going to do soon as I get in that new house?
BENEATHA: What?
RUTH: Honey—I'm going to run me a tub of water up to here . . . (*With her fingers practically up to her nostrils*) And I'm going to get in it—and I am going to sit . . . and sit . . . and sit in that hot water and the first person who knocks to tell *me* to hurry up and come out—
BENEATHA: Gets shot at sunrise.
RUTH (*laughing happily*):   You said it, sister! (*Noticing how large* BENEATHA *is absent-mindedly making the note*) Honey, they ain't going to read that from no airplane.

BENEATHA (*laughing herself*): I guess I always think things have more emphasis if they are big, somehow.

RUTH (*looking up at her and smiling*): You and your brother seem to have that as a philosophy of life. Lord, that man—done changed so 'round here. You know—you know what we did last night? Me and Walter Lee?

BENEATHA: What?

RUTH (*smiling to herself*): We went to the movies. (*Looking at* BENEATHA *to see if she understands*) We went to the movies. You know the last time me and Walter went to the movies together?

BENEATHA: No.

RUTH: Me neither. That's how long it been. (*Smiling again*) But we went last night. The picture wasn't much good, but that didn't seem to matter. We went—and we held hands.

BENEATHA: Oh, Lord!

RUTH: We held hands—and you know what?

BENEATHA: What?

RUTH: When we come out of the show it was late and dark and all the stores and things was closed up . . . and it was kind of chilly and there wasn't many people on the streets . . . and we was still holding hands, me and Walter.

BENEATHA: You're killing me.

(WALTER *enters with a large package. His happiness is deep in him; he cannot keep still with his new-found exuberance. He is singing and wiggling and snapping his fingers. He puts his package in a corner and puts a phonograph record, which he has brought in with him, on the record player. As the music, soulful and sensuous, comes up he dances over to* RUTH *and tries to get her to dance with him. She gives in at last to his raunchiness and in a fit of giggling allows herself to be drawn into his mood. They dip and she melts into his arms in a classic, body-melding "slow drag")*

BENEATHA (*regarding them a long time as they dance, then drawing in her breath for a deeply exaggerated comment which she does not particularly mean*): Talk about—olddddddddddd-fashioneddddddd—Negroes!

WALTER (*stopping momentarily*): What kind of Negroes? (*He says this in fun. He is not angry with her today, nor with anyone. He starts to dance with his wife again*)

BENEATHA: Old-fashioned.

WALTER (*as he dances with* RUTH): You know, when these *New Negroes* have their convention—(*Pointing at his sister*)—that is going to be the chairman of the Committee on Unending Agitation. (*He goes on dancing, then stops*) Race, race, race! . . . Girl, I do believe you are the first person in the history of the entire human race to successfully brainwash yourself. (BENEATHA *breaks up and he goes on dancing. He stops again, enjoying his tease*) Damn, even the N double A C P takes a holiday sometimes! (BENEATHA *and* RUTH *laugh. He dances with* RUTH *some more and starts to laugh and stops and pantomimes someone over an operating table*) I can just see that chick someday looking down at some poor cat on an operating table and before she starts to slice him, she says . . . (*Pulling his sleeves back maliciously*) "By the way, what are your views on civil rights down there? . . . "

(*He laughs at her again and starts to dance happily. The bell sounds*)

BENEATHA: Sticks and stones may break my bones but . . . words will never hurt me!

(BENEATHA *goes to the door and opens it as* WALTER *and* RUTH *go on with the clowning.* BENEATHA *is somewhat surprised to see a quiet-looking middle-aged white man in a business suit holding his hat and a briefcase in his hand and consulting a small piece of paper*)

MAN: Uh—how do you do, miss. I am looking for a Mrs.—(*He looks at the slip of paper*) Mrs. Lena Younger? (*He stops short, struck dumb at the sight of the oblivious* WALTER *and* RUTH)

BENEATHA (*smoothing her hair with slight embarrassment*):   Oh—yes, that's my mother. Excuse me (*She closes the door and turns to quiet the other two*) Ruth! Brother! (*Enunciating precisely but soundlessly:*   "There's a white man at the door!" *They stop dancing,* RUTH *cuts off the phonograph,* BENEATHA *opens the door. The man casts a curious quick glance at all of them*) Uh—come in please.

MAN (*coming in*):   Thank you.

BENEATHA: My mother isn't here just now. Is it business?

MAN: Yes . . . well, of a sort.

WALTER (*freely, the Man of the House*):   Have a seat. I'm Mrs. Younger's son. I look after most of her business matters.

(RUTH *and* BENEATHA *exchange amused glances*)

MAN (*regarding* WALTER, *and sitting*):   Well—My name is Karl Lindner . . .

WALTER (*stretching out his hand*):   Walter Younger. This is my wife—(RUTH *nods politely*)—and my sister.

LINDNER: How do you do.

WALTER (*amiably, as he sits himself easily on a chair, leaning forward on his knees with interest and looking expectantly into the newcomer's face*):   What can we do for you, Mr. Lindner!

LINDNER (*some minor shuffling of the hat and briefcase on his knees*):   Well—I am a representative of the Clybourne Park Improvement Association—

WALTER (*pointing*):   Why don't you sit your things on the floor?

LINDNER: Oh—yes. Thank you. (*He slides the briefcase and hat under the chair*) And as I was saying—I am from the Clybourne Park Improvement Association and we have had it brought to our attention at the last meeting that you people—or at least your mother—has bought a piece of residential property at—(*He digs for the slip of paper again*)—four o six Clybourne Street . . .

WALTER: That's right. Care for something to drink? Ruth, get Mr. Lindner a beer.

LINDNER (*upset for some reason*):   Oh—no, really. I mean thank you very much, but no thank you.

RUTH (*innocently*):   Some coffee?

LINDNER: Thank you, nothing at all.

(BENEATHA *is watching the man carefully*)

LINDNER: Well, I don't know how much you folks know about our organization. (*He is a gentle man; thoughtful and somewhat labored in his manner*) It is one of these community organizations set up to look after—oh, you know, things like block upkeep and special projects and we also have what we call our New Neighbors Orientation Committee . . .

BENEATHA (*drily*):   Yes—and what do they do?

LINDNER (*turning a little to her and then returning the main force to* WALTER):   Well—it's what you might call a sort of welcoming committee, I guess. I mean they, we—I'm the chairman of the committee—go around and see the new people who move into the neighborhood and sort of give them the lowdown on the way we do things in Clybourne Park.

BENEATHA (*with appreciation of the two meanings, which escape* RUTH *and* WALTER): Un-huh.

LINDNER: And we also have the category of what the association calls—(*He looks elsewhere*)—uh—special community problems . . .

BENEATHA: Yes—and what are some of those?

WALTER: Girl, let the man talk.

LINDNER (*with understated relief*):   Thank you. I would sort of like to explain this thing in my own way. I mean I want to explain to you in a certain way.

WALTER: Go ahead.

LINDNER: Yes. Well. I'm going to try to get right to the point. I'm sure we'll all appreciate that in the long run.

BENEATHA: Yes.

WALTER: Be still now!

LINDNER: Well—

RUTH (*still innocently*):   Would you like another chair—you don't look comfortable.

LINDNER (*more frustrated than annoyed*):   No, thank you very much. Please. Well—to get right to the point I—(*A great breath, and he is off at last*) I am sure you people must be aware of some of the incidents which have happened in various parts of the city when colored people have moved into certain areas—(BENEATHA *exhales heavily and starts tossing a piece of fruit up and down in the air*) Well—because we have what I think is going to be a unique type of organization in American community life—not only do we deplore that kind of thing—but we are trying to do something about it. (BENEATHA *stops tossing and turns with a new and quizzical interest to the man*) We feel—(*gaining confidence in his mission because of the interest in the faces of the people he is talking to*)—we feel that most of the trouble in this world, when you come right down to it—(*He hits his knee for emphasis*)—most of the trouble exists because people just don't sit down and talk to each other.

RUTH (*nodding as she might in church, pleased with the remark*):   You can say that again, mister.

LINDNER (*more encouraged by such affirmation*):   That we don't try hard enough in this world to understand the other fellow's problem. The other guy's point of view.

RUTH: Now that's right.

(BENEATHA *and* WALTER *merely watch and listen with genuine interest*)

LINDNER: Yes—that's the way we feel out in Clybourne Park. And that's why I was elected to come here this afternoon and talk to you people. Friendly like, you know, the way people should talk to each other and see if we couldn't find some way to work this thing out. As I say, the whole business is a matter of *caring* about the other fellow. Anybody can see that you are a nice family of folks, hard working and honest I'm sure. (BENEATHA *frowns slightly, quizzically, her head tilted regarding him*) Today everybody knows what it means to be on the outside of *something*. And of course, there is always somebody who is out to take advantage of people who don't always understand.

WALTER: What do you mean?

LINDNER: Well—you see our community is made up of people who've worked hard as the dickens for years to build up that little community. They're not rich and fancy people; just hard-working, honest people who don't really have much but those little homes and a dream of the kind of community they want to raise their children in. Now, I don't say we are perfect and there is a lot wrong in some of the things they want. But you've got to admit that a man, right or wrong, has the right to want to have the neighborhood he lives in a certain kind of way. And at the moment the overwhelming majority of our people out there feel that people get along better, take more of a common interest in the life of the community, when they share a common background. I want you to believe me when I tell you that race prejudice simply doesn't enter into it. It is a matter of the people of Clybourne Park believing, rightly or wrongly, as I say, that for the happiness of all concerned that our Negro families are happier when they live in their *own* communities.

BENEATHA (*with a grand and bitter gesture*):   This, friends, is the Welcoming Committee!

WALTER (*dumbfounded, looking at* LINDNER):   Is this what you came marching all the way over here to tell us?

LINDNER: Well, now we've been having a fine conversation. I hope you'll hear me all the way through.

WALTER (*tightly*):   Go ahead, man.

LINDNER: You see—in the face of all the things I have said, we are prepared to make your family a very generous offer . . .

BENEATHA: Thirty pieces and not a coin less!

WALTER: Yeah?

LINDNER (*putting on his glasses and drawing a form out of the briefcase*):   Our association is prepared, through the collective effort of our people, to buy the house from you at a financial gain to your family.

RUTH: Lord have mercy, ain't this the living gall!

WALTER: All right, you through?

LINDNER: Well, I want to give you the exact terms of the financial arrangement—

WALTER: We don't want to hear no exact terms of no arrangements. I want to know if you got any more to tell us 'bout getting together?

LINDNER (*taking off his glasses*):   Well—I don't suppose that you feel . . .

WALTER: Never mind how I feel—you got any more to say 'bout how people ought to sit down and talk to each other? . . . Get out of my house, man.

(*He turns his back and walks to the door.*)

LINDNER (*Looking around at the hostile faces and reaching and assembling his hat and briefcase*):   Well—I don't understand why you people are reacting this way. What do you think you are going to gain by moving into a neighborhood where you just aren't wanted and where some elements—well—people can get awful worked up when they feel that their whole way of life and everything they've ever worked for is threatened.

WALTER: Get out.

LINDNER (*at the door, holding a small card*):   Well—I'm sorry it went like this.

WALTER: Get out.

LINDNER (*almost sadly regarding* WALTER): You just can't force people to change their hearts, son.

(*He turns and put his card on a table and exits.* WALTER *pushes the door to with stinging hatred, and stands looking at it.* RUTH *just sits and* BENEATHA *just stands. They say nothing.* MAMA *and* TRAVIS *enter*)

MAMA: Well—this all the packing got done since I left out of here this morning. I testify before God that my children got all the energy of the *dead!* What time the moving men due?

BENEATHA: Four o'clock. You had a caller, Mama.

(*She is smiling, teasingly*)

MAMA: Sure enough—who?

BENEATHA (*her arms folded saucily*): The Welcoming Committee.

(WALTER *and* RUTH *giggle*)

MAMA (*innocently*): Who?

BENEATHA: The Welcoming Committee. They said they're sure going to be glad to see you when you get there.

WALTER (*devilishly*): Yeah, they said they can't hardly wait to see your face.

(*Laughter*)

MAMA (*sensing their facetiousness*): What's the matter with you all?

WALTER: Ain't nothing the matter with us. We just telling you 'bout the gentleman who came to see you this afternoon. From the Clybourne Park Improvement Association.

MAMA: What he want?

RUTH (*in the same mood as* BENEATHA *and* WALTER): To welcome you, honey.

WALTER: He said they can't hardly wait. He said the one thing they don't have, that they just *dying* to have out there is a fine family of fine colored people! (*To* RUTH *and* BENEATHA) Ain't that right!

RUTH (*mockingly*): Yeah! He left his card—

BENEATHA (*handing card to* MAMA): In case.

(MAMA *reads and throws it on the floor—understanding and looking off as she draws her chair up to the table on which she has put her plant and some sticks and some cord*)

MAMA: Father, give us strength. (*Knowingly—and without fun*) Did he threaten us?

BENEATHA: Oh—Mama—they don't do it like that any more. He talked Brotherhood. He said everybody ought to learn how to sit down and hate each other with good Christian fellowship.

(*She and* WALTER *shake hands to ridicule the remark*)

MAMA (*sadly*): Lord, protect us . . .

RUTH: You should hear the money those folks raised to buy the house from us. All we paid and then some.

BENEATHA: What they think we going to do—eat 'em?

RUTH: No, honey, marry 'em.

MAMA (*shaking her head*):   Lord, Lord, Lord . . .

RUTH: Well—that's the way the crackers crumble. (*A beat*) Joke.

BENEATHA (*laughingly noticing what her mother is doing*):   Mama, what are you doing?

MAMA: Fixing my plant so it won't get hurt none on the way . . .

BENEATHA: Mama, you going to take *that* to the new house?

MAMA: Un-huh—

BENEATHA: That raggedy-looking old thing?

MAMA (*stopping and looking at her*):   It expresses ME!

RUTH (*with delight, to* BENEATHA):   So there, Miss Thing!

(WALTER *comes to* MAMA *suddenly and bends down behind her and squeezes her in his arms with all his strength. She is overwhelmed by the suddenness of it and, though delighted, her manner is like that of* RUTH *and* TRAVIS)

MAMA: Look out now, boy! You make me mess up my thing here!

WALTER (*his face lit, he slips down on his knees beside her, his arms still about her*):   Mama . . . you know what it means to climb up in the chariot?

MAMA (*gruffly, very happy*):   Get on away from me now . . .

RUTH (*near the gift-wrapped package, trying to catch* WALTER'S *eye*):   Psst—

WALTER: What the old song say, Mama . . .

RUTH: Walter—Now?

(*She is pointing at the package*)

WALTER (*speaking the lines, sweetly, playfully, in his mother's face*):

　　I got wings . . . you got wings . . .

　　All God's Children got wings . . .

MAMA: Boy—get out of my face and do some work . . .

WALTER:

　　When I get to heaven gonna put on my wings,

　　Gonna fly all over God's heaven . . .

BENEATHA (*teasingly, from across the room*):   Everybody talking 'bout heaven ain't going there!

WALTER (*to* RUTH, *who is carrying the box across to them*):   I don't know, you think we ought to give her that . . . Seems to me she ain't been very appreciative around here.

MAMA (*eying the box, which is obviously a gift*):   What is that?

WALTER (*taking it from* RUTH *and putting it on the table in front of* MAMA):   Well—what you all think? Should we give it to her?

RUTH: Oh—she was pretty good today.

MAMA: I'll good you—

(*She turns her eyes to the box again*)

BENEATHA: Open it, Mama.

(*She stands up, looks at it, turns and looks at all of them, and then presses her hands together and does not open the package*)

WALTER (*sweetly*):   Open it, Mama. It's for you. (MAMA *looks in his eyes. It is the first present in her life without its being Christmas. Slowly she opens her package and lifts out, one by one, a brand-new sparkling set of gardening tools.* WALTER *continues, prodding*) Ruth made up the note—read it . . .

MAMA (*picking up the card and adjusting her glasses*): "To our own Mrs. Miniver—Love from Brother, Ruth and Beneatha." Ain't that lovely . . .

TRAVIS (*tugging at his father's sleeve*): Daddy, can I give her mine now?

WALTER: All right, son. (TRAVIS *flies to get his gift*)

MAMA: Now I don't have to use my knives and forks no more . . .

WALTER: Travis didn't want to go in with the rest of us, Mama. He got his own. (*Somewhat amused*) We don't know what it is . . .

TRAVIS (*racing back in the room with a large hatbox and putting it in front of his grandmother*): Here!

MAMA: Lord have mercy, baby. You done gone and bought your grandmother a hat?

TRAVIS (*very proud*): Open it!

(*She does and lifts out an elaborate, but very elaborate, wide gardening hat, and all the adults break up at the sight of it*)

RUTH: Travis, honey, what is that?

TRAVIS (*who thinks it is beautiful and appropriate*): It's a gardening hat! Like the ladies always have on in the magazines when they work in their gardens.

BENEATHA (*giggling fiercely*): Travis—we were trying to make Mama Mrs. Miniver—not Scarlett O'Hara!

MAMA (*indignantly*): What's the matter with you all! This here is a beautiful hat! (*Absurdly*) I always wanted me one just like it!

(*She pops it on her head to prove it to her grandson, and the hat is ludicrous and considerably oversized*)

RUTH: Hot dog! Go, Mama!

WALTER (*doubled over with laughter*): I'm sorry, Mama—but you look like you ready to go out and chop you some cotton sure enough!

(*They all laugh except* MAMA, *out of deference to* TRAVIS' *feelings*)

MAMA (*gathering the boy up to her*): Bless your heart—this is the prettiest hat I ever owned—(WALTER, RUTH *and* BENEATHA *chime in—noisily, festively and insincerely congratulating* TRAVIS *on his gift*) What are we all standing around here for? We ain't finished packin' yet. Bennie, you ain't packed one book.

(*The bell rings*)

BENEATHA: That couldn't be the movers . . . it's not hardly two good yet—

(BENEATHA *goes into her room.* MAMA *starts for door*)

WALTER (*turning, stiffening*): Wait—wait—I'll get it.

(*He stands and looks at the door*)

MAMA: You expecting company, son?

WALTER (*just looking at the door*): Yeah—yeah . . .

(MAMA *looks at* RUTH, *and they exchange innocent and unfrightened glances*)

MAMA (*not understanding*): Well, let them in, son.

BENEATHA (*from her room*): We need some more string.

MAMA: Travis—you run to the hardware and get me some string cord.

(MAMA *goes out and* WALTER *turns and looks at* RUTH. TRAVIS *goes to a dish for money*)

RUTH: Why don't you answer the door, man?

WALTER (*suddenly bounding across the floor to embrace her*):   'Cause sometimes it hard to let the future begin!

(*Stooping down in her face*)

I got wings! You got wings!
All God's children got wings!

(*He crosses to the door and throws it open. Standing there is a very slight little man in a not too prosperous business suit and with haunted frightened eyes and a hat pulled down tightly, brim up, around his forehead.* TRAVIS *passes between the men and exits.* WALTER *leans deep in the man's face, still in his jubilance*)

When I get to heaven gonna put on my wings,
Gonna fly all over God's heaven . . .

(*The little man just stares at him*)

Heaven—

(*Suddenly he stops and looks past the little man into the empty hallway*) Where's Willy, man?

BOBO: He ain't with me.

WALTER (*not disturbed*):   Oh—come on in. You know my wife.

BOBO (*dumbly, taking off his hat*):   Yes—h'you, Miss Ruth.

RUTH (*quietly, a mood apart from her husband already, seeing* BOBO):   Hello, Bobo.

WALTER: You right on time today . . . Right on time. That's the way! (*He slaps* BOBO *on his back*) Sit down . . . lemme hear.

(RUTH *stands stiffly and quietly in back of them, as though somehow she senses death, her eyes fixed on her husband*)

BOBO (*his frightened eyes on the floor, his hat in his hands*):   Could I please get a drink of water, before I tell you about it, Walter Lee?

(WALTER *does not take his eyes off the man.* RUTH *goes blindly to the tap and gets a glass of water and brings it to* BOBO)

WALTER: There ain't nothing wrong, is there?

BOBO: Lemme tell you—

WALTER: Man—didn't nothing go wrong?

BOBO: Lemme tell you—Walter Lee. (*Looking at* RUTH *and talking to her more than to* WALTER) You know how it was. I got to tell you how it was. I mean first I got to tell you how it was all the way . . . I mean about the money I put in, Walter Lee . . .

WALTER (*with taut agitation now*):   What about the money you put in?

BOBO: Well—it wasn't much as we told you—me and Willy—(*He stops*) I'm sorry, Walter. I got a bad feeling about it. I got a real bad feeling about it . . .

WALTER: Man, what you telling me about all this for? . . . Tell me what happened in Springfield . . .

BOBO: Springfield.

RUTH (*like a dead woman*):   What was supposed to happen in Springfield?

BOBO (*to her*):   This deal that me and Walter went into with Willy—Me and Willy was going to go down to Springfield and spread some money 'round so's we wouldn't have to wait so long for the liquor license . . . That's what we were going to do. Everybody said that was the way you had to do, you understand, Miss Ruth?

WALTER: Man—what happened down there?

BOBO (*a pitiful man, near tears*):   I'm trying to tell you, Walter.

WALTER (*screaming at him suddenly*):   THEN TELL ME, GODDAMMIT . . . WHAT'S THE MATTER WITH YOU?

BOBO: Man . . . I didn't go to no Springfield, yesterday.

WALTER (*halted, life hanging in the moment*):   Why not?

BOBO (*the long way, the hard way to tell*):   'Cause I didn't have no reasons to . . .

WALTER: Man, what are you talking about!

BOBO: I'm talking about the fact that when I got to the train station yesterday morning—eight o'clock like we planned . . . Man—*Willy didn't never show up.*

WALTER: Why . . . where was he . . . where is he?

BOBO: That's what I'm trying to tell you . . . I don't know . . . I waited six hours . . . I called his house . . . and I waited . . . six hours . . . I waited in that train station six hours . . . (*Breaking into tears*) That was all the extra money I had in the world . . . (*Looking up at* WALTER *with the tears running down his face*) Man, *Willy is gone.*

WALTER: Gone, what you mean Willy is gone? Gone where? You mean he went by himself. You mean he went off to Springfield by himself—to take care of getting the license—(*Turns and looks anxiously at* RUTH) You mean maybe he didn't want too many people in on the business down there? (*Looks to* RUTH *again, as before*) You know Willy got his own ways. (*Looks back to* BOBO) Maybe you was late yesterday and he just went on down there without you. Maybe—maybe—he's been callin' you at home tryin' to tell you what happened or something. Maybe—maybe—he just got sick. He's somewhere—he's got to be somewhere. We just got to find him—me and you got to find him. (*Grabs* BOBO *senselessly by the collar and starts to shake him*) We got to!

BOBO (*in sudden angry, frightened agony*):   What's the matter with you, Walter! *When a cat take off with your money he don't leave you no road maps!*

WALTER (*turning madly, as though he is looking for* WILLY *in the very room*):   Willy! . . . Willy . . . don't do it . . . Please don't do it . . . Man, not with that money . . . Man, please, not with that money . . . Oh, God . . . Don't let it be true . . . (*He is wandering around, crying out for* WILLY *and looking for him or perhaps for help from God*) Man . . . I trusted you . . . Man, I put my life in your hands . . . (*He starts to crumple down on the floor as* RUTH *just covers her face in horror.* MAMA *opens the door and comes into the room, with* BENEATHA *behind her*) Man . . . (*He starts to pound the floor with his fists, sobbing wildly*) THAT MONEY IS MADE OUT OF MY FATHER'S FLESH——

BOBO (*standing over him helplessly*):   I'm sorry, Walter . . . (*Only* WALTER's *sobs reply.* BOBO *puts on his hat*) I had my life staked on this deal, too . . .

(*He exits*)

MAMA (*to* WALTER):   Son—(*She goes to him, bends down to him, talks to his bent head*) Son . . . Is it gone? Son, I gave you sixty-five hundred dollars. Is it gone? All of it? Beneatha's money too?

WALTER (*lifting his head slowly*):   Mama . . . I never . . . went to the bank at all . . .

MAMA (*not wanting to believe him*):   You mean . . . your sister's school money . . . you used that too . . . Walter? . . .

WALTER: Yessss! All of it . . . It's all gone . . .

(*There is total silence.* RUTH *stands with her face covered with her hands;* BENEATHA *leans forlornly against a wall, fingering a piece of red ribbon from the mother's gift.* MAMA *stops and looks at her son without recognition and then, quite without thinking about it, starts to beat him senselessly in the face.* BENEATHA *goes to them and stops it*)

BENEATHA: Mama!

(MAMA *stops and looks at both of her children and rises slowly and wanders vaguely, aimlessly away from them*)

MAMA: I seen . . . him . . . night after night . . . come in . . . and look at that rug . . . and then look at me . . . the red showing in his eyes . . . the veins moving in his head . . . I seen him grow thin and old before he was forty . . . working and working and working like somebody's old horse . . . killing himself . . . and you—you give it all away in a day—(*She raises her arms to strike him again*)

BENEATHA: Mama—

MAMA: Oh, God . . . (*She looks up to Him*) Look down here—and show me the strength.

BENEATHA: Mama—

MAMA (*folding over*):   Strength . . .

BENEATHA (*plaintively*):   Mama . . .

MAMA: Strength!

Curtain

ACT III

An hour later.

At curtain, there is a sullen light of gloom in the living room, gray light not unlike that which began the first scene of Act One. At left we can see WALTER *within his room, alone with himself. He is stretched out on the bed, his shirt out and open, his arms under his head. He does not smoke, he does not cry out, he merely lies there, looking up at the ceiling, much as if he were alone in the world.*

In the living room BENEATHA *sits at the table, still surrounded by the now almost ominous packing crates. She sits looking off. We feel that this is a mood struck perhaps an hour before, and it lingers now, full of the empty sound of profound disappointment. We see on a line from her brother's bedroom the sameness of their attitudes. Presently the bell rings and* BENEATHA *rises without ambition or interest in answering. It is* ASAGAI, *smiling broadly, striding into the room with energy and happy expectation and conversation.*

ASAGAI: I came over . . . I had some free time. I thought I might help with the packing. Ah, I like the look of packing crates! A household in preparation for a journey! It depresses some people . . . but for me . . . it is another feeling. Something full of the flow of life, do you understand? Movement, progress . . . It makes me think of Africa.

BENEATHA: Africa!

ASAGAI: What kind of a mood is this? Have I told you how deeply you move me?

BENEATHA: He gave away the money, Asagai . . .

ASAGAI: Who gave away what money?

BENEATHA: The insurance money. My brother gave it away.

ASAGAI: Gave it away?

BENEATHA: He made an investment! With a man even Travis wouldn't have trusted with his most worn-out marbles.

ASAGAI: And it's gone?

BENEATHA: Gone!

ASAGAI: I'm very sorry . . . And you, now?

BENEATHA: Me? . . . Me? . . . Me, I'm nothing . . . Me. When I was very small . . . we used to take our sleds out in the wintertime and the only hills we had were the ice-covered stone steps of some houses down the street. And we used to fill them in with snow and make them smooth and slide down them all day . . . and it was very danger-ous, you know . . . far too steep . . . and sure enough one day a kid named Rufus came down too fast and hit the sidewalk and we saw his face just split open right there in front of us . . . And I remember standing there looking at his bloody open face thinking that was the end of Rufus. But the ambulance came and they took him to the hospital and they fixed the broken bones and they sewed it all up . . . and the next time I saw Rufus he just had a little line down the middle of his face . . . I never got over that . . .

ASAGAI: What?

BENEATHA: That that was what one person could do for another, fix him up—sew up the problem, make him all right again. That was the most marvelous thing in the world . . . I wanted to do that. I always thought it was the one concrete thing in the world that a human being could do. Fix up the sick, you know—and make them whole again. This was truly being God . . .

ASAGAI: You wanted to be God?

BENEATHA: No—I wanted to cure. It used to be so important to me. I wanted to cure. It used to matter. I used to care. I mean about people and how their bodies hurt . . .

ASAGAI: And you've stopped caring?

BENEATHA: Yes—I think so.

ASAGAI: Why?

BENEATHA (bitterly):   Because it doesn't seem deep enough, close enough to what ails mankind! It was a child's way of seeing things—or an idealist's.

ASAGAI: Children see things very well sometimes—and idealists even better.

BENEATHA: I know that's what you think. Because you are still where I left off. You with all your talk and dreams about Africa! You still think you can patch up the world. Cure the Great Sore of Colonialism—(Loftily, mocking it) with the Penicillin of Independence—!

ASAGAI: Yes!

BENEATHA: Independence and then what? What about all the crooks and thieves and just plain idiots who will come into power and steal and plunder the same as be-fore—only now they will be black and do it in the name of the new Independence—WHAT ABOUT THEM?!

ASAGAI: That will be the problem for another time. First we must get there.

BENEATHA: And where does it end?

ASAGAI: End? Who even spoke of an end? To life? To living?

BENEATHA: An end to misery! To stupidity! Don't you see there isn't any real progress, Asagai, there is only one large circle that we march in, around and around, each of us with our own little picture in front of us—our own little mirage that we think is the future.

ASAGAI: That is the mistake.

BENEATHA: · What?

ASAGAI: What you just said—about the circle. It isn't a circle—it is simply a long line—as in geometry, you know, one that reaches into infinity. And because we cannot see the end—we also cannot see how it changes. And it is very odd but those who see the changes—who dream, who will not give up—are called idealists . . . and those who see only the circle—we call *them* the "realists"!

BENEATHA: Asagai, while I was sleeping in that bed in there, people went out and took the future right out of my hands! And nobody asked me, nobody consulted me— they just went out and changed my life!

ASAGAI: Was it your money?

BENEATHA: What?

ASAGAI: Was it your money he gave away?

BENEATHA: It belonged to all of us.

ASAGAI: But did you earn it? Would you have had it at all if your father had not died?

BENEATHA: No.

ASAGAI: Then isn't there something wrong in a house—in a world—where all dreams, good or bad, must depend on the death of a man? I never thought to see *you* like this, Alaiyo. You! Your brother made a mistake and you are grateful to him so that now you can give up the ailing human race on account of it! You talk about what good is struggle, what good is anything! Where are we all going and why are we bothering!

BENEATHA: AND YOU CANNOT ANSWER IT!

ASAGAI (*shouting over her*):   I LIVE THE ANSWER! (*Pause*) In my village at home it is the exceptional man who can even read a newspaper . . . or who ever sees a book at all. I will go home and much of what I will have to say will seem strange to the people of my village. But I will teach and work and things will happen, slowly and swiftly. At times it will seem that nothing changes at all . . . and then again the sudden dramatic events which make history leap into the future. And then quiet again. Retrogression even. Guns, murder, revolution. And I even will have moments when I wonder if the quiet was not better than all that death and hatred. But I will look about my village at the illiteracy and disease and ignorance and I will not wonder long. And perhaps . . . perhaps I will be a great man . . . I mean perhaps I will hold on to the substance of truth and find my way always with the right course . . . and perhaps for it I will be butchered in my bed some night by the servants of empire . . .

BENEATHA: *The martyr!*

ASAGAI (*he smiles*):   . . . or perhaps I shall live to be a very old man, respected and esteemed in my new nation . . . And perhaps I shall hold office and this is what I'm trying to tell you, Alaiyo: Perhaps the things I believe now for my country will be wrong and outmoded, and I will not understand and do terrible things to have things my way or merely to keep my power. Don't you see that there will be young men and women—not British soldiers then, but my own black countrymen—to step out of the shadows some evening and slit my then useless throat? Don't you see they have always been there . . . that they always will be. And that such a thing as my own death will be an advance? They who might kill me even . . . actually replenish all that I was.

BENEATHA: Oh, Asagai, I know all that.

ASAGAI: Good! Then stop moaning and groaning and tell me what you plan to do.

BENEATHA: Do?

ASAGAI: I have a bit of a suggestion.

BENEATHA: What?

ASAGAI (*rather quietly for him*):   That when it is all over—that you come home with me—

BENEATHA (*staring at him and crossing away with exasperation*):   Oh—Asagai—at this moment you decide to be romantic!

ASAGAI (*quickly understanding the misunderstanding*):   My dear, young creature of the New World—I do not mean across the city—I mean across the ocean: home—to Africa.

BENEATHA (*slowly understanding and turning to him with murmured amazement*):   To Africa?

ASAGAI: Yes! . . . (*Smiling and lifting his arms playfully*) Three hundred years later the African Prince rose up out of the seas and swept the maiden back across the middle passage over which her ancestors had come—

BENEATHA (*unable to play*):   To—to Nigeria?

ASAGAI: Nigeria. Home. (*Coming to her with genuine romantic flippancy*) I will show you our mountains and our stars; and give you cool drinks from gourds and teach you the old songs and the ways of our people—and, in time, we will pretend that—(*Very Softly*)—you have only been away for a day. Say that you'll come—(*He swings her around and takes her full in his arms in a kiss which proceeds to passion*)

BENEATHA (*pulling away suddenly*):   You're getting me all mixed up—

ASAGAI: Why?

BENEATHA: Too many things—too many things have happened today. I must sit down and think. I don't know what I feel about anything right this minute.

(*She promptly sits down and props her chin on her fist*)

ASAGAI (*charmed*):   All right, I shall leave you. No—don't get up. (*Touching her, gently, sweetly*) Just sit awhile and think . . . Never be afraid to sit awhile and think. (*He goes to door and looks at her*) How often I have looked at you and said, "Ah—so this is what the New World hath finally wrought . . ."

(*He exits.* BENEATHA *sits on alone. Presently* WALTER *enters from his room and starts to rummage through things, feverishly looking for something. She looks up and turns in her seat*)

BENEATHA (*hissingly*):   Yes—just look at what the New World hath wrought! . . . Just look! (*She gestures with bitter disgust*) There he is! *Monsieur le petit bourgeois noir—* himself! There he is—Symbol of a Rising Class! Entrepreneur! Titan of the system! (WALTER *ignores her completely and continues frantically and destructively looking for something and hurling things to floor and tearing things out of their place in his search.* BENEATHA *ignores the eccentricity of his actions and goes on with the monologue of insult*) Did you dream of yachts on Lake Michigan, Brother? Did you see yourself on that Great Day sitting down at the Conference Table, surrounded by all the mighty bald-headed men in America? All halted, waiting, breathless, waiting for your pronouncements on industry? Waiting for you—Chairman of the Board! (WALTER *finds what he is looking for—a small piece of white paper—and pushes it in his pocket and puts on his coat and rushes out without ever having looked at her. She shouts after him*) I look at you and I see the final triumph of stupidity in the world!

(*The door slams and she returns to just sitting again.* RUTH *comes quickly out of* MAMA's *room*)

RUTH: Who was that?

BENEATHA: Your husband.

RUTH: Where did he go?

BENEATHA: Who knows—maybe he has an appointment at U.S. Steel.

RUTH (*anxiously, with frightened eyes*):   You didn't say nothing bad to him, did you?

BENEATHA: Bad? Say anything bad to him? No—I told him he was a sweet boy and full of dreams and everything is strictly peachy keen, as the ofay kids say!

(MAMA *enters from her bedroom. She is lost, vague, trying to catch hold, to make some sense of her former command of the world, but it still eludes her. A sense of waste overwhelms her gait; a measure of apology rides on her shoulders. She goes to her plant, which has remained on the table, looks at it, picks it up and takes it to the window sill and sets it outside, and she stands and looks at it a long moment. Then she closes the window, straightens her body with effort and turns around to her children*)

MAMA: Well—ain't it a mess in here, though? (*A false cheerfulness, a beginning of something*) I guess we all better stop moping around and get some work done. All this unpacking and everything we got to do. (RUTH *raises her head slowly in response to the sense of the line; and* BENEATHA *in similar manner turns very slowly to look at her mother*) One of you all better call the moving people and tell 'em not to come.

RUTH: Tell 'em not to come?

MAMA: Of course, baby. Ain't no need in 'em coming all the way here and having to go back. They charges for that too. (*She sits down, fingers to her brow, thinking*) Lord, ever since I was a little girl, I always remembers people saying, "Lena—Lena Eggleston, you aims too high all the time. You needs to slow down and see life a little more like it is. Just slow down some." That's what they always used to say down home—"Lord, that Lena Eggleston is a high-minded thing. She'll get her due one day!"

RUTH: No, Lena . . .

MAMA: Me and Big Walter just didn't never learn right.

RUTH: Lena, no! We gotta go. Bennie—tell her . . . (*She rises and crosses to* BENEATHA *with her arms outstretched.* BENEATHA *doesn't respond*) Tell her we can still move . . . the notes ain't but a hundred and twenty-five a month. We got four grown people in this house—we can work . . .

MAMA (*to herself*):   Just aimed too high all the time—

RUTH (*turning and going to* MAMA *fast—the words pouring out with urgency and desperation*):   Lena—I'll work . . . I'll work twenty hours a day in all the kitchens in Chicago . . . I'll strap my baby on my back if I have to and scrub all the floors in America and wash all the sheets in America if I have to—but we got to MOVE! We got to get OUT OF HERE!!

(MAMA *reaches out absently and pats* RUTH's *hand*)

MAMA: No—I sees things differently now. Been thinking 'bout some of the things we could do to fix this place up some. I seen a second-hand bureau over on Maxwell Street just the other day that could fit right there. (*She points to where the new furniture might go.* RUTH *wanders away from her*) Would need some new handles on it and then a little varnish and it look like something brand-new. And—we can put up them new curtains in the kitchen . . . Why this place be looking fine. Cheer us all up so that we forget trouble ever come . . . (*To* RUTH) And you could get some nice screens to put up in your room round the baby's bassinet . . . (*She looks at both of them, pleadingly*) Sometimes you just got to know when to give up some things . . . and hold on to what you got. . . .

(WALTER *enters from the outside, looking spent and leaning against the door, his coat hanging from him*)

MAMA: Where you been, son?

WALTER (*breathing hard*): Made a call.

MAMA: To who, son?

WALTER: To The Man. (*He heads for his room*)

MAMA: What man, baby?

WALTER (*stops in the door*): The Man, Mama. Don't you know who The Man is?

RUTH: Walter Lee?

WALTER: *The Man*. Like the guys in the streets say—The Man. Captain Boss—Mistuh Charley . . . Old Cap'n Please Mr. Bossman . . .

BENEATHA (*suddenly*): Lindner!

WALTER: That's right! That's good. I told him to come right over.

BENEATHA (*fiercely, understanding*): For what? What do you want to see him for!

WALTER (*looking at his sister*): We going to do business with him.

MAMA: What you talking 'bout, son?

WALTER: Talking 'bout life, Mama. You all always telling me to see life like it is. Well—I laid in there on my back today . . . and I figured it out. Life just like it is. Who gets and who don't get. (*He sits down with his coat on and laughs*) Mama, you know it's all divided up. Life is. Sure enough. Between the takers and the "tooken." (*He laughs*) I've figured it out finally. (*He looks around at them*) Yeah. Some of us always getting "tooken." (*He laughs*) People like Willy Harris, they don't never get "tooken." And you know why the rest of us do? 'Cause we all mixed up. Mixed up bad. We get to looking 'round for the right and the wrong; and we worry about it and cry about it and stay up nights trying to figure out 'bout the wrong and the right of things all the time . . . And all the time, man, them takers is out there operating, just taking and taking. Willy Harris? Shoot—Willy Harris don't even count. He don't even count in the big scheme of things. But I'll say one thing for old Willy Harris . . . he's taught me something. He's taught me to keep my eye on what counts in this world. Yeah—(*Shouting out a little*) Thanks, Willy!

RUTH: What did you call that man for, Walter Lee?

WALTER: Called him to tell him to come on over to the show. Gonna put on a show for the man. Just what he wants to see. You see, Mama, the man came here today and he told us that them people out there where you want us to move—well they so upset they willing to pay us *not* to move! (*He laughs again*) And—and oh, Mama—you would of been proud of the way me and Ruth and Bennie acted. We told him to get out . . . Lord have mercy! We told the man to get out! Oh, we was some proud folks this afternoon, yeah. (*He lights a cigarette*) We were still full of that old-time stuff . . .

RUTH (*coming toward him slowly*):   You talking 'bout taking them people's money to keep us from moving in that house?

WALTER: I ain't just talking 'bout it, baby—I'm telling you that's what's going to happen!

BENEATHA: Oh, God! Where is the bottom! Where is the real honest-to-God bottom so he can't go any farther!

WALTER: See—that's the old stuff. You and that boy that was here today. You all want everybody to carry a flag and a spear and sing some marching songs, huh? You wanna spend your life looking into things and trying to find the right and the wrong part, huh? Yeah. You know what's going to happen to that boy someday—he'll find himself sitting in a dungeon, locked in forever—and the takers will have the key! Forget it, baby! There ain't no causes—there ain't nothing but taking in this world, and he who takes most is smartest—and it don't make a damn bit of difference *how*.

MAMA: You making something inside me cry, son. Some awful pain inside me.

WALTER: Don't cry, Mama. Understand. That white man is going to walk in that door able to write checks for more money than we ever had. It's important to him and I'm going to help him . . . I'm going to put on the show, Mama.

MAMA: Son—I come from five generations of people who was slaves and sharecroppers—but ain't nobody in my family never let nobody pay 'em no money that was a way of telling us we wasn't fit to walk the earth. We ain't never been that poor. (*Raising her eyes and looking at him*) We ain't never been that—dead inside.

BENEATHA: Well—we are dead now. All the talk about dreams and sunlight that goes on in this house. It's all dead now.

WALTER: What's the matter with you all! I didn't make this world! It was give to me this way! Hell, yes, I want me some yachts someday! Yes, I want to hang some real pearls 'round my wife's neck. Ain't she supposed to wear no pearls? Somebody tell me—tell me, who decides which women is suppose to wear pearls in this world. I tell you I am a *man*—and I think my wife should wear some pearls in this world!

(*This last line hangs a good while and* WALTER *begins to move about the room. The word "Man" has penetrated his consciousness; he mumbles it to himself repeatedly between strange agitated pauses as he moves about*)

MAMA: Baby, how you going to feel on the inside?

WALTER: Fine! . . . Going to feel fine . . . a man . . .

MAMA: You won't have nothing left then, Walter Lee.

WALTER (*coming to her*):   I'm going to feel fine, Mama. I'm going to look that son-of-a-bitch in the eyes and say—(*He falters*)—and say, "All right, Mr. Lindner—(*He falters even more*)—that's *your* neighborhood out there! You got the right to keep it like you want! You got the right to have it like you want! Just write the check and—the house is yours." And—and I am going to say—(*His voice almost breaks*) "And you—you people just put the money in my hand and you won't have to live next to this bunch of stinking niggers! . . ." (*He straightens up and moves away from his mother, walking around the room*) And maybe—maybe I'll just get down on my black knees . . . (*He does so;*

RUTH *and* BENNIE *and* MAMA *watch him in frozen horror*) "Captain, Mistuh, Bossman— (*Groveling and grinning and wringing his hands in profoundly anguished imitation of the slow-witted movie stereotype*) A-hee-hee-hee! Oh, yassuh boss! Yasssssuh! Great white—(*Voice breaking, he forces himself to go on*)—Father, just gi' ussen de money, fo' God's sake, and we's—we's ain't gwine come out deh and dirty up yo' white folks neighborhood . . . " (*He breaks down completely*) And I'll feel fine! Fine! FINE! (*He gets up and goes into the bedroom*)

BENEATHA: That is not a man. That is nothing but a toothless rat.

MAMA: Yes—death done come in this here house. (*She is nodding, slowly, reflectively*) Done come walking in my house on the lips of my children. You what supposed to be my beginning again. You—what supposed to be my harvest. (*To* BENEATHA) You—you mourning your brother?

BENEATHA: He's no brother of mine.

MAMA: What you say?

BENEATHA: I said that that individual in that room is no brother of mine.

MAMA: That's what I thought you said. You feeling like you better than he is to-day? (BENEATHA *does not answer*) Yes? What you tell him a minute ago? That he wasn't a man? Yes? You give him up for me? You done wrote his epitaph too—like the rest of the world? Well, who give you the privilege?

BENEATHA: Be on my side for once! You saw what he just did, Mama! You saw him—down on his knees. Wasn't it you who taught me to despise any man who would do that? Do what he's going to do?

MAMA: Yes—I taught you that. Me and your daddy. But I thought I taught you something else too . . . I thought I taught you to love him.

BENEATHA: Love him? There is nothing left to love.

MAMA: There is *always* something left to love. And if you ain't learned that, you ain't learned nothing. (*Looking at her*) Have you cried for that boy today? I don't mean for yourself and for the family 'cause we lost the money. I mean for him: what he been through and what it done to him. Child, when do you think is the time to love somebody the most? When they done good and made things easy for everybody? Well then, you ain't through learning—because that ain't the time at all. It's when he's at his lowest and can't believe in hisself 'cause the world done whipped him so! When you starts measuring somebody, measure him right, child, measure him right. Make sure you done taken into account what hills and valleys he come through before he got to wherever he is.

(TRAVIS *bursts into the room at the end of the speech, leaving the door open*)

TRAVIS: Grandmama—the moving men are downstairs! The truck just pulled up.

MAMA (*turning and looking at him*):   Are they, baby? They downstairs?

(*She sighs and sits.* LINDNER *appears in the doorway. He peers in and knocks lightly, to gain attention, and comes in. All turn to look at him*)

LINDNER (*hat and briefcase in hand*):   Uh—hello . . .

(RUTH *crosses mechanically to the bedroom door and opens it and lets it swing open freely and slowly as the lights come up on* WALTER *within, still in his coat, sitting at the far corner of the room. He looks up and out through the room to* LINDNER)

RUTH: He's here.

(*A long minute passes and* WALTER *slowly gets up*)

LINDNER (*coming to the table with efficiency, putting his briefcase on the table and starting to unfold papers and unscrew fountain pens*):   Well, I certainly was glad to hear from you people. (WALTER *has begun the trek out of the room, slowly and awkwardly, rather like a small boy, passing the back of his sleeve across his mouth from time to time*) Life can really be so much simpler than people let it be most of the time. Well—with whom do I negotiate? You, Mrs. Younger, or your son here? (MAMA *sits with her hands folded on her lap and her eyes closed as* WALTER *advances.* TRAVIS *goes closer to* LINDNER *and looks at the papers curiously*) Just some official papers, sonny.

RUTH: Travis, you go downstairs—

MAMA (*opening her eyes and looking into* WALTER'S):   No. Travis, you stay right here. And you make him understand what you doing, Walter Lee. You teach him good. Like Willy Harris taught you. You show where our five generations done come to. (WALTER *looks from her to the boy, who grins at him innocently*) Go ahead, son—(*She folds her hands and closes her eyes*) Go ahead.

WALTER (*at last crosses to* LINDNER, *who is reviewing the contract*):   Well, Mr. Lindner. (BENEATHA *turns away*) We called you—(*There is a profound, simple groping quality in his speech*)—because, well, me and my family (*He looks around and shifts from one foot to the other*) Well—we are very plain people . . .

LINDNER: Yes—

WALTER: I mean—I have worked as a chauffeur most of my life—and my wife here, she does domestic work in people's kitchens. So does my mother. I mean—we are plain people . . .

LINDNER: Yes, Mr. Younger—

WALTER (*really like a small boy, looking down at his shoes and then up at the man*): And—uh—well, my father, well, he was a laborer most of his life. . . .

LINDNER (*absolutely confused*):   Uh, yes—yes, I understand. (*He turns back to the contract*)

WALTER (*a beat; staring at him*):   And my father—(*With sudden intensity*) My father almost *beat a man to death* once because this man called him a bad name or something, you know what I mean?

LINDNER (*looking up, frozen*):   No, no, I'm afraid I don't—

WALTER (*a beat. The tension hangs; then* WALTER *steps back from it*):   Yeah. Well—what I mean is that we come from people who had a lot of *pride*. I mean—we are very proud people. And that's my sister over there and she's going to be a doctor—and we are very proud—

LINDNER: Well—I am sure that is very nice, but—

WALTER: What I am telling you is that we called you over here to tell you that we are very proud and that this—(*Signaling to* TRAVIS) Travis, come here. (TRAVIS *crosses and* WALTER *draws him before him facing the man*) This is my son, and he makes the sixth generation our family in this country. And we have all thought about your offer—

LINDNER: Well, good . . . good—

WALTER: And we have decided to move into our house because my father—my father—he earned it for us brick by brick. (MAMA *has her eyes closed and is rocking back and forth as though she were in church, with her head nodding the Amen yes*) We don't want to make no trouble for nobody or fight no causes, and we will try to be good neighbors. And that's *all* we got to say about that. (*He looks the man absolutely in the eyes*) We don't want your money. (*He turns and walks away*)

LINDNER (*looking around at all of them*):   I take it then—that you have decided to occupy . . .

BENEATHA: That's what the man said.

LINDNER (*to* MAMA *in her reverie*):   Then I would like to appeal to you, Mrs. Younger. You are older and wiser and understand things better, I am sure . . .

MAMA: I am afraid you don't understand. My son said we was going to move and there ain't nothing left for me to say. (*Briskly*) You know how these young folks is nowadays, mister. Can't do a thing with 'em! (*As he opens his mouth, she rises*) Good-bye.

LINDNER (*folding up his materials*):   Well—if you are that final about it . . . there is nothing left for me to say. (*He finishes, almost ignored by the family, who are concentrating on* WALTER LEE. *At the door* LINDNER *halts and looks around*) I sure hope you people know what you're getting into.

(*He shakes his head and exits*)

RUTH (*looking around and coming to life*):   Well, for God's sake—if the moving men are here—LET'S GET THE HELL OUT OF HERE!

MAMA (*into action*):   Ain't it the truth! Look at all this here mess. Ruth, put Travis' good jacket on him . . . Walter Lee, fix your tie and tuck your shirt in, you look like somebody's hoodlum! Lord have mercy, where is my plant? (*She flies to get it amid the general bustling of the family, who are deliberately trying to ignore the nobility of the past moment*) You all start on down . . . Travis child, don't go empty-handed . . . Ruth, where did I put that box with my skillets in it? I want to be in charge of it myself . . . I'm going to make us the biggest dinner we ever ate tonight . . . Beneatha, what's the matter with them stockings? Pull them things up, girl . . .

(*The family starts to file out as two moving men appear and begin to carry out the heavier pieces of furniture, bumping into the family as they move about*)

BENEATHA: Mama, Asagai asked me to marry him today and go to Africa—

MAMA (*in the middle of her getting-ready activity*):   He did? You ain't old enough to marry nobody—(*Seeing the moving men lifting one of her chairs precariously*) Darling, that ain't no bale of cotton, please handle it so we can sit in it again! I had that chair twenty-five years . . .

(*The movers sigh with exasperation and go on with their work*)

BENEATHA (*girlishly and unreasonably trying to pursue the conversation*):   To go to Africa, Mama—be a doctor in Africa . . .

MAMA (*distracted*):   Yes, baby—

WALTER: *Africa!* What he want you to go to Africa for?

BENEATHA: To practice there . . .

WALTER: Girl, if you don't get all them silly ideas out your head! You better marry yourself a man with some loot . . .

BENEATHA (*angrily, precisely as in the first scene of the play*):   What have you got to do with who I marry!

WALTER: Plenty. Now I think George Murchison—

BENEATHA: *George Murchison!* I wouldn't marry him if he was Adam and I was Eve!

(WALTER *and* BENEATHA *go out yelling at each other vigorously and the anger is loud and real till their voices diminish.* RUTH *stands at the door and turns to* MAMA *and smiles knowingly*)

MAMA (*fixing her hat at last*):   Yeah—they something all right, my children . . .

RUTH: Yeah—they're something. Let's go, Lena.

MAMA (*stalling, starting to look around at the house*):   Yes—I'm coming. Ruth—

RUTH: Yes?

MAMA (*quietly, woman to woman*):   He finally come into his manhood today, didn't he? Kind of like a rainbow after the rain . . .

RUTH (*biting her lip lest her own pride explode in front of* MAMA):   Yes, Lena.

(WALTER*'s voice calls for them raucously*)

WALTER (*off stage*):   Y'all come on! These people charges by the hour, you know!

MAMA (*waving* RUTH *out vaguely*):   All right, honey—go on down. I be down directly.

(RUTH *hesitates, then exits.* MAMA *stands, at last alone in the living room, her plant on the table before her as the lights start to come down. She looks around at all the walls and ceilings and suddenly, despite herself, while the children call below, a great heaving thing rises in her and she puts her fist to her mouth to stifle it, takes a final desperate look, pulls her coat about her, pats her hat and goes out. The lights dim down. The door opens and she comes back in, grabs her plant, and goes out for the last time*)

Curtain

(1959)

QUESTIONS FOR REFLECTION

Experience

1. Did you find this play engaging or interesting? Why or why not? What makes it specifically an urban play? A "minority" play?
2. To what extent can you relate to the experiences of the play's characters?

Interpretation

3. Describe the relationship of Mama (Lena) with her daughter, Beneatha, and with her son, Walter. What expectations does she have for the future of each? Why?
4. Give two explanations for the primary conflicts of the play. What precipitates the various arguments and battles the characters wage with one another?
5. Explain the roles of Joseph Asagai and George Murchison. Does either character have thematic significance? Explain.
6. Identify and discuss a major theme of the play. Support your ideas with references to specific events and speeches.
7. Identify two important stage props and comment on their role in the play. Discuss whether either or both may be symbolic, and why.

8. Select a scene you find compelling and describe how to stage it.
9. Are you satisfied with the play's ending? Why or why not? How do you envision the future of the family, particularly of Ruth and Walter and of Beneatha?

Evaluation

10. Some readers consider this play a modern American classic. What do you think may have led them to such an assessment?
11. How is Hansberry's play a comment on the Langston Hughes poem that she uses as her epigraph?

TERRENCE MCNALLY

[b. 1939]

Terrence McNally has long been a fixture on and off Broadway. His plays have won wide acclaim for their wit, wisdom, and humanity. Among his numerous plays are *A Perfect Ganesh; Lips Together, Teeth Apart; Whisky; The Ritz;* and *Things That Go Bump in the Night.* McNally has also written screenplays, scripts for television, and the book for the musical adaptation of Manuel Puig's *The Kiss of the Spiderwoman.*

Andre's Mother was written as a script for television. It won the 1990 Emmy Award for Best Writing in a Miniseries or Special.

TERRENCE MCNALLY

Andre's Mother

CHARACTERS

CAL
ARTHUR
PENNY
ANDRE'S MOTHER

Four people enter. They are nicely dressed and carry white helium-filled balloons on a string. They are CAL, *a young man;* ARTHUR, *his father;* PENNY, *his sister; and* ANDRE'S MOTHER.

CAL: You know what's really terrible? I can't think of anything terrific to say. Goodbye. I love you. I'll miss you. And I'm supposed to be so great with words!

PENNY: What's that over there?

ARTHUR: Ask your brother.

CAL: It's a theatre. An outdoor theatre. They do plays there in the summer. Shakespeare's plays. (*To* ANDRE'S MOTHER.) God, how much he wanted to play Hamlet. It was his greatest dream. I think he would have sold his soul to play it. He would have gone to Timbuktu to have another go at that part. The summer he did it in Boston, he was so happy!

PENNY: Cal, I don't think she . . . ! It's not the time. Later.

ARTHUR: Your son was a . . . the Jews have a word for it . . .

PENNY (*Quietly appalled.*):   Oh my God!

ARTHUR: Mensch, I believe it is and I think I'm using it right. It means warm, solid, the real thing. Correct me if I'm wrong.

PENNY: Fine, dad, fine. Just quit while you're ahead.

ARTHUR: I won't say he was like a son to me. Even my son isn't always like a son to me. I mean . . . ! In my clumsy way, I'm trying to say how much I liked Andre. And how much he helped me to know my own boy. Cal was always two hands full but Andre and I could talk about anything under the sun. My wife was very fond of him, too.

PENNY: Cal, I don't understand about the balloons.

CAL: They represent the soul. When you let go, it means you're letting his soul ascend to Heaven. That you're willing to let go. Breaking the last earthly ties.

PENNY: Does the Pope know about this?

ARTHUR: Penny!

PENNY: Andre loved my sense of humor. Listen, you can hear him laughing. (*She lets go of her white balloon.*) So long, you glorious, wonderful, I-know-what-Cal-means-about-words . . . *man!* God forgive me for wishing you were straight every time I laid eyes on you. But if any man was going to have you, I'm glad it was my brother! Look how fast it went up. I bet that means something. Something terrific.

ARTHUR: (ARTHUR *lets his balloon go.*) Goodbye. God speed.

PENNY: Cal?

CAL: I'm not ready yet.

PENNY: Okay. We'll be over there. Come on, pop, you can buy your little girl a Good Humor.

ARTHUR: They still make Good Humor?

PENNY: Only now they're called Dove Bars and they cost 12 dollars.

(PENNY *takes* ARTHUR *off.* CAL *and* ANDRE'S MOTHER *stand with their balloons.*)

CAL: I wish I knew what you were thinking. I think it would help me. You know almost nothing about me and I only know what Andre told me about you. I'd always had it in my mind that one day we would be friends, you and me. But if you didn't know about Andre and me . . . If this hadn't happened, I wonder if he would have ever told you. When he was so sick, if I asked him once I asked him a thousand times, tell her. She's your mother. She won't mind. But he was so afraid of hurting you and of your disapproval. I don't know which was worse. (*No response. He sighs.*) God, how many of us live in this city because we don't want to hurt our mothers and live in mortal terror of their disapproval. We lose ourselves here. Our lives aren't furtive, just our feelings toward people like you are! A city of fugitives from our parent's scorn or heartbreak. Sometimes he'd seem a little down and I'd say, "What's the matter, babe?" and this funny sweet, sad smile would cross his face and he'd say, "Just a little homesick, Cal, just a little bit." I always accused him of being a country boy just playing at being a hot shot, sophisticated New Yorker. (*He sighs.*) It's bullshit. It's all bullshit. (*Still no response.*) Do you remember the comic strip Little Lulu? Her mother had no name, she was so remote, so formidable to all the children. She was just Lulu's mother. "Hello, Lulu's Mother," Lulu's friends would say. She was almost anonymous in her remoteness. You remind me of her. Andre's Mother. Let me answer the questions you can't ask and then I'll leave you alone and you won't ever have to see me again. Andre died of AIDS. I don't know how he got it. I tested negative. He died bravely. You would have been proud of him. The only thing that frightened him was you. I'll have everything that was his sent to you. I'll pay for it. There isn't much. You should have come up the summer he played Hamlet. He was magnificent. Yes, I'm bitter. I'm bitter I've lost him. I'm bitter what's happening. I'm bitter even now, after all this, I can't reach you. I'm beginning to feel your disapproval and it's making me ill. (*He looks at his balloon.*) Sorry, old friend. I blew it. (*He lets go of the balloon.*) Good night, sweet prince, and flights of angels sing thee to thy rest! (*Beat.*) Goodbye, Andre's Mother. (*He goes.* ANDRE'S MOTHER *stands alone holding her white balloon. Her lip trembles. She looks on the verge of breaking down. She is about to let go of the balloon when she pulls it down to her. She looks at it a while before she gently kisses it. She lets go of the balloon. She follows it with her eyes as it rises and rises. The lights are beginning to fade.* ANDRE'S MOTHER'*s eyes are still on the balloon. Blackout.*)

(*1988*)

QUESTIONS FOR REFLECTION

Experience

1. To what extent do you sympathize with Andre's Mother?

Interpretation

2. Why is the play entitled "Andre's Mother"? What effect does the playwright achieve by making the mother's part silent?
3. What is the significance of Cal's allusion to Lulu's mother?
4. What is the effect of Cal's references to *Hamlet*? What is conveyed through Cal's quoting from Shakespeare's play?
5. What is the significance of the helium balloons and of what the characters do with them?
6. What is the significance of the final stage direction?
7. What is the overall theme of *Andre's Mother*?

Evaluation

8. What does the play suggest about the values of Andre, his mother, and lover?

AUGUST WILSON

[b. 1945]

August Wilson was born and raised in Pittsburgh, Pennsylvania. He quit school at sixteen and worked at various odd jobs until moving to Minneapolis–St. Paul, where he founded the Black Horizons Theatre Company. Having dropped out of school, Wilson educated himself at the public library, discovering there the work of Ralph Ellison, Richard Wright, and Langston Hughes, three modern African-American writers whose work inspired him. Wilson is the author of *Ma Rainey's Black Bottom, Fences, Joe Turner's Come and Gone, The Piano Lesson,* and *Two Trains Running,* all notable for their depiction of the urban lives of African-Americans. The recipient of many awards, including two Pulitzer Prizes, a New York Drama Critics Circle Award, and Tony Award, Wilson continues to provide a window on the lives of Americans struggling for success, equality, and survival.

AUGUST WILSON

Fences

CHARACTERS

TROY MAXSON
JIM BONO, TROY's *friend*
ROSE, TROY's *wife*
LYONS, TROY's *oldest son by previous marriage*
GABRIEL, TROY's *brother*
CORY, TROY *and* ROSE's *son*
RAYNELL, TROY's *daughter*

Setting. *The setting is the yard which fronts the only entrance to the Maxson household, an ancient two-story brick house set back off a small alley in a big-city neighborhood. The entrance to the house is gained by two or three steps leading to a wooden porch badly in need of paint.*

   A relatively recent addition to the house and running its full width, the porch lacks congruence. It is a sturdy porch with a flat roof. One or two chairs of dubious value sit at one end where the kitchen window opens onto the porch. An old-fashioned icebox stands silent guard at the opposite end.

The yard is a small dirt yard, partially fenced, except for the last scene, with a wooden saw-horse, a pile of lumber, and other fence-building equipment set off to the side. Opposite is a tree from which hangs a ball made of rags. A baseball bat leans against the tree. Two oil drums serve as garbage receptacles and sit near the house at right to complete the setting.

The Play. *Near the turn of the century, the destitute of Europe sprang on the city with tenacious claws and an honest and solid dream. The city devoured them. They swelled its belly until it burst into a thousand furnaces and sewing machines, a thousand butcher shops and bakers' ovens, a thousand churches and hospitals and funeral parlors and money-lenders. The city grew. It nourished itself and offered each man a partnership limited only by his talent, his guile, and his willingness and capacity for hard work. For the immigrants of Europe, a dream dared and won true.*

The descendants of African slaves were offered no such welcome or participation. They came from places called the Carolinas and the Virginias, Georgia, Alabama, Mississippi, and Tennessee. They came strong, eager, searching. The city rejected them and they fled and settled along the riverbanks and under bridges in shallow, ramshackle houses made of sticks and tarpaper. They collected rags and wood. They sold the use of their muscles and their bodies. They cleaned houses and washed clothes, they shined shoes, and in quiet desperation and vengeful pride, they stole, and lived in pursuit of their own dream. That they could breathe free, finally, and stand to meet life with the force of dignity and whatever eloquence the heart could call upon.

By 1957, the hard-won victories of the European immigrants had solidified the industrial might of America. War had been confronted and won with new energies that used loyalty and patriotism as its fuel. Life was rich, full, and flourishing. The Milwaukee Braves won the World Series, and the hot winds of change that would make the sixties a turbulent, racing, dangerous, and provocative decade had not yet begun to blow full.

ACT I

Scene 1

It is 1957. TROY *and* BONO *enter the yard, engaged in conversation.* TROY *is fifty-three years old, a large man with thick, heavy hands; it is this largeness that he strives to fill out and make an accommodation with. Together with his blackness, his largeness informs his sensibilities and the choices he has made in his life.*

Of the two men, BONO *is obviously the follower. His commitment to their friendship of thirty-odd years is rooted in his admiration of* TROY*'s honesty, capacity for hard work, and his strength, which* BONO *seeks to emulate.*

It is Friday night, payday, and the one night of the week the two men engage in a ritual of talk and drink. TROY *is usually the most talkative and at times he can be crude and almost vulgar, though he is capable of rising to profound heights of expression. The men carry lunch buckets and wear or carry burlap aprons and are dressed in clothes suitable to their jobs as garbage collectors.*

BONO: Troy, you ought to stop that lying!

TROY: I ain't lying! The nigger had a watermelon this big.

He indicates with his hands.

Talking about . . . "What watermelon, Mr. Rand?" I liked to fell out!
"What watermelon, Mr. Rand?" . . . And it sitting there big as life.

BONO: What did Mr. Rand say?

TROY: Ain't said nothing. Figure if the nigger too dumb to know he carrying a watermelon, he wasn't gonna get much sense out of him. Trying to hide that great big old watermelon under his coat. Afraid to let the white man see him carrying it home.

BONO: I'm like you . . . I ain't got no time for them kind of people.

TROY: Now what he looks like getting mad cause he see the man from the union talking to Mr. Rand?

BONO: He come to me talking about . . . "Maxson gonna get us fired." I told him to get away from me with that. He walked away from me calling you a troublemaker. What Mr. Rand say?

TROY: Ain't said nothing. He told me to go down the Commissioner's office next Friday. They called me down there to see them.

BONO: Well, as long as you got your complaint filed, they can't fire you. That's what one of them white fellows tell me.

TROY: I ain't worried about them firing me. They gonna fire me cause I asked a question? That's all I did. I went to Mr. Rand and asked him, "Why? Why you got the white men driving and the colored lifting?" Told him, "what's the matter, don't I count? You think only white fellows got sense enough to drive a truck. That ain't no paper job! Hell, anybody can drive a truck. How come you got all whites driving and the colored lifting?" He told me "take it to the union." Well, hell, that's what I done! Now they wanna come up with this pack of lies.

BONO: I told Brownie if the man come and ask him any questions . . . just tell the truth! It ain't nothing but something they done trumped up on you cause you filed a complaint on them.

TROY: Brownie don't understand nothing. All I want them to do is change the job description. Give everybody a chance to drive the truck. Brownie can't see that. He ain't got that much sense.

BONO: How you figure he be making out with that gal be up at Taylors' all the time . . . that Alberta gal?

TROY: Same as you and me. Getting just as much as we is. Which is to say nothing.

BONO: It is, huh? I figure you doing a little better than me . . . and I ain't saying what I'm doing.

TROY: Aw, nigger, look here . . . I know you. If you had got anywhere near that gal, twenty minutes later you be looking to tell somebody. And the first one you gonna tell . . . that you gonna want to brag to . . . is gonna be me.

BONO: I ain't saying that. I see where you be eyeing her.

TROY: I eye all the women. I don't miss nothing. Don't never let nobody tell you Troy Maxson don't eye the women.

BONO: You been doing more than eyeing her. You done bought her a drink or two.

TROY: Hell yeah, I bought her a drink! What that mean? I bought you one, too. What that mean cause I buy her a drink? I'm just being polite.

BONO: It's all right to buy her one drink. That's what you call being polite. But when you wanna be buying two or three . . . that's what you call eyeing her.

TROY: Look here, as long as you known me . . . you ever known me to chase after women?

BONO: Hell yeah! Long as I done known you. You forgetting I knew you when.

TROY: Naw, I'm talking about since I been married to Rose?

BONO: Oh, not since you been married to Rose. Now, that's the truth, there. I can say that.

TROY: All right then! Case closed.

BONO: I see you be walking up around Alberta's house. You supposed to be at Taylor's and you be walking up around there.

TROY: What are you watching where I'm walking for? I ain't watching after you.

BONO: I see you walking around there more than once.

TROY: Hell, you liable to see me walking anywhere! That don't mean nothing cause you see me walking around there.

BONO: Where she come from anyway? She just kinda showed up one day.

TROY: Tallahassee. You can look at her and tell she one of them Florida gals. They got some big healthy women down there. Grow them right up out the ground. Got a little bit of Indian in her. Most of them niggers down in Florida got some Indian in them.

BONO: I don't know about that Indian part. But she damn sure big and healthy. Woman wear some big stockings. Got them great big old legs and hips as wide as the Mississippi River.

TROY: Legs don't mean nothing. You don't do nothing but push them out of the way. But them hips cushion the ride!

BONO: Troy, you ain't got no sense.

TROY: It's the truth! Like you riding on Goodyears!

ROSE *enters from the house. She is ten years younger than* TROY, *her devotion to him stems from her recognition of the possibilities of her life without him: a succession of abusive men and their babies, a life of partying and running the streets, the Church, or aloneness with its attendant pain and frustration. She recognizes* TROY's *spirit as a fine and illuminating one and she either ignores or forgives his faults, only some of which she recognizes. Though she doesn't drink, her presence is an integral part of the Friday night rituals. She alternates between the porch and the kitchen, where supper preparations are under way.*

ROSE: What you all out here getting into?

TROY: What you worried about what we getting into for? This is men talk, woman.

ROSE: What I care what you all talking about? Bono, you gonna stay for supper?

BONO: No, I thank you, Rose. But Lucille say she cooking up a pot of pigfeet.

TROY: Pigfeet! Hell, I'm going home with you! Might even stay the night if you got some pigfeet. You got something in there to top them pigfeet, Rose?

ROSE: I'm cooking up some chicken. I got some chicken and collard greens.

TROY: Well, go on back in the house and let me and Bono finish what we was talking about. This is men talk. I got some talk for you later. You know what kind of talk I mean. You go on and powder it up.

ROSE: Troy Maxson, don't you start that now!

TROY [*puts his arm around her*]:   Aw, woman . . . come here. Look here, Bono . . . when I met this woman . . . I got out that place, say, "Hitch up my pony, saddle up my mare . . . there's a woman out there for me somewhere. I looked here. Looked there.

Saw Rose and latched on to her." I latched on to her and told her—I'm gonna tell you the truth—I told her, "Baby, I don't wanna marry, I just wanna be your man." Rose told me . . . tell him what you told me, Rose.

ROSE: I told him if he wasn't the marrying kind, then move out the way so the marrying kind could find me.

TROY: That's what she told me. "Nigger, you in my way. You blocking the view! Move out the way so I can find me a husband." I thought it over two or three days. Come back—

ROSE: Ain't no two or three days nothing. You was back the same night.

TROY: Come back, told her . . . "Okay, baby . . . but I'm gonna buy me a banty rooster and put him out there in the backyard . . . and when he see a stranger come, he'll flap his wings and crow . . . " Look here, Bono, I could watch the front door by myself . . . it was that back door I was worried about.

ROSE: Troy, you ought not talk like that. Troy ain't doing nothing but telling a lie.

TROY: Only thing is . . . when we first got married . . . forget the rooster . . . we ain't had no yard!

BONO: I hear you tell it. Me and Lucille was staying down there on Logan Street. Had two rooms with the outhouse in the back. I ain't mind the outhouse none. But when that goddamn wind blow through there in the winter . . . that's what I'm talking about! To this day I wonder why in the hell I ever stayed down there for six long years. But see, I didn't know I could do no better. I thought only white folks had inside toilets and things.

ROSE: There's a lot of people don't know they can do no better than they doing now. That's just something you got to learn. A lot of folks still shop at Bella's.

TROY: Ain't nothing wrong with shopping at Bella's. She got fresh food.

ROSE: I ain't said nothing about if she got fresh food. I'm talking about what she charge. She charge ten cents more than the A&P.

TROY: The A&P ain't never done nothing for me. I spends my money where I'm treated right. I go down to Bella, say, "I need a loaf of bread, I'll pay you Friday." She give it to me. What sense that make when I got money to go and spend it somewhere else and ignore the person who done right by me? That ain't in the Bible.

ROSE: We ain't talking about what's in the Bible. What sense it made to shop there when she overcharge?

TROY: You shop where you want to. I'll do my shopping where the people been good to me.

ROSE: Well, I don't think it's right for her to overcharge. That's all I was saying.

BONO: Look here . . . I got to get on. Lucille going be raising all kind of hell.

TROY: Where you going, nigger? We ain't finished this pint. Come here, finish this pint.

BONO: Well, hell, I am . . . if you ever turn the bottle loose.

TROY [hands him the bottle]:   The only thing I say about the A&P is I'm glad Cory got that job down there. Help him take care of his school clothes and things. Gabe done moved out and things getting tight around here. He got that job. . . . He can start to look out for himself.

ROSE: Cory done went and got recruited by a college football team.

TROY: I told that boy about that football stuff. The white man ain't gonna let him get nowhere with that football. I told him when he first come to me with it. Now you come telling me he done went and got more tied up in it. He ought to go and get recruited in how to fix cars or something where he can make a living.

ROSE: He ain't talking about making no living playing football. It's just something the boys in school do. They gonna send a recruiter by to talk to you. He'll tell you he ain't talking about making no living playing football. It's a honor to be recruited.

TROY: It ain't gonna get him nowhere. Bono'll tell you that.

BONO: If he be like you in the sports . . . he's gonna be all right. Ain't but two men ever played baseball as good as you. That's Babe Ruth and Josh Gibson.* Them's the only two men ever hit more home runs than you.

TROY: What it ever get me? Ain't got a pot to piss in or a window to throw it out of.

ROSE: Times have changed since you was playing baseball, Troy. That was before the war. Times have changed a lot since then.

TROY: How in hell they done changed?

ROSE: They got lots of colored boys playing ball now. Baseball and football.

BONO: You right about that, Rose. Times have changed, Troy. You just come along too early.

TROY: There ought not never have been no time called too early! Now you take that fellow . . . what's that fellow they had playing right field for the Yankees back then? You know who I'm talking about, Bono. Used to play right field for the Yankees.

ROSE: Selkirk?

TROY: Selkirk! That's it! Man batting .269, understand? .269. What kind of sense that make? I was hitting .432 with thirty-seven home runs! Man batting .269 and playing right field for the Yankees! I saw Josh Gibson's daughter yesterday. She walking around with raggedy shoes on her feet. Now I bet you Selkirk's daughter ain't walking around with raggedy shoes on her feet! I bet you that!

ROSE: They got a lot of colored baseball players now. Jackie Robinson was the first. Folks had to wait for Jackie Robinson.

TROY: I done seen a hundred niggers play baseball better than Jackie Robinson. Hell, I know some teams Jackie Robinson couldn't even make! What you talking about Jackie Robinson. Jackie Robinson wasn't nobody. I'm talking about if you could play ball then they ought to have let you play. Don't care what color you were. Come telling me I come along too early. If you could play . . . then they ought to have let you play.

TROY *takes a long drink from the bottle.*

ROSE: You gonna drink yourself to death. You don't need to be drinking like that.

TROY: Death ain't nothing. I done seen him. Done wrassled with him. You can't tell me nothing about death. Death ain't nothing but a fastball on the outside corner. And you know what I'll do to that! Lookee here, Bono . . . am I lying? You get one of them fastballs, about waist high, over the outside corner of the plate where you can get the meat of the bat on it . . . and good god! You can kiss it goodbye. Now, am I lying?

BONO: Naw, you telling the truth there. I seen you do it.

TROY: If I'm lying . . . that 450 feet worth of lying!

Josh Gibson   (1911–1947) *powerful, black baseball player known in the 1930s as the Babe Ruth of the Negro leagues.*

Pause.

That's all death is to me. A fastball on the outside corner.

ROSE: I don't know why you want to get on talking about death.

TROY: Ain't nothing wrong with talking about death. That's part of life. Everybody gonna die. You gonna die, I'm gonna die. Bono's gonna die. Hell, we all gonna die.

ROSE: But you ain't got to talk about it. I don't like to talk about it.

TROY: You the one brought it up. Me and Bono was talking about baseball . . . you tell me I'm gonna drink myself to death. Ain't that right, Bono? You know I don't drink this but one night out of the week. That's Friday night. I'm gonna drink just enough to where I can handle it. Then I cuts it loose. I leave it alone. So don't you worry about me drinking myself to death. 'Cause I ain't worried about Death. I done seen him. I done wrestled with him.

Look here, Bono . . . I looked up one day and Death was marching straight at me. Like Soldiers on Parade! The Army of Death was marching straight at me. The middle of July, 1941. It got real cold just like it be winter. It seem like Death himself reached out and touched me on the shoulder. He touch me just like I touch you. I got cold as ice and Death standing there grinning at me.

ROSE: Troy, why don't you hush that talk.

TROY: I say . . . What you want, Mr. Death? You be wanting me? You done brought your army to be getting me? I looked him dead in the eye. I wasn't fearing nothing. I was ready to tangle. Just like I'm ready to tangle now. The Bible say be ever vigilant. That's why I don't get but so drunk. I got to keep watch.

ROSE: Troy was right down there in Mercy Hospital. You remember he had pneumonia? Laying there with a fever talking plumb out of his head.

TROY: Death standing there staring at me . . . carrying that sickle in his hand. Finally he say, "You want bound over for another year?" See, just like that . . . "You want bound over for another year?" I told him, "Bound over hell! Let's settle this now!"

It seem like he kinda fell back when I said that, and all the cold went out of me. I reached down and grabbed that sickle and threw it just as far as I could throw it . . . and me and him commenced to wrestling.

We wrestled for three days and three nights. I can't say where I found the strength from. Every time it seemed like he was gonna get the best of me, I'd reach way down deep inside myself and find the strength to do him one better.

ROSE: Every time Troy tell that story he find different ways to tell it. Different things to make up about it.

TROY: I ain't making up nothing. I'm telling you the facts of what happened. I wrestled with Death for three days and three nights and I'm standing here to tell you about it.

Pause.

All right. At the end of the third night we done weakened each other to where we can't hardly move. Death stood up, throwed on his robe . . . had him a white robe with a hood on it. He threw on that robe and went off to look for his sickle. Say, "I'll be back." Just like that. "I'll be back." I told him, say, "Yeah, but . . . you gonna have to find me!" I wasn't no fool. I wasn't going looking for him. Death ain't nothing to play with. And I know he's gonna get me. I know I got to join his army . . . his camp followers.

But as long as I keep my strength and see him coming . . . as long as I keep up my vigilance . . . he's gonna have to fight to get me. I ain't going easy.

BONO: Well, look here, since you got to keep up your vigilance . . . let me have the bottle.

TROY: Aw hell, I shouldn't have told you that part. I should have left out that part.

ROSE: Troy be talking that stuff and half the time don't even know what he be talking about.

TROY: Bono know me better than that.

BONO: That's right. I know you. I know you got some Uncle Remus* in your blood. You got more stories than the devil got sinners.

TROY: Aw hell, I done seen him too! Done talked with the devil.

ROSE: Troy, don't nobody wanna be hearing all that stuff.

LYONS *enters the yard from the street. Thirty-four years old,* TROY'*s son by a previous marriage, he sports a neatly trimmed goatee, sport coat, white shirt, tieless and buttoned at the collar. Though he fancies himself a musician, he is more caught up in the rituals and "idea" of being a musician than in the actual practice of the music. He has come to borrow money from* TROY, *and while he knows he will be successful, he is uncertain as to what extent his lifestyle will be held up to scrutiny and ridicule.*

LYONS: Hey, Pop.

TROY: What you come "Hey, Popping" me for?

LYONS: How you doing, Rose?

He kisses her.

Mr. Bono. How you doing?

BONO: Hey, Lyons . . . how you been?

TROY: He must have been doing all right. I ain't seen him around here last week.

ROSE: Troy, leave your boy alone. He come by to see you and you wanna start all that nonsense.

TROY: I ain't bothering Lyons.

Offers him the bottle.

Here . . . get you a drink. We got an understanding. I know why he come by to see me and he know I know.

LYONS: Come on, Pop . . . I just stopped by to say hi . . . see how you was doing.

TROY: You ain't stopped by yesterday.

ROSE: You gonna stay for supper, Lyons? I got some chicken cooking in the oven.

LYONS: No, Rose . . . thanks. I was just in the neighborhood and thought I'd stop by for a minute.

TROY: You was in the neighborhood all right, nigger. You telling the truth there. You was in the neighborhood cause it's my payday.

LYONS: Well, hell, since you mentioned it . . . let me have ten dollars.

TROY: I'll be damned! I'll die and go to hell and play blackjack with the devil before I give you ten dollars.

BONO: That's what I wanna know about . . . that devil you done seen.

Uncle Remus   *Black storyteller who recounts traditional black tales in the book by Joel Chandler Harris.*

LYONS: What . . . Pop done seen the devil? You too much, Pops.

TROY: Yeah, I done seen him. Talked to him too!

ROSE: You ain't seen no devil. I done told you that man ain't had nothing to do with the devil. Anything you can't understand, you want to call it the devil.

TROY: Look here, Bono . . . I went down to see Hertzberger about some furniture. Got three rooms for two-ninety-eight. That what it say on the radio. "Three rooms . . . two-ninety-eight." Even made up a little song about it. Go down there . . . man tell me I can't get no credit. I'm working every day and can't get no credit. What to do? I got an empty house with some raggedy furniture in it. Cory ain't got no bed. He's sleeping on a pile of rags on the floor. Working every day and can't get no credit. Come back here—Rose'll tell you—madder than hell. Sit down . . . try to figure what I'm gonna do. Come a knock on the door. Ain't been living here but three days. Who know I'm here? Open the door . . . devil standing there bigger than life. White fellow . . . got on good clothes and everything. Standing there with a clipboard in his hand. I ain't had to say nothing. First words come out of his mouth was . . . "I understand you need some furniture and can't get no credit." I liked to fell over. He say, "I'll give you all the credit you want, but you got to pay the interest on it." I told him, "Give me three rooms worth and charge whatever you want." Next day a truck pulled up here and two men unloaded them three rooms. Man that drove the truck give me a book. Say send ten dollars, first of every month to the address in the book and everything will be all right. Say if I miss a payment the devil was coming back and it'll be hell to pay. That was fifteen years ago. To this day . . . the first of the month I send my ten dollars, Rose'll tell you.

ROSE: Troy lying.

TROY: I ain't never seen that man since. Now you tell me who else that could have been but the devil? I ain't sold my soul or nothing like that, you understand. Naw, I wouldn't have truck with the devil about nothing like that. I got my furniture and pays my ten dollars the first of the month just like clockwork.

BONO: How long you say you been paying this ten dollars a month?

TROY: Fifteen years!

BONO: Hell, ain't you finished paying for it yet? How much the man done charged you.

TROY: Ah hell, I done paid for it. I done paid for it ten times over! The fact is I'm scared to stop paying it.

ROSE: Troy lying. We got that furniture from Mr. Glickman. He ain't paying no ten dollars a month to nobody.

TROY: Aw hell, woman. Bono know I ain't that big a fool.

LYONS: I was just getting ready to say . . . I know where there's a bridge for sale.

TROY: Look here, I'll tell you this . . . it don't matter to me if he was the devil. It don't matter if the devil give credit. Somebody has got to give it.

ROSE: It ought to matter. You going around talking about having truck with the devil . . . God's the one you gonna have to answer to. He's the one gonna be at the Judgment.

LYONS: Yeah, well, look here, Pop . . . let me have that ten dollars. I'll give it back to you. Bonnie got a job working at the hospital.

TROY: What I tell you, Bono? The only time I see this nigger is when he wants something. That's the only time I see him.

LYONS: Come on, Pop, Mr. Bono don't want to hear all that. Let me have the ten dollars. I told you Bonnie working.

TROY: What that mean to me? "Bonnie working." I don't care if she working. Go ask her for the ten dollars if she working. Talking about "Bonnie working." Why ain't you working?

LYONS: Aw, Pop, you know I can't find no decent job. Where am I gonna get a job at? You know I can't get no job.

TROY: I told you I know some people down there. I can get you on the rubbish if you want to work. I told you that the last time you came by here asking me for something.

LYONS: Naw, Pop . . . thanks. That ain't for me. I don't wanna be carrying nobody's rubbish. I don't wanna be punching nobody's time clock.

TROY: What's the matter, you too good to carry people's rubbish? Where you think that ten dollars you talking about come from? I'm just supposed to haul people's rubbish and give my money to you cause you too lazy to work. You too lazy to work and wanna know why you ain't got what I got.

ROSE: What hospital Bonnie working at? Mercy?

LYONS: She's down at Passavant working in the laundry.

TROY: I ain't got nothing as it is. I give you that ten dollars and I got to eat beans the rest of the week. Naw . . . you ain't getting no ten dollars here.

LYONS: You ain't got to be eating no beans. I don't know why you wanna say that.

TROY: I ain't got no extra money. Gabe done moved over to Miss Pearl's paying her the rent and things done got tight around here. I can't afford to be giving you every payday.

LYONS: I ain't asked you to give me nothing. I asked you to loan me ten dollars. I know you got ten dollars.

TROY: Yeah, I got it. You know why I got it? Cause I don't throw my money away out there in the streets. You living the fast life . . . wanna be a musician . . . running around in them clubs and things . . . then, you learn to take care of yourself. You ain't gonna find me going and asking nobody for nothing. I done spent too many years without.

LYONS: You and me is two different people, Pop.

TROY: I done learned my mistake and learned to do what's right by it. You still trying to get something for nothing. Life don't owe you nothing. You owe it to yourself. Ask Bono. He'll tell you I'm right.

LYONS: You got your way of dealing with the world . . . I got mine. The only thing that matters to me is the music.

TROY: Yeah, I can see that! It don't matter how you gonna eat . . . where your next dollar is coming from. You telling the truth there.

LYONS: I know I got to eat. But I got to live too. I need something that gonna help me to get out of the bed in the morning. Make me feel like I belong in the world. I don't bother nobody. I just stay with my music cause that's the only way I can find to live in the world. Otherwise there ain't no telling what I might do. Now I don't come criticizing you and how you live. I just come by to ask you for ten dollars. I don't wanna hear all that about how I live.

TROY: Boy, your mamma did a hell of a job raising you.

LYONS: You can't change me, Pop. I'm thirty-four years old. If you wanted to change me, you should have been there when I was growing up. I come by to see you . . . ask for ten dollars and you want to talk about how I was raised. You don't know nothing about how I was raised.

ROSE: Let the boy have ten dollars, Troy.

TROY [*to* LYONS]:   What the hell you looking at me for? I ain't got no ten dollars. You know what I do with my money.

To ROSE.

Give him ten dollars if you want him to have it.

ROSE: I will. Just as soon as you turn it loose.

TROY [*handing* ROSE *the money*]:   There it is. Seventy-six dollars and forty-two cents. You see this, Bono? Now, I ain't gonna get but six of that back.

ROSE: You ought to stop telling that lie. Here, Lyons. [*She hands him the money.*]

LYONS: Thanks, Rose. Look . . . I got to run . . . I'll see you later.

TROY: Wait a minute. You gonna say, "thanks, Rose" and ain't gonna look to see where she got that ten dollars from? See how they do me, Bono?

LYONS: I know she got it from you, Pop. Thanks. I'll give it back to you.

TROY: There he go telling another lie. Time I see that ten dollars . . . he'll be owing me thirty more.

LYONS: See you, Mr. Bono.

BONO: Take care, Lyons!

LYONS: Thanks, Pop. I'll see you again.

LYONS *exits the yard.*

TROY: I don't know why he don't go and get him a decent job and take care of that woman he got.

BONO: He'll be all right, Troy. The boy is still young.

TROY: The *boy* is thirty-four years old.

ROSE: Let's not get off into all that.

BONO: Look here . . . I got to be going. I got to be getting on. Lucille gonna be waiting.

TROY [*puts his arm around* ROSE]:   See this woman, Bono? I love this woman. I love this woman so much it hurts. I love her so much . . . I done run out of ways of loving her. So I got to go back to basics. Don't you come by my house Monday morning talking about time to go to work . . . 'cause I'm still gonna be stroking!

ROSE: Troy! Stop it now!

BONO: I ain't paying him no mind, Rose. That ain't nothing but gin-talk. Go on, Troy. I'll see you Monday.

TROY: Don't you come by my house, nigger! I done told you what I'm gonna be doing.

The lights go down to black.

Scene 2

The lights come up on ROSE *hanging up clothes. She hums and sings softly to herself. It is the following morning.*

ROSE [*Sings*]:   Jesus, be a fence all around me every day
        Jesus, I want you to protect me as I travel on my way.

Jesus, be a fence all around me every day.

TROY *enters from the house.*

Jesus, I want you to protect me
As I travel on my way.

[*To* TROY] 'Morning. You ready for breakfast? I can fix it soon as I finish hanging up these clothes?

TROY: I got the coffee on. That'll be all right. I'll just drink some of that this morning.

ROSE: That 651 hit yesterday. That's the second time this month. Miss Pearl hit for a dollar . . . seem like those that need the least always get lucky. Poor folks can't get nothing.

TROY: Them numbers don't know anybody. I don't know why you fool with them. You and Lyons both.

ROSE: It's something to do.

TROY: You ain't doing nothing but throwing your money away.

ROSE: Troy, you know I don't play foolishly. I just play a nickel here and a nickel there.

TROY: That's two nickels you done thrown away.

ROSE: Now I hit sometimes . . . that makes up for it. It always comes in handy when I do hit. I don't hear you complaining then.

TROY: I ain't complaining now. I just say it's foolish. Trying to guess out of six hundred ways which way the number gonna come. If I had all the money niggers, these Negroes, throw away on numbers for one week—just one week—I'd be a rich man.

ROSE: Well, you wishing and calling it foolish ain't gonna stop folks from playing numbers. That's one thing for sure. Besides . . . some good things come from playing numbers. Look where Pope done bought him that restaurant off of numbers.

TROY: I can't stand niggers like that. Man ain't had two dimes to rub together. He walking around with his shoes all run over bumming money for cigarettes. All right. Got lucky there and hit the numbers . . .

ROSE: Troy, I know all about it.

TROY: Had good sense, I'll say that for him. He ain't throwed his money away. I seen niggers hit the numbers and go through two thousand dollars in four days. Man bought him that restaurant down there . . . fixed it up real nice . . . and then didn't want nobody to come in it! A Negro go in there and can't get no kind of service. I seen a white fellow come in there and order a bowl of stew. Pope picked all the meat out the pot for him. Man ain't had nothing but a bowl of meat! Negro come behind him and ain't got nothing but the potatoes and carrots. Talking about what numbers do for people, you picked a wrong example. Ain't done nothing but make a worser fool out of him than he was before.

ROSE: Troy, you ought to stop worrying about what happened at work yesterday.

TROY: I ain't worried. Just told me to be down there at the Commissioner's office on Friday. Everybody think they gonna fire me. I ain't worried about them firing me. You ain't got to worry about that.

Pause.

Where's Cory? Cory in the house? [*Calls*] Cory?
ROSE: He gone out.

TROY: Out, huh? He gone out 'cause he know I want him to help me with this fence. I know how he is. That boy scared of work.

GABRIEL *enters. He comes halfway down the alley and, hearing* TROY*'s voice, stops.*

TROY [*continues*]:   He ain't done a lick of work in his life.

ROSE: He had to go to football practice. Coach wanted them to get in a little extra practice before the season start.

TROY: I got his practice . . . running out of here before he gets his chores done.

ROSE: Troy, what is wrong with you this morning? Don't nothing set right with you. Go on back in there and go to bed . . . get up on the other side.

TROY: Why something got to be wrong with me? I ain't said nothing wrong with me.

ROSE: You got something to say about everything. First it's the numbers . . . then it's the way the man runs his restaurant . . . then you done got on Cory. What's it gonna be next? Take a look up there and see if the weather suits you . . . or is it gonna be how you gonna put up the fence with the clothes hanging in the yard.

TROY: You hit the nail on the head then.

ROSE: I know you like I know the back of my hand. Go on in there and get you some coffee . . . see if that straighten you up. 'Cause you ain't right this morning.

TROY *starts into the house and sees* GABRIEL. GABRIEL *starts singing.* TROY*'s brother, he is seven years younger than* TROY. *Injured in World War II, he has a metal plate in his head. He carries an old trumpet tied around his waist and believes with every fiber of his being that he is the Archangel Gabriel. He carries a chipped basket with an assortment of discarded fruits and vegetables he has picked up in the strip district and which he attempts to sell.*

GABRIEL [*Singing*]:   Yes, ma'am, I got plums
You ask me how I sell them
Oh ten cents apiece
Three for a quarter
Come and buy now
'Cause I'm here today
And tomorrow I'll be gone

GABRIEL *enters.*

Hey, Rose!

ROSE: How you doing, Gabe?

GABRIEL: There's Troy . . . Hey, Troy!

TROY: Hey, Gabe.

Exit into kitchen.

ROSE [*to* GABRIEL]:   What you got there?

GABRIEL: You know what I got, Rose. I got fruits and vegetables.

ROSE [*looking in basket*]:   Where's all these plums you talking about?

GABRIEL: I ain't got no plums today, Rose. I was just singing that. Have some tomorrow. Put me in a big order for plums. Have enough plums tomorrow for St. Peter and everybody.

TROY *enters from kitchen, crosses to steps.*

[*To* ROSE] Troy's mad at me.

TROY: I ain't mad at you. What I got to be mad at you about? You ain't done nothing to me.

GABRIEL: I just moved over to Miss Pearl's to keep out from in your way. I ain't mean no harm by it.

TROY: Who said anything about that? I ain't said anything about that.

GABRIEL: You ain't mad at me, is you?

TROY: Naw . . . I ain't mad at you, Gabe. If I was mad at you I'd tell you about it.

GABRIEL: Got me two rooms. In the basement. Got my own door too. Wanna see my key?

He holds up a key.

That's my own key! Ain't nobody else got a key like that. That's my key! My two rooms!

TROY: Well, that's good, Gabe. You got your own key . . . that's good.

ROSE: You hungry, Gabe? I was just fixing to cook Troy his breakfast.

GABRIEL: I'll take some biscuits. You got some biscuits? Did you know when I was in heaven . . . every morning me and St. Peter would sit down by the gate and eat some big fat biscuits? Oh, yeah! We had us a good time. We'd sit there and eat us them biscuits and then St. Peter would go off to sleep and tell me to wake him up when it's time to open the gates for the judgment.

ROSE: Well, come on . . . I'll make up a batch of biscuits.

ROSE *exits into the house.*

GABRIEL: Troy . . . St. Peter got your name in the book. I seen it. It say . . . Troy Maxson, I say . . . I know him! He got the same name like what I got. That's my brother!

TROY: How many times you gonna tell me that, Gabe?

GABRIEL: Ain't got my name in the book. Don't have to have my name. I done died and went to heaven. He got your name though. One morning St. Peter was looking at his book . . . marking it up for the judgment . . . and he let me see your name. Got it in there under M. Got Rose's name . . . I ain't seen it like I seen yours . . . but I know it's in there. He got a great big book. Got everybody's name what was ever been born. That's what he told me. But I seen your name. Seen it with my own eyes.

TROY: Go on in the house there. Rose going to fix you something to eat.

GABRIEL: Oh, I ain't hungry. I done had breakfast with Aunt Jemimah. She come by and cooked me up a whole mess of flapjacks. Remember how we used to eat them flapjacks?

TROY: Go on in the house and get you something to eat now.

GABRIEL: I got to go sell my plums. I done sold some tomatoes. Got me two quarters. Wanna see?

He shows TROY *his quarters.*

I'm gonna save them and buy me a new horn so St. Peter can hear me when it's time to open the gates.

GABRIEL stops suddenly. Listens.

Hear that? That's the hellhounds. I got to chase them out of here. Go on get out of here! Get out!

GABRIEL exits singing.

> Better get ready for the judgment
> Better get ready for the judgment
> My Lord is coming down

ROSE enters from the house.

TROY: He gone off somewhere.

GABRIEL [*offstage*]:   Better get ready for the judgment

> Better get ready for the judgment morning
> Better get ready for the judgment
> My God is coming down

ROSE: He ain't eating right. Miss Pearl say she can't get him to eat nothing.

TROY: What you want me to do about it, Rose? I done did everything I can for the man. I can't make him get well. Man got half his head blown away . . . what you expect?

ROSE: Seem like something ought to be done to help him.

TROY: Man don't bother nobody. He just mixed up from that metal plate he got in his head. Ain't no sense for him to go back into the hospital.

ROSE: Least he be eating right. They can help him take care of himself.

TROY: Don't nobody wanna be locked up, Rose. What you wanna lock him up for? Man go over there and fight the war . . . messin' around with them Japs, get half his head blown off . . . and they give him a lousy three thousand dollars. And I had to swoop down on that.

ROSE: Is you fixing to go into that again?

TROY: That's the only way I got a roof over my head . . . cause of that metal plate.

ROSE: Ain't no sense you blaming yourself for nothing. Gabe wasn't in no condition to manage that money. You done what was right by him. Can't nobody say you ain't done what was right by him. Look how long you took care of him . . . till he wanted to have his own place and moved over there with Miss Pearl.

TROY: That ain't what I'm saying, woman! I'm just stating the facts. If my brother didn't have that metal plate in his head . . . I wouldn't have a pot to piss in or a window to throw it out of. And I'm fifty-three years old. Now see if you can understand that!

TROY gets up from the porch and starts to exit the yard.

ROSE: Where you going off to? You been running out of here every Saturday for weeks. I thought you was gonna work on this fence?

TROY: I'm gonna walk down to Taylors'. Listen to the ball game. I'll be back in a bit. I'll work on it when I get back.

He exits the yard. The lights go to black.

Scene 3

The lights come up on the yard. It is four hours later. ROSE *is taking down the clothes from the line.* CORY *enters carrying his football equipment.*

ROSE: Your daddy like to had a fit with you running out of here this morning without doing your chores.

CORY: I told you I had to go to practice.

ROSE: He say you were supposed to help him with this fence.

CORY: He been saying that the last four or five Saturdays, and then he don't never do nothing, but go down to Taylors'. Did you tell him about the recruiter?

ROSE: Yeah, I told him.

CORY: What he say?

ROSE: He ain't said nothing too much. You get in there and get started on your chores before he gets back. Go on and scrub down them steps before he gets back here hollering and carrying on.

CORY: I'm hungry. What you got to eat, Mama?

ROSE: Go on and get started on your chores. I got some meat loaf in there. Go on and make you a sandwich . . . and don't leave no mess in there.

CORY *exits into the house.* ROSE *continues to take down the clothes.* TROY *enters the yard and sneaks up and grabs her from behind.*

Troy! Go on, now. You liked to scared me to death. What was the score of the game? Lucille had me on the phone and I couldn't keep up with it.

TROY: What I care about the game? Come here, woman. [*He tries to kiss her.*]

ROSE: I thought you went down Taylors' to listen to the game. Go on, Troy! You supposed to be putting up this fence.

TROY [*attempting to kiss her again*]:   I'll put it up when I finish with what is at hand.

ROSE: Go on, Troy. I ain't studying you.

TROY [*chasing after her*]:   I'm studying you . . . fixing to do my homework!

ROSE: Troy, you better leave me alone.

TROY: Where's Cory? That boy brought his butt home yet?

ROSE: He's in the house doing his chores.

TROY [*calling*]:   Cory! Get your butt out here, boy!

ROSE *exits into the house with the laundry.* TROY *goes over to the pile of wood, picks up a board, and starts sawing.* CORY *enters from the house.*

TROY: You just now coming in here from leaving this morning?

CORY: Yeah, I had to go to football practice.

TROY: Yeah, what?

CORY: Yessir.

TROY: I ain't but two seconds off you noway. The garbage sitting in there overflowing . . . you ain't done none of your chores . . . and you come in here talking about "Yeah."

CORY: I was just getting ready to do my chores, now, Pop . . .

TROY: Your first chore is to help me with this fence on Saturday. Everything else come after that. Now get that saw and cut them boards.

CORY *takes the saw and begins cutting the boards.* TROY *continues working. There is a long pause.*

CORY: Hey, Pop . . . why don't you buy a TV?

TROY: What I want with a TV? What I want one of them for?

CORY: Everybody got one. Earl, Ba Bra . . . Jesse!

TROY: I ain't asked you who had one. I say what I want with one?

CORY: So you can watch it. They got lots of things on TV. Baseball games and everything. We could watch the World Series.

TROY: Two hundred dollars, huh?

CORY: That ain't that much, Pop.

TROY: Naw, it's just two hundred dollars. See that roof you got over your head at night? Let me tell you something about that roof. It's been over ten years since that roof was last tarred. See now . . . the snow come this winter and sit up there on that roof like it is . . . and it's gonna seep inside. It's just gonna be a little bit . . . ain't gonna hardly notice it. Then the next thing you know, it's gonna be leaking all over the house. Then the wood rot from all that water and you gonna need a whole new roof. Now, how much you think it cost to get that roof tarred?

CORY: I don't know.

TROY: Two hundred and sixty-four dollars . . . cash money. While you thinking about a TV, I got to be thinking about the roof . . . and whatever else go wrong around here. Now if you had two hundred dollars, what would you do . . . fix the roof or buy a TV?

CORY: I'd buy a TV. Then when the roof started to leak . . . when it needed fixing . . . I'd fix it.

TROY: Where you gonna get the money from? You done spent it for a TV. You gonna sit up and watch the water run all over your brand new TV.

CORY: Aw, Pop. You got money, I know you do.

TROY: Where I got it at, huh?

CORY: You got it in the bank.

TROY: You wanna see my bankbook? You wanna see that seventy-three dollars and twenty-two cents I got sitting up in there.

CORY: You ain't got to pay for it all at one time. You can put a down payment on it and carry it on home with you.

TROY: Not me. I ain't gonna owe nobody nothing if I can help it. Miss a payment and they come and snatch it right out your house. Then what you got? Now, soon as I get two hundred dollars clear, then I'll buy a TV. Right now, as soon as I get two hundred and sixty-four dollars, I'm gonna have this roof tarred.

CORY: Aw . . . Pop!

TROY: You go on and get you two hundred dollars and buy one if ya want it. I got better things to do with my money.

CORY: I can't get no two hundred dollars. I ain't never seen two hundred dollars.

TROY: I'll tell you what . . . you get you a hundred dollars and I'll put the other hundred with it.

CORY: All right, I'm gonna show you.

TROY: You gonna show me how you can cut them boards right now.

CORY *begins to cut the boards. There is a long pause.*

CORY: The Pirates won today. That makes five in a row.

TROY: I ain't thinking about the Pirates. Got an all-white team. Got that boy . . . that Puerto Rican boy . . . Clemente. Don't even half-play him. That boy could be something if they give him a chance. Play him one day and sit him on the bench the next.

CORY: He gets a lot of chances to play.

TROY: I'm talking about playing regular. Playing every day so you can get your timing. That's what I'm talking about.

CORY: They got some white guys on the team that don't play every day. You can't play everybody at the same time.

TROY: If they got a white fellow sitting on the bench . . . you can bet your last dollar he can't play! The colored guy got to be twice as good before he get on the team. That's why I don't want you to get all tied up in them sports. Man on the team and what it get him? They got colored on the team and don't use them. Same as not having them. All them teams the same.

CORY: The Braves got Hank Aaron and Wes Covington. Hank Aaron hit two home runs today. That makes forty-three.

TROY: Hank Aaron ain't nobody. That's what you supposed to do. That's how you supposed to play the game. Ain't nothing to it. It's just a matter of timing . . . getting the right follow-through. Hell, I can hit forty-three home runs right now!

CORY: Not off no major-league pitching, you couldn't.

TROY: We had better pitching in the Negro leagues. I hit seven home runs off of Satchel Paige.* You can't get no better than that!

CORY: Sandy Koufax. He's leading the league in strikeouts.

TROY: I ain't thinking of no Sandy Koufax.

CORY: You got Warren Spahn and Lew Burdette. I bet you couldn't hit no home runs off of Warren Spahn.

TROY: I'm through with it now. You go on and cut them boards.

Pause.

Your mama tell me you done got recruited by a college football team? Is that right?

CORY: Yeah. Coach Zellman say the recruiter gonna be coming by to talk to you. Get you to sign the permission papers.

TROY: I thought you supposed to be working down there at the A&P. Ain't you suppose to be working down there after school?

CORY: Mr. Stawicki say he gonna hold my job for me until after the football season. Say starting next week I can work weekends.

TROY: I thought we had an understanding about this football stuff? You suppose to keep up with your chores and hold that job down at the A&P. Ain't been around here all day on a Saturday. Ain't none of your chores done . . . and now you telling me you done quit your job.

CORY: I'm gonna be working weekends.

TROY: You damn right you are! And ain't no need for nobody coming around here to talk to me about signing nothing.

CORY: Hey, Pop . . . you can't do that. He's coming all the way from North Carolina.

TROY: I don't care where he coming from. The white man ain't gonna let you get nowhere with that football noway. You go on and get your booklearning so you can work yourself up in that A&P or learn how to fix cars or build houses or something, get you a trade. That way you have something can't nobody take away from you. You go on and learn how to put your hands to some good use. Besides hauling people's garbage.

Satchel Paige   (1960?–1982) legendary black pitcher in the Negro leagues.

CORY: I get good grades, Pop. That's why the recruiter wants to talk with you. You got to keep your grades to get recruited. This way I'll be going to college. I'll get a chance . . .

TROY: First you gonna get your butt down there to the A&P and get your job back.

CORY: Mr. Stawicki done already hired somebody else 'cause I told him I was playing football.

TROY: You a bigger fool than I thought . . . to let somebody take away your job so you can play some football. Where you gonna get your money to take out your girlfriend and whatnot? What kind of foolishness is that to let somebody take away your job?

CORY: I'm still gonna be working weekends.

TROY: Naw . . . naw. You getting your butt out of here and finding you another job.

CORY: Come on, Pop! I got to practice. I can't work after school and play football too. The team needs me. That's what Coach Zellman say . . .

TROY: I don't care what nobody else say. I'm the boss . . . you understand? I'm the boss around here. I do the only saying what counts.

CORY: Come on, Pop!

TROY: I asked you . . . did you understand?

CORY: Yeah . . .

TROY: What?!

CORY: Yessir.

TROY: You go on down there to that A&P and see if you can get your job back. If you can't do both . . . then you quit the football team. You've got to take the crookeds with the straights.

CORY: Yessir.

Pause.

Can I ask you a question?

TROY: What the hell you wanna ask me? Mr. Stawicki the one you got the questions for.

CORY: How come you ain't never liked me?

TROY: Liked you? Who the hell say I got to like you? What law is there say I got to like you? Wanna stand up in my face and ask a damn fool-ass question like that. Talking about liking somebody. Come here, boy, when I talk to you.

CORY *comes over to where* TROY *is working. He stands slouched over and* TROY *shoves him on his shoulder.*

Straighten up, goddammit! I asked you a question . . . what law is there say I got to like you?

CORY: None.

TROY: Well, all right then! Don't you eat every day?

Pause.

Answer me when I talk to you! Don't you eat every day?

CORY: Yeah.

TROY: Nigger, as long as you in my house, you put that sir on the end of it when you talk to me!

CORY: Yes . . . sir.

TROY: You eat every day.

CORY: Yessir!

TROY: Got a roof over your head.

CORY: Yessir!

TROY: Got clothes on your back.

CORY: Yessir.

TROY: Why you think that is?

CORY: Cause of you.

TROY: Ah, hell I know it's 'cause of me . . . but why do you think that is?

CORY [*hesitant*]:   Cause you like me.

TROY: Like you? I go out of here every morning . . . bust my butt . . . putting up with them crackers* every day . . . cause I like you? You about the biggest fool I ever saw.

Pause.

It's my job. It's my responsibility! You understand that? A man got to take care of his family. You live in my house . . . sleep you behind on my bedclothes . . . fill your belly up with my food . . . cause you my son. You my flesh and blood. Not 'cause I like you! Cause it's my duty to take care of you. I owe a responsibility to you! Let's get this straight right here . . . before it go along any further . . . I ain't got to like you. Mr. Rand don't give me my money come payday cause he likes me. He gives me cause he owe me. I gave you your life! Me and your mamma worked that out between us. And liking your black ass wasn't part of the bargain. Don't you try and go through life worrying about if somebody like you or not. You best be making sure they doing right by you. You understand what I'm saying, boy?

CORY: Yessir.

TROY: Then get the hell out of my face, and get on down to that A&P.

ROSE *has been standing behind the screen door for much of the scene. She enters as* CORY *exits.*

ROSE: Why don't you let the boy go ahead and play football, Troy? Ain't no harm in that. He's just trying to be like you with the sports.

TROY: I don't want him to be like me! I want him to move as far away from my life as he can get. You the only decent thing that ever happened to me. I wish him that. But I don't wish him a thing else from my life. I decided seventeen years ago that boy wasn't getting involved in no sports. Not after what they did to me in the sports.

ROSE: Troy, why don't you admit you was too old to play in the major leagues? For once . . . why don't you admit that?

TROY: What do you mean too old? Don't come telling me I was too old. I just wasn't the right color. Hell, I'm fifty-three years old and can do better than Selkirk's .269 right now!

ROSE: How's was you gonna play ball when you were over forty? Sometimes I can't get no sense out of you.

TROY: I got good sense, woman. I got sense enough not to let my boy get hurt over playing no sports. You been mothering that boy too much. Worried about if people like him.

---

crackers   *white people, often used to refer disparagingly to poor whites.*

ROSE: Everything that boy do . . . he do for you. He wants you to say "Good job, son." That's all.

TROY: Rose, I ain't got time for that. He's alive. He's healthy. He's got to make his own way. I made mine. Ain't nobody gonna hold his hand when he get out there in that world.

ROSE: Times have changed from when you was young, Troy. People change. The world's changing around you and you can't even see it.

TROY [*slow, methodical*]:   Woman . . . I do the best I can do. I come in here every Friday. I carry a sack of potatoes and a bucket of lard. You all line up at the door with your hands out. I give you the lint from my pockets. I give you my sweat and my blood. I ain't go no tears, I done spent them. We go upstairs in that room at night . . . and I fall down on you and try to blast a hole into forever. I get up Monday morning . . . find my lunch on the table. I go out. Make my way. Find my strength to carry me through to the next Friday.

Pause.

That's all I got, Rose. That's all I got to give. I can't give nothing else.

TROY *exits into the house. The lights go down to black.*

Scene 4

It is Friday. Two weeks later. CORY *starts out of the house with his football equipment. The phone rings.*

CORY [*calling*]:   I got it!

He answers the phone and stands in the screen door talking.

Hello? Hey, Jesse. Naw . . . I was just getting ready to leave now.

ROSE [*calling*]:   Cory!

CORY: I told you, man, them spikes is all tore up. You can use them if you want, but they ain't no good. Earl got some spikes.

ROSE [*calling*]:   Cory!

CORY [*calling to* ROSE]:   Mam? I'm talking to Jesse.

Into phone.

When she say that? [*Pause.*] Aw, you lying, man. I'm gonna tell her you said that.

ROSE [*calling*]:   Cory, don't you go nowhere!

CORY: I got to go to the game, Ma!

Into the phone.

Yeah, hey, look, I'll talk to you later. Yeah, I'll meet you over Earl's house. Later. Bye, Ma.

CORY *exits the house and starts out the yard.*

ROSE: Cory, where you going off to? You got that stuff all pulled out and thrown all over your room.

CORY [*in the yard*]:   I was looking for my spikes. Jesse wanted to borrow my spikes.

ROSE: Get up there and get that cleaned up before your daddy get back in here.

CORY: I got to go to the game! I'll clean it up *when I get back.*

CORY *exits.*

ROSE: That's all he need to do is see that room all messed up.

ROSE *exits into the house.* TROY *and* BONO *enter the yard.* TROY *is dressed in clothes other than his work clothes.*

BONO: He told them the same thing he told you. Take it to the union.

TROY: Brownie ain't got that much sense. Man wasn't thinking about nothing. He wait until I confront them on it . . . then he wanna come crying seniority.

Calls.

Hey, Rose!

BONO: I wish I could have seen Mr. Rand's face when he told you.

TROY: He couldn't get it out of his mouth! Liked to bit his tongue! When they called me down there to the Commissioner's office . . . he thought they was gonna fire me. Like everybody else.

BONO: I didn't think they was gonna fire you. I thought they was gonna put you on the warning paper.

TROY: Hey, Rose!

To BONO.

Yeah, Mr. Rand like to bit his tongue.

TROY *breaks the seal on the bottle, takes a drink, and hands it to* BONO.

BONO: I see you run right down to Taylors' and told that Alberta gal.

TROY [*calling*]:   Hey Rose! [*To* BONO] I told everybody. Hey, Rose! I went down there to cash my check.

ROSE [*entering from the house*]:   Hush all that hollering, man! I know you out here. What they say down there at the Commissioner's office?

TROY: You supposed to come when I call you, woman. Bono'll tell you that.

To BONO.

Don't Lucille come when you call her?

ROSE: Man, hush your mouth. I ain't no dog . . . talk about "come when you call me."

TROY [*puts his arm around* ROSE]:   You hear this, Bono? I had me an old dog used to get uppity like that. You say, "C'mere, Blue!" . . . and he just lay there and look at you. End up getting a stick and chasing him away trying to make him come.

ROSE: I ain't studying you and your dog. I remember you used to sing that old song.

TROY [*he sings*]:   Hear it ring! Hear it ring! I had a dog his name was Blue.

ROSE: Don't nobody wanna hear you sing that old song.

TROY [*sings*]:   You know Blue was mighty true.

ROSE: Used to have Cory running around here singing that song.

BONO: Hell, I remember that song myself.

TROY [*sings*]:   You know Blue was a good old dog.

Blue treed a possum in a hollow log.

That was my daddy's song. My daddy made up that song.

ROSE: I don't care who made it up. Don't nobody wanna hear you sing it.

TROY [*makes a song like calling a dog*]:   Come here, woman.

ROSE: You come in here carrying on, I reckon they ain't fired you. What they say down there at the Commissioner's office?

TROY: Look here, Rose . . . Mr. Rand called me into his office today when I got back from talking to them people down there . . . it come from up top . . . he called me in and told me they was making me a driver.

ROSE: Troy, you kidding!

TROY: No I ain't. Ask Bono.

ROSE: Well, that's great, Troy. Now you don't have to hassle them people no more.

LYONS *enters from the street.*

TROY: Aw hell, I wasn't looking to see you today. I thought you was in jail. Got it all over the front page of the *Courier* about them raiding Sefus' place . . . where you be hanging out with all them thugs.

LYONS: Hey, Pop . . . that ain't got nothing to do with me. I don't go down there gambling. I go down there to sit in with the band. I ain't got nothing to do with the gambling part. They got some good music down there.

TROY: They got some rogues . . . is what they got.

LYONS: How you been, Mr. Bono? Hi, Rose.

BONO: I see where you playing down at the Crawford Grill tonight.

ROSE: How come you ain't brought Bonnie like I told you. You should have brought Bonnie with you, she ain't been over in a month of Sundays.

LYONS: I was just in the neighborhood . . . thought I'd stop by.

TROY: Here he come . . .

BONO: Your daddy got a promotion on the rubbish. He's gonna be the first colored driver. Ain't got to do nothing but sit up there and read the paper like them white fellows.

LYONS: Hey, Pop . . . if you knew how to read you'd be all right.

BONO: Naw . . . naw . . . you mean if the nigger knew how to *drive* he'd be all right. Been fighting with them people about driving and ain't even got a license. Mr. Rand know you ain't got no driver's license?

TROY: Driving ain't nothing. All you do is point the truck where you want it to go. Driving ain't nothing.

BONO: Do Mr. Rand know you ain't got no driver's license? That's what I'm talking about. I ain't asked if driving was easy. I asked if Mr. Rand know you ain't got no driver's license.

TROY: He ain't got to know. The man ain't got to know my business. Time he find out, I have two or three driver's licenses.

LYONS [*going into his pocket*]:   Say, look here, Pop . . .

TROY: I knew it was coming. Didn't I tell you, Bono? I know what kind of "Look here, Pop" that was. The nigger fixing to ask me for some money. It's Friday night. It's my payday. All them rogues down there on the avenue . . . the ones that ain't in jail . . . and Lyons is hopping in his shoes to get down there with them.

LYONS: See, Pop . . . if you give somebody else a chance to talk sometime, you'd see that I was fixing to pay you back your ten dollars like I told you. Here . . . I told you I'd pay you when Bonnie got paid.

TROY: Naw . . . you go ahead and keep that ten dollars. Put in the bank. The next time you feel like you wanna come by here and ask me for something . . . you go on down there and get that.

LYONS: Here's your ten dollars, Pop. I told you I don't want you to give me nothing. I just wanted to borrow ten dollars.

TROY: Naw . . . you go on and keep that for the next time you want to ask me.

LYONS: Come on, Pop . . . here go your ten dollars.

ROSE: Why don't you go on and let the boy pay you back, Troy?

LYONS: Here you go, Rose. If you don't take it I'm gonna have to hear about it for the next six months.

He hands her the money.

ROSE: You can hand yours over here too, Troy.

TROY: You see this, Bono. You see how they do me.

BONO: Yeah, Lucille do me the same way.

GABRIEL is heard singing offstage. He enters.

GABRIEL: Better get ready for the Judgment! Better get ready for . . . Hey! . . . Hey! . . . There's Troy's boy!

LYONS: How are you doing, Uncle Gabe?

GABRIEL: Lyons . . . The King of the Jungle! Rose . . . hey, Rose. Got a flower for you.

He takes a rose from his pocket.

Picked it myself. That's the same rose like you is!

ROSE: That's right nice of you, Gabe.

LYONS: What you been doing, Uncle Gabe?

GABRIEL: Oh, I been chasing hellhounds and waiting on the time to tell St. Peter to open the gates.

LYONS: You been chasing hellhounds, huh? Well . . . you doing the right thing, Uncle Gabe. Somebody got to chase them.

GABRIEL: Oh, yeah . . . I know it. The devil's strong. The devil ain't no pushover. Hellhounds snipping at everybody's heels. But I got my trumpet waiting on the judgment time.

LYONS: Waiting on the Battle of Armageddon, huh?

GABRIEL: Ain't gonna be too much of a battle when God get to waving that Judgment sword. But the people's gonna have a hell of a time trying to get into heaven if them gates ain't open.

LYONS [*putting his arm around GABRIEL*]:   You hear this, Pop. Uncle Gabe, you all right!

GABRIEL [*laughing with LYONS*]:   Lyons! King of the Jungle.

ROSE: You gonna stay for supper, Gabe. Want me to fix you a plate?

GABRIEL: I'll take a sandwich, Rose. Don't want no plate. Just wanna eat with my hands. I'll take a sandwich.

ROSE: How about you, Lyons? You staying? Got some short ribs cooking.

LYONS: Naw, I won't eat nothing till after we finished playing.

Pause.

You ought to come down and listen to me play, Pop.

TROY: I don't like that Chinese music. All that noise.

ROSE: Go on in the house and wash up, Gabe . . . I'll fix you a sandwich.

GABRIEL [*to* LYONS, *as he exits*]:   Troy's mad at me.

LYONS: What you mad at Uncle Gabe for, Pop.

ROSE: He thinks Troy's mad at him cause he moved over to Miss Pearl's.

TROY: I ain't mad at the man. He can live where he want to live at.

LYONS: What he move over there for? Miss Pearl don't like nobody.

ROSE: She don't mind him none. She treats him real nice. She just don't allow all that singing.

TROY: She don't mind that rent he be paying . . . that's what she don't mind.

ROSE: Troy, I ain't going through that with you no more. He's over there cause he want to have his own place. He can come and go as he please.

TROY: Hell, he could come and go as he please here. I wasn't stopping him. I ain't put no rules on him.

ROSE: It ain't the same thing, Troy. And you know it.

GABRIEL *comes to the door.*

Now, that's the last I wanna hear about that. I don't wanna hear nothing else about Gabe and Miss Pearl. And next week . . .

GABRIEL: I'm ready for my sandwich, Rose.

ROSE: And next week . . . when that recruiter come from that school . . . I want you to sign that paper and go on and let Cory play football. Then that'll be the last I have to hear about that.

TROY [*to* ROSE *as she exits into the house*]:   I ain't thinking about Cory nothing.

LYONS: What . . . Cory got recruited? What school he going to?

TROY: That boy walking around here smelling his piss . . . thinking he's grown. Thinking he's gonna do what he want, irrespective of what I say. Look here, Bono . . . I left the Commissioner's office and went down to the A&P . . . that boy ain't working down there. He lying to me. Telling me he got his job back . . . telling me he working weekends . . . telling me he working after school . . . Mr. Stawicki tell me he ain't working down there at all!

LYONS: Cory just growing up. He's just busting at the seams trying to fill out your shoes.

TROY: I don't care what he's doing. When he get to the point where he wanna disobey me . . . then it's time for him to move on. Bono'll tell you that. I bet he ain't never disobeyed his daddy without paying the consequences.

BONO: I ain't never had a chance. My daddy came on through . . . but I ain't never knew him to see him . . . or what he had on his mind or where he went. Just moving on through. Searching out the New Land. That's what the old folks used to call it. See a fellow moving around from place to place . . . woman to woman . . . called it searching out the New Land. I can't say if he ever found it. I come along, didn't want no kids. Didn't know if I was gonna be in one place long enough to fix on them right as their daddy. I figured I was going searching too. As it turned out I been hooked up with Lucille near about as long as your daddy been with Rose. Going on sixteen years.

TROY: Sometimes I wish I hadn't known my daddy. He ain't cared nothing about no kids. A kid to him wasn't nothing. All he wanted was for you to learn how to walk so he could start you to working. When it come time for eating . . . he ate first. If there was anything left over, that's what you got. Man would sit down and eat two chickens and give you the wing.

LYONS: You ought to stop that, Pop. Everybody feed their kids. No matter how hard times is . . . everybody care about their kids. Make sure they have something to eat.

TROY: The only thing my daddy cared about was getting them bales of cotton in to Mr. Lubin. That's the only thing that mattered to him. Sometimes I used to wonder why he was living. Wonder why the devil hadn't come and got him. "Get them bales of cotton in to Mr. Lubin" and find out he owe him money . . .

LYONS: He should have just went on and left when he saw he couldn't get nowhere. That's what I would have done.

TROY: How he gonna leave with eleven kids? And where he gonna go? He ain't knew how to do nothing but farm. No, he was trapped and I think he knew it. But I'll say this for him . . . he felt a responsibility toward us. Maybe he ain't treated us the way I felt he should have . . . but without that responsibility he could have walked off and left us . . . made his own way.

BONO: A lot of them did. Back in those days what you talking about . . . they walk out their front door and just take on down one road or another and keep on walking.

LYONS: There you go! That's what I'm talking about.

BONO: Just keep on walking till you come to something else. Ain't you never heard of nobody having the walking blues? Well, that's what you call it when you just take off like that.

TROY: My daddy ain't had them walking blues! What you talking about? He stayed right there with his family. But he was just as evil as he could be. My mama couldn't stand him. Couldn't stand that evilness. She run off when I was about eight. She sneaked off one night after he had gone to sleep. Told me she was coming back for me. I ain't never seen her no more. All his women run off and left him. He wasn't good for nobody.

When my turn come to head out, I was fourteen and got to sniffing around Joe Canewell's daughter. Had us an old mule we called Greyboy. My daddy sent me out to do some plowing and I tied up Greyboy and went to fooling around with Joe Canewell's daughter. We done found us a nice little spot, got real cozy with each other. She about thirteen and we done figures we was grown anyway . . . so we down there enjoying ourselves . . . ain't thinking about nothing. We didn't know Greyboy had got loose and wandered back to the house and my daddy was looking for me. We down there by the creek enjoying ourselves when my daddy come up on us. Surprised us. He had them leather straps off the mule and commenced to whupping me like there was no tomorrow. I jumped up, mad and embarrassed. I was scared of my daddy. When he commenced to whupping on me . . . quite naturally I run to get out of the way.

Pause.

Now I thought he was mad cause I ain't done my work. But I see where he was chasing me off so he could have the gal for himself. When I see what the matter of it was, I lost all fear of my daddy. Right there is where I become a man . . . at fourteen years of age.

Pause.

Now it was my turn to run him off. I picked up them same reins that he had used on me. I picked up them reins and commenced to whupping on him. The gal jumped up and run off . . . and when my daddy turned to face me, I could see why the devil had never come to get him . . . cause he was the devil himself. I don't know what happened. When I woke up, I was laying right there by the creek, and Blue . . . this old dog we had . . . was licking my face. I thought I was blind. I couldn't see nothing. Both my eyes were swollen shut. I layed there and cried. I didn't know what I was gonna do. The only thing I knew was the time had come for me to leave my daddy's house. And right there the world suddenly got big. And it was a long time before I could cut it down to where I could handle it.

Part of that cutting down was when I got to the place where I could feel him kicking in my blood and knew that the only thing that separated us was the matter of a few years.

GABRIEL *enters from the house with a sandwich.*

LYONS: What you got there, Uncle Gabe?

GABRIEL: Got me a ham sandwich. Rose gave me a ham sandwich.

TROY: I don't know what happened to him. I done lost touch with everybody except Gabriel. But I hope he's dead. I hope he found some peace.

LYONS: That's a heavy story, Pop. I didn't know you left home when you was fourteen.

TROY: And didn't know nothing. The only part of the world I knew was the forty-two acres of Mr. Lubin's land. That's all I knew about life.

LYONS: Fourteen's kinda young to be out on your own. [*Phone rings.*] I don't even think I was ready to be out on my own at fourteen. I don't know what I would have done.

TROY: I got up from the creek and walked on down to Mobile. I was through with farming. Figured I could do better in the city. So I walked the two hundred miles to Mobile.

LYONS: Wait a minute . . . you ain't walked no two hundred miles, Pop. Ain't nobody gonna walk no two hundred miles. You talking about some walking there.

BONO: That's the only way you got anywhere back in them days.

LYONS: Shhh. Damn if I wouldn't have hitched a ride with somebody!

TROY: Who you gonna hitch it with? They ain't had no cars and things like they got now. We talking about 1918.

ROSE [*entering*]:   What you all out here getting into?

TROY [*to* ROSE]:   I'm telling Lyons how good he got it. He don't know nothing about this I'm talking.

ROSE: Lyons, that was Bonnie on the phone. She say you supposed to pick her up.

LYONS: Yeah, okay, Rose.

TROY: I walked on down to Mobile and hitched up with some of them fellows that was heading this way. Got up here and found out . . . not only couldn't you get a job . . . you couldn't find no place to live. I thought I was in freedom. Shhh. Colored folks living down there on the riverbanks in whatever kind of shelter they could find for themselves. Right down there under the Brady Street Bridge. Living in shacks made of sticks and tarpaper. Messed around there and went from bad to worse. Started stealing. First it was food. Then I figured, hell, if I steal money I can buy me some food. Buy me some shoes too! One thing led to another. Met your mama. I was young and anxious to be a man. Met your mama and had you. What I do that for? Now I got to worry about feeding you and her. Got to steal three times as much. Went out one day looking for somebody to rob . . . that's what I was, a robber. I'll tell you the truth. I'm ashamed of it today. But it's the truth. Went to rob this fellow . . . pulled out my knife . . . and he pulled out a gun. Shot me in the chest. It felt just like somebody had taken a hot branding iron and laid it on me. When he shot me I jumped at him with my knife. They told me I killed him and they put me in the penitentiary and locked me up for fifteen years. That's where I met Bono. That's where I learned how to play baseball. Got out that place and your mama had taken you and went on to make life without me. Fifteen years was a long time for her to wait. But that fifteen years cured me of that robbing stuff. Rose'll tell you. She asked me when I met her if I had gotten all that foolishness out of my system. And I told her, "Baby, it's you and baseball all what count with me." You hear me, Bono? I meant it too. She say, "Which one comes first?" I told her, "Baby, ain't no doubt it's baseball . . . but you stick and get old with me and we'll both outlive this baseball." Am I right, Rose? And it's true.

ROSE: Man, hush your mouth. You ain't said no such thing. Talking about, "Baby, you know you'll always be number one with me." That's what you was talking.

TROY: You hear that, Bono. That's why I love her.

BONO: Rose'll keep you straight. You get off the track, she'll straighten you up.

ROSE: Lyons, you better get on up and get Bonnie. She waiting on you.

LYONS [*gets up to go*]:   Hey, Pop, why don't you come on down to the Grill and hear me play?

TROY: I ain't going down there. I'm too old to be sitting around in them clubs.

BONO: You got to be good to play down at the Grill.

LYONS: Come on, Pop . . .

TROY: I got to get up in the morning.

LYONS: You ain't got to stay long.

TROY: Naw, I'm gonna get my supper and go on to bed.

LYONS: Well, I got to go. I'll see you again.

TROY: Don't you come around my house on my payday.

ROSE: Pick up the phone and let somebody know you coming. And bring Bonnie with you. You know I'm always glad to see her.

LYONS: Yeah, I'll do that, Rose. You take care now. See you, Pop. See you, Mr. Bono. See you, Uncle Gabe.

GABRIEL: Lyons! King of the Jungle!

LYONS *exits.*

TROY: Is supper ready, woman? Me and you got some business to take care of. I'm gonna tear it up too.

ROSE: Troy, I done told you now!

TROY [*puts his arm around* BONO]:   Aw hell, woman . . . this is Bono. Bono like family. I done known this nigger since . . . how long I done know you?

BONO: It's been a long time.

TROY: I done known this nigger since Skippy was a pup. Me and him done been through some times.

BONO: You sure right about that.

TROY: Hell, I done know him longer than I known you. And we still standing shoulder to shoulder. Hey, look here, Bono . . . a man can't ask for no more than that.

Drinks to him.

I love you, nigger.

BONO: Hell, I love you too . . . but I got to get home see my woman. You got yours in hand. I got to go get mine.

BONO *starts to exit as* CORY *enters the yard, dressed in his football uniform. He gives* TROY *a hard, uncompromising look.*

What you do that for, Pop?

He throws his helmet down in the direction of TROY.

ROSE: What's the matter? Cory . . . what's the matter?

CORY: Papa done went up to the school and told Coach Zellman I can't play football no more. Wouldn't even let me play the game. Told him to tell the recruiter not to come.

ROSE: Troy . . .

TROY: What you Troying me for. Yeah, I did it. And the boy know why I did it.

CORY: Why you wanna do that to me? That was the one chance I had.

ROSE: Ain't nothing wrong with Cory playing football, Troy.

TROY: The boy lied to me. I told the nigger if he wanna play football . . . to keep up his chores and hold down that job at the A&P. That was the conditions. Stopped down there to see Mr. Stawicki . . .

CORY: I can't work after school during the football season, Pop! I tried to tell you that Mr. Stawicki's holding my job for me. You don't never want to listen to nobody. And then you wanna go and do this to me!

TROY: I ain't done nothing to you. You done it to yourself.

CORY: Just cause you didn't have a chance! You just scared I'm gonna be better than you, that's all.

TROY: Come here.

ROSE: Troy . . .

CORY *reluctantly crosses over to* TROY.

TROY: All right! See. You done made a mistake.

CORY: I didn't even do nothing!

TROY: I'm gonna tell you what your mistake was. See . . . you swung at the ball and didn't hit it. That's strike one. See, you in the batter's box now. You swung and you missed. That's strike one. Don't you strike out!

Lights fade to black.

ACT II

Scene 1

The following morning. CORY *is at the tree hitting the ball with the bat. He tries to mimic* TROY, *but his swing is awkward, less sure.* ROSE *enters from the house.*

ROSE: Cory, I want you to help me with this cupboard.

CORY: I ain't quitting the team. I don't care what Poppa say.

ROSE: I'll talk to him when he gets back. He had to go see about your Uncle Gabe. The police done arrested him. Say he was disturbing the peace. He'll be back directly. Come on in here and help me clean out the top of this cupboard.

CORY *exits into the house.* ROSE *sees* TROY *and* BONO *coming down the alley.*

Troy . . . what they say down there?

TROY: Ain't said nothing. I give them fifty dollars and they let him go. I'll talk to you about it. Where's Cory?

ROSE: He's in there helping me clean out these cupboards.

TROY: Tell him to get his butt out here.

TROY *and* BONO *go over to the pile of wood.* BONO *picks up the saw and begins sawing.*

TROY [*to* BONO]:   All they want is the money. That makes six or seven times I done went down there and got him. See me coming they stick out their *hands.*

BONO: Yeah. I know what you mean. That's all they care about . . . that money. They don't care about what's right.

Pause.

Nigger, why you got to go and get some hard wood? You ain't doing nothing but building a little old fence. Get you some soft pine wood. That's all you need.

TROY: I know what I'm doing. This is outside wood. You put pine wood inside the house. Pine wood is inside wood. This here is outside wood. Now you tell me where the fence is gonna be?

BONO: You don't need this wood. You can put it up with pine wood and it'll stand as long as you gonna be here looking at it.

TROY: How you know how long I'm gonna be here, nigger? Hell, I might just live forever. Live longer than old man Horsely.

BONO: That's what Magee used to say.

TROY: Magee's a damn fool. Now you tell me who you ever heard of gonna pull their own teeth with a pair of rusty pliers.

BONO: The old folks . . . my granddaddy used to pull his teeth with pliers. They ain't had no dentists for the colored folks back then.

TROY: Get clean pliers! You understand? Clean pliers! Sterilize them! Besides we ain't living back then. All Magee had to do was walk over to Doc Goldblum's.

BONO: I see where you and that Tallahassee gal . . . that Alberta . . . I see where you all done got tight.

TROY: What you mean "got tight"?

BONO: I see where you be laughing and joking with her all the time.

TROY: I laughs and jokes with all of them, Bono. You know me.

BONO: That ain't the kind of laughing and joking I'm talking about.

CORY *enters from the house.*

CORY: How you doing, Mr. Bono?

TROY: Cory? Get that saw from Bono and cut some wood. He talking about the wood's too hard to cut. Stand back there, Jim, and let that young boy show you how it's done.

BONO: He's sure welcome to it.

CORY *takes the saw and begins to cut the wood.*

Whew-e-e! Look at that. Big old strong boy. Look like Joe Louis. Hell, must be getting old the way I'm watching that boy whip through that wood.

CORY: I don't see why Mama want a fence around the yard noways.

TROY: Damn if I know either. What the hell she keeping out with it? She ain't got nothing nobody want.

BONO: Some people build fences to keep people out . . . and other people build fences to keep people in. Rose wants to hold on to you all. She loves you.

TROY: Hell, nigger, I don't need nobody to tell me my wife loves me, Cory . . . go on in the house and see if you can find that other saw.

CORY: Where's it at?

TROY: I said find it! Look for it till you find it!

CORY *exits into the house.*

What's that supposed to mean? Wanna keep us in?

BONO: Troy . . . I done known you seem like damn near my whole life. You and Rose both. I done know both of you all for a long time. I remember when you met Rose. When you was hitting them baseball out the park. A lot of them old gals was after you then. You had the pick of the litter. When you picked Rose, I was happy for you. That was the first time I knew you had any sense. I said . . . My man Troy knows what he's doing . . . I'm gonna follow this nigger . . . he might take me somewhere. I been following you too. I done learned a whole heap of things about life watching you. I done learned how to tell where the shit lies. How to tell it from the alfalfa. You done learned me a lot of things. You showed me how to not make the same mistakes . . . to take life as it comes along and keep putting one foot in front of the other.

Pause.

Rose a good woman, Troy.

TROY: Hell, nigger, I know she a good woman. I been married to her for eighteen years. What you got on your mind, Bono?

BONO: I just say she a good woman. Just like I say anything. I ain't got to have nothing on my mind.

TROY: You just gonna say she a good woman and leave it hanging out there like that? Why you telling me she a good woman?

BONO: She loves you, Troy. Rose loves you.

TROY: You saying I don't measure up. That's what you trying to say. I don't measure up cause I'm seeing this other gal. I know what you trying to say.

BONO: I know what Rose means to you, Troy. I'm just trying to say I don't want to see you mess up.

TROY: Yeah, I appreciate that, Bono. If you was messing around on Lucille I'd be telling you the same thing.

BONO: Well, that's all I got to say. I just say that because I love you both.

TROY: Hell, you know me . . . I wasn't out there looking for nothing. You can't find a better woman than Rose. I know that. But seems like this woman just stuck onto me where I can't shake her loose. I done wrestled with it, tried to throw her off me . . . but she just stuck on tighter. Now she's stuck on for good.

BONO: You's in control . . . that's what you tell me all the time. You responsible for what you do.

TROY: I ain't ducking the responsibility of it. As long as it sets right in my heart . . . then I'm okay. Cause that's all I listen to. It'll tell me right from wrong every time. And I ain't talking about doing Rose no bad turn. I love Rose. She done carried me a long ways and I love and respect her for that.

BONO: I know you do. That's why I don't want to see you hurt her. But what you gonna do when she find out? What you got then? If you try and juggle both of them . . . sooner or later you gonna drop one of them. That's common sense.

TROY: Yeah, I hear what you saying, Bono. I been trying to figure a way to work it out.

BONO: Work it out right, Troy. I don't want to be getting all up between you and Rose's business . . . but work it so it come out right.

TROY: Ah hell, I get all up between you and Lucille's business. When you gonna get that woman that refrigerator she been wanting? Don't tell me you ain't got no money now. I know who your banker is. Mellon don't need that money bad as Lucille want that refrigerator. I'll tell you that.

BONO: Tell you what I'll do . . . when you finish building this fence for Rose . . . I'll buy Lucille that refrigerator.

TROY: You done stuck your foot in your mouth now!

TROY *grabs up a board and begins to saw.* BONO *starts to walk out the yard.*

Hey, nigger . . . where you going?

BONO: I'm going home. I know you don't expect me to help you now. I'm protecting my money. I wanna see you put that fence up by yourself. That's what I want to see. You'll be here another six months without me.

TROY: Nigger, you ain't right.

BONO: When it comes to my money . . . I'm right as fireworks on the Fourth of July.

TROY: All right, we gonna see now. You better get out your bankbook.

BONO *exits, and* TROY *continues to work.* ROSE *enters from the house.*

ROSE: What they say down there? What's happening with Gabe?

TROY: I went down there and got him out. Cost me fifty dollars. Say he was disturbing the peace. Judge set up a hearing for him in three weeks. Say to show cause why he shouldn't be recommitted.

ROSE: What was he doing that cause them to arrest him?

TROY: Some kids was teasing him and he run them off home. Say he was howling and carrying on. Some folks seen him and called the police. That's all it was.

ROSE: Well, what's you say? What'd you tell the judge?

TROY: Told him I'd look after him. It didn't make no sense to recommit the man. He stuck out his big greasy palm and told me to give him fifty dollars and take him on home.

ROSE: Where's he at now? Where'd he go off to?

TROY: He's gone on about his business. He don't need nobody to hold his hand.

ROSE: Well, I don't know. Seem like that would be the best place for him if they did put him into the hospital. I know what you're gonna say. But that's what I think would be best.

TROY: The man done had his life ruined fighting for what? And they wanna take and lock him up. Let him be free. He don't bother nobody.

ROSE: Well, everybody got their own way of looking at it I guess. Come on and get your lunch. I got a bowl of lima beans and some cornbread in the oven. Come on get something to eat. Ain't no sense you fretting over Gabe.

ROSE turns to go into the house.

TROY: Rose . . . got something to tell you.

ROSE: Well, come on . . . wait till I get this food on the table.

TROY: Rose!

She stops and turns around.

I don't know how to say this.

Pause.

I can't explain it none. It just sort of grows on you till it gets out of hand. It starts out like a little bush . . . and the next thing you know it's a whole forest.

ROSE: Troy . . . what is you talking about?

TROY: I'm talking, woman, let me talk. I'm trying to find a way to tell you . . . I'm gonna be a daddy. I'm gonna be somebody's daddy.

ROSE: Troy . . . you're not telling me this? You're gonna be . . . what?

TROY: Rose . . . now . . . see . . .

ROSE: You telling me you gonna be somebody's daddy? You telling your *wife* this?

GABRIEL enters from the street. He carries a rose in his hand.

GABRIEL: Hey, Troy! Hey, Rose!

ROSE: I have to wait eighteen years to hear something like this.

GABRIEL: Hey, Rose . . . I got a flower for you.

He hands it to her.

That's a rose. Same rose like you is.

ROSE: Thanks, Gabe.

GABRIEL: Troy, you ain't mad at me is you? Them bad mens come and put me away. You ain't mad at me is you?

TROY: Naw, Gabe, I ain't mad at you.

ROSE: Eighteen years and you wanna come with this.

GABRIEL [*takes a quarter out of his pocket*]:   See what I got? Got a brand new quarter.

TROY: Rose . . . it's just . . .

ROSE: Ain't nothing you can say, Troy. Ain't no way of explaining that.

GABRIEL: Fellow that give me this quarter had a whole mess of them. I'm gonna keep this quarter till it stop shining.

ROSE: Gabe, go on in the house there. I got some watermelon in the frigidaire. Go on and get you a piece.

GABRIEL: Say, Rose . . . you know I was chasing hellhounds and them bad mens come and get me and take me away. Troy helped me. He come down there and told them they better let me go before he beat them up. Yeah, he did!

ROSE: You go on and get you a piece of watermelon, Gabe. Them bad mens is gone now.

GABRIEL: Okay, Rose . . . gonna get me some watermelon. The kind with the stripes on it.

GABRIEL *exits into the house.*

ROSE: Why, Troy? Why? After all these years to come dragging this in to me now. It don't make no sense at your age. I could have expected this ten or fifteen years ago, but not now.

TROY: Age ain't got nothing to do with it, Rose.

ROSE: I done tried to be everything a wife should be. Everything a wife could be. Been married eighteen years and I got to live to see the day you tell me you been seeing another woman and done fathered a child by her. And you know I ain't never wanted no half nothing in my family. My whole family is half. Everybody got different fathers and mothers . . . my two sisters and my brother. Can't hardly tell who's who. Can't never sit down and talk about Papa and Mama. It's your papa and your mama and my papa and my mama . . .

TROY: Rose . . . stop it now.

ROSE: I ain't never wanted that for none of my children. And now you wanna drag your behind in here and tell me something like this.

TROY: You ought to know. It's time for you to know.

ROSE: Well, I don't want to know, goddamn it!

TROY: I can't just make it go away. It's done now. I can't wish the circumstance of the thing away.

ROSE: And you don't want to either. Maybe you want to wish me and my boy away. Maybe that's what you want? Well, you can't wish us away. I've got eighteen years of my life invested in you. You ought to have stayed upstairs in my bed where you belong.

TROY: Rose . . . now listen to me . . . we can get a handle on this thing. We can talk this out . . . come to an understanding.

ROSE: All of a sudden it's "we." Where was "we" at when you was down there rolling around with some godforsaken woman? "We" should have come to an understanding before you started making a damn fool of yourself. You're a day late and dollar short when it comes to an understanding with me.

TROY: It's just . . . She gives me a different idea . . . a different understanding about myself. I can step out of this house and get away from the pressures and problems . . . be a different man. I ain't got to wonder how I'm gonna pay the bills or get the roof fixed. I can just be a part of myself that I ain't never been.

ROSE: What I want to know . . . is do you plan to continue seeing her. That's all you can say to me.

TROY: I can sit up in her house and laugh. Do you understand what I'm saying. I can laugh out loud . . . and it feels good. It reaches all the way down to the bottom of my shoes.

Pause.

Rose, I can't give that up.

ROSE: Maybe you ought to go on and stay down there with her . . . if she's a better woman than me.

TROY: It ain't about nobody being a better woman or nothing. Rose, you ain't the blame. A man couldn't ask for no woman to be a better wife than you've been. I'm responsible for it. I done locked myself into a pattern trying to take care of you all that I forgot about myself.

ROSE: What the hell was I there for? That was my job, not somebody else's.

TROY: Rose, I done tried all my life to live decent . . . to live a clean . . . hard . . . useful life. I tried to be a good husband to you. In every way I knew how. Maybe I come into the world backwards, I don't know. But . . . you born with two strikes on you before you come to the plate. You got to guard it closely . . . always looking for the curve ball on the inside corner. You can't afford to let none get past you. You can't afford a call strike. If you going down . . . you going down swinging. Everything lined up against you. What you gonna do. I fooled them, Rose. I bunted. When I found you and Cory and a halfway decent job . . . I was safe. Couldn't nothing touch me. I wasn't going back to the penitentiary. I wasn't gonna lay in the streets with a bottle of wine. I was safe. I had me a family. A job. I wasn't gonna get that last strike. I was on first looking for one of them boys to knock me in. To get me home.

ROSE: You should have stayed in my bed, Troy.

TROY: Then when I saw that gal . . . she firmed up my backbone. And I got to thinking that if I tried . . . I just might be able to steal second. Do you understand after eighteen years I wanted to steal second.

ROSE: You should have held me tight. You should have grabbed me and held on.

TROY: I stood on first base for eighteen years and I thought . . . well, goddamn it . . . go on for it!

ROSE: We're not talking about baseball! We're talking about you going off to lay in bed with another woman . . . and then bring it home to me. That's what we're talking about. We ain't talking about no baseball.

TROY: Rose, you're not listening to me. I'm trying the best I can to explain it to you. It's not easy for me to admit that I been standing in the same place for eighteen years.

ROSE: I been standing with you! I been right here with you, Troy. I got a life too. I gave eighteen years of my life to stand in the same spot with you. Don't you think I ever wanted other things? Don't you think I had dreams and hopes? What about my life? What about me. Don't you think it ever crossed my mind to want to know other men? That I wanted to lay up somewhere and forget about my responsibilities? That I wanted someone to make me laugh so I could feel good? You not the only one who's got wants and needs. But I held on to you, Troy. I took all my feelings, my wants and needs, my dreams . . . and I buried them inside you. I planted a seed and watched and prayed over it. I planted myself inside you and waited to bloom. And it didn't take me no eighteen years to find out the soil was hard and rocky and it wasn't never gonna bloom.

But I held on to you, Troy. I held you tighter. You was my husband. I owed you everything I had. Every part of me I could find to give you. And upstairs in that room . . . with the darkness falling in on me . . . I gave everything I had to try and erase the doubt that you wasn't the finest man in the world. And wherever you was going . . . I wanted to be there with you. Cause you was my husband. Cause that's the only way I was gonna survive as your wife. You always talking about what you give . . . and what you don't have to give. But you take too. You take . . . and don't even know nobody's giving!

ROSE turns to exit into the house. TROY grabs her arm.

TROY: You say I take and don't give!
ROSE: Troy! You're hurting me!
TROY: You say I take and don't give.
ROSE: Troy . . . you're hurting my arm! Let go!
TROY: I done give you everything I got. Don't you tell that lie on me.
ROSE: Troy!
TROY: Don't you tell that lie on me!

CORY enters from the house.

CORY: Mama!
ROSE: Troy. You're hurting me.
TROY: Don't you tell me about no taking and giving.

CORY comes up behind TROY and grabs him. TROY, surprised, is thrown off balance just as CORY throws a glancing blow that catches him in the chest and knocks him down. TROY is stunned, as is CORY.

ROSE: Troy. Troy. No!

TROY gets to his feet and starts at CORY.

Troy . . . no. Please! Troy!

ROSE pulls on TROY to hold him back. TROY stops himself.

TROY [*to* CORY]: All right. That's strike two. You stay away from around me, boy. Don't you strike out. You living with a full count. Don't you strike out.

TROY exits out the yard as the lights go down.

Scene 2

It is six months later, early afternoon. TROY enters from the house and starts to exit the yard. ROSE enters from the house.

ROSE: Troy, I want to talk to you.
TROY: All of a sudden, after all this time, you want to talk to me, huh? You ain't wanted to talk to me for months. You ain't wanted to talk to me last night. You ain't wanted no part of me then. What you wanna talk to me about now?

ROSE: Tomorrow's Friday.

TROY: I know what day tomorrow is. You think I don't know tomorrow's Friday? My whole life I ain't done nothing but look to see Friday coming and you got to tell me it's Friday.

ROSE: I want to know if you're coming home.

TROY: I always come home, Rose. You know that. There ain't never been a night I ain't come home.

ROSE: That ain't what I mean . . . and you know it. I want to know if you're coming straight home after work.

TROY: I figure I'd cash my check . . . hang out at Taylors' with the boys . . . maybe play a game of checkers . . .

ROSE: Troy, I can't live like this. I won't live like this. You livin' on borrowed time with me. It's been going on six months now you ain't been coming home.

TROY: I be here every night. Every night of the year. That's 365 days.

ROSE: I want you to come home tomorrow after work.

TROY: Rose . . . I don't mess up my pay. You know that now. I take my pay and I give it to you. I don't have no money but what you give me back. I just want to have a little time to myself . . . a little time to enjoy life.

ROSE: What about me? When's my time to enjoy life?

TROY: I don't know what to tell you, Rose. I'm doing the best I can.

ROSE: You ain't been home from work but time enough to change your clothes and run out . . . and you wanna call that the best you can do?

TROY: I'm going over to the hospital to see Alberta. She went into the hospital this afternoon. Look like she might have the baby early. I won't be gone long.

ROSE: Well, you ought to know. They went over to Miss Pearl's and got Gabe today. She said you told them to go ahead and lock him up.

TROY: I ain't said no such thing. Whoever told you that is telling a lie. Pearl ain't doing nothing but telling a big fat lie.

ROSE: She ain't had to tell me. I read it on the papers.

TROY: I ain't told them nothing of the kind.

ROSE: I saw it right there on the papers.

TROY: What it say, huh?

ROSE: It said you told them to take him.

TROY: Then they screwed that up, just the way they screw up everything. I ain't worried about what they got on the paper.

ROSE: Say the government send part of his check to the hospital and the other part to you.

TROY: I ain't got nothing to do with that if that's the way it works. I ain't made up the rules about how it work.

ROSE: You did Gabe just like you did Cory. You wouldn't sign the paper for Cory . . . but you signed for Gabe. You signed that paper.

The telephone is heard ringing inside the house.

TROY: I told you I ain't signed nothing, woman! The only thing I signed was the release form. Hell, I can't read, I don't know what they had on that paper! I ain't signed nothing about sending Gabe away.

ROSE: I said send him to the hospital . . . you said let him be free . . . now you done went down there and signed him to the hospital for half his money. You went back on yourself, Troy. You gonna have to answer for that.

TROY: See now . . . you been over there talking to Miss Pearl. She done got mad cause she ain't getting Gabe's rent money. That's all it is. She's liable to say anything.

ROSE: Troy, I seen where you signed the paper.

TROY: You ain't seen nothing I signed. What she doing got papers on my brother anyway? Miss Pearl telling a big fat lie. And I'm gonna tell her about it too! You ain't seen nothing I signed. Say . . . you ain't seen nothing I signed.

> ROSE *exits into the house to answer the telephone. Presently she returns.*

ROSE: Troy . . . that was the hospital. Alberta had the baby.

TROY: What she have? What is it?

ROSE: It's a girl.

TROY: I better get on down to the hospital to see her.

ROSE: Troy . . .

TROY: Rose . . . I got to go see her now. That's only right . . . what's the matter . . . the baby's all right, ain't it?

ROSE: Alberta died having the baby.

TROY: Died . . . you say she's dead? Alberta's dead?

ROSE: They said they done all they could. They couldn't do nothing for her.

TROY: The baby? How's the baby?

ROSE: They say it's healthy. I wonder who's gonna bury her.

TROY: She had family, Rose. She wasn't living in the world by herself.

ROSE: I know she wasn't living in the world by herself.

TROY: Next thing you gonna want to know if she had any insurance.

ROSE: Troy, you ain't got to talk like that.

TROY: That's the first thing that jumped out your mouth. "Who's gonna bury her?" Like I'm fixing to take on that task for myself.

ROSE: I am your wife. Don't push me away.

TROY: I ain't pushing nobody away. Just give me some space. That's all. Just give me some room to breathe.

> ROSE *exits into the house.* TROY *walks about the yard.*

TROY [*with a quiet rage that threatens to consume him*]: All right . . . Mr. Death. See now . . . I'm gonna tell you what I'm gonna do. I'm gonna take and build me a fence around this yard. See? I'm gonna build me a fence around what belongs to me. And then I want you to stay on the other side. See? You stay over there until you're ready for me. Then you come on. Bring your army. Bring your sickle. Bring your wrestling clothes. I ain't gonna fall down on my vigilance this time. You ain't gonna sneak up on me no more. When you ready for me . . . when the top of your list say Troy Maxson . . . that's when you come around here. You come up and knock on the front door. Ain't nobody else got nothing to do with this. This is between you and me. Man to man. You stay on the other side of that fence until you ready for me. Then you come up and knock on the front door. Anytime you want. I'll be ready for you.

The lights go down to black.

Scene 3

The lights come up on the porch. It is late evening three days later. ROSE *sits listening to the ball game waiting for* TROY. *The final out of the game is made and* ROSE *switches off the radio.* TROY *enters the yard carrying an infant wrapped in blankets. He stands back from the house and calls.*

ROSE *enters and stands on the porch. There is a long, awkward silence, the weight of which grows heavier with each passing second.*

TROY: Rose . . . I'm standing here with my daughter in my arms. She ain't but a wee bittie little old thing. She don't know nothing about grown-ups' business. She innocent . . . and she ain't got no mama.

ROSE: What you telling me for, Troy?

She turns and exits into the house.

TROY: Well . . . I guess we'll just sit out here on the porch.

He sits down on the porch. There is an awkward indelicateness about the way he handles the baby. His largeness engulfs and seems to swallow it. He speaks loud enough for ROSE *to hear.*

A man's got to do what's right for him. I ain't sorry for nothing I done. It felt right in my heart.

To the baby.

What you smiling at? Your daddy's a big man. Got these great big old hands. But sometimes he's scared. And right now your daddy's scared cause we sitting out here and ain't got no home. Oh, I been homeless before. I ain't had no little baby with me. But I been homeless. You just be out on the road by your lonesome and you see one of them trains coming and you just kinda go like this . . .

He sings as a lullaby.

Please, Mr. Engineer let a man ride the line
Please, Mr. Engineer let a man ride the line
I ain't got no ticket please let me ride the blinds

ROSE *enters from the house.* TROY *hearing her steps behind him, stands and faces her.*

She's my daughter, Rose. My own flesh and blood. I can't deny her no more than I can deny them boys.

Pause.

You and them boys is my family. You and them boys and this child is all I got in the world. So I guess what I'm saying is . . . I'd appreciate it if you'd help me take care of her.

ROSE: Okay, Troy . . . you're right. I'll take care of your baby for you . . . cause . . . like you say . . . she's innocent . . . and you can't visit the sins of the father upon the child. A motherless child has got a hard time.

She takes the baby from him.

From right now . . . this child got a mother. But you a womanless man.

    ROSE *turns and exits into the house with the baby. Lights go down to black.*

Scene 4

    It is two months later. LYONS *enters from the street. He knocks on the door and calls.*

LYONS: Hey, Rose! [*Pause.*] Rose!

ROSE [*from inside the house*]:   Stop that yelling. You gonna wake up Raynell. I just got her to sleep.

LYONS: I just stopped by to pay Papa this twenty dollars I owe him. Where's Papa at?

ROSE: He should be here in a minute. I'm getting ready to go down to the church. Sit down and wait on him.

LYONS: I got to go pick up Bonnie over her mother's house.

ROSE: Well, sit it down there on the table. He'll get it.

LYONS [*enters the house and sets the money on the table*]:   Tell Papa I said thanks. I'll see you again.

ROSE: All right, Lyons. We'll see you.

    LYONS *starts to exit as* CORY *enters.*

CORY: Hey, Lyons.

LYONS: What's happening, Cory. Say man, I'm sorry I missed your graduation. You know I had a gig and couldn't get away. Otherwise, I would have been there, man. So what you doing?

CORY: I'm trying to find a job.

LYONS: Yeah I know how that go, man. It's rough out here. Jobs are scarce.

CORY: Yeah, I know.

LYONS: Look here, I got to run. Talk to Papa . . . he know some people. He'll be able to help get you a job. Talk to him . . . see what he say.

CORY: Yeah . . . all right, Lyons.

LYONS: You take care. I'll talk to you soon. We'll find some time to talk.

LYONS *exits the yard.* CORY *wanders over to the tree, picks up the bat, and assumes a batting stance. He studies an imaginary pitcher and swings. Dissatisfied with the result, he tries again.* TROY *enters. They eye each other for a beat.* CORY *puts the bat down and exits the yard.* TROY *starts into the house as* ROSE *exits with* RAYNELL. *She is carrying a cake.*

TROY: I'm coming in and everybody's going out.

ROSE: I'm taking the cake down to the church for the bake sale. Lyons was by to see you. He stopped by to pay you your twenty dollars. It's laying in there on the table.

TROY [*going into his pocket*]:   Well . . . here go this money.

ROSE: Put it in there on the table, Troy. I'll get it.

TROY: What time you coming back?

ROSE: Ain't no use in you studying me. It don't matter what time I come back.

TROY: I just asked you a question, woman. What's the matter . . . can't I ask you a question?

ROSE: Troy, I don't want to go into it. Your dinner's in there on the stove. All you got to do is heat it up. And don't you be eating the rest of them cakes in there. I'm coming back for them. We having a bake sale at the church tomorrow.

ROSE *exits the yard.* TROY *sits down on the steps, takes a pint bottle from his pocket, opens it, and drinks. He begins to sing.*

TROY: Hear it ring! Hear it ring!
   Had an old dog his name was Blue
   You know Blue was a mighty true
   You know Blue was a good old dog
   Blue trees a possum in a hollow log
   You know from that he was a good old dog

BONO *enters the yard.*

BONO: Hey, Troy.

TROY: Hey, what's happening, Bono?

BONO: I just thought I'd stop by to see you.

TROY: What you stop by and see me for? You ain't stopped by in a month of Sundays. Hell, I must owe you money or something.

BONO: Since you got your promotion I can't keep up with you. Used to see you every day. Now I don't even know what route you working.

TROY: They keep switching me around. Got me out in Greentree now . . . hauling white folks' garbage.

BONO: Greentree, huh? You lucky, at least you ain't got to be lifting them barrels. Damn if they ain't getting heavier. I'm gonna put in my two years and call it quits.

TROY: I'm thinking about retiring myself.

BONO: You got it easy. You can *drive* for another five years.

TROY: It ain't the same, Bono. It ain't like working the back of the truck. Ain't got nobody to talk to . . . feel like you working by yourself. Naw, I'm thinking about retiring. How's Lucille?

BONO: She all right. Her arthritis get to acting up on her sometime. Saw Rose on my way in. She going down to the church, huh?

TROY: Yeah, she took up going down there. All them preachers looking for somebody to fatten their pockets.

Pause.

Got some gin here.

BONO: Naw, thanks. I just stopped by to say hello.

TROY: Hell, nigger . . . you can take a drink. I ain't never known you to say no to a drink. You ain't got to work tomorrow.

BONO: I just stopped by. I'm fixing to go over to Skinner's. We got us a domino game going over his house every Friday.

TROY: Nigger, you can't play no dominoes. I used to whup you four games out of five.

BONO: Well, that learned me. I'm getting better.

TROY: Yeah? Well, that's all right.

BONO: Look here . . . I got to be getting on. Stop by sometime, huh?

TROY: Yeah, I'll do that, Bono. Lucille told Rose you bought her a new refrigerator.

BONO: Yeah, Rose told Lucille you had finally built your fence . . . so I figured we'd call it even.

TROY: I knew you would.

BONO: Yeah . . . okay. I'll be talking to you.

TROY: Yeah, take care, Bono. Good to see you. I'm gonna stop over.

BONO: Yeah. Okay, Troy.

BONO *exits.* TROY *drinks from the bottle.*

TROY: Old Blue died and I dig his grave
         Let him down with a golden chain
         Every night when I hear old Blue bark
         I know Blue treed a possum in Noah's Ark.
         Hear it ring! Hear it ring!

CORY *enters the yard. They eye each other for a beat.* TROY *is sitting in the middle of the steps.* CORY *walks over.*

CORY: I got to get by.

TROY: Say what? What's you say?

CORY: You in my way. I got to get by.

TROY: You got to get by where? This is my house. Bought and paid for. In full. Took me fifteen years. And if you wanna go in my house and I'm sitting on the steps . . . you say excuse me. Like your mama taught you.

CORY: Come on, Pop . . . I got to get by.

CORY *starts to maneuver his way past* TROY. TROY *grabs his leg and shoves him back.*

TROY: You just gonna walk over top of me?

CORY: I live here, too!

TROY [*advancing toward him*]:   You just gonna walk over top of me in my own house?

CORY: I ain't scared of you.

TROY: I ain't asked if you was scared of me. I asked you if you was fixing to walk over top of me in my own house? That's the question. You ain't gonna say excuse me? You just gonna walk over top of me?

CORY: If you wanna put it like that.

TROY: How else am I gonna put it?

CORY: I was walking by you to go into the house cause you sitting on the steps drunk, singing to yourself. You can put it like that.

TROY: Without saying excuse me???

CORY *doesn't respond.*

I asked you a question. Without saying excuse me???

CORY: I ain't got to say excuse me to you. You don't count around here no more.

TROY: Oh, I see . . . I don't count around here no more. You ain't got to say excuse me to your daddy. All of a sudden you done got so grown that your daddy don't count around here no more . . . Around here in his own house and yard that he done paid for with the sweat of his brow. You done got so grown to where you gonna take over. You gonna take over my house. Is that right? You gonna wear my pants. You gonna go in there and stretch out on my bed. You ain't got to say excuse me cause I don't count around here no more. Is that right?

CORY: That's right. You always talking this dumb stuff. Now, why don't you just get out my way.

TROY: I guess you got someplace to sleep and something to put in your belly. You got that, huh? You got that? That's what you need. You got that, huh?

CORY: You don't know what I got. You ain't got to worry about what I got.

TROY: You right! You one hundred percent right! I done spent the last seventeen years worrying about what you got. Now it's your turn, see? I'll tell you what to do. You grown . . . we done established that. You a man. Now, let's see you act like one. Turn your behind around and walk out this yard. And when you get out there in the alley . . . you can forget about this house. See? 'Cause this is my house. You go on and be a man and get your own house. You can forget about this. 'Cause this is mine. You go on and get yours 'cause I'm through with doing for you.

CORY: You talking about what you did for me . . . what'd you ever give me?

TROY: Them feet and bones! That pumping heart, nigger! I give you more than anybody else is ever gonna give you.

CORY: You ain't never gave me nothing! You ain't never done anything but hold me back. Afraid I was gonna be better than you. All you ever did was try and make me scared of you. I used to tremble every time you called my name. Every time I heard your footsteps in the house. Wondering all the time . . . what's Papa gonna say if I do this? . . . What's he gonna say if I do that? . . . What's Papa gonna say if I turn on the radio? And Mama, too . . . she tries . . . but she's scared of you.

TROY: You leave your mama out of this. She ain't got nothing to do with this.

CORY: I don't know how she stand you . . . after what you did to her.

TROY: I told you to leave your mama out of this!

He advances toward CORY.

CORY: What you gonna do . . . give me a whupping? You can't whip me no more. You're too old. You just an old man.

TROY [*shoves him on his shoulder*]:   Nigger! That's what you are. You just another nigger on the street to me!

CORY: You crazy! You know that?

TROY: Go on now! You got the devil in you. Get on away from me!

CORY: You just a crazy old man . . . talking about I got the devil in me.

TROY: Yeah, I'm crazy! If you don't get on the other side of that yard . . . I'm gonna show you how crazy I am! Go on . . . get the hell out of my yard.

CORY: It ain't your yard! You took Uncle Gabe's money he got from the army to buy this house and then you put him out.

TROY [TROY *advances on* CORY]:   Get your black ass out of my yard!

TROY*'s advance backs* CORY *up against the tree.* CORY *grabs up the bat.*

CORY: I ain't going nowhere! Come on . . . put me out! I ain't scared of you.

TROY: That's my bat!

CORY: Come on!

TROY: Put my bat down!

CORY: Come on, put me out.

CORY *swings at* TROY, *who backs across the yard.*

What's the matter? You so bad . . . put me out!

TROY *advances toward* CORY.

CORY [*backing up*]:   Come on! Come on!

TROY: You're gonna have to use it! You wanna draw that bat back on me . . . you're gonna have to use it.

CORY: Come on! . . . Come on!

CORY *swings the bat at* TROY *a second time. He misses.* TROY *continues to advance toward him.*

TROY: You're gonna have to kill me! You wanna draw that bat back on me. You're gonna have to kill me.

CORY, *backed up against the tree, can go no further.* TROY *taunts him. He sticks out his head and offers him a target.*

Come on! Come on!

CORY *is unable to swing the bat.* TROY *grabs it.*

TROY: Then I'll show you.

CORY *and* TROY *struggle over the bat. The struggle is fierce and fully engaged.* TROY *ultimately is the stronger and takes the bat from* CORY *and stands over him ready to swing. He stops himself.*

Go on and get away from around my house.

CORY, *stung by his defeat, picks himself up, walks slowly out of the yard and up the alley.*

CORY: Tell Mama I'll be back for my things.

TROY: They'll be on the other side of that fence.

CORY *exits.*

TROY: I can't taste nothing. Helluljah! I can't taste nothing no more. [TROY *assumes a batting posture and begins to taunt Death, the fastball on the outside corner.*] Come on! It's between you and me now! Come on! Anytime you want! Come on! I be ready for you . . . but I ain't gonna be easy.

The lights go down on the scene.

Scene 5

The time is 1965. The lights come up in the yard. It is the morning of TROY's *funeral. A funeral plaque with a light hangs beside the door. There is a small garden plot off to the side. There is noise and activity in the house as* ROSE, GABRIEL, *and* BONO *have gathered. The door opens and* RAYNELL, *seven years old, enters dressed in a flannel nightgown. She crosses to the garden and pokes around with a stick.* ROSE *calls from the house.*

ROSE: Raynell!

RAYNELL: Mam?

ROSE: What you doing out there?

RAYNELL: Nothing.

ROSE comes to the door.

ROSE: Girl, get in here and get dressed. What you doing?

RAYNELL: Seeing if my garden growed.

ROSE: I told you it ain't gonna grow overnight. You got to wait.

RAYNELL: It don't look like it never gonna grow. Dag!

ROSE: I told you a watched pot never boils. Get in here and get dressed.

RAYNELL: This ain't even no pot, Mama.

ROSE: You just have to give it a chance. It'll grow. Now you come on and do what I told you. We got to be getting ready. This ain't no morning to be playing around. You hear me?

RAYNELL: Yes, mam.

ROSE exits into the house. RAYNELL continues to poke at her garden with a stick. CORY enters. He is dressed in a Marine corporal's uniform, and carries a duffel bag. His posture is that of a military man, and his speech has a clipped sternness.

CORY [*to* RAYNELL]:   Hi.

Pause.

I bet your name is Raynell.

RAYNELL: Uh huh.

CORY: Is your mama home?

RAYNELL runs up on the porch and calls through the screendoor.

RAYNELL: Mama . . . there's some man out here. Mama?

ROSE comes to the door.

ROSE: Cory? Lord have mercy! Look here, you all!

ROSE and CORY embrace in a tearful reunion as BONO and LYONS enter from the house dressed in funeral clothes.

BONO: Aw, looka here . . .

ROSE: Done got all grown up!

CORY: Don't cry, Mama. What you crying about?

ROSE: I'm just so glad you made it.

CORY: Hey Lyons. How you doing, Mr. Bono.

LYONS goes to embrace CORY.

LYONS: Look at you, man. Look at you. Don't he look good, Rose. Got them Corporal stripes.

ROSE: What took you so long.

CORY: You know how the Marines are, Mama. They got to get all their paperwork straight before they let you do anything.

ROSE: Well, I'm sure glad you made it. They let Lyons come. Your Uncle Gabe's still in the hospital. They don't know if they gonna let him out or not. I just talked to them a little while ago.

LYONS: A Corporal in the United States Marines.

BONO: Your daddy knew you had it in you. He used to tell me all the time.

LYONS: Don't he look good, Mr. Bono?

BONO: Yeah, he remind me of Troy when I first met him.

Pause.

Say, Rose, Lucille's down at the church with the choir. I'm gonna go down and get the pallbearers lined up. I'll be back to get you all.

ROSE: Thanks, Jim.

CORY: See you, Mr. Bono.

LYONS [*with his arm around* RAYNELL]: Cory . . . look at Raynell. Ain't she precious? She gonna break a whole lot of hearts.

ROSE: Raynell, come and say hello to your brother. This is your brother, Cory. You remember Cory.

RAYNELL: No, Mam.

CORY: She don't remember me, Mama.

ROSE: Well, we talk about you. She heard us talk about you. [*To* RAYNELL.] This is your brother, Cory. Come on and say hello.

RAYNELL: Hi.

CORY: Hi. So you're Raynell. Mama told me a lot about you.

ROSE: You all come on into the house and let me fix you some breakfast. Keep up your strength.

CORY: I ain't hungry, Mama.

LYONS: You can fix me something, Rose. I'll be in there in a minute.

ROSE: Cory, you sure you don't want nothing. I know they ain't feeding you right.

CORY: No, Mama . . . thanks. I don't feel like eating. I'll get something later.

ROSE: Raynell . . . get on upstairs and get that dress on like I told you.

ROSE *and* RAYNELL *exit into the house.*

LYONS: So . . . I hear you thinking about getting married.

CORY: Yeah, I done found the right one, Lyons. It's about time.

LYONS: Me and Bonnie been split up about four years now. About the time Papa retired. I guess she just got tired of all them changes I was putting her through.

Pause.

I always knew you was gonna make something out yourself. Your head was always in the right direction. So . . . you gonna stay in . . . make it a career . . . put in your twenty years?

CORY: I don't know. I got six already, I think that's enough.

LYONS: Stick with Uncle Sam and retire early. Ain't nothing out here. I guess Rose told you what happened with me. They got me down the workhouse. I thought I was being slick cashing other people's checks.

CORY: How much time you doing?

LYONS: They give me three years. I got that beat now. I ain't got but nine more months. It ain't so bad. You learn to deal with it like anything else. You got to take the crookeds with the straights. That's what Papa used to say. He used to say that when he struck out. I seen him strike out three times in a row . . . and the next time up he hit the ball over the grandstand. Right out there in Homestead Field. He wasn't satisfied hitting in the seats . . . he want to hit it over everything! After the game he had two hundred people standing around waiting to shake his hand. You got to take the crookeds with the straights. Yeah, Papa was something else.

CORY: You still playing?

LYONS: Cory . . . you know I'm gonna do that. There's some fellows down there we got us a band . . . we gonna try and stay together when we get out . . . but yeah, I'm still playing. It still helps me to get out of bed in the morning. As long as it do that I'm gonna be right there playing and trying to make some sense out of it.

ROSE [*calling*]:   Lyons, I got these eggs in the pan.

LYONS: Let me go on and get these eggs, man. Get ready to go bury Papa.

Pause.

How you doing? You doing all right?

CORY *nods.* LYONS *touches him on the shoulder and they share a moment of silent grief.* LYONS *exits into the house.* CORY *wanders about the yard.* RAYNELL *enters.*

RAYNELL: Hi.

CORY: Hi.

RAYNELL: Did you used to sleep in my room?

CORY: Yeah . . . that used to be my room.

RAYNELL: That's what Papa call it. "Cory's room." It got your football in the closet.

ROSE *comes to the door.*

ROSE: Raynell, get in there and get them good shoes on.

RAYNELL: Mama, can't I wear these? Them other one hurt my feet.

ROSE: Well, they just gonna have to hurt your feet for a while. You ain't said they hurt your feet when you went down to the store and got them.

RAYNELL: They didn't hurt then. My feet done got bigger.

ROSE: Don't you give me no backtalk now. You get in there and get them shoes on.

RAYNELL *exits into the house.*

Ain't too much changed. He still got that piece of rag tied to that tree. He was out here swinging that bat. I was just ready to go back in the house. He swung that bat and then he just fell over. Seem like he swung it and stood there with this grin on his face . . . and then he just fell over. They carried him on down to the hospital, but I knew there wasn't no need . . . why don't you come on in the house?

CORY: Mama . . . I got something to tell you. I don't know how to tell you this . . . but I've got to tell you . . . I'm not going to Papa's funeral.

ROSE: Boy, hush your mouth. That's your daddy you talking about. I don't want to hear that kind of talk this morning. I done raised you to come to this? You standing there all healthy and grown talking about you ain't going to your daddy's funeral?

CORY: Mama . . . listen . . .

ROSE: I don't want to hear it, Cory. You just get that thought out of your head.

CORY: I can't drag Papa with me everywhere I go. I've got to say no to him. One time in my life I've got to say no.

ROSE: Don't nobody have to listen to nothing like that. I know you and your daddy ain't seen eye to eye, but I ain't got to listen to that kind of talk this morning. Whatever was between you and your daddy . . . the time has come to put it aside. Just take it and set it over there on the shelf and forget about it. Disrespecting your daddy ain't gonna make you a man, Cory. You got to find a way to come to that on your own. Not going to your daddy's funeral ain't gonna make you a man.

CORY: The whole time I was growing up . . . living in his house . . . Papa was like a shadow that followed you everywhere. It weighed on you and sunk into your flesh. It would wrap around you and lay there until you couldn't tell which one was you anymore. That shadow digging in your flesh. Trying to crawl in. Trying to live through you. Everywhere I looked, Troy Maxson was staring back at me . . . hiding under the bed . . . in the closet. I'm just saying I've got to find a way to get rid of that shadow, Mama.

ROSE: You just like him. You got him in you good.

CORY: Don't tell me that, Mama.

ROSE: You Troy Maxson all over again.

CORY: I don't want to be Troy Maxson. I want to be me.

ROSE: You can't be nobody but who you are, Cory. That shadow wasn't nothing but you growing into yourself. You either got to grow into it or cut it down to fit you. But that's all you got to make life with. That's all you got to measure yourself against that world out there. Your daddy wanted you to be everything he wasn't . . . and at the same time he tried to make you into everything he was. I don't know if he was right or wrong . . . but I do know he meant to do more good than he meant to do harm. He wasn't always right. Sometimes when he touched he bruised. And sometimes when he took me in his arms he cut.

When I first met your daddy I thought . . . Here is a man I can lay down with and make a baby. That's the first thing I thought when I seen him. I was thirty years old and had done seen my share of men. But when he walked up to me and said, "I can dance a waltz that'll make you dizzy," I thought, Rose Lee, here is a man that you can open yourself up to and be filled to bursting. Here is a man that can fill all them empty spaces you been tipping around the edges of. One of them empty spaces was being somebody's mother.

I married your daddy and settled down to cooking his supper and keeping clean sheets on the bed. When your daddy walked through the house he was so big he filled it up. That was my first mistake. Not to make him leave some room for me. For my part in the matter. But at that time I wanted that. I wanted a house that I could sing in. And that's what your daddy gave me. I didn't know to keep up his strength I had to give up little pieces of mine. I did that. I took on his life as mine and mixed up the pieces so that you couldn't hardly tell which was which anymore. It was my choice. It was my life and I didn't have to live it like that. But that's what life offered me in the way of being a woman and I took it. I grabbed hold of it with both hands.

By the time Raynell came into the house, me and your daddy had done lost touch with one another. I didn't want to make my blessing off of nobody's misfortune . . . but I took on to Raynell like she was all them babies I had wanted and never had.

The phone rings.

Like I'd been blessed to relive a part of my life. And if the Lord see fit to keep up my strength . . . I'm gonna do her just like your daddy did you . . . I'm gonna give her the best of what's in me.

RAYNELL [*entering, still with her old shoes*]:   Mama . . . Reverend Tollivier on the phone.

ROSE *exits into the house.*

RAYNELL: Hi.

CORY: Hi.

RAYNELL: You in the Army or the Marines?

CORY: Marines.

RAYNELL: Papa said it was the Army. Did you know Blue?

CORY: Blue? Who's Blue?

RAYNELL: Papa's dog what he sing about all the time.

CORY [*singing*]:   Hear it ring! Hear it ring!
> I had a dog his name was Blue
> You know Blue was mighty true
> You know Blue was a good old dog
> Blue treed a possum in a hollow log
> You know from that he was a good old dog.
> Hear it ring! Hear it ring!

RAYNELL *joins in singing.*

CORY *and* RAYNELL: Blue treed a possum out on a limb
> Blue looked at me and I looked at him
> Grabbed that possum and put him in a sack
> Blue stayed there till I came back
> Old Blue's feets was big and round
> Never allowed a possum to touch the ground.
>
> Old Blue died and I dug his grave
> I dug his grave with a silver spade
> Let him down with a golden chain
> And every night I call his name
> Go on Blue, you good dog you
> Go on Blue, you good dog you

RAYNELL: Blue laid down and died like a man
> Blue laid down and died . . .

BOTH: Blue laid down and died like a man
> Now he's treeing possums in the Promised Land
> I'm gonna tell you this to let you know
> Blue's gone where the good dogs go
> When I hear old Blue bark
> When I hear old Blue bark
> Blue treed a possum in Noah's Ark,
> Blue treed a possum in Noah's Ark.

ROSE *comes to the screen door.*

ROSE: Cory, we gonna be ready to go in a minute.

CORY [*to* RAYNELL]:   You go on in the house and change them shoes like Mama told you so we can go to Papa's funeral.

RAYNELL: Okay, I'll be back.

RAYNELL *exits into the house.* CORY *gets up and crosses over to the tree.* ROSE *stands in the screen door watching him.* GABRIEL *enters from the alley.*

GABRIEL [*calling*]:   Hey, Rose!

ROSE: Gabe?

GABRIEL: I'm here, Rose. Hey Rose, I'm here!

ROSE *enters from the house.*

ROSE: Lord . . . Look here, Lyons!

LYONS: See, I told you, Rose . . . I told you they'd let him come.

CORY: How you doing, Uncle Gabe?

LYONS: How you doing, Uncle Gabe?

GABRIEL: Hey, Rose. It's time. It's time to tell St. Peter to open the gates. Troy, you ready? You ready, Troy. I'm gonna tell St. Peter to open the gates. You get ready now.

GABRIEL, *with great fanfare, braces himself to blow. The trumpet is without a mouthpiece. He puts the end of it into his mouth and blows with great force, like a man who has been waiting some twenty-odd years for this single moment. No sound comes out of the trumpet. He braces himself and blows again with the same result. A third time he blows. There is a weight of impossible description that falls away and leaves him bare and exposed to a frightful realization. It is a trauma that a sane and normal mind would be unable to withstand. He begins to dance. A slow, strange dance, eerie and life-giving. A dance of atavistic signature and ritual.* LYONS *attempts to embrace him.* GABRIEL *pushes* LYONS *away. He begins to howl in what is an attempt at song, or perhaps a song turning back into itself in an attempt at speech. He finishes his dance and the gates of heaven stand open as wide as God's closet.*

That's the way that go!

(*1986*)

QUESTIONS FOR REFLECTION

Experience

1. To what extent can you relate to the situations of Wilson's characters? Why or why not?

Interpretation

2. How does Wilson establish the world of his play? What kinds of details help readers and viewers orient themselves?

3. Identify the play's most important references to religion, and explain their function.
4. How does Wilson make his characters believable? Which of them do you understand best? Why?
5. What metaphors do Troy and Rose use to make sense of their lives? How does the playwright use these metaphors for expressive purposes?
6. Identify the various kinds of "fences" the play includes. Explain the significance of the title.
7. Select one longer speech or one important exchange of dialogue, and explain its significance to the play's theme.
8. Select one scene or part of a scene, and explain how you would stage it.

Evaluation

9. Identify the values each of the characters lives by. Whose values does the play seem to endorse?

WENDY WASSERSTEIN

[b. 1950]

Wendy Wasserstein was born and raised in New York City. She was educated at Smith College and at Mount Holyoke College, from which she graduated with a B.A. in 1971. Two years later she earned a master's degree in playwriting from City College of New York. From 1973 until 1976 she studied at the Yale School of Drama, from which she received a master of fine arts. In 1989 she won the Pulitzer Prize and a Tony Award for Best Play for *The Heidi Chronicles,* and in 1993 she won an Outer Circle Critics Award and a Tony nomination for *The Sisters Rosenzweig.* In addition to plays, she has written for public television and film.

Tender Offer, which was written and produced in 1977, is a one-act play that captures the relationship between a father and his teen-age daughter. The play's economy and its humor belie its underlying seriousness.

WENDY WASSERSTEIN

Tender Offer

A girl of around nine is alone in a dance studio. She is dressed in traditional leotards and tights. She begins singing to herself, "Nothing Could Be Finer Than to Be in Carolina." She maps out a dance routine, including parts for the chorus. She builds to a finale. A man, PAUL, around thirty-five, walks in. He has a sweet, though distant, demeanor. As he walks in, LISA notices him and stops.

PAUL: You don't have to stop, sweetheart.

LISA: That's okay.

PAUL: Looked very good.

LISA: Thanks.

PAUL: Don't I get a kiss hello?

LISA: Sure.

PAUL [*Embraces her.*]:   Hi, Tiger.

LISA: Hi, Dad.

PAUL: I'm sorry I'm late.

LISA: That's okay.

PAUL: How'd it go?

LISA: Good.

PAUL: Just good?

LISA: Pretty good.

PAUL: "Pretty good." You mean you got a lot of applause or "pretty good" you could have done better.

LISA: Well, Courtney Palumbo's mother thought I was pretty good. But you know the part in the middle when everybody's supposed to freeze and the big girl comes out. Well, I think I moved a little bit.

PAUL: I thought what you were doing looked very good.

LISA: Daddy, that's not what I was doing. That was tap-dancing. I made that up.

PAUL: Oh. Well it looked good. Kind of sexy.

LISA: Yuch!

PAUL: What do you mean "yuch"?

LISA: Just yuch!

PAUL: You don't want to be sexy?

LISA: I don't care.

PAUL: Let's go, Tiger. I promised your mother I'd get you home in time for dinner.

LISA: I can't find my leg warmers.

PAUL: You can't find your what?

LISA: Leg warmers. I can't go home till I find my leg warmers.

PAUL: I don't see you looking for them.

LISA: I was waiting for you.

PAUL: Oh.

LISA: Daddy.

PAUL: What?

LISA: Nothing.

PAUL: Where do you think you left them?

LISA: Somewhere around here. I can't remember.

PAUL: Well, try to remember, Lisa. We don't have all night.

LISA: I told you. I think somewhere around here.

PAUL: I don't see them. Let's go home now. You'll call the dancing school tomorrow.

LISA: Daddy, I can't go home till I find them. Miss Judy says it's not professional to leave things.

PAUL: Who's Miss Judy?

LISA: She's my ballet teacher. She once danced the lead in *Swan Lake,* and she was a June Taylor dancer.

PAUL: Well, then, I'm sure she'll understand about the leg warmers.

LISA: Daddy, Miss Judy wanted to know why you were late today.

PAUL: Hmmmmmmmmm?

LISA: Why were you late?

PAUL: I was in a meeting. Business. I'm sorry.

LISA: Why did you tell Mommy you'd come instead of her if you knew you had business?

PAUL: Honey, something just came up. I thought I'd be able to be here. I was looking forward to it.

LISA: I wish you wouldn't make appointments to see me.

PAUL: Hmmmmmmmm.

LISA: You shouldn't make appointments to see me unless you know you're going to come.

PAUL: Of course I'm going to come.

LISA: No, you're not. Talia Robbins told me she's much happier living without her father in the house. Her father used to come home late and go to sleep early.

PAUL: Lisa, stop it. Let's go.

LISA: I can't find my leg warmers.

PAUL: Forget your leg warmers.

LISA: Daddy.

PAUL: What is it?

LISA: I saw this show on television, I think it was WPIX Channel 11. Well, the father was crying about his daughter.

PAUL: Why was he crying? Was she sick?

LISA: No. She was at school. And he was at business. And he just missed her, so he started to cry.

PAUL: What was the name of this show?

LISA: I don't know. I came in in the middle.

PAUL: Well, Lisa, I certainly would cry if you were sick or far away, but I know that you're well and you're home. So no reason to get maudlin.

LISA: What's maudlin?

PAUL: Sentimental, soppy. Frequently used by children who make things up to get attention.

LISA: I am sick! I am sick! I have Hodgkin's disease and a bad itch on my leg.

PAUL: What do you mean you have Hodgkin's disease? Don't say things like that.

LISA: Swoosie Kurtz, she had Hodgkin's disease on a TV movie last year, but she got better and now she's on *Love Sidney*.

PAUL: Who is Swoosie Kurtz?

LISA: She's an actress named after an airplane. I saw her on *Live at Five*.

PAUL: You watch too much television; you should do your homework. Now, put your coat on.

LISA: Daddy, I really do have a bad itch on my leg. Would you scratch it?

PAUL: Lisa, you're procrastinating.

LISA: Why do you use words I don't understand? I hate it. You're like Daria Feldman's mother. She always talks in Yiddish to her husband so Daria won't understand.

PAUL: Procrastinating is not Yiddish.

LISA: Well, I don't know what it is.

PAUL: Procrastinating means you don't want to go about your business.

LISA: I don't go to business. I go to school.

PAUL: What I mean is you want to hang around here until you and I are late for dinner and your mother's angry and it's too late for you to do your homework.

LISA: I do not.

PAUL: Well, it sure looks that way. Now put your coat on and let's go.

LISA: Daddy.

PAUL: Honey, I'm tired. Really, later.

LISA: Why don't you want to talk to me?

PAUL: I do want to talk to you. I promise when we get home we'll have a nice talk.

LISA: No, we won't. You'll read the paper and fall asleep in front of the news.

PAUL: Honey, we'll talk on the weekend, I promise. Aren't I taking you to the theater this weekend? Let me look. [*He takes out appointment book.*] Yes. Sunday. *Joseph and the Amazing Technicolor Raincoat* with Lisa. Okay, Tiger?

LISA: Sure. It's Dreamcoat.

PAUL: What?

LISA: Nothing. I think I see my leg warmers. [*She goes to pick them up, and an odd-looking trophy.*]

PAUL: What's that?

LISA: It's stupid. I was second best at the dance recital, so they gave me this thing. It's stupid.

PAUL: Lisa.

LISA: What?

PAUL: What did you want to talk about?

LISA: Nothing.

PAUL: Was it about my missing your recital? I'm really sorry, Tiger, I would have liked to have been here.

LISA: That's okay.

PAUL: Honest?

LISA: Daddy, you're prostrastinating.

PAUL: I'm procrastinating. Sit down. Let's talk. So. How's school?

LISA: Fine.

PAUL: You like it?

LISA: Yup.

PAUL: You looking forward to camp this summer?

LISA: Yup.

PAUL: Is Daria Feldman going back?

LISA: Nope.

PAUL: Why not?

LISA: I don't know. We can go home now. Honest, my foot doesn't itch anymore.

PAUL: Lisa, you know what you do in business when it seems like there's nothing left to say? That's when you really start talking. Put a bid on the table.

LISA: What's a bid?

PAUL: You tell me what you want and I'll tell you what I've got to offer. Like Monopoly. You want Boardwalk, but I'm only willing to give you the Railroads. Now, because you are my daughter I'd throw in Water Works and Electricity. Understand, Tiger?

LISA: No. I don't like board games. You know, Daddy, we could get Space Invaders for our home for thirty-five dollars. In fact, we could get an Osborne System for two thousand. Daria Feldman's parents . . .

PAUL: Daria Feldman's parents refuse to talk to Daria, so they bought a computer to keep Daria busy so they won't have to speak in Yiddish. Daria will probably grow up to be a homicidal maniac lesbian prostitute.

LISA: I know what that word prostitute means.

PAUL: Good. [*Pause.*] You still haven't told me about school. Do you still like your teacher?

LISA: She's okay.

PAUL: Lisa, if we're talking try to answer me.

LISA: I am answering you. Can we go home now, please?

PAUL: Damn it, Lisa, if you want to talk to me . . . Talk to me!

LISA: I can't wait till I'm old enough so I can make my own money and never have to see you again. Maybe I'll become a prostitute.

PAUL: Young lady, that's enough.

LISA: I hate you, Daddy! I hate you! [*She throws her trophy into the trash bin.*]

PAUL: What'd you do that for?

LISA: It's stupid.

PAUL: Maybe I wanted it.

LISA: What for?

PAUL: Maybe I wanted to put it where I keep your dinosaur and the picture you made of Mrs. Kimbel with the chicken pox.

LISA: You got mad at me when I made that picture. You told me I had to respect Mrs. Kimbel because she was my teacher.

PAUL: That's true. But she wasn't my teacher. I liked her better with the chicken pox. [*Pause.*] Lisa, I'm sorry. I was very wrong to miss your recital, and you don't have to become a prostitute. That's not the type of profession Miss Judy has in mind for you.

LISA [*Mumbles.*]:   No.

PAUL: No. [*Pause.*] So Talia Robbins is really happy her father moved out?

LISA: Talia Robbins picks open the eighth-grade lockers during gym period. But she did that before her father moved out.

PAUL: You can't always judge someone by what they do or what they don't do. Sometimes you come home from dancing school and run upstairs and shut the door, and when I finally get to talk to you, everything is "okay" or "fine." Yup or nope?

LISA: Yup.

PAUL: Sometimes, a lot of times, I come home and fall asleep in front of the television. So you and I spend a lot of time being a little scared of each other. Maybe?

LISA: Maybe.

PAUL: Tell you what. I'll make you a tender offer.

LISA: What?

PAUL: I'll make you a tender offer. That's when one company publishes in the newspaper that they want to buy another company. And the company that publishes is called the Black Knight because they want to gobble up the poor little company. So the poor little company needs to be rescued. And then a White Knight comes along and makes a bigger and better offer so the shareholders won't have to tender shares to the Big Black Knight. You with me?

LISA: Sort of.

PAUL: I'll make you a tender offer like the White Knight. But I don't want to own you. I just want to make a much better offer. Okay?

LISA [*Sort of understanding.*]:   Okay. [*Pause. They sit for a moment.*] Sort of, Daddy, what do you think about? I mean, like when you're quiet what do you think about?

PAUL: Oh, business usually. If I think I made a mistake or if I think I'm doing okay. Sometimes I think about what I'll be doing five years from now and if it's what I hoped it would be five years ago. Sometimes I think about what your life will be like, if Mount Saint Helen's will erupt again. What you'll become if you'll study penmanship or word processing. If you'll speak kindly of me to your psychiatrist when you are in graduate school. And how the hell I'll pay for your graduate school. And sometimes I try and think what it was I thought about when I was your age.

LISA: Do you ever look out your window at the clouds and try to see which kinds of shapes they are? Like one time, honest, I saw the head of Walter Cronkite in a flower vase. Really! Like look don't those kinda look like if you turn it upside down, two big elbows or two elephant trunks dancing?

PAUL: Actually still looks like Walter Cronkite in a flower vase to me. But look up a little. See the one that's still moving? That sorta looks like a whale on a thimble.

LISA: Where?

PAUL: Look up. To your right.

LISA: I don't see it. Where?

PAUL: The other way.

LISA: Oh, yeah! There's the head and there's the stomach. Yeah! [LISA *picks up her trophy.*] Hey, Daddy.

PAUL: Hey, Lisa.

LISA: You can have this thing if you want it. But you have to put it like this, because if you put it like that it is gross.

PAUL: You know what I'd like? So I can tell people who come into my office why I have this gross stupid thing on my shelf, I'd like it if you could show me your dance recital.

LISA: Now?

PAUL: We've got time. Mother said she won't be home till late.

LISA: Well, Daddy, during a lot of it I freeze and the big girl in front dances.

PAUL: Well, how 'bout the number you were doing when I walked in?

LISA: Well, see, I have parts for a lot of people in that one, too.

PAUL: I'll dance the other parts.

LISA: You can't dance.

PAUL: Young lady, I played Yvette Mimieux in a *Hasty Pudding Show.*

LISA: Who's Yvette Mimieux?

PAUL: Watch more television. You'll find out. [PAUL *stands up.*] So I'm ready. [*He begins singing.*] "Nothing could be finer than to be in Carolina."

LISA: Now I go. In the morning. And now you go. Dum-da.

PAUL [*Obviously not a tap dancer.*]:   Da-da-dum.

LISA [*Whines.*]:   Daddy!

PAUL [*Mimics her.*]:   Lisa! Nothing could be finer . . .

LISA: That looks dumb.

PAUL: Oh, yeah? You think they do this better in *The Amazing Minkcoat?* No way! Now you go—da da da dum.

LISA: Da da da dum.

PAUL: If I had Aladdin's lamp for only a day, I'd make a wish. . . .

LISA: Daddy, that's maudlin!

PAUL: I know it's maudlin. And here's what I'd say:

LISA *and* PAUL: I'd say that "nothing could be finer than to be in Carolina in the moooooooooooornin'."

(1977)

QUESTIONS FOR REFLECTION

Experience

1. To what extent can you identify with the situation depicted in Wasserstein's play? Why?

Interpretation

2. How would you characterize the relationship between Lisa and Paul?
3. Examine the play's dialogue for shifts of direction. Account for the conversational logic of these shifts and explain their dramatic effects.
4. Explain the significance of Paul and Lisa's discussion of the meaning of "procrastination" and "maudlin."
5. What is the function of Paul's inaccuracy in naming the title of the Broadway play *Joseph and the Amazing Technicolor Dreamcoat*?
6. Explain the various meanings of the "tender offer" Paul makes Lisa.
7. Consider how you would direct the actors in staging the play's final scene—the father/daughter dance routine.
8. What is the theme of the play?

Evaluation

9. How effectively does Wasserstein characterize a father-daughter relationship? Where is her depiction most convincing, least convincing, and why?

JOSEFINA LÓPEZ

Josefina López wrote her first play at the age of seventeen. *Simply María* was produced in San Diego and later aired on PBS. A surreal exploration of the development of a Mexican woman growing up in the United States, the play's action occurs mostly as a dream sequence. In exploring social and gender values, *Simply María* uses irony and satire to illuminate cultural differences and evaluate cultural mythologies.

JOSEFINA LÓPEZ

Simply María

or

The American Dream

CHARACTERS

Principals:
MARÍA, *daughter of Carmen and Ricardo*
CARMEN, *mother of María*
RICARDO, *father of María*
JOSÉ, *María's husband*
PRIEST

In order of appearance:
GIRL 1
GIRL 2
GIRL 3
MOTHER, *Carmen's mother*
WOMAN
NARRATOR
IMMIGRANT 1
IMMIGRANT 2
IMMIGRANT 3
IMMIGRANT 4
STATUE OF LIBERTY
MEXICAN MAN
MEXICAN WOMAN
POSTMAN
PERSON 1
VENDOR 1
VENDOR 2
BAG LADY
PROTESTOR
MAN 1
DIRTY OLD MAN
CHOLO 2
VALLEY GIRL 1
VALLEY GIRL 2

CHOLO 1
PERSON 2
PERSON 3
PERSON 4
ANGLO BUYER
MYTH
MARY
MARÍA 2
REFEREE
ANNOUNCER
FLOOR MANAGER
HUSBAND
WIFE
SALESMAN
HEAD NURSE
NURSE 2
NURSE 3
NURSE 4
BAILIFF
JUDGE
PROSECUTOR
JUROR 1
JUROR 2

Note: *Many of the above characters can be played by the same actor/actress.*

Place. *The play begins in an unspecified town in Mexico and moves to downtown Los Angeles.*
Time. *Over a period of years chronicling the growth of María from birth to her womanhood.*

SCENE ONE

There is a long thin movie screen on the top and across the stage that will be used to display slides of titles for a couple of seconds each. Lights rise. MARÍA, *a young woman with a suitcase, enters. She goes to the center and remains still.* THREE GIRLS *enter and stand behind her.*

GIRL 3 (*Loud introduction.*):   Romeo and Juliet elope. Or, where's the wedding dress?

(*Lights slowly fade. Then dim lights slowly rise.* RICARDO, *a tall, dark and handsome young Mexican man enters. He tries to hide in the darkness of the night. He whistles carefully, blending the sound with the noises of the night.*)

CARMEN (*From her balcony.*):   Ricardo, ¿eres tú?
RICARDO: Yes! Ready?

CARMEN: Sí. (*She climbs down from her balcony, then runs to* RICARDO, *kissing and consuming him in her embrace.*) Where's the horse?

RICARDO: What horse?

CARMEN: The one we are going to elope on.

RICARDO: You didn't say to bring one. All we agreed on was that I would be here at midnight.

CARMEN: I would have thought that you would have thought to . . .

RICARDO: Shhhh!!! ¡Mira! (*Points to* CARMEN's *room.*)

CARMEN: ¡Mi madre! Let's go! And on what are we going?

RICARDO: On this. (*Brings an old bike.*)

CARMEN: ¡Qué! On that? No! How could . . . Everyone knows that when you elope, you elope on a horse, not on a . . . Ricardo, you promised!

MOTHER (*Discovering* CARMEN *gone.*): ¡Carmencita! Carmen! She's gone!

CARMEN: Oh, no! Hurry! Let's go!

RICARDO (*Hops on the bike.*): Carmen, hurry! Get on!

CARMEN: We won't fit!

MOTHER: ¡M'ija! Where are you?

CARMEN: We better fit! (*Jumps on, and they take off. She falls and then quickly hops back on.*) Ricardo, marry me! (*Crickets are heard, lights dim. Fade out.*)

SCENE TWO

THREE WOMEN *enter a church with candles. A fourth, much older, enters with a lighted candle and lights the other candles. The* THREE WOMEN *then transform into statues of the saints in the church.* PRIEST *comes downstage, waiting for a wedding to begin.* CARMEN *enters, pregnant.*

PRIEST: Will he be here soon?

CARMEN: Soon. He promised.

PRIEST: I was supposed to start half an hour ago.

WOMAN (*Enters with a note.*): Is there anyone here named Carmen?

CARMEN: Yes . . . Is it from Ricardo? (*Reading the note.*) "I haven't been able to get a divorce. It will be some time soon, believe me . . . Just wait. I'm working hard so that I can save money to buy a little house or a ranch for the three of us. If you wait, good things will come." (*To* PRIEST.) There won't be a wedding today.

(*Exits crying with* PRIEST. *The statues become* WOMEN *and they all ad lib malicious gossip about the pregnant bride.* CARMEN *enters again, holding baby.* PRIEST *enters.* WOMEN *become statues again.*)

PRIEST: Will he be here? (RICARDO *enters.*)

CARMEN: He is here.

PRIEST: Good. Now we can start.

CARMEN (*To* RICARDO.): I thought you wouldn't show up.

PRIEST: (*Begins his speech, which is more or less mumbled and not heard except for:*) Do you, Carmen, accept Ricardo as your lawfully wedded husband?

CARMEN: I do.

PRIEST: Do you, Ricardo, accept Carmen as your lawfully wedded wife?

RICARDO: I do.

PRIEST: Under the Catholic Church, in the holy House of God, I pronounce you husband and wife. (*Takes baby from* CARMEN, *and sprinkles holy water on baby.*) Under the Catholic Church, in the holy House of God, this child shall be known as María.

The PRIEST *puts the baby on the center of the stage.* CARMEN, RICARDO *and* PRIEST *exit. On the screen the following title is displayed:* **The Making of a Mexican Girl.**

NARRATOR: The making of a Mexican girl.

(*The statues now transform into* THREE ANGELIC GIRLS *who begin to hum, then sing beautifully with only the word "María." They come center stage and deliver the following, facing the audience:*)

ALL: María.

GIRL 1:   As a girl you are to be

GIRL 2:   Nice,

GIRL 3:   forgiving,

GIRL 1:   considerate,

GIRL 2:   obedient,

GIRL 3:   gentle,

GIRL 1:   hard-working,

GIRL 2:   gracious.

GIRL 3:   You are to like:

GIRL 1:   Dolls,

GIRL 2:   kitchens,

GIRL 3:   houses,

GIRL 1:   cleaning,

GIRL 2:   caring for children,

GIRL 3:   cooking,

GIRL 1:   laundry,

GIRL 2:   dishes.

GIRL 3:   You are not to:

GIRL 1:   Be independent,

GIRL 2:   enjoy sex,

GIRL 3:   but must endure it as your duty to your husband,

GIRL 1:   and bear his children.

GIRL 2:   Do not shame your society!

GIRL 3:   Never,

GIRL 1:   never,

GIRL 2:   never,

ALL: Never!!!!

GIRL 1:   Your goal is to reproduce.

GIRL 2:   And your only purpose in life is to serve three men:

GIRL 3:   Your father,

GIRL 1:   your husband,

GIRL 2:   and your son.

GIRL 3:   Your father. (RICARDO *enters.*)

RICARDO: Carmen, I must go.

CARMEN: Ricardo, don't go. Not after all the time I've waited.

RICARDO: I don't want to leave you, but we need the money. There's no work here. I must go to el norte, so I can find work and send for you.

CARMEN: I don't want to be alone.

RICARDO: You have María. I'm going so that we can have the things we don't have.

CARMEN: I would prefer to have you and not the things I don't have.

RICARDO: I want something else besides a life on this farm.

CARMEN: María will not see you.

RICARDO: She will. When I am on the other side, I will send for you. She will be very proud of me.

CARMEN: You promise?

RICARDO: I promise.

CARMEN: Well, then I will wait; we will wait.

RICARDO: I will write. (*Kisses* CARMEN *on the forehead.*)

CARMEN: Ricardo, remember that I love you. (RICARDO *leaves.*) Don't forget to write.

(*Fade out.*)

SCENE THREE

NARRATOR: Yes, write a lot; they will miss you. All who are in search of opportunity go to the same place: America. And America belongs to those who are willing to risk.

(*A giant sail enters the stage brought on by* FOUR EUROPEAN IMMIGRANTS.)

IMMIGRANT 1: All for a dream.

IMMIGRANT 2: Ciao, mia Italia!

IMMIGRANT 3: Auf Wiedersehen, mein Deutschland!

IMMIGRANT 4: Au revoir, mon France!

IMMIGRANT 2: Hello, America!

(*In the background* "America the Beautiful" *plays, the music growing louder. The* STATUE OF LIBERTY *enters.*)

IMMIGRANT 3: The Lady!

IMMIGRANT 4: Up high in the sky, incapable of being brought down.

IMMIGRANT 2: And like her . . .

IMMIGRANT 3: . . . we carry . . .

IMMIGRANTS 2 & 4: . . . a similar torch.

ALL: A torch of hope.

STATUE OF LIBERTY: Give me your tired, your poor, your huddled masses yearning to breathe free . . .

(*At the bottom of the* STATUE OF LIBERTY *are* THREE MEXICAN PEOPLE [RICARDO *is one of them*] *trying to go across the stage as if it is the border. They run around hiding, sneaking, and crawling, trying not to get spotted by the border patrol.*)

RICARDO: ¡Vénganse! ¡Por aquí!

MEXICAN MAN: ¿Y ahora qué hacemos?

MEXICAN WOMAN: What do we do now?

MEXICAN MAN: ¡Vámonos! ¡Por allá!

MEXICAN WOMAN: ¡Nos nortearon!

RICARDO: Let's go back.

(*They go to hide behind the* EUROPEAN IMMIGRANTS. *The* STATUE OF LIBERTY *composes herself and continues.*)

STATUE OF LIBERTY: I give you life, liberty and the pursuit of happiness for the price of your heritage, your roots, your history, your relatives, your language . . . Conform, adapt, bury your past, give up what is yours and I'll give you the opportunity to have what is mine.

MEXICAN MAN: Pues bueno, if we have to.

MEXICAN WOMAN: Sounds good.

IMMIGRANT 4:   Look, fireworks!

RICARDO: ¡Nos hicimos!

(*"America the Beautiful" becomes overwhelming; lights flash, representing the fireworks. A few seconds later the same lights that adorn the celebration for* EUROPEAN IMMIGRANTS *become the lights from the helicopters hunting after the* MEXICAN PEOPLE. *Hound dogs are also heard barking, and the* MEXICAN PEOPLE *scatter and try to hide.*)

RICARDO: ¡La migra!

MEXICAN MAN: The immigration!

MEXICAN WOMAN: ¡Córranle!

(*The* EUROPEAN IMMIGRANTS *and the* STATUE OF LIBERTY *all keep pointing at the* MEXICAN PEOPLE *so that they can be caught. The* MEXICAN PEOPLE *run offstage, and with the sail tilted down, they charge after them. Fade out.*)

SCENE FOUR

POSTMAN (*Throwing in paper airplane.*):   Air mail for Carmen García.

CARMEN (CARMEN *enters and reads letter.*):   "Mi querida Carmen, how are you? How is María? I've sent you some more money. This is the last letter I write to you because I am now sending for you. I fixed my papers with the help of a friend, and I got an apartment where we can live. Tell María I love her, and to you I send all my love . . . " María! . . . "Leave as soon as possible . . . " Leave as soon as possible . . . María, ¡ven acá!

MARÍA (MARÍA *enters.*):   Yes, Mami.

CARMEN: María get ready; we're going.

MARÍA: Going where?

CARMEN: To join your father in the city of the angels.

MARÍA: Angels?

(MARÍA *puts on her coat for the journey. Fade out.*)

SCENE FIVE

On the screen the following title is displayed: **Los Angelitos Del Norte.** *The following is the making of a city. Actors will take on many roles. It will be organized chaos. Noises of police and firetruck sirens, along with other common city noises are heard. The lights rise on* VENDORS *selling on the streets, and all sorts of unusual and not so unusual* PEOPLE *found in downtown L.A. on Broadway.* CARMEN *and* MARÍA *are engulfed in the scene, appalled to see what they have come to.*

PERSON 1:   Broadway! Downtown L.A.!

VENDOR 1:   Cassettes, ¡cartuchos, dos dólares!

VENDOR 2:   Anillos de oro sólido. Solid gold. Not plated.

CARMEN: Perdone, señora, could you tell me . . .

BAG LADY: Get out of my way!

PROTESTOR: Homosexuality is wrong! No sex! No sex! ¡Se va a acabar el mundo! The world is coming to an end!

(*Separates* CARMEN *from* MARÍA.)

CARMEN: María! María, where are you?! (*Searches frantically.*)

MARÍA: Mami! Mami! (*Cries for* CARMEN.)

WOMAN 1:   Buy this! ¿Sombras para verte como estrella de cine?

WOMAN 2:   Hair brushes, all kinds, a dollar!

WOMAN 3:   You want to buy handbags?

WOMAN 4:   ¡Vámonos! Here comes the police.

(*All the* VENDORS *on the street run away.*)

MAN 1:   Jesus loves you! (*Hands* CARMEN *a pamphlet.*) He died for our sins!

CARMEN: ¿Qué?

WOMAN 1:   That RTD bus is late again!

DIRTY OLD MAN: Hey! Little girl! You want to get married? The world is coming to an end and you don't want to die without having experienced it.

CARMEN: María! María! ¿Dónde estás, hija mia?

CHOLO 2:   East L.A.!

TWO VALLEY GIRLS: We love it!

CHOLO 1:   Hey, bato!

TWO VALLEY GIRLS: Party and let party!

CHOLO 2:   ¡Oye, mi carnal!

PERSON 2:   ¡Viva la huelga! Boycott grapes!

PERSON 3:   Chicano Power!

TWO VALLEY GIRLS: We love it.

PERSON 3:   Chicano Power!

TWO VALLEY GIRLS: We love it.

PERSON 4:   A little culture for the gringuitos. ¡Tostadas, frijoles!

ANGLO BUYER: How much? ¿Cuánto? ¿Salsa? ¿Cerveza?

CARMEN: María!

(MARÍA *runs scared and bumps into* CARMEN. *They hug each other.* RICARDO, *dressed in a charro outfit enters and gives some yells as if ready to sing a corrido. All the chaos of the city stops, and all the city people recoil in fear.* RICARDO *becomes the hero rescuing* CARMEN *and* MARÍA *from their nightmare.*)

TWO VALLEY GIRLS: We love it!

CARMEN: ¡Ayyy! What a crazy city! It's so awful! People here are crazy! (*Almost about to cry, she embraces* RICARDO.) But Ricardo, I'm so happy to be here.

MARÍA (*Trying to get attention.*):   An ugly man chased me!

RICARDO: But you are all right?

MARÍA: Sí. Now that you are here.

RICARDO: Carmen, we are finally together like I promised.

CARMEN: Ricardo, where's our home?

RICARDO: Follow me.

(*They leave the stage. Fade out. Props for next scene are set up quickly.*)

SCENE SIX

NARRATOR: They are going to the housing projects; Pico Aliso, Ramona Gardens, Estrada Courts. No one likes it there, but it's cheap. Es Barato. (*On the screen the following title is displayed:* **Little House in The Ghetto.**) Little house in the ghetto.

RICARDO: Here we are.

CARMEN: ¿Aquí?

RICARDO: Yes, I hope it's all right. It's only for now.

MARÍA (*Smiling.*):   I like it! Look, Mami! There are swings and grass.

RICARDO: There are a lot of kids in the neighborhood you can play with.

MARÍA: Really, Papi? Would they want to play with me?

RICARDO: Sure. (*Noticing* CARMEN's *displeasure.*) What's wrong? You don't like it?

CARMEN: Oh. No, I'm just tired from the trip.

RICARDO: How was the trip?

MARÍA (*Cutting in.*):   It was great!

CARMEN: Great? You threw up on me the whole way here.

MARÍA: Except, I don't understand why the bus never got off the ground. Where are the angels? And where are the clouds? And the gate? And the music . . . Like in the stories Mami used to tell me. I thought we were going to heaven. I thought you had been called to heaven because you are an angel. Are you an angel?

RICARDO: Yes, I'm your angel always.

MARÍA: So if this isn't heaven and you're an angel, what are we doing here?

RICARDO: María, I brought you to America so that you can have a better life. It wasn't easy for me. I was hiding in a truck with a lot of other people for hours. It was so hot and humid that people preferred to get caught by the migra than die of suffocation. But I was going to make it because I knew that I had a daughter to live for. I did it for you. In America, the education is great! You can take advantage of all the opportunities offered to you. You can work hard to be just as good as anybody. You can be anything you want to be! (*Pause.*) Carmen, let me show you the kitchen. (CARMEN *and* RICARDO *exit.*)

MARÍA: America, I don't even know you yet and I already love you! You're too generous. Thank you. I'll work hard. I can be anything I want to be! (*Starts changing clothes to end up wearing a casual shirt and pants when she finishes the following:*) America, I'm ready to play the game. I'm gonna show those boys in this neighborhood how to really play football!

(*She makes some football moves. Then she runs out.* CARMEN *enters.*)

CARMEN: María, ¡ven aquí! (MARÍA *enters.*)
MARÍA: Yes, Mami.
CARMEN: La señora Martínez told me you were playing football with the boys.
MARÍA: Yes, Mami; I was.
CARMEN: I don't want you playing football with the boys. It's not proper for a lady.
MARÍA: But I'm good at sports. I'm better than some of the boys.
CARMEN: It doesn't look right. ¿Qué van a decir?

(*In the background appear the* THREE GIRLS *who are only seen and heard by* MARÍA. *They whisper to her.*)

GIRL 1:   Never shame your society.
GIRL 2:   Never,
GIRL 3:   never,
GIRL 1:   never,
ALL: NEVER!!!
MARÍA: But my Papi said . . .
CARMEN: You are not going to play with boys! (CARMEN *exits.*)
MARÍA: I don't understand. Papi tells me to compete, Mami tells me it doesn't look right. I like to compete, too. (MARÍA *exits to her room.*)
RICARDO (*To* MARÍA.):   María, ¡ven aquí! Who were you walking home with today?
MARÍA: A friend.
RICARDO: A boyfriend?
MARÍA: No, just a friend I have in my last class. He lives close by.
RICARDO: I don't want you walking home with or talking to boys. Study!
MARÍA (*Dares to ask.*):   Papi, why?
RICARDO: You're thirteen and you are very naïve about boys. The only thing on their minds is of no good for a proper girl. They tell girls that they are "special," sweet things, knowing that girls are stupid enough to believe it. They make pendejas out of them. They get them pregnant, and shame their parents . . . Go to your room!

(*The* THREE GIRLS *appear again and whisper to* MARÍA.)

GIRL 1:   Never shame your society!
GIRL 2:   Never,
GIRL 3:   (*Does not continue, but slowly walks away from the two girls.*)
GIRL 1:   Never,
GIRL 1 AND 2:   Never!!

(*Spotlight on* MARÍA. MARÍA *goes to the mirror,* GIRL 3 *appears in the mirror.* MARÍA *brushes her hair and so does* GIRL 3. *Then* GIRL 3 *begins to touch herself in intimate ways, discovering the changes through puberty, while* MARÍA *remains still, not daring to touch herself. Finally, when* MARÍA *does dare to touch herself,* CARMEN *comes into the room and discovers her. Lights quickly come back on.*)

CARMEN: María, what are you doing?

MARÍA: Nothing.

CARMEN: María, were you . . . (*Before* MARÍA *can answer.*) It is a sin to do that. Good girls don't do that. (GIRL 3 *goes behind* MARÍA.)

GIRL 3 (*Whispering.*):   Why? Why? Why?

MARÍA: Why?

CARMEN (*Somewhat shocked.*):   Because it is dirty! Sex is dirty.

GIRL 3:   Why is it dirty? What makes it dirty?

MARÍA (*Suppresses and ignores* GIRL 3.):   I'm sorry, I didn't know what I was doing.

CARMEN: María, I'm telling you for your own good. Women should be pure. Men don't marry women who are not unless they have to. Quieren vírgenes. It's best that way, if you save yourself for your wedding night. Be submissive.

GIRL 3:   Why? Why? Why?

MARÍA: Yes, but . . . Why?

CARMEN: That's the way it is. I know it's not fair, but women will always be different from men. Ni modo.

MARÍA AND GIRL 3:   I don't understand. Why must a woman be submissive? Why is sex dirty? (GIRL 1 *appears.*)

GIRL 1:   María, stop questioning and just accept.

GIRL 3:   No, María! God gave you a brain to think and question. Use it!

GIRL 1:   But it is not up to us to decide what is right and what is wrong. Your parents know best, María. They love you and do things for you.

GIRL 3:   María, they are not always right . . .

RICARDO (*Interrupting the argument.*):   María! Come and help your mother with dinner right now!

MARÍA: All right! (*She goes to the table and chairs.*)

RICARDO: What do you do in your room? You spend so much time in there.

MARÍA: I was doing my homework.

RICARDO: It takes you all that time? (RICARDO *has the mail and pulls out a letter from the pile.*)

MARÍA: Yes, I want my work to be perfect so that I can win an award . . .

RICARDO: All for an award? How about if I give you a trophy for washing the dishes when you are supposed to, and for doing the laundry right?

(*He begins to read the letter.* MARÍA *searches through the pile. She finds a letter, reads it and becomes excited.*)

CARMEN (*To* RICARDO.):   Who's the letter from?

RICARDO: My cousin, Pedro.

CARMEN: What are you going to tell him?

RICARDO: The truth. I'm going to tell him his Martita did pendejadita and is due in three months. (*To* MARÍA.) What do I tell you?

CARMEN: Ayy, ¡qué vergüenza!

RICARDO: ¡Tanto estudio y para nada! It's such a waste to educate women. How is all that education helping her now. She's pregnant and on welfare . . . What's that smell? The tortillas are burning!

MARÍA: Ayyy!!!! (MARÍA *runs to the kitchen.*)

CARMEN: When you get married, what is your husband going to say?

MARÍA: I'm sorry; I completely forgot.

CARMEN: You can't cook, you can't clean . . .

MARÍA: I try to do all the chores you ask.

CARMEN: You can't do anything right. Not even the tortillas.

MARÍA: I really try . . .

RICARDO: No Mexican man is going to marry a woman who can't cook.

CARMEN: You're almost eighteen! (*Looks to* RICARDO.) I married your father when I was eighteen and I already knew how to do everything.

MARÍA: Mamá, papá, there are other more important things . . . (*She holds the letter, but decides not to say anything.*) I just don't care for housework.

(MARÍA *goes to her room. Spotlight on* MARÍA. *She looks at the letter and* GIRL 3 *appears. They look at the letter and* GIRL 3 *reads.*)

GIRL 3:   "Congratulations! You are eligible for a four-year scholarship . . . Please respond as soon as possible . . . "

(MARÍA *jumps up in excitement. She then gets a typewriter and begins to type her response. The typewriter is not working. She goes outside to look for her father. Fade out.*)

SCENE SEVEN

RICARDO *and* MARÍA *enter.*

MARÍA: Papá . . . ¿Está ocupado?

RICARDO: I'm reading the paper.

MARÍA: Do you think . . . well . . . maybe when you have finished reading you can fix this for me? Here is the manual.

(*She shows it to him. He pretends to look, but cannot understand it.*)

RICARDO: Go get my tool box. I'll do it my way.

(RICARDO *begins to check the typewriter carefully.* MARÍA *looks attentively and also tries to think of a way to introduce the subject of college.* GIRL 1 *appears.*)

GIRL 1:   There is no one who can take the place of my father, who loves me but cannot show it any other way. If I wasn't scared, I would hold you. I love you.

(RICARDO *finishes fixing the typewriter and hands it to* MARÍA.)

CARMEN: ¡Ayy! ¡Qué huebona! Where is María?

RICARDO: She's in her room typing. I fixed her typewriter.

CARMEN: What is she typing?

RICARDO: I don't know. Ask her.

CARMEN (*She goes to* MARÍA's *room.*):   María, come help me fold the clothes.

MARÍA: I'm busy!

CARMEN: Busy? Busy! Can't it wait? I have things to do, too.

MARÍA: All right. (*They start folding the clothes.* RICARDO *enters.*)

CARMEN: María, your birthday is almost here. Do you want me to make you a beautiful dress for your birthday? Maybe you can wear it for your graduation? Oh, our neighbor, la señora Martínez, told me today her daughter Rosario is graduating from a good business school. She says she already has a good job as a secretary.

MARÍA: Mamá, Papá, I don't want to be a secretary. (*Pause.*) I want to go to college.

RICARDO: What?

CARMEN: It's too expensive.

MARÍA (*Quickly.*):   I was awarded a big, four-year scholarship!

RICARDO: ¿Que? College? Scholarship?

CARMEN: ¿Para qué?

MARÍA: I want to be educated . . . (*Courageously.*) I want to be an actress.

RICARDO: You want to go to college to study to be an actress? ¿Estás loca?

CARMEN: Ayyy, María, you are crazy! You don't know what you want.

RICARDO: I didn't know you had to study to be a whore.

CARMEN: What have we done to make you want to leave us? We've tried to be good . . .

MARÍA: Nothing. It's not you. I want to be something.

RICARDO: Why don't you just get married like most decent women and be a housewife?

CARMEN: That's something.

RICARDO: That's respectable.

MARÍA: I don't understand what you are so afraid of . . .

RICARDO: I don't want you to forget that you are a Mexican. There are so many people where I work who deny they are Mexican. When their life gets better they stop being Mexican! To deny one's country is to deny one's past, one's parents. How ungrateful!

MARÍA: Papi, I won't. But you said that with an education I could be just as good as anybody. And that's why you brought me to America.

RICARDO: No. Get married!

MARÍA: I will. But I want a career as well. Women can now do both.

RICARDO: Don't tell me about modern women. What kind of wife would that woman make if she's busy with her career and can't tend to her house, children and husband.

MARÍA: And that's all a woman is for? To have children? Clean a house? Tend to her husband like a slave? And heat his tortillas?

RICARDO: ¡Qué atrevida! Why do you make it seem as if it would be some sort of nightmare? (*Sarcastically.*) Women have always gotten married and they have survived.

MARÍA: But surviving is not living.

CARMEN: María, listen to your father.

MARÍA: Papi, I listened to you. That's why! You encouraged me when I was young, but now you tell me I can't. Why?

RICARDO (*Trying to find an answer.*):   Because . . . you are a woman.

MARÍA: Papi, you're not being fair.

RICARDO (*Trying to keep face and control.*):   You ungrateful daughter! I don't want to see you. Get out of my face! (MARÍA *runs to her room, crying.*)

CARMEN: Ricardo, why don't you even let her try, ¿por favor? (*She goes to* MARÍA's *room.* RICARDO *stands, and then exits. Lights change to* MARÍA's *room.*) María, don't cry. Don't be angry at us either, and try to understand us. ¡M'ija! We are doing this for you. We don't want you to get hurt. You want too much; that's not realistic. You are a Mexican woman, and that's that. You can't change that. You are different from other women. Try to accept that. Women need to get married, they are no good without men.

MARÍA: Mami, I consider myself intelligent and ambitious, and what is that worth if I am a woman? Nothing?

CARMEN: You are worth a lot to me. I can't wait for the day when I will see you in a beautiful white wedding dress walking down the aisle with a church full of people. This is the most important event in a woman's life.

MARÍA: Mother, we are in America. Don't you realize you expect me to live in two worlds? How is it done? Can't things be different?

CARMEN: No sé. That's the way your father is. Ni modo.

MARÍA: Ni modo? Ni modo! Is that all you can say? Can't you do anything? (*Gives up on her and just explodes.*) ¡¡Ayy!! Get out! Get out!

(CARMEN *leaves and* MARÍA *continues to pound on her pillow with rage.* MARÍA *slowly begins to fall asleep. Fade out.*)

SCENE EIGHT

On the screen the following title is displayed: **The Dream.** GIRL 2, *who will now portray* MYTH, *appears. She wears a spring dress and looks virginal. She goes to* MARÍA.

MYTH (*Shaking* MARÍA *lightly.*):   María, get up and come see.

MARÍA: Who are you?

MYTH: I'm Myth. María, come see what can be.

MARÍA: What do you mean? What's going on?

MYTH: María, you are dreaming the American Dream. You can be anything you want to be. Follow me.

(*The sound of a horse is heard.*)

MARÍA: Is that a horse I'm hearing?

MYTH: See . . .

(A PRINCE *appears and he and* MYTH *begin to dance to a sweet melody. Just as they are about to kiss, the fierce sound of a whip accompanied by loud and wild cries of the horse running off are heard.*)

PRINCE (*In a very wimpy voice.*):   My horse! My horse!

(Runs off to catch his horse.)

MARÍA: What happened?

MYTH: I don't know.

(Another crack of the whip is heard, but now GIRL 3, who will portray "MARY," appears with the whip.)

MARY: Sorry to spoil the fairy tale, but Prince Charming was expected at the castle by Cinderella . . . Hello, María.

MARÍA: And who are you?

MARY: My name is Mary. It's my turn now, so get lost Myth!

(She snaps her finger and a large hook pulls MYTH offstage.)

MYTH: You're such a meanie!

MARY: Control, that's the thing to have. So come along and follow me!

MARÍA: Where are you taking me?

MARY: To liberation! Self independence, economic independence, sexual independence. We are free! María, in America, you can be anything you want to be. A lawyer. A doctor. An astronaut. An actress!!! The Mayor. Maybe even the President . . . of a company. You don't have to be obedient, submissive, gracious. You don't have to like dolls, dishes, cooking, children and laundry. Enjoy life! Enjoy liberation! Enjoy sex! Be free!

(GIRL 1, who will portray "MARÍA 2," appears brandishing a broom.)

MARÍA 2:   You bad woman! You bitch!

MARY: I'm not!

MARÍA 2:   You American demon. You are. You are. You just want to tempt her, then hurt her.

MARÍA *(Throwing MARY her whip.)*:   Mary, catch!

MARY: Thanks! Now we will see!

(MARÍA 2 and MARY have a mock sword combat, until a man blows a whistle and becomes a referee for a wrestling match.)

REFEREE *(Taking away the broom and the whip.)*:   All right, c'mon girls. I don't want weapons. Give them. *(The women push him away and charge at each other. MARY tries some dirty tricks.)* I told you I wanted this to be a clean fight. What were you using?

MARY: Nothing! I'm so innocent.

REFEREE: Now come over here and shake hands.

MARÍA 2 *(Asking the audience.)*:   Should I? Should I?

(Gets MARY's hand and twists it. They wrestle wildly, with MARY winning, then MARÍA 2. The REFEREE finally steps in.)

REFEREE: Break! Break! *(He holds MARY and pulls her out.)*

MARY *(Barely able to speak.)*:   María, before you are a wife, before you are a mother, first you are a woman! I'll be back.

(She's dragged out. MARÍA 2, who won the fight, acknowledges the cheers of the crowd, then gestures for MARÍA to kneel and pray. MARÍA 2 puts a wedding veil on MARÍA.)

MARÍA 2:   A woman's only purpose in life is to serve three men. Her father, her husband and her son. Her father.

(RICARDO *appears. He picks up* MARÍA *and escorts her to the church. The bells and the wedding march are heard. The following title is displayed:* **White Wedding.** MARÍA *walks down the aisle; the groom enters.*)

MARÍA 2:   Her husband.

(*The couple kneels and a wedding lasso is put around them.*)

PRIEST (*Same as first* PRIEST.):   Dearly beloved, we are gathered here, under the Catholic Church, in the holy House of God, to unite these two people in holy matrimony. Marriage is sacred. It is the unification of a man and a woman, their love and commitment, forever, and ever, and ever; no matter what! Well, then, let's begin . . . María, do you accept José Juan González García López as your lawfully wedded husband to love, cherish, serve, cook for, clean for, sacrifice for, have his children, keep his house, love him even if he beats you, commits adultery, gets drunk, rapes you lawfully, denies you your identity, money, love his family, serve his family, and in return ask for nothing?

MARÍA (*Thinks about it and turns to her parents.*):   I do.

PRIEST: Very good. Now, José. Do you accept María García González López as your lawfully wedded wife to support?

JOSÉ: I do.

PRIEST: Good. Well, if there is anyone present who is opposed to the union of these two people, speak now, or forever hold your truth. (RICARDO *stands up, takes out a gun and shows it to the audience.*) Do you have the ring? (JOSÉ *takes out a golden dog collar. The* PRIEST *gives it his blessings.*) Five, six, seven, eight. By the power vested in me, under the Catholic Church, in the holy House of God, I pronounce you husband and wife.

(*The* THREE GIRLS *take away* MARÍA*'s veil and bouquet. They place the dog collar around* MARÍA*'s neck. Then they get the lasso and tie it around her to make the collar work like a leash. To* JOSÉ.) You may pet the bride. (*The lasso is given to* JOSÉ. *He pulls* MARÍA, *who gets on her hands and knees. They walk down the aisle like dog and master. The wedding march plays, people begin to leave. Fade out.*)

SCENE NINE

A table and two chairs are placed in the center of the stage. MARÍA, *pregnant, walks in uncomfortably. She turns on the television, then the ensemble creates the television setting, playing roles of T.V. producer, director, make-up people, technicians, as if the actual studio is there. Brief dialogue is improvised to establish on-set frenzy.*

ANNOUNCER: And here is another chapter of your afternoon soap opera, "HAPPILY EVERAFTER." Our sultry Eliza Vázquez decides to leave Devero in search of freedom!

FLOOR MAN: Okay everyone, tape rolling, standby in ten seconds. Five, four, three, two . . .

(*He cues.*)

ACTRESS: Devero, I'm leaving you.
ACTOR: Eliza, why?
ACTRESS: I don't love you anymore. Actually, I never did.
ACTOR: Eliza, but I love you.
ACTRESS: I faked it, all of it. I did it because I had to. But now I must go and be free!

(MARÍA *claps loudly in excitement for her.*)

FLOOR MANAGER: Cut! (*To* MARÍA.) What are you doing here?
MARÍA: This is my living room.
FLOOR MANAGER: Oh, sure it is. Well go into the kitchen, make yourself a snack; we'll have the carpet cleaned in an hour. (*Pushes her aside.*) I know, I'm sorry . . . Standby. Five, four, three, two, one.
ACTRESS: . . . But now I must go and be free!
ACTOR: You can't do this to me!
ACTRESS: Oh, yes I can!
ACTOR: But I've given you everything!
ACTRESS: Everything but an identity! Well, Devero, Devero, Devero, I've discovered I no longer need you. There are unfulfilled dreams I must pursue. I want adventure.
FLOOR MANAGER: And . . . cut! That's a take. Roll commercial. Five seconds. Four, three, two, one.

(*The soap opera ends.* MARÍA *claps approvingly. A commercial quickly begins, with the ensemble creating a similar on-set frenzy. In the commercial a man comes home with a bottle of Ajax as a gift for his wife.*)

HUSBAND: Honey, I'm home! I brought you something. (*Hides the can treating it as if he had flowers.*)
WIFE: Hi, darling! (*They give each other a peck on the mouth from a distance.*) How was work?
HUSBAND: Fine . . . Ta–Dah! (*Presents the can.*)
WIFE: You shouldn't have. Oh, thank you! I need all the cleaning power I can get!
HUSBAND: I can smell you've been cleaning.
WIFE: Yes! I've mopped the floors, done the dishes, the laundry; this house is spotless.
HUSBAND: What a wife! (*They give each other another peck on the mouth from a distance.*) You're a good wife!

(MARÍA *goes to turn off the television. The doorbell rings. She goes to answer the door. It's her husband who grunts at her and comes in, asks for his dinner and sits at the table.*)

JOSÉ: María! María! I'm home. I'm hungry.
MARÍA: José, how was work? Dinner is ready. I made your favorite dish. Do you want to eat now? (JOSÉ *doesn't answer.*) Well, I'll serve you then. (MARÍA *places a plate on the table.*) My mother came to visit today and she asked me what we are going to name the baby. She thought it would be nice to call her Esperanza. (JOSÉ *grunts.*) Of course

it isn't going to be a girl. It's going to be a boy, and we'll name him after you. That would be nice, wouldn't it? (MARÍA *feels pains.*) Ayyy! How it hurts. I hope after the baby is born, I will be better. I've been getting so many pains, and I have a lot of stretchmarks . . . I know you don't like me to ask for money, but I need the money to buy a dress that fits. I have nothing I can wear anymore.

JOSÉ (*After a spoonful.*):   My dinner is cold.

MARÍA: Oh, is it cold? Well, I'll heat it up right now. It will only take a minute.

(MARÍA *runs to the kitchen.* JOSÉ *leaves the table and stares at the bed. The following title is displayed:* **The Sex Object.**

JOSÉ: María! ¡Mi amor! Come here, baby! . . . Come on, m'ijita. I won't hurt you . . .

(*He continues to try to persuade her. Eventually he gets his way. There are sounds of lust and pain. Finally,* MARÍA *gives out a loud scream of pain.*)

JOSÉ: What is it?

MARÍA: The baby!

(*Fade out.*)

SCENE TEN

The lights rise after the scream. MARÍA *spreads her legs wide open, covering herself with a white sheet.* THREE NURSES *run in. On the screen the following title is displayed:* **The Reproducing Machine or Be Fruitful.** *Dolls will be used as babies.*)

SALESMAN: Here we have it. Direct from Mexico. The Reproducing Machine. You can have one by calling our toll-free number. Get your pencil.

HEAD NURSE: Now, relax. Just breathe like this. (*Example.*) Ahhh!! All in good rhythm. Good! Don't worry, millions of women have children, especially Mexican women, they have millions. But you'll get used to it. After your fourth child, they'll just slide right on out.

MARÍA: 'Amá! Mamá!

HEAD NURSE: There's nothing I can do. I went through it myself. Now, isn't the pain great? You're giving birth! Why, it's the most satisfying feeling a woman can feel. Okay, I think it's coming! Push, Push, Push.

(*A baby pops up, flying into the air. It is caught by one of the nurses. She presents the baby to the* HEAD NURSE.)

HEAD NURSE: Oh, it's a girl.

NURSE 2 (*Presenting the baby to* JOSÉ.):   Here's your baby daughter.

JOSÉ: A daughter? How could you do this to me? Well, I'll have to call her Sacrifice.

(MARÍA *screams again.*)

HEAD NURSE: What is it?

MARÍA: There's another one inside; I can feel it!

HEAD NURSE: Nahhh! Well, I'll check just in case. (*She peeps under the sheet.*) Well, I'll be! Yeah, there's another one. Push! Push! Push!

(*Another baby pops into the air.* NURSE 3 *catches the baby.*)

NURSE 2 (*Presenting it to* JOSÉ.):   Here's another lovely daughter.

JOSÉ: Another daughter? I'll have to call her Abnegation.

SALESMAN (*Appearing from nowhere.*):   Here we have this amazing machine. The world renowned Reproducing Machine!

(MARÍA *screams again.*)

HEAD NURSE: What is it?

MARÍA: There's another one!

SALESMAN: Ahh, but if you were watching earlier, you saw the other amazing function. It can also be used as a sex object.

HEAD NURSE: Push! Push! Push!

(*Another baby pops up.*)

NURSE 4 (*Catching baby.*):   I got it.

SALESMAN: Yes siree! You can be the boss. It's at your disposal. Hours of pleasure. And if it ever does go out of control, a kick and a few punches will do the job and it will be back to normal.

NURSE 2:   Here's another one.

JOSÉ: Another girl? Why are you doing this to me? I'll call her Obligation.

SALESMAN: It's made in Mexico. It's cheap! It cooks! It cleans!

(MARÍA *screams again.*)

HEAD NURSE: Push! Push! Push!

(THREE BABIES *pop up into the air. Some land in the audience. All the nurses are busy collecting them.*)

SALESMAN: Its stretchmarks can stretch all the way from here to Tijuana. Not even a Japanese model can beat this one.

NURSE 2 (*To* JOSÉ.):   Guess what?

JOSÉ: No, don't tell me; another girl?

NURSE 2:   Surprise!

JOSÉ (*See babies.*):   Three girls! I'll call them Frustration, Regret, and Disappointment.

SALESMAN: It delivers up to twenty-one children. It feeds on beans, chile, and lies.

HEAD NURSE: Are there any more babies in that Mexican oven of yours?

MARÍA: I don't think so.

HEAD NURSE: See you in nine months for your next Mexican litter.

SALESMAN: You can have your own reproducing machine! Call the number on your screen now!

(*Fade out.*)

SCENE ELEVEN

Lights rise after a brief pause. On the stage is a table which serves as a crib for the six crying babies. On the screen the following title is displayed: **The Nightmare.** MARÍA *tries to quiet the babies by holding each one at a time, then by the bunch.* CARMEN, RICARDO *and* JOSÉ *enter. They stand behind her like demons.*

JOSÉ: Shut those babies up!

CARMEN: You're a bad wife!

RICARDO: This house is a mess!

CARMEN: You can't cook, you can't clean!

JOSÉ: Where's my dinner?

RICARDO: The dishes?

JOSÉ: My tortillas?

RICARDO: You're a bad wife!

CARMEN: I did it all my life!

JOSÉ: Bad wife!

MARÍA: No! I'm not! I'm a good wife! I try. I really do!

(MARÍA *goes to get the laundry and begins to fold it quickly, but nicely and carefully. Suddenly, the clothes begin to take on a life of their own. There is a giant coat, and a pair of pants surrounding* MARÍA. *They start pushing her around, then her wedding dress appears and heads towards* MARÍA's *neck. They wrestle on the ground.*)

CARMEN: Martyr!

(MARÍA *manages to get away, and runs upstage. As she is running, a giant tortilla with the Aztec Calendar emblem falls on her, smashing her to the ground.*)

MARÍA: Help!

RICARDO: Martyr!

(MARÍA *manages to get out from under the tortilla; as she escapes, she is attacked by a storm of plates.*)

MARÍA: Help!

RICARDO, CARMEN, *and* JOSÉ: Martyr!!! Martyr!!! Martyr!!!

MARÍA (*Becomes uncontrollably mad.*):   Enough! Do you want your dishes cleaned? I've got the perfect solution for them. (MARÍA *gestures. Sounds of dishes being smashed are heard.*) Now you don't have to worry. I'll buy you a million paper plates! Ohhhh! And the tortillas. Mamá! I'm going to show you how they should be done. (*She gets a bag of tortillas and begins tossing them into the audience like frisbees.*) Are these good enough? I hope so! I tried to get the top side cooked first . . . or was it last? Anyway, who cares! Here are the tortillas! (*Attacks her mother with a couple of tortillas.*) I hate doing the dishes! I hate doing the laundry! I hate cooking and cleaning! And I hate all housework because it offends me as a woman! (*There is a piercing moment of silence.*) That's right. I am a woman . . . a real woman of flesh and blood. This is not the life I want to live; I want more! And from now on I am directing my own life! Action!

(*Lights come fully on.* TWO GIRLS *grab and pull* MARÍA *harshly to take her to another place. The stage now becomes a courtroom.* MARÍA *is sat next to the* JUDGE. *The following title is displayed:* **The Trial.** *The courtroom is filled with people who create a lot of commotion. The* JUDGE, *the* BAILIFF, *and the* PROSECUTOR *enter.*)

BAILIFF: Please rise, the honorable hang-judge presiding.

JUDGE (*Bangs his gavel until everyone quiets down.* JUDGE *will be done by same actor who does* PRIEST.):   Quiet in my courtroom! I am warning you, anyone who causes any such commotion like this again will be thrown out! Is that understood! Let's begin!

BAILIFF: We are here today to give trial to María who is being accused by her husband of rebellion toward her implied duties of marriage.

JUDGE: How do you plead?

MARÍA: Plead? Innocent! Guilty! I don't know!

JUDGE: Are you making a joke out of my question?

MARÍA: No . . . Sir.

JUDGE: It sounds to me like you wish to challenge these laws.

MARÍA: I don't understand why I am on trial. What real laws have I broken?

JUROR 1:   She knows what she's guilty of.

JUROR 2:   She knows what laws not to break!

MARÍA: Who are they?

BAILIFF: Your jury.

MARÍA: But they are women, Mexican, traditional . . . They can't possibly be objective.

BAILIFF: They are a good jury.

MARÍA: This is unjust! I must speak up to this . . .

BAILIFF: You have no voice.

MARÍA: Where's my lawyer? I do get one, don't I?

(*The courtroom fills with cruel laughter, which quickly stops.*)

JUDGE: No, you defend yourself.

MARÍA: How do I defend myself when I can't speak?

PROSECUTOR (*To* MARÍA.):   You're dead meat, shrimp. (*To audience.*) This trial is meant to help preserve the institution of marriage. Ladies and gentlemen of the jury . . . in this case, ladies of the jury. A man's home is his castle. Where he has his foundation. It is the place where he comes home to his family, and he becomes the king of his castle. But this poor man comes home one evening and finds his children unattended, his house a mess, his dinner unprepared and his wife sitting back, watching soap operas!

MARÍA: I object!

JUDGE: You have no voice.

MARÍA: You said I was to defend myself.

JUDGE: Not now!

PROSECUTOR: What we are going to try to do is prove the guilt of this woman . . .

MARÍA: I object!

JUDGE: Shut up!

MARÍA: I won't!

JUDGE: Mister Prosecutor, call your first witness!

PROSECUTOR: I call Ricardo García to the witness stand. (RICARDO *takes the stand.*) Tell us about your daughter.

RICARDO: She was very obedient when she was young, but when she came to the United States she began to think of herself as "American" . . . She studied a lot, which is good, but she almost refused to do her chores because she thought herself above them.

PROSECUTOR: Could you tell us what happened that evening your daughter rebelled?

RICARDO: I'd rather not . . . That evening María was hysterical. She threw dishes, tortillas . . .

PROSECUTOR: Thank you, that will be all. My next witness will be Carmen García. (CARMEN *takes the stand.*) Tell us about your daughter.

CARMEN: She's really a good girl. She's just too dramatic sometimes. She's such a dreamer, forgive her.

PROSECUTOR: Could you tell us what you saw that evening?

CARMEN: Well, she was a little upset, so she did a few things she didn't mean to do.

MARÍA: No, Mamá! I meant it!

JUROR 1:   She admits it!

JUROR 2:   She's guilty!

ALL: Guilty!

CARMEN: No, she's just unrealistic.

MARÍA: I'm guilty then!

(*The whole courtroom becomes chaotic. Everyone yells out "guilty."* CARMEN *becomes so sad she begins to cry.*)

MARÍA: Mami, don't cry!

(*The lights go on and off and everyone disappears. Fade out.*)

SCENE TWELVE

MARÍA *begins to regain consciousness and wakes up from her dream. She is awakened by* CARMEN's *actual crying, which continues and grows.* MARÍA *gets up and listens to* CARMEN *and* RICARDO *arguing in the kitchen.*

RICARDO: ¡Cállate! Don't yell or María will hear you.

CARMEN: Then tell me, is it true what I am saying?

RICARDO: You're crazy! It wasn't me.

CARMEN: Con mis propios ojos I saw you and la señora Martínez meet in the morning by the park. You have been taking her to work and who knows what! Tell me, is it true? If you don't, I'm going to yell as loud as I can and let this whole neighborhood know what's going on.

RICARDO: Okay. It was me! ¿Estás contenta?

CARMEN: ¿Por qué? Why do you do this to me? And with our neighbor? She lives right in front of us.

RICARDO: Look, every man sooner or later does it.

CARMEN: Do you think I don't know about all of your affairs before la señora Martínez? She is not your first! I never said anything before because I was afraid you would send us back to Mexico. But now I don't care! You break it with that bitch or . . . I'll kill her and you. ¡Ayyy! Ricardo, I've endured so much for you. I knew you were no angel when we ran off together, but I thought you would change. You would change, because you loved me. I love you, Ricardo! But I can no longer go on living like this or I'll be betraying myself and I'll be betraying María.

RICARDO: Carmen, ¡ven aquí! Carmen, wait!

(CARMEN *and* RICARDO *exit. The* THREE GIRLS *enter.* GIRL 3 *hands* MARÍA *a piece of paper and a pen.*)

MARÍA: "Dear Mamá and Papá. Last night I heard everything. Now I know that your idea of life is not for me—so I am leaving. I want to create a world of my own. One that combines the best of me. I won't forget the values of my roots, but I want to get the best from this land of opportunities. I am going to college and I will struggle to do something with my life. You taught me everything I needed to know. Goodbye."

GIRL 1:   Los quiero mucho. Nunca los olvidaré.

GIRL 2:   Mexico is in my blood . . .

GIRL 3:   And America is in my heart.

MARÍA: "Adiós."

(*Fade out.*)

(*1994*)

QUESTIONS FOR REFLECTION

Experience

1. To what extent can you identify with either the minority or gender experience depicted in Lopéz's play?

Interpretation

2. Explain how López distinguishes among her two groups or types of characters.
3. Explain the effect of the play's opening scene. What does the allusion to Shakespeare's *Romeo and Juliet* accomplish?
4. What stereotypes about Mexican men and women does López present in Scene 2? What is her attitude toward these cultural stereotypes?
5. What political ideas emerge from Scene 3? What distinction is made between European and Mexican immigrants in America?
6. What images of America does the play present? How does María see America and her place in it?
7. Identify and explain the function of three types of sound effects included in the play.
8. Explain the relevance of Scene 8—the "dream scene." Comment on the names of the characters who appear in this scene. Compare the marriage vows and ceremony in Scene 8 with those of Scene 2.

9. Explain the function of the screen and the titles projected on it throughout the play.

Evaluation

10. What conflicting values does the play describe? What perspective is offered on the conflict between Mexican and American cultural attitudes toward sex, for example, toward gender roles, and toward self-fulfillment?
11. What images of marriage and motherhood does the play present? What perspectives are offered on them?

Critical Perspectives and Research

PART FOUR

CHAPTER TWENTY-TWO

Critical Theory: Approaches to the Analysis and Interpretation of Literature

READINGS FOR ANALYSIS

WILLIAM CARLOS WILLIAMS
[1883–1963]

The Use of Force

They were new patients to me, all I had was the name, Olson. Please come down as soon as you can, my daughter is very sick.

When I arrived I was met by the mother, a big startled looking woman, very clean and apologetic who merely said, Is this the doctor? and let me in. In the back, she added. You must excuse us, doctor, we have her in the kitchen where it is warm. It is very damp here sometimes.

The child was fully dressed and sitting on her father's lap near the kitchen table. He tried to get up, but I motioned for him not to bother, took off my overcoat and started to look things over. I could see that they were all very nervous, eyeing me up and down distrustfully. As often, in such cases, they weren't telling me more than they had to, it was up to me to tell them; that's why they were spending three dollars on me.

The child was fairly eating me up with her cold, steady eyes, and no expression to her face whatever. She did not move and seemed, inwardly, quiet; an unusually attractive little thing, and as strong as a heifer in appearance. But her face was flushed, she was breathing rapidly, and I realized that she had a high fever. She had magnificent blonde hair, in profusion. One of those picture children often reproduced in advertising leaflets and the photogravure sections of the Sunday papers.

She's had a fever for three days, began the father, and we don't know what it comes from. My wife has given her things, you know, like people do, but it don't do no good. And there's been a lot of sickness around. So we tho't you'd better look her over and tell us what is the matter.

As doctors often do I took a trial shot at it as a point of departure. Has she had a sore throat?

Both parents answered me together, No . . . No, she says her throat don't hurt her.

Does your throat hurt you? added the mother to the child. But the little girl's expression didn't change, nor did she move her eyes from my face.

Have you looked?

I tried to, said the mother, but I couldn't see.

As it happens, we had been having a number of cases of diphtheria in the school to which this child went during that month and we were all, quite apparently, thinking of that, though no one had as yet spoken of the thing.

Well, I said, suppose we take a look at the throat first. I smiled in my best professional manner and asking for the child's first name I said, come on, Mathilda, open your, mouth and let's take a look at your throat.

Nothing doing.

Aw, come on, I coaxed, just open your mouth wide and let me take a look. Look, I said opening both hands wide. I haven't anything in my hands. Just open up and let me see.

Such a nice man, put in the mother. Look how kind he is to you. Come on, do what he tells you to. He won't hurt you.

At that I ground my teeth in disgust. If only they wouldn't use the word "hurt" I might be able to get somewhere. But I did not allow myself to be hurried or disturbed, but speaking quietly and slowly I approached the child again.

As I moved my chair a little nearer, suddenly with one catlike movement both her hands clawed instinctively for my eyes and she almost reached them too. In fact she knocked my glasses flying and they fell, though unbroken, several feet away from me on the kitchen floor.

Both the mother and father almost turned themselves inside out in embarrassment and apology. You bad girl, said the mother, taking her and shaking her by one arm. Look what you've done. The nice man. . . .

For heaven's sake, I broke in. Don't call me a nice man to her. I'm here to look at her throat on the chance that she might have diphtheria and possibly die of it. But that's nothing to her. Look here, I said to the child, we're going to look at your throat. You're old enough to understand what I'm saying. Will you open it now by yourself or shall we have to open it for you?

Not a move. Even her expression hadn't changed. Her breaths however were coming faster and faster. Then the battle began. I had to do it. I had to have a throat culture for her own protection. But first I told the parents that it was entirely up to them. I explained the danger but said that I would not insist on a throat examination so long as they would take the responsibility.

If you don't do what the doctor says you'll have to go to the hospital, the mother admonished her severely.

Oh yeah? I had to smile to myself. After all, I had already fallen in love with the savage brat, the parents were contemptible to me. In the ensuing struggle they grew more and more abject, crushed, exhausted while she surely rose to magnificent heights of insane fury of effort bred of her terror of me.

The father tried his best, and he was a big man but the fact that she was his daughter, his shame at her behavior and his dread of hurting her made him release her just at the critical moment several times when I had almost achieved success, till I wanted to kill him. But his dread also that she might have diphtheria made him tell me to go on, go on though he himself was almost fainting, while the mother moved back and forth behind us raising and lowering her hands in an agony of apprehension.

Put her in front of you on your lap, I ordered, and hold both her wrists.

But as soon as he did the child let out a scream. Don't, you're hurting me. Let go of my hands. Let them go I tell you. Then she shrieked terrifyingly, hysterically. Stop it! Stop it! You're killing me!

Do you think she can stand it, doctor! said the mother.

You get out, said the husband to his wife. Do you want her to die of diphtheria?

Come on now, hold her, I said.

Then I grasped the child's head with my left hand and tried to get the wooden tongue depressor between her teeth. She fought, with clenched teeth, desperately! But now I also had grown furious—at a child. I tried to hold myself down but I couldn't. I know how to expose a throat for inspection. And I did my best. When finally I got the wooden spatula behind the last teeth and just the point of it into the mouth cavity, she opened up for an instant but before I could see anything she came down again and gripping the wooden blade between her molars she reduced it to splinters before I could get it out again.

Aren't you ashamed, the mother yelled at her. Aren't you ashamed to act like that in front of the doctor?

Get me a smooth-handled spoon of some sort, I told the mother. We're going through with this. The child's mouth was already bleeding. Her tongue was cut and she was screaming in wild hysterical shrieks. Perhaps I should have desisted and come back in an hour or more. No doubt it would have been better. But I have seen at least two children lying dead in bed of neglect in such cases, and feeling that I must get a diagnosis now or never I went at it again. But the worst of it was that I too had got beyond reason. I could have torn the child apart in my own fury and enjoyed it. It was a pleasure to attack her. My face was burning with it.

The damned little brat must be protected against her own idiocy, one says to one's self at such times. Others must be protected against her. It is social necessity. And all these things are true. But a blind fury, a feeling of adult shame, bred of a longing for muscular release are the operatives. One goes to the end.

In a final unreasoning assault I overpowered the child's neck and jaws. I forced the heavy silver spoon back of her teeth and down her throat till she gagged. And there it was—both tonsils covered with membrane. She had fought valiantly to keep me from knowing her secret. She had been hiding that sore throat for three days at least and lying to her parents in order to escape just such an outcome as this.

Now truly she was furious. She had been on the defensive before but now she attacked. Tried to get off her father's lap and fly at me while tears of defeat blinded her eyes.

EMILY DICKINSON
[1830–1886]

I'm "wife"—I've finished that—
That other state—
I'm Czar—I'm "Woman" now—
It's safer so—

How odd the Girl's life looks
Behind this soft Eclipse—
I think that Earth feels so
To folks in Heaven—now—

This being comfort—then
That other kind—was pain—
But why compare?
I'm "Wife"! Stop there!

THE CANON AND THE CURRICULUM

Interpreting literature is an art and a skill that readers develop with experience and practice. Regular reading of stories, poems, plays, and essays will give you opportunities to become a skillful interpreter. Simply reading the literary works, however, is not enough, not if you wish to participate in the invigorating critical conversations teachers and other experienced readers bring to their discussion of literature. To develop a sense of the interpretive possibilities of literary works, you will need to know something of the various critical perspectives that literary critics use to analyze and interpret literature. This chapter introduces you to a number of major critical perspectives, including historical, biographical, psychological, and sociological approaches (among others), each of which approaches the study of literature a different way.

This discussion of critical perspectives aims to provide you with a set of ideas about how literature can be analyzed and interpreted. It is not designed to explain the history of literary criticism. Nor is its goal to convert you to a particular critical approach. Neither has any attempt been made to present the intricacies and variations in interpretive analysis developed by proponents of the various critical perspectives. And although you will find in this chapter discussions of ten critical perspectives, still other approaches to literary interpretation are available, both older ones that have currently declined in use and newer approaches that are still emerging.

Before considering the first of our critical perspectives, that of formalist criticism, we should review some basic questions currently being debated, sometimes heatedly, throughout the educational establishment. You may have already heard about the controversy surrounding the literary "canon" or list of works considered suitable for study in a university curriculum. There is now considerable disagreement about just what books should be read in college courses, why they should be read, and how they should be read. As a way of putting the ten critical perspectives in context, we will take up each of these questions in a brief overview of the current debate about the university literature curriculum.

What We Read

The notion of a literary canon or collection of accepted books derives from the idea of a biblical canon—those books accepted as official scriptures. A scriptural canon contains those works deemed to represent the moral standards and religious beliefs of a particular group, Jews for example, or Muslims, Hindus, or Christians. A canon of accepted works also contains, by implication, its obverse or flip side— that some works are excluded from the canon. Just as certain works, such as the Book of Maccabees, were not accepted into the Hebrew Scriptures and the Gospel of Thomas was denied entry into the Christian New Testament, not every book or literary work written can become part of an officially sanctioned literary canon or a university curriculum. Certain works inevitably will be omitted while others just as necessarily are selected for inclusion. The central question revolves around which works should be included in the canon, and why.

As you may know, certain "classics" for a long time have dominated the canon of literature for study in university courses—epic poems by Homer and Dante, for example, plays by Ibsen and Shakespeare, poems by writers from many countries, but especially those from Europe and America, novels such as Charles Dickens's *Great Expectations,* Jane Austen's *Pride and Prejudice,* Mark Twain's *The Adventures of Huckleberry Finn*, Emily Bronte's *Wuthering Heights,* and many others. In the last two decades, however, there has been a movement to alter the canon of classical works, most of which have been written by white males of European ancestry, in the more or less distant past. Some of the changes in what we read have come from adding works by writers long omitted, such as those by minority writers—African Americans, Native Americans, Asian Americans, and other writers from around the world beyond Europe, those from Australia, India, and Africa, for example. The works added by minority writers have been largely, though not exclusively, modern and contemporary ones.

Still other changes in the literary canon have come from the rediscovery or recovery of older works, many from the Renaissance and the nineteenth century, especially works by women, which had for a long time been considered unworthy of serious study and of inclusion in college literature curricula. Such works were considered not to have withstood the test of time, lasting decades or centuries, as have the classics. What needs to be remembered, however, is that "time" is an abstraction that itself accomplishes nothing. It is, rather, individuals throughout time who make the choices about which books are to be taught in schools and universities. And it is people today of both genders and of various cultures, races, ethnicities, and sexual dispositions who are debating not only what works should be part of the canon of literature but whether the very idea of a canon is viable at all. In other words, what is a canon for? Is a literary canon inevitable? Is it even necessary?

Why We Read

These changes in what we read are related to a debate about why we read. Classic novels and plays, stories and poems have long been read because the lessons they are presumed to teach are considered valuable. The meanings of certain American canonical works, for example, have been viewed as educationally and morally good for readers to assimilate, largely because the works are believed to reflect values central to the American way of life. They reflect values relating to the importance of friendship, responsible behavior, and hard work, for example, or values relating to decency, justice, and fair play. Of course, other works accepted into the literary canon taught in American colleges and universities do not reflect such views, both works written by American writers and works by writers of other nationalities and literary traditions, many of which are included in this book.

It is certainly the case that regardless of the language(s) and tradition(s) represented by a canon of literary works, those works are often canonized because they are believed to perpetuate a tradition of moral beliefs, cultural attitudes, and social dispositions. What is interesting to note, however, is that canonical literary works of many traditions and genres—Henrik Ibsen's *A Doll House,* for example, or Emily Dickinson's lyric poems—disrupt and run counter to many traditional literary, social, religious, and cultural values. And works such as Shakespeare's tragedies and Keats's and Wordsworth's poetry harbor ideas and attitudes about which common readers and professional critics have long disagreed, a disagreement that derives partly from varying critical perspectives used to interpret the works and partly from their richness and complexity, which makes it impossible to say once and for all just what those enticing and intellectually provocative works mean.

Another reason for the continuity of the traditional canon is that it is easier to preserve the status quo than to initiate change. Change is neither welcomed nor embraced, even when it is inevitable. Moreover, later generations read the books of former ones because earlier generations want their descendants to read and value what they read and valued. Those earlier generations have the power to enforce such a decision since they hold the positions of authority in schools and on councils that design curricula and create reading lists for school programs and university courses.

Today, however, many of these assumptions have been reevaluated by teachers and critics from a wide range of political persuasions. With the demographic changes that have been occurring in educational institutions in the past quarter century have come additional reasons for reading. Minority groups that now form a significant population in university classrooms, minority teachers, younger faculty raised in a much altered political environment, large numbers of women faculty—all insist on the need for multiple perspectives, varying voices, different visions of experience. They argue that literary works should be read to challenge conventional ways of behaving and orthodox ways of thinking. (Some educators say that there is nothing new in this, and that, in fact, traditional canonical works have long been read this way.) For some of these other readers, however, literature exists less for moral instruction or cultural education than to help inaugurate political and social change, a view that is less widely endorsed than the view that literary works should invite critical scrutiny and stimulate questioning and debate.

How We Read

That brings us to the important question of how we read. Just how do we read? Do we simply "just read"? And if we do, then what do we mean by "just reading"? Most often just reading means something on the order of reading for pleasure, without worrying about analysis and interpretation. From the standpoint of more analytical reading, "just reading" refers to interpreting the words on the page, making sense of them in a way that seems reasonable.

But a number of assumptions lie behind this notion. One such assumption is that the meaning of a literary work is available to anyone willing to read it carefully. Another is that literary works contain layers or levels of meaning, that they have to be analyzed to understand their complex meanings. Still another is that although different readers all bring their unique experience as members of particular genders, races, religions, and nationalities to their interpretation of literary works, they finally understand the meaning of those works in the same way. In this view, literary works such as *Hamlet* or *The Scarlet Letter* mean the same thing to every reader.

Each of these assumptions, however, has been challenged by literary theorists in the past two decades, to the extent that many serious readers find them untenable. It doesn't take long, for example, to realize that though we share some understanding of Shakespeare's play or Hawthorne's novel, we invariably see different things in them and see them differently. The differences we make of literary works and the different ways we understand them are related to the varying assumptions about literature and life that we bring to our reading. The different ways these assumptions have been modified and the different emphases and focuses serious readers and literary critics bring to bear on literary works can be categorized according to various approaches or critical perspectives. Ten critical perspectives are here presented, though others could be added. These ten, however, reflect critical positions that many academic readers find useful, whether they are reading works new to the canon or older established ones.

For each critical perspective you will find an overview that introduces the critical approach, an application of the critical perspective to the Williams short story and the Dickinson poem reprinted at the beginning of this chapter, and a list of questions you can use to apply the critical perspective to other literary works. A set of selected readings concludes each section.

Think of these ten critical perspectives as a kind of critical smorgasbord, a set of intellectual dishes you can sample and taste. Those you find most appealing you may wish to partake of more heartily, partly by applying them in your own analytical writing, partly by reading from the list of selected books. Or your instructor may encourage you to work with ones he or she believes are especially valuable. The important thing to realize, however, is that you always interpret a literary work from a theoretical standpoint, however hidden or implicit it may be. Understanding the assumptions and procedures of the various theoretical perspectives is crucial for understanding what you are doing when you interpret literature, how you do it, and why you do it that way.

In his lively book introducing college students to literary theory, *Falling Into Theory* (1994), David H. Richter of Queens College CUNY summarizes the important issues concerning literary studies today in a series of provocative questions. Richter organizes his questions according to the categories I have borrowed from him for this introductory overview: *why we read, what we read, how we read.* Keep Richter's guiding questions in mind as you read the discussion of the various critical perspectives.

> *Why we read.* What is the place of the humanities and literary studies in society? Why should we study literature? Why do we read?
> *What we read.* What is literature and who determines what counts as literature? Is there a core of "great books" that every student should read? What is the relationship of literature by women and minority groups to the canon? Are criteria of quality universal, or are literary values essentially political?
> *How we read.* How do we and how should we read texts? Does meaning reside in the author, the text, or the reader? To what degree is the meaning of a text fixed? What ethical concerns do we bring to texts as readers, and how do these concerns reshape the texts we read? What do we owe the text and what does it owe us? How do the politics of race and gender shape our reading of texts? Do political approaches to literature betray or shed light on them?

Canon and Curriculum: Selected Readings

To learn more about the controversy surrounding the literary canon and the college English curriculum, the following books provide a variety of perspectives on the issues.

Alter, Robert. *The Pleasures of Reading in an Ideological Age.* 1989.

Atlas, James. *The Battle of the Books.* 1990.

D'Souza, Dinesh. *Illiberal Education: The Politics of Sex and Race on Campus.* 1991.

Eagleton, Terry. *Literary Theory: An Introduction.* 1983.

Graff, Gerald. *Beyond the Culture Wars.* 1992.

Greenblatt, Stephen, and Giles Gunn. *Redrawing the Boundaries: The Transformation of English and American Literary Studies.* 1992.

Kimball, Roger. *Tenured Radicals: How Politics Has Corrupted Higher Education.* 1990.

Lauter, Paul. *Canons and Contexts.* 1991.

Lentricchia, Frank. *Criticism and Social Change.* 1983.

Levine, George et al. *Speaking for the Humanities.* 1989.

Richter, David. *Falling Into Theory.* 1994.

Scholes, Robert. *Textual Power.* 1985.

FORMALIST PERSPECTIVES

An Overview of Formalist Criticism

Formalist critics view literature as a distinctive art, one that uses the resources of language to shape experience, communicate meaning, and express emotion. Formalists emphasize the form of a literary work to determine its meaning, focusing on literary elements such as plot, character, setting, diction, imagery, structure, and point of view. Approaching literary works as independent systems with interdependent parts, formalists typically subordinate biographical information or historical data in their interpretations. Underlying formalist critical perspectives is the belief that literary works are unified artistic wholes that can be understood by analyzing their parts.

According to the formalist view, the proper concern of literary criticism is with the work itself rather than with literary history, the life of the author, or a work's social and historical contexts. For a formalist, the central meaning of a literary work is discovered through a detailed analysis of the work's formal elements rather than by going outside the work to consider other issues, whether biographical, historical, psychological, social, political, or ideological. Such additional considerations, from the formalist perspective, are extrinsic, or external, and are of secondary importance. What matters most to the formalist critic is how the work comes to mean what it does—how its resources of language are deployed by the writer to convey meaning. Implicit in the formalist perspective, moreover, is that readers can indeed determine the meanings of literary works—that literature can be understood and its meanings clarified.

Two other tenets of formalist criticism deserve mention: (1) that a literary work exists independent of any particular reader—that is, that a literary work exists outside of any reader's re-creation of it in the act of reading; (2) that the greatest literary works are "universal," their wholeness and aesthetic harmony transcending the specific particularities they describe.

The primary method of formalism is a close reading of the literary text, with an emphasis, for example, on a work's use of metaphor or symbol, its deployment of irony, its patterns of image or action. Lyric poetry lends itself especially well to the kinds of close reading favored by formalist critics because its language tends to be more compressed and metaphorical than the language of prose—at least as a general rule. Nonetheless, formal analysis of novels and plays can also focus on close reading of key passages (the opening and closing chapters of a novel, for example, or the first and last scenes of a play, or a climactic moment in the action of drama, poetry, or fiction). In addition, formalist critics analyze the large-scale structures of longer works, looking for patterns and relationships among scenes, actions, and characters.

One consistent feature of formalist criticism is an emphasis on tension and ambiguity. Tension refers to the way elements of a text's language reflect conflict and opposition. Ambiguity refers to the ways texts remain open to more than a single, unified, definitive interpretation. Both tension and ambiguity as elements of formalist critical approaches were picked up and elaborated to serve different interpretive arguments by critics employing the methodologies of structuralism and deconstruction.

The previous chapters of *Literature* titled "Elements" in particular illustrate and apply techniques of formal analysis. In Chapter Three, "Elements of Fiction," in the section "Setting," for example, a paragraph from William Faulkner's short story "A Rose for Emily" is analyzed to show how one literary element—setting—functions in the story as a whole. In the same section of that chapter, the setting of Kate Chopin's "The Story of an Hour" is described in symbolic terms. Analogously, for poetry, in the chapter "Elements of Poetry," in the section "Diction," the connotation of Wordsworth's diction in "I wandered lonely as a cloud" is analyzed to show how Wordsworth's language relates to the image patterns he creates and how diction and imagery contribute to the poem's meaning. Throughout *Literature* you will find numerous examples of formal analysis. You can use the many focused brief analyses in these chapters in particular to model your own close readings of works in each of the three literary genres in terms of formalist criticism.

Thinking from a Formalist Perspective

A formalist critic reading William Carlos Williams's "The Use of Force" might consider how the story begins and ends, contrasting its opening matter-of-fact objective description with its concluding shift of perspective and heightening of language. A formalist perspective would typically include observations about the relations among the characters, particularly the doctor, who is clearly an outsider among the poor parents, and who is invited in among them only because they are desperate to help their sick daughter. Character relations are of paramount interest in Williams's story since a conflict occurs between the doctor and his patient, one that is resolved only through the use of force. The relations between the doctor and the parents are equally interesting, since their surface behavior contrasts with their feelings about each other.

Other aspects of the story of interest from a formalist perspective would include the writer's use of first-person narration, especially the way the narrator's thoughts are made known to readers (less through dialogue than through a kind of interior monologue that readers "overhear"). A formalist critic might ask what difference it would make if the story were told in the third person, or if the narrator's ideas were to be voiced in direct dialogue. At a key moment—a climactic one, in fact—the story shifts from internal report of the doctor's thoughts to direct dialogue. A formalist would be interested in the effects of this shift, especially in its artistic effectiveness.

A formalist critic reading Emily Dickinson's "I'm 'wife'" would note its neat division into three stanzas and consider the focus of each. A formalist perspective would consider why, in fact, the poem is cast in three stanzas and not one or two, four, or six. A consideration of the relationship between form and meaning might help readers notice how the poem's rhyme scheme and its sentence patterns reinforce or subvert its stanza organization.

Other considerations formalist critics would be likely to raise about the poem might include the connotations of "Czar" for the speaker. Of particular importance in this regard would be the language used to describe the "Girl's life" in the second stanza, especially how it is described as existing behind a "soft Eclipse." Readers following a formalist agenda might also question how the slant rhymes of the poem contribute to its idea and its effect.

Such questions, however, are only a starting point toward a formal analysis of Williams's story and Dickinson's poem.

A CHECKLIST OF FORMALIST CRITICAL QUESTIONS

1. How is the work structured or organized? How does it begin? Where does it go next? How does it end? What is the work's plot? How is its plot related to its structure?
2. What is the relationship of each part of the work to the work as a whole? How are the parts related to one another?
3. Who is narrating or telling what happens in the work? How is the narrator, speaker, or character revealed to readers? How do we come to know and understand this figure?
4. Who are the major and minor characters, what do they represent, and how do they relate to one another?
5. What are the time and place of the work—its setting? How is the setting related to what we know of the characters and their actions? To what extent is the setting symbolic?

6. What kind of language does the author use to describe, narrate, explain, or otherwise create the world of the literary work? More specifically, what images, similes, metaphors, symbols appear in the work? What is their function? What meanings do they convey?

Formalist Criticism: Selected Readings

Brooks, Cleanth. *The Well Wrought Urn: Studies in the Structure of Poetry.* 1947.
Burke, Kenneth. *Counterstatement.* 1930.
Eliot, T. S. *Selected Essays.* 1932.
Empson, William. *Seven Types of Ambiguity.* 1930.
Ransom, John Crowe. *The New Criticism.* 1941.
Wellek, Rene, and Austin Warren. *Theory of Literature.* 1949, 1973.
Wimsatt, W. K. *The Verbal Icon.* 1954.

BIOGRAPHICAL PERSPECTIVES

Overview of Biographical Criticism

To what extent a writer's life should be brought to bear on an interpretation of his or her work has long been a matter of controversy. Some critics insist that biographical information at best distracts from and at worst distorts the process of analyzing, appreciating, and understanding literary works. These critics believe that literary works must stand on their own, stripped of the facts of their writers' lives.

Against this view, however, can be placed one that values the information readers gain from knowing about writers' lives. Biographical critics argue that there are essentially three kinds of benefits readers acquire from using biographical evidence for literary interpretation: (1) readers understand literary works better since the facts about authors' experiences can help readers decide how to interpret those works; (2) readers can better appreciate a literary work for knowing the writer's struggles or difficulties in creating it; and (3) readers can better assess writers' preoccupations by studying the ways they modify and adjust their actual experience in their literary works.

Knowing, for example, that Shakespeare was an actor who performed in the plays he wrote provides an added dimension to our appreciation of his genius. It also might invite us to look at his plays from the practical standpoint of a performer rather than merely from the perspective of an armchair reader, a classroom student, or a theatergoer. Or to realize that Ernest Hemingway's stories derive from experiences he had in Africa hunting big game and from World War I, and his numerous marriages may lead readers to see just how the life and work are related, especially to see how Hemingway selected from and shaped his actual experience to create his short stories. Again the more circumscribed life led by Emily Dickinson may bear on our reading of her work. Considering biographical information and using it to analyze the finished literary work can be illuminating rather than distracting or distorting. Thinking about the different alternative titles a writer may have considered can also lead readers to focus on different aspects of a work, especially to emphasize different incidents and to value the viewpoints of different characters. As with any critical approach, however, a biographical perspective should be used judiciously, keeping the focus on the literary work and using the biographical information to clarify understanding and to develop an interpretation.

A biographical critic can focus on a writer's works not only to enhance understanding of them individually but also to enrich a reader's understanding of the artist. In an essay on the relations between literature and biography, Leon Edel, author of an outstanding biography of Henry James, suggests that what the literary biographer seeks to discover about the subject are his or her characteristic ways of thinking, perceiving, and feeling that may be revealed more honestly and thoroughly in the writer's work than in his or her conscious nonliterary statements. In addition, what we learn about writers from a judicious study of their work can also be linked with an understanding of the writer's world, and thus serve as a bridge to an appreciation of the social and cultural contexts in which the writer lived.

Thinking from a Biographical Perspective

Whether one focuses on formalist questions to analyze "The Use of Force" or on other issues such as the doctor's psychological impulses or the power struggles among doctor, patient, and parents, biographical information can add to a reader's appreciation of the story. In addition to being a writer, William Carlos Williams was a doctor, a pediatrician with a practice in Rutherford, New Jersey. Williams never gave up medicine for literature, as some other writers did. Instead he continued to treat patients all his life. In fact, he acquired some of the raw material for his poetry, fiction, and essays directly from his practice of medicine.

Another biographical fact of interest is that Williams did some of his writing between seeing patients. He would typically jot notes, write lines of poems, sketch outlines for stories, record dialogue, and otherwise fill the gaps in his time with his writing. Some have suggested that Williams's many short sketches, brief stories, and short poems result directly from this method of composing. Of course, Williams did not do all of his writing in the short bursts of time between seeing his patients. He also wrote during vacations and more extended blocks of time. And Williams did, in fact, write one of the longest American poems of the century, *Paterson,* a book-length poem in five long sections, written and published over a period of more than twenty years.

Of biographical interest regarding Dickinson's "I'm 'wife'" is the fact that Dickinson never married. A critic with a biographical bent might see in this early poem themes and concerns that became important preoccupations for the poet, issues of gender and power, concerns about the relationship between men and women in marriage, both a marriage she may have wanted for herself and the marriage of her brother, a marriage that some biographers argue was a disappointment to her, though one she initially encouraged. Biographical questions of interest would focus on whether Dickinson's poem was based on her own experience, perhaps on frustrated hopes, or whether it was simply a metaphor she played with poetically to deflect the circumstances of everyday reality.

A CHECKLIST OF BIOGRAPHICAL CRITICAL QUESTIONS

1. What influences—persons, ideas, movements, events—evident in the writer's life does the work reflect?
2. To what extent are the events described in the work a direct transfer of what happened in the writer's actual life?
3. What modifications of the actual events has the writer made in the literary work? For what possible purposes?
4. Why might the writer have altered his or her actual experience in the literary work?
5. What are the effects of the differences between actual events and their literary transformation in the poem, story, play, or essay?
6. What has the author revealed in the work about his or her characteristic modes of thought, perception, or emotion? What place does this work have in the artist's literary development and career?

Biographical Criticism: Selected Readings

Edel, Leon. *Henry James,* 5 vols. 1953–1972.
Farr, Judith. *The Passion of Emily Dickinson.* 1992.
Mariani, Paul. *William Carlos Williams: A New World Naked.* 1981.
Sewall, Richard B. *The Life of Emily Dickinson,* 2 vols. 1974.
Williams, William Carlos. *Autobiography.* 1951, 1967.
Wolff, Cynthia Griffin. *Emily Dickinson.* 1986.

HISTORICAL PERSPECTIVES

An Overview of Historical Criticism

Historical critics approach literature in two ways: (1) they provide a context of background information necessary for understanding how literary works were perceived in their time; (2) they show how literary works reflect ideas and attitudes of the time in which they were written. These two general approaches to historical criticism represent methods and approaches that might be termed "old historicism" and "new historicism" respectively.

The older form of historical criticism, still in use today, insists that a literary work be read with a sense of the time and place of its creation. This is necessary, insist historical critics, because every literary work is a product of its time and its world. Understanding the social background and the intellectual currents of that time and that world illuminate literary works for later generations of readers.

Knowing something about the London of William Blake's time, for example, helps readers better appreciate and understand the power of Blake's protest against horrific social conditions and the institutions of church and state Blake held responsible for permitting such conditions to exist. In his poem "London," Blake refers to chimney sweepers, who were usually young children small enough to fit inside a chimney, and whose parents sent them to a kind of work that drastically curtailed not only their childhood but also their lives. Or, to take another example, understanding something about the role and position of women in late nineteenth-century America helps readers of the late twentieth century better understand the protagonist of Kate Chopin's "The Story of an Hour." Readers might appreciate why, for example, Mrs. Mallard feels the need to escape from her marriage and why her feelings are described by turns as exhilarating and "monstrous."

Thinking from a New Historicist Perspective

Like earlier historical approaches, a more contemporary approach identified as "new historicism" considers historical contexts of literary works essential for understanding them. A significant difference, however, between earlier historical criticism and new historicism is the newer variety's emphasis on analyzing historical documents with the same intensity and scrutiny given foregrounded passages in the literary works to be interpreted. In reading Williams's "The Use of Force," for example, a new historicist might pay as much attention to Williams's and other doctors' medical records of the 1920s and 1930s as to the details of incident and language in the story itself. Similarly, in interpreting Dickinson's "I'm 'wife'" new historicist critics would concern themselves with diaries of women written during the early 1860s, when the poem was written. In both instances the records and diaries would be read to ascertain prevailing cultural attitudes about doctor–patient relationships and middle-class marriage respectively. In addition, new historicist critics might also typically compare prevailing cultural attitudes about these issues today with those of the times in which the story and poem were written. In fact, one common strategy of new historicist critics is to compare and contrast the language of contemporaneous documents and literary works to reveal hidden assumptions, biases, and cultural attitudes that relate the two kinds of texts, literary and documentary, usually to demonstrate how the literary work shares the cultural assumptions of the document.

An important feature of new historicist criticism is its concern with examining the power relations of rulers and subjects. A guiding assumption among many new historicist critics is that texts, not only literary works but also documents, diaries, records, even institutions such as hospitals and prisons, are

ideological products culturally constructed from the prevailing power structures that dominate particular societies. Reading a literary work from a new
historicist perspective thus becomes an exercise in uncovering the conflicting
and subversive perspectives of the marginalized and suppressed, as, for example, the perspective and voice of the young patient in "The Use of Force,"
and the vision and values of the speaker in Dickinson's "I'm 'wife,'" whose
perspectives tend to be undervalued because they are females.

While appropriating some of the methods of formalist and deconstructive
critics, new historicists differ from them in a number of important ways. Most
importantly, unlike critics who limit their analysis of a literary work to its language and structure, new historicists spend more time analyzing nonliterary
texts from the same time in which the literary work was written. New historicists, however, do apply the close reading strategies of formalist and deconstructive perspectives, but their goal is not, like the formalists, to show how the
literary work manifests universal values or how it is unified. Nor is the new historicist goal to show how the text undermines and contradicts itself, an emphasis of deconstructive perspectives. Instead, new historicists analyze the
cultural context embedded in the literary work and explain its relationship
with the network of the assumptions and beliefs that inform social institutions
and cultural practices prevalent in the historical period when the literary work
was written. Finally, it is important to note that for new historicist critics, history does not provide mere "background" against which to study literary
works, but is, rather, an equally important "text," one that is ultimately inseparable from the literary work, which inevitably reveals the conflicting power relations that underlie all human interaction, from the small-scale interactions
with families to the large-scale interactions of social institutions.

One potential danger of applying historical perspectives to literature is that
historical information and documents may be foregrounded and emphasized
so heavily that readers lose sight of the literary work the historical approach is
designed to illuminate. When the prism of history is used to clarify and explain elements of the literary work, however, whether in examining intellectual currents, describing social conditions, or presenting cultural attitudes,
readers' understanding of literary works can be immeasurably enriched. The
challenge for historical understanding, whether one uses the tools of the older
historicist tradition or the methods of the new historicism, is to ascertain what
the past was truly like, how its values are inscribed in its cultural artifacts, including its literature. Equally challenging is an exploration of the question,
What was it possible to think or do at a particular moment of the past, including possibilities that may no longer be available to those living today?

A CHECKLIST OF HISTORICAL AND NEW HISTORICIST
CRITICAL QUESTIONS

1. When was the work written? When was it published? How was it received by the
   critics and the public? Why?

2. What does the work's reception reveal about the standards of taste and value during the time it was published and reviewed?

3. What social attitudes and cultural practices related to the action of the work were prevalent during the time the work was written and published?

4. What kinds of power relations does the work describe, reflect, or embody?

5. How do the power relations reflected in the literary work manifest themselves in the cultural practices and social institutions prevalent during the time the work was written and published?

6. What other types of historical documents, cultural artifacts, or social institutions might be analyzed in conjunction with particular literary works? How might a close reading of such a nonliterary "text" illuminate those literary works?

7. To what extent can we understand the past as it is reflected in the literary work? To what extent does the work reflect differences from the ideas and values of its time?

Historical and New Historicist Criticism: Selected Readings

Armstrong, Nancy. *Desire and Domestic Fiction.* 1987.
Dollmore, Jonathan, and Alan Sinfield. *Political Shakespeare.* 1985.
Geertz, Clifford. *The Interpretation of Cultures.* 1973.
Greenblatt, Stephen. *Learning to Curse: Essays in Early Modern Culture.* 1990.
Greenblatt, Stephen. *Marvellous Possessions.* 1991.
Kenner, Hugh. *The Pound Era.* 1971.
Levinson, Marjorie, et al. *Rethinking Historicism.* 1989.
Lindenberger, Herbert. *Historical Drama.* 1975.
Veeser, H. Aram. *The New Historicism.* 1989.
Veeser, H. Aram. *The New Historicism: A Reader.* 1994.

PSYCHOLOGICAL PERSPECTIVES

An Overview of Psychological Criticism

Psychological criticism approaches a work of literature as the revelation of its author's mind and personality. Psychological critics see literary works as intimately linked with their author's mental and emotional characteristics. Critics who employ a psychological perspective do so to explain how a literary work reflects its writer's consciousness and mental world, and they use what they know of writers' lives to explain features of their work. Some psychological critics are more interested in the creative processes of writers than in their literary works; these critics look into literary works for clues to a writer's creative imagination. Other psychological critics wish to study not so much a writer's creative process as his or her motivations and behavior; these critics may study a writer's works along with letters and diaries to better understand not just what a writer has done in life but why the writer behaved in a particular manner. Still other critics employ methods of

Freudian psychoanalysis to understand not only the writers themselves, such as Shakespeare or Kafka, but the literary characters they create, Iago, for example, or Gregor Samsa.

Psychoanalytic criticism derives from Freud's revolutionary psychology in which he developed the notion of the "unconscious" along with the psychological mechanisms of "displacement," "condensation," "fixation," and "manifest and latent" dream content. Freud posited an unconscious element of the mind below consciousness, just beneath awareness. According to Freud, the unconscious harbors forbidden wishes and desires, often sexual, that are in conflict with an individual's or society's moral standards. Freud explains that although the individual represses or "censors" these unconscious fantasies and desires, they become "displaced" or distorted in dreams and other forms of fantasy, which serve to disguise their real meaning.

The disguised versions that appear in a person's conscious life are considered to be the "manifest" content of the unconscious wishes that are their "latent" content, which psychoanalytic critics attempt to discover and explain. Psychoanalytic critics rely heavily on symbolism to identify and explain the meaning of repressed desires, interpreting ordinary objects such as clocks and towers and natural elements such as fire and water in ways that reveal aspects of a literary character's sexuality. These critics also make use of other psychoanalytic concepts and terms such as "fixation," or "obsessive compulsion," attaching to feelings, behaviors, and fantasies that individuals presumably outgrow yet retain in the form of unconscious attractions.

Among the most important of the categories derived from Freud that psychoanalytic critics employ are those Freud used to describe mental structures and dynamics. Freud recognized three types of mental functions, which he designated the "id," the "ego," and the "superego." Freud saw the id as the storehouse of desires, primarily libidinal or sexual, but also aggressive and possessive. He saw the superego as the representative of societal and parental standards of ethics and morality. And he saw the ego as the negotiator between the desires and demands of the id and the controlling and constraining force of the superego, all influenced further by an individual's relationship with other people in the contexts of actual life. These few but important psychoanalytic concepts have been put to varied uses by critics with a wide range of psychological approaches. Freud himself analyzed Sophocles' tragic drama *Oedipus Rex* to explain how Oedipus harbored an unconscious desire to kill his father and marry his mother, events the play accounts for. Other critics have used Freud's insights—which, by the way, Freud himself says he derived from studying literary masters such as Sophocles, Shakespeare, and Kafka—to analyze the hidden motivations of literary characters. One of the most famous of all literary characters, Hamlet, has stimulated psychological critics of all persuasions to explain why he delays killing King Claudius. In his book *Hamlet and Oedipus,* Ernest Jones uses Freud's theory of the "Oedipus complex" to explain Hamlet's delay, which Jones sees, essentially, as Hamlet's inability to punish Claudius for what he, Hamlet, unconsciously wanted to do himself.

Thinking from a Psychoanalytic Perspective

We can use a psychoanalytic perspective to make a few observations about the behavior of the characters in Williams's "The Use of Force" and the marital situation described in Dickinson's "I'm 'wife.'"

The doctor in "The Use of Force" can be seen as repressing his real desire to humiliate his young female patient under the guise of inspecting her throat for signs of illness. The girl's refusal can be seen as an unwillingness to expose herself to this strange overbearing man, who is forcing himself upon her. Her mouth can be interpreted as a displacement for her vagina, and the doctor's attempt to open it by force as a kind of rape. Even the parents' actions might be explained in psychoanalytic terms in that they act as voyeurs, alternately frightened and sexually excited by what they are witnessing.

Dickinson's speaker experiences no such overt violation. Her subjugation is more acceptable because she seems to fulfill a socially sanctioned role as "wife." What is interesting from a psychoanalytic standpoint, however, is the way she subverts that role by comparing herself to a "Czar," a powerful emperor, which seems to conflict with her role as "wife" and "Woman." Moreover, the speaker's comparison between the "Girl's life" and the wife's, which is elaborated with the analogy of differences experienced between those on Earth and in Heaven, can be seen as a displacement of her poetic ambition onto the image of a wife, which the speaker endows with spiritual and temporal powers.

A CHECKLIST OF PSYCHOLOGICAL CRITICAL QUESTIONS

1. What connections can you make between your knowledge of an author's life and the behavior and motivations of characters in his or her work?
2. How does your understanding of the characters, their relationships, their actions, and their motivations in a literary work help you better understand the mental world and imaginative life, or the actions and motivations, of the author?
3. How does a particular literary work—its images, metaphors, and other linguistic elements—reveal the psychological motivations of its characters or the psychological mindset of its author?
4. To what extent can you employ the concepts of Freudian psychoanalysis to understand the motivations of literary characters?
5. What kinds of literary works and what types of literary characters seem best suited to a critical approach that employs a psychological or psychoanalytical perspective? Why?
6. How can a psychological or psychoanalytic approach to a particular work be combined with an approach from another critical perspective—for example, that of biographical or formalist criticism, or that of feminist or deconstructionist criticism?

Psychological and Psychoanalytic Criticism: Selected Readings

Bloom, Harold. *The Anxiety of Influence.* 1973.

Chodorow, Nancy. *Feminism and Psychoanalytic Theory.* 1990.

Crews, Frederick. *The Sins of the Fathers: Hawthorne's Psychological Themes.* 1966.

Crews, Frederick. *Skeptical Engagements.* 1986.

Felman, Soshana. *Jacques Lacan and the Adventure of Insight.* 1987.

Freud, Sigmund. *The Interpretation of Dreams.* 1900.

Freud, Sigmund. *Introductory Lectures on Psychoanalysis.* 1917–1918.

Freud, Sigmund. *New Introductory Lectures on Psychoanalysis.* 1933.

Hoffman, Frederick J. *Freudianism and the Literary Mind.* 1957.

Holland, Norman. *The Dynamics of Literary Response.* 1968.

Jones, Ernest. *Hamlet and Oedipus.* 1949.

Manheim, Leonard, and Eleanor Manheim, eds. *Hidden Patterns: Studies in Psychoanalytic Literary Criticism.* 1966.

Mitchell, Juliet. *Psychoanalysis and Feminism.* 1975.

Nelson, Benjamin, ed. *Sigmund Freud on Creativity and the Unconscious.* 1958.

Skura, Meredith. *The Literary Use of the Psychoanalytic Process.* 1981.

Trilling, Lionel. *The Opposing Self.* 1955.

Wilson, Edmund. *The Wound and the Bow.* 1941.

Wright, Elizabeth, ed. *Psychoanalytic Criticism.* 1984.

SOCIOLOGICAL PERSPECTIVES

An Overview of Sociological Criticism

Like historical and biographical critics, sociological critics argue that literary works should not be isolated from the social contexts in which they are embedded. And also like historical critics, especially those who espouse new historicist perspectives, sociological critics emphasize the ways power relations are played out by varying social forces and institutions. Sociological critics focus on the values of a society and how those values are reflected in literary works. At one end of the sociological critical spectrum, literary works are treated simply as documents that either embody social conditions or are a product of those conditions. Critics employing a sociological perspective study the economic, political, and cultural issues expressed in literary works as those issues are reflected in the societies in which the works were produced.

A sociological approach to the study of Shakespeare's *Othello* could focus on the political organization of the Venetian state as depicted in the play and its relation to the play's depiction of authority, perhaps considering as well the breakdown of authority in the scenes set in Cyprus. Another sociological perspective might focus on the play's economic aspects, particularly how money and influence are used to manipulate others. Still other sociological issues that could be addressed include the role of women in the play and the issue of

Othello's race. How, for example, does Shakespeare portray the power relations between Othello and Desdemona, Iago and Emilia, Cassio and Bianca? To what extent is each of these women's relationship with men considered from an economic standpoint? Or, to what extent is Othello's blackness a factor in his demise, or is his race a defining characteristic in other characters' perceptions of him?

Two significant trends in sociological criticism have had a decisive impact on critical theory: Marxist criticism and feminist criticism. Proponents of each of these critical perspectives have used some of the tools of other critical approaches such as the close reading of the formalists and deconstructionists and the symbolic analysis of the psychoanalytic critics to espouse their respective ideologies in interpreting literature.

Marxist Critical Perspectives

In the same way that many psychoanalytic critics base their approach to literature on the theoretical works of Sigmund Freud, Marxist critics are indebted to the political theory of Karl Marx and Friedrich Engels. Marxist critics examine literature for its reflection of how dominant elite and middle-class/bourgeois values lead to the control and suppression of the working classes. Marxist critics see literature's value in promoting social and economic revolution, with works that espouse Marxist ideology serving to prompt the kinds of economic and political changes that conform to Marxist principles. Such changes would include the overthrow of the dominant capitalist ideology and the loss of power by those with money and privilege. Marxist criticism is concerned both with understanding the role of politics, money, and power in literary works, and with redefining and reforming the way society distributes its resources among the classes. Fundamentally, the Marxist ideology looks toward a vision of a world not so much where class conflict has been minimized but one in which classes have disappeared altogether.

Marxist critics generally approach literary works as products of their era, especially as influenced, even determined by the economic and political ideologies that prevail at the time of their composition. The literary work is considered a "product" in relation to the actual economic and social conditions that exist at either the time of the work's composition or the time and place of the action it describes.

Marxist analyses of novels focus on the relations among classes. In British and European novels of the nineteenth century, for example, class is a significant factor in the rise and fall of the characters' fortunes. Novels such as Charles Dickens's *Little Dorritt, Dombey and Son,* and *Oliver Twist,* George Eliot's *Middlemarch,* Anthony Trollope's *The Eustace Diamonds,* and William Makepiece Thackery's *Vanity Fair* portray a panoramic vision of society with characters pressing to move up in social rank and status. These and numerous other novels from the eighteenth through the twentieth century provide abundant territory for Marxist perspectives to investigate the ways political and economic forces conspire to keep some social, ethnic, and racial groups in power and others out. In fact, the Marxist critical perspective has been brought to bear most often on the novel, next most often on drama, and least often on poetry, where issues of power, money, and political influence are not nearly as pervasive.

Thinking from a Marxist Perspective

In applying a Marxist critical perspective to a work like Williams's "The Use of Force," one would consider the ways in which power relations are played out in the story. It seems clear that the doctor is the privileged individual who wields the power over both the girl and her family. Since he can refuse to treat the girl, insist on being paid more for his services, or berate the parents for their ineptitude (though he actually does none of these things), the parents are cowed by his presence. The girl, though defiant, is at his mercy since he is physically stronger and psychologically more powerful than she is. In addition to such observations, a Marxist critic might consider the story's action from an economic standpoint, in which the doctor performs a service for a fee, with the entire situation viewed strictly as an economic transaction. Moreover, the parents are apparently poor, and one could surmise that they and their daughter might not receive the quality of medical service or the courteous delivery of medical care they would get were they more economically prosperous.

A CHECKLIST OF MARXIST CRITICAL QUESTIONS

1. What social forces and institutions are represented in the work? How are these forces portrayed? What is the author's attitude toward them?
2. What political economic elements appear in the work? How important are they in determining or influencing the lives of the characters?
3. What economic issues appear in the course of the work? How important are economic facts in influencing the motivation and behavior of the characters?
4. To what extent are the lives of the characters influenced or determined by social, political, and economic forces? To what extent are the characters aware of these forces?

Marxist Criticism: Selected Readings

Baxandall, Lee, and Stefan Morawski, eds. *Marx and Engels on Literature and Art.* 1973.
Benjamin, Walter. *Illuminations.* 1968.
Eagleton, Terry. *Marxism and Literary Criticism.* 1976.
Jameson, Fredric. *Marxism and Form.* 1971.
Lukacs, George. *Realism in Our Time.* 1972.
Trotsky, Leon. *Literature and the Revolution.* 1924.
Williams, Raymond. *Marxism and Literature.* 1977.

Feminist Critical Perspectives

Feminist criticism, like Marxist and new historicist criticism, examines the social and cultural aspects of literary works, especially for what those works reveal about the role, position, and influence of women. Like other socially minded critics, feminist critics consider literature in relation to its social, economic, and political contexts, and indeed look to analyze its social, economic, and political content. Feminist critics also typically see literature as an arena to contest for power and control, since as sociological critics, feminist critics also see literature as an agent for social transformation.

Moreover, feminist critics seek to redress the imbalance of literary study in which all important books are written by men or the only characters of real interest are male protagonists. Feminist critics have thus begun to study women writers whose works have been previously neglected. They have begun to look at the way feminine consciousness has been portrayed in literature written by both women and men. And they have begun to change the nature of the questions asked about literature that reflect predominantly male experience. In these and other ways feminist critical perspectives have begun to undermine the patriarchal or masculinist assumptions that have dominated critical approaches to literature until relatively recently. For although feminist critics can trace their origins back to nineteenth-century politics and cite as formative influences the works of Margaret Fuller, Mary Wollstonecraft Godwin, John Stuart Mill, and Elizabeth Cady Stanton, feminist perspectives only began to be raised in literary circles with Virginia Woolf's *A Room of One's Own* (1929), which describes the difficult conditions under which women writers of the past had to work, and with Simone de Beauvoir's *The Second Sex* (1949), which analyzes the biology, psychology, and sociology of women and their place, role, and influence in Western culture. It is only in the late 1960s and early 1970s, however, that feminist criticism *per se* began to emerge with the publication of Mary Ellman's *Thinking About Women* (1968), Kate Millet's *Sexual Politics* (1970), and a host of other works that have followed for more than a quarter century and show no signs of abating.

In his influential and widely used *Glossary of Literary Terms,* M. H. Abrams identifies four central tenets of much feminist criticism, summarized in the following list.

> 1. Western civilization is pervasively patriarchal (ruled by the father)—that is, it is male-centered and controlled, and is organized and conducted in such a way as to subordinate women to men in all cultural domains: familial, religious, political, economic, social, legal, and artistic.
>
> 2. The prevailing concepts of *gender*—of the traits that constitute what is masculine and what is feminine—are largely, if not entirely, cultural constructs that were generated by the omnipresent patriarchal biases of our civilization.
>
> 3. This patriarchal (or "masculinist," or "androcentric") ideology pervades those writings which have been considered great

literature, and which until recently have been written almost
entirely by men for men.

4. The traditional aesthetic categories and criteria for analyzing
and appraising literary works . . . are in fact infused with masculine assumptions, interests, and ways of reasoning, so that the
standard rankings, and also the critical treatments, of literary
works have in fact been tacitly but thoroughly gender-biased.*

It should be noted, however, that Abrams's list, though helpful, tends to blur
distinctions among the many different varieties of feminist criticism as currently practiced. Thus the ways these assumptions are reflected in feminist criticism vary enormously from the reader-response approaches used by feminist
critics, such as Judith Fetterley and Elizabeth Flynn, to the cultural studies approaches used by Jane Tompkins and Eve Kosovsky Sedgwick, to the Lacanian
psychoanalytic approaches employed by Helene Cixous and Julia Kristeva. It
would be better to think of feminist criticism in the plural as the criticism of
feminists rather than to envision it as a singular monolithic entity.

Thinking from a Feminist Perspective

In applying the perspective of feminist criticism to "I'm 'wife,'" we might consider the way the roles of woman and wife are suggested in the poem. A feminist reading would be alert for other signs of power contestation in the poem,
why for example the speaker compares herself to a "Czar," and what that means
in terms of her ability to exert her will and control her destiny. Feminist readers would also ask what the masculine term "Czar" signifies in the poem, and
whether there is a feminine counterpart.

Feminist readers might also interrogate the poem to ask why the state of
wifehood brings "comfort" and "That other" state—of girlhood—"was pain."
They would probe beyond the text of the poem to consider the extent to
which such differences in experience and feeling obtained in marriages during
Dickinson's lifetime, thus sharing an interest with new historicist critics. Moreover, they might also wonder whether the poem's abrupt ending "I'm 'Wife'!
Stop there!" with its insistent tone might not mask an undercurrent of fear or
powerlessness.

A CHECKLIST OF FEMINIST CRITICAL QUESTIONS

1. To what extent does the representation of women (and men) in the work reflect the
   place and time in which the work was written?
2. How are the relations between men and women, or those between members of the
   same sex, presented in the work? What roles do men and women assume and perform and with what consequences?

*M. H. Abrams. *A Glossary of Literary Terms,* 6th ed., 1993, pp. 234–35.

3. Does the author present the work from within a predominantly male or female sensibility? Why might this have been done, and with what effects?
4. How do the facts of the author's life relate to the presentation of men and women in the work? To their relative degrees of power?
5. How do other works by the author correspond to this one in their depiction of the power relationships between men and women?

Feminist Criticism: Selected Readings

Baym, Nina. *Woman's Fiction.* 1978.
Buck, Claire. *The Bloomsbury Guide to Women's Literature.* 1992.
Cixous, Helene. *The Laugh of the Medusa.* 1976.
Fetterley, Judith. *The Resisting Reader.* 1978.
Gallop, Jane. *The Daughter's Seduction: Feminism and Psychoanalysis.* 1982.
Gates, Henry L., Jr. *Reading Black, Reading Feminist.* 1990.
Gilbert, Sandra, and Susan Gubar. *The Madwoman in the Attic.* 1979.
Heilbrun, Carolyn. *Toward a Recognition of Adrogyny.* 1973.
Moers, Ellen. *Literary Women.* 1976.
Rich, Adrienne. *On Lies, Secrets, and Silence.* 1980.
Ruthven, K. K. *Feminist Literary Studies: An Introduction.* 1984.
Schweickart, Patricinio, and Elizabeth Flynn. *Gender and Reading.* 1986.
Showalter, Elaine. *A Literature of Their Own.* 1977.
Showalter, Elaine. *The New Feminist Criticism.* 1986.
Smith, Barbara. *Toward a Black Feminist Criticism.* 1977.

READER-RESPONSE PERSPECTIVES

An Overview of Reader-Response Criticism

Reader-response criticism raises the question of where literary meaning resides—in the literary text, in the reader, or in the interactive space between text and reader. Reader-response critics differ in the varying degrees of subjectivity they allow into their theories of interpretation. Some, like David Bleich, see the literary text as a kind of mirror in which readers see themselves. In making sense of literature, readers recreate themselves. Other reader-response critics, like Wolfgang Iser, focus on the text rather than on the feelings and reactions of the reader. Text-centered reader-response critics emphasize the temporal aspect of reading, suggesting that readers make sense of texts over time, moving through a text sentence by sentence, line by line, word by word, filling in gaps and making inferences about what is being implied by textual details as they read.

Still other reader-response critics like Norman Holland focus on the psychological dynamics of reading. Holland argues that every reader creates a specific identity theme unique to him or her self in reading any literary work. He suggests that to make sense of a literary work readers must find in it, or create through the process of reading it, their identity themes.

One of the earliest and most influential reader-response critics, Louise Rosenblatt, argues against placing too much emphasis on the reader's imagination, identity, or feelings in literary interpretation. Like Iser, Rosenblatt keeps the focus on the text, though she is more concerned than is Iser with the dynamic relationship between reader and text, since it is in that interrelationship that Rosenblatt believes literary meanings are made.

For Rosenblatt, as for other reader-response critics, the meaning of a literary work cannot exist until it is "performed" by the reader. Until then literary meaning is only potential. It becomes actual when readers realize its potential through their acts of reading, responding, and interpreting.

As you might expect, reader-response critics respect not only the intellectual acts of analysis and comprehension that readers perform but also their subjective responses and their emotional apprehension of literary works. This distinction between intellectual comprehension and emotional apprehension of literature is explored earlier in this book for each of the three literary genres—fiction, poetry, and drama.

One benefit of using reader-response perspectives to interpret literary works is that you begin with what is primary and basic—your initial reactions, your primary responses. Of course, as you read, you may change your mind about your reaction to a work. You may experience opposite or different feelings. Or you may make sense of the work differently because of discoveries you make later in the process of reading. What you read in the last chapter of a novel, for example, may change your understanding of what you read in the first chapter or in a middle chapter, which you had interpreted one way until you reached the end. What's important for reader-response critics is just this kind of active reading dynamic, in which a reader's changing ideas and feelings are foregrounded. These critics describe the recursiveness of the reading process, the way in which our minds anticipate what is coming in the text based on what we have already read and, simultaneously, the way we loop back retrospectively to reconsider earlier passages in light of later ones that we read. The literary text does not disappear for reader-response critics. Instead it becomes part of readers' experience as they make their way through it.

Reader-response criticism thus emphasizes process rather than product, an experience rather than an object, a shifting subjectivity rather than a static and objective text and meaning. For reader-response critics the text is not a "thing"; it does not stand still, for it lives only in its readers' imaginations. For these critics, then, literary works do not have an independent objective meaning that is true once and for all and that is identical for all readers. Instead, they argue that readers *make* meaning through their encounters with literary texts. And the meanings they make may be as varied as the individuals who read them.

Reader-response critics emphasize two additional points about the range and variety of readers' interpretations. First, an individual reader's interpretation of a work may change, in fact, probably will change over time. Reading Shakespeare's *Julius Caesar* in high school can be a very different experience from reading it in college or later as an adult. Second, historically, readers from different generations and different centuries interpret books differently. The works say different things to readers of different historical eras based on their particular needs, concerns, and historical circumstances. In both the individual cases and the larger historical occasions, changes occur, changes that affect how individuals perceive, absorb, and understand what they read at different times of their lives.

The crucial thing for readers is to acknowledge their own subjectivity in the act of reading and to be aware that they come to literary works with a set of beliefs, ideas, attitudes, values—with all that makes them who and what they are. Being aware of our predispositions when we read can prevent our biases and prejudices from skewing our interpretations of literary works. At the same time, we need to pay attention to the details of the text. We cannot make words and sentences mean anything at all. There are limits and boundaries to what is acceptable, limits and boundaries that are subject to negotiation and debate. For most reader-response theorists, interpretation has both latitude and limits. Negotiating between them in a delicate balancing act allows readers to exercise their subjectivity while recognizing the significance of the words on the page.

Perhaps an analogy will clarify the double-sided nature of literary interpretation from a reader-response perspective, one that recognizes both the reader's freedom and the text's limits. You might think of a text as a musical score, one that is brought to life in performance. Readers make the potential meanings of a text come to life in much the same way that a musician brings a piece of music to life in performance. When musicians play a score or readers read a literary work, they cannot change the notes of the score or the words of the text. Both readers and musicians are limited by what is on the page. Yet there is room for differing interpretations and varied responses. Two interpretations of a literary work, like two musical performances, are likely to differ, sometimes in significant ways. The varying interpretations will be valid insofar as they respect the words or notes on the page, and insofar as they represent a reasonable and logically defensible approach to the work.

Thinking from a Reader-Response Perspective

In reading "The Use of Force," reader-response critics would consider a reader's emotional reactions to the story's action. They might ask how a reader responds to the doctor, how he or she reacts to the doctor's acknowledgment of his feelings about the parents and the child, how readers respond to the way he opens the girl's mouth. Like feminist critics, they would consider the extent to which female readers might respond differently from males, though the important thing for a reader-response perspective would be the intensity and nature of a particular reader's response.

Some reader-response critics would also examine the reader's responses at different points in the text, focusing on particular words and phrases that might signal a shift in the story's tone and hence a change in the reader's response. The doctor's response to the parents calling him a "nice man" is to grind his teeth in disgust. His remark to the girl after she knocks his glasses off is "Will you open it now by yourself or shall we have to open it for you?" And his reference to his contempt for the parents and to the child as a "little brat" are places for readers to consider their responses.

In reading Dickinson's "I'm 'wife,'" reader-response critics might point to the way the poem's language associates "wife" with "Woman" and with "Czar" and invite readers to consider the extent to which these terms reflect their experience or understanding of marriage. They might ask whether the idea of marriage reflected in the poem reminds you of your own relatives' marriages, of the marriage of your parents. If so, why, a reader-response critic might ask, and, if not, why not?

Reader-response critics would also ask about readers' responses to the men who are implied but not explicitly named in the poem, and to the analogy made in the second stanza, which uses the contrast between Earth and Heaven to suggest a difference between the speaker's life before and after marriage. These critics might ask readers to explore their feelings about such an analogy and invite them to consider ways in which their own lives involve a difference such as that describing the speaker's before and after states. The emphases of reader-response critics essentially, then, would be two: (1) the reader's direct experience of the language and details of the poem in the process of reading it; (2) the reader's actual experience outside the poem which he or she brings to the reading and which is used to interpret it. Where formalist critics would play down this experiential connection to the poem and encourage readers to focus solely on the words on the page, reader-response critics want to extend the readers' perceptions about the poem and deepen their response to it by deliberately evoking actual experiences of readers that they can bring to bear on both their apprehension and their comprehension of the poem.

A CHECKLIST OF READER-RESPONSE CRITICAL QUESTIONS

1. What is your initial emotional response to the work? How did you feel upon first reading it?
2. Did you find yourself responding to it or reacting differently at any point? If so, why? If not, why not?
3. At what places in the text did you have to make inferences, fill in gaps, make interpretive decisions? On what bases did you make these inferential guesses?
4. How do you respond to the characters, the speaker, or the narrator? How do you feel about them? Why?
5. What places in the text caused you to do the most serious thinking? How did you put the pieces, sections, parts of the work together to make sense of it?
6. If you have read a work more than once, how has your second and subsequent readings differed from earlier ones? How do you account for those differences, or for the fact that there are no differences in either your thoughts or your feelings about the work?

Reader-Response Criticism: Selected Readings

Bleich, David. *Readings and Feelings.* 1975.
Bleich, David. *Subjective Criticism.* 1968.

Clifford, John, ed. *The Experience of Reading*. 1991.
Eco, Umberto. *The Open Work*. 1989.
Fish, Stanley. *Is There a Text in This Class?* 1980.
Freund, Elizabeth. *The Return of the Reader*. 1987.
Holland, Norman. *The Dynamics of Literary Response*. 1968.
Holland, Norman. *Poems in Persons*. 1973.
Iser, Wolfgang. *The Act of Reading*. 1978.
Mailloux, Steven. *Interpretive Conventions*. 1982.
Rabinowitz, Peter. *Before Reading*. 1987.
Rosenblatt, Louise. *Literature as Exploration*. 1939, 1975.
Rosenblatt, Louise. *The Reader, The Text, The Poem: A Transactional Theory of the Literary Work*. 1978.
Steig, Michael. *Stories of Reading*. 1989.
Suleiman, Susan R., and Inge Crosman, eds. *The Reader in the Text*. 1980.
Tompkins, Jane, ed. *Reader-Response Criticism*. 1980.
Wimmers, Inge Crosman. *Poetics of Reading*. 1988.

MYTHOLOGICAL PERSPECTIVES

An Overview of Mythological Criticism

In general terms a "myth" is a story that explains how something came to be. Every culture creates stories to explain what it considers important, valuable, and true. Thus the Greek myth of Persephone, who was kidnapped by Pluto, the god of the underworld, and allowed to return to her mother Demeter every year, explains the changes of the seasons. Or the Biblical story of Eve's temptation by the serpent in the book of Genesis, which concludes with God's curse of the serpent, explains, among other things, why snakes crawl on their bellies.

Myth criticism, however, is not concerned with stories that explain origins so much as those that provide universal story patterns that recur with regularity among many cultures and in many different times and places. The patterns myth critics typically identify and analyze are those that represent common, familiar, even universal human experiences, such as being born and dying, growing up and crossing the threshold into adulthood, going on a journey, engaging in sexual activity. These familiar patterns of human action and experience, however, are of interest to myth critics not primarily in and of themselves, but rather for how they represent religious beliefs, social customs, and cultural attitudes.

Birth, for example, is of interest as a symbolic beginning and death as a symbolic ending. A journey is a symbolic venturing out into the world to explore and experience what it has in store for the traveler. Sleeping and dreaming are not simply states of ordinary experience but symbolic modes of entrance into another realm and an envisioning of unusual and perhaps strange possibilities unimagined in waking life. So too with physical contests, sexual encounters, and other forms of experience, which many times are occasions for individuals to be tested, challenged, and perhaps initiated into an advanced or superior state of being—becoming a warrior, for example, a mother, a prophet, or a king.

Myth critics discover in literature of all times and places stories with basic patterns that can be explained in terms of *archetypes,* or universal symbols, which some mythological critics believe are part of every person's unconscious mind, a kind of a collective unconscious that each of us inherits by virtue of our common humanity. Besides the fundamental facts of human existence, other archetypes include typical literary characters such as the Don Juan or womanizer, the *femme fatale* or dangerous female, the trickster or con artist, the damsel in distress, the rebel, the tyrant, the hero, the betrayer. Creatures real and imaginary can also be archetypal symbols. The lion, for example, can represent strength, the eagle independence, the fox cunning, the unicorn innocence, the dragon destruction, the centaur the union of matter and spirit, animality and humanity, or even humanity and divinity.

It is on plot or the sequence of causally related incidents and actions, however, that myth criticism focuses most heavily. The archetypal images, creatures, and characters exist within stories that themselves exhibit patterns of recurrence. So, for example, there are stories of the arduous quest fraught with perils which a protagonist must survive, perhaps to rescue an innocent victim, perhaps to prove superior courage or morality, perhaps to save others from destruction. There are stories of vengeance, of death and rebirth, of resurrection, of transformation from one state of being into another, stories of enlightenment, of devastation, of lost paradises. Many such stories can be found in the religious literature of cultures around the world. The Bible, for example, contains stories of creation (Adam and Eve), fraternal rivalry and murder (Cain and Abel), destruction (Noah) and forgiveness (the ark and the covenant), wandering and enslavement (the exodus), death and resurrection (Jesus' life and ministry)—and so on. This list can be multiplied by consulting, for example, the Taoist and Confucian religious traditions of China, the Hindu traditions of India, the Buddhist traditions of Japan, and the Islamic tradition of the Middle East.

Myth critics approach the study of literary works and the study of a culture's myths in many ways. The Canadian critic Northrop Frye, for example, explains the traditional literary genres, including the novel, the drama, and epic, with reference to the recurrence in them of mythic patterns such as death and rebirth, departure and return, ignorance and insight. Frye, in fact, associates the genres of comedy, romance, tragedy, and irony or satire with the cycle of the seasons, each genre representing the natural events associated with a particular season (comedy with the fertility of spring, for example, and tragedy with the decline of the year in autumn). The French critic, Claude Lévi-Strauss, who employs the strategies of structuralist and semiotic analysis, treats cultural myths as signs whose meanings are not understood by the cultures that create those myths. His work is grounded in structural anthropology and owes much to the linguistic theory of Ferdinand de Saussure, who had a profound effect on the development of French and American structuralist perspectives on literary analysis and interpretation. And the American critic of popular culture, John Cawelti, to cite still another approach, analyzes the mythic impulse and mythic elements in forms of popular literature such as the western.

Thinking from a Mythological Perspective

What a mythological critic does with archetypal characters, stories, creatures, and even natural elements such as sun and moon, darkness and light, fire and water, is to link them up with one another, to see one literary work in relation to others of a similar type. Thus, for example, Hamlet's revenge of his father's death can be linked with myths from other cultures that include a son's avenging his father. Or the story of Hamlet can be linked with others in which the corruption poisoning a country has been eliminated through some action taken by the hero. Or, to take a different example, the story of the prodigal son could be linked with other stories of sons wasting their inheritance, of fathers forgiving their children, or of one brother envying another.

In considering Williams's "The Use of Force" from a mythological perspective, a myth critic might consider the doctor as an intruder who comes to menace a helpless and innocent family. Or he might be seen as a hero who battles against the odds to save the life of a helpless victim. A myth critic might consider the role of Dickinson's "wife" and her rank as "Czar" in the poem "I'm 'wife'" in relation to prominent female characters from myth and legend, whether human or divine. Myth critics would probably take note too of the references to Heaven and Earth in developing an explanation of the transformation undergone by the speaker of the poem.

A CHECKLIST OF MYTHOLOGICAL CRITICAL QUESTIONS

1. What incidents in the work seem common or familiar enough as actions that they might be considered symbolic or archetypal? Are there any journeys, battles, falls, reversals of fortune?
2. What kinds of character types appear in the work? How might they be typed or classified?
3. What creatures, elements of nature, or man-made objects play a role in the work? To what extent might they be considered symbolic?
4. What changes do the characters undergo? How can those changes be characterized or named? To what might they be related or compared?
5. What religious or quasi-religious traditions with which you are familiar might the work's story, characters, elements, or objects be compared to or affiliated with? Why?

Mythological Criticism: Selected Readings

Bodkin, Maud. *Archetypal Patterns in Poetry.* 1934.
Campbell, Joseph. *The Hero with a Thousand Faces.* 1949.
Cawelti, John. *Adventure, Mystery, Romance.* 1976.
Chase, Richard. *Quest for Myth.* 1949.
Fiedler, Leslie. *Love and Death in the American Novel.* 1964.

Frazer, James G. *The Golden Bough,* rev. 1911.
Frye, Northrop. *Anatomy of Criticism.* 1957.
Graves, Robert. *The White Goddess.* 1948.
Jung, Carl Gustav. *Modern Man in Search of a Soul.* 1933.
Lévi-Strauss, Claude. *Structural Anthropology.* 1968.
Vickery, John B., ed. *Myth and Literature,* 1966.

STRUCTURALIST PERSPECTIVES

An Overview of Structuralist Criticism

It is important to distinguish the general meaning of "structure" as used by critics of varying persuasions from its use by adherents of structuralist criticism. In the traditional and most general sense, the word "structure" refers to the organization of a literary work—to its arrangement of incident and action (plot); its division into sections, chapters, parts, stanzas, and other literary units; its employment of repetition and contrast; its patterns of imagery (light and dark images, for example) and sound (its patterns of rhythm and rhyme).

For structuralist critics, however, the notion of "structure" has another meaning, one which derives from linguistics and anthropology and which refers to the systems of signs that designate meaning. To understand the structuralist perspective one needs to understand what structuralists mean by "signs" and how language is an arbitrary system of such signs. We can illustrate with a familiar example—the word "dog," which represents the four-legged animal many of us have as a pet. Why do the letters D-O-G, when put together, signify the creature who barks at the mail carrier and wags its tail while running off with our sneakers? The answer, of course, is because of a particular set of linguistic conventions that operate due to common usage and agreement. Such use and agreement, such a convention, however, is arbitrary. That is, it could have been otherwise. In fact, in languages such as French and Italian, the word "dog" means nothing. In those languages the furry four-footed barker is respectively *chien* (pronounced sheYEN) and *cane* (pronounced CAHnay), a word that looks like the English "cane," or walking stick, but which is a sign, in Italian, for what we call a dog.

But there is one additional linguistic element of importance—that of difference. We have just seen how the English word "cane" differs from the Italian *cane* and the French *chien* and how the two languages designate the faithful canine companion, perhaps named "Fido," in different ways. In both languages (as in all languages) words are differentiated from one another by sound and by spelling. Thus, in English C-A-N-E refers to a walking stick, but C-O-N-E and C-A-P-E to entirely different things. The same is true in Italian, where *cane,* our equivalent of dog, differs from *cani* (CAHknee), the Italian plural, meaning "dogs." This notion of difference is critical to the way structuralism analyzes systems of signs, for it is through differences that languages, literatures, and other social systems convey meaning.

One technique structuralist critics rely on heavily in analyzing difference is "binary opposition," in which a text's contrasting elements are identified and examined. In employing binary opposition as an analytical instrument, structuralist literary critics imitate what structural anthropologists do when they analyze societies to determine which of their social habits and customs are meaningful. The founder of structuralist anthropology, Claude Lévi-Strauss, an important influence on literary structuralism, has explained how a society's most important values can be deciphered by analyzing such binary oppositions as the distinction between "the raw and the cooked," which became a title for one of his books.

Structuralist critics find all kinds of opposition in literature, from small-scale elements, such as letters and syllables; through symbols, such as light and dark; to motions or directions (up and down), times (before and after), places (inside and outside), distances (far and near); to elements of plot and character, such as changes of feeling and reversals of fortune. Such differences are significant structural elements requiring interpretation, whether the differences are explicit or implicit, described or only hinted at.

Semiotics

Semiotics is the study of signs and sign systems; it is, more importantly, the study of codes, or the systems we use to understand the meaning of events and entities, including institutions and cultural happenings as well as verbal and visual texts—from poems to songs to advertisements, and more. Situated on the border between the humanities and the social and behavioral sciences, semiotics is concerned with how the workings of sign systems in various disciplines such as literature and psychology enable us to understand the richly textured significations of all kinds of cultural texts, from action films and television game shows and situation comedies to professional football games to parades and fourth of July celebrations; from religious rituals such as bar mitzvahs and marriage ceremonies to social occasions such as annual company picnics and New Year's parties.

Although semiotic perspectives derive from the theoretical foundations of structuralist and poststructuralist thought, semiotics does not limit itself to the goals and methods of those critical approaches. And though semiotic analysis is sometimes presented in logical symbols and mathematical terminology, it is not restricted to those forms of language. In fact, one of the strengths of a semiotic perspective is its ability to analyze the ways various discourses convey meaning, whether these discourses employ words or communicate, as does fashion, for example, by means of other signs and symbols.

Thinking from a Structuralist Perspective

We can analyze virtually anything from a structuralist perspective—a baseball or football game, an aerobics class, a restaurant menu or a three-course dinner, fashion shows, movies, MTV videos, newspaper cartoons. The possibilities are endless, and, in fact, one critic, Roland Barthes in his book *Mythologies,* has provided a series of brilliant structuralist analyses of foods, fashions, and sports, including wrestling.

Fairy tales and folktales have been a popular source of interpretations for structuralist critics, for such basic stories contain plots and character elements that lend themselves well to binary analysis, and they often reveal much about the values of the cultures that created them. Think of Cinderella, for example, and how she exists in opposition to her stepsisters (she is beautiful while they are ugly; she is poor while they are rich; she is a servant, they her masters). Remember how she loses one slipper while retaining the other, how her coach turns into a pumpkin and her footmen into mice (or is it the other way around)? Difference functions throughout the story on many levels, including the all-important one of the reversal of her fortune with that of her stepsisters and of a prince replacing her nasty stepmother as her future companion. You may also wish to consider books and movies that make use of the "Cinderella plot," where a metaphorical Prince Charming rescues a poor common girl from an oppressive and unhappy life. The films *An Officer and a Gentleman* and *Pretty Woman* provide two examples.

Structuralist analysis is used at a number of places in *Literature.* Look again, for example, in Chapter Three at the discussion of setting in Kate Chopin's "The Story of an Hour" and William Faulkner's "A Rose for Emily." Chopin's story is seen as having a number of meaningful oppositions, including that between the enclosed inner space of Mrs. Mallard's bedroom and the open free space outside her home, an opposition that reflects the tension between her present marital subjugation and her yearning to be "free," as well as a difference between the natural world of birds and trees and her human world bound by ties of obligation. Faulkner's story, on the other hand, posits an opposition between the story's past and present, a time before the significant changes brought by twentieth-century modern ways, when Miss Emily Grierson could live according to a different code of values represented by an earlier time.

A structuralist perspective of "The Use of Force" would consider the difference between the doctor's initial thoughts as he enters the house and his later feelings as the parents call him a "nice" man—including the fact that he sees himself as different from their view of him. It would attend to the difference between the doctor's inner thoughts and his spoken dialogue, as well as to differences between how the doctor had hoped to attend to his patient and what he actually does to get her to open her mouth. It would also analyze the binary oppositions that exist in the story, including doctor/patient, adult/child, sickness/health, helping/hurting, and so on.

Dickinson's "I'm 'wife'" invites structuralist analysis as well. Not only do the poem's first and last lines begin with the words "I'm 'wife,'" which gives the poem something of a circular movement, but the term "Girl's life" is contrasted with the words "wife" and "Woman," and the state of being "wife" is set off against "That other state," which is unnamed but implied. In addition there is a contrast between "comfort" and "pain" and another posited between "Earth" and "Heaven." All these oppositions would be viewed by structuralist critics as key elements of signification.

A CHECKLIST OF STRUCTURALIST CRITICAL QUESTIONS

1. What are the elements of the work—words, stanzas, chapters, parts, for example— and how can these be seen as revealing "difference"?
2. How do the characters, narrators, speakers, or other voices heard in the work reveal difference?
3. How do the elements of the work's plot or overall action suggest a meaningful pattern? What changes, adjustments, transformations, shifts of tone, attitude, behavior, or feeling do you find?
4. How are the work's primary images and events related to one another? What elements of differentiation exist, and what do they signify?
5. What system of relationships governs the work as a whole?
6. What system of relations could be used to link this work with others of its kind? With different kinds of things with which it shares some similarities?

Structuralist Criticism: Selected Readings

Barthes, Roland. *Elements of Semiology.* 1967.
Culler, Jonathan. *Structuralist Poetics.* 1975.
Genette, Gerard. *Figures.* 1966.
Hawkes, Terence. *Structuralism and Semiotics.* 1977.
Lévi-Strauss, Claude. *The Raw and the Cooked.* 1966.
Macksey, Richard, and Eugenio Donato, eds. *The Structuralist Controversy.* 1970.
Scholes, Robert. *Semiotics and Interpretation.* 1982.
Scholes, Robert. *Structuralism in Literature: An Introduction.* 1974.
Smith, Barbara Herrnstein. *On the Margins of Discourse.* 1978.
Todorov, Tzvetan. *The Poetics of Prose,* trans. 1977.

DECONSTRUCTIVE PERSPECTIVES

An Overview of Deconstructive Criticism

Deconstruction arose as a further development of structuralism. Like structuralist critics, deconstructive critics look for opposition in literary works (and in other kinds of "texts" such as films, advertisements, and social institutions, including schools and hospitals). Like structuralism, deconstruction emphasizes difference, or the structure of constituent opposition in a text or any signifying system (for example, male/female, black/white, animate/inanimate). For deconstructionist critics, any meaning is constructed as the result of an opposition, which can be read as ideologically grounded. This is the case with the use of language itself, which creates meaning by opposition (the difference in meaning between the English words "cap" and "cup," for example, is based on a difference between their middle letters). The difference is significant as the words refer to different things.

Deconstruction differs from structuralism, however, in describing at once both a pair of equally valid conflicting oppositions, and in identifying a prevailing ideology that needs to be subverted, undermined, challenged, or otherwise called into question—an ideological view, for example, that suggests that one race or gender is superior to another, or a conviction that the poor are happy with their lot. We can distinguish the more explicitly politicized type of deconstruction, "deconstructionist criticism," from a less politically animated type, "deconstructive criticism," in which the ideological impulse is implicit rather than explicit, latent rather than overtly expressed.

Through a careful analysis of a text's language, deconstructive critics unravel the text by pointing to places where it is ambivalent, contradictory, or otherwise ambiguous. Critics who employ deconstruction as a critical method actually would say that the text deconstructs itself, and that critics do not deconstruct the text so much as show how the text contradicts itself and thereby dismantles itself. They would argue that the contradictions found in any verbal text are inherent in the nature of language, which functions as a system of opposition or differences. And since language itself is radically oppositional and thereby inherently ideological, then all discourse is, first, oppositional and hence subject to deconstruction, and, second, ideological, and indicative of power differentiation. In addition, deconstructionist critics also posit the existence of absent textual qualities or characteristics by suggesting that these absent elements have been suppressed by the dominant ideology that controls the apparent meaning of the work.

Deconstructionist critics operate on the premise that language is irretrievably self-contradictory and self-destroying. They argue that since language is unstable, it cannot be controlled by writers. As a result, literary works mean more than their authors are aware of, and their meanings are as unstable as the language of which they are constructed. The aim of deconstructive analysis is to demonstrate the instability of language in texts, thereby revealing how a text's conflicting forces inevitably destroy its apparently logical or meaningful structure and how its apparently clear meaning splits into contradictory, incompatible, and ultimately undecidable possibilities.

Deconstructionist criticism favors terms like "unmasking," "unraveling," "recovering," "suppression," and "contradiction." Unlike formalist criticism, which it resembles in its scrupulous attention to textual detail and its insistence on analyzing the text as a self-contained world, deconstructionist criticism attempts to dismantle the literary work and show that it does not mean what it appears to mean. Deconstructionist criticism includes a penchant for showing how literary texts "subvert" and "betray" themselves, an elevation of criticism to an equal stature with literary creation (so that a deconstructive critical essay on "The Use of Force," for example, is as valuable an artistic production as the original story), and its radical skepticism about the ability of language to communicate anything except contradictions.

A crucial notion for deconstructionist criticism is that of difference, or "différence," as the seminal deconstructionist philosopher and critic Jacques Derrida spells it. By différence, Derrida means to suggest both the usual meaning of difference (dissimilarity) and the additional idea of deferral, both derived from the two meanings of the French verb "différer," which means "to differ" and "to defer" or "postpone." The kind of difference meant by Derrida is, specifically, a deferral of meaning that is never completed or finished because a spoken utterance or a written text means whatever it means as a function of differences among its elements. The result is that its meaning cannot be established as single or determinate. Meaning, thus, is indefinitely postponed, endlessly deferred.

This kind of playing with language is further exemplified by Derrida's explanation of the "self-effacing trace," his notion that a network of differences of meaning is implied even though those differences are not actually present in an utterance or a text. The explicit meaning, which is present, carries with it "traces" of the absent implied meanings, which for ideological reasons are suppressed, though other implications are "there" as inescapable alternative possibilities because they can be construed or imagined.

Thinking from a Deconstructive Perspective

"The Use of Force" yields a number of oppositions that deconstructionist critics would describe to unmask a prevailing ideology in need of subversion. Primary in importance among them is the conflict between doctor and patient, in which "doctor" is the privileged term and "patient" the submissive and submerged one. The doctor is the agent who acts upon the passive patient. In this story, however, we find that the patient is neither patient nor submissive. She is impatient with her parents and with the doctor. She actively knocks his glasses off and splinters the wooden tongue depressor he puts in her mouth by crushing it with her teeth. In this and other ways, the story reflects a tissue of contradictory attitudes and impulses, including the doctor's ambivalent feelings for the girl, whom he both hates and admires, his conflicted feelings toward her parents, whom he pities yet can barely tolerate, and his ambivalence about his own actions, which he both wants and does not want to perform. Other oppositions include those between male and female, older and younger, privileged and unprivileged, all located in the same doctor/patient relationship.

A deconstructive analysis of Dickinson's "I'm 'wife'" would include consideration of the binary oppositions noted in the discussion of "Thinking from a Structuralist Perspective" mentioned earlier. The deconstructive strategy would be to show how the terms "wife," "Woman," "Czar," and "Girl's life" cancel each other out so that a single determinate meaning of the poem is impossible to establish. Deconstructionist critics would, in addition, attempt to show how the poem's inherent contradictions privilege one pair of terms, "wife" for example, over "Girl['s]," while undermining the apparent authority and privileged status of "wife" and the state to which it refers. They would also consider absent terms suggested but not stated directly, such as "Husband."

A CHECKLIST OF DECONSTRUCTIVE CRITICAL QUESTIONS

1. What oppositions exist in the work? Which of the two opposing terms of each pair is the privileged or more powerful term? How is this shown in the work?
2. What textual elements (descriptive details, images, incidents, passages) suggest a contradiction or alternative to the privileged or more powerful term?
3. What is the prevailing ideology or set of cultural assumptions in the work? Where are these assumptions most evident?
4. What passages of the work most reveal gaps, inconsistencies, or contradictions?
5. How stable is the text? How decidable is its meaning?

Deconstructive Criticism: Selected Readings

Attridge, Derek, ed. *Acts of Literature.* 1992.
Bloom, Harold, ed. *Deconstruction and Criticism.* 1979.
Culler, Jonathan. *On Deconstruction.* 1982.
de Man, Paul. *Allegories of Reading.* 1979.
Derrida, Jacques. *Writing and Difference.* 1978.
Johnson, Barbara. *A World of Difference.* 1987.
Miller, J. Hillis. *Fiction and Repetition.* 1982.
Norris, Christopher. *Deconstruction: Theory and Practice.* 1982.
Scholes, Robert. *Protocols of Reading.* 1989.
Taylor, Mark C., ed. *Deconstruction in Context.* 1986.

CULTURAL STUDIES PERSPECTIVES

An Overview of Cultural Studies

The term "cultural studies" indicates a wide range of critical approaches to the study of literature and society. It is a kind of umbrella term that not only includes approaches to the critical analysis of society such as Marxism, feminism, structuralism, deconstruction, and new historicism, but also refers to a wide range of interdisciplinary studies, including women's studies, African-American studies, Asian, Native American, Latino studies, and other types of area studies.

Like deconstruction, feminism, and new historicism, cultural studies perspectives are multidisciplinary. These and other forms of cultural criticism typically include the perspectives of both humanistic disciplines, such as literature and art, and the social and behavioral sciences, such as anthropology, economics, and psychology. The idea of cultural studies, however, is broader than any of the particular critical perspectives described in this chapter. Cultural studies are not restricted, for example, to structuralist or deconstructionist critical procedures, nor are they solely concerned with feminist issues or Marxist causes.

As a critical perspective in the late twentieth century, cultural studies employs a definition of culture that differs from two other common ways of considering it. Traditionally, and especially from the perspective of anthropology, culture has been considered as the way of life of a people, including its customs, beliefs, and attitudes, all of which cohere in a unified and organic way of life. This traditional anthropological notion has coexisted with another idea, one of culture as representing the best that a civilization has produced—in its institutions, its political and philosophical thought, its art, literature, music, architecture and other lasting achievements.

Both of these ways of viewing culture are contested by the newer forms of cultural studies, which look not at the stable coherences of a society or a civilization's history, but at its dissensions and conflicts. For the newer versions of cultural criticism, the unifying concerns and values of older forms of cultural study are suspect, largely because they avoid issues of political and social inequality. In fact, one way of viewing the current debate over the humanities described in an earlier section of this chapter, "The Canon and the Curriculum," is as a conflict between the older view of cultural studies that emphasizes a kind of normative national cultural consensus, and newer versions, which challenge such norms and values and question the very idea of cultural consensus. Moreover, the different goals and procedures of these contrasting cultural studies perspectives, along with the differences among the critical perspectives described earlier, powerfully illustrate how nearly everything now associated with literate culture has become contested. These areas of contestation include not only the meaning of "culture," but the meaning of teaching, learning, reading, and writing, along with notions of text, author, meaning, criticism, discipline, and department. Cultural studies perspectives breach the traditional understanding of these terms, in the process redrawing the boundaries that formerly separated them.

The notion of boundaries, in fact, is one of the more helpful metaphors for thinking about the new cultural studies. That some new emergent critical schools overlap or that critical perspectives may combine forces suggests how disciplinary borders are being crossed and their boundaries reconfigured. In addition to crossing geographical and intellectual boundaries (as well as those between high and popular culture), the new cultural studies also envision a plurality of cultures rather than seeing "Culture" with a capital "C" as singular, monolithic, or universal.

Thinking from a Cultural Studies Perspective

In considering literary works and other kinds of canonical and noncanonical texts from the various standpoints of cultural studies, it is important to note that no single approach, method, or procedure prevails. There is, then, no single "cultural studies" perspective on Williams's "The Use of Force" or Dickinson's "I'm 'wife'." Rather there are various ways of thinking about the cultural and social issues embedded in these works. Some of these issues have been raised in the explanations of feminist, Marxist, new historicist, structuralist, and deconstructionist critical perspectives.

One additional cultural studies perspective that has recently gained prominence is that of *gender criticism,* more specifically gay and lesbian studies. Gender criticism and studies overlap, to some extent, with feminist critical perspectives. In addition to studying the relations between and among men, gender criticism also explores such intra-gender issues of women as lesbian sexuality and female power relations.

One of the central problems of gender studies is the way gender is defined. To what extent, for example, does gender overlap with sex? To what extent is gender a cultural category and sex a biological one? To what extent do the language of sexuality used in the past and the current uses of both "sex" and "gender" as categories reflect biological, psychological, and socially constructed elements of sexual difference? Related to these overlapping questions are others, especially considerations of what some gender critics see as heterosocial or heterosexist bias in the very concept of gender and gender relations.

Gender critics share with adherents of other socially oriented perspectives a concern for analyzing power relations and for discerning ways in which homophobic discourse and attitudes prevail in society at large. Through analysis of various forms of historical evidence and through acts of political agency, gender critics have challenged perspectives that view homosexual acts and unions as "sinful" or "diseased." They have questioned the way AIDS has been represented in the mainstream media and have opened up discussion about what constitutes such apparently familiar notions as "family," "love," and "sexual identity."

A CHECKLIST OF GENDER STUDIES CRITICAL QUESTIONS

1. What kinds of sexual identity, behavior, and attitudes are reflected in the work? Is there any overtly or covertly expressed view of homosexuality or lesbianism?
2. To what extent does the work accommodate, describe, or exemplify same-sex relationships? To what extent are same-sex sexual relationships either in the foreground or background of the work?
3. With what kinds of social, economic, and cultural privileges (or lack thereof) are same-sex unions or relationships depicted? With what effects and consequences?

Cultural Studies: Selected Readings

Butler, Judith. *Gender Trouble.* 1989.
Comley, Nancy, and Robert Scholes. *Hemingway's Genders.* 1994.
Giroux, Henry. *Border Crossings.* 1992.
Gunn, Giles. *The Culture of Criticism and the Criticism of Culture.* 1987.
Sedgwick, Eve Kosofsky. *Between Men: English Literature and Male Homosexual Desire.* 1985.
Sedgwick, Eve Kosofsky. *Epistemology of the Closet.* 1990.
Tompkins, Jane. *Sensational Designs: The Cultural Work of American Fiction 1790–1860.* 1985.
Torgovnick, Marianna DeMarco. *Crossing Ocean Parkway.* 1994.

USING CRITICAL PERSPECTIVES AS HEURISTICS

One of your more difficult decisions regarding critical theory will be in choosing a critical perspective that is suitable and effective in analyzing a particular literary work. You might be able to offer, for example, a Marxist, deconstructionist, or feminist reading of "Humpty Dumpty" or "Little Bo Peep," even though these nursery rhymes may not be conventionally approached from any of those critical perspectives. You will need to decide whether one of those approaches offers a richer yield than a more traditional approach, such as formalism or myth criticism. The same is true of your approach to Williams's "The Use of Force" and Dickinson's "I'm 'wife.'" Although both works have been analyzed in this chapter from ten critical perspectives, you probably found that certain critical perspectives made a better interpretive fit than others for Williams's story or Dickinson's poem.

Another thing to remember is that you can combine critical perspectives. There is no rule of interpretation that says you must limit yourself to the language and method of a single critical approach or method. You may wish, for example, to combine formalist and structural perspectives in analyzing "I'm 'wife,'" while also raising feminist critical questions in your interpretation. Or in interpreting "The Use of Force," you may wish to combine new historicist critical concerns with those of a biographical, psychological, or structuralist approach. In some ways, in fact, various concerns of the critical perspectives explained in this chapter overlap. Feminists raise historical questions as well as psychological and biographical ones. Reader-response critics attend to structuralist and formalist issues. And new historicist critics may employ formalist or deconstructionist methods of close reading.

A danger in using any critical approach to literature is that literary texts are read with an eye toward making them conform to a particular critical theory rather than using that critical theory to illuminate the text. In the process, critics may distort the text of a literary work by quoting from it selectively or by ignoring aspects of it that do not fit their theoretical approach or conform to their interpretive perspective. Some critics, moreover, apply their favorite critical perspective in a mechanical way, so that every work of literature is read with an eye toward proving the same ideological point, regardless of how important the issue is in one work as compared with another. Or critics may put all works of literature through an identical ideological meat grinder with every work emerging ground into the same kind of critical hamburger.

The various critical perspectives you have been learning about should be used as ways to think about literary works rather than as formulas for grinding out a particular kind of interpretation. Try to see the various critical perspectives as interpretive possibilities, as intellectual vistas that open up literary works rather than as stultifying formulas that limit what can be seen in them. Try, as well, to experience the element of intellectual playfulness, the imaginative energy and resourcefulness used in thinking with and through these critical perspectives.

Perhaps the best way to consider these and other critical perspectives is as *heuristics,* or methods for generating ideas, in this case, ideas about literature. A heuristic often takes the form of a set of questions. Writers and speakers use a sequence of questions to think through a topic in preparation for writing or speaking about it. Greek and Roman rhetoricians developed heuristics for generating ideas and for developing and organizing their thinking by using sets of questions that would enable them to think through a subject from a variety of perspectives. They used questions that invited comparison and contrast, definition and classification, analysis and division of a topic.

You can do the same with the critical perspectives described in this chapter. Instead of the classical questions that encourage comparison or causal analysis, use the questions that accompany each of the critical perspectives. Rather than deciding at first just which critical perspective is best suited to your chosen literary work, jot down answers to the questions for each of the approaches. As you think and write, you will begin to see which critical perspectives yield the most helpful ideas, which, that is, prompt your best thinking. In the course of using the critical questions to stimulate your thinking, you will also decide whether to use one critical perspective or to combine a few. You will also decide what you wish to say about the work. And you will begin to discover why you see it as you do, what you value in it, and how you can substantiate your way of seeing and experiencing it.

In addition, try to consider these critical perspectives as opportunities to engage in a play of mind. Viewing a literary work (or other cultural artifact) from a variety of critical perspectives will enable you to see more of its possibilities of signification. It will also give you a chance to live inside a variety of critical methods, to put on a number of different critical hats. Try to enjoy the experience.

CHAPTER TWENTY-THREE

Writing with Sources

WHY DO RESEARCH ABOUT LITERATURE?

One reason to do research about the literary works you read and study is to understand them better. Another is to see how they have been interpreted over the years, perhaps even centuries, since they were written. Moreover, scholars who have devoted their lives to the study of particular authors, periods, and genres can provide insights that can enrich your understanding and deepen your appreciation of literature.

Reading and studying literature in an academic environment also often requires research. You may be required to read books and articles about an author or a work, using your research in an essay on a literary topic. This is a fairly standard requirement in both general introductory literature courses and in more specialized courses for literature majors.

Even if research on the literature you read is not a requirement, you may find that what others who have read the same works have to say provides a stimulus for your own ideas. For example, you can use *The Humanities Index,* the *MLA Bibliography,* or your library's computerized catalog (see "Using Computerized Databases" in this chapter) to find articles about many of the selections in this book. You can also use *The New York Times Index* and *Book Review Digest* to find reviews of collections of short stories, essays, poems, or plays.

Locate several articles or reviews on a work you have read and, as you read them, notice when you have a particularly strong reaction. You may disagree with what you read, you may be surprised by a new point of view, or you may find your own opinions reinforced in a way you had not expected. You may find that one or more of the works consulted provides the spark for a fully developed essay of your own.

Research materials consist of two general kinds: primary sources and secondary sources. *Primary sources* are firsthand accounts, such as historical documents, diaries, journals, letters, and original literary works, including novels, stories, poems, plays, and essays. Primary sources constitute raw evidence you can use for your research paper. *Secondary sources* are materials written about primary sources. Secondary sources include critical writing that expresses opinions, draws conclusions, or explains an issue. Secondary sources include books, articles, pamphlets, and reviews.

CLARIFYING THE ASSIGNMENT

It is critical that you understand thoroughly the requirements of the assignment. Does your instructor expect you to write a three-page paper or a twenty-page paper—or, as is more likely, something in between? Are you expected to type your paper double-spaced? Are you required to use primary sources, secondary sources, or both? How many words, how many pages, and how many sources are required?

Are you expected to focus on a single work using only one or two sources, on a single work using multiple sources, on multiple works by an author—or something else? Are you expected to document your sources and to provide a list of works you cite in the paper? Be sure that you clarify the specific requirements of the assignment.

SELECTING A TOPIC

Instructors sometimes provide topics, either by assigning everyone the same topic (or some variation of it) or by giving individual students assigned topics of their own. If that is your situation, you can skip down to the next section on finding and using sources. Most often, however, you will need to choose your own topic for a paper utilizing literary research.

You can do a number of things to simplify the task of finding a topic. First, ask your instructor for suggestions. Second, look over your class notes and your reading notes for key points of emphasis, recurrent concerns, and interesting questions and ideas. Third, talk with other students, both with your classmates and with students who have already written papers for the course you are taking. Fourth, you can consult other sources with information about the author and work (or works) you will be writing about. Any or all of these can provide guidance and suggestions about viable topics for your paper.

A *viable topic* is one you can manage in the allotted number of pages required for the assignment. It should also be a topic you can say something about in detail and with specificity. Once you have settled on a topic, it's a good idea to clear it with your instructor. Once your instructor sees what you're interested in, he or she can help you shape the topic, perhaps by narrowing or broadening it in ways that might make it more manageable or potentially more interesting, or both.

You can also get ideas for topics by consulting the ideas for writing suggestions in Chapters Four, Eleven, and Seventeen. In those chapters on fiction, poetry, and drama, you will find additional guidelines for writing about literary works. As a general guideline for all literary papers, however, try to turn your topic into a question that your research paper answers. This question need not be explicit in your topic, but it should emerge in the opening paragraphs of your paper, either explicitly or implicitly, as you present your thesis. When you read the student papers later in this chapter, notice how the focused topics lead naturally into a manageable thesis, allowing for specific observations to be developed into a cogent argument.

FINDING AND USING SOURCES

Researchers have a number of tools available for finding secondary sources—critical studies of authors, analyses of their works, and relevant biographical, social, and historical background material. Your school library's computer databases of books and articles provide comprehensive listings of such sources. But even before tapping into those databases you can consult books in the library reference room as a preliminary step. General reference works about literature can give you an overview of an author's life and work, an introduction to a genre, such as tragedy or epic, or an understanding of a critical approach, such as new historicism, or provide some other kind of generalized prelude to the more focused search you will undertake once you have refined your topic and decided how to proceed with your research.

Works you may find helpful as preliminary guides to literary research include the following:

Columbia Literary History of the United States. Ed. Emory Elliot et al. New York: Columbia University Press, 1988.

An Encyclopedia of Continental Women Writers. Ed. Karharina Wilson. 2 vols. New York: Garland, 1991.

Encyclopedia of World Literature in the Twentieth Century. Ed. Leonard S. Klein. 5 vols. Rev. ed. New York: Continuum, 1983–1984.

European Writers. George Stade and William T. Jackson. 7 vols. New York: Macmillan, 1983–1985.

Longman Companion to Twentieth-Century Literature. Ed. A. C. Ward. 3rd ed. New York: Longman, 1981.

MLA International Bibliography. Available on line and on CD-ROM. New York: MLA, 1921–.

The New Cambridge Bibliography of English Literature. 5 vols. Cambridge: Cambridge UP, 1967–1977.

The New Guide to Modern World Literature. Ed. Martin Seymour-Smith. 4 vols. New York: Peter Bedrick Books, 1985.

The New Princeton Encyclopedia of Poetry and Poetics. Ed. Alex Preminger and T.V.F. Brogan. Princeton: Princeton UP, 1993.

The Oxford History of English Literature. 13 vols. Oxford: Oxford UP, 1945–.

A Research Guide for Undergraduate Students: English and American Literature. By Nancy L. Baker. 2nd ed. New York: MLA, 1985.

Research Guide to Biography and Criticism: Literature. Ed. Walton Beacham. 2 vols. Osprey, FL: Beacham, 1985.

You can find some or all of these sources in the reference sections of many college libraries.

USING COMPUTERIZED DATABASES

You may have access to your university library with a link from your room, your home, your residence hall, or your school's computer center. You may also be able to access the library's holdings through computer terminals located in the library proper. One of the first things you should do is learn how to use the library's computerized catalog to access bibliographic information. You can get a friend to help you. You can get assistance from the library staff. Your school may even provide formal instructions in use of their on-line services.

All on-line catalogs are organized in a similar way. The information that is retrieved and displayed on the computer screen depends on the format you use in making your request. Most programs offer at least three search options: author, title, and subject. For example, suppose you know that you want to write about Ernest Hemingway. You don't have a precise topic in mind, and want to consult some books *about* Ernest Hemingway. To find out what books the library has about Hemingway, you would search for "Hemingway, Ernest," as subject. (The program will give you on-screen instructions on how to start the search.) Following is what one university library's on-line catalog lists for Hemingway as subject:

1.	Hemingway, Ernest 1898		1 entry
2.	Hemingway, Ernest 1899–1961		52 entries
3.	Hemingway, Ernest 1899–1961	Appreciation	1 entry
4.	Hemingway, Ernest 1899–1961	Appreciation—Germany	1 entry
5.	Hemingway, Ernest 1899–1961	Bibliography	10 entries
6.	Hemingway, Ernest 1899–1961	Biography	12 entries
7.	Hemingway, Ernest 1899–1961	Juvenile letters	1 entry
8.	Hemingway, Ernest 1899–1961	Biography—Marriage	4 entries

Notice that category 2 includes fifty-two items. Since the category has no heading, to determine the kinds of books included within it, you would press 2 and scan the listings. If you press 8, Biography—Marriage, four listings appear:

1.	Along with Youth	Griffin, Peter
2.	Hadley	Diliberto, Gioia
3.	The Hemingway Women	Kert, Bernice
4.	How It Was	Hemingway, Mary Welsh

If you want more data on one of these books, press the appropriate number. You will be provided with information about the length and size of the book, its publication date, and location. Most systems also provide information about the book's availability.

In browsing in one of these books about Hemingway's personal life, you might get an idea for a research paper that focuses on the home life depicted in "Soldier's Home." Reading that story in the context of secondary biographical sources would be one way to gain added insight into the story. Another would be to consult critical secondary sources that are less biographical than analytical and interpretive. Here you would return to that large category of 52 items and begin scanning for titles that appeared promising. One such recent title is Paul Smith's *A Reader's Guide to the Short Stories of Ernest Hemingway* (Boston: G. K. Hall, 1989). After locating a few such sources, you are ready to read and take notes as you work toward refining your topic and developing a thesis for your paper. To do that you should use the techniques of note taking described earlier—especially annotation and the double-entry notebook—to develop a critical perspective.

USING THE INTERNET FOR RESEARCH

Through the Internet you can connect to the World Wide Web (WWW), a system of linked electronic documents. Navigating the Web involves connecting to electronic pathways within and between Web pages and Web sites. Accessing various Web sites for information requires either a specific Internet address or use of a search engine, such as Yahoo or InfoSeek, which allows you to enter key words for the topic you wish to research.

To make use of the Internet for your literary research, follow these guidelines:

- Link your computer to the Internet, open your Web browser, and call up the browser's home page.
- Go to the browser's search options and select a search engine.
- Enter the words you want to search (key words for your topic).
- Survey the list of "hits" the search engine provides.
- Click on any related hyperlinks that seem interesting.
- Skim each site and download those that appear promising. (Store their addresses for future use.)

Using the Internet for research can be fun. But it can also prove a formidable challenge. One problem you may confront is a large number of hits or potential sources. Deciding which of these are of most value requires careful analysis. This is due largely to the openness of the World Wide Web. Since anyone can put up a Web site and place any information on that site, you cannot be certain that the site's information is accurate, current, or unbiased.

Therefore, you must evaluate Internet sources for their reliability. You can use the following guidelines to do so.

- Consider the source of the electronic information you discover. Consider the credentials of the source provider. Is the source maintained by a reputable provider, such as a university or corporation?

• Compare your electronic sources with your print sources. Evaluate your electronic sources for range and depth as well as accuracy and currency of information.
• Ask yourself whether you are sufficiently confident of the source's reliability to cite it in your research paper.

For guidance in documenting electronic sources, see pp. 1403–1405.

DEVELOPING A CRITICAL PERSPECTIVE

How can you use outside critical sources to develop a critical perspective? Let us say, for example, that you are required to write a five- or six-page paper analyzing and interpreting a particular literary work. Let us speculate further that you are required to read and cite in your paper two or three outside sources. And let us also imagine that you have been asked to select critical sources that provide different interpretive perspectives on the work you will be writing about. What will you do? How will you go about writing this paper?

Here is where annotation and the double-entry notebook are particularly helpful. Let's assume that you have found the relevant articles or sections of books you need. If you can photocopy the appropriate pages, do that. Then annotate those pages the same way you annotated the literary work itself. (Before you actually read any criticism, however, do some preliminary writing—annotating, listing, journal keeping.) In your journal or notebook summarize in a few sentences the thesis or main idea of each source. Opposite your summaries, jot down a set of responses. When you record your summaries of the articles and your responses leave plenty of room, as you will want to add other things that you notice on rereading them.

Still another technique useful for writing critical papers is quoting key passages and commenting on their significance or validity. In writing a paper about Hemingway's "Soldier's Home," for example, you could (and perhaps should) quote a bit of the story directly. Or you might select a few such passages for direct quotation. Of more importance than your apt selection of such passages, however, is the way you relate them in your comments explaining their significance. The place to get a start on this crucial process is in your reading journal or double-entry notebook, where you can record the relevant passages verbatim and practice commenting on their significance. These comments will provide the germ from which your paper will grow.

In using outside critical sources you will find yourself usually doing one of two things. Either you will agree with the critic and use his or her comments to bolster your interpretation. Or you will disagree and take exception to the critic's ideas by arguing against them in your paper. Both are acceptable ways to proceed. In fact, given a requirement to include more than two sources, it is highly unlikely that you will agree entirely with the positions taken in all of them. Thus even if you agree in part, you will need to make distinctions and to express qualified approval as you modify their viewpoints and express the reservations necessary to make them congruent with your own ideas.

DEVELOPING A THESIS

You should be able to state your thesis in a single direct sentence. Your thesis concentrates in a sentence nutshell what you wish to emphasize—your central idea, the point you wish to make about your topic. Your essay overall elaborates your thesis, providing evidence in the form of textual support.

In general, when you develop your thesis, try to make it as specific as you can. At the same time, try to avoid oversimplifying your idea by setting up mutually exclusive "black and white" categories. Introduce qualifying terms as necessary. Words such as "although," "however," "but," and "rather" suggest an approach that reflects thoughtful consideration of the issues.

Consider the theses of two of the three student papers included later in this chapter. In one paper, Lucienne Retelle analyzes Alice Walker's story "Everyday Use" in the context of a critical article she read about the work. Here is her thesis:

> In relating the story ["Everyday Use"] to the Biblical Prodigal Son, Patricia Kane shows thoughtfulness and insight; however, in her eagerness to expose what she sees as differences in male/female values, she demonstrates a superficial understanding of the Gospel parable and misses the central message: one of repentance and forgiveness.

Notice how Ms. Retelle takes issue with the critical perspective offered by Patricia Kane. She uses the critic's view as a springboard from which to launch her own analysis of the story as one whose central concerns are the prodigal son's repentance and his father's forgiveness. Her thesis is clear, direct, and specific. We know what she thinks. It remains for her to flesh out her interpretation and to refute Patricia Kane's argument.

In a second paper, Michelle Carerra discusses James Joyce's short novel, "The Dead." Her topic is the "awakening" or enlightenment of its main character, Gabriel Conroy. Here is her thesis:

> Like the stories in *Dubliners* that lead up to it, "The Dead" dramatizes a moment of self-realization. The story portrays the gradual awakening of Gabriel Conroy, whose vision of his wife, Gretta, at the end of the story, is at once a frustrating disappointment and a touching movement toward understanding and love.

Notice how Ms. Carerra's thesis is elaborated over two sentences. The first generalized sentence links "The Dead" with the stories that precede it in Joyce's linked collection of short stories, *Dubliners*. Her second sentence elaborates the thesis in more detail, specifying what she believes happens to Joyce's protagonist. Such detail is necessary in a thesis. Without detail, readers can have only a vague sense of the writer's idea.

DRAFTING AND REVISING

In writing your research paper, follow the guidelines for drafting and revising your paper just as you would for an interpretive paper in which you do not use secondary sources. Set aside sufficient time to work out the basic argument of your research paper. This will involve the extra time necessary for tracking down sources, taking notes, and reflecting on their significance for your overall argument.

In your preliminary draft you should try to articulate your argument without your sources. Get your ideas down as clearly as you can. Provide the textual support you need as evidence from the work(s) you are analyzing or otherwise discussing. Then write a second draft in which you incorporate the relevant sources either to support your idea or as representing antithetical views that you attempt to refute.

Leave time for a third draft in which you further refine your thinking, taking into consideration additional evidence you find in the text or in the secondary sources. Use this third draft also to provide precise documentation for your sources—accurate parenthetical citations and precise page references.

In general, approach the drafting of a research essay or paper as you would any other essay or assignment. Make sure you get your own ideas into the initial draft before you begin relying on your secondary sources. This is critical if you want to avoid letting your sources take over the voice and content of your research essay.

CONVENTIONS

In writing about literary works you need to observe a number of conventions, including those regarding quotations, verb tenses, manuscript form, and the strict avoidance of plagiarism.

Using Quotations

In writing about literature you will need to quote lines from poems, dialogue from plays and stories, and descriptive and explanatory passages from prose fiction and nonfiction. For quoted prose passages that exceed four typed lines in your paper, begin a new line and indent ten spaces from the left margin for each line of the quotation. This format, called block quotation, does not require quotation marks because the blocked passage is set off visually from the rest of your text.

Michelle Carerra uses two block quotations in her research paper (included later in this chapter) on Joyce's "The Dead," both from the text of the short novel. In her research essay on E. B. White (see the last student paper in this chapter), Radhika A. Jones uses three block quotations, two from White's works—an essay and a novel—and one from a secondary source.

When quoting poetry, separate the lines of poetry with slashes. Include a space before and after each slash.

> Lorraine Hansberry derived the title of her best-known play, *A Raisin in the Sun,* from a poem by Langston Hughes. In "Dream Deferred," the speaker asks, "What happens to a dream deferred? / Does it dry up / like a raisin in the sun?"

Chapter Eleven contains examples of student writers quoting from the poems they write about. For additional examples of students introducing quotations from literature into their analytical essays, see Chapters Four (on fiction) and Seventeen (on Drama).

Verb Tense Conventions in Literary Papers

In writing about literature, you will often need to describe a story, novel, poem, or play. In doing so you will use present tense, past tense, or both. In most instances, it is conventional to use present tense when describing what happens in a literary work. Consider the following examples:

> In Robert Hayden's "Those Winter Sundays," the speaker <u>reflects</u> on his father and <u>realizes</u> how much his father <u>loved</u> the family.

The present tense is used to describe the speaker's actions of reflecting and realizing. The past tense is used to describe the father's action, which occurred in the past, well before the speaker's present acts of reflecting and realizing.

> Ibsen's <u>A Doll House</u> <u>portrays</u> a conventional middle-class environment and a conventional middle-class family. In displaying a strong concern for money and for authority, Ibsen's characters <u>reveal</u> their middle-class values. Ibsen often <u>portrayed</u> characters with everyday problems of the middle class.

The verbs describing what the play does are in the present tense. Those describing what the dramatist did are in past tense.

Manuscript Form

In preparing your paper for submission, observe the following guidelines:

1. Type your essay double-spaced on 8 1/2-inch by 11-inch paper.
2. Leave 1-inch margins at the top and bottom, and on both sides.

3. Beginning in the upper left corner 1 inch below the top and 1 inch from the left side, type the following on separate lines:
   (a) your name
   (b) your instructor's name
   (c) course title, number, and section
   (d) date
4. Double-space below the date and center your title. It is not necessary to put quotation marks around your title or to underline or italicize it. It is necessary to underline titles of books and plays used in your title. And it is necessary to put quotation marks around the titles of short stories, poems, and essays.
5. Be sure your printer's ink supply or your typewriter ribbon is adequate for clear, readable copy.
6. If your printer feeds connected sheets of paper, be sure to separate them before submitting your essay.
7. Number each page consecutively beginning with the second page, 1/2 inch from the upper-right corner.
8. Clip or staple the paper, making sure the pages are right side up and in the correct numerical order.

Plagiarism

Plagiarism is the act of using someone else's words, ideas, or organizational patterns without crediting the source. Plagiarism may be the result of careless note taking, or may be deliberate. To avoid plagiarism, it is necessary to clearly indicate what you have borrowed so your reader can distinguish your own language and ideas from those of your sources.

Research essays and papers written with little original thought and containing many long passages of quoted and summarized material strung together may include plagiarized words and ideas. Be sure to credit each source you use at the point of borrowing, even in the midst of a paragraph or the middle of a sentence. Be sure not only to acknowledge using the source but also, if you have used exact language from the source, to put quotation marks around the borrowed words and phrases—even if you have separated some of the borrowed material and interspersed your own language.

Plagiarism is a serious offense. A form of academic theft, plagiarism is not tolerated in colleges and universities. Some have stringent policies, including failure for the course in which the plagiarism occurs and even expulsion from school.

To avoid plagiarism observe the following guidelines in writing your research essays and papers.

• Develop your own ideas about the works you read. Keep notes of your ideas separate from the notes you take from sources.

- Jot the title, author, and page number of a source on the page or notecard you use for your notes pertaining to material from that source.
- Put quotation marks around quoted material you copy from sources into your notes.
- When you summarize and paraphrase a source, be sure to use your own words. Avoid having the source open before you when you summarize and paraphrase.
- If you introduce any quotations from a source into your summaries and paraphrases of them, put quotation marks around the quoted words and phrases.
- Make sure that your own ideas and your own voice are the controlling centers in your research essays and papers. Use your sources to support, illustrate, and amplify your own thinking presented in your own words.
- Observe the conventions for documentation provided in the following section of this book, in your college handbook, and in the *MLA Handbook for Writers of Research Papers,* 4th ed. (1995).

DOCUMENTING SOURCES

If you incorporate the work of others into your paper, it will be necessary to credit your sources through documentation. You should always provide source credit when quoting directly, paraphrasing (rewriting a passage in your own words), borrowing ideas, or picking up facts that aren't general knowledge.

By crediting your sources, you are participating honestly and correctly in shared intellectual activity. You are showing your reader that your knowledge of a text includes some insights into what others have thought and said about it. And you are assisting your reader, who may want to consult the sources that you found valuable.

Established conventions for documenting sources vary from one academic discipline to another. For research essays and papers in literature and language the preferred style is that of the Modern Language Association (MLA). MLA documentation style has established conventions for citing sources within the text of research essays, papers, and articles. It also has established conventions for the list of works you use in preparing your research writing—usually called "List of Works Cited" or "Works Cited."

In the current MLA style, parenthetical citations within the text indicate that a source has been used. These citations refer the reader to a reference list, which should start on a new page at the end of the paper. In the "alternate" or "old" MLA style, references are marked by raised numbers in the text that correspond to numbered notes either at the foot of the page (footnotes) or the end of the paper (endnotes). Both the reference list and the endnotes and footnotes contain bibliographic information about the sources; however, the arrangement, punctuation, and capitalization of the sources differs between the two reference styles.

New MLA Style: Parenthetical Citations Paired with a Reference List

When you refer to a specific section of a work in the body of your paper, provide your reader with the author and page numbers of your source. Place the page numbers in parentheses, and add the author's name if it isn't contained in your sentence.

> According to Lawrence Lipking (30–39), a poet's life involves much more than his or her literal biography.

> A recent critic argues that a poet's life involves much more than his or her literal biography (Lipking 30–39).

If your paper includes two or more works by the same author, add the title of the work before the page number(s). The following are examples of other kinds of citations commonly found in literature papers.

A work in an anthology:

> Bacon's "Of Revenge" affords us a glimpse at his view of human nature: "There is no man doth a wrong for the wrong's sake, but thereby to purchase himself profit, or pleasure, or honor, or the like" (1565).

(The author and title of the anthologized selection should be listed in the *Works Cited*.)

A classic verse play or poem:

> "She loved me for the dangers I had passed," recounts Othello, "And I loved her that she did pity them" (I.iii.166–67).

(Act, scene, and line numbers are used instead of page numbers. Arabic numbers may also be used for the act and scene.)

> Tennyson's Ulysses compares a dull existence to a dull sword when he says: "How dull it is to pause, to make an end, / To rust unburnished, not to shine in use!" (22–23).

(Line numbers are used instead of page numbers. Note the use of a slash [/] to indicate the end of a line.)

Styling a Works Cited List

The items in a works cited list should be alphabetically arranged. The following are typical kinds of entries for a literature paper.

A book by a single author:

> Lipking, Lawrence. *The Life of the Poet: Beginning and Ending Poetic Careers.* Chicago: U of Chicago P, 1981.

(The second line is indented five spaces.)
An article in a book:

> Williams, Sherley Anne. "The Black Musician: The Black Hero as Light Bearer." *James Baldwin: A Collection of Critical Essays.* Ed. Kenneth Kinnamon. Englewood Cliffs, NJ: Prentice-Hall, 1974. 147-54.

(The page numbers "147-54" refer to the entire article. References to specific pages would appear in parenthetical citations.)
A journal article:

> Walker, Janet. "Hardy's Somber Lyrics." *Poetry* 17 (1976): 25-39.

(The article appeared in issue 17 of the journal *Poetry*. The page numbers refer to the entire article.)
A work in an anthology:

> Bacon, Francis. "Of Revenge." *Literature: Reading Fiction, Poetry, Drama, and the Essay.* 2nd ed. Ed. Robert DiYanni. New York: McGraw-Hill, 1990. 1565-1655.

(The page numbers refer to the entire essay.)
Cite the anthology itself if you are using more than one selection from it. The selections can simply be cited without repeating the anthology title and publication data.

> DiYanni, Robert, ed. *Literature: Reading Fiction, Poetry, Drama, and the Essay.* 4th ed. New York: McGraw-Hill, 1998.
> Tennyson, Alfred, Lord. "Ulysses." DiYanni. 649-50.

A multivolume work; a second edition:

> Daiches, David. *A Critical History of English Literature.* 2nd ed. 2 vols. New York: Ronald, 1970.

A translation:

> Auerbach, Erich. *Mimesis: The Representation of Reality in Western Literature.* Trans. Willard Trask. Princeton: Princeton UP, 1953.

Alternate MLA Style: Note Numbers Paired with Endnotes/Footnotes

Using Note Numbers

Raised note numbers, in consecutive order, follow the quotation or information being cited. They belong *after* all punctuation, except a dash.

> "She loved me for the dangers I had passed," recounts Othello,
> "And I loved her that she did pity them."[1]

If you include several quotations from the same text in your paper, you may switch to parenthetical citations after the first note. This will reduce the number of footnotes or endnotes.

> Emilia tells Desdemona that jealousy is "a monster begot upon
> itself, born on itself" (III.iv.155-56).

Using Endnotes/Footnotes

Each raised note number corresponds to a footnote or endnote. The only difference between footnotes and endnotes is their placement in the paper. Footnotes appear at the bottom of the page on which the reference occurs: quadruple-space between the last line of text and the first note. Endnotes are grouped together on a separate page immediately following the last page of text.

The following are the same sources given above, but now in endnote form. Note that specific page references are given for each entry; these page references would be contained in parentheses in new MLA style.

[1]Lawrence Lipking, *The Life of the Poet: Beginning and Ending Poetic Careers* (Chicago: U of Chicago P, 1981) 30-39.

[2]Sherley Anne Williams, "The Black Musician: The Black Hero as Light Bearer," in *James Baldwin: A Collection of Critical Essays,* ed. Kenneth Kinnamon (Englewood Cliffs, NJ: Prentice-Hall, 1974) 147.

[3]Janet Walker, "Hardy's Somber Lyrics," *Poetry* 17 (1976): 35.

[4]Francis Bacon, "Of Revenge," *Literature: Reading Fiction, Poetry, Drama, and the Essay,* 2nd ed., ed. Robert DiYanni (New York: McGraw-Hill, 1990) 1565-66.

[5]David Daiches, *A Critical History of English Literature,* 2nd ed., 2 vols. (New York: Ronald, 1970) 2: 530.

[6]Erich Auerbach, *Mimesis: The Representation of Reality in Western Literature,* trans. Willard Trask (Princeton: Princeton UP, 1953) 77.

Noting Subsequent References

It is usually enough simply to list the author's name and the appropriate page(s) in subsequent references to a source.

> [7]Lipking 98.

DOCUMENTING ELECTRONIC SOURCES

The MLA Handbook for writers of Research Papers, 5th ed., distinguishes electronic citation forms according to whether the material is available on a CD-ROM or whether it is available online. Because electronic media are continually changing, the details of citations may evolve even as the basic needs for citing references remain the same.

Source on CD-ROM

Citations for electronic sources are distinguished according to whether the material was published once, like a book, or whether it is published in regularly updated periodical form.

CD Produced as a One-Time Publication

Author's name followed by the title underlined or italicized; editor, compiler, or translator if relevant. Publication medium; edition, release, or version if relevant; place of publication; name of publisher; date of publication.

> French, William P., ed. *Database of African-American Poetry,*
> *1760–1900.* CD-ROM. Alexandria, VA: Chadwyck-
> Healy, 1995.

If you wish to cite part of a work, place quotation marks around the part or section you cite. Underline or italicize the title of the work as a whole. If you are not provided with an author, begin your citation with the title.

> "Modernism." *The Oxford English Dictionary.* 2nd ed. CD-ROM.
> Oxford: Oxford UP, 1992.

CD Updated Periodically

Author or institution name followed by a period. Article's title and original date or inclusive dates in quotation marks. Database name underlined followed by type of source (CD, for example). Locator and provider or the vendor of the database if available; date of publication.

Smith, Dinitia. "Hollywood Adopts the Canon." *New York Times*
10 Now. 1996: D4. *New York Times Ondisc.* CD-ROM.
UMI–Proquest. Dec. 1996.

If you cite a CD-ROM multidisk publication, include the total number of
disks if you use them all, or the disk number(s) for the one(s) you wish to cite.

Patrologia Latina Database. CD-ROM. 5 discs. Alexandria, VA:
Chadwyck-Healey, 1995.

Online Sources

When citing Internet sources include the Internet address or URL (uniform
resource locator) in angle brackets < >. Provide the entire address, including
the access-mode identifier (http, ftp, gopher, telnet, news).

Online Scholarly Project or Reference Database

Title underlined or italicized; editor if given followed by electronic publication
information, date or latest update, and name of sponsoring institution if provided. Date of access and electronic address in angle brackets.

African American Women Writers of the Nineteenth Century. Ed.
Thomas P. Lukas. 1999. Digital Schomburg, New York
Public Library. 11 May 1999
http.//digital.nypl.org/schomburg/writers_aal9/>.

Online Professional or Personal Site

Name of person who created the site, title of site underlined or italicized; if no
title is given, provide a title such as Home Page. Name of institution or organization associated with the site, date of access, and electronic address.

Pace University Home Page. Pace. 3 Dec. 1998
<http://www.pace.edu/>.

Online Book

Author's name, title underlined or italicized; name of editor, compiler, or translator if relevant. City of publication, publisher, year of publication. Date of access and electronic address.

Alice Dunbar-Nelson. *The Goodness of St. Rocque and Other Sto-
ries.* New York: Dodd, Mead, 1899. *African American
Women Writers of the Nineteenth Century.* Ed. Thomas P.
Lukas. 1999. Digital Schomburg, New York Public
Library. 11 May 1999
<http://digilib.nypl.org/dynaweb/
digs-f/wwm976/@Generic_BookView>.

Online Periodical Article

Author, title of article, title of journal or magazine, volume, number, year, and
date for scholarly journal; date for magazine; electronic address.

Scholarly Journal

Pereira, Edimilson de Almeida. "Survey of African–Brazilian Literature." *Callaloo* 18.4 (1995): 875–80. 11 Apr. 1997
   <http://muse.jhu.edu/journals/callaloo/v018/18.4de_
   almeida_pereira9.html>.

Magazine

Landsburg, Steven E. "Who Shall Inherit the Earth?" *Slate* 1 May
   1997. 2 May 1997 <http://slate.com/Economics/97-
   05-01/Economics.asp>.

THREE STUDENT ESSAYS INCORPORATING RESEARCH

A Student Essay Using One Source as a Stimulus

The following essay, "The Prodigal Daughter in Alice Walker's 'Everyday Use,'"
was discovered by Lucienne Retelle, a student who wanted to read what others had to say about Walker's story. When Lucienne found this article, she remembered reading "The Prodigal Son" in Chapter One of this text and
became intrigued with the idea of relationships between "Everyday Use" and
the Biblical parable. You may want to reread Walker's story (page 357) as well
as "The Prodigal Son" (page 21). Then read Patricia Kane's article and finally
Lucienne Retelle's evaluation of that article. How convincing do you find
Kane's argument? Retelle's responding argument? How do you think Kane
might answer Retelle?

PATRICIA KANE

The Prodigal Daughter in Alice Walker's "Everyday Use"

"Everyday Use," Alice Walker's variation on the archetypal prodigal child story not
only amuses with its deft humor, it also pleases by ending with the equivalent of the
fatted calf remaining with the stay-at-home. Walker's tale, one of those collected in *In

Love and Trouble, displays a world in which a mother comes to see both the humbug in the returning daughter's new appreciation of the mother's realm and the everyday worth of her younger daughter. The reversals and variations from the Biblical prodigal son story suggest that when women make the choices, the tale expresses different values.

The story, narrated by the mother, begins as she awaits a visit from her older daughter, Dee. Immediately her tone establishes the values of her realm as she declares that the swept yard in which she sits is "more comfortable than most people know" (47). As she sits comfortably in her yard, she muses on her daughters. Dee, older, better looking, and brighter than Maggie, scorned the everyday world of rural blacks and went away to school. Maggie, scarred in a fire Dee may have set to destroy a house she hated, will marry a local man and remain in the familiar life. When the mother describes her life and work, including killing hogs and calves, she pictures a realm in which any special meals to mark reconciliation will be more personal than those provided through the orders of the Biblical father.

Prodigal children value what they once rejected, and the returned Dee now finds her scorned past to be fashionable. Her mother, though bemused by her exclaiming over chitlins and other familiar food, agrees to let her take the butter churn to use for a centerpiece. She humors her wish to be known as Wangero although she reminds Dee that she was named for her aunt and grandmother, not any oppressor. The elements of the familiar story seem to be in place. Although chitlins have replaced the calf at the meal, the butter churn evokes calves, and Dee/Wangero seems to now appreciate her mother's world. The matter of the name, however, which shows the mother confident of who she is while Wangero/Dee takes her sense of style from others, provides a variation in the theme and foreshadows the central scene.

Wangero/Dee claims two quilts handmade by her grandmother and earmarked for Maggie on her marriage. Wangero/Dee, who refused a quilt when she went away to college because they were out of style, proclaims these to be priceless. She will value them, she says, by hanging them whereas Maggie would "be backward enough to put them to everyday use" (57). Maggie, although this was "her portion," responds by agreeing to let her sister have the quilts because such "was the way she knew God to work" (58).

God, however, in the person of the mother, suddenly feels something like she does when the spirit of God touches her in church. She hugs Maggie for the first time and returns her portion to her. Realizing not only the worth of her daughter of everyday use, but also that even if her use of the quilts will wear them out, their value lies in use not display, she bestows the riches of her domestic kingdom not on the prodigal but on the familiar daughter. Maggie is the now-embraced lost child of this tale.

After the prodigal child leaves, the mother and Maggie sit in the yard "just enjoying" (59) in the realm of everyday use.

Work cited:
  Walker, Alice. "Everyday Use." *In Love & Trouble.* New York: HBJ, 1973. 47–59.

Has the Prodigal Daughter Really Returned?

Lucienne Retelle
Introduction to Fiction
Prof. Judith Stanford

Patricia Kane, in her response to Alice Walker's "Everyday Use," states that this story is a variation on the theme of the Biblical story, "The Prodigal Son." She proposes that the mother in Alice Walker's story is the feminine equivalent to the father of the Prodigal Son, and as such, they both represent God. Kane suggests, however, that the male and female express different values, and that when God is represented as female, he/she makes different choices. Kane concludes that Walker exemplifies this through Mama who ultimately "bestows the riches of her domestic kingdom not on the prodigal but on the familiar daughter," and Maggie becomes the embraced lost child.

In relating the story to the Biblical Prodigal Son, Patricia Kane shows thoughtfulness and insight; however, in her eagerness to expose what she sees as differences in male/female values, she demonstrates a superficial understanding of the Gospel parable and misses the central message: one of repentance and forgiveness.

At first glance Kane's thesis is appealing and perhaps convincing; but when you compare the two stories carefully, the actions and responses of both parents have basic similarities. In both stories, the mother and father freely give their children their "portion" as they need and/or request it. The Biblical father gives his younger son his portion of property which enables him to go off to a distant place to live as he wishes. Mama in "Everyday Use" works hard to raise money from her church which enables her daughter Dee to go away to school; and she offers her a quilt as well. The father is rich and the mother is poor, but the portions they give are relatively equal based upon their means.

The Prodigal Son rejects his inheritance, just as Dee rejects part of her portion, the quilt, because at the time it held no value for her. Both the Prodigal Son and Dee, the prodigal daughter, repudiate the values of their parents, and they leave home to pursue their own way of life.

The mother's and father's responses to their children when they come back are different in character: the father is fully open and receiving, while the mother is somewhat reticent. This is *not*, as Kane suggests, because they have different values, but because the children come back for different reasons and under different circumstances. The prodigal son has not been successful in his worldly life, and comes back weary and destitute, longing for the comforts of his father's home. In contrast, Dee comes back flaunting her success and new worldly values. She is elaborately dressed while the son is probably in rags. He comes back humbly, hoping to be received; she comes back confidently, intending to take.

While their actual responses may be different in character, Mama and Biblical father both demonstrate similar parental desires and feelings for their "lost" children. The father waits for his son, sees him a long way off and is deeply moved at his return. They greet warmly and the father has no words of reproach. He immediately orders the cooking of a fatted calf by way of celebration. Similarly, Mama also "waits." She has a recurring dream in which she and Dee publicly reunite with arms around each other, Dee with tears in her eyes, grateful to her mother saying she couldn't have done anything without her mother's help. But their reunion doesn't happen as it does in Mama's dream. Dee arrives with haughty airs, gives her mother a perfunctory greeting, and immediately busies herself with her camera. Nevertheless, Mama has prepared to celebrate. She has made her yard clean and wavy and prepares the "fatted calf" represented by pork, collards, chitlins, and corn bread.

Kane observes that because the Biblical father "orders" others to do the cooking while Mama prepares her own, the mother's feast is more personal, suggesting that a woman's mark of reconciliation is "better" or has a higher value than the male's. This judgment is irrelevant to the message: both parents demonstrate acceptance and desire for reconciliation through their welcome and through offering the celebration meal. Their different styles of doing so, whether due to male/femaleness, lifestyles, or personal habits, do not alter the quality of the reconciliation. Their messages are the same; the setting and cultures are different.

A secondary theme of the Prodigal Son parable is the attitude of the older brother who stayed at home with his father. Kane does not address this theme, nor does she make a comparison between this brother and Maggie, which is critical if we are to understand more fully Mama's behavior.

In the Biblical story, the older brother is angry and resentful at his father's lavish display of welcome for his returning brother. The father pleads with him to join in the celebration and reassures his son by saying the older son is always with him and everything the father has is also the son's.

In contrast, Maggie is shy and cowers in the presence of her returning sister. No anger or resentfulness is implied on her part. In her own way she is present and participates in the celebration. Moreover, she does *not* show resentfulness, and when Dee demands the quilts, Maggie tells her she can have them. The quality of Maggie's generosity is great, considering her comparative lack of life's gifts. She is neither as intelligent, nor as attractive, nor as well educated as Dee.

Just as the Biblical father reassured his older son, Mama has a protective attitude toward Maggie; she takes back the quilts from Dee, and hugs Maggie to her. Mama has already given Dee the butter churner, which in its own way is just as important and symbolic a portion. It too has intrinsic, sentimental and "everyday use" value.

Both parents demonstrate love for their "lost" children, both waited for their return, and both celebrated. The fact that Mama gives Maggie the quilts does not take away from Dee: Dee long ago rejected this portion, so it became Maggie's.

Finally, to approach the two stories as an in toto variation on the theme of the Biblical story, based on differences in male/female values as Kane has done, is inappropriate, for two reasons: first, as previously described, the stay-at-home children are very different from one another, and Mama's attitude is clearly related to the kind of person Maggie is. Second, and more significant, Dee has not truly "returned" as the prodigal son has, and therefore a direct comparison cannot be made. Dee does not come back seeking forgiveness and does not indicate she has anything to repent. She is still "out there" in the world, breaking away, and the story ends with her leaving again.

I suggest, however, that if Alice Walker had written her story differently—according to Mama's dream—Mama's attitude and response assuredly would have been akin to the Biblical father's. She would have been tearfully and overwhelmingly joyful at Dee's return. In addition, she would have had no need to protect Maggie from her sister's demand for her "portion"—because, most likely, Dee wouldn't have demanded it in the first place.

Reference Sources:

Kane, Patricia. "The Prodigal Daughter in Alice Walker's 'Everyday Use.'" *Notes on Contemporary Literature.* 15.2 (1985): 7.

The New American Bible. Jean Marie Hiesberger, gen. ed. New York: Oxford, 1995.

A RESEARCH PAPER ON A SINGLE WORK USING MULTIPLE SOURCES

The following paper was prepared for a writing and literature course in which students were given a choice of works to research and write about. They were asked to focus on an issue in the work or an aspect of it and to develop a research essay that explained their idea, using at least three secondary sources in addition to the text of the work itself.

The writer focuses on one character, the protagonist of James Joyce's short novel "The Dead," the culminating work in a collection of short stories entitled *Dubliners*. She directs her attention to the central concern of the work, which she identifies as the "awakening" of Gabriel Conroy. Her paper explains what this awakening is, what it means for the protagonist, and why it is important.

In the course of her research essay, the writer summarizes her sources, quotes directly from them, and quotes from the story, sometimes briefly and occasionally more extensively in block form. She summarizes scenes from the work and explains their significance for her topic. Essentially an analysis of character, the paper contrasts the character of the protagonist with two other characters to better illuminate his. In the conclusion the writer broadens the scope of her analysis to implicate the reader by suggesting ways that the protagonist's experience may correspond to our own.

Michelle Carerra
Prof. Krickstein
October 15, 1994
English 120

The Awakening of Gabriel Conroy

Like the stories in <u>Dubliners</u> that lead up to it, "The Dead" dramatizes a moment of self-realization. The story portrays the gradual awakening of Gabriel Conroy, whose vision of his wife, Gretta, at the end of the story is at once a frustrating disappointment and a touching movement toward understanding and love. Robert Adams voices the view of more than one critic when he writes of "The Dead" that this "greatest of the stories in <u>Dubliners</u> stands apart from the rest, being warmer in tonality, richer in the writing, and more intimate in its subject matter" (83). Florence Walzl concurs when she writes that "The Dead is markedly different from the earlier stories [. . .] . It is not only a longer, more fully developed narrative, but it presents a more kindly view of Ireland" (428).

In one sense the "dead" of the title are all those who have lived and died, those who have gone before the festive inhabitants of Dublin who celebrate the Christmas season, Gabriel Conroy and Gretta among them. In another sense the dead are all those who, though alive and breathing, have lost their naturalness, their spontaneity, and most importantly, their passion. Gabriel, one of these, has lost touch with his past and with traditional Irish values. He looks instead toward continental Europe, toward the future, and toward change for an escape from the outmoded and restrictive attitudes of the past (Ellmann 395).

We glimpse Gabriel arriving at the party as a man coming in from the dark, here the symbolic darkness of Gabriel's ignorance (Walzl 433). Gabriel appears to be something of a generous gentleman, as he slips a coin into the hand of the servant Lily. With this gesture of holiday good will, Gabriel attempts to buy his way out of further conversation with Lily, but she makes him uncomfortable by commenting that "The men that is now is only all palaver and what they can get out of you." It is a remark, Joyce's narrator notes, that Lily delivers "with great bitterness" (178).

Gabriel deflects further discussion by attending to his coat and scarf and shoes. He then presses the tip into the girl's hand and disappears up the stairs. Our first impression of Gabriel is of someone who though cultivated and cultured, is

nonetheless naive. This small scene sets the tone for
Gabriel's more serious errors in understanding, which Joyce
saves for a later revelation.

Early in the story, Gabriel is distinguished from his wife,
Gretta, his emotional opposite. Gabriel describes Gretta as
someone who would walk home in the snow if she were allowed.
Gabriel, on the other hand, will not go out in snow or rain
without his galoshes. Unlike her more cultured husband, Gretta
is without pretention, and she is more spontaneous. She
retains the youthful romantic nature she possessed when a
young man named Michael Furey died, according to her version
of the event, for love of her. Even in middle age, Gretta
appears more comfortable with the memory of the boy from her
past than with the presence of her more cultivated husband.

Gabriel's difference from the others at the party is
revealed during a conversation with Miss Ivors. When Miss
Ivors suggests that Gabriel and Gretta accompany her and some
friends on a vacation to the primitive Irish-speaking Aran
islands off the western coast of Ireland, Gabriel does not
accept. He tells her that he has already planned to travel in
the other direction—east to France and Belgium. These
countries represent for Gabriel the world of culture and
civilization. The Irish islands, by contrast, represent what
he considers uncivilized and repugnant. Ironically, however,
his wife's family come from one of those islands—a fact that
Gabriel prefers to ignore.

During his conversation with Miss Ivors, Gabriel confesses
his disgust with Ireland this way: "O, to tell you the truth
. . . I'm sick of my own country, sick of it" (189). When
pressed for an explanation, however, Gabriel declines to
provide one. He feels superior to his ignorant countrymen, and
is out of sympathy with their restrictive political, religious
and cultural values. To say so, however, would be distasteful
and uncomfortable. It would also be discourteous. And so
Gabriel is silent.

Other important scenes put Gabriel on display, increasing
our perception of him as more concerned with surface than with
substance, more impressed by the sound of his voice than the
truth of his words or the value of his actions. Gabriel's
clichéd after-dinner speech, for example, is filled with
outlandish praise of his old aunts, whom he flatters beyond
their comprehension. Gabriel sees the old Irish past as dead,
paying it only a token and insincere tribute. His thoughts and
energies are directed elsewhere—to the future and to the
Continent. Yet Gabriel points ironically toward what seems
most true—the power of the past to continue living into the
future; the inability of individuals to completely escape

their past and their cultural roots. In rejecting those
things, Gabriel is rejecting the essential part of himself. It
is unclear how much of this he understands. At the time he
gives his speech, however, it seems clear that he believes
none of his lofty sentiments.

We begin to see just how much Gabriel is shut out of his
wife's inner life in still another scene at the party. After
dinner there is singing by Mr. Darcy. When he sings an Irish
ballad called "The Lass of Aughrim," Gretta listens
enraptured, lost in memory:

> She was standing right under the dusty fanlight and
> the flame of the gas lit up the rich bronze of her
> hair which he had seen her drying at the fire a few
> days before. She was in the same attitude and seemed
> unaware of the talk about her. At last she turned
> towards them and Gabriel saw that there was colour
> on her cheeks and that her eyes were shining. (212)

At this moment Gabriel feels an immense tenderness towards
his wife and also a strong sexual desire for her. Both his
tenderness and his desire grow as the party winds down and
Gabriel accompanies Gretta to the hotel. Gabriel's desire
increases further as he rehearses mentally how he will
approach Gretta and how he will express his feelings.

The critical point of this scene concerns the thoughts Gretta
has as Gabriel watches her. He expects her to tell him that she
has been thinking of him and of their life together. Instead,
she tells Gabriel about Michael Furey, whose image she had
conjured up when Mr. Darcy sang "The Lass of Aughrim," a song
Michael Furey himself sang before he died. As Gabriel listens
to Gretta reminisce about the poor delicate boy with the big
sad eyes, he experiences with a shock a moment of self-
realization:

> Gabriel felt humiliated by the failure of his irony
> and by the evocation of this figure from the dead, a
> boy in the gasworks. While he had been full of
> memories of their secret life together, full of
> tenderness and joy and desire, she had been comparing
> him in her mind with another. A shameful
> consciousness of his own person assailed him. He saw
> himself as a ludicrous figure, acting as a pennyboy
> for his aunts, a nervous well-meaning sentimentalist,
> orating to vulgarians and idealising his own clownish
> lusts, the pitiable fatuous fellow he had caught a
> glimpse of in the mirror. Instinctively he turned his

> back more to the light lest she might see the shame
> that burned upon his forehead. (219-20)

Gabriel's humiliation is increased further when he learns
the circumstances of Michael Furey's death. With that
knowledge comes a second revelation accompanied by Joyce's
description of the snow falling over all of Ireland. The
beauty of the language, which matches the beauty of the snow-
filled scene, also suggests the beauty of Gabriel's perception
that all people share life and death, that the dead live and
the living shall join the dead in a shared humanity. "The time
had come," as the narrator puts it, "for Gabriel to set out on
his journey westward" (223), a statement that has been
characterized as "an enigmatic sentence that has bothered many
readers of 'The Dead'" (Benstock 167).

But as Joyce's biographer Richard Ellmann has explained
(396), it is not really so puzzling. According to Ellmann,
this westward journey is the journey back to Gabriel's past,
to his cultural roots. The tone of Joyce's sentence suggests
resignation and relinquishment, as Gabriel gives up his "sense
of the importance of civilized thinking, of Continental
tastes" (Ellmann 397) and other nice distinctions he prides
himself in making. Moreover, this journey westward is also the
ultimate journey toward the setting sun, toward the closing of
life. For Gabriel, the journey toward what he previously saw
as death is really a journey into life, the real life of
feeling as experienced by those more sincere and authentic
than he has ever been. For although Gabriel Conroy had indeed
been sick of his country, as he had told Miss Ivors, he
nevertheless finds himself drawn to it. The story, ultimately,
turns on a paradox: that to go forward one has to go back.
Gabriel's soul swoons as he hears the snow "falling faintly
through the universe and faintly falling, like the descent of
their last end, upon all the living and the dead" (224).

During Gabriel's vision, Joyce slows down the narrative pace
(Loomis 150). Time slows as we are presented a vision of
humanity's common fate. It is a vision that we share rather
than one we merely analyze. For we too know that like Gabriel
and Gretta and Michael Furey, everyone is subject to the
experiences of love and sorrow, pain and joy, passion and
tenderness, living and dying. And, like Gabriel, in realizing
and reminding ourselves of the inevitability of this simple
truth, our sympathies are enlarged and deepened for Gabriel,
for Gretta, for Michael Furey, and for one another as well.

Works Cited

Adams, Robert. <u>James Joyce</u>. New York: Octagon Books, 1980.

Benstock, Bernard. "The Dead." In <u>"Dubliners": Critical Essays</u>. Ed. Clive Hart. London: Faber and Faber, 1969. 156-69.

Ellmann, Richard. "The Backgrounds of 'The Dead.'" <u>Dubliners: Text, Criticism, and Notes</u>. Ed. Robert Scholes and A. Walton Litz. New York: Viking, 1969. 388-403.

Joyce, James. "The Dead." <u>Dubliners: Text, Criticism, and Notes</u>. Ed. Robert Scholes and A. Walton Litz. New York: Viking, 1969. 175-224.

Loomis, C. C. "Structure and Sympathy in Joyce's 'The Dead.'" <u>PMLA</u> 75 (1960): 149-51.

Walzl, Florence. "Gabriel and Michael: The Conclusion of 'The Dead.'" <u>Dubliners: Text, Criticism, and Notes</u>. Ed. Robert Scholes and A. Walton Litz. New York: Viking, 1969. 423-79.

A RESEARCH PAPER USING MULTIPLE WORKS AND MULTIPLE SOURCES

In her essay on E. B. White, Radhika A. Jones presents a view of the writer's work that focuses on the way the egg functions as image and symbol of White's central themes. The writer announces her focus in the opening paragraph and highlights the way eggs pervade White's work signifying "the sanctity, the beauty, and the fragility of life." This idea the writer complicates and enriches as she develops her essay, as for example in the final sentence of paragraph 4 where she remarks that eggs are "at once sources of stability and continuity; they are links in a natural chain"; and again near the end of paragraph 8 where she sees White's recognition of eggs as sources not only of continuity but also of "subtle change." The writer also links the symbolism of the egg to White's concern with time and change and with his irrepressible idealism.

One of the more impressive aspects of Ms. Jones's essay is the way she moves back and forth among White's works she cites as evidence. Instead of treating each work once and then moving on to another, she weaves two, three, sometimes four different works into a single paragraph, showing how each illustrates or enforces the point she is making at the time. In her third paragraph, for example, she refers to two novels and two essays to explain her point. Although other features of the essay might be held up as exemplary, we might mention the writer's aptly chosen epigraph, which points toward the idea she develops in the essay. In addition, mention might be made of the way her conclusion brings the essay full circle in a return to its title.

Radhika A. Jones

Essentially Egg-Shaped

> I don't know of anything in the entire
> world more wonderful to look at than a nest
> with eggs in it. An egg, because it
> contains life, is the most perfect thing
> there is. It is beautiful and mysterious.
> An egg is a far finer thing than a tennis
> ball or a cake of soap. A tennis ball will
> always be just a tennis ball. A cake of
> soap will always be just a cake of soap—
> until it gets so small nobody wants it and
> they throw it away. But an egg will someday
> be a living creature.
>   (E.B. White, The Trumpet of the Swan)

The reverent admiration that Sam Beaver, young hero of The Trumpet of the Swan, has for eggs can only be rivalled by that of his creator. E. B. White's work, from his essays to his children's literature, is replete with eggs—as objects of natural beauty and as sources of life. A relatively small and simple object with an infinite number of thematic associations, the egg as subject matter perfectly reflects White's ability to transform concrete observations into clear, universal conclusions. White's eggs are rich with meaning; they are links in a never-ending cycle of life; they are sources of continuity in a world fragmented by passing time. And even in those works that do not figure literal eggs, the sanctity, the beauty, and the fragility of life that they represent pervades White's work.

Perhaps only a writer so attuned to simplicity and detail could write an essay that is just about brown and white eggs, as is White's "Riposte." In this essay he takes issue with an Englishman who believes that Americans prefer white eggs to brown because white eggs seem more hygienic and brown eggs more countrified. "My goodness" is White's comment (Essays 60): "there is no such thing as an *unnatural* egg" (Essays 61). Mr. Priestley (the Englishman) has missed the point altogether—an egg is an egg; its color is irrelevant to its identity. That White would devote an entire essay to discussing this topic is a testimonial to his interest in the egg. He would not have it misjudged.

In and of themselves eggs—oval shells of calcium carbonate—
are not terribly exciting, but as sources of new life they
hold magical and exhilarating properties. In the spectrum of
White's work, eggs hatch right and left and White revels in
each birth. One pictures White as his own character Sam
Beaver, sitting awed and motionless as he witnesses the
miracle of the cygnets' birth (Trumpet 29-30). Or as Charlotte
the spider, offering her "sincere congratulations" on the
occasion of the newly hatched barnyard goslings (Web 44). In
"The Geese" White appoints himself caretaker of three goslings
and meticulously looks after their eggs as a tribute to a
goose acquaintance who had died of old age (145-49). "Spring"
finds him caring for "254 little innocents"—chicks for whom
he and his stove act as mother-hen (Meat 234-37). In short,
White hails eggs as producers of life; in his writing and in
his life they are objects to be revered and tended
appropriately.

It would not be enough, however, simply to say that White is
a writer with a healthy respect for the wonder of an egg: to
do so would be to take the egg out of context. White's eggs
are very much in context; they are part of the natural cycle
of life, of development. The hatching of eggs is not a once-
in-a-lifetime occurrence. It happens every spring and every
spring it brings the renewal of youth and hope. "Each spring,"
writes White in Charlotte's Web, "there were new little
spiders hatching out to take the place of the old" (183).
Likewise, the three new goslings and their offspring in "The
Geese" continue the tradition of the original pair of geese
with whom White had "an acquaintance of such long standing—
long standing and loud shouting" (145). Eggs come as
dependably as the seasons; they are at once sources of
stability and continuity; they are links in a natural chain.

Indeed, if White can be said to have a central
preoccupation, then it is certainly the mystery of time's
cyclic nature, and the precarious yet precious relationships
that ensue. His literal tales of hatching eggs are only a few
of his many essays and stories that address the topic of
passing time and chronicle the natural cycles of life. Such
is clearly the case in Charlotte's Web, which begins with the
birth of Wilbur the pig and follows him into old age, while
also telling the story of his spider friend Charlotte and her
descendants. Wilbur is saved from an untimely, unnatural
death by the resourceful and clever Charlotte; he lives out
his life as Nature intended, as does she. But Charlotte's Web
is more than a story of animal progeny; it is a tale of how
the love between two friends enriched both of their lives.
White has taken us beyond the simple hatching of eggs to life
outside the egg-shell, where we can see his joy for life

reflected in the relationships he creates among living things.

"Once More to the Lake" and "The Ring of Time" move to the realm of human relationships and life cycles, away from literal eggs. "Once More to the Lake" involves the time lapse between being a son and then becoming a father of one's own son, and depicts the change in temperament that naturally accompanies those passing years. White so vividly remembers the summers when he was a boy that he is lulled into thinking "there had been no years," but as he gradually notices subtle changes in the lake and in himself—the cacaphonous sounds of the new outboard motors, his reluctance to swim in the rain as he would have done long ago—he realizes that life may be cyclic but it spirals ever forward. He has aged and there have undeniably been years (Essays 191-202).

"The Ring of Time" addresses the illusion of the young that time has no ramifications. "She is at that enviable moment in life," White writes of a young circus performer who is riding her horse around the ring, "when she believes she can go once around the ring, make one complete circuit, and at the end be exactly the same age as at the start" (Essays 145). Later in the essay he refers to this feeling as "true seduction" and a "delusion," for "time has not stood still for anybody but the dead, and even the dead must be able to hear the acceleration of little sports cars and know that things have changed" (Essays 148-49).

Eggs may come every spring, in other words, but they are not the same eggs. Charlotte's children and grand-children cannot really replace Charlotte in Wilbur's eyes. White recognizes the new eggs each spring for what they are worth—sources of continuity yet also subtle change. Life is not merely seasonal repetition, even though this spring may be reminiscent of the last.

The egg is a tiny microcosm of life, and as such it is a perfect example of White's tendency to look to the smaller things in order to facilitate a better understanding of the larger issues of his day. "Who has the longer view of things, anyway, a prime minister in a closet or a man on a barn roof?" he asks in "Clear Days" (Meat 20), written slightly before the outbreak of World War II. Later, in 1941, he writes, "I sometimes think I am crazy—everybody else fighting and dying or working for a cause or writing to his senator, and me looking after some Barred Rock chickens" (Meat 236). White is clearly concerned with the topic of war, but he continues to write about it in the context of his experiences on his farm.

In his review of One Man's Meat, Benjamin DeMott dismisses White's subjects because they are so ordinary. He lists them as "Maine, progress as disaster, frustrations of urban life, and so on" (63) as if it bores him to include them at all. But I am more inclined to agree with the reviewer who wrote, "It is the gift of the poetic imagination to shape commonplace things into conclusions of considerable weight" (DeVane 164). To the attentive artist no place does not lend itself to observation, no topic is too mundane. White commits himself to reporting what he sees and thinking about what meaning he can derive from his observations, not to merely musing on grandiose abstractions. Likewise, he commits himself to preserving and protecting what life there is around him, instead of lamenting the lives he cannot save in Europe.

> I soon knew that the remaining warmth in this stubborn stove was all I had to pit against the Nazi idea of *Frühling* [. . .] . Countries are ransacked, valleys drenched with blood. Though it seems untimely I still publish my belief in the egg, the contents of the egg, the warm coal, and the necessity for pursuing whatever fire delights and sustains you. (Meat 237)

White invests in the egg the ultimate sanctity of human life, and he will go to great lengths to uphold it. He works within his sphere of influence to comment on more universal themes; his sight and his actions lead to insight and speculation (144).

> "Look," he [Templeton] began in his sharp voice, "you say you have seven goslings. There were eight eggs. What happened to the other egg? Why didn't it hatch?"
> "It's a dud, I guess," said the goose. (White, Web 45)

E. B. White does not write fairy-tales; not all of his eggs hatch. White's world has a dual nature, where happiness and sorrow co-exist peacefully, naturally. Perhaps this co-existence is the reason children recognize him as a wonderful writer for he does not hide from them what well-meaning adults would. White has the ability to gently exploit the contradictions in life; his essays and stories probe the reality of not-so-happy endings.

When I was eight I cried for Charlotte, who died alone at the Fair Grounds. I felt that it was grossly unfair that she who had worked so hard should perish so soon after her triumph—felt that she should at least be able to return home with Wilbur. Now I realize that White has too much respect for Nature to have permitted me that miracle. Charlotte was a spider with a spider's life span; such things cannot be altered, and certainly not by a writer as familiar with and respectful of life cycles as E. B. White.

However much White might want to promote life among his fellow creatures, he is not idealistic enough to suppose that he can always be successful. In "The Geese" he expresses a desire to hatch the old goose's three eggs as a tribute to her, but he finds himself not obsessed enough to devote himself to an incubator for the necessary thirty days. Instead, he purchases three new-born goslings from a neighbor (145-46). Where there is life, there is also, so to speak, non-life, and White presents this contrast directly: "Summer was upon us, the pond was alive again. I brought the three eggs up from the cellar and dispatched them to the town dump" (147). We are not told what to make of this incongruence, we are merely given it, and we know by the startling juxtaposition of those two sentences that White is thinking about it himself. His closing sentence is along similar lines: "I don't know anything sadder than a summer's day" (149). Summer days in "Once More to the Lake" are tinged with sadness as well, as the son prepares to bathe in the rain, the father feels "the chill of death" (<u>Essays</u> 202). But on the other hand, those same summer days are also replete with the joy of new life—the three goslings nurtured by White, the son who feels no chill of death. White's world is by no means pessimistic, nor is it idealistically optimistic. It is a depiction of reality as seen through the eyes of a man who acknowledges the unfortunate, yet is always willing to "publish his belief in the egg" (White, <u>Meat</u> 237).

> The world White loves is more than a collection of things, natural and man-made, or a fascinating organization of reassuring cyclical, ongoing processes: it is a world in which the motive for creating, nurturing, teaching, encouraging, singing, and celebrating is love. (Elledge 303)

This love pervades White's works: it is implicit in all of his essays, his children's stories. It motivates him to take his son to visit his old haunt in "Once More to the Lake"; it motivates him to keep a vigil by the stove that warms the chicks in "Spring"; it motivates him to raise three goslings in memory of the old goose in "The Geese." In short, it motivates him to cherish life, and to cherish the eggs, symbolic and literal, that bring life into the world. In

White's world, life is nothing short of a miracle, and "to him a miracle was essentially egg-shaped" (Elledge 25).

Works Cited

DeMott, Benjamin. "Books: Pick of the List." Rev. of <u>Essays of E. B. White</u>, by E. B. White. <u>Saturday Review</u> 20 Aug. 1977: 63.

DeVane, William C. "A Celebration of Life." Rev. of <u>One Man's Meat</u>, by E. B. White. <u>The Yale Review</u> 1942: 163-65.

Elledge, Scott. <u>E. B. White: A Biography</u>. New York: Norton, 1984.

Hoy, Pat C. II, and Robert DiYanni. "E. B. White." Introduction. <u>Prose Pieces: Essays and Stories, Sixteen Modern Writers</u>. New York: Random, 1988. 143-45.

White, E. B. <u>Charlotte's Web</u>. New York: Harper & Brothers, 1952.

---. <u>Essays of E. B. White</u>. New York: Harper & Row, 1977.

---. "The Geese." <u>Prose Pieces: Essays and Stories, Sixteen Modern Writers</u>. Ed. Pat C. Hoy and Robert Di Yanni. New York: Random, 1988. 145-49.

---. <u>One Man's Meat</u>. 2nd ed. New York: Harper & Row, 1944.

---. <u>The Trumpet of the Swan</u>. New York: Harper & Row, 1970.

APPENDIX

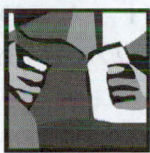

Writers' Lives

LEE K. ABBOTT
(b. 1947)

Lee K. Abbott was raised in southern New Mexico in the small town of Las Cruces. He received a B.A. (1970) and M.A. (1973) from New Mexico State University, and an M.F.A. from the University of Arkansas in 1977. In 1989 he became a professor of English at the Ohio State University. His stories, collected in five volumes, have appeared in a variety of magazines and literary journals, including *Harper's* and *The Kenyon Review.* Abbott has been awarded numerous prizes, and his stories have been included in *Best American Short Stories* (1985 and 1987), the *Pushcart Prize* volumes (1987 and 1989), and the *O. Henry Prize Stories* (1984). His work has also been twice nominated for a Pulitzer prize.

MARGARET ATWOOD
(b. 1939)

Margaret Atwood, one of Canada's foremost writers, was born in Ottawa. She graduated from the University of Toronto and received an M.A. from Radcliffe College in 1962. The recipient of many awards and fellowships, Atwood has won international acclaim for her critical writing and fiction. One of her most widely known novels, *The Handmaid's Tale,* which was made into a film, describes life in a future world where women suffer severe repression. Her numerous stories, novels, and poems are complemented by her editorial and critical work, which includes the *Oxford Book of Canadian Verse.*

1425

W. H. AUDEN
(1907–1973)

Wystan Hugh Auden was born in England but emigrated to America in 1939, becoming a U.S. citizen in 1946. As a young English poet his early work reflected Marxist and Freudian thinking as well as a droll wit. His later work revealed a more conservative political strain and a Christian sympathy. Auden was a prolific editor, anthologist, and translator as well as one of the twentieth century's most renowned poets.

ELIZABETH BISHOP
(1911–1979)

Elizabeth Bishop was born and raised in Worcester, Massachusetts. As a consequence of her father's early death and her mother's mental illness, Bishop, at age six, went to live with her grandmother in Nova Scotia. After graduating from boarding school and Vassar College, she moved to Key West, Florida, and then to Brazil, where she lived for fifteen years. Returning to the United States, she taught at the University of Washington and at Harvard. She published her first volume of poems, *North and South,* in 1946 and later won both the Pulitzer prize and the National Book Award. Her last collection, *Complete Poems 1927–1979,* won the National Book Critics Circle Award.

WILLIAM BLAKE
(1757–1827)

William Blake was born in London and was apprenticed to an engraver there at the age of fourteen. At age twenty-two Blake entered the Royal Academy as an engraving student, but clashes over artistic differences precipitated his return to private study of such Renaissance masters as Raphael, Durer, and Michelangelo. A revolutionary at heart, Blake moved in a circle of radical thinkers including William Godwin, Thomas Paine, and Mary Wollstonecraft. His poems, which he published himself, and for which he supplied engravings and water colors, include *Songs of Innocence* (1789), *Songs of Experience* (1794), and the prophetic *Marriage of Heaven and Hell* (1790), among others. His work is visionary and unconventional.

JORGE LUIS BORGES
(1899–1986)

Born in Buenos Aires, Argentina, Borges' first language was English, though he wrote poetry and fiction in Spanish. Besides doing his own extensive writing, Borges anthologized Argentine literature and served as director of Argentina's National Library. His intricately plotted stories often explore philosophical themes, which frequently employ images of mirrors and mazes. Borges' poor eyesight eventuated in blindness, an occasional subject in his work. His most popular work includes the stories in his books *Fictions* and *Labyrinths*.

KAY BOYLE
(b. 1902)

Born in Minnesota, Kay Boyle lived in England, Austria, and France for nearly twenty years, until the onset of World War II. From 1946 to 1953 she was a correspondent for *The New Yorker* magazine. The author of more than fifteen novels, seven short-story collections, books of poetry, and stories for children, Boyle has also translated books from French into English. Although some of her works depict the human spirit in conflict with oppressive forces, a number of her stories and novels explore the human need for love.

ROBERT BROWNING
(1812–1889)

Robert Browning was born in a London suburb and educated primarily through reading in his father's extensive library. Browning's first poems were printed in his early twenties, but he did not achieve fame as a poet until he was in his fifties. Browning was married to the poet Elizabeth Barrett, with whom he lived in Italy, returning to England after her death. The work that made him famous, *The Ring and The Book* (1868–69), which is based on a seventeenth-century Roman murder trial, represents the poetic form for which he is best known—the dramatic monologue. The form weds the character revelations of drama with the lyricism of poetry. Among Browning's most successful examples of the genre is "My Last Duchess."

RAYMOND CARVER
(1939–1988)

Originally from Oregon where he was raised in a working-class milieu, Raymond Carver lived in Washington and spent much of his life in California. After working at a series of low-paying odd jobs, Carver worked as an editor and as a college teacher at the University of California at Berkeley, the University of Iowa, the University of Texas at El Paso, and Syracuse University. Carver's fictional mentors include James Joyce, Ernest Hemingway, and above all, Anton Chekhov, whose stories Carver admired above those of all other writers. His best stories are lean and spare and touch deeply on central human problems.

ANTON CHEKHOV
(1860–1904)

Born in southern Russia and trained to become a doctor, Anton Chekhov during his university years wrote short pieces for newspapers and magazines. By the time he received his medical degree, he was already well known as a writer, and he would eventually write hundreds of stories and half a dozen of the most important plays of the modern theater, including *Uncle Vanya, The Three Sisters, The Seagull,* and *The Cherry Orchard*. His short stories' style has been considered a model by successive generations of writers.

KATE CHOPIN
(1851–1904)

Born and raised in St. Louis, Kate Chopin spent the years after her marriage in Louisiana as a society matron and mother of six. Business setbacks and the death of her husband in 1883 led her to assume control of the family business. Subsequently devoting herself to writing, she published short stories in magazines along with a novel, *The Awakening* (1899), now considered a formative work of female self-assertion. At the time, however, this work, like some of her short stories, was condemned for its highly charged eroticism and its guiltless adultery.

E. E. CUMMINGS
(1894–1962)

Edward Estlin Cummings was born in Cambridge, Massachusetts. After attending Harvard University, he joined the Red Cross Ambulance Corps in France during World War I. Comments critical of the French army in his letters got him imprisoned, but he was released after four months. His poems, which began appearing in the 1920s, are identifiable by their unusual typography and punctuation. In addition to poetry, Cummings wrote essays and a novel, *The Enormous Room,* based on his experiences in France. He also produced graphic art, including paintings.

JOHN DONNE
(1572–1631)

John Donne was both a poet and a prelate, who made his name as a preacher at St. Paul's Cathedral in London. Before his conversion from Roman Catholicism to Anglicanism and his ordination as an Anglican priest, Donne wrote worldly love lyrics at the court of Queen Elizabeth I. His poems, which circulated in manuscript, were justly famous, and were later collected under the title *Songs and Sonnets.* Donne's poetry is justly celebrated for its striking and unusual imagery, its strong and direct language, and its probing analyses of the experiences of religious faith and doubt and of secular and sacred love.

T. S. ELIOT
(1888–1965)

Thomas Stearns Eliot was born in St. Louis, Missouri, but moved to England in 1914 and became a British citizen in 1927. Though he had been raised in the southwestern United States, Eliot traced his family's roots to New England, where he vacationed. He studied at the Sorbonne in Paris and at Merton College, Oxford, England. Instead of pursuing an academic life, Eliot turned to business and poetry, working as a clerk for Lloyd's Bank of London and as editor and director of the London publishing house Faber and Faber, all the while writing the poems that were to make him famous. The most explosive of these was *The Waste Land,* which burst upon the literary scene in 1922, becoming for a long time the most famous modern poem in English. Earlier, Eliot had written "The Love Song of J. Alfred Prufrock," a dramatic monologue that portrays the life of a timid, inhibited man.

RALPH ELLISON
(1914–1994)

Ralph Waldo Ellison, who was named after the important nineteenth-century writer and intellectual Ralph Waldo Emerson, was born in Oklahoma and educated at the Tuskegee Institute in Alabama, where he studied music. His short stories and his novel, *Invisible Man,* for which he won the National Book Award in 1953, employ musical motifs and stylistic elements, which he describes in his essays on music, collected in *Shadow and Act.* This book also contains essays and interviews about race and race relations, the central subjects of Ellison's work.

WILLIAM FAULKNER
(1897–1962)

William Faulkner was born into a Mississippi family whose influence and wealth had disappeared during the Civil War. Faulkner lived most of his life in the South he memorialized in his fiction, writing about the Oxford, Mississippi, of his actual life in his fictional Yoknapatawpha County. Faulkner won a Nobel prize for Literature in 1949, along with a National Book Award and two Pulitzer prizes. His major novels include *The Sound and the Fury, As I Lay Dying,* and *Absalom, Absalom!* "A Rose for Emily," his best-known and perhaps best-loved story, portrays the results of change in the post–Civil War South.

LAWRENCE FERLINGHETTI
(b. 1919)

Lawrence Ferlinghetti was both a poet and a publisher who founded the City Lights bookstore in San Francisco, the country's first paperback bookstore. He also edited City Lights Books, a feature of the San Francisco poetry revival of the 1950s. Along with Allen Ginsberg, whose poem "Howl" he published, which led to his being charged with obscenity, Ferlinghetti was a central figure in the group of writers known as the "Beats." His poetry often centers on political concerns and typically reflects anti-bourgeois tendencies and attitudes. His best-known volume, however, *A Coney Island of the Mind* (1958), contains his more lyrical and freely imaginative poems.

GABRIEL GARCIA MARQUEZ
(b. 1938)

Gabriel Garcia Marquez was born in Colombia and studied law in Bogota before working as a full-time journalist until 1965. He received the Nobel prize for literature in 1982, and has won numerous international literary awards. One of the members of "El Boom," the flowering of fictional writers in South America in the 1950s and 1960s, he published his first novel, *In Evil Hour* (1962), to critical acclaim. *One Hundred Years of Solitude* (1967) brought him international recognition. Through the use of "magic realism"—the embellishing of a realistic setting with surrealistic imagery and events—he created what has been described as "the greatest revolution in the Spanish language since *Don Quixote* of Cervantes."

CHARLOTTE PERKINS GILMAN
(1860–1935)

Charlotte Perkins Gilman was born in Hartford, Connecticut. Raised in semi-poverty, Gilman's early education was sparse, though she took up commercial art at the Rhode Island School of Design in 1878. After marriage and the birth of a daughter, Gilman experienced a deep depression, the cure by rest which became the basis of her short story "The Yellow Wallpaper." Gilman became an essayist and public speaker, who espoused feminist themes. Her book *Women and Economics* (1898) was one of the earliest to urge that women take a significant place in the working world. Her feminist ideas were also expressed in her Utopian novel *Herland,* which describes a world of women without men.

THOMAS HARDY
(1840–1928)

Thomas Hardy, English Victorian novelist and poet, was born in Dorsetshire, the region of England he later called Wessex in his novels. Hardy trained as an architect and began to practice in 1867, but he soon turned his attention to writing, initially poetry, then fiction, for which he became famous. His first published poetry, however, was not available until 1898, when *Wessex Poems* appeared, after he had given up his career as the novelist who had penned *Jude the Obscure* and *Tess of the D'Urbervilles.* Hardy's poetry ranges widely in style and form, as he experimented with image and idiom throughout his thirty-year career as a poet.

NATHANIEL HAWTHORNE
(1804–1864)

Nathaniel Hawthorne lived most of his life in New England, the setting for many of his works, including his famous masterpiece, *The Scarlet Letter*. During the administration of American President Franklin Pierce, Hawthorne served as American consul in Liverpool, England. He traveled in Europe, most notably in Italy, and he lived for a while in Rome, the setting for his novel *The Marble Faun*. Besides his handful of novels, Hawthorne wrote many tales and short stories that have become classics of American literature. "Young Goodman Brown" is one of his most famous and one of his finest stories, particularly in its reflection of the Puritan frame of mind, which absorbed Hawthorne's literary imagination.

SEAMUS HEANEY
(b. 1939)

Seamus Heaney was born and raised in Northern Ireland, an area torn for decades by political, religious, and civil strife. He was educated at Queens College, Belfast, where he later taught. His first collection of poetry, *Death of a Naturalist* (1966), led a new generation of Irish poets in civil war–torn Northern Ireland. His poems, which touch on themes of nature and history as well as politics, are among the most celebrated of the century, as Heaney has been hailed as the successor to William Butler Yeats as the most important Irish poet of the later modern era.

ERNEST HEMINGWAY
(1899–1961)

Born in Illinois, Ernest Hemingway was both a Nobel prize and a Pulitzer prize winner for his fiction. His career was nourished by the twentieth century's major cultural and political events, including World War I, the Spanish Civil War, and the flourishing of the arts in Paris in the 1920s. Like many American writers, Hemingway worked originally as a newspaper reporter. He also fought in Italy during World War I, was wounded, and used his war experiences in his early book of stories and sketches, *In Our Time* (1925), and in his novel *A Farewell to Arms* (1929). He lived in Paris, where he met Gertrude Stein and Ezra Pound. An avid sportsman and big-game hunter, Hemingway reveled in competition and pursuits that pitted him against nature. His direct and unadorned writing style has been much imitated by subsequent writers.

GEORGE HERBERT
(1593–1633)

George Herbert, English poet and Anglican priest, after serving as a University of Cambridge orator, became a parson in charge of a country parish. His prose work, *The Country Parson,* was recognized as a valuable source of wise guidance for devout and useful Christian living. His poetry, collected after his death by his friend Nicholas Ferrar, was printed in 1633 as *The Temple.* Herbert's poems, while ranging widely in imagery like those of his contemporary John Donne, offer a more homely and familiar window on religious experience.

ROBERT HERRICK
(1591–1674)

Robert Herrick is an English poet best known for his pastoral and love lyrics. Herrick attended Cambridge University and became an Anglican cleric in 1627. Though a clergyman, Herrick was a lover of London's society of poets and wits, who initially regarded his work in rural England as a form of exile. Herrick was a classicist, who was influenced by his Roman predecessors. His verse is formal and refined. His best-known poem, "To the Virgins, to Make Much of Time," celebrates the theme of *carpe diem,* or seize the day.

GERARD MANLEY HOPKINS
(1844–1889)

Gerard Manley Hopkins was an English poet gifted not only in his poetic resourcefulness but also in music and art. Hopkins was born in Essex, outside London. As a student at Oxford University he studied classic Greek and Roman literature. At the age of twenty-two Hopkins converted from Anglicanism to Roman Catholicism and became a Jesuit priest. He spent several years in working-class parishes until he was appointed Professor of Greek at University College in Dublin in 1877. His poetry is distinguished by an intricate form of rhythm, which he called "sprung rhythm" and by an intense musicality.

A. E. HOUSMAN
(1859–1936)

Alfred Edward Housman, British poet and scholar, was an eminent classical scholar and translator and a professor of Latin at Cambridge University from 1911 to 1936. He achieved general fame with his book *A Shropshire Lad* (1896), a collection of poems that stressed the brevity and fragility of youth and love. His lyrics, which celebrate nature, are set against the background of the English countryside and reveal the influence of English ballads and classical verse. Among his most famous poems are "When I Was One-and-Twenty" and "To an Athlete Dying Young."

BEN JONSON
(1573–1637)

Ben Jonson was born and educated in London, where he received a strong grounding in classical Greek and Latin. He worked as a bricklayer and a soldier before becoming a playwright and poet. Jonson was famed for his wit and his ability to engage others in contests of poetry, and he was well known at The Mermaid Tavern in London for the weekly literary discussions, during which he would match wits with rival poets, including William Shakespeare. Jonson's followers called themselves the "tribe of Ben" in his honor. He was crowned as the first poet Laureate of England in 1619.

JAMES JOYCE
(1882–1941)

James Joyce is best known as the author of *Ulysses,* one of the most important literary works of the twentieth century. Joyce was born in Ireland, but left his home country to escape the stultifying influence of his country's social system, especially as reflected in institutional Catholicism. After a brief return to Ireland, Joyce moved permanently to Europe, living in Italy, France, and Switzerland, supporting his writing by giving language lessons. His short-story collection, *Dubliners,* describes the lives of ordinary people living in the Irish capital. His novel *A Portrait of the Artist as a Young Man* exemplifies Joyce's use of stream-of-consciousness, a technique that became popular among a number of the world's writers. His masterpiece, *Ulysses* (1920), brought Joyce both international acclaim and financial freedom.

JOHN KEATS
(1795–1821)

John Keats, who was born in London, experienced the loss of both his parents when he was still a child. After being apprenticed to a medical doctor, Keats received his own license to practice medicine, but gave up that career for poetry. At an early age Keats was stricken with tuberculosis, and he went to Italy in the hope of regaining his health. He died in Rome at the age of twenty-five, but not before producing a small but significant body of enduring poems, including the great "Ode to a Nightingale" and "Ode on a Grecian Urn."

JAMAICA KINCAID
(b. 1949)

Jamaica Kincaid was born and educated on the island of Antigua. She left Antigua for the United States, where she began writing and publishing stories in magazines as diverse as *Rolling Stone* and *The New Yorker,* where she later became a staff writer. Her first book, *At the Bottom of the River,* won a prize, and since then she has received widespread recognition for her unusual essays, short stories, and novels, which dispense with standard plots, characters, and dialogue. Her work is saturated in the life and culture of the British West Indies.

BOBBIE ANN MASON
(b. 1940)

Bobbie Ann Mason was born in Kentucky, and she draws her fictional material from the lives of rural and working-class people from that part of the United States. *Shiloh and Other Stories* (1962), Mason's first book, deals with the impact of the outside world via television on people whose lives do not include knowledge and experience that most Americans take for granted. Her writing vividly conveys the regionalisms and sense of place of her native Kentucky. Before becoming a fiction writer, Mason worked as a college teacher, having earned a doctorate at the University of Connecticut.

BOB McKENTY
(b. 1935)

Bob McKenty is a retired businessman, who worked for many years for the Equitable Life Assurance Company as a computer specialist. He has written light verse for as long as he can remember, getting serious about humor some years ago when he established a newsletter of light verse entitled *Lighten Up!* He lives happily in Matawan, New Jersey, with his wife, Mary.

JOHN MILTON
(1608–1674)

John Milton was born to be a poet. He was educated under private tutors at home before entering St. Paul's School and Cambridge University, where he studied Greek and Latin and mastered modern languages in his spare time. He then spent five years of independent study followed by a two-year tour of Europe all in preparation for his vocation as a poet. During the Puritan Interregnum, Milton served as a secretary to Oliver Cromwell, who ran the Commonwealth until the restoration of the English kings. Milton's poetry is vastly learned and heavily allusive, especially in his long magisterial epic poems *Paradise Lost* and *Paradise Regained*. But Milton also wrote a number of memorable poems on a smaller scale, including some of the finest sonnets in English.

FRANK O'CONNOR
(1903–1966)

Frank O'Connor was born Michael O'Donovan in Cork, Ireland. As a short-story writer and playwright, O'Connor was an important element in the Irish Literary Revival that followed Ireland's independence from English rule in 1921. O'Connor worked initially as a librarian, while the stories he wrote were published in the *Irish Statesman*. In 1935 he became codirector, with William Butler Yeats, of Dublin's Abbey Theatre. His stories contain vivid use of Irish speech and manners. His literary criticism includes *The Lonely Voice* (1966), a fine study of the short story.

TILLIE OLSEN
(b.1913)

Tillie Olsen was born in Nebraska, where she was raised and educated in the public schools, leaving school in the eleventh grade. Her fiction has received wide recognition for its portrayal of the lives of women, especially their struggles with working-class poverty. Olsen has also often been cited for her role in guiding young writers. Her best-known works are a short-story collection, *Tell Me a Riddle* (1961), from which "I Stand Here Ironing" is taken, and *Silences* (1978), which examines the forces that silence art.

LUIGI PIRANDELLO
(1867–1936)

Luigi Pirandello was born in Sicily and moved to Rome as a young man to pursue a writing career. In 1904 he was forced by a change in his family's fortunes to begin teaching to earn a living. Novels and short stories flowed from his pen. Later, he wrote radically innovative plays that profoundly affected the development of modern theater. His best known plays are *Six Characters in Search of an Author* (1921), *Henry IV* (1922), and *It Is So If You Think So!* (1923), which reflects the difficulty of establishing truth. He spent the last years of his life traveling from country to country, having turned over his publishing royalties and possessions to his children.

EDGAR ALLAN POE
(1809–1849)

Edgar Allan Poe was born in Boston, and orphaned at the age of two and adopted by a wealthy family. Poe was forced to make his own way, however, after causing a breach with his family during his later school years. He supported himself as a literary editor and a writer, producing *Tales of the Grotesque and Arabesque* (1840) and *The Raven and Other Poems* (1845). Poe is best known for his stories of horror and of crime and detection. A great influence on the French symbolist poets and unique among the American writers of his day, Poe was, after his death, the subject of a malicious biography, which strove to link his life with his brilliantly grotesque literary creations.

ALEXANDER POPE
(1688–1744)

Alexander Pope was born a Roman Catholic at a time when England was violently anti-Catholic and was educated largely at home. A childhood accident deformed his spine and retarded his physical growth, which led the young Alexander Pope to pursue a bookish life. He was a skillful poet early on, having written his *Pastorals* by the age of sixteen. In his mid-twenties he translated Homer's *Iliad* and *Odyssey,* edited Shakespeare's plays, and published *An Essay on Criticism,* a highly regarded work of critical thought in poetic form. Pope is best known, however, for his witty and satirical poems written in heroic couplets, *The Dunciad* and *The Rape of the Lock.*

KATHERINE ANNE PORTER
(1890–1960)

Katherine Anne Porter, short-story writer and novelist, was awarded the Pulitzer prize and National Book Award in 1966 for *The Collected Stories.* Born in Texas, Porter spent time living in Europe and Mexico. Her short-story collections include *Flowering Judas and Other Stories* (1935) and *Pale Horse, Pale Rider* (1939). Her novel, *Ship of Fools,* on which she worked for twenty years, brought her wide acclaim before it was made into a movie. Her basic concern in writing was to examine human motives and portray human experience as she had come to understand it.

ADRIENNE RICH
(b. 1929)

Adrienne Rich was born in Baltimore. She attended Radcliffe College, publishing her first book of poems, *A Change of World* (1951), while a student there. After studying at Oxford University, she married an economist and raised a family of sons, before becoming radicalized and emerging as a lesbian-feminist political activist. She has taught at a number of colleges and universities, including Brandeis, Smith, Douglass, Columbia, and the City College of New York. She has published prose as well as poetry, with *Of Woman Born* (1976) and *On Lies, Secrets and Silence,* two of her more important works. Her poetry continues to receive a wide readership as Rich herself remains a highly influential figure in feminist circles.

E. A. ROBINSON
(1869–1935)

Edwin Arlington Robinson was raised in Gardiner, Maine, the "Tilbury Town" of such poems as "Miniver Cheevy" and "Richard Cory." He attended Harvard for two years, but had to leave because of the failure of his father's lumber business. Widely read in English and American literature, Robinson was drawn to the dark vision of novelist and poet Thomas Hardy, whose starkness of perspective can be detected in some of Robinson's ironic poems. Robinson won three Pulitzer prizes, with special acknowledgment of the success of his dramatic monologues.

THEODORE ROETHKE
(1908–1963)

Theodore Roethke was born in Saginaw, Michigan, where his father oversaw a substantial greenhouse. After attending the University of Michigan and Harvard University, Roethke taught poetry at a number of schools before settling at the University of Washington. His influence extended to other poets, who studied with him there, including James Wright. Roethke's first book of poems, *Open House* (1941), shows his extensive knowledge of flowers and vegetation. His second volume, *The Lost Son* (1948), includes the lyric "My Papa's Waltz." He earned a Pulitzer prize in 1953 for *The Waking*.

ANNE SEXTON
(1928–1974)

Anne Sexton was born and raised in Massachusetts, where she later worked in the Boston literary milieu. She taught creative writing at a number of universities, and was recognized early on as a poet of considerable talent and raw power. She suffered from mental illness and depression, experiences which are reflected in her work. Before taking her own life at age forty-six, Sexton published *Live or Die* (1966), which was awarded the Pulitzer prize for poetry.

WILLIAM SHAKESPEARE
(1564–1616)

William Shakespeare was born and raised, lived and died, in Stratford-on-Avon, a country town nearly a hundred miles outside London. Although Shakespeare is best known as a playwright, considered by many to be the greatest dramatist that ever lived, he was also a gifted poet, both in the songs and speeches from his plays and in his narrative poems *Venus and Adonis* (1593) and *The Rape of Lucrece* (1594). Shakespeare's *Sonnets,* composed between 1593 and 1601 and published in 1609, remain the height of achievement in this genre. Their densely metaphorical language, their formal elegance, and their psychological penetration make them among Shakespeare's finest poetic accomplishments.

LESLIE SILKO
(b. 1948)

A Native American, Leslie Marmon Silko was brought up in Laguna Pueblo, New Mexico. She has taught at the University of Arizona and the University of New Mexico, and she has been honored with a MacArthur Fellowship. Her essays, poems, and stories center on the traditions of the Navajo People, and celebrate Native-American culture and traditions, especially a respect for the land and for the past. Her books include *Ceremony* (1970), her first novel; *Storyteller* (1981), a collection of tribal folktales, family anecdotes, photographs, poems, and stories; *The Almanac of the Dead* (1993); and *Sacred Water* (1993), a collection of poems.

ISAAC BASHEVIS SINGER
(b. 1904)

Isaac Bashevis Singer, who won the Nobel prize in Literature in 1978, was born in Poland and has lived in the United States since 1935. His short stories and novels in Yiddish deal with a society and way of life now passed out of European experience. His milieu is the world of the Eastern European shtetl, in which the characters pursue spiritual quests yet struggle with demons and other evil forces or succumb to material temptations. From a family of rabbis, Singer has drawn on that cultural background for his trilogy, which follows the course of a rabbinical family from 1800 to the Nazi takeover. His short story output is prolific, consisting of more than twelve collections, including *Gimpel the Fool* (1957) and *The Spinoza of Market Street* (1961). His stories have appeared in the *Jewish Daily Forward, Commentary, Esquire,* and *The New Yorker.*

JEAN STAFFORD
(1914–1993)

An American novelist and short-story writer, Jean Stafford is especially noted for her evocative presentations of childhood and adolescence. Her first novel, *Boston Adventure* (1944), depicts Boston as perceived by the young daughter of an immigrant family. A later novel, *The Mountain Lion* (1947), is a study of a brother and sister in the years between childhood and adolescence. Her three collections of stories includes *Bad Characters* (1966); she was awarded a Pulitzer prize for her *Collected Stories* in 1969.

WALLACE STEVENS
(1879–1955)

Wallace Stevens was born in Reading, Pennsylvania, and studied at Harvard before taking a law degree from New York University. For nearly forty years Stevens was associated with the Hartford Accident and Indemnity Company, where he became a vice president. In college Stevens wrote poetry and served as president of the literary magazine and the literary society. During his years of practicing law and working as an insurance industry executive, Stevens wrote and published many poems. His first volume, *Harmonium,* was published in 1923. His *Collected Poems* (1955) won both the Pulitzer prize and the National Book Award.

MAY SWENSON
(1919–1989)

May Swenson was born in Utah of Swedish parents, and moved to New York City after attending college. She performed editorial jobs and taught poetry while writing her own poems and winning awards for them. Her first book, *A Cage of Spines* (1958), was followed by *Half Sun Half Sleep* (1967), which includes witty descriptions of life in New York City along with translations from six Swedish poets. Swenson was a poetic experimenter who played with poetic forms, as in her shaped verse, exemplified by "Women."

AMY TAN
(b. 1952)

Amy Tan was born in Oakland, California, three years after her parents left China during the Maoist revolution. She attended schools in California and in Switzerland and received an M.A. at the University of California at Berkeley. Before devoting herself to writing fiction and memoir, Tan worked as a writer of computer manuals. Her writing draws on her experience as a Chinese-American with a dual cultural heritage. She is best known for her novel *The Joy Luck Club* (1989), which was made into a successful film, and from which the story "Rules of the Game" has been taken.

ALFRED, LORD TENNYSON
(1809–1892)

Alfred, Lord Tennyson, one of the best known and liked Victorian poets, became Poet Laureate in 1850. His early poetry is influenced by the English Romantic poets, especially by John Keats. Among his more highly recognized work is the twelve-part narrative poem, *Idylls of the King,* based on King Arthur and his Round Table, which occupied Tennyson from 1859 to 1888. Tennyson, however, is justly honored as a lyric poet of exquisite musicality and deep feeling as exemplified by his long elegiac poem, *In Memoriam* (1850), inspired by the death of his friend Arthur Hallam.

DYLAN THOMAS
(1914–1953)

Dylan Thomas was born in coastal Wales, the son of an English teacher. His poetry, which centers on themes of birth and death, innocence, childhood, and sex, reflects his Welsh heritage and his rural upbringing. Thomas lacked a university education and thus instead of supporting himself and his family by teaching, he made broadcasts for BBC radio and went on extended poetry reading tours in the United States, where he was a wildly popular figure, with a reputation for being a prodigious drinker as well as a fine performer of poems. His handful of highly regarded poems is complemented by some memorable short stories and a play for voices, *Under Milk Wood* (1954).

JOHN UPDIKE
(b. 1932)

John Updike, American novelist, short-story writer, and poet, was born and raised in Pennsylvania. Following his graduation from Harvard, Updike worked at *The New Yorker* before devoting himself full time to writing. Updike has long been a versatile writer, publishing criticism, essays, poetry, novels, and short stories for more than forty years. He is best known for his portrayals of suburban life and for characters who experience the anxieties, tensions, and frustrations of middle-class existence.

ALICE WALKER
(b. 1944)

Alice Walker, recipient of the Pulitzer prize and National Book Award for her novel *The Color Purple* (1982), was born in Georgia, one of eight children. She received a B.A. from Sarah Lawrence College and has held numerous teaching posts at American universities. In her short-story collections *In Love and Trouble* (1973) and *You Can't Keep a Good Woman Down* (1981), she focuses on black American women, whose struggles are the result of their race and their gender. Among the many honors Walker has received for her fiction and poetry are a Guggenheim Fellowship, a National Endowment for the Arts grant, and the American Academy and Institute of Arts and Letters Award.

EUDORA WELTY
(b. 1909)

Eudora Welty was born in Jackson, Mississippi, and attended the Mississippi State College for Women and the University of Wisconsin. She is best known for her portraits of people and life in the deep South. During World War II she was on the staff of the *New York Times Book Review,* testimony to the insatiable appetite for reading she developed as a child. She began publishing collections of stories in 1941 with *Curtain of Green* and won a Pulitzer prize in 1980 for *The Collected Stories,* which contains work from her numerous collections of short fiction spanning forty years. Welty has also written novels, such as *The Optimist's Daughter,* which won the Pulitzer prize in 1982, and criticism, collected in *The Eye of the Story* (1977). Her memoir, *One Writer's Beginnings,* describes her early experience with literature including her literary influences.

WALT WHITMAN
(1819–1892)

Walt Whitman was born in Huntington, New York, and was educated in the Brooklyn public schools. In his youth he worked successively as an office boy and clerk for a doctor, lawyer, and printer. After teaching school from 1836 to 1841, he began a journalistic career, which involved, at various stages, writing, typesetting, and editing the *Brooklyn Daily Eagle* and *Daily Times,* among other newspapers. During the Civil War, Whitman served as a nurse and worked briefly as a clerk in the Bureau of Indian Affairs. His wide range of experiences is reflected in his deeply democratic vision in poems remarkable for their formal freedom, their freshness of idiom, and their profound compassion.

WILLIAM CARLOS WILLIAMS
(1883–1963)

William Carlos Williams, poet, novelist, short-story writer, was born in Rutherford, New Jersey, where, after earning an M.D., he pursued a medical career as a pediatrician. In the early years of his medical practice there was little time for writing, so Williams concentrated on short forms. His poetic output, which was both innovative and prodigious, was part of a modernist literary revolution that sent poetry in new directions. His fiction is collected in *Making Light of It, The Knife of the Times,* and *The Farmer's Daughter and Other Stories,* from which "The Use of Force" is taken.

WILLIAM WORDSWORTH
(1770–1850)

William Wordsworth was born in the Lake District of northern England, which is central to many of his poems. Along with Samuel Taylor Coleridge, Wordsworth was the earliest and most influential of the English Romantic poets. With Coleridge, he published *Lyrical Ballads* (1798), which essentially launched the Romantic movement in England, calling for a poetry written in a language really used by common people and about matters reflective of everyday life. Wordsworth's sister Dorothy was a constant companion and inspiration. It was from her notebook entries that he later culled the details for his poem "I Wandered Lonely as a Cloud." As with much of Wordsworth's poetry, this lyric reflects his deep love of nature, his vision of a unified world, and his celebration of the power of memory and imagination.

JAMES WRIGHT
(*1927–1980*)

James Wright was born in Martins Ferry, Ohio, and received his Ph.D. at the University of Washington, where he studied with Theodore Roethke. In 1966, he began teaching at Hunter College in New York, where he taught until his death. In addition to his own poetry, which first appeared in the volume *A Green Wall* (1957) and was last collected in *Above the River: The Complete Poems* (1990), Wright was also a translator of the works of Cesar Valejo, Pablo Neruda, and George Trakl.

WILLIAM BUTLER YEATS
(*1865–1939*)

William Butler Yeats was born in Dublin, Ireland, son of the well-known Irish painter, John Butler Yeats. W. B. Yeats himself studied painting for three years, and art would become one of the three dominant themes in his poetry, along with Irish nationalism and the occult. Yeats's interest in Irish folklore was reflected in his early poetry and in the plays he wrote based on Irish legend, especially about Cuchulain. His occult interests appear in his book *The Celtic Twilight* (1893) and *The Secret Rose* (1897). His love for things Irish is revealed throughout his work, which spans a period of nearly half a century, during which he reinvented himself as a poet numerous times, and developed a range of varying styles, voices, and perspectives. Yeats is generally considered the greatest Irish poet of the twentieth century and one of the finest poets of modern times.

Glossary

Allegory   A symbolic narrative in which the surface details imply a secondary meaning. Allegory often takes the form of a story in which the characters represent moral qualities.

Alliteration   The repetition of consonant sounds, especially at the beginning of words.

Anapest   Two unaccented syllables followed by an accented one, as in cŏmprĕhend or ĭntĕrvene.

Antagonist   A character or force against which a main character struggles.

Argumentative essay   An essay that puts forth a claim directly and explicitly supports it with evidence.

Aside   Words spoken by an actor directly to the audience, which are not "heard" by the other actors on stage.

Assonance   The repetition of similar vowel sounds in a sentence or a line of poetry as in "I rose and told him of my woe."

Aubade   A love lyric in which the speaker complains about the arrival of the dawn, when he must part from his lover.

Ballad   A narrative poem written in four-line stanzas, characterized by swift action and narrated in a direct style.

Blank verse   A line of poetry or prose in unrhymed iambic pentameter.

Caesura   A strong pause within a line of verse.

Catastrophe   The action at the end of a tragedy that initiates the denouement.

Catharsis   The purging of the feelings of pity and fear that, according to Aristotle, occur in the audience of tragic drama.

Character   An imaginary person that lives in a literary work. Literary characters may be major or minor, static or dynamic.

Characterization   The means by which writers present and reveal character.

Chorus   A group of characters in Greek tragedy who comment on the action of a play without participating in it. Their leader is the choragos.

Climax   The turning point of the action in the plot of a play or story. The climax represents the point of greatest tension in the work.

Closed form   A type of form or structure in poetry characterized by regularity and consistency in such elements as rhyme, line length, and metrical pattern.

Comedy   A type of drama in which the characters experience reversals of fortune, usually for the better. In comedy things work out happily in the end. Comic drama may be either romantic—characterized by a tone of tolerance and geniality—or satiric. Satiric plays offer a darker vision of human nature, one that ridicules human folly.

Comic relief   The use of a comic scene to interrupt a succession of intensely tragic dramatic moments. The comedy of scenes offering comic relief typically parallels the tragic action the scenes interrupt.

Complication   An intensification of the conflict in a story or play.

Conflict   A struggle between opposing forces in a story or play, usually resolved by the end of the work.

Connotation   The personal and emotional associations called up by a word that go beyond its dictionary meaning.

Convention   A customary feature of a literary work such as the use of a chorus in Greek tragedy or an explicit moral in a fable.

Couplet   A pair of rhymed lines that may or may not constitute a separate stanza in a poem.

Dactyl   A stressed syllable followed by two unstressed ones, as in flút-tĕr-ĭng or blúe-bĕr-řy.

Denotation   The dictionary meaning of a word.

Denouement   The resolution of the plot of a literary work.

Deus ex machina   A god who resolves the entanglements of a play by supernatural intervention (literally, a god from the machine) or any artificial device used to resolve a plot.

Dialogue   The conversation of characters in a literary work.

Diction   The selection of words in a literary work.

Dramatic monologue   A type of poem in which a speaker addresses a silent listener.

Dramatis Personae   The characters or persons of the play.

Elegy   A lyric poem that laments the dead.

Elision   The omission of an unstressed vowel or syllable to preserve the meter of a line of poetry.

Enjambment   A run-on line of poetry in which logical and grammatical sense carries over from one line into the next. An enjambed line differs from an end-stopped line in which the grammatical and logical sense is completed within the line. In the opening lines of Robert Browning's "My Last Duchess," for example, the first line is end-stopped and the second enjambed:

> That's my last Duchess painted on the wall,
> Looking as if she were alive. I call
> That piece a wonder, now. . . .

Epic   A long narrative poem that records the adventures of a hero. Epics typically chronicle the origins of a civilization and embody its central values.

Epigram   A brief witty poem, often satirical.

Exposition   The first stage of a fictional or dramatic plot in which necessary background information is provided.

Expository essay   An essay that advances an idea in a direct manner. Its primary purpose is to provide information.

Fable   A brief story with an explicit moral, often including animals as characters.

Falling action   In the plot of a story or play the action following the climax of the work that moves it towards resolution.

Falling meter   Poetic meters such as trochaic and dactylic that move or fall from a stressed to an unstressed syllable.

Fiction   An imagined story.

Figurative language   A form of language use in which writers and speakers convey something other than the literal meaning of their words. See *hyperbole, metaphor, metonymy, simile, synecdoche,* and *understatement.*

Flashback   An interruption of a work's chronology to describe or present an incident that occurred prior to the main time frame of the action.

Foil   A character who contrasts and parallels the main character in a play or story.

Foot   A metrical unit composed of stressed and unstressed syllables. For example, an *iamb* or *iambic foot* is represented by ˘ ´, that is, an unaccented syllable followed by an accented one.

Foreshadowing   Hints of what is to come in the action of a play or story.

Fourth wall   The imaginary wall of the box theater setting, supposedly removed to allow the audience to see the action.

Free verse   Poetry without a regular pattern of meter or rhyme.

Gesture   The physical movement of a character during a play.

Hyperbole   A figure of speech involving exaggeration.

Iamb   An unstressed syllable followed by a stressed one, as in tŏdáy.

Image   A concrete representation of a sense impression, a feeling, or an idea. Imagery refers to the pattern of related details in a work.

Imagery   The pattern of related comparative aspects of language in a literary work.

Irony   A contrast or discrepancy between what is said and what is meant or between what happens and what is expected to happen. In verbal irony characters say the opposite of what they mean. In irony of circumstance or situation the opposite of what is expected happens. In dramatic irony a character speaks in ignorance of a situation or event known to the audience or to other characters.

Literal language   A form of language in which writers and speakers mean exactly what their words denote.

Lyric poem   A type of poem characterized by brevity, compression, and the expression of feeling.

Metaphor   A comparison between essentially unlike things without a word such as *like* or *as.* An example: "My love is a red, red rose."

Meter   The measured pattern of rhythmic accents in poems.

Metonymy   A figure of speech in which a closely related term is substituted for an object or idea. An example: "We have always remained loyal to the crown."

Monologue   A speech by one character.

Narrative essay   A type of essay in which an idea is illustrated by means of a story or a series of incidents.

Narrative poem   A poem that tells a story.

Narrator   The voice and implied speaker of a fictional work, to be distinguished from the actual living author.

Octave   An eight-line unit, which may constitute a stanza or a section of a poem, as in the octave of a sonnet.

Ode   A long, stately poem in stanzas of varied length, meter, and form. Usually a serious poem on an exalted subject.

Onomatopoeia   The use of words to imitate the sounds they describe. Words such as *buzz* and *crack* are onomatopoetic.

Open form   A type of structure or form in poetry characterized by freedom from regularity and consistency in such elements as rhyme, line length, and metrical pattern.

Parable   A brief story that teaches a lesson often ethical or spiritual.

Parody   A humorous, mocking imitation of a literary work.

Pathos   A quality of a play's action that stimulates the audience to feel pity for a character.

Personification   The endowment of inanimate objects or abstract concepts with animate or living qualities. An example: "The yellow leaves flaunted their color gaily in the wind."

Plot   The unified structure of incidents in a literary work.

Point of view   The angle of vision from which a story is narrated.

Props   Articles or objects that appear on stage during a play.

Protagonist   The main character of a literary work.

Quatrain   A four-line stanza in a poem.

Recognition   The point at which a character understands his or her situation as it really is.

Resolution   The sorting out or unraveling of a plot at the end of a drama or narrative.

Reversal   The point at which the action of the plot turns in an unexpected direction for the protagonist.

Rhetorical question   A question to which an overt answer is not expected. Writers use rhetorical questions to set up an explanation they are about to provide and to trigger a reader's mental response.

Rhyme   The matching of final vowel or consonant sounds in two or more words.

Rhythm   The recurrence of accent or stress in lines of verse.

Rising action   A set of conflicts and crises that constitute that part of a play's plot leading up to the climax.

Rising meter   Poetic meters such as iambic and anapestic that move or ascend from an unstressed to a stressed syllable.

Romance   A type of narrative fiction or poem in which adventure is a central feature and in which an idealized vision of reality is presented.

Satire   A literary work that criticizes human misconduct and ridicules vices, stupidities, and follies.

Sestet   A six-line unit of verse constituting a stanza or section of a poem; the last six lines of an Italian sonnet.

Sestina   A poem of thirty-nine lines written in iambic pentameter. Its six-line stanzas repeat in an intricate and prescribed order the six last words of each line in the opening stanza. After the sixth stanza there is a three-line *envoi* (or envoy) which uses the six repeating words, two to a line.

Setting   The time and place of a literary work that establish its context.

Simile   A figure of speech involving a comparison between unlike things using *like, as,* or *as though.* An example: "My love is like a red, red rose."

Soliloquy   A speech in a play which is meant to be heard by the audience but not by other characters on the stage. If there are no other characters present the soliloquy represents the character's thinking aloud.

Sonnet   A fourteen-line poem in iambic pentameter. The *Shakespearean* or *English sonnet* is arranged as three quatrains and a couplet, rhyming *abab cdcd efef gg.* The *Petrarchan* or *Italian sonnet* divides into two parts: an eight-line octave and a six-line sestet, rhyming *abba abba cde cde* or *abba abba cd cd cd.*

Speculative essay   A meditative essay generally loose in structure concerned with exploring an idea, a perception, or a feeling.

Spondee   A metrical foot represented by two stressed syllables such as kníck-knáck.

Stage direction   A playwright's descriptive or interpretive comments that provide readers (and actors) with information about the dialogue, setting, and action of a play.

Staging   The spectacle a play presents in performance, including the positions of actors on stage, the scenic background, the props and costumes, and the lighting and sound effects.

Stanza   A division or unit of a poem that is repeated in the same form—with similar or identical patterns of rhyme and meter.

Structure   The design or form of a literary work.

Style   The way an author chooses words, arranges them in sentences or in lines of dialogue or verse, and develops ideas and actions *with* description, imagery, and other literary techniques.

Subject   What a story or play is about; to be distinguished from plot and theme.

Subplot   A subsidiary or subordinate or parallel plot in a play or story that coexists with the main plot.

Symbol   An object or action in a literary work that means more than itself, that stands for something beyond itself.

Synecdoche   A figure of speech in which a part is substituted for the whole. An example: "Lend me a hand."

Syntax   The grammatical order of words in a sentence or line of verse or dialogue.

Tale   A story that narrates strange happenings in a direct manner, without detailed descriptions of character.

Tempo   The variation in pace in which a scene is acted.

Tercet   A three-line stanza.

Theme   The idea of a literary work abstracted from its details of language, character, and action, and cast in the form of a generalization.

Tone   The implied attitude of a writer toward the subject and characters of a work.

Tragedy   A type of drama in which the characters experience reversals of fortune, usually for the worse. In tragedy, catastrophe and suffering await many of the characters, especially the hero.

Tragic flaw   A weakness or limitation of character resulting in the fall of the tragic hero.

Tragic hero   A privileged, exalted character of high repute, who by virtue of a tragic flaw and fate suffers a fall from glory into suffering.

Tragicomedy   A type of play that contains elements of both tragedy and comedy.

Understatement   A figure of speech in which a writer or speaker says less than what he or she means; the converse of exaggeration.

Unities   The idea established by Aristotle that a play should be limited to a specific time, place, and story. The events of the plot should occur within a twenty-four-hour period, should occur within a given geographic locale, and should tell a single story.

Villanelle   A nineteen-line lyric poem that relies heavily on repetition. The first and third lines alternate throughout the poem, which is structured in six stanzas—five tercets and a final quatrain.

Acknowledgments

Fiction

LEE ABBOTT   "The View of Me from Mars" from *Dreams of Distant Lives* by Lee K. Abbott.

MARGARET ATWOOD   "Rape Fantasies" by Margaret Atwood. © O.W. Toad Ltd., 1991. Reprinted by permission of Margaret Atwood.

JORGE LUIS BORGES   "The Garden of Forking Paths" by Jorge Luis Borges, translated by Donald A. Yates, from *Labyrinths*. Copyright © 1962, 1964 by New Directions Publishing Corp. Reprinted by permission of New Directions Publishing Corp.

KAY BOYLE   "Astronomer's Wife" by Kay Boyle.

RAYMOND CARVER   From *Cathedral* by Raymond Carver. Copyright © 1981 by Raymond Carver. Reprinted by permission of Alfred A. Knopf, Inc.

SANDRA CISNEROS   "Eleven," "Barbie-Q," and "There Was a Man, There Was a Woman" from *Woman Hollering Creek* by Sandra Cisneros. Copyright © 1991 by Sandra Cisneros. Published by Vintage Books, a division of Random House, Inc., New York and originally in hardcover by Random House, Inc. Excerpt from "Straw Into Gold" by Sandra Cisneros. Copyright © 1987 by Sandra Cisneros. First published in *The Texas Observer*, September 1987. Reprinted by permission of Susan Bergholz Literary Services, New York. All rights reserved.

RALPH ELLISON   "Battle Royal" from *Invisible Man* by Ralph Ellison. Copyright © 1948 by Ralph Ellison. Reprinted by permission of Random House, Inc.

LOUISE ERDRICH   "American Horse" by Louise Erdrich.

WILLIAM FAULKNER   From "A Rose for Emily" from *Collected Stories of William Faulkner* by William Faulkner. Copyright © 1930 and renewed 1958 by William Faulkner. Reprinted by permission of Random House, Inc.

ERNEST HEMINGWAY   "Soldiers Home" from *The Short Stories of Ernest Hemingway* by Ernest Hemingway.

JAMES JOYCE   "Araby" from *Dubliners* by James Joyce. Copyright 1916 by B.W. Heubsch. Definitive text Copyright © 1967 by the Estate of James Joyce. Used by permission of Viking Penguin, a division of Penguin Putnam Inc.

JAMAICA KINCAID   "Girl" from *At the Bottom of the River* by Jamaica Kincaid. Copyright © 1983 by Jamaica Kincaid. Reprinted by permission of Farrar, Straus & Giroux, Inc.

D.H. LAWRENCE   "The Blind Man," copyright 1933 by the Estate of D.H. Lawrence; renewal © 1961 by Angelo Ravagli and C. Montague Weekley, Executors of the Estate of Frieda Lawrence Ravagli, "The Horse-Dealers Daughter" copyright 1922 by Thomas B. Seltzer, Inc., renewed 1950 by Frieda Lawrence. "The Rocking-Horse Winner" by D.H. Lawrence, copyright 1933 by the Estate of D.H. Lawrence, renewed © 1961 by Angelo Ravagli and C.M. Weekley, Executors of the Estate of Frieda Lawrence, from *Complete Short Stories of D.H. Lawrence* by D.H. Lawrence. Used by permission of Viking Penguin, a division of Penguin Putnam Inc. From "Morality and the Novel" from *Phoenix: The Posthumous Papers of D.H. Lawrence* by D.H. Lawrence and edited by Edward McDonald. Copyright 1936 by Frieda Lawrence, renewed © 1964 by The Estate of the late Frieda Lawrence Ravagli. Used by permission of Viking Penguin, a division of Penguin Putnam Inc.

GABRIEL GARCIA MARQUEZ   "A Very Old Man with Enormous Wings" from *Leaf Storm and Other Stories* by Gabriel Garcia Marquez.

BOBBIE ANN MASON   "Shiloh" from *Shiloh and Other Stories* by Bobbie Ann Mason.

FLANNERY O'CONNOR   "Good Country People," copyright 1955 by Flannery O'Connor and renewed 1983 by Regina O'Connor and "A Good Man Is Hard to Find" copyright 1953 by Flannery O'Connor and renewed 1981 by Regina O'Connor from *A Good Man Is Hard to Find and Other Stories* reprinted by permission of Harcourt Brace & Company. "O'Connor on 'Good Country People'" from "Writing Short Stories" and "The Nature Aim of Fiction" from *Mystery and Manners* by Flannery O'Connor edited by Sally & Robert Fitzgerald, 1969.

FRANK O'CONNOR   "Guests of the Nation" from *Collected Stories* by Frank O'Connor. Copyright © 1981 by Harriet O'Donovan Sheehy, Executrix of the Estate of Frank O'Connor. Reprinted by permission of Alfred A. Knopf, Inc., and arrangement with Harriet O'Donovan Sheehy, c/o Joan Daves Agency as agent for the proprietor. Copyright 1966 by Frank O'Connor.

TILLIE OLSEN   "I Stand Here Ironing," copyright © 1956, 1957, 1960, 1961 by Tillie Olsen, from *Tell Me A Riddle* by Tillie Olsen. Introduction by John Leonard. Used by permission of Delacorte Press/Seymour Lawrence, a division of Random House, Inc.

PETRONIUS   "The Widow of Ephesus" by Petronius from *The Satyricon* by Petronius, translated by William Arrowsmith. Translation copyright © 1959, renewed 1987 by William Arrowsmith. Used by permission of Dutton Signet, a division of Penguin Putnam Inc.

LUIGI PIRANDELLO   "War" from *The Medals and Other Stories* by Luigi Pirandello. Reprinted by permission of the Pirandello Estate and Toby Cole, Agent. © E.P. Dutton, N.Y., 1939.

KATHERINE ANNE PORTER   "Magic," "The Jilting of Granny Weatherall" from *Flowering Judas and Other Stories,* copyright 1930 and renewed 1958 by Katherine Anne Porter, reprinted by permission of Harcourt Brace & Company.

LESLIE SILKO   "Yellow Woman" by Leslie Silko. Copyright © 1973 by Leslie Marmon Silko, as printed in *The Man to Send Rain Clouds.* No changes shall be made to the text of the above work without the express written consent of the Wylie Agency, Inc. Reprinted by permission.

ISAAC BASHEVIS SINGER   "Gimpel the Fool" by Isaac Bashevis Singer, translated by Saul Bellow, copyright 1953, 1954 by The Viking Press Inc., renewed © 1981, 1982 by Viking Penguin Inc., from *A Treasury Of Yiddish Stories* by Irving Howe and Eliezer Greenberg. Used by permission of Viking Penguin, a division of Penguin Putnam Inc.

JEAN STAFFORD   "Bad Characters" from *Bad Characters* by Jean Stafford. Copyright © 1964 by Jean Stafford. Copyright renewed © 1992 by Nora Cosgrove. Reprinted by permission of Farrar, Straus & Giroux Inc.

AMY TAN "The Rules of the Game," from *The Joy Luck Club* by Amy Tan. Copyright © 1989 by Amy Tan. Used by permission of Putnam Berkley, a division of Penquin Putnam Inc.

JOHN UPDIKE "A & P" from *Pigeon Feathers and Other Stories* by John Updike. Copyright © 1962 by John Updike. Reprinted by permission of Alfred A. Knopf, Inc.

ALICE WALKER "Everyday Use" by Alice Walker from *In Love & Trouble: Stories of Black Women* by Alice Walker. Copyright © 1973 by Alice Walker, reprinted by permission of Harcourt, Inc.

EUDORA WELTY "A Worn Path" from *A Curtain of Green and Other Stories,* copyright 1941 and renewed 1969 by Eudora Welty, reprinted by permission of Harcourt Brace & Company.

Poetry

FREDERICK ASALS From *Flannery O'Connor: The Imagination of Extremity* by Frederick Asals. Reprinted by permission of The University of Georgia Press.

MARGARET ATWOOD "This Is a Photograph of Me" from *The Circle Game* by Margaret Atwood, 1965. Reprinted with the permission of Stoddart Publishing Co., Limited, Don Mills, Ontario, Canada.

W. H. AUDEN "The Unknown Citizen," "Musee des Beaux Arts," and "In Memory of W. B. Yeats" from *W. H. Auden; Collected Poems* by W. H. Auden, edited by Edward Mendelson. Copyright © 1940 and renewed 1968 by W. H. Auden. Reprinted by permission of Random House, Inc.

JIMMY SANTIAGO BACA "Section XVII from Meditations on the South Valley" by Jimmy Santiago Baca, from *Martin and Meditations on The South Valley.* Copyright © 1987 by Jimmy Santiago Baca. Reprinted by permission of New Directions Publishing Corp.

RICHARD BARKSDALE From *Langston Hughes* by Richard K. Barksdale.

ELIZABETH BISHOP "First Death in Nova Scotia" and "Sestina" from *The Complete Poems 1927–1979* by Elizabeth Bishop. Copyright © 1979, 1983 by Alice Helen Methfessel. Reprinted by permission of Farrar, Straus and Giroux, LLC.

NEAL BOWERS "Driving Lessons" by Neal Bowers as appeared in *Shenandoah,* 42:2 (Summer 1992), pp. 42–43. Reprinted by permission of the author.

GWENDOLYN BROOKS "The Mother" and "First fight. Then fiddle." from *Blacks* by Gwendolyn Brooks.

RAYMOND CARVER "Photograph of My Father in His Twenty-second Year" by Raymond Carver, © 1984 by Raymond Carver; © 1988 by Tess Gallagher. Reprinted by permssion of ICM. All rights reserved.

ROSARIO CASTELLANOS "Chess" as translated by Maureen Ahern from *A Rosario Castellanos Reader* by Rosario Castellanos, edited by Maureen Ahern, translated by Maureen Ahern and others. Copyright © 1988. By permission of Maureen Ahern, Fondo de Cultura Economica and the University of Texas Press.

C.P. CAVAFY "The City" by C.P. Cavafy from *Collected Poems, Revised Edition,* translated by Edmund Keeley and Philip Sherrard. Copyright © 1992 by Edmund Keeley and Philip Sherrard. Reprinted by permission of Princeton University Press.

HELEN CHASIN From *Coming Close and Other Poems* by Helen Chasin, 1968. Reprinted by permission of Yale University Press.

LUCILLE CLIFTON "Homage to My Hips" by Lucille Clifton. Copyright © 1980 by The University of Massachusetts Press. First appeared in *Two-Headed Woman,* published by the University of Massachusetts Press. Now appears in *Good Woman: Poems and a Memoir 1969–1980,* published by BOA Editions, Ltd. Reprinted by permission of Curtis Brown, Ltd.

JUDITH ORTIZ COFER "The Idea of Islands" by Judith Ortiz Cofer is reprinted with permission from the publisher of *Terms of Survival* (Houston: Arte Publico Press—University of Houston, 1987).

GREGORY CORSO "Marriage" by Gregory Corso, from *The Happy Birthday of Death*. Copyright © 1960 by New Directions Publishing Corp. Reprinted by permission of New Directions Publishing Corp.

E.E. CUMMINGS "I(a," "Me up at does," "anyone lived in a pretty how town," "Buffalo Bill's," and "i thank You God for most this amazing" from *Complete Poems: 1904–1962* by E.E. Cummings, edited by George J. Firmage. Copyright 1923, 1925, 1926, 1931, 1935, 1938, 1939, 1940, 1944, 1945, 1946, 1947, 1948, 1949, 1950, 1951, 1952, 1953, 1954, © 1955, 1956, 1957, 1958, 1959, 1960, 1961, 1962, 1963, 1966, 1967, 1968, 1972, 1973, 1974, 1975, 1976, 1977, 1978, 1979, 1980, 1981, 1982, 1983, 1984, 1985, 1986, 1987, 1988, 1989, 1990, 1991, by the Trustees for the E.E. Cummings Trust. Copyright © 1973, 1976, 1978, 1979, 1981, 1983, 1985, 1991 by George James Firmage. Reprinted by permission of Liveright Publishing Corporation.

EMILY DICKINSON "Because I Could Not Stop for Death," #712, "I'm 'wife'—I've finished that," #199, "I taste a liquor never brewed," #214, "I like a look of Agony," #241, "Wild Nights—Wild Nights!" #249, "There's a certain Slant of light," #258, "I felt a Funeral, in my Brain," #280, "Some keep the Sabbath going to Church," #324, "I dreaded that first Robin, so," #348, "Much Madness is divinest Sense," #435, "I died for Beauty—but was scarce," #449, "I heard a Fly buzz-when I died," #465, "The Heart asks Pleasure—first," #536, "Pain—has an Element of Blank," #650, "Remorse—is Memory—awake," #744, "I like to see it lap the Miles," #585, "The Bustle in a House," #1078, "The last Night that She lived," #1100, "A narrow Fellow in the Grass," #986, "Further in Summer than the Birds," #1068, "A Route of Evanescence," #1463, "Apparently with no surprise," #1624, "My life closed twice before its close," #1732, "The Soul Selects her own Society," #303, "The Wind begun to knead the Grass" and "Wind begun to rock the Grass," #824, "Crumbling is not an instant's Act," #997, and Poems #632, #650, by Emily Dickinson. Reprinted by permission of the publishers and the Trustees of Amherst College from *The Poems of Emily Dickinson*, Thomas H. Johnson, ed., Cambridge, Mass.: The Belknap Press of Harvard University Press, Copyright © 1951, 1955, 1979, 1983 by the President and Fellows of Harvard College. "Tell all the Truth but tell it slant," #1129, and "I'm 'wife'—I've finished that," #199 by Emily Dickinson. Reprinted by permission of the publisher from *The Passion of Emily Dickinson* by Judith Farr, Cambridge, Mass.: Harvard University Press, Copyright © 1997 by the President and Fellows of Harvard College. "After great pain, a formal feeling comes," #341, by Emily Dickinson. "We grow accustomed to the Dark," #419, by Emily Dickinson. "There is a pain—so utter," #599, by Emily Dickinson. "My Life had stood—a Loaded Gun," #754, by Emily Dickinson. "I Dance upon my toes," #326, by Emily Dickinson.

HILDA DOOLITTLE "Heat, part II of Garden" by H.D., from *Collected Poems, 1912–1944*. Copyright © 1982 by The Estate of Hilda Doolittle. Reprinted by permission of New Directions Publishing Corp.

RITA DOVE "Canary" from *Grace Notes* by Rita Dove. Copyright © 1989 by Rita Dove. Reprinted by permission of the author and W.W. Norton & Company, Inc.

T.S. ELIOT "Journey of the Magi" from *Collected Poems 1909–1962* by T.S. Eliot, copyright 1936 by Harcourt Brace & Company, copyright © 1964, 1963 by T.S. Eliot, reprinted by permission of the publisher, and Faber and Faber, Ltd. "The Love Song of J. Alfred Prufrock" by T.S. Eliot from *Collected Poems 1909–1962* by T.S. Eliot. Reprinted by permission of Faber and Faber Ltd.

LOUISE ERDRICH "Indian Boarding School: The Runaways" from *Jacklight* by Louise Erdrich.

ROBERT FAGLES "The Starry Night" by Robert Fagles from *I, Vincent: Poems from the Pictures of Van Gogh* by Robert Fagles. Reprinted by permission of Professor Robert Fagles.

LAWRENCE FERLINGHETTI "Constantly Risking Absurdity" by Lawrence Ferlinghetti from *A Coney Island of the Mind*. Copyright © 1958 by Lawrence Ferlinghetti. Reprinted by permission of New Directions Publishing Corp. "Short Story on a Painting of Gustav Klimt" by Lawrence Ferlinghetti, from *Endless Life*. Copyright © 1976 by Lawrence Ferlinghetti. Reprinted by permission of New Directions Publishing Corp.

ROBERT FROST "Dust of Snow," "Stopping by Woods on a Snowy Evening," "The Silken Tent," "The Span of Life," "Fire and Ice," "For Once, Then, Something," "Two Look at Two," "Once by the Pacific," "Acquainted with the Night," "Tree at My Window," "Departmental," "Desert Places," "Design," "Provide, Provide," "The Most of It," "Sentence Sounds," "The Figure a Poem Makes," "The Road Not Taken," "Mowing," "Mending Wall," "Birches," and "Putting in the Seed" from *The Poetry of Robert Frost* by Robert Frost. "The Unmade Word," "The Tuft of Flowers," "Home Burial," and "Hyla Brook" from *Collected Poems, Prose, and Plays by Robert Frost*. Reprinted by permission of the Executor of the Robert Frost Estate.

DAVID GEWANTER Goya's "The Third of May, 1808" by David Gewanter. Copyright 1997 by The University of Chicago. All rights reserved. Reprinted by permission.

NIKKI GIOVANNI "Ego Tripping" from *The Women And The Men* by Nikki Giovanni. Copyright © 1970, 1974, 1975 by Nikki Giovanni. By permission of William Morrow and Company, Inc.

ROBERT GRAVES "Symptoms of Love" by Robert Graves from *Collected Poems* by Robert Graves, 1975. Reprinted by permission of Carcanet Press Limited.

DONALD HALL "My son my executioner" by Donald Hall. Copyright Donald Hall. Reprinted by permission of the author.

GARY LAYNE HATCH "Terrier Torment: or Mr. Hopkins and His Dog" by Gary Layne Hatch, 1995. Reprinted by permission of the author.

ROBERT HAYDEN "Those Winter Sundays" copyright © 1966 by Robert Hayden, from *Angle of Ascent: New and Selected Poems* by Robert Hayden. Reprinted by permission of Liveright Publishing Corporation.

SEAMUS HEANEY "Mid-Term Break" and "Digging" from *Open Ground: Selected Poems 1966–1996* by Seamus Heaney. Reprinted by permission of Farrar, Straus and Giroux, LLC.

E. WARD HERLANDS "When Edward Hopper Was Painting" by E. Ward Herlands, *Midstream* 37:4 (May 1991). Reprinted by permission of the author.

LANGSTON HUGHES "Dream Deferred," "Same in Blues," "Dream Boogie," "The Negro Speaks of Rivers," "Mother to Son," "I, Too," "My People," "The Weary Blues," "Young Gal's Blues," "Morning After," "Trumpet Player," "Madam and the Rent Man," "Theme for English B," "Aunt Sue's Stories," "Let America Be America Again," by Langston Hughes. From *Collected Poems* by Langston Hughes. Copyright © 1994 by the Estate of Langston Hughes. Reprinted by permission of Alfred A. Knopf Inc.

VICENTE HUIDOBRO "Ars Poetica" by Vicente Huidobro, translation by David M. Guss, from *The Selected Poems of Vicente Huidobro*. Copyright © 1963 by Empreza Editoria Zig Zag, S.A., © 1981 by David M. Guss. Reprinted by permission of New Directions Publishing Corp.

JANE KENYON "Notes from the Other Side" copyright 1996 by the Estate of Jane Kenyon. Reprinted from *Otherwise: New & Selected Poems* with the permission of Graywolf Press, Saint Paul, Minnesota.

GALWAY KINNELL "Saint Francis and the Sow" from *Three Books* by Galway Kinnell. Copyright © 1993 by Galway Kinnell. Previously published in *Mortal Acts, Mortal Words* (1980). Reprinted by permission of Houghton Mifflin Co. All rights reserved.

KENNETH KOCH "Variations on a Theme by William Carlos Williams" by Kenneth Koch. Copyright © by Kenneth Koch, 1994. Reprinted by permission of the author.

YUSEF KOMUNYAKAA "Facing It" from *Dien Cai Dau* © 1988 by Yusef Komunyakaa, Wesleyan University Press by permission of University Press of New England.

JOSEPH LANGLAND "Hunters in the Snow: Breughel" from *The Greed Town* by Joseph Langland, Scribners, 1956.

PHILIP LARKIN "A Study of Reading Habits" from *Collected Poems* by Philip Larkin. Reprinted by permission of Faber and Faber Ltd.

D.H. LAWRENCE "The Piano" and "Piano" by D.H. Lawrence from *The Complete Poems of D.H. Lawrence* by D.H. Lawrence, edited by V. de Sola Pinto & F.W. Roberts. Copyright © 1964, 1971 by Angelo Ravagli and C.M. Weekley, Executors of the Estate of Frieda Lawrence Ravagli. Used by permission of Viking Penguin, a division of Penguin Putnam Inc.

DENISE LEVERTOV "O Taste and See" by Denise Levertov, from *Poems 1960–1967*. Copyright © 1964 by Denise Levertov. Reprinted by permission of New Directions Publishing Corp.

AUDRE LORDE "Hanging Fire" from *The Black Unicorn* by Audre Lorde. Copyright © 1978 by Audre Lorde. Reprinted by permission of W.W. Norton & Company, Inc.

ARCHIBALD MACLEISH "Ars Poetica" from *Collected Poems 1917–1982* by Archibald MacLeish. Copyright © 1982 by The Estate of Archibald MacLeish. Reprinted by permission of Houghton Mifflin Company. All rights reserved.

BOB MCKENTY "Snow on Frost" and "Adam's Song" by Bob McKenty, 1993. Reprinted by permission of the author.

PETER MEINKE "Advice to my Son" from *Liquid Paper: New and Selected Poems* by Peter Meinke, © 1991. Reprinted by permission of the University of Pittsburgh Press.

TOM MOLITO "Cosmic Simplicities" by Tom Molito. Reprinted by permission of the author.

MARIANNE MOORE Reprinted with the permission of Simon & Schuster from *The Collected Poems of Marianne*. Copyright 1935 by Marianne Moore; copyright renewed © 1963 by Marianne Moore and T.S. Eliot.

HOWARD MOSS "Shall I Compare Thee to a Summer's Day?" from *A Swim Off the Rocks* by Howard Moss. Reprinted by permission of the Executor for Howard Moss.

SHARON OLDS "Size and Sheer Will" from *The Dead And The Living* by Sharon Olds. Copyright © 1983 by Sharon Olds. Reprinted by permission of Alfred A. Knopf, Inc.

JEMIE ONWUCHEKWA From *Langston Hughes: An Introduction to the Poetry* by Jemie Onwuchekwa.

WILFRED OWEN "Dulce et Decorum Est" by Wilfred Owen, from *The Collected Poems of Wilfred Owen*. Copyright © 1963 by Chatto & Windus, Ltd. Reprinted by permission of New Directions Publishing Corp.

LINDA PASTAN "Ethics" from *Waiting For My Life* by Linda Pastan. Copyright © 1981 by Linda Pastan. Reprinted by permission of W.W. Norton & Company, Inc.

MARGE PIERCY "A Work of Artifice" from *Circles On The Water* by Marge Piercy. Copyright © 1982 by Marge Piercy. Reprinted by permission of Alfred A. Knopf, Inc.

EZRA POUND "The River Merchant's Wife: A Letter" by Ezra Pound from *Personae*. Copyright © 1926 by Ezra Pound. Reprinted by permission of New Directions Publishing Corp.

JACQUES PREVERT "Family Portrait" by Jacques Prevert translated by Harriet Zinnes.

ARNOLD RAMPERSAD From "Introduction" by Arnold Rampersad from *Collected Poems* by Langston Hughes. Copyright © 1994 by the Estate of Langston Hughes. Reprinted by permission of Alfred A. Knopf Inc.

JOHN CROWE RANSOM "Piazza Piece" from *Selected Poems* by John Crowe Ransom. Copyright 1927 by Alfred A. Knopf, Inc., and renewed 1955 by John Crowe Ransom. Reprinted by permission of the publisher.

HENRY REED   "Naming of Parts" from *A Map of Verona* by Henry Reed.

ADRIENNE RICH   "Aunt Jennifer's Tigers" and "Rape" from *The Fact of A Doorframe: Poems Selected and New 1950–1984* by Adrienne Rich. Copyright © 1984 by Adrienne Rich. Copyright © 1975, 1978 by W.W. Norton & Company, Inc. Copyright © 1981 by Adrienne Rich. Reprinted by permission of the author and W.W. Norton & Company, Inc.

ALBERTO RIOS   "A Dream of Husbands" by Alberto Rios from *Whispering to Fool the Wind*.

THEODORE ROETHKE   "Elegy for Jane," copyright 1950 by Theodore Roethke, "My Papa's Waltz," copyright 1942 by Hearst Magazines, Inc., "The Waking," copyright 1953 by Theodore Roethke, from *The Collected Poems of Theodore Roethke* by Theodore Roethke. Used by permission of Doubleday, a division of Random House Inc.

KRAFT ROMPF   "Waiting Table" by Kraft Rompf. Reprinted by permission of the author.

NATALIE SAFIR   "Matisse's Dance" by Natalie Safir.

GJERTRUD SCHNACKENBERG   "Signs" from *The Lamplit Answer* by Gjertrud Schnackenberg. Copyright © 1985 by Gjertrud Schnackenberg. Reprinted by permission of Farrar, Straus and Giroux, LLC.

ANNE SEXTON   "Her Kind" from *To Bedlam and Part Way Back* by Anne Sexton. Copyright © 1960 by Anne Sexton, © renewed 1988 by Linda G. Sexton. "The Starry Night" from *All My Pretty Ones* by Anne Sexton. Copyright © 1962 by Anne Sexton, © renewed 1990 by Linda G. Sexton. "Two Hands" from *The Awful Rowing Toward God* by Anne Sexton. Copyright © 1975 by Loring Conant, Jr., Executor of the Estate of Anne Sexton. Reprinted by permission of Houghton Mifflin Co. All rights reserved.

LOUIS SIMPSON   "The Battle" reprinted by permission of Louis Simpson from *Good News of Death and Other Poems*. Copyright © 1955 by Louis Simpson.

STEVIE SMITH   "Mother, Among the Dustbins" by Stevie Smith, from *Collected Poems of Stevie Smith*. Copyright © 1972 by Stevie Smith. Reprinted by permission of New Directions Publishing Corp.

GARY SOTO   "Behind Grandma's House" from *New and Selected Poems* by Gary Soto. © 1995, published by Chronicle Books. Reprinted by permission.

WILLIAM STAFFORD   "Traveling through the Dark" by William Stafford, copyright 1962, 1998 by the Estate of William Stafford. Reprinted from *The Way It Is: New & Selected Poems* with the permission of Graywolf Press, Saint Paul, Minnesota.

WALLACE STEVENS   "Thirteen Ways of Looking at a Blackbird" from *Collected Poems* by Wallace Stevens. Copyright 1923, and renewed 1951 by Wallace Stevens. Reprinted by permission of Alfred A. Knopf, Inc.

MURIEL STUART   "In the Orchard" from *Selected Poems* by Muriel Stuart.

MAY SWENSON   "Women" by May Swenson. From her *Iconographs* and used with permission of the Literary Estate of May Swenson. "The Universe" by May Swenson. From her *New And Selected Things Taking Place* and used with permission of The Literary Estate of May Swenson.

DYLAN THOMAS   "Fern Hill" by Dylan Thomas from *The Poems of Dylan Thomas*. Copyright © 1945 by The Trustees for the Copyrights of Dylan Thomas. Reprinted by permission of New Directions Publishing Corp. and David Higham Associates. "Do Not Go Gentle Into That Good Night" by Dylan Thomas from *The Poems of Dylan Thomas*. Copyright © 1952 by Dylan Thomas. Reprinted by permission of New Directions Publishing Corp. and David Higham Ltd.

JEAN TOOMER   "Reapers" from *Cane* by Jean Toomer and "Song of the Son." Copyright 1923 by Boni & Liveright, renewed 1951 by Jean Toomer. Reprinted by permission of Liveright Publishing Corporation.

ROBERT WALLACE   "The Double-Play" © 1961 by Robert Wallace. Reprinted from *Views From A Ferris Wheel* by permission of the author.

and the rights of translation into foreign languages, are strictly reserved. Particular emphasis is laid upon the matter of readings, permission for which must be secured from the Author's agent in writing. Inquiries concerning rights should be addressed to: William Morris Agency, Inc., 1325 Ave. of the Americas, New York, NY 10019, Attn: Gilbert Parker. *Andre's Mother* was originally produced by The Manhattan Theatre Company.

ARTHUR MILLER   From *Death of a Salesman* by Arthur Miller. Copyright 1949, renewed © 1977 by Arthur Miller. Used by permission of Viking Penguin, a division of Penguin Putnam Inc.

WILLIAM SHAKESPEARE   From *The Tragedy of Othello* by William Shakespeare, edited by Alvin Kernan. Copyright © 1963 by Alvin Kernan. Used by permission of Dutton Signet, a division of Penguin Putnam Inc. "Hamlet, Prince of Denmark" by William Shakespeare, from *Introduction to Shakespeare* edited by Hardin Craig and David Bevington, 1975. Reprinted by permission of David Bevington, the Phyllis Fay Horton Professor in the Humanities Dept. at the University of Chicago.

WENDY WASSERSTEIN   *Tender Offer* by Wendy Wasserstein. Copyright © 1991 by Wendy Wasserstein. First published in *Antaeus Issue #66, Plays In One Act,* Spring 1991. No part of this material may be reproduced in whole or in part without the express written permission of the author or her agent. Reprinted by permission of Rosenstone/Wender.

AUGUST WILSON   From *Fences* by August Wilson. Copyright © 1986 by August Wilson. Used by permission of Dutton Signet, a division of Penguin Putnam Inc.

Critical Perspective:

JOHN ASHWORTH   From "Olivier, Freud, and Hamlet" by John Ashworth as appeared in *The Atlantic Monthly,* April 1949.

MAURICE CHARNEY   From "Shakespeare's Villains" by Maurice Charney from *How to Read Shakespeare* by Maurice Charney.

EMILY DICKINSON   From "On 'Wild Nights'" by Judith Farr. Reprinted by permission of the publisher from *The Passion of Emily Dickinson* by Judith Farr, Cambridge, Mass.: Harvard University Press, Copyright © 1997 by the President and Fellows of Harvard College.

GERALD ELSE   From *Poetics* by Aristotle, translated by Gerald F. Else, 1967. Reprinted by permission of the University of Michigan Press.

KATHLEEN FEELEY   From "On 'Good Country People'" by Kathleen Feeley from *Flannery O'Connor: Voice of the Peacock* by Kathleen Feeley. Reprinted by permission of the author.

ROBERT FROST   From "The Unmade Word" by Robert Frost from *Collected Poems, Prose, and Plays* by Robert Frost. Reprinted by permission of the Executor of the Robert Frost Estate.

CAROLYN HEILBRUN   From *Hamlet's Mother and Other Women* by Carolyn Heilbrun. Copyright © 1990 Columbia University Press. Reprinted with permission of the publisher.

NORMAN HOLLAND   From The Brain of Robert Frost by Norman Holland. Reprinted by permission of Sterling Lord Literistic, Inc. Copyright 1988 by Norman Holland.

BERNARD KNOX   "Sophocles' Oedipus" from *Word and Action: Essays on the Ancient Theater* by Bernard Knox, pp. 956–958. Reprinted by permission of Johns Hopkins University Press.

MAYNARD MACK   Reprinted from *Everybody's Shakespeare: Reflections Chiefly On The Tragedies* by Maynard Mack by permission of the University of Nebraska Press. © 1993 by Maynard Mack.

DOROTHY TUCK MCFARLAND   Excerpt from "On 'Everything That Rises Must Converge'" from Flannery O'Connor by Dorothy Tuck McFarland. (Frederick Ungar, 1976) Reprinted by permission of The Continuum Publishing Corp.

HELEN MCNEIL   Excerpt from *Emily Dickinson* by Helen McNeil, 1986. Reprinted by permission of Virago Press.

A.D. NUTTALL   From "Othello" by A.D. Nuttall from *A New Mimesis* (Methuen).

FLANNERY O'CONNOR   From *The Habit of Being: Selected Letters of Flannery O'Connor* by Flannery O'Connor, edited by Sally Fitzgerald, 1979.

RICHARD POIRIER   From "On 'Stopping by Woods'" and "On 'Mending Wall'" from *Robert Frost: The Work of Knowing* edited by Richard Poirier. Copyright © 1977 by Richard Poirier. Used by permission of Oxford University Press, Inc.

ADRIAN POOLE   From *Tragedy: Shakespeare and the Greek Example* by Adrian Poole. Reprinted by permission of Blackwell Publishers.

WILLIAM PRITCHARD   From *Frost: A Literary Life Reconsidered* edited by William Pritchard. Copyright © 1984 by William Pritchard. Used by permission of Oxford University Press, Inc.

W.D. SNODGRASS   "A Rocking Horse: Symbol, Pattern, Way to Live" by W.D. Snodgrass, *The Hudson Review,* Summer 1958. © W.D. Snodgrass. Reprinted by permission of the author.

ALLEN TATE   "Dickinson and Knowledge" and "On 'Because I Could Not Stop for Death'" from "Emily Dickinson" from *Collected Essays* by Allen Tate, Swallow, 1959. Reprinted by permission of Mrs. Helen Tate.

WILLIAM CARLOS WILLIAMS   "The Use of Force" by William Carlos Williams, from *The Collected Stories of William Carlos Williams.* Copyright © 1938 by William Carlos Williams. Reprinted by permission of New Directions Publishing Corp.

YVOR WINTERS   "Robert Frost: or, the Spiritual Drifter as Poet" by Yvor Winters from *The Function of Criticism.* Reprinted with the permission of Ohio University Press/Swallow Press, Athens, Ohio.

Poems and Paintings

VINCENT VAN GOGH   *The Starry Night,* photograph © 1997 the Museum of Modern Art, New York.

EDWARD HOPPER   *Sunday,* photograph © 1997 the Museum of Modern Art, New York.

HENRI MATISSE   *Dance (First Version),* © 1998 Succession H. Matisse, Paris/Artists Rights Society (ARS), New York. Photograph © 1997 the Museum of Modern Art, New York.

PABLO PICASSO   *Girl with a Mandolin (Fanny Tellier),* © 1998 Estate of Pablo Picasso/Artists Rights Society (ARS). New York. Photograph © 1997 the Museum of Modern Art, New York.

PABLO PICASSO   *Still Life with Pitcher, Bowl, & Fruit,* © 1998 Estate of Pablo Picasso/Artists Rights Society (ARS), New York.

Index

of Authors, Titles, and First Lines

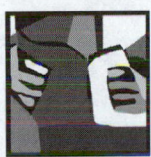

Selection titles appear in italics, and first lines of poems appear in roman type. Page numbers in roman type indicate the opening page of a selection; italic numbers indicate discussion. Bold page numbers indicate complete sections on specific authors.